ECONOMICS

PRINCIPLES, PROBLEMS, DECISIONS, Second Edition

W • W • NORTON & COMPANY • INC • NEW YORK

EDWIN MANSFIELD

UNIVERSITY OF PENNSYLVANIA

ECONOMICS

PRINCIPLES, PROBLEMS, DECISIONS

SECOND EDITION

To Edward Deering Mansfield (1801–1880)
and his brother-in-law Charles Davies (1798–1876),
neither of whom should be held responsible
for the views expressed here.

Published simultaneously in Canada by George J. McLeod Limited, Toronto. Printed in the United States of America.

ISBN 0 393 09112 0

1 2 3 4 5 6 7 8 9 0

Permission from the following sources to reprint photographs is hereby gratefully acknowledged: Mansell Collection (p. 22, 394); New York Port Authority (pp. 92); The Department of the Treasury (pp. 128); Edward C. Topple, New York Stock Exchange Photographer (pp. 139); British Airways (pp. 166); United Press International (pp. 237, 364, 791); Board of Governors of the Federal Reserve System (pp. 338, 341); New York Times (p. 357); Dow Chemical U.S.A. (425); Time-LIFE Picture Agency (p. 430); Sloan's Supermarkets (p. 473); Ford Archives (p. 491); Photoreporters, Inc. (p. 580); Jacques E. Levy (p. 636), from his book, *Cesar Chavez, Autobiography of La Causa;* Merritt Associates Inc. (Realtors), Larchmont, New York (p. 656; German Information Center (pp. 728, 764); Swiss Bank Corporation (p. 751); Inter Nationes (800). Picture Research by Liesel Bennett

CONTENTS

PART THREE NATIONAL OUTPUT, INCOME, AND EMPLOYMENT

PART SEVEN MARKET STRUCTURE AND ANTITRUST POLICY

PART EIGHT DISTRIBUTION OF INCOME AND GENERAL EQUILIBRIUM

PREFACE

Several aims converged in the planning and preparation of this new edition. Foremost was the need to examine the pressures exerted on economic theory by shock waves of inflation, high unemployment, and a relentless demand on the world's supply of natural resources. The turbulence that beset the domestic and international economies over the past few years has forced economists to rethink some of their favorite constructs, to modify others. A time of ferment, however, has its uses, and I have sought to give maximum exposure in this revision to the fresh thinking stimulated under stress. A second aim has been once again to take theory beyond the classroom and demonstrate how economics can be, and has been, utilized by decision makers in both the private and public sectors. With record numbers of students enrolling in the introductory course, an economics text that concentrates exclusively on principles will fail to tap the surge of new interest in the field. While economics has its share of elegant theories, I continue to believe that their elegance is enhanced, not diminished, by application to real problems of the economy.

No matter how carefully conceived and developed, a textbook requires the seasoning that only course use can give it. This volume is no exception. And so a third major concern in this edition was to respond to the reports, comments, and suggestions generously provided by teachers and students from many of the campuses where the first edition was used. I have worked hard to iron out wrinkles without singeing the fabric in the process. No page or paragraph has escaped reconsideration. While the structure and proportion of the text may not have been significantly altered, much of the content has. It almost goes without saying that extensive updating was necessary throughout in the text, tables, and diagrams. But this new edition also gave me an opportunity to clarify points and to improve over-all readability.

Such changes are not cosmetic. Though sometimes they involve only a sentence or two, often they have led to the rewriting of entire sections. In the paragraphs that follow, I provide a brief guided tour of the areas that have undergone the most substantial reworking.

First, the material on the determination of national income, fiscal policy, money, monetary policy, and the debate between the monetarists and Keynesians has been extensively rewritten, extended, and deepened. Consumption, saving, and investment now are taken up in an entirely separate chapter. The original exposition has been bolstered by the leakage-injections approach to the determination of national output, an expanded and simplified treatment of the multiplier, and new sections on the paradox of thrift and the permanent-income hypothesis. In Chapter 11, the material on fiscal policy now includes the balanced-budget multiplier, an analysis of the case where taxes are independent of NNP, and more discussion of the effects of how a deficit or surplus is financed, while in Chapter 12 a closer look is given to the accuracy of forecasting models. In Part Four, considerably more space is devoted to the demand for money, the effects of the money supply on NNP, and the discussion of monetary policy. The sections on the Keynesian-monetarist debate have been refined in the light of new empirical findings, stagflation is accorded far more attention, and the Phillips curve comes under extended and critical scrutiny.

Second, at several points in the text, aspects of theory that are relatively advanced have been shifted to chapter appendices. Specifically, *IS* and *LM* curves, though accorded a much fuller exposition, now form an appendix to Chapter 16. Practically all of the material on indifference curves, budget lines, isoquants, and isocost curves has been put in appendices to Chapters 21 and 22. The treatment of linear programming is now an appendix to Chapter 23. For those instructors who want to include these topics, this material is just as accessible as it was in the first edition. For those who do not, the current position of these topics makes them less obtrusive and they can be skipped without loss of continuity.

Third, the introductory chapters have been altered so that the student encounters many key analytical concepts in economics, and the nature of fundamental economic problems, more quickly. Chapter 1 now has major sections on resources, scarcity, choice, and opportunity costs (together with several case studies), as well as a discussion of the functions of any economic system and the major principles of economic organization. Chapter 2 now has some new material on the Industrial Revolution and a basic treatment of graphs. Chapter 3 takes up the law of increasing cost, Chapter 4 deals at greater length with price ceilings and floors, Chapter 5 has a better analysis of the effects of external economies and diseconomies, and Chapter 6 explores in greater depth tax incidence, the public debt, and alternative ways of financing government expenditures.

Fourth, the chapters on income distribution have undergone major revision. The discussion of the firm's demand for labor has been simplified, and material concerning farm workers' unions and unions of public employees has been added. The chapter on interest, rent, and profits has been extended to include sections on the present value of future income, new results on the returns from human capital, the present value of lifetime earnings in specific occupations, and the functional distribution of income. In the chapter on income inequality, a more detailed description is provided of tax loopholes, social security, and recent theories of John Rawls and others.

Fifth, formerly given brief mention, our nation's energy problems now occupy nearly half of Chapter 19. Included are substantial discussions about the Organization of Petroleum Exporting Countries, the relationship between energy and economic growth, the ways that our energy choices can affect the environment, and the shortage of natural gas. Close examination is given to policy measures that might be adopted, such as a tax on fuel, and on new energy technologies, such as oil from shale, coal gasification, and solar energy.

Sixth, the discussion of the theory of consumer behavior and the theory of the firm has been rewritten so that there is no necessity to use indifference curves or isoquants. The material on marginal utility has been expanded, while indifference curves and isoquants are now in appendices (and the latter part of Chapter 20, which can be omitted without loss of continuity).

Seventh, recent developments on the international stage have demonstrated that the United States economy cannot be examined *in vacuo*. Much of the new content in Part Nine is a direct outgrowth of these events. The treatments of terms of trade and of nontariff barriers have been made less cryptic, and the discussion of SDRs has been expanded. New sections have been added on our experience with floating exchange rates, on the interpretation of the balance of payments under a regime of floating exchange rates, on the Trade Act of 1974 and on the Tokyo Round, on U.S.-USSR technology transfers, and on the likelihood that OPEC will become a model for other less developed countries.

Eighth, many more one-page inserts have been added to provide in-depth commentaries on timely and important issues and topics. Among the new topics taken up are New York's fiscal crisis, income-tax loopholes, the stock market, international comparisons of inflation and unemployment, indexation, Cesar Chavez's farm workers union, the alleged capital crisis, misrepresentation of consumer goods, a case study of an actual monopolistically competitive firm, estate-tax loopholes, and Eurodollars. These inserts add spice to the discussion, as well as insight into important topics.

Ninth, the questions at the end of each chapter have been increased in number with greater emphasis given to problem solving. These questions should be useful both for review and examination purpose as well as bases for classroom discussion.

Since instructors differ considerably in their choice and ordering of topics, this book is organized for maximum flexibility. Many instructors take up microeconomics before macroeconomics. This book will work just as well for these instructors as for those who prefer to present macroeconomics first. (A suggested ordering of chapters is presented for them on p. XXII.) As an alternative to reversing the chapter sequence in the one-volume editions, some instructors may want to consider the two-volume paperbound version, *Principles of Microeconomics* and *Principles of Macroeconomics*, second editions.

This book can also be adapted for use in one-semester courses. Pages XXIII–XXIV present outlines for a one-semester course stressing microeconomics, a one-semester course stressing macroeconomics, and a one-semester course covering both.

As supplements to this text, I have prepared both a book of readings and a study guide containing problems and exercises. *Economics: Readings, Issues, and Cases*, second edition, provides a substantial set of supplementary articles, carefully correlated with the text for instructors who want to introduce their students to the writings of major contemporary economists. It is designed to acquaint the student with a wide range of economic analysis, spanning the spectrum from the classics to the present-day radicals. The emphasis, as in the text, is on integrating theory, measurement, and applications.

The *Study Guide*, second edition, contains, in addition to concepts, cases, and tests, a far greater percentage of problems that require the student to work with quantitative matter in applying concepts to practical situations. Each chapter now includes a completely new section on Behavioral Objectives, a number of Discussion Questions drawn from economic issues in the news, and some Extension Questions to encourage students to develop their ability to extend economic reasoning to sort out and select among alternative courses of action. Major efforts have been made to root out the less effective questions and insert ones that work better.

Finally, it is a pleasure to acknowledge the debts that I owe to the many teachers at various colleges and universities who have commented in detail on various parts of the manuscript. The first edition benefited greatly from the advice I received from the following distinguished economists, none of whom is responsible, of course, for the outcome: Bela Balassa, Johns Hopkins; Robert Baldwin, University of Wisconsin (Madison); Arthur Benavie, North Carolina; William Branson, Princeton; Martin Bronfenbrenner, Duke; Edward Budd, Penn State; Richard Cooper, Yale; F. Trenery Dolbear, Brandeis; Robert Dorfman, Harvard; James Duesenberry, Harvard; David Fand, Wayne State; Robert Gordon, Northwestern; Herschel Grossman, Brown; Albert Hirschman, Harvard; Ronald Jones, Rochester; John Kareken, Minnesota; Ann Krueger, Minnesota; Robert Kuenne, Princeton; Simon Kuznets, Harvard; Raymond Lubitz, Columbia and the Federal Reserve; Sherman Maisel, University of California (Berkeley); Thomas Mayer, University of California (Davis); Arthur Okun, Brookings Institution; Lloyd Orr, Indiana; Roger Ransom, University of California (Berkeley); Albert Rees, Princeton; Vernon Ruttan, Minnesota; David Schulze, Florida; Nicolas Spulber, Indiana; Michael Taussig, Rutgers; and Fred Westfield, Vanderbilt.

Among the teachers who contributed comments and suggestions for changes in the first edition are: Wallace Atherton, California State University at Long Beach; James Duesenberry, Harvard; Richard Easterlin, University of Pennsylvania; Judith Fernandez, University of California (Berkeley); David Gay, University of Arkansas; Howard A. Gilbert, South Dakota State University; Judy Herman, Queens College; Alan Heston, University of Pennsylvania; Ronald Jones, University of Rochester; Leonard Martin, Cleveland State University; Thomas Mayer, University of California (Davis); William McEachern, University of Connecticut; Steven Morrison, University of California (Berkeley); E. Dwight Phaup, Union College; Charles Ratliff, Davidson College; Anthony Romeo, University of Connecticut; Warren St. James, Nassau County Community College; Stephen Sacks, University of Connecticut; Allen Sanderson, William and Mary; Richard Sutch, University of California (Berkeley); Frank Tansey, City University of New York; Thomas Tidrick, Clayton Junior College; Simon Whitney, Iona College; William Whitney, University of Pennsylvania; and Harold Williams, Kent State University.

I would like to thank Elisabeth Allison of Harvard University for contributing the inserts that appear (over her initials) in various chapters, and Donald S. Lamm and Mary Shuford of W. W. Norton for their efficient handling of the editorial and publishing end of the work. As always, my wife, Lucile, has contributed an enormous amount to the completion of this book.

Philadelphia, 1977 E.M.

Outline of a One-Year Course with Macroeconomics Following Microeconomics.

1 Economic Problems, Policies, and Decisions
2 Economic Analysis: Models and Measurement
3 The American Economy: Our Mixed Capitalist System
4 The Price System: Consumers, Firms, and Markets
5 The Economic Role of the Government
6 Government Expenditures, Taxation, and the Public Debt
7 The Business Firm: Organization, Motivation, and Technology
20 Consumer Behavior and Rational Choice
21 Market Demand
22 Optimal Input Decisions and Cost Analysis
23 Optimal Output Decisions and Market Supply
24 Perfect Competition and Monopoly
25 Monopolistic Competition and Oligopoly
26 Industrial Organization and Antitrust Policy
27 Determinants of Wages
28 Interest, Rent, and Profits
29 Income Inequality, Poverty, and Discrimination
30 General Equilibrium and Welfare Economics
8 Unemployment, Inflation, and National Output
9 Consumption, Saving, and Investment
10 The Determination of National Output
11 Fiscal Policy and National Output
12 Business Fluctuations and Economic Forecasting
13 The Role and Importance of Money
14 The Banking System and the Quantity of Money
15 Monetary Policy
16 Problems of Economic Stabilization Policy
17 Economic Growth
18 American Economic Growth: History, Policies, Problems, and Prospects
19 Environmental and Energy Problems
31 International Trade
32 Exchange Rates and the Balance of Payments
33 International Finance: History, Problems, and Policies
34 The Less Developed Countries
35 The Communist Countries, Marxism, and Radical Economics

Outline of a One-Semester Course Emphasizing Microeconomics.

1 Economic Problems, Policies, and Decisions
2 Economic Analysis: Models and Measurement
3 The American Economy: Our Mixed Capitalist System
4 The Price System: Consumers, Firms, and Markets
5 The Economic Role of the Government
7 The Business Firm: Organization, Motivation, and Technology
20 Consumer Behavior and Rational Choice
21 Market Demand
22 Optimal Input Decisions and Cost Analysis
23 Optimal Output Decisions and Market Supply
24 Perfect Competition and Monopoly
25 Monopolistic Competition and Oligopoly
26 Industrial Organization and Antitrust Policy
29 Income Inequality, Poverty, and Discrimination [optional]
8 Unemployment, Inflation, and National Output
9 Consumption, Saving, and Investment
10 The Determination of National Output
11 Fiscal Policy and National Output
13 The Role and Importance of Money[1]
14 The Banking System and the Quantity of Money
15 Monetary Policy

[1] Also, assign the beginning sections of Chapter 12.

Outline of a One-Semester Course Emphasizing Macroeconomics.

1 Economic Problems, Policies, and Decisions
2 Economic Analysis: Models and Measurement
3 The American Economy: Our Mixed Capitalist System
4 The Price System: Consumers, Firms, and Markets
5 The Economic Role of the Government
6 Government Expenditures, Taxation, and the Public Debt
7 The Business Firm: Organization, Motivation, and Technology
8 Unemployment, Inflation, and National Output
9 Consumption, Saving, and Investment
10 The Determination of National Output
11 Fiscal Policy and National Output
12 Business Fluctuations and Economic Forecasting
13 The Role and Importance of Money
14 The Banking System and the Quantity of Money
15 Monetary Policy
16 Problems of Economic Stabilization Policy
17 Economic Growth
18 American Economic Growth: History, Policies, Problems, and Prospects
31 International Trade
32 Exchange Rates and the Balance of Payments
34 The Less Developed Countries

Outline of a One-Semester Course Emphasizing Both Macroeconomics and Microeconomics.

1 Economic Problems, Policies, and Decisions
2 Economic Analysis: Models and Measurement
3 The American Economy: Our Mixed Capitalist System
4 The Price System: Consumers, Firms, and Markets
5 The Economic Role of the Government
6 Government Expenditures, Taxation, and the Public Debt
7 The Business Firm: Organization, Motivation, and Technology
8 Unemployment, Inflation, and National Output
9 Consumption, Saving, and Investment
10 The Determination of National Output
11 Fiscal Policy and National Output
12 Business Fluctuations and Economic Forecasting
13 The Role and Importance of Money
14 The Banking System and the Quantity of Money
15 Monetary Policy
16 Problems of Economic Stabilization Policy
20 Consumer Behavior and Rational Choice
21 Market Demand
22 Optimal Input Decisions and Cost Analysis
23 Optimal Output Decisions and Market Supply
29 Income Inequality, Poverty, and Discrimination

PART ONE

Introduction to Economics

1 Economic Problems, Policies, and Decisions

A French sage had a point when he said, "I finally know what distinguishes man from the other beasts: economic worries." Rich people, poor people, beggars, and kings: all have economic worries, though not of equal degree. And so do all the nations of the world. This is the nature of the human condition—and the basic reason why economics enters into a vast array of everyday activities, and plays an important role in the solution of national problems. Perhaps the best way to get an idea of what economics is all about is to look at some of the problems it can help solve. In these opening pages you will encounter six fairly typical economic problems. Although this is only a small sample, it is designed to give you a reasonable first impression of how the study of economics bears directly on the real world.

Economic Problems: A Sampler

Unemployment and Inflation

The history of the American economy is for the most part a story of growth. Our output—the amount of goods and services we produce annually—has grown rapidly over the years, giving us a standard of living that could not have been imagined a century ago. For example, output per person in the United States was about \$7,000 in 1975; in 1909 it was about \$1,840. Nonetheless, the growth of output has not been steady or uninterrupted; instead, our output has tended to fluctuate—and so has unemployment. In periods when output has fallen, thousands, even millions, of people have been thrown out of work. In the Great Depression of the 1930s, for example, over 20 percent of the labor force was unemployed (see Figure 1.1). Unemployment on this scale results in enormous economic waste and social misery.

The first of our sample of economic problems is: *What determines the extent of unemployment in the American economy, and what can be done to reduce it?* This problem is complicated by a related phenomenon: the level of prices may rise when we reduce the level of unemployment. In other words, inflation may occur. Thus, the problem is not only to curb unemployment, but to do this without producing an inflation so ruinous to the nation's economic health that the cure proves more dangerous than the ailment. As Figure 1.2 shows, we have experienced considerable inflation since 1929; the dollar has lost about ¾ of its purchasing power during this period. Moreover, in the 1970s, our economy has been bedeviled by "stagflation"—that is, a combination of high unemployment and high inflation.

During the past 50 years, economists have learned a great deal about the factors that determine the extent of unemployment. Since, contrary to earlier opinion, our economy has no automatic regulator that keeps it moving quickly and dependably toward minimal unemployment with stable prices, the American people, as well as people in other lands, have given their government the responsibility of promoting conditions favoring a high level of employment without serious inflation. Economists have developed useful techniques to help the government do this job. In particular, they have shown how government can use its control over the money supply and interest rates, as well as its power to spend and tax, to pro-

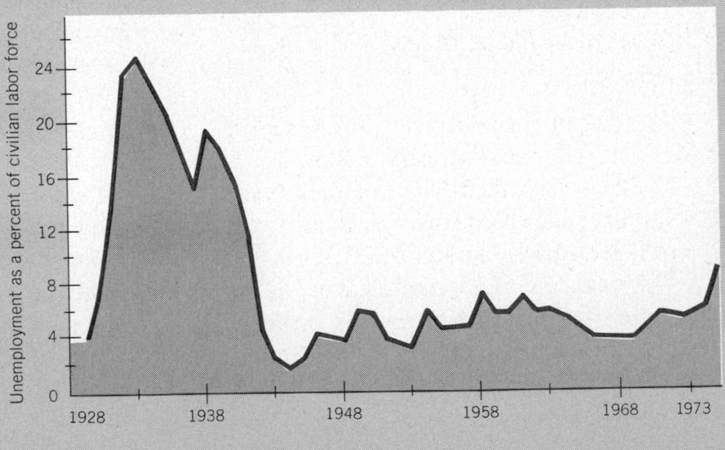

Figure 1.1
Unemployment Rates, United States, 1929–75
The unemployment rate has varied substantially from year to year. In the Great Depression, it reached a high of about 25 percent. In 1975, it rose to 8½ percent.

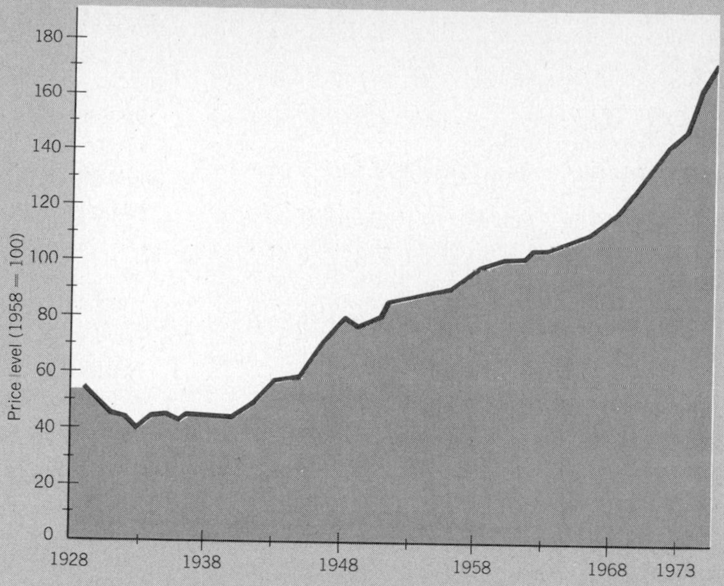

Figure 1.2
Changes in Price Level, United States, 1929–75
The price level has increased steadily since the 1930s, and is now about four times as high as it was in 1935.

mote high employment with reasonably stable prices. As a responsible citizen, you must be interested in this matter. To judge how well Congress and the president are doing their jobs, and to determine how you should vote, you must know what the government can do to reduce unemployment and how much it is doing. Also, to understand the fallacies in many apparently simple remedies for the complex economic problems in this area, you need to know some economics.

Government Regulation of Business

The 100 largest manufacturing firms control about ½ of all manufacturing assets in the United States (and their share of total assets seems to have increased since World War II). In certain industries, like automobiles, the four largest firms account for over 90 percent of the market (see Table 1.1). Nonetheless, although the large corporations obviously wield considerable power in their markets, the American economic system is built on the idea that firms should compete with one another. In particular, the producers of steel, automobiles, oil, toothpicks, and other goods are expected to set their prices independently and not to collude. Certain acts of Congress, often referred to as the antitrust laws, make it illegal for firms to get together and set the price of a product.

Our second example of an economic problem is: *Why is competition of this sort socially desirable?* More specifically, why should we be in favor of the antitrust laws? What reasons are there to believe that such laws will result in a more efficient economic system? (And what do we mean by "efficient"?) To a business executive, lawyer, government official, or judge, these questions are very important, since it is likely that at one time or another these people will be concerned with an antitrust case. But these issues also matter to every citizen, because they deal with the basic rules of the game for firms in our economy. Of course, one reason why Americans have traditionally favored competition over collusion, and relatively

Table 1.1
Market Share of Four Largest Firms, Selected Manufacturing Product Markets, United States, 1972.

Industry	Market share of four largest firms (percent)
Automobiles	93
Cigarettes	84
Soap	62
Tires	73
Aircraft	66
Metal cans	66
Blast furnaces and steel plants	45

Source: Statistical Abstract of the United States.

small firms over giant ones, is that they have mistrusted the concentration of economic power, and obviously, this mistrust was based on both political and economic considerations. But beyond this, you should know when competition generally benefits society, and when it does not.

One way that society has attempted to control the economic power of corporations that dominate an entire industry is through public regulation. Take the case of radio and TV. The Federal Communications Commission, a government agency, monitors the activities of broadcasting stations and networks to prevent misuse of the airwaves. Other regulatory commissions supervise the activities of the power companies, the airlines, the railroads, and other industries where it is felt that competition cannot be relied on to produce socially desirable results.

The regulatory commissions and the principles they use are currently a subject of tremendous controversy. Many observers feel that they tend to be lax, or, worse still, to be captured by the industries they are supposed to regulate. Since these regulated industries produce about 10 percent of national income, we all have a big stake in understanding how they operate and whether they are being regulated properly. This is another aspect of the same general problem of how industries should be organized.

The Elimination of Poverty

As pointed out by Philip Wicksteed, a prominent twentieth-century British economist, "A man can be neither a saint, nor a lover, nor a poet, unless he has comparatively recently had something to eat." Although relatively few people in the United States lack food desperately, about 25 million American people, about 12 percent of the population of the United States, live in what is officially designated as poverty. These people have frequently been called invisible in a nation where the average yearly income per person is about $7,000; but the poor are invisible only to those who shut their eyes, since they exist in ghettos in the wealthiest American cities like New York, Chicago, and Los Angeles, as well as near Main Street in thousands of small towns. They can also be found in areas where industry has come and gone, as in the former coal-mining towns of Pennsylvania and West Virginia, and in areas where decades of farming have depleted the soil.

Table 1.2 shows the distribution of income in the United States in 1974. Clearly, there are very substantial differences among families in income level. Indeed, the cats and dogs of the very rich eat better than some human beings. You as a citizen and a human being need to understand the social mechanisms underlying the distribution of income, both in the United States and in other countries, and how reasonable and just they are. Our third economic problem is: *Why does poverty exist in the world today, and what can be done to abolish it?* To help the poor effectively, we must understand

Table 1.2
Percentage Distribution of Families, by Income, United States, 1974.

Money income (dollars)	Percent of all families
Under 2,000	3
2,000– 3,999	6
4,000– 6,999	13
7,000– 9,999	14
10,000–14,999	24
15,000–24,999	28
25,000 and over	12
Total	100

Source: Statistical Abstract of the United States.

the causes of poverty. Does it make sense, for example, to pour billions of dollars into programs often denounced by politicians and even the recipients themselves as a "welfare mess"?

Since poverty is intimately bound up with our racial problems and the decay of our cities, the success or failure of measures designed to eradicate poverty may also help us determine whether we can achieve a society where equality of opportunity is more than a slogan and where people do not have to escape to the suburbs to enjoy green space and fresh air. Nor does the economist's concern with poverty stop at our shoreline. One of the biggest problems of the world today is the plight of the poor countries of Asia, Africa, and Latin America—the so-called less developed countries. The industrialized countries of the world, like the United States, Western Europe, Japan, and the Soviet Union, are really just rich little islands surrounded by seas of poverty. Over two billion people live in countries where income per person is less than $750 per year. These countries lack equipment, technology, and education; sometimes (but by no means always) they also suffer from overpopulation. Economists have devoted considerable attention to the problems of the less developed countries, and to developing techniques to assist them.

Pollution and Energy Problems

The poor seem always to be with us; and in our industrialized world, so too is pollution. For many years, people in the United States paid relatively little attention to the environment and what they were doing to it, but this attitude has changed markedly in the past decade. Now the public is really concerned about environmental pollution.

You may have seen the considerable air pollution in Los Angeles, New York, or many other cities. Chances are that a river near you is no longer fit for swimming or an abundant fish life, even if it is not as badly polluted as Cleveland's Cuyahoga, which was so full of wastes that it literally caught fire in 1969. In response to the pollution problem, the government and interested groups of private citizens are trying to control pollution, whether from auto exhausts, combustion of fossil fuels, solid-waste disposal, or the noise of sirens and jackhammers. But this is a difficult task, not unlike the job performed by Hercules in the Augean stables.

Besides pollution, another problem we face is concerned with energy. In early 1974, the major oil-exporting countries in the Middle East, Africa, and South America raised the price of crude oil very sharply, helping to increase inflation here and transferring tens of billions of dollars from the oil-consuming nations to the oil-exporting nations. The American people have become increasingly uneasy about their growing dependence on foreign oil. Some observers, rightly or wrongly, believe that we must reduce our current rate of energy consumption. Our energy and environmental problems are intertwined. Many suggested solutions to our energy problems would result in further environmental deterioration; many suggested solutions to our environmental problems would make our energy problems worse.

Our fourth example of an economic problem is: *What causes environmental pollution, and how can we reduce it to the proper levels? What is the nature of our energy problems, and how can they be resolved?* Economists have devoted substantial attention to questions like these in recent years. Of course, these questions entail technological considerations as well as purely economic ones. For example, in dealing with our energy problems, one must know something about the costs of producing electricity in nuclear plants and the possible hazards involved. But technological considerations are not the only ones. To a considerable extent, our environmental and energy problems are economic problems—and economics must play an important role in any attempted solution.

The Planned Economies and East-West Relations

Roughly ⅓ of the world's people live and work under a set of economic rules quite different from ours. The object of the game—achieving material prosperity and living the good life—may be broadly similar, but differences in how it is played account for a distinct cleavage between Communist and capitalist countries. Some of these differences can be spotted at once. For example, the steel mills of the Soviet Union are owned and operated by the government, whereas the steel mills of Gary, Indiana, or Pittsburgh belong to private corporations. Under the Communist system, the productive activities of a country are planned by a small group of bureaucrats in government ministries. In the capitalist world, industrial decision making is dispersed among many firms, each sizing up the demand for its products and choosing its own methods of production.

For many years, there has been intense economic, political, and ideological rivalry between the West and the Communist countries. During the 1970s, the United States, as part of its policy of *détente* with the Soviet Union, began to increase its trade with the Soviets. Particularly in fields of advanced technology such as electronics, the United States entered into a number of cooperative programs with the Soviet Union, the purpose being to share and exchange technological information. Many American firms and government agencies have taken part in this program, which has been an important aspect of East-West relations in the 1970s.

Our fifth example of an economic problem is: *How do the economic systems of the Communist countries work? Have they been performing as well as our economic system in recent years? What are the potential costs of greater technological and economic cooperation with the Soviets? What are the potential benefits?* Economics helps you to understand the differences between Communism and capitalism, and the relationships between them. Economists, here and in the Communist countries, have devoted considerable time and effort to studying each other's economic systems, in the process laying to rest many pernicious myths. This is all to the good, because sensible dealings with other nations must rest on fact, not myth. It will be a long time before the tensions between the Communist and capitalist blocs are eliminated, but a realistic understanding of the Communist systems is bound to promote the chances of harmonious international relations.

Organizational Efficiency

The problems discussed in previous sections are problems that concern our entire society. Obviously, they merit study by economists. But much of economics deals with narrower problems, such as the operations of the business firm. Consider, for example, the cost calculations that must be made by the management of Continental Air Lines to determine how many flights to run between Houston and Los Angeles. Or take the case of the International Business Machines Corporation (IBM), which must decide how to make, market, and price its next generation of electronic computers. These firms face very difficult problems, often involving millions of dollars. It is important, both to the firms themselves and to society at large, that they make the best decisions possible.

This is our sixth example of an economic problem: *How should a firm decide what to produce, how much to produce, and how to produce it?* Economics can give you tools that will help you solve such managerial problems, whatever sort of career you choose. For example, one large newsprint company with six mills in Canada and two hundred customers in various parts of the United States had to decide how much newsprint to ship from each mill to each customer. The sorts of economic techniques described in subsequent chapters enabled it to find the optimal solution. Moreover, many of these principles and tools are just as applicable in government as in business. For example, they have been used to determine whether programs designed to reduce the dropout rates in high schools are worth the amounts spent on them, and whether a government dam should be built at one site or another.

What Is Economics?

Resources, Scarcity, and Choice

Now that we have looked at a number of specific economic problems, we are in a position to set forth and probe the following basic definition: *economics is concerned with the way resources are allocated among alternative uses to satisfy human wants.* This definition will help get you oriented, but to understand it fully, you must know what resources are, why they are scarce and how choices are made as to their use and allocation.

To economists, a ***resource*** is a material or service used to produce goods or services that can be used to satisfy human wants. For present purposes, all that we want to emphasize about resources is that for the most part, they are scarce. No matter how rich any society may be, it has only a limited amount of resources. Even the United States, which is clearly among the richest of nations, has only a finite amount of resources. Not all resources are scarce: ***Free resources,*** such as air, are so abundant that they can be obtained without charge. But the number of free resources is actually quite limited. For instance, although the earth contains a huge amount of water, it is not a free resource to the typical urban or suburban homeowner, who must pay a local water authority for providing and maintaining his water supply. Despite the reassuring lyrics of the old ballad, "The Best Things In Life Are Free," a great many resources are not free at all.

Those resources that are scarce are called ***economic resources.*** The test of whether a resource is an economic resource or a free resource is price: economic resources command a nonzero price but free resources do not. Economists often classify economic resources into three categories: ***land, labor,*** and ***capital.***

Land. A shorthand expression for natural resources, land includes minerals, as well as plots of ground. Clearly, land is an important and valuable resource in both agriculture and industry. In addition, it is a major part of our environment, and it provides enjoyment above and beyond its contribution to agricultural and industrial output.

Labor. Human efforts, both physical and mental, are included in the category of labor. Thus, when you study for a final examination or make out an income tax return, this is as much labor as if you were to dig a ditch. The available supply of labor is, of course, an important resource in any society.

Capital. Buildings, equipment, inventories, and other nonhuman producible resources that contribute to the production, marketing, and distribution of goods and services all fall within the economist's definition of capital. Examples of capital are blast furnaces, oil refineries, machine tools, and warehouses. But not all types of capital are big or bulky. For example, a hand calculator, or a pencil for that matter, is a type of capital.

The amount of goods and services that can be obtained from the amount of resources at hand is dependent upon the existing technology. ***Technology*** is society's pool of knowledge concerning the industrial arts. It includes knowledge, needed in industry, of the principles of social and physical phenomena (such as the laws of motion and the properties of fluids); knowledge regarding the application of these principles to production (such as applying various aspects of genetic theory to the breeding of new plants); and knowledge regarding the day-to-day operation of productive processes (such as the rules of thumb of the skilled craftsman). Note that technology is different from the techniques in use, since not all that is known is likely to be applied. Also, technology is different from pure science, although the distinction is not very precise. Pure science is directed toward understanding, whereas technology is directed toward use.

Given the existing technology, the fact that resources are scarce means that only a limited amount of goods and services can be produced from them. In other words, the capacity to produce goods and services is limited—*far more limited than human wants.* ***Human wants*** are the goods, services, and circumstances people desire. Wants vary greatly among individuals, and, for a given individual, they vary greatly over time. Some people like to ride horseback, others like to read. Some want to carouse until 3:00 A.M.; others follow Ben Franklin's maxim of early to bed, early to rise. For present purposes, the important thing to note about human wants is that they seem to be insatiable in the aggregate (even though an individual's desire for a particular good in a particular period of time is not infinite). In part, this is because wants arise from cultural factors—advertising, social pressures, education, and emulation of other people—as well as the basic human drives for food, shelter, and clothing. In other words, people's wants tend to increase and multiply as they see ads for products that look attractive, and as they hear about and come into contact with affluent people. Although many people claim to prefer the simple life, it often turns out they mean a steak fixed simply in a simple $80,000 split-level house in the suburbs.

Since the amount of goods and services that can be produced is less than what is wanted, there arises the necessity for ***choice.*** Somehow or other, a choice must be made as to how the available resources will be used (or if they will be used at all). Somehow or other, a choice must be made as to how the output produced from these resources will be distributed among the population. Economics is concerned with how such choices are made. Economists have spent a great deal of time, energy, and talent (their own and other peoples') trying to determine how such choices *are* made in various circumstances, and how they *should* be made. Indeed, as we shall see in the next section, the basic questions that economics deals with are problems of choice of this sort. Note that these problems of choice go beyond the problems of particular individuals in choosing how to allocate their own resources; they are problems of social choice.

Central Questions in Economics

Economists are particularly concerned with four basic questions regarding the working of any economic system—ours or any other. These questions are: (1) What determines what is produced? (2) What determines how it is produced? (3) What determines how the society's output is distributed among the members? (4) What determines the rate at which the society's productive capacity will grow? These questions lie at the core of economics, because they are directed at the most fundamental characteristics of economic systems.

To illustrate the nature and basic importance of these questions, suppose that, because of war or natural catastrophe, your town is isolated from the adjoining territory. No longer is it possible for the town's inhabitants to leave, or for people or goods to enter. (Lest you regard this as fanciful, it is perhaps worthwhile to note that Leningrad was under siege in World War II for over two years.) In this situation, you and your fellow townspeople must somehow resolve each of these questions. You must decide what goods and services will be produced, how each will be produced, who will receive what, and how much provision there will be for increased output in the future.

In a situation of this sort, your very survival will depend on how effectively you answer these questions. If a decision is made to produce too much clothing and too little food, some of the townspeople may starve. If a decision is made to produce wheat from soil that is inappropriate for wheat, but excellent for potatoes, much the same result may occur. If a decision is made to allot practically all of the town's output to friends and political cronies of the mayor, those who oppose him may have a very rough time. And if a decision is made to eat, drink, and be merry today, and not to worry about tomorrow, life may be very meager in the days ahead.

Because we are considering a relatively small and isolated population, the importance of these questions may seem more obvious than in a huge country like the United States, which is constantly communicating, trading, and interacting with the rest of the world. But the truth is that these questions are every bit as important to the United States as to the isolated town. And, for this reason, it is important that we understand how these decisions are made, and whether they are being made effectively. Just as in the hypothetical case of the isolated town, your survival depends on these decisions—but in the United States the situation isn't hypothetical!

Three Basic Principles of Economic Organization

Based on their studies of how various societies have gone about answering these four basic questions, economists have found that the methods used fall into three categories—tradition, command, and the price system. Throughout all history, societies have relied on one of these three methods (or some mixture of them) to answer the basic economic questions. In view of the fact that human ingenuity seems to have been able to construct only these three methods, it is worthwhile describing each of them briefly.

Tradition. For much of recorded time, tradition was the basic principle of economic organization. A host of procedures, inherited from the far distant past and frequently hallowed by religion and enforced by law, guided the behavior of individuals and groups. For example, in ancient societies, sons frequently followed the occupations of their fathers. You were born into a particular station in life, and tradition dictated that you stayed in that station. In India, such a caste system remained in existence until quite recently. In many parts of the world, tradition continues to play a major role in determining how the economic system functions. Tradition is a particularly important determinant of economic behavior in many of the less developed countries.

Command. Throughout human history, various kinds of political authorities have imposed their will on society to determine how the basic economic questions would be answered. In ancient times, the Roman emperors decreed that the economic system would respond in particular ways to their desires. In modern times, the governments of China and the Soviet Union have brought about radical changes in the economic order. In the Soviet Union, for example, the government has pushed industrialization at a rapid pace, and has tried hard to catch up with the West. In every economy, the basic economic questions are answered to some extent by command, but in a democratic society the commands are in accord with, and in response to, majority opinion.

Price system. Of the three basic ways to organize an economy, the price system is in many respects the most difficult to understand; and for that reason we shall devote considerable attention to the price system in subsequent chapters. At this point, it is sufficient to point out that, under the price system, consumers are free to buy what they please, firms are free to sell what they please, and resource owners are free to use them as they please. Under the price system, the four basic economic questions are answered through the working of free markets.

It is worth emphasizing that the United States relies on a combination of all three of these methods. Tradition unquestionably plays a role, although less than in many other societies. For example, some families, like the Adamses or Kennedys, have had a tradition of going into public service; and others, like the Pattons, have gone into the military. Command plays a major role too. For example, the government decides how much is spent on defense. (As we shall see in subsequent chapters, the government intervenes in our economic affairs in myriad ways, often to the applause of liberals and the consternation of conservatives.) And although it is not allowed to operate unfettered, the price system plays a central role in our economy. Thus, even though our economy relies more heavily on the price system than many other economies do, command and (to some extent) tradition are also important.

The Basic Problem of Choice

In a previous section, we illustrated the nature of the basic economic questions by taking up the case of a town that is isolated from the adjoining territory, because of a war or natural catastrophe. To show some essential elements of any problem of choice, let's return to this illustration. Suppose that you are a member of the town council that is organized to determine how the town's resources should be utilized. To keep things simple, suppose that only two goods—food and clothing—can be produced. (This is an innocuous assumption that allows us to strip the problem to its essentials.) You must somehow figure out how much of each good should be produced. How can you go about solving this problem?

Clearly, the first step toward a solution is to list the various resources contained within the town. Using the technology available to the townspeople, each of these resources can be used to produce either food or clothing. Some of these resources are much more effective at producing one good than the other. For example, a tailor probably is better able to produce clothing than to produce food. But nonetheless most resources can be adapted to produce either good. For example, the tailor can be put to work on a farm, even though he may not be very good at farming.

After listing the various available resources and having determined how effective each is at producing food or clothing, the next step is to see how much food the town could produce per year, if it produced nothing but food, and how much clothing it could produce per year, if it produced nothing but clothing. Also, you should determine, if various amounts of food are produced per year, the maximum amount of clothing that the town can produce per year. For example, if the town produces 100 tons of food per year, what is the maximum amount of clothing it can produce per year? If the town produces 200 tons of food per year, what is the maximum amount of clothing it can produce per year? And so on.

Having carried out this step, suppose that the results are as shown in Table 1.3. According to this table, the town can produce (at most) 200 tons of clothing per year if it produces nothing but clothing. It can produce (at most) 180 tons of clothing per year if it produces 100 tons of food per year. It can produce (at most) 150 tons of clothing per year, if it produces 200 tons of food per year. It can produce (at most) 100 tons of clothing per year, if it produces 300 tons of food per year. And it can produce (at most) 400 tons of food per year, if it produces no clothing at all. (These five possible combinations of food output and clothing output are labeled *A* to *E* in Table 1.3.)

The data in Table 1.3 put in bold relief the basic problem of choice facing you and the other members of the town council. Because the town's resources are limited, the town can only produce limited amounts of each good. There is no way, for example, that the town can produce 200 tons of clothing per year and 200 tons of food per year. This is beyond the capacity of the town's resources. If the town wants to produce 200 tons of clothing, it can produce no food—which is hardly a pleasant prospect. And if the town wants to produce 200 tons of food, it can produce 150 (not 200) tons of clothing per year. Table 1.3 shows what combinations of food and clothing outputs are attainable.

A very important fact illustrated by Table 1.3 is that, whenever the town increases its production of one good, it must cut back its production of the other good. For example, if the town increases its production of food from 100 to 200 tons per year, it must cut back its production of clothing from 180 to 150 tons per year. Thus, in a very real sense, *the cost to the town of increasing its food output from 100 to 200 tons per year is that it must reduce its clothing output from 180 to 150 tons per year.*

Table 1.3
Combinations of Output of Food and Clothing That the Town Can Produce Per Year.

Possibility	Amount of food produced per year (tons)	Amount of clothing produced per year (tons)
A	0	200
B	100	180
C	200	150
D	300	100
E	400	0

Economists refer to this cost as ***alternative cost***; it is one of the most fundamental concepts in economics. *The alternative cost of using resources in a certain way is the value of what these resources could have produced if they had been used in the best alternative way.* In this case, the alternative cost of the extra 100 tons of food per year is the 30 tons of clothing per year that must be given up.

Finally, based on the data in Table 1.3, you and the other members of the town council must determine which combination of food and clothing output is best. To come to a conclusion on this score, you must decide, explicitly or implicitly, the relative importance—that is, the relative value to the townspeople—of food and clothing. In other words, you must decide at what point an increase in the output of one good is no longer worth what it costs in terms of reduced output of the other good. For example, the town council may agree that it is worthwhile to increase food output from 100 to 200 tons per year, because the extra 100 tons of food is worth more to the town's welfare than the 30 tons of clothing that is given up. But the town council may feel that it is unwise to increase food output beyond this point (from 200 to 300 tons per year), because the extra 100 tons of food is not worth as much to the town's welfare as the 50 tons of clothing that is given up by doing so.

On Parks and Schooling: Applications of Alternative Costs

As an example of the application of the concept of alternative costs to contemporary social issues, consider a case where a bill is presented to Congress to set aside certain wilderness areas as national parks. At first glance, it may appear that such a step entails no cost to society, since the land is not being utilized and the resources required to designate the areas as national parks are trivial. But using the concept of alternative cost, it is clear that this step may have very substantial costs to society. For instance, if these lands are made part of the national park system, the minerals, timber, and other natural resources contained within the areas cannot be extracted nor can the lands be used as sites for factories or processing plants. As pointed out in the previous section, the alternative cost of using resources in one way is the value of what these resources could have produced had they been used in the best alternative way. Suppose that if these lands are not turned into national parks, their most valuable alternative use is for development of copper mines which would produce benefits amounting to $25 million per year to the society. Then the actual cost to society of using these lands and parks is $25 million per year, since this is the amount that society is giving up when it uses them in this way (rather than selecting the most valuable alternative). Thus, whether these lands should be used as parks depends on whether the society believes that it is worth $25 million or more to do so.

Besides being applicable to social issues, the concept of alternative cost has direct relevance to the decision-making process of private citizens. For example, consider the case of a student who must decide whether or not a college education is worth its cost. In making this decision, the student should recognize that the true cost of going to college is considerably in excess of the out-of-pocket expenses because one can obtain wages by working rather than attending classes and studying. In other words, the time spent in school has alternative costs, since it could be devoted to a job rather than to education. For the sake of concreteness, let's assume that the student could earn $5,000 during each school year if he or she works rather than goes to college. Also, let's assume that the student goes to a college where the annual tuition and fees equal $2,500, and additional expenses amount to $2,000. Under these rather arbitrary assumptions (which may be quite different from your own situation), Table 1.4 shows that the total annual cost—including the alternative cost of the student's time—of a college education amounts to $9,500. This, of course, is much higher than the annual out-of-pocket cost which is $4,500. Whether or not the cost is worthwhile depends on how much the student's subsequent earnings will be raised by a college diploma—and how much enjoyment he or she will get from the experience at college and the knowledge obtained there.

Table 1.4
Annual Cost (dollars) to the Student of a College Education: A Hypothetical Case

Out-of-pocket costs:	
Tuition and fees	2,500
Books, travel, and other expenses	2,000
Alternative cost of student's time	5,000
Total	9,500

Note: These figures vary greatly from college to college and from individual to individual. Also, the "other expenses" cited in the second line include living expenses in excess of those which would have been incurred whether or not the student went to college.

In recent years, economists have carried out a number of important studies concerned with actual policy making in fields such as conservation of natural resources and education, often utilizing the concept of alternative costs in the process. This may come as a surprise to many who assume that economics deals only with subjects that are closely related to the market place.

Some Important Characteristics of Economic Problems

As stressed in previous sections, economic problems generally involve choice. Several common threads often characterize these problems of choice.

Forecasting. To choose among a number of feasible solutions to an economic problem, it frequently is necessary to forecast what will occur if each solution is adopted. This emphasis on the future necessarily entails some uncertainty. For example, in a period of substantial unemployment, the government can reduce the extent of unemployment in a variety of ways: it can reduce taxes, increase its expenditures, or increase the amount of money in circulation, among other methods. Which measure is best depends on the magnitude and nature of the effects of each one, which must be forecasted. Unfortunately, economic forecasting is by no means an exact science, but there is no way to avoid making such forecasts. One way or another, a choice will be made, and any choice involves a forecast, explicit or implicit. Each year, thousands of studies are carried out by economists in an effort to improve their ability to forecast various phenomena. Judging by the available evidence, these efforts have been paying off, and economic forecasting has become increasingly reliable. However, it would be foolish to claim that forecasts of this sort are anything other than rough guides to the future.

Role of Government. Many economic problems involve choices concerning the role of government in economic affairs. Consider the problem of stemming inflation. Should the government impose wage and price controls, or should the government leave prices and wages to private bargaining and markets? Or, how much government intervention to reduce pollution should be accepted? Should the Environmental Protection Agency be given the power to impose regulations of various kinds on the extent to which any firm or individual can pollute the environment, or should we allow firms and individuals to make these decisions themselves?

Turn to a different area: the antitrust laws, which are designed to stimulate and preserve competition and to discourage monopoly. In the Von's Grocery case of 1965, the Supreme Court disallowed a merger between two supermarkets that together had less than 8 percent of the Los Angeles market. Is this carrying government intervention too far? Or consider the regulation of natural gas prices by the Federal Power Commission. When it instructed the Commission to regulate these prices, the Supreme Court said that the producers of natural gas had appreciable power over the market; but there are thousands of natural gas producers, and many observers believe that the industry is highly competitive. Is governmental regulation of this sort justified?

Interdependence. Many economic problems cannot be considered in isolation, because attempts to solve one problem may worsen another problem. For example, measures designed to reduce the rate of inflation may increase unemployment, unless the government is very careful. Similarly, stepping up the rate of increase of national output may also increase environmental pollution, and attempts to reduce pollution may worsen the poverty problem, because the antipollution programs may hurt the poor more than the rich. Needless to say, an attempt to solve a particular problem does not always aggravate another problem. However, since it *may* make another problem worse, we must determine its side effects before we act.

Economics in Action

The Role of Economics in Public Policy

The problems we have touched on in this chapter are only a sample of the ways economics affects your life as a citizen, administrator, worker, investor, or consumer. But even this small sample makes it clear that some economic problems are problems facing our entire society. For example, avoiding excessive unemployment is not a task that can be assigned to a particular individual, family, or firm. It requires the concerted effort of our entire society. In other words, it is a problem of public policy—a problem that is considered and debated in the political arena. As citizens, we are all entitled to take part in making public policy—and we are all affected by the policies adopted.

Economics, and economists, play an extremely important role in the formulation of public policy. Skim through the articles in a daily newspaper. Chances are that you will find a report of an economist testifying before Congress, perhaps on the costs and benefits of a program to reduce unemployment among black teenagers in the Bedford-Stuyvesant area of New York City, or on the steps that can be taken to make American goods more competitive with those produced by Japan or West Germany. Still another economist may crop up on the sports page, arguing that professional athletes should be allowed to sell their talents to any team, not merely the team that has acquired the right to negotiate with them through a players' draft.

Economics and economists play a key role at the highest levels of our government. The president, whether Democrat or Republican, relies heavily on his economic advisers in making the decisions that help to shape the future of the country. Like his predecessors in the White House, President Carter works closely and continually with his economic advisers, some of whom were involved in his successful campaign for the presidency in 1976. In addition, economics plays a very important role in the decisions made by individual government agencies. For example, the Energy Research and Development Administration (ERDA) is charged with the responsibility of devising a program of research and development to help us overcome our energy problems. To carry out this responsibility, ERDA must take careful account of economic factors, and use economic techniques to allocate its multi-billion-dollar budget efficiently.

In the Congress, too, economics plays a major role. Economists are frequent witnesses before congressional committees, staff members for the committees, and advisers to individual congressmen and senators. Many congressional committees focus largely on economic matters. For example, some, including the powerful Ways and Means Committee of the House of Representatives, deal with taxes. In recent years, tax reform has been a hot subject, as the public has clamored for the reduction of various loopholes in the tax laws. (These loopholes frequently favor the rich at the expense of the poor.) The Congress also decides how much the government will spend each year on various programs. There is frequently considerable politicking over the size and distribution of government expenditures. For example, in 1976, many congressmen fought hard against President Ford's attempt to keep a tight lid on government spending, and there was considerable debate over the adequacy of the amounts allotted for antipoverty, health, and educational programs.

Finally, perhaps the most dramatic evidence of the importance of economics in the formulation of public policy is provided during presidential elections, when each candidate—with his or her own cadre of economic advisers supplying ideas and reports—stakes out a position on the major economic issues of the day. This position can be of crucial importance in determining victory or defeat, and you, the citizen, must know some economics to understand whether a candidate is talking sense or nonsense (or merely evading an issue). For example, if a candidate promises to increase government expenditures, lower taxes, and reduce the federal deficit, you can be pretty certain that he is talking through his hat. This may not be obvious to you now, but it should be later on.

The Role of Economics in Private Decision Making

Not all economic problems affect all, or even a major part, of our society: some affect a particular individual, household, or firm, and are largely a matter of private decision making. Because these problems tend to be narrow and localized, they are sometimes viewed as less important or interesting than those involving public policy. But this is not the case. If individuals, households, and firms do a reasonably good job of solving their own problems, many social problems are solved automatically. Moreover, most of us spend most of our lives wrestling with these narrower questions. Thus we all have an interest in learning how to cope better with them.

Economics and economists play an extremely important role in private decision making. Their role in the decision-making process in business firms is particularly great, since many of the nation's business executives have studied economics in college or in postgraduate programs, and many of the nation's larger corporations hire professional economists to forecast their sales, reduce their costs, increase their efficiency, negotiate with labor and government, and carry out a host of other tasks. Judging from the fancy salaries business economists are paid, the firms seem to think they can deliver the goods; and in fact the available evidence seems to indicate that they do provide important guidance to firms in many areas of their operations.

As an illustration, consider the Magnavox Company, a major manufacturer of television sets. In 1971, Magnavox's president, Robert Platt, decided to move slowly in converting Magnavox's TV sets from electron tubes to all solid-state sets, because he did not believe that the solid-state sets would catch on quickly with the public, and because he wanted to wait until an improved picture tube was available in 1973 before making the transition. This was a mistake. Consumers rushed to buy the solid-state sets, and Magnavox's sales fell to $226 million in 1972, down 36 percent from their peak in 1968. Economics is concerned with decisions of this sort, and although it cannot insure success or prevent mistakes, it can shed important light on the way such decisions should be made.

Finally, economics and economists influence the decision making of households as well as firms. Few households—other, perhaps, than the Rockefellers and the Gettys—can afford to hire their own professional economist, but this does not mean that many households do not receive and use a considerable amount of economic advice. On the contrary, most households take magazines and newspapers that contain a great deal of economic information. The *Wall Street Journal* is packed with it; so are the financial pages of the *New York Times* and other leading newspapers. Even a general news magazine like *Time* now has a board of economic advisers—and puts an economist on its cover from time to time. (*Newsweek*, its competitor, features columns by economists.) Based on information provided in such publications, households can make more informed decisions on their investments and expenditures. Through this channel, among others, economics can play a major role in their decision making.

Summary

Economics helps you to understand the nature and organization of our society (and other societies), the arguments underlying many of the great public issues of the day, and the operation and behavior of business firms and other economic decision-making units. It is no exaggeration to say that everyone must know something about economics to function responsibly and effectively as a citizen, administrator, worker, or consumer.

According to one standard definition, economics is concerned with the way resources are allocated among alternative uses to satisfy human wants. A resource is a material or service used to produce goods or services. Not all resources are scarce. Free resources, such as air, are so abundant that they can be obtained without charge. Those resources that are scarce are called economic resources. The test of whether a resource is an economic resource or a free resource is price: economic resources command a nonzero price but free resources do not. Economists often classify economic resources into three categories: land, labor, and capital.

Since economic resources are scarce, only a limited amount of goods and services can be produced from them, and there arises the necessity for choice. For example, if an isolated town has a certain amount of resources, it must choose how much of each good it will produce from these resources. If it increases the amount produced of one good, it must reduce the amount produced of another good. The alternative cost of using resources to increase the production of the one good is the reduction in the output of the other good. To illustrate the use of the concept of alternative cost, which is one of the most important in economics, we discussed the cases of public parks and a college education.

Economists are particularly concerned with four basic questions regarding the working of any economic system, ours or any other. These questions are: (1) What determines what is produced? (2) What determines how it is produced? (3) What determines how the society's output is distributed among the members? (4) What determines the rate at which the society's productive capacity will grow? To answer these questions societies have relied on one of three methods (or some mixture of them): tradition, command, and the price system. The American economy relies more heavily on the price system than many other economies do, but command and (to some extent) tradition are important too.

CONCEPTS FOR REVIEW

Economics	Government regulation	Planned economy	Free resources
Unemployment	Poverty	Interdependence	Land
Inflation	Pollution	Resources	Capital
Forecasting	Economic resources	Labor	Technology
Choice			

QUESTIONS FOR DISCUSSION AND REVIEW

1. Alfred Marshall, the great British economist, defined economics as follows: "Economics is a study of men as they live and move and think in the ordinary business of life. But it concerns itself chiefly with those motives which affect, most powerfully and most steadily, man's conduct *in the business part of his life*. . . . [The] steadiest motive to ordinary business work is the desire for the pay which is the material reward of work."[1] Does this definition encompass all of the examples of economic analysis and problems contained in this chapter? Do you agree with this definition? If not, how would you modify it?

2. Herbert Spencer, the English philosopher, wrote that "the poverty of the incapable, the distresses that come upon the imprudent, the starvation of the idle, and those shoulderings aside of the weak by the strong, which leave so many 'in shallows and in miseries,' are the decrees of a large, far-seeing benevolence." Interpret and explain this view. Do you agree with it? Why or why not?

3. "Resources are scarce and once a decision is made to use them for one purpose, they are no longer available for another. One opportunity cost of reading [an] . . . article, for example, is not simultaneously being able to read [another article]."[2] Explain, and relate to the question of how much society should spend on defense.

4. "The analytical approach to choice is the hallmark of the [economics] profession. It is the essence of the discipline to focus on, and especially to quantify, the dimensions of choice—the costs, the benefits, and the alternative ways to achieve a given result."[3] Give three specific situations where data concerning the annual costs of operating a car would throw important light on a problem of choice faced by a household or firm.

5. Suppose that it costs a college student $1,000 per year more for room and board than if he or she works (and lives at home). If this assumption is correct, why is this amount, rather than the full cost of room and board, the proper amount to use in Table 1.4?

6. "Modern economics can and has successfully prescribed the means of preventing large-scale unemployment without bringing on major inflation."[4] Explain what this statement means, and suggest ways to test whether it is true.

[1] A. Marshall, *Principles of Economics*, London: Macmillan, 1920.
[2] D. Eastburn, "Economic Man in Conflict with His Economic Self," *New York Times Magazine*, July 26, 1970.
[3] A. Okun, *The Political Economy of Prosperity*, New York: Norton, 1970.
[4] C. Schultze, "Is Economics Obsolete? No, Underemployed," *Saturday Review*, January 22, 1972.

7. In this chapter, we described four basic questions that any economic system must answer. Which of these questions is involved in each of the following specific problems: (a) Should the United States use natural gas to produce ammonia? (b) Should taxes on the poor be lower? (c) Should American consumers save more? (d) Should more of our nation's industry be used to produce food?

8. Consider "a Melanesian native group, the Aztec empire, a Greek city state, an English medieval manor, modern America, or modern Russia. Each of these economic systems represents a configuration of institutions almost totally unlike that of any of the others, yet each has a practicable means by which the fundamental tasks of the economic order have been accomplished."[5] What are these fundamental tasks? In which of these cases do you think that tradition played the biggest role? In which of these cases do you think that command played the biggest role? In which of these cases do you think that the price system played the biggest role?

9. "Unemployment can be cured by public employment. In other words, the government can give a job to anyone who wants it." Do you agree? What problems do you see in this approach to the problem?

10. "Inflation is of little consequence. If prices go up, wages must go up commensurately, so who cares if prices go up?" Comment in detail, and explain why you agree or disagree.

[5] H. Bowen, *Toward Social Economy*, New York: Holt, Rinehart, and Winston, 1948.

2 Economic Analysis: Models and Measurement

As a formal field of study, economics is a Johnny-come-lately. Copernicus paved the way for modern astronomy 400 years ago, and Newton started his revolution in physics in the seventeenth century. By contrast, modern economics is generally said to have begun in 1776, the same year as the American Revolution, with the publication of Adam Smith's *The Wealth of Nations,* and to have developed into a science only a century or so ago. But despite its relative youth, economics has influenced generations of statesmen, philosophers, and ordinary citizens, and has played a significant role in shaping our society today. To understand the great ideas that underlie important parts of our civilization and to appreciate great segments of our intellectual heritage, you must understand some economics.

Apart from its value as an intellectual discipline, economics provides keys that help to interpret the broad sweep of the world's history. Economic forces have strongly influenced the course of human events. It would be a gross oversimplification to argue that taxes levied by the British on the American colonies were the sole cause of the American Revolution; yet the movement for independence cannot be understood without some knowledge of the economic ties of the colonies to the mother country. Few historians would call the triumph of Nazism in the 1930s solely a consequence of raging inflation; yet Hitler used the economic plight of Germany as a lever in his rise to power.

In 1960, John F. Kennedy's pledge "to get the economy moving ahead" scored effectively at the political box office. In 1976, Jimmy Carter's promise to reduce unemployment helped him defeat Gerald Ford for the presidency. It is safe to say that many elections have turned on economic issues, that many wars have resulted from economic causes, and that many revolutions have occurred because of economic discontent. Of course, economics is only one key to history; political, social, religious, and cultural factors are extremely important too. But to understand much about history—either the history of ideas or the history of events—you need to know something about economics.

The Industrial Revolution and Adam Smith

The Industrial Revolution

To illustrate the importance of economics in understanding the history of events, let's consider one of the most fundamental and remarkable developments in human history, the so-called Industrial Revolution. Until the middle of the eighteenth century, industry, as distinct from agriculture or commerce, played a small role in the economies of Europe or America. But during the late eighteenth and early nineteenth centuries, a host of important technological innovations, such as James Watt's steam engine and Richard Arkwright's spinning jenny, made possible a very rapid growth in the output of industrial goods (like textiles and pig iron). And accompanying this growth of industrial output was the advent of the factory—a social and economic institution that is taken for granted today, but which was largely unknown prior to the Industrial Revolution.

Economics is important in understanding the effects of the Industrial Revolution and the conditions that made it possible. The Industrial Revolution was characterized by major improvements in technology and by large increases in the amount of capital resources available to society. (Recall from the previous chapter that capital resources include buildings, equipment, and other nonhuman producible resources.) Both the improvements in technology and the additional capital made it possible for England (where the Industrial Revolution first took hold) to increase its total output. Why? Because improved technology made possible greater output from a given amount of resources, and because more capital constituted an increase in resources. Due to the increased output, the standard of living in England, as measured by per capita income, grew at an unprecedented rate. As the Industrial Revolution spread, this rise in living standards occurred too on the European continent and in the United States; it remained one of the lasting effects of industrialization.

However, this long-term increase in the standard of living took many years to be achieved. In the short run, the Industrial Revolution was marked by considerable human suffering (but perhaps not much more so than in previous years). Although a small segment of European society led rich lives in city drawing rooms or on country estates, the great bulk of the population at that time lived in abject poverty. To take one small example, in some coal mines, both men and women worked, often half-naked, for long hours; children worked in the mines too—and some seldom saw daylight for months. In the factory towns, as in the mines, the hours were long, and children often spent their early years at work. Shifts of 10 to 12 hours a day were not uncommon, and wages were very low.

As stressed above, the Industrial Revolution was characterized by considerable increases in capital. How did England (and other countries) bring about this increase in capital? By saving. In other words, the English people had to set aside some of their resources, and to say in effect, "These resources will not be used to satisfy the current needs of our population for food, clothing, and other forms of consumption. Instead, they will be used to produce capital—factories, machines, equipment, railroads, and canals—which will increase our future productive capacity." Much more will be said about this saving process in subsequent chapters. For now, the essential point is that this saving process was one of the necessary conditions that made possible the Industrial Revolution.

Adam Smith, Father of Modern Economics

To illustrate the importance of economics in understanding the history of ideas, let's consider Adam Smith (1723–90), the man who is often called the father of modern economics. Smith lived during the Industrial Revolution, and was one of the first scholars to understand many of the central mechanisms of a free, or unplanned, economy. Much of his life was spent as professor of moral philosophy at the University of Glasgow in Scotland. In 1759, he published *The Theory of Moral Sentiments,* which established him as one of Britain's foremost philosophers, but this was not the book for which he is famous today. His masterpiece, published in 1776 (while the American colonists were brewing rebellion), was *The Wealth of Nations,*[1] a long, encyclopedic book 12 years in the writing. It was not an instant success, but the laurels it eventually won undoubtedly compensated for its early neglect. It is unquestionably one of the most influential books ever written.

Much of *The Wealth of Nations* seems trite today, because it has been absorbed so thoroughly into modern thought, but it was not trite when it was written. On the contrary, Smith's ideas were revolutionary. *He was among the first to describe how the price system works and how a free, competitive economy can function—without central planning or government interference—to allocate resources efficiently. He recognized the virtues of the "invisible hand" that leads the private interests of firms and individuals toward socially desirable ends, and he was properly suspicious of firms that are sheltered from competition, since he recognized the potentially undesirable effects on resource allocation.*

In addition, Smith—with the dire poverty of his times staring him in the face—was interested in the forces that determined the evolution of the economy—that is, the forces determining the rate of growth of average income per person. Although Smith did not approve of avarice, he felt that saving was good because it enabled society to invest in machinery and other forms of capital. Accumulating more and more capital would, according to Smith, allow output to grow. In addition, he emphasized the importance of increased specialization and division of labor in bringing about economic progress. Moreover, he recognized that the rate of population increase was an important determinant of a country's economic development.

All in all, Smith's views were relatively optimistic, in keeping with the intellectual climate of his time—the era of Voltaire, Diderot, Franklin, and Jefferson, the age of the Enlight-

[1] Adam Smith, *The Wealth of Nations,* New York: Modern Library, 1937.

ADAM SMITH

on the "Invisible Hand" and Specialization

It is only for the sake of profit that any man employs [his] capital in the support of industry, and he will always, therefore, endeavor to employ it in the support of that industry of which the produce is likely to be of greatest value, or to exchange for the greatest quantity either of money or of other goods. But the annual revenue of every society is always precisely equal to the exchangeable value of the whole annual produce of its industry, or rather is precisely the same thing with that exchangeable value. As every individual, therefore, endeavors as much as he can both to employ his capital in the support of domestic industry, and so to direct that industry that its produce may be of the greatest value, every individual necessarily labors to render the annual revenue of the society as great as he can: He generally, indeed, neither intends to promote the public interest, nor knows how much he is promoting it. . . . He intends only his own security; and by directing that industry in such a manner as its produce may be of the greatest value, he intends only his own gain, and *he is in this, as in many other cases, led by an invisible hand to promote an end which was no part of his intention.* Nor is it always the worse for the society that it was no part of it. *By pursuing his own interest he frequently promotes that of the society more effectually than when he really intends to promote it.* I have never known much good done by those who affected to trade for the public good. It is an affectation, indeed, not very common among merchants, and very few words need be employed in dissuading them from it. . . .

It is the maxim of every prudent master of a family, never to attempt to make at home what it will cost him more to make than to buy. The tailor does not attempt to make his own shoes, but buys them of the shoemaker. The shoemaker does not attempt to make his own clothes, but employs a tailor. The farmer attempts to make neither the one nor the other, but employs those different artificers. All of them find it for their interest to employ their whole industry in a way in which they have some advantage over their neighbors, and to purchase with a part of its produce, or with the price of a part of it, whatever else they have occasion for.

Adam Smith, *The Wealth of Nations,* London: George Routledge, 1900, p. 345. Originally published in 1776. (Italics added.)

enment, when men believed so strongly in rationality. Leave markets alone, said Smith, and beware of firms with too much economic power and government meddling. If this is done, there is no reason why considerable economic progress cannot be achieved.

Economics: A Social Science

In the previous chapter, we tried to indicate the practical importance of economics. But economics is much more than a bag of techniques for solving practical problems. *Like any other natural or social science, it is concerned with explaining and predicting observed phenomena, whether or not these explanations and predictions have any immediate practical application.* One only need look at some of the books economists write for each other—books bristling with complicated mathematical formulas and highly theoretical arguments—to realize that not all economics is a search for immediate answers to the world's ailments. Instead, many fields of economics pursue abstract truth, immediately useful or not.

Thus much economic research is directed at questions like these: What determines the level of national output? (Why did the total amount of goods and services produced in the United States plummet by about 30 percent between 1929 and 1933?) What determines the price of various commodities? (Why are lamb chops more expensive than hot dogs?) What determines the over-all price level? (Why is the average level of prices so much higher now than it was 40 years ago?) What determines how much a worker makes? (Why are brain surgeons paid more than pipefitters?) What determines the rate of increase of per capita output? (Why has Japan's per capita output increased so much more rapidly than other industrialized countries' in recent years?) What determines how a consumer allocates his or her income among various commodities? (How will an increase in the price of honeydew melons influence the quantity you buy?) What determines the goods a country exports and those it imports? (Why do we export electronic computers and import transistor radios?) What determines the value of foreign money? (Why was a British pound worth about $1.60 in October 1976?)

As these questions and their parenthetical accompaniments stand, they are not in the form of practical problems. Yet a knowledge of the answers to these questions is obviously of interest and of value. In this respect, many branches of economics recall mathematics. Pure mathematics is not concerned with day-to-day affairs, but various branches of mathematics are very valuable in solving practical problems, and some knowledge of mathematics is indispensable for understanding the world around us and for professional and technical training. Or think of physics. Although many of its branches are rather far removed from practical application, a general knowledge of physics has proved necessary to solve many types of practical problems; and certain branches, like solid-state physics, have had enormous practical impact on technology and industry.

The crucial consideration is that *economics is a science*. Like other sciences, it formulates and tests basic propositions that can be used to predict and explain the phenomena we observe in the world around us. This does not mean it cannot be useful; but because it is a science—a social science—economics goes beyond problem-solving *to deal with the basic principles and mechanisms that make economic systems work as they do.*

Also, it is important to recognize that economics, although probably the most highly developed of the social sciences, is still far from being able to solve many of the pressing social issues we face. Nor will a knowledge of economics insure that your bank balance will soar. Economics can help solve important social problems, and it can help you come to better decisions, but it is no panacea. As you will see below, there are many economic questions that are unsettled and debated by the experts. Consequently, one should not expect too much. But even the most demanding student would probably admit that, to be valuable, a subject need not provide reliable answers to all interesting questions.

How Successful Are Economics and Economists?

Accuracy of Economic Propositions

Economics has come a long way since Adam Smith. Due to the efforts of such great figures as David Ricardo, Thomas Malthus, John Stuart Mill, Alfred Marshall, and John Maynard Keynes, as well as the work of countless other talented people, our understanding of the workings of the economic system has improved continually and significantly. But you may still have some doubts about how much of a science economics is, and whether it will give you valid, useful answers, or just ivory-tower concoctions with little or no applicability to the real world. These questions deserve an answer, although finding a concise one is not easy. One reason for the difficulty is that some aspects of economics are not as well understood as others, in part because less research has been done on them. Any discipline—physics, chemistry, or biology, for example—has such areas. Another reason is that all scientific predictions contain some error. Thus, the real question isn't whether economic predictions and propositions are accurate, but *how* accurate they are.

Even in this more meaningful form, the question is not easy to answer, however, since, as noted above, some economic predictions and propositions are much more accurate than others. For example, advances in economics and related disciplines in the postwar period have allowed economists to figure out more efficient ways for firms to run many aspects of their operations. Linear programming and related economic techniques have been applied to petroleum refineries, for example, to determine the minimum-cost blend of gasoline stocks and the most profitable outputs of regular and premium gasoline, enabling firms to increase their profits substantially. Short-range forecasting of changes in business conditions is another area where economics has proved very useful. Such forecasts are used by the government, as well as a host of firms, to guide major decisions involving billions of dollars.

On the other hand, economic knowledge in other areas is very limited. For example, economists are still uncertain about many effects of the government's monetary and fiscal policies. Most economists believe that both *monetary policy* (the government's policy concerning the money supply and interest rates) and *fiscal policy* (the government's policy concerning spending and taxes) play an important role in determining the size of national output, the extent of unemployment, and the rate of inflation. But an influential minority of the economics profession believes monetary policy to be far more important than fiscal policy, and the available evidence is too weak to show conclusively whether they are right or wrong. Our knowledge of the modern process of inflation is also limited. This the Nixon administration found out in the late 1960s when it tried to control the inflation occurring then. The standard remedies it applied did not work as many distinguished economists predicted they would.

However, even though economic knowledge in some areas is much more limited than we would like, you should recognize this important fact: *judging from all available evidence, a knowledge of economics will enable you to solve economic problems better than you would without it. Even though economic predictions and propositions are not always very precise, they tend to work better than predictions and propositions not based on economics.* And this, if you think about it, is really the crucial consideration.

Signals of Progress

One important signal that economics had become a full-fledged science was the establishment in 1969 of a Nobel Prize in economics. The beginning of these awards was an indication that economics was the first of the social sciences to "arrive." The first Nobel Prizes went to Professors Ragnar Frisch of Norway and Jan Tinbergen of Holland. Paul Samuelson, Simon Kuznets, Kenneth Arrow, Wassily Leontief, Tjalling Koopmans, and Milton Friedman were the first Americans to receive these prizes. All these scholars have contributed greatly to economics, but each in a quite different way: Samuelson, Arrow, and Koopmans have been responsible primarily for theoretical advances, while Kuznets has done basic empirical work, and Frisch, Tinbergen, Leontief, and Friedman have pioneered in the blending of theoretical and statistical techniques. Like any science, economics requires advances of many types–theoretical, empirical, statistical–to develop and flourish.

Another clear signal that economics has become a useful science is the very high salaries economists pull down in industry and government. Years ago, the taunt may have been, "If you're so smart, why aren't you rich?" Today the reply could be, "Those economists who are interested in making money seem to be doing very well indeed!" Of course, this does not mean that most economists in universities are making loads of money. Like other academic scientists, they are willing to earn less than they could in industry or government in order to enjoy the freedom to do research and teach. But if an economist wants to make lots of money, he certain has the opportunity.

The Methodology of Economics

Model Building in Economics

By now, you may think it worthwhile to devote a little time to economics, but you still don't know anything about how economists approach their subject or the methods they use. In the rest of this chapter, we will provide a general description of the methodology of economics. Like other types of scientific analysis, economics is based on the formulation of ***models***. *A model is a theory. It is composed of a number of assumptions from which conclusions–or predictions–are deduced.* If an astronomer wants to formulate a model of the solar system, he might represent each planet by a point in space and assume that each would change position in accord with certain mathematical equations. Based on this model, he might predict when an eclipse would occur, or estimate the probability of a planetary collision. The economist proceeds along similar lines when he sets forth a model of economic behavior.

There are several important aspects of models. First, *to be useful, a model must in general simplify and abstract from the real situation.* The assumptions made by a model need not be exact replicas of reality. If they were, the model would be too complicated to use. The basic reason for using a model is that the real world is so complex that masses of detail often obscure underlying patterns. The economist faces the familiar problem of seeing the forest, as distinct from just the trees. Other scientists must do the same; physicists work with simplified models of atoms, just as economists work with simplified models of markets. However, this does not mean that *all* models are good or useful. A model may be so oversimplified and distorted that it is utterly useless. The trick is to construct a model so that irrelevant and unimportant considerations and variables are neglected, but the major factors–those that seriously affect the phenomena the model is designed to predict—are included.

Second, *the purpose of a model is to make predictions about the real world, and in many respects the most important test of a model is how well it predicts.* In this sense, a model that predicts the price of copper within plus or minus $.01 a pound is better than a model that predicts it within plus or minus $.02 a pound. Of course, this does not mean that a model is useless if it cannot predict very accurately. We do not always need a very accurate prediction. For example, a road map is a model that can be used to make predictions about the route a driver should take to get to a particular destination. Sometimes, a very crude map is good enough to get you where you want to go, but such a map would not, for instance, serve the hiker who needs to know the characteristics of the terrain through which he plans to walk. How detailed a map you need depends on where you are going and how you want to get there.

Third, *if one wants to predict the outcome of a particular event, he will be forced to use the model that predicts best, even if this model does not predict very well.* The choice is not between a model and no model; it is between one model and another. After all, if one must make a forecast, he will use the most accurate device available—and any such device is a model of some sort. Consequently, when economists make simplifying assumptions and derive conclusions that are only approximately true, it is somewhat beside the point to complain that the assumptions are simpler than reality or that the predictions are not always accurate. This may be true, but if the predictions based on the economists' model are better than those obtained on the basis of other models, their model must, and will, be used until something better comes along. Thus, if a model can predict the price of copper to within plus or minus $.01 per pound, and no other model can do better, this model will be used even if those interested in the predictions bewail the model's limitations and wish it could be improved.

Economic Measurement

To utilize and test economic models, economists need facts of many kinds. As Lord William Beveridge said almost 40 years ago, "There can be no science of society until the facts about society are available. . . . It matters little how wrong we are with our existing theories, if we are honest and careful with our observations." As economics has become more of a science, more and more economists have spent more and more time digging out the facts and seeing what their implications are. Each economic model yields predictions, and to determine whether these predictions are accurate enough to be worth anything, economists must continually collect data to see how accurate the predictions are. For example, if a model predicts that the price of copper should be $.03 a pound higher in 1978 than in 1977, it is important to determine what price change really occurred, and how close the model's predictions were to reality.

At the outset, note that, to a very large extent, economics is not an experimental, or laboratory, science. In other words, economists, unlike physicists, chemists, or biologists, cannot generally carry out experiments under carefully controlled conditions. Consequently, they usually cannot study the effects of varying one factor, while holding constant other factors that may influence the outcome. Such controlled experiments are common in the natural sciences and in technology. For example, a controlled experiment might be performed in agriculture to learn the effect of various amounts of fertilizer on the amount of wheat produced on an acre of land. A sample of plots of ground might be planted with wheat, the amount of fertilizer varying from plot to plot. Then the yield obtained from each plot might be related to the amount of fertilizer used on that plot.

Since controlled experimentation of this sort is often, but not always, impossible in economics, economists must rely on data generated by the economic system. For example, to test a model of consumer behavior, an economist may set out to estimate the effect of a household's income on the amount of money it spends per year on clothing. To make such an estimate, the economist cannot perform an experiment in which he varies the income of a household and sees the effect on its clothing expenditures. Instead, he must gather data concerning the incomes and clothing expenditures of a large number of households, and study the relationship between them. The relationship he finds may, for example, resemble that shown in Figure 2.1: The line *AA′* represents an average relationship between household income and household clothing expenditure. If this relationship is in accord with the model, he will accept this model (at least tentatively); if not, he will reject it, and search for a better model.

Graphs and Relationships

Economists find it useful to present data and relationships between variables in graphs, such as Figure 2.1. Several things should be noted concerning graphs. First, a graph has a horizontal axis and a vertical axis, each of which has a scale of numerical values. For example, in Figure 2.1, the horizontal axis shows a household's annual income, and the vertical axis shows the annual amount spent by the household on clothing. The intersection of the two axes is called the origin, and is the point where both the variable measured along the horizontal axis and the variable measured along the vertical axis are zero. In Figure 2.1, the origin is at the lower lefthand corner of the figure, labeled *0*.

Second, to show the relationship between two variables, one can plot the value of one variable against the value of the other variable. Thus, in Figure 2.1, each family is represented by a dot. For example, the dot for the Buchanan family is in the position shown in Figure 2.1, because its income was $5,000 and its clothing expenditure was $400. Clearly, the relationship, *AA′* does not fit all the families exactly, since all the points do not fall on the line. *AA′* does, however, give the average clothing

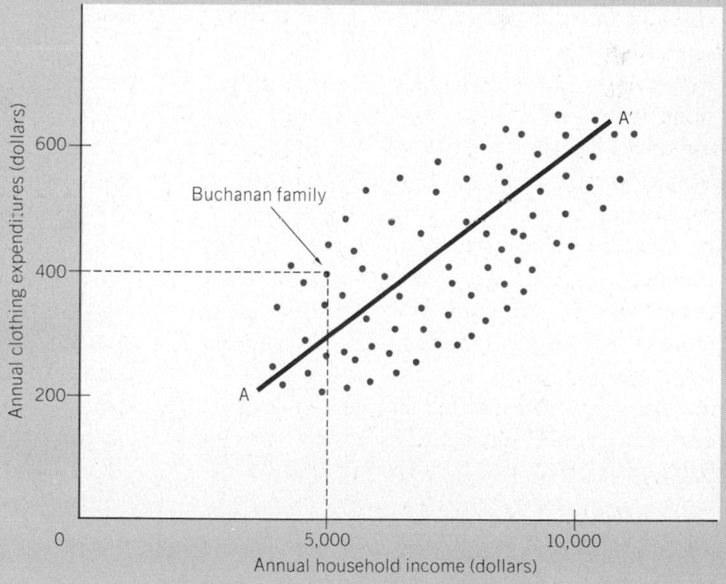

Figure 2.1
Relationship between Annual Clothing Expenditures and Annual Household Income
The line *AA′* represents an average relationship. Each family is represented by a dot. Clearly, *AA′* does not fit all families exactly, since all the points do not fall on the line. *AA′* does, however, give average clothing expenditure for each income level.

Figure 2.2
Relationship between Quantity Demanded and Price of Tennis Balls (as shown in Table 2.1).

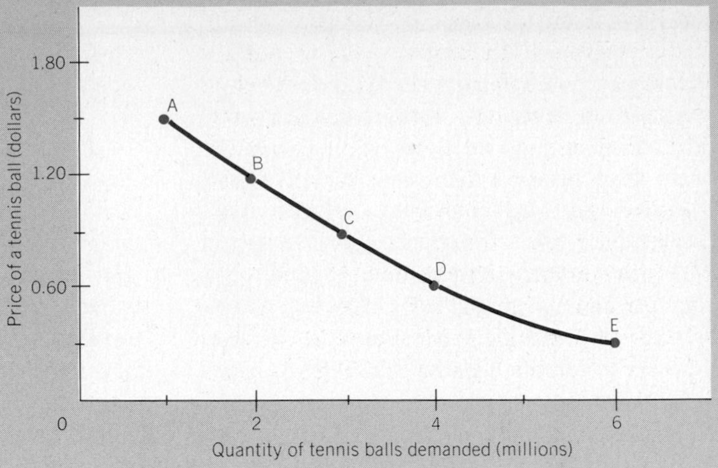

expenditure for each level of income: it is an average relationship.

Third, the relationship between two variables is *direct* if, as in Figure 2.1, the line of average relationship is upward sloping. In other words, if the variable measured along the vertical axis tends to increase (decrease) in response to increases (decreases) in the variable measured along the horizontal axis, the relationship is direct. On the other hand, if the line of average relationship is downward sloping, as in Figure 2.2, the relationship is *inverse.* In other words, if the variable measured along the vertical axis tends to decrease (increase) in response to increases (decreases) in the variable measured along the horizontal axis, the relationship is inverse.

To illustrate how one can graph a relationship between two variables, consider Table 2.1, which shows the amount of tennis balls demanded in a particular market at various prices. Putting price on the vertical axis and quantity demanded on the horizontal axis, one can plot each combination of price and quantity in this table as a point on a graph; and that is precisely what has been done in Figure 2.2 (points *A* to *E*). Note that, in contrast to the line in Figure 2.1, the line in Figure 2.2 goes through all of the points.

Table 2.1
Quantity of Tennis Balls Demanded in a Particular Market at Various Prices

Price of a tennis ball (dollars)	Quantity of tennis balls demanded (millions)
1.50	1
1.20	2
0.90	3
0.60	4
0.30	6

Statistical Tests and Quantitative Models

Based on the study of relationships like those shown in Figures 2.1 and 2.2, economists determine how well various models fit reality. In other words, they perform statistical tests to see whether a particular model is satisfactory. Two types of error can be made: they can reject a satisfactory model, or they can accept an unsatisfactory one. Which of these errors is more important will depend, of course, on the costs involved. For example, if the cost of accepting an unsatisfactory model is low, while the cost of rejecting a satisfactory model is high, then one should worry more about the latter type of error than the former. Using standard statistical methods, economists formulate their tests so that the probability that they will commit each type of error is roughly commensurate with the costs. Generally, it is impossible to eliminate completely the probability of error; the expense of doing so would be prohibitive.

Measurements like those in Figures 2.1 and 2.2 enable economists to ***quantify*** their models: in other words, they enable them to construct models that predict *how much* effect one variable has on another. For example, economists could be content with a model that predicts that higher household income results in higher household clothing expenditures; but this model would not be interesting or useful, since you don't need an economist to tell you that. A more valuable model is one that is quantitative, that predicts *how much* clothing expenditure will increase if household income increases by a certain amount.

A model of this sort might predict that clothing expenditures tend to increase by $60 when income increases by $1,000. Judging by Figure 2.1, such a model would be reasonably accurate, at least for households with incomes between $5,000 and $10,000 per year. Such quantitative models, tested against data like those in Figure 2.1, can be extremely valuable to firms that sell clothing and related products, to government agencies concerned with consumer expenditures, and to economists and other social scientists interested in consumer behavior.[2]

[2] It is worth noting that, although it is useful to see how well a model would have fit the historical facts, this is no substitute for seeing how well it will predict the future. As a distinguished mentor of mine once observed, "It's a darned poor person who can't predict the past."

Examples of Economic Models

The Pricing of Urban Transportation: A Case Study

For a first glimpse of the practical importance of economic models, consider the situation faced by the Boston and Maine Railroad in the early 1960s. The Boston and Maine wanted to discontinue its unprofitable railroad passenger commuter service into Boston. According to the railroad, the revenues it obtained from its commuter operations did not and could not meet the costs of providing the service. However, the Mass Transportation Commission of Massachusetts was not at all sure that such service had to be unprofitable for the Boston and Maine. The commission thought that lowering the price of commuter tickets might increase the service's profitability. This issue was of considerable importance both to the railroad and to Boston commuters.

To understand the Commission's view, we need the concept of a demand curve. Assuming that the incomes and tastes of the Boston commuting public, as well as the cost of commuting by alternative means of transportation, remain constant, it is extremely likely that the number of commuter tickets sold by the Boston and Maine will be inversely related to the price it charges for a ticket. In other words, holding constant these other factors, the lower the price, the greater the quantity of tickets sold. *This relationship between price and quantity of tickets sold can be represented graphically by a* ***demand curve,*** *which shows the number of tickets that will be sold at each price.*

The Commission suspected that the demand curve might be shaped like BB' in Figure 2.3, in which case the quantity of tickets sold would increase very substantially in response to a price cut. If BB' is the demand curve, and if

Figure 2.3
Demand Curve for Commuter Tickets, the Commission's View and the Skeptics' View
The commission suspected the demand curve might be *BB′*; the skeptics thought it might be *AA′*.

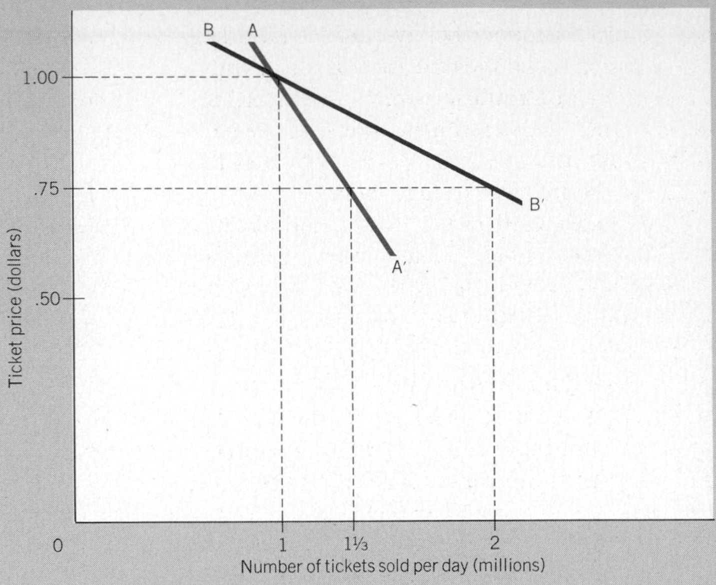

the price of a ticket is reduced from $1 to $.75, the quantity of tickets sold per day increases from 1 million to 2 million, with the result that the railroad's total revenue from suburban passenger service increases from $1 million per day (if the ticket price is $1) to $1.5 million per day (if the ticket price is $.75).[3] Since the extra $500,000 per day in revenue is greater than the extra cost of carrying the extra million passengers per day, such a price reduction would increase the railroad's profits. Indeed, according to the Commission, it might increase the Boston and Maine's profits enough to push its suburban passenger service into the black.

On the other hand, skeptics had a different model of the situation. According to their model, the demand curve was shaped like *AA′* in Figure 2.3, in which case the quantity of tickets sold does not increase very much in response to price cuts. If the price of a ticket is reduced from $1 to $.75, the quantity of tickets sold per day increases only from 1 million to 1⅓ million, with the result that the total revenues of the railroad remain constant at $1 million per day. Since it will cost the railroad more to transport 1⅓ million people than 1 million people per day, it follows that the railroad will make less money by reducing the price of a ticket. Thus, according to the skeptics, a price cut of this sort would not make the Boston and Maine's suburban passenger service profitable. On the contrary, it would make it more unprofitable.

Which model was correct? The Commission's or the skeptics'? As in any science, a question of this sort must be answered by an appeal to facts. Measurements must be made, and data gathered to shed light on the shape of this demand curve. Once such data are in hand, statistical tests can be carried out to see which model is closer to reality. The Commission asked the Boston and Maine to experiment with a reduction in ticket prices to see its effect on the quantity of tickets sold. This experiment, made in 1963, indicated that the skep-

[3] The total revenue equals 1 million tickets times $1 when the price is $1, and 2 million tickets times $.75 when the price is $.75. Thus it is $1 million in the former case and $1.5 million in the latter. Of course, the demand curves in Figure 2.3 (and the other numbers in this example) are hypothetical, but they illustrate the essential point.

tics' model was more nearly correct than the Commission's, and the railroad continued with its petition to terminate commuter passenger service when the experiment ended. However, public subsidies eventually were instituted to keep the service from terminating.

The models used in the Boston and Maine case were very simple, relative to most others employed by economists. All economic models are not this straightforward. Moreover, in this brief sketch we cannot do justice to all the subtleties and nuances involved in interpreting and testing these models: there are lots of problems and pitfalls. Yet, even so, this case study is a useful introduction to the construction and use of economic models.

The Battle against Unemployment: Another Case Study

Turning to more complicated economic models, let's look at some techniques used by government economists to combat unemployment. In early 1975, when the national unemployment rate exceeded 8 percent and was the highest in over 30 years, President Ford and the Congress both expressed grave concern. Fortunately, decades of research by economists all over the world had produced models that indicated the factors influencing the unemployment rate—among them, the level of taxes, government expenditures, and the money supply. These models indicated a number of ways by which the government could reduce the unemployment rate. One was to increase government expenditure, another was to reduce taxes. Having made their own evaluations of the advantages and disadvantages of each approach, the Congress and the Ford administration decided on a tax cut. A $23 billion tax cut was passed in March 1975. During late 1975 and early 1976, unemployment fell, and the tax cut was given considerable credit for it.

This was by no means the first time that models of this sort had been used. For example, when the Kennedy administration took office in 1961, it was confronted with a relatively high unemployment rate. (About 7 percent of the labor force was unemployed in mid-1961.) Based on these same kinds of economic models, Walter W. Heller, chairman of President Kennedy's Council of Economic Advisers, and other administration officials argued strongly for a tax cut, which was passed in 1964. According to available studies, this measure seemed to work: unemployment fell, as the models predicted it would. Of course, the models used by Heller and his colleagues may have been wrong; perhaps unemployment fell for reasons other than the tax cut. One cannot rule out this possibility, but it seems unlikely.[4]

Values and Decisions

Positive Economics versus Normative Economics

Economists make an important distinction between positive economics and normative economics. ***Positive economics*** *contains descriptive statements, propositions, and predictions about the world.* For instance, an economic model may predict that the price of copper will increase by $.01 a pound if income per person in the United States rises by 10 percent; this is positive economics. Positive economics tells us only what will happen under certain circumstances. It says nothing about whether the results are good or bad—or about what we should do. ***Normative economics,*** *on the other hand, makes statements about what ought to be, or about what a person, organization, or nation ought to do.* For instance, a model might say

[4] However, it should be noted that some prominent economists—the monetarists—feel that the models used by Heller and his colleagues were wrong, at least in part. To understand this issue, you need to know more about fiscal and monetary policy, discussed in Chapters 11 and 15.

that Chile should nationalize its copper industry and use the profits to reduce poverty; this is normative economics.

Clearly, positive economics and normative economics must be treated differently. Positive economics is science in the ordinary sense of the word. Propositions in positive economics can be tested by an appeal to the facts. Needless to say, in a nonexperimental science like economics, it is sometimes difficult to get the facts you need to test particular propositions. For example, if income per person in the United States does not rise by 10 percent, it may be difficult to tell what the effect of such an increase would be on the price of copper. Moreover, even if per capita income does increase by this amount, it may be difficult to separate the effect of the increase in income per person on the price of copper from the effect of other factors. But nonetheless, we can, in principle, test propositions in positive economics by an appeal to the facts.

In normative economics, however, this is not the case. *In normative economics, the results you get depend on your values or preferences.* For example, if you believe that reducing unemployment is more important than maintaining the purchasing power of the dollar, you will get one answer to certain questions; whereas if you believe that maintaining the purchasing power of the dollar is more important than reducing unemployment, you are likely to get a different answer to the same questions. This is not at all strange. After all, if people desire different things (which is another way of saying that they have different values), they may well make different decisions and advocate different policies. It would be strange if they did not.

The Role of Values

People sometimes make fun of economists because they disagree, and their differences are sometimes held up as evidence that economics is really not a science at all. In truth, of course, they prove nothing of the kind. *Because economists—like physicists, mathematicians, lawyers, and plumbers—differ in their preferences and values, they come to different conclusions when they enter the realm of normative economics.* Thus liberal economists often differ from conservative economists in their conclusions on public policy, and the disagreements can be over means as well as ends. *However, there is very substantial agreement on most of the propositions of positive economics.* Of course, this does not mean that everything is settled, but the areas of disagreement are generally relatively narrow. And this, it should be noted, is the important thing, since the pure science of economics is positive economics.

This book will spend a lot of time on the principles of positive economics—the principles and propositions concerning the workings of the economic system about which practically all economists tend to agree. Also, normative economics will be treated as well, since we must discuss questions of policy—and all policy discussions involve individual preferences, not solely hard facts. In these discussions, we shall try to indicate how the conclusions depend on one's values. Then you can let your own values be your guide. The purpose of this book is not to convert you to a particular set of values. It is to teach you how to obtain better solutions to economic problems, whatever set of values you may have.

Methodological Hazards in Economics

There are lots of impediments to straight thinking in economics that are not present in other disciplines like chemistry or biology. Some of the most important impediments are the following:

Bias. People have preconceptions about economic matters that they don't have about chemical or biological matters. Few people have a long-standing bias against two hydrogen atoms combining with an oxygen atom to form water, but some people grow up with the idea that profits are a bad thing or that unions are a social evil. These biases get in the way of objective analysis, because people tend to believe what they want to believe. If you want to learn any economics, you must respect facts, unpleasant though they may be at times.

Loaded words. Another hazard in economics is the use of loaded, emotional words. Unless you school yourself to look carefully at what words mean—and don't mean—you can be gulled by misleading terminology. For example, Marxists often refer to the exploitation of labor by capitalists, which sounds bad, since no one can be in favor of exploitation. But you must remember that labels can be misleading. What the Marxists call exploitation, most Western economists do not regard as exploitation at all.

Jargon. Social scientists are often and justly accused of using unfamiliar words, or jargon, to describe common phenomena. Economists do not escape this charge. You would probably not refer to your checking account in a bank as a demand deposit: economists do. What is more, economists define some terms in a different way from the man on the street. You will find out that rent to the economist is not an amount paid each month for an apartment, but a payment for a resource that is fixed in supply. Of course, economists have a right to define terms as they please, but you can be confused if you assume that seemingly familiar terms mean what you think they mean.

Post hoc ergo propter hoc. Still another pitfall is to assume that, because one event follows another, the former event is caused by the latter. The Romans had a phrase for this kind of reasoning: *post hoc ergo propter hoc* ("after this, therefore because of this"). This fallacy occurs all the time. Consider the people who attributed a spell of bad weather that occurred after the first moon landing to the astronauts' trip to the moon. The bad weather followed the lunar trip—therefore it must have been caused by it. Needless to say, this sort of reasoning is treacherous indeed, since many events occur on the heels of other events without being caused by them. To jump to the conclusion that an event following another event is caused by the earlier event is clearly to court disaster.

Fallacy of composition. Some people assume that what is true of part of a system must be true for the whole system. This can be quite wrong. For example, it may be true that a farmer will gain from producing a larger crop. But it may not be true that farmers as a whole will gain if all produce a larger crop. Or consider another case: a business firm will go bankrupt by continuing to spend more than it takes in, but it does not follow that an entire nation will go bankrupt if its government spends more than it takes in. The fallacy of composition—that what is true of the part must be true of the whole—lies in wait for the unwary student of economics, and for the experienced economist too. Grievous errors can be avoided by keeping clear of this fallacy's clutches.

Myopic specialization. Since economic factors are closely intertwined with social, psychological, and political factors, there is no well defined border between economics and the other social sciences—sociology, anthropology, psychology, and political science. To understand many problems in society, one must consider the sociological and political, as well as economic angles. For example, noneconomic factors are important in explaining why some countries are richer than others. Even in solving narrower problems, such as why consumers buy a particular product, psychological as well as economic factors must be considered. Thus, the economist must continually keep abreast of the advances made in other fields, since they can help him solve his own problems. Conversely, political scientists, psychologists, and other social scientists can often use economic techniques in their work. A myopic refusal to cross disciplinary boundaries can result in poor or misleading results.

Summary

Economics—and economists—have played a significant role in shaping the present nature of society. A knowledge of economics is necessary to understand the history of human events, and the masterpieces of economics produced in the past are important segments of our intellectual heritage. The methodology used by economists is much the same as that used in any other kind of scientific analysis. The basic procedure is the formulation and testing of models. A model must in general simplify and abstract from the real world. Its purpose is to make predictions concerning phenomena in the real world, and in many respects the most important test of a model is how well it predicts these phenomena. One illustration of the construction and use of an economic model was the discussion concerning the Boston and Maine's decision to discontinue suburban passenger service. Another example of the use of economic models was the decision made by the Congress and the Ford administration to pass a tax cut in 1975 to reduce unemployment.

To test and quantify their models, economists gather data and utilize various statistical techniques. Economists often distinguish between positive economics and normative economics. Positive economics contains descriptive statements, propositions, and predictions about the world; whereas normative economics contains statements about what ought to be, or about what a person, organization, or nation ought to do. In normative economics, the results you get depend on your basic values and preferences; in positive economics, the results are testable, at least in principle, by an appeal to the facts.

Although economics plays an important role in helping to solve basic social and private problems, you should not jump to the conclusion that economics is wholly a bag of techniques designed to solve practical problems; this is far from the case. Economics—like any natural or social science—is concerned with explaining and predicting observed phenomena, whether or not these explanations or predictions have any immediate application to practical problems. Also, it is important to recognize that, although economics can help solve social and private problems, it is no panacea. Nor is economics able to answer every important question about the workings of the economic system. As we shall see, our understanding of some questions is far from adequate. Nonetheless, a knowledge of economics is very useful and important in understanding the world around us.

CONCEPTS FOR REVIEW

Model
Measurement
Demand curve
Positive economics
Normative economics
Fallacy of composition

QUESTIONS FOR DISCUSSION AND REVIEW

1. In Adam Smith's words, "I have never known much good done by those who affected to trade for the public good." Did he mean that public officials do little good? Or didn't he include them among those who "trade"? Some American corporations claim to support many activities, such as the arts, because they are "for the public good." Does this contradict Smith's statement? How valid do you regard his statement to be?

2. Companies that invest a relatively large amount in research and development frequently tend to have relatively high rates of growth of sales. Does this mean that large expenditures on research and development *cause* high rates of growth of sales? Can you think of other explanations for the observed correlation? (Hint: Firms that spend a great deal on research and development may tend to have relatively progressive managements.)

3. Suppose that the quantity of corn demanded annually by American consumers at each price of corn is as follows:

Price (dollars per bushel)	Quantity of corn (millions of bushels)
1	2.0
2	1.0
3	0.5
4	0.4

How much will farmers receive for their corn crop if it is 2 million bushels? If it is 1 million bushels? If you owned all of the farms producing corn, would you produce 2 million bushels? Why or why not?

4. Plot the relationship between price and quantity demanded in Question 3 in a graph. Is the relationship direct or inverse? Based on your graph, estimate how much corn is likely to be demanded if the price is (a) \$1.50, (b) \$2.50, and (c) \$3.50.

5. Suppose that you wanted to construct a model to explain and predict the breakfast food that your neighbor will choose tomorrow. What factors would you include? How well do you think you could predict?

6. Suppose that you were given the job of estimating the demand curve for commuter tickets in metropolitan Boston. How would you proceed? What sorts of difficulties would you anticipate?

7. "If one firm cuts its price, it will make more money, so if all firms cut their price, they will make more money." Do you agree? If so, prove that it is true. If not, cite the kind of methodological error that is committed.

8. "Models are useless because they cannot include all of the variables that influence the phenomenon we want to predict." Comment.

9. On the basis of positive economics alone, which of the following statements can be determined to be true or false: (a) The tax cut of 1975 reduced unemployment in the United States by 1 percent. (b) The tax cut was timed improperly. (c) The tax cut was a less equitable way of reducing unemployment than a program whereby the unemployed were hired by the government to perform important social functions.

10. "For its unwillingness to indulge in sociopolitical 'guesswork,' out of fear of transgressing the limits of proper scientific procedure, economics is placed in a position in which its findings *must* be partial and imcomplete and very possibly erroneous."[5] Comment.

[5] R. Heilbroner, "On the Limited 'Relevance' of Economics," *The Public Interest,* 1970.

PART TWO

The Private Sector and the Public Sector: an Overview

3 The American Economy: Our Mixed Capitalist System

The economy of the United States is beset by many problems. As pointed out in Chapter 1, the mid-seventies have been a period of excessive unemployment and excessive inflation. Also, we are confronted by serious environmental, energy, and poverty problems, among others. Yet, despite these problems, the American economy is clearly among the most prosperous in the world. The typical American family has plenty of food, clothing, housing, appliances, and luxuries of many kinds, and the typical American worker is well educated and well trained. The tremendous strength and vitality of the American economy should be recognized, as well as its shortcomings. Nothing is gained by overlooking either the successes or the faults of our system.

As a first step toward understanding why we are so well off in some respects and so lacking in others, we need to understand how our economy works. Of course, this is a big task. Indeed, you could say that this whole book is devoted to discussing this subject. So we will not try to present a detailed picture of the operation of the American economy at this point. All we shall do now is give a preliminary sketch, a basic blueprint of some of the highlights. The details will be provided later, as they are needed.

The American Economy: Some Salient Facts

To begin with, let's take up a few elementary facts about the American economy. First, it is huge. The United States contains over 210 million people, about 95 million of whom are in the labor force. Table 3.1 shows how large our population is, relative to other major nations. In addition, the American economy contains over 12 million business firms, and thousands of local and state governments, as well as the enormous federal government with its many departments and agencies. By practically any standard, ours is one of the biggest economic shows on earth.

Second, the American economy is very rich and productive. In 1975, our income per capita was about $7,000 per year. In other words, if you take the total amount of income that Americans made that year and divide by the number of Americans in existence (including all ages), the result equals about $7,000. Table 3.2 shows some rough estimates of income per capita in selected countries in 1976; the results put the United States at the top of the list. Moreover, the United States produces an enormous amount of such basic products as steel, petroleum, chemicals, electric power, automobiles, electronic computers, and a myriad of other goods. For example, we lead the world in steel production, electric energy production, and computer production, three basic indices of industrial might.

Table 3.1
Population, 1974, Selected Countries

Country	Population (millions of people)
China	800
India	586
Soviet Union	251
United States	211
Japan	110
Germany	62
United Kingdom	56
Italy	56

Source: United Nations.

Table 3.2
Income Per Capita, 1976, Selected Countries

Country	Income per capita (dollars)
United States	7,700
Canada	7,500
Sweden	7,100
France	6,400
Germany	6,200
Japan	4,900
United Kingdom	4,800
Italy	4,000
Soviet Union	3,700
Egypt	700
India	500
China	400

These estimates are rough, because of problems in converting other currencies into dollars, and for other reasons. Nonetheless, they should provide reasonable indications of relative orders of magnitude.

Third, our economy is based heavily on freedom of choice. Consumers can buy what they like, and reject what they do not like; workers can take jobs when and where they please, and quit if they please; firms can produce whatever products they want to produce, and use whatever techniques they want to use. Of course, this freedom is not unlimited. For example, there are laws to prevent people and firms from engaging in antisocial dealings. Moreover, this freedom is not all it might be. For example, it is sometimes difficult for a firm to enter a market, or for a person to get a particular type of job. Yet relative to other countries, our economy is very free.

Fourth, the American economy is rich in economic resources. As you will recall from Chapter 1, economic resources are the land, labor, and capital used to produce the goods and services that people want. The United States is blessed with a big, industrious, well-educated labor force, as well as a large amount of plant and equipment. Also, the United States has a great deal of fertile soil and natural resources. Even in the case of energy resources, where fear has been expressed that we shall become increasingly dependent on foreign sources of supply, the United States is by no means poor. We lead the world in coal reserves, and have a considerable amount of oil.

Finally, the American economy is noted for its sophisticated and advanced technology. In contrast to pure science (where, until World War II, the United States was not a leader), the United States has long been a leader in many areas of technology. This technological lead seems to have narrowed somewhat in recent decades, but it still exists. According to data collected by the National Science Board and the Organization for Economic Cooperation and Development, the United States has been responsible for a very large share of the major new processes and products introduced since World War II.

The Tasks of an Economic System

Although many of the statistics concerning the American economy are impressive, we cannot evaluate how well an economic system (or any system) is working unless we know what it is meant to do. Basically, as we saw in Chapter 1, there are four things that any economic system—*ours or any other*—must do. First, *it must determine the level and composition of society's output.* That is, it must answer questions like: To what extent should society's resources be used to produce new destroyers and missiles? To what extent should they be used to produce sewage plants to reduce water pollution? To what extent should they be used to produce swimming pools for the rich? To what extent should they be used to produce low-cost housing for the poor? Pause for a moment to think about how important—and how vast—this function is. Most people simply take for granted that somehow it is decided what we as a society are going to produce, and far too few people really think about the social mechanisms that determine the answers to such questions.

Second, *an economic system must determine how each good and service is to be produced.* Given existing technology, a society's resources can be used in various ways. Should the skilled labor in Birmingham, Alabama, be used to produce cotton or steel? Should a particular machine tool be used to produce aircraft or automobiles? The way questions of this sort are answered will determine the way each good and service is produced. In other words, it will determine which resources are used to produce which goods and services. If this function is performed badly, society's resources are put to the wrong uses, resulting in less output than if this function is performed well.

Third, *an economic system must determine*

how the goods and services that are produced are to be distributed among the members of society. In other words, how much of each type of good and service should each person receive? Should there be a considerable amount of income inequality, the rich receiving much more than the poor? Or should incomes be relatively equal? Take your own case: somehow or other, the economic system determines how much income you will receive. In our economic system, your income depends on your skills, the property you own, how hard you work, and prevailing prices, as we shall see in succeeding chapters. But in other economic systems, your income might depend on quite different factors. This function of the economic system has generated, and will continue to generate, heated controversy. Some people favor a relatively egalitarian society where the amount received by one family varies little from that received by another family of the same size. Other people favor a less egalitarian society where the amount a family or person receives varies a great deal. Few people favor a thoroughly egalitarian society, if for no other reason than that some differences in income are required to stimulate workers to do certain types of work.

Fourth, *an economic system must determine the rate of growth of per capita income.* An adequate growth rate has come to be regarded as an important economic goal, particularly in the less developed countries of Africa, Asia, and Latin America. There is very strong pressure in these countries for changes in technology, the adoption of superior techniques, increases in the stock of capital resources, and better and more extensive education and training of the labor force. These are viewed as some of the major ways to promote the growth of per capita income. In the industrialized nations, the goal of economic growth has become somewhat more controversial. Some observers claim that we have become rich enough, while others point out that since so many of the world's people, here and abroad, are poor, it seems hard to believe that extra output would not be useful.

The Economic System: A Simple Introductory Model

The Product Transformation Curve and the Determination of What Is Produced

In the previous chapter, we said that economists use models to throw light on economic problems. At this point, let's try our hand at constructing a simple model to illuminate the basic functions any economic system, ours included, must perform. To keep things simple, suppose that society produces only two goods, food and tractors. This, of course, is unrealistic, but, as we stressed in the previous chapter, a model does not have to be realistic to be useful. Here, by assuming that there are only two goods, we eliminate a lot of unnecessary complexity and lay bare the essentials. In addition, we suppose that society has at its disposal a certain amount of resources, and that this amount is fixed for the duration of the period in question. This assumption is quite realistic. So long as the period is relatively short, the amount of a society's resources is relatively fixed (except, of course, under unusual circumstances, such as if a country annexes additional land). Finally, we suppose as well that society's technology is fixed. So long as the period is relatively short, this assumption too is realistic.

Under these circumstances, it is possible to figure out the various amounts of food and tractors that society can produce. Specifically, we can proceed as in Chapter 1, where we determined the amounts of food and clothing that an isolated town could produce. Let's begin with how many tractors society can produce if all resources are devoted to tractor production:

Table 3.3
Alternative Combinations of Outputs of Food and Tractors That Can Be Produced

Possibility	Food (millions of tons)	Tractors (millions)
A	0	15
B	2	14
C	4	12
D	6	10
E	8	7
F	10	4
G	12	0

According to Table 3.3, the answer is 15 million tractors. Next, let's consider the opposite extreme, where society devotes all its resources to food production: According to Table 3.3, it can produce 12 million tons of food in this case. Next, let's consider cases where both products are being produced: Such cases are represented by possibilities *B* to *F* in the table. As emphasized in Chapter 1, the more of one good that is produced, the less of the other good can be produced. Why? Because to produce more of one good, resources must be taken away from the production of the other good, lessening the amount of the other good produced.

Figure 3.1 shows how we can use a graph (based on the principles in Chapter 2) to show the various production possibilities society can attain. It is merely a different way of presenting the data in Table 3.3; the output of food is plotted on the horizontal axis and the output of tractors on the vertical axis. The curve in Figure 3.1, which shows the various combinations of output of food and tractors that society can produce, is called a ***product transformation curve.*** Economists are fond of inelegant labels of this sort. Like Eliza Doolittle, heroine of *My Fair Lady* (and *Pygmalion,* in her earlier incarnation), economics is sometimes guilty of "cold-blooded murder of the English tongue." But so are other sciences. You just have to roll with the punches—and learn what these strange-sounding terms mean.

The product transformation curve is a useful indicator of the economic tasks facing any society. It shows the various production possibilities open to society. For example, in Figure

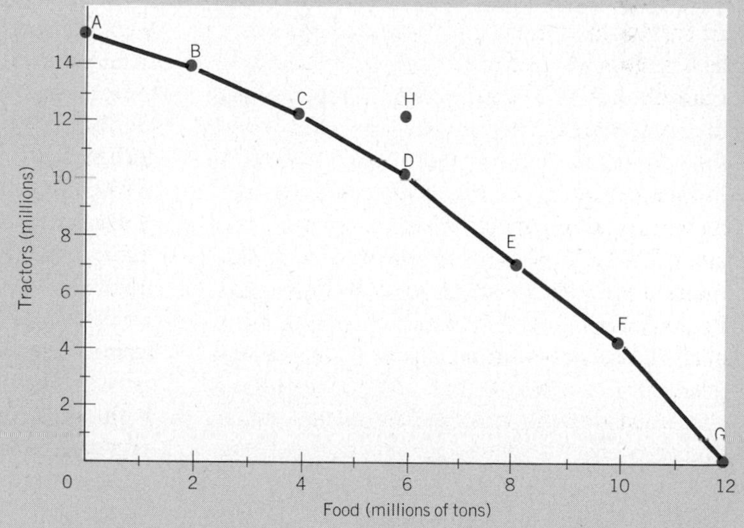

Figure 3.1
Product Transformation Curve
This curve shows the various combinations of tractors and food that can be produced efficiently with given resources and technology. Point *H* is unattainable.

3.1, society can choose to produce 4 million tons of food and 12 million tractors (point *C*), or 6 million tons of food and 10 million tractors (point *D*), but it cannot choose to produce 6 million tons of food and 12 million tractors (point *H*). Point *H* is inaccessible with this society's resources and technology: Perhaps it will become accessible if the society's resources increase or if its technology improves, but for the present, point *H* is out of reach.

Since society must wind up somewhere on the product transformation curve, it is clear that *the first function of any economic system—to determine the level and composition of society's output—is really a problem of determining at what point along the product transformation curve society should be.* Should society choose point *A, B, C, D, E, F,* or *G?* In making this choice, one thing is obvious from the product transformation curve: *you cannot get more of one good without giving up some of the other good.* In other words, you cannot escape the problem of choice. So long as resources are limited and technology is less than magic, you must reckon with the fact (emphasized in Chapter 1) that more of one thing means less of another. The old saw that you don't "get something for nothing" is hackneyed, but true, so long as resources are fully and efficiently utilized.

The Law of Increasing Cost

In the previous section, we stressed that an increased output of one good (say, food) means a decreased output of the other good (say, tractors). This amounts to saying (in the language of Chapter 1) that the alternative cost of producing more food is the output of tractors that must be forgone. In this section, we go a step further: we point out that, *as more and more of a good is produced, the production of yet another unit of this good is likely to entail a larger and larger alternative cost* and we explain why this is true.

This so-called law of increasing cost can be demonstrated in Figure 3.1. What is the cost of increasing food output from 0 to 2 million tons? It is 1 million tractors (since this is the amount that tractor output must be reduced if this increase in food output takes place). What is the cost of increasing food output from 2 to 4 million tons? It is 2 million tractors. What is the cost of increasing food output from 4 to 6 million tons? It is 2 million tractors. What is the cost of increasing food output from 6 to 8 million tons? It is 3 million tractors. Similarly, the cost of increasing food output from 8 to 10 million tons is 3 million tractors, and the cost of increasing food output from 10 to 12 million tons is 4 million tractors.

The important point here is that, as more and more food is produced, the cost of increasing food output by 2 million tons increases. To see this, note that the *first* 2 million tons of food cost 1 million tractors, the *second* 2 million tons of food cost 2 million tractors, the *third* 2 million tons of food cost 2 million tractors, the *fourth* 2 million tons of food cost 3 million tractors, the *fifth* 2 million tons of food cost 3 million tractors, and the *sixth* 2 million tons of food cost 4 million tractors. Clearly, the more food that is already being produced, the greater the cost of producing an additional 2 million tons.

Why is this the case? Basically, it is because resources are not as effective in producing one good as in producing the other. When society only produces a small amount of food, it can use in food production those resources that are well suited to producing food and not so well suited to producing tractors. But as society produces more and more food, it tends to run out of such resources, and must absorb into food production those resources that are less suited to producing food and better suited to producing tractors. To increase food output by 2 million tons with the latter type of resources, a greater reduction must occur in tractor output than when the 2-million-ton increase in food output occurred with the resources that were well suited to food production (and not so well suited to producing tractors). Thus the cost of producing an additional 2 million tons of food tends to increase as more food is already being produced.

This law of increasing cost explains why a product transformation curve has the shape shown in Figure 3.1. That is, it explains why the product transformation curve has the "bowed-out" shape (rather than the "bowed-in" shape) indicated in Figure 3.2. Because the cost of increasing food output by a certain amount increases as more of it is already produced, the product transformation curve tends to fall more steeply as one moves from left to right along the horizontal axis—which explains why the product transformation curve has the "bowed-out" shape.

The Product Transformation Curve and the Determination of How Goods Are Produced

Let's turn now to the second basic function of any economic system: to determine how each good and service should be produced. In Table 3.3, we assumed implicitly that society's resources would be fully utilized and that the available technology would be applied in a way that would get the most out of the available resources. In other words, we assumed that the firms making food and tractors were as efficient as possible and that there was no unemployment of resources. But if there is widespread unemployment of people and machines, will society still be able to choose a point on the product transformation curve? Clearly, the answer is no. Since society is not using all of its resources, it will not be able to produce as much as if it used them all. Thus, *if there is less than full employment of resources, society will have to settle for points inside the product transformation curve.* For example, the best society may be able to do under these circumstances is to attain point K in Figure 3.3. Clearly, K is a less desirable point than C or D—but that is the price of unemployment.

Suppose, on the other hand, that there is full employment of resources but that firms are inefficient. Perhaps they promote relatives of the boss, regardless of their ability; perhaps the managers are lazy or not much interested in efficiency; or perhaps the workers like to take long coffee breaks and are unwilling to work hard. Whatever the reason, will society still be able to choose a point on the product transformation curve? Again, the answer is no. Since society is not getting as much as it could out of its resources, it will not be able to produce as

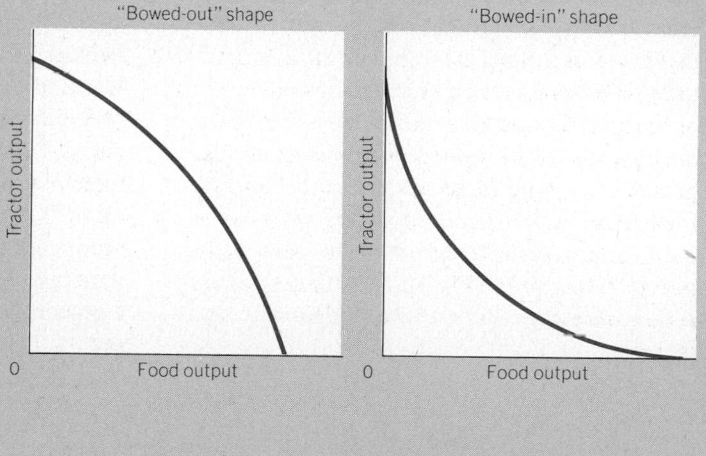

Figure 3.2
Shape of the Product Transformation Curve.
So long as the law of increasing cost holds true, the product transformation curve will have the shape on the left ("bowed-out"), *not* the shape on the right ("bowed-in").

Figure 3.3
Product Transformation Curve
This curve, like Figure 3.1, shows the various combinations of tractors and food that can be produced efficiently with given resources and technology. Point *K* is less desirable than points *C* or *D*, because less output is produced at this point. But because of unemployment or inefficiency, society may wind up at point *K*.

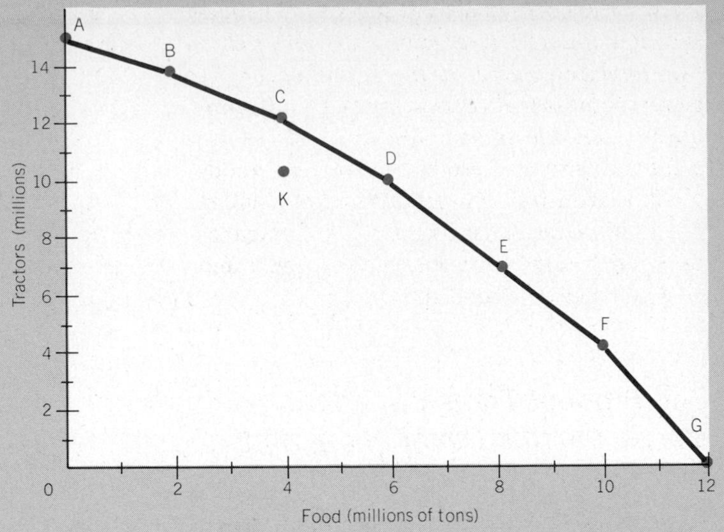

much as it would if its resources were used efficiently. Thus, *if resources are used inefficiently, society will have to settle for points inside the product transformation curve.* Perhaps in these circumstances, too, the best society can do may be point *K* in Figure 3.3. This less desirable position is the price of inefficiency.

At this point, it should be obvious that our model at least partially answers the question of how each good and service should be produced. The answer is to *produce each good and service in such a way that you wind up on the product transformation curve, not on a point inside it.* Of course, this is easier said than done, but at least our model indicates a couple of villains to watch out for: unemployment of resources and inefficiency. When these villains are present, we can be sure that society is not on the product transformation curve. Also, the old saw is wrong and it is possible to "get something for nothing" when society is inside the product transformation curve. That is, society can increase the output of one good without reducing the output of another good in such a situation. Society need not give up anything—in the way of production of other goods—to increase the production of this good under these circumstances.

This simple model helps illuminate the sequence of events in various countries at the beginning of World War II. In certain countries, like the Soviet Union, the war effort meant a substantial decrease in the standard of living on the home front. Resources had to be diverted from the production of civilian goods to the production of military goods, and the war struck a severe blow at the living standards of the civilian population. In other countries, like the United States, it was possible to increase the production of military goods without making such a dent in the living standards of the civilian population. This happened because the United States at the beginning of World War II was still struggling to emerge from the Great Depression, and several million people were still unemployed. The same was not true in the Soviet Union. Thus, we could increase the production of both guns and butter, whereas they could not.

Suppose that we divide all goods into two

classes: war goods and civilian goods. Then, as shown in Figure 3.4, *we were inside our product transformation curve at the beginning of the war, while the Russians were not.* Consequently, for the reasons discussed above, we could increase our production of war goods without reducing our production of civilian goods, while the Russians could not. (Note that in Figure 3.4, the two goods are war goods and civilian goods, not food and tractors).

The Product Transformation Curve, Income Distribution, and Growth

Let's return now to the case where our economy produces food and tractors. The third basic function of any economic system is to distribute the goods and services that are produced among the members of society. Each point on the product transformation curve in Figure 3.3 represents society's total pie, but to deal with the third function, we must know how the pie is divided up among society's members. Since the product transformation curve does not tell us this, it cannot shed light on this third function.

Fortunately, the product transformation curve is of more use in analyzing the fourth basic function of any economic system: to determine the society's rate of growth of per capita income. Suppose that the society in Figure 3.3 invests a considerable amount of its resources in developing improved processes and products. For example, it might establish agricultural experiment stations to improve farming techniques and industrial research laboratories to improve tractor designs. As shown in Figure 3.5, the product transformation curve will be pushed outward. This will be the result of improved technology, enabling more food and/or more tractors to be produced from the same amount of resources. Thus one way for an economy to increase its output—and its per capita income—may be to invest in research and development.

Another way is by devoting more of its resources to the production of capital goods rather than consumers' goods. ***Capital goods*** consist of plant and equipment that are used to make other goods; ***consumers' goods*** are items that consumers purchase like clothing, food, and drink. Since capital goods are themselves resources, a society that chooses to produce lots of capital goods and few consumers'

Figure 3.4
Effect of Increased Production of War Goods at the Beginning of World War II
Because the United States was at a point inside its product transformation curve, we could increase our production of war goods without reducing production of civilian goods. Because the Russians were on their product transformation curve, they could increase their output of war goods only by reducing output of civilian goods.

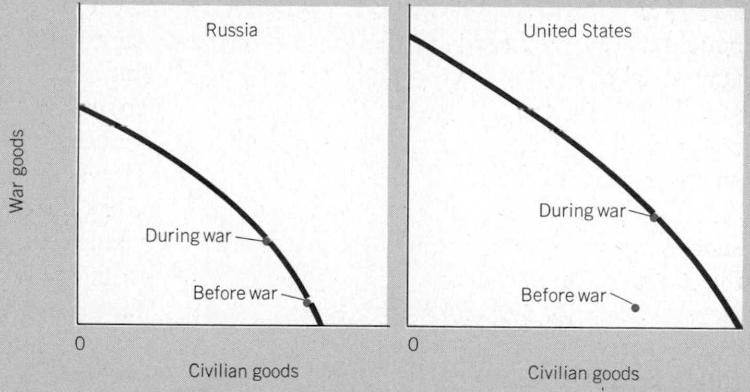

Figure 3.5
Effect of Improvement in Technology on Product Transformation Curve
An improvement in technology results in an outward shift of the product transformation curve.

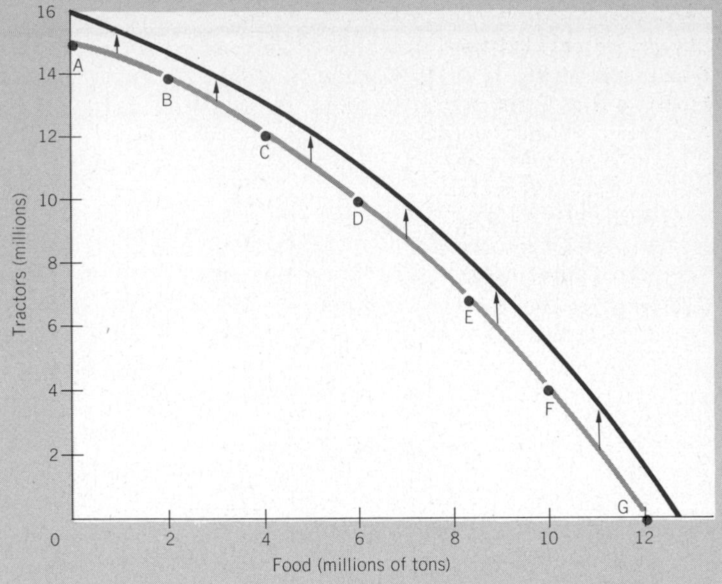

goods will push out its product transformation curve much farther than a society that chooses to produce lots of consumers' goods and few capital goods.

To illustrate this point, consider our simple society that produces food and tractors. The more tractors (and the less food) this society produces, the more tractors it will have in the next period; and the more tractors it has in the next period, the more of both goods—food and tractors—it will be able to produce then. Thus the more tractors (and the less food) this society produces, the farther out it will push its product transformation curve—and the greater the increase in output (and per capita income) that it will achieve in the next period. For example, if this society chooses point *F* (shown in Figures 3.5, 3.3, or 3.1), the effect will be entirely different than if it chooses point *C*. If it chooses point *F*, it produces 4 million tractors, which we assume to be the number of tractors worn out each year. Thus, if it chooses point *F*, it adds nothing to its stock of tractors: it merely replaces those that wear out. Since it has no more tractors in the next period than in the current period, the product transformation curve does not shift out at all if point *F* is chosen. On the other hand, if point *C* is chosen, the society produces 12 million tractors, which means that it has 8 million additional tractors at the beginning of the next period. Thus, as shown in Figure 3.6, the product transformation curve is pushed outward. By producing more capital goods (and less consumers' goods) our society has increased its production possibilities and its per capita income.

Essentially, this is the saving process described in Chapter 2 in connection with the Industrial Revolution. As pointed out there, England (and the other countries where the Industrial Revolution occurred) set aside some of its resources during the late eighteenth and early nineteenth centuries, and used them to produce capital goods, not consumption goods. In this way, the productive capacity of the nation was increased. But this was not the only reason for such an increase in productive capacity at that time. In addition, there were a

Figure 3.6
Effect of Increase in Capital Goods on Product Transformation Curve
An increase in the amount of capital goods results in an outward shift of the product transformation curve. The choice of point *C* means the production of more capital goods than the choice of point *F*.

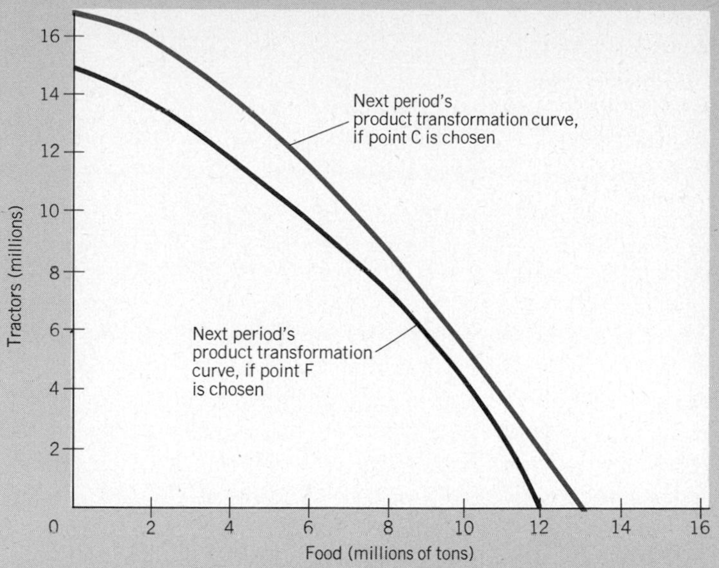

host of important technological advances, such as the steam engine and the spinning jenny, which also pushed the product transformation curve outward. Thus both the process of capital formation (illustrated in Figure 3.6) and the process of technological change (illustrated in Figure 3.5) were at work.

Capitalism: An Economic System

What Is Capitalism?

The particular kind of economic system the United States has adopted to carry out the four basic economic functions is ***capitalism.*** Capitalism is one of those terms that is frequently used but seldom defined, and even less frequently understood. Its operation is complex, but its principal characteristics can be lumped into four major categories.

Private ownership of capital. Under capitalism you or I can buy the tools of production. We can own factories, equipment, inventories, and other forms of capital. In a capitalistic system, somebody owns each piece of capital—and receives the income from it. Each piece of equipment has some sort of legal instrument indicating to whom it belongs. (If it belongs to a corporation, its owners basically are the stockholders who own the corporation.) Moreover, each piece of capital has a money market value. This system is in marked contrast to a Communist or socialist state where the government owns the capital. In these states, the government decides how much and what kinds of capital goods will be produced; it owns the capital goods; and it receives and distributes the income they produce. In the Soviet Union or China, no one can buy or put up a new steel plant: it simply isn't allowed.

The United States is basically a capitalistic system, but there are certain areas where the government, not individuals, owns capital, and where individual property rights are limited in various ways by the government. The government owns much of the tooling used in the defense industries; it owns dams and the Tennessee Valley Authority; and it owns research laboratories in such diverse fields as atomic energy, space exploration, and health. Further, the government determines how much of a man's assets can go to his heirs when he dies. (The rest goes to the government in the form of estate and inheritance taxes.) Also, the government can make a person sell his property to allow a road or other public project to be built. There are many such limitations on property rights. Ours is basically a capitalistic system, but it must be recognized that the government's role is important. More will be said on this score in subsequent sections.

Freedom of choice and enterprise. Another important characteristic of capitalism is freedom of choice and freedom of enterprise. ***Freedom of choice*** means that consumers are free to buy what they please and reject what they please; that laborers are free to work where, when, and if they please; and that investors are free to invest in whatever property they please. By ***freedom of enterprise,*** we mean that firms are free to enter whatever markets they please, obtain resources in whatever ways they can, and organize their affairs as best they can. Needless to say, this does not mean that firms can run roughshod over consumers and workers. Even the strongest champions of capitalism are quick to admit that the government must set "rules of the game" to prevent firms from engaging in sharp or unfair practices. But granting such limitations, the name of the game under capitalism is economic freedom.

Freedom to do what? Under capitalism, individuals and firms are free to pursue their own self-interest. Put in today's idiom, each individual or firm can do his, her, or its own thing. However, it is important to note that this freedom is circumscribed by one's financial resources. Consumers in a capitalistic system can buy practically anything they like—if they have the money to pay for it. Similarly, workers can work wherever or whenever they please—if they don't mind the wages. And a firm can run its business as it likes—if it remains solvent. Thus an important regulator of economic activity under capitalism is the pattern of income and prices that emerges in the market place.

Competition. Still another important characteristic of capitalism is ***competition.*** Firms compete with one another for sales. Under perfect competition, there are a large number of firms producing each product; indeed, there are so many that no firm controls the product's price. Because of this competition, firms are forced to jump to the tune of the consumer. If a firm doesn't produce what consumers want—at a price at least as low as other firms are charging—it will lose sales to other firms. Eventually, unless it mends its ways, such a firm will go out of business. Of course, in real-life American markets, the number of producers is not always so large that no firm has any control over price. (Much more will be said on this score below.) But in the purest form of capitalism, such imperfections do not exist. Also, lest you think that competition under capitalism is confined to producers, it must be remembered that owners of resources also compete. They are expected to offer their resources—including labor—to the buyer who gives them the best deal, and buyers of resources and products are supposed to compete openly and freely.

Reliance upon markets. Finally, another very important characteristic of capitalism is its reliance upon markets. *Under pure capitalism, the market—the free market—plays a central role.* Firms and individuals buy and sell products and resources in competitive markets. Some firms and individuals make money and prosper; others lose money and fail. Each firm or individual is allowed freedom to pursue his interests in the market place, while the government guards against shady and dishonest dealings. Such is the nature of the economic system under pure capitalism.

How Does Capitalism Perform the Four Basic Economic Tasks?

The ***price system*** lies at the heart of any capitalist economy. In a purely capitalist economy, it is used to carry out the four basic economic functions discussed above. The price system is a way to organize an economy. Under such a system, every commodity and every service, including labor, has a price. Everyone receives money for what he sells, including labor, and uses this money to buy the goods and services he wants. If more is wanted of a certain good, the price of this good tends to rise; if less is wanted, the price of the good tends to fall. Producers base their production decisions on the prices of commodities and inputs. Thus increases in a commodity's price generally tend to increase the amount of it produced, and decreases generally tend to decrease the amount produced. In this way, firms' output decisions are brought into balance with consumers' desires.

The very important question of how the price system performs the basic economic functions we discussed above will be answered in some detail in the next chapter. All we can do here is provide a preliminary sketch of the way the price system carries out each of these four tasks. First, consider the determination of what the society will produce. In a substantially capitalistic economy, such as ours, consumers choose the amount of each good that they want, and producers act in accord with these decisions. The importance consumers attach to a good is indicated by the price they are willing to pay for it. Of course, the principle of ***consumer sovereignty***—producers dancing to the tune of consumers' tastes—should not be viewed as always and completely true, since producers do attempt to manipulate the tastes of consumers through advertising and other devices, but it is certainly a reasonable first approximation.

In its second fundamental task, the price system helps determine how each good and service will be produced by indicating the desires of workers and the relative value of various types of materials and equipment as well as the desires of consumers. For example, if plumbers are scarce relative to the demand for them, their price in the labor market—their wage—will be bid up, and they will tend to be used only in the places where they are productive enough so that their employers can afford to pay them the higher wages. The forces that push firms toward actually carrying out the proper decisions are profits and losses. Profits are the carrot and losses are the stick used to eliminate the less efficient and less alert firms and to increase the more efficient and the more alert.

How does the price system accomplish its third task, of determining how much in the way of goods and services each member of the society is to receive? In general, an individual's income depends largely on the quantities of resources of various kinds that he owns and the prices he gets for them. For example, if a man both works and rents out farm land he owns, his income is the number of hours he works per year times his hourly wage rate plus the number of acres of land he owns times the annual rental per acre. Thus the distribution of income depends on the way resource ownership—including talent, intelligence, training, work habits, and, yes, even character—is distributed among the population. Also, to be candid, it depends on just plain luck.

Finally, how does the price system determine the nation's rate of growth of per capita income? A nation's rate of growth of per capita income depends on the rate of growth of its resources and the rate of increase of the efficiency with which they are used. In our economy, the rate at which labor and capital resources are increased is motivated, at least in part, through the price system. Higher wages for more skilled work are an incentive for an individual to undergo further education and training. Capital accumulation occurs in response to the expectation of profit. Increases in efficiency, due in considerable measure to the advance of technology, are also stimulated by the price system.

Our Mixed Capitalist System

The Role of Government

Since the days of Adam Smith, economists have been fascinated by the features of a purely capitalistic economic system—an economy that relies entirely on the price system. Smith, and many generations of economists since, have gone to great pains to explain that in such an economic system, *the price system, although it is not controlled by any person or small group, results in economic order, not chaos.* The basic economic tasks any economy must perform can, as we have said, be carried out in such an economic system by the price system. It is an effective means of coordinating economic activity through decentralized decision making based on information disseminated through prices and related data.

But does this mean that the American economy is purely capitalistic? As we have noted repeatedly in previous sections, the answer is no. A purely capitalistic system is a useful model of reality, not a description of our economy as it exists now or in the past. It is useful because a purely capitalistic economy is, for some purposes, a reasonably close fit to our own. However, this does not mean that such a model is useful for all purposes. Many American markets are not entirely competitive and never will be; they are dominated by a few producers or buyers who can influence price and thus distort the workings of the price system. Moreover, *the American economy is a mixed capitalistic economy, an economy where both government and private decisions are important.* The role of the government in American economic activity is very large indeed. Although it is essential to understand the workings of a purely capitalistic system, any model that omits the government entirely cannot purport to be adequate for the analysis of many major present-day economic issues.

To create a more balanced picture of the workings of the American economy, we must recognize that, although the price system plays an extremely important role, it is not permitted to solve all of the basic economic problems of our society. Consumer sovereignty does not extend—and cannot realistically be extended—to all areas of society. For example, certain public services cannot be left to private enterprise. The provision of fire protection, the operation of schools, and the development of weapons systems are examples of areas where we rely on political decision making, not the price system alone. Moreover, with regard to the consumption of commodities like drugs, society imposes limits on the decisions of individuals.

In addition, certain consequences of the price system are, by general agreement, unacceptable. Reliance on the price system alone does not assure a just or equitable or optimal distribution of income. It is possible, for example, that one person will literally have money to burn while another person will live in degrading poverty. Consequently, the government modifies the distribution of income by imposing taxes that take more from the rich than the poor, and by welfare programs that try to keep the poor from reaching the point where they lack decent food, adequate clothing, or shelter. Besides providing public services and maintaining certain minimum income standards, the government also carries out a variety of regulatory functions. Industries do not police the actions of their constituent firms, so it falls to the government to establish laws that impose limits on the economic behavior of firms. For example, these laws say that firms must not misrepresent their products, that child labor must not be employed, and that firms must not collude and form monopolies to interfere with the proper functioning of the price system. In this way, the government tries, with varying effectiveness, to establish the "rules of the game"—the limits within which the economic behavior of firms (and consumers) should lie.

Capital, Specialization, and Money: Other Characteristics of the American Economy

Finally, we must point out three additional characteristics of the American economy: the use of a great deal of capital per worker, specialization, and the use of money. These characteristics are common to all modern, industrialized nations, not just the United States, and they are so obvious that you may take them for granted. But they are too important to be ignored.

First, consider the enormous amount of capital American labor has to work with. Think of the oil refineries in New Jersey and Philadelphia, the blast furnaces and open hearths in Pittsburgh and Cleveland, the railroad yards of Chicago and Wichita, the aircraft plants in California and Georgia, the skyscrapers of New York, and the host of additional types of capital that we have and use in this country. To understand this idea fully, stop and think about what we mean by capital. As noted in Chapter 1, to the economist capital is not the same as money. A man with a hot-dog stand who has $100 in his pocket may say that he has $100 in capital. But his definition is different from that of the economist, who would include in the man's capital the value of his stand; the value of his equipment; the value of his inventories of hot dogs, buns, and mustard; and the value of other nonlabor resources (other than land) that he uses.

Defining capital as economists do, it is evident that American workers have an enormous amount of capital to work with. And it is evident as well that this enormous amount of capital, together with an advanced technology, and a well-trained labor force, is responsible for the tremendous amount of goods and services the American economy produces. All this capital contributes to increased production because it is often more efficient to adopt ***roundabout methods of production.*** For example, it is often more efficient to build a blast furnace and open hearth to produce steel rather than to try to produce steel directly. On the other hand, harking back to our discussion of Figure 3.6, it is also true that the production of capital goods means that less consumers' goods can be produced in the current period. In other words, although a greater amount of capital means greater production, consumers must be willing—or forced—to forgo current consumption of goods and services to produce this capital.

Next, consider the tremendous amount of specialization in the American economy. You may decide to specialize in tax law (and a particular branch of tax law at that), a classmate may specialize in brain surgery, another may specialize in repairing hi-fi sets, and another in monitoring certain types of equipment in an oil refinery. In contrast to more primitive economies, where people specialize much less, the American economy is characterized by an intricate web of specialization. What does it accomplish? As stressed by Adam Smith over two centuries ago, it results in much greater output than if people attempted to be Jacks-of-all-trades. Because of this specialization, people can concentrate on the tasks they do best. For example, Bobby Fischer, the world champion chess player, can concentrate on chess and leave the hi-fi repairs to people who understand more about woofers and tweeters. However, it should be recognized that this specialization also results in great interdependence. Because each of us performs such specialized tasks, each of us depends on others for most of the things he needs. For example, unless you are much better at farming than I am, you would lose a lot of weight—and not because you wanted to—if farmers decided that they no longer wanted to provide us city folks with the fruits (and vegetables) of their labor.

Finally, the use of money is another important characteristic of all economies, including the American economy. Unquestionably you take the use of money as much for granted as you do the fact that the moon revolves about the earth. But money is a social invention. There is no evidence that Adam and Eve were created with the idea of money. They, or their descendants, had to think it up themselves, and this took time, as evidenced by the fact that extremely primitive cultures resorted to barter, which meant that to get a particular commodity, you had to swap a commodity that you owned for it. Since the exchange of commodities and services by barter was very difficult, the use of money has made trade and exchange much, much easier and facilitated the specialization of labor.

Summary

The product transformation curve, which shows the various production possibilities a society can attain, is useful in indicating the nature of the economic tasks any society faces. The task of determining the level and composition of society's output is really a problem of determining at what point along the product transformation curve society should be. Society, in performing this task, has to recognize that it cannot get more of one good without giving up some of another good, if resources are fully and efficiently used. However, if they are not fully and efficiently used, society will have to settle for points inside the product transformation curve—and it will be possible to obtain more of one good without giving up some of another good.

Clearly, the task of determining how each good and service should be produced is, to a considerable extent, a problem of keeping society on its product transformation curve, rather than at points inside the curve. The product transformation curve does not tell us anything about the distribution of income, but it does indicate various ways that a society can promote growth in per capita income. By doing research and development, or by producing capital goods (rather than consumers'goods), society may push its product transformation curve outward, thus increasing per capita income.

The American economy is one of the richest in the world. Based on freedom of enterprise, the American economy is rich in resources—land, labor, and capital—and American technology is among the most advanced in the world. Ours is a capitalistic economy, an economic system in which there is private ownership of capital, freedom of choice, freedom of enterprise, competition, and reliance upon markets. Many countries do not have a capitalistic economy, and even ours is not a purely capitalistic system. Under pure capitalism, the price system is used to perform the four basic economic tasks. Although it is not controlled by any person or small group, the price system results in order, not chaos.

A purely capitalistic system is a useful model of reality, not a description of our economy as it exists now or in the past. The American economy is a mixed capitalistic economy, in which both government and private decisions are important. For example, certain public services, like fire protection and schools, cannot be left to private enterprise. In addition, society has said that certain consequences of the price system—like the existence of abject poverty—are unacceptable. For this reason and others, the government carries out a long and impressive array of additional functions, many of which are discussed in subsequent chapters.

CONCEPTS FOR REVIEW

Product transformation curve
Capital goods
Consumers' goods
Capitalism
Capital
Consumer sovereignty
Money

QUESTIONS FOR DISCUSSION AND REVIEW

1. In a famous passage from *The Wealth of Nations,* Adam Smith said that "the great increase of the quantity of work, which, in consequence of the division of labor, the same number of people are capable of performing, is owing to three different circumstances; first, to the increase of dexterity in every particular workman; secondly, to the saving of the time which is commonly lost in passing from one species of work to another; and lastly, to the invention of a great number of machines which facilitate and abridge labor, and enable one man to do the work of many." Taking medicine, law, engineering, or some other profession, describe in detail how specialization tends to increase productivity. Then indicate whether more and more specialization is a good thing. (Beyond some point, is more specialization counterproductive?)

2. "[How] does New York City each day obtain about the quantity of milk that it demands? Of the thousands of people engaged in supplying New York with milk, almost none knows how much the city consumes or how much is being produced.[1]"

3. "The English obtain about twice as many bushels of wheat per acre as do the Americans, but we obtain about twice as many bushels per man.[2]" Why do you think this is true? Does it indicate that the price system is not working properly in the United States, England, or both?

4. According to Karl Marx, "the division of labor seizes upon not only the economic but every other sphere of society and everywhere lays the foundation of that all-engrossing system of specializing and sorting men, that development in a man of one single faculty at the expense of all other faculties, which caused A. Ferguson, the master of Adam Smith, to exclaim: 'We make a nation of helots, and have no free citizens.' " Comment.

5. "Libertarians fail to realize that the price system is, and ought to be, a method of coercion. . . . The very term 'rationing by the purse" illustrates the point. Economists defend such forms of rationing, but they have to do so primarily in terms of its efficiency and its fairness."[3] Comment.

6. "The great advantage of the [price system] . . . is that it permits wide diversity. It is, in political terms, a system of proportional representation. Each man can vote, as it were, for the color of tie he wants and get it; he does not have to see what color the majority wants and then, if he is in the minority, submit."[4] Comment.

[1] S. Slichter, *Modern Economic Society,* New York: Holt, 1928.
[2] *Ibid.*
[3] P. Samuelson, "The Economic Role of Private Activity," *A Dialogue on the Proper Economic Role of the State,* Chicago: University of Chicago Press, 1963.
[4] M. Friedman, *Capitalism and Freedom,* Chicago: University of Chicago Press, 1962, p. 15.

7. Suppose that a society's product transformation curve is as follows:

	Output (per year)	
Possibility	Food (millions of tons)	Tractors (millions)
A	0	30
B	4	28
C	8	24
D	12	20
E	16	14
F	20	8
G	24	0

(a) Is it possible for the society to produce 30 million tons of food per year? (b) Can it produce 30 million tractors per year? (c) Suppose this society produces 20 million tons of food and 6 million tractors per year. Is it operating on the product transformation curve? If not, what factors might account for this?

8. Plot the product transformation curve in Question 7 in a graph. At what point along the horizontal axis does the curve cut the axis? At what point along the vertical axis does the curve cut the axis?

9. Suppose that, because of important technological improvements, the society in Question 7 can double its production of tractors at each level of food production. If so, is this society on its new product transformation curve if it produces 20 million tons of food and 16 million tractors? Plot the new product transformation curve. At what point along the horizontal axis does the new curve cut the axis? At what point along the vertical axis does it cut the axis?

10. Given its present resources, a university like Harvard or Yale can choose to accept and graduate more graduate students and less undergraduates, or less graduate students and more undergraduates. Show how the concept of the product transformation curve can be used to represent the choices open to such a university.

4 The Price System: Consumers, Firms, and Markets

Capitalist economies use the price system to perform the four basic tasks any economic system must carry out. Of course, as we pointed out in the previous chapter, the American economy is a mixed capitalist system, not a pure one. But this does not mean that the price system is unimportant. On the contrary, the price system plays a vital role in the American economy, and to obtain even a minimal grasp of the workings of our economic system, one must understand how the price system operates. This chapter takes up the nature and functions of the price system, as well as some applications of our theoretical results to real-life problems. For example, we show how the price system determines the quantity produced of a commodity like wheat, and how the pricing policies of the Broadway theater hurt show business in a variety of ways. These applications should help illustrate the basic theory and indicate its usefulness.

Consumers

We begin by describing and discussing consumers and firms, the basic building blocks that make up the private, or nongovernmental, sector of the economy. What is a consumer? Sometimes—for example, when a person buys a beer on a warm day—the consumer is an individual. In other cases—for example, when a family buys a new car—the consumer may be an entire household. Consumers purchase the goods and services that are the ultimate end-products of the economic system. When a man buys tickets to a ball game, he is a consumer; when he buys himself a Coke at the game, he is a consumer; and when he buys his wife a book on baseball for their twentieth wedding anniversary, he is also a consumer.

Consumers—whether individuals or households—are an extremely varied lot. To get some idea of the variation, let's look at two families, the Rockefellers and the Ríoses. First, consider the Rockefeller family. *Fortune* magazine has credited seven Rockefellers with a minimum combined wealth of $1 billion, and a maximum of $1.9 billion. These descendants of John D. Rockefeller, who amassed an enormous fortune in the oil business (and founded Standard Oil), live in regal style. The grandsons of John D.—including former Governor and Vice-President Nelson Rockefeller and David Rockefeller, chairman of the Chase Manhattan Bank—each have a large house on the Rockefeller estate of over 4,000 acres at Pocantico Hills, New York. The estate has scores of buildings, including a $1 million recreation facility that contains bowling alleys, a tennis court, a swimming pool, and a squash court. Further, the Rockefeller brothers have New York City homes, and plantations in Venezuela, Hawaii, and elsewhere. Certainly, the Rockefellers consume on a mammoth scale. And they can afford it. Since they are estimated to be worth at least $1 billion, even if they put their money in a savings account at 5 percent interest, they would have more than $50 million per year coming in. Clearly, the Rockefellers have kept the wolf at a remarkable distance from the door!

In contrast, let's look at the Ríoses, a Puerto Rican family living in La Esmeralda, a slum section of San Juan. There are three branches of the Ríos family. One is headed by a man who works as a messenger and makes about $1,700 a year, another by a woman who works as a barmaid and makes about $1,500 a year, and another by a woman who makes about $500 a year. The Ríoses consume relatively little. They live in crowded quarters with inadequate sanitary facilities, none of them has a refrigerator, and on the average, the members of this family have spent about four years in school. Excluding clothing, the total value of the possessions of these households is $436, $149, and $120; and the total value of each household's clothing is $496, $70, and $53.[1] Clearly, the Ríos family, which is quite typical of the families in La Esmeralda, is an example of abject poverty. To compare the level of consumption of the Rockefellers with that of the Ríoses is to compare an ocean liner with a frail canoe: yet both are consumers.

Firms

There are over 12 million firms in the United States. About $\frac{9}{10}$ of the goods and services produced in this country are produced by firms. (The rest are provided by government and not-for-profit institutions like universities and hospitals.) A firm is an organization that produces a good or service for sale. In contrast to not-for-profit organizations, firms attempt to make a profit. It doesn't take great analytical power to see that an economy like ours is centered around the activities of firms.

Like consumers, firms are extremely varied in size, age, power, and purpose. Consider two examples, Peter Amacher's drugstore on Chi-

[1] Oscar Lewis, *La Vida,* New York: Random House, 1966.

cago's South Side and the General Motors Corporation. The Amacher drugstore, started in 1922 by Mr. Amacher's father-in-law, is known in the retail drug trade as an independent, because it has no affiliation with a chain-store organization. Mr. Amacher and two other pharmacists keep the store open for business 13 hours a day, except on Sundays. The store sells about $150,000 worth of merchandise per year. Prescriptions account for about 25 percent of total sales, and cosmetics and greeting cards are the other principal sales items. Amacher's drugstore is an example of the small-business segment of the American business community.

In contrast, General Motors is one of the giants of American industry. It is the largest manufacturer of automobiles in the United States, with sales in 1975 of over $35 billion. Besides cars, it makes trucks, locomotives, aircraft engines, household applicances, and other products. Its total assets amounted to about $22 billion in 1975; and its total employment was about 700,000. General Motors, which was formed by merger, was set up as a holding company in 1908 by William C. Durant, owner of the Buick Motor Car Company. Durant acquired about 50 auto companies and parts manufacturers and put them all together as General Motors. Its present share of the market is greater than it was in 1908, when it produced about 25 percent of all cars in this country. In 1974, for example, it produced abut 50 percent of all domestically produced cars.[2]

Markets

Consumers and firms come together in a market. The concept of a market is not quite as straightforward as it may seem, since most markets are not well defined geographically or physically. For example, the New York Stock Exchange is an atypical market because it is located principally in a particular building. For present purposes, *a* ***market*** *can be defined as a group of firms and individuals that are in touch with each other in order to buy or sell some good.* Of course, not every person in a market has to be in contact with every other person in the market. A person or firm is part of a market even if it is in contact with only a subset of the other persons or firms in the market.

Markets vary enormously in their size and procedures. For some toothpastes, most people who have their own teeth (and are interested in keeping them) are members of the same market; while for other goods like Picasso paintings, only a few dealers, collectors, and museums in certain parts of the world may be members of the market. And for still other goods, like lemonade sold by neighborhood children for a nickel a glass at a sidewalk stand, only people who walk by the stand—and are brave enough to drink the stuff—are members of the market. Basically, however, all markets consist primarily of buyers and sellers, although third parties like brokers and agents may be present as well.

Markets also vary in the extent to which they are dominated by a few large buyers or sellers. For example, in the United States, there was for many years only one producer of aluminum. Clearly this firm, the Aluminum Corporation of America, had great power in the market for aluminum. In contrast, the number of buyers and sellers in some other markets is so large that no single buyer or seller has any power over the price of the product. This is true in various agricultural markets, for example. When a market for a product contains so many buyers and sellers that none of them can influence the price, economists call the market ***perfectly competitive.*** In these introductory chapters, we make the simplifying assumptions that markets are perfectly competitive. We will relax that assumption later.

[2] L. Weiss, *Economics and American Industry,* New York: Wiley, 1961, p. 329; and General Motors' 1975 annual report.

Demand and Supply

The Demand Side of a Market

There are two sides of every market, just as there are of every argument. A market has a demand side and a supply side. *The* ***demand*** *side can be represented by a market demand curve, which shows the amount of the commodity buyers demand at various prices.* Consider Figure 4.1, which shows the demand curve for wheat in the American market during the middle 1970s.[3] The figure shows that about 1,850 million bushels of wheat will be demanded annually if the farm price is $3 per bushel, about 1,650 million bushels will be demanded annually if the farm price is $4 per bushel, and about 1,500 million bushels will be demanded annually if the farm price is $5 per bushel. The total demand for wheat is of several types: to produce bread and other food products for domestic use, as well as for feed use, for export purposes, and for industrial uses. The demand curve in Figure 4.1 shows the total demand—including all these components—at each price. Any demand curve pertains to a particular period of time, and its shape and position depend on the length of this period.

Take a good look at the demand curve for wheat in Figure 4.1. This simple, innocent-looking curve influences a great many people's lives. After all, wheat is the principal grain used for direct human consumption in the United States. To states like Kansas, North Dakota, Oklahoma, Montana, Washington, Nebraska, Texas, Illinois, Indiana, and Ohio, wheat is a mighty important cash crop. Note that the demand curve for wheat slopes downward to the right. In other words, the quantity of wheat demanded increases as the price falls. This is true of the demand curve for most commodities: they almost always slope downward to the right. This makes sense; one would expect increases in a good's price to result in a smaller quantity demanded.

What determines the position of the demand curve for a commodity? Why isn't the demand curve for wheat higher or lower, and what factors will cause it to shift? Although the position of the demand curve for a commodity depends on many and varied factors, those discussed below are generally of primary importance.

Consumer tastes. If consumers show an increasing preference for a product, the demand curve will shift to the right; that is, at each price, consumers will desire to buy more than previously. On the other hand, if consumers show a decreasing preference for a product, the demand curve will shift to the left, since, at each price, consumers will desire to buy less than previously. Take wheat. If consumers become convinced that foods containing wheat prolong life and promote happiness, the demand curve may shift, as shown in Figure 4.2; and the greater the shift in preferences, the larger the shift in the demand curve.

Income level of consumers. For some types of products, the demand curve shifts to the right if per capita income increases; whereas for other types of commodities, the demand curve shifts to the left if per capita income rises. Economists can explain why some goods fall into one category and other goods fall into the other, but, at present, this need not concern us. All that is important here is that changes in per capita income affect the demand curve, the size and direction of this effect varying from product to product. For example, in the case of wheat, a 10 percent increase in per capita income would probably have a relatively small effect on the demand curve, as shown in Figure 4.3.

Number of consumers in the market. Compare Austria's demand for wheat with America's. Austria is a small country with a population of about 7 million; the United States is a huge country with a population of about 211 million. Clearly, at a given price of wheat, the quantity

[3] I am indebted to officials of the U.S. Department of Agriculture for providing me with this information. Of course, these estimates are only rough approximations, but they are good enough for present purposes.

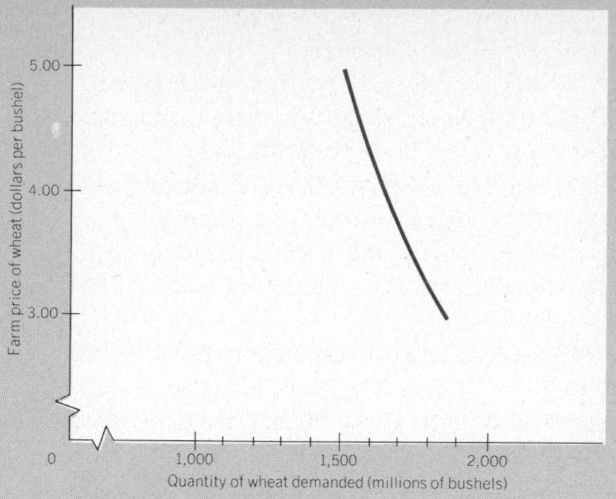

Figure 4.1
Market Demand Curve for Wheat, Middle 1970s
The curve shows the amount of wheat buyers would demand at various prices. At \$3.00 per bushel, over 20 percent more wheat can be sold than at \$5.00 per bushel.

Figure 4.2
Effect of Increased Preference for Wheat on Market Demand Curve
An increased preference for wheat would shift the demand curve to the right.

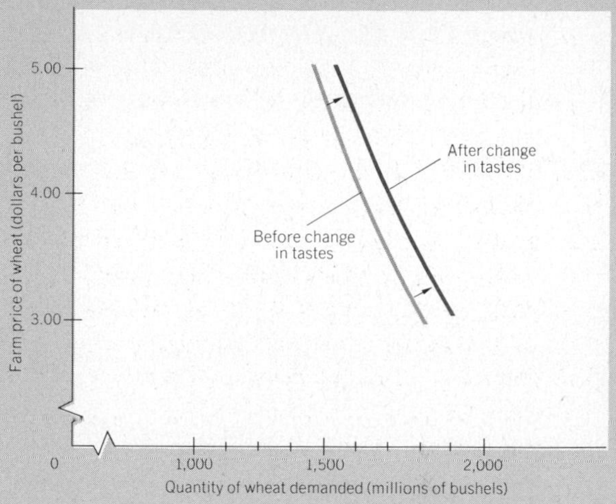

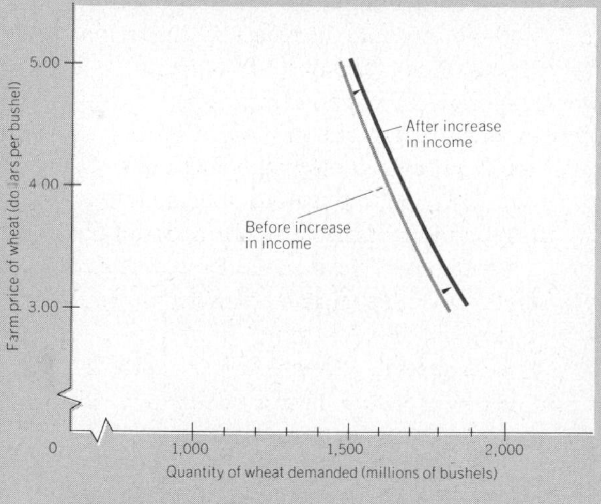

Figure 4.3
Effect of Increase in Income on Market Demand Curve for Wheat
An increase in income would shift the demand curve for wheat to the right, but only slightly.

Figure 4.4
Market Demand Curve for Wheat, Austria and the United States
Since the United States has far more consumers than Austria, the demand curve in the United States is far to the right of Austria's.

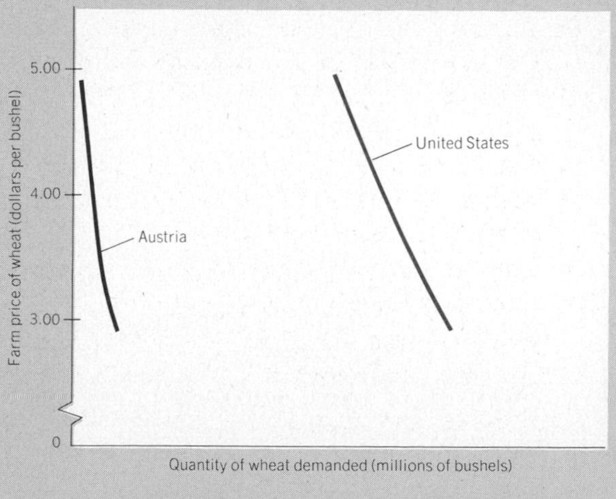

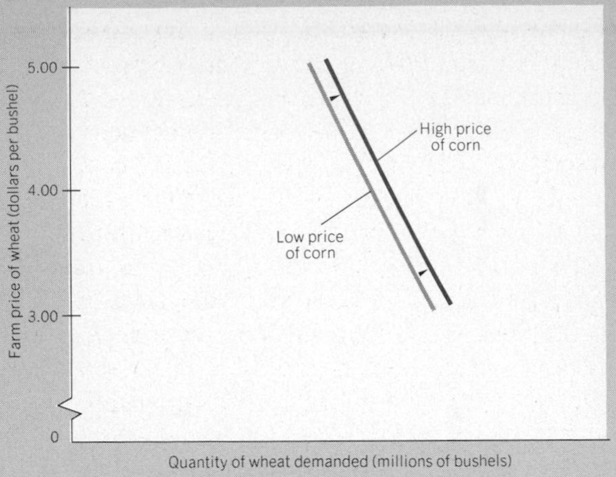

Figure 4.5
Effect of Price of Corn on Market Demand Curve for Wheat
Price increases for corn will shift the demand curve for wheat to the right.

Figure 4.6
Market Supply Curve for Wheat, Middle 1970s
The curve shows the amount of wheat sellers would supply at various prices. At $5.00 per bushel, over ⅓ more wheat would be supplied than at $3.00 per bushel.

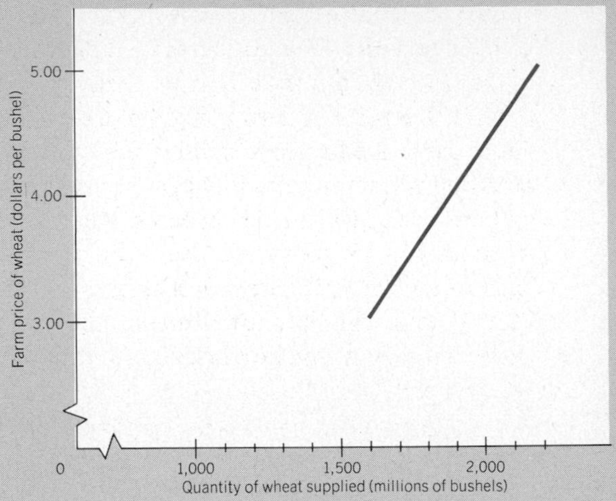

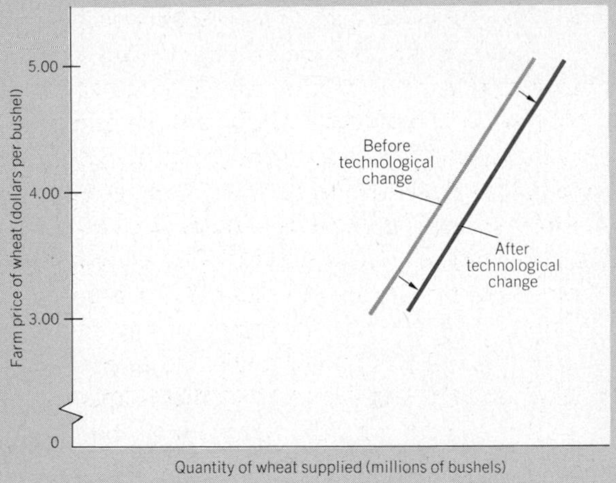

Figure 4.7
Effect of Technological Change on Market Supply Curve for Wheat
Improvements in technology often shift the supply curve to the right.

Figure 4.8
Effect of Increase in Farm Wage Rates on Market Supply Curve for Wheat
An increase in the wage rate might shift the supply curve to the left.

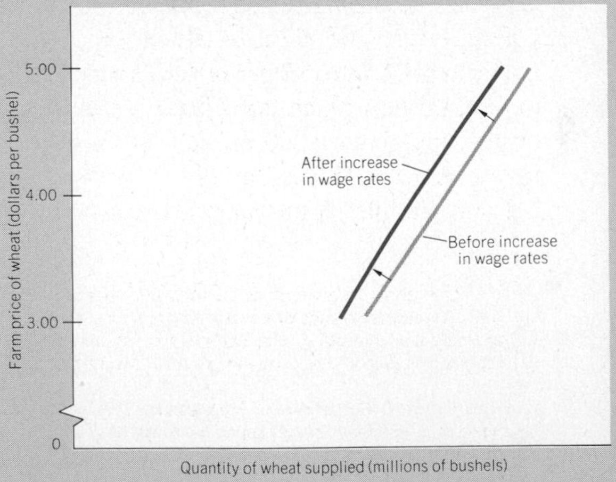

demanded by American consumers will greatly exceed the quantity demanded by Austrian consumers, as shown in Figure 4.4. Even if consumer tastes, income, and other factors were held constant, this would still be true simply because the United States has so many more consumers in the relevant market.[4]

Level of other prices. Since wheat can be substituted to some extent for corn as livestock feed, the quantity of wheat demanded depends on the price of corn as well as on the price of wheat. If the price of corn is high, more wheat will be demanded since it will be profitable to substitute wheat for corn. If the price of corn is low, less wheat will be demanded since it will be profitable to substitute corn for wheat. Thus, as shown in Figure 4.5, increases in the price of corn will shift the demand curve for wheat to the right, and decreases in the price of corn will shift it to the left.

The Supply Side of a Market

So much for our first look at demand. What about the other side of the market: supply? *The* ***supply*** *side of a market can be represented by a market supply curve that shows the amount of the commodity sellers will supply at various prices.* Let's continue with the case of wheat. Figure 4.6 shows the supply curve for wheat in the United States in the middle 1970s, based on estimates made informally by government experts.[5] According to the figure, about 1,600 million bushels of wheat would be supplied if the farm price were $3 per bushel, about 1,900 million bushels if the farm price were $4 per bushel, and about 2,200 million bushels if the farm price were $5 per bushel.

Look carefully at the supply curve shown in Figure 4.6. Although it looks innocuous enough, it summarizes the potential behavior of thousands of American wheat farmers—and their behavior plays an important role in determining the prosperity of many states and communities. Note that the supply curve for wheat slopes upward to the right. In other words, the quantity of wheat supplied increases as the price increases. This seems plausible, since increases in price give a greater incentive for farms to produce wheat and offer it for sale. Empirical studies indicate that the supply curves for a great many commodities share this characteristic of sloping upward to the right.

What determines the position of the supply curve for a commodity? As you might expect, it depends on a host of factors. But the following stand out.

Technology. Recall that technology was defined in Chapter 1 as society's pool of knowledge concerning the industrial arts. As technology progresses, it becomes possible to produce commodities more cheaply, so that firms often are willing to supply a given amount at a lower price than formerly. Thus technological change often causes the supply curve to shift to the right. For example, this certainly has occurred in the case of wheat, as shown in Figure 4.7. There have been many important technological changes in wheat production, ranging from advances in tractors to the development of improved varieties, like semidwarf wheats.

Input prices. The supply curve for a commodity is affected by the prices of the resources (labor, capital, and land) used to produce it. Decreases in the price of these inputs make it possible to produce commodities more cheaply, so that firms may be willing to supply a given amount at a lower price than they formerly would. Thus decreases in the price of inputs may cause the supply curve to shift to the right. On the other hand, increases in the price of inputs may cause it to shift to the left. For example, if the wage rates of farm labor increase, the supply curve for wheat may shift to the left, as shown in Figure 4.8.

[4] Note that no figures are given along the horizontal axis in Figure 4.4. This is because we do not have reasonably precise estimates of the demand curve in Austria. Nonetheless, the hypothetical demand curves in Figure 4.4 are close enough to the mark for present purposes.

[5] Officials of the U.S. Department of Agriculture provided me with these estimates. Although rough approximations, they are good enough for present purposes.

The Determination of Price

Equilibrium Price

The two sides of a market, demand and supply, interact to determine the price of a commodity. Recall from the previous chapter that prices in a capitalistic system are important determinants of what is produced, how it is produced, who receives it, and how rapidly per capita income grows. It behooves us, therefore, to look carefully at how prices themselves are determined in a capitalist system. As a first step toward describing this process, we must define the equilibrium price of a product. At various points in this book, you will encounter the concept of an equilibrium, which is very important in economics, as in many other scientific fields.

Put briefly, *an* ***equilibrium*** *is a situation where there is no tendency for change;* in other words, it is a situation that can persist. Thus, *an* ***equilibrium price*** *is a price that can be maintained.* Any price that it is not an equilibrium price cannot be maintained for long, since there are basic forces at work to stimulate a change in price. The best way to understand what we mean by an equilibrium price is to take a particular case, such as the wheat market. Let's put both the demand curve for wheat (in Figure 4.1) and the supply curve for wheat (in Figure 4.6) together in the same diagram. The result, shown in Figure 4.9, will help us determine the equilibrium price of wheat.

We begin by seeing what would happen if various prices were established in the market. For example, if the price were $4 per bushel, the demand curve indicates that 1,650 million bushels of wheat would be demanded, while the supply curve indicates that 1,900 million bushels would be supplied. Thus, if the price were $4 a bushel, there would be a mismatch between the quantity supplied and the quantity demanded per year, since the rate at which wheat is supplied would be greater than the rate at which it is demanded. Specifically, as shown in Figure 4.9, there would be an *excess supply* of 250 million bushels. Under these circumstances, some of the wheat supplied by farmers could not be sold, and as inventories of wheat built up, suppliers would tend to cut

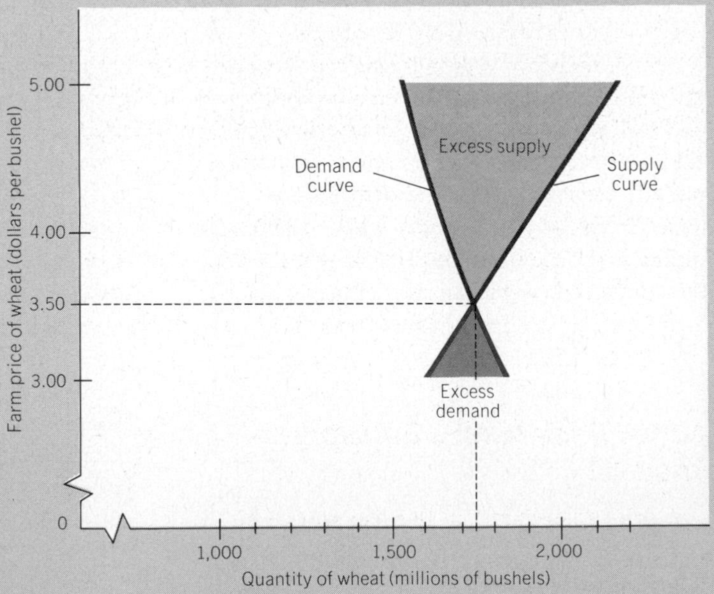

Figure 4.9
Determination of the Equilibrium Price of Wheat, Middle 1970s
The equilibrium price is $3.50 per bushel, and the equilibrium quantity is 1,750 million bushels. At a price of $4.00 per bushel, there would be an excess supply of 250 million bushels. At a price of $3.00 per bushel, there would be an excess demand of 250 million bushels.

their prices in order to get rid of unwanted inventories. Thus a price of $4 per bushel would not be maintained for long—and for this reason, $4 per bushel is not an equilibrium price.

If the price were $3 per bushel, on the other hand, the demand curve indicates that 1,850 million bushels would be demanded, while the supply curve indicates that 1,600 million bushels would be supplied. Again we find a mismatch between the quantity supplied and the quantity demanded per year, since the rate at which wheat is supplied would be less than the rate at which it is demanded. Specifically, as shown in Figure 4.9, there would be an *excess demand* of 250 million bushels. Under these circumstances, some of the consumers who want wheat at this price would have to be turned away empty-handed. There would be a shortage. And given this shortage, suppliers would find it profitable to increase the price, and competition among buyers would bid the price up. Thus, a price of $3 per bushel could not be maintained for long—so $3 per bushel is not an equilibrium price.

Under these circumstances, the equilibrium price must be the price where the quantity demanded equals the quantity supplied. Obviously, this is the only price at which there is no mismatch between the quantity demanded and the quantity supplied; and consequently the only price that can be maintained for long. In Figure 4.9, the price at which the quantity supplied equals the quantity demanded is $3.50 per bushel, the price where the demand curve intersects the supply curve. Thus $3.50 per bushel is the equilibrium price of wheat under the circumstances visualized in Figure 4.9, and 1,750 million bushels is the equilibrium quantity.

Actual Price versus Equilibrium Price

The price that counts in the real world, however, is the actual price, not the equilibrium price, and it is the actual price that we set out to explain. In general, economists simply assume that the actual price will approximate the equilibrium price, which seems reasonable enough, since the basic forces at work tend to push the actual price toward the equilibrium price. Thus, if conditions remain fairly stable for a time, the actual price should move toward the equilibrium price.

To see that this is the case, consider the market for wheat, as described by Figure 4.9. What if the price somehow is set at $4 per bushel? As we saw in the previous section, there is downward pressure on the price of wheat under these conditions. Suppose the price, responding to this pressure, falls to $3.75. Comparing the quantity demanded with the quantity supplied at $3.75, we find that there is still downward pressure on price, since the quantity supplied exceeds the quantity demanded at $3.75. The price, responding to this pressure, may fall to $3.60, but comparing the quantity demanded with the quantity supplied at this price, we find that there is still a downward pressure on price, since the quantity supplied exceeds the quantity demanded at $3.60.

So long as the actual price exceeds the equilibrium price, there will be a downward pressure on price. Similarly, so long as the actual price is less than the equilibrium price, there will be an upward pressure on price. Thus there is always a tendency for the actual price to move toward the equilibrium price. But it should not be assumed that this movement is always rapid. Sometimes it takes a long time for the actual price to get close to the equilibrium price. Sometimes the actual price never gets to the equilibrium price because by the time it gets close, the equilibrium price changes. All that safely can be said is that the actual price will move toward the equilibrium price. But of course this information is of great value, both theoretically and practically. For many purposes, all that is needed is a correct prediction of the direction in which the price will move.

Changes in the Demand and Supply Curves

Heraclitus, the ancient Greek philosopher, said you cannot step in the same stream twice: everything changes, sooner or later. One need not be a disciple of Heraclitus to recognize that demand curves and supply curves shift. Indeed, we have already seen that demand curves shift in response to changes in tastes, income, population, and prices of other products, and that supply curves shift in response to changes in technology and input prices. Any supply-and-demand diagram like Figure 4.9 is essentially a snapshot of the situation during a particular period of time. The results in Figure 4.9 are limited to a particular period because the demand and supply curves in the figure, like any demand and supply curves, pertain only to a certain period.

Changes in the demand curve. What happens to the equilibrium price of a product when its demand curve changes? This is an important question because it sheds a good deal of light on how the price system works. Suppose that consumer tastes shift in favor of foods containing wheat, causing the demand curve for wheat to shift to the right. This state of affairs is shown in Figure 4.10, where the demand curve shifts from DD' to D_1D_1'. It is not hard to see the effect on the equilibrium price of wheat. When DD' is the demand curve, the equilibrium price is OP. But when the demand curve shifts to D_1D_1', a shortage of $(OQ_2 - OQ)$ develops at this price: that is, the quantity demanded exceeds the quantity supplied at this price by $(OQ_2 - OQ)$. Consequently, suppliers raise their prices. After some testing of market reactions and trial-and-error adjustments, the price will tend to settle at OP_1, the new equilibrium price, and quantity will tend to settle at OQ_1. On the other hand, suppose that consumer demand for wheat products falls off, perhaps because of a great drop in the price of corn products. The demand for wheat now shifts to the left. Specifically, as shown in Figure 4.11, it shifts from DD' to D_2D_2'. What will be the effect on the equilibrium price of wheat? Clearly, the new equilibrium price will be OP_2, where the new demand curve intersects the supply curve.

In general, *a shift to the right in the demand curve results in an increase in the equilibrium price, and a shift to the left in the demand curve results in a decrease in the equilibrium price.* This is the lesson of Figures 4.10 and 4.11. Of course, this conclusion depends on the assumption that the supply curve slopes upward to the right, but, as we noted in a previous section, this assumption is generally true.

At this point, since all of this is theory, you may be wondering how well this theory works in practice. In 1972 and 1973, there was a vivid demonstration of the accuracy of this model in various agricultural markets, including wheat. Because of poor harvests abroad and greatly increased foreign demand for American wheat, the demand curve for wheat shifted markedly to the right. What happened to the price of wheat? In accord with our model, the price increased spectacularly, from about \$1.35 a bushel in the early summer of 1972 to over \$4 a year later. Anyone who witnessed this phenomenon could not help but be impressed by the usefulness of this model.

Changes in the supply curve. Suppose that because of technological advances in wheat production, wheat farmers are willing and able to supply more wheat at a given price than they used to. Specifically, suppose that the supply curve shifts from SS' to S_1S_1' in Figure 4.12. What will be the effect on the equilibrium price? Clearly, it will fall from OP (where the SS' supply curve intersects the demand curve) to OP_3 (where the S_1S_1' supply curve intersects the demand curve). On the other hand,

Figure 4.10
Effect on the Equilibrium Price of a Shift to the Right of the Market Demand Curve
A shift to the right from *DD′* to D_1D_1' results in an increase in the equilibrium price from *OP* to OP_1 and an increase in the equilibrium quantity from *OQ* to OQ_1.

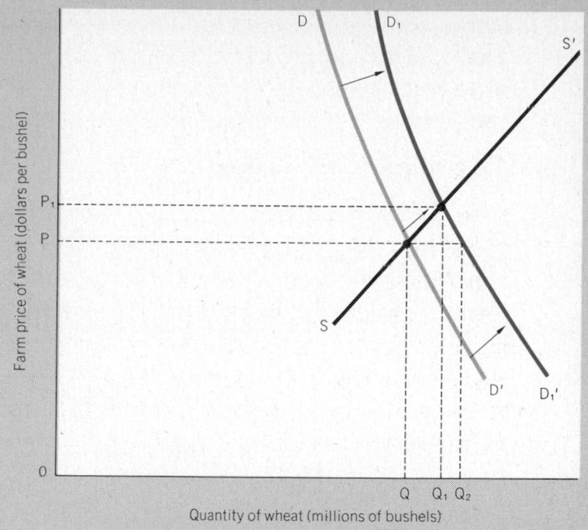

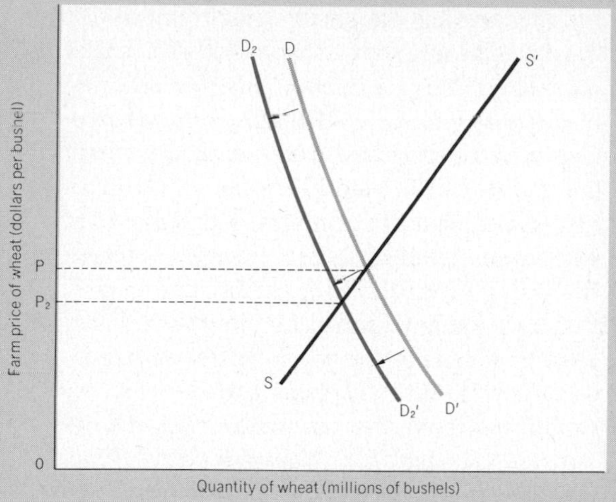

Figure 4.11
Effect on the Equilibrium Price of a Shift to the Left of the Market Demand Curve
A shift to the left from *DD′* to D_2D_2' results in a decrease in the equilibrium price from *OP* to OP_2 and a decrease in the equilibrium quantity.

Figure 4.12
Effects on the Equilibrium Price of Shifts in the Market Supply Curve
A shift to the right from *SS′* to S_1S_1' results in a decrease in the equilibrium price from *OP* to OP_3. A shift to the left from *SS′* to S_2S_2' increases the equilibrium price from *OP* to OP_4.

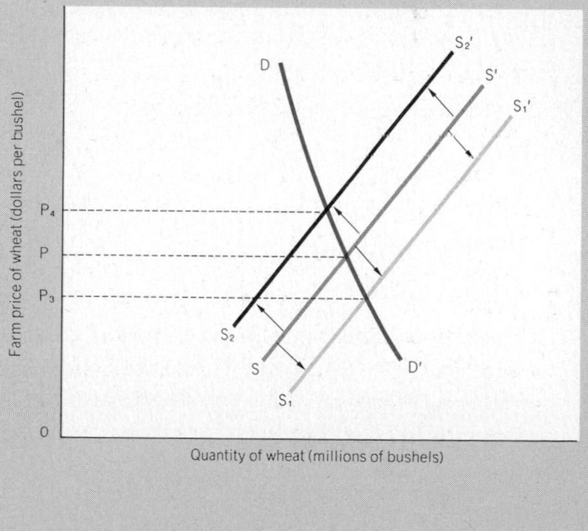

suppose that the weather is poor, with the result that the supply curve shifts to the left. Specifically, suppose that the supply curve shifts from SS' to S_2S_2' in Figure 4.12. Clearly, the equilibrium price will increase from OP (where the SS' supply curve intersects the demand curve) to OP_4 (where the S_2S_2' supply curve intersects the demand curve).

In 1976, American consumers of coffee were shown vividly what a shift to the left in the supply curve of a commodity will do. There were three major reasons for this shift in the supply curve for coffee: (1) A frost in Brazil killed over 500 million coffee trees, and damaged many more. (2) A civil war in Angola, a major supplier of coffee, cut back its crop. (3) An earthquake in Guatemala disrupted the flow of coffee. The result was just what our theory would predict: a big jump in coffee prices. For example, Brazilian coffee, upon arrival in New York, sold for $1.25 per lb. in May 1976, compared with 69 cents per lb. a year before.

In general, *a shift to the right in the supply curve results in a decrease in the equilibrium price, and a shift to the left in the supply curve results in an increase in the equilibrium price.* Of course, this conclusion depends on the assumption that the demand curve slopes downward to the right, but, as we noted in a previous section, this assumption is generally true.

How the Price System Functions

The Price System and the Determination of What Is Produced

Having described how prices are determined in free markets, we can now describe somewhat more fully how the price system goes about performing the four basic tasks that face any economic system. (In the previous chapter, we sketched out the functions of the price system, but in a very cursory manner.) Let's begin by considering the determination of what society will produce: How does the price system carry out this task? As pointed out in the previous chapter, consumers indicate what goods and services they want in the market place, and producers try to meet these wants. More specifically, the demand curve for a product shows how much of that product consumers want at various prices. If consumers don't want much of it at a certain price, its demand curve will indicate that fact by being positioned close to the vertical axis at that price. In other words, the demand curve will show that, at this price for the product, the amount consumers will buy is small. On the other hand, if consumers want lots of the product at this price, its demand curve will be far from the vertical axis.

A product's demand curve is an important determinant of how much firms will produce of the product, since it indicates the amount of the product that will be demanded at each price. From the point of view of the producers, the demand curve indicates the amount they can sell at each price. In a capitalist economy, firms are in business to make money. Thus the manufacturers of any product will turn it out only if the amount of money they receive from consumers exceeds the cost of putting the product on the market. Acting in accord with the profit motive, firms are led to produce what the consumers desire. For example, we saw in the previous section that if consumers' tastes shift in favor of foods containing wheat, the demand curve for wheat will shift to the right, which will result in an increase in the price of wheat. This increase will stimulate farmers to produce more wheat. For example, when the demand curve shifts from DD' to D_1D_1' in Figure 4.10, the equilibrium quantity produced increases from OQ to OQ_1. Given the shift in the demand curve, it is profitable for firms to step up their production. Acting in their own self-interest, they are led to make production decisions geared to the wants of the consumers.

Thus the price system uses the self-interest of the producers to get them to produce what consumers want. Consumers register what they want in the market place by their purchasing decisions—shown by their demand curves. Producers can make more money by responding to consumer wants than by ignoring them. Consequently, they are led to produce what consumers want—and are willing to pay enough for to cover the producers' costs. Note that costs as well as demand determine what will be produced, and that producers are not forced by anyone to do anything. They can produce air conditioners for Eskimos if they like—and if they are prepared to absorb the losses. The price system uses prices to communicate the relevant signals to producers, and metes out the penalties and rewards in the form of losses or profits.

The Price System and the Determination of How Goods Are Produced

Next, consider how society determines how each good and service is produced. How does the price system carry out this task? As pointed out in the previous chapter, the price of each resource gives producers an indication of how scarce this resource is, and how valuable in other uses. Clearly, firms should produce goods and services at minimum cost. Suppose that there are two ways of producing tables: Technique *A* and Technique *B*. Technique *A* requires 4 man-hours of labor and $10 worth of wood per table, whereas Technique *B* requires 5 man-hours of labor and $8 worth of wood. If the price of a man-hour of labor is $4, Technique *A* should be used since a table costs $26 with this technique, as opposed to $28 with Technique *B*.[6] In other words, Technique *A* uses fewer resources per table.

The price system nudges producers to opt for Technique *A* rather than Technique *B* through profits and losses. If each table commands a price of $35, then by using Technique *A*, producers make a profit of $35 − $26 = $9 per table. If they use Technique *B*, they make a profit of $35 − $28 = $7 per table. Thus producers, if they maximize profit, will be led to adopt Technique *A*. Their desire for profit leads them to adopt the techniques that will enable society to get the most out of its resources. No one commands firms to use particular techniques. Washington officials do not order steel plants to substitute the basic oxygen process for open hearths, or petroleum refineries to substitute catalytic cracking for thermal cracking. It is all done through the impersonal market place.

You should not, however, get the idea that the price system operates with kid gloves. Suppose all firms producing tables used Technique *B* until this past year, when Technique *A* was developed: in other words, Technique *A* is based on a new technology. Given this technological change, the supply curve for tables will shift to the right, as we saw in a previous section, and the price of a table will fall. Suppose it drops to $27. If some firm insists on sticking with Technique *B*, it will lose money at the rate of $1 a table; and as these losses mount, the firm's owners will become increasingly uncomfortable. The firm will either switch to Technique *A* or go bankrupt. The price system leans awfully hard on producers who try to ignore its signals.

The Price System and the Determination of Who Gets What

Let's turn now to how society's output will be distributed among the people: How does the price system carry out this task? How much a

[6] To obtain these figures, note that the cost with Technique *A* is 4 man-hours times $4 plus $10, or $26, while the cost with Technique *B* is 5 man-hours times $4 plus $8, or $28.

person receives in goods and services depends on his money income, which in turn is determined under the price system by the amount of various resources that he owns and by the price of each resource. Thus, under the price system, each person's income is determined in the market place: he comes to the market place with certain resources to sell, and his income depends on how much he can get for them.

The question of who gets what is solved at two levels by the price system. Consider an individual product—for example, the tables discussed in the previous section. For the individual product, the question of who gets what is solved by the equality of quantity demanded and quantity supplied. If the price of these tables is at its equilibrium level, the quantity demanded will equal the quantity supplied. Consumers who are willing and able to pay the equilibrium price (or more) get the tables, while those who are unwilling or unable to pay it do not get them. It is just as simple—and as impersonal—as that. It doesn't matter whether you are a nice guy or a scoundrel, or whether you are a connoisseur of tables or someone who doesn't know good workmanship from poor: all that matters is whether you are able and willing to pay the equilibrium price.

Next, consider the question of who gets what at a somewhat more fundamental level. After all, whether a consumer is able and willing to pay the equilibrium price for a good depends on his money income. Thus the Rockefellers can pay the equilibrium price for an astonishing variety of things, whereas the Ríos family can scrape up the equilibrium price for very little. As we have already seen, a consumer's money income depends on the amount of resources of various kinds that he owns and the price that he can get for them. Some people have lots of resources: they are endowed with skill and intelligence and industry, or they have lots of capital or land. Other people have little in the way of resources. Moreover, some people have resources that command a high price, while others have resources that are of little monetary value. The result is that, under the price system, some consumers, like the Rockefellers, get a lot more of society's output than other consumers, like the Ríos family.

The Price System and Economic Growth

Let's turn now to the task of determining a society's rate of growth of per capita income. How does the price system do this? As pointed out in the previous chapter, a nation's rate of increase of per capita income depends on the rate of growth of its resources and the rate of increase of the efficiency with which they are used. First, consider the rate of growth of society's resources. The price system controls the amount of new capital goods produced much as it controls the amount of consumer goods produced. Similarly, the price system influences the amount society invests in educating, training, and upgrading its labor resources. To a considerable extent, the amount invested in such resource-augmenting activities is determined by the profitability of such investments, which is determined in turn by the pattern of prices.

Next, consider the rate of increase of the efficiency with which a society's resources are used. Clearly, this factor depends heavily on the rate of technological change. If technology is advancing at a rapid rate, it should be possible to get more and more out of a society's resources. But if technology is advancing rather slowly, it is likely to be difficult to get much more out of them. The price system affects the rate of technological change in a variety of ways: it influences the profitability of investing in research and development, the profitability of introducing new processes and products into commercial practice, and the profitability of accepting technological change—as well as the losses involved in spurning it.

The price system establishes strong incentives for firms to introduce new technology. Any firm that can find a cheaper way to produce an existing product, or a way to produce a better product, will have a profitable jump on its competitors. Until its competitors can do the same thing, this firm can reap higher profits than it otherwise could. Of course, these higher profits will eventually be competed away, as other firms begin to imitate this firm's innovation. But lots of money can be made in the period during which this firm has a lead over its competitors. These profits are an important incentive for the introduction of new technology.

Two Case Studies

The Price System in Action behind Enemy Lines

Just as general discussions of tennis will take a neophyte only so far, after which he or she must watch and participate in a few matches, so a general discussion of the price system will take a student only so far. Then he should look at real-life examples of the price system at work. Our first illustration of the price system in operation is a prisoner-of-war camp in World War II. This case is not chosen because of its inherent importance, but because of its simplicity. Just as certain elementary forms of life illustrate important biological principles in a simple way, so the economic organization of a prisoner-of-war camp is an elementary form of economic system that illustrates certain important economic principles simply and well.

The prisoner-of-war camp was so elementary because no goods were produced there. All commodities were provided by the country running the camp, by the Red Cross, and by other outside donors. Each prisoner received an equal amount of food and supplies—canned milk, jam, butter, cookies, cigarettes, and so on. In addition, private parcels of clothing, cigarettes, and other supplies were received, with different prisoners, of course, receiving different quantities. Because no goods were produced in the prisoner-of-war camp, the first two tasks of an economic system (What will be produced? How will it be produced?) were not relevant; neither was the fourth task (What provision is to be made for growth?)

All that did matter in this elementary economic system was the third task: to determine who would consume the various available goods. At first blush, the answer may seem obvious: each prisoner would consume the goods he received from the detaining country, the Red Cross, and private packages. But this assumes that prisoners would not trade goods back and forth ("I'll swap you a cigarette for some milk"), which is clearly unrealistic. After all, some prisoners smoked cigarettes, others did not; some liked jam and didn't like canned beef, others liked canned beef and didn't like jam. Thus there was bound to be exchange of this sort, and the real question is in what way and on what terms such exchange took place.

How did the prisoners go about exchanging goods? According to one observer, the process developed as follows:

> Starting with simple direct barter, such as a nonsmoker giving a smoker friend his cigarette issue in exchange for a chocolate ration, more complex exchanges soon became an accepted custom. . . . Within a week or two, as the volume of trade grew, rough scales of exchange values came into existence. [Some prisoners], who had at first exchanged tinned beef for practically any other foodstuff, began to insist on jam and margarine. It was realized that a tin of jam was worth one-half pound of margarine plus something else, that a cigarette issue was worth several chocolate issues, and a tin of diced carrots was worth practically nothing. . . . By the end of the month, there was a lively trade in all com-

> modities and their relative values were well known, and expressed not in terms of one another—one didn't quote [jam] in terms of sugar—but in terms of cigarettes. The cigarette became the standard of value.[7]

Thus the prisoners used the price system to solve the problem of allocating the available supply of goods among consumers. A market developed for each good. This market had, of course, both a demand and a supply side. Each good had its price—but this price was quoted in cigarettes, not dollars and cents. These markets were not started in a self-conscious, deliberate way. No one said, "Let's adopt the price system to allocate available supplies," or "Let's vote on whether or not to adopt the price system." Instead, the system just evolved . . . and it worked.

To see how the supply of a particular good—jam, say—was allocated, look at Figure 4.13, which shows the market supply curve for jam, *SS′*. In the short run, this supply was fixed, so *SS′* is a vertical line. Figure 4.13 also provides the market demand curve for jam, *DD′*, which shows the amount of jam the prisoners wanted to consume at various prices of jam—expressed in terms of cigarettes. For example, *DD′* shows that the prisoners wanted OQ_1 tins of jam when a tin of jam cost OP_1 cigarettes, and OQ_2 tins of jam when a tin of jam cost OP_2 cigarettes. For the quantity demanded to equal the available supply, the price of a tin of jam had to be *OP* cigarettes: one tin of jam had to exchange for *OP* cigarettes. At this price, the available supply of jam was rationed, without resort to fights among prisoners or intervention by the prison authorities. Those prisoners who could and would pay the price had the jam—and there were just enough such consumers to exhaust the available supply. Moreover, this held true for each of the other goods (including cigarettes) as well.

[7] R. A. Radford, "The Economic Organization of a P.O.W. Camp," reprinted in E. Mansfield, *Economics: Readings, Issues, and Cases,* 2d ed., New York: Norton, 1977.

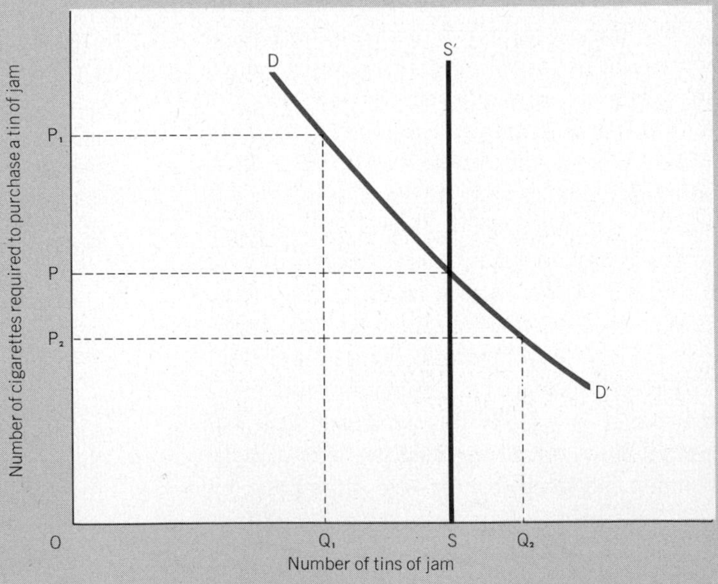

Figure 4.13
Determinants of Equilibrium Price of a Tin of Jam (in terms of cigarettes) in a P.O.W. Camp
The market supply for jam is fixed at *OS* tins. The market demand curve is *DD′*. Thus the equilibrium price of a tin of jam is *OP* cigarettes. If the price were OP_1, OQ_1 tins would be demanded; if the price were OP_2, OQ_2 tins would be demanded.

The Price System in Action on the Great White Way

It is a long way from a prisoner-of-war camp to the Broadway theater, but economics, like any good tool of analysis, applies to a very wide variety of problems. In this section, we discuss the theater's pricing problems—and the role of the price system in helping to solve these problems. Prices for tickets to Broadway shows are established at levels that are much the same whether the show is a success or a flop. For example, an orchestra ticket to *Kelly* (which managed to hold out for one performance before closing) cost about as much as an orchestra ticket to such hits as *Fiddler on the Roof* or *A Chorus Line*. And once a play opens, the price of a ticket remains much the same whether the play is greeted with universal praise or with discontented critics and customers.

Because of these pricing methods, the Broadway theater has been beset for many years by serious problems. Here they are described by two veteran observers of the Broadway stage:

> For centuries the sale of theater tickets has brought on corruption and confusion. When there are more buyers than sellers, a black market results. The so-called "retail" price, the price printed on the ticket, becomes meaningless. Speculation doubles, triples, or quadruples the "real" as opposed to the "legal" asking price. A smash hit on Broadway means "ice"—the difference between the real and legal prices—a well-hidden but substantial cash flow that is divided among shadowy middlemen. Ticket scandals break out in New York as regularly as the flu. The scenario is familiar. A play opens and becomes a superhit. Tickets become difficult, then impossible, to obtain. There are letters to the newspapers. . . . Shocking corruption is discovered. Someone . . . is convicted of overcharging and accepting illegal gratuities. Someone may even go to jail. The black market, valiantly scotched, *never stops for a single moment.*[8]

[8] S. Little and A. Cantor, *The Playmakers,* New York: Norton, 1970, p. 220.

Besides enriching crooked box-office men and managers, as well as other shadowy elements of society, the black market for theater tickets has the additional undesirable effect of excluding the authors, composers, directors, and stars of the play from participation in the premium revenue. Almost all of these people receive a percentage of the play's revenues; and if the revenues at the box office are less than the customers pay for their seats (because of "ice"), these people receive less than they would if no black market existed. The amount of "ice" can be substantial. For example, Rodgers and Hammerstein estimated that, at one performance of their play, *South Pacific,* the public probably paid about $25,000 for tickets with a face value of $7,000, the amount turned in at the box office.

To focus on the problem here, let's look at the market for tickets to a particular performance of *My Fair Lady* (one of Broadway's all-time big hits) when it was at the height of its popularity. Since the supply of tickets to a given performance is fixed, the market supply curve, *SS′* in Figure 4.14, is a vertical line at the quantity of tickets corresponding to the capacity of the theater. The price set officially on the price of a ticket was $8. But because the show was enormously popular, the market demand curve was *DD′* in Figure 4.14, and the equilibrium price for a ticket was $50.[9]

Figure 4.14 makes the nature of the problem apparent: at the official price of $8, the quantity of tickets demanded is much greater than the quantity supplied. Supply and demand don't match. Obviously, there is an incentive for people to buy the tickets from the box office at $8 and sell them at the higher prices customers are willing to pay. There is also an incentive for box-office men to sell them surreptitiously at higher prices and turn in only $8. The price system cannot play the role it did in the prisoner-of-war camp for jam and

[9] This figure is an estimate based on an article in *Variety.*

Figure 4.14
Equilibrium Price for Tickets to *My Fair Lady*
The market supply for tickets is fixed at *OS* per performance. If the demand curve is *DD′*, the equilibrium price of a ticket is \$50. (If the demand curve is D_1D_1', the equilibrium price is \$7.) If the demand curve is *DD′* and the price of a ticket is \$8, the quantity of tickets demanded will far exceed the quantity supplied.

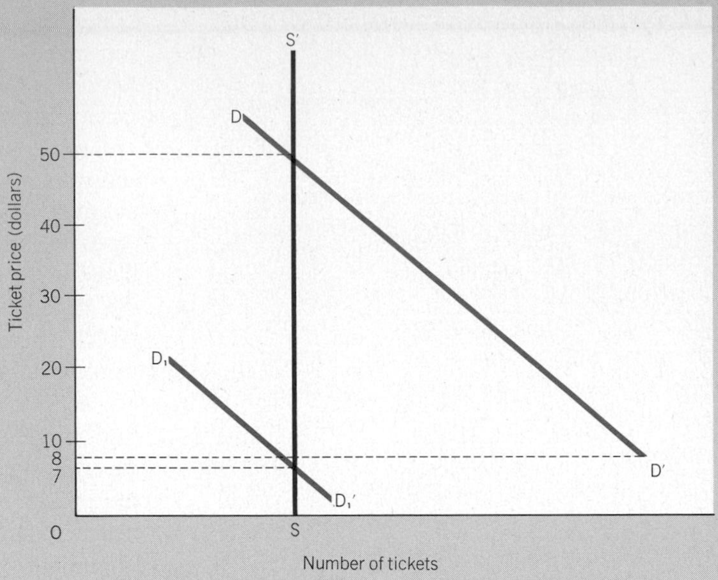

other goods. It cannot act as an effective rationing device because, to do so, the price of tickets would have to increase to its equilibrium level, \$50.

Many theater experts believe that the solution to Broadway's pricing problems lies in allowing the price system to work more effectively by permitting ticket prices to vary depending on a show's popularity. For example, the official ticket price would be allowed to rise to \$50 for *My Fair Lady.* On the other hand, if *My Fair Lady* had been much less popular and its market demand curve had been D_1D_1' in Figure 4.14, its official ticket price would have been allowed to fall to \$7. In this way, the black market for tickets would be eliminated, since the equilibrium price—which equates supply and demand—would be the official price. "Ice" would also be eliminated, since there would be no difference between the official and the actual price paid, and the people responsible for the show would receive its full receipts, not share them with crooked box-office men and illegal operators.[10]

Price Ceilings and Price Supports

During national emergencies, the government sometimes puts a lid on prices, not allowing them to reach their equilibrium levels. For example, during World War II, the government did not allow the prices of various foodstuffs to rise to their equilibrium levels, because it felt that this would have been inequitable (and highly unpopular). Under such circumstances, the quantity demanded of a product exceeds the quantity supplied. In other words, the situation is like that in Figure 4.14, where the quantity demanded of tickets for *My Fair*

[10] In the mid-1970s, a step was taken toward somewhat greater price flexibility for Broadway shows. A booth was established in Times Square where tickets to some shows were on sale at (approximately) half of the official ticket price. In this way, a show was enabled to cut its price, if it was unable to fill the theater at the official ticket price. Apparently, this innovation has worked quite well, both for the producers of the shows and the theater-going public.

Lady exceeds the quantity supplied at a price of \$8. There is a shortage.

Since the price system is not allowed to perform its rationing function, some formal system of rationing or allocating the available supply of the product may be required. Thus, in World War II, families were issued ration coupons which determined how much they could buy of various commodities. And in late 1973, when supplies of gasoline seemed to be cut by the curtailment of Arab exports of oil to the United States, there was serious talk that gasoline and oil might be rationed in a similar way. Such rationing schemes may be justified in emergencies (of reasonably short duration), but they can result eventually in serious distortions, since prices are not allowed to do the job normally expected of them.

To illustrate the sorts of problems that can arise when price ceilings are imposed, consider the rent ceilings that exist on some apartments in New York City. Originally imposed to prevent dwelling costs from soaring during World War II, these ceilings have been defended on the ground that they help the poor, at least in the short run. Although this may be so, they have also resulted in a shortage of housing in New York City. Because they have pushed the price of housing below the equilibrium price, less housing has been supplied than has been demanded. The depressed price of housing has discouraged investors from building new housing, and has made it unprofitable for some owners of existing housing to maintain their buildings. Thus, although it would be socially desirable to channel more resources into New York housing, the rent ceilings have prevented this from occurring.

Government authorities may also impose price floors—or price supports, as they often are called. These floors are generally defended on the ground that they enable the producers of the good in question to make a better living. For example, the federal government imposed price supports on a wide range of agricultural commodities until 1973, the purpose being to increase farm incomes. Just as in the case in Figure 4.14 where the demand curve is D_1D_1' and where a price floor of \$8 exists, the result is that the quantity supplied exceeds the quantity demanded at the support price. Thus there is a surplus of the commodity—and, in the case of agricultural commodities, the government had to buy up and store these surpluses. As in the case of a price ceiling, the result is that the price system is not allowed to do the job expected of it.

Whether price ceilings or floors are socially desirable depends on whether the loss in social efficiency resulting from them is exceeded by the gain in equity they achieve. As indicated above, their purpose is to help or protect particular parts of the population which would be treated inequitably by the unfettered price system. Since one person's views of what is equitable differ from another person's, this is an area of considerable controversy. More will be said about both price ceilings and floors in subsequent chapters, particularly Chapters 5 and 16.

The Circular Flows of Money and Products

So far we have been concerned largely with the workings of a single market—the market for wheat or tables or jam or tickets to *My Fair Lady*. But how do all of the various markets fit together? This is a very important question. Perhaps the best way to begin answering it is to distinguish between product markets and resource markets. As their names indicate, ***product markets*** *are markets where products are bought and sold; and* ***resource markets*** *are markets where resources are bought and sold.* Let's first consider product markets. As shown in Figure 4.15, firms provide products to consumers in product markets, and receive money in return. The money the firms receive is their receipts; to consumers, on the other hand, it represents their expenditures.

Next, let's consider resource markets. Figure 4.15 shows that consumers provide resources—including labor—to firms in resource markets, and they receive money in return. The money the consumers receive is their income; to firms, on the other hand, it represents their costs. Note that the flow of resources and products in Figure 4.15 is counterclockwise: that is, *consumers provide resources to firms which in turn provide goods and services to consumers.* On the other hand, the flow of money in Figure 4.15 is clockwise: that is, *firms pay money for resources to consumers who in turn use the money to buy goods and services from the firms.* Both flows—that of resources and products, and that of money—go on simultaneously and repeatedly.

So long as consumers spend all their income, the flow of money income from firms to consumers is exactly equal to the flow of expenditure from consumers to firms. Thus these circular flows, like Ole Man River, just keep rolling along. As a first approximation, this is a perfectly good model. But as we pointed out in Chapter 1, capitalist economies have experienced periods of widespread unemployment and severe inflation that this model cannot explain. Also, note that our simple economy in Figure 4.15 has no government sector. In the following chapter, we shall bring the government into the picture. Under pure capitalism, the government would play a limited role in the economic system, but in the mixed capitalistic system we have in the United States, the government plays an important role indeed.

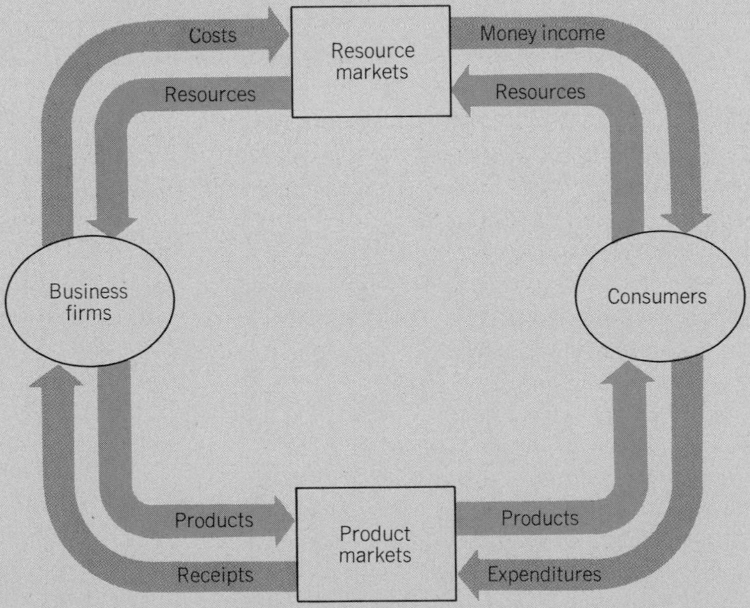

Figure 4.15
The Circular Flows of Money and Products
In product markets, consumers exchange money for products and firms exchange products for money. In resource markets, consumers exchange resources for money and firms exchange money for resources.

Summary

Consumers and firms are the basic units comprising the private sector of the economy. Consumers, whether individuals or households, purchase the goods and services that are the ultimate end-products of the economic system. Consumers are obviously an extremely varied lot, as a brief comparison of the Rockefeller and Ríos families indicates. A firm is a unit that produces a good or service for sale. About $^9/_{10}$ of the goods and services produced in the United States are produced by firms, which number in the millions. Like consumers, they are extremely varied in size, age, power, and purpose, as illustrated by a comparison of Amacher's drugstore and General Motors. A market is a group of firms and individuals that are in touch with each other in order to buy or sell some commodity or service. When a market for a homogeneous product contains so many buyers and sellers that none of them can influence the price, economists call it a perfectly competitive market.

There are two sides of every market: the demand side and the supply side. The demand side can be represented by the market demand curve, which almost always slopes downward to the right and whose location depends on consumer tastes, the number and income of consumers, and the prices of other commodities. The supply side of the market can be represented by the market supply curve, which generally slopes upward to the right and whose location depends on technology and resource prices. The equilibrium price and equilibrium quantity of the commodity are given by the intersection of the market demand and supply curves. If conditions remain reasonably stable for a time, the actual price and quantity should move close to the equilibrium price and quantity. Changes in the position and shape of the demand curve–in response to changes in consumer tastes, income, population, and prices of other commodities–result in changes in the equilibrium price and equilibrium output of a product. Similarly, changes in the position and shape of the supply curve–in response to changes in technology and resource prices, among other things–also result in changes in the equilibrium price and equilibrium output of a product.

To determine what goods and services society will produce, the price system sets up incentives for firms to produce what consumers want. To the extent that they produce what consumers want and are willing to pay for, firms reap profits; to the extent that they don't, they experience losses. Similarly, the price system sets up strong incentives for firms to produce these goods at minimum cost. These incentives take the form of profits for firms that minimize costs and losses for firms that operate with relatively high costs. To determine who gets what, the price system results in each person's receiving an income that depends on the quantity of resources he owns and the prices that they command. The price system also establishes incentives for activities that result in increases in a society's per capita income. The very simple case of a prisoner-of-war camp and the more complicated case of the Broadway theater provide real illustrations of the price system in action.

There are circular flows of money and products in a capitalist economy. In product markets, firms provide products to consumers and receive money in return. In resource markets, consumers provide resources to firms, and receive money in return. The flow of resources and products is as follows: consumers provide resources to firms which in turn provide goods and services to consumers. The flow of money is as follows: firms pay money for resources to consumers who in turn use the money to buy goods and services from firms. Both flows go on simultaneously and repeatedly.

CONCEPTS FOR REVIEW

Consumer	Supply	Equilibrium price
Firm	Perfect competition	Product market
Market	Market demand curve	Resource market
Demand	Market supply curve	Actual price

QUESTIONS FOR DISCUSSION AND REVIEW

1. Assume that the market for electric toasters is competitive, and that the quantity supplied per year depends as follows on the price of a toaster:

Price of a toaster (dollars)	Number of toasters supplied (millions)
6	4.0
8	5.0
10	5.5
12	6.0
14	6.3

Plot the supply curve for toasters. Is this a direct or inverse relationship? Are supply curves generally direct or inverse relationships?

2. Suppose that the quantity of toasters demanded per year depends as follows on the price of a toaster:

Price of toaster (dollars)	Number of toasters demanded (millions)
6	7.0
8	6.5
10	6.2
12	6.0
14	5.8

Plot the demand curve for toasters. If the price is $8, will there be an excess demand of toasters? If the price is $14, will there be an excess demand? What is the equilibrium price of a toaster? What is the equilibrium quantity? (Use the data in Question 1.)

3. Suppose that the government imposes a price ceiling on toasters. In particular, suppose that it decrees that a toaster cannot sell for more than $8. Will the quantity supplied equal the quantity demanded? What sorts of devices may come into being to allocate the available supply of toasters to consumers? What problems will the government encounter in keeping the price at $8? What social purposes, if any, might such a price ceiling serve? (Use the data in Questions 1 and 2.)

4. Suppose that the government imposes a price floor on toasters. In particular, suppose that it decrees that a toaster cannot sell for less than $14. Will the quantity supplied equal the quantity demanded? How will the resulting supply of toasters be taken off the market? What problems will the government encounter in keeping the price at $14? What social purposes, if any, might such a price floor serve? (Use the data above.)

5. Will each of the following tend to shift the demand curve for toasters to the right, to the left, or not at all? (a) Consumer incomes rise by 20 percent. (b) The price of bread falls by 10 percent. (c) The price of electricity increases by 5 percent. (d) Medical reports indicate that toast prevents heart attacks. (e) The cost of producing a toaster increases by 10 percent.

6. Will each of the following tend to shift the supply curve for toasters to the right, to the left, or not at all? (a) The wage of workers producing toasters increases by 5 percent. (b) The price of the metal used to make toasters falls by 10 percent. (c) The price of bread falls by 10 percent. (d) Consumer incomes rise by 20 percent. (e) New technology makes toaster production much more efficient.

7. If both the demand and supply curve for a product shift to the right, can one predict whether the product's equilibrium price will increase or decrease? Can one predict whether its equilibrium quantity will increase or decrease?

8. According to W. Allen Wallis, "Not only do prices convey information on how an individual should act, but they provide at the same time a powerful inducement for him to do so." Do you agree? If you do, explain why it is true. If you don't, explain where it is wrong.

9. Suppose that you were appointed head of a blue-ribbon commission to recommend changes in pricing practices for the entertainment industry. Would you recommend a free market for tickets for Broadway shows? For tickets to the San Francisco Opera? For the Dallas Cowboys games? In each case, why or why not?

10. Suppose that the American public becomes convinced that beets are more desirable, and string beans are less so. Describe the shifts that will occur in the demand and supply curves in the relevant markets, and the mechanisms that will signal and trigger a redeployment of resources.

11. (Advanced) If the demand curve for butter is $Q_D = 20 - 4P$ (where Q_D is the quantity demanded and P is the price of butter) and the supply curve for butter is $Q_S = 2P$ (where Q_S is the quantity supplied), what is the equilibrium price? What is the equilibrium quantity? (Both Q_D and Q_S are measured in millions of pounds, and price is measured in dollars per pound.)

5 The Economic Role of the Government

To state that the United States is a mixed capitalist system, in which both government decisions and the price system play important roles, is hardly to provoke a controversy. But going a step beyond, as we shall in this chapter, takes us into areas where viewpoints often diverge. The proper functions of government and the desirable size and nature of government expenditures and taxes are not matters on which all agree. Indeed, the question of how big government should be, and what its proper functions are, is hotly debated by conservatives and liberals throughout the land. Of course, this is only a preliminary airing of many of these issues. As the base of economic analysis is broadened in subsequent chapters, much more will be said on these matters, and you will be in a far better position to judge them for yourself.

In the latter part of this chapter, we describe

the nature and causes of our farm problem, and indicate the extent to which government programs seem to have solved this problem. This is an interesting application of the supply and demand theory presented in the previous chapter, as well as an example of the economic role of the government. Whether you are from the city or the country, you should be interested in the nature and success of our farm programs—if for no other reason than that you and your tax-paying and food-consuming friends and relatives pay for them.

Limitations of the Price System

Despite its many advantages, the price system suffers from serious limitations. Because these limitations are both prominent and well known, no one believes that the price system, left to its own devices, can be trusted to solve our society's basic economic problems. Indeed, some economists argue that the price system's limitations are so great that it should be scrapped. In fact, however, we have not scrapped it. Instead, we have charged the government with the responsibility for correcting many of its shortcomings. Thus, to a considerable extent, the goverment's role in the economy has developed in response to the limitations of the price system, which are described below.

Distribution of income. There is *no* reason to believe that the distribution of income generated by the price system is *fair* or, in some sense, *best.* Some rich families receive much more income in a day than the Ríos family does in a year. Most people feel that the distribution of income generated by the price system should be altered to suit humanitarian needs; in particular, that help should be given to the poor. Both liberals and conservatives tend to agree on this score, although there are arguments over the extent to which the poor should be helped and the conditions under which they should be eligible for help. But the general principle that the government should step in to redistribute income in favor of the poor is generally accepted in the United States today.[1]

Public goods. Some goods and services *cannot be provided through the price system because there is no way to exclude a citizen from consuming the good whether he pays for it or not.* For example, there is no way to prevent a citizen from benefiting from national expenditures on defense, whether he pays money toward defense or not. Consequently, the price system cannot be used to provide such goods; no one will pay for them since they will receive them whether they pay or not. Further, some goods, like the quality of the environment and national defense (and others cited below), *can be enjoyed by one person without depriving others of the same enjoyment.* Such goods are called ***public goods.*** The government provides many public goods. Such goods are consumed collectively or jointly, and it is inefficient to try to price them in a market. They tend to be indivisible; thus, they frequently cannot be split into pieces and be bought and sold in a market.

External economies and diseconomies. In cases where *the production or consumption of a good by one firm or consumer has adverse or beneficial uncompensated effects on other firms or consumers, the price system will not operate effectively.* An ***external economy*** is said to occur when consumption or production by one person or firm results in uncompensated benefits to another person or firm. A good example of an external economy exists where fundamental research carried out by one firm is used by another firm. (To cite one such case, there were external economies from the Bell Telephone Laboratories' invention of the transistor.)

[1] Also, because the wealthy have more "dollar votes" than the poor, the sorts of goods and services that society produces will reflect this fact. Thus luxuries for the rich may be produced in larger amounts and necessities for the poor may be produced in smaller amounts than some critics regard as sensible and equitable. This is another frequently encountered criticism of the price system.

Where external economies exist, it is generally agreed that the price system will produce too little of the good in question and that the government should supplement the amount produced by private enterprise. This is the basic rationale for much of the government's huge investment in basic science. An ***external diseconomy*** is said to occur when consumption or production by one person or firm results in uncompensated costs to another person or firm. A good example of an external diseconomy occurs when a firm dumps pollutants into a stream and makes the water unfit for use by firms and people downstream. Where activities result in external diseconomies, it is generally agreed that the price system will tolerate too much of the activity and that the government should curb it. For example, as we shall see in Chapter 19, the government, in keeping with this doctrine, has involved itself increasingly in environmental protection and the reduction of air and water pollution.[2]

What Functions Should the Government Perform?

There are wide differences of opinion on the proper role of government in economic affairs. Although it is generally agreed that the government should redistribute income in favor of the poor, provide public goods, and offset the effects of external economies and diseconomies, there is considerable disagreement over how far the government should go in these areas, and what additional areas the government should be responsible for. Some people feel that "Big Government" is already a problem; that government is doing too much. Others believe that the public sector of the economy is being undernourished and that government should be allowed to do more. This is a fundamental question, and one that involves a great deal more than economics.

Conservative view. On the one hand, conservatives, such as the University of Chicago's recent Nobel laureate, Milton Friedman, believe that the government's role should be limited severely. They feel that economic and political freedom is likely to be undermined by excessive reliance on the state. Moreover, they tend to be skeptical about the government's ability to solve the social and economic problems at hand. They feel that the prevailing faith in the government's power to make a substantial dent in these problems is unreasonable, and they call for more and better information concerning the sorts of tasks government can reasonably be expected to do—and do well. They point to the slowness of the government bureaucracy, the difficulty in controlling huge government organizations, the inefficiencies political considerations can breed, and the difficulties in telling whether government programs are successful or not. On the basis of these considerations, they argue that the government's role should be carefully circumscribed.

The flavor of the conservative position on this question, as well as a generous helping of sarcasm and wit, is evident in the remarks of George Stigler, another distinguished economist at the University of Chicago:

> I consider myself courageous, or at least obtuse, in arguing for a reduction in governmental controls over economic life. You are surely desirous of improving this world, and it assuredly needs an immense amount of improvement. No method of displaying one's public-spiritedness is more popular than to notice a problem and pass a law. It combines ease, the warmth of benevolence, and a suitable disrespect for a less enlightened era. What I propose is, for most people, much less attractive: close study of the comparative performance of public and private economy, and the dispassionate appraisal of special reme-

[2] The effects of external economies and diseconomies can also be taken care of by legal arrangements that assign liabilities for damages and compensate for benefits. However, such arrangements often are impractical or too costly to be used.

dies that is involved in compassion for the community at large.[3]

Liberal view. To such remarks, liberals respond with very telling salvos of their own. Just as conservatives tend to be skeptical of the government's ability to solve important social and economic problems, so liberals tend to be skeptical about the price system's ability to solve these problems. They point to the important limitations of the price system, discussed above, and they assert that the government can do a great deal to overcome these limitations, by regulating private activity, and by subsidizing and providing goods and services that the private sector produces too little of.

According to some distinguished liberals, like Harvard's John Kenneth Galbraith, the public sector of the economy has been starved of needed resources, while the private sector has catered to relatively unimportant wants. In his best-selling book, *The Affluent Society,* Galbraith argued that consumers are led by advertising and other promotional efforts to purchase more and more goods of marginal significance to them. On the other hand, in his opinion, the nation is suffering because too little is spent on government services like education, transportation, and urban renewal.[4] In the next chapter, we shall discuss this proposition in more detail.

Liberals tend to be less concerned than conservatives about the effects of greater governmental intervention in the economy on personal freedom. They point out that the price system also involves coercion, since the fact that the price system awards the available goods and services to those who can pay their equilibrium price can be viewed as a form of coercion. Moreover, some people are awarded only a pittance by the price system: in a real sense, they are coerced into discomfort and malnutrition.[5]

A Legal, Social, and Competitive Framework

Although there is considerable disagreement over the proper role of the government, both conservatives and liberals agree that it must do certain things. The first of these is to establish the "rules of the game"—that is, a legal, social, and competitive framework enabling the price system to function as it should. Specifically, the government must see to it that contracts are enforced, that private ownership is protected, and that fraud is prevented. Clearly, these matters must be tended to if the price system is to work properly. Also, the government must maintain order (through the establishment of police and other forces), establish a monetary system (so that money can be used to facilitate trade and exchange), and provide standards for the weight and quality of products.

As an example of this sort of government intervention, consider the Pure Food and Drug Act. This act, originally passed in 1906 and subsequently amended in various ways, protects the consumer against improper and fraudulent activities on the part of producers of foods and drugs. It prohibits the merchandising of impure or falsely labeled food or drugs, and it forces producers to specify the quantity and quality of the contents on labels. These requirements strengthen the price system. Without them, the typical consumer would be unable to tell whether food or drugs are pure or properly labeled. Unless the con-

[3] G. Stigler, "The Government of the Economy," *A Dialogue on the Proper Economic Role of the State,* University of Chicago, Graduate School of Business, Selected Paper no. 7, reprinted in E. Mansfield, *Economics: Readings, Issues, and Cases,* 2d ed., New York: Norton, 1977. Also, see M. Friedman, *Capitalism and Freedom,* Chicago: University of Chicago Press, 1962.

[4] J. K. Galbraith, *The Affluent Society,* Boston: Houghton Mifflin, 1958.

[5] See P. Samuelson, "The Economic Role of Private Activity," *A Dialogue on the Proper Economic Role of the State,* University of Chicago, Graduate School of Business, Selected Paper no. 7, reprinted in E. Mansfield, *Economics: Readings, Issues, and Cases.*

sumer can be sure that he is getting what he is paying for, the basic logic underlying the price system breaks down. Similar regulation and legislation have been instituted in fields other than food and drugs—and for similar reasons.

Besides establishing a legal and social framework that will enable the price system to do its job, the government must also see to it that markets remain reasonably competitive. Only if they are will prices reflect consumer desires properly. If, on the other hand, markets are dominated by a few sellers (or a few buyers), prices may be "rigged" by these sellers (or buyers) to promote their own interests. For example, if a single firm is the sole producer of aluminum, it is a safe bet that this firm will establish a higher price than if there were many aluminum producers competing among themselves. The unfortunate thing about prices determined in noncompetitive markets—rigged prices, if you will—is that they give incorrect signals concerning what consumers want and how scarce resources and commodities are. Producers, responding to these incorrect signals, do not produce the right things in the right quantities. Consumers respond to these incorrect signals by not supplying the right resources in the right amounts, and by not consuming the proper amounts of the goods that are produced. Thus the price system is not permitted to solve the four basic economic problems properly in the absence of reasonable competition.

To try to encourage and preserve competition, the Congress has enacted a series of antitrust laws, such as the Sherman Antitrust Act and the Clayton Act, and it has established the Federal Trade Commission. The antitrust laws make it illegal for firms to collude or to attempt to monopolize the sale of a product. Both conservative and liberal economists, with some notable exceptions, tend to favor the intent and operation of the antitrust laws. In addition, the government tries to control the activities of firms in markets where competition cannot be expected to prevail (as in the telephone industry, where efficient operations would be destroyed if more than a very few firms got in the act). In industries of this sort, the government often establishes commissions to regulate prices and standards of service. Such regulatory commissions are common in the communications, transportation, electric, and gas industries.

Redistribution of Income

We have already noted at several points the general agreement that the government should redistribute income in favor of the poor. In other words, it is usually felt that help should be given to people who are ill, handicapped, old and infirm, disabled, and unable for other reasons to provide for themselves. To some extent, the nation has decided that income—or at least a certain minimum income—should be divorced from productive services. Of course, this doesn't mean that people who are too lazy to work should be given a handout. It does mean that people who cannot provide for themselves should be helped. To implement this principle, various payments are made by the government to needy people—including the aged, the handicapped, the unemployed, pensioners, and veterans.

These welfare payments are to some extent a "depression baby," for they grew substantially during the Great Depression of the 1930s, when relief payments became a necessity. But they also represent a feeling shared by a large segment of the population that human beings should be assured that, however the Wheel of Fortune spins and whatever number comes up, they will not starve and their children will not be deprived of a healthy environment and basic schooling. Of course, someone has to pay for this. Welfare payments allow the poor to take more from the nation's output than they produce. In general, the more affluent members of society contribute some of their claims on output to pay for these programs, their contributions being in the form of taxes. By using its expenditures to help certain groups and by taxing other groups to pay for these programs, the government accomplishes each year, without revolt and without bayonets, a substantial redistribution of income. This is a crucial aspect of the government's role in our economy.

It should not be assumed, however, that all government programs transfer income from the rich to the poor. On the contrary, some programs, intentionally or unintentionally, soak the poor to give to the rich. Some government programs fatten the purses of rich farmers, some tax loopholes allow the affluent to dodge taxes through the creation of trusts and other legal devices, and some important taxes—such as sales taxes—hit the poor harder than the rich. Nonetheless, the best available evidence indicates that, when all its activities are taken into account, the government does take from the rich to give to the poor. In other words, taking account of both its expenditures and the taxes it levies, the government redistributes income in favor of the poor. Whether it goes as far as it should in this direction is a more nettlesome question, the answer to which will depend on your own ethical values.

Economic Stabilization

It is also generally agreed that the government should see to it that the economy maintains reasonably full employment with reasonably stable prices. Capitalist economies have tended to alternate between booms and depressions in the past. The Great Depression of the 1930s hit the American economy—and the world economy—a particularly devastating blow, putting millions of people out of work and in desperate shape. When World War II ended, the American people vowed that they would not let a depression of this sort occur again. The Congress passed the Employment Act of 1946, which stated that it was the responsibility of the federal government to maintain full employment in the United States. In particular, the federal government was not supposed to tolerate unemployment of the sort that materialized during severe depressions in the past.

Of course, it is one thing to charge the federal government with the responsibility for maintaining full employment and quite another thing to tell the federal government how to achieve this goal. Without a good deal of economic knowledge, this law would have been as empty as Atlantic City in December—since it is useless to tell the federal government to do something no one knows how to do. Fortunately, advances in economic knowledge during the 1930s made it much more likely that the federal government could carry out the responsibility of maintaining full employment. The man who contributed much of this new economic knowledge was John Maynard Keynes, one of the great figures of modern economics, whom we will discuss in some detail in Chapter 9.

Besides maintaining full employment, the government must also maintain a reasonably stable price level. No economy can function well if prices are gyrating wildly. Through its control of the money supply and its decisions regarding expenditures and taxation, the government has considerable impact on the price level, as well as on the level of employment.

Public Goods

As we have indicated, the government provides many public goods. Let's consider the nature of public goods in more detail. One hallmark of a public good is that it can be consumed by one person without diminishing the amount that other people consume of it. Public goods tend to be relatively indivisible: they often come in such large units that they cannot be broken into pieces that can be bought or sold in ordinary markets. Also, once such goods are produced, there often is no way to bar certain citizens from consuming them. Whether or not a citizen contributes toward their cost, he benefits from them. As pointed out in a previous section, this means that the price system cannot be used to handle the production and distribution of such goods.

An obvious example of a public good is a lighthouse. There might be general agreement that the cost of building a particular lighthouse would be more than justified by the benefits (saving of lives, fewer shipwrecks, cheaper transportation). Nonetheless, no firm or person would build and operate such a lighthouse because they could not find any way to charge the ships using the lighthouse for the service. Nor would any single user gain enough from the lighthouse to warrant constructing and operating it. Moreover, voluntary contributions are very unlikely to support such a lighthouse because each user is likely to feel that his contribution will not affect whether or not it is built, and that he will be able to use the lighthouse whether or not he contributes. Consequently, the lighthouse will be established and operated only if the government intervenes.

National defense is another example. The benefits of expenditure on national defense extend to the entire nation. Extension of the benefits of national defense to an additional citizen does not mean that any other citizen gets less of these benefits. Also, there is no way of preventing a citizen from benefiting from them, whether he contributes to their cost or not. Thus there is no way to use the price system to provide for national defense. Since it is a public good, national defense must be provided by the government. Similarly with flood control, roads, police and fire protection, public parks, and a host of other such services. In each case, although the people who benefit may not contribute to the costs of these services voluntarily, they may feel better off when the government taxes them to make such services possible.

Other services, such as education and health, can be provided by private enterprise on a fee basis, but much of the population feels that the government should intervene to see to it that everyone, regardless of income level, receives a certain minimum amount of education and health care. Free public education has, of course, been an important and conspicuous part of American society, and in recent years the government has begun to play a more significant role in the health field. Both in health and education, an important argument for government intervention has been that the social benefits of these services exceed the private benefits. However, opponents of such intervention assert that it is paternalistic and that it results in less efficiency in education and health. This is an area of controversy.

Essentially, deciding how much to produce of a public good is a political decision. The citizens of the United States elect senators and congressmen who decide how much should be spent on national defense or education, and how it should be spent. These elected representatives are responsive to special-interest groups, as well as to the people as a whole. Many special-interest groups lobby hard for the production of certain public goods. For example, an alliance of military and industrial groups presses for increased defense expenditures, and other interested groups promote expenditures on highways, health, education, and other functions.

The tax system is used to pay for the production of public goods. In effect, the government says to each citizen, "Fork over a certain amount of money to pay for the expenses incurred by the government." The amount a particular citizen is assessed may depend on his income (as in the income tax), the value of all or specific types of his property (as in the property tax), the amount he spends on certain types of goods and services (as in the sales tax), or on still other criteria. Much more will be said about the tax system in a later section of this chapter and in the next chapter.

Externalities

It is generally agreed that the government should encourage the production of goods and services that entail external economies and discourage the production of those that entail external diseconomies. Take the pollution of air and water. When a firm or individual dumps wastes into the water or air, other firms or individuals often must pay all or part of the cost of putting the water or air back into a usable condition. Thus the disposal of these wastes entails external diseconomies. Unless the government prohibits certain kinds of pollution, or enforces air and water quality standards, or charges polluters in accord with the amount of waste they dump into the environment, there will be socially undesirable levels of pollution.

To see how such externalities affect the social desirability of the output of a competitive industry, consider Figure 5.1, where the industry's demand and supply curves are contained in the top panel. As shown there, the equilibrium output of the industry is OQ_0. If the industry results in no external economies or diseconomies, this is likely to be the socially optimal output. But what if the industry results in external diseconomies, such as the pollution described above? Then the industry's supply curve, SS', does not fully reflect the true social costs of producing the product. The supply curve that reflects these social costs is S_1S_1', which, as shown in the middle panel of Figure 5.1, lies to the left of SS'. The optimal output of the good is OQ_1, which is less than the competitive output, OQ_0.

What can the government do to correct the situation? There are a variety of ways that it can intervene to reduce the industry's output from OQ_0 to OQ_1. For example, it can impose

Figure 5.1
Effect of External Economies and Diseconomies on the Optimal Output of a Competitive Industry
The optimal output is OQ_0 if neither external economies nor diseconomies are present. If there are external diseconomies, S_1S_1' reflects the true social costs of producing the product, and OQ_1 is the optimal output. If there are external economies, D_1D_1' reflects the true social benefits of producing the product, and OQ_2 is the optimal output.

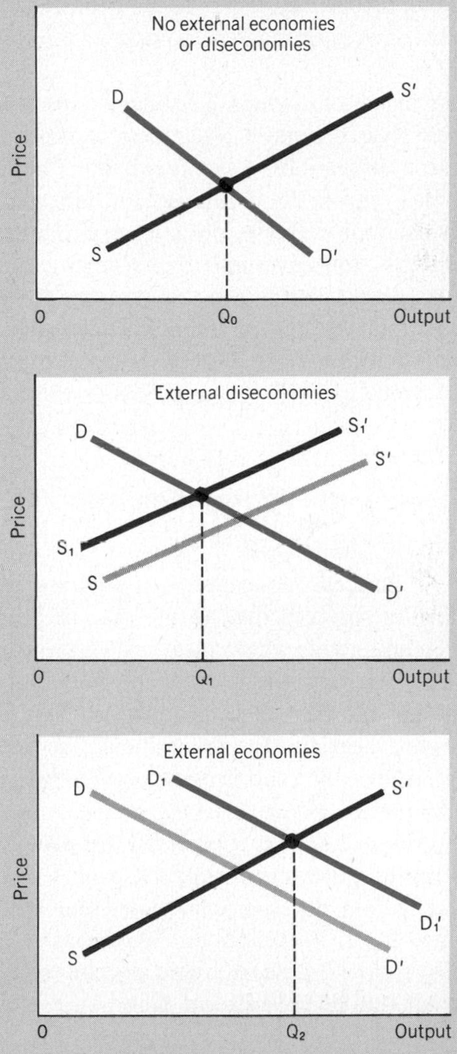

taxes on the industry, as we shall see in Chapter 6. If these taxes are of the right type and amount, they will result in the desired reduction of output.

What if the industry results in external economies? For example, what if the manufacture of one industrial product makes it cheaper to produce other products? Then the industry's demand curve, DD', underestimates the true social benefits of producing the product. The demand curve that reflects these social benefits correctly is D_1D_1', which, as shown in the bottom panel of Figure 5.1, lies to the right of DD'. The optimal output of the good is OQ_2, which is greater than the competitive output, OQ_0.

As in the case where the industry results in external diseconomies, the government can intervene in various ways to change the industry's output. But in this case, the object is to increase, not decrease, its output. To accomplish this, the government can, among other things, grant subsidies to the industry. If they are of the right type and amount, they can be used to increase the industry's output from OQ_0 to OQ_2.

Government Production and "Creeping Socialism"

As we pointed out in previous sections, it is generally accepted that, in the case of public goods and goods where there are very important externalities, the government should intervene to influence their production. But this does not mean that the government must actually produce the good in question. On the contrary, *the government does not produce most of the goods and services it provides.* For example, the federal government supports over ½ of the research and development carried out in the United States, but only about 30 percent of federally supported research and development is carried out in government laboratories. The rest is carried out by firms and universities working under government contracts.[6]

Some of the areas in which our government actually becomes involved in the production of goods and services are familiar. In the United States the post office, the airports, and many water, gas, and electric companies are publicly owned and operated. In these cases it would be inefficient to have many producers, and since competition is not feasible, the courts have held that such industries must be publicly owned or regulated. But there is no very clear line between them and other industries that have not been publicly owned. For example, many other countries have publicly owned telephone, telegraph, railroad, airline, and broadcasting industries. These industries are not under public ownership in the United States for historical and cultural reasons, as well as because the feeling exists that public ownership tends to result in too much bureaucracy and inefficiency.

For many years, this country has been suspicious of anything smacking of "creeping socialism." As we explained in Chapter 3, socialism means government ownership and operation of plants, farms, and mines. Clearly, *there has been little movement toward public ownership in the United States,* despite occasional cries to the contrary on the hustings and in the press. Perhaps the most important and controversial area where government ownership has been extended appreciably in the last 40 years has been in electric power. During the administration of Franklin D. Roosevelt, the Tennessee Valley Authority, Bonneville Dam, and Hoover Dam, among others, were established. But this was hardly a widespread thrust toward public ownership—and it took place several decades ago.

However, although there has been little

[6] Edwin Mansfield, "Federal Support of R and D Activities in the Private Sector," *Priorities and Efficiency in Federal Research and Development,* Joint Economic Committee of Congress, 1976.

movement toward government ownership and operation, *there has been a tendency in certain fields for the boundaries between the private sector and the public sector to become extremely blurred.* Particularly in the field of defense, it is difficult to know how to categorize some organizations. To what extent is a firm like Lockheed Aircraft Corporation really part of the private sector? Although it is privately owned, most of its output (92 percent in 1971) goes to a single customer—the government. Much of its supply of tools is provided by the government, and government officials play an important role in influencing its decisions, auditing its books, regulating its profits, and so forth. The same tendency toward blurred boundaries between the private and public sectors has occurred in atomic energy, space exploration, and other areas. To a certain extent, it appears that—in the words of Don Price, dean of Harvard's Kennedy School of Government—the government "has learned to socialize without assuming ownership."[7] This blurring of the boundaries between the private and public sectors is an important recent development, with repercussions on many aspects of our daily life.

Size and Nature of Government Activities

How Big Is the Government?

Up to this point, we have been concerned primarily with the reasons why the government must intervene in our economy—and the types of role it should play—but we have made little or no attempt to describe its role in quantita-

[7] Don Price, *The Scientific Estate*, Cambridge, Mass.: Belknap Press, 1965, p. 43.

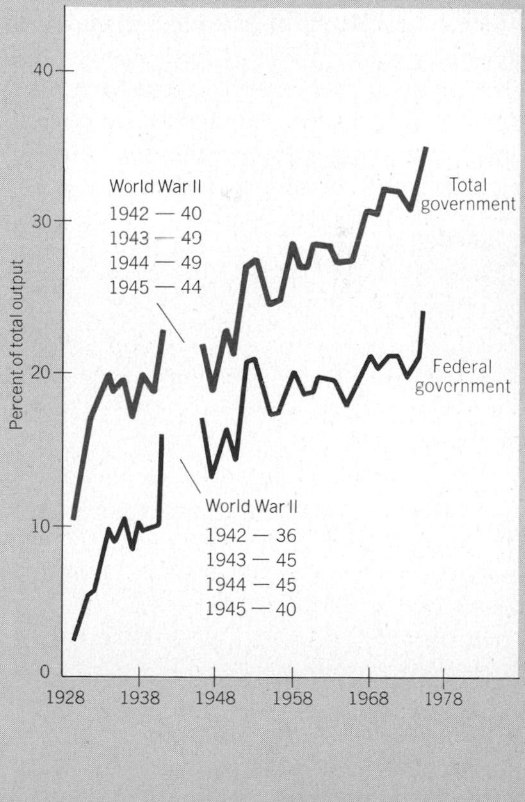

Figure 5.2
Government Spending as a Percent of Total Output, United States.
Government expenditures—federal, state, and local—totaled about $525 billion in 1975. These expenditures, which include transfer payments, have grown more rapidly than total output in this period.

tive terms. It is time now to turn to some of the relevant facts. One useful measure of the extent of the government's role in the American economy is the size of government expenditures, both in absolute terms and as a percent of our nation's total output.

The sum total of government expenditures—federal, state, and local—was about \$525 billion in 1975. Since our nation's total output was about \$1.5 trillion, this means that government expenditures were about $\frac{1}{3}$ of our total output. The ratio of government expenditures to total output in the United States has not always been this large, as Figure 5.2 shows. In 1929, the ratio was about 10 percent, as contrasted with about 35 percent in 1975. (Of course, the ratio of government spending to total output is smaller now than during World War II, but in a wartime economy, one would expect this ratio to be abnormally high.)

There are many reasons why government expenditures have grown so much faster than total output. Three of these are particularly important. First, the United States did not maintain anything like the kind of military force in pre-World-War-II days that it does now. In earlier days, when weapons were relatively simple and cheap, and when we viewed our military and political responsibilities much more narrowly than we do now, our military budget was relatively small. The cost of being a superpower in the days of nuclear weaponry is high by any standards. Second, there has been a long-term increase in the demand for the services provided by government, like more and better schooling, more extensive highways, more complete police and fire protection, and so forth. As incomes rise, people want more of these services. Third, ***government transfer payments***—payments in return for no products or services—have grown substantially. For example, various types of welfare payments have increased markedly. Since transfer payments do not entail any reallocation of resources from private to public goods, but a transfer of income from one private citizen or group to another, Figure 5.2 is, in some respects, an overstatement of the role of the public sector.

Table 5.1
Taxes as Percentages of Total Output, 1970

Country	Percentage
Sweden	43
France	39
West Germany	35
United Kingdom	35
Canada	32
United States	32
Japan	21
India	15
Nigeria	9

When in Table 5.1 we compare the size of government spending in the United States (relative to total output) with that in other countries, we learn that the governments of Sweden, France, West Germany, and the United Kingdom spend more—as a percent of total output—than we do. In part, of course, this is because of the extensive welfare programs in Sweden and the United Kingdom. It is interesting, however, that, despite our huge military programs, we do not spend more (relative to total output) than these countries. It is also noteworthy that poor countries like Nigeria—ones with little industry and at a relatively early stage of economic development—spend the least on government services. This is understandable, since such countries must devote more of their output to the basic necessities of life. In many cases, as we saw in Chapter 1, they have a difficult time merely feeding their populations.

What the Federal, State, and Local Governments Spend Money On

There are three levels of government in the

United States—federal, state, and local. The state governments spend the least, while the federal government spends the most. This was not always the case. Before World War I, the local governments spent more than the federal government. In those days, the federal government did not maintain the large military establishment it does now, nor did it engage in the many programs in health, education, welfare, and other areas that it currently does. Figure 5.2 shows that federal spending is now a much larger percentage of the total than it was 40 years ago. Table 5.2 shows how the federal government spends its money. *About ⅓ of the federal expenditures goes for defense and other items connected with international relations and national security. About ½ goes for welfare (and other income security) programs, health, and education. The rest goes to support farm, transportation, housing, and other such programs, as well as to run Congress, the courts, and the executive branch of the federal government.*

What about the local and state governments? On what do they spend their money? Table 5.3 shows that *the biggest expenditure of the state and local governments is on schools.* After the end of World War II, these expenditures increased greatly because of the baby boom—the increase in the number of school-age children. Traditionally, schools in the United States have been a responsibility of local governments—cities and towns. *State governments spend most of their money on highways; welfare,*

Table 5.2
Federal Expenditures, Fiscal 1977.

Purpose	Amount (billions of dollars)	Percent of total
National defense	101	26
International affairs and finance	7	2
Veterans' benefits	17	4
General science, space, and technology	4	1
Agriculture	2	[b]
Education, training, employment, and social services	17	4
Health	34	9
Natural resources, environment, and energy	14	4
Commerce and transportation	17	4
Community and regional development	6	1
Interest	41	11
General government	3	1
Income security	137	35
Law enforcement and justice	3	1
Revenue sharing	7	2
Allowances	2	1
Offsetting receipts	−19	−5
Total[a]	394	100

[a] Because of rounding errors, the figures may not sum to the totals.
[b] Less than ½ of 1 percent.
Source: The Budget in Brief, 1977. These are estimates made in 1976.

Table 5.3
Expenditures of State and Local Governments, United States, 1973

Type of expenditure	Amount (billions of dollars)	Percent of total
Education	93.0	41.7
Highways	21.6	9.7
Natural resources	3.4	1.5
Health and hospitals	14.9	6.7
Public welfare	31.4	14.1
Housing and urban renewal	3.3	1.5
Interest on debt	6.8	3.0
Other	48.3	21.8
Total	222.7	100.0

Source: Statistical Abstract of the United States.

Urban Fiscal Crisis: The Case of New York City

On June 16, 1975, *Time* magazine's cover read, "How New York Went Broke." It was hard for people (both New Yorkers and others) to believe, but New York City was in danger of defaulting on its obligations. It had to borrow huge sums of money to meet its expenses, pay its workers, and refinance its mammoth debt—and the banks were no longer willing to lend the city the money. How did New York get into this fix? First, it has taken responsibility for many services and programs not undertaken by most other major cities, and its pays relatively high wages (and fringe benefits) and has a large municipal work force. (In 1973, its per capita expenditures were about $1,400, as opposed to about $400 in Los Angeles, Philadelphia, and Detroit.) Second, as the poor have moved in and the rich have moved out, New York, like many large cities, has not been able to increase its taxes commensurately. Third, instead of bringing expenditures into better balance with revenues, the city resorted to various kinds of accounting sleight-of-hand to make it appear that its budget was closer to a balance than in fact it was. By 1975, the city had borrowed so much money that about 17 percent of its budget went for debt service—and the banks were unwilling to lend any more.

In response to the crisis, state and city officials established the Municipal Assistance Corporation (called "Big Mac") to convert some of the city's short-term debt into long-term bonds.* But despite a valiant effort on the part of "Big Mac," investors were unwilling to buy the required amount of such bonds. In September 1975, when it appeared that New York City would be unable to meet its financial obligations, the New York state legislature created an Emergency Financial Control Board to impose budgetary reform on the city. At the same time, the state helped the city meet its most pressing obligations. This put the state's financial position in considerable jeopardy and many observers claimed that, if New York City defaulted (that is, if it failed to pay its debts when due), it would not be long before New York State defaulted too.

Both city and state officials petitioned the federal government for help. They pointed out that, if the city or state defaulted, this would make it difficult, if not impossible, for many other local governments throughout the nation to borrow money. Both President Gerald Ford and Secretary of the Treasury William Simon replied that it was a local matter, and that it would be improper for the federal government to intervene. However, in October 1975, Simon softened his stand a bit, saying that if the state as well as the city were forced to default, "that would add a new dimension to the problem that would require close scrutiny."

Finally, in November 1975, a financial package was put together by Governor Hugh Carey of New York, some of the major banks which held the city's debt, the unions of municipal employees, the state legislature, and President Ford. Its major provisions were as follows: First, the pension funds of the municipal employees agreed to purchase $2.5 billion in city debt. Second, the banks agreed to refinance $1 billion of the city's maturing notes (which are short term debt). Third, there was a moratorium on the payment of $1.6 billion in maturing city notes. (Holders of these notes could exchange them for long-term bonds issued by "Big Mac," or they could hold them and receive 6 percent interest, but they could not get their principal for three years and perhaps longer.) Fourth, New York City taxes were increased by $200 million per year. Fifth, New York state agreed to advance the city $800 million. Sixth, President Ford asked the Congress to approve a loan of $2.3 billion to the city. This loan was to enable the city to get past seasonal problems in matching income with outgo, and was supposed to be repaid at the end of each year.

In November 1976, this financial package came apart when New York's highest court ruled that the moratorium on payment of $1.6 billion in notes was illegal. According to this court, it was an unconstitutional avoidance of the fact that the city owed the money and didn't pay it when due. How New York City will surmount its financial problems is by no means obvious, even to its highest officials. But, regardless of how it gets through its short-term problems, two things are clear. First, investors will never again look on municipal notes and bonds with the same confidence that they did in the past. Second, New York City will have to walk on a financial tightrope for some time to come.

The extent to which the city will continue to impose cutbacks on its services will depend, of course, on the behavior of the Carter administration. Many New Yorkers hope that President Carter and the Congress will help the city out of its fiscal predicament. Only time will tell how much aid of this sort will be forthcoming.

* Basically, a bond is an IOU issued either by a private or public entity. More will be said about bonds in Chapter 7.

old age, and unemployment benefits; and providing help to localities to cover the cost of education, as well as supporting education directly. In addition, the local and state governments support hospitals, redevelopment programs, and courts, police, and fire departments.

Table 5.4
Federal Receipts, by Tax, Fiscal 1977

Type of tax	Amount (billions of dollars)	Percent of total
Personal income tax	154	40
Corporation income tax	50	14
Employment taxes	113	32
Excise taxes	18	5
Estate and gift taxes	6	2
Other revenues	11	3
Total[a]	351	100

[a] Because of rounding errors, the figures may not sum to the totals.
Source: The Budget in Brief, 1977. These are estimates made in 1976.

Changes in View of Government Responsibilities

We have already seen that government expenditures in the United States have grown considerably, both in absolute amount and as a percentage of our total output. It must be recognized that this growth in government expenditure has been part of a general trend in the United States toward a different view of the government's role. Two hundred years ago, it was not uncommon for people to believe in the slogan "That government governs best which governs least." There was considerable suspicion of government interference and meddling, freedom was the watchword, and governments were viewed as potential tyrants. In the nineteenth century, the United States prospered mightily under this *laissez-faire* system, but gradually—and not without considerable protest—the nation began to interpret the role of the government more broadly.

Responding to the dangers of noncompetitive markets, states were given the power to regulate public utilities and railroads. The Interstate Commerce Commission was established in 1887 to regulate railroads operating across state lines; and the Sherman Antitrust Act was passed in 1890 to curb monopoly and promote competition. To help control recurring business fluctuations and financial panics, banking and finance were regulated. In 1913, the Federal Reserve System was established as a central bank controlling the member commercial banks. In 1933, the Federal Deposit Insurance Corporation was established to insure bank deposits. And in 1934, the Securities and Exchange Commission was established to watch over the financial markets. Responding to the "buyer-beware" attitudes of unscrupulous and careless sellers, the Pure Food and Drug Act was passed by Congress in 1906 to insure proper quality for drugs and food.

In addition, the government's role in the fields of labor and welfare expanded considerably. For example, in the 1930s, minimum wage laws were enacted, old-age pensions and unemployment insurance were established, and the government became an important force in collective bargaining and labor relations. Furthermore, the power of government has been used increasingly to insure that citizens will not fall below a certain economic level. Food-stamp programs and programs that provide aid to dependent children have been established. *In general, the broad trend in the United States in the past century has been for the government to be used to a greater and greater extent to achieve social objectives.*

Recall from your study of American history the programs of Theodore Roosevelt, Franklin D. Roosevelt, John F. Kennedy, and Lyndon

B. Johnson. Although they were quite different sorts of presidents faced with quite different sorts of situations, they all had one thing in common: they promoted a broader view of government responsibilities. Theodore Roosevelt's "Square Deal," Franklin D. Roosevelt's "New Deal," John F. Kennedy's "New Frontier," and Lyndon B. Johnson's "Great Society" all extended government responsibilities. Some of these extensions were highly controversial at the time. For example, the ill-feeling generated by FDR's "wild-eyed schemes" is legendary. Yet, when the Republicans took office subsequently, these schemes were not repudiated. This has been the typical pattern. Although the rate at which government involvement has grown has depended heavily on who was in power, neither political party has reversed the direction of change. As you would expect, conservatives view this trend with suspicion and alarm, while liberals view it with favor and satisfaction. Your own view will depend inevitably on your own political beliefs and preferences.

What the Federal, State, and Local Governments Receive in Taxes

To get the money to cover most of the expenditures discussed in previous sections, governments collect taxes from individuals and firms. As Table 5.4 shows, at the federal level the personal income tax is the biggest single money raiser. It brings in about ⅖ of the tax revenue collected by the federal government. The next most important taxes at the federal level are the Social Security, payroll, and employment taxes, and the corporation income tax. Other important taxes are excise taxes—levied on the sale of tobacco, liquor, imports, and certain other items—and death and gift taxes. (Even when the Grim Reaper shows up, the Tax Man is not far behind.)

At the local level, on the other hand, the most important form of taxation and source of revenue is the property tax (see Table 5.5). This is a tax levied primarily on real estate. Other important local taxes—although dwarfed

Table 5.5
State and Local Tax Revenues, by Source, 1973

	State		Local	
Source	Revenues (billions of dollars)	Percent of total	Revenues (billions of dollars)	Percent of total
General sales tax	20	29	3	6
Property tax	1	2	44	83
Selective excise taxes	17	25	2	3
Personal income tax	16	23	2	5
Corporate income tax	5	8	—	—
Motor vehicle licenses	3	5	—	—
Estate and gift taxes	1	2	—	—
Other taxes	4	6	2	3
Total[a]	68	100	53	100

[a] Because of rounding errors, the figures may not sum to the totals.
Source: Statistical Abstract of the United States.

in importance by the property tax—are local sales taxes and local income taxes. Many cities—for example, New York City—levy a sales tax, equal to a certain percent—4 percent in New York City—of the value of each retail sale. The tax is simply added on to the amount charged the customer. Also, many cities—for example, Philadelphia and Pittsburgh—levy an income (or wage) tax on their residents and even on people who work in the city but live outside it. At the state level, sales (and excise) taxes are the biggest money raisers, followed by income taxes and highway user taxes. Highway user taxes include taxes on gasoline and license fees for vehicles and drivers. Often they exceed the amount spent on roads, and the balance is used for a variety of nonhighway uses.

The Role of Government in American Agriculture

Thus far, we have been discussing the government's role in the American economy in rather general terms. Now we need to consider in some detail a particular example of the economic programs carried out by our government. The government's farm programs are a logical choice, because they illustrate the usefulness of the supply-and-demand analysis presented in the previous chapter. It is important to recognize at the outset that these farm programs are not being held up as a representative sample of what the government does. There are a host of other government economic programs—poverty programs, urban programs, defense programs, research programs, education programs, transportation programs, fiscal programs, monetary programs, and many more. Most of these programs will be discussed at some point in this book.

Agriculture is an enormously important sector of the American economy. Even though its size has been decreasing steadily—and this contraction has been going on for many decades—agriculture still employs about 4 million Americans. Its importance, moreover, cannot be measured entirely by its size. You need only think about how difficult it would be to get along without food to see the strategic role agriculture plays in our economic life. Also, when it comes to technological change, agriculture is one of the most progressive parts of the American economy. Output per man-hour has grown more rapidly there than in any other major sector of the American economy, in considerable part because of government-financed agricultural research programs. The efficiency of American agriculture is admired throughout the world.

Nonetheless, it is widely acknowledged that American agriculture has had serious problems. Perhaps the clearest indication of these problems is shown by a comparison of per capita income of American farmers with per capita income among the rest of the population. Until the past few years, it is clear that farm incomes have tended to be much lower than nonfarm incomes. For example, in 1970, per capita income on the farms was about 20 percent below that for the nonfarm population. Moreover, a large proportion of the rural population is poor. Thus the National Advisory Commission on Rural Poverty found that "rural poverty is so widespread, and so acute, as to be a national disgrace."[8] Of course, this does not mean that all farmers are poor: on the contrary, many do very well indeed. But a large percentage of the nation's farmers are poor by any standard.

This farm problem is nothing new. During the first two decades of the twentieth century, farmers enjoyed relatively high prices and relatively high incomes. But in 1920, the country experienced a sharp depression that jolted agri-

[8] National Advisory Committee on Rural Poverty, *The People Left Behind,* Washington, D.C., 1967, part of which is reprinted in E. Mansfield, *Economics: Readings, Issues, and Cases.*

culture as well as the rest of the economy. Whereas the Roaring Twenties saw a recovery and boom in the nonfarm sector of the economy, agriculture did not recover as completely, and the 1930s were dreadful years; the Great Depression resulted in a sickening decline in farm prices and farm incomes. World War II brought prosperity to agriculture, but in the postwar period, farm incomes continually have been well below nonfarm incomes. All in all, agriculture has been experiencing difficulties for several decades. In 1973, as we shall see, prosperity began to return to the farms. How long-lived it will be is anyone's guess.

Causes of the Farm Problem

In Chapter 1, we claimed that relatively simple economic models are of considerable use in understanding important public and private problems. To back up this claim, we will apply the simple models of market behavior presented in the previous chapter—the models involving market demand curves and market supply curves—to explain the basic causes of the problems that, until 1973, besieged agriculture. Let's start with the market demand curve for farm products. If you think about it for a moment, you will agree that this market demand curve must have two important characteristics. First, its shape must reflect the fact that food is a necessity and that the quantity demanded will not vary much with the price of food. Second, the market demand curve for food is unlikely to shift to the right very much as per capita income rises, because consumption of food per capita faces natural biological and other limitations.

Next, consider the market supply curve for farm products. Again, you should be aware of two important characteristics of this market supply curve. First, the quantity of farm products supplied tends to be relatively insensitive to price, because the farmers have only limited control over their output. (Weather, floods, insects, and other such factors are very important.) Second, because of the rapid technological change emphasized in the previous section, the market supply curve has been shifting markedly and rapidly to the right.

If you understand these simple characteristics of the market demand curve and market supply curve for farm products, it is no trick at all to understand why we had the sort of farm problem just described. Figure 5.3 shows the market demand and market supply curves for farm products at various points in time. As you would expect, the market demand curve for farm products shifts rather slowly to the right

Figure 5.3
Shifts over Time in Market Demand and Supply Curves for Farm Products
The market demand curve has shifted rather slowly to the right (from DD' to D_1D_1' to D_2D_2'), whereas the market supply curve has shifted rapidly to the right (from SS' to S_1S_1' to S_2S_2'), with the result that the equilibrium price has declined (from OP to OP_1 to OP_2).

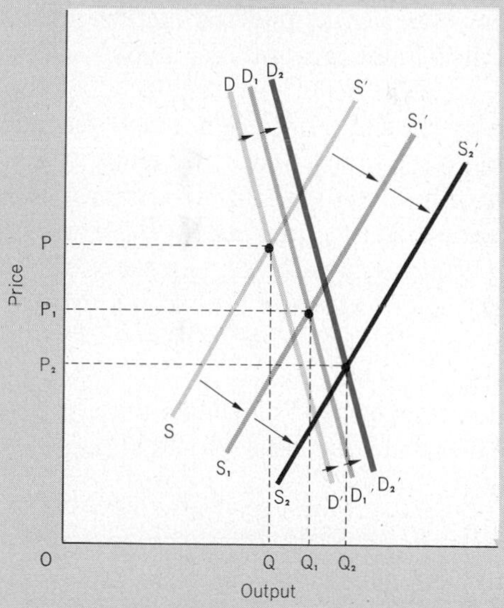

as incomes (and population) grow over time. Specifically, the market demand curve shifted from DD' in the first period to D_1D_1' in the second period to D_2D_2' in the third period. On the other hand, the market supply curve for farm products shifted rapidly to the right as technology improved over time. Specifically, it shifted from SS' in the first period to S_1S_1' in the second period to S_2S_2' in the third period.

What was the consequence of these shifts in the market demand and supply curves for food products? Clearly, *the equilibrium price of food products fell* (*relative to other products*). Specifically, the equilibrium price fell from OP to OP_1 to OP_2 in Figure 5.3. This price decrease was, of course, a large part of the farm problem. If we correct for changes in the general level of prices (which have tended to rise over time), there was, until 1973, a declining trend in farm prices. That is, agricultural prices generally fell, relative to other prices, in the last 60 years. Moreover, *given this fall in farm prices, farm incomes tended to fall, because, although lower prices were associated with greater amounts sold, the reduction in price was much greater than the increase in quantity sold,* as shown in Figure 5.3.[9]

Thus the simple model of market behavior described in the previous chapter makes it possible to explain the fact that, until recently, farm prices and farm incomes have tended to fall in the United States. Certainly there is nothing mysterious about these trends. Given the nature and characteristics of the market demand curve and market supply curve for farm products, our simple model shows that these trends are as much to be expected as parades on the Fourth of July.

However, one additional fact must be noted to understand the farm problem: *people and nonhuman resources have been relatively slow to move out of agriculture in response to these trends.* Recall from the previous chapter that the price system uses such trends—lower prices and lower incomes—to signal producers that they should use their resources elsewhere. Farmers have been loath to move out of agriculture (even though they often could make more money elsewhere)—and this was a primary cause of the farm problem that existed over most of the past 40 years. If more people and resources had left farming, agricultural prices and incomes would have risen, and ultimately farm incomes would have come closer to nonfarm incomes. (Poor education and color were, of course, significant barriers to migration.)

Nonetheless, even though farmers have been slow to move out of agriculture, they have left the farm in the long run. For example, in 1930 the farm population was about 30 million, or 25 percent of the total population; in 1950, it was about 23 million, or 15 percent of the total population; and in 1974, it was about 9 million, or 4 percent of the total population. Thus the price system has had its way. Resources have been moving out of agriculture in response to the signals and pressures of the price system. This movement of people and nonhuman resources unquestionably has contributed to greater efficiency and production for the nation as a whole. But during most of the past 40 years, we have continued to have a "surplus" of farmers—and this has been the root of the farm problem.

Government Aid to Agriculture

Traditionally, farmers have had a disproportionately large influence in Congress; and faced with declining economic fortunes, they appealed to the government for help. They extolled the virtues of rural life, emphasized that agriculture is a competitive industry, and claimed that it was unfair for their prices to fall relative to the prices they have had to pay. In

[9] The amount farmers receive is the amount they sell times the price. Thus, in Figure 5.3, the amount farmers receive in income is $OP \times OQ$ in the first period, $OP_1 \times OQ_1$ in the second period, and $OP_2 \times OQ_2$ in the third period. Clearly, since the price is decreasing much more rapidly than the quantity is increasing, farm incomes are falling.

addition, they pointed out that the movement of resources out of agriculture has entailed large human costs, since this movement, although beneficial to the nation as a whole, has been traumatic for the farm population. For reasons of this sort, they argued that the government should help farmers; and in particular, that the government should act to bolster farm prices and farm incomes.

Their voices were heard. In the Agricultural Adjustment Act of 1933, the Congress announced the concept of parity as the major objective of American farm policy. This concept acquired great importance—and must be clearly understood. Put in its simplest terms, the concept of ***parity*** says that a farmer should be able to exchange a given quantity of his output for as much in the way of nonfarm goods and services as he could at some time in the past. For example, if a farmer could take a bushel of wheat to market in 1912 and get enough money to buy a pair of gloves, today he should be able to get enough money for a bushel of wheat to buy a pair of gloves.

To see what the concept of parity implies for farm prices, suppose that the price of gloves triples. Obviously, if parity is to be maintained, the price of wheat must triple too. Thus the concept of parity implies that farm prices must increase at the same rate as the prices of the goods and services farmers buy. Of course, farmers buy lots of things besides gloves, so in actual practice the parity price of wheat or other farm products is determined by the changes over time in the average price of all the goods and services farmers buy.

Two major points should be noted about parity. First, to use this concept, one must agree on some base period, such as 1912 in the example above, during which the relationship of farm to nonfarm prices is regarded as equitable. Obviously, the higher farm prices were relative to nonfarm prices in the base period, the higher farm prices will be in subsequent periods if parity is maintained. It is interesting to note that 1910–14 was used for many years as the base period. Since this was a period of relatively high farm prices and of agricultural prosperity, the farm bloc must have wielded considerable political clout on this issue. Second, note that the concept of parity is an ethical, not a scientific proposition. It states what the relative economic position of a bushel of wheat ought to be—or more precisely, it states one particular view of what the relative economic position of a bushel of wheat should be. Based on purely scientific considerations, there is no way to prove (or disprove) this proposition, since it is based on one's values and political preferences. Using the terminology of Chapter 2, it is a proposition in normative, not positive economics.

Price Supports and Surplus Controls

During the four decades up to 1973, the concept of parity was the cornerstone of a system of government price supports. In many cases, the government did not support farm prices at the full 100 percent of parity. For example, Congress may have enacted a bill saying that the secretary of agriculture could establish a price of wheat, corn, cotton, or some other product that is between 65 and 90 percent of parity. But whatever the exact level of the price supports, the idea behind them was perfectly simple: it was to maintain farm prices above the level that would result in a free market.

Using the simple supply-and-demand model developed in the previous chapter, we can see more clearly the effects of these price supports. The situation is shown in Figure 5.4. A support price, OP', was set by the government. Since this support price was above the equilibrium price, OP, the public bought *less* of farm products (OQ_2 rather than OQ) and paid a *higher* price for them. Farmers gained from the price supports, since the amount they received for their crop under the price support was equal to $OP' \times OQ_1$, a greater amount than what they would have received in a free market, which was $OP \times OQ$.

Note, however, that since the support price exceeded the equilibrium price, the quantity supplied of the farm product, OQ_1, exceeded the quantity demanded, OQ_2. That is, *there was a surplus of the farm product in question,* which the government had to purchase, since no one else would. These surpluses were an embarrassment, both economically and politically. They showed that society's scarce resources were being utilized to produce products consumers simply did not want at existing prices. Moreover the cost of storing these surpluses was very large indeed: in some years, these storage costs alone hit the $1 billion mark.

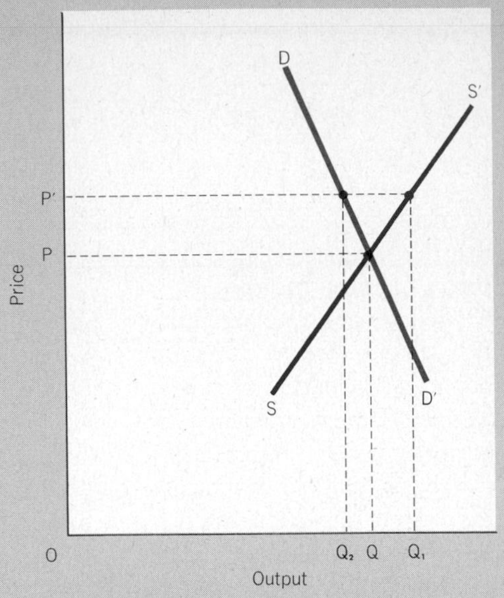

Figure 5.4
Effects of Farm Price Support Program
The support price, OP', is above the equilibrium price, OP, so the public buys OQ_2, farmers supply OQ_1 units of output, and the government buys the difference $(OQ_1 - OQ_2)$.

To help reduce these surpluses, the government followed two basic strategies. First, it tried to restrict output of farm products. In particular, the government established an acreage allotment program, which said that farmers had to limit the number of acres they planted in order to get price supports on their crops. The Department of Agriculture estimated how much of each product would be demanded by buyers (other than the government) at the support price, and tried to cut back the total acreage planted with this crop to the point where the quantity supplied equaled the quantity demanded. These output restrictions did not eliminate the surpluses, because farmers managed to increase the yields from acreage they were allowed to plant, but undoubtedly they reduced the surpluses. With these restrictions, the situation was as shown in Figure 5.5, where OQ_3 was the total output that could be grown on the acreage that could be planted with the crop. Because of the imposition of this output control, the surplus—which the government had to purchase—was reduced from $(OQ_1 - OQ_2)$ to $(OQ_3 - OQ_2)$. Farmers continued to benefit from price supports because the amount they received for their crop—$OP' \times OQ_3$—was still greater than they would have received in a free market, because the amount demanded of farm products was not very sensitive to their price.

Second, the government tried to shift the demand curve for farm products to the right. An effort was made to find new uses for various farm products. Also, various antipoverty programs, such as the food-stamp program, used our farm surpluses to help the poor. In addition, the government tried to expand the export markets for American farm products. Western Europe and Japan increased their demand for food, and the Communist countries purchased our farm products to offset their own agricultural deficiencies. Moreover, the less developed countries were permitted by

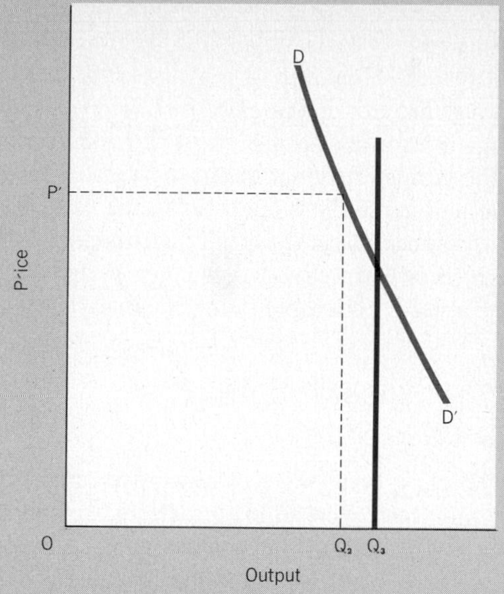

Figure 5.5
Effects of Price Supports and Output Restrictions
The government restricts output to OQ_3, with the result that it buys $(OQ_3 - OQ_2)$ units of output.

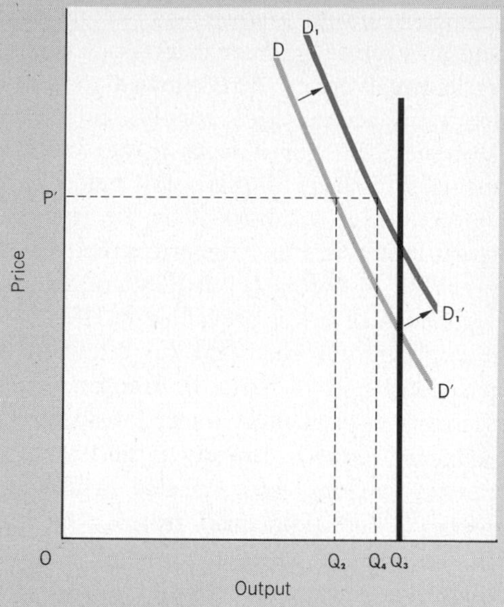

Figure 5.6
Effects of Price Supports, Output Restrictions, and a Shift to the Right in the Demand Curve for Farm Products
By shifting the demand curve from DD' to D_1D_1', the goverment reduces the surplus from $(OQ_3 - OQ_2)$ to $(OQ_3 - OQ_4)$ units of output.

Public Law 480 to buy our farm products with their own currencies, rather than dollars. The result was a reduction in farm surpluses, as shown in Figure 5.6. Since the market demand curve for farm products shifted from DD' to D_1D_1', the surplus was reduced from $(OQ_3 - OQ_2)$ to $(OQ_3 - OQ_4)$. Because of these demand-augmenting and output-restricting measures, surpluses during the late 1960s and early 1970s were considerably smaller than they were during the late 1950s and early 1960s.

The 1973 Farm Bill and More Recent Developments

In 1973, farm prices increased markedly, due partly to very great increases in foreign demand for American agricultural products. This increase in foreign demand was due partly to poor harvests in the Soviet Union, Australia, Argentina, and elsewhere, as well as to devaluations of the dollar. (In 1972–73, the Soviet Union alone bought over $1 billion of grain—on terms that provoked considerable controversy in the United States.) As a result, farm incomes reached very high levels, farm surpluses disappeared, and for the first time in 30 years the government was trying to stimulate farm production rather than restrict it.

Taking advantage of this new climate, Congress passed a new farm bill which ended price supports. This bill, the Agriculture and Consumer Protection Act of 1973, aimed at reducing government involvement in agriculture and at a return to freer markets. Specifically, agricultural prices were allowed to fluctuate freely in accord with supply and demand. However, the government makes cash payments to farmers if prices fall below certain "target" levels established by the law. These target levels are above the prices that generally prevailed in the past, but they are below the high levels of prices prevailing in 1973.

A program of this kind was originally proposed in 1949 by Charles F. Brannan, who was secretary of agriculture under President Harry Truman. Farm organizations and their supporters in Congress succeeded in killing the proposal. One important reason why it was passed in 1973 was that farm prices were so high. This meant that a program of this sort would cost little or nothing, so long as prices remained above the target levels. However, it must be recognized that, if prices fall back to their pre-1973 levels, this program will be very expensive to the taxpayers. More will be said about the Brannan plan in Chapter 21.

Besides establishing these new forms of subsidies, the 1973 farm bill limited total subsidy payments to any individual farmer to $20,000 per year. This provision is meant to deal more effectively than did the prior law with the problem of very large subsidies being paid to wealthy farmers. Also, the 1973 law states that whether or not land is taken out of production is at the discretion of the secretary of agriculture. In 1974, Secretary Earl Butz said that none should be taken out of production, and encouraged farmers to produce as much as they wanted. Nonetheless, in 1974, American crop production as a whole suffered its biggest setback in almost 40 years, due primarily to bad weather. Coupled with continued strong foreign demand for farm products, as well as domestic demand, the result was another year of high farm prices.

By 1975, it appeared to many knowledgeable observers that the farm sector no longer was suffering from overcapacity, and that, in this respect at least, an equilibrium had been achieved. However, it is too soon to be at all sure that this is the case. Just as one swallow doesn't make a spring, so a few good years for the farmers may not mean a new era. Nonetheless, it certainly is true that in the mid-1970s, excess agricultural capacity declined, and crop reserves were drawn down. As we have seen, this was a noticeable change from earlier years.

The Wheat Program: A Case Study

To get a better idea of how government programs have worked in agriculture, we will narrow our focus to the case of wheat. In the previous chapter, we described how the price of wheat would be determined in a free market. But the market for wheat has been influenced by government programs for many decades. Let's begin our brief account of the wheat program with the situation after World War II. During the war, a rural political coalition succeeded in getting guarantees of 100 percent of parity price. After the war, there was some movement away from rigid price supports by important government officials, including President Eisenhower's secretary of agriculture, Ezra Taft Benson, who wanted the government to reduce its involvement in the farm economy, both because he felt that the government's programs were not succeeding and because he wanted to see a reversal of "the trend toward government invasion of farm freedoms." [10]

During Secretary Benson's eight years in office (1953–61), there was a chronic mismatch between the quantity supplied and quantity demanded of wheat. Because of rapid advances in agricultural technology, wheat farmers were able to maintain production in the face of seri-

[10] D. Hadwiger, *Federal Wheat Commodity Programs,* Ames: Iowa State University Press, 1970, Chapter 8.

ous droughts, production controls, and moderate reductions in wheat prices. The government was forced to buy up enormous surpluses of wheat. A big issue in the 1950s was whether price supports should remain at the high levels established during World War II. Rural interests, which included commercial wheat farmers, wanted price supports to stay high: specifically, they wanted them to be at least 90 percent of parity. Secretary Benson, on the other hand, wanted to institute flexible support levels so that they could be used to help reduce overproduction. He succeeded in reducing price support levels—as well as in alienating farmers, farm leaders, and many political liberals.

In 1960, with the election of John F. Kennedy as president, Orville Freeman became secretary of agriculture. In contrast to Benson, Secretary Freeman felt that the government should play a major role in American agriculture. Faced with the prospect of continuing large surpluses of wheat, he pushed for great reductions in acreage, which was held at little more than half its postwar high. Also, he urged the export of wheat to the less developed countries, both to help promote their economic growth and to stave off famine. Rather than attempt to maintain 90 percent of parity, Freeman adopted the more modest goal of maintaining 100 percent of parity prices *on the production used for domestic food* (less than half the total crop in the 1960s).

The Cotton-Wheat Act of 1964 established a voluntary wheat-marketing certificate program for 1964 and 1965, later extended with only limited changes to 1969. Under this program, farmers who complied with acreage allotments and agreed to participate in a land-diversion program received price supports, marketing certificates, and payments for land diversion, but farmers who did not comply did not receive benefits. During 1964 to 1969, the price of wheat ranged from about $1.15 to $1.74 per bushel. However, the total price to farmers was more than this, because participants in the wheat program also got direct marketing certificate payments amounting to $.65 per bushel in 1969. During the early 1970s, the wheat program remained conceptually the same, although some modifications were made.[11]

In August 1973, the wheat program, like other agricultural programs, changed drastically. Price supports were ended, and, as we know from the previous section, the government pledged to make cash payments to farmers if the price fell below a certain target level—$2.05 per bushel in 1975. The price of wheat exceeded $4 per bushel in 1973, and was well above the target level. In contrast to previous years, the secretary of agriculture imposed no restrictions on the acreage that wheat farmers could plant in 1974. Given the enormous increase in the demand for American wheat, the emphasis was on expanding, not curtailing production.

Evaluation of Government Farm Programs

It is obviously hard to evaluate the success of the government's farm programs. Farmers will certainly take a different view of price supports and other measures than their city cousins. Nonetheless, from the point of view of the nation as a whole, these farm programs have received considerable criticism. To understand these criticisms, we must hark back to our discussion earlier in this chapter of the proper functions of government, and ask what justification there is for the government's intervening in this way in agriculture. Perhaps the most convincing justification is that the government ought to help the rural poor. As we saw in previous sections, most people agree that the gov-

[11] See G. Shepherd and G. Futrell, *Marketing Farm Products,* Ames: Iowa State University Press, 1969, p. 417; and W. Rasmussen and G. Baker, "Programs for Agriculture, 1933–1965," *Agriculture Economics Research,* July 1966.

ernment should redistribute income in this way.

Unfortunately, however, *our farm programs have done little for the farmers most in need of help,* because the amount of money a farmer has gotten from these programs has depended on how much he produced. Thus the big farmer has gotten the lion's share of the subsidies—and he, of course, needed help least. On the other hand, the small farmer, the farmer who is mired most deeply in poverty, has received little from these programs. Recognizing this fact, many observers have pointed out that, if these programs are really aimed at helping the rural poor, it would be more sensible to channel the money to them through direct subsidies, than to finance programs where much of the benefits go to prosperous commercial farmers.

It must also be recognized that *our farm programs have not dealt with the basic causes of the farm problem.* In the past at least, we have had too many people and resources in agriculture. This, as we stressed in previous sections, is why farmers' incomes have tended to be low. Yet the government's farm programs have been directed more toward supporting farm prices and incomes (and stabilizing a sector of the economy that historically has been unstable), rather than toward promoting the needed movement of people and resources out of agriculture. Indeed, some people would say that the government's farm programs have made it more difficult for the necessary adjustments to take place.

Given these defects, many proposals have been made to alter our farm programs. In the view of many observers, agriculture should return to something more closely approximating free markets, and the price system should be allowed to work more freely. The changes that occurred in 1973 are in that direction, but it is important to note that the government is still intervening heavily in agriculture. (Moreover, it should be emphasized that if farm prices recede from the high levels prevailing since 1973, the taxpayers may have to pay very heavy subsidies to farmers, according to the new law.) Although further movements toward a free market in agriculture may not be popular among many farm groups, there are signs that such changes may occur in the years ahead.

Finally, before closing this chapter, we must point out a fundamental moral of our farm programs: *the government, like the price system, can bungle the job of organizing a nation's economic activities.* We began this chapter by stressing the fact that the price system breaks down under some circumstances, and that the government must intervene. It is also worth stressing that the government sometimes intervenes when it shouldn't—and that even when it should intervene, it sometimes does so in a way that wastes resources. This, of course, doesn't mean that the government should play no part in the American economy. On the contrary, the government must—and does—play an enormously important role. What it does mean is that, just as the price system is no all-purpose cure-all, neither is the government.

Summary

The price system, despite its many virtues, suffers from serious limitations. There is no reason to believe that the distribution of income generated by the price system is equitable or optimal. Also, there is no way for the price system to handle public goods, and because of external economies or diseconomies, the price system may result in too little or too much of certain goods being produced. To a considerable extent, the government's role in the economy has developed in response to these limitations of the price system. There is considerable agreement that government should redistribute income in favor of the poor, provide public goods, and offset the effects of external economies and diseconomies. Also, it is generally felt that the government should establish a proper legal, social, and competitive framework for the price system, and that it should see to it that the economy maintains relatively full employment with reasonably stable prices. Beyond this, however, there are wide differences of opinion on the proper role of government in economic affairs. Conservatives tend to be suspicious of "big government" while liberals are inclined to believe that the government should do more.

In the past 50 years, government spending has increased considerably, both in absolute terms and as a percent of total output. (It is now about $\frac{1}{3}$ of our total output.) To a large extent, this increase has been due to our greater military responsibilities, as well as to the fact that, as their incomes have risen, our citizens have demanded more schools, highways, and other goods and services provided by government. The growth in government expenditures has also been part of a general trend in the United States whereby, more and more, the power of the government has been used to achieve social objectives. To get the money to cover most of these expenditures, governments collect taxes from individuals and firms. At the federal level, the most important form of taxation is the personal income tax.

One example of the role of government in the American economy is the farm program. American agriculture has been plagued by relatively low incomes. Until 1973, the demand for farm products grew slowly, while rapid technological change meant that the people and resources currently in agriculture could supply more and more farm products. Because people and resources did not move out of agriculture as rapidly as the price system dictated, farm incomes tended to be relatively low. In response to political pressures from the farm blocs, the government set in motion a series of programs to aid farmers. A cornerstone of these programs was the concept of parity, which said that the prices farmers receive should increase at the same rate as the prices of the goods and services farmers buy. The government instituted price supports to keep farm prices above their equilibrium level. But since the support prices exceeded the equilibrium prices, there was a surplus of the commodities that the government had to purchase and store. To help reduce these surpluses, the government tried to restrict the output of farm products and expand the demand for them.

These farm programs received considerable criticism. From the point of view of income redistribution, they suffered from the fact that they did little for the farmers most in need of help. As tools of resource allocation, they suffered because they dealt more with the symptoms of the farm problem than with its basic causes. In 1973, price supports were ended, but the government pledged to make cash payments to farmers if farm prices fall below certain target levels. The government's farm programs illustrate the fact that government intervention, like the price system, has plenty of limitations. Neither the price system nor government intervention is an all-purpose cure all.

CONCEPTS FOR REVIEW

Public goods
External economy
External diseconomy
Transfer payments
Antitrust laws
Welfare payments
Price supports
Parity
Depression
Private sector
Public sector
Income tax
Sales tax
Property tax

QUESTIONS FOR DISCUSSION AND REVIEW

1. "The government that governs least governs best." What does this mean? Does it have any implications for economic policy? If so, what? Do you agree with this proposition? Is it testable? If so, how?

2. "I believe the government should do only that which private citizens cannot do for themselves, or which they cannot do so well for themselves." Interpret and comment. Indicate how one might determine in practice what the legitimate functions of government are, according to this proposition.

3. "The ideal public policy, from the viewpoint of the state, is one with identifiable beneficiaries, each of whom is helped appreciably, at the cost of many unidentifiable persons, none of whom is hurt much."[12] Interpret and comment. Indicate how this proposition might be used to help predict government behavior.

4. Suppose that the demand and supply curves for paper are as shown below.

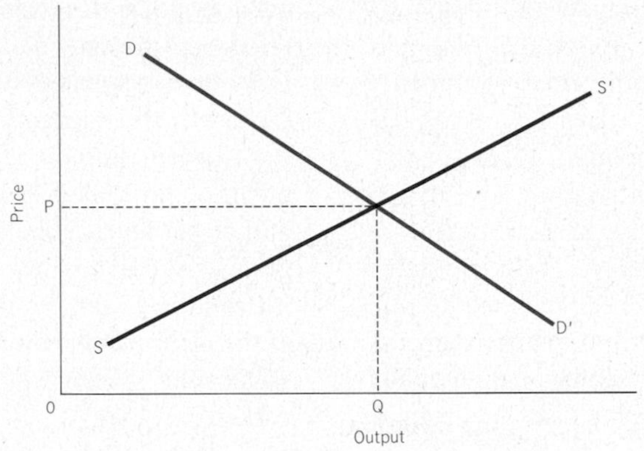

If paper production results in serious pollution of rivers and streams, is the socially optimal output of paper less than, greater than, or equal to *OQ*? Does the supply curve reflecting the true social costs of producing paper lie to the right of *SS'*, to the left of *SS'*, or at *SS'*? Why?

[12] G. Stigler, "The Government of the Economy," in E. Mansfield, *Economics: Readings, Issues, and Cases.*

5. Suppose that paper production results in some important uncompensated benefits to other industries. If there are major external economies of this sort (and if paper production no longer results in any pollution), is the socially optimal output of paper less than, greater than, or equal to *OQ* in Question 4? Does the demand curve reflecting the true social benefits from paper output lie to the right of *DD′*, to the left of *DD′*, or at *DD′*? Why?

6. "An uncrowded bridge is an example of a public good." Do you agree? Why or why not? Can this good—or more accurately, this service—be provided by private firms? Why or why not?

7. What are some of the major factors that have tended to reduce the rate at which people and resources have moved out of agriculture? Consider the cultural factors, relevant differences in birth rates, and institutions of land tenure and ownership.

8. Suppose that the demand curve for corn is as follows:

Price (dollars per bushel)	Quantity demanded per year (millions of bushels)
1	70
2	65
3	60
4	55
5	50
6	45

If the government supports the price of corn at $4 per bushel, and if it restricts output to 60 million bushels per year, how much corn will the government have to buy each year? If the government stopped supporting the price of corn, what would its price be?

9. "During the mid-1970s, the American agricultural problem turned from one of overcapacity to shortage." Explain whether you agree or disagree, and cite the evidence that leads you to whichever conclusion you reach. Be sure to define "overcapacity" and "shortage."

10. "The sharp increases in the price of wheat during the mid-1970s have been due primarily to shifts in the supply curve for wheat." Comment.

11. "I cannot get the amount of national defense I want and you, a different amount."[13] Explain. Is this true of all public goods?

12. Is delivery of the mail a public good? Why should the government provide this service? What are the arguments against its providing it?

[13] M. Friedman, *Capitalism and Freedom*.

6 Government Expenditures, Taxation, and the Public Debt

The government plays an extremely important role in the American economy. It is obvious that it influences our economic lives and fortunes in countless ways. At this point, we must look in detail at how decisions are made concerning the level and distribution of government expenditures. Also, we must discuss the principles of taxation. These topics are of central importance in understanding the public sector of our economy.

In addition, we must discuss some of the salient issues concerning the public sector, including the so-called military-industrial complex, tax reform, and revenue sharing. Further, we must describe in some detail the nature, size, and burden of the public debt, a subject that has been surrounded by as many myths as any in economics.

Government Expenditures

The Federal Budgetary Process

Determining how much the federal government should spend is a mammoth undertaking, involving literally thousands of people and hundreds of thousands of man-hours. Decisions on expenditures are part of the budgetary process. The ***budget*** is a statement of the government's anticipated expenditures and revenues. The federal budget is for a fiscal year, from October 1 to September 30. Let's consider the budget for the fiscal year beginning October 1, 1976. In the summer of 1975, the various agencies of the federal government began to prepare their program proposals. By the fall they had made detailed budget requests which the president, with his Office of Management and Budget, went over from October to December 1975. Since the agencies generally wanted more than the president wanted to spend, he usually cut down their requests.

In January 1976, the president submitted his budget to Congress, which then spent several months in intensive deliberation and negotiation. Congressional committees concerned with particular areas like defense or education recommended changes in the president's budget. The Congressional Budget Office, headed by Alice Rivlin (formerly an economist at the Brookings Institution), made various types of economic analyses to help congressmen evaluate alternative programs. By mid-May, the Congress passed a resolution setting tentative targets for over-all spending and revenues; this resolution was based on the joint recommendations by the House and Senate Budget Committees. The targets in the resolution had to be kept in mind by the various congressional committees dealing with specific spending or tax actions. If these actions added up to bigger totals than the resolution called for, the budget committees and the Congress had to decide how the discrepancies were to be reconciled: by changes in expenditures, taxes, or initial targets. Before late September 1976, the Congress adopted a second resolution, setting final ceilings for over-all expenditure and a floor on revenues.

This budgetary procedure is new. The Congressional Budget and Impoundment Control Act of 1974 established this series of steps that Congress must go through in considering the president's budget. Prior to the middle 1970s, the decision-making process in Congress was fragmented. Separate committees and subcommittees of the Appropriations Committees considered various parts of the president's recommended budget, and it was hard for Congress to establish any over-all policy for total government expenditure and taxes. Moreover, the Congressional Budget Office did not exist, and Congress lacked the staff required to analyze and examine the benefits and costs of various proposed programs. This new procedure attempted to bolster Congress's role in the budgetary process, and to force Congress to look at the over-all budgetary picture so that the total would be more than the sum of largely uncoordinated parts.

Benefit-Cost Analysis

How much should the government spend on various activities and services? Basically, the answer must be provided by the nation's political processes. For example, with regard to the provision of public goods

> voting by ballot must be resorted to in place of dollar voting. . . . Decision making by voting becomes a substitute for preference revelation through the market. The results will not please everybody, but they will approximate—more or less perfectly, depending on the efficiency of the voting process and the homogeneity of preferences—the community's preferences.[1]

[1] Richard and Peggy Musgrave, *Public Finance in Theory and Practice*, New York: McGraw Hill, 1973, p. 8.

Under certain circumstances, particular types of economic analysis can prove helpful to the policy makers and citizens who must determine how much the government should spend on various programs. Let's begin by supposing that we can measure the benefits and costs of each such program. What is the optimal amount to spend on each one? The answer, clearly enough, is that *spending on the program should be pushed to the point where the extra benefit from an extra dollar spent is at least equal to the dollar of cost.* This would insure that the amount spent on each government program yields a benefit at least as great as the value of output forgone in the private sector. This would also make sure that one government program is not being expanded at the expense of other programs that would yield greater benefits if they were expanded instead.

The principle that extra benefit should be compared with extra cost is valuable—and, as we shall see in the next section, widely applicable—but it can solve only a small part of the problem of allocating resources in the public sector. Why? Because it is impossible to measure the benefits from defense or police protection or the courts in dollars and cents. Only in certain cases can benefits be quantified at all precisely. And it is not only a question of the amount of the benefits and costs; it is also a question of who benefits and who pays. Nonetheless, it is difficult to see how rational choices can be made without paying attention to costs and benefits—even if they are measured imprecisely, and are by no means the whole story.[2]

Preventing School Dropouts: A Case Study[3]

Despite the difficulties involved, in recent years more and more benefit-cost analyses have been carried out to help guide public policy. For example, consider the following study, by the University of Wisconsin's Burton Weisbrod, of a program to reduce the dropout rate in a high school in St. Louis. In this program, potential dropouts were given counseling and help in getting part-time jobs. It cost over $500 per student. The question, of course, was whether the program did enough good to be worth the cost. To help answer this question, the experience of the students in the program was compared with the experience of a control group of comparable students who were not included in the program. It turned out that, despite the help they received, 44 percent of the students in the program dropped out of school before graduation, while 52 percent of the students in the control group dropped out before graduation. Thus the program seemed to reduce the dropout rate by 8 percentage points.

How much was this benefit worth? Weisbrod pointed out that one principal gain was the increased income earned by students who complete high school. A high school graduate earns about $2,750 more than a dropout over a lifetime. Let us use this figure—$2,750—as a measure of the benefit of preventing a student from dropping out. Was the program worthwhile? Since the program reduced the probability of dropping out by 8 percentage points, the average benefit per student was .08 times $2,750, or $220. Since this was less than the cost per student, the program did not seem worthwhile. Of course, one can object that the measure of the benefit from preventing a student from dropping out is incomplete. It does not include the psychic and social benefits from putting people in a position to earn their own keep rather than to be prime candidates for public assistance, and even perhaps jail. Nonetheless, this study raised important questions and had significant effects.

---

[2] See Charles Schultze, *The Politics and Economics of Public Spending,* Washington, D.C.: Brookings Institution, 1968. Also, see Bernard Herber, *Modern Public Finance,* Homewood, Ill.: Irwin, 1971, pp. 389–91.

[3] This section is based on Burton Weisbrod, "Preventing High School Dropouts," in Robert Dorfman, ed., *Measuring Benefits of Government Investments,* Washington, D.C.: Brookings Institution, 1965. A brief discussion of this study is also provided in Otto Eckstein, *Public Finance,* Englewood Cliffs, N.J.: Prentice-Hall, 1967.

Benefit-cost analyses have proved useful in many areas of government. In particular, they have been used for many years in the Department of Defense. Decisions to develop one weapons system rather than another, or to procure a certain amount of a given weapon, have been based in part on such studies. Other areas where benefit-cost analyses have been used extensively are water projects (irrigation, flood control, hydroelectric, and other projects), transportation projects, and urban renewal, recreation, and health projects. For example, in water projects, benefit-cost analysis has frequently been used by the Corps of Engineers and others to determine whether it is worthwhile to spend additional money on flood control, and if so, how much extra expenditure is justified.

A highly simplified example of a benefit-cost analysis of the construction of a dam is shown in Table 6.1. The alternative policies are to build a low dam or a high dam. Table 6.1 shows the annual costs and benefits associated with each of these policies. Clearly, the high dam should be built because the extra cost involved ($150,000 more than for the low dam) is more than outweighed by the extra benefits received ($200,000 more than for the low dam). Note, however, that this is a very simple case. In general, data on costs and benefits are not laid out so straightforwardly. Instead, there are very wide bands of uncertainty about the relevant costs and benefits.

Table 6.1
Benefit-Cost Analysis for Constructing a Dam

Alternative policies	Annual cost (dollars)	Annual benefit (dollars)
Build a low dam	600,000	650,000
Build a high dam	750,000	850,000

Government Expenditures and the Problem of Social Balance

It is not easy to decide how large government expenditures should be. As we saw in Chapter 5, opinions differ widely on the proper role of government in economic affairs, and it is often impossible to measure the costs and benefits of government programs with dependable accuracy. Nonetheless, some economists—led by Harvard's John Kenneth Galbraith—believe that the public sector of the economy has been deprived of needed resources, whereas the private sector has catered to relatively unimportant wants. For example, in *The Affluent Society,* Galbraith argued that consumers are led by advertising and other promotional efforts to purchase more and more goods of marginal importance to them. On the other hand, in his opinion, the nation is suffering from too little spending on government services. Thus he writes,

> In the years following World War II, the papers of any major city . . . told daily of the shortages and shortcomings in the elementary municipal and metropolitan services. The schools were old and overcrowded. The police force was understrength and underpaid. The parks and playgrounds were insufficient. Streets and empty lots were filthy, and the sanitation staff was underequipped and in need of men. Access to the city by those who work there was uncertain and painful and becoming more so. Internal transportation was overcrowded, unhealthy, and dirty. So was the air. Parking on the streets had to be prohibited, and there was no space elsewhere. These deficiencies were not in new and novel services, but in old established ones.[4]

Many economists agree with Galbraith. Particularly among liberals, there is a widespread feeling that resources are being malallocated, too much going for deodorants, comic books,

[4] John Kenneth Galbraith, *The Affluent Society,* Boston: Houghton Mifflin, 1958, p. 252. Incidentally, Galbraith opposed the tax cut of 1964 because he felt that government spending should be increased instead.

and mouth wash, and too little going for schools and public services. But this feeling is not shared by all economists. Galbraith's critics point out that expenditures often benefit particular interest groups, which lobby hard for them in federal and state legislatures. The result is that spending programs may be carried beyond the optimal point. Further, they point out that Galbraith's assertion that private wants are becoming more and more trivial and synthetic is not scientifically verifiable and that, in any case, it ignores the large number of people living in very modest circumstances, indeed, even in dire poverty.

Economic theory alone cannot settle this basic question. It is obviously a matter of politics as well as economics. However, in trying to reach an opinion, bear in mind that both sides may be partly correct. For certain types of government services, you may agree with Galbraith and his followers that too little is being spent, but for other types of government services you may agree with his critics that too much is being spent. For example, you may feel that too little is being spent on pollution control and urban problems, but that too much is being spent on agricultural subsidies (many of which go to wealthy farmers) and subsidies to the merchant marine (which are meant to keep the American shipping industry competitive with other nations).

Finally, it is important to distinguish between decisions concerning the *scope* of government activities and decisions concerning the *efficiency* of government. Thus far in this section we have been discussing the proper scope of government. Assume that we can divide all goods into public goods and private goods, and that Figure 6.1 shows the society's product transformation curve. In other words, as you recall from Chapter 3, Figure 6.1 shows the maximum amount of public goods that can be produced, given each quantity produced of private goods. Then the question that we have been discussing is: At what point along the product transformation curve should society be? For example, should society choose point *A* (where more public goods and less private goods are produced) or point *B* (where less public goods and more private goods are produced)?

But there is another important question: How can we attain a point *on* the product transformation curve, rather than one (like point *C*) that is *inside* it? As we know from Chapter 3, inefficiency will result in society's being on a point inside the product transformation curve. Thus, to attain a point on the

Figure 6.1
Product Transformation Curve, Public versus Private Goods
At point *B*, society produces less public goods and more private goods than at point *A*. Thus, a movement from point *A* to point *B* reduces government expenditures by reducing the *scope* of government services. At point *C*, society is producing inefficiently, and a movement from point *C* to point *B* or point *A* can be attained by increasing the *efficiency* of government (and/or private) operations.

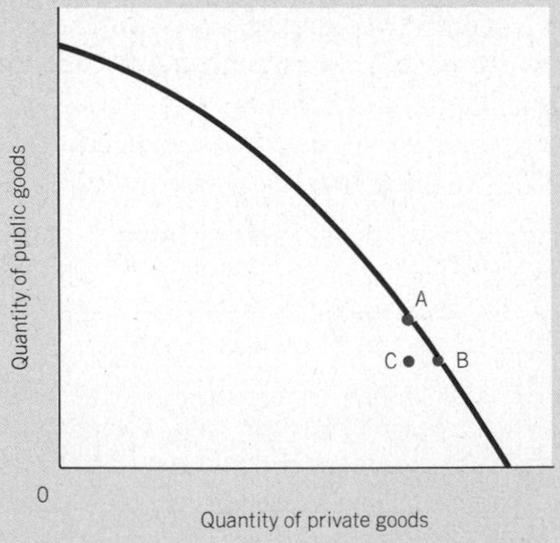

product transformation curve, government officials (and others) must do their best to eliminate inefficiency. By doing so, society can get more from the available resources. For example, it can attain points *A* or *B* rather than point *C*. Whether society wants to use its added efficiency to attain point *A* or point *B* is then a political question. However, regardless of how this question is decided, society is better off to eliminate inefficiency.

Two Case Studies: Defense and Coal Research

Military Spending and the Military-Industrial Complex

At this point, it is worthwhile to look briefly at two federal agencies, the Department of Defense and the Office of Coal Research (formerly in the Department of Interior, and now part of the Energy Research and Development Administration). Although these two agencies cannot be held up as typical, they do represent interesting case studies. On the one hand, the Department of Defense has repeatedly been charged with overspending. But since it is hard to tell what level of defense capability is optimal, it is equally difficult to tell whether defense spending is too much or too little. However, there can be no doubt about the enormous size of our defense expenditures. In 1970, American military expenditures were more than $80 billion, which means that they constituted over 40 percent of national output. (Moreover, this figure excludes defense-related spending by the Energy Research and Development Administration and National Aeronautics and Space Administration.) Some people claim that this exaggerates the cost of defense, because if defense expenditures were cut appreciably, our national output would fall. But this assumes that other forms of government spending would not be substituted for defense, or that fiscal and monetary policies could not keep the economy at a high employment level without defense spending—both very unrealistic assumptions.

However, some forms of defense and space spending, particularly on research and development, do provide important benefits to the civilian economy. The electronic computer, numerical control, integrated circuits, atomic energy, synthetic rubber, and many other significant inventions stemmed at least partly from military R and D. Moreover, there is undoubtedly considerable opportunity for such spillover from current military and space R and D. Nonetheless, there seems to be a widespread feeling that the spillover per dollar of military-space R and D is unlikely to be as great as in the past, because the capabilities that are being developed and the environment that is being probed are less intimately connected with civilian activities than formerly. For example, the devices needed to send a man to the moon may have relatively little applicability in the civilian economy because they "oversatisfy" civilian requirements and few people or firms are willing to pay for them.

There is considerable evidence that the weapons acquisition process has not been as efficient as it might have been. There have been spectacular overruns in development and production costs. For example, the cost of the Lockheed C5A transport plane increased from the $3.4 billion estimated in 1965 to $5.3 billion in 1968. To some extent, such cost increases reflect the fact that new weapons systems tend to push the state of the art, so that unexpected problems must be expected. But in addition, the firms that develop and produce these weapons systems often submit unrealistically low bids to get a contract, knowing that they are likely to get approval for cost increases later on. According to some observers, like Merton J. Peck of Yale University and F. M. Scherer of Northwestern University, these cost overruns have also been due to "inadequate attention to the efficient utilization of technical, production, and administrative manpower—areas in which major cost reductions are possible."[5]

In addition, some observers believe that the major defense contractors, in conjunction with the military services, apply undue political pressure in support of high defense budgets. For example, President Dwight D. Eisenhower, himself a distinguished military commander, warned of the dangers involved in this "military-industrial complex." In his last speech to the nation as president, he said, "In the councils of government, we must guard against the acquisition of unwarranted influence, whether sought or unsought, by the military-industrial complex. The potential for the disastrous rise of misplaced power exists and will persist." It seems unlikely that there is any real conspiracy, but military contractors, with their political allies, are undoubtedly a powerful lobby for defense spending.

In a world marked by international tensions, few people argue that our defense establishment should be dismantled. Many, indeed, argue that we should be careful to avoid a decline in our military strength relative to our potential adversaries. But this is no argument for inefficiency. Almost all agree that, given the size of the defense budget, sound economic controls must be exercised by Pentagon officials to prevent waste of resources on a mammoth scale.

The Office of Coal Research

Just as it is sometimes charged that certain agencies, like the Department of Defense, may have been spending too much, so it is sometimes charged that other agencies, like the Office of Coal Research, may have been spending too little. In recent years, there has been considerable discussion and alarm over the so-called energy crisis, a situation where a marked shortage seems to have arisen in clean domestic fuels. One way to avoid such a crisis is to develop new technologies to convert our relatively plentiful coal supplies into a clean gas or other forms of fuel that would be less polluting than coal. The Office of Coal Research was responsible for financing research of this kind, and in accord with President Nixon's energy message of June 4, 1971, it was charged with accelerating the coal gasification program to develop a process or processes to produce clean, high-quality gas from coal on a commercial scale by 1980.

The expenditures of the Office of Coal Research (OCR) increased very substantially during the early 1970s. Its budget was about $60 million in 1974, about $30 million in 1972, and about $15 million in 1970. Much of this money was spent for coal gasification work; about $30 million was spent in 1973 on this program, ⅔ being funded by OCR and about ⅓ by industry. The Office of Coal Research helped to finance several approaches to coal gasification, including the Institute of Gas Technology's HYGAS pilot plant, the Consolidation Coal Company's CO_2 Acceptor pilot plant, FMC Corporation's COED pilot plant, and others. Each of these pilot plants cost millions of dollars. Because it was felt that the social returns from the information gained from them would exceed the private returns to the companies operating them, the government subsidized this research and development.

Despite the increase in OCR's expenditures, many knowledgeable people felt that such work should be expanded even more rapidly. For example, in 1973 Senator Henry Jackson of Washington called for a 10-year R and D program on coal gasification costing $660 million (60 percent to be paid for by government, 40 percent by industry), and a 12-year R and D program on coal liquefaction costing $750 mil-

[5] M. J. Peck and F. M. Scherer, *The Weapons Acquisition Process,* Cambridge, Mass.: Harvard University Press, 1962, p. 594.

lion (75 percent to be paid for by government). Also, the Office of Science and Technology's Energy Advisory Panel called in 1972 for an expanded R and D program for coal liquefaction, as well as continued emphasis on coal gasification.

During the mid-1970s, the amount spent on coal research did increase dramatically—from the $60 million spent in 1974 to about $280 million in 1976. Besides the coal gasification program, the Energy Research and Development Administration (which now includes what formerly was the Office of Coal Research) is carrying out considerable research concerning coal liquefaction and direct combustion of coal. The United States has over 300 billion tons of coal reserves, more than any other country in the world. In view of this fact, and our recent energy problems, many observers feel that this increase in government support for coal research was justified and perhaps overdue.

Taxation and Government Revenues

The Federal Tax Legislative Process

It is one thing for the federal government to decide how much to spend and on what; it is another to raise the money to underwrite these programs. This section describes how the federal government decides how much to tax. Of course, this problem is not solved from scratch every year. Instead, the government takes the existing tax structure as given and changes it from time to time as seems desirable. Frequently the major initiative leading to a change in the tax laws comes from the president, who requests tax changes in his State of the Union message, his budget message, or a special tax message. Much of the spadework underlying his proposals will have been carried out by the Treasury Department, particularly the Treasury's Office of Tax Analysis, Office of the Tax Legislative Counsel, and Internal Revenue Service.

The proposal of a major tax change generally brings about considerable public debate. Representatives of labor, industry, agriculture, and other economic and social groups present their opinions. Newspaper articles, radio shows, and television commentators analyze the issues. By the time the Congress begins to look seriously at the proposal, the battle lines between those who favor the change and those who oppose it are generally pretty clearly drawn. The tax bill incorporating the change is first considered by the Ways and Means Committee of the House of Representatives, a very powerful committee composed of members drawn from both political parties. After public hearings, the committee goes into executive session and reviews each proposed change with its staff and with the Treasury staff. After careful study, the committee arrives at a bill it recommends—though this bill may or may not conform to what the president asked for. Then the bill is referred to the entire House of Representatives for approval. Only rarely is a major tax bill recommended by the committee turned down by the House.

Next, the bill is sent to the Senate. There it is referred to the Finance Committee, which is organized like the House Ways and Means Committee. The Finance Committee also holds hearings, discusses the bill at length, makes changes in it, and sends its version of the bill to the entire Senate, where there frequently is considerable debate. Ultimately, it is brought to a vote. If it does not pass, that ends the process. If it does pass (and if it differs from the House version of the bill, which is generally the case), then a conference committee must be formed to iron out the differences between the House and Senate versions. Finally, when this compromise is worked out, the result must be passed by both houses and sent to the president. The president rarely vetoes a tax bill, although it has occasionally been done.[6]

Principles of Taxation

According to the English political philosopher, Edmund Burke, "To tax and to please, no more than to love and to be wise, is not given to men." What constitutes a rational tax system? Are there any generally accepted principles to guide the nation in determining who should pay how much? The answer is that there are some principles most people accept, but they are so broad and general that they leave plenty of room for argument and compromise. Specifically, two general principles of taxation command widespread agreement.

Benefit principle. The first principle is that *people who receive more from a certain government service should pay more in taxes to support it.* Certainly few people would argue with this idea. However, it is frequently difficult, if not impossible, to apply. For example, there is no good way to measure the amount of the benefits received by a particular taxpayer from many public services, such as police protection.

Ability-to-pay principle. The second principle is that *people should be taxed so as to result in a socially desirable redistribution of income.* In practice, this has ordinarily meant that the wealthy have been asked to pay more than the poor. This idea, too, has generally commanded widespread assent—although this, of course, has not prevented the wealthy from trying to avoid its application to them.

It follows from these principles that if two people are in essentially the same circumstances (their income, purchases, utilization of public services are the same), then they should pay the same taxes. This is an important rule, innocuous though it may seem. It says that equals should be treated equally—*whether one is a Republican and the other is a Democrat, or whether one is a friend of the president and the other is his enemy, or whether one has purely salary income and the other has property income, they should be treated equally.* Certainly, this is a basic characteristic of an equitable tax system.

It is easy to relate most of the taxes in our tax structure to these principles. For example, the first principle—the benefit principle—is the basic rationale behind taxes on gasoline and license fees for vehicles and drivers. Those who use the roads are asked to pay for their construction and upkeep. Also, the property tax, levied primarily on real estate, is often supported on these grounds. It is argued that property owners receive important benefits—fire and police protection, for example—and that the extent of the benefits is related to the extent of their property.

The personal income tax is based squarely on the second principle—ability to pay. A person with a large income pays a higher proportion of income in personal income taxes than does a person with a smaller income. For example, in 1975, if a couple's income (after deductions but before exemptions) were $10,000, their federal income tax would be $1,430, whereas if their income were $50,000, their federal income tax would be $16,250. (However, the wealthy can avoid taxes in various perfectly legal ways, as we shall see in a later section.) Also, estate and inheritance taxes hit the rich much harder than the poor; but again, it is possible to take some of the sting out of them if you have a good lawyer.

The principles cited above are useful and important, but they do not take us very far toward establishing a rational tax structure. They are too vague and leave too many ques-

[6] For an excellent discussion of the federal tax legislative process, see J. Pechman, *Federal Tax Policy,* rev. ed., New York: Norton, 1970, part of which is reprinted in E. Mansfield, *Economics: Readings, Issues, and Cases,* 2d ed., New York: Norton, 1977.

tions unanswered. For example, if I use about the same amount of public services as you do, but my income is twice yours, how much more should I pay in taxes? Twice as much? Three times as much? Fifty percent more? These principles throw no real light on many of the detailed questions that must be answered by a real-life tax code.

The Personal and Corporate Income Taxes

The federal personal income tax brings in over $150 billion a year. Yet a great many people are perhaps unaware of just how much they are contributing because it is deducted from their wages each month or each week, so that they owe little extra when April 15 rolls around. (Indeed, they may even be due a refund.) This pay-as-you-go scheme reduces the pain, but, of course, it does not eliminate it: taxes are never painless.

Obviously, how much a family has to pay in personal income taxes depends on the family's income. The tax schedule (as of 1975) is as shown in Table 6.2. The second column shows how much a couple would have to pay if their income was the amount shown in the first column. For example, at an income of $5,000, their income tax would be $475; at an income of $20,000, their income tax would be $3,900. Clearly, the percentage of income owed in income tax increases as income increases, but this percentage does not increase indefinitely. The percentage of income going for personal income taxes never exceeds 70 percent, no matter how much money the couple makes. (And on income from wages and personal effort, it never exceeds 50 percent.)

It is instructive to look further at how the "tax bite" increases with income. In particular, let's ask ourselves what proportion of an *extra* dollar of income the couple will have to pay in personal income taxes. In other words, what is the ***marginal tax rate***—the tax on an extra dollar of income? The fourth column of Table 6.2 shows that the marginal tax rate is 17 percent if the couple's income is $5,000, 28 percent if their income is $20,000, 50 percent if their income is $50,000, and 70 percent if their income is $1 million. Thus, the greater the couple's income, the greater the proportion of

Table 6.2
Federal Personal Income Tax, Couple without Children, 1975[a]

Income (after deductions but before personal exemptions) (dollars)	Personal income tax (dollars)	Average tax rate (percent)	Marginal tax rate (percent)
Below 1,500	0	0	0
3,000	155	5.2	15
5,000	475	9.5	17
10,000	1,430	14.3	22
20,000	3,900	19.5	28
50,000	16,250	32.5	50
100,000	44,220	44.2	60
1,000,000	669,870	67.0	70

[a] If a family contained dependent children and its income was less than $8,000 per year, it could get a credit of up to $400, which might wipe out any income tax liability and result in a cash payment to the family.

an extra dollar that goes for personal income taxes.

Clearly, the personal income tax tends to reduce the inequality of after-tax income, since the rich are taxed more heavily than the poor. However, the personal income tax does not bear down as heavily on the rich as one might surmise from Table 6.2. This is because, as we shall see in a subsequent section, there are a variety of perfectly legal ways for people to avoid paying taxes on their incomes. Current tax laws are favorable to homeowners, who can deduct the payment of local real estate taxes and the interest on their mortgage from their income to get the adjusted level of income on which they pay income taxes. Also, money a person makes on the stock market or from some other situation where his assets go up in value, known as a ***capital gain,*** is subject to lower personal income tax rates than other income. Interest paid by state and local governments on their bonds is not taxable at all by the federal government. In addition, of course, there is some illegal tax evasion, such as underreporting of income, fake expenses, and imaginary dependents. But evasion is much less important than legal tax avoidance, despite Will Rogers's quip that the income tax has made more liars among the American public than golf.

The federal government imposes a tax on the incomes of corporations as well as of people. Corporations must pay 20 percent of their first $25,000 of annual profits, 22 percent of their second $25,000 of annual profits, and 48 percent of the rest as corporate income tax. For example, a corporation with annual profits of $150,000 would pay $58,500 in corporate income tax—$5,000 (20 percent of the first $25,000) plus $5,500 (22 percent of the next $25,000) plus $48,000 (48 percent of the remaining $100,000). The corporate income tax involves double taxation. The federal government taxes a corporation's earnings both through the corporate income tax (when the corporation earns the profits) and through the personal income tax (when the corporation's earnings are distributed to the stockholders as dividends).

It is generally agreed that the personal income tax is paid by the person whose income is taxed: he or she cannot shift this tax to someone else. But the incidence of the corporate income tax is not so clear. To some extent, corporations may pass along some of their income tax bill to customers in the form of higher prices or to workers in the form of lower wages. Some economists feel that a corporation shifts much of the tax burden in this way; others disagree. This is a controversial issue that has proved very difficult to resolve.

Fiscal Relations between Federal, State, and Local Government

It is important to recognize that there are several levels of government in the United States—federal, state, and local—and that each level of government spends and taxes. Thus all levels of government, not just the federal government, play a role in our economic affairs. Unfortunately, however, there has been limited coordination between the spending and tax decisions of the federal government and those of the state and local governments. From the point of view of promoting full employment without inflation, it would be desirable for the federal, state, and local governments to work in unison, or at least in the same direction, to fight excessive unemployment or inflation. But in fact they often have worked at cross-purposes.

In this country the state and local governments are traditionally entrusted with the responsibility for some of the services that have had to be expanded most rapidly—education, highways, municipal facilities, and so forth. Yet the kinds of taxes the state and local governments rely on—notably sales and property taxes—do not provide a yield that increases very rapidly with increases in income. Thus a basic question arises: How can the state and local governments get the money they need to expand their services at the desired rate? Presently, the state and local governments are caught in a fiscal bind. Their expenditures are being pushed up more rapidly than their revenues. On the other hand, because the personal income tax generates a great deal of additional money as income increases, the federal government is in the fortunate position of having its revenues increase at a relatively rapid rate.

Recognizing that it has access to greater sources of revenue, the federal government has been making more and more grants to states and—on a smaller scale—to local governments. These grants have been earmarked primarily for highways, welfare, and education, the major expenditure areas for state and local governments. One effect of these grants is to offset the considerable regional differences in income. Since some states—particularly those in the Deep South—are poor, less tax revenue is generated there than in richer states even if tax rates are the same. Thus, to equalize the extent and quality of public services, the federal government in effect takes from the richer states—like New York and California—and gives to the poorer states—like Mississippi and Alabama.

Revenue Sharing

In recent years, a great deal of attention has been given to ***revenue sharing***—large and unconditional grants by the federal government to the state and local governments. Initially suggested by Walter W. Heller of the University of Minnesota and Joseph Pechman of the Brookings Institution, this idea was accepted by the Nixon administration, and eventually by Congress. At first it was opposed on the ground that those who spend money should have the responsibility of raising it, since the divorce of expenditure from financing responsibilities might lead to wasteful expenditures. Initially, other objections were raised as well. But the fiscal plight of the state and local governments is serious and undesirable: there is a mismatch between their responsibilities and their resources. Recognizing that some device must be adopted to help the local and state governments, Congress passed the first revenue-sharing bill in 1972.

However, this bill did not establish revenue sharing as a permanent program. Instead, it was given a termination date of December 31, 1976, to be sure that it would be examined in the light of several years of experience to see how effective revenue sharing proved in practice. There are great difficulties in making such an examination (since the effects of revenue sharing are hard to measure), but the studies carried out to date seem to suggest that the program has been working out reasonably well. According to Richard Nathan of the Brookings Institution, the adoption of revenue sharing has helped to promote a desirable decentralization of government power. To improve the program, he feels that the formula for dividing the shared funds between state and local governments should be made more flexible. At present, local governments *in each state* receive \$2 for every \$1 received by the state government. In late 1976, Congress and the Ford administration extended the program (with little modification) to 1980.

The Property Tax and the Sales Tax

The ***property tax*** is the fiscal bulwark of our local governments. The way it works is simple enough. Most towns and cities estimate the amount they will spend in the next year or two, and then determine a property tax based on the assessed property values in the town or city. For example, if there is \$500 million in assessed property values in the town and the town needs to raise \$5 million, the tax rate will be 1 percent of assessed property value. In other words, each property owner will have to pay 1 percent of the assessed value of his property. There are well-known problems in the administration of the property tax. First, assessed values of property often depart significantly from actual market values; the former are typically much lower than the latter. And the ratio of assessed to actual value is often lower among higher-priced pieces of property; thus wealthier people tend to get off easier. Second, there is widespread evasion of taxes on ***personal property***—securities, bank accounts, and so on. Many people simply do not pay up. Third, the property tax is not very flexible: assessments and rates tend to change rather slowly.

The ***sales tax,*** of course, is a bulwark of state taxation. It provides a high yield with relatively low collection costs. As Table 6.3 indicates, most of the states have some form of general sales tax, the rate being usually between 3 and 5 percent. Retailers add to the price of goods sold to consumers an amount equal to 3 to 5 percent of the consumer's bill. This extra amount is submitted to the state as the general sales tax. Some states exempt food purchases from this tax, and a few exempt medical supplies. Where they exist, these exemptions help reduce the impact of the sales tax on the poor; but in general the sales tax imposes a greater burden relative to income on the poor than on the rich, for the simple reason that the rich save a larger percentage of their income. Practically all of a poor family's income may be subject to sales taxes; a great deal of a rich family's income may not be, because it is not spent on consumer goods, but is saved.

Who really pays the property tax or the sales tax? To what extent can these taxes be shifted to other people? The answer is not as straightforward as one might expect. For the property tax, the owner of unrented residential property swallows the tax, since there is no one else to shift it to. But the owner of rented property

Table 6.3
State Retail Sales Tax Rates, 1975

State	Percentage	State	Percentage	State	Percentage
Alabama	4	Louisiana	3	Oklahoma	2
Arizona	4	Maine	5	Pennsylvania	6
Arkansas	3	Maryland	4	Rhode Island	5
California	4¾	Massachusetts	3	South Carolina	4
Colorado	3	Michigan	4	South Dakota	4
Connecticut	7	Minnesota	4	Tennessee	3½
District of Columbia	5	Mississippi	5	Texas	4
Florida	4	Missouri	3	Utah	4
Georgia	3	Nebraska	2½	Vermont	3
Hawaii	4	Nevada	3	Virginia	3
Idaho	3	New Jersey	5	Washington	4½
Illinois	4	New Mexico	4	West Virginia	3
Indiana	4	New York	4	Wisconsin	4
Iowa	3	North Carolina	3	Wyoming	3
Kansas	3	North Dakota	4		
Kentucky	5	Ohio	4		

Source: Advisory Commission on Intergovernmental Relations.

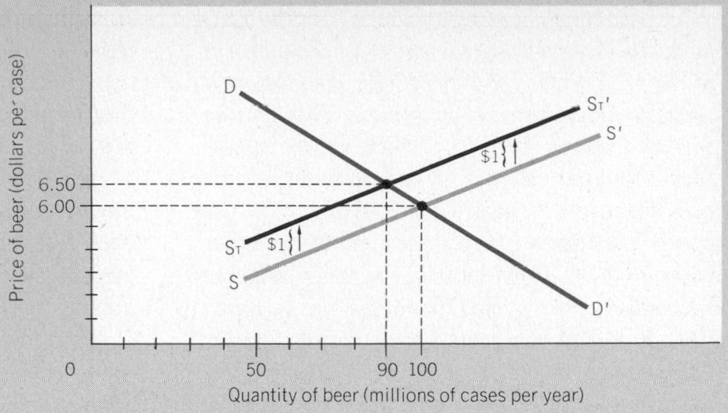

Figure 6.2
Effect of a $1.00 Tax on a Case of Beer.
The tax shifts the supply curve upward by $1.00 (from *SS′* to $S_T S_T'$). Since the demand curve is unaffected, the equilibrium price of beer increases from $6.00 to $6.50 per case.

may attempt to pass along some of the tax to the tenant. In the case of a general sales tax, it is generally concluded that the consumer pays the tax. But if the tax is imposed on only a single commodity, the extent to which it can be shifted to the consumer depends on the demand and supply curves for the taxed commodity. The following section explains in some detail why this is the case.

Tax Incidence

Suppose that a sales or excise tax is imposed on a particular good, say beer. In Figure 6.2, we show the demand and supply curves, *DD′* and *SS′*, for beer before the imposition of the tax. Obviously, the equilibrium price of a case of beer is $6, and the equilibrium quantity is 100 million cases. If a tax of $1 is imposed on each case produced, what is the effect on the price of each case? Or to see it from the beer guzzler's perspective, how much of the tax is passed on to the consumer in the form of a higher price?

Since the tax is collected from the sellers, the supply curve is shifted upward by the amount of the tax. In Figure 6.2, the posttax supply curve is $S_T S_T'$. For example, if the pretax price had to be $5 a case to induce sellers to supply 80 million cases of beer, the posttax price would have to be $1 higher—or $6 a case—to induce the same supply. Similarly, if the pretax price had to be $6 a case to induce sellers to supply 100 million cases of beer, the posttax price would have to be $1 higher—or $7 a case—to induce the same supply. The reason why the sellers require $1 more per case to supply the pretax amount is that they must pay the tax of $1 per case to the government. Thus, to wind up with the same amount as before (after paying the tax), they require the extra $1 per case.

Figure 6.2 shows that, after the tax is imposed, the equilibrium price of beer is $6.50, an increase of $.50 over its pretax level. Consequently, in this case, ½ of the tax is passed on to consumers, who pay $.50 per case more for beer. And ½ of the tax is swallowed by the sellers, who receive (after they pay the tax) $.50 per case less for beer. But it is not always true that sellers pass half of the tax on to consumers and absorb the rest themselves. On the contrary, in some cases, consumers may bear almost all of the tax (and sellers may bear practically none of it), while in other cases consumers may bear almost none of the tax (and sellers may bear practically all of it). The result will depend on how sensitive the quantity demanded and the quantity supplied are to the price of the good.

In particular, holding the supply curve constant, *the less sensitive the quantity demanded is to the price of the good, the bigger the portion of the tax that is shifted to consumers.* To illustrate this, consider Figure 6.3, which shows the effect of a $1 per case tax on beer in two markets, one where the quantity demanded (D_1D_1') is much more sensitive to price than in the other case (D_2D_2'). As is evident, the price increase to consumers resulting from the tax is much greater in the latter case than in the former. And the amount of the tax that is absorbed by producers is much less in the latter case (where D_2D_2' prevails) than in the former (where D_1D_1' prevails).

It can also be shown that, holding the demand curve constant, *the less sensitive the quantity supplied is to the price of the good, the bigger the portion of the tax that is absorbed by producers.* To illustrate this, consider Figure 6.4, which shows the effect of a $1 per case tax on beer in two markets, one where the quantity supplied (S_1S_1') is much more sensitive to price than in the other case (S_2S_2'). As is evident, the price increase to consumers resulting from the tax is much greater in the former case than in the latter. And the amount of the tax that is absorbed by producers is much less in the former case (where S_1S_1' prevails) than in the latter case (where S_2S_2' prevails).

Finally, note that the tax reduces the equilibrium quantity of the good that is taxed—beer in this case. One reason why governments impose taxes on goods like cigarettes and liquor is that they are regarded (in some circles at least) as socially undesirable. Clearly, the more sensitive the quantity demanded and quantity supplied are to price, the larger the reduction in the equilibrium quantity. Thus, if the government imposes a tax of this sort to reduce the quantity consumed of the good, the effect will be greater if both the quantity demanded and the quantity supplied are relatively sensitive to price.

Tax Reform

Because the tax structure of the United States contains so many exemptions and loopholes, there is continual pressure for tax reform. Sen-

Figure 6.3
Effect on Tax Incidence of the Sensitivity of the Quantity Demanded to Price
Before the tax, the equilibrium price is OP_0, regardless of whether D_1D_1' or D_2D_2' is the demand curve. After the tax, the equilibrium price is OP_1, if the demand curve is D_1D_1', or OP_2 if the demand curve is D_2D_2'. Clearly, the increase in price to the consumer is greater if the quantity demanded is less sensitive to price (D_2D_2') than if it is more sensitive (D_1D_1').

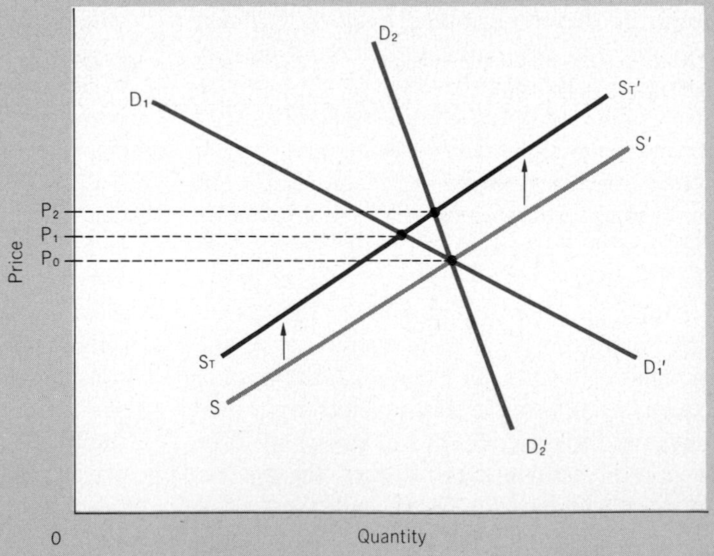

ator George McGovern, in his bid for the presidency in 1972, stressed the importance of tax reform, stating, "The tax code ... is riddled with loopholes, special exemptions, and shelters.... Income which is earned on an assembly line or in an office should no longer be more heavily taxed than profits from oil or securities." President Carter, in his 1976 presidential campaign, also emphasized tax reform. In particular, there are questions about the equity of the relatively low tax rates on capital gains, the tax-free status of interest on state and local bonds, and other aspects of the tax code.

Because there are so many exemptions, exclusions, and deductions, a surprisingly small percentage of all income is subject to the federal personal income tax. In 1960, only about $\frac{3}{7}$ of personal income in the United States was subject to the income tax. This erosion of the tax base, lamented frequently by experts on public finance, means that tax rates must be higher than they would be if the tax base were broader. In other words, if a larger proportion of all income were subject to the personal income tax, a smaller tax could be imposed on each dollar of income subject to tax. Many tax experts feel strongly that the erosion of the tax base should be stopped, and that the tax base should be broadened appreciably. But it is difficult to take away the various exemptions and deductions that have been granted in the past.

When the time seems ripe for a change in tax rates to stabilize the economy, there is often a tendency to try to accomplish tax reform as well. For example, if a tax cut seems advisable to reduce excessive unemployment, there may be an attempt to combine tax reform with tax reduction. Although the attempt to kill two birds—economic stabilization and tax reform—with one stone seems laudable in theory, in practice it can spell trouble. For example, here is how Thomas Dernburg of American University and Duncan McDougall of the University of Kansas describe the attempts in the early 1960s to mix tax reduction and tax reform:

> During the debate of the early 1960s, the Treasury proposed that the tax bill contain a comprehensive package of reform. Aware that congress-

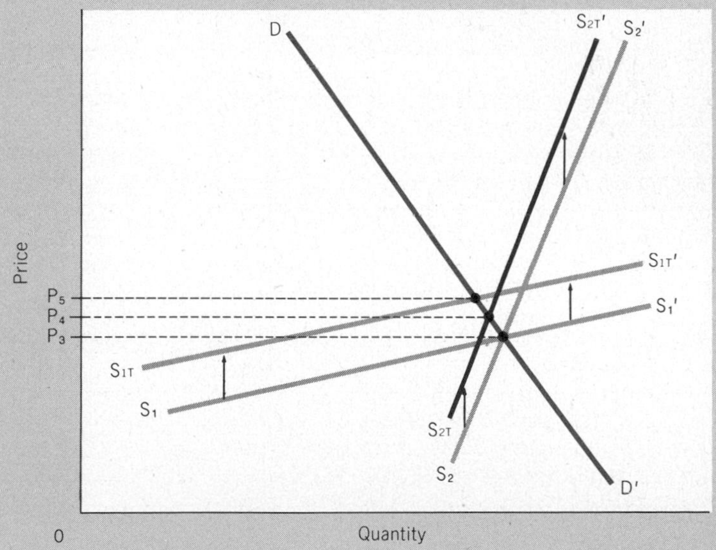

Figure 6.4
Effect on Tax Incidence of the Sensitivity of the Quantity Supplied to Price
Before the tax, the equilibrium price is OP_3, regardless of whether S_1S_1' or S_2S_2' is the pretax supply curve. After the tax, the equilibrium price is OP_4, if the (pretax) supply curve is S_2S_2', or OP_5 if the (pretax) supply curve is S_1S_1'. Clearly, the increase in price to the consumer is greater if the quantity supplied is more sensitive to price (S_1S_1') than if it is less sensitive (S_2S_2').

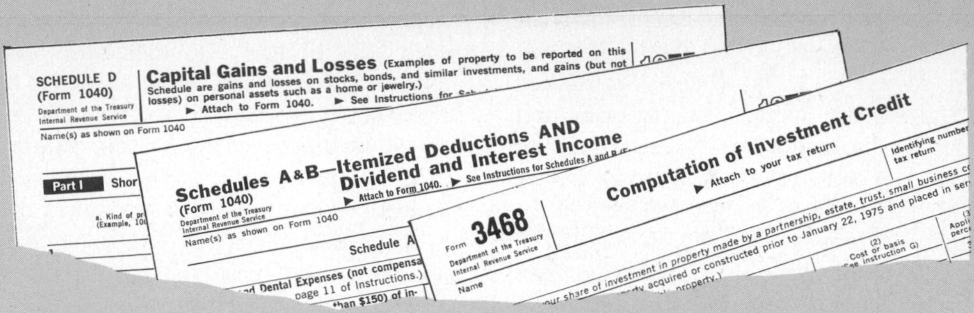

How People Reduce Their Income Tax without Cheating

Lawyers and accountants like to distinguish between tax *avoidance* and tax *evasion.* Tax avoidance occurs when a taxpayer takes legal steps to minimize his tax bill. Tax evasion occurs when a taxpayer misreports his income or takes other illegal steps to cut down on what he pays Uncle Sam. Tax avoidance is a particularly profitable pastime of the well-to-do. With the help of a good lawyer or accountant, one frequently can cut his or her income taxes considerably. To illustrate, consider the following three cases.

George Adams has savings of $50,000, which he has invested in stocks. The dividends from these stocks amount to $3,000 per year. Since his marginal income tax rate is 28 percent, he pays $840 per year in federal income tax on his dividend income. (Why? Because he must pay 28 cents in taxes on every extra dollar of income he receives. Thus 0.28 times $3,000, or $840, is the amount of tax he must pay on an extra $3,000 of income.) If he invests his $50,000 in state and local bonds instead, he can obtain $2,800 per year in interest. Since the interest from state and local bonds is exempt from federal income taxes, he can cut his income tax bill by $840—and, allowing for the fact that he receives $200 less in income per year, he will increase his after-tax income by $640.

William Smith has an 8-year-old daughter. Each year, he saves $1,000, which he invests in stocks in her name. The income from these stocks is not taxable, since his daughter can receive up to $750 per year in income without having to file any federal income tax return. Thus, by the time that she is 18 (and he has given her $10,000 in stocks), the annual income from these stocks will be $700, if the stocks yield 7 percent. And, assuming that his marginal federal income tax rate is 30 percent, he will avoid $210 per year (.30 times $700) in federal income taxes. Why? Because, if he had bought the stocks in his own name, he would have had to pay this much in taxes on this income. At age 18, his daughter can apply this money to her college bills, rather than have him provide it.

Now take the actual case of a wealthy socialite who took a job as an editor. Because of this job, she may be able to deduct many expenses that she would have incurred anyhow. For example, if she takes a trip to Europe, many of her expenses may be deductible, if she can argue (convincingly) that the trip is somehow related to the development of a book. A deduction is an item that is subtracted from one's income to obtain the net income figure on which the amount of income tax is figured. If you can deduct an expense that otherwise would not be deductible, this reduces your income tax by an amount equal to your marginal income tax rate times the expense. Thus, in the case of the socialite, if she spends $5,000 on a trip to Europe, and if her marginal tax rate is 60 percent, she will save $3,000 in income taxes (that is, $.60 \times \$5,000$) if she can convince the Internal Revenue Service that the trip pertained to her business interests.

Many economists feel that the tax system would be more equitable if the tax code were simplified and if many of these ways to avoid income taxes were eliminated. Clearly, some people are better able to take advantage of these loopholes than others. In particular, the wealthy frequently are in a better position to benefit from them than the poor. For this reason, among others, the personal income tax does not bear down as heavily on the rich as one might presume from the official tax rates.

men cannot be interested in reforms that penalize wealthy constituents and potential campaign contributors, the Treasury attempted to tack the reform package onto the tax reduction proposed by the President. The hope was that the tasty carrot of a tax reduction might be strong enough to drag along the refractory donkey of reform. Tax reform got nowhere in Congress. Realizing that the entire bill was in jeopardy, the Administration eventually gave up on reform, and the final bill represented rate reduction and not much else. Undoubtedly, the attempt to gain reform was one factor making for delay in obtaining passage of the tax bill.[7]

Government Debt

The National Debt: Size and Growth

No subject in economics has more confused the public than the national debt. When the federal government spends more than it receives in taxes, it borrows money to cover the difference. The national debt–composed of bonds, notes, and other government IOUs of various kinds–is the result of such borrowing. These IOUs are held by individuals, firms, banks, and public agencies. There is a large and very important market for government securities, which are relatively riskless and highly liquid. If you look at the *New York Times* or *Wall Street Journal*, for example, you can find each day the prices at which each of a large number of issues of these bonds, notes, and bills are quoted.

How large is the national debt? In 1975, as shown in Figure 6.5, it was almost $600 billion. This certainly seems to be a large amount, but it is important to relate the size of the national debt to the size of our national output. After all, a $600 billion debt means one thing if our annual output is $1 trillion, and another thing if our annual output is $100 billion. As a percent of output, the national debt is smaller now than in 1939, and no larger now than shortly after the Civil War. In 1975, the debt was about 40 percent of output; in 1939, it was about 50 percent of output; and in 1868, it was about 40 percent of output. The debt–expressed as a percentage of output–is shown in Figure 6.6. Surely the figures do not seem to provide any cause for alarm. The popular misconception that the national debt is growing at a dangerous rate seems hard to square with the facts.

It is obvious from Figure 6.5 that the size of our national debt is due largely to one thing: World War II. In 1939, the national debt was less than $50 billion; by 1945, it was close to $300 billion. This huge increase occurred to finance the war. Since 1945, the national debt has not grown fast. Indeed, as a percent of national output, it has decreased substantially since 1945. Consequently, as Richard and Peggy Musgrave point out, "The specter of an ever-rising debt to [output] ratio, which so agitated the public only a few decades ago, has become of more or less anthropological interest, a striking example of the demise of a once burning issue."[8]

Burdens and Advantages of the National Debt

Although a discussion of many aspects of the national debt must be postponed to later chapters, it is essential that we look more closely at why the public has been so agitated about the debt's size. One important reason has been that they have felt that the debt was a burden that was being thrust on future generations. To evaluate this idea it is important to recognize that a public debt is not like your debt or mine, which must be paid off at a certain time in the

[7] Thomas Dernburg and Duncan McDougall, *Macroeconomics*, New York: McGraw-Hill, 1972, p. 414.

[8] Richard and Peggy Musgrave, *Public Finance in Theory and Practice*, p. 587. Note too that much of the public debt is in the hands of government agencies, not held by the public. For example, in 1975 only about $350 billion was held by private investors.

Figure 6.5
Size of the National Debt, United States, 1929–75
The national debt, currently almost $600 billion, is due largely to World War II.

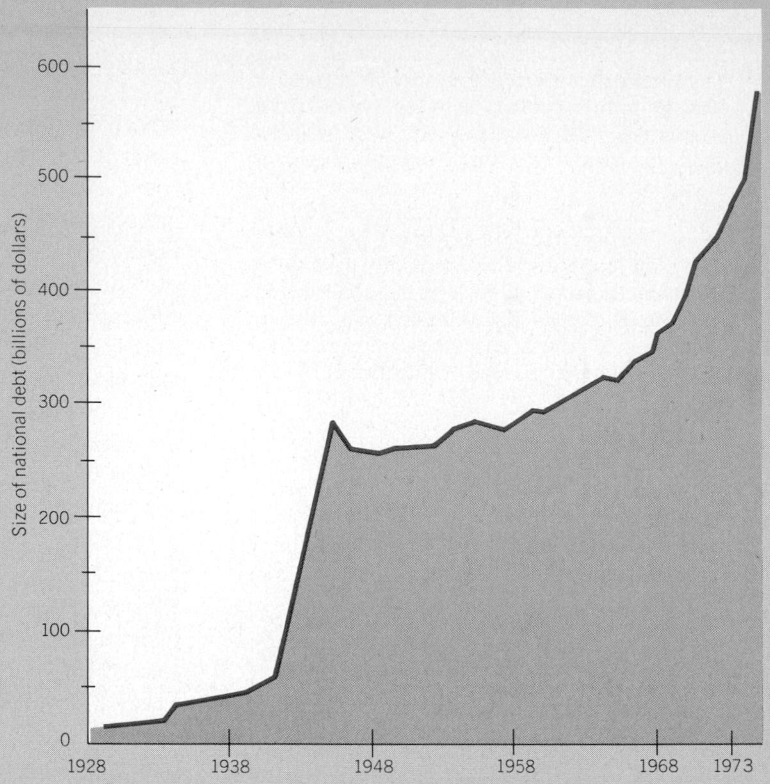

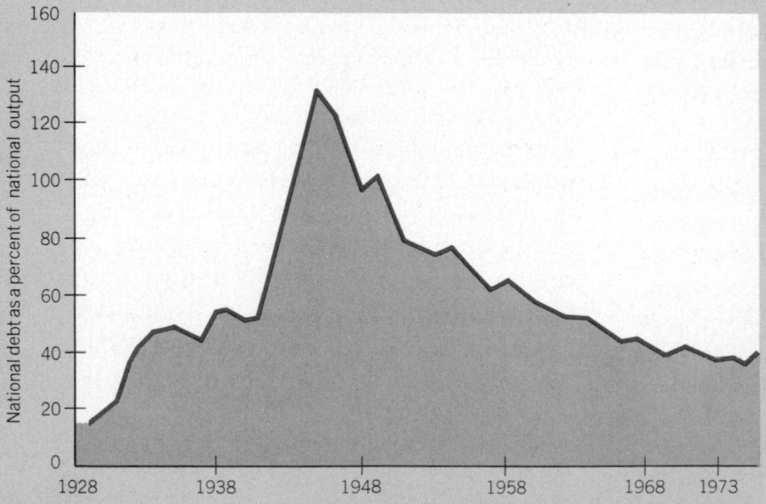

Figure 6.6
National Debt as a Percent of National Output, United States, 1929–75
As a percent of national output, the national debt has declined steadily since World War II.

future. In practice, new government debt is floated to pay off maturing public debt. There never comes a time when we must collectively reach into our pockets to pay off the debt. And even if we did pay it off, the same generation would collect as the one that paid.

Of course, this does not mean that the debt is of no economic consequence. On the contrary, to the extent that the debt is held by foreigners, we must send goods and services overseas to pay the interest on it. This means that less goods and services are available for our citizens. Thus, if we finance a particular government activity by borrowing from foreigners, the costs may be transferred to future generations, since they must pay the interest. But from the point of view of the world as a whole, the current generation sacrifices goods and services, since the lending country forgoes current goods and services. Also, it must be recognized that, if the debt is incurred to purchase capital goods, they may produce enough extra output to cover the interest payments.

Even if the debt is internally held, it may have some undesirable effects. Taxes must be collected from the public at large to pay interest to the holders of government bonds, notes, and other obligations. To the extent that the bondholders receiving the interest are wealthier than the public as a whole, there is some redistribution of income from the poor to the rich. To the extent that the taxes needed to obtain the money to pay interest on the debt reduce incentives, the result also may be a smaller national output.

Beyond this, the existence of all those government bonds, notes, and so forth in the portfolios of people and firms may make them feel richer, and this may make them spend more. Whether this is good or bad depends upon whether we are at less than full employment. If so, it is a good thing; if not, it is bad. In addition, the existence of a large, broadly marketed national debt enables the Federal Reserve System to buy and sell government securities to help stabilize the economy, as we shall see in Chapter 15. This is a good thing—or at least a convenience.

A final word should be added about the idea that the national debt imposes a burden on future generations. *The principal way in which one generation can impose such a burden on another is by using up some of the country's productive capacity or by failing to add a normal increment to this capacity.* This, of course, is quite different from incurring debt. For example, World War II would have imposed a burden on subsequent generations whether or not the national debt was increased. However it was financed, the war would have meant that our resources had to be used for tanks and war planes rather than for keeping up and expanding our productive capacity during 1941–45. And this imposed a burden, a real burden, on Americans living after 1945—as well, of course, as on those living during the war.

Alternative Ways of Financing Government Expenditures—and Their Effects

To complete the present discussion of public finance, it is important to recognize that there are three ways that the federal government can finance any expenditure. The first way is to *raise taxes* to cover the expenditure. The effect of this method of financing the expenditure is straightforward: purchasing power is transferred from the people paying the extra taxes to the government. Thus the costs are borne by the taxpayer. The second way is to *borrow the money* from willing lenders. In this case, too, the effect is straightforward: purchasing power is transferred from the lenders to the government. The current costs of the government programs are borne by the lenders, who receive interest subsequently in return.

The third way the federal government can finance any expenditure is to *create new money.* In other words, it can print extra currency (or

The Department of the Treasury and the National Debt

The average U.S. citizen has very little direct contact with the Department of the Treasury. If he works for the federal government, he receives a bimonthly check; if he is so fortunate as to have overpaid his income tax, he may receive a lovely green refund check. In fact, the processing of checks is (at least, to the nonrecipient economist) much less important than many other functions of the Treasury. Should the Congress or the president wish technical advice on the effect of a new tax measure, the Treasury Department will supply the analysis. In addition, it represents American interests in negotiations over international monetary arrangements with other countries; and, through the Internal Revenue Service and the Customs Service, it collects most federal taxes.*

But from an economist's point of view, one of the most interesting tasks the Treasury performs may be the management of the national debt. Imagine yourself with a debt of about $350 billion (held by private investors), with a few billion coming due each week. Obviously, much of the Treasury's time must be spent scratching for new Peters in order to pay old Pauls. This may not sound like an easy task; and, in fact, it isn't. Over the years the Treasury has developed a bewildering array of devices—refinancing Series E bonds, U.S. savings bonds, short-term bills, long-term bonds—for coaxing new lenders to release their cash, or persuading old lenders to defer collection. The most important of these instruments is U.S. Treasury bills, which in 1973 amounted to almost $103 billion. (Should you ever have a spare $10,000, the smallest denomination in which Treasury bills are sold, their current prices can be found in the financial pages of any major newspaper.)

Almost every month the undersecretary of the Treasury for monetary affairs must decide in what form the portion of the debt coming due should be refinanced. Are interest rates going up? If so, he might refinance by selling long-term bonds, locking up money at the present low rate. Will interest rates fall? If so, he might prefer the 90-day bill. Before an issue is floated, he gets a reading of market conditions from committees of the American Bankers Association and the Investment Bankers Association. But cost is not his only problem. He must also worry about the effect of Treasury operations on financial markets and must have developed future refunding policies. In any case, an elaborate financial network of banks, big insurance companies, pension funds, and investment houses is always waiting to respond to the Treasury's next offering.

E.A.

* Moreover, faithful television fans may realize that, through its Bureau of Customs, the Treasury is responsible for controlling the importation of narcotics.

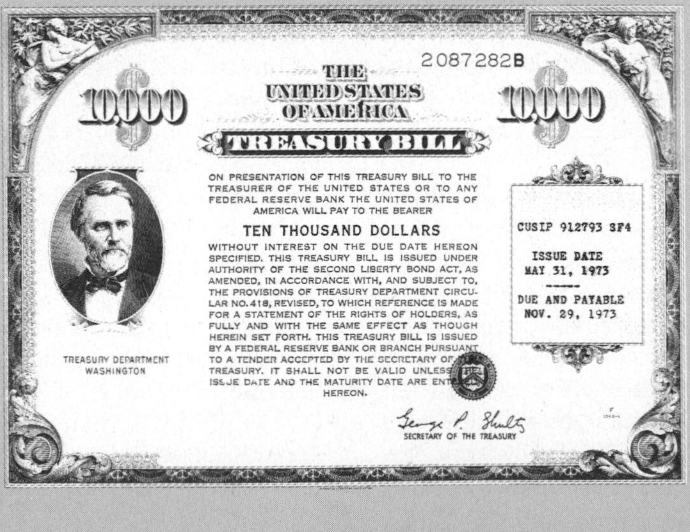

create new money in other ways that will be described in Chapters 13 to 15). If the economy is already at full employment, this procedure is likely to cause inflation. The increase in the price level will mean that households and firms will have to buy less than would otherwise have been the case. At the same time, the government will use the new money to finance the expenditure (and obtain the resources it wants). Thus purchasing power is transferred from the consumers and firms whose incomes and receipts do not keep pace with inflation to the government. One disadvantage of this means of finance is that these consumers and firms are often the weakest and least able to bear this burden.

If the economy is not at full employment, the alternative costs of government programs may be much less than if the economy is at full employment. Recall from Chapter 1 that the alternative cost of using resources in a particular way is the value of the output that could have been obtained if these resources had been used in some other way. Clearly, if the resources used in a particular government program would have been unemployed if this program had not been started, society is giving up very little by using these resources in this program. Why? Because they would have been idle otherwise. On the other hand, if there is full employment, these resources would not have been idle, and the alternative costs of the program would be the value of what they could produce elsewhere.

Summary

The spending decisions of the federal government take place in the context of the budgetary process. The president submits his budget, which is a statement of anticipated expenditures and revenues, to Congress, which votes appropriations. Basically, the amount that the government spends on various activities and services must be decided through the nation's political processes. Voting by ballots must be substituted for dollar voting. In making such decisions, it is important to distinguish between changes in government expenditure that alter the scope of government and changes in government expenditures due to changes in efficiency.

Spending on each government program should be pushed to the point where the extra benefit from an extra dollar spent is at least equal to the dollar of cost. In some areas, benefit-cost analyses have proved useful in determining which of a variety of projects can accomplish a particular goal most economically, and whether any of them is worth carrying out. However, accurate measurement of the relevant benefits and costs is frequently difficult.

The Ways and Means Committee of the House of Representatives and the Senate Finance Committee play important roles in the federal tax legislative process. It is generally agreed that people who receive more in benefits from a certain government service should pay more in taxes to support it. It is also generally agreed that people should be taxed so that the result is a socially desirable redistribution of income, and that equals should be treated equally. But these general principles, although useful, cannot throw light on many of the detailed questions a real-life tax code must answer.

The personal and corporate income taxes are very important sources of federal revenue, the sales tax is an important source of state revenues, and the property tax is an important source of local revenues. In recent years, there has been continual pressure for tax reform, since the tax structure of the United States contains many exemptions and loopholes. Also, recognizing the mismatch between the responsibilities and resources of the state and local governments, the federal government has begun a program of revenue sharing.

When the government spends more than it receives in revenues, the difference is called a deficit. The national debt is the result of previous deficits, since the government borrows money to cover a deficit. It could simply print money for this purpose, but it has chosen to borrow a considerable proportion of what was needed. Despite much public worry about the size of the national debt, as a percentage of national output it has been declining over the past 25 years. There are important differences between government debt and private debt. Although the size of the debt is certainly of consequence, it is not true that it somehow transmits a serious burden to future generations or that it may lead to bankruptcy.

CONCEPTS FOR REVIEW

Benefit-cost analysis	Tax reform	Capital gains
Revenue sharing	Benefit principle	Tax incidence
Military-industrial complex	Personal income tax	Public debt
Marginal tax rate	Sales tax	Tax evasion
	Ability to pay	Tax avoidance

QUESTIONS FOR DISCUSSION AND REVIEW

1. "Cost-benefit analysis necessarily involves groping and the making of subjective judgments, not just briskly proceeding with dispassionate scientific measurements."[9] Suppose that such an analysis were made to determine which of a number of roads should be built. Indicate the kinds of subjective judgments that would have to be made.

2. Suppose that the government is trying to determine whether it should build a road from *A* to *B*, or whether it should build one that goes from *B* to *C* as well. The annual costs and benefits from the two alternative projects are as follows:

	Road from *A* to *B*	Road from *A* to *B* to *C*
Annual cost (millions of dollars)	10	15
Annual benefit (millions of dollars)	20	22

Which project, if any, should the government accept? Why?

3. Can you be sent to jail for tax avoidance? Why do people often prefer to receive capital gains rather than ordinary forms of income? If a person's marginal income tax rate is 25 percent and he receives $100 in tax-free income, how much does this equal in before-tax income?

[9] R. McKean, "The Nature of Cost-Benefit Analysis," in E. Mansfield, *Microeconomics: Selected Readings,* 2d ed. New York: Norton, 1975, p. 371.

4. Suppose that if it produces the indicated amount of private goods, the maximum amount of public goods that a society can produce is as follows:

Quantity of private goods	Quantity of public goods
0	12
1	11
5	6
8	1
10	0

If this society produces 5 units of private goods and 5 units of public goods, is it being as efficient as it could be? If not, can we tell whether the inefficiency occurs in the private or public sector? And if so, how?

5. "The national debt is of little or no economic consequence because we owe it to ourselves." Comment and evaluate.

6. Is it possible to test Galbraith's proposition that too little is being spent on government services? What sorts of tests would you propose? In 1973, President Nixon proposed a greatly expanded program of energy research and development. What sorts of information would you look at in order to decide whether the president's proposal should have been accepted or rejected?

7. Make a detailed set of recommendations concerning changes that should be made in the American tax system. With regard to every change that you propose, state your reasons for advocating the change.

8. Suppose that the supply curve for gin is as follows:

Price of gin (dollars per quart)	Quantity supplied (millions of quarts)
4	10
5	9
6	8
7	7
8	6
9	5

Plot the supply curve on graph paper. Suppose that the government imposes a tax of $2 per quart on gin, and that the tax is collected from the sellers. Plot the posttax supply curve on graph paper.

9. Under the circumstances described in Question 8, suppose that the quantity of gin demanded is 7 million quarts, regardless of the price (so long as it is between $4 and $9 per quart). What will be the equilibrium price of gin before the tax, and after it? How much of the tax is passed on to the consumer?

10. Under the circumstances described in Question 8, suppose that the demand curve for gin is a horizontal line at $6 per quart. If this is the case, what will be the equilibrium price of gin before the tax, and after it? How much of the tax is passed on to the consumer?

7

The Business Firm: Organization, Motivation, and Technology

It is hard to overstate the importance of business firms in the American economy. They produce the bulk of our goods and services, hire most of the nation's workers, and issue stocks and bonds that represent a large percentage of the nation's wealth. Judged by any yardstick—even less complimentary ones like the responsibility for environmental pollution—business firms are an extremely important part of the American economy. In this chapter, we discuss the various types of business firms, such as proprietorships and corporations. Then we describe the various types of securities—common stock, bonds, and so forth—issued by firms, and discuss the workings of the stock market. Next, we take up the motivation and structure of firms, as well as their technology. Finally, we provide some essential elements of accounting. This material is a necessary introduction to the workings of the business enterprise, absolutely essential to anyone who works for, manages, or invests in a firm.

Types and Functions of Firms

General Motors: A Case Study

In Chapter 4, when we first discussed the role of the business firm in the American economy, we cited two examples of American business firms: Peter Amacher's drugstore and the General Motors Corporation. Now that we are considering the operations of the business firm in more detail, let's look more closely at the General Motors Corporation. A description of its formation and vicissitudes should give you a better feel for what firms do and the sorts of problems they face.

General Motors was formed in 1908 by William C. Durant, an energetic and imaginative businessman who made over a million dollars in the carriage business before he was 40. After taking over the bankrupt Buick Motor Company in 1904, Durant built it into a very successful operation. Then, in 1908, he gained control of a number of small automobile companies (including Cadillac and Olds), several truck firms, and ten parts and accessory firms. The resulting amalgamation was General Motors.

In 1910, General Motors' sales fell below scheduled production, and Durant lacked the funds to pay his work force and suppliers. To get the money he needed, he went to a banking syndicate, which lent him $15 million—but required him to turn over the management of the company to them. By 1915, Durant had acquired another auto producer, Chevrolet, and had picked up formidable financial allies in the Du Ponts, the owners of the famous chemical firm. Using both these levers, Durant regained full control of General Motors in 1916; and between 1916 and 1920, he concentrated on expanding the productive capacity of the General Motors Corporation. A man of extraordinary vision, he recognized, as did few of his contemporaries, a great potential demand for moderately priced cars, and devoted his energy to putting General Motors in a position to satisfy this demand.

Although Durant was a man of great vision, he was not the sort of administrator who created a tidy organizational structure. The General Motors Corporation under Durant was a very large agglomeration of companies in a variety of product lines, with somewhat tangled lines of communication and diffuse control. When automobile sales did not come up to expectations in 1920, the firm suffered a reduction in profits. The ensuing crisis resulted in Durant's retirement as president of General Motors, and the adoption by the firm of a new organizational plan created by Alfred Sloan, a young M.I.T.-trained engineer, who soon became president. This plan divided General Motors into a number of divisions: the Buick division, the Chevrolet division, the accessory division, and so forth. Each division was given considerable freedom, but greater attention was devoted to central control and coordination than under Durant's more anarchic organization. Sloan's organizational plan, an important innovation in its day, has remained in effect with little change from 1920 to the present: Figure 7.1 shows the organization of General Motors today.

During the 1920s General Motors prospered: its sales rose from $600 million in 1920 to $1,500 million in 1929, and its profits rose from about $38 million in 1920 to about $248 million in 1929. The next decade was different: the 1930s were the years of the Great Depression, when sales and profits of most firms, including General Motors, were hard hit. But during the 1940s General Motors entered another period of prosperity and growth. Its sales rose from about $1.8 billion in 1940 to about $5.7 billion in 1949, and its profits rose from about $196 million in 1940 to about $656 million in 1949. The 1950s and 1960s saw the prosperity of General Motors continue. Of course there were short intervals when sales

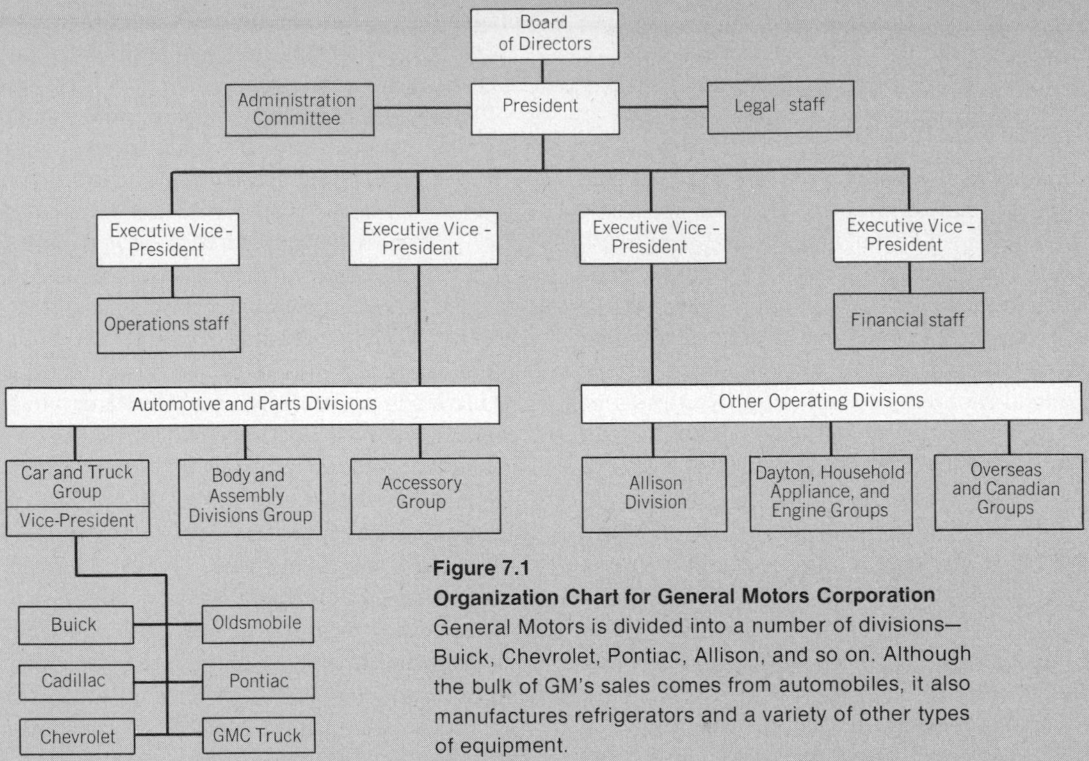

Figure 7.1
Organization Chart for General Motors Corporation
General Motors is divided into a number of divisions—Buick, Chevrolet, Pontiac, Allison, and so on. Although the bulk of GM's sales comes from automobiles, it also manufactures refrigerators and a variety of other types of equipment.

and profits fell, but the trend was upward—in part because of population growth and because higher incomes have meant bigger sales of automobiles. The firm has experienced no prolonged period of low profits or considerable excess capacity, as was the case in the 1930s. By 1975, General Motors had sales of over $35 billion. The somewhat jumbled organization William Durant assembled in 1908 had become one of the biggest industrial companies in the United States, a symbol of industrial might around the world.

Characteristics of American Firms: Some Salient Facts

General Motors is an economic colossus—a huge organization with almost 700,000 employees. Of course it is not typical of American business firms. If we broaden our focus to take in the entire population of business firms in the United States, the first thing we note is their tremendous number; according to government statistics, there are over twelve million. The vast majority of these firms, as one would expect, is very small. There are lots of grocery stores, gas stations, auto dealers, drugstores (like Mr. Amacher's), clothing shops, restaurants, and so on. You see hundreds of them as you walk along practically any downtown city street. But these small firms, although numerous, do not control the bulk of the nation's productive capacity. The several hundred largest firms have great economic power, measured by their sales, assets, employment, or other such indices. The small firms tend to be weak and short-lived. On the average, they tend to go out of business before they have been in existence seven years.

The next thing to note is that most of the nation's business firms are engaged in agriculture, services, and retail trade. Table 7.1 shows that almost 3/4 of the firms in the United States are in these industries, an understandable figure since these industries tend to have lots and lots of small businesses. Although manufacturing firms constitute only about 3 percent of all American firms, they account for more than 1/3 of all business receipts. On the other hand, agriculture (including forestry and fisheries) includes about 30 percent of the nation's business firms, but accounts for only 3 percent of the total receipts. Clearly, this is because manufacturing firms tend to be much bigger, in terms of receipts, employment, and assets, than agricultural firms. Think, for example, of the steel plants in Pittsburgh or Cleveland, or of the aircraft plants in California or Georgia. They dwarf the typical farm—and they are only parts of a manufacturing firm.

Finally, note that most of the nation's business firms are proprietorships: indeed, almost 4/5 fall into this category, while about 13 percent are corporations, and about 8 percent are partnerships. You often hear the terms *proprietorship, partnership, corporation.* What do these terms mean?

Proprietorships

A proprictorship is a legal form of business organization—the most common form, as we saw in the previous section, and also the simplest. Specifically, a ***proprietorship*** is a firm owned by a single individual. A great many of the nation's small businesses are proprietorships. For example, the corner drugstore may well be one. If so, it has a single owner. He hires the people he needs to wait on customers, deliver orders, do the bookkeeping, and so forth. He borrows, if he can, whatever money he feels he needs. He reaps the profits, or incurs the losses. All his personal assets—his house, his furniture, his

Table 7.1
Number and Receipts of Business Firms, by Industry, United States, 1972

Industry	Number of firms (millions)	Receipts of firms (millions of dollars)
Agriculture, forestry, and fisheries	3.4	77
Mining	0.1	25
Construction	1.0	143
Manufacturing	0.4	855
Transportation, communication[a]	0.4	172
Wholesale trade	0.6	349
Retail trade	2.3	470
Financial	1.5	148
Services	3.2	146
Total	12.9	2,385

Source: Statistical Abstract of the United States.
[a] Includes electric and gas.

car—can be taken by creditors to meet the drugstore's bills: that is, he has unlimited liability for the debts of the business.

What Lincoln said about the common man applies as well to proprietorships: God must love them, or He wouldn't have created so many of them. If proprietorships didn't have advantages over other legal forms of business organization under many sorts of circumstances, there wouldn't be so many of them. What are these advantages? First, the owner of a proprietorship has complete control over the business. He doesn't have to negotiate with partners or other co-owners. He is the boss—and the only boss. Anyone who has been in a position of complete authority knows the joy it can bring: many proprietors treasure this feeling of independence. Second, a proprietorship is easy and inexpensive to establish: all you have to do is hang out your shingle and announce you are in business. This too is a great advantage.

But proprietorships have important disadvantages as well—and for this reason, they are seldom found in many important industries. One disadvantage is that it is difficult for a proprietor to put together enough financial resources to enter industries like automobiles or steel. No one in the world has enough money to establish, by himself, a firm of General Motors' present size. Another disadvantage is that the proprietor is liable for all of the debts of the firm. If his business fails, his personal assets can be taken by his creditors, and he can be completely wiped out.

Partnerships

A ***partnership*** is somewhat more complicated than a proprietorship. As its name implies, it is a form of business organization where two or more people agree to own and conduct a business. Each partner agrees to contribute some proportion of the capital and labor used by the business, and to receive some proportion of the profits or losses. There are a variety of types of partnerships. In some cases, one or more of the partners may be "silent partners," who put up some of the money, but have little or nothing to do with the operations of the firm. The partnership is a common form of business organization in some industries and professions, like the law. But as we saw in a previous section, partnerships are found less frequently than proprietorships or corporations in the United States.

A partnership has certain advantages. Like a proprietorship, it can be established without great expense or legal red tape. (However, if you ever go into partnership with someone, you would be well advised to have a good lawyer draw up a written agreement establishing such things as the salaries of each partner and how profits are to be shared.) In addition, a partnership can avoid some of the problems involved in a proprietorship. It can usually put together more financial resources and specialized know-how than a proprietorship—and this can be an important advantage.

But the partnership also has certain drawbacks. First, each partner is liable without limit for the bills of the firm. For example, even if one partner of a law firm has only a 30 percent share of the firm, he may be called upon to pay all the firm's debts if the other partners cannot do so. Second, there is some red tape in keeping a partnership in existence. Whenever a partner dies or withdraws, or whenever a new partner is admitted, a new partnership must be established. Third, like the proprietorship, the partnership is not a very effective way to obtain the large amounts of capital required for some modern industries. A modern automobile plant may cost $500 million, and not many partnerships could assemble that much capital. For these reasons, as well as others discussed in the next section, the corporation has become the dominant form of business organization.

Corporations

A far more complicated form of business organization than either the proprietorship or partnership, the ***corporation*** is a fictitious legal person, separate and distinct from its owners. A businessman forms a corporation by having his lawyer draw up the necessary papers stating (in general terms) what sorts of activities he and the other owners of the corporation intend to engage in. The owners of the corporation are the stockholders. ***Stock,*** pieces of paper signifying ownership of the corporation, is issued to the owners, generally in exchange for their cash. Ordinarily, each ***share*** of stock gives its owner one vote. The corporation's ***board of directors,*** which is responsible for setting over-all policy for the firm, is elected by the stockholders. Any of the firm's owners can, if he is dissatisfied with the company's policies or thinks he has better opportunities elsewhere, sell his stock to someone else, assuming, of course, that he can find a buyer.

The corporation has many advantages over the partnership or proprietorship. In particular, each of the corporation's owners has limited, not unlimited, liability. If I decide to become one of the owners of General Motors and if a share of General Motors common stock sells for $65 a share, I can buy ten shares of General Motors stock for $650. And I can be sure that, if General Motors falls on hard times, I cannot lose more than the $650 I paid for the stock. There is no way that I can be assessed beyond this. Moreover, the corporation, unlike the partnership or proprietorship, has unlimited life. If several stockholders want to withdraw from the firm, they simply sell their stock. The corporation goes on, although the identity of the owners changes. For these reasons, the corporation is clearly a better device for raising large sums of money than the partnership or proprietorship. This is an enormous advantage of the corporation, particularly in industries like automobiles and steel, which could not otherwise finance their operations.

Without question, the corporation is a very important social invention. It permits people to assemble the large quantities of capital required for efficient production in many industries. Without limited liability and the other advantages of the corporation, it is doubtful that the opportunities and benefits of large-scale production could have been reaped. However, this does not mean that the corporate form will work for all firms. In many cases, a firm requires only a modest amount of capital, and there is no reason to go to the extra trouble and expense of establishing a corporation. Moreover, one disadvantage of the corporation is ***double taxation of income,*** since, as you will recall from Chapter 6, corporations pay income taxes—and the tax rate is often about ½ of every extra dollar earned. Thus every dollar earned by a corporation and distributed to stockholders is taxed twice by the federal government—once when it is counted as income by the corporation, and once when the remainder is counted as income by the stockholders. This disadvantage of the corporation must be balanced against the advantage that the top tax rates for corporations are less than those that may apply to unincorporated businesses.

The Modern Corporation: Financing, Organization, and Power

Corporate Securities

The corporation raises money by issuing various kinds of securities; of these, three kinds—common stock, preferred stock, and bonds—are particularly significant. Each of these types of securities is important to the workings of the corporation and to people's investment decisions. ***Common stock*** is the ordinary certificate of ownership of the corporation. A holder of common stock is an owner of the firm. He shares in the firm's profits—if there are any profits. At frequent intervals, the board of directors of the firm may declare a dividend of so much per share for the common stockholders. For example, the common stockholders of General Motors received dividends of $2.40 per share in 1975. ***Dividends*** are thus the income the owners of common stock receive. (In addition, of course, common stockholders may make money by selling their stock for more than they paid for it; as noted in the previous chapter, such income is called ***capital gains.***) Common stock is generally regarded as more risky than preferred stock or bonds, for reasons that will be explained.

Preferred stock is a special kind of certificate of ownership that pays at most a stated dividend. For example, owners of one type of General Motors preferred stock receive $5 a share per year, as long as the firm makes enough to pay this dividend. To protect the owners of preferred stock, it is stipulated that no dividends can be paid on the common stock unless the dividends on the preferred stock are paid in full. Since the common stockholders cannot receive their dividends unless the preferred stock's dividends have been paid, common stock is obviously more risky than preferred stock. But by the same token, the amount preferred stockholders have to gain if the company prospers is less than the amount common stockholders have to gain, since however high its profits may be, the firm will pay only the stated dividend—for example, $5 per share per year in the case of General Motors—to the owners of preferred stock.

Bonds are quite different from both common and preferred stocks. ***Bonds*** are debts of the firm; in other words, they are IOUs issued by the firm. In contrast to stockholders, the bondholders are not owners of a firm: they are its creditors, and receive interest, not dividends. Specifically, a bond is a certificate bearing the firm's promise to pay the interest every six months until the bond matures, at which time the firm also promises to pay the bondholder the principal (the amount he lent the firm) as well. Often, bonds are sold in $1,000 denominations. For example, one type of bond issued by General Motors is a $3\frac{1}{4}$ percent bond, due in 1979. The owner of each such bond receives $32.50 per year in interest, and General Motors promises to pay him the principal of $1,000 when the bond falls due in 1979. A firm must pay the interest on the bonds and the principal when it is due, or it can be declared bankrupt. In other words, the bondholders are legally entitled to receive what is due them before the stockholders can get anything.

Thus, from the point of view of the investor, bonds are generally considered less risky than preferred stock, and preferred stocks are considered less risky than common stock. But we have ignored another fact: inflation. The tendency for the price level in the United States to increase over time has meant that bondholders have been paid off with dollars that were worth less than those they lent. For this reason, together with the fact that owners of common stocks reaped substantial capital gains during the 1960s and early 1970s, many investors in recent years have tended to favor common stocks. Indeed, during the 1960s, a "cult of equities" developed; these were the years when it appeared that stock prices were headed only one way—ever higher. It became very fashionable to buy common stock. But in the middle 1970s, the public's infatuation with common stocks seemed to fade, as stock prices fell. To understand why the value of stocks can gyrate so considerably, it is necessary to look briefly at the workings of thc stock market.

The Stock Market

In general, large corporations do not sell stock directly to the investor. Instead, the investor

Buying and Selling Common Stocks

Over 30 million Americans own common stocks, which indicates that you don't have to be wealthy to be an investor. Suppose that you are interested in buying General Motors stock. To determine its current price, you need only look at the financial pages of any major newspaper. For example, on April 24, 1976, the *New York Times* showed the following information concerning General Motors common stock:

1976				Sales				
High	*Low*	*Stock*	*Div*	*100s*	*High*	*Low*	*Last*	*Net Change*
72¾	57¾	Gn Mot	2.40	1513	70½	69¾	69⅞	−⅝

Reading from left to right, $72.75 and $57.75 are the highest and lowest prices of GM stock in 1976 (up to this date), Gn Mot is the symbol used for General Motors, and $2.40 is the level of GM's dividends in the previous year. The last five figures show the number of shares sold (151,300), the highest price ($70.50), the lowest price ($69.75), and the final price ($69.87½) of a share on the previous day, as well as the change in the price from the day before (down $.62½ per share). Knowing what these symbols mean, you can tell at a glance what GM common stock sold for yesterday. (And any broker will be glad to give you current quotations.)

To determine whether GM common stock is a good buy, you would be well advised to look at GM's recent earnings record and to obtain as much information as you can concerning the firm's earnings prospects in the future. This is because, as a firm's earnings (per share of common stock) go up, the price of its stock tends to go up too. Some economists and business analysts have gone so far as to publish formulas by which one can determine, on the basis of forecasts of what a firm's earnings will be, how much the stock is worth. They believe that one should buy if the current price of the stock is below this measure of the stock's intrinsic value and sell if the price is above it.

In contrast, other economists believe that the movement of stock prices has more to do with psychology than with financial valuation of this sort. As John Maynard Keynes put it, "[Most persons] are concerned, not with what an investment is really worth to a man who buys it 'for keeps,' but with what the market will value it at, under the influence of mass psychology, three months or a year hence. . . . For it is not sensible to pay 25 for an investment of which you believe the prospective yields to justify a value of 30, if you also believe that the market will value it at 20 three months hence." As Princeton's Burton Malkiel observes, "This theory might . . . be called the 'greater-fool theory.' It's perfectly all right to pay three times what a stock is worth as long as later on you can find some innocent to pay five times what it's worth."*

There is no simple, foolproof way to determine whether GM common stock is a good buy. Certainly, the firm's earnings prospects are of basic importance, but it is difficult, even for the firm itself, to predict what its earnings will be. And psychological factors can outweigh earnings changes in any event. Since even the most astute traders on Wall Street frequently do no better than one could do by buying the Dow-Jones average, you would do well to approach the stock market with caution. More than one economic savant has lost his or her shirt.

* B. Malkiel, *A Random Walk Down Wall Street,* New York: Norton, 1973.

buys stock on the stock market. Two major stock exchanges in the United States are the New York Stock Exchange and the American Stock Exchange, both in New York City. On these and similar exchanges in other cities, the common stocks of thousands of corporations are bought and sold. The price of each common stock fluctuates from day to day, indeed from minute to minute. Basically, the factors responsible for these price fluctuations are the shifts in the demand curve and supply curve for each kind of common stock. For example, if a strike breaks out at a General Motors plant, this may cause the demand curve for General Motors stock to shift downward to the left, since the strike is liable to mean lower profits for General Motors. Because of this downward, or leftward, shift in the demand curve, the price of General Motors common stock will tend to fall, as in fact happened during a United Auto Workers strike in 1974.

Occasionally, the stock market gets a case of jitters over economic conditions, stock prices tumble, and old investors think back to the Great Crash of 1929. The 1920s witnessed a feverish interest in investing in the stock market. Along with raccoon coats, Stutz Bearcats, and the Charleston, common stocks were the rage. Both the professionals on Wall Street and the neophytes on Main Street bought common stocks and more common stocks. Naturally, as the demand curves for common stocks shifted upward to the right, their prices rose, thus whetting the appetites of investors for still more common stocks. This upward spiral continued until 1929, when the bubble burst. Suddenly the prices of common stocks fell precipitously—and continued to drop during the early 1930s. The most famous average of industrial stock prices, the Dow-Jones average, fell from 381 in 1929 to 41 in 1933. Many investors, large and small, were wiped out.

The Great Crash made investors wary of common stocks for many years. But by the 1960s confidence in them was fully restored, and there certainly was no tendency for investors to shy away from them. In the 1970s, although many small investors (and some large ones) lost their shirts, the stock market remained a major outlet for savings. Judging from historical experience, the public's taste for common stocks seems to be justified. Studies show that, during the course of a lifetime, the typical investor would have done better to invest in common stocks than in the best-quality bonds, because stock prices have tended to rise. This tended to apply in a great many cases, even for investors who lived through the Great Crash. And it has certainly been borne out during the past 40 years. Thus, although common stocks are riskier in some respects than bonds or preferred stocks, they seem to have performed better, on the average, at least in recent times.

During periods when the average of stock prices is going up, such as the 1920s and much of the 1950s and 1960s, it is relatively easy to be a financial wizard, whether by luck or calculation. A much more exacting test of your financial acumen is how well you can pick which stocks will outperform the averages. If you can predict that increases will occur in a certain firm's profits, and if other people don't predict the same thing, you may be able to pass this test. However, the sobering truth is that "playing the stock market" is much more an art than a science. The stock market is affected by psychological as well as economic considerations. Moreover, when you try to spot stocks that will increase in price, you are pitting your knowledge and experience against those of skilled professionals with big research staffs and with friends and acquaintances working for the companies in question. And even these professionals can do surprisingly poorly at times.

Do economists have a nose for good investments? John Maynard Keynes was an extremely successful speculator who made millions of dollars. Other economists have been far less successful. Certainly, a knowledge of basic economics is not sufficient to enable you to make money on the stock market, but insofar as the market reflects economic realities, a knowledge of basic economics should be helpful.

The Giant Corporation

Much of the trading on the stock market centers around the relatively small number of giant corporations that control a very substantial percentage of the total assets and employment in the American economy. And well it might, for the largest 100 manufacturing corporations control about ½ of this country's manufacturing assets. These firms have tremendous economic and political power. They include the giant automobile manufacturers (General Motors, Ford, and Chrysler), the big oil firms (Exxon, Gulf, Standard Oil of Indiana, Mobil, Standard Oil of California, Texaco, Atlantic-Richfield), the big steel firms (U.S. Steel, Bethlehem, Jones and Laughlin, Armco), the big computer and office machinery producers (IBM and Xerox), the leading tobacco firms (American Brands, R. J. Reynolds, Philip Morris), and many others.

The large corporation is generally organized into various operating divisions. We saw in Figure 7.1 how General Motors is divided along various product lines. An automotive division like Buick is part of the Car and Truck Group, the head of which reports to an executive vice-president, who reports in turn to the president of General Motors. Usually, the president is the chief operations officer in the firm, although sometimes the chairman of the board of directors fills this role. As for the board of directors, some members are chosen for their reputations and contacts, while others are chosen for their knowledge of the firm, the industry, or some profession or specialty. Usually, the board contains at least one representative of the financial community, and a university president or former government official is often included to show that the firm is responsive to broad social issues. Members of GM's board include Charles Townes, a professor at the University of California, John Connor, a former secretary of commerce; and Leon Sullivan, pastor of Zion Baptist Church of Philadelphia. The board of directors is concerned with over-all policy. Since it meets only a few times a year, it seldom becomes involved in day-to-day decisions; and it usually goes along with management's policies, so long as management retains the board's confidence.

An interesting and important feature of the large corporation is the fact that it is owned by many, many people, practically all of whom have little or no detailed information about the firm's operations. For example, the owners of the American Telephone and Telegraph Company, the giant public utility, number several million but most of them know relatively little about what is going on in the firm. Moreover, because of the wide diffusion of ownership, working control of a large corporation can often be maintained by a group with only ⅕ or less of all the voting stock. The result is a *separation of ownership from control.* In other words, the owners control the firm in only a limited and somewhat sporadic sense.

So long as a firm's management is not obviously incompetent or corrupt, it is difficult for insurgent stockholders to remove the management from office. Most stockholders do not go to the annual meetings to vote for members of the firm's board of directors. Instead, they receive *proxies,* which, if returned, permit the management to exercise their votes. Usually enough shareholders mail in their proxies to give management the votes it needs to elect a friendly board of directors. In recent years, the Securities and Exchange Commission, which oversees and regulates the financial markets, has attempted to make the giant corporations more democratic by enabling insurgent groups to gain access to mailing lists of stockholders and so forth. But there is still a noteworthy and widespread separation of ownership from control.

The New Industrial State

The large corporation is a subject of considerable debate among economists. Many feel that bigness can be a detriment to society, whereas others are more impressed by its virtues. One view of the large corporation that has received considerable attention in recent years can be found in John Kenneth Galbraith's *The New Industrial State.*[1] Galbraith is less concerned than most economists with the disadvantages of the large corporation; indeed, he feels that large corporations are required for much of society's business. According to Galbraith, the large corporation is free of most of the restraints imposed by the market place. It can, by a judicious mixture of advertising and other devices, influence the demand for its own products. Indeed, according to Galbraith, it can control its demand curve to a very considerable extent. In addition, the management of the large corporation is, in Galbraith's view, largely emancipated from the control of the stockholders, since there is a considerable separation of ownership from control. Moreover, the large corporation is free from the obligation to borrow in the capital markets, since it can reinvest its own earnings.

Under these circumstances, who runs the large corporation, and for what purpose? Galbraith's answer is that the large corporation is run by the ***"technostructure"***—the professional managers, engineers, and technicians who are the corporate bureaucracy—and the large corporation's overriding goal is its own survival and autonomy. Consequently, the large corporation tries to avoid risk, and emphasizes planning and stability. It is interested in corporate growth, even if this means some sacrifice of profits. Moreover, it is often interested in technological leadership. Galbraith does not view this situation as bad. Instead, he regards it as inevitable since, in his view, modern technology requires that huge amounts of money and huge organizations dominate the modern economy. Whether you like it or not, he says, this is the way it must be.

Although Galbraith's book has generated much useful and interesting discussion, it has not escaped criticism by the economics profession. For one thing, as Robert Solow of M.I.T. has pointed out, the large corporation does not dominate many parts of the American economy. Nor is it at all clear that modern technology requires very large firms in many industries. Nor is Galbraith's assumption that firms attempt to maximize their rate of growth of sales necessarily better than the more conventional assumption that firms maximize their profits. As we shall see, most economists seem to regard profit maximization as the more fruitful assumption.

[1] John Kenneth Galbraith, *The New Industrial State,* Boston: Houghton Mifflin, 1967.

Motivation and Technology of the Firm

Profit Maximization

What determines the behavior of the business firm? As a first approximation, *economists generally assume that firms attempt to maximize* ***profits,*** *which are defined as the difference between the firm's revenue and its costs.* In other words, economists generally assume, contrary to Galbraith, that firms try to make as much money as possible. This assumption certainly does not seem unreasonable: most businessmen appear to be interested in making money. Nonetheless, the assumption of profit maximization oversimplifies the situation. Although businessmen certainly want profits, they are interested in other things as well. For example, some firms claim that they want to promote better cultural activities or better racial relations in their community. At a less lofty level, other firms say that their aim is to increase their share of the market. Whether or not one takes these self-proclaimed goals very seriously, it is clear that firms are not interested *only* in making money—often for the same reason that Dr. Johnson gave for not becoming a philosopher: "because cheerfulness keeps breaking in."[2]

In a large corporation, there are some fairly obvious reasons why firms may not maximize profits. Various groups within such firms develop their own party lines, and intrafirm politics is an important part of the process determining firm behavior. Whereas in a small firm it may be fairly accurate to regard the goals of the firm as being the goals of the proprietor, in the large corporation the decision on the goals of the firm is a matter of politics, with various groups within the organization struggling for power. In addition, because of the separation of ownership from control, top management usually has a great deal of freedom as long as it seems to be performing reasonably well. Under these circumstances, the behavior of the firm may be dictated in part by the interests of the management group, resulting in higher salaries, more perquisites, and a bigger staff for their own benefit than would otherwise be the case.

Also, in a world of risk and uncertainty, it is difficult to know exactly what profit maximization means, since the firm cannot be sure that a certain level of profit will result from a certain action. Instead, the best the firm can do is to estimate that a certain probability distribution of profit levels will result from a certain action. Under these circumstances, the firm may choose less risky actions, even though they have a lower expectation of profit than other actions. In a world where ruin is ruinous, this may be perfectly rational policy.

Nonetheless, profit maximization remains the standard assumption in economics. As we agreed in our discussion of model building in Chapter 2, to be useful models need not be exact replicas of reality. Economic models based on profit maximization have been very useful indeed. For one thing, they help to show how the price system functions. For another, in the real world, they suggest how a firm should operate if it wants to make as much money as possible. Even if a firm does not want to maximize profit, these theories can be utilized. For example, they can show how much the firm is losing by taking certain courses of action. In recent years, the theory of the profit-maximizing firm has been studied more and more for the sake of determining profit-maximizing rules of business behavior.

Technology and Inputs

The decisions a firm should make in order to maximize its profits are determined by the current state of technology. Technology, it will be recalled from Chapter 1, is the sum total of society's knowledge concerning the industrial arts. Just as the consumer is limited by his income, the firm is limited by the current state of technology. If the current state of technology is such that we do not know how to produce more than 40 bushels of corn per year from an acre of land and 2 man-years of labor, then this is as much as the firm can produce from this combination of land and labor. In making its decisions, the firm must take this into account.

In constructing his model of the profit-maximizing firm, the economist must somehow represent the state of technology and include it in his model. As a first step toward this end, we must define an ***input.*** Perhaps the simplest definition of an input is that it is anything the

[2] This quote is taken from R. Solow, "The New Industrial State, or Son of Affluence," *The Public Interest,* Fall 1967. Since footnotes are so often used to cite dreary material, it seems worthwhile to use them occasionally to cite humor as well.

firm uses in its production process. For example, some of the inputs of a farm producing corn might be seed, land, labor, water, fertilizer, various types of machinery, as well as the time of the people managing the farm. In analyzing production processes, we suppose that all inputs can be classified into two categories: fixed and variable inputs.

A ***fixed input*** is one whose quantity cannot change during the period of time under consideration. This period will vary: it may be six months in one case, six years in another case. Among the most important inputs often included as fixed are the firm's plant and equipment—that is, its factory and office buildings, its machinery, its tooling, and its transportation facilities. A ***variable input*** is one whose quantity can be changed during the relevant period. For example, it is generally possible to increase or decrease the number of workers engaged in a particular activity (although this is not always the case, since they may have long-term contracts). Similarly, it frequently is possible to alter the amount of raw material that is used.

The Short Run and the Long Run

Whether an input is considered variable or fixed depends on the length of the period under consideration. The longer the period, the more inputs are variable, not fixed. Although the length of the period varies from case to case, economists have found it very useful to focus special attention on two time periods: the short run and the long run. The ***short run*** is defined as the period of time in which some of the firm's inputs are fixed. More specifically, since the firm's plant and equipment are among the most difficult inputs to change quickly, *the short run is generally understood to mean the length of time during which the firm's plant and equipment are fixed.* On the other hand, *the* ***long run*** *is that period of time in which all inputs are variable.* In the long run, the firm can make a complete adjustment to any change in its environment.

To illustrate the distinction between the short run and the long run, let's return to the General Motors Corporation. Any period of time during which GM's plant and equipment cannot be altered freely is the short run. For example, a period of one year is certainly a case of the short run, because in a year GM could not vary the quantity of its plant and equipment. It takes longer than a year to construct an automotive plant, or to alter an existing plant to produce a new kind of automobile. For example, the tooling phase of the model changeover cycle currently takes about 2 years. On the other hand, any period of time during which GM can vary the quantity of all inputs is the long run: for example, a period of 50 years is certainly a case of the long run. Whether a shorter period of time—10 years, say—is a long-run situation depends on the problem at hand. If all the relevant inputs can be varied, it is a long-run situation; if not, it is a short-run situation.

The Production Function

Having defined an input and distinguished between the short and long runs, we can now describe how economists represent the state of technology. The basic concept economists use for this purpose is the production function. For any commodity, *the* ***production function*** *is the relationship between the quantities of various inputs used per period of time and the maximum quantity of the commodity that can be produced per period of time.* More specifically, the production function is a table, a graph, or an equation showing the maximum output rate that can be achieved from any specified set of usage rates of inputs. The production function summarizes the characteristics of existing technology at a given point in time. It shows the technological constraints the firm must reckon with.

To see more clearly what we mean by a production function, consider the Milwaukee Machine Company, a hypothetical machine shop that produces a simple metal part. Suppose that we are dealing with the short run. The firm's basic plant and equipment are fixed, and the only variable input is the amount of labor used by the machine shop. Suppose that the firm collects data showing the relationship between the quantity of its output and the quantity of labor it uses. This relationship, shown in Table 7.2, is the firm's production function. It shows that, when 1 worker is employed, 100 parts are produced per month; when 2 workers are employed, 210 parts are produced per month; and so on.

Table 7.2
Production Function, Milwaukee Machine Company

Quantity of labor used per month (number of men employed)	Output per month (number of parts)
0	0
1	100
2	210
3	315
4	415
5	500

To illustrate what a production function looks like in a real case, let's consider a crude oil pipeline that transports petroleum from oilfields and storage areas over hundreds of miles to major urban and industrial centers. We begin by noting that the output of such a pipeline is the amount of oil carried per day, and that the two principal inputs are the diameter of the pipeline and the horsepower applied to the oil carried. Both inputs are important. Clearly, the bigger the diameter of the pipe, the more oil the pipeline can carry, holding constant the horsepower applied. And the greater the horsepower applied, the more oil the pipeline can carry, holding constant the diameter of the pipeline.

The production function shows the maximum output rate that can be derived from each combination of input rates. Thus, in this case, the production function shows the maximum amount of oil carried per day as a function of the pipeline's diameter and the amount of horsepower applied. On the basis of engineering estimates, one can derive the production function for crude oil pipelines. For example, Leslie Cookenboo of the Exxon Corporation derived such a production function, assuming that the pipeline carries Mid-Continent crude, has ¼-inch pipe throughout the lines, has lines 1,000 miles in length with a 5 percent terrain variation, and no net gravity flow in the line.[3] Some of his results are shown in Table 7.3. For example, the production function shows that if the diameter of the pipeline is 22 inches and the horsepower is 40,000, the pipeline can carry 215,000 barrels per day. Certainly, any firm operating a pipeline or considering the construction of one is vitally interested in such information. The production function plays a strategic role in the decision making of any firm.

Elements of Accounting

The Firm's Balance Sheet

In a previous section, we stated that economists generally assume that firms attempt to maximize profits. Viewed as a first approximation, this assumption does not seem too hard to swallow, but exactly what do we mean by profit? This is an important question, of inter-

[3] L. Cookenboo, *Crude Oil Pipe Lines and Competition in the Oil Industry,* Cambridge: Harvard University Press, 1955.

Table 7.3
Production Function, Crude Oil Pipeline[a]

Line diameter (inches)	Horsepower (thousands)				
	20	30	40	50	60
	Output rate (thousands of barrels per day)				
14	70	90	95	100	104
18	115	140	155	165	170
22	160	190	215	235	250
26	220	255	290	320	340

Source: Leslie Cookenboo, *Crude Oil Pipe Lines and Competition in the Oil Industry,* Cambridge: Harvard University Press, 1955.
[a]The output rates given in this table are only approximate, since they were read from Cookenboo's graph on p. 16.

est to businessmen and investors as well as to economists. The accounting profession provides the basic figures that are reported in the newspapers and in a firm's annual reports to its stockholders. If General Motors reports that it made $1.5 billion last year, this figure is provided by GM's accountants. How do the accountants obtain this figure? What are its limitations?

Basically, accounting concepts are built around two very important statements: the balance sheet and the profit and loss statement. *A firm's* ***balance sheet*** *shows the nature of its assets, tangible and intangible, at a certain point in time.* For example, let us return to the Milwaukee Machine Company. Its balance sheet might be as shown in Table 7.4. The lefthand side of the balance sheet shows the assets of the firm as of December 31, 1976. ***Current assets*** are assets that will be converted into

Table 7.4
Balance Sheet, Milwaukee Machine Company, as of December 31, 1976

Assets (dollars)		Liabilities and net worth (dollars)	
Current assets:		Current liabilities:	
Cash	20,000	Accounts payable	20,000
Inventory	120,000	Notes payable	40,000
Fixed assets:		Long-term liabilities:	
Equipment	160,000	Bonds	160,000
Buildings	180,000		
		Net worth:	
		Preferred stock	100,000
		Common stock	100,000
		Retained earnings	60,000
Total	480,000	Total	480,000

cash relatively quickly (generally within a year), whereas ***fixed assets*** generally will not be liquidated quickly. The firm has $20,000 in cash, $120,000 in inventory, $160,000 in equipment, and $180,000 in buildings. At first glance, these figures may seem more accurate than they are likely to be. It is very difficult to know how to value various assets. For example, should they be valued at what the firm paid for them, or at what it would cost to replace them? More will be said about these problems in the next section.

The righthand side of the firm's balance sheet shows the claims by creditors on the firm's assets and the value of the firm's ownership. For example, in Table 7.4, the Milwaukee Machine Company has total liabilities—or debts—of $220,000. There is $60,000 in ***current liabilities,*** which come due in less than a year; and $160,000 in ***long-term liabilities,*** which come due in a year or more. Specifically, there is $20,000 in ***accounts payable,*** which are bills owed for goods and services that the firm bought; $40,000 in ***notes payable,*** short-term notes owed to banks, finance companies, or other creditors; and $160,000 in ***bonds payable,*** or bonds outstanding.

The difference between the value of a firm's assets and the value of its liabilities is its ***net worth,*** which is the value of the firm's owners' claims against the firm's assets. In other words, the value of the firm to its owners is the total value of its assets less the value of the debts owed by the firm. Since

total value of assets − total liabilities = net worth,

it follows that

total value of assets = total liabilities + net worth.

That is, *the sum of the items on the lefthand side of the balance sheet must equal the sum of the items on the righthand side.* This, of course, must be true because of the way we define net worth. In the case of the Milwaukee Machine Company, the firm's net worth—the difference between its assets and its liabilities—is $260,000. Specifically, there is $100,000 worth of preferred stock and $100,000 worth of common stock; there is also $60,000 in retained earnings, which we shall explain below.

The Firm's Profit and Loss Statement

A firm's ***profit and loss statement*** *shows its sales during a particular period, its costs incurred in connection with these sales, and its profits during this period.* Table 7.5 shows the Milwaukee Machine Company's profit and loss statement during the period January 1, 1977 to December 31, 1977. Sales during this period were $240,000. The cost of manufacturing the items made during this period was $110,000—$30,000 for materials, $40,000 for labor, $34,000 for depreciation (discussed below), and $6,000 for miscellaneous operating expenses.

However, because the firm has reduced its inventory from $120,000 to $110,000 during the period, the cost of manufacturing the items *made* during the period does not equal the cost of manufacturing the items *sold* during the period. To find the *cost of goods sold*—which is the amount that logically should be deducted from sales to get the profits made from the sale of these goods—we must add the decrease in the value of inventory to the total manufacturing cost. (Why? Because the firm sold more items than it produced during this period. Thus the cost of the items it sold equals the cost of the items it produced during this period plus the cost of the items it sold from its inventory. Since the cost of the items it sold from its inventory equals the decrease in the value of its inventory, the cost of the items it sold equals the cost of the items it produced during this period plus the decrease in inventory.) Putting

Table 7.5
Profit and Loss Statement, Milwaukee Machine Company, January 1, 1977, to December 31, 1977 (dollars)

Net Sales		240,000
Manufacturing cost of goods sold		120,000
Materials	30,000	
Labor	40,000	
Depreciation	34,000	
Miscellaneous operating cost	6,000	
Total	110,000	
Plus beginning inventory	120,000	
Less closing inventory	−110,000	
Adjusted total	120,000	
Selling and administrative costs		20,000
Fixed interest charges and state and local taxes		10,000
Net earnings before income taxes		90,000
Corporation income taxes		40,000
Net earnings after taxes		50,000
Dividends on preferred stock		4,000
Net profits of common stockholders		46,000
Dividends paid on common stock		20,000
Addition to retained earnings		26,000

it another way, we must add the beginning inventory and subtract the closing inventory, as shown in Table 7.5. The resulting figure for cost of goods sold is $120,000.

But manufacturing costs are not the only costs the firm incurs. To estimate the firm's profits, we must also deduct from sales its selling and administrative expenses, its interest charges, and its state and local taxes, as well as its federal income taxes. Table 7.5 shows that the Milwaukee Machine Company's after-tax earnings during 1977 were $50,000. This is the amount left for the owners of the business. The profit and loss statement also shows what the owners do with what is left. For example, Table 7.5 shows that the Milwaukee Machine Company used $4,000 to pay dividends to holders of preferred stock. When this was done, the holders of common stock were free to distribute some of the profits to themselves. According to Table 7.5, they distributed $20,000 to themselves in dividends on the common stock, and plowed the rest—$26,000—back into the business as retained earnings.

Before leaving the profit and loss statement, we should explain one element of manufacturing cost—***depreciation.*** While the other elements of manufacturing cost are self-explanatory, this one is not. The idea behind depreciation is that the buildings and equipment will not last forever; eventually they will have to replaced. Clearly, it would be foolish to charge the entire cost of replacing them to the year when they are replaced. Instead, a better picture of the firm's true profitability will be drawn if the cost of replacing them is spread gradually over the life of buildings and equipment, thus recognizing that each year's output has a hand in wearing them out. One frequently used technique is so-called ***straight-line depreciation,*** which spreads the cost of buildings and equipment (less their scrap value) evenly over their life. Thus, if the Milwaukee Machine Company buys a piece of equipment for $20,000 and if it is expected to last ten years (its scrap value being zero), it would charge depreciation of $2,000 per year for this machine (for ten years after its purchase). The $34,000 charge for depreciation in Table 7.5 is the sum of such charges. Clearly, this is only a rough way to estimate the true depreciation charges, but it is good enough for many purposes.

Relationship between the Balance Sheet and Profit and Loss Statement

The balance sheet and profit and loss statement are closely related. To see the relationship, let's compare the Milwaukee Machine Company's balance sheet at the end of the period covered by the profit and loss statement in Table 7.5 with the balance sheet at the beginning of this period. The balance sheet at the beginning of the period was shown in Table 7.4. The balance sheet at the end of the period is now given in Table 7.6. At first glance, it may not be obvious how the two balance sheets and the profit and loss statement are related; but after a little reflection, it should be clear that the firm's net worth as shown by the end-of-period balance sheet must equal the firm's net worth as shown by the beginning-of-period balance sheet plus the addition to retained earnings shown in the profit and loss statement.

The reason for this lies in the definition of ***addition to retained earnings.*** This is the amount the common stockholders plow back into the firm; in other words, the amount they add to the net worth of the firm. Since this is so, the increase (or decrease, if addition to retained earnings is negative) in the net worth of the firm must equal the addition to retained earnings (assuming, of course, that the net worth of the firm is not changed by altering the amount of stock outstanding).[4] Thus, for example, in the case of the Milwaukee Machine Company, the firm's net worth had to increase by $26,000 during 1977; and since it was $260,000 at the beginning of 1977, it must

[4] This statement also makes some other assumptions. For a more complete treatment, see any college accounting textbook.

Table 7.6
Balance Sheet, Milwaukee Machine Company, as of December 31, 1977

Assets (dollars)		Liabilities and net worth (dollars)	
Current assets:		Current liabilities:	
Cash	36,000	Accounts payable	10,000
Inventory	110,000	Notes payable	40,000
Fixed assets		Long-term liabilities	
Equipment	170,000	Bonds	160,000
Buildings	180,000		
		Net worth:	
		Preferred stock	100,000
		Common stock	100,000
		Retained earnings	86,000
Total	496,000	Total	496,000

have been \$286,000 at the end of 1977. Where on the balance sheet does this \$26,000 show up? What part of net worth increased by \$26,000? The answer is that ***retained earnings,*** which shows the total amount that the stockholders have plowed back into the firm in the past, went up by \$26,000.

Economic versus Accounting Profits

The previous sections described the nature of profit, as defined by accountants. This is the concept on which practically all published figures in business reports are based. But economists define profits somewhat differently. In particular, the economist does not assume that the firm attempts to maximize the current, short-run profits measured by the accountant. Instead he assumes that the firm will attempt to maximize the sum of profits over a long period of time.[5] Also, when the economist speaks of profits, he means profit after taking account of the capital and labor provided by the owners. Thus, suppose that the owners of the Milwaukee Machine Company, who receive profits but no salary or wages, put in long hours for which they could receive \$30,000 in 1977 if they worked for someone else. Also suppose that if they invested their capital somewhere other than in this firm, they could obtain a return of \$22,000 on it in 1977. Under these circumstances, economists would say that the firm's after-tax profits in 1977 were \$50,000 − \$30,000 − \$22,000, or − \$2,000, rather than the \$50,000 shown in Table 7.5. In other words, the economist's concept of profit includes only what the owners make above and beyond what their labor and capital employed in the business could have earned elsewhere. In this case, that amount is negative.

[5] The profits earned at various points in time should be *discounted* before being added together, but, for simplicity's sake, we neglect this point here. For some relevant discussion, see Chapter 28.

To a considerable extent, the differences between the concepts used by the accountant and the economist reflect the difference in their functions. The accountant is concerned with controlling the firm's day-to-day operations, detecting fraud or embezzlement, satisfying tax and other laws, and producing records for various interested groups. On the other hand, the economist is concerned primarily with decision making and rational choice among prospective alternatives. Although the figures published on profits almost always conform to the accountant's, not the economist's, concept, the economist's concept is the more relevant one for many kinds of decisions. (And this, of course, is recognized by sophisticated accountants.) For example, suppose the owners of the Milwaukee Machine Company are trying to decide whether they should continue in business. If they are interested in making as much money as possible, the answer depends on the firm's profits as measured by the economist, not the accountant. If the firm's economic profits are greater than zero, the firm should continue in existence; otherwise, it should not. Thus the Milwaukee Machine Company should not stay in existence if 1977 is a good indicator of its future profitability.

The Financial Statements of General Motors: A Case Study

To conclude this chapter, let's return once again to General Motors, and examine its financial statements—its balance sheet and profit and loss statement. These are a bit more detailed than the hypothetical statements of the Milwaukee Machine Company, but they are constructed on the same principles. Each year, General Motors issues an annual report to its stockholders, which includes these financial statements. Table 7.7 reproduces GM's balance sheet as of December 31, 1974; and Table 7.8 reproduces GM's profit and loss statement

Table 7.7
Balance Sheet, General Motors Corporation, as of December 31, 1974

Assets (millions of dollars)		Liabilities and net worth (millions of dollars)	
Current assets:		Current liabilities:	
Cash	401	Accounts payable	3,600
Government securities	938	Taxes owed	2,499
Accounts receivable	3,001	Other	3
Inventories	6,405		
		Long-term liabilities	
Fixed Assets:		Bonds	122
		Other	1713
Investments	1,552		
Real estate, plant, and equipment	6,215	Net worth:	
Other	1,956	Preferred stock	284
		Common stock	479
		Retained earnings[a]	11,769
Total	20,468	Total	20,468

Source: Moody's.
[a] Includes capital surplus.

Table 7.8
Profit and Loss Statement, General Motors Corporation, January 1, 1974, to December 31, 1974 (millions of dollars)

Net sales (and other income)		31,861
Manufacturing cost of goods sold		28,624
Materials, labor, and miscellaneous operating costs	28,147	
Depreciation	1,705	
Total	29,852	
Plus beginning inventory	5,177	
Less closing inventory	−6,405	
Adjusted total	28,624	
Selling and administrative costs (and interest charges)		1,560
Net earnings before U.S. and foreign taxes		1,677
U.S. and foreign taxes		727
Net earnings after taxes		950
Dividends on preferred stock		13
Net profits of common stockholders		937
Dividends paid on common stock		973
Addition to retained earnings		−36

Source: Moody's.

for 1974. Take a close look at these tables, and see if you understand what each item means. For example, Table 7.7 says that GM had $3,001 million in accounts receivable at the end of 1974. What are accounts receivable? (Bills its customers owe General Motors.) It also says that GM had $284 million in preferred stock at the end of 1974. What is preferred stock? (If you don't recall, turn back to the section on "Corporate Securities.") According to Table 7.8, GM incurred depreciation costs of $1,705 million in 1974. What is depreciation? (Turn back to "The Firm's Profit and Loss Statement" if you need to.) Also, GM's addition to retained earnings was negative in 1974. What does this mean? (See the section on "Relationship between Balance Sheet and Profit and Loss Statement.")

Financial analysts spend an enormous amount of time poring over the financial statements of various companies to estimate whether their stock is a good or bad investment. Banks look at a firm's financial statements when they decide whether or not to grant the firm a loan. The financial pages of the major newspapers, as well as magazines specializing in financial and business news, are sprinkled liberally with summaries of these financial statements. You would do well to make sure you understand the basic definitions and principles of accounting presented in previous sections. In dealing with practical problems, this information will serve you well.

Summary

There are three principal types of business firms: proprietorships, partnerships, and corporations. The corporation has many advantages over the other two—limited liability, unlimited life, and greater ability to raise large sums of money. The corporation raises money by issuing various kinds of securities, of which three kinds—common stock, preferred stock, and bonds—are particularly important. A relatively small number of giant corporations control a very substantial proportion of the total assets and employment in the American economy. In the large corporation, ownership and control tend to be separated. So long as a firm's management is not obviously incompetent or corrupt, it is difficult for insurgent stockholders to remove the management from office.

As a first approximation, economists generally assume that firms attempt to maximize profits. In large part, this is because it is a close enough approximation to reality for many of the most important purposes of economics. Also, economists are interested in the theory of the profit-maximizing firm because it provides rules of behavior for firms that do want to maximize profits. In constructing his model of the profit-maximizing firm, the economist must somehow represent the state of technology and include it in his model. He classifies inputs used by the firm into two categories: fixed and variable. He also differentiates between the short run and the long run. Then, to summarize the characteristics of existing technology at a given point in time, he uses the concept of the production function, which shows the maximum output rate of a given commodity that can be achieved from any specified set of usage rates of inputs.

Accounting concepts are built around two very important statements: the balance sheet and the profit and loss statement. The balance sheet shows the nature of the firm's assets and liabilities at a given point in time. The difference between its assets and its liabilities is its net worth, which is the value of the firm's owners' claims against its assets. A firm's profit and loss statement shows its sales during a particular period, its costs incurred in connection with these sales, and its profits during the period. The balance sheet and the profit and loss statement are closely related. Economists define profits somewhat differently than accountants do. In particular, the economist excludes from profit the value of the capital and labor provided by the owners, and he is interested in longer periods than those to which accounting statements apply. Although the profit figures that are published almost always conform to the accountant's concept, the economist's concept is the more relevant one for many kinds of decisions.

CONCEPTS FOR REVIEW

Proprietorship	Preferred stock	Production function
Partnership	Bond	Balance Sheet
Corporation	Profit	Current Assets
Liability	Input	Fixed Assets
Board of directors	Fixed input	Profit and loss statement
Common stock	Variable input	Depreciation

QUESTIONS FOR DISCUSSION AND REVIEW

1. Which of the following are inputs in the steel industry? (a) coke, (b) iron ore, (c) labor, (d) bread, (e) capital, (f) water, (g) oxygen, (h) yeast.

2. "Modern technology, says Galbraith, makes planning essential, and the giant corporation is its chosen instrument. This planning, in turn, requires the corporation to eliminate risk and uncertainty, to create for itself an environment of stability and security, and to free itself from all outside interference with its planning function."[6] Comment.

3. "The long run in one industry or situation may be shorter than the short run in another industry or situation." Explain and evaluate. If you agree, give several specific examples.

4. Assume that a partnership wanted to enter the automobile industry. What problems would such a legal form of organization impose upon the potential entrants? Are there any partnerships that produce automobiles? Why?

5. The great English economist, John Maynard Keynes, said that investing in stocks was like "entering a newspaper beauty-judging contest in which you have to select the six prettiest faces out of 100 photographs. The prize goes to the person whose selections most nearly conform to those of the group as a whole."[7] Explain and evaluate.

[6] W. Adams, "Another View of the New Industrial State," in E. Mansfield, *Economics: Readings, Issues, and Cases,* 2d ed., New York: Norton, 1977.

[7] B. Malkiel, *A Random Walk Down Wall Street.*

6. Suppose that a firm's balance sheet is as follows:

Assets (dollars)		Liabilities and net worth (dollars)	
Current assets		Current liabilities	
Cash	200,000	Accounts payable	100,000
Inventory	300,000	Notes payable	______
Fixed Assets		Long-term liabilities	
Equipment	______	Bonds	400,000
Buildings	800,000		
		Net Worth	400,000
Total	2,000,000	Total	______

Fill in the three blanks. What is the total amount that the firm owes? How much have the owners contributed? What is the difference between current assets and fixed assets?

7. Suppose that a firm's accounting profits for 1976 are $20,000. The firm is a proprietorship, and the owner worked 500 hours managing the business during 1976, for which he received no compensation other than the profits. If he could have gotten $10 an hour working for someone else, how much were his economic profits during 1976? Suppose that he also contributed $50,000 in capital to the firm, and that he could have obtained 6 percent interest on this capital if he had invested it elsewhere. In this case, how much were his economic profits?

8. Do you think that General Motors maximizes profits? What do you think William C. Durant would have replied if you had asked him this question? For economic models to be useful, must firms maximize profits?

9. Suppose that a friend offered to sell you some stock in a small company. How would the firm's balance sheet and profit and loss statement be useful in evaluating how much the stock is worth?

10. Based on the data in Table 7.3, if line diameter is held constant and horsepower is increased, does an extra 1,000 horsepower seem to increase the output of a pipeline by the same amount, regardless of how many horsepower are already applied? Why or why not?

PART THREE

National Output, Income, and Employment

8 Unemployment, Inflation, and National Output

Three of the most important indicators of the health of any nation's economy are its unemployment rate, its rate of inflation, and the size of its national output. Every government, including our own, watches these indicators with great interest. Moreover, most societies today are committed to policies designed to influence each of them, in particular to keeping unemployment and inflation to a reasonable minimum, and to promoting the growth of national output. These social goals certainly seem sensible, since high rates of unemployment can cause enormous social waste and private hardship. Also, most societies seem to believe that the benefits of greater national output outweigh the costs, and that serious inflation should not be tolerated.

In this chapter, we begin to study unemployment, inflation, and national output. Our first objective is to discuss the nature of unemployment and inflation, and how the rate of inflation is related to the rate of unemployment.

Then we turn to a detailed examination of how national output is measured, our purpose being to describe such concepts as gross national product and its components: consumption, investment, government spending, and net exports. Finally, we discuss how the gap between actual and potential output is related to the level of unemployment.

Unemployment

Types of Unemployment

Almost a century ago, Pope Leo XIII said, "Among the purposes of a society should be to arrange for a continuous supply of work at all times and seasons."[1] The word *unemployment* is one of the most frightening in the English language–and for good reason. Unemployed people become demoralized, suffer loss of prestige and status, and their families tend to break apart. Sometimes they are pushed toward crime and drugs; often they feel terrible despair. Their children are innocent victims too. Indeed, perhaps the most devastating effects of unemployment are on children, whose education, health, and security may be ruined. After a few minutes' thought, most people would agree that in this or any other country every citizen who is able and willing to work should be able to get a job.

Of course we are not saying that all unemployment, whatever its cause or nature, should be eliminated. According to the U.S. government, *any person 16 years old or more who does not have a job and is looking for one is* ***unemployed.*** Since this definition is necessarily quite broad, it is important that we distinguish among several quite different kinds of unemployment.

Frictional unemployment. This sort of unemployment is related to the entrance of new workers into the labor market and the movement of workers from one position to another. For example, Tom Smith may quit his job after the boss calls him a fathead. It may take him a month to find another job, perhaps because he is unaware of job opportunities or perhaps because the boss was right. During this month, he is numbered among the unemployed. It would not make much sense to try to eliminate all such temporary unemployment. On the contrary, a free labor market could not function without a certain amount of frictional unemployment.

Structural unemployment. Unemployment of this kind exists when jobs are available for qualified workers, but the unemployed do not have the necessary qualifications. This sort of unemployment results from a mismatch between job requirements and the skills of the unemployed, as in the case of a 58-year-old cotton picker thrown out of work by the introduction of mechanical cotton pickers who lacks the skills needed to get a job in another field. To some extent, structural unemployment can be reduced by monetary and fiscal policies of the sort described in the following chapters. But in many cases, the principal way to attack it is by retraining workers whose skills are no longer in demand for jobs in other occupations, industries, or areas.

Cyclical unemployment. This type of unemployment occurs when, because of an insufficiency of aggregate demand, there are more workers than jobs. Cyclical unemployment is associated with business fluctuations, or the so-called business cycle. Industrialized capitalistic economies have been subject to fluctuations, with booms often succeeding busts and vice versa. Before World War II the American economy periodically went through serious depressions, during which unemployment was very high. The Great Depression of the 1930s was particularly long and severe, and when World War II ended, the American people resolved that the gigantic social costs of the enormous unemployment of the 1930s must

[1] Pope Leo XIII, *Encyclical Letter on the Conditions of Labor,* May 15, 1891.

not be repeated in the postwar period. To avoid this, Congress passed the Employment Act of 1946, which says,

> It is the continuing policy and responsibility of the Federal Government to use all practicable means . . . [to create and maintain] conditions under which there will be afforded useful employment opportunities, including self-employment, for those able, willing, and seeking to work and to promote maximum employment, production, and purchasing power.

The Employment Act of 1946 was an extremely important piece of legislation, for it committed the federal government to combat cyclical unemployment.

How Much Unemployment Is There?

To get some idea of the extent of unemployment, we can consult Figure 8.1, which shows the percent of the labor force unemployed during each year from 1929 to 1975. Note the wide fluctuations in the unemployment rate, and the very high unemployment rates during the 1930s. Fortunately, unemployment since World War II has never approached the tragically high levels of the Great Depression of the 1930s. In 1949 and 1950, and again in 1954, the unemployment rate pushed up toward 6 percent, but in general it remained at about 4 percent or less until 1958, when it increased to almost 7 percent. Between 1958 and 1964, it averaged about 6 percent, and then declined steadily until it fell below 4 percent in 1966–69. In 1970–74, it bounced back up to 5 or 6 percent, and then rose to $8\frac{1}{2}$ percent in 1975, after which it receded. Although many of these variations in the unemployment rate may seem small, they are by no means unimportant. Any administration, Democratic or Republican, watches these figures closely, and tries to avoid significant increases in unemployment.

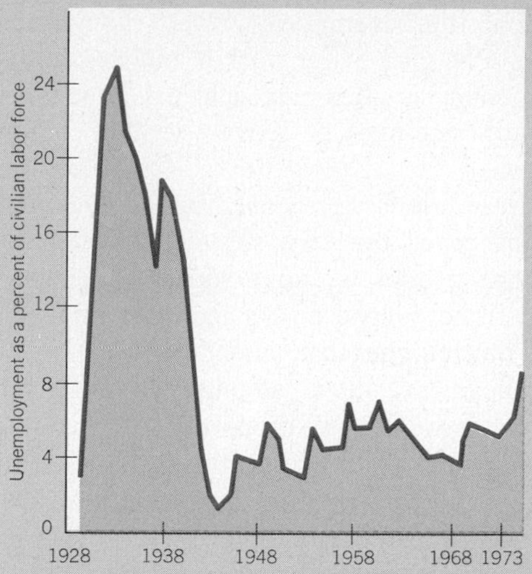

Figure 8.1
Unemployment Rates, United States, 1929–75
The unemployment rate has varied substantially. Fortunately, since World War II it has not approached the very high levels of the Great Depression of the 1930s. But the recent recession of 1974–75 showed that the nation is not immune to severe bouts of unemployment.

The importance of unemployment statistics makes it worthwhile to see how they are collected. The federal government periodically conducts a scientific survey of the American people, asking a carefully selected sample of the population whether they have a job, and, if not, whether they are looking for one. According to most expert opinion, the resulting figures are quite reliable within certain limits. One of these is that they do not indicate the extent to which people are ***underemployed.*** Some people work only part-time, or at jobs well below their level of education or skill, but the government figures count them as fully employed. Also, some people have given up looking for a job and are no longer listed among the unemployed, even though they would be glad to get work if any was offered. To count as unemployed in the government figures, one must be actively seeking employment.

In addition, aggregate figures on unemployment cover up very substantial differences among groups within a society. Unemployment rates among blacks and other minorities are much higher than among whites. Also, unemployment rates among teenagers and women tend to be disproportionately high. For example, in 1975, although the unemployment rate for all workers was 8.5 percent, it was 19.9 percent among people 16 to 19 years of age and 13.9 percent among nonwhites. Consequently, since unemployment tends to be concentrated in particular segments of the population, overall unemployment rates can be somewhat misleading.

Finally, some critics of the official unemployment statistics would use a definition of unemployment that focuses attention on "serious" cases of joblessness. They would exclude unemployed people with a working spouse, unemployed teenagers living with a parent with a job, and unemployed people who have been out of work less than a month. Also, they would have the government try harder to find out whether those who say they are unemployed are making a serious effort to find work. Officials of the Bureau of Labor Statistics reply that such a change in definition would convert the statistics into a measure of hardship rather than of unemployment.

Unemployment: A Case Study

Since general descriptions of the plight of the unemployed often have relatively little impact, a real-life case study may give you a better feel for what unemployment is like. Consider Joseph Torrio, a New Haven factory worker who was laid off after 18 years on the job. He describes in his own words how he spent several mornings:

> Up at seven, cup of coffee, and off to Sargent's. Like to be there when the gang comes to work, the lucky devils. Employment manager not in. Waited in his outer office. . . . Three others waiting, two reporting for compensation. Other one laid off two weeks ago and said he called at office every day. He inquired what I was doing and when I said "looking for work" he laughed. "You never work here? No? What chance you think you got when 400 like me who belong here out?" Employment manager showed up at 9:30. I had waited two hours. My time has no value. A pleasant fellow; told me in a kind but snappy way business was very bad. What about the future, would he take my name? Said he referred only to the present. Nothing more for me to say, so left. Two more had drifted into office. Suppose they got the same story. Must be a lot of men in New Haven that have heard it by now.
>
> [On May 21], interview with sales manager of the Real Silk Hosiery Mills. Had seen their ads for salesmen in the paper. Sales manager approached me with his hand sticking out, the first one who had offered to shake hands with me. I told him my name and inquired about the position. He took me into his private office, well furnished, and asked me if I had had any selling experience. I told him that I hadn't any but I thought I could do the work. . . . Asked me to report at 9 A.M. the next morning for further instructions. . . . [On May 22], I kept my appointment with the sales manager. Spent the morning learning about different kinds of stockings. Made another appointment for the afternoon which I did not keep because he wanted me to bring along $6 as security on a bag and some stock. I did not have the $6.[2]

No single case study can give you an adequate picture of the impact on people of being without a job. There are a wide variety of responses to unemployment. Some people weather it pretty well, others sink into despair; some people have substantial savings they can

[2] E. W. Bakke, *The Unemployed Worker*, Hamden, Conn.: Archon, 1969, pp. 168, 169, 174, and 175.

draw on, others are hard pressed; some people manage to shield their families from the blow, others allow their misfortunes to spread to the rest of the family. But despite these variations, being without work deals a heavy blow to a person's feeling of worth. It hits hard at a person's self-image, indicating that he or she is not needed, cannot support a family, is not really a full and valuable member of society. It can strike a cruel blow at men and women alike, since many women are vitally interested in achievement outside the home, sometimes because they are the family breadwinners. The impact of widespread and persistent unemployment is most clearly visible at present among the blacks and other racial minorities, where unemployment rates are much higher than among the white population. Unquestionably, the prevalence of unemployment among blacks greatly influences how the blacks view themselves, as well as the way they interact with the rest of the community.

Inflation

Nature and Effects of Inflation

It is hard to find anyone these days who does not know the meaning of inflation firsthand. Try to think of commodities you regularly purchase that cost less now than they did several years ago. Chances are that you can come up with precious few. ***Inflation** is a general upward movement of prices.* In other words, inflation means that goods and services that currently cost $10 may soon be priced at $11 or even $12, and wages and other input prices increase as well. It is essential to distinguish between the movements of individual prices and the movement of the entire price level. As we saw in Chapter 4, the price of an individual commodity can move up or down with shifts in the commodity's demand or supply curve. If the price of a particular good—corn, say—goes up, this need not be inflation, since the prices of other goods may be going down at the same time, so that the over-all price level—the general average level of prices—remains much the same. Inflation occurs only if most prices for goods and services in the society move upward—that is, if the average level of prices increases.

Inflation may seem no more than a petty annoyance: after all, most people care about relative, not absolute, prices. For example, if wages (the price of labor) increase at the same rate as prices, a family may be no better or worse off under inflation than under a constant price level. But this view ignores the people—civil service employees, teachers, and many others—who cannot increase their wages to compensate for price increases because they work under long-term contracts, among other reasons. These people and people living on pensions and other fixed incomes take a considerable beating from inflation.

Also, inflation hurts lenders and benefits borrowers, since it results in the depreciation of money. A dollar is worth what it will buy, and what it will buy is determined by the price level. If the price level increases, a dollar is worth less than it was before. Consequently, if you lend Bill Jones $100 in 1977 and he pays you $100 in 1987—when a dollar will buy much less than in 1977—you are losing on the deal. In terms of what the money will buy, he is paying you less than what he borrowed. Of course, if you anticipate considerable inflation, you may be able to recoup by charging him a high enough interest rate to offset the depreciation of the dollar, but it is not so easy to forecast the rate of inflation and protect yourself.

Unlike unemployment, inflation (at least in small doses) does not seem to reduce national output: in the short run, output may increase. The principal effect of inflation is on the distribution of income and wealth. Many inflations are not anticipated; and even if they are, we have just noted that many people are not knowledgeable enough to protect themselves.[3] The poor worker who has put aside some money for his old age, only to find that it will buy a fraction of what he hoped, has been victimized by inflation. Why should he bear this loss? As Arthur Okun, a former chairman of the Council of Economic Advisers, has put it, " 'sharpies' . . . make sophisticated choices and often reap gains on inflation which do not seem to reflect any real contribution to economic growth. On the other hand, the unsophisticated saver who is merely preparing for the proverbial rainy day becomes a sucker."[4]

Citizens and policy makers generally agree that inflation, like unemployment, should be minimized. For example, when President Ford convened a national Summit Conference of business people, labor leaders, and others in the fall of 1974, almost all agreed that inflation was "Public Enemy Number One," or close to it. However, such sentiment has not prevented the United States from suffering from considerable inflation. As shown in Figure 8.2, the price level has tended to increase considerably in the United States during the past 40 years. Substantial inflation followed World War II; the price level increased by about 33 percent between 1945 and 1948. Bursts of inflation recurred during the Korean War and then during the Vietnam War. And in the 1960s and 1970s, despite the government's efforts, inflation has continued. (Indeed, during 1974, prices rose by about 12 percent.) Our government's policy is to avoid both excessive unemployment and excessive inflation, but this goal, like many desirable social objectives, is by no means easy to achieve. Indeed, under certain circumstances, it may be impossible to have both stable prices and high employment, as we shall see in the next section.

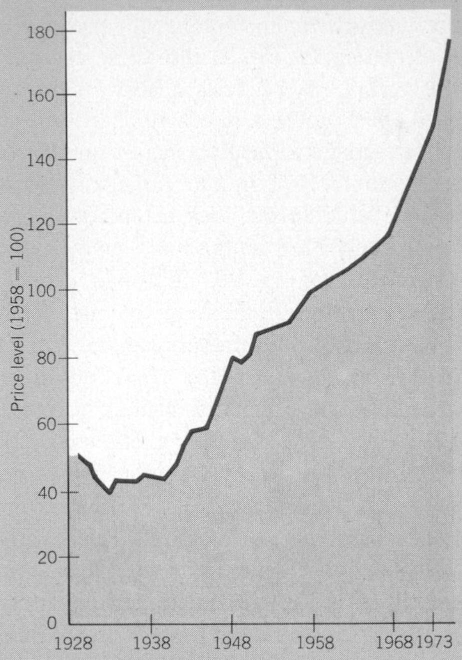

Figure 8.2
The Price Level, United States, 1929–75
The price level has increased considerably in the United States during the past 40 years. In recent years, inflation has been a stubborn problem.

The Relationship between Inflation and Unemployment

According to many economists, in the short run the unemployment rate is inversely related to the rate of inflation: that is, the lower the unemployment rate, the higher the rate of inflation. This relationship is by no means fixed and immutable, and the factors underlying its shape and position are still matters of debate. But, as a first approximation, we assume that this relationship is like that shown in Figure

[3] Economists often distinguish between anticipated and unanticipated inflation because if inflation is anticipated, people may be able to compensate for it by charging higher interest rates and by similar devices.

[4] Arthur Okun, "The Costs of Inflation," in his *The Battle against Unemployment*, rev. ed., New York, Norton, 1972.

8.3. In Chapter 16, we shall discuss in detail the reasons why many economists believe this relationship exists (and some recent controversies over its existence). At this point, it is sufficient to point out that both the unemployment rate and the inflation rate are determined by the total level of spending on the goods and services produced by the economy. Consumers, firms, and governments all spend money on the goods and services the nation produces. The level of output in our economy depends on how much money they spend. If their expenditures are very low, this means that the economy will operate in Range *A* in Figure 8.4, where national output is far below its maximum. Because the low level of expenditure means a low level of demand for the nation's goods and services, firms cannot sell enough goods and services to make it profitable to hire many of the workers who want to work. Thus employment is low, and the unemployment rate is high. As for the inflation rate, it is low, since there are plenty of excess capacity and unemployed resources. It is no time to raise prices.

Under these circumstances, suppose that an increase occurs in the total level of spending. National output and employment will rise, and the unemployment rate will fall, but there will be little or no increase in the price level since output can be increased without bidding up the prices of labor and other inputs. When the level of expenditure increases to the point where output and employment are in Range *B*, the unemployment rate will be substantially lower than in Range *A*, but the price level will begin to rise. Why? Because bottlenecks occur in some parts of the economy, and labor pushes harder for wage increases (and firms are more willing to agree to such increases). Finally, if the level of spending increases to the point where output and employment are in Range *C*, there will be no further decreases in the unemployment rate, since national output, which has reached its maximum, can grow no longer. In this range, the rate of inflation is very high, since total spending far exceeds the value of national output at initial prices. There are "too many dollars chasing too few goods."

As indicated in Figure 8.4, the inflation rate is likely to increase as output and employment

Figure 8.3
Relationship between Unemployment Rate and Rate of Inflation
According to many economists, there is an inverse short-run relationship between the unemployment rate and the rate of inflation. If the relationship is as shown here, a 6 percent unemployment rate means a 7 percent rate of inflation, a 7 percent unemployment rate means a 5.5 percent rate of inflation, and an 8 percent unemployment rate means a 4.5 percent rate of inflation.

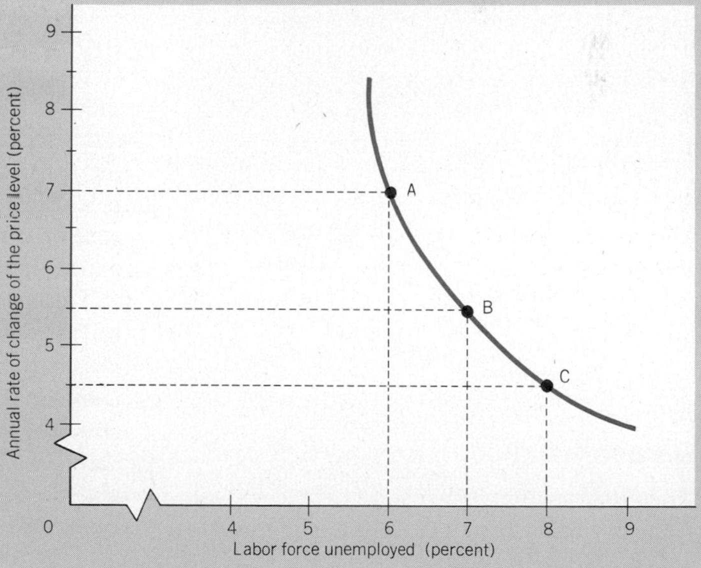

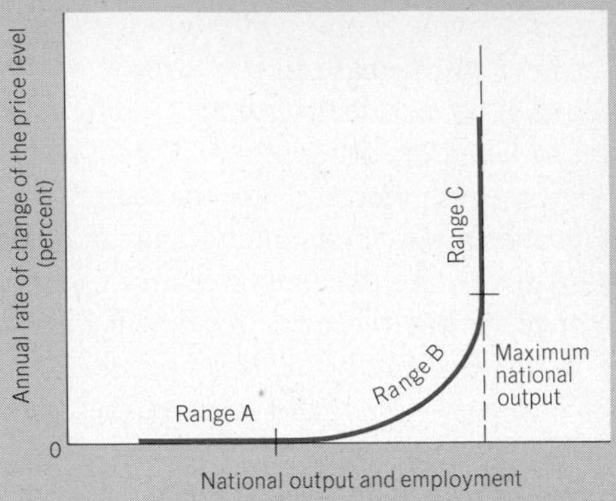

Figure 8.4
Output, Employment, and the Rate of Inflation
Chapter 3 pointed out that any economy can only produce so much, given its resources and the existing technology. The maximum output level, if all the economy's resources are fully and efficiently employed, is shown by the broken vertical line. In Range *A*, where national output is far below this maximum, the rate of inflation is very low but the unemployment rate is very high. In Range *B*, the unemployment rate is substantially less than in Range *A*, but the price level begins to rise. In Range *C*, national output is at its maximum, and increases in total spending result only in inflation.

increase—which means that it is likely to increase as unemployment decreases. Thus there may be the inverse relationship between the unemployment rate and the inflation rate shown in Figure 8.3.

Shifts in the Inflation-Unemployment Relationship

The curve in Figure 8.3 is a fascinating tool. At first glance it may seem that the government can simply aim at any point along the curve. For example, it might choose point *A* (where the unemployment rate is 6 percent and the inflation rate is 7 percent) or point *C* (where the unemployment rate is 8 percent and the inflation rate is 4½ percent). To reach point *A* or point *C*, monetary and fiscal policies can be used, as we shall see in subsequent chapters.

If the curve remains fixed, this choice among points on the curve is a real one—and a relevant one. Some administrations are more inclined than others to tolerate more unemployment in order to stem inflation. Some are more willing than others to tolerate inflation in order to reduce unemployment. The target you choose depends, of course, on your evaluation of the relative social costs associated with unemployment and inflation. The more importance you give to the costs of unemployment, and the less importance to the costs of inflation, the farther *up* the curve you will want to be. (For example, you will prefer point *A* to point *B*.) The more importance you attach to the costs of inflation, and the less to the costs of unemployment, the farther *down* on the curve you will want to be. (For example, you will prefer point *C* to point *B*.)

But fortunately or unfortunately, government policy making is not as simple as this. Perhaps the most important reason is that the curve in Figure 8.3 shifts. For example, it shifted upward during the early 1970s, as shown in Figure 8.5, for reasons that will be discussed in Chapter 16. Because of this shift the American economy was confronted simultaneously with excessive unemployment and excessive inflation—an uncomfortable combination known as "stagflation."

To repeat, *although there may be an inverse relationship in the short run between inflation and unemployment, this relationship may shift, with the result that one cannot be sure that increased unemployment will mean an eventual decline in inflation, or that increased inflation will mean an eventual decline in unemployment.* For example, if the relationship shifts in the

Figure 8.5
Shift in Relationship Between Unemployment Rate and Rate of Inflation
If the relationship between the unemployment rate and the inflation rate shifts from position 1 to position 2, the economy may move from point *D* to point *E*, in which case increased inflation is associated with increased unemployment.

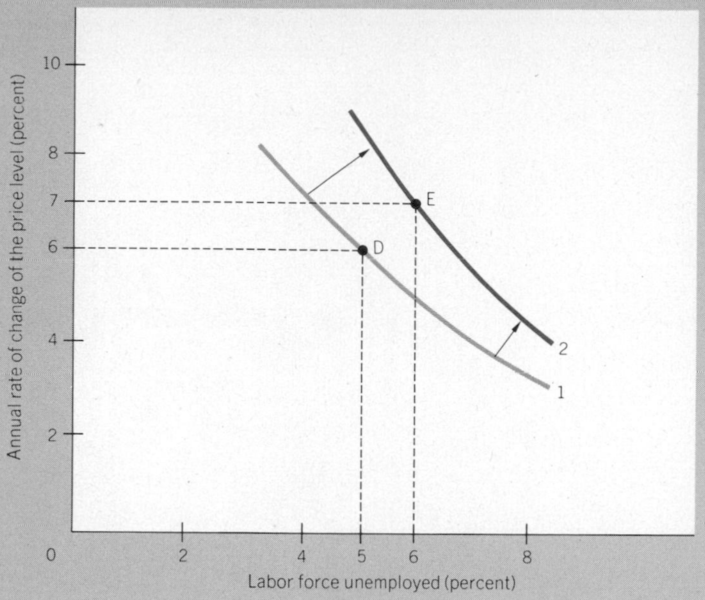

way shown in Figure 8.5, the inflation rate may increase from 6 to 7 percent, even though the unemployment rate increases from 5 to 6 percent. To see why, note that an unemployment rate of 5 percent means an inflation rate of 6 percent when the relationship is in its original position—position 1 in Figure 8.5. But after the relationship shifts to position 2, an unemployment rate of 6 percent means an inflation rate of 7 percent. Thus the economy can move from point *D* to point *E* in Figure 8.5, in which case increased inflation is associated with increased unemployment. The fact that shifts of this sort can occur in this relationship means that it is less useful than might appcar at first glance in guiding public policy.

Gross National Product

Estimates of Gross National Product: Uses and History

Unemployment and inflation statistics help us gauge how well an economy is performing. In addition, there is another major measuring rod that reflects the nation's over-all economic condition: the gross national product. Put in the simplest terms, *the **gross national product**—or **GNP**, as it is often called—is a measure of the total amount of goods and services produced by our economy during a particular period of time.* This measure is important both for its own sake, and because it helps us to understand both inflation and unemployment. The federal government and the business community watch the GNP figures avidly. Government officials, from the president down, are interested because these figures indicate how prosperous we are, and because they are useful in forecasting the future health of the economy. Politicians are well aware that the political party in power generally gets clobbered when GNP falls substantially. Business executives are also extremely interested in the GNP figures because the sales of their firms are related to the level of GNP, and so the figures are useful in forecasting the future health of their businesses. All in all, it is no exaggeration to say that the gross national product is one of the most closely watched numbers in existence.

Unemployment and Inflation: An International Overview

Economic problems, like smugglers, have no respect for international boundaries. In the mid-1970s, unemployment and inflation afflicted most of the industrialized world. As shown in the accompanying table, the unemployment rate in the fall of 1975 was about 8 percent in the United States and Canada, about 4 percent in France, Germany, Italy, and Britain, and about 2 percent in Japan. Compared with previous experience since World War II, these unemployment rates were very high. For example, in 1969, West Germany's unemployment rate was only 0.9 percent, as compared with 4.5 percent in late 1975.

A comparison of the U.S. unemployment rate with that in other countries shows that our unemployment rate (and Canada's) tends to be higher than the others, both in 1975 and 1969. To some extent, this is due to the fact that unemployment is defined differently in one country than in another. For example, in some countries, to be counted as unemployed, you must register with government unemployment exchanges. Another reason for the international differences in unemployment rates is that institutional and cultural arrangements differ from country to country. Thus, in Japan, many large firms commit themselves to a policy of lifetime employment for workers. This is one reason for Japan's relatively low unemployment rates. Still another reason for the international differences in unemployment rates is differences among countries in their fiscal and monetary policies (discussed in Chapters 11 and 15).

Lest you jump to the conclusion that present-day unemployment means starvation, note that there are substantial unemployment benefits in all of these countries. The percentage of workers covered by such plans in each country is: United States, 95; Canada, 99; Britain, 80; West Germany, 93; France, 61; Italy, 51; and Japan, 45. In the case of some U.S. auto workers who were laid off in 1974, unemployment benefits were almost equal to what they made when they were working. But this is the exception, not the rule. In general, although jobless benefits are an important cushion, they are far from big enough to prevent the unemployed from taking a substantial cut in income.*

* In the United States, unemployment insurance typically replaces only ⅓ to ½ of an unemployed worker's previous before-tax wages. But it replaces a great deal more of his or her *after-tax* income, because jobless benefits are exempt from taxes. Thus, according to Martin Feldstein of Harvard University, unemployment insurance increases unemployment, since it encourages (or at least enables) the jobless to remain unemployed longer than they otherwise would. Many economists agree with Feldstein, but there is considerable argument over the extent of this effect. Stephen Marston of the Brookings Institution estimates that unemployment insurance increases the unemployment rate by about 0.25 percentage points, while Feldstein estimates the increase at about 1.25 percentage points.

Unemployment Rate and Inflation Rate in the United States and Six Other Major Countries

Country	Unemployment rate[a] 1975	1969	Inflation rate[b] 1975	1974
United States	8.4	3.5	7.1	12.2
Canada	7.2	4.7	10.0	12.5
France	4.0	1.7	10.1	21.5
Germany	4.5	0.9	6.0	5.9
Italy	3.4	3.4	10.2	25.0
Japan	1.7	1.1	19.8	21.5
Great Britain	4.7	2.4	28.7	19.2

[a] The number of people unemployed as a percentage of the labor force. 1975 figures pertain to the third quarter.
[b] Annual percentage rate of increase of consumer prices. 1975 figures pertain to the first three quarters of the year.

As for the rate of inflation, the accompanying table shows that the price level increased at a rapid rate during 1974 and 1975 in all of these countries. The U.S. performance actually seemed somewhat better than in the other countries. While Great Britain, Canada, France, and Italy experienced increases in consumer prices of 10 percent per year or more during the first three quarters of 1975, we managed to keep the rate of inflation down to an average of 7 percent per year during that period. But a 7 percent annual rate of inflation is hardly anything to brag about. Many economists, and citizens as well, would be glad to return to the days when the price level seldom rose at more than a few percentage points per year—and unemployment rarely exceeded 4 or 5 percent.

In view of their importance, it is noteworthy that estimates of the gross national product are of comparatively recent vintage. The Department of Commerce first made such estimates in 1932, after experiments at various universities and at the National Bureau of Economic Research. A leading pioneer in this field was Nobel laureate Simon Kuznets, then at the University of Pennsylvania. The concepts that Kuznets and others developed are often called the ***national income accounts,*** and the Bureau of Economic Analysis of the U.S. Department of Commerce compiles these figures on a continuing basis. Just as the accounts of a firm are used to describe and analyze its financial health, so the national income accounts are used to describe and analyze the economic health of the nation as a whole.

Measuring Gross National Product

The American economy produces millions of types of goods and services. How can we add together everything from lemon meringue pie to helicopters, from books to houses? The only feasible answer is to use money as a common denominator and to make the price of a good or service—the amount the buyer is willing to pay—the measure of value. In other words, we add up the value in money terms of the total output of goods and services in the economy during a certain period, normally a year, and the result is the gross national product during that period.

At the outset, we must note several important points about the gross national product. First, it does not include the value of *all* goods and services produced: it includes only the value of *final* goods and services produced. ***Final goods and services*** are goods and services destined for the ultimate user. For example, flour purchased for family consumption is a final good, but flour to be used in manufacturing bread is an ***intermediate good,*** not a final good. Clearly, we would be double counting if we counted both the bread and the flour used to make the bread as output. Thus the output of intermediate goods—goods that are not destined for the ultimate user, but are used as inputs in producing final goods and services—must not be included in gross national product. For example, steel used in the production of automobiles and cotton used in the production of blue jeans must not be included. To avoid double counting, we include only the value of final goods and services in gross national product.

Second, some final goods and services that must be included in gross national product are not bought and sold in the market place, so they are valued at what they cost. For example, consider the services performed by government—police protection, fire protection, the use of the courts, defense, and so forth. Such services are not bought and sold in any market (despite the old saw about the New Jersey judge who was "the best that money could buy"). Yet they are an important part of our economy's final output. Economists and statisticians have decided to value them at what they cost the taxpayers. This is by no means ideal, but it is the best practical solution advanced to date.

Third, it is necessary for practical reasons to omit certain types of final output from gross national product. In particular, some nonmarketed goods and services, such as the services performed by housewives, are excluded from the gross national product. This is not because economists fail to appreciate these services, but because it would be extremely difficult to get reasonably reliable estimates of the money value of a housewife's services. At first glance, this may seem to be a very important weakness in our measure of total output, but so long as the value of these services does not change much (in relation to total output), the variation in gross national product will provide a reasonably accurate picture of the variation in total output—and, for many purposes, this is all that is required.

Fourth, purely financial transactions are excluded from the gross national product. Such financial transactions include government transfer payments, private transfer payments, and the sale and purchase of securities. ***Government transfer payments*** are payments made by the government to individuals who do not contribute to production in exchange for them. Payments to welfare recipients are a good example of government transfer payments. Since these payments are not for production, it would be incorrect to include them in GNP. ***Private transfer payments*** are gifts or other transfers of wealth from one person or private organization to another. Again these are not payments for production, so there is no reason to include them in GNP. The sale and purchase of securities are not payments for production, as you will recall from our discussion in Chapter 7, so they too are excluded from GNP.

Finally, the sale of secondhand goods is also excluded from the gross national product. The reason for this is clear. When a good is produced, its value is included in GNP. If its value is also included when it is sold on the secondhand market, it will be counted twice, thus leading to an overstatement of the true GNP. For example, suppose that you buy a new bicycle and resell it a year later. The value of the new bicycle is included in GNP when the bicycle is produced. But the resale value of the bicycle is not included in GNP; to do so would be double counting.

Gross National Product: Adjusting for Price Changes

In discussing inflation, we stressed that the general price level has changed over time. Since gross national product values all goods and services at their current prices, it is bound to be affected by changes in the price level as well as by changes in total output. If all prices doubled tomorrow, this would produce a doubling of gross national product. Clearly, if gross national product is to be a reliable measure of changes in total output, we must correct it somehow to eliminate the effects of such changes in the price level.

To make such a correction, economists choose some ***base year*** and express the value of all goods and services in terms of their prices during the base year. For example, if 1970 is taken as the base year and if the price of beef was $1 per pound in 1970, beef is valued at $1 per pound in all other years. Thus, if 200 million pounds of beef were produced in 1975, this total output is valued at $200 million even though the price of beef in 1975 was actually higher than $1 per pound. In this way, distortions caused by changes in the price level are eliminated.

It is customary to express gross national product either in current dollars or in constant dollars. Figures expressed in ***current dollars*** are actual dollar amounts, whereas those expressed in ***constant dollars*** are corrected in this way for changes in the price level. Expressed in current dollars, gross national product is affected by changes in the price level. Expressed in constant dollars, gross national product is not affected by the price level because the prices of all goods are maintained at their base-year level. GNP, after being corrected for changes in the price level, is called ***real GNP.*** Inflation has caused GNP expressed in current dollars to increase more rapidly than GNP in constant dollars (Figure 8.6).

It is often useful to have some measure of how much prices have changed over a certain period of time. One way to obtain such a measure is to divide the value of a set of goods and services expressed in current dollars by the value of the same set of goods and services expressed in constant (or base-year) dollars. For example, suppose that a set of goods and services costs $100 when valued at 1977 prices, but $70 when valued at 1970 prices. Apparently, prices have risen an average of 43

Figure 8.6
Gross National Product, Expressed in Current Dollars and in 1958 Dollars, United States, 1929–75
Because of inflation, GNP expressed in current dollars has increased more rapidly in recent years than GNP in constant (1958) dollars. This has been particularly true in the mid-1970s, reflecting the price surge then.

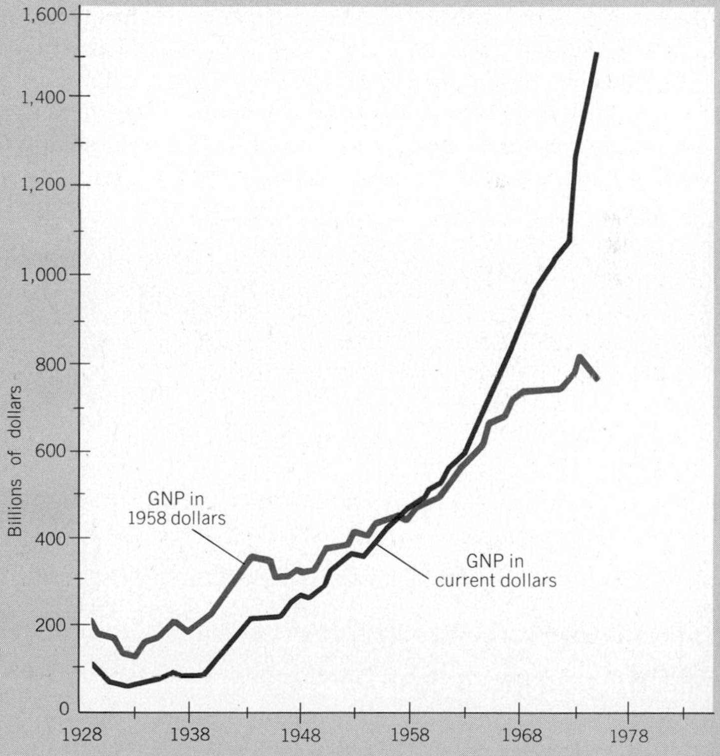

percent for this set of goods between 1970 and 1977. How do we get 43 percent? The ratio of the cost in 1977 prices to the cost in 1970 prices is 100 ÷ 70 = 1.43; thus prices must have risen on the average by 43 percent for this set of goods.

The ratio of the value of a set of goods and services in current dollars to the value of the same set of goods and services in constant (base-year) dollars is a ***price index.*** Thus 1.43 is a price index in the example above. An important function of a price index is to convert values expressed in current dollars into values expressed in constant dollars. This conversion, known as ***deflating,*** can be achieved simply by dividing values expressed in current dollars by the price index. For example, in the illustration above, values expressed in 1977 dollars can be converted into constant (i.e., 1970) dollars by dividing by 1.43. This procedure is an important one, with applications in many fields other than the measurement of gross national product. For example, firms use it to compare their output in various years. To correct for price changes, they deflate their sales by a price index for their products.

To illustrate how a price index can be used to solve such problems, suppose that we want to measure how much the output of bread rose ***in real terms***—that is, in constant dollars—between 1973 and 1977. We know that the value of output of bread in current dollars during each year was as shown in the first column of Table 8.1, and that the price of bread during each year was as shown in the second column. To determine the value of output of bread in 1973 dollars, we form a price index with 1973 as base year, as shown in the third column. Then dividing the figures in the first column by this price index, we get the value of output of bread during each year in 1973 dollars, shown in the fourth column. Thus the fourth column shows how much the output of bread has grown in real terms. For example, the real output of bread has risen by 19 percent—(1,900 − 1,600) ÷ 1,600—between 1973 and 1977.

Intermediate Goods, Value-Added, and Net National Product

We have pointed out that gross national product includes the value of only the final goods and services produced. Obviously, however, the output of final goods and services is not due solely to the efforts of the producers of the final goods and services. The total value of an automobile when it leaves the plant, for example, represents the work of many industries besides the automobile manufacturers. The steel, tires, glass, and many other components of the

Table 8.1
Use of Price Index to Convert from Current to Constant Dollars

Year	(1) Output of bread in current dollars	(2) Price of bread (dollars)	(3) Price index (price ÷ 1973 price)	(4) Output of bread in 1973 dollars[a]
1973	1,600 million	0.50	1.00	1,600 million
1974	1,768 million	0.52	1.04	1,700 million
1975	1,980 million	0.55	1.10	1,800 million
1976	2,090 million	0.55	1.10	1,900 million
1977	2,204 million	0.58	1.16	1,900 million

[a]This column was derived by dividing column 1 by column 3.

Table 8.2
Value-added by Various Industries, United States, 1975

Industry	Value-added (billions of dollars)
Agriculture, forestry, and fisheries	55
Mining	38
Construction	67
Manufacturing	346
Transportation	57
Communication	38
Electricity, gas, and sanitation	37
Wholesale and retail trade	272
Finance, insurance, and real estate	209
Other services	182
Government[a]	201
Rest of the world	11
Gross national product	1,516[b]

[a] Equals wages and salaries of government workers.
[b] Because of rounding errors, figures do not sum to total.
Source: Survey of Current Business, July 1976.

automobile were not produced by the automobile manufacturers. In reality, the automobile manufacturers only added a certain amount of value to the value of the intermediate goods—steel, tires, glass, and so forth—they purchased. This point is basic to an understanding of how the gross national product is calculated.

To measure the contribution of a firm or industry to the final output, we use the concept of value-added. ***Value-added*** means just what it says: *the amount of value added by a firm or industry to the total worth of the product.* It is a measure in money terms of the extent of production taking place in a particular firm or industry. Suppose that $160 million of bread was produced in the United States in 1976. To produce it, farmers harvested $50 million of wheat, which was used as an intermediate product by flour mills, which turned out $80 million of flour. This flour was used as an intermediate product by the bakers who produced the $160 million of bread. What is the value-added at each stage of the process? For simplicity, assume that the farmers did not have to purchase any materials from other firms in order to produce the wheat. Then the value-added by the wheat farmers is $50 million, the value-added by the flour mills is $30 million ($80 million − $50 million); and the value-added by the bakers is $80 million ($160 million − $80 million). Of course, the total of the value-added at all stages of the process ($50 million + $30 million + $80 million) must equal the value of the output of final product ($160 million), because each stage's value-added is its contribution to this value.

Table 8.2 shows the value-added by various industrial groups in the United States in 1975. Since the total of the value-added by all industries must equal the value of all final goods and services, which, of course, is gross national product, it follows that $1,516 billion—the total of the figures in Table 8.2—must have been equal to gross national product in 1975. It is interesting to note that most of the value-added in the American economy in 1975 was not contributed by manufacturing, mining, construction, transportation, communication, or electricity or gas. Instead, most of it came from services—wholesale and retail trade, finance, insurance, real estate, government services, and other services. This is a sign of a basic change taking place in the American economy, which is turning more and more toward producing services, rather than goods.

Gross national product has one drawback as a measure that must now be faced: it does not take into account the fact that plant and equipment wear out with use, and that a certain amount of each year's national output must be devoted to replacing the capital goods worn out in producing the year's output. Economists have therefore developed another important measure, net national product (or NNP), that recognizes what every accountant knows—the relevance of depreciation. (Recall the discussion in Chapter 7.) Specifically, ***net national product*** *equals gross national product minus depreciation.* To obtain net national product, government statisticians estimate the amount of depreciation—the amount of the nation's plant, equipment, and structures that are worn out during the period—and deduct it from gross national product. Net national product is a more accurate measure of the economy's output than gross national product because it takes depreciation into account, but estimates of net national product contain whatever errors are made in estimating depreciation (which is not easy to measure). As we shall see in succeeding chapters, data on gross national product are more often used, even if net national product may be a somewhat better measure. Actually, since GNP and NNP move together quite closely, which one you use doesn't matter much for most practical purposes.

The Limitations of Gross National Product and Net National Product

It is essential that the limitations of both gross national product and net national product be understood. Although they are very useful, these figures are by no means ideal measures of economic well-being. At least five limitations of these measures must always be borne in mind:

Population. GNP and NNP are not very meaningful unless one knows the size of the population of the country in question. For example, the fact that a particular nation's GNP equals $50 billion means one thing if the nation has 10 million inhabitants, and quite another thing if it has 500 million inhabitants. To correct for the size of the population, GNP per capita—GNP divided by the population—is often used as a rough measure of output per person in a particular country.

Leisure. GNP and NNP do not take account of one of mankind's most prized activities, leisure. During the past century, the average work week in the United States has decreased substantially. It has gone from almost 70 hours in 1850 to about 40 hours today. As people have become more affluent, they have chosen to substitute leisure for increased production. Yet this increase in leisure time, which surely contributes to our well-being, does not show up in GNP or NNP. Neither does the personal satisfaction (or displeasure and alienation) people get from their jobs.

Quality changes. GNP and NNP do not take adequate account of changes in the quality of goods. An improvement in a product is not reflected accurately in GNP and NNP unless its price reflects the improvement. For example, if a new type of drug is put on the market at the same price as an old drug, and if the output and cost of the new drug are the same as the old drug, GNP will not increase, even though the new drug is twice as effective as the old one. Because GNP and NNP do not reflect such increases in product quality, it is sometimes argued that the commonly used price indices overestimate the amount of inflation, since, although prices may have gone up, quality may have gone up too.

Value and distribution. GNP and NNP say nothing about the social desirability of the composition and distribution of the nation's output. Each good and service produced is valued at its price. If the price of a Bible is $5 and the price of a pornographic novel is $5, both are valued at $5, whatever you or I may think about their respective worth. Moreover, GNP and NNP measure only the total quantity of goods and services produced. They tell us nothing about how this output is distributed among the people. If a nation's GNP is $500 billion, this is its GNP whether 90 percent of the output is consumed by a relatively few rich families or whether the output is distributed relatively equally among the citizens.

Social costs. GNP and NNP do not reflect some of the social costs arising from the production of goods and services. In particular, they do not reflect the environmental damage resulting from the operation of our nation's factories, offices, and farms. It is common knowledge that the atmosphere and water supplies are being polluted in various ways by firms, consumers, and governments. Yet these costs are not deducted from GNP or NNP, even through the failure to do so results in an overestimate of our true economic welfare.

Economists are beginning to correct the GNP figures to eliminate some of these problems. For example, William Nordhaus and James Tobin at Yale University have tried to correct the GNP figures to take proper account of the value of leisure, the value of housewives' services, and the environmental costs of production, among other things.[5] They have found that, when these corrections were made, the increase in economic well-being since World War II has been much less than is indicated by the growth of uncorrected GNP per capita. Unquestionably, more work along this line is needed, and will be done. However, it is also worth noting that many of these adjustments and corrections are necessarily quite rough, since there is no accurate way to measure the relevant values and costs.

[5] W. Nordhaus and J. Tobin, "Is Growth Obsolete?" *Fiftieth Anniversary Colloquium,* New York: National Bureau of Economic Research, 1972.

Measures of National Income

Gross National Income Equals GNP

We have been dealing with the measurement of national product, or output. Now we must recognize *the identity between gross national product and gross national income.* ***Gross national income*** is the total annual flow of income paid out (or owed) as wages, rent, interest, and profits, plus two other items: indirect business taxes and depreciation. (*Indirect business taxes* are sales taxes, excise taxes, and other such taxes that firms view as part of their costs.) In other words, gross national income exactly equals the total claims on output—the sum total of the wages of the workers who participated in the productive efforts, the interest paid to the investors who lent money to the firms that produced the output, the profits of the owners of the firms who produced the output, and the rents paid the owners of land used to produce the output, as well as indirect business taxes and depreciation. If you think back to the circular flows of money and products described in Chapter 4, you can see (at least vaguely) why gross national income must equal gross national product.

To provide you with a real proof that this equality must hold, let's start with a single firm, the General Electric Corporation, a huge producer of electrical equipment, appliances, and other products. By the simple rules of accounting discussed in Chapter 7,

$$\text{profit} = \text{sales} - \text{costs}. \qquad (8.1)$$

Thus it follows that

$$\text{sales} = \text{costs} + \text{profit}. \qquad (8.2)$$

Table 8.3
Sales, Costs, and Profit, General Electric Company, 1974

Sales (millions of dollars)		Costs and profit (millions of dollars)	
Sales:	13,599	Employee compensation	5,223
		Interest and rent	180
		Depreciation	376
		Indirect business taxes	123
		Intermediate products bought from other firms	6,696
		Total costs	12,598
		Profits	1,001
Total	13,599	Total	13,599

Source: Moody's.

Suppose we put the value of General Electric's output (i.e., its sales) on the lefthand side of Table 8.3 and its costs and profits on the righthand side. Clearly, by Equation (8.2), the total of the righthand side must equal the total of the lefthand side.

Now, suppose that we deduct one element of costs, "Intermediate products bought from other firms," from both sides of Table 8.3, and present the results in Table 8.4. Since the lefthand total equals the righthand total in Table 8.3, the same must hold in Table 8.4. The total of the lefthand side of Table 8.4 equals value-added, since General Electric's value-added equals its sales minus its expenditures on intermediate goods bought from other firms. The total of the righthand side of Table 8.4 equals the total claims against General Electric's output, which is the total of income paid out (or owed) by the firm—wages, interest, rent, profits—plus indirect business taxes and depreciation. And, as pointed out above, the total of the lefthand side must equal the total of the righthand side of Table 8.4.

Next, imagine constructing a table like Table 8.4 for each employer in the economy, putting sales less intermediate products bought from other firms on the left and costs plus profits less intermediate products bought from other firms on the right. For every employer,

Table 8.4
Value-added and Claims against Output, General Electric Company, 1974

Value-added (millions of dollars)		Claims against output	
Sales:	13,599	Employee compensation	5,223
		Interest and rent	180
Subtract: Intermediate products bought from other firms:	6,696	Profits	1,001
		Depreciation	376
		Indirect business taxes	123
Value-added	6,903	Total	6,903

Source: Moody's.

the total of the left side must equal the total of the right side. Thus, if we add up the total of the lefthand sides for all employers in the economy, the result must equal the total of the righthand sides for all the employers in the economy. But what is the total of the left hand sides for all employers in the economy? It is the sum of value-added for all employers, which, as we saw in a previous section, equals gross national product. And the total of the righthand sides for all employers in the economy is the total of all income paid out (or owed) in the economy—wages, interest, rent, profits—plus indirect business taxes and depreciation. Consequently, gross national product must equal the total of all income paid out (or owed) in the economy plus indirect business taxes and depreciation.

Table 8.5 shows the total amounts of various types of income paid out (or owed) in the American economy during 1975. It also shows depreciation and indirect business taxes. You can see for yourself that the total of these items equals gross national product. Besides helping to prove the point stated at the beginning of this section, this table is an interesting description of the relative importance of various types of income. For example, it shows the great importance of wages and salaries in the total income stream in the United States. In 1975, roughly 60 percent of gross national income was paid out in wages and salaries.

Table 8.5
Gross National Income, United States, 1975

Type of claim on output	Amount of claim (billions of dollars)
Employee compensation	929
Rental income	22
Net interest	75
Income of proprietors and professionals	90
Corporate profits	92
Indirect business taxes	139
Depreciation	161
Statistical discrepancy[a]	8
Gross national income	1,516

[a] This also includes some minor items that need not be of concern here. See the source.
Source: Survey of Current Business, July 1976.

National Income, Personal Income, and Disposable Income

There is more to gross national income than the total amount of income paid out (or owed) by employers (including government). As noted in the previous section, it also includes indirect business taxes and depreciation. We are sometimes interested only in the total amount of income paid out (or owed) by employers, an amount called ***national income.*** Clearly, it is easy to derive national income if you know gross national income. All you have to do is subtract indirect business taxes and depreciation from gross national income. Or putting it another way, all you have to do is subtract indirect business taxes from net national product, since gross national income minus depreciation equals net national product.[6] Table 8.6 shows the result for 1975.

For some purposes, we also need to know how much the people of a nation receive in income. This is ***personal income,*** and it differs from national income in two ways. First, some people who have a claim on income do not actually receive it. For example, although all a firm's profits belong to the owners, not all of its profits are paid out to them. As we saw in

[6] Two other small items must also be taken into account. As shown in Table 8.6, we must subtract *business transfer payments*—pensions and other payments made by firms that are transfer payments—and add *subsidies less surpluses of government enterprises,* which corrects for the fact that some government agencies pay out more to income recipients than they produce in value-added. In addition, of course, there is a statistical discrepancy that must be recognized. It is purely a statistical matter. (Also, there are some miscellaneous items totaling only $4 billion that need not be specified in detail here.)

Table 8.6
Gross National Product, Net National Product, National Income, Personal Income, and Disposable Income, United States, 1975

Measure	Amount (billions of dollars)
Gross national product	1,516
Subtract: Depreciation	161
Net national product	1,355
Subtract: Indirect business taxes	139
Business transfers	6
Statistical discrepancy	4
Add: Subsidies less surpluses of government enterprises	2
National income	1,208
Subtract: Corporate profits	92
Contributions for social insurance	110
Add: Government transfers to persons	169
Dividends	32
Interest paid by government	33
Business transfers	6
Other items	4
Personal income	1,250
Subtract: Personal taxes	169
Disposable personal income	1,081

Source: Survey of Current Business, July 1976.

Chapter 7, part of the profits are plowed back into the business, and part go to the government for corporate income taxes. Also, wage earners do not actually receive the amounts they and their employers pay currently for Social Security. Second, some people receive income that is not obtained in exchange for services rendered. You will recall from an earlier section that government transfer payments are made to welfare recipients, people receiving unemployment compensation or Social Security, and so forth. Also, there are business transfer payments—pensions and other payments made by firms that are not in exchange for current productive services.

If you know national income, it is easy to derive personal income. You begin by subtracting profits from national income and adding dividends to the result. This will correct for the fact that profits not distributed as dividends do not actually enter people's hands. Then you must deduct contributions for social insurance, and add government and business transfer payments. (Note that interest paid by governments on their debt is regarded as a transfer payment, on the grounds that it is not a payment for current goods and services.) These calculations are shown in detail in Table 8.6.

Finally, it is also useful for many purposes to know how much the people of a nation receive in income and get to keep after personal income taxes. This is ***disposable income.*** If you know what personal income is, you can easily obtain disposable income by deducting personal income taxes from personal income, as shown in Table 8.6. Disposable income plays a very important role in subsequent chapters because it has a major influence on how much consumers spend. According to Table 8.6, disposable income equaled about 71 percent of gross national product (gross national income) in 1975.

Measures of National Expenditure

Consumption, Investment, Government Expenditure, and Net Exports

Up to this point, we have been concerned with national output and national income. Now we take up ***national expenditure.*** At the outset, note that if we include business spending for increased inventories as a form of expenditure, *the total amount spent on final goods and services must equal the total value of final goods and services produced.* In other words, *gross national expenditure must equal gross national product,* because all goods produced must either be bought by someone or added to the producer's inventories. In either case, the value of the goods is included in gross national expenditure.

Table 8.7
Expenditure on Final Goods and Services, United States, 1975[a]

Type of Expenditure		Amount (billions of dollars)
Personal consumption		973
Durable goods	132	
Nondurable goods	409	
Services	432	
Gross private domestic investment		184
Expenditures on plant and equipment	147	
Residential structures	51	
Increase in inventories	−15	
Net exports		20
Exports	148	
Imports	128	
Government expenditures		339
Federal	124	
State and local	215	
Gross national product		1,516

[a] Because of rounding errors, figures sometimes do not sum to total.
Source: Survey of Current Business, July 1976.

The total amount spent on final goods and services is generally broken down into four parts, described below.

Consumption. This is the amount spent by households on durable goods, nondurable goods, and services. For example, consumption includes your expenditures on meals and clothing, and your family's expenditures on a car or on an electric washer and dryer. Table 8.7 shows that in 1975 consumption accounted for about 64 percent of the total amount spent on final goods and services in the United States. Expenditure on consumer durable goods is clearly much less than on consumer nondurable goods or services.

Investment. This is the amount spent by firms for new plant and equipment, new housing, and increases in inventories, as well as the amount spent by households for new housing. (One reason why houses are treated as investment goods is that they can be rented out.) Table 8.7 shows that in 1975 investment accounted for about 12 percent of the total amount spent on final goods and services in the United States. This is ***gross investment,*** the gross amount of money spent on new plant, equipment, buildings, and extra inventory, not the net amount. Why? Because during the period in question, some plant, equipment, and so forth wore out: there was depreciation. Thus, to determine ***net investment*** we must deduct depreciation from gross investment. Net investment measures the change (net of depreciation) in the quantity of the nation's capital goods. If net investment is positive, the nation's productive capacity, as gauged by its capital stock, is growing. If net investment is negative, the nation's productive capacity, as gauged by its capital stock, is declining.

Government purchases of goods and services. This includes the expenditures of the federal, state, and local governments for the multitude of functions they perform: defense, education, police protection, and so forth. It does not include transfer payments, since they are not payments for current production. Table 8.7 shows that government spending in 1975 accounted for about 22 percent of the total amount spent on final goods and services in the United States. State and local expenditures are bigger than federal expenditures. As you recall

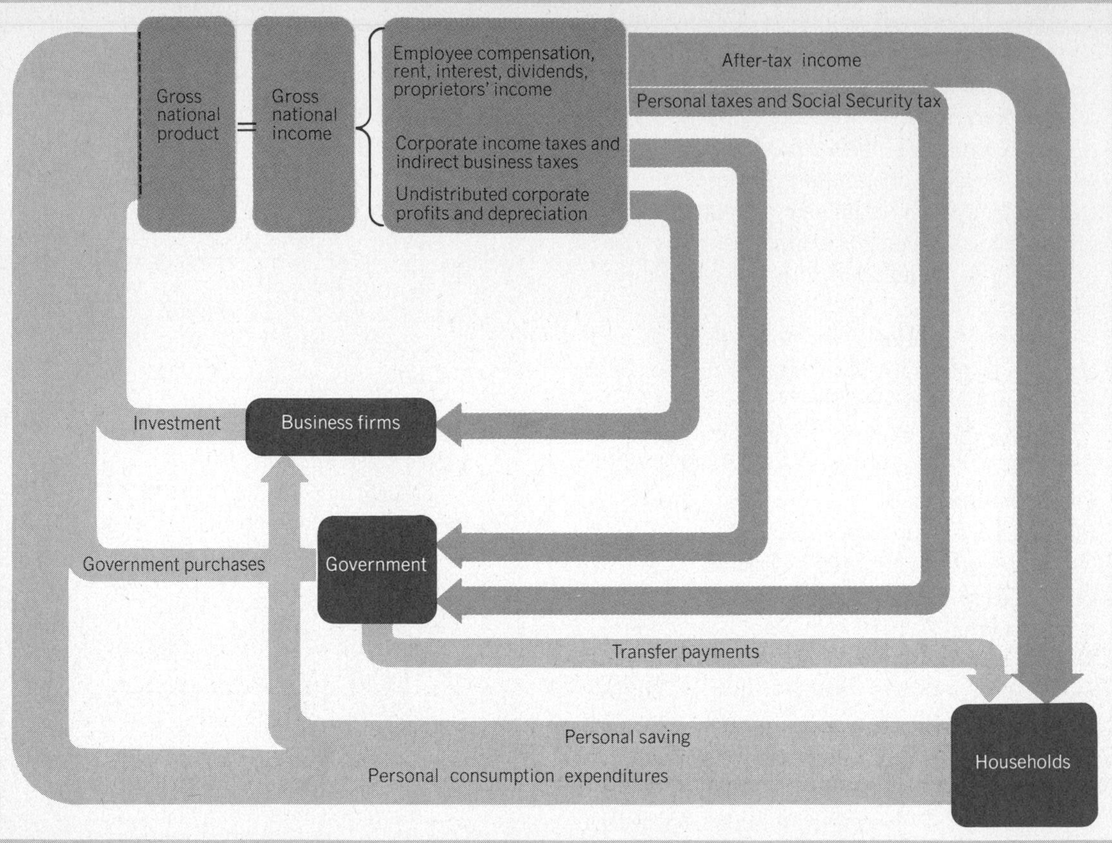

Figure 8.7
Flows of Output, Income, and Expenditures in the National Economy
This diagram shows that (1) gross national income equals GNP; (2) part of gross national income goes to households, part goes to firms, and part goes to government; and (3) households, firms, and government spend these receipts on GNP.

from Chapter 5, many of the expenditures of the federal government are connected with national defense, while at the state and local levels the biggest expenditure is for education.

Net exports of goods and services. This equals the amount spent by foreigners on our goods and services less the amount we spent on other nations' goods and services. Obviously, this factor must be included since some of our national output is destined for foreign markets, and since we import some of the goods and services we consume. There is no reason why this component of spending cannot be negative, since imports can exceed exports. The quantity of net exports tends to be quite small. Table 8.6 shows that net exports in 1975 were equal to about 1 percent of the total amount spent on final goods and services in the United States. Because net exports are so small, we shall generally ignore them until Chapters 31 to 33, when we shall focus attention exclusively on international trade and finance.

Finally, to see how these flows of expenditures are related to the flows of output and income, look carefully at Figure 8.7, which shows diagrammatically the relationships among them. Beginning at the top lefthand side of the figure, we see that gross national income equals GNP. Then moving to the right, we see that part of the gross national income goes to firms, part goes to the government, and the rest goes to households. These receipts are then used by households, firms, and the government to buy the gross national product, as shown on the lefthand side of the figure. (For simplicity, this figure assumes that net exports are zero and that the government has a balanced budget.)

The National Economy: Three Basic Facts

The measures of national output, national income, and national expenditure discussed above are some of the basic figures economists look at when trying to analyze the state of the economy. Using these measures, it is easy to demonstrate the following three facts, each of which will be needed in succeeding chapters. First, *disposable income, although it goes up and down with gross national product, does not fluctuate as much as gross national product.* This is shown in Figure 8.8. As we shall soon see, disposable income has a smoother path because our tax system and our social insurance programs, as well as other mechanisms, tend to dampen the effect of changes in gross national product on disposable income. When total output declines, the amount of after-tax income people receive does not go down so much; and when total output increases, the amount of after-tax income they receive does not go up so much. This, of course, cushions the effect of changes in GNP on people's expenditures.

Second, *consumption expenditure seems to depend closely on—and vary directly with—disposable income.* This observation, shown in Figure 8.9, is neither strange nor surprising. On the contrary, it would be odd if the amounts households spend on goods and services were *not* closely related to their after-tax income, for consumers can do only two things with their after-tax income: spend it or save it.

Third, *investment varies much more than the*

Figure 8.8
Relationship between Disposable Income and Gross National Product, United States, 1929–75
Disposable income, although it goes up and down with gross national product, does not fluctuate as much as GNP. To see this, note that the disposable income curve is smoother than the GNP curve.

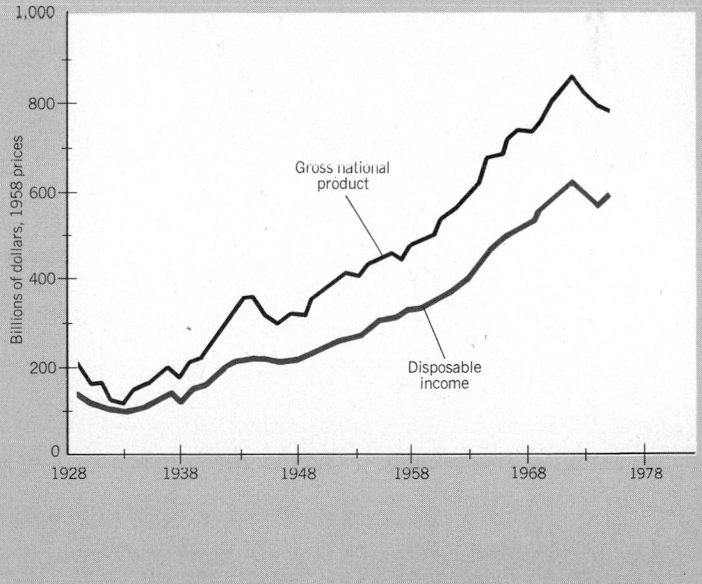

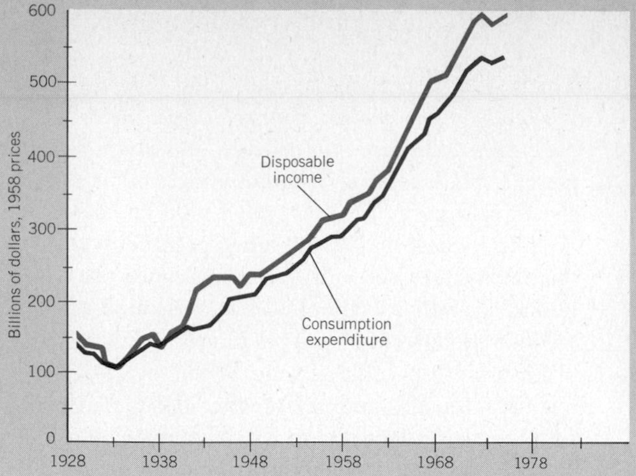

Figure 8.9
Relationship between Consumption and Disposable Income, United States, 1929–75
Consumption expenditure seems to depend closely on, and vary directly with, disposable income.

Figure 8.10
Consumption Expenditure, Gross Private Domestic Investment, and Government Expenditures, United States, 1929–75
Investment varies more than the other components of total spending. Also, because of wars, government spending moves up and down rather erratically.

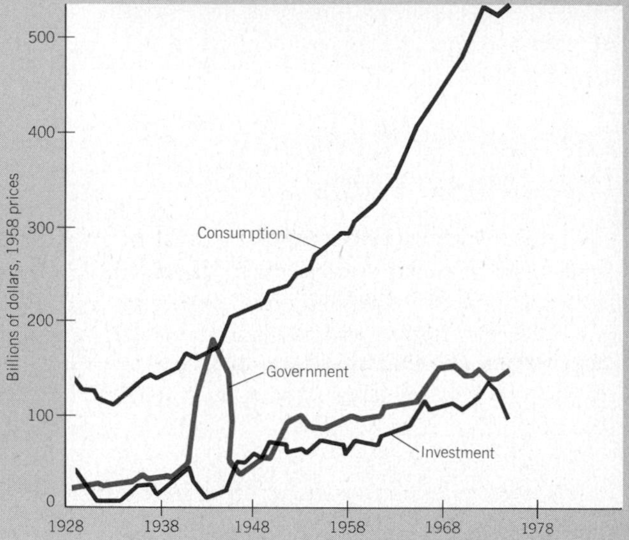

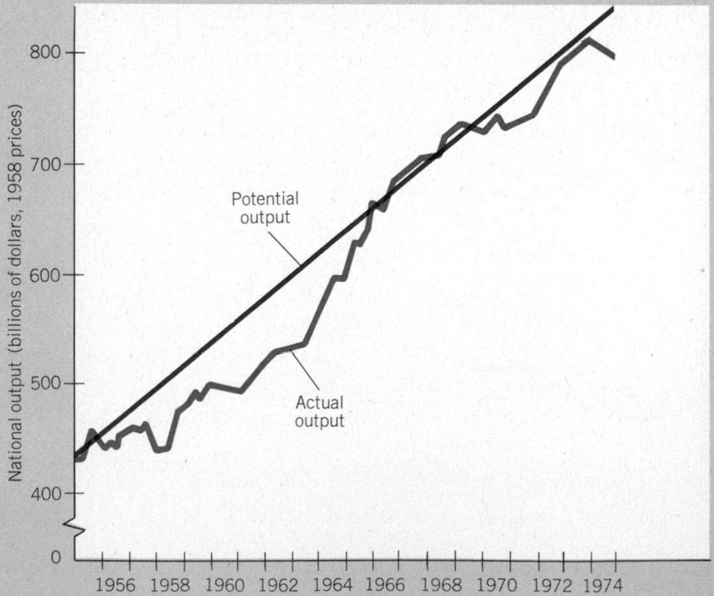

Figure 8.11
Actual and Potential Output, United States, 1955–74
The gap measures what it costs society each year, in output forgone, to tolerate an unemployment rate above 4 percent.

other components of total spending. Figure 8.10 shows that investment goes up and down, while consumption moves along with only slight bumps and dips, and government expenditures do not move up and down very much except when war breaks out.[7] (Note the bulges in government spending during World War II, the Korean War, and the Vietnam War.) The volatility of investment is an important factor in explaining the changes in national output over time. Also, the wartime bulges in government spending have been major causes of changes in national output. We shall have considerably more to say on this score in the next few chapters.

The Gap between Actual and Potential Output

Gross national product is a measure of the value of final goods and services produced in a given period: in other words, GNP measures actual output. Besides being concerned about actual output, economists are also interested in potential output. Specifically, they are interested in estimating how high the gross national product could have been *if the unemployment rate had been quite low, say 4 percent* (which is a common definition of full employment). An economy's potential output is determined by the size of its labor force, the average number of hours a worker is on the job per year, and the average amount of goods and services a worker can produce per hour. The average amount of goods and services a worker can produce per hour depends in turn on the extent and quality of the capital he has to work with, the level of technology, and his skill and schooling.

More specifically, the ***potential GNP*** is estimated by multiplying 96 percent of the labor force times the normal hours of work per year times the average output per man-hour at the relevant time. In the past few years, there has been some criticism of this definition of potential GNP on the grounds that an unemployment rate of 5 percent is a more realistic measure of full employment than 4 percent because there now are more young people, women, and minority workers in the labor force. All of these groups find it relatively difficult to find jobs. Since this debate is unresolved, we shall stick with the conventional definition, but the apparent difficulties in this measure should be noted.

If potential GNP is defined in this way, the gap between actual and potential GNP depends on the difference between the actual unemployment rate and 4 percent. Specifically, the gap will grow larger and larger as the unemployment rate exceeds 4 percent by greater and greater amounts. Figure 8.11 shows the estimated size of the gap between actual and potential GNP from 1955 to 1974. (Note that both actual and potential GNP are expressed in 1958 prices.) This gap is an extremely important measure of what it costs society to tolerate an unemployment rate above 4 percent. Besides the psychic costs of unemployment described in a previous section, society produces less than it could, so that human wants are less effectively fulfilled than they could be.

For example, consider 1975, a recession year when unemployment was about $8\frac{1}{2}$ percent. According to Walter W. Heller, a former chairman of the Council of Economic Advisers, the gap between potential and actual GNP in 1975 was equal to about 12 percent of potential GNP. Although this estimate is very rough, it is accurate enough to suggest the social waste that accompanies large-scale unemployment. Clearly we must learn to curb the forces responsible for such waste. The following chapters will discuss some of the basic fac-

[7] Net exports are excluded from Figure 8.10. They were almost always under $10 billion during this period.

tors that cause excessive unemployment and excessive inflation, as well as various measures that can be taken to combat them.

Summary

Unemployment inflicts enormous social costs. Recognizing this fact, the Congress passed the Employment Act of 1946, which commits the federal government to combat excessive unemployment. Inflation is a general upward movement of prices. Since inflation results in an arbitrary and often inequitable redistribution of income, government policy makers attempt to curb inflation. Unfortunately, there may be an inverse relationship in the short run between the unemployment rate and the rate of inflation, because it is easier for unions and unorganized labor to increase wages and for firms to increase prices when there is little unemployment. What you regard as the optimal combination of unemployment and inflation depends on your political preferences and values. However, the relationship between unemployment and inflation is by no means fixed. In the middle 1970s, this relationship shifted upward, with the result that increased unemployment coexisted with increased inflation, this mixture being called "stagflation."

Besides unemployment and inflation, another very important indicator of the health of any economy is its gross national product, which measures the total value of the final goods and services it produces in a particular period. Since gross national product is affected by the price level, it must be deflated by a price index to correct for price-level changes. Gross national product is the sum of value-added by all industries. Net national product is gross national product minus depreciation. It indicates the value of net output when account is taken of capital used up.

Gross national product equals gross national income. Gross national income equals the sum of the total claims against output, including indirect business taxes and depreciation. National income is the total amount of income paid out (or owed) by employers; personal income is the total amount people actually receive in income; and disposable income is the total amount they get to keep after taxes.

Gross national product also equals gross national expenditure. Gross national expenditure equals the total amount spent on final goods and services, including business spending for increased inventories. The total amount spent on final goods and services is generally broken down into four parts: consumption, investment, government purchases, and net exports.

Based on the official data, investment appears to vary much more over time than other types of expenditure. As we shall see, this volatility is an important clue to the causes of change in national output. Also, there have been large variations in government expenditures associated with wars; these too have caused major changes in national output.

Clearly, one of the major social costs of unemployment is the fact that less goods and services are produced than could be produced with full employment. Estimates have been made of how the gap between actual and potential output is related to the unemployment rate. According to a rough estimate made by Walter Heller, this cost totaled about 12 percent of potential GNP in 1975.

CONCEPTS FOR REVIEW

Frictional unemployment
Structural unemployment
Cyclical unemployment
Gross national product
Intermediate good
Value-added
Current dollars
Constant dollars
Price index
Net national product
Gross national income
Personal income
Transfer payments
Disposable income
Inflation
National income
Consumption
Investment
Net exports

QUESTIONS FOR DISCUSSION AND REVIEW

1. "Unemployed workers make about as much as when they were employed because of unemployment insurance, so the nation need not worry about the unemployed." Specify at least two fundamental errors in this statement.

2. "The Employment Act of 1946 should be amended to include the goal of stabilizing the purchasing power of the dollar as well as the goal of maintaining high-level employment."[8] Comment and evaluate.

3. Suppose that if the unemployment rate in a particular nation is 5 percent, the inflation rate is 6 percent per year. In the short run, the inflation rate goes down by 1 percent if the unemployment rate goes up by 1 percent (so long as the unemployment rate is between 4 and 8 percent). Plot the relationship between inflation and unemployment in this nation on a graph, and discuss the policy choices open to its government in the short run. Can this relationship shift? If so, what effect will this have on the government's policy choices?

4. "Inflation is a necessary cost of economic progress." Comment and evaluate.

5. The following table shows the value of GNP in the nation of Puritania. The figures shown are in millions of 1960 dollars and current dollars. Fill in the blanks.

Year	GNP in millions of 1960 dollars	GNP in millions of current dollars	Price index [current price level / 1960 price level]
1960	1,000	—	1.00
1965	—	1,440	1.20
1970	1,300	—	1.40
1975	1,500	—	1.60
1976	—	2,720	1.70

[8] J. Backman, "The Case against Creeping Inflation," *New York Times Magazine,* May 3, 1959.

6. Given the following data (in millions of dollars) concerning the Puritanian economy in 1974, compute its gross national product and net national product.

Gross private domestic investment	400
Personal consumption expenditure	1,000
Exports	300
Imports	100
Government expenditures	300
Increase in inventories	50
Depreciation	100

7. An economic historian, after careful research, makes the following estimates (in millions of dollars) concerning the Puritanian economy in 1910.

Disposable personal income	400
Business transfer payments	0
Statistical discrepancy	0
Subsidies less surpluses of government agencies	0
Net national product	600
National income	550
Personal income	460

How much were personal income taxes and indirect business taxes in Puritania in 1910?

8. Which of the following items are included in Puritania's gross national income? (a) The income of a lawyer, (b) interest received on government bonds, (c) the value of a housewife's services, (d) the allowance received by a ten-year-old, (e) donations to the Puritanian branch of the Salvation Army, (f) interest on corporate bonds, (g) dividends, (h) Social Security payments made by the Puritanian government, (i) the value of a 20-year-old house that is sold to a new owner, (j) the value of ten shares of U.S. Steel stock sold by one Puritanian citizen to another.

9. According to the September 1932 issue of *Fortune* magazine, "About 1,000,000 out of [New York City's] 3,200,000 working population are unemployed." What effect did this have on the city's population? During the past 30 years, has this experience been repeated? About how many New Yorkers are presently unemployed?

10. Suppose that you were given the job of estimating the gross national product of Monaco. How would you proceed?

9 Consumption, Saving, and Investment

In early 1975, the American economy was in the midst of a severe recession. Gross national product was well below its potential level, and unemployment in May 1975 reached 9 percent, the highest in decades. Early 1973, on the other hand, was a time of economic boom. GNP was moving ahead rapidly, and the unemployment rate was receding to less than 5 percent. Why the pronounced difference between these two periods? To answer this question, as well as to understand the causes of severe unemployment and inflation, and what can be done to avoid these problems, we must understand how the level of a nation's output is determined.

In this chapter, we take up some important elements of the modern theory of output and employment. To begin with, we describe the classical and Marxian views of unemployment, and Keynes's objections to these views. Then we discuss the determinants of consumption expenditure and investment. In the following chapter, we show how these elements are combined to form a model of the determination of national output—a model that lies at the heart of modern economics.

Theories of Unemployment

The Classical View of Unemployment

Until the 1930s, most economists were convinced that the price system, left to its own devices, would hold unemployment to a reasonable minimum. Thus most of the great names of economics in the nineteenth and early twentieth centuries—including John Stuart Mill, Alfred Marshall, and A. C. Pigou[1]—felt that there was no need for government intervention to promote a high level of employment. To be sure, they recognized that unemployment was sometimes large, but they regarded these lapses from high employment as temporary aberrations that the price system would cure automatically. We begin by taking an initial, brief look at why the classical economists felt this was true. (More will be said concerning their theories below and in later chapters.)

The classical economists recognized the fact, cited in the previous chapter, that the level of total spending determines the unemployment rate. They believed that total spending was unlikely to be too small to purchase the full-employment level of output, because of ***Say's Law*** (named after the nineteenth-century French economist, J. B. Say). According to this law, the production of a certain amount of goods and services results in the generation of an amount of income precisely sufficient to buy that output. (Recall the circular flow discussed in Chapters 4 and 8). In other words, *supply creates its own demand, since the total amount paid out by the producers of the goods and services to resource owners must equal the value of the goods and services. Thus, if this amount is spent, it must be sufficient to purchase all of the goods and services that are produced.*

But what if resource owners do not spend all of their income, but save some of it instead? How then will the necessary spending arise to take all of the output off the market? The answer the classical economists offered is that each dollar saved will be invested. Therefore, investment (made largely by business firms) will restore to the spending stream what resource owners take out through the saving process. Recall that the economist's definition of investment is different from the one often used in common parlance. To the economist, investment means expenditure on plant, equipment, and other productive assets. The classical economists believed that the amount invested would automatically equal the amount saved because the interest rate—the price paid for the use of money—would fluctuate in such a way as to maintain equality between them. In other words, there is a market for loanable funds, and the interest rate will vary so that the quantity of funds supplied equals the quantity demanded. Thus, since funds are demanded to be used—that is, invested—the amount saved will be invested.

Further, the classical economists said that the amount of goods and services businessmen can sell depends upon the prices businessmen charge, as well as on total spending. For example, $1 million in spending will take 200 cars off the market if the price is $5,000 per car, and 400 cars off the market if the price is $2,500 per car. Recognizing this, the classical economists argued that firms would cut prices to sell

[1] The ideas of John Stuart Mill (1806-73) and his arguments in support of individual freedom are particularly famous. He was one of the great philosophers of the nineteenth century. He was also a great economist; his *Principles of Political Economy* (1848) is his best-known work. He advocated many social reforms, including shorter working hours and tax reform.

Alfred Marshall (1842-1924) played an important role in the construction of the theories of supply and demand, the use of partial equilibrium techniques, and other major developments in economics. His *Principles of Economics* (1890), which had eight editions, was a leading economics text for many years.

A. C. Pigou (1877-1959) a student of Marshall, was professor of economics at Cambridge University from 1908 to 1943. His *Economics of Welfare* (1932) was a pathbreaking work that dealt in an important way with various aspects of welfare economics.

their output. Competition among firms would prod them to reduce their prices in this way, with the result that the high-employment level of output would be taken off the market.

Looking at this process more closely, it is obvious that the prices of resources must also be reduced under such circumstances. Otherwise firms would incur losses because they would be getting less for their product, but paying no less for resources. The classical economists believed that it was realistic to expect the prices of resources to decline in such a situation. Indeed they were quite willing to assume that the wage rate—the price of labor—would be flexible in this way. They expected this flexibility because of competition among laborers. Through the processes of competition, they felt that wage rates would be bid down to the level where everyone who really wanted to work could get a job.

The Views of Karl Marx

Quite a different view of unemployment was held by Karl Marx (1818-83), the intellectual father of communism. A man of unquestioned genius, he became an object of quasi-religious devotion to a large part of the world and a hated (and sometimes feared) revolutionary figure to another large part of the world. Because Marx the revolutionary has had such an enormous effect on modern history, it is difficult to discuss Marx the economist. But he was a very profound and influential economist. A meticulous German scholar who spent much of his life in poverty-ridden circumstances in Britain, he wrote a huge, four-volume work on economics, *Das Kapital.*[2] Eighteen years in the making, it remains one of the most influential books ever written.

To understand Marx, we need to know something about the times in which he lived. The period was characterized by revolutionary pressures against the ruling classes. In most of the countries of Europe, there was little democracy, as we know it. The masses participated little, if at all, in the world of political affairs, and very fully in the world of drudgery. For example, at one factory in Manchester, England, in 1862, people worked an average of about 80 hours per week. For these incredibly long hours of toil, the workers generally received small wages. They often could do little more than feed and clothe themselves. Given the circumstances of the times, it is little wonder that revolutionary pressures were manifest.

Marx, viewing the economic system of his day, believed that capitalism was doomed to collapse. He believed that the workers were exploited by the capitalists—the owners of factories, mines, and other types of capital. And he believed that the capitalists, by introducing new labor-saving technology, would throw more and more workers into unemployment. This army of unemployed workers, by competing for jobs, would keep wages at a subsistence level. As machinery was substituted for labor, Marx felt that profits would fall. Unemployment would become more severe. Big firms would absorb small ones. Eventually the capitalistic system was bound to collapse.

To get the flavor of his reasoning and emotions, consider the following passage from *Das Kapital,* a famous passage describing his vision of the death knell of the capitalist system:

> Along with the constantly diminishing number of the magnates of capital, who usurp and monopolize all advantages of this process of transformation, grows the mass of misery, oppression, slavery, degradation, exploitation; but with this too grows the revolt of the working-class, a class always increasing in numbers, and disciplined, united, organized by the very mechanism of the process of capitalist production itself . . . Centralization of the means of production and socialization of labor at last reach a point where they become incompatible with their capitalist integument. This integument bursts asunder. The knell of capitalist private property sounds. The expropriators are expropriated.[3]

[2] Karl Marx, *Das Kapital,* New York: Modern Library, 1906.

[3] Karl Marx, *Das Kapital,* pp. 836-37.

According to Marx, the inevitable successor to capitalism would be socialism, an economic system with no private property. Instead, property would be owned by society as a whole. Socialism, constituting a "dictatorship of the proletariat," would be only a transitional step to the promised land of communism. Marx did not spell out the characteristics of communism in detail. He was sure that it would be a classless society where everyone worked and no one owned capital, and he was sure that the state would "wither away," but he did not attempt to go much beyond this in his blueprint for communism. In Chapter 35, we shall discuss Marx's doctrines, and their limitations, in detail. The important point here is that, although the classical view (discussed in the previous section) was the dominant one, it did not go unchallenged, even in the nineteenth century.

John Maynard Keynes and the Great Depression

The man who was responsible for much of the modern theory of the determination of national product was John Maynard Keynes (1883-1946). Son of a British economist who was justly famous in his own right, Keynes was enormously successful in a variety of fields. He published a brilliant book on the theory of probability while still a relatively young man. Working for a half-hour in bed each morning, he made millions of dollars as a stock market speculator. He was a distinguished patron of the arts and a member of the Bloomsbury set, a group of London intellectuals who were the intellectual pace-setters for British society. He was a faculty member at Cambridge University, and a key figure at the British Treasury. In short, he was an extraordinarily gifted and accomplished man.

Keynes lived and worked almost a century after Marx. His world was quite different from Marx's world; and Keynes himself—polished, successful, a member of the elite—was quite different from the poverty-stricken, revolutionary Marx. But the two great economists were linked in at least one important respect: both were preoccupied with unemployment and the future of the capitalistic system. As we saw in the previous section, Marx predicted that unemployment would get worse and worse, until at last the capitalist system would collapse. In the 1930s, when Keynes was at the height of his influence, the Great Depression seemed to many people to be proving Marx right.

In 1936, while the world was still in the throes of this economic disaster, Keynes published his masterpiece, *The General Theory of Employment, Interest, and Money.*[4] His purpose in this book was to explain how the capitalist economic system could get stalled in the sort of depressed state of equilibrium that existed in the 1930s. He also tried to indicate how governments might help to solve the problem. Contrary to the classical economists, Keynes concluded that no automatic mechanism in a capitalistic society would generate a high level of employment—or, at least, would generate it quickly enough to be relied on in practice. Instead, the equilibrium level of national output might for a long time be below the level required to achieve high employment. His reasons for believing that this could be the case are discussed in detail in this and subsequent chapters.

To push the economy toward a higher level of employment, Keynes advocated the conscious, forceful use of the government's power to spend and tax. As we shall see in Chapter 11, many years passed before these powers became accepted tools of national economic policy, but it was Keynes who provided much of the intellectual stimulus. And in so doing, he helped

[4] John Maynard Keynes, *The General Theory of Employment, Interest, and Money,* New York: Harcourt, Brace, 1936.

falsify the predictions of Marx. Keynes and his many followers showed how severe unemployment could be tamed, and how a capitalistic economy could be managed to avoid the sorts of debacles Marx predicted. It is no exaggeration to say that Keynes made a major contribution to saving the capitalist system.

Flaws in the Classical View

There were at least two basic flaws in the classical model, as Keynes and his followers pointed out. First, *there is no assurance that desired saving will equal desired investment at a level insuring high employment.* The people and firms who save are often not the same as the people and firms who invest, and they often have quite different motivations. In particular, a considerable amount of saving is done by families who want to put something aside for a rainy day or for a car or appliance. On the other hand, a considerable amount of investment is done by firms that are interested in increasing their profits by expanding their plants or by installing new equipment. Desired saving may not equal desired investment at a level insuring high employment. Instead, they may be equal at a level corresponding to considerable unemployment (or to considerable inflation). Thus a purely capitalist economic system, in the absence of appropriate government policies, has no dependable rudder to keep it clear of the shoals of serious unemployment or of serious inflation.

Second, *Keynes and his followers pointed out the unreality of the classical economists' assumption that prices and wages are flexible.* Contrary to the classical economists' argument, the modern economy contains many departures from perfect competition that are barriers to downward flexibility of prices and wages. In particular, many important industries are dominated by a few producers who try hard to avoid cutting price. Even in the face of a considerable drop in demand, such industries have sometimes maintained extraordinarily stable prices. Moreover, the labor unions fight tooth and nail to avoid wage cuts. In view of these facts of life, the classical assumption of wage and price flexibility seems unrealistic indeed. And it seems unlikely that price and wage reductions can be depended on to maintain full employment.

The Great Depression of the 1930s struck a severe blow against the classical view. When it continued for years, and millions and millions of people continued to be unemployed, it became increasingly difficult to accept the idea that unemployment was only a temporary aberration that the market economy would cure automatically in a reasonable length of time. Nonetheless, the diehard followers of the classical economists did not change their tune. They claimed that the economy would get back to high employment if the labor unions would allow more wage flexibility, if the big corporations would allow more price flexibility, and if President Franklin D. Roosevelt and his New Dealers would quit interfering with free markets.

Finally, when Keynes's *General Theory* appeared in 1936, it seemed to offer a more satisfactory model, even though, at first, only a minority of the economics profession was converted to the Keynesian view. Within 10 or 15 years of its publication, most economists were convinced that Keynes's theory was essentially sound; and his ideas now are generally accepted, although they have been refined and extended by his followers. Whether Republican or Democrat, any modern economist relies heavily on Keynesian ideas and concepts. But, of course, not all economists share Keynes's views on proper public policy. Moreover, as we shall see in subsequent chapters, under certain circumstances, more complicated models are likely to outperform the simple Keynesian model presented in this and the following chapters.

The Consumption Function: A Major Element of the Modern Theory

Keynes's *General Theory of Employment, Interest, and Money* is impenetrable for the general reader. Even among professional economists, it is not noted for its lucidity or liveliness. But the basic ideas that Keynes presented–and that subsequent economists have refined, extended, and reworked–are really quite simple. In the remainder of this chapter, we shall describe several of the most important elements of the modern theory of the determination of national output. The first such element to be discussed is the ***consumption function,*** *which is the relationship between consumption spending and disposable income.* Keynes emphasized that *consumption expenditures–whether those of a single household or the total consumption expenditures in the entire economy–are influenced heavily by income.* For individual households, Figure 9.1 shows that families with higher incomes spend more on consumption than families with lower incomes. Of course, individual families vary a good deal in their behavior; some spend more than others even if their incomes are the same. But, on the average, a family's consumption expenditure is tied very closely to its income.

What is true for individual families also holds for the entire economy: total consumption expenditures are closely related to disposable income. This fact, noted in the previous chapter, is shown in detail in Figure 9.2, a "scatter diagram" that plots total consumption expenditure in each year (from 1929 to 1974) against disposable income in the same year (from 1929 to 1974). The points fall very near the straight line drawn in Figure 9.2, but not right on it. For most practical purposes, however, we can regard the line drawn in Figure 9.2 as representing the relationship between total consumption expenditures and disposable income. In other words, we can regard this line as the consumption function.

The consumption function, the importance of which was stressed by John Maynard

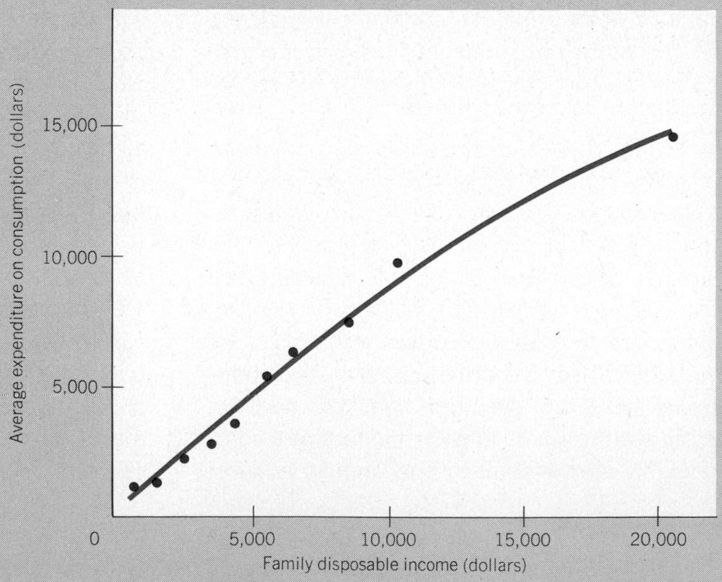

Figure 9.1
Relation between Family Expenditures on Consumption and Family Disposable Income, United States
Families with higher incomes spend more on consumption than families with lower incomes.

Figure 9.2
Relationship between Consumption Expenditure and Disposable Income, United States, 1929–74
There is a very close relationship between consumption expenditure and disposable income in the United States. In this figure a dot is given for each year. The dot's horizontal distance from the origin measures the disposable income that year, and its vertical position from the origin measures the consumption expenditure that year. As you can see, the dots generally are very close to the line.

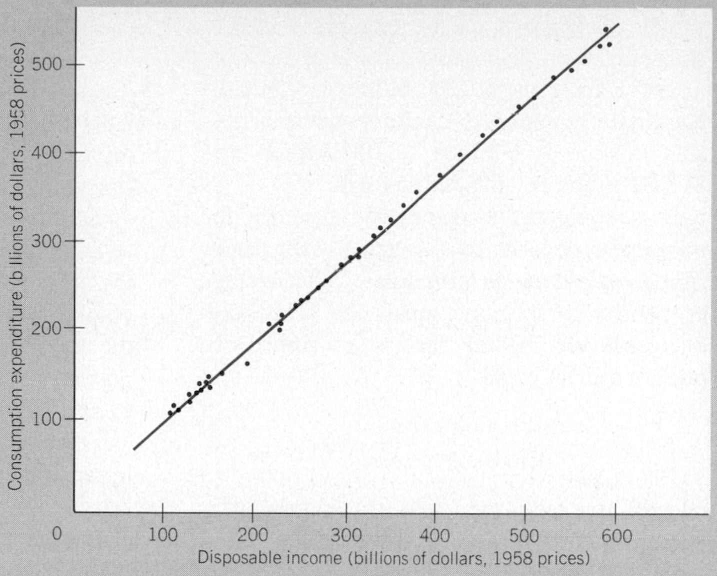

Keynes, is at the heart of the modern theory of the determination of national output. It is a working tool that is used widely and often by economists to analyze and forecast the behavior of the economy. There have been many statistical studies of the consumption function. Some of these studies have been based on cross-section data—comparisons of the amount spent on consumption by families at various income levels. (Figure 9.1 is based on cross-section data.) Others have been based on time-series data—comparisons of the total amount spent on consumption in the economy with total income over various periods of time. (Figure 9.2 is based on time-series data.)

The Marginal Propensity to Consume

Suppose that we know what the consumption function for a given society looks like at a particular point in time. For example, suppose that it is given by the figures for disposable income and consumption expenditure in the first two columns of Table 9.1. Based on our knowledge of the consumption function, we can determine the *extra* amount families will spend on consumption if they receive an *extra* dollar of disposable income. *This amount—the fraction of an extra dollar of income that is spent on consumption—is called the* ***marginal propensity to consume.*** For reasons discussed in subsequent sections of this chapter, the marginal propensity to consume, shown in column 4 of Table 9.1, plays a major role in the modern theory of national output determination.

To make sure that you understand exactly what the marginal propensity to consume is, consult Table 9.1. What is the marginal propensity to consume when disposable income is between $1,000 billion and $1,050 billion? The second column shows that, when income rises from $1,000 billion to $1,050 billion, consumption rises from $950 billion to $980 billion. Consequently, the fraction of the extra $50 billion of income that is consumed is $30 billion ÷ $50 billion, or 0.60. Thus, the marginal propensity to consume is 0.60.[5] Based on

[5] Students with some knowledge of mathematics will recognize that this is an approximation since $50 billion is a substantial change in income, whereas the marginal propensity to consume pertains to a small change in income. But this is an innocuous simplification. Similar simplifications are made below.

similar calculations, the marginal propensity to consume when disposable income is between \$1,050 billion and \$1,100 billion is 0.60; the marginal propensity to consume when disposable income is between \$1,100 billion and \$1,150 billion is 0.60; and so forth.

It is important to distinguish between the marginal propensity to consume and the ***average propensity to consume.*** The average propensity to consume equals the proportion of disposable income that is consumed. In other words, it equals

$$\frac{\text{consumption expenditure}}{\text{disposable income}}$$

Clearly, this will not in general equal the marginal propensity to consume, which is

$$\frac{\text{change in consumption expenditure}}{\text{change in disposable income}}$$

The point is that the marginal propensity to consume is the proportion of *extra* income consumed, and this proportion generally is quite different from the proportion of *total* income consumed. For example, in Table 9.1, the average propensity to consume when disposable income is \$1,100 billion is 0.92; but the marginal propensity to consume when disposable income is between \$1,050 billion and \$1,100 billion is 0.60.

The marginal propensity to consume can be interpreted geometrically as the slope of the consumption function. The slope of any line is, of course, the ratio of the vertical change to the

Table 9.1
The Consumption Function

Disposable income (billions of dollars)	Consumption expenditure (billions of dollars)	Average propensity to consume	Marginal propensity to consume	Saving (billions of dollars)	Marginal propensity to save
1,000	950	.95		50	
			$\frac{30}{50}$ = .60		$\frac{20}{50}$ = .40
1,050	980	.93		70	
			$\frac{30}{50}$ = .60		$\frac{20}{50}$ = .40
1,100	1,010	.92		90	
			$\frac{30}{50}$ = .60		$\frac{20}{50}$ = .40
1,150	1,040	.90		110	
			$\frac{30}{50}$ = .60		$\frac{20}{50}$ = .40
1,200	1,070	.89		130	
			$\frac{30}{50}$ = .60		$\frac{20}{50}$ = .40
1,250	1,100	.88		150	
			$\frac{30}{50}$ = .60		$\frac{20}{50}$ = .40
1,300	1,130	.87		170	

horizontal change when a small movement occurs along the line. As shown in Figure 9.3, the vertical change is the change in consumption expenditure, and the horizontal change is the change in disposable income. Thus the ratio of the vertical change to the horizontal change must equal the marginal propensity to consume.

In general, the marginal propensity to consume can differ, depending on the level of disposable income. For example, the marginal propensity to consume may be higher at lower levels than at higher levels of disposable income. Only if the consumption function is a straight line, as in Figure 9.2 and Table 9.1, will the marginal propensity to consume be the same at all levels of income. For simplicity, we assume in much of the subsequent analysis that the consumption function is a straight line, but this assumption can easily be relaxed without affecting the essential aspects of our conclusions.

The Saving Function and the Marginal Propensity to Save

If people don't devote their disposable income to consumption expenditure, what else can they do with it? Of course, they can save it. When families refrain from spending their income on consumption goods and services—that is, when they forgo present consumption to provide for larger consumption in the future—they save. Thus we can derive from the consumption function the total amount people will save at each level of disposable income. All we have to do is subtract the total consumption expenditure at each level of disposable income from disposable income. The difference is the total amount of saving at each level of disposable income. This difference is shown in the next to last column of Table 9.1. We can plot the total amount of saving against disposable income, as in Figure 9.4. The resulting rela-

Figure 9.3
The Marginal Propensity to Consume, Interpreted Geometrically as the Slope of the Consumption Function
The slope of the consumption function between points *A* and *B* equals the vertical change (which is the change in consumption expenditure) divided by the horizontal change (which is the change in disposable income). Since the marginal propensity to consume equals the change in consumption expenditure divided by the change in disposable income, it follows that the slope equals the marginal propensity to consume.

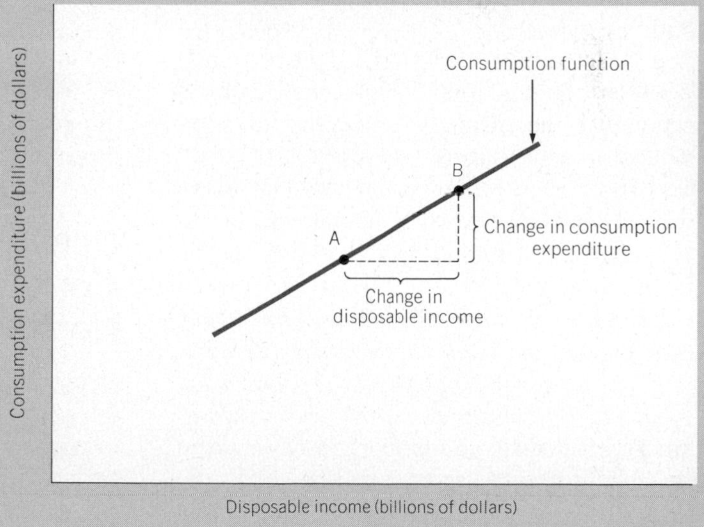

Figure 9.4
The Saving Function
The saving function describes the total amount of saving at each level of disposable income. The slope of the saving function equals the change in saving divided by the change in disposable income. Thus, the slope of the saving function equals the marginal propensity to save.

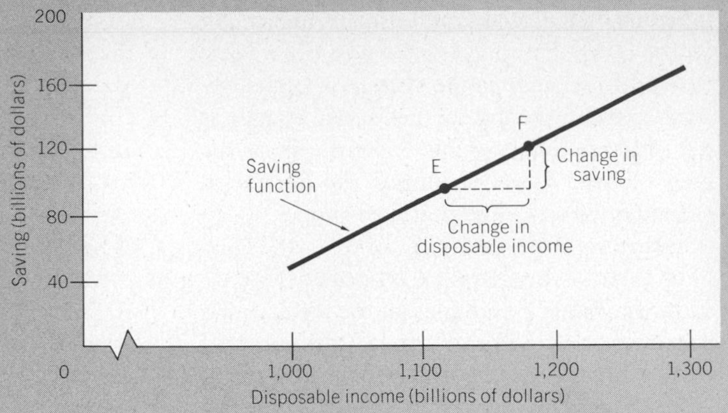

tionship between total saving and disposable income is called the ***saving function.*** Like the consumption function, it plays a major role in the modern theory of national output determination.

If we know the saving function, we can calculate the marginal propensity to save at any level of disposable income. The ***marginal propensity to save*** *is the proportion of an extra dollar of disposable income that is saved.* To see how to calculate it, consult Table 9.1 again. The fifth column shows that, when income rises from \$1,000 billion to \$1,050 billion, saving rises from \$50 billion to \$70 billion. Consequently, the fraction of the extra \$50 billion of income that is saved is \$20 billion ÷ \$50 billion, or 0.40. Thus the marginal propensity to save is 0.40. Similar calculations show that the marginal propensity to save when disposable income is between \$1,050 billion and \$1,100 billion is 0.40; the marginal propensity to save when disposable income is between \$1,100 billion and \$1,150 billion is 0.40; and so forth.

Note that, *at any particular level of disposable income, the marginal propensity to save plus the marginal propensity to consume must equal one.* By definition, the marginal propensity to save equals the proportion of an extra dollar of disposable income that is saved, and the marginal propensity to consume equals the proportion of an extra dollar of income that is consumed. The sum of these two proportions must equal one, for, as stated above, the only things that people can do with an extra dollar of disposable income are consume it or save it. Table 9.1 shows this fact quite clearly.

Finally, it is worth noting that the marginal propensity to save equals the slope of the saving function—just as the marginal propensity to consume equals the slope of the consumption function. As pointed out above, the slope of a line equals the vertical distance between any two points on the line divided by the horizontal distance between them. Since (as shown in Figure 9.4) the vertical distance is the change in saving and the horizontal distance is the change in disposable income, the slope of the saving function must equal the marginal propensity to save.

Determinants of Consumption and Saving: Nonincome Factors

In previous sections, we have been concerned solely with the effect of changes in disposable income on total consumption expenditure and saving. It is important to recognize that many other factors besides disposable income also have an effect on total consumption expenditure and saving. Holding disposable income constant, total consumption expenditure is likely to vary with the amount of wealth in the hands of the public, the ease and cheapness with which consumers can borrow money, the expectations of the public, the amount of durable goods on hand, the income distribution, and the size of the population. In this section, we discuss the effects of these nonincome factors on consumption and saving.

Amount of wealth. Holding disposable income constant, it is clear that total consumption expenditure will be higher if the public has a large amount of wealth—stocks, bonds, savings accounts, and so on—than if it has a small amount. Why? Because people are more willing to spend out of current income when they have large assets to tide them over if their incomes fall. Thus, if the Merriwether family has $100,000 in stocks and bonds, it is more likely to spend a large percentage of its income than if it has little or nothing in wealth.

Ease and cheapness of borrowing. Holding disposable income constant, it is clear that total consumption expenditure will be higher if the public can borrow money easily and cheaply. This is particularly important for expenditures on consumer durables like automobiles and appliances. If required down payments are increased, and interest rates go up, some potential buyers will be persuaded (or forced) to postpone purchases of such items. For example, the Merriwethers may want a new car, and they may be quite willing to borrow the money to pay for it at 10 percent per year. But if the interest rate is raised to 15 percent per year, they may decide to stick with their old car until it is run into the ground.

Expectations. Holding disposable income constant, total consumption expenditure may be higher if the public feels that price increases are in the wind or that goods will become harder to get. Why? Because the public may want to stock up on goods before their prices rise and while they are still available. (In recent years, the expectation of price rises with regard to such items as autos and sugar seems to have had such an effect.) On the other hand, the expectation of price increases may have the opposite effect if the public is alarmed by the inflation, and wants to build up its savings to cushion it against hard times ahead. Recent experience, according to the Council of Economic Advisers, seems to indicate that consumers react to heightened inflationary expectations of this sort by cutting back their consumption expenditures.

Amount of durable goods on hand. Holding disposable income constant, total consumption expenditure may be higher if the public has few durable goods on hand. For example, during World War II, very few automobiles were produced for ordinary civilian purposes. When such goods became available once again immediately after the war, there was an increase in the proportion of disposable income spent on durable goods, particularly since the public came out of the war with considerable savings and liquid assets. More will be said about this in the next chapter.

Distribution of income. Holding disposable income constant, total consumption expenditure would be expected to increase as a nation's income becomes more nearly equally distributed. Why? Because one would expect that the marginal propensity to consume would be higher (and the marginal propensity to save would be lower) among poor families than among rich ones. Thus, if a dollar of income is transferred from a rich family to a poor one, the poor family would be expected to save a smaller proportion of this extra dollar than the rich family from whom it was taken. Consequently, total consumption expenditure would be expected to increase as a result of transfers of income of this sort.

Size of population. Holding disposable income constant, total consumption expenditure would be expected to increase as a nation's population increases. As there are more and more mouths to feed, bodies to clothe, and families to house, one would expect that more would be spent on consumption goods, and less would be saved.

Shifts in the Consumption and Saving Functions

Suppose that a change occurs in one of the factors discussed in the previous section. For example, suppose that there is a marked increase in the amount of wealth in the hands of the public. What effect will this have on the consumption function? Obviously, it will shift the consumption function upward, as from position 1 to position 2 in panel A of Figure 9.5. Or suppose that it becomes more difficult and expensive for consumers to borrow money. What effect will this have on the consumption function? Obviously, it will shift the consumption function downward, as from position 1 to position 3 in panel A of Figure 9.5.

It is important to distinguish between a *shift* in the consumption function and a *movement along* a given consumption function. A shift in the consumption function means that the public wants to spend a different amount on consumption goods out of a given amount of disposable income than in the past. Thus, if the consumption function shifts to position 2 in panel A of Figure 9.5, this means that the public wants to spend more on consumption goods out of a given amount of disposable income than when the consumption function was at position 1. And if the consumption function shifts to position 3 in panel A of Figure 9.5, this means that the public wants to spend less on consumption goods out of a given amount of disposable income than when the consumption function was at position 1.

In contrast, a movement along a given consumption function is a change in total consumption expenditure induced by a change in disposable income, with no change in the relationship between total consumption expenditure and disposable income. For example, the movement from point A to point B is a movement along a consumption function (in position 1). Similarly, the movement from point C to point D is a movement along a consumption function (in position 2). As we shall see in the next chapter, this distinction between a shift in the consumption function and a movement along a consumption function is important in many aspects of the theory of output and employment.

Note too that an *upward* shift in the consumption function must be accompanied by a *downward* shift in the saving function. If the public wants to spend *more* on consumption goods out of a given amount of disposable income, it must want to save *less* out of that amount of disposable income. (Why? Because consumption expenditure plus saving equals disposable income). Thus, if the consumption function shifts upward from position 1 to position 2 in panel A of Figure 9.5, the saving function must shift downward from position 4 to position 5 in panel B of Figure 9.5.

Also, a *downward* shift in the consumption function must be accompanied by an *upward* shift in the saving function. If the public wants to spend *less* on consumption goods out of a given amount of disposable income, it must want to save *more* out of that amount of disposable income. (Why? Because consumption expenditure plus saving equals disposable income.) Thus, if the consumption function shifts downward from position 1 to position 3 in panel A of Figure 9.5, the saving function must shift upward from position 4 to position 6 in panel B of Figure 9.5.

The Permanent-Income and Life-Cycle Hypotheses

The consumption function, as described in

Figure 9.5
Shifts in Consumption and Saving Functions
If the consumption function moves from position 1 to position 2 (or position 3), this is a *shift* in the consumption function. A movement from *A* to *B* (or from *C* to *D*) is a *movement along* a given consumption function.

An *upward* shift in the consumption function (as from position 1 to position 2 in panel A) is accompanied by a *downward* shift in the saving function (from position 4 to position 5 in panel B). A *downward* shift in the consumption function (as from position 1 to position 3 in panel A) is accompanied by an *upward* shift in the saving function (from position 4 to position 6 in panel B).

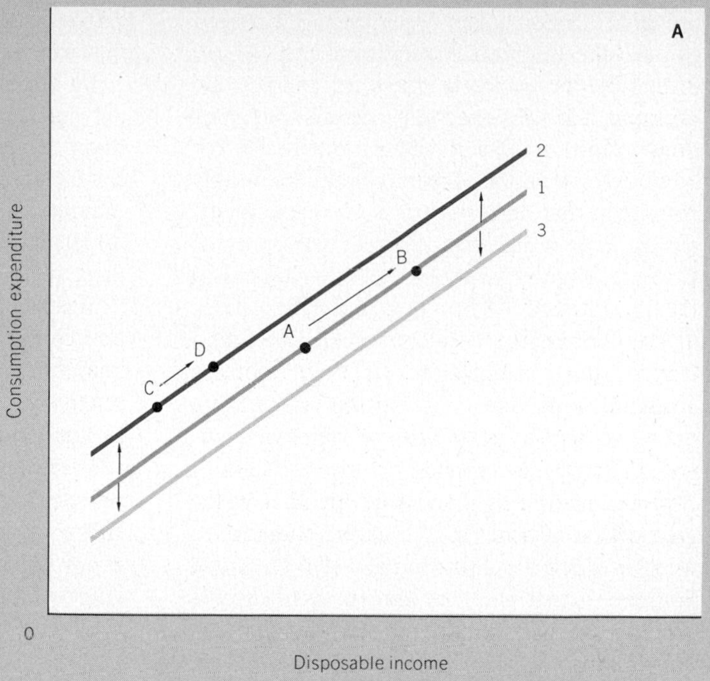

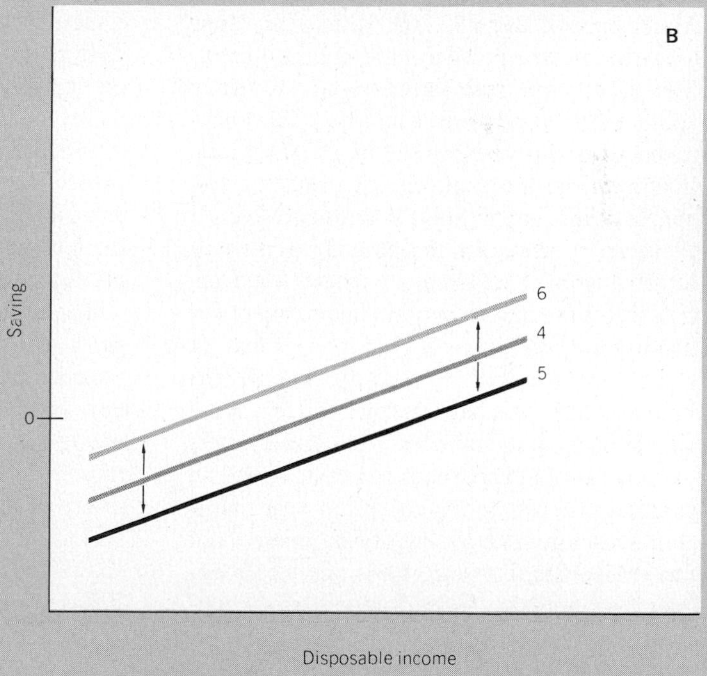

previous sections, is a relationship between *current* consumption expenditure and *current* disposable income. In Figures 9.1 and 9.2, for example, it is presumed that current consumption expenditure in a given period, whether for a family or a nation, depends upon disposable income in that same period. Some economists, led by Milton Friedman of the University of Chicago, Franco Modigliani of the Massachusetts Institute of Technology, and Albert Ando of the University of Pennsylvania, have challenged this presumption. In their view, a household's current consumption expenditure does not depend upon current disposable income; instead, it depends on the household's expected stream of disposable income over a long period of time (as well as the household's wealth, which we discussed above). Thus two households that have the same current disposable income may spend quite different amounts on consumption goods, if their expected income streams over the long term are quite different.

To illustrate what these economists mean, consider two hypothetical families: the Smiths and the Does. Although both Mr. Smith and Mr. Doe will earn $12,000 this year, their long-run income prospects are quite different. Mr. Smith is a businessman who ordinarily makes $50,000 per year, but whose income is much lower this year because of a foolish decision by one of his employees that caused a sizable one-time loss to Smith's firm. Based on all available evidence, Smith's annual income will return to about $50,000 in the future. Mr. Doe, on the other hand, has been unemployed for many years, and there is no prospect that he will return to work. His $12,000 income this year was due to his having won a lottery. What Friedman, Modigliani, and Ando are saying is that one would expect each family to spend an amount on consumption goods this year that is commensurate with its long-term income, not just its income this year. Thus one would expect the Smiths to spend a lot more on consumption goods than the Does, even though their current incomes are the same.

Although Friedman's theory (often called the permanent-income hypothesis) differs in many respects from the Modigliani-Ando theory (often called the life-cycle hypothesis), the differences need not concern us here. What is important for present purposes is that both of these theories predict that a transitory change in income may not have much impact on a household's consumption expenditure, if the household's long-run income prospects remain relatively unaffected. In contrast, the basic Keynesian consumption function assumes that consumption expenditure is dependent on current disposable income. To keep the analysis as simple as possible, we shall use the basic Keynesian consumption function in subsequent chapters; but the fact that it is a simplification should be recognized.

Determinants of Investment

In the previous chapter, we stressed that investment consists largely of the amount firms spend on new buildings and factories, new equipment, and increases in inventory. Investment plays a central role in the modern theory of output and employment. To understand this theory, it is essential that you understand the factors determining the level of net investment (which is gross investment less depreciation). Basically, there are two broad determinants of the level of net investment—the expected rate of return from capital, and the interest rate.

The ***expected rate of return from capital*** is the perceived rate of return that businessmen believe they can obtain if they put up new buildings or factories, add new equipment, or increase their inventories. Each of these forms of investment requires the expenditure of money. The rate of return measures the profitability of such an expenditure; it shows the annual profits to be obtained per dollar invested. Thus a rate of return of 10 percent means that, for every dollar invested, an annual profit of 10 cents is obtained. Clearly, the higher the expected rate of return from a particular investment, the more profitable the investment is expected to be.

The ***interest rate*** is the cost of borrowing money. More specifically, it is the annual amount that a borrower must pay for the use of a dollar for a year. Thus, if the interest rate is 8 percent, a borrower must pay 8 cents per year for the use of a dollar. And if the interest rate is 12 percent, a borrower must pay 12 cents per year for the use of a dollar. Anyone with a savings account knows what it is to earn interest; anyone who has borrowed money from a bank knows what it is to pay interest.

To determine whether to invest in a particular project (a new building, piece of equipment, or other form of investment), a firm must compare the expected rate of return from the project with the interest rate. If the expected rate of return is less than the interest rate, the firm will lose money if it borrows money to carry out the project. For example, if the firm invests in a project with a 10 percent rate of return and borrows the money to finance the project at 12 percent interest, it will receive profits of 10 cents per dollar invested and pay out interest of 12 cents per dollar invested. So it will lose 2 cents (12 cents minus 10 cents) per dollar invested.

Even if the firm does not borrow money to finance the project, it will be unlikely to invest in a project where the expected rate of return is less than the interest rate. Why? Because, if the firm can lend money to others at the prevailing interest rate, it can obtain a greater return from its money by doing this than by investing in the project. Thus, if the interest rate is 12 percent and an investment project has an expected rate of return of 10 percent, a firm will do better, if it has a certain amount of money, to lend it out at 12 percent than to earn 10 percent from the investment project.

Since firms are likely to invest only in projects where the expected rate of return exceeds the interest rate, it is obvious that *the level of investment depends on the total volume of investment projects where the expected rate of return exceeds the interest rate.* For example, if the interest rate is 10 percent, the level of investment depends on the total volume of investment projects where the expected rate of return exceeds 10 percent. The more such projects there are, the higher will be the level of (gross and net) investment. The fewer such projects there are, the lower will be the level of (gross and net) investment. In the next two sections, we discuss a number of factors that influence how many such projects there are.

Technological Change and the Existing Stock of Capital

The rate of technological change can have an important influence on the volume of investment projects where the rate of return exceeds the interest rate. New technology frequently opens up profitable investment opportunities. For example, DuPont, after successfully developing nylon in 1938, found it profitable to invest millions of dollars in new plant and equipment to produce this new synthetic fiber. In other words, the invention of nylon resulted in an additional number of investment projects where the rate of return was high enough to induce firms to invest. Another case of this sort was the continuous wide strip mill, one of the most important developments in steel technology in this century. After the invention of the continuous wide strip mill by Armco in the 1920s, American steel producers invested huge sums in new rolling mills to replace the old hand mills.

In general, *a more rapid rate of technological change is likely to result in a greater number of investment projects where the rate of return exceeds the interest rate. Thus a more rapid rate of technological change is likely to increase the level of investment.*

Another factor that influences the volume of investment projects where the rate of return exceeds the interest rate is the existing stock of capital. As a firm's sales go up, its need for plant, equipment, and inventories clearly goes up as well. Beyond some point, increases in sales result in pressure on the capacity of existing plant and equipment, so that the firm finds it profitable to invest in additional plant and equipment. Clearly, the crucial relationship is between a firm's sales and its stock of capital goods—that is, its stock of plant, equipment, and inventories. If its sales are well below the amount it can produce with its stock of capital goods, there is little pressure on the firm to invest in additional capital goods. But if its sales are at the upper limit of what can be produced with its capital goods, the firm is likely to view the purchase of additional capital goods as yielding a high rate of return.

In general, *the smaller the existing stock of capital goods—relative to present and prospective sales levels—the greater the number of investment projects where the expected rate of return exceeds the interest rate.* Conversely, *the bigger the existing stock of capital goods—relative to present and prospective sales levels—the smaller the number of investment projects where the expected rate of return exceeds the interest rate.*

Business Expectations and the Interest Rate

Still another factor that influences the number of investment projects where the expected rate of return exceeds the interest rate is the state of business expectations. Sometimes businessmen are optimistic; sometimes they are pessimistic. If they believe that their sales are about to drop dramatically, they will be unlikely to invest much in additional capital goods. On the other hand, if they believe that their sales are about to increase greatly, they may be led to invest heavily in capital goods. Firms must make investment decisions on the basis of forecasts. There is no way any firm can tell exactly what the future will bring, and the investment decisions it makes will be influenced by how optimistic or pessimistic its forecasts are. This in turn will depend on existing business conditions, as well as on many other factors. Sometimes government actions and political developments have an important impact on business expectations. Sometimes unexpected changes in the fortune of one industry have a major effect on expectations in other industries.

In general, *the more optimistic business expectations are, the larger the number of investment projects where the expected rate of return exceeds the interest rate. Conversely, the more pessimistic business expectations are, the smaller the number of investment projects where the expected rate of return exceeds the interest rate.*

Finally, the number of investment projects where the expected rate of return exceeds the interest rate clearly depends on the level of the interest rate. The higher the interest rate, the smaller the number of projects that have expected rates of return exceeding the interest rate. The lower the interest rate, the larger the number of projects that have expected rates of return exceeding the interest rate. To illustrate this fact, suppose that a firm is considering the six investment projects shown in Table 9.2. If the interest rate is 6 percent, all of them have expected rates of return exceeding the interest

Table 9.2
Expected Rates of Return from Investment Projects Considered by a Firm

Project	Expected rate of return (percent)
A	12
B	14
C	8
D	11
E	7
F	10

rate. If the interest rate is 10 percent, only three of them (projects *A, B,* and *D*) have expected rates of return exceeding the interest rate. And if the interest rate is 15 percent, none of them has an expected rate of return exceeding the interest rate.

In general, *increases in the interest rate tend to reduce investment, while decreases in the interest rate tend to increase investment.*

Why Is Investment So Volatile?

In the previous chapter, we pointed out the important fact that investment tends to be relatively unstable. That is, it varies from year to year by greater percentages than does consumption expenditure. Based on our discussion in the last few sections, it is easy to see why this is the case. First, technological innovation occurs irregularly—that is, in fits and starts—not at a constant rate. Thus investment (which, as we have seen, is dependent on the rate of technological change) also tends to occur irregularly. For example, investment booms seem to have occurred in response to major innovations like the railroad and the automobile.

Second, because capital goods tend to be quite durable, firms frequently can postpone investment decisions. For example, they can postpone the replacement of a piece of equipment by repairing it and extending its life. Or they can postpone the construction of a new building by tolerating crowded conditions in their existing buildings. Since many investment decisions are postponable, the exact time when projects are accepted may depend on the state of business expectations and the level of firms' profits, both of which are highly variable. Also, since the optimism or pessimism of business expectations tends to be contagious, firms often tend to invest at the same time.

Third, there are great differences from one year to the next in the extent to which existing productive capacity is being utilized. In some years, sales are so great that firms are working their plants at full capacity. In other years, sales are so slack that firms have plenty of excess capacity. In periods when the existing stock of capital goods is more than sufficient to meet current sales, the level of investment will tend to be lower than in periods when the existing stock of capital goods is only barely sufficient to meet current sales. Because of the year-to-year variation in the extent to which sales levels press against productive capacity, there is considerable variation in the level of investment.

Summary

Until the 1930s, most economists were convinced that the price system, left to its own devices, would insure the maintenance of full employment. They thought it unlikely that total spending would be too small to purchase the full-employment level of output, and argued that prices would be cut if any problem of this sort developed. A notable exception was Karl Marx, who felt that the capitalistic system would suffer from worse and worse unemployment, leading to its eventual collapse. John Maynard Keynes, in the 1930s, developed a theory to explain how the capitalist economic system remained mired in the Great Depression, with its tragically high levels of unemployment. Contrary to the classical economists, Keynes concluded that there was no automatic mechanism in a capitalistic system to generate and maintain full employment—or, at least, to generate it quickly enough to be relied on in practice. Keynes's ideas form the core of the modern theory of output and employment.

The consumption function—the relation between consumption expenditures and disposable income—is at the heart of this theory. There have been many studies of the consumption function, some based on cross-section data, some based on time-series data. From the consumption function, one can determine the marginal propensity to consume, which is the proportion of an extra dollar of income that is spent on consumption, as well as the saving function (the relationship between total saving and disposable income) and the marginal propensity to save (the proportion of an extra dollar of income that is saved).

Holding disposable income constant, total consumption expenditure is likely to depend on the amount of wealth in the hands of the public, the ease and cheapness with which consumers can borrow money, the expectations of the public, the amount of durable goods on hand, the income distribution, and the size of the population. Changes in these factors are likely to cause shifts in the consumption function. Also, it is widely accepted that current consumption expenditure does not depend solely on disposable income in the current period. Instead, as stressed by the permanent-income and life-cycle hypotheses, it depends on the expected stream of disposable income over a long period of time.

The level of investment is determined by the expected rate of return from capital and the interest rate. The expected rate of return from capital is the perceived rate of return that businessmen believe they can obtain if they put up new buildings, add new equipment, or increase their inventories. The interest rate is the cost of borrowing money. The level of investment is directly related to the expected rate of return from capital, and inversely related to the interest rate. The expected rate of return from capital is itself dependent upon the rate of technological change, the size of the existing stock of capital goods (relative to present and prospective sales levels), and the optimism or pessimism of businessmen's expectations.

CONCEPTS FOR REVIEW

Say's law	Marginal propensity to save	Permanent-income hypothesis
Consumption function	Average propensity to consume	Interest rate
Saving function	Average propensity to save	Expectations
Marginal propensity to consume	Wealth	Expected rate of return

QUESTIONS FOR DISCUSSION AND REVIEW

1. "If the government will leave things alone, competition in the product and input markets will cure a recession." Comment and evaluate.

2. Describe Say's Law in as much detail as you can. Explain the arguments given by the classical economists, and the counterarguments given by Keynes and his followers. Indicate what sorts of tests economists could conduct to determine which of these models is closer to the truth.

3. Suppose that only three families inhabit a nation and that each family spends 90 percent of its income on consumption goods. For the nation as a whole, what is the marginal propensity to save? How much difference is there between the marginal propensity to consume and the average propensity to consume? To what extent does the nation's marginal propensity to consume depend on the distribution of income? Is this realistic?

4. Assume that the consumption function is as follows:

Disposable income (billions of dollars)	Consumption expenditure (billions of dollars)
900	750
1,000	800
1,100	850
1,200	900
1,300	950
1,400	1,000

(a) How much will be saved if disposable income is $1,000 billion? (b) What is the average propensity to consume if disposable income is $1,000 billion? (c) What is the marginal propensity to consume if disposable income is between $1,000 billion and $1,100 billion? (d) What is the marginal propensity to save if disposable income is between $1,000 billion and $1,100 billion?

5. Suppose that the relationship between consumption expenditure and disposable income in the United States were as follows:

Consumption (billions of dollars)	Disposable income (billions of dollars)
750	700
830	800
910	900
970	1,000
1,030	1,100
1,100	1,200

Draw the consumption function on a graph. On another graph, draw the saving function. Is the marginal propensity to consume constant, or does it vary with the level of disposable income? Does the average propensity to consume rise or fall as disposable income arises?

6. "Unless firms make profits, they cannot invest in plant and equipment. Profits set an upper limit on how much they can invest." Comment and evaluate.

7. What effect would each of the following have on the position of the consumption function? That is, would each raise it, lower it, or have no effect on it? (a) An increase in interest rates; (b) expectations of greater inflation; (c) a catastrophe that wiped out half the nation's assets; (d) a marked increase in liquid assets held by people; (e) a rumor that major shortages of goods are about to occur.

8. What effect would each of the following have on the amount of investment? That is, would each increase it, decrease it, or have no effect on it? (a) Expectations of greater likelihood of impending recession by firms; (b) a decrease in interest rates; (c) increased rate of invention of important new synthetic materials; (d) a marked reduction in the percent of existing plant that is utilized; (e) an increase in the perceived profitability of building up inventories.

10 The Determination of National Output

National output varies substantially from year to year, as we have seen in previous chapters. One of the most important tasks of economic theory is to explain why these changes occur. Having explored the determinants of consumption and investment in the previous chapter, we now bring them together in the most basic Keynesian model to show how national output is determined. National output is defined as net national product in this chapter, since it is the best measure of how much the economy is producing when depreciation is taken into account. But since net national product and gross national product differ by relatively little, and since they move up and down together, this theory will also enable us to explain movements in gross national product, and to help forecast them.

In this chapter, we shall make three major simplifying assumptions. First, we assume that there are no government expenditures and that the economy is closed (no exports or imports).

Thus *total spending on final output—that is, on net national product—in this simple case equals consumption expenditure plus net investment.* (Why? Because the other two components of total spending—government expenditures and net exports—are zero.)

Second, we assume that there are no taxes, no transfer payments, and no undistributed corporate profits. Thus *NNP equals disposable income in this simple case,* because the items in Table 8.6 that are taken from, or added to, NNP to get disposable income total zero. Later chapters relax this and the first assumption.

Third, in most of this chapter, we shall assume that the total amount of desired investment is *independent* of the level of net national product. This, of course, is only a rough simplification, since, as we noted in the previous chapter, the amount firms invest will be affected by the level of output in the economy. But this simplification is very convenient and not too unrealistic. Moreover, as we shall show at the end of this chapter, it is relatively easy to extend the model to eliminate this assumption.

The Equilibrium Level of Net National Product

As stressed in Chapter 4, an equilibrium is a situation where there is no tendency for change; in other words, it is a situation that can persist. In Chapter 4, we studied the equilibrium value of a product's price. Here we are interested in the equilibrium value of net national product. In Chapter 4, we saw that price is at its equilibrium value when the quantity demanded equals the quantity supplied. Here we shall see that NNP is at its equilibrium value when the flow of income (generated by this value of NNP) results in a level of spending that is just sufficient (not too high, not too low) to take this level of output off the market.

To understand this equilibrium condition, it is essential to keep three points in mind. First, *the production of goods and services results in a flow of income to the workers, resource owners, and managers that help to produce them.* Each level of NNP results in a certain flow of income. More specifically, under the assumptions made here, NNP equals disposable income. Thus whatever the level of NNP may be, we can be sure that the level of disposable income will be equivalent to it.

Second, *the level of spending on final goods and services is dependent on the level of disposable income.* As we saw in the previous chapter, consumption expenditure depends on the level of disposable income. (For the moment, we assume that investment is independent of the level of output in the economy.) Thus, if we know the level of disposable income, we can predict what level of spending will be forthcoming.

Third, *the level of production is dependent mainly on the level of spending.* If producers find that they are selling goods faster than they are producing them, their inventories will decline. If they find that they are selling goods slower than they are producing them, their inventories will rise. *If NNP is at its equilibrium value, the desired level of spending must be just equal to NNP.* Why? Because otherwise there will be an undesired increase or decrease in producers' inventories—a situation which cannot persist. Much more will be said on this score in the sections that follow.

Aggregate Supply and Demand

Let's look in more detail at the process whereby national output (that is, NNP) determines the level of income, which in turn determines the level of spending. Suppose that the first column of Table 10.1 shows the various possible output levels—that is, the various possible values of NNP—that the economy might produce this year. This column is an ***aggregate supply*** schedule for the economy as a whole. It shows the various output levels that

Table 10.1
Determination of Equilibrium Level of Net National Product (billions of dollars)

(1) Net national product (= disposable income)	(2) Desired consumption expenditure	(3) Desired saving	(4) Desired investment	(5) Total desired spending (2) + (4)	(6) Tendency of national output
1,000	950	50	90	1,040	Upward
1,050	980	70	90	1,070	Upward
1,100	1,010	90	90	1,100	No change
1,150	1,040	110	90	1,130	Downward
1,200	1,070	130	90	1,160	Downward
1,250	1,100	150	90	1,190	Downward

might be produced, *if producers expect that there will be enough spending to take this much output off the market.*

Since NNP equals disposable income (under our current assumptions), the first column of Table 10.1 also shows the level of disposable income corresponding to each possible level of NNP. From this, it should be possible to determine the level of spending corresponding to each level of NNP. Specifically, suppose that the consumption function is as shown in Table 9.1 on page 192. In this case, desired consumption expenditure at each level of NNP will be as shown in column 2 of Table 10.1. And suppose that firms want to invest $90 billion (net of depreciation) regardless of the level of NNP. Under these circumstances, total desired spending at each level of NNP will be as shown in column 5 of Table 10.1. (Since total desired spending equals desired consumption expenditure plus desired investment, column 5 equals column 2 plus column 4.)

Column 5 of Table 10.1 is an ***aggregate demand*** schedule for the economy as a whole. It shows the level of total desired spending at each level of national output (and income). *If NNP is at its equilibrium value, aggregate demand must equal aggregate supply.* In other words, *if NNP is at its equilibrium value, desired spending must equal NNP.* The easiest way to show this is to show that, if desired spending is not equal to NNP, NNP is *not* at its equilibrium value. The following discussion provides such a proof. First we show that, if desired spending is greater than NNP, NNP is not at its equilibrium level. Then we show that, if desired spending is less than NNP, NNP is not at its equilibrium level.

If desired spending is *greater* than NNP, what will happen? Since the total amount that will be spent on final goods and services exceeds the total amount of final goods and services produced (the latter being, by definition, NNP), firms' inventories will be reduced. Consequently, firms will increase their output rate to avoid continued depletion of their inventories and to bring their output into balance with the rate of aggregate demand. Since an increase in the output rate means an increase in NNP, it follows that NNP will tend to increase if desired spending is greater than NNP. NNP therefore is not at its equilibrium level.

On the other hand, what will happen if desired spending is *less* than NNP? Since the total amount that will be spent on final goods and services falls short of the total amount of final goods and services produced (the latter being, by definition, NNP), firms' inventories will increase. As inventories pile up unexpectedly, firms will cut back their output to bring it into better balance with aggregate demand. Since a reduction in output means a reduction in NNP, it follows that NNP will tend to fall if desired spending is less than NNP. Once again, NNP is not at its equilibrium level.

Thus, if NNP tends to increase when desired spending is greater than NNP, and if NNP tends to decrease when desired spending is less than NNP, clearly NNP will be at its equilibrium level only if desired spending is equal to NNP.

The Process Leading toward Equilibrium: A Tabular Analysis

To get a better idea of why NNP tends to the level where desired spending on NNP equals NNP, consider three possible values of NNP—$1,050 billion, $1,100 billion, and $1,150 billion—and see what would happen in our simple economy (in Table 10.1) if these values of NNP prevailed. First, what would happen if firms were to produce $1,050 billion of final goods and services? Given our assumptions, disposable income would also equal $1,050 billion (since disposable income equals NNP), so that consumers would spend $980 billion on consumption goods and services. (This follows from the nature of the consumption function: see column 2 of Table 10.1). Since firms want to invest $90 billion, total desired spending would be $1,070 billion ($980 billion + $90 billion, as shown in column 5). But the total amount spent on final goods and services under these circumstances would exceed the total value of final goods and services produced by $20 billion ($1,070 billion − $1,050 billion), so that firms' inventories would be drawn down by $20 billion. Clearly, this situation could not persist very long. As firms become aware that their inventories are becoming depleted, they would step up their production rates, so that the value of output of final goods and services—NNP—would increase.

Second, what would happen if firms were to produce $1,150 billion of final goods and services? Given our asumptions, disposable income would also equal $1,150 billion (since disposable income equals NNP), with the result that consumers would spend $1,040 billion on consumption goods and services. (Again, this follows from the consumption function: see column 2 of Table 10.1). Since firms want to invest $90 billion, total spending would be $1,130 billion ($1,040 billion + $90 billion, as shown in column 5). But the total amount spent on final goods and services under these circumstances would fall short of the total value of final goods and services produced by $20 billion ($1,150 billion − $1,130 billion), so that firms' inventories would increase by $20 billion. Clearly, this situation, like the previous one, could not continue very long. When firms see that their inventories are increasing, they reduce their production rates, causing the value of output of final goods and services—NNP—to decrease.

Finally, consider what would happen if firms were to produce $1,100 billion of final goods and services? Disposable income would also equal $1,100 billion (since disposable income equals NNP), so that consumers would spend $1,010 billion on consumption goods and services. (Once again, this follows from the consumption function: see column 2 of Table 10.1.) Since firms want to invest $90 billion, total spending would be $1,100 billion ($1,010 billion + $90 billion, as shown in column 5). Thus the total amount spent on final goods and services under these circumstances would exactly equal the total value of final goods and services produced. Consequently, there would be no reason for firms to alter their production rates. Thus this would be an equilibrium situation—a set of circumstances where there is no tendency for NNP to change—and the equilibrium level of NNP in this situation would be $1,100 billion.

These three cases illustrate the process that pushes NNP toward its equilibrium value. So long as NNP is below its equilibrium value, the situation is like that described in our first case. So long as NNP is above its equilibrium value, the situation is like that described in our second case. Whether NNP is below or above its equilibrium value, there is a tendency for production rates to be altered so that NNP moves toward its equilibrium value. Eventually, NNP will reach its equilibrium value, and the situation will be like that described in our third case. The important aspect of the third case—the equilibrium situation—is that, for it to occur, desired spending must equal NNP.

A Graphical Analysis

For the sake of absolute clarity, we can represent the same argument in a diagrammatic, rather than tabular, analysis. Let's show again that the equilibrium level of NNP is at the point where desired spending equals NNP, but now using a graph. Since disposable income equals net national product in this simple case, we can plot consumption expenditure (on the vertical axis) versus net national product (on the horizontal axis), as shown in Figure 10.1. This is the consumption function. Also, we can plot the sum of consumption expenditure and investment expenditure against NNP, as shown in Figure 10.1. This relationship, shown by the $C + I$ line, indicates the level of total desired spending on final goods and services for various amounts of NNP. Finally, we can plot a 45-degree line, as shown in Figure 10.1. This line contains all points where the amount on the horizontal axis equals the amount on the vertical axis. Thus, since NNP is on the horizontal axis and desired spending is on the vertical axis, it contains all points where total desired spending equals net national product.

The equilibrium level of net national product will be at the point where total desired spending equals NNP. Consequently, the *equilibrium level of NNP will be at the point on the horizontal axis where the C + I line intersects the 45-degree line—$1,100 billion in Figure 10.1.* Under the conditions assumed here, no other level of NNP can be maintained for any considerable period of time. Let's begin by

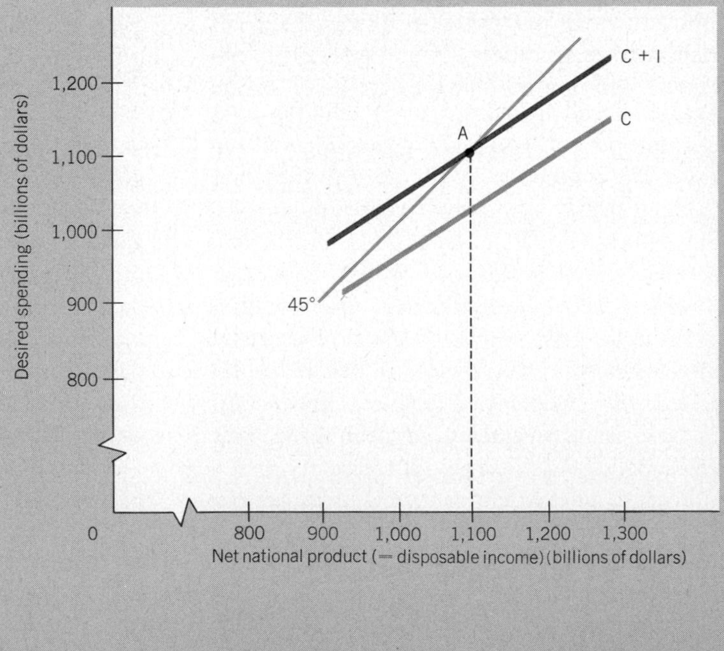

Figure 10.1
Determination of Equilibrium Value of Net National Product
The consumption function is *C*, and the sum of consumption and investment expenditure is *C* + *I*. The equilibrium value of NNP is at the point where the *C* + *I* line intersects the 45-degree line, here $1,100 billion. The *C* + *I* line shows aggregate demand and the 45-degree line shows aggregate supply.

proving that the point where the $C + I$ line intersects the 45-degree line is indeed the point where desired spending equals NNP. This is easy, since a 45-degree line is, by construction, a line that includes all points where the amount on the horizontal axis equals the amount on the vertical axis. In this case, as noted above, desired spending is on the vertical axis and NNP is on the horizontal axis. Thus at point A, the point where the $C + I$ line intersects the 45-degree line, desired spending must equal NNP, because such a point is on the 45-degree line.

Next, let's see why the equilibrium level of NNP must be at $1,100 billion, the point on the horizontal axis where the $C + I$ line intersects the 45-degree line. If NNP exceeds $1,100 billion the $C + I$ line lies below the 45-degree line. Since the $C + I$ line shows how much people desire to spend with a particular level of disposable income, this shows that total desired spending is less than NNP. Consequently, some production will not be sold, inventories will build up, production will be cut back, and NNP will decrease. If NNP is less than $1,100 billion, the $C + I$ line lies above the 45-degree line, which shows that total desired spending is greater than NNP. Consequently, inventories will decrease, production will be stepped up, and NNP will increase. Thus, since NNP tends to fall when it exceeds $1,100 billion, and to rise when it falls short of $1,100 billion, its equilibrium value must be $1,100 billion.

Leakages and Injections: Another Approach

In studying any topic, it helps to look at it from more than one angle. Another approach to the determination of national output is the so-called leakage-injection approach. The basic idea underlying this approach is that, under our assumptions, the production of a particular level of output (that is, NNP) results in a level of disposable income that is equivalent to this level of NNP. But, as we know from our previous discussions, not all of this disposable income is spent by households; some of it is saved. This saving is a ***leakage*** from the spending stream, because it withdraws spending from the flow of income and expenditure. Such a leakage tends to reduce the equilibrium value of NNP because, unless it is offset, it results in total spending being too small to take the entire output (that is, NNP) off the market.

But firms do not sell their whole output to consumers. As we know from previous chapters, some of NNP (including items like blast furnaces and oil refineries) is sold to firms, this spending being called investment. Investment is an ***injection*** into the spending stream, because it adds spending to the flow of income and expenditure. That is, it is a supplement to consumption expenditure. Such an injection tends to increase the equilibrium value of NNP because it offsets the leakage of saving. If desired investment is less than desired saving, it is only a partial offset of this leakage. If desired investment is greater than desired saving, it more than offsets this leakage.

The equilibrium value of NNP is the one where the leakages equal the injections. Why? Because desired spending will equal NNP only if the desired amount of income not spent on output (leakages) equals the desired spending on output that is a supplement to consumer expenditure (injections). If leakages are greater than injections, NNP is above its equilibrium value, since desired spending will be too small to take the existing NNP off the market. If leakages are less than injections, NNP is below its equilibrium value, since desired spending will be more than sufficient to take the existing NNP off the market.

To illustrate the use of the leakage-injection approach, consider Table 10.2, which is based on the same data as Table 10.1. Column 3 shows desired saving at each level of NNP.

Saving is, as we have seen, a leakage. Thus the total leakages at each level of NNP are given in column 3. Column 4 shows desired investment at each level on NNP. Investment is, as we have seen, an injection. Thus the total injections at each level of NNP are given in column 4.

If NNP is *less* than $1,100 billion, Table 10.2 indicates that the total leakages are less than the total injections. The desired amount withdrawn from the expenditure stream via saving is less than the desired amount added via investment. Thus total desired spending is greater than NNP, and, as we saw in previous sections, this will result in an increase in NNP. For example, suppose that NNP equals $1,050 billion. At this level of NNP, desired saving is $70 billion, whereas desired investment is $90 billion. Consumers want to withdraw $70 billion from the expenditure stream via saving, while firms want to add $90 billion to it via investment. Consequently, total desired spending exceeds NNP by $90 billion minus $70 billion, or $20 billion. Since firms' inventories are drawn down by $20 billion, there is a tendency for NNP to increase, as we saw in a previous section.

If NNP is *greater* than $1,100 billion, Table 10.2 indicates that the total leakages are more than the total injections. The desired amount withdrawn from the expenditure stream via saving is more than the desired amount added via investment. Thus total desired spending is less than NNP, and, as we saw in previous sections, this will result in a decrease in NNP. For example, suppose that NNP equals $1,150 billion. At this level of NNP, desired saving is $110 billion, whereas desired investment is $90 billion. Consumers want to withdraw $110 billion from the expenditure stream via saving, while firms want to add $90 billion to it via investment. Consequently, total desired spending falls short of NNP by $110 billion minus $90 billion, or $20 billion. Since firms' inventories increase by $20 billion, there is a tendency for NNP to fall, as we saw in a previous section.

Only when NNP *equals* $1,100 billion will there be no tendency for NNP to rise or fall. As shown in Table 10.2, this is the value of NNP where the total leakages equal the total injections. (Specifically, both desired saving and desired investment equal $90 billion at this level of NNP). Thus, as pointed out above, the equilibrium value of NNP is the one where the total leakages equal the total injections.

Note that the equilibrium value of NNP, as determined by the leakage-injection approach, is the same as the one determined by the approach used in the previous section. Using either approach, we get the same answer—an

Table 10.2
The Leakage-Injection Approach to the Determination of Net National Product (billions of dollars)

(1) Net national product (= disposable income)	(2) Desired consumption expenditure	(3) Leakages (desired saving)	(4) Injections (desired investment)	(5) Tendency of national output
1,000	950	50	90	Upward
1,050	980	70	90	Upward
1,100	1,010	90	90	No change
1,150	1,040	110	90	Downward
1,200	1,070	130	90	Downward
1,250	1,100	150	90	Downward

Figure 10.2
Determination of Equilibrium Value of Net National Product
The saving function is SS' and the investment function is II'. The equilibrium value of NNP is at the point where SS' intersects II', which here is \$1,100 billion. At this point, the total leakages equal the total injections, since the saving function represents the leakages and the investment function represents the injections.

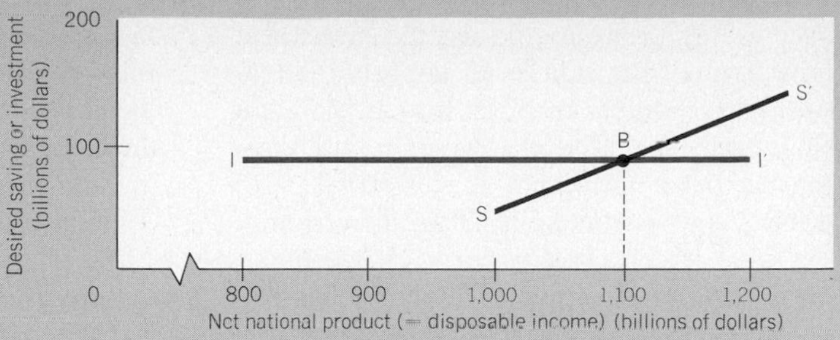

equilibrium NNP of \$1,100 billion. This will always be true. To see why, recall that according to the approach used in the previous section, NNP is at its equilibrium value when total desired spending on output equals NNP. It is easy to show that this condition will be met if and only if the total leakages (desired saving) equal the total injections (desired investment). Since

total desired spending = desired consumption expenditure + desired investment,

and

NNP = desired consumption expenditure + desired saving,

it follows that total desired spending will equal NNP if and only if desired saving equals desired investment. Thus, if we use one approach, we will get the same answer as if we use the other approach.

Leakages and Injections: A Graphical View

Graphs can be used to determine the equilibrium value of NNP when the leakage-injection approach is used. To do so, all that we have to do is plot the saving function and the investment function on the same graph. (The ***investment function*** is the relationship between NNP and desired investment.) The equilibrium value of NNP is the value of NNP at which these two functions intersect. Why? Because at the value of NNP at which they intersect, the total leakages (represented by the saving function) equal the total injections (represented by the investment function).

Based on the data in Table 10.2, the saving function (SS') and investment function (II') are as shown in Figure 10.2. Thus the equilibrium value of NNP must be \$1,100 billion, since this is the point where the two functions intersect. For the reasons given in the previous section, the equilibrium value of NNP, as determined by a graph of this sort, must be the same as the one determined by Figure 10.1. And in accord with this fact, both Figures 10.1 and 10.2 yield the same answer—namely, that the equilibrium value of NNP is \$1,100 billion.

Usefulness of the Leakage-Injection Approach

Why bother to look at the determination of NNP in terms of the leakage-injection approach? After all, as we have stated repeatedly, we can get the same answer by comparing total desired spending on final goods and services with NNP. One important reason for looking at the determination of NNP in terms of desired saving (leakage) and desired investment (injection) is that it helps to lay bare the reasons why equilibrium NNP may be different from the level of NNP that would result in reasonably full employment at reasonably stable prices. As we pointed out in our discussion of the flaws in the classical view of unemployment, these reasons revolve about the fact that desired saving and desired investment are carried out by different parts of society and for different reasons. Households do much of the saving. They abstain from consuming now in order to provide for retirement, college educations for their children, emergencies, and other ways of consuming later. Firms, on the other hand, do most of the investing. They build plants and equipment and expand their inventories in response to profit opportunities. Because of this cleavage between the savers and the investors, *there is no assurance that desired saving will equal desired investment at a level of NNP that results in reasonably full employment at reasonably stable prices.*[1]

Saving and Investment: Desired and Actual

In the previous sections, we stressed that desired saving need not equal desired investment. This is an important fact, which must be understood. At the same time, however, it must be recognized that, whether or not desired saving equals desired investment, *actual saving must always equal actual investment.* In other words, although the amount people *set out to save* during a particular year may not equal the amount firms *set out to invest,* the *actual amount saved* will always equal the *actual amount invested.* This must be true because, as pointed out in the previous chapter, NNP has to equal consumption plus net investment;[2] and it also has to equal consumption plus saving. Subtracting consumption from each of these expressions for NNP, saving must equal investment.

To see why, consider the case (in Table 10.1) where NNP is $1,050 billion. In this case, desired saving is $70 billion but desired investment is $90 billion. How does it turn out that actual saving equals actual investment? As pointed out in a previous section, there is an unintended ***disinvestment*** (i.e., negative investment) of −$20 billion in inventories if NNP is $1,050 billion. (Recall from Chapter 8 that a build-up of inventories is a form of investment, so a $1 billion increase in inventories equals $1 billion of investment.) Thus the actual investment is $90 billion (in intended investment) minus $20 billion (in unintended disinvestment), or $70 billion. Actual saving equals desired saving, or $70 billion. Thus actual saving equals actual investment.

As a further illustration, consider the case where NNP is $1,150 billion. In this case, desired saving is $110 billion but desired investment is $90 billion. How does it turn out that actual saving equals actual investment? As pointed out in a previous section, there is an unintended investment in inventories of $20 billion (because total spending falls short of NNP by this amount). Thus actual investment turns out to equal the desired investment of $90 billion plus the unintended investment of $20 billion, or $110 billion in all. Since actual saving also equals $110 billion, actual saving equals actual investment.[3]

In general, actual saving always must equal

[1] Note that, under the simplifying assumptions made in this chapter, there is only one leakage (saving) and one injection (investment). In subsequent chapters, we shall be concerned with models where other leakages (taxes and imports) and injections (government expenditures and exports) are involved.

[2] Recall from Chapter 8 that net national product equals consumption plus government expenditures plus net exports plus net investment. Since government expenditures and net exports are assumed to be zero, it follows that net national product equals consumption plus net investment.

[3] Note that we assume here that actual saving will equal desired saving and that unintended changes in inventories will make actual investment conform to actual and desired saving. There are other ways for adjustments to take place. The important thing is that, one way or another, actual saving will equal actual investment.

actual investment, even though desired saving does not always equal desired investment.

Effects of Change in Desired Investment

The Multiplier: A Geometric Formulation

In Chapter 8, we pointed out that investment is a particularly volatile form of expenditure. It is subject to large variations from year to year. For example, in 1975, business fixed investment was 12 percent (in real terms) below its 1974 level. Looking at the highly simplified model we have constructed, what is the effect of a change in the amount of desired investment? Specifically, if firms increase their desired investment by \$1 billion, what effect will this increase have on the equilibrium value of net national product? This is a very important question, the answer to which sheds considerable light on the reasons for changes in national output. We devote the next several sections to answering this question.

Let's begin by noting once again that, if NNP is at its equilibrium level, desired saving must equal desired investment. Then let's apply the sort of graphical analysis that we used in Figure 10.2 to determine the effect of an increase in desired investment on equilibrium NNP. If the saving function in our simplified economy is SS' in Figurc 10.3 and desired investment is shown by the horizontal line I_1I_1', what will be the effect of a \$1 billion increase in desired investment on equilibrium NNP? Before the increase in desired investment, equilibrium NNP was cqual to Y_0. The increase of \$1 billion in desired investment will shift the investment function up by \$1 billion, to the new position (I_2I_2') shown in Figure 10.3. This shift in the investment function will increase the equilibrium level of NNP, but by how much?

The resulting increase in equilibrium NNP, ΔY, can be derived by the following geometrical reasoning. First, the slope of SS' times the change in equilibrium NNP must equal the increase in desired investment, \$1 billion. This follows from the definition of the slope of a line: The slope of SS' equals the vertical distance between any two points on SS' divided by the horizontal difference between them. The vertical distance between points A and B in Figure 10.3 is the increase in desired investment (ΔI), and the horizontal distance between points A and B is the change in equilibrium NNP (ΔY). Consequently, the change in equilibrium NNP must equal the increase in desired investment divided by the slope of SS'.

Figure 10.3
The Multiplier
If investment increases by ΔI, the equilibrium valuc of NNP increases by ΔY. Clearly $\frac{\Delta I}{\Delta Y}$ equals the slope of the saving function between A and B. Since this slope equals the marginal propensity to save (MPS), $\frac{\Delta I}{\Delta Y}$ = MPS. Thus, $\Delta Y = \frac{\Delta I}{\text{MPS}}$ and if ΔI = 1, $\Delta Y = \frac{1}{\text{MPS}}$.

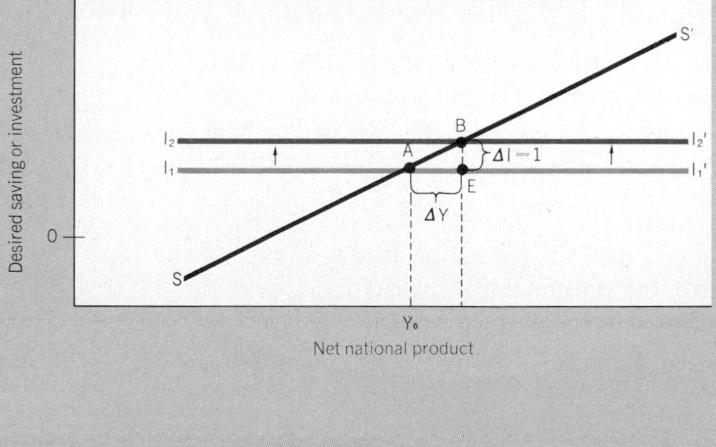

Since the slope of SS' is the marginal propensity to save—as pointed out in the previous chapter—it follows that *the change in equilibrium NNP equals the increase in desired investment divided by the marginal propensity to save. Thus a $1 billion increase in desired investment will result in an increase in equilibrium NNP of* $\left(\frac{1}{MPS}\right)$ *billions of dollars, where MPS is the marginal propensity to save.*

This is a very important conclusion. To understand more clearly what it means, let's consider a couple of numerical examples. For example, if the marginal propensity to save is $\frac{1}{3}$, a $1 billion increase in desired investment will increase equilibrium NNP by $1 \div \frac{1}{3}$ billion dollars; that is, by $3 billion. Or take a somewhat more complicated case. If the consumption function is as shown in the first two columns of Table 10.1, what is the effect of an increase in desired investment from $90 billion to $91 billion? The first step in answering this question is to determine the marginal propensity to consume—which is 0.60 in Table 10.1. Then it is a simple matter to determine the marginal propensity to save—which must be $1 - 0.60$ or 0.40. Finally, since the marginal propensity to save is 0.40, it follows from the previous paragraph that a $1 billion increase in desired investment must result in an increase in equilibrium NNP of $\frac{1}{0.40}$ billion dollars. That is, equilibrium NNP will increase by $2½ billion.

Since a dollar of extra desired investment results in $\left(\frac{1}{\text{MPS}}\right)$ dollars of extra NNP, $\left(\frac{1}{\text{MPS}}\right)$ is called the ***multiplier.*** If you want to estimate the effect of a given increase in desired investment on NNP, all you have to do is multiply the increase in desired investment by $\left(\frac{1}{\text{MPS}}\right)$: the result will be the resulting increase in NNP. Moreover, it is easy to show that the same multiplier holds for decreases in desired investment as well as for increases. That is, a dollar less of desired investment results in $\left(\frac{1}{\text{MPS}}\right)$ dollars less of NNP. Consequently, if you want to estimate the effect of a given change in desired investment (positive or negative) on NNP, all you have to do is multiply the change in desired investment by $\left(\frac{1}{\text{MPS}}\right)$.

It is important to note that, since MPS is less than one, the *multiplier must be greater than one.* In other words, an increase in desired investment of $1 will result in an increase in NNP of more than $1. This means, of course, that NNP is relatively sensitive to changes in desired investment. Moreover, since the multiplier is the reciprocal of the marginal propensity to save, the smaller the marginal propensity to save, the higher the multiplier—and the more sensitive is NNP to changes in desired investment. As we shall see, this result has important implications for public policy. For example, because our system of taxes and transfer payments tends to increase the marginal propensity to save out of NNP, the destabilizing effect of a sharp change in investment expenditures is reduced.

The Multiplier: An Algebraic Interpretation[4]

Equations speak more clearly to some than words, and so for those with a taste for (elementary) algebra, we will show how the results of the previous section can be derived algebraically. If you have trouble with equations, or if you feel that you already understand the material, go on to the next section. We begin by recalling that the equilibrium value of NNP is attained at the point where NNP equals total desired spending on output. This condition can be expressed in the following equation:

$$\text{NNP} = C + I, \tag{10.1}$$

[4] This section is optional and can be omitted without loss of continuity.

Figure 10.4
Consumption Function
The consumption function is derived from the data in Table 10.1. The marginal propensity to consume is 0.6, so the slope is 0.6.

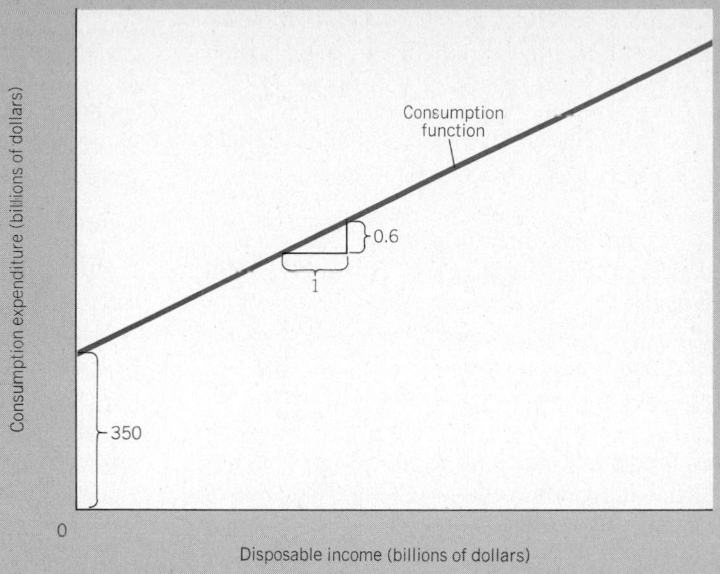

which says that NNP must equal desired expenditure on consumption goods (C) plus desired investment (I). Since desired consumption expenditures plus desired investment equals total desired spending, it follows that this equation states that NNP must equal total desired spending.

Next, let's introduce a friend from this and the previous chapter, the consumption function. The consumption function in the first two columns of Table 10.1 can be represented by the following equation:

$$C = 350 + 0.6D \tag{10.2}$$

which says that desired consumption equals \$350 billion plus 0.6 times disposable income (D). Figure 10.4 shows the consumption function. As you can see, \$350 billion is the intercept on the vertical axis, while 0.6 is the slope of the consumption function. Since—as we noted in the previous chapter—the slope of the consumption function equals the marginal propensity to consume, 0.6 equals the marginal propensity to consume.

The next step is to substitute the righthand side of equation (10.2) for C in Equation (10.1). The result is:

$$\text{NNP} = 350 + 0.6D + I. \tag{10.3}$$

But recall that disposable income is equal to NNP in our simplified economy. Consequently, we can substitute NNP for D in this equation, to get

$$\text{NNP} = 350 + 0.6\text{NNP} + I. \tag{10.4}$$

And going a step further, we can subtract 0.6 times NNP from both sides of Equation (10.4), which gives

$$\text{NNP} - 0.6\text{NNP} = 350 + I, \tag{10.5}$$

or, collecting terms,

$$0.4\text{NNP} = 350 + I. \tag{10.6}$$

Finally, dividing both sides by 0.4, we have

$$\text{NNP} = \frac{350}{0.4} + \frac{I}{0.4}. \tag{10.7}$$

Now we can see what happens to NNP if there is a \$1 billion increase in I. In other words, suppose that I is increased from some amount, $X billion, to $(X + 1) billion. How much will this increase NNP? From Equation (10.7), it is clear that NNP will equal

$$\frac{350}{0.4} + \frac{X}{0.4}$$

if desired investment equals $X billion. It is also clear from Equation (10.7) that NNP will equal

$$\frac{350}{0.4} + \frac{(X+1)}{0.4}$$

if desired investment is equal to $ (X + 1) billion. Consequently the increase in NNP due to the $1 billion increase in desired investment is equal to

$$\left[\frac{350}{0.4} + \frac{(X+1)}{0.4}\right] - \left[\frac{350}{0.4} + \frac{X}{0.4}\right]$$

$$= \frac{X+1}{0.4} - \frac{X}{0.4} = \frac{X}{0.4} + \frac{1}{0.4} - \frac{X}{0.4} = \frac{1}{0.4}$$

That is, a $1 billion increase in desired investment will result in an increase of $\frac{1}{0.4}$ billion dollars in NNP. Recalling that 0.6 is the marginal propensity to consume—and that the sum of the marginal propensity to consume and the marginal propensity to save equals one—it follows that *a $1 billion increase in desired investment will result in an increase of* $\left(\frac{1}{MPS}\right)$ *billions of dollars in NNP, where MPS is the marginal propensity to save—0.4 in this case.*

This is precisely the same conclusion we arrived at in the previous section. Thus we have derived the value of the multiplier by an algebraic route rather than the geometric route used before.

The Multiplier and the Spending Process

Now that we have shown in two ways that the multiplier equals $\frac{1}{\text{MPS}}$, we can leave the realm of graphs and equations and examine the operation of the multiplier in the real world. Specifically, what process in the real world insures that a $1 billion change in desired investment results in a change of $\left(\frac{1}{\text{MPS}}\right)$ billions of dollars in equilibrium NNP? It is worthwhile spelling this out in some detail.

If there is a $1 billion increase in desired investment, the effects can be divided into a number of stages. In the first stage, firms spend an additional $1 billion on plant and equipment. This extra $1 billion is received by workers and suppliers as extra income, which results in a second stage of extra spending on final goods and services. How much of their extra $1 billion in income will the workers and suppliers spend? If the marginal propensity to consume is 0.6, they will spend 0.6 times $1 billion, or $.6 billion. This extra expenditure of $.6 billion is received by firms and disbursed to workers, suppliers, and owners as extra income bringing about a third stage of extra spending on final goods and services. How much of this extra income of $.6 billion will be spent? Since the marginal propensity to consume is 0.6, they will spend 60 percent of this $.6 billion, or $.36 billion. This extra expenditure of $.36 billion is received by firms and disbursed to workers, suppliers, and owners as extra income, which results in a fourth stage of spending, then a fifth stage, a sixth stage, and so on.

Table 10.3 shows the total increase in expenditure on final goods and services arising from the original $1 billion increase in desired investment. The total increase in expenditures is the increase in the first stage, plus the increase in the second stage, plus the increase in the third stage, and so on. Since there is an endless chain of stages, we cannot list all the increases. But because the successive increases in spending get smaller and smaller, we can determine their sum, which in this case is $2.5

Table 10.3
The Multiplier Process

Stage	Amount of extra spending (billions of dollars)
1	1.00
2	.60
3	.36
4	.22
5	.13
6	.08
7	.05
8	.03
9 and beyond	.03
Total	2.50

billion. Thus the $1 billion increase in desired investment results—after all stages of the spending and respending process have worked themselves out—in a $2.5 billion increase in total expenditures on final goods and services. In other words, it results in a $2.5 billion increase in NNP.

It is important to note that this spending and respending process results in the same multiplier as indicated in previous sections. This happens because, if 0.6 is the marginal propensity to consume, a $1 billion increase in desired investment will result in increased total spending of $(1 + .6 + .6^2 + .6^3 + \ldots)$ billions of dollars. This is evident from Table 10.3, which shows that the increased spending in the first stage is $1 billion, the increased spending in the second stage is $.6 billion, the increased spending in the third stage is $$.6^2$ billion, and so on. But it can be shown that $(1 + .6 + .6^2 + .6^3 + \ldots) = \frac{1}{1 - .6}$ (See footnote 5.)[5] Consequently, since $(1 - .6)$ is equal to the marginal propensity to save, a $1 billion increase in desired investment results in an increase of $\left(\frac{1}{\text{MPS}}\right)$ billions of dollars in NNP. Thus, however we look at it, the answer remains the same: the multiplier equals $\left(\frac{1}{\text{MPS}}\right)$.

Application of the Multiplier: A Case Study[6]

Now that we have discussed the modern theory of the determination of NNP in the abstract, it is time to look at a specific application of this theory. Consider a famous incident that occurred at the end of World War II. Economists, using the best models then available, had been able to forecast the pace of the economy reasonably well during the war. When the war was coming to an end, they were charged with forecasting the level of national product in 1946, the year immediately after the war. This was an important task, since the government was worried that the economy might suffer severe postwar unemployment. The Great Depression of the 1930s was a recent—and still bitter—memory.

A group of economists in Washington was given the responsibility for this forecast. They made it in terms of gross national product, not net national product, but they used essentially the same theory as that discussed in previous sections. To forecast gross national product in

---

[5] To see this, let's divide 1 by $(1 - m)$, where m is less than 1. Using the time-honored rules of long division, we find that

$$\begin{array}{r@{}l} & 1 + m + m^2 + m^3 + \ldots \\ 1 - m \,\big)\!\!\!\! & \overline{\,1\qquad\qquad\qquad\qquad} \\ & \underline{1 - m} \\ & \quad m \\ & \quad \underline{m - m^2} \\ & \qquad m^2 \\ & \qquad \underline{m^2 - m^3} \\ & \qquad\quad m^3 \\ & \qquad\quad \underline{m^3 - m^4} \\ & \qquad\qquad m^4 \end{array}$$

Thus letting $m = 0.6$, it follows that 1 divided by $(1 - .6)$ equals $1 + .6 + .6^2 + .6^3 + \ldots$

[6] This account is based on Michael Sapir, "Review of Economic Forecasts for the Transition Period," *Conference on Research in Income and Wealth,* vol. 11, Princeton: National Bureau of Economic Research, 1949; and Lawrence Klein, "A Post-Mortem on Transition Predictions of National Product," *Journal of Political Economy,* August 1946.

Figure 10.5
Shift in the Consumption Function
If the consumption function shifts from C_1C_1' to C_2C_2' this means that, at each level of disposable income, consumers desire to spend $1 billion more on consumption goods and services. Such a shift results in an increase of $\left(\frac{1}{MPS}\right)$ billion of dollars in equilibrium NNP, as shown in Figure 10.6.

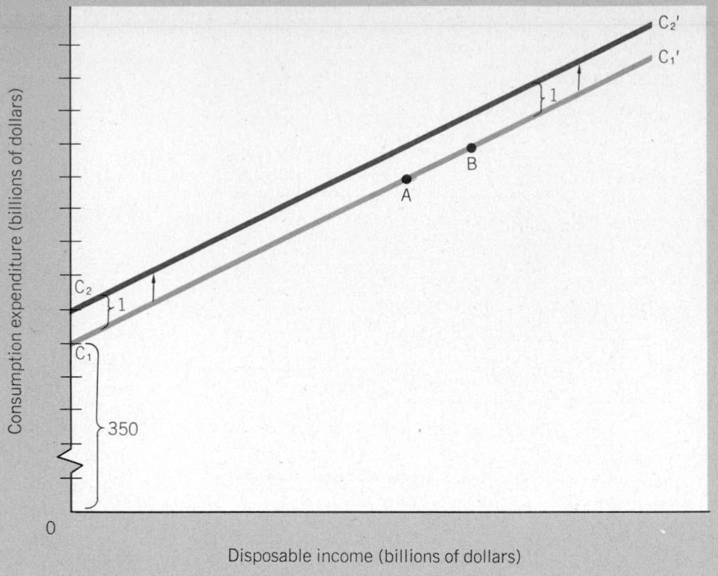

1946, these Washington economists began by using prewar data to estimate the consumption function. Then they estimated the amount of investment that would take place in 1946. Finally, to forecast gross national product in 1946, they performed the sort of calculations shown in Equation (10.7). In other words, they computed the multiplier $\left(\frac{1}{MPS}\right)$ and multiplied it by their estimate of investment for 1946. Then they added an amount analogous to the first term on the righthand side of Equation (10.7); and since their model—unlike ours—included government spending and taxes, other calculations, which will be discussed in Chapter 11, had to be made as well. The result was a forecast of a gross national product in 1946 of about $170 billion. This forecast received considerable attention and publicity inside and outside the government.

Before discussing the accuracy of this forecast, an important empirical question must be considered: in real-world studies like this, what is the estimated value of the multiplier? Judging from our findings in the previous sections, we would guess a figure of at least $2\frac{1}{2}$, since the marginal propensity to consume should be at least 0.6. But these results are based on the assumption of no taxation. For reasons discussed in Chapter 11, the multiplier will be lower if there is taxation. Including the effects of taxation (and other factors like imports) most estimates of the multiplier seem to center around a value of 2. But these estimates can vary considerably, depending, of course, on the shape of the consumption function and other factors.

Effects of Shifts in the Consumption Function

Before discussing the accuracy of this forecast for 1946, we must look at the effects of shifts in the consumption function. So far, we have been concerned only with the effects of changes in desired investment on NNP. We have shown—repeatedly and in various ways—that changes in desired investment have an amplified effect on NNP, with the extent of the

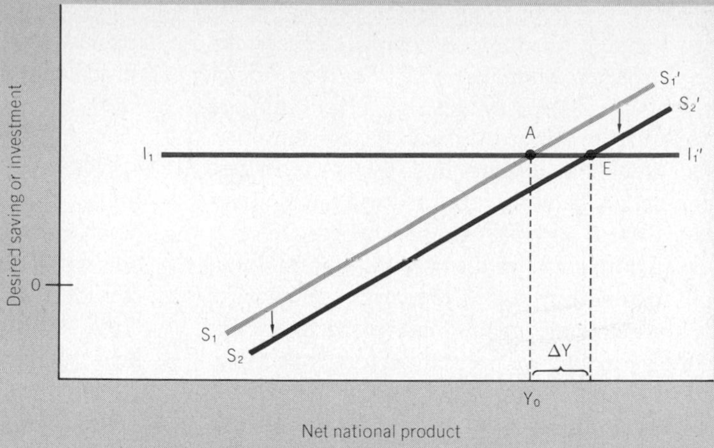

Figure 10.6
Effect of a Downward Shift of the Saving Function
A \$1 billion upward shift in the consumption function results in a \$1 billion downward shift in the saving function. Thus, if the consumption function shifts from C_1C_1' to C_2C_2' in Figure 10.5, the saving function shifts downward from S_1S_1' to S_2S_2', as shown here. The point where the saving function intersects the investment function shifts from *A* to *E*, and the equilibrium value of NNP increases by ΔY, which is the same amount that it increases when desired investment increases by \$1 billion. (See Figure 10.3.)

amplification measured by the multiplier. But it is important to note at this point that a shift in the consumption function will also have such an amplified effect on NNP. For example, in Figure 10.5, if the consumption function shifts from C_1C_1' to C_2C_2', this means that at each level of disposable income, consumers desire to spend \$1 billion more on consumption goods and services than they did before. It is easy to show that *this \$1 billion upward shift in the consumption function will have precisely the same effect on equilibrium NNP as a \$1 billion increase in desired investment.*

To see that this is the case, recall from Chapter 9 that an upward shift in the consumption function results in a downward shift in the saving function. Specifically, a \$1 billion upward shift in the consumption function means that the saving function shifts downward by \$1 billion (because, if consumers desire to spend \$1 billion *more* out of each level of disposable income than before, they must desire to save \$1 billion *less* out of each level of disposable income than before). As shown in Figure 10.6, a \$1 billion downward shift in the saving function results in an increase in the equilibrium value of NNP. And this increase is the same as when desired investment increases by \$1 billion, the situation we observed in Figure 10.3. In either case, the increase equals $\left(\frac{1}{MPS}\right)$ billions of dollars.[7]

[7] For those of more mathematical bent, it may be worthwhile to use some simple algebra to prove that this is the case. Let's recall that in Equation (10.7), we showed that the equilibrium value of NNP equals

$$\frac{350}{0.4} + \frac{I}{0.4},$$

where 350 is the intercept on the vertical axis of the consumption function, 0.4 is the marginal propensity to save, and I is desired investment. A \$1 billion shift upward in the consumption function causes the intercept to increase from its former amount, \$350 billion, to \$351 billion. What is the effect of this increase in the intercept on the equilibrium value of NNP? If the intercept is \$350 billion, the equilibrium value of NNP will equal

$$\frac{350}{0.4} \times \frac{I}{0.4}.$$

If the intercept is \$351 billion, the equilibrium value of NNP will equal

$$\frac{351}{0.4} + \frac{I}{0.4}.$$

Consequently, the increase in NNP from the \$1 billion upward

Moreover, *a $1 billion downward shift in the consumption function will have precisely the same effect on equilibrium NNP as a $1 billion decrease in desired investment.* Thus both upward and downward shifts in the consumption function—from changes in tastes, assets, prices, population, and other factors—will have a magnified effect on NNP. In other words, NNP is sensitive to shifts in the consumption function in the same way that it is sensitive to changes in desired investment. This is an important point. Finally, to prevent misunderstanding, recall from Chapter 9 that a *shift* in the consumption function is quite different from a *movement along* a given consumption function. (An example of the latter would be the movement from point *A* to point *B* in Figure 10.5.) We are concerned here with shifts in the consumption function, not movements along a given consumption function.

The Accuracy of the Postwar Forecasts

We can now pick up the GNP forecasts for 1946 where we left off several paragraphs back. The government forecasters' estimate of a GNP of about $170 billion caused a severe chill in many parts of the government, as well as among businessmen and consumers. A GNP of only about $170 billion would have meant a great deal of unemployment in 1946. Indeed, according to some predictions, about eight million people would have been unemployed in the first quarter of 1946.

---

shift in the consumption function is

$$\left[\frac{351}{0.4} + \frac{I}{0.4}\right] - \left[\frac{350}{0.4} + \frac{I}{0.4}\right] = \frac{351}{0.4} - \frac{350}{0.4} = \frac{1}{0.4}$$

That is, a $1 billion upward shift in the consumption function results in an increase of $\frac{1}{0.4}$ billions of dollars in NNP. Recalling that 0.4 = MPS, it follows that *a $1 billion upward shift in the consumption function will result in an increase of* $\left(\frac{1}{MPS}\right)$ *billions of dollars in NNP.*

Unfortunately for the forecasters—but fortunately for the nation—the GNP in 1946 turned out to be not $170 billion, but about $190 billion. And unemployment was only about ⅓ of the forecasted amount. These are very large errors in practically anyone's book—so big that they continue to embarrass the economics profession 30 years later. Of course, our knowledge of the economy has expanded considerably over the past 30 years, and an error of this magnitude is much less likely now. Moreover, even at the end of World War II, some economists forecasted GNP in 1946 pretty well. Not everyone, by any means, agreed with the forecast of $170 billion. But it is worth bearing this notable mistake in mind when considering economic forecasts of this sort. Economics is not as exact a science as physics or chemistry—and mischief can result if one assumes otherwise.

What went wrong in the Washington economists' forecast? To a considerable extent, the answer lies in the topic of the previous section: a shift in the consumption function. When World War II ended, households had a great deal of liquid assets on hand. They had saved money during the war. There had been rationing of many kinds of goods, and other goods—like automobiles or refrigerators—could not be obtained at all. When the war ended and these goods flowed back on the market, consumers spent more of their income on consumption goods than in the previous years. In other words, there was a pronounced upward shift of the consumption function.

To see why this shift in the consumption function caused the forecasters to underestimate GNP in 1946, recall from the previous section that an upward shift of $1 billion in the consumption function will result in an increase of $\left(\frac{1}{MPS}\right)$ billions of dollars in national product. Bearing this in mind, suppose the forecasters assumed that the consumption function remained fixed, when in fact there was a $8 billion shift upward. Then if the multiplier—$\frac{1}{\text{MPS}}$—was $2\frac{1}{2}$, national product would turn out to be \$20 billion higher than the forecasters expected. (Since $\frac{1}{\text{MPS}}$ is assumed to be $2\frac{1}{2}$, national product will increase \$2.5 billion for every \$1 billion shift in the consumption function, so an \$8 billion shift in the consumption function will result in a \$20 billion increase in national product.) Of course, these figures—a multiplier of $2\frac{1}{2}$ and an \$8 billion shift in the consumption function—are only illustrative, not precise estimates of the actual situation. For one thing, as noted above, the multiplier is wrong because it assumes no taxation. But they indicate the sort of thing that occurred, and they show dramatically the effects of a shift in the consumption function.

The Paradox of Thrift

Now that we understand more fully the effects on NNP of a shift in the consumption function, we can appreciate the so-called paradox of thrift. Despite all of the praise heaped upon it by moral philosophers, thrift (as spendthrifts have long suspected) can be a dangerous thing. If society as a whole desires to save more, the result may well be a decrease in national output and no increase in saving. To see why this is so, consider Figure 10.7, which shows a situation where the saving function shifts upward from S_1S_1' to S_3S_3'. Since the investment function remains constant at II', the equilibrium level of NNP falls from Y_1 to Y_3. And despite the public's attempt to save more, saving remains fixed at \$80 billion, the amount that it equaled before the public's attempt to increase it.

Of course, the fact that an upward shift in the saving function is likely to cause a decrease in the equilibrium value of NNP is really no news. As we pointed out in the previous chapter, an upward shift in the saving function is accompanied by a downward shift in the consumption function. (Recall Figure 9.5.) And as we saw in an earlier section of this chapter, a downward shift in the consumption function will result in a decrease in the equilibrium value of NNP.

The important point here is that, *although thrift may be a private virtue, it can be a problem from the viewpoint of society as a whole.* Suppose, for example, that a recession occurs, with the result that NNP falls and unemployment rises. Under such circumstances, the public may well be inclined to cut back on its

Figure 10.7
The Paradox of Thrift
If the saving function shifts upward from S_1S_1' to S_3S_3', the equilibrium value of NNP falls from Y_1 to Y_3—and, despite its attempt to save more, the public still saves \$80 billion, just as it did before. All that results is a reduction in NNP.

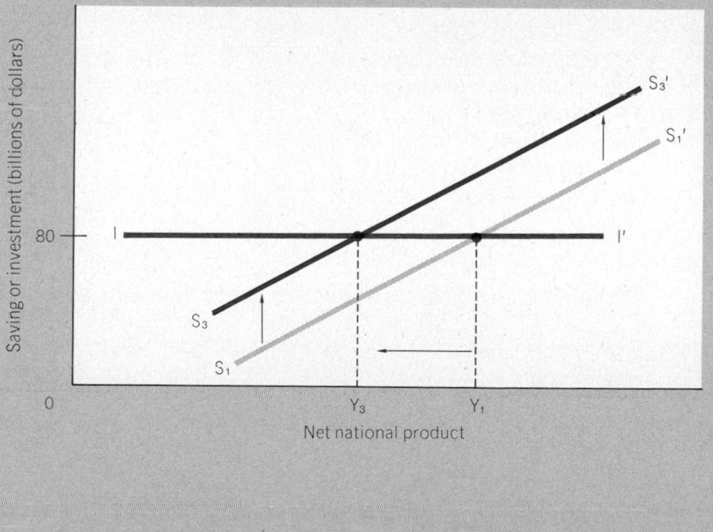

spending. That is, faced with economic storm signals, the public may try to save more. But what will be the unintended result? As indicated in Figure 10.7, the equilibrium value of NNP will be reduced, thus aggravating the recession. And to add insult to injury, the public may not be able to accomplish its goal of increasing saving. Thus all that will be achieved is an undesirable reduction in national ouput (and employment).

Induced Investment

Before concluding this chapter, one final point is worth noting. In previous sections, we have assumed that desired net investment is a certain amount, regardless of the level of NNP. This assumption has been reflected in the fact that the investment function—for example, in Figures 10.2 and 10.3—is horizontal. Although this assumption may be a useful first approximation, it neglects the fact that firms are much more likely to invest in plant and equipment when NNP is high than when it is low. After all, NNP measures output; and the greater the output of the economy, the greater the pressure on the capacity of existing plant and equipment—and the greater the pressure to expand this capacity by investing in additional plant and equipment.

It is relatively simple to extend the theory to take account of the fact that, to some extent, increases in NNP may increase desired investment. Rather than portraying the investment function as a horizontal line, we need only assume that it is positively sloped, as in Figure 10.8. Then, as before, the equilibrium level of NNP is at the point where the saving function intersects the investment function—that is, at point *A*, the point where desired saving equals desired investment. Much more will be said about *induced investment*—investment stimulated by increases in NNP—in Chapter 12.

Summary

The equilibrium level of net national product will be at the point where desired spending equals NNP. If desired spending exceeds NNP, NNP will tend to increase. If desired spending falls short of NNP, NNP will tend to fall.

Another way to describe this equilibrium condition is to say that NNP is at its equilibrium level if desired saving equals desired investment. This is the so-called leakage-injection approach. Because of the cleavage between

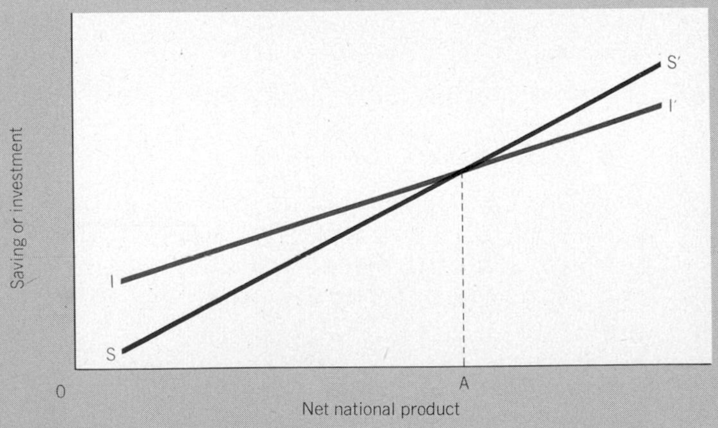

Figure 10.8
Determination of Equilibrium Value of Net National Product, with Induced Investment
If the level of investment depends on NNP, the investment function, *II'*, is positively sloped, and the equilibrium level of NNP is at the point where *II'* intersects *SS'*, the saving function.

savers and investors, there is no assurance that desired saving will equal desired investment at a level of NNP that results in reasonably full employment at stable prices. But actual saving and actual investment always must turn out to be equal.

A $1 billion change in desired investment will result in a change in equilibrium NNP of $\left(\frac{1}{MPS}\right)$ billions of dollars, where MPS is the marginal propensity to save. In other words, the multiplier is $\frac{1}{MPS}$. The multiplier can be interpreted in terms of—and derived from—the successive stages of the spending process. An example of the use of the multiplier was the formulation at the end of World War II of GNP forecasts for 1946.

A shift in the consumption function will also have an amplified effect on NNP, a $1 billion shift in the consumption function resulting in a change of $\left(\frac{1}{MPS}\right)$ billions of dollars in NNP. To a considerable extent, the large error in government forecasts of GNP in 1946 was due to an unanticipated shift in the consumption function. Responding to large accumulated wartime savings and pent-up wartime demands, consumers spent more of their income on consumption goods than in previous years.

Although thrift may be a private virtue, it can be a problem from the viewpoint of society as a whole. If society as a whole desires to save more, the result may well be a decrease in national output—and no increase in saving. This is the so-called paradox of thrift.

CONCEPTS FOR REVIEW

Aggregate demand	Desired investment	Shifts in the consumption function
Aggregate supply	Desired saving	45-degree line
Leakage-injection approach	Multiplier	Paradox of thrift
	Induced investment	

QUESTIONS FOR DISCUSSION AND REVIEW

1. Suppose that the consumption function in a particular economy is given by the following table:

Disposable income (billions of dollars)	Consumption expenditure (billions of dollars)
400	300
500	360
600	410
700	440
800	470

If firms want to invest $140 billion, what is the equilibrium value of NNP? Can we be sure that this is the full-employment value of NNP? Why or why not? (The full-employment value of NNP is defined as the value of NNP that can be produced if the unemployment rate is about 4 percent.)

2. Using the data in Question 1, plot the consumption function and the $C + I$ line on a graph, and derive the equilibrium value of NNP graphically. Is the consumption function a straight line? Does the answer to this question affect the validity of the analysis in any way?

3. Using the data in Question 1, plot the saving function and the investment function, and show how they can be used to determine the equilibrium value of NNP. Does desired saving equal desired investment if NNP equals $800 billion? If NNP were $800 billion, show how actual saving would turn out to equal actual investment.

4. Suppose that desired investment increases by $1 billion in Question 1. Using a graph like that derived in Question 2, show what effect this will have on the equilibrium value of NNP. Next, use a graph like that derived in Question 3 to do the same thing. Do you get the same answer? Why?

5. Suppose that consumers want to spend $50 billion more at each level of disposable income than indicated in Question 1. Using a graph like that derived in Question 2, show what effect this will have on the equilibrium value of NNP. Next, use a graph like that derived in Question 3 to do the same thing. Do you get the same answer? Why?

6. Suppose that the consumption function in a certain economy is $C = 100 + 0.8D$, where C is consumption expenditure and D is disposable income. If desired investment equals 10, what is the equilibrium value of NNP? What is the value of the multiplier? Is this a realistic figure for the United States?

7. In Question 6, suppose that desired investment falls from 10 to 6. What effect will this have on the equilibrium value of NNP? By how much, and in what direction, would the consumption function have to shift to offset this effect?

8. "The investment function is a horizontal line, so there must be a great deal of induced investment." Comment and evaluate.

9. (Advanced) In a certain economy, the average propensity to consume is always equal to the marginal propensity to consume. If the equilibrium level of NNP equals $300 billion and if desired investment equals $100 billion, what is the equation for the consumption function in this economy?

11

Fiscal Policy and National Output

In the period since World War II, the idea that the government's power to spend and tax should be used to stabilize the economy—that is, to reduce unemployment and fight inflation—has gained acceptance throughout the world. In many countries, including the United States, this acceptance was delayed by a fear of government deficits and of increases in the public debt, but with the passage of time these fears have receded or been put in proper perspective. However, time has also revealed that fiscal policy is no panacea. Witness the severe inflationary pressures and the high unemployment rates that have plagued the American economy in the mid-1970s. Both the power and the limitations of fiscal policy must be recognized.

This chapter presents a first look at fiscal policy, in the context of the simplest Keynesian model. In effect, we assume here that the money supply is fixed, and that the interest rate is not affected by changes in total desired spending (or that, if it is affected, it has little effect on total desired spending). In Chapter 16 (and its Appendix), a more sophisticated analysis of fiscal policy is presented, with money and financial assets included in the model.

Government Expenditure and Net National Product

In the previous chapter, we showed how the equilibrium level of net national product was determined in a simplified economy without government spending or taxation. We must now extend this theory to include both government spending and taxation. As we shall see, the results form the basis for much of our nation's past and present economic policy. In this section, we incorporate government spending into the theory of the determination of net national product. In so doing, we assume that government spending will not affect the consumption function or the level of desired investment. In other words, we assume that government spending does not reduce or increase private desires to spend out of each level of income. (Government includes here federal, state, and local.)

Suppose that the government purchases $50 billion worth of goods and services and that it will purchase this amount whatever the level of NNP. (Note that only government purchases, not transfer payments, are included here.) Clearly, adding this public expenditure to the private expenditures on consumption and investment results in a higher total level of desired spending. In an economy with government spending (but no net exports), total desired spending on output equals desired consumption expenditure plus desired investment expenditure plus desired government expenditure. Thus, since an increase in government expenditure (like increases in consumption or investment expenditure) results in an increase in total desired spending, and since the equilibrium value of net national product is at the point where total desired spending equals NNP, it follows that an increase in government expenditure, as well as the induced increase in private spending, brings about an increase in the equilibrium value of NNP.

To see the effects of government expenditure on the equilibrium value of NNP, we can use a simple graph similar to those introduced in the previous chapter. We begin by plotting the consumption function, which shows desired consumption expenditure at each level of

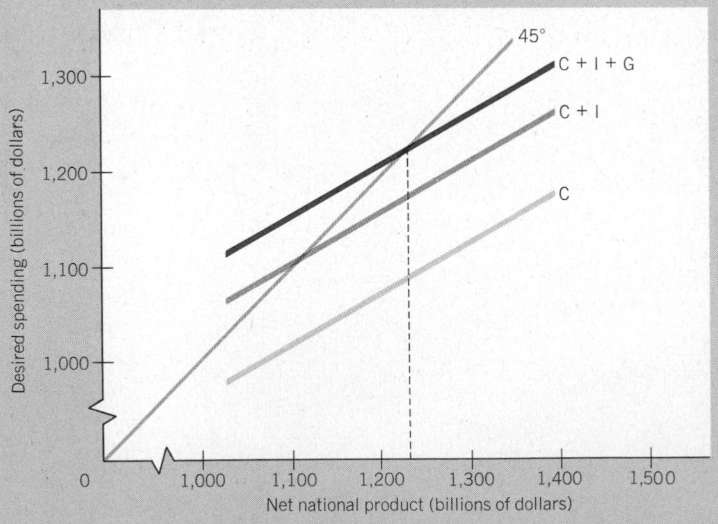

Figure 11.1
Determination of Net National Product, Including Government Expenditure
The consumption function is *C*, the sum of consumption and investment expenditures is $C + I$, and the sum of consumption, investment, and government expenditures is $C + I + G$. The equilibrium value of NNP is at the point where the $C + I + G$ line intersects the 45-degree line, which here is $1,225 billion. The $C + I + G$ line shows aggregate demand, and the 45-degree line shows aggregate supply.

NNP (since NNP equals disposable income under our assumptions): the result is line C in Figure 11.1. Then, as in the previous chapter, we can plot the sum of desired consumption expenditure and investment expenditure at each level of NNP: the result is line $C + I$. Next, we plot the sum of desired consumption expenditure, investment expenditure, and government expenditure at each level of NNP, to get line $C + I + G$. Since the $C + I + G$ line shows total desired spending, and since, as we stressed in the previous chapter, the equilibrium value of NNP is at the point where total desired spending equals NNP, it follows that the equilibrium value of NNP is at the point where the $C + I + G$ line intersects the 45-degree line. This is at an output of $1,225 billion.

What happens to the equilibrium level of NNP if government expenditure increases? Figure 11.2 shows the results of a $5 billion increase in government spending. Obviously, the increased government expenditure (G_1) will raise the $C + I + G$ line by $5 billion, as the figure shows. Since the $C + I + G_1$ line must intersect the 45-degree line at a higher level of NNP, increases in government expenditure result in increases in the equilibrium level of NNP. In Figure 11.2, the $5 billion increase in government expenditure raises the equilibrium value of NNP from $1,225 billion to $1,237.5.

Figure 11.2 also shows what happens when government spending goes down by $5 billion (to G_2). The new $C + I + G_2$ line is $5 billion lower than the old $C + I + G$ line. Since the new $C + I + G_2$ line intersects the 45-degree line at a lower level of NNP, decreases in government expenditure result in decreases in the equilibrium level of NNP. In Figure 11.2, the $5 billion decrease in government expenditure reduces the equilibrium value of NNP from $1,225 billion to $1,212.5 billion.

How sensitive is the equilibrium level of NNP to changes in government spending? In the previous chapter, we found that a $1 billion change in desired investment—or a $1 billion shift in the consumption function—results in a change in equilibrium NNP of $\left(\frac{1}{MPS}\right)$ bil-

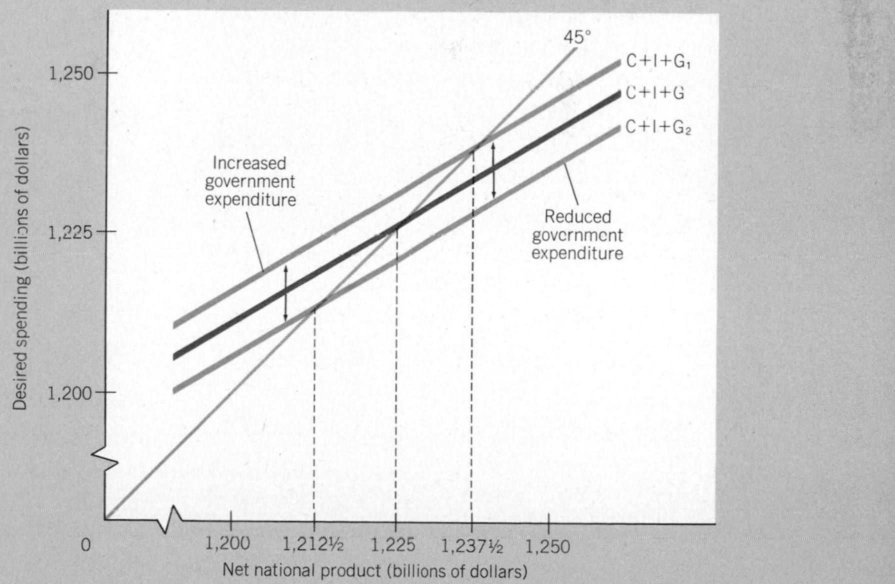

Figure 11.2
Effects on Equilibrium Net National Product of a $5 Billion Increase and Decrease in Government Expenditure
A $5 billion increase raises the equilibrium value of NNP from $1,225 billion to $1,237.5 billion. A $5 billion decrease reduces the equilibrium value of NNP from $1,225 billion to $1,212.5 billion.

lions of dollars, where MPS is the marginal propensity to save. The effect of a $1 billion change in government expenditure is exactly the same. In other words, *it will result in a change in equilibrium NNP of* $\left(\frac{1}{MPS}\right)$ *billion dollars.* Thus *a change in government expenditure has the same multiplier effect on NNP as a change in investment or a shift in the consumption function.* For example, if the marginal propensity to consume is 0.6, an extra $1 billion in government expenditure will increase equilibrium NNP by $2.5 billion.

The mathematically inclined reader may be interested in proving that a $1 billion change in government expenditure will result in a change in equilibrium NNP of $\left(\frac{1}{\text{MPS}}\right)$ billions of dollars.* To prove this proposition, recall that the equilibrium value of NNP is at the point where desired spending—$C + I + G$—equals NNP. Thus,

$$NNP = C + I + G. \qquad (11.1)$$

Assuming that the consumption function is as given in Table 9.1 (and Table 10.1), it follows that

$$C = 350 + 0.6\ NNP$$

where 0.6 is the marginal propensity to consume. (Note that NNP equals disposable income. This is because there are no taxes, no transfer payments, and no undistributed corporate profits. Taxes are brought into the picture in the next section.) Substituting the righthand side of equation (11.2) for C in Equation (11.1), we have

$$NNP = 350 + 0.6\ NNP + I + G \qquad (11.3)$$

Thus

$$(1 - 0.6)\ NNP = 350 + I + G \quad (11.4)$$

$$NNP = \frac{350}{0.4} + \frac{I}{0.4} + \frac{G}{0.4}$$

What happens to NNP when G increases from $\$X$ billion to $\$(X + 1)$ billion? How much will this increase the equilibrium value of NNP? From Equation (11.4), it is clear that equilibrium NNP will be

$$\frac{350}{0.4} + \frac{I}{0.4} + \frac{X}{0.4}$$

if government expenditure equals $\$X$ billion. And it is equally clear from Equation (11.4) that NNP will equal

$$\frac{350}{0.4} + \frac{I}{0.4} + \frac{(X + 1)}{0.4}$$

if government expenditure is $\$(X + 1)$ billion. Consequently the increase in NNP due to the $1 billion increase in government spending is

$$\left[\frac{350}{0.4} + \frac{I}{0.4} + \frac{(X + 1)}{0.4}\right] - \left[\frac{350}{0.4} + \frac{I}{0.4} + \frac{X}{0.4}\right],$$

which equals

$$\frac{X + 1}{0.4} - \frac{X}{0.4} = \frac{1}{0.4}.$$

That is, a $1 billion increase in government expenditure will result in an increase of $\frac{1}{0.4}$ billion dollars of NNP—which is equal to $\left(\frac{1}{\text{MPS}}\right)$ billions of dollars of NNP, since $0.4 = \text{MPS}$. This is what we set out to prove.

* The material in this box can be skipped without loss of continuity.

Taxation and Net National Product

The previous section added government expenditures to our theory, but it did not include taxes. Here we assume taxes to be net of transfer payments. For simplicity, it is assumed that all tax revenues stem from personal taxes. How do tax collections influence the equilibrium value of net national product? For example, if consumers pay 16⅔ percent of their income to the government in taxes, what effect does this have on NNP? Clearly, the imposition of this tax means that, for each level of NNP, people have less disposable income than they would with no taxes. In particular, disposable income now equals 83⅓ percent of NNP, whereas without taxes it equaled NNP. Thus the relationship between consumption expenditure and NNP is altered by the imposition of the tax. Before the tax was levied, the relationship was given by line C_0 in Figure 11.3; after the imposition of the tax, it is given by line C_1.

The relationship between consumption expenditure and national output changes in this way because consumption expenditure is determined by the level of disposable income. For instance, in the case in Figure 11.3, consumption expenditure equals $350 billion plus 60 percent of disposable income. Thus, since the tax reduces the amount of disposable income at each level of NNP, it also reduces the amount of consumption expenditure at each level of NNP. In other words, since people have less after-tax income to spend at each level of NNP, they spend less on consumption goods and services at each level of NNP. This seems eminently reasonable. It is illustrated in Figure 11.3, where, at each level of NNP, consumption expenditure after the tax (given by line C_1) is less than before the tax (given by line C_0).

Because the imposition of the tax influences the relationship between consumption expenditure and NNP, it also influences the equilib-

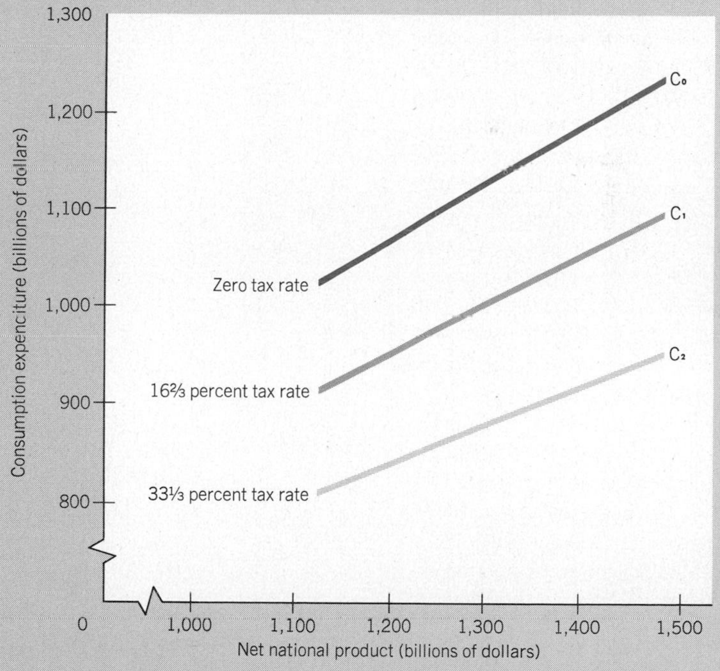

Figure 11.3
Relationship between Consumption Expenditure and Net National Product, Given Three Tax Rates
If taxes are zero, C_0 is the relationship between consumption expenditure and NNP. If consumers pay 16⅔ percent of their income in taxes, C_1 is the relationship; and if consumers pay 33⅓ percent of their income in taxes, C_2 is the relationship. Clearly, the higher the tax rate, the less consumers spend on consumption from a given NNP.

rium value of NNP. As we have stressed repeatedly, the equilibrium value of NNP is at the point where desired spending on output equals NNP. Lines C_0 and C_1 in Figure 11.3 show desired consumption expenditure at each level of NNP, before and after the tax. Adding desired investment and government expenditure to each of these lines, we get the total desired spending before and after the tax. The results are shown in Figure 11.4, under the assumption that the sum of desired investment and government spending equals \$140 billion. The $C_0 + I + G$ line shows desired spending before the tax, while the $C_1 + I + G$ line shows desired spending after the tax.

Note that the equilibrium level of NNP is lower after the imposition of the tax than before. Specifically, as shown in Figure 11.4, it is \$980 billion after the imposition of the tax and \$1,225 billion before. The tax reduced the equilibrium level of NNP because it lowered the $C + I + G$ line from $C_0 + I + G$ to $C_1 + I + G$. It did this because, as pointed out above, it reduced the amount people wanted to spend on consumption goods at each level of NNP. People still wanted to spend the same amount *from each (after-tax) income level,* but because of the tax, their spending decisions had to be based on a *reduced (after-tax) income,* so that they spent less on consumption goods and services at each level of NNP.

Going a step further, *the higher the tax rate, the lower the equilibrium value of NNP; and the lower the tax rate, the higher the equilibrium value of NNP.* This is a very important proposition, as we shall see in subsequent sections. To demonstrate it, let's see what will happen to the equilibrium value of NNP when the tax rate is increased from 16⅔ percent of NNP to 33⅓ percent of NNP. If the tax rate is 33⅓ percent, total desired spending at each level of NNP will be given by line $C_2 + I + G$ in Figure 11.5. Since the equilibrium value of NNP will be at the point where the $C_2 + I + G$ line

Figure 11.4
Determination of Equilibrium Value of Net National Product, with Zero and 16⅔ Percent Tax Rates

The tax rate influences the relationship between consumption expenditure and NNP. (C_0 is this relationship with a zero tax rate, while C_1 is the relationship with a 16⅔ percent tax rate. See Figure 11.3.) The $C_0 + I + G$ line shows total desired spending at each level of NNP if the tax rate is zero, and the $C_1 + I + G$ line shows total desired spending at each level of NNP if the tax rate is 16⅔ percent. Consequently, the equilibrium value of NNP is \$1,225 billion if the tax rate is zero, and \$980 billion if it is 16⅔ percent.

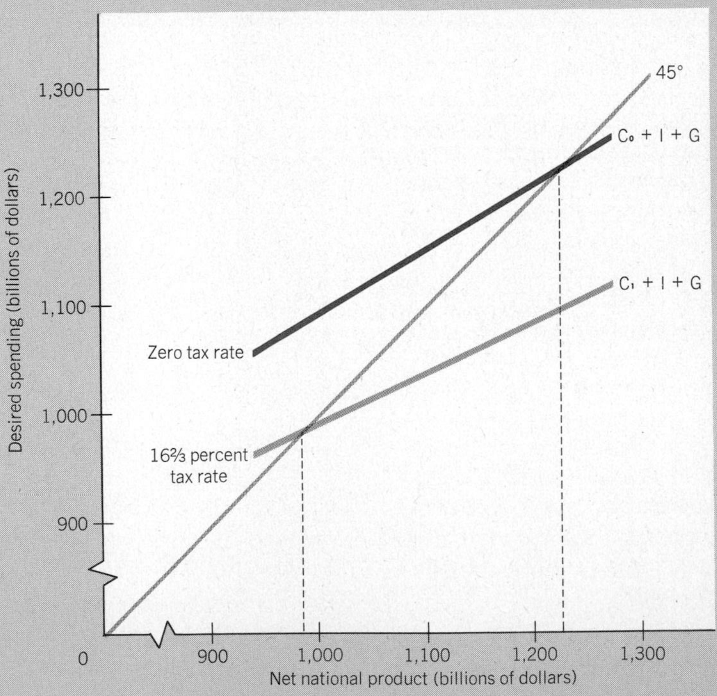

Figure 11.5
Determination of Equilibrium Value of Net National Product, with 16⅔ Percent and 33⅓ Percent Tax Rates
The $C_1 + I + G$ line shows total desired spending at each level of NNP if the tax rate is 16⅔ percent, and the $C_2 + I + G$ line shows total desired spending at each level of NNP if the tax rate is 33⅓ percent. Consequently, the equilibrium value of NNP is $980 billion if the tax rate is 16⅔ percent and $816⅔ billion if it is 33⅓ percent.

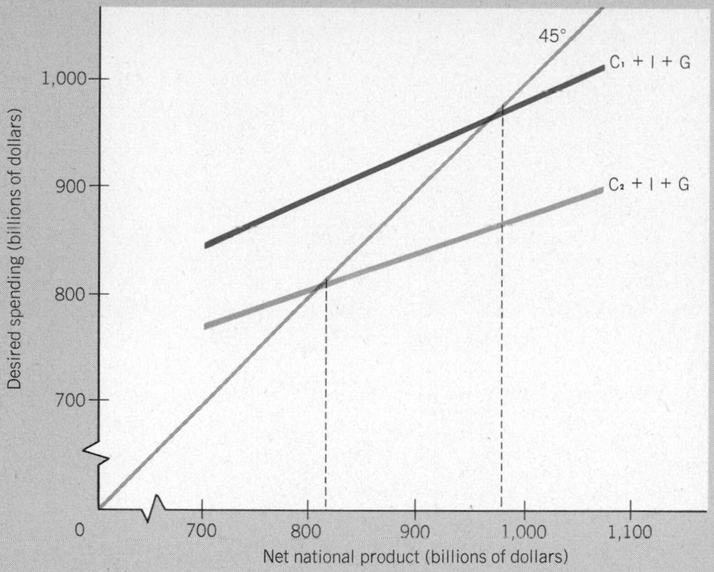

intersects the 45-degree line, the equilibrium value of NNP will be $816⅔ billion, rather than $980 billion (which was the equilibrium value when the tax rate was 16⅔ percent). Thus the increase in the tax rate will reduce the equilibrium value of NNP. By reducing the amount people want to spend on consumption at each level of NNP, it will lower the $C + I + G$ line from $C_1 + I + G$ to $C_2 + I + G$.

On the other hand, suppose that the tax rate is lowered from 16⅔ percent of NNP to a lesser amount. What will happen to the equilibrium value of NNP? If the tax rate is less than 16⅔ percent, the desired spending on output at each level of NNP will be given by a $C + I + G$ line that lies between $C_0 + I + G$ and $C_1 + I + G$ line in Figure 11.4. Since the equilibrium value of NNP will be at the point where this line intersects the 45-degree line, the equilibrium value of NNP will be greater than $980 billion. Thus the decrease in the tax rate will increase the equilibrium value of NNP. By increasing the amount people want to spend on consumption at each level of NNP, it will raise the $C + I + G$ line from $C_1 + I + G$ to a higher level.[1]

---

[1] Note that the slope of the relationship between consumption and NNP increases as the tax rate decreases. This means that the "marginal propensity to consume out of NNP" increases as the tax rate decreases. Consequently, the multiplier—the amount by which NNP changes if desired investment changes (or the consumption function shifts, or government expenditures change)—increases as the tax rate goes down, and conversely decreases as the tax rate goes up. In other words, as the tax rate increases, NNP becomes less sensitive to changes in investment, government spending, and the consumption function.

To see this, the mathematically inclined reader is encouraged to work through the following proof. Suppose that the consumption function is a straight line:

$$C = \alpha + \beta(1 - T)Y,$$

where Y = NNP, T equals the tax rate, i.e., the proportion of NNP consumers pay in taxes, α is the intercept of the consumption function, and β is the marginal propensity to consume. By definition,

$$Y = C + I + G.$$

Thus substituting for C,

$$Y = \alpha + \beta(1 - T)Y + I + G,$$

which means that

$$[1 - \beta(1 - T)]Y = \alpha + I + G,$$

or

$$Y = \frac{\alpha}{1 - \beta(1 - T)} + \frac{I}{1 - \beta(1 - T)} + \frac{G}{1 - \beta(1 - T)}.$$

Thus a $1 billion increase in α, I, or G results in an increase of $\left[\frac{1}{1 - \beta(1 - T)}\right]$ billions of dollars in NNP. In other words, the multiplier is $\left[\frac{1}{1 - \beta(1 - T)}\right]$. But $\left[\frac{1}{1 - \beta(1 - T)}\right]$ gets bigger as T gets smaller; and conversely, $\left[\frac{1}{1 - \beta(1 - T)}\right]$ gets smaller as T gets bigger. This completes the proof.

Table 11.1
Determination of Equilibrium Level of Net National Product (billions of dollars)

(1) Net national product	(2) Taxes	(3) Disposable income (1)−(2)	(4) Desired consumption expenditure	(5) Desired saving (3)−(4)	(6) Desired invest-ment	(7) Government expenditure	(8) Total desired spending (4)+(6)+(7)	(9) Tendency of national output
1,000	50	950	920	30	90	50	1,060	Upward
1,050	50	1,000	950	50	90	50	1,090	Upward
1,100	50	1,050	980	70	90	50	1,120	Upward
1,150	50	1,100	1,010	90	90	50	1,150	No change
1,200	50	1,150	1,040	110	90	50	1,180	Downward
1,250	50	1,200	1,070	130	90	50	1,210	Downward
1,300	50	1,250	1,100	150	90	50	1,240	Downward

A Tabular Illustration

To illustrate how one can determine the equilibrium level of NNP when both government expenditure and taxation are included in our model, consider the numerical example shown in Table 11.1. The numbers in this table are the same as in Table 10.1, except that we now assume that the government spends $50 billion per year on goods and services and that it receives $50 billions in taxes per year. (For simplicity, we assume in this table that the amounts of both government expenditure and taxes are independent of the level of NNP. This is in contrast to the previous section where we assumed that taxes were proportional to NNP.) Column 1 of the table shows various possible levels of NNP. To obtain the level of disposable income corresponding to each level of NNP, we must subtract taxes (in column 2) from NNP, the result being shown in column 3.

Since the consumption function is assumed to be the same as in Table 10.1 (and Table 9.1), the desired consumption expenditure at each level of disposable income is as shown in column 4. Note that disposable income no longer equals NNP, as it did in Table 10.1, because taxes have entered the picture; this means that the relationship between desired consumption expenditure and NNP is also different. But since the consumption function is unchanged, the relationship between desired consumption expenditure and disposable income is the same as in Table 10.1.

Columns 5 to 8 of the table seem self-evident. Since desired saving equals disposable income less desired consumption expenditure, column 5 equals column 3 minus column 4. Column 6 shows desired investment, which is $90 billion. Column 7 shows government expenditure, which is $50 billion. And column 8 shows total desired spending on output at each level of NNP. Since total desired spending equals desired consumption expenditure plus desired investment expenditure plus desired government expenditure, column 8 equals column 4 plus column 6 plus column 7.

As emphasized in previous discussions (in this and the previous chapter), *national output will be at its equilibrium value only if total desired spending is equal (no more, no less) to NNP.* Thus, based on the data in Table 11.1, it is clear that the equilibrium value of NNP is $1,150 billion. Why? Because a comparison of columns 1 and 8 in Table 11.1 shows that this is the only value of NNP at which total desired spending (column 8) equals NNP (column 1).

If NNP is *less* than $1,150 billion, there will be a tendency for it to increase. Total spending will exceed the value of output produced, the result being that firms' inventories will be depleted. Firms will respond by raising their production rates, thus increasing NNP. If NNP is *greater* than $1,150 billion, there will be a tendency for it to decline. Total spending will fall short of the value of output produced, the result being that firms' inventories will mount. Firms will respond by lowering their production rates, thus decreasing NNP.

Finally, the leakage-injection approach described in the previous chapter is an alternative way of determining the equilibrium level of NNP. To use this approach, two points must be understood. First, *taxes are a leakage because they withdraw spending from the flow of income and expenditure.* After all, money that goes for taxes cannot be spent on output. Second, *government expenditure is an injection since it adds spending to the flow of income and expenditure.* It is a supplement to consumption expenditure and investment.

Since taxes are a leakage, the total leakages in Table 11.1 are desired saving plus taxes, or column 5 plus column 2. And since government expenditure is an injection, the total injections in Table 11.1 are desired investment plus government expenditure, or column 6 plus column 7. According to our discussion in the previous chapter, *the equilibrium value of NNP must be the value of NNP at which total leakages equal total injections*—in other words, the value of NNP at which desired saving plus taxes (column 5 plus column 2) equals desired investment plus government expenditure (column 6 plus column 7). Table 11.1 shows that this value of NNP is $1,150 billion. Of course, the answer obtained by the leakage-injection approach coincides, as it must, with that obtained by comparing the value of total desired spending (column 8) with the value of NNP (column 1).

The Balanced-Budget Multiplier

According to our previous conclusions, increases in government expenditures tend to increase NNP, while increases in tax receipts tend to reduce NNP. What will be the result when *both* government expenditures and tax receipts are increased *by the same amount?* Clearly, the increase in government expenditures will push NNP up, while the tax increase will push NNP down. But which force will prevail? According to an economic proposition called the balanced-budget multiplier, the result will be an *increase* in equilibrium NNP—and under the assumptions made in Table 11.1, this increase equals the increase in both government expenditures and taxes. (Although it is not very difficult to prove that this is the case, the proof involves some mathematics, and so will be omitted here.)

On the other hand, suppose that both government expenditures and tax receipts are *decreased* by the same amount. What will be the effect on NNP? Clearly, the decrease in government expenditures will push NNP down, while the tax cut will push NNP up. But which force will prevail? According to the balanced-budget multiplier, the result will be a *decrease* in equilibrium NNP—and under the assumptions made in Table 11.1, this decrease equals the decrease in both government expenditures and taxes.

To illustrate the application of this proposition, consider a proposal made by President Ford in 1975 to cut both taxes and government expenditures by $28 billion. Assuming that both the expenditure and tax cuts went into effect at the same time, this would have reduced NNP, as we have just seen. (However, if the tax cut occurred before the expenditure cut, as some observers claimed it would, the proposal might not have had this effect at all. Recall that the balanced-budget multiplier is concerned with a *simultaneous* change in government receipts and tax revenues.)

Recessionary and Inflationary Gaps

In this and the previous chapter, we have shown how the equilibrium level of net national product is determined. But it is of central importance to recognize that *this equilibrium level of NNP may not correspond to full employment.* As pointed out in Chapter 9, a basic theme of modern economics is that there is no automatic tendency for NNP to equal its full-employment level. For example, in Table 11.1, there is no assurance that $1,150 billion is the level of NNP corresponding to full employment. It may be below the full-employment level, in which case the unemployment rate will exceed 4 or 5 percent (the figures generally used to define full employment). Or it may be above the full-employment level, in which case there will be considerable inflation.

For simplicity, suppose that, so long as total spending does not exceed the value (at initial prices) of the full-employment level of output, the price level remains constant. (As pointed out in Chapter 8, this really is not true, but it is a useful simplification in the present context.) Then if the equilibrium NNP is *below* the full-employment level, the ***recessionary gap*** *is the increase in desired spending required to push the equilibrium NNP up to the full-employment level.* For example, if the full-employment level of NNP is Q_1 in Figure 11.6, the recessionary gap is $40 billion. Why? Because this is the amount by which desired spending must be increased if NNP is to rise from its current equilibrium level, Q_0, to Q_1. In other words, as shown in Figure 11.6, this is the amount by which the $C + I + G$ line must be raised in order to increase the equilibrium level of NNP from Q_0 to Q_1. *To prevent excessive unemployment, such a recessionary gap should be eliminated.*

Figure 11.6
Recessionary Gap
The equilibrium level of NNP, Q_0, is too low to result in full employment. The level of NNP corresponding to full employment is Q_1. To raise the equilibrium level of NNP from Q_0 to Q_1, desired spending must be increased by $40 billion. In other words, the $C + I + G$ line must be raised by $40 billion. This amount—the *vertical* distance between the 45-degree line and the $C + I + G$ line *at the full-employment level of NNP*—is called the *recessionary gap.*

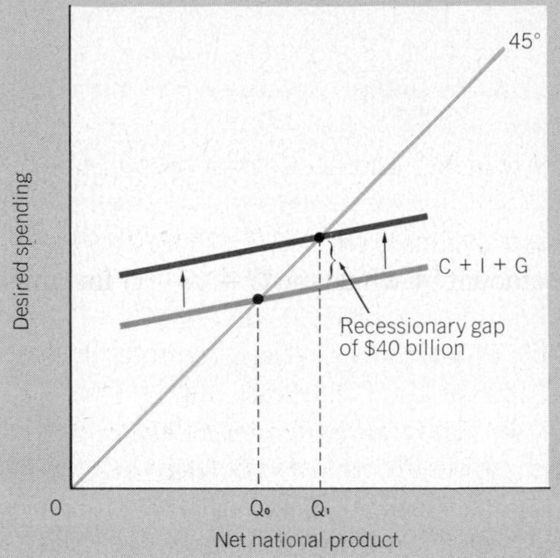

On the other hand, if the equilibrium NNP is *above* the full-employment level, the ***inflationary gap*** *is the reduction in desired spending required to push the equilibrium NNP down to the full-employment level.* For example, if the full-employment level of NNP is Q_2 in Figure 11.7, the inflationary gap is $40 billion. Why? Because this is the amount by which desired spending must be reduced if NNP is to fall from its current equilibrium level, Q_3, to Q_2.

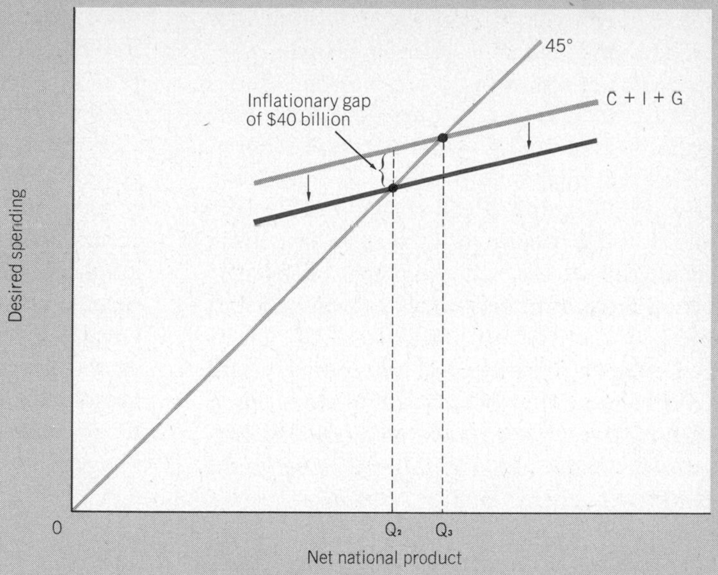

Figure 11.7
Inflationary Gap
For simplicity, assume that Q_2, the full-employment level of NNP, is the *maximum* value of *real* NNP (*in initial prices*) that can be achieved; thus any increase of *money* NNP above Q_2 is due entirely to inflation. To reduce the equilibrium NNP from Q_3 (its current level) to Q_2, desired spending must be reduced by $40 billion. In other words, the $C + I + G$ line must be lowered by $40 billion. This amount—the *vertical* distance between the 45-degree line and the $C + I + G$ line *at the full-employment level of NNP*—is called the *inflationary gap.*

In other words, as shown in Figure 11.7, this is the amount by which the $C + I + G$ line must fall in order to reduce the equilibrium level of NNP from Q_3 to Q_2. Assuming that Q_2 is the maximum value of real NNP (in initial prices) that can be achieved, any increase of money NNP above Q_2 is due entirely to inflation. Thus, *to curb inflationary pressures, such an inflationary gap should be eliminated.*

The Nature and Objectives of Fiscal Policy

Our discussions in previous sections make it easy to understand the basic ideas underlying modern fiscal policy. For example, suppose that the economy is suffering from an undesirably high unemployment rate. What should the government do? Since there is a recessionary gap, the economy needs increased spending. In other words, as shown in Figure 11.6, the economy needs an upward shift of the $C + I + G$ line, which by increasing NNP will increase employment as well. There are three ways that the government can try to bring this about. First, it can reduce taxes, which, as shown in a previous section, will shift the relation between consumption expenditure and NNP—and consequently the $C + I + G$ line—upward. Second, it can increase government expenditures, which will also shift the $C + I + G$ line upward. Third, the government can encourage firms to invest more, perhaps by enacting tax credits to make investment more profitable for them; an increase in desired investment will shift the $C + I + G$ line upward too.

On the other hand, perhaps we are suffering from an undesirably high rate of inflation. What should the government do? Since there is an inflationary gap, the economy needs reduced spending. In other words, what is required is a downward shift of the $C + I + G$ line, as shown in Figure 11.7. The government has three ways to try to bring this about. First, it can increase taxes; this, as shown in a previous section, will shift the relation between consumption expenditure and NNP—and consequently the $C + I + G$ line—downward. Second, it can cut government expenditures, which will also shift the $C + I + G$ curve downward. Third, it can change the tax laws and do other things to discourage firms from investing in plant and equipment or inventories; a decrease in desired investment will shift the $C + I + G$ line downward too.

Certainly, these ideas do not seem very hard to understand. Put bluntly, all we are saying is that, *if there is too much unemployment, the government should promote, directly or indirectly, additional public and/or private spending, which will result in additional output and jobs.* On the other hand, *if there is too much inflation, the government should reduce, directly or indirectly, spending (public and/or private); this will curb the inflationary pressure on prices.* Surely these propositions seem reasonable enough. And they are useful—although by themselves they cannot deal as effectively as one would like with times like the mid-1970s, when excessive unemployment and inflation have occurred together. We shall discuss such situations in detail in Chapter 16.

Perhaps the most surprising thing about these ideas is that they have been understood and accepted only very recently. Until the appearance of John Maynard Keynes's work in the 1930s, the economics profession really did not understand the effects of fiscal policy at all well. And once Keynes showed his fellow economists the way, it took over 20 years to convince congressmen, presidents, and other officials that these ideas were valid. Moreover, the educational process is still going on. Perhaps the most important reason why it has been so difficult to get across such simple ideas is that, until recently, the conventional wisdom passed down from father to son was that the government is no different from any other large enterprise: businesses must balance income against outgo, so should the government. In other words, it should spend no more than what it collects in taxes. This proposition is at odds with the ideas presented above. If those ideas are accepted, it may be necessary for the government to run a deficit or a surplus, depending on the economic situation. A ***deficit*** occurs when the government spends more than it collects in taxes; a ***surplus*** occurs when it spends less. It has taken a long time to convince people that full employment and stable prices—not a balanced budget—should be our goals. Some people still believe that the road to economic destruction is lined with unbalanced budgets.

Makers of Fiscal Policy

When you go to a ball game, you generally get a program telling you who on each team is playing each position. To understand the formulation and implementation of fiscal policy in the United States we need the same kind of information. Who are the people who establish our fiscal policy? Who decides that in view of the current and prospective economic situation, tax rates or government expenditures should be changed? This is not a simple question because lots of individuals and groups play an important role. In the Congress, the House and Senate Budget Committees—as well as the Congressional Budget Office—have been charged with important responsibilities in this area. Also, the Appropriations Committees, the House Ways and Means Committee, and the Senate Finance Committee have considerable influence. In addition, another congressional committee is of importance—the Joint Economic Committee of Congress. Established by the Employment Act of 1946, this committee goes over the annual Economic Report of the President on the state of the economy, and, through its hearings, provides a major forum for review of economic issues.

The Council of Economic Advisers

Before World War II, there was relatively little place in the government for economists. The Treasury had a small number, the antitrust division of the Justice Department a handful, but there was no place for economists who aspired to give advice on broad policy matters. The Employment Act of 1946 changed that situation by creating a council to "gather timely and authoritative information . . . to develop and recommend to the President national economic policies . . . and to make and furnish studies . . . as the President may request."

But as demonstrated by the first chairman, Edwin Nourse, the act was really a hunting license for a chairman to peddle his good counsel. Nourse, who believed that the Council's role was to "interpret literal facts . . . without becoming involved in any way in the advocacy of particular measures," found that such services were rarely required by the president. It is hard to find any trace of the Nourse era on the economic policies of the late forties.

THE FIRST COUNCIL OF ECONOMIC ADVISERS, EDWIN NOURSE, CHAIRMAN, AT LEFT.

Nourse's successor, Leon Keyserling, hunted so avidly that Congress almost suspended his license. Keyserling was temperamentally and politically inclined to activism. His advocacy of expansionist policies to a conservative Congress and a president concerned primarily with containing the Korean War inflation led to a bill reducing the CEA's budget by 25 percent. The Council was saved by the persuasiveness of a new chairman, Arthur F. Burns, and the support of a few senators. But the limits of independent advocacy had been established.

The Eisenhower years were quiet years for the Council. Even the election of John F. Kennedy, who was eager to increase the U.S. rate of economic growth, did not insure the Council's future. Kennedy was inclined to fiscal conservatism and less interested in domestic than in foreign affairs. It was Walter Heller, the new chairman under Kennedy, who made the CEA an integral part of the New Frontier. The tax cut of 1964, which Heller sold to a president committed to balanced budgets, is a tribute to his success in making a body without formal powers or legislative prerogatives an integral part of the policy-making process. The new-found status of the Council was acknowledged in Washington by the establishment of a Quadriad, made up of representatives of the Council, the Bureau of the Budget, the Treasury, and the Federal Reserve, which met periodically to discuss economic affairs.

The Council's influence has risen and ebbed in recent years with both the state of the economy and with other pressures on the president. In 1966, as the Vietnam War intensified, the Council urged a tax increase; Lyndon Johnson, more attuned to the political realities, did not take action on the proposal until 1967. The Council's position in the Nixon administration further exemplified this process. Led by Paul McCracken and Herbert Stein, the Council championed restraint in fiscal and monetary policies early in Nixon's first term. But faced with mounting inflationary pressures, the Council members reluctantly joined other administration economists in setting up wage and price controls. In the Ford administration, the CEA played an important role, although the secretary of the Treasury, William Simon, often was the administration's leading economic spokesman. During 1974 and 1975, the Council had to help the president combat both double-digit inflation and the most severe recession since the thirties. In the Carter administration, the CEA has continued to play a major role in policy formation. E.A.

In the executive branch of government, the most important person in the establishment of fiscal policy is, of course, the president. Although he must operate in the context of the tax and expenditure laws passed by Congress, he and his advisers are the country's principal analysts of the need for fiscal expansion or restraint and its leading spokesmen for legislative changes to meet these needs. Needless to say, he doesn't pore over the latest economic data and make the decisions all by himself. The Office of Management and Budget, which is part of the Executive Office of the President, is a very powerful adviser to the president on expenditure policy, as is the Treasury Department on tax policy. In addition, there is the ***Council of Economic Advisers,*** which is part of the Executive Office of the President. Established by the Employment Act of 1946, its job is to help the president carry out the objectives of that act.

During the past 30 years, the Council of Economic Advisers, headed by a series of distinguished economists who left academic and other posts to contribute to public policy, has become a very important actor on the national economic policy stage. Its position has been well described by Stanford's G. L. Bach:

> Fundamentally, it is responsible for overseeing the state of the economy, for continually checking on the appropriateness of government policies for stable economic growth, and for working intimately with the President and other parts of the executive branch in developing overall legislative policy in the economic field. Some Council chairmen have worked closely with Congressional committees; others have remained more in the background as Presidential advisers. But for macroeconomic policy, the Council is now perhaps the President's most important single advisory group. It is *his* council and more specifically *his* part of the government than are the regular executive branch departments.[2]

[2] G. L. Bach, *Making Monetary and Fiscal Policy,* Washington, D.C.: Brookings Institution, 1971, pp. 30-31.

Automatic Stabilizers

Now that we have met some of the major players, we must point out that they get help from some ***automatic stabilizers***—some structural features of our economy that tend to stabilize national output. Although these economic stabilizers cannot do all that is required to keep the economy on an even keel, they help a lot. As soon as the economy turns down and unemployment mounts, they give the economy a helpful shot in the arm. As soon as the economy gets overheated and inflation crops up, they tend to restrain it.

Tax revenues. Changes in tax revenues are an important automatic stabilizer. One of the major points emphasized in Chapter 5 was that our federal system relies heavily on the income tax. The amount of income tax collected by the federal government goes up with increases in NNP and goes down with decreases in NNP. Moreover, because the income tax is progressive, the average tax rate goes up with increases in NNP, and goes down with decreases in NNP. This, of course, is just what we want to occur. When output falls off and unemployment mounts, tax collections fall off too, so disposable income falls less than NNP. This means less of a fall in consumption, which tends to brake the fall in NNP. When output rises too fast and the economy begins to suffer from serious inflation, tax collections rise too—which tends to brake the increase in NNP. Of course, corporation income taxes, as well as personal income taxes, play a significant role here.

Unemployment compensation and welfare payments. Unemployment compensation is paid to workers who are laid off, according to a system that has evolved over the past 40 years. When an unemployed worker goes back to work, he stops receiving unemployment compensation. Thus, when NNP falls off and unemployment mounts, the tax collections to finance unemployment compensation go down (because of lower employment), while the amount paid out to unemployed workers goes up. On the other hand, when NNP rises too fast and the economy begins to suffer from serious inflation, the tax collections to finance unemployment compensation go up, while the amount paid out goes down because there is much less unemployment. Again, this is just what we want to see happen. Spending is bolstered when unemployment is high and curbed when there are serious inflationary pressures. Various welfare programs have the same kind of automatic stabilizing effect on the economy.

Corporate dividends, family saving, and farm programs. Since corporations tend to maintain their dividends when their sales fall off, and moderate the increase in their dividends when their sales soar, their dividend policy tends to stabilize the economy. This is very important. Also, to the extent that consumers tend to be slow to raise or lower their spending in response to increases or decreases in their income, this too tends to stabilize the economy. Finally, there are the agricultural support programs, described in Chapter 5. The government has buttressed farm prices and incomes when business was bad and unemployment was high. When output was high and inflation occurred, the government distributed the commodities in its warehouses and received dollars. In both cases, these programs acted as stabilizers.

Having painted such a glowing picture of the economy's automatic stabilizers, we are in danger of suggesting that they can stabilize the economy all by themselves. It would be nice if this were true, but it isn't. All the automatic stabilizers do is *cut down* on variations in unemployment and inflation, not *eliminate* them. Discretionary tax and spending programs are needed to supplement the effects of these automatic stabilizers. Some economists wish strongly that it were possible to set well-defined rules for government action, rather than leave things to the discretion of policy makers. Indeed, Milton Friedman, among others, forcefully argues for greater reliance on such rules, but most economists feel that it is impossible to formulate a set of rules flexible and comprehensive enough to let us do away with the discretionary powers of policy makers. Instead their concern is with sharpening the tools available to government economic decision makers.

The Tools of Discretionary Fiscal Policy

Suppose that the Council of Economic Advisers, on the basis of information concerning recent economic developments, believes that national output may decline soon, causing serious unemployment, and that other agencies, like the Treasury and the Federal Reserve System, agree. What specific measures can the Council recommend that the government take under such circumstances?

First, *the government can vary its expenditure for public works and other programs.* If increased unemployment seems to be in the wind, it can step up outlays on roads, urban reconstruction, and other public programs. Of course, these programs must be well thought out and socially productive. There is no sense in pushing through wasteful and foolish public works programs merely to make jobs. Or if, as in 1969, the economy is plagued by inflation, it can (as President Nixon ordered) stop new federal construction programs temporarily.

Second, *the government can vary welfare payments and other types of transfer payments.* For example, a hike in Social Security benefits may provide a very healthy shot in the arm for an economy with too much unemployment. An increase in veterans' benefits or in aid to dependent children may do the same thing. The federal government has sometimes helped the states to extend the length of time that the unemployed can receive unemployment compensation; this too will have the desired effect. On the other hand, if there is full employment and inflation is a dangerous problem, it may be worthwhile to cut back on certain kinds of transfer payments. For example, if it is agreed that some veterans' benefits should be reduced, this reduction might be timed to occur during a period when inflationary pressures are evident.

Third, *the government can vary tax rates.* For example, if there is considerable unemployment, the government may cut tax rates, as it did in 1975. Or if inflation is the problem, the government may increase taxes, as it did in 1968 when, after considerable political maneuvering and buckpassing, the Congress was finally persuaded to put through a 10 percent tax surcharge to try to moderate the inflation caused by the Vietnam War. However, temporary tax changes may have less effect than permanent ones, since, as pointed out in Chapter 9, consumption expenditure may be influenced less by transitory changes in income than by permanent changes.

Of course there are advantages and disadvantages in each of these tools of fiscal policy. One of the big disadvantages of public works and similar spending programs is that they take so long to get started. Plans must be made, land must be acquired, and preliminary construction studies must be carried out. By the time the expenditures are finally made and have the desired effect, the dangers of excessive unemployment may have given way to dangers of inflation, so that the spending, coming too late, does more harm than good. To some extent, this problem may be ameliorated by having a backlog of productive projects ready to go at all times. In this way, at least a portion of the lag can be eliminated.

In recent years, there has been a widespread feeling that government expenditures should be set on the basis of their long-run desirability and productivity and not on the basis of short-term stabilization considerations. The optimal level of government expenditure is at the point where the value of the extra benefits to be derived from an extra dollar of government expenditure is at least equal to the dollar of cost. This optimal level is unlikely to change much in the short run, and it would be wasteful to spend more—or less—than this amount for stabilization purposes when tax changes could be used instead. Thus many economists believe that tax cuts or tax increases should be the primary fiscal weapons to fight unemployment or inflation.

However, one of the big problems with tax changes is that it is difficult to get Congress to take speedy action. There is often considerable debate over a tax bill, and sometimes it becomes a political football. Another difficulty with tax changes is that it generally is much easier to reduce taxes than it is to get them back up again. To politicians, lower taxes are attractive because they are popular, and higher taxes are dangerous because they may hurt a politician's chances of re-election. In discussing fiscal policy (or most other aspects of government operations, for that matter), to ignore politics is to risk losing touch with reality.

Two Hits and a Miss: Recent Applications of Economic Analysis

The Tax Cut of 1964

With some knowledge of the players and the plays they can call, we can look now at three examples of fiscal policy in action. When the Kennedy administration took office in 1961, it was confronted with a relatively high unemployment rate—about 7 percent in mid-1961. By 1962, although unemployment was somewhat lower (about 6 percent), the president's advisers, led by Walter W. Heller, chairman of the Council of Economic Advisers, pushed for a tax cut to reduce unemployment further. The president, after considerable discussion of the effects of such a tax cut, announced in June 1962 that he would propose such a measure to the Congress; and in January 1963, the bill was finally sent to Congress.

The proposed tax bill was a victory for modern ideas on fiscal policy. Even though it would mean a deliberately large deficit, the president had been convinced to cut taxes to push the economy closer to full employment. But the Congress was not so easily convinced. Many congressmen labeled the proposal irresponsible and reckless. Others wanted to couple tax reform with tax reduction. It was not until 1964, after President Kennedy's death, that the tax bill was enacted. It took a year from the time the bill was sent to Congress for it to be passed, and during this interval, there was a continuous debate in the executive branch and the Congress. The secretary of the Treasury, Douglas Dillon, the chairman of the Federal Reserve Board, William M. Martin, and numerous congressmen—all powerful and all initially cool to the proposal—were eventually won over. The result was a tax reduction of about $10 billion per year.

The effects of the tax cut are by no means easy to measure, but in line with the theory presented in earlier sections, consumption expenditure did increase sharply during 1964. Moreover, the additional consumption undoubtedly induced additional investment. According to some estimates, the tax cut resulted in an increase in GNP of about $24 billion in 1965 and more in subsequent years.[3] The unemployment rate, which had been about 5½ to 6 percent during 1962 and 1963, fell to 5 percent during 1964 and to 4.7 percent in the spring of 1965. It is fair to say that most economists were extremely pleased with themselves in 1965. Fiscal policy based on their theories seemed to work very well indeed! Unfortunately, however, this pleasure did not last very long, there being another, and sadder, tale to tell.

The Tax Surcharge of 1968

In late July 1965, President Lyndon Johnson announced that the United States would send 50,000 more men to Vietnam. From fiscal 1965 to fiscal 1966, defense expenditures rose from $50 billion to $62 billion—a large increase in government expenditure, and one that took place at a time of relatively full employment. On the basis of the theory presented earlier in this chapter, such an increase in government expenditure would be expected to cause inflationary pressures. The Council of Economic Advisers recognized this danger, and recommended in late 1965 that the president urge Congress to increase taxes. Johnson was reluctant. The inflationary pressures mounted during 1966, and little was done by fiscal policy makers to quell them.

Even in 1967, the Congress was unwilling to raise taxes. The case for fiscal restraint was, it felt, not clear enough. As for the president, he said, "It is not a popular thing for a President to do . . . to ask for a penny out of a dollar to pay for a war that is not popular either."[4] Finally, in mid-1968, a 10 percent surcharge on income taxes, together with some restraint in government spending, was enacted. This increase in taxes was obviously the right medicine, but it was at least two years too late, and its effects were delayed and insufficient.

The Tax Cut of 1975

In late 1974, the unemployment rate began to mount. Whereas it was 5.5 percent in August, it reached 7.2 percent in December. Although economists were rather slow to recognize that the economy was slumping into a severe recession, by early 1975 it was clear that some stimulus was needed. Inflation, which President

[3] Arthur Okun, "Measuring the Impact of the 1964 Tax Reduction," in Walter W. Heller, *Perspectives on Economic Growth,* New York: Random House, 1968, p. 33.

[4] Arthur Okun, *The Political Economy of Prosperity,* New York: Norton, 1970, p. 88.

Ford had labeled "Public Enemy Number One" in the fall of 1974, continued to be a problem, but most policy makers felt that unemployment rates were reaching intolerable levels. By March 1975, the unemployment rate was 8.7 percent, the highest level in over 30 years, and something clearly had to be done to lower it.

In early 1975, President Ford proposed a $16 billion tax cut. As his Council of Economic Advisers stated, its purpose was "to halt the decline in production and employment so that growth of output can resume and unemployment can be reduced."[5] In March 1975, Congress passed a $23 billion tax cut, which provided rebates (of $100 to $200) on 1974 personal income taxes as well as reductions in 1975 income taxes. Both personal and corporate income taxes were cut. Personal tax liabilities were reduced through a $30 credit for each taxpayer and each dependent, as well as through increased standard deductions and low-income allowances. Corporate tax liabilities were reduced through a liberalization of the investment tax credit, as well as changes in tax rates.

The evidence seems to indicate that the tax cut was the right kind of medicine. In accord with our theories, national output did, in fact, increase in the latter half of 1975, and unemployment eased somewhat. By the end of 1975, the recovery was well under way—due in part, according to most economists, to the tax cut.

Based on the histories of all three of these tax changes (1964, 1968, and 1975), it is clear that, although we know a great deal more than we used to about how fiscal policy should be employed to avoid inflation or considerable unemployment, there is no guarantee that it will be used in this way. In the early 1960s and in 1974-75, policy makers seemed to make reasonably correct choices; in 1965-68, they did not. Without question, mistakes will continue to be made: all that we can do is try to learn from past mistakes.

[5] Council of Economic Advisers, *1975 Annual Report,* Washington, D.C.: Government Printing Office, 1975.

Deficit and Surplus Financing

Now that you have studied the basic elements of fiscal policy, let's see how well you would fare with some of the problems that confront our nation's top policy makers. Suppose that, through some inexplicable malfunctioning of the democratic process, you are elected president of the United States. Your Council of Economic Advisers reports to you that, on the basis of various forecasts, national output is likely to drop next year, and unemployment is likely to be much higher. Naturally, you are concerned; and having absorbed the ideas presented in this chapter, you ask your advisers—the Council of Economic Advisers, the Treasury, and the Office of Management and Budget—what sort of fiscal policy should be adopted to head off this undesirable turn of events. On the basis of their advice, you suggest to Congress that taxes should be cut and government expenditures should be increased.

When they receive your message, a number of key congressmen point out that if the government cuts taxes and raises expenditures it will operate in the red. In other words, government revenue will fall short of government spending—there will be a deficit. They warn that such fiscal behavior is irresponsible, since it violates the fundamental tenet of public finance that the budget should be balanced: income should cover outgo. For further clarification on this point, you call in your advisers, who deny that the budget should be balanced each year. They point out that if a deficit is run in a particular year, the government can borrow the difference; and they claim that the national debt is in no sense dangerously large in the United States at present. Whose advice would you follow—that of your economic advisers or that of the congressmen?

Or suppose your advisers tell you that inflation is a growing problem and that you should cut back government spending and raise taxes. Since this advice seems eminently sensible, based on the principles set forth in this chapter, you propose this course of action to Congress. Some prominent newspapers point out that by raising taxes and cutting expenditures, the government will take in more than it spends. In other words, there will be a surplus. They say that there is no reason for the government to take more money from the people than it needs to pay for the services it performs, and argue that taxes should not be increased because the government can cover its expenditures without such an increase. Whose advice would you follow—that of your economic advisers or that of the newspapers?

You would be wise to go along with your economic advisers in both cases. Why? Because there is nothing particularly desirable about a balanced budget. Although it may well be prudent for individuals and families not to spend more than they earn, this does not carry over to the federal government. When we need to stimulate the economy and raise national output, it is perfectly legitimate and desirable for the federal government to run a deficit, provided it gets its full money's worth for what is spent. All that happens is that the government borrows the difference, and—as we pointed out in Chapter 6—there is no indication that the national debt is dangerously large. Thus, in the first case, you should not have been worried by the fact that a deficit would result. And in the second case, while it is true that the government could support its expenditures with lower taxes, this would defeat your purpose. What you want to do is to cut total spending, public and private, and raising taxes will cut private spending.

Deficit Spending in the 1930s: A Case Study

Some people—fewer than there used to be, but still some—are dead set against deficit spending by the government. Many, when pressed to explain their opposition, retort that it was tried by Franklin D. Roosevelt during the Great Depression of the 1930s and that it failed to eliminate the high levels of unemployment that prevailed then. This is both bad history and bad economics. The federal government did spend more than it took in during the Roosevelt administration, but the deficit was far too small to have much effect. GNP fell from about $100 billion in 1929 to less than $60 billion in 1933. Federal deficits in the 1930s were only a few billion dollars per year at most, and in many years these deficits were offset by surpluses run by the state and local governments. The situation somewhat resembled that described by the columnist Heywood Broun, when he wrote, "I have known people to stop and buy an apple on the corner and then walk away as if they had solved the whole unemployment problem."[6]

In a careful study of the effects of fiscal policy in the 1930s, Professor E. Cary Brown of M.I.T. concluded that fiscal policy "seems to have been an unsuccessful recovery device in the thirties—not because it did not work, but because it was not tried."[7] For those who know something of the political history of the period, this is not surprising. Few government officials of that day understood the power and effects of fiscal policy. The federal government did run a deficit, but largely in spite of itself. In that era, the golden rule of fiscal responsibility was a balanced budget, and deficits were regarded as unfortunate aberrations. If you contrast this attitude with the attitude of the federal government toward the tax cuts of 1964 and 1975, you will see how far the nation has come in its understanding of fiscal policy.

[6] Heywood Broun, *It Seems to Me,* 1933. Of course, this does not mean that the Roosevelt administration did not attempt to reduce unemployment. What we are saying is that the history of the period is not a very good test of the effectiveness of deficit spending.

[7] E. Cary Brown, "Fiscal Policy in the Thirties: A Reappraisal," *American Economic Review,* December 1956, pp. 865–66.

Alternative Budget Policies

At least three policies concerning the government budget are worthy of detailed examination. The first policy says that *the government's budget should be balanced each and every year.* This is the philosophy that generally prevailed, here and abroad, until the advent of Keynesian economics in the 1930s. Superficially, it seems eminently reasonable. After all, won't a family or firm go bankrupt if it continues to spend more than it takes in? Why should the government be any different? However, the truth is that the government has economic capabilities, powers, and responsibilities that are entirely different from those of any family or firm, and it is misleading–sometimes even pernicious–to assume that what is sensible for a family or firm is also sensible for the government.

If this policy of balancing the budget is accepted, the government cannot use fiscal policy as a tool to stabilize the economy. Indeed, if the government attempts to balance its budget each year, it is likely to make unemployment or inflation worse rather than better. For example, suppose that severe unemployment occurs because of a drop in national output. Since incomes drop, tax receipts drop as well. Thus, if the government attempts to balance its budget, it must cut its spending and/or increase tax rates, both of which will tend to lower, not raise, national output. On the other hand, suppose that inflation occurs because spending increases too rapidly. Since incomes increase, tax receipts increase too. Thus, for the government to balance its budget, it must increase its spending and/or decrease tax rates, both of which will tend to raise, not lower, spending.[8]

A second budgetary philosophy says that *the government's budget should be balanced over the course of each "business cycle."* As we shall see in Chapter 12, the rate of growth of national output tends to behave cyclically. As shown in Figure 8.6, it tends to increase for a while, then drop, increase, then drop. Unemployment also tends to ebb and flow in a similar cyclical fashion. This is the so-called business cycle. According to this second budgetary policy, the government is not expected to balance its budget each year, but is expected to run a big enough surplus during periods of high employment to offset the deficit it runs during the ensuing period of excessive unemployment. This policy seems to give the government enough flexibility to run the deficits or surpluses needed to stabilize the economy, while at the same time allaying any public fear of a chronically unbalanced budget. It certainly seems to be a neat way to reconcile the government's use of fiscal policy to promote noninflationary full employment with the public's uneasiness over chronically unbalanced budgets.

Unfortunately, however, it does contain one fundamental flaw: there is no reason to believe that the size of the deficits required to eliminate excessive unemployment will equal the size of the surpluses required to moderate the subsequent inflation. For example, suppose that national output falls sharply, causing severe and prolonged unemployment; then regains its full-employment level only briefly; then falls again. In such a case, the deficits incurred to get the economy back to full employment are likely to exceed by far the surpluses run during the brief period of full employment. Thus there would be no way to stabilize the economy without running an unbalanced

[8] In sophisticated circles, there is some support for this philosophy of a balanced budget, based on the idea that it makes it easier for the Office of Management and Budget to keep expenditures within reasonable limits. Once this philosophy is abandoned completely, it is feared that the individual departments and agencies of the government can challenge OMB's estimate of how big a surplus or deficit is appropriate, and argue that more spending on their part would be a good thing. In other words, it makes it easier to control spending.

Another point that is frequently made is that the government, through inappropriate fiscal or monetary policies, is often responsible for problems of unemployment and inflation. To many economists, the practical problem seems to be how to prevent the government from creating disturbances, rather than how to use the government budget (and monetary policy) to offset disturbances arising from the private sector. Unfortunately, as we noted in connection with the inflation arising from the Vietnam War, there is sometimes a good deal of truth to this.

budget over the course of this business cycle. If this policy were adopted, and if the government attempted to balance the budget over the course of each business cycle, this would interfere with an effective fiscal policy designed to promote full employment with stable prices.

Finally, a third budgetary policy says that *the government's budget should be set so as to promote whatever attainable combination of unemployment and inflation seems socially optimal,* even if this means that the budget is unbalanced over considerable periods of time. This policy is sometimes called ***functional finance.***[9] Proponents of functional finance point out that, although this policy may mean a continual growth in the public debt, the problems caused by a moderate growth in the public debt are small when compared with the social costs of unemployment and inflation.

Certainly, the history of the past 40 years has been characterized by enormous changes in the nation's attitude toward the government budget. Forty years ago, the prevailing attitude was that the government's budget should be balanced. The emergence of the modern theory of the determination of national output and employment shook this attitude, at least to the point where it became respectable to advocate a balanced budget over the business cycle, rather than in each year. Then, as modern ideas regarding fiscal policy have become accepted by more and more people, the idea that the budget should be balanced over the business cycle has been largely abandoned, and the government budget is now viewed as a means to reduce undesirable unemployment and inflation.

The Full-Employment Budget

Some of the misconceptions about budget deficits and surpluses can be avoided by the use of the ***full-employment budget,*** which shows the difference between tax revenues and government expenditures that would result if we had full employment, which is generally defined as 4 percent unemployed. For example, in 1958, the Eisenhower administration ran a deficit of over $10 billion—a reasonably large deficit by historical standards. Basically, the reason for this deficit was that, with the unemployment rate at about 7 percent, there was a substantial gap between actual and potential output. Net national product fell from 1957 to 1958, and, as a result, incomes and federal tax collections fell, and the government ran a deficit. But this $10 billion deficit was entirely due to the high level of unemployment the country was experiencing.

Had we been at full employment, there would have been a surplus of about $5 billion in 1958. NNP, incomes, and federal tax receipts would all have been higher. Government spending and the tax rates in 1958 were not such as to produce a deficit if full employment had been attained. On the contrary, the full-employment budget shows that, if full employment had prevailed, tax receipts would have increased so that federal revenues would have exceeded expenditure by about $5 billion. It is important to distinguish between the full-employment budget and the actual budget. When, as in 1958, the actual budget shows a deficit but the full-employment budget does not, most economists feel that fiscal policy is not too expansionary, since at full employment the federal government would be running a surplus.

Recognizing these considerations, recent administrations have officially adopted the full-employment budget as their measure of the stabilization impact of the budget. As you can see in Figure 11.8, President Nixon ran a full-employment surplus during his first term in office to combat inflation. In 1972, there was a full-employment deficit, but in 1973, and to a greater extent 1974, there were full-employment surpluses. This is in contrast to the actual budget, which was in deficit for most

[9] See Abba Lerner, *Economics of Control,* New York: Macmillan, 1944.

Figure 11.8
Full-Employment and Actual Budget Deficits and Surpluses, 1956–75.
The full-employment budget shows the difference between tax revenues and government expenditures that would result if there was full employment, which is generally defined as 4 percent unemployed. The Nixon administration was the first to officially adopt the full-employment budget as a measure of the stabilization impact of the budget.

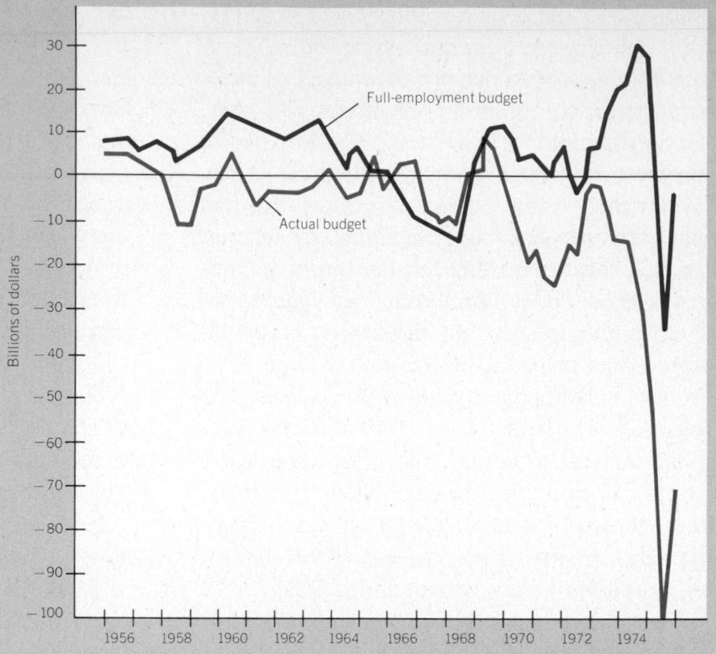

of these years. President Ford ran a substantial full-employment deficit in 1975 to promote recovery from the recession. As you can see in Figure 11.8, the full-employment budget can differ substantially from the actual budget. To understand whether fiscal policy is restrictive or stimulative, you must understand the difference.

Effects of How a Deficit Is Financed, or How a Surplus Is Used

Before leaving the topic of budget deficits and surpluses, it is important to note that the effect of a deficit may depend on how it is financed, as well as on its size. One way for the government to finance a deficit is *to borrow from consumers and business firms.* (Such borrowing results in increases in the national debt, discussed in Chapter 6.) When the government borrows from consumers and business firms, it takes funds from them that might otherwise be spent on consumption or investment goods. Thus, some of the expansionary effect of a budget deficit may be offset by reduced private spending, if a deficit is financed by borrowing from the public.

A second way for the government to finance a budget deficit is *to create new money.* For example, the government can simply print additional money to meet the deficit. (As will become clearer in Chapter 15, a similar result may be obtained if the government borrows from the central bank—the Federal Reserve in the United States.) When the government spends newly created money, it does not use funds that might otherwise be spent by the private sector. Consequently, *the expansionary effects of a deficit may be greater if it is financed by the creation of new money than if it is financed by borrowing from the public.*

Similarly, the effect of a surplus may depend on how it is used, as well as on its size. One way that the government can use a surplus is *to buy back some of its bonds from the public.* (Such purchases reduce the national debt.) When the government buys back some of its bonds, it provides the sellers of these bonds (consumers and firms) with additional spendable funds. Thus some of the anti-inflationary effects of a surplus may be offset by additional private spending. Another way that the government can use a surplus is to *impound the funds,* that is, keep the funds idle. Since this latter use of the surplus does not provide the private sector with additional spendable funds, there is no such offset to the surplus's anti-inflationary effect. Consequently, *the anti-inflationary effects of a surplus may be greater if the surplus is impounded than if it is used to reduce the national debt.*

Recent American Experience with Fiscal Policy

It should be evident by now that much more is known today about the impact of fiscal policy than at the time when the economy was staggered by the Great Depression. But this does not mean that economists have all the answers. Enough is known to keep the economy from careening off a bumpy road; avoiding the potholes is another matter.

The hard choices faced by economists in the top councils of government can be demonstrated by a close inspection of the recent attempts to give the economy a smoother ride. Let's begin with the situation in the late 1960s, when there was mounting inflation due partly to government spending on the Vietnam War. During 1969 and 1970, the administration restricted government expenditures and tried to run a surplus. As the administration's restrictive fiscal policies took hold, the nation's level of real output began to rise more slowly; and in 1970, gross national product in constant dollars fell below its 1969 level. Unemployment, which had been only 3.5 percent of the civilian labor force in 1969, rose to 4.9 percent in 1970 and to 5.9 percent in 1971.

During 1970 and 1971, many liberal economists accused the administration of being so absorbed with reducing inflation that it was creating serious unemployment. Yet despite the administration's efforts, the rate of inflation was not decreasing as fast as desired. Between 1969 and 1970, the index of consumer prices rose by about 6 percent. During the first half of 1971, it rose at an annual rate of about $4\frac{1}{2}$ percent. Although this was an improvement, the inflationary process was proving difficult to quell.

In August 1971, the Nixon administration, reversing its previous attitudes, established controls on prices, wages, and rents. This was the first time that such controls had been adopted by an American government in peacetime. At the same time, the administration switched to a more expansionary fiscal policy in order to reduce the relatively high level of unemployment. Specifically, the president called for a tax reduction of about $7 or $8 billion. Included in his tax package was an investment tax credit, which encouraged investment by business firms, as well as a reduction in personal income taxes. This so-called New Economic Policy also was the subject of criticism, both from the left and the right. Some economists welcomed the shift to a more expansionary policy as long overdue; others viewed it as a mistake. Also, both the tax reduction and the controls were criticized on the grounds that they benefited business more than labor. But the unemployment rate did drop slightly, to $5\frac{1}{2}$ percent in late 1972, and the rate of inflation declined to about 3 percent during the year.

After his re-election in November 1972, President Nixon indicated that he wanted to keep a tight lid on government spending, both to reduce inflation and to trim some programs that he regarded as secondary or of dubious value. In particular, he stressed the desirability of a $250 billion ceiling on federal spending. Critics of the president's economic policies claimed that his emphasis on restricting public expenditures was a mistake. In early 1973, the president phased out the wage and price controls he had imposed in 1971. Inflation, which never had been quelled, increased after the phaseout of the controls, and during early 1973 the economy was in the midst of a boom. In June 1973, the president imposed another price freeze, this time for 60 days. Then he instituted a program which attempted to limit price increases to an amount equal to cost increases. This program was largely ineffectual, and was phased out in 1974.

In early 1974, the price of foreign oil was increased very substantially by the OPEC countries. This price increase, as well as considerable increases in farm prices (recall Chapter 5), spearheaded a bewildering inflationary spurt. During 1974, consumer prices rose by about 12 percent! From the point of view of inflation, this was the worst year in decades. At the same time, the nation's real output fell, as the economy dropped into the most serious recession since World War II. The result was a marked increase in unemployment. By March 1975, the unemployment rate was 8.7 percent, as compared with 4.9 percent in December 1973.

Faced with a combination of excessive unemployment and excessive inflation, President Ford proposed a $16 billion tax cut, and, as we saw above, Congress passed a $23 billion tax cut in March 1975. Since federal expenditures increased considerably from 1974 to 1975, and federal receipts fell (because of the tax cut), there was a very large deficit in 1975—about $70 billion. But the full-employment deficit was only about $8 billion. As we have seen before, the economy began to revive in mid-1975, and unemployment fell from 8.7 percent in March 1975 to 7.5 percent in March 1976. However, "stagflation"—the combination of a high unemployment rate and a high rate of inflation—was by no means vanquished. On the contrary, both unemployment and inflation continued to be excessive in mid-1976.

Clearly, judging from our recent history, fiscal policy is no panacea. Policy makers are continually confronted with difficult choices, and the tools of fiscal policy, at least as they are currently understood and used, are not sufficient to solve or dispel many of the problems at hand. However, it is important to recognize that fiscal policy is not the only available means by which policy makers attempt to stabilize the economy. There is also monetary policy, which we shall discuss in detail in Chapter 15. Really, a sensible fiscal policy can be formulated only in conjunction with monetary policy, and although it is convenient to discuss them separately, in real life they must be coordinated. Also, lest you become overly pessimistic, you should note that, despite the problems that remain unsolved, our improved understanding of fiscal and monetary policy has enabled us to steer a better and more stable course than in the days before World War II. So far at least, bouts of severe unemployment and double-digit inflation have been moderated by government action.

Summary

The equilibrium level of net national product is the level where desired consumption plus desired investment plus desired government spending equals net national product. A $1 billion change in government expenditure will result in a change in equilibrium NNP of the same amount as a $1 billion change in desired investment or a $1 billion shift in the relation between consumption expenditures and NNP. In any of these cases, there is a multiplier effect. An increase in the tax rate shifts the relationship between consumption expenditure and NNP downward, thus reducing the equilibrium value of NNP. A decrease in the tax rate shifts the relationship upward, thus increasing the equilibrium value of NNP.

The equilibrium level of NNP may not be the level corresponding to full employment. A recessionary gap is the increase in desired spending required to push the equilibrium NNP up to the full-employment level. An inflationary gap is the decrease in desired spending required to push the equilibrium NNP down to its full-employment level (at initial prices).

Policy makers receive a lot of help in stabilizing the economy from our automatic stabilizers—automatic changes in tax revenues, unemployment compensation and welfare payments, corporate dividends, family saving, and farm aid. However, the automatic stabilizers can only cut down on variations in unemployment and inflation, not eliminate them. Discretionary programs are needed to supplement the effects of these automatic stabilizers. Such discretionary actions include changing government expenditure on public works and other programs, changing welfare payments and other such transfers, and changing tax rates. An important problem with some of these tools of fiscal policy is the lag in time before they can be brought into play.

At least three policies concerning the government budget have received considerable attention. First, the budget can be balanced each and every year. Second, the budget can be balanced over the course of the business cycle. Third, the budget can be set in a way that will promote full employment with stable prices whether or not this means that the budget is unbalanced over considerable periods of time. The history of the past 40 years has seen enormous changes in the public's attitude toward the government budget. Forty years ago, the prevailing doctrine was that the budget should be balanced each year; now the attitude seems to be that the budget should be used as a tool to reduce unemployment and inflation. Some of the popular misconceptions concerning budget deficits and budget surpluses can be avoided by the use of the full-employment budget, which shows the difference between tax revenue and government expenditure that would result if we had full employment.

CONCEPTS FOR REVIEW

$C + I + G$ line	Full-employment budget	Discretionary fiscal policy
Deficit	Functional finance	Balanced budget
Surplus	Automatic stabilizers	Recessionary gap
		Inflationary gap

QUESTIONS FOR DISCUSSION AND REVIEW

1. Suppose that the consumption function in a particular economy is given by the following table:

Disposable income (billions of dollars)	Consumption expenditure (billions of dollars)
400	350
500	425
600	500
700	575
800	650

Assuming that no taxes are imposed, what is the equilibrium value of NNP if government expenditures are \$50 billion and desired investment is \$50 billion?

2. Based on the data in Question 1, plot the $C + I + G$ line in a graph. Using a graph of this sort, estimate the effect on the equilibrium level of NNP of a $10 billion increase in government spending.

3. Suppose that taxes are 20 percent of NNP. Using the data in Question 1, fill in the blanks below.

NNP (billions of dollars)	Consumption expenditure (billions of dollars)
—	350
—	425
—	500
—	575
—	650

4. Using the data in Question 3, what is the equilibrium value of NNP if government expenditures are $50 billion and desired investment is $50 billion? How does this result compare with that in Question 1? Explain the difference between these two results.

5. Using the data in Question 3, is the government's budget balanced at the equilibrium level of NNP if government expenditures are $50 billion and desired investment is $50 billion? If not, how big is the surplus or deficit?

6. Describe the balanced-budget multiplier. If both government expenditures and taxes rise by the same amount, what is the effect, according to the balanced-budget multiplier?

7. "An important advantage of public works as a tool of fiscal policy is that they can be started quickly. An important advantage of tax rate changes is that they almost never get embroiled in partisan politics." Comment and evaluate.

8. "The full-employment budget is just a lot of hocum to persuade the public that big deficits are smaller and less inflationary than they really are." Comment and evaluate.

9. According to Joseph Pechman, "Among taxes, the federal individual income tax is the leading [automatic] stabilizer." Explain why, and discuss the significance of this fact. He also says that "on the expenditure side, the major built-in stabilizer is unemployment compensation." Again, explain why, and discuss the significance of this fact.

10. According to Maurice Stans, "The federal government should have a balanced budget; its expenditures, especially in times like these, should not exceed its income." Do you agree? Why or why not?

12

Business Fluctuations and Economic Forecasting

The American economy has not grown at a constant rate: instead, output has expanded rapidly in some periods; little, if at all, in others; and actually contracted in still others. Our history indicates that national output, employment, and the price level tend to fluctuate. These fluctuations, often mild, sometimes violent, are frequently called business cycles. The average citizen, as well as the government official or the business executive, needs to know why these fluctuations occur and whether they can be avoided. This chapter summarizes some of the leading theories advanced to answer these questions.

We also take up a related question of great practical importance: can business fluctuations be forecasted? More and more, economic models are being used by government and industry to forecast changes in GNP and other economic variables. Economic forecasting has become a very important part of the economist's job. Although no reputable economist would claim that economic forecasting is very precise or reliable, the forecasts produced by relatively sophisticated models are watched closely by decision makers around the world. In the latter part of this chapter, we describe some of the more widely used forecasting techniques, and see how accurate they have proved in the past.

Business Fluctuations

To illustrate what we mean by "business fluctuations"—or the "business cycle"—let's look at how national output has grown in the United States since World War I. Figure 12.1 shows the behavior of real GNP (in constant dollars) in the United States since 1919. It is clear that output has grown considerably during this period; indeed, GNP is more than 5 times what it was 50 years ago. It is also clear that this growth has not been steady. On the contrary, although the long-term trend has been upward, there have been periods—like 1919-21, 1929-33, 1937-38, 1944-46, 1948-49, 1953-54, 1957-58, 1969-70, and 1973-75—when national output has declined.

Let's define the full-employment level of GNP as the total amount of goods and services that could have been produced if the unemployment rate had been 4 percent. Figure 12.1 shows that national output tends to rise and approach its full-employment level for a while, then falter and fall below this level, then rise to approach it once more, then fall below it again, and so on. For example, output remained close to the full-employment level in the prosperous mid-1920s, fell far below this level in the depressed 1930s, and rose again to this level once we entered World War II. This movement of national output is sometimes called the ***business cycle,*** but it must be recognized that these cycles are far from regular or consistent. On the contrary, they are very irregular.

Each cycle can be divided into four phases, as shown in Figure 12.2. The ***trough*** is the point where national output is lowest relative to its full-employment level. ***Expansion*** is the subsequent phase during which national output rises. The ***peak*** occurs when national output is highest relative to its full-employment level. Finally, ***recession*** is the subsequent phase during which national output falls.[1] Besides these four phases, two other

[1] More precisely, the peak and trough are generally defined in terms of deviations from the long-term trend of national output, rather than in terms of deviations from the full-employment level of national output. But the latter definition tends to be easier for beginners to grasp.

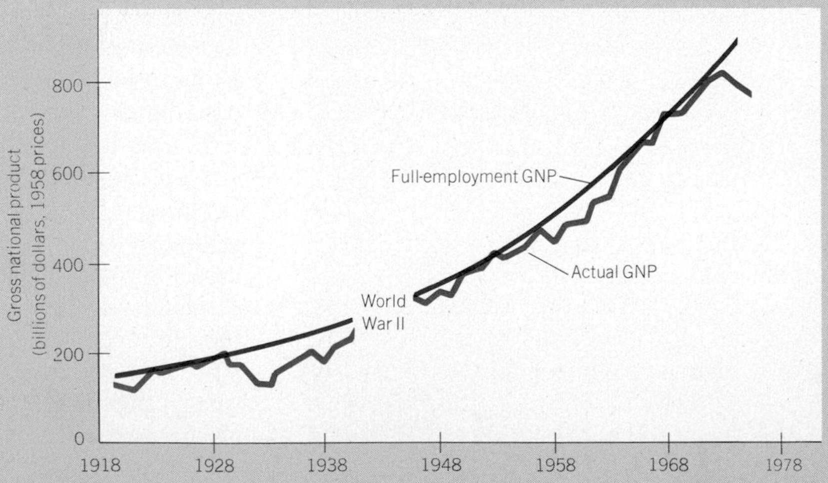

Figure 12.1
Gross National Product (in 1958 dollars), United States, 1918–74, Excluding World War II
Real GNP has not grown steadily. Instead, it has tended to approach its full-employment level, then to falter and fall below this level, then to rise once more, and so on. This movement of national output is sometimes called the business cycle.

Figure 12.2
Four Phases of Business Fluctuation
Each cycle can be divided into four phases: trough, expansion, peak, and recession.

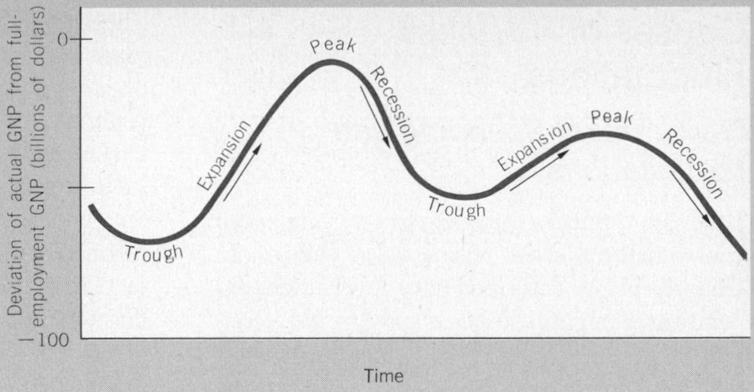

terms are frequently used to describe stages of the business cycle. A ***depression*** is a period when national output is well below its full-employment level; it is a severe recession. Depressions are, of course, periods of excessive unemployment. ***Prosperity*** is a period when national output is close to its full-employment level. Prosperity, if total spending is too high relative to potential output, can be a time of inflation. Of course, in some business cycles, the peak may not be a period of prosperity because output may be below its full-employment level, or the trough may not be a period of depression because output may not be far below its full-employment level.

Since World War II, peaks have occurred in 1948, 1953, 1957, 1960, 1969, and 1973, while troughs have occurred in 1949, 1954, 1958, 1961, 1970, and 1975. None of these recessions has been very long or very deep (although the 1974–75 recession was more severe than the others). We have done better since the war at avoiding and cushioning recessions, partly because of improvements in economic knowledge of the causes and cures of business cycles. Note that, although these cycles have certain things in common, they are highly individualistic. For certain classes of phenomena, it may be true that "if you've seen one, you've seen them all," but not for business cycles; they vary too much in length and nature. Moreover, the basic set of factors responsible for the recession and the expansion differs from cycle to cycle.[2] This means that any theory designed to explain them must be broad enough to accommodate their idiosyncracies.

It is also worth stressing that investment seems to be the component of total spending that varies most over the course of a business cycle. Investment goes down markedly during recessions and increases markedly during expansions; on the other hand, consumption generally moves along with only slight bumps and dips.[3] The volatility of investment, together with the reasons for this volatility, are important clues to the cause of many business cycles. We shall see that this variation in investment plus our old friend (of Chapter 10), the multiplier, can produce the sorts of business fluctuations that have occurred in the United States.

[2] For example, there is some evidence that every so often, a business boom, or peak, takes place at about the same time as a boom in building construction; thus such a peak is buoyed further by this favorable conjuncture—and every so often, a trough is lowered by it. These long swings in building (and other phenomena), lasting 15 to 25 years, are called Kuznets cycles after Harvard's Nobel laureate, Simon Kuznets, who has devoted considerable study to them. See Alvin Hansen, *Business Cycles and National Income,* New York: Norton, 1962.

[3] However, expenditure on consumer durables is more volatile than other consumption expenditure. Moreover, the consumption function can shift, as it did after World War II. (Recall the discussion of this shift in Chapter 10.)

Causes of Business Fluctuations

Government Spending and Expectations

Like investment, *government spending* too can sometimes cause business fluctuations. In Chapter 11, we described how government expenditures might be used to stabilize the economy. The unfortunate fact is that in the past the government's spending—particularly during and after wars—has sometimes been a major destabilizing force, resulting in business fluctuations. Recall from Chapter 8 the great bulge in government spending during World War II and the lesser bulges during the Korean and Vietnam Wars. These increases in spending produced strong inflationary pressures. The price level rose over 50 percent during 1940-46 (World War II), and major inflationary spurts also occurred during the wars in Korea and Vietnam.

Government spending has been a destabilizing force after, as well as during, wars. The recession in 1953-54 was caused primarily by the reduction in government expenditures when the Korean War came to a close. When hostilities terminated, government expenditures were reduced by more than $10 billion. Government spending sometimes has also had the same destabilizing effect in other than wartime or postwar situations. The recession in 1957-58 was aggravated by a drop in defense expenditures in late 1957. Faced with this drop, the defense contractors cut their inventories and expenditures for plant and equipment.

Another factor is the nature and behavior of *expectations.* For example, in the recession of 1974-75, businessmen's expectations became decidedly more pessimistic. Capital spending was cut by over $15 billion and inventory investment by over $17 billion. (Fortunately, the economy began to move upward in mid-1975.) Firms' expectations play a significant role in amplifying business fluctuations. Decisions made at any point in time depend on expectations concerning the future. For example, when a firm builds a new warehouse, it has certain expectations concerning the extent of its sales in the future, the price it will have to pay for labor and transportation, and so on. In forming their expectations, businessmen often tend to follow the leader. As more and more businessmen and analysts predict a rosy future, others tend to jump on the bandwagon. This means that, as the economy advances from a trough, optimistic expectations concerning sales and profits tend to spread, slowly at first, then more and more rapidly. These expectations generate investment, which in turn increases national output. Thus the rosy expectations are self-fulfilling, at least up to a point. (In this area, even if "wishing won't make it so," expecting may turn the trick!) The result is that the expansion is fueled by self-fulfilling and self-augmenting expectations.

Eventually, however, these expectations are not fulfilled, perhaps because full-employment ceilings cause national output to grow at a slower rate, perhaps because the government cuts back its spending (as in 1953-54), perhaps for some other reason. Now the process goes into reverse. Pessimistic expectations appear; and as national output begins to decline, these expectations spread more and more rapidly. These expectations also tend to be self-fulfilling. Businessmen, feeling that the outlook for sales and profits is unfavorable, cut back on their investing, which in turn reduces national output. Thus the recession is made more serious by the epidemic of gloom. In any theory of business fluctuations, it is necessary to recognize the importance of self-fulfilling expectations.

The Acceleration Principle

Investment in plant and equipment, as we know, varies considerably over the course of the business cycle. One of the most important reasons for this variation is illustrated by the following example. Suppose that the Johnson Shoe Corporation, a maker of women's shoes, requires 1 machine to make 50 pairs of shoes per year. Since each machine (and related plant and facilities) costs $2,000 and each pair of shoes costs $20, it takes $2 worth of plant and equipment to produce $1 worth of output per year. In 1968, we suppose that the quantity of the firm's plant and equipment was exactly in balance with its output. In other words, the firm had no excess capacity; sales were $10,000 and the actual stock of capital was $20,000. The firm's sales in subsequent years are shown in Table 12.1. For example, in 1969 its sales increased to $12,000; in 1970 they increased to $14,000; and so forth.

Table 12.1 also shows the amount the firm will have to invest each year in order to produce the amount it sells. Let's begin with 1969. To produce $12,000 worth of product, the firm must have $24,000 worth of capital. This means that it must increase its stock of capital from $20,000—the amount it has in 1968—to $24,000.[4] In other words, it must increase its stock of capital by $4,000, which means that its net investment in plant and equipment must equal $4,000. But this is not the same as its gross investment—the amount of plant and equipment the firm must buy—because the firm must also replace some plant and equipment that wears out. Suppose that $1,000 of plant and equipment wear out each year: then gross investment in 1969 must equal net investment ($4,000) plus $1,000, or $5,000.

Next, let's look at 1970. The firm's sales in that year are $14,000. To produce this much output, the firm must have $28,000 of capital, which means that it must increase its stock of capital by $4,000—from $24,000 to $28,000. In addition, there is $1,000 of replacement investment to replace plant and equipment that wear out in 1970. In all, the firm's gross investment must be $5,000. In 1971, the firm's sales are $15,000. To produce this output, this firm

[4] Note that the firm's stock of capital is an entirely different concept than its common stock or preferred stock. See Chapter 7.

Table 12.1
Relationship between Sales and Investment, Johnson Shoe Corporation

Year	Sales (thousands of dollars)	Needed stock of capital (thousands of dollars)	Actual stock of capital (thousands of dollars)	Replacement investment (thousands of dollars)	Net investment (thousands of dollars)	Gross investment (thousands of dollars)
1968	10	20	20	1	0	1
1969	12	24	24	1	4	5
1970	14	28	28	1	4	5
1971	15	30	30	1	2	3
1972	16	32	32	1	2	3
1973	16	32	32	1	0	1
1974	15	30	31	0	−1	0
1975	15	30	30	0	−1	0
1976	15	30	30	1	0	1
1977	17	34	34	1	4	5

must have $30,000 of capital, which means that it must increase its stock of capital by $2,000—from $28,000 to $30,000. In addition, there is $1,000 of replacement investment. In all, the firm's gross investment must be $3,000. Table 12.1 shows the results for subsequent years.

What conclusions can be drawn from Table 12.1? First, *changes in sales can result in magnified percentage changes in investment.* For example, between 1968 and 1969 sales went up by 20 percent, whereas gross investment went up by 400 percent. Between 1976 and 1977, sales went up by about 13 percent, whereas gross investment went up by 400 percent. The effect of a decrease in sales is even more spectacular because it tends to drive net investment to zero (or to negative values, as in 1974). Indeed, even gross investment may be driven to zero, as in 1974, if the firm wants to reduce the value of its plant and equipment. To accomplish this, the firm simply does not replace the plant and equipment that wear out.

Second, *the amount of gross investment depends on the rate of increase of sales.* In particular, for gross investment to remain constant year after year, the rate of increase of sales must also remain constant. You can see this in 1969 and 1970. In each of these years, since sales increased from the previous year by the same amount ($2,000), gross investment remained constant at $5,000 per year. It is very important to note that *gross investment will fall when sales begin to increase at a decreasing rate.* The fact that sales are increasing does not insure that gross investment will increase; on the contrary, if sales are increasing at a decreasing rate, gross investment will fall. This is a very important point.

This effect of changes in sales on gross investment is often called the ***acceleration principle,*** since changes in sales result in accelerated, or magnified, changes in investment, and since an increase in investment results from an increase in the growth rate (an ***acceleration***) of sales. The acceleration principle applies to kinds of investment other than plant and equipment. For example, it is easy to show that it applies to inventories and housing as well, since firms often try to maintain a certain amount of inventory for each dollar of sales—just as they often maintain a certain amount of plant and equipment for each dollar of sales.

The Interaction between the Acceleration Principle and the Multiplier

Economists—led by Nobel laureates Paul Samuelson and Sir John Hicks[5]—have shown that the acceleration principle combined with the multiplier may produce business cycles like those experienced in the real world. The basic idea is easy. Suppose that national output is increasing, and the economy is moving up toward full employment. Sales are increasing at an increasing rate. Because of the acceleration principle, the increases in sales result in a high level of investment. And via the multiplier, the high level of investment promotes further increases in national output. Thus the accelerator and multiplier tend to reinforce one another, resulting in a strong upward movement of national output. The economy is in an expansion. It is a good time to be president of the United States, president of a major corporation, or an average citizen.

Eventually, however, the economy nears full employment; and since we have only a certain amount of land, labor, and capital, it simply is impossible to increase national output at the rate experienced during the recovery. Sales, which cannot increase forever at the old rate, begin to increase more slowly. But as we saw in the previous section, the reduction in the rate of increase of sales is the kiss of death for in-

[5] Paul A. Samuelson, "The Interaction between the Multiplier Analysis and the Acceleration Principle," *Review of Economics and Statistics,* 1939; and John Hicks, *A Contribution to the Theory of the Trade Cycle,* Oxford: Oxford University Press, 1950. Also, see R. F. Harrod, *The Trade Cycle,* Oxford: Oxford University Press, 1936.

vestment. Even though sales continue to increase, the drop in the rate of increase means decreasing investment. And this reduction in investment sounds the death knell for the boom, since it reduces national output directly and via the multiplier. The reduction in national output means a reduction in sales, and the reduction in sales means a drastic reduction in investment, through the acceleration principle. The drastic reduction in investment means a further reduction in national output. The economy is in a recession. Everything is moving downward, with the notable exception of unemployment. People are getting increasingly nervous—including the president of the United States, the presidents of major corporations, and many average citizens.

Eventually, however, firms reduce their stock of capital to the point where it is in balance with their reduced sales. In other words, they go through the sort of process shown in Table 12.1 during 1974-75, when the Johnson Shoe Corporation reduced its stock of capital by refusing to replace worn-out plant and equipment. At the end of this process, the stock of capital is in balance with sales. To keep this balance, firms must now replace worn-out equipment, which means an increase in gross investment. Via the multiplier, this increase in investment results in an increase in national product, which means an increase in sales. Via the acceleration principle, this increase in sales results in an increase in investment, which in turn increases national product. The economy is once again in the midst of a recovery. It is again a good time to be president of the United States, president of a major corporation, or an average citizen. As moviegoers put it, this is where we came in.

This theory, although highly simplified, provides a great many insights into the nature of business fluctuations. One aspect of the theory in particular should be noted: business cycles are self-starting and self-terminating. Recession, trough, recovery, peak—each phase of the business cycle leads into the next. This theory shows that one need not look outside the economic system for causes of the upper and lower turning points—that is, the points where the economy begins to turn down after a recovery or begins to turn up after a recession. These turning points can occur for the reasons we have just indicated.

Inventory Cycles

Inventories also play an important role in business fluctuations. Indeed, the "minor" or "short" business cycle, lasting about two to four years, is sometimes called an ***inventory cycle*** because it is often due largely to variations in inventories. This cycle proceeds as follows. Businessmen, having let their inventories decline during a business slowdown, find that they are short of inventories. They increase their inventories, which means that they produce more than they sell. This investment in inventories has a stimulating effect on national output. So long as the rate of increase of their sales holds up, firms continue to increase their inventories at this rate.[6] Thus inventory investment continues to stimulate the economy. But when their sales begin to increase more slowly, firms begin to cut back on their inventory investment. This reduction in inventory investment has a depressing effect on national output. As their sales decrease, firms cut back again on their inventory investment, further damping national output. Then when inventories are cut to the bone, the process starts all over again.

As an illustration, consider the recession of 1974-75. During the fourth quarter of 1974, inventories were still increasing at an annual rate of about $10 billion. Then because of a drop in sales, businessmen found themselves

[6] As noted above, the acceleration effect discussed in previous sections applies to inventories as well as plant and equipment, since firms often try to maintain inventories equal to a certain percentage of sales. Thus the *rate of increase* of sales will affect the rate of investment in inventories as well as plant and equipment.

with excess inventories. They cut back their orders from suppliers, which in turn had to reduce output and employment. Inventories were reduced at an annual rate of about $20 billion during early 1975. This inventory liquidation played a major role in the recession. Production plummeted. Fortunately, the reduction in inventories all but ceased in the second half of 1975, and production and employment picked up.

Innovations and Random External Events

Let's turn now to a different sort of explanation of business fluctuations. Clearly, the acceleration principle is only one factor influencing gross investment. Since a firm will invest in any project where the returns exceed the costs involved, many investment projects are not triggered by changes in sales. For example, a new product may be invented, and large investments may be required to produce, distribute, and market it. Consider the automobile industry, currently one of America's largest industries. It took big investments by the pioneers in the auto business to get the automobile to the point where it was an important item in the average consumer's budget. Or consider nylon, which Du Pont spent several million dollars to develop. It took large investments before nylon was on its way.

Major innovations do not occur every day; neither do they occur at a constant rate. There are more in some years than in others, and sheer chance influences the number of innovations in a given year. Similarly, chance greatly influences the timing of many other types of events that bear on the level of output and investment. These include crop failures, hurricanes, and other such natural disasters, as well as man-made events, like strikes in major industries and financial panics, which also affect output and investment.

Let's suppose that these events—innovations and other occurrences that have a major effect on investment—occur more or less at random. Because so many factors influence the timing of each such event, we cannot predict how many will occur in a particular year. Instead, the number is subject to chance variation, like the number thrown in a dice game or the number of spades in a poker hand. In particular, suppose that the chance that one of these events occurs in one year is about the same as in another year.

If this is the case, economists—led by Norway's Nobel laureate, Ragnar Frisch[7]—have shown that business cycles are likely to result. The basic idea is simple enough. The economy, because of its internal structure, is like a pendulum or rocking chair. If it is subjected to random shocks—like pushing a rocking chair every now and then—it will move up and down. These random shocks are the bursts of investment that arise as a consequence of a great new invention or of the development of a new territory, or for some other such reason. These bursts play the role of the forces hitting the pendulum or the rocking chair. To a considerable extent, they may be due to noneconomic events or forces, but whatever their cause, they bang into the economy and shove it in one direction or another.

Of course, the occurrence of these shocks is not the whole story. Business fluctuations in this model do not occur only because of the random events that affect investment. In addition, the economy must respond to—and amplify—the effects of these stimuli. The economy must be like a rocking chair, not a sofa. (If you whack a sofa every now and then, you are likely to hurt your hand, but not to move the sofa much.) Frisch showed that the economy is likely to respond to, and amplify, these shocks. This model explains the fact, stressed in a previous section, that although cycles bear some

[7] Ragnar Frisch, "Propagation Problems and Impulse Problems in Dynamic Economics," *Economic Essays in Honor of Gustav Cassel*, London: Allen and Unwin, 1933.

family resemblance, no two are really alike. Thus the model has the advantage of not explaining more than it should. It does not imply that business fluctuations are more uniform and predictable than they are.

This theory provides valuable insight into the nature of business fluctuations. Like the theory of the interaction of the acceleration principle and the multiplier, it contains important elements of truth, although it obviously is highly simplified. Each of these theories focuses on factors that may be partly responsible for business fluctuations. They complement one another, in the sense that both processes—the interaction of the multiplier and the acceleration principle, and the random external stimuli to investment—may be at work. There is no need to choose between these theories: both help to explain business fluctuations, and both are far from the whole truth.

Monetary Factors

Finally, we must stress that *monetary factors are of great importance in causing business fluctuations.* By monetary factors we mean the rate at which the money supply grows, the rate of interest, and the availability of credit. The Federal Reserve System has major powers over these factors in the United States. As we shall see in Chapter 15, these factors figured significantly in slowing down the boom of the late 1960s and in reducing inflationary pressures during the 1970s. These factors are so important that we shall devote the next several chapters entirely to them. In economics as in other aspects of life, money counts.

Can Business Fluctuations Be Avoided?

Now that we have looked at some theories designed to explain business fluctuations, we are led to ask whether they (the fluctuations, not the theories) can be avoided in the future. To some extent, a discussion of this question is premature, since we have not yet taken up monetary policy. But there is no reason to postpone answering it in general terms, waiting for subsequent chapters to provide more detailed discussions of various aspects of the answer.

On the basis of our increased knowledge of the reasons for business fluctuations and the growing acceptance of modern monetary and fiscal policy, some people seem to think the business cycle has been licked. That is, they feel that we can now use monetary and fiscal policy to head off a recession or a boom, and in this way offset the processes and events that destabilize the economy. This is a rather optimistic view, although the evidence does indicate that we have been able to reduce the severity and frequency of major recessions in recent years. Our record in this regard has been distinctly better than in pre-World-War-II days, although the 1973–75 recession was rather severe.

Does this mean that a major depression—like that experienced in the 1930s—is impossible? The answer is no. Even though we now know how to prevent a depression, one could still occur through stupidity or some weird sequence of events. But the probability of such a depression is very, very small, given our automatic stabilizers and the fact that policy makers—and the electorate—know now that fiscal policy and monetary policy can be used to push the economy toward full employment.

It seems unlikely, however, that the small recessions—the "dips" and "pauses"—are a thing of the past. There will be ups and downs in spending on plant and equipment, there will be fluctuations in inventories, there will be military build-ups and cutbacks, and changes in government spending and in tax rates. All these things can be destabilizing, and existing economic knowledge is not sufficiently precise to allow policy makers to iron out the resulting small deviations of national output from its long-term upward trend. Although there has been a certain amount of optimistic talk about "fine-tuning" of the economy, the truth is that we lack the knowledge or the means to do it.

Finally, the prospect for inflation is not so bright. The recent record of the United States has not been particularly encouraging. We have just about learned that a balanced budget is not the touchstone of fiscal policy, but we have still to learn how to maintain reasonably full employment with reasonably stable prices. This is a very difficult problem, and an important one, which we shall discuss in much greater detail in Chapters 13, 15, and 16.

Can Business Fluctuations Be Forecasted?

How useful are modern economic theories in forecasting NNP? This is a perfectly reasonable question. After all, when you study physics or chemistry, you expect to come away with certain principles that will enable you to predict physical or chemical phenomena. To the extent that economics is a science, you have a right to expect the same thing, since an acid test of any science is how well it predicts.

This question is also of great practical importance. Government officials are enormously interested in what NNP is likely to be in the next year or so, since they must try to anticipate whether excessive unemployment or serious inflationary pressures are developing. Business executives are equally interested, since their firms' sales, profits, and needs for equipment depend on NNP. For these reasons, forecasting is one of the principal jobs of economists in government and industry.

The first thing that must be said is that, in forecasting as in most other areas, economics is not an exact science. If an economist tells you he can predict exactly what NNP will be next year, you can be pretty sure that he is talking through his hat. Of course, by luck, he may be able to predict correctly, but lucky guesses do not a science make. However, although economic forecasting is not perfectly accurate, economic forecasts are still useful. Since governments, firms, and private individuals must continually make decisions that hinge on what they expect will happen, there is no way that they can avoid making forecasts, explicit or implicit. Really the only question is how best to make them.

There is considerable evidence that, even though forecasts based on economic models are sometimes not very good, they are better—on the average—than those made by noneconomists. There is no substitute for economic analysis in accurate forecasting over the long haul. Of course, this really isn't very surprising. It would be strange if economists, whose profession it is to study and predict economic phenomena, were to do worse than those without this training—even if the others are tycoons or politicians. Further, it would be strange if government and industry were to hire platoons of economists at fancy prices—which they do—if they couldn't predict any better than anyone else.

In the realm of economic forecasting, what is a good batting average? According to M.I.T.'s Paul Samuelson,

> In economic forecasting of the direction of change, we ought to be able to do at least .500 just by tossing a coin. And taking advantage of the undoubted upward trend in all modern economies, we can bat .750 or better just by parrot-like repeating, "Up, Up." The difference between the men and the boys, then, comes between an .850 performance and an .800 performance. Put in other terms, the good forecaster, who must in November make a point-estimate of GNP for the calendar year ahead, will over a decade, have an average error of perhaps one percent, being in a range of $12 billion with reality being $6 billion on either side of the estimate. And a rather poor forecaster may, over

the same period, average an error of $1\frac{1}{2}$ percent. When we average the yearly results for a decade, it may be found that in the worst year the error was over 2 percent, compensated by rather small errors in many of the years not expected to represent turning points.[8]

Economists have no single method for forecasting NNP or GNP. They vary in their approaches just as physicians, for example, differ in theirs. But reputable economists tend to use one of a small number of forecasting techniques, each of which is described below. Of course, many economists do not restrict themselves to one technique, but rely on a combination of several, using one to check on another.

Leading Indicators

Perhaps the simplest way to forecast business fluctuations is to use ***leading indicators,*** which are certain economic series that typically go down or up before national output does. The National Bureau of Economic Research, founded by Wesley C. Mitchell (1874–1948), has carried out detailed and painstaking research to examine the behavior of various economic variables over a long period of time, in some cases as long as 100 years. The Bureau has attempted to find out whether each variable goes down before, at, or after the peak of the business cycle, and whether it turns up before, at, or after the trough. Variables that go down before the peak and up before the trough are called ***leading series.*** Variables that go down at the peak and up at the trough are called ***coincident series.*** And those that go down after the peak and up after the trough are called ***lagging series.***

It is worthwhile examining the kinds of variables that fall into each of these three categories, since they give us important facts concerning the anatomy of the cycle. According to the Bureau, some important leading series are business failures, new orders for durable goods, average work week, building contracts, stock prices, certain wholesale prices, and new incorporations. These are the variables that tend to turn down before the peak and turn up before the trough.[9] Coincident series include employment, industrial production, corporate profits, and gross national product, among many others. Some typical lagging series are retail sales, manufacturers' inventories, and personal income.

Economists sometimes use leading series as forecasting devices. There are good economic reasons why these series turn down before a peak or up before a trough. In some cases, they indicate changes in spending in strategic areas of the economy, while in others they indicate changes in businessmen's and investors' expectations. Both to guide the government in determining its economic policies and to guide firms in their planning, it is important to try to spot turning points—peaks and troughs—in advance. This, of course, is the toughest part of economic forecasting. Economists sometimes use these leading indicators as evidence that a turning point is about to occur. If a large number of leading indicators turn down, this is viewed as a sign of a coming peak. If a large number turn up, this is thought to signal an impending trough.

Unfortunately, the leading indicators are not very reliable. It is true that the economy has seldom turned down in recent years without a warning from these indicators. This is fine. But unfortunately these indicators have turned down on several occasions—1952 and 1962, for example—when the economy did not turn down subsequently. Thus they sometimes provide false signals. Also, in periods of expansion, they sometimes turn down too long be-

[8] Paul A. Samuelson, "Economic Forecasting and Science," in his *Readings in Economics,* New York: McGraw-Hill, 1970, pp. 112–13, and reprinted in E. Mansfield, *Economics: Readings, Issues, and Cases,* 2d ed., New York: Norton, 1977.

[9] Of course, business failures turn *up* before the peak and *down* before the trough.

fore the real peak. And in periods of recession, they sometimes turn up only a very short while before the trough, so that we've turned the corner before anything can be done. Nonetheless, these indicators are not worthless. They are watched closely and used to supplement other, more sophisticated forecasting techniques.

Simple Keynesian Models

Leading indicators are used primarily to spot turning points—peaks and troughs. They are of little or no use in predicting GNP (or NNP). To forecast GNP, we need a more sophisticated approach, one more firmly rooted in economic theory. (Leading indicators are largely the product of strictly empirical analysis.) To forecast GNP, it is worthwhile bringing into play the theory we described in Chapters 9 to 11. After all, if the theory is any good, it should help us to forecast GNP. This theory can be used in a variety of ways to help prepare such forecasts, and a first course in economics can provide no more than the most basic introduction to these methods.

One simple way of trying to forecast GNP is to treat certain components of total spending as given and to use these components to forecast the total. This method is sometimes used by the Council of Economic Advisers, among others. For example, suppose that we decide to forecast private investment and government expenditures as a first step, after which we will use these forecasts to predict GNP.[10] Private investment is made up of three parts: expenditures on plant and equipment, residential construction, and changes in inventories. The most important of these parts is expenditure on plant and equipment. To forecast it, the results of surveys of firms' expenditure plans for the next year are helpful. The Department of Commerce and the Securities and Exchange Commission send out questionnaires (at the beginning of each year) to a large number of firms, asking them how much they plan to spend on plant and equipment during the year. The results, which appear in March in the *Survey of Current Business* (a Department of Commerce publication), are pretty accurate. For example, the average error in 1951-63 was only about 3 percent.

These surveys can help us forecast business expenditures on plant and equipment, but what about the other parts of private investment—residential construction and changes in inventories? Lots of techniques are used to forecast them. Some people use construction contracts and similar indicators as the basis for forecasts of residential construction. For inventory changes, some people watch surveys (like those that have been carried out by *Fortune* magazine and the Commerce Department) which ask companies about their inventory plans.

Next, we need a forecast of government expenditures. At the federal level, it is possible to forecast government expenditures on the basis of the president's proposed budget or Congress's appropriations (although these forecasts can sometimes be quite wrong, as in the case of the Vietnam build-up when expenditures were higher than expected). At the state and local level, it is often possible to extrapolate spending levels reasonably well.

Suppose that, having studied as many relevant factors as we can, we finally conclude that in our best estimate private investment plus government expenditure will equal $600 billion next year. How do we go from this estimate to an estimate of GNP? Suppose that consumers in the past have devoted about 90 percent of their disposable income to consumption expenditure, and that disposable income has been about 70 percent of GNP. Assuming that this will also be true again next year, it follows that consumption expenditure will equal 63 percent (90 percent times 70 percent) of GNP. In other words,

[10] We continue to ignore net exports in this part of the book because they are quite small. Chapters 31-33 will study them in some detail.

$$C = .63Y, \tag{12.1}$$

where C is consumption expenditure and Y is GNP. Also, by definition,

$$Y = C + I + G,$$

where I is gross private investment and G is government expenditure. Since $I + G = 600$, it follows that

$$Y = C + 600. \tag{12.2}$$

Substituting the righthand side of Equation (12.1) for C,

$$Y = .63Y + 600,$$

or

$$\begin{aligned} Y - .63Y &= 600 \\ .37Y &= 600 \\ Y &= \frac{600}{.37} \\ &= 1{,}622. \end{aligned}$$

Thus our forecast for GNP next year is $1,622 billion.

At this point, our job may seem to be over. But it really isn't; we must check this forecast in various ways. For example, it implies that consumption expenditures next year will be $1,022 billion. (Since $C = .63Y$, according to Equation (12.2), and Y equals 1,622, C must equal 1,022.) Does this seem reasonable? For example, how does it compare with the latest results of the survey of consumer buying plans carried out at the Survey Research Center at the University of Michigan? Also, the forecasted level of GNP must be compared with the productive capacity of the economy. Do we have the physical capacity to produce this much at stable prices? To what extent will the general price level be pushed upward? Moreover, our assumptions concerning investment and government spending must be re-examined in the light of our forecast of GNP. If GNP is $1,622 billion, is it reasonable to assume that I will be the amount we initially forecasted? Or do we want to revise our forecast of investment? A great many steps must be carried out before we finally put forth a GNP forecast, if we are conscientious and professional in our approach. Moreover, even after the forecast is made, it is often updated as new information becomes available, so the process goes on more or less continuously.

Econometric Models

In recent years, more and more emphasis has been placed on econometric models. Twenty years ago, econometric models were in their infancy, but now the Council of Economic Advisers, the Treasury, the Federal Reserve Board, and other parts of the federal government pay attention to the forecasts made by econometric models—and sometimes construct their own econometric models. Business firms too hire economists to construct econometric models for them, to forecast both GNP and their own sales. ***Econometric models*** are systems of equations estimated from past data that are used to forecast economic variables. There are many kinds of econometric models. For example, some are designed to forecast wage rates; others are designed to forecast the sales of a new product; and still others are designed to forecast a particular company's share of the market. We are concerned here only with econometric models designed to forecast GNP.

The essence of any econometric model is that it blends theory and measurement. It is not merely a general, nonquantitative theory. Useful as such a theory may be, it does not in general permit quantitative or numerical forecasts. Nor is an econometric model a purely empirical result based on little or no theoretical underpinning. Although such results may also be useful, they generally are untrustworthy once the basic structure of the economic situation changes. Most econometric models designed to forecast GNP are built, at least in part, on the theoretical foundations described in previous chapters. In other words, they contain a number of equations, one of which is designed to explain consumption expenditures, one to explain investment expenditures, and so forth.

To see what is involved in the construction of an econometric model, let's consider just one of the equations, the consumption equation. The first step in formulating this equation is to ask ourselves what variables influence consumption expenditure. We know from Chapter 9 that one important determinant of consumption expenditure is disposable income. Thus, if the ratio of disposable income to GNP remains constant, consumption expenditure should be closely related to GNP. To keep things simple, let's suppose that this is the only factor that determines consumption expenditure. Needless to say, this is not the case, but it makes it easier to see what is involved in constructing an econometric model.

Economic theory—and hunch and intuition based on experience and insight—suggest the explanatory variables to be used in an equation, but they alone cannot supply the numbers to be used. For example, if the relationship between consumption expenditure and GNP can be represented by a straight line, it follows that

$$C = a + bY, \qquad (12.3)$$

where C is consumption expenditure and Y is gross national product. But what are the numerical values of a and b? At this point, statistical techniques of various sorts come into play. In the simple case considered here, we can plot consumption expenditure (C) against gross national product (Y) in various years in the past, as shown in Figure 12.3. Then we can pick the values of a and b that fit the data best. For example, as shown in Figure 12.3, an equation based on $a = -1{,}400$ and $b = 2$ does not fit the data at all well, while an equation based on $a = 20$ and $b = .6$ does much better. There are standard statistical methods, known as regression techniques, that can be used to determine which values of a and b fit the data best. These values, once determined, can be inserted into Equation (12.3).

A Small Econometric Model[11]

Econometric models, like many of the good things in life, come in various sizes. Some are composed of lots of equations; some contain only a few. Bigger models are not necessarily

[11] This section, and the following one, are optional and can be omitted without loss of continuity.

Figure 12.3
Relationship between Consumption Expenditure and Gross National Product, 1964–74.
The line $C = 20 + .6Y$ fits the data (indicated by the dots) far better than the line $C = -1{,}400 + 2Y$. (C is consumption expenditure and Y is GNP.) No one needs a Ph.D. in mathematical statistics to see this.

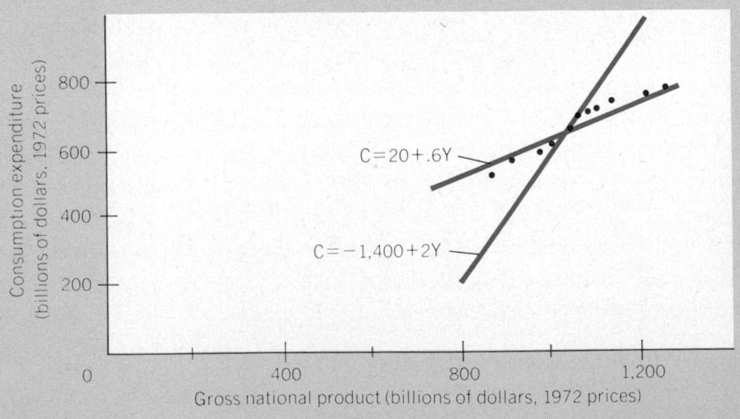

to be preferred to smaller ones, or vice versa. The sort of model that is best for a particular purpose depends on which one predicts best and how costly it is to operate. The best way to get a feel for the nature of an econometric model is to examine one. Let's take a look at a small one designed by Irwin Friend and Paul Taubman of the University of Pennsylvania's Wharton School.[12] Because it contains only five equations, it is an easy one for a student to begin on. More complicated models are discussed in the next section.

Although the discussion in this section and the next one is at an elementary level, the nature of the analysis requires familiarity with the idea of, and notation for, a set of equations. Readers who do not have this familiarity can skip these two sections without losing the thread of the argument.

One of the hardest things to keep track of in econometric models is what each symbol stands for. Let's begin by spelling this out for the Friend-Taubman model. There are nine variables used in the model, and the symbol for each is as follows:

Y = gross national product
C = consumption expenditure
E = plant and equipment expenditures
E^e = expected plant and equipment expenditures, according to surveys
H = residential construction expenditure
L = housing starts (lagged a quarter)
I = inventory investment
S^e = expected business sales, according to surveys
G = government expenditure plus net exports.

Y, C, E, E^e, H, I, G, and S^e are measured in billions of 1954 dollars. L is measured in hundreds of thousands of units. Another symbol that must be explained is Δ, which means the change in a particular variable. For example, ΔY means "the change in Y," or since Y is GNP, it means "the change in GNP." Still another symbol is the subscript $_{-1}$. Any variable with a subscript $_{-1}$ means the value of the variable in the preceding period. Thus a change with a subscript $_{-1}$ means a change occurring between the previous two periods. For example, ΔC_{-1} means the change in consumption expenditure between the last period and the period before. In this model, each period is six months.

Having disposed of the preliminaries, let's look at the model. The first equation explains ΔC, the change in consumption expenditure between this period and last period. According to this equation,

$$\Delta C = 2.18 + .37\Delta Y + .10\Delta C_{-1}. \qquad (12.4)$$

In other words, the change in consumption expenditures equals 2.18 billion (1954) dollars plus .37 times the change in GNP between this period and last period plus .10 times the change in consumption expenditures between last period and the period before. Certainly it is reasonable to expect that the change in consumption will be directly related to the change in GNP. This follows from our discussion of the consumption function in Chapter 9. It is also reasonable to expect that the change in consumption between this period and the last will depend on the change in consumption between the last period and the one before. Basically the reason for this is that there is likely to be a lag in adjustment. The numbers in Equation (12.4), like those in all the equations in the model, were estimated from past data.

The second equation explains ΔE, the change in expenditures on plant and equipment between this period and the last period. According to this equation,

$$\Delta E = -.82 + .63(E^e - E_{-1}) + .08(\Delta Y + \Delta Y_{-1}). \qquad (12.5)$$

[12] Irwin Friend and Paul Taubman, "A Short-Term Forecasting Model," *Review of Economics and Statistics*, August 1964. This model has been revised since publication, and is presented for illustrative purposes only.

In other words, the change in expenditure on plant and equipment equals −.82 billion (1954) dollars plus .63 times the difference between expected expenditure on plant and equipment (based on surveys) and actual expenditure on plant and equipment in the previous period, plus .08 times the sum of the change in GNP between this period and the last period and the change in GNP between the last period and the previous period. One would suppose, of course, that the change in actual expenditure on plant and equipment would be directly related to the change indicated by businessmen's expectations concerning their expenditures on plant and equipment. Also, based on the acceleration principle, one would suppose that the amount spent on plant and equipment would be directly related to the rate of change of GNP. Both suppositions are included in Equation (12.5) because neither theory by itself does as well historically as a mixture of both.

The third equation explains ΔH, the change in residential construction between this period and last period. According to this equation,

$$\Delta H = .35 + .58\Delta L + .06(\Delta Y - \Delta Y_{-1}) - .16(E^e - E_{-1}). \tag{12.6}$$

In other words, the change in expenditure on residential construction equals .35 billion (1954) dollars plus .58 times the change in housing starts (lagged a quarter) plus .06 times the change in the rate of change of GNP minus .16 times the expected change in expenditure on plant and equipment (based on surveys). One would suppose, of course, that the change in expenditure on construction would be directly related to the change in housing starts (lagged a quarter). Also, from the acceleration principle, one would suppose that the amount spent on residential construction would be directly related to the rate of change of GNP. Thus the change in the amount spent on residential construction would be assumed to vary directly with the change in the rate of change of GNP, which of course equals $\Delta Y - \Delta Y_{-1}$. Finally, the change in residential construction is likely to be inversely related to the change in expected expenditures on plant and equipment because if there is a great increase (decrease) in the latter, this will mean higher (lower) interest rates and greater (less) competition for resources which may discourage (encourage) residential construction.

The fourth equation explains ΔI, the change in inventory investment between this period and the last period. According to this equation,

$$\Delta I = 1.51 + .025\Delta S^e + 1.70(E^e - E_{-1}) - 1.15I_{-1}. \tag{12.7}$$

In other words, the change in inventory investment equals 1.51 billion (1954) dollars plus .025 times the change in total sales expected by businessmen (as given by surveys) plus 1.70 times the difference between expected expenditure on plant and equipment (as given by surveys) and actual expenditure on plant and equipment in the previous period minus 1.15 times the inventory investment in the previous period. The authors of the model argue that the change in inventory investment will be directly related to the change in expected sales, since firms generally want to keep their inventories more or less proportional to their sales. Also, they believe that the change in inventory investment will be directly related to the expected change in expenditure on plant and equipment, since the latter is a good indicator of the general economic outlook. In addition, they state that the change in inventory investment will be inversely related to the level of inventory investment in the previous period. According to their model, if inventory investment was high (low) in the previous period, there will be a smaller (bigger) change in inventory investment than if it was low (high) in the previous period.

Finally, the fifth equation merely states the

obvious fact that the change in GNP must equal the change in consumption expenditures plus the change in each of the parts of gross private investment (expenditures on plant and equipment, residential construction, and inventories) plus the change in government expenditures (plus net exports). In other words,

$$\Delta Y = \Delta C + \Delta E + \Delta H + \Delta I + \Delta G. \quad (12.8)$$

This must be true because Y = consumption + gross private investment + government expenditures (plus net exports). Since gross private investment equals $E + H + I$, it follows that $Y = C + E + H + I + G$. Thus the change in Y must equal the sum of the changes in C, E, H, I, and G.

Econometric models—even small ones like this—are fairly complicated. It is easy to get so engrossed in the details of each equation that we lose sight of the basic purpose of the model—to forecast GNP, in this case. How can we use this model to forecast GNP? As a first step, let's substitute the righthand side of Equation (12.4) for ΔC in Equation (12.8). Also, let's substitute the righthand side of Equation (12.5) for ΔE in Equation (12.8). Let's substitute the righthand side of the Equation (12.6) for ΔH in Equation (12.8), and the righthand side of Equation (12.7) for ΔI in Equation (12.8). All of these substitutions give us an expression for ΔY. In particular,

$$\Delta Y = 3.22 + 2.00\Delta G + 4.34(E_e - E_{-1}) - 2.30I_{-1} + .05\Delta S^e + 1.15\Delta L + .037\,\Delta Y_{-1} + .19\Delta C_{-1}. \quad (12.9)$$

This equation can be used to forecast ΔY—the change in gross national product between the *next* period and the *present* period. To do so, one must insert the appropriate values of ΔC_{-1}, ΔY_{-1}, $(E^e - E_{-1})$, ΔL, ΔS^e, I_{-1}, and ΔG into Equation (12.9). For example, if the change in consumption between this period and the last period was \$1 billion, we would substitute 1 for ΔC_{-1} in Equation (12.9). And if the change in gross national product between this period and the last period was \$2 billion, we would substitute 2 for ΔY_{-1}, and so on for the other variables on the righthand side of Equation (12.9). When the value of each of the variables has been inserted into Equation (12.9), we are the proud possessor of a forecast of ΔY—the change in gross national product between the next period and the present period.

Large Econometric Models

The econometric model just presented is a small one designed to forecast changes in GNP over the next six months. The economists who constructed it did not intend it to be used to estimate the effects of government policy—for example, changes in tax rates or government expenditures—or to forecast prices, income distribution, unemployment, capital utilization, and so forth. In recent years, there has been a remarkable amount of activity in the economics profession here and abroad, aimed at the construction of larger econometric models, which may be able to represent the behavior of the economy in richer and more complete detail. The leading figure in the development of such models has been Lawrence Klein of the University of Pennsylvania. Two of the models that he has constructed—or helped to construct—are known as the Wharton model and the Brookings model.

The original Wharton model, published in 1967, contained about 50 equations: 3 equations that explain various components of consumer spending (consumer nondurable goods, automobiles, and other consumer durable goods), 6 equations to explain various components of private investment (expenditure on plant and equipment, residential housing, and inventory changes), 4 explaining depreciation, 4 explaining tax receipts and transfer payments, 5 explaining the level of output in various sectors of the economy, 7 explaining price level changes in various sectors of the economy, and other equations explaining hours worked, wage rates, unemployment, interest rates, profits, and other variables. This model was used to make quarterly forecasts of GNP, unemployment, changes in the price level, and other variables a year or more ahead. It was also used to forecast the effects on the economy of alternate government policies—for example, to estimate the effects of changes in tax rates on GNP and unemployment. Its forecasts were watched closely and publicized widely in the business commmunity and in government.[13] In recent years, the Wharton model has been extended and refined in numerous ways. It currently contains over 200 equations.

The Brookings model—more formally, the Brookings Quarterly Econometric Model of the United States—was also composed of well over 200 equations. Produced by a team of over 20 well-known economists, headed by Klein and Harvard's James Duesenberry, work on this model went on for over 10 years, and although it was designed largely for experimental purposes, it provided economists with many useful results.[14] Another large model is the Federal Reserve Board-Massachusetts Institute of Technology-Pennsylvania model, which contains over 125 equations. It emphasizes the financial variables that are of importance to the Federal Reserve System.[15] In addition, large econometric models have been built by Data Resources, Inc., Chase Econometrics, the University of Michigan, UCLA, and the Bureau of Economic Analysis of the Department of Commerce, among others.

[13] Michael Evans and Lawrence Klein, *The Wharton Econometric Forecasting Model*, Philadelphia: University of Pennsylvania Press, 1967.

[14] J. Duesenberry, G. Fromm, L. Klein, and E. Kuh, *The Brookings Quarterly Econometric Model of the United States*, Chicago: Rand McNally, 1965.

[15] Some econometric models, such as those developed at the Federal Reserve Bank of St. Louis, have been built largely on monetary factors. In the following three chapters, we shall discuss the effects of monetary factors on national output, employment, and the price level.

Table 12.2
Predictive Record of Some Leading Economic Forecasting Techniques

		Error (in billions of dollars)				
Year	Actual GNP	Average general forecast (Federal Reserve Bank of Philadelphia)	Council of Economic Advisers	Michigan model	Friend-Taubman model	Wharton model
1959	484	−13	—	−19	—	
1960	504	4	—	−10	—	
1961	520	− 7	—	2	—	
1962	560	4	14	4	—	1
1963	591	−11	− 6	− 6	4	1
1964	632	− 7	− 4	− 4	5	1
1965	685	−10	− 6	−14	−3	−4
1966	748	− 7	−10	− 7	—	−4
1967	790	4	6	13	—	3
Average error (1963–67)		7.8	6.4	8.8	4.0	2.8

Source: Michael Evans, *Macroeconomic Activity*, New York: Harper & Row, 1969, p. 516.

Econometric Forecasts: The Track Record

How well can econometric models forecast? Table 12.2 compares the success of the Wharton model, the Friend-Taubman model, and a model constructed at the University of Michigan's Research Seminar in Quantitative Economics in predicting GNP during 1959-67 with the forecasts of the Council of Economic Advisers and a composite forecast of GNP from about 50 economists which is tabulated each year by the Federal Reserve Bank of Philadelphia. With the exception of the Friend-Taubman model, these forecasts were made at the end of the previous year. The Friend-Taubman forecasts were made in mid-March.

In this period, the econometric models seemed to do better than the average forecast of general economists. While the general economists were off, on the average, by about $8 billion during the period, the econometric models were off by an average of about $5 billion. The performance of the Wharton model in this period was particularly impressive. Its average error was only about $3 billion—or less than ½ of 1 percent. In this ball game, that is a very fancy batting average: recall Samuelson's remarks quoted earlier.

However, before you jump to the conclusion that the problem of economic forecasting is now solved, let's turn to the predictive performance of various models in more recent years. Table 12.3 shows how well six well-known models—those of the Bureau of Economic Analysis, Chase Econometrics, Data Resources, Inc., Ray C. Fair, and General Electric, as well as the Wharton model—performed during 1970-74. Also, it shows the performance of the average forecast obtained from the American Statistical Association and National Bureau of Economic Research (ASA-NBER) Survey of a large number of general economists. The figures in Table 12.3 are all average errors. For example, the top line in the table shows that, in forecasting one quarter ahead, the ASA-NBER Survey was in error, on the average, by 1.4 percentage points in forecasting the rate of increase of GNP (in money terms), by 1.8 percentage points in forecasting the rate of increase of GNP (in real terms), by 0.1 percentage points in forecasting the unemployment rate, and by 1.7 percentage points in forecasting the rate of increase of prices.

In this period, there seems to be less difference between the accuracy of the econometric models and that of the average forecast of general economists than in the earlier period. For example, although the Wharton model sometimes has a smaller average error than the ASA-NBER Survey, the reverse is sometimes true. But the date when the various forecasts were made was not the same, and so the results are not entirely comparable. More important is the fact that the GNP forecasts in this later period seem considerably poorer than in the earlier one. Whereas the most accurate models in the earlier period had an average error of only about ½ of 1 percent, the average error in the later period was much higher. In particular, after mid-1973, the forecasting performance of both the econometric models and the general economists declined considerably.

An important reason for this decline in performance was the difficulty in incorporating the effects of the Arab oil embargo, the drastic oil price increase, and the high inflation rate of 1973-74 into such models. The assumption underlying any econometric model is that the basic structure of the economy—the numbers in the equations of the model—will not change much. If this assumption does not hold, the model is in trouble. After all, any econometric model is powered by past data, not magic. Another reason why the models did better during 1959-67 was that this was a period of sustained prosperity. It is easier to forecast GNP during a period when it is steadily rising (or steadily falling) than at a turning point in the business cycle, such as 1970 or 1974. Unfortunately, the turning points are often of major significance to policy makers.

Table 12.3
Average Error (in percentage points) of Forecasts of the Rate of Increase of GNP, the Unemployment Rate, and the Rate of Price Increase, Seven Forecasters, 1970–74.

Forecaster	Rate of increase of GNP (in money terms)	Rate of increase of GNP (in real terms)	Unemployment rate	Rate of price increase
		Forecasts of one quarter ahead		
ASA-NBER Survey	1.4	1.8	0.1	1.7
Bureau of Economic Analysis	1.5	1.6	0.1	1.4
Chase Econometrics	1.3	1.5	0.2	1.4
Data Resources, Inc.	1.7	2.0	0.2	1.8
Ray C. Fair	2.2	2.6	0.2	2.0
General Electric	1.4	1.7	0.1	1.1
Wharton	2.0	1.8	0.2	1.1
		Forecasts of two quarters ahead		
ASA-NBER Survey	1.5	1.4	0.2	1.7
Bureau of Economic Analysis	1.1	1.4	0.2	1.5
Chase Econometrics	1.4	1.5	0.3	1.8
Data Resources, Inc.	1.2	1.6	0.2	1.8
Ray C. Fair	1.9	2.4	0.3	2.1
General Electric	1.3	1.4	0.2	1.4
Wharton	1.3	1.3	0.3	1.6
		Forecasts of three quarters ahead		
ASA-NBER Survey	1.4	1.2	0.3	1.7
Bureau of Economic Analysis	1.3	1.5	0.2	1.7
Chase Econometrics	1.0	1.2	0.3	1.8
Data Resources, Inc.	1.1	1.3	0.2	1.7
Ray C. Fair	1.6	1.9	0.4	2.1
General Electric	1.0	1.3	0.4	1.4
Wharton	1.3	1.2	0.3	1.8
		Forecasts of one year ahead		
ASA-NBER Survey	1.3	1.3	0.3	1.7
Bureau of Economic Analysis	1.2	1.5	0.3	1.7
Chase Econometrics	1.0	1.2	0.3	1.6
Data Resources, Inc.	1.3	1.2	0.3	1.7
Ray C. Fair	1.5	1.9	0.4	2.1
General Electric	1.0	1.2	0.3	1.3
Wharton	1.3	1.0	0.4	1.8

Source: Stephen McNees, "How Accurate Are Economic Forecasts?" *New England Economic Review,* November 1974.

Despite the rather large errors in some recent economic forecasts, neither government nor industry can swear off forecasting. For decades, economic forecasting has played an important role in the decision-making process, both in government and industry. For example, in the recession of 1953-54, President Eisenhower asked Arthur Burns, chairman of the Council of Economic Advisers, to appear at every meeting of the Cabinet until further notice, and summarize developments and prospects. During the 1960s and 1970s, Presidents Kennedy, Johnson, Nixon, Ford, and Carter also paid close attention to economic forecasts. So do most corporation presidents. This isn't because these forecasts are always very good. It's because they are the best available. As Thomas Huxley put it, "If a little knowledge is dangerous, who is the man who has so much as to be out of danger?"

Summary

Changes in sales can result in magnified or accelerated changes in investment; the amount of gross investment depends on the rate of increase of sales. The fact that sales are increasing does not insure that gross investment will increase. On the contrary, if sales are increasing at a decreasing rate, gross investment is likely to fall. This effect of sales on investment is called the acceleration principle. The interaction of the acceleration principle with the multiplier can cause business cycles. Thus turning points can be generated within the economic system. Investment is also determined by many events that occur more or less at random, like innovations, wars, and so on. The effects of these random shocks can also cause business fluctuations. The short cycles are generally inventory cycles. The acceleration principle also applies to inventories.

Although we are not in a position to erase the small dips and pauses in economic activity, it seems extremely unlikely that we will have another depression of the severity of the 1930s. The reason is that policy makers—and the electorate—know that monetary and fiscal policy can be used to push the economy back toward full employment. However, the prospect for price stability is not so bright.

Although economics is by no means an exact science, economic forecasts are useful for many purposes. This does not mean that these forecasts are always very accurate. It means only that they are better than noneconomists' forecasts. Economists have a number of techniques for forecasting. One makes use of leading indicators—variables that historically have turned up or down before GNP. Although of some use, these leading indicators are not very reliable. Another technique is based on the use of simple Keynesian models plus surveys and other data. For example, investment and government expenditures (and net exports) are sometimes estimated as a first step. Then, using the historical relationship between consumption and GNP, it is possible to forecast GNP. A third technique is based on econometric models, which are systems of equations estimated from past data. Econometric models blend theory and measurement.

Econometric models may be big or small. An example of a small model is the Friend-Taubman model; an example of a large model is the Wharton model. During the 1960s, econometric models seemed to do somewhat better than the average forecasts of general economists. However, it is important to recognize that econometric models—like any forecasting device in the social sciences—are quite fallible. During the 1970s, the forecasting performance of both the econometric models and general economists seemed to decline. Nonetheless, economic forecasts continue to receive considerable attention from heads of state and heads of firms. This isn't because these forecasts are always very good: it's because they are the best available.

CONCEPTS FOR REVIEW

Business cycle
Trough
Expansion
Peak
Recession
Depression
Prosperity
Inventory cycle
Net investment
Gross investment
Acceleration principle
Leading indicators
Coincident series
Lagging series
Econometric models
Expectations

QUESTIONS FOR DISCUSSION AND REVIEW

1. "What goes up must come down. There is a cycle in economic activity just as in many other things, and one can use this cycle to forecast quite accurately." Comment and evaluate.

2. Suppose that a firm requires \$3 in capital for every \$1 of its sales. Suppose that none of its capital ever wears out, and that it had \$450,000 in capital at the end of 1970. Its sales in subsequent years were as follows:

Year	Sales (dollars)
1971	150,000
1972	180,000
1973	210,000
1974	220,000
1975	225,000
1976	220,000

How much did the firm invest each year?

3. Describe how the multiplier and acceleration principle can interact to result in business fluctuations. To what extent do you think that this interaction is an adequate explanation of recent fluctuations in the American economy?

4. List the dozen technological innovations that you would regard as being the most important in this century. What effect did each have on the American economy, and to what extent did they contribute to business fluctuations?

5. "The government itself is frequently the cause of business fluctuations." Comment and evaluate.

6. "Many short cycles are basically due to inventory fluctuations." Explain and evaluate. Also, describe how the acceleration principle can be applied to inventories.

7. On p. 261, seven leading series are listed. Explain why each of them would be expected to be a leading series, rather than a coincident or lagging series.

8. Suppose that consumption expenditure was \$100 billion in 1970 and \$105 billion in 1971, and that GNP increased by \$10 billion per year from 1971 to 1976. Based on Equation (12.4), what was the value of consumption expenditure from 1972 to 1976?

PART FOUR

Money, Banking, and Stabilization Policy

13

The Role and Importance of Money

According to the maxim of an ancient Roman, "Money alone sets all the world in motion." Although a statement that leaves so little room for the laws of physics or astronomy may be a mite extravagant, no one would deny the importance of money in economic affairs. The quantity of money is a very significant factor in determining the health and prosperity of any economic system. Inadequate increases in the quantity of money may bring about excessive unemployment, while excessive increases in the quantity of money may result in serious inflation. To some economists, a discussion of business fluctuations and economic stabilization that ignores the money supply is like a performance of *Hamlet* that omits the prince. Most economists would not go quite that far, but almost all would agree that the money supply is very important.

In this chapter, we are concerned with the nature and value of money, as well as with the relationship between a nation's money supply and the extent of unemployment and inflation. In particular, we consider questions like: What is money? What determines its value? What factors influence the demand for money, and what factors influence its quantity? What is the relationship between the quantity of money and the price level? What is the relationship between the quantity of money and the level of net national product? To understand the workings of our economy and the nature of our government's economic policies, you must be able to answer these questions.

What Is Money?

We must begin by defining money. At first blush, it may seem natural to define it by its physical characteristics. You may be inclined to say that money consists of bills of a certain size and color with certain words and symbols printed on them, as well as coins of a certain type. But this definition would be too restrictive, since money in other societies has consisted of whale teeth, wampum, and a variety of other things. Thus it seems better to define money by its functions than by its physical characteristics. Like beauty, money is as money does.

Money's first function is to act as a *medium of exchange.* People exchange their goods and services for something called money, and then use this money to buy the goods and services they want. To see how important money is as a medium of exchange, let's suppose that it did not exist. To exchange the goods and services they produce for the goods and services they want to consume, people would resort to *barter,* or direct exchange. If you were a wheat farmer, you would have to go to the people who produce the meat, clothes, and other goods and services you want, and swap some of your wheat for each of these goods and services. Of course this would be a very cumbersome procedure, since it would take lots of time and effort to locate and make individual bargains with each of these people. To get some idea of the extent to which money greases the process of exchange in any highly developed economy, consider all the purchases your family made last year—cheese from Wisconsin and France, automobiles from Detroit, oil from Texas and the Middle East, books from New York, and thousands of other items from all over the world. Imagine how few of these exchanges would have been feasible without money.

Second, money acts as a *standard of value.* It is the unit in which the prices of goods and services are measured. How do we express the price of coffee or tea or shirts or suits? In dollars and cents, of course. Thus money prices tell us the rates at which goods and services can be exchanged. For example, if the money price of a shirt is $12 and the money price of a tie is $4, a shirt will exchange for 3 ties. Put differently, a shirt will be "worth" 3 times as much as a tie.

Money also acts as a *store of value.* A person can hold on to money and use it to buy things later. You often hear stories about people who hoard a lot of money under their mattresses or bury it in their back yards. These people have an overdeveloped appreciation of the role of money as a store of value. But even those of us who are less miserly often use this function of money by carrying some money with us, and keeping some in the bank to make future purchases.

Finally, it should be recognized that money is a social invention. It is easy to assume that money has always existed, but this is not the case. Someone had to get the idea, and people had to come to accept it. Nor has money always had the characteristics it has today. In ancient Greece and Rome, money consisted of gold and silver coins. By the end of the seventeenth century, paper money was established in England; but this paper currency, unlike today's currency, could be exchanged for gold. Only recently has the transition been made to money that is not convertible into gold or silver. But regardless of its form or characteristics, anything that is a medium of exchange, a standard of value, and a store of value is money.

Three Kinds of Money

Like Caesar's Gaul, all money in modern economies is divided into three parts—coins, currency, and demand deposits. ***Coins*** are not really a very large proportion of the total quantity of money in the United States. In all, they amount to only about $8 billion, or about 2 to 3 percent of the total money supply. This is mainly because coins come in such small denominations. It takes a small mountain of pennies, nickels, dimes, quarters, and half-dollars to make even a billion dollars. Of course, the metal in each of these coins is worth less than the face value of the coin; otherwise people would melt them down and make money by selling the metal. In the 1960s, when silver prices rose, the government stopped using silver in dimes and quarters to prevent coins from meeting this fate.

Currency—paper money like the $5 and $10 bills everyone likes to have on hand—constitutes a second and far larger share of the total money supply than coins. Together, currency and coins outstanding totaled about $74 billion in 1975, as shown in Table 13.1. The Federal Reserve System, described in the next chapter, issues practically all of our currency in the form of Federal Reserve notes. Before 1933, it was possible to exchange currency for gold, but this is no longer the case. All American currency (and coin) is presently "fiat" money. It is money because the government says so and because the people accept it. There is no real metallic backing of the currency anymore. But this does not mean that we should be suspicious of the soundness of our currency, since gold backing is not what gives money its value. (In fact, to some extent, cause and effect work the other way: the use of gold to back currencies has in the past increased the value of gold.) Basically, the value of currency depends on its acceptability by people and on its scarcity.

Table 13.1
Money Supply, December 31, 1975, Seasonally Adjusted

	Amount (billions of dollars)
Demand deposits	222.6
Currency and coins	73.8
Total	296.4

Source: Economic Report of the President.

Third, bank deposits subject to payment on demand—so-called ***demand deposits***—are quantitatively by far the biggest part of our money supply, as shown in Table 13.1. At first you may question whether these demand deposits—or checking accounts, as they are commonly called—are money at all. In everyday speech, they often are not considered money. But economists include demand deposits as part of the money supply, and for good reason. After all, you can pay for goods and services just as easily by check as with cash. Indeed, the public pays for more things by check than with cash. This means that checking accounts are just as much a medium of exchange—and just as much a standard of value and a store of value—as cash. Thus, since they perform all of the functions of money, they should be included as money.

Figure 13.1 shows how the money supply—the sum total of coins, paper currency, and demand deposits—has behaved since World War II. You can see that the quantity of money has generally increased from one year to the next, and that the increase has been at an average rate of about 3 or 4 percent per year. However, the rate of increase of the quantity of money

Figure 13.1
Behavior of Money Supply, United States, 1947–75
The money supply, about $300 billion in 1975, has generally increased from year to year, but the rate of increase has by no means been constant.

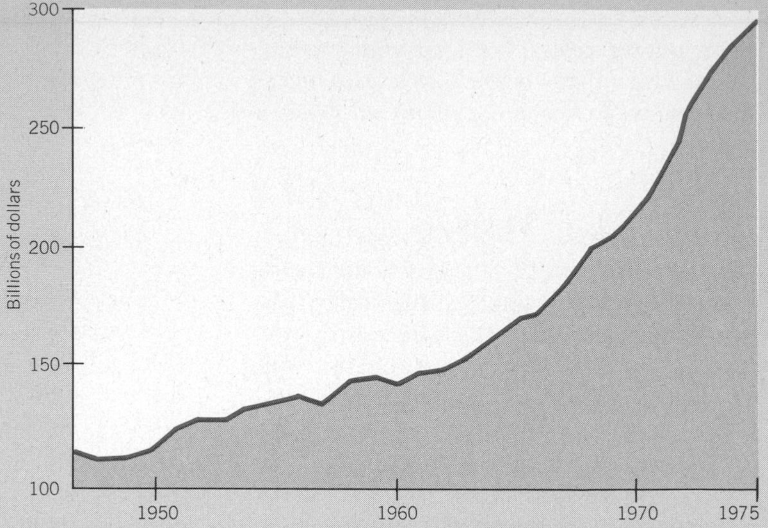

has by no means been constant. In some years, like 1972, the quantity of money increased by about 9 percent; in others, like 1975, it increased by about 4 percent. A great deal will be said later about the importance and determinants of changes in the quantity of money.

Near-Monies

We have just stated that all money is of three kinds—coins, currency, and demand deposits. This is the money supply, narrowly defined. It is not the only definition. There is also the money supply, broadly defined, which includes time or savings deposits as well as coins, currency, and demand deposits. The money supply, narrowly defined, is often called M_1, while the money supply, broadly defined, is often called M_2. Although economists usually use the narrow definition—and when we refer to the money supply in this book, we shall mean this definition—it is sometimes useful to work with the broad definition as well.

Time or savings deposits are excluded from the narrow definition of money because, in most instances, you cannot pay directly for anything with them. For example, suppose that you have a savings account at a commercial bank. You cannot draw a check against it, as you can with a demand deposit. And to withdraw your money from the account, you may have to give the bank a certain amount of notice (although in practice this right may be waived and the bank will ordinarily let you withdraw your money when you want).

On the other hand, economists who use the broad definition feel that time or savings deposits should be included in the money supply because, even if they do not constitute a medium of exchange, they can readily be transformed into cash. You may intend to buy a house sometime in the next year and you may want to keep $5,000 on hand to use as a down payment. You could leave this $5,000 in your checking account, or you could put it in a savings account, where it would earn some interest. Because ordinarily you can withdraw the money from a savings account on short notice, you may decide on this alternative. Since this savings account can so readily be transformed into cash, it is almost like a checking account. Not quite, but almost.

In recent years, the emergence of negotiable order of withdrawal (NOW) accounts has meant that the distinction between checking and savings accounts is even more blurred than in the past. NOW accounts are essentially interest-bearing checking accounts at savings banks and other thrift institutions and banks. First created in 1972 by a Massachusetts savings bank, such accounts are becoming legal in more and more states, particularly in the Northeast. Although they amounted to only about $1.5 billion in 1976, many observers expect them to grow in size. If so, it will no longer be possible to ignore them in the (narrow) definition of the money supply.

Many other assets can also be transformed into cash without much difficulty—though not quite as easily as savings deposits. For example, it is not difficult to convert government bonds into cash. There is no simple way to draw a hard-and-fast dividing line between money and nonmoney, since many assets have some of the characteristics of money. Consequently, there are still other definitions of the money supply that are more inclusive than M_2. But most economists feel that, although assets like government bonds have some of the properties of money, it would be stretching things too far to include them in the money supply. (For one thing, their price varies as interest rates change.)

Economists call such assets ***near-money,*** and recognize that the amount of near-money in the economy has an important effect on spending habits. There is some disagreement among economists as to exactly what is and what isn't near-money, but this needn't concern us here. The major point we want to make is that any dividing line between money and nonmoney must be arbitrary.

The Value of Money

Let's go back to one very important point that was mentioned briefly in a previous section: there is no gold backing for our money. In other words, there is no way that you can exchange a $10 bill for $10 worth of gold. (If you look at a $10 bill, you will see that it says nothing about what the government will give you in exchange for it.) Currency and demand deposits are really just debts, or IOUs. Currency is the debt of the government, while demand deposits are the debts of the commercial banks. Intrinsically, neither currency nor demand deposits have any real value. A $10 bill is merely a small piece of paper, and a demand deposit is merely an entry in a bank's accounts. And, as we have seen, even coins are worth far less as metal than their monetary value.

All this may make you feel a bit uncomfortable. After all, if our coins, currency, and demand deposits have little or no intrinsic value, doesn't this mean that they can easily become worthless? To answer this question, we must realize that basically, *money has value because people will accept it in payment for goods and services.* If your university will accept your check in payment for your tuition, and your grocer will accept a $20 bill in payment for your groceries, your demand deposit and your currency have value. You can exchange them for goods and services you want. And your university or your grocer accepts this money only because they have confidence that they can spend it for goods and services they want.

Thus money is valuable because it will buy things. But how valuable is it? For example, how valuable is $1? Clearly, *the value of a dollar is equivalent to what a dollar will buy. And what a dollar will buy depends on the price level.* If all prices doubled, the value of a dollar would be cut in half, because a dollar would be able to buy only half as many goods and services as it formerly could. On the other hand, if all prices were reduced by 50 percent, the value of a dollar would double, because a dollar would be able to buy twice as many goods and services as it formerly could. You often hear people say that today's dollar is worth only

$.50. What they mean is that it will buy only half what a dollar could buy at some specified date in the past.

It is interesting and important to see how the value of the dollar, as measured by its purchasing power, has varied over time. Figure 13.2 shows how an index of the price level in the United States has changed since 1779. Over time, prices have fluctuated sharply, and the greatest fluctuations have resulted from wars. For example, the price level fell sharply after the Revolutionary War, and our next war—the War of 1812—sent prices skyrocketing, after which there was another postwar drop in prices. The period from about 1820 to about 1860 was marked by relative price stability, but the Civil War resulted in an upward burst followed by a postwar drop in prices. After a period of relative price stability from 1875 to 1915, there was a doubling of prices during World War I and the usual postwar drop. World War II also caused an approximate doubling, but there was no postwar drop in prices.

Clearly, the value of money is inversely related to the price level. In inflationary times, the value of money decreases; the opposite is true when the price level falls (an infrequent phenomenon in the past three decades). Thus the wartime periods when the price level rose greatly were periods when the value of the dollar decreased greatly. The doubling of prices during World War II meant that the value of the dollar was chopped in half. Similarly, the postwar periods when the price level fell greatly were periods when the value of the dollar increased. The 50 percent decline in prices after the Civil War meant a doubling in the value of the dollar. Given the extent of the variation of the price level shown in Figure

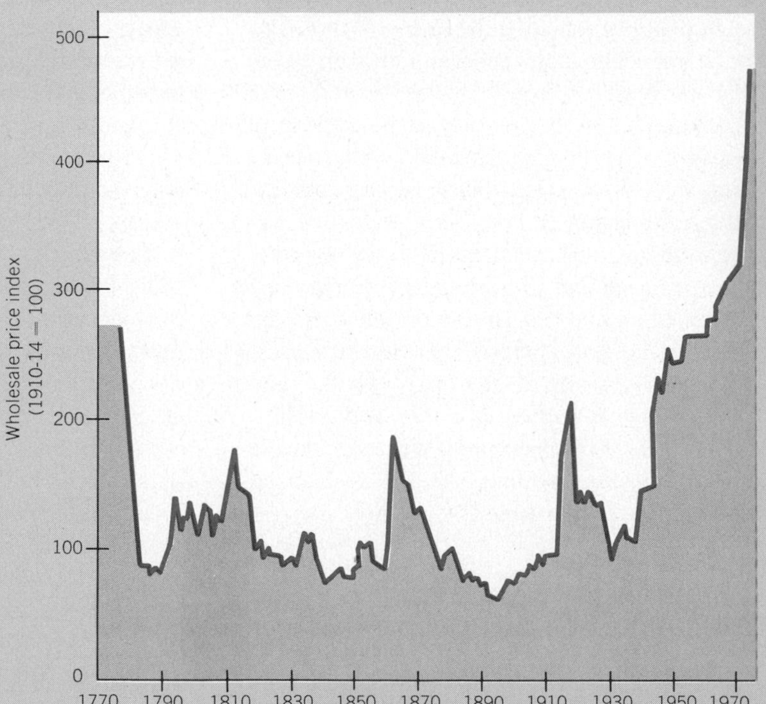

Figure 13.2
Index of Wholesale Prices, United States, 1779–1975 (1910–14 = 100)
The price level has fluctuated considerably, sharp increases generally occurring during wars. Since World War II, the price level has tended to go only one way—up.

13.2, it is clear that the value of the dollar has varied enormously during our history.

Inflation

Runaway Inflation: A Case Study

In periods of inflation, the value of money is reduced. Since inflation means an increase in the price level, and since an increase in the price level means a reduction in the value of money, this proposition seems clear enough. But remember that inflations vary in severity: ***runaway inflations*** wipe out the value of money quickly and thoroughly, while ***creeping inflations*** erode its value gradually and slowly. There is a lot of difference between a runaway inflation and a creeping inflation.

The case of Germany after World War I is a good example of runaway inflation. Germany was required to pay large reparations to the victorious Allies after the war. Rather than attempting to tax its people to pay these amounts, the German government merely printed additional quantities of paper money. This new money increased total spending in Germany, and the increased spending resulted in higher prices because the war-devastated economy could not increase output substantially. As more and more money was printed, prices rose higher and higher, reaching utterly fantastic levels. By 1923, it took a *trillion* marks (the unit of German currency) to buy what one mark would buy before the war. The effect of this runaway inflation was to disrupt the economy. Prices had to be adjusted from day to day. People rushed to the stores to spend the money they received as soon as possible, since very soon it would buy much less. Speculation was rampant. This inflation was a terrible blow to Germany. The middle class was wiped out; its savings became completely worthless. It is no wonder that Germany has in recent years been more sensitive than many other countries to the evils of inflation.

Runaway Inflation and the Quantity of Money

Needless to say, this is not the only case in history of runaway inflation. Our own country suffered from runaway inflations during the Revolutionary War and the Civil War. You may have heard the expression that something is "not worth a continental." It comes from the fact that the inflated dollars in use during the Revolutionary War were called continentals. There have also been runaway inflations in China and Eastern Europe and other parts of the world. Generally, such inflations have occurred because the government increased the money supply at an enormously rapid rate. It is not hard to see why a tremendous increase in the quantity of money will result in a runaway inflation. Other things held constant, increases in the quantity of money will result in increases in total desired spending, and once full employment is achieved, such increases in desired spending will bring about more and more inflation. Eventually, when the inflation is severe enough, households and businesses may refuse to accept money for goods and services because they fear that it will depreciate significantly before they have a chance to spend it. Instead, they may insist on being paid in merchandise or services. Thus the economy will turn to barter, with the accompanying inconveniences and inefficiency.

To prevent such an economic catastrophe, the government must manage the money supply responsibly. As we have stressed in previous sections, the value of money depends basically on the public's willingness to accept it, and the public's willingness to accept it depends on money's being reasonably stable in value. If the government increases the quantity of money at a rapid rate, thus causing a severe inflation and an accompanying precipitous fall in the value of money, public confidence in money will be shaken, and the value of money will be destroyed. The moral is clear: *the gov-*

Is Indexation the Answer to Inflation?

In the mid-1970s, when inflation in the United States was excessive in the eyes of practically all observers, some economists, like Milton Friedman of the University of Chicago, proposed a device called *indexation* to ameliorate the effects of inflation. Indexation is another word for the use of price-escalator clauses in private and public contracts. For example, in many industries, wages now rise automatically in accord with increases in the price level. And many government pensions now have similar provisions. What these economists were proposing was that such provisions be extended throughout the economy, or at least throughout much of it. For example, a person's income tax liability would be geared to the value of his or her income, after correcting for the effects of price-level changes. And interest rates would rise automatically with the rate of inflation.

Without question, indexation would help to reduce some of the harmful effects of inflation. For example, if the U.S. Treasury were to issue bonds where the principal and interest were adjusted to compensate for rises in the price level, it would be possible for small savers to put aside some money for the future, without being victimized by inflation. To see how such bonds might work, suppose that you invested $1,000 in them, and that you cashed them in two years after you bought them. If the price level then was 20 percent higher than when you bought them, you would receive $1,200 in principal plus interest. (Why $1,200? Because, since the price level was 20 percent higher, $1,200 at the time you cashed in the bonds would be the same as $1,000 at the time when you invested in them.)

Indexation really is not a new idea. Such great names of economics as Alfred Marshall of Cambridge and Irving Fisher of Yale were interested in the idea earlier in this century. And it has been tried on a limited scale in Canada and Israel, and to a greater extent in Brazil. But it has not received widespread support in the United States. Undoubtedly, one reason is that many people feel that indexation represents a surrender in the fight against inflation. In their view, it is better to quell inflation than to try to live with it. Also, some people are worried that "indexation will make it easier for the public to recognize changes in the rate of inflation, will thereby reduce the time lag in adapting to such changes, and so will make the . . . price level more sensitive and variable."*

Further, some observers believe that indexation of a comprehensive sort simply is not feasible. For example, as the Council of Economic Advisers has pointed out, "A major obstacle is that many current dollar payment obligations have been incurred in past periods. Furthermore, individuals can hardly be forced to index their future contracts if . . . they wish to make other allowances for the price movements they expect."† As inflation abated somewhat in 1976, talk of indexation died down. But that does not mean that the idea has been abandoned: it might be revived and even applied if the nation suffers more bouts of double-digit inflation.

* Milton Friedman, "Using Escalators to Help Fight Inflation," *Fortune*, July 1974, p. 176.
† Council of Economic Advisers, *Annual Report*, 1975, p. 141.

ernment must restrict the quantity of money, and conduct its economic policies so as to maintain a reasonably stable value of money.

Creeping Inflation and the Value of Money

For the past 40 years, the price level in the United States has tended to go one way only—up. Year after year, prices have risen. Since 1950, there hasn't been a single year when the price level has fallen, and in the 1940s it fell only in 1949. Certainly, this has not been a runaway inflation, but it has resulted in a very substantial erosion in the value of the dollar. Like a beach slowly worn away by the ocean, the dollar has slowly lost a considerable portion of its value. Specifically, prices now tend to be about 4 times what they were 40 years ago. Thus the dollar now is worth about ¼ of what it was worth then. Although a creeping inflation of this sort is much less harmful than a runaway inflation, it has a number of unfortunate social consequences.

For one thing, people with fixed incomes are hit hard by inflation. Although a creeping inflation does not hurt them as much as a runaway inflation, its cumulative effect over a period of years can be substantial. Old people often suffer, since they tend to have fixed incomes derived from public and private pensions, and interest on their savings. In addition, as we pointed out in Chapter 8, inflation hurts lenders and savers. The results can be both devastating and inequitable. The family that works hard and saves for retirement (and a rainy day) finds that its savings are worth far less, when it finally spends them, than the amount it saved. For example, consider the well-meaning souls who invested $1,000 of their savings in United States savings bonds in 1939. By 1949, these bonds were worth only about 800 1939 dollars, including the interest received in the 10-year period. Thus these people had $200 taken away from them, in just as real a sense as if someone picked their pockets.

Although a mild upward creep of prices at the rate of a few percent per year is not likely to result in very disastrous social consequences, any major inflation is a real social problem. (And inflation in the mid-1970s could be more appropriately designated as sprinting, rather than creeping; in 1974, the price level rose by about 12 percent.) Because it has proved difficult to bring inflation under control, some people have argued in recent years that inflation is not as bad as it looks. This, of course, seems quite sensible to those who have gained from inflation. But it does not do justice to the many people, including a disproportionate number of the elderly, who have been "suckered" by inflation. Why should these people have been subjected to such an arbitrary and inequitable tax on their savings and incomes? Moreover, this is not the only consideration. According to some respected economists, inflation tends to feed on itself. That is, a 2 percent rate of inflation tends to grow to a 3 percent rate of inflation, which tends to grow to a 4 percent rate of inflation, and so on. Although the available evidence is too weak to demonstrate this proposition, the possibility should nonetheless be borne in mind.

Inflation has a bad name, both among economists and with the general public. The novelist Ernest Hemingway, overstating his case more than a bit, wrote, "The first panacea for a mismanaged nation is inflation of currency: the second is war. . . . Both are the refuge of political and economic opportunists." [1] Yet we must recognize that under some conditions, full employment can be achieved only if a moderate amount of inflation is tolerated. For example, as we shall see, this seems to have been the case in the 1970s. Under such circumstances, the nation is faced with a painful decision: Should it allow a moderate amount of inflation in order to promote full employment? The im-

[1] Ernest Hemingway, "Notes on the Next War," *Esquire*, September 1935.

portance of maintaining full employment was described in detail in Chapter 8. The answer you give to this question will depend on your own ethical values and political preferences.

Unemployment and the Quantity of Money

In the last two sections, we have been concerned primarily with what happens when the quantity of money grows too rapidly. As we have seen, the result is inflation. But this is only part of the story. The quantity of money can grow too slowly as well as too rapidly; and when this happens the result is increased unemployment. If the money supply grows very slowly, or decreases, there will be a tendency for total desired spending to grow very slowly or decrease. This in turn will cause national output to grow very slowly or decrease, thus causing unemployment to increase. The result will, of course, be the social waste and human misery associated with excessive unemployment.

According to many economists, the recession of 1974-75 was due partly to an inadequate growth of the money supply. The Federal Reserve, trying to stem the inflationary tide in 1974, cut back on the rate of increase of the money supply. Looking back over past business fluctuations, it appears that an inadequate rate of increase in the quantity of money was responsible, at least in part, for many recessions. For example, according to Harvard's James Duesenberry, "Every major depression has been accompanied by a substantial decline in the money supply, and often by a complete collapse of the banking system. Among the many causes responsible for our major depressions, money and banking difficulties have always been prominent."[2] Recall that in our discussion of business fluctuations in the previous chapter, we stressed the importance of monetary factors. In this chapter, as well as Chapters 14 to 16, we will study these factors in detail.

[2] J. S. Duesenberry, *Money and Credit: Impact and Control,* Englewood Cliffs, N.J.: Prentice-Hall, 1972, p. 3.

Determinants of the Quantity of Money

Judging from our discussion thus far, it is clear that to avoid excessive unemployment or excessive inflation, the quantity of money must not grow too slowly or too fast. But what determines the quantity of money? We have already seen that money is of three types: coins, paper currency, and demand deposits. Let's begin by considering the quantity of coins and paper currency in circulation. They make up about ¼ of the total money supply. Practically all the currency is Federal Reserve notes, issued by the Federal Reserve Banks. When the United States was on the gold standard, the amount of money in circulation was determined by the amount of monetary gold in the country. When gold flowed into the country, the money supply increased; when it flowed out, the money supply decreased. This is no longer the case, since we are no longer on the gold standard—and neither is any other major nation.

If gold doesn't determine the amount of coins and currency in circulation, what does? The answer is that this amount responds to the needs of firms and individuals for cash to use or hoard. When people want more coins and currency, they go to their banks and exchange their demand deposits for coins and currency: in other words, they convert part of their checking accounts into cash. When they want less coins and currency, they take their cash to the banks and exchange it for demand deposits, thus converting some of their cash into checking accounts. Although the Federal Reserve System controls the size of the entire money supply, it allows the share of money in coin and currency to be determined by the public's wishes.

Next, consider the quantity of demand deposits, which is of obvious importance, since the bulk of our money supply is composed of demand deposits, not coin and paper currency. Demand deposits are created by commercial banks.[3] The question of how much money banks can create is both fundamental and complicated, and most of the next chapter will be required to present an adequate answer. For the moment, it is sufficient to say that the Federal Reserve System limits the amount of demand deposits the banks can create.

Thus the supply of money is determined to a considerable degree by the Federal Reserve System, which, as we have noted before, is our nation's central bank. Within limits, the Federal Reserve can and does control the quantity of money. But to some extent the private sector of the economy also determines the quantity of money. For example, the nation's commercial banks, through their lending (and other) decisions, can influence the money supply. In the remainder of this chapter, we shall make the simplifying assumption that the money supply is governed solely by the Federal Reserve. In the following chapter, we shall see how the commercial banks also play an important role in this regard.

The Demand for Money

We have discussed in general terms how changes in the quantity of money affect the tempo of economic activity. Now let's look in detail at how changes in the quantity of money affect net national product. The first step in doing this is to discuss the demand for money.

[3] Of course, banks do not create money all by themselves. The public's preferences and actions, as well as bank behavior, influence the amount of demand deposits. Also, commercial banks may not be as unique in this respect as it appears at first sight. See James Tobin, "Commercial Banks as Creators of Money" in D. Carson, ed., *Banking and Monetary Studies,* Homewood, Ill.: Irwin, 1963.

Why does a family or firm want to hold money? Certainly, a family can be wealthy without holding much money. We all know stories about very rich men who hold very little money, since virtually all of their wealth is tied up in factories, farms, and other nonmonetary assets. Unlike assets that yield profits or interest, money produces no direct return; so why do people and firms want to hold money, rather than other kinds of assets? Basically, there are the following three reasons:

Transactions demand for money. To carry out most transactions, money is required. Thus people and firms like to keep some money on their person and in their checking accounts to buy things. Clearly, the higher a person's income—in dollar, not real terms—the more money he or she will want to hold for transactions purposes. For example, in 1976, when a doctor makes about $50,000 a year, the average physician will want to keep more money on hand for transactions purposes than in the days—many, many years ago—when a doctor made perhaps $10,000 a year. Because the quantity of money demanded by a household or firm increases with its income, it follows that the total quantity of money demanded for transactions purposes in the economy as a whole is directly related to net national product. That is, the higher (lower) the level of NNP, the greater (less) the quantity of money demanded for transactions purposes.

Precautionary demand for money. Besides the transactions motive, households and firms like to hold money because they are uncertain concerning the timing and size of future disbursements and receipts. Unpredictable events often require money: for example, people get sick, and houses need repairs. Also, receipts frequently do not come in exactly when expected. To meet such contingencies, people and firms like to put a certain amount of their wealth into money and near-money. In the economy as a whole, the total quantity of money demanded for precautionary purposes (like the quantity demanded for transactions purposes) is likely to vary directly with NNP. For example, if NNP goes up, households and firms will want to hold more money for precautionary purposes, because their incomes and sales will be higher than before the increase in NNP.

Speculative demand for money. Finally, people like to hold some of their assets in a form in which they can be sure of its monetary value and can take advantage of future price reductions. The amount of money individuals and firms will keep on hand for speculative reasons will vary with their expectations concerning future price movements. In particular, if people feel that the prices of bonds and stocks are about to drop soon, they are likely to demand a great deal of money for speculative purposes. By holding money, they can obtain such securities at lower prices than at present. On the other hand, if they believe that the prices of bonds and stocks are about to rise, they are likely to demand much less money for these purposes. Rather than holding money, they will tend to hold these securities, and reap the profit arising from their increase in price.

The Interest Rate and the Demand for Money: The Liquidity Preference Function

Up to this point, we have discussed why individuals and firms want to hold money. But we must recognize that there are disadvantages, as well as advantages, in holding money. One is that the real value of money will fall if inflation occurs. Another is that an important cost of holding money is the interest or profit one loses, since instead of holding money, one might have invested it in assets that would have yielded interest or profit. For example, the annual cost of holding $5,000 in money if one can obtain 6 percent on existing investments, is $300, the amount of interest or profit forgone.

With NNP constant, the amount of money held by individuals and firms is *inversely* related to the interest rate. *The higher the interest rate, the smaller the amount of money demanded. The lower the interest rate, the greater the amount of money demanded.* This is because the cost of holding money increases as the interest rate or yield on existing investments increases. For example, if the interest rate were 7 percent rather than 6 percent, the cost of holding $5,000 in money for one year would be $350 rather than $300. Thus, as the interest rate or profit rate increases, people try harder to minimize the amount of money they hold. So do firms: big corporations like General Motors or U.S. Steel are very conscious of the cost of holding cash balances.

Another reason why the interest rate may be inversely related to the quantity of money demanded is that *bond prices are inversely related to the rate of interest.* If the interest rate goes up, bond prices go down; if the interest rate goes down, bond prices go up. (To see why, suppose that a very long-term bond pays interest of $300 per year. This bond is worth $3,000 if the prevailing interest rate is 10 percent, and $6,000 if it is 5 percent, because with a 10 percent interest rate one can get $300 per year by investing $3,000, whereas with a 5 percent interest rate one must invest $6,000 to get $300 per year.) Thus, if the interest rate is low, bond prices may be so high (relative to speculators' expectations) that speculators may hold money rather than buy bonds. And if the interest rate is high, bond prices may be so low (relative to speculators' expectations) that speculators will want to buy them rather than hold money. Consequently, a high (low) interest rate may result in a lesser (greater) quantity of money demanded.

Figure 13.3 summarizes two important conclusions of our discussion in this and the previous section. Panel A of Figure 13.3 shows that, *holding the interest rate constant, the quantity of money demanded is directly related to NNP.* As

Figure 13.3
The Demand for Money
Holding the interest rate constant, the quantity of money demanded is *directly* related to NNP, as shown in panel A. Holding NNP constant, the quantity of money demanded is *inversely* related to the interest rate, as shown in panel B. The latter relationship is known as the *liquidity preference function.*

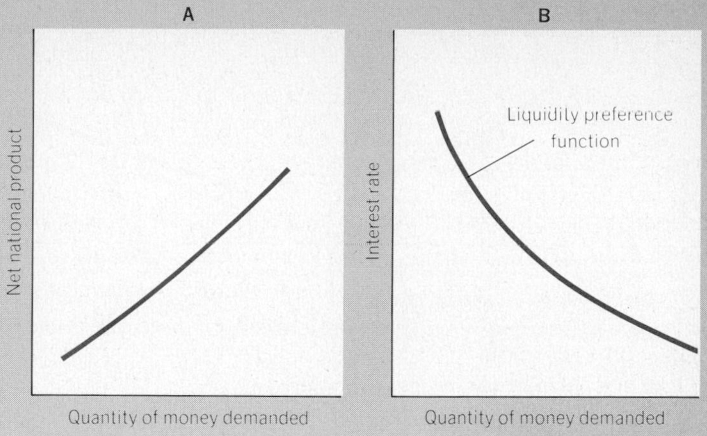

we explained in the previous section, the higher (lower) the level of NNP, the greater (less) the quantity of money demanded. Panel B of Figure 13.3 shows that, *with NNP constant, the quantity of money demanded is inversely related to the interest rate.*[4] This latter relationship, described in this section, is called the ***liquidity preference function.***

Changes in the Money Supply and National Output

Effects of an Increase in the Money Supply: The Keynesian Model

Now that we have investigated the demand for money, we are ready to show how changes in the quantity of money influence the value of NNP. Given the liquidity preference function, it is a simple matter to show how the money supply can be inserted into the Keynesian model (in Chapters 10 and 11) that explains the level of NNP.

To begin with, let's trace the effects of an increase in the money supply from $200 billion to $250 billion. If the liquidity preference function is as shown in panel A of Figure 13.4, the result will be a *decrease in the interest rate* from *d* percent to *c* percent. Why? Because, if the interest rate is *d* percent, people will demand only $200 billion in money, not the $250 billion that is supplied. Having more money on hand than they want, they will invest the excess in bonds, stocks, and other financial assets, with the result that the prices of bonds, stocks, and other financial assets will rise.[5] As pointed out in the previous section, such a price rise is equivalent to a fall in the rate of interest. When the interest rate has fallen to *c* percent, people will be willing to hold the $250 billion in money. At this interest rate, the quantity of money demanded will equal the quantity of money supplied.

The decrease in the interest rate from *d* percent to *c* percent affects the investment func-

[4] However, this relationship between the quantity of money and the interest rate is only short-run. In the long run, increases in the money supply, if they result in increased inflation, may *raise* interest rates, because lenders will require a greater return to offset the greater rate of depreciation of the real value of the dollar. Still, however, the *real* rate of interest—the rate of interest adjusted for inflation—may decline.

[5] For simplicity, we assume that when people have excess money balances, they use the money to buy financial assets. (In the next section, we assume that when people have smaller money balances than they want, they sell financial assets to get more money.) A more complete analysis is provided in Chapter 16. The results are the same as those provided here.

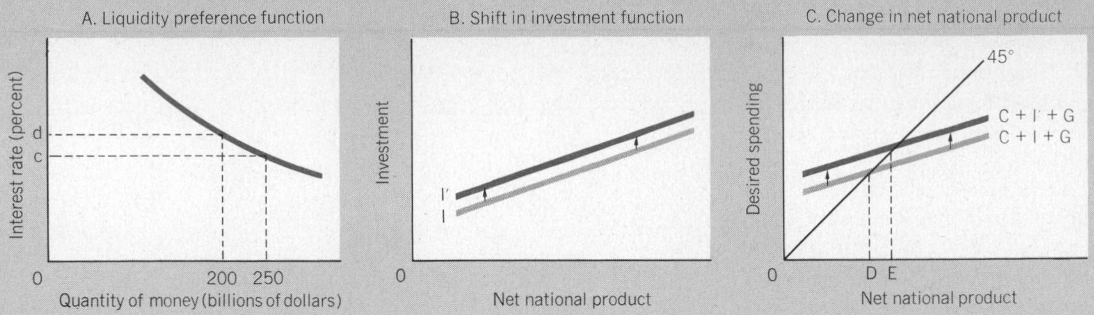

Figure 13.4
Effect of an Increase in the Money Supply.
If the money supply increases from $200 billion to $250 billion, the interest rate drops from *d* percent to *c* percent (panel A). Because of the decrease in the interest rate, the investment function shifts upward (panel B), and the equilibrium level of NNP increases from *D* to *E* (panel C).

tion.[6] Recall from Chapter 9 that the level of investment is inversely related to the interest rate. Because it is less costly to invest—and because credit is more readily available[7]—*the investment function will shift upward,* as shown in panel B of Figure 13.4. This occurs because at each level of net national product, firms will want to invest more, since investment is more profitable (because of the cut in the interest rate) and funds are more readily available.[8]

[6] Changes in the money supply, interest rates, and credit availability affect the consumption function and government spending, as well as the investment function. For example, *increases (decreases) in interest rates shift the consumption function and the level of government spending downward (upward).* These factors augment the effect of monetary policy described in the text. We focus attention on the investment function in Figures 13.4 and 13.5 merely because this simplifies the exposition.

[7] Note that it is not just a matter of interest rates: Availability of credit is also important. In times when money is tight, some potential borrowers may find that they cannot get a loan, regardless of what interest rate they are prepared to pay. In times when money is easy, people who otherwise might find it difficult to get a loan may be granted one by the banks. To repeat, both availability and interest rates are important.

[8] Many firms depend to a considerable extent on retained earnings to finance their investment projects. Thus, since they do not borrow externally, the effect on their investment plans of changes in interest rates and credit availability is slight. This factor may reduce the effects of changes in the money supply.

This shift in the investment function then affects the equilibrium level of net national product. As shown in panel C of Figure 13.4, *the equilibrium level of net national product will increase* from *D* to *E*, in accord with the principles discussed in Chapter 10. (Recall that the equilibrium value of NNP is at the point where the $C + I + G$ line intersects the 45-degree line.) Thus *the effect of the increase in the money supply is to increase net national product.*

This, in simplified fashion, is how an increase in the money supply affects NNP, according to the Keynesian model. To summarize, *the increase in the money supply results in a reduction in the interest rate, which results in an increase in investment, which results in an increase in NNP.* Obviously, this theory is of great importance in helping us to understand more completely why our economy behaves the way it does. For example, we can now understand better why vast increases in the quantity of money will result in runaway inflation. Total spending will be pushed upward at a very rapid rate, driving the price level out of sight.

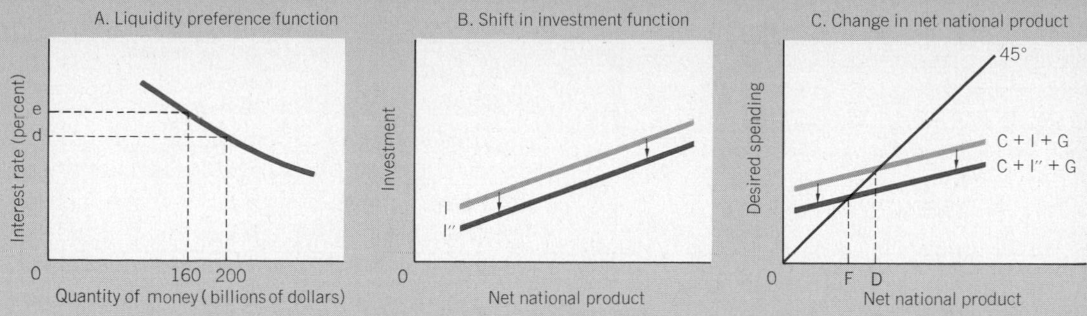

Figure 13.5
Effect of a Decrease in the Money Supply
If the money supply decreases from $200 billion to $160 billion, the interest rate increases from *d* percent to *e* percent (panel A). Because of the increase in the interest rate, the investment function shifts downward (panel B) and the equilibrium level of NNP decreases from *D* to *F* (panel C).

Effects of a Decrease in the Money Supply: The Keynesian Model

Next, let's trace the effects of a decrease in the money supply from $200 billion to $160 billion. If the liquidity preference function is as shown in panel A of Figure 13.5, the result will be an *increase in the interest rate* from *d* percent to *e* percent. Why? Because, if the interest rate is *d* percent, prople will demand $200 billion in money, not the $160 billion that is supplied. Having less money on hand than they want, they will sell some of their bonds, stocks, and other financial assets to build up their money balances, with the result that the prices of bonds, stocks, and other financial assets will fall. As pointed out above, such a fall in price is equivalent to an increase in the interest rate. When the interest rate has increased to *e* percent, people will be willing to hold only the $160 billion in money. At this interest rate, the quantity of money demanded will equal the quantity of money supplied.

The increase in the interest rate from *d* percent to *e* percent affects the investment function. Because it is more costly for firms to invest—and more difficult to obtain credit—*the investment function will shift downward,* as shown in panel B of Figure 13.5. This shift occurs because, at every level of net national product, firms want to invest less. The reasons why an increase in the interest rate reduces investment were given in detail in Chapter 9.

This downward shift in the investment function has an effect in turn on the equilibrium level of net national product. As shown in panel C of Figure 13.5, *the equilibrium level of net national product will decrease from* D *to* F (since the equilibrium level of NNP is at the point where the $C + I + G$ line intersects the 45 degree line). Thus *the effect of the decrease in the money supply is to decrease net national product.*

This, in simplified fashion, is how a decrease in the money supply affects NNP, according to the Keynesian model. To summarize, *the decrease in the money supply results in an increase in the interest rate, which results in a decrease in investment, which results in a decrease in NNP.*

This theory helps to explain, among other things, why an inadequate rate of growth of the money supply can lead to excessive unemployment. If the money supply is too small, NNP will not reach its full employment level.

The Monetarists

Some prominent economists, led by Milton Friedman of the University of Chicago, believe that the quantity of money affects NNP in a different way than was indicated in the previous sections. These economists rely on a theoretical framework generally labeled monetarism; hence they are called monetarists. In their view, monetarism provides more effective tools for forecasting or controlling nominal NNP than the Keynesian model described in Chapters 9 and 10. (***Nominal NNP*** means NNP in money, not real terms. In other words, nominal NNP is NNP measured in current, not constant, dollars.)

Monetarists regard the rate of growth of the money supply as the principal determinant of nominal, or money, net national product. Indeed, they go so far as to say that fiscal policy, although it will alter the composition of net national product, may have little or no long-run effect on the size of nominal NNP unless it influences the money supply. This latter view, explained in more detail in Chapter 16, is not now accepted by most economists.

The monetarists have had a great impact on economic thought in the postwar period, even though theirs remains a minority view. Professor Friedman's most severe critics admit that his research in this area has been pathbreaking and extremely important. According to his findings,

> the rate of change of the money supply shows well-marked cycles that match closely those in economic activity in general and precede the latter by a long interval. On the average, the rate of change of the money supply has reached its peak nearly 16 months before the peak in general business and has reached its trough over 12 months before the trough in general business.[9]

Clearly, findings of this sort must be taken seriously. Moreover, research carried out at the Federal Reserve Bank of St. Louis has shown a close relationship between short-run changes in the quantity of money and short-run changes in NNP. Based on this relationship, the St. Louis Bank has constructed some simple econometric models that have had some success in forecasting NNP. These results have also strengthened the hand of the monetarists. (However, in the 1970s, research suggests that models of this sort have not forecasted as well as the models described in Chapter 12.)

The Velocity of Money and the Equation of Exchange

The monetarists have revived interest in the so-called quantity theory of money, which was developed many years ago by such titans of economics as Alfred Marshall of Cambridge and Irving Fisher at Yale. To understand this theory, it is useful to begin by defining a new term: the velocity of circulation of money. The ***velocity of circulation of money*** is the rate at which the money supply is used to make transactions for final goods and services. That is, it equals the average number of times per year that a dollar is used to buy the final goods and services produced by the economy. In other words,

$$V = \frac{\text{NNP}}{M}, \qquad (13.1)$$

where V is velocity, NNP is the nominal net national product, and M is the money supply. For example, if our nominal net national product is $1 trillion and our money supply is $200

[9] Milton Friedman, testimony before the Joint Economic Committee, "The Relationship of Prices to Economic Stability and Growth," 85th Congress, 2d Session, 1958.

billion, the velocity of circulation of money is 5, which means that, on the average, each dollar of our money consummates \$5 worth of purchases of net national product.

Nominal net national product can be expressed as the product of real net national product and the price level: In other words,

$$\text{NNP} = P \times Q, \tag{13.2}$$

where P is the price level—the average price at which final goods and services are sold—and Q is net national product in real terms. For example, suppose that national output in real terms consists of 200 tons of steel. If the price of a ton of steel is \$100, then nominal NNP equals $P \times Q$, or \$100 × 200, or \$20,000.[10]

If we substitute $P \times Q$ for NNP in Equation (13.1), we have

$$V = \frac{P \times Q}{M}. \tag{13.3}$$

That is, velocity equals the price level *(P)* times real NNP *(Q)* divided by the money supply *(M)*. This is another way to define the velocity of circulation of money—a way that will prove very useful.

Now that we have a definition of the velocity of circulation of money, our next step is to present the so-called equation of exchange. The ***equation of exchange*** is really nothing more than a restatement, in somewhat different form, of our definition of the velocity of circulation of money. To obtain the equation of exchange, all we have to do is multiply both sides of Equation (13.3) by M. The result, of course, is

$$MV = PQ. \tag{13.4}$$

[10] Since real NNP is measured here in physical units (tons), P is the price level. If real NNP had been measured in constant dollars, P would have been a price index. In either event, our conclusions would be basically the same.

To understand exactly what this equation means, let's look more closely at each side. *The righthand side equals the amount received for final goods and services during the period,* because Q is the output of final goods and services during the period and P is their average price. Thus the product of P and Q must equal the total amount received for final goods and services during the period—or nominal NNP. For example, if national output in real terms equals 200 tons of steel, and if the price of a ton of steel is \$100, then \$100 × 200—that is, $P \times Q$—must equal the total amount received for final goods and services during the period.

The lefthand side of Equation (13.4) equals the total amount spent on final goods and services during the period. Why? Because the lefthand side equals the money supply—M—times the average number of times during the period that a dollar was spent on final goods and services—V. Obviously, $M \times V$ must equal the amount spent on final goods and services during the period. For example, if the money supply equals \$10,000 and velocity equals 2, the total amount spent on final goods and services during the period must equal \$10,000 × 2, or \$20,000.

Thus, since the *amount received for* final goods and services during the period must equal the *amount spent on* final goods and services during the period, the lefthand side must equal the righthand side.

The equation of exchange—Equation (13.4)—is what logicians call a tautology: it holds by definition. Yet it is not useless. On the contrary, economists regard the equation of exchange as very valuable, because it sets forth some of the fundamental factors that influence NNP and the price level. This equation has been used by economists for many years. It is the basis for the crude quantity theory of money used by the classical economists, as well as the recent theories put forth by the monetarists.

The Crude Quantity Theory of Money and Prices

The classical economists discussed in Chapter 9 assumed that both V and Q were constant. They believed that V was constant because it was determined by the population's stable habits of holding money, and they believed that Q would remain constant at its full employment value.[11] On the basis of these assumptions, they propounded the ***crude quantity theory*** of money and prices, a theory that received a great deal of attention and exerted considerable influence in its day.

If these assumptions hold, it follows from the equation of exchange—Equation (13.4)—that the price level (P) must be proportional to the money supply (M), because V and Q have been assumed to be constant. (In the short run, the full-employment level of real net national product will not change much.) Thus we can rewrite Equation (13.4) as

$$P = \left(\frac{V}{Q}\right) M, \qquad (13.5)$$

where (V/Q) is a constant. So P must be proportional to M if these assumptions hold.

The conclusion reached by the crude quantity theorists—namely, *that the price level will be proportional to the money supply*—is very important, if true. To see how they came to this conclusion, one must recognize that they stressed the transaction motive for holding money. Recall from an earlier section that, based on this motive, one would expect the quantity of money demanded to be directly related to the level of nominal NNP. The crude quantity theorists went so far as to assume that it was *proportional* to the level of nominal NNP. This amounted to assuming that velocity was constant.

Suppose that a 10 percent increase occurs in the quantity of money. Why would the crude quantity theorists predict a 10 percent increase in the price level? To begin with, they would assert that, since the quantity of money has increased relative to the value of nominal NNP, households and firms now hold more money than they want to hold. Further, they would argue that households and firms will spend their excess money balances on commodities and services, and that the resulting increase in total desired spending will increase the nominal value, but not the real value of NNP (since full employment is assumed). In other words, the increase in aggregate demand will bid up prices. More specifically, they would argue that prices will continue to be bid up until they have increased by 10 percent, since only then will the nominal value of NNP be big enough so that households and firms will be content to hold the new quantity of money.

[11] In some cases, they did not really assume continual full employment; instead, they were concerned with the long-run changes in the economy, and compared the peaks of the business cycle, where full employment frequently occurs.

Evaluation of the Crude Quantity Theory

The crude quantity theory is true to its name: it is only a crude approximation to reality. One important weakness is its assumption that velocity is constant. Another is its assumption that the economy is always at full employment, which we know from previous chapters to be far from true. But despite its limitations, the crude quantity theory points to a very important truth: if the government finances its expenditures by a drastic increase in the money supply, the result will be drastic inflation. For example, if the money supply is increased tenfold, there will be a marked increase in the price level. If we take the crude quantity theory at face value, we would expect a tenfold increase in the price level; but that is a case of spurious accuracy. Perhaps the price level will go up only eightfold. Perhaps it will go up twelvefold. The important thing is that it will go up a lot.

There is a great deal of evidence to show that the crude quantity theory is a useful predictor during periods of runaway inflation, such as in Germany after World War I. The German inflation occurred because the German government printed and spent large bundles of additional money. You often hear people warn of the dangers in this country of the government's "resorting to the printing presses" and flooding the country with a vast increase in the money supply. It is a danger in any country. And one great value of the crude quantity theory is that it predicts correctly what will occur as a consequence: rapid inflation.

There is also considerable evidence that the crude quantity theory works reasonably well in predicting long-term trends in the price level. For example, during the sixteenth and seventeenth centuries, gold and silver were imported by the Spanish from the New World, resulting in a great increase in the money supply. The crude quantity theory would predict a great increase in the price level, and this is what occurred. Or consider the late nineteenth century, when the discovery of gold in the United States, South Africa, and Canada brought about a considerable increase in the money supply. As the crude quantity theory would lead us to expect, the price level rose considerably as a consequence.

A More Sophisticated Version of the Quantity Theory

The crude quantity theory was based on two simplifying assumptions, both of which are questionable. One assumption was that real net national product (Q) remains fixed at its full-employment level; the other was that the velocity of circulation of money (V) remains constant. A more sophisticated version of the quantity theory can be derived by relaxing the first assumption. This version of the quantity theory recognizes that the economy is often at less than full employment and consequently that real net national product (Q) may vary a good deal for this reason.

So long as velocity remains constant, the equation of exchange—Equation (13.4)—can be used to determine the relationship between net national product in current dollars and M, even if Q is allowed to vary. On the basis of the equation of exchange, it is obvious that $P \times Q$ should be proportional to M, if the velocity of circulation of money (V) remains constant. Since $P \times Q$ is the nominal net national product, it follows that, if this assumption holds, *the nominal net national product should be proportional to the money supply.* In other words,

$$\text{NNP} = aM, \qquad (13.6)$$

where NNP is the nominal net national product and V is assumed to equal a constant—a. Thus, if the money supply increases by 10 percent, the nominal value of NNP should increase by 10 percent. If the money supply increases by 20 percent, the nominal value of NNP should increase by 20 percent. And so forth.

If velocity is constant, this version of the quantity theory should enable us to predict nominal net national product if we know the money supply. Also, if velocity is constant, this version of the quantity theory should enable us to control nominal net national product by controlling the money supply. Clearly, if velocity is constant, Equation (13.6) is an extremely important economic relationship—one that will go a long way toward accomplishing the goals of Chapter 9 to 12, which were to show how net national product could be forecasted and controlled. But is velocity constant? Since Equation (13.6) is based on this assumption, we must find out.

Figure 13.6
Velocity of Circulation of Money, United States, 1920–75
The velocity of circulation of money has generally been between 2.5 and 5.0, except during World War II.

Figure 13.6 shows how the velocity of circulation of money has behaved since 1920.[12] Obviously velocity has not been constant. But on the other hand, it has not varied enormously. Excluding the war years, it has generally been between 2.5 and 5.0 in the United States. Over the long run, it has been reasonably stable, but it has varied a good deal over the business cycle. As shown in Figure 13.6, velocity tends to decrease during depressions and increase during booms. *All in all, one must certainly conclude that, although velocity is fairly stable over the long run, it is not so stable that Equation (13.6) alone can be used in any precise way to forecast or control net national product.*

However, this does not mean that Equation (13.6) is useless, or that the more sophisticated quantity theory is without value. On the contrary, this version of the quantity theory points out a very important truth, which is that *the money supply has an important effect on net national product (in money terms): increases in the quantity of money are likely to increase nominal NNP, while decreases in the quantity of money are likely to decrease nominal NNP.* Because velocity is not constant, the relationship between the money supply and net national product is not as neat and simple as that predicted by Equation (13.6), but there is a relationship—as shown in Figure 13.7[13]

The Importance of Money

Whether one is a Keynesian using the model presented in Figures 13.4 and 13.5 or a monetarist using the more sophisticated form of

[12] The velocity figures in Figure 13.6 are based on gross national product, not net national product. But for present purposes, this makes little real difference.

[13] As we shall see in Chapter 16, sophisticated monetarists often relax the assumption that V is constant, and claim that it is possible to predict V as a function of other variables, like the frequency with which people are paid and the level of business confidence. However, many economists feel that changes in V reflect, rather than cause, changes in NNP.

quantity theory makes a considerable difference, as we shall see in Chapter 16. But it is important to underscore the fact that *the effect of the money supply on nominal NNP is qualitatively the same in both the Keynesian and monetarist models.* Whatever theory you look at, you get the same qualitative result: increases in the money supply would be expected to increase nominal NNP, and decreases in the money supply would be expected to decrease nominal NNP. Thus, whether the Keynesian (majority) view of the world or the monetarist (minority) view of the world is correct, the quantity of money would be expected to influence nominal NNP—and push it in the same direction.

Furthermore, no matter which view is accepted, it would be expected that, as the economy approaches full employment, a bigger and bigger share of the increase in nominal NNP due to increases in the money supply will reflect price increases, not increases in real output. *If the economy is at considerably less than full employment, increases in the money supply would be expected to increase real NNP, while decreases in the money supply would be expected to reduce real NNP.* However, *once full employment is approached, increases in the money supply result more and more in increases in the price level, as distinct from increases in real NNP.*

These expectations are shared both by the monetarists and the Keynesians, which is fortunate since, as we shall see, they are important guides to the formulation of monetary policy, both here and abroad.

Summary

Money performs several basic functions. It serves as a medium of exchange, a standard of value, and a store of value. There are three kinds of money—coins, currency, and demand deposits. Economists include demand deposits as part of the money supply because you can pay for goods and services about as easily by check as with cash. Besides this narrow definition of money, a broader definition includes

Figure 13.7
Relationship between Money Supply and National Product, United States, 1929–75
There is a reasonably close relationship between the money supply and the money value of national product. As one goes up, the other tends to go up too.

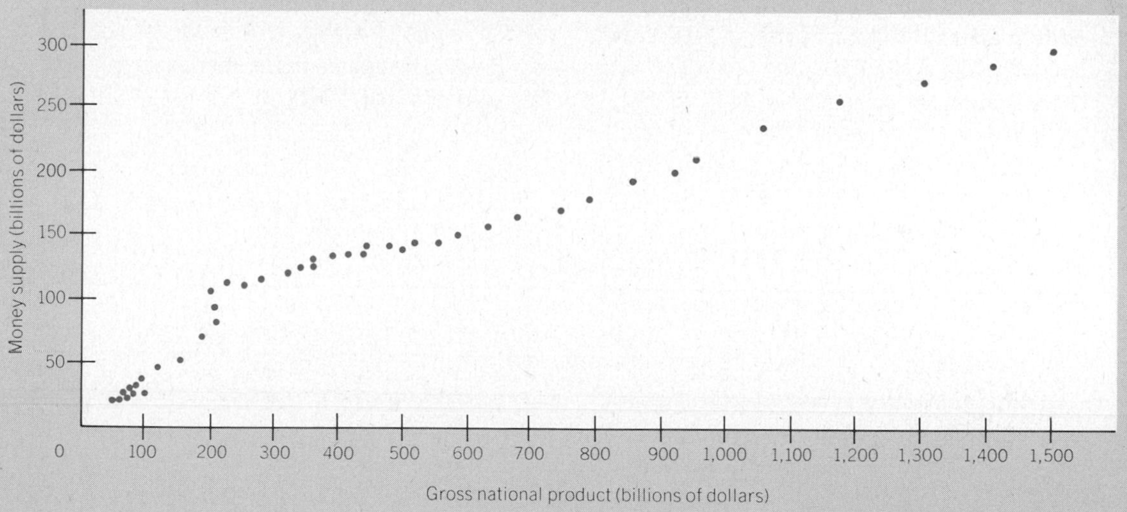

saving and time deposits. Of course, there are lots of other assets–for example, government bonds–that can be transformed without much difficulty into cash. It is not easy to draw a line between money and nonmoney, since many assets have some of the characteristics of money.

America's history has seen many sharp fluctuations in the price level. Wars have generally been periods of substantial inflation, and prices have dropped in the postwar periods. Since World War II, prices have tended to go one way only–up. Although a mild upward creep of prices at the rate of a few percent per year is not likely to result in any disastrous social consequences, runaway inflation is a real social evil that disrupts the economy very seriously. Generally, such inflations have occurred because the government expanded the money supply far too rapidly. However, too small a rate of growth of the money supply can also be a mistake, resulting in excessive unemployment.

Most economists believe that the lower the interest rate, the greater the amount of money demanded. Thus increases in the quantity of money result in lower interest rates, which result in increased investment (and other types of spending), which results in a higher NNP. Conversely, decreases in the quantity of money result in higher interest rates, which result in decreased investment (and other types of spending), which results in a lower NNP. This is the Keynesian approach.

The equation of exchange is $MV = PQ$, where M is the money supply, V is velocity, P is the price level, and Q is net national product in real terms. The velocity of circulation of money is the rate at which the money supply is used to make transactions for final goods and services. Specifically, it equals NNP in money terms divided by the money supply.

If the velocity of circulation of money remains constant and if real net national product is fixed at its full employment level, it follows from the equation of exchange that the price level will be proportional to the money supply. This is the crude quantity theory, which is a reasonably good approximation during periods of runaway inflation, and works reasonably well in predicting long-term trends in the price level.

A more sophisticated version of the quantity theory recognizes that real net national product is often at less than full employment, with the result that Q is not fixed. Thus, if velocity remains constant, net national product in money terms should be proportional to the money supply. In fact, velocity has by no means remained stable over time. However, nominal NNP has been fairly closely related to the money supply.

The monetarists, led by Milton Friedman, prefer the quantity theory over the Keynesian model. There are many important disagreements between the monetarists and the Keynesians, but both approaches agree that increases in the money supply will increase nominal NNP while decreases in the money supply will decrease nominal NNP.

CONCEPTS FOR REVIEW

Demand deposits
Currency
Time deposits
Near-money
Runaway inflation
Transactions demand
Precautionary demand
Speculative demand
Velocity of circulation
Equation of exchange
Crude quantity theory
Liquidity preference function
Federal Reserve notes

QUESTIONS FOR DISCUSSION AND REVIEW

1. "Money, in and of itself, has no value whatsoever. It is valuable only because of what it can buy." Comment and evaluate.

2. Explain in detail why the following items are not money: (a) government bonds, (b) U.S. Steel stock, (c) gold, (d) uranium.

3. Give some reasons why time deposits should be regarded as money. Give some reasons why they should not. Which side of the argument do you find more convincing?

4. Why is the interest rate regarded as the "price" of holding money? What factors will shift the liquidity preference function to the right? To the left?

5. "Creeping inflation inevitably leads to runaway inflation." Comment and evaluate.

6. If the value of NNP (in money terms) increases 10 percent and the money supply remains fixed, does velocity increase? Why or why not? What are some of the factors that might cause an increase in velocity?

7. "The history of the United States is an account of one inflation after another. The currency is being debased further and further. Soon we may experience a runaway inflation." Comment and evaluate.

8. According to Milton Friedman, the monetarists "have always stressed that money matters a great deal for the development of nominal [i.e., money] magnitudes, but not over the long run for real magnitudes." What does he mean? Do you agree or disagree?

9. Describe how the quantity of money influences nominal and real NNP according to (a) the Keynesian model, (b) the crude quantity theory, and (c) the more sophisticated quantity theory. What sorts of tests might be performed to determine which of these models works best?

14 The Banking System and the Quantity of Money

Banking is often viewed as a colorless, dull profession whose practitioners are knee-deep in deposit slips and canceled checks. Also, when the time comes to reject a loan application, the banker is often viewed as a heartless skinflint—even if he advertises that "you have a friend at Chase Manhattan." Yet despite these notions, most people recognize the importance of the banks in our economy, perhaps because the banks deal in such an important and fascinating commodity—money.

In this chapter, we look in detail at how commercial banks operate. We begin by discussing the Federal Reserve System and the functions of commercial banks. Then we describe the nature of commercial banks' loans and investments, as well as the important concept of reserves. After looking into legal reserve requirements we go on to describe how commercial banks create money—a very important and commonly misunderstood process. Finally, we take up the effects of currency

Figure 14.1
Organization of Federal Reserve System
The Federal Reserve System contains about 6,000 commercial banks, the 12 regional Federal Reserve Banks, and the Board of Governors, as well as the Federal Open Market Committee and various advisory councils and committees.

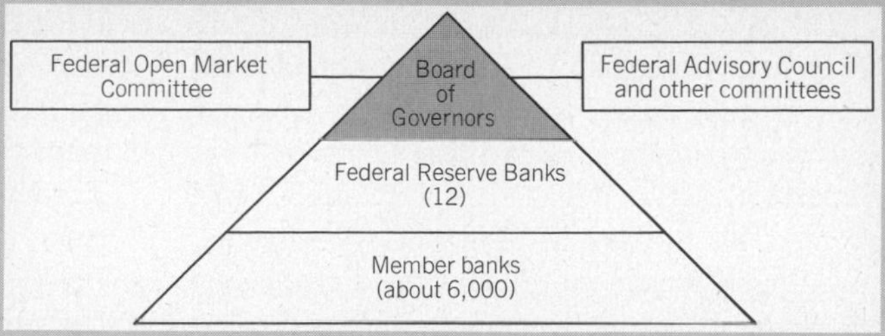

withdrawals and excess reserves on our results. The purpose of this chapter is to introduce you to the operations of the banking system, which is neither as colorless nor as mysterious as is sometimes assumed.

The Federal Reserve System

Any nation must exercise control over the quantity of money. In the United States, the Federal Reserve System is charged with this responsibility. The Federal Reserve System—or "Fed," as it is called by the *cognoscenti*—plays a central role in the American banking system and in the economy as a whole. After a severe financial panic in 1907, when a great many banks failed, there was strong public pressure to do something to strengthen our banking system. At the same time, there was great fear of centralized domination of the nation's banks. The result—after six years of negotiation and discussion—was the establishment by Congress of the ***Federal Reserve System*** in 1913. As shown in Figure 14.1, the organization of this system can be viewed as a triangle. At the base are the commercial banks that belong to the system—the ***member banks.*** All ***national banks*** (so called because they receive their charters from the federal government) have to be members, and many of the larger ***state banks*** (chartered by the states) are members too. Member banks, which number about 6,000 out of the nation's almost 15,000 commercial banks, hold about 80 percent of the nation's demand deposits.

Federal Reserve Banks. In the middle of the triangle in Figure 14.1 are the 12 Federal Reserve Banks, each located in a Federal Reserve district. The entire nation is divided into 12 Federal Reserve districts, with Federal Reserve Banks in New York, Chicago, Philadelphia, San Francisco, Boston, Cleveland, St. Louis, Kansas City, Atlanta, Richmond, Minneapolis, and Dallas. Each of these banks is a corporation owned by the member banks, but, despite this fact, the member banks do not in any sense act as owners of the Federal Reserve Bank in their district. Instead, each Federal Reserve Bank is a public agency. These Federal Reserve Banks act as "bankers' banks," performing much the same sorts of functions for commercial banks that commercial banks perform for the public. That is, they hold the deposits of member banks and make loans to them. In addition, as noted in previous chapters, the Federal Reserve Banks perform a function no commercial bank can perform: they issue Federal Reserve notes, which are the nation's currency.

The Board of Governors. At the top of the triangle in Figure 14.1 is the Board of Governors of the Federal Reserve System. Located in Washington, this board—generally called the Federal Reserve Board—has 7 members appointed by the president for 14-year terms. The board, which coordinates the activities of the Federal Reserve System, is supposed to be independent of partisan politics and to act to promote the nation's general economic welfare. It is responsible for supervising the operation of the money and banking system of the United States. The board is assisted in important ways by the Federal Open Market Committee, which establishes policy concerning the purchase and sale of government securities. The Federal Open Market Committee is composed of the board plus 5 presidents of Federal Reserve Banks. The board is also assisted by the Federal Advisory Council, a group of 12 commercial bankers that advises the board on banking policy.

Functions of the Federal Reserve

The Federal Reserve Board, with the 12 Federal Reserve Banks, constitute the central bank of the United States. Every major country has a central bank: for example, England has the Bank of England, and France has the Bank of France. ***Central banks*** are very important organizations, whose most important function is to help control the quantity of money. One interesting feature of our central bank is that its principal allegiance is to Congress, not to the executive branch of the federal government. This came about because Congress wanted to protect the Fed from pressure by the president and the Treasury Department. Thus the Fed was supposed to be independent of the executive branch. In fact, although the Fed has sometimes locked horns with the president, it has generally cooperated with him and his administration, as we shall see in Chapter 15.

To repeat, any central bank's most important function is to control the money supply. But this is not its only function: a central bank also handles the government's own financial transactions, and coordinates and controls the country's commercial banks. Specifically, the Federal Reserve System is charged with these responsibilities: First, the Federal Reserve Banks hold deposits, or reserves, of the member banks. As we shall see, these reserves play an important role in the process whereby the Fed controls the quantity of money. Second, the Federal Reserve System provides facilities for check collection. In other words, it enables a bank to collect funds for checks drawn on other banks. Third, the Federal Reserve Banks supply the public with currency through the issuance of Federal Reserve notes. Fourth, the Federal Reserve Banks act as fiscal agents for the federal government—they hold some of the checking accounts of the U.S. Treasury, and aid in the purchase and sale of government securities. Finally, the Federal Reserve Banks supervise the operation of the member commercial banks. More will be said about the nature of bank supervision and regulation later in the chapter, and much more will be said about the functions of the Federal Reserve in the next chapter.

Commercial Banks in the United States

In 1975, there were almost 15,000 commercial banks in the United States. This testifies to the fact that, in contrast to countries like England, where a few banks with many branches dominate the banking scene, the United States has promoted the growth of a great many local banks. In part, this has stemmed from a traditional suspicion in this country of "big bankers." ("Eastern bankers" are a particularly suspect breed in some parts of the country.) Most of our banks are state, not national, banks: there are over 9,000 state banks, but only about 5,000 national banks.

Commercial banks have two primary functions. First, *banks hold demand deposits and permit checks to be drawn on these deposits.* This function is familiar to practically everyone. Most people have a checking account in some commercial bank, and draw checks on this account. Second, *banks lend money to industrialists, merchants, homeowners, and other individuals and firms.* At one time or another, you will probably apply for a loan to finance some project for your business or home. Indeed, it is quite possible that some of the costs of your college education are being covered by a loan to you or your parents from a commercial bank.

In addition, commercial banks perform a number of other functions. Often they hold time or savings accounts. You will recall that these accounts bear interest and, although technically one must give a certain amount of notice before withdrawal, in practice they can usually be withdrawn whenever their owner likes. Commercial banks also sell money orders and traveler's checks, and handle estates and trusts. Because of their work with trusts, some banks—for example, the First Pennsylvania Bank and Trust Company, a large Philadelphia bank—include the word *trust* in their title. In addition, commercial banks rent safe-deposit boxes and provide a variety of services for customers.

Needless to say, commercial banks are not the only kind of financial institution. Mutual savings banks and savings and loan associations hold savings and time deposits; "consumer finance" companies lend money to individuals; insurance companies lend money to firms and governments; "factors" provide firms with working capital; and investment bankers help firms sell their securities to the public. All these types of financial institutions play an important role in the American economy. In general, they all act as intermediaries between savers and investors; that is, they all turn over to investors money that they received from savers. As we saw in Chapter 10, this process of converting savings into investment is very important in determining net national product.[1]

The Bank of America: A Case Study

We can learn something about banking in the United States from the history of a particular bank—the Bank of America, the nation's largest commercial bank. In 1904, Amadeo Peter Giannini, a 34-year-old son of an Italian immigrant, founded the Bank of Italy in the Italian district of San Francisco. Giannini was a man of enormous energy and drive. At the age of 12, he had gone to school by day, while working in his stepfather's produce firm for much of each night. At 19, he was a full-fledged member of the produce firm, and at 31 had become rich enough to retire from the produce business—and eventually to turn to banking.

Giannini showed the sort of entrepreneurial zeal in banking that would be expected from his previous track record. As an illustration, consider the following episode:

> In 1906, the city of San Francisco was rocked by earthquake and swept by fire. As the flames approached the little Bank of Italy, the young banker piled his cash and securities into a horse-drawn wagon and with a guard of two soldiers took them to his home at San Mateo, twenty miles from San Francisco, where he buried them in the garden; and then while the ruins of the city were still smoking he set up a desk in the open air down by the waterfront, put up a sign over the desk which read BANK OF ITALY, and began doing business again—the first San Francisco bank to resume.[2]

[1] The relationships among the various types of financial institutions are governed in part by law. In the middle 1970s, legislation has been proposed, and sometimes enacted, that would narrow some of the differences between commercial banks and other financial institutions. For example, in 1976, Congress passed, and President Ford signed, a bill approving NOW accounts for thrift institutions. And the Senate passed a bill in late 1975 to permit commercial banks to pay interest on demand deposits.

[2] Frederick Lewis Allen, *The Lords of Creation,* New York: Harper and Bros., 1935, p. 320. Much of this section is based on Allen's account.

Clearly, Giannini was a banker who did not observe banker's hours.

Giannini's bank prospered and grew. By the time he was 50, it had over 25 branches. During the 1920s, he acquired more and more branches, until old-line California bankers began to realize that the Bank of Italy had become a factor to be reckoned with. They did their best to prevent its further expansion, but to no avail. A man who can turn an earthquake to his advantage is unlikely, after all, to submit to such pressures. Indeed, by 1929, Giannini had 453 banking offices in California alone, as well as a considerable number elsewhere. His was the fourth largest commercial bank in the country.

In 1930, Giannini's bank was renamed the Bank of America. The 1930s were not particularly kind to it, any more than they were to the rest of the economy. But in the past 35 years, the Bank of America has grown and grown. In 1940, its loans (and discounts) totaled $778 million; in 1950, $3.3 billion; in 1960, $6.7 billion; and in 1970, $16 billion. Clearly, the Bank of America was on the move. By 1975, it had deposits of over $50 billion, and was the largest commercial bank in the United States. (The ten largest banks in the United States, in terms of deposits, are listed in Table 14.1.) It had come a long way since the days of the open-air desk on the waterfront.

How Banks Operate

The Bank of America, the biggest in the country, is hardly a typical commercial bank. It has had a remarkable history and a gifted founder. Many commercial banks are very small, as you would guess from the fact that there are almost 15,000 of them in the United States. And there is a great deal of variation among banks in their operating procedures and styles. Some are principally for firms; they do little business with individuals. Others are heavily engaged in lending to consumers. Nonetheless, although it is difficult to generalize about the operations of commercial banks because they vary so much, certain principles and propositions generally hold.

First, *banks generally make loans to both firms and individuals, and invest in securities, particularly the bonds of state and local governments, as well as federal government bonds.* The relationship between a business firm and its bank is often a close and continuing one. The firm keeps a reasonably large deposit with the bank for long periods of time, while the bank provides the firm with needed and prudent loans. The relationship between an individual and his or her bank is much more casual, but banks like consumer loans because they tend to be relatively profitable. In addition, besides lending to firms and individuals, banks buy

Table 14.1
The Ten Largest Commercial Banks in the United States in Terms of Deposits, June 30, 1975

Bank and location	Deposits (billions of dollars)
Bank of America, San Francisco	53.9
First National City Bank, New York	47.1
Chase Manhattan Bank, New York	34.2
Manufacturers Hanover Trust Company, New York	23.2
Chemical Bank, New York	19.2
Morgan Guaranty Trust Company, New York	18.6
Bankers Trust Company, New York	15.1
First National Bank, Chicago	13.8
Continental Illinois National Bank, Chicago	13.7
Security Pacific National Bank, Los Angeles	11.6

Source: American Banker.

large quantities of government bonds. For example, in the early 1970s, commercial banks held about $60 billion of state and local government bonds.

Second, *banks, like other firms, are operated to make a profit.* They don't do it by producing and selling a good, like automobiles or steel. Instead, they perform various services, including lending money, making investments, clearing checks, keeping records, and so on. They manage to make a profit from these activities by lending money and making investments that yield a higher rate of interest than they must pay their depositors. For example, the Bank of America may be able to get 10 percent interest on the loans it makes, while it must pay only 6 percent interest to its depositors. (Commercial banks do not pay interest on demand deposits, but they do pay interest on time deposits.[3] Also, they provide services at less than cost to holders of demand deposits.) If so, it receives the difference of 4 percent, which goes to meet its expenses—and to provide it with some profits.

Third, *banks must constantly balance their desire for high returns from their loans and investments against the requirement that these loans and investments be safe and easily turned into cash.* Since a bank's profits increase if it makes loans or investments that yield a high interest rate, it is clear why a bank favors high returns from its loans and investments. But those that yield a high interest rate often are relatively risky, which means that they may not be repaid in full. Because a bank lends out its depositors' money, it must be careful to limit the riskiness of the loans and investments it makes. Otherwise it may fail.

Until about 40 years ago, banks used to fail in large numbers during recessions, causing depositors to lose their money. Even during the prosperous 1920s, over 500 banks failed per year. It is no wonder that the public viewed the banks with less than complete confidence. Since the mid-1930s, bank failures have been rare, in part because of tighter standards of regulation by federal and state authorities. For example, bank examiners audit the books and practices of the banks. In addition, confidence in the banks was strengthened by the creation in 1934 of the Federal Deposit Insurance Corporation, which insures over 99 percent of all commercial bank deposits. At present, each deposit is insured up to $40,000.

[3] Legislation passed by the Senate in late 1975 would allow banks to pay interest on checking accounts. (See footnote 1.) More will be said on this score in Chapter 15.

The Balance Sheet of an Individual Bank

A good way to understand how a bank operates is to look at its balance sheet. Figure 14.2 shows the Bank of America's balance sheet as

Figure 14.2
Balance Sheet, Bank of America, January 1, 1975

Assets (billions of dollars)		Liabilities and net worth (billions of dollars)	
Cash	15.0	Demand deposits	13.5
Securities	7.6	Savings and time deposits	37.2
Loans	31.3	Other liabilities	7.3
Other assets	6.5	Net worth	2.4
Total	60.4	Total	60.4

Source: Moody's.

of the beginning of 1975. The lefthand side shows that the total assets of the Bank of America were $60.4 billion, and that these assets were made up as follows: $15.0 billion in cash, $7.6 billion in bonds and other securities, $31.3 billion in loans, and $6.5 billion in other assets. In particular, note that the loans included among the assets of the Bank of America are the loans it made to firms and individuals. As we have emphasized repeatedly, lending money is one of the major functions of a commercial bank.

The righthand side of the balance sheet says that the total liabilities–or debts–of the Bank of America were $58.0 billion, and that these liabilities were made up of $50.7 billion in deposits (both demand and time), and $7.3 billion in other liabilities. Note that the deposits at the Bank of America are included among its liabilities, since the Bank of America owes the depositors the amount of money in their deposits. It will be recalled from the previous sections that maintaining these deposits is one of the major functions of a commercial bank. Returning to the balance sheet of the Bank of America, the difference between its total assets and its total liabilities–$2.4 billion–is, of course, its net worth.

One noteworthy characteristic of any bank's balance sheet is the fact that *a very large percentage of its liabilities must be paid on demand.* For example, if all the depositors of the Bank of America tried to withdraw their demand deposits, over ⅕ of its liabilities would be due on demand. Of course, the chance of everyone wanting to draw out his or her money at once is infinitesimally small. Instead, on a given day some depositors withdraw some money, while others make deposits, and most neither withdraw nor deposit money. Consequently, any bank can get along with an amount of cash to cover withdrawals that is much smaller than the total amount of its deposits. For example, the Bank of America's cash equaled about ⅓ of its total deposits. Note that "cash" here includes the bank's deposit with the Federal Reserve System and its deposits with other banks, as well as cash in its vault.

The Bank of America's practice of holding an amount of cash–including its deposits with the Federal Reserve and with other banks–much less than the amount it owes its depositors may strike you as dangerous. Indeed, if you have a deposit at the Bank of America, you may be tempted to go over and withdraw the money in your account and deposit it in some bank that does have cash equal to the amount it owes its depositors. But you won't be able to do this because *all banks hold much less cash than the amount they owe their depositors.* Moreover, this is a perfectly sound banking practice, as we shall see.

Fractional-Reserve Banking

To understand the crucial significance of ***fractional-reserve banking,*** as this practice is called, let's compare two situations–one where a bank must hold as reserves an amount equal to the amount it owes its depositors, another where its reserves do not have to match the amount it owes its depositors. In the first case, the bank's balance sheet might be as shown in Figure 14.3, if demand deposits equal $2 million and net worth equals $500,000. The bank's loans and investments in this case are made entirely with funds put up by the owners of the bank. To see this, note that loans and investments equal $500,000, and that the bank's net worth also equals $500,000. Thus, if some of these loans are not repaid or if some of these investments lose money, the losses are borne entirely by the bank's stockholders. The depositors are protected completely because every cent of their deposits is covered by the bank's reserves.

Now let's turn to the case of fractional-reserve banking. In this case, the bank's balance sheet might be as shown in Figure 14.4, if deposits equal $2 million and net worth equals

Figure 14.3
Bank Balance Sheet: Case Where Reserves Equal Demand Deposits

Assets (millions of dollars)		Liabilities and net worth (millions of dollars)	
Reserves	2.0	Demand deposits	2.0
Loans and investments	0.5	Net worth	0.5
Total	2.5	Total	2.5

$500,000. Some of the loans and investments made by the bank are not made with funds put up by the owners of the bank, but with funds deposited in the bank by depositors. Thus, though depositors deposited $2 million in the bank, the reserves are only $400,000. What happened to the remaining $1.6 million? Since the bank (in this simple case) only has two kinds of assets, loans (and investments) and reserves, the bank must have lent out (or invested) the remaining $1.6 million.

The early history of banking is the story of an evolution from the first to the second situation. The earliest banks held reserves equal to the amounts they owed depositors, and were simply places where people stored their gold. But as time went on, banks began to practice fractional-reserve banking. It is easy to see how this evolution could take place. Suppose that you owned a bank of the first type. You would almost certainly be struck by the fact that most of the gold entrusted to you was not demanded on any given day. Sooner or later, you might be tempted to lend out some of the gold and obtain some interest. Eventually, as experience indicated that this procedure did not inconvenience the depositors, you and other bankers might make this practice common knowledge.

You might use several arguments to defend this practice. First, you would probably point out that none of the depositors had lost any money. (To the depositors, this would be a rather important argument.) Second, you could show that the interest you earned on the loans made it possible for you to charge depositors less for storing their gold. Consequently, you would argue that it was to the depositors' advantage (because of the savings that accrued to them) for you to lend out some of the gold. Third, you would probably argue that putting the money to work benefited the community and the economy. After all, in many cases, firms can make highly productive investments only if they can borrow the money, and by lending out your depositors' gold, you would enable such investments to be made.

Legal Reserve Requirements

Arguments of this sort have led society to permit fractional-reserve banking. In other words,

Figure 14.4
Bank Balance Sheet: Fractional Reserves

Assets (millions of dollars)		Liabilities and net worth (millions of dollars)	
Reserves	0.4	Demand deposits	2.0
Loans and investments	2.1	Net worth	0.5
Total	2.5	Total	2.5

a bank is allowed to hold less in reserves than the amount it owes its depositors. But what determines the amount of reserves banks hold? For example, the Bank of America, according to Figure 14.2, held cash equal to about 30 percent of its total deposits. Probably it could get away with holding much less in reserves, so long as there is no panic among depositors and it makes sound loans and investments. One reason why the Bank of America held this much cash is very simple: *the Federal Reserve System requires every commercial bank that is a member of the system to hold a certain percentage of its deposits as reserves.* This percentage varies with the size of the bank. As of 1976, each member bank had to hold as reserves $7\frac{1}{2}$ percent of its first $2 million of demand deposits, 10 percent of its next $8 million, 12 percent of its next $90 million, 13 percent of its next $300 million, and $16\frac{1}{2}$ percent of its demand deposits in excess of $400 million. These are ***legal reserve requirements;*** they exist for time deposits too, but are lower than for demand deposits.

The Federal Reserve System in recent years has dictated that the average bank should hold about $1 in reserves for every $6 of demand deposits. Most of these reserves are held in the form of deposits by banks at their regional Federal Reserve Bank. Thus, for example, a great deal of the Bank of America's reserves are held in its deposit with the Federal Reserve Bank of San Francisco. In addition, some of any bank's reserves are held in cash on the bank's premises. However, its legal reserves are less than the "cash" entry on its balance sheet since its deposits with other banks do not count as legal reserves. Of course, these legal reserve requirements are binding only on members of the Federal Reserve System, and, as we noted in a previous section, although all national banks are members, not all state banks are. But the banks outside the Federal Reserve System hold only about 20 percent of the nation's deposits, and the Fed seems to believe that it includes a large enough proportion of the banks to accomplish its goals.

The most obvious reason why the Fed imposes these legal reserve requirements would seem to be to keep the banks safe, but in this case the obvious answer isn't the right one. Instead, *the most important reason for legal reserve requirements is to control the money supply.* It will take some more discussion before this becomes clear.

To close with a historical sidelight, until 1972 legal reserve requirements were higher for big-city banks than for small-town banks. Back when the Federal Reserve System was formed, big-city banks often held the reserves of the small-town banks, and thus it seemed reasonable to enforce higher reserve requirements for the big-city banks. But nowadays reserves of all member banks—in big cities or in small towns—are held by the Federal Reserve Banks. Consequently, this difference in legal reserve requirements was like the human appendix and wisdom teeth: a somewhat illogical and useless inheritance from the past. Finally, in 1972, it was jettisoned.

The Safety of the Banks

We have just argued that the reserve requirements imposed by the Federal Reserve System exceed what would be required under normal circumstances to insure the safety of the banks. To support our argument, we might cite some authorities who claim that a bank would be quite safe if it only had reserves equal to about 2 percent of its deposits. Under these circumstances it would be able to meet its depositors' everyday demands for cash. Obviously this level of reserves is much lower than the legally required level.

At the same time, one should recognize that high reserve requirements will not by themselves insure bank safety. For example, suppose that a bank lends money to every budding inventor with a scheme for producing perpetual-motion machines—and that it grants particularly large loans to those who propose to market these machines in the suburbs of Missoula, Montana. This bank is going to fail eventually, even if it holds reserves equal to 20 percent—or 50 percent for that matter—of its demand deposits. It will fail simply because the loans it makes will not be repaid, and eventually these losses will accumulate to more than the bank's net worth. In other words, if the bank is sufficiently inept in making loans and investments it will lose all the owners' money and some of the depositors' money besides.

To promote its safety, a bank must make sensible loans and investments. In addition, it must protect itself against short-term withdrawals of large amounts of money. Although larger-than-usual withdrawals are not very likely to occur, the bank must be prepared to meet a temporary upswing in withdrawals. One way is to invest in securities that can readily be turned into cash. For example, the bank may invest in short-term government securities that can readily be sold at a price that varies only moderately from day to day. Such securities are often referred to as *secondary reserves.*

There can be no doubt that banks are much safer today than they were 50 or 100 years ago. The reason is that the government has put its power squarely behind the banking system. It used to be that "runs" occurred on the banks. Every now and then, depositors, frightened that their banks would fail and that they would lose some of their money, would line up at the tellers' windows and withdraw as much money as they could. Faced with runs of this sort, banks were sometimes forced to close because they could not satisfy all demands for withdrawals. Needless to say, no fractional-reserve banking system can satisfy demands for total withdrawal of funds.

Runs on banks are a thing of the past, for several reasons. One is that the government—including the Federal Deposit Insurance Corporation (FDIC), the Fed, and other public agencies—has made it clear that it will not stand by and tolerate the sorts of panics that used to occur periodically in this country. The FDIC insures the accounts of depositors in practically all banks so that, even if a bank fails, the depositor will get his money back—up to $40,000. Another reason is that the banks themselves are better managed and regulated. For example, bank examiners are sent out to look over the bankers' shoulders and see whether they are solvent. It is a far cry from the situation 60-odd years ago that led to the creation of the Federal Reserve System.

Nonetheless, this does not mean that bank regulation is all that it might be. In the middle 1970s, three big banks—Franklin National, U.S. National, and Security National—failed, and many observers felt that the regulating agencies, such as the FDIC and the Fed, were not doing a proper job. For example, Arthur Burns, chairman of the Fed, cited a "competition in laxity" among the regulators. One criticism was that banks were relying too heavily on debt and too little on equity capital. Some congressional leaders called for the creation of a Federal Bank Commission, which would combine the regulatory functions of the Fed, FDIC, and the Comptroller of the Currency. Despite the advances made in the past 60 years, bank regulation is still an area of some national concern.

The Lending Decision: A Case Study

To get a better feel for the workings of a bank, let's look at an actual decision faced by Robert Swift, the assistant vice-president of the Lone Star National Bank of Houston, Texas. Mr. Swift received a call from Ralph Desmond, president of the Desmond Engineering Corporation. Mr. Desmond wanted to change his bank; he was dissatisfied with the amount he could borrow from his present bank. He wanted to borrow $30,000 from the Lone Star to pay what he owed to his present bank, pay some bills coming up, and buy some material needed to fulfill a contract. Mr. Swift asked Mr. Desmond to come to his office with various financial statements regarding the Desmond Engineering Corporation and its prospects. These included recent profit and loss statements and balance sheets, as well as a variety of other data, including information indicating how rapidly the firm collected its bills and the quality of the debts owed the firm.

Mr. Swift forwarded Mr. Desmond's loan application to the credit department of the bank for further analyses. The credit department added comments on the Desmond Engineering Corporation's solvency and prospects. Besides being secured by a mortgage on some equipment owned by the Desmond Engineering Corporation, this loan was to be personally endorsed by Mr. Desmond and another principal stockholder in the firm. Consequently, Mr. Swift obtained information on the extent and nature of the personal assets of Mr. Desmond and the other stockholder. This information was used, together with all the other data on the firm, to determine whether the bank would make the loan. After a reasonable amount of time, Mr. Swift recommended the acceptance of Mr. Desmond's loan application. In his view, Mr. Desmond had a very good chance of repaying the loan.[4]

[4] This case comes from Leonard Marks and Alan Coleman, *Cases in Commercial Bank Management,* New York: McGraw-Hill, 1962, pp. 168-76. However, the outcome is purely conjectural.

Note two things about this decision. First, if the bank grants Mr. Desmond the loan, it will create a demand deposit for him. In other words, it will create some money. Second, the bank can do this only if it has reserves exceeding the legal reserve requirements. Both of these points are important enough to dwell on for a while.

Two Ways Banks Cannot Create Money

Genesis tells us that God created heaven and earth. Economists tell us that banks create money. To many people, the latter process is at least as mysterious as the former. Even bankers themselves have been known to fall into serious error by claiming that they do not create money. Yet the way banks create money is a relatively simple process, which the next few sections will describe in detail. Suppose that someone receives $10,000 in newly printed currency and deposits it in his local bank. Before we see how the bank can create more than $10,000 from this deposit, we will describe two ways in which banks *cannot* create new money. Since people often jump to the conclusion that one or the other of these two processes is the correct one, it is a good idea to kill off these heresies at the outset.

First, suppose that ours is not a fractional-reserve banking system. In other words, assume that every bank has to maintain reserves equal to its deposits. In this case, the bank receiving the $10,000 deposit cannot create any

Figure 14.5
Changes in Bank Balance Sheet, Where Reserves Equal Demand Deposits

Assets (dollars)		Liabilities and net worth (dollars)	
Reserves	+10,000	Demand deposits	+10,000
Loans and investments	No change	Net worth	No change
Total	+10,000	Total	+10,000

new money. You may be inclined to think that it can be done, but it can't. To see why not, consider the changes in the bank's balance sheet, shown in Figure 14.5. When the $10,000 is deposited in the bank, the bank's deposits go up $10,000. Since the bank must hold $10,000 in reserves to back up the new $10,000 deposit, it must put the $10,000 it receives from the depositor into its reserves. Thus the bank's demand deposits go up by $10,000, and its reserves go up by $10,000. Since demand deposits are on the righthand side of the balance sheet and reserves are on the lefthand side, the balance sheet continues to balance. *No new money is created. All that happens is that the depositor gives up $10,000 in one form of money—currency—and receives $10,000 in another form of money—a demand deposit.*

Next, let's turn to a second way banks cannot create money. Suppose that we have a fractional-reserve banking system and that the legal reserve requirement is $16\frac{2}{3}$ percent. In other words, the bank must hold $1 in reserves for every $6 of demand deposits. Suppose that the bank decides to take the crisp, new $10,000 in currency that is deposited and add it to its reserves, thus increasing its reserves by $10,000. Then suppose it reasons (incorrectly) that it can increase its deposits by $50,000, since it has $10,000 in additional reserves. Why $50,000? Because the $10,000 in additional reserves will support $60,000 in demand deposits; and since the person who deposited the $10,000 has a demand deposit of $10,000, this means that it can create additional demand deposits of $60,000 minus $10,000, or $50,000.

The bank will create these additional demand deposits simply by making loans or investments. Thus when a person comes in to the bank for a loan, all the banker has to do is give him a demand deposit—a checking account—that didn't exist before. In other words, the banker can say to his staff, "Establish a checking account of $50,000 for Mr. Smith. We have just lent him this amount to buy a new piece of equipment to be used in his business." At first, this whole process looks a bit like black magic, perhaps even larceny. After all, how can checking accounts be established out of thin air? But they can, and are. In essence, this is how banks create money.

But we prefaced this example by saying that it contains an error: the error is the supposition that the bank can create an additional $50,000 of demand deposits on the basis of the $10,000 deposit. To see why this won't work, consider the changes in the bank's balance sheet, shown in Figure 14.6. After the bank received the $10,000 deposit, its demand deposits and its reserves both increased by $10,000, as shown in the first panel of Figure 14.6. Then, as we noted above, the bank made a $50,000 loan and (in the process of making the loan) created $50,000 in new deposits, as shown in the second panel. So far, so good. The bank's balance sheet continues to balance—in accord with common sense and accounting (in that order). The bank's reserves are $\frac{1}{6}$ of its demand deposits; they satisfy the legal reserve requirements established by the Fed.

So what is the problem? None, unless the money lent by the bank is spent. If the man who received the loan—Mr. Smith—never used the money he borrowed, the bank could act this way and get away with it. But people who borrow money are in the habit of spending it; why pay interest on money one doesn't use? Even if Mr. Smith, the recipient of this loan, spent the money, the bank could act in accord with this example and get away with it if the people who received the money from Mr. Smith deposited it in this same bank. But the chances of this occurring are very small. The equipment Mr. Smith plans to buy is likely to be produced by a firm in some other city; and even if it is located in the same city, the firm may well have an account at another bank.

To see the problem that results when the loan is spent, suppose that Mr. Smith spends

Figure 14.6
Changes in Bank Balance Sheet: Fractional Reserves

	Assets (dollars)		Liabilities and net worth (dollars)	
Bank receives deposit	Reserves	+10,000	Demand deposits	+10,000
	Loans and investments	No change	Net worth	No change
	Total	+10,000	Total	+10,000
Bank makes loan	Reserves	No change	Demand deposits	+50,000
	Loans and investments	+50,000	Net worth	No change
	Total	+50,000	Total	+50,000
Mr. Smith spends $50,000	Reserves	−50,000	Demand deposits	−50,000
	Loans and investments	No change	Net worth	No change
	Total	−50,000	Total	−50,000
Total effect	Reserves	−40,000	Demand deposits	+10,000
	Loans and investments	+50,000	Net worth	No change
	Total	+10,000	Total	+10,000

the $50,000 on a machine produced by the Acme Corporation, which has an account at the First National Bank of Boston. He sends the Acme Corporation a check for $50,000 drawn on our bank. When the Acme Corporation receives Mr. Smith's check, it deposits this check to its account at the First National Bank of Boston, which, using the facilities of the Federal Reserve System, presents the check to our bank for payment. Our bank must then fork over $50,000 of its cash—its reserves—to the First National Bank of Boston. Consequently, once the $50,000 check is paid, the effect on our bank's balance sheet is as shown in the third panel of Figure 14.6. Taken as a whole, the bank's demand deposits have increased by $10,000, and its reserves have decreased by $40,000, as shown in the bottom panel of Figure 14.6.

At this point, the error in this example is becoming clear. *If the bank was holding $1 in reserves for every $6 in demand deposits before the $10,000 deposit was made, these transactions must cause the bank to violate the legal reserve requirements.* This is simple to prove. Suppose that, before the $10,000 deposit, our bank had $\$X$ in demand deposits and $\$\frac{X}{6}$ in reserves. Then, after the transactions described above, it must have ($\$X + \$10{,}000$) in demand deposits and $\left(\$\frac{X}{6} - \$40{,}000\right)$ in reserves. Certainly, the reserves $\left(\text{which equal } \$\frac{X}{6} - \$40{,}000\right)$ are now less than $\frac{1}{6}$ of the demand deposits (which equal $\$X + \$10{,}000$). This must be true whatever value X has. (Try it and see.) Thus no bank can create money in this way because, if it did, it would violate the legal reserve requirements after the newly created demand deposits were used. However, as we shall see later, a monopoly bank—that is, the only bank in the country—could create money like this. But monopoly banks do not exist in the United States.

How Banks Can Create Money

Now that you have learned two ways that banks *cannot* create money, let's describe how they *can* create money. Imagine the following scenario. First, suppose once again that someone deposits $10,000 of newly printed money in our bank, which we'll call Bank *A*. Second, suppose that Bank *A* lends Mr. Smith $8,333, and that Mr. Smith uses this money to purchase some equipment from Mr. Jones, who deposits Mr. Smith's check in his account at Bank *B*. Third, Bank *B* buys a bond for $6,944 from Mr. Stone, who deposits the check from Bank *B* to his account at Bank *C*. Fourth, Bank *C* lends $5,787 to Mr. White, who uses the money to buy a truck from the local General Motors dealer, Mr. Black, who deposits Mr. White's check for $5,787 to his account at Bank *D*. Fifth, Bank *D* lends Mr. Cohen $4,823 which Mr. Cohen uses to buy some lumber from Mr. Palucci, who deposits Mr. Cohen's check to his account at Bank *E*. Admittedly, this is a somewhat complicated plot with a substantial cast of characters, but life is like that.

The first step in our drama occurs when someone deposits $10,000 in newly printed money in Bank *A*. The effect of this deposit is shown in the first panel of Figure 14.7: Bank *A*'s demand deposits and its reserves both go up by $10,000. Now Bank *A* is far too smart to pull the sort of trick described in the last section. It does not try to make a $50,000 loan, lest it wind up with less reserves than dictated by the legal reserve requirements. When Mr. Smith asks one of the loan officers of the bank for a loan to purchase equipment, the loan officer approves a loan of $8,333, not $50,000. Mr. Smith is given a checking account of $8,333 at Bank *A*.

How can Bank *A* get away with this loan of $8,333 without winding up with less than the legally required reserves? The answer is given in the rest of Figure 14.7. The second panel of this figure shows what happens to Bank *A*'s balance sheet when Bank *A* makes the $8,333 loan and creates a new demand deposit of $8,333. Obviously, both demand deposits and loans go up by $8,333. Next, look at the third panel of Figure 14.7, which shows what happens when Mr. Smith spends the $8,333 on equipment. As pointed out above, he purchases this equipment from Mr. Jones. Mr. Jones deposits Mr. Smith's check to his account in Bank *B* which presents the check to Bank *A* for payment. After Bank *A* pays Bank *B* (through the Federal Reserve System), the result—as shown in the third panel—is that Bank *A*'s deposits go down by $8,333 since Mr. Smith no longer has the deposit. Bank *A*'s reserves also go down by $8,333 since Bank *A* has to transfer these reserves to Bank *B* to pay the amount of the check.

As shown in the bottom panel of Figure 14.7, the total effect on Bank *A* is to increase its deposits by the $10,000 that was deposited originally and to increase its reserves by $10,000 minus $8,333, or $1,667. In other words, reserves have increased by $\frac{1}{6}$ as much as demand deposits. This means that Bank *A* will meet its legal reserve requirements. To see this, suppose that before the deposit of $10,000, Bank *A* had demand deposits of $\$X$ and reserves of $\$\frac{X}{6}$. Then after the full effect of the transaction occurs on Bank *A*'s balance sheet, Bank *A*'s demand deposits will equal ($\$X + \$10{,}000$) and its reserves will equal $\left(\$\frac{X}{6} + \$\,\frac{10{,}000}{6}\right)$, since $\$1{,}667 = \frac{\$10{,}000}{6}$. Thus Bank *A* continues to

Figure 14.7
Changes in Bank *A*'s Balance Sheet

	Assets (dollars)		Liabilities and net worth (dollars)	
Bank receives deposit	Reserves	+10,000	Demand deposits	+10,000
	Loans and investments	No change	Net worth	No change
	Total	+10,000	Total	+10,000
Bank makes loan	Reserves	No change	Demand deposits	+ 8,333
	Loans and investments	+ 8,333	Net worth	No change
	Total	+ 8,333	Total	+ 8,333
Mr. Smith spends $8,333	Reserves	− 8,333	Demand deposits	− 8,333
	Loans and investments	No change	Net worth	No change
	Total	− 8,333	Total	− 8,333
Total effect	Reserves	+ 1,667	Demand deposits	+10,000
	Loans and investments	+ 8,333	Net worth	No change
	Total	+10,000	Total	+10,000

hold $1 in reserves for every $6 in demand deposits, as required by the Fed.

Impact on Other Banks

It is important to recognize that *Bank* A *has now created $8,333 in new money.* To see this, note that Mr. Jones winds up with a demand deposit of this amount that he didn't have before; and this is a net addition to the money supply, since the person who originally deposited the $10,000 in currency still has his $10,000, although it is in the form of a demand deposit rather than currency. But this is not the end of the story. The effects of the $10,000 deposit at Bank *A* are not limited to Bank *A*. Instead, as we shall see, other banks can also create new money as a consequence of the original $10,000 deposit at Bank *A*.

Let's begin with Bank *B*. Recall from the previous section that the $8,333 check made out by Mr. Smith to Mr. Jones is deposited by the latter in his account at Bank *B*. This is a new deposit of funds at Bank *B*. As pointed out in the previous section, Bank *B* gets $8,333 in reserves from Bank *A* when Bank *A* pays Bank *B* to get back the check. Thus the effect on Bank *B*'s balance sheet, as shown in the first panel of Figure 14.8, is to increase both demand deposits and reserves by $8,333. Bank *B* is in much the same position as was Bank *A* when the latter received the original deposit of $10,000. Bank *B* can make loans or investments of $6,944. (The way we derive $6,944 is explained in footnote 5 below.)[5] Specifically, it decides to buy a bond for $6,944 from Mr. Stone, who deposits the check from Bank *B* to his account in Bank *C*. Thus, as shown in the

[5] Since Bank *B* has to hold $\frac{\$8,333}{6}$, or $1,389, in legally required reserves, it can lend $8,333 minus $1,389, or $6,944. If it lends more than this amount, it may wind up with less than the legally required reserves.

second panel of Figure 14.8, the effect of this transaction is to increase Bank *B*'s investments by $6,944 and to increase its demand deposits by $6,944 when Bank *B* buys the bond. This transaction increases Bank *B*'s demand deposits by $6,944 because the bank creates a demand deposit of $6,944 to pay for the bond. In other words, the bank in effect creates a deposit for itself and uses it to pay Mr. Stone for the bond. Then Bank *B*'s demand deposits and its reserves are decreased by $6,944 when it transfers this amount of reserves to Bank *C* to pay for the check. When the total effects of the transaction are summed up, Bank *B*, like Bank *A*, continues to meet its legal reserve requirements, since its increased reserves ($1,389) equal ⅙ of its increased demand deposits ($8,333).

Bank B *has also created some money—$6,944 to be exact.* Mr. Stone has $6,944 in demand deposits that he didn't have before; and this is a net addition to the money supply since the person who originally deposited the currency in Bank *A* still has his $10,000, and Mr. Jones still has the $8,333 he deposited in Bank *B*, and this is still not the end of the story. Bank *C* has experienced an increase of $6,944 in its demand deposits and in its reserves. Thus it—like Banks *A* and *B* before it—can increase its loans and investments. By how much? At this point, the pattern is becoming clear; *it can lend the amount by which its reserves exceed the legally required reserves.* In other words, since Bank *C* must hold $\$\frac{6,944}{6}$, or $1,157, in legally required reserves against the new deposit of $6,944, it can lend $6,944 minus $1,157, or $5,787.

According to our plot, Bank *C* lends $5,787 to Mr. White, who buys a truck from the local General Motors dealer, Mr. Black. Mr. Black deposits Mr. White's check for $5,787 to his account at Bank *D*. Figure 14.9 traces out the effects on Bank *C*'s balance sheet. The top panel shows the original increase in its demand deposits and in its reserves of $6,944. The second panel shows the increase of $5,787 in its loans stemming from its loan to Mr. White, as well as the accompanying increase in its demand deposits of $5,787 representing the demand deposit it gave to Mr. White. The third panel shows the $5,787 decrease in demand de-

Figure 14.8
Changes in Bank *B*'s Balance Sheet

	Assets (dollars)		Liabilities and net worth (dollars)	
Bank receives deposit	Reserves	+8,333	Demand deposits	+8,333
	Loans and investments	No change	Net worth	No change
	Total	+8,333	Total	+8,333
Bank buys bond	Reserves	No change	Demand deposits	+6,944
	Loans and investments	+6,944	Net worth	No change
	Total	+6,944	Total	+6,944
Mr. Stone deposits money in Bank *C*	Reserves	−6,944	Demand deposits	−6,944
	Loans and investments	No change	Net worth	No change
	Total	−6,944	Total	−6,944
Total effect	Reserves	+1,389	Demand deposits	+8,333
	Loans and investments	+6,944	Net worth	No change
	Total	+8,333	Total	+8,333

Figure 14.9
Changes in Bank *C*'s Balance Sheet

	Assets (dollars)		Liabilities and net worth (dollars)	
Bank receives deposit	Reserves	+6,944	Demand deposits	+6,944
	Loans and investments	No change	Net worth	No change
	Total	+6,944	Total	+6,944
Bank makes loan	Reserves	No change	Demand deposits	+5,787
	Loans and investments	+5,787	Net worth	No change
	Total	+5,787	Total	+5,787
Mr. White spends $5,787	Reserves	−5,787	Demand deposits	−5,787
	Loans and investments	No change	Net worth	No change
	Total	−5,787	Total	−5,787
Total effect	Reserves	+1,157	Demand deposits	+6,944
	Loans and investments	+5,787	Net worth	No change
	Total	+6,944	Total	+6,944

posits when Mr. White checked out the whole of his account, and the $5,787 decrease in reserves when Bank *C* transferred this amount of reserves to Bank *D* to pay for the check. The bottom panel shows the total effect. As in the case of Banks *A* and *B*, Bank *C* continues to meet the legal reserve requirements when the full effects of the transaction have made themselves felt.

Bank C *also has created some money—$5,787, to be exact.* To see why, note that Mr. Black has $5,787 in demand deposits that he didn't have before; and this is a net addition to the money supply since the original depositor in Bank *A* still has his $10,000, Mr. Jones still has the $8,333 in Bank *B*, and Mr. Stone still has the $6,944 in Bank *C*. But this is still not the end of the story. Bank *D* has experienced an increase of $5,787 in its demand deposits and its reserves. Thus it—like Banks *A, B,* and *C* before it—can increase its loans and investments by the amount of its ***excess reserves*** (those in excess of legal requirements). Since it must hold $\frac{\$5,787}{6} = \$964$ as legal reserves against its increase in deposits of $5,787, its excess reserves are $5,787 minus $964, or $4,823. Thus Bank *D* can increase its loans and investments by $4,823. As we saw at the beginning of this saga, it decides to lend Mr. Cohen $4,823 to buy some lumber from Mr. Palucci. Mr. Cohen pays Mr. Palucci with a check for $4,823 drawn on Bank *D* and Mr. Palucci deposits the check to his account at Bank *E*. As shown in Figure 14.10, Bank *D* winds up with no excess reserves after it transfers reserves to Bank *E* to pay for the check. (To check your grasp of the material in this section, see if you can fill in the numbers in the top three panels of Figure 14.10; the correct answer is given at the bottom of the facing page.) But Mr. Palucci winds up with a demand deposit of $4,823 that he didn't have before. Thus *Bank* D *also creates some money—$4,823, to be exact.*

The Total Effect of the Original $10,000 Deposit

How big an increase in the money supply can the entire banking system support as a conse-

Figure 14.10
Changes in Bank *D*'s Balance sheet

	Assets (dollars)		Liabilities and net worth (dollars)	
Bank receives deposit	Reserves		Demand deposits	
	Loans and investments		Net worth	
	Total		Total	
Bank makes loan	Reserves		Demand deposits	
	Loan and investments		Net worth	
	Total		Total	
Mr. Cohen spends $4,823	Reserves		Demand deposits	
	Loans and investments		Net worth	
	Total		Total	
Total effect	Reserves	+ 964	Demand deposits	+5,787
	Loans and investments	+4,823	Net worth	No change
	Total	+5,787	Total	+5,787

quence of the original $10,000 deposit in Bank *A*? Clearly, the effects of the original deposit spread from one bank to another, since each bank hands new reserves (and deposits) to another bank, which in turn hands them to another bank. For example, Bank *E* now has $4,823 more in deposits and reserves and so can create $4,019[6] in new money by making a loan or investment of this amount. This process goes on indefinitely, and it would be impossible to describe each of the multitude of steps involved. Fortunately, it isn't necessary to do so. We can figure out the total amount of new money the entire banking system can support as a consequence of the original $10,000 deposit in Bank *A* without going through all these steps.

We do this by computing how much new money each bank creates. Besides the original $10,000, Bank *A* creates $8,333—which is $\frac{5}{6}$ of $10,000. Then Bank *B* creates an additional $6,944—$(\frac{5}{6})^2$ of $10,000. Then Bank *C* creates an additional $5,787—$(\frac{5}{6})^3$ of $10,000. Then Bank *D* creates an additional $4,823—$(\frac{5}{6})^4$ of

6 Why $4,019? Because it must hold $\frac{\$4,823}{6} = \$804$ as reserves to support the new demand deposit of $4,823. Thus it has excess reserves of $4,019, and it can create another new demand deposit of this amount.

The missing numbers in Figure 14.10 are:

	Assets (dollars)		*Liabilities and net worth (dollars)*	
Bank receives deposit	Reserves	+5,787	Demand deposits	+5,787
	Loans and investments	No change	Net worth	No change
	Total	+5,787	Total	+5,787
Bank makes loan	Reserves	No change	Demand deposits	+4,823
	Loans and investments	+4,823	Net worth	No change
	Total	+4,823	Total	+4,823
Mr. Cohen spends $4,823	Reserves	−4,823	Demand deposits	−4,823
	Loans and investments	No change	Net worth	No change
	Total	−4,823	Total	−4,823

Table 14.2
Increase in Money Supply Resulting from $10,000 Increase in Reserves

Source	Amount (dollars)
Original deposit	10,000
Created by Bank *A*	8,333
Created by Bank *B*	6,944
Created by Bank *C*	5,787
Created by Bank *D*	4,823
Created by Bank *E*	4,019
Created by Bank *F*	3,349
Created by Bank *G*	2,791
Created by Bank *H*	2,326
Created by Bank *I*	1,938
Created by Bank *J*	1,615
Created by other banks	8,075
Total	60,000

$10,000. Then Bank *E* creates an additional $4,019–$(5/6)^5$ of $10,000. The amount of money created by each bank is less than that created by the previous bank, so that the total amount of new money created by the original $10,000 deposit–$10,000 + $8,333 + $6,944 + $5,787 + $4,823 + $4,019 + . . . –tends to a finite limit as the process goes on and on. Elementary algebra tells us what this sum of terms will be. *When the process works itself out, the entire banking system can support $60,000 in money as a consequence of the original $10,000 deposit of new funds.*[7] For a demonstration of this fact, see Table 14.2 and Figure 14.11. Table 14.2 shows the amount of new demand deposits created at each stage of this process, while Figure 14.11 plots the cumulative expansion in demand deposits.

We must note that the banking system as a whole has accomplished what we said in a previous section that an individual bank–Bank *A*–could not do. It has created an additional $50,000 of demand deposits on the basis of the original $10,000 deposit. In other words, given the additional $10,000 in reserves, the banking system can create $60,000 in money. Certainly this seems sensible, since each $1 of reserves can back up $6 in demand deposits. But for the reasons discussed in a previous section, an individual bank cannot do this, unless, of course, it is a monopoly bank. If it is, it need have no fear of losing reserves to other banks, because there are no other banks; so it can behave this way. However, banking in the United States is not monopolized.

In general, *if a certain amount of additional reserves is made available to the banking system, the banking system as a whole can increase the money supply by an amount equal to the amount of additional reserves multiplied by the reciprocal of the required ratio of reserves to deposits.* In other words, to obtain the total increase in the money supply that can be achieved from a certain amount of additional reserves, multiply the amount of additional reserves by the reciprocal of the required ratio of reserves to deposits–or, what amounts to the same thing, *divide the amount of additional reserves by the legally required ratio of reserves to deposits.* Putting it in still another way, the banking system as a whole can increase the money supply by $(1/r)$ dollars–where r is the required ratio of reserves to deposits–for every $1 increase in reserves.[8]

Let's apply this proposition to a couple of specific cases. Suppose that the banking system's reserves increase by $10,000 and that the required ratio of reserves to deposits is $1/6$. To determine how much the banking system can increase the money supply, we must divide the

[7] The proof of this is as follows: the total amount of money supported by the $10,000 in reserves is $10,000 + $8,333 + $6,944 + $5,787 + . . . , which equals $10,000 + 5/6 × $10,000 + (5/6)² × $10,000 + (5/6)³ × $10,000 + . . . , which equals $10,000 ×

$$(1+5/6+(5/6)^2+(5/6)^3+\ldots)=\$10{,}000\times\frac{1}{1-(5/6)}=\$60{,}000,$$

since $1 + 5/6 + (5/6)^2 + (5/6)^3 + \ldots = \frac{1}{1-(5/6)}$.

[8] The total amount of money supported by $1 of additional reserves is

$$1 + (1-r) + (1-r)^2 + (1-r)^3 + \ldots = \frac{1}{1-(1-r)} = \frac{1}{r}$$

We reach this conclusion by the same method we used in footnote 7.

Figure 14.11
Cumulative Expansion in Demand Deposits on Basis of $10,000 of New Reserves and Legal Reserve Requirement of 16⅔ Percent
The original deposit was $10,000. In the first stage of the expansion process, Bank *A* created an additional $8,333. In the second stage, Bank *B* created an additional $6,944. In the third stage, Bank *C* created an additional $5,787. This process goes on until the final result is $60,000 of demand deposits.

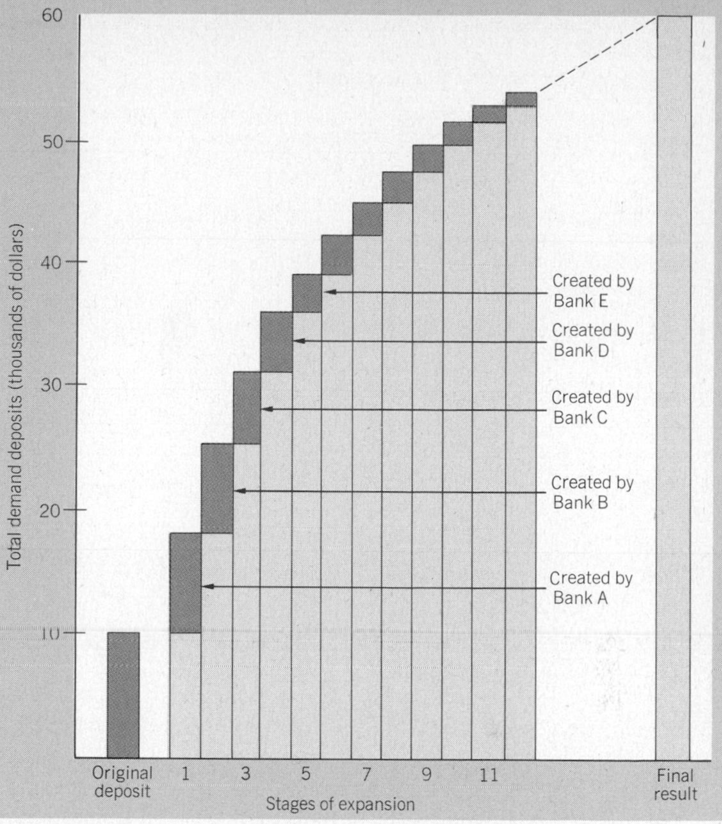

amount of the additional reserves—$10,000—by the required ratio of reserves to deposits—⅙—to get the answer, $60,000. Note, with proper satisfaction, that this answer checks with our earlier results. Now suppose that the required ratio of reserves to deposits is ⅕. By how much can the banking system increase the money supply? Dividing $10,000 by ⅕, we get the answer: $50,000. Note that the higher the required ratio of reserves to deposits, the smaller the amount by which the banking system can increase the money supply on the basis of a given increase in reserves. More will be said about this in the next chapter.

Finally, an increase in reserves generally affects a great many banks at about the same time. For expository purposes, it is useful to trace through the effect of an increase in the reserves of a single bank—Bank *A* in our case. But usually this is not what happens. Instead, lots of banks experience an increase in reserves at about the same time. Thus they all have excess reserves at about the same time, and they all make loans or investments at about the same time. The result is that, when the people who borrow money spend it, each bank tends both to gain and lose reserves. Thus, on balance, each bank need not lose reserves. In real life the amount of bank money often expands simultaneously throughout the banking system until the legally required ratio of deposits to reserves is approached.

The Effect of a Decrease in Reserves

Up to this point, we have been talking only about the effect of an increase in reserves.

Figure 14.12
Change in Your Bank's Balance Sheet

	Assets (dollars)		Liabilities and net worth (dollars)	
You withdraw deposit	Reserves	−10,000	Demand deposits	−10,000
	Loans and investments	No change	Net worth	No change
	Total	−10,000	Total	−10,000
Bank sells bond and gets funds from Bank *Q*	Reserves	+ 8,333	Demand deposits	No change
	Loans and investments	− 8,333	Net worth	No change
	Total	No change	Total	No change
Total effect	Reserves	− 1,667	Demand deposits	−10,000
	Loans and investments	− 8,333	Net worth	No change
	Total	−10,000	Total	−10,000

What happens to the quantity of money if reserves decrease? For example, suppose that you draw $10,000 out of your bank and hold it in the form of currency, perhaps by sewing it in your mattress. You thus reduce the total reserves of the banking system by $10,000. Let us begin with the effect on your bank. Clearly, it will experience a $10,000 decrease in deposits (because of your withdrawal) and, at the same time, a $10,000 decrease in reserves. Thus, if it was holding $1 in reserves for every $6 in deposits before you withdrew the money, it now holds less than the legally required reserves. If its deposits go down by $10,000, its reserves must go down by $1,667, not $10,000, if the 6:1 ratio between deposits and reserves is to be maintained. To observe the legal reserve requirements, your bank must increase its reserves by $10,000 minus $1,667, or $8,333. It has several ways to get this money, one being to sell securities. It may sell a municipal bond to Mrs. Cherrytree for $8,333. To pay for the bond, she writes a check on her bank, Bank *Q*, for the $8,333. Thus, as shown in Figure 14.12, your bank's investments decrease by $8,333, and its reserves increase by $8,333 when Bank *Q* transfers this amount to your bank to pay for the check.

But this is not the end of the story. Because Bank *Q* has lost $8,333 in deposits and $8,333 in reserves, its reserves are now less than the legal minimum. To maintain the legally required reserves, its reserves should have gone down by $\frac{\$8{,}333}{6}$, or $1,389—not by $8,333. Thus Bank *Q* must increase its reserves by $8,333 minus $1,389, or $6,944. To do so, it sells a bond it holds for $6,944. But when the person who buys the bond gives Bank *Q* his check for $6,944 drawn on Bank *R*, Bank *R* loses $6,944 in deposits and $6,944 in reserves. Thus Bank *R*'s reserves are now below the legal requirement. To maintain the legally required reserves, its reserves should have gone down by $\frac{\$6{,}944}{6}$, or $1,157—not by $6,944. So Bank *R* must increase its reserves by $6,944 minus $1,157, or $5,787. And on and on the process goes.

Let us consider the over-all effect on the money supply of the $10,000 decrease in reserves. Your bank's demand deposits decreased by $10,000, Bank *Q*'s demand deposits decreased by $8,333 ($\frac{5}{6}$ of $10,000), Bank *R*'s demand deposits decreased by $6,944 ($(\frac{5}{6})^2$ of $10,000), and so on. The total decrease in the money supply—$10,000 + $8,333 + $6,944 + . . . —tends to a finite limit as the proccss goes on and on. This limit is $60,000. Thus, *when the process works itself out, the entire banking system will reduce the money supply by $60,000 as a consequence of a $10,000 decrease in reserves.* More generally, *if the banking system's reserves decrease by a certain amount, the banking system as a whole will reduce demand deposits by an amount equal to the reduction in reserves multiplied by the reciprocal of the required ratio of reserves to deposits.*

In other words, to obtain the total decrease in demand deposits resulting from a reduction in reserves, *divide the reduction in reserves by the legally required ratio of reserves to deposits.* Putting it another way, the banking system as a whole will reduce demand deposits by $(1/r)$ dollars—where r is the required ratio of reserves to deposits—for every $1 decrease in reserves. Of course, there is often a simultaneous contraction of money on the part of many banks, just as there is often a simultaneous expansion. But this doesn't affect the result.

Let's apply this proposition to a particular case. Suppose that the banking system experiences a decrease in reserves of $10,000 and that the required ratio of reserves to deposits is $\frac{1}{6}$. Applying this rule, we must divide the reduction in reserves—$10,000—by the required ratio of reserves to deposits—$\frac{1}{6}$—to get the answer, which is a $60,000 reduction in demand deposits. This answer checks with the result in the next to last paragraph.

Note that the effect of a $1 decrease in reserves is equal in absolute terms to the effect of a $1 increase in reserves. Whether the change is an increase or a decrease, a $1 change in reserves leads to a $$(1/r)$ change in demand deposits. Or, more precisely, this is the case if certain assumptions, discussed in the next section, are true. To complete our discussion of how banks create money, we turn now to these assumptions.

Currency Withdrawals and Excess Reserves

In discussing the amount of additional demand deposits that can be created by the banking system as a result of injecting $10,000 of new reserves, we made the important assumption that everyone who received the new demand deposits—from Mr. Palucci back to the person who originally deposited his money in Bank *A*—wants to keep this money in the form of demand deposits rather than currency. However, this clearly may not be the case. Some people who receive new demand deposits may choose to withdraw some part of this money as currency. For example, Mr. Palucci may decide to withdraw $1,000 of his new demand deposit in cash.

What effect will this withdrawal of currency have on the amount of demand deposits the banking system can create? To begin with, note that this withdrawal of currency from the entire banking system reduces the reserves of the banking system by $1,000. Applying the results of the previous section, this means that the banking system can create $6,000 less in demand deposits ($1,000 divided by $\frac{1}{6}$) than it could if the currency had not been withdrawn. Consequently, the banking system can create $60,000 minus $6,000, or $54,000, from the combination of the original $10,000 injection of reserves and the $1,000 withdrawal of currency. In other words, the banking system can create an amount of demand deposits equal to the amount of additional reserves *left perma-*

nently with the banking system ($10,000 minus $1,000, or $9,000 in this case) divided by the required ratio of reserves to demand deposits.

Similarly, in discussing how much demand deposits will be reduced as a consequence of a $10,000 reduction in reserves, we made the important assumption that everyone who buys a security from a bank pays the bank by check. But some people may pay partly or in full with currency, and this will affect how much the amount of demand deposits must be reduced by the banking system. If somebody pays $1,000 in currency to one of the banks, this restores $1,000 of the $10,000 in reserves that the banking system lost. Thus the banking system really loses $9,000, not $10,000. Then, applying the rule set forth in the previous section, the banking system must reduce its demand deposits by $54,000 ($9,000 divided by $1/6$), not $60,000 ($10,000 divided by $1/6$). In general, whether the change in reserves is an increase or a decrease, the change in demand deposits equals the change in reserves *left permanently with the banking system* ($9,000 in these cases) divided by the required ratio of reserves to demand deposits. Thus *whether or not a change in reserves has the maximum effect on demand deposits depends on how much of these reserves the public leaves in the banking system.*[9]

Another important assumption lies behind our discussion of the effects of $10,000 of additional reserves—or a $10,000 reduction in reserves—on the amount of demand deposits: *we have assumed that no bank holds excess reserves.* In other words, we have assumed that, whenever a bank has enough reserves to make a loan or investment, it will do so. Recall Bank *A*, which received a new deposit of $10,000. The new deposit enabled Bank *A* to increase its loans and investments by $8,333 without winding up with less than the legally required reserves. Thus we assumed that it would go ahead and make this much in additional loans and investments. In general, this seems to be a reasonable assumption, for the simple reason that loans and investments bring profits (in interest) into the bank while excess reserves bring none. But the matter is not as simple as all that. If a bank cannot find loans and investments it regards as attractive, it may decide to make no such loans. After all, there isn't much profit to be made on a loan that is not repaid. Also, if interest rates are very low, the bank may feel that it isn't losing much by not lending money. During the Great Depression of the 1930s, for example, banks held large excess reserves for this reason. In addition, banks can benefit by maintaining excess reserves, since they constitute insurance against deposit losses.

What difference does it make whether banks hold excess reserves? The answer is plenty. If, for example, Bank *A* decides to lend less than the full $8,333, this will mean that an increase in reserves will have a smaller effect on the amount of demand deposits than we indicated previously. Similarly, if banks hold excess reserves, a decrease in reserves is likely to have a smaller effect on the amount of demand deposits than we indicated above. Thus *whether or not a change in reserves has the maximum effect on demand deposits depends on the lending policies of the bankers. If they do not lend out as much as they can, the effect on demand deposits will be diminished accordingly.*

[9] Note too that people can convert demand deposits into time deposits, and vice versa. There are legal reserve requirements against time deposits, but they are lower than those against demand deposits. The conversion of demand deposits into time deposits will influence how much money can be supported by a certain amount of reserves. Thus the banking system can support an amount of demand deposits equal to the amount of additional reserves divided by the legally required ratio of reserves to demand deposits (no more, no less) only if there is no conversion of demand deposits into time deposits. In other words, we assume that all the demand deposits created by the banking system are converted into neither cash nor time deposits.

Summary

The Federal Reserve System is responsible for regulating and controlling the money supply. Established in 1913, the Fed is composed of the member banks, 12 regional Federal Reserve Banks, and the Federal Reserve Board, which coordinates the activities of the system. The Federal Reserve System is the central bank of the United States. Commercial banks have two primary functions. First, they hold demand deposits and permit checks to be drawn on them. Second, they lend money to firms and individuals.

Most of our money supply is not coin and paper currency, but bank money—demand deposits. This money is created by banks. Whereas the earliest banks held reserves equal to demand deposits, modern banks practice fractional-reserve banking: that is, their reserves equal only a fraction of their demand deposits. The Federal Reserve System requires every commercial bank that is a member of the system to hold a certain percentage of its demand deposits as reserves; the percentage varies with the size of the bank. Although they increase the safety of the banks, the major purpose of these legal reserve requirements is to control the money supply. Banks have become much safer in recent years, due in part to better management and regulation, as well as to the government's stated willingness to insure and stand behind their deposits. However, bank failures still occur, and bank regulation is not as stringent as it might be.

A bank creates money by lending or investing its excess reserves. If banks had to keep reserves equal to their deposits, they could not create money. A bank cannot lend or invest more than its excess reserves, unless it is a monopoly bank, because it will wind up with less than the legally required reserves. However, the banking system as a whole can support demand deposits equal to its total reserves divided by the legally required ratio of reserves to deposits. Thus, if reserves somewhere in the banking system increase by a certain amount, the banking system as a whole can increase demand deposits by the amount of the increase in reserves divided by the legally required ratio of reserves to deposits.

Similarly, if there is a decrease in reserves somewhere in the banking system, the system as a whole must decrease demand deposits by the amount of the decrease in reserves divided by the legally required ratio of reserves to deposits. Demand deposits are decreased by banks' selling securities or refusing to renew loans, just as demand deposits are increased by banks' making loans and investments.

Our argument so far has assumed that when additional reserves were made available to the banking system, there was no withdrawal of part of them in the form of currency, and that when reserves are decreased, no currency is deposited in banks. If such changes in the amount of currency take place, the change in demand deposits will equal the change in reserves left permanently with the banking system divided by the legally required ratio of reserves to deposits. We have also assumed that the banks hold no excess reserves. Since banks make profits by lending money and making investments, this assumption is generally sensible. But when loans are risky and interest rates are low—for example, in the Great Depression of the 1930s—banks have been known to hold large excess reserves. Clearly, changes in reserves will not have their full, or maximum, effect on demand deposits if the banks do not lend and invest as much as possible.

CONCEPTS FOR REVIEW

Fractional-reserve banking
Legal reserve requirements
Excess reserves
Simultaneous expansion

QUESTIONS FOR DISCUSSION AND REVIEW

1. Suppose that John Smith deposits $50,000 in newly printed currency to his account at Bank *A*. What is the effect on Bank *A*'s balance sheet? Fill in blanks below.

Assets (dollars)		Liabilities and net worth (dollars)	
Reserves	______	Demand deposits	______
Loans and investments	______	Net worth	______
Total	______	Total	______

2. If the legal reserve requirement is that Bank *A* must hold $1 in reserves for every $5 in demand deposits, by how much can Bank *A* increase its loans (after the deposit described in Question 1), if it is not a monopoly bank? By how much can it increase its loans if it is a monopoly bank?

3. Suppose that Bank *A* lends the Bugsbane Music Box Company $30,000. What is the effect on Bank *A*'s balance sheet of both the deposit described in Question 1 and this loan? Fill in the blanks below.

Assets (dollars)		Liabilities and net worth (dollars)	
Reserves	______	Demand deposits	______
Loans and investments	______	Net worth	______
Total	______	Total	______

4. After the Bugsbane Music Box Company receives the $30,000 loan, it uses the money to buy a new piece of equipment from the XYZ Tool Company. The XYZ Tool Company deposits Bugsbane's check on Bank *A* to its account at the Bank of America. What is the total effect on Bank *A*'s balance sheet of the deposit described in Question 1, the loan in Question 3, and the purchase described here? Fill in the blanks below.

Assets (dollars)		Liabilities and net worth (dollars)	
Reserves	______	Demand deposits	______
Loans and investments	______	Net worth	______
Total	______	Total	______

5. If Bank *A* had no excess reserves prior to the transactions described in Questions 1, 3, and 4, and if the legal reserve requirement is as described in Question 2, does Bank *A* have excess reserves after these transactions? If so, how large are these excess reserves?

6. "Banks do not create money. After all, they can only lend out money that they receive from depositors." Comment and evaluate.

7. Suppose that the legally required ratio of reserves to deposits is $\frac{1}{5}$. If the banking system's reserves shrink by $50 million, by how much will the money supply change? What assumptions are you making about excess reserves and currency withdrawals?

8. "Demand deposits are increased by banks when they call in loans and sell investments." Comment and evaluate.

9. Describe the way in which the banking system can create money if there is a single monopoly bank in the nation.

10. Suppose that you were the president of the Bank of America. What rules would you ask your executives to follow in making loans? In other words, what information should they look at, and how should they use this information, to decide whether or not to grant a particular loan?

15 Monetary Policy

Like fiscal policy, monetary policy is no panacea, but it is a very important tool for stabilization of the economy. In recent years, monetary policy has been the subject of considerable controversy. For example, in 1974, when the Federal Reserve held a tight rein on the money supply, many economists claimed that improper monetary policy was pushing the United States into a recession, while others argued that a restrictive monetary policy of this sort was needed to combat the very high rate of inflation. Without doubt, such controversies will continue in the future, since one thing is certain: economists of all persuasions agree that monetary policy has a major impact on the economy.

In this chapter, we are concerned with a variety of basic questions about monetary policy: Who makes monetary policy? What sorts of tools can be employed by monetary policy makers? How does monetary policy affect our national output and the price level? What are some of the problems involved in formulating effective monetary policy? What has been the nature of monetary policy in the United States in recent decades?

The Aims of Monetary Policy

Monetary policy is concerned with the money supply and interest rates. We described in Chapter 13 how the money supply influences net national product and the price level. If the economy is at considerably less than full employment, increases in the money supply tend to increase real NNP, and decreases in the money supply tend to decrease real NNP, with little or no effect on the price level. As full employment is approached, increases in the money supply tend to affect the price level, as well as real output. Finally, once full employment is reached, increases in the money supply result primarily in increases in the price level, since real output cannot increase appreciably.

In formulating monetary policy, the government's objectives are to attain and maintain reasonably full employment without excessive inflation. In other words, when a recession seems imminent and business is soft, the monetary authorities are likely to increase the money supply and push down interest rates. That is, they will "ease credit" or "ease money," as the newspapers put it. This tends to increase net national product. On the other hand, when the economy is in danger of overheating and serious inflation threatens, the monetary authorities will probably rein in the money supply and push up interest rates—in newspaper terms, they will "tighten credit" or "tighten money." This tends to reduce spending, and thus curb the upward pressure on the price level.

At this point, you may be muttering to yourself, "But the aims of monetary policy are essentially the same as those of fiscal policy!" Of course, you are right. Monetary policy and fiscal policy are both aimed at promoting full employment without inflation. But they use different methods to attain this goal. Fiscal policy uses the spending and taxing powers of the government, whereas monetary policy uses the government's power over the money supply.

The Central Role of Bank Reserves

As you will recall from Chapter 13, there is a difference of view concerning the processes by which changes in the money supply affect NNP and the price level. On the one hand, monetarists use the quantity theory of money to link changes in the money supply directly to changes in nominal NNP. On the other hand, Keynesians believe that an increase (decrease) in the money supply decreases (increases) the interest rate, which in turn shifts the investment function upward (downward). This shift in the investment function tends to increase (decrease) national product.[1]

Regardless of which view is closer to the truth, it is essential that we understand how the monetary authorities can promote their aims, since both Keynesians and monetarists acknowledge the importance of monetary policy. Economists of all persuasions would agree that a fundamental and key question is: How can the monetary authorities influence the money supply? And they would agree that the answer is: *by managing the reserves of the banking system.*

To see what this means in practice, suppose that the monetary authorities think that a recession is about to develop, and that, to prevent it, they want to increase the money supply more rapidly than they would otherwise. How can they realize this objective? By increasing the reserves of the banks. As we saw in the previous chapter, an increase in bank reserves enables the banks to increase the money supply.

[1] Keynesians also recognize that spending by consumers and state and local governments, as well as investment, is likely to be affected by changes in the quantity of money. See Chapter 13.

Indeed, we learned that if there were no excess reserves and no currency withdrawals, the banks could increase the money supply by $6 for every $1 of additional reserves.[2] (The ways in which the monetary authorities can increase the reserves of the banking system are discussed at length in subsequent sections.)

On the other hand, suppose that the monetary authorities smell a strong whiff of unacceptable inflation in the economic wind, and so decide to cut back on the rate of increase of the money supply. To do so, they can slow down the rate of increase of bank reserves. As we saw in the previous chapter, this will force the banks to curtail the growth of their demand deposits, by easing off on their loans and investments. Indeed, if the monetary authorities go so far as to reduce the reserves of the banking system, this will tend to reduce the money supply. Under the assumptions made in the previous chapter, the banks must cut back the money supply by $6 for every $1 reduction in reserves.

Makers of Monetary Policy

Who establishes our monetary policy? Who decides that, in view of the current and prospective economic situation, the money supply should be increased (or decreased) at a certain rate? As in the case of fiscal policy, this is not a simple question to answer; many individuals and groups play an important role. Certainly, however, *the leading role is played by the Federal Reserve System—in particular, by the members of the Federal Reserve Board and the Federal Open Market Committee.* The chairman of the Federal Reserve Board is often the chief spokesman for the Federal Reserve System. The recent chairmen—Arthur F. Burns and William McChesney Martin—undoubtedly have had considerable influence over monetary policy.

Although the Federal Reserve is responsible to Congress, Congress has established no clear guidelines for its behavior. Thus the Federal Reserve has had wide discretionary powers over monetary policy. But the Fedeal Reserve System is a huge organization, and it is not easy to figure out exactly who influences whom and who decides what. Formal actions can be taken by a majority of the board and of the Federal Open Market Committee (which is composed of the 7 members of the board plus 5 of the presidents of the 12 regional banks). However, this obviously tells only part of the story.

To get a more complete picture, it is essential to note too that many agencies and groups other than the Fed have an effect on monetary policy, although it is difficult to measure their respective influences. The Treasury frequently has an important voice in the formulation of monetary policy. The Fed must take into account the problems of the Treasury, which is faced with the task of selling huge amounts of government securities each year. Also, congressional committees hold hearings and issue reports on monetary policy and the operations of the Federal Reserve. These hearings and reports cannot fail to have some effect on Fed policy. In addition, beginning in 1975, the Congress has stipulated that the Fed must publish its long-term targets for growth in the money supply, the purpose being to establish somewhat more control over monetary policy. Finally, the president may attempt to influence the Federal Reserve Board. To keep the board as free as possible from political pressure, members are appointed for long terms—14 years—and a term expires every 2 years. But since members frequently do not serve out their full terms, a president may be able to name more than two members during each of his terms in office.

[2] Of course, this assumes that the legal reserve requirement is $16\frac{2}{3}$ percent. If the legal reserve requirement were 20 percent, a $5 increase in the money supply could be supported by $1 of additional reserves. Also, as pointed out in the previous chapter, a much smaller increase in the money supply may result from an extra dollar of reserves if banks hold excess reserves and if currency is withdrawn.

Figure 15.1
Consolidated Balance Sheet of the 12 Federal Reserve Banks, March 31, 1976 (billions of dollars).

Assets		Liabilities and net worth	
Gold certificates[a]	12	Reserves of member banks	28
Securities	90	Treasury deposits	7
Loans to commercial banks	1	Outstanding Federal Reserve notes	76
Other assets	18	Other liabilities and net worth	10
Total	121	Total	121

Source: Federal Reserve Bulletin.
[a] Cash is included here too.

The Federal Reserve Banks: Their Consolidated Balance Sheet

We know from a previous section that the Federal Reserve controls the money supply largely by controlling the quantity of member bank reserves. To understand how the Federal Reserve can control the quantity of member bank reserves, one must begin by examining the consolidated balance sheet of the 12 regional Federal Reserve Banks. Such a consolidated balance sheet is shown in Figure 15.1; it pertains to March 31, 1976.

As shown in Figure 15.1, the assets of the Federal Reserve Banks are largely of three kinds: gold certificates, securities, and loans to commercial banks. *Gold certificates* are warehouse receipts issued by the Treasury for gold bullion. Most important for present purposes are *securities* and *loans to commercial banks.* The securities listed on the Federal Reserve Banks' balance sheet are government bonds, notes, and bills. By buying and selling these securities, the Federal Reserve establishes considerable leverage on the quantity of member bank reserves (as we shall see below). The loans to commercial banks listed on the Federal Reserve Banks' balance sheet are loans of reserves that the Fed has made to commercial banks. As pointed out in the previous chapter, the Fed can make such loans if it wants to.

According to the righthand side of the balance sheet in Figure 15.1, the liabilities of the Federal Reserve Banks are largely of three kinds: outstanding Federal Reserve notes, Treasury deposits, and reserves of member banks. The outstanding *Federal Reserve notes* are the paper currency that we use. Since these notes are debts of the Federal Reserve Banks, they are included among the Banks' liabilities. *Treasury deposits* are the deposits which the U.S. Treasury maintains at the Federal Reserve Banks. The Treasury draws checks on these deposits to pay its bills. Finally, the *reserves of member banks* have been discussed in some detail in the previous chapter. Note that, although these reserves are assets from the point of view of the commercial banks, they are liabilities from the point of view of the Federal Reserve Banks.

Tools of Monetary Policy

Open Market Operations

Figure 15.1 shows that government securities constitute about 75 percent of the assets held by the Federal Reserve Banks. As we saw in Chapter 6, the market for government securities is huge and well developed. The Federal Reserve is part of this market: sometimes it buys government securities, sometimes it sells

Figure 15.2
Effect of Fed's Purchasing $1 Million of Government Securities

A. Effect on Fed's balance sheet:

Assets (millions of dollars)		Liabilities and net worth (millions of dollars)	
Government securities	+ 1	Member bank reserves	+ 1

B. Effect on balance sheet of the Chase Manhattan Bank:

Assets (millions of dollars)		Liabilities and net worth (millions of dollars)	
Reserves	+ 1	Demand deposits	+ 1

them. Whether it is buying or selling—and how much—can have a heavy impact on the quantity of bank reserves. Indeed, the most important means the Federal Reserve has to control the quantity of bank reserves are ***open market operations,*** which is the name given to the purchase and sale by the Fed of U.S. government securities in the open market.

Buying securities. Suppose that the Federal Reserve buys $1 million worth of government securities in the open market, and that the seller of these securities is General Motors.[3] To determine the effect of this transaction on the quantity of bank reserves, let's look at the effect on the balance sheet of the Fed and on the balance sheet of the Chase Manhattan Bank, General Motors' bank.[4] In this transaction, the Fed receives $1 million in government securities and gives General Motors a check for $1 million. When General Motors deposits this check to its account at the Chase Manhattan Bank, the bank's demand deposits and reserves increase by $1 million. Thus, as shown in Figure 15.2, the lefthand side of the Fed's balance sheet shows a $1 million increase in government securities, and the righthand side shows a $1 million increase in bank reserves. The lefthand side of the Chase Manhattan Bank's balance sheet shows a $1 million increase in reserves, and the righthand side shows a $1 million increase in demand deposits. Clearly, *the Fed has added $1 million to the banks' reserves.* The situation is entirely analogous to the $10,000 deposit at Bank *A* in the previous chapter.

Selling securities. Suppose that the Federal Reserve sells $1 million worth of government securities in the open market. They are bought by Merrill Lynch, Pierce, Fenner, and Smith, a huge brokerage firm. What effect does this transaction have on the quantity of bank reserves? To find out, let's look at the balance sheet of the Fed and the balance sheet of Merrill Lynch's bank, which we again assume to be the Chase Manhattan. When Merrill Lynch buys the government securities from the Fed, the Fed gives Merrill Lynch the securities in exchange for Merrill Lynch's check for $1 million. When the Fed presents this check to the Chase Manhattan Bank for payment, Chase Manhattan's demand deposits and reserves decrease by $1 million. Thus, as shown in Figure 15.3, the lefthand side of the Fed's balance sheet shows a $1 million decrease in government securities, and the righthand side shows a $1 million decrease in reserves. The lefthand side of the Chase Manhattan Bank's balance sheet shows a $1 million decrease in reserves,

[3] Large corporations often hold quantities of government securities.

[4] For simplicity, we assume that General Motors has only one bank, the Chase Manhattan Bank. Needless to say, this may not be the case, but it makes no difference to the point we are making here. We make a similar assumption regarding the investment firm of Merrill Lynch in the next paragraph.

Figure 15.3
Effect of Fed's Selling $1 Million of Government Securities

A. Effect on Fed's balance sheet:

Assets (millions of dollars)		Liabilities and net worth (millions of dollars)	
Government securities	−1	Member bank reserves	−1

B. Effect on balance sheet of the Chase Manhattan Bank:

Assets (millions of dollars)		Liabilities and net worth (millions of dollars)	
Reserves	−1	Demand deposits	−1

and the righthand side shows a $1 million decrease in demand deposits. Clearly, *the Fed has reduced the reserves of the banks by $1 million.*

The Federal Open Market Committee

Thus the Federal Reserve adds to bank reserves when it buys government securities and reduces bank reserves when it sells them. Obviously, the extent to which the Federal Reserve increases or reduces bank reserves depends on the amount of government securities purchased or sold. The greater the amount, the greater the increase or decrease in bank reserves. As noted above, open market operations are the Fed's most important technique for controlling the money supply. The power to decide on the amount of government securities the Fed should buy or sell at any given moment rests with the *Federal Open Market Committee.* This group wields an extremely powerful influence over bank reserves and the nation's money supply. Every three or four weeks, the Federal Open Market Committee meets to discuss the current situation and trends, and gives instructions to the manager of the Open Market Account at the Federal Reserve Bank of New York, who actually buys and sells the government securities.

To get some insight into the nature of these discussions, consider the meeting of the Federal Open Market Committee (FOMC) that was held on May 26, 1970. According to Sherman Maisel, a former member of the Federal Reserve Board and one of the participants, much of the meeting was devoted to a discussion of whether the money supply was increasing too rapidly.

> The money supply and bank credit had grown far faster than appeared consistent with the 4 percent growth rate set as policy by prior votes [of the Committee]. The FOMC would now have to make a choice.... If the money supply were held to a 4 percent growth rate, interest rates would continue to rise and perhaps at an accelerating rate.... Was this what the Committee wanted, or would it prefer to allow reserves and money to grow more rapidly in order to avoid the unsettling effect of a still more rapid run-up in interest rates?... As in many similar situations, the Committee was sharply divided in its views.... The FOMC finally agreed that it would not change its basic policy stance. Monetary growth above 4 percent was not desirable.[5]

Although no single meeting can be regarded as typical, this brief description gives you some idea of the sort of discussion that takes place every three or four weeks in the meetings of the Federal Open Market Committee.

[5] Sherman Maisel, *Managing the Dollar,* New York: Norton, 1973. A section of this book dealing with Federal Reserve decision making is reprinted in E. Mansfield, *Economics: Readings, Issues, and Cases,* 2d ed., New York: Norton, 1977.

Changes in Legal Reserve Requirements

Open market operations are not the only means the Federal Reserve has to influence the money supply. Another way is *to change the legal reserve requirements.* In other words, *the Federal Reserve Board can change the amount of reserves banks must hold for every dollar of demand deposits.* In 1934, Congress gave the Federal Reserve Board the power to set—within certain broad limits—the legally required ratio of reserves to deposits for both demand and time deposits. From time to time, the Fed uses this power to change legal reserve requirements. For example, in 1958 it cut the legally required ratio of reserves to deposits in big city banks from 17½ percent to 16½ percent, and the ratio remained there until 1968, when it was raised to 17 percent. Table 15.1 shows the change in legal reserve requirements during 1951–73.

Table 15.1
Changes in Legal Reserve Requirements for Demand Deposits in Reserve City Banks, 1951–73.

Year	Reserve requirement (percent of deposits)
1951	20
1953	19
1954	18
1958	16½–17½[a]
1968	17
1969	17½
1973	18

[a] The reserve requirement was reduced from 17½ to 17 to 16½ percent during the year.

The obvious effect of an increase in the legally required ratio of reserves to deposits is that banks must hold larger reserves to support the existing amount of demand deposits. This in turn means that banks with little or no excess reserves will have to sell securities, refuse to renew loans, and reduce their demand deposits to meet the new reserve requirements. For example, suppose that a member bank has \$1 million in reserves and \$6 million in demand deposits. If the legal reserve requirement is 16 percent, it has excess reserves of \$1 million minus \$960,000 (.16 × \$6 million), or \$40,000. It is in good shape. If the legal reserve requirement is increased to 20 percent, this bank now needs \$1.2 million (.20 × \$6 million) in reserves. Since it only has \$1 million in reserves, it must sell securities or refuse to renew loans.

Consider now what happens to the banking system as a whole. Clearly, an increase in the legally required ratio of reserves to deposits means that, with a given amount of reserves, the banking system can maintain less demand deposits than before. For example, if the banking system has \$1 billion in total reserves, it can support $\frac{\$1 \text{ billion}}{.16}$, or \$6.25 billion in demand deposits when the legal reserve requirement is 16 percent. But it can support only $\frac{\$1 \text{ billion}}{.20}$, or \$5 billion in demand deposits when the legal reserve requirement is 20 percent. (See Figure 15.4.)[6] Thus, *increases in the legal reserve requirement tend to reduce the amount of demand deposits—bank money—the banking system can support.*

What is the effect of a decrease in the legally required ratio of reserves to deposits? Obviously, it means that banks must hold less reserves to support the existing amount of demand deposits, which in turn means that banks will suddenly find themselves with excess reserves. For example, if the banking system has \$1 billion in reserves and \$5 billion in demand deposits, there are no excess reserves when the legal reserve requirement is 20 percent. But

[6] We assume arbitrarily in Figure 15.4 that the total net worth of the banks is \$2 billion. Obviously, this assumption concerning the amount of total net worth makes no difference to the point we are making here.

suppose the Federal Reserve lowers the legal reserve requirement to 16 percent. Now the amount of legally required reserves is $800 million ($5 billion × .16), so that the banks have $200 million in excess reserves—which means that they can increase the amount of their demand deposits. Thus *decreases in the legal reserve requirements tend to increase the amount of demand deposits—bank money—the banking system can support.*

Changes in legal reserve requirements are a rather drastic way to influence the money supply—they are to open market operations as a cleaver is to a scalpel, and so are made infrequently. For example, for about ten years—from April 1958 to January 1968—no change at all was made in legal reserve requirements for demand deposits in city banks. Nonetheless, the Fed can change legal reserve requirements if it wants to. And there can be no doubt about the potential impact of such changes. Large changes in reserve requirements can rapidly alter bank reserves and the money supply.

Changes in the Discount Rate

Still another way that the Federal Reserve can influence the money supply is through changes in the discount rate. As shown by the balance sheet of the Federal Reserve Banks (in Figure 15.1), commercial banks that are members of the Federal Reserve System can borrow from the Federal Reserve when their reserves are low (if the Fed is willing). This is one of the functions of the Federal Reserve. The interest rate the Fed charges the banks for loans is called the ***discount rate,*** and the Fed can increase or decrease the discount rate whenever it chooses. Increases in the discount rate discourage borrowing from the Fed, while decreases in the discount rate encourage it.

The discount rate can change substantially and fairly often (Table 15.2). For example, take 1968: the discount rate was changed from $4\frac{1}{2}$ to 5 percent in March, from 5 to $5\frac{1}{2}$ percent in April, and from $5\frac{1}{2}$ to $5\frac{1}{4}$ percent in August. When the Fed increases the discount rate, it obviously makes it more expensive for

Figure 15.4

Consolidated Balance Sheet of All Member Banks, before and after an Increase (from 16 to 20 percent) in the Legal Reserve Requirement

A. Before the increase in the legal reserve requirement:

Assets (billions of dollars)		Liabilities (billions of dollars)	
Reserves	1.00	Demand deposits	6.25
Loans and investments	7.25	Net worth	2.00
Total	8.25		8.25

B. After the increase in the legal reserve requirement:

Assets (billions of dollars)		Liabilities (billions of dollars)	
Reserves	1.00	Demand deposits	5.00
Loans and investments	6.00	Net worth	2.00
Total	7.00		7.00

Table 15.2
Average Annual Value of the Discount Rate, 1960–75

Year	Discount rate (percent)
1960	3.53
1961	3.00
1962	3.00
1963	3.23
1964	3.55
1965	4.04
1966	4.50
1967	4.19
1968	5.17
1969	5.87
1970	5.95
1971	4.88
1972	4.50
1973	6.44
1974	7.83
1975	6.25

Source: Economic Report of the President.

banks to augment their reserves in this way; hence it tightens up a bit on the money supply. On the other hand, when the Fed decreases the discount rate, it is cheaper for banks to augment their reserves in this way, and hence the money supply eases up a bit. However, note that the Fed is largely passive in these relations with the banks. It cannot make the banks borrow. It can only set the discount rate and see how many banks show up at the "discount window" to borrow. Also, it must be recognized that the Fed will not allow banks to borrow on a permanent or long-term basis. They are expected to use this privilege only to tide themselves over for short periods. To discourage banks from excessive use of the borrowing privilege, the discount rate is kept more or less in line with short-term market interest rates.

Most economists agree that changes in the discount rate have relatively little direct impact, and that the Fed's open market operations can and do offset easily the amount the banks borrow. Certainly changes in the discount rate cannot have anything like the direct effect on bank reserves of open market operations or changes in legal reserve requirements. *The principal importance of changes in the discount rate lies in their effects on people's expectations.* When the Fed increases the discount rate, this is generally interpreted as a sign that the Fed will tighten credit and the money supply. A cut in the discount rate is generally interpreted as a sign of easier money and lower interest rates. For example, when in 1969 the Federal Reserve announced an increase in the discount rate, the effect was a sharp drop in the prices of stocks and bonds. People interpreted this increase in the discount rate as a sure sign that the Fed was going to keep the money supply under tight reins to fight inflation.

Other Tools of Monetary Policy

In addition, the Federal Reserve has several other tools it can use, each of which is discussed below. These tools are generally less important than open market operations, changes in legal reserve requirements, and changes in the discount rate.

Moral suasion. This is a fancy term to describe various expressions of pleasure or displeasure by the Fed. In other words, the Fed tells the banks what it would like them to do or not do, and exhorts them to go along with its wishes. It may appeal to the patriotism of the bankers, or it may make some statements that could be regarded as threats. Of course, the Fed does not have the power to force banks to comply with its wishes, but the banks don't want to get into difficulties with the Fed. Thus moral suasion can have a definite impact, particularly for short periods. But banks are profit-oriented enterprises, and when the Fed's wishes conflict strongly with the profit motive, moral suasion may not work very well.

Interest-rate ceilings. The Fed can vary the maximum interest rate commercial banks can pay on time deposits. Since the 1930s, the Fed has had the power, under ***Regulation Q,*** to establish a ceiling on the interest rates commercial banks can pay.[7] And the level at which this ceiling is set can have an important influence on the flow of funds into time deposits, savings and loan associations, and other financial institutions. In particular, by preventing commercial banks from paying more than a certain rate of interest on time deposits, the Fed can protect the savings and loan associations, which are important sources of funds for the construction industry. In other words, the Fed can prevent the commercial banks from drawing too many deposits away from the savings and loan associations. Because it is aimed so directly at the construction industry, Regulation Q is often regarded as a selective credit control, not as a general tool of monetary policy. (A ***selective credit control*** is a control aimed at the use of credit for specific purposes.) Most economists favor the elimination of such interest ceilings on the grounds that they interfere with the functioning of free markets for funds. The Ford administration pressed for passage of legislation, introduced in Congress in 1973, that would phase out these ceilings.

Stock market credit. Another of the Fed's tools is to vary the margin requirements for the purchase of stocks. ***Margin requirements*** set the maximum percentage of the price of stocks that a person can borrow. For example, in the early 1960s, you could borrow 50 percent of the cost of such securities from your broker, but in late 1972, you could borrow only 35 percent from your broker. This is another example of a selective credit control. It may seem odd that margin requirements for the purchase of stocks were singled out for special treatment, but the severity of the stock market crash in 1929 was attributed partly to the fact that people in those days could borrow a large percentage—sometimes even 90 percent—of the value of the stock they purchased. (When stock prices slid, their small equity vanished quickly, and they had to sell out.) Consequently, after the crash, margin requirements were imposed.

Real estate and consumer credit. During and immediately after World War II, the Fed also had two other powers—regulation of mortgage terms and of installment contracts. Until 1953, the Fed could vary the size of down payments for houses and the number of years mortgages could run. This was an effective tool to influence the pace of residential construction. Increases in the size of down payments and decreases in the length of mortgages tended to discourage construction, while decreases in the size of down payments and increases in the length of mortgages tended to encourage construction. Until 1952, the Fed, under Regulation W, could also establish minimum amounts a person had to put up when he bought appliances, automobiles, and other items; and it could impose other restrictions on installment buying. After the Korean War, these restrictions became unpopular, and this power of the Fed was not continued.

When Is Monetary Policy Tight or Easy?

Everyone daydreams about being powerful and important. It is a safe bet, however, that few people under the age of 21 daydream about being members of the Federal Reserve Board or the Federal Open Market Committee. Yet the truth is that the members of the board and

[7] Since the 1930s, no commercial banks have been permitted to pay interest on demand deposits. Some people felt that many of the banks' problems in the 1920s and 1930s were due to too much competition: hence this law. It is easy to see why bankers felt that their earnings would be improved if none of them were allowed to compete for deposits by paying interest, but this is hardly consistent with a competitive philosophy. Legislation passed by the Senate in late 1975 would enable the banks to pay interest on demand deposits.

the committee are among the most powerful people in the nation. Suppose you were appointed to the Federal Reserve Board. As a member, you would have to decide–month by month, year by year–exactly how much government securities the Fed should buy or sell, as well as whether and when changes should be made in the discount rate, legal reserve requirements, and the other instruments of Federal Reserve policy. How would you go about making your choices?

Obviously you would need lots of data. Fortunately, the Fed has a very large and able research staff to provide you with plenty of the latest information about what is going on in the economy. But what sorts of data should you look at? Clearly, one thing you would want is some information on the extent to which monetary policy is inflationary or deflationary–that is, the extent to which it is "tight" or "easy." This is not simple to measure, but there is general agreement that the members of the Federal Reserve Board–and other members of the financial and academic communities–have often used the following four variables as measures.

The level of short-term interest rates. High interest rates are interpreted as meaning that monetary policy is tight; low interest rates are usually thought to mean that monetary policy is easy. The Fed can influence the level of interest rates through its open market operations and other policies. The level of interest rates has been used by the Fed and by the financial and academic communities as a major indicator of the effect of monetary policy on the economy, and the Fed has set as a target increases, decreases, or stability in interest rates. However, to know what the proper interest rate is, you need a forecast of the strength or weakness of investment demand, and an estimate of the extent to which a high interest rate is required to offset inflation. Thus the level of interest rates may be an ambiguous indicator.

The rate of increase of the money supply. When the money supply is growing at a relatively slow rate (much less than 4 or 5 percent per year), this is often interpreted as meaning that monetary policy is tight. A relatively rapid rate of growth in the money supply (much more than 4 or 5 percent per year) is often taken to mean that monetary policy is easy. During the 1960s and 1970s, this has become an increasingly important indicator of the effects of monetary policy on the economy. Its popularity is due to the influence of the monetarists. This indicator has the disadvantage of being influenced by the decisions of the banks and the public about how they want to hold their assets. And it is difficult to know whether the proper definition of the money supply is M_1, M_2, or something else.

The rate of increase of the monetary base. The ***monetary base,*** which by definition equals bank reserves plus currency outstanding, is important because the total money supply is dependent upon–and made from–it. Moreover, as an indicator of the effects of monetary policy, the monetary base has the advantage of being almost completely under the control of the Federal Reserve. A relatively slow growth rate in the monetary base (much less than 4 or 5 percent per year) is often interpreted as a sign of tight monetary policy. A relatively rapid rate of growth (much more than 4 or 5 percent per year) is often taken to mean that monetary policy is easy. This indicator is currently influential, particularly among the monetarists. Before 1960, it was seldom emphasized.

The level of free reserves. ***Free reserves*** are the excess reserves of the banks minus the amounts borrowed by the banks from the Federal Reserve.[8] When free reserves are negative, and the banks owe more to the Fed than they have in excess reserves, this has been used as an indicator that monetary policy is tight. Large and positive free reserves have been used as an

[8] Another measure of money market conditions is the interest rate on federal funds, the interest rate banks receive when they make an overnight loan of reserves to another bank.

indicator that monetary policy is easy. During the 1950s, the Fed used the amount of free reserves as its principal indicator of the effect of monetary policy on the economy, but this method is much less important today. Its shortcomings have been pointed out by many observers. In particular, the banks can influence the amount of free reserves by their lending and borrowing policies.

Decision Making at the Fed: A Case Study

Let's continue to assume that you have been appointed to the Federal Reserve Board, and that the economy suddenly is confronted with what seems to be a dangerously inflationary situation. What sort of action would you recommend? One appropriate action would be to sell a considerable amount of government securities, which would reduce bank reserves. You might also recommend an increase in the discount rate or even an increase in legal reserve requirements. To see how well you were doing, you would watch the variables discussed in the previous section. Specifically, you would look at the rate of increase of the money supply, as well as the rate of increase of the monetary base, and try to reduce both. At the same time you would try to increase interest rates.

Let's compare your recommendations with what the Fed really did in a similar situation. You will recall that the large military build-up associated with the Vietnam War created strong inflationary pressures during the middle and late 1960s. Fiscal policy was not used to curb this inflation, since government spending was highly destablizing and tax changes were painfully slow in coming. Consequently, much of the responsibility for fighting inflation fell to the Federal Reserve. What actions did it take?

In July 1965, when President Johnson announced that 50,000 more men would be sent to Vietnam, it was evident that inflationary pressures would mount unless appropriate fiscal or monetary policies were adopted. William M. Martin, chairman of the Federal Reserve Board, discussed these dangers with administration policy makers during the summer and fall of 1965, and argued publicly for a tax increase. But no such tax increase was in the cards. On December 4, 1965, the Fed decided to fire a highly visible volley against inflation. *The Federal Reserve Board voted to increase the discount rate from 4 to 4½ percent.* President Johnson and many Democrats in Congress were openly critical of this action, but many businessmen and economists agreed with the board's decision to act against inflation.

During 1965, the price level rose by 3 percent. During 1966, inflationary pressures continued unabated, and the government's large expenditures on Vietnam and domestic programs led to a huge budget deficit. As the hopes for a tax increase became dimmer, the Federal Reserve began to resort to sterner and more powerful measures to stem the inflationary tide. During early 1966, the Fed tried to tighten money, but there was a controversy within the board over the proper indicator. Using interest rates as an indicator, money was tight; but the money supply seemed to indicate that money was easy. By the summer of 1966, *the Fed allowed no increase in the monetary base, and the rate of increase in the money supply was cut to zero.* In other words, the Fed did not permit the money supply to increase at all. *Interest rates climbed to very high levels,* in part because of an increase in the demand for credit as people and firms began to fear that soon they would be unable to get credit. Money became extremely tight.

The effects on the financial and housing markets were devastating. Money for mortgages was extremely scarce, and for a time virtually no buyers could be found for municipal bonds. Knowledgeable people began to talk about an impending financial panic. By September 1966, when a crisis seemed imminent, the Fed assured all banks that it would lend them reserves so long as they made only legitimate and socially desirable loans. In addition, the Fed used its open market operations to increase bank reserves, and thus allow some increase in the money supply. By late September, the financial markets were operating reasonably well again.

Clearly, the Fed did pretty much what you would have recommended, and its policies had the intended effect. Indeed, this episode—the so-called credit crunch of 1966—indicates dramatically the potency of monetary policy. For that matter, according to some economists, the Fed may have gone too far. The job of the Fed is often described as "leaning against the wind," and in this case it leaned so heavily that it may almost have caused a panic. However, in its defense it must be pointed out that the Fed was faced with the problem of undoing the mischief caused by inadequate fiscal policies. It was dealt a very bad hand by the fiscal policy makers.

Monetary Policy in the United States

Experience during the 1950s to 1970s

For a more complete—and more balanced—picture of monetary policy in the United States, let's look briefly at the formulation of monetary policy in the past 25 years. When the Eisenhower administration took office in 1952, the economy was prosperous, but the Korean War was ending and the economy would soon have to adapt to peacetime conditions. At first, the Federal Reserve viewed inflation as the big danger, and in January 1953 it raised the discount rate and used open market operations to cut bank reserves. But by the middle of 1953, the Fed changed its course and increased bank reserves by its open market operations and by reducing the legal reserve requirements. This was fortunate because the reduction in government expenditures on the war helped to push the economy into a recession in mid-1953. During this recession, the Fed maintained a stimulative monetary policy.

In 1954, the economy came out of the recession; and by late 1954 and 1955, inflation began to reappear. In late 1955 the Fed moved toward credit restraint. In the middle of 1957, the economy turned down again, partly because of a drop in investment and defense expenditures. Once this became evident, the Fed quickly eased credit; the money supply was permitted to increase more rapidly; and interest rates fell. The recession was short-lived, and by late 1958 the economy was rising once more. But almost as soon as the recovery was under way, both the monetary and fiscal authorities began to put on the brakes. Interest rates rose substantially during much of 1958 and all of 1959. As a consequence of these monetary (and fiscal) policies, the economy began to turn soft once more, and in 1960 another recession began. In early 1960, the Federal Reserve began to ease credit somewhat.

When the Kennedy administration took office in 1961, it inherited a soft economy. To stimulate it, the Federal Reserve added to bank reserves, thus permitting rapid growth in the money supply. However, monetary policy did not play a leading role in economic policy in the Kennedy years. Instead, as described in Chapter 11, the Kennedy administration pushed hard for the tax cut, which was the cornerstone of its economic policy. Monetary policy played a supporting role. Leading administration economists felt that the money supply should grow in such a way as to accommodate the desired growth in national product, but that the growth in national product was to be brought about largely by the tax cut.[9] In fact,

[9] During much of the 1960s, monetary policy was formulated with one eye on the balance of payments, discussed in Chapter 32. If the Fed had attempted to stimulate the economy, interest rates would have fallen, and capital would have gone abroad in response to higher yields there. The result would have been a worsening of our balance of payments problems. In Chapter 32, we discuss the effect of balance of payments problems on domestic economic policy.

the Federal Reserve expanded the money supply during the early 1960s at a substantially higher average annual rate than during the late 1950s. In later years, some monetarists—like Milton Friedman—were to argue that this increase in the money supply, and not the tax cut, was responsible for the growth of national product in the mid-1960s.

When government spending in Vietnam began to skryrocket in 1965, monetary policy began to push itself to the fore. As described in the previous section, the Federal Reserve Board, faced with strong inflationary pressures stemming from a highly destabilizing fiscal policy, committed itself to a strong deflationary stance. The result, as we have seen, was the credit crunch of 1966, after which the Fed eased credit considerably. Indeed, in a rapid about-face, the Fed began to expand credit very rapidly in 1967 and 1968. In the latter part of 1967, the money supply was increasing at 10 percent per year. The tax surcharge was expected (incorrectly) to reduce spending so much that the Fed was encouraged to increase the money supply to offset it partially. Alarmed by this apparent shift to an inflationary posture, critics in Congress and elsewhere belabored the Fed for its "stop-go" policies.

When the Nixon administration came into office in 1969, inflation was unquestionably the nation's principal economic problem. Thus practically everyone, both Republicans and Democrats, agreed that monetary policy should be tight. In accord with this view, the Federal Reserve kept a close rein on the money supply during 1969. The result, however, was to slow the growth of national output and to increase unemployment.

Early in 1970, the Federal Reserve stated that it would adhere to a policy of maintaining steady growth in the money supply. Apparently the target was a 4 percent annual increase in the quantity of money. This decision was in part a reaction to the many criticisms of the Fed's previous "stop-go" policies. During most of 1970, the Fed succeeded in expanding the money supply at this relatively constant rate. During the first half of 1971, the money supply was allowed to expand rapidly: from January to June 1971, the quantity of money increased at a rate of 12 percent. But the second half of 1971 saw little growth in the money supply.

In August 1971, President Nixon announced his New Economic Policy, which, as you will recall from Chapter 11, entailed direct controls of prices, wages, and rents, as well as an expansionary fiscal policy. In line with the more expansionary tone of his economic policies, the president announced in early 1972, that "the Federal Reserve has taken steps to create the monetary conditions necessary for rapid economic expansion." In fact, the money supply grew by about 8 percent in 1972.

After price and wage controls were largely removed in 1973, open inflation occurred with a vengeance. In the *single month* of June 1973, wholesale prices increased by 2.4 percent. President Nixon responded by slapping a 60-day freeze on most prices (but not wages) beginning in mid-June of 1973. And the Federal Reserve tightened money considerably. For example, on June 8, 1973, the Fed raised the discount rate to 6½ percent, its highest level since 1921.

During 1973 and 1974, the Federal Reserve cut back on the rate of increase in the money supply. During 1973, the money supply grew by about 6 percent; during 1974, it grew by about 5 percent. Interest rates reached unprecedented heights in 1974. On the average, the discount rate was almost 8 percent during the year. And the prime bank rate, the interest rate that commercial banks charge their best customers, exceeded 12 percent for a time. Many critics of the Nixon and Ford administrations charged that the Federal Reserve was taking too strong a stance in its fight against inflation.

In the fourth quarter of 1974, there was a sharp, and largely unexpected, drop in real

William McChesney Martin and Arthur F. Burns

According to an old saying, "Where you stand depends on where you sit." This is no less true at 20th and Constitution, the location of the Federal Reserve Board, than elsewhere in Washington. But while internal and external constraints determine the broad outlines of monetary policy, whatever baggage the chairman brings to the job weighs also in setting the Fed's stances vis-à-vis the rest of the government and its stand on specific issues. Consider, for example, former Chairman William McChesney Martin and present Chairman Arthur F. Burns.

Martin associated himself with the New York financial community. Indeed he had served as president of the New York Stock Exchange during the thirties. He believed that good monetary policy required a "feel" for credit markets, an instinct presumably inbred and possibly cultivated, but certainly not acquired by examining thousands of statistics on M_1 and M_2. More importantly, Martin held that the primary responsibility of the Fed was to preserve a sound currency: to stand firm while others were pandering to popular sentiment and calling for cheap money. While elected officials played to the crowd with promises of more employment, the Fed would fight the good fight—against inflation. In order to assure the independence necessary to pursue such a course, Martin virtually removed the Fed from all but the most formal and infrequent contact with the Treasury, the CEA, and Budget Bureau during the Eisenhower administration.

WILLIAM MCCHESNEY MARTIN

ARTHUR F. BURNS

Burns brought a different set of baggage to his new job. Having spent much of his professional life as an economist at Columbia University and with the National Bureau of Economic Research, he was at home, not in a Wall Street club, but with a page of statistics. Thus his chairmanship has meant much more systematic collection and analysis of data on money markets and interest rate movements. (One veteran banker commented, "They may not be making better policy now, but they can certainly tell you better why they're making it.") More significantly, under Burns the Fed became a more active member of the Quadriad and he himself has given informal economic counsel to the president.

In 1974, Burns led the Fed in a very hard fight against the double-digit inflation that occurred then. The rate of growth of the money supply was cut back, and interest rates rose to record levels. Conservatives tended to applaud Burns. (As the president of the Philadelphia National Bank put it, "If the Fed fails again, we will be fighting inflation three years from now at 20 percent.") Liberals criticized him vehemently for helping to bring on the recession that began in the latter part of 1974. Faced with this recession, Burns cautioned that the policy goal should be one of "moderation" and "steadiness" in the expansion of money and credit. Before the Senate Banking Committee, he said that the money supply (M_1) would be allowed to grow by between 5 and 7½ percent in the year ending March 1976. Many of his critics felt that this was an inadequate rate of monetary growth. In 1976, there were signs that the Fed was begining to loosen up on monetary policy, as inflation showed at least a temporary drop.

E.A.

NNP. The United States entered the deepest recession in decades. During the first quarter of 1975, there was little or no growth in the money supply, but in subsequent quarters the Fed permitted the money supply to grow more rapidly, with the result that the money supply increased by about 4 percent during the year as a whole. Interest rates declined during the latter part of 1974, and remained relatively stable during 1975. Critics of the Fed maintained that it increased the money supply much too slowly in 1975, thus impeding the recovery. Even in terms of the Fed's own announced targets, the growth in the money supply seemed rather low. In his 1976 campaign, President Carter belabored Arthur F. Burns and the Fed on these grounds, and once Carter became president, there was speculation that he and Burns might clash. Only time will tell how the Fed will behave during the Carter administration.

Problems in Formulating Monetary Policy

Before attempting to evaluate the Fed's record, we must recognize the three major kinds of decisions it must continually make. First, the Fed must maintain a constant watch on the economy, checking for signs that the economy is sliding into a recession, being propelled into an inflationary boom, or growing satisfactorily. As we saw in Chapter 12, there is no foolproof way to forecast the economy's short-term movements. Recognizing the fallibility of existing forecasting techniques all too well, the Fed must nonetheless use these techniques as best it can to guide its actions.

Second, having come to some tentative conclusion about the direction in which the economy is heading, the Fed must decide to what extent it should tighten or ease money. The answer depends on the Fed's estimates of when monetary changes will take effect and the magnitude of their impact, as well as on its forecasts of the economy's future direction. Also, the answer depends on the Fed's evaluation of the relative importance of full employment and price stability as national goals. If it regards full employment as much more important than price stability, it will probably want to err in the direction of easy money. On the other hand, if it thinks price stability is at least as important as full employment, it may want to err in the direction of tight money.

Finally, once the Fed has decided what it wants to do, it must figure out how to do it. Should open market operations do the whole job? If so, how big must be the purchase or sale of government securities? Should a change be made in the discount rate, or in legal reserve requirements? How big a change? Should moral suasion be resorted to? These are the operational questions the Fed continually must answer.

In answering these questions, the Fed must reckon with two very inconvenient facts, both of which make life difficult. First, *there is often a long lag between an action by the Fed and its effect on the economy.* Although the available evidence indicates that monetary policy affects some types of expenditures more rapidly than others, it is not uncommon for the bulk of the total effects to occur a year or more after the change in monetary policy.[10] Thus the Fed may act to head off an imminent recession, but find that some of the consequences of its action are not felt until later, when inflation—not recession—is the problem. Conversely, the Fed may act to curb an imminent inflation, but find that the consequences of its action are not felt until some time later, when recession, not inflation, has become the problem. In either case, the Fed can wind up doing more harm than good.

[10] For example, see Frank de Leeuw and Edward Gramlich, "The Channels of Monetary Policy: A Further Report on the Federal Reserve–MIT Econometric Model," *Federal Reserve Bulletin,* June 1969. However, there is considerable disagreement concerning the length of this lag.

Second, *experts disagree about which of the available measures—such as interest rates, the rate of increase of the money supply, or the rate of increase of the monetary base—is the best measure of how tight or easy monetary policy is.* Fortunately, these measures often point in the same direction; but when they point in different directions, the Fed can be misled. For example, during 1967-68, the Fed wanted to tighten money somewhat. Using free reserves and interest rates as the primary measures of the tightness of monetary policy, it reduced free reserves and increased interest rates. However, at the same time, it permitted a substantial rate of increase in the money supply and the monetary base. By doing so, the Fed—in the eyes of many experts—really eased, not tightened, money.

How Well Has the Fed Performed?

Given the difficult problems the Federal Reserve faces and the fact that its performance cannot be measured by any simple standard, it would be naïve to expect that its achievement could be graded like an arithmetic quiz. Nonetheless, just as war is too important to be left to the generals, so monetary policy is too important to be left unscrutinized to the monetary authorities. According to recent studies of Federal Reserve policy making, what have been the strengths and weaknesses of the Fed's decisions?

Forecasting. If one takes into account the limitations in existing forecasting techniques, the Fed seems to have done a reasonably good job in recent years of recognizing changes in economic conditions. As noted in previous sections, it sometimes was a bit slow to see that the economy was sinking into a recession, or that inflationary pressures were dominant. But hindsight is always much clearer than foresight, which is why Monday morning quarterbacks make so few mistakes—and get paid so little. Because the Fed did a creditable job of recognizing changes in economic conditions, the time interval between changes in economic conditions and changes in policy was rather short, particularly when compared with the corresponding time interval for fiscal policy.

Recognition of lags. The Fed does not seem to have taken much account of the long—and seemingly quite variable—lags between changes in monetary policy and their effects on the economy. Instead, it simply reacted quickly to changes in business conditions. As pointed out in a previous section, such a policy can in reality be quite destabilizing. For example, the Fed may act to suppress inflationary pressures, but find that the consequences of its action are not felt until some time later when recession—not inflation—is the problem. Unfortunately, the truth is that, despite advances in knowledge in the past decade, economists do not have a firm understanding of these lags. Thus the Fed is only partly to blame.

Coordination. With a few notable exceptions, there generally seems to have been reasonably good coordination between the Federal Reserve and the executive branch (the Treasury and the Council of Economic Advisers, in particular). This is important because monetary policy and fiscal policy should work together, not march off in separate directions. Of course, the fact that the Fed and the executive branch have generally been aware of one another's views and probable actions does not mean that there has always been agreement between them. Nor does it mean that, even when they agreed, they could always point monetary and fiscal policy in the same direction. But at least the left hand had a pretty good idea of what the right hand was doing.

Measures. The Fed has been criticized for paying too much attention during the 1950s to free reserves and interest rates as measures of the tightness or looseness of monetary policy, and giving too little attention to the rate of

Is There an Independent Federal Reserve? Should There Be?

A MEETING OF THE FEDERAL OPEN MARKET COMMITTEE.

Some say the Fed is responsible to Congress. Its enabling legislation was passed by Congress in 1913, and it could presumably be reorganized should it sufficiently rouse Congress's wrath. But Congress moves with nothing if not deliberate speed, and not since 1935 has it sought to influence the Federal Reserve through new legislation. The president fills vacancies on the Board of Governors, but since terms on the board run for 14 years, presidents have had to wait until their second terms to appoint a majority of the board.

In fact, as knowledgeable observers often agree, there are two groups that, without appearing prominently on the organization chart, exercise considerable influence over the policies of the Fed. One is the business community—a group with a definite interest in preserving the value of a dollar. The second is the board's professional staff of senior economists. Administrations come and go, but the staff economist remains, and his uniquely detailed knowledge of the workings of the Fed assures him a hearing at 20th and Constitution.

Does it matter that the Fed is a focal point for the forces in the economy who fear inflation and are willing to accept somewhat higher unemployment in the hopes prices will not rise as rapidly? It may matter less than the formal structure suggests. Virtually since its inception, the Federal Reserve has had a crop of antagonistic observers in Congress. Former Secretary of the Treasury John Connally compared one of the Fed's perennial congressional foes to a cross-eyed discus thrower: "He'll never set any records for distance but he certainly keeps the crowd on its toes."

Both William McChesney Martin and the present chairman, Arthur Burns, have been sensitive to the ultimate vulnerability of the Fed's independence, and so have been reluctant to buck administration policy too dramatically. Whether the Federal Reserve's current procedures can survive the general call for more accountability is an open question. In early 1975, Congress passed a resolution that the Federal Reserve must publish its targets for growth in the money supply. But the extent to which this will tie the Fed's hands is by no means clear.

E.A.

growth of the money supply and the monetary base. During the 1960s and 1970s, however, the Fed has paid much more attention to the rate of growth of the money supply and the monetary base. Again, the fault is only partly the Fed's, since the experts cannot agree on the relative importance that should be attached to each measure. But wherever the fault, if any, may lie, the Fed's performance is bound to suffer if it acts on the basis of unreliable measures.

Emphasis. The Fed is often criticized for putting too much emphasis on preventing inflation and too little on preventing unemployment. According to various studies, it probably is true that the Fed has been more sensitive to the dangers of inflation than has the Congress or the administration. Liberals, emphasizing the great social costs of excessive unemployment, tend to denounce the Fed for such behavior. Without question, the costs of unemployment are high, as stressed in Chapter 8. Conservatives, on the other hand, often claim that governments are tempted to resort to inflation in order to produce the short-term appearance of prosperity, even though the long-term effects may be undesirable. They say that, in the short run (when the next election is decided), unemployment is more likely than inflation to result in defeat at the polls. Whether you think that the Fed has put too much emphasis on restraining inflation will depend on the relative importance that you attach to reducing unemployment, on the one hand, and reducing inflation, on the other.[11]

Should the Fed Be Governed by a Rule?

As we have just seen, important criticisms can be made of Federal Reserve policy making. The monetarists, led by Milton Friedman, go so far as to say that the Fed's attempts to "lean against the wind"—by easing money when the economy begins to dip and tightening money when the economy begins to get overheated—really do more harm than good. In their view, the Fed actually intensifies business fluctuations by changing the rate of growth of the money supply. Why? Partly because the Fed sometimes pays too much attention to measures other than the money supply. But more fundamentally, it is because the Fed tends to overreact to ephemeral changes, and because the effects of changes in the money supply on the economy occur with a long and highly variable lag. In their view, this lag is so unpredictable that the Fed—no matter how laudatory its intent—tends to intensify business fluctuations.

According to Professor Friedman and his followers, the Fed should abandon its attempts to "lean against the wind." *They propose that the Fed conform to a rule that the money supply should increase at some fixed, agreed-upon rate, such as 4 or 5 percent per year. The Fed's job would be simply to see that the money supply grows at approximately this rate.* The monetarists do not claim that a rule of this sort would prevent all business fluctuations, but they do claim that it would work better than the existing system. In particular, they feel that it would prevent the sorts of major depressions and inflations we have experienced in the past. Without major decreases in the money supply (such as occurred during the crash of 1929–33), major depressions could not occur. Without major increases in the money supply (such as occurred during World War II), major inflations could not occur. Of course, it would be nice if monetary policy could iron out minor business fluctuations as well, but in their view this simply cannot be done at present.

This proposal has received considerable attention from both economists and politicians. A number of studies have been carried out to try to estimate what would have happened if Friedman's rule had been used in the past. The

[11] For a good discussion of recent monetary and fiscal policy, see G. L. Bach, *Making Monetary and Fiscal Policy,* Washington, D.C.: Brookings Institution, 1971. Also, see the papers by Milton Friedman and Walter W. Heller in E. Mansfield, *Economics: Readings, Issues and Cases,* 2d ed., New York: Norton, 1977.

results, although by no means free of criticism, seem to indicate that such a rule might have done better than discretionary action did in preventing the Great Depression of the 1930s and the inflation during World War II. But in the period since World War II, the evidence in favor of such a rule is less persuasive. Most economists seem to believe that it would be a mistake to handcuff the Fed to a simple rule of this sort. They think that a discretionary monetary policy can outperform Friedman's rule.

Nonetheless, the debate over rules versus discretionary action goes on, and the issues are still very much alive. Professor Friedman has been able to gain important converts, including the Federal Reserve Bank of St. Louis and members of the Joint Economic Committee of Congress. Indeed, after the Fed's "stop-go" policies of 1966-68 (when the Fed tightened money sharply in 1966 and loosened it rapidly in 1967-68), the Joint Economic Committee urged the Fed to adopt a rule of the sort advocated by Friedman. In 1968, the committee complained that its advice was not being followed, and special hearings were held. The Council of Economic Advisers and the secretary of the Treasury sided with the Fed against adopting such a rule. Some academic economists favor such a rule, others oppose it, and considerable economic research is being carried out to try to clarify and resolve the questions involved.

Monetary Policy: Advantages and Disadvantages

Just as sensible wine drinkers value both Bordeaux and Burgundy (and both France and California), so most economists believe that both monetary and fiscal policy can and should play an important role in our nation's economic stabilization policies. However, this does not mean, of course, that monetary policy does not have certain advantages over fiscal policy, and vice versa. One disadvantage of monetary policy, according to many economists, is that it may be less dependable than fiscal policy when the government wants to stimulate the economy. All that monetary policy can do is to increase bank reserves. The monetary authorities cannot make the banks lend out the excess reserves—as illustrated by the situation during the 1930s when banks held huge excess reserves. And if the banks don't lend them out or invest them, there is little or no stimulation to the economy. Thus monetary policy may be less effective as a stimulant than as a rein on the economy. However, the 1970s are not the 1930s, and this assymetry may be less pronounced than has sometimes been assumed.

On the other hand, one of the most important advantages of monetary policy is that the monetary authorities can react much more quickly to changed economic conditions than can the fiscal authorities. Changes in monetary policy can be put into effect relatively quickly if the Fed wants to do so, but no matter what the Treasury, the Council of Economic Advisers, and other administration officials want to do, changes in tax and expenditure policy must be approved by the Congress. Proposed fiscal policies can be delayed and even made into a political football, as happened to the tax surcharge of 1968, which had been kicked around for a couple of years before it finally was enacted.

According to some observers, another advantage of monetary policy is that it is nondiscriminatory. In other words, the Fed does not favor particular classes of borrowers or activities; it just tightens or eases money and credit, and lets the market determine which people and industries will be benefited or hurt. But other observers retort that monetary policy is highly discriminatory, since it can hit a particular group or industry or type of borrower harder than anyone would intend. For example, the home construction industry has sometimes been clobbered by tight monetary policy.

Because of the importance of mortgage funds to the construction industry, tight money can have a big impact on its output and profits.

Summary

Monetary policy is concerned with the money supply and interest rates. Its purpose is to attain and maintain full employment without inflation. When a recession seems imminent and business is soft, the monetary authorities are likely to increase the money supply and reduce interest rates. On the other hand, when the economy is in danger of overheating and inflation threatens, the monetary authorities are likely to rein in the money supply and push up interest rates. Monetary policy and fiscal policy are aimed at much the same goals, but they use different methods to promote them. One advantage of monetary policy is that the lag between decision and action is relatively short. In view of the time involved in getting tax (and spending) changes enacted, this is an important point.

Although monetary policy is influenced by Congress, the Treasury, and other parts of the government and the public at large, the chief responsibility for the formulation of monetary policy lies with the Federal Reserve Board and the Federal Open Market Committee. To a very large extent, monetary policy operates by changing the quantity of bank reserves. The most important tool of monetary policy is open market operations, which involve the buying and selling of government securities in the open market by the Federal Reserve. When the Fed buys government securities, this increases bank reserves. When the Fed sells government securities, this reduces bank reserves. The Fed can also tighten or ease money by increasing or decreasing the discount rate or by increasing or decreasing legal reserve requirements. In addition, the Fed can use moral suasion, and it has power over maximum interest rates on time deposits and margin requirements for the purchase of stock.

As indicators of how tight or easy monetary policy is, the Fed has looked at the level of short-term interest rates, the quantity of free reserves, the rate of growth of the money supply, and the rate of growth of the monetary base. During the 1950s, the Fed paid most attention to the first two indicators; in the 1960s and 1970s, the Fed increased the amount of attention paid to the last two. To provide some idea of how monetary policy has been used, we presented a brief description of the nature and course of monetary policy during the past two decades. Also, to provide a richer picture of the use of monetary policy to stem inflation, we described in some detail the credit crunch of 1966. This episode (like the developments in 1974) is a dramatic example of the potency of monetary policy.

The Federal Reserve is faced with many difficult problems in formulating and carrying out monetary policy. It must try to see where the economy is heading, and whether—and to what extent—it should tighten or ease money to stabilize the economy. This task is made very difficult by the fact that there is often a long—and highly variable—lag between an action by the Fed and its effect on the economy. There is also considerable disagreement over the best way to measure how tight or easy monetary policy is.

There has been criticism of various kinds regarding the performance of the Federal Reserve. Often, the Fed is criticized for paying too little attention to the long lags between its actions and their effects on the economy. Also, some critics claim that the Fed puts too much emphasis on fighting inflation and too little on preventing unemployment. Some monetarists, led by Milton Friedman, believe that monetary policy would be improved if discretionary policy were replaced by a rule that the Fed should increase the money supply at some fixed, agreed-on rate, such as 4 or 5 percent per year.

The Fed, the Council of Economic Advisers, the Treasury, and many academic economists have argued against the adoption of such a rule, but Friedman's proposal has won some support in the Joint Economic Committee and elsewhere. The debate over rules versus discretionary policy goes on, and is one of the liveliest in present-day economics.

CONCEPTS FOR REVIEW

Monetary policy
Federal Reserve Board
Federal Open Market Committee
Discount rate
Changes in legal reserve requirements
Easy money
Moral suasion
Selective credit control
Free reserves
Monetary base
Margin requirements
Credit crunch
Tightening money

QUESTIONS FOR DISCUSSION AND REVIEW

1. Suppose that the Federal Reserve buys $5 million worth of government securities from U.S. Steel. Insert the effects in the blanks below.

Effects on Fed's balance sheet:

Assets	Liabilities and Net Worth
Securities ______	Member bank reserves ______

Effects on balance sheet of U.S. Steel's bank:

Assets	Liabilities and net worth
Reserves ______	Demand deposits ______

2. Suppose that the Federal Reserve sells $5 million worth of government securities to U.S. Steel. What is the effect on the quantity of bank reserves?

3. "When the Fed increases legal reserve requirements, it loosens credit, because the banks have more reserves." Comment and evaluate.

4. "Regulation Q interferes with the functioning of free markets, and should be abandoned. By establishing a floor under interest rates, it promotes inflation." Comment and evaluate.

5. Suppose that you have $5,000 to invest. At a restaurant you overhear someone saying that the Fed is almost certain to increase the discount rate dramatically. If this rumor is correct, do you think that you should invest now, or wait until after the increase in the discount rate? Or doesn't it matter? Be sure to explain the reasons for your preference (or lack of it) in this regard.

6. "The Fed should keep interest rates low to promote prosperity. Unfortunately, however, it is dominated by bankers who like high interest rates because they increase bank profits." Comment and evaluate.

7. "The Fed is like a driver whose steering wheel takes about a minute to influence the car's wheels." Comment and evaluate.

8. According to Walter W. Heller, "In the imperfect world in which we actually operate, beset by all sorts of rigidities, . . . [Friedman's] money supply rule might, in fact, be destabilizing."[12] Comment and evaluate.

9. According to Henry Wallich, a member of the Fed's Board of Governors, although "monetary policy has so often been wrong that it [may seem] preferable to deprive it of discretion and subject it to a fixed rule, . . . this reasoning is fallacious."
Do you agree? Why or why not? How would you go about testing this proposition?

10. According to Sherman Maisel, William McChesney Martin, former chairman of the Federal Reserve Board, felt "that the primary function of the Federal Reserve Board was to determine what was necessary to maintain a sound currency. . . . [To Martin] it is as immoral for a country today to allow the value of its currency to fall as it was for kings of old to clip coinage." Do you agree with Martin's views? Why or why not?

[12] Milton Friedman and Walter W. Heller, *Monetary vs. Fiscal Policy,* New York: Norton, 1969.

16 Problems of Economic Stabilization Policy

Despite the advances in economic knowledge during the past 30 years, the United States, like other countries, finds it very difficult to achieve full employment with stable prices. Monetary policy is an important means toward that end. And in the eyes of most economists, so is fiscal policy. Yet, despite the power of monetary and fiscal policies, we are still a long way from the desired degree of economic stability. Judging from the experience of the past 30 years, we have learned how to avoid very serious depressions, but we have not yet learned how to attain full employment with stable prices. Excessive unemployment and excessive inflation persist.

Two important reasons why our performance has been less than satisfactory are evident. First, economists are still uncertain about many effects of monetary and fiscal policies. For one thing, as pointed out in previous chapters, the views of the monetarists differ from those of the Keynesians. Second, if some of the inflationary pressures in our society stem from an upward push of costs (or profits), some form of incomes policy may be needed to quell undesirable inflation. In this chapter, we discuss both of these problems at length.

The General Problem of Achieving Economic Stability

As a first step, let's review how fiscal and monetary policies can be used to promote full employment without inflation. We begin with fiscal policy. With a given level of potential output or capacity, actual net national product is determined by desired spending. Fiscal policy uses the government's expenditures and taxes to influence desired spending. Specifically, when NNP is at less than its full-employment level, increases in government expenditures or reductions in taxes can be used to push it up to this level, and thus reduce excessive unemployment. Or when there is excessive inflation, decreases in government expenditures or increases in taxes can reduce total spending, and thus curb inflation.

Monetary policy uses the government's power over the quantity of money to influence NNP. Increases in the money supply tend to increase the money value of NNP, whereas reductions in the money supply tend to reduce the money value of NNP. The route by which the quantity of money has this effect on NNP is a subject of controversy. The majority, or Keynesian, view is that increases in the money supply reduce interest rates, which stimulates investment, which increases NNP. Conversely, decreases in the money supply increase interest rates, which cuts investment, which reduces NNP. (Many Keynesians, at least in more recent years, also recognize that changes in the money supply influence the net worth of consumers, and thus have an impact on consumption expenditures.) Monetarists, relying heavily on the quantity theory of money, relate changes in the money supply more directly to changes in nominal, or money, NNP.

The controversy between the monetarists and the Keynesians has received so much attention in recent years that one might think that, if it were resolved, the problem of formulating monetary and fiscal policies to achieve full employment with stable prices would be licked. This is by no means true. However the controversy is resolved, no existing economic model can give policy makers reliable quantitative estimates of how much the money supply should be altered, or government expenditures should be changed, or tax rates should be modified, to achieve full employment with stable prices. To a considerable extent, the knowledge we have is qualitative, not quantitative. Until we can better estimate the quantitative effects of policy changes of various magnitudes, it will be unreasonable to expect that monetary and fiscal policies can be used with precision to achieve our national goals.

In addition, it must be emphasized that both the Keynesian and the monetarist models are just that—models. In other words, they are convenient and useful simplifications; and, as such, they abstract from many important aspects of reality. In particular, they take little or no notice of the possibility that inflation may arise because of an upward push of costs, and they tell us very little about what to do when there is both excessive unemployment and excessive inflation. Nor do they say much about the extent of the lags between the time when policy makers want to act and the time when such action is approved and taken, or the lags between the time when action is taken and the time when its economic effects are felt.

Further, it must be recognized that government decisions are not dictated by considerations of economic stabilization alone. Thus, even if economic models were completely accurate and the government knew how to achieve full employment at stable prices, it would not always choose to do so. For example, the political party in power may be committed to a particular policy designed to alleviate a certain social ill, like poverty or discrimination. To carry out this objective, it may increase government expenditures at a time when, from the point of view of economic stabilization, it would be better to reduce them. Or in wartime, modern military needs require enormous outlays, but the political party in power may not be willing to take the unpopular step of raising taxes, even though this would be desirable for economic stabilization. Or consider an upcoming presidential election. The incumbent president may initiate or expand programs to make people feel prosperous in the short run, even though this may be destabilizing in the longer run. After all, the important thing is to win the election and prevent that other fellow, whoever he may be, from ruining the country!

Monetarists versus Keynesians

The debate between the monetarists and the Keynesians has not been limited to the classroom and scholarly gatherings. It has spilled over onto the pages of the daily newspapers and aroused considerable interest in Congress and other parts of the government. At heart, the argument is over what determines the level of output, employment, and prices. The Keynesians put more emphasis on the federal budget than do the monetarists, who put more emphasis on the money supply than do the Keynesians. To understand this debate fully, we need to know something about the recent development of economic thought. Up until the Great Depression of the 1930s, the prevailing theory was that NNP, expressed in real terms, would tend automatically to its full-employment value. (Recall from Chapter 9 the classical economists' reasons for clinging to this belief.) Moreover, the prevailing theory was that the price level could be explained by the crude quantity theory of money. In other words, the price level, P, was assumed to be proportional to the quantity of money, M, because $MV = PQ$, and real NNP, Q, and the velocity of money, V, were thought to be essentially constant.

During the Great Depression of the 1930s, this body of theory was largely discredited and abandoned. Clearly, NNP was not tending automatically toward its full-employment level. And the crude quantity theory seemed to have little value. In contrast, Keynes's ideas, which stressed the importance of fiscal policy, seemed to offer the sort of theoretical guidance and policy prescriptions that were needed. Keynesians did not neglect the use of monetary policy entirely, but they felt that it played a subsidiary role. Particularly in depressions, monetary policy seemed to be of relatively little value, since "you can't push on a string." In other words, monetary policy can make money available, but it cannot insure that it will be spent.

During the 1940s, 1950s, and early 1960s, the Keynesian view was definitely predominant, here and abroad. But by the mid-1960s, it was being challenged seriously by the monetarists, led by Professor Milton Friedman and his supporters. The monetarist view harked back to the pre-Keynesian doctrine in many respects. In particular, it emphasized the importance of the equation of exchange as an analytical device and the importance of the quantity of money as a tool of economic policy. The monetarist view gained adherents in the late 1960s. Partly responsible was the long delay in passing the surtax of 1968, for the reluctance of the administration to propose and of Congress to enact the new levy vividly illustrated some of the difficulties in using fiscal policy for stabilization. In contrast, monetary policy seemed to assure only a short lag between policy decisions and their implementation. Another factor favoring the monetarists was that the economy was plagued by inflation, not unemployment. Monetary policy, by controlling the quantity of money, can quite effectively restrain inflation, even if, under certain circumstances, it may not be so effective in reducing unemployment. "You may be able to pull on a string," even if "you can't push on a string."

Causes of Business Fluctuations: The Opposing Views

Monetarists and Keynesians tend to disagree over the basic causes of business fluctuations. As seen by monetarists, major depressions, such as the Great Depression of the 1930s, are due to decreases in the money supply. In the Great Depression, for example, the money supply contracted by over ¼. Similarly, major inflations, in their view, are due to increases in the money supply. Looking at recent developments, they assert that the inflation of the late 1960s and early 1970s was due to the increases that occurred in the money supply.

Keynesians, on the other hand, reject the monetarist view that money is the predominant factor accounting for business fluctuations. To the Keynesians, this view is simplistic and inadequate. The Keynesian view is that both monetary and nonmonetary factors cause business fluctuations. Among the important nonmonetary factors are changes in desired investment or shifts in the consumption function. (We have discussed many of these nonmonetary factors in Chapter 12.) The Keynesians do not deny that there is a correlation between changes in the money supply and changes in NNP, but they believe that the monetarists tend to mix up cause and effect. The Keynesians argue that increases in desired spending may bring about a greater demand for money, which in turn causes the money supply to increase. Under these circumstances, the line of causation may be the opposite of that posited by the monetarists.

Monetarists and Keynesians also tend to differ over the extent to which our economy is stable. The monetarists are generally more inclined to believe that, if the money supply is managed properly by the government, the free-market economy will tend automatically toward full employment with reasonably stable prices. Although the monetarists are by no means unanimous in this respect, they tend to emphasize the self-regulating characteristics of a free-enterprise economy. In their view, business fluctuations must often be laid at the door of the monetary authorities, whose well-meaning attempts to stabilize the economy frequently do more harm than good.

In contrast, the Keynesians are convinced that a free-enterprise economy has relatively weak self-regulating mechanisms. Like Keynes himself, they argue that the equilibrium level of national output may remain for a long time below the level required for full employment. (See Chapter 9 for Keynes's views.) Also, they argue that there is nothing in the modern economy to prevent considerable inflation, even if the money supply does not increase greatly. Thus, in their view, the government has a much more positive discretionary role to play in stabilizing the economy than visualized by the monetarists.

Effects of the Interest Rate: The Opposing Views

Many of the basic disagreements between the Keynesians and monetarists center about the quantitative effects of the interest rate.[1] These disagreements are of three kinds:

Demand for money. The first disagreement is over the demand for money. Recall from Chapter 13 that, because the cost of holding money is the interest forgone, the quantity of money demanded goes down as the interest

[1] Both the Keynesian and monetarist groups contain a variety of opinions; thus it is somewhat misleading to refer to *the* Keynesian view or *the* monetarist view. All that we can do here is summarize and contrast one major version of each of these theories, leaving a more detailed treatment to more advanced texts.

Figure 16.1
Keynesian and Monetarist Assumptions Concerning the Demand for Money
Keynesians tend to believe that the quantity of money demanded is more sensitive to the interest rate than do monetarists. Thus, if the interest rate falls from r to r', the quantity of money demanded increases from D_0 to D_3 under Keynesian assumptions, but only from D_1 to D_2 under monetarist assumptions.

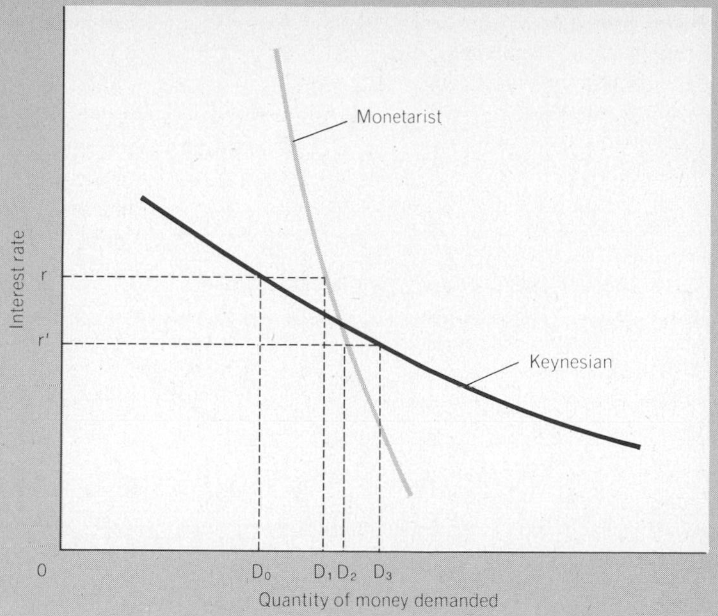

rate goes up—as shown in Figure 13.3. *According to the monetarists, the quantity of money demanded is relatively insensitive to changes in the interest rate; whereas to Keynesians, it is very sensitive to such changes.* Thus, as shown in Figure 16.1, monetarists believe that the relationship between the quantity of money demanded and the interest rate is more nearly vertical than do Keynesians. The reason is that the monetarists believe that the transactions motive for holding money is particularly important, and the interest rate is less important than people's incomes in determining the transactions demand for money. Keynesians, on the other hand, put more emphasis on the speculative motive for holding money, where the interest rate plays a major role.

Supply of money. The second disagreement is over the extent to which the supply of money is influenced by the interest rate. *According to the monetarists, the supply of money is relatively insensitive to changes in the interest rate; whereas to Keynesians, it is quite sensitive to such changes.* In other words, the monetarists believe that the relationship between the money supply and the interest rate shown in Figure 16.2 is nearly vertical, whereas the Keynesians do not. The reason is the monetarists believe that banks will generally keep few excess reserves, with the result that they will be unable to vary the money supply in response to changes in loan demand and in interest rates. Keynesians, on the other hand, believe that banks generally hold considerable excess reserves during depressions, and that they can and do increase the money supply when loan demand and interest rates are high.

Total desired spending. The third disagreement is over the extent to which total desired spending is sensitive to changes in the interest rate. *According to the monetarists, total expenditure is very sensitive to changes in the interest rate; whereas to some Keynesians, it is not so sensitive to such changes.* Thus the monetarists believe that the relationship between total desired spending and the interest rate shown in Figure 16.3 is close to horizontal, whereas the Keynesians believe that it is closer to vertical. The

Figure 16.2
Keynesian and Monetarist Assumptions Concerning the Supply of Money
Keynesians tend to believe that the supply of money is more sensitive to the interest rate than do monetarists. Thus, if the interest rate falls from r to r', the supply of money drops from S_3 to S_0 under Keynesian assumptions, but only from S_2 to S_1 under monetarist assumptions.

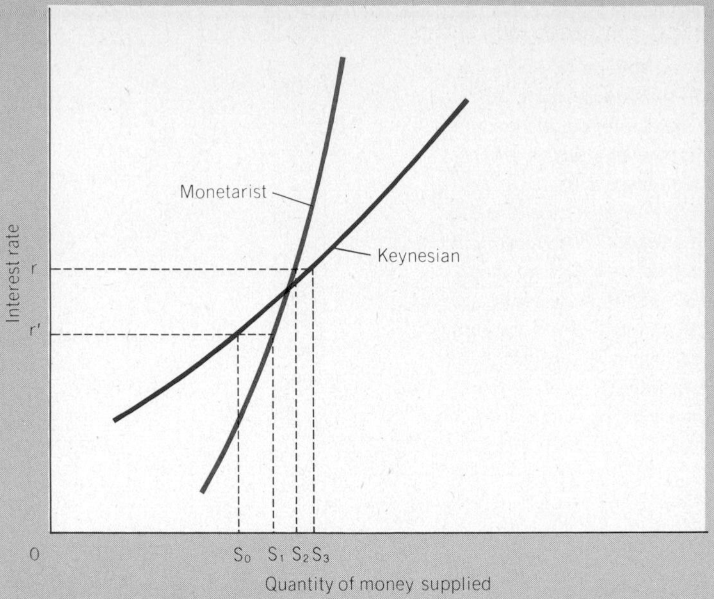

reason is that the monetarists are convinced that firms' investment decisions, as well as investment in residential housing and expenditure on consumer durable goods, depend considerably on the interest rate, whereas the Keynesians feel that, although the interest rate has an effect, it is smaller than the monetarists assume. According to the Keynesians, other factors, such as existing business conditions and businessmen's expectations, are far more important than the interest rate in determining total expenditure.

The Effect of Monetary Policy: The Opposing Views

Given the three disagreements described in the preceding section, it is easy to see why monetarists believe that monetary policy is of preeminent importance, whereas Keynesians tend to believe that it is of lesser importance. As a first step toward understanding why this is so, one must recognize that *the equilibrium interest rate must be at the level where the quantity of money demanded equals the quantity of money supplied.* If the public wants to hold less money than is supplied, the interest rate will tend to decline in order to encourage people to demand more money. If the public wants to hold more money than is supplied, the interest rate will tend to increase in order to make people cut back on their demand for money. Only if the quantity of money demanded equals the quantity of money supplied is the interest rate at its equilibrium level.

Suppose that the monetary authorities increase the money supply, with the result that the *money supply curve* (that is, the relationship between the money supply and the interest rate in Figure 16.2) shifts to the right. Under both the Keynesian and monetarist assumptions, there will be a fall in the equilibrium interest rate, since the quantity of money supplied will exceed the quantity of money demanded at the existing interest rate. But, as shown in Figure 16.4, there will be a greater fall in the interest rate under the monetarist assumptions (shown in panel B of Figure 16.4) than under the Keynesian assumptions (shown in panel A). Under the monetarist assumptions, the interest

Figure 16.3
Keynesian and Monetarist Assumptions Concerning the Effect of the Interest Rate on Total Desired Spending
Keynesians tend to believe that total desired spending is less sensitive to the interest rate than do monetarists. Thus, if the interest rate falls from *r* to *r′*, total desired spending increases from T_0 to T_3 under monetarist assumptions, but only from T_1 to T_2 under Keynesian assumptions.

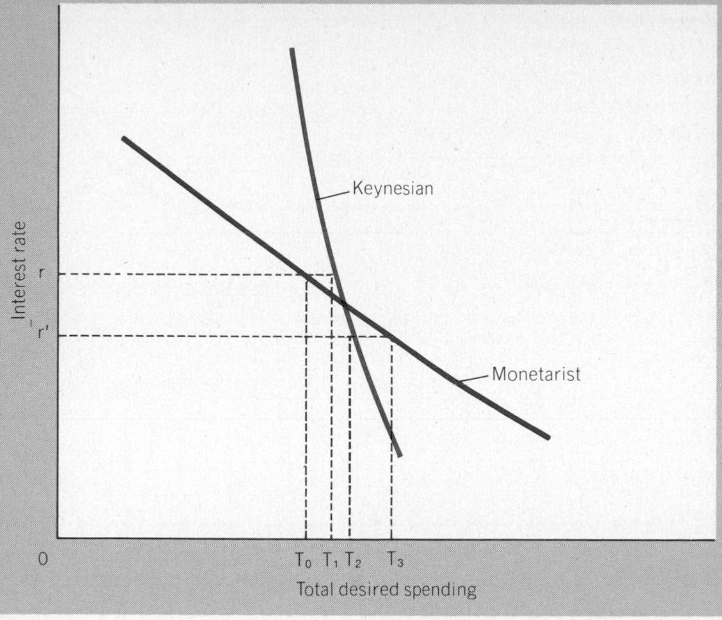

rate will fall to r_1, whereas under the Keynesian assumptions, it will fall to r_2.

Further, the resulting fall in the interest rate will have a greater effect on total expenditure under the monetarist assumptions than under the Keynesian assumptions. Under the monetarist assumptions, the fall in the interest rate to r_1 results in total expenditure increasing to X_1. Under the Keynesian assumptions, the fall in the interest rate to r_2 results in total expenditure increasing to X_2. Clearly, *the effect of the increase in the money supply on total expenditure is greater under the monetarist assumptions than under the Keynesian assumptions*—and it is not hard to see why monetarists tend to be more enthusiastic about the effects of monetary policy than are the Keynesians.[2]

The Effect of Fiscal Policy: The Opposing Views

The monetarists attack the Keynesian view that fiscal policy works in the way we described in Chapter 11. According to the monetarists, whether the government runs a surplus or deficit has little or no long-run effect on NNP, except insofar as the government finances the surplus or deficit in a way that affects the stock of money. For example, if the government runs a deficit and finances it by borrowing from the public, the money supply will be unchanged. Thus the monetarists would argue that such a deficit has little or no long-run expansionary effect on NNP. On the other hand, if the government finances its deficit by increasing the money supply, the monetarists would expect NNP to increase, but as a result of the expansion of the money supply, not of the deficit. Thus the monetarists claim that the expansion of NNP after the tax cut of 1964 was due to considerable increases in the money supply, not to the tax cut.

Given the assumptions that they make, it is not difficult to see why the monetarists come to this conclusion. Suppose, for example, that an increase occurs in government expenditure. The result, of course, will be a shift to the right of the expenditure function in the righthand

[2] In Figure 16.4, the analysis is simplified in a number of respects. For a more complete analysis of the topics discussed in this and the following sections, see the Appendix to this chapter.

Figure 16.4
Effects of Monetary Policy under Keynesian and Monetarist Assumptions
An increase in the money supply results in a bigger drop in the interest rate, and a bigger increase in spending, under monetarist assumptions than under Keynesian assumptions.

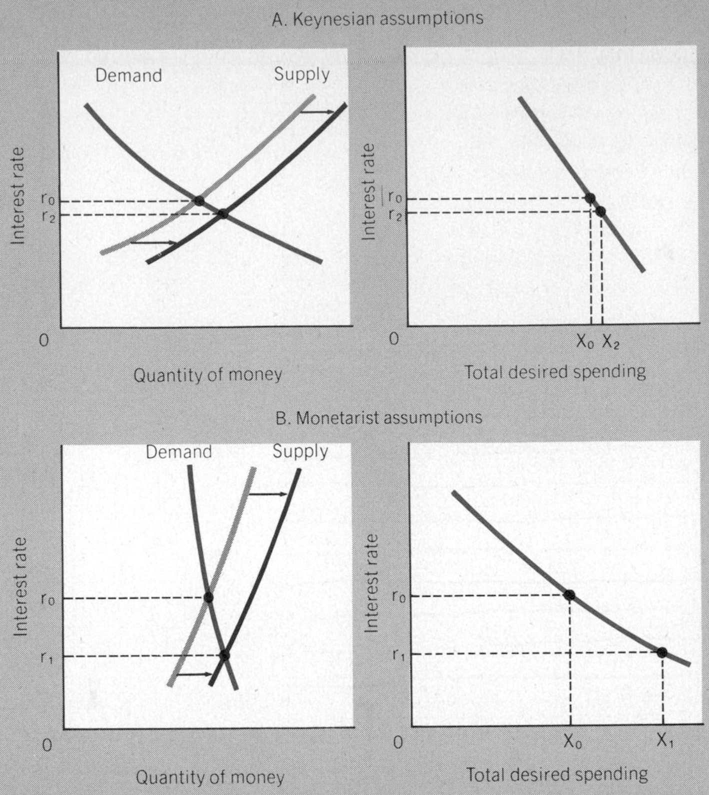

panel of Figure 16.5B. (Note that the B panels in Figure 16.5 are the relevant ones here, since we are concerned with the monetarist assumptions.) If this function shifts from E_1 to E_2, the public will demand more money for transaction purposes, and the *demand curve for money*—that is the relationship between the quantity of money demanded and the interest rate (which we called the liquidity preference function in Chapter 13)—will shift to the right, as shown in the lefthand panel of Figure 16.5B. Thus the interest rate will increase to r_3. This relatively great increase in the interest rate will cut private expenditure on consumption goods and investment, and total expenditure will be X_3. (If the interest rate had not risen, total expenditure would have been X_5.) Since X_3 is not appreciably greater than X_0, the increase in government expenditure has little effect on total expenditure: its principal effect is to substitute public for private expenditure.

Based on their own quite different assumptions, the Keynesians conclude, of course, that fiscal policy is very effective. To see why, assume once again that an increase occurs in government expenditure, the result being a shift from E_1 to E_2 of the expenditure function in the righthand panel of Figure 16.5A. (This time, the A panels are the relevant ones, since they contain the Keynesian assumptions.) Once again, as total expenditure rises, the public will demand more money for transactions purposes, thus increasing the interest rate. But according to the Keynesians the increase in the interest rate will be relatively small, since there will be an expansion in the money supply and the quantity of money demanded is relatively sensitive to the interest rate. Thus the interest

Figure 16.5
Effects of Fiscal Policy under Keynesian and Monetarist Assumptions.
An increase in government expenditure results in a bigger rise in the interest rate, and a smaller increase in spending, under monetarist assumptions than under Keynesian assumptions.

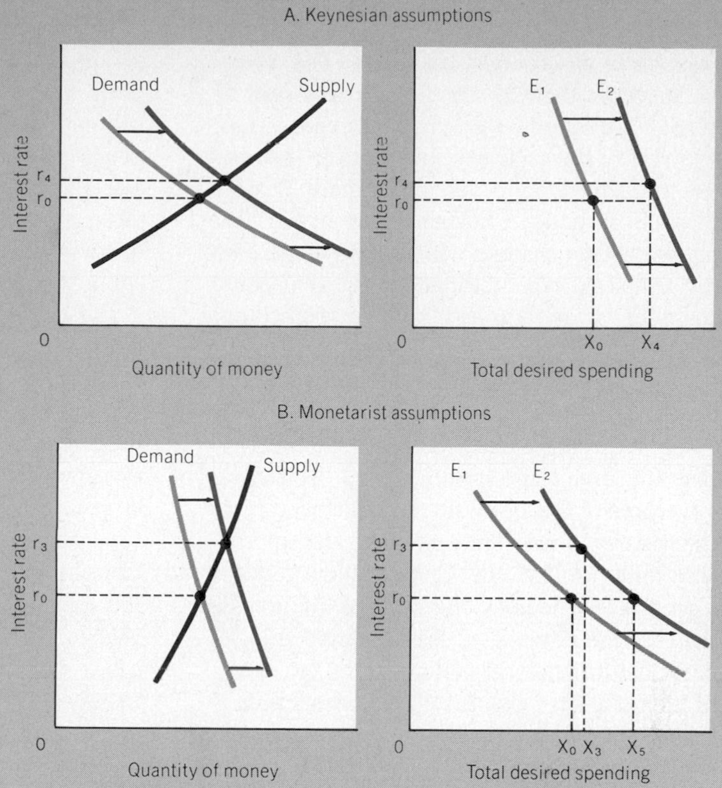

rate rises only to r_4, and total expenditure will be X_4. Since X_4 is much greater than X_0, the increase in government expenditure has a great effect on total expenditure, based on the Keynesian assumptions.

Policy Recommendations: Keynesians and Monetarists

Many, but not all, leading monetarists advocate the establishment of a rule to govern monetary policy. In the previous chapter, we discussed the arguments of Friedman and his supporters for such a rule. You will recall their charge that the Federal Reserve's monetary policies have often caused economic instability. Because of the difficulties in forecasting the future state of the economy and the fairly long and variable time lag in the effect of changes in the money supply, the Fed, in the eyes of many leading monetarists, frequently has caused excessive inflation or unemployment by its discretionary policies. According to the monetarists, we would be better off with a rule stipulating that the money supply should grow steadily at a constant rate, say 4 or 5 percent per year.

The Keynesians retort that such a rule would handcuff the monetary authorities and contribute to economic instability, since discretionary monetary policies are required to keep the economy on a reasonably even keel. The Keynesians grant that the Fed sometimes makes mistakes, but they assert that things would be worse if the Fed could not pursue the policies that a given set of circumstances seems to call for.

The monetarists and Keynesians also differ

over many aspects of fiscal policy. The monetarists claim that the Congress is very slow to change tax rates and government expenditures to stabilize the economy, and that for this reason monetary policy is much more flexible than fiscal policy. Further, they argue that temporary tax changes will have little effect on consumption expenditures because household spending is determined by permanent, not transitory, income. Recall the permanent-income hypothesis regarding the consumption function, discussed in Chapter 9.

To these arguments, the Keynesians reply that the budgetary machinery in the federal government has been altered considerably in the past few years. The new budgetary apparatus, built around the Congressional Budget Committees and the Congressional Budget Office, has the potential at least to sharpen legislative action on fiscal policy. As for the effects of temporary tax changes, the Keynesians deny that such changes have little or no effect on consumer spending. In particular, they tend to feel that expenditures on consumer durable goods are affected considerably by such tax changes.

An Overview of the Debate

The debate between the monetarists and the Keynesians is important and illuminating. It has forced the entire economics profession to review its thinking about the effects of monetary and fiscal policies. This is the sort of ferment that keeps a discipline healthy and vital. Chances are that it will be many years before the issues are completely resolved, but in the past decade, considerable strides have been taken toward understanding the real differences between these two schools of thought.

The Keynesian theory, in its simplest form, emphasizes that the economy will be in equilibrium only when consumers are spending at the rate they desire, given their income, and when firms are investing at the rate they desire. The monetarist theory, in its simplest form, emphasizes that the economy will be in equilibrium only when consumers and firms are willing to hold the existing quantity of money, given their income and the quantity of other assets that they hold. In truth, of course, both these conditions for equilibrium must be fulfilled: neither alone is sufficient to guarantee equilibrium.

For example, what happens when the government increases the quantity of money by handing out some newly printed money to the public? Let's begin with the public's asset holdings. Since the public has more money than before, it will rearrange its portfolio of assets, assuming that it had the portfolio it desired prior to the increase in the money supply. Consumers and firms, finding themselves with more money than they want to hold, will exchange money for other types of assets. In other words, they will spend some of their money holdings—and will continue to spend money until, once again, their portfolio of assets is balanced so as to maximize their satisfaction.

Second, consider how the increase in the public's income due to the increase in the money supply will affect spending. The people who receive the newly printed money, finding that their disposable incomes have risen, want to spend more on consumption goods. Firms that receive the new money are also likely to want to increase their investment expenditures. Both consumers and firms will continue to spend more until, once again, their expenditures are in the desired relationship to their incomes. Note that this adjustment process, stressed by Keynesian theory, goes on simultaneously with the adjustment process described in the previous paragraph, which is related to the monetarist theory.

Once one recognizes that both processes go on simultaneously, it is easy to see that much of the debate between the Keynesians and monetarists is really over which of two simplifications is more fruitful—or does less violence

Milton Friedman versus Walter W. Heller

Seldom do the *New York Times,* the *Wall Street Journal,* and *Vogue* cover a debate between two economists. That they covered the seventh annual Arthur K. Salomon Lecture at New York University in November 1968 is a tribute to the impact each of the protagonists—Milton Friedman and Walter W. Heller—has had on presidents, potential presidents, and public opinion in the monetary versus fiscal debate.

Friedman, a professor at the University of Chicago, has written on as wide a range of subjects as any living economist. A staunch conservative, he nevertheless originated such "liberal" proposals as the educational voucher (used experimentally in Vermont and North Dakota districts) and the negative income tax. In keeping with his conservative philosophy, he has attacked the evils of Social Security and the minimum wage, praised the virtues of abolishing licensing of professions, and argued the intimate connection between capitalism and freedom. Although never a full-time government employee since his World War II stint with the Treasury Department, he has served in his spare time as economic adviser to presidential candidate Barry Goldwater and to President Nixon (before Nixon left the faith and imposed price and wage controls).

FRIEDMAN-HELLER DEBATE, NOVEMBER 1968.

But Friedman is most prominently identified, at least within the economics profession, as the defender (and in large part the creator) of monetarism. While Keynesianism triumphant swept the economics profession in the postwar years, Friedman and a few University of Chicago colleagues were investigating the historical connection between money and U.S. economic history, eventually persuading the Federal Reserve Bank of St. Louis to gather and publish statistics using their concepts and fortifying the monetarist arguments until the inflation of the late sixties made monetarism fashionable again. In 1976, Friedman won the Nobel Prize for his work.

By contrast, Walter W. Heller, a professor at the University of Minnesota, has been a liberal and a political activist (at least by economists' standards). As chairman of the Council of Economic Advisers under both Presidents Kennedy and Johnson, he was a principal architect of the 1962 investment tax credit and the 1964 tax cut. He enjoyed a close and sympathetic relationship with the New Frontiersmen, and as a consequence, the council assumed a broader, more activist role than it has enjoyed before or since. He was a leading spokesman for the use of fiscal and monetary policies, not merely to avoid major depressions and inflations, but to smooth out the smaller fluctuations in the economy.

In their debate, Heller posed many basic questions concerning monetarism: "Which money-supply indicator do you believe? Can one read enough from money supply without weighing also shifts in demand and interest rates? Don't observed variations in monetary time lags and velocity cast serious doubt on any simple relation between money supply and GNP? Can a rigid monetary rule find happiness in a world beset with rigidities and rather limited adjustment capabilities? That is, is the rigid Friedman rule perhaps a formula made in heaven, that will work only in heaven?" These questions remain at the heart of the continuing debate between Keynesians and monetarists. E.A.

to reality. According to the Keynesians, the multiplier is more stable than the velocity of money, so that changes in taxes or government spending have a more predictable effect on total spending than changes in the quantity of money.[3] According to the monetarists, the velocity of money is more predictable than the multiplier, which means that the effects of changes in the quantity of money on total spending are more predictable than changes in taxes or government spending. Much econometric work is being done at present to try to resolve this issue. Although the evidence as yet is inconclusive, it is reasonable to expect that in the foreseeable future we will be much better able to answer this question.

Cost-Push Inflation and the Phillips Curve

Whether they lean toward the monetarist or the Keynesian route to economic stability, policy makers have found inflation to be a stubborn foe. In previous chapters, we described ***demand-pull inflation,*** a situation in which there is too much aggregate spending. The $C + I + G$ line is too high, resulting in inflationary pressure. Or, put in terms of the equation of exchange, $M \times V$ is too high, so that P is pushed up: too much money is chasing too few goods. This kind of inflation stems from the demand or spending behavior of the nation's consumers, firms, and government. We have had many inflations of this kind. The major inflations during the Revolutionary and Civil Wars were basically caused by demand-pull factors; and so, much more recently, was the inflation arising from the Vietnam War. In these extreme cases, the rise in the price level can be treated as a matter of arithmetic: with all resources fully utilized, national output is fixed, and prices rise in proportion to the increase in total spending.

However, in the view of many economists, demand-pull inflation is not the only kind of inflation. There is also a different kind—***cost-push inflation.*** The process underlying cost-push inflation is not as well understood as it should be, but, according to many economists, it works something like this: costs are increased, perhaps because unions push up wages, and in an attempt to protect their profit margins, firms push up prices. These price increases affect the costs of other firms and the consumer's cost of living. As the cost of living goes up, labor feels entitled to, and obtains, higher wages to offset the higher living costs. Firms again pass on the cost increase to the consumer in the form of a price increase. This so-called ***wage-price spiral*** is at the heart of cost-push inflation.

Basically, in cost-push inflation, *the culprits are unions and firms with considerable market power.* In a world of perfect competition, both in product and input markets, cost-push inflation could not occur. In such a world, labor could not increase wages in the face of appreciable unemployment. If it tried, competition would bring wages back down. Nor could firms increase prices to protect their profits. Competition would put a tight ceiling on their pricing policy. Under perfect competition, inflation could occur (make no mistake about that), but it would have to be of the demand-pull type. Whether big labor or big business initiates the wage-price spiral is very difficult to determine in practice, and may well vary from case to case. But whoever makes the first move, the result is inflation.

In some cases, increases in materials prices may play a major role in cost-push inflation. When the oil-producing countries increased the price of crude oil in early 1974, this resulted in price increases in a wide variety of

[3] Data we have seen (recall Figure 13.6) confirm that velocity is far from constant. For one thing, it varies with interest rates and with people's expectations. However, sophisticated monetarists would say that the velocity function—a functional relationship derived from the demand for money—is stable. This is different from saying that velocity as a calculated number is stable.

products that are made (directly or indirectly) from petroleum. Because these price increases were not offset by price reductions elsewhere in the economy, the over-all price level increased (and at a very rapid rate) in 1974. Of course, the price hike for crude oil (and other materials) was by no means the sole reason for this inflation. But unquestionably it did play a noteworthy role in exacerbating it. More will be said on this score in subsequent sections.

Generally it is difficult, if not impossible, to sort out cost-push inflation from demand-pull inflation. However, one case of fairly pure cost-push inflation occurred in the late 1950s. This was a period of considerable slack in the economy. You will recall from Chapter 12 that a recession occurred in 1957–58. By 1958 6.8 percent of the labor force was unemployed. Nonetheless, wage increases took place during the late 1950s—and at a rate in excess of the rate of increase of labor productivity (output per man-hour).[4] For example, average earnings (outside agriculture) went up by 4 percent between 1957 and 1961, while labor productivity went up by 2½ percent. Moreover, prices increased each year—by 3 percent from 1956 to 1957, and by 2 percent from 1957 to 1958.

Certainly this seemed to be a different phenomenon than the demand-pull inflation described in previous chapters. There was no evidence that too much money was chasing too few goods. Instead, this was apparently a case of cost-push inflation. Commenting on the situation in the middle and late 1950s, the Council of Economic Advisers concluded, "The movement of wages during this period reflected in part the power exercised in labor markets by strong unions and the power possessed by large companies to pass on higher wage costs in higher prices."[5]

[4] In the next section, we shall discuss the importance of the rate of increase of output per man-hour. For present purposes, it is sufficient to note that the greater the rate of increase of output per man-hour, the larger the rate of increase of cost per man-hour that can be absorbed without an increase in unit cost.

[5] *1962 Annual Report of the Council of Economic Advisers*, Washington, D.C.: Government Printing Office, p. 175.

The Phillips Curve

What determines the rate at which labor can push up wages? If you think about it for a while, you will probably agree that *labor's ability to increase wages depends on the level of unemployment. The more unemployment, the more difficult it is for labor to increase wages.* Although perfect competition by no means prevails in the labor market, there is enough competition so that the presence of a pool of unemployed workers puts some damper on wage increases. In nonunion industries and occupations, workers are much less inclined to push for wage increases—and employers are much less inclined to accept them—when lots of people are looking for work. In unionized industries and occupations, unions are less likely to put their members through the hardship of a strike—and firms have less to lose from a strike—when business is bad and unemployment is high.

Because wages tend to be increased at a greater rate when unemployment is low, one would expect the rate of increase of wages in any year to be inversely related to the level of unemployment. This expectation is borne out by the available evidence. In a particular period of time in the United States, suppose that the rate of increase in wages tends to be related to the level of unemployment in the way shown in Figure 16.6. According to this figure, which is based on hypothetical, but reasonable, numbers, wages tend to rise by about 7 percent per year when 9 percent of the labor force is unemployed, by about 8½ percent per year when 7 percent of the labor force is unemployed, and by about 10 percent per year when 6 percent of the labor force is unemployed. *The relationship between the rate of increase of wages and the level of unemployment is the* ***Phillips curve.*** It was named after A. W. Phillips, the British economist who first called attention to it.

Given the Phillips curve in Figure 16.6 it is

Figure 16.6
The Phillips Curve
The Phillips curve shows the relationship between the rate of increase of wages and the level of unemployment. This curve is drawn on the assumption that little or no inflation is expected.

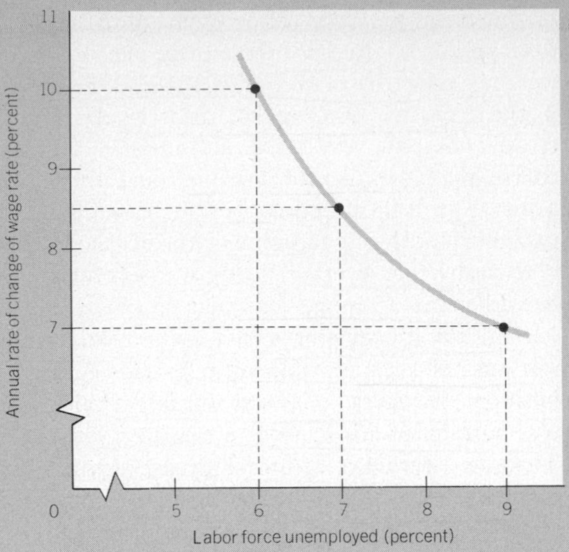

a simple matter to determine the relationship between the rate of inflation and the level of unemployment. If C is the total cost—wage and nonwage—per man-hour, the total cost per unit of output equals $C \times M \div O$, where M is the total number of man-hours worked and O is total output. This says no more than that total cost per unit of output equals total cost per man-hour times the number of man-hours divided by the number of units of output. Thus total cost per unit of output equals total cost per man-hour divided by output per man-hour. (Output per man-hour is often called ***labor productivity.***) Since the rate of increase of a ratio is the rate of increase of the numerator minus the rate of increase of the denominator, it follows that the *rate of increase of total cost per unit of output equals the rate of increase of total cost per man-hour minus the rate of increase of output per man-hour.*

Suppose that the rate of increase of prices equals the rate of increase of total cost per unit of output, and that the rate of increase of total cost per man-hour equals the rate of increase of wages. Then *the rate of increase of prices equals the rate of increase of wages minus the rate of increase of output per man-hour.* Suppose too that the rate of increase of output per man-hour (that is, labor productivity) is 3 percent per year. Then the rate of increase of prices equals the rate of increase of wages minus 3 percent. Consequently, the relationship between the rate of increase in prices and the level of unemployment is as shown in Figure 16.7.

There is, of course, a simple relationship between the curve in Figure 16.6 and the curve in Figure 16.7. The curve in Figure 16.7 (which shows the relationship between *price* increases and unemployment) is always 3 percentage points below the curve in Figure 16.6 (which shows the relationship between *wage* increases and unemployment). Why? Because the rate of increase of prices—under the assumptions set forth above—always equals the rate of increase of wages minus 3 percent.

At this point it should be clear that the curve in Figure 16.7 is none other than the curve encountered before, in Figure 8.3. Our present discussion has added an account of how this relationship is related to, and based on, the Phillips curve.

Shifts in the Phillips Curve

Before we get too impressed by the apparent accuracy of the Phillips curve, we must remind ourselves that the world is more complicated than Figure 16.7 indicates. In fact, predictions based on this curve may be quite wrong. Why? *Because the Phillips curve tends to be unstable.* For example, it may shift from position 1 to position 2 in Figure 16.8, thus causing the relationship between the rate of price increase and unemployment to shift from position 1 to position 2 in Figure 16.9. If you make a prediction based on the curve's being in position 1 in Figure 16.9, when in fact it is in position 2, you can make a substantial mistake. For example, suppose that you want to predict the rate of price increase if unemployment is 7 percent. Assuming that the curve is in position 1, you will predict a 6 percent increase in prices, but in fact there will be an 8 percent increase. The moral is clear enough: we need to look at the factors that can cause the Phillips curve to move.

Education. An important factor that can shift the Phillips curve is education or training. As more and more of the labor force is trained and equipped with relevant and basic skills, there is less upward pressure on wages at any level of unemployment. An important reason why wages are pushed upward as unemployment falls is that the economy tends to run out of skilled workers, so that poorly educated and untrained workers constitute a large percentage of the unemployed. When aggregate demand gets strong enough to absorb these workers, other workers experience so strong a demand that their wages are pushed up. Thus it follows that programs to train the labor force, particularly the unemployed, will shift the Phillips curve downward. That is, the rate of increase of wages associated with a given level of unemployment will fall.

Mobility. Increased mobility of workers will also shift the Phillips curve. As the labor force becomes able and willing to move from place to place, there is less pressure on wages at any level of unemployment. Thus it follows that measures designed to increase the mobility of workers—such as employment services and preferential tax treatment of moving expenses—tend to shift the Phillips curve downward.

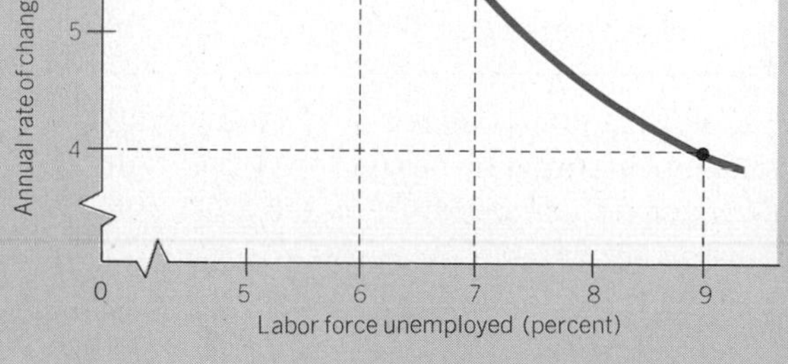

Figure 16.7
Relationship between Unemployment Rate and Rate of Inflation
This relationship can, under the conditions specified in the text, be deduced from the Phillips curve.

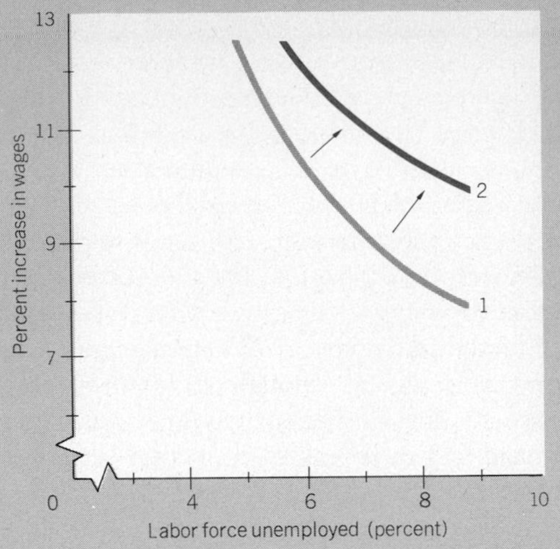

Figure 16.8
Shift in Phillips Curve
The Phillips curve can shift over time, as from position 1 to position 2.

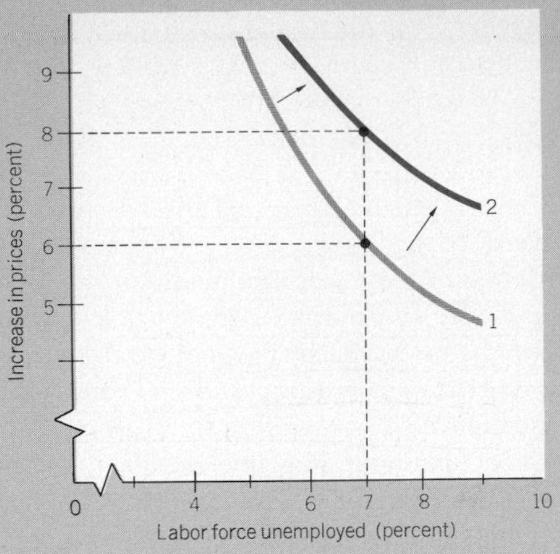

Figure 16.9
Shift in Relationship between Price Increase and Unemployment Rate
If the Phillips curve shifts, as in Figure 16.8, the relationship between the unemployment rate and the rate of inflation will shift from position 1 to position 2.

Discrimination. Still another factor that will shift the Phillips curve is reduced discrimination against blacks, women, and others who historically have fared poorly in the labor force. With intense discrimination, labor markets must be very tight (and wages must be under considerable upward pressure) to make employers willing to hire women, blacks, and other minorities. With less discrimination, there is less upward pressure on wages at any level of unemployment, because the minorities are now in a position to compete on a more equal basis with other workers. Thus reductions in discrimination tend to shift the Phillips curve downward.

Demography and unions. The Phillips curve can also be shifted by changes over time in the demographic composition of the labor force (such as the proportion of women, teenagers, or blacks), as well as by changes in the bargaining power of unions.

Expectations. Finally, shifts occur in the Phillips curve because of changes in people's expectations. If people expect a great deal of inflation, this will be reflected in the wage demands of labor (and the pricing policies of management). Thus wages will rise more rapidly at a given unemployment level than if people expect less inflation. In other words, the more inflation people expect, the further upward and out from the origin the Phillips curve is likely to be. And the less inflation people expect, the further downward and close to the origin the Phillips curve will be. If we experience a great deal of inflation—as we have in the 1970s—the Phillips curve is likely to be pushed upward because it is likely that people will come to expect inflation to continue. This phenomenon undoubtedly was important in explaining our experience with high unemployment and high rates of inflation in the 1970s.

The Phillips Curve: Short versus Long Run

According to some economists, among them Milton Friedman of the University of Chicago and Edmund Phelps of Columbia, the Phillips curve in Figure 16.6 is only a short-run relationship. In the long run, the Phillips curve is vertical, as shown in panel A of Figure 16.10. Thus expansionary monetary and fiscal policies that result in inflation will only reduce unemployment temporarily. The only permanent way to reduce it is through manpower and training policies that will make the unemployed better suited to the available jobs. This is because labor comes to recognize that its wage gains are being eroded by inflation, so that it builds its expectations of inflation into its wage demands, thus pushing the Phillips curve upward and outward from the origin. Eventually, labor bargains with reference to the real, not the money wage.

This challenge to the conventional Phillips curve has itself been challenged by many economists. (This entire area is one of continuing controversy.) As indicated by panel B of Figure 16.10, there may be a range of unemployment, perhaps above 5 percent, where an inverse relationship exists in the long run between unemployment and inflation; but below this range, the Phillips curve may be essentially vertical. This view has been put forth by Yale's James Tobin and Northwestern University's Robert Gordon, among others. If this is the case, monetary and fiscal policies may not be the right tools to reduce unemployment in the range where the curve is essentially vertical. Manpower and retraining programs might be emphasized instead.

"Stagflation"

In recent years, and particularly during the mid-1970s, the American economy has been characterized by "stagflation"—a combination of high unemployment and high inflation. (The term *stagflation* was coined by putting together *stag*nation and in*flation*.) Apparently, the Phillips curve shifted upward; that is, at a given unemployment rate, the inflation rate has been higher than it formerly was. Why did this shift occur? Economists are by no means in agreement on this score. Indeed, the combination of excessive unemployment and excessive inflation in the mid-1970s has been an embarrass-

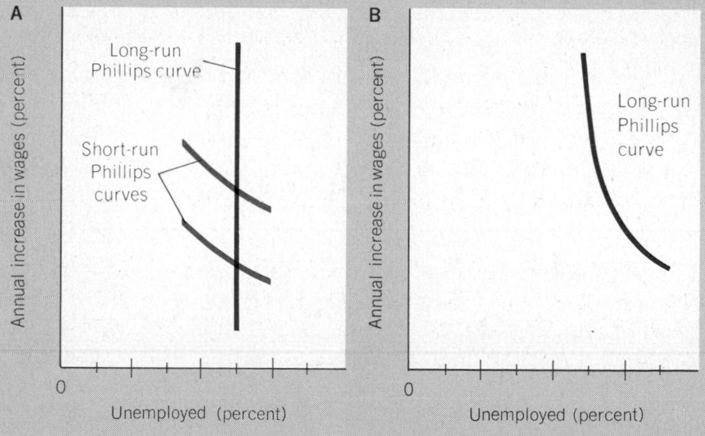

Figure 16.10
The Phillips Curve, Short and Long Run
Some economists argue that the long-run Phillips curve is vertical, as in panel A; others argue that it is shaped like that in panel B.

ment to economists, since they have neither a universally accepted explanation for it nor a well-developed cure for it. Nonetheless, the following account seems to be a reasonably accurate sketch of what occurred during the mid-1970s.

Let's begin in the summer of 1972. Although the economy was not in rosy shape then, it was far healthier than in the next few years. The unemployment rate then was about 5 percent, and the inflation rate in 1972 was about 3 percent. What occurred to propel the economy into the subsequent stagflation? Basically, several factors were at work. First, food prices shot up, beginning in late 1972, because of bad crops around the world (and the disappearance of Peruvian anchovies, which caused a drop in the fish catch off the South American coast). Second, many other raw material prices increased rapidly, due to a world-wide expansion of economic activity and the devaluation of the dollar. Third, the price of crude oil increased greatly in 1974, as pointed out in a previous section. These three factors together with a relatively great increase in the money supply in late 1972, were responsible for pushing the inflation rate up to 9 percent in 1973 and 12 percent in 1974.

At the same time, these three factors set in motion serious recessionary forces. The oil price hike acted like an excise tax levied on the consumer; it reduced the amount that consumers could spend on other things. The general inflation raised people's money incomes, thus pushing them into higher income tax brackets and increasing the amount they had to pay in taxes. (Similarly, the inflation swelled the paper profits of many firms, and increased their tax bills.) Because of the oil price increase and the effective increase in taxes, as well as other factors like the decline in the stock market, consumers cut back on their spending. Thus the $C + I + G$ line was pushed downward, and the equilibrium value of NNP fell.

This scenario can explain our being afflicted simultaneously with both the highest inflation rate (12 percent in 1974) and the highest unemployment rate ($8\frac{1}{2}$ percent in 1975) in postwar history. And many economists believe this to be the explanation. But other economists emphasize additional factors as well, such as changes in the structure of the American economy. To explain the evident upward shift in the Phillips curve, it is frequently claimed that our economy does not work the way it used to. According to this view, there is less competition than formerly, and a more pervasive public expectation that inflation may accelerate. As pointed out above, such factors could push the Phillips curve upward. The extent to which they in fact have done so is largely unknown.

Attacks on Market Power and Controls on Prices: Two Suggested Remedies

The government would, of course, like to shift the Phillips curve downward, for example from position C to position D in Figure 16.11. Programs to train manpower, increase labor mobility, reduce discrimination, and change expectations can have this effect. Unfortunately, however, programs of this sort take a considerable amount of time to make an impact, and, as we have seen in the previous section, the evidence of recent years seems to indicate that the Phillips curve has shifted upward, not downward. In this section, we take up two other remedies—the reduction of market power, and price and wage controls.

Reduction of market power. Since the market power of unions and firms is the basic cause of cost-push inflation, it would seem logical to attack cost-push inflation in this way. To some extent, the government is, of course, committed to a policy of this sort. Antitrust policy is a basic part of our nation's economic policy. But as we shall see in Chapter 26, antitrust policy is

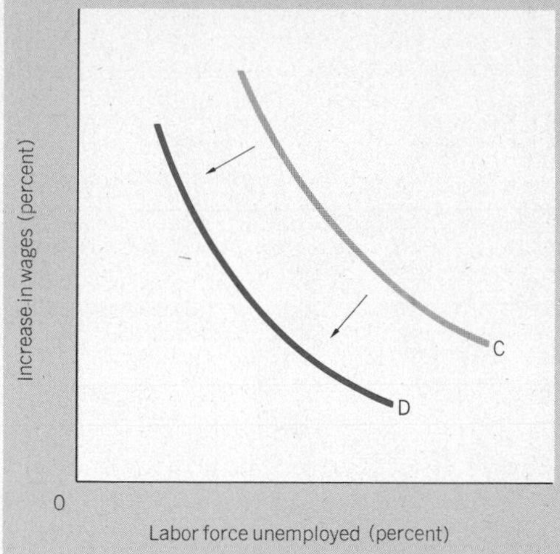

Figure 16.11
Shift in Phillips Curve
The government would like to shift the Phillips curve downward, as from position *C* to position *D*.

not designed to root out market power in all forms and degrees. This would be foolish in any case, because economies of scale and other considerations require that firms in many industries–to be efficient and innovative–must have a certain amount of market power. Moreover, even when the existing size of firms or concentration of industries cannot be defended on these grounds, the government is not seriously attempting to break up existing firms. Some economists would favor such a policy, both to quell cost-push inflation and to obtain the other advantages (discussed in Chapters 26 and 30) of a competitive economy. But it does not seem at all likely that such a radical–and politically difficult–policy will be adopted.

Price and wage controls. During World War II–and other wartime emergencies–the government has imposed controls on wages and prices. In other words, the government intervened directly in the market place to see that wages and prices did not increase by more than a certain amount. Some distinguished economists argue that price and wage controls should also be used to control cost-push inflation in peacetime. According to a former president of the American Economic Association,

> A complete attack on inflation requires that both causes of inflation–both the excess of demand or spending, and the wage-price spiral–be brought under control. . . . The defense against the wage-price spiral (i.e., cost-push inflation) . . . is the direct control over prices and wages. These direct controls are not a substitute for a strong fiscal policy; they perform a different task. . . . To tie down the wage-price spiral, with reasonable justice and equity, we need to do three things. They are (1) Effectively stabilize basic living costs. This is necessary if wages are to be stabilized. (2) Maintain a general ceiling on wages and prices in that part of the economy where wages are determined by collective-bargaining contracts and where prices normally move in response to wage movements. I have reference here to what may properly be called the great industrial core of the American economy–the steel, automobile, electrical goods, construction, transport, and like industries. (3) As a contribution to over-all stability, place firm ceiling prices on basic raw materials.[6]

But most economists do not share this view. The economics profession has little enthusiasm for direct controls of wages and prices, for several reasons. First, such controls are likely to result in a distortion of the allocation of resources. Recall from Chapter 4 our discussion of the functions of the price system in allocating resources. Price and wage controls do not permit prices to perform these functions, and the result is inefficiency and waste. Second, such controls are likely to be expensive to administer. For example, during the Korean War, the Economic Stabilization Agency had 16,000 employees; and even so, it was difficult to prevent violation or evasion of the controls.

[6] John Kenneth Galbraith, testimony before the Joint Committee on the Economic Report, 82d Congress, 1st Session.

Are Price and Wage Controls Desirable? Inevitable?

According to some respected economists, such as Robert Lekachman of the City University of New York, price and wage controls are desirable. In his view, there is a need for a permanent federal agency to establish and apply criteria concerning wages and prices. As he puts it, "The continuing concentration of economic power and the proliferation of conglomerates and multinational corporations as recent embodiments of that power dictate the creation of a countervailing source of power operating in the public interest. Hence, the sooner economists and politicians shed the delusion that controls are required only in exceptional circumstances, the better."*

Most economists, however, are skeptical of the desirability of such controls. As C. Jackson Grayson, Jr., of Southern Methodist University (and former chairman of President Nixon's Price Commission) has said, "The lessons of history seem pretty clear. . . . In A.D. 301, the emperor Diocletian imposed the first extensive price-wage program. His edict (referred to as 'commanded cheapness') set schedules for 76 different wage categories and for 890 different price categories (222 of which were for food!). The penalty for an offense was death. Thirteen years later, the program, in shambles, was abandoned."† Turning from ancient Rome to modern times, the recent experience with incomes policies has not been very encouraging either. As Lloyd Ulman and Robert Flanagan of the University of California concluded from their study of Western European experiences after World War II, "Incomes policy, to generalize from the experience of the countries in this account, has not been very successful. . . . Experience . . . suggests that in none of the variations so far turned up has incomes policy succeeded in . . . making full employment consistent with a reasonable degree of price stability."‡

Perhaps the most frequent criticism of controls is that they interfere with the price system's ability to allocate resources, the result being bottlenecks, shortages, and waste. Other points emphasized by critics of controls are that a wage-price controls program will not work unless both labor and business cooperate, and that incomes policies will not work for long, since they erode with time. According to Grayson, voluntary programs have limited success, with the result that they tend to become mandatory, and getting into controls is easier than getting out. Both critics and defenders of controls accept that, unless monetary and fiscal policies are formulated responsibly, controls can have little durable effect. As Lekachman says, "Controls will fail except in the context of appropriate fiscal, monetary, and employment programs."[§]

Although they differ in their evaluation of the desirability of controls, both defenders of them, like Lekachman, and critics, like Grayson, feel that, for better or worse, controls will eventually be tried again in this country. Thus Grayson predicts that "We will turn again in the United States, in desperation, to some form of controls over wages and prices—just as people have done over the centuries. And the answer will still be the same—they make some short-term gains, but at the expense of the long-run welfare."[‖] It is also a safe bet that the controversy over the desirability of controls will continue for a long time to come, since inflationary pressures are unlikely to disappear.

* R. Lekachman, "The Inevitability of Controls," *Challenge,* November–December 1974.
† C. J. Grayson, "Controls Are Not the Answer," *Challenge,* November–December 1974.
‡ L. Ulman and R. Flanagan, *Wage Restraint: A Study of Incomes Policies in Western Europe,* Berkeley: University of California Press, 1971.
§ Lekachman.
‖ Grayson.

Third, there is widespread opposition to detailed government regulation and control of this sort, on the grounds that it impairs our economic freedom. The Council of Economic Advisers undoubtedly spoke for most of the economics profession when it said in 1968,

> The most obvious—and least desirable—way of attempting to stabilize prices is to impose mandatory controls on prices and wages. While such controls may be necessary under conditions of an all-out war, it would be folly to consider them as a solution to the inflationary pressures that accompany high employment under any other circumstance. . . . Although such controls may be unfortunately popular when they are not in effect, the appeal quickly disappears once people live under them.[7]

Wage and Price Controls under the Nixon Administration: A Case Study

Despite the disadvantages of price controls, the Nixon administration adopted them in the summer of 1971. Wholesale prices were rising then at about 5 percent per year. The wage-price spiral was very much in evidence. Collective bargaining agreements were reached calling for wage increases far in excess of productivity increases, and there was no question but that firms would boost prices in an attempt to cover the resulting increase in costs. Since it took office in 1969, the Nixon administration had been opposed to wage and price guidelines, or wage and price controls, although a number of congressmen and others had suggested the adoption of controls or some form of incomes policy. However, in August 1971, President Nixon reversed his previous stand. He froze wages and prices for a three-month period. Then he appointed a 15-member Pay Board and a 7-member Price Commission, both of which were supervised by the government's Cost of Living Council.

The Pay Board was given the responsibility of administering wage controls, and the Price Commission was to administer price controls. In November 1971, these two bodies announced their initial policies. The Pay Board stated that pay increases had to be kept under 5.5 percent per year. A company could increase some employees' pay by more than this amount, but other employees would have to get less since total increases could not exceed this figure. The Price Commission ruled that

[7] *1968 Annual Report of the Council of Economic Advisers,* Washington, D.C.: Government Printing Office, p. 119.

price increases had to be kept under 2.5 percent. Both for prices and wages, exceptions could be made in some areas. Large firms were required to notify the Pay Board and Price Commission of intended wage or price increases.

From November 1971 to January 1973, this program of price and wage controls continued. Although it did not eliminate inflation, prices seemed to go up more slowly than before the freeze. (The consumer price index went up by about 3 percent during 1972.) By early 1973, it appeared that controls might safely be relaxed. In January 1973, the Pay Board and the Price Commission became part of the Cost of Living Council, headed by Harvard's labor economist, John Dunlop. And controls were eliminated or relaxed for most prices and wages, with the major exceptions of the health, food, and construction industries. To a considerable extent, the Nixon administration phased out the first peacetime wage and price controls in our history.

Unfortunately, inflation occurred subsequently at a bewildering pace. During the first half of 1973, wholesale prices of farm products and processed foods and feeds rose at the unbelievable rate of 48 percent per year. At the same time, the prices of lumber, fuel, and other industrial goods rose at alarming rates. President Nixon responded by imposing a 60-day freeze on prices (but not wages), beginning in mid-June of 1973. This was only a breather, an interim measure designed to give the administration some time to deal with the serious inflationary pressures that were evident through the economy.

In August 1973, the administration announced that price increases could not exceed cost increases. This was the core of the new postfreeze program. But it soon became obvious that this new program was not proving effective, and that there was growing criticism and skepticism concerning price controls. In April 1974, Congress allowed the control authority to expire. This phase of the program was widely acknowledged to be a failure.

It is difficult to evaluate the effects of the price and wage controls established between 1971 and 1974. According to many observers, the price level rose, once controls were relaxed, to the level that it would have attained in any event, if there had been no controls. Thus, to these observers, the effects of the controls were short-term and largely cosmetic. To other observers, the controls had a significant longer-term effect. According to the Council of Economic Advisers, "regardless of the overall effect of the program, whatever contribution it may have made was probably concentrated in its first 16 months, when the economy was operating well below its potential. As various industrial sectors reached capacity operations in 1973 under the stimulus of a booming domestic and world economy, the controls system began to obstruct normal supplier-purchaser relationships, and in some cases the controls became quite unworkable."[8] Still others maintained that the administration, by frequently voicing its distaste for controls, had a hand in undermining its own program.

Incomes Policies

Most economists regard neither direct controls not the reduction of market power as effective, practical devices to fight cost-push inflation. Faced with this fact, there has been considerable interest, both here and abroad, in using incomes policies to stem cost-push inflation. According to one common definition, an ***incomes policy*** contains three elements. *First, it has some targets for wages (and other forms of income) and prices for the economy as a whole.* For example, the target may be to stabilize the price level, or to permit the consumer price

[8] *1975 Annual Report of the Council of Ecomonic Advisers,* Washington, D.C.: Government Printing Office, pp. 228–29.

index to increase by less than 2 percent per year, or to allow wage increases not exceeding a certain percentage.

Second, an incomes policy gives particular firms and industries some more detailed guides for decision making on wages (and other forms of income) and prices. These guides are set in such a way that the over-all targets for the entire economy will be fulfilled. For example, if the aim is price stability, these guides tell firms and unions what kinds of decisions are compatible with this target. To be useful, the guides must be specific and understandable enough to be applied in particular cases. There obviously is little point in telling firms and unions to avoid "inflationary" wage and price decisions if they don't know whether a particular decision is "inflationary" or not.

Third, an incomes policy contains some mechanisms to get firms and unions to follow the guides. An incomes policy differs from price and wage controls in that it seeks to induce firms and unions to follow these guides voluntarily. But if it is to have any effect, clearly the government must be prepared to use certain forms of "persuasion" beyond moral suasion. In fact, governments sometimes have publicly condemned decisions by firms and unions that were regarded as violating the guides. Government stockpiles of materials and government purchasing policies have also been used to penalize or reward particular firms and industries. Other pressures too have been brought to bear in an attempt to induce firms to follow the established guides. Thus the difference between an incomes policy and price and wage controls is one of degree and emphasis, not a clear-cut difference in kind.

An example of an incomes policy in the United States was the so-called Kennedy-Johnson guidelines. Although earlier administrations (for example, the Eisenhower and Truman Administrations) had often appealed to business and labor to limit wage and price increases, the first systematic attempt at a fairly specific incomes policy in the United States occurred during the Kennedy administration. In 1961, President Kennedy's Council of Economic Advisers issued the following wage-price guidelines:

> The general guide for noninflationary wage behavior is that the rate of increase in wage rates (including fringe benefits) in each industry be equal to the trend rate of *over-all productivity advance.* General acceptance of this guide would maintain stability of labor cost per unit of output for the economy as a whole—though not of course for individual industries. The general guide for noninflationary price behavior calls for price reduction if the industry's rate of productivity increase exceeds the over-all rate—for this would mean declining unit labor costs; it calls for an appropriate increase in price if the opposite relationship prevails; and it calls for stable prices if the two rates of productivity increase are equal. [Note once again that productivity equals output per man-hour.][9]

To see just what this meant, let's consider prices and wages in the auto industry. Suppose that labor productivity in the economy as a whole was increasing at 3.2 percent per year. Then according to the guidelines, *wages in the automobile industry should increase by 3.2 percent per year.* If labor productivity in the auto industry increased by 4.2 percent per year, then, if the auto makers applied this guideline, the labor cost of producing a unit of output would decrease by 1 percent per year in the auto industry (since the 3.2 percent rate of increase of wages minus the 4.2 percent rate of increase of labor productivity equals −1 percent). Thus the guidelines specified that *prices in the auto industry should decrease,* perhaps by about 1 percent per year.

The Council of Economic Advisers specified several situations where these general guidelines would have to be modified. In particular, if there was a shortage of labor in a particular industry or if an industry's wages were

[9] *1962 Annual Report of the Council of Economic Advisers,* Washington, D.C.: Government Printing Office, p. 189.

lower than those earned elsewhere by similar labor, higher wage increases (than specified in general) would be warranted. Or if an industry's profits were insufficient to attract needed infusions of capital, or if an industry's nonwage costs rose greatly, higher price increases than specified in general would be justified. However, the Council did not attempt to set forth detailed, quantitative provisions about the extent to which higher wages or prices would be warranted under these circumstances.

The Steel Price Increase of 1962: A Case Study

To conform to our definition of an incomes policy, the Kennedy-Johnson wage-price policy had to have an over-all target, more detailed guides for wage and price decisions, and a mechanism to get firms and unions to observe these guides. The over-all target was the stabilization of prices, and the more detailed guides for price and wage decisions were described in the previous section. But what about the mechanisms to induce acceptance of these guides? How did the government get industry and labor to go along?

The famous confrontation in 1962 between President Kennedy and the steel industry is an interesting case study of how pressure was brought to bear. Before the wage-price guidelines were issued, President Kennedy asked the major steel companies to avoid raising prices, and no price increases occurred. Then, after the issuance of the guidelines, he asked the steel union for restraint in the wage negotiations coming up in March 1962. Arthur Goldberg, Kennedy's secretary of labor, played an important role in persuading the union to accept a 2.5 percent increase in compensation, which was clearly noninflationary. At this point, government and the press felt quite optimistic about the apparent success of the president's program.

In the week following the wage agreement, however, the United States Steel Corporation increased all its prices by $3\frac{1}{2}$ percent, and most of the major steel companies followed suit. The price increase was clearly a violation of the president's guidelines. It almost seemed as if the steel companies were trying to demonstrate once and for all that pricing was up to them, and them alone. Their action elicited a wrathful speech by the president publicly denouncing them. Roger M. Blough, chairman of the United States Steel Corporation, tried to rebut the president's arguments by claiming that U.S. Steel's profits were too low to attract new capital.

Three of the major steel producers—Armco, Inland, and Kaiser—did not follow U.S. Steel's lead in the day or so after its price increase. Government officials, noting this fact as well as prior public arguments against price increases by Inland officials, quickly began to apply pressure on these three producers to hold their prices constant. Government officials who knew executives of these firms called them and tried to persuade them to do so. The firms were also informed that government contracts would be directed to firms that held their prices constant. Apparently, the government's campaign succeeded. Inland and Kaiser made public statements that they would not raise prices. Faced with this fact, the other steel companies had no choice but to rescind the price increase.

This is an example of how presidential pressure can induce firms to go along with the guidelines. Often the Council of Economic Advisers tried to head off price increases before they were announced. In one way or another, sometimes from the companies themselves, the Council often learned of an impending price increase. The Council then asked the firms to meet to discuss the situation. In these meetings, the Council explained the importance of price stability and both parties discussed the proposed increase. It is difficult, of course, to measure the impact of such discussions, but, according to the Council, they sometimes resulted in the postponement or reduction of the planned price increases.

The Kennedy-Johnson Guidelines: Criticism and Experience

Soon after the announcement of the guidelines, critics began to point out problems in them. The criticism was of several types:

Inefficiency. Some observers feared that the guidelines would result in inefficiency and waste. In a free-enterprise economy, we rely on price changes to direct resources into the most productive uses and to signal shortages or surpluses in various markets. If the guidelines were accepted by industry and labor, prices would not be free to perform this function. Of course, the guidelines specified that modifications of the general rules could be made in case of shortages, but critics of the guidelines felt that this escape hatch was too vague to be very useful.

Freedom. Many observers were concerned about the reduction in economic freedom. Of course, the guidelines were presented in the hope that they would be observed voluntarily. But a time was sure to come when they would be in serious contradiction with the interests of firms and unions. In such a situation, what would happen if the firms or unions decided not to follow them? To the extent that the government applied pressure on the firms or unions, there would certainly be a reduction in economic freedom; and to some observers, it seemed likely that the next step might well be direct government controls. Moreover, the nonlegislated character of the guidelines and the arbitrary choice of whom to pursue by the government raised important questions of a political nature.

Feasibility. Many people felt that the guidelines really were not workable. In other words, even if the public would go along with them, in many cases they would be impossible to use, because accurate and relevant data on changes in labor productivity in particular industries were often unobtainable, and the situations where exceptions were allowed were so vaguely specified.

Symptoms. Some economists felt that reliance on the guidelines was dangerous because it focused attention on symptoms rather than causes of inflation. In their view, inflation was largely the result of improper monetary and fiscal policies. In other words, the basic causes had to be laid at the government's own door. But by setting up guidelines, the government seemed to be saying that the fault lay with industry and labor. Thus some critics felt that the guidelines tended to cloud the real issues and so let the government escape responsibility for its actions.

After the government's bout with the steel industry in 1962, there was no major public fight over wages and prices for a couple of years; and the government claimed that the guideposts were working well. To a considerable extent, this may have been because the economy still had considerable slack, as well as because of the noninflationary expectations of firms and individuals engendered by several years of relative price stability. By 1965, as labor markets tightened and prices rose in response to the Vietnam build-up (see Chapter 11), it became much more difficult to use the guidelines. Union leaders fought the guidelines tooth and nail, mainly because consumer prices were rising. In various important labor negotiations, unions demanded and got higher wage increases than the guidelines called for. For example, the airline machinists got a 4.9 percent increase in 1966. By 1968, the guidelines were dead: no one was paying any attention to them.

What effect did the guidelines have? Some people claim that they had no real effect at all, while others claim that they reduced cost-push inflation in the early 1960s by a considerable amount. Since it is difficult to separate the effects of the guidelines from the effects of other factors, there is considerable dispute over the question. Considering the level of unemployment in the early 1960s, wages increased less rapidly then than in earlier or later periods. Prices too increased less rapidly during that period—holding unemployment constant—than earlier or later. But whether these developments were due to the guidelines, or to noninflationary expectations or some other factor, is very hard to say.

Perhaps the most important reason why the guidelines broke down was that they could not deal with the strong demand-pull inflation of the late 1960s. Even the strongest defenders of the guidelines are quick to point out that they are no substitute for proper monetary and fiscal policy. *If fiscal or monetary policy is generating strong inflationary pressures, such as existed in the late 1960s, it is foolish to think that guidelines can save the situation.* Perhaps they can cut down on the rate of inflation for a while; but in the long run, the dike is sure to burst. If the guidelines are voluntary, as in this case, firms and unions will ignore them, and the government will find it difficult, if not impossible, to do anything about it. *Even price and wage controls are no adequate antidote to strong inflationary pressures by an overly expansive fiscal or monetary policy. Such controls may deal temporarily with the symptoms of inflation, but over the long haul these inflationary pressures will have an effect.*

Economic Stabilization: Where We Stand

Where do we stand in the struggle to achieve full employment without inflation? Clearly, we know much more than we did 30 years ago about how to use monetary and fiscal policies to attain this objective. Given the more advanced state of economics, it is very, very unlikely that a catastrophe like the Great Depression of the 1930s will occur again. But on the other hand, economists were overly optimistic in the mid-1960s when they talked about "fine-tuning" the economy. Our experience since then makes it clear that we have a long way to go before we understand the workings of the economy well enough to achieve continuous full employment without inflation. Equally important, we have seen that, even if the advice of its economists were always correct, the government might still pursue destabilizing policies, as it did in the late 1960s.

The mid-1970s have been characterized by both excessive inflation and excessive unemployment. Throughout the Western industrialized world, governments have been perplexed by this phenomenon of "stagflation." The standard economic remedies—monetary and fiscal policy—are not very effective in dealing with this combination of ailments. Although they can deal with either excessive unemployment or excessive inflation, they are not well designed to deal simultaneously with both of them.

To some economists, the answer (or at least a partial answer) is to rely more heavily on some form of incomes policy to fight inflation. But the evidence, here and abroad, seems to emphasize the problems in formulating an effective incomes policy. The unfortunate truth is that we do not have an adequate understanding of the factors causing "stagflation." Until we obtain a better basic understanding of this phenomenon, the chances are that policy makers, both here and abroad, will continue to have problems with regard to economic stabilization—and that there will be a good deal of floundering. If we experience severe inflation (á la 1974) once again, it is likely that some form of incomes policy will be applied in the United States. But it must be recognized that such policies have had limited success in restraining inflation in the past, in the United States as in other countries.

Summary

An important debate has been going on between the monetarists and Keynesians. The monetarists believe that changes in the money supply are the basic reason for business fluctuations. Keynesians believe that both monetary and nonmonetary factors cause business fluctuations. Many of the basic disagreements between the Keynesians and monetarists center about the quantitative effects of the interest rate. (1) According to the monetarists, the quantity of money demanded is relatively insensitive to changes in the interest rate; whereas to Keynesians, it is very sensitive to such changes. (2) According to the monetarists, the supply of money is relatively insensitive to changes in the interest rate; whereas to Keynesians, it is quite sensitive to such changes. (3) According to the monetarists, total expenditure is very sensitive to changes in the interest rate; whereas to some Keynesians, it is not so sensitive to such changes.

Because of these differing points of view, monetarists believe that monetary policy is of pre-eminent importance, whereas Keynesians tend to believe that it is of lesser importance. There also are differences of view concerning the effects of fiscal policy. The monetarists attack the Keynesian view that fiscal policy works as described in Chapter 11. According to the monetarists, whether the government runs a surplus or a deficit does not have much long-run effect on NNP, except insofar as the government finances the deficit or surplus in a way that alters the quantity of money. Monetarists and Keynesians come to quite different policy conclusions. In particular, many leading monetarists favor the establishment of a rule to govern monetary policy, an idea most Keynesians oppose.

An important barrier to achieving economic stability through monetary and fiscal policy is cost-push inflation. The Phillips curve shows the relationship between the rate of increase of wages and the level of unemployment. Given the Phillips curve, it is a simple matter to determine the relationship between the rate of inflation and the level of unemployment. If the Phillips curve remains fixed, it poses an awkward dilemma for policy makers. To the extent that they use fiscal and monetary policy to fight unemployment, they fuel the fires of inflation; to the extent that they use monetary and fiscal policy to fight inflation, they contribute to greater unemployment.

The available evidence indicates that the Phillips curve is unstable. The Phillips curve shifts in response to increased education or training of the work force, increased mobility of workers, reduced discrimination, demographic changes, changes in union bargaining power, and changes in people's expectations. Also, it can shift, at least temporarily, in response to various government policies, such as wartime controls on wages and prices. Although a few economists favor such controls during peacetime, most do not agree. Such controls are likely to distort the allocation of resources, to be difficult to administer, and to run counter to our desire for economic freedom. Another way to shift the Phillips curve is to attack market power, but although many economists favor some such action, it does not seem practically or politically feasible.

Many countries have experimented with various kinds of incomes policies. An incomes policy contains targets for wages and prices for the economy as a whole, more detailed guides for wage and price decisions in particular industries, and some mechanisms to get firms and unions to follow these guides. The Kennedy-Johnson guidelines were one form of incomes policy. Further, wage and price controls have been instituted in some countries. For the first time, the United States resorted to such controls in peacetime in 1971–74. Although controls of this sort have a short-term effect on the price level, how much effect they have in the long run is hard to say.

In recent years, and particularly during the mid-1970s, the American economy has been characterized by "stagflation," a combination of high unemployment and high inflation. Apparently, the Phillips curve shifted upward; that is, at a given unemployment rate, the inflation rate has been higher than it formerly was. Among the most important factors responsible for this shift were bad crops, the devaluation of the dollar, and the marked increase in the price of crude oil in the early and mid-1970s. These factors combined both to cause serious inflation and severe recession. In addition, according to some economists, there is less competition than formerly, and a more pervasive public expectation that inflation will go on. These factors, too, could have pushed the Phillips curve upward.

CONCEPTS FOR REVIEW

Monetarists	Cost-push inflation	Incomes policy
Keynesians	Wage-price spiral	Price freeze
Demand-pull inflation	Phillips curve	

QUESTIONS FOR DISCUSSION AND REVIEW

1. According to Juanita Kreps, "It is the function of manpower programs to improve the terms of the tradeoff—that is, to shift the Phillips curve to the left." Suggest as many kinds of manpower programs as you can that might help in this regard. What sorts of manpower programs have been launched in this country?

2. According to Milton Friedman, "It is far better that inflation be open than that it be suppressed [by price guidelines]." Do you agree? Why or why not?

3. "The Kennedy-Johnson guidelines for noninflationary price behavior called for price reduction if an industry's rate of productivity increase exceeded the over-all rate. It is unrealistic to expect price cuts of this sort." Do you agree? Why or why not?

4. "The inflations arising from the Revolutionary, Civil, and Vietnam Wars were largely cost-push." Comment and evaluate.

5. "Keynesians believe that the demand curve for money is close to vertical; consequently, they feel that monetary policy has less effect on NNP than monetarists." Comment and evaluate.

6. Suppose that the relationship between the annual rate of change of the wage rate and the percent of the labor force unemployed is as shown below:

Rate of change of wage rate (percent per year)	Unemployment rate (percent)
5	8
6	7
7	6
8	5

Plot the Phillips curve on a graph. Would Milton Friedman accept this curve as a long-run Phillips curve? Why or why not?

7. Suppose that output per man-hour is growing at 2 percent per year. Based on the data in Question 6, plot the relationship between the annual rate of change of the price level and the unemployment rate. State the assumptions you are making.

8. "The Phillips curve shifts position so much that it is an unreliable tool for the determination of public policy." Comment and evaluate.

9. "Reliance on incomes policies is dangerous because it looks at symptoms, not the basic causes of our problems." Comment and evaluate.

10. John Kenneth Galbraith has written that "the defense against the wage-price spiral . . . is the direct control over prices and wages." Using the experience of the United States with such controls during the early 1970s as a guide, evaluate Galbraith's position. Would Galbraith accept such evidence as conclusive? Why or why not?

APPENDIX: *IS* and *LM* Curves—A More Complete Model

To understand more completely the argument between the Keynesians and the monetarists, it is worthwhile to enlarge the model of national output determination in Chapters 10 and 11 to include monetary factors. The simplest extension of this sort involves the use of *IS* and *LM* curves, both of which will be discussed in detail below. These curves, originated by Oxford's Nobel laureate, Sir John Hicks, help to put the debate between the monetarists and the Keynesians into somewhat deeper perspective.

Before describing how *IS* and *LM* curves are constructed, it is important to be clear concerning the basic assumptions that are being made. First, it is assumed that the price level is fixed, and that the public has a fixed demand curve for real money balances, a fixed consumption function, and a fixed investment function. Second, foreign trade is ignored. Third, the money supply is fixed by the monetary authorities, and does not vary with NNP or the interest rate. Fourth, tax rates are fixed, and fiscal policy takes the form of varying government expenditure.

The IS *Curve: Definition and Derivation*

The IS *curve shows, for each possible level of the interest rate, the level of NNP that will satisfy the equilibrium condition that desired spending on output must equal NNP.* (If this equilibrium condition is a bit hazy, review Chapter 10.) This equilibrium condition is equivalent to saying that the public must be spending the desired amount relative to its income. (We put a great deal of stress on this equilibrium condition in Chapter 10.) To construct the *IS* curve,

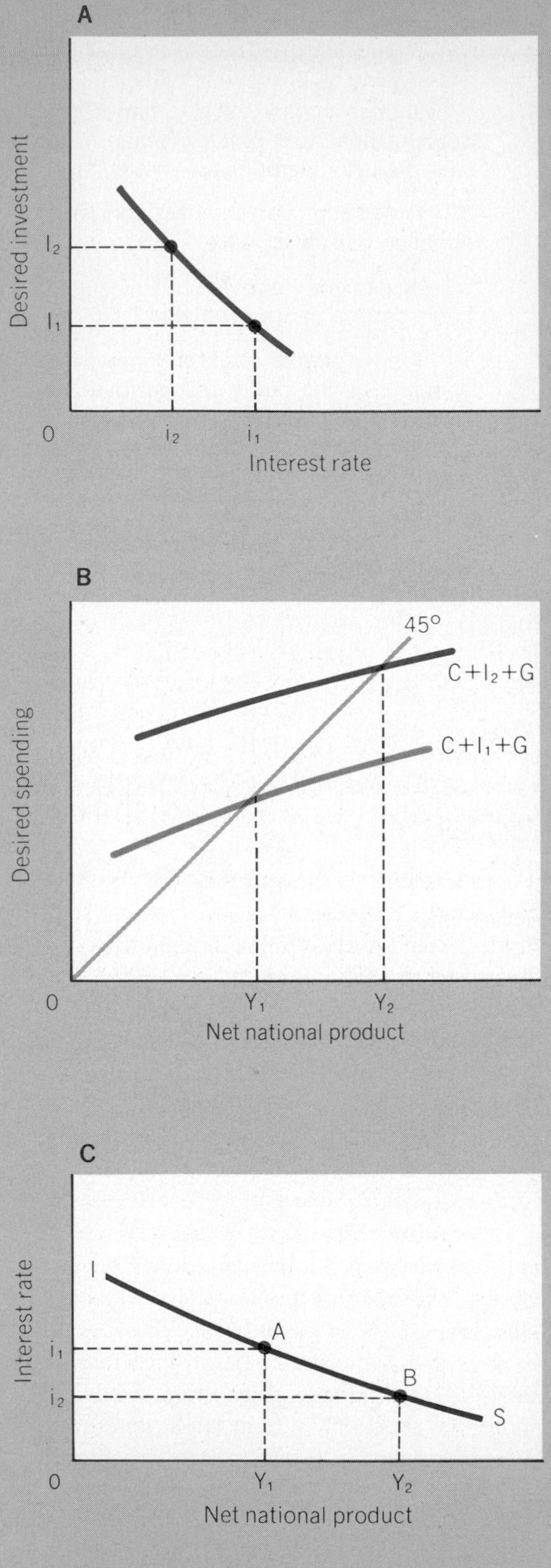

Figure 16.12
Derivation of the *IS* Curve
If the interest rate is i_1, desired investment is I_1. If the interest rate is i_2, desired investment is I_2.

If desired investment is I_1, equilibrium NNP is Y_1. If desired investment is I_2, equilibrium NNP is Y_2.

The *IS* curve shows, for each level of the interest rate, the level of NNP that will satisfy the equilibrium condition that desired spending on output must equal NNP. Points *A* and *B* are derived in the panels above, which show that equilibrium NNP equals Y_1 if the interest rate is i_1 and Y_2 if the interest rate is i_2.

it is essential to recognize two things. First, the level of desired investment is inversely related to the interest rate. (In other words, for reasons described in Chapter 9, the higher the rate of interest, the lower the amount of desired investment, as shown in panel A of Figure 16.12.) Second, the level of desired investment (as well as consumption and government expenditure) will determine the equilibrium level of NNP. (See panel B of Figure 16.12.) Thus, since the interest rate determines the level of desired investment, and the level of desired investment determines the equilibrium level of NNP, there will be a relationship between the level of the interest rate and the equilibrium level of NNP; this relationship is the *IS* curve, shown in panel C of Figure 16.12.

To see more precisely what the *IS* curve is, it is useful to derive some points on such a curve. Let's derive two points—*A* and *B*—on the *IS* curve in panel C of Figure 16.12. To derive point *A*, note that, if the interest rate is i_1, desired investment will be I_1, according to panel A of Figure 16.12. And if desired investment is I_1, total desired spending at each level of NNP will be as shown by the $C + I_1 + G$ line in panel B of Figure 16.12, with the result that the equilibrium level of NNP will be Y_1. Thus, if the interest rate is i_1, the equilibrium level of NNP is Y_1—which explains the coordinates of point *A*.

To explain point *B*, note that if the interest rate is i_2, desired investment will be I_2, according to panel A of Figure 16.12. And if desired investment is I_2, total desired spending at each level of NNP will be as shown by the $C + I_2 + G$ line in panel B of Figure 16.12, with the result that the equilibrium level of NNP will be Y_2. Thus, if the interest rate is i_2, the equilibrium level of NNP is Y_2—which explains the coordinates of point *B*.

Note that *the* IS *curve slopes downward to the right.* That is, the lower the interest rate, the higher the level of NNP on the *IS* curve. For example, when the interest rate fell from i_1 to i_2 in Figure 16.12, panel A, desired investment increased from I_1 to I_2. And when desired investment rose from I_1 to I_2, the equilibrium level of NNP increased from Y_1 to Y_2, as shown in panel B of Figure 16.12. More generally, since the level of desired investment is inversely related to the interest rate, but directly related to the equilibrium level of NNP, it follows that the interest rate must be inversely related to the level of NNP on the *IS* curve.

The LM *Curve: Definition and Derivation*

The LM *curve shows, for each possible level of the interest rate, the level of NNP that will satisfy the equilibrium condition that the public be satisfied to hold the existing quantity of money.* We have stressed the importance of this equilibrium condition, and have pointed out that two of the principal reasons why the public wants to hold cash is the transaction motive and the speculative motive. Clearly, the quantity of money demanded for transactions purposes is dependent upon the value of NNP. Further, the quantity of money demanded for speculative (and other) purposes is dependent on the rate of interest. Thus, as stressed in Chapter 13, the total quantity of money demanded by the public is dependent both on the value of NNP and on the interest rate.

More specifically, the total quantity of money demanded by the public is *directly* related to the value of NNP and *inversely* related to the interest rate. (Recall the discussion in Chapter 13.) As NNP increases (and incomes rise), people want to keep more money on hand to buy things. Thus the quantity of money demanded by the public is directly related to the value of NNP (as shown in panel A of Figure 16.13). On the other hand, the higher the inter-

Figure 16.13
Derivation of the *LM* Curve
Holding constant the interest rate, *i*, the quantity of money demanded increases as NNP increases. Holding constant NNP, the quantity of money demanded increases as the interest rate decreases. If $i = .04$ and NNP $= Y_3$, the quantity of money demanded equals $1 trillion. If $i = .06$ and NNP $= Y_4$, the quantity of money demanded equals $1 trillion. These correspond to points *C* and *D* in panel B.

The *LM* curve shows, for each possible level of the interest rate, the level of NNP that will satisfy the equilibrium condition that the quantity of money demanded equal the supply of money. Points *C* and *D* are derived in panel A.

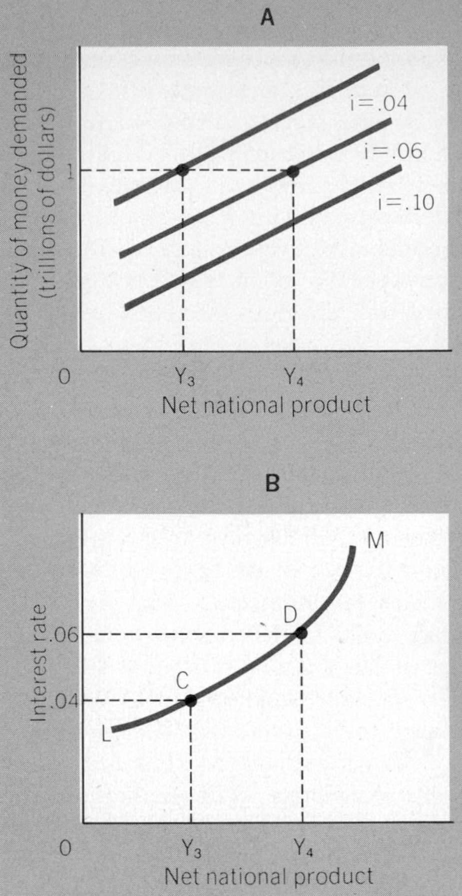

est rate, the more costly it is to hold money (because the more interest is forgone by holding money rather than investing it). Thus the higher the interest rate the smaller the amount of money that is demanded. In other words, the quantity of money demanded by the public is inversely related to the interest rate. (This is shown in panel A of Figure 16.13 by the fact that, if NNP is held constant, the quantity of money demanded increases as *i* decreases.)

Let's derive two points, *C* and *D*, on the *LM* curve, shown in panel B of Figure 16.13. Recall that any *LM* curve is based on the supposition that the money supply is *fixed*, and that the money supply must be just equal to the quantity of money demanded (for an equilibrium to occur). The *LM* curve in panel B of Figure 16.13 shows, for each interest rate, the value of NNP that will result in the public demanding this fixed amount of money, say $1 trillion. If the relationships in panel A of Figure 16.13 hold, the quantity of money demanded will equal $1 trillion if the interest rate is 4 percent and NNP is Y_3. Thus, if the interest rate is 4 percent, NNP (on this *LM* curve) must be Y_3—which explains the coordinates of point *C*. Panel A of Figure 16.13 shows that the quantity of money demanded will also equal $1 trillion if the interest rate is 6 percent and the NNP is Y_4. Thus, if the interest rate is 6 percent, NNP (on this *LM* curve) must be Y_4—which explains the coordinates of point *D*.

Note that to maintain the quantity of money demanded equal to the fixed money supply ($1 trillion in this case), an increase in the interest rate must be accompanied by an increase in NNP. Why? Because, holding NNP constant, an increase in the interest rate will reduce the quantity of money demanded, as shown in panel A of Figure 16.13. Thus, unless NNP is increased, the quantity of money demanded will be less than the fixed money supply. To bring it back into equality with the fixed money supply, and thus to maintain the equilibrium on which the *LM* curve is based, NNP must be increased. Similarly, a decrease in the interest rate must be accompanied by a decrease in NNP, if the quantity of money demanded is to equal the fixed money supply. For these reasons, *the* LM *curve slopes upward to the right.* That is, the higher the interest rate, the higher the level of NNP that satisfies the equilibrium condition underlying the *LM* curve.

The Equilibrium Level of NNP

As pointed out in an earlier section of this chapter, a full-scale equilibrium requires *both* that households and firms be spending the desired amounts relative to their incomes *and* that they be satisfied to hold the existing amount of money. In other words, both the equilibrium condition underlying the *IS* curve and the equilibrium condition underlying the *LM* curve must be satisfied. For this to be so, the equilibrium combination of NNP and interest rate must be at a point lying both on the *IS* curve (which means that it satisfies the equilibrium condition underlying this curve) and on the *LM* curve (which means that it satisfies the equilibrium condition underlying this curve).

If we plot the IS *and* LM *curves on the same diagram, as in Figure 16.14, the equilibrium combination of NNP and interest rate must therefore be the one that is given by the intersection of the two curves.* Only this combination

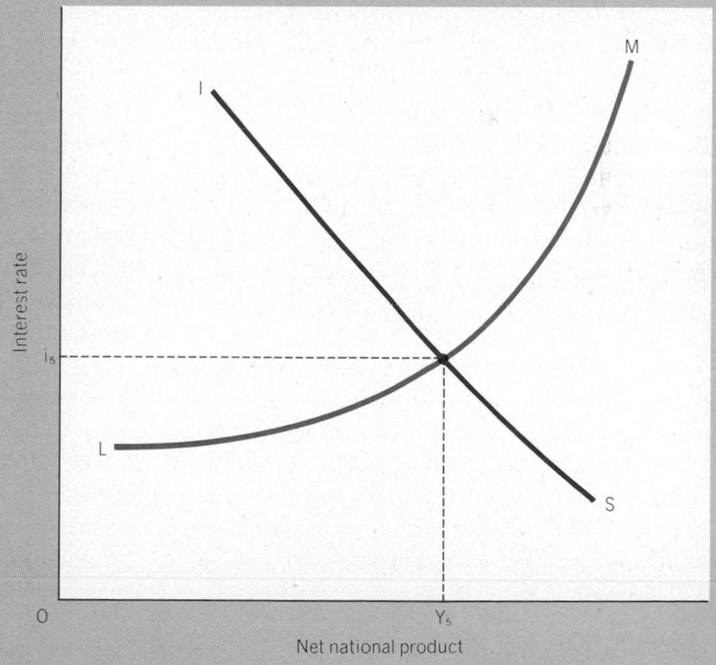

Figure 16.14
Determination of Equilibrium NNP and Interest Rate
The equilibrium level of NNP (and of the interest rate) must be at the intersection of the *IS* and *LM* curves. The equilibrium NNP equals Y_5, and the equilibrium interest rate equals i_5.

Figure 16.15
Effect of a $10 Billion Increase in Government Expenditures on *IS* Curve
If government expenditures are increased by $10 billion, and the interest rate is i_1, equilibrium NNP increases from Y_1 to Y_1'. If the interest rate is i_2, it increases from Y_2 to Y_2'. Since the level of NNP on the *IS* curve corresponding to any level of the interest rate is increased, the effect of the increase in government expenditures must be to shift the *IS* curve to the right.

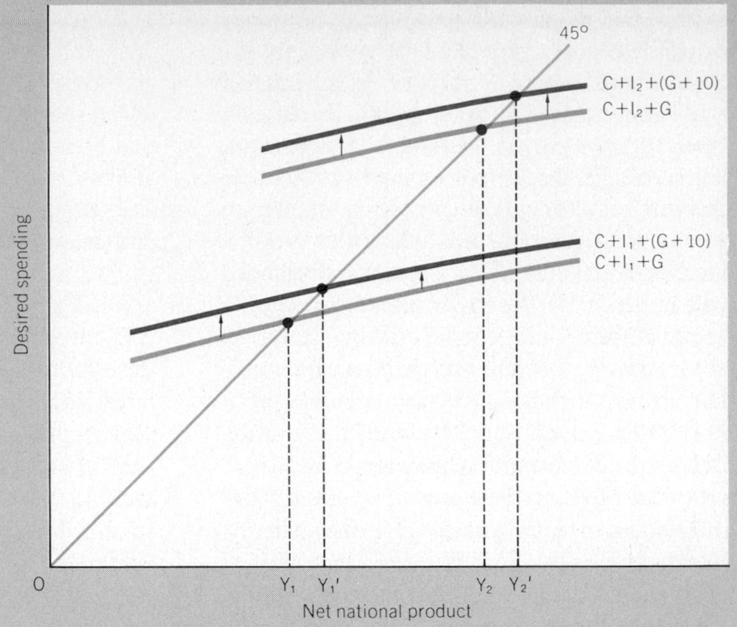

lies on both curves, and thus satisfies both equilibrium conditions. For example, in Figure 16.14, the equilibrium level of NNP must be Y_5, and the equilibrium level of the interest rate must be i_5. This is the only combination of NNP and interest rate that will satisfy both equilibrium conditions, given that the money supply, the public's demand curve for money, its consumption function, its investment function, and government expenditures (and taxes) remain fixed.

Effects of Fiscal and Monetary Policy on the IS *and* LM *Curves*

The IS *curve will shift to the right if government expenditures increase or taxes decrease.* The reason why these factors shift the *IS* curve to the right is that, holding the interest rate constant, each of these factors increases the level of NNP that satisfies the equilibrium condition underlying the *IS* curve.

To see why this is so, take as an example the effect of a $10 billion increase in government expenditures in Figure 16.12. Before the increase occurs, what is the equilibrium level of NNP corresponding to an interest rate of i_1? As we saw in Figure 16.12, it is Y_1. But after the increase occurs, it is no longer Y_1. Due to the increased government expenditure, the $C + I + G$ line in panel B of Figure 16.12 is raised from $C + I_1 + G$ to $C + I_1 + (G + 10)$, as shown in Figure 16.15. Thus the equilibrium level of NNP is increased to Y_1', as shown in Figure 16.15. Similarly, if the interest rate is i_2, the equilibrium level of NNP is increased to Y_2'. Since the level of NNP on the *IS* curve corresponding to each level of the interest rate is increased, the effect of the increase in government expenditure is to shift the *IS* curve to the right.

The LM *curve will shift to the right if the monetary authorities increase the money supply, and it will shift to the left if they decrease the money supply.* To see why, consider first an increase in the money supply. Under such circumstances, if the interest rate stays the same, NNP must increase in order to bring the quantity of money demanded into equality with the new money supply. Why? Because the quantity of money demanded, if it is to equal the new money supply, must increase, and an increase in NNP will result in such an increase in the quantity of money demanded. Thus, since the level of NNP where this equality holds (the interest rate being unchanged) is greater than before, the effect of the increase in the money supply must be to shift the *LM* curve to the right.

Next, consider a decrease in the money supply. If the interest rate stays the same, NNP must decrease in order to bring the quantity of money demanded into equality with the new money supply. Why? Because decreases in NNP will decrease the quantity of money demanded, which is required if the quantity of money demanded is to equal the diminished money supply. Thus, since the level of NNP where this equality holds (the interest rate being unchanged) is smaller than before, the effect of the decrease in the money supply must be to shift the *LM* curve to the left.

Effects of Fiscal Policy on NNP

To understand the difference between Keynesian and monetarist views concerning the effects of fiscal policy on NNP, it is useful to consider three alternative assumptions. First, let's assume that the economy is operating at a point where *the* LM *curve has a positive slope and is neither close to being vertical nor close to being horizontal.* Since an increase in government expenditures shifts the *IS* curve to the right, an expansionary fiscal policy will increase both NNP and the interest rate, if the *LM* curve has such a shape. Panel A of Figure 16.16 shows that this is the case. A shift to the right of the *IS* curve (such as from I_1S_1 to $I_1'S_1'$) increases both NNP (from Y_6 to Y_7) and the interest rate (from i_6 to i_7).

Second, let's assume that the economy is operating at a point where *the* LM *curve is close to being vertical.* Indeed, to make things simple, let's assume that it is vertical. If so, an expansionary fiscal policy results in an increase in the interest rate, but no increase in NNP. For example, in panel B of Figure 16.16, a shift to the right of the *IS* curve (such as from I_2S_2 to $I_2'S_2'$) increases the interest rate (from i_8 to i_9), but not NNP. This is the so-called *classical range* of the *LM* curve, where fiscal policy cannot increase NNP.

Third, let's assume that the economy is operating at a point where *the* LM *curve is horizontal (or nearly so).* If so, an expansionary fiscal policy results in an increase in NNP, but no increase in the interest rate. For example, in panel C of Figure 16.16, a shift to the right of the *IS* curve (such as from I_3S_3 to $I_3'S_3'$) increases NNP (from Y_8 to Y_9), but not the interest rate. This is sometimes called the *liquidity-trap range.*

Although both a perfectly vertical and a perfectly horizontal *LM* curve are polar extremes, they are useful in indicating the differences between the monetarists and the Keynesians. *The monetarists believe that the* LM *curve is close to vertical, whereas the Keynesians believe that it is much closer to horizontal.* (Why? Because of the differences in their assumptions, indicated in Figures 16.1 to 16.3.) Given their different views concerning the shape of the *LM* curve, it is easy to see why they come to quite different conclusions concerning the effects of fiscal policy on NNP. Clearly, the monetarists, based on their assumptions, will conclude that fiscal policy has less impact on NNP than will the Keynesians.

Effects of Monetary Policy on NNP

To understand the difference between Keynesian and monetarist views concerning the effects of monetary policy on NNP, it is useful to consider three alternative assumptions.

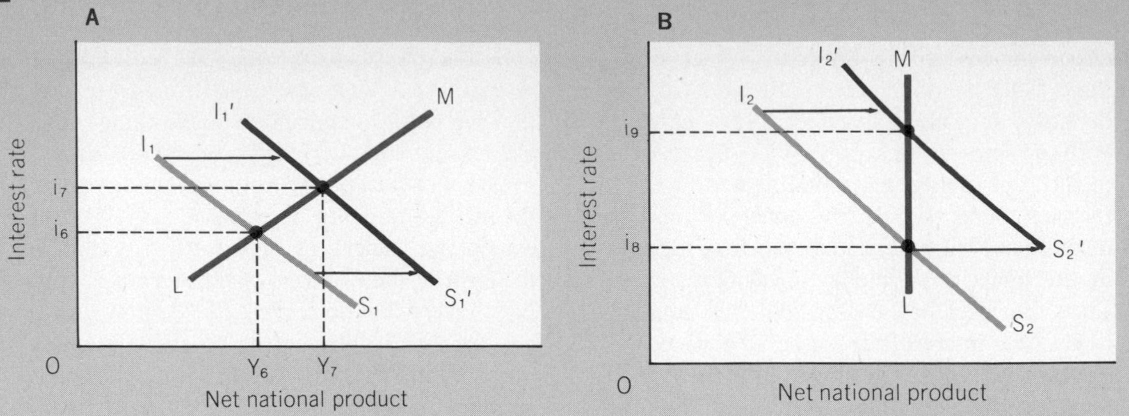

Figure 16.16
Effects of Fiscal Policy
An expansionary fiscal policy shifts the *IS* curve to the right. If the *LM* curve is upward sloped (as in panel A), the result of an expansionary fiscal policy will be an increase in both NNP and the interest rate. If the *LM* curve is vertical (as in panel B), the result will be an increase in the interest rate, but no increase in NNP. If the *LM* curve is horizontal (as in panel C), the result will be an increase in NNP, but no increase in the interest rate. The monetarists believe that the *LM* curve is close to vertical, whereas the Keynesians believe that it is closer to horizontal.

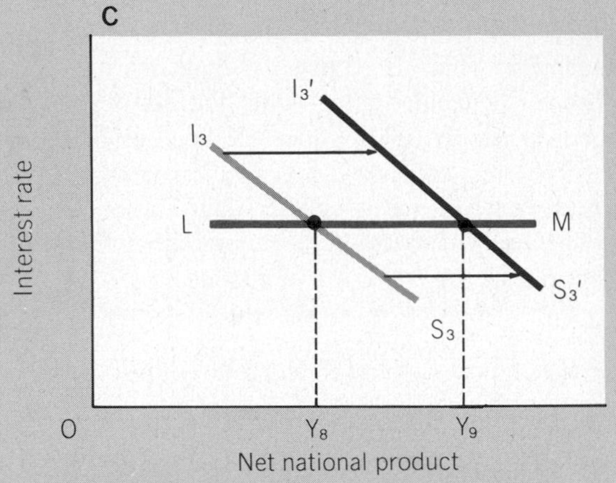

First, let's assume that the economy is operating at a point where the IS *curve has a negative slope and is neither close to being horizontal nor close to being vertical.* Since an increase in the money supply shifts the *LM* curve to the right, an expansionary monetary policy will increase NNP and reduce the interest rate, if the *IS* curve has this shape. Panel A of Figure 16.17 shows that this is the case. A shift to the right of the *LM* curve (from L_1M_1 to $L_1'M_1'$) increases NNP (from Y_{10} to Y_{11}) and reduces the interest rate (from i_{10} to i_{11}).

Second, let's assume that the economy is operating at a point where *the* IS *curve is horizontal (or very nearly so).* If so, expansionary monetary policy results in an increase in NNP, but little or no decrease in the interest rate. For example, in panel B of Figure 16.17, a shift to the right of the *LM* curve (from L_2M_2 to $L_2'M_2'$) increases NNP (from Y_{12} to Y_{13}) but does not reduce the interest rate.

Third, let's assume that the economy is operating at a point where *the* IS *curve is close to being vertical.* If so, an expansionary mone-

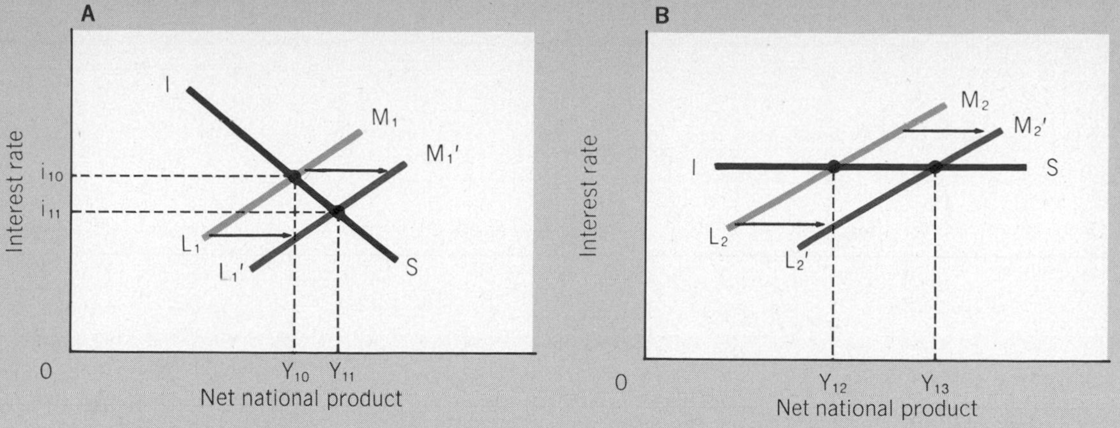

Figure 16.17
Effects of Monetary Policy
An increase in the money supply shifts the *LM* curve to the right. If the *IS* curve is downward sloped (as in panel A), an increase in the money supply will increase NNP and reduce the interest rate. If the *IS* curve is horizontal (as in panel B), it will increase NNP, but have no effect on the interest rate. If the *IS* curve is vertical (as in panel C), it will reduce the interest rate, but have no effect on NNP. The monetarists believe that the *IS* curve is close to horizontal, whereas some Keynesians believe that it is closer to vertical.

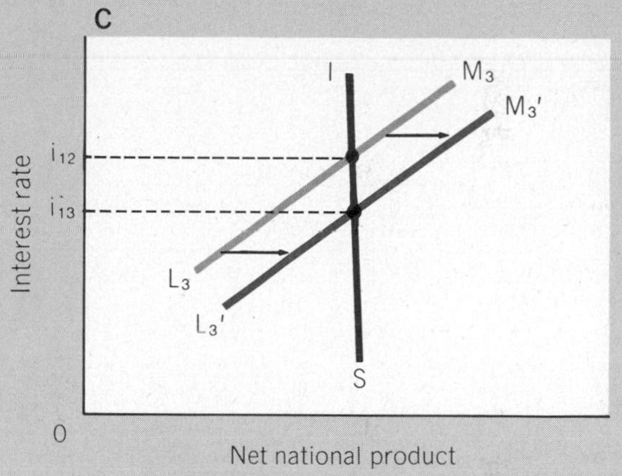

tary policy results in a decrease in the interest rate, but little or no increase in NNP. For example, in panel C of Figure 16.17, a shift to the right of the *LM* curve (from L_3M_3 to $L_3'M_3'$) decreases the interest rate (from i_{12} to i_{13}), but does not affect NNP.

Although both a perfectly horizontal and a perfectly vertical *IS* curve are polar extremes, they are useful in indicating the differences between the monetarists and the Keynesians. *Some Keynesians believe that the* IS *curve is close to vertical, whereas the monetarists believe that it is closer to horizontal.* (Why? Because of the differences in their assumptions, indicated in Figures 16.1 to 16.3.) Given their different views concerning the shape of the *IS* curve, it is easy to see why they come to different conclusions concerning the effects of monetary policy on NNP. Clearly, the monetarists, based on their assumptions, will conclude that monetary policy has a greater impact on NNP than will the Keynesians.

PART FIVE

Economic Growth, Energy, and the Environment

17

Economic Growth

Until fairly recently in human history, poverty was the rule, not the exception. As Sir Kenneth Clark puts it in his famous lectures on *Civilisation*,

> Poverty, hunger, plagues, disease: they were the background of history right up to the end of the nineteenth century, and most people regarded them as inevitable—like bad weather. Nobody thought they could be cured: St. Francis wanted to sanctify poverty, not abolish it. The old Poor Laws were not designed to abolish poverty but to prevent the poor from becoming a nuisance. All that was required was an occasional act of charity.[1]

Clearly, the human condition has changed considerably during the past century, at least in the industrialized nations of the world. Rising living standards have brought a decline in poverty, though by no means its disappearance. How has this increase in per capita output been achieved? This question has fascinated econo-

[1] K. Clark, *Civilisation*, New York: Harper & Row, 1970.

mists for a long time. Although we still are far from completely understanding the process of economic growth, our knowledge has increased considerably through the efforts of economic researchers, here and abroad. In this chapter, we discuss the process of economic growth in industrialized countries. A discussion of economic growth in less developed countries will be presented in Chapter 34.

Economic Growth: Definition and Evaluation

What Is Economic Growth?

There are two common measures of the rate of economic growth. The first is the rate of growth of a nation's real gross national product (or net national product),[2] which tells us how rapidly the economy's total real output of goods and services is increasing. The second is the rate of growth of *per capita* real gross national product (or net national product), which is a better measure of the rate of increase of a nation's standard of living. We shall use the second measure unless we state otherwise.

Two aspects of the rate of growth of per capita real gross national product should be noted from the start. First, *this measure is only a very crude approximation to the rate of increase of economic welfare.* For one thing, gross national product does not include one good that people prize most highly—leisure. For another, gross national product does not value at all accurately new products and improvements in the quality of goods and services, and does not allow properly either for noneconomic changes in the quality of life or for the costs of environmental pollution. Nor does gross national product take account of how the available output is distributed. Clearly, it makes a difference whether the bulk of the population gets a reasonable share of the output, or whether it goes largely to a favored few.

Second, *small differences in the annual rate of economic growth can make very substantial differences in living standards a few decades hence.* For example, per capita GNP in the United States was about $7,000 in 1975. If it grows at 3 percent per year, it will be about $14,600 (1975 dollars) in the year 2000, whereas if it grows at 4 percent per year, it will be about $18,700 (1975 dollars) in the year 2000. Thus an increase of 1 percentage point in growth rate means a $4,100—or 30 percent—increase in per capita GNP in the year 2000. Even an increase of ¼ of 1 percentage point can make a considerable difference. If the growth rate increases from 1¾ percent to 2 percent per year, per capita GNP in the year 2000 will increase from $10,800 to $11,500. Of course, this is no more than simple arithmetic, but that doesn't make it any less important.

Economic Growth as a Policy Objective

Following World War II, governments throughout the world became much more involved in trying to stimulate economic growth. In the United States, the government was not much inclined to influence the growth rate before the war. Of course, the government did many things that had some effect on the rate of economic growth, and in a general sort of way was interested in promoting economic growth. But it was normally taken for granted that, left to its own devices, our economy would manage to grow at more or less the proper rate. In the late 1950s and early 1960s, the climate of opinion began to change. To a considerable extent, this was because the U.S. rate of economic growth during the 1950s was rather low compared to that of other industrialized nations. From 1950 to 1959, per capita GNP grew by

[2] Either net national product or gross national product will do. As pointed out in Chapter 8, NNP has certain conceptual advantages, but GNP is more frequently used. It makes little difference since they do not differ by much. We use gross national product in this chapter, because data on GNP are more easily available.

about 2 percent per year in the United States, whereas it grew by about 6 percent in Japan, 5 percent in Italy and Germany, 4 percent in France, and 3 percent in the Netherlands, Norway, and Sweden. Moreover, our growth rate seemed to be less than that of the Soviet Union, the leading economic power in the Communist world.

The Call for Faster Economic Growth

During the late 1950s and early 1960s, many American economists and politicians drew attention to these facts, and called for an explicit public policy designed to increase our growth rate. In response, President Kennedy set as a target the attainment of a $4\frac{1}{2}$ percent annual increase in total output during the 1960s. Three principal arguments were given at that time for government stimulation of the rate of economic growth. First, it was argued that we had to increase our rate of economic growth to stay ahead of the Communist countries, the Soviet Union in particular. Economic growth was regarded as important for national defense and national prestige. In 1958, a report by the Rockefeller Brothers Fund concluded that growth was the most feasible way to provide for the defense outlays it envisioned as necessary in the future.

Second, it was argued that we should increase our rate of economic growth in order to increase public expenditures for schools, urban renewal, transportation, hospitals, and other such services. As we saw in Chapter 6, some observers, led by John Kenneth Galbraith, believed that there was a serious underinvestment in the public sector. Since it is very difficult politically to increase the percentage of GNP devoted to such services, it was felt that the only realistic way to remedy the situation was to increase the GNP. Then the absolute amount spent on the public sector could increase even if its percentage of GNP remained much the same.

Third, it was argued that we should increase our rate of economic growth in order to impress the neutral nations, many of which are relatively poor, with the benefits of our type of society. The emphasis here, as in the first argument, was on economic competition with the Communist world. According to many observers, the neutral countries were watching the growth rates of the Communist and capitalist countries, and the results would help decide which way these countries jumped. As the Council of Economic Advisers put it in 1962, "The less developed nations . . . need a further demonstration of the ability of a free economy to grow."[3]

During the 1970s, the enthusiasm for growth abated somewhat, for reasons discussed in the next section. But growth was by no means abandoned as a policy objective, in the United States or elsewhere. One important reason was that growth was viewed as a means by which poverty, here and abroad, might be reduced. If output per capita is rising, it is more likely that the electorate will vote to redistribute some of its income to the poor than if output per capita is constant. With growth, such a redistribution means that the poor can be made better off without cutting into the living standards of the more affluent. Without growth, this is impossible.

Skepticism toward Growth

Not all economists and policy makers agree that the government should alter the growth rate. Particularly in the past few years, there has been increasingly a feeling among economists (as well as the public at large) that economic growth should not be force-fed. Those who feel this way fall into two broad groups. One school of economists—including people like the University of Rochester's W. Allen Wallis, a prominent adviser to Presidents

[3] *1962 Annual Report of the Council of Economic Advisers,* Washington, D.C.: Government Printing Office, p. 110.

Nixon and Eisenhower—believes that the proper rate of economic growth is that which would emerge from private decisions. In their view, there is no reason to "force" growth on the economy, since there is no real possibility that the USSR will catch up with us soon, and the "unmet social needs" argument is little more than a slogan.

Another group of economists—led by E. J. Mishan of the London School of Economics—feels that economic growth, as usually measured, is a mirage. In their view, it has resulted in the degradation of the environment, the congestion and noise of our cities, the ugliness of some of the countryside, and the dullness of much of our work. They argue that the added production is not really of much value to society, and that people must be convinced by producers (through advertising and other sales techniques) that they want it. This viewpoint has appealed to many young people in recent years. However, it should be noted that if we are to reduce poverty, clean up the environment, and improve the quality of life, we shall need productive capacity, and economic growth is an important way to get it.

Whether or not the government should increase the rate of economic growth is, of course, a political decision; and your opinion of such a government policy will depend on many things, including your attitude toward present sacrifice for future material gain. As we shall see in subsequent sections, *a more rapid rate of growth can often be achieved only if consumers are willing to give up some consumption now so that they and their children can have more goods and services in the future.* To the extent that you believe that private decisions place too little weight on the future and too much weight on the present, you may be inclined to support a government policy designed to increase the growth rate. Otherwise you may not favor such a policy. In the next chapter, we shall discuss the pros and cons of economic growth in much more detail. Here we are concerned with its determinants.

The Aggregate Production Function

Economic Growth and the Product Transformation Curve

To represent the process of economic growth, it is convenient to use the product transformation curve which, as you will recall from Chapter 3, shows all efficient combinations of output an economy can produce. For example, suppose that a society produces only two goods, food and tractors. Then if this society has at its disposal a fixed amount of resources and if technology is fixed, the product tranformation curve (like the one in Figure 17.1) shows the maximum quantity of food that can be produced, given each amount of tractors produced.

Clearly, *a nation's potential output increases when its product transformation curve shifts outward,* for example, from position *A* to position *B* in Figure 17.2. This happens because the society can produce (and consume) more of one good without having to produce (and consume) less of the other good. Thus its productive capacity must be greater. If the product transformation curve shifts outward, if the economy is efficient, and if population remains constant, per capita GNP increases and economic growth occurs. Moreover, the faster the product transformation curve shifts outward, the greater the rate of economic growth.

Even if a nation's product transformation curve does not shift outward, economic growth can occur if unemployment or inefficiency is reduced. If a nation allows some of its resources to be unemployed or underutilized because of an insufficiency of desired spending, this will cause the economy to operate at a point *inside* the product transformation curve rather than *on* the curve. The same thing will happen if a nation allocates its resources inefficiently. Clearly, a nation can achieve some economic growth by getting closer to the product transformation curve through a reduction in unemployment or inefficiency.

A nation's potential output is directly related to the amount of resources it possesses and the extent to which they are used. These resources, or inputs, are of various kinds, including labor, capital, and land. The relationship between the amount used of each of these inputs and the resulting amount of potential output is often called the ***aggregate production function.*** It is analogous to the production function discussed in Chapter 7, which is the relationship between a firm's inputs and its output. However, the aggregate production function pertains to the entire economy, not a single firm.

Given that a nation's potential output depends on the amount of labor, capital, and land it uses, then the rate of growth of a nation's potential output must depend, in part at least, on the changes that occur in the amount of each of these inputs that is used. For example, if a nation invests heavily in additional capital, we would expect this to result in a substantial increase in potential output. Thus *a nation's rate of economic growth depends on the extent of the changes in the amounts of the various inputs used.* In addition, *a nation's rate of economic growth depends on the rate of technological change.* The aggregate production function is constructed on the assumption that technology is fixed. Changes in technology result in shifts in the production function, since more output is obtained from a given amount of resources.

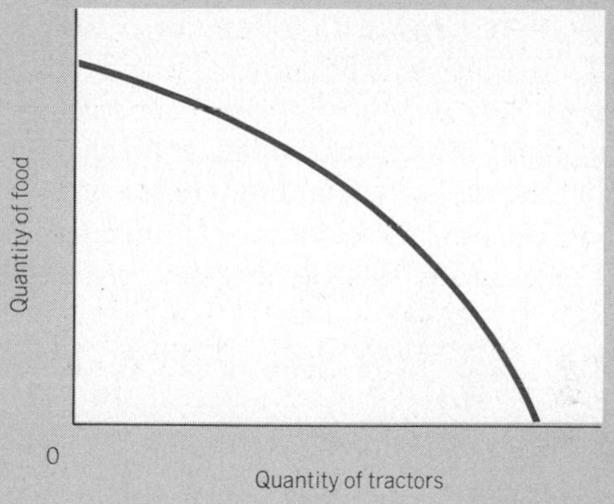

Figure 17.1
Product Transformation Curve
The product transformation curve shows all efficient combinations of output an economy can produce.

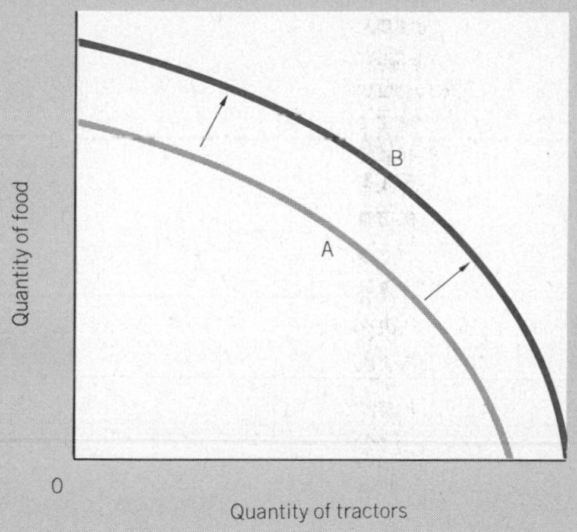

Figure 17.2
Outward Shift of Product Transformation Curve
A nation's potential output increases when its product transformation curve shifts outward, for example, from position *A* to positon *B*.

The Law of Diminishing Marginal Returns

If a nation's land, labor, and capital increase, one would certainly expect its output to increase as well. But suppose the nation cannot increase the amount used of all of its resources at the same rate. Instead, suppose it can increase the quantity of one resource, say labor, while the amount of other resources, like land, is held constant. In this situation, what will be the effect on output if the nation uses more and more of the resource that can be augmented? This is an important question, which occurs both in the present context and in the study of the production processes of the business firm.

To help answer it, economists have formulated the famous ***law of diminishing marginal returns,*** which states that, *if more and more of a resource is used, the quantities of other resources being held constant, the resulting increments of output will decrease after some point has been reached.* To see what this means, suppose that we obtain data concerning the amounts of output resulting from the utilization of various amounts of one resource, holding constant the amounts of other resources. For example, suppose that data are obtained concerning the amounts of output resulting from various amounts of labor, holding constant the amounts of capital and land. Then suppose that we determine the *extra* amount of output resulting from the addition of each *extra* unit of labor. According to the law of diminishing marginal returns, this extra amount of output will eventually *decrease,* as more and more labor is utilized with the fixed amounts of capital and land. In other words, beyond some point, *an additional unit of labor will add less and less to total output.*

To illustrate the workings of this law, consider Table 17.1, which shows the total output—or GNP—of a simple agricultural society under a set of alternative assumptions concerning the number of man-hours of labor used. For simplicity, we assume that this society produces only one product, corn, so that total output can be measured in bushels of corn. Also, we assume that the amount of land and capital that can be used is fixed in quantity. Column 1 in the table shows various alternative numbers of man-hours of labor that can be used with this fixed amount of land and capital. Column 2 shows the total output in each case.

Column 3 shows the additional output resulting from the addition of an extra man-hour of labor; this is called the ***marginal product***

Table 17.1
The Law of Diminishing Marginal Returns

(1) Man-hours of labor (millions)	(2) Bushels of corn (millions)	(3) Marginal product of labor (bushels per man-hour)	(4) Average product of labor (bushels per man-hour)
1	1.5		1.50
		2.0	
2	3.5		1.75
		2.5	
3	6.0		2.00
		3.0	
4	9.0		2.25
		2.0	
5	11.0		2.20
		2.0	
6	13.0		2.17
		1.0	
7	14.0		2.00
		0.0	
8	14.0		1.75

of labor. For example, if the quantity of labor is between 2 million man-hours and 3 million man-hours, the marginal product of labor is 2.5 bushels per man-hour of labor, because each extra man-hour of labor results in an extra 2.5 bushels of output.

In Table 17.1, the marginal product of labor increases as more and more labor is used, but only up to a point: beyond 4 million man-hours of labor, the marginal product of labor goes down as more and more labor is used. Specifically, the marginal product of labor reaches a maximum of 3.0 bushels per man-hour when between 3 and 4 million man-hours of labor are used. Then it falls to 2.0 bushels per man-hour when between 4 and 5 million man-hours of labor are used, remains at 2.0 bushels per man-hour when between 5 and 6 million man-hours of labor are used, and falls once again to 1.0 bushel per man-hour when between 6 and 7 million man-hours of labor are used.

Thus, as predicted by the law of diminishing marginal returns, *the marginal product of labor eventually declines.* Moreover, as shown in column 4 of Table 17.1, the ***average product*** of labor, which is defined as total output per man-hour, also falls beyond some point as more and more labor is used with a fixed amount of other resources. This too stems from the law of diminishing marginal returns.

It is easy to see why the law of diminishing marginal returns must be true. For example, imagine what would happen in the simple economy of Table 17.1 if more and more labor were applied to a fixed amount of land. Beyond a point, as more and more labor is used, the extra labor has to be devoted to less and less important tasks. If enough labor is used, it even becomes increasingly difficult to prevent the workers from getting in one another's way! For such reasons, one certainly would expect that, beyond some point, extra amounts of labor would result in smaller and smaller increments of output.

Finally, note several important things about this law. First, at least one resource must be fixed in quantity. The law of diminishing marginal returns does not apply to cases where there is a proportional increase in all resources. Second, technology is assumed to be fixed. Third, the law of diminishing marginal returns is an empirical generalization, not a deduction from physical or biological laws.

Thomas Malthus and Population Growth

A nation's rate of economic growth depends on, among other things, how much the quantities of inputs of various kinds increase. To illuminate the nature of the growth process, we discuss the effect on the rate of economic growth of increasing each kind of input, holding the others constant. We begin by looking at the effects of changes in the quantity of labor. Economists have devoted a great deal of attention to the effects of population growth on the rate of economic growth. The classic work was done by Thomas Malthus (1776–1834), a British parson who devoted his life to academic research. The first professional economist, he taught at a college established by the East India Company to train its administrators—and was called "Pop" by his students behind his back. Whether "Pop" stood for population or not, Malthus's fame is based on his theories of population growth.

Malthus believed that the population tends to grow at a geometric rate. In his *Essay on the Principle of Population,* published in 1798, he pointed out the implications of such a constant rate of growth:

> If any person will take the trouble to make the calculation, he will see that if the necessities of life could be obtained without limit, and the number of people could be doubled every twenty-five years, the population which might have been produced from a single pair since the

THOMAS MALTHUS
on Population

Throughout the animal and vegetable kingdoms Nature has scattered the seeds of life abroad with the most profuse and liberal hand; but has been comparatively sparing in the room and the nourishment necessary to rear them. . . . Necessity, that imperious, all-pervading law of nature, restrains them within the prescribed bounds. The race of plants and the race of animals shrink under this great restrictive law; and man cannot by any efforts of reason escape from it.

In plants and irrational animals, the view of the subject is simple. . . . The effects of this check on man are more complicated.

It may safely be pronounced that population, when unchecked, goes on doubling itself every twenty-five years, or increases in a geometrical ratio. The rate according to which the productions of the earth may be supposed to increase, will not be so easy to determine. Of this, however, we may be perfectly certain, that the ratio of their increase in a limited territory must be of a totally different nature from the ratio of the increase of population. A thousand millions are just as easily doubled every twenty-five years by the power of population as a thousand. But the food to support the increase from the greater number will by no means be obtained with the same facility. Man is necessarily confined in room. When acre has been added to acre til all the fertile land is occupied, the yearly increase of food must depend upon the melioration of the land already on possession. This is a fund, which, from the nature of all soils, instead of increasing, must be gradually diminishing. But population, could it be supplied with food, would go on with unexhausted vigor; and the increase of one period would furnish the power of a greater increase the next, and this without any limit. . . .

It may be fairly pronounced, therefore, that considering the present average state of the earth, the means of subsistence, under circumstances the most favorable to human industry, could not possibly be made to increase faster than in an arithmetical ratio. . . . The ultimate check to population appears then to be a want of food, arising necessarily from the different ratios according to which population and food increase.

Thomas Malthus, *An Essay on the Principle of Population,* London: Reeves and Turner, 1888, pp. 4–6. Originally published in 1798.

> Christian era, would have been sufficient, not only to fill the earth quite full of people, so that four should stand in every square yard, but to fill all the planets of our solar system in the same way, and not only them but all the planets revolving around the stars which are visible to the naked eye, supposing each of them . . . to have as many planets belong to it as our sun has.[4]

In contrast to the human population, which tends to increase at a geometric rate,[5] the supply of land can increase slowly if at all. And land, particularly in Malthus's time, was the source of food. Consequently, it seemed to Malthus that the human population was in danger of outrunning its food supply: "Taking the whole earth," he wrote, ". . . and supposing the present population to be equal to a thousand millions, the human species would increase as the numbers 1, 2, 4, 8, 16, 32, 64, 128, 256, and subsistence as 1, 2, 3, 4, 5, 6, 7, 8, 9. In two centuries, the population would be to the means of subsistence as 256 to 9; in three centuries as 4096 to 13, and in two thousand years the difference would be incalculable."[6]

Certainly, Malthus's view of humanity's prospects was bleak, as he himself acknowledged (in a masterpiece of British understatement) when he wrote that "the view has a melancholy hue." Gone is the optimism of Adam Smith: according to Malthus, the prospects for economic progress are very limited. Given the inexorable increase in human numbers, the standard of living will be kept at a minimum level required to keep body and soul together. If it exceeds this level, the population will increase, driving the standard of living back down. On the other hand, if the standard of living is less than this level, the population will decline because of starvation. Certainly, the long-term prospects were anything but bright. Thomas Carlyle, the famous historian and essayist, called economics "the dismal science." To a considerable extent, economics acquired this bad name through the efforts of Parson Malthus.

Malthus's theory can be interpreted in terms of the law of diminishing marginal returns. Living in what was still largely an agricultural society, he emphasized the role of land and labor as resources, and assumed a relatively fixed level of technology. Since land is fixed, increases in labor—due to population growth—will eventually cause the marginal product of

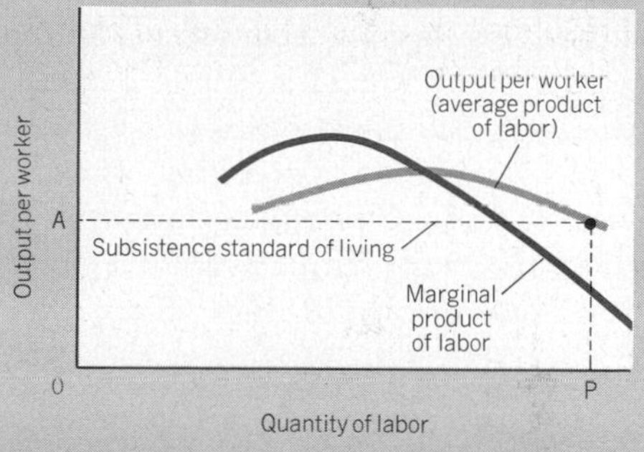

Figure 17.3
Diminishing Marginal Returns and the Effect of Population Growth
According to Malthus, the labor force will tend to *OP* because, if output per worker exceeds *OA*, population will increase, and if output per worker is less than *OA*, starvation will reduce the population.

[4] T. Malthus, *Essay on the Principle of Population,* as quoted by R. Heilbroner, *The Worldly Philosophers,* New York: Simon and Schuster, 1961, p. 71. For those who would like to read more concerning the history of economic thought, Heilbroner's book is highly recommended.

[5] Of course, it does not matter to Malthus's argument whether the population doubles every 25 years or every 40 years: the important thing is that it increases at a geometric rate.

[6] T. Malthus, "The Principle of Population Growth," reprinted in E. Mansfield, *Economics: Reading, Issues, and Cases,* 2d ed., New York: Norton, 1977. See also the full *Essay on the Principle of Population,* Philip Appleman, ed. New York: Norton, 1976, which contains critical commentary from Malthus's own time to the present.

labor to get smaller and smaller because of the law of diminishing marginal returns. In other words, because of this law, the marginal product of labor will behave as shown in Figure 17.3, with the result that continued growth of the labor force will ultimately bring economic decline—that is, a reduction in output per worker. This happens because as the marginal product of labor falls with increases in the labor force, the average product of labor will eventually fall as well—and the average product of labor is another name for output per worker.

Of course, Malthus recognized that various devices could keep the population down—war, famine, birth-control measures, among others. In fact, he tried to describe and evaluate the importance of various checks on population growth. For example, suppose that population tends to grow to the point where output per worker is at a subsistence level—just sufficient to keep body and soul together. If this is the case, and if the subsistence level of output per worker is *OA,* then the labor force will tend to equal *OP* in Figure 17.3. Why? Because, as noted above, Malthus believed that if the standard of living rises appreciably above *OA,* population will increase, thus forcing it back toward *OA.* On the other hand, if the standard of living falls below *OA,* some of the population will starve, thus pushing it back toward *OA.*

Effects of Population Growth

Was Malthus right? Among the less developed nations of the world, his analysis seems very relevant today. During the past 30 years, the population of the less developed nations has grown very rapidly, in part because of the decrease in death rates attributable to the transfer of medical advances from the industrialized countries to the less developed countries. Between 1940 and 1970, the total population of Asia, Africa, and Oceania almost doubled. There has been a tendency for growing populations to push hard against food supplies in some of the countries of Africa, Latin America, and Asia; and the Malthusian model can explain important elements of the situation.

However, Malthus's theory seems far less relevant or correct for the industrialized countries. In contrast to his model, population has not increased to the point where the standard of living has been pushed down to the subsistence level. On the contrary, the standard of living has increased dramatically in all of the industrialized nations. The most important mistake Malthus made was to underestimate the extent and importance of technological change. Instead of remaining fixed, the marginal-product-of-labor curve in Figure 17.3 moved gradually to the right, as new methods and new products increased the efficiency of agriculture. In other words, the situation was as shown in Figure 17.4. Thus, as population

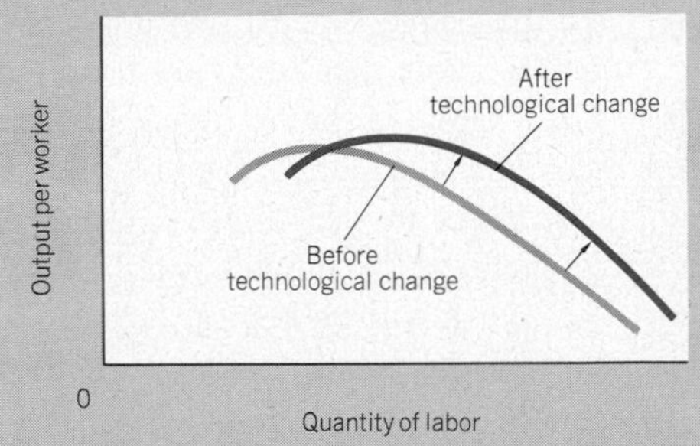

Figure 17.4
Shift over Time in the Marginal Product of Labor
Technological change has shifted the marginal-product-of-labor curve to the right.

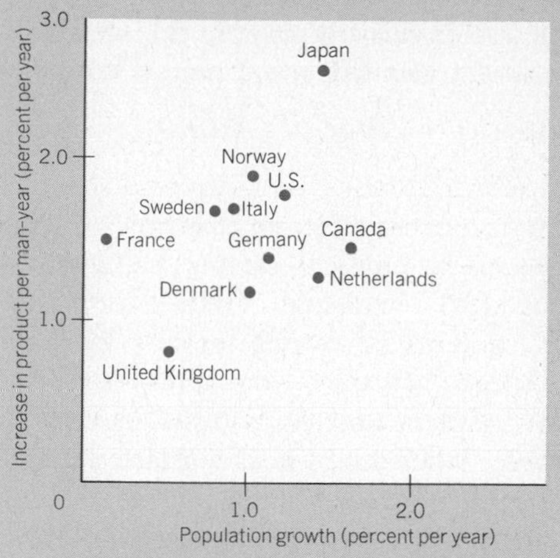

Figure 17.5
Relationship between Population Growth and Increases in National Product per Man-year, 11 Industrialized Nations, 1913–59
In industrialized nations, there is little or no relationship between a nation's rate of population growth and its rate of economic growth.

increased, the marginal product of labor did not go down. Instead, technological change prevented the productivity of extra agricultural workers from falling.

Among the industrialized nations, have countries with relatively high rates of growth of population had relatively low—or relatively high—rates of economic growth? In general, there seems to be little or no relationship between a nation's rate of population increase and its rate of economic growth. For example, Figure 17.5 plots the rate of population increase against the rate of growth of output per man-year in 11 industrialized nations between 1913 and 1959. The results suggest that there is little or no relation between them; and the relationship that exists appears to be direct rather than inverse.

David Ricardo and Capital Formation

Ricardo on Trade and Economic Growth

A contemporary and good friend of Malthus's who also contributed to the theory of economic growth was David Ricardo (1772–1823). Of all the titans of economics, he is probably least known to the general public. Smith, Malthus, Marx, and Keynes are frequently encountered names. Ricardo is not, although he made many brilliant contributions to economic thought. An extremely successful stockbroker who retired at the age of 42 with a very large fortune, he devoted much of his time to highly theoretical analyses of the economic system and its workings. In contrast to Malthus, who was reviled for his pessimistic doctrines. Ricardo and his writings were widely admired in his own time. He was elected to the House of Commons and was highly respected there.

Ricardo was concerned in much of his work with the distribution of income. Unlike Adam Smith, who paid much less attention to the conflict among classes, Ricardo emphasized the struggle between the industrialists—a relatively new and rising class in his time—and the landowners—the old aristocracy that resisted the rise of the industrial class. This clash was reflected in the struggle in Britain around 1800 over the so-called Corn Laws (*corn* being a general term covering all types of grain). Because of the increase in population, the demand for grain increased in Britain, causing the price of grain to rise greatly. This meant higher profits for the landowners. But the industrialists complained bitterly about the increase in the price of food, because higher food prices meant that they had to pay higher wages. As the price of grain increased, merchants began to import cheap grain from abroad. But the landowners, who dominated Parliament, passed legislation—the Corn Laws—to keep cheap grain out of Britain. In effect, the Corn Laws imposed a high tariff or duty on grain.

According to Ricardo's analysis, the landlords were bound to capture most of the benefits of economic progress, unless their control of the price of grain could be weakened. As national output increased and population expanded, poorer and poorer land had to be brought under cultivation to produce the extra food. As the cost of producing grain increased, its price would increase too—and so would the rents of the landlords. The workers and the industrialists, on the other hand, would benefit little, if at all. As the price of grain increased, the workers would have to get higher wages—but only high enough to keep them at a subsistence level (since Ricardo agreed entirely with his friend Malthus on the population issue). Thus the workers would be no better off; and neither would the industrialists, who would wind up with lower profits because of the increase in wage rates.

Ricardo felt that the Corn Laws should be repealed and that free trade in grain should be permitted. In a beautiful piece of theoretical analysis that is still reasonably fresh and convincing 150 years after its publication, he laid out the basic principles of international trade and pointed out the benefits to all countries that can be derived by specialization and free trade. For example, suppose that England is relatively more efficient at producing textiles, and France is relatively more efficient at producing wine. Then, on the basis of Ricardo's analysis, it can be shown that each country is likely to be better off by specializing in the product it is more efficient at producing—textiles in England, wine in France—and trading this product for the one the other country specializes in producing. In Chapter 31, we shall discuss this argument in considerable detail; it is a very important part of economics.

Ricardo's View of Capital Formation

Let's turn to the effect on economic growth of increases in physical capital, holding other inputs and technology fixed. Ricardo constructed some interesting theories concerning the effects of capital formation—i.e., investment in plant and equipment—on economic growth. Other things held constant, a nation's output depends on the amount of plant and equipment that it has and operates. Moreover, one can draw a curve showing the marginal product of capital—the extra output that would result from an extra dollar's worth of capital—under various assumptions about the total amount of capital in existence. This curve will slope downward to the right, as shown in Figure 17.6, because of the law of diminishing marginal returns. As more and more capital is accumulated, its marginal product eventually must decrease. For example, if $100 billion is the total investment in plant and equipment (or total capital), the extra output to be derived from an extra dollar of investment is worth $*A*; whereas if the total investment is increased to $150 billion, the economy must resort to less productive investments, and the extra output to be derived from an extra dollar of investment is only worth $*B*.

The curve in Figure 17.6 leads to the conclusion that investment in plant and equipment, although it will increase the growth rate up to some point, will eventually be unable to increase it further. As more and more is invested in new plant and equipment, less and less productive projects must be undertaken. Finally, when all the productive projects have been carried out, further investment in plant and equipment will be useless. At this point—

Figure 17.6
Marginal Product of Capital
This curve shows the marginal product of capital, under various assumptions concerning the total amount of capital. For example, if there is \$100 billion of capital, the marginal product of capital is \$*A*, whereas if there is \$150 billion of capital, the marginal product of capital is \$*B*.

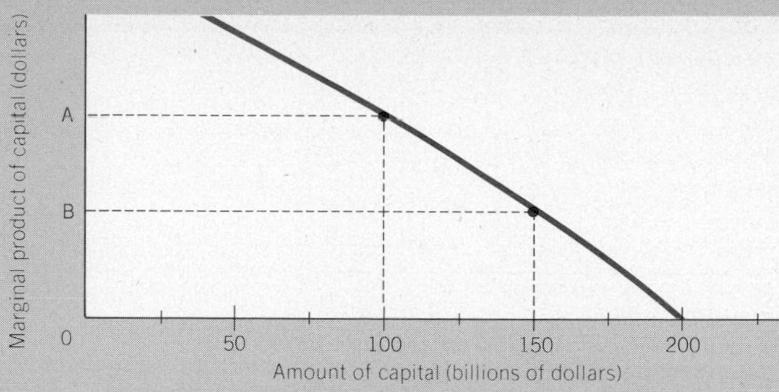

\$200 billion of total capital in Figure 17.6—further investment in plant and equipment will not increase output at all.

This kind of analysis led Ricardo to the pessimistic conclusion that the economy would experience decreases in the profitability of investment in plant and equipment, and eventual termination of economic growth. Also, he expected increases in the ratio of capital to output, because he expected increases in the total amount of capital to be accompanied by decreases in the marginal product of capital. To illustrate this, suppose that an economy's output equals \$1 trillion and its total capital is \$3 trillion. Suppose too that \$100 billion of extra capital will result in \$30 billion in extra output, another \$100 billion of extra capital will result in \$20 billion in extra output, and still another \$100 billion in extra capital will result in \$10 billion in extra output. Then the amount of capital per dollar of output will be (3,000 + 100)/(1,000 + 30) if \$100 billion is invested, (3,000 + 200)/(1,000 + 50) if \$200 billion is invested, and (3,000 + 300)/(1,000 + 60) if \$300 billion is invested. Since the marginal product of capital is decreasing, the amount of capital per dollar of output is increasing—from 3 to 3.01 to 3.05 to 3.11.

Was Ricardo right? Have we seen increases in the amount of capital per dollar of output, decreases in the profitability of investment in plant and equipment, and eventual termination of economic growth? Clearly, no. Ricardo, like Malthus, was led astray by underestimating the extent and impact of future changes in technology. Suppose that, because of the development of major new products and processes, lots of new opportunities for profitable investment arise. Obviously, the effect on the curve in Figure 17.6 is to shift it to the right, because there are more investment opportunities than before above a certain level of productivity. But if this curve shifts to the right, as shown in Figure 17.7, we may be able to avoid Ricardo's pessimistic conclusions.

To see how this can occur, note that, if XX' in Figure 17.7 is the relevant curve in a particular year and if \$100 billion is the total amount of capital, an extra dollar of investment in plant and equipment would have a marginal product of \$*C*. A decade later, if YY' is the relevant curve and if the total amount of capital has grown to \$150 billion, the marginal product of an extra dollar of investment in plant and equipment is still \$*C*. Thus there is no reduction in the productivity of investment opportunities despite the 50 percent increase in the total amount of capital. Because of technological change and other factors, productive and profitable new investment opportunities are opened up as fast as old ones are invested in.

Figure 17.7
Effects of Technological Change on the Marginal Product of Capital
Technological change has shifted the marginal-product-of-capital curve to the right. (Actually, Ricardo's variable input was a combined dose of capital and labor.)

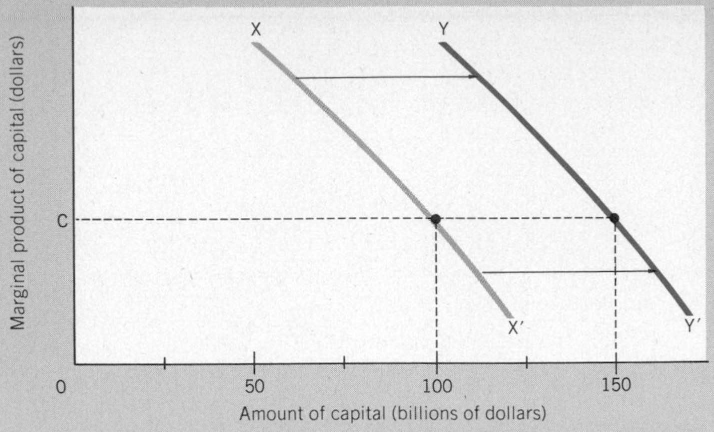

The history of the United States is quite consistent with this sort of shift in investment opportunities over time. Even though we have poured an enormous amount of money into new plant and equipment, we have not exhausted or reduced the productivity or profitability of investment opportunities. The rate of return on investment in new plant and equipment has not fallen. Instead, it has fluctuated around a fairly constant level during the past 70 years. Moreover, the amount of capital per dollar of output has remained surprisingly constant. It has not increased.

Effects of Capital Formation

To see more clearly the role of investment in the process of economic growth, let's extend the Keynesian model we discussed in Chapter 10. Suppose we ignore the government and consider only the private sector of the economy. Suppose that the full-employment, noninflationary NNP this year is $1,000 billion, and that the consumption function is such that consumption expenditure is $900 billion if NNP is $1,000 billion. If desired investment this year is $100 billion, with the result that NNP is in fact $1,000 billion, *next year's full-employment NNP will increase because this year's investment will increase the nation's productive capacity.* In other words, this year's investment increases next year's full-employment NNP. The amount of the increase in full-employment NNP depends on the ***capital-output ratio,*** which is the number of dollars of extra investment required to produce an extra dollar of output. For example, if the capital-output ratio is 2, $2 of investment is required to increase full-employment NNP by $1.

Let's look more closely at the effect of investment on full-employment NNP. If the capital-output ratio is 2, full-employment NNP will increase by $50 billion as a consequence of the $100 billion of investment: thus full-employment NNP next year is $1,050 billion. On the other hand, suppose that this year's investment is $200 billion rather than $100 billion, and that the consumption function is such that consumption expenditure is $800 billion rather than $900 billion if NNP is $1,000 billion. What will full-employment NNP be next year? If the capital-output ratio is 2, it will be $1,100 billion. Why? Because the $200 billion in investment will increase full-employment NNP by $100 billion—from $1,000 billion to $1,100 billion.

Thus the full-employment NNP will be

larger if investment is $200 billion than if it is $100 billion. Similarly, the full-employment NNP will be larger if investment is $300 billion than if it is $200 billion. If the capital-output ratio is 2, the full-employment NNP will be $1,150 billion next year, if investment is $300 billion. Why? Because the $300 billion in investment will increase full-employment NNP by $150 billion—from $1,000 billion to $1,150 billion.

In general, the greater the percent of NNP that the society devotes to investment this year, the greater will be the increase in its full-employment NNP. Thus, *so long as the economy sustains noninflationary full employment and the capital-output ratio remains constant, the rate of growth of national output will be directly related to the percent of NNP devoted to investment.*[7]

Certainly, this result seems sensible enough. If a country wants to increase its growth rate, it should produce more blast furnaces, machine tools, and plows, and less cosmetics, household furniture, and sports cars. But all this is theory. What do the facts suggest? Table 17.2 shows the rate of investment and the growth rate in the six major industrialized nations of the non-Communist world in 1955-64. The growth rate was highest in Japan, so was the investment rate. The growth rates were lowest in the United States and the United Kingdom, and so were the investment rates. Of course, this does not prove that there is any simple cause-and-effect relationship between the investment rate and the growth rate, but it certainly is compatible with the view that investment influences growth.

Table 17.2
Rate of Growth of Output per Man and Percent of GNP Invested in Physical Capital, 1955-64

Nation	Rate of growth of output per man (percent)	Percent of GNP Invested
	Annual Average	
France	4.7	15.7
Germany	4.4	20.1
Italy	5.7	16.9
Japan	8.8	30.2
United Kingdom	2.6	13.7
United States	1.9	13.9

Source: Angus Maddison, *Lloyds Bank Review*, January 1966, and E. Phelps, *The Goal of Economic Growth*, rev. ed., New York: Norton, 1969.

As revealed in the historical record of the United States, between 1929 and 1947 the amount of U.S. plant and equipment increased at about the same rate as the labor force. On the other hand, between 1947 and 1965, the amount of U.S. plant and equipment increased much more rapidly than the labor force. These facts would lead one to expect that the rate of economic growth would be more rapid in the latter period; and, in keeping with the theory, this turns out to be true. Again, one must be cautious about interpreting such comparisons. Lots of other things besides the investment rate were different in 1947-65 than in 1929-47, and these other things, not the investment rate, may have been responsible for the difference in growth rates. However, it seems likely that the difference in investment rates was at least partially responsible.

The Role of Human Capital

A nation's rate of economic growth is influenced by the rate at which it invests in

[7] It can be shown that the rate of growth of NNP equals s/b, where s is the proportion of NNP that is saved (and invested), and b is the capital-output ratio, assuming that both s and b are constant and that full employment is maintained. For example, if b is 2 and $s = .10$, NNP will grow at 5 percent per year, since $.10/2 = .05$. This result is part of the so-called Harrod-Domar growth model developed by Sir Roy Harrod of Oxford and Evsey Domar of M.I.T. Although useful, this result must be used with caution since it is based on highly simplified assumptions.

human capital as well as physical capital. It may seem odd to speak of *human* capital, but every society builds up a certain amount of human capital through investments in formal education, on-the-job training, and health programs. You often hear people talk about investing in their children's future by putting them through college. For the economy as a whole, the expenditure on education and public health can also be viewed—at least partly—as an investment, because consumption is sacrificed in the present in order to make possible a higher level of per capita output in the future.

The United States invests in human capital on a massive scale. For example, in 1960 expenditures for schools at all levels of education were about $25 billion, or about 5 percent of our gross national product. Moreover, our total investment in the education of the population—the "stock" of educational capital—has grown much more rapidly than has the stock of plant and equipment. For example, whereas the stock of physical capital was about 4 times as big in 1956 as in 1900, the stock of educational capital was about 8 times as big. These enormous and rapidly growing investments in human capital have unquestionably increased the productivity, versatility, and adaptability of our labor force. They have certainly made a major contribution to economic growth.

Income tends to rise with a person's education. Using this relationship to measure the influence of education on a person's productivity, some economists, notably the University of Chicago's Theodore Schultz and Gary Becker, have tried to estimate the profitability, both to society and to the person, of an investment in various levels of education. For example, Becker has tried to estimate the rate of return from a person's investment in a college education. According to his estimates, the typical urban white male in 1950 received about a 10 percent return (after taxes) on his investment in tuition, room, books, and other college expenses (including the earnings he gave up by being in college rather than at work). This was a relatively high return—much higher, for example, than if the student (or his family) simply put the equivalent amount of money in a savings bank or in government bonds.

By the mid-1970s, however, the return from the investment in a college education seemed to have fallen considerably. According to Richard Freeman of Harvard University and Herbert Hollomon of M.I.T., it declined from about 11 or 12 percent in 1969 to about 7 or 8 percent in 1974. In part, this was due to the increase in college tuition, as well as the recession experienced by the economy that year. Also, the income differential between college-educated and other workers seems to have narrowed. For example, in 1969, full-time, male workers with four years of college earned 53 percent more than male workers with only four years of high school, but in 1974, the differential was only about 40 percent. Whether this decrease in the return from a college education is temporary is hard to say.

The Role of Technological Change

A nation's rate of economic growth depends on the rate of technological change, as well as on the extent to which quantities of inputs of various kinds increase. Indeed, the rate of technological change is perhaps the most important single determinant of a nation's rate of economic growth. Recall from Chapter 1 that technology is knowledge concerning the industrial and agricultural arts. Thus technological change often takes the form of new methods of producing existing products; new designs that make it possible to produce goods with important new characteristics; and new techniques of organization, marketing, and management. Two examples of technological change are new ways of producing power (for example, atomic energy) and new fibers (for example, nylon or dacron).

We have already seen that technological change can shift the curves in both Figure 17.4 and 17.7, thus warding off the law of diminishing marginal returns. But note that new knowledge by itself has little impact. *Unless knowledge is applied, it has little effect on the rate of economic growth.* A change in technology, when applied for the first time, is called an ***innovation,*** and the firm that first applies it is called an ***innovator.*** Innovation is a key stage in the process leading to the full evaluation and utilization of a new process or product. The innovator must be willing to take the risks involved in introducing a new and untried process, good, or service; and in many cases, these risks are high. Once a change in technology has been applied for the first time, the ***diffusion process***—the process by which the use of the innovation spreads from firm to firm and from use to use—begins. How rapidly an innovation spreads depends heavily on its economic advantages over older methods or products. The more profitable the use of the innovation is, the more rapidly it will spread.

Joseph Schumpeter, Harvard's distinguished economist and social theorist, stressed the important role played by the innovator in the process of economic growth. In Schumpeter's view, the innovator is the mainspring of economic progress, the man with the foresight to see how new things can be brought into being and the courage and resourcefulness to surmount the obstacles to change. For his trouble, the innovator receives profit; but this profit eventually is whittled down by competitors who imitate the innovator. The innovator pushes the curves in Figure 17.4 and 17.7 to the right, and once his innovation is assimilated by the economy, another innovator may shove these curves somewhat further to the right. For example, one innovator introduces vacuum tubes, a later innovator introduces semiconductors; one innovator introduces the steam locomotive, a later innovator introduces the diesel locomotive. This process goes on and on—and is a main source of economic growth.

The Electronic Computer: A Case Study[8]

To get a better feel for the nature of technological change and the process of innovation, let's consider one of the most important technological advances of the twentieth century—the electronic computer. Many of the basic ideas underlying the computer go back to Charles Babbage, a brilliant nineteenth-century British inventor; but not until 1946 was the first electronic computer, the ENIAC, designed and constructed. John Mauchly and J. Presper Eckert, both professors at the Moore School of Electrical Engineering at the University of Pennsylvania, were responsible for the ENIAC's design and construction. The work was supported by the U.S. Army. John von Neumann, a famous mathematician at the Institute for Advanced Study at Princeton, added the important concepts of stored programming and conditional transfer.

After the war, Mauchly and Eckert established a small firm to produce electronic computers. Their firm was acquired by Remington Rand, which in 1951 marketed the Univac I, a machine used by the Census Bureau. The International Business Machines Corporation (IBM), the leading company in office machinery and data processing, which before this had been cautious about the potential market for computers, was spurred into action by Remington Rand's success. Once it entered the field, IBM's financial resources, strong marketing organization, and engineering strength enabled it to capture a very large share of the

[8] This and the following section are based to a considerable extent on E. Mansfield, *The Economics of Technological Change,* New York: Norton, 1968; and my paper in the International Economic Association's *Science and Technology in Economic Growth,* London: Macmillan, 1973.

computer market, here and abroad. In the United States, IBM's share of the market grew to about 90 percent during the 1960s.

The electronic computer has been an extremely important stimulus to economic growth. By 1966, the total number of computers installed in the Western world exceeded 50,000 at a total value of about $20 billion. These computers have had important effects on production techniques in many industries. For example, in the chemical, petroleum, and steel industries, digital computers were an important step in the evolution of control techniques. Computers helped to determine and enforce the best conditions for process operation, as well as acting as data loggers. They could also be programmed to help carry out the complex sequence of operations required to start up or shut down a plant. They have increased production, decreased waste, improved quality control, and reduced the chance of damage to equipment. In another quite different industry, banking, computers have had an important effect too. They have made it possible to eliminate conventional machines and processes for sorting checks, balancing accounts, and computing service charges. With high-speed sorters, it is possible now to process more than 1,500 checks per minute.

Obviously, the electronic computer has enabled us to produce more output from a given amount of resources. In other words, it has enabled us to push the product transformation curve outward, thus increasing our rate of economic growth. But it must be recognized that the process by which the computer has had this effect has by no means been simple or straightforward. Many people in many countries were involved in the development of the basic ideas. Many organizations, public and private, funded the experimental work. Firms of various types were the innovators with respect to particular aspects of the modern computer. And countless individuals and organizations had to be willing to accept, work with, and invest in computers.

Technological Change: Determinants and Measurement

What determines the rate of technological change and the rate at which changes in technology are applied and spread? Clearly, the nature and extent of a nation's scientific capability, and the size and quality of its educational system are of fundamental importance. The first thing that must be said about the influence of a nation's scientific capability on its rate of technological change is that science and technology are two quite different things that have drawn together only recently. Until the twentieth century, it simply was not true that technology was built on science. Even today, many technological advances rely on little in the way of science. However, in more and more areas of the economy (such as aircraft, electronics, and chemicals), the rapid application of new technology has come to depend on a strong scientific base. Merely to imitate or adapt what others have developed, a firm in these areas needs access to high-caliber scientists.

A nation's educational system also has a fundamental influence on the rate of technological change. First, and perhaps most obviously, it determines how many scientists and engineers are graduated, and how competent they are. Clearly, the rate of technological change depends on the quantity and quality of scientific and engineering talent available in the society. Second, the educational system influences the inventiveness and adaptability of the nation's work force. Despite the closer links between technology and science, workers and independent inventors remain important sources of inventions in many areas. Third, the educational system also influences the rate of technological change and innovation via the training of managers.

Industrial managers are a key agent in the innovative process. We must emphasize that the proper management of innovation is much more than establishing and maintaining a research and development laboratory that produces a great deal of good technical output. In many industries, most important innovations are not based in any significant degree on the firms' research and development. And even when the basic idea does come from a firm's own R and D, the coupling of R and D with marketing and production is crucial. Many good ideas are not applied properly because the potential users do not really understand them, and many R and D projects are technically successful but commercially irrelevant because they were not designed with sufficient comprehension of market realities. Typically, successful technological innovations seem to be stimulated by perceived production and marketing needs, not by technological opportunities. In other words, most of the time it takes a market-related impetus to prompt work on a successful innovation.

In addition, the rate of technological change depends on the organization of industry and the nature of markets. Although a certain amount of industrial concentration may promote more rapid technological change, increases in concentration beyond a moderate level probably reduce rather than increase the rate of technological change. The rate of technological change also depends on the scale and sophistication of available markets. The scale of the market influences the extent to which a firm can spread the fixed costs of developing and introducing an innovation. This factor has often been cited as a reason for America's technological lead over many other countries. Finally, it is extremely important to note that a country that is not a technological leader can still achieve considerable technological change by borrowing and transferring technology from the leaders.

It is difficult to measure the rate of technological change. Perhaps the most frequently used measure is the rate of growth of labor productivity—that is, the rate of growth of output per man-hour. Unfortunately, this measure is influenced by lots of other factors besides the rate of technological change. Nonetheless, despite its inadequacies, it is worthwhile to look briefly at how rapidly productivity has increased in the United States over the long run. Since about 1890, the nation's real output per man-hour increased by about 2 percent per year—and these productivity gains were widely diffused, real hourly earnings growing about as rapidly, on the average, as output per man-hour.

In part because of differing rates of technological change, there have been considerable

Table 17.3
Average Annual Rates of Increase of Labor Productivity, Selected Manufacturing Industries, 1947–73.

Industry	Productivity increase (percent per year)
Canning and preserving	3.2
Flour	4.1
Bakery products	2.4
Sugar	4.2
Candy	3.2
Malt liquors	5.1
Soft drinks	3.5
Tobacco products	3.1
Hosiery	5.4
Paper	4.0
Boxes	3.4
Man-made fibers	5.7
Drugs[a]	4.9
Paints	2.5
Petroleum refining	5.8
Tires	3.9
Footwear	1.3
Glass containers	1.7
Cement	4.5
Steel	1.8
Copper, lead, and zinc	2.3
Aluminum	4.5
Household appliances	5.3
Motor vehicles	3.9

Source: National Commission on Productivity and Work Quality, *Fourth Annual Report*, March 1975.
[a]1960–73.

differences among industries in the rate of growth of output per man-hour. As shown in Table 17.3, labor productivity increased after World War II in some industries—like man-made fibers—by more than 5 percent per year, and in other industries—like footwear—by only about 1 percent per year. To some extent, these differences can be explained by interindustry differences in the amount spent on *research and development.* In addition, a number of other factors—like the amount spent by *other industries* to improve the capital goods and other inputs the industry uses, the extent of *competition* in the industry, the attitudes of *unions* toward change, and the quality of *management*—undoubtedly played important roles too in explaining these interindustry differences in productivity increase.

Entrepreneurship and the Social Environment

Still another set of basic factors influencing a nation's level of potential output and its rate of economic growth is the economic, social, political, and religious climate of the nation. It is difficult, if not impossible, to measure the effect of these factors, but there can be no doubt of their importance. Some societies despise material welfare and emphasize the glories of the next world. Some societies are subject to such violent political upheavals that it is risky, if not foolish, to invest in the future. Some societies are governed so corruptly that economic growth is frustrated. And some societies look down on people engaged in industry, trade, or commerce. Obviously, such societies are less likely to experience rapid economic growth than others with a more favorable climate and conditions.

The relatively rapid economic growth of the United States was undoubtedly stimulated in part by the attitude of its people toward material gain. It is commonplace to note that the United States is a materialistic society, a society that esteems business success, that bestows prestige on the rich, that accepts the Protestant ethic (which, crudely stated, is that work is good), and that encourages individual initiative. The United States has been criticized over and over again for some of these traits—often by nations frantically trying to imitate its economic success. Somewhat less obvious is the fact that, because the United States is a young country whose people came from a variety of origins, it did not inherit many feudal components in the structure of society. This too was important.

The United States has also been characterized by great economic and political freedom, by institutions that have been flexible enough to adjust to change, and by a government that has encouraged competition in the market place. This has meant fewer barriers to new ideas. Also, the United States has for a long time enjoyed internal peace, order, and general respect for property rights. There have been no violent revolutions since the Civil War, and for many years we were protected from strife in other lands by two oceans—which then seemed much broader than they do now. All these factors undoubtedly contributed to rapid economic growth.

The American economy also seems to have been able to nurture a great many entrepreneurs and a vast horde of competent businessmen. During the nineteenth century, American entrepreneurs were responsible for such basic innovations as the system of interchangeable parts, pioneered by Eli Whitney and others. In many areas, the United States gained a technological lead over other nations, and the available evidence seems to indicate that, to a significant extent, this lead has been maintained. It must be recognized that much of this lead has come from superior management as well as superior technological resources. For example, the Organization for Economic Cooperation and Development recently concluded, "In the techniques of *management*, including the management of research, and of combined technological and market forecasting, the United States appears to have a significant lead."[9]

The Gap between Actual and Potential Output

Up to this point, our discussion of economic growth has centered on the factors that determine how rapidly a nation's potential output grows—factors like technological change, increased education, investment in plant and equipment, and increases in the labor force. Now we must examine the factors that determine how close a nation's actual output comes to its potential output. As we already know, a nation's potential output is its output under full employment. Thus, as we also know, whether or not the economy operates close to full employment is determined by the level of the $C + I + G$ line. If the $C + I + G$ line is too low, the economy will operate with considerable unemployment, and actual output will be substantially below potential output. Or, in terms of the equation of exchange, if $M \times V$ is too small, the economy will operate with considerable unemployment, and actual output will be substantially below potential output.

From previous chapters, we also know how the government can use fiscal and monetary policies to push actual output close to potential output. Cuts in tax rates, increases in government spending, incentives for private investment in plant and equipment, increases in the money supply, reductions in interest rates; all these devices can be used to push actual output closer to potential output. Such devices promote economic growth, in the sense that actual per capita output is increased. However, only so much growth can be achieved by squeezing the slack out of the economy. For example, if there is a 7 percent unemployment rate, output per capita can be increased by perhaps 9 percent simply by reducing the unemployment rate to 4 percent, as we saw in Chapter 8. *But this is a one-shot improvement.* To get any further growth, the nation must increase its potential output.

Of course this doesn't mean that it isn't important to maintain the economy at close to full employment. On the contrary, as we stressed in Chapter 8, one of the major objectives of public policy must be full employment, and a reduction of unemployment will have a significant effect on the rate of economic growth in the short run. (Much of the economic growth in the United States in the early 1960s was caused by the transition to full employment.) But the point we are making is that, once the economy gets to full employment, no further growth can occur by this route. If a nation wants further growth, it must influence the factors responsible for the rate of growth of potential output.

Japan: A Case Study of Rapid Economic Growth

Japan has experienced a very high rate of economic growth for a long time. Especially after World War II, the Japanese economy increased per capita GNP very rapidly. For example, between 1955 and 1964 gross national product per man increased at an average rate of 8.8 percent per year. Some of the most important reasons for this rapid growth are as follows:[10]

High investment. After World War II, the

[9] Organization for Economic Cooperation and Development, *Technology Gap: General Report*, Paris, 1968, p. 25. However, according to many observers, our lead in this respect is being reduced.

[10] For further discussion, see K. Ohkawa and H. Rosovsky, "Recent Japanese Growth in Historical Perspective," *American Economic Review*, May 1963, pp. 578–88; and M. Peck (with the collaboration of S. Tamura), "Infusion of Technology and the Mysteries of the Catch-Up," unpublished, 1974.

rate of investment in plant and equipment was extremely high. For example, in 1954 the Japanese devoted over 20 percent of their GNP to the formation of physical capital; and in 1961 and 1964, they devoted 35 and 33 percent, respectively. While this high rate of capital formation was due, particularly in the early postwar years, to the dislocations caused by the war, this was not the only reason. To a considerable extent, the rate was high because Japan was catching up with technological developments elsewhere in the world. Japan invested heavily in newer industries based on innovations in other countries—television, electronic devices, synthetics, and others—as well as in older industries like steel, machinery, and chemicals.

Technological transfer. A second very important contributor to Japan's economic growth was the borrowing and application of technology developed in other countries. The Japanese were skilled borrowers of Western technology. Their success illustrates a very important point often overlooked by nations interested in increasing their growth rates. To benefit from technology, a nation does not have to develop or invent it. Conversely, because a country develops or invents a new product or process, it does not follow that the product or process will do much for its rate of economic growth. If another country is quicker to apply and exploit the innovation, it may get more of the economic benefits. The Japanese concentrated their energies and resources on transferring Western technology rather than developing or inventing their own. This strategy paid off well.

Education and other factors. Japan has also had an abundant supply of educated labor, which has made it much easier to assimilate new technology. The importance of such an investment in human capital has been emphasized in previous sections. And Japan undoubtedly benefited from the fact that its burden of national defense was largely assumed by the United States, so that Japanese resources could be devoted to economic development rather than to defense. Last, Japan's level of per capita GNP was lower than that of most of the nations with which it is generally compared. It is often argued that countries at a relatively low level of economic development find it easier to achieve a high growth rate than do more affluent societies. In other words, a high rate of growth may be easier to achieve from a low economic base.

In conclusion, it is worth noting that the recession of the mid-1970s hit Japan, as it did other major industrialized countries. Despite the emphasis in Japan upon lifetime employment, firms had to lay off many workers; indeed, the unemployed swelled to 1.2 million in January 1976, a postwar high. Some Japanese seemed to believe that the days of rapid growth were over. But as is clear from the previous section, whether or not this is true depends to a considerable extent on how fast Japan can get back to full employment. If the Japanese can squeeze the slack out of their economy relatively quickly, their growth rate may not suffer greatly over the long run.

Summary

Economic growth is measured by the increase of per capita real gross national product, an index that does not measure accurately the growth of economic welfare, but is often used as a first approximation. In the recent past, many economists and politicians called for an explicit public policy designed to increase our growth rate. A nation's rate of economic growth depends on the increase in the quantity and quality of its resources (including physical and human capital) and the rate of technological change. In addition, the rate of economic growth depends on the extent to which a society maintains full employment and on the efficiency with which its resources are allocated and managed.

One factor that may influence a nation's rate of economic growth is the rate at which its population grows. In Malthus's view, population growth, unless checked in some way, ultimately meant economic decline, since output could not grow in proportion to the growth in population. The law of diminishing marginal returns insured that beyond some point, increases in labor, holding the quantity of land constant, would result in smaller and smaller increments of output. However, Malthus underestimated the extent and importance of technological change, which offset the law of diminishing marginal returns.

Another factor that determines whether per capita output grows rapidly or slowly is the rate of expenditure on new plant and equipment. Without technological change, more and more of this sort of investment would result in increases in the amount of capital per dollar of output and decreases in the profitability of investment in plant and equipment, as Ricardo pointed out. But because of technological change, none of these things has occurred. According to the available evidence, a nation's rate of economic growth seems directly related to its rate of investment in plant and equipment.

To a considerable extent, economic growth here and abroad has resulted from technological change. A change in technology, when applied for the first time, is called an innovation, and the firm that first applies it is called an innovator. Innovation is a key stage in the process leading to the full evaluation and utilization of a new process or product. Unless knowledge is used, it has little effect on the rate of economic growth. The rate of technological change and the rate at which new technology is applied depend on a number of factors, including the nature and extent of a nation's scientific capability, the size and quality of its educational system, the quality of its managers, the attitude and structure of its firms, the organization of its industries, and the nature of its markets.

Another factor with an important effect on a nation's rate of economic growth is the rate at which it invests in human capital. The United States invests in human capital on a massive scale, and these enormous and rapidly growing investments have unquestionably increased the productivity, versatility, and adaptability of our labor force. Still another set of basic factors influencing the rate of economic growth is the economic, social, and political climate of the nation. Some societies despise material welfare, are subject to violent political upheavals, and are governed by corrupt groups. Such societies are unlikely to have a high rate of economic growth. Finally, the rate of economic growth is also affected by the extent and behavior of the gap between actual and potential GNP. However, once a nation gets to full employment, it cannot grow further by reducing this gap.

CONCEPTS FOR REVIEW

Economic growth
Capital formation
Population increase
Marginal product of labor
Average product of labor
Law of diminishing marginal returns
Technological change
Innovation
Innovator
Diffusion process
Aggregate production function

QUESTIONS FOR DISCUSSION AND REVIEW

1. Suppose that a society produces only two goods, food and tractors, and that its product transformation curve in 1976 and 1977 is given below:

Quantity of food (millions of tons)	Quantity of tractors (thousands of tractors)
0	9
1	8
2	7
3	5
4	3
5	0

If this society produces 4,000 tractors and 3 million tons of food in 1976 and 5,000 tractors and 3 million tons of food in 1977 (its population remaining constant), has any economic growth occurred between 1976 and 1977? If so, to what is it due?

2. Suppose that the society in Question 1 produces 6,000 tractors and 3 million tons of food in 1978 (its population remaining the same as in 1977), has any economic growth occurred between 1977 and 1978? If so, is it due entirely to a shift in the product transformation curve? How can you tell?

3. Suppose that a society produces only one commodity, wheat, and that it has the following aggregate production function:

Man-hours of labor (millions)	Bushels of wheat (millions)
0	0
1	2
2	4
3	6
4	7
5	7

What is the marginal product of labor when between 1 and 2 million man-hours of labor are used? When between 2 and 3 million man-hours of labor are used? When between 4 and 5 million man-hours of labor are used? Do the results conform to the law of diminishing marginal returns? Why or why not?

4. Suppose that an advance in technology doubles the output that can be obtained from each amount of labor in Question 3. Under these new conditions, what is the marginal product of labor when between 1 and 2 million man-hours of labor are used? When between 4 and 5 million man-hours of labor are used? Do the results conform to the law of diminishing marginal returns? Why or why not?

5. In Question 3, suppose that the subsistance wage was 1,400 bushels of wheat. According to Malthus, what would have been the equilibrium labor force? What factors would push the labor force toward this level? What would be the effect of the technological advance in Question 4 on the equilibrium labor force?

6. Suppose that a society's full-employment NNP increases between 1975 and 1976 by $100 billion. During the same period, its corporations floated $20 billion in stocks and bonds, and it invested $200 billion. What is the capital-output ratio in this society? Will the capital-output ratio in this society always be the same? Why or why not?

7. Suppose that a society's capital-output ratio is 3 and that it invests 10 percent of its NNP. If full employment is maintained, by what percentage will its NNP grow?

8. "Ricardo's pessimistic view of the prospects for economic growth stemmed from his assumptions concerning the capital-output ratio. If he had recognized that it was not fixed, he would have been closer to correct." Comment and evaluate.

9. In 1971, Herbert Stein wrote, "During the past 4 years the rates of growth in productivity . . . slowed down." What are some possible reasons why this occurred? What is the significance of this slowdown?

10. Describe in as much detail as you can the ways in which capital formation, population growth, technological change, and education are interrelated. Show how these interrelationships make it difficult to sort out the effect of each of these factors on the rate of economic growth.

18 American Economic Growth: History, Policies, Problems, and Prospects

About a century ago, Benjamin Disraeli, the famous British prime minister, said that "increased means and increased leisure are the two civilizers of man." Although one might add to Disraeli's list of "civilizers," there can be little doubt that economic growth has helped to improve man's lot. Since World War II, the rate of economic growth has become a major index, both here and abroad, of how well an economy is performing; and many governments have tried to increase their rate of economic growth. In 1960 John F. Kennedy ran for president on a platform emphasizing the need for faster economic growth in the United States; and in subsequent elections—here and abroad—economic growth frequently has been a campaign issue.

However, bigger may not always be better. More and more often, observers in recent years have stressed that economic growth may not be an unalloyed blessing. It too has its costs. Indeed, the pros and cons of more rapid economic growth have been the subject of much debate. In this chapter, we are concerned with four basic questions about economic growth in the United States. What has been our rate of economic growth in the past? What are the advantages and disadvantages of a faster rate of economic growth? If faster growth is desired, what measures can the government take to promote it? And, assuming that present trends continue, what rate of economic growth can we expect in the future?

Economic Growth in the United States

Let's begin by looking at the salient facts about the rate at which the American economy has grown in the past. Soon after its emergence as an independent nation, the United States reached a relatively high level of economic development. By 1840, it ranked fourth in per capita income, behind England, France, and Germany. During the next 30 years, the United States experienced relatively rapid economic growth. By 1870, it ranked second only to England in per capita income. In the next 40 years, the American economy continued to grow rapidly. National product per person employed grew by about 2.2 percent per year between 1871 and 1913. This growth rate was higher than for practically any other major industrialized nation; and well before the turn of the century, income per capita was greater in the United States than in any other nation in the world.

Between 1913 and 1959, the American growth rate was somewhat lower than in previous years. National product per person employed grew by about 1.8 percent per year. Nonetheless, although we grew less rapidly than in earlier years, we pulled further ahead of most other industrialized countries, because we continued to grow faster than they did. Of course, our rate of economic growth varied from decade to decade: economic growth does not proceed at a steady rate. In some decades (like the 1920s), our economy grew rapidly, while in others (like the 1930s), it grew little, if at all. During periods of recovery and prosperity, the growth rate was high; during depressions, it was low. In the 1950s, the growth rate in the United States was lower than in many other countries. As pointed out in the previous chapter, this caused considerable controversy and some alarm.

During the 1960s, our growth rate increased perceptibly. But our present growth rate is by no means the highest among the major industrialized nations. That honor belongs to Japan, which, as we saw in the previous chapter, has long experienced rapid economic growth. Table 18.1 shows the annual rates of growth of per capita real GNP in the United States and other major Western industrialized countries during the last century. You can see that, for the period as a whole, per capita real GNP in the United States grew at an average rate of about 2 percent per year. Compared with Germany, France, Italy, Canada, and the United Kingdom, our growth rate was quite impressive. In recent years, however, many industrialized countries have shown growth rates larger than or equal to ours.

Table 18.1
Average Annual Growth Rates of Per Capita Real GNP, Selected Western Industrialized Countries (percent)

Country	1870–1964	1929–70
United States	1.9	1.9
Canada	1.7	2.1
France	1.5	2.0
Germany	1.7	3.0
Italy	1.4	2.5
United Kingdom	1.3	1.7

Source: U.S. Department of Commerce, *Long-Term Economic Growth,* 1966, and *Statistical Abstract of the United States.*

Figure 18.1
Population and Labor Force, United States, 1900–75.
The American population in 1975 was over double what it was in 1920, and about triple what it was in 1900.

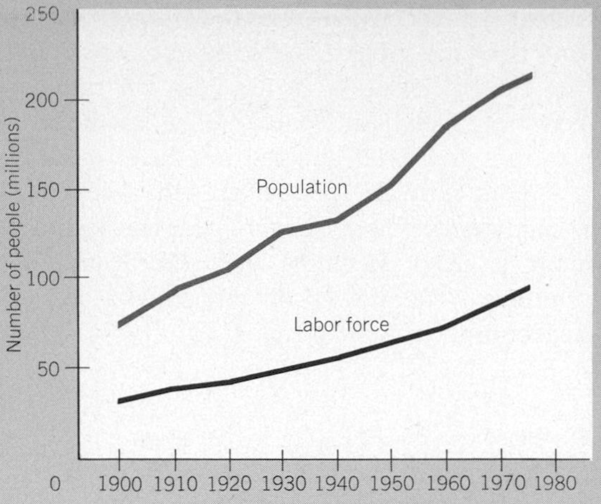

Population and Human Resources

As we have seen, a nation's rate of economic growth is influenced, among other things, by its rate of population growth and the extent of its investment in human capital. As shown in Figure 18.1, the population of the United States has grown substantially during our history, because of a fairly high birth rate as well as considerable immigration from other parts of the world.[1] Indeed, our population in 1975 was over double what it was in 1920, and about triple what it was in 1900.

In the past 15 or 20 years, the birth rate has fallen considerably, due partly to changes in attitudes toward women's role in society. However, according to official forecasts, the American population will continue to grow for at least the next 10 or 20 years, and perhaps for much longer. Of course, increases in population do not necessarily bring about economic growth. As we saw in the previous chapter, population increases, carried beyond a certain point, can lower per capita GNP, unless they are offset by other factors, such as advances in technology.

Equally important, it is not sheer numbers alone that count. The quality as well as the quantity of the population determines how much is produced. Measured by its education and skill, the quality of the American population is among the highest in the world. Moreover, as indicated by Table 18.2, the educational level of the population has increased dramatically during the past 70 years. To a considerable extent, our economic growth seems to have been due to this large investment in human capital.

Is it possible to make any quantitative estimate of the contribution of increased education to economic growth in the United States? Because the effects of education, technological change, and investment in plant and equipment intertwine in various ways, it is very difficult to sort out any one of them. Yet it is worthwhile to give the best estimates currently available. According to Edward Denison of the Brookings Institution, increased education seemed to account for about ⅛ of the growth in real output in the United States during 1909–29, and for about ¼ of this growth during 1929–57.

[1] As shown in Figure 18.1, the percent of the population in the labor force does not remain constant over time, and changes in this percentage can, of course, influence a country's rate of economic growth. Increases in the number of years of schooling and more liberal attitudes toward working wives, as well as changes in the age distribution of the population and in income levels, will influence this percentage.

Table 18.2
Percent of 17-Year-Olds That Graduated from High School, United States, 1900–80

Year	Percent graduated from high school
1900	6.4
1920	16.8
1940	50.8
1950	59.0
1960	65.1
1970	78.0
1980 (projected)	82.5

Source: Statistical Abstract of the United States, 1972.

Moreover, he forecasts that increased education will account for about 1/10 of this growth during 1969–80. Thus, if these estimates, shown in Table 18.3, can be trusted, increased education has been a major contributor to economic growth in the United States.

Technological Change

America's economic growth has also been due in very considerable part to technological change. For example, as shown in Table 18.3, Denison concludes that the "advance of knowledge" contributed about 1/8 of the growth in real output during 1909–29, and about 1/5 of this growth during 1929–57. Also, he forecasts that it will contribute about 1/4 of this growth during 1969–80. Such estimates are rough, but useful. It is very difficult to separate the effects on economic growth of technological change from those of investment in physical capital, since to a considerable extent new technology must be embodied in physical capital—new machines and equipment—to be used. For example, a nuclear power plant must obviously be built to take advantage of nuclear power plant technology. Nor can the effects of technological change easily be separated from those of education. After all, the returns from increased education are enhanced by technological change, and, as we saw in the previous chapter, the rate of technological change is influenced by the extent and nature of a society's investment in education.

In interpreting America's economic growth, we must recognize that the United States has long been a technological leader. Even before 1850, scattered evidence gives the impression that the United States was ahead of other countries in many technological areas. And after 1850, the available evidence indicates that productivity was higher in the United States than in Europe, that the United States had a strong export position in technically progressive industries, and that Europeans tended to

Table 18.3
Estimated Sources of Growth in Real National Income in the United States, 1909–80

Source	Period 1909–29	1929–57	1969–80
	[Percent of total growth]		
Increase in quantity of labor	39	27	26
Increase in quantity of capital	26	15	25
Improved education and training	13	27	7
Technological change	12	20	28
Other factors	10	11	14
Total	100	100	100

Source: E. Denison, *The Sources of Economic Growth in the United States,* New York: Committee for Economic Development, 1962, and his paper in T. Khachaturov, ed., *Methods of Long-Term Planning and Forecasting,* London: Macmillan, 1976.

Table 18.4
Expenditures on Research and Development, United States, 1945–74 (millions of dollars)

Year	Total R and D expenditure	Sources of funds: Government	Industry	Universities and nonprofit institutions
1945	1,520	1,070	430	20
1950	2,870	1,610	1,180	80
1955	6,270	3,490	2,510	270
1960	13,551	8,752	4,508	291
1965	20,439	13,033	6,539	519
1974[a]	32,045	16,955	13,916	1,174

Source: Statistical Abstract of the United States, 1970, and National Science Foundation, *Science Indicators,* 1974. The data for the earlier years may not be entirely comparable with those for the later years.
[a]Estimated by National Science Foundation.

imitate American techniques. Needless to say, the United States did not lead in all fields, but it appears to have held a technological lead in many important aspects of manufacturing. This was in contrast to pure science where, until World War II, the United States was not a leader.

Toward the end of the nineteenth century, as the connection between science and technology gradually became closer, commercial research laboratories began to appear. The first organized research laboratory in the United States was established by Thomas Edison in 1876. Eastman Kodak (1893), B. F. Goodrich (1895), General Electric (1900), DuPont (1902), and the Bell Telephone System (1907) were some of the earliest firms to establish laboratories. The industrial R and D laboratory constituted a significant departure from the past, when invention was mainly the work of independent inventors like Eli Whitney (interchangeable parts and cotton gin), Robert Fulton (steamboat), Samuel Morse (telegraph), Charles Goodyear (vulcanization of rubber), and Cyrus McCormick (reaper). These men were responsible for a very rich crop of inventions, some of which established whole new industries. Since the advent of the industrial laboratory, the relative importance of independent inventors seems to have declined, but they continue to produce a significant share of the important inventions in many areas. For example, xerography was invented by an independent inventor, Chester Carlson.

Recent decades have witnessed a tremendous growth in the amount spent on research and development. Table 18.4 shows that R and D expenditures in the United States in 1974 were over 20 times what they were in 1945. Although the bulk of these expenditures go for rather minor improvements rather than major advances, this vast increase in research and development has generated much economic growth. But, as the table shows, the federal government is the source of most R and D funds, which are heavily concentrated on defense and space technology. In the eyes of many economists, this vast investment in R and D would probably have had a bigger impact on the rate of economic growth if more of it had been directed at civilian rather than military and political objectives.

Capital Formation and Natural Resources

As pointed out in the previous chapter, a nation's rate of economic growth depends partially on how much of its GNP is invested in new plant and equipment. In recent years, we have devoted over 10 percent of our GNP to this purpose. In the United States, the average worker has more equipment to work with than his counterpart in any other country of the world. In manufacturing, for example, the average American worker has at his disposal about $30,000 worth of plant and equipment. Moreover, the government has invested huge amounts in highways, harbors, dams, and other forms of social capital; and the public has invested heavily in residential construction.

America's great natural resources have also been an important factor underlying our economic growth. We have an abundance of fertile soil and of various kinds of ores and minerals; a reasonably good climate; and coal, oil, and other sources of power. Few nations have as plentiful a supply of natural resources, and obviously they have been a great boon to our economic development. Although countries with limited natural resources can offset this limitation by importing raw materials, by irrigation and drainage projects, and by the use of modern technology, a good supply of natural resources is a valuable asset in achieving rapid economic growth.

In recent years, some fear has been expressed that if the world economy continues to grow at current rates, we shall begin to run out of basic raw materials. For example, in 1972, Dennis and Donella Meadows and their colleagues at M.I.T. conducted a study sponsored by the Club of Rome on *The Limits to Growth,*[2] in which they concluded that unless we curb our growth rate the world will run out of raw materials in the foreseeable future. However, this ignores the fact that the price system encourages producers to conserve raw materials as they become increasingly scarce, and that it provides a strong incentive for producers to invent and adopt new techniques that use less of these resources. The price system accomplishes these things simply by seeing to it that the price of a raw material increases as it becomes scarcer. More will be said about these "doomsday models" in a subsequent section of this chapter.

[2] For example, see Donella Meadows, Dennis Meadows, J. Randers, and William Behrens, "The Limits to Growth," reprinted in E. Mansfield, *Economics: Readings, Issues, and Cases,* 2d ed., New York: Norton, 1977.

The Social and Entrepreneurial Environment, the GNP Gap, and Allocative Efficiency

As we stressed in the previous chapter, America's relatively rapid long-term economic growth has also been a result of its social and entrepreneurial environment. In general, American society places considerable emphasis on materialistic considerations, values hard work, allows a great deal of economic and political freedom, and is flexible enough to adjust to change. Also, the United States has not been wracked (in the past century) by internal armed conflict or widespread confiscation of private property. These factors have been important in promoting economic growth. In addition, the price system, which has been relied on to channel resources into the proper uses, seems to have worked quite well. It has provided the incentives required to get labor, land, and capital to move from less productive to more productive uses.

However, not all aspects of the American economy have been conducive to rapid economic growth. For one thing, as we saw in Chapter 8, in many periods actual GNP fell short of potential GNP because desired spending was too low. For example, in the Great Depression of the 1930s, actual GNP was far below our potential GNP. When a large gap develops between actual and potential GNP, this reduces the growth rate, as we saw in the previous chapter. Moreover, it has indirect as well as direct effects. As this gap grows, and there is substantial unemployment, firms are discouraged from investing in new technology or capital formation, and unions are more inclined to resist adopting new techniques that might replace men with machines, so that the growth rate in subsequent years may be reduced as well.

Another factor that can reduce our economic growth rate is the increased strength of monopolistic forces that prevent resources from being allocated efficiently. For example, some labor unions resist the adoption of new techniques that would increase productivity and growth. Thus the compositors' union has restricted the use of the teletypesetter by requiring that the machine be operated by a journeyman printer or apprentice. Also, groups that are adversely affected by changes that would promote economic growth often try to convince the government to stop or offset them. For example, the farm programs discussed in Chapter 5 impeded past economic growth by making it more difficult to transfer resources out of agriculture and into more productive uses. Also, many industries that cannot compete with foreign producers lobby for and obtain tariffs, with the result that resources are misallocated.

Finally, if resources tend to be more immobile, this too will hamper economic growth. As tastes, technology, and population change, resources often should move from one use or location to another, if society's output is to be maximized. But there are many barriers to the mobility of resources. In the case of labor, people often are reluctant to pick up stakes; sever their ties to friends, family, and neighbors; and move to another location. Similarly, they often are unwilling or unable to learn a new occupation or trade, even though it might increase their income. The immobility of capital is even more obvious. A particular piece of capital is built for specific purposes—for example, to cut metal or to refine oil—and cannot be used for other purposes. However, when this piece of capital wears out, it can be replaced with capital of another type.

The Pros and Cons of Economic Growth

Past and Present Views of Economic Growth

Despite an imperfect record, the American economy has strongly adhered to a pattern of growth. Should we try to increase our rate of economic growth? Some economists answer yes, some answer no. Before presenting the issues, several points should be noted about the attitudes of economists, past and present, toward economic growth. First, the great economists of the past were deeply concerned with the poverty and economic misery of their times; and they tried in various ways to help set humanity on a course whereby output per capita might rise. Smith, Malthus, and Ricardo all wanted to ameliorate the meager lot of the average Englishman of their day; Marx was distressed and angered by the misery of the working classes; and Keynes spent much of his time and energy trying to find a way out of the poverty and misery arising from the Great Depression.

Second, except for Smith and Keynes, these great economists of the past were not very optimistic about how much output per capita could be increased. Malthus and Ricardo were about as pessimistic as one reasonably could get. In their view, population would expand whenever the standard of living poked its head above the subsistence level, with the result that more and more people would be working a relatively fixed amount of land. Given the law of diminishing marginal returns, it appeared certain to them that output per capita would eventually fall. As for Marx, we have seen that he believed the capitalistic system was headed for collapse, and that the bulk of the population was doomed to increased misery so long as capitalism survived.

With all the advantages of hindsight, it is relatively easy to see where the pessimists went wrong, at least for the industrialized nations. As pointed out in the previous chapter, Malthus and Ricardo vastly underestimated the power of technological change. They could not visualize the sorts of innovations that were to occur. New techniques and new products were destined to offset the dreaded law of diminishing marginal returns and to allow food supplies to more than keep pace with increases in population. Moreover, because of innovations in birth control and changes in attitudes, population has not grown as rapidly as many people forecasted. Marx could not visualize the sorts of changes that were to occur in capitalism. Nor could he avoid the consequences of the basic flaws in his economic theories, which are discussed further in Chapter 35.

It is important to recognize that, for a variety of reasons, the attitudes of most economists today are quite different from the attitudes of their great predecessors. The difference does not lie in a lack of concern for the underprivileged. Most economists today are just as interested in eradicating poverty as were Smith or Marx. *The big difference is that today's economists are reasonably confident that we can increase output per capita. Indeed, they expect, almost as a matter of course, that output per capita will increase in the industrialized nations of the world.* Of course, some wish that it could be made to increase a little faster (and some would like to slow it down) but, in general, the present view is decidedly optimistic.

The Case for Economic Growth

Having reached a level of affluence that would have astonished Smith, Ricardo, Malthus, or Marx (but not Keynes), the industrialized nations are now at a point where some observers question the wisdom of further economic growth. For example, in the United States, the attitude toward economic growth has changed perceptibly in the decade or so since President Kennedy made it a target of public policy. More emphasis is placed today on the "costs" of economic growth. There are more statements to the effect that we really are rich enough, and more questions about the desirability of technological change, which is one of the principal mainsprings of economic growth. But many people continue to favor rapid economic growth. What arguments do they use?

Higher living standards. It is often argued that economic growth means a higher standard of living, which is important in and of itself. But before accepting this uncritically, one should stress the limitations of the customary growth measures. A decade or so ago, people tended uncritically to accept increases in per capita GNP as a measure of increases in economic welfare, despite the many warnings of economists. People now are more conscious of the frailties of the GNP—the fact that it does not count as "product" many benefits that are a part of the productive process (such as increased leisure) and that it does not count as "costs" many problems (such as the human and environmental costs) that arise as a consequence of the productive process. Some economists are currently trying to improve the statistics to take better account of some of these factors, such as environmental pollution (see Chapter 8). But since it is unlikely that we will ever have very precise measures of economic welfare, the available figures need to be treated with caution.

Reduction of poverty. It is argued that economic growth provides the means to reduce poverty and attain other national objectives. In the words of Peter Passell and Leonard Ross,

> "Growth is the only way that America will ever reduce poverty. . . . While the relative share of income that poor people get seems to be frozen, their incomes do keep pace with the economy. . . . Even allowing for inflation, the average income of the bottom 10th of the population has increased about 55 percent since 1950. Twenty more years of growth could do for the poor what the Congress won't do."[3]

[3] P. Passell and L. Ross, "Don't Knock the $2-Trillion Economy," *New York Times*, March 5, 1972.

Also, it is argued that economic growth makes it easier to achieve other national goals, because they can be achieved without reducing the production and consumption of other goods and services. For example, as mentioned in the previous chapter, it has been maintained that economic growth makes it easier to expand needed government and social services, since such an expansion can be achieved without cutting private consumption.

Defense and prestige. Many maintain that economic growth contributes to national prestige and national defense. As pointed out in the previous chapter, this was one of the most important reasons for the emphasis on economic growth in the early 1960s. People were worried that we were losing the "growth race" to the Soviet Union, and that Premier Nikita Khrushchev's claim that the Russians would "bury" us economically might be more than an idle boast. In recent years, as our relations with the Communist countries have improved, these reasons for economic growth have been given less importance, but they still are cited by some proponents of economic growth.

The Case against Economic Growth

Basically, there are four arguments made by those who question the wisdom of further economic growth in our society:

Quality of life. It is argued that increases in per capita GNP really will not make us any happier: on the contrary, they will only be achieved by reducing the quality of our lives. For example, according to E. J. Mishan of the London School of Economics, economic growth results in "the appalling traffic congestion in our towns, cities, and suburbs, . . . the erosion of the countryside, the 'uglification' of coastal towns, . . . and a wide heritage of natural beauty being wantonly destroyed."[4] In his view, to strain for further economic growth is simply to put ourselves on a meaningless treadmill, since it prevents us from enjoying what we have. Relatively few economists share this rather extreme view.

Pollution. It is argued that economic growth is likely to result in additional environmental pollution. Of course, increases in per capita GNP do not necessarily have to entail increases in pollution. On the contrary, as we shall see in the next chapter, it is possible to increase output without increasing pollution. Nonetheless, the fact seems to be that economic growth in the past has been associated with increases in pollution, and some observers feel that this association is likely to persist in the future. Thus they regard increases in environmental pollution as a likely "cost" of economic growth. Among those who argue against further economic growth on environmental grounds is biologist Barry Commoner of Washington University, who concludes that

> in most of the technological displacements which have accompanied the growth of the economy since 1946, the new technology has an appreciably greater environmental impact than the technology which it has displaced, and the postwar technological transformation of productive activities is the chief reason for the present environmental crisis. . . . If we are to survive economically as well as biologically, much of the technological transformation of the United States economy since 1946 will need to be, so to speak, redone in order to bring the nation's productive technology much more closely into harmony with the inescapable demands of the ecosystem.[5]

Solving social and political problems. It is argued that economic growth is not the solver of social problems that its proponents claim. For example, critics point out that we are rich enough now to solve the problem of poverty in the United States. In their view, what we need is the will and courage to eliminate poverty,

[4] E. Mishan, *Technology and Growth,* New York: Praeger, 1969.

[5] B. Commoner, "The Environmental Costs of Economic Growth," in R. and N. Dorfman, *Economics of the Environment,* 2d ed., New York: Norton, 1977.

not extra output. In reply to the argument that economic growth is needed for reasons of national prestige and defense, the critics retort that it is not the size of a country's GNP, but its composition, that counts in determining military strength. For example, the Soviet Union's military strength is roughly equal to ours, although its GNP is about 50 percent smaller. Moreover, the critics question whether the less developed countries are much impressed by a simple comparison of our growth rate with that of the Soviet Union.

Current sacrifices. It is pointed out that, to increase our growth rate, it may be necessary for us to make sacrifices now. For example, we may have to sacrifice leisure or postpone the consumption of goods and services in order to invest in capital goods. Many economists have stressed that one cannot make the naïve assumption that more growth is costless, or that it will always be worth the sacrifices involved. Thus some economists argue that there is no reason to "force" growth on the economy. To them, the proper rate of economic growth is that which would emerge from private decisions. Whether the increase in the growth rate is worth the sacrifices depends upon the tastes and preferences of the people: it is a political issue.

Is Doomsday at Hand?

Most critics of economic growth believe that it is not worth its costs, for the sorts of reasons discussed above. But some go further and argue that *sustained economic growth for an additional century will not be possible.* This arresting conclusion has been put forth by Dennis and Donella Meadows and their colleagues in the book, *The Limits to Growth.* Specifically, they say that

> if the present growth trends in world population, industrialization, pollution, food production, and resource depletion continue unchanged, the limits to growth on this planet will be reached sometime within the next one hundred years. The most probable result will be a rather sudden and uncontrollable decline in both population and industrial capacity.[6]

In view of the world-wide interest in their study, it is worth looking in some detail at the model they use. (This model is related closely to the work of Jay Forrester at M.I.T.) According to this model, per capita output is determined by the supply of natural resources and the amount of capital per worker. Technological change doesn't enter into the model, and the supply of resources is seen as largely fixed. There is no allowance for the fact that new resources may be discovered, that resources may be made more useful by new technologies, or that plentiful resources may be substituted for scarce ones. Given these assumptions, it is easy to see why they came to their very pessimistic conclusions.

Critics have directed a great many salvoes at these so-called doomsday models. For one thing, they point out that the assumption of no technological change is at odds with reality, and that it tends to insure that economic growth will slow down. As we saw in the last chapter, increases in capital will eventually result in diminishing marginal returns. Unless technological change occurs, less and less productive projects must be undertaken as more and more is invested in capital. The eventual result is a cessation of economic growth. But this result is due to the assumption of no technological change–a strange assumption for M.I.T. faculty members to make.

Another disturbing assumption is that there is a relatively small and readily exhaustible amount of resources. This assumption seems to ignore the fact that, as particular resources become increasingly scarce, their prices go up, and there is an incentive to find more of them, to find substitutes for them, and to economize on their use. Given this assumption, it is not hard to see why economic growth eventually

[6] D. Meadows et al, "The Limits to Growth."

will be impossible, according to the model. After all, if there is only a finite amount of resources, and if economic growth means using them at current rates, we eventually will run out of them. No question about it.

But this assumption seems oversimplified and overly pessimistic. As Peter Passell and Leonard Ross point out,

> before we run out of Arabian oil, we will begin extracting petroleum from the vast reserves of oil-shale rocks and tar sands. And long before we run out of those reserves, cars will be powered with other sources of energy. Appeals to faith in technical change are more than a cheap debating trick to counter the Forrester school. The technology of substituting plentiful materials for scarce ones grows every day. Silicates made from sand replace copper and silver radio circuitry; European cattle feeds are enriched with nutrients made of natural gas converted by bacteria; mattresses are filled with polyurethane which never was closer to a Liberian rubber tree than Bayonne, N.J.[7]

Perhaps the most fundamental criticism of their model is that it fails to recognize the workings of the price system. As Robert Solow has pointed out, the price system leads us to economize on various raw materials as they become scarce.

> Higher and rising prices of exhaustible resources lead competing producers to substitute other materials that are more plentiful and therefore cheaper. To the extent that it is impossible to design around or find substitutes for expensive natural resources, the prices of commodities will rise relative to the prices of other goods and services that don't use up a lot of resources. Consumers will be driven to buy fewer resource-intensive goods and more of other things. All of these effects work automatically . . . to reduce resource requirements per unit of GNP.[8]

Because of these criticisms, most economists do not accept the conclusions of the doomsday models. However, Dennis and Donella Meadows and their colleagues unquestionably have focused attention on some very important issues, and for this we must be grateful. But until their models are free of the objections noted above, they will have difficulty in convincing economists of the wisdom of their policy recommendations—which are to curb economic growth and population growth drastically.

Public Policies to Stimulate Economic Growth

Although the critics of growth have made some headway, there has been no renunciation of economic growth as a goal of public policy. On the contrary, most government officials, in the United States and elsewhere, continue to press for further economic growth. All nations have important social objectives that seem more likely to be attained if they can increase per capita output. Thus most would like to effect such an increase, notwithstanding Mishan's views concerning the hollowness of it all. But the more sophisticated question of how far the government should go in promoting or forcing growth is not easy to answer. And as you would expect, there are very substantial differences of opinion on this score among politicians in this country (and other countries as well). Whether or not we should stimulate growth is essentially a political question, and your own view will depend on your political preferences.

But whether you are for or against the stimulation of growth, you should know how the government's policies can influence the growth rate. Suppose that the American people, registering their opinions through the proper democratic process, indicate that they want to increase the nation's rate of economic growth. What sorts of programs would lead to that goal?

First, the nation might *increase expenditures on research and development* (R and D), since

[7] P. Passell and L. Ross, "Don't Knock the $2-Trillion Economy."
[8] R. Solow, "Is the End of the World At Hand?" in E. Mansfield, *Economics: Readings, Issues, and Cases,* 2d ed., New York: Norton, 1977.

increases in such expenditures are likely to increase the rate of technological change, which in turn will increase the growth rate.[9] The government can either increase R and D expenditures by directly financing more R and D, or it can provide tax credits or other inducements to get private firms to increase their R and D expenditures. It is important to recognize, however, that the added R and D must be carried out in areas where the social payoffs are high: otherwise there will be little impact on the growth rate. Moreover, we must also note that the government can stimulate the growth rate by encouraging the application and diffusion of existing technology, as well as by encouraging the development of new technology.

Second, measures might be taken to *increase investment in education and training.* If there is a high rate of return from such an investment, increased education and training would increase the nation's potential output considerably. To foster such increases, the federal government could spend larger amounts on scholarships and provide more loans for potential students. (Since 1965, the Department of Health, Education, and Welfare has helped students with grants, loans, and loan guarantees.) Also, the government could provide more financial support to the nation's colleges and universities. But a major question is how high the rate of return from increased education really is. Until the early 1970s, the evidence indicated that it was relatively high, but, as we saw in the previous chapter, recent studies suggest that it now may be lower than it used to be.

Third, steps might be taken to *increase investment in plant and equipment.* Increases in aggregate investment will increase the growth rate, assuming, of course, that the extra investment is in areas of high productivity. Again, we must recognize that this policy, like the others described above, imposes costs. Increases in investment can occur—under full employment—only at the expense of current consumption. Assuming that the people understand these costs and are willing to pay them, the government can increase investment in plant and equipment by keeping interest rates low (to encourage investment) and personal tax rates high (to choke off consumption). Also, the government can give tax credits for investment in plant and equipment and allow firms to depreciate their plant and equipment more rapidly.[10]

Fourth, if the economy is operating at considerably less than full employment, the government might step in *to narrow the gap between actual and potential output.* As we saw in the previous chapter, this can be a very effective way to grow, at least in the short run. To do it, the government must use its fiscal and monetary policies to reduce unemployment. The goal of full employment is widely accepted—more widely, for that matter, than the goal of increasing the rate of economic growth. Unfortunately, however, when the economy approaches full employment, there may be a tendency for the goal of full employment to conflict with the goal of price stability, as we saw in Chapter 8. Thus an attempt to close completely the gap between actual and potential output may lead to undesirable inflationary pressures.

Policies for Economic Growth in the Early 1960s: A Case Study

As we have noted, in the early 1960s, the Kennedy administration set out to spur the rate of economic growth in the United States. We

[9] It is interesting to contrast this attitude toward R and D with the view of the French revolutionaries, who said, as they led the famous scientist, Lavoisier, to the guillotine, "The Republic has no need of scientists." Clearly, scientists are viewed differently—and treated more gently—today.

[10] A tax credit is a device whereby a firm's income tax liability is smaller if it invests a great deal in plant and equipment than if it invests little. Obviously, such a tax credit increases the profitability of investing in plant and equipment. More rapid depreciation of plant and equipment also encourages investment because, if a firm can write off a new piece of equipment more rapidly for tax purposes, the new piece of equipment is more profitable to the firm than it otherwise would be.

now can take a closer look at the set of economic policies designed to accomplish this goal. These policies were formulated by members of the Council of Economic Advisers, and others, inside and outside the government. To be put into effect, some of these policies and programs had to be approved by the Congress.

For research and development, the Kennedy administration proposed a Civilian Industrial Technology program to encourage and support additional R and D in industries that it regarded as lagging technologically. It also proposed an industrial extension service—analogous to the agricultural extension service that distributes technological information and advice—to increase the rate of diffusion of innovations. Congress eventually approved the industrial extension service,[11] but not the Civilian Industrial Technology program. An important reason for its defeat was that some industrial groups feared that government sponsorship of industrial R and D could upset existing competitive relationships.

In the field of education too, the administration proposed new measures. For example, in his 1962 *Economic Report,* President Kennedy stated,

> Public education has been the great bulwark of equality of opportunity in our democracy for more than a century. . . . There can be no better investment in equity and democracy—and no better instrument for economic growth. For this reason, I urge action by the Congress to provide Federal aid for more adequate public school facilities, higher teachers' salaries, and better quality in education. I urge early completion of congressional action on the bill to authorize loans for construction of college academic facilities and to provide scholarships for able students who need help. The talent of our youth is a resource which must not be wasted.[12]

To encourage investment in plant and equipment, the administration pushed through an "investment tax credit" that permitted firms to deduct from their income tax statements 7 percent of the amount they invested in new plant and equipment. Obviously, this made such investment more profitable. Also, the administration revised the depreciation schedules so that firms could write off such investments more quickly for tax purposes, thus increasing their profitability still more. But it did not lower interest rates or increase taxes to choke off consumption. In its *1962 Annual Report,* the Council of Economic Advisers recognized that such actions might promote growth, but felt that other considerations, such as our balance of payments (discussed in Chapter 32), ruled them out.

Finally, turning to the reduction of the gap between actual and potential output, the administration used fiscal and monetary policies to push the economy toward full employment. An important part of this policy in the eyes of most economists was the tax cut of 1964, described in Chapter 11. Between 1962 and 1966, the United States achieved a high rate of growth, in considerable part because of the reduction of the gap between actual and potential output.

Thus, taken as a whole, the Kennedy administration's policies to stimulate economic growth conformed to the elementary principles discussed in this and the previous chapter. In the area of growth policy—just as in fiscal, monetary, and incomes policy—the basic principles of economics take you a long way toward understanding the policies of government, whether Democratic or Republican.

Adjustment to Technological Change

Technological Unemployment

Up to now, we have stressed that rapid technological change is an important stimulus to economic growth. But this stimulus to growth can

[11] The industrial extension service, embodied in the State Technical Services Act, was passed in 1965, but was later killed.

[12] *Economic Report of the President,* Washington, D.C.: Government Printing Office, 1962, p. 10.

Is There a Capital Crisis?

Assuming that the American people desire continued economic growth, American firms must invest an enormous amount in plant, equipment, and other forms of capital in the next decade. For example, according to Roger Brinner and Allen Sinai of Data Resources, Inc., about $1.9 trillion will have to be invested in machinery between 1975 and 1985, compared with about $670 billion invested in this way between 1965 and 1975. This accelerated rate of investment is due partly to the fact that our investment rate was not very high during the past decade, partly to the increased capital requirements to satisfy the antipollution and safety regulations that recently have been enacted, and partly to a variety of other factors.

If these estimates are at all reliable, the required investment is enormous by any standards. And many people, particularly in industry and on Wall Street, are worried that we won't be able to augment our capital stock at the required rate. One reason for this concern is inflation. According to some economists, many companies will have trouble increasing their capital stock at the desired rate because their allowances for depreciation will be too small to permit them to replace worn-out equipment. (Why? Because, as we saw in Chapter 7, depreciation allowances are based on historical cost—and in times of rapid inflation, historical cost is much less than the cost of replacing equipment.) Moreover, they will have a difficult time borrowing money for this purpose, because they already have amassed a very large amount of debt. According to some estimates, American firms in 1975 had about $2 of owner-provided capital per $1 of debt, whereas in 1965 they had about $4 of owner-provided capital per $1 of debt.

Some economists believe that these apparent problems can be avoided if the federal government runs a surplus in the late 1970s. Among the leading supporters of this view are James Duesenberry of Harvard University and Barry Bosworth and Andrew Carron of the Brookings Institution.* The reason why a surplus tends to ease the situation is that the government, if it runs a surplus, is spending less than it takes in. Thus a surplus, like individual or corporate saving, results in resources being available for investment. However, critics of this view point out that the federal budget has generally been biased toward deficits, not surpluses.

Other economists, like Robert Eisner of Northwestern University, are inclined to minimize the seriousness of this whole matter. In their view, no capital crisis exists. They point out that, if the quantity of capital supplied is less than the quantity demanded, then interest rates should rise to induce more saving. And if markets are working properly, there is no reason, they say, why the quantity demanded should be less than the amount that is socially optimal. As evidence that there is no capital shortage, some people cite the fact that the rate of return on invested capital has been falling during the late 1960s and early 1970s. They say that, if there were a shortage of capital, it should be rising. But other economists, such as Federal Reserve Board member Henry Wallich, point out that the rate of return from newly invested capital may be higher than that from old capital.

Thus far there is no indication that the Congress will reduce taxes on business to encourage firms to invest more, even though some of the Ford administration's highest officials, notably Secretary of the Treasury William Simon, have clamored for greater incentives for capital formation.

* B. Bosworth, J. Duesenberry, and A. Carron, *Capital Needs in the Seventies,* Washington, D.C.: Brookings Institution, 1975.

be offset, at least partially, if rapid technological change results in technological unemployment. Economists have long recognized that new technology can throw people out of work. Karl Marx, in particular, gave technological change—and technological unemployment—a significant role in his theoretical system. (As we saw in Chapter 9, he believed that capitalists would adopt new technologies that would result in more and more technological unemployment.) Workers too have long recognized and feared technological unemployment. As long ago as the mid-1700s, a mob of worried English spinners entered James Hargreaves's mill and smashed the first workable multispindle frames.

Although the dread of technology-induced mass unemployment is not new, it was revived with great effect in the late 1950s and early 1960s. The new scare word was *automation.* For example, Professor Crossman of Oxford University, addressing an international conference in 1964, said that "unemployment due to automation will grow steadily over the next four decades, perhaps centuries, and in the end it is likely to reach a very high figure, say 90 percent of the labor force, unless radical changes are made in the present pattern of working."[13] Although ***automation*** means different things to different people, it generally refers to processes designed to mechanize the the human cognitive, conceptual, and informational processes.

Do increases in the rate of technological change necessarily result in increases in aggregate unemployment? To make a long story short, the answer is *no.* Rapid technological change need not have this effect if the government increases total spending at the proper rate. When total spending rises too slowly, increased aggregate unemployment takes place. If it rises too rapidly and resources are already fully employed, inflation will result. As we know, the job of choosing and carrying out appropriate fiscal and monetary policies is not easy; but used with reasonable finesse, such policies should prevent any large increase in aggregate unemployment from technological change.

To see how large-scale technological unemployment can occur—and how it can be avoided—consider Figure 18.2, which shows the $C + I + G$ line at a particular point in time. (If you are a bit hazy about the meaning and significance of this line, review Chapter 11.) Since this line intersects the 45-degree line at point A, the equilibrium level of net national product is \$400 billion. If the high-employment level of net national product is also \$400 billion, the economy enjoys a high level of employment. Now suppose that there is a significant amount of technological change. What will be the result? To begin with, the advance in technology will almost certainly result in an increase in productivity. In other words, it will enable the labor force to produce more than it formerly could. Thus the high-employment level of net national product will increase—say to \$450 billion. Given this increase, it is obvious that there will be substantial unemployment if the $C + I + G$ line stays put. This is obvious enough. After all, if output remains the same and output per man-hour increases, fewer workers will be needed and there will be unemployment.

But there is no reason why the $C + I + G$ *line should remain constant.* The advance in technology itself may increase the profitability of investment, thus raising I. Moreover, the advance in technology may result in new consumer products, which prompt consumers to spend more of a given level of income, thus raising C. Suppose that, by virtue of these changes in C and I, the $C + I + G$ line shifts to $C' + I' + G'$ (shown in panel B of Figure 18.2). The new equilibrium level of net national product is \$425 billion, as shown in

[13] Organization for Economic Cooperation and Development, *The Requirements of Automated Jobs,* Paris, 1965, p. 21.

Figure 18.2
Possible Effects of Technological Change on Equilibrium Level of Net National Product.

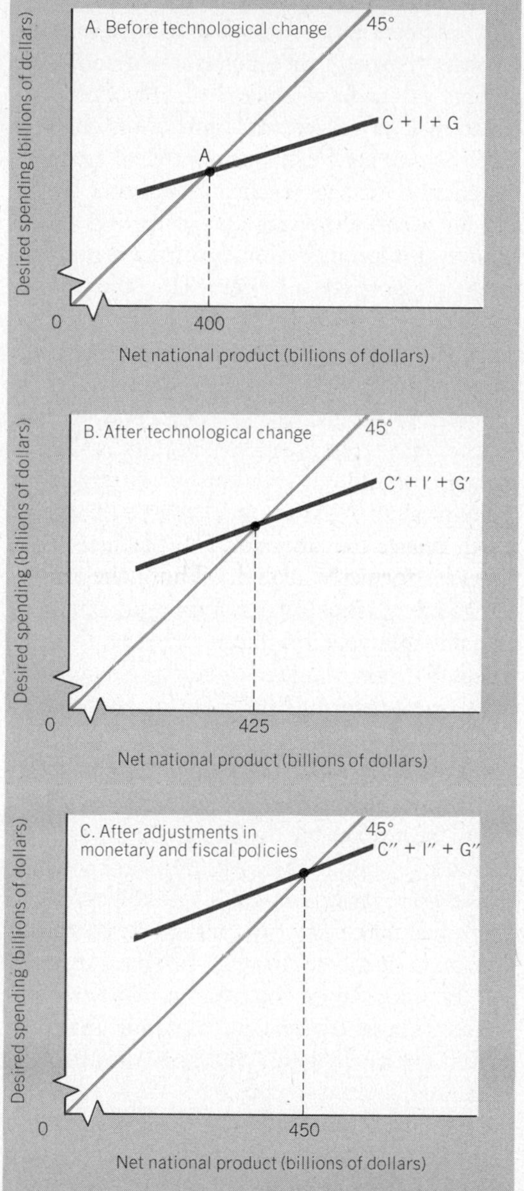

panel B. Unfortunately, in this particular case (but not necessarily in other cases), the new equilibrium level of NNP is less than the new high-employment level of NNP. Thus, without some change in public policy, there would be some technological unemployment. But as we know, the Federal Reserve can increase I by increasing the money supply and reducing interest rates, and the government can push C upward by reducing tax rates and increase G by increasing its own expenditures. Thus there is no reason why the government cannot raise the $C + I + G$ line to the point where it intersects the 45-degree line at $450 billion. For example, the government might nudge the $C + I + G$ line up to $C'' + I'' + G''$ in panel C of Figure 18.2. And if it does this, the equilibrium level of net national product equals the high-employment level of net national product. Thus it should be possible to avoid large amounts of technological unemployment, although transitional problems, discussed in a subsequent section, will remain.

Structural Unemployment

The considerable concern during the 1950s and early 1960s that technological change would result in massive technological unemployment was heightened by fears that workers and jobs were becoming more and more mismatched. According to one group of economists, technological change and other factors were increasing the skill and educational requirements of available jobs, and making it more likely that shortages of highly educated workers would coexist with unemployed pools of unskilled workers. Unemployment of this sort—unemployment that occurs because the workers available for employment do not possess the qualities that employers require—is called ***structural unemployment.*** The economists who asserted that structural unemployment was growing in the late 1950s and early 1960s were often called the structuralists.

In opposition to the structuralists, another

large group of economists denied that structural unemployment was increasing. An important and lively debate took place, both inside and outside the government, over the important question of how unemployment would respond to an increase in total spending. If an increase in total spending would reduce unemployment, then evidently at least that much unemployment was not structural. If it would fail to reduce unemployment, then the unemployment that remained could be called structural. To put the issue to a test, attempts were made to compare various periods when the general pressure of total spending was about the same, to see whether the level of unemployment was higher or more strongly concentrated in certain skill categories, industries, or regions in more recent periods than in the past.

Although neither side had a monopoly on the truth, the results of these tests, as well as the course of events after the 1964 tax cut, provided little support for the structuralist view. There was no evidence that unemployment was becoming more concentrated in particular geographic regions. Moreover, after adjusting for the effect of the over-all unemployment rate on the unemployment rate in particular occupations and industries, very few occupations or industries showed an unambiguous tendency for unemployment to increase with time. Also, after adjusting for the effects of the over-all unemployment rate, there was no significant tendency for unemployment rates among blacks to rise during the late 1950s and early 1960s. Thus, although a substantial portion of all unemployment may have been structural, there was no evidence that unemployment of this type increased greatly during that period.

Labor Displacement

Economic growth often occurs as a consequence of innovation and the redeployment of resources, which in turn means that *people—* workers, managers, owners of capital—*must adapt to these innovations and redeployments of resources.* Some people lose their jobs, some must move to other places, and some must enter new occupations. For example, consider the movement of people from agricultural to urban areas in the United States—a movement that has been part of the process of economic growth. During the postwar period, the number of farm owners and farm workers declined by over 40 percent. Innovations in agriculture—ranging from chemical fertilizers and insecticides to the mechanical cotton picker and huge harvesting combines—have contributed to this exodus, although they are by no means the only reason. Of those who left agriculture, many wound up in urban ghettos, many lacked the skills and education needed to fill urban jobs, and many who adapted to their new surroundings did so at considerable cost in psychological and emotional terms. Such human costs do not show up in the gross national product. Yet they are important costs, or disadvantages, of economic growth.

Although an adequate level of total spending can go a long way toward assuring that aggregate unemployment will not exceed a socially acceptable minimum, it cannot prevent labor from being displaced from particular occupations, industries, and regions, and being drawn to others. Nor would we want to eliminate all such movements of labor, without which it would be impossible to adjust to changes in technology, population, and consumer tastes. However, regardless of the long-run benefits of this adjustment process, important problems may arise in the short run, and great distress may be imposed on the workers who are displaced. These movements of labor must be carried out as efficiently and painlessly as possible.

The most serious adjustment problems have occurred when massive displacement has occurred in isolated areas among workers with specialized skills and without alternative sources of employment. Coal miners are a good example. About ⅔ of the nation's bituminous coal miners in 1960 were located in West Virginia, Pennsylvania, and Kentucky, and most of the coal mining was concentrated in isolated towns. Employment in bituminous coal started to decline after World War II, partly because of shifting demand and the adoption of new techniques. Between 1947 and 1959, total employment in the industry declined by more than 60 percent, leading to an unemployment rate of roughly 10 percent of the labor force in 5 major bituminous coal areas during most of the 1950s. In 25 smaller areas where there were few job opportunities outside coal mining, the unemployment rate was even higher.

Displaced older workers have encountered particularly serious problems. Seniority rights have helped hold down the displacement of older workers; but once unemployed, they are less likely than younger workers to be reemployed. For example, one year after the shutdown of the Packard automobile plant in Detroit, 77 percent of the workers under 45 were working at another job, whereas the percentages were 67 for the 45-to-54 age group and 62 for the 55-to-64 age group. Even if skill is held constant, the older workers had more serious unemployment problems than the younger workers, at least as measured by length of unemployment. Another study obtained similar results for a period when the general level of employment was higher than in the Packard case. It is easy to understand why older workers have more trouble finding another job. Many of their skills are specific to a particular job, and much of their income and status may be due to seniority, so that they cannot command as high a wage on the open market as they previously earned. Moreover, employers naturally are reluctant to invest in hiring and training a worker who will only be available for a relatively few years and who often has relatively limited education. Finally, because of their roots in the community, older workers are less likely to move to other areas where jobs are more plentiful.

Displaced black workers seem to find it even more difficult than older workers to obtain suitable re-employment at their previous status and earnings. For example, among workers who had been earning the same wage at Packard, blacks experienced a higher average length of unemployment than whites. Moreover, the prestige and economic level of the new job were more likely to be lower for blacks than whites. Needless to say, prejudice often plays an important role in preventing displaced blacks from obtaining new jobs.

Manpower and Training Policies

Beyond insuring an adequate level of total spending, perhaps the most important way that the government can facilitate adjustment to the adoption of new techniques is by promoting the necessary adaptability of the labor force through education and training. Education can increase the versatility and flexibility of the work force and increase its ability to adjust to change. It can open up greater opportunities and improve the productivity of workers at any level of skill or ability. The available evidence indicates the importance of a broad-based, secondary education rather than a narrow vocational education. The training for many—perhaps most—specific jobs can and should be done on the job.

Turning from the education of tomorrow's work force to the retraining of today's, it is generally agreed that the government should help workers who are casualties of technological (and other) change to obtain the skills required to return to productive employment. A coordinated, integrated system of adult retraining, which takes proper account of nationwide needs and supplies and reaches the underprivileged and hard-core unemployed, is useful and important. However, it should be recognized that industry quite properly plays the predominant role in the vocational training and retraining of the work force, and that the government plays only a residual role. The dif-

JOHN MAYNARD KEYNES

on "Economic Possibilities for Our Grandchildren"

Let us, for the sake of argument, suppose that a hundred years hence we are all of us, on the average, eight times better off in the economic sense than we are today. Assuredly there need be nothing here to surprise us.

Now it is true that the needs of human beings may seem to be insatiable. But they fall into two classes—those needs which are absolute in the sense that we feel them whatever the situation of our fellow human beings may be, and those which are relative in the sense that we feel them only if their satisfaction lifts us above, makes us feel superior to, our fellows. Needs of the second class, those which satisfy the desire for superiority, may indeed be insatiable; for the higher the general level, the higher still are they. But this is not so true of the absolute needs—a point may soon be reached, much sooner perhaps than we are all of us aware of, when these needs are satisfied in the sense that we prefer to devote our further energies to non-economic purposes.

Now, for my conclusion, which you will find, I think, to become more and more startling to the imagination the longer you think about it.

I draw the conclusion that, assuming no important wars and no important increase in population, the *economic problem* may be solved, or be at least within sight of solution, within a hundred years. This means that the economic problem is not—if we look into the future—*the permanent problem of the human race.*

Why, you may ask, is this so startling? It is startling because—if, instead of looking into the future we look into the past—we find that the economic problem, the struggle for subsistence, always has been hitherto the primary, most pressing problem of the human race—not only of the human race, but of the whole of the biological kingdom from the beginnings of life in its most primitive forms.

Thus we have been expressly evolved by nature—with all our impulses and deepest instincts—for the purpose of solving the economic problem. If the economic problem is solved, mankind will be deprived of its traditional purpose.

Will this be a benefit? If one believes at all in the real values of life, the prospect at least opens up the possibility of benefit. Yet I think with dread of the readjustment of the habits and instincts of the ordinary man, bred into him for countless generations, which he may be asked to discard within a few decades.

John Maynard Keynes, *Essays in Persuasion,* London: Macmillan, 1933. Originally published in 1930.

ficulties faced by government-sponsored training programs are considerable, given the limitations of capacity of the vocational education system and the lack of basic education among the trainees.

The government can also promote greater efficiency of labor markets and better adjustment to change by providing better labor market information and by experimenting, in its role as employer, with new adjustment techniques. Job seekers typically have relatively little information about alternative job openings. The federal government should do what it can to expand the amount and quality of available information—keeping in mind that the costs incurred must bear a reasonable relationship to the benefits attained. As well as exploring new ways of disseminating information to those who need and want work, the government might also investigate new education technologies to recognize individual potential and to promote faster and better learning.

Visions of the Economic Future

Finally, let's turn to the rate of economic growth in the future. What sort of economic growth rate is the United States likely to experience between now and the year 2000? Long-range economic forecasting is a hazardous business—unless, of course, the forecaster is so old and the forecast so far in the future that he can be sure of being dead before anyone can tell whether the forecast was right or wrong. As we saw in Chapter 12, it is difficult enough to forecast what will happen next year, let alone 20 years from now. Nonetheless, for some purposes, long-range economic forecasts are useful and need to be made. What do they indicate about the future rate of economic growth in the United States?

In 1967, Herman Kahn, the well-known physicist and strategic theorist, collaborated with sociologist Anthony Wiener to produce some forecasts of what the world will be like by the year 2000. In their view, economic growth will probably have resulted in a per capita gross national product of at least $17,000 (in terms of 1975 prices) in the United States. This is a very, very high standard of living. For comparison, recall that per capita GNP in 1975 was about $7,000. Thus Kahn and Weiner believe that per capita GNP will be more than twice as high in 2000 as in 1975. In their view the United States will have become a "postindustrial society." There will be a reduction in society's emphasis on efficiency and production, less attention paid to traditional work-oriented values, much more leisure, and a much looser relationship between work and income.[14]

Certainly, if these are truly the characteristics of the future, it is not at all what was anticipated by many of the great economists of the past. Malthus and Ricardo never dreamed of such affluence, and Marx never dreamed it could happen under capitalism. Only Keynes, who lived much later than the others, could see the handwriting on the wall. In a famous article written in 1930, he concluded that "assuming no important wars and no important increase in population, the *economic problem* may be solved, or be at least within sight of solution, within a hundred years."[15] Specifically, he hazarded the guess that we might then be eight times better off economically than at the time he was writing.

At first glance, it may seem that if Keynes and Kahn and Wiener are right, we are on the threshold of solving practically all our problems. But upon closer examination, one cannot escape the feeling that there are likely to be important problems in adjusting to such a level of affluence. As Keynes put it so well,

> I think with dread of the readjustment of the habits and instincts of the ordinary man, bred into him for countless generations, which he may be asked to discard within a few decades. . . .

[14] Herman Kahn and Anthony J. Weiner, *The Year 2000,* New York: Macmillan, 1967.

[15] John Maynard Keynes, "Economic Possibilities for our Grandchildren," reprinted in *Essays in Persuasion.*

> [For] the first time since his creation man will be faced with his real, his permanent problem—how to use his freedom from pressing economic cares, how to occupy his leisure, which science and compound interest will have won for him, to live wisely and agreeably and well.

Nonetheless, one must be very pessimistic about the intelligence and imagination of our people if he regards such problems as outweighing the benefits of this economic freedom. Admittedly, the rich have their problems, but there are few poor people who wouldn't trade places with them. In time, is it too much to expect that we will learn how to use these riches to build a better life than we, or others, have known before? I think not. In time, is it too much to expect that we will become more willing and able to share these riches with the poorer nations of the world? I hope not. On this latter point, it is important to understand that the forecasts of milk and honey by the year 2000 are for the industrialized countries, not the less developed countries. The prospects for the latter are less cheerful, as we shall see in Chapter 34.

Summary

Compared with that of other major industrial countries, America's rate of economic growth has been quite impressive over the past century, although in recent years many industrialized countries have experienced higher growth rates than we have. Our relatively rapid economic growth has been due to a variety of important factors, such as rapid technological change, increases in education and training, investment in plant and equipment, plentiful natural resources, and our social and entrepreneurial climate. However, not all aspects of the American economy have been conducive to rapid economic growth. Actual GNP has fallen short of potential GNP, and monopolies and immobilities have prevented efficient resource allocation.

Having reached a level of affluence that would have astonished Smith, Ricardo, Malthus, or Marx (but not Keynes), the industrialized nations are now at a point where some observers question the wisdom of further economic growth. The critics of growth assert that more output does not bring more happiness, that economic growth is likely to result in additional environmental pollution, that we are rich enough now to solve our major social problems, and that extra growth is not worth the sacrifices it requires. On the other hand, the proponents of growth argue that it will bring higher living standards, that it will enable us to solve such national problems as poverty, and that it is important for reasons of national defense and national prestige. Although the critics of growth have made some headway, there has been no renunciation of economic growth as a goal of public policy. To stimulate the rate of economic growth, governments encourage investment in technology, education, and plant and equipment, as well as reduce the gap between actual and potential GNP.

Although rapid technological change is an important stimulus to economic growth, it can also result in technological unemployment. If the government increases total spending at the proper rate, there is no reason why technological unemployment should be large. But an adequate level of total spending cannot prevent labor from being displaced from particular occupations, industries, and regions, and being drawn to others. This adjustment process, which results in long-run benefits, may impose great distress on the workers who are involved. It is important that these movements of labor be carried out as efficiently and painlessly as possible. Through its manpower and training policies, the government can help to distribute the "costs of change" more equitably. Finally, according to various long-term forecasts, per capita real GNP in the United States is likely to be more than twice as high in 2000 as in 1975. If this turns out to be true, many economic problems will be solved, but many will still remain.

CONCEPTS FOR REVIEW

Benefits from economic growth
Costs of economic growth
Limits to economic growth
Automation
Structural unemployment
Technological unemployment
Investment tax credit

QUESTIONS FOR DISCUSSION AND REVIEW

1. "Increases in population mean increases in output, because more people can produce more. Further, they mean economic growth because, with more people, there can be greater specialization of labor." Comment and evaluate.

2. During the middle-1970s, there was much public concern that the United States might experience a "capital shortage." According to *Business Week,* "the capital shortage problem . . . [is] part of the whole question of economic growth, and once the capital shortage is looked at in this way, it begins to take on some real meaning." Explain. Do you agree? Why or why not?

3. According to some scientists and engineers, the United States is losing its technological lead over other countries in many areas of industrial technology. If this is true, what, if anything, does it portend for our rate of economic growth?

4. "The world has only a fixed amount of copper, manganese, tin, iron, and other resources. If we continue using them at current rates, we're bound to run out of them. Thus it is inevitable that economic growth can only be sustained for a limited amount of time." Comment and evaluate.

5. "The arguments against economic growth are foolish. Who can be against higher living standards?" Comment and evaluate.

6. Discuss the effects on the U.S. economic growth rate of each of the following: (a) the investment tax credit, (b) government support of higher education, (c) the development of birth-control pills, (d) government support of basic research, (d) increases in featherbedding.

7. "Technological change almost always results in a loss of jobs. No wonder organized labor opposes it." Comment and evaluate.

8. Contrast the views of Karl Marx and John Maynard Keynes concerning economic growth in the non-Communist world. Whose views have been closer to correct?

9. According to E. J. Mishan, "If the moving spirit behind economic growth were to speak, its motto would be 'Enough does not suffice.' " Comment and evaluate.

10. According to Robert Solow, "The Doomsday Models [by Forrester et al.] . . . say that continued economic growth is impossible . . . because (a) the earth's natural resources will soon be used up; (b) increased industrial production will soon strangle us in pollution; and (c) increased population will eventually outrun the world's capacity to grow food." Do you agree with these models? Why or why not?

19

Environmental and Energy Problems

Environmental pollution and energy are two important problems in the United States—and both are related to economic growth. According to many scientists and social observers, one of the costs of economic growth is environmental pollution. For many years, people in the United States paid relatively little attention to the environment and what they were doing to it, but this attitude has changed markedly in the last decade. Now the public seems genuinely concerned about environmental problems. However, in the effort to clean up the environment, choices are not always clear, nor solutions easy. In particular, the energy crisis that surfaced in the fall of 1973 has brought home the fact that a cleaner environment is not costless. Many measures that would reduce pollution would increase the demand for energy.

America's energy problems are related only partly to environmental matters. To a considerable extent, they stem from the fact that oil reserves in this country are being depleted, and that we face increasing dependence on foreign sources of oil—a rather worrisome prospect, since these foreign sources have banded together in an international cartel which raised the price of crude oil enormously in 1974. Also, there is the related question of developing safe and reliable alternatives to fossil fuels. In this chapter, we consider the economic aspects of both environmental decay and the nation's energy needs. Our purpose is to indicate the extent and seriousness of these problems, the factors that are responsible for them, and the sorts of public policies that might be adopted to help deal with them.

Our Environmental Problems

The Nature and Extent of Environmental Pollution

To see what we mean by environmental pollution, let's begin with one of the most important parts of man's environment, our water supplies. As a result of human activities, large amounts of pollutants are discharged into streams, lakes, and the sea. Chemical wastes are released by industrial plants and mines, as well as by farms and homes when fertilizers, pesticides, and detergents run off into waterways. Oil is discharged into the waters by tankers, sewage systems, oil wells, and other sources. Organic compounds enter waterways from industrial plants and farms, as well as from municipal sewage plants; and animal wastes, as well as human wastes, contribute substantially to pollution.

To reduce the ill effects of water pollution, waste water is sometimes subjected to a treatment process, in which the water is separated from the solid waste, and both are treated so as to protect public health and in-stream life. Generally, the treatment occurs in one or two phases. Primary treatment takes large particles out of the water and lets some of the smaller particles settle out as sludge before releasing the water to a nearby stream or river. Secondary treatment employs a controlled sequence of aeration and settling processes. According to the Environmental Protection Agency, the wastes of about 30 percent of the population served by sewerage facilities received only primary treatment (or no treatment at all) in 1973.

Obviously, we cannot continue to increase the rate at which we dump wastes into our streams, rivers, and oceans. A river, like everything else, can bear only so much. The people of Cleveland know this well: in 1969, the Cuyahoga River, which flows through Cleveland, literally caught fire, so great was its concentration of industrial and other wastes. Of course, the Cuyahoga is an extreme case, but many of our rivers, including the Hudson and the Ohio, are badly polluted, as Table 19.1 shows. Water pollution is a nuisance and perhaps a threat: for example, according to the Public Health Service, we may be approaching a crisis with respect to drinking water.[1]

If clean water is vital to man's survival, so too is clean air. Yet the battle being waged against air pollution in most of our major cities has not been won. Particles of various kinds are spewed into the air by factories that utilize combustion processes, grind materials, or produce dust. Motor vehicles release lead compounds from gasoline and rubber particles worn from tires, helping to create that unheavenly condition known as smog. Citizens of Los Angeles are particularly familiar with smog, but few major cities have escaped at least periodic air pollution. No precise measures have been developed to gauge the effects of air pollution on public health and enjoyment, but some rough estimates suggest that perhaps 25 percent of all deaths from respiratory disease

[1] See *Fortune,* February 1970; D. Rohrer, D. Montgomery, M. Montgomery, D. Eaton, and M. Arnold, *The Environment Crisis,* Skokie, Ill.: National Textbook, 1970; and Enviromental Protection Agency, *The Economics of Clean Water, 1973,* Washington, D.C.: Government Printing Office, 1973.

Table 19.1
Water Pollution for Major Drainage Areas, United States, 1970 and 1971

Major watershed	Stream miles	Polluted miles 1970	Polluted miles 1971	Polluted miles Change
Ohio	28,992	9,869	24,031	+14,162
Southeast	11,726	3,109	4,490	+ 1,381
Great Lakes	21,374	6,580	8,771	+ 2,191
Northeast	32,431	11,895	5,823	− 6,072
Middle Atlantic	31,914	4,620	5,627	+ 1,007
California	28,277	5,359	8,429	+ 3,070
Gulf	64,719	16,605	11,604	− 5,001
Missouri	10,448	4,259	1,839	− 2,420
Columbia	30,443	7,443	5,685	− 1,758
United States	260,324	69,739	76,299	+ 6,560

Source: Council on Environmental Quality, *Third Annual Report,* August 1972.

could be avoided by a 50 percent reduction in air pollution.

One of the most important contributors to air pollution is the combustion of fossil fuels, particularly coal and oil products: by-products of combustion comprise about 85 percent of the total amount of air pollutants in the United States. Most of these pollutants result from impure fuels or inefficient burning. Among the more serious pollutants are sulphur dioxide, carbon monoxide, and various oxides of nitrogen. Table 19.2 shows the total amount of major air pollutants emitted by various sources, and Figure 19.1 shows the upward trend in the amount of these emissions. According to some observers, the worst air pollution threat for the future lies in the tremendous growth of the electric power industry. Of course, nuclear energy, which may provide more of our future energy needs, does not pollute the air. However, the rate of growth of nuclear power is hard to forecast (for reasons

Table 19.2
Estimated Emissions of Air Pollutants by Weight, Nationwide, 1971

Source	Carbon monoxide	Particulates	Sulphur oxides	Hydrocarbons	Nitrogen oxides
	(millions of tons per year)				
Transportation	77.5	1.0	1.0	14.7	11.2
Fuel combustion in stationary sources	1.0	6.5	26.3	0.3	10.2
Industrial processes	11.4	13.6	5.1	5.6	0.2
Solid waste disposal	3.8	0.7	0.1	1.0	0.2
Miscellaneous	6.5	5.2	0.1	5.0	0.2
Total	100.2	27.0	32.6	26.6	22.0

Source: Council on Environmental Quality, *Fourth Annual Report,* August 1973.

Figure 19.1
Weight of Emission of Air Pollutants, United States, 1940–70
Among the most serious air pollutants are carbon monoxide, sulphur oxides, nitrogen oxides, particulates, and hydrocarbons. In the past 30 years, the amount of these pollutants emitted in the United States has increased.

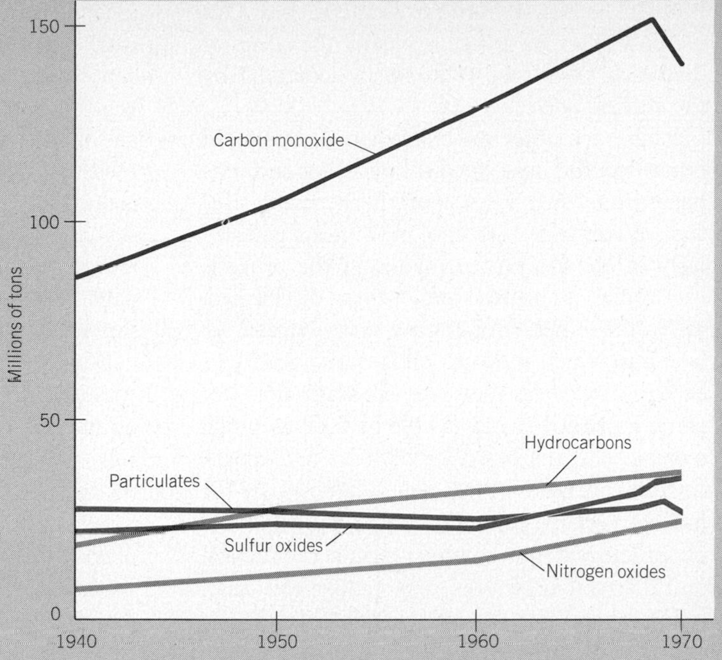

discussed below), and in any event nuclear energy is not free of environmental difficulties. Nuclear reactors can cause thermal pollution of rivers and streams, and radiation may be a threat despite various preventive measures.

At present, the automobile is the principal source of air pollution in the United States. According to some estimates, human activities pump into the air over 200 million tons of waste each year, and automobiles can be credited with the dubious honor of contributing about 40 percent of this figure. Spurred on by the public interest in pollution control, some technologists have been hard at work on substitutes for the internal combustion engine. Attempts have been—and are being—made to devise economical and convenient electric and steam-driven automobiles. To date, however, these efforts have not succeeded. Thus it seems likely that in the near future at least, we shall have to rely heavily on modifications of the internal combustion engine and its fuel to reduce air pollution.[2] (More use of nonpolluting transport like bicycles and feet would help too.)

Unfortunately, the air and water are not the only parts of man's environment that are being polluted. Each year, we produce an enormous amount of solid waste. Junk heaps testify to the quantity of superannuated cars left, like mechanical corpses, to mar the scenery. Each year industry produces literally mountains of waste and refuse. And picnic lovers and beer drinkers the world over are engaged in what sometimes seems a conspiracy to distribute cans, bottles, and other trash in every conceivable quarter. (Indeed, they sometimes even deposit some in a trash basket!) And it must be noted that the

[2] Ibid. Also, see L. Lave and E. Seskin, "Air Pollution and Human Health," *Science*, August 21, 1970.

problem is not merely an aesthetic one. Our nation's cities are buckling under the strain of disposing of all the solid waste generated by the affluent society.

There are other problems too. In many of our cities, the noise level is annoying and perhaps dangerous. Then there is thermal pollution. Water is used to cool machinery, particularly in electric power plants; in the process, the water is heated and, when discharged, raises the water temperature in the stream or lake into which it flows. Thus the solubility of certain substances may rise, the water may become more toxic and unable to hold as much oxygen, and the behavior patterns and reproductive capacities of fish may be altered. As for fish, so perhaps for man. There are questions about the extent to which man's production and disposal of wastes may render the earth uninhabitable for various kinds of life. To be sure, many of the most pessimistic and shocking predictions are probably little more than science fiction, but the questions are too important to be dismissed without careful consideration.

The Important Role of External Diseconomies

The reason why our economic system has tolerated pollution of the environment lies largely in the concept of external diseconomies, which we mentioned in Chapter 5. An ***external diseconomy*** occurs when one person's (or firm's) use of a resource damages other people who cannot obtain proper compensation. When this occurs, a market economy is unlikely to function properly. The price system is based on the supposition that the full cost of using each resource is borne by the person or firm that uses it. If this is not the case and if the user bears only part of the full costs, then the resource is not likely to be directed by the price system into the socially optimal use.

To understand why, we might begin by reviewing briefly how resources are allocated in a market economy. As we saw in Chapter 4, resources are used in their socially most valuable way because they are allocated to the people and firms who find it worthwhile to bid most for them, assuming that prices reflect true social costs. For example, under these circumstances, a paper mill that maximizes its profits will produce the socially desirable output of paper and use the socially desirable amounts of timber, labor, capital, and other resources.

Suppose, however, that because of the presence of external diseconomies people and firms do not pay the true social costs for resources. For example, suppose that some firms or people can use water and air for nothing, but that other firms or people incur costs as a consequence of this prior use. In this case, the ***private costs*** of using air and water differ from the ***social costs:*** *the price paid by the user of water and air is less than the true cost to society.* In a case like this, users of water and air are guided in their decisions by the private cost of water and air—by the prices they pay. Since they pay less than the true social costs, water and air are artificially cheap to them, so that they will use too much of these resources, from society's point of view.

Note that the divergence between private and social cost occurs if and only if the use of water or air by one firm or person imposes costs on other firms or persons. Thus, if a paper mill uses water and then treats it to restore its quality, there is no divergence between private and social cost. But when the same mill dumps wastes into streams and rivers (the cheap way to get rid of its by-products), the towns downstream that use the water must incur costs to restore its quality. The same is true of air pollution. An electric power plant uses the atmosphere as a cheap and convenient place to dispose of wastes, but people living and working nearby may incur costs as a result, since the incidence of respiratory and other diseases may increase.

We said above that pollution-causing activities that result in external diseconomies represent a malfunctioning of the market system. At this point, the nature of this malfunctioning should be clear. *Firms and people dump too much waste material into the water and the atmosphere. The price system does not provide the proper signals because the polluters are induced to use our streams and atmosphere in this socially undesirable way by the artificially low price of disposing of wastes in this manner. Moreover, because the polluters do not pay the true cost of waste disposal, their products are artificially cheap, so that too much is produced of them.*

Consider two examples. Electric power companies do not pay the full cost of disposing of wastes in the atmosphere. They charge an artificially low price, and the public is induced to use more electric power than is socially desirable. Similarly, since the owners of automobiles do not pay the full cost of disposing of exhaust and other wastes in the atmosphere, they pay an artificially low price for operating an automobile, and the public is induced to own and use more automobiles than is socially desirable.[3]

The Polluted Hudson and the Tin Can: Two Case Studies[4]

Richmond is a village of about 2,000 people about 10 miles south of Albany. It is situated at a very badly polluted place on the Hudson River. The water is brown with the human and industrial wastes of Albany, Troy, and other cities upstream, as well as with the wastes dumped into the river locally. In the area immediately around Richmond, two of the principal polluters are the village of Richmond itself and the Smith Paper Company. The village's sewer mains dump their contents into the river, and the Smith Paper Company discharges its untreated wastes into a creek that flows into the river.

The people of Richmond have dragged their heels about building a sewage treatment system because they have felt that unless towns upstream took action, their own efforts would be fruitless. After some prodding by New York State, a referendum was held in 1968 to vote on a sewer district, but it was turned down by the voters. Needless to say, part of the reason was that the people of the village would have to pay about $85 per family per year for the water treatment system. Despite the state's nudging, the officials of Richmond admit that it will be a long time before the problem is taken care of.

The Smith Paper Company has also been slow to do anything about water pollution. State health officials ordered it to clean up its effluent by July 1970, but the company did not formulate a preliminary plan for a treatment system until April 1970. According to many reports, the Company was not in healthy financial condition, and Smith's treatment costs, according to some of its engineers, could run as high as $300,000—or about 10 percent of the value of its plant. Obviously, one reason why this plant remains in business is that it does not pay the full social costs of waste disposal. Obviously, too, the price of its paper is artificially low for this reason. This is no criticism of the company. In a free enterprise economy, firms are expected to be motivated by profit. The problem is that, because of external diseconomies, the market system does not insure that the private costs of waste disposal equal the social costs. The result is a polluted river.

Richmond is an example of one type of pollution. To understand how external diseconomies can result in another type of pollution, consider the cans and bottles that are so conspicuous a part of our nation's litter problem.

[3] L. Ruff, "The Economic Common Sense of Pollution," *The Public Interest,* Spring 1970; R. Solow, "The Economist's Approach to Pollution and Its Control," *Science,* August 6, 1971; and M. Goldman, *Controlling Pollution,* Englewood Cliffs, N.J.: Prentice-Hall, 1967.

[4] The names Richmond and Smith are fictitious, but otherwise the case study given in the first part of this section, taken from an article in the *New York Times,* is factual.

Years ago, beer, soft drinks, and other such liquids came in relatively expensive bottles on which there was a deposit. Typically, when you purchased a bottle of beverage, you had to deposit $.05 for the bottle. If you didn't bring back the bottle, you didn't get the $.05 back. If someone else found—or stole—your bottle, he could take it back and get the money. Since $.05 was a significant amount in those days, there were few bottles lying around as unsightly litter. Kids—and more than a few adults—were only too glad to pick them up and take them back to the store to get the deposit. Thus, in those days, the system worked in such a way that the purchaser of the beverage paid for the cost of bringing the bottle back to the store. Either he took it back himself (and got his deposit back), or in effect he paid someone else $.05 to do it for him.

But this situation changed abruptly about 40 years ago, when producers of beer and soft drinks introduced a packaging innovation: the can. Unlike the old-fashioned bottle, there was no deposit on the can. Indeed, one of the advantages to consumers was that they didn't have to bother to take the cans back; they could simply throw them away. Consumers preferred the can for its convenience, and bottle manufacturers were forced to develop a cheaper no-deposit bottle to compete with cans. The result has been trash and litter, because there is no longer the same incentive to pick up cans and bottles or to return them to stores or manufacturers. Moreover, since bottles are no longer used over and over, there are more bottles and cans to dispose of.

It is important to note that, once the cans and no-deposit bottles were introduced, the consumer of beverages no longer had to pay for the cost of disposing of the cans or bottles. Basically, this was the reason for the litter problem. In other words, there was now an external diseconomy, since purchasers and consumers of beverages imposed costs on other people, who had to bear the expense of disposing of the litter. Of course, this was not always the case, since many people were public-spirited enough to dispose of their own cans and bottles, even without financial incentive. But our highways and parks testify to the fact that many people are not so public-spirited; as a result, certain states (like Oregon and Vermont) have passed laws requiring the sale of deposit bottles.

Economic Growth and Environmental Pollution

According to many authorities, economic growth—defined as increases in total economic output per capita—has been associated with increases in the level of environmental pollution. This is not very surprising, since practically all the things that are produced must eventually be thrown away in one form or another. Thus, as output per capita goes up, the level of pollution is likely to go up as well. For example, as we grow more affluent and increase the number of automobiles per capita, we also increase the amount of such air pollutants as nitrogen oxide and tetraethyl lead, both of which are emitted by automobiles. We also increase the number of automobiles that eventually must be scrapped.

But it is important to recognize that pollution is not tied inextricably to national output. Although increases in national output in the past have been associated with increases in pollution, there is no reason why this correlation must continue unchanged in the future. Clearly, we can produce things that are heavy polluters of the environment—like electric power and automobiles—or we can produce things that do not pollute the environment nearly so much—like pianos and bicycles.

In recent years, some people have suggested that we curtail our economic growth in order to reduce pollution: ***Zero Economic Growth*** is their goal. Very few economists seem to favor such a policy. Opponents of Zero Economic Growth point out that more productive capacity would help produce the equipment required to reduce pollution. As we shall see, this equipment will not be cheap. Moreover, with proper public policies, we should be able to increase output without increasing pollution, if this is what our people want. In addition, as pointed out by Walter Heller of the University of Minnesota,

> Short of a believable threat of extinction, it is hard to believe that the public would accept the tight controls, lowered material living standards, and large income transfers required to create and manage a [no-growth] state. Whether the necessary shifts could be accomplished without vast unemployment and economic dislocation is another question. It may be that the shift to a no-growth state would throw the fragile ecology of our economic system so out of kilter as to threaten its breakdown. Like it or not, economic growth seems destined to continue.[5]

Some people have also argued that technological change is the real villain responsible for pollution, and that the rate of technological change should be slowed. Certainly, technological change has made people more interdependent, and brought about more and stronger external diseconomies. Technological change also results in ecological changes, some of which are harmful. For example, detergents have contained phosphate, which induced water pollution by causing heavy overgrowths of algae.

But technological change is also a potential hero in the fight against pollution, because the creation of new technology is an important way to reduce the harmful side effects of existing techniques—assuming, of course, that we decide to use our scientists and engineers to this end. Contrary to some people's views, pollution is not the product of some mindless march of technology, but of human action and inaction. There is no sense in blaming technology, when pollution is due basically to economic, social, and political choices and institutions.

Finally, it is frequently suggested that, as our population increases, we must expect more pollution. Many who advocate a policy of ***Zero Population Growth*** advance the argument that it would help reduce the level of pollution. The available evidence indicates some relationship between a nation's population and its pollution levels. But there are important differences in the amount of pollution generated by people in various countries. The average American is responsible for much more pollution than the average citizen of most other countries, because the average American is a much bigger user of electric power, detergents, pesticides, and other such products. It has been estimated that the United States, with less than $1/10$ of the world's population, produces about $1/3$ of the wastes discharged into the air and water. Clearly, much more than economics is involved in the discussion of the optimal level of poulation. Although it is only one of a number of important factors, a nation's population does affect the level of pollution; but as we shall see in subsequent sections, pollution can be reduced considerably even if our population continues to grow.[6]

Public Policy toward Pollution

Pollution is caused by defects in our institutions, not by malicious intent, greed, or corruption. In cases where waste disposal causes significant external diseconomies, economists generally agree that government intervention may be justifiable. But how can the govern-

[5] W. Heller, "Economic Growth and Ecology—An Economist's View," *Monthly Labor Review*, November 1971.

[6] It must also be noted that pollution is not confined to capitalist countries; the Soviet Union and other Communist countries are afflicted by serious pollution problems. Nor is pollution anything new: for example, the ancient Romans complained of water pollution.

ment intervene? Perhaps the simplest way is ***direct regulation,*** through the issuance of certain enforceable rules for waste disposal. For example, the government can prohibit the burning of trash in furnaces or incinerators, or the dumping of certain materials in the ocean; and make any person or firm that violates these restrictions subject to a fine, or perhaps even imprisonment. Also, the government can ban the use of chemicals like DDT, or require that all automobiles meet certain regulations for the emission of air pollutants. Further, the government can establish quality standards for air and water.

The government can also intervene by establishing effluent fees. An ***effluent fee*** is a fee a polluter must pay to the government for discharging waste. In other words, a price is imposed on the disposal of wastes into the environment; and the more a firm or individual pollutes, the more he must pay. The idea behind the imposition of effluent fees is that they can bring the private cost of waste disposal closer to the true social costs. Faced with a closer approximation to the true social costs of his activities, the polluter will reduce the extent to which he pollutes the environment. Needless to say, many practical difficulties are involved in carrying out this seemingly simple scheme, but many economists believe that this is the best way to deal with the pollution problem.[7]

Still another way for the government to intervene is to establish ***tax credits*** for firms that introduce pollution-control equipment. There are, of course, many types of equipment that a plant can introduce to cut down on pollution—for example, "scrubbers" for catching poisonous gases, and electrostatic precipitators for decreasing dust and smoke. But such pollution-control equipment costs money, and firms are naturally reluctant to spend money on purposes where the private rate of return is so low. To reduce the burden, the government can allow firms to reduce their tax bill by a certain percentage of the amount they spend on pollution-control equipment. Tax incentives of this sort have been discussed widely in recent years, and some have been adopted.

[7] Another possibility is for the government to issue a certificate or license to pollute. The government might issue a limited number of certificates, to be auctioned off to the highest bidders. Although it has theoretical possibilities, this technique is not being used to any appreciable extent at present.

Direct Regulation

Let's look more closely at the advantages and disadvantages of each of these major means by which the government can intervene to remedy the nation's pollution problems. At present we rely mostly on direct regulation of waste disposal (and the quality of the environment); and despite the many problems involved, it has undoubtedly done much good. As Allen Kneese, one of the country's top experts in this area, says about water pollution, "The control of water discharges through administrative orders regulating individual waste disposers has been a useful device and cannot be abandoned until we have a better substitute."[8]

However, economists agree that direct regulation suffers from some serious disadvantages. First, such regulations have generally taken the form of general, across-the-board rules. For example, if two factories located on the same river dump the same amount of waste material into the river, such regulations would probably call for each factory to reduce its waste disposal by the same amount. Unfortunately, although this may appear quite sensible, it may in fact be very inefficient. Suppose, for example, that it is much less costly for one factory to reduce its waste disposal than for the other. Clearly, in such a case, it would be more efficient to ask the factory that could reduce its wastes more cheaply to cut down more on its waste disposal than the other factory. For reasons of this sort, reductions in pollution are

[8] A. Kneese, "Public Policy toward Water Pollution," in E. Mansfield, *Microeconomics: Selected Readings,* 2d ed., New York: Norton, 1975, p. 467.

likely to be accomplished at more than minimum cost, if they are accomplished by direct regulation.

Second, to formulate such regulations in a reasonably sensible way, the responsible government agencies must have access to much more information than they are likely to obtain or assimilate. Unless the government agencies have a detailed and up-to-date familiarity with the technology of hundreds of industries, they are unlikely to make sound rules. Moreover, unless the regulatory agencies have a very wide jurisdiction, their regulations will be evaded by the movement of plants and individuals from localities where regulations are stiff to localities where they are loose. In addition, the regulatory agencies must view the pollution problem as a whole, since piecemeal regulation may simply lead polluters to substitute one form of pollution for another. For example, New York and Philadelphia have attempted to reduce water pollution by more intensive sewage treatment. However, one result has been the production of a lot of biologically active sludge that is being dumped into the ocean—and perhaps causing problems there.[9]

Effluent Fees

The use of effluent fees is the approach most economists seem to prefer, for the following reasons: First, it obviously is socially desirable to use the cheapest way to achieve any given reduction in pollution. A system of effluent fees is more likely to accomplish this objective than direct regulation, because the regulatory agency cannot have all the relevant information (as we noted above), whereas polluters, reacting in their own interest to effluent fees, will tend to use the cheapest means to achieve a given reduction in pollution.

To see why this is the case, consider a particular polluter. Faced with an effluent fee—that is, a price it must pay for each unit of waste it discharges—the polluter will find it profitable to reduce its discharge of waste so long as the cost of doing so is less than the effluent fees it saves. Thus, if this firm can reduce its discharge of wastes relatively cheaply, it will be induced to make such a reduction by the prospect of increased profits. On the other hand, if it cannot reduce its discharge of wastes at all cheaply, it will not make such a reduction, since the costs will exceed the saving in effluent fees. Thus a system of effluent fees induces firms that can reduce waste disposal more cheaply to cut down more on their waste disposal than firms where such a reduction is more expensive. This means that a given reduction of pollution will occur at a relatively low cost.

Economists also favor effluent fees because this approach requires far less information in the hands of the relevant government agencies than does direct regulation. After all, when effluent fees are used, all the government has to do is meter the amount of pollution a firm or household produces (which admittedly is sometimes not easy) and charge accordingly. It is left to the firms and households to figure out the most ingenious and effective ways to cut down on their pollution and save on effluent fees. This too is a spur to inventive activities aimed at developing more effective ways to reduce pollution. Also, economists favor the use of effluent fees because financial incentives are likely to be easier to administer than direct regulation. Witness the case of Richmond, which illustrates the gap between regulation and enforceable performance.

To illustrate how effluent fees can produce more efficient ways to reduce pollution, consider a recent proposal by the state of Washington for reducing emission of sulphur oxides. The proposed regulation would oblige copper smelters to control 90 percent of the sulphur content of ore entering smelters. There is considerable disagreement over the cost of the regulation. The state says it would

[9] Solow, "The Economist's Approach."

cost the smelters about \$.02 per pound of copper to comply, whereas the smelters say it is technologically impossible to comply. Some people have suggested that one way to resolve this controversy might be to impose a fee equivalent to \$.03 per pound of copper if the emission of sulphur oxide were not controlled. Then if the smelters could achieve 90 percent control for \$.02 per pound, they would have every incentive to do so, thus increasing their profits. If they could not reach the goal, they would have an incentive to adopt other control measures or to develop new and less costly control devices.

While economists tend to favor the use of effluent fees, they are not always against direct regulation. Some ways of disposing of certain types of waste are so dangerous that the only sensible thing to do is to ban them. For example, a ban on the disposal of mercury or arsenic in places where human beings are likely to consume them—and die—seems reasonable enough. In effect, the social cost of such pollution is so high that a very high penalty—imprisonment—is put on it. In addition, of course, economists favor direct regulation when it simply is not feasible to impose effluent fees—for example, in cases where it would be prohibitively expensive to meter the amount of pollutants emitted by various firms or households.

The Ruhr: A Case Study[10]

Let's consider a well-known case of effluent fees in use—the Ruhr valley in West Germany. The Ruhr is one of the world's most industrialized areas. It includes about ⅓ of West Germany's industrialized capacity, and about 70 to 90 percent of West Germany's coal, coke, and iron and steel outputs. It contains about 10 million people and about 4,300 square miles. Water supplies in the Ruhr are quite limited: 5 small rivers supply the area. The amazing amount of waste materials these rivers carry is indicated by the fact that the average annual natural low flow is less than the volume of effluent discharged into the rivers. Yet the local water authorities have succeeded in making this small amount of water serve the needs of the firms and households of this tremendous industrial area, and at the same time the streams have been used for recreation. Moreover, all this has been achieved at a remarkably low cost. The success of water management in the Ruhr seems to be due in considerable part to institutional arrangements that allowed the German water managers to plan and operate a relatively efficient regional system. Collective water quality improvement measures are used. Water quality is controlled by waste treatment in over 100 plants, regulation of river flow by reservoir, and a number of oxidation lakes in the Ruhr itself.

Effluent fees are an integral part of the institutional arrangements governing water quality. The amount a firm has to pay depends upon how much waste—and what kind—it pumps into the rivers. A formula has been devised to indicate how much a polluter must pay to dispose of a particular type of waste. In simple terms, the formula bases the charge on the amount of clean water needed to dilute the effluent in order to avoid harm to fish. Using this formula, the local authorities can determine, after testing the effluent of any firm, the amount the firm should pay. Specifically, the amount depends on the amount of suspended materials that will settle out of the effluent, the amount of oxygen consumed by bacteria in a sample of effluent, the results of a potassium permanganate test, and the results of a fish toxicity test. You need not understand the nature or specific purposes of these measurements and tests. The important thing is that you understand their general aim—which is to measure roughly the amount of pollution caused by various kinds of wastes. Having made these

[10] This section is based on A. Kneese and B. Bower, *Managing Water Quality: Economics, Technology, Institutions,* Washington, D.C.: Resources for the Future, 1968, Chapter 12.

measurements and tests, the local authorities use their formula to determine how much a firm must pay in effluent fees.

Tax Credits for Pollution-Control Equipment

Many tax inducements to encourage firms and individuals to install pollution-control equipment have been proposed. A typical suggestion is that the government offer a tax credit equal to 20 percent of the cost of pollution-control equipment, and allow a firm to depreciate such equipment in only one to five years. In this way, the government would help defray some of the costs of the pollution-control equipment by allowing a firm that installed such equipment to pay less taxes than if no such tax inducements existed.

However, such schemes have a number of disadvantages. For one, subsidies to promote the purchase of particular types of pollution-control equipment may result in relatively inefficient and costly reductions in pollution. After all, other methods that don't involve special pollution-control equipment—such as substituting one type of fuel for another—may sometimes be a more efficient way to reduce pollution. Also, subsidies of this sort may not be very effective. Even if the subsidy reduces the cost to the firm of reducing pollution, it may still be cheaper for the firm to continue to pollute. In other words, subsidies of this sort make it a little less painful for polluters to reduce pollution; but unlike effluent fees, they offer no positive incentive.

Furthermore, it seems preferable on grounds of equity for the firms and individuals that do the polluting—or their customers—to pay to clean up the mess that results. Effluent fees work this way, but with tax credits for pollution-control equipment, the government picks up part of the tab by allowing the polluter to pay lower taxes. In other words, the general public, which is asked to shoulder the additional tax burden to make up for the polluters' lower taxes, pays part of the cost. But is this a fair allocation of the costs? Why should the general public be saddled with much of the bill?

Pollution-Control Programs in the United States

In recent years, there has been considerable growth in government programs designed to control pollution. To take but one example, federal expenditures to reduce water pollution increased in the period from the mid-1950s to 1970 from about $1 million to $300 million annually. To curb water pollution, the federal government has for years operated a system of grants-in-aid to state, municipal, or regional agencies to help construct treatment plants; and grants are made for research on new treatment methods. In addition, the 1970 Water Quality Improvement Act authorizes grants to demonstrate new methods and techniques and to establish programs to train people in water control management. (The federal government has also regulated the production and use of pesticides.) The states, as well as the federal government, have played an important role in water pollution control. They have set standards for allowable pollution levels, and many state governments have provided matching grants to help municipalities construct treatment plants.

In 1969, the Congress established a new agency—the Council on Environmental Quality—to oversee and plan the nation's pollution control programs. Modeled to some extent on the Council of Economic Advisers, the Council on Environmental Quality, which has three members, is supposed to gather information on considerations and trends in the quality of the environment, review and evaluate the federal government's programs in this area, develop appropriate national policies, and conduct needed surveys and research on environmental quality. The tasks assigned to the council are obviously important ones. The extent to which this relatively new agency can carry out these tasks is difficult to say. It will be some time before the council's effectiveness can be appraised at all fully.

In 1970, the federal government established another new agency, the Environmental Protection Agency (EPA). Working with state and local officials, this agency establishes standards for desirable air and water quality, and devises rules for attaining these goals. The 1970 Clean Air Amendments directed EPA to establish minimum ambient standards for air quality, and it set limits on the emission of carbon monoxide, hydrocarbons, and nitrous oxides from automobiles. But after a number of clashes between EPA and the auto makers, the EPA relaxed the deadlines when these limits were supposed to be met. The 1972 amendments to the Water Pollution Act authorized EPA to set effluent standards for both privately and publicly owned plants. A stated goal of the amendments was to eliminate the discharge of pollutants into water by 1985, but, for reasons discussed in the next section, this goal seems unrealistically stringent. In general, recent legislation has emphasized direct regulation, although there has been some study of the use of effluent fees. For example, the government has considered imposing a fee on the emission of sulphur oxide into the air.

Some people believe that public policy is moving too rapidly in this area; others believe that it is moving too slowly. It is not easy to determine how fast or how far we should go in attempting to reduce pollution. Those who will bear the costs of pollution-control projects—towns like Richmond, firms like the Smith Paper Company—have an understandable tendency to emphasize (and perhaps inflate) the costs and discount the benefits of such projects. Those who are particularly interested in enjoying nature and outdoor recreation—like the Sierra Club—are understandably inclined to emphasize (and perhaps inflate) the benefits and discount the costs of such projects. Politics inevitably plays a major role in the outcome of such cases. The citizens of the United States must indicate, through the ballot box as well as the market place, how much they are willing to pay to reduce pollution. We must also decide at what level of government the relevant rules are to be made. Since many pollution problems are local, it often seems sensible to determine the appropriate level of environmental quality locally. (However, there are obvious dangers in piecemeal regulation, as pointed out above.)

How Clean Should the Environment Be?

One of the most fundamental questions about pollution control is: How clean do we want the air, water, and other parts of our environment to be? At first glance, it may seem that we should restore and maintain a pristine pure environment, but this is not a very sensible goal, since the costs of achieving it would be enormous. The Environmental Protection Agency has estimated that it would cost about $60 billion to remove 85 to 90 percent of water pollutants from industrial and municipal sources by the mid-1980s. This is hardly a trivial amount, but it is far less than the cost of achieving zero discharge of pollutants, which would be about $320 billion—a truly staggering sum.

Fortunately, however, there is no reason to aim at so stringent a goal. It seems obvious that, as pollution increases, various costs to society increase as well. Some of these costs were described at the beginning of this chapter. For example, we pointed out that increases in air pollution result in increased deaths, and that increases in water pollution reduce the recreational value of rivers and streams. Suppose that we could get accurate data on the cost to society of various levels of pollution. Of course, it is extremely difficult to get such data, but if we

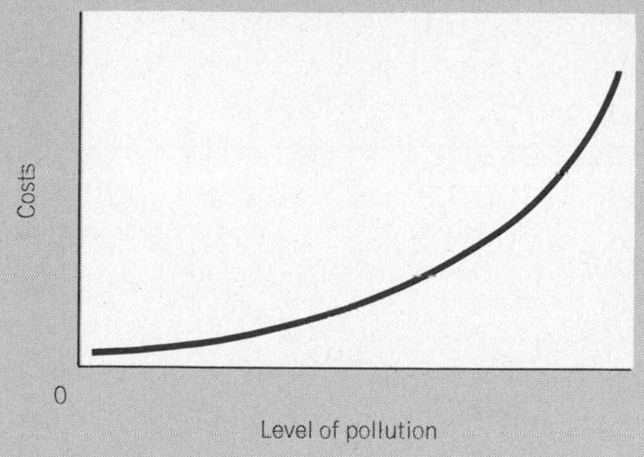

Figure 19.2
Costs to Society of Pollution
The costs to society of pollution increase with the level of pollution.

could, we could determine the relationship between the amount of these costs and the level of pollution. Clearly, it would look like the hypothetical curve in Figure 19.2: the greater the level of pollution, the higher these costs will be.

But these costs are not the only ones that must be considered. We must also take into account the costs of controlling pollution. In other words, we must look at the costs to society of maintaining a certain level of environmental quality. These costs are not trivial, as we saw at the beginning of this section. To maintain a very low level of pollution, it is necessary to invest heavily in pollution-control equipment and to make other economic sacrifices.[11] If we could get accurate data on the cost to society of controlling pollution, we could find the relationship between the amount of these costs and the level of pollution. Clearly, it would look like the hypothetical curve in Figure 19.3; the lower the level of pollution, the higher these costs will be.

At this point, it should be obvious why we should not try to achieve a zero level of pollution. *The sensible goal for our society is to minimize the sum of the costs of pollution and the costs of controlling pollution.* In other words, we should construct a graph, as shown in Figure 19.4, to indicate the relationship between the sum of these two types of costs and the level of pollution. Then we should choose the level of pollution at which the sum of these two types of costs is a minimum. Thus, in Figure 19.4, we should aim for a pollution level of *A*. There is no point in trying for a lower level; such a reduction would cost more than it would be worth. For example, the cost of achieving a zero pollution level would be much more than it would be worth. Only when the pollution level exceeds *A* is the extra cost to society of the additional pollution greater than the cost of

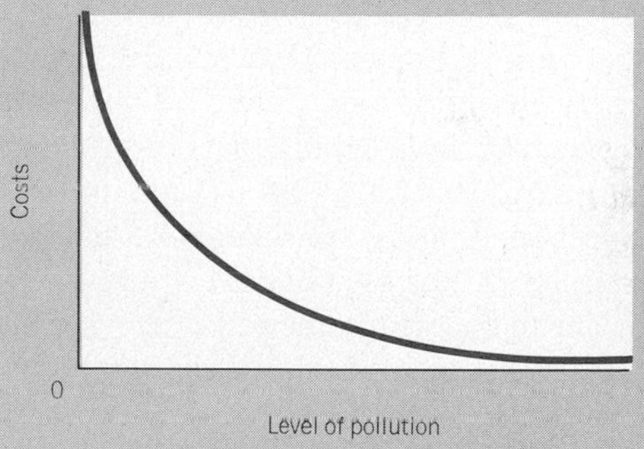

Figure 19.3
Costs to Society of Pollution Control
The more pollution is reduced, the higher are the costs to society of pollution control.

[11] It is important to recognize that the costs of pollution control extend far beyond the construction of more and better water treatment plants, or the more extensive control of gas emission, or other such steps. A serious pollution-control program can put firms out of business, put people out of work, and bring economic trouble to entire communities. Further, a pollution-control system can result in a redistribution of income. For example, automobiles, electric power, and other goods and services involving considerable pollution are likely to increase in price relative to other goods and services involving little pollution. To the extent that polluting goods and services play a bigger role in the budgets of the poor than of the rich, pollution controls hurt the poor and help the rich.

Figure 19.4
Determining Optimal Level of Pollution
The optimal level of pollution is at point *A*, since this is where the total costs are a minimum. Below point *A*, the cost to society of more pollution is less than the cost of preventing it. Above point *A*, the cost to society of more pollution is greater than the cost of preventing it.

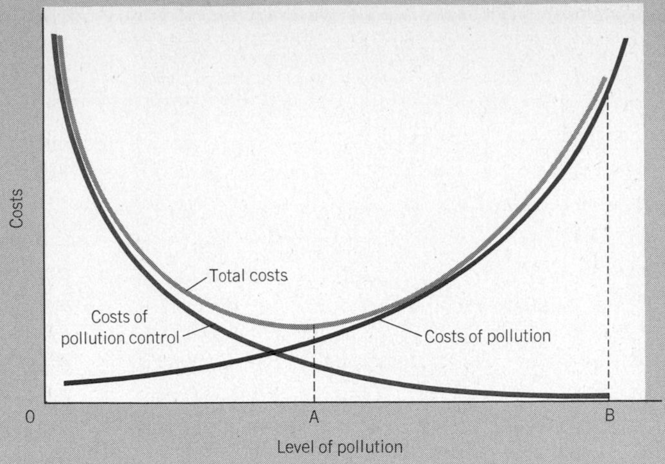

preventing it. For example, the cost of allowing pollution to increase from A to B is much greater than the cost of prevention.

It is easy to draw hypothetical curves, but not so easy actually to measure these curves. Unfortunately, no one has a very clear idea of what the curves in Figure 19.4 really look like—although we can be sure that their general shapes are like those shown there. Thus no one really knows just how clean we should try to make the environment. Under these circumstances, expert opinion differs on the nature and extent of the programs that should be carried out. Moreover, as pointed out in the previous section, political considerations and pressures enter in. But one thing is for sure: we will continue to live with some pollution—and that, for the reason just given, will be the rational thing to do.

Our Energy Problems

OPEC and the Energy Crisis

During the early 1970s, even as it began to dawn on Americans that our environment was not indestructible, other urgent concerns arose about our natural resources. A nation that had taken its abundant energy supplies for granted suddenly was confronted by the prospect of shortages. In late 1973, there was the Arab oil embargo; then in 1974, there was a tremendous increase in the price of imported crude oil. In September 1973, imported crude oil cost American petroleum refiners about $4.50 per barrel; a year later, it cost them about $12.50 per barrel. This great and sudden increase in the price of imported crude oil had a very substantial effect on both the national and international economy. It helped to create inflation at home, and transferred tens of billions of dollars from the oil-consuming nations to the oil-producing nations.

Why did the price of imported crude oil increase so spectacularly? Because the Organization of Petroleum Exporting Countries (OPEC) upped the price of crude oil. OPEC is an international cartel—that is, an association of national petroleum producers that gets together and sets prices for oil.[12] In other words, OPEC operates like a monopoly, or close to it. Formed in the early 1960s, OPEC's charter says that "members shall study and formulate a

[12] Although many of the oil-exporting countries are in the Middle East, OPEC also includes countries in Africa, Latin America, and other continents.

system to ensure the stabilization of prices by, among other means, the regulation of production, with due regard to the interests of the producing and the consuming nations, and to the necessity of securing a steady income to the producing countries." In the 1960s, OPEC gained strength; in the 1970s, it lowered the boom on the oil-consuming nations.

The Arab oil embargo in late 1973 called attention to another aspect of our energy problems—the fact that the United States is coming to depend to an increasing extent on foreign sources of supply of crude oil. Gross imports of petroleum and petroleum products were about 36 percent of U.S. consumption in 1974, as compared to about 21 percent in 1965. Some people are disturbed that we may be approaching the point where our national security might be imperiled by a cutoff of foreign oil. They assert that a sudden interruption of oil imports would disrupt our economy and perhaps have military consequences as well. They are particularly fearful on this score, since many of the oil producers are Arab nations, hostile to Israel, a country we have supported.

The argument that we should try to avoid being dependent on foreign sources of oil is by no means new. Until 1973, this argument was used to justify the adoption of oil import quotas in the United States. These import quotas set a limit on the amount of foreign oil that could be imported. Many economists were opposed to these quotas because they increased the price of petroleum and petroleum products to consumers. (See Chapter 31.) Whether self-sufficiency with regard to energy is as important a goal as some policy makers seem to believe is hard to say. But recent events—the Arab oil embargo in particular—have made the potential threat more credible.

Energy and Economic Growth

U.S. policy makers have proclaimed the importance of guaranteeing energy supplies that will meet the nation's growing energy demands. According to some observers, such as the authors of the *Limits to Growth*[13] (discussed in the previous chapter), this will not be possible. Why? Because there is only a finite supply of energy resources like oil and coal. If economic growth continues, the demand for these resources will increase exponentially. Eventually, according to these observers, we shall run out of such resources, with the result that both output and production will decline. Moreover, although this outcome is not around the corner, it is not so far off either: in their view, it will occur in the next 100 years.

Many people regard this as one of the most serious and fundamental of our energy problems. However, few economists accept the assumptions underlying these arguments. In the first place, economists charge that the authors of *Limits to Growth* underestimate very substantially the amount of the world's energy resources. Between 1944 and 1969, total world economic reserves of crude oil increased by about 12 times, due to producers' efforts to find and develop new sources of supply. Since annual world consumption rose about 6 times, this meant that reserves more than kept pace with oil consumption. Yet the authors of *Limits to Growth* assumed that known economic reserves of energy resources would increase only 5 times between now and the year 2100.

More fundamentally, economists charge that the authors of *Limits to Growth* do not take proper account of the workings of the price system. When the supply of a resource becomes tight, its price rises, with the result that firms have a greater financial incentive to find more of it. Also, as the price of this resource rises, firms have an incentive to develop new technology that permits less of this resource to be used. These mechanisms have resulted in the elimination of many apparent

[13] Dennis and Donella Meadows et al, *The Limits to Growth,* New York: New American Library, 1972.

shortages in the past, and most economists tend to believe that they will play a major role in attacking our energy problems as well.[14]

Energy and the Environment

Still another aspect of our current energy problem is related to the environment. As stressed in earlier sections of this chapter, energy production is responsible for a considerable amount of environmental pollution. One senator has put it this way: "Airborne pollutants, concentration of nuclear wastes, oil spills, thermal pollution from power plants, extensive modification of the landscape by the increased construction of transmission lines, refineries, pumped storage facilities, and marine transmission facilities are illustrative causes of environmental problems related to energy production and use."[15] In recent years, it has become increasingly obvious that our environmental and energy problems are intertwined.

To illustrate, consider the case of the trans-Alaskan pipeline. Atlantic-Richfield and Exxon discovered the Prudhoe Bay oil field, the largest known field in North America, in 1967. The cheapest way to deliver this oil seemed to be to build a 900-mile pipeline from the North Slope to Valdez. However, there were objections from environmentalists, who argued that a trans-Canadian pipeline would result in less ecological damage. The Interior Department, after issuing the required environmental impact statement in March 1972, recommended that the trans-Alaskan pipeline be built. This ruling was appealed to the courts. Finally, in late 1973, Congress passed legislation to end the legal battle and to go ahead with the trans-Alaskan pipeline, which was supposed to get oil flowing from Alaska by 1978.

The choice here was between building the trans-Alaskan pipeline or a 2,500-mile pipeline across Canada into the Midwest (assuming Canada approved). What were the arguments for the trans-Alaskan pipeline? The most important seemed to be that construction costs would be about $3 billion less than for the trans-Canadian pipeline, and that the trans-Canadian pipeline would take one to three years longer to complete. Unquestionably, these were important arguments. However, as some environmentalists pointed out, oil prices tend to be much higher in the Midwest (where the trans-Canadian pipeline would deliver oil) than on the West Coast (where the trans-Alaskan pipeline would deliver oil). This fact might have helped to offset the higher delivery costs associated with the trans-Canadian route.

The arguments against the trans-Alaskan pipeline were environmental in considerable part. The trans-Alaskan pipeline will go through earthquake-prone regions, and the oil will have to be carried by tanker from Valdez to the West Coast. Thus the danger of an oil spill is much larger than if the trans-Canadian pipeline were built. Supporters of the trans-Alaskan pipeline argued that mandatory safety measures would reduce this danger to a very low level, whereas its critics challenged this claim. When the final decision had to be made, it was to build the trans-Alaskan pipeline. Only time will tell what the environmental consequences will be.

The Shortage of Natural Gas

Still another facet of our recent energy problems has been a reported shortage of one of our most important fuels, natural gas. As shown in Table 19.3, natural gas accounts for about 30 percent of total energy consumption in the United States. It is a very desirable fuel because it is relatively nonpolluting. According to many economists, this shortage is due to the regulatory policies of the Federal Power Commission. Only recently has the Federal Power Commission been required to set prices of gas

[14] This section, as well as others in this chapter, are based in part on R. Mancke, *The Failure of U.S. Energy Policy*, New York: Columbia University Press, 1974.
[15] Ibid., p. 43.

Table 19.3
Total Gross Consumption of Energy, and Percent from Each Major Source, United States, 1966–74

Year	Total energy consumption (quadrillion Btus)	Oil	Natural gas	Coal	Hydropower	Nuclear
				(percent of total)		
1966	56.4	43.2	30.9	22.1	3.7	0.1
1968	61.8	43.8	31.7	20.5	3.8	0.2
1970	67.1	44.0	32.8	18.9	4.0	0.3
1972	71.9	45.8	32.0	17.3	4.1	0.8
1973	74.7	46.4	30.6	17.9	3.9	1.2
1974	72.7	46.0	30.1	18.3	4.2	1.4

Source: Economic Report of the President, 1975.

producers in sales to pipelines. Before 1954, there was no such regulation. But in that year, the Supreme Court found that the Federal Power Commission should determine whether prices of gas sold in interstate commerce were "reasonable." Since then, there has been continual controversy over whether such regulation is really necessary or desirable, and if so, over what form it should take.

The Supreme Court ruled that the price of natural gas should be regulated because it felt that the price was not determined under competitive conditions. It believed that the producers of natural gas had appreciable monopoly power. However, this belief was not shared by many observers, including a number of distinguished academic economists. For example, Morris Adelman of M.I.T. testified that "it is my conclusion that the production of natural gas is a competitive industry." Adelman's view was based in part on the fact that the industry contains thousands of producers and that there is relatively little concentration of employment or sales. Nonetheless, other eminent economists argued that the industry did contain serious monopolistic elements, and the court seemed to agree.

In response to its new responsibility, the Federal Power Commission established "area prices" for each of 23 natural-gas-producing regions of the United States. Any producer of gas was allowed to agree to a contract for a price less than or equal to the "area price" for his region. If he wanted a higher price, he had to prove its "necessity and convenience" to the commission. According to many observers, the commission set these "area prices" in such a way as to keep the price of natural gas artificially low. In other words, the commission has been accused of "freezing" the price at less than its equilibrium level. At first glance, this may seem to be a boon to the nation and the consumer. After all, who can be against low prices? But the truth is that a price that is too low can be just as bad for society as one that is too high.

To see what is wrong with a price that is too low, we must hark back to our discussion of how the price system works. Recall that a product's price influences how much of it firms will supply. Clearly, if the price set by the commission is lower than would be the case in a competitive market, firms will supply less natural gas in the long run than they would under competition. That is, they will invest fewer resources in exploring for natural gas, with the result that there may be a "shortage" of natural gas, in the sense that the quantity supplied may be less than the quantity demanded. In other words, the situation would be like that in Figure 19.5, where OP_r is the price set by the commission. At this price, the quantity supplied is less than the quantity demanded. According to some observers, the remedy is to end the regulation of natural gas prices. More will be said on this score below.[16]

Public Policy toward Energy

Reduction of Energy Demand

What can we do to help solve our energy problems? One suggestion made by some economists is that we should reduce our demand for energy. Without question, there are many areas where energy could be saved with little inconvenience. One way that a reduction in energy demand could be accomplished is through the imposition of a tax on fuel. A number of economists have suggested such a measure. To see how it might work, consider Figure 19.6, which shows the demand and supply curves for fuel. Without the tax, the price of fuel would be OP_0, and the quantity consumed would be OQ_0.

Suppose that a tax of \$.20 per gallon[17] of fuel were imposed. If so, the supply curve would shift upward by the amount of the tax. To see why, note that, if the pretax price had to be OP_0 per gallon to induce sellers to supply OQ_0 gallons of fuel, the posttax price would have to be \$.20 higher to induce the same supply. Similarly, if the pretax price had to be OP_1 per gallon to induce sellers to supply OQ_1 gallons of fuel, the posttax price would have to be \$.20 higher to induce the same supply. The reason why the sellers require \$.20 more per gallon to supply the pretax amount is that they must pay the tax of \$.20 per gallon to the gov-

[16] Note that in 1975 the Federal Power Commission abandoned the establishment of area rates, and that in the summer of 1976 it raised the nation-wide price of gas to \$1.42 per 1,000 cubic feet, pending court review. Nonetheless, there is continuing pressure for deregulation. For a more complete discussion, see P. MacAvoy, *Crisis of the Regulatory Commission*, New York: Norton, 1970. In Chapters 24 and 30, we discuss other aspects of pricing by regulated industries.

[17] We assume here that fuel is measured in gallons. For some fuels (like coal), this is not the case; but this simplification can easily be removed. It is used here only for convenience.

Figure 19.5
Shortage of Natural Gas
If the regulated price of natural gas is OP_r, the quantity supplied will be OQ_S and the quantity demanded will be OQ_D. Since the quantity demanded exceeds the quantity supplied, there is a shortage. This is because OP_r is below the equilibrium price, OP.

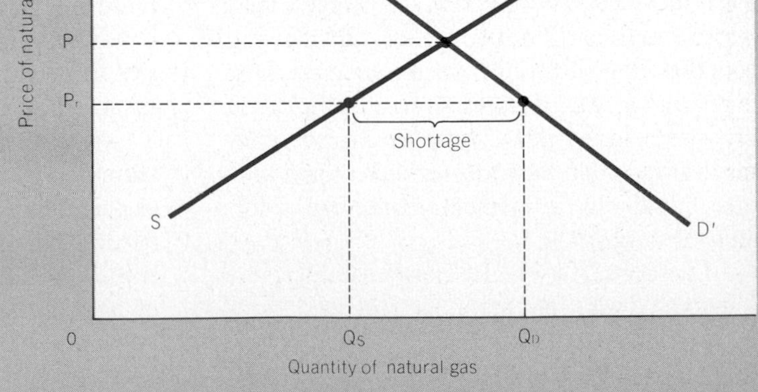

Figure 19.6
Effect of a Tax on Fuel
If a tax of $.20 per gallon is imposed on fuel, the supply curve for fuel shifts from SS' to S_1S_1'. Since the demand curve for fuel is DD', the quantity of fuel consumed is cut from OQ_0 to OQ_2.

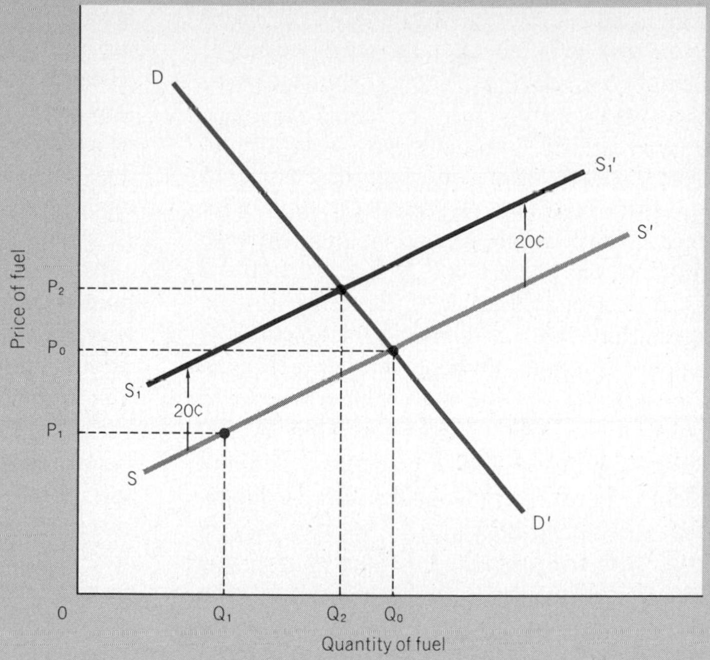

ernment. Thus they need the extra $.20 to wind up with the same amount as before.

Since the tax shifts the supply curve upward by $.20, the posttax supply curve is S_1S_1'—and the posttax equilibrium price and quantity are OP_2 and OQ_2, respectively. The effect of the tax on the quantity of fuel consumed is just what one would expect: it reduces fuel consumption. In Figure 19.6, the reduction is from OQ_0 to OQ_2. According to calculations by Dale Jorgensen of Harvard University and Edward Hudson of Data Resources, Inc., a tax equal to 3 percent of sales in 1985 and increasing gradually to about 15 percent in the year 2000 would result in no growth whatsoever in the quantity of energy consumed between 1985 and 2000. However, it is by no means clear that the United States should seek to maintain energy consumption at a constant level. For one thing, such a policy would reduce our rate of economic growth, although considerable growth would still occur.

Development of New Energy Technologies

Another way that we can avoid increased dependence on foreign oil is to develop new technologies that can produce energy economically from our domestic resources. One important resource of this kind is shale, which is found in Colorado, Wyoming, and Utah. For many years, shale has been regarded as a promising source of synthetic oil, but so far the costs of producing oil by this route have been too high to make it economical. Also, there are many unresolved environmental problems, since it is difficult to dispose of the spent shale. In Canada, a potentially important source of synthetic oil is the tar sands located in Alberta. Here too, the costs of producing oil in this way are relatively high—about $9 per barrel in 1975, according to some estimates. But some production is occurring. In both the cases of shale and tar sands, perhaps additional investments in research and development can solve the problems that presently prevent these resources from being a more economical source of synthetic oil.

The United States has vast quantities of coal. To some extent, it should be possible to substitute our relatively plentiful coal for other fuels. However, one important problem with much of our Eastern coal is that it contains a great deal of sulphur, with the result that its combustion leads to a rise in the emission of sulphur dioxide, an important air pollutant. One way to cope with this problem is to scrub most of this chemical from power plants' flue stacks. Unfortunately, however, there does not seem to be any technology that can do this effectively and economically. Another way to cope with the problem is to convert coal to a clean gas. A number of technologies have been developed to do this, but many are still in the pilot-plant stage. Here is another area where research and development have a promising role to play.

Still another promising source of energy is the sun. Techniques for harnessing solar energy have been known for a long time. For example, flat plate collectors can be used to heat water or air, which can then be used to heat buildings. But solar energy is still very costly, and there are problems in storing it for use on cloudy days and at night. According to some experts, solar energy is potentially of great economic significance, and too little has been invested to try to develop it and reduce its cost. This is an obvious area for further research and development.

Is Nuclear Power the Answer?

In 1938, Otto Hahn and Fritz Strassmann "discovered" nuclear fission in their studies of the substances obtained when neutrons impinge on the uranium nucleus. Their work, as well as that of Fermi, Bohr, Wheeler, and others, formed the basis for nuclear reactors. A nuclear reactor produces electricity by producing heat. Generally, a reactor will contain fissionable material, control rods, a moderator, shielding, and structural materials and mechanisms for removing the heat that is generated. The capital cost of a nuclear power reactor tends to be high because of the complexity of the plant.

Atomic energy came into being for military purposes during World War II, and for some time, private industry in the United States was prohibited from developing nuclear power. The Atomic Energy Commission Act of 1954 permitted private industry to own and operate nuclear reactors, but the ownership of nuclear fuels (and certain important elements of nuclear technology) resided with the government. In 1964, the AEC Act was amended to allow private ownership of nuclear fuels. The first commercial nuclear power plant in the United States was Duquesne Light Company's Shippingport plant in Pennsylvania, which began operations in 1957.

The federal government and private industry have invested billions of dollars in nuclear power, and by 1974, it accounted for almost 7 percent of the nation's electrical generating capacity. (See Figure 19.7.) Yet nuclear power remains controversial. For one thing, there has been considerable discussion of possible dangers to the environment and to public safety. As critics of nuclear power point out, reactors release some amount of irradiated wastes, the disposal of nuclear wastes can cause problems, and thermal pollution can pose an environmental threat. Further, there are possible dangers associated with the use of fissionable materials to make bombs, and with the sabotage of nuclear power plants by terrorists. Although the probability of these disastrous events unquestionably is low, some citizens regard it as too high to be acceptable. Others, however, feel that the risks have been greatly exaggerated.

In addition, there has been considerable con-

Figure 19.7
Nuclear Capacity as a Percent of All Installed Electrical Generating Capacity, United States, 1959–74
Government and private investment since 1959 in nuclear power has resulted in its increase to almost 7 percent of U.S. electrical generating capacity. *Source: Statistical Abstract of the United States and Federal Power Commission.*

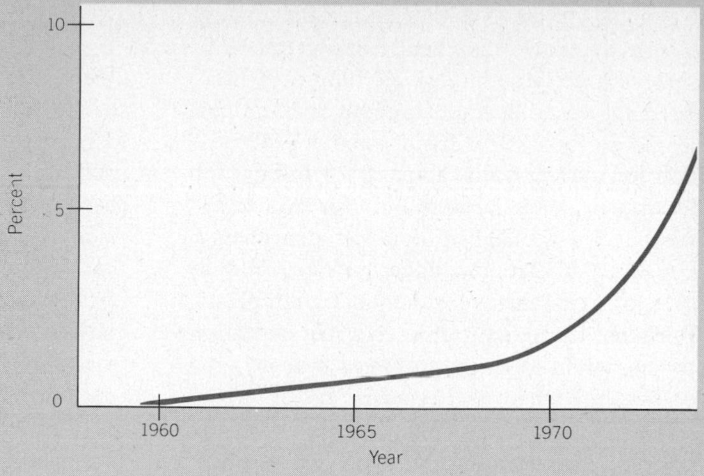

troversy over how the production costs of nuclear power compare with those of conventional power. Many advocates of nuclear power have insisted that it is competitive with conventional power—or that it soon would be. Critics, on the other hand, have claimed that this is not true. For example, Philip Sporn estimated in 1970 that the cost of switchboard delivered nuclear power was 7.06 mills per kilowatt-hour as against 6.65 mills for coal-fired energy, with coal at $.25 per Btu. And in the mid-1970s, many electric utilities began canceling or postponing orders for nuclear plants, as they re-examined the economics of nuclear power.

Due both to the environmental and economic uncertainties surrounding nuclear power, it appears that it is a very incomplete answer to our energy problems. However, here too advances in technology may alter the picture considerably. The federal government has invested huge sums in the development of a Liquid Metal Fast Breeder Reactor, which, if successful, could produce more plutonium than it consumes. Also, the government has invested considerable sums in research concerning fusion. However, according to expert opinion, neither the breeder reactor nor the fusion reactor could affect the energy picture in an important way before the end of this century.[18]

Government Policies and Proposals

Faced with the energy problems described above, the government has taken or proposed a number of actions. First, it has tried in a variety of ways to encourage the conservation of fuel. For example, President Ford recommended in 1975 that the price of oil, some of which was under federal controls, be allowed to increase, thus reducing oil consumption and stimulating oil output. But this suggestion was viewed with considerable skepticism in Congress, since it would aggravate existing inflationary pressures. Faced with congressional opposition, the Ford administration did not push hard for removing federal controls in 1975, although action along this line may occur in the future.

Second, the government has increased its expenditures on energy research and development. In President Ford's revised request to

[18] Parts of this section are taken from my "The Diffusion of Eight Major Industrial Innovations in the United States," in *The State of Science and Research: Some New Indicators,* Washington, D.C., National Planning Association, 1975.

Congress, he asked authority for the Energy Research and Development Administration to sign contracts for almost $2 billion in fiscal 1976. Of this total amount, about $620 million would go for nuclear fission, about $140 million for nuclear fuels, about $620 million for fossil fuels, about $260 million for nuclear fusion, and about $80 million for solar energy. However, in 1976, the House defeated a bill to give loan guarantees for demonstration plants. President Carter has proposed a reorganization of the nation's energy programs, but it is too early to say what its effects may be.

Third, there have been proposals that the price of natural gas should be decontrolled. President Ford, the Federal Energy Administration, and the Federal Power Commission have favored such a step on the grounds that it would end the natural gas shortage and result in a less wasteful use of gas. On the other hand, congressional liberals and consumers groups have resisted, arguing that the market for natural gas is not competitive. As Michigan's Senator Philip Hart put it, "I can't agree that we can lift price regulation in the natural gas industry until we take steps to make this a competitive market."

Finally, some observers have proposed a variety of measures to weaken the power of the OPEC oil cartel. One proposal is that the major oil-consuming nations should get together and bargain collectively with OPEC in an effort to reduce oil prices. However, the prevailing view seems to be that this is not feasible (even if it would work, which is by no means clear) since several major oil-consuming nations do not want to join such a group. Another proposal is that the United States should try to drive a wedge among the various members of OPEC and get them to compete with one another. Although some ingenious schemes have been put forth to help accomplish this, there was little evidence (up to 1976, at least) that OPEC was so disunited that the price of oil was about to crumble.

Summary

One of the major social issues of the 1970s is environmental pollution. To a considerable extent, environmental pollution is an economic problem. Waste disposal and other pollution-causing activities result in external diseconomies. Specifically, the firms and individuals that pollute the water and air (and other facets of the environment) pay less than the true social costs of disposing of their wastes in this way. Part of the true social cost is borne by other firms and individuals who must pay to clean up the water or air, or who must live with the consequences. Because of the divergence of private from social costs, the market system does not result in an optimal allocation of resources. Firms and individuals create too much waste and dispose of it in excessively harmful ways. Because the polluters do not pay the full cost of waste disposal, their products are artificially cheap, with the result that too much is produced of them.

The government can intervene in several ways to help remedy the breakdown of the market system in this area. One way is to issue regulations for waste disposal and other activities influencing the environment. Another is to establish effluent fees, charges a polluter must pay to the government for discharging wastes. In recent years, there has been considerable growth in government programs designed to control pollution. It is extremely difficult to determine how clean the environment should be. Of course, the sensible goal for society is to permit the level of pollution that minimizes the sum of the costs of pollution and the costs of controlling pollution; but no one has a very clear idea of what these costs are, and to a large extent the choices must be made through the political process.

Another major issue of the 1970s has been energy. There are several aspects of this issue. First, the Arab oil embargo in late 1973 and OPEC's huge price increase in early 1974 called attention to the growing dependence of the United States on foreign sources of crude oil. Second, according to some observers (but few economists), we will "run out" of energy resources unless we cut back on energy consumption. Third, energy production is responsible for a considerable amount of environmental pollution. Fourth, according to some economists and public officials, the regulatory policies of the Federal Power Commission have resulted in a shortage of natural gas.

A variety of policy measures have been carried out or proposed to help deal with our energy problems. One proposal is that we enact a tax on fuel to reduce energy demand. Another approach is to develop new energy technologies that can produce energy economically from our domestic energy resources. The Energy Research and Development Administration has begun work along this line. Still another proposal is that the price of natural gas be decontrolled. Finally, a variety of measures has been proposed to try to weaken the power of the OPEC oil cartel.

CONCEPTS FOR REVIEW

External diseconomies	Primary treatment	Thermal pollution
Private costs	Secondary treament	Noise pollution
Social costs	Air pollution	Effluent fees
Water pollution		

QUESTIONS FOR DISCUSSION AND REVIEW

1. Suppose that the paper industry emits wastes into rivers and streams, and that municipalities or firms downstream must treat the water to make it usable. Do the paper industry's private costs equal the social costs of producing paper? Why or why not?

2. Suppose that each ton of paper produced results in pollution that costs municipalities and firms downstream $1.00, and that a law is passed that requires the paper industry to reimburse the municipalities and firms downstream for these costs. Prior to this law, the supply curve for paper was:

Price of paper (dollars per ton)	Quantity supplied (million tons)
1.00	10.0
2.00	15.0
2.50	17.5
3.00	20.0
4.00	25.0

After the law takes effect, what will be the quantity supplied at each price?

3. If the demand curve for paper is as shown below, what will be the equilibrium output of paper before and after the paper industry has to reimburse the municipalities and firms downstream (as indicated in Question 2)?

Price of paper (dollars per ton)	Quantity demanded (million tons)
1.00	30.0
2.00	25.0
3.00	20.0
3.50	17.5
4.00	15.0

4. In Question 3, which output—the one prevailing before the industry has to reimburse others, or the one prevailing afterward—is socially more desirable? Why?

5. Suppose that the social cost (in billions of dollars) due to pollution equals $5P$, where P is the level of pollution, and that the cost (in billions of dollars) of pollution control equals $10 - 2P$. What is the optimal level of pollution?

6. "A tax on fuel will reduce the quantity consumed by a greater amount if the quantity of fuel demanded is relatively insensitive to its price than if it is relatively sensitive to it." Comment and evaluate.

7. "The apparent shortage of natural gas really has been due to the fact that natural gas producers, expecting higher prices in the future, have been holding supplies off the market." Comment and evaluate.

8. "The only dependable way to cut down on pollution is to ban certain kinds of polluting activities." Do you agree? Why or why not?

9. The *1971 Annual Report of the Council of Economic Advisers* states that "new rules for use of the environment are bound to affect competitive relationships within and among industries, localities, and nations." Give examples of these effects, and ways that society can make the transition easier.

10. Smoke is a classic case of an external diseconomy. (It was cited by Alfred Marshall and others.) Describe what actions can and should be taken to eliminate socially undesirable effects of smoke.

PART SIX

Consumer Behavior and Business Decision Making

20

Consumer Behavior and Rational Choice

To a considerable extent, consumers, voting with their pocketbooks, are the masters of our economic system. No wonder, then, that economists spend much of their time describing and analyzing how consumers act. In addition, economists are interested in determining how consumers, as well as other decision-making units, should go about making rational choices. In this chapter, we present the basic model economists use to analyze consumer behavior.

After describing this model, we shall show how it can be used to promote better decision making, both by consumers and by government agencies and other organizations. After all, as we stressed in Chapter 1, one of the reasons why anyone should take the trouble to study economics is that it helps him or her to make better decisions. These applications should make the basic economic theory more interesting and understandable, as well as provide concepts and data we will need in subsequent chapters.

Consumer Expenditures

The Walters of San Diego

Since we are concerned here with consumer behavior, perhaps the best way to begin is to look at the behavior of a particular consumer. It is hard to find any consumer who is "typical." There are hundreds of millions of consumers in the United States, and as we saw in Chapter 4, they vary enormously. (Recall the princely Rockefellers and the poverty-stricken Ríoses.) Nonetheless, it is instructive to look at how a particular American family—the Edward Walters of San Diego[1]—spends its money. The Walters are in their mid-thirties, have two children (ages eight and six), and have Mrs. Walter's younger brother living with them. They own their own home, and both work. Mr. Walter manages a small clothing firm in San Diego, and Mrs. Walter is a designer at the same firm. Together, the Walters make about $25,000 a year.

How do the Walters spend their money? For most consumers, we cannot answer this question with any accuracy, because the people in question simply do not tell anyone what they do with their money. But because the Walters and their buying habits were scrutinized in a series of articles in a national magazine, it is possible to describe quite accurately where their money goes. As shown in Table 20.1, the Walters, who own their own home, spend about $735 a month—about 35 percent of their income—on housing. In addition, they spend about $300 a month—about 14 percent of their income—on food and drink. Also, they spend about $150 a month—about 7 percent of their income—on domestic help, which is needed since both parents work.

In addition, as shown in Table 20.1, the Walters spend about $150 a month—about 7 percent of their income—on private schools and other lessons for their children. Another $150 a month goes for entertainment and clothing. Because of the mild weather in San Diego (and perhaps because they can get clothing at a discount since they are in the clothing business), their expenditures on clothing are not very large. Medical, dental, and insurance expenses consume about $145 a month—again, about 7 percent of income—and $50 a month—or about 3 percent of their income—is spent on transportation. Finally, the Walters allocate about $420 a month—about 20 percent of their income—for taxes and savings.

This, in a nutshell, is how the Walters spend their money. The Walters exchange their resources—mostly labor—in the resource markets for $25,000 a year. They take this money into the product markets and spend about ⅘ of it for the goods and services described above. The remaining ⅕ of their income goes for taxes and saving. The Walters, like practically

Table 20.1
Monthly Spending Pattern of Mr. and Mrs. Walter of San Diego, California

Item	Amount (dollars)	Percent of income
Housing	735	35
Food and drink	300	14
Domestic help	150	7
Private school and education	150	7
Entertainment and clothing	150	7
Medical, dental, and insurance expenses	145	7
Transportation	50	3
Taxes and savings[a]	420	20
Monthly income	2,100	100

[a] Estimated by deducting other items from monthly income.

[1] For obvious reasons, we have changed the name and residence of the family in question. Otherwise, however, the facts given in the following paragraphs are as they were stated in a national magazine.

Table 20.2
Allocation of Income by U.S. Households, 1973

	Percent of total
Personal taxes	15
Personal saving	5
Consumption expenditures	
Autos and parts	6
Furniture and household equipment	5
Other durable goods	2
Food and drink	16
Clothing and shoes	7
Gasoline and oil	3
Other nondurable goods	7
Housing	11
Household operations	5
Transportation	2
Other services	16
Total income[a]	100

[a] Personal income net of interest payments. See Chapter 8.
Source: Survey of Current Business.

every family, keep a watchful eye on where their money goes and what they are getting in exchange for their labor and other resources. So do we all: as stressed in Chapter 3, the basic purpose of our economic system is to satisfy the wants of consumers.

Aggregate Data for the United States

How does the way that the Walters spend their money compare with consumer behavior in general? In Table 20.2, we provide data on how all consumers allocated their aggregate income in 1973. These data tell us much more about the typical behavior of American consumers than our case study of the Walters. Note first of all that American households paid about 15 percent of their income in taxes. This, of course, is the price of the government services we described in Chapter 5. In addition, American households saved about 5 percent of their income. In other words, they refrained from spending 5 percent of their income on goods and services; instead, they put this amount into stocks, bonds, bank accounts, or other such channels for saving.

American consumers spent the remaining 80 percent of their income on goods and services. Table 20.2 makes it clear that they allocated much of their expenditures to housing, food and drink, and transportation. Spending on housing, household operations, and furniture and other durable household equipment accounted for about 20 percent of American consumers' total income. Spending on food and alcoholic beverages accounted for about 16 percent of total income. Spending on automobiles and parts, gasoline and oil, and other transportation accounted for about 10 percent of total income. Thus taxes, savings, housing, food and drink, and transportation accounted for almost 70 percent of the total income of all households in the United States.

The data in Table 20.2 make it obvious that the Walter family is not very typical of American consumers. For example, it spends a much larger percentage of its income on housing, domestic help, and education than do consumers as a whole. To some degree, this is because the Walters are more affluent than most American families, but this is only part of the reason. To a large extent, it simply reflects the fact that people want different things. Looking around you, you see considerable diversity in the way consumers spend their money. Take your own family as an example. It is a good bet that your family spends its money quite differently than the nation as a whole. If your parents like to live in a big house, your family may spend much more than the average on housing. Or if they like to go to sports events, their expenditures on such entertainment may be much higher than average.

A Model of Consumer Behavior

Why do consumers spend their money the way they do? The economist answers this question with the aid of a ***model of consumer behavior,*** which is useful both for analysis and for decision making, and which is not difficult to understand, despite some unfamiliar and strange-sounding terminology. We shall soon see how it can be used to help solve real problems in both the private and public sectors of the economy.

To construct this model, the economist obviously must consider the tastes of the consumer. As Henry Adams put it, "Everyone carries his own inch-rule of taste, and amuses himself by applying it, triumphantly, wherever he travels." Certainly, it takes no genius to figure out that the amount a consumer purchases of a particular commodity is influenced by his tastes. Some people like beef, others like pork. Some people like the opera, others would trade a ticket to hear Joan Sutherland for a ticket to the Dallas Cowboys game any day of the week. Three assumptions, which seem reasonable for most purposes, underlie the economist's model of consumer preferences.

First, it is assumed that *the consumer when confronted with two alternative market baskets, can decide whether he prefers the first to the second, the second to the first, or whether he is indifferent between them.* For example, suppose Mrs. Walter, the San Diego designer, is confronted with a choice between a market basket containing 3 chocolate bars and a ticket to the movies and another market basket containing 2 chocolate bars and a record of the Tabernacle Choir singing Chopin's Minute Waltz. Despite the rather bizarre composition of these two market baskets, we assume that she can somehow decide whether she prefers the first market basket to the second, the second market basket to the first, or whether she is indifferent between them.

Second, it is assumed that *the consumer's preferences are transitive.* The meaning of transitive in this context is simple enough. Suppose that Mrs. Walter prefers an ounce of Chanel No. 5 perfume to an ounce of Blue Grass perfume, and that she prefers an ounce of Blue Grass perfume to an ounce of Sortilège perfume. Then, if her preferences are transitive, she must prefer an ounce of Chanel No. 5 perfume to an ounce of Sortilège perfume. The reason for this assumption is clear. If the consumer's preferences were not transitive, the consumer would have inconsistent or contradictory preferences. Although some people may have preferences that are not transitive, this assumption seems to be a reasonable first approximation—for the noninstitutionalized part of the population at least.

Third, it is assumed that *the consumer always prefers more of a commodity to less.* For example, if one market basket contains 3 bars of soap and 2 monkey wrenches and a second contains 3 bars of soap and 3 monkey wrenches, it is assumed that the second market basket is preferred to the first. To a large extent, this assumption is justified by the definition of a commodity as something the consumer desires. Of course, this does not mean that certain things are not a nuisance. For example, if one market basket contains 3 bars of soap and 2 rattlesnakes, we would not be at all surprised if the consumer did *not* prefer this market basket to one containing 3 bars of soap and no rattlesnakes. But to such a consumer, a rattlesnake would not be desired—and thus would not be a commodity. Instead, the absence of a rattlesnake would be desired—and would be a commodity.

Total and Marginal Utility

In Chapter 2, we pointed out that a model, to be useful, must omit many unimportant factors, concentrate on the basic factors at work, and simplify in order to illuminate. So that we focus on the important factors at work here, let's assume that there are only two goods, food and clothing. This is an innocuous assumption, since the results we shall obtain can be generalized to include cases where any number of goods exists. For simplicity, food is measured in pounds, and clothing is measured in number of pieces of clothing.

Consider Mrs. Walter, making choices for her family. Undoubtedly, she regards certain market baskets—that is, certain combinations of food and clothing (the only commodities)—to be more desirable than others. For example, she certainly regards 2 pounds of food and 1 piece of clothing to be more desirable than 1 pound of food and 1 piece of clothing. For simplicity, suppose that it is possible to measure the amount of satisfaction that she gets from each market basket by its utility. *A* ***utility*** *is a number that represents the level of satisfaction that the consumer derives from a particular market basket.* For example, the utility attached to the market basket containing 2 pounds of food and 1 piece of clothing may be 10 utils, and the utility attached to the market basket containing 1 pound of food and 1 piece of clothing may be 6 utils. (A util is the traditional unit in which utility is expressed.)

It is important to distinguish between total utility and marginal utility. The total utility of a market basket is the number described in the previous paragraph, whereas *the* ***marginal utility*** *measures the additional satisfaction derived from an additional unit of a commodity.* To see how marginal utility is obtained, let's take a close look at Table 20.3. The total utility the Walter family derives from the consumption of various amounts of food is given in the middle column of this table. (For simplicity, we assume for the moment that the Walters consume only food.) The marginal utility, shown in the righthand column, is the extra utility derived from each amount of food over and above the utility derived from 1 less pound of food. Thus it equals the difference

Table 20.3
Total Utility and Marginal Utility Derived by the Walters from Consuming Various Amounts of Food per Day

Pounds of food	Total utility	Marginal utility[a]
0	0	—
1	3	3 (= 3 − 0)
2	7	4 (= 7 − 3)
3	9	2 (= 9 − 7)
4	10	1 (= 10 − 9)

[a] These figures pertain to the interval between the indicated number of pounds of food and one pound less than the indicated number. This table assumes that no clothing is consumed.

between the total utility of a certain amount of food and the total utility of 1 less pound of food.

For example, as shown in Table 20.3, the *total* utility of 3 pounds of food is 9 utils, which is a measure of the total amount of satisfaction that the Walters get from this much food. In contrast, the *marginal* utility of 3 pounds of food is the extra utility obtained from the third pound of food—that is, the total utility of 3 pounds of food less the total utility of 2 pounds of food. Specifically, as shown in Table 20.3, it is 2 utils. Similarly, the *total* utility of 2 pounds of food is 7 utils, which is a measure of the total amount of satisfaction that the Walters get from this much food. In contrast, the *marginal* utility of 2 pounds of food is the extra utility from the second pound of food—that is, the total utility of 2 pounds of food less the total utility of 1 pound of food. Specifically, as shown in Table 20.3, it is 4 utils.

The Law of Diminishing Marginal Utility

Economists generally assume that, as a person consumes more and more of a particular com-

Figure 20.1
The Law of Diminishing Marginal Utility
Beyond some point (*OA* in this case), the marginal utility of a commodity declines as the consumer consumes more and more of it. This is the so-called law of diminishing marginal utility.

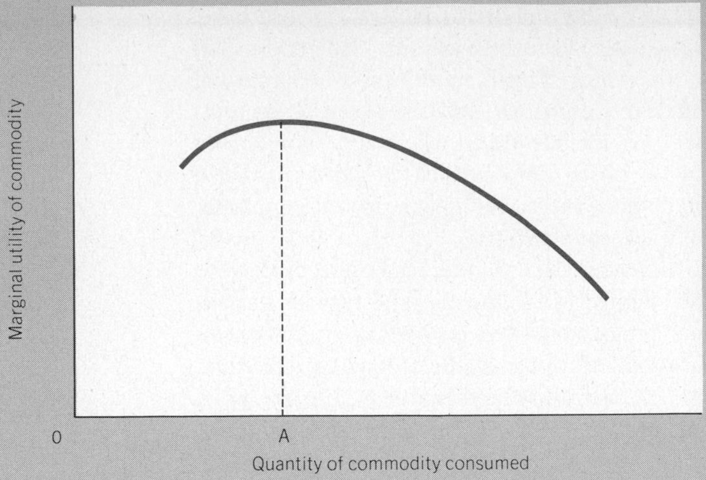

modity, there is, beyond some point, a decline in the extra satisfaction derived from the last unit of the commodity consumed. For example, if the Walters consume 2 pounds of food in a particular period of time, it may be just what the doctor ordered. If they consume 3 pounds of food in the same period of time, the third pound of food is likely to yield less satisfaction than the second. If they consume 4 pounds of food in the same period of time, the fourth pound of food is likely to yield less satisfaction than the third. And so on.

This assumption or hypothesis is often called the law of diminishing marginal utility. This law states that, *as a person consumes more and more of a given commodity (the consumption of other commodities being held constant), the marginal utility of the commodity eventually will tend to decline.* In other words, it states that the relationship between the marginal utility of a commodity and the amount consumed will be as shown in Figure 20.1. As you can see, the marginal utility declines as the amount consumed increases (beyond *OA*). Finally, note that the figures concerning the Walter family in Table 20.3 are in accord with this law. Once the consumption of food exceeds 2 pounds, the marginal utility of food declines.

The Equilibrium Market Basket

Preferences alone do not determine the consumer's actions. *Besides knowing the consumer's preferences, we must also know his income and the prices of commodities to predict which market basket he will buy.* The consumer's money income is the amount of money he can spend per unit of time. Clearly, his choice of a market basket is constrained by the size of his money income. For example, although Mr. Walter may regard a Hickey Freeman as his favorite suit, he may not buy it because he may have insufficient funds (as the bankers delicately put it). Also, the market basket the consumer chooses is influenced by the prices of commodities. For example, if the Hickey Freeman suit were offered by a discount store at $100, rather than its list price of $350, Mr. Walter might purchase it after all.

Given the consumer's tastes, economists assume that he attempts to maximize utility. In other words, *the consumer is assumed to be rational in the sense that he chooses the market basket—or more generally, the course of action—that is most to his liking.* Of course, as previously noted, the consumer is generally unable to reach the most preferred position—the market basket he would choose if his money income were unlimited and if prices did not matter. Instead, he must maximize his utility subject to the constraints imposed by the size of his money income and the nature of commodity prices.

What is the optimal market basket, the one that maximizes utility subject to these constraints? It is the one where *the consumer's income is allocated among commodities so that, for every commodity purchased, the marginal utility of the commodity is proportional to its price.* Thus, in the case of the Walter family, the optimal market basket is the one where

$$\frac{MU_F}{P_F} = \frac{MU_C}{P_C} \tag{20.1}$$

where MU_F is the marginal utility of food, MU_C is the marginal utility of clothing, P_F is the price of a pound of food, and P_C is the price of a piece of clothing.

To understand why the rule in Equation (20.1) is correct, it is convenient to begin by pointing out that $MU_F \div P_F$ is the marginal utility of the *last dollar's worth* of food and that $MU_C \div P_C$ is the maginal utility of the *last dollar's worth* of clothing. To see why this is so, take the case of food. Since MU_F is the extra utility of the *last pound* of food bought, and since P_F is the price of this *last pound,* the extra utility of the *last dollar's worth* of food must be $MU_F \div P_F$. For example, if the last pound of food results in an extra utility of 4 utils and this pound costs $2, then the extra utility from the last dollar's worth of food must be 4 ÷ 2, or 2 utils. In other words, the marginal utility of the last dollar's worth of food is 2 utils.

Since $MU_F \div P_F$ is the marginal utility of the last dollar's worth of food and $MU_C \div P_C$ is the marginal utility of the last dollar's worth of clothing, what Equation (20.1) really says is that *the rational consumer will choose a market basket where the marginal utility of the last dollar spent on all commodities purchased is the same.* To see why this must be so, consider the numerical example in Table 20.4, which shows the marginal utility the Walters derive from various amounts of food and clothing. Rather than measuring food and clothing in physical units, we measure them in Table 20.4 in terms of the amount of money spent on them.

Table 20.4
Marginal Utility Derived by the Walters from Various Quantities of Food and Clothing

	Dollars worth				
Commodity	1	2	3	4	5
	Marginal utility (utils)				
Food	20	16	12	10	7
Clothing	12	10	7	5	3

Given the information in Table 20.4, how much of each commodity should Mrs. Walter buy if her money income is only $4 (a ridiculous assumption but one that will help to make our point)? Clearly, the first dollar she spends should be on food since it will yield her a marginal utility of 20. The second dollar she spends should also be on food since a second dollar's worth of food has a marginal utility of 16. (Thus the total utility derived from the $2 of expenditure is 20 + 16 = 36.)[2] The marginal utility of the third dollar is 12 if it is spent on more food—and 12 too if it is spent on clothing. Suppose that she chooses more food. (The total utility derived from the $3 of expenditure is 20 + 16 + 12 = 48.) What about the final dollar? Its marginal utility is 10 if it is spent on more food and 12 if it is spent on clothing; thus she will spend it on clothing. (The total utility derived from all $4 of expenditure is then 20 + 16 + 12 + 12 = 60.)

Clearly, Mrs. Walter, if she is rational, will allocate $3 of her income to food and $1 to clothing. This is the equilibrium market basket, the market basket that maximizes con-

[2] Since the marginal utility is the extra utility obtained from each dollar spent, the total utility from the total expenditure must be the sum of the marginal utilities of the individual dollars of expenditure.

sumer satisfaction. The important thing to note is that this market basket demonstrates the principle set forth earlier in this section. As shown in Table 20.4, the marginal utility derived from the last dollar spent on food is equal to the marginal utility derived from the last dollar spent on clothing. (Both are 12.) Thus this market basket has the characteristic described above: the marginal utility of the last dollar spent on all commodities purchased is the same. In the next section, we show that this will always be the case for market baskets that maximize the consumer's utility. If it were not true, the consumer could obtain a higher level of utility by changing the composition of his or her market basket.

Further Proof of the Budget Allocation Rule

In the previous section, we stated the proposition that the consumer, to maximize utility, will choose a market basket where the marginal utility of the last dollar spent on all commodities purchased is the same. In this section, we show that, if this budget allocation rule is not followed, the consumer cannot be maximizing utility. This is offered as further proof of the proposition in the previous section. For simplicity, we assume that the consumer buys only two commodities, food and clothing.

Suppose that the marginal utility of the last dollar spent on food is 5 utils whereas the marginal utility of the last dollar spent on clothing is 3 utils. Clearly, the consumer is not maximizing utility, because spending $1 more on food will increase total utility by 5 utils,[3] and spending $1 less on clothing will reduce total utility by 3 utils. Thus the transfer of $1 of expenditure from clothing to food will increase total utility by 2 utils—which means that the consumer currently isn't maximizing utility. More generally, a transfer of expenditure from clothing to food will always increase a consumer's utility so long as the marginal utility of the last dollar spent on food exceeds the marginal utility of the last dollar spent on clothing. Thus *the consumer will not be maximizing utility if the marginal utility of the last dollar spent on food exceeds the marginal utility of the last dollar spent on clothing.*

Suppose that the situation is reversed, the marginal utility of the last dollar spent on food being 3 utils and the marginal utility of the last dollar spent on clothing being 5 utils. Clearly, the consumer is not maximizing utility, because spending $1 more on clothing will increase total utility by 5 utils,[4] and spending $1 less on food will reduce total utility by 3 utils. Thus the transfer of $1 of expenditure from food to clothing will result in a net increase of utility of 2 utils—which means that the consumer currently isn't maximizing utility. More generally, a transfer of expenditure from food to clothing will always increase total utility so long as the marginal utility of the last dollar spent on clothing exeeds the marginal utility of the last dollar spent on food. Thus *the consumer will not be maximizing utility if the marginal utility of the last dollar spent on clothing exceeds the marginal utility of the last dollar spent on food.*

In the previous paragraph, we showed that the consumer will *not* be maximizing utility if the marginal utility of the last dollar spent on food *is less than* the marginal utility of the last dollar spent on clothing. In the paragraph before last, we showed that the consumer will *not* be maximizing utility if the marginal utility of the last dollar spent on food *exceeds* the marginal utility of the last dollar spent on clothing. Consequently, it follows that the consumer will be maximizing utility only when the marginal utility of the last dollar spent on food

[3] We assume here that the extra utility from an *extra* dollar spent on food equals the extra utility from the *last* dollar spent on food. This is an innocuous assumption.

[4] We assume here that the extra utility from an *extra* dollar spent on clothing equals the extra utility from the *last* dollar spent on clothing. This, like the assumption in footnote 3, is innocuous.

equals the marginal utility of the last dollar spent on clothing. This is what we set out to prove.

Usefulness of the Model of Consumer Behavior

Of what practical use is this model, other than to help you pass courses in economics? In Chapter 21, we shall describe how this model of consumer behavior helps us interpret and analyze market demand curves, but for now we want to emphasize that, apart from its usefulness as a theoretical tool, this model of consumer behavior can be applied to practical decision making. Many problems people and organizations face are of the following type: *the person or organization has a certain amount of money to spend, and must decide how much to allocate to a number of different uses.* For example, a person may have a certain money income, and the problem is how much to spend on various goods and services. Or a philanthropic foundation like the Ford Foundation must determine how much of its money to allocate each year to various kinds of research and educational purposes. Or a government agency like the Department of Health, Education, and Welfare must allocate its funds to medical research, medical education, and so on.

Faced with a problem of this sort, the economist's model of consumer behavior can be of some help. All these problems are basically the same as that facing the consumer, and the economist's model of consumer behavior shows the rational approach to their solution. Thus this model does not apply only to consumers. It can be useful in any situation where a person or organization must allocate a fixed amount of money among alternative uses. *This model is much more than a theory of consumer behavior: it is a theory of rational choice.*

A model like this is useful because it shows what factors are important to the decision maker, and how these factors should be combined to come to a decision. At first glance, this statement may not mean much, but put yourself in the position of the person making the decision. There are lots of factors that he might weigh and try to measure in coming to a decision. There is a good chance that he will look at the wrong factors, or give some factors improper weight. The economist's model of consumer behavior can be very useful in indicating which factors are relevant and how they should be combined.

Purchasing a Sprinkler System: A Case Study

Consider a very simple decision, the sort that must be made frequently by practically everyone. Mr. Walter, whom we met earlier, must buy a sprinkler system for his lawn. He finds that there are two possibilities: either he can purchase a sprinkler system that will cost $500 and that will spray 500 gallons of water per hour on his lawn, or he can purchase a sprinkler system that will cost $300 and that will spray 200 gallons of water per hour on his lawn. The owner of the firm that sells sprinkler systems advises Mr. Walter to buy the more expensive system because the cost per gallon of water sprayed on his lawn per hour will be less than with the less expensive system. For this reason, the owner of the firm regards the more expensive system as the better buy.

You may find it difficult to see how the model of consumer behavior can help Mr. Walter come to a decision. But think for a moment about the choice he faces. If he buys the less expensive sprinkler system, he will save $200, but he will be able to put 300 fewer gallons of water on his lawn per hour. The more expensive sprinkler system will cost $200 more, but he will be able to put 300 more gallons of water on his lawn per hour. Clearly, according to the model, Mr. Walter should maximize his utility, not minimize the cost per gallon of water put on his lawn per hour. Thus his decision should depend on whether the extra utility from the $200 is greater or less than the extra utility to be gained from being able to put 300 extra gallons of water on his lawn per hour. If he has a big lawn or if he wants to be able to water it quickly, the extra capability may be worth at least $200 to him. In this case, he should buy the more expensive system, since this will increase his total utility. On the other hand, if he has a small lawn or if he doesn't care how long it takes to water it, the extra capability may not be worth $200 to him. In this case, he should buy the less expensive system, which will increase his total utility.

In conclusion, then, Mr. Walter should not necessarily take the advice of the owner of the firm that sells sprinkler systems. The owner is using the wrong model. He is assuming that Mr. Walter wants to minimize the average cost of a gallon of water put on his lawn per hour, whereas Mr. Walter really wants to maximize utility. In a problem of this sort, the model of consumer behavior can provide the decision maker with the criteria or principles to guide his decision. Here it tells him his decision should depend on whether the capability of putting 300 extra gallons of water on the lawn per hour is worth the extra $200, not on whether one system has a lower cost per gallon per hour than the other system. In general, this is the sort of role this model can be expected to play—and it is an important role. Many important decisions (by consumers and others) are made improperly, often with wasteful and sometimes disastrous consequences, because people base their decisions on the wrong criteria.

Allocating Government Expenditures: Another Case Study

In contrast to the previous example, which involved a decision of no momentous importance by one consumer, this model of consumer behavior is also applicable to the allocation of government expenditures, where decisions involve billions of dollars. For example, decision makers in the Department of Health, Education, and Welfare must decide how much of the department's expenditures are to go for medical research, medical education, the promotion of good medical practices, and a host of other purposes. Billions of dollars are involved in these decisions. To what extent can our model be used by these decision makers?

Let's begin by examining how such decisions have often been made in the past. Many parts of the government have tended in the past to adopt a ***priorities approach*** to the allocation of a specified budget. That is, various items have been ranked according to the "urgency" with which they were needed. For example, the Department of Defense might have put a new supersonic bomber first on the list, indicating that it was to receive top priority. A main battle tank might be second, indicating next highest priority, and so on. In recent years, the military services have sometimes formulated lists of this kind that included several hundred weapons and items. Since such decisions involve huge sums, it is fair to ask whether this is a sensible approach to the problem of allocating funds. Based on the model of consumer behavior and rational choice, the answer is no. As Charles Hitch and Roland McKean put it, in their well-known book on defense economics, "The 'priorities approach' does not solve the allocation problem and can even trap us into adopting foolish policies."[5]

What is wrong with the priorities approach? In the first place, it is not clear exactly what a priority ranking means. Does it mean that money should be spent on the highest priority item until no more is needed, then on the second highest priority item until no more is

[5] C. Hitch and R. McKean, *The Economics of Defense in the Nuclear Age,* Cambridge, Mass.: Harvard University Press, 1965, p. 123.

Table 20.5
Hypothetical Case of Budget Allocations between Medical Education and Medical Research

Amount spent on: Medical education	Medical research	Total	Contribution to HEW goals of the last dollar spent on: Medical education	Medical research
(billions of dollars)			(units)	
2.0	0.0	2.0	1	11
1.8	0.2	2.0	2	11
1.6	0.4	2.0	3	10
1.4	0.6	2.0	4	9½
1.2	0.8	2.0	5	9
1.0	1.0	2.0	6	8
0.8	1.2	2.0	7	7
0.6	1.4	2.0	8	6
0.4	1.6	2.0	9	4
0.2	1.8	2.0	10	2
0.0	2.0	2.0	10	1

needed, and so on? Certainly not; one probably could continue spending on the highest priority item almost without limit and not reach the point where the usefulness of further units of the item was zero.

Nor does a list of priorities provide the information required to make a rational allocation of the budget. The information needed is precisely the sort required by the model of consumer behavior and rational choice—the utility to be derived from various amounts spent on particular items. Given this information, the principle that should be used to allocate the budget is precisely the one we discussed in the previous section: the amount spent on each item should be set in such a way that the marginal utility of the last dollar spent on each item is the same.

A government decision maker's problem in allocating an agency's budget is quite similar to that of our consumer, Mrs. Walter. The government decision maker is given a certain budget, which is analogous to the consumer's money income. He, like the consumer, is faced with prices attached to each of the items he is interested in buying. Like the consumer, he attaches a utility to each of the possible market baskets he could purchase. But, unlike the consumer, this utility is not (or should not be) a measure of his personal satisfaction; instead, it is an index of the contribution of the market basket to the agency's goals. He must try to maximize this utility.

For example, suppose that the Department of Health, Education, and Welfare has $2 billion, which must be spent on medical education or medical research. How can it decide how much to spend on each? Table 20.5 shows various allocations of this budget between medical education and medical research. The top line shows the case where all the money is devoted to medical education and nothing is devoted to medical research; the second line shows the case where $1.8 billion is devoted to medical education and $0.2 billion is devoted to medical research; and so on. For each such allocation, Table 20.5 shows the marginal contribution to HEW's goals of the last dollar spent on medical education and the marginal contribution to HEW's goals of the last dollar spent on medical research. For instance, if $1.8 billion were to go for medical education and $0.2 were to go for medical research, the last dollar spent on medical education would add 2 units to HEW's goals, whereas the last dollar spent on medical research would add 11 units to HEW's goals. (For present purposes, it is not essential to specify what these units might be. More will be said below on this score.)

Using the same reasoning as in the model of consumer choice, *the government decision maker should allocate his budget so that the marginal utility of the last dollar spent on all items purchased—that is, on medical education and medical research—is the same.* That is, he should spend $0.8 billion on medical education and $1.2 billion on medical research, based on the figures in Table 20.5. Why? Because this is the budget allocation where the marginal utilities—that is, the marginal contributions to HEW goals—of the last dollar spent on each are equal. (Both are 7 units.) Admittedly, *it may prove difficult to specify or agree on marginal utilities of this sort, but this is the right kind of approach to the problem.*

During the 1960s, the federal government turned increasingly from priority lists and other such crude devices to more sophisticated economic analysis in the allocation of funds. According to many observers, this considerably improved decision making. Although much of this analysis is far too complicated to be presented here, the basic principles involved in the newer analysis were essentially those of the model of consumer behavior and rational choice. This model is a guide to rational allocation of funds, whether the funds are being spent by consumers or governments. As we have seen, the fundamental rule is: given a fixed budget to be spent, the amount spent on each item in the budget should be set so that the marginal utility of the last dollar spent on each item is the same.

This is a very useful and powerful rule. As Edmund Burke said two centuries ago, "Economy is a distributive virtue, and consists not in saving but in selection." In other words, the basic problem for decision makers in both the private and public sectors of the economy is how to select those things on which they should spend money, and to decide how much to spend on each. The model of consumer behavior and rational choice provides the fundamental principles on which such decisions should be based.

Protecting the Consumer

A major assumption underlying the economist's model of consumer behavior and rational choice is that people know what they like and what they want. In general, this assumption is sensible, but sometimes the consumer is led to believe—by false advertising, improper grading of materials, and other such deceptive practices—that he is buying something he is not buying at all. The Federal Trade Commission has encountered practices of this sort in the lumber industry:

> The masquerading of low-grade lumber for high-grade lumber has bilked consumers of millions of dollars, has lowered the margin of structural safety in innumerable dwellings and, in the affected market areas, has impaired competitive mores among surviving wholesalers, retailers, and contractors.[6]

Similar improper practices have been discovered in other industries. For example, Ralph Nader testified before a Senate subcommittee concerning the packaging of sausage:

> What is on the labels is not all that is in the meat product. Last year, *Consumer Reports* tested fresh pork sausage—including leading brands—and found some distressing things. One-eighth

[6] R. Nader, testimony before the Senate Subcommittee on Executive Reorganization of the Committee on Government Operations, 91st Congress, 1st Session, 1969, reprinted in E. Mansfield, *Economics: Readings, Issues, and Cases,* 2d ed., New York: Norton, 1977.

Do You Know What You're Really Buying?

Caveat emptor—a Latin phrase meaning "Let the buyer beware"—is the rule that some merchants live by. In a variety of ways, they trick and cheat the consumer. For example, take the case of food. Stores sometimes soak turkeys and hams in water to increase their weight, thus charging the consumer high prices for water. Or they may attach a lead weight under the weighing pan to increase the indicated weight on the scales. Such practices have been going on for centuries. In 1481, Louis XI of France issued the following edict: "Anyone who sells butter containing stones or other things [to add to the weight] will be put into our pillory, then said butter will be placed on his head until entirely melted by the sun. Dogs may lick him and people offend him with whatever defamatory epithets they please without offense to God or King."

Like Louis XI, the federal government has tried to reduce such trickery (but without the benefit of pillory). For example, in 1966, the Congress passed the Fair Packaging and Labeling Act which requires that the labels of all consumer products that are covered must contain a statement of the net contents and the net quantity per serving. But even such information can be less than what the consumer really needs. For example, according to *Consumer Reports,* although a can of peaches may have a labeled weight of 16 ounces, this does not mean that the can contains 16 ounces of peaches. Instead, it contains an unspecified amount of syrup. Indeed, in a sample of brands studied in 1972, almost 40 percent of the labeled weight was syrup.

Another reason why it is difficult for consumers to get what they want (and pay for) is that the quality of a product is often so difficult to measure. Is there a simple way a consumer can measure whether one brand of piano really is better than another? Even in cases where the government grades products, the grading system often is unknown or confusing to the public. For example, did you know that the top grade of apple is "U.S. Extra Fancy," the second grade is "U.S. Fancy," and the third grade is "U.S. No. 1," and the fourth grade is "U.S. Utility"? Probably not. And if you do know this grading system, you may be dismayed to find that the system for other kinds of produce is quite different. Whereas "U.S. No. 1" is the third grade of apple, it is the first grade of pear (summer and fall).

Due to dishonest merchandising practices, improper labeling, and confusion concerning product quality, consumers have sometimes been led to improper choices—choices that fell far short of maximizing their utility. However, it is important to recognize that consumers also learn and that, at least for the more flagrant kinds of cheating, they avoid being exploited more than once by the same firms or people. Further, it is important to note that most firms, like most people, are honest, and that they should not be tarred because a minority engages in shady practices. Nonetheless, if you want to maximize your own utility, you are well advised to pay close attention to labels and to watch out for commercial trickery.*

* But you would be foolish to devote too much time acquiring information concerning what you are buying. Why? Because beyond some point, the extra utility stemming from better information may be outweighed by the costs of obtaining this information. For further discussion, see R. Miller, *Economic Issues for Consumers.* New York: West Publishing, 1975.

of the federally inspected sausage and more than one-fifth of the nonfederally inspected sausage contained "insect fragments, insect larvae, rodent hairs, and other kinds of filth." In typical samples, *Consumer Reports* found that 30 percent of the federally inspected sausage and 40 percent of the sausage subject only to infrequent Illinois inspection failed the tests for absence of filth or acceptable low bacteria counts. *Consumer Reports* stated that such findings suggest "unclean packinghouses, unsanitary ingredients, and inadequate inspection."[7]

Of course, such practices are the exception, not the rule, but there are enough problems of this sort to warrant a government program of consumer protection. For example, as we saw in Chapter 5, the federal government has long been charged by the Pure Food and Drug Act with the responsibility of seeing that adulterated and misbranded drugs and foods are not put on the market. In addition, the Federal Trade Commission is supposed to act against misleading advertising, and the 1969 Truth-in-Lending Act requires lenders to state more clearly the exact costs of borrowing, thus protecting the consumer when he borrows money. Unless consumers know what they are buying, they cannot make proper choices. In other words, they cannot maximize their satisfaction if they are lied to or misled about the nature of the goods and services for sale. For the price system to work well, the consumer must be protected against such deception and fraud.

Indifference Curves[8]

In the rest of this chapter, we show how the theory of consumer behavior can be used in cases where one cannot assume that marginal utility is measurable. Generally, of course, it is exceedingly difficult to formulate meaningful measures of a person's extra satisfaction from an extra amount of a particular good. We shall show that the theory remains useful even if such measures cannot be obtained. Once again, we assume for simplicity that there are only two goods, food and clothing, since this allows us to use simple two-dimensional diagrams to illustrate the model. Since there are only these two commodities, we can represent every possible combination of goods purchased by a consumer by a point in Figure 20.2, which measures the amount of food purchased along the vertical axis and the amount of clothing purchased along the horizontal axis.

Consider Mrs. Walter, making choices for her family. Certain market baskets—that is, certain combinations of food and clothing (the only commodities)—will be equally desirable to her. For example, she may be indifferent between a market basket containing 100 pounds of food and 5 pieces of clothing and a market basket containing 200 pounds of food and 2 pieces of clothing. These two market baskets can be represented by two points, *X* and *Y*, in Figure 20.2. In addition, other market baskets—each of which can be represented by a point in Figure 20.2—are just as desirable to Mrs. Walter as those represented by points *X* and *Y*. If we connect all of these points, we get a curve that represents market baskets that are equally desirable to the consumer. In our case, Mrs. Walter is indifferent among all of the market baskets represented by points on *AA′* in Figure 20.2. *AA′* is therefore called an ***indifference curve.***

There are three important things to note about any consumer's indifference curve. First, *any consumer has lots of indifference curves, not just one.* If Mrs. Walter is indifferent among all the market baskets represented by points on *BB′* in Figure 20.2, *BB′* is another of her indifference curves. Moreover, one thing is certain: she prefers any market basket on *BB′* to any market basket on *AA′*, since *BB′* in-

[7] Ibid.

[8] The rest of this chapter may be omitted without loss of continuity. An understanding of subsequent chapters does not depend on a reading of this material on indifference curves. Only the Appendices to Chapters 21, 22, and 23 are related to this material.

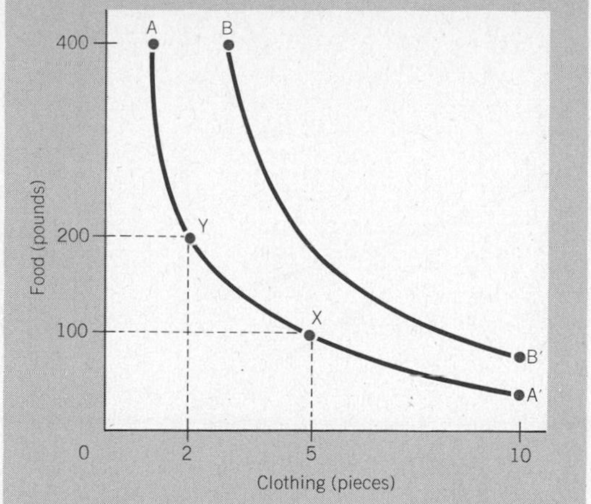

Figure 20.2
Two of Mrs. Walter's Indifference Curves
AA' and BB' are two of Mrs. Walter's indifference curves. Each shows market baskets that are equally desirable to Mrs. Walter. For example, she is indifferent between 200 pounds of food and 2 pieces of clothing (point *Y*) and 100 pounds of food and 5 pieces of clothing (point *X*).

cludes market baskets with as much clothing and more food (or as much food and more clothing) than the market baskets on AA'. (Remember that commodities are defined so that more of them are preferred to less.) Consequently, it must always be true that market baskets on higher indifference curves like BB' must be prefered to market baskets on lower indifference curves like AA'.

Second, *every indifference curve must slope downward and to the right,* to reflect the fact that commodities are defined so that more of them are preferred to less. If one market basket has more of one commodity than a second market basket, it must have less of the other commodity than the second market basket—assuming that the two market baskets are to yield equal satisfaction to the consumer. You can prove this to yourself. Suppose that you have a choice between two snacks and that you are indifferent between them. One snack consists of 1 piece of apple pie and 2 glasses of milk. The other consists of 2 pieces of apple pie and a certain number of glasses of milk. If you prefer more apple pie to less, and if you prefer more milk to less, can the number of glasses of milk in the latter snack be as large as 2? Clearly, the answer must be no.

Third, *indifference curves cannot intersect.* If they did, this would contradict the assumption that more of a commodity is preferred to less. For example, suppose that AA' and BB' in Figure 20.3 are two indifference curves and that they intersect. If this is the case, the market basket represented by point *D* is equivalent in the eyes of the consumer to the one represented by point *E,* since both are on indifference curve AA'. Moreover, the market basket represented by point *F* is equivalent in the eyes of the consumer to the one represented by point *E,* since both are on indifference curve BB'. And this means that the market basket represented by point *F* must be equivalent in the eyes of the consumer to the one represented by point *D.* (Remember that consumer preferences are assumed to be transitive!) But this is impossible because market basket *F* contains the same amount of food and 6 more pieces of clothing than does market basket *D.* Since more of a commodity is preferred to less, market basket *F* must be preferred to market basket *D.*

Indifference Curves and Utility

To continue building this new version of our model of consumer behavior, we need to return to the concept of utility. Since all market baskets on a particular indifference curve yield the same satisfaction to the consumer, they all must have the same utility. For example, all market baskets on indifference curve AA' in Figure 20.2 must have the same utility. More-

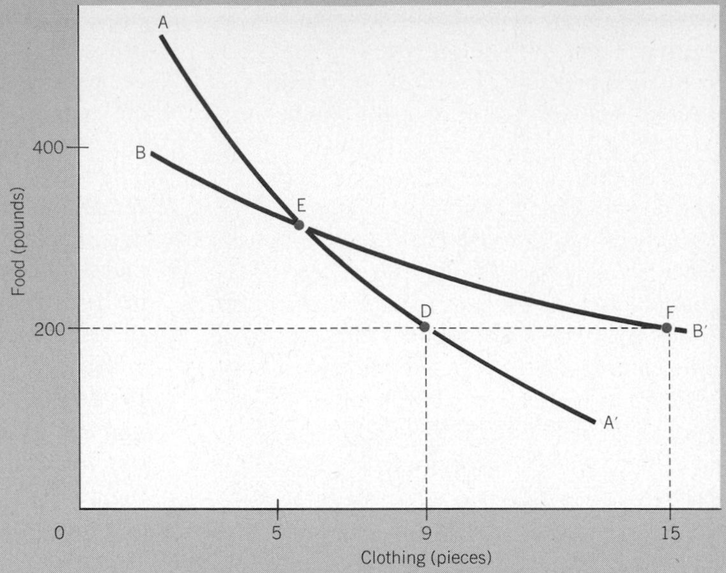

Figure 20.3
Intersecting Indifference Curves: A Contradiction
Indifference curves cannot intersect. If they did, the consumer would be indifferent between *D* and *E*, since both are on indifference curve *AA′*; and between *F* and *E*, since both are on indifference curve *BB′*. But this implies that he must be indifferent between *D* and *F*, which is impossible since *F* contains the same amount of food and 6 more pieces of clothing than *D*.

over, market baskets on higher indifference curves must have higher utilities than market baskets on lower indifference curves. For example, all market baskets on indifference curve *BB′* in Figure 20.2 must have higher utilities than market baskets on indifference curve *AA′*.

Given a group of indifference curves for a certain consumer, it is easy to establish an index of the utility obtained from any market basket by this consumer. *All that we have to do is attach a number to each indifference curve, this number being larger for higher indifference curves than for lower indifference curves. The utility index for any market basket is then the number attached to the indifference curve on which this market basket is located.* The resulting utility index shows at a glance which market baskets the consumer will pick over other market baskets. The rational consumer will, of course, try to pick the market basket that maximizes this index of utility.

Note that this utility index is not unique. Any set of numbers that increases as one goes from successively lower to higher indifference curves will constitute a suitable set of indices. Thus no assumption is made that we can obtain a meaningful measure of marginal utility. But it is possible to construct a utility index of this sort, so long as the three basic assumptions underlying the theory of consumer demand (described in an earlier section on "A Model of Consumer Behavior") are met.

The Budget Line

The consumer wants to maximize his or her utility, which means that he or she wants to achieve the highest possible indifference curve. But whether or not a particular indifference curve is attainable depends on the consumer's money income and on commodity prices. Exactly what constraints are imposed on the consumer by the size of his money income and the nature of commodity prices? To make things concrete, let's return to Mrs. Walter. Suppose that her total income is $400 per month, and that she can spend this amount only on two commodities, food and clothing. Needless to say, it is unrealistic to assume that there are only two commodities in existence, but this, as we have seen, makes it easier to present the model, and the results can easily be generalized to cases where more than two commodities exist.

Given these conditions, the answer to how much of each commodity Mrs. Walter can buy depends on the price of a pound of food and the price of a piece of clothing. Suppose the price of a pound of food is $1 and the price of a piece of clothing is $40. Then if she spent all of her income on food, she could buy 400 pounds of food per month. On the other hand, if she spent all of her income on clothing, she could buy 10 pieces of clothing per month. Or she could, if she wished, buy some food and some clothing. There are a large number of combinations of amounts of food and clothing that she could buy, and each such combination can be represented by a point on the line *CC′* in Figure 20.4 This line is called her ***budget line.***

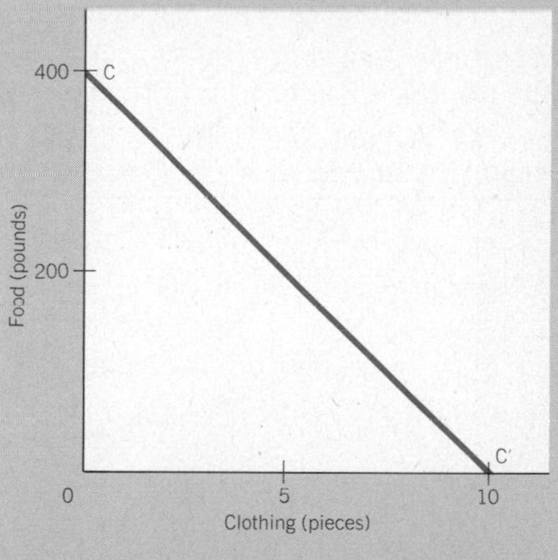

Figure 20.4
Mrs. Walter's Budget Line
The consumer's budget line shows the market baskets that can be purchased, given the consumer's income and prevailing commodity prices. This budget line assumes that Mrs. Walter's income is $400 per month, that the price of a pound of food is $1, and that the price of a piece of clothing is $40.

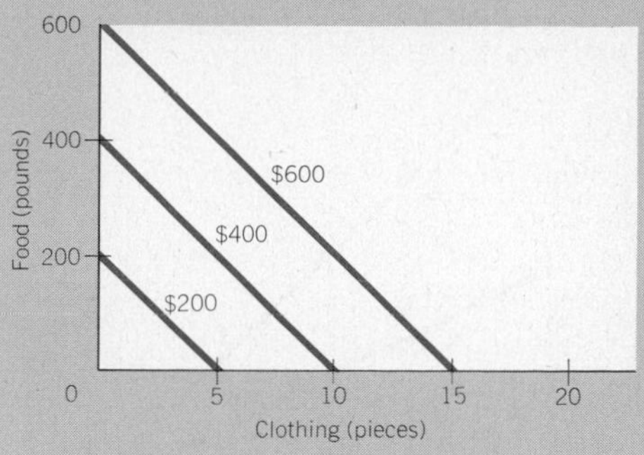

Figure 20.5
Mrs. Walter's Budget Line at Money Incomes of $200, $400, and $600 per Month
The higher the consumer's money income, the higher the budget line. Holding commodity prices constant, the budget line's slope remains constant.

Of course, the consumer's budget line depends on the consumer's money income and on commodity prices. In particular, an increase in money income means that the budget line rises, and a decrease in money income means that the budget line falls. This is illustrated in Figure 20.5, which shows Mrs. Walter's budget line at money incomes of $200, $400, and $600 per month. As you can see, her budget line moves upward as her income rises.

Commodity prices too affect the budget line: a decrease in a commodity's price causes the budget line to cut this commodity's axis at a point farther from the origin. Figure 20.6 shows Mrs. Walter's budget line when the price of a pound of food is $1 and when it is $2. You can see that the budget line cuts the vertical, or food, axis farther from the origin when the price of food is $1 per pound.

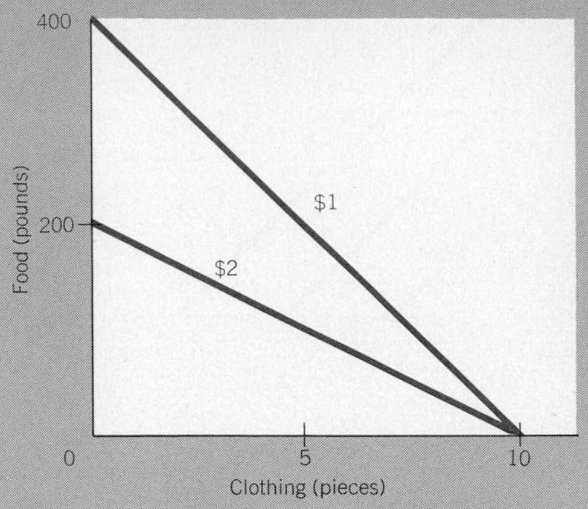

Figure 20.6
Mrs. Walter's Budget Line at Food Prices of $1 and $2 per Pound
Holding constant Mrs. Walter's money income at $400 per month and the price of a piece of clothing at $40, the budget line cuts the vertical axis farther from the origin when the price of food is $1 than when it is $2.

The Equilibrium Market Basket

With information on the consumer's indifference curves and his budget line, we are in a position to determine the consumer's ***equilibrium market basket***—the market basket that, among all those his income and prices permit him to purchase, yields the maximum utility. The first step is to combine the indifference curves with the budget line on the same graph. For example, Figure 20.7 brings together Mrs. Walter's indifference curves (from Figure 20.2) and her budget line (from Figure 20.4). Given the information assembled in Figure 20.7, it is a simple matter to determine her equilibrium market basket. *Her indifference curves show what she wants:* specifically, she wants to attain the highest possible indifference curve. Thus she would rather be on indifference curve *BB′* than on indifference curve *AA′*, and on indifference curve *DD′* than on indifference curve *BB′*. But, as we have pointed out repeatedly, she cannot choose any market basket she likes. *The budget line shows which market baskets her income and commodity prices permit her to buy.* Thus she must choose some market basket on her budget line, *CC′*.

Consequently, *the consumer's choice boils down to choosing that market basket on the budget line that is on the highest indifference curve. This is the equilibrium market basket.* For example, Mrs. Walter's equilibrium market bas-

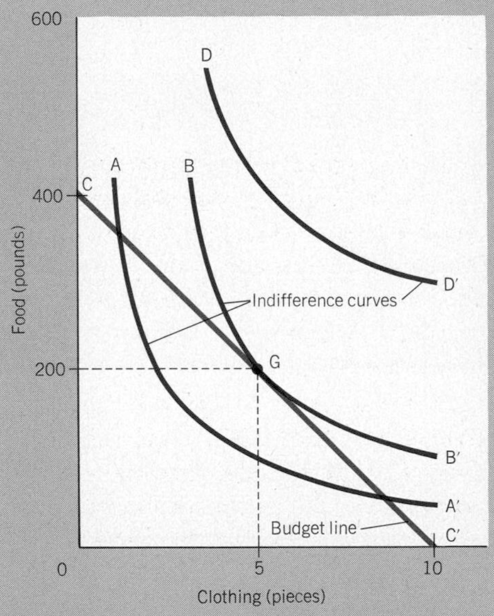

Figure 20.7
Mrs. Walter's Equilibrium Market Basket
Mrs. Walter's equilibrium market basket is at point *G*, containing 200 pounds of food and 5 pieces of clothing. This is the point on her budget line *CC′*, that is on the highest indifference curve, *BB′*, she can attain.

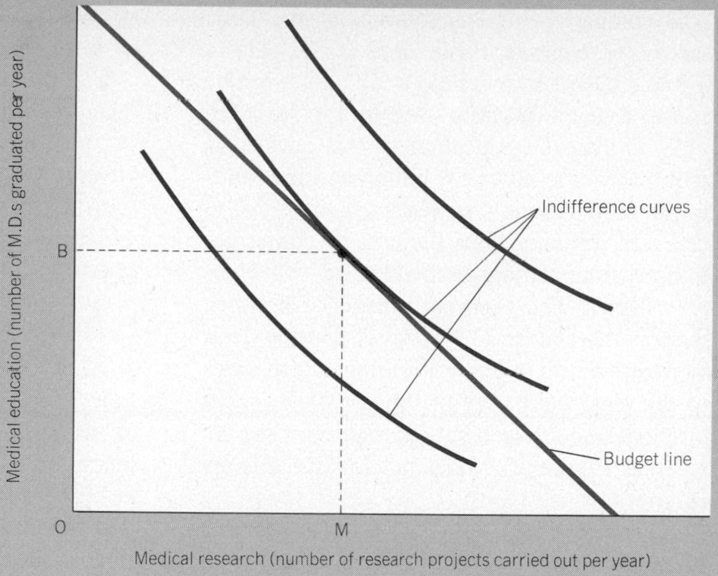

Figure 20.8
Budget Allocation of Department of Health, Education, and Welfare
The optimal allocation of the budget between medical research and medical education is to support the education of *OB* physicians and the funding of *OM* medical research projects.

ket is clearly at point *G* in Figure 20.7; it consists of 200 pounds of food and 5 pieces of clothing per month. This is her equilibrium market basket because any other market basket on the budget line *CC′* is on a lower indifference curve than point *G* is. But will the consumer choose this market basket? Admittedly, it may take some time and fumbling for the consumer to find out that this is the best market basket for him under the circumstances. Consumers, after all, do make mistakes. But they also learn, and eventually one would expect a consumer to come very close to acting in the predicted way.

Indifference Curves and Budget Allocation

Finally, let's show how this second version of our model of consumer behavior can be used by decision makers to help allocate their budgets. In an earlier section, we pointed out that the Department of Health, Education, and Welfare must allocate funds between medical research and medical education. Government officials, like the consumer, have indifference curves showing various combinations of items that have equal utility, in the sense that they make an equal contribution to the agency's goals. For example, if HEW's budget must be allocated between medical education and medical research, the indifference curves might be as shown in Figure 20.8.

The budget line—determined by the prices of medical education and medical research, as well as the total amount that the agency can spend—is also shown in Figure 20.8. Thus, using the same reasoning as in our model of the consumer, the government decision maker should support the education of *OB* physicians and the funding of *OM* medical research projects. Of course, *it is not easy to measure the indifference curves in Figure 20.8;* we do not pretend that it is. But the approach is right. As we have emphasized throughout this chapter, the model of consumer behavior and rational choice provides the basic principles on which budget allocation decisions of this sort should be based.

Finally, how does our solution in Figure

20.8 compare with our solution of the same sort of problem in Table 20.5? If the data in Table 20.5 are correct (and available), it can be shown that the solutions will be the same. In other words, the education of *OB* physicians will turn out to cost \$0.8 billion and the funding of *OM* research projects will turn out to cost \$1.2 billion. Thus there is no contradiction or disagreement between these two types of analysis. The essential difference between them is that Table 20.5 assumes that the decision maker can prepare meaningful estimates of the marginal utility of the last dollar spent on medical education and on medical research, whereas Figure 20.8 does not involve this assumption.

Summary

In our economic system, consumer wants and desires are a basic determinant of the nature and quantity of the goods and services produced. As a first step toward understanding consumer behavior, it is useful to look at how consumers spend their income. Recent government figures show that consumers spend about 80 percent of their income on goods and services; the rest goes for taxes and saving. Much of their expenditures for goods and services go for housing, food and drink, and transportation. To explain how a particular consumer allocates his or her income among various commodities, economists have formulated a model of consumer behavior and rational choice. This model is very important both for theoretical purposes and as a guide to practical decision making.

The amount of a particular commodity a consumer purchases is clearly influenced by his preferences. The model of consumer behavior assumes that the consumer's preferences are transitive and that commodities are defined so that more of them are preferred to less. Utility is a number that indexes the level of satisfaction derived by the consumer from a particular market basket. Market baskets with higher utilities are preferred over market baskets with lower utilities.

The model of consumer behavior and rational choice recognizes that preferences alone do not determine the consumer's actions. Given the consumer's preferences, the choices open to him are dictated by the size of his money income and the nature of commodity prices. If the consumer maximizes his utility, his income is allocated among commodities so that, for every commodity he buys, the marginal utility of the commodity is proportional to its price. In other words, the marginal utility of the last dollar spent on each commodity is made equal for all commodities.

This principle is a useful guide for practical decision making. For example, in the allocation of government expenditures, there has often been a tendency in the past to adopt a priorities approach. As has been recognized more and more in recent years, such an approach is likely to be less effective than an application of the simple principles underlying the model of consumer behavior and rational choice.

If we drop the assumption that marginal utility is measurable, a consumer's preferences can be represented by a set of indifference curves. Every indifference curve must slope downward and to the right; indifference curves cannot intersect; and higher are preferred to lower indifference curves. Market baskets with equal utility are on the same indifference curve. The consumer's budget line shows which market baskets his income and commodity prices permit him to buy. He is assumed to choose the market basket on the relevant budget line that is on the highest indifference curve. This is the equilibrium market basket.

Finally, we must remember that this model assumes that consumers know what they like and what they want. Sometimes consumers are misled by false advertising and other deceptive practices. For the price system to work well, the consumer must be protected against such deception and fraud.

CONCEPTS FOR REVIEW

Utility
Indifference curve
Transitive
Commodity
Budget line
Equilibrium market basket
Marginal utility
Law of diminishing marginal utility
Priorities approach
Consumer protection

QUESTIONS FOR DISCUSSION AND REVIEW

1. Some people judge the quality of a good by its price. If a consumer does this, how does it affect the model presented in this chapter?

2. Suppose that the total utility attached by Ms. Johnson to various quantities of hamburgers consumed (per day) is as follows:

Number of hamburgers	Total utility (utils)
0	0
1	5
2	12
3	15
4	17
5	18

Between 3 and 4 hamburgers, what is the marginal utility of a hamburger? Between 4 and 5 hamburgers, what is the marginal utility of a hamburger? Do these results conform to the law of diminishing marginal utility?

3. If Ms. Johnson is maximizing her satisfaction, and if the marginal utility of a hot dog is twice that of a bottle of beer, what must the price of a hot dog be if: (a) the price of a bottle of beer is $.75, (b) the price of a bottle of beer is $1? (Assume that Ms. Johnson consumes both beer and hot dogs.)

4. "A good's price is related to its marginal utility, not its total utility. Thus a good like water or air may be cheap, even though its total utility is high." Comment and evaluate.

5. Suppose that Ms. Johnson obtains equal satisfaction from each of the following combinations of meat and potatoes:

Combination	Meat (pounds)	Potatoes (pounds)
A	1	6
B	2	3
C	3	2
D	5	1

Plot the indifference curve on which these combinations lie.

6. Suppose that the indifference curve in Question 5 intersects an indifference curve on which lies a combination of 3 pounds of meat and 3 pounds of potatoes. Why does this contradict the assumptions underlying the theory of consumer behavior?

7. Suppose that Ms. Johnson has $6 to spend on meat and potatoes and that meat is $3 per pound and potatoes are $.30 per pound. Plot the budget line.

8. Faced with a number of alternative choices, people sometimes base their choice on the wrong criteria. According to Roland McKean, "One error, the use of the ratio of benefits to costs, is . . . a perennial favorite." What is wrong with using this ratio as a criterion?

9. According to Ralph Nader, "A negligently maintained, leaky pipeline blew up . . . , taking 41 lives and seriously burning over 100 other persons. . . . No law and no order was applied to the gas company and its induced violence." If consumers were misled concerning the safety of the pipeline, were their choices optimal? If not, in what way were they distorted?

10. If the marginal utility of one good is 3 and its price is $1, while the marginal utility of another good is 6 and its price is $3, is the consumer maximizing his or her satisfaction, given that he or she is consuming both goods? Why or why not?

21 Market Demand

What do Corfam (DuPont's synthetic leather) and the Edsel (the new make of automobile Ford introduced in the 1950s) have in common? Both were new products that were unsuccessful because the market demand for them was too small. In a capitalist economy, market demand is a fundamental determinant of what is produced and how. The market demand curve for a commodity plays an important role in the decision-making process within each firm producing the commodity, as well as in the economy as a whole. It is no exaggeration to say that firms spend enormous time and effort trying to cater to, estimate, and influence market demand.

In this chapter, we discuss the factors influencing the market demand curve for a commodity, as well as the measurement of market demand curves and their role in decision making by private business firms and government agencies. We consider questions like: How can we measure market demand curves? What is the price elasticity of demand? What role does the price elasticity of demand play in various practical problems facing the private and public sectors of the economy? What factors underlie the market demand curve for a commodity? These are important questions, from both a theoretical and a practical point of view.

Market Demand Curves: Role and Importance

Let's review what a market demand curve is. You will recall from Chapter 4 that a commodity's market demand curve shows how much of the commodity will be purchased during a particular period of time at various prices. Figure 21.1 ought to be familiar; it is the market demand curve for wheat in the middle 1970s, which figured prominently in our discussion of the price system in Chapter 4. Among other things, it shows that during the middle 1970s about 1,850 million bushels of American wheat would have been purchased per year if the price was $3.00 per bushel, that about 1,650 million bushels would have been purchased per year if the price was $4.00 per bushel, and that about 1,500 million bushels would have been purchased if the price was $5.00 per bushel.

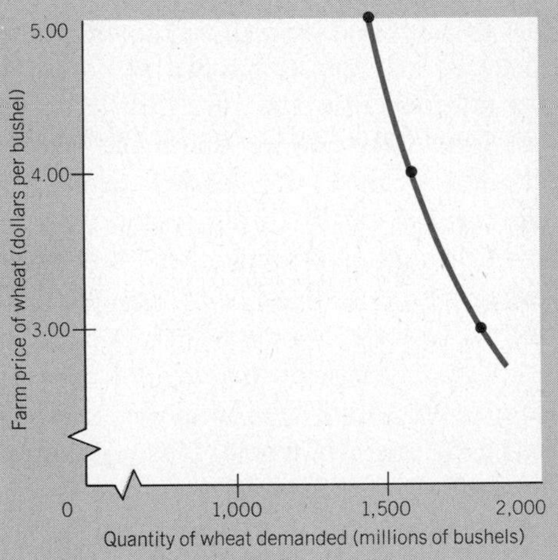

Figure 21.1
Market Demand Curve for Wheat, Middle 1970s
This curve shows how much wheat would be purchased at various prices.

Since the market demand curve reflects what consumers want and are willing to pay for, when the market demand curve for wheat shifts upward to the right this indicates that consumers want more wheat at the existing price. On the other hand, when the curve shifts downward to the left, this indicates that consumers want less wheat at the existing price. Such shifts in the market demand curve for a commodity trigger changes in the behavior of the commodity's producers. For example, when the market demand curve shifts upward to the right, the price of wheat will tend to rise, thus inducing farmers to produce more wheat, because they will find that, given the price increase, their profits will increase if they raise their output levels. The same process occurs in other parts of the economy: shifts in the demand curve reflecting the fact that consumers want more (less) of a commodity set in motion a sequence of events leading to more (less) production of the commodity.

Beyond playing a central role in the functioning of the price system, market demand curves are of enormous importance to firms and industries. In some industries, like wheat, there are lots of producers, no one of whom has any real influence over the price. In such industries, firms must base many important decisions on the price they expect to receive in the future. To forecast this price, they have to estimate the market demand curve, explicitly or implicitly. In other industries, like steel or petroleum, there are few producers, and these firms have considerable influence over the price they charge. In such industries, firms cannot make rational pricing decisions unless they take proper account of the market demand curve for their product. In Chapters 24 and 25, we shall describe the specific way in which such decisions should be made if firms want to maximize their profits.

Market demand curves are also very important to government agencies. The Department of Agriculture is continually engaged in intensive and sophisticated studies to estimate the market demand curves for various farm products. This information is essential to the department's work. In the case of wheat, for example, to estimate how changes in price will affect the amount of wheat that is purchased by buyers (other than the government), the department must have estimates of the market demand curve for wheat. Many other government agencies are vitally interested in other market demand curves. For example, the Federal Power Commission is concerned with the market demand curves for natural gas, oil, and other fuels. And the Federal Communications Commission is concerned with the market demand curve for telephone service, among other products. Without some knowledge of these demand curves, they are in no position to regulate these industries.

Measuring Market Demand Curves

To be of practical use, market demand curves must be based on careful measurements. Let's look briefly at some of the techniques used to estimate the market demand curve for particular commodities. At first glance, a quick and easy way to estimate the demand curve might seem to be interviewing consumers about their buying habits and intentions. However, although more subtle variants of this approach sometimes may pay off, simply asking people how much they would buy of a certain commodity at particular prices does not usually seem very useful, since off-the-cuff answers to such questions are rarely very accurate. Thus marketing researchers and econometricians interested in measuring market demand curves have been forced to use more complex procedures.

One such procedure is the ***direct market experiment.*** Although the designs of such experiments vary greatly and are often quite complicated, the basic idea is simple: to see the effects on the quantity demanded of actual variations in the price of the product. (Of course, researchers attempt to hold other market factors constant or to take into account whatever changes may occur.) For example, the Parker Pen Company conducted an experiment a number of years ago to estimate the demand curve for their ink, Quink. They increased the price from $.15 to $.25 in four cities, and found that the quantity demanded was quite insensitive to the price. Experiments like this are frequently made to try to estimate a product's market demand.

Still another technique is to use statistical methods to estimate demand curves from historical data on price and quantity purchased of the commodity. For example, one might plot the price of slingshots in various periods in the past against the quantity sold, as shown in Figure 21.2. Judging from the results, *DD′* seems a reasonable approximation to the demand curve. Although this simple analysis provides some insight into how statistical methods are used to estimate demand curves from historical data, it is a vast oversimplification. For one thing, the market demand curve may have shifted over time, so that *DD′* is not a proper estimate. Fortunately, modern statistical techniques recognize this possibility and allow us to estimate the position and shape of this curve (at each point in time) in spite of it.

Hundreds, perhaps thousands, of studies have been made to estimate the demand curves for particular commodities. In view of the importance of the results for decision making, this is not surprising. To illustrate the role played by such studies in the formulation of

Figure 21.2
Estimated Demand Curve for Slingshots
One very crude way to estimate the market demand curve is to plot the amount sold of a commodity in each year against its price in that year, and draw a curve, like *DD′*, that seems to fit the points reasonably well. However, this technique is generally too crude to be reliable.

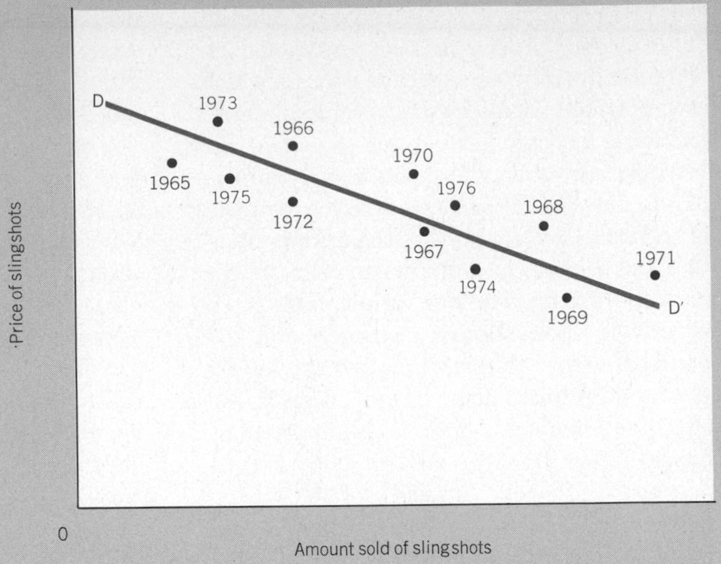

public policy, let's return to the case of the Boston and Maine Railroad, which we considered briefly in Chapter 2.

Railroad Transportation in Metropolitan Boston: A Case Study

As you will recall from Chapter 2, in the early 1960s the Boston and Maine Railroad wanted to discontinue passenger commuter service into Boston because it felt such service was unprofitable. In 1963, the Mass Transportation Commission of Massachusetts contracted with the Boston and Maine to establish a demonstration project to estimate the effect of a lowering of fares on the quantity of commuter tickets sold. The Boston and Maine was requested not to file a petition for the discontinuance of commuter service into Boston until after the experiment. During the experiment, which lasted about a year, fares were reduced about 28 percent on the average. The result was, of course, an increase in the number of tickets sold. However, the more important thing to the railroad and the commission was the *extent* to which the fare cut would increase the number of tickets sold. *How great* would be the resulting increase in the number of tickets sold? This was the important question because to increase the railroad's profits, a fare cut had to increase the railroad's revenues more than it increased its costs. And unless the price cut increased the number of tickets sold by a greater percentage than the reduction in price, it would not increase the railroad's revenues at all.

A comparison of the Boston and Maine's commuter revenues in 1963 with those in 1962 showed that this large fare reduction resulted in only a 0.6 percent increase in the railroad's revenues. Thus the price reduction increased the railroad's revenues by little or nothing. Since the reduction in fares increased the railroad's costs—because it was more costly to handle the larger volume of traffic—and increased its revenues scarcely at all, it did not increase the railroad's profits. Thus, after the experiment, the Boston and Maine decided to continue with its petition to terminate commuter service.[1] (Eventually, however, public subsidies were instituted to keep the service going.)

This is a fairly typical example of a direct market experiment designed to obtain information on relevant aspects of a market demand curve. Note the problems experiments of this sort must face. First, the experiment can be very costly if it alienates customers or reduces the firm's profits. Second, it is difficult to hold other relevant variables constant. For example, the effect of price changes was mixed up, to some extent, with the effect of increased service in the Boston and Maine case. Third, it is hard to conduct an experiment of this sort over a long enough period to estimate long-run effects. Thus, in the Boston and Maine case, the effect of the fare reduction on the number of tickets sold might have been much greater if the experiment had lasted longer. Nonetheless, despite these problems, experiments of this sort can produce useful evidence on the location and shape of a product's market demand curve. They are an important supplement to statistical analysis of historical data to estimate market demand curves.

The Price Elasticity of Demand

Market demand curves, like people, do not all look alike. Clearly, the shape of a commodity's market demand curve will vary from commodity to commodity. For example, the quantity demanded of some commodities, like beef in Figure 21.3, is fairly sensitive to changes in the commodity's price. That is, changes in price result in significant changes in quantity demanded. On the other hand, the quantity demanded of other commodities, like cotton in Figure 21.3, is not at all sensitive to changes in the price. Large changes in price result in small changes in the quantity demanded. Economists, government officials, businessmen, and labor leaders are all interested in the sensitivity of the quantity demanded of a particular good to changes in its price. Indeed, even the Congress, in its hearings, has shown considerable interest in this subject. There have been, for example, congressional investigations of the sensitivity of the quantity demanded of autos and steel to changes in their prices.

To promote unambiguous discussion of this subject, we must have some measure of the sensitivity of quantity demanded to changes in price. The measure customarily used for this purpose is the ***price elasticity of demand,*** defined as the percentage change in quantity demanded resulting from a 1 percent change in price. For example, suppose that a 1 percent reduction in the price of slingshots results in a 2 percent increase in the quantity demanded.

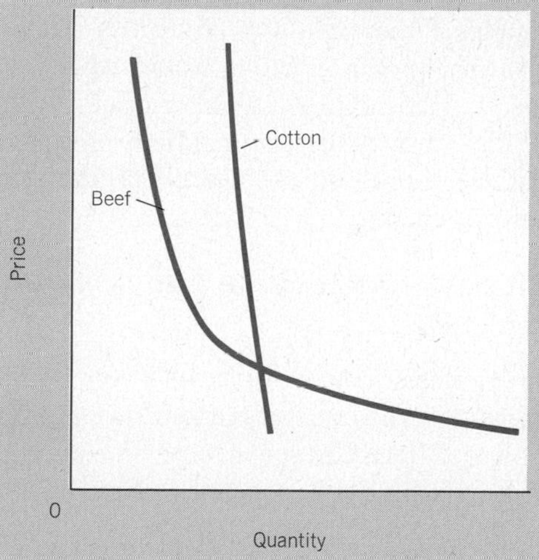

Figure 21.3
Market Demand Curves, Beef and Cotton
The quantity demanded of beef is much more sensitive to price than is the quantity demanded of cotton.

[1] See *Mass Transportation in Massachusetts,* Boston: Mass Transportation Commission, 1964.

Then, using this definition, the price elasticity of demand for slingshots is 2. (Convention dictates that we give the elasticity a positive sign even though the change in price is negative and the change in quantity demanded is positive.) Clearly, the price elasticity of demand is likely to vary from one point to another on the market demand curve. For example, the price elasticity of demand for slingshots may be higher when a slingshot costs a dollar than when it costs a quarter.

Note that the price elasticity of demand is expressed in terms of *relative*—i.e., proportional or percentage—changes in price and quantity demanded, not *absolute* changes in price and quantity demanded. Thus, in studying the slingshot market, we looked at the *percentage* change in quantity demanded resulting from a 1 *percent* change in price. This is because absolute changes depend on the units in which price and quantity are measured. For example, if the price of a product is reduced by \$1, this price reduction would equal 100, 1, or .01, depending on whether price is measured in cents, dollars, or hundreds of dollars. Relative changes do not depend on the units of measurement.

Table 21.1
Market Demand for Wheat, Early 1960s

Farm price of wheat (dollars per bushel)	Quantity of wheat demanded (millions of bushels)
1.00	1,500
1.20	1,300
1.40	1,100
1.60	900
1.80	800
2.00	700
2.20	675

Source: K. Fox, V. Ruttan, and L. Witt, *Farming, Farmers, and Markets for Farm Goods*, New York: Committee for Economic Development, 1962.

Calculating the Price Elasticity of Demand

The price elasticity of demand is a very important concept and one that economists use often, so it is worthwhile to spend some time explaining exactly how it is computed. Suppose that you have a table showing various points on a market demand curve. For example, Table 21.1 shows the quantity of wheat demanded at various prices, as estimated by Professor Karl Fox of Iowa State University during the early 1960s.[2] Given these data, how do you go about computing the price elasticity of demand for wheat? Clearly, the price elasticity of demand for any product generally varies from point to point on its market demand curve; so you must first determine at what point on the demand curve you want to measure the price elasticity of demand.

Let us assume that you want to estimate the price elasticity of demand for wheat when the price of wheat is between \$2.00 and \$2.20 per bushel. One way is to use the following formula:

$$\text{price elasticity} = -\left(\frac{Q_2 - Q_1}{Q_1}\right) \div \left(\frac{P_2 - P_1}{P_1}\right), \qquad (21.1)$$

where Q_2 is the quantity demanded when the price is P_2, and Q_1 is the quantity demanded when the price is P_1. If $P_2 = \$2.20$, it follows from Table 21.1 that $Q_2 = 675$, and if $P_1 = \$2.00$, it follows from Table 21.1 that $Q_1 = 700$. Thus, substituting these values into Equation (21.1), we have

$$\text{price elasticity} = -\left(\frac{675 - 700}{700}\right) \div \left(\frac{2.20 - 2.00}{2.00}\right) = .36.$$

The price elasticity of demand is estimated to be .36.

But we could just as well have estimated the

[2] Note that Table 21.1 pertains to the early 1960s whereas Figure 21.1 pertains to the middle 1970s. Consequently, the demand curves are quite different, as you can see.

price elasticity of demand in this range in a somewhat different way:

$$\text{pricc clasticity} = -\left(\frac{Q_1 - Q_2}{Q_2}\right) \div \left(\frac{P_1 - P_2}{P_2}\right), \qquad (21.2)$$

where P_1, P_2, Q_2, and Q_1 are as defined above. The answer would be

$$\text{price elasticity} = -\left(\frac{700 - 675}{675}\right) \div \left(\frac{2.00 - 2.20}{2.20}\right) = .41,$$

which is somewhat different from the answer we got in the previous paragraph.

To get around this difficulty, the generally accepted procedure is to use the average values of P and Q in place of Q_1 and P_1 in the denominators in Equation (21.1), and in place of P_2 and Q_2 in the denominators in Equation (21.2). In other words, we use as an estimate of the price elasticity of demand:

$$\text{price elasticity} = -\frac{(Q_2 - Q_1)}{\left(\frac{Q_1 + Q_2}{2}\right)} \div \frac{(P_2 - P_1)}{\left(\frac{P_1 + P_2}{2}\right)} \qquad (21.3)$$

This is the so-called ***arc elasticity of demand.*** In the specific case we are considering, the arc elasticity is

$$\text{price elasticity} = -\frac{(675 - 700)}{\left(\frac{675 + 700}{2}\right)} \div \frac{(2.20 - 2.00)}{\left(\frac{2.20 + 2.00}{2}\right)} = .38.$$

This is the answer to our problem.

Determinants of the Price Elasticity of Demand

Many studies have been made of the price elasticity of demand for particular commodities. Table 21.2 reproduces the results of some of them. Note the substantial differences among products. For example, the estimated price elasticity of demand for women's hats is about 3.00, while for cotton it is only about 0.12. Think for a few minutes about these results, and try to figure out why these differences exist. If you rack your brains for a while, chances are that you will agree that the following factors are important determinants of whether the price elasticity of demand is high or low.

Number and closeness of available substitutes. If a commodity has many close substitutes, its demand is likely to be highly elastic, i.e., the price elasticity is likely to be high. If the price of the product increases, a large proportion of its buyers will turn to the close substitutes that are available. If its price decreases, a great many buyers of substitutes will switch to this product. Naturally, the closeness of the substi-

Table 21.2
Estimated Price Elasticities of Demand for Selected Commodities, United States

Commodity	Price elasticity
Beef	0.92
Women's hats	3.00
Gasoline	0.20
Sugar	0.31
Corn	0.49
Cotton	0.12
Hay	0.43
Potatoes	0.31
Oats	0.56
Barley	0.39
Buckwheat	0.99
Shoes	0.40
Newspapers	0.10
Radio and TV sets	1.20
Tires	0.60

Source: H. Schultz, *Theory and Measurement of Demand,* Chicago: University of Chicago Press, 1938; M. Spencer and L. Siegelman, *Managerial Economics,* Homewood, Ill.: Irwin, 1959; and H. Houthakker and L. Taylor, *Consumer Demand in the United States, 1929–1970,* Cambridge, Mass.: Harvard, 1966.

tutes depends on how narrowly the commodity is defined. In general, one would expect that as the definition of the product becomes narrower and more specific, the product has more close substitutes and its price elasticity of demand is higher. Thus the demand for a particular brand of oil is more price elastic than the over-all demand for oil, and the demand for oil is more price elastic than the demand for fuel as a whole. If a commodity is defined so that it has perfect substitutes, its price elasticity of demand approaches infinity. Thus, if one farmer's wheat is exactly like that grown by other farmers and if he raises his price slightly (to a point above the market level), his sales will be reduced to nothing.

Importance in consumers' budgets. It is often asserted that the price elasticity of demand for a commodity is likely to depend on the importance of the commodity in consumers' budgets. For example, the demand for commodities like pepper and salt may be quite inelastic. The typical consumer spends a very small portion of his income on pepper and salt, and the quantity he demands may not be influenced much by changes in price within a reasonable range.

The length of the period to which the demand curve pertains. Every market demand curve pertains, you will recall, to a certain time interval. In general, demand is likely to be more sensitive to price over a long period than over a short one. The longer the period, the easier it is for consumers and business firms to substitute one good for another. If, for example, the price of oil should decline relative to other fuels, oil consumption in the month after the price decline would probably increase very little. But over a period of several years, people would have an opportunity to take account of the price decline in choosing the type of fuel to be used in new and renovated houses and businesses. In the longer period of several years, the price decline would have a greater effect on the consumption of oil than in the shorter period of one month.

Price Elasticity and Total Money Expenditure

Many important decisions hinge on the price elasticity of demand for a commodity. One reason why this is so is that the price elasticity of demand determines whether a given change in price will increase or decrease the amount of money spent on a commodity—often a matter of basic importance to firms and government agencies. (Recall the case of the Boston and Maine Railroad.) In this section, we show how the price elasticity of demand determines the effect of a price change on the total amount spent on a commodity.

As a first step, we must define three terms: price elastic, price inelastic, and unitary elasticity. The demand for a commodity is ***price elastic*** if the price elasticity of demand is *greater than 1.* The demand for a commodity is ***price inelastic*** if the price elasticity of demand is *less than 1.* And the demand for a commodity is of ***unitary elasticity*** if the price elasticity of demand *equals 1.* As indicated below, the effect of a price change on the total amount spent on a commodity depends on whether the demand for the commodity is price elastic, price inelastic, or of unitary elasticity. Let's consider each case:

Demand is price elastic. In this case, if the price of the commodity is *reduced,* the total amount spent on the commodity will *increase.* To see why, suppose that the price elasticity of demand for hi-fi sets is 2 and that the price of the hi-fi sets is reduced by 1 percent. Because the price elasticity of demand is 2, the 1 percent reduction in price results in a 2 percent increase in quantity of hi-fi sets demanded. Since the total amount spent on hi-fi sets equals the quantity demanded times the price, the 1 percent reduction in price will be more than offset by the 2 percent increase in quantity demanded: the result of the price cut will be an increase in the total amount spent on hi-fi sets.

Henry Ford and the Price Elasticity of Demand for Autos

HENRY FORD IN HIS FIRST AUTOMOBILE, 1903.

In 1905 the average automobile produced in the U.S. cost more than the average Datsun seventy years later. Many of the firms in the auto industry were warmed-over buggy makers who handcrafted rich men's toys. But change was in the air. *Motor Age,* the industry's first trade magazine, prophesied that "the simple car is the car of the future—. A golden opportunity awaits some bold manufacturer of a simple car."

It remained for Henry Ford, the son of a Wisconsin farmer, to translate these words into a car—the Model T. Ford, commenting on his rural youth, declared, "It was life on the farm that drove me into devising ways and means to better transportation." Turning from the kid glove and checkbook set, he saw the potential market—at the right price—for car sales in the agricultural community.

The Model T was introduced in 1909. A few numbers indicate its phenomenal progress.

YEAR	PRICE	CARS SOLD
1909	$900	58,022
1914	$440	472,350
1916	$360	730,041

However, all good things come to an end. By the twenties, Ford's unwillingness to alter the Model T in any fashion (cosmetic or mechanical), as well as increased competition from other manufacturers, and the development of trade-in and installment buying (which reduced the price elasticity of demand for automobiles) brought the Model T to an end. But the record profits of the Ford Motor Company between 1910 and 1920 vindicated Henry Ford in his belief that "it is better to sell a large number of cars at a reasonably small margin than to sell fewer cars at a larger margin of profit. Bear in mind that when you reduce the price of the car without reducing the quality you increase the possible number of purchases. There are many men who will pay $360 for a car who would not pay $440. I figure that on the $360 basis we can increase the sales to 800,000 cars for the year—less profit on each car, but more cars, more employment of labor and in the end, we get all the profit we ought to make."*

E.A.

* *Henry Ford,* ed. John B. Rae, Englewood Cliffs, N.J.: Prentice-Hall, 1969, p. 112.

On the other hand, if the price of the commodity is *increased,* the total amount spent on the commodity will *fall.* For example, if the price of hi-fi sets is raised by 1 percent, this will reduce the quantity demanded by 2 percent. The 2 percent reduction in the quantity demanded will more than offset the 1 percent increase in price, the result being a decrease in the total amount spent on hi-fi sets.

Demand is price inelastic. In this case, if the price is *reduced,* the total amount spent on the commodity will *decrease.* To see why, suppose that the price elasticity of demand for corn is 0.5 and that the price of corn is reduced by 1 percent. Because the price elasticity of demand is 0.5, the 1 percent price reduction results in a ½ percent increase in the quantity demanded of corn. Since the total amount spent on corn equals the quantity demanded times the price, the ½ percent increase in the quantity demanded will be more than offset by the 1 percent reduction in price: the result of the price cut will be a decrease in the total amount spent on corn.

Table 21.3
Effect of an Increase or Decrease in the Price of a Commodity on the Total Expenditure on the Commodity

Commodity's price elasticity of demand	Effect on total expenditure of: Price decrease	Price increase
Price elastic (which means that elasticity is greater than 1)	Increase	Decrease
Price inelastic (which means that elasticity is less than 1)	Decrease	Increase
Unitary elasticity (which means that elasticity equals 1)	No change	No change

On the other hand, if the price of the commodity is *increased,* the total amount spent on the commodity will *increase.* For example, if the price of corn is raised by 1 percent, this will reduce quantity demanded by ½ percent. The 1 percent price increase will more than offset the ½ percent reduction in quantity demanded, the result being an increase in the total amount spent on corn.

Demand is of unitary elasticity. In this case, a price increase or decrease results in no difference in the total amount spent on the commodity. Why? Because a price decrease (increase) of a certain percentage always results in a quantity increase (decrease) of the same percentage, so that the product of the price and quantity is unaffected. Table 21.3 summarizes the results of this section. It should help you review our findings.

The Farm Problem and the Price Elasticity of Demand

To illustrate the importance of the price elasticity of demand, let's return to the nation's farm problems. One of the most difficult problems for farmers is that, under a free market, farm incomes vary enormously between good times and bad, the variation being much greater than for nonfarm incomes. This is so because farm prices vary a great deal between good times and bad, whereas farm output is much more stable than industrial output. Why is agriculture like this?

The answer lies in considerable part with the price elasticity of demand for farm products. As we emphasized in Chapter 5, food is a necessity with few good substitutes. Thus we would expect the demand for farm products to be price inelastic. And as Table 21.2 suggests, this expectation is borne out by the facts. Given that the demand curve for farm products is price inelastic—and that the quantity supplied of farm products is also relatively in-

Figure 21.4
Instability of Farm Prices and Incomes
Because the demand curve in panel A is much less elastic than that in panel B, a small shift in the demand curve has a much bigger impact on price in panel A than in panel B.

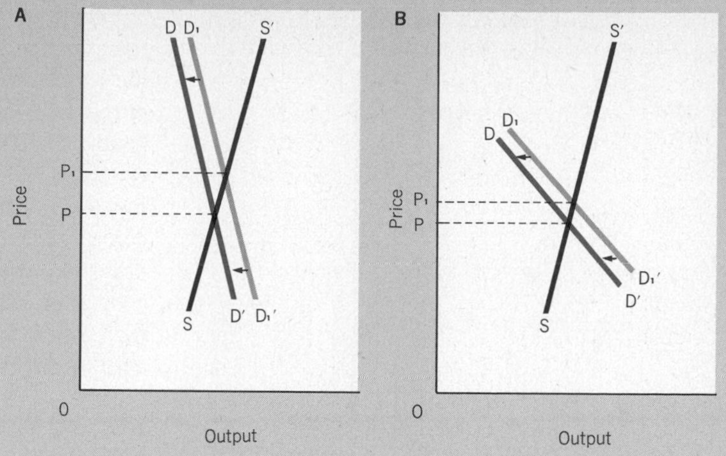

sensitive to price—it follows that relatively small shifts in either the supply curve or the demand curve result in big changes in price. This is why farm prices are so unstable. For example, panel A of Figure 21.4 shows a market where the demand curve is much more inelastic than in panel B. As you can see, a small shift in the demand curve from D_1D_1' to DD' results in a much bigger drop in price in panel A than in panel B.

This is not the only role the price elasticity of demand plays in our farm problems. Many other questions involve it. For example, consider the plan proposed after World War II by Charles Brannan who served as President Truman's secretary of agriculture. The plan was later supported in somewhat modified form by Ezra Taft Benson, secretary of agriculture in the Eisenhower administration. But it drew fire from many farmers, and not until 1973, after nearly three decades of controversy, was the plan approved by Congress.

According to the Brannan plan, a floor is established under the price received by farmers. Suppose that the market price is below this target level. If the target level is OP' in Figure 21.5, and if the output quota is OQ_3, this plan lets the competitive market alone, so that the output of OQ_3 is sold at a price of OP_2. Then according to this plan, the government issues subsidy checks to farmers to cover the difference between the market price and the target price, OP'.

Clearly, the cost to the government under the Brannan plan would be $(OP' - OP_2) \times OQ_3$. An important question is: Will the cost to the U.S. Treasury under this plan be greater than under a system whereby the price is supported at OP', and the government buys the amount—$(OQ_3 - OQ_2)$—that private buyers do not purchase at that price? The answer can be shown to depend on our friend, the price elasticity of demand. The cost to the Treasury under the latter system is $OP'(OQ_3 - OQ_2)$. Thus the cost under the Brannan plan would be greater than under the latter system if $(OP_2 \times OQ_3) < (OP' \times OQ_2)$.[3] But since $OP_2 \times OQ_3$ is the total money expenditure at price OP_2 and $OP' \times OQ_2$ is the total money expenditure at price OP', it follows from the pre-

[3] The cost to the government under the Brannan plan is $(OP' - OP_2) \times OQ_3 = OP' \times OQ_3 - OP_2 \times OQ_3$, while the cost under the other system is $OP' \times (OQ_3 - OQ_2) = OP' \times OQ_3 - OP' \times OQ_2$. Thus, the difference between the former cost and the latter is $OP' \times OQ_2 - OP_2 \times OQ_3$, which means that the cost under the Brannan plan would be greater than under the system if $OP_2 \times OQ_3 < OP' \times OQ_2$.

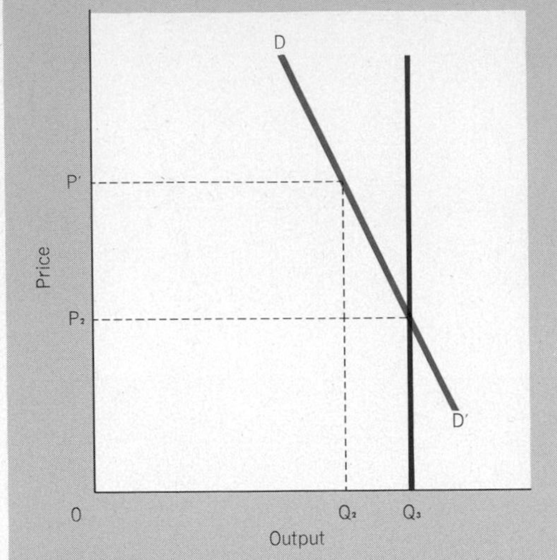

Figure 21.5
Effect of the Brannan Plan
Under the Brannan plan, the competitive market would be let alone, so that, if output were OQ_3, the price would be OP_2. Then the government would pay farmers the difference between this price and the target price, OP'.

vious section that $OP_2 \times OQ_3$ will be less than $OP' \times OQ_2$ if the price elasticity of demand is less than 1. (Why? Because the total amount spent on a commodity will be less at a lower price (such as P_2) than at a higher price (such as P') if demand is price inelastic.) Thus, since the elasticity of demand for farm products is in fact less than 1, the cost to the Treasury will be greater under the Brannan plan than under a system whereby the price is supported at OP', with the government clearing the market of the farm products not purchased by the private sector at that price.

Of course this is not necessarily an overwhelming argument against the Brannan plan. Clearly, the total cost to consumers and taxpayers is the same, whether the Brannan plan or the latter system is adopted. What is different is the burden on different segments of the population. The significant fact for present purposes is not whether the Brannan plan is good or bad, but the importance of the price elasticity of demand in discussing this plan, just as in discussing the instability of farm income and prices. Moreover, the price elasticity of demand is equally as important in problems concerning the industrial and service sectors of the economy as in problems concerning agriculture.

Deriving the Market Demand Curve

The Consumer's Demand Curve

Up to this point, we have simply taken the market demand curve for a commodity as given. Let's look now at the factors underlying the market demand curve. We begin with the behavior of a particular consumer, Mrs. Walter, the San Diego designer we introduced in Chapter 20. Let's examine the relationship between the price of food and the amount of food she will buy per month. Applying the theory of consumer behavior presented in Chapter 20 makes it easy to derive this relationship, which economists call the consumer's ***individual demand curve.***

Assuming that food and clothing are the only goods, that Mrs. Walter's monthly income is \$400, and that the price of clothing is \$40 per piece of clothing, we confront Mrs. Walter with a variety of prices of food. First, we confront her with a price of \$1 per pound of food. How much food will she buy? Next, we confront her with a price of \$2 per pound of food. How much food will she buy? The theory of consumer behavior shows how, under each of these sets of circumstances, she will allocate her income between food and clothing. Suppose that she will buy 200 pounds of food when the price is \$1 per pound, and 100 pounds of food when the price is \$2 per pound. These are two points on Mrs. Walter's individual demand curve for food—those corresponding to prices of \$1 and \$2 per pound. Figure 21.6 shows these two points, *X* and *Y*.

It is no trick to obtain more points on her individual demand curve for food. All that we have to do is confront her with other prices of food, and see how much food she buys at each price. Plotting the amount of food she buys against the price, we obtain new points on her individual demand curve for food. Connecting up all these points, we get her complete individual demand curve for food, shown in Figure 21.6. (In the Appendix to this chapter, a more detailed derivation of the individual demand curve, based on indifference curves, is given.)

Clearly, *the location and shape of an individual demand curve depend on the tastes of the consumer*. For example, if Mrs. Walter values

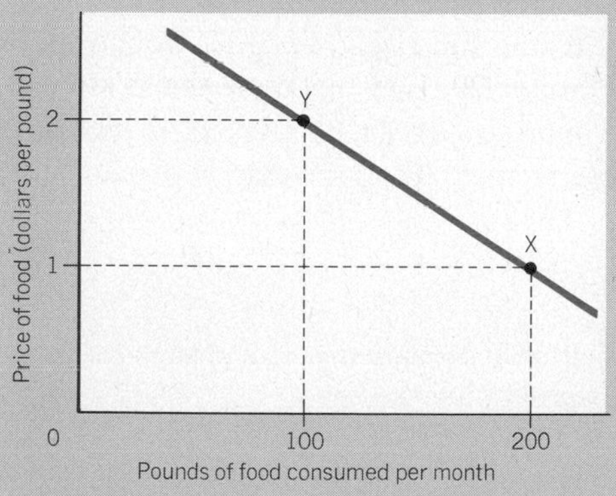

Figure 21.6
Mrs. Walter's Individual Demand Curve for Food
The consumer's individual demand curve for a commodity shows the amount of the commodity the consumer will buy at various prices. (Points *X* and *Y* on Mrs. Walter's individual demand curve for food are derived in Figure 21.11 in the Appendix to this chapter.)

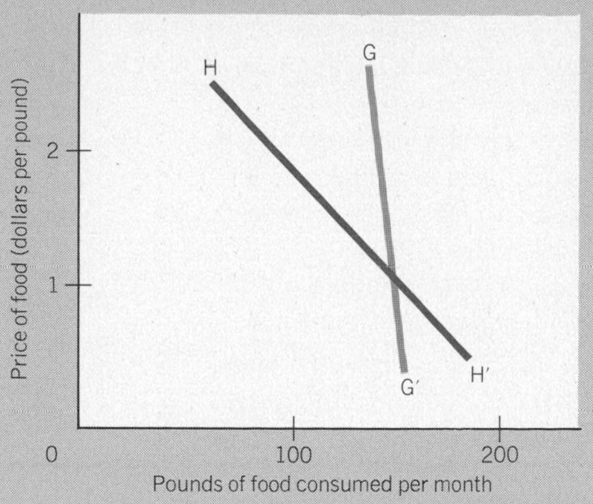

Figure 21.7
Hypothetical Individual Demand Curves
If Mrs. Walter values food so much that she is determined to buy much the same amount regardless of its price, her individual demand curve for food may look like *GG′*; but if she is less determined to maintain her family's food consumption, her individual demand curve for food may look like *HH′*.

food so much that she is determined to maintain her family's consumption of this commodity regardless of its price, her individual demand curve for food will look like *GG′* in Figure 21.7. But if she is less determined to maintain her family's food consumption, it may look like *HH′* in Figure 21.7.

Besides the consumer's tastes, other factors determining the location and shape of the consumer's individual demand curve are the income of the consumer and the prices of other goods. For example, Mrs. Walter's individual demand curve for food in Figure 21.6 is based on the assumption that her income is \$400 per month and that the price of a piece of clothing is \$40. If her income or the price of clothing changes, her individual demand curve for food will change as well. Thus her individual demand

Figure 21.8
Effect of Changes in Income and in Price of Clothing on Mrs. Walter's Individual Demand Curve for Food
The consumer's individual demand curve for a commodity depends on his money income and the price of other commodities. Mrs. Walter's individual demand curve for food may be D_0D_0' if her income is $300 per month and the price of a piece of clothing is $40, D_1D_1' if her income is $500 per month and the price of a piece of clothing is $40, and D_2D_2' if her income is $500 per month and the price of a piece of clothing is $50.

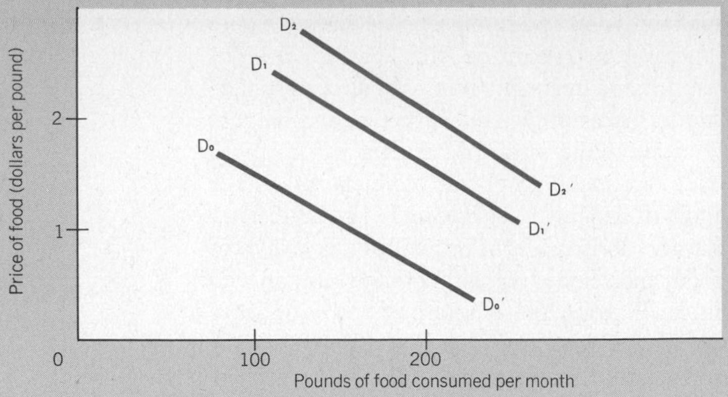

curve for food may be D_0D_0' in Figure 21.8 if her income is $300 per month and the price of a piece of clothing is $40, D_1D_1' if her income is $500 per month and the price of a piece of clothing is $40, and D_2D_2' if her income is $500 per month and the price of a piece of clothing is $50.

Transition to the Market Demand Curve

In Chapter 4, we discussed what we meant by a market. As a working definition, we decided that a market could be regarded as a group of firms and individuals that are in touch with each other in order to buy or sell some commodity. *The market demand curve for a commodity bears a very simple relationship to the individual demand curves of all the consumers in the market: it is the horizontal sum of all the individual demand curves.* In other words, to find the total quantity demanded in the market at a certain price, we add up the quantities demanded by the individual consumers at that price.

For example, Table 21.4 shows the individual demand curves for food of four families: the Walters, Joneses, Smiths, and Kleins. For simplicity, suppose that these four families constitute the entire market for food. (This assumption can easily be relaxed; it just makes things simple.) Then the market demand curve

Table 21.4
Individual Demand Curves and Market Demand Curve for Food

Price of food (dollars per pound)	Individual demand				Market demand
	Jones	Klein	Smith	Walter	
	(hundreds of pounds per month)				
1.00	50.0	45.0	5.0	2.0	102
1.20	43.0	44.0	4.2	1.8	93
1.40	36.0	43.0	3.4	1.6	84
1.60	30.0	42.0	2.6	1.4	76
1.80	25.0	41.4	2.4	1.2	70
2.00	20.0	41.0	2.0	1.0	64

for food is shown in the last column of Table 21.4. Figure 21.9 shows the families' individual demand curves for food, as well as the resulting market demand curve. To illustrate how the market demand curve is derived from the individual demand curves, suppose that the price of food is $1 per pound. Then the total quantity demanded in the market is 102 hundreds of pounds per month, since this is the sum of the quantities demanded at this price by the four families. (As shown in Table 21.4, this sum equals 50.0 + 45.0 + 5.0 + 2.0, or 102.)

Individual demand curves almost always slope downward to the right: that is, the consumer almost always responds to an increase in a commodity's price by reducing the amount of it he consumes. Or, put the other way around, a commodity's price almost always must be reduced to persuade the consumer to buy more of it. One way to explain this fact is by an appeal to the law of diminishing marginal utility, which (you will recall from Chapter 20) states that, as a person consumes more and more of a particular commodity, the commodity's marginal utility declines. Since the marginal utility—the extra utility derived from an extra unit of the commodity—declines, the price the consumer is willing to pay for an extra unit of the commodity must decline too.

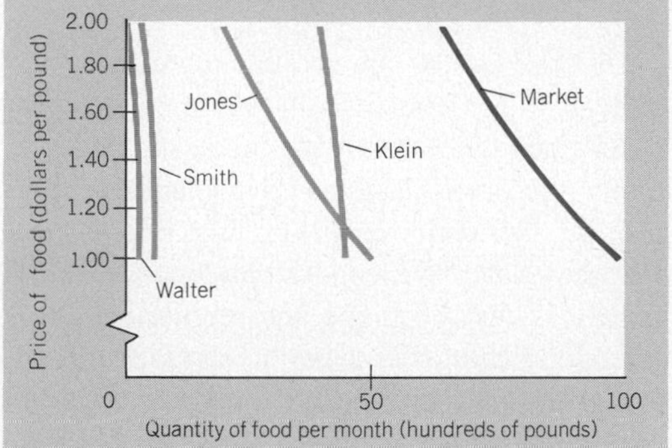

Figure 21.9
Individual Demand Curves and Market Demand Curves for Food
The market demand curve is the horizontal sum of all the individual demand curves.

This explanation relies on the assumption that marginal utility is measurable. Another way to explain the same thing makes no such assumption. According to this explanation, an increase in a commodity's price has two kinds of effects on the consumer—a substitution effect and an income effect. The ***substitution effect*** is what happens to the consumer's behavior if the commodity becomes dearer relative to other commodities: clearly, the consumer tends to buy less of the good. But this is not the only effect of the price increase. At the same time, there is also an ***income effect,*** the effect on the consumer's behavior of the fact that his real income is lower now that the price of the commodity has become higher. The income effect may prompt the consumer to buy more or less of the commodity. However, unless the income effect is very strange indeed—small increases in real income resulting in very large decreases in the consumption of the good—the total effect of a price increase (i.e., the substitution effect plus the income effect) will be a reduction of the quantity demanded of the commodity.

Since individual demand curves for a commodity almost always slope downward to the right, it follows that market demand curves too almost always slope downward to the right. (Why? Because, as stressed above, the market demand curve is the horizontal sum of all of the individual demand curves.) However, as emphasized repeatedly here and in Chapter 4, the shape and location of the market demand curve vary greatly from commodity to commodity and from market to market. For example, the quantity demanded of some commodities is quite sensitive to changes in their price; for other commodities, the quantity demanded varies only slightly with price changes. These differences stem from differences in consumer tastes, the number of consumers in the market, the income of consumers, and the prices of other commodities.

The Demand Curve for Automobiles: A Case Study

Some congressional committees have asserted that important industries in the American economy have tended to underestimate the price elasticity of demand, so that they have not been sufficiently prone to reduce prices. According to the critics, the industries in question should, in their own interest as well as the public's, reduce their prices. Among those charged with such an underestimation is the automobile industry, unquestionably one of the biggest industries in the entire American economy.

How great is the price elasticity of demand for automobiles? This is a very important question both to the automobile industry and to those, like the congressional committees, who have some responsibility for evaluating our economy's over-all performance. Perhaps the first major study of this question was carried out in 1939 by C. F. Roos and V. von Szeliski for the General Motors Corporation. On the basis of data for 1919–37, their statistical analysis indicated that the price elasticity of demand for new automobiles was about 1.5. In other words, a 1 percent reduction in price would result in about a 1.5 percent increase in the quantity demanded of new automobiles.

Several more recent studies of the price elasticity of demand for automobiles have been carried out by academic economists. Although there has been some controversy over particular aspects of these investigations, they seem to indicate that the price elasticity of demand for automobiles is at least 1.2. In other words, a 1 percent reduction in price brings about at least a 1.2 percent increase in the quantity demanded. Thus these studies, carried out by L. J. Atkinson, Gregory Chow, and D. B. Suits, seem generally to agree rather well with the earlier study by Roos and von Szeliski.

Two aspects of these studies should be noted. First, in contrast to the case of the Boston and Maine Railroad, the estimates obtained by these researchers were based on detailed statistical analysis of past data on price, quantity demanded, income, and a variety of other variables, not on the sort of direct market experiment the Boston and Maine carried out. Second, because automobiles are durable goods, these investigators had to recognize that the basic demand is for automobile ownership, not new cars. As Princeton's Gregory Chow put it,

> People buy automobiles because they want to use automobiles, and their wants are satisfied not only by the new cars that they have just bought but by the total number of cars in existence. So the demand for automobile services actually is a demand for automobile ownership rather than the demand for purchase. The demand for purchase is derived from the demand for automobile ownership.[4]

On the basis of the available evidence, it is difficult to tell conclusively whether the automobile manufacturers have tended to underestimate the price elasticity of demand for their product. But suppose for the sake of argument that they have. Why should anyone care? The answer is that both the automobile manufacturers and the general public should care, because, by underestimating the price elasticity of demand, the companies are underestimating the gain in sales from a price reduction. Thus they are inclined to maintain the price at too high a level, to the detriment of their own profits as well as the consumer's pocketbook.

[4] Senate Subcommittee on Antitrust and Monopoly, "The Price Elasticity of Demand for Automobiles," reprinted in E. Mansfield, *Microeconomics: Selected Readings*, 2d ed., New York: Norton, 1971.

Industry and Firm Demand Curves

Up to this point, we have been dealing with the market demand curve for a commodity. *The market demand curve for a commodity is not the same as the market demand curve for the output of a single firm that produces the commodity, unless, of course, the industry is composed of only a single firm.* If the industry is composed of more than one firm, as is usually the case, the demand curve for the output of each firm producing the commodity will usually be quite different from the demand curve for the commodity. For example, the demand curve for the output of Farmer Brown's wheat is quite different from the market demand curve for wheat. *In particular, the demand curve for the output of a particular firm is generally more price elastic than the market demand curve for the commodity,* because the products of other firms in the industry are close substitutes for the product of this firm. As pointed out earlier, products with many close substitutes have relatively high price elasticities of demand.

If there are many, many firms selling a homogeneous product, the individual firm's demand curve becomes *horizontal,* or essentially so. To see this, suppose that 100,000 firms sell a particular commodity and that each of these firms is of equal size. If any one of these firms were to triple its output and sales, the total industry output would change by only .002 percent—too small a change to have any perceptible effect on the price of the commodity. Consequently, each firm can act as if variations in its output—within the range of its capabilities—will have no real impact on market price. In other words, the demand curve facing the individual firm is horizontal, as in Figure 21.10.

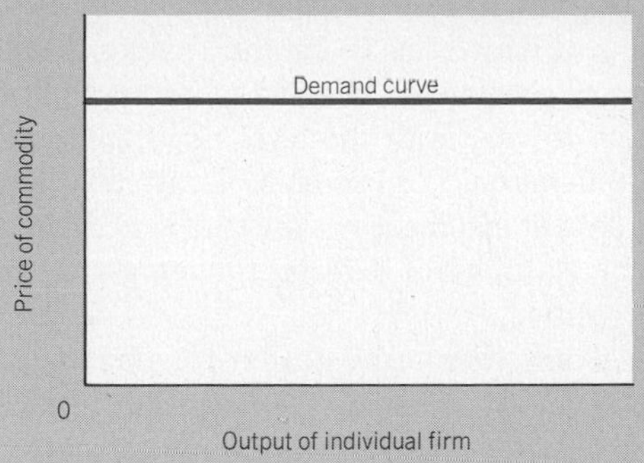

Figure 21.10
Demand Curve for Output of an Individual Firm: The Case of a Great Many Sellers of a Homogeneous Commodity
If there are many, many firms selling a homogeneous product, the demand curve facing an individual firm is horizontal.

Income Elasticity of Demand

So far this chapter has dealt almost exclusively with the effect of a commodity's price on the quantity demanded of it in the market. But price is not, of course, the only factor that influences the quantity demanded of the commodity. Another important factor is the level of money income among the consumers in the market. The sensitivity of the quantity demanded to the total money income of all of the consumers in the market is measured by the ***income elasticity of demand,*** which is defined as the percentage change in the quantity demanded resulting from a 1 percent increase in total money income (all prices being held constant).

A commodity's income elasticity of demand may be positive or negative. For many commodities, increases in income result in increases in the amount demanded: such commodities, like steak or caviar, have positive income elasticities of demand. For other commodities, increases in income result in decreases in the amount demanded: these commodities, like margarine and poor grades of vegetables, have negative income elasticities of demand. However, be careful to note that the income elasticity of demand of a commodity is likely to vary with the level of income under consideration. For example, if only families at the lowest income levels are considered, the income elasticity of demand for margarine may be positive.

Luxury items tend to have higher income elasticities of demand than necessities. Indeed, one way to define luxuries and necessities is to say that luxuries are commodities with high income elasticities of demand, and necessities are commodities with low income elasticities of demand.

Many studies have been made to estimate the income elasticity of demand for particular commodities, since, like the price elasticity of demand, it is of great importance to decision makers. In making long-term forecasts of industry sales, for example, firms must take the income elasticity of demand into account. Thus, if the income elasticity of demand for a product is high, and if incomes increase considerably during the next 20 years, the product's sales will tend to increase greatly during that period. On the other hand, if the income elasticity of demand for a product is close to zero, one would expect the product's sales not to increase very much on account of such increases in income.

To illustrate the findings of empirical studies in this area, consider the following results obtained by Herman Wold, a distinguished Swedish economist. According to his estimates, the income elasticity of demand is 0.37 for eggs, 0.34 for cheese, 0.42 for butter, 1.00 for liquor, –0.20 for margarine, 0.07 for milk and cream, and 1.48 for restaurant consumption of food. Certainly, these estimates seem reasonable. One would expect the income elasticity of demand to be negative for margarine, because consumers tend to view margarine as an inferior good, and as their incomes rise, they tend to switch from margarine to butter. Also, it is not surprising that the income elasticity of demand for milk and cream is close to zero, since people tend to view milk and cream as necessities, particularly for children. In addition, it is quite reasonable that the income elasticity of demand for liquor and restaurant consumption of food is higher than for the other commodities. Liquor and restaurant meals tend to be luxury items for most people.

Finally, let's look once again at the market demand for automobiles, considering the income elasticity of demand this time. To develop and exercise your economic intuition, think about the demand for automobiles, and try to guess what the income elasticity of demand for automobiles is likely to be. Is it likely to be positive or negative? If positive, is it likely to be above or below 1? This sort of exercise is extremely useful. Just as it is important that you be able to come up with a reasonable guess concerning the answer to an arithmetic problem, so you should be able to make a reasonable guess at a product's income elasticity of demand—or its price elasticity of demand, for that matter.

What are the facts? According to the early study by Roos and von Szeliski, the income elasticity of demand for automobiles is about 2.5: in other words, a 1 percent increase in income will result in about a 2.5 percent increase in the quantity demanded of automobiles. According to the later studies by Atkinson, Chow, and Suits, it is about 3.0: in other words, a 1 percent increase in income will result in about a 3.0 percent increase in the quantity demanded of automobiles. Needless to say, despite the advances that have been made in statistical and econometric methods, it is hard to estimate income elasticities or price elasticities with pinpoint accuracy. Fortunately, however, pinpoint accuracy seldom is necessary. In this case, the knowledge that the answer probably lies between 2.5 and 3.0 is of great value for many practical purposes.

Cross Elasticity of Demand

Besides the price of the commodity and the level of total money income—the factors discussed primarily in previous sections of this chapter—the quantity demanded of a commodity also depends on the prices of other commodities. For example, if the price of butter is held constant, the amount of butter demanded will be influenced by the price of margarine. The ***cross elasticity of demand,*** defined as the percentage change in the quantity demanded of one commodity resulting from a 1 percent change in the price of another commodity, is used to measure the sensitivity of the former commodity's quantity demanded to changes in the latter commodity's price.

Pairs of commodities are classified as ***substitutes*** or ***complements,*** depending on the sign of the cross elasticity of demand. If the cross elasticity of demand is positive, two commodities are substitutes. For example, butter and margarine are substitutes because a decrease in the price of butter will result in a decrease in the quantity demanded of margarine—many margarine eaters really prefer the "higher-priced spread." On the other hand, if the cross elasticity of demand is negative, two commodities are complements. For example, gin and tonic may be complements since a decrease in the price of gin may increase the quantity demanded of tonic. The reduction in the price of gin will increase the quantity demanded of gin, thus increasing the quantity demanded of tonic since gin and tonic tend to be used together.

Many studies have been made of the cross elasticity of demand for various pairs of commodities. After all, it frequently is very important to know how a change in the price of one commodity will affect the sales of another commodity. For example, what would be the effect of a 1 percent increase in the price of pork on the quantity demanded of beef? According to Herman Wold's estimates, the effect would be a .28 percent increase in the quantity demanded of beef—since he estimates that the cross elasticity of demand for these two commodities is 0.28. What effect would a 1 percent increase in the price of butter have on the quantity demanded of margarine? According to Wold, the effect would be a .81 percent increase in the quantity demanded of margarine—since he estimates that the cross elasticity of demand for these two commodities is 0.81.

Criticisms and Extensions of the Model

The theory of consumer behavior and market demand has not been without its critics. Among the most articulate (and severe) is Harvard's John Kenneth Galbraith, who argues that it is naïve and misleading to assume that consumer tastes arise from within the consumer, and that producers dance to the tune of consumer preferences. Instead, in Galbraith's view, producers, through their advertising and other selling activities, play an important role in molding consumer tastes and in getting consumers to want more and more of whatever they are producing. The following quotation indicates the spirit (and wit) of Galbraith's attack:

> Were it so that a man on arising each morning was assailed by demons which instilled in him a passion sometimes for silk shirts, sometimes for kitchenware, sometimes for chamber pots, and sometimes for orange squash, there would be every reason to applaud the effort to find the goods, however odd, that quenched this flame. But should it be that . . . production creates the wants it seeks to satisfy, or if the wants emerge *pari passu* with the production, then the urgency of the wants can no longer be used to defend the urgency of the production. Production only fills a void that it has itself created.[5]

[5] J. K. Galbraith, *The Affluent Society,* Boston: Houghton Mifflin, 1958, reprinted in E. Mansfield, *Economics: Readings, Issues, and Cases,* 2d ed., New York: Norton, 1977.

Of course, Galbraith is certainly correct in pointing out that consumer tastes are affected by advertising and other types of promotional efforts by producers. However most economists seem to feel that he goes too far in portraying the consumer as a docile animal producers lead around by the nose, and they are skeptical of his argument that acquired desires or tastes must be less important than those that are innate. For example, as Nobel laureate Friedrich von Hayek has stated,

> Professor Galbraith's argument could be easily employed, without any change of the essential terms, to demonstrate the worthlessness of literature or any form of art. Surely an individual's want for literature is not original with himself in the sense that he would experience it if literature were not produced. Does this then mean that the production of literature cannot be defended as satisfying a want because it is only the production which provokes the demand?[6]

Even such Marxist economists as Paul Baran feel that Galbraith goes too far. Baran writes that "to be sure, it does not follow, as some business economists like to assert, that the barrage of advertising and salesmanship to which the consumer is continually exposed has *no* influence on the formation of his wants. But neither is it true that these business practices constitute *the* decisive factor in making the consumer want what he wants."[7] To Baran, the crucial issue is over the kinds of values and preferences that are instilled into people by these processes, and whether they are good or bad, not whether such processes go on. Much more will be said on this score in Chapter 35.

Another criticism of the theory of consumer behavior and market demand is that it pays too little attention to the fact that what one consumer wants depends on what other consumers buy. For example, if the Walters associate with people who have big houses and beach cottages, they may come to want them too. However, it is possible to extend the model of consumer behavior and market demand to include such interdependencies, or "demonstration effects," as they are called by economists. Moreover, it is possible to extend the model to include the fact that some people may prefer expensive goods to cheaper ones, either because they like to show off their wealth or because they judge quality by price. Also, it is possible to include the effects of advertising in such a model. Interested students are referred to more advanced textbooks, where these extensions properly belong.

[6] F. A. Hayek, "*The Non Sequitur* of the Dependence Effect," *Southern Economic Journal,* April 1961, reprinted in E. Mansfield, *Economics: Readings, Issues, and Cases.*

[7] Paul Baran, *The Political Economy of Growth,* New York: Monthly Review Press, 1957.

Summary

The market demand curve, which is the relationship between the price of a commodity and the amount of the commodity demanded in the market, is one of the most important and frequently used concepts in economics. The market demand curve is the horizontal sum of the individual demand curves of all the consumers in the market. Individual demand curves almost always slope downward to the right because of the so-called law of decreasing marginal utility. Or, to avoid the use of marginal utility measures, one can explain this same thing in terms of the substitution and income effects of a price change. Since individual demand curves almost always slope downward to the right, market demand curves will do so too. The shape and position of a product's market demand curve depend on consumers' tastes, consumer incomes, the price of other goods, and the number of consumers in the market.

The price elasticity of demand measures the sensitivity of the amount demanded to changes in price. Whether a price increase results in an increase or decrease in the total amount spent on a commodity depends on the price elasticity of demand. The income elasticity of demand measures the sensitivity of the amount demanded to changes in total income. A commodity's income elasticity of demand may be positive or negative. Luxury items are generally assumed to have higher income elasticities of demand than necessities. The cross elasticity of demand measures the sensitivity of the amount demanded to changes in the price of another commodity. If the cross elasticity of demand is positive, two commodities are substitutes; if it is negative, they are complements.

The market demand curve for a commodity is not the same as the demand curve for the output of a single firm that produces the commodity, unless the industry is composed of only one firm. In general, the demand curve for the output of a single firm will be more elastic than the market demand curve for the commodity. Indeed, if there are many, many firms selling a homogeneous commodity, the individual firm's demand curve becomes horizontal.

There are many techniques for measuring demand curves, such as interview studies, direct experiments, and the statistical analysis of historical data. An example of a direct experiment was the demonstration project carried out by the Boston and Maine Railroad.

CONCEPTS FOR REVIEW

Market demand curve	Unitary elasticity	Substitute
Arc elasticity of demand	Price elastic	Infinitely elastic
Price elasticity of demand	Price inelastic	Brannon plan
Income elasticity of demand	Individual demand curve	Substitution effect
Cross elasticity of demand	Complement	Income effect

QUESTIONS FOR DISCUSSION AND REVIEW

1. An econometric analysis of the market for slingshots concludes that the price elasticity of demand for slingshots is 0.80, when the price is between $1 and $2 per slingshot. From this information alone, can you draw the demand curve for slingshots? Why or why not? If you know the quantity demanded at a price of $1, can you draw the market demand for slingshots (between a price of $1 and $2)?

2. Suppose that each of the four corners of an intersection contains a gas station, and that the gasoline is essentially the same. Do you think that the price elasticity of demand for each station's gasoline is above or below 1? Why? Do you think that it is less than or greater than the price elasticity of demand for all gasoline in the United States?

3. The Bugsbane Music Box Company is convinced that an increase in its price will reduce the total amount of money spent on its product. Can you tell from this whether the demand for its product is price elastic or price inelastic?

4. Suppose that there are five people who are the only members of a particular market. The amount that each person will buy of the product in question (at each price) is shown below. Determine five points on the market demand curve for the product.

Price	First person	Second person	Third person	Fourth person	Fifth person
(dollars)			(Quantity demanded)		
1	5	4	2	8	7
2	4	4	2	7	6
3	3	4	1	6	5
4	2	3	0	5	4
5	1	3	0	5	2

5. What is the sign of the cross elasticity of demand for each of the following pairs of commodities: (a) tea and coffee, (b) tennis rackets and tennis balls, (b) whisky and gin, (c) fishing licenses and fishing poles, (d) nylon rugs and wool rugs.

6. Do you think that the price elasticity of demand for subway service in New York City is above or below 1. If the price of subway rides were increased, do you think that the subway's total revenues would increase or decrease (or stay the same)?

7. On page 491, we saw that the quantity of Model T's sold increased from about 472,000 to about 730,000 when its price was reduced from $440 in 1914 to $360 in 1916. How can this fact be reconciled with recent studies which indicate that the price elasticity of demand for automobiles is about 1.2 to 1.5?

8. According to S. M. Sackrin's study for the Department of Agriculture of the demand for cigarettes, the price elasticity of demand is between 0.3 and 0.4, and the income elasticity of demand is about 0.5. If you were an economist at one of the major tobacco companies, how might you use these data?

9. Suppose that the relationship between the price of aluminum and the quantity of aluminum demanded is as follows:

Price (dollars)	Quantity
1	8
2	7
3	6
4	5
5	4

What is the arc elasticity of demand when price is between $1 and $2? Between $4 and $5?

10. According to the U.S. Department of Agriculture, the income elasticity of demand for coffee is about 0.23. If incomes rose by 1 percent, what effect would this have on the quantity demanded of coffee?

Appendix: Using Indifference Curves to Derive the Individual Demand Curve

In this Appendix, we show how indifference curves can be used to derive the consumer's demand curve. In particular, let's return to the case of Mrs. Walter, and show how her demand curve for food can be derived.

Assuming that food and clothing are the only goods, that Mrs. Walter's monthly income is $400, and that the price of clothing is $40 per piece of clothing, Mrs. Walter's budget line is budget line 1 in Figure 21.11, when the price of food is $1 per pound. Thus, as we saw in the previous chapter, Mrs. Walter will buy 200 pounds of food per month under these conditions.

If, however, the price of food increases to $2 per pound, her income and the price of clothing remaining constant, her budget line will be budget line 2 in Figure 21.11, and she will attain her highest indifference curve, *AA′*, by choosing the market basket corresponding to point *I*, a market basket containing 100 pounds of food per month. Thus, if the price of food is $2 per pound, she will buy 100 pounds of food per month.

We have derived two points on Mrs. Walter's individual demand curve for food—those corresponding to prices of $1 and $2 per pound. Figure 21.6 shows these two points, *X* and *Y*. To obtain more points on her individual demand curve for food, all we have to do is assume a particular price for food, construct the budget line corresponding to this price (holding her income and the price of clothing constant), and find the market basket on this budget line that is on her highest indifference curve. Plotting the amount of food in this market basket against the assumed price of food, we obtain a new point on her individual demand curve for food. Connecting up all these points, we get her complete individual demand curve for food, shown in Figure 21.6.

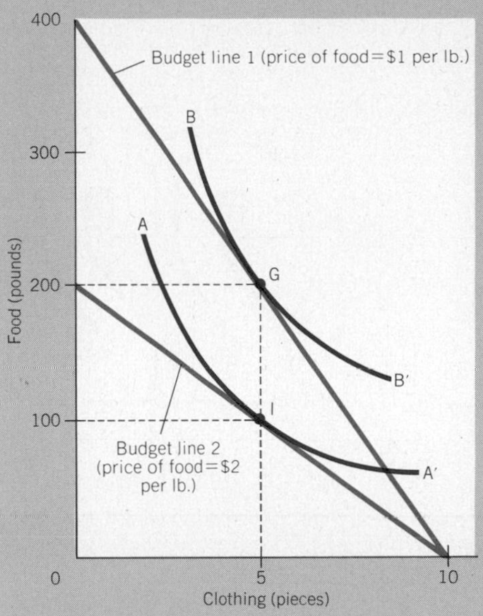

Figure 21.11
Effect of Change in Price of Food on Mrs. Walter's Equilibrium Market Basket
If the price of a pound of food is $1, Mrs. Walter's budget line is such that her equilibrium market basket is at point *G*, where she buys 200 pounds of food per month. If the price of a pound of food is $2, Mrs. Walter's budget line is such that her equilibrium market basket is at point *I*, where she buys 100 pounds of food per month.

22 Optimal Input Decisions and Cost Analysis

In economies based largely on free enterprise, like our own, the managers of business firms are given considerable responsibility for deciding where, when, and how various resources are used. Thus the manager's job is a central one, from both a social and private point of view. Fortunately, the United States has been able to develop large cadres of effective managerial talent, in large part because management and business have been highly esteemed professions in the United States. As Calvin Coolidge put it, with characteristic brevity and uncharacteristic overstatement, "The business of America is business." This is quite a different sentiment from that expressed by the ancient Roman historian, Tacitus, who said that Sabinus "had talents equal to business, and aspired no higher."

In this chapter, we shall take a closer look at the decision-making process within the firm. After discussing the organization, motivation, and technology of the firm in Chapter 7, we now discuss some of the central questions involved in its management and operation. In particular, if a firm attempts to maximize profits, what production technique—i.e., what combination of inputs—should it choose to produce a particular quantity of output? What are its costs? How do various types of costs vary with the firm's output rate? These questions are of the utmost importance, both for the managers of a firm and for society as a whole.

Average and Marginal Products

If the United States Steel Corporation decides to produce a certain quantity of steel, it can do so in many ways. It can use open hearth furnaces, or basic oxygen furnaces, or electric furnaces; it can use various types of iron ore; and it can use various types of coke. Which of these many ways will maximize U.S. Steel's profits? The management of U.S. Steel—and every business firm—devotes considerable time and energy to answering this kind of question. Let's restate it in the economist's terms: given that a firm is going to produce a certain quantity of output, what production technique—i.e., what combination of inputs—should it choose to maximize its profits?

As a first step toward answering this question, recall the characteristics of a firm's production function; namely, that it shows the most output that existing technology permits the firm to extract from each quantity of inputs. For example, the production function for an oil pipeline, described in Chapter 7, shows the maximum amount of oil a pipeline can carry, given that it has a certain diameter and that a certain number of horsepower are applied. From the production function, we can compute an input's average product and its marginal product. The ***average product of an input*** is the firm's total output divided by the amount of input used to produce this amount of output. For example, consider the simple case of a wheat farm with 1 acre of land (a fixed input). The relationship between the amount of labor used per year by this farm (a variable input) and the farm's output are shown in Table 22.1. This is the farm's production function. And the average product of labor is 30 bushels per man-year of labor when 1 man-year of labor is used, 35 bushels per man-year of labor when 2 man-years are used, $33\frac{1}{3}$ bushels per man-year of labor when 3 man-years are used, and so forth.

As the amount of labor used on the farm increases, so does the farm's output, but the amount of extra output from the addition of an extra man-year of labor varies depending on how much labor is already being used. The extra output from the addition of the first man-year of labor is $30 - 0 = 30$ bushels per man-year of labor. The extra output due to the addition of the second man-year of labor is $70 - 30 = 40$ bushels per man-year of labor. And the extra output from the addition of the fifth man-year of labor is $145 - 125 = 20$ bushels per man-year of labor. The ***marginal product of an input*** is the addition to total output due to the addition of the last unit of input, the quantity of other inputs used being held constant. Thus the marginal product of labor is 30 bushels when between 0 and 1 man-years of labor are used, 40 bushels when between 1 and

Table 22.1
Relationship between Labor Input and Output on One-Acre Wheat Farm

Number of man-years of labor	Bushels of wheat produced per year
0	0
1	30
2	70
3	100
4	125
5	145

Table 22.2
Average and Marginal Products of Labor, One-Acre Wheat Farm

Number of man-years of labor	Average product (bushels per man-year)	Marginal product[a] (bushels per man-year)
1	30	30
2	35	40
3	33⅓	30
4	31¼	25
5	29	20

[a] These figures pertain to the interval between the indicated number of man-years of labor and one man-year less than the indicated number.

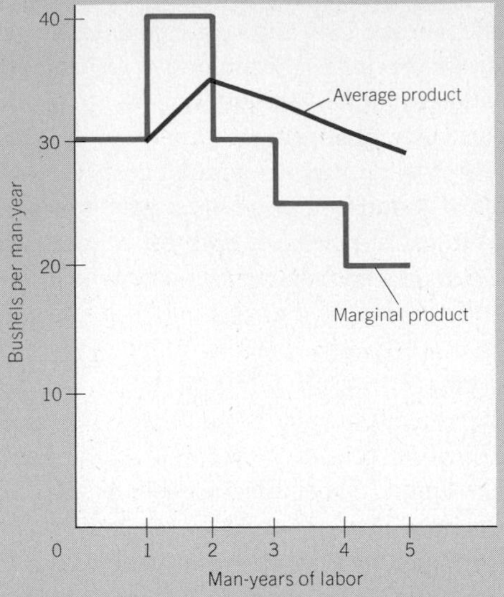

Figure 22.1
Average and Marginal Products of Labor, One-Acre Wheat Farm
Both the average product and the marginal product of labor rise, reach a maximum, and fall.

2 man-years of labor are used, and so on.

Table 22.2 shows the average and marginal products of labor at various levels of utilization of labor; Figure 22.1 shows the same thing graphically. As is generally the case for production processes, the average product of the variable input—labor in this case—rises, reaches a maximum, and then falls. The marginal product of labor also rises, reaches a maximum, and falls; this too is typical of many production processes. Why do average and marginal product behave in this way? Because of the law of diminishing marginal returns, to which we now turn.

The Law of Diminishing Marginal Returns

Perhaps the best-known—and certainly one of the least understood—laws of economics is the so-called ***law of diminishing marginal returns.*** Put in a single sentence, this law states that *if equal increments of an input are added, the quantities of other inputs held constant, the resulting increments of product will decrease beyond some point;* that is, the marginal product of the input will diminish. This law is illustrated by Table 22.2; beyond 2 man-years of labor, the marginal product of labor falls. Certainly, it seems entirely reasonable that, as more and more of a variable input (in this case, labor) is combined with a fixed amount of another input (in this case, land), the additional output to be derived from an additional unit of the variable input will eventually decrease. For example, in the case of Table 22.2, one would expect that, as more and more labor is added, the extra workers' functions eventually would become less and less important and productive.

This law plays a part in determining the firm's optimal input combination and the shape of the firm's cost functions, as we shall see below. To prevent misunderstanding and confusion, several points about this law should be stressed. First, it is assumed that technology remains fixed. If technology changes, the law of diminishing marginal returns cannot predict the effect of an additional unit of input. Second, at least one input must be fixed in quantity, since the law of diminishing marginal returns is not applicable to cases where there is a proportional increase in all inputs. Third, it must be possible, of course, to vary the proportions in which the various inputs are utilized. This is generally possible in industry and agriculture.

To illustrate how the law of diminishing marginal returns operates in real-life situations, let's return to the case of a 1,000-mile-long crude oil pipeline. Recall from Chapter 7 that the output of such a pipeline is the amount of oil carried per day, and that the two principal inputs are the diameter of the pipeline and the horsepower applied to the oil it carries. It makes sense, of course, that the pipeline's output will depend heavily on its diameter and the horsepower applied to the oil. The exact relationship between the quantities of these inputs and the quantity of output was given in the production function shown in Table 7.3. For convenience, this production function is reproduced in Tablc 22.3. Using thc production function, we can estimate the marginal product of each input.

Table 22.3
Production Function, Crude Oil Pipeline

Line Diameter (inches)	Horsepower (thousands) 20	30	40	50	60
Output rate (thousands of barrels per day)					
14	70	90	95	100	104
18	115	140	155	165	170
22	160	190	215	235	250
26	220	260	300	320	340

Source: See Table 7.3.

Figure 22.2 shows the marginal product of horsepower if the diameter of the pipeline is 18 inches. For example, when horsepower is between 20,000 and 30,000, the marginal product is (140,000 − 115,000) ÷ (30,000 − 20,000)–or 2.5 gallons of oil (per day) per horsepower. Why? Because in this range, an extra horsepower results in 2.5 extra gallons of oil carried per day. Similarly, the marginal product is 1.5 gallons when horsepower is between 30,000 and 40,000, 1.0 gallons when horsepower is between 40,000 and 50,000, and 0.5 gallons when horsepower is between 50,000 and 60,000. Thus, in accord with thc law of diminishing marginal returns, the marginal product of horsepower decreases as more

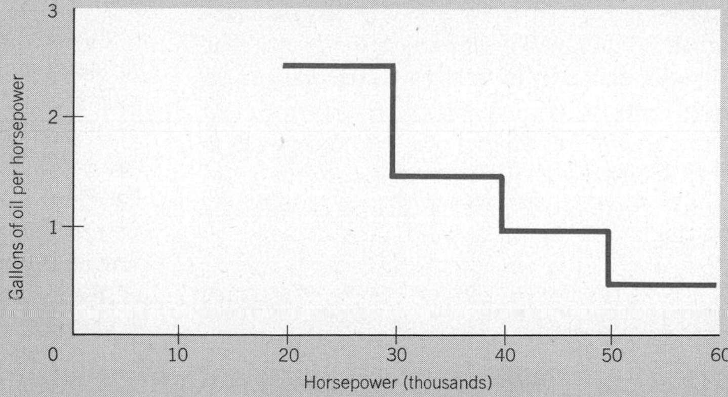

Figure 22.2
Marginal Product of Horsepower, Crude Oil Pipeline, 18-Inch Diameter
The graph shows the marginal product curve in an actual case. Note that the results agree with the law of diminishing returns.

Figure 22.3
Marginal Product of Line Diameter, Crude Oil Pipeline, 50,000 Horsepower
In this range, the marginal product of pipeline diameter does not decrease as the diameter increases, but this does not contradict the law of diminishing returns since the law states that the marginal product will decrease eventually, not in any particular range.

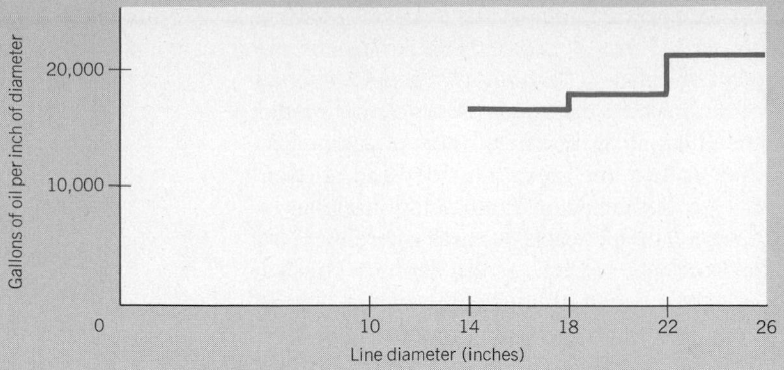

and more horsepower is used. Moreover, this is true for every pipe diameter, not just 18 inches.

Figure 22.3 shows the marginal product of pipeline diameter, given that the horsepower is 50,000. For example, when the diameter is between 14 and 18 inches, the marginal product is (165,000 − 100,000) ÷ (18 − 14)—or 16,250 gallons of oil (per day) per inch of pipeline diameter. This is so because in this range, an extra inch of diameter results in 16,250 extra gallons of oil carried per day. Similarly, the marginal product is 17,500 gallons when the diameter is between 18 and 22 inches, and 21,250 gallons when the diameter is between 22 and 26 inches. Thus the marginal product of pipeline diameter does not decrease as the diameter increases. However, this does not contradict the law of diminishing marginal returns because the law states only that the marginal product will decrease *eventually,* not that it will decrease in any particular range. In other words, the law says that, if diameter is increased more and more (and if horsepower is held constant at 50,000), *eventually* the marginal product of pipeline diameter will decrease.[1]

[1] Also, the inputs associated with line diameter may be gauged more appropriately by measures other than diameter. This too may influence the results.

The Optimal Input Decision

Now we are in a position to answer the question posed at the beginning of this chapter: Given that a firm is going to produce a particular quantity of output, what production technique—i.e., what combination of inputs—should it choose to maximize profits? Note first that if the firm maximizes its profits, it must minimize the cost of producing this quantity of output. This seems obvious enough. But what combination of inputs (that will produce the required quantity of output) will minimize the firm's costs? The answer can be stated like this: *the firm will minimize cost by combining inputs in such a way that the marginal product of a dollar's worth of any one input equals the marginal product of a dollar's worth of any other input used.*

Another way to say the same thing is: *the firm will minimize cost by combining inputs in such a way that, for every input used, the marginal product of the input is proportional to its price.* Why does this say the same thing? Because the marginal product of a dollar's worth of an input equals the marginal product of the input divided by its price. For example, if the marginal product of a man-year of labor is 40 units of output, and if the price of labor is $4,000 per man-year, the marginal product of a dollar's worth of labor is 40 ÷ 4,000 = .01 units of output. Thus, if the firm is satisfying the rule for cost minimization in the previous paragraph—that is, if it is combining inputs so that the marginal product of a dollar's worth of any one input equals the marginal product of a dollar's worth of any other input used—it must at the same time be combining inputs so that, for every input used, the marginal product of the input is proportional to its price.

To illustrate the application of this rule, let's take a numerical example from the wheat farm cited above. Suppose that the farm can vary the amount of labor and land it uses. Table 22.4 shows the marginal product of each input when various combinations of inputs (all combinations being able to produce the specified quantity of output) are used. Suppose that the price of labor is $4,000 per man-year and that the annual price of using land is $1,000 per acre. (We assume that the firm takes the prices of inputs as given and that it can buy all it wants of the inputs at these prices.) For each combination of inputs, Table 22.4 shows the marginal product of each input divided by its price. Based on our rule, the optimal input combination is 4.1 acres of land and 1 man-year of labor, since this is the only combination (capable of producing the required output) where the marginal product of labor divided by the price of labor equals the marginal product of land divided by the price of land. (See Table 22.4.)

Is this rule correct? Does it really result in a least-cost combination of inputs? Let's look at the cost of the various input combinations in Table 22.4. The first combination (0.5 man-years of labor and 7 acres of land) costs $9,000; the second combination (1.0 man-years of labor and 4.1 acres of land) costs $8,100; and so on. An examination of the total cost of each input combination shows that the input combination chosen by our rule—1.0 man-years of labor and 4.1 acres of land—is indeed the least-cost input combination, the one for the profit-maximizing firm to use.

A More General Proof

Of course, one example really does not prove that the rule results in minimum costs; it only demonstrates that it does so in this particular case. In this section, we prove that this rule generally is valid. To do so, we show that, if this rule is violated (and the firm combines inputs so that the marginal product of a dollar's worth of one input does *not* equal the marginal product of a dollar's worth of some other input used), the firm is not minimizing its costs. Specifically, we take the case of the wheat farm, and proceed in two steps: (1) We show that if the marginal product of a dollar's

Table 22.4
Determination of Optimal Input Combination

Amount of input used: Labor (man-years)	Amount of input used: Land (acres)	Marginal product: Labor	Marginal product: Land	Marginal product ÷ Price of input: Labor	Marginal product ÷ Price of input: Land	Total cost (dollars)
0.5	7.0	50	5	50 ÷ 4,000	5 ÷ 1,000	9,000
1.0	4.1	40	10	40 ÷ 4,000	10 ÷ 1,000	8,100
1.5	3.0	30	30	30 ÷ 4,000	30 ÷ 1,000	9,000
2.5	2.0	20	50	20 ÷ 4,000	50 ÷ 1,000	12,000

worth of labor is *greater* than the marginal product of a dollar's worth of land, the firm is not minimizing costs. (2) We show that if the marginal product of a dollar's worth of labor is *less* than the marginal product of a dollar's worth of land, the firm is not minimizing costs.

Suppose that *the marginal product of a dollar's worth of labor is greater than the marginal product of a dollar's worth of land.* Since the marginal product of a dollar's worth of labor is greater than the marginal product of a dollar's worth of land, it must follow that the wheat farm can increase its output, *without increasing its costs,* if it substitutes a dollar's worth of labor for a dollar's worth of land. For example, suppose that the marginal product of a dollar's worth of labor is 2 bushels of wheat, whereas the marginal product of a dollar's worth of land is 1 bushel of wheat. Then, if it substitutes a dollar's worth of labor for a dollar's worth of land, the wheat farm can increase its output by 1 bushel of wheat without increasing its costs. (Why? Because the addition of an extra dollar's worth of labor increases output by 2 bushels, while the subtraction of the dollar's worth of land reduces output by 1 bushel—and the net effect is an increase in output of 1 bushel.) Thus, since the firm can increase its output without increasing its costs, it must be able to reduce its costs, if it maintains the same output. In other words, it must not be minimizing its costs.

Suppose that *the marginal product of a dollar's worth of labor is less than the marginal product of a dollar's worth of land.* Since the marginal product of a dollar's worth of labor is less than the marginal product of a dollar's worth of land, it must follow that the wheat farm can increase its output, *without increasing its costs,* if it substitutes a dollar's worth of land for a dollar's worth of labor. For example, suppose that the marginal product of a dollar's worth of labor is 1 bushel of wheat, whereas the marginal product of a dollar's worth of land is 2 bushels of wheat. Then, if it substitutes a dollar's worth of land for a dollar's worth of labor, the wheat farm can increase its output by 1 bushel of wheat without increasing its costs. (Why? Because the addition of an extra dollar's worth of land increases output by 2 bushels, while the subtraction of a dollar's worth of labor reduces output by 1 bushel—and the net effect is an increase in output of 1 bushel.) Thus, since the firm can increase its output without increasing its costs, it must be able to reduce its costs, if it maintains the same output. In other words, it must not be minimizing its costs.

Since the firm is not minimizing the cost of producing its current output when the marginal product of a dollar's worth of labor is greater than, or less than, that of a dollar's worth of land, it must be true that *the firm is minimizing its costs only when the marginal product of a dollar's worth of labor equals that of a dollar's worth of land.* This, of course, is what we set out to prove.

Determining the Optimal Input Combination: A Case Study

If by now you wonder about the practical payoff from this sort of analysis, consider how a distinguished agricultural economist, Earl Heady of Iowa State University has used these methods to help farmers make better production decisions. Table 22.5 shows the various amounts of land and fertilizer that will produce 82.6 bushels of corn on Kansas Verdigras soil. As you can see, this amount of corn can be produced if 1.19 acres of land and no fertilizer are used, or if 1.11 acres of land and 20 pounds of fertilizer are used, or if .99 acres of land and 60 pounds of fertilizer are used, and so forth.

The third column of Table 22.5 shows the ratio of the marginal product of a pound of fertilizer to the marginal product of an acre of land, when each of these input combinations is used. For example, when 1.19 acres of land and no fertilizer are used, this ratio equals .0045.

Table 22.5
Combinations of Fertilizer and Land Required to Produce 82.6 Bushels of Corn, and Ratio of Marginal Products at Each Such Combination.

Amount of input used: Fertilizer (pounds)	Land (acres)	Marginal product of fertilizer ÷ Marginal product of land
0	1.19	.0045
20	1.11	.0038
40	1.04	.0030
60	0.99	.0019
80	0.96	.0010
100	0.95	.0003

Source: E. Heady and L. Tweeten, *Resource Demand and Structure of the Agricultural Industry,* Ames: Iowa State University Press, 1963, p. 111.

Based on the rule discussed in previous sections, a firm, if it minimizes costs, must set this ratio equal to the ratio of the price of a pound of fertilizer to the price of an acre of land. Why? Because the rule discussed above stipulates that the firm should choose an input combination so that

$$\frac{\text{marginal product of fertilizer}}{\text{price of fertilizer}} = \frac{\text{marginal product of land}}{\text{price of land}}$$

So if we multiply both sides of this equation by the price of fertilizer, and divide both sides by the marginal product of land, we get

$$\frac{\text{marginal product of fertilizer}}{\text{marginal product of land}} = \frac{\text{price of fertilizer}}{\text{price of land}}$$

Thus, to minimize costs, a firm should set the ratio in the third column of Table 22.5 equal to the ratio of the price of fertilizer to the price of land.

Heady and his coworkers, having obtained the results in Table 22.5, used this technique to determine the optimal input combination farmers should use to minimize their costs.[2] Of course, the optimal input combination depends on the price of land and the price of fertilizer. Suppose that a pound of fertilizer costs .003 times as much as an acre of land. Under these circumstances, the minimum-cost input combination would be 40 pounds of fertilizer and 1.04 acres of land—since, as shown in Table 22.5, this is the input combination where the ratio of the marginal product of fertilizer to the marginal product of land is .003. No matter what the ratio of the price of fertilizer to the price of land may be, the least-cost input combination can be derived this way.

Clearly, such results are of considerable practical value to farmers. Moreover, the same kind of analysis can be used by organizations in other sectors of the economy, not just agriculture. Studies of how the Defense Department could reduce its costs have utilized concepts and techniques of essentially this sort. In a more peaceful vein, this same kind of analysis has been used in various kinds of manufacturing firms. For example, steel firms have made many such studies to determine least-cost ways to produce steel, and auto firms have made similar studies to reduce their own costs.

What Are Costs?

Previous sections have discussed how we can determine the input combination that minimizes costs. But what do we mean by costs? Although this question may seem foolishly simple, it is in fact tricky. *Fundamentally, the **cost** of a certain course of action is the value of the best alternative course of action that could have been adopted instead.* For example, the

[2] E. Heady and L. Tweeten, *Resource Demand and Structure of the Agricultural Industry,* Ames: Iowa State University Press, 1963. It is assumed that a certain amount of labor is used, this amount being proportional to the number of acres of land.

cost of producing automobiles is the value of the goods and services that could be obtained elsewhere from the manpower, equipment, and materials used currently in automobile production. The costs of inputs to a firm are their values in their most valuable alternative uses. As we pointed out in Chapter 1, this is the so-called ***alternative cost,*** or ***opportunity cost*** doctrine.

Suppose that a firm's owner devotes 50 hours a week to the firm's business, and that, because he is the owner, he pays himself no salary. According to the usual rules of accounting, as we saw in Chapter 7, the costs of his labor are not included in the profit and loss statement. But according to the economist's alternative cost doctrine, the cost of his labor is by no means zero! Instead, this cost equals whatever amount he could obtain if he worked 50 hours a week for someone else. Both economists and sophisticated accountants agree that alternative costs are the relevant costs for many types of problems, and that failure to use the proper concept of cost can result in serious mistakes.

Costs for the individual firm are the necessary payments to the owners of resources to get them to provide these resources to the firm. To obtain these resources as inputs, the firm must bid them away from alternative uses. The payments made to the owners of these resources may be either explicit or implicit costs. If a payment is made to a supplier, laborer, or some other resource owner besides the firm's owner, this is an explicit cost, which is paid for in an explicit way. But if a resource is owned by the firm's owner, there may be no explicit payment for it, as in the case of the labor of the owner who paid himself no salary. The costs of such owner-supplied resources are called ***implicit costs.*** As we stressed above, such implicit costs equal what these resources could bring if they were used in their most valuable alternative employments. And the firm's profits (or losses), as defined by the economist, are the difference between the firm's revenues and its total costs, both explicit and implicit.

It should also be noted that the ***social costs*** of producing a given commodity do not always equal the ***private costs.*** That is, *the costs to society do not always equal the costs to the individual producer.* When a chemical plant discharges waste products into a nearby river the cost to the plant of disposing of the wastes is simply the amount paid to pump them to the river. However, if the river becomes polluted and its recreational uses are destroyed and the water becomes unfit for drinking, additional costs are incurred by other people. Differences of this sort between social and private costs may call for remedial government action, as we have seen in Chapter 5.

Short-Run Cost Functions

Total Costs in the Short Run

In previous sections, we showed how to determine the least-cost combination of inputs to produce any quantity of output. With this information at our disposal, it is easy to determine the minimum cost of producing each quantity of output. Knowing the (minimum) cost of producing each quantity of output, we can define and measure the firm's ***cost functions,*** which show how various types of costs are related to the firm's output. A firm's cost functions will vary, depending on whether they are based on the short or long run. In the short run, the firm cannot vary the quantities of plant and equipment it uses. These are the firm's fixed inputs, and they determine the scale of its operations.

Three kinds of costs are important in the short run: total fixed cost, total variable cost, and total cost. ***Total fixed cost*** is the total expenditure per period of time by the firm for fixed inputs. Since the quantity of the fixed inputs is unvarying (by definition), the total fixed cost will be the same whatever the firm's

Table 22.6
Fixed, Variable, and Total Costs, Bugsbane Music Box Company

Number of music boxes produced per day	Total fixed cost	Total variable cost (dollars)	Total cost
0	1,000	0	1,000
1	1,000	40	1,040
2	1,000	70	1,070
3	1,000	105	1,105
4	1,000	145	1,145
5	1,000	190	1,190
6	1,000	240	1,240
7	1,000	300	1,300
8	1,000	400	1,400
9	1,000	720	1,720

level of output. Among the firm's fixed costs in the short run are property taxes and interest on bonds issued in the past. To inject a whimsical note into a subject not otherwise noted for its amusement value, consider a hypothetical firm: the Bugsbane Music Box Company. This firm produces a high-priced line of music boxes that, when opened, play your favorite aria, show tune, or hymn, and emit a deadly gas that kills all insects, rodents, or pests—and alas, occasionally a frail Chihuahua—within a 50-foot radius. Table 22.6 shows that Bugsbane's fixed costs are $1,000 per day; the firm's total fixed cost function is shown in Figure 22.4.

Total variable cost is the firm's total expenditure on variable inputs per period of time. Since higher output rates require greater utilization of variable inputs, they mean a higher total variable cost. Thus, if Bugsbane increases its daily production of music boxes, it must increase the amount it spends per day on metal (for the components), wood (for the outside of the boxes), labor (for the assembly of the boxes), and other variable inputs. Table 22.6 shows Bugsbane's total variable costs at various output rates; Figure 22.5 shows the

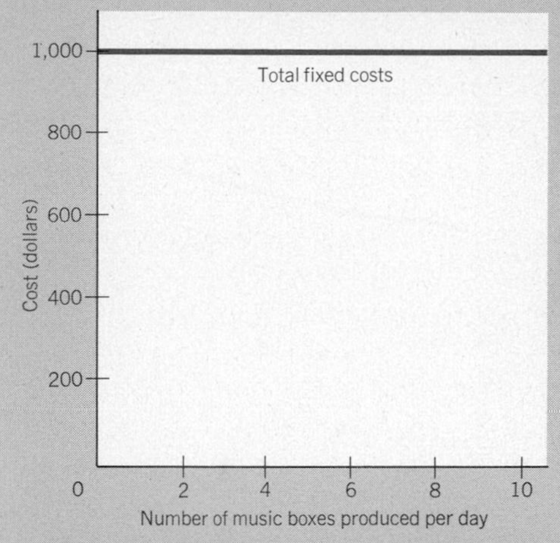

Figure 22.4
Total Fixed Costs, Bugsbane Music Box Company
The total fixed cost function is always a horizontal line, since fixed costs do not vary with output.

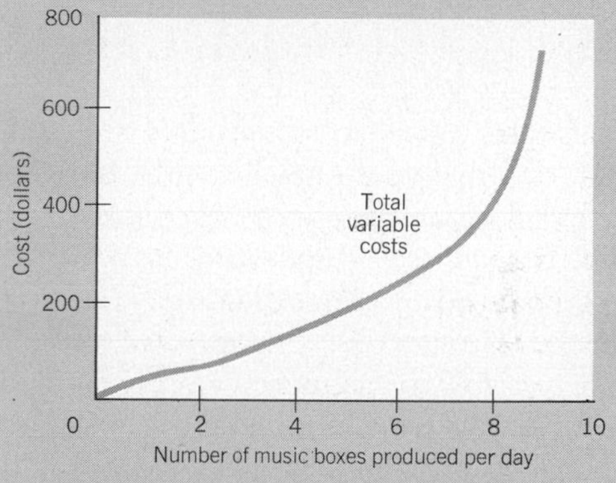

Figure 22.5
Total Variable Costs, Bugsbane Music Box Company
Total variable cost is the total expenditure per period of time on variable inputs. Due to the law of diminishing marginal returns, total variable cost increases first at a decreasing rate, then at an increasing rate.

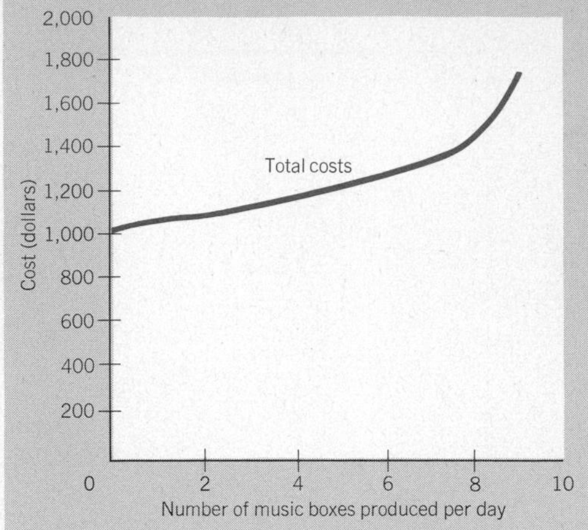

Figure 22.6
Total Costs, Bugsbane Music Box Company
Total cost is the sum of total fixed cost and total variable cost. It has the same shape as the total variable cost curve, since they differ by only a constant amount (equal to total fixed cost).

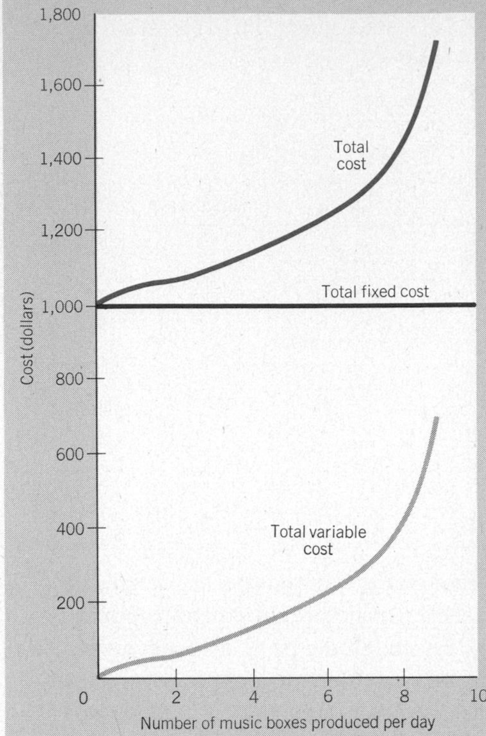

Figure 22.7
Fixed, Variable, and Total Costs, Bugsbane Music Box Company
All three cost functions, presented in Figures 22.4–22.6, are brought back for a curtain call.

firm's total variable cost function.

Up to the output rate of 2 music boxes per day, total variable cost increases at a decreasing rate; beyond that output rate, total variable cost increases at an increasing rate. It is important to understand that this characteristic of the total variable cost function results from the operation of the law of diminishing marginal returns. At small output rates, increases in the utilization of variable inputs may bring about increases in their productivity, causing total variable cost to increase with output, but at a decreasing rate. Beyond a point, however, there are diminishing marginal returns from the variable input, with the result that total variable costs increase at an increasing rate.

Total cost is the sum of total fixed cost and total variable cost. Thus, to obtain the Bugsbane Company's total cost at a given output, we need only add its total fixed cost and its total variable cost at that output. The result is shown in Table 22.6, and the corresponding total cost function is shown in Figure 22.6. Since the total cost function and the total variable cost function differ by only a constant amount (equal to total fixed cost), they have the same shape, as shown in Figure 22.7, which brings together all three of the total cost functions (or curves as they are often called).

Table 22.7
Average Fixed Cost, Average Variable Cost, and Average Total Cost, Bugsbane Music Box Company

Number of music boxes produced per day	Average fixed cost (dollars)	Average variable cost (dollars)	Average total cost (dollars)
1	1,000 (= 1000 ÷ 1)	40 (= 40 ÷ 1)	1,040 (= 1040 ÷ 1)
2	500 (= 1000 ÷ 2)	35 (= 70 ÷ 2)	535 (= 1070 ÷ 2)
3	333 (= 1000 ÷ 3)	35 (= 105 ÷ 3)	368 (= 1105 ÷ 3)
4	250 (= 1000 ÷ 4)	36 (= 145 ÷ 4)	286 (= 1145 ÷ 4)
5	200 (= 1000 ÷ 5)	38 (= 190 ÷ 5)	238 (= 1190 ÷ 5)
6	167 (= 1000 ÷ 6)	40 (= 240 ÷ 6)	207 (= 1240 ÷ 6)
7	143 (= 1000 ÷ 7)	43 (= 300 ÷ 7)	186 (= 1300 ÷ 7)
8	125 (= 1000 ÷ 8)	50 (= 400 ÷ 8)	175 (= 1400 ÷ 8)
9	111 (= 1000 ÷ 9)	80 (= 720 ÷ 9)	191 (= 1720 ÷ 9)

Average Costs in the Short Run

The president of Bugsbane unquestionably cares about the average cost of a music box as well as the total cost incurred; so do economists. Average cost tells you how much a product costs per unit of output. There are three average cost functions, one corresponding to each of the three total cost functions. Let's begin with ***average fixed cost,*** which is simply the total fixed cost divided by the firm's output. Table 22.7 and Figure 22.8 show the average fixed cost function for the Bugsbane Music Box Company. Clearly, average fixed cost must decline with increases in output, since it equals a constant—total fixed cost—divided by the output rate.

The next type of average cost is ***average variable cost,*** which is total variable cost divided by output. For Bugsbane, the average variable cost function is shown in Table 22.7 and Figure 22.9. At first, increases in the output rate result in decreases in average variable cost, but beyond a point, they result in higher average variable cost. This is because the law of diminishing marginal returns is in operation. As more and more of the variable inputs

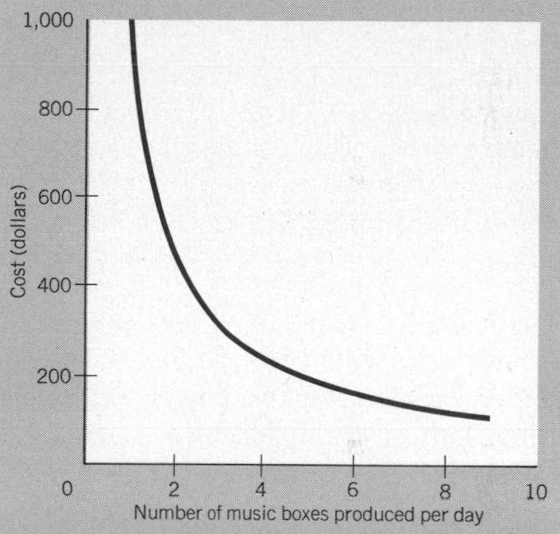

Figure 22.8
Average Fixed Costs, Bugsbane Music Box Company
Average fixed cost is total fixed cost divided by the firm's output. Since it equals a constant (total fixed cost) divided by the output rate, it must decline with increases in output.

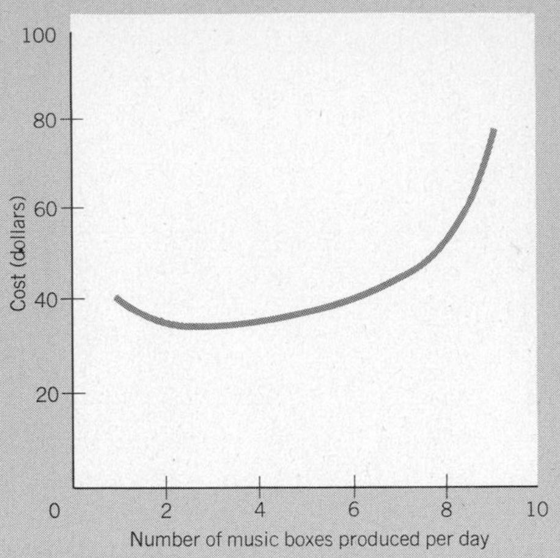

Figure 22.9
Average Variable Costs, Bugsbane Music Box Company
Average variable cost is total variable cost divided by the firm's output. Beyond a point, it increases as output increases because of the law of diminishing marginal returns.

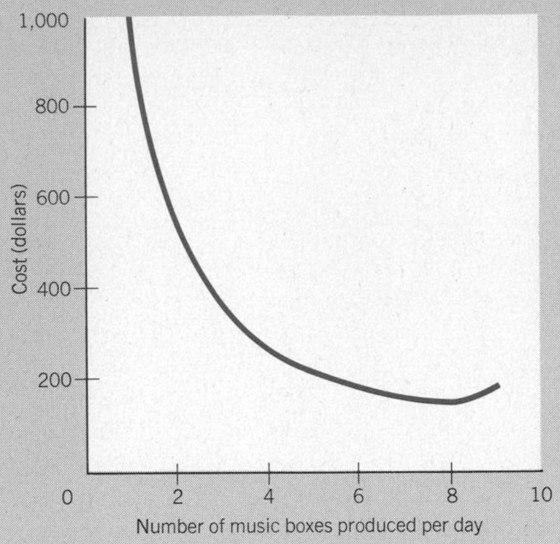

Figure 22.10
Average Total Costs, Bugsbane Music Box Company
Average total cost is total cost divided by output. It equals average fixed cost plus average variable cost; and beyond a point, it increases as output increases because of the law of diminishing marginal returns.

are utilized, the extra output they produce declines beyond some point, so that the amount spent on variable input per unit of output tends to increase.

The third type of average cost is ***average total cost,*** which is total cost divided by output. For Bugsbane, the average total cost function is shown in Table 22.7 and Figure 22.10. At any level of output, average total cost equals average fixed cost plus average variable cost. This is easy to prove:

$$\text{average total cost} = \frac{\text{total cost}}{\text{output}}$$

$$= \frac{\text{total fixed cost} + \text{total variable cost}}{\text{output}},$$

since total cost = total fixed cost + total variable cost. Moreover,

$$\frac{\text{total fixed cost} + \text{total variable cost}}{\text{output}}$$

$$= \frac{\text{total fixed cost}}{\text{output}} + \frac{\text{total variable cost}}{\text{output}}$$

and the righthand side of this equation equals average fixed cost plus average variable cost. Thus we have proved what we set out to prove.

The fact that average total cost is the sum of average fixed cost and average variable cost helps explain the shape of the average cost function. If, as the output rate goes up, both average fixed cost and average variable cost decrease, average total cost must decrease too. But beyond some point, average total cost must increase because increases in average variable cost eventually more than offset decreases in average fixed cost. However, average total cost achieves its minimum after average variable cost, because the increases in average variable cost are for a time more than offset by decreases in average fixed cost. All the average cost functions are shown below in Figure 22.12.

Marginal Cost in the Short Run

No one can really be said to understand the operations of a business firm without understanding the concept of ***marginal cost,*** the addition to total cost resulting from the addition of the last unit of output. To see how marginal cost is calculated, look at Table 22.8, which shows the total cost function of the Bugsbane Music Box Company. When output is between 0 and 1 music box per day, the firm's marginal cost is $40, since this is the *extra cost* of producing the first music box per day. In other words, $40 equals marginal cost in this situation because it is the difference between the total cost of producing 1 music box per day ($1,040) and the total cost of producing 0 music boxes per day ($1,000).

Table 22.8
Calculation of Marginal Cost, Bugsbane Music Box Company

Number of music boxes produced per day	Total cost (dollars)	Marginal cost[a] (dollars)
1	1,040	40 (= 1040 − 1000)
2	1,070	30 (= 1070 − 1040)
3	1,105	35 (= 1105 − 1070)
4	1,145	40 (= 1145 − 1105)
5	1,190	45 (= 1190 − 1145)
6	1,240	50 (= 1240 − 1190)
7	1,300	60 (= 1300 − 1240)
8	1,400	100 (= 1400 − 1300)
9	1,720	320 (= 1720 − 1400)

[a] These figures pertain to the interval between the indicated output rate and one unit less than the indicated output rate.

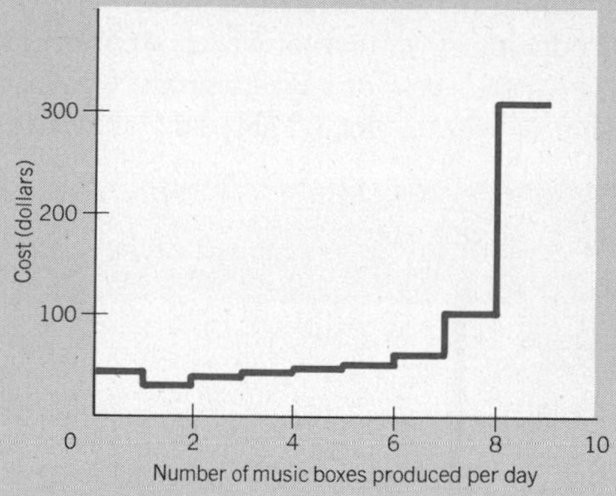

Figure 22.11
Marginal Costs, Bugsbane Music Box Company
Marginal cost is the addition to total cost resulting from the addition of the last unit of output. Beyond a point, it increases as output increases because of the law of diminishing marginal returns.

In general, marginal cost will vary depending on the firm's output level. Thus Table 22.8 shows that at Bugsbane marginal cost is $30 when the firm produces between 1 and 2 music boxes per day, $50 when the firm produces between 5 and 6 music boxes per day, and $320 when the firm produces between 8 and 9 music boxes per day. Table 22.8—and Figure 22.11, which shows the marginal cost function graphically—indicate that marginal cost, after decreasing with increases in output at low output levels, increases with further increases in output. In other words, beyond some point it becomes more and more costly for the firm to produce yet another unit of output.

The reason why marginal cost increases beyond some output level is to be found in the law of diminishing marginal returns. Clearly, if (beyond some point) increases in variable inputs result in less and less extra output, it follows that a larger and larger quantity of variable inputs must be added to produce an extra unit of output. For example, return for a moment to the wheat farm in Table 22.1. If it is producing 70 bushels of wheat, it requires an extra $1/30$ man-year of labor to produce an extra bushel of wheat—since Table 22.1 shows that the marginal product of a man-year of labor is 30 bushels of wheat if the farm's output is 70 bushels of wheat. But if it is producing 100 bushels of wheat, an extra $1/25$ man-year of labor is needed to produce an extra bushel of wheat, since Table 22.1 shows that the marginal product of a man-year of labor is 25 bushels of wheat if the farm's output is 100 bushels of wheat. *Since more and more of the variable input is required to produce an extra unit of output, the cost of producing an extra unit of output increases as output rises.*

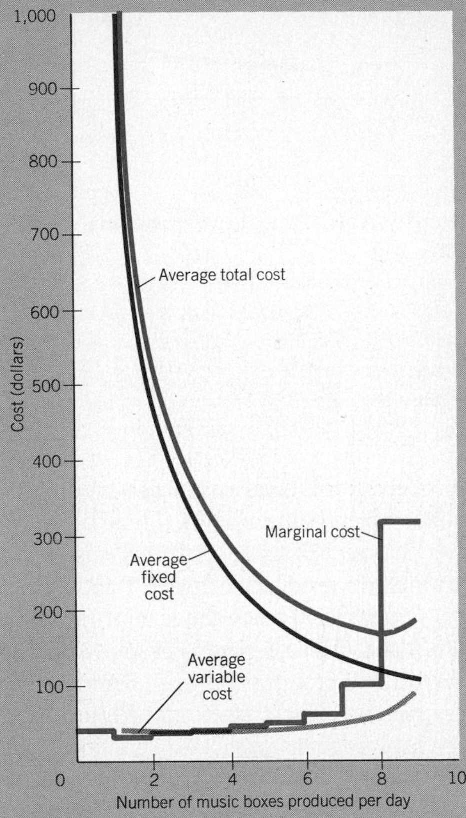

Figure 22.12
Average Fixed Costs, Average Variable Costs, Average Total Costs, and Marginal Costs, Bugsbane Music Box Company
All the curves presented in Figures 22.8–22.11 are brought together for review. Note that the marginal cost curve intersects both the average variable cost curve and the average total cost curve at their minimum points.

In addition, the relationship between the marginal cost function and the average cost functions must be noted. Figure 22.12 shows the marginal cost curve together with the three average cost curves. *The marginal cost curve intersects both the average variable cost curve and the average total cost curve at their minimum points.* The reason for this is simple. If the extra cost of a unit of output is greater (less) than the average cost of the units of output already produced, the addition of the extra unit of output clearly must raise (lower) the average cost of production. Thus, if marginal cost is greater (less) than average cost, average cost must be rising (falling). And if this is so, average cost can be a minimum only when it equals marginal cost. (The same reasoning holds for both average total cost and average variable cost, and for the short and long runs.)

To make sure that you understand this point, consider the following numerical example. Suppose that the average total cost of producing 4 units of output is \$10, and that the marginal cost of the fifth unit of output is less than \$10. Will the average total cost be less for 5 units of output than for 4 units? Clearly, it will be less, because the fifth unit's cost will pull down the average. On the other hand, if the marginal cost of the fifth unit of output had been greater than \$10, the average total cost for 5 units of output would have been greater than for 4 units of output, because the fifth unit's cost would pull up the average. Thus, average total cost will fall when it is above marginal cost, and it will rise when it is below marginal cost. Consequently, when it is a minimum, average total cost must equal marginal cost, as shown in Figure 22.12.

Finally, note the analogy between marginal cost and marginal utility, which we discussed in Chapter 20. Recall that marginal utility is the extra utility resulting from the consumption of an additional unit of a commodity. Substitute "cost" for "utility" and "production" for "consumption" in the previous sentence, and you get a perfectly valid definition of marginal cost. Economics is chock-full of marginal "thises" and marginal "thats," and you should be aware of their general family traits by now.

Short-Run Cost Functions of a Crude Oil Pipeline: A Case Study

Cost functions are not academic toys, but eminently practical analytical devices that play a major role in decision making by business executives and government agencies. To illustrate the nature and use of short-run cost functions, we will take up the real-world case of crude oil pipelines where we left off (earlier in this chapter). In the short run, it is reasonable to assume that the diameter of a pipeline is fixed. Given the production function in Table 22.3, it is easy to figure out the total cost of carrying various amounts of oil per day, with a pipeline of given diameter. In other words, we assume that the company that owns the pipeline can vary the horsepower by varying the number and type of pumping stations, but that the diameter of the pipeline is fixed.[3] Under these circumstances, if the diameter of the pipeline is 18 inches, what will the pipeline's cost functions look like?

Figures 22.13 and 22.14 answer this ques-

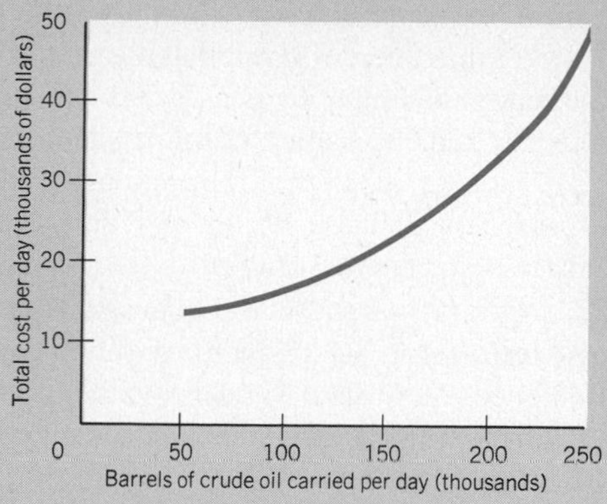

Figure 22.13
Total Cost Function, Crude Oil Pipeline, 18-Inch Diameter
This graph shows the total cost function in an actual case. Note that it is shaped as economic theory would predict.

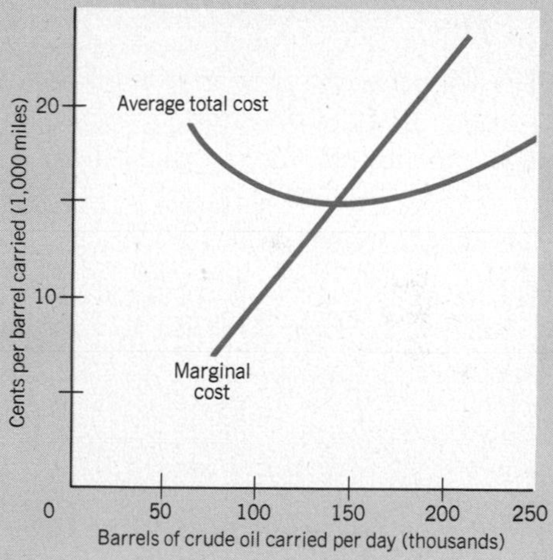

Figure 22.14
Average Total Cost Function and Marginal Cost Function, Crude Oil Pipeline, 18-Inch Diameter
This graph shows the average cost and marginal cost functions in an actual case. Note that their shape follows economic theory.

[3] Because the number and type of pumping stations must be altered, Leslie Cookenboo refers to this as the "intermediate run." See Cookenboo, *Crude Oil Pipe Lines and Competition in the Oil Industry,* Cambridge, Mass.: Harvard University Press, 1955.

tion. Figure 22.13 shows the ***total cost function*** for an 18-inch pipeline: the total daily cost of operating it, given that it carries various amounts of crude oil per day. If the pipeline carries 200,000 barrels of oil per day, the total daily cost is $33,000; if the amount of oil is increased to 250,000 barrels per day, the total daily cost rises to $48,000.

Figure 22.14 shows the ***average total cost function*** for an 18-inch pipeline: the total daily cost per barrel for the pipeline, given that it carries various amounts of crude oil per day. For example, according to Figure 22.14, the total daily cost per barrel for this pipeline to carry 200,000 barrels per day is $.16½, and the total daily cost per barrel for it to carry 250,000 barrels per day is $.19⅕. Figure 22.14 also shows the ***marginal cost function*** for such a pipeline: the additional daily cost of carrying an extra barrel of crude oil per day. For example, when this pipeline is carrying 200,000 barrels per day, the marginal cost runs to about $.23.

To the operators of the pipeline, a knowledge of these cost functions can mean the difference between profit and loss. For example, suppose that the operators of a particular 18-inch pipeline are thinking about increasing the amount of oil the pipeline will carry per day. Specifically, suppose that the pipeline can now carry 200,000 barrels per day and that the operators are thinking about adding enough horsepower so that it can carry 250,000 barrels per day. Suppose that according to the best estimates available, the pipeline can get $5 million in additional revenue each year if it carries the additional 50,000 barrels per day. Should the operators increase in this way the amount of oil the pipeline can carry?

If they want to increase profits, they should decide against this increase in the amount of horsepower. According to the total cost function in Figure 22.13, the pipeline's daily costs would increase by $15,000 per day if horsepower were increased so that 250,000, rather than 200,000, barrels of oil could be carried per day, while the extra oil carried would increase daily revenues by $5 million ÷ 365, or about $14,000 per day. Thus the extra costs would exceed the extra revenue, which means that the pipeline's profit would be reduced by increasing the amount of horsepower. Clearly, in making decisions of this sort (and they must make them repeatedly!), managers must rely heavily on information about the relevant cost functions.

Figure 22.15
Short-Run Average Cost Curves and Long-Run Average Cost Curve
The short-run average total cost functions for three plants—small, medium, and large—are *AA′*, *BB′*, and *DD′*. The long-run average cost function is *AUVD′*, if these are the only three types of plant that can be built.

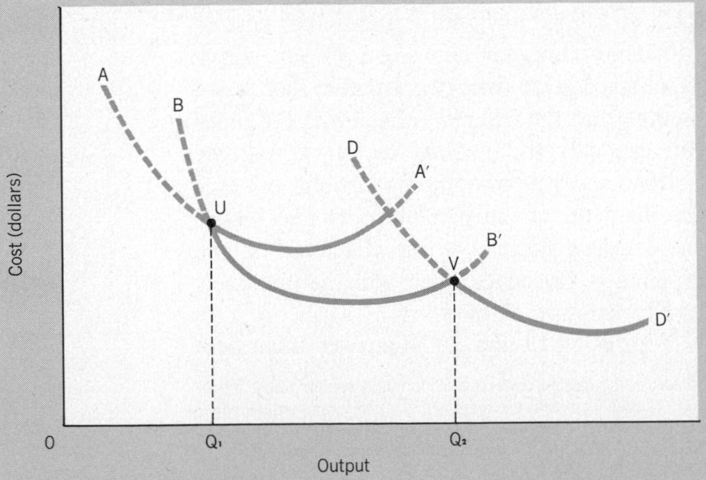

Long-Run Cost Functions

The Long-Run Average Cost Function

We have held to last one additional kind of cost function that plays a very important role in economic analysis. This is the firm's ***long-run average cost function,*** which shows the minimum average cost of producing each output level *when any desired type or scale of plant can be built.* Unlike the cost functions discussed in the previous three sections, this cost function pertains to the long run—to a period long enough that all inputs are variable and none is fixed. A useful way to look at the long run is to consider it a *planning horizon:* the firm must continually be planning ahead and trying to decide its strategy in the long run.

For example, a firm may be able to build plants of three sizes: small, medium, and large. The short-run average total cost functions corresponding to these plants are AA', BB', and DD' in Figure 22.15. If the firm is still in the planning stage of plant construction it can choose whichever plant has the lowest costs. Consequently, the firm will choose the small plant if it believes its output rate will be smaller than OQ_1, the medium plant if it believes its output rate will be above OQ_1, but below OQ_2, and the large plant if it believes that its output rate will be above OQ_2. Thus the long-run average cost curve is $AUVD'$. And if, as is generally the case, there are many possible types of plants, the long-run average cost curve looks like LL' in Figure 22.16. (Only a few of the short-run average cost curves are shown in Figure 22.16.)

The usefulness of the long-run average cost function can be illustrated by the familiar case of crude oil pipelines. Figure 22.17 shows the long-run average cost function for these pipelines, as well as selected short-run average cost functions (corresponding to diameters of 8, 10, 12, 14, 16, 18, 20, 24, 26, 30, and 32 inches). Note that long-run average cost—that is, cost per barrel—decreases as more and more oil is carried per day, at least up to 400,000 barrels per day. Thus it appears that costs are reduced when the greatest possible quantities of oil are transported in large-diameter pipelines. This fact is important in evaluating the effects of various kinds of market structure in the pipeline industry. If long-run average costs decrease with increases in output up to an output representing all, or nearly all, of the market, it

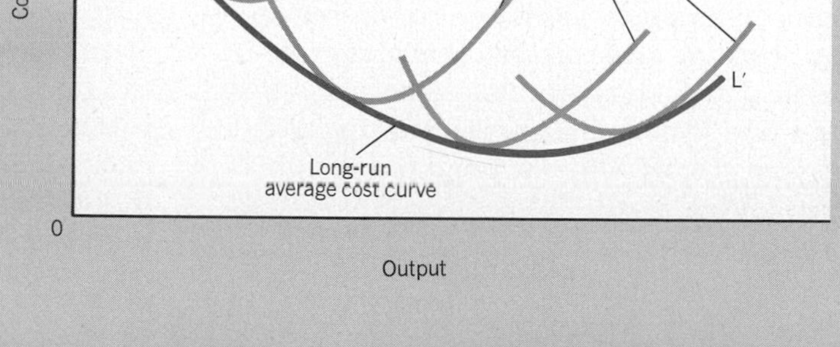

Figure 22.16
Long-Run Average Cost Curve
If many possible types of plants can be built, the long-run average cost function is LL'.

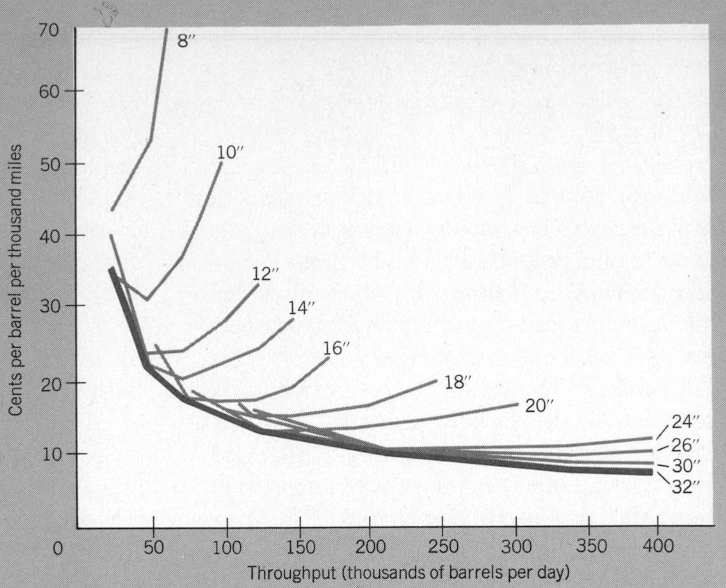

Figure 22.17
Costs per Barrel of Operating Crude Oil Trunk Pipelines
This graph shows the long-run average cost curve (and the revelant short-run average cost curves) in an actual case. Note that in this range at least, long-run average cost decreases as output increases.

is wasteful to force competition in such an industry, since costs would be greater if the industry output were divided among a number of firms than if it were produced by only one or two firms. More will be said on this score in Chapter 24.

Returns to Scale

What determines the shape of the long-run average cost function in a particular industry? Obviously, its shape must depend upon the characteristics of the production function—specifically, upon whether there are increasing, decreasing, or constant returns to scale. To understand what these terms mean, consider a long-run situation and suppose that the firm increases the amount of all inputs by the same proportion. What will happen to output? If output increases by a larger proportion than each of the inputs, this is a case of ***increasing returns to scale.*** If output increases by a smaller proportion than each of the inputs, this is a case of ***decreasing returns to scale.*** If output increases by the same proportion as each of the inputs, this is a case of ***constant returns to scale.***

There are many reasons why increasing returns to scale may exist in a particular industry. For example, one large plant may be more efficient than two smaller plants of the same total capacity because it is big enough to use certain techniques that the smaller plants cannot use. Moreover, increasing returns can result from certain geometric relations. For example, since friction is related to the surface area of a pipeline, whereas the amount a pipeline can carry is related to its volume, there are increasing returns to scale in pipelines. Also, greater specialization can result in increasing returns to scale. For example, as more machines and men are used to perform a certain activity, it is possible to subdivide tasks and allow various inputs to specialize.

On the other hand, there also are reasons why decreasing returns to scale may occur. As a firm gets bigger and bigger, one would expect that the problems of coordinating activities and conveying information promptly and accurately would multiply, and that decreasing returns to scale would eventually set in. There is also the possibility of constant returns to scale, although it may not occur as frequently as many economic theorists would like. In constructing economic models, theorists often find it convenient to assume constant returns to scale, but it is by no means clear that this assumption is justifiable in many situations where it is made.

Whether there are increasing, decreasing, or constant returns to scale in a particular situation must be settled case by case. Moreover, the answer is likely to depend on the particular range of output considered. For example, there frequently are increasing returns to scale up to some level of output, then perhaps constant returns to scale up to a higher level of output, beyond which there may be decreasing returns to scale. This pattern is responsible for the *U*-shaped long-run average cost function in Figure 22.16.

As we shall see in the following section, this *U*-shaped pattern is not found in all industries. Within the range covered by the available data, there is little or no evidence in many industries that long-run average cost increases as output rises. But this may be because the data do not cover a wide enough range. Eventually, one would expect long-run average cost to rise because of problems of coordination, increased red tape, and reduced flexibility. Firms as large as General Motors or U.S. Steel are continually bedeviled by the very real difficulties of enormous size.

Measurement of Cost Functions and Break-Even Charts

Countless studies have been made to estimate cost functions in particular firms and industries. Many of these have been based on the relationship over time between cost and output. For example, Figure 22.18 shows the total costs of a hypothetical firm in various years plotted against the firm's output in these years. Based on the data, a reasonable approximation to the firm's total cost function might be *CC′*.

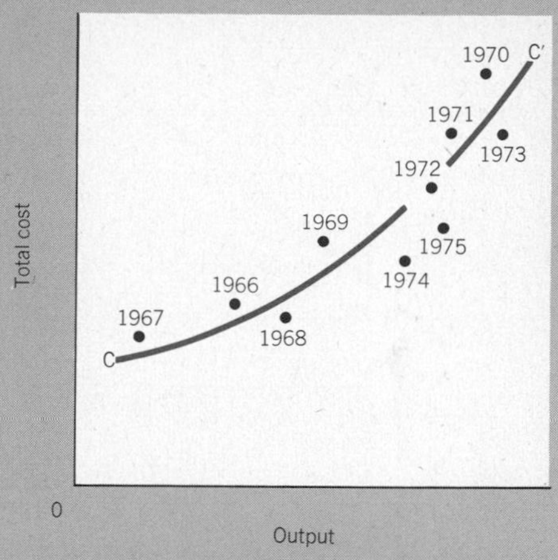

Figure 22.18
Relationship between Total Cost and Output: Time Series for a Particular Firm
One very crude way to estimate the total cost curve is to plot total cost in each year against total output in that year, and draw a curve, like *CC′*, that fits the points reasonably well. However, this technique is generally too crude to be reliable.

However, there are a number of difficulties in this simple procedure. For one thing, the firm's cost function may not have remained fixed throughout this period. For another, accounting data on costs may not be as accurate as one would like.[4] For these and other reasons, economists and statisticians have devised more sophisticated techniques to estimate cost functions.

To illustrate the sorts of results that have been obtained, Figure 22.19 shows the total cost function, average total cost function, and marginal cost function for a leather belt shop. Note that the total cost function appears linear, that is, a straight line, in the relevant range.

[4] Some of the difficulties are that the depreciation of an asset is often determined by the tax laws rather than economic criteria, many inputs are valued at historical, rather than alternative, cost, and accountants sometimes use arbitrary allocations of overhead and joint costs.

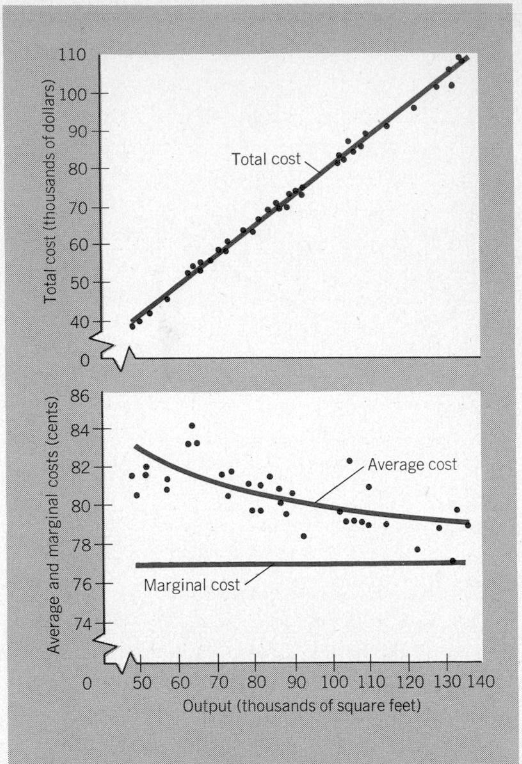

Figure 22.19
Total, Average, and Marginal Cost Functions of a Leather Belt Shop
This graph shows the short-run total, average, and marginal cost curves in an actual case. Note that marginal cost is constant in this case.

These results were obtained over 30 years ago by one of the pioneers in this field, Joel Dean of Columbia University.[5] Since that time, a great deal of evidence has been amassed on the shape of the cost functions of individual firms and industries. Two findings are particularly worth noting. First, within the range of observed data, the long-run average cost curve in many industries seems to be *L*-shaped (as in Figure 22.20), not *U*-shaped (as in Figure 22.16). That is, there is no evidence that it turns upward, rather than remains horizontal, at high output levels. Second, many empirical studies indicate that marginal cost in the short run tends to be constant in the relevant output range. However, this really does not contradict our assertions in previous sections, because the data used in these studies often do not cover periods when the firm was operating at peak capacity.

Estimated cost functions are used in a variety of ways by firms and government agencies. One important practical application of cost functions is to so-called ***break-even charts.*** To construct a break-even chart, the firm's total revenue must be plotted on the same chart with its total cost function. It is generally assumed that the price the firm receives for its product will not be influenced by the amount it sells, so that total revenue is proportional to output. Thus the total revenue curve is a straight line through the origin. Also, it is generally assumed that the firm's average variable cost—and marginal cost—are constant *in the*

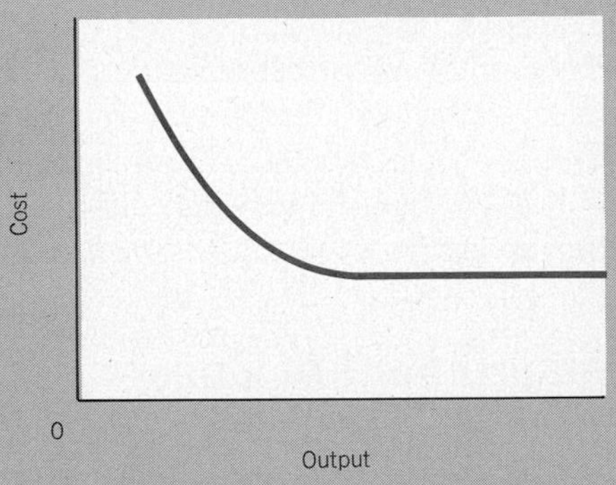

Figure 22.20
Apparent Shape of Many Long-Run Average Cost Curves
Within the range of observed data, there is no evidence in many industries that the long-run average cost curve turns upward, rather than remains horizontal, at high output levels.

[5] Joel Dean, *The Relation of Cost to Output for a Leather Belt Shop,* New York: National Bureau of Economic Research, 1941.

relevant output range, meaning that the firm's total cost function is also assumed to be a straight line.

Panel A of Figure 22.21 shows the break-even chart for an actual cable manufacturing firm.[6] The sales price of each unit of its output was $200. The firm's fixed costs were $50,000 per month and its average variable cost per unit of output was $20. The break-even chart shows the monthly profit or loss that will result from each sales level. For example, panel A (Figure 22.21) shows that the firm would have lost $14,000 per month if it had sold 200 units per month. On the other hand, it would have made a profit of $22,000 per month if it had sold 400 units per month. The chart also shows the ***break-even point,*** the output level that must be reached if the firm is to avoid losses. In panel A, the break-even point is 278 units of output per month.

Break-even charts are used very extensively by firms and other groups to estimate the effect of the sales rate on costs, receipts, and profits. A firm may use a break-even chart to determine the effect on profits of a projected increase in sales, or how many units of a particular product it must sell in order to break even. For instance, the cable manufacturing firm wanted to find out, among other things, how its break-even point would be affected if it installed new equipment that would increase its fixed costs to $60,000 per month and reduce its average variable cost to $10. Panel B of Figure 22.21 shows that under these circumstances the firm's break-even point would be 316, rather than 278, units of output per month. This information is, of course, of considerable value to the firm. It means that, if the firm installs the new equipment, it must sell at least 316 units of output per month to stay in the black.

[6] See Charles Stokes, *Managerial Economics: A Case Book,* New York: Random House, 1969. However, I have changed the numbers to make them easy to work with.

Summary

If a firm is going to produce a certain output, what combination of inputs should it choose to maximize its profits? As a first step toward answering this question, we describe the law of diminishing marginal returns, which states that, if equal increments of an input are added, the quantities of other inputs held constant, the resulting increments of product will decrease beyond some point; that is, the marginal prod-

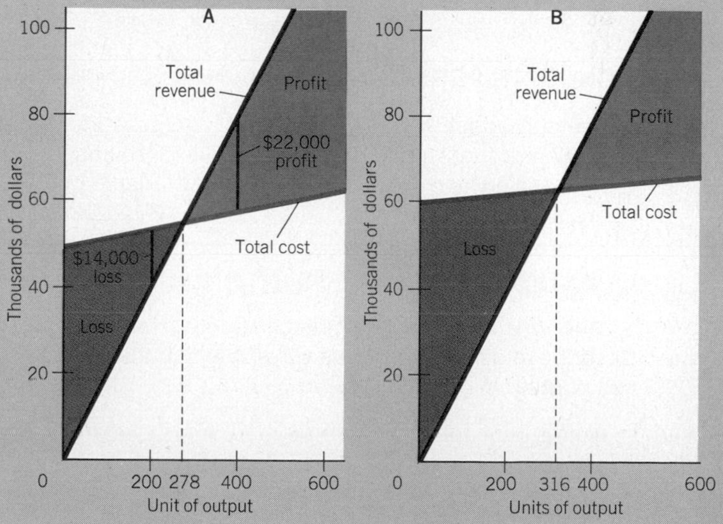

Figure 22.21
Break-Even Chart, Cable Manufacturing Firm
In panels A and B, the sales price of each unit of output is $200. In panel A, the firm's fixed costs are $50,000 per month, and its average variable cost per unit of output is $20. In panel B, the firm's fixed costs are $60,000 per month, and its average variable cost per unit of output is $10. In panel A, the firm's break-even point is 278 units of output per month, whereas in panel B it is 316 units of output per month.

uct of the input will diminish. The marginal product of an input is the addition to total output due to the addition of the last unit of the input, the amount of other inputs used being held constant. Also, it is useful to define an input's average product, which is the firm's total output divided by the amount of the input used to produce this amount of output.

To minimize its costs (and maximize its profits) a firm must choose its input combination so that the marginal product of a dollar's worth of any one input equals the marginal product of a dollar's worth of any other input used. Put differently, the firm should combine inputs so that, for every input used, the marginal product of the input is proportional to its price. As an illustration, we showed how this sort of model can be used to determine the optimal combination of fertilizer and land in the production of Kansas corn.

The cost of a certain course of action is the value of the best alternative course of action that could have been pursued instead. This is the doctrine of alternative, or opportunity, cost. Three kinds of total cost functions are important in the short run—total fixed cost, total variable cost, and total cost. In addition, there are three kinds of average cost functions (corresponding to each of the total cost functions)—average fixed cost, average variable cost, and average total cost. Also, marginal cost—the addition to total cost due to the addition of the last unit of output—is of enormous significance. Because of the law of diminishing marginal returns, marginal cost tends to increase beyond some output level. The firm's long-run average cost curve shows the minimum average cost of producing each output level when any desired type or scale of plant can be built. The shape of the long-run average cost curve is determined by whether there are increasing, decreasing, or constant returns to scale.

Cost functions play a very important practical role in economics and management. There have been countless studies to estimate cost functions in particular firms and industries. We have illustrated the sorts of results that have been obtained: for example, we have presented actual cost functions for a crude oil pipeline, as well as relevant aspects of the pipeline's production function. Cost functions can be used to help solve important sorts of managerial problems, as well as problems of public policy. We have shown how estimates of cost functions have been used to construct break-even charts, a commonly used practical application of cost functions. An actual case study of a cable manufacturing firm was employed to illustrate the use of these charts.

CONCEPTS FOR REVIEW

Marginal product	Opportunity cost	Average total cost
Average product	Fixed cost	Marginal cost
Law of diminishing marginal returns	Variable cost	Planning horizon
Average variable cost	Average fixed cost	Break-even chart

QUESTIONS FOR DISCUSSION AND REVIEW

1. Suppose that you were the president of a firm that operates a crude oil pipeline. Describe in detail the various ways in which the production and cost functions given in this chapter might be useful to you.

2. Suppose that you were given the job of estimating the cost functions for your college or university. How would you go about estimating the relationships between costs and number of students? Is there a difference between the long run and the short run? In this context, what is meant by variable and fixed costs? How might your results be used?

3. Suppose that a firm's short-run total cost function is as follows:

Output (number of units per year)	Total cost per year (dollars)
0	20,000
1	20,100
2	20,200
3	20,300
4	20,500
5	20,800

What are the firm's total fixed costs? What are its total variable costs when it produces 4 units per year?

4. In Question 3, what is the firm's marginal cost when between 4 and 5 units are produced per year? Does marginal cost increase beyond some output level?

5. In Question 3, what is the firm's average cost when it produces 1 unit per year? 2 units per year? 3 units per year? 4 units per year? 5 units per year?

6. "Decreasing returns to scale occur when increased scale allows efficiencies of various sorts." Comment and evaluate.

7. "A prerequisite for competition in a particular industry is that the long-run average cost curve be downward-sloped at all levels of output." Comment and evaluate.

8. Suppose that a firm has the following production function:

Man-hours of labor per year (thousands)	Output per year (thousands)
0	0
1	2
2	8
3	12
4	14
5	15

Plot on a graph the marginal product of labor at various levels of utilization of labor.

9. Using the data in Question 8, plot the average product of labor at various levels of utilization of labor.

10. Suppose that a cost-minimizing firm in a perfectly competitive market uses two inputs: labor and capital. If the marginal product of capital is twice the marginal product of labor, and if the price of a unit of labor is $4, what must be the price of a unit of capital?

Appendix: Isoquants, Isocost Curves, and the Optimal Input Combination

In this Appendix, we present a somewhat different way of finding a firm's optimal input combination. This approach is based on the use of isoquants and isocost curves. There are advantages in being acquainted with this approach, as well as the one presented earlier, but an understanding of this approach is not essential for beginning students.

Isoquants

In the case of a crude oil pipeline, a given amount of oil can be carried per day either by using a large diameter of pipe and relatively small horsepower or by using a smaller diameter of pipe and greater horsepower. Similar opportunities to vary inputs to achieve a given output rate exist in practically all industries. To describe these opportunities, economists use the concept of an isoquant. An ***isoquant*** is a curve showing all possible efficient combinations of inputs capable of producing a certain quantity of output. An *inefficient* combination of inputs is one that includes more of at least one input, and as much of other inputs, as some other combination of inputs that can produce the same quantity of output. Inefficient combinations clearly cannot minimize costs or maximize profits. For example, on a wheat farm, it may be possible to produce 1 unit of output with 2 units of land and 3 units of labor. It may also be possible to produce 1 unit of output with 3 units of land and 3 units of labor. The second input combination—which is inefficient—cannot be the least-cost input combination, so long as land has a *positive* price. Only *efficient* input combinations are worth bothering with in the present circumstances, and they alone are included in an isoquant.

There is an isoquant pertaining to each level of production. Figure 22.22 shows some isoquants for a wheat farm. These isoquants show the various combinations of inputs that can produce 100, 200, and 300 bushels of wheat per period of time. For instance, consider the isoquant for 100 bushels of wheat per period of time. According to this isoquant, the farm can attain this output rate if OL_1 units of labor and OD_1 units of land are used per period of time. Alternatively, this output rate can be attained with OL_2 units of labor and OD_2 units of

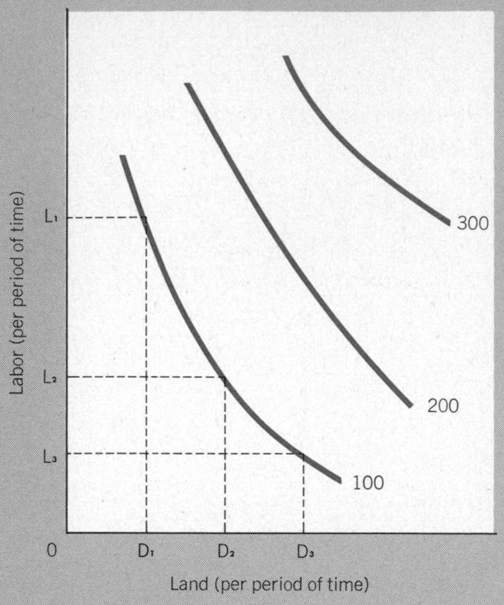

Figure 22.22
Isoquants, Wheat Farm
An isoquant shows all possible efficient combinations of inputs capable of producing a certain quantity of output. These isoquants show the various combinations of inputs that can produce 100, 200, and 300 bushels of wheat per period of time. For example, 100 bushels of wheat can be produced with OL_1 units of labor and OD_1 units of land, with OL_2 units of labor and OD_2 units of land, or with OL_3 units of labor and OD_3 units of land.

land—or OL_3 units of labor and OD_3 units of land—per period of time.

The shape and position of a firm's isoquants are derived from the firm's production function. Indeed, one way to represent the firm's production function is by showing its isoquants. Thus the firm's isoquants, like its production function, show the firm's technological possibilities—the various efficient input-output combinations that can be achieved with existing technology. The shape of an isoquant is typically like that shown in Figure 22.22; that is, it slopes downward to the right, but *its slope becomes less and less steep.* This fact stems from the operation of the law of diminishing returns.

To illustrate what isoquants in an actual firm look like, consider once again our crude oil pipeline. Figure 22.23 shows the isoquants corresponding to 100,000, 200,000, and 300,000 barrels of crude oil carried per day. For example, the isoquant corresponding to 100,000 barrels per day shows all the combinations of line diameter and horsepower that permit a pipeline to carry 100,000 barrels per day (for 1,000 miles). Note that each of these isoquants slopes downward to the right. Moreover, comparing these isoquants with Table 22.3, you can readily see that, if Table 22.3 contained more detailed data on the production function, it would be simple to derive the isoquants from the data regarding the production function in Table 22.3. How? By determining from this more detailed version of Table 22.3 the various input combinations that can produce each output rate. For example, to derive the isoquant corresponding to 100,000 barrels of crude oil carried per day, one could determine from such a table the various input combinations that can produce this output rate.

Isocost Curves and the Optimal Input Decision

To determine the combination of inputs that will minimize the firm's costs, one can use the isoquant concept. All input combinations that can efficiently produce the specified level of output can be represented by the isoquant corresponding to this level of output. For example, the isoquant in Figure 22.24 shows all the input combinations a wheat farm can use to produce a certain amount of wheat. The optimal input combination must lie on this isoquant, but where? A simple way to determine the optimal input combination is to draw a number of ***isocost curves,*** as shown in Figure 22.24. Each isocost curve shows the input

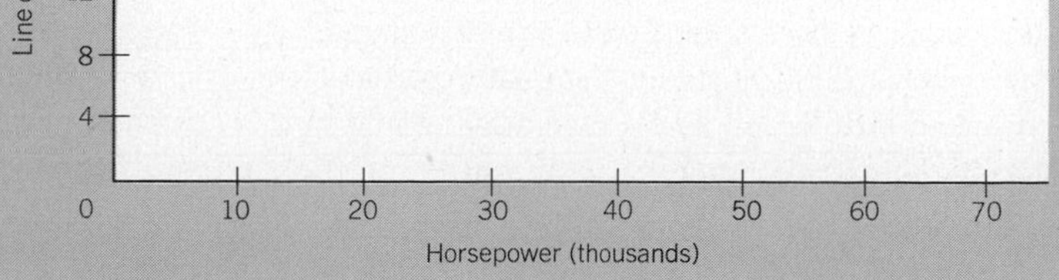

Figure 22.23
Isoquants for 100,000, 200,000, and 300,000 Barrels of Crude Oil Carried per Day, Crude Oil Pipeline
This graph shows the isoquants in an actual case. Note that they are shaped as economic theory would predict.

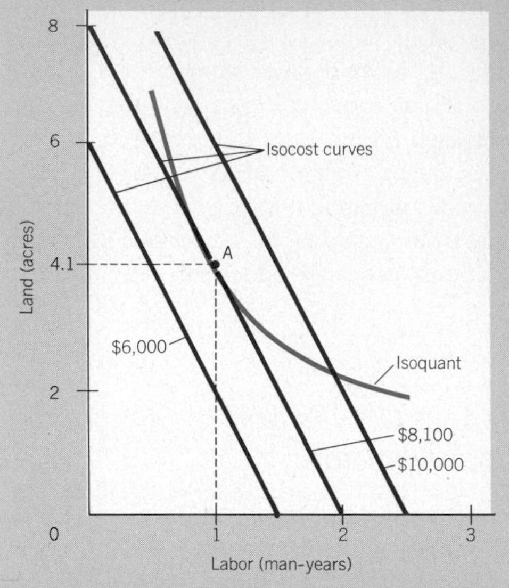

Figure 22.24
Least-Cost Input Combination
The least-cost input combination is at point *A*, where 4.1 acres of land and 1 man-year of labor are used. The isoquant shows all input combinations that can be used to produce the required amount of wheat, and the isocost curves show the input combinations costing $6,000, $8,100, and $10,000, respectively.

combinations the firm can obtain for a given expenditure. For example, the isocost curves corresponding to expenditures of $6,000, $8,100, and $10,000 are shown in Figure 22.24.

In Figure 22.24, the price of labor is $4,000 per man-year, and the annual price of using land is $1,000. Given the price of each input, it is, of course, a simple matter to draw each isocost curve. For example, take the case of the isocost curve corresponding to annual expenditures of $6,000. If this expenditure were devoted entirely to labor, 1½ man-years could be hired. Thus this isocost curve must cut the horizontal axis in Figure 22.24 at 1½ man-years of labor. Similarly, if this expenditure were devoted entirely to land, 6 acres of land could be hired. Thus this isocost curve must cut the vertical axis at 6 acres of land. Finally, if we connect the point where the isocost curve cuts the vertical axis to the point where it cuts the horizontal axis, we obtain the entire isocost curve.

Given both the isoquant and the isocost curves, one can readily determine the input combination that will minimize the firm's costs. This input combination corresponds to *that point on the isoquant that lies on the lowest isocost curve*—in other words, point *A* in Figure 22.24. Input combinations on lower isocost curves (like that corresponding to $6,000) that lie below *A* are cheaper than *A*, but cannot produce the desired output. Input combinations on isocost curves (like that corresponding to $10,000) that lie above *A* will produce the desired output but at a higher cost than *A*.

What is the relationship between the input combination determined in this way and the input combination determined by means of the rule described earlier in this chapter? Reassuringly enough, these input combinations will always be the same, since the rule described earlier in this chapter, will always give the same answer as this geometric technique. In general, *if you find the combination of inputs where the marginal product of a dollar's worth of any one input equals the marginal product of a dollar's worth of any other input used, this will give you the same answer as if you find the point on the isoquant that lies on the lowest isocost curve.*

Finding the Optimal Input Combination: A Case Study

To illustrate the use of isoquants and isocost curves to identify optimal input combinations, let's go back to Earl Heady's study of the production of corn, discussed earlier in this chapter. Figure 22.25 shows an isoquant that

Figure 22.25
Isoquant for the Production of 82.6 Bushels of Corn in Kansas
This graph shows how economic analysis has been used to help farmers make better production decisions. Given the assumed conditions, the optimal input combination would be 40 pounds of fertilizer and 1.04 acres of land.

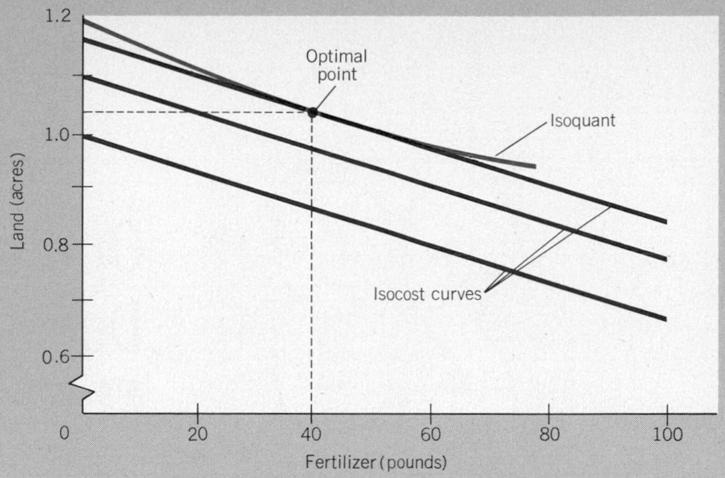

Heady and his coworkers estimated from the production of corn on Kansas Verdigras soil. This isoquant shows the amount of land and fertilizer that will produce 82.6 bushels of corn. It indicates that this amount of corn can be produced if 1.19 acres of land and no fertilizer are used, or if 1.11 acres of land and 20 pounds of fertilizer are used, or if .99 acres of land and 60 pounds of fertilizer are used, and so forth. (The same data are shown in Table 22.5.)

After estimating isoquants of this sort, Heady and his coworkers derived the optimal input combination farmers should use to minimize their costs. Suppose that a pound of fertilizer costs .003 times as much as an acre of land: then the isocost curves would be as shown in Figure 22.25. Clearly, under these circumstances, the minimum-cost combination would be 40 pounds of fertilizer and 1.04 acres of land. (Of course, this finding agrees with the results obtained earlier in the chapter, when we took up this same case.) No matter what the ratio of the price of fertilizer to the price of land may be, the least-cost input combination can be derived this way.

23 Optimal Output Decisions and Market Supply

In the previous chapter, we showed how the profit-maximizing firm determines the input combination it uses to produce any specified quantity of output. We now ask the second question that must be answered if a firm desires to maximize profits: What quantity of output should the firm produce? This chapter shows the way the profit-maximizing firm answers this question, and derives the firm's and the industry's supply curve. Here again, economic theory can aid the decision maker, as we shall see in the approach an airline took to scheduling its flights between two major cities. Finally, in the Appendix to this chapter, we show how the firm's production decisions can be viewed from a somewhat different standpoint: that of linear programming, a relatively new technique that enables economists to solve many important problems of industry and government that were beyond their reach only a few decades ago.

Table 23.1
Costs and Revenues, Allegro Piano Company

Output per week (pianos)	Price	Total revenue	Total fixed cost (dollars)	Total variable cost	Total cost	Total profit
0	1,000	0	1,000	0	1,000	−1,000
1	1,000	1,000	1,000	200	1,200	− 200
2	1,000	2,000	1,000	300	1,300	700
3	1,000	3,000	1,000	500	1,500	1,500
4	1,000	4,000	1,000	1,000	2,000	2,000
5	1,000	5,000	1,000	2,000	3,000	2,000
6	1,000	6,000	1,000	3,200	4,200	1,800
7	1,000	7,000	1,000	4,500	5,500	1,500
8	1,000	8,000	1,000	7,200	8,200	− 200

The Output of the Firm

What determines the output rate of a profit-maximizing firm? For simplicity, we will assume that the firm cannot affect the price of its product and that it can sell any amount it wants at this price. In other words, this is a ***perfectly competitive firm.*** Also, we will consider a short-run situation in which the firm can expand or contract its output rate by increasing or decreasing its utilization of variable inputs. The situation in the long run will be reserved for Chapter 24.

To illustrate the nature of the problem, suppose that your rich uncle dies and leaves you his business, the Allegro Piano Company. Once you take over the business, your first problem is to decide how many pianos (each of which has a price of $1,000) the firm should produce per week. Having a good deal of economic intuition, you instruct your accountant to estimate the company's total revenue and total costs (as well as fixed and variable costs) at various output levels. He estimates the firm's total revenue at various output rates and its total cost function (as well as its total fixed cost function and total variable cost function), with the results shown in Table 23.1. Subtracting the total cost at a given output rate from the total revenue at this output rate, you obtain the total profit at each output rate, which is shown in the last column of Table 23.1. Since the maximum profit is obtained at an output level of either 4 or 5 pianos per week, this is the output level you choose.

Figure 23.1 gives a somewhat more vivid picture of the firm's situation by plotting the relationship between total revenue and total cost, on the one hand, and output on the other. The vertical distance between the total revenue curve and the total cost curve is, of course, the profit at a corresponding output rate. Below an output rate of 2 pianos per week and above a rate of 7 pianos per week, the total revenue curve lies *below* the total cost curve, indicating that profits are negative—that is, there are losses. Both Table 23.1 and Figure 23.1 show that the output rate that will maximize the firm's profits is either 4 or 5 pianos per week. At either of these rates, the firm will make a profit of $2,000 per week, which is more than it can make at any other output rate.

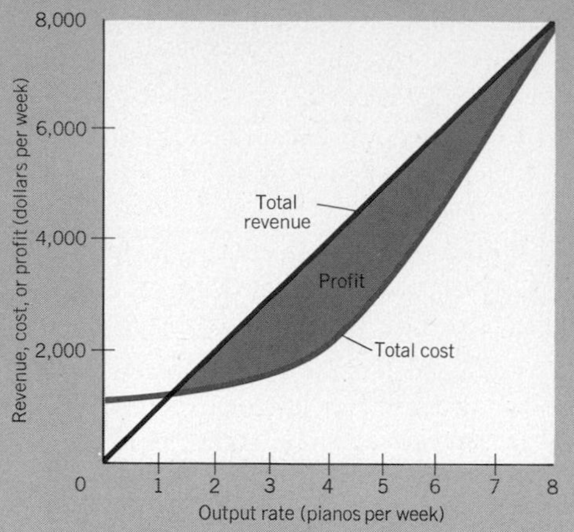

Figure 23.1
Costs, Revenue, and Profits, Allegro Piano Company
The output rate that will maximize the firm's profits is either 4 or 5 pianos per week.

Table 23.2
Marginal Cost and Price, Allegro Piano Company

Output per week (pianos)	Marginal cost[a] (dollars)	Price
1	200	1,000
2	100	1,000
3	200	1,000
4	500	1,000
5	1,000	1,000
6	1,200	1,000
7	1,300	1,000
8	2,700	1,000

[a] This is the marginal cost between the indicated output level and 1 unit less than the indicated output level.

There is an alternative way to analyze the firm's situation. Rather than looking at total revenue and total cost, let's look at price and marginal cost. Table 23.2 and Figure 23.2 show the product price and marginal cost at each output rate. It turns out that the maximum profit is achieved at the output rate where price equals marginal cost. In other words, both Table 23.2 and Figure 23.2 indicate that price equals marginal cost at the profit-maximizing output rates of 4 or 5 pianos per week. This raises a question: Will price usually equal marginal cost at the profit-maximizing output rate, or is this merely a coincidence?

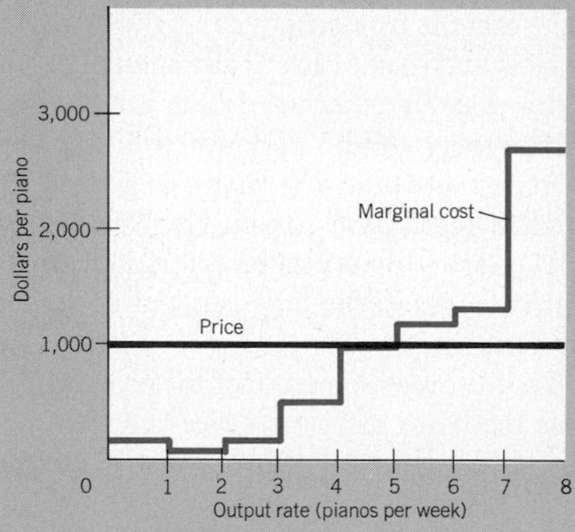

Figure 23.2
Marginal Cost and Price, Allegro Piano Company
At the profit-maximizing output rate of 4 or 5 pianos per week, marginal costs equal price.

The Golden Rule of Output Determination

Readers familiar with television scripts and detective stories will have recognized that the question just posed can only be answered in one way without ruining the plot. The equality of marginal cost and price at the profit-maximizing output rate is no mere coincidence. It will usually be true if the firm takes the price of its product as given. Indeed, the Golden Rule of Output Determination for a perfectly competitive firm is: *choose the output rate at which marginal cost is equal to price.*

To prove that this rule maximizes profits, consider Figure 23.3, which shows a typical short-run marginal cost function, MM'. Suppose that the price is OP_1. At any output rate less than OQ_1, price is greater than marginal cost.[1] This means that increases in output will increase the firm's profits since they will add more to total revenues than to total costs. Why? Because an extra unit of output adds an amount equal to price to total revenue and an amount equal to marginal cost to total cost. Thus, since price exceeds marginal cost, an extra unit of output adds more to total revenue than to total cost. For example, this is the case for the Allegro Piano Company when it is producing 3 pianos per week. As shown in Table 23.2, the extra cost of producing a fourth piano is $500, while the revenue brought in by producing and selling it is $1,000. Consequently, it pays the Allegro Piano Company to produce more than 3 pianos per week.

At any output rate above OQ_1, price is less than marginal cost. This means that decreases in output will increase the firm's profits since they will subtract more from total costs than from revenue. This happens because one less unit of output subtracts an amount equal to price from total revenue and an amount equal to marginal cost from total cost. Thus, since price is less than marginal cost, one less unit of output subtracts more from total cost than from total revenue. Such a case occurs, for instance, when the Allegro Piano Company is producing 7 pianos per week. As shown in Table 23.2, the extra cost of producing the seventh piano is $1,300, while the extra revenue it brings in is $1,000. So it pays the Allegro Piano Company to produce less than 7 pianos per week.

[1] Except perhaps for an irrelevant range where marginal cost decreases with increases in output.

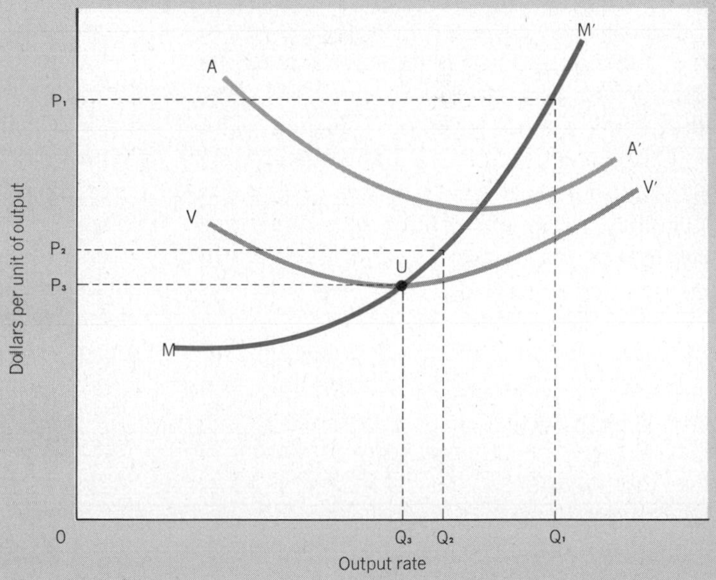

Figure 23.3
Short-Run Average and Marginal Cost Curves
If price is OP_1, the profit-maximizing output rate is OQ_1. If price is OP_2, the profit-maximizing output rate is OQ_2, even though the firm will incur a loss. If the price is below OP_3, the firm will discontinue production.

Since increases in output will increase profits if output is less than OQ_1, and decreases in output will increase profits if output is greater than OQ_1, it follows that profits must be maximized at OQ_1, the output rate at which price equals marginal cost. After all, if increases in output up to this output rate *(*OQ_1*,)* result in increases in profit and further increases in output result in decreases in profit, OQ_1 must be the profit-maximizing output rate. For the Allegro Piano Company, this output rate is 4 or 5 pianos per week, as we just saw.

Does It Pay to Be a Dropout?

All rules—even the Golden Rule we just mentioned—have exceptions. Under some circumstances, the perfectly competitive firm will not maximize its profits if it sets marginal cost equal to price. Instead, it will maximize profits only if it becomes an economic dropout by discontinuing production. Let's demonstrate that this is indeed a fact. The first important point is that even if the firm is doing the best it can, it may not be able to earn a profit. For example, if the price is OP_2, in Figure 23.3, short-run average cost, AA', exceeds the price, OP_2 at all possible output rates. Thus the firm cannot earn a profit whatever output it produces. Since the short run is too short for the firm to alter the scale of its plant, it cannot liquidate its plant in the short run. Its only choice is to produce at a loss or discontinue production.

Under what conditions will the firm produce at a loss, and under what conditions will it discontinue production? *If there is an output rate where price exceeds average variable cost, it will pay the firm to produce, even though price does not cover average total cost. If there is no such output rate, the firm is better off to produce nothing at all.* This is true because even if the firm produces nothing, it must pay its fixed cost. Thus, if the loss resulting from production is less than the firm's fixed cost, the firm is better off producing than not producing. On the other hand, if the loss resulting from production is greater than the firm's fixed cost, the firm is better off not to produce.

In other words, the firm will find it advantageous to produce if

$$\text{total losses} < \text{total fixed cost},$$

or (since total losses = total cost − total revenue) if

$$\text{total cost} - \text{total revenue} < \text{total fixed cost}.$$

Dividing each side of this inequality by output, the firm is better off to produce if:

$$\frac{\text{total cost}}{\text{output}} - \frac{\text{total revenue}}{\text{output}} < \frac{\text{total fixed cost}}{\text{output}}.$$

Since total revenue = price × output, this means that the firm is better off to produce if

$$\text{average total cost} - \text{price} < \text{average fixed cost},$$

or (adding price to both sides)

$$\text{average total cost} < \text{average fixed cost} + \text{price},$$

or (subtracting average fixed cost from both sides)

$$\text{average variable cost} < \text{price}.$$

Once again, we have proved what we set out to prove: that the firm will maximize profits by producing *nothing* if there is no output rate at which price exceeds average variable cost. Of course, if such an output rate does exist, the Golden Rule applies: the firm will set its output rate at the point where marginal cost equals price.

To illustrate the conditions under which it pays a firm to drop out, suppose that the cost functions of the Allegro Piano Company are as shown in Table 23.3. Clearly, in this case, there exists no output rate such that average variable cost is less than price—which, you will

Table 23.3
Costs and Revenues, Allegro Piano Company

Output per week (pianos)	Price	Total revenue	Total fixed cost	Total variable cost (dollars)	Average variable cost	Total cost	Total profit
0	1,000	0	1,000	0	—	1,000	– 1,000
1	1,000	1,000	1,000	1,200	1,200	2,200	– 1,200
2	1,000	2,000	1,000	2,600	1,300	3,600	– 1,600
3	1,000	3,000	1,000	4,200	1,400	5,200	– 2,200
4	1,000	4,000	1,000	6,000	1,500	7,000	– 3,000
5	1,000	5,000	1,000	8,000	1,600	9,000	– 4,000
6	1,000	6,000	1,000	10,200	1,700	11,200	– 5,200
7	1,000	7,000	1,000	12,600	1,800	13,600	– 6,600
8	1,000	8,000	1,000	15,200	1,900	16,200	– 8,200

recall, is $1,000 per piano. Thus, according to the results of the last paragraphs, the Allegro Piano company should discontinue production under these conditions. The wisdom of this course of action is shown by the last column of Table 23.3, which demonstrates that the profit-maximizing–or, what amounts to the same thing, the loss-minimizing–output rate is zero.

Sometimes, as in the present case, the best thing to do is nothing. The situation is analogous to the common experience of leaving a movie after the first ten minutes indicate that it is not going to be a good one, even though the admission price is not refundable. One ignores the fixed costs (the admission price), and finding that the variable cost (the pleasure gained from activities that would be forgone by seeing the rest of the show) is going to exceed the benefits of staying, one leaves.

In 1973, many meat-processing plants discontinued production for essentially this reason. The federal government, in an attempt to control inflation, froze the price of their product, but allowed the prices of the inputs they used to go up, with the result that their average variable costs exceeded price at all possible output levels. The consequence, as our theory would predict, was that many plants closed down. For example, in Chicago, the American Meat Institute announced that 16 plants closed down in the second quarter of 1973. As the president of Detroit's Crown Packing company put it, "Frankly, we closed down so that we would lose less money."

Decision Making at Continental Air Lines: A Case Study

In showing how the profit-maximizing firm should determine its output rate, we have repeatedly used this simple principle: *undertake a particular activity if, and only if, the additional revenues stemming from the activity exceed the additional costs.* Clearly, this principle underlies our Golden Rule of Output Determination. Recall that the Golden Rule dictates that an extra unit of output be produced so long as its price exceeds its marginal cost. Since its price equals the additional revenue stemming from the production of the additional unit and since its marginal cost equals the additional cost stemming from the production of the additional unit, the Golden Rule can be derived from this principle. This principle also underlies our discussion of the conditions under which it pays a firm to discontinue production.

It is remarkable how often this simple principle can be helpful in real-life problems—and even more remarkable how often managers fail to apply it, with the result that their firms make less money than they could. This doesn't mean, of course, that business executives are stupid or incompetent. It does mean that they often receive information in a form that makes it difficult to apply this rule. Also, they sometimes have the habit of applying rules of thumb which, if carefully examined, violate this principle.

To illustrate the sorts of cases that arise, consider Continental Air Lines, the nation's tenth largest airline. Continental, like other airlines, must continually decide whether or not to run an extra flight from one city to another. For example, Continental may be contemplating an extra daily flight from Houston to Los Angeles. To reach its decision, Continental must compare the costs of the extra flight with the revenues it is likely to bring in. Suppose that the extra revenues are estimated to be $3,100, that the extra out-of-pocket costs are $2,000, and that the fully allocated costs of the flight are $4,500. If you were the president of Continental, would you decide to run the extra flight?

Obviously, the first thing you need is a clear definition of "out-of-pocket cost" and "fully allocated cost." Suppose your accountants tell you that the ***out-of-pocket costs*** of the extra flight are the actual dollars Continental has to pay out to run the flight: the costs of the extra crew, the extra fuel, and the other extra inputs. On the other hand, the ***fully allocated costs*** are the out-of-pocket costs plus a specified share of Continental's overhead, depreciation, insurance, and other fixed costs. Given these definitions, if you were a clear-headed profit maximizer, you would run the flight. The extra costs incurred by the flight are the out-of-pocket costs, not the fully allocated costs, and the out-of-pocket costs are less than the extra revenue the new flight will produce. Thus the flight will increase the firm's profit—by $3,100 less $2,000, or $1,100 per day.

Why is the out-of-pocket cost, rather than fully allocated cost, the relevant measure of the flight's cost? Because the extra cost incurred by the flight is the out-of-pocket cost—and only that. The firm's fixed costs (including overhead, depreciation, insurance, and so forth) will be the same whether the extra flight is run or not. (Remember that fixed costs are fixed *in the short run!*) Consequently, it is incorrect to use the fully allocated cost, which includes a share of the firm's fixed costs, to measure the extra costs of the flight.

The case described here was an actual one. And in accord with the principles described above, Continental made the proper decision: it ran the extra flight. Unfortunately, however, not all firms are as sophisticated in this regard, with the result that profitable opportunities are sometimes missed. Any aspiring executive would do well to bear in mind the simple principle that additional revenues should be compared with additional costs (and that out-of-pocket and fully allocated costs can be quite different). According to *Business Week,* a leading magazine for business executives, "Getting management to accept and apply . . . [this principle] is the chief contribution any economist can make to his company."[2] Perhaps this is an overstatement, but unquestionably it has a core of truth.

The Firm's Supply Curve and the Market Supply Curve

In Chapter 4, we described some of the factors

[2] *Business Week,* "An Airline Takes the Marginal Route," April 20, 1963, reprinted in E. Mansfield, *Economics: Readings, Issues, and Cases,* 2d ed., New York: Norton, 1977.

Figure 23.4
Horizontal Summation of Short-Run Supply Curves of Firms
The market supply curve is *OSGG′*, if the firm supply curves are *OSBB′*, *OSDD′*, and *OSFF′*. However, if input prices are influenced by the output of the industry, the market supply curve may be *OSHH′* rather than *OSGG′*.

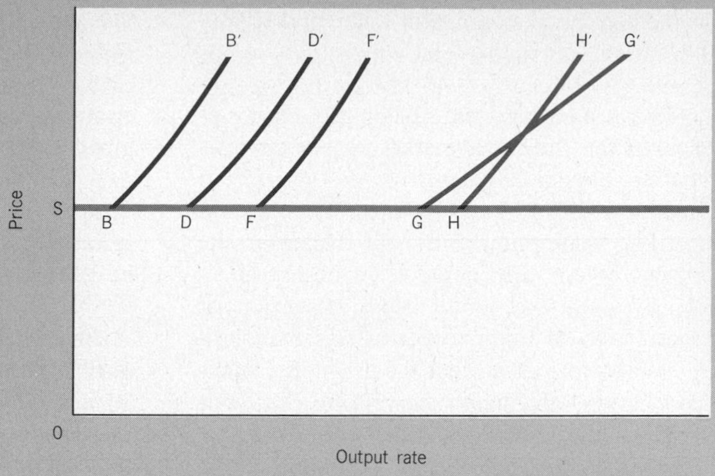

underlying a commodity's market supply curve, but we could not go into much detail. Now we can, because our Golden Rule of Output Determination underlies the market supply curve. As a first step, let's derive the firm's ***supply curve,*** which shows how much the firm will want to produce at each price. Assuming that the firm takes the price of its product as given (and can sell all it wants at that price), we know from the previous sections that the firm will choose the output level at which price equals marginal cost. Or if the price is below the firm's average variable cost curve at every output level, the firm will produce nothing. These results are all we need to determine the firm's supply curve.

For example, suppose that the firm's short-run cost curves are as shown in Figure 23.3. The marginal cost curve, *MM′*, must, of course, intersect the average variable cost curve, *VV′*, at the latter's minimum point, *U*. If the price of the product is less than OP_3, the firm will produce nothing, because there is no output level where price exceeds average variable cost. If the price of the product exceeds OP_3, the firm will set its output rate at the point where price equals marginal cost. Thus, if the price is OP_1, the firm will produce OQ_1; if the price is OP_2, the firm will produce OQ_2; and so forth. Consequently, it is obvious that *the firm's supply curve is exactly the same as the firm's marginal cost curve for prices above the minimum value of average variable cost* (OP_3). For prices at or below the minimum value of average variable cost, the firm's supply curve corresponds to the price axis, the desire to supply at these prices being uniformly zero. Thus the firm's supply curve is OP_3UM'.

Our next step is to derive the market supply curve from the supply curves of the individual firms. If one assumption holds, *the market supply curve can be regarded as the horizontal summation of the supply curves of all the firms producing the product.* For example, if there were 3 firms in the industry and their supply curves were *OSBB′*, *OSDD′*, and *OSFF′* in Figure 23.4, the market supply curve would be *OSGG′*, since *OSGG′* shows the *total* amount of the product that all of the firms together would supply at various prices. Of course, if there were only 3 firms, the market would not be perfectly competitive, but we can ignore this inconsistency. Figure 23.4 is designed to illustrate the fact that the market supply curve is the horizontal summation of thc firm supply curves, at least under one important assumption.

The assumption underlying this construction of the short-run market supply curve is that *increases or decreases in output by all firms simultaneously do not affect input prices.* This is a strong assumption. Although changes in the output of one firm alone often cannot affect input prices, the simultaneous expansion or contraction of output by all firms may well alter input prices, so that the individual firm's cost curves—and supply curve—will shift. For instance, an expansion of the whole industry may bid up the price of certain inputs, with the result that the cost curves of the individual firms will be pushed upward. In the aerospace industry, for example, a sudden expansion of the industry might well increase the price of certain inputs like the services of aerospace scientists and engineers.

If, contrary to the assumption underlying Figure 23.4 input prices *are* increased by the expansion of the industry, what will happen to the short-run market supply curve? The effect will be to make the amount supplied less sensitive to price changes than is indicated by $OSGG'$. In the relevant price range, the curve might be more like HH' than GG'. To see why, note that expansion of the industry causes the short-run average cost curve and the short-run marginal cost curve of each firm to move upward, because of the resulting increase in input prices. But if the marginal cost curve moves upward, price will equal marginal cost at a lower output than it would have if the marginal cost curve had not moved.

Returning now to the question posed at the beginning of this section, what factors determine the market supply curve? First, since the market supply curve is derived from the marginal cost curves of the firms in the industry, *the shape of the short-run supply curve is determined by the size of the firm's plants, the level of input prices, the nature of technology, and the other factors determining the shape of the marginal cost curve for each firm.* In particular, the short-run market supply curve generally slopes upward to the right because marginal cost curves (in the relevant range) generally slope upward to the right. Second, as we have seen in previous paragraphs, *the shape of the supply curve is influenced by the effect of changes in industry output on input prices.* Third, *the shape of the short-run supply curve is determined by the number of firms in the industry.* The supply curve in Figure 23.4 would be located farther to the right if there were more firms in the industry.

Measurement of Market Supply Curves and the Price Elasticity of Supply

In many situations, major decisions must be based on predictions of the effect of a commodity's price on the amount of the commodity that will be supplied. For example, recall the agricultural programs described in Chapter 5. Clearly, decision makers in the U.S. Department of Agriculture must be concerned with the market supply curve for many basic agricultural commodities. Nor is the importance of market supply curves confined to agriculture. In other parts of the economy, people must be vitally concerned with the location and shape of the market supply curve for various commodities.

Attempts to measure market supply curves have been aided greatly by modern advances in statistical and econometric techniques. Basically, these techniques rely on analyzing historical data on price and output to estimate the relationship between price and the quantity supplied. There are still many difficulties and hazards in estimating market supply curves, just as with market demand curves. It is not a business for the neophyte. But based on careful

Figure 23.5
Market Supply Curves for Watermelons, Periods of Varying Length
Panel A shows the market supply curve in a period of a few hours or a day. Panel B refers to a year or so. Panel C refers to 10 to 20 years.

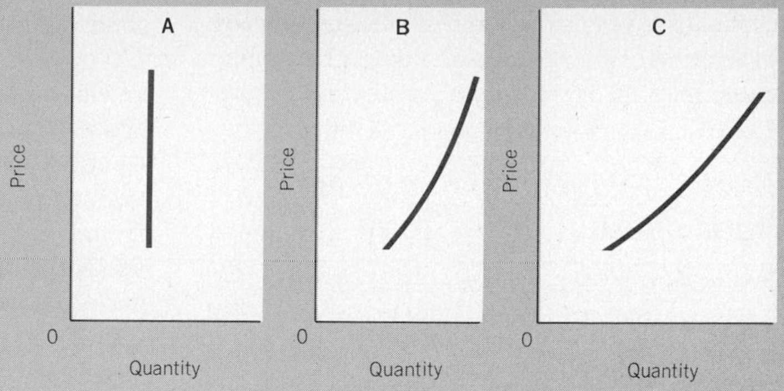

professional analysis, useful measurements can be made of market supply (and demand) curves.

Market supply curves vary, of course, in their shape. For some commodities, the quantity supplied is very sensitive to changes in the commodity's price. For others, the quantity supplied is not at all sensitive to changes in price. To measure the sensitivity of quantity supplied to changes in price, economists use the ***price elasticity of supply,*** which is defined as the percentage change in quantity supplied resulting from a 1 percent change in price. For example, suppose that a 1 percent reduction in the price of slingshots results in a 1.5 percent reduction in the quantity supplied. Then the price elasticity of supply for slingshots (in the neighborhood of the existing price) is 1.5. Clearly, the price elasticity of supply is likely to vary from one point to another on the market supply curve. For example, the price elasticity of supply for slingshots may be higher when the price of a slingshot is $2 than when it is $1.

The same factors that influence the location and shape of the market supply curve also determine the price elasticity of supply. But to these factors previously mentioned—the number of plants, input prices, and the nature of technology, among others—another important factor should be added: the length of the time period to which the supply curve pertains. *Market supply curves, like market demand curves, tend to be more price elastic if the time period is long rather than short.* For example, consider the market for watermelons. If we are dealing with a very short period—a few hours or a day—the supply of watermelons may be fixed, as in panel A of Figure 23.5. That is, the market supply curve may be perfectly inelastic, the price elasticity of supply being zero, because the period is too short to grow any more watermelons or transport any more watermelons into the market.

Suppose now that we lengthen the period of time to a year or so. In this period, farmers can alter the size of their watermelon crop in response to variations in price. Thus the price elasticity of supply will be higher than in the very short period of a few hours or a day. In this longer period, the price elasticity of supply has been estimated to be about .30; and the supply curve may be as shown in panel B of Figure 23.5.[3]

Finally, suppose that we lengthen the period further—to 10 or even 20 years. In this period, farmers can take land out of watermelon production or put land into watermelon production. Indeed, they can make all reasonable adjustments to changes in price. So the price elasticity of supply will be higher than in a

[3] D. Suits, "An Econometric Model of the Watermelon Market," *Journal of Farm Economics,* May 1955; and W. L'Esperance, "A Case Study in Prediction," *Econometrica,* 1964.

period of a year or so—and much higher than in a period of a few hours or a day. The supply curve may be as shown in panel c of Figure 23.5.

Price Elasticities of Supply in Agriculture: A Case Study

For various leading commodities, what are the best available estimates of the price elasticity of supply? Marc Nerlove of Northwestern University has done some important studies of the price elasticity of supply of agricultural commodities, in both the short and long runs. He concludes that, although the short-run price elasticity of supply for commodities like cotton and corn may be quite low, their price elasticity of supply in the long run is substantially higher. Specifically, estimates of the short-run price elasticities of supply are about 0.2 for cotton and about 0.1 for corn; but in the long run, Nerlove estimates the price elasticity of supply to be about 0.7 for cotton and about 0.2 for corn.[4]

Table 23.4 shows estimates by Nerlove and William Addison of the short-run and long-run price elasticities of supply for a number of vegetables produced for fresh market in the United States. The short-run elasticity is defined as the elasticity over one production period. In the short run, the price elasticity of supply tends to be about 0.1 to 0.3 for these vegetables, but in the long run, it generally is 1.0 or more. Thus, once again, we see that the short-run elasticities are considerably lower than the long-run elasticities.

Table 23.4
Estimated Price Elasticities of Supply, Short Run and Long Run, Selected Vegetables, United States

Vegetable	Price Elasticity Short run	Price Elasticity Long run
Green lima beans	0.10	1.70
Cabbage	0.36	1.20
Carrots	0.14	1.00
Cucumbers	0.29	2.20
Onions	0.34	1.00
Green peas	0.31	4.40
Green peppers	0.07	0.26
Tomatoes	0.16	0.90
Cauliflower	0.14	1.10
Celery	0.14	0.95
Spinach	0.20	4.70

Source: M. Nerlove and W. Addison, "Statistical Estimation of Long-Run Elasticities of Supply and Demand," *Journal of Farm Economics,* November 1958.

Summary

This chapter has shown how the profit-maximizing firm chooses its output level in the short run, when it takes the price of each of its inputs and outputs as given. If it maximizes profit, it should set its output rate in the short run at the level where marginal cost equals price, so long as price exceeds average variable cost. If there is no output rate at which price exceeds average variable cost, the firm should discontinue production. These are the basic rules the firm must follow to maximize profits. From these rules it follows that the firm's supply curve coincides with its marginal cost curve for prices exceeding the minimum value of average variable cost. For prices that are less than or equal to the minimum value of average variable cost, the firm's supply curve coincides with the price axis.

As a first approximation, the market supply curve can be viewed as the horizontal summation of the supply curves of all of the firms producing the product. This assumes that increases or decreases in output by all firms simultaneously do not affect input prices—a strong assumption. In general, the market sup-

[4] M. Nerlove, "Estimates of the Elasticities of Supply of Selected Agricultural Commodities," *Journal of Farm Economics,* May 1956.

ply curve of a product is determined by the size of the firms' plants, the level of input prices, the nature of technology, and the other factors determining the shape of the firms' marginal cost curves, as well as by the effect of changes in the industry output on input prices and by the number of firms producing the product. The sensitivity of the quantity supplied to changes in price is measured by the price elasticity of supply, defined as the percentage change in quantity supplied resulting from a 1 percent change in price. In general, the price elasticity of supply is greater if the time interval is long rather than short.

CONCEPTS FOR REVIEW

Supply curve of a firm
Market supply curve
Perfectly competitive firm
Fully allocated cost
Out-of-pocket cost
Price elasticity of supply

QUESTIONS FOR DISCUSSION AND REVIEW

1. A merchant named Lapidus said that he lost money on every item that he sold, but that he made it up on volume. Does this seem reasonable? Why or why not?

2. Describe various ways that estimates might be made of the price elasticity of supply of wheat, and indicate how these estimates might be of practical use to the U.S. Department of Agriculture.

3. Suppose that the total costs of a perfectly competitive firm are as follows:

Output rate	Total cost (dollars)
0	40
1	60
2	90
3	130
4	180
5	240

If the price of the product is $50, what output rate should the firm choose?

4. If the price elasticity of supply for corn is about 0.1 in the short run, as estimated by Marc Nerlove of Northwestern University, a 1 percent increase in the price of corn would have approximately what impact on the quantity supplied?

5. Suppose that the firm in Question 3 experienced an increase of $30 in its fixed costs. Plot its new total cost function. What effect will this increase in its fixed costs have on the output it will choose?

6. After the increase in fixed costs described in Question 5, what does the firm's marginal cost curve look like? Plot it on a graph. Does it differ from what it was before the increase in fixed costs? Why or why not?

7. After the increase in fixed costs described in Question 5, what output rate would the firm choose if the price of its product were $40? $50? $60? $70?

Appendix: Linear Programming

In this Appendix, we look at the theory of the firm from a somewhat different angle—that of ***linear programming.*** Linear programming is the most famous of the mathematical programming methods that have come into existence since World War II. It is a technique that permits decision makers to solve maximization and minimization problems where there are certain constraints on what can be done. First used shortly after World War II to help schedule the procurement activities of the United States Air Force, linear programming has become an extremely important part of economic theory and a very powerful tool for solving managerial problems. Its remarkable growth has been helped along by the development of computers, which can handle the many computations required to solve large linear programming problems.

There are at least two reasons why it is important to re-examine the theory of the firm in terms of linear programming. First, the programming analysis is more fundamental in one respect than the conventional analysis presented up to this point. The conventional theory is based on the production function, which assumes that the efficient production processes have been determined and given to the economist before he attacks the problem. But in the real world, the economist is usually confronted with a number of *feasible* production processes, and it is very difficult to tell which ones—or which combinations—are *efficient.* The choice of the optimal combination of production processes is an extremely important decision, and it can be analyzed more fully by linear programming.

Second, the programming analysis seems to conform more closely to the way businessmen view production. The language and concepts of linear programming, though abstract and by no means the same as those of management, seem to be closer to those of managers and engineers than the ones used by conventional theory. This means that often it is easier to apply linear programming to many types of production problems in industry and government.

The Linear-Programming View of the Firm

To the economist who uses linear programming, the technology available to a firm consists of a finite number of ***processes,*** each of which uses inputs and produces one or more outputs. General Motors can choose among a number of different processes to manufacture an automobile, and U.S. Steel can use a number of processes to manufacture steel. Typically, a firm can use various alternative processes to do a particular job. An important assumption in linear programming is that each process uses inputs in fixed proportions. Consider the case of an automobile manufacturer that, among other things, assembles truck engines. Suppose that one process it can employ is Process X, which uses 10 hours of labor and 1 hour of machine time to assemble 1 truck engine. If this process uses inputs in fixed proportions—as assumed in linear programming—this 10:1 ratio of labor time to machine time must be maintained. It cannot be altered.

Any process can be operated at various activity levels; the ***activity level*** of a process is the number of units of output produced with the process. For example, if Process X is used to assemble 3 truck engines, its activity level is 3; if it is used to assemble 100 truck engines, its activity level is 100. If the output of any process is varied, it is assumed that the inputs used by the process vary proportionately with the output of the process. Consequently, the amount of any input used by a process equals the activity level of the process—i.e., the number of units of output produced with the process—times the number of units of input the process requires to produce a unit of output. In our example, the amount of labor used by Process X to assemble 5 truck engines is 50 man-hours, since the process is operated at an activity level of 5, and Process X requires 10 man-hours of labor to assemble each truck engine.[5]

Linear programming views the firm's production problem as follows: *The firm has certain fixed amounts of a number of inputs at its disposal. A manufacturing firm, for example, has available a limited amount of land, managerial labor, raw materials, and equipment of various kinds. (These limitations on the amounts of various inputs that the firm can use are called* ***constraints.****) Each unit of output resulting from a particular process yields the firm a certain amount of profit. This amount of profit varies in general from process to process. Knowing the profit to be made from a unit of output from each process and bearing in mind the limited amounts of inputs at its disposal, the firm must determine the activity level at which each process should be operated to maximize profit.* This is the firm's problem in a nutshell—a linear-programming nutshell, that is.

Removing Defects from Sheet Metal: A Case Study

No general description of linear programming can give more than a very incomplete idea of the nature of linear programming and its power to solve real-life problems. We can get a somewhat better idea from a simple case study which concerns a metalworking firm that removes defects from sheet metal. Suppose that there are three processes the firm can use: Processes A, B, and C. Process A requires 2 man-hours of labor and 1 hour of machine time to remove the defects from 1 square foot of sheet metal, Process B does the same job with 1.5 man-hours of labor and 1.5 hours of machine time, and Process C requires 1.1 man-hours of labor and 2.2 hours of machine time. The same kind of machine is used for each process.

Assume that the firm has contracted to remove the defects from 100 square feet of sheet metal per week, and that it will receive a price of $10 a square foot for this service. Also assume that the firm must pay $3 per man-hour for labor and that the cost of an hour of machine time is $2. Given these circumstances, the firm must decide which process or processes it should use to satisfy this contract. Should it use any single process to remove the defects from all 100 square feet of sheet metal per week? If so, which process should it use? Should it use some combination of processes, such as Process A for 50 square feet and Process B for the rest? Which of the myriad of possibilities will maximize the firm's profits?

Since the firm receives $1,000 a week for the work (100 square feet × $10 per square foot) regardless of which processes it uses, the firm will clearly maximize its profit by minimizing its costs. Thus, in this simple case,[6] the problem boils down to determining which process or processes can do the job at least cost. We begin by assuming that the firm can hire all the labor that it wants and that it has plenty of the necessary machines. (This assumption is contrary to our earlier statement that linear programming views the firm as having limited amounts of certain inputs, but we relax this assumption in a later section.) Letting Q_1 be the number of square feet of sheet metal subjected to Process A, Q_2 be the number of square feet subjected to Process B, and Q_3 be the number of square feet subjected to Process C, the firm's problem can be regarded as the following simple linear programming problem: choose the lowest possible value for

$$\text{total cost} = 8.0\, Q_1 + 7.5\, Q_2 + 7.7\, Q_3 \qquad (23.1)$$

subject to the constraints.

$$Q_1 + Q_2 + Q_3 = 100 \qquad (23.2)$$
$$Q_1 \geq 0;\ Q_2 \geq 0;\ Q_3 \geq 0. \qquad (23.3)$$

Why should the firm seek the lowest possible value for the expression in Equation (23.1)? Because this expression equals the firm's total

[5] It is also assumed that, when two or more processes are used simultaneously, they do not interfere with one another or make each other more productive.

[6] Of course, in general the problem of maximizing profit does not boil down to the minimization of cost because the firm's total revenue is not fixed as it is in this simple case.

weekly costs of doing thc job. The cost of each square foot of sheet metal subjected to Process A is \$8.00, since Process A requires 2 man-hours of labor (at \$3 per man-hour) and 1 hour of machine time (at \$2 per hour). Thus the total cost of the sheet metal subjected to Process A is 8.0 Q_1. Similarly, the total cost of sheet metal subjected to Process B is 7.5 Q_2, since the cost of each square foot of sheet metal subjected to Process B is \$7.50. And the total cost of the sheet metal subjected to Process C is 7.7 Q_3, since the cost of each square foot subjected to Process C is \$7.70. Clearly, the total cost of the job is the sum of whatever costs are incurred using each of the processes, which is the expression in Equation (23.1).

Why must the firm conform to the constraints in Equation (23.2) and Inequality (23.3)? Obviously, Equation (23.2) must hold if the firm is to meet its contract, since it states that the sum of the amounts of sheet metal subjected to each process must equal 100 square feet. That is, $Q_1 + Q_2 + Q_3$ must equal 100. Also, the inequalities in (23.3) must hold: all they say is that the number of square feet of sheet metal subjected to each process must be either zero or more than zero, which certainly must be true. (If you wonder why such an obvious constraint must be specified, remember that electronic computers won't recognize it as being true unless they are told.)

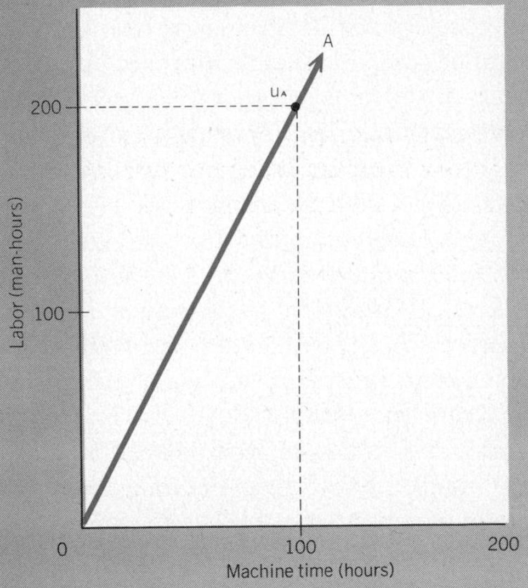

Figure 23.6
Graphical Representation of Process A
The ray *OA* includes all points where labor time is combined with machine time in the ratio of 2:1, since this is the ratio used by Process A. The point U_A corresponds to an output of 100 square feet of sheet metal per week. (Why? Because Process A uses 2 man-hours of labor and 1 hour of machine time per square foot of sheet metal. Thus 200 man-hours of labor and 100 hours of machine time are required to produce an output of 100 square feet.)

Solving the Problem: No Constraints on Inputs

It is convenient to begin solving the problem by providing a graphic representation of each of the three processes. Since a process is defined to have fixed input proportions and since all points where input proportions are unchanged lie along a straight line through the origin, we can represent each process by such a line, or ***ray.*** In Figure 23.6, the ray *OA* represents Process A. Process A uses 2 man-hours of labor and 1 hour of machine time per square foot of sheet metal—in other words, 2 man-hours of labor for every hour of machine time. Consequently, the ray *OA* includes all points where labor time is combined with machine time in the ratio of 2:1.

Two things should be noted about ray *OA*. First, each point on this ray implies a certain output level. For example, point U_A, where 200 man-hours of labor and 100 hours of machine time are used, implies an output of 100 square feet of sheet metal per week. Second, every possible output rate corresponds to some point on this ray. This is true because all possible points at which labor time is combined with machine time in the ratio of 2:1 are included in the ray *OA*.

Figure 23.7
Graphical Representation of Processes A, B, and C
Ray *OA* pertains to Process A, ray *OB* to Process B, and ray *OC* to Process C. Based on these rays, we derive the isoquant corresponding to an output of 100 square feet per week, $U_AU_BU_C$. (Since Process B uses 1.5 man-hours of labor and 1.5 hours of machine time per square foot of sheet metal, point U_B is at 150 man-hours of labor and 150 hours of machine time. Since Process C uses 1.1 man-hours of labor and 2.2 hours of machine time per square foot of sheet metal, point U_C is at 110 man-hours of labor and 220 hours of machine time.)

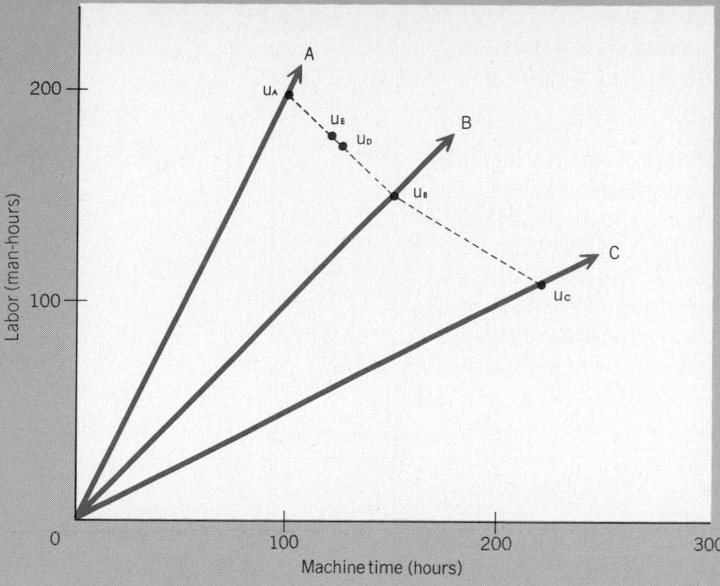

In Figure 23.7, we show the rays corresponding to all three processes: *OA* corresponds to Process A, *OB* to Process B, and *OC* to Process C. Each ray is constructed in the same way. Using these rays, we can draw the isoquant corresponding to the output of 100 square feet of sheet metal processed—the curve that includes all input combinations that can produce this amount of output. Focusing first on Processes A and B, point U_A is the point corresponding to an output of 100 square feet of sheet metal with Process A, and point U_B corresponds to an output of 100 square feet with Process B. Thus U_A and U_B are points on the isoquant corresponding to an output of 100 square feet of sheet metal.

Moreover, any point on the line segment joining U_A and U_B is also on this isoquant, because the firm can simultaneously use both Process A and Process B to remove defects from a total of 100 square feet of sheet metal. For example, point U_D corresponds to the case in which Processes A and B are each used to remove defects from 50 square feet of the metal; and point U_E corresponds to the case in which Process A is used for 60 square feet and Process B for 40 square feet. By varying the proportion of the total output subjected to each of these two processes, one can obtain all points on the line segment that joins U_A to U_B.

To complete the isoquant, we must recognize the existence of Process C, too. In Figure 23.7, U_C is the point corresponding to the use of Process C to remove defects from 100 square feet of sheet metal. Thus U_C is also a point on this isoquant. Moreover, any point on the line segment joining U_B and U_C is also on this isoquant, because the firm can simultaneously use both Process B and Process C to remove defects from a total of 100 square feet of sheet metal.[7] Consequently, the entire isoquant is $U_AU_BU_C$. Note that this isoquant, like all in linear programming, consists of connected line segments, and, while not smooth, has the same basic shape as the isoquants of conventional theory.

Given the isoquant $U_AU_BU_C$, it is simple to solve the firm's problem. All we have to do is

[7] At first glance, one might wonder why the line segment joining U_A to U_C is not part of the isoquant. After all, it too represents various combinations of labor time and machine time that can remove the defects from 100 square feet of sheet metal. This line segment is excluded because the points on it are inefficient: they use as much of one input and more of the other input than some point on $U_AU_BU_C$. Recall from the Appendix of Chapter 22 that an isoquant contains only efficient combinations of inputs.

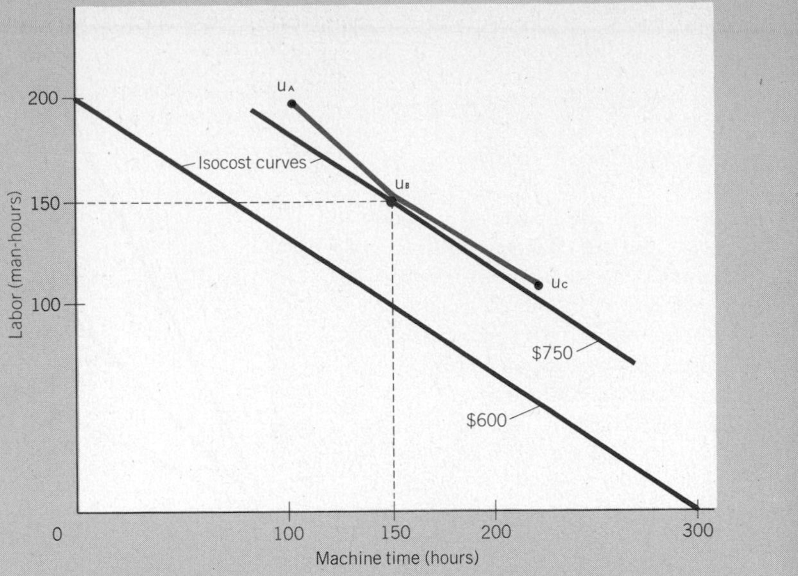

Figure 23.8
Isoquant and Isocost Curves
The point on the isoquant $U_A U_B U_C$ that is on the lowest isocost curve is point U_B. (The $600 isocost curve shows all combinations of labor and machine time that can be obtained for $600. The $750 isocost curve shows all combinations of labor and machine time that can be obtained for $750.)

construct Figure 23.8, which contains this isoquant as well as some isocost curves, each of which shows all input combinations that cost the firm the same amount. The isocost curves corresponding to $600 and $750 are shown in Figure 23.8. To find the input combination that minimizes the cost of removing defects from 100 square feet of sheet metal, we need only follow the procedure recommended in the Appendix to Chapter 22: find the point on the isoquant that is on the lowest isocost curve. Clearly, this is U_B—the point corresponding to the use of Process B alone. Thus the firm should use only Process B, its total costs will be $750, and it will make a profit of $250 per week on the contract, which is the best it can do.

Solving the Problem: Constraint on Machine Time

The foregoing problem is extremely simple—so simple that it can easily be solved outside the framework of linear programming.[8] Let's complicate the problem a bit and make it somewhat more realistic. In the previous section, we assumed that the firm could use all the machine time it wanted—at $2 per hour. But in the short run, the firm is likely to have only a certain number of machines available. It therefore is constrained to use no more than a certain number of machine hours per week. Specifically, suppose that the firm can use no more than 120 hours of machine time per week; this is the maximum capacity of the machines it owns or to which it has access. Now which process or processes should be used to satisfy the contract?

This problem recognizes that the firm has limited amounts of certain inputs in the short run; thus it contains constraints of the sort visualized in the linear-programming view of the firm. The objective is still to minimize the expression in Equation (23.1), and the constraints in Equation (23.2) and Inequality (23.3) must still be met, but there is now a new constraint:

$$Q_1 + 1.5\,Q_2 + 2.2\,Q_3 \leq 120 \qquad (23.4)$$

[8] All this problem really entails is a choice among three methods of production, the average costs of production being constant for each process and no constraint being placed on the amount that can be produced with a certain process. In such a case, the answer is obvious: produce the required volume of output with the process with the lowest average cost. Of course, the simplicity of this case does not detract from its usefulness as a first step in the discussion of the nature of linear programming.

Why? Because the number of hours of machine time per week must be less than (or equal to) 120, and the total number of hours of machine time used per week equals $Q_1 + 1.5Q_2 + 2.2Q_3$.

To see that this is so, recall that the removal of defects from each square foot of sheet metal by Process A requires 1 hour of machine time; thus, since Q_1 is the number of square feet of sheet metal treated per week by Process A, the number of hours of machine time per week used on Process A must also equal Q_1. Similarly, the number of hours of machine time per week used on Process B must equal 1.5 Q_2 since the removal of defects from each square foot of sheet metal by Process B requires 1.5 hours of machine time. Moreover, the number of hours of machine time per week used on Process C must equal 2.2 Q_3 since Process C requires 2.2 hours of machine time per square foot of metal. Thus the *total* amount of machine time used per week on *all* processes must be $Q_1 + 1.5\,Q_2 + 2.2\,Q_3$.

How can this problem be solved? The constraint in Inequality (23.4) means that many of the points in Figure 23.8 are no longer feasible, because they require more than 120 hours per week of machine time. These nonfeasible points are shown in the shaded area of Figure 23.9. To solve the problem, we must find that *feasible* point on the isoquant $U_A U_B U_C$ that is on the lowest isocost curve. The feasible points on this isoquant are all on line $U_A U_E$ in Figure 23.9. Isocost curves representing costs of \$600 and \$780 are also shown in Figure 23.9. It is evident that the point on $U_A U_E$ that is on the lowest isocost curve is U_E. Thus the firm should use 180 man-hours of labor and 120 machine hours per week—which means that Process A should be used on 60 square feet of sheet metal per week and Process B on 40 square feet.[9] The firm's total cost is \$780, and it makes \$220 per week—which is the best it can do under these circumstances.

[9] Since the total amount of man-hours used equals 180 hours, $2Q_1 + 1.5Q_2 = 180$. And since the total amount of machine time used equals 120 hours, $Q_1 + 1.5Q_2 = 120$. Solving these two equations simultaneously, $Q_1 = 60$ and $Q_2 = 40$. Thus Process A should be used on 60 square feet and Process B on 40 square feet.

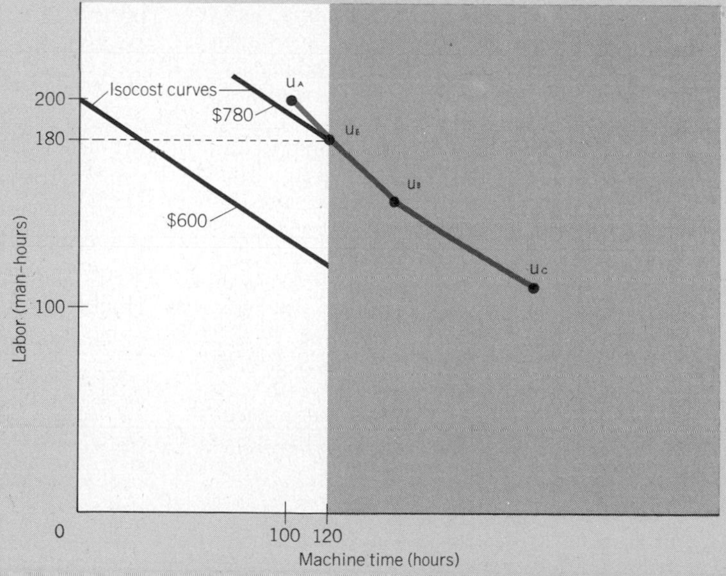

Figure 23.9
Isoquant (with constraint on machine time) and Isocost Curves
If the firm cannot use more than 120 hours of machine time per week, the shaded area is no longer feasible, so the feasible point on the isoquant that is on the lowest isocost curve is U_E. (The \$780 isocost curve, which is the lowest isocost curve touching the line U_AU_E, shows all combinations of labor and machine time that can be obtained for \$780.)

Applications of Linear Programming and Management Science

Since it is impossible to review all the many situations where linear programming has been applied, we restrict our attention here to two reasonably representative cases, as described by Robert Dorfman of Harvard. The first pertains to the petroleum refining industry; the second to the newsprint industry. Both are practical examples of how linear programming is actually used. Here are Dorfman's descriptions of these two cases:

> [In oil refining, one] application was to a moderate-sized refinery which produces premium and regular grades of automotive gasoline. The essential operation studied was blending. In blending, ten chemically distinct kinds of semirefined oil, called blending stocks, are mixed together. The result is a salable gasoline whose characteristics are approximately the weighted average of the characteristics of the blending stocks. For example, if 500 gallons of a stock with octane rating of 80 are blended with 1,000 gallons of a stock with octane rating of 86, the result will be $500 + 1{,}000 = 1{,}500$ gallons of product with octaine rating of $(\frac{1}{3} \times 80) + (\frac{2}{3} \times 86) = 84$.
>
> The significant aspect of gasoline blending for our present purposes is that the major characteristics of the blend—its knock rating, its vapor pressure, its sulphur content, etc.—can be expressed as linear functions of the quantities of the various blending stocks used. So also can the cost of the blend if each of the blending stocks has a definite price per gallon. Thus the problem of finding the minimum cost blend which will meet given quality specifications is a problem in mathematical programming.
>
> An entirely different kind of problem, also amenable to mathematical programming, arises in newsprint production. Freight is a major element in the cost of newsprint. One large newsprint company has six mills, widely scattered in Canada, and some two hundred customers, widely scattered in the United States. Its problem is to decide how much newsprint to ship from each mill to each customer so as, first, to meet the contract requirements of each customer, secondly, to stay within the capacity limits of each mill, and third, to keep the aggregate freight bill as small as possible. This problem involves 1,200 variables (6 mills × 200 customers), in contrast to the two- or four-variable problems we have been discussing. In the final solution most of these variables will turn out to be zero—the question is which ones. This problem is solved by mathematical programming and, though formidable, is not really as formidable as the count of variables might indicate.[10]

Of course, there is a great deal more to learn about linear programming than we can—or should—provide here. To understand the details, you must know some mathematics. Consequently, the detailed construction and solution of linear programming models are generally a matter for the expert, not the neophyte. But just as war is too important to be left to the generals, so linear programming is too useful to be left to the experts. In facing many problems, it is helpful to be familiar with the existence of linear programming and what it can reasonably be expected to do. Indeed, in many situations, this really is enough, since the rest can be delegated to others.

Linear programming is only one of a number of analytical tools that have been developed in the past 30 years to aid decision making in the private and public sectors of the economy. These techniques form the core of ***management science*** or ***operations research,*** a very rapidly growing and exciting field that draws on economics and other disciplines. Although management is still very much an art, the development and application of techniques like linear programming are making it more and more a science. Many problems that were "solved" only 10 or 20 years ago by guesswork and seat-of-the-pants judgment are now being handled by linear programming and other such techniques, with the result that decisions are better, firms are more efficient, and society gets more out of its available resources.

[10] R. Dorfman, "Mathematical, or 'Linear,' Programming," *American Economic Review,* December 1953, reprinted in Edwin Mansfield. *Microeconomics: Selected Readings,* 2d ed., New York: Norton, 1975.

PART SEVEN

Market Structure and Antitrust Policy

24

Perfect Competition and Monopoly

Even a country as rich as the United States cannot afford to waste resources, particularly when many of its citizens are poor and much of the world is hungry. One of the important determinants of how a society's resources are used is how its markets are organized. Thus, if the market for wheat contained few sellers rather than many, it would certainly use resources quite differently. Or if 20 firms, rather than one, provide telephone service in Chicago, resources would be used differently. Some forms of market organization tend to minimize social waste, whereas other forms promote it.

In this chapter, we examine the way resources are allocated and prices are set under perfect competition and monopoly. These two types of market organization—or market structures, as they are often called—are polar cases which seldom, if ever, occur in a pure form in the real world. But they are extremely useful models that shed much light on market structure's effects on resource allocation. Moreover, these models lie at the heart of many of our nation's policies toward business, including such important areas as our antitrust laws and the regulation of public utilities. Anyone who wants to understand how markets work in a capitalistic economy—or why our public policies toward business are what they are—must understand perfect competition and monopoly.

Market Structure and Economic Performance

Many economists have come to the conclusion, based on their studies of the workings of markets, that certain kinds of market organization are better, from society's point of view, than others. This is a much stronger statement than merely saying, as we did in the previous paragraph, that market structure influences market behavior. This statement is based on some set of values and preferences, explicit or implicit, and on certain economic models that predict that "better" behavior is more likely if markets are organized in certain ways than in other ways. Although there is considerable controversy on this score, many economists believe that, from society's point of view, market structures should be as close as possible to perfect competition, for reasons given below.

Economists have generally found it useful to classify markets into four broad types: perfect competition, monopoly, monopolistic competition, and oligopoly. Each of these terms describes a particular type of market structure or organization, a classification based largely, but not completely, on the number of firms in the industry that supplies the product. In perfect competition and monopolistic competition, there are *many* sellers, each of which produces only a small part of the industry's output. In monopoly, on the other hand, the industry consists of only a *single* seller. Oligopoly is an intermediate case where there are a *few* sellers. Each of these terms will be defined in detail in subsequent sections of this and the following chapter.

Perfect Competition

When a businessman speaks of a highly competitive market, he often means one in which each firm is keenly aware of its rivalry with a few others and in which advertising, styling, packaging, and other such commercial weapons are used to attract business away from them. In contrast, the basic feature of the economist's definition of ***perfect competition*** is its *impersonality.* Because there are so many firms in the industry, no firm views another as a competitor, any more than one small tobacco farmer views another small tobacco farmer as a competitor.

More specifically, a market must satisfy the following three conditions to be perfectly competitive. First, *the product of any one seller must be the same as the product of any other seller.* This condition insures that buyers do not care from which seller they purchase the goods, so long as the price is the same. Second, *each participant in the market, whether buyer or seller, must be so small in relation to the entire market that he cannot affect the product's price.* That is, all buyers and sellers must be "price takers," not "price makers." Third, *all resources must be able to switch readily from one use to another, and consumers, firms, and resource owners must have complete knowledge of all relevant economic and technological data.*

Clearly, no industry in the real world, now or in the past, satisfies all these conditions completely; thus no industry is perfectly competitive. Some agricultural markets may be reasonably close, but even they do not meet all the requirements. But this does not mean that it is useless to study the behavior of a perfectly competitive market. The conclusions derived from the model of perfect competition have proved very helpful in explaining and predicting behavior in the real world. Indeed, as we shall see, they have permitted a reasonably accurate view of resource allocation in many important segments of our economy.

Price and Output under Perfect Competition: The Market Period and the Short Run

How much of a particular product will be produced if the market is perfectly competitive, and what will the price be? The answers depend on the length of the time period. To begin with, let's consider the relatively short period of time when the supply of the relevant good is *fixed.* This period of time is called the ***market period.*** In the market period, as in the short and long runs, the price of a good in a perfectly competitive market is determined by the market demand and market supply curves. However, in the market period, the market supply curve is a vertical line, as shown in Figure 24.1.

Thus, in the market period, output is unaffected by price. In Figure 24.1, output is OQ—and regardless of price, it cannot be changed. *Given the supply, price is set by demand alone.* For example, price is OP_1 if the demand curve is D_1D_1', and OP_2 if the demand curve is D_2D_2'. The role of the price as a rationing device is particularly obvious in the market period, where this is the major function of price. The allocation of jam in the prisoner-of-war camp and the allocation of tickets to *My Fair Lady,* both taken up in Chapter 4, are among the examples you have encountered earlier of how price rations output in the market period. These cases can be regarded as taking place in the market period because the supply is fixed in each case.

Let's turn now to the short run, the period during which each firm's plant and equipment are fixed. What determines the price and output of a good in a perfectly competitive market in the short run? The answer once again is the market demand and market supply curves. However, the position and shape of these curves will generally be different in the short run than in the market period. In particular, the market supply curve in the short run will not be a vertical line; it will generally slope upward to the right, as in Figure 24.2. Thus, *in*

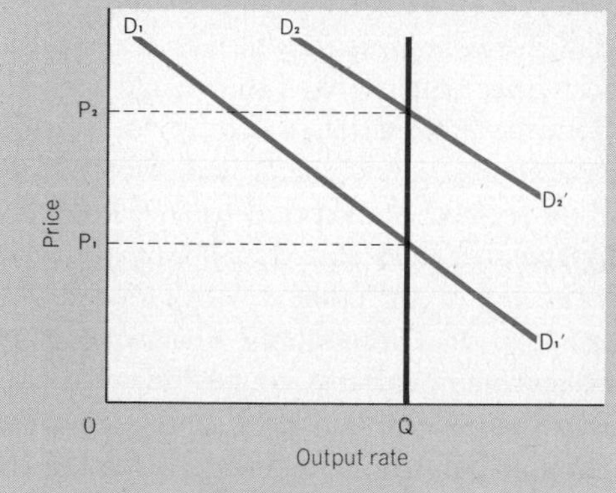

Figure 24.1
Price Determination in the Market Period
In the market period, supply is fixed at OQ. Equilibrium price is OP_1 if the demand curve is D_1D_1' and OP_2 if the demand curve is D_2D_2'.

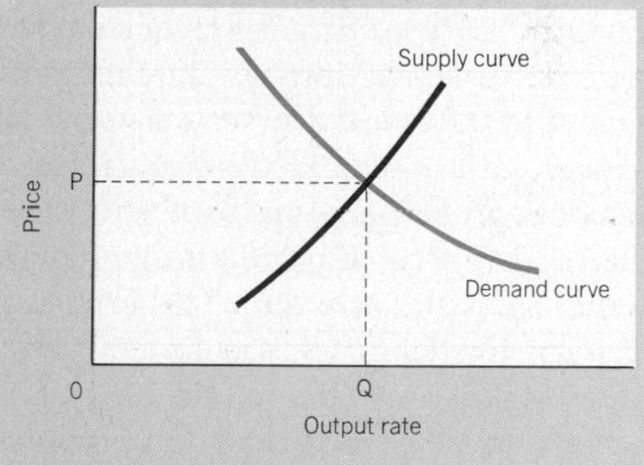

Figure 24.2
Price Determination in the Short Run
Equilibrium price is OP, and equilibrium output is OQ.

the short run, price influences, as well as rations, the amount supplied. In Figure 24.2, the equilibrium price and output in the short run are *OP* and *OQ*.

To illustrate the nature of the short-run supply curve, consider the bituminous coal industry, which in many respects comes reasonably close to perfect competition. According to Hubert Risser of the University of Kansas, the short-run supply curve for bituminous coal is very price elastic, so long as output stays within the range of existing capacity.[1] In other words, if output is less than existing capacity, small variations in price will result in large variations in output. Thus the situation in the short run is quite different from that in the market period, where output is fixed and unaffected by price. But of course the basic fact remains that equilibrium price and equilibrium output are determined by the intersection of the relevant demand and supply curves, in both the market period and the short run.

Price and Output under Perfect Competition: The Long Run

In the long run, what determines the output and price of a good in a perfectly competitive market? In the long run, a firm can change its plant size, which means that established firms may leave an industry if it has below-average profits, or that new firms may enter an industry with above-average profits. Equilibrium is achieved in the long run when enough firms—no more, no less—are in the industry so that "economic profits"—the excess of a firm's profits over what it could make with its resources in other industries—are zero. This condition is necessary for long-run equilibrium because new firms will enter the industry if there are economic profits, and existing firms will leave if there are economic losses.

Note that the existence of economic profits or losses in an industry brings about a shift in the industry's short-run supply curve. If there are economic profits, new firms will enter the industry, and so shift the short-run supply curve to the right. On the other hand, if there are economic losses in the industry (i.e., if the industry's profits are less than could be obtained elsewhere), existing firms will leave the industry, causing the short-run supply curve to shift to the left. Only if economic profits are zero will the number of firms in the industry—and the industry's short run supply curve—be stable. Putting this equilibrium condition another way, the long-run equilibrium position of the firm is at the point at which its long-run average costs equal price. If price exceeds average total costs, economic profits are being earned; and if price is less than average total costs, economic losses are being incurred.

Going a step further, *long-run equilibrium requires that price equal the lowest value of long-run average total costs.* In other words, firms must be producing at the *minimum point* on their long-run average cost curves, because to maximize their profits they must operate where price equals long-range marginal cost,[2] and at the same time they also have to operate where price equals long-run average cost. But if both these conditions are satisfied, long-run marginal cost must equal long-run average cost—since both equal price. And we know that long-run marginal cost equals long-run average cost only at the point at which long-run average cost is a minimum.[3] Consequently, if long-run marginal cost equals long-run average cost, the firm must be producing at the minimum point on the long-run average cost curve.

This equilibrium position is illustrated in Figure 24.3. When all adjustments are made, price equals *OP*. The equilibrium output of

[1] H. Risser, *The Economics of the Coal Industry,* Lawrence: University Press of Kansas, 1958, p. 155.

[2] The reasons why marginal cost must be equal to price, if profits are to be maximized, are given in Chapter 23.

[3] The previous discussion of this point on p. 520 concerned short-run cost functions, but the argument applies just as well to long-run cost functions.

Figure 24.3
Long-Run Equilibrium of a Perfectly Competitive Firm
In long-run equilibrium, output is *OQ* and the firm's plant corresponds to short-run average and marginal cost curves, *AA'* and *MM'*. At *OQ*, long-run marginal cost equals short-run marginal cost equals price; also, long-run average cost equals short-run average cost equals price. These conditions assure that the firm is maximizing profits and that economic profits are zero.

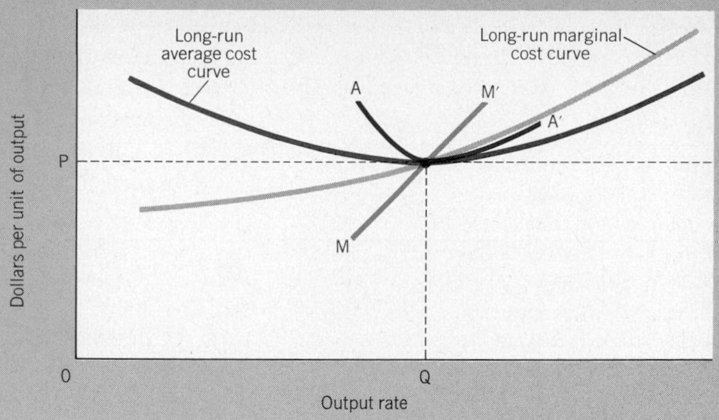

the firm is *OQ*, and its plant corresponds to short-run average and marginal cost curves *AA'* and *MM'*. At this output and with this plant, long-run marginal cost equals short-run marginal cost equals price: this insures that the firm is maximizing profit. Also, long-run average cost equals short-run average cost equals price: this insures that economic profits are zero. Since the long-run marginal cost and long-run average cost must be equal, the firm is producing at the minimum point on its long-run average cost curve.

To illustrate the process of entry and exit in an industry that approximates perfect competition, let's return to the bituminous coal industry. Entry into this industry is relatively easy, but exit is relatively difficult, for at least two reasons. First, it is costly to shut down a mine and reopen it later. Second, because of corrosion and water damage, it is hard to shut down a mine for longer than two years unless it is to be abandoned entirely. For these reasons, mines tend to stay open and produce even though short-term losses are incurred. For example, in the period before World War II, the demand for coal fell substantially, but although the industry suffered substantial losses, mines were slow to close down. Nonetheless, the competitive process had its way. Slowly, but surely, the number of mines fell markedly in response to these losses.[4] Thus, despite the barriers to rapid exit, firms eventually left the industry, just as the model would predict.

Constant, Increasing, and Decreasing Cost Industries

Perfectly competitive industries can be categorized into three types: constant cost industries, increasing cost industries, and decreasing cost industries. In a ***constant cost industry*** an expansion of output does not result in a change in input prices. Figure 24.4 shows the long-run equilibrium in a constant cost industry. Panel A shows the short- and long-run cost curves of a typical firm in the industry. Panel B shows the demand and supply curves in the market as a whole, *DD'* being the original demand curve and *SS'* being the original short-run supply curve. It is assumed that the industry is in long-run equilibrium, with the result that the price line is tangent to the long-run (and short-run) average cost curve at its minimum point. The price is *OP*.

Let's assume that the demand curve shifts from *DD'* to D_1D_1'. In the short run, with the

[4] J. B. Hendry, "The Bituminous Coal Industry," in W. Adams, *The Structure of American Industry*, New York: Macmillan, 1961.

Figure 24.4
Long-Run Equilibrium: Constant Cost Industry
If the demand curve shifts from DD' to D_1D_1', the price will increase in the short run from OP to OP_1. Each firm will expand output from OQ to OQ_1, and entry will occur, thus shifting the supply curve from SS' to S_1S_1'. The long-run supply curve in a constant cost industry is horizontal.

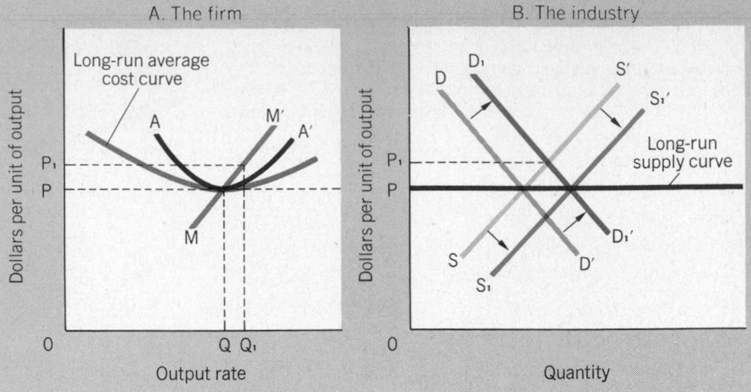

number of firms fixed, the price of the product will rise from OP to OP_1; each firm will expand output from OQ to OQ_1; and each firm will be making economic profits since OP_1 exceeds the short-run average costs of the firm at OQ_1. The consequence is that firms will enter the industry and shift the short-run supply curve to the right. In a constant cost industry, the entrance of the new firms does not affect the costs of the existing firms. The inputs used by this industry are used by many other industries as well, and the appearance of the new firms in this industry does not bid up the price of inputs (and consequently raise the costs of existing firms). Thus *a constant cost industry has a horizontal long-run supply curve.* Since output can be varied by varying the number of firms producing OQ units at an average cost of OP, the long-run supply curve is horizontal at OP.

Most economists seem to regard increasing, not constant, cost industries as the most prevalent of the three types. An ***increasing cost industry*** is one where the price of inputs increases with the amount the industry uses. The situation in such an industry is shown in Figure 24.5. The original conditions are the same as those in Figure 24.4, and we suppose again that the demand curve shifts from DD' to D_1D_1', with the result that the price of the product increases and firms earn economic profits, thus attracting new entrants. More and more inputs are required by the industry, and in an increasing cost industry the price of inputs increases with the amount the industry uses. Consequently, the cost of inputs increases for the established firms as well as the new entrants. The long-run average cost curves are pushed up from LL' to L_1L_1'. Thus the new equilibrium price is OP_2 and each firm produces OQ_2 units, the new short-run supply curve being S_2S_2'. *An increasing cost industry has a positively sloped long-run supply curve,* as shown in Figure 24.5. That is, after long-run equilibrium is achieved, increases in output require increases in the price of the product.

Decreasing cost industries are the most unusual situation, although quite young industries may sometimes fall into this category. In a ***decreasing cost industry,*** the expansion of the industry results in a decrease in the costs of the established firms.[5] Thus *a decreasing cost industry has a negatively sloped long-run supply curve.* That is, after long-run equilibrium is reached, increases in output are accompanied by decreases in price.

Whether an industry is a constant cost in-

[5] Certain *external economies,* which are cost reductions that occur when an industry expands, may be responsible for the existence of decreasing cost industries. An example of such an external economy is an improvement in transportation that is due to the expansion of an industry and that reduces the costs of each firm in the industry (see Chapter 5).

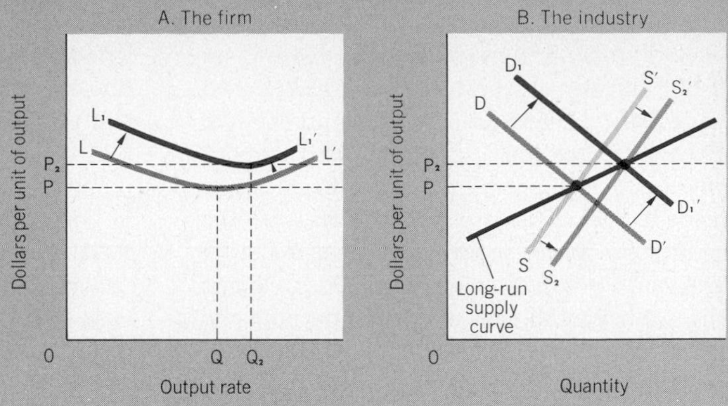

Figure 24.5
Long-Run Equilibrium: Increasing Cost Industry
If the demand curve shifts from DD' to D_1D_1', the price will increase in the short run. Entry will occur, and the price of inputs will increase, thus pushing the long-run average cost curve upward (from LL' to L_1L_1'). The new short-run supply curve will be S_2S_2'. The long-run supply curve in an increasing cost industry slopes upward to the right.

dustry, an increasing cost industry, or a decreasing cost industry is an empirical question that must be settled case by case. In trying to determine whether a particular industry is an increasing or constant cost industry, one important consideration is whether it is a relatively large user of certain inputs. For example, because the automobile industry uses a great deal of the nation's steel, an expansion of the automobile industry might well cause an increase in the price of steel; but an expansion of the paper-clip industry, which uses very little of the nation's steel, would be unlikely to raise the price of steel.

The Allocation of Resources under Perfect Competition: A More Detailed View

At this point, it is instructive to describe the process by which a perfectly competitive economy—one composed of perfectly competitive industries—would allocate resources. In Chapters 3 and 4, we stressed that the allocation of resources among alternative uses is one of the major functions of an economic system. Equipped with the concepts of this and previous chapters, we can now go much farther in describing how a perfectly competitive economy shifts resources in accord with changes in tastes, technology and other factors.

To be specific, suppose that a change occurs in tastes. Consumers become more favorably disposed toward wheat and less favorably disposed toward corn than in the past.[6] In the short run, the increase in the demand for wheat increases the price of wheat, and results in some increase in the output of wheat. However, the output cannot be increased very substantially because the industry's capacity cannot be expanded in the short run. Similarly, the fall in the demand for corn reduces the price of corn, and results in some reduction in output. But the output will not be curtailed greatly because firms will continue to produce as long as they can cover variable costs.

The change in the relative prices of wheat and corn tells producers that a reallocation of resources is called for. Because of the increase in the price of wheat and the decrease in the price of corn, wheat producers are earning economic profits and corn producers are showing economic losses. This will trigger a new de-

[6] Since we assume here that the markets for wheat and corn are perfectly competitive, it is also assumed that there is no government intervention in these markets.

ployment of resources. If some variable inputs in corn production can be used as effectively in the production of wheat, they may be switched from corn production to wheat production. Even if no variable inputs are used in both wheat and corn production, adjustment can be made in various interrelated markets, with the result that wheat production gains resources and corn production loses resources. When short-run equilibrium is attained in both the wheat and corn industries, the reallocation of resources is not yet complete since there has not been enough time for producers to build new capacity or liquidate old capacity. In particular, neither industry is operating at minimum average cost. The wheat producers are operating at greater than the output level where average cost is a minimum; and the corn producers are operating at less than this level.

What will happen in the long run? The shift in consumer demand from corn to wheat will result in greater adjustments in production and smaller adjustments in price than in the short run. In the long run, existing firms can leave corn production and new firms can enter wheat production. Because of short-run economic losses in corn production, some corn land and related equipment will be allowed to run down, and some firms engaged in corn production will be liquidated. As firms leave corn production, the supply curve shifts to the left, causing the price to rise above its short-run level. The transfer of resources out of corn production will stop when the price has increased, and costs have decreased, to the point where losses are avoided.

While corn production is losing resources, wheat production is gaining them. The prospect of positive economic profits in wheat production will cause new firms to enter the industry. The increased demand for inputs will raise input prices and cost curves in wheat production, and the price of wheat will be depressed by the movement to the right of the supply curve because of the entry of new firms. Entry ceases when economic profits are no longer being earned. At that point, when long-run equilibrium is achieved, more resources will be used in the industry than in the short run.

Finally, long-run equilibrium is established in both industries, and the reallocation of resources is complete. It is important to note that this reallocation can affect industries other than wheat and corn. If corn land and equipment can be easily adapted to the production of wheat, corn producers can simply change to wheat production. If not, the resources used in corn production are converted to some use other than wheat, and the resources that enter wheat production come from some use other than corn production.

Bituminous Coal: A Case Study

To illustrate how resources are allocated in the long run, we will look in more detail at the bituminous coal industry. Although it does not have all the characteristics of a perfectly competitive industry, it has enough of them so that the perfectly competitive model predicts many aspects of its behavior reasonably well. From the turn of the century until about 1923, the bituminous coal industry expanded rapidly. Between 1903 and 1923, the price of coal increased from $1.24 to $2.68 per ton, in considerable part because of the marked upward shift to the right of the demand curve for coal, an important fuel in this period of general industrial growth. In addition, the high prices of the period were sometimes the result of temporary shortages caused by strikes and insufficient railroad transportation. Thus temporary upward shifts to the left of the supply curve for coal, as well as shifts of the demand curve, were responsible for the increases in price.

Given the very high coal prices of 1917–23, coal mining was very profitable. Indeed, after-tax income in 1920 was about 20 percent of invested capital for all bituminous coal companies—and much higher for particular companies. These high profits signaled that more resources should be invested in the industry. And just as the perfectly competitive model would predict, more resources were invested; the number of bituminous coal firms increased by over 130 percent in nine key states between 1903 and 1923, and the industry's capacity grew by over 50 percent between 1913 and 1923.

Unfortunately, the demand for coal dropped considerably from 1923 to 1933, plunging the industry into a severe economic crisis. The downward shift to the left of the demand curve for coal during the early 1930s was due in considerable part to the fall in national output during the Great Depression. It was accompanied by a marked decrease in the price of coal: from $2.68 in 1923, the price per ton fell to $1.34 in 1933. Needless to say, this tremendous drop meant losses for bituminous coal producers. Indeed, in every year between 1925 and 1940, the bituminous coal industry as a whole showed losses.

These economic losses signaled that resources should be withdrawn from the bituminous coal industry and used elsewhere in the economy where they could be more valuably employed. And as the perfectly competitive model would predict, resources were in fact taken out of bituminous coal. Between 1923 and 1933, there was a reduction of over 40 percent in the number of coal companies operating in nine key states. And the industry's capacity fell by almost 40 percent between 1923 and 1933. Despite the difficulties in exit that we described in a previous section, the competitive process had its way. Its signals were heeded. Consequently, the industry began to move closer and closer to a position of long-run equilibrium, and although the industry remained on the nation's sick list, it began to show much smaller losses. By the onset of World War II, many of the basic adjustments had taken place.

Monopoly

At the opposite extreme from perfect competition is monopoly. Under a monopolistic market structure, what sort of behavior can we expect? How much of the product will be produced, and at what level will its price be set? To begin with, recall what is meant by ***monopoly:*** *a market where there exists one, and only one, seller.* Monopoly, like perfect competition, seldom corresponds more than approximately to conditions in real industries, but it is a very useful model.

In several respects, monopoly and perfect competition stand as polar opposites. The firm in a perfectly competitive market has so many rivals that competition becomes entirely impersonal. The firm is a price taker, an inconspicuous seller in a sea of inconspicuous sellers. The firm under monopoly has no direct competitors at all; it is the sole supplier. However, the monopolist is not entirely free of rivals. Even he is affected by certain indirect and potential forms of competition. For example, even if a firm managed to obtain a monopoly on wheat production, it would have to worry about competition from corn and other agricultural commodities that could be substituted for wheat. Moreover, the wheat monopolist would also have to take into account the possibility that new firms might arise to challenge its monopoly if it attempted to extract conspicuously high profits. Thus even the monopolist is subject to some restraint imposed by competitive forces.

Causes of Monopoly

There are many reasons why monopolies, or market structures that closely approximate monopoly, may arise.

Patents. A firm may acquire a monopoly over the production of a good by having patents on the product or on certain basic processes used in its production. The patent laws of the United States give an inventor the exclusive right to make a certain product or to use a certain process for 17 years. The purpose of the patent system is, of course, to encourage invention and innovation and to discourage industrial secrecy. Many firms with monopoly power achieved it in considerable part through patents. For example, the United Shoe Machinery Company became the sole supplier of certain important kinds of shoemaking equipment through control of basic patents. United Shoe was free to dominate the market until 1954, when, after prosecution under the antitrust laws, the firm was ordered to license its patents. And in 1968, when this remedy seemed insufficient, a divestiture program was agreed upon.

Inputs. A firm may become a monopolist by obtaining control over the entire supply of a basic input required to manufacture a product. For example, the International Nickel Company of Canada controls about $^9/_{10}$ of the proven nickel reserves in the world. Since it is hard to produce nickel without nickel, the International Nickel Company obviously has a strong monopoly position. Similarly, the Aluminum Company of America (Alcoa) kept its dominant position for a long time by controlling practically all the sources of bauxite, the ore used to make aluminum. However, as we shall see in Chapter 26, Alcoa's monopoly was broken in 1945 when the Supreme Court decided that Alcoa's control of practically all the industry's output violated the antitrust laws.

Government. A firm may become a monopolist because it is awarded a market franchise by a government agency. For example, the government may give a particular firm the franchise to sell a particular product in a public facility. Or it may give a particular company the right to provide a service, such as telephone service, to people in a particular area. In exchange for this right, the firm agrees to allow the government to regulate certain aspects of its operations. The form of regulation does not matter here; the important point for now is that the monopoly is created by the government.

Declining Cost. A firm may become a monopolist because the average costs of producing the product reach a minimum at an output rate that is large enough to satisfy the entire market (at a price that is profitable). In a case like this, a firm obviously has an incentive to expand until it produces all the market wants of the good. (Its costs fall as it continues to expand). Thus competition cannot be maintained in this case. If there are a number of firms in the industry, the result is likely to be economic warfare—and the survival of a single victor, the monopolist.[7]

Cases where costs behave like this are called ***natural monopolies.*** When an industry is a natural monopoly, the public often insists that its behavior be regulated by the government. For example, electric power is an industry where there seem to be great economies of scale—and thus decreasing average costs. Fuel consumed per kilowatt hour is lower in larger power generating units, and there are economies in combining generating units at a single site.[8] Because of these factors, it would be foolish to force competition in the industry, since it would be grossly wasteful. Instead, as we describe later, the market for electric power in a particular area is a regulated monopoly.

Naturally, the likelihood that the long-run average cost curve will decrease up to a point that satisfies the entire market depends on the size of the market. The smaller the market, the more likely it is. For example, in Figure 24.6, the industry is a natural monopoly if the demand curve is DD', but not if it is D_1D_1'. This is an important point. One of the disadvantages of tariffs is that they create separate little markets that can more easily be monopolized.

[7] Note that economies of scale are different from the external economies discussed in note 5: the individual firm has no control over external economies.

[8] Leonard W. Weiss, *Case Studies in American Industry,* New York: Wiley, 1967, pp. 90–91.

Figure 24.6
Natural Monopoly
The industry is a natural monopoly, if the demand curve is DD', but not if it is D_1D_1'.

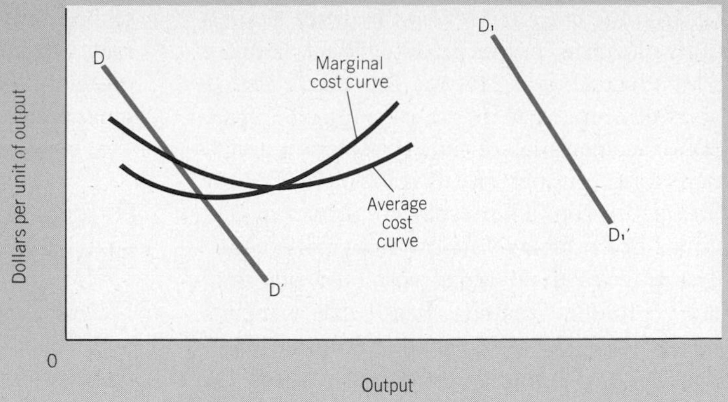

Conversely, one of the advantages claimed for the Common Market in Europe was that it would create a larger market that could support more efficient production and more competitive industries. More will be said on this score in Chapter 31. For now, the important point to recognize is that, just as stagnant marshes breed mosquitos, so small, insulated markets breed monopoly.

Demand Curve and Marginal Revenue under Monopoly

Before we can make any statements about the behavior of a monopolistic market, we must point out certain important characteristics of the demand curve facing the monopolist. Since the monopolist is the only seller of the commodity, the demand curve facing him is, of course, the market demand curve for the product. Since the market demand curve is almost always downward-sloping to the right, the monopolist's demand curve must also be downward-sloping to the right. This is quite different from perfect competition, where the firm's demand curve is horizontal. To illustrate the situation faced by a monopolist, consider the hypothetical case in Table 24.1. The price at which each quantity (shown in column 1) can be sold by the monopolist is shown in column 2. The firm's ***total revenue***—its total dollar sales volume—is shown in column 3. Obviously, column 3 is the product of the first two columns. Column 4 contains the firm's ***marginal revenue,*** defined as the addition to total revenue attributable to the addition of one unit to sales. (Thus if $R(q)$ is total revenue when q units are sold and $R(q-1)$ is total revenue when $(q-1)$ units are sold, the marginal revenue between q units and $(q-1)$ units is $R(q) - R(q-1)$.)

Marginal revenue is very important to the monopolist. We can estimate it from the figures in the first three columns of Table 24.1.

Table 24.1
Demand and Revenue of a Monopolist

Quantity	Price	Total revenue (dollars)	Marginal revenue
1	100	100	—
2	90	180	80
3	80	240	60
4	70	280	40
5	60	300	20
6	50	300	0
7	40	280	−20
8	30	240	−40

[a] These figures pertain to the interval between the indicated quantity of output and 1 unit less than the indicated quantity of output.

Clearly, the marginal revenue between 1 and 2 units of output per month is $180 – $100, or $80; the marginal revenue between 2 and 3 units of output per month is $240 – $180, or $60; the marginal revenue between 3 and 4 units of output per month is $280 – $240, or $40; and so on. The results are shown in column 4 of the table. Note that marginal revenue is analogous to marginal cost (and marginal utility, for that matter). Recall that marginal cost is the extra cost resulting from an extra unit of production. Substitute "revenue" for "cost" and "sales" for "production" in the previous sentence, and what do you get? A perfectly acceptable definition of marginal revenue.

Marginal revenue will always be *less than price* if the firm's demand curve is downward sloping (as it is under monopoly and other market structures that are not perfectly competitive). For example, in Table 24.1, the extra revenue from the second unit of output is $80 whereas the price of this unit is $90. The basic reason is that the firm must reduce the price of *all* units of output, not just the extra unit, in order to sell the extra unit. Thus, in Table 24.1, the extra revenue from the second unit of output is $80 because, while the price of the second unit is $90, the price of the first unit must be reduced by $10 in order to sell the second unit. Thus the extra revenue (that is, marginal revenue) is $90 – $10, or $80.

Table 24.2
Costs of a Monopolist

Quantity	Total variable cost (dollars)	Fixed cost	Total cost	Marginal cost[a]
1	40	100	140	40
2	70	100	170	30
3	110	100	210	40
4	150	100	250	40
5	200	100	300	50
6	260	100	360	60
7	350	100	450	90
8	450	100	550	109

[a] These figures pertain to the interval between the indicated quantity of output and 1 unit less than the indicated quantity of output.

Price and Output under Monopoly: The Short Run

We are now in a position to determine how output and price behave under monopoly. If the monopolist is free to maximize his profits, he will, of course, choose the price and output

Table 24.3
Profits of a Monopolist

Quantity	Total revenue (dollars)	Total cost	Total profit
1	100	140	−40
2	180	170	10
3	240	210	30
4	280	250	30
5	300	300	0
6	300	360	−60
7	280	450	−170
8	240	550	−310

Table 24.4
Marginal Cost and Marginal Revenue of a Monopolist

Quantity	Marginal cost[a]	Marginal revenue[a]	Total profit
1	40	—	−40
2	30	80	10
3	40	60	30
4	40	40	30
5	50	20	0
6	60	0	−60
7	90	−20	−170
8	100	−40	−310

[a] These figures pertain to the interval between the indicated quantity of output and one unit less than the indicated quantity of output.

at which the difference between total revenue and total cost is greatest. For example, if the firm's costs are as shown in Table 24.2 and if the demand curve it faces is as shown in Table 24.1, the firm will choose an output of either 3 or 4 units per period of time and a price of $80 or $70. This is evident from Table 24.3, which shows the firm's total profit at each output rate. Figure 24.7 shows the same thing graphically.

In Chapter 23, we set forth the Golden Rule of Output Determination for a perfectly competitive firm. We can now formulate a Golden Rule of Output Determination for a monopolist: *set the output rate at the point where marginal revenue equals marginal cost.* Table 24.4 and Figure 24.8 show that this rule results in a maximum profit in this example. It is easy to prove that this is generally a necessary condition for profit maximization. At any output rate at which marginal revenue exceeds marginal cost, profit can be increased by increasing output, since the extra revenue will exceed the extra cost. At any output rate at which marginal revenue is less than marginal cost, profit can be increased by reducing output, since the decrease in cost will exceed the decrease in revenue. Thus, since profit will not be a maximum when marginal revenue exceeds marginal cost

Figure 24.7
Total Revenue, Cost, and Profit of Monopolist
The output rate that will maximize the firm's profits is either 3 or 4 units per period of time. And based on the demand curve for its product (shown in Table 24.1), it must set a price of $80 or $70 to sell either 3 or 4 units per period of time.

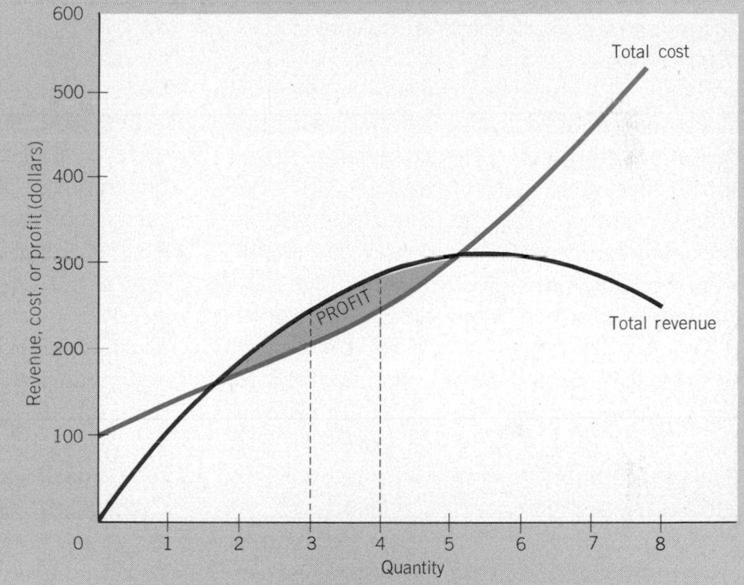

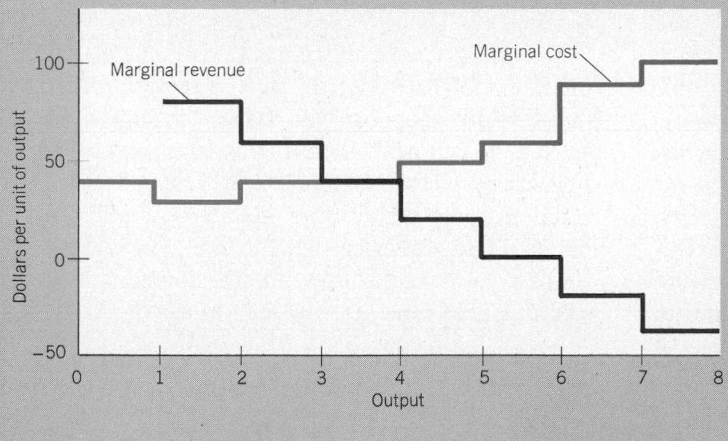

Figure 24.8
Marginal Cost and Marginal Revenue of Monopolist
At the profit-maximizing output rate of 3 or 4 units per period of time, marginal cost equals marginal revenue.

Figure 24.9
Equilibrium Position of Monopolist
The monopolist sets its output rate at *OQ*, where the marginal revenue curve *RR′* intersects the marginal cost curve *MM′*. At this output, price must be *OP*. And profit per unit of output equals *CP*, since average cost equals *OC*.

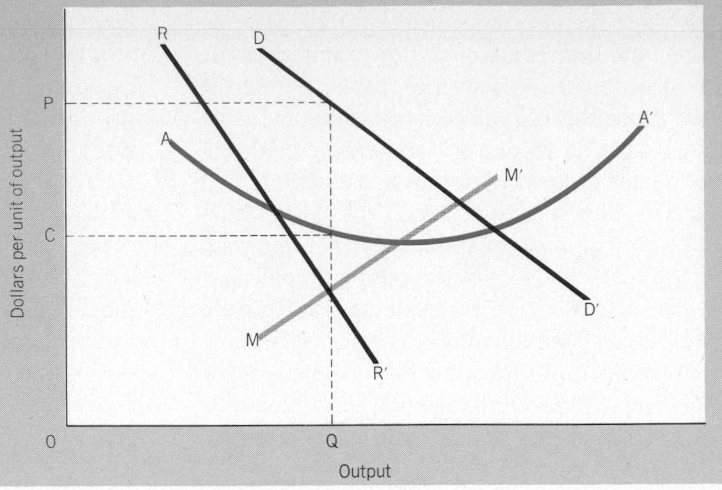

or falls short of marginal cost, it must be a maximum only when marginal revenue equals marginal cost.

Figure 24.9 shows the equilibrium position of a monopolist in the short run, *DD′* being the demand curve for its product, *AA′* the firm's short-run average cost curve, and *MM′* the firm's short-run marginal cost curve. *RR′* is the marginal revenue curve—the curve that shows the firm's marginal revenue at each output level. Short-run equilibrium will occur at the output, *OQ*, where the *MM′* curve intersects the *RR′* curve. And if the monopolist is to sell *OQ* units per period of time, the demand curve shows that it must set a price of *OP*. Thus the equilibrium output and price are *OQ* and *OP*, respectively.

It is interesting to compare the Golden Rule of Output Determination for a monopolist (set the output rate at the point where marginal revenue equals marginal cost) with that for a perfectly competitive firm (set the output rate at the point where price equals marginal cost). The latter is really the same as the former because, *for a perfectly competitive firm, price equals marginal revenue.* Since the perfectly competitive firm can sell all it wants at the market price, each additional unit sold increases the firm's total revenue by the amount of the price. Thus, *for both the monopolist and the perfectly competitive firm, profits are maximized by setting the output rate at the point where marginal revenue equals marginal cost.*

From the previous chapter, we know that perfectly competitive firms sometimes find it preferable to shut down rather than follow this rule; is this true for a monopolist as well? The answer is yes. *Just as a perfectly competitive firm will discontinue production if it will lose more money by producing than by shutting down, so a monopolist will do the same thing, and for the same reasons.* In other words, if there is no output such that price exceeds average variable costs, the monopolist, like a perfect competitor, will discontinue production. Certainly this makes sense. If by producing, the monopolist incurs greater losses than his fixed costs, he will "drop out," i.e., produce nothing.

Finally, note two misconceptions concerning monopoly behavior. First, it is sometimes said that a monopolist will charge "as high a price as he can get." Clearly, this is nonsense. For example, the monopolist in Table 24.1 could charge a higher price than $70 or $80, but to do so would be foolish since it would result in lower profits. Second, it is sometimes said that a monopolist will seek to maximize his profit per unit of output. This too is nonsense, since the monopolist is interested in his total profits and his return on capital, not on the profit per unit of output. A rational monopolist will not sacrifice his total profits to increase his profit per unit of output.

Price and Output under Monopoly: The Long Run

In contrast to the situation under perfect competition, the long-run equilibrium of a monopolistic industry may not be marked by the absence of economic profits. If a monopolist earns a short-run economic profit, he will not be confronted in the long run with competitors, unless the industry ceases to be a monopoly. The entrance of additional firms into the industry is, of course, incompatible with the existence of monopoly. Thus the long-run equilibrium of an industry under monopoly may be characterized by economic profits.

On the other hand, if the monopolist incurs a short-run economic loss, he will be forced to look for other, more profitable uses for his resources. One possibility is that his existing plant is not optimal and that he can earn economic profits by appropriate alterations to its scale and characteristics. If so, he will make these alterations in the long run and remain in the industry. However, if there is no scale of plant that will enable him to avoid economic losses, he will leave the industry in the long run. It should be obvious that the mere fact of having a monopoly over the production of a certain commodity does not mean that the firm must be profitable. For example, a monopoly over the production of cut-glass spittoons would be unlikely to catapult a firm into financial glory—or even allow it to avoid losses.

To illustrate the long-run behavior of a monopolist, consider the prewar policy of the Aluminum Company of America (Alcoa). Until after World War II, Alcoa was virtually the sole producer of aluminum in the United States. According to various observers, Alcoa recognized the dangers involved in potential competition, and adopted a policy of keeping its price low enough to ward off potential entrants. Naturally, it wanted to make money—and it did. But it was smart enough to see that, if it charged very high prices, it might encourage other firms to enter the aluminum industry. So it set a price high enough to permit it to make plenty of economic profits, but not so high that it would have to wrestle with competitors. Some other firms with monopoly power think the same way and act accordingly, but by no means all are so clever. On the contrary, some monopolists, like some newlyweds, think the *status quo* will last forever. And just as for newlyweds, sometimes it does, but sometimes it doesn't.

Perfect Competition and Monopoly: A Comparison

At the beginning of this chapter, we said that a market's structure would be likely to affect the behavior of the market; in other words, that a market's structure would influence how much was produced and the price that would be set. If we could perform an experiment in which an industry was first operated under conditions of perfect competition and then under conditions of monopoly (assuming that the demand for the industry's product and the industry's cost functions would be the same in either case[9]), we would find that the equilibrium price and output would differ under the two sets of conditions.

Specifically, if the product demand curve and the industry's cost functions are the same, *the output of a perfectly competitive industry*

[9] However, the cost and demand curves need not be the same. For example, the monopolist may spend money on advertising, thus shifting the demand curve. It should be recognized that the assumption that they are the same is stronger than it appears at first glance.

Figure 24.10
Comparison of Long-Run Equilibria: Perfect Competition and Monopoly
Under perfect competition, OQ_C is the industry output and OP_C is the price. Under monopoly, OQ_M is the industry output and OP_M is the price. Clearly, output is higher and price is lower under perfect competition than under monopoly.

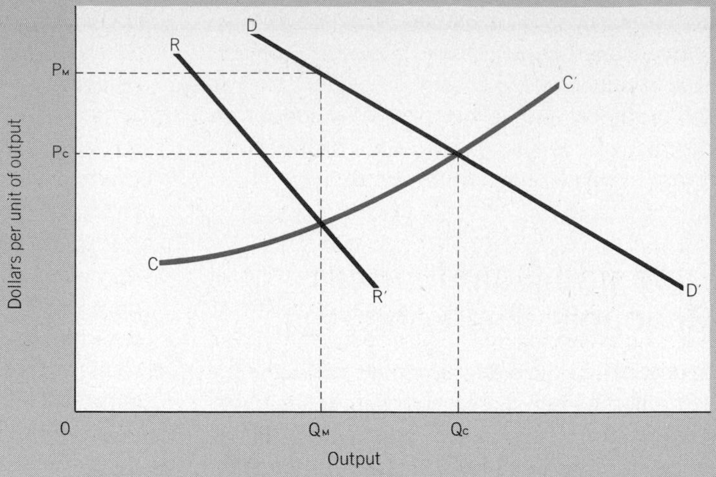

tends to be greater and the price tends to be lower than under monopoly. We see this in Figure 24.10, which shows DD', the industry's demand curve, and CC', the horizontal sum of the marginal cost curves of the perfectly competitive firms. If the industry is perfectly competitive, CC' is the industry supply curve. Since price and output under perfect competition are given by the intersection of the demand and supply curves, OQ_C is the industry output and OP_C is the price. But what if all of the competitive firms are bought up by a single firm, which operates as a pure monopolist? Under these conditions, CC' is the monopolist's marginal cost curve,[10] and DD' is the demand curve he faces. Moreover, RR' is his marginal revenue curve. Since the monopolist chooses the output where marginal cost equals marginal revenue, the industry output will be OQ_M and the price will be OP_M. Clearly, OQ_M is less than OQ_C, and OP_M is greater than OP_C—which is what we set out to prove.

Of course, all this is theory. But there is plenty of evidence that monopolists restrict output and charge higher prices than under competition. For example, take the case of tungsten carbide, which sold for \$50 per pound until a monopoly was established in 1927 by General Electric. Then the price went to between \$225 and \$453 per pound, until the monopoly was broken by the antitrust laws in 1945. The price then dropped back to between \$27 and \$45 per pound.[11] This case was extreme, but by no means unique. Indeed, for centuries people have observed that when monopolies are formed, output tends to be restricted, and price tends to be driven up.

Moreover, it has long been felt that the allocation of resources under perfect competition is socially more desirable than under monopoly. Society might be better off if more resources were devoted to producing the monopolized good in Figure 24.10, and if the competitive, not the monopolistic, output were produced. For example, in the *Wealth of Nations,* published about 200 years ago, Adam Smith stressed that when competitive forces are thwarted by "the great engine . . . of monopoly," the tendency for resources to be used "as

[10] The monopolist will operate the various plants that would be independent under perfect competition as branches of a single firm. It can be shown that the marginal cost curve of a multiplant monopoly is the horizontal sum of the marginal cost curves of the individual plants.

[11] W. Adams, *The Structure of American Industry,* p. 537.

nearly as possible in the proportion which is most agreeable to the interest of the whole society" is thwarted as well.

Why do many economists believe that the allocation of resources under perfect competition is more socially desirable than that under monopoly? This is not a simple question, and like most hard questions can be answered at various levels of sophistication. Put most simply, many economists believe that firms under perfect competition are induced to produce quantities of goods that are more in line with consumer desires, and that firms under perfect competition are induced to use the least costly methods of production. In Chapter 26, we shall indicate in detail why they believe that these things are true—and provide a much more complete discussion of the pros and cons of monopoly and competition.

Public Regulation of Monopoly

One way that society has attempted to reduce the harmful effects of monopoly is through ***public regulation.*** For example, suppose that the long-run cost curve in a particular industry is such that competition is not feasible. In such a case, society may permit a monopoly to be established, but a commission or some other public body is also established to regulate the monopoly's behavior. Among the many such regulatory commissions in the United States are the Federal Power Commission, the Federal Communications Commission, and the Interstate Commerce Commission. They regulate the behavior of firms with monopoly power in the electric power, telephone, transportation, and other industries. These industries are big as well as important, taking in about 10 percent of the national output. Thus we need to know how these commissions operate and make decisions on prices and other matters.

Regulatory commissions often set the price—or the maximum price—at the level at which it equals average total cost, including a "fair" rate of return on the firm's investment. For example, in Figure 24.11, the price would be established by the commission at *OP,* where the demand curve, *DD′*, intersects the average total cost curve, *AA′*, the latter including what the commission regards as a fair profit per unit of output.

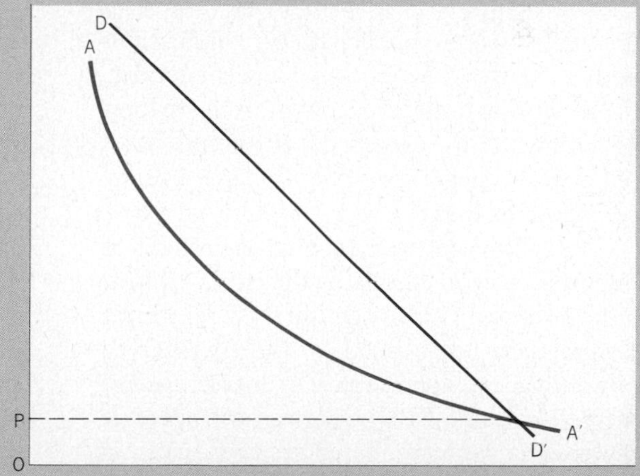

Figure 24.11
Regulation of Monopoly
The price established by a commission might be *OP*, where the demand curve *DD′* intersects the average total cost curve *AA′*. Costs here include what the commission regards as a fair profit per unit of output.

put. Needless to say, there has been considerable controversy over what constitutes a fair rate of return. Frequently, commissions have settled on 7 to 9 percent. In addition, there has been a good deal of controversy over what should be included in the company's "investment" on which the fair rate of return is to be earned. A company's assets can be valued at ***historical cost*** or at ***reproduction cost***—at what the company paid for them or at what it would cost to replace them. If the price level does not change much, these two approaches yield much the same answer. But if prices are rising—as they have been during most of the past 40 years—replacement cost will be greater than historical cost, with the result that the company will be allowed higher profits and rates if replacement cost is used. Most commissions now use historical cost.

To illustrate the public regulation of monopoly, consider the electric power industry in the United States. From its inception, the industry has been regulated, but this regulation has taken various forms. In the latter part of the nineteenth century, local governments issued franchises to attract power companies to their areas. As time went on, these franchises attempted to introduce more control over the companies, but city officials were often inexpert and corruption was frequent. At the turn of the century, there was a widespread cry for reform. Shortly before World War I, most of the states set up public utility commissions with the power to set rates and regulate service, the idea being to transfer control from the local governments to expert commissions. Most public utility regulation is in the hands of state commissions today.

The federal government also has played an important role in regulating the electric power industry since 1935, when the Federal Power Commission (established in 1920) was given power over rates and service in interstate commerce. Also, the FPC was given considerable power over accounting and security issues in the wake of the financial problems of the 1920s and the relative impotence of the state commissions in handling them. Although state commissions still have the principal responsibility for regulating electric power companies, the FPC has introduced many important new policies and methods. For example, it has been stricter in various areas of accounting. Indeed, some firms have tried to get out from under federal regulations by getting rid of their interstate connections. Although conflicts have arisen between the FPC and the state commissions, the FPC's orders generally supplement, rather than override, those of the state commissions.[12]

The regulatory commissions and the principles they use have become extremely controversial. Many observers feel that the commissions are lax, and that they tend to be captured by the industries they are supposed to regulate. For these and other reasons, some economists believe that regulation has little effect on prices. For example, George Stigler and Claire Friedland of the University of Chicago found that the level of electricity prices in a state does not seem to be affected by whether or not the state has a regulatory commission.[13] Moreover, it is frequently charged that the regulated industries have too little incentive to cut costs and to develop and accept innovations, and that they tend to favor uneconomical techniques because of the way prices are regulated. It is extremely difficult to measure the effects of regulation, and equally difficult to specify reasonable alternatives to existing practices that are both politically feasible and likely to be a substantial improvement. The odds are that this problem will remain with us for many years to come.

New Drugs: A Case Study

One of the most interesting and important illustrations of the controversies swirling

[12] L. Weiss, *Case Studies in American Industry,* pp. 96–98.

[13] G. Stigler and C. Friedland, "What Can Regulators Regulate? The Case of Electricity," *The Journal of Law and Economics,* 1962.

around the regulatory process is the case of pharmaceuticals. During the past 40 years, a wide variety of important new pharmaceuticals has been developed to ease pain and extend life. Among the most heralded of these new drugs have been penicillin, streptomycin, the polio vaccine, tranquilizers, and oral contraceptives. The Food and Drug Administration is charged with the regulatory responsibility of determining whether a new drug should be marketed in the United States. Obviously, the public should be protected from the sale of unsafe or harmful pharmaceutical products. Before 1962, the FDA was required to determine whether or not a new drug was unsafe, but not whether it was effective in its intended use. In other words, if a new drug was not really effective, but if it was safe, it would have been approved prior to 1962.

In 1962, the law was changed. No longer was safety the sole consideration; now the FDA had to be shown that a new drug was also effective. The reason for this change in the law was that according to hearings held by Senator Estes Kefauver and others, it appeared that much drug innovation was socially wasteful. As one former drug company medical director testified before the Kefauver hearings,

> Industry spokesmen would have us believe that all research is on wonder drugs or better medicinal products. They stress that there are many failures for each successful drug. This is true. . . . The problem arises out of the fact that they market so many of their failures. . . . Most [industries] must depend on selling only their successes. . . . [But] with a little luck, proper timing, and a good program, a bag of asafetida with a unique chemical side chain can be made to look like a wonder drug. The illusion may not last, but it frequently lasts long enough. By the time the doctor learns what the company knew at the beginning it has two new products to take the place of the old one.

Recently, there has been a considerable amount of controversy among economists as to whether or not this 1962 change in the law was beneficial. According to Sam Peltzman of the University of Chicago, it has been a bad thing. Because it is more costly and time-consuming to prove the efficacy, as well as safety, of a new drug, the cost of developing and bringing to market a new drug has increased, the result being that fewer new drugs have been marketed. Peltzman calculates that the reduced flow of new drugs (due to the change in the law) has cost consumers about $300 million. Included in this figure is the amount that consumers would have been willing to pay for the new drugs that would have been marketed under the old regulations, but that were not marketed under the new ones.

However, not all economists find Peltzman's calculation to be persuasive. According to T. McGuire, R. Nelson, and T. Spairns of Yale University, "Peltzman's analysis provides no real evidence on which one can rest a judgment of this sort." Also, the Food and Drug Administration has tried to rebut many of Peltzman's charges. For example, the director of FDA's Bureau of Drugs claimed that most of the decrease in the flow of new drugs "is accounted for by the marked decline in marketing of [drugs] . . . considered by experts to be incompatible with the practice of sound therapeutics."

This is an area where controversy is likely to continue, since the facts are hard to get and those that can be gotten are difficult to interpret. Economics certainly has a role to play in resolving this controversy, as witnessed by the contributions of Peltzman and others. But the findings of economists must be tied to research efforts of pharamacologists and other scientists. As so frequently is the case in developing sound regulatory policies, a variety of disciplines must be called upon by the FDA in trying to safeguard the nation's health, comfort, and longevity.[14]

[14] For a more complete discussion, see S. Peltzman, *Regulation of Pharmaceutical Innovation,* Washington, D.C.: American Enterprise Institute, 1974. Also, P. MacAvoy, *The Crisis of the Regulatory Commissions,* New York: Norton, 1970. In Chapter 30, we discuss the use of marginal-cost pricing by regulated industries.

Summary

Economists generally classify markets into four types: perfect competition, monopoly, monopolistic competition, and oligopoly. Perfect competition requires that the product of any seller be the same as the product of any other seller, that no buyer or seller be able to influence the price of the product, and that resources be able to switch readily from one use to another. Price and output under perfect competition are determined by the intersection of the market supply and demand curves. In the market period, supply is fixed; thus price, which is determined by demand alone, plays the role of the allocating device. In the short run, price influences as well as rations the amount supplied.

In the long run, equilibrium is achieved under perfect competition when enough firms—no more, no less—are in the industry so that economic profits are eliminated. In other words, the long-run equilibrium position of the firm is at the point where its long-run average cost equals price. But since price must also equal marginal cost (to maximize profit), it follows that the firm must be operating at the minimum point on the long-run average cost curve. Perfectly competitive industries can be categorized into three types: constant cost industries (horizontal long-run supply curves) increasing cost industries (upward-sloping long-run supply curves), and decreasing cost industries (downward-sloping long-run supply curves). Finally, we described in some detail how perfectly competitive industries go about shifting resources in accord with changes in consumer demand.

A pure monopoly is a market with one, and only one, seller. Monopolies may occur because of patents, control over basic inputs, and government action, as well as because of decreasing average costs up to the point where the market is satisfied. If average costs reach their minimum at an output rate large enough to satisfy the entire market, perfect competition cannot be maintained; and the public often insists that the industry (a natural monopoly) be regulated by the government. Since the monopolist is the only seller of the product, the demand curve facing the monopolist is the market demand curve, which slopes downward (rather than being horizontal as in perfect competition). The unregulated monopolist will maximize profit by choosing the output where marginal cost equals marginal revenue, marginal revenue being defined as the addition to total revenue attributable to the addition of one unit to sales. This rule for output determination also holds under perfect competition, since price equals marginal revenue under perfect competition. However, if the monopolist cannot prevent losses from exceeding fixed costs, he, like a perfect competitor, will discontinue production. In contrast to the case in perfect competition, the long-run equilibrium of a monopolistic industry may not be marked by the absence of economic profits.

The output of a perfectly competitive industry tends to be greater and the price tends to be lower than under monopoly. Under certain circumstances, it can be shown that society would be better off if more resources were devoted to the production of the good than under monopoly, the competitive output being best. One way that society has attempted to reduce the harmful effects of monopoly is through public regulation. Commissions often set price at the level at which it equals average total cost, including a fair rate of return on the firm's investment. To illustrate the public regulation of monopoly, we described briefly the history of electric power regulation in the United States, and discussed some of the issues regarding the regulation of new drugs. There is a great deal of controversy over current practices of the regulatory commissions; many economists view them as lax and/or ill-conceived.

CONCEPTS FOR REVIEW

Monopoly
Perfect competition
Monopolistic competition
Oligopoly
Market period
Constant cost industry
Increasing cost industry
Decreasing cost industry
Natural monopoly
Patents
Historical cost
Reproduction cost
Economic profit
Marginal revenue

QUESTIONS FOR DISCUSSION AND REVIEW

1. Compare the long-run equilibrium of a perfectly competitive industry with that which would occur if all the firms were to be merged into a single monopolistic firm. Is there any reason for society to prefer one equilibrium over the other?

2. If you were the president of a firm that had a monopoly on a certain product, would you choose an output level where demand for the product was price inelastic?

3. "Perfect competition requires that each participant in the market be able to affect the product's price." Comment and evaluate.

4. Suppose that the demand curve for onions is: $P = 10 - 3Q$, where P is the price of a pound of onions and Q is the quantity demanded (in millions of pounds). If the supply of onions in the market period is $3\frac{1}{6}$ million pounds, what is the equilibrium price of onions in the market period? What does the supply curve for onions look like in the market period?

5. In the short run, suppose that the demand curve for onions is as given in Question 4, and that the supply curve is: $P = Q/3$. What is the equilibrium price of onions in the short run? What does the supply curve for onions look like in the short run?

6. Suppose that a monopolist's demand curve is as follows:

Quantity demanded (per year)	Price (dollars)
8	1,000
7	2,000
6	3,000
5	4,000
4	5,000
3	6,000
2	7,000
1	8,000

Plot the firm's marginal revenue curve.

7. Suppose that the monopolist in Question 6 has fixed costs of $10,000 and average variable cost of $4,000. The average variable cost is the same for outputs of 1 to 10 units per year. What output rate will the firm choose? What price will it set?

8. Plot the marginal cost curve of the firm in Question 7. Where does this curve intersect the marginal revenue curve you drew in Question 6?

9. Suppose that the firm in Question 7 experienced a 50 percent increase in both its fixed and average variable costs. If the demand curve in Question 6 remains valid, what effect will this cost increase have on the output rate and price that the firm will choose?

25 Monopolistic Competition and Oligopoly

The industries encountered in the real world are seldom perfectly competitive or monopolistic. Although perfect competition and monopoly are very useful models that shed much valuable light on the behavior of markets, they are polar cases. Economists have developed other models that portray more realistically the behavior of many modern industries. The model of monopolistic competition, for example, helps to explain market behavior in such retail trades as gasoline stations and barber shops, while the model of oligopoly pertains to industries like steel, oil, and automobiles.

In this chapter, we examine how resources are allocated and prices are set under monopolistic competition and oligopoly. We also compare the behavior of monopolistically competitive and oligopolistic markets with the behavior of perfectly competitive and monopolistic markets. The results are of considerable significance, both because they give us a better understanding of how many markets work, and because they provide valuable information on the social desirability of monopolistic competition and oligopoly.

Monopolistic Competition and Oligopoly: Their Major Characteristics

A good way to begin studying monopolistic competition and oligopoly is to compare them with the market structures we have already encountered, perfect competition and monopoly. This we do in Table 25.1. According to this table, ***monopolistic competition*** *occurs where there are many sellers (as in perfect competition) but where there is product differentiation. In other words, the firms' products are not the same.* It does not matter whether the differences among products are real or imagined; what is important is that the consumer regards the products as different.

According to Table 25.1, ***oligopoly*** *occurs in markets where there are few sellers.* There are two types of oligopolies, one where all sellers produce an identical product, and one where the sellers produce somewhat different products. Examples of the first type—***pure oligopoly***—are the markets for steel, cement, tin cans, and petroleum. Examples of the second type—***differentiated oligopoly***—are the markets for automobiles and machinery. In contrast to the extremes of perfect competition and monopoly, monopolistic competition and oligopoly are intermediate cases that include an element of competition and an element of monopoly—an advantage from the point of view of realism.

Monopolistic Competition

The key feature of monopolistic competition is ***product differentiation.*** In contrast to perfect competition, where all firms sell an identical product, firms under monopolistic competition sell somewhat different products. Each producer differentiates his product from that of the next producer. This, of course, is the case in many American markets. For example, in many parts of retail trade, each producer tries to make his product a little different, by altering the product's physical make-up, the services he offers, and other such variables. Other differences—which may be spurious—are

Table 25.1
Types of Market Structure

Market structure	Number of producers	Product differentiation	Power over price	Marketing methods	Examples
1. Perfect competition	Many	None	None	Exchange or auction	Parts of agriculture are reasonably close
2. Monopolistic competition	Many	Considerable	Some	Advertising and product variation	Retail trade
3. Oligopoly	Few	Sometimes	Some	Advertising and product variation	Autos, steel, machinery
4. Monopoly	One	Unique product	Considerable	Institutional advertising	Public utilities

based on brand name, image making, advertising claims, and so forth. In this way, each producer has some monopoly power, but it usually is small, because the products of other firms are very similar.

In perfect competition, the firms included in an industry are easy to determine because they all produce the same product. But if product differentiation exists, it is no longer easy to define an industry, since each firm produces a somewhat different product. Nevertheless, it may be useful to group together firms that produce similar products and call them a ***product group.*** For example, we can formulate a product group called "toothpaste" or "toilet soap" or "chocolate bars." Of course, the process by which we combine firms into product groups is bound to be somewhat arbitrary, since there is no way to decide how close a pair of substitutes must be to belong to the same product group. However, it is assumed that meaningful product groups can be established.

Besides product differentiation, other conditions must be met for an industry to qualify as a case of monopolistic competition. First, *there must be a large number of firms in the product group.* In other words, the product must be produced by perhaps 50 to 100 or more firms, with each firm's product a fairly close substitute for the products of the other firms in the product group. Second, *the number of firms in the product group must be large enough so that each firm expects its actions to go unheeded by its rivals and is unimpeded by possible retaliatory moves on their part.* If there is a large number of firms, this condition will normally be met. Third, *entry into the product group must be relatively easy, and there must be no collusion, such as price fixing or market sharing, among firms in the product group.* Of course, if there are a large number of firms, collusion generally is difficult, if not impossible.

Price and Output under Monopolistic Competition

Under monopolistic competition, what determines how much output a firm will produce, and what price it will charge? If each firm produces a somewhat different product, it follows that the demand curve facing each firm slopes downward to the right. That is, if the firm raises its price slightly it will lose some, but by no means all, of its customers to other firms. And if it lowers its price slightly, it will gain some, but by no means all, of its competitors'

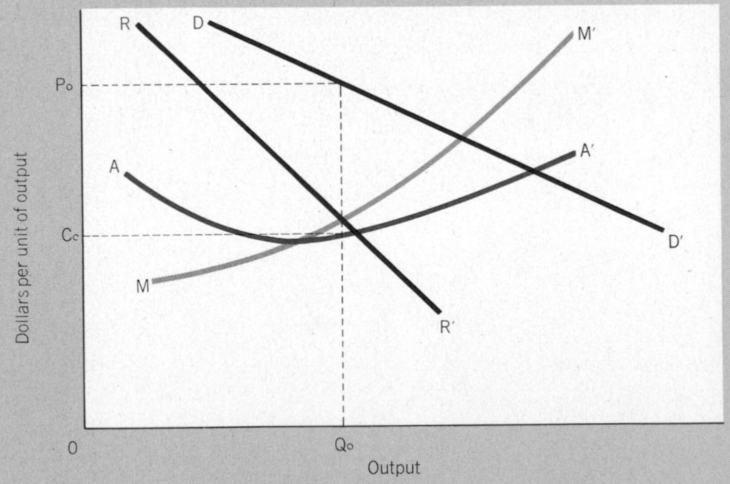

Figure 25.1
Short-Run Equilibrium: Monopolistic Competition
The firm will set price at OP_0 and its output rate at OQ_0 since marginal cost, MM', equals marginal revenue, RR', at this output. It will earn a profit of C_0P_0 per unit of output.

customers. This, of course, is in contrast to perfect competition, where the demand curve facing each firm is horizontal.

Figure 25.1 shows the short-run equilibrium of a monopolistically competitive firm. Its demand curve is DD', its marginal revenue curve is RR', its short-run marginal cost curve is MM', and its short-run average total cost curve is AA'. Given this demand curve and these cost curves, the firm in the short run will set its price at OP_0 and its output rate at OQ_0, since this combination of price and output will maximize its profits. We can be sure that this combination of price and output maximizes profit because marginal cost equals marginal revenue at this output rate. Economic profits will be earned because price, OP_0, exceeds average total costs, OC_0, at this output rate.

What will the equilibrium price and output be in the long run? Clearly, one condition for long-run equilibrium is that each firm be making no economic profits or losses, since entry or exit of firms will occur otherwise—and entry and exit are incompatible with long-run equilibrium. Another condition for long-run equilibrium is, of course, that each firm be maximizing its profits. At what price and output will both these conditions be fulfilled? Figure 25.2 shows that the long-run equilibrium is at a price of OP_1 and an output of OQ_1. The zero-economic-profit condition is met at this combination of price and output since the firm's average cost at this output equals the price, OP_1. And the profit-maximization condition is met since the marginal revenue curve, RR', intersects the marginal cost curve, MM', at this output rate.

A famous conclusion of the theory of monopolistic competition is that *a firm under this form of market organization will tend to operate with excess capacity.* In other words, the firm will construct a plant smaller than the minimum-cost size of plant and operate it at less than the minimum-cost rate of output. Why? Because, as shown in Figure 25.2, the long-run average cost curve must be tangent in long-run equilibrium to the demand curve. Thus, since the demand curve is *downward-sloping,* the long-run average cost curve must also be *downward-sloping* at the long-run equilibrium output rate. Consequently, the firm's output must be less than OQ_2, the output rate at which long-run average costs are minimized, since the long-run average cost curve slopes downward only at output rates less than OQ_2.

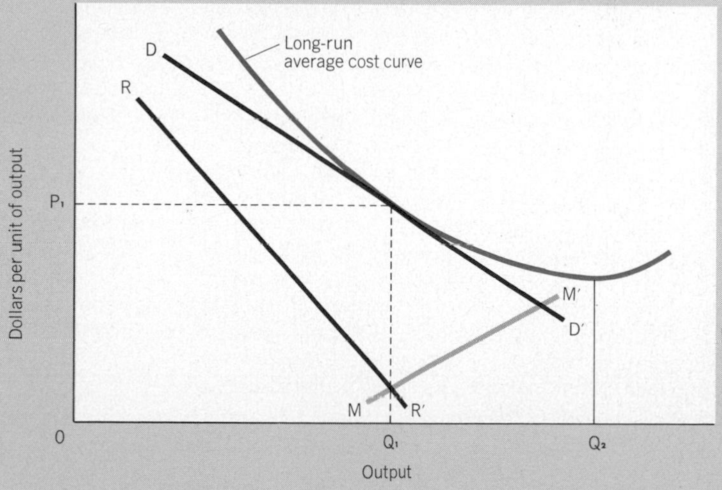

Figure 25.2
Long-Run Equilibrium: Monopolistic Competition
The long-run equilibrium is at a price of OP_1 and an output of OQ_1. There are zero profits since long-run average cost equals price. Profits are being maximized since marginal cost (MM') equals marginal revenue (RR') at this output.

A Monopolistic Competitor Par Excellence

Nowhere is product differentiation more obvious—and more important from the individual firm's point of view—than in clothes. There are thousands of American firms that produce clothing of various kinds. Each firm produces a somewhat different garment from the next firm—and each hopes that its designs will capture the fancy of the consumer. Since there are few barriers to entry, every successful fad is quickly imitated by a host of firms, the result being that profits are kept low, and the mortality rate of garment firms is very high. According to some estimates, perhaps $\frac{1}{5}$ of such firms go under in a typical year.

The Ultrawear Corporation,* a family firm, is an example of the firms populating the garment industry. It designs, produces, and markets women's clothes, which are shown to buyers from department stores and other retail outlets at markets in Los Angeles, Chicago, Dallas, and New York. In Dallas's Apparel Mart, for example, about $\frac{1}{4}$ million styles of women's and children's apparel and accessories—including Ultrawear's—are shown to 12,000 buyers from the Southwest at seasonal shows. Since each of the dresses (and other items) it sells is somewhat different from those of its competitors, the demand curve for each such dress is downward sloping. If Ultrawear cuts its price, it will increase the amount it will sell, but only within limits. If Ultrawear raises its price, it will reduce the amount that it will sell, but only within limits.

Like all monopolistically competitive firms, Ultrawear must worry constantly about competition from imitators. It must try to spot the trends in consumer preferences before its competitors. To do this, it monitors computer printouts from a sample of department stores to see what styles are "breaking out" and which ones are dying. And it pays close attention to the remarks of buyers from retail outlets. For example, several years ago, a buyer from a leading department store said that his store might be interested in a particular kind of pants for women. Ultrawear convinced him to stock some of the item and see how well it would sell. When the results seemed very favorable, Ultrawear produced lots of the item quickly—and sold over 50,000 in the next six months. By the time that its competitors were geared up for production of the item, Ultrawear had already made a handsome profit.

Because rivalry is keen, Ultrawear must try to cut its costs to the bone. On the average, its costs for patterns, cutting, insurance, contractor labor, and other incidentals are about $18 per garment. To this, it adds a 30 percent markup resulting in a wholesale price of $23.50. This markup contains an allowance for rent, clerical, sales, and transportation expenses. After deducting these expenses, it makes a profit of about $1.80 per garment, which is high relative to the rest of the industry. As noted above, the industry is characterized by the low profits one would expect under monopolistic competition. Ultrawear has managed to survive and prosper since its formation in 1945, due apparently to good management. How long it will be able to maintain its position is an open question.

* The name of the company is fictitious; otherwise, the account, which is factual, is based on "Anatomy of a Garment-Center Firm," *New York Times*, September 14, 1975.

This is a very important conclusion, since it suggests that monopolistically competitive industries will be overcrowded with firms. There will be too many firms (from society's point of view), each of which is smaller than required to minimize its unit costs. For this conclusion, as well as much of the entire theory of monopolistic competition, we are indebted to Edward Chamberlin of Harvard University, whose pathbreaking book on the subject first appeared in 1933.[1]

Comparisons with Perfect Competition and Monopoly

Market structure is important because it influences market behavior. We need to know how the behavior of a monopolistically competitive industry differs from that of a perfectly competitive industry or a monopoly. For example, suppose that there exists a magician who can transform an industry's structure by a wave of his wand. (John D. Rockefeller was a real-life magician who transformed the structure of the oil industry in the late 1800s—but he seemed to favor mergers, mixed with some ungentlemanly tactics, over wands.) Suppose that the magician makes an industry monopolistically competitive, rather than perfectly competitive or monopolistic. What difference would it make in the behavior of the industry? Or, to take a less fanciful case, what difference would it make if government action or technological change resulted in such a change in an industry's market structure? Of course, it is difficult to say how the industry's behavior would be affected, because output would be heterogeneous in one case and homogeneous in the other, and its cost curves would probably vary with its organization. But many economists seem to believe that differences of the following kind can be expected.

[1] E. Chamberlin, *The Theory of Monopolistic Competition,* Cambridge, Mass.: Harvard University Press, 1933.

First, *the firm under monopolistic competition is likely to produce less, and charge a higher price, than under perfect competition.* The demand curve confronting the monopolistic competitor slopes downward to the right. Consequently, as we saw in the previous chapter, marginal revenue must be less than price. Thus, under monopolistic competition, marginal cost must also be less than price, since marginal revenue must equal marginal cost at the firms' profit-maximizing output rate. But if marginal cost is less than price, the firm's output rate must be smaller—and the price higher—than if marginal cost equals price, which is the case under perfect competition. On the other hand, *relative to monopoly, monopolistically competitive firms are likely to have lower profits, greater output, and lower price.* For example, the firms in a product group might obtain positive economic profits if they were to collude and behave as a monopolist. Of course, the increase in profits resulting from the monopoly would benefit the producers, but consumers would be worse off because of the higher prices and smaller output of goods.

Also, as noted in the previous section, *a firm under monopolistic competition may be somewhat inefficient because it tends to operate with excess capacity.* Each firm builds a smaller than minimum-cost plant and produces a smaller than minimum-cost output. More firms exist than if there were no excess capacity, resulting in some overcrowding of the industry. Of course, inefficiences of this sort would not be expected under perfect competition. These inefficiencies may not be very great, since the demand curve confronting the monopolistically competitive firm is likely to be highly elastic; and the more elastic it is, the less excess capacity the firm will have. But many observers seem to believe that excess capacity of this sort is a serious problem in many important industries, including textiles.

Finally, *firms under monopolistic competition will, of course, offer a wider variety of styles, brands, and qualities than firms under perfect competition. Moreover, they will spend much more on advertising and other selling expenses than a perfectly competitive firm would.* Whether this diversity is worth its cost is hard to say. Some economists are impressed by the apparent waste in monopolistic competition. They think it results in too many firms, too many brands, too much selling effort, and too much spurious product differentiation. But if the differences among products are real and are understood by consumers, the greater variety of alternatives available under monopolistic competition may be very valuable to consumers. The proper evaluation of the social advantages and disadvantages of product differentiation is a problem economists have not solved.

Retailing: A Case Study[2]

To illustrate the case of monopolistic competition, consider retailing in the United States. An example of a retailer is, of course, Peter Amacher, the drugstore owner described in Chapter 4. Each retailer has a certain amount of monopoly power because his location, his product lines, his personality, and his salespeople are somewhat different from those of his competitors. In other words, his product is differentiated. But the extent and strength of his monopoly power is generally quite limited because he faces many competitors reasonably similar to himself in these respects. That is, lots of other firms sell products that are close substitutes for his own product. The goods carried by one drugstore, grocery store, or clothing shop are close substitutes for those carried by another drugstore, grocery store, or clothing shop. Moreover, entry into retail trade tends to be quite easy, as indicated by the fact that firms are continually entering various lines of retailing, and that the capital and skill required for entry are generally rather modest.

All in all, retailing seems to have many of the most important characteristics of monopolistic competition. Assuming that the retail industry can be approximated reasonably well by our model of monopolistic competition, we would expect that there would be some overcrowding of firms, that firms would try hard to differentiate their product through advertising and other selling expenses, and that long-run profits in the industry would tend to be low. Let us see to what extent these conditions do prevail.

There seems to be considerable evidence of overcrowding. More firms exist in retail trade than would be the case if each were operating at a point where unit costs were a minimum. But the extent of this excess capacity may not be very great, since the price elasticity of demand in retailing is normally very high—typically about 5.0, according to Leonard Weiss of the University of Wisconsin. Also, in accord with the model, firms in retail trade spend a great deal on various selling expenses, notably advertising. About $\frac{1}{4}$ of the total expenditure on advertising in the United States is spent by retailers. Usually these ads are local and provide a valuable source of information on sales and specials in a particular neighborhood. (It is the exceptional person who does not spend some part of each week scanning the retail ads in a local newspaper.) Retail stores spend a lot on other selling expenses too—attractive decor, free parking, trading stamps, clerks to hover over the customer, and so forth. These expenses add to the prices they charge for the products they carry.

The level of profits in retail trade also accords with what theory would lead us to expect: it is low. Except for a few years right after World War II (when there was a relative scarcity of retail outlets), profits seem to have been consistently lower in retailing than in manufacturing. Moreover, this can hardly be

[2] For a much more extensive discussion of retailing, see Leonard Weiss, *Case Studies in American Industry,* New York: Wiley, 1967.

attributed to less risk in retailing than in manufacturing, since retailing's bankruptcy rate has been exceptionally high—much higher than in other parts of the nonfarm economy. The facts seems to correspond quite well with the theory's prediction of no economic profits in the industry.[3]

Oligopoly

Oligopoly (domination by a few firms) is a common and important market structure in the United States; many industries, like steel, automobiles, oil, and electrical equipment, are oligopolistic. An example of an oligopolist is General Motors, described in Chapter 7. The key characteristic of oligopoly is interdependence, actual and perceived, among firms. Each oligopolist formulates its policies with an eye to their effect on its rivals. Since an oligopoly contains a small number of firms, any change in one firm's price or output influences the sales and profits of its competitors. Moreover, since there are only a few firms, each must recognize that changes in its own policies are likely to result in changes in the policies of its rivals as well.

What factors are responsible for oligopoly? First, in some industries, *low production costs* cannot be achieved unless a firm is producing an output equal to a substantial portion of the total available market, with the consequence that the number of firms will tend to be rather small. Second, there may be economies of scale in *sales promotion* in certain industries, and this too may promote oligopoly. Third, entry into some industries may be blocked by the requirement that a firm build and maintain a large, complicated, and *expensive plant,* or have access to *patents* or *scarce raw materials.* Only a few firms may be in a position to obtain all these necessary prerequisites for membership in the club.

The automobile industry is a good example of the impact of economies of scale in production. According to studies made by Joe Bain of the University of California, an automobile plant of minimum efficient size can provide almost 10 percent of the total national market.[4] Thus it simply is not economical to have a great many automobile firms. It might be possible to have a dozen automobile firms rather than the four we currently have without sacrificing productive efficiency, but because of economies of scale, it would not be feasible to have 50 or 100.

The automobile industry is also a good example of economies of scale in sales promotion. To be effective, advertising must often be carried out on a large scale, the result being that the advertising cost per unit of output decreases with increases in output, at least up to some point. For example, according to Leonard Weiss of the University of Wisconsin, General Motors and Ford each spent about $27 on advertising per car sold during 1954–57, whereas the smaller companies—Chrysler, Studebaker-Packard, and American Motors—spent about $50 or more per car sold. Also, car buyers like to deal with firms with a large, dependable dealer network. Since it takes a lot of money to establish such a network, and since the better dealers are attracted by the more popular brands, the smaller automobile manufacturers are at a substantial disadvantage.

In addition, the automobile industry offers a good example of barriers to entry due to large financial requirements. An automobile plant of minimum efficient size costs about $500 million to build and put into operation. This is an enormous amount of money, beyond the reach of practically all individuals. It takes the help of major financial interests and financial insti-

[3] Before leaving the subject of monopolistic competition, it should be recognized that Professor Chamberlin's theory has been subjected to considerable criticism. For example, the definition of the product group is ambiguous. See G. Stigler, *Five Lectures on Economic Problems,* London: Longmans Green, 1949.

[4] J. Bain, *Barriers to New Competition,* Cambridge, Mass.: Harvard University Press, 1956.

tutions to break into the automobile business. Since World War II, no new firms have obtained a foothold in the American automobile industry.

The availability of raw materials can also be a barrier to entry. Such is the case in the steel industry, where a few big firms have most of the available iron ore, partly through foresight and partly because they were the only organizations that could afford to spend the vast sums required to obtain the ore. Also, patents can be a very big barrier to entry. The electric light industry is a famous example: General Electric was able to dominate the industry from 1892 to 1930 through the acquisition of the basic Edison patents and then the acquisition of patents on many of the improvements.[5]

Mergers and Oligopoly

Mergers between firms often contribute to the movement toward oligopoly in particular industries. There have been three major waves of mergers in the American economy. The first occurred between 1887 and 1904, the second between 1916 and 1929, and the third after World War II. The first wave in 1887-1904 saw the formation of such giants as U.S. Steel and John D. Rockefeller's Standard Oil. The mergers in this period tended to be ***horizontal;*** that is, among firms producing essentially the same product. Such was the case with U.S. Steel, formed in 1901 from a combination of about 785 plants. During the second wave of mergers in 1916-29, the emphasis was more on ***vertical mergers*** (mergers among firms at various stages in the production process) and ***conglomerate mergers*** (mergers among firms producing entirely different products). During the third wave of mergers in the 25 years following World War II, a very large number of firms were absorbed and assimilated by others. Of the 1,000 largest manufacturing firms in existence at the end of 1950, 216 had disappeared by merger by 1963.

There are a host of reasons why firms merge. Sometimes they do it to reduce competition. For example, Thomas Edison was forthright when he said in 1892 about the formation of General Electric, "The consolidation of the companies . . . will do away with a competition which has become so sharp that the product of the factories has been worth little more than ordinary hardware."[6] Other mergers are made so that promoters can earn profits from corporate marriages. In still other cases, mergers occur because firms need the people or ideas other firms have, or because the owners want to sell out, or because there appear to be beneficial synergetic effects arising from complementary resources owned by the merging firms.

Whatever the reasons, many oligopolies have been created by a series of mergers. For example, consider U.S. Steel, which, as we have seen, was formed by combining about 785 plants. Just before the turn of the century, a large number of mergers resulted in the consolidation of more than 200 iron and steel firms into 20 much bigger firms. Then J. P. Morgan, the famous financier, organized the merger of 12 of these bigger firms into U.S. Steel—and received about $62 million in promotional profits for his labor. Or consider the electrical equipment industry. In 1892, General Electric was formed through the merger of Edison General Electric (itself a product of a number of mergers) and Thomson-Houston (it too the product of numerous mergers). As an example of an oligopolist that has grown through conglomerate mergers, consider International Telephone and Telegraph (ITT). Beginning as an operator of overseas telephone systems, this firm acquired a variety of seemingly unrelated businesses, such as the Sheraton hotel chain, the Hartford Fire Insurance Company, the Avis car rental agency, and the

[5] F. M. Scherer, *Industrial Market Structure and Economic Performance,* Skokie, Ill.: Rand McNally, 1970, pp. 391-92.

[6] Ibid., p. 113.

Continental baking company. Through these mergers, Harold Geneen, ITT's head, created a multibillion dollar enterprise in the 1960s.

Oligopoly Behavior and the Stability of Prices

Unlike perfect competition, monopoly, and monopolistic competition, there is no single unified model of oligopoly behavior. Instead, there are a number of models, each based on a somewhat different set of assumptions concerning the relationships among the firms that make up the oligopoly. Basically, no single model exists because economists have not yet been able to devise one that would cover all the relevant cases adequately. Economics, like all sciences, continues to grow; perhaps someone—indeed, perhaps someone reading this book—may be able to develop such a model before too long. However, it doesn't exist now.

Let's start with a model that sheds light on the stability of oligopolistic prices. Empirical studies of pricing in oligopolistic markets have often concluded that prices in such markets tend to be rigid. A classic example occurred in the sulphur industry. From 1926 to 1938, the price of sulphur remained at $18 a ton, despite great shifts in demand and production costs.[7] This example is somewhat extreme, but it illustrates the basic point: prices in oligopolistic industries commonly remain unchanged for fairly long periods. A well-known model designed to explain this price rigidity was advanced by Paul Sweezy, who asserted that, *if an oligopolist cuts his price, he can be pretty sure that his rivals will meet the reduction. On the other hand, if he increases his price, his rivals may not change theirs.*

Figure 25.3 shows the situation. The oligopolist's demand curve is represented by *DAD′* and the current price is *OP*. There is a "kink"

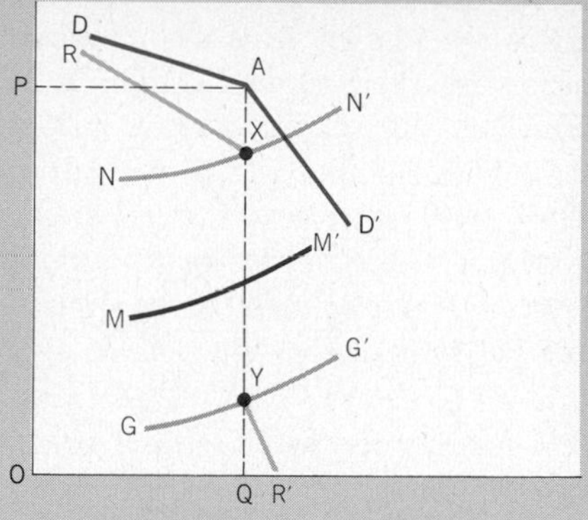

Figure 25.3
The Kinked Oligopoly Demand Curve
The oligopolist's demand curve is *DAD′*, the current price being *OP*. Because of the kink in the demand curve, the marginal revenue curve consists of two segments *RX* and *YR′*. Since the marginal cost curve is *MM′*, the most profitable output is *OQ*. Moreover, it remains the most profitable output—and *OP* the most profitable price—even if the marginal cost curve shifts to *NN′* or *GG′* or if the demand curve shifts considerably.

in the demand curve because *under the postulated circumstances the demand curve for the oligopolist's product is much less elastic for price decreases than for price increases.* Why is it less elastic for price decreases than for price increases? Because price decreases will be met by the firm's rivals, which means that the firm will not be able to take any appreciable amount of sales away from its rivals by such decreases. The effect of such decreases will be to increase the quantity demanded of the firm's product, since the total quantity demanded of the entire industry's product will increase due to the price reduction. But the increase in the quantity demanded of the firm's product will be relatively modest. On the other hand, if the firm raises its price, it is assumed that its rivals do not follow suit. Thus the quantity demanded

[7] Marshall Colberg, William Bradford, and Richard Alt, *Business Economics: Principles and Cases*, Homewood, Ill. Irwin, 1957, p. 276.

of the firm's product will fall considerably.

Because of the kink in the demand curve, the marginal revenue curve is not continuous: it consists of two segments, RX and YR'. Given that the firm's marginal cost curve is MM', the most profitable output is OQ, where the marginal cost curve intersects the vertical line, XY. Moreover, *OQ remains the most profitable output—and OP the most profitable price—even if the marginal cost curve shifts considerably (even to NN' or GG') or if the demand curve shifts (within limits).* One would expect price to be quite rigid under these circumstances, since many types of changes in cost and demand will not alter the price that maximizes profits.

This theory, although useful in explaining why price tends to remain at a certain level (OP in Figure 25.3), is of no use at all in explaining why this level, rather than another, currently prevails. It simply takes the current price as given; it does not explain why it is OP in Figure 25.3, for example. Thus this theory is an incomplete model of oligopoly pricing. Nonetheless, it seems to square with many of the relevant facts. For this and other reasons, Sweezy's model certainly has a place in the theory of oligopoly.

The Theory of Games

Another useful model is one that stresses the gamelike characteristics of oligopoly. As in a game, in oligopoly each firm must take account of its rivals' reactions to its own actions. For this reason, an oligopolistic firm cannot tell what effect a change in its output will have on the price of its product and on its profits unless it can guess how its rivals will respond to the change. To understand game theory,[8] you have to know what a ***game*** is: it is a competitive situation where two or more persons pursue their own interests and no person can dictate the outcome. Poker is a game, and so is a situation in which two firms are engaged in competitive advertising campaigns. A game is described in terms of its players, rules, payoffs, and information conditions. These elements are common to all conflict situations.

More specifically, a ***player,*** whether a single person or an organization, is a decision-making unit. Each player has a certain amount of resources, and the ***rules of the game*** describe how these resources can be used. For example, the rules of poker indicate how bets can be made and which hands are better than others. A ***strategy*** is a complete specification of what a player will do under each contingency in the playing of the game. For example, a corporation president might tell his subordinates how he wants an advertising campaign to start, and what should be done at subsequent times in response to various actions of competing firms. The game's outcome clearly depends on each player's strategies. A player's ***payoff*** varies from game to game: it is win, lose, or draw in checkers, and various sums of money in poker.

For simplicity we will restrict our attention to ***two-person games,*** i.e., those with only two players, and to ***zero-sum games,*** in which the amount one player wins exactly equals the amount the other player loses. The relevant features of a two-person, zero-sum game can be shown by constructing a ***payoff matrix.*** To illustrate, consider the case of two big soap producers, Procter and Gamble and Lever Brothers. Suppose that these two firms are about to stage rival advertising campaigns and that each firm has a choice of strategies. Procter and Gamble can choose to concentrate on either television ads or magazine ads; Lever Brothers has the same choice. Table 25.2 shows what will happen to the profits of each firm when each combination of strategies is chosen. For example, if both firms concentrate on TV ads, Procter and Gamble gains $3 million and Lever Brothers loses $3 million. If Procter and Gamble concentrates on TV ads

[8] One of the most interesting developments in the theory of oligopoly in the postwar period was the appearance of the classic volume: J. von Neumann and O. Morgenstern, *Theory of Games and Economic Behavior,* Princeton: Princeton University Press, 1944.

Table 25.2
Payoff Matrix

Possible strategies for Procter and Gamble	Possible Strategies for Lever Brothers: Concentrate on TV	Possible Strategies for Lever Brothers: Concentrate on magazines
Concentrate on TV	P and G gains $3 million, and Lever loses $3 million	P and G gains $2 million, and Lever loses $2 million
Concentrate on magazines	P and G gains $1 million, and Lever loses $1 million	P and G gains $1.5 million, and Lever loses $1.5 million

and Lever Brothers concentrates on magazine ads, Procter and Gamble gains $2 million and Lever Brothers loses $2 million. And so on.

Given the payoff matrix in Table 25.2, there is a definite optimal choice for each firm. To see that this is the case, let's begin by looking at the situation from Procter and Gamble's point of view. If Procter and Gamble concentrates on magazine ads, Lever Brothers will respond by choosing to concentrate on TV ads. Why? Because Lever Brothers will lose less ($1 million) than if it too concentrates on magazine ads (in which case its loss will be $1.5 million). Thus *Procter and Gamble, if it concentrates on magazine ads, will gain $1 million.*

What if Procter and Gamble concentrates on TV ads? In this case, Lever Brothers will respond by choosing to concentrate on magazines. Why? Because Lever Brothers will lose less ($2 million) than if it too concentrates on TV ads (in which case its losses will be $3 million). Thus *Procter and Gamble, if it concentrates on TV ads, will gain $2 million.*

Consequently, if both firms know the payoff matrix, *Procter and Gamble will choose the strategy of concentrating on TV ads, since it provides Procter and Gamble with a greater gain ($2 million) than if it concentrates on magazine ads (in which case the gain is $1 million).*

Now let's look at the situation from the point of view of Lever Brothers. If Lever Brothers concentrates on TV ads, Procter and Gamble will respond by also concentrating on TV ads. Why? Because Procter and Gamble will gain more ($3 million) than if it concentrates on magazine ads (in which case it will gain $1 million). Thus *Lever Brothers, if it concentrates on TV ads, will lose $3 million.*

What if Lever Brothers concentrates on magazine ads? In this case, Procter and Gamble will respond by choosing to concentrate on TV ads. Why? Because Procter and Gamble will gain more ($2 million) than if it concentrates on magazine ads (in which case it will gain $1.5 million). Thus *Lever Brothers, if it concentrates on magazine ads, will lose $2 million.*

Consequently, if both firms know the payoff matrix, *Lever Brothers will choose the strategy of concentrating on magazine ads, since it provides Lever Brothers with a smaller loss ($2 million) than if it concentrates on TV ads (in which case the loss will be $3 million).*

At this point, the solution of this game is clear: *Procter and Gamble will concentrate on TV ads, and Lever Brothers will concentrate on magazine ads.* In this way Procter and Gamble gains $2 million, Lever Brothers loses $2 million. By adopting these strategies, Procter and Gamble can guarantee itself a gain of this amount, and Lever Brothers can guarantee that its loss will not exceed this amount.

Note that each firm is assumed to maximize its payoff under the assumption that its opponent will adopt the strategy most damaging to itself. Many economists feel that this is an unnecessarily pessimistic outlook for the firm, and wonder whether such an attitude is a realistic representation of how firms actually view competitive situations. The firm that adopts this viewpoint, while his competitor does not, is likely to forgo considerable profit. Despite this and other limitations, the theory of games is a useful addition to economic theory because it provides a suggestive framework for analysis. One can structure formerly intractable problems and think about them in terms of this theory. However, in its present state, game theory cannot be used to derive specific predictions of the behavior of oligopolists; the world is much more complicated than simple examples like this one.

Collusion and Cartels

Up to this point, we have assumed that oligopolists do not collude, but conditions in oligopolistic industries tend to promote collusion, since the number of firms is small and the firms recognize their interdependence. The advantages of collusion to the firms seem obvious: increased profits, decreased uncertainty, and a better opportunity to prevent entry. Not all collusion is disguised from the public or secret. In contrast to illicit collusion, a ***cartel*** is an open, formal collusive arrangement among firms. In many countries in Europe, cartels are common and legally acceptable. In the United States, most collusive arrangements, whether secret or open cartels, were declared illegal by the Sherman Antitrust Act, which was passed in 1890. However, this does not mean that such arrangements do not exist. For example, widespread collusion to fix prices occurred among American electrical equipment manufacturers during the 1950s, and when the collusion was uncovered a number of high executives were tried, convicted, and sent to jail. Moreover, collusion of this sort is not limited to a single country: some cartels, like that in quinine in the early 1960s or in crude oil in the 1970s, are international in scope.[9]

If a cartel is etablished to set a uniform price for a particular product, what price will it charge? As a first step, the cartel must estimate the marginal cost curve for the cartel as a whole. If input prices do not increase as the cartel expands its output, this marginal cost curve is the horizontal sum of the marginal cost curves of the individual firms. Suppose that the resulting marginal cost curve for the cartel is MM' in Figure 25.4. If the demand curve for the industry's product is DD', the relevant marginal revenue curve is RR', and the output that maximizes the total profit of the cartel members is OQ. Thus, if it maximizes cartel profits, the cartel will choose a price of OP, which, of course, is the monopoly price. In short, *the cartel acts like a monopolist with a number of plants or divisions, each of which is a member firm.*

How will the cartel allocate sales among the member firms? If its aim is to maximize cartel profits, it will allocate sales to firms in such a way that the sum of the firms' costs is minimized. But this allocation is unlikely to occur in reality. The allocation process is a bargaining process, and firms with the most influence and the shrewdest negotiators are likely to receive the largest sales quotas, even though this decreases the total profits of the cartel. Moreover, high-cost firms are likely to receive larger

[9] See "Collusion among Electrical Equipment Manufacturers" and "Quinine: An International Cartel" in Edwin Mansfield, *Microeconomics: Selected Readings,* 2d ed., New York: Norton, 1975.

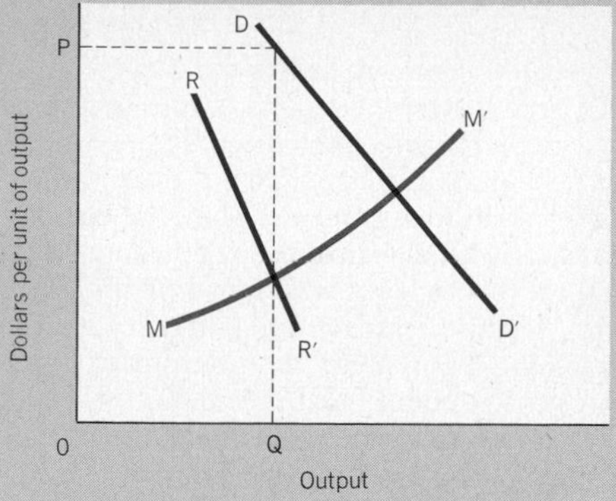

Figure 25.4
Price and Output of a Cartel
MM′ is the horizontal sum of the marginal cost curves of the firms in the cartel. If *DD′* is the demand curve, and *RR′* is the marginal revenue curve, the output that maximizes the total profit of the cartel members is *OQ*. The corresponding price is *OP*.

sales quotas than would be the case if total cartel profits were maximized, since they would be unwilling otherwise to stay in the cartel. In practice, it appears that cartels often divide markets geographically or in accord with a firm's level of sales in the past.

To illustrate how firms collude, consider the electrical equipment manufacturers we mentioned above. During the 1950s, there was widespread collusion among about 30 firms selling turbine generators, switchgear, transformers, and other products with total sales of about $1.5 billion per year. Representatives of these firms got together and agreed upon prices for many products. The available evidence indicates that both prices and profits tended to be increased by the collusive agreements—or at least until the firms were prosecuted under the antitrust laws by the Department of Justice. The following statement by F. M. Scherer of Northwestern University is a good description of some of the procedures used by these firms:

> Some of the most elaborate procedures were devised to handle switchgear pricing. As in the case of generators, book prices served as the initial departure point. Each seller agreed to quote book prices in sales to private buyers, and meetings were held regularly to compare calculations for forthcoming job quotations. Sealed-bid competitions sponsored by government agencies posed a different set of problems, and new methods were worked out to handle them. Through protracted negotiation, each seller was assigned a specific share of all sealed-bid business, e.g., General Electric's share of the high voltage switchgear field was set at 40.3 per cent in late 1958, and Allis-Chalmers' at 8.8 per cent. Participants then coordinated their bidding so that each firm was low bidder in just enough transactions to gain its predetermined share of the market. In the power switching equipment line, this was achieved for a while by dividing the United States into four quadrants, assigning four sellers to each quadrant, and letting the sellers in a quadrant rotate their bids. A "phases of the moon" system was used to allocate low-bidding privileges in the high voltage switchgear field, with a new seller assuming low-bidding priority every two weeks. The designated bidder subtracted a specified percentage margin from the book price to capture orders during its phase, while others added various margins to the book price. The result was an ostensibly random pattern of quotations, conveying the impression of independent pricing behavior.[10]

Barriers to Collusion

The fact that oligopoly often can lead to collusion is not new. Nor is it newly understood. Back in 1776, Adam Smith warned that "people of the same trade seldom meet together even for merriment and diversion, but the conversation ends in a conspiracy against the public, or in some contrivance to raise prices." However, it must be borne in mind that collu-

[10] F. M. Scherer, *Industrial Market Structure and Economic Performance,* p. 160.

sive arrangements are often difficult to accomplish and maintain for long. In particular, there are several important barriers to collusion:

Legal problems. The antitrust laws forbid outright collusion and price fixing. Of course, this does not mean that firms do not break those laws; witness the electrical equipment manufacturers just described. But the antitrust laws are an important obstacle to collusion.

Technical problems. Collusion is often difficult to achieve and maintain because an oligopoly contains an unwieldy number of firms, or the product is quite heterogeneous, or the cost structures of the firms differ considerably. It is clear that a collusive agreement will be more difficult to achieve and maintain if there are a dozen oligopolists than if there are three or four. Moreover, if the products sold by the oligopolists differ substantially, it will probably be more difficult for them to find a common price strategy that will be acceptable to all. Similarly, if the firms' cost structures differ, it will be more difficult to get agreement, since the low-cost firms will be more inclined to cut price. For example, National Steel, after introducing low-cost continuous strip mills in the 1930s, became a price cutter in the steel industry.

Cheating. There is a constant temptation for oligopolists to cheat on any collusive agreement. If other firms stick to the agreement, any firm that cheats—by cutting its price below that agreed to under the collusive arrangement—can take a lot of business away from the other firms and increase its profits substantially, at least in the short run. This temptation is particularly great when an industry's sales are depressed and its profits are low. Every firm is hungry for business, and it is difficult to resist. Moreover, one firm may be driven to cheating because it hears that another firm is doing so, with the eventual result that the collusive agreement is torn apart.

To illustrate the problems of maintaining a collusive agreement, let's return to the electrical equipment manufacturers. As the *Wall Street Journal* summed it up,

> One of the great ironies of the conspiracies was that no matter how hard the participants schemed, no matter how friendly their meetings and communications might be, there was an innate tendency to compete. Someone was always violating the agreements to get more business and this continually called for new illegal plans. For example, price-cutting in sales of power switching equipment to government agencies was getting out of hand in late 1958. This led to the "quadrant" system of dividing markets [described in the previous section].

As one executive of General Electric complained, "No one was living up to the agreements and we . . . were being made suckers. On every job some one would cut our throat; we lost confidence in the group." Given that these agreements were illegal, it is remarkable that such a complaint was uttered with a straight face.

Price Leadership

In order to coordinate their behavior without outright collusion, some industries contain a ***price leader.*** It is quite common in oligopolistic industries for one or a few firms to set the price and for the rest to follow their lead. Two types of price leadership are the dominant-firm model and the barometric-firm model. The ***dominant-firm*** model applies to cases where the industry has a single large dominant firm and a number of small firms. The dominant firm sets the price for the industry, but it lets the small firms sell all they want at that price. The ***barometric-firm*** model applies to cases where one firm usually is the first to make changes in price that are generally accepted by other firms in the industry. The barometric firm may not be the largest, or most powerful, firm. Instead, it is a reasonably accurate interpreter of changes in basic cost and demand conditions in the industry as a whole.

In the past, the steel industry has been a good example of price leadershp of the dominant-firm variety. The largest firm in the industry is U.S. Steel, which, as we know, was formed in 1901 by the merger of a number of companies. Judge Elbert Gary, the first chairman of the board of U.S. Steel, sought the cooperation of the smaller firms in the industry. He inaugurated a series of so-called "Gary dinners," attended by all the major steel producers, which made declarations of industry policy on pricing and other matters. Since any formal pricing agreements would have been illegal, they made no such agreements. But, generally speaking, U.S. Steel set the pricing pattern and other firms followed. Moreover, this relationship continued long after Judge Gary had gone to his reward. According to Walter Adams of Michigan State University, U.S. Steel typically set the pace, "and the other companies follow in lockstep—both in their sales to private customers and in their secret bids on government contracts."[11]

Illustrating the attitude of other firms was the statement by the president of Bethlehem Steel to a congressional committee in 1939 that "in the main we . . . await the [price] schedules of the [U.S.] Steel Corporation." However, there was some secret price-cutting, particularly during depressions. On at least one occasion, U.S. Steel responded to such price-cutting by announcing publicly that it would meet any price reduction it heard of. In this way, it attempted to discourage under-the-counter price cutting. In more recent times, U.S. Steel no longer seems to be the price leader it once was. In 1962, it drew a great deal of criticism from President Kennedy for being the first steel firm to raise prices. Subsequently, smaller steel firms have often been the first. Indeed, in 1968 the world was treated to the amusing spectacle of Bethlehem announcing a price cut in order to counter some secret price-cutting by the former price leader, U.S. Steel.[12]

[11] W. Adams, *The Structure of American Industry,* New York: Macmillan, 1961, p. 168.

Cost-Plus Pricing

There is one further model of oligopoly behavior to consider. According to studies of business behavior, ***cost-plus*** pricing is used by many oligopolists. It occurs in two steps. First, the firm estimates the cost per unit of output of the product. Since this cost will generally vary with the output rate, the firm must base this computation on some assumed output rate—often ⅔ or ¾ of the firm's capacity. Second, the firm adds a markup to the estimated average cost. This markup is meant to include certain costs that cannot be allocated to any specific product and to provide a return on the firm's investment. The size of the markup depends, of course, on the rate of profit the firm believes it can earn. Some firms, like General Electric and General Motors, have set a ***target rate of return*** figure they hope to earn, which determines the markup.

Unquestionably, many firms do compute prices on the basis of this sort of procedure. However, the cost-plus pricing model is incomplete unless it specifies more precisely what determines the size of the markup. Although firms may construct these markups to yield a certain target rate of return, the firms' profit and loss statements show that these markups do not prevail, since the firms' actual rates of return frequently vary considerably from the target rate of return. Moreover, to many economists this form of pricing seems naïve, since it takes no account, explicitly at least, of the extent or elasticity of demand or of the size of marginal, rather than average, costs.

Consider General Motors, which has been using cost-plus pricing for over 40 years. Gen-

[12] For a much more extensive discussion of the steel industry, see Weiss, *Case Studies in American Industry;* Adams, *Structure of American Industry;* Scherer, *Industrial Market Structure and Economic Performance.*

eral Motors starts by stating an objective of earning a profit of about 15 percent (after taxes) on total invested capital. Then it assumes that it will sell enough cars in the next year to operate at about 80 percent of its capacity; and on the basis of this assumption, it figures what its cost per car will be. Then it adds to this cost a markup big enough to produce the desired return on investment. The result is the so-called standard price. General Motors' high-echelon price policy committee takes this standard price as a first approximation, and makes small adjustments to reflect competitive conditions, long-run goals of the firm, and other things. Typically, these adjustments are quite small, and the actual price winds up close to the standard price.

Needless to say, there is no assurance that General Motors will earn the desired 15 percent of total invested capital. If it sells fewer cars than it needs to sell in order to operate at 80 percent of capacity, its unit costs will be higher than expected and its profits—both total and per unit of output—will be less than expected. On the other hand, if it sells more cars than it needs to sell in order to operate at 80 percent of capacity, its profits will be higher than expected. In general, since World War II, General Motors has achieved sales levels that permitted it to operate at more than 80 percent of capacity, with the result that it has earned substantially more, on the average, than the target rate of 15 percent of invested capital. But this was not the case in 1974 and 1975.

Nonprice Competition

Oligopolists tend to compete more aggressively through advertising and product differentiation than through direct price reductions. In other words, when we observe the behavior of major oligopolies, we find that firms try hard to get business away from their rivals by outdoing them with better advertising campaigns and with improvements in the product; but it is less common for oligopolists to slug it out, toe to toe, with price reductions. This is an important characteristic of oligopoly. In contrast to the case of perfect competition, nonprice competition plays a central role in oligopoly. It is worthwhile, therefore, to note a few salient points about the advertising and product development strategies of oligopolists.

Advertising is a very big business: currently about $20 billion per year is spent on it in the United States. One important purpose of advertising is, of course, to convince the consumer that one firm's product is better than another's. In industries where there is less physical differentiation of the product, advertising expenditures often are larger than in industries where the product varies more. Thus the cigarette, liquor, and soap industries spend over 10 percent of their gross revenues (excluding excise taxes) on advertising, whereas the automobile industry spends less than 1 percent of its gross revenues on advertising. The social desirability of much of this advertising is debatable, and much debated. While advertising can serve an important purpose by keeping the consumer better informed, some advertising is more misleading than informative. Unfortunately, it is difficult to make reliable estimates of the extent to which oligopolists may be overinvesting, from society's point of view, in advertising.

The development of new and improved products is also a very big business in the United States. Currently firms spend over $14 billion per year on research and development. In many industries, R and D is a central part of oligopolistic competition. For example, a spectacular case in the drug industry was the effect of American Cyanamid's Achromycin tetracycline, introduced in 1953, on sales of Aureomycin chlortetracycline, which had been marketed since late 1948. After an almost continuous upward trend in 1950-53, Aureomycin sales dropped by nearly 40 percent during the first full year of the sale of Achromycin.

Hardly a typical case, this nonetheless illustrates how one firm can take sales away from its rivals through new product development.

It is important to add, however, that much of industry's R and D is aimed at fairly minor improvements in products and processes. Moreover, a good deal of the engineering efforts of many important industries is aimed largely at style changes, not basic improvements in the product. For example, the automobile industry spends an enormous amount to produce the model changes that are familiar to car buyers throughout the land. Specifically, according to three economists—Frank Fisher, Zvi Griliches, and Carl Kaysen—such model changes in the automobile industry cost about $5 billion per year during the late 1950s.[13] From society's point of view, it is not at all clear that such huge expenditures are justifiable.

Perhaps the main reason why oligopolists would rather compete through advertising and product differentiation than through price is that a firm's rivals can easily and quickly match a price reduction, whereas they may find it difficult to match a clever advertising campaign or an attractive product improvement. For example Eastman Kodak had to work over six years to develop the instant camera it introduced in 1976 to compete with Polaroid's instant camera. Thus oligopolists tend to feel that they have a better chance of improving their long-run profits at the expense of their rivals in the arena of nonprice competition than by price cutting.

The Automobile Industry: A Case Study

To see in more detail how oligopoly works, let's examine the automobile industry. Its history can be divided into three stages. First, there was the period of growth and experimentation, which lasted until about 1910. During this period, dozens of firms entered the automobile industry, and there was widespread experimentation with various kinds of car designs. No single firm dominated the market, which was growing by leaps and bounds. Second, there was the period from about 1911 to about 1918, during which a mass market for automobiles was developed, through the genius of Henry Ford, who developed the assembly-line technique of production that is commonplace today. Exploiting the great economies of scale associated with this production technique, Ford reduced costs substantially, and adopted a strategy of reducing the price to broaden the market, cutting the price of the Model T from $900 in 1909 to $290 in 1925. (Recall our discussion in Chapter 21.)

Following World War I, there began the third stage in the industry's history, during which the number of automobile firms declined and the industry became concentrated in the hands of a few firms. Firms other than the Big Three—General Motors, Ford, and Chrysler—found it difficult to stay alive, largely for lack of capital. Moreover, new firms were effectively barred from entering the industry by the substantial economies of scale (both for production and sales promotion) and large capital requirements described earlier. The result was a drastic decline in the number of firms, eventually producing the present industry structure. Today there are only four automobile firms, and the Big Three have over 90 percent of the market for domestic automobiles. General Motors, which took the lead away from Ford after World War I, leads the industry in sales.

How are prices determined in the automobile industry? According to Richard Caves of Harvard University, the answer is as follows:

> The automobile industry fits [the] pattern of "tacit collusion" exceptionally well. Its product differentiation is there for all to see. The 3 lead-

[13] F. Fisher, Z. Griliches, and C. Kaysen, "The Costs of Automobile Model Changes since 1949," *Journal of Political Economy,* 1962.

ing producers accounted for almost 90 per cent of domestic output of cars in the 1930's and for more than 90 per cent in the post-war period. Each firm seems to use the same basic type of formula in setting prices annually for its various models. [General Motors' formula is discussed in a previous section.] These prices, once announced, normally stay unchanged through a whole model year (except for standard discounts to dealers to "clean up" what remains at the end of the year.)

Each firm, figuring the prices to announce for forthcoming models, naturally looks at trends in its own production and model-change costs and at general developments in the economy. It also pays close attention to its rivals' costs and what they may be expected to charge. In this game the firm likely to prefer the lowest price has a good deal of leverage to determine the general range of prices announced for any given type of car. The firms in this industry, as in others, dislike getting caught with an overpriced model more than they fear being slightly under the market. In the 1930's Ford tended to prefer the lowest prices and hence drew close attention from its rivals. In more recent years General Motors has been closely watched.

The prices announced for a given class of vehicle (e.g., full-size four-door sedans with the least luxurious trim) do not come out identical, nor is one firm among the Big Three (Ford, General Motors, Chrysler) typically either high or low. But the announced prices are close enough so that seldom does any adjustment occur after the first announcement. In both 1955 and 1956 (the 1956 and 1957 model years), however, Ford's prices missed those announced later by General Motors by a wide enough margin to lead Ford to make a change, down in 1955 and up in 1956. In each case, it ended up within a few dollars of GM's announced price.[14]

Comparison of Oligopoly with Perfect Competition

We have seen that economists have constructed a number of types of models of oligopoly behavior—the Sweezy model, the game-theoretic models, cartel models, price leadership models, cost-plus pricing models, and others—but there is no agreement that any of these models is an adquate general representation of oligopoly behavior. For this reason, it is difficult to estimate the effects of an oligopolistic market structure on price, output, and profits. Nonetheless, if a perfectly competitive industry were turned overnight into an oligopoly, it seems likely that certain changes would occur.

First, *price would probably be higher than under perfect competition.* The difference between the oligopoly price and the perfectly competitive price will depend, of course, on the number of firms in the industry and the ease of entry: the larger the number of firms and the easier it is to enter the industry, the closer the oligopoly price will be to the perfectly competitive level. Also, prices will tend to be more inflexible under oligopolistic conditions than under perfect competition.

Second, if the demand curve is the same under oligopoly as under perfect competition, it also follows that *output will be less under oligopoly than under perfect competition.* However, it is not always reasonable to assume that the demand curve is the same in both cases, since the large expenditures for advertising and product variation incurred by some oligopolies may tend to shift the demand curve to the right. Consequently in some cases both price and output may tend to be higher under oligopoly than under perfect competition.

Third, *oligopolistic industries tend to spend more on advertising, product differentiation, and style changes than perfectly competitive industries.* The use of some resources for these purposes is certainly worthwhile, since advertising provides buyers with information, and product variation allows greater freedom of choice. Whether oligopolies spend too much for these purposes is by no means obvious. However, there is a widespread feeling among economists, based largely on empirical studies (and

[14] R. Caves, *American Industry: Structure, Conduct, Performance,* Englewood Cliffs, N.J.: Prentice-Hall, 1967, p. 45.

hunch), that in some oligopolistic industries such expenditures have been expanded beyond socially optimal levels.

Fourth, one would expect on the basis of the models presented in this chapter that the *profits earned by oligopolists would be higher, on the average, than the profits earned by perfectly competitive firms.* This conclusion is supported by substantial statistical evidence. For example, Joe Bain of the University of California has found that firms in industries in which the largest few firms had a high proportion of total sales tended to have higher rates of return than firms in industries in which the largest few firms had a small proportion of total sales.[15]

These conclusions would be accepted by most economists, though certainly not by all. For example, some distinguished economists are impressed by the fact that big oligopolists must constantly confront big labor and big government.[16] They emphasize the importance of ***countervailing power,*** the check on a big firm that arises from the fact that it deals with other big organizations. Put crudely, the idea is that big firms must sit across the negotiating table from other big firms, as well as big unions and big government. Confronted with these big customers and suppliers, the large oligopolistic firm is, according to this view, unable to capitalize on its market power, since it encounters countervailing power from its customers and suppliers. The result is that the behavior of the big oligopolist is closer to the behavior of a perfectly competitive firm than would otherwise be the case. Within the economics profession, this idea has been received skeptically, although it has had an undeniable impact. Critics have pointed out that it is not clear that entrenched power breeds countervailing power. Nor is it clear that two oligopolists confronting one another will act to eliminate, rather than redistribute, their oligopolistic gains.

[15] J. Bain, "Relation of Profit Rate to Industry Concentration: American Manufacturing, 1936–1940," *Quarterly Journal of Economics,* August 1951. However, there has been some disagreement on this score. See L. Weiss, "The Concentration-Profits Relationship and Antitrust," in H. Goldschmid, H. M. Mann, and J. F. Weston, *Industrial Concentration: The New Learning,* Boston: Little Brown, 1974.

[16] John Kenneth Galbraith, *American Capitalism,* Boston: Houghton Mifflin, 1952.

Summary

Monopolistic competition occurs where there are many sellers whose products are not the same. Thus the demand curve facing each firm slopes downward to the right. The conditions for long-run equilibrium are that each firm is maximizing profits and that economic profits are zero. A famous conclusion of the theory of monopolistic competition is that firms under this form of market organization will tend to operate with excess capacity. The firm under monopolistic competition is likely to produce less, and charge a higher price, than under perfect competition. Relative to pure monopoly, monopolistically competitive firms are likely to have lower profits, greater output and lower prices. Firms under monopolistic competition will, of course, offer a wider variety of styles, brands, and qualities than will firms under perfect competition. Retailing provides an interesting illustration of monopolistic competition.

Oligopoly is characterized by a small number of firms and a great deal of interdependence, actual and perceived, among them. Oligopoly is a common market structure in the United States. According to empirical studies, prices tend to be rigid in oligopolistic industries. A well-known theory designed to explain this phenomenon is Sweezy's model, based on the kinked demand curve. This theory is an incomplete model of oligopoly pricing, even though it may be of use in explaining the rigidity of prices. One of the most interesting postwar developments in oligopoly theory is the theory of games, a suggestive framework for analysis in which one can structure formerly intractable problems. However, in its present state, game theory cannot be used to derive specific predictions concerning the behavior of oligopolists.

Conditions in oligopolistic industries tend to promote collusion. A cartel is an open, formal, collusive arrangement. A profit-maximizing cartel will act like a monopolist with a number of plants or divisions, each of which is a member firm. However, in practice, output is unlikely to be allocated among the member firms to minimize total costs, since the allocation process is basically a matter of bargaining. Collusive arrangements often occur, although there are important barriers to effective collusion. Price leadership is quite common in oligopolistic industries, one or a few firms apparently setting the price and the rest following their lead. Two types of price leadership are the dominant-firm model and the barometric-firm model. An example of the former kind of price leadership was the steel industry until a decade or so ago.

According to numerous studies of business behavior, cost-plus pricing is used by many oligopolists. However, a cost-plus model of pricing is incomplete unless it specifies more precisely the determinants of the size of the markup. Relative to perfect competition, it seems likely that both price and profits will be higher under oligopoly. Moreover, oligopolistic industries will tend to spend more on advertising, product differentiation, and style changes than perfectly competitive industries.

CONCEPTS FOR REVIEW

Monopolistic competition	Game theory	Cartel
Oligopoly	Player	Collusion
Pure oligopoly	Strategy	Dominant firm
Differentiated oligopoly	Countervailing power	Barometric firm
Product differentiation	Payoff	Cost-plus pricing
Product group	Zero-sum game	Markup
	Payoff matrix	Target rate of return

QUESTIONS FOR DISCUSSION AND REVIEW

1. Make a detailed comparison of the long-run equilibrium in (a) a perfectly competitive industry, (b) a monopolistic industry, (c) a monopolistically competitive industry, and (d) an oligopolistic industry. Are there any reasons for believing that society should prefer one of these equilibria over the others?

2. In 1973, the Federal Trade Commission accused the nation's eight largest oil firms of pursuing "a common course of action" that kept the profits from the sale of crude petroleum artificially high. Would such behavior be in accord with oligopolistic theories? How would you go about proving or disproving the FTC's accusation?

3. "Monopolistic competition occurs in markets where there are few sellers, and oligopoly occurs where there are many sellers." Comment and evaluate.

4. "Monopolistic competition is wasteful because too much product differentiation occurs." How would you test this proposition?

5. "The kinked oligopoly demand curve is not a very effective tool of analysis because oligopolists frequently do raise their price in response to a price increase by a rival." Comment and evaluate.

6. "The theory of games is unrealistic because oligopolists seldom take account of how their rivals will respond to their actions. After all, there is no way to tell what their rivals will do in response to a particular action." Comment and evaluate.

7. Suppose that a cartel consists of four firms, each of which has a horizontal marginal cost curve. For each firm, marginal cost equals \$4. Suppose that the marginal revenue curve for the cartel is $MR = 10 - 2Q$, where MR is marginal revenue (in dollars) and Q is the cartel's output per year (in thousands of units). What output rate will the cartel choose?

8. According to the Senate Subcommittee on Antitrust and Monopoly, "Some system of marketing quotas, whether overt or carefully hidden, must underlie any price-fixing agreement." Comment and evaluate.

9. Discuss the incentives that each firm in Question 7 would have to cheat on the collusive agreement described there.

10. Suppose that a firm engages in cost-plus pricing. Assuming that it will operate next year at 80 percent of capacity, it estimates its average costs at that output rate. Then it adds a certain percentage to this average cost figure to get its price. But suppose that the demand curve shifts to the left during the next year, and that the firm can only operate at 40 percent of capacity if it maintains this price. What factors will govern whether the firm sticks with this price? What does this indicate about cost-plus pricing?

26 Industrial Organization and Antitrust Policy

Monopoly and *monopolist* have long been dirty words—or at least slightly derogatory ones. The public has tended to view monopolists with suspicion at least since Adam Smith's famous attack on monopolies in the eighteenth century. Smith preached and generations of economists since have taught that a monopolist charges a price in excess of the price that would prevail under perfect competition. But why is it so bad that price is higher, and output lower, than under perfect competition?

In this chapter we deal with this and other issues of public policy toward market structure and industrial organization. The opening sections present the case against monopoly power, as well as the defense made by some economists. Then, after describing the extent of industrial concentration in the United States, we discuss the nature, history, and effectiveness of antitrust policy in the United States, together with the problems in constructing standards for antitrust policy. Finally, we describe some laws in this country that restrict, rather than promote, competition.

The Case against Monopoly

Monopoly and the Misallocation of Resources

Many people oppose monopolies on the grounds that they "gouge" the consumers by charging a higher price than would otherwise exist–a price that can be sustained only because monopolists artificially limit the supply. In other words, these people claim that monoplists reap higher profits than would be possible under perfect competition and that these profits are at the expense of consumers, who pay higher prices than under perfect competition. Is their claim accurate? Certainly, as we saw in Chapter 24, a monopolist will reap higher profits than under perfect competition and consumers will pay higher prices under monopoly than under perfect competition. But is this bad?

To the extent that the monopolist is rich and the consumers are poor, we are likely to answer yes. Also, to the extent that the monopolist is less deserving than the consumers, we are likely to answer the same thing. But suppose the monopolist is a selfless philanthropist who gives to the poor, is monopoly still socially undesirable? The answer remains yes, because *monopoly imposes a burden on society by misallocating resources. In the presence of monopoly, the price system cannot be relied on to decide what is to be produced, how the output is to be produced, and to whom it should be distributed.*

To see more precisely how monopoly interferes with the proper functioning of the price system, suppose that all industries other than the shoe industry are perfectly competitive. The shoe industry, however, has been monopolized. How does this cause a misallocation of resources? Under fairly general circumstances, a good's price can be taken as a measure of the social value of an extra unit of the good. For example, if the price of a pair of socks is $1, the value to the consumer of an extra pair of socks can be taken to be $1. Moreover, under fairly general circumstances, a good's marginal cost can be taken as a measure of the cost to society of an extra unit of the good. For example, if the marginal cost of a pair of shoes is $30, the cost to society of producing an extra pair of shoes can be taken to be $30.

In perfectly competitive industries, price is set equal to marginal cost, as we saw in Chapter 24. Thus each of the competitive industries produces up to the point where the social value of an extra unit of the good (which equals price) is set equal to the cost to society of producing an extra unit of the good (which equals marginal cost). This is the amount each of these industries should produce: the output rate that will result in an optimal allocation of resources.

To see that this is the optimal output rate, consider what happens when an industry produces up to the point where the social value of an extra unit of the good is *more* than the cost to society of producing an extra unit. This isn't the socially optimal output rate because a one-unit increase in the output rate will increase the social value of output by more than the social cost of production, which means that it will increase social welfare. Thus, since a one-unit increase in the output rate will increase social welfare, the existing output rate cannot be optimal.

Next, consider what happens when an industry produces up to the point where the social value of an extra unit of the good is *less* than the cost to society of producing the extra unit. This isn't the socially optimal output rate because a one-unit decrease in the output rate will decrease the social value of output by less than the social cost of production, which means that it will increase social welfare. Thus, since a one-unit decrease in the output rate will increase social welfare, the existing output rate cannot be optimal.

Putting together the results of the previous two paragraphs, it follows that the socially optimal output rate must be at the point where the social value of an extra unit of the good *equals* the social cost of producing an extra unit of the good. Why? Because if the output rate is not optimal when the social value of an extra unit of the good exceeds or falls short of the cost to society of producing the extra unit, it must be optimal only when the two are equal.

Now let's return to the shoe industry—the sole monopolist.[1] Is the shoe industry producing the optimal amount of shoes? The answer is no. Like any monopolist, it produces at the point where marginal revenue equals marginal cost, as we saw in Chapter 24. Thus, since marginal revenue is *less* than price (as was proved there), the monopolist produces at a point where price is *greater* than marginal cost. Consequently, *the monopolistic industry produces at a point where the social value of an extra unit of the good (which equals price) is greater than the cost to society of producing the extra unit (which equals marginal cost).* As we saw in a previous paragraph, this means that the monopolist's output rate is too small. A one-unit increase in the output of shoes will increase the social value of output by more than the social cost of production.

Here lies the economist's principal complaint against monopoly: it results in a misallocation of resources. Too little is produced of the monopolized good. Society is less well off—in terms of its own tastes and potentialities—than it could be. The price system, which would not lead to, or tolerate, such waste if all industries were perfectly competitive, is not allowed to perform as it should. These inefficiencies caused by monopoly are described further and in more detail in Chapter 30.

Income Distribution and Efficiency

Misallocation of resources is only part of the economist's brief against monopoly. As we have already pointed out, *monopoly redistributes income in favor of the monopolists.* In other words, the monopolist can fatten his own purse by restricting his output and raising his price. Admittedly, there is no scientific way to prove that monopolists are less deserving than the rest of the population, but it is also pretty difficult to see why they are more deserving.

In addition, *since monopolists do not have to face direct competition, they are likely to be less diligent in controlling costs and in using resources efficiently.* As Sir John Hicks put it, "The best of all monopoly profits is a quiet life."[2] Certainly we all dream at times of being able to take life easy. It would be strange if the monopolist, having succeeded in insulating himself from direct competition, did not take advantage of the opportunity—not open to firms in perfectly competitive markets—to relax a bit and worry less about pinching pennies. For this reason, economists fear that, to use Adam Smith's pungent phrase, "Monopoly . . . is a great enemy to good management."

Further, *it is often claimed that monopolists are slow to innovate and adopt new techniques and products.* This lethargy stems from the monopolist's freedom from direct competition. Innovation tends to be disruptive, while old ways, like old shoes, tend to be comfortable. The monopolist may be inclined, therefore, to stick with "time-honored" practices. Without question, competition is an important spur to innovation and to the rapid diffusion of innovations. But there are well-known arguments on the other side as well: some economists argue that substantial monopoly power promotes innovation and technological change. Much more will be said below on this score.

The Case against Oligopoly and Monopolistic Competition

Thus far, we have discussed the case against monopoly. Although economists are more con-

[1] Are puns really the lowest form of humor?

[2] J. Hicks, "Annual Survey of Economic Theory: The Theory of Monopoly," *Econometrica,* 1935.

cerned about monopoly than about oligopoly or monopolistic competition, this does not mean that they give either oligopoly or monopolistic competition a clean bill of health. Even though oligopoly has aroused less public indignation and opposition than out-and-out monopoly, an oligopoly can obviously be just as deleterious to social welfare. After all, if oligopolists engage in collusion, open or tacit, their behavior with regard to price and output may resemble a monopolist's. Only if there is real competition among the oligopolists can we expect price to be pushed closer to marginal cost under oligopoly than under monopoly. If oligopolists "cooperate" and "maintain orderly markets," the amount of social waste may be no less than under monopoly.

Also, the inflexibility of prices under oligopoly tends to interfere with the effective functioning of the price system. In a perfectly competitive industry, price will decline when the demand curve shifts to the left, thus prompting resources to move out of the industry. (We examined this process in Chapter 24, using coal and corn as examples.) But in an oligopolistic industry, price tends to remain constant when demand shifts to the left, with the result that output falls and much of the industry's plant is left idle. Although resources leave the oligopolistic industry, as they should, the resources that are stuck in the industry in the short run are not utilized adequately. And the fact that prices are not allowed to decline contributes to cost-push inflation.

Monopolistic competition can also be a socially wasteful form of market organization. As we saw in Chapter 25, monopolistically competitive markets are characterized by overcrowding and excess capacity. There are more firms than would exist under perfect competition, and each firm produces less than the minimum-cost output rate. Thus the industry's output is produced inefficiently: more resources are used than are really necessary. Of course, the extent of this waste may not be very great if the demand curve facing each firm is very elastic, but there is no reason to believe that the demand curve will always be so elastic as to insure that the waste is small.

In addition, price under monopolistic competition—as well as under monopoly and oligopoly—will exceed marginal cost, although the difference between price and marginal cost may be smaller than under monopoly or oligopoly. Thus monopolistic competition, like monopoly and oligopoly, results in a misallocation of resources. The argument leading to this conclusion is exactly like that given earlier for monopoly. Also, monopolistic competition, as well as oligopoly, may allow waste arising from too much being spent (from society's point of view) on product differentiation, advertising, and other selling expenses. This is very difficult to prove, although many economists suspect it is so.

The moral is that many economists look with disfavor on serious departures from perfect competition, whether these departures are in the direction of monopoly, oligopoly, or monopolistic competition. Judged against the perfectly competitive model, all may lead to social waste and inefficiency. However, monopoly is generally presumed to be the greatest evil, with the result that economists usually look with most disfavor on markets dominated by one, or a very few, sellers—or buyers.[3]

The Defense of Monopoly Power

Not all economists agree that monopoly power is a bad thing. On the contrary, some respected voices in the economics profession have been raised to praise monopoly, not bury it. In the previous sections, we have assumed that technology is fixed and independent of an industry's market structure. Some economists like Joseph Schumpeter and John Kenneth

[3] Monopsony, where a single buyer exists, is taken up in Chapter 27.

Galbraith of Harvard University have asserted that the rate of technological change is likely to be higher in an imperfectly competitive industry (i.e., monopoly, oligopoly, etc.) than in a perfectly competitive industry. Since the rate of technological change affects productivity and living standards, in their view a perfectly competitive economy is likely to be inferior in a dynamic sense to an economy containing many imperfectly competitive industries.

But is their assertion true? This question has been debated at great length. On the one hand, Schumpeter and Galbraith argue that firms under perfect competition have fewer resources to devote to research and experimentation than do firms under imperfect competition. Because profits are at a relatively low level, it is difficult for firms under perfect competition to support large expenditures on research and development. Moreover, they argue that unless a firm has sufficient control over the market to reap the rewards from an innovation, the introduction of the innovation may not be worthwhile. If competitors can imitate the innovation very quickly, the innovator may be unable to make any money from it.

Defenders of perfect competition retort that there is likely to be less pressure for firms in imperfect markets to introduce new techniques and products, since such firms have fewer competitors. Moreover, firms in imperfect markets are better able to drive out entrants who, uncommitted to present techniques, are likely to be relatively quick to adopt new ones. (Entrants, unlike established producers, have no vested interest in maintaining the demand for existing products and the profitability of existing equipment.) Also, there are advantages in having a large number of independent decision-making units. There is less chance that an important technological advance will be blocked by the faulty judgment of a few men.

It is very difficult to obtain evidence to help settle the question, if it is posed in this way, since perfect competition is, of course, a hypothetical construct that does not exist in the real world. However, it does seem unlikely that a perfectly competitive industry (if such an industry could be constructed) would be able in many areas of the economy to carry out the research and development required to promote a high rate of technological change. Moreover, if entry is free and rapid, firms in a perfectly competitive industry will have little motivation to innovate. Although the evidence is not at all clear-cut, at least this much can be granted the critics of perfect competition.

Monopoly Power, Big Business, and Technological Change

But some economists go much further than the assertion that a certain amount of market imperfection will promote a more rapid rate of technological change. They say that an industry composed of or dominated by a few large companies is the best market structure for promoting rapid technological change. For example, Galbraith has said that the "modern industry of a few large firms [is] an almost perfect instrument for inducing technical change."[4] And in some circles, it is accepted as an obvious fact that giant firms with their financial strength and well-equipped laboratories are absolutely necessary to maintain a rapid rate of technological change.

Suppose that, for a market of given size, we could replace the largest firms by a larger number of somewhat smaller firms—and thus reduce the extent to which the industry is dominated by the largest firms. Is there any evidence that this would decrease the rate of technological change, as is sometimes asserted? The evidence currently available is much more limited than one would like, but the available studies—based on detailed data concerning research expenditures, patents, important inven-

[4] John Kenneth Galbraith, *American Capitalism,* Boston: Houghton Mifflin, 1952, p. 91.

tions and innovations, and the diffusion of innovation—do not indicate that such a decrease in industrial concentration would reduce the rate of technological change in most industries.

Specifically, the available studies do not show that total research and development expenditures in most industries would decrease if the largest firms were replaced by somewhat smaller ones. Nor do they indicate that the research and development expenditures carried out by the largest firms are generally more productive (or more fundamental or more risky) than those carried out by somewhat smaller firms. Moreover, they do not suggest that greater concentration of an industry results in a faster diffusion of innovations. However, if innovations require a large amount of capital, they do suggest that the substitution of a larger number of smaller firms for a few large ones may lead to slower commercial introduction of the innovations.[5]

Thus, *contrary to the allegations of Galbraith and others, there is little evidence that industrial giants are needed in most industries to insure rapid technological change and rapid utilization of new techniques.* Of course this does not mean that industries composed only of small firms would necessarily be optimal for the promotion and diffusion of new techniques. On the contrary, there seem to be considerable advantages in a diversity of firm sizes. Complementarities and interdependencies exist among large and small firms. There is often a division of labor. Smaller firms may focus on areas requiring sophistication and flexibility and cater to specialized needs, while bigger firms concentrate on areas requiring large production, marketing, or technological resources. However, there is little evidence in most industries that firms considerably smaller than the biggest firms are not big enough for these purposes.

[5] Edwin Mansfield, *Technological Change,* New York: Norton, 1971, and the literature cited there.

Monopoly, Big Business, and Economic Power

The discussion in previous sections makes it clear that the case against monopoly power is not open-and-shut. On the contrary, a certain amount of monopoly power is inevitable in practically all real-life situations, since perfect competition is a model that can only be approximated in real life. Moreover, a certain amount of monopoly power may be needed to promote desirable technological change. The difficult problem is to determine how much monopoly power is optimal under various circumstances (and how this power is to be measured). Some economists (like Galbraith) are convinced that a great deal of monopoly power is both inevitable and desirable. Others believe the opposite. And the economic arguments are not strong enough to resolve the differences of opinion.

Some critics of monopoly power and big business are concerned about the centralization of power in the hands of a relatively few firms. Although this is only partly an economic matter, it is obviously relevant to public policy makers. Economic power in the United States is distributed very unevenly; a few hundred corporations control a very large share of the total assets of the nonfarm economy. Moreover, within particular industries, there is considerable concentration of ownership and production, as we shall see in the next section. This concentration of power has been viewed with concern by observers like A. A. Berle, who asserted that the largest several hundred firms "each with its own dominating pyramid within it—represent a concentration of power over economies which makes the medieval feudal system look like a Sunday School party. In sheer economic power this has gone far beyond anything we have yet seen."[6]

[6] A. A. Berle, *Economic Power and the Free Society,* New York: Fund for the Republic, p. 14.

It is important to note that this distrust of power leads to a distrust of giant firms, whether or not they have substantial monopoly power. Even if General Motors had little power over prices, it would still have considerable economic—and political—power because of its sheer size. Note too that a firm's size is not necessarily a good indicator of the extent of its monopoly power. A small grocery store in a remote community may be a monopolist, but a large merchandising firm with many rivals may have little monopoly power.

Let's look at the biggest 100 manufacturing firms in the United States. Recognizing that bigness is not the same as monopoly power, what percentage of the nation's assets do these firms control, and is this percentage increasing or decreasing over time? According to the latest available figures, the 100 largest manufacturing firms control about ½ of all manufacturing assets in the United States, and this percentage seems to have increased considerably since the end of World War II. For example, Willard Mueller of the University of Wisconsin points out that, of the total assets of manufacturing firms, "the share held by the top one hundred companies rose from 39.3 percent to 49.3 percent [between 1947 and 1968], and the share of the top 200 rose from 47.2 percent to 60.9 percent. In other words, by 1968 the top one hundred companies held a greater share than that held by the top 200 in 1947."[7] Thus there can be no doubt about the vast economic power of the 100 largest firms—and no doubt that, since World War II, they have increased their share of the nation's manufacturing assets.

Industrial Concentration in the United States

Economists and policy makers are interested in market structure because it influences market performance. But how can one measure an industry's market structure? How can one tell how close an industry is to being a monopoly or a perfectly competitive industry? An important measure economists have devised is the ***market concentration ratio,*** which shows the percentage of total sales or production accounted for by the biggest 4 firms. Clearly, the higher the market concentration ratio, the more concentrated the industry is in a very few hands. Of course, basing this measure on 4 firms is arbitrary. You can use 5, 6, 7, or any number of firms you like. But the figures issued by the government are generally based on 4 firms.

Table 26.1 shows the market concentration ratios for selected industries. Clearly, these ratios vary widely from industry to industry. For example, the automobile industry is a tight oligopoly, with the concentration ratio about as high as it can get—93 percent. On the other

Table 26.1
Concentration Ratios in Selected Manufacturing Product Markets, 1972

Industry	Market share of 4 largest firms (percent)
Automobiles	93
Photographic equipment	74
Tires	73
Aircraft	66
Blast furnaces and steel plants	45
Industrial organic chemicals	43
Petroleum refining	31
Bread and cake	29
Pharmaceuticals	26
Radio and TV equipment	19
Newspapers	17
Commercial printing	4

Source: Statistical Abstract of the United States.

[7] W. Mueller, *A Primer on Monopoly and Competition,* New York: Random House, 1970, p. 26.

hand, there is very little industrial concentration in the commercial printing industry: its concentration ratio is only 4 percent. Table 26.2 shows the number and size of industries that have concentration ratios of various magnitudes. Over ½ of the manufacturing industries in the United States have concentration ratios of less than 40 percent, but a substantial number (which account for 8 percent of the total shipments) have concentration ratios of 80 percent or more.

Most economists who have studied trends in industrial concentration seem to agree that remarkably little change has occurred in the past 70 years in the average level of concentration in the United States. As Morris Adelman of M.I.T. puts it, "Any tendency either way, if it exists, must be at the pace of a glacial drift."[8] Also, the available evidence seems to indicate that the levels of market concentration are lower in the United States than in other major industrialized countries, with the possible exception of Great Britain and Japan.

Interestingly, there is a tendency for industries that have high (or low) levels of concentration in one country also to have high (or low) levels of concentration in another country. This suggests that certain basic factors, such as barriers to entry, play an important role in determining an industry's level of concentration in all countries. Very substantial barriers to entry, such as economies of scale and large capital requirements, tend to promote high levels of concentration.

Finally, it is important to recognize that the concentration ratio is only a rough measure of an industry's market structure. Certainly, to provide a reasonably adequate description, it must be supplemented with data on the extent and type of product differentiation in the industry, as well as on barriers to entry. Moreover, even with these supplements, it is still a crude measure. (Among other things, it takes no account of competition from foreign suppliers.) Nonetheless, the concentration ratio has proved to be a valuable tool to economists, and it has turned out to have some predictive value. For example, in accord with the models described in Chapters 24 and 25, there seems to be a relationship between the level of concentration in an industry and the industry's profit rate. As these models would predict, the profit rate seems to be higher in industries where the concentration ratio is higher.

[8] M. Adelman, "The Measurement of Industrial Concentration," *Review of Economics and Statistics,* 1951.

Table 26.2
Number and Relative Value of Shipments of Industries with Various Levels of Concentration, 1970

Concentration ratio (percent)	Number of industries	Percent of total shipments
80–100	27	8
60–79	51	11
40–59	99	23
20–39	161	38
Less than 20	71	20
Total	409	100

The Antitrust Laws

National policies are too ambiguous and rich in contradictions to be summarized neatly and concisely. Consequently, it would be misleading to say that the United States has adopted a policy of promoting competition and controlling monopoly. To a large extent, it certainly is true that "competition is our fundamental national policy," as the Supreme Court said in 1963. But it is also true that we have adopted many measures to promote monopoly and to limit competition, as we shall see in subsequent sections. On balance, however, we probably have gone further in promoting competition than other major industrialized countries, and the principal pieces of legislation designed to further this objective are the ***antitrust laws.***

In 1890, the first antitrust law, the Sherman Act, was passed by Congress. Although the common law had long outlawed monopolistic practices, it appeared to many Americans in the closing years of the nineteenth century that legislation was required to discourage monopoly and to preserve and encourage competition. The formation of "trusts"—monopolistic combines that colluded to raise prices and restrict output—brought the matter to a head. The heart of the Sherman Act lies in the following two sections:

> Sec. 1. Every contract, combination in the form of trust or otherwise, or conspiracy, in restraint of trade or commerce among the several states or with foreign nations, is hereby declared to be illegal. Every person who shall make any such contract or engage in any such combination or conspiracy, shall be deemed guilty of a misdemeanor . . .
>
> Sec. 2. Every person who shall monopolize, or attempt to monopolize or combine or conspire with any other person or persons, to monopolize any part of the trade or commerce among the several States, or with foreign nations shall be deemed guilty of a misdemeanor.

The first 20 years of experience with the Sherman Act were not very satisfying to its supporters. The ineffectiveness of the Sherman Act led in 1914 to passage by Congress of two additional laws: the Clayton Act and the Federal Trade Commission Act. The Clayton Act tried to be more specific than the Sherman Act in identifying certain practices that were illegal because they would "substantially lessen competition or tend to create a monopoly." In particular, the Clayton Act outlawed unjustified ***price discrimination,*** a practice whereby one buyer is charged more than another buyer for the same product. It also outlawed the use of a ***tying contract,*** which makes the buyer purchase other items to get the product he wants. Further, it outlawed mergers that substantially lessen competition; but since it did not prohibit one firm's purchase of a competitor's plant and equipment, it really could not stop mergers. In 1950, this loophole was closed by the Celler-Kefauver Anti-Merger Act.

The Federal Trade Commission Act created the Federal Trade Commission to investigate unfair and predatory practices and to issue cease-and-desist orders. The act stated that "unfair methods of competition in commerce are hereby declared unlawful." However, the commission—composed of 5 commissioners, each appointed by the president for a term of 7 years—was given the unenviable task of defining exactly what was "unfair." The courts took away much of the commission's power; but in 1938, the commission acquired the function of outlawing untrue and deceptive advertising. Also, the commission has authority to carry out economic investigations of the structure and conduct of American business.

The language of the antitrust laws does not tell you a great deal about their meaning or effect; the words are vague and slippery. What these laws mean must be determined by the courts, which obviously have considerable freedom in interpreting them. Nor do these laws enforce themselves. Thus their effect is determined by the action or inaction of the Department of Justice, which is responsible for enforcing them.

The Courts and the Justice Department

The antitrust laws, like any laws, are enforced in the courts. Typically, charges are brought against a firm or group of firms by the Antitrust Division of the Department of Justice, a trial is held, and a decision is reached by the judge. In key cases, appeals are made that eventually reach the Supreme Court. Clearly, the real impact of the antitrust laws depends on how the courts interpret them. And the judicial interpretation of these laws has changed considerably over time. The first major set of antitrust cases took place in 1911 when the Standard Oil Company and the American Tobacco Company were forced to give up a large share of their holdings of other companies. In these cases, the Supreme Court put forth and used the famous ***rule of reason***—that only unreasonable combinations in restraint of trade, not all trusts, required conviction under the Sherman Act. In 1920, the rule of reason was used by the Supreme Court in its finding that U.S. Steel had not violated the antitrust laws even though it had tried to monopolize the industry—since the Court said it had not succeeded. Moreover, U.S. Steel's large size and its potential monopoly power were ruled beside the point since "the law does not make mere size an offense. It . . . requires overt acts."

During the 1920s and early 1930s the courts, including a conservative Supreme Court, interpreted the antitrust laws in such a way that they were as toothless as a new-born babe. Although Eastman Kodak and International Harvester controlled very substantial shares of their markets, the Court, using the rule of reason, found them innocent on the grounds that they had not built up their near-monopoly position through overt coercion or predatory practices. Moreover, the Court reiterated that mere size was not an offense, no matter how great the unexerted monopoly power might be.

In the late 1930s, this situation changed very greatly, with the prosecution of the Aluminum Corporation of America (Alcoa). This case, decided in 1945 (but begun in 1937), reversed the decisions in the U.S. Steel and International Harvester cases. Alcoa had achieved its 90 percent of the market by means that would have been considered "reasonable" in the earlier cases—keeping its price low enough to discourage entry, building capacity to take care of increases in the market, and so forth. (Recall our discussion of Alcoa in Chapter 24.) Nonetheless, the court decided that Alcoa, because it controlled practically all the industry's output, violated the antitrust laws. Thus *the Court used market structure rather than market conduct as a test of legality: monopoly, not just monopolizing, was attacked.*

The impact of the antitrust laws is determined by the vigor with which the Antitrust Division of the Justice Department prosecutes cases. If the Antitrust Division does not prosecute, the laws can have little effect. Like the judicial interpretation of the laws, the extent to which the Justice Department has prosecuted cases has varied from one period to another. Needless to say, the attitude of the political party in power has been an important determinant of how vigorously antitrust cases have been prosecuted. When the Sherman Act was first passed, it was of singularly little value. For example, President Grover Cleveland's attorney general did not agree with the law and would not prosecute under it. "Trust-busting" was truly a neglected art until President Theodore Roosevelt devoted his formidable energies to it. In 1903, he established the Antitrust Division of the Justice Department. Moreover, his administration started the major cases that led to the Standard Oil, American Tobacco, and U.S. Steel decisions.

Subsequently, there was a long lull in the prosecution of antitrust cases, reflecting the Supreme Court's rule of reason doctrine and a strong conservative tide in the nation. The lull continued for about 25 years, until 1937, when there was a significant upsurge in activity on the antitrust front. Led by Thurman Arnold, the Antitrust Division entered one of the most vigorous periods of antitrust enforcement to date. Arnold went after the glass, cigarette, cement, and other industries, the most important case being that against Alcoa. The Antitrust Division attempted in this period to reopen cases that were hopeless under the rule of reason doctrine. With the change in the composition of the Supreme Court and the less business-oriented administration, Arnold's activism turned out to be effective.

Post-World-War-II Developments

The period since World War II has been a vigorous one from the viewpoint of antitrust, with at least three notable developments. First, one of the biggest cases in the history of antitrust occurred in 1961 when, as you will recall from the previous chapter, the major electrical equipment manufacturers were convicted of collusive price agreements. Executives of General Electric, Westinghouse, and other firms in the industry admitted that they met secretly in hotels and communicated by mail in order to maintain prices, share the market, and eliminate competition. Some of the executives were sentenced to jail on criminal charges, and the firms had to pay large amounts to customers to make up for the overcharges. In particular, 1,800 triple damage suits against the firms resulted in payments estimated at between $400 and $600 million. Even the most zealous antitrusters will admit that this was no slap on the wrist!

Second, following the enactment of the Celler-Kefauver Anti-Merger Act, horizontal mergers—mergers of firms making essentially the same good—have become increasingly likely to run afoul of the antitrust laws. In 1962, Chief Justice Earl Warren went so far as to say that a merger that resulted in a firm having 5 percent of the market might be undesirable. In the Von's Grocery case in 1965, the court disallowed a merger between two supermarkets that together had less than 8 percent of the Los Angeles market. (In this case, the court emphasized the trend toward increasing concentration in grocery retailing in Los Angeles.) Also, vertical mergers—mergers of firms that supply or sell to one another—have been viewed with a jaundiced eye by the courts. For example, in the Brown Shoe case, the Supreme Court said that the merger of Brown with R. G. Kinney would mean that other shoe manufacturers would be frozen out of a substantial part of the retail shoe market.

Third, one of the leading problems confronting the Justice Department in recent years has been conglomerate mergers—mergers of firms in unrelated industries. Conglomerate firms like Litton Industries, International Telephone, and Ling-Temco-Vought were regarded very highly by investors during the 1960s. Inspired by their apparent success, other firms began to merge with firms in other industries in order to become conglomerates themselves. Supporters of these mergers claimed that they enabled weak companies to be revitalized by superior management, bigger research facilities, and so on. However, this merger movement was opposed by many other observers on the grounds that conglomerates were obtaining too much power in the economy. To some extent, this problem has diminished in importance since the conglomerates began to show relatively disappointing earnings in the late 1960s. But the Justice Department continues to keep a watchful eye on conglomerate mergers. For example, in 1967 it succeeded in preventing a conglomerate merger between Procter and Gamble, the big soap manufacturer, and Clorox, a maker of liquid bleach. And in 1971 it made some attempt to force ITT to divest itself of the Hartford Fire Insurance Company (which, as we saw in the previous chapter, ITT had acquired), but the case was dropped.

Standards for Antitrust Policy

There are at least two fairly distinct approaches to antitrust policy. *The first looks primarily and directly at market performance—the industry's rate of technological change, efficiency, and profits, the conduct of individual firms, and so on.* Advocates of this approach argue that, in deciding antitrust cases, one should review in detail the performance of the firms in question to see how well they have served the economy. If they have served well, they should not be held in violation of the antitrust laws simply because they have a large share of the market. This test, as it is usually advocated, relies heavily on an evaluation of the technological "progressiveness" and "dynamism" of the firms in question. Although this approach seems quite sensible, it has a number of disadvantages. In particular, it is very difficult to tell at present whether a particular industry's performance is "good" or "bad." Economists simply do not have the sorts of measuring rods that would be required to obtain reasonably accurate and well-accepted readings on an industry's performance. In view of the vagueness of the criteria and the practical realities of the antitrust environment, adopting this approach would probably invite nonenforcement of the laws.

The second approach emphasizes the importance of an industry's market structure—the number and size distribution of buyers and sellers in the market, the ease with which new firms can enter, and the extent of product differentiation. According to this approach, one should look to market structure for evidence of undesirable monopolistic characteristics. The basic idea behind this approach, as George Stigler puts it, is that "an industry which does not have a competitive structure will not have competitive behavior." Two leading authorities on antitrust law, Carl Kaysen of M.I.T. and Donald Turner of Harvard (and formerly head of the Antitrust Division under President Johnson), are strong advocates of this approach. They believe that, if for 5 years or more, one firm has accounted for 50 percent or more of annual sales in a market, or if 4 or fewer firms have accounted for 80 percent of such sales, it should be presumed that "market power" exists. And they propose that such "market power" be declared illegal, unless such concentration can be defended by economies of scale or some other such justification. If it cannot be defended, divestiture and dissolution would constitute possible remedies.[9]

Although respected economists favor each of these approaches, the second is probably preferred by most experts in this field. Moreover, the Justice Department adopted this approach in its 1968 merger guidelines, which stated that mergers would ordinarily be challenged when the firms involved had more than specified shares of the market.[10] However, this does not mean that the market structure approach does not have lots of critics. On the contrary, many economists and lawyers feel that the relationship between market structure and market performance is so weak that it is a mistake to choose, more or less arbitrarily,

[9] C. Kaysen and D. Turner, *Antitrust Policy,* Cambridge, Mass.: Harvard University Press, 1959.

[10] For example, in the case of horizontal mergers, the guidelines stated that a horizontal merger would ordinarily be challenged when:

1. The 4-firm concentration ratio in the appropriate market is approximately 75 percent or more, and the firms involved in the merger account for the following percentages of the market:

Larger or acquiring firm	Smaller or acquired firm
4 percent	4 percent or more
10 percent	2 percent or more
15 percent	1 percent or more

2. The 4-firm concentration ratio is less than approximately 75 percent, and the firms involved in the merger account for the following percentages of the market:

Larger or acquiring firm	Smaller or acquired firm
5 percent	5 percent or more
10 percent	4 percent or more
15 percent	3 percent or more
20 percent	2 percent or more
25 percent	1 percent or more

(Under both 1 and 2, percentages not shown in the table should be interpolated between those given.)

3. In industries in which the concentration ratio for any group of firms from the 2 largest to the 8 largest has increased 7 percent or more in the last 5 to 10 years, the department will challenge any merger involving a firm whose market share is roughly 2 percent or more.

Source: U.S. Department of Justice, "Merger Guidelines" (mimeo), issued May 30, 1968.

some level of concentration and to say that, if concentration exceeds this level, market performance is likely to be undesirable. For example, the editors of *Fortune* magazine went so far in 1966 as to propose that Congress should amend the antitrust laws to make it clear that "it is not national policy to prefer any particular size, shape, or number of firms to any other size, shape, or number; and that mergers—horizontal, vertical, or conglomerate—are entirely legal unless they spring from a manifest attempt to restrain trade.[11]

The Effectiveness of Antitrust Policy

How effective have the antitrust laws been? Obviously it is difficult to tell with any accuracy, since there is no way to carry out an experiment in which American history is rewritten to show what would have happened if the antitrust laws had not been on the books. Many experts seem to feel that the antitrust laws have not been as effective as they might—or should—have been, largely because they do not have sufficient public support and there is no politically powerful pressure group pushing for their enforcement. But although some experts feel that the antitrust laws have had little effect, others believe that the evidence, although incomplete and unclear, suggests that they have had a significant impact on business behavior and markets. For example, Edward Mason of Harvard University has pointed out that their effectiveness is due "not so much to the contribution that particular judgments have made to the restoring of competition as it is to the fact that the consideration of whether or not a particular course of action may or may not be in violation of the antitrust acts is a persistent factor affecting business judgment, at least in large firms."[12] This same idea is summed up in the old saying that the ghost of Senator Sherman sits as an *ex officio* member of every firm's board of directors.

Some indication of the effects of our antitrust laws can perhaps be obtained by looking at experience in other countries, since Britain, Germany, and many other European countries (as well as Japan) took a very tolerant view of monopoly power for a long time. After World War II, there was pressure to break up some of the powerful combines in Germany and Japan, but this pressure has been somewhat relaxed more recently—although antitrust practices seem to be gaining ground in the European Common Market. Foreign experience seems to indicate that the antitrust laws have helped prevent American firms from adopting many restrictive and predatory practices common elsewhere. However, this does not mean that antitrust legislation and enforcement have managed to break up many of our giant corporations. One of the most important problems is that it is more difficult to attack existing concentration in an industry than to stop further concentration firms attempt to bring about through merger. As John Kenneth Galbraith puts it, "If a firm is already large, it is substantially immune under the antitrust laws."[13]

Certainly, there is little prospect that our giant corporations will soon be broken up. In part, this reflects the fact that much of the public is not really sold on the idea of breaking up big oligopolists, even though it may not be quite comfortable with them. Also, the effectiveness of the antitrust laws is limited by the amount of resources the Antitrust Division is given to carry out its job. Until the 1930s, the Antitrust Division received an annual appro-

[11] See "A New 'Worst' in Antitrust" and "The Antitrust Chief Replies," reprinted in E. Mansfield, *Economics: Readings, Issues, and Cases,* 2d ed., New York: Norton, 1977.

[12] Edward Mason, Preface to Carl Kaysen and Donald Turner, *Antitrust Policy* (and reprinted in E. Mansfield, *Monopoly Power and Economic Performance,* 3d ed. New York: Norton, 1974).

[13] J. K. Galbraith, "The New Industrial State," in E. Mansfield, *Economics: Readings, Issues, and Cases.*

priation of less than $300,000, which permitted it to bring only a few cases to court a year. More recently, the division's budget has increased considerably—it was about $6 million in 1963—but it is still unable to bring more than about 50 cases annually, a small number by practically any standard. Moreover, most of these tend to be open and shut cases of price-fixing conspiracies, frequently in food processing and distribution, building materials, and the service trades.

Yet despite the difficulties, the Antitrust Division brought action during the 1970s against International Business Machines Corporation and American Telephone and Telegraph, two of the biggest firms in the United States. And the Federal Trade Commission went after the big ready-to-eat cereal manufacturers. Even the U.S. Senate showed a surprising penchant for trust-busting when 45 senators voted for an unsuccessful bill proposed in 1975 that would have required the major oil companies (like Exxon, Texaco, and Mobil) to divest themselves of their production and transportation arms. (And as of 1976, this divestiture movement in oil is by no means dead.) Thus, while there is little prospect that many of our giant corporations will soon be split up, the history of the 1970s suggests that (for better or worse) such dissolution is not impossible either.

The Pabst Case: Antitrust in Action

Perhaps the most effective way to learn certain things about the antitrust field is to try to decide an actual antitrust case. Suppose that, over the protests of the American Bar Association, you are appointed a district court judge and that your first job is to hear a case (actually brought by the government in 1958) to prevent Pabst Brewing Company from acquiring the Blatz Brewing Company. According to the government, the effect of this merger "may be substantially to lessen competition, or to tend to create a monopoly" in the production and sale of beer in the state of Wisconsin, the three-state area of Wisconsin, Illinois, and Michigan, and the United States. A fundamental issue in any case of this sort is the definition of market and industry boundaries. Market boundaries must be broad enough to include all relevant competitors but not so broad as to include products that are not reasonable substitutes. The delineation of market and industry boundaries—in terms of "line of commerce" and "section of the country"—is bound to involve judgment, there being no simple, mechanical rule to settle it.

In the Pabst case, both the government and Pabst agreed "that the line of commerce involved the production, sale, and distribution of beer and that the continental United States is a relevant geographic market." However, there was disagreement over the government's use of Wisconsin and the three-state area of Wisconsin, Illinois, and Michigan as separate geographical markets. Pabst and Blatz claimed that there was no good reason to single out these particular areas as distinct markets. The government, on the other hand, claimed that they were distinct markets because the two firms competed most intensively in these areas. Pabst was the nation's eleventh largest seller of beer; its sales were 2.67 percent of the national market and about 11 percent of the sales in Wisconsin. Blatz was the nation's thirteenth largest seller of beer, its sales being 2.04 percent of the national market and about 13 percent of the sales in Wisconsin. Thus, if you look at the smaller geographical area (Wisconsin and the three-state area), the two firms account for a substantial proportion of the market—about 24 percent in Wisconsin. But if you look at the national market as a whole, they account for a small proportion—less than 5 percent.

As the district judge how should you decide the case? Should you agree with the government that Wisconsin and the three-state area are relevant markets? Or should you agree with Pabst and Blatz that they are not relevant markets in themselves, but just parts of a market? Moreover, if you agree with the government concerning the market definition, should you also agree that two firms with a total of 24 percent of Wisconsin sales should not be allowed to merge? Or if you agree with Pabst and Blatz concerning the market definition, should you allow a merger between two firms that together account for about 5 percent of the national market? It is a tough problem, isn't it? To demonstrate just how tough it is, the district judge decided one way, while the Supreme Court decided the other way. The district court, agreeing with Pabst and Blatz that Wisconsin and the three-state area should not be treated as distinct relevant areas, dismissed the government's complaint. But the district court's decision was reversed by the Supreme Court, which agreed with the government's position that the smaller areas should be treated as relevant, distinct markets.

The antitrust field is characterized by many complexities and uncertainties, as well as by legal and economic vagueness and ambiguity. This case illustrates how difficult it is even to decide what the relevant market is![14]

The Patent System

In a previous section, we pointed out that our national economic policies are by no means free of contradiction. In particular, although many of our policies are designed to promote competition and limit monopoly, one should not assume that all of them are meant to promote these objectives. On the contrary, quixotic as it may seem, some are designed to do just the opposite: to restrict competition. Among the most important of these policies are our laws concerning patents, which grant the inventor exclusive control over the use of his invention for 17 years. That is, the inventor is given a temporary monopoly over the use of his invention.

Since Congress passed the original patent act in 1790, the arguments used to justify the existence of the patent laws have not changed very much. First, these laws are regarded as an important incentive to induce the inventor to put in the work required to produce an invention. Particularly in the case of the individual inventor, it is claimed that patent protection is a strong incentive. Second, patents are regarded as a necessary incentive to induce firms to carry out the further work and make the necessary investment in pilot plants and other items that are required to bring the invention to commercial use. If an invention became public property when made, why should a firm incur the costs and risks involved in attempting to develop, debug, and perfect it? Another firm could watch, take no risks, and duplicate the process or product if it were successful. Third, it is argued that, because of the patent laws, inventions are disclosed earlier than otherwise, the consequence being that other inventions are facilitated by the earlier dissemination of the information. The resulting situation is often contrasted with the intense secrecy about processes that characterized the medieval guilds and which undoubtedly retarded technological progress and economic growth.

Not all economists agree that the patent system is beneficial. A patent represents a monopoly right, although as many inventors can testify, it may be a very weak one. Critics of the patent system stress the social costs arising from the monopoly. After a new process or product has been discovered, it may cost very little for other persons who could make use of this knowledge to acquire it. The patent

[14] For further discussion of the Pabst case, see Henry Einhorn and William Smith, *Economic Aspects of Antitrust: Readings and Cases*, New York: Random House, 1968.

gives the inventor the right to charge a price for the use of the information, with the result that the knowledge is used less widely than is socially optimal. Critics also point out that patents have been used to create monopoly positions, which were sustained by other means after the original patents had expired. They cite as examples the aluminum, shoe machinery, and plate-glass industries. In addition, the cross-licensing of patents often has been used by firms as a vehicle for joint monopolistic exploitation of their market.

Critics also question the extent of the social gains arising from the system. They point out that the patent system was designed for the individual inventor, but that over the years most research and development has been institutionalized. They assert that patents are not really important as incentives to the large corporation, since it cannot afford to fall behind in the technological race, whether or not it receives a patent. Also, they say that because of long lead times, most of the innovative profits from many innovations can be captured before imitators have a chance to enter the market, whether or not the innovator is granted a patent. Finally, they claim that firms keep secret what inventions they can, and patent those they cannot.

These questions concerning the effects and desirability of the patent system have proven extremely difficult to settle. But most observers seem to agree that, despite its faults, it is difficult to find a realistic substitute for the patent system. However, over the past 30 years, there has been a discernible trend for the courts and Congress to resolve conflicts between the patent system and antitrust policy more and more in favor of the latter. The courts have found more and more patents invalid; Congress has set higher standards of patentability; and the courts have curtailed the extension of the effects of the patent beyond the invention described in the patent claim.

Other Policies Designed to Restrict Competition

The reasons why laws are enacted to restrict, rather than promote, competition are not difficult to understand. Everyone wants competition for the other guy, but not for himself. Moreover, certain sectors of the economy seem to need help, and have the political muscle to get it—partly in the form of laws designed to take some of the competitive heat off them. A case of this sort is retail trade, where the small independent retailers felt threatened by the advent of the chain store. The chain stores were able to reduce the costs of distribution below those of the smaller retailers, with the result that the total number of grocery stores and drug stores fell considerably in the 1920s and 1930s. The small retailers charged that their smaller numbers were due to the predatory tactics of the chain stores. They took their charges to Congress and succeeded in getting the Robinson-Patman Act enacted in 1936.

The Robinson-Patman Act says that sellers must not discriminate in price among purchasers of similar grade and quality where the effect might be to drive competitors out of business. The act was aimed at preventing price discrimination in favor of chain stores that buy goods in large quantities. Most economists do not regard the Robinson-Patman Act with enthusiasm because it attempts to keep competitors in existence even if they are inefficient. (Needless to say, the social virtues of the competitive system do not lie in maintaining a lot of inefficient small businessmen in operation.) Moreover, most observers seem to believe that the act has had the effect of reducing the vigor of price competition in retail trade.

Another law designed to limit competition in retail trade was the Miller-Tydings Act of 1937, which exempted from the antitrust laws the use of resale price maintenance agreements in states permitting such agreements. ***Resale price maintenance agreements*** permitted manufacturers of a trademarked or branded item to establish the retail price of the item by contracts with retailers. Moreover, the Miller-Tydings Act permitted the manufacturer to bind *all* retailers in a state to a contract simply by signing such a contract with *any one* of the retailers in the state. Of course, the result was to reduce the amount of price competition in retail trade. In 1975, Congress passed a bill nullifying such agreements.

Finally, you should recognize that policies designed to limit competition are found in many other areas besides retail trade. In Chapter 5, we saw that our national farm policies have been aimed at keeping the prices of agricultural products at a level exceeding what they would be under competition. In Chapter 27, we shall see that the government has promoted the growth of strong labor unions, which try to raise wages above competitive levels. In the field of international trade, the Webb-Pomerene Act of 1918 allowed American exporters to get together to form export trade associations, which, according to some observers, may have tended to reduce competition. Even in the bituminous coal industry, which we looked at in some detail in Chapter 24, Congress passed the Bituminous Coal Act of 1937 to establish minimum prices and reduce "cutthroat" competition, though in 1943 the act was not renewed.

Thus it simply is erroneous to think that the United States has opted decisively for competition. On the contrary, although the antitrust laws are clearly designed to promote competition and limit monopoly, a number of other laws are designed to do just the opposite. In many of the industries where laws designed to restrict competition have been enacted—for example, agriculture, retail trade, and bituminous coal—the basic problem has been that too many people and too much capital were tied up in the industry. Economists generally believe that it would be wiser to encourage people and capital to leave these industries than to attempt to limit competition. (Recall, for example, our discussion in Chapter 5 of pre-1973 American farm policies.)

Summary

The most important reason why economists oppose monopoly is that it imposes a burden on society by misallocating resources. A monopolistic industry produces up to the point where the social value of an extra unit of the good is greater than the cost to society of producing an extra unit of the good—which means that too little is produced of the monopolized good. Society is less well off than it could be. Oligopoly can be as bad as monopoly if oligopolists engage in collusion; and even if they don't collude, inefficiencies are likely to result. Monopolistic competition can also be a socially wasteful form of market organization.

In defense of monopoly power, some economists have asserted that the rate of technological change is likely to be greater in an imperfectly competitive industry than under perfect competition. It does seem unlikely that a perfectly competitive industry would be able—and have the incentive—to carry out the research and development required to promote a rapid rate of technological change in many sectors of the economy. But contrary to the allegations of Galbraith and others, there is little evidence that giant firms are needed to insure rapid technological change in a great many sectors of the economy. The situation is much more complex than such statements indicate, and the contributions of smaller firms are much greater than is commonly recognized.

Economic power in the United States is distributed very unevenly; 100 corporations control about $\frac{1}{2}$ the total manufacturing assets of the economy. Moreover, many individual industries are dominated by a few firms. This concentration of power is viewed with concern by many economists and lawyers. In 1890, the Sherman Act was passed; it outlawed any contract, combination, or conspiracy in restraint of trade and made it illegal to monopolize or attempt to monopolize. In 1914, Congress passed the Clayton Act, and the Federal Trade Commission was created. A more recent antitrust development was the Celler-Kefauver Anti-Merger Act of 1950.

The real impact of the antitrust laws depends on the interpretation placed on these laws by the courts. In its early cases, the Supreme Court put forth and used the famous rule of reason—that only unreasonable combinations in restraint of trade, not all trusts, required conviction under the Sherman Act. The situation changed greatly in the 1940s when the Court decided that Alcoa, because it controlled practically all of the nation's aluminum output, was in violation of the antitrust laws. The impact of the antitrust laws is also determined by the vigor with which the Antitrust Division of the Justice Department prosecutes cases. This too has varied from period to period.

There are at least two fairly distinct approaches to antitrust policy. One looks primarily and directly at market performance; the other emphasizes market structure. Although there are respected economists in favor of each of these approaches, the second is probably preferred by most experts in this field. Many observers seem to feel that the antitrust laws have not been as effective as they might—or should—have been, largely because they do not have sufficient public support. Others feel that the evidence, although incomplete and unclear, suggests that they have had a significant effect on business behavior and markets.

Finally, it is important to note that not all our laws are designed to promote competition and restrict monopoly. On the contrary, some laws are designed to do just the opposite. For example, the patent system confers a temporary monopoly on inventors. And the Robinson-Patman Act and many other laws have been designed to restrict competition. The truth is that, despite some protests to the contrary, our nation is by no means fully committed to promoting competition and preventing monopoly.

CONCEPTS FOR REVIEW

Concentration ratio	Conglomerate merger	Line of commerce
Rule of reason	Resale price maintenance	Section of the country
Horizontal merger	Market performance	Patent system
Vertical merger	Market structure	Robinson-Patman Act

QUESTIONS FOR DISCUSSION AND REVIEW

1. According to John Kenneth Galbraith, "The antitrust laws effectively protect the large business from social pressure or regulation by maintaining the myth that the market does the regulating instead." Do you agree? Why or why not?

2. According to *Fortune* magazine, "Congress should amend the antitrust statutes to make it clear . . . that it is not national policy to prefer any particular size, shape, or number of firms to any other size, shape, or number." Do you agree? Why or why not?

3. "The real impact of the antitrust laws depends on judicial interpretation." Comment and evaluate.

4. "Perfect competition results in optimal efficiency and an optimal distribution of income. This is why the United States opts for a perfectly competitive economy." Comment and evaluate.

5. Suppose that an industry is composed of five firms. The market share of each firm is given below:

Firm	Market share (percent)
A	10
B	10
C	20
D	25
E	35

What is the concentration ratio for this industry?

6. Suppose that firm *E* loses ½ of its sales to firm *C*. If the sales of the other firms remain constant, what is the effect on the concentration ratio in Question 5?

7. According to the Ford administration's attorney general, Edward Levi, "The general impression of the public is that monopoly is inevitable, and since it is inevitable, it is silly to try to prevent it."[15] Comment and evaluate.

8. Chief Justice Hughes observed, "Good intentions will not save a plan otherwise objectionable, but knowledge of actual intent is an aid in the interpretation of facts and prediction of consequence." Relate this to the construction of standards for antitrust policy.

9. Edward S. Mason has written, "Monopoly (or monopoly power) 'without more' is still no offense under the antitrust laws, but the 'more' is being attenuated into what mathematicians might call the second order of smalls."[16] What does he mean? Do you agree? Why?

10. What sorts of empirical tests can you devise to shed light on the extent to which the patent system increases the rate of technological change and whether its social benefits exceed its social costs?

[15] "The Effectiveness of the Antitrust Laws," in E. Mansfield, *Monopoly Power and Economic Performance*, p. 146.
[16] Ibid., p. 179.

PART EIGHT

Distribution of Income and General Equilibrium

27

Determinants of Wages

Everyone has a healthy—indeed, sometimes an unhealthy—interest in income: organizations as holy as the church and as unholy as the Mob exhibit an interest in this subject. Surely we all need to look carefully at the social mechanisms underlying the distribution of income in our society. Most income is in the form of wages and salaries: that is, it is labor income. What determines the price paid for a particular kind of labor? For example, why is the wage rate for surgeons frequently in the neighborhood of $50 an hour, while the wage rate for relatively unskilled labor is frequently in the neighborhood of $3 or $4 an hour? Or why is the wage rate for a secretary higher in 1977 than in 1960?

Economists frequently classify inputs into three categories: labor, capital, and land. The disadvantage of this simple classification is that each category contains an enormous variety of inputs. For example, the services of labor include the work of a football star like O. J.

Simpson, a salesman like Willy Loman, and a knight like Don Quixote. But it does have the important advantage of distinguishing between quite different classes of inputs. In this chapter, we are concerned with the determinants of the price of labor. The next chapter will deal with the determinants of the prices of capital and land, as well as profits.

The Labor Force and the Price of Labor

At the outset it is important to note that, to the economist, labor includes a great deal more than the organized labor that belongs to trade unions. The secretary who works at General Motors, the young account executive at Merrill Lynch, the auto mechanic at your local garage, the professor who teaches molecular biology, all put forth labor. Table 27.1 shows the occupational distribution of the labor force in the United States. You can see that almost ⅔ of the people employed are white-collar workers (such as salesmen, doctors, secretaries, or managers) and service workers (such as waiters, bartenders, or cooks), while only about ⅓ are blue-collar workers (such as carpenters, mine workers, or foremen) and farm workers.

It is also worthwhile to preface our discussion with some data concerning how much people actually get paid. As shown in Table 27.2, average weekly earnings vary considerably from one industry to another. For example, in 1975, workers in manufacturing averaged about $190 a week, while construction workers averaged $265 a week, and workers in retail trade averaged $108 a week. Also, average weekly earnings vary considerably from one period to another. Table 27.2 shows that average weekly earnings in manufacturing in 1965 were only $108, as contrasted with $190 in 1975. In subsequent sections, we shall investigate the reasons for these differences in wages, both among industries and among periods of time.

More broadly, we shall be concerned in subsequent sections with the price of labor, which includes a great many forms of remuneration other than what are commonly regarded as wages. As noted above, economists include as labor the services performed by professional people (such as lawyers, doctors, and professors) and self-employed businessmen (such as

Table 27.1
Occupational Composition of the Employed Labor Force, United States, 1974

	Percent of employed labor force	
White-collar workers		48.6
Professional and technical	14.4	
Managers and administrators	10.4	
Sales workers	6.3	
Clerical workers	17.5	
Blue-collar workers		34.6
Craftsmen and foremen	13.4	
Operatives	16.2	
Nonfarm laborers	5.1	
Service workers		13.2
Farm workers		3.5
Total		100.0

Source: Bureau of Labor Statistics.

Table 27.2
Average Weekly Earnings, Selected Industries, 1955–75 (dollars)

Year	Manufacturing	Construction	Retail trade
1955	76	91	49
1960	90	113	58
1965	108	138	67
1970	134	195	82
1975	190	265	108

Source: U.S. Department of Labor.

electricians, mechanics, and barbers). Thus the amount such people receive per unit of time is included here as a particular sort of price of labor, even though these amounts are often called fees or salaries rather than wages.

Finally, it is important to distinguish between *money* wages and *real* wages. Whereas the money wage is the amount of money received per unit of time, the real wage is the amount of real goods and services that can be bought with the money wage. Obviously, the real wage depends on the price level for goods and services as well as on the magnitude of the money wage. In recent years, the inflation we have experienced has meant that real wages have increased less than money wages; thus the increases in earnings in Table 27.2 exaggerate the increase in real wages. In subsequent sections, since we shall assume that product prices are held constant, our discussion will be in terms of real wages.

The Equilibrium Wage and Employment under Perfect Competition

The Firm's Demand Curve for Labor

Let's begin by discussing the determinants of the price of labor under perfect competition. That is, we assume that firms take the prices of their products, as well as the prices of all inputs as given; and we assume that owners of inputs take input prices as given. Under these circumstances, what determines how much labor an individual firm will hire (at a specified wage rate)? Once we answer this question, we can derive a firm's demand curve for labor. A ***firm's demand curve for labor*** is the relationship between the price of labor and the amount of labor utilized by the firm. That is, it shows, for each price, the amount of labor that the firm will use.

Let us assume that we know the firm's production function, and that labor is the only variable input. Given the production function, we can determine the marginal product of labor when various quantities are used. The results of such a calculation are as shown in Table 27.3. If the price of the firm's product is $10, let's determine the value to the firm of each additional worker it hires per day. According to Table 27.3, the firm achieves a daily output of 7 units when it hires the first worker; and since each unit is worth $10, this brings the firm's daily revenues up to $70. By hiring the second worker, the firm increases its daily output by 6 units; and since each unit is worth $10, the resulting increase in the firm's daily revenues is $60. Similarly, the increase in the firm's daily revenues from hiring the third worker is $50, the increase from hiring the fourth worker is $40, and so on.

How many workers should the firm hire per

Table 27.3
The Firm's Demand for Labor under Perfect Competition

Number of workers per day	Total output per day	Marginal product of labor	Value of marginal product (dollars)
0	0		
		7	70
1	7		
		6	60
2	13		
		5	50
3	18		
		4	40
4	22		
		3	30
5	25		

day if it wants to maximize profit? Clearly, it should hire more workers as long as each extra worker results in at least as great an addition to revenues as he does to costs. For example, if the price of a worker is $50 per day, it is profitable for the firm to hire the first worker since this adds $70 to the firm's daily revenues but only $50 to its daily costs. Also, it is profitable to hire the second worker, since this adds $60 to the firm's daily revenues but only $50 to its daily costs. The addition of the third worker does not reduce the firm's profits. But beyond 3 workers per day, it does not pay the firm to hire more labor. (The addition of a fourth worker adds $50 to the firm's daily costs but only $40 to its daily revenues.)

Thus the optimal number of workers per day for this firm is 3. Table 27.3 shows that this is the number of workers at which the value of the marginal product of labor is equal to the price of labor. What is the ***value of the marginal product of labor?*** It is the marginal product of labor multiplied by the product's price. For example, in Table 27.3, the value of the marginal product of labor is $70 when between 0 and 1 workers are used per day. Why? Because the marginal product of labor is 7 units of output, and the price of a unit of output is $10. Thus their product—7 times $10—equals $70.

To maximize profit, the value of the marginal product of labor must be set equal to the price of labor, because if the value of the marginal product is greater than labor's price, the firm can increase its profit by increasing the quantity used of labor; while if the value of the marginal product is less than labor's price, the firm can increase its profit by reducing the quantity used of labor. Thus *profits must be at a maximum when the value of the marginal product is equal to the price of labor.*

Given the results of this section, it is a simple matter to derive the firm's demand curve for labor. Specifically, its demand curve must be the value-of-marginal-product schedule in the last column of Table 27.3. For example, if the daily wage of a worker is between $51 and $60, the firm will demand 2 workers per day; if the daily wage of a worker is between $41 and $50, the firm will demand 3 workers per day; and so forth. Thus *the firm's demand curve for labor is its value-of-marginal-product curve,* which shows the value of labor's marginal product at each quantity of labor used. This curve is shown in Figure 27.1.[1]

Profit Maximization and the Firm's Demand Curve for Labor

In the previous section, we said that *a perfectly competitive firm will employ labor in an amount such that the value of the marginal product of labor—labor's marginal product multiplied by the product's price—equals the price of labor.* This is a fundamental result, the basis of the firm's demand curve for labor. Let's show how this result can be derived from the principles of profit maximization presented in Chapter 22. Recall that the firm, if it minimizes costs, will pick a combination of inputs in which the ratio

[1] Strictly speaking, the firm's demand curve is the same as the curve showing the value of the input's marginal product only if this input is the only variable input. For a discussion of the more general case, see my *Microeconomics: Theory and Applications,* 2d ed., New York: Norton, 1975, Chapter 12.

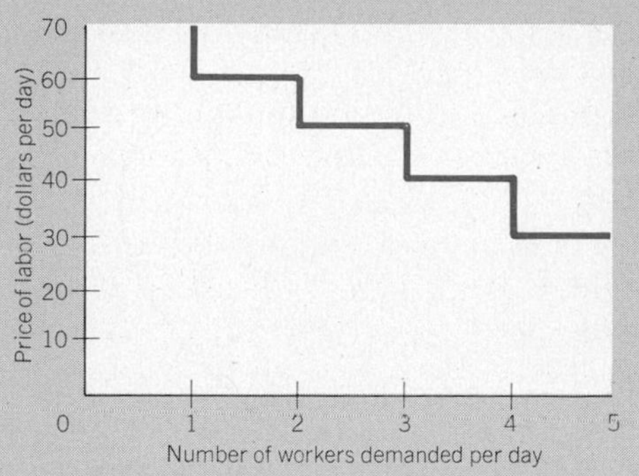

Figure 27.1
The Firm's Demand Curve for Labor under Perfect Competition
The firm's demand curve for labor is the firm's value-of-marginal-product curve, which shows the value of labor's marginal product at each quantity of labor used. The data for this figure come from Table 27.3.

of each input's marginal product to its price is equal. That is, it will set

$$\frac{MP_A}{P_A} = \frac{MP_B}{P_B} = \frac{MP_C}{P_C}, \qquad (27.1)$$

where MP_A is the marginal product of input A, P_A is the price of input A, MP_B is the marginal product of input B, P_B is the price of input B, and so on. If Equation (27.1) does not hold, the firm can always reduce costs by altering the utilization of certain inputs. For example, if the marginal product of a unit of input A is 2 units of output, the price of a unit of input A is \$1, the marginal product of a unit of input B is 6 units of output, and the price of a unit of input B is \$2, the firm can reduce its costs by using 1 unit less of input A—which reduces output by 2 units and cost by \$1—and by using ⅓ unit more of input B—which increases output by 2 units and cost by \$.67. This substitution of input B for input A has no effect on output but reduces the total cost of production by \$.33.

Going a step further, it can be shown that the perfectly competitive firm, if it maximizes profit, must be operating at a point where each of the ratios in Equation (27.1) equals the reciprocal of the product's price.[2] In other words,

$$\frac{MP_A}{P_A} = \frac{MP_B}{P_B} = \ldots = \frac{1}{P},$$

where P is the product's price. Rearranging terms,

$$MP_A \cdot P = P_A \qquad (27.2a)$$
$$MP_B \cdot P = P_B \qquad (27.2b)$$
$$MP_C \cdot P = P_C \qquad (27.2c)$$

Thus we find that each input's marginal product multiplied by the product's price should be set equal to the input's price. This is precisely the result that we obtained for labor in the previous section. As you can see, it holds for any input or combination of inputs, and can be derived from the principles of profit maximization in Chapter 22.

The Market Demand and Supply Curves for Labor

In previous sections, we were concerned with

[2] To see why, note that each of the ratios in Equation (27.1) equals the reciprocal of the firm's marginal cost. To prove that this is so, consider any input, say input A. What is the cost of producing an extra unit of output if this extra unit of output is achieved by increasing the utilization of input A, while holding constant the utilization of other inputs? Since an extra unit of input A results in MP_A extra units of output, $(1/MP_A)$ units of input A will result in 1 unit of extra output. Since $(1/MP_A)$ units of input A will cost $(1/MP_A)\ P_A$, it follow that $P_A \div MP_A$ equals marginal cost. The same type of reasoning can be used for any input, not just input A.

As we know from Chapter 24, a perfectly competitive firm, if it maximizes profit, sets price equal to marginal cost. Thus, since each of the ratios in Equation (27.1) equals the reciprocal of marginal cost, it must also equal the reciprocal of the product's price. This is what we set out to show.

the demand curve of a single firm for labor. But many firms, not just one, are part of the labor market, and the price of labor depends on the demands of all of these firms. The situation is analogous to the price of a product, which depends on the demands of all consumers. *The **market demand curve for labor** shows the relationship between the price of labor and the total amount of labor demanded in the market: that is, it shows, for each price, the amount of labor that will be demanded in the entire market.* The market demand curve for labor, like any other input, is quite analogous to the market demand curve for a consumer good, which we discussed in detail in Chapter 21. But there is at least one important difference. *The demand for labor and other inputs is a **derived demand,** since inputs are demanded to produce other things, not as an end in themselves.* This fact helps to explain why the price elasticity of demand is higher for some inputs than for others. In particular, the larger the price elasticity of demand for the product the input helps produce, the larger the price elasticity of demand for the input. (In addition, the price elasticity of demand for an input is likely to be greater in the long run than in the short run, and greater if other inputs can readily be substituted for the input in question.)

We have already seen that a product's price depends on its market supply curve as well as its market demand curve. This is equally true for labor. Its ***market supply curve*** is *the relationship between the price of labor and the total amount of labor supplied in the market.* When an individual supplies labor, he is supplying something he himself can use, since the time that he does not work can be used for leisure activities. (As Charles Lamb, the famous English essayist, put it, "Who first invented work, and bound the free and holiday-rejoicing spirit down ... to that dry drudgery at the desk's dead wood?"[3]) Because of this fact, the market supply curve for labor, unlike the supply curve for inputs supplied by business firms, may be ***backward bending,*** particularly for the economy as a whole. That is, *beyond some point, increases in price may result in smaller amounts of labor being supplied.*

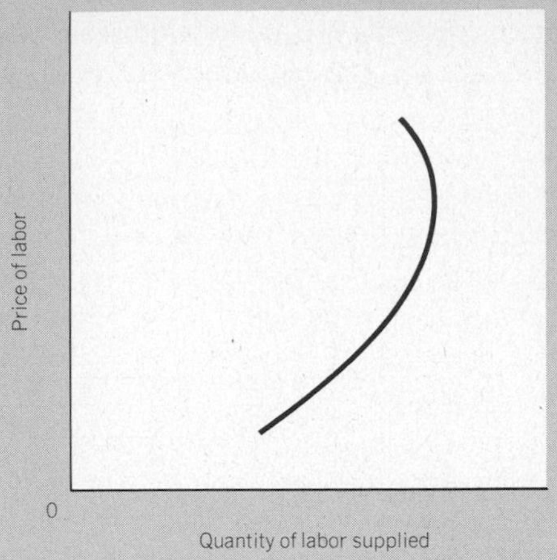

Figure 27.2
Backward-Bending Supply Curve for Labor
Beyond some point, increases in the price of labor may result in smaller amounts of labor being supplied. The reason for a supply curve of this sort is that, as the price of labor increases, the individual supplying the labor becomes richer and wants to increase his amount of leisure time.

An example of a backward-bending supply curve is provided in Figure 27.2. What factors account for a curve like this? Basically, the reason is that as the price of labor is increased, the individual supplying the labor becomes richer. And when he becomes richer, he wants to increase his amount of leisure time, which means that he wants to work less. Even though the amount of money per hour he gives up by not working is greater than when the price of labor was lower, he nonetheless chooses to increase

[3] The answer to Lamb's question is perhaps to be found in Genesis 3:19.

his leisure time. This sort of tendency has shown up quite clearly in the last century. As wage rates have increased and living standards have risen, the average work week has tended to decline.

Note that there is no contradiction between the assumption that the supply curve of labor or other inputs *to an individual firm* is horizontal under perfect competition and the fact that the *market* supply curve for the input may not be horizontal. For example, unskilled labor may be available to any firm in a particular area at a given wage rate in as great an amount as it could possibly use. But the total amount of unskilled labor supplied in this area may increase relatively little with increases in the wage rate. The situation is similar to the sale of products. As we saw in Chapter 21, any firm under perfect competition believes that it can sell all it wants at the existing price. Yet the total amount of the product sold in the entire market can ordinarily be increased only by lowering the price.

Equilibrium Price and Quantity of Labor

Labor's price (or wage rate) is determined under perfect competition in essentially the same way that a product's price is determined: by supply and demand. *The price of labor will tend toward equilibrium at the level where the quantity of labor demanded equals the quantity of labor supplied.* Thus, in Figure 27.3, the equilibrium price of labor is *OP*. If the price were higher than *OP*, the quantity supplied would exceed the quantity demanded and there would be downward pressure on the price. If the price were lower than *OP*, the quantity supplied would fall short of the quantity demanded and there would be upward pressure on the price. By the same token, *the equilibrium amount of labor utilized is also given by the intersection of the market supply and demand curves.* For example, in Figure 27.3, *OQ* units of labor will be utilized in equilibrium in the entire market.

Graphs such as Figure 27.3 are useful, but it is important to look behind the geometry, and to recognize the factors that lie behind the demand and supply curves for labor. For example, consider the market for surgeons and that for unskilled labor. As shown in Figure 27.4, the demand curve for the services of surgeons is to the right of the demand curve for unskilled labor (particularly at high wage rates).

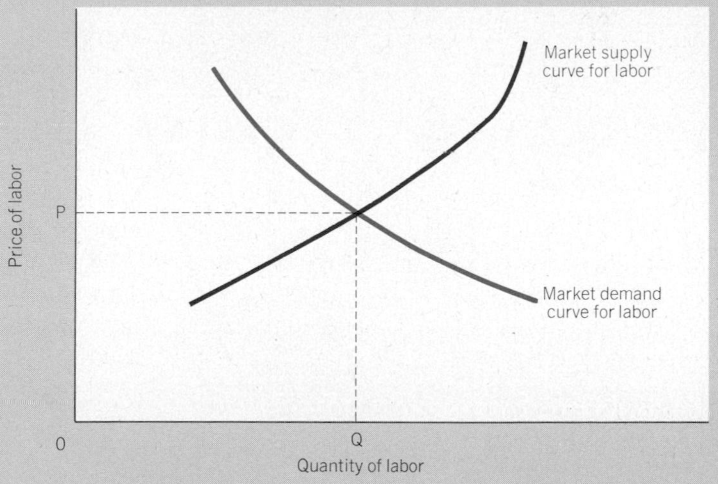

Figure 27.3
Equilibrium Price and Quantity of Labor
The equilibrium price of labor is *OP*, and the equilibrium quantity of labor used is *OQ*.

Why is this so? Because an hour of a surgeon's services is worth more to people than an hour of an unskilled laborer's services. In this sense, surgeons are more productive than unskilled laborers. Also, as shown in Figure 27.4, the supply curve for the services of surgeons is far to the left of the supply curve for unskilled labor. Why is this so? Because very few people are licensed surgeons, whereas practically everyone can do unskilled labor. In other words, surgeons are much more scarce than unskilled laborers.

For these reasons, surgeons receive a much higher wage rate than do unskilled laborers. As shown in Figure 27.4, the equilibrium price of labor for surgeons is much higher than for unskilled labor. If unskilled laborers could quickly and easily turn themselves into competent surgeons, this difference in wage rates would be eliminated by competition, since unskilled workers would find it profitable to become surgeons. But unskilled workers lack the training and often the ability to become surgeons. Thus surgeons and unskilled labor are examples of ***noncompeting groups.*** Wage differentials can be expected to persist among noncompeting groups because people cannot move from the low-paid to the high-paid jobs. But this is not the only reason for wage differentials, as we shall see in the next section.

Wage Differentials

Everyone realizes that, even in the same occupation, some people get paid more than others. One reason for such wage differentials is that people differ in productive capacity. For example, some machinists are more skillful than others. Suppose that there are two types of machinists: class *A* and class *B*. Then, to maximize profit, a firm should hire each type of machinist up to the point at which

$$MP_A \cdot P = P_A \tag{27.3a}$$
$$MP_B \cdot P = P_B \tag{27.3b}$$

where MP_A is the marginal product of Class *A* machinists, MP_B is the marginal product of class *B* machinists, P_A is the wage rate for class *A* machinists, P_B is the wage rate for class *B* machinists, and *P* is the price of the firm's product. This follows directly from Equation (27.2). Thus the differential in wages between more skilled and less skilled machinists will equal the differential in their marginal products, since $P_A \div P_B = MP_A \div MP_B$.

In general, however, one cannot divide workers into two homogeneous groups, because each worker differs from the next in the value of his output. Under these circumstances, the difference in wages paid to workers

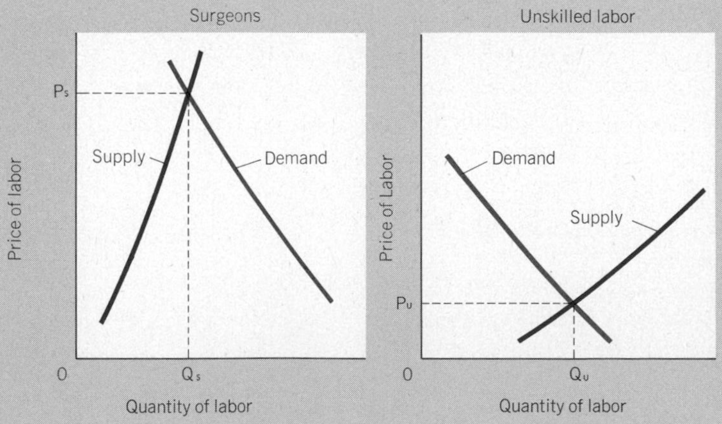

Figure 27.4
The Labor Market for Surgeons and Unskilled Labor
The wage for surgeons is higher than for unskilled labor because the demand curve for surgeons is farther to the right and the supply curve for surgeons is farther to the left than the corresponding curves for unskilled labor.

will equal the difference in the total value of their output. Consider the case of two lathe operators: Arnold and Leo. Arnold works for firm *X* and Leo works for firm *Y*. Arnold (together with the appropriate tools and materials) can produce output worth $1,000 per month and Leo (with the same tools and materials) can produce output worth $900 per month. In equilibrium, Arnold will earn $100 more per month than Leo. If the difference in wages were less than $100, Leo's employer would find it profitable to replace Leo with Arnold, since this would increase the value of output by $100 and cost less than $100. If the difference were more than $100, Arnold's employer would find it profitable to replace Arnold with Leo; although this would reduce the value of output by $100, it would reduce costs by more than $100.

Besides differences in productive capacity and ability, there are many other reasons for wage differentials. Even if all workers were of equal ability, these differentials would still exist to offset differences in the characteristics of various occupations and areas. For example, some occupations require large investments in training, while other occupations require a much smaller investment in training. A chemist must spend about eight years in undergraduate and graduate training. During each year of training, he incurs direct expenses for books, tuition, and the like, and he loses the income he could make if he were to work rather than go to school. Clearly, if his net remuneration is to be as high in chemistry as in other jobs he might take, he must make a greater wage when he gets through than a person of comparable age, intelligence, and motivation whose job requires no training beyond high school. The difference in wages must be at least sufficient to compensate for his investment in extra training.

Similarly, members of some occupations must bear larger occupational expenses than others. For example, a psychologist may have to buy testing materials and subscribe to expensive journals. For net compensation to be equalized, such workers must be paid more than others. Also, some jobs are more unstable than others. For example, some types of construction workers are subject to frequent layoffs and have little job security, whereas many government employees (but not the top ones) are assured stable and secure employment. If the former jobs are to be as attractive as the latter, they must pay more. In addition, other differences among jobs must be offset by wage differentials if the net remuneration is to be equalized. For instance, there are differences among regions and communities in the cost of living. (Living costs are generally lower in small towns than in big cities.)

The All-Volunteer Army: A Case Study

In recent years, there has been considerable controversy concerning the advantages and disadvantages of an all-volunteer army, the system used in this country since the early 1970s. Many economists have argued that recruiting an all-volunteer army is more efficient and equitable than relying on the draft, which through a complicated system of deferments and exemptions, as well as a lottery system, selected a certain number of young men for military service. Proponents of an all-volunteer army point out that it is more compatible with freedom of choice than the draft. In addition, they say that military personnel are used more effectively because the price of such personnel is a more realistic indicator of its value in alternative uses. Further, they point out that the cost of military manpower is distributed more equitably among the members of society. Under the draft a small group of draftees bore a large share of the cost, because they received less in wages than would have been required to induce them to volunteer.

Other economists and social observers oppose an all-volunteer army. They point out that the present system can hardly be expected to produce the necessary military manpower in a full-scale war. They also contend that an army of "paid mercenaries" might constitute a political danger by attempting to gain improper power. Some claim too that an all-volunteer army relies disproportionately on the black population, since young blacks constitute a much larger percentage of those without civilian jobs than their white counterparts.

How did the all-volunteer army come into being? In 1964, President Johnson asked that a study be made to determine whether it would be possible to shift from reliance on the draft to a system in which defense manpower needs would be met entirely by volunteers. A team of economists attempted to learn what it would cost.[4] Essentially they applied the kind of analysis described in this chapter. The basic approach was to estimate the supply curve for labor to the Department of Defense.

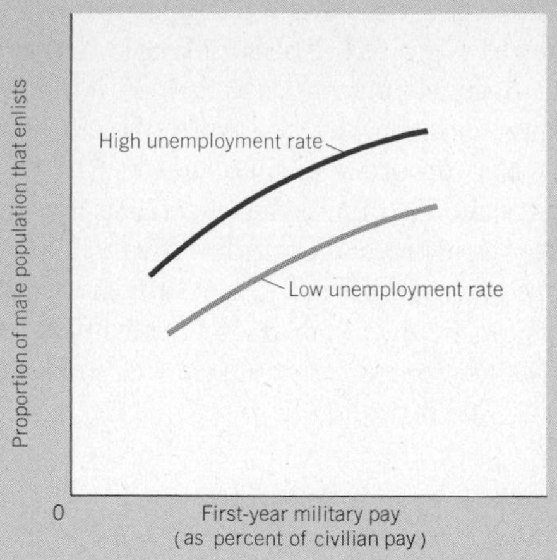

Figure 27.5
Relationship between Military Pay and Number of Enlistments
Holding the unemployment rate constant, the proportion of the male population that enlists is directly related to the level of military pay (as a percent of civilian pay). Using this supply curve, economists determined the level of military pay required to bring forth the extra enlistments needed to eliminate the draft.

Figure 27.5 shows the relationship between the proportion of the male population that enlists and the level of military pay (as a percent of civilian pay), the unemployment rate being held constant at two alternative levels. As would be expected, the number of enlistments increases with the level of military pay and the unemployment rate. Using this supply curve, which was estimated by the economists, one could determine (for given values of the unemployment rate) the level of military pay that was required to bring forth the number of extra enlistments needed to eliminate the draft.

According to the economists, a 60 to 90 percent increase in enlistments was needed to eliminate the draft. To bring forth these extra enlistments, they estimated on the basis of the supply curve that first-term military pay for enlisted men had to be increased by about 110 percent (if the unemployment rate were 5.5 percent). Using 1964 military earnings as a base, increases in first-term pay for enlisted men had to be about $3,000 to attract enough volunteers to maintain a 2.65-million-man defense force. Multiplying 2.65 million men by the average increase in pay, the economists estimated that the increased cost to the Defense Department would be about $5 billion per year.[5] This estimate was very crude, as the economists stressed, since many noneconomic factors influenced the enlistment rate and the data and underlying assumptions were rough.

[4] See S. Altman and A. Fechter, "The Supply of Military Personnel in the Absence of a Draft," *American Economic Review,* May 1967; and literature cited there.

[5] Note that the average increase in pay is less than the average increase in first-term pay. The way Altman and Fechter proceed from the latter to the former is described in their work. Also, note that the costs to the Defense Department, which are estimated here, may be quite different from the social costs of switching to an all-volunteer army.

By 1973, the draft was no longer being used to obtain military manpower. Whether it will be reactivated in the near future is hard to say. For present purposes, the important point is that economic analysis, based on the fundamental concepts in this chapter, played a very significant role in the discussion and resolution of this major issue. And if conditions or attitudes change so that this issue must be reconsidered, you can be sure that economics will continue to play a significant role in its resolution.

Monopsony

In previous sections, we have assumed that perfect competition exists in the labor market. In some cases, however, ***monopsony*** exists instead. *A monopsony is a market structure where there is a single buyer.* For example, a single firm may hire all the labor in an isolated "company town," such as exists in the coal mining regions of West Virginia and Kentucky. What determines the price of labor under monopsony? Suppose the firm's demand curve for labor is *DD′* in Figure 27.6 and the supply curve of labor is *SS′*. Because the firm is the sole buyer of labor, it takes into account the fact that to acquire more labor it must pay a higher wage to *all* workers, not just the extra workers. For example, if the firm wants to increase the number of workers it employs from 5 to 6, it may have to pay the sixth an hourly wage of $5. If the supply curve of labor slopes upward to the right, this wage is more than was required to obtain the first 5 workers. Since the firm must pay all workers the same wage to avoid labor unrest, it must raise the wages of the first 5 workers to the level of the sixth, if it hires the sixth worker. Thus *the cost of hiring the sixth worker exceeds the wage that must be paid this worker.*

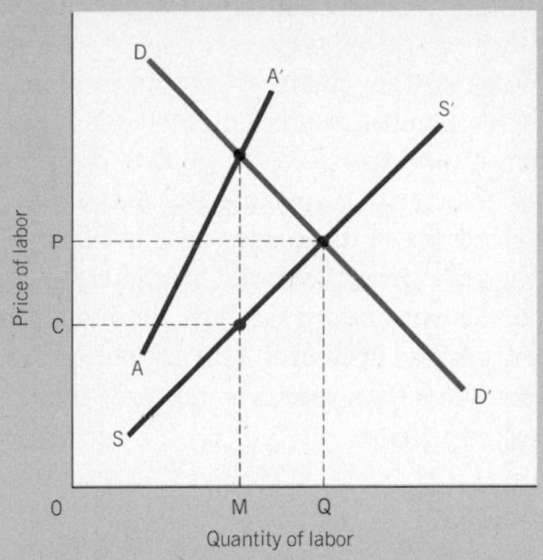

Figure 27.6
Equilibrium Wage and Quantity of Labor under Monopsony
The monopsonistic firm, if it maximizes profit, will hire laborers up to the point where the extra cost of adding an extra laborer, shown by *AA′*, equals the extra revenue from adding the extra laborer, shown by *DD′*.

The supply curve for labor, *SS′* in Figure 27.6, shows the cost of hiring an additional worker if workers already employed do *not* have to be paid a higher wage when the additional worker is hired. Thus *SS′* does *not* show the true additional cost to the monopsonist of hiring an additional worker, for the reasons given in the previous paragraph. Instead, *AA′*, which includes the extra wages that must be paid to the workers already employed, shows the true additional cost. For the reasons given above, *AA′* lies above *SS′*.

If profit is maximized, the monopsonistic firm will hire labor up to the point at which the extra cost of adding an additional laborer (shown by *AA′*) equals the extra revenue from adding the additional laborer (shown by *DD′*). Thus the quantity of labor purchased will be *OM* and the price of labor will be *OC* in Figure 27.6. In contrast, under perfectly competitive conditions the equilibrium quantity and price would be at the intersection of the demand and supply curves. That is, the quantity of labor purchased would be OQ and the price of labor would be OP.

What is the effect of monopsony on the wage rate and the amount of labor hired? In general, *the wage rate, as well as the quantity hired, is lower under monopsony than under perfect competition.* This is the case in Figure 27.6, and it will generally hold true. Certainly this makes sense. One would expect a monopsonist, free from the pressures of competition, to pay workers less than would be required under perfect competition.

Labor Unions

About 1 in 4 nonfarm workers in the United States belong to unions, and the perfectly competitive model does not apply to these workers any more than it does to monopsonistic labor markets. Obviously, then, we must discuss labor unions in some detail. There are about 200 national unions in the United States; the biggest are the Teamsters, the United Auto Workers, and the United Steelworkers, each with over a million members. Next come the Electrical Workers, the Machinists, the Carpenters, the Mine Workers, and the Retail Clerks, each with over 500,000 members.

The national unions[6] are of great importance in the American labor movement. The supreme governing body of the national union is the convention, which is held every year or two. The delegates to the convention have the authority to set policy for the union. However, considerable power is exercised by the national union's officers. Union presidents—men like Leonard Woodcock of the Auto Workers, I. W. Abel of the Steelworkers, and Frank Fitzsimmons of the Teamsters—exercise great power.

[6] Sometimes they are called international unions because some locals are outside the United States—for example, in Canada.

A national union is composed of local unions, each in a given area or plant. Some local unions have only a few members, but others have thousands. The local union, with its own president and officers, often plays an important role in collective bargaining. The extent to which the local unions maintain their autonomy varies from one national union to another. In industries where markets are localized (like construction and printing), the locals are more autonomous than in industries where markets are national (like steel, automobiles, and coal).

Finally, there is the AFL-CIO, a federation of national unions created by the merger of the American Federation of Labor and the Congress of Industrial Organizations in 1955. The AFL-CIO does not include all national unions. For example, the United Mine Workers refused to join the AFL-CIO, the Auto Workers left it in 1968, and the Teamsters were kicked out (because of corruption). The AFL-CIO is a very important spokesman for the American labor movement; but because the national unions in the AFL-CIO have given up relatively little of their power to the federation, its authority is limited.

The American Labor Movement

Early History of American Labor Unions

To understand the nature and behavior of labor unions, it is necessary to look briefly at the history of the American labor movement. Unions arose, of course, because workers recognized that acting together gave them more bargaining power than acting separately. They frequently felt that they were at the mercy of their employers, and they formed fraternal societies and unions to promote economic and social benefits for the members. The first recorded case of collective bargaining in the United States took place in 1799, when Philadelphia shoemakers negotiated collectively with their employers.

However, until the 1930s unions in the United States were not very strong, partly because of employers' efforts to break up unions, and partly because the courts held that the unions' attempts to increase wages and influence working conditions were conspiracies in restraint of trade. It is not difficult to understand the antiunion feelings of management, but it is difficult to exonerate the ruthlessness with which some managements attempted to stamp out unionism. Not only were prounion workers fired and blacklisted; they were sometimes beaten up or locked out of the plant. And when strikes occurred, strike breakers were sometimes hired to teach the striking workers a lesson.

The courts were also hostile to unions. The prevailing doctrine in much of the nineteenth century was that unions were criminal conspiracies, and even when this doctrine was abandoned the courts frequently regarded strikes, picketing, and other such union tactics as illegal. In addition, they sometimes used the Sherman Act of 1890 to stop unions, on the grounds that unions were conspiracies to restrain trade. Moreover, the courts often issued ***injunctions,*** which are cease-and-desist orders, to prevent unions from striking, boycotting, picketing, or carrying out other activities against the interests of their employers. In this way, the courts prevented unions from utilizing their potential power effectively.

In 1886, the *American Federation of Labor* came into existence. In contrast to many early unions, which were aimed at political goals, the AFL, led by Samuel Gompers, concentrated on economic issues. Basically, the AFL was an association of national craft unions, each of which was autonomous; but although it had limited power over the national unions, Gompers was a very important spokesman for the American labor movement.

The AFL came to be the dominant federation in American labor history, and its philosophy exerted great influence on the development of trade unionism in the United States. This philosophy was built on several tenets. First, Gompers and his associates felt that it would be a mistake to promote the development of a labor party in the United States. The AFL would try to elect its friends and defeat its enemies, but it would not form a third party and it would not align itself with either of the two major political parties. Second, the AFL would concentrate its efforts on bread-and-butter economic issues, not on attempts to alter the basic form of society. Higher wages and better working conditions, not social revolution or elimination of private property, were its aims. Third, the AFL was suspicious of government regulation. It felt that the interests of labor would be served best if the government interfered as little as possible in collective bargaining.

The AFL was relatively successful in increasing union membership; total union membership was about 2 million in 1904 and about 5 million in 1920. In part, this increase resulted from tight labor markets and the government's support of collective bargaining during World War I in return for labor's help in the war effort. After the war, union membership dropped from more than 5 million to about 2.6 million in 1933 (due in part to the onset of the Great Depression). The period after World War I was marked by strong antiunion sentiments. Employers resisted unions strenuously—and successfully. For example, in 1919 the U.S. Steel Corporation—led by our old friend from Chapter 25, Elbert Gary—crushed a strike resulting from an attempt to organize its plants. Firms pushed hard for an "American Plan" under which union members would not be hired. Certainly the 1920s were a difficult period for American labor unions.

The New Deal and World War II

During the early 1930s, the tide began to turn. To a great extent, this was because of government encouragement of unions, in which the first important step was the *Norris-LaGuardia Act* of 1932. This act made it much more difficult for courts to issue injunctions against unions, and it made ***yellow-dog contracts***—agreements in which a worker promised his employer not to join a union—unenforceable in federal courts. The next important step occurred in 1935, when Congress passed the ***Wagner Act,*** which made it an unfair labor practice for employers to refuse to bargain collectively with unions representing a majority of their workers, or to interfere with their workers' right to organize. In addition, this act established the *National Labor Relations Board* to investigate unfair labor practices, to issue orders enforceable in federal courts, and to hold elections to determine which, if any, union would represent various groups of employees. The Wagner Act was a very important factor in encouraging the growth of labor unions in the United States—so important that it has often been called American labor's Magna Carta.

Another important factor in the growth of unions during the 1930s was the emergence of industrial unions. The more favorable atmosphere for union organization and growth led to the creation in 1935 of a new federation, the ***Congress of Industrial Organizations.*** The unions that created and formed the CIO rebelled against the AFL's apparent inability to take advantage of the opportunity to organize the mass production industries like autos and steel. The AFL was composed primarily of unions organized along craft lines: the carpenters had one union, the machinists had another union, and so on for other crafts. This is in contrast to industrial unions, which include all workers in a particular plant or industry.

The young CIO, led by the United Mine Workers' president, John L. Lewis, set out to establish industrial unions in the mass-production industries.[7] The CIO was very successful in its organization drives during the late 1930s. In 1937 U.S. Steel, formerly a bulwark of antiunionism, recognized the Steelworkers as bargaining agent for its more than 200,000 workers. Using the sit-down strike—in which strikers occupy the plant—as a weapon, workers in the automobile and rubber industries organized CIO unions too. In addition, the CIO organized unions in electrical machinery, petroleum refining, textiles, meat packing, longshoring, and other industries.[8]

The 1930s were a period of spectacular union growth. Aided by the prounion attitude of the Roosevelt administration, the new legislation, and the energy of its leaders, total union membership rose from less than 3 million in 1933 to more than 10 million in 1941. World War II witnessed a further growth in total union membership. Stimulated by the increase in total employment and the government's favorable attitude toward their growth, unions increased their membership from over 10 million in 1941 to almost 15 million—or about 36 percent of all nonfarm workers—in 1945. As in World War I, the government helped unions gain recognition in exchange for union cooperation in promoting war production. By the end of World War II, labor unions were conspicuous and powerful features of the economic landscape.

The United Automobile Workers: A Case Study[9]

To illustrate the growth of the labor move-

[7] Before leaving the AFL, Lewis emphasized the strength of his convictions by knocking down and bloodying up his principal opponent, William Hutcheson, president of the Carpenters' Union, on the floor of the 1935 AFL convention.

[8] Confronted with the CIO's successes, the AFL also organized new industrial unions, although craft unions remained by far the most important part of the federation.

[9] This section is based in considerable part on A. Paradis, *Labor in Action,* New York: Messner, 1963.

ment in the 1930s and early 1940s, consider the history of the United Automobile Workers, currently one of the nation's largest unions. The UAW was organized in August 1935 and affiliated with the CIO in 1936, but was not recognized by either General Motors or Ford until 1937. In late 1936, a sit-down strike occurred in some of General Motors' factories, with the result that other GM factories were closed for lack of parts. GM got an injunction that ordered the men to vacate the plants, but when it was determined that the judge who issued the injunction had over $200,000 worth of GM stock, the injunction was declared invalid.

Faced with this situation, GM president Alfred P. Sloan, Jr.—an acquaintance of ours from Chapter 7—said, "General Motors will never recognize any union as the sole bargaining agency for all its employees." On January 11, 1937 violence broke out between the police and the strikers, when the police tried to stop the delivery of food to the sit-down strikers occupying the plants. On the following day, the governor of Michigan sent the National Guard to maintain the peace. Finally, on February 11, 1937, General Motors agreed to recognize the union as the bargaining agency for its workers, and the union agreed to end the strike. The union leaders hailed the agreement as a tremendous victory.

However, the Ford Motor Company was still unorganized. Henry Ford was dead set against the unionization of his employees and used strong tactics to discourage it. For example, in 1937 Walter Reuther, a young union organizer who was later to become president of the UAW, received a savage beating from Ford's men. In 1938, the UAW reported various unfair practices of the Ford Motor Company to the National Labor Relations Board. Although Ford succeeded in delaying a final decision until 1941, the company was finally ordered to rehire and pay back wages to over 2,000 employees who had been illegally fired for union membership. In 1941, Ford signed a contract with the UAW, thus completing the unionization of the major automobile producers.

From these violent beginnings there gradually has developed a viable system of collective bargaining in the automobile industry. During the 1940s the relationship between labor and management was sometimes closer to an armed truce than a permanent peace treaty, but time has mellowed this relationship considerably. And as the UAW grew older, it also got richer. By the 1960s it had over $50 million in assets. Moreover, it became an important factor in politics, particularly in Michigan. Through the efforts of Reuther and his colleagues, the UAW became a major force in the American economy.

Postwar Developments

Creation and Structure of the AFL-CIO

In 1955, a merger occurred between the AFL and the CIO. Given the acrimony marking the relationship between these two organizations in the 1930s, the merger may seem surprising. But the differences in their attitudes toward the question of organization along industrial versus craft lines had diminished in importance over the years. And the old leaders, including those like Lewis of the Mine Workers and Hutcheson of the Carpenters who had traded blows in earlier days, had died—or, as in Lewis's case, were no longer in either federation.[10]

Moreover, the merger had advantages. The labor movement, despite large-scale organization drives in the South after the war, was unable to increase union membership appreciably during the 1950s. Many unions attributed this

[10] Lewis resigned from the presidency of the CIO because workers would not follow his lead and vote for Wendell Willkie for president of the United States in 1940. Later he took his union back into the AFL, but withdrew from the AFL in 1947 because the AFL did not boycott the National Labor Relations Board in an effort to defeat the Taft-Hartley Act.

fact to the rivalry between the AFL and the CIO and argued that a united front would result in increased membership. Also, and perhaps most important, Congress passed several pieces of legislation, including the Taft-Hartley Act of 1947, that were heartily disliked by the unions, and it was felt that the merger would increase labor's political clout.

The AFL-CIO is organized along the lines indicated in Figure 27.7. The organization closely resembles that of the AFL (the larger of the merging federations). The constitution of the AFL-CIO puts supreme governing power in the hands of a biennial convention. The national unions are represented at these conventions on the basis of their dues-paying membership. Between conventions, the AFL-CIO's business is directed by its president and secretary-treasurer, as well as by various committees and councils composed of representatives of various national unions or people elected at the convention. The AFL-CIO contains seven trade and industrial departments, such as building trades, food and beverage trades, maritime trades, and so forth. Also, as indicated by Figure 27.7, a few local unions are not affiliated with a national union, but are directly affiliated with the AFL-CIO.

Internal Problems in Labor Unions

As unions have grown older and more secure and powerful, there has been more and more concern about the nature of their internal practices and leadership. After all, they are no longer the underdogs that they were 50 years ago. They are huge organizations with immense power. Both in this country and in Europe, observers have charged that unions are often far from democratic. Members are frequently apathetic, for there is less interest in union affairs now than in the early days when unions were fighting for survival; and the leadership of some unions has become entrenched and bureaucratic. Moreover, there are frequent charges that unions engage in racial and other forms of discrimination.

The leadership of a union, like the management of a large corporation, is not easy to overturn. The leadership controls a staff, the union paper, and other levers to help maintain itself in power. These advantages, together with worker apathy, enable leaders to stay in power for many years without being very responsive to majority rule. As Clark Kerr, former president of the University of California and a distinguished labor economist, put it, "Unions

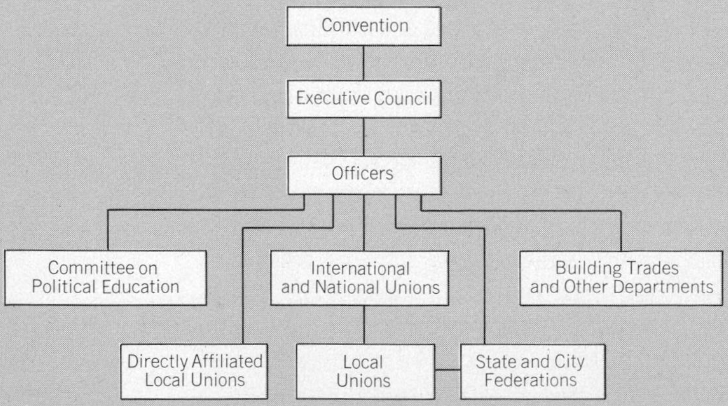

Figure 27.7
Structure of AFL-CIO
The AFL-CIO, which resulted from a merger of the AFL and CIO in 1955, is organized with the governing power in the hands of a biennial convention.

have usually ended up by being a business serving the members, but sometimes with the members having little more influence over the conduct of the business than the stockholders have over a corporation. Unions have almost never ended up as a town meeting."[11]

It is important, however, that this problem not be exaggerated. Union leaders know that they must produce results that are roughly satisfactory to at least a substantial number of their membership. Although local union meetings are seldom attended by more than 10 percent of the members, the rest always *can* show up. Moreover, although there are difficulties in overturning an entrenched leadership, it is seldom impossible. Just as the management of a large corporation will be sacked if it departs sufficiently from the wishes of the stockholders, so the leaders of a union will be kicked out of office if they depart sufficiently from the wishes of the members. In recent years, the presidents of the United Steelworkers; International Union of Electrical Workers; State, County, and Municipal Employees; and United Mine Workers have been defeated in contested elections.

Another problem is corruption within labor unions. In the 1950s, a Senate committee—the so-called McClellan Committee—conducted lengthy and revealing investigations which showed, for example, that the leaders of the Teamsters Union had misused union funds, had questionable relations with the underworld, and had "shamefully betrayed their own members." Other unions were also accused of corrupt practices. It is important, however, to avoid smearing the entire labor movement. Although racketeering and fraud unquestionably are problems, they tend to be localized in a relatively few industries—particularly the building trades, trucking, longshoring, laundries, and hotels. Many responsible and honest leaders of the labor movement have tried hard to rid the labor movement of these unsavory practices.

[11] Clark Kerr, *Unions and Union Leaders of Their Own Choosing*, New York: Fund for the Republic, 1957, p. 10.

Postwar Labor Legislation

After World War II, public sentiment turned somewhat against unions. Strikes and higher prices got under the skin of the consumer as well as the employer, and there began to be a lot of talk in Congress and elsewhere about the prewar Wagner Act having been too one-sided, giving the advantages to labor and the penalties to the employer. In 1947, despite bitter labor opposition, the ***Taft-Hartley Act*** was passed, with the purpose of redressing the balance between labor and employers. The act established standards of conduct for unions as well as employers, defined unfair union practices, and stated that unions can be sued for acts of their agents. Also, the act outlawed the closed shop, which requires that firms hire only workers who are already union members, and stipulated that, unless the workers agree in writing, the ***checkoff*** is illegal. (The checkoff is a system in which the employer deducts union dues from each worker's pay and hands them over to the union.)

In addition, the act tried to increase protection against strikes in which the public's safety and health are involved. If the president decides that an actual or impending strike imperils the national health or safety, he can appoint a fact-finding committee to investigate the situation. After receiving the committee's report, he can tell the attorney general to obtain an injunction forbidding a strike for 80 days, during which the parties can continue to negotiate. A Federal Mediation Service was established to help the parties settle such negotiations. The act does not forbid a strike at the end of the 80 days, if no agreement has been reached.

In response to the evidence of union corruption presented by the McClellan Committee, Congress passed the ***Landrum-Griffin Act***

CESAR CHAVEZ

A Strike in the Roses

Cesar Chavez is the founder and leader of the United Farm Workers of America. Unlike the powerful giant unions like the Teamsters and Autoworkers, his is a new and struggling union. In the following paragraphs, he describes in his own words the first strike that his union carried out. It is an interesting account of some of the problems he faced, as he saw them.

We had our first strike in the spring of 1965. While we didn't win, it gave us a good indication of what to expect in other strikes, how labor contractors and police would be used against us.

Epifanio Camacho, a farm worker from McFarland, just south of Delano, came and told us of all the abuses in the rose industry there. We worked with those workers for more than a month until we had them tightly organized. Grafting roses is highly skilled work. Grafters crawl on their knees for miles slitting mature rose bushes and inserting buds at top speed. The slightest miscalculation means the bud will not take and the bush will be useless. Although they were promised $9 a thousand plants, grafters of roses were actually getting between $6.50 and $7 a thousand. After a series of meetings to prepare the strike, we chose the biggest company, Mount Arbor, which employed about eighty-five workers, not counting the irrigators and supervisors. We voted not to have a picket line, because everyone pledged not to break the strike. We had a pledge ceremony on Sunday, the day before the strike started. Dolores [Huerta] held the crucifix, and the guys put their hands on it, pledging not to break the strike.

Early Monday morning we sent out ten cars to check the people's homes. We found lights in five or six places and knocked on the doors. The men were getting up.

"Where are you going?" we asked them.

Most of them were embarrassed. "Oh, I was just getting up, you know."

"You're not going to work, are you?"

"Of course not!"

A day or so later, we had a hunch two or three workers living in one house were going to break the strike. So Dolores drove up to their driveway in a green truck, killed the motor, put it in gear, set the brake, locked the windows and doors, took the keys, and hid them so they couldn't drive out. Even though she was alone, she refused to move.

Then a group of Mexican workers from Tangansiguiero helped break the strike. Everybody was angry, and we sent a letter to the mayor of Tangansiguiero denouncing them. In those little Mexican towns, they have an old building where people go to read the news. On one side they list things like stray animals, and on the other they have a list of criminals. The mayor was so upset, he put our letter on the side with the criminals, in effect classifying them as such.

Labor contractors were used to break the strike. Under the California Labor Code, a worker can't be recruited to a strike zone unless he's been warned that a strike is in progress. In this case, they were not told, and we turned the information in to the labor commissioner's office. His office in Delano did what I thought was a beautiful job of documenting a case where one employer lent all of his crew to Mount Arbor. I went with the agent of the labor commissioner's office to the district attorney in Kern County, who refused to accept the information or issue a citation. So we knew immediately what would be the pattern from then on. Without labor contractors, we'd win every strike in California.

Because it's so hard to find good rose grafters, however, we were able to get a wage increase after four days. But we never got a contract.*

* This passage is adapted from Jacques Levy, *Cesar Chavez: Autobiography of La Causa,* New York: Norton, 1975, pp. 179–80.

in 1959. This act attempts to protect the rights of individual union members from abuse by union leaders. It contains a "bill of rights" for labor guaranteeing that each member can participate in union elections, that elections be held by secret ballot, and that other steps be taken to protect the rights of the members. It also requires unions to file financial reports, forbids payments (beyond wages) by employers to union representatives, and prohibits loans exceeding $2,000 by unions to union officials.

Recent Trends in Union Membership

In recent years, union membership has increased rather modestly; indeed, during the late 1950s and early 1960s, it didn't increase at all. To some extent, this has been due to dissension within the labor movement and to a diminution of the zeal that characterized the movement in earlier years. Also, rightly or wrongly, unions have lost a certain amount of public sympathy and respect because of racial discrimination, unpopular strikes, evidence of corruption, and the belief that they are responsible in considerable part for cost-push inflation. But these factors only partly explain this lack of growth. In addition, important changes in the labor force have tended to reduce union membership.

Specifically, the increasing proportion of *white-collar workers* seems to have raised important problems for unions. To date, unions have made relatively little progress in organizing white-collar workers. For example, in the early 1960s, only about 3 percent of engineers, and about 9 percent of office workers were union members. One reason for this lack of progress is that white-collar employees tend to identify with management. Also, the increasing proportion of *women* in the labor force seems to raise important problems for unions. It is sometimes claimed that female workers are harder to organize because they do not stay in the labor force very long and because they are concentrated in jobs—clerical and sales positions—that are difficult to organize. Nonetheless, almost 1 in 5 union members in 1962 were women; and the majority of the Retail Clerks, the Clothing Workers, and the International Ladies' Garment Workers were women.

However, even though union membership has not been growing in recent years, it would be a mistake to jump to the conclusion that the American labor movement is stagnant or that unions are declining in importance. For one thing, membership is not a very good measure of power. A small union can sometimes bring an enormous amount of pressure to bear if it is located strategically in the economy. Also, union membership has been growing rapidly in some areas, notably ***public employment.*** Between 1956 and 1968, union membership among public employees grew from 915,000 to 2,155,000, with the bulk of the membership in six unions, three of federal employees and three of state and local employees.[12] For many years, there was a tradition, as well as legal prohibitions, against strikes by public employees. But during the 1960s, when these workers seemed to be left behind economically, various executive orders and legislative enactments encouraged unionism among public employees.

Unionizing Public Employees

The largest union of state and local employees is the American Federation of State, County, and Municipal Employees (AFSCME). In 1975, its total national membership was 700,000, and some observers were predicting that in the next decade it would overtake the Teamsters as the largest union in the country.

[12] The three unions of federal employees are the American Federation of Government Employees, the National Association of Letter Carriers, and the United Federation of Postal Clerks. The three unions of state and local employees are the American Federation of State, County, and Municipal Employees; the American Federation of Teachers; and the International Association of Firefighters.

To illustrate its rapid growth, consider the situation in Pennsylvania, where it has won a major victory. The impetus for unionization of public employees in Pennsylvania came in 1970 when the state legislature gave such employees the right to bargain collectively. Since 1970, 105,000 out of 116,000 eligible state employees have joined unions, as have 34 percent of Pennsylvania's county employees, 83 percent of its city employees, 56 percent of its borough employees, 46 percent of its township employees, and 90 percent of its school-district employees. Although not all belong to the AFSCME, many do.

A nettlesome problem regarding the unionization of public employees is related to strikes. Since such employees man vital public services, a strike can bring a community or state to its knees. In four states—Pennsylvania, Hawaii, Oregon, and Vermont—strikes of this sort are legal. But the fact that they are forbidden by law in other states, such as New York, does not prevent walkouts by teachers, sanitation workers, or other state and local employees from being a fairly common occurrence. The public, naturally, becomes indignant when strikes of this sort occur, and the question of whether or not public employees should be able to walk off the job provokes heated debate.

Another feature of labor negotiations in this area is the mixture of unionism and politics. Public officials, sensitive to the political pressures of the unions, have found it difficult to resist many union requests for increased pay and fringe benefits. To a certain extent, they have tried to buy labor peace. In New York, for example, the unions have become a potent political force. As Columbia University's Raymond Horton put it, "The union members by no means vote in a bloc, but the mayor can't take the risk that they won't." Much of this potency has waned since the onset of New York's financial crisis, but some of it remains.

Due in part to the growing pressure of the unions, the gap in wages between the private and public sectors has been decreasing. Between 1955 and 1973, the average annual earnings of state and local workers increased by 165 percent, compared with a 129 percent increase for all private employees. According to the unions, this represents merely an adjustment for the fact that the wages of public employees were far too low in prior years. Unquestionably, this is at least partly true. But according to some observers, the gap that existed in the past has at this point been closed.

How Unions Increase Wages

Clearly, unions wield considerable power, and economists must include them in their analysis if they want their models of the labor market to reflect conditions in the real world. We shall now see how this is done. Let us begin by supposing that a union wants to increase the wage rate paid its members. How can it accomplish this objective? In other words, how can it alter the market supply curve for labor, or the market demand curve for labor, so that the price of labor—its wage—will increase?

First, the union may try to *shift the supply curve of labor to the left.* For example, it may shift the supply curve in Figure 27.8 from SS' to S_1S_1', with the result that the price of labor will increase from OP to OP_1. (Of course, DD' is the demand curve for labor.) How can the union cause this shift in the supply curve? Craft unions have frequently forced employers to hire only union members, and then restricted union membership by high initiation fees, reduction in new membership, and other devices. In addition, unions have favored legislation to reduce immigration, shorten working hours, and limit the labor supply in other ways.

Second, *the union may try to get the employers to pay a higher wage, while allowing some of the supply of labor forthcoming at this higher wage to find no opportunity for work.* For ex-

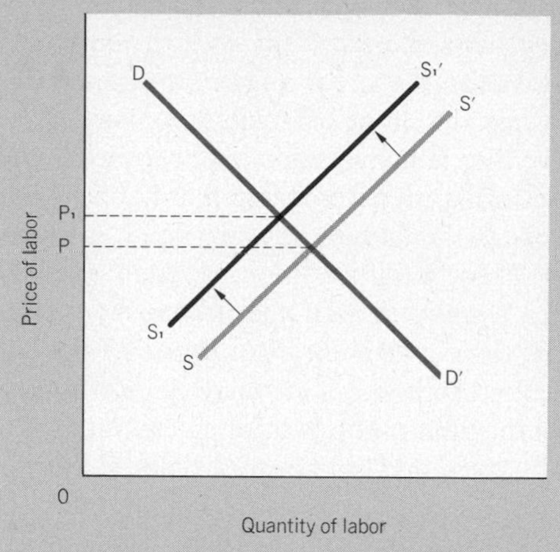

Figure 27.8
Shift of Supply Curve for Labor
A union may shift the supply curve from SS' to S_1S_1' by getting employers to hire only union members and then restricting union membership, or by other techniques.

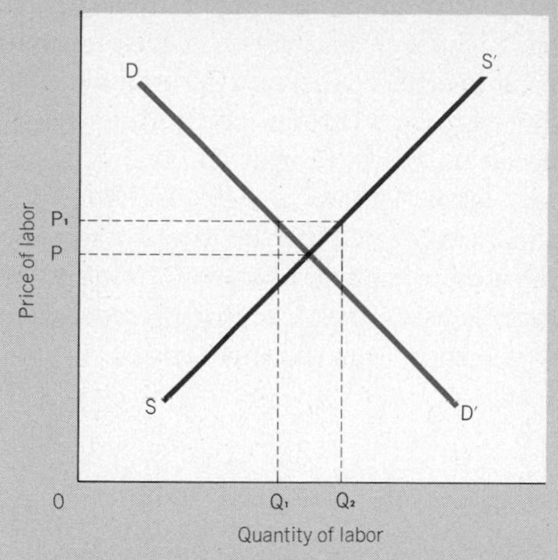

Figure 27.9
Direct Increase in Price of Labor
A union may get the employer to raise the wage from OP to OP_1, and let the higher wage reduce the opportunity for work. This is commonly done by strong industrial unions.

ample, in Figure 27.9, the union may exert pressure on the employers to raise the price of labor from OP to OP_1. At OP_1, not all of the available supply of labor can find jobs. The quantity of labor supplied is OQ_2, while the amount of labor demanded is OQ_1. The effect is the same as in Figure 27.8, but in this case the union does not limit the supply directly. It lets the higher wage reduce the opportunity for work. Strong industrial unions often behave in this fashion. Having organized practically all the relevant workers and controlling the labor supply, the union raises the wage to OP_1. This is a common and important case.

Third, *the union may try to shift the demand curve for labor upward and to the right.* For example, in Figure 27.10, it might try to shift the demand curve from DD' to D_2D_2', with the result that the price of labor will increase from

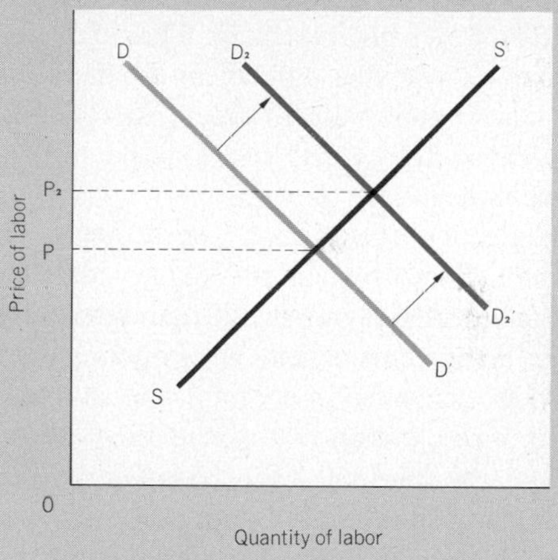

Figure 27.10
Shift in Demand Curve for Labor
A union may shift the demand curve for labor from DD' to D_2D_2' by featherbedding or other devices, thus increasing the wage from OP to OP_2.

OP to OP_2. To cause this shift in the demand for labor, the union may resort to "featherbedding." That is, it may try to restrict output per worker in order to increase the amount of labor required to do a certain job. For example, the railroad unions have insisted on much unnecessary labor. Unions also try to shift the demand curve by helping the employers compete against other industries, or by helping to make Congress pass legislation that protects the employers from foreign competition.

Collective Bargaining

Collective bargaining is the process of negotiation between the union and management over wages and working conditions. Representatives of the union and management meet periodically to work out an agreement or contract; this process generally begins a few months before the old labor contract runs out. Typically, each side asks at first for more than it expects to get, and compromises must be made to reach an agreement. The union representatives take the agreement to their members, who must vote to accept or reject it. If they reject it, they may vote to strike or to continue to negotiate.

Collective bargaining agreements vary greatly. Some pertain to only a single plant while others apply to an entire industry. However, an agreement generally contains the following elements: it specifies the extent and kind of recognition that management gives the union, the level of wage rates for particular jobs, the length of the workweek, the rate of overtime pay, the extent to which seniority will determine which workers will be first to be laid off, the nature and extent of management's prerogatives, and how grievances between workers and the employer will be handled.

Historically, industries and firms have extended recognition to unions by accepting one of three arrangements: the closed shop, the union shop, or the open shop. In a ***closed shop,*** a worker must be a union member before he can be hired. This gives the union more power than if there is a ***union shop,*** in which the employer can hire nonunion workers who must then become union members in a certain length of time after being hired. In an ***open shop,*** the employer can hire union or nonunion labor, and nonunion workers need not, once employed, join the union. As we have seen, the closed shop was banned by the Taft-Hartley Act. The Taft-Hartley Act also says that the union shop is legal unless outlawed by state laws; and in about 20 states there are "right-to-work" laws that make the union shop illegal. Needless to say, these right-to-work laws are hated by organized labor, which regards them as a threat to its security and effectiveness.

Besides the kind of recognition accorded the union, collective bargaining deals with a variety of issues concerning employee compensation. Should workers be paid by the hour, or should they receive a certain amount of pay for each unit they produce? If they are paid by the hour, how much should each occupation receive per hour, and how much variation in this amount should be permitted to compensate for extra merit or skill? How much should each worker receive in the way of fringe benefits: paid holidays, medical insurance, sick leave, and so forth? What should be the standard work week, and what should be the overtime rate paid for work exceeding the standard work week? These and other related questions are obviously of great importance, both to the workers and to the employers.

In addition, collective bargaining agreements generally provide for some way to iron out grievances and disagreements between the workers and management during the life of the contract. It would be unrealistic to assume that such problems will not occur. Often, it is stipulated that disagreements that cannot be resolved by the parties will be settled by submitting them to an arbitrator whose decision will be final. The arbitrator, who is impartial and acceptable to both sides, will hear the case at issue and decide what, in the light of the written contract, seems to be an appropriate resolution of the problem.

Strikes and Pattern Bargaining

Most contracts are settled without resort to a discontinuance of work. But not always. If the union stops work, it is called a ***strike,*** whereas if the employer precipitates the work stoppage, it is called a ***lockout.*** Whoever is immediately responsible, the result is the same: the workers lose income and the employer loses output and profits. The threat of a work stoppage is a potent force encouraging both sides to reach agreement. Strikes occur less frequently than is generally recognized; only about 0.2 percent of all man-days is lost through strikes. (The amount of time lost through strikes is much less than the time spent on coffee breaks!) Without the right to strike, labor's bargaining powers would be greatly weakened. However, when strikes take place in strategic areas involving the nation's health and safety, the government must step in to protect the interests of the public. No government will let a crippling strike go on very long. Presidents, both Republican and Democratic, have used the provisions of the Taft-Hartley Act to stop strikes in important areas. As noted in a previous section, the increasing unionization of public employees—firemen, air controllers, teachers—makes such strikes more and more of a problem.

Collective bargaining is a power struggle. At each point in their negotiations, both the union and the employer must compare the costs (or benefits) of agreeing with the other party with the costs (or benefits) of continuing to disagree. The costs of disagreement are the costs of a strike, while the costs of agreement are the costs of settling on terms other than one's own. These costs are determined by basic market forces. For example, during periods when demand is great, employers are more likely to grant large wage increases because the costs of disagreement seem higher (a strike will prove more costly) than those of settlement. The outcome of the negotiations will depend on the relative strength of the parties. The strength of the employer depends on his ability to withstand a strike. The strength of the union depends on its ability to keep out nonunion workers and to enlist the support of other unions, as well as on the size of its financial reserves.

It is important to note that a union's wage demands are likely to be influenced by what other unions are getting for their memberships. If some unions are getting increases of $1 an hour, another union may feel that it must do at least as well to show its membership that it can produce for them. For this reason, wage negotiations in a few important industries like steel and autos may set a pattern for other industries. Right after World War II, the pattern setters were the auto, mine, steel, electrical, and rubber unions. Within an industry, *pattern bargaining* often exists. Once a contract is signed with one major producer, the other firms in the industry accept—and are given—essentially identical terms.

The Pros and Cons of Big Unions

Finally, we should discuss briefly some of the criticisms that are made of the big unions. These criticisms are based largely on their monopoly power. Critics charge that by exerting such power, unions push up the price of labor and reduce the level of employment in various industries. This results in badly allocated resources, since wage rates no longer signal accurately the relative scarcity of labor of various types. Moreover, it is argued that the resulting upward pressure on wages is an important element in cost-push inflation. Opponents of big unions have proposed at least four policies designed to reduce their power: first, that the antitrust laws be applied to unions as well as firms; second, that industry-wide bargaining, which allows a union to shut down an entire industry, be banned; third, that the union shop be banned; and fourth, that big unions be broken up into a number of smaller ones.

On the other hand, many economists feel that labor unions are an important positive force in the American economy. They argue that it is foolish to believe that without unions labor markets would be perfectly competitive—and that the price of labor would be the proper one from the point of view of resource allocation. They point out that unions tend to be an antidote to the monopsonistic power held by some employers in the labor market. And they argue that unions are not really the prime movers in cost-push inflation, but rather that unions often respond to prior price increases by firms. Thus economists are divided in their attitudes toward the growth and power of big unions.

Summary

Assuming perfect competition, a firm will employ each type of labor in an amount such that its marginal product times the product's price equals its wage. In other words, the firm will employ enough labor so that the value of the marginal product of labor equals labor's price. Consequently, the firm's demand curve for labor—which shows, for each price of labor, the amount of labor the firm will use—is the firm's value-of-marginal-product curve (if labor is the only variable input). The market demand curve for labor shows the relationship between its price and the total amount of labor demanded in the market.

Labor's price depends on its market supply curve as well as on its market demand curve. Labor's market supply curve is the relationship between the price of labor and the total amount of labor supplied in the market. (Labor's market supply curve may be backward bending.) An input's price is determined under perfect competition in essentially the same way that a product's price is determined: by supply and demand. The price of labor will tend in equilibrium to the level at which the quantity of labor demanded equals the quantity of labor supplied. By the same token, the equilibrium amount of labor utilized is also given by the intersection of the market supply and demand curves.

If there are qualitative differences among workers, the differential in their wages will reflect the differential in their marginal products. Some of the differences in the wage rates workers receive are due to differences of this sort. However, even if all workers were of equal ability, there would still be differences in wage rates to offset differences in the characteristics of various occupations and areas. For example, occupations differ in the cost of training and stability of earnings, and geographical areas differ in the cost of living.

There are about 200 national unions in the United States, the biggest being the Teamsters, the Auto Workers, and the Steelworkers. Each national union is composed of local unions, which operate within the context of the constitution of the national union. The AFL-CIO is a federation of national unions created by the merger in 1955 of the American Federation of Labor and the Congress of Industrial Organizations. The AFL-CIO is a very important spokesman for the American labor movement, but because the national unions in the AFL-CIO have given up relatively little of their power to the federation, its authority is limited.

The American Federation of Labor was founded in 1886 and was led by Samuel Gompers. The AFL's philosophy of "bread-and-butter" unionism became the dominant philosophy of American labor. During the 1930s the tide began to turn in favor of unions with the passage of the Norris-LaGuardia Act and the Wagner Act. The late 1930s saw great increases in union membership and power. After World War II, public sentiment turned somewhat against unions, and both the Taft-Hartley Act and the Landrum-Griffin Act were passed over union opposition. In recent years, union membership has increased rather modestly.

There are several ways that unions can increase wages—by shifting the supply curve of labor to the left, by shifting the demand curve for labor to the right, and by influencing the wage directly. Collective bargaining is the process of negotiation between union and management over wages and working conditions. An agreement generally specifies the extent and kind of recognition that management gives the union—such as the closed shop, union shop, or open shop. In addition, it specifies the level of wage rates for particular jobs, the length of the workweek, the rate of overtime pay, the extent to which seniority will determine which workers will be first to be laid off, the nature and extent of management's prerogatives, and how grievances between workers and the employer will be handled. The union's power is based to a considerable extent on its right to strike.

Critics of big unions charge that they possess considerable monopoly power, and that, by pushing up the price of labor and reducing the level of employment, they cause a malallocation of resources and contribute to cost-push inflation. Opponents of big unions often suggest that the antitrust laws be applied to them and that other measures be adopted to curb their power. Supporters of big unions reply that it is foolish to believe that the price of labor would be the proper one from the point of view of resource allocation if there were no big unions. Moreover, they argue that unions are needed to offset the monopsonistic power of employers, and they deny that unions are the prime movers in cost-push inflation.

CONCEPTS FOR REVIEW

Local union
National union
Monopsony
Derived demand
Backward-bending supply curve
American Federation of Labor
Injunction
Norris-LaGuardia Act
Yellow-dog contract
Wagner Act
National Labor Relations Board
Congress of Industrial Organizations
Craft union
Industrial union
Taft-Hartley Act
Closed shop
Landrum-Griffin Act
Strike
Lockout
Pattern bargaining
Featherbedding
Union shop
Open shop

QUESTIONS FOR DISCUSSION AND REVIEW

1. Suppose that you were the president of a small firm that hired nonunion labor. How would you go about estimating the marginal product of a certain worker, or of certain types of workers? Would it be easy? If not, does this mean that the theory of wage determination is incorrect or useless?

2. Describe the various ways that labor unions can influence the wage rate. Do you think that they attempt to maximize the wage rate? If not, what do you think their objectives are?

3. Suppose that the marginal product of skilled labor to a perfectly competitive firm is 2 units and the price of skilled labor is $4 an hour, while the marginal product of unskilled labor is 1 unit and the price of unskilled labor is $2.50 an hour. Is the firm minimizing its costs? Explain.

4. "The national unions in the AFL-CIO have given up none of their power to the federation." Comment and evaluate.

5. Suppose that a perfectly competitive firm's production function is as follows:

Quantity of labor (man-years)	Output per year (thousands of units)
0	0
1	3.0
2	5.0
3	6.8
4	8.0
5	9.0

The firm is a profit maximizer, and the labor market is competitive. Labor must be hired in integer numbers and for a year (no more, no less). If the firm hires 4 man-years of labor, and if the price of a unit of the firm's product is $3, one can establish a range for what the annual wage prevailing in the labor market must be. What is the maximum amount it can be? What is the minimum amount? Why? Do these numbers seem realistic? Why or why not?

6. Based on the data in Question 5, plot the marginal product of labor at various utilization rates of labor. Also, plot the value of labor's marginal product at each quantity of labor used.

7. Suppose that the firm in Question 5 were a monopsonist. Do you think that it would pay a lower, higher, or the same wage rate as under the conditions described in Question 5? Why?

8. "John Jones is twice as good a bricklayer as Bill Bailey, so he ought to get twice as much money." For this statement to be true, how should terms like *good, ought,* and *money* be defined?

9. "The unions should not be exempt from the antitrust laws." Comment and evaluate.

10. State the principal provisions of: (a) the Wagner Act, (b) the Taft-Hartley Act, (c) the Landrum-Griffin Act, and (d) the Norris-LaGuardia Act.

28

Interest, Rent, and Profits

Not all income is received in the form of wages. The school teacher who has a savings account at the Bank of America receives income in the form of *interest.* The widow who rents out 100 acres of rich Iowa land to a farmer receives income in the form of *rent.* And the engineer who founds and owns a firm that develops a new type of electronic calculator receives income in the form of *profit.* All of these types of income—interest, rent, and profit—are forms of property income. That is, they are incomes received by owners of property. In this chapter, we are concerned with the determinants of interest, rent, and profit. Also, we try to explain the social functions of each of these types of property income.

The Nature of Interest

Charles Lamb, the famous English essayist, said, "The human species, according to the best theory I can form of it, is composed of two distinct races, the men who borrow and the men who lend." Whether or not such a cleavage exists, most of the human species, at one time or another, are borrowers or lenders of money. Thus practically everyone is familiar with ***interest,*** which is a payment for the use of money. More specifically, *the rate of interest is the amount of money one must pay for the use of a dollar for a year.* Thus, if the interest rate is 5 percent, you must pay 5 cents for the use of a dollar for a year.

Everyone who borrows money pays interest. Consumers pay interest on personal loans taken out to buy appliances, mortgages taken out to buy houses, and many other types of loans. Firms pay interest on bonds issued to purchase equipment and on short-term bank loans taken out to finance inventories. And governments pay interest on bonds issued to finance schools, highways, and other public projects.

Interest rates vary, depending on the nature of the borrower and the type of loan. One of the most important determinants of the rate of interest charged a particular borrower is the *riskiness* of the loan. Naturally, if the lender has doubts about his chances of getting his money back, he will charge a higher interest rate than if he is sure of being repaid. Thus small, financially rickety firms have to pay higher interest rates than large blue-chip firms; and the large, well-known firms have to pay higher interest rates than the federal government. Another factor that influences the interest rate is the *cost of bookkeeping and collection.* If a firm makes many small loans and must hound the borrowers to pay up, these costs are a great deal larger than if it makes one large loan. Consequently the interest rate that must be charged for such small loans is often considerably higher than for bigger loans.

Despite the diversity of interest rates encountered at any point in time in the real world, it is analytically useful to speak of the ***pure rate of interest,*** which is the interest rate on a riskless loan. The rate of interest on U.S. government bonds—which are about as safe as one can get in this world—comes close to being a pure rate of interest. Actual interest rates will, of course, vary from the pure rate, depending on the riskiness of the loan together with other factors, but the configuration of actual interest rates will tend to move up and down with the pure interest rate.

The Determination of the Interest Rate

The Demand for Loanable Funds

Since the interest rate is the price paid for the use of loanable funds, it—like any price—is determined by demand and supply. The ***demand curve for loanable funds*** shows the quantity of loanable funds demanded at each interest rate. Of course, the demand for loanable funds is a demand for what these funds will buy. Money is not wanted for its own sake, since it cannot, for example, build factories or equipment. Instead, it can provide command over resources—men and equipment and materials—to do things like build factories or equipment.

As shown in Figure 28.1, the demand curve slopes downward to the right, indicating that more loanable funds are demanded at a lower rate of interest than at a higher rate of interest. A very large demand for loanable funds stems from firms who want to borrow money to invest in capital goods like machine tools, buildings, and so forth. At a particular point in time a firm has available a variety of possible investments, each with a certain rate of return, which indicates its profitability or net produc-

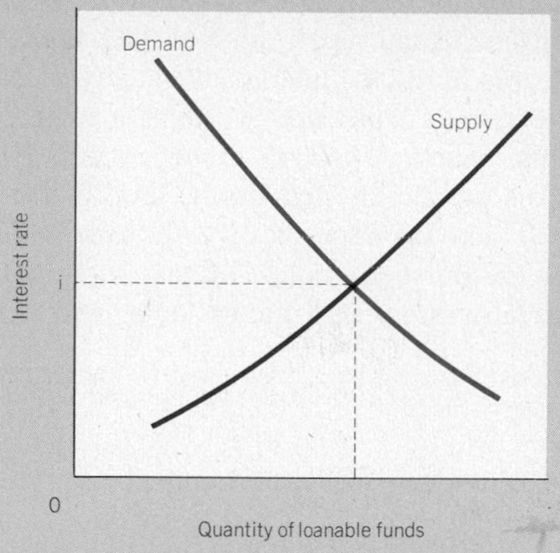

Figure 28.1
Determination of Equilibrium Rate of Interest
The interest rate is determined by the demand and supply of loanable funds, the equilibrium level of the interest rate being *Oi*.

tivity. At higher interest rates, a firm will find it profitable to borrow money for fewer of these projects than if interest rates are lower.

To be more specific, *an asset's* ***rate of return*** *is the interest rate earned on the investment in the asset.* For example, suppose that a piece of equipment costs $10,000 and yields a permanent return to its owner of $1,500 per year.[1] (This return allows for the costs of maintaining the machine). The rate of return on this piece of capital is 15 percent. Why? Because if an investment of $10,000 yields an indefinite annual return of $1,500, the interest rate earned on this investment is clearly 15 percent.

If a firm maximizes profit, it will borrow to carry out investments where the rate of return, adjusted for risk, exceeds the interest rate. For example, it is profitable for a firm to pay 10 percent interest to carry out a project with a 12 percent rate of return, but it is not profitable to pay 15 percent interest for this purpose. (More will be said on this score in a subsequent section.) Consequently, the higher the interest rate, the smaller the amount that firms will be willing to borrow.

Large demands for loanable funds are also made by consumers and the government. Consumers borrow money to buy houses, cars, and many other items. The government borrows money to finance the building of schools, highways, housing, and many other types of public projects. As in the case of firms, the higher the interest rate, the smaller the amount that consumers and governments will be willing to borrow. Adding the demands of firms, consumers, and government together, we find the aggregate relationship at a given point in time between the pure interest rate and the amount of funds demanded—which is the demand curve for loanable funds. For the reasons given above, this demand curve looks the way a demand curve should: it is downward-sloping to the right.

The Supply of Loanable Funds

The ***supply curve for loanable funds*** is the relationship between the quantity of loanable funds supplied and the pure interest rate. The supply of loanable funds comes from households and firms that find the available rate of interest sufficiently attractive to get them to save. In addition, the banks play an extremely important role in influencing the supply of loanable funds. Indeed, banks can actually create or destroy loanable funds (but only within limits set by the Federal Reserve System, our central bank).

The equilibrium value of the pure interest rate is given by the intersection of the demand and supply curves. In Figure 28.1, for example, the equilibrium rate of interest is *Oi*. Fac-

[1] Of course, it is unrealistic to assume that the yield continues indefinitely, but it makes it easier to understand the principle involved.

tors that shift the demand curve or supply curve for loanable funds tend to alter the interest rate. For example, if people become more willing to postpone consumption to future time periods, the supply curve for loanable funds will shift to the right, and the interest rate will decline. Or if inventions result in very profitable new investment possibilities, the demand curve will shift to the right and the interest rate will increase. (See Figure 28.2.)

However, this is only part of the story. Because of the government's influence on both the demand and supply sides of the market for loanable funds, the interest rate at any point in time is to a considerable extent a matter of public policy. A nation's monetary policy can have a significant effect on the level of the interest rate. More specifically, when the Federal Reserve pursues a policy of easy money, this generally means that interest rates tend to fall

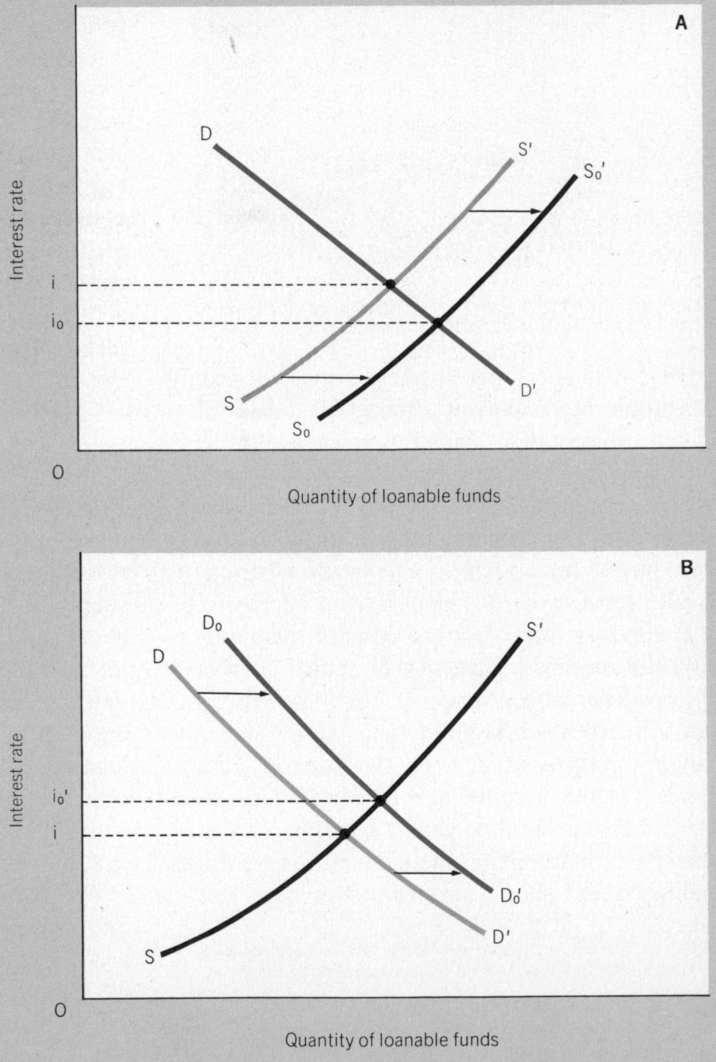

Figure 28.2
Effects on the Equilibrium Interest Rate of Shifts in the Demand or Supply Curves for Loanable Funds
If people become more willing to postpone consumption to future time periods, the supply curve will shift from *SS'* to S_0S_0', and the equilibrium interest rate will fall from *i* to i_0.

If very profitable new investment opportunities are opened up, the demand curve will shift from *DD'* to D_0D_0', and the equilibrium interest rate will rise from *i* to i'_0.

in the short run because the Fed is pushing the supply curve for loanable funds to the right. On the other hand, when the Federal Reserve pursues a policy of tight money, interest rates generally tend to rise in the short run because the Fed is pushing the supply curve for loanable funds to the left. (See Figure 28.3.)

The government is also an important factor on the demand side of the market for loanable funds, because it is a big borrower, particularly during wartime. Between 1941 and 1945, it borrowed almost $200 billion to help finance World War II. At the present time, total federal debt (excluding the debt of state and local governments) held by the public is about ⅙ as big as total private debt. The total amount of federal debt in 1975 was about $575 billion.

Finally, note that the equilibrium level of the pure interest rate can be determined by John Maynard Keynes's ***liquidity preference theory,*** as well as by the loanable funds theory described in this section. The liquidity preference theory focuses attention on all money, not just loanable funds, and says that the interest rate is determined by the demand and supply of all money in the economy. The two approaches are not contradictory; rather, they complement one another.

Functions of the Interest Rate

Interest has often been a relatively unpopular and somewhat suspect form of income. Even Aristotle, who was hardly noted for muddle-headedness, felt that money was "barren" and that it was improper to charge interest. And in the Middle Ages, church law outlawed usury, even though interest continued to be charged. In real life and in fiction, the money lender is often the villain, almost never the hero. Yet it is perfectly clear that *interest rates serve a very important function: they allocate the supply of loanable funds.*

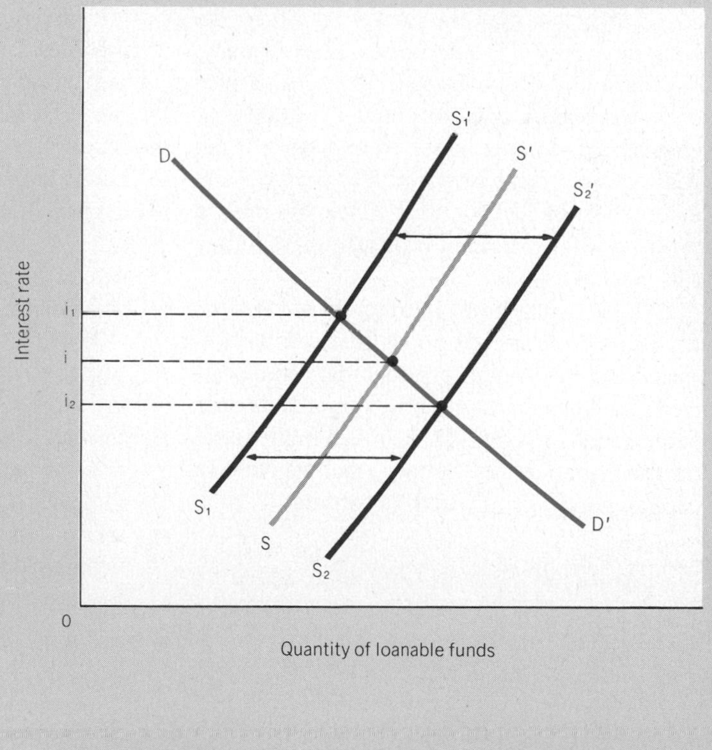

Figure 28.3
Effects on the Equilibrium Interest Rate of Federal Reserve Policies Influencing the Supply Curve for Loanable Funds
When the Federal Reserve pushes the supply curve to the right (from *SS'* to S_2S_2'), the equilibrium interest rate falls from i to i_2. When the Federal Reserve pushes the supply curve to the left (*SS'* to S_1S_1'), the equilibrium interest rate increases from i to i_1.

At a given point in time, funds that can be used to construct new capital goods are scarce, and society faces the problem of allocating these scarce funds among alternative possible uses. One way to allocate the loanable funds is through freely fluctuating interest rates. When such funds are relatively scarce, the interest rate will rise, with the result that only projects with relatively high rates of return will be carried out since the others will not be profitable. On the other hand, when such funds are relatively plentiful, the interest rate will fall, and less productive projects will be carried out because they now become profitable.

The advantage of using the interest rate to allocate funds is that only the most productive projects are funded. To see why, assume that all investments are riskless. *If firms can borrow all the money they want at this rate of interest, and if they maximize their profits, they obviously will buy all capital goods and accept all investment opportunities where the rate of return on these capital goods or investment opportunities exceeds the interest rate at which they can borrow.*[2] The reason for this is clear enough. If one can borrow money at an interest cost that is less than the rate of return on the borrowed money, clearly one can make money. For example, if you borrow $1,000 at 3 percent per year interest and buy a $1,000 machine that has a rate of return of 4 percent per year, you receive a return of $40 per year and incur a cost of $30 per year. Since you make a profit of $10 per year, it obviously pays to buy this machine.

At a particular point in time, there is a variety of possible capital goods that can be produced and investment projects that can be carried out. Their rates of return vary a great deal; some goods or projects have much higher rates of return than others. Suppose that we rank the capital goods or projects according to their rates of return, from highest to lowest. If only a few of the goods or projects can be accepted, only those at the top of the list will be chosen. But as more and more can be accepted, society and private investors must go further and further down the list, with the consequence that projects with lower and lower rates of return will be chosen. How many of these capital goods and investment projects will be carried out? As noted above, firms will continue to invest as long as the rate of return on these goods or projects exceeds the interest rate at which they can borrow. Thus it follows that *the most productive projects—all those with rates of return exceeding the interest rate—will be carried out.*

Although interest is sometimes represented as a product of greedy capitalists, even socialist and Communist economies must use something like an interest rate to help allocate funds. After all, the socialists and Communists face the same sort of allocation problem that capitalists do. And when they try to screen out the less productive projects and to accept only the more productive ones, they must use the equivalent of an interest rate in their calculations, whether they call it that or not. (However, they do not, of course, pay interest income.) In the Soviet Union there have been published acknowledgments that a misallocation of resources resulted from decisions made in earlier years when interest rates—or their equivalent—were ignored. At present, Soviet decision makers use what amount to interest rates in their calculations to determine which capital investments should be made and which should not.

Finally, besides its role in allocating the supply of loanable funds, the interest rate plays another important part in our economy: *it influences the level of investment, and thus the level of net national product.* Increases in the interest rate tend to reduce aggregate investment, thereby reducing total spending, whereas decreases in the interest rate tend to increase aggregate investment, thereby in-

[2] We assume here that the investment opportunities are independent in the sense that the rate of return from each opportunity is not influenced by whether some other opportunity is accepted.

creasing total spending. Through its monetary policies, the government attempts to influence the interest rate (and the quantity of money) so that total spending pushes net national product towards its full-employment level with reasonably stable prices.

Capital Budgeting

The principles discussed in the previous section can be applied to individual firms as well as entire societies. In particular, they help to indicate how a firm should make decisions on the choice of investment projects. Suppose, for example, that the Bugsbane Music Box Company believes that it will have $10 million from internal sources—primarily retained earnings and depreciation allowances—to invest next year. *To decide which investment projects to accept, it should estimate the rate of return from each one.* Suppose that it finds that it can invest $2 million in projects with rates of return of 30 percent, that it can invest $4 million in projects with rates of return of 25 percent, and so on, as shown in Table 28.1. Applying the principles just discussed, Bugsbane can maximize its profits by allocating the $10 million available from internal sources as follows: all projects yielding rates of return of 20 percent or more should be accepted; and all projects yielding less than 20 percent should not be undertaken. In other words, the projects with the highest rates of return—and with a total cost of $10 million—should be chosen.

Table 28.1
Investment Opportunities for Bugsbane Music Box Company

Rate of return (percent)	Amount of money the firm can invest at given rate of return (dollars)
30	2 million
25	4 million
20	4 million
15	6 million
10	7 million

This is a very useful step toward solving the firm's problem, but it assumes that the firm is unable or unwilling to borrow. If this is true, then nothing more needs to be said. But, as shown in Table 28.1, the firm has investment opportunities yielding 15 percent per year that it is not undertaking. It would pay the firm to undertake these projects even if it had to pay 10 or 12 percent interest—or anything less than 15 percent, for that matter. If the firm can borrow all the money it wants (within reason), but must pay 12 percent interest, what investment opportunities should it accept? Clearly, all whose rate of return exceeds 12 percent. Thus, looking at Table 28.1, we see that the firm should invest its $10 million from internal sources and borrow an additional $6 million in order to undertake projects totaling $16 million.

This is an extremely simple case, but it illustrates how the interest rate and the concept of an asset's rate of return are used in practical business situations. ***Capital budgeting***—the term applied to this area—has become an extremely important part of a firm's operations, as businessmen have relied more and more on economic concepts in allocating their firms' resources. Unaided hunch and intuition will no longer do in most major firms. Instead, most big firms insist that the prospective rate of return be estimated for each proposed investment, and that, making allowances for differences in risk, funds be allocated to the projects with the highest rates of return.[3] Of course, it is often difficult to make such estimates, but if funds are to be allocated rationally, it is essential that an analysis of this sort be carried out, formally or on the back of an envelope.

[3] In practice, firms often base their decisions on discounted cash flow rather than rates of return. The present discussion is necessarily simplified. For a more complete treatment, see any managerial economics text.

Capital and Roundabout Methods of Production

Labor and land are often called the ***primary inputs*** because they are produced outside the economic system. Labor is created by familiar biological processes (which usually are not economically oriented, one would hope), and land is supplied by nature. *Capital*, on the other hand, *consists of goods that are created for the purpose of producing other goods.* Factory buildings, equipment, raw materials, inventories—all are various types of capital. In contrast to labor and land, capital is an input produced by the economic system itself.[4] A machine tool is capital; so is a boxcar or an electric power plant. These inputs are produced by firms, and they are purchased and used by firms. But they are not final consumption goods; instead, they are used to produce the final goods and services consumed by the public.

Our economy devotes a considerable amount of its productive capacity to the production of capital. The giant electrical equipment industry produces generators used by the electric power industry. The machine tool industry produces the numerically controlled tools used by the automobile, aircraft, and hundreds of other industries. The result in many sectors of the economy is a *roundabout method of production.* Consider the stages that lead to the manufacture of an automobile. Workers dig iron ore to be used to make pig iron to be used to make steel to be used to make machine tools to be used to make cylinders to be used to make a motor to be used to make the automobile.

Why does the economy bother to produce capital? After all, it may seem unnecessarily circuitous to construct capital to produce the goods and services consumers really want. Why not produce the desired goods and services—and *only* the desired goods and services—directly? For example, why produce plows to help produce agricultural crops? Why not forget about the plows and just produce the crops the consumers want? The answer is, of course, that the other inputs—labor and land—can produce more of the desired consumer goods and services when they are used in combination with capital than when they are used alone. A given amount of labor and land can produce more crops when used in combination with plows than when used alone.

The production and use of lots of capital make the other inputs—labor and land—more productive. But this does not mean that any society would be wise to increase without limit its production and use of capital. After all, the only way a society can produce more capital is to produce less goods and services of direct use to consumers. (For society as a whole, there are no free lunches, if resources are used fully and efficiently.) As the production of capital increases, consumers must cut further and further into their level of consumption at the present time in order to increase their capacity to produce in the future. Beyond a point, the advantage of having more in the future is overbalanced by the disadvantage of having less now. At this point, a society should stop increasing its production of capital goods.

The process by which people give up a claim on present consumption goods in order to receive consumption goods in the future is called ***saving.*** Just as a child may (infrequently) give up a lollipop today in order to get a lollipop and a candy cane next week, so an entire society may give up the present consumption of automobiles, food, tobacco, clothing, and so forth in order to obtain more of such goods and services later on. Saving, which (as we saw in Chapter 2) was so essential in promoting the Industrial Revolution, continues to play a

[4] Obviously, this distinction requires qualification. After all, land can be improved, and the quality of labor can be enhanced (by training and other means). Thus land and labor have some of the characteristics of capital since to some extent they can be "produced"—or at least enhanced—by the economic system. More will be said about human capital in a later section.

major role in the promotion of economic growth today.[5]

Capitalization of Assets

In a capitalist economy, each capital good has a market value. How can we determine what this value is? How much money is a capital good worth? To keep things reasonably simple, suppose that you can get 5 percent on various investments open to you; specifically, you can get 5 percent by investing your money in the stock of a local firm. That is, for every \$1,000 you invest, you will receive a permanent return of \$50 a year—and this is the highest return available. Now suppose that you have an opportunity to buy a piece of equipment that will yield you a permanent return of \$1,000 per year. This piece of equipment is worth \$1,000 ÷ .05 = \$20,000 to you. Why? Because this is the amount you would have to pay for any other investment open to you that yields an equivalent amount—\$1,000—per year. (If you must invest \$1,000 for every \$50 of annual yield, \$20,000 must be invested to obtain an annual yield of \$1,000.)

In general, if a particular asset yields a permanent amount—X dollars—each year, how much is this asset worth? In other words, how much should you be willing to pay for it? If you can get a return of $100 \times r$ percent per year from alternative investments, you would have to invest $X \div r$ dollars in order to get the same return as this particular asset yields. Consequently, this asset is worth

$$\frac{\$X}{r}.$$

[5] In a more poetic vein, this process of saving has been described as follows by William M. Thackeray:

Though small was your allowance,
You saved a little store;
And those who save a little
Shall get a plenty more.

If it does nothing else, the foregoing helps explain why Thackeray is better known as a novelist than a poet.

For example, if the rate of return on alternative investments had been 3 percent rather than 5 percent in the example above, the worth of the piece of equipment would have been \$1,000 ÷ .03 = \$33,333 (since X = \$1,000 and r = .03). This is the amount you would have to pay for any other investment open to you that yields an equivalent amount—\$1,000—per year. To see this, note that, if you must invest \$1,000 for every \$30 (not \$50, as before) of annual yield, \$33,333 (not \$20,000, as before) must be invested to obtain an annual yield of \$1,000.

This process of computing an asset's worth is called ***capitalization.*** Note one important point about an asset's capitalized value. Holding constant an asset's annual returns, the asset's worth is higher, the lower the rate of return available on other investments. Thus the piece of equipment discussed above was worth \$33,333 when you could get a 3 percent return on alternative investments, but only \$20,000 when you could get a 5 percent return on alternative investments. This makes sense. After all, the lower the rate of return on alternative investments, the more you must invest in them in order to obtain annual earnings equivalent to those of the asset in question. Thus the more valuable is the asset in question.

This principle helps to explain why in securities markets bond prices fall when interest rates rise, and rise when interest rates fall. As we pointed out in Chapter 7, a bond is a piece of paper that states that the borrower will pay the lender a fixed amount of interest each year (and the principal when the bond comes due). Suppose that this annual interest is \$100, and that the interest rate equals $100 \times r$ percent per year. Then, applying the results of the previous paragraphs, this bond will be worth $100 \div r$ dollars, if the bond is due a great many years hence. For example, if the interest rate is 5 percent, it is worth \$2,000. But if the interest rate rises to 10 percent, it will be worth only \$1,000, and if the interest rate falls to 4 percent, it will be worth \$2,500. Securities dealers make these sorts of calculations all the time, for they recognize that the value of the bond will fall when interest rates rise, and rise when interest rates fall.

The Present Value of Future Income

In the previous section, we determined the value of an asset that yields a perpetual stream of earnings. Now let's consider a case where an asset will provide you with a single lump sum at a certain time in the future. For example, suppose that you are the heir to an estate of \$100,000, which you will receive in two years. How much is that estate worth now?

To answer this question, we must recognize the basic fact that *money now is worth more than money later.* Why? Because one can always invest money that is available now and obtain interest on it, the result being that a dollar now is worth more in the future. For example, suppose that the interest rate is 6 percent. If so, a dollar received now is equivalent to \$1.06 received a year hence. Why? Because if you invest the dollar now, you'll get 1.06 in a year. Similarly, *a dollar received now is equivalent to* $(1.06)^2$ *dollars two years hence.* Why? Because if you invest the dollar now, you'll get 1.06 dollars in a year; and if you reinvest this amount for another year at 6 percent, you'll get $(1.06)^2$ dollars.

Thus, if the interest rate is 6 percent, the estate is worth $100{,}000 \div (1.06)^2$ dollars now. Since $(1.06)^2 = 1.1236$, it is worth

$$\frac{\$100{,}000}{1.1236} = \$88{,}100.$$

In general, *if the interest rate is* $100 \times r$ *percent per year, a dollar received now is worth* $1 \div (1 + r)^2$ *dollars two years from now.* Thus, whatever the value of the interest rate may be, the estate is worth

$$\frac{\$100{,}000}{(1 + r)^2}.$$

The principle that money now is worth more than money later is of fundamental importance. If you don't understand it, you don't understand a basic precept of the world of finance. Although the example considered in previous paragraphs pertains only to a two-year period, this principle remains valid no matter how long the period of time we consider. Table 28.2 shows the present value of a

Table 28.2
Present Value of a Future Dollar

Number of years hence (that dollar is received)	Interest rate (percent) 4	6	8	10
	(cents)			
1	96.2	94.3	92.6	90.9
2	92.5	89.0	85.7	82.6
3	89.0	83.9	79.4	75.1
4	85.5	79.2	73.5	68.3
5	82.3	74.7	68.1	62.0
10	67.6	55.8	46.3	38.5
15	55.5	41.7	31.5	23.9
20	45.6	31.1	21.5	14.8

dollar received at various points of time in the future. As you can see, its present value declines with the length of time before the dollar is received (so long as the interest rate remains constant).

Rates of Return from Investing in Human Capital

In recent years, economists have shown a great interest in *human capital.* Certainly it is true that many expenditures on education and training, as well as on other things like health, can be viewed as investments, because these expenditures, like an investment in physical capital, result in deferred increases in income. In other words, just as a firm may invest in a machine in order to increase its future earnings, so a student (or his parents) may invest in his education to increase his future earnings. Moreover, just as a firm can estimate the rate of return from its investment in the machine, so the student can estimate the rate of return from his investment in his education. In this way the student, like the firm, can determine whether this investment is more profitable than others he might make instead.

How big an investment does a student make when he attends college? As we saw in Chapter 1, this investment includes both out-of-pocket costs (such as tuition, books, and extra living expenses) and another cost that students often forget to include: the forgone earnings the student could make if he worked instead of going to college. How much does a college education increase the student's prospective earnings? Perhaps the simplest way to answer this question is to compare the average income of high school graduates with the average income of college graduates of the same age. The difference between these two averages is a rough measure of the increase in income, at each age level, from a college education.

Based on estimates of this sort, economists have calculated that the rate of return from the investment in a college education has been about 10 percent. (Current studies suggest that the figure may be closer to 8 percent in the middle 1970s.) This is an interesting result, both for private decision-making and for public policy, but it is important to note its limitations. First, this is an average figure for white males only, which may differ a great deal from the figure pertaining to any particular individual. Further, some of the increase in income attributed to a college education may result from the fact that the people who graduated from college were abler, more conscientious, more highly motivated, or better prepared at home than those who did not go to college. It is very difficult to sort out the effects of the college education from the effects of other factors.

Nonetheless, the idea of viewing education as a form of investment in human capital is a fruitful one. For one thing, it permits deeper insight into the reasons why some people get paid more than others. Thus people who invest a great deal in their education—like doctors, dentists, and lawyers—must receive higher incomes after graduation to make this investment worthwhile. Also, this concept is useful in analyzing ways in which a society can increase its level of per capita income. If the rate of return to a society from additional investment in human capital is high, one way to increase per capita income is to increase the investment in education and other forms of human capital.

The Present Value of Lifetime Earnings in Science and Engineering

In a previous section, we showed how one can determine the present value of a dollar received at various points of time in the future. Let's apply these results to questions like: Do chemists make more money than physicists?

What Does That Dream House Really Cost?

The biggest investment you'll probably ever make is in a house. Most people can't afford to buy a house for cash, for the simple reason that they don't have enough money in their bank accounts—or stuffed in the mattress. (A typical suburban house now costs $40,000 or more in many areas, although prices vary greatly from location to location.) Thus the ordinary procedure is for a house buyer to take out a mortgage, often from a savings and loan association or a bank. A mortgage is a loan; the house itself becomes security (or collateral) for the loan. If you fail to meet the mortage payments, the lender can foreclose the mortgage, which means that the lender is entitled to take possession of the house.

To figure out how much your payments must be each month, the lender determines how much you must pay so that, when the mortgage terminates, you will have repaid the amount you borrowed and paid the stipulated interest on your debt. The size of the monthly mortgage payment depends on three things: (1) the amount you borrow, (2) how long the mortgage extends, and (3) the interest rate. Clearly, the more that you borrow, the higher your monthly payment, holding all other things equal. And the higher the interest rate and the shorter the period of the mortgage, the higher your monthly payment.

To be more specific, look at the accompanying table, which shows the monthly payment per $1,000 borrowed. As you can see, the monthly payment is $7.76 per $1,000 borrowed, if the mortgage extends for 20 years and the interest rate is 7 percent. Thus, if you take out a $20,000 mortgage (at 7 percent for 20 years), the monthly payment is 20 times $7.76, or $155.20. Or take a case where the mortgage extends for 25 years and the interest rate is 9

Monthly Mortgage Payments (per $1,000 borrowed)

Interest rate (percent)	Length of mortgage (years) 15	20	25	30
	(dollars)			
7	8.99	7.76	7.07	6.66
7½	9.28	8.06	7.39	7.00
8	9.56	3.37	7.72	7.34
8½	9.85	8.68	8.06	7.69
9	10.15	9.00	8.40	8.05
9½	10.45	9.33	8.74	8.41
10	10.75	9.66	9.09	8.78

percent. In this case, if you take out a $20,000 mortgage, the monthly payment is 20 times $8.40, or $168.00.

As noted above, much of the monthly payment is used to repay part of the principal of the loan. The rest goes for interest on the portion of the loan that is not yet repaid. Over the lifetime of a mortgage, a very substantial amount is paid by the borrower for interest. For example, if you take out a 20-year, $20,000 mortgage at an interest rate of 7½ percent, you will pay $18,650 in interest over the life of the mortgage. And the higher the interest rate, the bigger the amount that you will pay in interest. Thus, if the interest rate is 9½ percent (rather than 7½ percent), you will pay $24,660 (rather than $18,650) in interest over the life of a 20-year, $20,000 mortgage. As you can see, *a difference of 2 percentage points in the interest rate increases the total interest payments by over $6,000!* Finally, note that when these interest costs are included, the total cost of a $40,000 house will really be about $60,000. For example, if the buyer takes out a 20-year, $20,000 mortgage at 9½ percent, his total payments over the life of the mortgage will be $40,000 + $24,660, or $64,660.

Do electrical engineers make more money than mechanical engineers? Do psychologists with B.A. degrees make more money than psychologists with Ph.D.s? These are important questions, which can have implications for one's choice of career. To answer these questions, economists calculate the average income of people in each profession at each age level. For example, they may find that the average income of a Ph.D. chemist is as follows at various age levels:

Age (years)	Average income (dollars)
26	20,000
27	21,000
28	23,000
.	.
.	.
.	.
65	33,000

Then they determine the *present value* of these earnings to a person that is entering the profession.

To see what is meant by the present value of a stream of earnings, let's draw on some figures presented earlier in Table 28.2. At an interest rate of 6 percent, a dollar one year hence is worth 94.3 cents now. Thus to a 26-year-old Ph.D. chemist, the expectation of $21,000 one year hence (when he is 27) is worth $21,000 x 0.943 or $19,803, to him at present. Similarly, Table 28.2 shows that a dollar received two years hence is worth 89.0 cents now (if the interest rate is 6 percent). Thus the expectation of $23,000 two years hence (when he is 28) is worth $23,000 x 0.89, or $20,470, to him at present. Similarly, one can obtain the present value of his expected earnings three years hence, four years hence, and for each year up to his retirement. The sum of these values is the present value of his entire lifetime stream of earnings. This is the figure that economists use to measure the lifetime income level in various professions.

Early in the 1970s, Richard Freeman of Harvard University calculated such figures for scientists and engineers. His results are shown in Table 28.3. As you can see, Ph.D. physicists tend to make more than other scientists, the present value of their lifetime earnings being about $212,000. The lowest-paid Ph.D.s are those in geography, linguistics, and sociology, where the present value of the lifetime earnings is about $150,000. Among engineers, the highest-paid Ph.D.s seem to be the mechanical engineers, where the present value of lifetime earnings is about $235,000.

Besides presenting data for Ph.D. scientists and engineers, Freeman also gives data for those with B.A.s and M.A.s. A comparison of the figures for the B.A.s with those for the M.A.s and Ph.D.s indicates the areas where graduate education is likely to be most profitable. In chemistry, for instance, the present value of lifetime earnings is much higher for Ph.D.s than for B.A.s ($203,000 versus $168,000). But in economics, the present value of lifetime earnings is lower for Ph.D.s than for B.A.s To a considerable extent, this is because the Ph.D.s in economics tend to work in universities or in the government, whereas the B.A.s work in industry. The Ph.D.s are willing to accept lower monetary incomes because of the nonmonetary benefits such as opportunities for research, satisfactions derived from teaching, and participation in the making of public policy.

Rent: Nature and Significance

Besides interest, another type of property in-

Table 28.3
Present Value of Lifetime Income, by Field of Science or Engineering and Degree Level

Field of science or engineering	Ph.D.	Degree level M.A. (thousands of dollars)	B.A.
Agriculture	170	147	148
Biology	172	136	139
Chemistry	203	179	168
Earth Science	167	170	179
Economics	179	185	218
Geography	145	n.a.	n.a.
Linguistics	149	n.a.	n.a.
Mathematics	180	179	228
Statistics	191	192	193
Physics	212	189	203
Psychology	166	150	165
Sociology	155	n.a.	n.a.
Civil engineering	210	179	188
Electrical engineering	230	223	208
Industrial engineering	229	194	192
Mechanical engineering	235	190	201

Source: R. Freeman, *The Market for College-Trained Manpower,* Cambridge, Mass.: Harvard University Press, 1971. The figures pertain to the 1960s, and the data for scientists are not comparable in some respects with those for engineers.

come is rent. To understand rent, one must understand what economists mean by land. ***Land*** is defined by economists as *any input that is fixed in supply, its limits established by nature.* Thus, since certain types of minerals and natural resources are in relatively fixed supply, they are included in the economist's definition of land. Suppose that the supply of an input is completely fixed. Increases in its price will not increase its supply and decreases in its price will not decrease its supply. Following the terminology of the classical economists of the nineteenth century, *the price of such an input is **rent.*** Note that rent means something quite different to an economist than to the man in the street, who considers rent the price of using an apartment or a car or some other object owned by someone else.

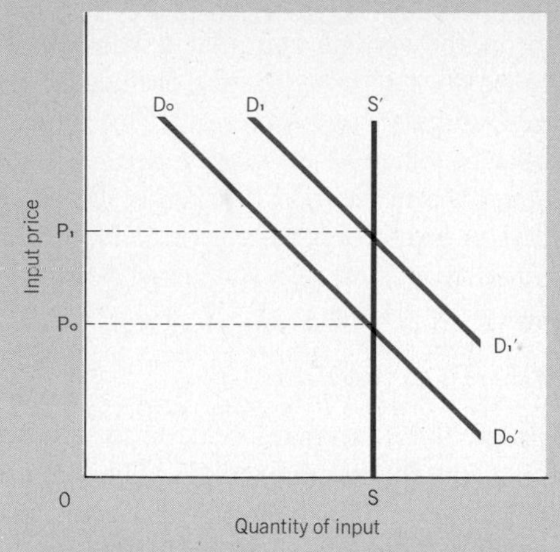

Figure 28.4
Rent
Rent is the price of an input in fixed supply. Since its supply curve is vertical, the price of such an input is determined entirely by the demand curve for the input. If the demand curve is D_0D_0', the rent is OP_0; if the demand curve is D_1D_1', the rent is OP_1.

If the supply of an input is fixed, its supply curve is a vertical line SS' as shown in Figure 28.4. Thus the price of this input, its rent, is determined entirely by the demand curve for the input. For example, if the demand curve is D_0D_0', the rent is OP_0; if the demand curve is D_1D_1', the rent is OP_1. Since the supply of the input is fixed, the price of the input can be lowered without influencing the amount supplied. Thus *a rent is a payment above the minimum necessary to attract this amount of the input.*[6]

Why is it important to know whether a certain payment for inputs is a rent? Because a reduction of the payment will not influence the availability and use of the inputs if the payment is a rent; whereas if it is not a rent, a reduction of the payment is likely to change the allocation of resources. For example, if the government imposes a tax on rents, there will be no effect on the supply of resources to the economy.

In 1879, Henry George (1839–97) published a book, *Progress and Poverty,* in which he argued that rents should be taxed away by the government. In his view, owners of land were receiving substantial rents simply because their land happened to be well situated, not because they were doing anything productive. Since this rent was unearned income and since the supply of land would not be influenced by such a tax, George felt that it was justifiable to tax away such rent. Indeed, he argued that a tax of this sort should be the only tax imposed by the government.

Critics of George's views pointed out that land can be improved, with the result that the supply is not completely price-inelastic. More-

[6] In recent years, there has been a tendency among economists to extend the use of the word *rent* to encompass all payments to inputs above the minimum required to make these inputs available to the industry or to the economy. To a great extent these payments are costs to individual firms; the firms must make such payments to attract and keep these inputs, which are useful to other firms in the industry. But if the inputs have no use in other industries, these payments are not costs to the industry as a whole (or to the economy as a whole) because the inputs would be available to the industry whether or not these payments are made.

over, they argued that if land rents are unearned so are many other kinds of income. In addition, they pointed out that it was unrealistic to expect such a tax to raise the needed revenue. George's single-tax movement gained a number of adherents in the last decades of the nineteenth century, and he even made an unsuccessful bid to become mayor of New York. Arguments in favor of a single tax continue to surface from time to time.

Rent: An Example

To make the concept of rent more concrete, consider the following example. There is a lot at the corner of Third Avenue and Winchester Street in a California suburb; this property is on the edge of the town. What will be the rent for this lot? It has various possible uses. It could be the location of a store or restaurant, a small farm, a site for an apartment building, or used for some other purpose. In each possible use, this lot has a certain value as an input.

In a competitive market, this lot will tend to rent for an amount equal to its value in its most productive use. That is, if the value of its marginal product is highest when it is used as the location for a store, a store will be built on it, and the lot will command a rent equal to the value of its marginal product. In this way, the lot will be drawn into the use that seems to yield the highest returns to the renter. From society's point of view, this has much to recommend it, since the use that yields the highest returns is likely to be the one consumers value most highly.

Classical economists viewed rent as a differential that had to be paid for the utilization of better rather than poorer land. They argued as follows: if land becomes scarce, the better lands will receive a nonzero price before the poorer lands. The rent on any acre will rise to the point where it is equal to the difference in productivity between this acre and an acre of no-rent land. Why? Because, as we saw in Equation (27.3) in Chapter 27, the price differential between two inputs will equal the differential in their marginal products.

Profits

Besides interest and rent, another important type of property income is profit. Profit is not new to us. In Chapter 7, we discussed at some length the economist's concept of profit and how it varies from the accountant's concept. According to the accountant, profit is the amount of money the owner of a firm has left after paying wages, interest, and rent—and after providing proper allowance for the depreciation of buildings and equipment. The economist dissents from this view; his position is that the alternative costs of the labor, capital, and land contributed by the owner should also be deducted.

Profit Statistics

Available statistics concerning profits are based on the accountant's concept, not the economist's. Before taxes, corporation profits average about 10 percent of gross national income. Profits—expressed as a percent of either net worth or sales—vary considerably from industry to industry and from firm to firm. (For example, the drug industry's profits in the postwar period have frequently been about 15-20 percent of net worth—considerably higher than in most other manufacturing industries.) Also, profits vary greatly from year to year, and are much more erratic than wages. They fall more heavily in recessions and rise more rapidly in recoveries than wages do. Table 28.4 shows profit as a percent of stockholders' equity in each major manufacturing industry in the United States in 1974.

To some extent, the measured differences in profits among firms come about because the profit figures are not corrected for the value of the inputs contributed by the owners. Because they are smarter and more resourceful, some

Table 28.4
Annual Rates of Profit (after taxes) on Stockholders' Equity, Selected Industries, United States, 1974.

Industry	Rate of profit (percent)
All manufacturing	14.9
Nondurable goods:	17.2
Food	14.0
Tobacco	15.6
Textiles	8.2
Paper	17.8
Printing	13.2
Chemicals	18.2
Petroleum	21.0
Rubber	14.4
Durable goods:	12.6
Motor vehicles	6.9
Aircraft	10.6
Electrical Equipment	11.1
Other machinery	13.2
Other fabricated metal products	16.6
Primary metals	16.4
Stone, clay, and glass	10.6
Instruments	16.1

Source: World Almanac

owners provide managerial labor of a much higher quality than other owners do. Profits arising from this fact are, at least in part, wages for superior management. Similarly, some owners put up a lot of the capital and work long hours. Profits arising from these sources are, at least in part, interest on capital and wages for time spent working in the firm.

Innovation, Uncertainty, and Monopoly Power

Why do profits—as the economist defines them—exist? Three important factors are innovation, uncertainty, and monopoly power. Suppose that an economy was composed of perfect competitive industries, that entry was completely free, and that no changes in technology—no new processes, no new products, or other innovations—were permitted. Moreover, suppose that everyone could predict the future with perfect accuracy. Under these conditions, there would be no profits, because people would enter industries where profits exist, thus reducing these profits eventually to zero, and leave industries where losses exist, thus reducing these negative profits eventually to zero. This sort of no-profit equilibrium has already been discussed in Chapter 24.

But in the real world, innovations of various kinds are made. For example, DuPont introduces a new product like nylon, or Henry Ford introduces the assembly line, or Marconi introduces the radio. The people who carry out these bold schemes are the ***innovators,*** the men with vision and the daring to back it up. The innovators are not necessarily the inventors of new techniques or products, although in some cases the innovator and the inventor are the same. Often the innovator takes another man's invention, adapts it, and introduces it to the market. According to economists like the late Joseph Schumpeter of Harvard, profits are the rewards earned by innovators. Of course, the profits derived from any single innovation eventually erode with competition and imitation, but other innovations replace them, with the result that profits from innovation continue to be made.

In the real world, uncertainty also exists. Indeed, one of the real hazards in attempting to be an innovator is the risk involved. According to a theory set forth several decades ago by Frank Knight of the University of Chicago, all economic profit is due to uncertainty. Profit is the reward for risk bearing. Assuming that people would like to avoid risk, they will prefer relatively stable, sure earnings to relatively unstable, uncertain earnings—*if the average level of earnings is the same.* Consequently, to induce people to take the risks involved in owning businesses in various industries, a profit—a premium for risk—must be paid to them. This is similar to the higher wages that, according to the previous chapter, must be paid for jobs where earnings are unstable or uncertain.

Still another reason for the existence of profits is the fact that markets are not perfectly competitive. Under perfect competition, there will, of course, be a tendency in the long run for profits to disappear. But, as we have seen, this will not be the case if an industry is a monopoly or oligopoly. Instead, profits may well exist in the long run in such imperfectly competitive industries. And, as we know from Chapter 26, much of our entire economy is composed of imperfectly competitive industries. Monopoly profits are fundamentally the result of "contrived scarcities." Since a firm's demand curve is downward-sloping if competition is imperfect, it pays the firm to take account of the fact that the more it produces, the smaller the price it will receive. In other words, the firm realizes that it will spoil the market if it produces too much. Thus it pays firms to limit their output, and this contrived scarcity is responsible for the existence of the profits they make as a consequence.

The Functions of Profits

To many people, profit seems to be "something for nothing." They do not recognize the innovative or risk-bearing functions of the owners of the firm, and consequently see no reason for the existence of profits. Other people, aware that profits arise because of imperfect competition, ignore the other functions of profit and regard it as entirely the ill-gotten gain of fat monopolists, often smoking big cigars and properly equipped with a rapacious leer. But no group is more hostile to profits than the followers and disciples of Karl Marx. According to Marx, laborers in a capitalist system receive a wage that is barely enough to cover the minimum amount of housing, food, clothing, and other commodities needed for survival. The difference between the amount the employers receive for their products and the amount they pay the laborers that produce them is "surplus value." And, according to Marx, this "surplus value," which includes what we would call profit, is a measure of, and consequence of, exploitation of labor by owners of firms.

Marx's views and those of others who look on profits with suspicion and even distaste are rejected by most economists, who feel that profits play a legitimate and very important role in a capitalistic system. In such a system, each consumer, each supplier of inputs, and each firm tries to advance his own interests. Workers try to maximize their earnings, capitalists look for the highest interest returns, landlords try to get the highest rents, and firm owners seek to maximize their profits. At first glance, this looks like a chaotic, dog-eat-dog situation; but, as we have seen, it actually turns out to be an orderly and efficient system—if competition is present.

Profits and losses are mainsprings of this system, for several reasons. First, *they are signals that indicate where resources are needed and where they are too abundant.* When there are economic profits in an industry, this is the signal for resources to flow into it; when economic losses exist in an industry, this is the signal for resources to leave it.

Second, *profits are very important incentives for innovation and for betting on the future.* For an entrepreneur like Joseph Wilson of Xerox, profits are the bait society dangles before him to get him to take the risks involved in marketing a new product, like xerography. If his judgment turns out to be faulty, losses—negative profits—are the penalties society imposes on him.

Third, *profits are society's reward for efficiency.* Firms that use inefficient techniques or produce an inappropriate amount or type of product are penalized by losses. Firms that are particularly alert, efficient, and adaptive receive profits. Further, profits enable firms to embark on new projects. For example, the profits that Xerox earned on xerography are currently being used to support its new ventures into other types of business machines.

The importance of profits in a free enterprise economy is clear enough. However, this does not mean that all profits are socially justified or that the system as a whole cannot be improved. Clearly, monopoly profits may not be socially justified, and a competitive system, despite its advantages, may produce many socially undesirable effects—for example, an undesirable income distribution. Much more will be said on this score in the next chapter.

The Functional Distribution of Income

In this and the previous chapter, we have been concerned with wages, interest, rent, and profit. How is the total income of the nation as a whole divided among these categories? In other words, what proportion of all income goes to employees? What proportion goes for interest? For rent? For profits? In this section, we take up these questions.

Table 28.5 shows the proportion of national income going for (1) wages and salaries, (2) proprietors' income, (3) corporate profits, (4) interest, and (5) rent.[7] It is clear that wages and salaries are by far the largest of these five income categories. In 1975, for example, about ¾ of national income went for wages and salaries (including employer contributions to Social Security and pensions). Moreover, this is an understatement of the share of employee compensation in national income, because part of proprietors' income is really wages. As we pointed out in an earlier section, a portion of what the proprietor of the corner drugstore or the local shoestore makes is compensation for his labor, not profit as defined by the economist.

The figures in Table 28.5 indicate a marked reduction over time in the proportion of national income going to proprietors, and a marked increase over time in the proportion going for

[7] The concept of rent on which these figures are based is different from the one presented in this chapter, but this does not affect the conclusions presented below.

Table 28.5
Percentage Shares of National Income, 1900–75

Period	Wages and salaries	Proprietors' income	Corporate profits	Interest	Rent	Total
			(percent)			
1900–09	55	24	7	5	9	100
1910–19	54	24	9	5	8	100
1920–29	60	18	8	6	8	100
1930–39	67	15	4	9	5	100
1939–48	65	17	12	3	3	100
1949–58	67	14	13	3	3	100
1963–70	70	12	11	4	3	100
1975	76	7	8	7	2	100

Source: I. Kravis, "Income Distribution: Functional Share," *International Encyclopedia of the Social Sciences,* New York: Macmillan, 1968, and *Annual Reports of the Council of Economic Advisers.* These figures may not be entirely comparable over time, but they are sufficiently accurate for present purposes.

wages and salaries. Part of this shift is due to the fact that the corporation has become a more dominant organizational form, with the result that many people who would have been individual proprietors owning their own small businesses 50 years ago now work as employed managers for corporations. Another fact that may help to explain this shift is the long-term shift from agriculture (where labor's share of income is low) to manufacturing and services (where labor's share is higher).

Some economists are impressed by the constancy of the share of national income going to labor. Using definitions that are somewhat different than those underlying Table 28.5, they come up with numbers indicating that labor's share has not varied much over time. Other economists, using somewhat different definitions, conclude that labor's share has varied considerably. But one thing is for sure: there is no evidence that a bigger share of the economic pie is going to capitalists in the form of interest, rent, or profits. Perhaps the figures in Table 28.5 exaggerate the extent to which labor's share has increased, but there is certainly no evidence that it has decreased.

Summary

Interest is a payment for the use of money. Interest rates vary a great deal, depending on the nature of the borrower and the type and riskiness of the loan. The pure interest rate—the interest rate on riskless loans—is, like any price, determined by the interaction of supply and demand. However, because of the influence of the government on both the demand and supply sides of the market, it is clear that the pure interest rate is to a considerable extent a matter of public policy. One very important function of interest rates is to allocate the supply of loanable funds.

Capital is composed of inputs produced by the economic system itself. Our economy uses very roundabout methods of production and devotes a considerable amount of its productive capacity to the production of capital. If more and more capital is produced during a particular period, consumers must cut further and further into their consumption during that period. This process is called saving.

In a capitalist system, each capital good has a market value that can be determined by capitalizing its earnings. Holding constant an asset's annual return, the asset's worth is higher, the lower the rate of return available on other investments. Any piece of capital has a rate of return, which indicates its net productivity. An asset's rate of return is the interest rate earned on the investment in the asset. If firms maximize profits, they must carry out all projects where the rate of return exceeds the interest rate at which they can borrow.

Rent is the return derived by inputs that are fixed in supply. Since the supply of the input is fixed, its price can be lowered without influencing the amount supplied. It is important to know whether a certain payment is a rent because a reduction of the payment will not influence the availability and use of the inputs if the payment is a rent. If it is not a rent, however, a reduction of the payment is likely to change the allocation of resources. Thus, if the government imposes taxes on rents, there will be no effect on the supply of resources to the economy.

Another important type of property income is profits. Available statistics on profits are based on the accountant's concept, not the economist's, with the result that they include the alternative costs of the labor, capital, and land contributed by the owners of the firm. Profits play a very important and legitimate role in a free enterprise system. Two of the important factors responsible for the existence of profits are innovation and uncertainty: profits are the rewards earned by innovators and a payment for risk-bearing. Still another reason for the existence of profits is monopoly power; due to contrived scarcity, profits are made by firms in imperfectly competitive markets.

CONCEPTS FOR REVIEW

Rate of interest	Rate of return	Liquidity preference
Pure rate of interest	Risk	Saving
Primary inputs	Capital budgeting	Land
Capitalization	Rent	Innovator

QUESTIONS FOR DISCUSSION AND REVIEW

1. Suppose that the demand curve for loanable funds is as follows:

Quantity demanded (billions of dollars)	Interest rate (percent)
50	4
40	6
30	8
20	10

Plot the demand curve on a graph. Describe the various kinds of borrowers that are on the demand side of the market for loanable funds.

2. Suppose that the supply curve for loanable funds is as follows:

Quantity supplied (billions of dollars)	Interest rate (percent)
20	4
25	6
30	8
35	10

Plot the supply curve on the same graph you used to answer Question 1. What is the equilibrium rate of interest? If usury laws do not permit interest rates to exceed 6 percent, what do you think will happen in this market?

3. Assume that you inherit $1,000, which will be paid to you in two years. If the interest rate is 8 percent, how much is this inheritance worth now? Why?

4. "The supply curve for iron ore is horizontal, so its price is a rent." Comment.

5. "Based on the available data concerning changes over time in labor's share of total income in the United States, it is evident that labor is getting so powerful that it is receiving more and more of the total. This is an important reason for the shortage of capital in the United States." Comment and evaluate.

6. Do you agree with Henry George's view that rents should be taxed away by the government? Why or why not?

7. Describe the social functions of the interest rate. Do you agree with Aristotle that it is improper to charge interest?

8. Suppose that a candidate for president proposes that all profits be taxed away. Would you support his proposal? Why or why not?

9. Suppose that you can get 10 percent per year from alternative investments and that, if you invest in a particular business, you will get $1,000 per year indefinitely. How much is this investment worth to you?

10. If a firm can borrow money at 10 percent per year and will accept only (riskless) investments that yield 12 percent per year or more, is the firm maximizing profit?

29 Income Inequality, Poverty, and Discrimination

Although the United States is one of the richest countries on earth, it is not a land of milk and honey to all its inhabitants. Some Americans are poor—so poor that they suffer from malnutrition—and while poverty may not be a sin, it is no less an inconvenience to the poor. Given the affluence of American society, one is led to ask why poverty exists and whether it cannot be abolished by proper public policies. One purpose of this chapter is to examine these questions.

Poverty does not exist in a social vacuum; for example, it is intimately bound up with the problems of discrimination that have played an important role in American life for many years. Unquestionably, discriminatory barriers have tended to depress the incomes of females, nonwhites, and other minority groups. Besides looking at poverty in the United States, this chapter also discusses some relevant aspects of discrimination.

Inequality of Income

One doesn't have to be a very perceptive social observer to recognize that there are great differences in income levels in the United States. But a person's idea of what the distribution of income looks like depends on the sort of family and community he comes from. A child brought up in Lake Forest, a wealthy suburb of Chicago, is unlikely to be as aware of the incidence of poverty as a child brought up on Chicago's poor South Side. For a preliminary glimpse of the extent of income inequality in the United States, scan Table 29.1, which shows the percentage of all families in the United States that were situated in various income classes in 1974. According to the table, 22 percent of the nation's families received an income of less than $7,000 in 1974. On the other hand, 12 percent of the nation's families received an income of $25,000 or more in 1974.

It may come as a surprise to some that so large a percentage of the nation's families made less than $7,000 and that so few families made more than $25,000. The image of the affluent society projected in the Sunday supplements and on some television programs is strangely out of tune with these facts. Yet, to put these figures in world perspective, it should be recognized that Americans are very rich relative to other peoples. This fact is shown clearly by Table 29.2, which gives for various countries the 1974 level of income per person, which is the total income of each nation divided by its population. The United States is among the leaders in this table.

Nonetheless, recognizing that our poor are better off than the bulk of the population in many other countries, the fact remains that there is substantial inequality of income in this country. Why is this the case? Based on our discussion of labor and property incomes in previous chapters, this question is not hard to answer. One reason is that some people possess greater abilities than others. For example, since Catfish Hunter has extraordinary skill as a baseball player, it is easy to understand why

Table 29.1
Percentage Distribution of Families, by Income, 1974

Money income (dollars)	Percent of all families	Percent of total income received	Percent of families with this and lower incomes	Percent of income received by families with this and lower incomes
Under 2,000	3	[a]	3	[a]
2,000– 3,999	6	1	9	1
4,000– 6,999	13	4	22	5
7,000– 9,999	14	8	36	13
10,000–14,999	24	18	60	31
15,000–24,999	28	33	88	64
25,000 and over	12	36	100	100
Total	100	100		

Source: Department of Commerce.
[a] Less than 0.5 percent.

Table 29.2
Selected Countries Grouped by Approximate Level of Income per Capita, 1974

I. Countries with income per capita exceeding $5,000		
United States	Denmark	Sweden
Canada	Germany	Switzerland
II. Countries with income per capita between $3,000 and $5,000		
Australia	Japan	France
Soviet Union	United Kingdom	Norway
III. Countries with income per capita between $1,000 and $3,000		
Greece	Italy	Argentina
Spain	Israel	Venezuela
IV. Countries and regions with income per capita less than $1,000		
India	Much of the Middle East	Most of Africa
China	Much of Latin America	Most of Asia

he makes a lot of money. Another reason is differences in the amount of education and training people receive. Thus physicians or lawyers must receive a higher income than people in occupations requiring little or no training. (Otherwise it would not pay people to undergo medical or legal training.) Still another reason is that some people own large amounts of property. For example, because of a shrewd choice of ancestry, the Fords, Rockefellers, and Mellons get high incomes from inherited wealth. Still other reasons are that some people have managed to obtain monopoly power, and others have had an extraordinary string of good luck.

A Measure of Income Inequality

To what extent has income inequality in the United States decreased in recent years? Some people say that because of the advent of the "welfare state" the nation is moving rapidly toward greater equality of income. Others say that the rich are getting richer and the poor are getting poorer. Who is right? To answer this question, we need some way to measure the degree of income inequality. The most commonly used technique is the ***Lorenz curve,*** which plots the percentage of people, going from the poorest up, on the horizontal axis, and the percentage of total income they get on the vertical axis.

For example, the Lorenz curve based on the figures in Table 29.1 is shown in Figure 29.1. To see how this diagram was constructed, note that in Table 29.1 families with incomes under $4,000 accounted for 9 percent of all families, but only 1 percent of all income. Thus, plotting 9 percent on the horizontal axis against 1 percent on the vertical axis, we get point *A*. The table also indicated that families with incomes under $7,000 accounted for 22 percent of all families, but only 5 percent of all income. Plotting these figures in the same way, we get point *B*. Connecting up all points like *A* and *B*, we obtain the Lorenz curve in Figure 29.1.

Two extreme cases must be understood to see how the Lorenz curve is used. First, *if incomes were the same for all families* (or whatever kinds of recipients are under consideration), the Lorenz curve would be a straight line connecting the origin of the diagram with its upper righthand corner. That is, it would be *OP* in Figure 29.1. To see this, note that if incomes are distributed equally, the lowest 10 percent of the families receive 10 percent of the total income, the lowest 20 percent of the families receive 20 percent of the total income,

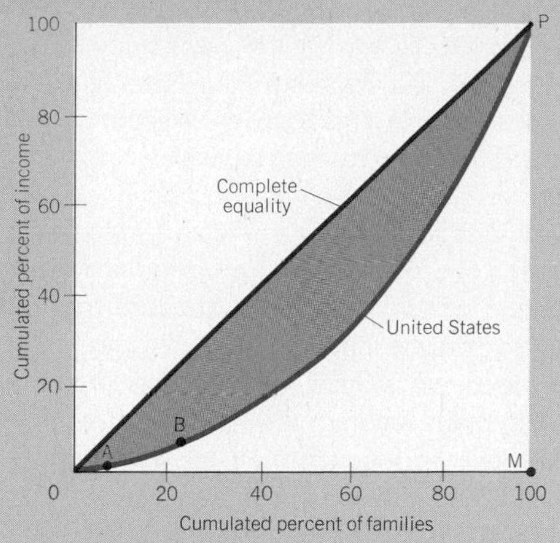

Figure 29.1
Lorenz Curve for Family Income, United States, 1974
OP is the Lorenz curve if income were distributed equally. The shaded area between this hypothetical Lorenz curve and the actual Lorenz curve is a measure of income inequality.

and so forth. Plotting 10 percent on the horizontal axis against 10 percent on the vertical axis, 20 percent on the horizontal axis against 20 percent on the vertical axis, and so forth, one gets a Lorenz curve of *OP*.

Second, *if incomes were distributed completely unequally*—that is, if one person had all of the income and the rest had none—the Lorenz curve would lie along the horizontal axis from *O* to *M* and along the vertical line from *M* to *P*. It would be *OMP* in Figure 29.1. Why? Because the lowest 10 percent of the families have zero percent of the total income, the lowest 20 percent of the families have zero percent of the total income, and so, in fact, do the lowest 99 percent of the families. Plotting 10 percent on the horizontal axis against zero percent on the vertical axis, 20 percent on the horizontal axis against zero percent on the vertical axis, and so on, one gets a Lorenz curve that lies along the horizontal axis from *O* to *M*. But since 100 percent of the families must receive 100 percent of the income, the Lorenz curve must then jump up from *M* to *P*.

These two examples make it clear that *the shaded area in Figure 29.1*—the deviation of the actual Lorenz curve from the Lorenz curve corresponding to complete equality of income—*is a measure of income inequality.* The larger this shaded area, the greater the extent of income inequality. For example, Figure 29.2 shows the Lorenz curve for the income distributions in three countries: *D*, *E*, and *F*. As reflected in the Lorenz curves, income inequality is greater in *F* than in *E*, and greater in *E* than in *D*. Why? Because the area between the actual Lorenz curve and the Lorenz curve corresponding to complete equality is greater in *F* than in *E*, and greater in *E* than in *D*.

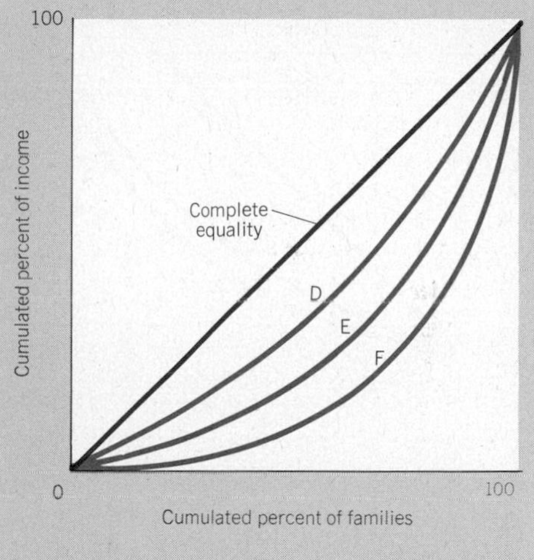

Figure 29.2
Lorenz Curves for Countries *D*, *E*, and *F*
Income inequality is greater in country *F* than in country *E*, and greater in country *E* than in country *D*.

Trends in Income Inequality

Let us now return to the question posed at the beginning of the previous section: To what extent has income inequality in the United States decreased in recent years? Figure 29.3 shows the Lorenz curves for the income distributions in 1929 and 1962. These curves make it clear that there has been a considerable reduction in income inequality. For example, the share of income going to the top 20 percent declined by ⅕ between 1929 and 1962. This change, described by some writers as an "income revolution," did not occur gradually throughout the period. Instead, essentially all the reduction in income inequality occurred before the end of World War II. Since then, there has been little change in the degree of income inequality.

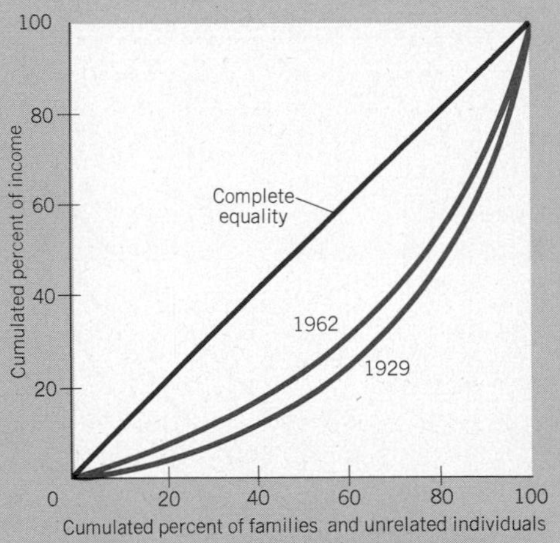

Figure 29.3
Changes over Time in Lorenz Curves for Family Income in the United States
Income inequality in the United States has decreased over time, as indicated by the Lorenz curves for 1929 and 1962.

One of the reasons for the reduction in income inequality between 1929 and the end of World War II was the increased importance of wages and salaries relative to other sources of income: wages and salaries are more equally distributed than income from self-employment and property. Also, many public programs were established to provide income for the poor. (The details of these programs are described below.) In addition, the shift from substantial prewar unemployment to the full employment of World War II narrowed wage differentials among various types of workers.[1] Further, the inequality in the distribution of wealth was reduced during this period.

Finally, it is interesting to compare the extent of income inequality—and the rate of change of income inequality—in the United States with that in other countries. For example, reasonably comparable data are available for the United Kingdom, Germany, Sweden, and the Netherlands. During the 1930s, the United States had a slightly more unequal distribution of pretax income than the United Kingdom, about the same as the Netherlands, and a somewhat more equal distribution than Germany or Sweden. In all these countries, there has been a movement toward equality. However, in the United Kingdom, the Netherlands, and Sweden, this movement seems to have continued during the postwar period. This has not been the case in the United States.

The United States now has a more equal distribution of income than the Netherlands and West Germany, about the same as the United Kingdom, and somewhat less equal than Sweden. Data for the less developed countries, like India or Sri Lanka, are sparse and not very reliable, but they seem to indicate that these countries often have greater income inequality than heavily industrialized countries

[1] See Selma Goldsmith, "Changes in the Size Distribution of Income," *American Economic Review,* May 1957; and Robert Solow, "Income Inequality since the War," in *Postwar Economic Trends in the United States,* ed. Ralph Freeman, Cambridge, Mass.: M.I.T. Press, 1960.

like the United States or the United Kingdom. The contrast between a very rich minority and the very poor masses seems much more striking in many less developed countries than in the United States.

Effects of the Tax Structure on Income Inequality

So far we have looked at the distribution of before-tax income. But we must also consider the effect of the tax system on income inequality. Let's begin with the personal income tax. Figure 29.4 shows that income is more equally distributed after personal income taxes are deducted. However, the effect of the federal income tax, although noteworthy, is not as large as some people believe. For example, the top 20 percent of families received 45.5 percent of the before-tax income and 43.7 percent of the after-tax income—a difference of only about 2 percentage points.[2] The federal income tax is ***progressive,*** since the rich pay a higher proportion of their income for this tax than the poor. In contrast, some other taxes, like sales taxes, are ***regressive:*** the rich pay a lower proportion of their income for these taxes than do the poor.

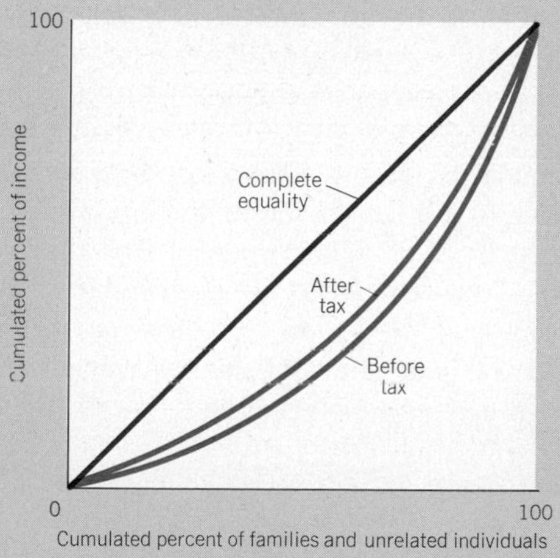

Figure 29.4
Effect of Federal Income Tax on Lorenz Curve, United States
In the United States, inequality of after-tax income is less than inequality of before-tax income.

Needless to say, people who feel that the tax system should promote a redistribution of income from rich to poor favor progressive, not regressive taxes. Besides the personal income tax, other progressive taxes are inheritance or estate taxes. (The federal government levies a gift tax to prevent wealthy people from circumventing the estate tax by giving their money away before death.) State governments also levy inheritance taxes (on persons who inherit money) and estate taxes (on the deceased's estate). All of this is applauded by reformers who oppose accumulation and preservation of inherited wealth. But, as in the case of the personal income tax, the portion of an estate subject to taxes can be reduced through clever use of various loopholes, all quite legal. Thus the estate tax is not as progressive as it looks.

Not all taxes are progressive; examples of regressive taxes are not hard to find. General sales taxes of the sort used by most states and some cities are regressive, since high-income people pay a smaller percentage of their income in sales taxes than do low-income people. The Social Security and payroll tax is also regressive. So is the property tax, according to estimates by Richard Musgrave of Harvard University. In the mid-1950s, he estimated that this tax took about 5 percent of incomes under \$2,000, but about 3½ percent of incomes over \$10,000. It is difficult to tell whether the corporation income tax is progressive or re-

[2] See Edward Budd, *Inequality and Poverty,* New York: Norton, 1967, pp. xiii and xiv.

gressive. At first glance, it seems progressive because the owners of corporations—the stockholders—tend to be wealthy people; and to the extent that the corporate income tax is paid from earnings that might otherwise be paid to the stockholders, one might conclude that it is progressive. But this ignores the possibility that the corporation may pass the tax on to the consumer by charging a higher price; in this case the tax may not be progressive.

Who Pays the Taxes—and Receives the Services?

To get a better picture of the extent to which the government—in terms of both the money it spends and the taxes it levies—takes from the rich and gives to the poor, studies have been carried out to determine how much people in various income brackets pay in taxes and receive in services. The results of one important study of this sort are shown in Figure 29.5. They indicate that the percentage of income paid in federal taxes increases gradually from the $5,000 to $20,000 income levels. At the state and local level, taxes as a percent of income go down steadily as income increases. Thus, if we add up federal, state, and local taxes and consider their sum, the entire tax structure is regressive up to an income level of about $10,000.

But this gives only a partial and distorted picture of the effects of government, because it only considers taxes and ignores expenditures. When government expenditures are considered too, it turns out—as shown in Figure 29.5—that people with incomes below about $5,000 receive more in benefits from government expenditures than they pay in taxes. From $5,000 to $10,000, the ***net tax rate*** (taxes minus benefits as a percent of income) rises from about 10 percent to about 25 percent. Beyond $10,000, the net tax rate does not seem to increase greatly as income rises.

These figures are very interesting, but it must be recognized that they are based on a number of rather arbitrary assumptions about how the benefits of government expenditures are allocated between rich and poor. Also, it is difficult to predict the ***incidence*** of some taxes—that is, it is difficult to know who *really* pays them. Of course, the incidence of certain taxes is relatively easy to determine, as we saw in Chapter 6. For example, it is generally accepted that the personal income tax is paid by the person whose income is taxed. But there are other cases—such as the corporation income taxes we just mentioned—where it is difficult to tell how much of the tax burden the firm shifts to the consumer.[3] For these and other reasons, there is considerable controversy over the extent to which the spending and taxing activities of the government really are progressive or regressive.

Figure 29.5
Burden of Taxes, by Income Level, United States
People with income below about $5,000 received more in benefits from government expenditures than they paid in taxes. Above about $10,000, the net tax rate does not seem to increase greatly as income rises.

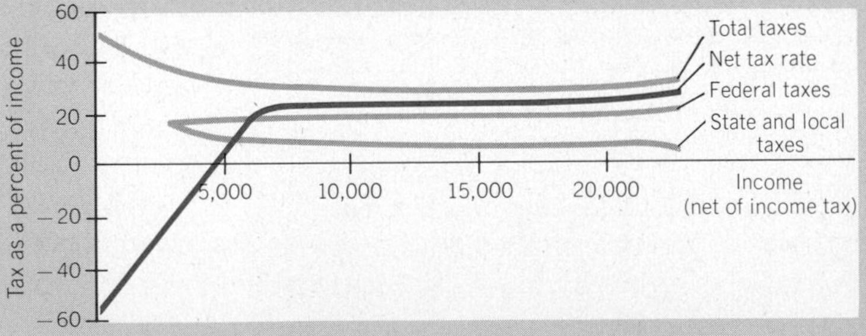

Income Inequality: The Pros and Cons

The Case against Income Inequality

Many distinguished social philosophers have debated the merits and demerits of making the income distribution more equal. We cannot consider all the subtler points, but those who favor greater equality make four main arguments. First, *they say that inequality of income lessens total consumer satisfaction because an extra dollar given to a poor man provides him with more extra satisfaction than the loss of a dollar takes away from a rich man.* For example, according to A. C. Pigou, "It is evident that any transference of income from a relatively rich man to a relatively poor man of similar temperament, since it enables more intense wants to be satisfied at the expense of less intense wants, must increase the aggregate sum of satisfactions."[4]

A problem in this very appealing argument is its assumption that the rich man and the poor man have the same capacities to gain enjoyment from income. Most economists believe that there is no scientific way to make such comparisons, as we shall see in the next chapter. They deny that the satisfaction one person derives from an extra dollar of income can be measured against the satisfaction another person derives from an extra dollar. Although such comparisons may be drawn, they rest on ethical, not scientific, grounds.

Second, *it is argued that income inequality is likely to result in unequal opportunities for young people to gain advanced education and training.* The children of the rich can get an education, while the children of the poor often cannot. The result is that some able and productive people may be denied an education simply because their parents happen to be poor. Clearly, this is a waste of resources.

Third, *it is argued that income inequality is likely to lead to political inequality.* The rich may well influence legislation and political decisions more heavily than the poor, and there is likely to be one kind of justice for the rich and another kind for the poor.

Fourth, in the past few years, the arguments for income equality have been carried a step forward by John Rawls, the Harvard philosopher. He says that, *if people were framing a constitution for society without knowing what their class position would be, they would opt for equality.* And he argues that "all social values . . . are to be distributed equally unless an unequal distribution . . . is to everyone's advantage"—that is, unless an unequal distribution is to the advantage of society's least privileged group. Although Rawls' book, *A Theory of Justice,* has had considerable impact, many economists have pointed out that his prescription for society might not appeal to people who were willing to take risks. For example, suppose that you were framing a social constitution and that you could establish a society that guaranteed every family $15,000 a year (no more, no less) or one where 99 percent of all families would receive $20,000 and 1 percent would receive $12,000. You might choose the latter kind of society because, although there is a small chance that you would do worse than in the egalitarian case, the chance of doing better seems worth this risk.

---

[3] To see how the burden of a tax can be shifted, recall our discussion in Chapter 6 of the effects of an *excise* tax—a tax imposed on each unit sold of a particular product. The federal government imposes excise taxes on liquor and tobacco, among many other products. The immediate effect of these taxes is to raise the price of the commodity since the supply function will be shifted upward and to the left. If demand is price inelastic, most of the burden of the tax is shifted to the consumer. Under these circumstances, firms sell almost as many units of the product as before the tax was imposed, despite the higher price induced by the tax. On the other hand, if supply is relatively inelastic, the burden is borne mainly by the producer. Usually, the aim of excise taxes is to put the burden on consumers. For example, in the case of liquor and tobacco there clearly is a feeling that drinking and smoking smack of sin, and sinners should pay, in this world and the next. For a discussion of excise taxes, see Joseph Pechman, *Federal Tax Policy,* rev. ed., New York: Norton, 1970.

[4] A C. Pigou, *Economics of Welfare,* 4th ed., London: Macmillan, 1948, p. 89.

How the Rich Have Avoided Estate Taxes

Federal Estate Tax, 1975

Taxable estate[a] (dollars)	Federal estate tax[b] (dollars)
20,000	1,600
40,000	4,800
60,000	9,500
100,000	20,700
250,000	65,700
500,000	145,700
1,000,000	325,700
4,000,000	1,838,200
8,000,000	4,568,200
10,000,000	6,088,200

[a] This excludes the first $60,000 of assets.
[b] Besides federal estate taxes, there are also state estate and inheritance taxes.

The accompanying table suggests that the United States has had a stiff estate tax. If, for example, a former captain of industry died with a taxable estate of about $4 million, the table shows that about $1.8 million of his estate went to Uncle Sam for estate taxes. Or if the local physician died with a taxable estate of $500,000, the table shows that $145,700 of his estate went for estate taxes. But appearances can be deceiving. In fact, there are a variety of ways that the rich have cut down on the estate taxes they paid. By availing themselves of these perfectly legal devices, the rich have passed a sizable portion of their wealth on to their heirs.

To begin with, any citizen has been allowed to leave as much as ½ of his or her property to a surviving spouse free of tax. To see what this means, consider the ex-captain of industry. If he had assets worth $8 million, he could leave $4 million to his wife, and pay no estate tax on this amount. Thus his taxable estate was only $4 million (less $60,000, since there was an exemption of this amount), although his total estate was $8 million. In this way, he cut his estate tax from about $4.5 million (the tax on a taxable estate of about $8 million) to about $1.8 million (the tax on a taxable estate of about $4 million). Clearly, our multimillionaire industrialist has been able to salvage a substantial part of his estate with this marital deduction.

Another way to reduce estate taxes has been through the creation of trusts. For example, suppose that a husband with an estate of $120,000 has wanted to provide for a wife and daughter, neither of whom has any property. He has been able to leave $60,000 to his wife and put the remainder of his estate in a trust. The trust has been set up so that the income from the trust has gone to his wife during her lifetime, and the assets in the trust have gone to his daughter when his wife dies. Under this arrangement, there has been no estate tax when the husband dies. And when the wife dies, and leaves $60,000 to the daughter, there has been no estate tax either (because of the $60,000 exemption).

Still another way to avoid estate taxes has been to make gifts. Suppose that the local physician with the $500,000 taxable estate had a wife and six children. Each year, he could give up to $3,000 to each child, without incurring any gift tax.* (With his wife's consent, he could give $6,000.) Also, he and his wife each had a lifetime exemption from gift taxes of $30,000. Consequently, by the end of ten years, he could give his children a total of $420,000. Since this amount would not be part of his estate when he died, no estate tax would be paid on it.

In late 1976, the laws governing federal estate taxes were changed in a variety of ways, and some of these procedures to avoid estate taxes are no longer as effective as before. But there still are plenty of ways to avoid paying estate taxes, as evidenced by a recent statement in *Business Week* that "starting in 1981, estates up to $425,000 can be passed to heirs free of any estate and gift taxes." Of course, this is a highly technical subject, and one where lawyers, not economists, are the best authority. But this brief discussion should help to explain why large estates frequently have managed to pass relatively unscathed from generation to generation—and why the estate tax, though very progressive in appearance, has been less so in practice.

* There is a federal tax on gifts. Without such a tax, it would be easy to avoid estate taxes through gifts.

The Case for Income Inequality

In general, people who favor income inequality also make four arguments. First, *they argue that income inequality is needed to give people an incentive to work and create.* After all, if everyone receives the same income, why bother to increase your production, or to try to invent a new process, or to work overtime? Whatever you do, your income will be the same. This is an important point, though it overlooks the fact that nonmonetary incentives like pride in a job well done can be as important as monetary incentives. One often hears that progressive taxation is dampening incentives for effort and risk taking, but statistical studies do not seem to turn up any clear-cut evidence of the extent of this effect.

Second, *advocates of income inequality claim that it permits greater savings, and thus greater capital formation.* Although this seems reasonable, it is not hard to cite cases where countries with greater inequality of income invest less, not more, than countries with less inequality of income. For example, some Middle Eastern countries with great income inequality have not had relatively high investment rates.

Third, *advocates of income inequality say that the rich have been important patrons of new and high-quality products that benefit the entire society.* They argue that there are social advantages in the existence of certain people with the wherewithal to pioneer in consumption and to support art and culture. In their view, a completely egalitarian society would be a rather dull affair.

Fourth, *advocates of income inequality point out that even if everyone received the same income, the poor would not be helped a great deal, because the wealthy are relatively few.* If the riches of the rich were transferred to the poor, each poor person would get only a little, because there are so many poor and so few rich.

This is an age-old argument that involves

much more than economics. Whether you favor greater or less income inequality depends on your ethical and political beliefs. It is not a matter economics alone can settle. What economists can do is assess the degree of income inequality in a country and suggest ways to alter the gap between the haves and have-nots in accord with the dictates of the people or their leaders. In recent years, economists in and out of government have devoted much effort to designing programs aimed at reducing poverty. To understand these programs, we must discuss what poverty is, and who the poor are.

Our Poverty Problems

What Is Poverty?

Some people are fond of saying that everything is relative. Certainly this is true of poverty. Relative to the Rockefeller family, practically all of us are poor; but relative to the Ríos family (discussed in Chapter 4), practically all of us are rich. Moreover, poverty is certainly subjective. For example, consider the average young executive making $20,000 a year. After a bad day at the office or a particularly expensive family shopping spree, he is likely to tell anyone who will listen that he is as poor as a church mouse.

There is no well-defined income level that can be used in all times and places as a touchstone to define poverty. Poverty is partly a matter of how one person's income stacks up against that of others. What most people in America today regard as stark poverty would have seemed like luxury to many Americans of 200 years ago—and would seem like luxury in parts of Asia and Africa today. Consequently, one must be careful not to define poverty in such a way that it cannot be eliminated—and then try to eliminate it. If, for example, poverty is defined as being in the bottom 10 percent of the income distribution, how can a war against poverty ever be won? Regardless of what measures are taken, there will always be a bottom 10 percent of the income distribution, unless all income inequality is eliminated (which is highly unlikely).

Perhaps the most widely accepted definition of poverty in the United States today is the one developed by the Social Security Administration. It begins by determining the cost of a *minimal* nutritionally sound food plan (given by the Department of Agriculture). Then, since low-income families spend about ⅓ of their incomes on food, this food cost is multiplied by 3 to obtain an income level that is used as a criterion for poverty. Families with less income are regarded as "living below the poverty level."

Based on these computations, an urban family of four needed an income of about $5,400 to make it barely over the Social Security Administration's poverty line in 1975. (Since farm families typically have lower food costs, the estimates for them are somewhat lower.) Although one could quarrel with this figure on various counts, most people would agree that families with income below this level are poor—as indicated by the fact that this income only permits a family to spend about $.45 per person on each meal.[6]

Particular cases of poverty are generally more illuminating and impressive than discussions in the abstract. Consider the following two actual cases in New York City (though the names, of course, are fictitious). First, there is the Smith family. The Smiths—Christopher, 47, and Irene, 35—opened a small restaurant after years of saving. Within a month, Christopher had a severe heart attack and was laid up in the hospital. The Smiths lost the restaurant, and Irene went to work as a nurse's aide to supplement her husband's small disability benefits. After about a year of working and try-

[6] The basic figures come from the Department of Commerce's *Current Population Reports*, which explain in detail the way in which these figures are derived. The method described in the text is crude, but it provides results that are quite close to those of more complicated methods.

ing to take care of her husband and two children—John, 13, and Deborah, 12—Irene collapsed from the strain and had to enter a mental hospital. While she was away, a relative took care of Christopher and the children. After getting out of the hospital, Irene learned that her husband had cancer and required expensive surgery. She became so upset that the doctor called in one of the city's charity agencies, which tried to help this troubled and impoverished family as best it could.

Second, consider the Jones family. Jean Jones, 35, is trying to raise seven children. Her husband, an unskilled laborer, never made much money. He drank a lot, terrified Mrs. Jones and the children with his abuse, and was an unfaithful husband. Four years ago, Mrs. Jones separated from him. She gets along as best she can on public assistance, but is having a difficult time. Two of the children have been arrested for theft; two others are in trouble in school; and one daughter is pregnant out of wedlock. Mrs. Jones feels beaten. In recent months, through the help of neighbors, she has consulted a community service bureau where the social workers have given her help and encouragement. But she obviously needs a great deal of aid if she and her family are to get their heads above water.

Neither of these cases is typical. Since they were cited by the *New York Times* as being among New York's 100 neediest cases, it is fair to say that their plight is probably worse than that of the great bulk of America's poor. But they provide some idea of just how bad things can get; and one has to be headhearted indeed not to feel compassion for people like the Smiths and Mrs. Jones.

The Characteristics of the Poor

Because college students tend to come from relatively well-off families, they often are unaware of the number of families in the United States whose incomes fall below the Social Security Administration's poverty line. According to estimates made by the federal government in 1974, about 12 percent of the population in the United States was below this line. In absolute terms, this means that over 24 million people were poor—usually not as poor as the Smiths or Mrs. Jones, but poor enough to fall below the criterion described above.

Fortunately, the incidence of poverty (measured by this criterion) has been declining in the United States. In 1947, about 30 percent; in 1960, about 20 percent; and in 1974, about 12 percent of the people were poor by this definition. Of course, this is what we would expect. As the average level of income rises, the proportion of the population falling below the poverty line (which is defined by a relatively fixed dollar amount of income) will tend to decrease. Nonetheless, the fact that poverty is being eliminated in the United States does not mean that this process is going on as fast as it should. Many observers feel, as we shall see in subsequent sections, that poverty could and should be eradicated more rapidly.

Naturally, the poor are not confined to any particular demographic group, but some types of families are much more likely than others to be below the poverty line. In particular, *blacks are much more likely to be poor than whites.* In 1974, 28 percent of black heads of families were poor, whereas 7 percent of white heads of families were poor. Also, *families headed by females are much more likely to be poor than families headed by males.* Of people in families headed by females 37 percent were poor, opposed to 6 percent of people in families headed by males. In addition, very large families—7 persons and over—are much more likely than others to be poor.

Poverty strikes a particularly hard blow at children. Even the most hardhearted citizens are prone to agree that the young should be shielded from the crippling impact of dire poverty. According to a government survey carried out in 1975, *over 8 million children under*

16 in the United States were being raised in families below the poverty line. This is a very striking fact indeed.

To a considerable extent, the reasons why families are poor lie beyond the control of the families themselves. About ⅓ of the poor adults have suffered a disability of some sort, or the premature death of the family breadwinner, or family dissolution. Some have had to face a smaller demand for their occupation (because of technological or other change) or the decline of their industry or geographical area. Some have simply lived "too long"—their savings have given out before their minds and bodies did. Another instrumental factor in making some families poor is discrimination of various kinds. The most obvious type is racial, but others exist as well: discrimination based on sex, religion, age, residence, education, and seniority. In addition, of course, some people are poor because they have very limited ability or little or no motivation. These factors should not be overlooked.

There are important barriers which tend to separate the poor from the rest of society. As the University of Wisconsin's Robert Lampman points out,

> Barriers, once established, tend to be reinforced from the poverty side by the alienated themselves. The poor tend to be cut off from not only opportunity but even from information about opportunity. A poverty subculture develops which sustains attitudes and values that are hostile to escape from poverty. These barriers combine to make events nonrandom: e.g., unemployment is slanted away from those inside the feudalistic walls of collective bargaining, disability more commonly occurs in jobs reserved for those outside the barriers, the subculture of poverty invites or is prone to self-realizing forecasts of disaster.[7]

Most of the heads of poor families do not have jobs. For example, in 1966, about 40 percent did not work at all, and another 27 percent worked only part of the year. However, it is worth noting that almost ⅓ of the heads of poor families worked all year round, but simply could not make enough to get above the poverty line. Judging from the available evidence, poverty tends to be self-perpetuating. Families tend to be poor year after year, and their children tend to be poor. Because the families are poor, the children are poorly educated, poorly fed, and poorly cared for, and poverty is transmitted from one generation to the next. It is a vicious cycle.

[7] Robert Lampman, "Approaches to the Reduction of Poverty," *American Economic Review,* May 1965.

Social Insurance

Old-Age Insurance

Until about 40 years ago, the federal government played little or no role in helping the poor. Private charity was available in limited amounts, and the state and local governments provided some help, but the general attitude was "sink or swim." Self-reliance and self-support were the watchwords. The Great Depression of the 1930s, which changed so many attitudes, also made a marked change in this area. In 1935, with the passage of the Social Security Act, the federal government established a social insurance system providing compulsory old-age insurance for both workers and self-employed people, as well as unemployment insurance. By 1975, about 32 million Americans were receiving over $67 billion in benefits from the resulting system of old-age and survivors' insurance.

Every wage earner covered under the Social Security Act pays a tax, which in 1975 amounted to 5.85 percent of the first $14,100 of his or her annual earnings. The employer also pays a tax, which is equal to that paid by the employee. Table 29.3 indicates how much at present one can expect to receive each month in ***old-age insurance*** benefits. As you can see, the size of the benefits depends on

Table 29.3
Monthly Social Security Benefits, 1975[a]

Average annual earnings (after 1950)(dollars)	Retired worker 65 years old	Retired worker 62 years old	Wife 65 years old	Wife 62 years old
	(dollars)			
3,000	210	168	105	79
5,000	286	229	143	93
8,000	402	322	201	151

Source: World Almanac.
[a]These figures show the maximum benefits payable, if a person has achieved the indicated age at retirement.

one's average yearly earnings after 1950. Also, the size of the benefits depends on the number of years one has worked. (In the table, it is assumed that the wage earner has worked—and paid Social Security taxes—for at least 10 years.) The benefits in the table are a retirement annuity. In other words, they are paid to the wage earner from the date of retirement to the time he or she dies. In addition, when a wage earner dies, Social Security provides payments to his or her spouse, to dependent parents, and to children until they are 18 years of age (21 if they are in school). Further, payments are made to a wage earner (and dependents), if he or she is totally disabled and unable to work.

There are a number of controversial aspects of the Social Security program. First, *if you work past the retirement age of 65, you can be penalized considerably.* For every dollar in wages that you earn above and beyond $2,400 per year, you lose 50 cents in Social Security benefits. Thus, since you must pay taxes on your earnings, you get to keep well under ½ of every extra dollar that you earn in wages (over $2,400 per year). But you can earn any amount of interest or dividends or pensions without your Social Security benefits being reduced. To some observers, this is unfair discrimination against older people who want to hold down jobs.

Second, *so long as you have worked 10 years, the amount of benefits you receive is the same, whether you have worked only this length of time or much longer.* Thus people who begin work relatively late in life (often the more prosperous) tend to pay less in Social Security taxes than those who begin work early, but they receive the same annual benefits. Some people are disturbed that the benefits one receives bear so little relationship to the amount one pays in taxes.

Third, *the Social Security tax is regressive,* since those with annual earnings above $14,100 pay a smaller proportion of their income in Social Security taxes than do those with annual earnings below $14,100. For this and other reasons, many observers believe that the system is not as generous to the poor as it should be.

Fourth, *some people are disturbed that the Social Security system is not really an ordinary insurance system at all.* An ordinary insurance program must have assets that are sufficient to finance all of the benefits promised to the people in the program: This is not the case for Social Security. But this does not mean that you won't receive your Social Security benefits. What it does mean is that the Social Security system is a means of transferring income each year from the working young and middle-aged to the retired old people. It will be up to future Congresses to determine what these benefits will be. Perhaps you will receive much more than the amounts in Table 29.3—but then again, perhaps you won't. Only time will tell.

Fifth, *some people are disturbed that Social Security is mandatory.* For example, Milton Friedman is concerned that the government interferes with an individual's freedom to plan for the future by forcing him or her to be a member of the Social Security system. (Workers might be able to obtain larger pensions by investing the money that they contribute to Social Security in investments of their own choosing.) Other observers retort that without a mandatory system, some workers would make inadequate provision for their old age and might become public charges.

Medicare, Unemployment Insurance, and Other Programs

In 1965, the Congress extended the Social Security program to include ***Medicare,*** a compulsory hospitalization insurance plan plus a voluntary insurance plan covering doctors' fees for people over 65. The hospitalization insurance pays for practically all the hospital costs of the first 90 days of each spell of illness, as well as some additional costs. The voluntary plan covers about 80 percent of doctors' fees after the first $50. The cost of the compulsory insurance is included in the taxes described above. This program is also an important factor in preventing and alleviating poverty. The incidence of illness is relatively high among the elderly; and with the rapid rise in medical costs, it has become more and more difficult for them to afford decent care.

Besides instituting old-age, survivors, and medical insurance, the Social Security Act also encouraged the states to set up systems of ***unemployment insurance.*** Such systems now exist in all states, financed by taxes on employers. Once an insured worker is unemployed, he can obtain benefits after a short waiting period, generally a week. In most states, the weekly benefits are about $\frac{1}{2}$ of the worker's pretax wage, up to a maximum ranging (in 1976) from $60 in Indiana to $139 in the District of Columbia. (Since these benefits are not subject to income taxes, these figures understate the value of the benefit to the recipient.) In most states, there is a 26-week ceiling on the duration of benefits, but in 1975, there was a temporary extension of benefits to a maximum duration of 65 weeks. Clearly, unemployment insurance is another important device to keep people from falling below the poverty line.

Finally, in 1974, a new program was created to replace federal grants to the states to help the aged, the blind, and the disabled. This program, called the ***Supplemental Security Income*** program, establishes a uniform national minimum income for people in these categories who are unable to work. (Also, many states supplement these federal payments.) In 1974, over 3 million people received income from this program.

Antipoverty Programs

According to the great English poet and essayist, Samuel Johnson, "A decent provision for the poor is the true test of civilization." There is general agreement that our social insurance programs, although useful in preventing and alleviating poverty, are not an adequate or complete antipoverty program. For one thing, they focus largely on the elderly, which means that they do not aid many poor people. They do not help the working poor; and even for the unemployed, they provide only limited help for a limited period of time.

Consequently, the government has started a number of additional programs specifically designed to help the poor, although many of them are aimed more at the symptoms of poverty than at its basic causes. For example, there are programs that provide goods and services to the poor. Perhaps the most important of these are the ***food programs,*** which distribute food to needy families. (Before 1973, this food generally came from surpluses due to the farm programs described in Chapter 5.) The federal government gives stamps that can be used to buy food to local agencies, which sell them (at less than the equivalent of market prices) or give them to low-income families. In 1975, over 17 million people were participating in the food-stamp program, and the cost to the federal government exceeded $4 billion. On the whole, this program reached people that were truly needy, but critics pointed out that some recipients, like college students from well-off families, qualified for the program and received this subsidy. In 1975, President Ford proposed a law to curtail the provision of benefits to higher income families.

More important in quantitative terms than programs that give particular commodities to the poor are programs that provide them with cash. These are what people generally have in mind when they refer to welfare. There are advantages, of course, to cash payments. They allow a family to adapt its purchases to its own needs and circumstances. There are obvious disadvantages too, since the money may be spent on liquor and marijuana rather than on food and milk. The most important single program of cash payments gives ***aid to families with dependent children.*** In 1975, this program alone paid out almost $9 billion to over 11 million beneficiaries.

To qualify for this program, a family must contain dependent children who are without the support of a parent (usually the father) through death, disability, or absence (and in some states, through unemployment as well). The amount paid to a family under this program varies from state to state, since each state administers its own program and sets its own schedule of payments—as well as contributes part of the cost of the program, with the federal government providing the balance. In 1972, the average payment was about $3,000 for a family of four, but it was higher in states like New York and Massachusetts and lower in states like Mississippi and Alabama. To determine eligibility, the family's affairs are examined; and while receiving aid the family may be under the surveillance of a social worker who supervises its housekeeping and child care.

Many additional programs are aimed at alleviating poverty. For example, our vast investment in public education is certainly a very important weapon in any war on poverty. Beyond this, a number of new antipoverty programs were started in the 1960s and 1970s. For example, the *Manpower Development and Training Act* has provided federal subsidies for the training of unemployed workers; the *Work Incentives Program* has provided training and employment for people on welfare; and the *Job Opportunities in the Business Sector* program has granted subsidies to firms that give on-the-job training to the poor. Manpower programs of this sort have included millions of Americans in the 1970s.

The Negative Income Tax

There is widespread dissatisfaction with current antipoverty—or welfare—programs. The cost of these programs has risen alarmingly; the programs themselves are judged by many experts to be inefficient; and, in some people's view, the welfare recipients are subjected to unnecessary meddling and spying. Moreover, there is little incentive for many people to get off welfare. Both Republicans and Democrats seem to agree that current welfare programs need improvement. What changes might be made? One suggestion that has received serious consideration is the negative income tax, an idea proposed by the University of Chicago's Milton Friedman (an adviser to presidential candidate Barry Goldwater in 1964 and to President Nixon) and Yale's James Tobin (an adviser to President Kennedy).

A ***negative income tax*** would work as follows: just as families with reasonably high incomes *pay* taxes, families with low incomes would *receive* a payment. In other words, the

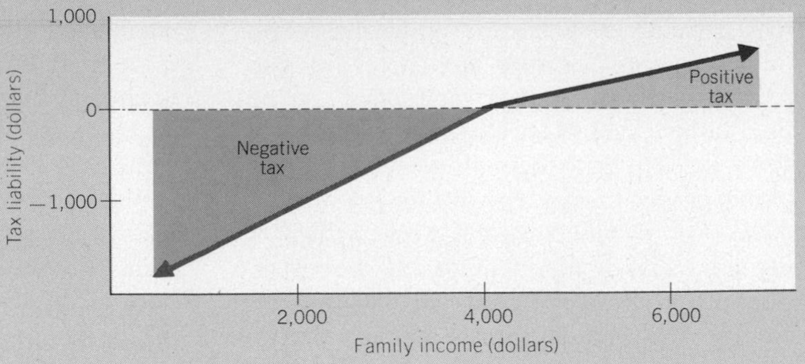

Figure 29.6
Example of Negative Income Tax
A family with more than $4,000 in income pays taxes; for example, a family with an income of $6,000 pays $500 in taxes. A family with an income less than $4,000 receives a payment; for example, a family with an income of $1,000 is paid $1,500.

poor would pay a *negative* income tax. Figure 29.6 illustrates how a negative income tax might work; it shows the amount a family of four would pay—or receive—in taxes for incomes at various levels. According to Figure 29.6, $4,000 is the ***break-even income***—the income at which a family of four neither pays nor receives income taxes. Above $4,000, a family pays taxes; for example, a family with an income of $6,000 pays $500 in taxes. Below $4,000 a family receives a payment; for example, a family with an income of $1,000 is paid $1,500.

There are several advantages of a negative income tax. First, it would give people on welfare more incentive to work. As indicated in Figure 29.6, for every extra dollar it earns, the family receives only $.50 less from the government under this kind of negative income tax. Thus the family gets to keep half of every extra dollar (up to $4,000) it earns, which is a larger portion of this extra dollar than under the present system. Second, there would be no "means tests" and no regulations that cut off welfare payments if the husband remains with his family. In the past, the welfare system has given families an incentive to break up, and encroached on the dignity of poor people. Third, it might cost less to administer the negative income tax than the present system, and differences among states in benefits might be reduced.

Despite these advantages, many citizens remain skeptical about the negative income tax. For one thing, they are antagonistic to the idea of giving people an income without requiring any work in return. They also are unwilling to transfer large amounts from rich to poor. The amount would depend, of course, on how high the break-even income was set and on the negative tax rates. In the late 1960s, it was estimated that a negative income tax based on the sort of plan described in Figure 29.6 would have meant that those above the break-even income level would transfer about $25 billion to those below the break-even level. Despite the attractive features of a negative income tax, a transfer of this magnitude has proved unacceptable in many quarters.[8]

The Problems of Discrimination

Racial Discrimination

Poverty, discrimination, and race are closely intertwined. Despite recent improvements, the sad fact is that racial discrimination occurs in many walks of life in many areas of the United

[8] For further discussion of the negative income tax, see James Tobin, "On Improving the Economic Status of the Negro" in E. Mansfield, *Economics: Readings, Issues, and Cases,* 2d ed., New York: Norton 1977.

States. Table 29.4 shows certain aspects of the relative position of the white and nonwhite populations in the United States. The average income of nonwhites is only about ⅔ that of whites. About ¼ of the nonwhite population are below the poverty line, compared to only about $1/10$ of the white population. On the average, whites complete about 12 years of schooling, while nonwhites complete only about 11 years. About 19 percent of whites who are 25 to 34 years old are college graduates, compared to only about 8 percent of nonwhites in the same age range.

There is considerable agreement that at least part of these economic differences is the result of discrimination. Nonwhites are often prevented from reaching certain occupational or managerial levels. For example, it is rare to find a black in the higher reaches of management in a major corporation. To a considerable extent, of course, they are cut off from job opportunities at this level by lack of education.

Table 29.4
Economic Characteristics of Whites and Nonwhites, United States, 1973

	White	Nonwhite
Median income (dollars)	12,600	7,600
Percent of persons in poverty	10	27
Percent unemployed (men)	3	6
Percent unemployed (women)	4	8
Percent unemployed (teenagers)	13	31
Median years of school completed[a]	12	11
Percent of persons 25–34 years old who are college graduates	19	8

Source: Bureau of the Census and Bureau of Labor Statistics.
[a]Men 25 years or older.

But even at much lower levels, they are kept out of certain occupations by union policy (the building trades are a good example); and even when nonwhites do essentially the same kind of work as whites, there is sometimes a tendency to pay nonwhites less.

Some important effects of racial discrimination can be demonstrated by using the theory of wages discussed in Chapter 27. (The general point of this discussion holds true whether discrimination is on racial or other grounds.) The important thing to recognize at the outset is that nonwhite labor is not allowed to compete with white labor. This results in two different labor markets, one for whites and one for nonwhites. As shown in Figure 29.7, the demand curve for nonwhite labor is quite different from the demand curve for white labor, reflecting the fact that nonwhites are not allowed to enter many of the more productive occupations. Because of the difference in the demand (and supply) curves, the equilibrium wage for nonwhites (P_B) is lower than for whites (P_w).

How does this equilibrium differ from a situation of no discrimination? If nonwhites and whites competed in the same labor market, the total demand for labor—regardless of color—would be D_TD_T', the total supply of labor—regardless of color—would be S_TS_T', and the wage for all labor—regardless of color—would be P_T. A comparison of P_T with P_B shows that the wage rate of nonwhites would be increased considerably. A comparison of P_T with P_w shows that the wage rates of whites would be decreased slightly. The slight cut in white wages would be much smaller than the considerable increase in nonwhite wages, since the nation's total production (and income) would increase because nonwhites could be put to more productive use.

Thus the effect of discrimination is to exploit nonwhites—by reducing their wages relative to whites—and to lower the nation's total output. Fortunately, there is evidence that racial discrimination is lessening. In part because

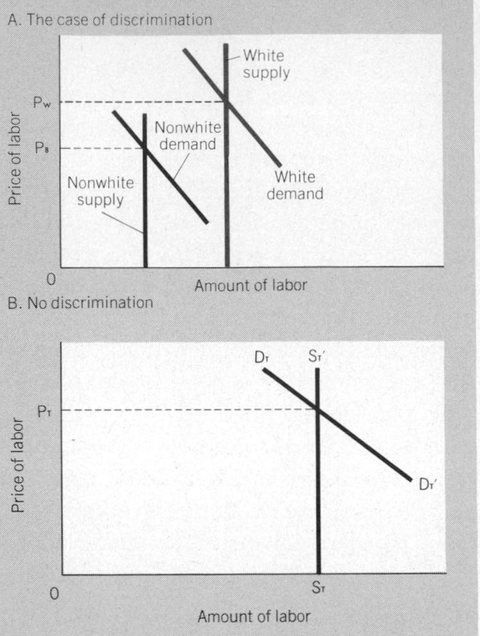

Figure 29.7
Racial Discrimination
Under discrimination, the demand curve for white labor is quite different from that for nonwhite labor, and the supply curve of white labor is quite different from that of nonwhite labor, so that the equilibrium wage for nonwhites (P_B) is lower than for whites (P_W). If there were no discrimination, the wage for all labor, nonwhite or white, would be P_T.

of changing attitudes among whites, the growing restiveness of the nonwhites, and the coming of age of new leadership, the old patterns of segregation and discrimination are breaking down. For example, blacks are now being recruited actively by many prestigious colleges, and they are being hired and promoted to responsible positions in firms where formerly they remained at a relatively menial level. The ratio of nonwhite to white average income rose from about 50 percent in the 1950s to about 60 percent in the 1970s. Progress is slow, but it unquestionably exists.

What opportunities exist for nonwhites to become entrepreneurs, to start and develop their own firms? Because of lack of funds and education, relatively few blacks own the stores and shops in the black ghettos. The white storeowners are often regarded as exploiters by the blacks, and it is sometimes suggested that the blacks displace the whites as owners of these stores and businesses. However, many influential and well-informed observers, both black and white, feel that the potential gains from such a policy are not very great. The stores and businesses that are involved are currently not very profitable, and it is doubtful that they could be made much more so by new and relatively inexperienced ownership. Also, it is argued that any such movement toward black separation will work to the disadvantage of blacks as well as whites.

Nonetheless, steps could be taken to encourage nonwhite enterprise. Perhaps the most important is to help nonwhites develop basic business skills. In addition, of course, the government could insure that promising nonwhite businesses have adequate access to capital. Measures of this sort have been suggested by government officials, but thus far only limited progress seems to have been made.

Discrimination against Women

Needless to say, discrimination is not limited to nonwhites—blacks, Puerto Ricans, Mexican-Americans, and American Indians. There is also some discrimination against older workers. Even more widespread is discrimination against women. Figure 29.8 shows that, holding age and education constant, women earn much less than men. To some extent, this difference in earnings arises because women work shorter hours and often have less experience in their jobs than men. But even after adjusting for factors such as education, work experience

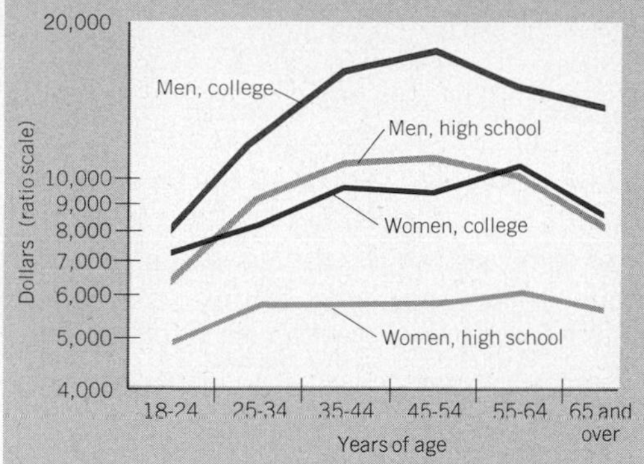

Figure 29.8
Annual Income, by Age, for Male and Female High School and College Graduates
At the same age and with the same level of education, women tend to be paid appreciably less than men.

during the year, and lifetime work experience, there remains a differential of about 20 percent between the earnings of men and women. To a considerable extent, this differential is probably the result of discrimination, the nature of which is well described by the following passage from the *1973 Annual Report of the Council of Economic Advisers:*

> There is clearly prejudice against women engaging in particular activities. Some patients reject women doctors, some clients reject women lawyers, some customers reject automobile saleswomen, and some workers reject women bosses. Employers also may have formulated discriminatory attitudes about women, exaggerating the risk of job instability or client acceptance and therefore excluding women from on-the-job training which would advance their careers. In fact, even if employers do estimate correctly the average job turnover of women, women who are strongly committed to their jobs may suffer from "statistical discrimination" by being treated as though their own behavior resembled the average. The extent to which this type of discrimination occurs depends on how costly it is for employers to distinguish women who will have a strong job commitment from those who will not. Finally, because some occupations restrict the number of newcomers they take in and because women move in and out of the labor force more often, more women than men tend to fall into the newcomer category and to be thus excluded. For example, restrictive entry policies may have kept women out of the skilled crafts.
>
> On the other hand, some component of the earnings differential and of the occupation differential stems from differences in role orientation which start with differences in education and continue through marriage, where women generally are expected to assume primary responsibility for the home and subordinate their own outside work to their household responsibilities. It is not now possible to distinguish in a quantitative way between the discrimination which bars women from jobs solely because of their sex, and the role differentiation whereby women, either through choice or necessity, restrict their careers because of the demands of their homes. Some may label the latter as a pervasive societal discrimination which starts in the cradle; nonetheless, it is useful to draw the distinction.[9]

In various ways, the government has set out to discourage discrimination against women. For example, the Equal Pay Act of 1963 requires employers to pay men and women equally for the same work, and Title VII of the Civil Rights Act of 1964 bars discrimination in hiring, firing, and other aspects of employment. In addition, a number of women have been appointed to high-ranking government jobs, including economists Marina Whitman of the University of Pittsburgh, who has served as a member of the President's Council of Economic Advisers, and Alice Rivlin, who has headed the Congressional Budget Office. An Advisory Committee on the Economic Role of Women has also been organized by the president. All these measures undoubtedly will have a beneficial effect, but it must be recognized that eliminating discrimination of this kind

[9] *The Economic Report of the President,* 1973, pp. 106–7.

will require basic changes in the attitudes of both males and females. The problem of discrimination against women is likely to be with us for a long time.[10]

Summary

Lorenz curves are used to measure the extent of income inequality. They make it clear that there has been a considerable reduction in income inequality in the United States since the late 1920s. Practically all this reduction occurred before the end of World War II. Many factors are responsible for existing income differentials. Some people are abler, better educated, or luckier than others. Some people have much more property, or more monopoly power, than others.

Critics of income inequality argue that it lessens total consumer satisfaction because an extra dollar given to a poor man provides him with more extra satisfaction than the loss of a dollar takes away from a rich man. Also, they argue that income inequality leads to social and political inequality. Defenders of income inequality point out that it is scientifically impossible to make interpersonal comparisons of utility, and argue that income inequality is needed to provide incentives for people to work and create, and that it permits greater capital formation.

There is no well-defined income level that can be used in all times and all places to determine poverty. Perhaps the most widely accepted definition of poverty in the United States today is the one developed by the Social Security Administration, according to which about 12 percent of the population in the United States—over 24 million people—fall below the poverty line. The incidence of poverty has been declining, but many observers feel that poverty could and should be eradicated more quickly. Nonwhite families, families headed by a female, and very large families are more likely than others to be poor. To a considerable extent, the reasons for their poverty lie beyond the control of the poor people. About 1/3 of poor adults have suffered a disability of some sort, or the premature death of the family breadwinner, or family dissolution. Most heads of poor families do not have jobs.

Because private charity is inadequate, the nation has authorized its government to carry out various public programs to aid the poor. There are programs to provide them with goods and services—for example, food-stamp programs. Other programs, like aid to families with dependent children, give them cash. There is widespread dissatisfaction with existing antipoverty—or welfare—programs. They are judged to be inefficient; their costs are increasing at an alarming rate; and they provide little incentive for people to get off welfare. One suggestion to remedy these problems is a negative income tax. Although this scheme has attractive features, in most of the forms put forth it involves a transfer of income that may be beyond the present realm of political feasibility.

Despite recent improvements, the sad fact is that racial discrimination occurs in many walks of life in many areas of the United States. Nonwhites often are cut off from educational and job opportunities; and even when nonwhites do essentially the same kind of work as whites, there is sometimes a tendency to pay them less. The effects of discrimination are to exploit nonwhites by reducing their wages relative to whites and to lower the nation's total output. There is also much discrimination against women, making them less likely than men to enter the better paying occupations. Even after adjusting for factors such as education and work experience, women earn about 20 percent less than men.

[10] See Barbara Bergmann, "The Economics of Women's Liberation," and Marilyn Power Goldberg, "The Economic Exploitation of Women," in E. Mansfield, *Economics: Readings, Issues, and Cases.*

CONCEPTS FOR REVIEW

Poverty
Negative income tax
Welfare
Aid to dependent children
Discrimination
Lorenz curve
Progressive tax
Regressive tax
Net tax rate
Medicare
Social Security
Supplemental Security Income

QUESTIONS FOR DISCUSSION AND REVIEW

1. "Since there cannot be two different prices for a homogeneous input, the existence of discrimination can be expected to disappear over time due to market forces." Comment and evaluate.

2. "The poor are responsible for their own poverty, and those that are worthy can pull themselves up by their bootstraps." Comment and evaluate.

3. Suppose that the following data pertain to the income distribution in the nation of Upper Usher in 1976:

Income (dollars)	Percent of families with indicated income
2,000	40
4,000	30
6,000	20
10,000	10

Plot the Lorenz curve for this nation in 1976.

4. In 1977, suppose that the income distribution in Upper Usher is as follows:

Income (dollars)	Percent of families with indicated income
2,000	20
4,000	40
6,000	35
10,000	5

Plot the 1977 Lorenz curve, and compare it with the 1976 Lorenz curve. Did income inequality in this nation increase or decrease between 1976 and 1977?

5. "The Social Security system is actuarially unsound. The amounts currently collected in Social Security taxes do not equal the amounts currently paid out in benefits. We cannot keep this up!" Comment and evaluate.

6. According to some economists, Social Security should be voluntary, not mandatory. Present the arguments on each side of this issue in as much detail as you can.

7. According to James Tobin, "The defects of present categorical assistance programs could be . . . greatly reduced by adopting a system of basic income allowances integrated with and administered in conjunction with the federal income tax [in other words, a negative income tax]." Do you agree? Why or why not?

8. According to Marilyn Power Goldberg, capitalism "is inherently exploitative" of women, and "women cannot successfully defeat their exploitation within the context of the present economic system." Do you agree? Why or why not?

30 General Equilibrium and Welfare Economics

A number of years back, a cigarette ad proclaimed that "Kent gets it all together." Without judging the validity of this claim, we can say with considerable justification that the study of general equilibrium and welfare economics "gets together" much of what we have already discussed concerning consumers, firms, inputs, and markets. It shows how various markets for products and inputs interact. Rather than focusing on a single market, industry, firm, or consumer, it looks at the economic system as a whole. It also examines the nature of the policy recommendations economists can make. It goes beyond mere analysis and description of the workings of the economic system to indicate that certain ways of allocating society's resources are better than others. For many economists, these conclusions concerning the optimal allocation of resources are much of the real "pay dirt" from economic analysis.

General Equilibrium Analysis

Partial Equilibrium versus General Equilibrium Analysis

In previous chapters, we looked in detail at the behavior of individual decision-making units and the workings of individual markets. We looked at consumers, at firms, and at various types of product markets and input markets. We almost always viewed each single market in isolation. According to the models we have used, the price and quantity in each such market are determined by supply and demand curves, with these curves drawn on the assumption that other prices are given. Each market is regarded as independent and self-contained for all practical purposes. In particular, it is assumed that *changes in price in the market under consideration do not have serious repercussions on the prices in other markets.* This is ***partial equilibrium analysis.***

General equilibrium analysis recognizes that *changes in price may affect other prices, and that the changes in other prices may have an impact on the market under consideration.* No market can adjust to a change in conditions without causing *some* change in other markets, and in some cases this change may be substantial. For example, suppose that an upward shift occurs in the demand for barley. In previous chapters, it was generally assumed that when the price and output of barley changed in response to this change in conditions, the prices of other products would remain fixed. However, the market for barley is not sealed off from the markets for rye, corn, wheat, and other foodstuffs. (For that matter, it is not completely sealed off from the markets for nonfood products like sewing machines and autos.) Thus the market for barley cannot adjust without disturbing the equilibrium of other markets *and having these disturbances feed back on itself.*

Both partial and general equilibrium analysis are very useful, each in its own way. Partial equilibrium analysis is perfectly adequate when a change in conditions in one market has little repercussion on prices in other markets. For example, in studying the effects of a proposed excise tax on the production of a certain commodity, we often can assume that prices of other commodities are fixed and remain close to the truth. However, if a change in conditions in one market has important repercussions on other prices, a general equilibrium analysis may be required.

Suppose that the tastes of consumers shift toward barley products and away from rye products, causing an upward shift in the demand for barley and a downward shift in the demand for rye. To determine the effects on the prices of the two commodities, the economist must look simultaneously at the market for barley and the market for rye, as well as the relationships between them. To do so, he employs general equilibrium analysis, which shows that the immediate effect is a rise in the price of barley (because of the upward shift in the demand curve for barley) and a drop in the price of rye (because of the downward shift in its demand curve).

This is the response in the market period. What happens in the short run when firms can adjust their output? Assuming that both the barley industry and the rye industry were in long-run equilibrium before the pattern of demand changed, the immediate result of the price rise in the barley industry is to increase barley production. Firms will find it profitable to produce up to the point where marginal cost equals the new, higher price level. Similarly, in the rye industry, the result of the price decrease is to cut production because firms will find it profitable to produce only up to the point where marginal cost equals the new, lower price level. If some of the inputs used in rye production can be adapted to barley production, they may be transferred directly from the rye industry to the barley industry. Otherwise, adjustments occur in various related markets, with the result that the barley industry gains resources while the rye industry loses them.

So much for the short run. In the long run, when firms can enter or leave each industry, they will enter the barley industry, since economic profits are being earned there. The increased demand for inputs will raise input prices and cost curves in barley production, and the price of barley will be depressed by the movement to the right of the supply curve because of the entry of new firms. Eventually, when economic profits are no longer earned, entry will cease. Meanwhile, in the rye industry, firms will leave rye production since economic losses are being incurred there. As they leave, the supply curve shifts to the left, causing the price to rise. The transfer of resources out of rye will stop when losses there no longer occur. (Recall our discussion of similar cases in Chapter 24.)

General equilibrium analysis is concerned with problems like this one, where more than one market is involved. Often, it is necessary to look at a fairly large number of markets simultaneously to do justice to the problem. We have simplified matters considerably by confining our attention to the markets for barley and rye, since in all likelihood the markets for other foodstuffs, as well as various input markets, would also be affected. Cases of this sort often call for the solution of a complex system of equations to estimate the equilibrium price and quantity in each market.

Input-Output Analysis

Input-output analysis, due largely to Nobel laureate Wassily Leontief, puts general equilibrium analysis in a form that is operationally useful to governments and firms faced with a variety of important practical problems. An important feature of input-output analysis is its emphasis on the *interdependence* of the economy. Each industry uses the outputs of other industries as its inputs, and its own output may be used as an input by the same industries whose output it uses. Recognizing this interdependence, input-output analysis attempts to determine the amount each industry must produce so that a specified amount of various final goods will be turned out by the economy. This type of analysis has been used to help predict production requirements to meet estimated demands. For example, economic planners have applied it to military mobilization and to problems of economic development in less developed countries.

To put general equilibrium analysis in a usable form, input-output analysis makes a number of simplifying assumptions. Thus it generally uses as variables the *total* quantity of a particular good demanded or supplied, rather than the quantity demanded by a particular consumer or supplied by a particular firm. This reduces enormously the number of variables and equations in the analysis. Also, in the simpler versions of input-output analysis, it is assumed that consumer demand for all commodities is known. Input-output analysis attempts to find out what can be produced, and the amount of each input and intermediate good that must be employed to produce a given output. It views these questions as largely a matter of technology.

Finally, input-output analysis assumes that inputs are used in *fixed proportions* to produce any product and that there are *constant returns to scale.* This is a key assumption of Leontief's input-output system. For example, in the production of steel, Leontief would assume that, for every ton of steel produced, a certain amount of iron ore, a certain amount of coke, a certain amount of fuel and so on would be required. The amount of each input required per unit of output is assumed to be the same, whatever the level of output. For example, if a certain amount of iron ore is required to produce

Table 30.1
Amount of Each Input Used per Dollar of Output (dollars)

Type of input	Type of output: Electric power	Coal	Chemicals
Electric power	.10	.30	.00
Coal	.50	.10	.00
Chemicals	.20	.00	.90
Labor	.20	.60	.10
Total	1.00	1.00	1.00

1 million tons of steel, it is assumed that 10 times that amount is required to produce 10 million tons of steel.[1]

With some basic algebra, the essentials of input-output analysis are quickly grasped. Suppose that the economy consists of only three industries: coal, chemicals, and electric power. Each industry uses the products of the other industries in the proportions shown in Table 30.1. For instance, the second column of Table 30.1 states that every dollar's worth of coal requires \$.30 worth of electric power, \$.10 worth of coal, and \$.60 worth of labor. (Of course one could just as well carry out the analysis with inputs and outputs measured in physical units–man-hours or tons per year–as in money.)

This economy has set consumption targets of \$100 million of electric power, \$50 million of coal, and \$50 million of chemicals. Input-output analysis takes up the question: *How much will have to be produced by each industry in order to meet these targets?* Let's begin with coal. If electric power output is E, chemical output is C, and coal output is X (E, C, and X are measured in millions of dollars), it follows from Table 30.1 that

$$X = .5E + .1X + 50 \qquad (30.1)$$

if the target is met. Why? Because the electric power industry needs an amount of coal equal in value to $.5E$, the coal industry needs an amount equal in value to $.1X$, and an amount equal in value to 50 must be produced for consumption. Thus the total output of coal must be equal to the sum of these three terms, as shown in Equation (30.1).

If we construct similar equations for electric power output and chemical output, we find that

$$E = .1E + .3X + 100 \qquad (30.2)$$
$$C - .2E + .9C + 50 \qquad (30.3)$$

if the targets are to be met. For example, Equation (30.3) must hold because chemical output must equal the amount needed by the electric power industry ($.2E$) plus the amount needed by the chemical industry itself ($.9C$) plus 50 for consumption.

Since Equations (30.1) to (30.3) are three equations in three unknowns, X, E, and C, we can solve for the unknowns, which turn out to be $X = 144$, $E = 159$, and $C = 818$. We have answered our question: *\$144 million of coal, \$159 million of electric power, and \$818 million of chemicals must be produced to meet the consumption targets.* We can also find out how much labor will be required to meet these targets, since (according to Table 30.1) the total value of labor required equals

$$.2E + .6X + .1C \qquad (30.4)$$

Substituting the 144, 159, and 818 for X, E, and C, respectively, in (30.4), we find that \$206 million of labor is required. If this does not exceed the available labor supply, the solution is

[1] In previous chapters, we said that the proportion in which inputs are combined can generally be altered. This, of course, is a direct contradiction of the assumption of fixed proportions in input-output analysis. But it often takes a fair amount of time for changes to be made and they are often gradual, with the result that Leontief's assumption of fixed proportions may work reasonably well in the short run.

feasible; otherwise the targets must be scaled downward.

This simple example illustrates the fundamentals of input-output analysis. It also suggests why the assumption that inputs are used in fixed proportions is so convenient. Without this assumption, the input-output table in Table 30.1 would not hold for each output level of the industries. Instead, the numbers in the table would vary depending on how much of each commodity was produced. The added complexity that would arise (without this assumption) is obvious. Even with this assumption, the computational and estimation problems involved in solving large input-output models can be substantial. Government agencies, such as the Departments of Commerce and Labor, have constructed a model of the U.S. economy involving several hundred industries. Usually, however, far fewer industries are included in such models.

Applicability of Input-Output Analysis

Whether input-output analysis can be applied fruitfully in a particular situation depends in part on whether the ***production coefficients***—the numbers in Table 30.1—remain constant. (See footnote 1.) There are at least two important factors that might cause changes over time in such coefficients. First, changes in technology may change the relative quantities of inputs used. For example, the amount of coal required to produce many goods decreased considerably in the years since World War II. Second, changes in the relative prices of inputs may result in changes in production coefficients as cheaper inputs are substituted for more expensive ones.

Since World War II, much has been done to implement and extend input-output analysis. Basic research has been conducted by academic economists interested in the quantitative significance of various types of economic interdependence. Applied research has been devoted to formulating techniques that would be useful in decision making in government and business. For example, in 1973-74, Anne Carter of Brandeis University and Clopper Almon of the University of Maryland used input-output analysis to estimate the effect of the Arab oil embargo on the level of unemployment in various industries. Other countries have used input-output analysis to determine the relationship of imports and exports to domestic production, as well as to analyze various problems of economic development. Also, business firms have used input-output analysis to forecast their sales.[2]

To illustrate how input-output analysis can help solve important problems of public policy, consider the economic effects of disarmament. If the United States were to reduce its military budget by $1 billion, what would be the effect on sales and employment in various industries? Clearly, one can determine from the composition of the military budget the effect of such a reduction on the sales and employment of each industry. Moreover, one can determine the net effect on each industry if this reduction in the military budget is counterbalanced by a $1 billion increase in civilian demand. Based on input-output analysis, Leontief and his associates concluded that, in 1958, an $8 billion reallocation of military purchases to civilian demand would result in an 18 percent reduction in aircraft employment, a 6 percent reduction in radio employment, a 1 percent increase in automobile employment, and a 1 percent increase in textile employment, among other things.

Welfare Economics

The Nature of Welfare Economics

One of the great goals of economics is to determine how best to allocate society's scarce re-

[2] W. Leontief, *Input-Output Economics,* New York: Oxford University Press, 1966; and H. Chenery and P. Clark, *Interindustry Economics,* New York: Wiley, 1959.

sources. Questions concerning the optimal allocation of inputs among industries and the optimal distribution of commodities among consumers are general equilibrium problems, since the optimal usage of any input cannot be determined by looking at the market for this input alone, and the optimal output of any commodity cannot be determined by looking at the market for this commodity alone. On the contrary, the optimal allocation of resources between two products depends on the relative strength of the demands for the products and their relative production costs.

The term ***welfare economics*** covers the branch of economics that studies policy issues concerning the allocation of resources. (Do not confuse welfare economics with the various government "welfare" programs you read about in the previous chapter.) It should be stressed from the start that welfare economics, although useful, is certainly no panacea. By itself, welfare economics can seldom provide a clear-cut solution to issues of public policy. But in combination with other disciplines, it can frequently show useful ways to structure and analyze these issues.

Perhaps the most important limitation of welfare economics stems from the fact that *there is no scientific way to compare the utility level of different individuals.* There is no way to show scientifically that a bottle of Château Haut-Brion will bring you more satisfaction than it will me, or that your backache is worse than mine. This is because there is no scale on which we can measure pleasure or pain so that interpersonal comparisons can be made scientifically. For this reason, the judgment of whether one distribution of income is better than another must be made on ethical, not scientific, grounds. For example, if you receive twice as much income as I do, economists cannot tell us whether this is a better distribution of income than if I receive twice as much income as you do. This is an ethical judgment.

However, most problems of public policy involve changes in the distribution of income. A decision to increase the production of jet aircraft and to reduce the production of railroad locomotives may mean that certain stockholders and workers will gain, while others will lose. Because it is so difficult to tell whether the resulting change in the distribution of income is good or bad, it is correspondingly difficult to conclude whether such a decision is good or bad.

Faced with this problem, economists have adopted a number of approaches, all of which have significant shortcomings. Some economists have simply paid no attention to the effects of proposed policies on the income distribution. Others have taken the existing income distribution as optimal, while still others have asserted that less unequal income distributions are preferable to more unequal ones. Purists have argued that we really cannot be sure a change is for the better unless it hurts no member of society, while others have suggested that we must accept the judgment of Congress (or the public as a whole) on what is an optimal distribution of income.

For now, the major thing to note is that the conditions for an optimal allocation of resources, described in the following section, are incomplete, since they say nothing about the optimal income distribution. Whatever the income distribution you or I may consider best on ethical or some other (nonscientific) grounds, the conditions below must be met if resources are to be allocated optimally. Remember, however, that there may be many allocations of resources that meet these conditions, and the choice of which is best will depend on one's feelings about the optimal income distribution.

Conditions for Optimal Resource Allocation

Fundamentally, there are three necessary conditions for optimal resource allocation. The first pertains to the optimal allocation of commodities among consumers, and states that *the ratio of the marginal utilities of any two goods must be the same for any two consumers who consume both goods.* That is, if the marginal utility of good A is twice that of good B for one consumer, it must also be twice that of good B for any other consumer who consumes both goods. The proof that this condition is necessary to maximize consumer satisfaction is quite simple. We need only note that, if this ratio were unequal for two consumers, both consumers could benefit by trading.

Thus assume that the ratio of the marginal utility of good A to that of good B is 2 for one consumer, but 3 for another consumer. This means that the first consumer regards an additional unit of good A as having the same utility as 2 extra units of good B, whereas the second consumer regards an additional unit of good A as having the same utility as 3 extra units of good B. Then, if the first consumer trades 1 unit of good A for 2.5 units of good B from the second consumer, both are better off. (Why? Because the first consumer receives 2.5 units of good B, which he prefers to 1 unit of good A, and the second consumer receives 1 unit of good A, which he prefers to 2.5 units of good B.)

The second condition, which pertains to the optimal allocation of inputs among producers, states that *the ratio of the marginal products of two inputs must be the same for any pair of producers that use both inputs.* That is, if the marginal product of input 1 is twice that of input 2 in one firm, it must also be twice that of input 2 in any other firm that uses both inputs. If this condition does not hold, total production can be increased merely by reallocating inputs among firms.

To illustrate this, suppose that for the first producer the marginal product of input 1 is twice that of input 2, whereas for the second producer the marginal product of input 1 is three times that of input 2. Then, if the first producer gives 1 unit of input 1 to the second producer in exchange for 2.5 units of input 2, both firms can expand their output. To see this, suppose that the marginal product of input 1 is M_1 for the first producer and M_2 for the second producer. Then the output of the first producer is reduced by M_1 units because of its loss of the unit of input 1, but it is increased by $2.5 \times M_1/2$ units because of its gain of the 2.5 units of input 2, so that on balance its output increases by $M_1/4$ units because of the trade. Similarly, the output of the second producer is increased by M_2 units because it gains the 1 unit of input 1, but it is decreased by $2.5 \times M_2/3$ units because it loses the 2.5 units of input 2, with the consequence that on balance its output increases by $M_2/6$ units because of the trade.

The third condition pertains to the optimal output of a commodity. It states that *any commodity's output level, if it is optimal, must be such that the marginal social benefit from an extra unit of the commodity is equal to its marginal social cost.* If this condition is violated, social welfare can be increased by altering the output level of the commodity. Specifically, if the marginal social benefit from an extra unit of the commodity exceeds its marginal social cost, an increase in the output of the commodity will increase social welfare. (Why? Because the extra social benefit resulting from an extra unit of the commodity outweighs the extra social cost.) And if the marginal social benefit from an extra unit of the commodity is less than marginal social cost, a decrease in the output of the commodity will increase social welfare.

Optimal Resource Allocation: A Case Study

Let's turn now to a case study of how these conditions can be applied to one of our most important commodities—water. If the first condition is to hold, the ratio of the marginal utility of water to that of any other good must be the same for all consumers. To be specific, suppose that the other good is money. Then the ratio of the marginal utility of water to the marginal utility of money must be the same for all consumers. That is, if resources are allocated optimally, *the amount of money a consumer will give up to obtain an extra unit of water must be the same for all consumers.* This follows because the ratio of the marginal utility of good A to the marginal utility of good B equals the number of units of good B that the consumer will give up to get an extra unit of good A.

The common sense underlying this condition has been described well in a study of water resources done at the RAND Corporation:

> Suppose that my neighbor and I are both given rights (ration coupons, perhaps) to certain volumes of water, and we wish to consider whether it might be in our mutual interest to trade those water rights between us for other resources—we might as well say for dollars, which we can think of as a generalized claim on other resources like clam chowders, babysitting services, acres of land, or yachts. . . . Now suppose that the last acre-foot of my periodic entitlement is worth $10 at most to me, but my neighbor would be willing to pay anything up to $50 for the right. . . . Evidently, if I transfer the right to him for any compensation between $10 and $50, we will both be better off in terms of our own preferences. . . . But this is not yet the end. Having given up one acre-foot, I will not be inclined to give up another on such easy terms (and) my neighbor is no longer quite so anxious to buy as he was before, since his most urgent need for one more acre-foot has been satisfied. . . . Suppose he is now willing to pay up to $45 (for another acre-foot), while I am willing to sell for anything over $15. Evidently, we should trade again. Obviously, the stopping point is where the last (or marginal) unit of water is valued equally (in terms of the greatest amount of dollars we would be willing to pay) by the two of us. . . . At this point no more mutually advantageous trades are available—and efficiency has been attained.[3]

[3] J. Hirshleifer, J. Milliman, and J. DeHaven, *Water Supply,* Chicago: University of Chicago Press, 1960, p. 38, reprinted in E. Mansfield, *Microeconomics: Selected Readings,* 2d ed., New York: Norton, 1975.

If people can trade water rights freely—as in this hypothetical case—an efficient allocation of water rights will be achieved. But what if water rights cannot be traded freely, because certain kinds of water uses are given priority over other types of uses, and it is difficult, even impossible, for a low-priority user to purchase water rights from a high-priority user? Clearly, the effect is to prevent water from being allocated so as to maximize consumer satisfaction. Unfortunately, this question is not merely an academic exercise: it focuses attention on a very practical problem. In fact, there is a wide variety of limitations on the free exchange of water rights in the United States. For example, some legal codes grant certain types of users priority over other types of users, and free exchange of water is limited. Experts believe that these limitations are a serious impediment to the optimal allocation of water resources.

Perfect Competition and Welfare Maximization

One of the most fundamental findings of economic theory is that a perfectly competitive economy satisfies the three sets of conditions for welfare maximization set forth in the section before last. An argument for competition can be made in various ways. Some people favor it simply because it prevents the undue concentration of power and the exploitation of consumers. But to the economic theorist, the basic argument for a perfectly competitive economy is that such an economy satisfies these three conditions. In this section we prove that this is indeed a fact.

Condition 1: The ratio of the marginal utilities of any pair of commodities must be the same for all consumers buying both commodities. Recall that under perfect competition consumers choose their purchases so that the marginal utility of a commodity is proportional to its price. Since prices, and thus price ratios, are the same for all buyers under perfect competition, it follows that the ratio of the marginal utilities between any pair of commodities must be the same for all consumers. For example, if every consumer can buy bread at $.25 a loaf and butter at $1 a pound, each one will arrange his purchases so that the ratio of the marginal utility of butter to that of bread is 4. Thus the ratio will be the same for all consumers: 4 for everyone.

To make sure you understand this point, let's consider any two goods, *A* and *B*. Based on our discussion in Chapter 20, we know that each consumer will buy amounts of these goods so that

$$\frac{MU_A}{P_A} = \frac{MU_B}{P_B},$$

where MU_A is the marginal utility of good *A*, MU_B is the marginal utility of good *B*, P_A is the price of good *A*, and P_B is the price of good *B*. Multiplying both sides of this equation by $P_A \div MU_B$, it follows that

$$\frac{MU_A}{MU_B} = \frac{P_A}{P_B},$$

Since $P_A \div P_B$ is the same for all consumers, $MU_A \div MU_B$ must also be the same for all of them, which means this condition is satisfied.

Condition 2: The ratio of the marginal products of any pair of inputs must be the same for all producers using both inputs. We have already seen in an earlier chapter that under perfect competition producers will choose the quantity of each input so that the ratio of the marginal products of any pair of inputs equals the ratio of the prices of the pair of inputs. Since input prices, and thus price ratios, are the same for all producers under perfect competition, it follows that the ratio of the marginal products must be the same for all producers. For example, if every producer can buy labor services at $4 an hour and machine tool services at $8 an hour, each one will arrange the quantity of its inputs so that the ratio of the marginal product of machine tool service to that of labor is 2. Thus the ratio will be the same for all producers: 2 for each.

To make sure you understand this point, let's consider any two inputs, *X* and *Y*. Based on our discussion in Chapter 22, we know that each firm will buy amounts of these inputs so that

$$\frac{MP_X}{P_X} = \frac{MP_Y}{P_Y},$$

where MP_X is the marginal product of input *X*, MP_Y is the marginal product of input *Y*, P_X is the price of input *X*, and P_Y is the price of input *Y*. Multiplying both sides of the equation by $P_X \div MP_Y$, it follows that

$$\frac{MP_X}{MP_Y} = \frac{P_X}{P_Y}.$$

Since $P_X \div P_Y$ is the same for all firms, $MP_X \div MP_Y$ must also be the same for all of them, which means this condition is satisfied.

Condition 3: The marginal social benefit from an extra unit of any commodity must be equal to its marginal social cost. Recall from Chapter 23 that under perfect competition firms will choose their outputs so that price equals marginal cost. If a commodity's price is an accurate measure of the marginal social benefit from producing an extra unit of it, and if its marginal cost is an accurate measure of the marginal social cost of producing an extra unit of it, the fact that price is set equal to marginal cost insures that this condition will be met.

Thus, in summary, *all three conditions for optimal resource allocation are satisfied under perfect competition.* This is one principal reason why many economists are so enamored of perfect competition and so wary of monopoly and other market imperfections. If a formerly competitive economy is restructured so that some industries become monopolies, these conditions for optimal resource allocation are no longer met. As we know from Chapter 24, each monopolist produces less than the perfectly competitive industry that it replaces would have produced. Thus too few resources are devoted to the industries that are monopolized, and too many resources are devoted to the industries that remain perfectly competitive. This is one of the economist's chief charges against monopoly. It wastes resources because it results in overallocation of resources to competitive industries and underallocation of resources to monopolistic industries. The result is that society is less well off. Similarly, oligopoly and monopolistic competition are charged with wasting resources, since the conditions for optimal resource allocation are not met there either.

However, in evaluating this result and judging its relevance, one must be careful to note that it stems from a very simple model that ignores such things as technological change and other dynamic considerations, risk and uncertainty, and external economies and diseconomies. Also, there is the so-called *theory of the second-best,* which states that unless *all* of the conditions for optimal resource allocation are met, it may be a mistake to increase the number of such conditions that are fulfilled. Thus piecemeal attempts to preserve or impose competition may do more harm than good.

Marginal Cost Pricing

The previous section showed that the conditions for optimal resource allocation are satisfied under perfect competition. Economists interested in the functioning of planned, or socialist, economies have pointed out that a price system also could be used to increase social welfare in such economies. According to economists like Abba Lerner[4] of the City University of New York, rational economic organization could be achieved in a socialist economy that is decentralized, as well as under perfect competition. For example, the socialist government might solve the system of equations that is solved automatically in a perfectly competitive economy, and obtain the prices that would prevail under perfect competition. Then the government might publish this price list, together with instructions for consumers to maximize their satisfaction and for producers to maximize profit. (Of course, the wording of the instructions to consumers might be a bit less heavy-handed than "Maximize your satisfaction!")

Under a socialist system of this sort, the government does not have to become involved in the intricate and detailed business of setting production targets for each plant. It need only compute the proper set of prices. In following the rules to maximize "profits," plant managers will choose the proper production levels. Thus decentralized decision making, rather than detailed centralized direction, could be used, thus reducing administrative costs and bureaucratic disadvantages.

The prices the government would publish, like those prevailing in a perfectly competitive economy, would equal marginal cost. Many economists have recommended that government-owned enterprises in basically capitalist economies also adopt ***marginal cost pricing,*** i.e., that they set price equal to marginal cost. Taking the case of a bridge where the marginal cost (the extra cost involved in allowing an additional vehicle to cross) is zero, Harold Hotelling argued in a famous article that the socially optimal price for crossing the bridge is zero, and that its costs should be defrayed by general taxation. If a toll is charged, the conditions for optimal resource use are not met.[5]

Marginal cost pricing has fascinated economists during the 40 years that have elapsed

[4] Abba Lerner, *The Economics of Control,* New York: Macmillan, 1944.

[5] Harold Hotelling, "The General Welfare in Relation to Problems of Taxation and of Railway and Utility Rates," *Econometrica,* 1938.

since Hotelling's article,[6] but there are a number of problems in the application of this idea. One of the most important is that if the firm's average costs decrease with increases in its scale of output (as is frequently the case in public utilities), it follows from the discussion in Chapter 22 that marginal cost must be less than average cost, with the consequence that the firm will not cover its costs if price is set equal to marginal cost.[7] This means that marginal cost pricing must be accompanied by some form of subsidy if the firm is to stay in operation—and the collection of the funds required for the payment of the subsidy may also violate the conditions for optimal resource allocation. This subsidy also means that there is a change in the income distribution favoring users of the firm's output and penalizing nonusers. The difficulties in determining whether such a change is good or bad have already been stressed.

Marginal Cost Pricing: A Case Study

To illustrate the reasoning that underlies marginal cost pricing, consider once more the case of water supplies. We saw earlier that economic efficiency requires that the amount of money a consumer will give up to obtain an extra unit of water must be the same for all consumers. In other words, the price of water must be the same for all consumers. But what determines the level at which this price should be set?

> Suppose that at a certain moment in time [consumers are willing to pay] $30 per unit. Then, if the community as a whole can acquire and transport another unit of water for, say, $20, it would clearly be desirable to do so; in fact, any of the individual customers to whom the unit of water is worth $30 would be happy to pay the $20 cost, and none of the other members of the community would be made worse off thereby. We may say that, on efficiency grounds, additional units should be made available so long as any members of the community are willing to pay the additional or marginal costs incurred. . . . So the . . . rule is to make the price equal to marginal cost and equal for all customers.[8]

Unfortunately, it seems that water pricing practices do not often conform to this rule. For example, some types of water users are commonly charged lower prices than other types of water users, although the marginal cost of the water is the same. According to the study carried out at the RAND Corporation,

> In Los Angeles, for example, there is an exceptionally low rate for irrigation use. Domestic, commercial, and industrial services are not distinguished as such, but they are differentially affected by the promotional volume rates. More serious, because much more common, is the system of block rates, with reductions [in price] for larger quantities used. . . . [This system leads] to wasteful use of water by large users, since small users would value the same marginal unit of water more highly if delivered to them. . . . The customer paying the lower price will on the margin be utilizing water for less valuable purposes than it could serve if transferred to the customer paying the higher price.

External Economies and Diseconomies

Up to this point, we have assumed (implicitly or explicitly) in this chapter that there is no difference between private and social benefits, or between private and social costs. For example, costs to producers have been assumed to be costs to society, and costs to society have been assumed to be costs to producers. Benefits to producers have been assumed to be benefits to society, and benefits to society have

[6] For example, see J. Nelson, *Marginal Cost Pricing in Practice,* Englewood Cliffs, N.J.: Prentice-Hall, 1964.

[7] Recall from Chapter 22 that an increase in output results in a reduction in average cost only when marginal cost is less than average cost. Since the firm's receipts will cover its costs only if price is at least equal to average cost, it follows that, under these circumstances, the firm cannot cover its costs if it sets price equal to marginal cost.

[8] Hirshleifer, Milliman, and DeHaven, *Water Supply,* pp. 40–41.

been assumed to be benefits to producers. In many instances, however, these assumptions do not hold. Instead, producers sometimes confer benefits on other members of the economy but cannot obtain payment for these benefits, and they sometimes act in a way that harms others without having to pay the full costs. In these cases, the pursuit of private gain will not promote the social welfare.

It is convenient and customary to classify divergences between private and social returns into four types. First, there are external economies of production. As we know from Chapter 5, an external economy occurs when an action results in uncompensated benefits to others. When such benefits are the result of an increase in a firm's production, they are called ***external economies of production.*** The firm may benefit others directly. For example, it may train workers who eventually go to work for other firms, which do not have to pay the training costs. Or the firm may benefit other firms indirectly because its increased output may reduce the cost of services provided to other firms in the industry. For example, a great expansion in an aircraft firm may make it possible for aluminum producers to take advantage of economies of scale, thus enabling other metal fabricating firms to get cheaper aluminum. In either case, there is a difference between private and social returns; the gains to society are greater than the gains to the firm.

Second, there are ***external economies of consumption,*** which occur when an action taken by a consumer, rather than a producer, results in an uncompensated benefit to others. For example, if I maintain my house and lawn, this benefits my neighbors as well as myself. If I educate my children and make them more responsible citizens, this too benefits my neighbors as well as myself (and my children). The list of external economies of consumption could easily be extended, but the idea should be clear now.

Third, there are external diseconomies of production. As we know from Chapter 5, an external diseconomy occurs when an action results in uncompensated costs to others. When such costs are due to increases in a firm's production, they are called ***external diseconomies of production.*** For example, a firm may pollute a stream by pumping out waste materials, or it may pollute the air with smoke or other emissions. Such actions result in costs to others. For instance, Chesapeake Bay's oyster beds and Long Island's clam beds are being threatened by water pollution. However, the private costs of waste disposal paid by the firms and cities responsible for the pollution are not equal to the full social costs, because they are not charged for their contribution to poorer water and their harm to industries dependent on good water. There are many examples of external diseconomies of production, such as traffic congestion and the defacement of scenery.

Fourth, there are ***external diseconomies of consumption,*** which occur when an action taken by a consumer results in an uncompensated cost to others. Some external diseconomies of consumption can be fairly subtle. For example, a family that feels that a three-year-old Chevrolet is perfectly adequate may become dissatisfied after moving to a community where everyone drives a new Pontiac.

At first glance, these instances of divergences between social and private costs and benefits may not seem very important. But when all these types of external economies and diseconomies are considered, their aggregate significance can be substantial. In the case of water pollution, the wastes discharged into a river by a single firm may not seriously harm the water quality but the combined effect of many firms' actions will. The importance of various types of external economies of production is also clear, and it is equally obvious that consumer tastes and well-being are determined by the tastes and well-being of other members of society.

How do these external economies and diseconomies alter the optimality of resource allocation under perfect competition? If a person (or firm) takes an action that contributes to society's welfare but results in no payment for him, he will probably take this action less frequently than would be socially optimal. Thus, if the production of a certain good, say beryllium, creates external economies, less than the socially optimum amount of beryllium will be produced under perfect competition. The producers are unlikely to increase output simply because the increase will reduce the costs of other companies. By the same token, if a person (or firm) takes an action resulting in costs to others that he is not forced to pay, he is likely to take this action more frequently than is socially desirable. Thus, if the production of a certain good is responsible for external diseconomies, more of this good will probably be produced under perfect competition than is socially optimal.[9]

The Planning of Urban Land Use

To illustrate the importance of external economies and diseconomies, consider urban land use in the United States. Americans have become more and more concerned about the plight of their cities in recent years. To a considerable extent, of course, urban problems are closely related to poverty and racial problems. The poor tend to huddle together in the central cities. Often these slums are inhabited largely by nonwhites, resulting in ghettos in the heart of the city. But there are other aspects of our urban problems too. Crime and delinquency are prevalent and highly visible in the densely populated urban core, urban transportation is often criticized as being slow and inefficient, and our metropolitan areas are viewed by some as characterized by a suburban sprawl that is both inefficient and socially unhealthy.

To help solve some of the city's problems, urban planners have attempted to influence the allocation of land in the metropolitan area. There are a number of useful legal devices at their disposal. First, there is *zoning.* In most areas, local governments can deny a citizen the right to develop land as he chooses; instead, a proposed use must be in accord with the community's over-all plan. Second, there is *code enforcement,* by which the government sees to it that minimum standards of maintenance and construction are met. Third, the government can *condemn private property* and use it for public purposes, including urban renewal. Fourth, the government can *invest directly* in structures (e.g., public housing). Fifth, it can influence the use of land by changing its *tax rates.*

Although these are powerful tools, it is obvious that most of the basic decisions on land use are made by families and firms. So long as we maintain anything approaching a free enterprise system, this must remain true. Thus the planner's influence on urban land use is considerably circumscribed. Moreover, the city planner typically does not control all the powers mentioned above. Instead, these powers reside in various parts of a local government, and there is no assurance that the planner's view will be accepted by other local officials. The planner's job is further complicated by the difficulty of defining goals and by the multitude of governments in most metropolitan areas.

During the past 20 years, the federal government has promoted and encouraged the redevelopment of the inner core of our major cities. Old tenements have been knocked down and new buildings have taken their place. Both federal loans and capital grants (covering up to ⅔ of the net cost of the project) have been pro-

[9] It should be noted that private costs and benefits can in many instances be made to equal social costs and benefits by legal requirements that assign liabilities for damages and compensate for benefits. However, such systems often are impractical or too costly to be useful. See G. Stigler, *The Theory of Price,* New York: Macmillan, 1966, pp. 110–14; R. Coase, "The Problem of Social Cost," *Journal of Law and Economics,* 1961; and W. Baumol, *Economic Theory and Operations Analysis,* Englewood Cliffs, N.J.: Prentice-Hall, 1965, pp. 368–71 and 375–80, on which this section is partly based.

vided. In all, over 100,000 housing units, most of them substandard, were demolished–and tens of thousands of new housing units were constructed–by urban renewal programs between 1950 and 1960 alone.

Urban renewal rests on the idea that the market mechanism does not work properly for urban land use. Why is this idea reasonable? Why do profit-maximizing individuals not find it worthwhile to keep up their property? The answer lies in the fact that the value of a piece of property depends on the neighborhood in which it is situated as well as on its own characteristics and state of repair. The enjoyment people get from a piece of property depends on its surroundings. In other words, in the jargon of the previous section, there are important external economies and diseconomies with regard to land use.

To see why this fact can cause urban blight, consider two adjacent properties. Suppose that the two owners, *A* and *B*, are each trying to determine whether to invest some money to redevelop their properties. The rate of return on the investment by each owner is shown in Table 30.2. This rate of return depends on whether the other owner redevelops his property as well. If both redevelop, each will make 7 percent on their investment. If neither redevelops, each can obtain 4 percent by investing the money in some other type of investment. If one redevelops but the other does not, the owner who redevelops makes only 3 percent since little is accomplished as long as the other owner does not redevelop. The owner who does not redevelop earns 10 percent on his investment because his property benefits (at no cost) from the improvements in the other property.

Table 30.2
Returns from Investment, Two Property Owners

		Owner *B* Invest	Owner *B* Not invest
		Owner *A*'s rate of return	
Owner *A*	Invest	.07	.03
	Not invest	.10	.04
		Owner *B*'s rate of return	
Owner *A*	Invest	.07	.10
	Not invest	.03	.04

Source: O. Davis and A. Whinston, "The Economics of Urban Renewal," *Law and Contemporary Problems,* Winter 1961, reprinted in E. Mansfield, *Economics: Readings, Issues, and Cases,* 2d ed., New York: Norton, 1977.

Under these circumstances, *neither owner will redevelop his property.* For example, take owner *A*. If owner *B* redevelops, owner *A* receives a higher return if he does not redevelop than if he redevelops. If owner *B* does not redevelop, owner *A* also receives a higher return if he does not redevelop than if he redevelops. In either case, owner *A* believes that he is better off not to redevelop. The situation is similar for owner *B*. Nevertheless, from society's point of view or from the point of view of the two owners' acting together as a unit, redevelopment may be desirable. Needless to say, this example is highly simplified and rather extreme, but it does illustrate the basic point that external economies and diseconomies may prevent redevelopment, even though it is socially desirable.

One need only look at portions of New Haven, Philadelphia, Atlanta, or other cities to recognize that urban renewal has been beneficial in many respects. Unfortunately, however, not all its effects have been good. For example, it has sometimes hurt the poor. When old tenements are knocked down, the people who lived in them often have a hard time finding another place to live, since the people who occupy the new buildings that displace the tenements are often middle class. Unless proper attention is paid to rehousing those whose homes are being demolished, the dispossessed–typically poor and often nonwhite–will be victimized by what seems at first glance to be a very desirable development.

Summary

An analysis that takes account of the interrelations among various markets is called a general equilibrium analysis. Whereas partial equilibrium analysis assumes that changes in price do not have serious repercussions on other prices (which in turn affect the market under consideration), general equilibrium analysis deals explicitly with the effect of one market on another, as well as with the feedback from the second market to the first.

Input-output analysis is a technique that makes the general equilibrium model empirically useful. It assumes that inputs are used in fixed proportions in producing any product and that there are constant returns to scale. An important feature of input-output analysis is its emphasis on the interdependence of the economy. Using simultaneous linear equations, input-output analysis answers questions like: If consumption targets for each of a number of industries are given, how much will have to be produced by each industry to meet these targets; and given the available resources, can these production levels be achieved?

Welfare economics deals with the optimal allocation of resources. A major limitation of welfare economics is that there is no scientific way to compare the utility levels of different individuals, so that the question of whether one distribution of income is better than another must be settled on ethical, not scientific, grounds. Putting aside income distribution, three conditions must be met if resources are to be allocated optimally. First, the ratio of the marginal utilities of two commodities must be the same for any two consumers buying both commodities. Second, the ratio of the marginal products of two inputs must be the same for any pair of producers using both inputs. Third, the marginal social benefit from an extra unit of any commodity must be equal to its marginal social cost.

A perfectly competitive economy satisfies all three of these sets of conditions for welfare maximization. This is one of the fundamental arguments for a perfectly competitive economy. In principle, a price system could be used in a similar way in planned, or socialist, economies. The prices set would equal marginal cost. Many economists have recommended that government-owned or government-regulated enterprises in basically capitalistic economies also adopt marginal cost pricing. However there are a variety of practical problems involved in applying it.

External economies occur when the actions of a firm or consumer result in uncompensated benefits to third parties. External diseconomies occur when the actions of a firm or consumer result in uncompensated costs to third parties. If external economies or diseconomies exist, a perfectly competitive economy is unlikely to result in an optimal allocation of resources. For example, urban renewal is based on the idea that the market mechanism does not work properly for urban land use, because the value of a piece of property depends on the neighborhood in which it is located, as well as on its own characteristics and state of repair.

CONCEPTS FOR REVIEW

Partial equilibrium analysis
General equilibrium analysis
Input-output analysis
Welfare economics
Efficient allocation of resources
Marginal cost pricing

QUESTIONS FOR DISCUSSION AND REVIEW

1. Suppose that the Sleepy Hollow Fife and Drum Company is the sole monopolist in the land of Upper Usher, all other markets being perfectly competitive. How will resource allocation differ from that in a perfectly competitive economy? How will the distribution of income differ?

2. The antitrust authorities of Upper Usher try to break up the Sleepy Hollow Fife and Drum Company on the grounds that it will result in a better distribution of income. Comment and evaluate.

3. "My idea of the perfect house is one with a very small lot that is situated next to a large lot that is maintained with great care by my neighbor." Are there external economies involved here? Are external diseconomies involved too? Can your neighbor charge you for his services? Explain.

4. "Input-output analysis is of limited use because the production coefficients used in any such analysis are assumed to be constant." Comment and evaluate.

5. Over the past 40 years, nylon has displaced silk in many uses, and has been substituted for many other natural fibers. Trace the impact of this displacement and substitution on various firms, groups, and markets in as much detail as you can.

6. Suppose that a consumer buys oranges but not apples. To maximize welfare, must the ratio of the marginal utility of an apple to that of an orange equal the ratio of the price of an apple to that of an orange? Why or why not?

7. "When an economist draws a demand curve and a supply curve for a particular market, and finds the equilibrium price, this is an example of general equilibrium analysis." Comment and evaluate.

8. Suppose that you are given the job of forecasting the amount produced by each of the industries in Table 30.1 in the year 2000. Do you think that input-output analysis would be useful in this context? What would be some of the key problems in using it?

9. Should American Telephone and Telegraph use marginal cost pricing? Why or why not?

10. According to Edward Banfield, " 'Doing good' is becoming—has already become—a growth industry, like other forms of mass entertainment." Do you agree? Why or why not? What has welfare economics got to do with "doing good"? How can one tell whether or not he is "doing good"?

PART NINE

International Economics

31

International Trade

It takes the average human being little time to realize that he is not an island unto himself and that he benefits from living with, working with, and trading with other people. Exactly the same is true of nations. They too must interact with one another, and they too benefit from trade with one another. No nation can be an island unto itself—not even the United States. To understand how the world economy functions, you must grasp the basic economic principles of international trade.

This chapter discusses many of the fundamental questions about international trade. What is the nature of American foreign trade? What are the effects of international trade? What determines the sorts of goods a nation will import or export? What are the advantages of free trade and the arguments against it? What are the social costs of tariffs and quotas, and what has been their history in the United States? What are some of the major issues regarding protectionism in the United States today? Some of these questions have occupied the attention of economists for hundreds of years; some are as current as today's newspaper.

America's Foreign Trade

America's foreign trade, although small relative to our national product, plays a very important role in our economic life. Many of our industries depend on other countries for markets or for raw materials (like coffee, tea, or tin). Our ***exports***—the things we sell to other countries—amount to about 5 to 10 percent of our gross national product, which seems small relative to other countries like Germany, France, Italy, and the United Kingdom, where exports are about 15 to 20 percent of gross national product. But this is because our domestic market is so large. In absolute terms, and relative to those of other countries, our exports seem very large indeed. In recent years, they have represented about 15 percent of total world trade. Without question, our way of life would have to change considerably if we could not trade with other countries.

When we were a young country, we exported raw materials primarily. For example, during the 1850s about 70 percent of our exports were raw materials and foodstuffs. But the composition of our exports has changed with time. More are now finished manufactured goods and less are raw materials. In the 1960s, about 60 percent of our exports were finished manufactured goods, and only about 20 percent were raw materials and foodstuffs. Table 31.1 shows the importance of machinery and industrial supplies in our merchandise exports. Table 31.2 indicates to whom we sell: Western Europe and Canada take almost ½ of our exports, and Latin America takes about 15 percent.

What sorts of goods do we buy from abroad? About 10 percent of our ***imports*** are agricultural commodities like coffee, sugar, bananas, and cocoa. Almost 30 percent are petroleum and its products. But a considerable proportion is neither raw materials nor foodstuffs. Over ⅓ of our imports, as shown in Table 31.3, are manufactured goods like bicycles from England or color TVs from Japan. Just as we sell more to Canada and Western Europe than any other area, so we buy more from these countries too (see Table 31.4). But the pattern varies, of course, from product to product. For example, Canada is our leading foreign source for wood pulp and nonferrous metals, while Latin America is our leading source of imported coffee and sugar.

Finally, several general observations on the pattern of world trade are worth making. First, *much of world trade involves the industrialized richer countries.* This is no surprise, since these countries account for so large a share of the world's productivity and purchasing power. Second, *the industrialized, richer countries of the world tend to trade with one another, while the nonindustrialized, poorer countries tend to trade with the industrialized countries, not with one another.* The reasons for this are clear enough. The nonindustrialized countries supply the industrialized countries with raw materials and foodstuffs, and receive manufactures in return. The nonindustrialized countries have little reason to trade with one another since they cannot get from one another the manufactures they need. Third, *neighboring nations tend to trade with one another.* This too is predictable: lower transportation costs and greater familiarity tend to promote trade between neighbors.

Specialization and Trade

We have discussed the extent and nature of our trade with other countries, but not *why* we trade with other countries. Do we—and our trading partners—benefit from this trade? And if so, what determines the sorts of goods we

Table 31.1
U.S. Merchandise Exports, 1975

Product	Amount (millions of dollars)
Food, feed, and beverages	19,239
Industrial supplies and materials	30,776
Machinery	29,193
Automotive vehicles and parts	10,599
Consumer goods (excluding autos)	6,563
Aircraft	3,225
Other	7,589
Total	107,184

Source: Survey of Current Business, March 1976. These figures exclude military items.

Table 31.2
U.S. Exports, by Area, 1975

Country	Amount (millions of dollars)
Japan	9,570
Australia, New Zealand, and South Africa	3,509
Latin America	17,096
Canada	23,635
Eastern Europe	2,859
United Kingdom	4,807
European Economic Community	17,862
Other Western Europe	7,595
Other	20,251
Total	107,184

Source: See Table 31.1.

Table 31.3
U.S. Merchandise Imports, 1975

Product	Amount (millions of dollars)
Food, feed, and beverages	9,683
Petroleum and oil products	26,522
Other industrial supplies and materials	24,694
Capital goods	9,693
Automotive vehicles and parts	11,871
Consumer goods (excluding autos)	13,739
Other	1,937
Total	98,139

Source: See Table 31.1.

Table 31.4
U.S. Imports, by Area, 1975

Country	Amount (millions of dollars)
Japan	11,257
Australia, New Zealand, and South Africa	2,243
Latin America	16,177
Canada	21,877
Eastern Europe	737
United Kingdom	3,737
European Economic Community	12,151
Other Western Europe	4,883
Other	25,077
Total	98,139

Source: See Table 31.1.

should export and import? These are very important questions, among the most fundamental in economics. The answers are by no means new. They have been well understood for considerably more than a century, due to the work of such great economists as David Hume, David Ricardo, Adam Smith, and John Stuart Mill.

As a first step, it is useful to recognize that the benefits *nations* receive through trade are essentially the same as those *individuals* receive through trade. Consider the hypothetical case of John Barrister, a lawyer, with a wife and two children. The Barrister family, like practically all families, trades continually with other families and with business firms. Since Mr. Barrister is a lawyer, he trades his legal services for money which he and his wife use to buy the food, clothing, housing, and other goods and services his family wants. Why does the Barrister family do this? What advantages does it receive through trade? Why doesn't it attempt to be self-sufficient?

To see why the Barrister family is sensible indeed to opt for trade rather than self-sufficiency, let's compare the current situation—where Mr. Barrister specializes in the production of legal services and trades the money he receives for other goods and services—with the situation if the Barrister family attempted to be self-sufficient. In the latter case, the Barristers would have to provide their own transportation, telephone service, foodstuffs, clothing, and a host of other things. Mr. Barrister is a lawyer—a well-trained, valuable, productive member of the community. But if he were to try his hand at making automobiles—or even bicycles—he might be a total loss. Thus, if the Barrister family attempted to be self-sufficient, it might be unable to provide many of the goods it now enjoys.

Clearly, *trade permits specialization, and specialization increases output:* this is the advantage of trade, both for individuals and for nations. In our hypothetical case, it is obvious that, because he can trade with other families and with firms, Mr. Barrister can specialize in doing what he is good at—law. Consequently, he can be more productive than if he were forced to be a Jack-of-all-trades, as he would have to be if he could not trade with others. The same principle holds for nations. For example, because the United States can trade with other nations, it can specialize in the goods and services it produces particularly well. Then it can trade them for goods that other countries are especially good at producing. Thus both we and our trading partners benefit.

Some countries have more and better resources of certain types than others. Saudi Arabia has oil, Canada has timber, Japan has a skilled labor force, and so on. *International differences in resource endowments, and in the relative quantity of various types of human and nonhuman resources, are important bases for specialization.* For example, countries with lots of fertile soil, little capital, and much unskilled labor are likely to find it advantageous to produce agricultural goods, while countries with poor soil, much capital, and highly skilled labor will probably do better to produce capital-intensive, high-technology goods. We must recognize, however, that the bases for specialization do not remain fixed over time. Instead, as technology and the resource endowments of various countries change, the pattern of international specialization changes as well. For example, as we saw in the previous section, the United States specialized more in raw materials and foodstuffs about a century ago than it does now.

Absolute Advantage

To clarify the benefits of trade, consider the following example. Suppose that the United States can produce 2 electronic computers or 5,000 cases of wine with 1 unit of resources.

Suppose that France can produce 1 electronic computer or 10,000 cases of wine with 1 unit of resources. Given the production possibilities in each country, are there any advantages in trade between the countries? And if so, what commodity should each country export, and what commodity should each country import? Should France export wine and import computers, or should it import wine and export computers?

To answer these questions, assume that the United States is producing a certain amount of computers and a certain amount of wine—and that France is producing a certain amount of computers and a certain amount of wine. If the United States shifts 1 unit of its resources from producing wine to producing computers, it will increase its production of computers by 2 computers and reduce its production of wine by 5,000 cases of wine. If France shifts 1 unit of resources from the production of computers to the production of wine, it will increase its production of wine by 10,000 cases and reduce its production of computers by 1 computer.

Table 31.5 shows the *net* effect of this shift in the utilization of resources on *world* output of computers and of wine. World output of computers increases (by 1 computer) and world output of wine increases (by 5,000 cases) as a result of the redeployment of resources in each country. Thus *specialization increases world output.*

Table 31.5
Case of Absolute Advantage

	Increase or decrease in output of: Computers	Wine (thousands of cases)
Effect of U.S.'s shifting 1 unit of resources from wine to computers	+2	− 5
Effect of France's shifting 1 unit of resources from computers to wine	−1	+10
Net effect	+1	+ 5

Moreover, if world output of each commodity is increased by shifting 1 unit of American resources from wine to computers and shifting 1 unit of French resources from computers to wine, it follows that world output of each commodity will be increased further if each country shifts *more* of its resources in the same direction. This is because the amount of resources required to produce each good is assumed to be constant, regardless of how much is produced.

Thus, in this situation, one country—the United States—should specialize in producing computers, and the other country—France—should specialize in producing wine. This will maximize world output of both wine and computers, permitting a rise in both countries' standards of living. Of course, complete specialization of this sort is somewhat unrealistic, since countries often produce some of both commodities, but this simple example illustrates the basic principles involved.

Comparative Advantage

The case just described is a very special one, since one country (France) has an absolute advantage over another (the United States) in the production of one good (wine), whereas the second country (the United States) has an absolute advantage over the first (France) in the production of another good (computers). What do we mean by the term *absolute advantage*? Country *A* has an ***absolute advantage*** over Country *B* in the production of a good when Country *A* can produce a unit of the good with less resources than can Country *B*. Since the

United States can produce a computer with fewer units of resources than France, it has an absolute advantage over France in the production of computers. Since France requires fewer resources than the United States to produce a given amount of wine, France has an absolute advantage over the United States in the production of wine.

But what if one country is more efficient in producing both goods? If the United States is more efficient in producing both computers and wine, is there still any benefit to be derived from specialization and trade? At first glance, you are probably inclined to answer no. But if this is your inclination, you should reconsider—because you are wrong.

To see why specialization and trade have advantages even when one country is more efficient than another at producing both goods, consider the following example. Suppose the United States can produce 2 electronic computers or 5,000 cases of wine with 1 unit of resources, and France can produce 1 electronic computer or 4,000 cases of wine with 1 unit of resources. In this case, the United States is a more efficient producer of both computers and wine. Nonetheless, as we shall see, world output of both goods will increase if the United States specializes in the production of computers and France specializes in the production of wine.

Table 31.6 demonstrates this conclusion. If 2 units of American resources are shifted from wine to computer production, 4 additional computers and 10,000 fewer cases of wine are produced. If 3 units of French resources are shifted from computer to wine production, 3 fewer computers and 12,000 additional cases of wine are produced. Thus the combined effect of this redeployment of resources in both countries is to increase world output of computers by 1 computer and to increase world output of wine by 2,000 cases. Even though the United States is more efficient than France in the production of both computers and wine,

Table 31.6
Case of Comparative Advantage

	Increase or decrease in output of: Computers	Wine (thousands of cases)
Effect of U.S.'s shifting 2 units of resources from wine to computers	+4	−10
Effect of France's shifting 3 units of resources from computers to wine	−3	+12
Net effect	+1	+ 2

world output of both goods will be maximized if the United States specializes in computers and France specializes in wine.

Basically, this is so because, although the United States is more efficient than France in the production of both goods, it has a greater advantage in computers than in wine. It is twice as efficient as France in producing computers, but only 25 percent more efficient than France in producing wine. To derive these numbers, recall that 1 unit of resources will produce 2 computers in the United States, but only 1 computer in France. Thus the United States is twice as efficient in computers. On the other hand, 1 unit of resources will produce 5,000 cases of wine in the United States, but only 4,000 cases in France. Thus the United States is 25 percent more efficient in wine.

A nation has a ***comparative advantage*** in those products where its efficiency relative to other nations is highest. Thus, in this case, the United States has a comparative advantage in the production of computers and a comparative disadvantage in the production of wine. So long as a country has a comparative advantage in the production of some commodities and a comparative disadvantage in the production of others, it can benefit from specialization and trade. A country will specialize, of course, in products where it has a comparative advantage, and import those where it has a comparative disadvantage. The point is that *specialization and trade depend on comparative, not absolute advantage.* One of the first economists to understand the full significance of this fact was David Ricardo, the famous English economist of the early nineteenth century.

A Geometric Representation of Comparative Advantage

The principle of comparative advantage, like so many important economic concepts, can be displayed diagrammatically. Again, we suppose that in the United States 1 unit of resources will produce 2 electronic computers or 5,000 cases of wine. Consequently, the ***product transformation curve*** in the United States—the curve that shows the maximum number of computers that can be produced, given various outputs of wine—is the one in panel A of Figure 31.1. The United States must give up 1 computer for every additional 2,500 cases of wine that it produces; thus the slope of the American product transformation curve is $-\frac{1}{2{,}500}$.[1] Also, as in the previous section, we suppose that in France 1 unit of resources will produce 1 electronic computer

[1] As we know from Chapter 3, the product transformation curve shows the maximum amount of one commodity that can be produced, given various outputs of the other commodity. Since the United States must give up 1/2,500 computer for each additional case of wine that it produces, the slope must be −1/2,500.

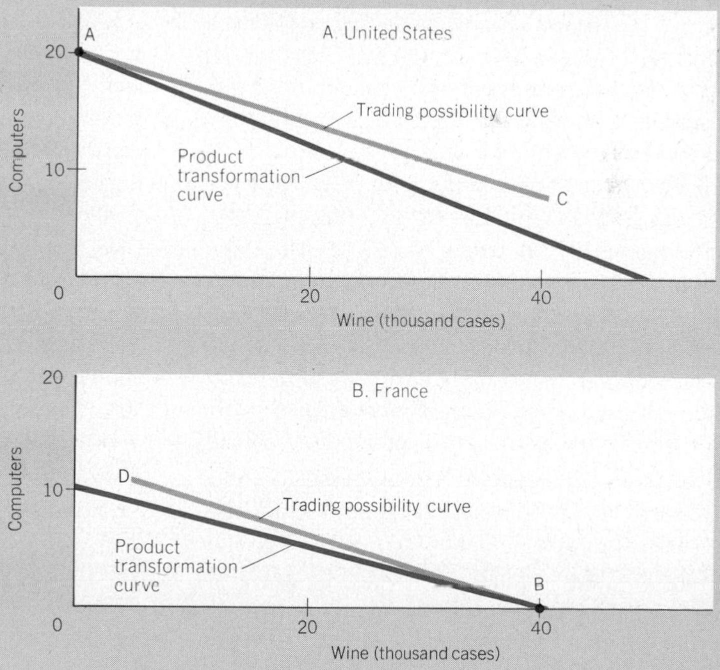

Figure 31.1
Benefits of Specialization and Trade
AC represents the various amounts of computers and wine that the United States can end up with, if it specializes in computers and trades them for French wine. The slope of *AC* equals −1 times the ratio of the price of a case of wine to the price of a computer, assumed to be $\frac{1}{3{,}333}$. *BD* represents the various amounts of computers and wine that France can wind up with, if it specializes in wine and trades for U.S. computers. *AC* lies above America's product transformation curve and *BD* lies above France's product transformation curve. Thus both countries can have more of both commodities by specializing and trading than by attempting to be self-sufficient.

or 4,000 cases of wine. Thus the product transformation curve in France is as shown in panel B of Figure 31.1. France must give up 1 computer for every additional 4,000 cases of wine it produces; thus the slope of France's product transformation curve is $-\frac{1}{4,000}$.

Now suppose that the United States uses all its resources to produce computers and that France uses all its resources to produce wine. In other words, the United States operates at point A on its product transformation curve and France operates at point B on its product transformation curve. Then suppose that the United States trades its computers for France's wine. AC in panel A of Figure 31.1 shows the various amounts of computers and wine the United States can end up with if it specializes in computers and trades them for French wine. AC is called the ***trading-possibility curve*** of the United States. The slope of AC is minus 1 times the ratio of the price of a case of wine to the price of a computer, since this ratio equals the number of computers the United States must give up to get a case of French wine. Similarly, the line BD in panel B of Figure 31.1 shows France's trading-possibility curve. That is, BD represents the various amounts of computers and wine France can wind up with if it specializes in wine and trades it for U.S. computers.

The thing to note about both panels of Figure 31.1 is that each country's trading-possibility curve—AC in panel A, BD in panel B—lies above its product transformation curve. This means that *both countries can have more of both commodities by specializing and trading than by trying to be self-sufficient*—even though the United States is more efficient than France at producing both commodities. Thus Figure 31.1 shows what we said in the previous section: if countries specialize in products where they have a comparative advantage and trade with one another, each country can improve its standard of living.

The Terms of Trade and Incomplete Specialization

The ***terms of trade*** are defined as the quantity of domestic goods that a country must give up in order to get a unit of imported goods. Thus, in Figure 31.1, the terms of trade are measured by the ratio of the price of a computer to the price of a case of wine—since this ratio shows how many cases of its wine France must give up to get an American computer. In Figure 31.1, we assume that this ratio equals 3,333:1. It is important to note that this ratio must be somewhere between 2,500:1 and 4,000:1. By diverting its own resources from computer production to wine production, the United States can exchange a computer for 2,500 cases of wine. Since this is possible, it will not pay the United States to trade a computer for less than 2,500 cases of wine. Similarly, since France can exchange a case of wine for 1/4,000 of a computer by diverting its own resources from wine to computers, it clearly will not be willing to trade a case of wine for less than 1/4,000 of a computer.

But where will the price ratio lie between 2,500:1 and 4,000:1? The answer depends on *world supply and demand for the two products.* The stronger the demand for computers (relative to their supply) and the weaker the demand for wine (relative to its supply), the higher the price ratio. On the other hand, the weaker the demand for computers (relative to their supply) and the stronger the demand for wine (relative to its supply), the lower the price ratio.

Figure 31.1 shows that the United States should specialize completely in computers, and that France should specialize completely in wine. This result stems from the assumption that the cost of producing a computer or a case of wine is constant. If, on the other hand, the cost of producing each good increases with the amount produced, the result is likely to be incomplete specialization. In other words, although the United States will continue to specialize in computers and France will continue to specialize in wine, each country will also produce some of the other good as well. This is a more likely outcome, since specialization generally tends to be less than complete.

Comparative Advantage and Actual Trade Patterns: A Case Study

The principle of comparative advantage is useful in explaining and predicting the pattern of world trade, as well as in showing the benefits of trade. For example, consider the exports of Great Britain and the United States. Robert Stern of the University of Michigan compared British and American exports of 39 industries in 1950.[2] In some of these industries, Britain exported much more than we did, while in others we exported more than the British. In all these industries, labor productivity—output per man-hour—was higher in the United States than in Great Britain. But in some industries labor productivity in the United States was over three times as great as in Britain, whereas in other industries labor productivity was less than three times as great as in Britain. According to the principle of comparative advantage, the industries where the United States is most efficient relative to the British should be the ones where the United States exports more than the British.

To what extent is this hypothesis borne out by the facts? In 21 of the 24 industries where our labor productivity was more than three times that of the British, our exports exceeded British exports. In 11 of the 15 industries where our labor productivity was less than three times that of the British, our exports were less than British exports. Thus, in 32 out of 39 industries, the principle of comparative advantage, as interpreted by Stern, predicted correctly which country would export more. This is a high batting average, since labor is not the only input and labor productivity is an imperfect measure of true efficiency. Moreover, as we shall see in subsequent sections, countries raise barriers to foreign trade, preventing trade from taking place in accord with the principle of comparative advantage.

[2] Robert M. Stern, "British and American Productivity and Comparative Costs in International Trade," *Oxford Economic Papers*, October 1962.

International Trade and Individual Markets

We have emphasized that nations can benefit by specializing in the production of goods for which they have a comparative advantage and trading these goods for others where they have a comparative disadvantage. But how do a nation's producers know whether they have a comparative advantage or disadvantage in the production of a given commodity? Clearly, they do not call up the local university and ask the leading professor of economics (although that might not always be such a bad idea). Instead, as we shall see in this section, the market for the good provides the required signals.

To see how this works, let's consider a new (and rather whimsical) product—bulletproof suspenders. Suppose that the Mob, having run a scientific survey of gunmen and policemen, finds that most of them wear their suspenders over their bulletproof vests. As a consequence, the Mob's gunmen are instructed to render a victim immobile by shooting holes in his suspenders (thus making his trousers fall down and trip him). Naturally, the producers of suspenders will soon find it profitable to produce a new bulletproof variety, an innovation which, it is hoped, will make a solid contribution to law and order. The new suspenders are demanded only in the United States and England, since the rest of the world wears belts. The demand curve in the United States is *DD*, as shown in panel A of Figure 31.2, and the de-

Figure 31.2
Determination of Quantity Imported and Exported under Free Trade
Under free trade, price will equal \$4.95, or £3. The United States will export *XY* units, the English will import *UV* units, and *XY* = *UV*.

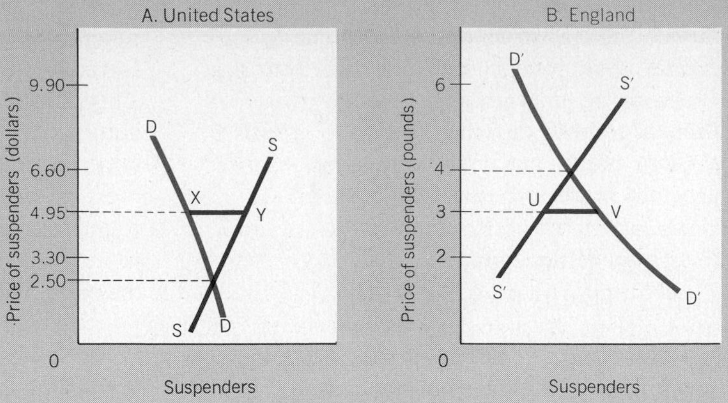

mand curve in England is *D′D′*, as shown in panel B. Suppose further that this product can be manufactured in both the United States and England. The supply curve in the United States is *SS*, as shown in panel A, and the supply curve in England is *S′S′*, as shown in panel B.

Take a closer look at Figure 31.2. Note that prices in England are expressed in pounds (£) and prices in the United States are expressed in dollars (\$). This, of course, is quite realistic. Each country has its own currency, in which prices in that country are expressed. As of early 1977, £1 was equal to \$1.65. In other words, you could exchange a pound note for \$1.65—or \$1.65 for a £1 note. For this reason, the two panels of Figure 31.2 are lined up so that a price of \$1.65 is at the same level as a price of £1, \$3.30 is at the same level as £2, and so on.

To begin with, suppose that bulletproof suspenders can not be exported or imported, perhaps because of a very high tariff (tax on imports) imposed on them in both the United States and England. (One can readily imagine members of both Congress and Parliament defending such a tariff on the grounds that a capacity to produce plenty of bulletproof suspenders is important for national defense.) If this happens, the price of bulletproof suspenders will, of course, be \$2.50 in the United States and £4 in England. Why? Because, as shown in Figure 31.2, these are the prices at which each country's demand curve intersects its supply curve.

Next, suppose that international trade in this product is permitted, perhaps because both countries eliminate the tariff. Now what will happen? Since the price is lower in the United States than in England, people can make money by sending this product from the United States to England. After all, they can buy it for \$2.50 in this country and sell it for £4 (= \$6.60) in England. But they will not be able to do so indefinitely. As more and more suspenders are supplied by the United States for the English market, the price in the United States must go up (to induce producers to produce the additional output) and the price in England must go down (to induce consumers to buy the additional quantity).

When an equilibrium is reached, *the price in the United States must equal the price in England.* If this did not happen, there would be an advantage in increasing American exports (if the price in England were higher) or in decreasing American exports (if the price in the United States were higher). Thus only if the prices are equal can an equilibrium exist.

At what level will this price—which is common to both countries—tend to settle? Obviously, *the price must end up at the level where the amount of the good one country wants to ex-*

port equals the amount the other country wants to import. In other words, it must settle at \$4.95 or £3. Otherwise, the total amount demanded in both countries would not equal the total amount supplied in both countries. And any reader who has mastered the material in Chapter 4 knows that such a situation cannot be an equilibrium.

At this point, we can see how market forces indicate whether a country has a comparative advantage or a comparative disadvantage in the production of a certain commodity. *If a country has a comparative advantage, it turns out—after the price of the good in various countries is equalized and total world output of the good equals total world demand for it—that the country exports the good under free trade and competition.* For example, in Figure 31.2, it turns out—as we've just seen—that the United States is an exporter of bulletproof suspenders under free trade, because the demand and supply curves in the United States and England take the positions they do. The basic reason why the curves take these positions is that the United States has a comparative advantage in the production of this good. Thus, to put things in a nutshell, a nation's producers can tell (under free trade) whether they have a comparative advantage in the production of a certain commodity by seeing whether it is profitable for them to export it. If they can make a profit, they have a comparative advantage.[3]

Economies of Scale, Learning, and Technological Change

Specialization and trade may be advantageous even if there is no difference among countries in the efficiency with which they can produce goods and services. In a case like this, although no nation has a technological advantage over any other, specialization and trade may still be of benefit, because there may be economies of scale in producing some commodities. Thus, if one country specializes in one good and another country specializes in another good, firms can serve the *combined* markets of both countries, which will make their costs *lower* than if they could only reach their domestic markets. This is a major argument for forming an international economic association like the European Common Market, discussed below.

Another reason for specialization is that it may result in learning. It is well known that the cost of producing many articles goes down as more and more of the articles are produced. For example, in the aircraft and machine tool industries, producers are well aware of the reduction in costs from learning. The unit costs of a new machine tool tend to be reduced by 20 percent for each doubling of cumulated output, due to improved efficiency through individual and organizational learning. Clearly, if such learning is an important factor in an industry, there are advantages in having one nation's producers specialize in a certain good. Specialization can reduce costs to a lower level than if each nation tries to be self-sufficient. Longer production runs cut costs since *the more a producer makes, the lower the unit costs.*

International trade also arises because of technological change. Suppose, for example, that a new product is invented in the United States and an American firm begins producing and selling it in the American market. It catches on, and the American innovator decides to export the new product to Europe and other foreign markets. If the new product meets European needs and tastes, the Europeans will import it from the United States; and later, when the market in Europe gets big enough, the American firm may establish a branch plant in Europe. For a time at least, Eu-

[3] In reality, of course, things are not quite so simple. For one thing, high transport costs are often involved in moving goods from one country to another. These costs can impede trade in certain commodities. Also, tariffs or quotas can be enacted by governments to interfere with free trade.

ropean firms do not have the technological know-how to produce the new product, which is often protected to some extent by patents.

Trade of this sort is based on a *technology gap* between countries. Consider the plastics industry. After the development of a new plastic, there is a period of 15 to 25 years when the innovating country has a decisive advantage and is likely to lead in per capita production and exports. It has a head start, as well as the benefits of patents and commercial secrecy. Production may be licensed to other countries, but usually on a limited scale and only after a number of years. Soon after the patents expire, a different phase begins. Imitation is easier, technical know-how spreads more readily, direct technical factors lose importance, and such other factors as materials costs become much more important. Industry from other countries may challenge the innovator in export markets, and sometimes in the innovator's home market as well, although the innovator still benefits to some extent from his accumulated knowledge and experience and his ongoing research and development.

The United States tends to export products with a high technological component—relatively new products based on considerable research and development. For example, if the 5 U.S. industries with the largest research programs are compared with the 14 other major industries, we see that the high-research industries export 4 times as much per dollar of sales as the others.[4] During the 1960s, Europeans expressed considerable concern over the technological gap between the United States and Europe. They asserted that superior know-how stemming from scientific and technical development in the United States had allowed American companies to obtain large shares of European markets in areas like aircraft, space equipment, computers, and other electronic products.

It is difficult to separate technical advantages from other competitive factors in explaining why American firms left their European rivals far behind in some fields. Differences in educational levels and managerial skills, economies of scale, and other such factors may have been very important. As we shall see in the following chapter, our technological lead seems to have narrowed in recent years, as the Japanese, Germans, and others have upgraded their technology. According to many observers, some American exports will be, and are being, hurt as a consequence.[5]

Multinational Firms

One of the most remarkable economic phenomena of the last 20 years has been the growth of multinational firms—firms that make direct investments in other countries and produce and market their products abroad. For example, Coca-Cola is produced and bottled all over the world. Most multinational firms are American, but companies like Shell in petroleum and Hoffman-LaRoche in drugs are examples of foreign-based multinational firms. The available data indicate that the multinational firms have grown by leaps and bounds, and that their shipments have become a bigger and bigger proportion of international trade. Indeed, according to economists like Lawrence Krause of the Brookings Institution, they are "now having a revolutionary effect upon the international economic system."[6]

[4] Charles Kindleberger, *International Economics*, Homewood, Ill.: Irwin, 1968, p. 67. Also, see R. Vernon, "International Investment and International Trade in the Product Cycle," *Quarterly Journal of Economics*, May 1966.

[5] Besides differences in technology, another reason for trade is a difference in national tastes. If Country *A* likes beef and Country *B* likes pork, it may pay both countries to produce beef and pork, and Country *A* may find it advantageous to import beef from Country *B* and Country *B* may find it advantageous to import pork from Country *A*.

[6] Lawrence Krause, "The International Economic System and the Multinational Corporation," *The Annals*, 1972. Some of this and the previous section is based on my "Technology and Technological Change" in J. Dunning, ed., *Economic Analysis and the Multinational Enterprise*, London: Allen and Unwin, 1974.

The reasons why firms have become multinational are varied. In some cases, firms have established overseas branches to control foreign sources of raw materials. In other cases, they have invested overseas in an effort to defend their competitive position. Very frequently, firms have established foreign branches to exploit a technological lead. After exporting a new product (or a cheaper version of an existing product) to foreign markets, firms have decided to establish plants overseas to supply these markets. Once a foreign market is big enough to accommodate a plant of minimum efficient size, this decision does not conflict with economies of scale. Moreover, transport costs often hasten such a decision. Also, in some cases, the only way a firm can introduce its innovation into a foreign market is through the establishment of overseas production facilities.

By carrying its technology overseas, the multinational firm plays a very important role in the international diffusion of innovations. A firm with a technological edge over its competitors often prefers to exploit its technology in foreign markets through wholly owned subsidiaries rather than through licensing or other means. To some extent, this is because of difficulties in using ordinary market mechanisms to buy and sell information. The difficulties of transferring technology across organizational, as well as national, boundaries also contribute to the decision. For these and other reasons, the innovating firm may find it advantageous to transfer its technology to other countries by establishing subsidiaries abroad.

One of the most important effects of the multinational firm has been to integrate the economies of the world more closely into a world-wide system. In other words, multinational firms have tended to break down some of the barriers between nations. Besides speeding the diffusion of new technology, they have linked the capital markets of many countries and promoted the international transfer of important managerial labor. However, a number of problems are also associated with multinational firms. One is the possibility that they will attain undesirable monopoly power in some industries. In addition, as we shall see in subsequent chapters, they may put undesirable stress on the international financial system and threaten the sovereignty of some nation-states. In the latter connection, recent evidence of their bribing foreign officials has not contributed to their popularity, here or abroad.

Arguments Against Tariffs and Quotas

The Social Costs of Tariffs

Despite its advantages, not everyone benefits from free trade. On the contrary, some firms and workers may feel that their well-being is threatened by foreign competition; and they may press for a ***tariff,*** a tax the government imposes on imports. The purpose of a tariff is to cut down on imports in order to protect domestic industry and workers from foreign competition. A secondary reason for tariffs is to produce revenue for the government.

To see how a tariff works, consider the market for wristwatches. Suppose that the demand and supply curve for wristwatches in the United States are *DD* and *SS,* as shown in panel A of Figure 31.3, and that the demand and supply curves for wristwatches in Switzerland are *D′D′* and *S′S′*, as shown in panel B. Clearly, Switzerland has a comparative advantage in the production of wristwatches, and under free trade the price of a wristwatch would tend toward $10 in the United States and toward 30 Swiss francs in Switzerland. (Note that 3 Swiss francs are assumed to equal $1.) Under free trade, the United States would import 10 million wristwatches from Switzerland.

Now if the United States imposes a tariff of

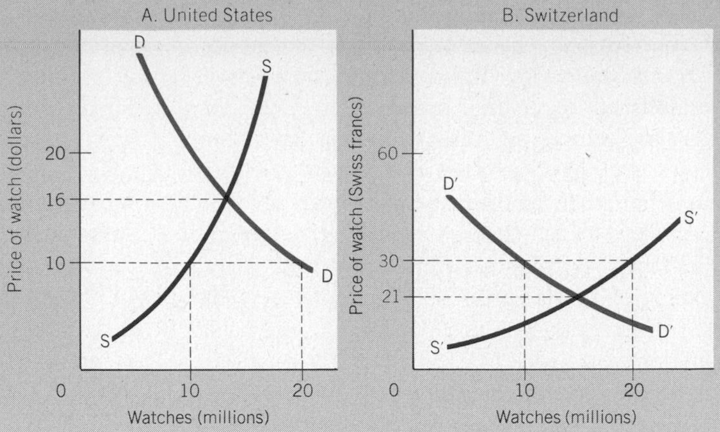

Figure 31.3
Effect of a Tariff on Swiss Watches
Under free trade, price would equal $10, or 30 Swiss francs. If a tariff of $10 is imposed on each watch imported from Switzerland, there will be a complete cessation of imports. Price in the U.S. will increase to $16, and price in Switzerland will fall to 21 Swiss francs.

$10 on each wristwatch imported from Switzerland, the imports will completely cease. Any importer who buys watches in Switzerland at the price (when there is no foreign trade) of 21 Swiss francs—which equals $7—must pay a tariff of $10; this makes his total costs $17 per watch. But this is more than the price of a watch in the United States when there is no foreign trade (which is $16). Consequently, there is no money to be made by importing watches—unless Americans can be persuaded to pay more for a Swiss watch than for an identical American watch.

What is the effect of the tariff? Clearly, the domestic watch industry receives a higher price—$16 rather than $10—than it would without a tariff. And the workers in the domestic watch industry may have more jobs and higher wages than without the tariff. The victim of the tariff is the American consumer, who pays a higher price for wristwatches.

Thus the domestic watch industry benefits at the expense of the rest of the nation. But does the general public lose more than the watch industry gains? In general, the answer is yes. The tariff reduces the consumption possibilities open to the nation. For example, suppose that wristwatches and bread were the only two commodities. A nation's ***consumption-possibility curve*** shows the various combinations of goods that can be consumed. Under free trade, the consumption-possibility curve is higher, as shown in Figure 31.4, than it is with the tariff. Clearly, the tariff reduces the consumption possibilities open to the nation.

The tariff in Figure 31.3 is a ***prohibitive tariff***—a tariff so high that it stops all imports of the good in question. Not all tariffs are pro-

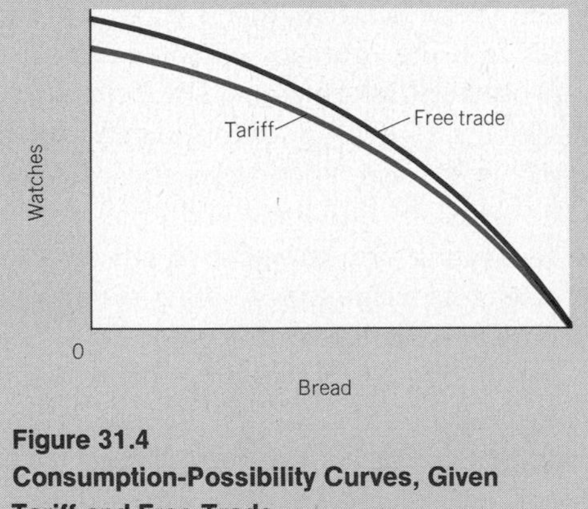

Figure 31.4
Consumption-Possibility Curves, Given Tariff and Free Trade
Under free trade, the consumption-possibility curve is farther from the origin than with the tariff. Consequently, society as a whole is better off under free trade.

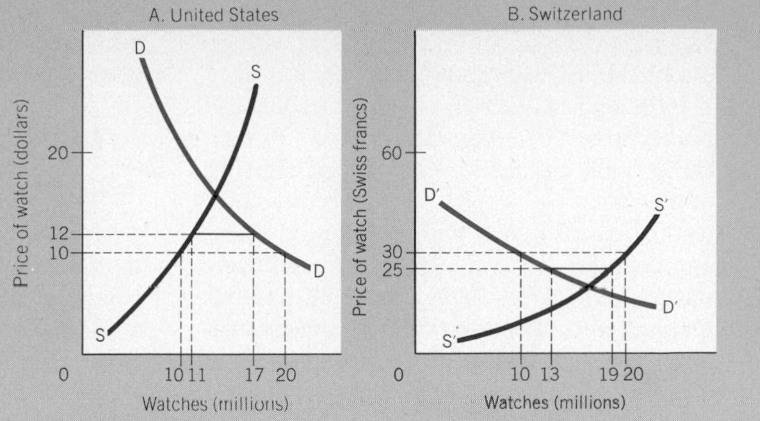

Figure 31.5
Effect of a Quota on Swiss Watches
Before the quota is imposed, the price is $10, or 30 Swiss francs. After a quota of 6 million watches is imposed, the price in the United States rises to $12, and the price in Switzerland falls to 25 Swiss francs.

hibitive. (If they were, the government would receive no revenue at all from tariffs.) In many cases, the tariff is high enough to stop some, but not all, imports; and, as you would expect, the detrimental effect of a nonprohibitive tariff on consumption possibilities and living standards is less than that of a prohibitive tariff. But this does not mean that nonprohibitive tariffs are harmless. On the contrary, they can do lots of harm to domestic consumption and living standards.

The detrimental effects of tariffs have long been recognized, even in detective stories. For example, in the course of solving the mystery concerning the Hound of the Baskervilles, Sherlock Holmes expressed his enthusiastic approval of a newspaper editorial that read as follows:

> You may be cajoled into imagining that your own special trade or your own industry will be encouraged by a protective tariff, but it stands to reason that such legislation must in the long run . . . lower the general conditions of life on this island.[7]

Of course, Holmes considered this point elementary (my dear Watson) but worth hammering home.

[7] Arthur Conan Doyle, *The Hound of the Baskervilles,* in *The Complete Sherlock Holmes,* Garden City, N.Y.: Garden City Publishing Co., 1938, p. 802.

The Social Costs of Quotas

Besides tariffs, other barriers to free trade are ***quotas,*** which many countries impose on the amount of certain commodities that can be imported annually. For example, the United States sets import quotas on sugar and exerts pressure on foreigners to get them to limit the quantity of steel and textiles that they will export to us. To see how a quota affects trade, production, and prices, let's return to the market for wristwatches. Suppose the United States places a quota on the import of wristwatches: no more than 6 million wristwatches can be imported per year. Figure 31.5 shows the effect of the quota. Before it was imposed, the price of wristwatches was $10 (or 30 Swiss francs), and the United States imported 10 million wristwatches from Switzerland. The quota forces the United States to reduce its imports to 6 million.

What will be the effect on the U.S. price? The demand curve shows that, if the price is $12, American demand will exceed American supply by 6 million watches; in other words, we will import 6 million watches. Thus, once the quota is imposed, the price will rise to $12, since *this is the price that will reduce our imports to the amount of the quota.* Clearly, a quota—like a tariff—increases the price of the good. (Note too that the price in Switzerland will fall to 25 francs. Thus the quota will reduce the price in Switzerland.)

Both a quota and a tariff reduce trade, raise prices, protect domestic industry from foreign competition, and reduce the standard of living of the nation as a whole. But most economists tend to regard quotas with even less enthusiasm than they do tariffs. Under many circumstances, a quota insulates local industry from foreign competition even more effectively than a tariff does. Foreigners, if their costs are low enough, can surmount a tariff barrier; but if a quota exists, there is no way they can exceed the quota. Moreover, a (nonprohibitive) tariff provides the government with some revenue, while quotas do not even do that. The windfall price increase from a quota accrues to the importer who is lucky enough or influential enough—or sufficiently generous with favors and bribes—to get an import license. (However, if the government auctions off the import licenses, it can obtain revenue from a quota.)

Export Subsidies and Other Barriers to Free Trade

Finally, ***export subsidies,*** another means by which governments try to give their domestic industry an advantage in international competition, are also a major impediment to free trade. Such subsidies may take the form of outright cash disbursements, tax exemptions, preferential financing or insurance arrangements, or other preferential treatment for exports. Export subsidies, and other such measures, frequently lead to countermeasures. For example, to counter foreign export subsidies, the U.S. government has imposed duties against such subsidies on goods sold here.

Other barriers to free trade include licensing requirements and unreasonable product quality standards. By granting few licenses (which are required in some countries to import goods) and by imposing unrealistically stringent product quality standards, governments discourage imports.

Arguments for Tariffs and Quotas

Given the disadvantages to society at large of tariffs and other barriers to free trade, why do governments continue to impose them? There are many reasons, some sensible, some irrational. One of the most convincing is the desirability of maintaining a domestic industry for purposes of *national defense.* For example, even if the Swedes had a comparative advantage in producing airplanes, we would not allow free trade to put our domestic producers of aircraft out of business if we felt that a domestic aircraft industry was necessary for national defense. Although the Swedes are by no means unfriendly, we would not want to import our entire supply of such a critical commodity from a foreign country, where the supply might be shut off for reasons of international politics. (Recall the Arab oil embargo of 1973.)

This is a perfectly valid reason for protecting certain domestic industries, and many protective measures are defended on these grounds. To the extent that protective measures are in fact required for national defense, economists go along with them. Of course the restrictions entail social costs (some of which were described in previous sections), but these costs may well be worth paying for enhanced national security. The trouble is that many barriers to free trade are justified on these grounds when in fact they protect domestic industries only tenuously connected with national defense. Moreover, even if there is a legitimate case on defense grounds for protecting a domestic industry, subsidies are likely to be a more straightforward and efficient way to do so than tariffs or quotas.

Besides national defense, there are other noneconomic reasons for protecting particular domestic industries. Some countries—Canada, for one—use a tariff to protect certain industries that they feel help them to be more independent of foreign domination and influence. Many Canadians, for understandable reasons, are intent on maintaining their traditions and values, and on resisting the penetration of American ways. Such noneconomic reasons for protection are perfectly reasonable if the nation as a whole understands the economic cost and agrees that the game is worth the candle (and if the reasons are sufficiently understood by foreigners that the measures do not provoke retaliation).

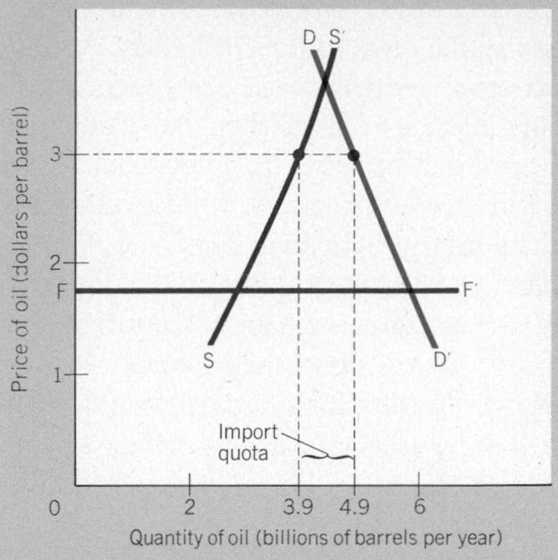

Figure 31.6
Effect of the pre-1973 Import Quota
SS′ is the supply curve for domestically produced petroleum, *FF′* is the supply curve for foreign produced petroleum, and *DD′* is the demand curve for petroleum in the United States. With an import quota of 1 billion barrels, the price will be $3; the price would be $1.75 if the import quota were removed.

The Pre-1973 Oil Import Quotas: A Case Study

As we pointed out in Chapter 19, the United States has been concerned about its energy supplies. To illustrate the nature and effect of barriers to free trade, as well as to shed light on this problem, let's consider the oil import quotas that existed until 1973 in the United States. These quotas were the subject of great controversy. First established by President Eisenhower in 1959, the Mandatory Oil Import Quota allowed firms to import only a certain amount of oil. Supporters of the quota argued that we could not afford to depend on foreigners for our oil because foreign sources might be cut off in war or other emergencies. Opponents argued that the costs to the consumer of these quotas were very high and that the oil requirements for national security were overstated.

Economists at Charles River Associates estimated the costs to the consumer in a study prepared for President Nixon's Office of Science and Technology.[8] Figure 31.6 shows the demand curve for petroleum in the United States, labeled *DD′*. The supply curve for domestically produced petroleum was *SS′*. The supply curve for foreign-produced petroleum at that time was *FF′*, a horizontal line at $1.75. Clearly, the price of petroleum under the import quota was set at the level—$3.00 per barrel—where the horizontal distance between the quantity demanded and the quantity supplied was equal to the import quota. If there were free trade, the price of petroleum would have been at the intersection of the *FF′* and *DD′* curves—or $1.75 per barrel.

Thus, in 1968, for example, consumers paid about $5.6 billion more for petroleum than they would have under free trade. We arrive at this figure by noting that consumers bought about 4.9 billion barrels of oil in 1968. If they paid $1.25 extra for each barrel, they paid 4.9

[8] James Burrows and Thomas Domencich, *An Analysis of the United States Oil Import Quota,* Lexington, Mass.: Heath, 1970.

billion times $1.25—or $5.6 billion—more than under free trade. Moreover, this does not include all the costs to the consumers. Additional costs arise because some consumers used less oil at the price of $3.00 than they would have if the price had been $1.75. They would have increased their satisfaction if they could have expanded their oil consumption.[9]

This was an enormous cost. Could it be justified on grounds of national security? It was difficult to tell, but many economists were doubtful. During his first term in office, President Nixon asked for a "full review of the nation's oil-import policies by the executive offices of the president." A task force—composed of the secretaries of labor, defense, state, interior, and commerce, as well as the director of the Office of Emergency Preparedness—was appointed to study the issue. Though many questions were raised concerning the merits of the oil import quota, it was continued nonetheless.

In 1973, when government officials became increasingly concerned about impending fuel shortages, opposition to the oil import quota mounted. Finally, in April 1973, President Nixon announced he was suspending direct control over the quantity of crude oil and refined products that could be imported. The oil import quota was dead. But in late 1973 and early 1974, the situation changed drastically, as the Arabs first cut back oil exports to us and then increased the price of oil by an enormous amount. No longer was FF' the supply curve for foreign oil; instead, the supply curve jumped off the graph. The days of relatively cheap foreign oil were over, at least for the foreseeable future.

Other Arguments for Tariffs

Besides national defense, several other arguments for tariffs or quotas can make sense. First, *tariffs or other forms of protection can be justified to foster the growth and development of young industries.* For example, suppose that Japan has a comparative advantage in the production of a certain semiconductor, but Japan does not presently produce this item. It may take Japanese firms several years to become proficient in the relevant technology, to engage in the learning described in a previous section and to take advantage of the relevant economies of scale. While this industry is "growing up," Japan may impose a tariff on such semiconductors, thus shielding its young industry from competition it can not yet handle. This "infant industry" argument for tariffs has a long history; Alexander Hamilton was one of its early exponents. Needless to say, it is *not* an argument for *permanent* tariffs, since infant industries are supposed to grow up—and the sooner the better. (Moreover, a subsidy for the industry would probably be better and easier to remove than a temporary tariff, according to many economists.)

Second, *tariffs sometimes may be imposed to protect domestic jobs and to reduce unemployment at home.* In the short run the policy may succeed, but we must recognize that other nations are likely to retaliate by enacting or increasing their own tariffs, so that such a policy may not work very well in the long run. A more sensible way to reduce domestic unemployment is to use the tools of fiscal and monetary policy described in Chapters 11 and 15 rather than tariffs. If workers are laid off by industries that cannot compete with foreign producers, proper monetary and fiscal policy, together with retraining programs, should enable these workers to switch to other industries that can compete.

Third, *tariffs sometimes may be imposed to prevent a country from being too dependent on only a few industries.* For example, consider a Latin American country that is a major producer of bananas. Under free trade, this

[9] Of course, one must distinguish between the costs to the consumer and the costs to the nation as a whole. For example, some of the costs to the consumer represented the transfer of money to the oil producers. See ibid.

country might produce bananas and little else, putting its entire economy at the mercy of the banana market. If, for instance, the price of bananas fell, the country's national income would decrease drastically. To promote industrial diversification, this country may establish tariffs to protect other industries, for example, certain types of light manufacturing. In a case like this, the tariff protects the country from having too many eggs—or bananas (if you want to avoid mixing a metaphor)—in a single basket.

Fourth, *tariffs may sometimes improve a country's terms of trade—that is, the ratio of its import prices to its export prices.* For example, the United States is a major importer of bananas. If we impose a tariff on bananas, thus cutting down on the domestic demand for them (because the tariff will increase their price), the reduction in our demand is likely to reduce the price of bananas abroad. Consequently, foreign producers of bananas will really pay part of the tariff. However, other countries may retaliate; and if all countries pursue such policies, few, if any, are likely to find themselves better off.

Frequently Encountered Fallacies

Although, as we have just seen, tariffs can be defended under certain circumstances, many of the arguments for them frequently encountered in political oratory and popular discussions are misleading. Although no field of economics is free of popular misconceptions and fallacies, this one is particularly rich in pious inanities and thunderous *non sequiturs.* For example, one frequently encountered fallacy is that, if foreigners want to trade with us, they must be benefiting from the trade. Consequently, according to this argument, we must be giving them more than we get—and it must be in our interest to reduce trade. This argument is, of course, entirely erroneous in its assumption that trade cannot be beneficial to *both* trading partners. On the contrary, as we have seen, the heart of the argument for trade is that it can be mutually beneficial.

Another fallacy one often encounters in polite conversation—and not-so-polite political debate—is that a tariff is required to protect our workers from low-wage labor in other countries. According to this argument, since American labor (at $5 an hour) clearly cannot compete with foreign labor (which works at "coolie" wage levels), we have no choice but to impose tariffs. If we do not, cheap foreign goods will throw our high-priced laborers out of work. This argument is wrong on two counts. First, *high wages do not necessarily mean high unit costs of production.* Because the productivity of American workers is high, unit labor costs in the United States are roughly in line with those in other countries. (Recall from Chapter 16 that unit labor cost equals the wage rate divided by labor productivity. Obviously, unit labor cost may be no higher here than abroad, even though the wage rate here is much higher, if labor productivity here is also much higher than abroad.) Second, *if our costs were out of line with those of other countries, there should be a change in exchange rates, which would tend to bring them back into line.* As we shall see in Chapter 32, exchange rates should move to bring our exports and imports into balance.

Still another fallacy that makes the rounds is that it is better to "buy American" because then we have both the goods that are bought and the money, whereas if we buy from foreigners we have the goods but they have the money. Like some jokes, this fallacy has an ancient lineage—and one that borders on respectability, since Abraham Lincoln is supposed to have subscribed to it. Basically, the flaw is the implicit assumption that money is somehow valued for its own sake. In reality, all the foreigners can do with the money is buy some of our goods, so that really we are just swapping some of our goods for some of theirs. If such a trade is mutually advantageous, fine.

Why do politicians (both Democrats and Republicans) sometimes utter these fallacies? No doubt an important reason is simply ignorance. There is no law that prevents people with little understanding of economics from holding public office. But this may not be the only reason. Special-interest groups—particular industries, unions, and regions—have a lot to gain by getting the government to enact protective tariffs and quotas. And Congress and the executive branch of the government are often sensitive to the pressures of these groups, which wield considerable political power.

Faced with a choice between helping a few powerful, well-organized groups and helping the general public—which is poorly organized and often ignorant of its own interests—politicians frequently tend to favor the special-interest groups. After all, these groups have a lot to gain and will remember their friends, while the general public—each member of which loses only a relatively small amount—will be largely unaware of its losses anyhow. Having decided to help these groups, a congressman or senator may not exert himself unduly to search out or expose the weakness in some of the arguments used to bolster their position. For example, there is the story of a well-known senator who, about to deliver a certain oration, wrote in the margin of one section of his speech: "Weak point here. Holler like hell."

Tariffs in the United States

How high are American tariffs, now and in the past? In our early years, we were a very protectionist nation. The argument for protecting our young industry from the competition of European manufacturers was, of course, the "infant industry" argument, which, as we saw above, can be perfectly sensible. However, our own industries understandably found it advantageous to prolong their childhood for as long as possible—and to press for continuation of high tariffs. During the nineteenth century and well into the twentieth, the industrial Northeast was particularly strong in its support of tariffs. Furthermore, the Republican party, which generally held sway in American politics between the Civil War and the New Deal, favored a high tariff. Thus, as shown in Figure 31.7, the tariff remained relatively high from about 1870 until the early 1930s. With the exception of the period around World War I, average tariff rates were about 40 to 50 percent. With the enactment of the Smoot-Hawley Tariff of 1930, the tariff reached its peak—about 60 percent. Moreover, these tariff rates understate the extent to which the tariff restricted trade: some goods were completely shut out of the country by the tariff, and do not

Figure 31.7
Average American Tariff Rates
The tariff generally remained high from about 1870 to the early 1930s; in recent years it has decreased substantially.

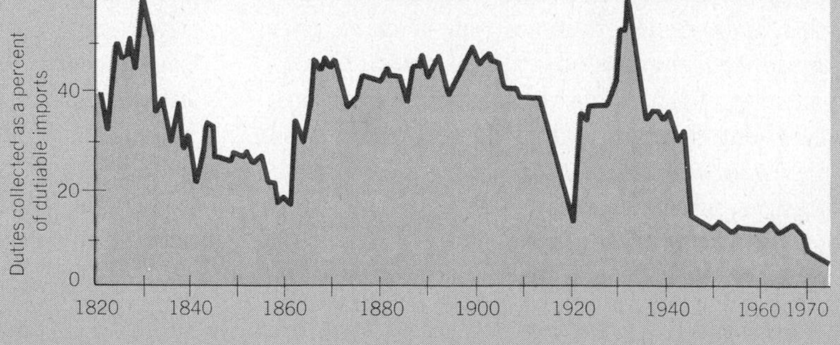

show up in the figures.

With the Democratic victory in 1932, a movement began toward freer trade. The Trade Agreements Act of 1934 allowed the president to bargain with other countries to reduce barriers to trade. He was given the power to lower U.S. tariffs by as much as 50 percent. In 1945, he was given the power to make further tariff reductions. Between 1934 and 1948, tariff rates fell substantially, as shown in Figure 31.7. By 1948, the United States was no longer a high-tariff country; the average tariff rate was only about 10 percent.

During the 1950s, there were no further decreases in the tariff—but there were no substantial increases either. The movement toward freer trade was continued by President Kennedy in 1962, and during the 1960s, the "Kennedy Round" negotiations took place among about 40 nations in an attempt to reduce tariffs. In 1967, the United States agreed to cut tariffs by about $\frac{1}{3}$ on a great many items.

The negotiations during the 1960s were prompted by the establishment of the European Economic Community—or "Common Market." The EEC was composed originally of Belgium, France, West Germany, Holland, Italy, and Luxembourg; and in the 1970s, Britain, Denmark, and Ireland joined. When the EEC was formed, the member countries agreed to reduce the tariff barriers against one another's goods—but not against the goods of other nations, including the United States.

The formation and success of the Common Market—and the likelihood that other European countries would join—posed a problem for the United States. The Common Market is a large and rich market, with over 200 million people and a combined gross national product exceeding $800 billion. With the reduction of tariff barriers *within* the Common Market, trade *among* the members of the Common Market increased rapidly, and prices of many items were cut. But American exporters were less than ecstatic about all of this, because the members of the Common Market still maintained their tariff barriers against American goods. While the "Kennedy Round" negotiations succeeded in reducing some of the tariff barriers between the United States and the Common Market, important tariff barriers remain, particularly for agricultural products.

In 1973, over 100 nations met in Tokyo to plan a new round of trade negotiations. The aim was to make further progress toward the reduction of tariffs and nontariff barriers to trade. In 1974, the Congress passed the Trade Reform Act of 1974, which enabled the president, after international negotiations, to reduce any tariff presently above 5 percent by $\frac{3}{5}$ and to abolish any tariff presently equal to 5 percent or less. Also, the act allowed workers, firms, and communities that are hurt by import competition to obtain payments and other forms of assistance. In 1975, a new round of negotiations was begun in Geneva. As in previous years, one of the important problem areas was agriculture, where the European Economic Community is reluctant to reduce tariffs.

Recent years have seen some increase in protectionist feelings in the United States. As Western Europe and Japan have become more formidable competitors abroad and at home, many industries have begun to press for quotas and higher tariffs. The textile and steel industries have been particularly vocal and have managed to increase trade barriers. Some unions have joined the protectionist forces in an effort to hold on to jobs. The Hartke-Burke bill, which attempted to increase trade barriers and to impede the international diffusion of technology, received considerable attention in Congress in the early 1970s. And the Trade Reform Act of 1974 was not free of protectionist features. It is to be hoped that this upsurge of protectionist spirit will be short-lived, and developments here and abroad will enable us and our trading partners to move closer to the realization of the benefits of free trade.

The European Economic Community

The EEC, born in the embers of World War II, was fathered by a desire to bind Germany to the rest of Europe. The success of the European Steel and Coal Community and the Benelux union encouraged the "Europeanists," and in 1957 the Treaty of Rome formally proclaimed the birth of a six-country free-trade area in which labor, capital, and goods were to move freely. None of this was to happen instantaneously, but the six countries—France, Germany, Italy, Belgium, the Netherlands, and Luxembourg—did agree on a timetable for the removal of centuries-old barriers and on a commission and council to manage the details of the process.

There are ample statistics to tell the story since 1958—growth rates of above 4 percent, increased competitiveness by European firms, increases in per capita incomes, and increased membership (including Great Britain). But the flavor of this customs union comes through best by seeing what it has meant to three prototype economic men.

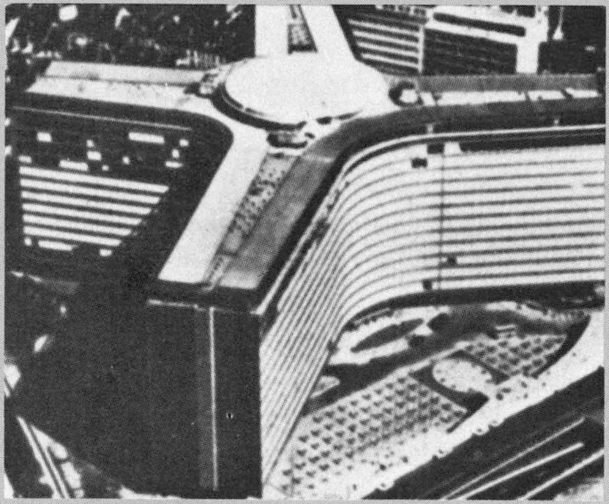

HEADQUARTERS OF THE EUROPEAN ECONOMIC COMMUNITY, BRUSSELS

Nino T. was born in southern Italy, where reported unemployment is 14 percent.* If disguised unemployment were included, the rate might run as high as double that. Wages, for those with jobs, averaged about $20 per week. In 1965, he migrated to Germany to work in an automobile plant in Frankfort, where he could make $75 a week, and send back $40 to his family. He planned to stay for another two years—perhaps until he had saved enough to buy a small business.

John C. works for a leather-goods firm in London. As a new member of the Common Market, he was able to migrate to the Continent and find a job, at considerably higher wages. He has no plans to do so, however, and when Britain joined the Common Market, his chief worry was that it would mean higher food prices. Why? Because the technologically inefficient but politically powerful French farmer was able to demand protection from cheap American and Canadian food. Thus, while French wheat would flow freely into Great Britain, the high external tariff would now keep out North American wheat.

Richard B., an American businessman, now lives in Paris, managing the French subsidiary of a large New-York-based corporation. He was moved to Paris about ten years ago, when company officials decided that the removal of internal barriers by the EEC would allow U.S. companies to operate on the scale to which they were accustomed. To stay competititve in the European market, they decided to build production facilities inside the EEC, rather than producing in the U.S. and shipping abroad. Richard now finds himself very much at home in France, and seriously considers living out his days in Paris. E.A.

* George Hildebrand, *The Italian Economy,* New York: Harper and Row, 1967, p. 337.

Summary

International trade permits specialization, and specialization increases output. This is the advantage of trade, both for individuals and for nations. Country *A* has an absolute advantage over Country *B* in the production of a good when Country *A* can produce a unit of the good with less resources than can Country *B*. Trade can be mutually beneficial even if one country has an absolute advantage in the production of all goods.

Specialization and trade depend on comparative, not absolute advantage. A nation is said to have a comparative advantage in those products where its efficiency relative to other nations is highest. Trade can be mutually beneficial if a country specializes in the products where it has a comparative advantage and imports the products where it has a comparative disadvantage.

The principle of comparative advantage is of use in predicting the pattern of world trade, as well as in showing its benefits. If markets are relatively free and competitive, producers will automatically be led to produce in accord with comparative advantage. If a country has a comparative advantage in the production of a certain good, it will turn out—after the price of the good in various countries is equalized and total world output of the good equals total world demand—that this country is an exporter of the good under free trade.

Specialization may occur because of economies of scale and learning. Also, some countries develop new products and processes, which they export to other countries until the technology becomes widely available.

A tariff is a tax imposed by the government on imports, the purpose being to cut down on imports in order to protect domestic industry and workers from foreign competition. Tariffs benefit the protected industry at the expense of the general public, and, in general, a tariff costs the general public more than the protected industry (and its workers and suppliers) gains. Quotas are another barrier to free trade. They too reduce trade, raise prices, protect domestic industry from foreign competition, and reduce the standard of living of the nation as a whole.

Tariffs, quotas, and other barriers to free trade can sometimes be justified on the basis of national security and other noneconomic considerations. Moreover, tariffs and other forms of protection can sometimes be justified to protect infant industries, to prevent a country from being too dependent on only a few industries, and to carry out other national objectives. But many arguments for tariffs are fallacious.

In our early years, we were a very protectionist country. Our tariff remained relatively high until the 1930s, when a movement began toward freer trade. Between 1934 and 1948, our tariff rates dropped substantially. Again during the 1960s, there was a significant reduction in our tariffs. But more recently, as some of our industries (like steel) have been hit hard by imports, there has been some tendency to push for more protectionist measures.

Although it has equaled only about 5 to 10 percent of our gross national product, foreign trade is of very considerable importance to the American economy. Many of our industries rely on foreign countries for raw materials or for markets, and our consumers buy many kinds of imported goods. In absolute terms, our exports are large and have represented about 15 percent of total world trade. Both our exports and imports are mostly finished manufactured goods.

CONCEPTS FOR REVIEW

Comparative advantage
Absolute advantage
Product transformation curve
Trading-possibility curve
Tariff
Quota
Prohibitive tariff
Export subsidy
Technology gap
Multinational firm
European Economic Community

QUESTIONS FOR DISCUSSION AND REVIEW

1. According to Hendrik Houthakker, "Our workers get high real income not because they are protected from foreign competition, but because they are highly productive, at least in certain industries." Do you agree? Why or why not?

2. According to Richard Cooper, "Technological innovation can undoubtedly strengthen the competitive position of a country in which the innovation takes place, whether it be one which enlarges exports or displaces imports." Give examples of this phenomenon, and discuss various ways that one might measure the effects of technological innovation on a country's competitive position.

3. Discuss the effects of the multinational firm on the world economy. Do you think that the activities of multinational firms should be regulated in new ways? If so, why?

4. Suppose that the United States can produce 3 electronic computers or 3,000 cases of wine with 1 unit of resources, while France can produce 1 electronic computer or 2,000 cases of wine with 1 unit of resources. Will specialization increase world output?

5. Suppose that the United States has 100 units of resources while France has 50 units. Based on the data in Question 4, draw the product transformation curve in each country. Without international trade, what will be the ratio of the price of an electronic computer to the price of a case of wine in each country?

6. Given the information in Questions 4 and 5, how will firms in France and the United States know whether they should produce wine or electronic computers? Must the government instruct them on this score? Why or why not?

7. Under the circumstances described in Questions 4 and 5, will each country specialize completely in the production of one or the other good? Why or why not? What factors result in incomplete specialization in the real world?

8. "The United States doesn't export electronic computers because we have a comparative advantage in producing them. It's because we're better at producing them than any other country." Comment and evaluate.

9. "The principle of comparative advantage doesn't work. The U.S. exports electronic computers to Japan and imports electronic consumer goods like TV sets from Japan." Comment and evaluate.

10. Would you favor a high tariff on imported steel if you were: (a) an automobile worker, (b) a steel worker, (c) an automobile buyer, (d) a plastics worker? Explain your reasoning in each case.

32 Exchange Rates and the Balance of Payments

During the early 1970s, any American at all acquainted with the financial or international news became aware that the United States was having "balance of payments difficulties"—or, a bit more specifically, we were experiencing deficits in our balance of payments. In response to these deficits, President Nixon devalued the dollar twice between 1971 and 1973, and then, together with the other major trading nations of the world, agreed in 1973 to allow exchange rates to "float." These were important developments by any standard. Even in the nation's less prestigious and more sensational newspapers, they managed to crowd the juiciest sports and criminal news off the front pages.

To understand these developments, we must consider several questions. What are exchange rates, and how are they determined? How are international business transactions carried out? Should there be fixed or flexible exchange rates? What is the balance of payments, and what is its significance? What problems has the United States had with its balance of payments in recent years? These questions, which are both fundamental and timely, are taken up in this chapter.

International Transactions and Exchange Rates

Suppose you want to buy a book from a German publisher, and that book costs 20 marks. (The German currency consists of marks, not dollars.) To buy the book, you must somehow get marks to pay the publisher, since this is the currency in which he deals. Or, if he agrees, you might pay him in dollars; but he would then have to exchange the dollars you give him for marks, since he must pay his bills in marks. Whatever happens, either you or he must somehow exchange dollars for marks, since international business transactions, unlike transactions within a country, involve two different currencies.

If you decide to exchange dollars for marks to pay the German publisher, how can you make the exchange? The answer is simple. You can buy German marks at a bank, just as you might buy lamb chops at a butcher shop. Just as the lamb chops have a price (expressed in dollars), so the German marks have a price (expressed in dollars). The bank may tell you that each mark you buy will cost you $.40. This makes the ***exchange rate*** between dollars and marks .4 to 1, since it takes .4 dollars to purchase 1 mark (or 2½ marks to purchase 1 dollar).

In general, *the exchange rate is simply the number of units of one currency that exchanges for a unit of another currency.* The obvious question is what determines the exchange rate. Why is the exchange rate between German marks and American dollars what it is? Why doesn't a dollar exchange for 10 marks, rather than 2½ marks? This basic question will occupy us in the next three sections.

Exchange Rates under the Gold Standard

As a starter, let's see how exchange rates were determined under the ***gold standard,*** which prevailed before the 1930s. *If a country was on the gold standard, a unit of its currency was convertible into a certain amount of gold.* For example, before World War I the dollar was convertible into $\frac{1}{20}$ ounce of gold, and the British pound was convertible into ¼ ounce of gold. Thus, since the pound exchanged for 5 times as much gold as the dollar, the pound exchanged for $5. The currency of any other country on the gold standard was convertible into a certain amount of gold in the same way; and *to see how much its currency was worth in dollars, you divided the amount of gold a unit of its currency was worth by the amount of gold ($\frac{1}{20}$ ounce) a dollar was worth.*

Why did the exchange rate always equal the ratio between the amount of gold a foreign currency was worth and the amount of gold a dollar was worth? For example, why did the price of a British pound stay at $5 before World War I? To see why, suppose that the price (in dollars) of a pound rose above this ratio—above $5. Instead of exchanging their dollars directly for pounds, Americans would have done better to exchange them for gold and then exchange the gold for pounds. By this indirect process, Americans could have exchanged $5 for a pound, so they would have refused to buy pounds at a price above $5 per pound.

Similarly, if the price of a pound fell below $5, the British would have refused to sell pounds, since they could have obtained $5 by converting the pound into gold and the gold into dollars. Thus, *because Americans would refuse to pay more than $5, and the British would refuse to accept less, for a pound, the price of a pound had to remain at about $5.* (In practice, the pound could be a few cents above or below $5, because it costs money to transport gold in order to carry out the conversion.)

But what insured that this exchange rate, dictated by the gold content of currencies, would result in a rough equality of trade between countries? For example, if one pound exchanged for $5, perhaps the British might find our goods so cheap that they would import a great deal from us, while we might find their goods so expensive that we would import little from them. Under these circumstances, the British would have to ship gold to us to pay for the excess of their imports from us over their exports to us, and eventually they would run out of gold. Could this happen? If not, why not? These questions occupied the attention of many early economists. The classic answers were given by David Hume, the famous Scottish philosopher, in the eighteenth century.

Hume pointed out that under the gold standard a mechanism insured that trade would be brought into balance and that neither country would run out of gold. This mechanism was as follows: If, as we assumed, the British bought more from us than we bought from them, they would have to send us gold to pay for the excess of their imports over their exports. As their gold stock declined, their price level would fall. (Recall the quantity theory of money.) As our gold stock increased, our price level would rise. Thus, because of our rising prices, the British would tend to import less from us; and because of their falling prices, we would tend to import more from them. Consequently, the trade between the two countries would tend toward a better balance. Eventually, when enough gold had left Britain and entered the United States, prices here would have increased enough, and prices in Britain would have fallen enough, to put imports and exports in balance.

Flexible Exchange Rates

The gold standard is long gone; and after many decades of fixed exchange rates (discussed in the next section), the major trading nations of the world began to experiment with flexible exchange rates in early 1973. Let's consider a situation where exchange rates are allowed to fluctuate freely, like the price of any commodity in a competitive market. In a case of this sort, exchange rates—like any price—are determined by supply and demand. There is a market for various types of foreign currency—German marks, British pounds, French francs, and so on—just as there are markets for various types of meat.

In the case of the German mark, the demand and supply curves may look like those shown in Figure 32.1. The demand curve shows the amount of German marks that people with dollars will demand at various prices of a mark. The supply curve shows the amount of German marks that people with marks will supply at various prices of a mark. Since the amount of German currency supplied must equal the

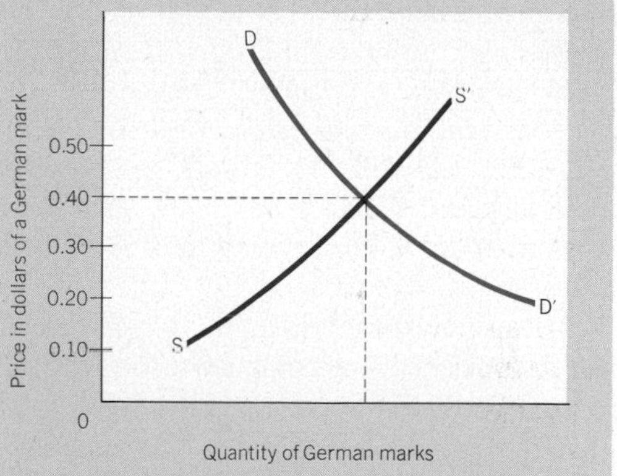

Figure 32.1
Determination of the Exchange Rate between Dollars and German Marks under Freely Fluctuating Exchange Rates
Under freely fluctuating exchange rates, the equilibrium price of a German mark would be $.40 if *DD'* is the demand curve for marks and *SS'* is the supply curve.

amount demanded in equilibrium, *the equilibrium price (in dollars) of a German mark is given by the intersection of the demand and supply curves.* In Figure 32.1, this intersection is at $.40.

Let's look in more detail at the demand and supply sides of this market. On the *demand* side are people who want to import German goods (like the book you want to buy) into the United States, people who want to travel in Germany (where they'll need German money), people who want to build factories in Germany, and others with dollars who want German currency. The people on the *supply* side are those who want to import American goods into Germany, Germans who want to travel in the United States (where they'll need American money), people with marks who want to build factories in the United States, and others with marks who want American currency.

Thus it is obvious that *when Americans demand more German cameras or Rhine wine (causing the demand curve to shift upward and to the right), the price (in dollars) of the German mark will tend to increase.* Conversely, *when the Germans demand more American cars or computers (resulting in a shift of the supply curve downward and to the right), the price (in dollars) of the German mark will tend to decrease.*

To see why an increase in German demand for American cars or computers shifts the supply curve downward and to the right, recall that the supply curve shows the amount of marks that will be supplied at each price of a mark. Thus a shift downward and to the right in the supply curve means that more marks will be supplied at a given price (in dollars) of the mark. Given the posited increase in German demand for American goods, such a shift in the supply curve would be expected.

Changes in Exchange Rates: Determinants and Effects

Under a system of flexible exchange rates, changes in tastes, among other things, affect the equilibrium level of the exchange rate, as shown by the usual sorts of supply-and-demand diagrams that we introduced in Chapter 4. For example, as we have just seen, if Americans become fonder and fonder of German goods and less fond of their domestic goods, there will be an increase in the demand for goods imported from Germany, and an attendant increase in the demand for German marks. As shown in Figure 32.2, the demand curve for marks shifts from *DD′* to *EE′*, causing a rise in the price (in dollars) of a German mark from $.40 to $.44.

Also, differences between the two countries in many other factors, including the rate of inflation and the rate of economic growth, will affect the exchange rate. *If the rate of inflation in the United States is relatively high, this is likely to result in an increase in the price (in dollars) of a German mark, because of its effect on these supply and demand curves.* On the other

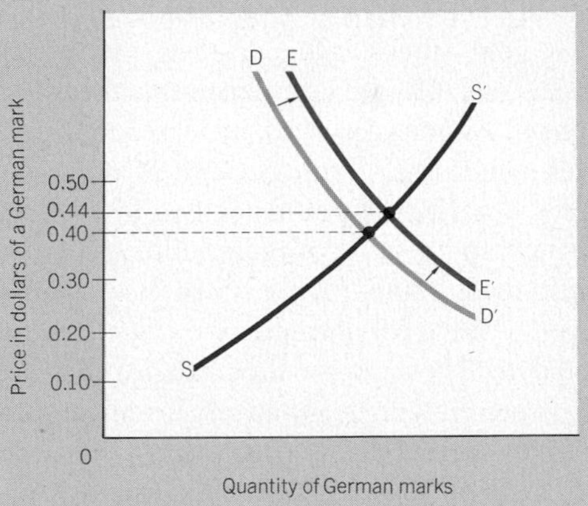

Figure 32.2
Effect of Shift in Demand Curve for German Marks
If the demand curve shifts from *DD′* to *EE′*, the equilibrium price of a German mark increases from $.40 to $.44.

hand, *a relatively low rate of inflation in the United States, and a high rate of inflation in Germany, is likely to cause a decrease in the price (in dollars) of a German mark.*

Two terms frequently encountered in discussions of exchange rates are ***appreciation*** and ***depreciation.*** When Country *A*'s currency becomes more valuable relative to Country *B*'s currency, Country *A*'s currency is said to appreciate relative to that of Country *B*, and Country *B*'s currency is said to depreciate relative to that of Country *A*. In Figure 32.2, the mark appreciated relative to the dollar and the dollar depreciated relative to the mark. This use of terms makes sense. Since the number of dollars commanded by a mark increased, the mark clearly became more valuable relative to the dollar and the dollar became less valuable relative to the mark.

Note that such a change in exchange rates would not have been possible under the gold standard. Unless a country changed the amount of gold that could be exchanged for a unit of its currency, exchange rates were fixed under the gold standard. Sometimes governments did change the amount of gold that could be exchanged for their currencies. For example, in 1933 the United States increased the price of gold from $21 an ounce to $35 an ounce. When a country increases the price of gold, this is called a ***devaluation*** of its currency.

Under flexible exchange rates, what insures a balance in the exports and imports between countries? The situation differs, of course, from that described by David Hume, since Hume assumed the existence of the gold standard. Under flexible exchange rates, the balance is achieved through changes in exchange rates. For example, suppose once again that for some reason Britain is importing far more from us than we are from Britain. This will mean that the British, needing dollars to buy our goods, will be willing to supply pounds more cheaply. In other words, the supply curve for British pounds will shift downward and to the right from S_1S_1' to S_2S_2', as shown in Figure 32.3. This will cause the price of a pound to decline from P_1 dollars to P_2 dollars. Or, from Britain's point of view, the price (in pounds) of a dollar will have been bid up by the swollen demand for imports from America.

Because of the increase in the price (in pounds) of a dollar, our goods will become more expensive in Britain. Thus the British will tend to reduce their imports of our goods. At the same time, since the price (in dollars) of a pound has decreased, British goods will become cheaper in the United States, and this, of course, will stimulate us to import more from Britain. Consequently, as our currency appreciates in terms of theirs—or, to put it another way, as theirs depreciates in terms of ours—the British are induced to import less and export

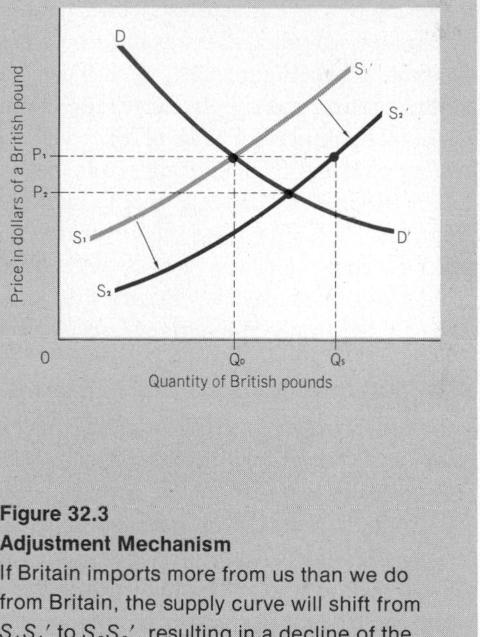

Figure 32.3
Adjustment Mechanism
If Britain imports more from us than we do from Britain, the supply curve will shift from S_1S_1' to S_2S_2', resulting in a decline of the price of the pound from P_1 to P_2 dollars. If Britain tries to maintain the price at $\$P_1$, the British government will have to exchange dollars for $(Q_S - Q_D)$ pounds.

more. Thus there is an automatic mechanism (just as there was under the gold standard) to bring trade between countries into balance.

Fixed Exchange Rates

Although many economists believed that exchange rates should be allowed to fluctuate, very few exchange rates really did so in the period from the end of World War II up to 1973. Instead, *most exchange rates were fixed by government action and international agreement.* Although they may have varied slightly about the fixed level, the extent to which they were allowed to vary was small. Every now and then, governments changed the exchange rates, for reasons discussed below; but for long periods of time, they remained fixed.

If exchange rates remain fixed, the amount demanded of a foreign currency may not equal the amount supplied. For example, consider the situation in Figure 32.4. If *DD′* and *SS′* are the demand and supply curves for German marks, the equilibrium price of a mark is $.40. But suppose the fixed exchange rate between dollars and marks is .35 to 1: that is, each mark exchanges for $.35. Unless the government intervenes, more German marks will be demanded at a price of $.35 per mark than will be offered. Specifically, the difference between the quantity demanded and the quantity supplied will be $Q_D - Q_S$. Unless the government steps in, a black market for German marks may develop, and the real price may increase toward $.40 per mark.

To maintain exchange rates at their fixed levels, governments can intervene in a variety of ways. For example, they may reduce the demand for foreign currencies by reducing defense expenditures abroad, by limiting the amount that their citizens can travel abroad, and by curbing imports from other countries. Thus, in the case depicted in Figure 32.4, the American government might adopt some or all

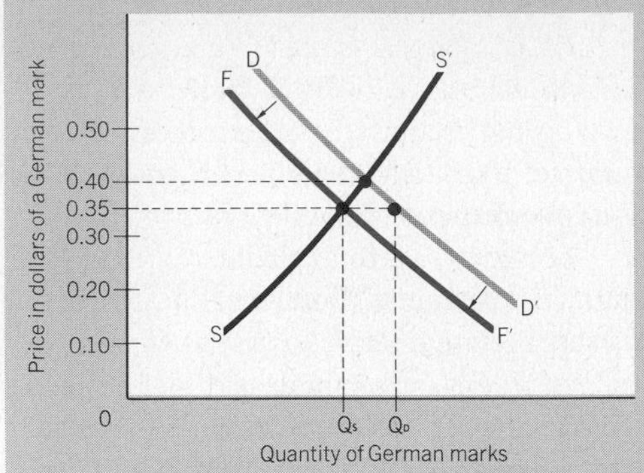

Figure 32.4
Fixed Exchange Rate
The equilibrium price of a German mark is $.40, if *DD′* is the demand curve. If $.35 is the fixed exchange rate, the U.S. government may try to shift the demand curve for marks from *DD′* to *FF′*, thus bringing the equilibrium exchange rate into equality with the fixed exchange rate.

of these measures to shift the demand curve for German marks downward and to the left. If the demand curve can be pushed from *DD′* to *FF′*, the equilibrium price of a German mark can be reduced to $.35, the fixed exchange rate. For the time being, there will no longer be any mismatch between the quantity of marks demanded and the quantity supplied.

However, when exchange rates are fixed, such mismatches cannot be eliminated entirely and permanently. To deal with temporary mismatches of this sort, governments enter the market and buy and sell their currencies in order to maintain fixed exchange rates. This happened in post-World-War-II Britain. At times the amount of British pounds supplied exceeded the amount demanded. Then the British government bought up the excess at the fixed exchange rate. At other times, when the quantity demanded exceeded the amount supplied, the British government supplied the pounds desired at the fixed exchange rate. As long as the equilibrium exchange rate was close to (sometimes above and sometimes below) the fixed exchange rate, the amount of its currency the government sold at one time equaled, more or less, the amount it bought at another time.

But in some cases governments tried to maintain a fixed exchange rate far from the equilibrium exchange rate. For example, the British government might have tried to maintain the price (in dollars) of the pound at P_1 in the situation in Figure 32.3, when the supply curve for British pounds was S_2S_2'. Since the quantity of British pounds supplied exceeded the quantity demanded at that exchange rate, the British government would have to buy the difference. That is, it would have to buy ($Q_S - Q_D$) pounds with dollars. Moreover, it would have to keep on exchanging dollars for pounds in these quantities for as long as the demand and supply curves remained in these positions. Eventually, the government would run out of dollars and would have to impose restrictions to shift the supply or demand curves (as described above) or change the exchange rate. How long it could maintain the price of the pound at P_1 would depend on how big its reserves of foreign currency were.

Fixed versus Flexible Exchange Rates

Why, until 1973, did most countries fix their exchange rates, rather than allow them to fluctuate? One important reason was the feeling that flexible exchange rates might vary so erratically that it might be difficult to carry out normal trade. For example, an American exporter of machine tools to Britain might not know what British pounds would be worth six months from now, when he would collect a debt in pounds. According to the proponents of fixed exchange rates, fluctuating rates would increase uncertainties for people and firms engaged in international trade and thus reduce the volume of such trade. Moreover, they argued that the harmful effects of speculation over exchange rates would increase if exchange rates were flexible, because speculators could push a currency's exchange rate up or down, and destabilize the exchange market. Further, they argued that flexible exchange rates might promote more rapid inflation, for reasons described in the next chapter.

Many economists disagreed, feeling that flexible exchange rates would work better. They asked why flexible prices are used and trusted in other areas of the economy, but not in connection with foreign exchange. They pointed out that a country would have more autonomy in formulating its fiscal and monetary policy if exchange rates were flexible, and they claimed that speculation regarding exchange rates would not be destabilizing. But until 1973, the advocates of flexible exchange rates persuaded few of the world's central bankers and policy makers.

However, considerable attention was devoted to a compromise between fixed and completely flexible exchange rates—the so-called *crawling peg*. According to the crawling peg (which admittedly sounds more like an insect than a system of exchange rates), the exchange rate between currencies would be allowed to change, but only up to a certain amount—perhaps 1 or 2 percent per year. Thus, if supply and demand dictated that the dollar should depreciate relative to the German mark, the price (in dollars) of the mark could increase 10 or 20 percent over a decade.

The advantage of the crawling peg is, of course, that it allows exchange rates to move in a way that eventually results in international equilibrium. However, in contrast to flexible exchange rates, the crawling peg insures that changes in exchange rates will be gradual enough to preserve many of the benefits of fixed exchange rates. In particular, the risks and uncertainties involved in international

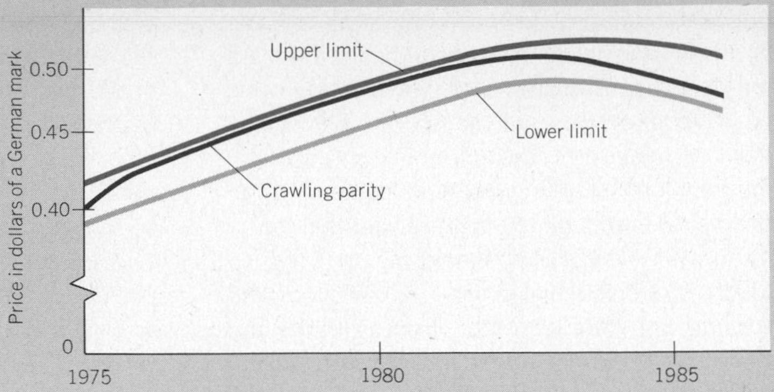

Figure 32.5
The Crawling Peg
According to the crawling peg, the exchange rate can vary by a certain amount each year. The upper and lower limits and crawling parity are shown here for a hypothetical case. Supply and demand can push the exchange rate between the upper limit and lower limit.

trade might be less than under flexible rates (see Figure 32.5).

In early 1973, after a series of attempts to alter the system of fixed exchange rates to maintain its viability, the major trading nations of the world agreed to allow exchange rates to fluctuate—in other words, to float. However, they did not go so far as to establish completely flexible exchange rates. Instead, the float was to be managed. Central banks would step in to buy and sell their currency. For example, the United States agreed that "when necessary and desirable" it would support the value of the dollar. Also, some European countries decided to maintain fixed exchange rates among their own currencies, but to float jointly against other currencies. This new system of fluctuating exchange rates seems to have worked reasonably well, despite the fact that the international monetary system received some major jolts, such as the oil crisis (described below) in the mid-1970s.

Experience with the Gold Standard and Gold Exchange Standard

What has been our experience with various types of exchange rates? During the latter part of the nineteenth century, the gold standard seemed to work very well, but serious trouble developed after World War I. After going off the gold standard during World War I, for reasons we will discuss in the next chapter, some countries tried to re-establish the old rates of exchange in the postwar period. Because the wartime and postwar rates of inflation were greater in some countries than in others, under the old exchange rates the goods of some countries were underpriced and those of other countries were overpriced. According to the doctrines of David Hume, this imbalance should have been remedied by increases in the general price level in countries where goods were underpriced and by reductions in the general price level in countries where goods were overpriced. But wages and prices proved to be inflexible, and, as one would expect, it proved especially difficult to adjust them downward. When the adjustment mechanism failed to work quickly enough, the gold standard was abandoned.

During the 1930s, governments tried various schemes. This was, of course, the time of the Great Depression, and governments were trying frantically to reduce unemployment. Sometimes a government allowed the exchange rate to be flexible for a while, and when it found what seemed to be an equilibrium level, fixed the exchange rate there. Sometimes a government depreciated the value of its own currency relative to those of other countries in an attempt to increase employment by making its goods cheap to other countries. Of course, when one country adopted such policies, others retaliated, causing a reduction in international trade and lending, but little or no benefit for the country that started the fracas.

In 1944, the Allied governments sent representatives to Bretton Woods, New Hampshire, to work out a more effective system for the postwar era. It was generally agreed that competitive devaluations, such as occurred in the 1930s, should be avoided. Out of the Bretton Woods conference came the ***International Monetary Fund*** (IMF), which was set up to maintain a stable system of fixed exchange rates and to insure that when exchange rates had to be changed because of significant trade imbalances, disruption was minimized.

The system developed during the postwar period is generally labeled the *gold-exchange standard*, as opposed to the gold standard. Under this system, the dollar—which had by this time taken the place of the British pound as the world's key currency—was convertible into gold at a fixed price (not, however, for monetary purposes by private American citizens, as we saw in Chapter 13). And since other currencies could be converted into dollars at fixed exchange rates, other currencies were convertible indirectly into gold at a fixed price.

During the early postwar period, this system worked reasonably well. However, throughout the 1960s our gold stock decreased substantially, as year in, year out, we had a deficit in our balance of payments, described below. To prevent speculators and others from depleting our gold stock, the major central banks agreed in 1968 to establish a ***"two-tier" gold system***—an ***official tier*** in which gold, used solely for monetary purposes, was traded back and forth between central banks at the official exchange rates, and a ***private tier*** in which the rest of the world's gold supply was traded on a free market. The central banks agreed not to sell gold to the private tier.

But this remedy could only postpone the breakdown of the gold-exchange standard. In August 1971, President Nixon announced that the United States would no longer convert dollars into gold for foreign central banks. Thus the link between gold and exchange rates was shattered. Also, pressure was exerted on other countries, particularly Japan and Germany, to allow their currencies to appreciate in terms of our own. Since this would make their goods more expensive to us and cut down on their exports, they resisted such changes. But eventually they allowed their currencies to become more expensive in terms of ours, and (what amounts to the same thing) we allowed our currency to become cheaper in terms of theirs. A new system of fixed exchange rates was approved in 1971, when representatives of the major trading nations met at the Smithsonian Institution.

Although President Nixon hailed the Smithsonian agreement as "the greatest international monetary agreement in the history of the world," events were to prove it unequal to the tasks it faced. In February 1973, scarcely more than a year after the agreement, the United States felt obliged to devalue the dollar again, as the outflow of dollars to other countries continued. Then, in March 1973, representatives of the major trading nations met in Paris to establish a system of fluctuating exchange rates, thus abandoning the Bretton Woods system of fixed exchange rates. This was a major break with the past, and one that was greeted with considerable apprehension as well as hope.

The Fight to Save the Pound: A Case Study

From this discussion it is clear that although exchange rates were generally fixed until 1973, from time to time they were altered to respond to changes in basic economic conditions. To illustrate how these alterations occurred, consider the case of Great Britain in the mid-1960s. Since 1949, the exchange rate between dollars and pounds had been 2.8 to 1, which meant that a British pound was worth $2.80. But at this exchange rate, Britain found it very difficult to export as much as she bought from foreigners. In other words, at this exchange rate the quantity of pounds supplied exceeded the quantity demanded. If the market for pounds had been free, the price of the pound would have dropped. That is, the pound would have depreciated relative to the dollar.

Britain's Labor government, elected in 1964, declared that it would not depreciate the pound. Prime Minister Harold Wilson claimed that maintaining the exchange rate at $2.80 was of primary importance and called the fight to maintain the exchange rate a "second battle of Britain." (The original battle of Britain occurred early in World War II, when Britain fought off air attacks by Nazi Germany.) In 1964, the government slapped a 15 percent tax on imports to shift the supply curve for pounds to the left. In 1965, the government restricted foreign travel and exports of capital. Finally, in 1966, the government froze wages, increased taxes, and cut government expenditures to curb inflation in an attempt to promote exports. All these measures were designed to push the equilibrium exchange rate—the rate at which the demand and supply curves for pounds intersect—up toward $2.80.

But it was to no avail. In 1967, the British were forced to devalue the pound. The exchange rate was reduced from $2.80 to $2.40, a depreciation of about 14 percent. It was hoped that this change would expand British exports, now cheaper to non-Britons, and discourage foreign imports, now more expensive to Britons. In other words, it was hoped that $2.40 was close to the equilibrium exchange rate. From 1967 to 1971, when the Smithsonian agreement took place, the exchange rate remained at this level. During 1975 and 1976, the pound fell once again, to below $1.65 in October 1976. But this decline occurred under a regime of floating, not fixed, exchange rates. In considerable degree, it reflected Britain's very high rate of inflation. (In early 1975, prices were rising at more than 30 percent per year.) As we noted above, a relatively high rate of inflation pushes down the value of a nation's currency when exchange rates are flexible.[1]

Experience with Floating Exchange Rates

From 1973 to date, exchange rates have been flexible, not fixed. As noted above, there has been some intervention by central banks to keep the movement of exchange rates between broad bounds, but this intervention generally has not been very great. The result has been considerable volatility in exchange rates. For example, the exchange rate between the dollar and the German mark has sometimes varied by 2 percent or more from one day to the next, and by 15 percent or more over a period of several months. Figure 32.6 shows the changes in the value of the dollar relative to selected foreign currencies during 1973–75. Clearly, the dollar depreciated considerably relative to the French franc, the German mark, the British pound, and the Italian lira in late 1974 and early 1975. But in late 1975, the dollar appreciated considerably relative to all of them, particularly the pound and the lira.

Unquestionably, the variations in exchange rates, some of which are erratic and without fundamental economic significance, have made international transactions more difficult. For example, Renault, the French auto manufacturer, is reported to have hesitated to launch an export drive into the U.S. market because of the erratic behavior of the dollar-franc ex-

[1] For further discussion, see Richard Cooper's contribution to R. Caves, *Britain's Economic Prospects,* Washington, D.C.: Brookings Institution, 1968, and J. B. Cohen, *Balance-of-Payments Policy,* Baltimore: Penguin, 1969.

Figure 32.6
Changes over Time in Foreign Exchange Rates, 1973–75
Since 1973, exchange rates have been floating. The dollar depreciated relative to the French franc, the German mark, the British pound, and the Italian lira in late 1974 and early 1975, but appreciated relative to them in late 1975.
Source: Board of Governors of the Federal Reserve System.

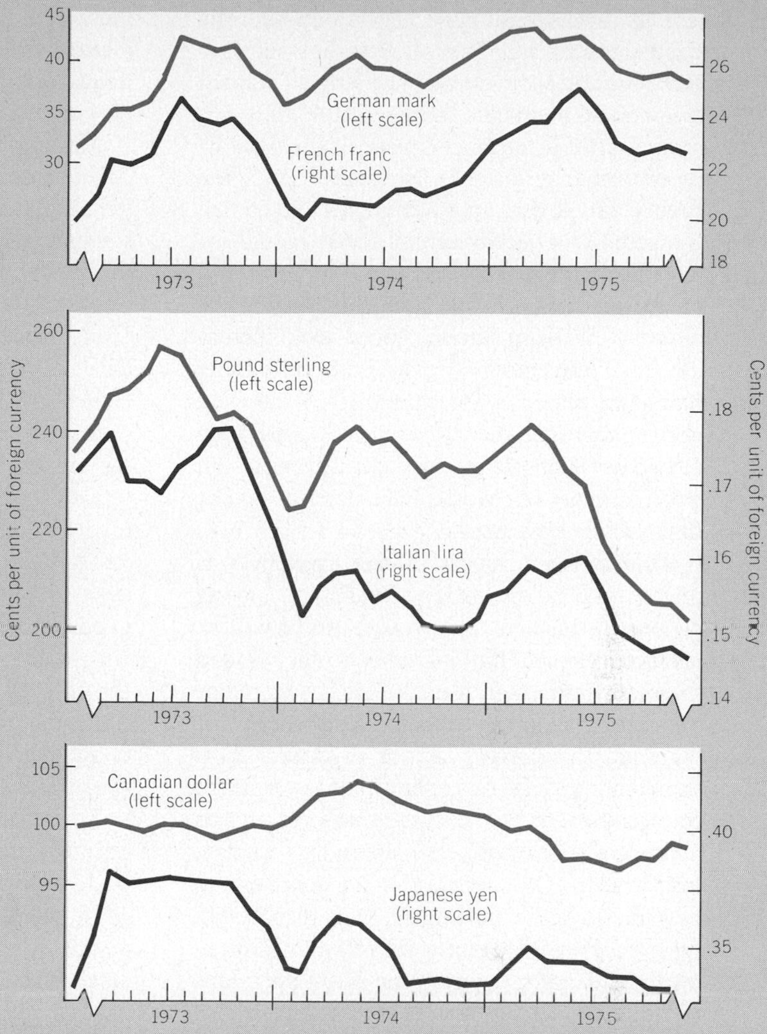

change rate. However, businessmen seem to have coped rather successfully with such exchange rate variation, as reflected in the following statement in late 1975 by the National Foreign Trade Council: "[Floating exchange rates have] . . . responded well to the shocks of the fast-moving developments of recent years, . . . [although] at times business has been unfavorably affected by sharp fluctuations of key currencies."

One of the greatest "shocks" of recent years was the increase in oil prices at the beginning of 1974. This sharp price increase meant that oil-importing countries suddenly had to pay unprecedented bills to the oil-producing countries, with the result that massive strain was put on the international financial system. Although the difficulties were not surmounted easily, the new system of floating exchange rates seems to have shown the required resilience to overcome this crisis.

During 1973 and 1974, there was considerable disagreement, particularly between the United States and France, over how flexible exchange rates should be. The French wanted to go back to fixed exchange rates; the U.S. wanted little or no impediment to the flexibility of exchange rates. In November 1975, the French and American governments agreed to a compromise whereby central banks would intervene to prevent "disorderly," or "erratic," fluctuations in exchange rates. Secretary of the Treasury William Simon defined such fluctuations as "movements that have no underlying economic reason." He said that in the year prior to this agreement, there were perhaps one or two occasions when the Federal Reserve did not intervene, but would have done so on the basis of this agreement.

An important aspect of this agreement is that it foreshadows more consultation among nations in this area. Every week, there will be contact between high Treasury officials and their counterparts in about a dozen other major countries to determine whether "disorderly" or "erratic" fluctuations are in evidence. This should allow decisions concerning government intervention in the exchange markets to be made on the basis of better and more complete information. Of course, it is too soon to tell how these new arrangements will turn out in practice. How frequently the relevant governments will agree to intervene is by no means obvious. But on the surface at least, this agreement seems to indicate somewhat more stability for exchange rates.

The Balance of Payments

We have referred repeatedly in this chapter to the balance of payments. Now we will discuss it in some detail. *Any country's* ***balance of payments*** *measures the flow of payments between it and other countries.* Consider the U.S. balance of payments in 1975, reproduced in Table 32.1. There are two types of items in the balance of payments: debit items and credit items. ***Debit items*** are items for which we must pay foreigners—items that use up the foreign currency we have. ***Credit items*** are items for which foreigners pay us—items that provide us with a stock of foreign currency. For example, if a French importer buys an American car to sell in France, this is a credit item in the U.S. balance of payments because a foreigner—the French importer—must pay us for the car. On the other hand, if an American importer buys some French wine to sell in the United States, this is a debit item in the U.S. balance of payments. We must pay the foreigner—the French winemaker—for the wine.

It is essential to understand at the outset that *the balance of payments always balances.* The total of credit items must always equal the total of debit items, because the sum of the debit items is the total value of goods, services, and assets we received from foreigners. These goods, services, and assets must be paid for with credit items, since credit items provide the foreign currency required by foreigners. Since the debit items must be paid for by the credit items, *the sum of the credit items must equal the sum of the debit items.*

To see exactly what the balance of payments tells us, let's look at each of the entries in Table 32.1, starting with the debits column. During 1975, we imported about $98 billion worth of merchandise. This, of course, is a debit item, since it requires payments to manufacturers abroad. Also, we spent about $1 billion for net military transactions, about $2 billion for remittances abroad (such as Social Security payments to Americans now living abroad), about $2 billion for net government grants and long-term capital outflows (such as our foreign aid programs and government finance for exports), about $9 billion for net private long-term capital outflows, about $3 billion for net nonliquid short-term private capital outflows, and about $6 billion for net liquid private capital outflows. These items (each of which will be described in some detail below) are all debit items, since they entail payments by us to foreigners.

Table 32.1
United States Balance of Payments, 1975

	Credit	Debit
	(billions of dollars)	
Goods and services		
Merchandise exports	107	
Merchandise imports		98
Net services (including travel and transportation)	2	
Net military transactions		1
Net investment income	6	
Transfers, capital movements, and movements of reserve assets		
Remittances		2
Net U.S. government grants and capital outflows		2
Net U.S. private long-term capital outflows		9
Net nonliquid short-term private capital outflows		3
Errors and omissions	4	
Net liquid private capital outflows		6
Net change in liabilities to foreign official agencies	3	
Net change in U.S. reserves		1
Total	122	122

Source: Survey of Current Business, March 1976.

To see how we paid for these debit items, we must look at the credits column. We exported about $107 billion worth of merchandise. This, of course, is a credit item, since it represents payments to us by foreign purchasers of American goods. Also, we received $2 billion (net) for services abroad, and about $6 billion in net income from foreign investments; both of these are credit items. Thus, adding up these credit items and these debit items (and noting that we must add $4 billion to the credit items to offset errors and omissions), our payments abroad totaled about $121 billion and payments to us equaled about $119 billion. The remaining items in the balance of payments show how we paid for the difference of $2 billion. As shown by the last two items in Table 32.1, foreigners accepted $3 billion in additional IOUs from us, and our reserves increased by $1 billion. This covered the $2 billion difference.

Goods and Services

Having looked briefly at the entire balance of payments, let's break the table into two parts: (1) goods and services; and (2) transfers, capital movements, and movements of reserve assets. First, consider goods and services. As you can see from Table 32.1, this part of the balance of payments shows the amount of goods and services we exported and imported. Note that exports and imports include *invisible* items, as well as *visible* items (that is, merchandise). Among the invisible items are transportation services, tourist expenditures, military sales and expenditures, and earnings on investments in other countries. They must be accounted for in the balance of payments, since they entail payments by one country to another. For example, when a British vessel carries our merchandise, we must pay for this service. Or when an American tourist stays at the George

V Hotel in Paris, we must pay for this service—and judging from the George V's rates, pay dearly at that. Or when foreigners lend us capital, we must pay them interest.

You will recall from the previous section that credit items supply us with foreign currency while debit items use up our foreign currency. Thus it is clear that when foreign carriers transport our goods or people, this is a debit item, but when we carry other countries' goods or people, this is a credit item in our balance of payments. Similarly, expenditures by American tourists traveling abroad are debit items, but money spent here by foreign tourists is a credit item. Further, interest we pay to foreigners on money they lent us is a debit item, but interest foreigners pay us on money we lent them is a credit item.

Besides the transactions made by private citizens, the government's transactions must be included too in our balance of payments. The United States government supports a vast network of military bases around the world. Every now and then, we become involved in "police actions" and other euphemisms and circumlocutions which, to the naked eye, look very much like wars. We also engage in a host of other government activities abroad (like the work of the United States Information Service, the Peace Corps, and so on), and all these programs affect our balance of payments. In the main, they result in debit items since they involve payments abroad. For example, money spent by U.S. military authorities stationed in Wiesbaden, Germany, to buy supplies from local German companies is a debit item.

We can tell a great deal about America's transactions with other countries by looking at the individual figures for goods and services in Table 32.1. First, it is clear that in 1975 we exported about $9 billion more merchandise than we imported. Second, we spent about $2 billion less on foreign transportation and other services and on tourism abroad than foreigners spent on our transportation and other services and on tourism here. Third, foreigners paid us far more—about $6 billion more—in interest and dividends on money we invested abroad than we paid foreigners for similar investments here. Fourth, the U.S. government spent (net) about $1 billion abroad for military transactions.

The Balance of Trade

The newspapers often mention the balance of trade. The ***balance of merchandise trade*** refers only to a part of the balance of payments. A nation is said to have a *favorable* balance of merchandise trade if its exports of merchandise are more than its imports of merchandise, and an *unfavorable* balance of merchandise trade if its exports of merchandise are less than its imports of merchandise. As Table 32.1 shows, the United States had a favorable balance of merchandise trade of about $9 billion in 1975. But obviously the balance of merchandise trade tells only part of what we want to know about a country's transactions with other countries. As shown in Table 32.1, there is much more to the balance of payments than a comparison of merchandise exports with merchandise imports. Moreover, a "favorable" balance of trade is not necessarily a good thing, since imports, not exports, contribute to a country's standard of living.

Also, note that the United States had a *net surplus with respect to goods and services* of about $16 billion in 1975. In other words, the credit items for goods and services added up to $115 billion, while the debit items added up to $99 billion. This means that we spent about $16 billion less on foreign goods and services than foreigners spent on our goods and services. Any surplus with respect to goods and services must be offset by a deficit in the rest of the balance of payments. This is because, as stressed in the previous section, the total of the debit items must equal the total of the credit items. Similarly, any deficit with respect to goods and services must be offset by a surplus in the rest of the balance of payments. In the following sections, we shall see exactly how the deficit with respect to goods and services was offset in 1975.

Transfers, Capital Movements, and Reserve Assets

Let's turn now to the rest of the balance of payments, which shows transfers (gifts, pensions, etc.), capital movements, and movements of reserve assets from one country to another. Take a close look at the second part of our 1975 balance of payments, reproduced in Table 32.2. You will see that the entries regarding capital movements are classified as transactions by the government or by private parties. This classification seems self-explanatory; for example, when an American lends money to a German firm by buying its long-term bonds, this is clearly a *private* capital outflow. In Table 32.2, the term, *capital outflow,* is used repeatedly. A capital outflow is a loan or investment abroad. For example, Americans may buy plants in foreign countries, or purchase the securities of foreign firms, or make deposits in foreign banks.

Recall from previous sections that a credit item supplies us with foreign currency and a debit item uses up our foreign currency. Let's apply this rule to a case where we lend money abroad. Clearly, such a transaction requires that we use foreign currency, since we will be buying foreign bonds or other securities. Thus lending abroad results in a debit item. On the other hand, borrowing from abroad supplies us with foreign currency, since foreigners pay us with their currency when they buy our bonds or other securities. Thus borrowing abroad results in a credit item.

Table 32.2 shows that in 1975 the United States government granted or lent (long-term) about $2 billion abroad (net of repayments), and private citizens and firms made long-term capital outflows of about $9 billion, net nonliquid short-term capital outflows of about $3 billion, and net liquid capital outflows of about $6 billion. Also, we sent $2 billion abroad in remittances—for example, gifts and pensions. As we just pointed out, these are all debit items. Combined with the $16 billion net surplus for goods and services (and the credit item of $4 billion to offset errors and omissions), this meant a total of about $2 billion of debits to be financed, one way or another, by the United States. This is frequently referred to as the "deficit on an official-settlements basis" in our balance of payments. The use of the term

Table 32.2
Transfers, Capital Movements, and Movements of Reserve Assets, 1975

	Credit	Debit
	(billions of dollars)	
Remittances		2
Net U.S. government grants and long-term capital outflows		2
Net U.S. private long-term capital outflows		9
Net nonliquid short-term private capital outflows		3
Errors and omissions	4	
Net liquid private capital outflows		6
Net change in liabilities to foreign official agencies	3	
Net change in U.S. reserves		1

Source: Table 32.1.

Table 32.3
Deficit in U.S. Balance of Payments, 1975

	Credit	Debit
	(billions of dollars)	
Merchandise exports	107	
Merchandise imports		98
Net services	2	
Net military transactions		1
Net investment income	6	
Remittances		2
Net U.S. government grants and capital outflows		2
Net U.S. private long-term capital outflows		9
Net nonliquid short-term private capital outflows		3
Errors and omissions	4	
Net liquid private capital outflows		6
Total	119	121

Deficit on official-settlements basis = \$121 billion − \$119 billion = \$2 billion

Source: Survey of Current Business, March 1976.

deficit does not mean that our entire balance of payments is in deficit. That could never be the case, since by definition the total of the debits must always equal the total of the credits. What this deficit really means is that we spent about \$2 billion more on foreign goods, services, and investments than foreigners spent on our goods, services, and investments. This is shown in Table 32.3.

Financing the Deficit

Next we must consider how this deficit (on an official-settlements basis) of about \$2 billion was financed. What credit items in other parts of the balance of payments offset this debit balance? To answer this question, we must look at the last two items in the balance of payments—net change in U.S. liabilities to foreign official agencies, and net change in U.S. reserves. First, consider the net change in U.S. liabilities to foreign central banks. As you can see from Tables 32.1 and 32.2, our debt to foreign central banks increased by about \$3 billion during 1975. In other words, foreign central banks built up their short-term investments here. They invested about \$3 billion in our short-term debt, which is how we financed the deficit.

Next, let's look at the change in the level of U.S. monetary reserves, including gold. Such changes are another way the deficit could have been financed. For example, in 1970, foreign central banks asked us for about \$3 billion in reserves. Thus the 1970 deficit was financed partly by transferring our reserves to other countries and partly by our increased liabilities. Of course, as noted above, the situation now is different than it was in 1970. The U.S. government will no longer exchange gold for dollars held by foreign central banks. But other reserve assets, including foreign exchange, can be used to make settlements. In 1975, however, there was no reduction in U.S. reserves; instead, our reserves increased by \$1 billion.

Finally, when we get down to the bottom of the balance of payments, we achieve the balance between debit items and credit items that logic—and arithmetic—assures us will prevail, since we must pay in cash or IOUs for what we get from other nations.[2]

Interpretation of a Deficit or Surplus: Fixed versus Floating Exchange Rates

To prevent confusion, it is important to point out that the interpretation of a deficit or surplus in our balance of payments is different under floating exchange rates than under fixed exchange rates. Under fixed exchange rates, a deficit (on an official-settlements basis) meant that foreign central banks had bought dollars because at the fixed exchange rates the private demand for dollars by foreigners was less than the available supply. This was viewed as a measure of pressure on the dollar in foreign exchange markets. Under floating exchange rates, on the other hand, exchange rates are allowed to change in response to such pressure. Thus a deficit of this sort can not be interpreted as evidence of such pressure. The size of the deficit is determined now by factors such as the preference of the oil-exporting countries (which garnered a huge amount of investable funds in the mid-1970s) for putting their funds in the United States. In May 1976, *the federal government stopped publishing figures on the deficit or surplus in our balance of payments because such figures no longer mean what they used to.*

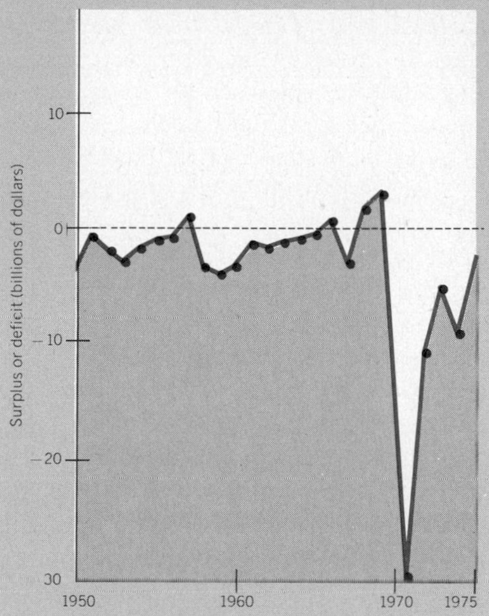

Figure 32.7
Deficit or Surplus in U.S. Balance of Payments, 1950–75

U.S. Balance of Payments Deficits, 1950–72

As noted in the previous section, when exchange rates were fixed, a balance of payments deficit was evidence of pressure on the dollar in foreign exchange markets. Figure 32.7 shows that, *during the period from 1950 to 1972 (the last full year when exchange rates were fixed), the United States showed a chronic deficit in its balance of payments.* This chronic deficit caused considerable uneasiness and concern, both here and abroad. Several factors were responsible for it.

Postwar recovery of Western Europe and Japan. As the Western European and Japanese economies recovered from the devastation of World War II, they adopted new technology, and became tough competitors. To cite but one example, the Japanese were particularly adept at absorbing modern electronic technology and

[2] However, even this certainty is clouded a bit by the fact that there are errors and omissions in the statistics that mean that a perfect balance is never achieved. But this only reflects the limitations of the data: logic dictates that if complete data could be obtained, a perfect balance would always be achieved.

at producing electronic goods for civilian markets. In many areas of technology, the United States continued to enjoy a lead, but the gap seemed to be narrowing. As productivity in Western Europe and Japan rose more rapidly than ours, their costs fell relative to ours, and they were able to undersell us much more in their own markets, third markets, and sometimes even our own market.

Military and foreign aid. We spent enormous amounts abroad for military purposes and for foreign aid. Our military expenditures abroad were particularly high during the Vietnam War. For example, they were about $4.5 billion in 1968. Not only did this war take a heavy toll in lives and in social disruption; it also helped keep our balance of payments in deficit. Note, however, that some of our government spending abroad has involved the use of "tied" funds, which can be used only to buy American goods. Since these programs result in exports that would not otherwise be made, the elimination of some of these programs would not reduce the deficit. If the government spending were cut, the exports it financed would be cut as well.

Private investment abroad. American firms invested enormous amounts of money abroad. U.S. investors acquired oil refineries, assembly lines, and hundreds of other types of plants. The rate of private investment abroad increased spectacularly during the 1950s and 1960s. In the early 1950s, new American private investment abroad was about $2 billion per year; in the late 1950s, over $3 billion per year; in the early 1960s, over $4 billion per year; and in the late 1960s, over $8 billion per year. The reason for this growth is fairly obvious. The markets of Western Europe (and other parts of the world) were growing rapidly and the construction of plants abroad was a profitable move. To help reduce our balance of payments deficit, the government introduced a voluntary program to limit such investment abroad in 1965, and made the program compulsory in 1968. (It lapsed in the 1970s.)

Inflation and discrimination. A number of other factors, including inflation in the United States and discrimination abroad against U.S. products, also contributed to our balance of payments deficits. Clearly, inflation in the United States—such as occurred in the late 1960s and early 1970s in particular—makes our exports more expensive abroad. It is true, of course, that inflation in the United States was not as great as in many other countries, but in many industries, like steel, our prices rose relative to those abroad. Also, foreigners maintained various quotas, tariffs, and other devices to keep out American exports. Many of these discriminatory regulations were enacted during earlier days when such policies were more understandable than during the period under consideration.

Autonomous and Accommodating Transactions

One of life's certainties is that the balance of payments of any nation will balance, but this, like many of the certainties of life, is merely a tautology. The important point is not that a balance is achieved, but *how it is achieved.* Sometimes a balance is achieved in a way that results in a stable equilibrium. In other cases, a balance is achieved in a way that results in disequilibrium, which, as we know, is a situation that cannot be maintained indefinitely. In the latter cases, something has to change; things cannot go on as they are. In the late 1960s and early 1970s, economists and bankers generally agreed that the U.S. balance of payments was in disequilibrium.

To see more clearly what disequilibrium means, it is convenient to distinguish between autonomous transactions and accommodating transactions. *Autonomous transactions* occur for reasons quite independent of the balance of payments. Exports, imports, and net capital movements occur because of people's tastes, comparative costs, and relative rates of return in various countries. Government expenditures abroad are made for military, political, and other reasons. Thus it is customary to treat these transactions as autonomous. On the other hand, *accommodating transactions* are made to bring about the necessary balance that must occur in the balance of payments. They compensate for differences between the total credits and total debits resulting from the autonomous transactions. For example, changes in a country's gold stock and other reserve assets, as well as short-term investments in the country's currency and other assets by foreigners, may be accommodating transactions.

Accommodating transactions are evidence of disequilibrium in a country's balance of payments. The United States's autonomous transactions–exports, imports, government expenditures abroad, long-term capital movements–resulted in a debit balance during the 1960s and early 1970s. This meant that certain accommodating transactions (reductions in our gold stock and other reserve assets, and increases in foreign investments in our currency and short-term investments) had to occur. These accommodating transactions were evidence of disequilibrium. They could not go on forever.

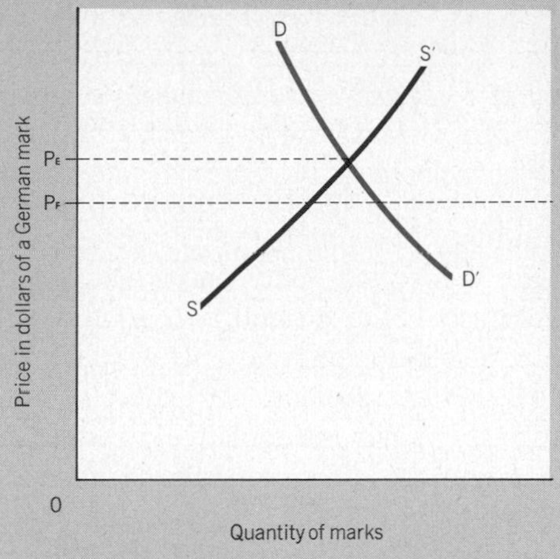

Figure 32.8
"Overvaluation" of the Dollar
Whereas the fixed exchange rate was only $\$P_F$ for a German mark, the equilibrium price was $\$P_E$.

Restoring Equilibrium in the Early 1970s

Under a regime of fixed exchange rates, what can a country do to restore equilibrium in its balance of payments? In general there are three routes it can take. (1) It can adjust its exchange rate. (2) It can change its price level. (3) It can adopt various kinds of controls to interfere with market forces. To illustrate each of these ways to restore equilibrium, consider the situation facing the United States in 1970. The dollar at that time was overvalued relative to other currencies, like the German mark. The situation was as shown in Figure 32.8, where *DD'* and *SS'* are the demand and supply curves for marks. In a free market for foreign exchange, the price (in dollars) of a German mark would have risen from the fixed exchange rate, P_F, to P_E. This would have discouraged American imports, encouraged American exports, and brought the U.S. balance of payments into equilibrium. In other words, it would have increased the autonomous transactions resulting in credits and decreased the autonomous transactions resulting in debits.

Thus one step the United States might have taken in 1970 to restore equilibrium was to *depreciate the dollar.* But the United States was reluctant to depreciate its currency relative to others. Depreciation of our currency would hurt friendly nations who had been willing to hold large dollar balances. The United States wanted to discourage speculation against the dollar. And there was a chance that depreciation of the world's leading currency would seriously disrupt the entire world monetary system. Also, it must be noted that depreciation would have required the cooperation of other countries. For example, unless the Germans were prepared to let the mark rise in value relative to the dollar, they could stop it by also depreciating the mark.

A second way to restore equilibrium was to *change the price level.* This was the sort of mechanism the gold standard used to restore equilibrium. In a country with a chronic deficit, like the United States, the remedy would be a lowering of its general price level relative to that of other countries. This would reduce our imports and promote our exports. In contrast to the previous alternative, it would not have meant any alteration in exchange rates. However, it might well have led to a depression in the United States. Because wages and prices are very difficult to push downward, any serious attempt to reduce aggregate spending in an effort to reduce the price level would probably cut output and increase unemployment. For this reason, economists were not enthusiastic about this route to equilibrium. However, they may well have counseled the president to keep inflation to a minimum—for balance of payments reasons as well as others discussed in previous chapters. In an inflationary world, all that the United States really had to do was have a lower inflation rate than other countries, not reduce its price level.

A third way to restore equilibrium was to *adopt various types of controls.* For example, a country might impose controls over the exchange market. Thus the United States government might have required all foreign exchange received by exporters (or others) to be sold to the government, and the government might have rationed this foreign exchange among importers and others who wanted it. By so doing, the government would see that equilibrium in the balance of payments was restored. However, this kind of scheme has many disadvantages. For example, it obviously limits freedom of choice and is difficult for the government to enforce.

Another type of government control is aimed at trade rather than the exchange markets. In this case, the government tries to influence imports and exports through quotas, tariffs, subsidies, and other such controls. For example, the United States might have raised tariffs and imposed quotas to cut its imports, and subsidized some of its exports to increase their volume. It might also have imposed limits on the amount American tourists could spend abroad. Of course, an important difficulty with such interference with free trade is that it reduces world efficiency, as we saw in Chapter 31.

In addition, the government might have discouraged American investment abroad—and in fact it did so in various ways, including the imposition in 1963 of an "interest equalization tax" of 15 percent (later reduced to 11½ percent) on any purchase of a foreign stock or bond by an American from a foreigner. Also, in the special circumstances facing the United States, one way to restore equilibrium to our balance of payments might have been to convince other countries to increase their share of the responsibilities for defense and foreign aid. For example, Western Europe might pay a larger share of the costs of maintaining a defensive shield that protects us all. The United States has been pressing for this for many years, with some success. Also, the United States might have tried to persuade other countries to remove discriminatory barriers to our goods. And finally, the United States might have tried to step up its rate of productivity increase and product innovation. This would have made our exports more competitive.

In fact, what did the United States do in the early 1970s to restore equilibrium in its balance of payments? As you might expect, we adopted many of the measures described above. In December 1971, we depreciated the dollar relative to all major foreign currencies. On the average, the dollar was depreciated by about 10 to 15 percent. Moreover, throughout

The International Money Game

Q: During the early 1970s, what contributed to, or aggravated, an international monetary crisis?

A: It's not a what, but a who. In periods of international financial stress, speculators moved vast sums of money out of weak currencies into strong currencies, and forced the central banks to intervene in order to maintain orderly foreign exchange markets.

Q: Why did speculators do a thing like that?

A: Because it was very profitable.

Q: Who were the speculators?

A: Right after the war (World War II, that is), the "in" speculator was a small Swiss banker (sometimes referred to as a Gnome of Zurich). More recently, much of the speculation business was rumored to be centered in OPEC (Organization of Petroleum Exporting Countries). As long as the U.S. kept exchanging billions of U.S. dollars for oil, the sheiks had plenty to speculate with.

Q: Were there other speculators?

A: Sure. Multinational corporations.

Q: I thought companies dealt in foreign exchange only to cover costs of their imports. Aren't they the honest merchants?

INTERNATIONAL MONEY DESK AT A SWISS BANK, ZURICH.

A: Some do. Most small companies deal in foreign exchange only when converting receipts from an overseas customer into dollars. But a select group of multinationals have come to be major powers in foreign exchange markets. The biggest 200 American-based MNFs (multinational firms) own about $25 billion in cash, and have another $100 billion or so in inventories and receivables. In comparison, West Germany's reserves—the largest of any Western nation—amount to about $31 billion. During the currency crises of the sixties, these MNFs learned that it was not wise to be caught in pounds sterling or dollars, and so began to move money on a large scale.

Q: By ship?

A: No, by prepayment and borrowings. For example, branches of a multinational continuously buy and sell from each other. If a treasurer saw an appreciation of the mark coming on, he urged the German subsidiaries to pay its sister subsidiaries as slowly as possible.

Q: It sounds unpatriotic.

A: Depends on whom you ask. The treasurer would claim enlightened profit-maximizing. Isn't that what you want a firm to do?

E.A.

the early 1970s a serious effort was made to contain inflation at home, and, for better or worse, some protectionist controls were established or continued. Also, the president's special assistant on international economic policy, Peter Peterson (later secretary of commerce), beat the drum for subsidies or encouragement for added research and development by American industry. In February 1973, the dollar was depreciated again, this time by about 10 percent. And when renewed speculation against the dollar caused a further crisis in March 1973, other countries decided to allow the dollar to float, and an international agreement was reached to this effect in Paris. Thus far, the new system of floating exchange rates seems to be working reasonably well, as we have seen in previous sections.

International Lending

Before concluding this chapter, we must discuss international capital movements in somewhat more detail. The factors underlying international transactions with regard to goods and services are clear enough. For example, we saw in the previous chapter why countries find it profitable to import and export goods and services. But we need to know more about the reasons why nations lend to one another. What factors are responsible for the capital movements shown in the balance of payments?

If the world were free of political problems and nationalist fervor, the answer would be easy. Because different parts of the world are endowed with different amounts and qualities of land and other resources, and have different population densities and amounts of capital, the rate of return to be derived from investments will vary from place to place. Consequently, nations where savings rates are high and investment opportunities are relatively poor will invest their capital in nations where the investment opportunities are better.

Such international lending helps both the lender and the borrower. The lender receives a higher rate of return than it would otherwise, and the borrower gains by having more capital to work with, so that the borrower's output and wages are higher than they would be otherwise. So long as the lender receives a relatively high return from the borrowing country, there is no reason why it should ask for repayment. It may continue to lend money to the borrowing country for years and years. For example, England was a net lender to the United States for about a century. To pay interest to the lender, the borrowing country must sell the lender more goods than it buys, thus building up a credit in its balance of payments that it can use to finance the interest, which is, of course, a debit item.

But the world is not free of political problems and nationalist fervor. Wars occur, governments topple, devastating inflations take place, property is confiscated. Only a fool contemplates investment in another country without taking some account of these and other risks; and because these risks are present, international lending that would otherwise be profitable and beneficial—and would take place if only economic considerations were involved—is sometimes stymied. Suppose that you had $1 million to invest, and that you could invest it at 15 percent interest in a country with an unstable government, where the chances were substantial that your investment would be confiscated and that you would get back only a fraction of the $1 million. Would you make the loan? Maybe; maybe not. Unfortunately, such risks discourage many international loans that would otherwise be advantageous to both lender and borrower.

America's Role as International Lender

As a country grows and develops, its balance of

payments tends to go through four stages. First, *a country, when it is relatively undeveloped, is often a net borrower with an "unfavorable" balance of trade.* Its imports exceed its exports, and it borrows from other countries to finance the difference between its imports and exports. It needs the goods, supplies, and equipment it imports to put it on the road to economic development. For example, during the first century of American history we were a substantial net borrower of capital from Europe. This capital helped fuel the early economic growth of the United States, described in Chapter 18.

Second, *as the country pays back more and more of its debts, it gets to the stage where debt repayment exceeds new borrowing, and its balance of trade becomes "favorable."* In other words, its exports exceed its imports, with the difference being used to reduce the country's outstanding debts and to pay interest on them. The United States entered this stage in the 1870s and remained in it for about half a century.

Third, *as the country becomes richer and more advanced, it becomes a net lender to other countries, and its balance of trade continues to be "favorable."* This excess of exports over imports is to be expected, since other countries borrow to finance such a net flow to them of goods and services. The United States entered this stage during and after World War I, when it lent huge amounts to its wartime allies for equipment and relief. Although the 1920s were a period when the United States erected high tariffs and barriers to imports, so long as we continued to lend abroad, foreigners could get the dollars to buy our exports. (However, when we cut back our foreign lending in the 1930s, serious trouble developed.)

Fourth, *the country becomes a mature creditor.* At this point, the interest it receives from its foreign investments is so great that it exceeds the new loans made to foreigners. Thus its balance of trade must become "unfavorable." Its imports will exceed its exports. In real terms, this difference represents payment of goods and services by foreigners for the use of capital. This "unfavorable" balance of trade is not unfavorable at all, since a country consumes imports, not exports. England reached this stage years ago; the United States is currently heading in this direction.

The United States is now the world's great creditor country—the great international lender. We continue to invest vast amounts abroad, both as private firms and individuals take advantage of profitable opportunities and as our government engages in large foreign aid and military programs. The United States is now entering the fourth stage; it is becoming a mature creditor. Our interest from foreign investments made in previous years helps to finance our net imports and our military and aid programs.

Summary

An important difference between international business transactions and business transactions within a country is that international business transactions involve more than one currency. The exchange rate is simply the number of units of one currency that exchanges for a unit of another currency. Before the 1930s, many major countries were on the gold standard, which meant that their currency was convertible into a certain amount of gold, and that the relative gold content of currencies determined exchange rates.

The gold standard is long gone. Another way to determine exchange rates is to allow the market for foreign exchange to function like any other free market, the exchange rate being determined by supply and demand. Under such a system, exchange rates, which are flexible, tend to move in a way that removes imbalances among countries in exports and imports. In 1973, many major countries, including the United States, allowed their currencies to float, resulting in much more flexibility of exchange rates.

Until 1973, when exchange rates became more flexible, most exchange rates were fixed by government action and international agreement. They were allowed to vary slightly, but only slightly, about the official rate. If exchange rates are fixed, the amount of a foreign currency demanded may not equal the amount supplied. To maintain exchange rates at the official levels, governments enter the market and buy and sell their currencies as needed. They also intervene by curbing imports, limiting foreign travel, and other measures. There has been considerable discussion over the relative advantages of fixed and flexible exchange rates.

A country's balance of payments measures the flow of payments between it and other countries. Debit items result in a demand for foreign currency, whereas credit items supply foreign currency. The total of the debit items must equal the total of the credit items because the total of the debit items is the total amount of goods, services, and assets we received from foreigners, and these goods, services, and assets must be paid for with credit items. The balance of merchandise trade refers only to part of the balance of payments. A nation is said to have a favorable (unfavorable) balance of merchandise trade if its exports of merchandise exceed (are less than) its imports of merchandise.

If a country's balance with regard to goods and services, transfers, and capital movements is negative, it is said to have a deficit in its balance of payments. The United States experienced a chronic deficit during the 1950s, 1960s, and early 1970s. This deficit—the result of the growing productivity of other economies, our large investments abroad, and our military and foreign aid expenditures abroad—was financed by reductions in our gold stock and by foreigners' acceptance of our short-term debt. Our balance of payments was in disequilibrium. To bring it into equilibrium, we could depreciate the dollar, curb inflation at home, impose controls of various kinds, or try to step up domestic productivity and innovation. Several steps along this line were attempted, including devaluations of the dollar in 1971 and 1973 and allowing the dollar to float in 1973. Under floating exchange rates, a deficit in our balance of payments is not an indication of pressure on the dollar in foreign exchange markets, because exchange rates are allowed to change in response to such pressure.

The United States is now the world's great creditor country. As a country develops, its balance of payments tends to go through four stages. The United States seems to be entering the fourth stage, where the balance of trade becomes "unfavorable."

CONCEPTS FOR REVIEW

Exchange rate
Devaluation of currency
Appreciation
Depreciation
Crawling peg
International Monetary Fund
Gold exchange standard
Official tier
Private tier
Balance of merchandise trade
Balance of payments
Gold standard
Deficit on an official-settlements basis
Autonomous transactions
Accommodating transactions
Debit items
Credit items

QUESTIONS FOR DISCUSSION AND REVIEW

1. Do you think that we should return to the gold standard? Why or why not? Do you think that this is a live possibility?

2. "Exports finance imports. Unless we export to other countries, we cannot get the imports we need." Comment and evaluate.

3. Suppose that the demand curve for German marks is as follows:

Quantity demanded (billions of marks)	Price (in dollars) of a mark
20	0.20
15	.30
10	.40
5	.50

Plot this demand curve on a graph. What sorts of groups, organizations, and individuals are part of the demand side of this market?

4. Suppose that the supply curve for German marks is as follows:

Quantity supplied (billions of marks)	Price (in dollars) of a mark
8	0.20
9	.30
10	.40
11	.50

Plot this supply curve on the same graph as the demand curve in Question 3. What sorts of groups, organizations, and individuals are part of the supply side of this market?

5. Based on the information in Questions 3 and 4, what is the equilibrium value of the exchange rate, if it is completely flexible? Why? Is the exchange rate between the U.S. dollar and the German mark completely flexible at present?

6. Suppose that the exchange rate is fixed, and that the price (in dollars) of a mark is set at $0.30. Based on the data in Questions 3 and 4, will the quantity of marks demanded equal the quantity supplied? What sorts of government actions will have to be taken?

7. The United States had an unfavorable balance of merchandise trade of about $7 billion in 1972. What does this mean? Of what importance is this fact?

8. Explain in detail why the balance of payments must balance. Indicate the significance of a payments deficit under a regime of fixed exchange rates.

9. During the 1950s and 1960s, the British government reacted to deficits in its balance of payments by adopting deflationary monetary and fiscal policies (temporarily at least). Was this sensible? Why or why not?

10. Under what circumstances would you be willing to invest $10,000 (if you had $10,000) in (a) Chile, (b) Angola, (c) Japan, (d) India? What interest rate would you expect? What guarantees would you expect? Why?

33 International Finance: History, Problems, and Policies

To many people, international finance is a rather esoteric subject. Nonetheless, one U.S. president after another has had to grapple with it, and many of the nation's leading private citizens have had to learn about it, as one international monetary crisis after another has occurred. No area of economics has received more attention in the press in recent years, and none has seemed more unsettled. We need to look in some detail at the evolution of international financial relationships in the recent past, since we cannot understand the present situation unless we know how we got where we are—and what was tried (and with how much success) in the past.

This chapter will describe the history of international financial relationships over the past 50 years and show how existing problems have developed. In addition, we will examine the effect of foreign trade on domestic output and employment; describe some of the organizations, such as the International Monetary

Fund, that have played a major role in international finance; and discuss proposed solutions to existing problems, as well as the formation of recent American policy.

Pre-World-War-II Days

The late nineteenth century and the period up to World War I were the heyday of the gold standard. Several dozen countries, including practically all the economically powerful ones, were on the gold standard. This was a period of international specialization, relatively low tariffs, relatively free trade, and a large volume of international transactions. Although it—like every period—had its problems and crises, it is often regarded as a golden age of international trade and finance, a period of harmonious and closely knit international economic relations. Unfortunately, this golden age, like the peace of the world, was shattered by the events of 1914.

During World War I, practically all the warring nations went off the gold standard to keep people from hoarding gold or from sending it to neutral countries. After the war, there was serious inflation in some European countries. (For example, you will recall Germany's runaway inflation from Chapter 13.) During the 1920s many countries went back on the gold standard, but after the economic troubles of the previous decade, the old exchange rates were no longer appropriate, and when the adjustment mechanism (based on changes in domestic price levels) failed to work quickly (and painlessly) enough, the gold standard was abandoned. In September 1931, England, in response to serious gold drains, went off the gold standard.

The 1930s were the years of the Great Depression. In response to the deep drop in output and swollen unemployment rolls, governments adopted protectionist policies like higher tariffs and import quotas. At the same time, confidence in the banks and the monetary system sank. Austria's biggest bank failed in 1931, followed by bank failures and runs on the banks in Germany and England. In the United States, President Roosevelt took gold out of circulation as money in 1933. Moreover, to stimulate American exports (and thus increase jobs), Roosevelt devalued the dollar by about 40 percent in early 1934, raising the price of gold from about $20 to $35 an ounce.

As would be expected, other countries reacted to our devaluation by retaliatory measures. They too devalued or went off the gold standard. In addition, they increased their tariffs and erected other barriers to our exports. It was a time when governments around the world adopted "beggar-thy-neighbor" policies that aimed at the "export" of unemployment. After all, an increase in net exports—like an autonomous increase in private investment or government spending—will increase a country's net national product, and thus increase its employment. Consequently, if a country can reduce its imports or increase its exports, it can increase its employment.

But the beggar-thy-neighbor policies of the 1930s did not achieve this end. They brought about retaliatory measures that prevented a country from increasing its net exports, and all that resulted was a mutually disadvantageous drying up of international trade.

The Effects of Foreign Trade on Net National Product

To understand more clearly what "beggar-thy-neighbor" policies were designed to achieve, let's look more closely at the effects of foreign trade on NNP and domestic employment. Recall from Chapter 8 that net national product = consumption + investment + government spending + net exports, where net exports equal exports minus imports. In other words,

$$Y = C + I + G + X, \qquad (33.1)$$

where Y is NNP, C is consumption, I is investment, G is government spending, and X is net exports. Recall too that *the equilibrium level of NNP will be at the point where desired spending on NNP—*which equals desired consumption + desired investment + desired government spending + desired net exports—*equals NNP.*

Thus, in Figure 33.1, the equilibrium level of NNP must be \$500 billion, since this is the level at which the $C + I + G + X$ line intersects the 45-degree line. To see this, note that we are merely carrying out a straightforward extension of the analysis in Chapter 11, where we assumed that net exports were zero. Once this assumption is relaxed, desired net exports must be added to the $C + I + G$ line to get total desired spending, and the equilibrium level of NNP is at the point where the resulting total-desired-spending line—$C + I + G + X$—intersects the 45-degree line.

We can also use the leakage-injection approach (described in Chapters 10 and 12) to show the effects of foreign trade on the equilibrium value of NNP. Clearly, *exports are an injection* since they add spending to the domestic flow of income and expenditure. In other words, foreign spending on American products results in additional output and jobs in the U.S. On the other hand, *imports are a leakage* because they withdraw spending from the domestic flow of income and expenditure. In other words, they constitute a use for income other than spending on U.S. goods and services.

Once this is understood, it is clear why governments during the 1930s wanted to increase their exports and decrease their imports.

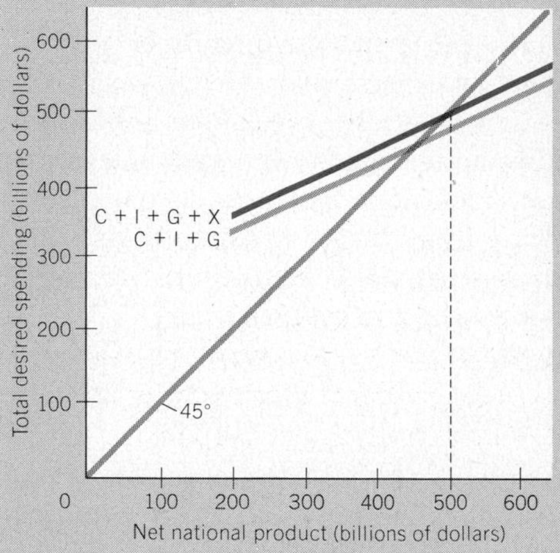

Figure 33.1
Effects of Foreign Trade on Net National Product
The equilibrium level of NNP is at the point where the $C + I + G + X$ line intersects the 45-degree line; in this case, \$500 billion.

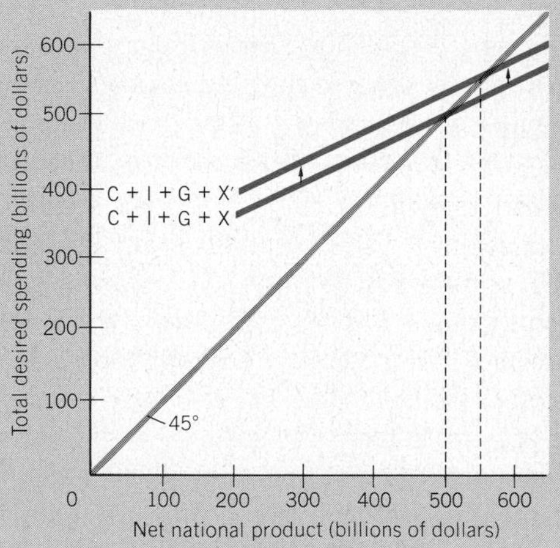

Figure 33.2
Effect of Increase in Net Exports on Net National Product
If net exports increase from X to X', the equilibrium level of *NNP* increases from \$500 billion to \$550 billion.

Spending on net exports results in increases in NNP. For example, if desired spending on net exports increases from X to X', as shown in Figure 33.2, the equilibrium level of NNP increases from $500 billion to $550 billion. Moreover, *increases in spending on net exports have a multiplier effect,* which is like the multiplier effect for investment or government spending. Thus a $1 increase in desired spending on net exports results in more than a $1 increase in NNP.[1] Since governments during the 1930s wanted desperately to increase their NNP to reduce unemployment, it is clear why they tried to increase their net exports. However, as emphasized in the previous section, all that resulted was a reduction in international trade, because of retaliatory measures.

The Impact of War and the Postwar Dollar Shortage

Major wars have a way of changing international economic relationships. Once World War II got under way, the combatants changed their trading patterns, with war materiel, not consumer goods, the paramount concern. Export industries were shifted to war production, while attempts were made to increase imports of strategic materials and equipment. The inevitable problem for the combatants was how to pay for these imports. For some time, the United States provided these items to its allies on the basis of loans and lend-lease programs. (In all, we contributed about $37 billion worth of goods in lend-lease.) Besides affecting trading patterns, wars also have an effect on the price levels of various countries. Some countries suffer from much greater inflation than others, with the result that countries with relatively high rates of inflation tend to incur deficits in their balance of payments unless changes occur in exchange rates.

Perhaps the most spectacular effect of World War II was on the productive capacities of most of the warring nations. Countries like Germany, France, and the United Kingdom suffered a great reduction in their capacity to produce goods and services. Their factories were bombed to the ground. Their towns and cities were shelled and sometimes overrun by enemy forces. Their farms were run down and in some cases turned into battlegrounds. Even factories that were not hit by enemy fire were old and dilapidated at the end of the war because there had been little wartime investment not related to the war.

When World War II finally ended, it was clear that international economic relationships would be subject to many strains and stresses in the postwar period, due in part to the ravages of the war. In addition, the Allies were seriously divided on ideological grounds. The Western nations distrusted the Communist nations and vice versa, and trade between the two blocs was cut substantially as the cold war proceeded. Also, there was a strong tide of nationalism among the less developed countries of the world. Many colonies became independent and tried to lessen their dependence upon the richer countries by adopting measures that reduced international trade. Further, most governments emerged from the war intent on following policies that would promote full employment at home. (Recall the Employment Act of 1946 in the United States.) Laudable as these objectives were, they were not always compatible with smooth international economic relationships.

Had you been studying economics right after World War II, one of the phrases you would have heard repeatedly was "the dollar shortage." Everyone—whether he knew what it meant or not—talked about the dollar shortage

[1] If we assume that exports, government expenditures, and tax receipts are the same at all levels of NNP, then a $1 increase in desired spending on net exports will result in an increase in equilibrium NNP of $\frac{1}{MPS + MPI}$ dollars, where MPS is the marginal propensity to save and MPI is the marginal propensity to import. (The *marginal propensity to import* is the proportion of an extra dollar of income that is spent on imports.) Note that the multiplier is smaller now than in the case of a closed economy (where MPI equals zero).

in the late 1940s and early 1950s. There *was* a dollar shortage in the sense that, at the official fixed exchange rate, foreigners could not get as many dollars as they wanted. The situation was like that shown in Figure 33.3. Given *DD′* and *SS′*, the existing demand and supply curves for dollars by foreigners, there was a gap between the quantity demanded and the quantity supplied at the existing price (in foreign currency) of a dollar. Had the exchange rate been allowed to fluctuate, the dollar would have been bid up considerably. That is, it would have appreciated relative to other currencies.

It is easy to see why foreigners wanted dollars so much. Other countries badly needed to rebuild their economies, and since the United States was the one major economic power that emerged relatively unscathed from the war, foreigners needed dollars to put their own economies back into reasonable order. The United States responded to their plight, not by allowing the dollar to appreciate in terms of other currencies, but by simply giving or lending dollars to those in need. Foreign countries then used various types of controls over foreign exchange and imports—of the sort described in the previous chapter—to direct the use of this American aid.

Aid Programs and the World Bank

Postwar Aid Programs

American financial assistance took several forms in the period after World War II. In the immediate postwar period, the primary objective was, of course, to help the populations of the war-ravaged countries and to get the European economies back on their feet. For example, the United Nations Relief and Rehabilitation Administration (UNRRA) provided $4 billion of food, clothing, and medical services, about ¾ of which was financed by the United States. In addition, other forms of relief, aid, and loans were extended. In all, the United States provided about $17 billion in aid between the war's end and 1948, about half in loans and about half in grants.

By 1948, it was clear that Europe needed a more comprehensive program to stimulate its economic recovery and political stability. Secretary of State George Marshall, in a famous address at Harvard in June 1948, set forth the outlines of a plan—the Marshall Plan—to speed Europe's recovery. This plan established the European Recovery Program, which poured

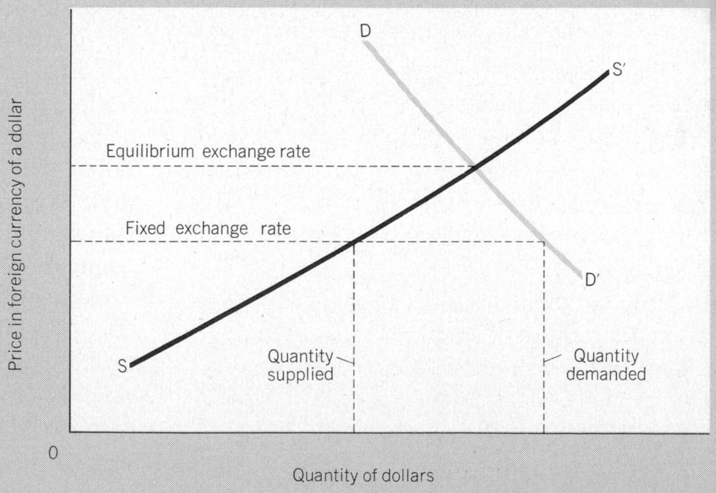

Figure 33.3
The Dollar Shortage
At the fixed exchange rate, the quantity demanded of dollars exceeded the quantity supplied. The equilibrium exchange rate exceeded the fixed exchange rate.

Table 33.1
U.S. Foreign Economic and Military Aid Program, 1946–74.

Year	Economic Loans	Economic Grants	Military Loans	Military Grants	Total
			(billions of dollars)		
1946–52	8.5	22.7	—	3.5	34.7
1953–61	5.9	18.2	0.2	23.2	47.4
1962–65	8.3	8.7	0.4	7.5	25.0
1966	2.2	2.5	0.3	1.8	6.9
1967	1.7	2.3	0.3	1.9	6.2
1968	1.8	2.3	0.3	2.2	6.6
1969	1.3	2.2	0.3	2.6	6.4
1970	1.4	2.3	0.1	2.7	6.4
1971	1.3	2.1	0.7	3.5	7.7
1972	1.6	2.3	0.6	4.3	8.8
1973	1.4	2.7	0.6	4.9	9.6
1974	1.2	2.8	1.4	3.6	8.9
Total	35.3	69.9	5.1	61.8	172.1

Source: Statistical Abstract of the United States.

over $10 billion in aid into Europe, much in the form of grants. Most observers regarded the Marshall Plan as a success: European productive capacity grew dramatically during the late 1940s and early 1950s.

By the early 1950s, Europe's economy was in pretty good shape, but this did not spell the end of our foreign aid programs. On the contrary, much of our aid shifted toward the less developed nations. Table 33.1 shows the total amount the United States spent on foreign aid between 1946 and 1974. During this period, we spent about $170 billion—a huge sum by any standard. About 40 percent of these expenditures have been for military purposes, about 60 percent have been for economic purposes. No nation has ever contributed as much to the economic development of poorer countries as we have.

Why have we engaged in these foreign aid programs? In part, because we wanted to keep people in faltering economies from espousing Communism. Starvation and misery are good breeding grounds for revolution. Also, we wanted to provide our friends and allies with modern and effective weapons. Thus one need not be a cynic to attribute a good deal of this aid to our own self-interest. But it is simplistic—and overly harsh—to dismiss many of these programs in this way. The truth is that the United States was also motivated by old-fashioned humanitarianism, which, reports to the contrary notwithstanding, is still alive (although sometimes embattled) in the United States, as well as other parts of the world.

The World Bank

In 1944, late in World War II, the major economic powers agreed to establish the International Bank for Reconstruction and Development, also known as the World Bank. Although its first loans were for postwar reconstruction, the bank's principal function now is to make long-term loans to the less developed countries—in Latin America, Asia, and elsewhere. They desperately need capital, while the rich, economically advanced countries have capital to lend. The World Bank's purpose was to channel funds from rich nations to poor, thus supplementing private investment, which was often scared off by the apparent risks. More specifically, the major economic powers contributed a certain amount of money to form the bank, with each country's share determined by its economic size. About $\frac{1}{3}$ of the total was put up by the United States. The Soviet Union helped organize the World Bank, but later declined to join.

Now over 30 years old, the World Bank still makes loans to people or governments with sound investment projects who have been unable to get private financing. Moreover, by floating its own bond issues it can lend money above and beyond what was originally put up by the major powers. In other words, the World Bank sells its own IOUs, which are considered safe by investors because they are guaranteed by member countries. In addition, it helps less developed countries get loans from private lenders by insuring the loans. That is, the World Bank can tell the lender that if the loan goes sour it will see that he is paid back.

Of course, this movement of capital from the capital-rich nations to the capital-poor nations should prove beneficial for both rich and poor. The poor countries are enabled to carry out projects that will result in economic returns high enough to pay off the lender with interest and have some net benefits left over. The rich countries are enabled to invest their capital at a higher rate of return than they could obtain at home. Thus both parties benefit, as long as the loans are economically sound.

The World Bank has established the International Development Agency to make "soft" loans, as well as the International Finance Corporation, which lends to foreign development banks. An increasing percentage of the bank's financing is being channeled through these two agencies. The bank is concerned with agriculture, as well as industry. In 1975, its spending on agriculture exceeded $1 billion, and was double the 1973 figure. According to Robert McNamara, the bank's president, its total annual lending (of all types) should reach $10 billion by 1980.

The International Monetary Fund

1944 was a vintage year for international financial institutions. It saw the basic agreements underlying both the World Bank and the International Monetary Fund. Both evolved from international conferences held at Bretton Woods, New Hampshire, where representatives of 16 countries met to try to establish a new international monetary system. Out of these historic conferences came a system that survived—with some crises and changes—for almost 30 years. A cornerstone of this system was the International Monetary Fund (IMF), established by 40 nations to insure reasonable stability of exchange rates. The Fund was composed initially of about $30 billion of gold and currency, contributed by the member countries. It has been enlarged greatly since then, and membership has grown to over 100 countries.

The IMF has three purposes. First, it provides a permanent mechanism for consultation by various countries on international financial problems. Second, it tries to promote the stability of exchange rates and to avoid competitive depreciation of currencies. Third, it is empowered to make temporary loans to member countries to give them time to correct disequilibria in their balances of payments, thus promoting smoother international financial adjustments.

Note that the Fund was built on a philosophy of *fixed* exchange rates. The men who met at Bretton Woods were impressed with the problems of flexible exchange rates, at least as they were used in the 1930s, and agreed that exchange rates should be reasonably stable. Of course, they recognized that from time to time changes in certain exchange rates would be required. (Among the people at Bretton Woods was John Maynard Keynes, which suggests that the conferees were hardly financial babes in the woods.) But changes in exchange rates should, they felt, be made only in response to persistent disequilibria. In this respect, the spirit behind the IMF differed substantially from the old gold standard. Whereas the IMF recognized that exchange rates should sometimes change, the gold standard emphasized exchange stability under all circumstances.

To see more precisely what the IMF was designed to do, suppose that a member country was in temporary difficulties with its balance of payments, which showed a large deficit. The IMF could lend foreign currencies to the country running the deficit. In any year, a country could readily borrow in foreign currencies up to $\frac{1}{4}$ of its quota at the Fund, which was determined by its contribution to the Fund. After formal consultation with the Fund, the country could borrow even more than this amount if it was working hard to cure the basic disequilibrium in its balance of payments. This allowed the country to make the necessary adjustments more gradually, and lessened the likelihood that it would be forced into a position where it had to depreciate its currency or impose controls over exchange or imports. The country was expected to pay back all the foreign currency that it borrowed in three to five years at most.

Suppose, however, that the basic disequilibrium in a country's balance of payments was so great that no reasonable action short of depreciating its currency would restore equilibrium. In such cases, members of the IMF were permitted to change their exchange rates after consultation with other members of the Fund. Since 1944, there have been numerous changes in exchange rates. For example, in 1949 the United Kingdom reduced the dollar value of the pound from $4.00 to $2.80. Moreover, the values of some currencies have increased, not decreased. For example, in 1973, West Germany increased the official value of its currency by about 5 percent.

How well has the IMF worked? During its early years, it did not have the resources or financial muscle to deal with the tremendous dollar shortage. From the mid-1950s to 1973, the IMF turned in a more impressive performance as a stabilizing force in international financial relationships, even though it could not cope with large disequilibria. The role of the Fund under the system of floating exchange rates adopted in 1973 has not yet become clear. In early 1976, the Interim Committee of the IMF recognized that the underlying economic and financial situation determines the degree of exchange rate stability that is possible. When formally approved by 60 percent of the member countries representing 80 percent of the votes, the Articles of Agreement of the IMF will be amended to reflect this and other agreements. For example, $\frac{1}{6}$ of the gold holdings of the IMF will be auctioned off (over a period of four years) to finance a Trust Fund for the poorer members of the IMF.

The IMF in Action: A Case Study

Let's consider an important case where the International Monetary Fund was involved in maintaining an exchange rate—the case of Great Britain in 1964. Britain ran a serious deficit in its balance of payments in the early 1960s; and in 1964, amid considerable speculation that devaluation would have to come, the British government fought to maintain the existing value of the pound. (Recall the discussion in Chapter 32.) It began by obtaining assistance from the central banks of Belgium, Canada, France, Italy, the Netherlands, Switzerland, Germany, and the United States. This assistance took the form of so-called swaps agreements and gave Britain about $200 million in aid by the end of September 1964. But

Eurodollars: The Bucks That Don't Stop Here

In recent years, the general public has slowly become aware of the existence of something called Eurodollars. One reason for their growing prominence was their importance in "recycling petrodollars"—that is, in channeling funds from the oil-exporting countries to borrowers. When the amounts of money received by the oil-exporting countries increased greatly in 1974, it was important that these funds be recycled in this way, and Eurodollars played a major role. But this has been only one of the major functions of Eurodollars, as we shall see.

A Eurodollar is simply an American dollar that is deposited in a foreign commercial bank. Suppose that Buck Croesus, a well-heeled cowboy actor, has $1 million in checking and savings accounts at American banks. To create 1 million Eurodollars, all Mr. Croesus has to do is to transfer his $1 million in bank accounts to a bank in Europe. He will than have a $1 million claim on the European bank, and the European bank will hold the $1 million accounts he transfered to it. The European bank can lend these dollars out, in which case it transfers their ownership to the borrower. When Mr. Croesus withdraws his dollar deposit from the European bank, he exchanges his dollar-denominated claim on the European bank for a dollar-denominated claim on an American bank.

How did Eurodollars come into being? According to the Council of Economic Advisers, the answer is as follows:

> The emergence and growth of the Eurodollar market may be viewed as a classic example of free market forces at work, overcoming obstacles created by regulations, and responding to market incentives to accommodate various needs. After World War II, when the dollar emerged as the major trading currency, the initial impetus to the growth of the Eurodollar market was given by certain Eastern European countries. Anxious to hold dollars to finance their badly needed imports from the West, but concerned that their dollar balances might be blocked or confiscated in retaliation for their expropriation of American-owned properties if such balances were held in banks under U.S. Government jurisdiction, these countries began placing their dollar balances with commercial banks in Western Europe. Since the late fifties, when most major countries removed restrictions on the holding of foreign exchange (including dollars) by their residents, higher interest rates offered by foreign banks, relative to interest rates offered by the U.S. banks, provided the main incentive for

holders of dollar funds to place these with foreign banks rather than banks located in the United States.

The ability and willingness of foreign banks to offer a more attractive return than U.S. banks has been predicated on several factors. The U.S. banking authorities do not allow commercial banks in the United States to pay interest on deposits of less than 30 days, and they regulate the rate of interest that may be paid on deposits of longer maturity. Commercial banks abroad are mostly exempt from such restrictions. Also, unlike U.S. banks, commercial banks in countries where the growth of the Eurodollar market has been the most spectacular are not subject to reserve requirements on their dollar-denominated liabilities. As a result, the net cost of such funds to these banks is reduced, and they can offer a higher yield.*

How large are the dollar liabilities of European banks? According to estimates made by the Bank of International Settlements, they were about $100 billion at the end of 1973. Eurodollars are not included in the statistics concerning the U.S. money supply, because they must be "converted" into deposits in American banks before they can become means of payment in this country. At times, the Federal Reserve has been quite concerned that Eurodollars were being borrowed by American banks to increase their reserves and thus thwart the Fed's attempts to reduce reserves and tighten monetary policy. For example, this was the case in 1969. To cut down on this source of reserves, the Fed imposed a 10 percent reserve requirement on Eurodollar borrowings (above a certain level), and increased it to 20 percent in 1971. In 1973, it was lowered to 8 percent.

* *1975 Annual Report of the Council of Economic Advisers,* Washington, D.C.: Government Printing Office, pp. 213–14

this aid was not enough. In addition, Britain turned to the International Monetary Fund.

At the beginning of December 1964, Britain borrowed $1 billion from the Fund. This drawing was made in the following currencies:

Currency	Millions of dollars worth
Austrian schillings	38
Belgian francs	57
Canadian dollars	69
German marks	273
French francs	163
Italian lire	23
Japanese yen	54
Netherland guilders	66
Spanish pesetas	40
Swedish kronor	27
U.S. dollars	200
Total	1,000

Thanks to this assistance, as well as to subsequent international aid to the British, the battle to maintain the British pound at $2.80 was won, at least temporarily. Thus the International Monetary Fund allowed the British a breathing spell to get their balance of payments in better shape. As we have noted, providing such breathing spells is one of the important functions of the IMF.

In this case, however, the breathing spell was not very long, and the battle, although temporarily won, was to be lost soon afterward. Despite the IMF action, the British still could not make the necessary adjustments to reduce the deficit in their balance of payments and were forced to devalue the pound from $2.80 to $2.40 in 1967. Fortunately, IMF assistance was able to overcome temporary disequilibria in many other cases—for example, that of Italy in 1964. In these cases the victories were longer lasting.[2]

[2] See Brian Tew, *International Monetary Cooperation,* London: Hutchinson University Library, 1965, pp. 197–98.

The Dollar Glut

The dollar shortage in the period immediately after World War II gradually disappeared, and was replaced by a dollar glut. The train of events that led to this change is quite clear. After World War II, American exports grew enormously and were financed only in part by our imports. Additional financing came from our foreign aid programs and private investment abroad. As the European economies got back on their feet, private investment abroad seemed more and more profitable. Moreover, our foreign aid programs—redirected toward the less developed countries and military assistance—continued.

During the 1950s, our balance of payments showed a persistent deficit, since our private investment abroad and our foreign aid more than offset the surplus of our exports over our imports. Since foreigners received more in payments from us than we did from them, they could either hold dollar balances or ask us for gold. In general, they took the dollar balances during the 1950s. Dollars were considered "as good as gold," since they could be exchanged for gold at $35 an ounce. And they had the advantage that bank balances held in the United States or short-term U.S. securities brought interest, while gold did not. However in the late 1950s, foreigners began to take more and more gold as their dollar balances became bigger and bigger (Figure 33.4).

By the late 1950s bankers and others, both here and abroad, expressed growing concern about the large deficit in our balance of payments. Foreigners warned us that confidence in the dollar was being impaired, and some members of our own financial community cautioned us to move toward eliminating our persistent deficit. By the 1960s, there was considerable feeling that the dollar would have to be depreciated or devalued, or both. This resulted in a sharp reduction in our gold stock, as shown in Figure 33.4. If the dollar were devalued, money could be made by buying gold. So investors exchanged dollars for gold.

Foreign central banks viewed dollar balances as reserves, since these balances could be converted into gold. But by the late 1960s these central banks had all the dollars they wanted. Indeed, they had more than they wanted. But many held dollars because they knew that if they tried to turn them into gold, the United States would have to end the convertibility of dollars into gold since our gold

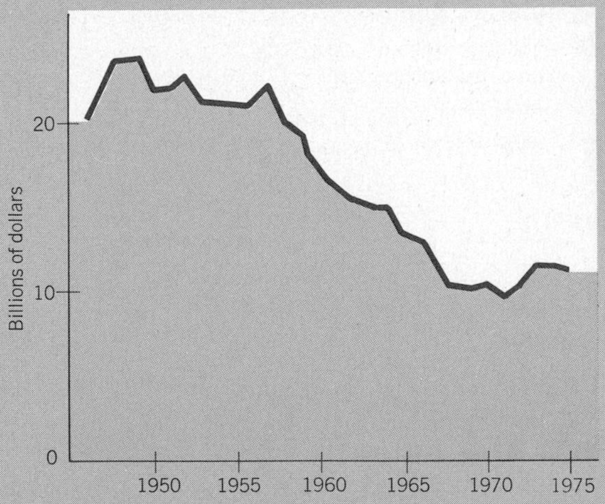

Figure 33.4
Size of U.S. Gold Reserves, 1946–75
Since the late 1950s the U.S. gold reserves have decreased considerably.

stocks were much less than foreign dollar balances.

It is worth emphasizing the fact that most nations (in the West) held their basic reserves in the form of both dollars and gold. This seemed perfectly reasonable since dollars were convertible into gold at $35 an ounce. The dollar was the "reserve currency"—the "key currency"—of the world. However, as foreign dollar balances spurted upward and the U.S. gold stock fell, it became increasingly questionable whether we could continue to stand behind the convertibility of dollars into gold.

In 1968, the ten leading Western economic powers met in Washington and Stockholm and agreed to introduce a two-tier gold system. As you will recall from the previous chapter, all the gold held by central banks at the time was included in the official tier. This gold was to be traded only for monetary purposes among central banks at the official rates. The rest of the world's gold supply was included in the private tier, where the price of gold was to be determined by supply and demand. No gold from the public tier was to be sold in the private tier.

The two-tier gold system was a step toward the reduction of gold's importance in the world's monetary system. Although there was some worry that governments might try to profit by buying gold at $35 an ounce in the official tier, this two-tier system seemed to work reasonably well for several years. (In 1973, it was abandoned.) But it was only an interim measure and in 1971, President Nixon announced that the United States would no longer sell gold to foreign governments. The convertibility of dollars into gold was suspended.

At a conference at the Smithsonian Institution in Washington in late 1971, the major Western nations agreed to a depreciation of the dollar against their currencies averaging about 10 to 15 percent. As part of the agreement, the United States agreed to devalue the dollar by about 9 percent. Also, the permissable limits for exchange-rate fluctuations were widened, thus allowing more flexibility. However, this agreement did not bring about the desired improvement of the U.S. payments deficit. Consequently, in 1973, the dollar was again depreciated, this time by about 10 percent.

Gold and Special Drawing Rights

Liquidity Shortage

As we have stressed, the short-term dollar balances held by foreigners were an important part of the reserves of foreign governments in the 1950s and 1960s. The U.S. balance of payments deficit, by providing these dollar balances, was providing the non-Communist world with an important part of its international monetary reserves. By the late 1960s, about $\frac{1}{3}$ of the non-Communist world's monetary reserves were in the form of U.S. short-term debt to foreign central banks and international monetary organizations. The rest was in the form of gold.

Obviously, as the volume of international trade increased, the volume of international monetary reserves had to increase as well. But the amount of gold to be used for reserves was determined in considerable measure by the amount of gold produced. And since the price of gold was maintained at $35 an ounce for many years, gold mining became less profitable as the costs of producing gold increased. The result was that the amount of gold reserves increased rather slowly. The rate of growth of dollar reserves depended on the size and growth of the U.S. balance of payments deficit. In a very real sense, our deficits provided other countries with reserves. Convenient as this may have been, however, it could not go on forever, since other countries were increasingly restless about the lack of discipline such a dollar-based reserve system implied for the United States.

Thus, since gold reserves were increasing slowly and our deficits could not be counted on to continue to provide new reserves, many economists during the 1960s feared that there would be a shortage of reserves. For example, the Council of Economic Advisers pointed out in 1968 that while world trade had increased by over 7 percent annually since 1960, international monetary reserves had increased by less than 3 percent annually. Moreover, the two-tier gold system made it all the more likely that international monetary reserves would not grow fast enough.

One suggested remedy was that the price of gold be increased. For example, it could have been increased from its level (at that time) of $35 an ounce to $70 an ounce. In this way, the dollar value of all international gold reserves would have doubled, thus easing the potential shortage of reserves. But this solution suffered from several problems. First, it would have hurt many friendly nations that held large amounts of dollars. In terms of gold, the value of their dollars would have been halved by this step. Second, it would have benefited those nations that hoarded or produced gold, since it would have doubled the value in dollars of their gold. Among these nations are the Soviet Union and South Africa, which many people felt should not be subsidized in this way. Third, it would have perpetuated the central role of gold as an international monetary reserve. Many economists pointed out how foolish it is to mine gold and cast it into ingots, only then to put it back in the ground as a monetary reserve. They ask why we could not replace gold with another form of reserve asset, such as special drawing rights, the topic we turn to next.

Special Drawing Rights

The leading Western economic powers agreed in 1968 to allow the International Monetary Fund to establish special drawing rights (SDRs). These SDRs are a new kind of reserve asset, which can be used by member countries much as they used gold in the past. New SDRs can be created by a vote of 85 percent of the IMF's membership. Unlike garden-variety IMF loans, SDRs do not have to be repaid to the IMF, but their allocation among countries must be in accord with IMF quotas. SDRs are sometimes called "paper gold." (Apparently international economists accomplished at long last what the alchemists tried so hard—and with so little luck—to achieve. They managed to create gold out of baser materials.) "Paper gold" is backed by nothing other than the member countries' pledge to accept it in exchange for currencies. It is much like our domestic money—which, as we know from Chapter 13, is not convertible into gold or silver. In 1970, over $3 billion worth of "paper gold" was created by the IMF. The United States received about $900 million, the United Kingdom received about $400 million, and France and Germany about $200 million each. More SDRs were issued in later years. By early 1976 about $7.7 billion of SDRs had been created, of which the United States got about $2.8 billion.

The establishment of SDRs certainly seemed a step toward a more sensible way to expand international reserves, although it will take much more time before the impact of SDRs can be fully assessed. There has been considerable disagreement among economists over the rate at which reserves should be increased. But this question is of less importance under floating exchange rates than under fixed exchange rates, because international adjustments now tend to occur through changes in exchange rates rather than through the transfer of reserves from one country to another. Thus there is less fear of a shortage of reserves.

How rapidly (and whether) SDRs will displace gold and foreign exchange as monetary reserves is by no means clear. By late 1974, they constituted 5 percent of all international reserve assets, and the stated intent was to end the central role of gold as a monetary reserve. Moreover, in January 1976, it was agreed that gold will no longer be a medium of settlement in International Monetary Fund transactions. But it is still possible for countries to revalue gold at market-related prices and to trade in gold at those prices. If this were done, existing gold reserves would increase substantially in value, and SDRs would become a smaller percentage of total reserve assets.

Problems of International Adjustment

The international financial system experienced some serious problems during the 1960s and early 1970s, with one crisis following another. Some of these crises reached the front pages of the newspapers, but many did not. One of the most serious problems was the difficulty in making international adjustments. The existing system did not provide a very effective way for countries to cure their balance of payments ills. Although in theory countries could change their exchange rates to cure chronic deficits (or surpluses), in practice exchange rates tended to be very rigid. The fact that a country could borrow from the IMF to ward off depreciation of its currency meant that the adjustment of exchange rates was postponed. Thus chronic deficits became more chronic, and the adjustments required to correct these deficits were delayed.

At the same time, governments, for understandable reasons, often refused to sacrifice major domestic objectives for international adjustment. For example, when a country with a balance of payments deficit had a soft domestic economy, it was likely to pursue a stimulative, expansionary policy even though this policy did not promote international adjustment. The United States did just this in the early 1960s. Of course, since no country can ignore its balance of payments problems, a nation's international problems will influence its domestic economic policy, but modern nations resist making great sacrifices on the domestic front for the sake of international adjustment.

However, international adjustments must ultimately be made, unless the system is to break down. A country with a chronic balance of payments deficit has only three choices: to get rid of its deficit, to persuade foreigners to hold more of its currency, or to fail to fulfill its obligations. Of course, if a country has enormous gold and currency reserves, as the United States did in the 1960s, it can avoid facing these choices for a long time. But eventually even the biggest reserves are depleted; and then, since it is foolish to expect foreigners to hold more and more of its currency, the nation must correct its deficit. This may be painful, since it may mean the sacrifice of some domestic objectives, but there is no alternative.

The Relation between International and Domestic Economic Policies

As an illustration of the conflict that sometimes exists between domestic objectives and international adjustment, consider the case of the United States during the early 1960s, a period when there was considerable slack in our economy. Responding to our relatively high unemployment (about 6 percent) and our relatively low rate of economic growth, President John F. Kennedy, newly elected, set out to redeem his campaign promise "to get this country moving again."

What sorts of domestic economic policies would promote this objective? Clearly, economic policy should stimulate the economy.

Fiscal policy should add to aggregate demand, and money should be easy. But what about our international financial problems? At that time, we also had serious difficulties with our balance of payments. What sorts of domestic economic policies would help reduce the chronic deficit in our balance of payments? According to our discussions in Chapter 32, the conventional answer would be that economic policy should be restrictive. Inflation should be fought hard, through a combination of tight fiscal and monetary policies.

Thus the sort of medicine that would help the nation's domestic problems would have unwanted international side effects, and vice versa. Faced with this unhappy choice, economic policy makers during the early 1960s generally opted for stimulating the economy. (Recall, for example, the tax cut of 1964.) They tried to "get this country moving again," even if it meant further trouble with our balance of payments. And given the high social costs of unemployment, this choice was quite understandable. (However, they continually had to take account of the effects of various actions on our balance of payments. For example, monetary policy during the 1960s reflected the fact that public officials felt that low interest rates would worsen our balance of payments problems.)

Of course, it should not be assumed that a country's domestic objectives are always at odds with its international objectives. This is by no means the case. At times there may be a conflict between them; at times they may be quite compatible. For example, in the United States in the late 1960s they were quite compatible. As you will recall from earlier chapters, inflation due to inadequate fiscal policies and monetary expansion became an increasingly serious problem in the United States in the late 1960s. There was widespread agreement among economists that a restrictive fiscal and monetary policy was the proper one to achieve our domestic objectives. Such a policy was also right from the point of view of our international economic problems.

Flexible Exchange Rates: A Remedy under Testing

During the 1960s and early 1970s, it was clear that the international monetary system badly needed repair. The response was a profusion of suggestions by economists and bankers. "Everybody has a plan," as Yale's James Tobin put it, with perhaps some pardonable exaggeration. As we have seen, one of the basic problems was to reconcile national autonomy in domestic economic policy with effective and reasonably prompt international economic adjustments. This problem was made more difficult in recent years by powerful multinational firms, which transferred large amounts of short-term capital from one country to another in response to differentials in interest rates and opportunities for speculative gains.

According to some economists, the answer to this problem was flexible exchange rates, which, as we saw in Chapter 32, are determined by supply and demand in a free market. Advocates of flexible exchange rates argued that they would bring about a quick and automatic equilibrium in each nation's balance of payments. For example, if a country began with a balance of payments deficit, flexible exchange rates would cause a reduction in the price of its currency—that is, a depreciation of its currency relative to other currencies. This in turn would increase its exports and reduce its imports, thus cutting its balance of payments deficit. The depreciation would go on until the deficit was eliminated.

Note that this international adjustment takes place under flexible exchange rates regardless of the sorts of domestic policies the various countries espouse. Even if one country is inflating recklessly, while another country is deflating itself into mass unemployment, international adjustment will still occur. To many economists, this is a great advantage of flexible exchange rates. They point out that flexible exchange rates allow governments much more leeway in formulating domestic economic policy. On the other hand, some critics of flexible exchange rates feel that this freedom from balance of payments discipline may lead to an unacceptable rate of inflation.

As we noted in Chapter 32, one of the principal arguments against flexible exchange rates is that they would make foreign trade more risky because no one would be able to predict what foreign currency would be worth. The result would be to reduce international trade. Those who support flexible exchange rates reply that it is possible to establish workable and efficient futures markets for foreign currencies, similar to the markets that exist for some commodities. In other words, one can buy or sell British pounds or German marks, to be delivered at a given date in the future.

In March 1973, the major world economic powers decided to experiment with the use of more flexible exchange rates. The American dollar, the Japanese yen, the German mark, and other important currencies were allowed to float. The resulting exchange rates were to be determined to a considerable extent by supply and demand. But it was agreed that the float would be managed. Governments would still buy and sell their currencies to keep exchange rates within broad limits. Moreover, fixed exchange rates continued to prevail between certain currencies, such as between some neighboring countries in Europe. As noted in Chapter 32, this system seems to have worked reasonably well to date, although some countries, notably France, have pressed for a return to fixed exchange rates.

The Formation of Recent American Policy

Let's look in more detail at the way decisions were made concerning exchange rates and the nation's balance of payments problems during the 1960s and 1970s. It is clear that the Kennedy, Johnson, Nixon, Ford, and Carter administrations all have been deeply concerned with these problems. At the beginning of his administration, President Kennedy set up a Cabinet Committee on Balance of Payments, consisting of the secretaries of treasury, state, commerce, defense, and agriculture, as well as the chairman of the Council of Economic Advisers. The chairman of the Fed was also invited to all of the meetings. This committee met often to consider our balance of payments problems. The people at the Treasury Department—particularly Secretary Douglas Dillon and Undersecretary Robert V. Roosa—were much more concerned about the problem than the people at the Council of Economic Advisers, like Walter Heller. But the president seemed to agree with Dillon and Roosa:

> "I know that everyone thinks that I worry about this too much," [President Kennedy] said as we pored over what seemed like the millionth report on [the balance of payments problem]. "But if there's ever a run on the bank, and I have to devalue the dollar or bring home our troops, as the British did, I'm the one who will take the heat. Besides it's the club that De Gaulle and all the others hang over my head. Any time there's a crisis or a quarrel, they can cash in all their dollars, and where are we?"[3]

In the Johnson administration, the Treasury Department continued to exert leadership in this area. President Johnson, in contrast to President Kennedy, had little interest in the technical aspects of the issues concerning our balance of payments. The Cabinet Committee established by President Kennedy became less important in the Johnson administration, while an informal committee of people from the

[3]Theodore Sorensen, *Kennedy,* New York: Harper & Row, 1965, p. 408, as quoted in G. L. Bach, *Making Monetary and Fiscal Policy,* Washington, D.C.: Brookings Institution, 1971, p. 133. Some of the material in this section is based on Bach's discussion.

Treasury, State, and Commerce Departments, the Federal Reserve, and the Council of Economic Advisers became more important.

Like their predecessors, the Nixon and Ford administrations were forced to spend much time and thought on our international financial problems. Secretary of the Treasury George Shultz and Federal Reserve Chairman Arthur Burns, as well as Undersecretary of the Treasury Paul Volcker and the Council of Economic Advisers, were particularly influential in the Nixon administration. For example, before the 10 percent depreciation of the dollar in February 1973, Paul Volcker traveled to Western Europe and Japan to make sure that such a move would be acceptable to various important foreign governments. In the Ford administration, Undersecretary of the Treasury Edwin Yeo did much of the negotiating leading up to the agreement with France in 1975 to prevent "disorderly" fluctuation of exchange rates. The quest for a solution to the world's international financial problems has consumed an appreciable portion of the time of the nation's leading economic policy makers. One can only hope that many of these problems will be resolved before too long.

Summary

The late nineteenth century and the period up to World War I were generally times of harmonious and close-knit economic relationships. The gold standard was in its heyday until World War I; and after the war many countries returned to it. But during the Great Depression of the 1930s, Britain and other countries were forced off the gold standard; and protectionist and beggar-thy-neighbor policies were adopted. Since changes in net exports have a multiplier effect on NNP, each country tried to increase net exports to reduce unemployment. But such policies resulted in retaliation, with the result that world trade diminished.

Once World War II got underway, the combatants changed their trading patterns, putting military, not civilian, objectives first. Loans and lend-lease programs were adopted by the United States to help finance some of our wartime exports of strategic materials and equipment. When World War II ended, some countries—like Germany, France, and the United Kingdom—had suffered a great reduction in their productive capacity. The United States embarked on a series of foreign aid programs to help the populations of the war-ravaged countries and to get the European economies back on their feet.

During the late 1940s and early 1950s, there was a severe dollar shortage. Given the existing demand and supply curves for dollars by foreigners, there was a gap between the quantity demanded and the quantity supplied at the existing price (in foreign currency) of dollars. Gradually, however, this situation changed, until recently there has been a dollar glut. For reasons discussed in the previous chapter, we have experienced a chronic deficit in our balance of payments.

The International Monetary Fund was established at the end of World War II to provide a permanent mechanism for international consultation, to promote stability of exchange rates, and to make temporary loans to member countries, giving them time to correct disequilibria in their balances of payments. The IMF, built largely on a philosophy of fixed exchange rates, has been a cornerstone of the postwar international monetary system.

The international monetary system had some serious problems during the 1960s and early 1970s. One was the difficulty of making international adjustments. Although in theory countries could change their exchange rates to cure chronic deficits (or surpluses) in their balance of payments, in practice exchange rates tended to be very rigid. Moreover, governments, for understandable reasons, often refused to sacrifice major national objectives for international adjustment. For example, when a country with a balance of payments deficit had a soft domestic economy, it was likely to pursue an expansionary policy even though this did not promote international adjustment.

Another basic problem was concerned with the rate of growth of international monetary reserves. Since gold reserves increased at a relatively slow pace and since U.S. balance of payments deficits could not be counted on to continue to provide new reserves, many economists were concerned during the 1960s that there would be a shortage of reserves. Special drawing rights—or "paper gold"—were established in 1968 to deal with the problem of inadequate reserves. SDRs can be created by the IMF and can be used much like gold by member countries.

In 1973, the major economic powers decided to experiment with the use of more flexible exchange rates. The American dollar, the Japanese yen, the German mark, and the other important currencies were allowed to float. The resulting exchange rates were to be determined to a considerable extent by supply and demand; but it was agreed that the float would be managed, meaning that governments would still buy and sell their currencies to keep exchange rates within broad limits. Although many economists and central bankers had grave reservations about such a system, it seems to have worked reasonably well to date, despite the shocks (such as the oil crisis) of recent years.

CONCEPTS FOR REVIEW

Fixed exchange rates
Flexible exchange rates
Dollar shortage
Dollar glut
World Bank
International Monetary Fund
Marshall Plan
Special drawing rights

QUESTIONS FOR DISCUSSION AND REVIEW

1. Suppose that the $C + I + G + X$ line in the nation of Upper Usher is as follows:

NNP (billions of dollars)	Total desired spending, or $C + I + G + X$ (billions of dollars)
50	60
60	65
70	70
80	75
90	80

What is the equilibrium level of NNP?

2. Suppose that all other elements of total desired spending in Question 1 (that is, consumption expenditure, investment, government expenditure, and imports) remain constant, but that desired exports increase by $5 billion at each level of NNP. What now is the equilibrium level of NNP?

3. Suppose that all other elements of total desired spending in Question 1 remain constant (including exports), but that desired imports increase by $5 billion at each level of NNP. What now is the equilibrium level of NNP?

4. "Foreign aid is an element of American foreign policy and should be used to promote American interests." Comment and evaluate.

5. "Foreign aid is a humanitarian measure designed to help poor people to the extent that we can." Comment and evaluate.

6. "Because they have no gold backing, SDRs are a highly suspect form of reserve asset." Comment and evaluate.

7. "Under floating exchange rates, reserves play a much less important role than under fixed exchange rates." What does this mean? Do you agree? Why or why not?

8. The French have argued strongly for a return to more stable exchange rates. What have their arguments been?

9. According to Milton Friedman, "It is not the least of the virtues of floating exchange rates that we would again be master in our own house." What does he mean? Do you agree or not? What are some other virtues of flexible exchange rates?

10. According to Henry Wallich, "The reason why flexible rates are inadvisable is that their successful functioning would require more self-discipline and mutual forbearance than countries today are likely to muster." What does he mean? Do you agree or not? What are some other arguments against flexible exchange rates?

34

The Less Developed Countries

Fresh from a raid on the well-stocked family refrigerator or comfortably placed in front of a television set, the average American finds it difficult to believe that hunger is a problem in the world. Yet it is. The industrialized countries—like the United States, Western Europe, Japan, and the USSR—are really just rich little islands surrounded by seas of poverty in Asia, Africa, and much of Latin America. This chapter deals with the problems of these so-called "less developed countries" (LDCs)—the poor countries of the world. We take up several questions. Which countries are poor and why? How badly do they need additional capital? How great is the danger of overpopulation? To what extent do they lack modern technology? How can they stimulate their rate of economic growth? What can the United States do to help them? These questions are crucial, both to the people in the less developed countries and to us.

Less Developed Countries: Definition and Characteristics

What Is a Less Developed Country?

Economics abounds with clumsy terms. A profession responsible for cross elasticity of demand and average propensity to consume cannot claim a prize for elegant language. The term *less developed country* is not a model of clarity. For a country to be less developed it must be poor, but *how* poor? Any answer has to be arbitrary. We shall define any country with a per capita income of $750 or less as less developed. Although the $750 cut-off point is arbitrary, it certainly is low enough so that any country unfortunate enough to qualify is most certainly poor. Recall that per capita income in the United States is about $7,000.

Table 34.1 shows that many countries have a per capita income of $750 or less. Thus much of the world is, by this definition, less developed. Indeed, *the staggering fact is that more people live in the less developed countries than in the developed countries (with per capita incomes of over $3,000) or the intermediate countries (with per capita incomes of $751 to $3,000).* Specifically, about ⅕ of the world's people live in the developed countries, about ⅛ live in the intermediate countries, and ⅔ live in the less developed countries.

Imagine what life might be like if you grew up in a country with per capita income of $750 or less per year.[1] Chances are that you would be illiterate. You would probably work on a farm with meager tools and little technology. You would have few possessions (and sometimes only enough food to keep body and soul

[1] It must be noted that these income figures *overestimate* the gap between the rich and poor nations, since the procedure used to translate local currencies into dollars is to look at prices of internationally traded goods, which are generally more expensive than goods and services consumed locally. Thus a per capita income of $750 or less isn't as low as it seems, but is still very low.

Table 34.1
Countries Classified by Level of Per Capita Income, 1974

A. Countries with per capita income exceeding $3,000			
Australia	Finland	Luxembourg	Sweden
Austria	France	Netherlands	Switzerland
Belgium	Germany	New Zealand	United Kingdom
Canada	Iceland	Norway	United States
Denmark	Japan	Soviet Union	
B. Countries with per capita income of $751 to $3,000			
Argentina	Hong Kong	Panama	Spain
Chile	Jamaica	Portugal	Uruguay
Costa Rica	Lebanon	Saudi Arabia	Venezuela
Greece	Malta	South Africa	
C. Countries with per capita income of $750 or less			
Afghanistan	China	Iraq	Peru
Algeria	Congo	Kenya	Philippines
Angola	Egypt	Laos	Sri Lanka
Bangladesh	Ethiopia	Malaysia	Thailand
Brazil	Ghana	Morocco	Turkey
Burma	India	Nigeria	Uganda
Cambodia	Indonesia	Pakistan	Zaire

Source: Agency for International Development.

together) and be likely to die young. This is the life in most of Asia, Africa, and Latin America.

The unpleasant fact is that this harsh existence—not the affluent way of life portrayed in *Better Homes and Gardens* or even the *Jersey City Journal*—is the lot of most earth dwellers. Of course this does not mean that the less developed countries do not have rich citizens: indeed they do. But the rich are a tiny minority surrounded by masses of poor people. Nor does it mean that many of these people do not live in cities. Bombay, for example, is the home of over 4 million, most of them poor.

It must also be recognized that many of the less developed countries have gained their political independence in recent years. Before World War II, the major European powers had substantial empires. For example, the British had colonies all over the globe. In the postwar period, many colonies have achieved independence. These new countries are often fiercely nationalistic. They resent what they regard as exploitation at the hands of the former European colonists and demand power and status. Although weak individually, together they represent a force that must be reckoned with.

Moreover, because of better communications and altered religious and cultural beliefs, the expectations and demands of people in less developed countries have changed enormously. Years ago, they were more likely to accept a life of privation and want, since their eye was on the next world. Now the emphasis has shifted to this world, and to material comforts—and getting them quickly. People in less developed countries have become aware of the high standards of living in the industrialized societies, and they want to catch up as fast as they can.

Although the available data on the less developed countries are not as accurate as one would like, these countries seem to have increased their per capita output in recent years. As Table 34.2 shows, the average rate of growth of per capita output in 15 major less developed countries was about 2½ percent per year during 1950-73. But since the average growth rate in the major developed countries was somewhat higher, *the gap between income per capita in the less developed countries and in the developed countries has been increasing*. This is a disturbing fact. Apparently, the gap between rich and poor will not decrease, unless recent trends are altered.

Table 34.2
Annual Rate of Growth of Per Capita National Product, 1950-67 and 1970-73

Less developed country	Average annual growth rate 1950-67	1970-73[a]
Brazil	2.1	3.9
Sri Lanka	0.8	-0.6
Colombia	1.3	2.8
Egypt	2.7	1.6
Ghana	1.3	5.1
India	1.6	-0.9
Malaya	0.8	n.a.
Mexico	2.8	3.5
Pakistan	1.5	-2.4
Peru	2.9	2.6
Philippines	1.8	3.1
South Korea	3.8	8.7
Taiwan	5.3	n.a.
Thailand	3.2	2.3
Turkey	2.8	5.9
Average	2.3	2.7

Source: A. Maddison, *Economic Progress and Policy in Developing Countries,* New York: Norton, 1970; and United Nations.
[a] Where figures for 1970-73 were unavailable, 1970-72 (or the most recent period for which data were available) was used.

A Closer Look at the LDCs

Needless to say, the less developed countries vary enormously. Some, like China, are huge; others, like Paraguay, are small. Some, like Taiwan, have lots of people jammed into every square mile of land; others, like Brazil, have relatively few people spread over lots of land. Some, like Iraq, have important natural resources (notably oil); others have few resources. Some, like India, have had great civilizations many, many centuries old; others have had ruder histories. Nonetheless, although it is not easy to generalize about the less developed countries, many of them, besides suffering from relatively low productivity, have the following characteristics:

Stress on agriculture. The less developed countries generally devote most of their resources to food production. Agriculture is by far their largest industry. This contrasts markedly with industrialized countries like the United States, where only a small percentage of output is food. Moreover, food makes up most of the goods consumed in less developed countries. They are so poor that the typical family has very little besides food, a crude dwelling, some simple clothing, and other such necessities.

Dual economy. Many less developed countries have two economies, existing side by side. One of these is a *market-oriented* economy much like that in developed countries. This economy is generally found in the big cities, where there may be some modern manufacturing plants, as well as government agencies, wholesale and retail outlets, and services for the small number of rich people in the country. Coexisting with this relatively modern economy is a *subsistence* economy based largely on barter, innocent of all but the crudest technology and capable of producing little more—and sometimes less—than a subsistence wage for the inhabitants. This subsistence economy often includes most of the rural areas. It has little or no capital, few decent roads, only the most rudimentary communications. Unfortunately, this is the economy in which the bulk of the population exists.

Political problems. Some of the less developed countries have relatively weak, unstable governments. Thus the climate for long-term investment and planning is relatively poor in such countries. Moreover, some governments are controlled by a small group of wealthy citizens or by other groups with a vested interest in resisting social change. Corruption among government officials is encountered too often, and honest officials are sometimes not very well trained or experienced in their duties. To some extent these problems stem from the relative youth of many of these countries. But whatever the reasons, they hamper the effect of government on economic development.

Income inequality. Most of the less developed countries have a relatively high degree of income inequality. Indeed, there is much more income inequality than in the industrialized countries. Typically, a few landowners or industrialists in a less developed country are rich, sometimes enormously rich. But all outside this tiny group are likely to be very poor. The middle class, so important in the industrialized countries, is very small in most less developed countries.

Barriers to Development and the Need for Capital Formation

Why are the less developed economies so poor, and what can they do to raise their income levels? These are very difficult questions, both because the answers vary from country to country and because the answers for any single country are hard to determine. A variety of factors generally is responsible for a country's poverty, and these factors are so intermeshed that it is difficult to tell which are most important. Nonetheless, certain factors stand out; among these is the lack of capital in less developed countries.

Without exception, the people in the less developed countries have relatively little capital to work with. There are few factories, machine tools, roads, tractors, power plants, miles of railroad, and so on. If you visited one of these countries, you would be struck by the absence of mechanical aids to production. Workers use their hands, legs, and simple tools, often as their ancestors did long ago.

There are several reasons why the less developed countries have not accumulated much capital. First, a country must usually reduce consumption to accumulate capital, but for the less developed countries, with their very low income levels, a reduction in consumption can be painful. Equally important, much of the saving that does go on in less developed countries is not utilized very effectively. Second, there are important barriers to domestic investment, such as the smallness of local markets, the lack of skilled labor, and the lack of qualified entrepreneurs (faced with the right incentives) who are willing and able to take the risks involved in carrying out investment projects. Third, fear that property will be confiscated deters industrialized countries from investing in the less developed countries. As we pointed out above, many of the less developed countries are relatively young nations, filled with nationalistic fervor and fearful of becoming economically dependent. They are suspicious of foreign investment in their countries—and in some cases are quite capable of confiscating foreign-owned property. Needless to say, this does not make foreigners particularly anxious to invest in some of them.

Recognizing their need for additional capital, the less developed countries have used three principal methods to increase investment. First, they have *taxed away part of the nation's resources and used them for investment purposes or made them available to private investors.* Second, they have tried to *mobilize "surplus labor" from agriculture to carry out investment projects.* Third, they have *increased government spending on investment projects without increasing taxes, thus producing inflation.* Although effective within limits, each of these methods has important limitations. Taxes may dull incentives and in any event are often evaded; "surplus labor" is difficult to transfer and utilize; and a little inflation may soon develop into a big inflation. (As shown in Table 34.3, the rate of inflation in some less developed countries has been impressive indeed.) Besides these three methods, a country can *use foreign aid to increase investment.* It too has its problems and limitations, but it is hard to see how many less developed countries can scrape up the capital they need without it.

Methods of this sort have enabled many less developed countries to increase the proportion of their national output devoted to capital formation. For example, Table 34.4 shows that in major LDCs the average proportion of national output devoted to capital formation was about 16 percent in 1973 (whereas it was less

Table 34.3
Annual Rate of Increase of the Domestic Price Level, 1950–65 and 1971–73

Country	Average annual rate of increase (percent) 1950–65	1971–73[a]
Brazil	30.1	21
Sri Lanka	−0.1	7
Colombia	9.3	18
Egypt	1.6	3
Ghana	5.7	9
India	2.3	9
Malaya	1.4	5
Mexico	6.2	9
Pakistan	2.3	5
Peru	8.2	8
Philippines	1.8	18
South Korea	19.8	10
Taiwan	6.6	n.a.
Thailand	1.6	6
Turkey	8.2	18
Average	7.1	10

Source: See Table 34.2.
[a] 1970–71 for Brazil and Pakistan.

Table 34.4
Gross Fixed Capital Formation as a Percentage of National Product, 1973[a]

Less developed countries		Developed countries	
Country	Percentage	Country	Percentage
Brazil	16	France	26
Sri Lanka	17	Germany	25
Colombia	19	Italy	19
Egypt	11	Japan	37
Ghana	9	United Kingdom	18
India	15		
Malaya	16	Average	24
Mexico	19		
Pakistan	13		
Peru	13		
Phillipines	18		
South Korea	24		
Thailand	20		
Turkey	18		
Average	16		

Source: United Nations.
[a] Where 1973 figures are unavailable, these data pertain to 1972, 1971, or whatever is the latest year for which data are given.

than 10 percent in 1950). This proportion is still significantly less than in the developed countries, where it averaged about 24 percent in 1973, but it is increasing. Needless to say, these figures are very rough, and not too much reliance should be placed on them. But they do indicate that the less developed countries are progressing in their attempts to increase their rate of capital formation.

The Population Explosion

Another very important reason why per capita income is so low in some (but by no means all) less developed countries is that they suffer from overpopulation. Many less developed countries have sizably increased their total output. In Latin America, Africa, and Southeast Asia, it may have grown at about 5 percent per year in recent years. If population in these areas had remained approximately constant, output per capita would also have increased at about 5 percent per year. But population has not remained constant. It has grown at almost 3 percent per year, so that output per capita has increased at only about 2 percent per year.

Table 34.5 shows the rate of population growth in a variety of less developed countries, as well as some major developed countries. Clearly the rate has been higher, without exception, in the less developed countries than in the developed ones. The most important reason is that modern methods of preventing and curing diseases have been introduced into the LDCs, thus reducing the death rate, particularly among children. It used to be that although the birth rate in the less developed countries was higher than in the developed countries, the death rate was also higher, so that the rate of population growth was about

Table 34.5
Annual Rates of Growth of Population, Less Developed and Developed Countries, 1950–67 and 1970–73 (percentages)

Less developed			Developed		
Country	1950–67	1970–73	Country	1950–67	1970–73
Brazil	3.1	2.8	France	1.1	0.9
Sri Lanka	2.5	1.9	Germany	1.2	0.7
Colombia	3.2	3.2	Italy	0.7	0.8
Egypt	2.5	2.2	Japan	1.1	1.3
Ghana	2.7	2.7	United Kingdom	0.5	0.3
India	2.2	2.1	United States	1.6	0.9
Malaya	3.0	3.7			
Mexico	3.3	3.5	Average	1.0	0.8
Pakistan	2.4	3.6			
Peru	2.6	3.2			
Philippines	3.2	3.0			
South Korea	2.8	2.0			
Taiwan	3.1	n.a.			
Thailand	3.0	3.2			
Turkey	2.7	2.5			
Average	2.8	2.8			

Source: See Table 34.2.

the same in the less developed countries as in the developed ones. But in recent years, the death rate in the LDCs has been reduced by better control of malaria and other diseases, whereas the birth rate has remained high. The result has been a population explosion. For example, in parts of Latin America the population is doubling every 20 years.

This growth of sheer numbers, which recalls the work of Thomas Malthus (Chapter 17), is only part of the problem. The populations of the less developed countries also tend to be illiterate and ill-nourished. Thus they do not have the skills required to absorb much modern technology. In addition, many workers have little or nothing to do. They live with their relatives and occasionally hold a job. Although they may not be included in the official unemployment figures, they represent a case of *disguised unemployment.* In sum, the population of many less developed countries is large (relative to the available capital and natural resources), fast-growing, of relatively poor economic quality, and poorly utilized.

The less developed countries have responded to the population explosion in at least two ways. Where birth control is opposed on religious or cultural grounds, the LDCs often concentrate on the widespread unemployment that results from population increase. The rapidly expanding labor force cannot be employed productively in agriculture, since there is already a surplus of farm labor in many LDCs, and the capital stock is not increasing rapidly enough to employ the growing numbers in industry. Governments faced with serious unemployment of this sort often are induced to *create public works programs and other projects to make jobs, even if these projects do not really promote economic growth.*

The LDCs have also responded to the population explosion by *attempting to lower the birth rate through the diffusion of contraceptive devices and other birth control techniques.* In many of the less developed countries, there is no religious barrier to the adoption of such techniques. For example, Hinduism does not frown on birth control. However, their adoption has been slow. One reason is the medical drawbacks of existing contraceptive devices. Also, there are obvious problems in communicating the necessary information to huge numbers of illiterate and often superstitious people. India has made considerable efforts to disseminate birth control information, but the problems are enormous. In some of the smaller LDC's, such as Singapore, South Korea, and Taiwan, birth control programs seem to have had a more definite effect on the rate of population increase.

Besides trying to cope with or influence the growth rate of their populations, the LDCs have also tried to increase the economic quality of their human resources. In other words, *they have been investing in human capital.* Such an investment seems warranted; educational and skill levels in many less developed countries have been quite low. Table 34.6 shows that in 15 major less developed countries, the proportion of the population aged 5 to 19 in primary or secondary school increased, on the average, from about 30 percent in 1950 to about 50 percent in 1964. This was certainly a step in the right direction, although enrollment in school is obviously only a crude measure of the quality of the labor force. In order to absorb and utilize, and eventually develop, modern technology, the LDCs must continue to invest in a more productive labor force.

Table 34.6
Percentage of Population Aged 5 to 19 Enrolled in Primary and Secondary Education, 1950 and 1964

Country	1950	1964
	(percentage)	
Brazil	22	46
Sri Lanka	54	65
Colombia	22	45
Egypt	20	41
Ghana	14	57
India	19	38
Malaya	35	50
Mexico	30	52
Pakistan	16	25
Peru	34	50
Philippines	59	57
South Korea	43	53
Taiwan	38	64
Thailand	38	48
Turkey	24	40
Average	31	52
United States	80	84

Source: Statistical Yearbook, UNESCO.

Technology: A Crucial Factor

Still another very important reason why per capita income is so low in the less developed countries is that these countries use rudimentary and often backward technology. In previous chapters, we have seen that to a considerable extent the increase in per capita income in the developed countries has resulted from the development and application of new technology. Too often, the less developed countries still use the technology of their forefathers—the agricultural and manufacturing methods of long, long ago. Why is this the case? Why don't the less developed countries copy the advanced technology of the industrialized countries, following the examples of the Japanese and Russians, among others, who promoted their economic development during the twentieth century by copying Western technology?

There are several reasons. One is that some types of modern technology require considerable capital. Modern petroleum refining technology, to choose one, cannot be used without lots of capital, which the less developed countries, with their low rates of investment, find difficult to scrape up. But many technological improvements do not require substantial capital. Indeed, some technological improvements are capital-saving. That is, they reduce the amount of capital needed to produce a given amount of output.

A second reason why the less developed countries find it difficult to copy and use modern technology is that they lack both a skilled labor force and entrepreneurs. Imagine the difficulties in transplanting a complicated technology—for example, that involved in steel production—from the United States to a less developed country where there are few competent engineers, fewer experienced and resourceful managers, and practically no laborers with experience in the demanding work required to operate a modern steel plant.

Even more fundamental is the fact that much of our advanced Western technology is really not very well suited to circumstances in the less developed countries. Because the industrialized countries have relatively great amounts of capital and relatively little labor, they tend to develop and adopt technology that substitutes capital for labor. But this technology may not be appropriate for less developed countries where there is little capital and lots of labor. Thus *it is very important that the less developed countries pick and choose among the technologies available in the industrialized countries, and that they adapt these technologies to their own conditions.* Mindless attempts to ape the technologies used in the industrialized countries can result in waste and failure.

In agriculture, important technological advances have taken place in the less developed countries in recent years. In particular, new types of seeds have been developed, increasing the yields of wheat, rice, and other crops. Some of this research was supported by the Rockefeller and Ford Foundations. The resulting increase in agricultural productivity has been so impressive that many observers call it a "green revolution." There is no question that wheat and rice production has increased greatly in countries like Mexico, the Philippines, Iran, Sri Lanka, India, and Pakistan. Plenty of opportunity remains for improvements in livestock yields as well, but religious beliefs and traditional prejudices are sometimes an important barrier to change.

In industry, most of the new technology adopted by the less developed countries is taken from the developed countries. Very little attempt is being made to devise new technologies more appropriate to conditions in the less developed countries, both because the less developed countries do not have the engineering and scientific resources to develop them, and because such attempts have not been very successful in the past. In countries where the private sector finds it unprofitable to carry out research and development, government research institutes sometimes try to fill the void, but these institutes frequently devote too much of their limited resources to projects not closely related to economic development. In addition, productivity centers have been created in some countries to teach managers and supervisory personnel how to make better use of new technology. Such centers have helped promote the diffusion of new technology in Mexico and Taiwan, among other countries.

Entrepreneurship, Social Institutions, and Natural Resources

Yet another important reason why per capita income is so low in the less developed countries is that they lack entrepreneurs and favorable social institutions. This point was noted in the previous section but needs more discussion. In some LDCs there is a rigid social structure. One "knows one's place" and stays in it, people distrust and resist change, and things are done in the time-honored way they have always been done (as far as anyone can remember). No wonder these countries lack entrepreneurs! The basic social and political institutions discourage entrepreneurship. Moreover, these institutions also are at least partially responsible for the ineffective utilizations of savings, relatively high birth rates, and difficulties in transferring technology noted above. As Richard Gill of Harvard University has put it, "In many underdeveloped countries, a complete social and political revolution is required while the industrial revolution is getting underway."

The governments of many less developed countries are relatively weak and unstable. It is difficult enough for any government to give these countries an effective tax system and a rational program of public expenditures, including proper provision for the highways, public utilities, communications, and other "social overhead capital" they need. But the problems are made even more difficult when the government is weak, unstable, and perhaps somewhat corrupt. Further, the population's value systems and attitudes sometimes do little to promote economic development. Again quoting Gill, "A sharp desire for material betterment, a willingness to work hard and in a regular, punctual manner, an awareness of the future benefits of present sacrifices—these attitudes may be the prerequisites of economic growth; yet they may be largely absent in many underdeveloped countries."[2]

Finally, it should also be pointed out that some of the LDCs have little in the way of natural resources. Moreover, technological change has made some of their resources less valuable, as in the case of synthetic rubber, which affected the market for natural rubber, an important natural resource of Malaya. But this is not true of all the less developed countries: Iraq and Indonesia, among others, are endowed with oil, which (as members of the OPEC cartel) they are using to propel themselves into affluence. In any event, the skimpiness of natural resources in some less developed countries does not mean that they are condemned to poverty. Neither Denmark nor Switzerland is endowed with great natural resources, but both are prosperous.

The important thing is how a country uses what it has. International trade allows a country to compensate, at least in part, for its deficiencies in natural resources. Thus, although some of the less developed countries have been dealt a poor hand by Mother Nature, this lack alone does not explain their poverty. Of course, they might have been more prosperous with more natural resources; but even with what they have, they might have done much better.

There are several ways for them to use their resources more effectively. In many of the less developed countries, a peasant may farm several strips of land that are very small and distant from one another, working a small patch here and a small patch there. Obviously, this procedure is very inefficient. If these small plots could be put together into larger farms, output and productivity could be increased. In other LDCs, huge farms are owned by landlords and worked by tenant farmers. This system too tends to be inefficient, because the tenant farmers have little incentive to increase productivity (since the extra output will accrue to the landlord) and the landlords have little incentive to invest in new technology (since they often fear that the tenant farmers will not know how to use the new equipment).

Land reform is a very lively—indeed an explosive—issue in many less developed countries, and one of the issues the Communists try to exploit. Recall that agriculture is a very important part of the economy of most of the less developed countries. Thus the land is the major form of productive wealth. No wonder

[2] Richard Gill, *Economic Development: Past and Present,* Englewood Cliffs, N.J.: Prentice-Hall, 1967, p. 87.

there is a bitter struggle in some countries over who is to own and work it.

The Role of Government

There are several opinions on the role the governments of the less developed countries should play in promoting economic growth. Some people go so far as to say that these countries would fare best if they allowed market forces to work with a minimum of government interference. But the less developed countries themselves believe a free enterprise system would produce results too slowly, if at all. Thus the prevailing view in the less developed countries is that the government must intervene—and on a large scale.

In some less developed countries—China, for example—the government exercises almost complete control over the economy. As we shall see in Chapter 35, China's economy is planned. The government makes the basic decisions on what is produced, how it is produced, and who gets it. But even in the non-Communist LDCs, such as India, the government makes many decisions on what sorts of investment projects will be undertaken, and it controls foreign exchange. And, needless to say, the government has the responsibility for providing the important social overhead capital—roads, public utilities, schools, and so on—that is so badly needed.

Further, the government may also foster social and political change. As Nobel laureate Simon Kuznets has put it, "The problem of strategy is essentially the problem of how fast you can change an inadequate set of social and political institutions, without provoking a revolution internally, or losing allies and partners externally. The question is to know what institutions you want to change, and how."

Most economists would agree that the government has a very important role to play in promoting economic development. But there is a tendency to put less weight on the government's role than in the past. Experience has made it clear that some of the less developed countries are plagued by incompetent and corrupt government officials and by a plethora of bureaucratic red tape. Moreover, many governments have gone on spending sprees that have resulted in serious inflation. Even those who are very mistrustful of free markets find it difficult to put their complete faith in such governments, well-intentioned though they may be. Recent years have seen more and more emphasis on self-interest and individual action as contributors to growth. (If Adam Smith is peering down from the Great Beyond, he probably is smiling in agreement.) But this in no way denies the fact that governments have a key role to play.

Balanced Growth

An important issue facing the governments of most less developed countries is the extent to which they want to maintain a balance between the agricultural and industrial sectors of the economy. That is, how much more rapidly should they expand industry than agriculture? According to some economists, less developed countries should invest heavily in industry, since the long-term trend of industrial prices is upward, relative to agricultural prices. In addition, advocates of unbalanced growth argue that the development of certain sectors of the economy will result in pressures for development elsewhere in the economy. Advocates of this approach point to the Soviet Union, which stressed industrialization in its growth strategy.

Other economists argue that industry and agriculture should be expanded at a more nearly equal rate. Successful industrial expansion requires agricultural expansion as well, because industry uses raw materials as inputs and because, as economic growth takes place, the people will demand more food. Balanced growth has other advantages. Various sectors of the economy are closely linked and an attempt to expand one sector in isolation is unlikely to succeed. Proponents of balanced growth deny that the long-term trend of industrial prices is upward, relative to agricultural prices. And to illustrate the wisdom of their approach, they cite as examples the United States and Britain, where industry and agriculture both expanded in the course of the development process.

In practically all of the 13 LDCs included in Table 34.7, industrial employment has increased more rapidly than agricultural employment in recent years. Without question, the less developed countries are expanding industry relative to agriculture. In some cases, such as India and Pakistan, it is generally agreed that more balance—more emphasis on agriculture—would have been preferable. Moreover, in many cases, the allocation of resources within industry could certainly have been improved. Countries have sometimes put too much emphasis on substituting their own production—even when it is not efficient—for imports. For example, Chile has prohibited the import of fully assembled cars to promote domestic production, but Chile's automobile plants have been uneconomic.

One reason why the less developed countries tend to push industrialization is that they see heavy industrialization in the wealthier countries. The United States, Western Europe, Japan, the USSR, all have lots of steel plants, oil refineries, chemical plants, and other kinds of heavy industry. It is easy for the less developed countries to jump to the conclusion that, if they want to become richer, they must become heavily industrialized too. It certainly

Table 34.7
Average Annual Rate of Growth of Product, by Sector, 1960–70

Country	Industry	Agriculture	Wholesale and retail trade
		(percentage)	
Brazil	6.4	3.9	5.3
Sri Lanka[a]	7.2	2.7	6.8
Colombia	5.5	3.6	5.4
Egypt	6.0	4.7	4.0
Ghana[b]	8.4	5.2	6.1
India	5.2	2.0	4.2
Mexico	9.3	3.9	8.2
Pakistan[c]	8.7	3.7	6.1
Peru[b]	4.6	6.1	n.a.
Phillipines	5.8	4.0	4.3
South Korea	16.6	4.5	10.2
Thailand	11.9	5.5	9.4
Turkey	10.3	2.5	8.7
Average	8.1	4.0	6.6

Source: United Nations.
[a]1963–70.
[b]1968–70.
[c]1960–69.

seems sensible enough—until you think about the theory of comparative advantage. After all, if the less developed countries have a comparative advantage in areas other than heavy industry, they may do better to put more of their resources where their comparative advantage lies.

Another reason why the leaders of some less developed countries are fascinated by steel plants, airlines, and other modern industries, is that they think such industries confer prestige on their countries and themselves. Such prestige may be costly. Given their current situation, many of these countries might be well advised to invest much of their scarce resources in promoting higher productivity in agriculture, where they have a comparative advantage. Of course, we are not saying that many of these countries should not attempt to industrialize. We *are* saying that some of them have pushed industrialization too far—and that many have pushed it in uneconomic directions.

Development Planning in Less Developed Countries

The governments of many LDCs have established development plans to specify targets or goals for the economy. In some countries, these goals are set forth in very specific, detailed form; in others, they are more generally formulated. An important purpose of these plans is to allocate scarce resources, such as capital, in order to achieve rapid economic growth (or whatever the country's social objectives may be). For example, in India, estimates have been made of the amount of capital that would be generated internally, as well as the capital that could be imported from abroad. Then the plan attempted to set a system of priorities for the use of this capital.

Some plans are merely window dressing, full of bold words and little else. But others are the result of careful investigation and hard work. Clearly, to be useful, a plan must set realistic goals, which take proper account of the country's resources, available capital, and institutions. An unrealistically ambitious plan, if actually put in effect, is likely to lead to inflation, while a plan that is too easily satisfied is likely to mean a less than optimal rate of economic growth.

A useful plan should specify the policies to be used to reach the plan's goals, as well as the goals themselves. It should also forecast carefully how the various components of gross national product will change over time, the extent to which inflationary pressures will develop, the adequacy of the supply of foreign exchange, and the effects of the development program on various regions and parts of the population.

Planning techniques have benefited from the application of many tools of modern economic analysis, among them linear programming and input-output analysis. Linear programming can be used to determine how resources should be allocated to maximize output, and input-output analysis can determine how much capacity there must be in various industries to satisfy certain consumption targets (see Chapters 23 and 30). These modern tools have undoubtedly helped in formulating development plans, but their importance should not be exaggerated. It would be a great mistake to think that making a good plan is merely a job for an electronic computer.

If the plan is realistic, it can be a useful tool, but unless it is implemented properly, it will achieve very little for the economy. How well it is implemented will depend on the government's ability to marshal resources through taxation and foreign aid, to work effectively with the private sector, and to pick productive public investment projects. In some countries, like India, "the plan" has sometimes become a political symbol, but in many others, like Mexico, planning has been politically less visible. Countries where economic growth has been most rapid seem to have viewed "the plan" less as holy writ, and planning has tended to be more modest and low-key.

Planning in Action: The Case of India

Perhaps the best way to understand the operation of development plans is to look at the nature of a particular country's plans and how they have been fulfilled. For example, consider the interesting case of India, which has had a series of five-year plans.[3] The First Five-Year Plan was for 1951–56. Its targets were to increase net investment in India from 5 to 6.75 percent of national income, to reduce income inequality, to cut the rate of population increase to 1 percent per year, and to lay the groundwork for a doubling of per capita output in a generation. To achieve these targets, the government relied heavily on capital formation. In particular, it sought to carry out many of the investment projects that had been discussed and planned under the British for 50 years or more. The First Five-Year Plan was accompanied by moderate growth. Per capita output grew by about 1.7 percent per year, and net investment rose from 5 to 8 percent of national income.

At the beginning of 1956, the Indian Planning Commission published its Second Five-Year Plan, which called for much heavier investments—and more emphasis on investment in industry and mining, rather than agriculture and power—than the First Plan. Moreover, the Second Plan relied more heavily on deficit financing than did the First Plan, and devoted much more attention to the expansion of employment opportunities, since unemployment was a considerable problem. Unfortunately, the Second Plan ran into severe difficulties. One big problem was the loss of foreign exchange, as imports grew much more rapidly—and exports less rapidly—than expected. But perhaps more important was the fact that output did not grow as rapidly as the plan called for. By the end of the Second Five-Year Plan, all sectors of the economy, other than the service sector, were producing less than the planned targets. Nonetheless, per capita output grew by about 1.8 percent per year.

India's Third Five-Year Plan—for 1961–66—involved bigger investments and somewhat more emphasis on agriculture than the Second Plan. Responding to the fact that agricultural imports had been much higher than expected under the Second Plan, the Third Plan called for more investment in agriculture. Unfortunately, however, agricultural production during the Third Plan did not come up to expectations. Indeed, India might have experienced a serious famine in 1966 if it had not received substantial food imports from the United States. During the course of the Third Plan, India did increase the percentage of national income devoted to investment from 11 to 14 percent, but a substantial proportion of her investment was financed by foreign aid. Unfortunately, India's output grew by $\frac{1}{6}$, instead of the planned $\frac{1}{3}$, during the Third Plan, and there was little or no increase in per capita output.

Although the failure of the Third Plan was due in considerable measure to India's involvement in two wars and to two bad harvests, it nonetheless shook many Indians' confidence in the planning process. There was a three-year delay before the Fourth Five-Year Plan was unveiled, and its political significance was played down. The Fourth Plan shifted the emphasis to agricultural development, including irrigation and fertilizers; it stressed a large birth control program; and it called for a $5\frac{1}{2}$ percent increase per year in national output, as

[3] It is worthwhile emphasizing that the development strategies of *small* LDCs, because of their necessarily greater reliance on foreign trade, must be quite different from that of *large* LDCs, like India.

well as further increases in investment. The Fourth Plan put somewhat more emphasis on the price system and somewhat less on detailed planning. In practice, however, the latter changes seemed to have been slow to occur.

In 1975, when Prime Minister Indira Gandhi declared a national emergency, she claimed that many of the stern measures taken at that time were designed to help improve India's economic condition. She put forth a 20-Point Economic Program which emphasized the reduction of inflation, the encouragement of agriculture, and the reduction of the birth rate. How much impact this program will have on India's serious economic problems is hard to say.[4]

Choosing Investment Projects in Less Developed Countries

Clearly, one of the crucial problems any less developed country must face is how the available capital should be invested. Countless investment projects could be undertaken—roads, irrigation projects, power plants, improvements in agricultural equipment, and so on. Faced with this menu of alternatives, how should a country choose?

One procedure often used is to accept projects resulting in high output per unit of capital invested. That is, projects are ranked by the ratio of the value of the output they produce to the capital they require. For example, if a project yields $2 million worth of output per year and requires $1 million of capital, its ratio would be 2. Projects with high values of this ratio are accepted. This procedure, which is crude but sensible, is based on the correct idea that capital is the really scarce resource in many of the less developed countries. It is aimed at maximizing the output to be derived from a certain amount of capital.

However, a better technique for choosing projects is the concept of rate of return, which is used by profit-maximizing firms to choose among alternative investment opportunities. A less developed country, like a firm, can compute the rate of return from each investment opportunity. That is, it can estimate the rate of interest that will be obtained from each investment. Then it, like a firm, should choose the *projects with the highest rates of return.*

In computing the rate of return from each investment project, it is necessary to attach values to the resources it uses and to the returns it produces. At first glance, it may seem adequate to use market prices of inputs and outputs as these values. For example, if unskilled labor's market price is $.10 an hour, this would be the value attached to unskilled labor. Unfortunately, there are some important pitfalls in using market prices in this way. In particular, *market prices of inputs in the less developed countries often do not indicate social costs properly.* For example, although the market price of unskilled labor may be $.10 an hour, there may be lots of unskilled labor doing essentially nothing in the countryside, with the result that the social cost—the true alternative cost—of using such labor is zero, not $.10 an hour. Moreover, *the market prices of some outputs may not indicate their social worth.* Because of tariffs and quotas, domestic prices may differ significantly from world prices, which may be closer to the appropriate price for some analyses of this sort.

Thus, when computing each project's rate of return, it is important to make proper adjustments so that inputs are valued at their social cost and outputs are valued at their social worth. This is easier said than done, but even crude adjustments in the right direction can be worthwhile.

[4] Much of the material in the section comes from Benjamin Higgins, *Economic Development,* New York: Norton, 1968; J. Bhagwati and P. Desai, *India: Planning for Industrialization,* Oxford: Oxford University Press, 1970; R. Gill, *Economic Development,* A. Maddison, *Economic Progress and Policy,* and W. Malenbaum, *Modern India's Economy,* Columbus, Ohio: Charles Merrill, 1971.

OPEC: A Model for Other Less Developed Countries?

The OPEC oil cartel, when it precipitously raised the price of crude oil, transformed a group of less developed countries, like Saudi Arabia, Iran, and Libya, from relative poverty to relative affluence. Some economists believe that other less developed countries will attempt to form cartels to raise the price of raw materials over which they have significant control. Indeed, there has already been some activity in this direction. For example, the seven leading bauxite exporters have formed the International Bauxite Association, and have pushed for significant increases in the price of this major raw material (used to make aluminum). And the leading tin producers have asked for substantial price increases.

The circumstances under which such cartels are likely to be successful are relatively easy to enumerate. First, the cartel must be able to control the supply of the commodity, or at least a very substantial portion of it. Unless the cartel can reduce the amount supplied, it cannot increase the price. Second, the members of the cartel must be able to agree on policy and coordinate their actions.

If some countries cheat on the cartel agreements and secretly cut prices, the cartel may fall apart. Third, the demand for the product must be relatively insensitive to price changes. If, for example, close substitutes exist for the product, the cartel may not find it worthwhile to raise prices very far.

The accompanying table lists the raw materials where the chances seem highest that a cartel of this sort might be successful. Let's look more closely at a few of the most likely cases—bauxite, copper, and tin. In the case of bauxite (and alumina), about 75 percent of the world's exports come from the seven members of the International Bauxite Association—Australia, Guinea, Guyana, Jamaica, Sierra Leone, Surinam, and Yugoslavia. Like OPEC, the members of this group have pressed for higher taxes on the multinational firms that process the raw material. In the view of many knowledgeable economists, this is the case where the probability of OPEC-type action is greatest.

With regard to copper, four leading producing countries have formed CIPEC (a French acronym for the copper council). They accounted for about ½ of the world's exports of copper in 1971, and if other less developed countries, like Papua, New Guinea, and the Philippines, joined CIPEC, its share would increase to about ⅔. Until 1975 at least, there was considerable disagreement among CIPEC members concerning the desirability of raising copper prices. Some economists think it unlikely that they will be able to achieve sufficient agreement to engage in OPEC-like action.

As for tin, only four countries—Bolivia, Indonesia, Malaysia, and Thailand—account for ⅘ of the non-Communist world's production of this metal. This, of course, makes collusion relatively easy. But there are many substitutes for tin, and the United States has a stockpile of it, both of which should discourage considerable price increases.

Faced with these prospects, what can the United States do? According to many economists, an important measure that we might take is to form a stockpile of each of these commodities equal to our total imports over one or two years. In this way, we could be sure that our economy would not be disrupted for a year or two, and by then the cartel (weakened by the reduced American market for its product) might no longer be effective. Other economists are not so optimistic. In their view, we are likely to be confronted with higher raw materials prices and possible interruptions of supply, due to OPEC-like action in some of these areas, the result being further inflationary pressures and discord in our relations with other countries.

Some Major Commodities with over ⅓ of U.S. Imports from Less Developed Countries.

Commodity	Major sources of U.S. imports	Projected annual rate of growth of U.S. demand	Net imports as percent of U.S. domestic use (1970)
			(percent)
Bauxite	Jamaica, Surinam, Canada, Australia	7	86
Chromium	South Africa, USSR, Turkey	5	100
Cobalt	Zaire, Zambia, Norway, Finland	2	96
Copper	Canada, Peru, Chile	4–5	30
Iron ore	Canada, Venezuela	2	30
Lead	Canada, Australia, Peru, Mexico	1.6	40
Manganese	Brazil, Gabon, South Africa, Zaire	3	94
Tin	Malaysia, Thailand, Bolivia	4	71
Tungsten	Canada, Bolivia, Peru, Australia, Thailand	8	50

Source: R. Mikesell, "More Third World Cartels Ahead?" *Challenge,* November 1974, p. 28.

Foreign Aid

American Programs

The plight of the less developed countries is of concern to Americans, both because it is good morality and good policy to help them. From the point of view of humanitarianism, the United States and the other rich nations have a moral responsibility to help the poor nations. From the point of view of our self-interest, the promotion of growth in the less developed countries should help to preserve and encourage political and international stability and to make them more effective trading partners.

How can the United States be of help? With regard to many of their problems, we can do relatively little. But one thing that we can do is to provide badly needed capital. Responding to that need, we have given and lent a substantial amount of capital to the less developed countries in the past 20 years.

One important type of foreign aid consists of loans and gifts made by the United States government. It has amounted to almost $200 billion since World War II. At first, the emphasis was on aid to Europe (recall the Marshall Plan, discussed in Chapter 33), but since the late 1950s, the emphasis has been on the less developed countries. About $\frac{1}{3}$ has been for military aid; about $\frac{2}{3}$ for nonmilitary aid. As noted in Chapter 32, much of this aid has been in the form of loans or grants that must be spent on American goods and services. Also, much of it consisted of our giving away part of what were then surplus stocks of food. (Recall the agricultural programs discussed in Chapter 5.) India has been a leading recipient of U.S. agricultural surpluses. Table 34.8 shows the flow of resources from the United States (and other developed non-Communist nations) to the LDCs in 1973. As you can see, American official development assistance amounted to about $3 billion in that year.

In addition, the United States has established various kinds of technical assistance programs designed to help the less developed countries borrow some of our technology, administrative techniques, medical knowledge, educational methods, and so on. The emphasis frequently is on training people from the less developed countries to the point where they can teach their fellow countrymen. Often the costs of these programs are shared by the United States and by the recipient of the aid. Most observers seem to believe that these technical assistance programs have been worthwhile and successful.

Some other aspects of American policy are also important, although they are not aid programs. For one thing, the United States and other developed countries can help the LDCs by reducing trade barriers, thus allowing them to increase their national incomes through trade. However, it seems unlikely that trade alone can substitute for aid, and the situation is clouded by the trade barriers the LDCs themselves have been erecting to protect their own industry. Another way that the United States can help is through private investment. American corporations have invested an enormous amount in the less developed countries—over $3 billion in 1973 alone, according to Table 34.8. To the less developed countries, this is a significant source of capital.

Besides providing capital, the multinational corporations have also been a source of needed technology. However, these firms have faced much more difficult problems in transmitting technology to less developed countries than to industrialized countries. Many of the techniques of the multinational firms are not very well suited to the less developed countries, with their plentiful unskilled labor, few skills, and little capital. Moreover, there is sometimes little incentive for multinational firms to adapt their products, production techniques, and marketing methods to the conditions present in developing countries. And when they do manage to make a technological transplant, its effects are often restricted to narrow segments of the economy. Still further, it should be noted that the multinational firms are often viewed with some suspicion and fear by the host governments.

In recent years, American foreign aid has been reduced because of considerable feeling in Congress and elsewhere that our aid programs were not working very well. During the early 1960s an average of about $4 billion per year was spent on such aid programs, but by the early 1970s this figure had been cut to about $3 billion. Foreign aid has been a controversial subject in the United States for some time. Many critics argue that the money could better be spent at home to alleviate domestic poverty. They claim that other industrialized countries—like Germany and Japan—should contribute a bigger share of the aid to the less developed countries. And they assert that our aid programs have not had much impact on the less developed countries so far.

Many suggestions have been made for ways to improve the effectiveness of our foreign aid. One prominent suggestion is that we go further in concentrating the bulk of our aid on a relatively few countries—those that really want to do what is necessary to develop, that can use the money well, and that are important from the point of view of size and international politics. Obviously adopting this suggestion means reducing aid to some other countries. Another suggestion is that, rather than impose political conditions on aid, we should give money with no strings attached. This suggestion entails a great deal more than economics. To evaluate it, one must decide what the goals of foreign aid should be. To what extent should it be aimed at raising the standard of living of the world's population, whatever the effect on the United States? To what extent should it be aimed at furthering American goals and American foreign policies? In practice, foreign aid has been bound up closely with our foreign policy. Given the political facts of life, it is difficult to see how it could be otherwise.

The World Bank and Other Aid Programs

The United States has provided a large percentage of the aid that has flowed from the industrialized countries to the less developed countries, but, as shown in Table 34.8, it has

Table 34.8
Flow of Resources from Individual Developed Market Economies to Less Developed Countries, 1973[a]

Country	Official development assistance	Other official flows of funds	Private capital	Total
		(millions of dollars)		
United States	2,993	318	3,733	7,044
Japan	988	1,216	3,522	5,726
France	1,487	93	1,186	2,766
Germany	965	150	251	1,366
United Kingdom	588	41	354	983
Canada	510	34	434	978

Source: United Nations.
[a] Note that these figures for the United States are based on different definitions than those in Table 33.1. For example, private capital flows are included here. Also, Tables 34.8 and 34.9 are based on the United Nations' definition of a less developed country.

by no means been the sole contributor. Other industrialized nations also have aid programs. For example, France contributed about $1.5 billion in official development assistance in 1973, and Japan and Germany contributed about $1 billion. Moreover, the Soviet Union has formulated a significant aid program. Table 34.9 shows that the Soviet Union committed over $1 billion in capital to the LDCs in 1973. Indeed, it is often claimed that the Russian programs have had more political effect than our own because they allow the recipient countries more freedom to build "prestige" projects like steel mills and because they make their aid look somewhat less like charity.[5]

In addition, the International Bank for Reconstruction and Development (the World Bank) has channeled large amounts of capital into the less developed countries. As you will recall from Chapter 33, the World Bank is set up to lend money to finance development projects and to insure private loans made for this purpose. In the late 1950s and early 1960s, the World Bank set up the International Finance Corporation and the International Development Association, affiliated agencies that have become increasingly important as sources of funds for the poor nations. The bank's activities have grown substantially: in 1965, its loan authorizations were about $1 billion; in 1974, they were about $4 billion. Nonetheless, despite its achievements, many economists believe that in the past the World Bank has sometimes been too conservative and that it should have been willing to take bigger risks. Since the late 1960s, when Robert McNamara became its head, the bank has become less conservative in this respect.

Table 34.10 shows the amount of aid received per capita by various countries in the early 1970s. The largest amounts were received by Israel and Vietnam, both political allies of the United States. Excluding these two countries, the amount of annual aid received per capita ranged from less than $1 in Brazil and Mexico to about $10 in South Korea.

To illustrate the size and nature of foreign aid, consider the case of India. In 1951, foreign aid equaled about 1 percent of India's national product; by 1958, it had risen to about 2.7 per-

[5] Since the mid-1970s, the oil-exporting countries have established aid programs too. As a percent of GNP, their programs are bigger than those of the industrialized countries.

Table 34.9
Bilateral Commitments of Capital by Centrally Planned Economies to Less Developed Countries

Source	1954–69	1970	1971	1972	1973
			(millions of dollars)		
Bulgaria	157	82	55	40	43
China	883	685	492	498	351
Czechoslovakia	1,166	55	14	100	303
East Germany	684	125	25	23	—
Hungary	375	79	42	45	148
Poland	529	25	65	100	243
Romania	373	10	141	385	36
Soviet Union	5,977	197	677	921	1,236
Total	10,144	1,258	1,511	2,112	2,360

Source: United Nations.

Table 34.10
Per Capita Disbursements to Individual Countries of Official Assistance from Developed Market Economies and Multilateral Institutions, 1971–73 Annual Average

Country	Amount of aid per person (dollars per year)	Country	Amount of aid per person (dollars per year)
Congo	8.80	Israel	37.07
Egypt	1.40	South Korea	9.98
Ethiopia	2.06	India	1.41
Ghana	5.70	Sri Lanka	4.18
Zaire	5.37	Peru	3.41
Brazil	0.93	Philippines	3.87
Chile	3.48	Thailand	1.52
Colombia	5.04	Pakistan	5.11
Mexico	0.31	Vietnam	25.80

Source: United Nations.

cent; and by 1965, it had increased to about 3.8 percent. Clearly, India has received vast amounts of foreign aid, most of it as loans, but some as grants and assistance under Public Law 480, which involved the transfer of commodities like wheat and was close to being a grant. An interesting feature of the foreign aid India has received is that it has come from so many sources. Non-Communist aid to India has been channeled in through the Aid-India Consortium, composed of Canada, Japan, the United Kingdom, the United States, West Germany, Belgium, France, Italy, Holland, the World Bank, and others. (In 1976, the consortium pledged $1.8 billion in aid.) Until 1971, the United States put up the bulk of the consortium's aid funds—over 70 percent in the First Plan, over 55 percent in the Second Plan, and over 58 percent in the Third Plan. India has also received some aid from the Soviet Bloc countries. During the Second Plan, about 6 percent of India's aid came from the Soviet Bloc, and during the Third Plan, about 12 percent came from this source. Soviet Bloc aid generally has been used for heavy industrial projects.

What are the maturity of the loans and the interest rate for the loan segment of India's aid? The average maturity for loans authorized during the Third Five-Year Plan was 36 years for American loans, 25 years for British loans, 17 years for German loans, 15 years for Japanese loans, and 12 years for Russian loans. The average interest rate was 1.9 percent for American loans, 4.4 percent for British loans, 4.8 percent for German loans, 5.8 percent for Japanese loans, and 2.5 percent for Russian loans. Thus American lenders set the easiest terms. Aside from commodity assistance, the bulk of the aid received by India has been used for power projects, harbor development, railroads, and industrial projects such as iron and steel plants. This reflects India's emphasis on industrialization. This emphasis also has meant that India has had to rely on substantial technical assistance programs to provide the necessary skills and training. The United States has provided much of this assistance, and the United Nations has sponsored trips to India by foreign experts, as well as fellowships enabling Indians to study and gain experience abroad.[6]

[6] For further discussion, see Bhagwati and Desai, *India.*

Summary

A country is defined here as a less developed country if its per capita income is $750 or less. Over 2 billion people live in the less developed countries, which include most of the countries in Asia, Africa, and Latin America. In recent years, there has been a great increase in the expectations and material demands of the people in these countries. The less developed countries vary greatly, but they generally devote most of their resources to the production of food, are composed of two economies (one market-oriented, the other subsistence), and often have relatively weak, unstable governments and a relatively high degree of income inequality.

One obvious reason why income per capita is so low is that the people in the less developed countries have so little capital to work with. The less developed countries, with their low incomes, do not save much, they lack entrepreneurs, and the climate for investment (domestic or foreign) often is not good. Also, some less developed countries suffer from overpopulation; and as total output has increased, these gains have been offset by population increases. Modern medical techniques have reduced the death rate, while the birth rate has remained high. The result is a population explosion.

Another very important reason why per capita income is so low in these countries is that they often use backward technology. The transfer of technology from one country to another is not as easy as it sounds, particularly when the recipient country has an uneducated population and little capital. Also, these countries lack favorable social institutions and sometimes have few natural resources.

To promote development, most of the less developed countries seem to believe that the government must intervene on a large scale. An important issue facing the governments of most less developed countries is the extent to which they want to maintain a balance between the agricultural and industrial sectors of the economy. Without question, the LDCs are expanding industry relative to agriculture. In some cases, such as India and Pakistan, more balance—less emphasis on industry, more on agriculture—would have been preferable. Moreover, some countries have put too much emphasis on substituting their own production for imports, even when their own production is uneconomic.

Many of the less developed countries have established development plans that specify targets or goals for the economy and policies designed to attain them. One criterion often used to determine whether a given investment project should be accepted or rejected is the ratio of the value of the output produced to the capital used. Only projects with high values of this ratio are accepted. A more sophisticated criterion is the rate of return from the project, the method used by firms in capital budgeting. However, when computing each project's rate of return, it is important that inputs be valued at their social cost and that outputs be valued at their social worth. Modern tools of economic analysis—like linear programming and input-output analysis—are used in formulating some plans.

The United States has been involved in a number of major aid programs to help the less developed countries. During the early 1960s, our government gave or lent about $4 billion per year to the LDCs and carried out a variety of technical assistance programs. In recent years, these aid programs have come under increasing attack, and expenditures have been reduced. One suggestion frequently made is that we go further in concentrating our aid on a relatively few countries that really want to do what is necessary to develop, can use the money well, and are important in terms of size and politics. Besides the United States, other countries—including the Soviet Union—have carried out significant aid programs. And the World Bank has channeled major amounts of capital into the less developed countries.

CONCEPTS FOR REVIEW

Less developed country	Birth control	Population explosion
Balanced growth	Development plan	International Finance Corporation
Green revolution	Foreign aid	International Development Association
Comparative advantage	World Bank	Multinational corporation

QUESTIONS FOR DISCUSSION AND REVIEW

1. Between 1950 and 1967, the annual rate of growth of per capita national product was 5.3 percent in Taiwan, and 1.6 percent in India. Suggest as many hypotheses as you can to explain this difference.

2. In 1950, gross nonresidential investment was 9.8 percent of national product in Taiwan, and 7.4 percent of national product in India. In 1966, it was 16.7 percent of national product in Taiwan, and 13.8 percent of national product in India. Does this help to explain the difference in Question 1? Why or why not?

3. Between 1950 and 1967, the annual rate of growth of population was 3.1 percent in Taiwan and 2.2 percent in India. Does this help to explain the difference in Question 1? Why or why not?

4. "It is always a good idea for less developed countries to substitute their own production for imports. This is the only way they can become economically independent." Comment and evaluate.

5. Why don't some market prices of inputs correspond closely to social costs in less developed countries? Give examples. What implications does this have for the economic analysis of investment projects in LDCs?

6. Angus Maddison has written that "the so-called crisis in planning which has caused so much heart-searching amongst Indian economists, is in reality a move towards a more sophisticated policy mix in which the price mechanism is being restored to a more realistic role." Explain and evaluate.

7. When the United States was a young country, was there disagreement among the founding fathers concerning the strategy we should adopt to promote economic development? If so, describe some of the positions taken by our leaders at that time.

8. "Foreign aid is of limited use; it goes into the pockets of the rich and powerful, not the poor." Comment and evaluate.

9. According to Simon Kuznets, "A substantial economic advance in the less developed countries may require modification in the available stock of material technology, and probably even greater innovations in political and social structure." What does he mean? If he is correct, what are the implications for the less developed countries? For the developed countries?

10. According to Hans Morgenthau, "Foreign aid for economic development has a chance to be successful only within relatively narrow limits which are raised by cultural and political conditions impervious to direct outside influence." Do you agree? If he is correct, what are the implications for the less developed countries? For the developed countries?

35 The Communist Countries, Marxism, and Radical Economics

Everybody talks and reads about communism. You hear the word frequently on television and see it frequently in the newspapers, but if you really know what it means, you are in the minority. It is a safe bet that most people have only a vague and distorted idea of what communism is, partly because the relationship in recent years between the Communist and non-Communist countries has been marked by suspicion, dissension, and sometimes war. Yet about $\frac{1}{3}$ of the world's population lives under Communist rule. The Soviet Union, China, Yugoslavia, Cuba, and many other countries are Communist. Clearly, you should know something about the nature of communism to understand what is going on in a large part of the world.

In this chapter, we describe and analyze the nature and workings of the economic system in various Communist countries, with our major emphasis on the Soviet Union. After a brief discussion of the doctrines of Karl Marx, the intellectual father of communism, we describe how the Soviet economy works. Since economic planning plays a major role in its functioning, the USSR's planning system is described in some detail. Next, we turn to the economies of China and Yugoslavia, and to some of the major differences between communism and democratic socialism. Finally, we describe briefly the nature of radical economics, a recent, and still very small, movement in the United States that draws heavily on Marx's views.

The Doctrines of Karl Marx

The Class Struggle

The name Karl Marx probably makes you think of revolutionaries meeting by candlelight in damp cellars to plot the overthrow of nineteenth-century European governments. If this is the picture you associate with the name, you are quite right! Karl Marx was a revolutionary who wanted the masses to revolt against the existing social order. In 1848, he and Friedrich Engels published the famous *Communist Manifesto,* the spirit of which is given by its closing lines:

> Communists . . . openly declare that their ends can be attained only by the forcible overthrow of all existing social conditions. Let the ruling classes tremble at a Communist revolution. The proletarians have nothing to lose but their chains. They have a world to win. Workers of the world, unite!

This is stirring language, no doubt about it. But why did Marx preach revolution, and what goals do the communists want to achieve?

To understand their aims, it is helpful to look at Marx's famous treastise, *Capital* (the first part of which was published in 1867), which states much of his economic and political thought. According to Marx, the fundamental causes of political and social change are socioeconomic factors. Changes in the ways goods and services are produced and distributed—and in the ways in which men enter into "productive relations" with one another (for example, the feudal lord with the serf under feudalism, or the capitalist with the worker under capitalism)—are responsible for the great political and social movements of history. History can be viewed as a series of class struggles. In ancient times, the struggle was between masters and slaves. In feudal times, it was between lords and serfs. And in modern times, it is between the ***capitalists,*** who own the means of production, and the workers, or ***proletariat.***

According to Marx, every economic system—ancient, feudal, or modern—develops certain defects or internal contradictions, which eventually cause it to give way to a new system. As the old system begins to weaken, the new system gains strength. Thus the feudal system grew out of the ancient system, and the modern system grew out of the feudal system. In Marx's view, *the struggle between the capitalists and the proletariat will eventually result in the defeat of the capitalists. This will set the stage for a new economic system—**socialism,** a transitional phase toward communism.* Communism, according to Marx, is the ultimate, perfect form of economic system.

The reasons for Marx's belief that in modern times there must be a struggle between capitalists and workers lie in his theory of value and wages. *According to Marx, the **value** of any commodity—that is, its price relative to other commodities—is determined by the amount of labor time used in its manufacture.* In other words, if a shirt requires twice as much labor time to produce as a tie, its price is twice that of a tie. By labor time, Marx meant both the amount of labor used in making a commodity and the amount of labor time "congealed" in the machinery used to make the commodity. According to Marx, wages tend to equal the lowest level consistent with the subsistence of the workers, because capitalists, driven by the profit motive, pay the lowest wage they can.

Combining his theory of value and his theory of wages, Marx concluded that workers

Karl Marx
on Capitalism

As soon as the laborers are turned into proletarians, their means of labor into capital, as soon as the capitalist mode of production stands on its own feet, then the further socialization of labor and further transformation of the land and other means of production into socially exploited and, therefore, common means of production, as well as the further expropriation of private proprietors, takes a new form. That which is now to be expropriated is no longer the laborer working for himself, but the capitalist exploiting many laborers. This expropriation is accomplished by the action of the immanent laws of capitalistic production itself, by the centralization of capital. One capitalist always kills many. Hand in hand with this centralization, or this expropriation of many capitalists by few, develop, on an ever extending scale, the co-operative form of the labor-process, the conscious technical application of science, the methodical cultivation of the soil, the transformation of the instruments of labor into instruments of labor only usable in common, the economizing of all means of production by their use as the means of production of combined, socialized labor, the entaglement of all peoples in the net of the work-market, and this, the international character of the capitalistic regime.

Along with the constantly diminishing number of the magnates of capital, who usurp and monopolize all advantages of this process of transformation, grows the mass of misery, oppression, slavery, degradation, exploitation; but with this too grows the revolt of the working-class, a class always increasing in numbers, and disciplined, united, organized by the very mechanism of the process of capitalist production itself. The monopoly of capital becomes a fetter upon the mode of production, which has sprung up and flourished along with, and under it. Centralization of the means of production and socialization of labor at last reach a point where they become incompatible with their capitalist integument. This integument is burst asunder. The knell of capitalist private property sounds. The expropriators are expropriated.

Karl Marx, *Capital*, New York: Modern Library, 1906, pp. 836–37. Originally published in 1867.

produce a ***surplus value***—a value above and beyond the subsistence wage they receive—which is taken by the capitalists. This surplus value arises because the capitalists make the workers labor for longer hours than are required to produce an amount of output equal to their wage. For example, a worker may be made to work 10 hours a day, even though his output in 6 hours equals the value of his wage. The output produced in the remaining 4 hours is surplus value.

According to Marx, surplus value is what makes the capitalist world tick. Indeed, the reason why capitalists engage in production is to make this surplus value, which they steal from the workers. Capitalists also use some of it to purchase new capital. Thus capital formation, in Marx's view, comes about as a consequence of surplus value. If the capitalist class is exploiting the workers in the way Marx visualized, it is not difficult to see why he felt that a class struggle between capitalists and workers was inevitable, and even easier to see why he was on the workers' side.

Marx's Vision of the Future

In Marx's view, capitalism would eventually reveal certain fundamental weaknesses that would hasten its demise. As more and more capital is accumulated, Marx felt that the profit rate would be driven down, that unemployment would increase (because of a rise in technological unemployment), that business cycles would become more severe (depressions becoming more devastating), and that monopoly would grow more widespread. As these developments imposed greater and greater hardships on the working class, the chance of revolution would increase. Eventually the workers, recognizing that they "have nothing to lose but their chains," would throw off the yoke of capitalism.

However, Marx did not visualize an immediate progression to communism. Instead, he saw socialism as a way station on the road to communism. *Socialism would be a "dictatorship of the proletariat."* The workers would rule. Specifically, they would control the government, which, according to Marx, is merely a tool of the propertied class under capitalism. Moreover, the socialist government would own the means of production—the factories, mines, and equipment. Under socialism each person would receive an amount of income related to the amount he produced.

Finally, after an unspecified length of time, Marx felt that socialism would give way to communism, his ideal system. Communism would be a classless society, with all men as brothers, everyone working, and no one owning capital or exploiting his fellow man. Under communism, the state would become obsolete and wither away. The principle of income distribution would be, "From each according to his ability, to each according to his needs." Marx was a visionary and a social prophet, and communism was his promised land, the ultimate goal for which he prodded the workers to revolt—and the land into which the forces of history would ultimately propel them.

Since Marx's doctrines have captured the imagination of huge numbers of people, and hundreds of millions now march under his banners, it is clear that Marx was a remarkable success as a social philosopher and political activist. But what about Marx the economist? Most economists feel that his economic theories have basic flaws, and that many of his economic predictions have gone badly astray. Although there is almost universal admiration for the power and originality of his mind, few economists in the non-Communist world buy his economic doctrines.

Specifically, there are the following problems with his theories: First, his labor theory of value simply will not hold water. As we have seen in previous chapters, the price of a commodity depends on nonlabor costs as well as labor costs. In particular, capital, land, and entrepreneurship contribute to production. Moreover, the price of a commodity depends on the demand for it as well as on its costs. (You will recall that price is determined by the intersection of the demand curve and the supply curve.)

Second, Marx's subsistence theory of wages has long been discredited. It simply isn't true that wages are set at the subsistence level. Far from being barely sufficient to keep the worker alive, wages in the United States are high enough to provide the typical worker with a car, television, travel, and a variety of other conveniences. Further, Marx's prediction that the working class would experience greater and greater misery has not been fulfilled. On the contrary, the standard of living of workers in the West has increased at a remarkable rate in the century since Marx wrote *Capital.*

Third, his prediction that the rate of profit would fall has been wrong. Instead, the rate of profit has moved up and down, with no clear trend in either direction. And his prediction of greater warfare between capitalists and workers has not materialized either. On the contrary, workers have tended to buy shares in corporations, thus joining the capitalist class. And the lines of demarcation between the working class and the capitalist class have been blurred, not accentuated, by time.

Nonetheless, despite these and other flaws in his theories, Marx was a very important figure in economics. He recognized some of the most important problems of capitalism—in particular the problems of unemployment, income inequality, and monopoly power—and analyzed these problems forcefully and originally. One need not agree with his ideas, or sympathize with some of his followers, to recognize his remarkable talents.

The Soviet Economy

Communism in the USSR

The economy of the Soviet Union provides an important example of the application of Marxian theories. By the beginning of the twentieth century, Marxism was an international political force of some significance. In 1917, a Marxist-oriented party established itself in Russia. This was the first time any major country went communist. With V. I. Lenin at its helm, the Communist party overthrew the Russian government in November 1917, and set up the Union of Soviet Socialist Republics several years later. The stated goal of the party was to establish Marxian socialism—and eventually communism—in the USSR. When Lenin died in 1924, his place was taken by Josef Stalin, who ruled until his death in 1953. Then Nikita Khrushchev, and more recently, Leonid Brezhnev, have become the Soviet leaders. Since the USSR is now by far the most economically advanced and militarily strongest Communist country, we need to understand how its economy works.

Two characteristics of the Soviet economy should be stressed at the outset. First, although Marx seemed to want the state eventually to wither away, the Soviet government is a remarkably hardy perennial. The Kremlin's influence over Russian life is well known. Power is centralized in the hands of a relatively few Communist officials who make the big decisions about what is to be produced, how it is to be produced, and who is to receive how much. This contrasts with capitalist economies like ours, where these decisions are made largely in the market place.

Second, in accord with Marx's views, most productive resources in the Soviet Union are publicly owned. The government owns the factories, mines, equipment, and so on. This too is quite different from the situation in the United States, where most productive resources are privately owned. Specifically, the Soviet government owns practically all industry, most retail and wholesale stores, and most urban housing. Some farms are government-owned, but most are collective farms. The principal case of private ownership in the Soviet Union is the small strip of land each family on a collective farm is allowed to work for itself. In addition, people are allowed to own furniture, clothing, utensils, and sometimes houses.

The Soviet Union's central planners decide what the country will produce. How do they go about making these decisions, what steps do they follow, and who is involved in this process? Before trying to answer these questions, it is important to recognize that the procedures followed by the central planners change from time to time as they recognize their mistakes and try to rectify them. Planning and controlling a vast economy like the Soviet Union's is enormously complicated. In the period immediately after the Russian Revolution of 1917, the Communists made some whopping mistakes, but as time went on, the planners became better able to carry out their jobs.

This is the general procedure that evolved: First, the principal officials of the Communist party made the fundamental decisions as to how much output would be allocated for consumption and how much for investment, which industries would be expanded and which would be cut back. Once these decisions were made, people at a lower level decided the details concerning how various plants should be operated. Then these decisions were transmitted to and carried out by managers, engineers, and workers. This decision-making process is clearly very centralized. During the 1960s, the Russians began to experiment with greater decentralization, delegating more of the planning to the individual plants and industries, and doing less of it centrally. But these reforms met with resistance, as we shall see below.

Several groups are involved in planning. The top officials of the Communist party establish the over-all goals for the economy. These goals are generally enunciated in a ***five-year plan,*** which shows where the economy should be in five years. Table 35.1 shows part of the Soviet Union's Ninth Five-Year Plan,

Table 35.1
The Ninth Five-Year Plan for the Soviet Union, 1971–75

Item	Actual output in 1970	Planned output for 1975
Electric power (billions of kilowatt hours)	740	1,030–1,070
Oil (million tons)	349	480–500
Natural gas (billion M^3)	198	300–320
Coal (million tons)	624	685–695
Steel (million tons)	116	142–150
Chemicals (billion rubles)	21	36
Plastics and synthetic resins (thousand tons)	1,672	3,457
Chemical fibers (thousand tons)	623	1,050–1,100
Pulp (thousand tons)	5,110	8,490
Paper (thousand tons)	4,185	5,560
Cement (million tons)	95	122–127
Motor vehicles (thousands)	916	2,000–2,100
Instruments (million rubles)	3,102	6,155
Farm machinery (million rubles)	2,115	3,500
Tractors (thousands)	458	575
Grain harvester combines (thousands)	99	138

Source: Directives of the 24th Congress of the Communist Party of the Soviet Union for the Five-Year Economic Development Plan of the U.S.S.R. for 1971–75, Moscow, 1971.

for 1971–75. For example, one goal was to increase electric power production by about 42 percent (about 8 percent per year).[1] When the broad goals are decided, the detailed production plans are drawn up by *Gosplan,* the State Planning Commission. Gosplan obtains enormous amounts of data from the ministries responsible for the performance of particular industries. These data describe production capacities of various productive units and available productive resources. On this basis, Gosplan formulates a tentative production plan.

Once Gosplan's tentative plan is formulated, a host of other groups enters the picture. A number of ministries, each concerned with a particular industry, report to Gosplan in the Soviet administrative hierarchy. These ministries review Gosplan's tentative plan, as do individual plant managers. The purpose of this evaluation is to make sure that the plan is realistic and feasible. Some plant managers will argue that the amount they are asked to produce is too high or that the amount of labor and materials they are allocated is too low. Negotiations take place, and suggestions for revision are sent back to Gosplan. Eventually Gosplan produces the final five-year plan.

Economic Planning: A Simple Illustration

The job faced by the Soviet planners is difficult and complex. Unless you have some appreciation of how tough it is, you cannot understand the difficulties any planned economy must face. Suppose you are handed the job of planning the performance of a small economy consisting of a chemical industry, a coal industry, and an electric power industry. To produce electric power, one needs coal, chemicals, electric power, and labor as inputs. To produce coal, one needs electric power, coal, and labor as inputs. To produce chemicals, one needs chemicals and labor as inputs. Suppose that the country's political rulers have said that in five years they want the country to consume $100 million of electric power, $50 million of coal, and $50 million of chemicals.

Clearly, it is not easy to decide what production targets to establish for each industry. For one thing, the output set for one industry must depend on the output set for another industry because each industry uses another's output. Thus, if you are not careful, one industry will be unable to achieve its target because another industry has produced too little. Suppose that each industry uses the products of the other industries in the proportions shown in Table 35.2. (The second column of figures, for example, states that every dollar's worth of coal requires $.30 worth of electric power, $.10 worth of coal, and $.60 worth of labor.) Under these circumstances, what should the production targets be? The answer certainly isn't obvious. Try it and see. (It can be shown that the production targets must be as follows: in five years, $144 million of coal, $159 million of electric power, and $818 million of chemicals must be produced. For a proof, see pages 691–92.)

This simple illustration gives you some inkling of the problems faced by the Soviet planners—but only an inkling. Our illustration has only three industries, while in fact the Russians have to deal with thousands. In the illustration, the input-output coefficients (in Table 35.2) were assumed known. In fact, these coefficients change over time and are not very accurately known. In this simple illustration, we can work out the production target for each industry, using straightforward mathematical techniques. The Soviet planning problem is so much bigger and more complicated that it is impossible, even with the most sophisticated mathematical techniques and the biggest computers, to solve their planning problem the way

[1] According to reports issued by the Soviet authorities in 1976, this goal was met. However, other goals of the plan, notably those for agriculture, were not met.

Table 35.2
Amount of Each Input Used per Dollar of Output

Type of input	Electric power	Type of output Coal	Chemicals
		(dollars)	
Electric	0.1	0.3	0.0
Coal	0.5	0.1	0.0
Chemicals	0.2	0.0	0.9
Labor	0.2	0.6	0.1
Total	1.0	1.0	1.0

we could solve it for the three-industry economy.

Soviet Economic Planning

To make the planning problem more tractable, the Soviets set higher priorities for certain production goals than for others. For example, they may set a goal for the production of houses and a goal for the production of missiles, but the production of missiles may be given higher priority. Thus, if trouble arises in meeting this production goal, the planners may take resources away from the housing industry to make sure the higher-priority goal is achieved. This makes the planner's job a little easier, but does not guarantee that the economy will be very efficient.

The best-laid plans can go awry. To make sure theirs do not, the Russians have a number of important organizations to check on the performances of plants and managers. First, there is the *Gosbank,* the state-run banking system. When the plan is published, the Gosbank gives each manager enough money to buy the resources—labor, materials, and so on—allocated to him. If the manager runs out of money, clearly he is using more resources than the plan called for. Also, when the manager sells his plant's output, he must deposit the receipts in the Gosbank. If he deposits less than the value of output specified in the plan, it is clear that he has produced less than the plan called for. In this way, the Gosbank keeps close tabs on the performance of various plants. Second, the *State Control Commission* has inspectors who visit plants and go over the records of the Gosbank. Third, officials of the Communist party are expected to report poor performance to the party bosses.

The Soviet economy is a ***command economy:*** people are told what to do. The manager of an industrial plant is told that to fulfill the plan, he must produce a certain amount, his ***quota.*** Moreover, he is authorized to spend a specific amount on wages (he is free to hire labor in the labor market), and to purchase a specified amount of raw materials and equipment. His job is to carry out these orders, but he is not told *how* to run his plant: that is up to him. The Soviets have introduced managerial incentives not too different from those in the West. If a manager is resourceful and diligent, he may be able to exceed his quota. In this case the Soviets—like good capitalists—reward him with extra pay, honors, and perhaps a promotion. If he is lazy, foolish, or unlucky, he may fall short of his quota, which may lead to a pay cut or disgrace.

However, because managers have generally been judged on whether they have met their quotas, certain problems have arisen. Managers have tried to underestimate what their plants could produce in order to get easy quotas. They have tried to hoard and conceal materials and labor so that they would appear to use less resources than they did. And they have sometimes allowed the quality of their product to decline in order to meet their quota. Moreover, managers have been loath to introduce new methods or other innovations because of the risks involved. If a new method did not pan out, it could mean Siberia for the manager. Better play it safe, even though this hurts productivity over the long run.

Soviet workers have considerable freedom to determine where they work. However, farm workers are not allowed to leave the farms, and personnel are not allowed to leave certain projects of great importance to the government. To get work of the right kind done to fulfill the plan, the planners set up wage differentials to induce people to do the needed work. This, of course, is quite similar to the sorts of incentives that prevail under capitalism. In addition, however, other pressures are used to get people to work hard and in accord with the plan. The government provides medals and awards to workers who do very well. The labor unions, which are really part of the state, push for higher productivity. And people who perform poorly may be fined or penalized in other ways. Nonetheless, labor problems of various kinds exist. For example, there are many complaints that Soviet workers are unnecessarily late and absent from their jobs, and that labor turnover is far higher than it should be.

Prices, Incomes, and Economic Growth

Prices in the USSR

As we have seen in earlier chapters, prices in a market economy allocate resources in a way that promotes the goals and satisfactions of the consumers. Obviously, prices in the Soviet Union do not function like this. On the contrary, they are set by the government to promote the goals of the state. Note that there are two fundamental differences here between the United States and the Soviet Union. Prices are set largely by the market in the United States; they are set by the government in the USSR. And prices should promote the goals of consumers in the United States, but promote the goals of the government in the USSR.

More specifically, how are prices set—and how are they used—in the Soviet Union? The answer varies depending on whether one adopts the point of view of a producer or a consumer. First, consider a producer: a plant producing shoes, say. The government sets the price of the shoes, as well as the prices of the labor, materials, and other inputs the producer uses. The government tries to set these prices so that a firm of average efficiency will run neither a profit nor a loss. Thus the system of prices is used to determine whether a producer is relatively efficient or relatively inefficient. If he makes a profit, this is evidence that he is efficient; a loss is evidence that he is inefficient.

This is no different from capitalism. But in the USSR, prices of inputs do not reflect the relative scarcity of inputs, as they do in capitalistic economies. Moreover, the price system in the USSR does not determine the output of each commodity, as it does under capitalism. Instead, as we saw in the previous section, government planning determines target output levels.

Next, let's consider the prices consumers must pay for goods and services. The function performed by these prices is quite different from that performed by the prices that producers must pay. While the prices facing producers are used to gauge the producers' efficiency (and how well they perform according to the plan), the prices facing consumers are used to ration the consumer goods that are produced. Thus the price of a commodity to the producer is likely to be quite different from its price to the consumer. For example, the price of a pair of shoes may be 10 rubles to the producer and 20 rubles to a consumer. Why 20 rubles to the consumer? Because 20 rubles is the price the government feels will equate the amount demanded with the amount being produced.

Consumer prices are set with an eye toward raising the planned revenue needed for investment. The gap between the price to the consumer and the price to the producer is the ***turnover tax.*** The turnover tax rate—100 percent in the case of the shoes, since the difference between the two prices, 10 rubles, is the same as the price to the producer—varies considerably from commodity to commodity. It provides a good deal of the Soviet government's revenue, and is a way to reduce inflationary pressures and make consumer spending fit in with the government's economic plan.

The Distribution of Income

At this point, recall that one of the fundamental tasks of any economic system is to distribute the society's output among the people. Does each citizen in the Soviet Union receive income in accord with his need, as Marx envisioned? The answer clearly is no. The Soviet planners set incomes in accord with the type of work a person does, how hard he works, and how productive he is. The result is a great deal of income inequality in the Soviet Union. If we look only at income from labor, the extent of income inequality is about as great there as in the United States. However, for all types of income (including interest, dividends, and capital gains, none of which exist in the Soviet Union), there is more income inequality in the United States.

It is important to recognize that about ¾ of all Soviet industrial workers are paid according to ***piece rates.*** The amount each of these workers receives is determined by how much output he or she turns out. Thus to a much greater extent than in the United States, income is tied directly to a person's production. This, of course, is an important reason for the considerable income inequality in the USSR. Moreover, the Soviet labor unions do not play the same role American unions do. Whereas wage differentials in the United States have often been narrowed by union pressures, such pressures have not been exerted by unions in the USSR. It is very interesting, and understandable, that the Communists have emphasized monetary incentives to coax people to produce more.

In the Soviet Union, as in the United States, occupations differ greatly in pay and status. Distinguished Soviet scientists and professors, leading ballet and opera stars, and important government officials and industrial managers are at the top of the heap. Their incomes are perhaps 20 times as high as that of an unskilled laborer, and they have the good housing, the plush vacations, the cars, and other luxuries that are scarce in the Soviet Union. The unskilled and semiskilled workers get the lowest incomes in the Soviet Union, as they do elsewhere. This doesn't mean, however, that various occupations cannot change their position in the salary scale. On the contrary, the Soviet planners push wages for various types of work up or down in order to get the labor required to help fulfill the plan.

To put a floor under the living standards of the poor, the Soviet government provides many free services, including education and health care. Also, the government provides other services at a very low price. For example, very low-rent housing—most of which is government owned—is available. These programs help reduce income inequality by supplementing the incomes of the poor. The turnover tax, discussed above, is used to finance these programs.

Economic Growth

A nation's rate of economic growth is often used as an indicator of its performance. Has the Soviet economy been growing more rapidly than the economies of the United States and other non-Communist countries? Before trying to answer this question, it is essential to recognize that the United States is far in front of the Soviet Union economically. *Our gross national product (in real terms) is about double that of the Soviet Union. Consequently, since our population is smaller than theirs, per capita gross national product in the United States is more than twice that in the Soviet Union.* When comparing the growth rates of the two countries, keep these facts in mind.

In the 1950s, the Soviet Union achieved a very rapid rate of economic growth. American observers watched with some uneasiness as the Soviet gross national product increased at about 7 percent per year, while our own increased much more slowly. This remarkable Soviet performance was partly responsible for President Kennedy's decision in the early 1960s to attempt to increase our own growth rate. One important reason for the rapid Soviet growth was the heavy investment by the Russians in plant and equipment. Investment constituted about 30 percent of gross national product, in contrast to about 15 percent in the United States. Soviet planners kept a tight lid on consumption. Indeed, consumption per capita grew little, if at all, from the late 1920s to the late 1950s. The Soviet consumer was not allowed to increase his standard of living. The increases in production went primarily to build factories and equipment and to build military power. Other reasons for the high Soviet growth rate were the fact that the Soviets could—and did—borrow Western technology, and that the Soviet system does not tolerate unemployment.

In the 1960s and early 1970s, the Soviet growth rate seemed to slump. This, together with the fact that people began to place somewhat less emphasis on the growth rate as a measure of economic performance, resulted in less concern in the United States over the Soviet growth rate, less pressure for government measures to increase our growth rate, and less talk about "growthmanship." According to leading Kremlin watchers, an important reason for the decline in the Soviet growth rate was the greater emphasis on consumption in the post-Stalin Soviet Union. The Communist leaders began to allocate more to the consumer, and this increase in consumption goods meant a decrease in the production of investment goods, which in turn lowered the growth rate.

It should now be clear that the social mechanisms determining the rate of economic growth in the Soviet Union are entirely different from those that determine the rate of economic growth in the United States. In the Soviet Union, the central planners attempt to determine the growth rate by their decisions on the rate of investment in various industries, the amount spent on research and development, and the rate of expansion of the educational system. In the United States, on the other hand, decision making is decentralized. The American growth rate is determined largely by countless decisions by consumers and producers, each attempting to reach his own goals.

Since per capita gross national product is so much lower in the Soviet Union than in the United States, it seems extremely doubtful that the Soviet Union will catch up with us for a long time. Even if the Soviet growth rate exceeds ours by a full percentage point, it will be sometime in the twenty-first century before their GNP catches up with ours, and since their population exceeds ours, it will be even further in the future before their per capita GNP equals ours. Moreover, as their economy grows, maintaining a high growth rate may become more difficult. In addition, an even more fundamental question is whether any real tragedy would ensue if the Russians did narrow the income gap considerably. Since gross national product is a poor measure of military power, an increase in Soviet GNP by itself certainly would not imperil American security.

Evaluation of the Soviet Economy

Soviet Economic Performance

In previous sections, we've described the salient features of the Soviet economy. Now let's try to evaluate its performance. Needless to say, any such evaluation must be incomplete. And since we look at the Soviet economy through American eyes, it is sure to be biased—at least in the eyes of the Soviets and other Communists. But we cannot avoid trying to make such an evaluation, despite the many formidable problems involved.

One's evaluation of the Soviet economy must depend fundamentally on the value one places on freedom. The USSR is a command economy; to us, its economy is not free. The planners decide what is produced, how it is produced, and who is to get what. A centrally planned economy of this sort may be able to push industrialization and economic growth at a rapid rate, but at a great cost in economic freedom and in living standards. The Soviet planners have decided to build tractors, not cars; dams, not housing; and blast furnaces, not refrigerators. Of course, this emphasis on investment has increased future living standards, but that may be small comfort to those called on to make these sacrifices—people who, it should be recalled, have had a much lower standard of living than their counterparts in the industrialized Western countries.

It is difficult to say much about the equity of the income distribution, since there is no scientifically valid way to say that one income distribution is better than another. This is an ethical question, which each person must answer for himself. Perhaps the most interesting aspect of the income distribution in the Soviet Union is that it contains so much inequality. There is less difference between the Soviet Union and the Western industrialized countries in the extent of income inequality than one might expect. Thus those who favor more income equality may find less to say for the Soviet economy than might be expected.

As for efficiency, it is clear that the Russian economy works—and that in many respects it works very well indeed. However, it is also plagued by problems. First, as noted above, incentives for innovation have been weak. Managers, fearful of not meeting their quotas, often resist new techniques. Second, since the planners, not the market, dictate what will be produced, goods consumers do not want are sometimes produced. The link between consumers and producers is not as firm as in the Western economies. Third, the use of production quotas and targets has led to inefficiency. For example, if the quota for a pencil factory is expressed in terms of number of pencils, the manager of the factory may reduce the quality or size of the pencils in order to meet his quota. Fourth, since input prices do not reflect relative scarcities, they may give improper signals to producers. Fifth, the Soviet Union has had many setbacks in agriculture. For example, its farms produced about 6 percent less in 1975 than in 1974, and about 4 percent less in 1974 than in 1973. To some extent, the poor performance of Soviet agriculture seems due to the fact that many farms are too big, and that there are too few incentives for efficiency.[2]

Changes in the Soviet Economy

The Soviet economy experienced a substantial decrease in its growth rate in the early 1960s. This led to a considerable amount of self-criticism by Soviet economists. Many of the problems just cited—resistance to innovation, mismatches between what is produced and what

[2] Responding to this situation, the United States, as well as Canada, Australia, and other countries, has sold grain to the Soviets. In 1972–73 we sold over $1 billion of grain to them, on terms that were controversial in the United States.

consumers want, inefficiency due to the stress on production quotas—were admitted by some Soviet economists, and there was much discussion of possible solutions. Among the most influential economists arguing for economic reforms was Professor Y. Liberman of Kharkov University, who proposed several kinds of changes. First, he favored more decentralized decision making. Plant managers should be allowed to decide on their work force, the wages they want to pay, the supplies they want to use, and the improvements they want to make in their equipment. Second, a plant's efficiency should be gauged by the ratio of its profit to its capital investment—a dangerously capitalistic concept. To prod managers and workers to increase efficiency, the bonuses received by managers and the benefits received by workers should vary with the plant's profits. Third, to promote a better match between the goods produced and what consumers want, the profits of a plant should be linked to the amount of goods sold rather than the amount of goods produced. Fourth, interest—long banished from the Communist world—should be resurrected. Recognizing that the interest rate is a device to ration scarce capital, Liberman proposed that interest charges, imposed as a tax, be made for the use of capital by plants.

During the early 1960s, the Communists began to experiment with changes of this sort. As favorable results were achieved by the decentralized decision making and emphasis on "profits" that Liberman proposed, these innovations spread throughout the economy. By 1968, perhaps ¼ of the Soviet economy was characterized by this "new look"—a remarkable shift toward decentralization and Western economic concepts. But the Soviets have had difficulties in operating an economy that is part planned and part market-oriented, and many of the Soviet central planners distrust the "new look." When the Soviet economy fell short of its production goals in the late 1960s, there was a shift back toward centralization. The future direction of the Soviet economy remains uncertain. It may move further toward greater decentralization and Western economic concepts, or it may revert to its older style of operation.

Détente and U.S.-USSR Technological Cooperation[3]

During the early 1970s, the United States, as part of its policy of *détente* with the Soviet Union, began to increase the extent of technological cooperation; an important step in this direction was the May 1972 U.S.-USSR Summit Agreement on Cooperation in the Fields of Science and Technology. This agreement set up a joint commission (under the cochairmanship of H. G. Stever, director of the U.S. National Science Foundation, and V. A. Kirillin, chairman of the USSR State Committee for Science and Technology), the aim of which was to promote technological transfer between the U.S. and USSR, and to do cooperative research and development in areas such as the application of computers to management, energy, and chemical catalysis.

This was an important step in U.S.-USSR relations. But it was by no means the first time that the Russians have imported Western technology. On the contrary, in the 1890s, there was a massive infusion of Western technology (and capital) into basic Russian industries like steel. Again in the late 1920s and early 1930s, there was a very significant import of Western technology concerning electrical equipment, machine tools, and other types of equipment. And in the 1950s, there was an absorption of processes to produce fertilizers and synthetic fibers. Now, as in these previous periods, the USSR seems to be intent on importing technology of various kinds, with particular em-

[3] This section is based partly on my "East-West Technological Cooperation and Competition," *NATO Review,* August 1975.

phasis on areas like computer technology and integrated circuits.

Despite its large investment in R and D and its high level of scientific accomplishment in many areas, the Soviet Union continues to lag behind the West in these and many other aspects of civilian technology. The Soviets have encountered important difficulties in getting new technology out of the laboratory and into widespread application, due, in part at least, to the rather sharp separation of R and D from production, which has tended to reduce the economic relevance of the R and D carried out and to thwart the transfer of technology. Also, as noted above, the incentive system facing Soviet managers seems to have discouraged innovation, as well as the transfer of many kinds of technology.

The advantages to the U.S. of increased U.S.-USSR technology transfer are generally regarded to be of three broad types. First, it is hoped that technological cooperation will result in improvements in political and diplomatic relations between the East and West. Second, it is hoped that increased technological cooperation will result in the West's gaining access to technology developed in the Soviet Union and Eastern Europe. Third, it is hoped that increased technological cooperation will result in increased U.S. exports to the Soviet Union and Eastern Europe. At the same time, of course, there is the danger that increased technology transfer will result in a major enhancement of Soviet military capabilities, or in increased competition from the Soviets in economic areas. Many American scientists and engineers believe that we should proceed cautiously in this area.

To the Soviet Union, American technology is a means of raising the Soviet economic growth rate. Soviet gross national product grew at an average annual rate of 6.4 percent in 1950–58, 5.3 percent in 1958–67, and 3.7 percent in 1967–73. Confronted by this decline in the rate of growth of GNP (and of the rate of growth of productivity), the Soviet leaders seem to be intent on obtaining advanced technology from the West to reverse this trend, which they view with some concern. Without question, technology transfer from the West can help the Soviets in this regard. What is less obvious is whether the Soviets will be able in the forseeable future to remove or offset the institutional barriers that seem to have prevented them from achieving a high rate of innovation (and rapid diffusion of innovation) outside the military and space fields.

The Chinese Economy

Communism in China

In 1949, another of the world's major powers—China—joined the Communist ranks. With Mao Tse-tung at its head, the Communist army entered Peking, the capital of a nation containing ¼ of the world's population. China was a poor country, with little capital, little technology, and little education—a less developed country par excellence, despite its ancient civilization. Further, the Communists inherited an economy marred by many years of war with the Japanese. Clearly, the country needed as much economic growth as possible, and quickly.

The Chinese Communists responded with a ruthless drive toward industrialization. China's Five-Year Plan of 1952–57 emphasized investment in heavy industry like steel and machinery and some expansion of light industry. It also called for a massive reorganization of agriculture, involving collective ownership of some farms and transfer of land from the rich to the poor. To permit the high rate of investment called for by the plan, the Chinese government pared consumption to the bone. The Chinese people were asked to work long and hard—for little return in goods and services.

Most observers agree that the plan achieved

its goal of rapid economic growth. Even though China's population increased considerably, output per capita increased by about 4 or 5 percent per year during the 1950s. This was an enormous achievement for a country whose economy had been stagnant for centuries. To accomplish these objectives, China adopted measures that seem stern even when compared with the Soviet Union. (China, like the USSR, operates a command economy, but this, of course, has not prevented the development of considerable tension between them. To buttress its own position, each nation claims that the other has abandoned the true faith of Marxism.)

Having succeeded in pushing the economy ahead in the Five-Year Plan of 1952–57, in 1958 China's leaders launched a more ambitious plan, called the Great Leap Forward. Its aim was to increase per capita output by 25 percent. The large number of underemployed workers in China were to be swept into the employed labor force, and there was to be a great increase in investment. It all sounded very impressive on paper, but it turned out to be a disaster. Despite all the slogans and propaganda, the plan was foolish and unrealistic. For example, literally millions of people were asked to produce steel in primitive furnaces in their back yards. The result, or course, was a lot of unusable scrap metal. Also, poor planning directed millions of workers to produce other goods of little or no value. And too many people were ordered to leave agriculture and enter factories, with the result that far too little food was produced.

By 1960, the Great Leap Forward was obviously a failure of catastrophic proportions, and China's leaders had little choice but to alter their policies. In 1961, they published their new economic plan, which called for more emphasis on agriculture and less on industry. For example, industries that contributed to agricultural productivity—like the tractor industry—would receive more capital, while less would be devoted to industries that did not affect agriculture. Also, higher priority was given to the production of consumer goods for the peasants. Despite the new emphasis, the gains in agricultural production and efficiency seem to have been modest during the 1960s. Apparently, the Great Leap Forward had wreaked so much havoc that it was difficult to get agriculture moving ahead.

The so-called Cultural Revolution that began in 1968 saw large-scale political disorders in Communist China. Because the data on Chinese economic performance are meager and unreliable, even the experts find it difficult to estimate the effects of this social turmoil on the economy. But by 1971, it seemed likely that the economy had recovered in large part from the economic disorders arising from the Cultural Revolution. According to recent estimates by Thomas Rawski, Chinese industrial production in 1971 was perhaps double what it had been in 1963.

Economic Life in China

Despite the economic gains it has achieved, China is still a less developed country. In 1970, the average wage in industry was about $270 per year, and the average wage in agriculture was about $200 per year. Over 50 percent of the typical wage earner's income goes for food, and many consumer goods, like rice and cloth, are rationed, so that a family can buy only a certain amount per month. Automobiles are uncommon in China; the bicycle is the usual means of private transportation in cities. Workers are divided into a number of strata, and wages are uniform within each strata. The government plays an important role in determining where and in what position a particular person works. Labor markets are not nearly as free as in the United States.

To step up its rate of economic growth, China devotes about 20 percent of its national output to capital formation. This is a high rate of investment, relative to developed countries as well as to other less developed countries. However, it must be recognized that this does not come from voluntary saving. Instead, it is due to government action. Because the educational and skill level of the population is low, it is difficult to invest this forced saving as productively as would otherwise be the case. The Russians, when they were on better terms with the Chinese, provided some technical assistance, but those days are long gone. At present, China finds it difficult to absorb the technology it so badly needs.

About ⅘ of China's population is engaged in agriculture, which contributes about 40 percent of GNP. Industrial production, which constitutes about ⅓ of GNP, has been growing more rapidly than agricultural output. Indeed, industrial output grew at about 10 percent per year in 1971, and at a somewhat lesser rate in 1972. But agriculture experienced a setback in 1972, when grain output was hard hit by drought in western and northern China, resulting in a 4 percent decrease in grain production from 1971 to 1972. Consequently, China increased her wheat imports from Canada, Australia, and the United States from 3.2 million tons in 1971 to 4.5 million tons in 1972.

The distribution of income in China is much less unequal than it was 30 years ago. Some economists, like John Gurley of Stanford University, believe that China has been able to eradicate abject poverty despite her economic adversities. According to Gurley,

> The basic, overriding economic fact about China is that for twenty years she has fed, clothed, and housed everyone.... Millions have not starved; sidewalks and streets have not been covered with multitudes of sleeping, begging, hungry, and illiterate human beings; millions are not disease-ridden.[4]

[4] John Gurley, "Maoist Economic Development," in E. Mansfield, *Economics: Readings, Issues, and Cases,* 2d ed., New York: Norton, 1977.

It is difficult, however, to obtain reliable information about living conditions in so huge and diverse a country, particularly when very few Americans were allowed in China before President Nixon's visit in 1972. Many economists are less enthusiastic than Gurley about China's economic performance.[5] Also, some call attention to the price the Chinese have paid in what we would regard as regimentation and lack of political and social freedom.

The Yugoslav Economy

After World War II, Yugoslavia, like China, entered the Communist ranks, led by Tito, the leader of its wartime resistance to the Nazis. The Yugoslavs, like the Chinese, have developed their own brand of economic system under Communism. During the late 1940s, the Yugoslavs tried to use Soviet-style central planning, but after deciding that it would not work well for them, they proceeded to develop an economic system that is much more decentralized and much closer to the market-directed economies than the Soviet Union's. However, it is important to recognize that Yugoslavia remains a one-party Communist country, dedicated to Communist goals.

The Yugoslav economy is a mixture of planning and decentralized decision making. Most of the productive resources are collectively owned, and much investment has been centrally planned. In other words, the central planners have decided where much of the investment funds, obtained by taxation, were to be spent. (For example, they have figured out whether the textile industry should be expanded or whether some other industry—perhaps machinery—should be expanded instead.) But since 1965, most of the country's investment has been allocated through firms, not central planning.

[5] For example, see James Tobin, "The Economy of China: A Tourist's View," in E. Mansfield, *Economics: Readings, Issues, and Cases.*

In agriculture, the Yugoslavs began by trying to collectivize the farms, but gave up this idea in the early 1950s. Most land was returned to private ownership, and the rest was made into cooperative farms. Since the Yugoslavs seem to have achieved a higher rate of growth of farm output than the Soviets, this policy seems to have been justified.

Yugoslavia's rate of economic growth has been among the highest in the world. Between 1950 and 1967, output per capita grew at an average rate of 5.6 percent per year, which is very high indeed. One important reason for this high rate of growth was that Yugoslavia devoted a relatively large proportion—about 20 percent—of its output to capital formation. Also, the Yugoslavs have channeled much surplus rural labor to the cities, where its productivity is higher. Foreign aid also contributed to Yugoslavia's economic growth. The United States, for example, gave Yugoslavia $2¼ billion up to 1964. Also, Yugoslavia has not experienced particularly rapid population growth. Its population increased by about 1.2 percent per year between 1950 and 1967, a lower rate of increase than that of the United States.

Despite its very significant economic advances, Yugoslavia is still a fairly poor and predominantly rural country. Income per capita was about $800 in 1965, and the Communist government has stressed the importance of continued economic growth. One consequence of Yugoslavia's rapid economic growth has been considerable inflationary pressure. In the period from 1950 to 1965, the domestic price level increased at an average rate of about 4.9 percent per year. In an attempt to reduce these pressures, the government has often imposed price controls. There also has been substantial unemployment in Yugoslavia, much of it because of the difficulty of finding work for people with very low technical skills.

A distinctive feature of the Yugoslav economy is its system of *workers' management.* Most firms in Yugoslavia are worker-managed, at least in theory. The workers own the firm where they work and choose the people who run it. Firms attempt to maximize profits, just as in the United States, and whatever profits remain after taxes may be distributed to the workers or plowed back into the firm. Each worker is guaranteed a certain minimum income. How much he receives above the minimum depends on the firm's profits. Thus there are monetary incentives for managers and workers to increase a firm's efficiency, cut its costs, increase its sales, and raise its profits.

Most observers seem to agree that the Yugoslav economic system has worked quite well, although its performance has been uneven. In particular, it seems to have achieved greater industrial democracy and to have relied less on administrative pressure than the Soviet Union, while at the same time doing a better job of catering to consumer tastes and tapping individual initiative. Although there is some skepticism concerning the amount of power actually exercised by the workers, many observers, both Communist and non-Communist, view the Yugoslav economy as an interesting alternative to the Russian or Chinese versions of Communism.

Democratic Socialism

We have described three brands of Communism—Russian, Chinese, and Yugoslav. And in previous chapters, we have described capitalism. But we must stress that there are other types of economic systems besides capitalism and Communism. One of the most important of these is ***democratic socialism,*** which has included Sweden's socialist government and Britain's Labor government, among others. In many ways, the democratic socialist economies occupy a middle ground between our more capitalist system and the Communist systems. They generally favor government ownership of heavy industry like coal and steel (although the fervor for nationalization of such industries has died down in recent years); heavy taxation of the rich; and extensive welfare programs (social security, medical care, and so on); as well as a certain amount of economic planning, rather than the unfettered play of market forces.

But in contrast to the Communists, the democratic socialists generally do not favor violent revolution. Instead, they believe that democratic means should be used to obtain power. A good example is the British Labor government, which came into office after World War II. During the 1920s and 1930s, the Labor party had worked within the existing political system and gained strength. Finally, after the war it got its hands on the reins. Since then the Labor party has remained a major influence in British politics (although it has been in and out of office). As it has gathered further experience, its goals have changed somewhat. For example, because government ownership of industry seems to have been inefficient, the socialists are much more tolerant of private property, and less interested in nationalizing industry, than they were 25 years ago.

To a considerable extent, the more capitalist countries—like the United States—have taken over many of the socialist programs. For example, the United States has moved a long way toward heavy taxation of the rich and toward extensive welfare programs. If Calvin Coolidge could be retrieved from the Great Beyond—and if Silent Cal could be induced to comment—he surely would be impressed (and perhaps dismayed) by how far the United States has traveled toward socialism since his presidency in the 1920s. Even though *planning* is viewed with suspicion in the United States, the government has become more and more involved in various aspects of our economic life, as we have seen in earlier chapters. The adoption by essentially capitalistic countries of many of their programs has taken some of the appeal—and some of the vitality and direction—from the socialists.

With regard to planning, it is worth noting that a group of economists, union leaders, business men, and legislators, headed by Wassily Leontief, Senator Hubert Humphrey, Leonard Woodcock of the United Auto Workers, and others, have proposed that the United States adopt a formal system of national economic planning. This proposal, submitted to Congress in 1975, would have an Office of Economic Planning established within the Executive Office of the President, with responsibilities for gathering the relevant data and formulating alternative plans for periods from 5 to 25 years in the future. This proposal has been viewed with great skepticism by some economists, particularly conservatives, since they feel that planning is unlikely to work well, and is likely to lead toward reduced economic freedom. Although this bill probably will not be adopted in the near future, it is an indication of the direction in which at least some influential liberal groups in the U.S. are moving.

Radical Economics

Radical Economics and the New Left

In the United States in recent years, a new force in economics has appeared—radical economics. The radical economists, mainly young and still in the process of shaping their own contributions to the field, draw heavily on the views of Karl Marx. Looking at the urban, racial, environmental, and poverty problems of today, they argue that the conventional tools of economics are too biased toward maintaining the *status quo* to analyze many of these problems properly. They challenge the methods and assumptions of conventional economics, criticize conventional economists for neglecting many important social problems, and question the reasonableness of many of our society's economic goals.

The analytical framework underlying radical economics consists largely of the following hypotheses. First, following Marx, the radical economists argue that the structure of any society is determined principally by the society's dominant mode of production, and that the most distinctive features of the mode of production under capitalism is the use of the wage-contract, the dominance of impersonal markets, and the private ownership of capital. Second, according to the radical economists, the pressure under capitalism for capital accumulation and riches tends to create a momentum in and of itself, which creates important contradictions and social problems. Third, according to the radical economists, the United States has reached a state of economic development where class struggles are not necessary or rational, since there is enough productive capacity so that all citizens can share adequately in wealth and leisure. To solve existing social problems, the radicals argue that the basic institutions of our society must change. In their eyes, nothing less will suffice.

The flavor of the radical position is well conveyed by this quotation from David Gordon:

> Radicals criticize capitalist society essentially because it evolves irrationally. Its basic mode of production and the structures of its institutions create conflicts which do not need to exist. In the language of economics, it forces "trade-offs" that are not necessary. Fundamentally, radicals argue, capitalism forces a conflict between the aggregate wealth of society (and obviously the enormous wealth of some individuals) and the freedom of most individuals. In another, truly democratic, humanist and socialist society, radicals argue, conditions could be forged in which increases in aggregate social wealth complemented the personal freedom of all individuals. Edwards and MacEwan mention some of the other unnecessary conflicts created (or sustained) by capitalist societies: "income growth versus a meaningful work environment, employment versus stable prices, private versus social costs, public versus private consumption, and income versus leisure." Other conflicts can be specified, but the criticisms gain force in the context of the radical vision of a "better" society. It should be emphasized in discussing the radical vision that many modern radicals, though socialist, do not view most modern socialist countries with great approval. To many Western radicals, the purposes and the realities of the socialist revolution in Cuba provide the closest manifest approximation to their ideals. Che Guevara, in many ways a more important ideologue of that revolution than Fidel Castro, has often expressed those ideals most eloquently.[6]

Response to Radical Economics

As you would expect, the economics profession has responded in a variety of ways to the emergence of radical economics, with its relatively small number of followers. Some economists have chosen to ignore them, while others, like Robert Solow of M.I.T., have responded sharply. In Solow's view,

> Radical economics may conceivably be the wave of the future, but I do not think that it is the wave of the present. In fact, to face the issue head on, I think that radical economics as it is practiced contains more cant, not less cant; more role-playing, not less role-playing; less facing of the facts, not more facing of the facts, than conventional economics. In short, we neglected radical economics because it is negligible. There is little evidence that radical political economics is capable of generating a line of normal science, or even that it wants to.[7]

Since radical economists are still engaged in the work that will tell whether theirs is really a contribution to science, it is premature to attempt to evaluate the accuracy or importance of their efforts. Admittedly, they have attracted considerable attention, despite the smallness of their numbers, but attention and agreement are two different things. The vast majority of the economics profession unquestionably would disagree with their conclusions. Most econo-

[6] D. Gordon, *Problems in Political Economy: An Urban Perspective,* Boston: Heath, 1971, p. 7.

[7] R. Solow, "The State of Economics," *American Economic Review,* May 1971.

mists do not believe that capitalism should be replaced. Nor do they agree with the radicals' view of how our society works, or with their indictment of conventional economics.

Most economists today do not seem to believe that our modern version of capitalism is about to wither on the vine. This is particularly noteworthy, since at the end of World War II, many distinguished non-Marxist economists and social seers, as well as the Marxists, were predicting the demise of capitalism and the rise of socialism. One of the most significant developments of the past 30 years has been the extent to which these prophecies have fallen flat on their faces. The essentially capitalistic economies of the West have shown a tremendous vitality, have grown at a relatively rapid rate, and have avoided any deep depressions (although stagflation has proved to be a persistent difficulty). This is a tremendous achievement, and one that should be recognized and appreciated. Of course it does not mean that we do not have many problems. On the contrary, much of this book has been devoted to the discussion of our important social problems. But it does mean that our modern version of capitalism seems to be more than holding its own in today's world.

Summary

Karl Marx was the intellectual father of communism. According to him, the fundamental causes of political and social change are socioeconomic factors. He viewed history as a series of class struggles, the present class struggle being between the capitalists, who own the means of production, and the workers. In Marx's view, the struggle will eventually result in the defeat of capitalism, which will be replaced by socialism, a transitional stage toward communism. To Marx, communism is the ultimate, perfect form of economic system. Capitalists and workers struggle because the workers are exploited. Marx, who subscribed to a labor theory of value, believed that the workers create a surplus value, the difference between the value of what they produce and the subsistence wage they receive. Capital formation, in Marx's view, comes about as a consequence of this surplus value.

According to Marx, the lot of the workers would inevitably get worse. Consequently, capitalism would eventually be overthrown and succeeded by socialism, then by communism. Socialism would be a "dictatorship of the proletariat." The workers would control the government, the government would own the means of production, and each person would receive an amount of income related to the amount he produced. After an unspecified period of time, Marx felt that socialism would give way to communism, which would be characterized by a classless society, the withering away of the state, and the distribution of income according to the principle: "From each according to his ability, to each according to his needs." Marx's economic theories have many flaws. For example, his labor theory of value and his subsistence theory of wages are discredited, and many of his predictions have been quite wrong. Nonetheless, Marx was an extremely important figure in economics, and his political and social theories have had an enormous impact on the world.

The Soviet Union, the first country to embrace Marxian socialism, has a command economy where power is concentrated in the hands of a relatively few Communist officials who make the big decisions on what is to be produced, how it is to be produced, and who is to receive how much. The government owns the factories, mines, equipment, and other means of production—and gives no evidence of withering away. The top officials of the Communist party establish the over-all goals for the economy. The detailed production plans to realize these broad goals are drawn up by Gosplan, the State Planning Commission. These plans are reviewed by individual industries and plants, and after negotiations and revision, Gosplan issues the final plan. To see to it that the plan is carried out, each plant manager is judged by how well he meets his production quota and whether he uses more or less resources than the plan calls for.

In the Soviet Union, the government, not the market, sets prices. Prices facing producers are set in such a way that a firm of average efficiency will make neither a profit nor a loss. Prices facing consumers are set to ration the consumer goods produced and to raise the planned revenue needed for investment. The difference between the price to the consumer and the price to the producer is the turnover tax. There is a great deal of income inequality in the Soviet Union. Monetary incentives are widely used to increase production, and about ¾ of all industrial workers are paid by piece rates.

In the 1950s, the Soviet Union achieved a very rapid rate of economic growth, largely because of a high rate of investment and the borrowing of Western technology. But in the 1960s and 1970s, the Soviet growth rate seemed to slump, due in part to a greater emphasis on consumption. Since per capita income in the Soviet Union is less than half of ours, it seems extremely doubtful that the Soviet Union will match our per capita income level in the near future. To increase the efficiency of the Russian economy, there was some movement toward decentralized (and more market-oriented) decision making in the 1960s.

Two other types of Communist systems are found in China and Yugoslavia. China is a very poor country despite its ancient civilization. China's first Five-Year-Plan was an ambitious and ruthless drive toward industrialization that seemed to achieve its objectives, but Mao's Great Leap Forward was a disaster that set back the country's economic development. More recently, China's industrial output seems to have grown relatively rapidly. Yugoslavia has developed an economic system that is much more decentralized and closer to the market-oriented economies than the USSR's. Most firms in Yugoslavia are worker-managed and profit-oriented. Yugoslavia's rate of economic growth has been among the highest in the world. Both China and Yugoslavia have devoted a relatively large percentage of national output to capital formation.

Marxian socialism—or communism—is not the only brand of socialism. There are many democratic socialist parties and governments in the world today. They occupy a middle ground between our more capitalistic system and the Communist systems. In the United States, a new force in recent years has been radical economics, which is based largely on Marxism. The radical economists challenge the methods and assumptions of conventional economics, and advocate basic institutional change. Many economists question whether radical economics is a contribution to science at all. At present, it is difficult to say, since radical economics is so new.

The essentially capitalist economies of the West have shown great vitality in the postwar period. They have grown at a relatively rapid rate, and have managed to avoid any deep depressions. Contrary to many predictions of 30 years ago by some distinguished social seers, our modern version of capitalism seems to be more than holding its own in the world of today, although it obviously is beset by many serious problems.

CONCEPTS FOR REVIEW

Communism
Marxism
Socialism
Capitalism
Proletariat
Surplus value
Capital
Command economy
Turnover tax
Democratic socialism
Radical economics
Gosplan
Gosbank

QUESTIONS FOR DISCUSSION AND REVIEW

1. In recent years, has the Soviet Union's rate of economic growth tended to decline? Has its rate of productivity growth (that is, the rate of growth of output relative to input) tended to decline as well? If so, why?

2. "It is a mistake for the United States to transfer its technology to the Soviet Union, since they may turn it against us." Comment and evaluate.

3. "Marx's labor theory of value is useful in explaining why profits are a socially legitimate type of income." Comment and evaluate.

4. Discuss the differences between the United States and the Soviet Union in the way in which prices are determined. What are some of the most important economic effects of these differences?

5. According to John Gurley, "Maoists believe . . . that development is not worth much unless everyone rises together." What does he mean? Do you agree with this Maoist belief? Why or why not?

6. "In a field where controlled experimentation is impossible, the relative performance of India and China gives some idea of whether a Communist or a democratic system results in faster economic development." Comment and evaluate.

7. Some economists argue that the differences between capitalistic and Communist economies will decline over the long run. According to this so-called *convergence hypothesis,* both kinds of economic systems will tend to adopt similar policies and institutions in response to similar problems and needs. Do you agree? What evidence can you present in support of this hypothesis? What evidence can you present against it?

8. According to some critics, like Assar Lindbeck, whereas either markets or centralized power can be used to organize a modern economy, the radical economists are against both. How then can an economy like ours be organized? What constructive suggestions, if any, have the radical economists put forth?

9. Compare the economic systems of the Soviet Union, China, and Yugoslavia. To what extent have they departed from Marx's teachings? To what extent are their economic institutions much the same? What are the major differences in the way economic decisions are made? Which of them seems to be performing best economically? Which of them seems to be performing worst?

10. Are the radical economists right in their indictments of conventional economics? What are the most important problems that the American economy will experience in the next 40 years? Can existing economic knowledge solve these problems? What kinds of research are most badly needed?

INDEX

Definitions of terms appear on pages set in **boldface** type.

minimal-like, shaped canvases. A number of these had to do with time and sequence. One set evolved from the idea of pages turned down and removed from a calendar: canvases "turned down" at one corner until the last rectangle was reduced to a triangle and the sequence of color changes brought to a halt.

The surfaces of these paintings were most often painted one color with a second acting as an accent. Later, thin, watercolor-like treatment emerged and there began references to nature—to woods, fields, and rivers. Nothing figurative though.

In turn this has given way to other series and sequences, but now off the stretcher and held firm by rods and sticks and rings and string or rope. Things are tied and sometimes the knots act as color comments. The over-all effect is like that of kites or sails on a Chinese junk, the canvas shaped into squares, rectangles or polygons and suspended in sequences fanned out along a wall like some huge hand of cards or from the ceiling like a chain of banners.

Smith's work has developed from a loud, aggressiveness to an almost oriental delicacy and subtleness. Now his color is more beautiful than ever and his "message" almost serene.

—Ralph Pomeroy

SMITH, Tony.

American. Born in South Orange, New Jersey, in 1912. Attended night classes at the Art Students League, New York, 1933–36; studied architecture, New Bauhaus, Chicago, 1937–38; architectural apprentice to Frank Lloyd Wright, 1938–40. Married: had 3 daughters. Worked as tool-maker and draftsman, New York, 1933–36; practicing architect, 1940–60; full-time sculptor and painter from 1960. Taught at New York University School of Education, 1946–50; Cooper Union and Pratt Institute, New York, 1950–53; Pratt Institute, Brooklyn, New York, 1957–58; Bennington College, Vermont, 1958–61; Hunter College, New York, 1962–74. Recipient: Longview Art Award, 1966; National Council for the Arts Award, 1966; Guggenheim Award, 1968; Fine Arts Medal, American Institute of Architects, New York, 1971; College Art Association Distinguished Teacher of Art Award, 1974; Creative Arts Award for Sculpture, Brandeis University, Waltham, Massachusetts, 1974. Agent: Pace Gallery, 32 East 57th Street, New York, New York 10022, U.S.A. *Died* (in Orange, New Jersey), *26 December 1980.*

Individual Exhibitions:

1966 *Two Exhibitions of Sculpture*, Wadsworth Atheneum, Hartford, Connecticut
Institute of Contemporary Art, Philadelphia
1967 Walker Art Center, Minneapolis
Galerie Müller, Stuttgart
Bryant Park, New York
1968 Galerie René Ziegler, Zurich
Galerie Yvon Lambert, Zurich
Donald Morris Gallery, Detroit
Fischbach Gallery, New York
Museum of Modern Art, New York (travelling exhibition)
1969 University of Hawaii, Honolulu
1970 Newark Museum, New Jersey
Montclair Art Museum, New Jersey
Art Museum, Princeton University, New Jersey
1971 *9 Sculptures*, New Jersey State Museum, Trenton (toured New Jersey)
Recent Sculpture, Knoedler Gallery, New York
Museum of Modern Art, New York
Painting and Sculpture, University of Maryland Art Gallery, College Park
1976 Fourcade/Droll Gallery, New York
1977 Susanne Hilberry Gallery, Birmingham, Michigan
1978 *Models and Drawings*, Montclair College, New Jersey
1979 *10 Elements and Throwback*, Pace Gallery, New York
1980 Richard Gray Gallery, Chicago
1981 Richard Gray Gallery, Chicago
1983 Pace Gallery, New York
1985 Paula Cooper Gallery, New York
Margo Leavin Gallery, Los Angeles
Xavier Fourcade Inc., New York

Selected Group Exhibitions:

1968 *Biennale*, Venice
Plus by Minus: Today's Half Century, Albright-Knox Art Gallery, Buffalo, New York
Minimal Art, Gemeentemuseum, The Hague
1969 *New York Painting and Sculpture 1940–1970*, Metropolitan Museum of Art, New York
1970 *Expo '70*, Osaka, Japan
1971 *L'Art Vivant Américain*, Fondation Maeght, St. Paul-de-Vence, France
Biennale of Outdoor Sculpture, Antwerp
1976 *200 Years of American Sculpture*, Whitney Museum, New York
1977 *New York: The State of the Art*, New York State Museum, New York
1980 *10 American Artists*, Wildenstein Gallery, London

Collections:

Museum of Modern Art, New York; Albright-Knox Art Gallery, Buffalo, New York; Memorial Art Gallery, University of Rochester, New York; Wadsworth Antheneum, Hartford, Connecticut; Princeton University, New Jersey; Corcoran Gallery of Art, Washington, D.C.; Detroit Institute of Art; Walker Art Center, Minneapolis; Institute of the Arts, Rice University, Houston; National Gallery of Canada, Ottawa.

Publications:

By SMITH: articles—"Talking with Tony Smith," interview, with Samuel Wagstaff, Jr., in *Artforum* (New York), December 1966; statement, in "Homage to the Square" in *Art in America* (New York), July 1967; "The Maze" in *Aspen* (New York), nos. 5–7, 1967; "Die" in *Art Now: New York*, November 1969; statement, in *Design Quarterly* (Minneapolis), nos. 78, 79, 1970; statement, in *Tony Smith: Two Exhibitions of Sculpture*, exhibition catalogue, Hartford, Connecticut 1966.

On SMITH: books—*Tony Smith: Two Exhibitions of Sculpture*, exhibition catalogue, by Samuel Wagstaff, Jr., Hartford, Connecticut 1966; *Tony Smith*, exhibition catalogue, by Renée Sabatello, New York 1968; *9 Sculptures by Tony Smith*, exhibition catalogue, with text by Eugene Goossen, Newark, New Jersey 1971; *Tony Smith: Recent Sculpture*, exhibition catalogue, by Martin Friedman and Lucy R. Lippard, New York 1971; *Tony Smith* by Lucy R. Lippard, London and Stuttgart, 1972; *Tony Smith: Painting and Sculpture*, exhibition catalogue, with a foreword by Eleanor Green, Baltimore 1974; *Tony Smith: 10 Elements and Throwback*, exhibition catalogue, with text by Sam Hunter, New York 1979; *Tony Smith: Paintings and Sculpture*, exhibition catalogue with text by Robert Hobbs, New York 1982.

Probably the most important sculptor to emerge from the minimal movement that surfaced in the 60's, Tony Smith seemed at the time to come from nowhere. Certainly his name was not known to any but a few fellow artists, and any "outsider" who had heard of him associated him with his work as an architect. Then he became famous, even being featured on the cover of *Time* magazine.

The reason for this, I think, is obvious. His sculpture was just too powerful not to demand immediate attention. Timing was also an important factor: when the world (or New York anyway) was ready for minimalism, Smith was ready for the world. His background as an architect gave him a mastery of the scale and placement so that his huge black forms—three-dimensional geometries—seemed powerful and elegant at the same time. This, even though his material was purposely "ugly." His sculptures were relatively inexpensive metaphors for steel and bronze made of ordinary plywood daubed with thick, irregular, greasy-looking black. Their surfaces suggested density, solidity, strength, and weight—at their scale, tons.

And yet there was also a freedom implied. Certain works got off the ground and even allowed us to walk under as well as between, within, and around them. Smith's stunning debut included a whole park full of black blocks, columns and pyramids especially thrilling covered partly by a fresh fall of snow. As a matter of fact the sculptures' curiously oriental quality was greatly underlined by the marvelous contrast of black, hard-edged, man-made forms with white, soft, rounded drifts and mounds—minimal coupled with minimal, so to speak. Ying and yang.

Later, in a series of small-scale, closely related pieces, Smith proved he could produce poetry in a non-natural way as truly as that produced by the arrangement of rocks in dry gardens by the Japanese. A further example of the paradoxes inherent in so reductive and abstract an art.

—Ralph Pomeroy

SMITHSON, Robert (Irving).

American. Born in Rutherford, New Jersey, 2 January 1938. Educated in New Jersey primary schools; attended evening classes while in high school, the Art Students League, New York, 1953; studied at Brooklyn Museum, New York, 1956. Served in the Army Reserve Forces, Special Services, Fort Knox, Kentucky, 1956. Married the artist Nancy Holt, *q.v.*, in 1963. Earth sculptor: settled in New York, 1956; visited Rome, 1961; experimented with drugs in 1961 and 1962, and withdrew temporarily from art; started to write, 1964; visited quarries frequently in the United States and Canada from 1965; Artist-Consultant, Tippetts-Abbett-McCarthy and Stratton, architects and engineers, 1966–1967; visited the Yucatan, Mexico, 1969; travelled in England and Wales, visiting Stonehenge and other ruins, 1969; spent years searching for island sites to buy: purchased island in Maine and site in Utah, 1971–72; proposed various schemes to interested mining companies: plans never fulfilled. Lecturer in Painting, Police Athletic League, New York, 1959; Visiting Lecturer, University of New Mexico, Albuquerque, 1973. Recipient: Art Institute of Chicago Award, 1972. *Died* (in airplane crash, in Amarillo, Texas) *20 July 1973.*

Individual Exhibitions:

1958 Artists Gallery, New York
1960 Richard Castelline Gallery, New York
1961 Galleria George Lester, Rome
1966 Dwan Gallery, New York (with Sol Lewitt and Leo Valledor)
1968 Galerie Konrad Fischer, Dusseldorf
Dwan Gallery, New York
1969 Galleria L'Attico, Rome
Dwan Gallery, New York
1970 Dwan Gallery, New York
Ace Gallery, Los Angeles (travelled to the Ace Gallery, Vancouver)
1974 *Drawings*, New York Cultural Center (toured the United States)
1976 John Weber Gallery, New York
1980 Galerie Ricke, Cologne
Sculpture, Herbert F. Johnson Museum of Art, Cornell University, Ithaca, New York (toured the United States, 1980–82)

Robert Smithson: ***Mirror/Salt Pieces*****, 1969**

Selected Group Exhibitions:

1965	*Current Art,* Institute of Contemporary Art, Philadelphia
1966	*Primary Structures,* Jewish Museum, New York
1967	*Color, Image and Form,* Detroit Institute of Arts
1968	*Minimal Art,* Gemeentemuseum, The Hague
1969	*When Attitude Becomes Form,* Kunsthalle, Berne (travelled to Museum Haus Lange, Krefeld, West Germany, and the Institute of Contemporary Arts, London)
1970	*Information,* Museum of Modern Art, New York
1971	*Elements of Art,* Museum of Fine Art, Boston
1972	*Documenta,* Kassel, West Germany
1973	*Contemporary Drawing,* Whitney Museum, New York

Collections:

Whitney Museum, New York; Museum of Modern Art, New York; Milwaukee Art Institute; Neue Galerie, Aachen, West Germany.

Publications:

By SMITHSON: book—*The Writings of Robert Smithson,* edited by Nancy Holt, New York 1979; articles—"Donald Judd" in *7 Sculptors,* exhibition catalogue, Philadelphia 1965; "The Crystal Land" in *Harper's Bazaar* (New York), May 1966; "Entropy and the New Monuments" in *Artforum* (New York), June 1966; "The Domain of the Great Bear," with Mel Bochner, in *Art Voices* (New York), Fall 1966; "Quasi-Infinities and the Waning of Space" in *Arts Magazine* (New York), November 1966; "Toward the Development of an Air Terminal" in *Artforum* (New York), June 1967; "Ultra-Moderne" in *Arts Magazine* (New York), September/October 1967; "Some Voice Thoughts on Museums" in *Arts Magazine* (New York), November 1967; "The Monuments of Passaic" in *Artforum* (New York), December 1967; "Dialogue with Allan Kaprow: What is a Museum?" in *Arts Yearbook*, New York 1967; "Strata: A Geophotographic Fiction" in *Aspen* (Colorado), no. 8, 1967; "A Museum of Language in the Vicinity of Art" in *Art International* (Lugano, Switzerland), March 1968; "The Establishment" in *Metro* (Venice), June 1968; "Minus Twelve" in *Minimal Art,* edited by Gregory Battcock, New York 1968; "A Sedimentation of the Mind: Earth Projects" in *Artforum* (New York), September 1968; "Aerial Art" in *Studio International* (London), February/April 1969; "Incidents of Mirror Travel in the Yucatan" in *Artforum* (New York), September 1969; "Tempo Concreto: Robert Smithson Has Been Interviewed in Rome" by Achille Bonito Oliva in *Domus* (Milan), December 1969; "Discussions with Heizer, Oppenheimer, Smithson" in *Avalanche* (New York), Fall 1970; "Symposium" in *Earth Art,* exhibition catalogue, Ithaca, New York 1970; "A Cinematic Atopia" in *Artforum* (New York), September 1971; "The Spiral Jetty" in *Arts of the Environment,* edited by G. Kepes, New York 1972; "Frederick Law Olmsted and the Dialectical Landscape" in *Artforum* (New York), February 1973; "Robert Smithson on Duchamp: An Interview" by M. Roth in *Artforum* (New York), October 1973; films—*The Spiral Jetty,* with Bob Fiore and Barbara Jarvis, 1970; *Swamp,* with Nancy Holt, 1971; videotape—*East Coast/West Coast,* with Nancy Holt, New York 1969.

On SMITHSON: books—*Arte Povera* by Germano Celant, Milan 1969; *The New Avant-Garde* by Gregoire Muller, Venice and London 1972; *Robert Smithson: Drawings,* exhibition catalogue, by Susan Ginsburg, New York 1974 (includes bibliography); *Robert Smithson: Sculpture,* exhibition catalogue, by Robert Hobbs, Ithaca, New York 1982; articles—"American Sculpture: The New Scene" by Gene Baro in *Studio International* (London), January 1968; "The Spiral Jetty is a Verb!" by D. Wheeler in *Artscanada* (Toronto), April/May 1971; "Robert Smithson's Development" by Lawrence Alloway in *Artforum* (New York), November 1972; "Amarillo Ramp" by Nancy Holt and Liza Bear in *Avalanche* (New York), Fall 1973; "For Robert Smithson" by Philip Leiden in *Art in America* (New York), November/December 1973; "Robert Smithson: Amarillo Ramp" by John Coplans in *Artforum* (New York), April 1974.

Simultaneous with DeMaria and Heizer, Robert Smithson formulated the art movement utilizing earth as sculptural material. "Spiral Jetty," the spiral ridge protrusion of earth and rocks dumped and sculptured in the Great Salt Lake, on last counts partially submerged, has been Smithson's most observed work. Another semi-submerged work, "Partially Buried Woodshed," at Kent State, Ohio, consists of a shed with earth and dirt encroaching upon the sagging structure. Smithson described the work as an experiment in "buried architecture."

Smithson's earthworks have always referred to the history of earth rituals. Particularly after his death, the works began to have a sense of the future as they wore away. To arrive at "Amarillo Ramp" is an indi-

viduated, long drive from main roads, and, without a knowledgeable guide, is a barely detectable structure, especially with the overgrowth of weeds and flowers and the weathering of the earth. Sculpture has recently gained such a quality of "found-ness," a sense that *physical detection,* through a process of discovery or categorization, is as important as sculptural *form.* Such sculptures are the Duchampian "found objects" of the 1970's and 1980's. Clearly Smithson's earthworks are not part of the later European art historical tradition, which tended to base sculpture on imagery from painting, rather than basing sculpture on physical relations and physical objects. Sculpture has now regained a physicality, which is always apparent in Smithson's work.

Smithson's "Amarillo Ramp," in Tecovas Lake, is located outside of the city of Amarillo. Amarillo houses the final assembly plant for American nuclear warheads. These two facts parallel each other in their respective fields of art and science. In science, the progress of metallurgy and the development of craft have led to the development of nuclear warheads. Concurrently, the development of art reaches an apex in Smithson's curved mound of earth and rocks. These two products are close in geographical proximity, yet exhibit hundreds of years of disagreement between the disciplines of science and art, and therefore possess the real secret between craft and artifice. Historically, science and art have exhibited characteristics now incorporated into the opposing discipline. Science historically included observations by way of outdoor mounds of earth, while art was a progress of formation of minerals, casting and bronzing. Herein lies the evident advancement of both fields.

—John Robinson

SNELSON, Kenneth.

American. Born in Pendleton, Oregon, 29 June 1927. Studied at the University of Oregon, Eugene, 1946–47; Black Mountain College, North Carolina, under Josef Albers, Buckminster Fuller, and Willem de Kooning, 1947–48; and Académie Montmartre, Paris, under Fernand Léger, 1949. Served in the United States Navy, 1945. Married Katherine Kaufmann in 1972; daughters: Andrea and Nicole. Independent sculptor, since 1960: lives and works in New York. Has taught at Cooper Union, New York; Pratt Institute, Brooklyn, New York; School of Visual Arts, New York; Southern Illinois University, Carbondale; and Yale University, New Haven, Connecticut. Member, Advisory Board, Public Arts Council, New York, since 1974. Recipient: Sculpture Award, New York State Council on the Arts, 1971; Reynolds Metals Sculpture Award, 1974; National Endowment for the Arts Grant, 1974; Prize, Iowa City Sculpture Competition, 1974; DAAD Fellowship, Berlin, 1975; National Endowment for the Arts Grant, 1975; American Institute of Architects Medal, 1981; American Institute of Arts and Letters Award, 1987. DHL: Rensselaer Polytechnic Institute, 1985. Agent: Zabriskie Gallery, 724 Fifth Avenue, New York, New York 10019; and 376 rue Quincampoix, 75004 Paris, France. Address: 140 Sullivan Street, New York, New York 10012, U.S.A.

Individual Exhibitions:

1962 Pratt Institute, Brooklyn, New York
1966 Dwan Gallery, New York
1967 Dwan Gallery, New York
1968 Dwan Gallery, New York
Bryant Park, New York
1969 Fort Worth Museum of Art, Texas
Rijksmuseum Kröller-Müller, Otterlo, Netherlands
1970 Kunsthalle, Dusseldorf
1971 Kunstverein, Hannover
1972 John Weber Gallery, New York
Galerie van der Voort, Ibiza, Spain
1974 Waterside Plaza, New York
1975 Galerie Buchholz, Munich
1977 Nationalgalerie, Berlin
Wilhelm-Lembruck-Museum, Duisburg, West Germany
Galerie de Gestlo, Hamburg
1978 *Portrait of an Atom,* Maryland Academy of Science, Baltimore
Sonnabend Gallery, New York
1981 Hirshhorn Museum, Washington, D.C.
Albright-Knox Art Gallery, Buffalo, New York
Zabriskie Gallery, New York
1982 University of Houston, Texas
University of Pittsburgh, Pennsylvania
Museum of Science and Industry, Tampa, Florida
North Carolina Museum of Life and Science, Durham
1983 Impression 5 Museum, Lansing, Michigan
Schenectady Museum, New York
1984 Zabriskie Gallery, New York
Columbus Museum of Art, Ohio
Galerie Zabriskie, Paris
De Cordova Museum, Lincoln, Massachusetts
1986 Zabriskie Gallery, New York
Galerie Zabriskie, Paris

Selected Group Exhibitions:

1964 *20th Century Engineering,* Museum of Modern Art, New York
1966 *Whitney Sculpture Annual,* Whitney Museum, New York
1967 *Sculpture of the 60's,* Los Angeles County Museum of Art

Kenneth Snelson: *Mozart,* 1982

1968 *The Pure and Clear: American Innovation*, Philadelphia Museum of Art
1969 *Contemporary American Sculpture*, Whitney Museum, New York
1970 *Salon International des Galeries Pilotes*, Lausanne, Switzerland
L'Art Vivant Americain, Fondation Maeght, St. Paul-de-Vence, France
1973 *Art in Space: Some Turning Points*, Detroit Institute of Arts
1977 *Panoramic Photography*, New York University
1983 *Big Pictures*, Museum of Modern Art, New York

Collections:

Museum of Modern Art, New York; Whitney Museum, New York; Hirshhorn Museum, Washington, D.C.; Hunter Museum of Art, Chattanooga, Tennessee; Art Institute of Chicago; Milwaukee Art Center; Rijksmuseum Kröller-Müller, Otterlo, Netherlands; Stedelijk Museum, Amsterdam.

Publications:

By SNELSON: articles—"A Design for the Atom" in *Industrial Design* (New York), February 1963; "Proprietary Protection" in *Progressive Architect* (New York), June 1964; "How Primary is Structure" in *Art Voices* (New York), Summer 1966; "An Interview with Kenneth Snelson," with John Coplans, in *Artforum* (New York), vol. V, no. 7, 1967.

On SNELSON: books—*Struktur und Spannung*, exhibition catalogue by Laszlo Glozer, Hannover 1971; *Kenneth Snelson*, exhibition catalogue with essay by Howard Fox, Washington, D.C. 1981; articles—"Kenneth Snelson: Dialogue Between Stress and Tension" by Gregory Battcock in *Arts Magazine* (New York), February 1968; "Kenneth Snelson: The Elegant Solution" by Stephen Kurtz in *Artnews* (New York), October 1968; "Snelson and Structure" by Deborah Perlberg in *Artforum* (New York), May 1975; "Kenneth Snelson: Straddling the Abyss Between Art and Science" by Richard Whelan in *Art News* (New York), February 1981; "Full Circle" by Charles Hagen in *Camera Arts* (New York), January/February 1982.

Michael Snow: *A Casing Shelved*, 1970

SNOW, Michael (James Aleck).
Canadian. Born in Toronto, Ontario, 10 December 1929. Educated at Upper Canada College, Toronto, 1946–51; studied at Ontario College of Art, Toronto, 1951–55. Married the artist and filmmaker Joyce Wieland, *q.v.* in 1959. Independent artist, musician, filmmaker and photographer, Toronto, since 1955. Professor of Advanced Film, Yale University, New Haven, Connecticut, 1970; Visiting Artist, Nova Scotia College of Art and Design, Halifax, 1970, 1974, and Ontario College of Art, Toronto, 1973, 1974, 1976. Also, a musician: member of the CCMC, Toronto, since 1974. Recipient: Purchase Award, *Winnipeg Exhibition*, 1958; Canada Council Arts Grant, 1959, and Senior Arts Grant, 1966, 1973, 1980; Henry Street Settlement Exhibition Award, New York, 1964; Guggenheim Fellowship, 1972; Independent Experimental Film Award, Los Angeles Film Critics Association, 1983. LL.D.: Brock University, St. Catherines, Ontario, 1975. Order of Canada, 1981. Agent: The Isaacs Gallery, Toronto. Address: c/o The Isaacs Gallery, 179 John Street, Toronto, Ontario M5T 1X3, Canada.

Individual Exhibitions:

1956 Hart House, University of Toronto
1957 Isaacs Gallery, Toronto (and 1958)
1959 Art Gallery of Ontario, Toronto
1960 Isaacs Gallery, Toronto (and 1962)
1963 Gallery XII, Montreal Museum of Fine Arts
Hart House, University of Toronto
1964 Isaacs Gallery, Toronto
Poindexter Gallery, New York
1965 Poindexter Gallery, New York
1966 20/20 Gallery, London, Ontario
Isaacs Gallery, Toronto
1967 *Retrospective '63–'66*, Vancouver Art Gallery
1968 Poindexter Gallery, New York
1969 Isaacs Gallery, Toronto
1970 *Michael Snow: A Survey*, Art Gallery of Ontario, Toronto
Canadian Pavilion, *Biennale*, Venice
Bykert Gallery, New York
1972 Center for Inter-American Relations, New York
Bykert Gallery, New York
1973 *Camera Works by Michael Snow*, University of Manitoba, Winnipeg
1974 *Projected Images*, Walker Art Center, Minneapolis
Isaacs Gallery, Toronto
1976 Museum of Modern Art, New York
1977 *7 Films et Plus Tard*, Centre Georges Pompidou, Paris (toured France, 1977–79)
1978 *Michael Snow*, Centre Georges Pompidou, Paris (travelled to the Kunstmuseum, Lucerne; Rheinisches Landesmuseum, Bonn; Städtische Galerie im Lenbachhaus, Munich; Musée des Beaux-Arts, Montreal; and the Vancouver Art Gallery, 1978–80)
1979 Isaacs Gallery, Toronto
Museum Boymans-van Beuningen, Rotterdam (with Richard Hefti)
1982 Isaacs Gallery, Toronto
1983 Canada House, London
University of California, Los Angeles
Agnes Etherington Art Centre, Kingston, Ontario (travelled to Ithaca, New York; Halifax, Nova Scotia; London, Ontario; Victoria, British Columbia; Toronto)
1984 Isaacs Gallery, Toronto
Vu Centre de la Photographie, Quebec City
1986 Isaacs Gallery, Toronto

Individual Film Screenings: Filmmakers Cinematique, New York, 1967, 1968, 1969; Gallery of Modern Art, New York, 1969; Whitney Museum, New York, 1969; Museum of Modern Art, New York, 1969, 1970; Edinburgh Film Festival, 1969, 1975; The Jewish Film Museum, New York, 1970; Pesaro Film Festival, Italy, 1973; *Rameau's Nephew*, world premiere, National Gallery, Ottawa, 1974; Cinematique Quebecoise, Montreal, retrospective, 1975; Museum of Modern Art, New York, retrospective, 1976; Anthology of Film Archives, New York 1975, 1976; Art Gallery of Ontario, Toronto, 1981; Osterreichisches Filmmuseum, Vienna, 1981; Canada House, London, 1983; University of California, Los Angeles, 1983.

Selected Group Exhibitions:

1957 *Biennial of Canadian Painting*, National Gallery of Canada, Ottawa (and 1959, 1965)

1962 *Canadian Painting Today,* J. B. Speed Museum, Louisville, Kentucky
1966 *The Satirical in Art,* York University, Toronto
1969 *Anti-Illusion: Procedures and Materials,* Whitney Museum, New York
1971 *Prospect 71,* Kunsthalle, Dusseldorf
1973 *Options and Alternatives,* Yale University, New Haven, Connecticut
1977 *Documenta 6,* Museum Fridericianum, Kassel, West Germany
1979 *Re-Visions,* Whitney Museum, New York
1985 *Aurora Borealis,* Centre d'Art Contemporain, Montreal

Collections:

National Gallery of Canada, Ottawa; Canada Council Art Bank, Ottawa; Art Gallery of Ontario, Toronto; Montreal Museum of Fine Arts; Winnipeg Art Gallery; Museum of Modern Art, New York; Philadelphia Museum of Art; Milwaukee Art Center, Wisconsin.

Publications:

By SNOW: books—*Place of Meeting,* with text by Ray Souster, Toronto 1962; *Michael Snow: A Survey,* with text by P. Adam Sitney, Toronto 1970; *Cover to Cover,* Halifax, Nova Scotia 1975; *High School,* Toronto 1980; article—"Passage" in *Artforum* (New York), September 1971; films—*A to Z,* 1956; *New York Eye and Ear Control (A Walking Woman Work),* 1964; *Short Shave,* 1965; *Wavelength,* 1967; *Standard Time,* 1967; *Back and Forth,* 1969; *One Second in Montreal,* 1969; *Dripping Water,* 1969; *Side Seat Paintings Slides Sound Films,* 1970; *La Region Centrale,* 1970–71; *Table Top Dolly,* 1972; *Rameau's Nephew by Diderot (Thanks to Dennis Young) by Wilma Schoen,* 1974; *Presents,* 1980; sound recordings—*The Artists Jazz Band,* 1974; *CCMC,* 5 vols., 1974–80; *Michael Snow: Music for Whistling, Piano, Microphone, and Tape Recorder,* 1975; *The Artists Jazz Band: Live at the Edge,* 1977.

On SNOW: books—*Expanded Cinema* by Gene Youngblood, New York, 1970; *Negative Space* by Manny Farber, New York 1971; *Experimental Cinema* by David Curtis London 1971; *Visionary Film* by P. Adams Sitney, New York 1974; *Une Histoire du Cinema* by Peter Kubelka and others, Paris 1976; *Documenta 6/Band 2,* exhibition catalogue, by Klaus Honnef and Evelyn Weiss, Cologne 1977; *Michael Snow,* exhibition catalogue, Lucerne 1979; *Snow Seen* by Regina Cornwell, Toronto 1980; *Michael Snow: Selected Photographic Works,* exhibition catalogue with essays by Pierre Theberge and Christopher Dewdney, Los Angeles 1983; *Walking Woman Works: Michael Snow 1961–67,* exhibition catalogue with text by Louise Dompierre, Kingston 1983.

A supremely cerebral artist, Michael Snow has produced an oeuvre marked by an almost philosophical examination of perception. Over the course of some thirty years—as painter, sculptor, filmmaker, musician, holographer and bookmaker—Snow has continually experimented in order to perceive the world without regard to convention and tradition. His artistic enterprise differs profoundly from other protean efforts in modern art; within his Renaissance scope of activities Snow, like Leonardo himself, is a skeptic—one who believes that increased knowledge only illuminates a vaster abyss. From his well-known, ubiquitous *Walking Woman* series (1961–67), in which a singular, virtually identical silhouette of a walking woman adorned some 200 works in assorted media, Snow has developed an art that, in its stylistic and technological diversity, questions the function of culture today.

Snow's film *Wavelength* (1967)—an obssessive 45-minute zoom across a loft space to a photograph of the sea—defined the artist's commitment to a "new cinema of structure." Eschewing the human subject and its intrinsic gaze, the artist was freer to examine the pure optical conditions of seeing—all the subliminal physiological experience hitherto subsumed by narrative.

Within this objective perceptual field, Snow began isolating certain characteristics specific to film (e.g., the contrast of stillness and movement), an activity that paralleled the kind of purity of medium espoused by Greenbergian late-moderism. For Snow, however, such formalism was neither exclusive nor to be experienced autonomously, unrelated to reality and to a developing critical, theoretical discourse. Works like *Wavelength* or *La Région Centrale* (1971)—a three-hour film consisting entirely of images shot in the bush in Quebec in which the main character is the camera itself—are as much about film as they are about narrative or representation. The artist's equation of *perception* with film allows a different type of psychology or subconscious to emerge. Of central importance, therefore, is the artist's device of framing, of asserting a disturbingly intractable perspective. In his video installation *De La* (1969–71), for example, a rotating mechanical sculpture—actually an elaborately engineered camera designed by the artist—projected images on four circumscribing video screens. The spectator's perceptual field was constantly challenged and exceeded by the swirling projection of images around him.

Snow's use of cinematic repetition, which parallels his 1960s collaborations with New Music composers Philip Glass and Steve Reich, elicits a hyperacute sensitivity from the viewer. Snow, in fact, has carried his photographic and film techniques to his own musical compositions. In the tradition of Duchamp and Cage, the artist's inclusion of chance and the "raw process" of art-making became part of the finished composition. His liner notes to his solo album *Music For Piano, Whistling, Microphone and Tape Recorder* (1975), for example, indicates that he placed a microphone on top of his piano and turned up the recording volume in order to make "a part of the recording process a part of the music" by allowing ambient sounds (such as a ringing telephone) to register on the master tape.

Sythesizing his earlier multiplicity of techniques, Snow has recently worked in holography. His installation at Vancouver's Expo 86—*The Spectral Image*—was seen in a vast cathedral-like hall illuminated by colored filters, a work that continues his implementation of the most advanced technology into his art. Snow's work in the recent exhibition *Visionary Apparatus* at the Massachusetts Institute of Technology's Hayden Gallery, like *The Spectral Image,* resounds with the added dimension of laser-pulse holographic illusionism, a sophisticated technology that once again attests to the artist's conviction in the mutually redemptive relationship between art and science.

—Mason Klein

SONDERBORG, K. R. H.

Danish. Born Karl Richard Horst Hofmann in Sonderborg, 5 April 1923; later adopted his name "Sonderborg." Studied painting, under Ewald Becker-Carus, in Hamburg, 1946, and at the Landeskunstschule, Hamburg, 1947–49; studied printmaking, under S. W. Hayter, at Atelier 17, Paris, 1953. Imprisoned by the Gestapo, Hamburg-Fuhlsbuttel, 1941–42; escaped, working as a salesman for an export company, Hamburg, 1942–45; full-time artist since 1949, in Hamburg, subsequently in New York and Copenhagen: Member, "Zen 49" artists group, 1953. Recipient: Lichtwark Preis, Hamburg, 1955; Karl-Ernst-Osthaus Preis, Hagen, West Germany, 1955. Agent: Galerie Karl Flinker, 25 rue de Tournon, 75006 Paris, France. Address: Kongens Nytorv 1, 1050 Copenhagen, Denmark.

Individual Exhibitions:

1956 Kestner-Gesellschaft, Hannover
Galleri Samlaren, Stockholm
1957 Kunstverein, Cologne
Galerie Springer, West Berlin
Galerie René Drouin, Paris
Galerie Van de Loo, Munich
1959 *Neue Bilder,* Galerie Van de Loo, Essen
1960 *Peintures, Dessins,* Galerie Karl Flinker, Paris
1961 Lefebre Gallery, New York
1962 Galerie Handschin, Basle
Galerie Schmela, Dusseldorf
Kunstverein, Freiburg
Galerie Müller, Stuttgart
Galerie Karl Flinker, Paris
1963 Galleri Blanche, Stockholm
1964 Tokyo Gallery
1965 Galerie Karl Flinker, Paris
Lefebre Gallery, New York
Gemalde, Zeichnungen, Kunstverein, Cologne
Stedelijk Museum, Amsterdam
Schilderijen, Tekeningen, Stedelijk Van Abbemuseum, Eindhoven, Netherlands
Tuschen, Gimpel und Hanover Galerie, Zurich
First British Exhibition, Stone Gallery, Newcastle upon Tyne
1966 Louisiana Museum, Humlebaek, Denmark
Galleria Stendhal, Milan
Hammerlunds Kunsthandel, Oslo
1967 Guggenheim Museum, New York
Carnegie Institute, Pittsburgh
1968 Galerie de France, Paris
Galerie Daniel Gervis, Paris
Manus-Presse, Stuttgart
1971 Galerie Daniel Gervis, Paris
1976 Galerie Daniel Gervis, Paris
1978 Kunstverein, Sonderborg, Denmark
1979 Galerie im Haus Behr, Stuttgart
Galerie am Markt, Schwabisch Hall, West Germany
1983 Galerie Hubert Winter, Vienna
1985 Kunstverein, Augsburg, West Germany
Galerie Nothhelfer, West Berlin
XPO Galerie, Hamburg
Staatsgalerie, Stuttgart
1986 Graphische Sammlung, Stuttgart

Selected Group Exhibitions:

1952 *Zen 49,* Galerie Bohler, Munich
1954 *Art After 1945,* Stedelijk Museum, Amsterdam
1958 *Biennale,* Venice
1959 *Documenta,* Kassel, West Germany
1960 *Guggenheim International,* Guggenheim Museum, New York
1963 *Bienal,* Sao Paulo
1965 *Painting Without a Brush,* Institute of Contemporary Art, Boston
1973 *Kunst In Deutschland 1898–1973,* Kunsthalle, Hamburg (travelled) to the Stadtische Galerie im Lenbachhaus, Munich)
1981 *Westkunst,* Messehallen, Cologne
1983 *Informel 1953–83,* Kunstverein, Lingen, West Germany

Collections:

Kunsthalle, Hamburg; Nationalgalerie, West Berlin; Wallraf-Richartz Museum, Cologne; Stedelijk Van Abbemuseum, Eindhoven, Netherlands; Louisiana Museum, Humlebaek, Denmark; Guggenheim Museum, New York.

Publications:

On SONDERBORG: books—*Sonderborg: Neue Bilder,* exhibition catalogue, with text by Carl Laszlo, Essen 1959; *Sonderborg: Peintures, Dessins,* exhibition catalogue, with text by Will Grohman, Paris 1960; *Sonderborg,* exhibition catalogue, with text by Annette Michelson, Paris 1962; *K. R. H. Sonderborg: VII Bienal de Sao Paulo 1963,* exhibition catalogue, with text by Werner Schmalenbach, Dusseldorf 1963; *Sonderborg,* exhibition catalogue, with text by Otto Hahn, New York 1965; *K. R. H. Sonderborg: Gemalde, Zeichnungen,* exhibition catalogue, with text by Werner Haftmann, Cologne 1965; *Sonderborg: Schilderijen, Tekeningen,* exhibition catalogue, with text by Werner Haftmann, Eindhoven, Netherlands 1965; *K. R. H. Sonderborg: First British Exhibition,* exhibition catalogue, with text by Friedrich Bayl, Otto Hahn and Thomas T. Ichinose, Newcastle upon Tyne 1965; *K. R. H. Sonderborg: Tuschen,* exhibition catalogue, Zurich

1965; *K. R. H. Sonderborg*, exhibition catalogue, with text by Willem Sandberg, Paris 1968; *Kunst in Deutschland 1898–1973*, exhibition catalogue, with text by Werner Hofmann, Hamburg 1973; *K. R. H. Sonderborg: Arbeiten auf Papier*, exhibition catalogue, with text by Hans Platschek, Kurt Leonhard and others, Stuttgart 1985.

The earliest painting by K. R. H. Sonderborg—on a canvas given to him by his father when he was 15 years old—was destroyed in an air raid over Hamburg. It probably has little bearing upon the subsequent development of this Danish-born artist but it does imply that Sonderborg's talent even from the start had a habit of cropping up in a variety of unlikely addresses. In a relatively short time he was able to install himself and his art in Cornwall, the Hebrides, Orkneys, Shetlands, Scotland, Paris and the United States. Perhaps something of this hither and thither existence is reflected in his pictures. They certainly have a staccato beat, a rhythm not unlike the clatter of a typewriter under the fingers of a fastmoving stenographer.

Sonderborg's nearest parallel in contemporary art is Erwin Bechthold, but even here there is no more than a superficial resemblance. Their approach is different. Only the end result shows some degree of kinship.

Three clues point to the sources of inspiration in Sonderborg's pictures—especially since his time in the United States. First there is his absorption in machinery and its operation. Then there is his hand-camera pressed into service whenever he sees a detail or element of the contemporary world that he believes to be visually worth recording (parts of machinery and angle shots of the industrial and urban scenes). And finally there are the scraps, clippings and cut-outs he can harvest from the media.

The salad he mixes out of all three is frequently the raw meat of his pictures, although all such ingredients undergo a Sonderborg change before they are finalised in pictorial form. Much of his work is basically black and white, but when colours are involved, these tend to cleave to the characteristics of a technical universe.

Not that they are always the portrait of technical imagery. It is just that the final Sonderborg transformation makes them appear so. A specific example of the stages through which this alchemic process can go is provided by four pictures based upon a newsprint photo of President Kennedy's golf kit. The first of these was painted in 1962, but execution of the entire series continued over four years. To give some idea of a Sonderborg synthesis it should be mentioned that in the second picture the JFK golf bag somehow became involved in and absorbed by the controls room of Karlsruhe's atomic energy plant.

Sonderborg is an inspired collector. He has gathered together many of the simplest mechanical statements—a metal coil, a spark, a cog—and set them up in contrast with some of the most complex contemporary mechanisms.

—Sheldon Williams

SONFIST, Alan.
American. Born in New York, 26 May 1946. Studied at the Art Students League, New York, 1963; studied painting and art education, Western Illinois University, Macomb, 1964–67, B.A. 1967; also studied at the Pratt Institute, New York, summers 1965, 1966, Ohio State University, Columbus, 1967–68, and painting and sculpture at Hunter College, New York, 1968–69, M.F.A. 1969. Independent artist, since 1970. Instructor at numerous universities and colleges, throughout the United States, since 1967. Recipient: Graham Foundation grants, 1971, 1972; Chase Manhattan Foundation for Environmental and Fine Arts Grant, 1975; National Endowment for the Arts grant, 1975, 1978, 1979, 1981; Creative Artists Public Service Grant, New York, 1977; United States Information Service Grant, to Paris, 1977; Con Edison Foundation Grant, New York, 1978; Citibank Foundation Grant, New York, 1978; Australian Arts Council Travel Grant, 1981; New Zealand Travel Grant, 1984. Address: 205 Mulberry Street, New York, New York 10012, U.S.A.

Individual Exhibitions:

1970 Reese Palley Gallery, New York
The Nature of Things, Harcus-Krakow Gallery, Boston
Star Chartings and Others, Deson-Zaks Gallery, Chicago
Outdoor Crystal Sculpture, Finch College Museum of Art, New York
Diagramma, Milan
1972 Institute of Contemporary Arts, London
Army Ants: Patterns and Structures, Automation House, New York
Sonfist Art, Akron Institute, Ohio
Lanscapes, Paley and Lowe Gallery, New York
1964 Carl Solway Gallery, Cincinnati, Ohio
Galerie Thelen, Cologne
1975 *Running Dead Animal*, Stefanotty Gallery, New York
Time-Landscape, Finch College Museum of Art, New York
Autobiography of Alan Sonfist, Herbert F. Johnson Museum of Art, Cornell University, Ithaca, New York
Autobiography of an Abandoned Animal Hole, Adiene Gallery, New York
1976 *Autobiography of Hemlock Forest*, Galerie Massimo Valsecchi, Milan
Galleria Cavallino, Venice
Adiene Gallery, New York
Autobiography of Time Landscape, 112 Greene Street Workshop, New York
Autobiography of Time Landscape, Centre Cultural Americain, Paris
1977 Carl Solway Gallery, Cincinnati, Ohio
Neue Galerie Sammlung Ludwig, Aachen, West Germany
Light Gallery, New York
Museum of Fine Arts, Boston
Galerie Bama, Paris
1978 *Public Monuments*, Neuberger Museum, Purchase, New York
Leo Castelli Gallery, New York
National Collection of Fine Arts, Smithsonian Institution, Washington, D.C.
1979 Multiples Gallery, New York
Monument to Atlanta, High Museum of Art, Atlanta
State University of New York, Stony Brook
1980 Albright-Knox Art Gallery, Buffalo, New York
1981 J. B. Speed Art Museum, Louisville, Kentucky
National Gallery of Art, Melbourne, Victoria
Marion Goodman Gallery, New York
1982 Carl Solway Gallery, Cincinnati
Lowe Art Museum, Coral Gables, Florida
1984 Corcoran Gallery of Art, Washington, D.C.
Galleria del Cavallino, Venice
1986 Diane Brown Gallery, New York
Nelson Museum, Kansas City, Missouri

Selected Group Exhibitions:

1969 *Invisible Image*, School of Visual Arts, New York
1971 *The Nature of Things*, Harcus-Krakow Gallery, Boston
1973 *Trees of Manhattan*, Finch College Museum of Art, New York
1974 *Projekt '74*, Wallraf-Richartz Museum, Cologne
1975 *Biennale*, Paris
1977 *Documenta*, Kassel, West Germany
1979 *Views of America*, Penthouse, Museum of Modern Art, New York
1981 *Natur-Skulptur*, Kunstverein, Stuttgart
1982 *Mapped Art*, Toledo Museum of Art, Ohio
1985 *The Artist as Social Designer*, Los Angeles County Museum of Art

Collections:

Museum of Modern Art, New York; Everson Museum, Syracuse, New York; Museum of Fine Arts, Boston; Akron Art Institute, Ohio; Allen Museum of Fine Arts, Oberlin College, Ohio; Museum of Contemporary Art, Chicago; High Museum, Atlanta; Museum of Fine Art, Dallas; Wallraf-Richartz Museum, Cologne; Power Institute of Fine Arts, Sydney.

Publications:

By SONFIST: videotapes—*Tiger-Chance-Kill*, 1976; *Nature's Time, Artificial Time*, 1976.

On SONFIST: books—*Science and Technology in Art Today* by Jonathan Benthall, New York 1972; *Art and the Future* by Douglas Davis, New York 1973; *Autobiography of Alan Sonfist*, exhibition catalogue, by Lawrence Alloway, Ithaca, New York 1975; *Unbuilt America*, edited by Carson and Sky, New York 1976; *The American Land* by Joshua C. Taylor, New York 1979; *Art of the Seventies* by Edward Lucie Smith, London 1980; *Overlay* by Lucy Lippard, New York 1983; *Artforms: An Introduction to the Visual Arts* by Duane and Sarah Preble, New York 1985.

My body is my museum; it's my history. It collects and absorbs observations-interactions. It is the deciphering of these recordings that I project into the outside world. My boundaries define the world of Art. I clarify my own common boundaries in relationship to the outside whether it be the room I exist in, the country I exist in, the universe I exist in. By adding other awareness, I am constantly redefining my boundaries and projecting these awarenesses into my art.

My work deals with the idea that the world is always in a state of flux. My art deals with the rhythm of the universe. The pieces are part of the rhythm. A plant grows in cycles—a man moves in cycles—my work tries to bring about awareness of these movements. My works are transitions—they provoke associations. One has to mediate with my work to gain understanding. It is not the beginning or the end that I am concerned with, but the energy that is given or received through communication with my art.

—Alan Sonfist

The links between nature and Alan Sonfist's art are varied and numerous. They include wet canvases in which mildew takes gradual possession of the linen surface and containers of micro-organisms, in which fungoid and bacterial growth generate changing displays. These are usually enclosed in sealed boxes, a form of containment extended into plexiglass columns with crystalline structures reactive to light, heat, and the spectator's presence. To quote the artist: "the growth of the work is characterized by patterns of indeterminacy, since a multiplicity of natural variables creates unforeseen occurrences." The technology involved and the neat craft should not obscure the fact that Sonfist's basic interest is in nature and not in the artifacts by which it is contained.

Another nature-based piece is the celebrated colony of army ants (1972) whose movements in search patterns for food revealed the graphic shape of a society. This notion recurs, in an extraordinary metamorphosis, in Sonfist's later work, "Abandoned Animal Hole," a cast of the warren of tunnels built by muskrats. The cement, pushed a section at a time into the burrows, converts hidden space into solid form in a way that constitutes a monument to the morphology of branching structure. It is an underground "tree." In these works Sonfist initiated processes and made them visible within a limited zone, such as a box, or a room, or a joined casting. In addition to the enactment of organic process he makes works that consist of objects removed from the unbounded field of the world. Here he subtracts from an existing endless process rather than beginning new ones, as in "Collection Bags," rows of soft containers for found objects. These consisted of things taken from the

Alan Sonfist: ***Wall of Earth*****, 1978**

ground: twigs from the forest floor, for example, not parts broken off growing trees, a restraint that is characteristic of Sonfist's approach to nature. These finds are sometimes accompanied by texts:

> I could feel the lines on my skin. The cold wind passed. The twigs formed their own lines moving back and forth from the rock.

He has also expressed a great kinship with Asher B. Durand, the Hudson River School painter. What touched Sonfist, leading him to visit the site in Troy of one of Durand's paintings, was a letter of 1881:

> All the license that the artist can claim or desire is to choose the time and place were Nature displays her chief perfections, whether of beauty or majesty, repose or action.

The interaction of artist and nature is the basis of Sonfist's interest in Durand. On sites similar to Durand's Sonfist collects small objects that are an equivalent of the plentitude of details in the landscape paintings of Durand.

In the works in which he uses material collected at the site Sonfist lovingly turns random samples into precious quotations. Nature is evoked as a limitless field, the found parts of which, the details, transported from the site by Sonfist are not restructured in ways that suggest their solidification. On the contrary, the "non-site," to use a term of Robert Smithson's, preserve a kind of serious nonchalance, as if the relics meant too much to change after the crucial acts of removal and storage. Placing the twigs, the stones, the feathers, is equivalent to preservation rather than to designing.

Sonfist's ability to reveal the forms of communities and processes and his participation in limitless nature have been recognized and well-discussed, but another aspect of his work is less familiar. To work with natural processes as media is of course to work in time, but the definition of time in his art is not restricted to this sense. There is also time as it relates the artist himself to his work, which is the central theme of the exhibition *The Autobiography of Alan Sonfist.* To understand the implication of this it helps to know that in 1970 he wanted to call his first exhibition *Retrospective,* but the gallery objected. The reason for using the word, which usually refers to an exhibition that summarizes a working life by looking backwards, is that this show represented, to quote the artist, "pieces of my past" and was thus the projection into the present of experiences that preceded the exhibition.

The extension of Sonfist's work in time is a central fact of his esthetic. To the extent that any work of art survives it is a projection of the past into what I shall call the unknown present. Sonfist is concerned with time beyond this and, in effect, dissolves the possibility of dating art at all, or at least reduces dating to an arbitrary convention. He does not use dates to indicate the time of production, but to indicate sequence. All his works can be viewed as 1946 *et seq.;* "my first experience was air." Sonfist considers that the materialization of a work of art, though obviously a crucial step if the work process is to be legible to others, has been over-emphasized. In his work he is "bringing back images of my past" and, therefore, "each piece will have its autobiography." His art is authenticated by its place in a continuum that includes all phases of the artist's life. Thus the act of dating has the effect of isolating art from the full range of genetic elements.

There is a sense in which genetic dating is applicable to all artists, on the principle of Whistler's incisive answer to the question of how long it took to do one of his paintings: "all my life." There is more to it than this, however, because the content of Sonfist's art is oriented, to a remarkable extent, toward memory and memories. Hence his anti-periodization protects his life as a continuum in which early experiences occur as survivals, reconstructions, and fantasies. Sonfist would not differentiate between these states: all are means to bind his experiences of life into unity. He writes: "My body is my museum, it's my history," and as such it is subject to the same changes in time as his work. Sonfist's offer of his body after death to the Museum of Modern Art to be preserved in the collection is a logical extension of

the fusion of the ideas of process and time. Supporting this view of the self as subject-matter is his temperamental inclination towards recollection, activated by surviving drawings, early diaries and scrap books, and what Sonfist calls "vague experiences" of growth and discovery as a child. Typically his tree pieces, which consist of flattened tracings of the trunks, were initiated by the rediscovery of a tree in the Bronx Park that he had climbed in childhood:

> The distances of my hand had changed and the surface of the tree had also. I can remember the feel—the smell—and the taste of the tree as I once had.

Art is not presumed to be complete when it is done: both the work's prior and subsequent history force us to a perpetual recontextualization. In the chronology of "Running Dead Animal," for example, Sonfist proposes such events as: "1953: upon tight-roping on a waterfall I woke up in a hospital with my face bandaged" and the period 1954–59 included monthly visits to the Museum of Natural History "to observe the stuffed animals." "1959: sat with an antelope in its cage. 1961: my brother shot a bird and I cried." Some of these events are repeated in genetic chronology of other works, some not. Thus the concept of art as the product of potent cause is diffused over the life of the artist. The only analogy to this historical layering of the work becoming the form of the work that I can think of is René Char's *Arrière-Histoire de Poème Pulverise,* in which annotations by the poet in a copy of a book become a book added to the original. Char records his hesitation about regarding the manuscript notes on equal terms with the poems, but he is wrong to feel that it was necessary to defend the primacy of the poems. What we get from the notes is a relationship, a connection between poetry and what Char calls "the awkward and untenable world that served in its making." "Each poem is accompanied by its confidential marginalia, like a whispering stream."

If we estimate Sonfist's art as beginning in 1946 we should not expect the chronologies to end with the production of the work and in fact the "autobiographies" that accompany each work must be revised, like the provenance of paintings, to bring them up to date. The work's meaning therefore is not something that emerges on its completion and exists thereafter in absolute form. On the contrary art demonstrates a principle of delayed coherence: it is a structure that can change and our knowledge of it changes also. Thus the "autobiographies" will gradually extend as they become a history of spectator-responses (interpretations) and itinerary (socially-conditioned distribution) attached to the work. In the earlier pieces the presence of the spectator initiated physical changes in Sonfist's work (crystal formation, movement of a school of fish), changes that occurred unpredictably but logically within the limits of the system prepared by the artist. The extension of the autobiography of the work incorporates the viewer in another way, drawing on our cognitive and social interaction with the artist via the work of art.

—Lawrence Alloway

Individual Exhibitions:

1966 Douglass College, New Brunswick, New Jersey
1968 Galerie Ricke, Cologne
1970 Leo Castelli Gallery, New York
Ace Gallery, Los Angeles
Stedelijk Van Abbemuseum, Eindhoven, Netherlands
1971 *Projects,* Museum of Modern Art, New York
Galerie Ricke, Cologne
1972 Leo Castelli Gallery, New York
Galerie Ricke, Cologne
1974 *Radio Mix,* Leo Castelli Gallery, New York
Seder-Creigh Gallery, Coronado, California
1975 Leo Castelli Gallery, New York
Galerie Ricke, Cologne
Ace Gallery, Los Angeles
1976 *ABACA Code,* Leo Castelli Gallery, New York
ABACA Code, Hand Cast Paper Sculpture and Other Work 1969–76, Seder/Creigh Gallery, Coronado, California
1977 Ace Gallery, Los Angeles
1978 Leo Castelli Gallery, New York (drawings)
Castelli Graphics, New York (lithographs)
Galerie Ricke, Cologne
Simultaneous Regional Editions, Rosamund Felsen Gallery, Los Angeles
Porte-Voix Audio Installation, The Clocktower, New York
1979 *BA-O-BA SEL Series,* Museum Haus Lange, Krefeld, West Germany
Expanded SEL Series, Leo Castelli Gallery, New York
AM/FM Radio Installation, Galerie Michele Lachowsky, Brussels
Porte-Voix, Eric Fabre Gallery, Paris
Porte-Vue, Centre Georges Pompidou, Paris
1980 *Pictographs,* Tony Shafrazi Gallery, New York
Galerie France Morin, Montreal
1981 *Runic Series 1980,* Galerie Ricke, Cologne
Dom Basor Series: India 1981, David Bellman Gallery, Toronto
Michele Lachowsky Gallery, Antwerp
Portland Center for the Visual Arts, Oregon
1982 *Rangoli: Aluminum Works Made in India 1981,* Rosamund Felsen Gallery, Los Angeles
Leo Castelli Gallery, New York
Galerie Eric Fabre, Paris
1983 Project Studio One, Long Island City, New York
1984 Galleria Schema, Florence (twice)
Carol Taylor Art, Dallas, Texas
Galerie Rolf Ricke, Cologne
Hara Museum of Contemporary Art, Tokyo (travelled to Nagoya and Osaka)
Leo Castelli Gallery, Greene Street, New York
Virginia Polytechnic Institute, Blacksburg
1985 Rosamund Felsen Gallery, Los Angeles
Susanna Hillberry Gallery, Birmingham, Michigan
Leo Castelli Gallery, Greene Street, New York
1986 Galerie Montenay Delsol, Paris
Tilden Foley Gallery, New Orleans
1987 Galerie Nature Morte, New York
Domaine de Kerguehennec, Rennes, France

Selected Group Exhibitions:

1970 *Information,* Museum of Modern Art, New York
1972 *Biennale,* Venice
1973 *Options and Alternatives: Some Directions in Recent Art,* Yale University Art Gallery, New Haven, Connecticut
1975 *Sculpture: American Directions 1945–1975,* National Collection of Fine Arts, Smithsonian Institution, Washington, D.C.
1978 *20th Century American Drawings: 5 Years of Acquisitions,* Whitney Museum, New York
1980 *Yesterday and After,* Museum of Fine Arts, Montreal
1982 *Americanische Zeichnungen der 70er Jahre,* Städtische Galerie, Munich
1984 *Neon, Fluorescent et Cie,* Institut Superieur d'Etude du Langue Plastique, Brussels
1986 *Temporary Contemporary,* Museum of Contemporary Art, Los Angeles
1987 *Tribute to Leo Castelli and His Artists,* Museo de Arte Contemporaneo, Mexico City

Collections:

Museum of Modern Art, New York; Whitney Museum, New York; Fogg Art Museum, Harvard University, Cambridge, Massachusetts; University of North Carolina, Greensboro; Moderna Museet, Stockholm; Ludwig Collection, Aachen, West Germany; Museum of Contemporary Art, Tehran; Australian National Gallery, Canberra.

Publications:

By SONNIER: books—*Object—Situation—Object 1969–70,* Cologne 1972; films—*Untitled,* 1969; *Untitled II,* 1969; *Negative-Positive,* 1970; *Rub Down,* 1970; *Untitled III,* 1970; *Painting Foot,* 1970; articles—"Keith Sonnier," interview with Liza Bear, in *Avalanche* (New York), May/June 1974; "An Interview with Keith Sonnier," with Calvin Harlan, in *Parachute* (Montreal), Spring 1977; "Keith Sonnier Interview," with Craig Gohlson, in *Interview* (New York), November 1977; "Interview with Keith Sonnier," with Bernard Lamarche-Vadel, in *Artiste* (Paris), October/November 1979.

On SONNIER: books—*Documenta 5,* exhibition catalogue by Harald Szeeman, Jean-Christophe Ammann and others, Kassel 1972; *Some Recent American Art,* exhibition catalogue by Jennifer Licht, New Haven 1973; *Keith Sonnier: Argon-und-Neon-Arbeiten,* exhibition catalogue, Krefeld 1979; *Keith Sonnier: Runic Serie 1980,* exhibition catalogue, Cologne 1981; *Keith Sonnier,* exhibition catalogue by Alanna Heiss, Long Island City 1983; articles—"Eccentric Abstraction" by David Antin in *Artforum* (New York), November 1966; "On Erotic Art" by Lucy Lippard in *Hudson Review* (New York), Spring 1967; "Primary Energy and the Microemotive Artists" by Piero Gilardi in *Arts Magazine* (New York), September 1968; "New York: Moving Out" by Ralph Pomeroy in *Art and Artists* (London), January 1969; "Le Neon dans l'Art Contemporain" by Beatrice Parent in *L'Art Vivant* (Paris), May 1971; review in *Flash Art* (Milan), December 1971; "Keith Sonnier: Video and Film as Color Field" by Robert Pincus-Witten in *Artforum* (New York), May 1972; "Keith Sonnier" by Jon Meyer in *Arts Magazine* (New York), September 1982; "Keith Sonnier at Nature Morte" by Stephen Ellis in *Art in America* (New York), June 1987.

SONNIER, Keith.

American. Born in Mamou, Louisiana, in 1941. Educated at the University of Southwestern Louisiana, Lafayette, 1959–63, B.A. 1963; travelled and studied in France, 1963–64; studied at Rutgers University, New Brunswick, New Jersey, 1965–66, M.F.A. 1966. Full-time artist: now lives and works in New York. Recipient: Guggenheim Fellowship, 1974; First Prize, *Tokyo Prints Biennale,* 1974. Agent: Leo Castelli Gallery, New York. Address: c/o Leo Castelli Gallery, 420 West Broadway, New York, New York 10012, U.S.A.

A study of Keith Sonnier's 1982 sculpture *Aesthesipol* resurrects the themes and concerns of his career. The word itself seems on the verge of signifying something, though it never quite resolves in specific meaning—for the artist invented it. *Aesthesipol* provides a summary of Sonnier's work: sculpture aimed at the process of language making. His primary concern, like that of many graffiti artists, is of inventing new ways to propel writing (and the meaning of writing) into vision. His favoured medium: technology. *Aesthesipol* is exemplary, a rambling glyph of extruded aluminium with a working pay phone attached to one of its three vertical members and a portable television attached to another. The sculpture assails the viewer with interacting and interchangeable waves of the aural, the visual, and the tactile. This type of pictured, rather than merely phonetic writing, is symptomatic in his work, and suggests a return to and reinvention of the moment when picturing and writing were one.

Pictured writing is grounded in touch, and establishing space and place for his sense of touch became Sonnier's first goal when he arrived in New York in 1966. His previous endeavours were limited by the isolating experiences in rural Louisiana where he lived in the unassimilated French community of the Cajuns until early adulthood. His early works stressed perfect symmetry and order. After studying in France for a year in 1963 he moved to New York where he abandoned the conventional techniques of figurative paintings of his student days in favour of a direct manipulation and exploration of a variety of materials ranging from satin to satellite.

From 1967 to 1969 Sonnier's work became a revelation—and invitation—to the pleasures of touch. Shreds of flesh-toned silk and satin, frequently com-

bined with pleated dacron screening, drape and drip off the wall and floor in soft sublimations of lingerie experience. He applies planes of latex to the wall which he either peels up and leaves hanging or peels down, attaching it to the floor with strings. The effect of the different planes comments on the nature of touch.

In 1969 Neon became Sonnier's primary medium. His first neon pieces are configured in gestural loops and curls that look like semi-conscious writing of doodles. He wraps neon around neon or incandescent light bulbs in a loose mirrored symmetry that creates the illusion of light reflecting itself. In these sculptures the light itself becomes the architecture. The gaseous flush of the neon thereafter thickens the surrounding atmosphere to the edge of tangibility.

The performance nature of much of Sonnier's work, his interest in dance, and his attraction to tactile light coupled with the new availability and portability of video hardware made television the next logical medium for him. During the '70s he introduced video tapes into his work. Like the neons, the tapes represented a distanced restraint that let the medium play with and against itself. In 1971 Sonnier isolated sound. *New Delhi Sound Piece* consisted of two speakers, one with a microphone attached to it causing feedback, another amplifying the sounds of passers by. These three new mediums incorporated the notion of feedback in Sonnier's subsequent work.

From 1977 to 1979 he intensified his pursuit of public communications. His efforts were almost solely devoted to researching and commandeering a satellite system, which resulted in his piece *Send-Receive* in 1979, a complex visual and verbal dialogue and feedback made possible by satellite technology. The piece consisted of a group of artists and performers in a San Francisco studio making a simultaneous exchange with a corresponding group in New York. San Francisco to New York, New York to San Francisco, dancer to dancer, musician to musician, speaker to speaker—layers of duets of visual and verbal cues, commands, and feedback mixed in material metaphor.

Sonnier, as much a writer as a sculptor, is in constant search of new mediums and new meanings. His pictured language, which thrives on technology, dares to expand past artistic conventions. His art speaks for itself; Sonnier's innovations of the '80s have continued to open new channels of communication.

—Carrie Baker

Keith Sonnier: *Expanded Sel III*, 1979

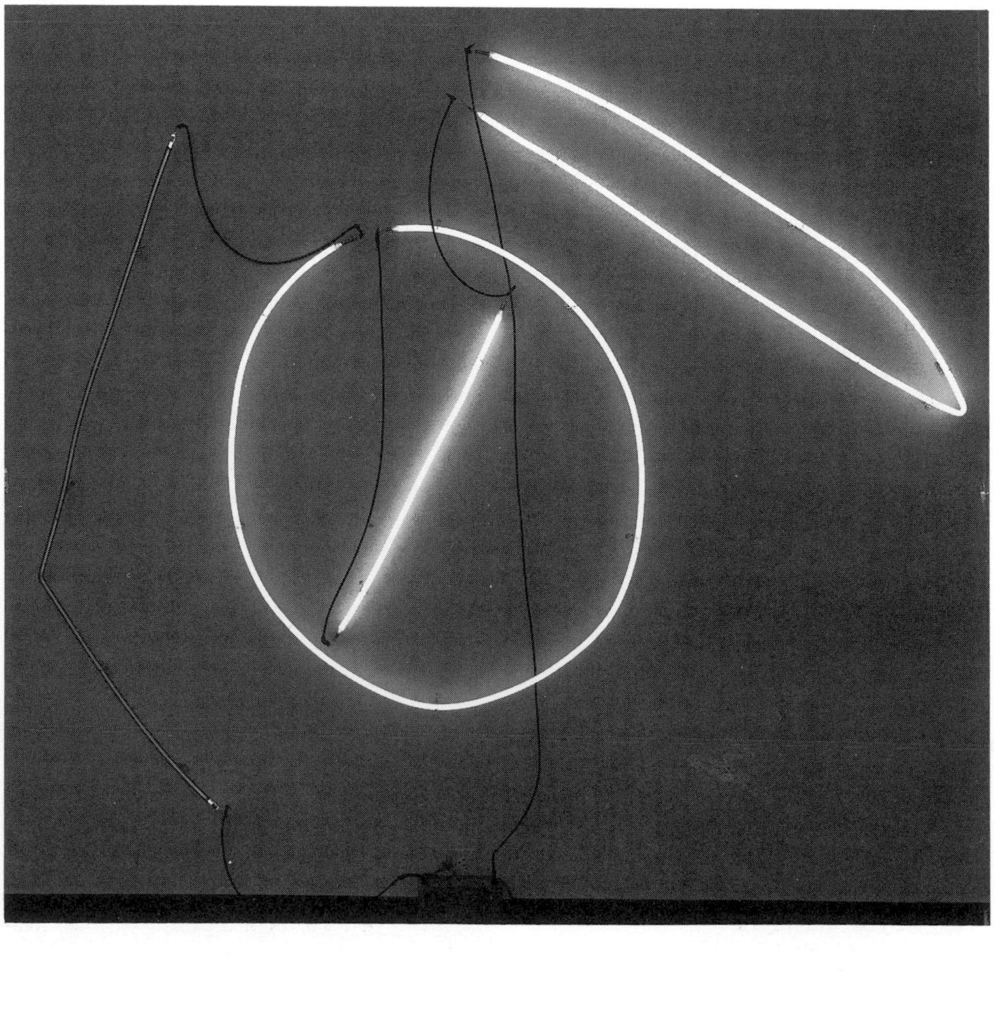

SORGE, Peter.

German. Born in Berlin, 14 April 1937. Educated in Mecklenburg, 1941–50, and in Dortmund, 1950–58; studied art-teaching at the Hochschule für Bildende Künste, West Berlin, 1958–64; studied painting, under Fred Thieler and Mac Zimmerman, in West Berlin, 1964–65. Married Maina-Miriam Munsky in 1970; son: Daniel. Independent "realist" painter, West Berlin, since 1964: Co-Founder, Ausstellungsgemeinschaft "Grossgorschen 35," West Berlin, 1964–69; Zehn Neun art association, 1969; Aspekt artists' group, 1972. Recipient: Second Burda-Preis, for graphics, Munich, 1968; Graphik-Preis der Stadt Wolfsburg, West Germany, 1969. Agent: Galerie Poll, Lutzowplatz 7, 1000 Berlin 30. Address: Clausewitzstrasse 7, 1000 Berlin 12, West Germany.

Individual Exhibitions:

1965 Grossgorschen 35, West Berlin
Galerie für Grafikfreunde, Frankfurt
Galerie Falazik, Bochum, West Germany
1966 Galerie Tobies und Silex, Cologne
Grossgorschen 35, West Berlin
1967 Galerie Ketterer, Kiel
1968 Galerie Klaus Groh, Oldenburg, West Germany
Galerie D. und R. Rothe, Wolfsburg, West Germany
Galerie Ostentor, Dortmund, West Germany
Galerie Poertner, Sennestadt, West Germany
Galerie Poll, West Berlin
1969 Galerie Schmucking, Braunschweig, West Germany
James-Bond-Oratorium, Akademie der Künste, West Berlin (with W. D. Siebert)
Galerie Klaus Groh, Oldenburg, West Germany
Diehl/Petrick/Sorge: Malerei, Graphik, Material, Haus am Waldsee, West Berlin (with Hans-Jürgen Diehl and Wolfgang Petrick; travelled to the Badischer Kunstverein, Karlsruhe)
1970 Kunstverein, Mannheim
Galerie Poll, West Germany
Galerie Kerlikowsky und Kneiding, Munich (with Hans-Jürgen Diehl and Wolfgang Petrick; toured Germany)
Galerie Ostentor, Dortmund, West Germany (with Munsky)
1971 Kunsthistorisches Institut, Groningen, Netherlands
Institut voor Industrielevoormgeving, Delft
Youth Center, Utrecht
Galerie de Tor, Amsterdam
Galerie Wentdorf und Swetec, Dusseldorf
Galerie im Espresso, Trier, West Germany
Galerie Kafseck, Paderborn, West Germany
Galerie Bauer und Pietschner, Bochum, West Germany
Kunstverein, Kassel, West Germany
1972 Kunstkreis, Gelsenkirchen, West Germany
Galerie Poll, West Berlin
Galleria Vinciana, Milan (with Hans-Jürgen Diehl and Wolfgang Petrick)
Galleria San Michele, Brescia, Italy (with Hans-Jürgen Diehl and Wolfgang Petrick)
1975 Kunsthalle, Nuremberg, West Germany
1976 Galerie Poll, West Berlin
1978 Galerie Art Moderna, Freiburg, West Germany
Goethe-Institut, Paris
1979 Galerie Zoellner, Bremen, West Germany
Galerie Poll, West Berlin
Kunstverein, Frechen, West Germany
1980 Kunstverein, Ludwigshafen, West Germany
1981 Galerie Peterson, Flensburg, West Germany
1982 Galerie im Judenturm, Coburg, West Germany
1984 Galerie Apex, Gottingen, West Germany
1985 Galerie Poll, West Berlin

Selected Group Exhibitions:

1961 *Junge Stadt sieht junge Kunst*, Städtische Museum, Wolfsburg, West Germany
1966 *Junge Berliner Kunstler*, Kunsthalle, Basle
1967 *Neue Realismus*, Haus am Waldsee, West Berlin
1968 *International Print Biennale*, City Museum and Art Gallery, Bradford, Yorkshire
1970 *Pop-Sammlung Beck*, Kunsthalle, Bonn (travelled to Darmstadt and Dortmund)
1971 *Biennale de Paris*, Parc Floral, Paris
1972 *Prinzip Realismus*, DAAD-Galerie, West Berlin
1978 *Funf Berliner Realisten*, Museum am Dom, Lubeck, West Germany
1980 *Berlin Realistisch 1890–1980*, Berlinische Galerie, West Berlin
1983 *Realistische Zeichnungen*, Nationalgalerie, West Berlin

Collections:

Kunstverein, Kassel, West Germany; Kunstverein, Mannheim; Berlinische Galerie, West Berlin; Nationalgalerie, West Berlin; Nationalgalerie/Kupferstichkabinett, East Berlin; Institut fur Auslandsbeziehungen, Stuttgart; Herzog Anton Ulrich-Museum, Braunschweig; Stadtische Kunstsammlungen, Bonn; Kunstverein fur die Rheinlande und Westfalen, Dusseldorf.

Publications:

By SORGE: books—*Zitate zur StVO*, Burgdorf, West Germany 1970; *Varspiele*, West Berlin 1972.

Peter Sorge: *Versuche uber die Grossstadt*, 1977

On SORGE: books—*Diehl/Petrick/Sorge: Malerei, Graphik, Material*, exhibition catalogue, West Berlin 1969; *Peter Sorge: Werkverzeichnis der Druckgraphik und Handzeichnungen 1963–70*, West Berlin 1970, rev. ed. 1972; *Deutsche Kunst der 60er Jahre: Malerei, Collage, Op-Art, Graphik* by Juliane Roh, Munich 1971; *Prinzip Realismus*, exhibition catalogue, West Berlin 1972; *Westberliner Realisten* by G. Strathmann, West Berlin 1979; *Peter Sorge*, exhibition catalogue with text by Lucius Grisebach, West Berlin 1985.

The terrors of engagierter Kunst receive their fullest freedom at the hands of Peter Sorge. His devastating (the correct word in this instance) realist style makes the most savage political and sociological cartoon look anaemic by comparison. It is not so much his expert control of narrative art that makes his works compelling and outstanding as the acid sense of drama which he is able to inject into them. The girl the soldiers picked up was the romantic figure in the first frame, but after they had taken her apart she features in the second half of the diptych-print as a broken disposable. Her two comrades (assailants) may not look so engaging in chapter two, but they at least are not smashed up like their poor victim.

Sorge makes the gun mean. No pistol in his prints could be less than villainous. Sorge firearms are not instruments for protective use; they are not even elements of martial equipment, a part of uniform. They are extensions of cruelty that will be brought into play if brute force fails to achieve objectives.

It is difficult to believe that this Berlin artist is just past 50 years of age. His technique and imagery suggest that he should either be much older (!), leaning back upon experience of a cruder past or at least reflecting or revivifying visions culled from the memoirs of a generation before—or, at the other extreme, he ought to be a "young" artist, gifted beyond his years, seeking to exhume the cruelties of a past era which he mercifully avoided.

The etchings and lithographs he makes of these nightmares are visually magnetic because of his inspired and accurate talent. His system of building up a graphic in compartments which often present a storyline need not always be the work pattern for horror, but it is significant that this artist will never sacrifice acid for saccharine. "How to achieve work and loveliness," for instance, is divided into three sections: top left—the rippling torso of a muscle man; top right—a faucet out of which descends a flow of water (like a single frame from a carefully made movie); bottom half—the flanks of a man and a woman; he hesitant, she inclining her pelvis toward his hip . . . a joint gesture of natural naked affection, except the half-lemon he is holding behind his back injects an acrid note.

—Sheldon Williams

SOTO, Jesus Rafael.

Venezuelan. Born in Ciudad Bolivar in 1923. Studied at the Academia de Bellas Artes, Caracas, 1942–47. Married in 1952. Painter: Director, Maracaibo School of Fine Arts, Venezuela, 1947–50; has lived and worked in Paris since 1950; also a musician. Recipient: Hatch Prize for Abstract Painting, Caracas, 1957; National Prize, Venezuela, 1960; Virgilio Cordo Prize, Caracas, 1960; Wolf Prize, *Bienal*, Sao Paulo, 1963; Premio David Bright, *Biennale*, Venice, 1964; First Prize, *Bienal America*, Cordova, Peru, 1964; Prize of the City of Cordova, 1964; First Prize, *Salon of Pan-American Painting*, Cali, Colombia, 1965; Medaglia d'Oro, Convegno Internazionale Studiosi d'Arte, Rimini, Italy, 1967. Agent: Galleria Naviglio, Milan. Address: c/o Galleria del Naviglio, Via Manzoni 45, 20121 Milan, Italy.

Individual Exhibitions:

1949	Atelier Libre de Arte, Caracas
1956	Galerie Denise René, Paris
1957	Galerie Aujourd'hui, Palais des Beaux-Arts, Brussels
	Museum of Modern Art, Caracas
1959	Galerie Iris Clert, Paris
1961	Museum of Modern Art, Caracas
	Galerie Rudolf, Zwirner, Essen
	Galerie Brusberg, Hannover
1962	Galerie Ad Libitum, Antwerp
	Galerie Edouard Loeb, Paris
1963	Museum Haus Lange, Krefeld, West Germany
1964	Galerie Müller, Stuttgart
1965	Galerie Edouard Loeb, Paris
	Kootz Gallery, New York
	Signals Gallery, London
1966	Galerie Schmela, Dusseldorf

Galleria del Naviglio, Milan
Galleria del Deposito, Genoa
Centre de l'Art Vivant, Trieste
Pfalzgalerie, Kaiserlautern, West Germany
1967 Galerie Denise René, Paris
1968 Galerie Francoise Mayer, Brussels
Kunsthalle, Berne
Stedelijk Museum, Amsterdam
Marlborough Galleria d'Arte, Rome
1969 Palais des Beaux-Arts, Brussels
Galleria Lorenzelli, Bergamo, Italy
Galleria Notizie, Turin
Galleria del Naviglio, Milan
Galleria Flori, Florence
Galleria Giraldi, Livorno
Galeria Estudio Actual, Caracas
Musée d'Art Moderne de la Ville, Paris
Svensk-Franska Kunstgalleriet, Stockholm
1970 Galerie Denise René, Paris
Galerie Godart Lefort, Montreal
Galerie Suvremene, Zagreb
Galleria de la Nova Loggia, Bologna
Galerie Semiha Huber, Zurich
Kunstverein, Mannheim
Marlborough Gallery, New York
Galerie Buchholz, Munich
Ulm Museum, West Germany
1971 Museum of Contemporary Art, Chicago
Galleria Rotta, Milan
Martha Jackson Gallery, New York
Galerie Denise Reneé-Hans Meyer, Dusseldorf
Kunstverein, Kaiserlautern, West Germany
Museo de Bellas Artes, Caracas
1972 Galerie Pauli, Lausanne, Switzerland
Galerie Beyeler, Basle
Galleria Levi, Milan
Museo de Arte Moderno, Bogota
1973 Galeria Tempora Calle, Bogota
Galleria Corsini, Rome
Universidad Central de Venezuela, Caracas
Estudio Dos, Valencia, Venezuela
Arte Contacto, Caracas
Galleria Godel, Rome
1974 Guggenheim Museum, New York (retrospective)
Denise René Gallery, New York
1975 Denise René Gallery, New York
1979 Museo de Arte Contemporaneo, Caracas
Centre Georges Pompidou, Paris
1981 Galeria Tempora Calle, Bogota
Galeria Theo, Madrid
Sala Celini, Madrid
1983 Museo de Arte de Caracas, Venzuela

Selected Group Exhibitions:

1943 *Annual Art Exhibition*, Caracas
1955 *Le Mouvement*, Galerie Denise René, Paris
1957 *Bienal*, Sao Paulo
1958 *World's Fair*, Brussels
Bienal, Sao Paulo
Biennale, Venice
1962 *Biennale*, Venice
1967 *International Exhibition*, Carnegie Institute, Pittsburgh
1969 *Middelheim Biennale*, Antwerp
1974 *Neuve Artistas Venezolanos*, Museo de Arte Contemporaneo, Caracas

Collections:

Cali Institute of Fine Arts, Colombia; University City, Caracas; Albright-Knox Art Gallery, Buffalo, New York; Stedelijk Museum, Amsterdam; Palais des Beaux-Arts, Brussels; Centre Georges Pompidou, Paris; Kunsthaus, Zurich; Moderna Museet, Stockholm; Louisiana Museum, Humlebaek, Denmark; National Gallery of Victoria, Melbourne.

Publications:

By SOTO: article—"Dialogue: Jesus Rafael Soto and Guy Brett" in *Museumjournaal* (Amsterdam), February 1969.

On SOTO: books—*Soto*, exhibition catalogue, by Jean Clay, Paris 1969; *Soto*, exhibition catalogue, by Guy Brett, New York 1970; *Soto* by Alfredo Boulton, Caracas 1973; *Soto*, exhibition catalogue, Caracas 1983; articles—"J. R. Soto" by Jean Clay in *Signals* (London), 1/10, 1965; "Soto" by Jean Clay in *Connaissance des Arts* (Paris), June 1969; "Soto dans le Labyrinthe" by Philippe Comte in *Opus International* (Paris), June 1969; "Soto's X Penetrables" by Jean Clay in *Studio International* (London), September 1969; "Soto's Logic" by Patrick d'Elme in *Cimaise* (Paris), May/August 1970; "Soto" by E. L. L. de Wilde in *Museumjournaal* (Amsterdam), October 1973.

Jesus Rafael Soto began as a painter and out of painting developed kinetic relief constructions which gradually grew into autonomous environments. In these, the spectator-turned-participant assumes a position so central that he is no longer divorceable from the work of art which without him remains incomplete. This process, traceable from phase to phase, took close to three decades of the artist's diligent and inventive life and gained for him an important place in post-war art.

As a student painter in Venezuela, where Soto was born, his first serious creative impetus came to him from a Cubist Braque still-life in a thrilling moment of comprehension, and his subsequent early work is an academic effort to learn from Cubism and from Cézanne the lessons of geometric simplification. When, as a youth of 27, Soto arrived in Paris, his avowed purpose was to find out what had happened in world art since Braque painted the still-life that had so moved him. Proceeding from a sense of stylistic continuity, he shortly thereafter determined to put his own shoulder to the wheel at the point at which the art-historical carriage seemed to him to be struck. Soto saw this point not in the prevalent area of tachist expression (which he dismissed as irrelevant) but, rather, within an investigative tradition concerned with the object's position in time and space. He correctly traced the modern origins of this issue to Picasso's constructions, the researches of Gabo and Moholy-Nagy, the spatially suggestive paintings of Mondrian and Malevich and, more immediately, to the kinetic mobile art of Alexander Calder.

The young Venezuelan showed implicit faith in the logical progression of art. As a young investigator, but no longer student, he found himself attracted, together with Agam and Tinguely, to the orbit of the Salon des Réalités Nouvelles, established in Paris in 1946, and to the Galerie Denise René, which had opened its doors two years earlier. The group's patron-saint was Vasarely, and each of the young men in his own way embarked upon research having as its objective the visual representation of movement. By the mid-50's, Soto and his friends had articulated their position and invented visual instruments for the expression of their principles.

Calder, as already mentioned, was the point of departure, but Soto's movement from the outset was different from that of the North American mobile maker. For Calder—the man who made sculpture move—did so mostly by letting carefully weighted, painted objects swing in the breeze, while Soto reduced physical motion to sensory vibration. The vibrating effect was either entirely based on optical responses to a physically static surface or further aided by the gentle movement of optically energetic suspended bodies as these came to act against similarly active optical surfaces. Leaving aside more distant antecedents, it may therefore be said that Soto related Calder's physical to Vasarely's optical kineticism, thereby combining palpable and visual kinetic elements into a new form language.

The environments that Soto created, at the outset in experimental modesty, developed their own momentum and eventually spilled over from his visual laboratory into the world at large. His planes, initially created to reflect vibrations, gradually grew into a striated cube large enough to accommodate the traffic of crowds, and eventually came to dwarf and submerge man as he literally made his way through resisting but penetrable mazes. The prime experience in Soto's later works is no longer optical, but tactile and sonorous as the human participant, through his act of penetration, agitates not only the real space before him but also our aural ambience. Quite logically, Soto's recent works are architectural. In his monumental factory interior for Renault in Paris, the decorative and the structural elements of his kinetic idiom merge.

Soto's art, then, gradually develops from a sensory and contemplative to a physical, and, in the case of the penetrable, to an athletic dimension: from the small laboratory experiment to monumental architectural scale: and from a self-contained aesthetic unity to one complementary to participatory activity by the viewer. Together with others, Soto has thus blurred the dividing line between the plastic and the performing arts: he has transformed the spectator outside the object to a central agent within the work itself; and reduced or radically altered the distance between art produced and consumed. Through these combined measures, for better or worse, Soto has greatly contributed to a perceptible shift away from art and toward life.

—Thomas Messer

SOULAGES, Pierre.

French. Born in Rodez, Aveyron, 24 December 1919. Educated at the Lycée Rodez until 1938; studied art at the Ecole des Beaux-Arts, Montpellier, 1941. Served in French Army, in Bordeaux and Nyons, 1939–41. Worked as a vineyard labourer, Montpellier, 1943–45; independent painter, Courbevoie, 1946, and in Paris, since 1947. Recipient: Painting Prize, *Bienal*, Sao Paulo, 1953; Grand Prize, *International Exhibition*, Tokyo, 1957; Grand Prize, *Graphics Biennale*, Ljubljana, Yugoslavia, 1959; Carnegie International Prize, Pittsburgh, 1964; Palette d'Or, *Festival International de Peinture*, Cagnes, 1972; Grand Prize des Arts de la Ville de Paris, 1975; Rembrandt Prize, Goethe-Institut, Basle, 1976; Grand Prix National des Arts, Paris, 1987. Agent: Galerie de France, 52 rue de la Verrerie, 75004 Paris. Address: 18 rue des Trois-Portes, 75005 Paris, France.

Individual Exhibitions:

1949 Galerie Lydia Conti, Paris
1951 Galleri Birch, Copenhagen
1952 Galerie Stangl, Munich
1954 Kootz Gallery, New York
1955 *Paintings*, Gimpel Fils, London
Arts Club of Chicago
Kootz Gallery, New York
1956 Galerie de France, Paris
Kootz Gallery, New York
1957 Galerie Berggruen, Paris
Kootz Gallery, New York
1958 Galerie Rosen, West Berlin
Kunstverein, Braunschweig, West Germany
Gimpel Fils, London
Howard Wise Gallery, Cleveland
1959 Kootz Gallery, New York
1960 Kestner-Gesellschaft, Hannover (retrospective)
Galerie de France, Paris
1961 Museum Folkwang, Essen (retrospective; travelled to the Hague and Zurich)
Museum of Modern Art, Ljubljana, Yugoslavia (graphics retrospective)
Kootz Gallery, New York
1962 Massachusetts Institute of Technology, Cambridge (retrospective)
Museum of Zagreb (graphics retrospective; toured Yugoslavia and Austria)
1963 *Malerier og Raderinger*, Ny Carlsberg Glyptotek, Copenhagen (retrospective)
Peintures sur Papier 1946–1963, Galerie de France, Paris

Pierre Soulages: *Peinture*, 1977

1964 Kootz Gallery, New York
1965 Kootz Gallery, New York
1966 Museum of Fine Arts, Houston (retrospective)
1967 Musée d'Art Moderne, Paris (retrospective)
Gimpel und Hanover Galerie, Zurich
Gimpel Fils, London
Galerie de France, Paris
1968 Museum of Art, Pittsburgh (retrospective; toured the United States and Canada)
Paintings since 1963, M. Knoedler Inc., New York
Comité d'Enterprise Credit Lyonnais, Paris
1971 Galerie Jobbe-Duval, Rennes, France
1972 University of Maryland, College Park (retrospective)
Galerie de France, Paris
Gimpel Fils, London
Galerie Protée, Toulouse
Galerie-Librairie La Hune, Paris
1973 Henie-Onstad Kunstsenter, Oslo
Nordyllands Kunstmuseum, Aalborg, Denmark
Gentofte Radhus, Denmark
Gimpel und Hanover Galerie, Zurich
Musée d'Art et d'Histoire, Neuchâtel, Switzerland
1974 Musée Dynamique, Dakar, West Africa (retrospective)
Maison des Arts et Loisirs, Montbeliard, France (graphics retrospective)
Galerie de France, Paris (graphics retrospective)
Galerie-Librairie La Hune, Paris
1975 Fundacao Gulbenkian, Lisbon (retrospective; travelled to Madrid and Montpellier)
Museo de Arte Moderno, Mexico City (retrospective)
1976 Museo de Bellas Artes, Caracas (retrospective; toured Brazil and Venezuela)
Musée d'Art et d'Industrie, St. Etienne, France (retrospective)
1977 Grand Palais, Paris (at *Foire International d'Art Contemporain*)
Galerie de France, Paris
1978 Galerie Ulysses, Vienna
Galerie Madoura, Vallauris, France
Institut Francais, Athens
1979 Galleri Birch, Copenhagen
Fondation Veranneman, Kruishoutem, Belgium
Peintures Récentes, Centre Georges Pompidou, Paris
1980 Musée de la Boverie, Liege, Belgium
Kunstlerhaus, Salzburg, Austria
1982 Galerie Ostertag, Frankfurt
Altes Schloss Museum, Giessen, West Germany
Galerie Ponce, Mexico City
Musee Charlottenburg, Copenhagen (retrospective; toured Denmark)
1983 Musée d'Unterlinden, Colmar, France
1984 Seibu Museum, Tokyo
1985 Pulchri Studio, The Hague
1986 Galerie de France, Paris
1987 Musée St. Pierre, Lyon, Frances
H.-Thoma Gesellschaft, Reutlingen, West Germany
Galerie E. Rieber, Munich

Selected Group Exhibitions:

1948 *Franzosisher Abstrakter Malerei,* Kunsthalle, Stuttgart (toured Germany)
1953 *Younger European Artists,* Guggenheim Museum, New York
1955 *The New Decade,* Museum of Modern Art, New York
1964 *Painting in France 1900–67,* National Gallery, Washington, D.C. (toured the United States)
1973 *Aspects of Contemporary Art,* South African National Gallery, Cape Town (toured South Africa)
1978 *Points de Repperes,* Palazzo Reale, Milan (travelled to Naples, Florence, Wroclaw, Poznan, Warsaw, Madrid, and Lisbon)
1981 *Westkunst,* Messehallen, Cologne
1986 *The Spiritual in Art,* Los Angeles County Museum of Art
1987 *Lumière de la Mediterranée,* Israel Museum, Jerusalem

Collections:

Centre Georges Pompidou, Paris; Nationalgalerie, West Berlin; Museum des 20. Jahrhundert, Vienna; Museum Boymans-van Beuningen, Rotterdam, Netherlands; Kunsthaus, Zurich; Galleria Civica d'Arte Moderna, Turin; Tate Gallery, London; Museum of Fine Arts, Montreal; Art Institute of Chicago; Museum of Modern Art, New York.

Publications:

On SOULAGES: books—*Abstrakte Franzosischer Malerei* by René Massat, Stuttgart 1948; *The Changing Forms of Art* by Patrick Heron, London 1955; *Pierre Soulages: Paintings,* exhibition catalogue, with text by Bernard Dorival, London 1955; *L'Art Abstrait* by Marcel Brion, Paris 1956; *Soulages* by R. van Gindertael, Paris 1957; *Musée de Poche: Pierre Soulages* by Hubert Juin, Paris 1958, as *Soulages,* New York 1959; *Pierre Soulages,* exhibition catalogue, with text by Werner Schmalenbach, Hannover 1960; *Soulages,* exhibition catalogue, with photo-reportage by Izis, Paris 1960; *Pierre Soulages,* exhibition catalogue, with text by Eduard Huttinger, Zurich 1961; *Les Peintures sur Papier de Soulages* by Michel Ragon, Paris 1962; *Soulages: Peintures sur Papier 1946–1963,* exhibition catalogue, Paris 1963; *Soulages: Malerier og Raderinger,* exhibition catalogue, with text by Haavard Rostrup, Copenhagen 1963; *Pierre Soulages,* exhibition catalogue, with text by Bernard Dorival, James Fitzsimmons and Werner Schmalenbach, Zurich 1967; *Soulages,* exhibition catalogue, with text by Bernard Dorival, Paris 1967; *Soulages: Paintings since 1963,* exhibition catalogue, with text by James Johnson Sweeney, New York 1968; *Soulages 1970–72,* exhibition catalogue, Paris 1972; *Pierre Soulages* by James Johnson Sweeney, Neuchâtel, Switzerland 1972, New York, London and Stuttgart 1973; *Pierre Soulages* by Michel Ragon, Paris 1974; *Soulages: Eaux-Fortes, Lithographies* by G. Duby and C. Labbaye, Paris 1974; *Pierre Soulages,* exhibition catalogue, with an interview by Bernard Ceysson, St. Etienne, France 1976; *Soulages: Peintres Récentes,* exhibition catalogue, with text by Alfred Pacquement, Paris 1979; *Soulages* by Bernard Ceysson, Nafels 1979; *Pierre Soulages,* exhibition catalogue with

texts by Alfred Pacquement and Ashido Okada, Tokyo 1984; *Pierre Soulages,* exhibition catalogue with texts by George Duby, Clement Rosset and others, Lyon 1987.

Prominent among the abstract painters of the School of Paris who won celebrity after 1945, Pierre Soulages has been consistent in his strength of expression, though the resources of his work have been restricted both in format and in palette. Colour as such is eliminated almost entirely, except where it is mixed with black. Black with brown, grey, green and blue dictates the mood of each painting. Handling of the oil pigment in varied thicknesses from quite high impasto to a transparent solution is always sensuous. By subtracting colour and mixing the pigment only in primarily tonal effectiveness, the imposition of the formal structure is emphasized.

Reflection is of the utmost importance in Soulages' paintings, not merely the reflection from the paint surface itself but in the diffusion of light in the chiaroscuro. Broad pathways of paint indicate the passages of intent, so that each canvas is a plan of tactile directions in which the reflections illuminate the plastic configuration of the paint. This plastic topography is, at first glance, strong in its negative saturation of the light, then grows in assertiveness as the subtle graduations of the shadowy reliefs are traversed. Activation of the picture space and an imaginary depth beyond it, implied by the lighter tones, expands the superficial limits of the non-objective image.

Soulages' contributions to theatre design in the 1949 sets for Graham Greene's *Heloise et Abelard* in Paris and in the 1952 ballet *Geste pour un genie* in honour of Leonardo's 500th anniversary demonstrate that his association with light and dark translate effectively in the proscenium frame. Those broad black bands, meeting and diagonally separating, construct dark and monolithic shapes that have their prototypes in memories of the ancient menhirs and the numinous sculptures of the old Romanesque churches abounding around Soulages' childhood home in the Massif Central. This solemn aura that broods over all of Soulages' work, either in paint or in prints, removed it from the context of ephemeral art styles and identifies it closely and specially with the rich and sensuous empathy of gesture, and the secret impulses of movements in the world of nature by night.

It is a magic and mysterious atmosphere that Soulages can conjure up, with no more than a personal Braille system of signs and reliefs in which the eye searches vainly for explicit directions and data. "Out of darkness came forth light," in the physical no less than the spiritual sense, is the import of Soulages' message. It also has the ambiguous paraphrase of the light that, dispelling our fears of the unknown, may also make clear the horrors the darkness has mercifully shrouded.

—G. S. Whittet

SPADARI, Giangiacomo.

Italian. Born in the Republic of San Marino, 4 April 1938. Lives and works in Milan. Address: viale Tunisia 23, 20124 Milan, Italy.

Individual Exhibitions:

1961 Galleria Spotorno, Milan
1965 Galleria Stefanoni, Lecco, Italy
Galleria Gianferrari, Milan
1966 Libreria Einaudi, Milan
1968 Galleria Bergamini, Milan
1969 Galleria Il Minotaura, Brescia, Italy
Fondacion Mendoza, Caracas
Galleria Il Punto, Turin
1970 Galleria Schwarz, Milan
Galerie Richard Foncke, Ghent
1971 Galleria Ciak, Rome
1972 Galleria Schwarz, Milan
Museo Civico, Modena, Italy
1973 Galerie Poll, Berlin
1974 Galleria Bocchi, Parma
1975 *Garibaldi e il Compromesso Storico,* Galleria Borgogna, Milan
1979 *1968: Tra Cronaca e Storia,* Centro Attività Visive, Palazzo dei Diamanti, Ferrara, Italy

Selected Group Exhibitions:

1968 *Biennale de l'Estampe,* Musée d'Art Moderne de la Ville, Paris
1969 *Salle Rouge pour le Vietnam,* Musée d'Art Moderne de la Ville, Paris
Kunst und Politik, Kunstverein, Karlsruhe, West Germany
1972 *Quadriennale,* Rome
1973 *Quattro Pittori: Una Città,* Palais des Beaux-Arts, Brussels (travelled to the Musée d'Art Moderne de la Ville, Paris)
1974 *Arts '74,* Helsinki

Publications:

By SPADARI: articles—"Giangiacomo Spadari" in *d'Ars* (Milan), December 1978; statement in *Giangiacomo Spadari: 1968: Tra Cronaca e Storia,* exhibition catalogue, Ferrara, Italy 1979.

On SPADARI: books—*Richerchi dopo l'Informale* by Enrico Crispolti, Rome 1968; *Giangiacomo Spadari: Garibaldi e il Compremesso Storico,* exhibition catalogue, by Mario Perazzi, Milan 1975; *Giangiacomo Spadari: 1968: Tra Cronaca e Storia,* exhibition catalogue, by Alik Cavaliere, Ferrara, Italy 1979; article—"Spadari: de la Chronique a l'Histoire" in *Opus International* (Paris), Spring 1978.

Giangiacomo Spadari: *Congresso,* 1969

SPAGNULO, Giuseppe.

Italian. Born in Grottaglie, Tarnato, 28 December 1936. Educated in Grottaglie primary and secondary schools; studied ceramic technology in father's worshop, Grottaglie, 1948–49; at the Scuola d'Arte, Faenza, Italy, 1953–55 and 1956–57; studied sculpture, under Marino Marini, at the Brera Accademia di Belle Arti, Milan, 1959–60. Served in the Italian Army Infantry, in Bari, Maddaloni and Milan, 1961–63. Married Clara Dalla Chiara in 1966; sons: Frederico and Andrea. Sculptor: worked as an assistant in sculpture, studio of Lucio Fontana, and of Gio and Arnaldo Pomodoro, Milan, 1959–60; produced first stone works, 1960–65; first wood and iron works, 1965–76; designed first stage sets, Bologna, 1975; has worked with cardboard, landscape, and archaeological themes, since 1976; spent year in Berlin, 1980. Lecturer in Sculpture, Istituto d'Arte, Monza, Italy, 1968–69. Recipient: Purchase Prize, *Mostra del Disegno,* Appiano Gentile, 1968; Purchase Prize for Drawing, Galleria delle Ore, Milan 1969; First Sculpture Prize, Seregno-Brianza, Italy, 1974. Agent: Studio Carlo Grossetti, via dei Piatti 9, 20123 Milan. Address: Viale Col de Lana 9, 20100 Milan, Italy.

Individual Exhibitions:

1965 Salone Annunciata, Milan
1968 Salone Annunciata, Milan
1969 Galleria Ferrari, Verona
Galleria Martano Due, Turin
1970 *Une Scultura nella Strada: Black Panther,* via Borgospesso, Milan
1971 Salone Annunciata, Milan
Studio Marconi, Milan
1972 *Ferri Spezzati,* Salone Annunciata, Milan
1973 *Scultura nella Città,* Nova Arte Moderna, Prato, Italy

Giuseppe Spagnulo: *Il Perseo* (detail), 1986

1974 Galerie Semiha Huber, Zurich
Galerie M, Bochum, West Germany
Studio Casati, Merate, Italy
1975 Galleria Schwarz, Milan
Salone Annunciata, Milan
1976 Galleria Il Sole, Bolzano, Italy
Galerie M, Bochum, West Germany
Galerie M, The Hague
Centro Sant'Elmo, Salò, Italy
Galleria 72, Bergamo, Italy
Galleria Il Segnappasi, Pesaro, Italy
Salone Annunciata, Milan (with Marco Gastini)
1977 Galleria Civica d'Arte Moderna, Turin
Salone Annunciata, Milan
Galerie Walter Storms, Munich
Newport Harbor Art Museum, Newport Beach, California
1978 Kunsthalle, Bielefeld, West Germany
Galleria Il Tritone, Biella, Italy
Studio Carlo Grossetti, Milan
Galerie D + C Müller-Roth, Stuttgart
Studio Casati, Merate, Italy
Galerie Walter Storms, Munich
1979 Galleria E Tre, Rome
Galerie Appel und Fertsch, Frankfurt
1980 Galerie Munro, Hamburg
Galerie Walter Storms, Munich (with Marco Gastini and Gilberto Zorio)
Studio Carlo Grossetti, Milan
Galerie Walter Storms, Villigen, West Germany
1981 Studio G 7, Bologna
Erotish, Rhetorisch, Heroisch, Nationgalerie, West Berlin
Kunstverein, Braunschweig, West Germany
1982 *L'Istinto e Sempre in Cerca di Anima,* Städtische Galerie im Lenbachhaus, Munich
1983 Studio Carlo Grossetti, Milan
Galerie Susanna Kulli, St. Gallen, Switzerland
Salone Villa Romana, Florence
1984 Galleria Civica, Modena, Italy
Galleria L'Isola, Rome
1985 Galleria Martano, Turin
Galleria Piero Cavellini, Milan
Wilhelm-Lehmbruck-Museum, Duisburg, West Germany
Kunstverein, Hamburg
Lunds Konsthall, Lund, Sweden
1986 Galerie Susanna Kulli, St. Gallen, Switzerland
Galerie Walter Storms, Munich
Spagnulo, at the *XLII Biennale,* Venice
Spagnulo, at the *XIX Biennale di Gubbio,* Italy
Galerie Hans Barlach, Cologne
1987 Galerie Hans Barlach, Hamburg
Galleri Nordenhake, Stockholm
Studio Carlo Grossetti, Milan

Selected Group Exhibitions:

1972 *Progetto/Intervento/Verifica,* Palazzo Reale, Milan
1975 *Empirica: L'Arte tra Addizione e Sottrazione,* Museo di Castelvecchio, Rimini
1977 *Arte in Italia 1969–1977,* Galleria Civica d'Arte Moderna, Turin
1979 *Le Stangze del Gioco,* Loggetta Lombardesca, Pinacoteca, Ravenna
1980 *Skulptur im 20. Jahrundert,* Wenkenpark, Riehen, near Basle
1981 *Linea della Ricerca Artistica in Italia 1960–1980,* Palazzo dell Esposizioni, Rome
1982 *Arte Italiana 1960–1982,* Hayward Gallery, London
1983 *L'Informale in Italia,* Galleria Comunale d'Arte Moderna, Bologna
1985 *A Generation of Italian Art,* Alvar Aalto Museum, Jyvaskyla, Finland (travelled to Pori, Finland)
1987 *Kunst RAI 87,* Amsterdam

Collections:

Galleria Civica d'Arte Moderna, Turin; Museo de Gibellina, Italy; Galleria Comunale d'Arte Moderna, Cagmiari, Italy; University of Parma; Nationalgalerie, West Berlin; Kunsthalle, Bielefeld, West Germany; Städtische Galerie im Lenbachhaus, Munich; Museum am Ostwall, Dortmund, West Germany; Bochum University, West Germany.

Publications:

On SPAGNULO: book—*Spagnulo e la Pratica Sociale della Scultura* by Tommaso Trini, Milan 1975; *Giuseppe Spagnulo: Erotisch, Rhetorisch, Heroisch,* exhibition catalogue, West Berlin 1981; *Giuseppe Spagnulo: L'Istinto e Sempre in Cerca di Anima,* exhibition catalogue, by Helmut Friedel, Munich 1982; articles—"Giuseppe Spagnulo" by Robert Sanesi in *Marcatre* (Milan), December 1966; "Spagnulo" by Zeno Birolli in *Nac* (Milan), June 1970.

One of the greatest stimuli to the work of Giuseppe Spagnulo at the start of his creative activity seems to have been the urge to overcome the weight of an inert material, to create a form that contradicts the true nature of the material used. This became evident when gigantic metal shapes (or even minute blocks of the same material) were bent in unlikely directions and fixed in a state of perpetual tension which made them dynamic. Later on, the evolution of Spagnulo's art was to become clearer with his approach to various materials, which made his aim more explicit. It can be recognized in his numerous series of *Cartoni:* raw cardboard, left in the natural state or just stained with lampblack, which can be folded and then pressed so as to achieve the desired form.

In the wake of the *Cartoni* came another interesting period, that of the series of works in clay (which Spagnulo christened "Landscapes"), in which another principle can be perceived, very much in keep-

ing with the moment in history through which we are passing today; that of extemporaneousness. These are works that the artist carries out with very simple, spare means: a surface of clay with pieces of tile or sheets of glass superimposed on them, on which he simply walks so as to give a wavy effect to the surface; this may even break the glass or drive the pieces of tile or stone into the clay. From these extempore works Spagnulo moved on most recently (1975–81) to another fascinating series, which he describes as "Archaeology." In these he works with solid iron plates with a deep groove in them; these are pressed on to similar iron plates which have been softened by heating, so as to obtain on the half-melted plate the impression of the groove in the first plate in relief. In this way it is possible to obtain works, always matched, which are presented as "traces of memory" (to use the sculptor's own well chosen expression). One plate is actually the "memory" of the other. The first is the matrix of the second, so that, rather than a "negative," what we have here is a sort of "twinning"—a double organism obtained from the interaction of the two aspects, one subordinate to and dependent on the other, a repeated record of what has its own form and yet is a mirror image of the other.

—Gillo Dorfles

Nancy Spero: *Shoot Out*, 1974

SPERO, Nancy.

American. Born in Cleveland, Ohio, 24 August 1926. Studied at the Art Institute of Chicago, 1945–49, B.F.A. 1949; Atelier André Lhote, and Ecole des Beaux-Arts, Paris, 1950–51. Married the artist Leon Golub, *q.v.*, in 1951; children: Stephen, Phillip, and Paul. Independent artist, since 1949: lived and worked in Ischia and Florence, 1956–57, and in Paris, 1959–64; now lives and works in New York. Co-Editor, *Rip-Off* magazine, ad hoc committee of women artists, since 1972. Guest Artist, Sacramento State University, California, 1974; Visiting Artist, School of the Art Institute of Chicago, 1974; and St. Lawrence University, Canton, New York, 1975. Recipient: Creative Artists Public Service Fellowship, New York State Council on the Arts, 1976; National Endowment for the Arts Grant, Washington, D.C., 1977. Agent: Josh Baer Gallery, 270 Lafayette Street, New York, New York 10012. Address: 530 La Guardia Place, New York, New York 10012, U.S.A.

Individual Exhibitions:

1962 Galerie Breteau, Paris
1965 Galerie Breteau, Paris
1968 Galerie Breteau, Paris
1971 University of California at San Diego
Mombaccus Art Center, New Paltz, New York
1973 A.I.R. Gallery, New York
1974 Women's Center, Williams College, Williamstown, Massachusetts
Douglass College Library, Rutgers University, New Brunswick, New Jersey
A.I.R. Gallery, New York
1977 Marianne Deson Gallery, Chicago
1978 Art Library, Queens College, New York
Herter Gallery, University of Massachusetts, Amsterdam
The Woman's Building, Los Angeles
1979 Peachtree Center Gallery, Atlanta
Hampshire College Art Center, Amherst, Massachusetts
Real Art Ways, Hartford, Connecticut
Picker Art Gallery, Colgate University, Hamilton, New York
A.I.R. Gallery, New York
1980 Livingston Gallery, Rutgers University, New Brunswick, New Jersey

1981 The Sarah Institute, New York
Ben Shahn Gallery, William Patterson College, Wayne, New Jersey
Herter Gallery, University of Massachusetts, Amherst
A.I.R. Gallery, New York
1982 *Nancy Spero/Leon Golub*, Florence Wilcox Gallery, Swarthmore College, Pennsylvania
Rockwell Kent Gallery, State University of New York at Plattsburgh
Francis Colburn Gallery, University of Vermont, Burlington
Vietnam War, Tweed Arts Group, Plainfield, New Jersey (with Leon Golub)
Galerie France Morin, Montreal
Matrix Gallery, Wadsworth Atheneum, Hartford, Connecticut
1983 University of New Mexico, Albuquerque (with Leon Golub)
Fire Station Gallery, Houston
Project Studio One, Long Island City, New York (with Leon Golub)
Art Galaxy, New York
A.I.R. Gallery, New York
Art for Social Change, New York
Brucknerhaus, Linz, Austria
Center for Creative Studies, Detroit (with Leon Golub)
Rhona Hoffman Gallery, Chicago
Willard Galleries, New York
1984 University of California, Berkeley
Riverside Studios, London
Cash Gallery, New York (with David Reynolds; travelled to A.R.C., Toronto)
Reed College, Portland, Oregon
University of Chicago, Champaign
1985 Lawrence Oliver Gallery, Philadelphia
Carnegie-Mellon University, Pittsburgh
University of Iowa, Iowa City
Powerhouse Gallery, Montreal
S. L. Simpson Gallery, Toronto
Coca Space, Seattle, Washington
Burnett Miller Gallery, Los Angeles
University of Connecticut, Storrs
1986 Hobart and William Smith Colleges, Geneva, New York (with Nicole Jolicoeur)
Museum Villa Stuck, Munich
Center Gallery, Carrboro, North Carolina
Greenville County Museum of Art, South Carolina (with Leon Golub)
Josh Baer Gallery, New York
Rhona Hoffman Gallery, Chicago
1987 Orchard Gallery, Derry, North Ireland
Fruit Market Gallery, Edinburgh
Institute of Contemporary Art, London
S. L. Simpson Gallery, Toronto
Washington Project for the Arts, Washington, D.C.
Josh Baer Gallery, New York
Lawrence Oliver Gallery, Philadelphia
Everson Museum of Art, Syracuse, New York (retrospective; travelled to New York City and Saskatoon, Canada)

Selected Group Exhibitions:

1963 *Salon International de Galeries Pilotes*, Musée Cantonal des Beaux-Arts, Lausanne, Switzerland
1972 *American Woman Artist Show*, Gedok-Kunsthaus, Hamburg
1977 *Words at Liberty*, Museum of Contemporary Art, Chicago
1979 *Feministische Kunst Internationaal*, Gemeentemuseum, The Hague (toured Holland)
1980 *Art of Conscience: The Art of the Last Decade*, Wright State University, Dayton, Ohio (toured the United States, 1981–82)
1981 *Crimes of Compassion*, Chrysler Museum, Norfolk, Virginia
1982 *Atomic Salon*, Ronald Feldman Gallery, New York
1984 *Content: A Contemporary Focus 1974–84*, Hirshhorn Museum, Washington, D.C.
1985 *Nude, Naked, Stripped*, Massachusetts Institute of Technology, Cambridge
1987 *Stations*, Centre International d'Art Contemporain, Montreal

Collections:

Judson Memorial Church, New York; Ramapo College, New Jersey; Institute of Technology, Boston.

Publications:

By SPERO: articles—"The Whitney Museum and Women" in *Art Gallery* (Ivoryton, Connecticut), January 1971; "Women's Speakout" in *New York Element*, February/March 1972; "Art: A Woman's Sensibility" in *California Institute of the Arts*, Valencia, California 1975; "Art Politics and Ethics: Interview with Leon Golub and Nancy Spero," with Derek Guthrie, in *New Art Examiner* (Chicago), April 1977; "Interview with Nancy Spero," with Donald Kuspit, in *Art in America* (New York), September/October 1977; "Ende" in *Women's Studies* (London), vol. 6, 1978; interview, with Nicole Jolicoeur and Nell Tenhaaf, in *Parachute* (Montreal), June/August 1985.

On SPERO: books—*American Sculpture in Process 1930–1970* by Wayne Andersen, Boston 1975; *From the Center* by Lucy Lippard, New York 1976; *Nancy Spero: The Black Paris Paintings*, exhibition catalogue with essay by Elaine King, Pittsburgh 1985; *Nancy Spero*, exhibition brochure with text by Rosetta Brooks, Philadelphia 1987; *Nancy Spero: Retrospective*, exhibition catalogue with essay by Jon Bird, London 1987; articles—"Bombs and Helicopters: The Art of Nancy Spero" by Leon Golub in *Caterpillar I* (New York), 1967; "Women Choose Women" by April Kingsley in *Artforum* (New York), March 1973; "Nancy Spero" by Donald Kuspit in *Art in America* (New York), July/August 1975; "Nancy Spero" by Lawrence Alloway in *Artforum* (New York), May 1976; "Women Ain't Losers" by John Perreault in the *Soho Weekly News* (New York), 23 September 1976; "Nancy Spero" by Corinne Robins in *Arts Magazine* (New York), November 1976; "Caring: 5 Political Artists" by Lucy Lippard in *Studio International* (London), vol. 193, no. 987, 1977; "Words and Images Through Time: The Art of Nancy Spero" by Corinne Robins in *Arts Magazine* (New York), December 1979; "Spero's Apocalypse" by Donald Kuspit in *Artforum* (New York), April 1980; "Nancy Spero" by Michael Newman in *Art Monthly* (London), September 1984; "Nancy Spero: Woman as Protagonist" by Jeanne Siegel in *Arts Magazine* (New York), September 1987.

From 1951 until 1965 I worked in oils on canvas. This group of existential works included lovers, prostitutes, mythological great mothers, etc.

From 1966 on I have worked exclusively on paper. 1966 to 1970: I made a series of over 100 war paintings. The paintings have messages, inscriptions, graffiti, i.e., S.E.A.R.C.H. and D.E.S.T.R.O.Y., L.O.V.E. TO H.A.N.O.I., etc. Victims are thrown from planes, the helicopter consumes its victims. "The Bomb," a human torso with obscene phallic heads spitting blood or fire—technological war.

"The Codex Artaud," 1971–72, have a cinematic quality—through extension (2 feet high and from 8 to 15 feet in length)—a fragmented and staccato positioning of the images of quotations. One has to change location, move in or distance oneself according to the scale of the images to follow the action. The rhythm of the whole is seemingly discordant and incomplete, relating to fractured time.

"Tortured in Chile," 1974, documents the torture of women political prisoners. From this work on I decided to represent "man" only through images of women.

"Torture of Women," 1976, extends in a continuous linear band, 20 inches high by 125 feet in length and contains case histories of women political prisoners from Latin American, Turkey, Iran, etc. (information from Amnesty International, etc.) combined with major references of mythological examples of the repression of women. The text is hand-painted with wood type alphabets and collaged bulletin style. Figures are collaged in to document and transcend the horror of immediate external realities.

"Notes on Women Part II—Women: Appraisals, Dance and Active Histories," 1979, is 20 inches high by 225 feet in length. A range of variously scaled hand-painted and collaged painted images weave through and interact with the 96 quotations and references, assembled from many cultures up to the present, defining aspects of existence with woman as the protagonist, an independent and positive force in a male-controlled world.

"The First Language," 1981, 20 inches high by 190 feet long, moves from war and rape to women's power, sexuality, grace and strength. There is no text in this piece, since gesture and movement are the earliest forms of human communication.

I use only images of women, to represent woman as protagonist and hero. This is a reversal of the typical art practice of portraying men as heroes and protagonists. I articulate women's situation and actions from repressed, victimized states to buoyant, self-confident stances.

These works are distanced from the Westernized notions of the personal subjective portrayal of individuality. The works deal with rhythm, stylization, contrast of body types, the juxtaposition of images past and present, varied historical references from disparate cultures, political information, etc.

I am not interested in individual physiognomies or personifications. The figures become generic in a somewhat similar way to, for example, the stylizations of Australian aboriginal art, early Greek vase painting, prehistoric art, etc. I combine in one work figures derived from various cultures whose extremely diverse and often disproportionate body sizes and types coexist in simultaneous time.

I use photographs informationally to derive images of contemporary women, for example, older Vietnamese women, a range of war and rape victims, youthful celebratory figures, who are depicted in stressed actions and symbolic representations. This is often emphasized by repeating the same figures but printed differently so that change between images is based on characteristics of tempo and time spans creating movement across the page. The repetition de-individualizes Western "subjectivity" in a non-hierarchical continuous presence.

—Nancy Spero

Nancy Spero's art/politics needs neither soap boxes nor labyrinthine rhetoric camouflaged in political jargon, to take control. Spero's images are ideographs montaged in staccato with verbal texts on long paper scrolls which become like personal holy scriptures. Since she knows all too well the effectiveness of hypnotic banality and subliminal ploys of the media, she rebukes them by using blunt dramatic symbols to confront the viewers. Traditional iconography would be inappropriate for her unconventional and sometimes harrowing messages about rape, murder, and political atrocities. Instead, she compresses information bits from hidden documents and the media, past and present, into verbal fragments. These are juxtaposed with figural analogies from the events. Spero demonstrates the persistence of these nightmarish occurrences throughout history. Beyond journalistic reportage, these collages grab the viewers in the way only art can.

More specifically, the history of torture, especially of women, is older than, but blasphemously aided by the *Bible*, the *Koran*, and all other generally respected sacred texts. Spero displays all kinds of tools of victimization with haunting beauty, with exquisite compassion and creative perspicacity.

A perfect example of this humanity is found in her work, "Codex Artaud." While Artaud had serious misogynistic tendencies, she empathized with his struggle to give birth to himself. She recognized in his struggles, his madness and spiritual anguish, a similarity to the history of women. The "Codex Artaud" had grown out of a preceding decade of work centering on anti-war responses to the Vietnam trauma. Phallic, tongue, and insectlike bombs spit death. The victims are seen licking the oppressor and vice-versa. Screeching slogans are scrawled on the paper as though in great desperation.

By 1974, Spero had come to the conclusion that the culprit of all the sado-sexual oppression grew out of

the Patriarchy and, thus, has devoted herself exclusively to themes of women and feminism ever since. It was also at this time that her unique usage of the collage medium was honed. Ways of seeing and methods of communication become synonymous in intensely compressed collages of figure fragments and label-printed type-scripts of personally and quoted texts. Exaggeratedly posed goddesses, classical figures, and monsters run, dance, kneel, and tumble as they stutter and shout the cacophony of horrific realities that compromise the "news." Since 1974 she has done works—"The Torture of Women" and "Notes on Women Part II: Women: Appraisals, Dance, and Active Histories"—which run rapid-fire through a gamut of themes: childbirth, girlhood, menstruation, and divorce. These are often spliced with themes of collective import such as: women's survival, male appraisals, racism, women's role in revolution, etc. New works evolve from unresolved ideas from past pieces and are expanded by the addition of more recent and profound insights.

While Spero's focus has widened over the years, there is a consistency and high-pitched concentration in her work that remains throughout. Though the visual and the verbal are interwoven in what seems like an erratic grouping of various sizes and scales, it is far from unplanned, and creates a sense of the rhythms of abuses. Snaps and snatches, jagged slashes of the stiletto, jolts of punctures and ballistic torment, all leave the viewers in a paralyzed free-fall through an angst-ridden existential abyss. And there is no sweet calm genesis after apocalypse; no consolation of death; no salvation. Instead, her "heretical" collages make it clear that any one of us is a potential victim of similarly gruesome offenses.

—Elise LaRose

Daniel Spoerri: *Table Sculpture*, 1964

SPOERRI, Daniel.

Swiss. Born Daniel Isaac Feinstein in Galati, Rumania, 27 March 1930; emigrated to Switzerland, and adopted by his uncle Theophile Spoerri, Zurich, 1942. Educated in Zurich schools; studied at the Ecole des Hautes Etudes Commercials, Basle, 1947–48; studied ballet at the School of Dance, Opera de Zurich, 1950–52; studied classical ballet, under Preobrajenska and Kniaseff, and mime, under Decroux and Marceau, Paris, 1952–53. Worked for Wacker Dance Studios, Paris, 1952–54; Principal Dancer, Berne Opera, 1953–57; assistant to Gustav-Rudolf Sellner, Landestheater, Darmstadt, 1957–59. Independent plastic artist, Paris, 1959–66, Symi, Greece, 1966–68, Dusseldorf, 1968–71, Cavigliano, Italy and Zurich, 1972–3, and in La Selle sur le Bied, France, since 1973: Founder-Member, with Pierre Restany, Yves Klein, Jean Tinguely, Martial Raysse, Arman and others, New Realists group, Paris, 1960; Organizer, with K. G. Pontus Hulten, *Bewogen Beweging* exhibition, Stedelijk Museum, Amsterdam, 1961; produced first tableau-pieds, 1961; first happenings and events, from 1962; "objets de magie à la noix" and exchanged objects according to emotional value ("feilschmarkt" works), from 1966; first eat-art events, from 1968. Also a poet, and choreographer and producer of "Autotheatre" works, mainly with Jean Tinguely, from 1953. Founder-Editor, *Material*, concrete poetry review, 5 issues, Darmstadt, 1957–59, Editions Mat (Multiplication d'Art Transformable), Paris, from 1959, and *Le Petit Colosse de Symi*, Greece, 1967–68; proprietor, with Carlo Schroter, Eat-Art Restaurant, 1968–71, and Eat-Art Galerie, Dusseldorf, 1970–71. Professor of Multimedia, Fachhochscule für Kunst and Design, Cologne, 1977; Guest Lecturer, San Francisco Art Institute, 1975; Lecturer, Hochscule für Bildende Künste, Hamburg, 1980. Recipient: DAAD Artist's Fellowship, West Berlin, 1978. Agent: Galerie Bonnier, 4 rue Saint Laurent, 1207 Geneva, Switzerland. Address: Moulin Boyard, 45210 La Selle sur le Bied, France.

Indiviual Exhibitions:

1961 *I Quadri a Trappola* Galleria Schwarz, Milan
Galleri Koepcke, Copenhagen
1962 Galerie Laurence, Paris
Galerie Lauhaus, Cologne
Studio F, Ulm, West Germany
1963 Galerie J, Paris
Galleria Schwarz, Milan
Galerie Rudolf Zwirner, Cologne
Galerie Dorothea Loehr, Frankfurt
Galerie Gerstner und Kutter, Basle
1964 Allan Stone Gallery, New York
Haus am Lutzowplatz, West Berlin
Galerie Rudolf Zwirner, Cologne
Galerie J, Paris
1965 Green Gallery, New York
Allan Stone Gallery, New York
Galleria Schwarz, Milan
Galerie Ad Libitum, Antwerp
City-Galerie, Zurich
Galerie Nachst St. Stephan, Vienna
1966 Galerie J, Paris (with Arman)
City Galerie, Zurich
1967 Spoerri House, Symi, Greece
1968 Galerie Gunar, Dusseldorf
Eat-Art Restaurant, Dusseldorf (opening event)
1969 Gegenverkehr, Aachen, West Germany
Galerie Handschin, Basle
1970 Eat-Art Galerie, Dusseldorf
Galleria al Vecchio Pastificio, Cavigliano, Italy
1971 Galerie Denise René-Hans Mayer, Dusseldorf
Eat-Art Gallery, Dusseldorf
Stedelijk Museum, Amsterdam (retrospective)
Galerie Seriaal, Amsterdam
Galerie Bischofberger, Zurich
Kunsthalle, Hamburg
1972 Centre National d'Art Contemporain, Paris
Helmhaus, Zurich
1974 Galerie Ben, Nice (with Claude Torey)
Galerie Germain, Paris
Kunsthalle, Dusseldorf
Galerie Günther Sachs, Hamburg
Schauspeilhaus, Bochum, West Germany (theatre decor for *Blue Angel*)
1975 Kunsthandel Brinkman, Amsterdam
Galerie Loeb, Berne
Galerie Bama, Paris
Galleria Multiphla, Milan
Galerie Bischofberger, Zurich
European Gallery, San Francisco
La Galerie Aberante, Plateau Beaubourg, Paris
1976 Spoerri Room, at *Dodspringet*, Charlottenborg, Copenhagen
1978 Galerie Levy, Hamburg
Spoerri Room, *Hammeraussetellung*, Kunsthalle, Basle
Deutsches Schauspielhaus, Hamburg (theatre decor for *A Winter's Tale*)
1979 Kölnischer Kunstverein, Cologne (for *Musée Sentimental*, with M. L. Plessen)
1981 Galerie Bonnier, Geneva
1987 Galerie Littman, Basle

Spoerri has also presented numerous banquets and Eat-Art events throughout Europe since 1970.

Selected Group Exhibitions:

1959 *Dynamo-Mouvement*, Hessenhuis, Antwerp
1960 *Festival d'Avant-Garde*, Musée d'Art Moderne, Paris
1961 *The Art of Assemblage*, Museum of Modern Art, New York
1962 *Dylaby*, Stedelijk Museum, Amsterdam
The New Realists, Sidney Janis Gallery, New York
1965 *MAT und MAT MOT*, Galerie der Spiegel, Cologne

1970 *Nouveau Realisme 1960–70,* Rotonda della Besana, Milan
1975 *Biennale,* Venice
1977 *Sucre d'Art,* Musée des Arts Décoratifs, Paris
1980 *Art Zanders '80,* Zanders Feinpapiere AG, Bergisch Gladbach, West Germany

Collections:

Sammlung Hahn, Museum für Moderne Kunst, Vienna; Kunstmuseum, Dusseldorf; Kaiser Wilhelm Museum, Krefeld, West Germany; Centre Georges Pompidou, Paris; Stedelijk Museum, Amsterdam; Kunsthaus, Zurich.

Publications:

By SPOERRI: books—*Topographie Anecdote du Hasard: An Anecdoted Topography of Chance,* with Robert Filliou, Paris 1961, new edition, with notes by Emmett Williams, New York 1966, with additional notes, by Dieter Rot, Neuwied 1968; *L'Optique Moderne,* with Francois Dufrene, edited by George Maciunas, New York 1962; *Gastronomisches Tagebuch,* Neuwied/West Berlin 1970; *My Mythological Travels,* New York 1970; *Sur les Keftedes,* Paris 1970; *Hommage à Isaac Feinstin—Motto: Daniel, du Apfel, falle weit vom Stamm,* exhibition catalogue, with an introduction by E. de Wilde, documents by Spoerri and others, Amsterdam 1971; *Krims Krams Magie,* Hamburg 1971; *Daniel Spoerri,* exhibition catalogue with Francois Dufrene, Paris 1972; *Die Bretonische Hausapotheke,* with M. L. Plessen, Cologne 1976; *Bretonische Heilquellen,* Cologne 1980; *Daniel Spoerri: Catalogue anecdote de seize oeuvres de l'Artiste de 1960 à 1964,* exhibition catalogue, Geneva 1981; film—*Resurrection,* with Tony Morgan, 1968.

On SPOERRI: books—*I Quadri a Trappola di Daniel Spoerri,* exhibition catalogue, with text by Alain Jouffroy, Milan 1961; *Daniel Spoerri,* exhibition catalogue, with text by Pierre Restany, Milan 1963; *Encyclopedie des Fraces, Attrapes et Mystifications* by N. Arnaud, Paris 1964; *Pop Art* by Lucy R. Lippard, New York and London 1966; *FOEW & ONBWHNW* by Dick Higgins, New York 1969; *Architektur, Concept Art* by Dick Higgins and Wolf Vostell, Dusseldorf 1969; *Pop Art et Cie* by Francois Pluchart, Paris 1971; *Daniel Spoerri,* exhibition catalogue, with texts by Claus Bremer and Marja Bloem, Zurich 1972, *Daniel Spoerri,* exhibition catalogue, Paris 1972.

Daniel Spoerri, who acted and danced when he was a youth, has a strong sense of theater, whether visual or in the actual performance.

His personal motto is: "Daniel, du Apfel falle weit vom Stamm."

In the mid 1950's he moved on from an appearance in the everlasting *Count of Luxembourg* to join the cast of the Berne Stadttheater's production of *Peter and the Wolf* (1956) and later produced and created the choreography for Tschumi ("Colour Ballet" in which he also danced).

Then he and Dieter Rot, with Pol Bury, Emmett Williams, Luca and Bremer published a review of concrete and ideogrammatic poetry called *Material.*

By 1960 this indefatigable and inventive Rumanian was staging exhibitions of his own works, having made contact with an assortment of other artists, including Duchamp, Albers, Soto and Agam. Later in Paris he joined forces with Gerstner, Man Ray, Tinguely and Vasarely. At this time he was deep into his MAT experiments (Multiplication/Art/Transformation).

Spoerri seems to have been at the centre of so many co-operative performances by contemporary artists (Luginbuhl, Ultvedt, Niki de Saint-Phalle, Rauschenberg and Raysse). What is so extraordinary about him and his *gauchiste* activities?

In 1962 it was typical of him and his works that he should have starred in Victor Musgrave's *Festival of Misfits* at London's Gallery One where the windows of 6 North Audley Street were covered with white sheets behind which the visual carnage was running riot. The other eight participants included Ben Vautier and Olof Ultvedt, but Spoerri's messy unfinished meals, dirty glasses and cigarette stubs attached to their uncleared tables made the deepest impression. Here was a terrible paradox—immediacy frozen into permanence. Litter and corruption were suddenly given art status. "The Bones of Szekely Gulyas—with the cooperation of rats" was offered as proof that actuality, even if it suffers the onslaught of time, *still matters.*

What happened to all this poignant disarray?

As usual with this artist, he operated on several levels simultaneously. The tables might be tidied up a bit and then "hung" like pictures on the wall, their bottles, plates, cutlery and napkins all firmly glued into place and perpetuity for the benefit of those who came to see them at the CNAC in Paris, or his admirers could join in a culinary frolic at Dusseldorf's Eat Art gallery where a special Spoerri triple-tiara cake presented to Pierre Restany amid art-debris like the *appetisers* he cooked in the manner of Arman and other artists, but for Seerials, the multiple-shop in Amsterdam, he had other aspects of anti-gravity and inverse-sociology to provide: "Le Pourboire de Madeleine" (a round tin tray with coins stuck to it so that it could be suspended picture-style from the wall) or his experiments with pairs of children's shoes (one lot suffering from rat urination, another showing how it had been deftly chewed, and in one case the calamity of the shoe caught in the mouse trap—all of them presented on trays of gravel). Spoerri's imagination is always heretical. His "Homage to an Unknown Soldier" is an erect penis with a crown like a stahlhelm, the whole trophy mounted like a big game hunter's prize on a wooden shield.

The artist is like the clown of contemporary art. All great clowns are artists.

—Sheldon Williams

STAECK, Klaus.

German. Born in Pulsnitz, Dresden, 28 February 1938. Educated in Bitterfeld, near Halle/Saale, 1944–56; studied law in Heidelberg, Hamburg, and West Berlin, 1957–64; self-taught in art. Independent artist, Heidelberg, since 1964: first prints and posters, 1960; first wood-prints, 1964–67; Founder, Edition Tangente, now Edition Staeck press, Heidelberg, 1965; Founder-Editor, with Peter Knorr and Siegfried Mahnert, *Tangente-Report* magazine, Heidelberg, 1965; worked with the artists Jochen Gerz, 1967, and Gerhard Steidl, 1970. Founder, Politischer Arbeitskreises, Student Association, Klausenpfad, Heidelberg, 1961; Candidate, Social Democratic Party (SPD) 1967; Chairman, Lawyer and Graphics Editor, Freie Hochschule für Kreativitat und Interdisziplinaire Forschung, Dusseldorf, 1973. Art tutor, Studenthochhausen, Klausenpfad, Heidelberg, 1967–69; Guest Instructor, Gesamthochschule, Kassel, West Germany, 1971; Professor, Gesamthochschule, Universitat Essen, 1981; Professor, Kunstakademie, Dusseldorf, 1986–88. Recipient: Zille-Preis, *Exhibition of Socio-Critical Art,* West Berlin, 1970; Pratt Center Prize, New York, 1968; Verkehrsburos prize, *Grafikbiennale,* Vienna, 1972; Forderpreis, *Intergrafik,* East Berlin, 1976; Kritikerpreis, West Berlin, 1979; Gold Medal, *Biennale für Fotomontage,* Gridziadz, Poland, 1979. Address: Ingrimstrasse 3/ Postfach 102063, 69 Heidelberg, West Germany.

Individual Exhibitions:

Staeck has had more than 3,00 one-man exhibitions at galleries, universities and institutes throughout Germany and Europe since 1960, including:

1965 Viola Gallery, Prague
1975 *Politick Affiches,* Stedelijk Van Abbemuseum, Eindhoven, Netherlands
1978 *Ruckblick in Sachen Kunst und Politik,* Kunstverein, Frankfurt (travelled to Heidelberg, Graz, West Berlin, Vienna, Aarhus, Russelheim and Hannover)
1979 Wilhelm-Lehmbruck-Museum, Duisburg, West Germany
1983 Henie-Onstad Kunstsenter, Hovikodden, Norway
1985 Konsthall, Malmo, Sweden
1986 Kunsthalle, Darmstadt, West Germany

Selected Group Exhibitions:

1967 *International Graphics Biennale,* Ljubljana, Yugoslavia
1969 *Intermedia 69,* Heidelberg
1970 *Kunst und Politik,* Badischer Kunstverein, Karlsruhe (toured Europe)
1971 *Biennale de Paris,* Parc Floral, Paris

Klaus Staeck: *Die Kunst ist Frei,* 1987

1972 *Documenta*, Kassel, West Germany
1973 *Kunst im Politischen Kampf*, Kunstverein, Hannover
1974 *Projekt 74*, Kunstverein, Cologne
1977 *Documenta 6*, Museum Fridericianum, Kassel, West Germany (and *Documenta 7*, 1982; *Documenta 8*, 1987)
1985 *Kunst in der Bundesrepublik 1945–85*, Nationalgalerie, West Berlin
1986 *Beuys zu Ehren*, Lenbachhaus, Munich

Collections:

Kunstverein, Heidelberg; Kunstverein, Dusseldorf; Kunsthalle, Cologne; Kaiser-Wilhelm-Museum, Krefeld, West Germany; Nationalgalerie, East Berlin; Kunstmuseum, Basle; Museum des 20. Jahrhunderts, Vienna; Stedelijk Van Abbemuseum, Eindhoven, Netherlands; Mahnsche Galerie, Brno, Czechoslovakia; Kulturhuset, Stockholm.

Publications:

By STAECK: books—*Intermedia 69*, exhibition catalogue, with Jochen Goetze, Heidelberg 1969; *Pornografie*, with Peter Gorsen, Giessen and Göttingen 1971; *Befragung der Documenta*, Göttingen, 1972; *Plakate Abreissen Verboten*, with Ingeborg Karst, Göttingen 1973; *Die Reichen mussen noch Reicher Werden*, with Ingeborg Karst, Reinbeck 1973; *Der Fall Staeck*, Göttingen 1975; *Die Kunst findet nicht im Saale statt*, with Dieter Adelmann, Reinbek 1976; *Eine Zensur findet gelegentlich statt*, with Dieter Adelmann, Göttingen 1977; *Gedichte/Collagen*, with Heinrich Boll, Göttingen 1979; *Die Gedanken sind frei*, East Berlin 1982; *Staeck's Umwelt*, Göttingen 1984.

On STAECK: books—*Kunst und Politik*, exhibition catalogue, with texts by G. Bussmann, Robert Kudielka, Herbert Marcuse and Gérald Gassiot-Talabot, Karlsruhe 1970; *Mail Art: Communications à Distance, Concept* by Jean-Marc Poinsot, with a preface by Jean Clair, Paris 1971; *Kunstjahrbuch 2*, edited by Jürgen Harten, Horst Richter, Karl Ruhrberg and Wieland Schmied, Hannover 1972; *Deutsch Kunst der 70er Jahre: Plastik, Objekte, Aktionen* by Jürgen Morschel, Munich 1972; *Projekt 74: Aspekte internationaler Kunst am Anfang der 70er Jahre*, exhibition catalogue, with texts by Dieter Ronte, Evelyn Weiss, Manfred Schneckenburger and others, Cologne 1974; *Klaus Staeck: Politik Affiches*, exhibition catalogue, Eindhoven, Netherlands, 1975; *Klaus Staeck: Ruckblick in Sachen Kunst und Politik*, exhibition catalogue, with texts by G. Bussman, Dieter Adelmann, Bazon Brock and others, Frankfurt 1978; *Documenta*, exhibition catalogue, 2 vols., edited by Rudi H. Fuchs, Kassel, West Germany 1982; *Documenta 8*, exhibition catalogue edited by Manfred Schneckenburger, Kassel, West Germany 1987.

With my work I would like to contribute towards exposing the untruthfulness of the excess of pictures surrounding us—I should like not to present what has been exposed, but to expose what has been presented.

As method I have chosen irony because to me the acridity and dullness that characterize most political discussions arouse fear. Dogmatism and oppression are often not far apart. To create a lasting alteration of consciousness in the direction of democratic socialism in the minds of those who hold differing political opinions, it is necessary to be inventive. Against an inert mass, cunning offers the only chance. I want to bring about necessary discussions on important political problems. I should like to place questions in such a way that they are hard to avoid. Irony helps me in this and is usually more effective than ponderous appeals or threats.

For me the attempt to reflect reality with pictorial means and to effect something in it represents rising above traditional art. An intensive study of the media is essential to any serious attempt at departure from the restrictions imposed by the encrusted art concept. In my case this led to posters, stickers, postcards and leaflets. It is with these media that I obtain access to the public, without which my work would be pointless. I convey my political ideas through posters which are made for the streets. Thus I reach everyone participating in daily life on the streets, in contrast to the past, when I had to rely on a small, elite circle of addresses.

The breakthrough out of boredom of the art ghettos, where paintings have stagnated to become pure decor, brought with it, though, along with problems of content, also new distributional and financial problems. Since then my work has largely drawn away from the business of art. It is mainly young people who employ my posters politically, but several hundred thousand posters and stickers have, for instance, been acquired by workers: those same workers that so many would like to get through to, but actually cannot. I know from representative inquiries which population groups I reach with my work: all groups feel themselves to be approached, though some more than others.

At present I am in the process of intensifying my contacts with the trade unions: numerous exhibitions in union headquarters, contributions to union newspapers and discussions with workers. At the same time I am increasingly engaged in collaboration with youth groups (e.g. exhibitions in youth centres and schools).

—Klaus Staeck

STAMOS, Theodoros.

American. Born in New York City, 31 December 1922. Educated in public schools, New York; studied sculpture, under Simon Kennedy and Joseph Kouzal, at the American Artist School, New York, 1936 (on scholarship). Painter: worked as hatblocker, florist, printer, and frame-maker, 1939–43; commission for work on *SS Argentina*, Moore McCormack Lines, New York, 1946; toured Western America, 1947; travelled to France, Italy, and Greece, 1948. Taught at Hartley Settlement House and Black Mountain College, North Carolina, 1950–54; Instructor, Art Students League, 1955; Lecturer, School of Fine Arts, Columbia University, New York, 1966; Professor, Brandeis University, Waltham, Massachusetts, 1967–68. Recipient: Tiffany Foundation Fellowship, 1951; National Institute of Arts and Letters Award, New York, 1956; Brandeis University Creative Arts Award, Waltham, Massachusetts, 1959; Mainichi Newspaper Prize, *Tokyo International*, 1967; National Arts Foundation Award, Washington, D.C., 1967. Agent: Louis K. Meisel Gallery, 141 Prince Street, New York, New York 10012. Address: 37 West 83rd Street, New York, New York 10024, U.S.A.

Individual Exhibitions:

1943 Wakefield Gallery, New York
1945 Mortimer Brandt Gallery, New York
1947 Betty Parsons Gallery, New York
1948 Betty Parsons Gallery, New York
1949 Betty Parsons Gallery, New York
1950 Phillips Memorial Gallery, Washington, D.C.
1951 Betty Parsons Gallery, New York
1953 Betty Parsons Gallery, New York
1954 Phillips Memorial Gallery, Washington, D.C.
1956 Betty Parsons Gallery, New York
1957 Philadelphia Art Alliance
Gump's Gallery, San Francisco
1958 André Emmerich Gallery, New York
Corcoran Gallery of Art, Washington, D.C. (retrospective)
1960 André Emmerich Gallery, New York
Gimpel Fils Gallery, London
McNay Art Institute, San Antonio, Texas
1961 André Emmerich Gallery, New York
Galleria del Naviglio, Milan
1962 André Emmerich Gallery, New York
1963 André Emmerich Gallery, New York
1964 André Emmerich Gallery, New York
1966 André Emmerich Gallery, New York
1967 Spingold Theater Arts Center Gallery, Waltham, Massachusetts
1968 André Emmerich Gallery, New York
1969 Waddington Fine Arts Gallery, Montreal
1970 André Emmerich Gallery, New York
1972 Marlborough-Gerson Gallery, New York
1973 Joslyn Art Museum, Omaha, Nebraska
1974 Athens Gallery
1977 Louis K. Meisel Gallery, New York
Galerie Le Portail, Heidelberg
Morgan Art Gallery, Shawnee Mission, Kansas
1978 Hokin Gallery, Palm Beach, Florida
Union College, Schenectady, New York
1979 Wichita State University, Kansas
1980 Munson-Williams-Proctor Institute, Utica, New York
State University of New York at New Paltz (retrospective)
1981 Martha White Gallery, Louisville, Kentucky
Louis K. Meisel Gallery, New York
1982 Karen and Jean Bernier Gallery, Athens
1984 Knoedler Gallery, Zurich
1985 Galerie Wurthle, Vienna
Kouros Gallery, New York
Ericson Gallery, New York

Selected Group Exhibitions:

1945 *Whitney Annual*, New York (and 1946)
1948 *Biennale*, Venice
1950 *Contemporary American Painting*, University of Illinois, Urbana
1952 *Carnegie International*, Carnegie Institute, Pittsburgh
1959 *Documenta*, Kassel, West Germany
1961 *Biennale*, Tokyo
1968 *Dada, Surrealism, and Their Heritage*, Museum of Modern Art (toured the United States)
1978 *Abstract Expressionism: The Formative Years*, Cornell University, Ithaca, New York
1980 *American Drawings*, Du Bose Gallery, Houston
1982 *A Curator's Choice 1942–63*, Rose Esman Gallery, New York

Collections:

Museum of Modern Art, New York; Whitney Museum, New York; Metropolitan Museum of Art, New York; Albright-Knox Art Gallery, Buffalo, New York; Hirshhorn Museum and Sculpture Garden, Smithsonian Institution, Washington, D.C.; Corcoran Gallery of Art, Washington, D.C., Walker Art Center, Minneapolis; Art Institute of Chicago; California Palace of the Legion of Honor, San Francisco; Tel Aviv Museum.

Publications:

On STAMOS: books—*Stamos*, exhibition catalogue, by B. B. Newman, New York 1947; *Theodoros Stamos* by Kenneth Sawyer, Paris 1960; *Stamos* by Ralph Pomeroy, New York 1971; *Theodoros Stamos* by Ralph Pomeroy, New York 1973; *Theodoros Stamos: Works from 1945 to 1984*, exhibition catalogue with essays by Barbara Cavaliere and Theodore F. Wolff, Zurich 1984; *Stamos*, exhibition catalogue with essay by Dore Ashton, New York 1985.

Younger by many years, but professionally their contemporary, Stamos (as he prefers being called) shared the explorations and discoveries of the American abstract painters who found their profound footing after the Second World War. Along with such painters as Baziotes and Rothko he depicted biomorphic subject matter in thin washes of pigment—in his case the sea and its creatures, rocks, plants and leaves. Which led to the abstraction of cultivated fields on Long Island and a series of works influenced by the Orient having mostly to do with the effect of light falling through semi-transparent screens: imaginary, non-literal tea houses. Fire and snow played their parts too along with the over-head viewpoint, turned toward river-bed-like channels of thick, rich paint—"landscapes" without any horizons--that occupied him in the 50s.

A long series of "sun boxes" followed. Paintings in which two rectangles suspended like reflections of

one another balanced in fields of radiant color. During this same period a group of wall hangings were produced after "cartoons" fashioned from the cut and torn paper, along with works on paper and a series of prints.

A trip to Greece resulted in a shift from the sunbox format—the "boxes" giving way to larger, more open rectangles with washes of paint sweeping into various parts of the canvas much like shallow waves. These paintings were an extension of an "Infinity Series" begun in the late 60s where an effort to push forms nearer and nearer to the periphery of the actual canvas led to emptier and emptier expanses of color. More or less in reaction to this, there then evolved paintings full of small, highly active forms, intricately composed, which are a little like the shapes found in the work of Arthur Dove (an artist much admired by Stamos).

A subtle, complex and powerful colorist, Stamos continues to probe the limits of abstraction in the last quarter of this century, firmly committed to the tradition of the easel picture and the painterly concerns which it has produced.

—Ralph Pomeroy

Peter Stämpfli: *Zeus*, 1980

STÄMPFLI, Peter.

Swiss. Born in Deisswil, Switzerland, 3 July 1937. Educated at Ecole des Arts et Métiers, Bienne, Switzerland, 1954–55; studied painting with Max von Muhlenen, Berne, 1954–59. Married Ana Maria Torello in 1961. Independent painter, Paris, since 1960: images of human body and food details, 1963–65; automobile and tyre details, 1966–70; tyre-track images, from 1970; first sculptures, 1985. Agent: Galerie Lelong, 13 rue de Teheran, 75008 Paris. Address: 54 rue Notre Dame de Lorette, 75009 Paris, France.

Individual Exhibitions:

1966 Galerie Bischofberger, Zurich
Galerie Rive Droite, Paris
1967 Galerie Tobies et Silex, Cologne
1968 Instituto Torcuato di Tella, Buenos Aires
1969 Galerie Rive Droite, Paris
Galerie Bischofberger, Zurich
1970 Galerie Rive Droite, Paris
1971 Galerie Rive Droite, Paris
Galerie Richard Foncke, Ghent
Galleria Christian Stein, Turin
1972 Palais des Beaux-Arts, Brussels
1974 Musée Galliera, Paris
1976 Galerie Jean Larcarde, Paris
Musée de l'Abbaye Sainte Croix, Les Sables-d'Olonne, France
1978 Galerie Jean Larcade, Paris
1979 Galerie Maeght, Zurich
Musée d'Art et d'Industrie, St. Etienne, France
1980 Centre Georges Pompidou, Paris
Galerie Maeght, Paris
1982 Galerie Maeght, Zurich
Kunsthaus, Aarau, Switzerland
Galerie Sapone, Nice, France
1987 Palais Municipal, Lyon, France
1988 Galerie Lelong, Paris

Selected Group Exhibitions:

1960 *42 Jung Schweizer*, Kunstmuseum, Leverkusen, West Germany
1963 *Biennale*, Paris
1967 *Bienal*, Sao Paulo
1969 *22 Jonge Zwitsers*, Stedelijk Museum, Amsterdam
1970 *Biennale*, Venice
1973 *Contemporary Swiss Art*, Tel Aviv Museum
1974 *Hyperrealistes Americains/Realistes Europeens*, Centre National d'Art Contemporain, Paris (travelled to Hannover; Rotterdam; Milan)
1976 *Aspects of Realism*, Rothmans Gallery, Stratford, Ontario (toured Canada)
1978 *Art Contemporain Suisse*, Helmhaus, Zurich
1985 *Dinge des Menschen*, Stadtische Kunsthalle, Recklinghausen, West Germany

Collections:

Kunsthaus, Zurich; Collection de la Peau de Lion, Zurich; Fonds National d'Art Contemporain, Paris; Centre Georges Pompidou, Paris; Kunstmuseum, Berne; Kunsthaus, Aarau; Fonds Regional d'Art Contemporain, Picardy; Musée d'Art et d'Industrie, St. Etienne; Musée de Dunquerque; Musée des Sables d'Olonne.

Publications:

On STÄMPFLI: books—*Le Peinture de Stämpfli* by Alain Jouffroy, Turin 1970: *Art in France* by Jean Clair, Paris 1972; *Peter Stampfli*, exhibition catalogue with essay by Bernard Ceysson, Aarau 1982; *Peter Stampfli: Vom Objektportrat zur geometrischen Struktur*, exhibition catalogue with preface by Fritz Billeter, Zurich 1982; *Le Pastel* by Genevieve Monnier, Geneva 1985; *25 Ans d'Art en France* by Jean Louis Pradel, Paris 1986.

All my work consists of seizing the image, the gesture, the objects which surround us, living what is going on around us, being sensitive to present events and translating them into painting.

I have taken a more particular interest in cars: I was dazzled by the object in its new, intact, self-advertising state, never by the used object. There was never the red print of lipstick on my glasses, never a trace of dirt on the wing of a car. I painted chrome bumpers, headlights, radiators, and then my attention fixed itself on the wheels. From the wheels I passed to the tyre, then to the tyre-mark . . . . The city is a part of all our lives. There was a period when painters depicted hunting scenes, portraits of kings. Today, the artist can only paint what he sees. I am not making an ironic proposal, I am simply seeking to draw up a report of a period. My images are in no instance reproductions; they are interpretations. The photograph is a starting-point, which I then translate into paint. It is very probable that one day I shall paint something other than tyres; it would take more than that to stop me from painting. The development of my plastic itinerary can appear extremely linear and logi-

cal: wheels-tyres-tyremarks-structures. But if someone had told it to me ten years ago I wouldn't have believed them.

—Peter Stämpfli

What immediately holds one's attention in Stämpfli's work is the imperious and absolute character of its forward progression. Nothing to cling to, to stop and take pleasure in: just series of pictures carried so implacably to their extreme consequences that, exclusively retaining the attention, they displace it from the preceding work, making of the oeuvre as a whole a phenomenon of perpetual actuality. What is more, the current language of the art world translates this state of fact perfectly: Stämpfli has been by turns, without anybody having emphasised these successive shifts, the painter of cars, the painter of wheels, the painter of tyres. He is , today, the painter of tyre-marks.

Between Stämpfli and James Rosenquist exists the same relationship as between Yves Klein and Mondrian: there has, indeed, been no lack of comparisons between Stämpfli's first pictures, painted at the same time as those of the initial generation of pop artists, and the works of Rosenquist. It was a way for critics to confine themselves to a thematic reading without noting the specificness of Stämpfli's work. Renouncing all montage of images, all relationships of an intellectual or emotional nature, isolating, on the contrary, the object on the white background of the canvas, he situates the object in an abstract space, depersonalises it. This dwindling of the context was given material form by Stämpfli when in 1966, in "Rouge Baiser" (Red Kiss), he cut out the picture following the exact shape of the lips. With "SS 396, No. 2" (1969) Stampfli's procedure marks a decisive step. The picture, in the shape of a wheel, is at once object and painting: the subject can be read simultaneously as realist painting, image of industrial civilization, and as concentric zones of colour, close to the works of Kenneth Noland, for example.

The reductive character which is clearly marked in Stämpfli's work, in his circumscribing his field of investigation from the wheel to the tyre alone, pushed this ambiguity of reading even further: the sculpted motif is at once both something real, everyday, identifiable in the repertoire of trademarks and industrial firms, and a structure which is abstract, repetitive, serial. The surface of the canvas assuming the precise form of the object, the identity is—except for volume—total. Perhaps it is in this slight distance—the perspectival crushing of an object reduced to the two-dimensional surface of the canvas—that the reason for the following stage should be sought.

The tyre-mark, the negative of the schema of the tyre, first combined with the picture, then independent, is a questioning of the classical structure of the picture: canvas of rectangular, square, or round format covered with paint. Through his personal language, Stämpfli joins up with the questions posed by an artist such as Frank Stella. He gives them, however, a more conceptual continuation as a result of the dialectic shift of the content of the work, in the absence of gratuitousness of the realist mode of writing finding its elements outside all formalism. The recent continuations of Stämpfli's work, all questioning of visual reality by means of perspective, the conflict with pictorial reality, place these apparently so specific paintings among those which are entering in the most penetrating fashion the debate being carried on by contemporary artists, that of the nature of art itself.

—Daniel Abadie

STANKIEWICZ, Richard (Peter).

American. Born in Philadelphia, Pennsylvania, 18 October 1922; moved with his family to Detroit, 1929. Educated at Cass Technical School, Detroit, M.I. 1940; studied at the Hans Hofmann School of Fine Arts, New York, 1948–50, and under Fernand Léger, 1950, and under Ossip Zadkine, 1950–51, in Paris. Served in the United States Navy, 1941–45. Married Patricia M. Doyle in 1961; children: Peter and Anthony. Sculptor: lived in Paris, 1950–51; settled in New York, 1952; Co-Founder, Hansa Gallery Cooperative, New York, 1952–58; lived in Worthington, Massachusetts, 1959 until his death in 1983. Artist-in-Residence, Tampa Art Institute, Florida, 1965; Lecturer, University of Miami, 1966. Professor of Art, State University of New York at Albany, 1967–82. Artist-in-Residence, Amherst College, Massachusetts, 1970–71; Salzman Visiting Artist, Brandeis University, Waltham, Massachusetts, 1973. Recipient: Brandeis University Creative Arts Award; National Arts Council Grant; Ford Foundation Grant. Agent: Zabriskie Gallery, 29 West 57th Street, New York, New York 10019. *Died* (Worthington, Massachusetts) *27 March 1983.*

Individual Exhibitions:

1953 Hansa Gallery, New York
1954 Hansa Gallery, New York
1955 Hansa Gallery, New York
1956 Hansa Gallery, New York
1957 Hansa Gallery, New York
1958 Hansa Gallery, New York
Frumkin Gallery, New York
Landau Gallery, Los Angeles
1959 Stable Gallery, New York
1960 Stable Gallery, New York
Galerie Neufville, Paris
1963 Robert Fraser Gallery, London
1965 Stable Gallery, New York
Tampa Art Institute, Florida
1969 Frank Walters Gallery, Sydney
National Gallery of Victoria, Melbourne
1971 Zabriskie Gallery, New York
1972 Zabriskie Gallery, New York
1973 Zabriskie Gallery, New York
1975 Zabriskie Gallery, New York
1977 Zabriskie Gallery, New York
1979 State University of New York at Albany (retrospective)
1981 Zabriskie Gallery, New York
1984 Zabriskie Gallery, New York
1987 Zabriskie Gallery, New York

Selected Group Exhibitions:

1958 *Biennale*, Venice
Carnegie Insternational, Carnegie Institute, Pittsburgh
1961 *Bienal*, Sao Paulo
Bewogene Bewegung, Stedelijk Museum, Amsterdam
4 Amerikanare, Moderna Museet, Stockholm (travelled to the Kunsthalle, Berne)
1963 *International Sculpture Exhibition*, Battersea Park, London
1964 *Recent American Sculptors*, Jewish Museum, New York
1968 *The Machine*, Museum of Modern Art, New York
1982 *3 Sculptors/3 Photographers*, Zabriskie Gallery, New York

Collections:

Guggenheim Museum, New York; Museum of Modern Art, New York; Whitney Museum, New York; Albright-Knox Art Gallery, Buffalo, New York; Philadelphia Museum of Art; Hirshhorn Museum and Sculpture Garden, Smithsonian Institution, Washington, D.C.; Dayton Art Institute, Ohio; Art Institute of Chicago; Centre Georges Pompidou, Paris; Moderna Museet, Stockholm.

Publications:

By STANKIEWICZ: articles—"Untitled" in *Art Now* (New York), no. 4, 1972.

On STANKIEWICZ: books—*Theories of Modern Art: A Source Book by Artists and Critics*, edited by Herschel B. Chipp, Berkeley, California 1970; *Icons and Images of the 60's*, edited by Nicolas and Elena Calas, New York 1971; *Richard Stankiewicz*, exhibition catalogue with essay by Fairfield Porter, New York 1987; articles—"2 New York Sculptors in Sydney" by Daniel Thomas in *Art in Australia* (Sydney), September 1969; "Letter from Australia" by Elwyn Lynn in *Art International* (Lugano, Switzerland), November 1969; "New York Letter" by A. Smith in *Art International* (Lugano, Switzerland), Summer 1972.

Richard Stankiewicz was born in Philadelphia in 1922 to a Polish emigrant family. In accordance with his family's wishes he studied engineering and worked in the tool industry in Detroit. Then, at the outbreak of the Second World War, he joined the U.S. Navy. So it was not until the age of 26 that he actually began his vocation: he enrolled at Hans Hofmann's school of painting in New York. On graduating in 1950 he lived for a while in Paris, where he studied with Léger and spent some time in Zadkine's workshop. He returned to New York and made his debut in 1953 at the Hansa Gallery, exhibiting spatial constructions made from welded scraps of industrial origin—pieces of pipe, wire, cable, chain, cogs, boilers, pistons, drums or unidentified pieces of used metal. The critics read meanings into these objects, conjecturing that the author was criticizing society's mechanical civilization and making fun of its technical arrogance. But the idea of using junk as a valuable artistic medium could also be said to involve the artist's memories of childhood, games on foundry slag heaps and refuse dumps. On an aesthetic level, the idea has precedence in Duchamp's *objets trouvés*, the "ready-mades" of Schwitters' "Merz" series, and from the use of chance as the antithesis of order—the mode of the avantgarde of the 1970's. It is easy to see the link between Stankiewicz and Dada. A kind of nonsense and a mockery of common sense and all logic appear in his work, similar to the collages and assemblages of Dada. On this basis, Stankiewicz's work is often considered a part of the neo-Dada movement that appeared in Europe and America at the end of the 1950's—for example, in the work of David Smith, John Chamberlain, or Mark di Suvero. Some critics have also pointed out all the similarity with abstract expressionism, since a reliance on the physical nature of materials, a spontaneity of gesture and a loosening of order and structure can all be seen in Stankiewicz's work.

By the 1960's Stankiewicz was already one of those sculptors whose formal ideas were of great interest; he was making a name for himself. The irony and element of subtle humor in his sculptures were particularly of note. For example: "Kabuki Dancer," 1954; "The Secretary," 1955; "Bird Lover," 1957; "The Candidate," 1960. This chapter in Stankiewicz's artistic biography was closed when he took part in the American Section of the 1958 Venice *Biennale* and gave his first one-man show in Paris in 1960. Few Americans abroad at that time succeeded in calling forth such a reaction. No one had displayed "junk" materials there before, and certainly not in such a way. It is likely that Tinguely, the creator of the "anti-machines" from junk, owes the impetus of many of his investigations in sculpture to Stankiewicz.

A break followed, filled with reflections and teaching. In 1969, Stankiewicz went on a journey to Australia. It made a great impression on his development and inaugurated changes in his workshop. The critic James R. Mellow has called these changes the road "from the comic to the classic." He was thinking about change from objects composed in an unconstrained manner, with a social message in the subtext, to rigorously abstract sculptured solids. The constructions were modelled from beams and plates of sectioned steel, from steel cylinders of varying size and diameter. Everything is compact, massive, credible in its reserved geometric silhouette. Objects arise, exhibiting geometry. Their basic element is a short, stumpy cylinder, wedged into its neighbor, hanging from it, placed at an angle to it. It can be seen that the artist is in some way verifying the physical laws gov-

erning solids—the balance and disturbance when a mass is displaced and the powers of gravity are negated. A fascination with matter, and anti-matter, the wedging of edges and levitation of solid figures, pulls the viewer into the play of pure form. This backing out of an outdated, restrained way of thinking and creating, without regard to the mainstream, is proof of this artist's courage and self-hood.

A surprise and a shock—the works of the second half of the 70's. They deny some of the axioms of sculpture—volume, mass, space—in the interests of linear form. Bas relief, contour, outline, open work instead of heavy, totemic masses—all of these works suggested new possibilities.

At the beginning of the 1980's the artist finds pleasure in placing contrasting materials next to one another—the flat with the 3-dimensional, the regular with the irregular, the smooth with the rough, new material with pieces of junk, natural rust with a treated surface. This expressively contrasted world of forms is seen across a frame forming a load-bearing construction. Square or rectangular frames here symbolize the aesthetic order so sought after in the "uncalm" art of our period.

The controversy accompanying all Stankiewicz's artistic work shows a link between his work and the traits of his personality, which tries to combine polarities of character. Perhaps this is why he needed to live outside noisy New York City in an area that is squeezed in between forested massifs that are scarcely populated.

—Szymon Bojko

STANLEY, Robert.
American. Born in Yonkers, New York, 3 January 1932. Studied at Oglethorpe University, Atlanta, 1949–53, B.A. 1953; High Museum of Art, Atlanta, 1952; Columbia University, New York, 1953; Art Students League, New York, 1953; Brooklyn Museum of Art School, New York (Max Beckman Scholarship), 1954–56. Married Jane Hutchinson in 1961 (divorced, 1968); married Marilyn Herzka in 1970. Independent artist known for very large figurative paintings: lives and works in New York. Instructor of Drawing and Painting, School of Visual Arts, New York, 1970–72; Visiting Artist, Louisiana State University, Baton Rouge, 1976; Visiting Lecturer, St. Lawrence University, Canton, New York, 1978; Visiting Artist, Syracuse University, New York, 1978; and Princeton University, New Jersey, 1979–80. Recipient: Cassandra Foundation Award, 1969; Igor Foundation Award for Painting, 1987. Agents: John Davis Gallery, 568 Broadway, New York, New York 10012; Bo Alveryd, 71 Avenue du Lac, 2028 Vaumarcus, Switzerland. Address: 3 Crosby Street, New York, New York 10013, U.S.A.

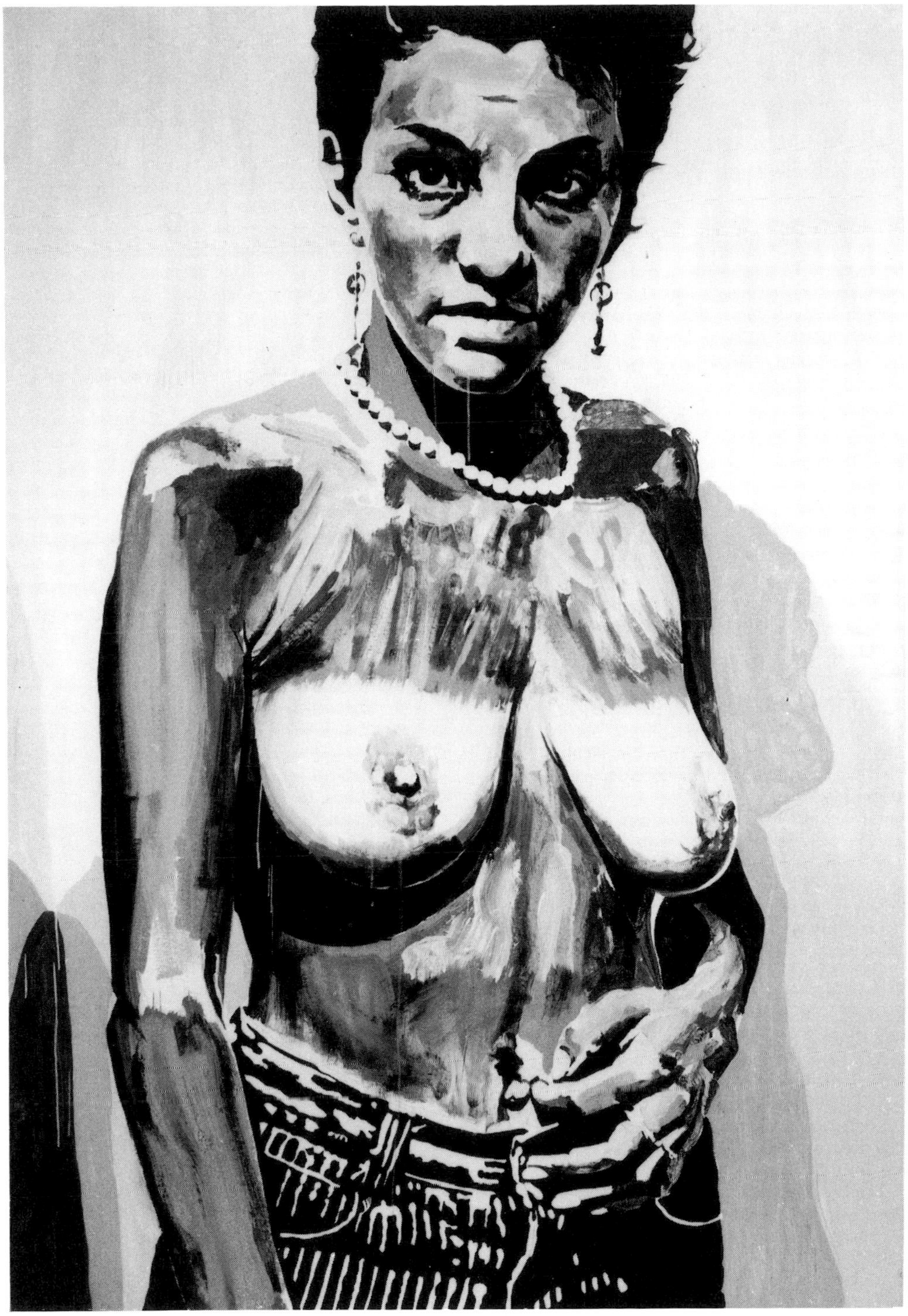

Robert Stanley: *Elena*, 1986

Individual Exhibitions:

1965 Bianchini Gallery, New York
1966 Bianchini Gallery, New York
Galerie Orez, The Hague
Contemporary Arts Center, Cincinnati, Ohio
Galerie Ricke, Kassel, West Germany
1967 Galerie Ricke, Kassel, West Germany
Galerie Kuckels, Bochum, West Germany
1968 Kleine Galerie, Frankfurt
1969 Gegenverkehr, Aachen, West Germany
On 1st, New York
1972 Warren Benedek Gallery, New York
1974 New York Cultural Center
1976 Union Gallery, Louisiana University, Baton Rougue
1977 P.S. 1, Long Island City, New York
1978 Hal Bromm Gallery, New York (photographs)
St. Thomas Aquinas College, Sparkill, New York
E. Weiner Gallery, New York
1980 E. Weiner Gallery, New York
Holly Keenberg Contemporary Art, Winnipeg, Manitoba (retrospective)
1983 Bucklew-Goehring Gallery, Tampa, Florida
1986 Le Consortium Centre d'Art Contemporain, Dijon, France
John Davis Gallery, New York
1987 Galerie Lavrov, Paris
New Arts Program, Kutztown, Pennsylvania
John Davis Gallery, New York

Selected Group Exhibitions:

1968 *Documenta 4,* Kassel, West Germany
1970 *Monumental Art,* Contemporary Arts Center, Cincinnati, Ohio
1973 *Biennial,* Whitney Museum, New York
1975 *The Nude in American Art,* New York Cultural Center
1977 *Outside the City Limits: Landscapes by New York City Artists,* Thorpe Intermedia Gallery, Sparkill, New York
1980 *The Director's Choice,* Fine Arts Gallery, University of Wisconsin at Milwaukee
1981 *Illusions of Light,* Worcester Art Museum, Massachusetts
1983 *Rutgers Archives for Printmaking,* Jane Voorhees Zimmerli Art Museum, Rutgers, New Jersey
1985 *A Decade of Visual Arts at Princeton,* Princeton Art Museum, New Jersey
1987 *Overtalk,* White Columns, New York

Collections:

Whitney Museum, New York; Metropolitan Museum of Art, New York; Housatonic Community College, Stratford, Connecticut; Fogg Art Museum, Cambridge, Massachusetts; Contemporary Art Center, Milwaukee, Wisconsin; Washing-

ton University, St. Louis, Missouri; Ludwig Collection, Aachen, West Germany.

Publications:

By STANLEY: books—*Tracks*, New York 1982; article—"Big Paintings: Bob Stanley," interview, with Robert Christgau, in *Cheetah* (New York), May 1968.

On STANLEY: books—*Erotic Art* by Phyllis and Eberhard Kronhausen, 2 vols., New York 1968, 1970; *Gordon/Lozano/Ryman/Stanley*, by Robert Christgau, Cincinnati, Ohio 1968; *Directions 2: Aspects of a New Realism*, by William Wilson, Milwaukee, Wisconsin 1969; *Robert Stanley*, exhibition catalogue, by Klaus Honnef, Aachen, West Germany 1969; *Bob Stanley's Louisiana Sweet* by Mario Amaya and Naomi Spector, New York 1978; articles—"The Flip Side" by David Bourdon in the *Village Voice* (New York), 17 June 1965; "The New Eroticism" by Douglas Davis in *Evergreen* (New York), September 1968; "Eros erinnert an Dharma" by John Anthony Thwaites in *Christ und Welt*, Dusseldorf 1969; "The Spectrum of Monochrome" by Lawrence Alloway in *Arts Magazine* (New York), December/January 1971; "Robert Stanley" by G. Gassiot-Talbot in *Opus International* (Paris), December 1971; "Bob Stanley" by John Lloyd Taylor in *Art International* (Lugano, Switzerland), September 1974; "Bob Stanley and Bart Wasserman at P.S. 1" by Carter Ratcliff in *Art in America* (New York), January/February 1978; "Paint Misbehavin'" by Peter Frank in the *Village Voice* (New York), 16 October 1978; "Bob Stanley" by William Zimmer in the *Soho Weekly News* (New York), 8 October 1980; "Bob Stanley" by Michael Florescu in *Arts Magazine* (New York), November 1980; "Parade in the Face of Death: the work of Robert Stanley" by Richard Artschwager in *Galeries* (Paris), Summer 1987.

Michael Florescu has said the following about my work:

"The work of Bob Stanley, it seems to me, is imbued with an old-fashioned morality, if not didacticism—a strange response, perhaps, to an artist whom Mario Amaya has dubbed 'that pirate of the Pop Art movement.' But in a time of pluralism in the visual arts, a phrase that has come to mean a time of multiple warring assertions, Stanley stands out as a questioner. His work is interrogative of the contemporary conventional wisdom rather than declarative. Uncharacteristically for a questioner, there is little humility about his paintings: they are big (not to mince works, they are enormous), and to quote Amaya again, they are 'as cyclical and all encompassing as the walls of an early Renaissance chapel.'"

—Robert Stanley

STAZEWSKI, Henryk.

Polish. Born in Warsaw, 9 January 1894. Educated at Kowalski's Secondary School, Warsaw; studied at the School of Fine Arts, Warsaw, under Stanislaw Lent, 1913–19. Painter: lived and worked in Warsaw from 1920; produced paintings and reliefs from 1920, neoplastic house interiors, 1923–32; Founder-Member, with Wladyslaw Strzeminski, Mieczyslaw Szulc, Henryk Berlewi and others, Blok artists group, Wilno, 1923–36; Editor, *Blok* magazine, nos. 1–5, 1924; Founder-Member, Praesens painters and architects group, Warsaw, 1926–29; Founder-Member, with Wladyslaw Strzeminski, Katarzyna Kobro, Julian Przybos and others, a.r. group, Lodz, 1929; Member, Michel Seuphor's Cercle et Carre group, Paris, 1930–31, and Abstraction-Creation group, Paris, 1931; Founder-Member, KAGR publicity graphic artists group, Warsaw, 1933; Member, Editorial Board, *Glos Plastykow* magazine, Warsaw, 1933; Founder-Member, Trade Union of Plastic Artists, Warsaw, 1935. Recipient: Ministry of Culture Prize, Warsaw, 1965; J. G. Herder Prize, University of Vienna. 1972. Member, Association Internationale des Arts Plastiques (A.I.A.P.), Paris, 1962. Golden Cross of Merit, Warsaw, 1955; Officer, Cross of the Order Polonia Restituta, Warsaw. Agents: Galerie Schlegel, Minervastrasse 119, 8000 Zurich, Switzerland; Crane Arts, 321 Kings Road, London S.W.3, England. *Died* (in Warsaw) *June 1988*.

Individual Exhibitions:

1921 Polonia Artists Club, Warsaw (with E. Miller and M. Szczuka)
1933 Art Propaganda Institute, Warsaw (with Karol Krynski)
1934 Art Propaganda Institute, Warsaw (with Wladyslaw Strzeminski)
1955 Polish Union of Writers Club, Warsaw
1956 Galleria Incontro, Rome (with Aleksander Winnicki)
1959 Kordegada, Warsaw
1960 Krzywekolo Gallery, Warsaw
1961 Castle of Lublin, Poland
Krzywekolo Gallery, Warsaw
1962 Krzywekolo Gallery, Warsaw
1963 *Reliefs and Collages*, Grabowski Gallery, London
1965 Galerija Zacheta, Warsaw
1966 Kazimir Gallery, Chicago
1967 Galerija Foksal, Warsaw
1969 Galerija Foksal, Warsaw
Museum of Fine Arts, Lodz, Poland
1970 Narodna Gallery, Prague
Galerija Foksal, Warsaw
Galerija Krzystofory, Cracow
1972 Mecatorhalle, Duisburg, West Germany
1974 Galerie 16, Paris
Wide White Space Gallery, Brussels
Galerie Polart, Dusseldorf
Biuro Wystawy Artystycznych, Lodz, Poland
Pape Ruddy Gallery, Los Angeles
Museum of Fine Arts, Lodz, Poland
1975 Galerie Schlegl, Zurich
1976 Galerija Wspolczesna, Warsaw
Galerija 72, Chelm, Poland
1977 Galerie Teufel, Cologne
1978 Galerija Zacheta, Warsaw
1979 Palazzo delle Esposizione, Rome (travelled to the Teatro del Falcone, Genoa, and the Museo d'Arte Moderna Ca Pesaro, Venice)
Recent Paintings, Fruit Market Gallery, Edinburgh (travelled to the Third Eye Centre, Glasgow)
Galerija Zapiecek, Warsaw
1980 Galerija Krytykow, Warsaw
Biuro Wystaw Artystycznych, Torun, Poland (retrospective)
Biuro Wystaw Artystycznych, Bydgoszcz, Poland
Galerie Quadrat, Bottrop, West Germany
1982 Galerie Denise René, Paris

Selected Group Exhibitions:

1922 *F9 Formist Artists Group: 3rd Exhibition*, Salon-Garlinski, Warsaw
1926 *Praesens Group*, Galerija Zacheta, Warsaw
1947 *1st Salon of ZPAP*, National Museum, Warsaw
1957 *Precurseurs d'Art Abstrait en Pologne*, Galerie Denise René, Paris
1961 *15 Polish Artists*, Museum of Modern Art, New York
1966 *Biennale*, Venice
1972 *The Non-Objective World 1939–55*, Annely Juda Fine Art, London (travelled to the Galerie Liatowisch, Basle, and the Galleria Milano, Milan)
1977 *Constructivisme Polonais 1923–36*, Musée d'Art Contemporain, Montreal
1978 *Abstraction-Creation 1931–36*, Westfälischer Landesmuseum, Münster, West Germany (travelled to the Musée d'Art Moderne de la Ville, Paris)
1980 *Polnische Kunst aus 3 Jahrzehnten*, Staatliche Kunstsammlungen, Dresden

Collections:

Museum of Fine Arts, Lodz, Poland; National Museum, Warsaw; National Museum, Cracow; Tate Gallery, London; Museum der Stadt, St. Gallen, Switzerland; Rijksmuseum Kröller-Müller, Otterlo, Netherlands, Stedelijk Museum, Amsterdam; Städtische Kunstgalerie, Bochum, West Germany; Museum of Modern Art, New York; Guggenheim Museum, New York.

Publications:

By STAZEWSKI: books illustrated—*Praesens Library no. 2: The Human Creative Mission in the Fine Arts* by Albert Gleizes, Warsaw 1927; *Praesens Library no. 3: Unism in Painting* by Wladyslaw Strzeminski, Warsaw 1928; *The Angelic Ruffian* by Anatol Stern, Warsaw 1928.

On STAZEWSKI: books—*Reliefs and Collages by Henryk Stazewski*, exhibition catalogue, with texts by Alan Bowness and Wieslaw Borowski, London 1963; *Contemporary Polish Painting: Henryk Stazewski* by Hanna Ptaskowska, Warsaw 1965; *Stazewski*, exhibition catalogue, with texts by Ryszard Stanislawski, Hanna Ptaszkowska and Wieslaw Borowski, Lodz, Poland 1969; *The Non-Objective World 1939–55*, exhibition catalogue, with text by George Rickey, London 1972; *Geometric Abstraction 1926–1942*, exhibition catalogue, with texts by Michel Seuphor and John Elderfield, Dallas 1972; *Henryk Stazewski: Malarstwo z lat 1923–1974*, exhibition catalogue Lodz, Poland 1974; *Henryk Stazewski*, exhibition catalogue, Brussels 1974; *Henryk Stazewski*, exhibition catalogue, Paris 1974; *Henryk Stazewski: Recent Paintings*, exhibition catalogue, with texts by Richard Demarco and Janina Ladnowska, Edinburgh 1979; *Henryk Stazewski*, exhibition catalogue, with texts by Ulrich Schumacher, Ryszard Stanislawski and Janina Ladnowska, Bottrop, West Germany 1980; *Stazewski*, exhibition catalogue, with text by Anka Ptaszkowska, Paris 1982.

Henryk Stazewski, a survivor of the heroic period of the Polish avant garde, and one of the promoters of abstraction (he was a member of Cercle et Carre), began his work as a painter and art theoretician in the 1920's. He was then in favor of the constituent elements of form—the independent roles of line and color, chiaroscuro and fracture: in his pictures the artist linked these elements equally. He wished to create an objectless world that would make the eye sensitive to only that which was universal—above all, to geometric form and to color.

Stazewski continued his pursuit of this problem after the war, in the 1950's. The idea of movement also concerned him at this time. Originally this was provoked by the structure of form which then developed in the sphere of "open structures."

In 1957 a new problem arose. The artist stopped painting pictures and turned to the construction of reliefs from flat smooth forms. He simultaneously executed radical simplifications, reducing form to a single element—the module; and color to black, white and grey. Stazewski then moved on to reliefs from smooth, polished metal. An artist whose creativity had drawn from the sources of abstraction—e.g., Mondrian—now developed a completely new kind of abstraction. In Mondrian's time the fixed relationships between the various respective elements were described in abstract pictures. In his reliefs, however, Stazewski introduced identical forms—modules (e.g., the square with concave sides, the ellipse with two ends cut off). Repeating these many times within the framework of a single picture, the artist removed their stamp of individuality; he "neutralized" them. Also, by repeating the same form-module, he focused attention not on form but on the various ways that it could be arranged.

The picture is thus constructed in an open manner which conceals potential changes of shape. As a result, the mid-1960s saw a sudden increase in interest in Stazewski's work. The possibilities of change inherent in his work prompted several critics to search for precursive elements with respect to the worldwide movement of visual art and the concepts of a neutral, anonymous art. Stazewski's work was thus suddenly regarded as of general importance; it could be re-created and given the greatest possible circulation.

In 1968 Strazewski returned to the problem of color. In a series of paintings from this period he analyzed color phenomena and the laws of visual perception. He based his research on scientific founda-

tions. Using squares marked on his canvases, he carried out a graduation of chromatic color of a section of the spectrum, achieving shades that differ so minimally that it is almost impossible to perceive the delineation.

In 1973 Stazewski created a series of white pictures the surfaces of which are divided simultaneously in rhythmical and unsettled sections with the help of parallel lines. The rhythms of the lines converge or diverge, change their course, undergo short jumps. In spite of these dynamizing moments, the artist achieves homogeneous surfaces by using one kind of method, the minimal mutations always taking place within the framework of one basic module.

A phenomenon of Stazewski's artistic personality is the fact that, although he was one of the pioneers of geometric abstraction, he was still very sensitive to the ephemera of nature. But he always sought a permanent form for that which is only transitory. An example of this is the cycle of work begun in 1975, inspired by the wintry landscape of a small town. In these works the artist uses only geometric designs of black lines on a white ground. At the same time he writes: "The artist ought to beware the ephemeral, but he can in art give certain observed ephemeral phenomena a permanence and an extension of their existence." He continues: "Creating art, one has no understanding of the transitoriness of that which one is doing. One is led by a false feeling of permanence without being aware of the withering of a rose." In other words, Stazewski, who always wanted to commemorate the world in universal and permanent forms, also had strong feelings about the impermanence of all that exists. The tension between that which is universal and that which is individual, between intellectual reflection and the sphere of emotion, protects his art from a dry one-sideness and marks it with strong personal sensitivity.

—Alicja Kepinska

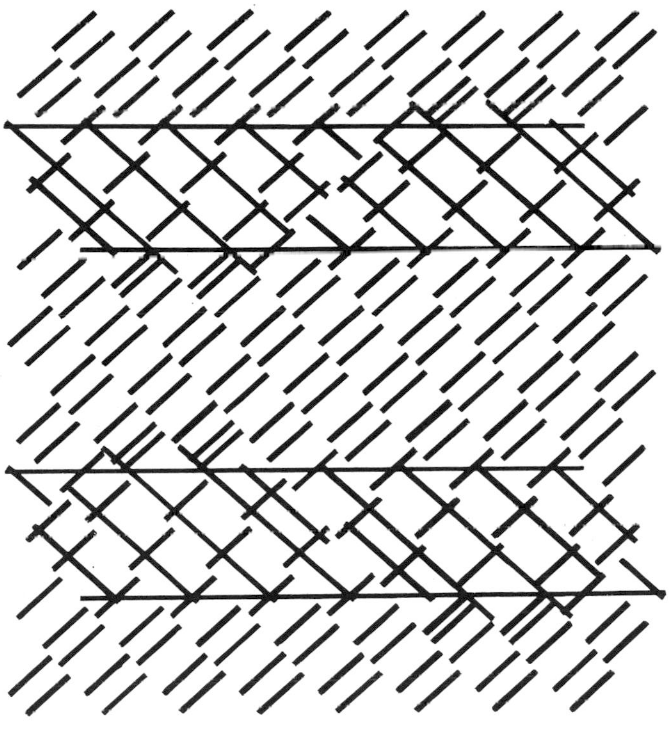

Jeffrey Steele: ***Sg III. 45*****, 1985**

STEELE, Jeffrey.

British. Born in Cardiff, South Wales, 3 July 1931. Studied at Cardiff College of Art, 1948–50; studied painting at Newport College of Art, South Wales, 1950–52; also studied at the Ecole des Beaux Arts, Paris, 1959–60. Married Glenda Reynolds in 1958 (divorced, 1966); children: Simon and Tamara; married Arja Nenonen in 1966 (divorced, 1976); daughter: Clara. Independent painter, since 1952. Worked as hospital porter, Cardiff, 1953–55; as cellarman, London, 1955–57; as radio operator, Cardiff, 1957–59. Co-Founder, Systems Group of Artists, London 1969 (dissolved, 1976). Lecturer, Barry Summer School, Glamorgan, South Wales, 1962–73; Lecturer in Painting, Newport College of Art, South Wales, 1965–68; Principal Lecturer, Portsmouth Polytechnic, since 1969. Recipient: French Government Scholarship, 1959; Welsh Arts Council Bursary, 1963; Painting Prize, Northern Ireland Arts Council, 1968; Painting Prize, *Welsh Arts Council Open Painting Exhibition,* Barry, Wales, 1968. Agents: Galerie Schoeller, Poststrasse 2, 4000 Dusseldorf 1, West Germany; Patricia Knight Fine Art, 21 Phipp Street, London EC2A 4NP, England; Galerie Media, rue des Moulines, 29, Neuchâtel, Switzerland. Address: 11a Eastern Villas Road, Portsmouth, Hampshire PO4 OSU, England.

Individual Exhibitions:

1961 Institute of Contemporary Arts, London
1963 Dillwyn Gallery, Swansea, South Wales
1964 Grabowski Gallery, London
Regional College of Art, Manchester
1966 McRoberts and Tunnard Gallery, London
1967 Sheffield University Arts Tower
City Art Gallery, Manchester (with Benjamin and Tyzack)
1974 *Current Work,* Lucy Milton Gallery, London
Galerie Media, Neuchâtel, Switzerland
1975 Galerie Jacomo-Santiveri, Paris (with Dilworth and Kidner)
1976 Le Disque Rouge, Brussels
1977 Galerie Gilles Gheerbrant, Montreal
Galerie Swart, Amsterdam
1978 Galerie Swart, Amsterdam
1979 Galerie Lydia Megert, Berne
1985 Kunsthaus, Nuremberg, West Germany

Selected Group Exhibitions:

1962 *The Geometric Environment,* Artist's International Association Gallery, London
1965 *The Responsive Eye,* Museum of Modern Art, New York (toured the United States)
1967 *Pittsburgh International,* Carnegie Institute, Pittsburgh
1968 *Cybernetic Serendipity,* Institute of Contemporary Arts, London
1969 *Systeemi,* Amos Andersonin Taidemuseo, Helsinki
1973 *Illusion in 20th Century Art,* University of Stirling, Scotland
1976 *System and Programme,* Palac Kultury i Nauki, Warsaw
1977 *Sul Concetto di Serie,* Museo Civico, Varese, Italy
1983 *Arte Programmata e Cinetica 1953–63,* Palazzo Reale, Milan
1986 *Arte e Scienza,* at the *42nd Biennale,* Venice

Collections:

Arts Council of Great Britain, London; British Council, London; Victoria and Albert Museum, London; Museum Boymans-van Beuningen, Rotterdam; Cabinet des Estampes, Geneva; Kunsthaus, Aarau, Switzerland; National Museum of Wales, Cardiff; Ateneum Art Museum, Helsinki; Museum Sztuki, Lodz, Poland.

Publications:

By STEELE: articles—"Towards a Non-Egocentric Art" in *ICA bulletin* (London), December 1966; "Statement of Kinetics" in *Studio International* (London), February 1967; "Cicerone" in *Anglo-Welsh Review* (Caerlean), Winter 1967; "Syntactic Art" in *Systeemi,* exhibition catalogue, Helsinki 1969; "Systems Theory and Syntactic Art" in *Systems,* exhibition catalogue, London 1972; "Structural Analysis of My Painting 'Solar Wind' " in *Review Integration* (Eschenau, West Germany), October 1972; "Note on My Current Work" in *Jeffrey Steele: Current Work,* exhibition catalogue, London 1974; "Note on the Relationship of Systematic-Constructivist Art to Architecture" in *Beispiele aus dem Grenzbereich Kunst-Architektur,* Berne 1975; "Portsmouth Fine Art Music" in *Experimental Music,* exhibition catalogue, by Gavin Bryars and Michael Nyman, London 1975; "Notes sur le Travail do Trevor Clarke" in *Media* (Neuchâtel, Switzerland), May 1976; "General Notes on Sg I . . . Drawings" in *Engelse en Nederlandse Rationele Tekeningen,* exhibition catalogue, Delft 1976; "Collaborative Work at Portsmouth" in *Studio International* (London), November/December 1976; "Core Conditions and Boundary Conditions" in *Artscribe* (London), July 1977; "The Identity Concept in the Constructive Context" in *Constructive Context* (London), 1978; "Notes Towards Some Theses Against the New Kitsch" in *Art Monthly* (London), July/August 1978; "Closing the Dossier on 'Pier and Ocean' " in *Art Monthly* (London), October 1980; "Vilification of Constructive Art" in *Art Monthly* (London), November 1982; "Die Kunstpraxis als Teil des grosseren Bereiches von linguistischer Praxis" in *Jeffrey Steele: Konkret Funf,* exhibition catalogue, Nuremberg 1985.

On STEELE: books—*Jeffrey Steele,* exhibition catalogue, by Sir Herbert Read, London 1964; *Jeffrey Steele,* exhibition catalogue, by Cyril Barrett, London 1966; *Optical Illusions and the Visual Arts* by Ronald G. Carracher and Jacqueline B. Thurston, New York and London 1966; *Constructivism* by

George Rickey, London 1967; *Op-Art* by Cyril Barrett, London 1969; *An Introduction to Optical Art* by Cyril Barrett, London 1971; *Introducing Op-Art* by John Lancaster, New York and London 1973; *Art since Pop* by John A. Walker, London 1975; *The Modern* by Terry Measham, Oxford 1976; *L'Ultima Avanguardia*, edited by Lea Vergine, Milan 1983; *Art & Science* by Ans van Berkum and Tom Blekkenhorst, Vlissingen 1986.

Since the year 1960 my general policy as an artist has been to attempt to instill a principle of necessity, to replace the subjective, contingent and random factors more normally associated with artistic production. This attempt has led to the elaboration of an appropriate formal system which, in conformity with the terminology used with the disciplines of semiology and linguistics, I call the *system* and designate "System Sy." Material works have the status of *representations* of this formal system in discrete states of its syntactic transformation, they stand in syntagmatic relation to it, and so I call them "Syntagms Sg" and number them in bureaucratic style: Sg I 1, Sg I 2, . . . Sg II 1, Sg III 1, 2, 3 and so forth.

Any given syntagm-figure is analysable into the momentary states of its component variables and each state of each variable is also given, as it is realized, an identifying number. I have found that this step-by-step method of research generates interesting data in the field of morphology, of topological connectivity, of serial and symmetry relations, etc.

Presentation of a sub-series of one or more of these syntagm-objects in a particular social context becomes a focus for cultural transactions; interaction amongst the sets of internal and external relations proper to the four different kinds of entity involved: the formal system, the material syntax, the percipient subject and the ideological state apparatus. A collective theoretical practice attempts to locate the content of these cultural transactions within a wider epistemological field.

—Jeffrey Steele

Jeffrey Steele is associated with a form of painting described as Systems. This, as its name implies, involves the use of some system in the construction of a picture.

There are two ways of using a system. One is to use it to generate some interesting visual image, but alter it in mid-stream, if it is not aesthetically satisfactory. The other, which is the course Steele follows, is to carry the system right through, and, if the result is aesthetically uninteresting, scrap it. Artistic control, thus, operates at the two ends, but not in the middle. There is a choice of system, and a verdict on the outcome of its use, but no tampering.

It may have been a coincidence, but Steele's early work had an optical-kinetic quality. He had been impressed by the work of Vasarely, though he felt that he had betrayed his original principles when, in the 1950's, he turned from black and white to colour and from art with optical pulsations to his more characteristic ambiguous figures, a kind of abstract Cubism.

Steele's own work in the 60's had great optical vibrancy. He, as so many other so-called Op artists, discovered to his surprise that by a regular repetition of forms he obtained this vibrancy unsolicited. What had motivated him in the late 50's was a desire to break with *tachisme*, "the individual artist's 'touch' or handwriting." He had been attracted to Neo-Plasticism and Constructivism, but was most impressed, while in Paris, with the work of Albers, Bill, Soto and Vasarely. But it was only on his return home that he hit on his own brand of optical effect.

The characteristic of his work in the 1960's was the intensification and movement of light which his structures induce. During this period he worked exclusively in black and white. The stark contrast of tones helped to enhance the luminous effect of his work. At times his pictures are rectilinear, as in "Divertissement" or "Lavolta." The first builds up to a great intensity of light in the centre; the second disperses light along its axes, and the light pulsates, and even rotates. But he was also producing curvilinear structures, such as "Baroque Experiment," a sort of limitless series of reflecting mirrors, slightly out of kilter, whose divergencies from the norm set up optical vibrations, of "Sub Rosa" which suggests the luminous flow of water.

Basically, however, Steele is concerned with structures. Even in those early paintings, such as "Divertissement" and "Lavolta," the structural element dominates: the hidden squares, the crossing axes, the undulations swimming against the current. In some cases these counter-structures are evident; in others they are so subtle as to escape the notice of the unperceptive.

In 1965 some of his paintings were used in fabric design, in particular a design for a bikini based on "Baroque Experiment." This was both flattering and embarrassing to Steele, particularly as a year later that same bikini was shown with the caption: "Take it off (this is last year's swimsuit)." This proves, if it proves anything, not that Steele's work at the time was ephemeral, but that fashion is fickle. The only ephemeral aspect of his work—the aspect which did not persist—is the optical effect, which was incidental anyway, even though it gave him public recognition. It was always his aim to counterbalance the optical effect.

In the late 60's Steele turned to colour and reverted entirely to his original interest in formal, as opposed to informal, structures. He developed an elaborate terminology to describe his systematic method of working, too elaborate to expound here. Each work is designated by a symbol (Sg) and a number: Sg I 1, I 2, etc. At present the symbol is Sg VI, but there is no reason why Steele should not revert to Sg I or Sg II which date from the early 1970's, and develop their possibilities further. An Sg (syntagm) is a material realization of a system (Sy) governed by operations, mappings, distributions, networks, syntaxes, etc. The terminology is drawn from linguistics. Steele believes that his systematic approach is a contribution to research in the field of morphology, topology, serial relations.

The earlier works put strong emphasis on the diagonal, and are very dynamic. The more recent works (Sg VI) consist of horizontal bands of rectangular areas of colour arranged on either side of a central axis, reminiscent of certain works of Lohse, for whom Steele has an undying admiration. They are imposing, even if they lack the dynamism and the over-lying structures of earlier works.

However interesting it may be to know the methods by which Steele arrives at his images, it is the images themselves which ultimately matter. Nevertheless the presence of an underlying structure based on a system makes itself felt if scarcely perceptibly: the visual stimulation is underwritten by a hidden order.

—D. C. Barrett

STEINBERG, Saul.

American. Born in Ramnicul-Sarat, near Bucharest, Rumania, 15 June 1914; emigrated to the United States, 1941: naturalised, 1943. Studied sociology and psychology at the University of Bucharest, 1932; studied architecture at the University of Milan, 1932. Served in the United States Navy, 1943–46. Cartoonist for *The New Yorker* since 1941; cartoons contributed to numerous other U.S. periodicals: his objects and drawings satirize contemporary society and the activity of making art. Artist-in-Residence, Smithsonian Institution, Washington, D.C., 1967. Agent: The Pace Gallery, New York. Address: c/o The Pace Gallery, 32 East 57th Street, New York, New York 10022, U.S.A.

Individual Exhibitions:

1943 Wakefield Gallery, New York
1945 Young Books Inc., New York
1948 Institute of Design, Chicago
1950 Rhode Island School of Design, Providence
Betty Parsons Gallery, New York
1951 Galleria l'Obelisco, Rome
1952 Galeria de Arte, São Paulo
Museu de Arte, São Paulo
Gump's Gallery, San Francisco
Institute of Contemporary Arts, London
Sidney Janis Gallery, New York
Kunsthalle, Wuppertal-Barmen, West Germany
Leopold-Hoesch-Museum, Düren, West Germany
Galleria l'Obelisco, Rome
Betty Parsons Gallery, New York
Frank Perls Gallery, Beverly Hills, California
1953 *Steinberg Drawings*, Arts Club of Chicago
Galerie Blanche, Stockholm
Galerie Maeght, Paris
Stedelijk Museum, Amsterdam
Virginia Museum of Fine Arts, Richmond
1954 Corcoran Gallery of Art, Washington, D.C.
Dallas Museum of Fine Arts
Museum am Ostwall, Dortmund, West Germany
Kunstkabinett, Frankfurt
Kestner-Gesellschaft, Hannover
Kunstmuseum, Basel
Santa Barbara Museum, California
1955 Harvard School of Design, Cambridge, Massachusetts
1956 Allan Frumkin Gallery, Chicago
1957 Institute of Contemporary Arts, London
1959 Musée d'Art Moderne, Brussels
1962 University of California at Santa Barbara
1965 Davison Art Center, Wesleyan University, Middletown, Connecticut
1966 Sidney Janis Gallery, New York
Galerie Maeght, Paris
Betty Parsons Gallery, New York
Wallraf-Richartz-Museum, Cologne
1967 B. C. Holland Gallery, Chicago
Museum Boymans-van Beuningen, Rotterdam
Obelisk Gallery, Boston
Aquarelles, Dessins et Collages 1955–1967, Musées Royaux des Beaux-Arts, Brussels
1968 Museo de Bellas Artes, Caracas
Zeichnungen und Collagen, Kunsthalle, Hamburg
Irving Galleries, Milwaukee
Louisiana Museum, Humlebaek, Denmark
Moderna Museet, Stockholm
1969 J. L. Hudson Gallery, Detroit
Sidney Janis Gallery, New York
Betty Parsons Gallery, New York
1970 Felix Landau Gallery, Los Angeles
1971 Richard Gray Gallery, Chicago
Ölbilder, Gouachen, Zeichnungen, Galerie Maeght, Zurich
1973 Galleria Galatea, Milan
Sidney Janis Gallery, New York
Galerie Maeght, Paris
Betty Parsons Gallery, New York
Steinberg at the Smithsonian, National Collection of Fine Arts, Smithsonian Institution, Washington, D.C.
1974 Institute of Contemporary Art, Boston
Galerie Maeght, Paris
Zeichnungen, Aquarelie, Collagen, Gemalde, Reliefs 1963–74, Kölnischer Kunstverein, Cologne (exhibition travelled throughout Germany and to Vienna)
1976 Sidney Janis Gallery, New York
Betty Parsons Gallery, New York
1977 Galerie Maeght, Paris and Zurich
1978 Whitney Museum, New York (retrospective; travelled to the Hirshhorn Museum, Smithsonian Institution, Washington, D.C.; Serpentine Gallery, London; and Fondation Maeght, St.-Paul-de-Vence, France)
1982 The Pace Gallery, New York
1983 Waddington Galleries, London
1986 Galerie Maeght Lelong, Paris
1987 Pace Gallery, New York

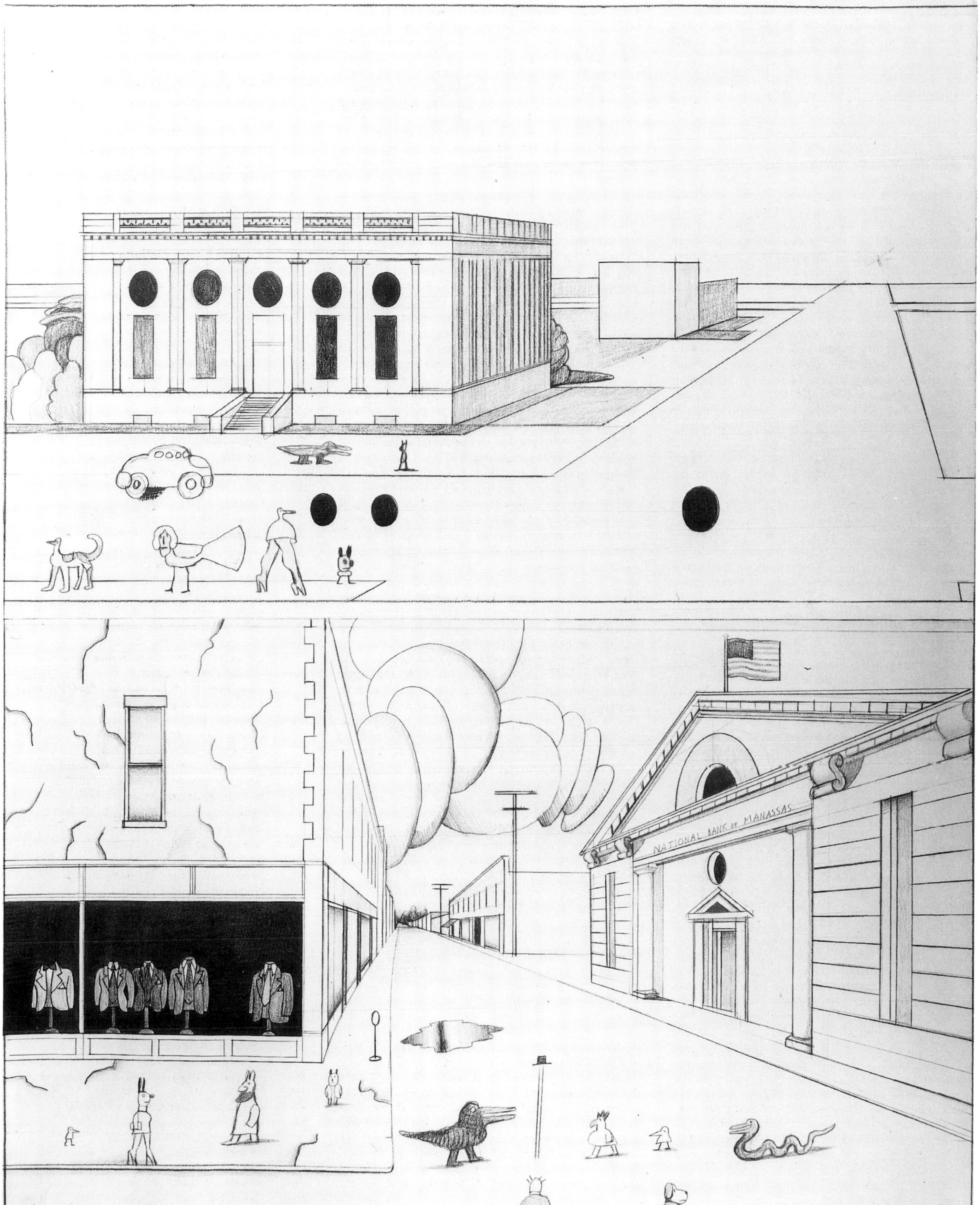

Saul Steinberg: ***Main Street, Manassas, Virginia*, 1978**

Selected Group Exhibitions:

1946 *14 Americans*, Museum of Modern Art, New York
1949 *An Exhibition for Modern Living*, Detroit Institute of Arts
1952 *Contemporary Drawings from 12 Countries 1945–1952*, Art Institute of Chicago
1954 *The Roy and Marie Neuberger Collection*, Whitney Museum, New York
1962 *American Drawing Annual XIX*, Norfolk Museum of Arts and Sciences, Virginia
1970 *L'Art Vivant aux États-Unis*, Fondation Maeght, St.-Paul-de-Vence, France
1971 *7 Enormously Popular American Artists*, Corcoran Gallery of Art, Washington, D.C.
1973 *American Drawing 1970–1973*, Yale University Art Gallery, New Haven, Connecticut
1974 *American Artists*, Cleveland Museum of Art
1977 *American Drawing 1927–1977*, Minnesota Museum of Art, St. Paul

Collections:

Museum of Modern Art, New York; Metropolitan Museum of Art, New York; Albright-Knox Art Gallery, Buffalo, New York; Fogg Museum, Harvard University, Cambridge, Massachusetts,; Detroit Institute of Arts; Victoria and Albert Museum, London.

Publications:

By STEINBERG: books—*All in Line*, New York 1945; *The Art of Living*, New York 1949; *The Passport*, New York 1954; *Steinberg's Umgang mit Menschen*, Hamburg 1954; *Dessins*, Paris 1956; *The Labyrinth*, New York 1960; *The Catalogue*, Cleveland 1962; *Steinberg's Paperback*, Hamburg 1964; *The New World*, New York 1965; *Le Masque*, with texts by Michel Butor and Harold Rosenberg, Paris 1966; *The Inspector*, New York 1973; articles—"Life in the Guatavir Line" in *Life* (New York), May 1940; "Mottoes Illustrated" in *Harper's* (New York), August 1946; "Recapitulation" in *Architectural Review* (London), December 1950; "Italy: Drawings" in *Harper's* (New York), February 1952; "Built in U.S.A.: Postwar Architecture, 1945–52" in *Artnews* (New York), February 1953; "Steinberg at the Bat" in *Life* (New York), 11 June 1955; "Drawings of Athens" in *Harper's* (New York), February 1956; "Steinberg U.S.A." in *Harper's* (New York), September 1960; "Statements and Documents" in *Daedalus* (New York), Winter 1960; "The Nose Problem" in *Location* (New York), Spring 1963; "Our False-Front Culture" in *Look* (New York), 9 January 1968.

On STEINBERG: books—*14 Americans*, exhibition catalogue, edited by Dorothy Miller, New York 1946; *Saul Steinberg*, exhibition catalogue, London 1952; *Saul Steinberg*, exhibition catalogue, Amsterdam 1953; *The Roy and Marie Neuberger Collection*, exhibition catalogue, New York 1954; *Steinberg*, exhibition catalogue, by Alfred Hentzen, Hannover 1954; *Conversations with Artists*, introduced by Alexander Eliot, New York 1961; *Steinberg Aquarelles, Dessins et Collages 1955–1967*, exhibition catalogue, Brussels 1967; *Steinberg*, exhibition catalogue, by Pierre Baudson, Rotterdam 1967; *Steinberg: Zeichnungen und Collagen*, exhibition catalogue, by Helmut Leppien, Pierre Baudson and Manuel Gasser, with an interview by André Parinaud, Hamburg 1968; *Saul Steinberg oder Philosophie der Zeichnung* by Franz Wittkamp, Mainz 1971; *Steinberg: Ölbilder, Gouachen, Zeichnungen*, exhibition catalogue, by Manuel Gasser, Zurich 1971; *Steinberg at the Smithsonian*, exhibition ctalogue, by John Hollander, Washington, D.C. 1973; *Saul Steinberg: Zeichnungen, Aquarelle, Collagen, Gemälde, Reliefs 1963–74*, exhibition catalogue, Cologne 1974; *Here at the New Yorker* by Brendan Gill, New York 1975; *The New Yorker Album of Drawings 1925–1975*, New York 1975; *American Drawings 1927–1977*, exhibition catalogue, by Paul Cummings, St. Paul, Minnesota 1977; *Saul Steinberg*, exhibition catalogue, by Harold Rosenberg, New York 1978; *Saul Steinberg: repères*, exhibition catalogue with introduction by Jean Fremon, Paris 1986; *Saul Steinberg's Gift*, exhibition catalogue with text by Adam Gopnik, New York 1987.

For many years Saul Steinberg has been placed in limbo by critics and the public, but the retrospective held at the Whitney Museum in 1978 must finally have confirmed him to be an artist rather than a cartoonist.

Steinberg's style is completely original. Noises, jokes, puns pervade his work. American society is made up of robots, mickey mouse ladies, growling dogs, majorettes and eagles. New York seems to envelop the world in the famous *New York* poster; Siberia appears only a few inches away. Buildings and monuments tower above the "little men." This recurrent figure reminds one of Chaplin in *Modern Times* and Meursault in *L'étranger.* Somehow things happen to these men; they do not have the power to form their own destiny. In "Graph Paper Building" the skyscraper dwarfs the tiny stick figures and the stucco buildings—it is an ugly, unnecessary intrusion. However, in "Piazza San Marco, Venice" the Italians inhabiting the pen and ink square scream and fight one another, while the tourists merely look at the architecture, never at each other.

From the paintings bursting with characters, Steinberg also goes on to draw individuals. The army man sits at a table and casually removes his nose. Simple immaculate lines convey this action; they are stamped with Steinberg's seal of officialdom. A minute horseman is chased by a massive boulder, which in turn is hounded by a crocodile down a steep hill. An outrageous situation—but one still hopes that the lone horseman will survive. One of my favourite and equally "crazy" paintings is "March-April 1966." Specific segments of land represent one month, and the cat/man bicycles across the bridge from March to April. The concept is witty and charming. Steinberg's vision of a taxi cab made up of crooked lines cannot help but give delight.

Among the most sombre but at the same time most exquisite paintings are "Anatolia" (1973) and "Camp II" (1960). In the former miniscule figures stare out at the horizon whose blue sky is interrupted by few clouds. Although the setting is perfect, there is a sense of doom, just as in *Waiting for Godot* one expects an explosion. In the latter the Camp is reminiscent of concentration camps, solid black towers dwarfing helpless people. "Kisumu", "Kunming", "Eastern Sunsets" and "African Postcards" have similar atmosphere and quality because of the free flowing watercolour technique.

Steinberg can paint with the eye of a child, producing simple yet ingenious pen and ink riddles, then in another moment paint landscapes that possess the beauty of Turner inhabited by the figures of Dali. He is a talented and deeply human painter.

—Carine Maurice

STELLA, Frank.

American. Born in Malden, Massachusetts, 12 May 1936. Studied painting, under Patrick Morgan, Phillips Academy, Andover, Massachusetts; under William Seitz and Stephen Greene, Princeton University, New Jersey. Married Barbara Rose in London, 1960 (divorced); children: Rachel and Michael. Painter: has lived and worked in New York since 1958. Artist-in-Residence, Dartmouth College, Hanover, New Hampshire, 1963; rejected Artist-in-Residence position, University of California at Irvine, by refusing to sign State's Loyalty Oath, 1965; Lecturer, Yale University, New Haven, Connecticut, 1965; Visiting Critic, Cornell University, Ithaca, New York, 1965; Art instructor, University of Saskatchewan, Saskatoon, Summer 1967, and Brandeis University, Waltham, Massachusetts, 1968. Recipient: First Prize, *International Biennial Exhibition of Paintings*, Tokyo, 1967. Agent: M. Knoedler and Company, 19 East 70th Street, New York, New York 10021. Address: 17 Jones Street, New York, New York 10013, U.S.A.

Individual Exhibitions:

1960 Leo Castelli Gallery, New York
1961 Galerie Lawrence, Paris
1962 Leo Castelli Gallery, New York
1963 Ferus Gallery, Los Angeles
Leo Castelli Gallery, New York
1964 Galerie Lawrence, Paris
Kasmin Gallery, London
Leo Castelli Gallery, New York
1965 Ferus Gallery, Los Angeles
3 American Painters, Harvard University, Cambridge, Massachusetts
1966 Leo Castelli Gallery, New York
Kasmin Gallery, London
David Mirvish Gallery, Toronto
Pasadena Art Museum, California
1967 Douglas Gallery, Vancouver
Seattle Art Museum
Galerie Bischofberger, Zurich
Leo Castelli Gallery, New York
1968 Gallery of Modern Art, Washington, D.C.
Kasmin Gallery, London
David Mirvish Gallery, Toronto
New Gallery, Bennington College, Vermont
Harcus-Krakow Gallery, Boston
Irving Blum Gallery, Los Angeles
1969 Leo Castelli Gallery, New York
Irving Blum Gallery, Los Angeles
University of Puerto Rico, Mayaguez
Recent Paintings, Rose Art Museum, Brandeis University, Waltham, Massachusetts
1970 Museum of Modern Art, New York
Hayward Gallery, London
1971 Lawrence Rubin Gallery, New York
1973 Leo Castelli Gallery, New York
1974 DM Gallery, London
Knoedler Gallery, New York
1975 Castelli Downtown Gallery, New York
Galerie Daniel Templon, Paris
Janie C. Lee Gallery, Houston
1976 Galerie André Emmerich, Zurich
Kunstmuseum, Basle
Sears Bank, Chicago
Koedler Contemporary Art, New York
David Mirvish Gallery, Toronto
B. R. Kornblatt Gallery, Baltimore
1977 Galerie M, Bochum, West Germany
Baltimore Museum of Art
Städtisches Kunsthaus, Bielefeld, West Germany
Museum of Modern Art, Oxford
Linda Farris Gallery, Seattle
Koedler Gallery Ltd., London
1978 School of Visual Arts, New York
Fort Worth Art Center, Texas (retrospective; toured the United States)
1979 Museum of Modern Art, New York
Brandeis University, Waltham, Massachusetts
Galerie Valeur, Nagoya, Japan
1980 Galerie 99, Bay Harbor Islands, Florida
1981 University of Arizona, Tucson
Swope Art Gallery, Terre Haute, Indiana
John C. Stoller, Minneapolis
M. Knoedler Company, New York
1982 Akira Ikeda Gallery, Tokyo
Leo Castelli Gallery, New York
Prints 1967–82, University of Michigan, Ann Arbor (toured the United States, 1982–85)
1983 Galerie Knoedler, Zurich
Akira Ikeda Gallery, Tokyo
San Francisco Museum of Modern Art
1985 M. Knoedler and Company, New York
Knoedler Kasmin Ltd., London
Greenberg Gallery, St. Louis
1986 Akira Ikeda Gallery, Tokyo
1987 Museum of Modern Art, New York
1988 L.A. Louver Gallery, Venice, California

Selected Group Exhibitions:

1964 *Biennale*, Venice
1965 *Bienal*, Sao Paulo
1966 *New Shapes of Colour*, Stedelijk Museum, Amsterdam
1969 *New York Painting and Sculpture 1940–70*, Museum of Modern Art, New York
1970 *Biennale*, Venice

Frank Stella: *C-Type*, 1984 Courtesy Museum of Contemporary Art, Chicago

1974 *Prints from Gemini G.E.L.*, Walker Art Center, Minneapolis (toured the United States)
1976 *20th Century American Drawing*, Guggenheim Museum, New York
1978 *Art about Art*, Whitney Museum, New York
1985 *Painterly Visions 1940–84*, Guggenheim Museum, New York
1988 *Contemporary American Art*, Sara Hilden Art Museum, Tampere, Finland (travelled to Oslo)

Collections:

Museum of Modern Art, New York; Whitney Museum, New York; Albright-Knox Art Gallery, Buffalo, New York; Walker Art Center,Minneapolis; Art Institute of Chicago; San Francisco Museum of Modern Art; Centre Georges Pompidou, Paris; Kaiser Wilhelm Museum, Krefeld, West Germany; Stedelijk Museum, Amsterdam; Stedelijk van Abbemuseum, Eindhoven, Netherlands.

Publications:

On STELLA: books—*3 American Painters*, exhibition catalogue, by Michael Fried, Cambridge, Massachusetts, April 1965; *Recent Paintings by Frank Stella*, exhibition catalogue, by William Seitz, Waltham, Massachusetts 1969; *Frank Stella*, exhibition catalogue, Amsterdam 1979; *Frank Stella*, exhibition catalogue, by William S. Rubin, New York 1970; *Frank Stella* by Robert Rosenblum, London 1971: *Frank Stella Prints 1967–1982*, catalogue raisonne by Richard H. Axsom, Ann Arbor 1982; *Frank Stella: Working Space*, Cambridge, Massachusetts 1986; *Frank Stella 1970–1987*, exhibition ctalogue with text by William Rubin, New York 1987.

When he had his first one-man show in New York in 1960, Frank Stella at 24 was not yet committed to a programme of irreversible iconoclasm. From his "Island" paintings of 1958 it was possible to detect some of the polarisation that had been effected by Jasper Johns in the large striped canvases and their enclosed square of pure colour. This welcome move away from the random impulses of Abstract Expressionism seen in de Kooning and Kline decided the subsequent moves on the board for Stella. Of the 1960 "Black Paintings," the emphasis was linear; metallic paints tracing enclosures of geometric shapes in large formats. The to-and-froing of the lines in parallel was given some rapid change of pace by stepping and switching through right angles to which the canvas stretcher was trimmed. These massive plans, hung vertically, had their strong two-dimensional presences as much by their rejection of the conventional shape of the support as their integration with mural space, using and adjusting to it as complementary to each work's internal proportions.

About 1962 the relative reticence of the stripes expanded so they became bands of pure and semi-transparent colour edged in white. Recession was accomplished by slightly varying the apex height of adjacent pyramids each formed by four triangles laid side by side. This contrast in colour none the less maintained the integrity of the plane. Other hexagonal motives divided by bands of colour retained their adhesion to the surface level.

Stella's arrowhead paintings of 1964, though large in scale, sacrifice something of their architectural integration in their green grounds hatched by light-toned metallic lines.

Up to 1965, the overall shape of the stretcher had decided the parallel of the design within it, but from here Stella alternated the important elements of the picture against a pure ground with a negative profile created from the shaping of the ground itself.

This return to the internal stresses of abstract cut-out shapes placed a greater strain on the applied colour weights, not only for themselves but for their contrapuntal effect on the wall against which they hung. The inverted V's and diagonally based triangles, cutting into a square as an off-centre Z, had the fragmenting dislocation of the plane to contend with, though here (as in all Stella's works) the flatness of the synthetic hues, together with the occasional use of fluorescent paint, preserves the integrity of surface in a bland non-reflective total.

By the early 1970's Stella had won an assured command of his means, often within both tall and wide formats of rectangular plan on which circles and hemispheres and wide band arcs performed progressive ballets on the one plane. Colours switched values as the eyes moved across the composition, and one colour area would merge irrevocably into its neighbour.

Interrelationships of parallel forms and complementary colours are conditions at the heart of Stella's statement, moving yet seeming static, monumental though momentarily in flux.

G. S. Whittet

STEPHENSON, Ian.

British. Born in Browney, near Meadowfield, County Durham, 11 January 1934. Early education in Blyth, Northumberland; studied, under Lawrence Gowing, King Edward VII School of Art, King's College, University of Durham, Newcastle upon Tyne, 1951–56, B.A. 1956 (Hatton Scholar, 1955–56; Art Editor, *Northerner* student magazine, 1955–57); Lecturer and Studio Demonstrator, King's College, 1956–58; designed, with Victor Pasmore, *The Developing Process*, a basic pedagogic course dedicated to a new creativity in art; Boise Scholar (University of London), in Italy, 1958–59. Married Kate Brown in 1959; children: Stephen and Stella. Painter: shared studio with Richard Hamilton, Newcastle upon Tyne, 1956–58; lived in London, 1959–66; participated in the film *Cubism and After*, BBC, London, 1962; contributed to the film, *Blow-Up*, by Michelangelo Antonioni, Metro-Goldwyn-Mayer, 1966; lived in Newcastle upon Tyne, 1966–70; abandoned easel painting for mural-scale abstracts on sectional canvases, 1966–70; returned London, 1970. Visiting Lecturer in Extempore Studies, London Polytechnic School of Art, 1959–62; Visiting Lecturer in Basic Design, and later in Painting, Chelsea School of Art, London, 1959–66; Director of Foundation Studies, Department of Fine Art, University of Newcastle, 1966–70. Director of Master's Degree Postgraduate Painting, Chelsea School of Art, since 1970. International Course Leader, Voss Summer School of Fine Arts, Norway, 1979. Member: Visual Arts Panel, Northern Arts Association, Newcastle upon Tyne, 1967–70; Fine Art Panel, National Council for Diplomas in Art and Design, London, 1972–74; Permanent Committee, New Contemporaries Association, London, 1973–75; Fine Art Board and Specialist Adviser, Council for National Academic Awards, London, 1974–75, 1980–83; Selection Juror, *British Painting Exhibition*, Hayward Gallery, London, 1974; Advisory Committee, *National Exhibition of Children's Art*, Manchester, since 1975; Working Party, *Jubilee Exhibition*, Royal Academy of Art, London, 1976–77; Selection Committee, Arts Council Awards, London, 1977. Recipient: Junior Section Prize, *John Moore's Exhibition*, Liverpool, 1957; Gulbenkian Foundation Purchase Award, London, 1960; Marzotto International Selection Prize, 1964; First Prize, *Northern Painters Exhibition*, Newcastle upon Tyne, 1966; Gold Medal and Diploma of Merit, Accademia Italia and Universita delle Arti, Parma, Italy, 1980–81. Honorary Member: Mark Twain Society, Missouri, 1978; Painting Faculty, British School, Rome, 1978; Contemporary Art Society, London, 1980; Accademia Italia delle Arti, Parma, Italy, 1980. Associate, 1975, Royal Academician, 1986, Royal Academy of Arts, London. Address: 49 Elm Park Gardens, London SW10 9PA, England.

Individual Exhibitions:

1958 New Vision Centre, London
1962 New Art Centre, London
1964 New Art Centre, London
1968 New Art Centre, London
1970 Laing Art Gallery, Newcastle upon Tyne
Laing Art Gallery, Newcastle upon Tyne (with John Martin)
1975 Hester van Royen Gallery, London
1977 *Paintings 1955–66 and 1966–77,* Hayward Gallery, London (toured the U.K.)
New Art Centre, London
1978 City Art Gallery, Birmingham (toured Wales)
1981 Editions Alecto, London
1983 Geolfrith Gallery, Sunderland
1985 Royal Academy, London
1987 Young Gallery, Salisbury, Wiltshire

Selected Group Exhibitions:

1964 *Mostra du Pittura Contemporanea,* Comunità Europea Club Unione, Valdagno, Italy (toured Europe)
1969 *Recent British Painting,* Tate Gallery, London (and world tour, 1969–75)
1973 *Recente Britse Tekenkunst,* Koninklijk Museum, Antwerp (toured West Germany)
1975 *Desenhos Britanicos Contemporaneos,* Museu de Arte Moderna, Sao Paulo (toured South America and Near East, 1975–82)
1976 *Arte Inglese Oggi 1960–1976,* Palazzo Reale, Milan
1977 *Color en la Pintura Britanica,* Museu de Arte Moderna, Rio de Janeiro (and world tour, 1977–83)
1981 *Deck of Cards,* British Council Gallery, Athens (toured the Greek Islands and Arabia)
1982 *Een Keuze uit de Hedendaagse Britse Kunst,* BP Gallery, Brussels
1983 *Mednarodni Bienale Grafike,* Moderna Galerija, Liubliana, Yugoslavia
1985 *Three Decades of British Painting 1946–72,* Turner House, Penarth, Wales

Collections:

Tate Gallery, London; Victoria and Albert Museum, London; Arts Council of Great Britain, London; Hatton Gallery, Newcastle upon Tyne; Whitworth Art Gallery, Manchester; Hunterian Museum and Art Gallery, University of Glasgow; National Museum of Wales, Cardiff; National Gallery of Victoria, Melbourne; Madison Art Center, Wisconsin.

Publications:

By STEPHENSON: articles—"Statements" in *Studio International* (London), September 1967; "Explanatory Note: Paintings 1968–79" in *Ian Stephenson,* exhibition catalogue, Newcastle upon Tyne 1970; "Remarks" in *One Magazine* (London), April 1974; "Correspondence: Without Recourse" in *Art Monthly* (London), November 1981.

On STEPHENSON: books—*Contemporary British Art* by Herbert Read, London 1964; *Private View* by John Russell, Bryan Robertson and Lord Snowdon, London 1965; *Adventure in Art,* edited by Hendrik Scheepmaker, New York 1969; *Ian Stephenson,* exhibition catalogue, by Andrew Forge, Newcastle upon Tyne 1970; *Ian Stephenson: Paintings 1955–56 and 1966–77,* exhibition catalogue, by William Feaver, London 1977; *Ian Stephenson: Ionic Variation Paintings on Paper 1961–1977* by Andrea Rose, Birmingham 1978; *Tendenze e Testimonianze dell'Arte Contemporanea,* edited by Nicolo Panepinto, Parma 1983.

Ian Stephenson, it seems, is hardly capable of laying paint on flat. Everything that he has done, from his earliest tentative studies to the 12 foot canvases, has in common a stippled surface. It is an obsession, and as such it is rooted at a far deeper level than the specialized preoccupations of a particular year. It is not, one might guess, just the consequence of a stylistic decision but the reflection of some ancient relationship, essential not only to his view of painting but of the world itself.

There are areas in his paintings—particularly the latest—where the numberless particles of paint are massed at random. The canvas is covered with layer upon layer of dots; individual colour differences are absorbed in the tonality of the mass. One is confronted by a cloud, spongy, shifting. We recognize sensations of distance—and its opposite as when with closed lids we contemplate the warm veiled greys and shifting points and sparks that are all one can see with one's eyes shut. There are no stepping stones in these last pictures, no anchorages with spaces in between. All is filled. All is void.

There is an analogy here with the filmy fields of Rothko. But the differences are extremely significant. When in front of a Rothko and one moves in close, the colour wraps round more closely. The expreience is heightened. The surface of the picture is a surface of semi-transparent colour, closer, more enveloping. Here, though, with Stephenson, the surface is not the same. The picture changes scale as one draws into it. The surface resolves itself into thousands and thousands of dots which one is far more clearly aware of outside oneself—at a distance—than before. To the oceanic sensations of the whole is added an awareness of multitude, sharpness, and the minute structure that the eye unravels in each inch of paint. The transitions from "cloud" to "myriad" and back again is available at will. There is no "correct" view of it.

Compare these paintings with the images on a TV screen, a newsprint photograph or a mezzotint. In all these cases the lines or dots are functional; in moving "in" to examine the system or "out" to read the image, we are crossing a distinct threshold in the quality of our attention. This journey does not span either/or alternatives: the work is a totality and each movement we make is an enlargement of our relationship to it, and indeed uncovers new dimensions of the subject-matter. The point is that the image is the upshot of how it is made.

This complexity is typical of the way Stephenson relates to painting himself: painting, one feels, encompasses a multiplicity of experience, widely contrasting sensations stemming from the same source, untrammelled choice. His pictures are the opposite of one-shot. They are difficult, demanding close and varied attention. There is much of the pedagogue in him, a tendency towards extreme conceptualization which shows particularly in some of the "Spray Studies," which are like laboratory demonstrations. At the same time doubt is always present, and the techniques and programmes he devises for himself are invariably open, wayward and humorous even, with room for endless speculation and revision. His ideas are rigorous; the processes they set in motion are subject to infinite nuance.

—Andrew Forge

STEVENSON, Harold.

American. Born in Idabel, Oklahoma, 11 March 1929. Studied at the University of Oklahoma, Norman; University of Mexico, Mexico City; and Art Students League, New York. Established residence in Paris, 1959; studio in Idabel, 1965; now lives in Long Island City, New York. Agent: Keith Green Gallery, 500 Park Avenue, New York, New York 10022. Address: 21-14 45th Avenue, Long Island City, New York 11101, U.S.A.

Individual Exhibitions:

1949 Hugo Gallery, New York
University of Oklahoma, Oklahoma City
Oklahoma Art Center, Oklahoma City
1958 Hugo Gallery, New York
1960 Galerie La Cour d'Ingres, Paris
1962 *Le Sensuel Fantastique,* Galerie Iris Clert, Paris
The Human Telescope, Robert Fraser Gallery, London
1963 *Adam Retrouvé,* Galerie Iris Clert, Paris
1964 Richard Feigen Gallery, New York (travelled to the Feigen Galleries in Chicago and Los Angeles)

Ian Stephenson: ***Ceolfrith Caper*****, 1984**

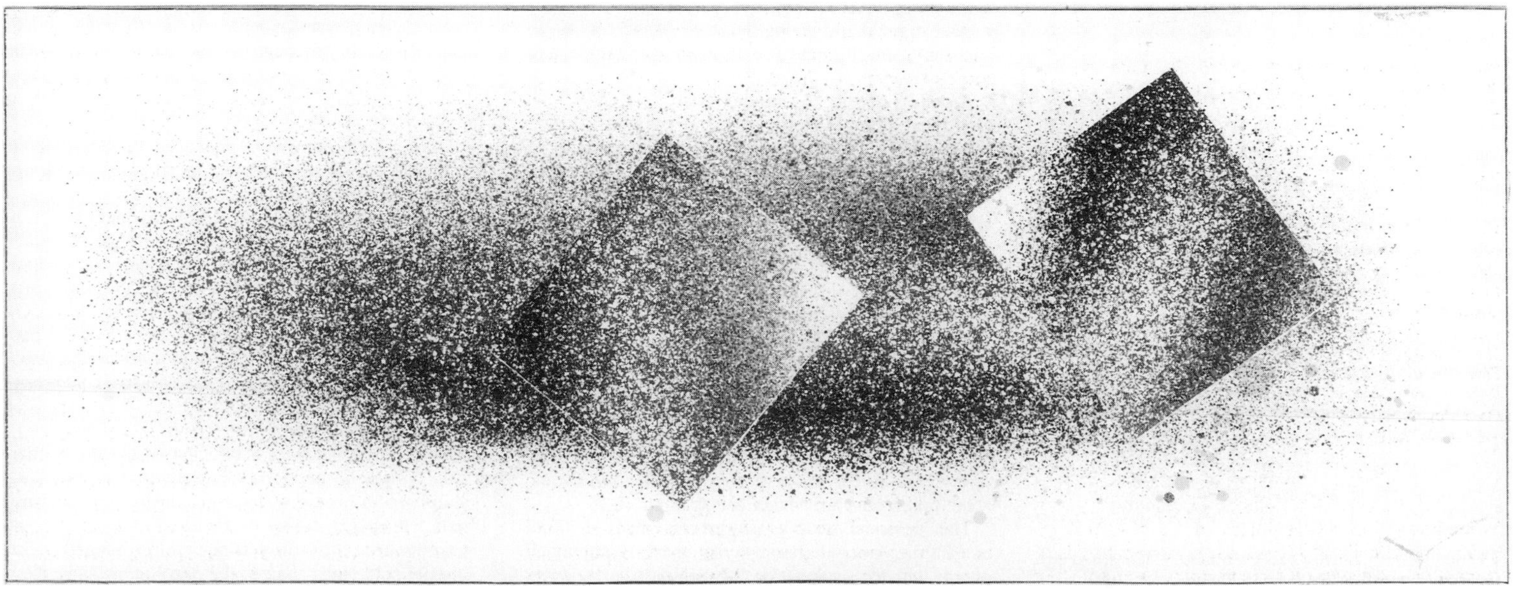

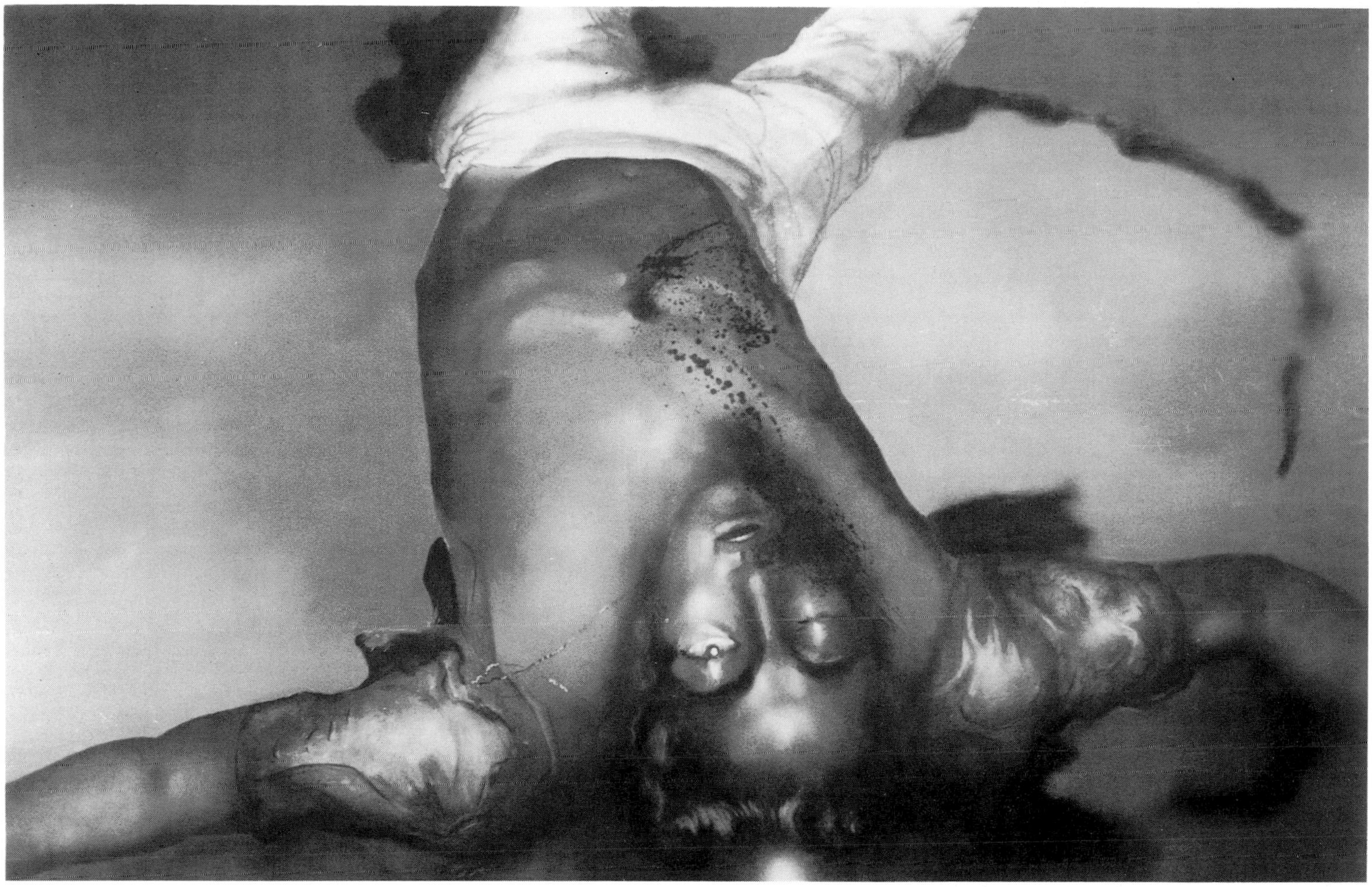

Harold Stevenson: ***Death at Tom*** **(*Memorial to Lightning Billy*), 1977**

1965 *The Idabel Paintings,* Alexander Iolas Gallery, New York
1968 *The Great Society,* Galerie Iris Clert, Paris
La Chasse, Galerie Iris Clert, Paris
1969 Galerie Hake, Kolo, West Germany
1970 Galleria La Medusa, Rome
1972 Alexander Iolas Gallery, New York
1973 Alexander Iolas Gallery, New York
Galleria La Medusa, Rome
ARA Pacis, Galerie Alexandre Iolas, Paris
Zoumboulakis Gallery, Athens
1974 *Black Fates,* Alexander Iolas Gallery, New York
1975 *Votives and Greek Themes,* Brooks Jackson-Iolas Gallery, New York
1976 *La Victoire and Death of the American Dream,* Brooks Brooks-Iolas Gallery, New York
1979 Galerie Iris Clert, Paris

Selected Group Exhibitions:

1962 *Piccola Biennale,* Venice
Annual Exhibition, Whitney Museum, New York
1965 *Pop Art,* Palais des Beaux-Arts, Brussels
1966 *Erotic Art '66,* Sidney Janis Gallery, New York
1968 *The Obsessive Image,* Institute of Contemporary Arts, London
Prospect '68, Dusseldorf
1972 *Pop Art,* Alexander Iolas Gallery, New York
1979 *Americans in Paris,* Centre Georges Pompidou, Paris
La Famille des Portraits, Musée du Louvre, Paris

Collections:

Whitney Museum, New York; Musée Nationale d'Art Moderne/Centre Georges Pompidou, Paris.

Publications:

On STEVENSON: books—*Pop Art* by Lucy Lippard, New York 1966; *Iris-Time* by Iris Clert, Paris 1978; *Le Milieu de l'Art,* with photographs by André Morain, Paris 1978; film—*Harold* by Andy Warhol, 1964.

My particular search for the spirit of Alexander began in Paris about 20 years ago, and by the late 1960's I had made several Alexander paintings. Iris Clert showed some of them, the Empress Farah Diba bought one, and after those first pictures dealing with the known historic images but making them monumental in scale and giving the stone likenessess flesh-like qualities, I found the problem got bigger and more evasive.

Brooks Jackson, Alexander Iolas, Iris Clert, and Bruni and Allen in Rome all asked for more Alexander pictures. They would be a long time coming. I had scratched the surface out of love and devotion, and to probe deeper meant a far more extensive involvement than I had ever anticipated.

In thinking back, I realize that I may have always been in love with the legend of Alexander the Great. The antique Greek world was dear to me even in my childhood; I knew instinctively what inspired Isadora Duncan; the ideal beauty of man seemed the most natural demand one should make; I dreamt of those ideals of beauty, freedom, democracy, diplomacy, fraternal passions, fidelity of the spirit . . . and all those gestures that inspired love in soldiers, jealousy in statesmen, fear in kings, insanity in the inner circle. Everyone I have ever loved personally has had for me some touch of Alexandrian beauty.

The personal search (in art) is such a time-consuming, over-all passion that there is not much energy left for explanations. I wouldn't be trying to say words now except out of a kind of frustration . . . I couldn't find anyone to capsule these many years.

How awkward it seems now after years of close association to place Alexander back into history. He is still so avant-garde, so modern, so untouched by the neurosis of our Judeo-Christian system (our system still wants to make him out to have been an alcoholic in need of a psychiatrist . . . how ludicrous!). It would appear to me that he is the model for men of the future; a man who dared to live his own singular destiny. What are all our worthless lives today amounting to? We conform, consume, take vitamins, get passports, vote, end up in nursing homes, die with social security numbers around our necks. The god-like quality of men is somehow lost in this conformist existence. Aristotle did not teach Alexander how to conquer the world; he taught him how to think.

I am a non-decorative painter; I do not paint to decorate anyone's existence, much less his "living room," nor do I paint for museums. My work is a matter of passion, and to live with my pictures means you have to live with my passion (in front of you). I am an old lover of Alexander, and what I don't understand about him does not make me love him less. Maybe I will understand him more in the future. Or, as one dear friend said shortly before he died, "I have loved you in this life, and I will love you in the next."

—Harold Stevenson

Alone, adrift, he rides across the vast plain in anarchic pursuit of the world's exploiters: moneylenders, shopkeepers, lawyers, bankers, businessmen, criminals. He stands outside of the law, feet apart, dressed to pronounce his virility, trigger-finger hungrily grazing the cold metal shaft of the pistol at his side. He is

the self-appointed nemesis to the injustices hiding in the legal system. He is Outlaw, he is Hero, he is a killer who enters battles to affirm his manhood through symbolic sexual rituals. Death and violence alone satisfy him. He is the Cowboy. He is a myth.

The Cowboy, a palpably sexual image—more accurately homosexual, derived as a response to the increasing confusion in sexual roles and male identity produced by industrialization and urbanization in America during the first decades of this century. Sensing his control over his own life weakening—indeed his masculine mastery and command, the American male created the Cowboy—a figure of super-masculinity and individual power—to combat his feelings of alienation. Harold Stevenson is one of the few American artists to recognize the myth's tenacious grip over the American imagination. His paintings comment on the continuing inability in the American male to reconcile what he would like to be with what he really is. Under the weight of his own inadequacies he is crushed, crushed by the compensatory myth of the Cowboy. Since the '50s Stevenson has been analysing and translating the physical and psychological consequence onto canvas, delivering a shocking, pornographic, sometimes unrecognizable portrait of the human condition as it really is.

Stevenson was born in a part of America that less than a century ago was populated by Indians until pioneers—among them an older generation of Stevenson's family—slaughtered and drove them from the land with fierce weapons. To this day his small home town, Idabel, Oklahoma remains a vacant, lonely region haunted by the memory of racial murder. Furthermore, for the few whites who live there, it is a land of alienation, one with no native history, for the rich oral culture of the Indians was forever lost through racial indifference and contempt. Consequentially, Stevenson relied on various foreign sources to provide the settings for his paintings. Of these he favoured the Roman or Greece warrior in classical form, for he could imbue it with all the sexual longing and the violence endemic to the Southwest of his boyhood.

Idabel, Oklahoma was the topic of his 1967 painting *The Great Society* which consisted of one hundred faces of various townspeople. The faces are a metaphor for the human race, the faces alienated from their bodies as Americans are from the land they possess. The artist blatantly avoids the townspeople's sexuality, seeing them rather as he did as a boy. For growing up in Idabel his own sexuality was denied, repressed, something sinful, which, because of this repression, is why sensuality is the exuberant force behind the majority of his work. *The Great Society,* however, invites no sexual fantasy, the bodies covered and their sexual energy passed forever like dead men. These are his people: once filled with the drive and excitement of violence, now repressed, anti-sexual, unfeeling, defeated.

Nearly all of Stevenson's paintings celebrate the relationship between male sexuality, violence and death. Part of the early romanticization of the male involved an intimacy between the three. And since the Cowboy is the preeminent symbol of masculinity in American culture, violence and death itself took on sexual attributes. His heroes thus become naked warriors pitted against death. This American idiom illustrates Stevenson's understanding of the darker aspects of American history; specifically, the anguish of disfigured manhood and the way in which it requires the romanticizing of violence. Equally, this illustrates his understanding of why Vietnam occurred, and why there might be more Vietnams.

The Altar of Peace (1973), probably Stevenson's best work to date, is a bitter and ironic commentary on the nature of war and throbs with references to Vietnam. Stevenson sets the piece in a pagan mode, appealing to a pre-Christian age to find his metaphor for the evil of Vietnam, an age without hope of redemption, a time before salvation. The stage is deliberately set outside of American history wherein he introduced American themes and images. The individual figures were taken from earlier works, then further developed and were finally collected on one canvas. Among them include a young boy embracing a black statue which has been mutilated, recalling a theme of the living male idealizing a hero. Right centre stands a warrior with a winged helmet passively watching the weeping youth whilst pressing his hands upon the buttocks of another warrior who is raping a woman. The gesture is ambiguous: he is either applauding the warrior or initiating his own sexual act upon his fellow. The scene rings with homosexuality as the warrior's attention is caught by the youth's grief—or his beauty. In the lower lefthand corner are two warriors, one of whom is sexually assaulting the other anally while his hand grips the base of a broken phallic monument. The monument is symbol of the defeated, as is the warrior being raped. A third warrior crouches behind a stone fragment watching the scene. Ironically his body seems to be becoming stone. The skin is ashen. His hair alone appears alive. He is the conquering warrior becoming Hero.

Altar of Peace suggests that war is mutilated male sexuality. It is violence without responsibility. It is the result of sexual confusion and inadequacy. Stevenson so adeptly summarizes this idea by castrating the defeated male; the Hero Death indifferently waves a broken arm or phallus. Winning is manhood; defeat is emasculation. War is the result of the inability to establish manhood and sexual competence nonviolently. It is the nature of Man in general and of the perversions and fantasies of the American male in specific Stevenson has recorded with such accuracy, an accuracy many viewers resist knowing.

—Carrie Barker

STEZAKER, John.

British. Born in Worcester in 1949. Studied at Nottingham School of Art; Slade School of Fine Art, London, 1967–73. Founder and Co-Editor, *Frameworks Magazine,* London. Former Lecturer, Chelsea School of Art, London. Lecturer, St. Martin's School of Art, London, since 1975. Agent: Nigel Greenwood Inc., 4 New Burlington Street, London W1. Address: 61 Praed Street, London W.10, England.

Individual Exhibitions:

1970 Sigi Krauss Gallery, London
Forum Stadtpark, Graz, Austria
1972 Nigel Greenwood Gallery, London
King's College, Cambridge
1973 Nigel Greenwood Gallery, London
Museum of Modern Art, Oxford
1974 Galerie December, Münster, West Germany
1975 Nigel Greenwood Gallery, London
Galleria Lia Rumma, Rome (travelled to Galleria Lia Rumma, Naples)
1976 Nigel Greenwood Gallery, London
Galerie Eric Fabre, Paris
1977 Nigel Greenwood Gallery, London
Spectro Arts, Newcastle upon Tyne
Galleria Schema, Florence
1978 The Photographers' Gallery, London
Ikon Gallery, Birmingham
City Museum, Southampton
1979 *Works 1973–1978,* Kunstmuseum, Lucerne
New '57 Gallery, Edinburgh

Selected Group Exhibitions:

1970 *Young Contemporaries,* London
3 Schools Exhibition, Royal Academy of Arts, London
1971 *Wall Show,* Lisson Gallery, London
1972 *The New Art,* Hayward Gallery, London
1973 *Critics' Choice,* Tooth's Gallery, London
1974 *Projekt '74,* Kunsthalle, Cologne
1975 *Structures and Codes,* Royal College of Art, London
1976 *Arte Inglese Oggi 1960–1976,* Palazzo Reale, Milan
1979 *Un Certain Art Anglais,* Musée d'Art Moderne de le Ville, Paris
1982 *Hayward Annual: British Drawing,* Hayward Gallery, London

Collections:

Victoria and Albert Museum, London; Tate Gallery, London

Publications:

By STEZAKER: book—*Beyond Art for Art's Sake: A Propos Mundas,* London 1973; articles—"3 Paradoxes and a Resolution" in *Studio International* (London), May 1972; "Conceptual Art" in *Studio International* (London), June 1972; interview, with Anne Seymour, in *The New Art,* exhibition catalogue, London 1972; "2 Instances of Institutional Determinancy of Art" in *Control Magazine* (London), no. 7, 1973; "Premises" in *Flash Art* (Milan), March/May 1973; "Post-Duchamp Reversal" in *Art and Artists* (London), December 1973; "Priorities I, II and III" in *Frameworks Journal* (London), vol. 1, nos. 1-3, 1974; "Ideal Types and Utopias" in *Control Magazine* (London), no. 8, 1974; "Conversation with Peter Smith" in *Studio International* (London), March/April 1975; "Social Expression: Social Reality" in *Meantime,* no. 1, 1977; interview in *Artlog* (London), January 1979.

On STEZAKER: books—*5 Collages by John Stezaker,* with text by John W. Walker, Birmingham 1978; *John Stezaker: Works 1973–1978,* exhibition catalogue, by B. Hatten and M. Kunz, Lucerne 1979; articles—"Problem Solving and Question Begging: The Works of Art-Language and John Stezaker" by Rosetta Brooks in *Studio International* (London), December 1973.

STILL, Clyfford.

American. Born in Grandin, North Dakota, 30 November 1904; moved with his family to Spokane, Washington, 1905. Educated in Spokane; enrolled at the Art Students League, New York, but withdrew after the first day, 1926; studied at Spokane University, Washington, 1926–27 and 1931–33, B.A. 1933; Fellow, Trask Foundation, Saratoga Springs, New York, 1934–35; studied art, philosophy and literary criticism, under Murray Bundy, Washington State University, Pullman, M.A. 1935 (Teaching Fellow). Married: daughters: Sandra and Diane. Painter: lived in Canada, 1927–31, then returned to Washington; worked in shipbuilding and aircraft industries, Oakland and San Francisco, 1941–45; settled in New York, 1945; Founder, with Mark Rothko, Robert Motherwell and others, Subjects of the Artist teaching group, New York, 1948–49; settled in Carroll County, near Westminster, and purchased a house in New Windsor, Maryland, 1966. Lecturer, 1935–40, and Assistant Professor of Fine Arts, 1940–41, Washington State University, Pullman; Professor, Richmond Professional Institute, Virginia, 1943–45; Lecturer, California School of Fine Arts, San Francisco, 1946–50; Summer School, Hunter College, City University of New York, 1951; and Brooklyn College, New York 1952–53; Visiting Artist and Lecturer, University of Colorado, Boulder, 1960. Recipient: Award of Merit Medal, American Academy of Arts and Letters, New York, 1972; Skowhegan Medal for Painting, Skowhegan School of Painting and Sculpture, Maine, 1974; Alumni Achievement Award, Washington State University, Pullman, 1975. D.F.A.: Maryland Institute, Baltimore, 1967; North Dakota State University, Fargo, 1972; San Francisco Art Institute, 1976. Honorary Member, Buffalo Fine Arts Academy, New York, 1962. Member, American Academy of Arts and Letters, New York, 1978. *Died* (in Baltimore, Maryland) *23 June 1980.*

Clyfford Still: ***Untitled*, 1957** Courtesy Whitney Museum, New York

Individual Exhibitions:

1943 San Francisco Museum of Art
1946 Art of This Century, New York
1947 Betty Parsons Gallery, New York
California Palace of the Legion of Honor, San Francisco
1950 Metart Gallery, San Francisco
Betty Parsons Gallery, New York
1951 Betty Parsons Gallery, New York
1959 Albright-Knox Art Gallery, Buffalo, New York
1963 Institute of Contemporary Art, University of Pennsylvania, Philadelphia
1966 *33 Paintings for the Albright-Knox Art Gallery,* Albright-Knox Art Gallery, Buffalo, New York
1969 Marlborough-Gerson Gallery, New York
1970 Marlborough-Gerson Gallery, New York
1976 San Francisco Museum of Modern Art
1979 Metropolitan Museum of Art, New York

Selected Group Exhibitions:

1935 *Annual Exhibition,* National Academy of Design, New York
1945 *Autumn Salon,* Art of This Century, New York
1952 *15 Americans,* Museum of Modern Art, New York
1956 *Modern Art in the United States,* Tate Gallery, London
1958 *The New American Painting,* travelling exhibition (toured Europe)
1959 *Documenta,* Kassel, West Germany
1965 *The New York School: The First Generation,* Los Angeles County Museum of Art
1969 *The New American Painting and Sculpture,* Museum of Modern Art, New York
1972 *Color Forum,* University Art Museum, Austin, Texas
1987 *American Painting: Abstract Expressionism and After,* San Francisco Museum of Modern Art

Collections:

Museum of Modern Art, New York; Whitney Museum, New York; Albright-Knox Art Gallery, Buffalo, New York; Hirshhorn Museum and Sculpture Garden, Smithsonian Institution, Washington, D.C.; Art Institute of Chicago; Museum of Fine Arts, Houston; San Francisco Museum of Modern Art; Tate Gallery, London; Kunsthalle, Basle.

Publications:

By STILL: articles—statement in *Americans,* exhibition catalogue, New York 1952; letter in *Paintings by Clyfford Still,* exhibition catalogue, Buffalo, New York 1959; "Comment" in *Albright-Knox Gallery Notes* (Buffalo, New York), Summer 1960; statement in *Clyfford Still,* exhibition catalogue, Philadelphia 1963; "An Open Letter to an Art Critic" in *Artforum* (San Francisco), December 1963; letter in *Artforum* (San Francisco), February 1964; statement in *33 Paintings for the Albright-Knox Art Gallery,* exhibition catalogue, by Katherine Kuh, Buffalo, New York 1966; "Notes by Clyfford Still" in *Clyfford Still,* exhibition catalogue, San Francisco 1976; "A Conversation with Clyfford Still" by Thomas Albright in *Artnews* (New York), March 1976; "Diary Notes and Letters" in *Clyfford Still,* exhibition catalogue, New York 1979.

On STILL: books—*Clyfford Still,* exhibition catalogue, by Ti-Grace Sharpless, Philadelphia 1963; *Clyfford Still,* exhibition catalogue, New York 1970; *Clyfford Still,* exhibition catalogue, by Katherine Kuh, New York 1979; articles—"Clyfford Still" by Hubert Crehan in the *San Francisco Chronicle,* July 1950; "U.S. Painters Today: Clyfford Still" by Kenneth Sawyer in *Portfolio and Art News Annual No. 2,* New York 1960; "The Outsider" by Thomas B. Hess in *Artnews* (New York), December 1969; "Still: The Enigma" by Katherine Kuh in *Vogue* (New York), February 1970; "Clyfford Still's Gift to the San Francisco Museum of Modern Art" by Henry T. Hopkins in *American Art Review,* January/February 1976; "Clyfford Still" by Clement Greenberg in *Arts Magazine* (New York), October 1980; "Regression and Color in Abstract Expressionism: Barnett Newman, Mark Rothko, Clyfford Still" by A. Gibson in *Arts Magazine* (New York), March 1981.

Though invariably linked with Newman and Rothko among the Founding Fathers of New York Abstract Expressionism, as early as 1944, Clyfford Still was capable of arriving at a sufficiently differentiated image to leave him identifiable from his colleagues while at the same time escaping a systematic formula of composition.

In these early pictures he maintained a contrast between those dark cloud-like outlines and the light tone of the ground on which they disported themselves. His common forms were of an organic base placed in an atmosphere of two-dimensional space on which they loomed. Then began the overloading of surface with pigment in dark weights of black and purples through which the light glinted as of a rosy dawn waking against an almost impenetrable night.

Despite an uncompromising commitment to colour

areas of unallusive significance, there came through in Still's works, especially those of mural scale, the inevitable visual comparisons with the massive backdrops of nature in mountain scenery. Yet in this giant environmental ambiance the paintings assumed elemental presences of their own on a positive and physically active spirit.

In consummation of paint worked and spread and played against its neighbour Still remained faithful to the concept of Action Painting in its crude evidence of sensual involvement. Refinement came in the choice of a limited palette that was flavoured of the fire-hot reds and yellows and sooty blacks and blues; Still's colours emerged not to rest but as alive in high impasto reliefs of chromatic textures akin to the molten debris of a furnace.

Realizing his own vision is Still's admitted assessment of the function of the artist; its apotheosis is reached in his many examples of total commitment to the evolution of a picture not from a process of rational addition but the superimposed stages of growth into a seemingly natural climax. This culmination of glowing and maturing areas until final abandonment epitomises the unique quality of Still; it is as though by the alchemy of prime selection of colours, few as they may be, and their spread on the support, each painting takes control of its own destiny, and the result is as much a fusion of conflicting impulses and forces as a pre-ordained exegesis of the artist's preformed image in his mind.

One was never under any illusion that for Clyfford Still painting was a succession of gestures applied in blanket saturation of the white ground, each laying on top of the previous coat in a woven chromatic depth of tactile subtle strength. Eye and finger-tip came together in appreciating Still in his joint impact where size too had its vital ingredient. Still's influence and effect were strong enough to persuade younger followers towards a greater self-confidence in the ability of a surface area to bear its own potentials of expansion outwards towards the spectator rather than away towards an imaginary horizon.

His paintings typically bore no names, merely being described as "Painting" or numbered. One catalogued as "Untitled" 1957 in the Whitney, New York, sums it up. It is a riven banner of blood stains and blob-splattered fabric, historic standard of a battle fought by American artists against the past and suffering defeat only when they themselves were overtaken by time.

—G. S. Whittet

STUART, Michelle.

American. Born in Los Angeles, California, 10 February 1938. Studied at Chouinard Art Institute, Los Angeles, 1954–55; Instituto de Bellas Artes, Mexico City, under Diego Rivera, 1955–56; and New School for Social Research, New York, 1958–60. Married Jose Barton in 1950 (divorced, 1974). Worked as a topographical draftswoman, Los Angeles, 1955; lived in Mexico, 1955–56, and in Paris, 1956–58; now a full-time artist, living and working in New York, since 1958. Adjunct Instructor, Pratt Institute School of Art and Design, New York, 1975–76, Parsons School of Design, New York, 1976–78, and Fordham University, New York, 1976–79. Recipient: MacDowell Fellowship, Peterborough, New Hampshire, 1974; National Endowment for the Arts Grant for Individual Artists, 1974–1977, 1980; Tamarind Institute Grant, 1974; New York Creative Artists Public Service Grant in Painting, 1974; Guggenheim Fellowship, 1975; Finnish Art Association Fellowship, Helsinki, 1985; Artists' Fellowship, New York Foundation for the Arts, 1987. Agents: Max Protetch Gallery, 560 Broadway, New York, New York 10012; Saxon/Lee Gallery, 7525 Beverly, Los Angeles, California 90036; Galerie Veda, Ginza Asahi Building, 6–6–7 Ginza, Chuo-ku, Tokyo 104, Japan; and Galerie Alfred Schmela, Mutter-Ey-Strasse 3, 4 Dusseldorf, West Germany. Address: 152 Wooster Street, New York, New York 10012, U.S.A.

Individual Exhibitions:

1973 Douglass College, Rutgers University, New Brunswick, New Jersey
Windham College, Putney, Vermont
1974 Max Hutchinson Gallery, New York
Galerie Alfred Schmela, Dusseldorf
1975 Max Hutchinson Gallery, New York
Fine Arts Center Gallery, State University at Oneonta, New York
Niagara Gorge Path Relocated, Lewiston, New York (site work)
1976 Galerie Alfred Schmela, Dusseldorf
Gallery of Fine Arts, State University of New York at Stony Brook
Galerie Farideh Cadot, Paris
Max Hutchinson Gallery, New York
Zolla/Lieberman Gallery, Chicago
East/West Wall Memory Relocated, P.S. 1, Institute for Art and Urban Resources, New York (site work)
1977 Massachusetts Institute of Technology, Cambridge
Williams College Museum of Art, Williamstown, Massachusetts
Galerie Munro, Hamburg
Strata: Graves/Hesse/Stuart/Winsor,, Vancouver Art Gallery
Galerie Alfred Schmela, Dusseldorf
Color/Time/Landform/Transformation, Tomkins Cove Quarry, Tomkins Cove, New York (site work and video project)
Incidents of Travel in Nature: A Space/Time Book and Video Project, Moore College of Art, Philadelphia
1978 University of New Mexico Art Gallery, Albuquerque
Incidents of Travel in Nature: A Space/Time Book and Video Project, Art Gallery, University of California at Long Beach (site work)
Fine Arts Gallery, Wright State University, Dayton, Ohio
Galerie Farideh Cadot, Paris
Centre d'Arts Plastiques Contemporains, Bordeaux
Zand Gallery, Teheran
Tanit Galerie, Munich
Zolla/Lieberman Gallery, Chicago
1979 Ehrensberger Gallery, Zurich
Droll/Kolbert Gallery, New York
Foster White Gallery, Seattle
Stone Alignments/Solstice Cairns, Portland Center for the Visual Arts, Oregon (permanent sculpture site work)
Galerie Schmela, Dusseldorf
Paperwork, Institute of Contemporary Arts, London
Janus Gallery, Venice, California
1980 Galerie Munro, Hamburg
Galerie Ahlner, Stockholm
Galleriet, Lund, Sweden
Galerie Aronowitsch, Stockholm
1981 *Correspondences,* Joslyn Art Museum, Omaha, Nebraska (audio visual room installation)
Galerie Tanit, Munich
Correspondences, P.S. 1, Institute for Art and Urban Resources, New York (audio visual room installation)
1982 *Correspondences,* St. Louis Art Museum (audio visual room installation)
Susan Caldwell Gallery, New York
Galerie Schmela, Dusseldorf
1983 Walker Art Center, Minneapolis
Janus Gallery, Los Angeles
Haags Gemeentemuseum, The Hague
Galleriet Anders Tornberg, Lund, Sweden
Galerie Ahlner, Stockholm
1984 *Sacred Precincts,* State University of New York, Purchase
Galerie Krista Mikkola, Helsinki
Gallery Ueda Warehouse and Ginza, Tokyo
1985 Long Island University, Greenvale, New York (travelled to Syracuse, New York; Boulder, Colorado; Binghamton, New York)
1986 Saxon/Lee Gallery, Los Angeles
Paradisi, Brooklyn Museum, New York
Arts Club of Chicago
Max Protetch Gallery, New York
1987 Thorden Wetterling Gallery, Goteborg, Sweden
Toni Birckhead Gallery, Cincinnati
Paintings and Prints, Anders Tornberg Gallery, Lund, Sweden
Malningar, Galerie Aronowitsch, Stockholm
Pfizer Inc., New York

Selected Group Exhibitions:

1972 *Outsize Drawings,* Loeb Art Center, New York University
1976 *Handmade Paper: Prints and Unique Work,* Museum of Modern Art, New York
1977 *Documenta,* Kassel, West Germany
1978 *Paper as Medium,* Smithsonian Institution, Washington, D.C.
1979 *The Presence of Nature,* Whitney Museum, New York
1980 *With Paper, About Paper,* Albright-Knox Art Gallery, Buffalo, New York
1981 *Le Moderna Museet de Stockholm à Bruxelles,* Palais des Beaux-Arts, Brussels
1982 *Sans Titre: 4 Années d'Acquisition au Musée de Toulon,* Musée d'Art, Toulon, France
1985 *Livres d'Artistes,* Centre Georges Pompidou, Paris
1987 *Sacred Spaces,* Everson Museum of Art, Syracuse, New York

Collections:

Museum of Modern Art, New York; Brooklyn Museum, New York; Albright-Knox Art Gallery, Buffalo, New York; Museum of Contemporary Art, Chicago; Walker Art Center, Minneapolis; Cincinnati Art Museum, Ohio; Kaiser-Wilhelm Museum, Krefeld, West Germany; Moderna Museet, Stockholm; Stadtisches Museum, Monchengladbach, West Germany; National Collection of Australia, Canberra.

Publications:

By STUART: books—*The Fall,* New York 1976; *A Complete Folk History of the United States at the Edge of the Century,* Dayton, Ohio and New York 1978; *From the Silent Garden,* Williamstown, Massachusetts 1979; *I-80 Series: Michelle Stuart,* exhibition catalogue, Omaha 1981; *Sacred Precincts: From Dreamtime to the South China Sea . . . ,* New York 1984; aritcles—"Project, Then/Now" in *Artforum* (New York), February 1980; "American Frontiers: The Photographs of Timothy O'Sullivan 1867-1874" in *The Print Collector's Newsletter* (New York), July/August 1982.

On STUART: books—*Michelle Stuart,* exhibition catalogue, with an essay by Lawrence Alloway, Oneonta, New York 1975; *From the Center* by Lucy Lippard, New York 1976; *Michelle Stuart,* exhibition catalogue, with an essay by Robert Hobbs, Cambridge, Massachusetts 1977; *Strata: Graves/Hesse/Stuart/Winsor,* exhibition catalogue, with an essay by Lucy Lippard, Vancouver 1977; *Michelle Stuart,* exhibition catalogue, with an essay by Jean-Pierre Sanchez, Bordeaux 1978; *Originals: American Women Artists* by Eleanor Munro, New York 1979; *Michelle Stuart: Paperwork,* exhibition catalogue, with text by Sarah Kent, London 1979; *With Paper, About Paper,* exhibition catalogue, with an essay by Carlotta Kotik, Buffalo, New York 1980; *La Peinture Américaine: Le Mythes et al Matière* by Madeleine Deschamps, Paris 1981; *Michelle Stuart: Place and Time,* exhibition catalogue, with text by Graham Beal, Minneapolis 1983; *The Pluralist Era: American Art 1968–81* by Corinne Robins, New York 1984; *Michelle Stuart: Voyages,* exhibition catalogue, with texts by Ted Castle and Judith Van Wagner, Greenvale, New York 1985; *Michelle Stuart,* exhibition catalogue, with text by Esther Sparks, Chicago 1986.

For some years I have been making large scale works concerned with the visual and conceptual experience in nature. The earlier ones were topographical renderings of cratered surfaces, sometimes with ele-

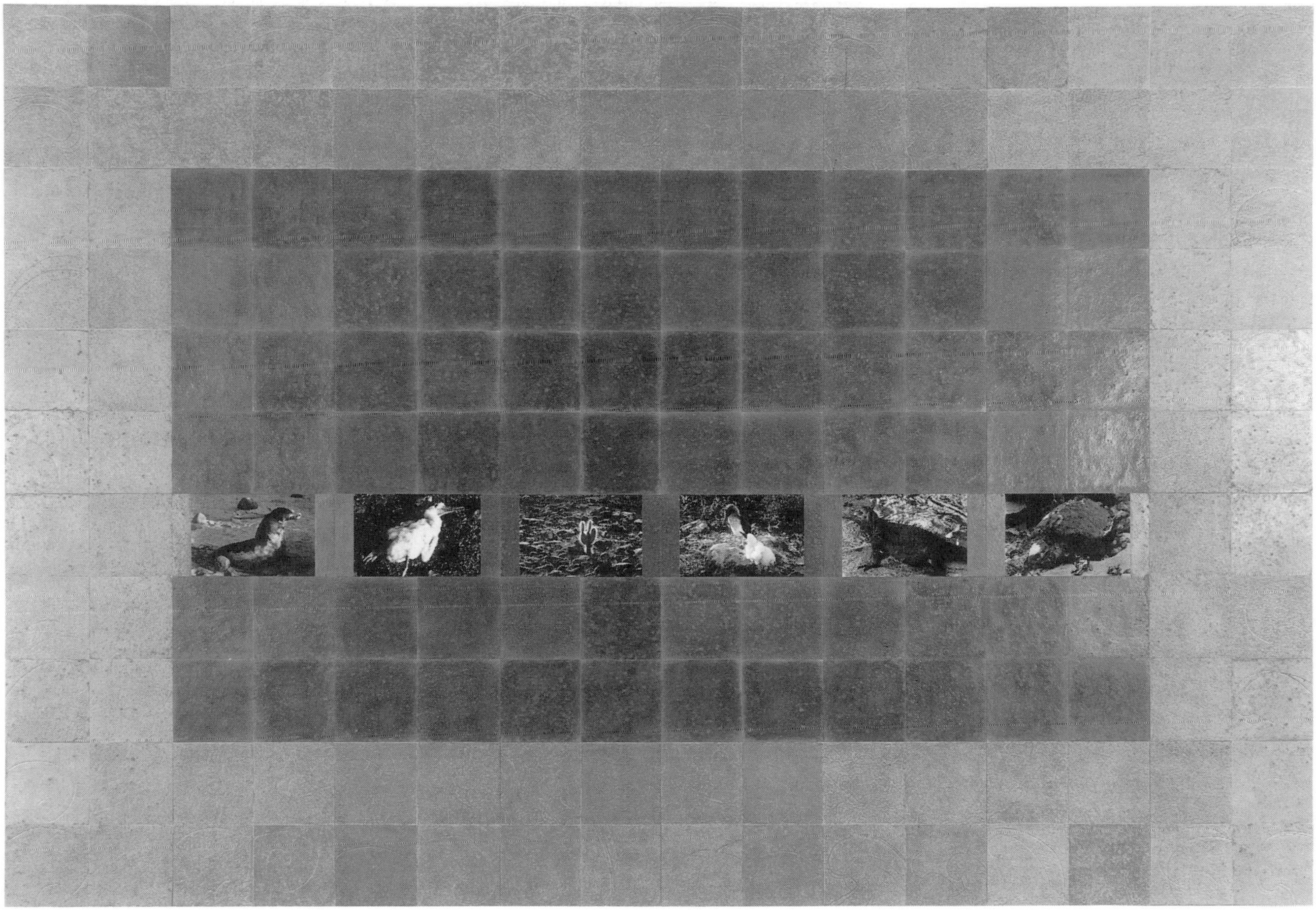

Michelle Stuart: *Islas Encantadas, Seymour Island Cycle,* 1982

ments suggesting waves and currents. The pieces that followed were multi-unit drawings in series that documented changes in nature using real geological surfaces. The marks were made with graphite on paper. The viewer moved physically with the piece. The units were two feet square with two inch intervals extending horizontally on the wall for as long as 12 feet. Parallel to the physical movement, passage of time was demonstrated in the sequence. It formed an open-ended continuum that described change.

During the last 8 years I have used rocks and earth as well as graphite, on muslin mounted rag paper. The height of the work is usually 9 to 12 feet by 5 feet wide. Most of the work is three-dimensional to some degree and some pieces move into the floor space. These pieces are a continuation of both the continuum and geological concepts, but deal directly with specific sites. They are made by violently indenting or impressing the paper repreatedly with rocks and layering and polishing the surface with earth from locations in which I feel strong sentient associations. The pulverized earth or mineral deposits color the paper and the rock marks become random events locked into the surface of the work. The process entails a continuous repetition of body movement. Each gesture varies from the preceding one and thus describes distinct patterns in time. Each repeated rock impression is configurationally infinite.

In special projects such as *Niagara Gorge Path Relocated,* executed at Artpark in Lewiston, New York, I worked in the same way, but the gorge was part of the piece. By relocating topographically the Niagara cascade to its original site I sought to evoke the perception of time and the flow of nature's processes. This piece included some public participation in the process.

In Project Studio 1 (an abandoned school now used for art projects) I made *East/West Wall Memory Relocated.* In this particular piece I sought to record the way in which memory shifts in time and space and a displacement occurs that re-forms our perceptions. In the two-part piece the texture of the wall's aging surface was rendered visible with graphite on paper and the parallel but opposite 13 foot by 5 foot wall units were interchanged.

Since the beginning of 1975 I have also been making intimate paper objects that I call "rock books." They are 'histories' of a place. 'Notebooks' relating to strata forms and time duration in nature. They are quiet, tactile explorations of the earth in specific geological sites. Some of them are handmade paper that in the process of making, I color with earth pigment. Some, tied with woven string, cannot be opened while others upon opening reveal the sequence of geologic processes that exist when the strata layers of an area are unveiled.

From 1977 to 1982 my work has continued to be involved with nature, but with the additional dimension of nature as a setting for man. This correspondence between the two, man and nature, inspired the passage work *Stone Alignments/Solstice Cairns,* a permanent outdoor sculpture made of boulders and stone that lies on a plateau overlooking the Columbia River Gorge in Oregon. The piece is 1000' x 600'. Also, the historical aspect was the idea behind a large audio-visual room installation called *Correspondences,* dealing with the perceptual relationship and marriage of two cultures, the Spanish and Maya in the Yucatan area of Mexico.

In addition the work during this period has included photographs, both black and white and color taken on the site by the artist. These photographs render narrative sequence both to nature cycles, such as "Islas Encantadas: Seymour Island Cycle" (The Galapagos Islands), and demonstrate symbolically or metaphorically man's inspiration from and use of natural resources such as stone and earth, and how, particularly with architecture, this influences his reality.

Recently, I have been doing large-scale paintings, installations and commissions in encaustic (wax) process with plants, earth and archaeological shards. I have also worked on large bronze site-specific commissions.

—Michelle Stuart

SUGA, Kishio.

Japanese. Born in Morioka, 19 February 1944. Studied at Tama Art College, Tokyo, 1964–68. Married Taeko Tomioka in 1969. Lives and works in Kawasaki. Travelled in Europe and the United States, 1970, in France, 1973. Recipient: First Prize, *Shell Art Exhibition,* Tokyo, 1967; Second Prize, Art Critics Competition, *Bijutsu-Techo* magazine, Tokyo, 1969; Grand Prize, *Japan Art Festival,* Tokyo, 1970. Agent: Tokyo Gallery, Japan. Address: c/o Tokyo Gallery, 8–16–18 Ginza, Chuo-ku, Tokyo, Japan.

Individual Exhibitions:

1968 Tsubaki Kindai Gallery, Tokyo
1969 Tamura Gallery, Tokyo

1970 Tamura Gallery, Tokyo
1971 Sato Gallery, Tokyo
1972 Tamura Gallery, Tokyo
Kinokuniya Gallery, Tokyo
Roppongi Building, Tokyo
1973 Tamura Gallery, Tokyo
Sato Gallery, Tokyo
City Hall, Morioka City, Japan
1974 Tamaru Gallery, Tokyo
Gallery 16, Kyoto
1975 Tokiwa Gallery, Tokyo
Maki Gallery, Tokyo (2 exhibitions)
Kaneko Art Gallery, Tokyo (2 exhibitions)
1976 Maki Gallery, Tokyo
Tokyo Gallery
International Christian University, Tokyo
1979 Tokyo Gallery

Selected Group Exhibitions:

1966 *International Young Artists Exhibition*, Tokyo
1967 *Shell Art Exhibition*, Shirokiya Department Store, Tokyo
1970 *Japan Art Festival, Tokyo*
Aspects of New Japanese Art, National Museum of Modern Art, Kyoto
1972 *Contemporary Japanese Graphics Exhibition*, Institute of Contemporary Arts, London
1973 *Biennale de Paris*
1974 *Japan: Tradition und Gegenwart*, Städtisches Kunsthalle, Dusseldorf
1975 *Materials Exhibition*, Stedelijk van Abbemuseum, Eindhoven, Netherlands
1976 *Kyoto Biennale*
International Open Encounter on Video, Museo de Arte Contemporaneo, Caracas

Publications:

By SUGA: articles—"Invisible Words in an Invisible World" in *Space Design* (Tokyo), October 1969; "The Starting Point of Disappearance" in *Space Design* (Tokyo), December 1969; "To Exist Beyond the Situation" in *Bijutsu-Techo* (Tokyo), February 1970; "Unnamable" in *Bijutsu-Techo* (Tokyo), May 1972.

On SUGA: articles—"Suga," special issue of *Kirokutai* (Tokyo), November 1972; "Current Critic" by Toshiaki Minemura in *Bijutsu-Techo* (Tokyo), June 1973; "In the Case of Suga's Work" by Toshiaki Minemura in *Sogetsu* (Tokyo), June 1973; "Thing's School" by Ichiro Haryu in *Asahi Journal* (Tokyo), no. 33, 1974; "Suga" by Toshikuni Maeno in *L'Art Vivant* (Paris), no. 45, 1974; "The Works of Kishio Suga" by Toshikuni Maeno in *Obararyusoka* (Tokyo), 1974; "Suga's Work with Natural Things" by Yusuke Nakahara in *Space Design* (Tokyo), March 1975; "Suga's Event in Tokiwa Gallery" by Yoshiaki Tono in *Obararyusoka* (Tokyo), June 1975; "Current Critic" by Toshiaki Minemura in *Obararyusoka* (Tokyo), October 1976.

I never intended to create "Art" in my work. "Art" or non-"Art" is just the result, and it is decided by other people, not by myself. I think about "Thing" and about the situation of an existing "Thing." I want to recognize the reality of "Thing" and its system. And, as "Thing" does not exist in isolation, I want to achieve its reality in Nature.

To achieve the situation of "Thing," I have to recognize "dependence" or being "dependent." this is one of my important concerns in deciding my position as regards the external world. I wish I had a window looking into my consciousness, just like the window of my room. I suppose a place in which to reflect my consciouness, which in this case, in my case, is Nature.

I am interested in each thing that is involved in the construction of nature. Each thing has an existence by itself, one by one, but nature has no center. Each thing is not a part of nature so much as it is a whole unto itself.

Various things are gathered together in nature, yet it seems that they have no relation to each other—but they are related: sometimes we can see it, sometimes we cannot.

I think that "relation" and "system" in nature are on the same level: seemingly separate relations have to be dependent on each other in order to be whole. That is to say, "system" in nature is a system of dependence, and it must be considered as a fact of "Thing." There is the absolute position of "Thing," which cannot be conveyed by fabricated rhetoric.

—Kishio Suga

In one of Kishio Suga's experiments can be seen the following work. A board is set across two walls horizontally in a corner, and a piece of cloth is folded and set upon it. The board is cut across to join the two walls, and the cloth is folded to make creases at the point where it touches the walls. What is interesting about the work is the feeling one has of the reversal of composition and external appearance. There is something wilful about setting the board across the corner and putting the cloth on top, but the folding of the cloth as it hits the wall at both ends seems to depend on something beyond this. From the middle upwards, it seems to depend on the state of physical contact with the wall as something exterior. But this folded part seems to be very artificial in physical appearance, while the upper cloth area seems to have been accomplished without this artificiality. This undoubtedly is because folding is the means employed, but this is accomplished forcibly as it were by the walls. Now if that be the case, this work of Suga shows the possibility of revealing how the act of making is regulated by means of the act being made. The corner is a space Suga is particularly fond of, and this work is characterized by the insertion into the work of a conversion power as against the act of that corner.

Obviously in whatever work of art the act of making can not overstep the physical conditions. And yet it is difficult to say that this fact is the same as determining a work through the conscious introduction of that area of letting something be made. Yet if we exaggerate this one point of letting something be made, we will inevitably end up with the result of bringing the material's physical qualities into prominence. It seems to me that the delicate balance between both poles is recovered in this cloth-corner work.

We can only wait in expectation to see how this kind of quality will appear in the other works, but it will be of deep interest to see how Suga suggests the work's possible expanse as the product that results from reversing the action of determining the work in a dislocation of the condition of this space.

—Yusuke Nakahara

Kishio Suga: *Extending Existence*, installation at the Maki Gallery, Tokyo, 1976

SUGAI, Kumi.

Japanese. Born in Kobe, Japan, 13 March 1919; has maintained residence in Paris since 1952. Educated at the School of Fine Arts, Osaka. Married to Mitsuko Sugai. Independent artist now practicing a spare, non-personal style of abstraction. Recipient: Grand Prize, *Triennal International de Gravure*, Grenchen, Switzerland, 1961; Grand Prize, *Biennal International de Gravure*, Cracow, 1966. Address: 91 rue de l'Amiral Mouchez, Pavillon 6, 75013 Paris, France.

Individual Exhibitions:

1954 Galerie Craven, Paris
Palais des Beaux-Arts, Brussels
1957 Galerie H. Le Grendre, Paris
1958 Galerie Creuzevaut, Paris
1959 Kootz Gallery, New York
1960 Städtisches Museum, Leverkusen, West Germany (retrospective)
1961 Kootz Gallery, New York
1962 Kootz Gallery, New York
1963 Galerie Creuzevaut, Paris
Kestner-Gesellschaft, Hannover (retrospective)
1964 Kootz Gallery, New York
Galerie Toni Brechbuhl, Grenchen, Switzerland
Die Insel, Hamburg (retrospective)
1965 American Art Gallery, Copenhagen
Galerie Bleu, Stockholm
Sundsvall Museum, Sweden
Kunsthallen, Gothenburg, Sweden
1967 Lefebre Gallery, New York
Kunstnernes Hus, Oslo (retrospective)
Galerie Brusberg, Hannover
1968 Galerie Defet, Nuremberg
Galerie Hilt, Basel
1969 Court Gallery, Copenhagen
Kunsthallen, Gothenburg, Sweden
Galerie Klipan, Stockholm
Tokyo Gallery, Tokyo

Kumi Sugai: *Femme et Homme B*, 1982

Minami Gallery, Tokyo
National Museum of Modern Art, Kyoto (retrospective)
1970 Galerie d'Eent N.V., Amsterdam
1971 Circle Gallery, London
Court Gallery, Copenhagen
Galerie Schottenring, Vienna
1972 Galerie Defet, Nuremberg
Galerie Hakken, Oslo
Galerie Christael, Helsinki
Galerie Hilt, Basel
1974 Galleria Annunciata, Milan
La Galerie Esplanade de la Défense, Paris
1976 Minami Gallery, Tokyo
1981 Satani Gallery, Tokyo
1983 Nantenshi Gallery, Tokyo
Seibu Museum of Art, Tokyo
1984 Seibu Hall, Ohtsu, Japan
Ohara Museum of Art, Kurashiki, Japan
1985 Nantenshi Gallery, Tokyo
1987 Nantenshi Gallery, Tokyo

Selected Group Exhibitions:

1956 *Salon Réalités Nouvelles*, Paris (and annually through 1982)
1957 *Salon de Mai*, Paris (and annually through 1982)
1959 *Biennal International de Gravure*, I jubljana, Yugoslavia (and annually through 1981)
Documenta, Kassel, West Germany
1961 *Trienal International de Gravure*, Grenchen, Switzerland
1962 *Biennale*, Venice
1964 *Painting and Sculpture of a Decade*, London
1966 *Salon Grands et Jeunes d'Aujourd'hui*, Paris (and annually through 1981)
1969 *Exposition Ars '69*, Helsinki
1972 *Biennal International de Gravure*, Norway

Collections:

Nationalgalerie, Berlin; Landesmuseum, Hannover; Centre Georges Pompidou, Paris; Galleria Nazionale d'Arte Moderna, Rome; Moderna Muséet, Stockholm; National Museum of Modern Art, Tokyo; National Museum of Modern Art, Kyoto; Museum of Modern Art, Toyama, Japan; Museum of Modern Art, New York; Art Institute of Chicago.

Publications:

By SUGAI: book of drawings—*Albam*, with poems by André Pieyre de Mandiargues, Paris 1960; books of prints—*La quête sans fin*, Paris 1957; *Repos goûte*, Paris 1964; *Sugai, ou la tension maxima*, Milan 1966; *Octobre*, Milan 1969; *Sugai*, Chikuma, Japan 1970; *Alea*, Paris n.d.; *Sugai gravure*, Tokyo n.d.

On SUGAI: books—*L'Aventure de l'art abstrait* by Michel Ragon, Paris 1956; *Kumi Sugai*, exhibition catalogue, Leverkusen, West Germany 1960; *Sugai* by André Pieyre de Mandiargues, Paris 1960; *Le voir dit* by Jean-Clarence Lambert, Paris 1962; *Kumi Sugai*, exhibition catalogue, by Wieland Schmidt and Irmtraud Schaarchmidt-Richter, Hannover 1963; *Kumi Sugai*, exhibition catalogue, by Hanns Theodor Flaemming, Hamburg 1964; *Kumi Sugai*, exhibition catalogue, by Fredrik Matheson and Oistein Parmann, Oslo 1967; *Japan: Tradition und Gegenwart*, exhibition catalogue, by J. Harten and others, Dusseldorf 1974; *Sugai*, Tokyo 1975; articles—"Sugai" by Jean-Clarence Lambert in *La jeune école de Paris*, Paris 1956; review by J. S. Byrd in *Art International* (Lugano, Switzerland), September 1965; "Kumi Sugai, Circle Gallery" by Peter Fuller in *Arts Review* (London), April 1971; "Sun King" in *Design* (London), June 1971; "Kumi Sugai" by A. P. de Mandiargues in *Le Arti* (Milan), May 1974.

Kumi Sugai's early abstract paintings were characterized by gloomy images suggestive of Japanese folklore, but clarity of composition and brightness of color came to dominate his work during the 1960's, infusing his paintings with freshness and dynamism. In addition to painting, Sugai is a printmaker who has won numerous prizes.

In 1969, at the age of 40, he returned from Paris and executed paintings for the walls of the new building of the National Museum of Modern Art, Tokyo. In this work Sugai demonstrated his excellent technique in composition by combining manifold elements covering an expansive area into a unified composite view.

Sugai's one-man show in 1976 (Minami Gallery, Tokyo) marked a new development for the ex-Ecole de Paris painter from Japan. A huge canvas in the show depicted an icon on a shiny Italian sportscar interlaced with bright-colored geometrical patterns. Sugai is now essentially uninterested in emotional hand-painted works and tends to hide his handtraces by mechanical non-personal expression.

In the 1980s, his geometric compositions began to break loose, and spread diagonally, leaving more vacant space in white. Clear-cut grey and black forms now dominated the canvases, with accentuated red shapes impressing themselves onto and integrating themselves into the formerly monochrome compositions.

—Yoshiaki Tono

SUGARMAN, George.

American. Born in New York City, 11 May 1912. Studied at City College of New York, 1934–38, B.A. 1938; Zadkine School of Sculpture, Paris, 1955–56. Served in the United States Navy, 1941–45. Sculptor: lives and works in New York: travelled in Europe and lived in Paris, 1951–55. Instructor, Hunter College Graduate School, New York, since 1960. Instructor, Yale University Graduate School of Art, New Haven, Connecticut, 1967–68. Recipient: Second Prize, *Carnegie International*, Pittsburgh, 1961; Longview Foundation Grant, 1961, 1962, 1963; National Endowment for the Humanities grant, 1966; Art Award, American Academy and Institute of Arts and Letters, 1985. Agent: Robert Miller Gallery, 41 East 57th Street, New York, New York 10022. Address: 21 Bond Street, New York, New York 10012, U.S.A.

Individual Exhibitions:

1958 Widdifield Gallery, New York
1961 Stephen Radich Gallery, New York
1964 Stephen Radich Gallery, New York
1965 Philadelphia Art Alliance
Stephen Radich Gallery, New York
1966 Dayton's Gallery, Minneapolis
Stephen Radich Gallery, New York
1967 Galerie Schmela, Dusseldorf
Galerie Ziegler, Zurich
Fischbach Gallery, New York
1969 *Plastiken, Collagen, Zeichnungen*, Kunsthalle, Basel (retrospective: travelled to Leverkusen, Berlin, and Amsterdam, 1969–70)
1970 Galerie Ziegler, Zurich
1971 Gallery 118, Minneapolis
1974 Zabriskie Gallery, New York
Dag Hammarskjold Plaza, New York
1977 Robert Miller Gallery, New York
1978 Robert Miller Gallery, New York
1979 Galerie Liatowitsch, Basel
1980 Robert Miller Gallery, New York
Galerie Rudolf Zwirner, Cologne
1981 Smith Gallery, Palo Alto, California
Galerie Ziegler, Zurich
1982 Robert Miller Gallery, New York
1984 Fuller Goldeen Gallery, San Francisco
1985 Robert Miller Gallery, New York
780 Third Avenue, New York (installation)
Whitney Museum, New York

Doris Freedman Plaza, Central Park, New York (installation)
1986 Whitney Museum, New York
1987 Todd Capp Gallery, New York
Helander Gallery, Palm Beach, Florida

Selected Group Exhibitions:

1952 *IV Salon de la Jeune Sculpture,* Musée Rodin, Paris
1956 *Sculptors Selected by Painters,* Tanager Gallery, New York
1963 *Bienal,* Sao Paulo
1967 *Sculpture of the 60's* Los Angeles County Museum of Art
1970 *Monumental Art,* Contemporary Arts Center, Cincinnati, Ohio
1975 *Sculpture: American Directions,* National Collection of Fine Arts, Washington, D.C.
1979 *The Decorative Impulse,* Institute of Contemporary Art, Philadelphia (travelled to San Diego, California; Minneapolis; Chicago)
1982 *Postminimalism,* Aldrich Museum of Contemporary Art, Ridgefield, Connecticut
1985 *Forms in Wood: American Sculpture of the 1950s,* Philadelphia Art Alliance, Pennsylvania
1987 *Sculpture: Exploration of Space,* Anchorage Museum of History and Art, Alaska

Publications:

By SUGARMAN: article—"Square Spiral" in *Art Now: New York,* January 1969.

On SUGARMAN: books—*Collage: Personalities, Concepts, Techniques* by Harriet Janis and Rudi Blesh. Philadelphia and New York 1962: *New York School. The First Generation: Paintings of the 1940s's and 1950's.* edited by Maurice Tuchman, Los Angeles 1965: *Constructivism: Origins and Evolution* by George Rickey, New York 1967; *Minimal Art: A Critical Anthology,* edited by Gregory Battcock, New York 1968; *George Sugarman: Plastiken, Collagen, Zeichnungen,* exhibition catalogue, by Amy Goldin and Peter F. Althaus, Basle 1969: *George Sugarman* exhibition catalogue, by Irving H. Sandler, Amsterdam 1970; *Icons and Images of the 60's* by Nicolas and Elena Calas, New York 1971: *Shape of Space: The Sculpture of George Sugarman* by Holliday T. Day, New York, 1981: *George Sugarman: Painted Wood Sculpture,* exhibition catalogue, New York 1985.

I believe that sculptural space is different from ordinary space, and each of my sculptures is an attempt to create, to define and to articulate an aesthetically significant space. And so, early on, I became interested in floor space, as in "Inscape" and horizontal extensions as in "Two in One." I have always avoided industrially available forms because I believe that they blur the particularity of the statement, so I have used as many different forms as I have been capable of imagining often within the same sculpture to create a rich and complex experience. These works ask such questions as "What is sculptural unity?" and "What are artistic relationships, not only within the work itself but also to the space it creates around it?"

Although most people respond to my use of color on a purely emotional basis and although it has been said that my work forms a bridge between painting and sculpture, my own reason for using the full range of color is purely formal, i.e. to help articulate the formal problem set in each sculpture.

Now that I am more concerned with outdoor, public sculpture, I have asked myself "What does *public* sculpture mean?" Certainly it has a different function than a gallery or museum-oriented work. Equally certain, it should be something more readily accessible to the general public. I think it is possible to do this and not only retain but even heighten all the aesthetic "high-art" values one believes in. My sculpture for the Federal Building in Baltimore shows my interest in the creation of a particularized, extended space, in interior volumes, in relationships between different forms, and it does it in ways appropriate only to outdoor sculpture: by its relation to the building it is placed in front of and by its function as a possible symbol of community.

—George Sugarman

George Sugarman has brought strong pictorial sensibility to contemporary sculpture. A student of Ossip Zadkine in Paris, Sugarman made sculptures in the early 1950's that had the deliberate, weighty and solid properties associated with his teacher's strong grounding in Cubism. By the late 1950's, however, Sugarman began to break away from the Cubist cube and to elaborate a more open and distinctively colorful approach to sculpture. As head of the New York-based New Sculpture Group, he was at the forefront of both the discussions and the practical investigations of new treatments of abstract sculpture, based on non-relational structures. In the sculptures of the late 1950's and early 1960's, he started to shape space

George Sugarman: *Baltimore Federal,* 1977

into a bold intrastructure of solids and voids, using juxtaposed arrangements of curved and straight edged forms as the means. For example, in *Yellow Top* (1960) a polychrome wood sculpture, different colors are used to articulate each separate element, drawing attention simultaneously, to the linear contours of the piece and its definition of space. It is during this period, also, that the sculptures begin to spill directly onto the floor and, even more forcefully, they stress the relationships of parts to parts in the bold but jungle-like compositions that Sugarman has continued to favor. In addition to the base and the floor, the wall has also occupied his attention. Strongly colored, his wall reliefs are volumetric and specifically structured forms that challenge cliché notions about the relationship of painting and sculpture.

In the late 1960's Sugarman began to interest himself in the demanding area of public art. Changing his materials from wood to metal, he has designed large-scaled and outdoor polychromed pieces, whose brightly colored, cut-out parts give a rich and varied experience of structure and space, wondrously accessible to the average user of the public places in which they stand. *Kite Castle* (1974), shown at the Hammarskjold Plaza in New York City, is revealing of the role of constructive animator which color—here the dominant tonal combination is red and blue—has in encouraging a positive reception to the piece. In his public art works, Sugarman aims to delight the viewer/stroller and to enhance the environment without overwhelming either one.

The exuberant qualities of his sculptures continued developing in the 1980s. *Big Ride* (1981), a relief collage with a dynamically angled multipart structure, shows increasing interest in heightening the illusion of movement through the juxtapositions of different shapes, colors and textured surfaces. In *Ariel* (1984), that illusion is so striking as to make the complex cut-out structure of this painted aluminum sculpture seem to rise up on the energy generated from the tensions within its various parts from the ground. In *Waltz* (1985), the organic flow to the rhythmical structure of this multipart form brings to mind the swaying configurations of flowers. References to nature serve to enhance the impact of much of Sugarman's recent work.

—Ronny Cohen

SUTHERLAND, Graham (Vivian).

British, Born in London, 24 August 1903; Educated in Sutton, and at Epsom College, Surrey; studied mathematics, Battersea Polytechnic, London, and apprenticed to Midland Railway Engineering Works, Derby, 1919–20; studied engraving techniques, under Stanley Anderson and Malcolm Osborn, Goldsmiths' College of Art. London, 1921–26. Served as Official War Artist, In England and France, 1941–44. Married Kathleen Frances Barry in 1927. Painter and designer: worked, with Clive Gardiner, on *Wembley International Exhibition* decorations, 1924; moved to Farningham, Kent, 1928, and to Eynsford, Kent, 1930; designed posters for Shell-Mex, London Passenger Transport Board, and the London Post Office, from 1930; moved to Sutton-at-Hone, and made first of several visits to Pembrokeshire, Wales, 1934; worked on china and glass designs, from 1935; moved to Trottiscliffe, 1936, and to Tetbury, Gloucestershire, 1939; designed sets and costumes for *The Wanderer* ballet by Frederick Ashton, Sadlers Wells Theatre, London, 1941; spent several months of each year in Southern France, from 1947; worked on designs for Coventry Cathedral tapestry, "Christ in Glory," 1954–57, woven in Felletin, 1958–62; purchased a house and settled in Menton, Southern France, but made frequent visits to England and Wales, from 1955: commissioned by Queen Elizabeth to paint composition for the President of Portugal on "the Common Interest of Portugal and England," 1957; visited New York, 1964; commissioned by Queen Elizabeth to paint picture for President Pompidou of France, 1972; innaugurated Graham Sutherland Gallery (now Graham and Kathleen Sutherland Foundation), under Picton Castle Trust, Haverfordwest, Wales, 1976. Lecturer in Engraving, 1928–32, and in Composition and Book Illustration, 1932–39, Chelsea School of Art, London; Lecturer in Painting, Goldsmiths' College of Art, London, 1946–47. Recipient: Acquisition Prize, Museum of Modern Art, Sao Paulo; Prize, *Biennale*, Venice, 1952; Foreign Minister's Prize, Tokyo, 1957; First Prize, *Biennale International d'Art*, Menton, 1972; Shakespeare Prize, Hamburg, 1974. D. Litt.: Oxford University, 1962; University of Leicester, 1965; University of Cardiff, 1979. Honorary Member, American Academy of Arts and Letters, 1972: Honorary Fellow, Accademia de San Luca, Rome, 1973; Commandeur des Arts et des Lettres, France, 1973; Honorary President, *Biennale Internationale d'Art*, Menton, 1974. Associate, Royal Society of Painters, Etchers and Engravers, 1925 (expelled, 1933); Trustee, Tate Gallery, London, 1949 (resigned, 1954). Order of Merit, 1960. *Died* (in London) *17 February 1980.*

Individual Exhibitions:

1925 XXI Gallery, London
1928 XXI Gallery, London
1938 Rosenberg and Helft Gallery, London
1940 Leicester Galleries, London (with Walter Goetz)
1941 Temple Newsom, Leeds (with Henry Moore and John Piper)
1946 Buchholz Gallery, New York
1947 Lefevre Gallery, London
Roland Browse and Delbanco, London
1948 Hanover Gallery, London
Buchholz Gallery, New York
1949 Stedelijk Museum, Amsterdam
1951 Institute of Contemporary Arts, London
Hanover Gallery, London
1952 Hanover Gallery, London
Redfern Gallery, London
Biennale, Venice (travelled to the Musée National d'Art Moderne, Paris)
1953 Kunsthaus, Zurich
Curt Valentin Gallery, New York
Tate Gallery, London
Stedelijk Museum, Amsterdam
1954 Akademie der Bildenden Künste, Vienna (toured Austria and West Germany)
1955 *Bienal*, Sao Paulo
1956 Roland Browse and Delbanco, London
1957 Kunstkabinett, Frankfurt
Hoffman Galerie, Hamburg
1958 Redfern Gallery, London
1959 Redfern Gallery, London
Arthur Jefress Gallery, London
Belfast Museum and Art Gallery
Paul Rosenberg Gallery, New York
1960 Roland Browse and Delbanco, London
1961 Arts Council Gallery, London (with Stanley Spencer and Ivon Hitchens)
Galleria Galatea, Turin (travelled to the Galleria Galatea, Milan)
1962 Marlborough Fine Art, London
1963 Galleria Fanti di Spade, Rome
Galleria Gallatea, Turin
Galleria II Centro, Naples (with Francis Bacon)
Prebendal House, Llandaff Cathedral, Cardiff
1964 Redfern Gallery, London
Paul Rosenberg Gallery, New York
1965 Galleria Civica d'Arte Moderna, Turin
Haus der Kunst, Munich
Gemeentemuseum, The Hague
Haus am Waldsee, West Berlin
Wallraf-Richartz Museum, Cologne
1966 Marlborough Fine Art, London
Kunsthalle, Basle
1967 Haus der Kunst, Munich (toured the Netherlands and West German)
1968 Marlborough Fine Art, London
1969 Kestner Gesellschaft, Hannover
Galleria II Fauno, Turin
Palais de l'Europe, Menton, France
Druikgraphik und Zeichnungen, Albrecht Dürer Gesellschaft, Nuremberg
1970 Marlborough Fine Art, London (with Pablo Picasso and Henry Moore)
1971 William West Gallery, London
1972 Galleria II Fauno, Turin
Galleria Narciso, Turin
Galleria Bergamini, Milan
1973 Marlborough Galerie, Zurich (travelled to Marlborough Fine Art, London)
1974 Marlborough Fine Art, London
Galleria d'Arte Sant'Ambrogio, Milan
1975 Lefevre Gallery, London
Alexander Postan Fine Art, London
1976 Redfern Gallery, London
Galleria dei Foscherari, Bologna
Palazzo Liceo Saracco, Acqui Terme, Italy
1977 Marlborough Fine Art, London
Portraits, National Portrait Gallery, London (retrospective)
1978 Graham Sutherland Gallery, Picton Castle Haverfordwest, Wales
1979 Marlborough Fine Art, London
Disegni di Guerra, Palazzo Reale, Milan
1980 Gawthorpe Hall, Padiham, Lancashire (with Oskar Kokoschka)
Le Point, Rome
1981 Palazzo delle Albere, Trento, Italy
Galleria Bergamini, Milan
1982 Tate Gallery, London
Imperial War Museum, London
Redfern Gallery, London
1986 Goldsmith's Gallery, London
1987 Galleria del Cavallino, Venice
Christopher Hall Gallery, London
1988 Galerie Patrice Trigano, Paris

Selected Group Exhibitions:

1935 *Exhibition of British Art*, Royal Academy of Arts, London
1936 *International Surrealist Exhibition*, New Burlington Galleries, London
1939 *Contemporary British Art*, at the *World's Fair*, New York
1941 *Britain at War*, Museum of Modern Art, New York
1955 *Documenta*, Kassel, West Germany
1960 *British Painting 1700–1960*, Pushkin Museum, Moscow (travelled to the Hermitage Museum, Leningrad)
1962 *British Art Today*, San Francisco Museum of Art (toured the United States)
1969 *British Drawings 1939–1949*, Scottish National Gallery, Edinburgh
1977 *British Painting 1952–1977*, Royal Academy of Arts, London

Collections:

Tate Gallery, London; Arts Council of Great Britain, London; Imperial War Museum, London; British Museum, London; Victoria and Albert Museum, London; Albertina Academy, Vienna; Centre Georges Pompidou, Paris; Kunstmuseum, Basle; National Gallery of Victoria, Melbourne; Art Gallery of Ontario, Toronto.

Publications:

By SUTHERLAND: book—*Graham Sutherland; Parafrasi della Natura e altre Corrispondenze*, edited by Roberto Tassi, Parma, Italy 1979; articles—"A Trend in English Draughtsmanship" in *Signature*, July 1936, "Graven Images; Line Engraving and the Illustrated Book" in *Signature* July 1937; "The Living Image; Art and Life" in the *Listener* (London), 13 November 1941; "Welsh Sketch Book" in *Horizon* (London), April 1942; "American Art Explained by American Artists, Part I" in *The Artist*, March 1944; letter, to H. P. Juda, in "thoughts on Painting" in *The Listener* (London), 6 September 1951; statement in *8 European Artists*, edited by

Felix H. Man, London, 1954; statement in *Conversations with Painters* by Noel Barber, London 1964; "Interview with Graham Sutherland" in *Druckgraphik und Zeichnungen mit dem Vollständigen Bestiarium*, exhibition catalogue, Nuremberg 1969; letter in the *Sunday Telegraph Magazine* (London), 10 September 1971; introduction to *The English Vision*, exhibition catalogue, London 1973; "Conversation with Paul Nicolls" in *Graham Sutherland*, exhibition catalogue, Turin 1976; "Conversation with Graham Sutherland" in *Portraits by Graham Sutherland*, exhibition catalogue, by John Hayes, London 1977; "The Nature of Poetry and Painting" in *The Sutherland Gift to the Nations*, exhibition catalogue, London 1979; statement, in *Sutherland— Disegni di Guerra*, exhibition catalogue, Milan 1979; books illustrated—*Henry IV: Part I* by Shakespeare, New York 1940; *Le Bestiare ou Cortege d'Orphée* by Guillaume Apollinaire, London 1979.

On SUTHERLAND: books—*Graham Sutherland* by Edward Scakville-West, London 1943, 1953; *The Imagery of Graham Sutherland* by Robert Melville, London 1950; *The Work of Graham Sutherland* by Douglas Cooper, London 1961; *Graham Sutherland: Das Graphische Werk 1922–1970* by Felix H. Man, Munich 1970; *Graham Sutherland* by Francesco Arcangeli, Milan 1973, New York 1975; *Sutherland Sketchbook*, London 1974; *Portraits by Graham Sutherland*, exhibition catalogue, by John Hayes, London 1977; *Graham Sutherland: Complete Graphic Work* by Roberto Tassi, London 1978; *Sutherland: Wartime Drawings* by Roberto Tassi, Milan 1979, London 1980; *The Art of Graham Sutherland* by John Hayes, Oxford 1980; *Graham Sutherland*, exhibition catalogue, by Ronald Alley, London 1982; *Graham Sutherland: The Early Years 1921–40*, exhibition catalogue with essay by Nannette Aldred, London 1986; *Graham Sutherland: Aquarelles et Dessins*, exhibition catalogue with text by Pierre Cabanne, Paris 1988; films—*Graham Sutherland* by John Read, BBC-TV, London 1954; *Graham Sutherland* by Margaret McCall, BBC-TV, London 1968; *Graham Sutherland: Lo Specchio e il Miraggio* by Pierpaolo Ruggerini, RAI-TV, Rome 1969; *Sutherland in Wales* by John Ormand, BBC-TV, London 1977; *Graham Sutherland* by Adriano Viale, 1977.

Although Graham Sutherland is usually thought of in terms of the neo-romantic naturalism that dominated the British art scene in the 1930's and 1940's, he was always a painter both firmly rooted in the native English tradition and fully aware of the complex development of modern European art. Yet the core of his own art is an attempt to express an essence which lies beyond sensible form, whether in the surrealistic appreciation of natural forms, or the imaginative symbolism of the Coventry Cathedral tapestry.

This was already apparent in his early etchings, which are in the tradition of the mystical Romanticism of Blake, or of Samuel Palmer's intense visionary landscapes. In the early 1930's he turned from engraving to oil and watercolour painting, and in the years up to the war worked chiefly on a series of Welsh landscapes which he described as imaginative paraphrases of the landscape of Pembrokeshire: "I felt I could express what I felt only by paraphrasing what I saw." These merge the English Romantic feeling for landscape with an imaginative freedom influenced by Surrealism, so could appropriately be exhibited in the 1936 *International Surrealist Exhibition*. They reveal Sutherland's fascination with the way in which organic forms undergo disturbing and sinister transformations, taking on an uncanny presence, which he also discovered in found objects: "Their sap may have gone out of them but their form remains . . . I am fascinated by the whole problem of the tensions produced by the power of growth."

He was therefore well-placed as an official war artist from 1941 to 1944 to capture the poignancy of the weird effects of destruction caused by bombing, with twisted iron and shattered masonry. This more cruel and violent vision he carried over into his spiky nature studies, which bring out the emotional meaning he found in the tortured forms of thistles, the gnarled branches of a tree, the spikes of a thorn bush, the jumbled masses of fallen rocks. The "Thorn Tree" paintings of 1946–7 and the "Standing" or "Hanging Forms" of the early 1950s contain all kinds of painterly ambiguity which make them seem charged with mysterious enigmatic presences, as though ghostly semi-human forms or monsters are about to emerge from them, paralleling Henry Moore's identification of the human figure with landscape.

In the 1960's Sutherland's particularly English blend of Surrealism and Romanticism made him the father-figure of a group of younger painters such as Keith Vaughan and John Minton. The sense of strangeness remained a constant factor in his own work, though after the war this greatly increased in diversity and variety, not only incorporating machine forms and depicting animals, birds and insects, but showing a new interest in the human figure both in his portraits and his series of religious pictures. The earliest of these, the 1944 "Crucifixion" for St. Matthew's Church, Northampton, is a tortured expressionistic work which fuses a modern idiom with the inspiration of old masters, especially Grünwald, combined with savage modern sufferings typified by Belsen. But the immense tapestry of "Christ in Glory" that he designed between 1954 and 1957 to occupy the entire east wall of the new Coventry Cathedral so that the whole vista leads up to this intentionally awe-inspiring creation, is a more Byzantine work, and its icon-like flattened space and compartmentalized composition recur in many of his later works.

As a portrait painter he showed a sharp eye for revealing detail which catches the essence of his sitters, as in the earliest in 1949, in which the folds and wrinkles of Somerset Maugham's face are emphasized almost to suggest the fibrous leaves of some tropical plant. The later highly dramatized portraits of Churchill (1955), Beaverbrook (1957) and Helena Rubinstein (1957) show similar symbolic transformations taking place, though carefully controlled by the demands of getting a reasonable external likeness as well as what Sutherland calls "pinning down a person's essence."

But landscape remained a continuing preoccupation, though Sutherland's move to the south of France seemed to mark a move towards a more "international" approach. However, he came to think that he was mistaken in making a prolonged break from renewing himself from the Welsh landscape which once so obsessed him, and from the late 60's he returned there at least two or three times a year to work in this "curiously charged atmosphere—at once calm and exciting." The relationship between artist and landscape finally reached what now seems the inevitable and logical conclusion with his donation of an important collection of his oils, watercolours and lithographs to form the new Graham Sutherland Gallery at Picton Castle near Haverford-west, within walking distance of the actual landscapes which were such a potent source of inspiration to him. Sutherland himself expressed his intentions exactly by saying "I believe that work done in a certain area is to be seen in that area."

—Lavinia Learmont

SUTTON, Philip.

British. Born in Poole, Dorset, 20 October 1928. Studied painting, under William Coldstream, at the Slade School of Fine Art, London, 1950–54. Served in the British Army, 1947–49. Married Heather Minifie Ellis Cooke in 1953; children: Jacob, Imogen, Saskia and Rebekah. Independent painter, in Snape, Suffolk, 1955–58, and in London since 1958: Member, London Group, 1956. Instructor, Slade School of Fine Art, London, 1956–75. Royal Academician, 1977. Agent: Browse and Darby Ltd., 19 Cork Street, London W1. Addresses: (studio) 7 Melbourne Grove, London SE22; (home) 10 Soudan Road, London SW11 4HH, England.

Individual Exhibitions:

1956	Roland, Browse and Delbanco, London
1958	Roland, Browse and Delbanco, London
1959	Geffrye Museum, London
1960	City Art Gallery, Leeds, Yorkshire
	Roland, Browse and Delbanco, London
1962	Stone Gallery, Newcastle upon Tyne
	Lane Gallery, Bradford, Yorkshire
	57 Gallery, Edinburgh
	Roland, Browse and Delbanco, London
1963	David Jones Gallery, Sydney
	Gallery A, Melbourne
	Rose Skinner Gallery, Perth, Western Australia
	Roland, Browse and Delbanco, London
	Battersea District Library, London
1965	*Paintings from Fiji*, Roland, Browse and Delbanco, London
1966	Curwen Gallery, London
	David Jones Gallery, Sydney
1967	*Recent Paintings*, Roland, Browse and Delbanco, London
	London Arts Gallery, Detroit
	David Jones Gallery, Sydney
	Arnolfini Gallery, Bristol
	Arts Centre, Folkestone, Kent
1969	Roland, Browse and Delbanco, London
	Hambledon Gallery, Blandford Forum, Dorset, England
1970	Park Square Gallery, Leeds
	Paintings/Drawings/Prints, Arnolfini Gallery, Bristol
	Paintings, Drawings, Prints and Sculptures, Arts Centre, Folkstone, Kent
	David Jones Gallery, Sydney
1971	Graves Art Gallery, Sheffield
	Roland, Browse and Delbanco, London
	Battersea District Library, London
	Oxford Gallery
	Park Square Gallery, Leeds
1972	Battersea District Library, London
	Studio Prints, London
	Compendium Galleries, Birmingham
1973	Roland, Browse and Delbanco, London
	David Jones Gallery, Sydney
	Peterloo Gallery, Manchester
1974	J. P. Lehmans Gallery, London
1975	Roland, Browse and Delbanco, London
1976	Orde Levinson, Johannesburg (travelled to Durban and Cape Town)
1977	Falmouth School of Art, Cornwall
	Royal Academy of Art, London
1979	Annex Gallery, Wimbledon, London
	Browse and Darby, London
	David Jones Gallery, Sydney
1980	Holsworthy Gallery, London
	Margaret Fisher Gallery, London
1981	Browse and Darby, London
	Minden Gallery, Jersey, Channel Islands
1982	Christopher Hall Gallery, London
	Browse and Darby, London
1983	John Brinkley Fellowship Exhibition, Norwich, Norfolk
	Beaux Art Gallery, Bath, Avon
1984	Shell Headquarters Gallery, London
	Browse and Darby, London
	Manor House Society, London
	Beaux Arts Gallery, Bath, Avon
	Bermondsey Gallery, London
1985	Lichfield Arts, Lichfield, Staffordshire
	Beaux Arts Gallery, Bath, Avon
	Dulwich Art Gallery, London
1986	Cambridge Art Gallery, Cambridge
	Municipal Gallery, Stoke-on-Trent, Staffordshire
	Poole Gallery, Dorset
	Newport Gallery, Isle of Wight
1987	Odette Gilbert Gallery, London
	Beaux Arts Gallery, Bath, Avon

Selected Group Exhibitions:

1952	*London Group*, Beaux-Arts Gallery, London
1955	*Critic's Choice*, Arthur Tooth and Sons, London
1956	*Contemporary British Painters*, Parsons Gallery, London
	6 Young Painters, Tate Gallery, London
1957	*Guggenheim International*, New York

1969 *English Landscape Tradition,* Camden Arts Centre, London
The Nude, New Grafton Gallery, London
1980 *Israel Observed,* Israel Museum, Jerusalem

Collections:

Arts Council of Great Britain, London: Tate Gallery, London; Ministry of Works, London; City Art Gallery, Birmingham; Cecil Higgins Museum and Gallery, Bedford; City Art Gallery, Leeds; Durban Museum, South Africa; National Gallery of South Australia, Adelaide; National Gallery of Victoria, Melbourne; Perth Art Gallery, Western Australia.

Publications:

On SUTTON: books—*Philip Sutton,* exhibition catalogue, London 1958; *Philip Sutton: Paintings from Fiji,* exhibition catalogue, London 1965; *Recent Paintings by Philip Sutton,* exhibition catalogue, with text by David Storey, London 1967; *Philip Sutton: Paintings/Drawings/Prints,* exhibition cards, with text by David Storey, Bristol 1970; *Philip Sutton: paintings, drawings, prints and sculptures,* exhibition catalogue, with text by David Storey, Folkestone 1970; *Philip Sutton,* exhibition catalogue, with texts by Frank Constantine and David Storey, Sheffield 1971; *Israel Observed,* exhibition catalogue, with text by Helene Marks, Jerusalem 1980.

Self-activation has always operated on Philip Sutton. After a spell in the R.A.F. he went to the Slade and became hooked on a lively figurative style without hang-ups on subject. He was exhibiting by 1952 and had his first one-man show in 1956. He was then 28 years old. Since that time he has worked in a progress of refinement and freshness of concentration on mood and colour. The early paintings were concerned with the use of medium, how to apply the paint so that it built up in an overall system of chords somewhat in the manner of an expressionist Cézanne. Colour was strong on key, the primaries especially the reds taking a predominant share. Generally the motives triggered off the painting, and sometimes in the landscapes there was a suspicion of the scene dictating too much in the organization of the composition. Exceptions were the interiors and the still life subjects where less complicated systems of pattern and colour became enriched by the freedom from detail. This conflict between truth to motive and unity of picture structure was to be resolved gradually in the flower pieces of 1957 and later when the ever-smiling ghost of Matisse encouraged the young Englishman.

After having lived in the Suffolk countryside for years, Sutton came to live in Battersea, a densely populated quarter of south London. Nature in its green growth was no longer pressing its vegetable lushness upon him, and he painted many interiors with his family of four and his wife as models. They took their places as broadly brushed passages centrally on the canvas, blues, pinks, deep cadmium reds and bright yellows all singing in euphoric harmony. This was a realism no less credible for its chromatic abandon. The colours were genuinely faithful to each other if not to local visual fact, and the drawing of the figures was portrayal of his offspring recognizably and unsentimentally abstracted in their outlines and broad summaries of their features and tonality.

For an artist who responds to the stimulus of his surroundings, Battersea seemed to lose even its intimate satisfactions, and in 1963 Sutton set off with his wife and four children to indulge what could be called a Gauguinesque dream. They ended up on one of the Fijian islands in the blue Pacific, and Sutton happily began painting; he made hundreds of oils, filled 30 sketchbooks and made many woodcuts.

The result, shown on his return to London, was an uncomplicated reflection of a peaceful locality where sun, sea and lush vegetation set up varied motives for pictures of a relaxed and pleasantly unpolluted atmosphere. This mood of relaxation is one that prevails in Sutton's paintings where only in the nudes is there any hint of tension, and this is implied by muscular pose rather than in any contrived conflict of tones or rhythms.

Sutton has the contemporary painter's engagement with the flat area of his surface totally; whether the central space defines a nude woman or a bunch of gladioli is important only for its contribution of colour and its form to the total experience. In this he is at one with both Bonnard and Matisse in the continued mood of optimism.

—G. S. Whittet

T

TADINI, Emilio.

Italian. Born in Milan, 5 June 1927. Studied art: received degree. Married Antonia Perazzoli in 1959; children: Francesco and Michele. Independent artist, Milan, since 1960. Art Instructor, Nuova Accademia Di Belle Arti, Milan, 1980–82. Agent: Studio Marconi, via Tadino 15, 20124 Milan. Address: via Jommelli 24, 20131 Milan, Italy.

Individual Exhibitions:

1961 Galleria del Cavallino, Venice
1966 Galleria II Punto, Turin
1967 Galleria del Minotaura, Brescia, Italy
Vita di Voltaire, Studio Marconi, Milan
1968 Galleria La Chiocciola, Padua
Gallerie Richard Foncke, Ghent
1969 Galleria Tempo, Bologna
Studio Condotti, Rome
1970 Studio Marconi, Milan
Gallerie Richard Foncke, Ghent
1971 *Viaggio in Italia,* Studio Marconi, Milan
Galleria San Michele, Brescia, Italy
1972 Studio Condotti, Rome
Galleria Quattro Venti, Palermo, Sicily
Galleria la Chiocciola, Padua
Gallerie Richard Foncke, Ghent
1973 Galleri A. H. Stockholm
1974 Galleria Europa, Bolzano, Italy
Estudio Actual, Caracas
La Struttura della Condensazione e dello Spostamento, Studio Marconi, Milan
1975 Galleria Torbandena, Treiste
Galleria II Triangolo, Pescara, Italy
Gallerie Rencontres, Paris
Galleria Quarta Dimensione, Arezzo, Italy
Università di Parma, Italy
Studio G7, Bologna
Gallerie Micha, Brussels
1976 Galleria Rizzardi, Milan
Galleria Cesarea, Genoa
Galleria Rondanini, Rome
Galleria Solferino, Milan
1977 Galleria Mercato del Sale, Milan
Museo Civico, Alessandria, Italy
Galleria d'Arte Contemporanea, Suzzara, Italy
1978 Galleria 72n, Bergamo, Italy
Studio Baleri, Bergamo, Italy
Studio Marconi, Milan
Gallerie C., Paris
1979 Galleria Torbandena, Trieste
Galleria 4M, Florence
Galleria Marin, Turin
Galleria Le Feu Vert, Cagliari, Italy
Centro Culturale Olivetti, Ivrea, Turin
Galleria La Chiocciola, Padua
D'Ars Agency, Milan
Galleria Greminger, Genoa
1980 Banca Popolare di Milano, Rome
Galleria II Disegno, Rome
Galleria II Triagono, Nola, Italy
Galerie Pieter van Coecke, Aalst, Belgium
Galerie Atmosphere, Brussels
Arte Incontri, Fara d'Adda, Italy
1981 Galleria La Bottega,, Parma
1982 Galerie J. L., Ostend, Belgium
Galleria Civica d'Arte Moderna, Suzzara, Italy

Selected Group Exhibitions:

1965 *Operazione Goldfinger,* Galleria Levi, Milan
1967 *Contemporary Italian Art,* Gemeentemuseum, The Hague
1970 *Studio Marconi at Felix Landau,* Felix Landau Gallery, Los Angeles
1971 *New Italian Art 1953–1971.* Walker Art Gallery, Liverpool
1973 *Pittura in Lombardia 1945–70,* Villa Reale, Monza, Italy
1977 *Quotidien, Histoire et Utopie,* Maison de la Culture, Grenoble, France
1978 *Biennale,* Venice (and 1982)
1979 *Testuale: Le Parole, le Immagini,* Rotonda di via Besana, Milan
1982 *L'Opera Dipinta,* Galleria La Pilotta, Parma, Italy (travelled to Rotonda di via Besana, Milan)
1986 *Aspects of Italian Art 1960–85,* Kunstverein, Frankfurt

Publications:

By TADINI: books—*Le Armi, l'Armore,* Milan 1963; *L'Opera,* Milan 1980.

On TADINI: books—*Emilio Tadini,* exhibition catalogue, with text by A. Martini, Venice 1961; *Emilio Tadini,* exhibition catalogue, with text by Guido Ballo, Turin 1966; *Tadini,* exhibition catalogue, with text by Roberto Sanesi, Brescia, Italy 1967; *Emilio Tadini: Vita di Voltaire,* exhibition catalogue, with texts by Henry Martin, Roberto Sanesi and Guido Ballo, Milan 1967; *Ricerche dopo l'Informale* by Enrico Crispolti, Rome 1968, *Emilio Tadini,* exhibition catalogue, with text by J. L. Schefer, Milan 1970; *Emilio Tadini: Viaggio in Italia,* exhibition catalogue, edited by Giorgio Marconi, Milan 1971; *New Italian Art 1953–1971,* exhibition catalogue, with text by Giovanni Carandente, Liverpool 1971; *Emilio Tadini: La Struttura della Condensazione e dello Spostamento,* exhibition catalogue, with text by Arturo Carlo Quintavalle, Milan 1974; *Emilio Tadini,* exhibition catalogue, with text by J. L. Schefer, Paris 1975; *Testuale: Le Parole, le Immagini,* exhibition catalogue, with texts by Flavio Caroli and Luciano Caramel, Milan 1979; *Emilio Tadini: Aquarelli,* exhibition catalogue, with texts by F. Vincitorio and others, Rome 1980.

Emilio Tadini took up painting during the 1960's, after having worked for years as a writer, critic and theorist of art, and as a novelist. His writing experience and literary acumen are in fact an important element in his painting. The 60's, characterized by the explosion of Pop Art, gave Tadini a feeling for flat colour, precise drawing, a vaguely advertisement-style of picture—generally, of a super-finished work. Where Pop Art was concerned to glorify consumer goods (Campbell's Soup), Tadini offers us literary goods (the Gate, The Cloth Column); where Pop Art chooses the film star (Marilyn Monroe), for subject, Tadini chooses the literary star (Voltaire, Goethe); where Pop Art illustrates the environment as a great supermarket, Tadini presents it as the place of nostalgically well educated babies.

There is a picture of his from 1975, called "Magasins Réunis," in which he tackles the theme of the supermarket, a subject that does suggest Pop Art themes; but it is a pretext for literature. From the godlike body of Superman there grows the head of a metaphysical manikin, Nembo Kid; surprised by this head, one asks about the present through the unrealized hopes of the past; a German helmet at the side reinterprets the tragedy of a recent past.

The past is injected into the present, as the historical symbols live together with the symbols of the present day. History and news coexist in a picture written on the canvas with the same sort of pleasure with which tin soldiers are paraded by children on the floor of a nursery.

The figures in Tadini's works, so definitely outlined as to look like coloured silhouettes, are combined with texts which do not name things but illustrate a kind of vocabulary where words and things each go their own way. Like a cosmos in miniature, a syllabary never completed, where words and pictures live only for the euphoria of a text meant only for looking at.

While we normally look at the pictures and read the words, Tadini shows us how it is possible to look at the alphabet too: an alphabet for the eyes which releases the letters from specific meaning and throws them on the table for visual feast.

Tadini's painting is a sort of Luna Park of words and pictures: a question mark makes a column ask a question: the word "house" is inscribed between, among other things, a table, a tricycle and a revolver. Pictures and words are used to portray an impossible literature, a literature that cannot exist in writing, a text that cannot be read, a writing that cannot be spoken but only looked at: it is the pleasure of painting.

Painting is presented, then, as an ever-open syllabary, a syllabary made from intimacy, archaeology, comments, travel, from cold gardens, from troubled holidays—a syllabary made to delight the eye. An eye which lingers equally on the particular and the universal, on words and on pictures, on history and on everyday life, but above all an eye that can never cease to narrate.

—Loredana Parmesani

TAJIRI, Shinkichi.

American. Born in Los Angeles, 7 December 1923. Studied at the Art Institute of Chicago, 1947–48, and with Ossip Zadkine and with Fernand Léger, Paris, 1948–50, and at the Académie de la Grande Chaumière, Paris, 1950–51. Served as volunteer in United States Armed Forces, 1943–46; awarded Purple Heart Medal. Married Denise Martin in 1951 (divorced, 1955); married Ferdina Jansen in 1957 (died, 1969); children: Giotta Fuyo and Ryu Vinci; married Suzanne van der Capellen in 1976. Worked as re-

Shinkichi Tajiri: *Square Knot*, 1973

storer of antiques, Chicago, 1946. Independent artist, since 1949: associated with *Cobra* group, 1949–1950; Co-Founder of Galerie 8, Paris, Paris. 1950; designer at Rasch Wallpaper, Bramsche, West Germany, 1952. Guest Lecturer Werkkunstschule, Wuppertal, West Germany, 1951–53; Visiting Professor, College of Art and Design, Minneapolis, 1964–65 and 1972. Professor of Fine Art, Hochschule der Künste, Berlin, since 1969. Recipient: First Prize, *International Wallpaper Exhibition*. Darmstadt, 1953; Golden Lion, *8th Amateur Film Festival*, Cannes, 1955; Copley Foundation Grant, 1959; Whitney Foundation Fellowship for Sculpture, 1960; Mainichi Shinbun Prize for Sculpture, Tokyo, 1963. Agent: Court Gallery, Ostergade 24, Copenhagen, Denmark. Address: Castle Scheres. 5991 NC Baarlo (Limburg), Netherlands.

Individual Exhibitions:

1951 Galerie Parnass, Wuppertal, West Germany
1953 Kunsthandel Martinet, Amsterdam (with Pierce Alechinsky)
1954 Galerie d'Aujourd'hui, Brussels
1955 Galerie Colette Allendy, Paris
1957 Galerie Parnass, Wuppertal, West Germany
1958 Kunstring, Rotterdam
Galerie Lucien Durand, Paris
1959 de Jong & Co., Hilversum, Netherlands
1960 Stedelijk Museum, Amsterdam
American Cultural Center, Paris
1961 Gemeentemuseum, Arnhem, Netherlands
1962 Galleria Odyssia, Rome
Galerie Parnass, Wuppertal, West Germany
1963 Tokyo Gallery
1964 Hamilton Gallery, London
American Art Gallery, Copenhagen
Galerie 20, Amsterdam
1965 Minneapolis Institute of Art
André Emmerich Gallery, New York
1966 Court Gallery, Copenhagen
1967 Stedelijk Museum, Amsterdam
1968 Palais des Beaux-Arts, Brussels
University of Economics, Tilburg, Netherlands
Von der Heydt Museum, Wuppertal, West Germany
1969 Kunsthalle, Basle
Galerie d'Espace, Amsterdam
1970 City Hall, Heerlen, Netherlands
1971 Konsthall Lund, Sweden
Norrkoping Museum, Sweden
1972 Sodertalie Konsthall, Sweden
Amos Andersons Taidemuseum, Helsinki
Vasterbotten Museum, Umea, Sweden
Kunstnernes Hus, Oslo
Aarhus Museum, Denmark
Galerie Judith Weingarten, Amsterdam
1974 Boymans Van Beunigen Museum, Rotterdam
Bonnefanten Museum, Maastricht, Netherlands
1976 *Tajiri's Daguerrotypes*, Stedelijk Museum, Amsterdam
Tajiri's Rediscovery of the Daguerrotype, Künstlerhaus Bethanien, Berlin
1977 Rheinisches Landersmuseum, Bonn
Van Abbemuseum, Eindhoven, Netherlands
Stadtisches Kunstahalle, Dusseldorf
Münchener Stadtmuseum, Munich
Kunstchau Böttcherstrasse, Bremen, West Germany
Rijksmuseum Kröller-Müller, Otterlo, Netherlands
1979 *Stereoscopic Views by Tajiri*, Stedelijk Museum. Amsterdam
Galerie Fiolet, Amsterdam
1980 Rijksmuseum Kröller-Müller, Otterlo, Netherlands
Kunstlerhaus Bethanien, Berlin
1981 Gemeentemuseum, Vlissingen, Netherlands
1982 Galerie Kunstbezit, Heerlen, Netherlands
1983 Collection d'Art, Amsterdam
1984 Galerie Wansink, Roermond, Netherlands
1985 Bonnefantenmuseum, Maastricht, Netherlands
1986 Galerij Paule Pia, Antwerp, Belgium
1987 Galerie Artline, The Hague

Selected Group Exhibitions:

1949 *International Exhibition of Experimental Art (COBRA)*, Stedelijk Museum, Amsterdam
1951 *COBRA*, Palais des Beaux-Arts, Liège, Belgium
1957 *Phases*, Stedelijk Museum, Amsterdam
1959 *Documenta 2*, Kassel, West Germany
1961 *Art of Assemblage*, Museum of Modern Art, New York
1968 *Science Fiction*, Kunstverein, Dusseldorf
1973 *Video*, Rotterdamsche Kunststichting, Rotterdam
1982 *Cobra*, Musée d'Art Moderne, Paris
1984 *L'Art a Paris 1945–66*, Centre National des Arts Plastiques, Paris
1987 *Paper as Medium*, Galerie Horst Dietrich, West Berlin

Publications:

By TAJIRI: books—*Ferdi*, Baarlo, Netherlands 1969; *Mayday I* and *II*, Baarlo, Netherlands 1970; *The Wall, Die Mauer, La Mur*, Berlin 1971; *Portrait, Self-Portrait and Measurements.* Berlin 1972; article—"Beyond Pornography" in *Suck* (Amsterdam), 1973; films-*The Vipers*, Paris 1955; *Ferdi*, 1955; *The Birth of Giotta Fuyo Tajiri, 6 June 1957*, 1957; *Bodil Joensen, A Summer Day*, Copenhagen 1970.

On TAJIRI: books—*Shinkichi Tajiri*, exhibition catalogue, by Aldo van Eyck, Amsterdam 1969; *Shinkichi Tajiri*, exhibition catalogue, by Dick Hillenius, Rotterdam 1974; *Tajiri's Daguerrotypes*, exhibition catalogue, by Ed van der Elsken, Amsterdam 1976; *Tajiri's Rediscovery of the Daguerrotype*, exhibition catalogue, by Michael Haerdter, Berlin 1976; *Stereoscopic Views by Tajiri*, exhibition catalogue, by Els Barent, Amsterdam 1979; *Tajiri*, exhibition catalogue by Nicole Gast, Maastricht 1985; film—*The World of Tajiri* by Ben Berbong, 1973.

My works are resumés of explorations into inner space.

—Shinkichi Tajiri

The strange mixture of cultural sources and influences in Shinkichi Tajiri's life seems to have given him great freedom of expression. Born in the United States of Japanese parents, his father a former member of the Samurai caste, Tajiri left his native country as a protest against the treatment of American Japanese during the war. He had previously studied with the famous sculptor Noguchi, who shares his mixed background, and in Paris became a pupil of both Léger and Zadkine. In Paris he was one of the pioneers of the junk-art school, his first impressive group of sculptures being based on bronze foundry droppings, welded into delicate, feathery torsos of vegetable forms.

The instinctive, elegant, oriental seductiveness is something Tajiri immediately rejects once it becomes dominant. A more acceptable inheritance is his fascination with technology and machinery; he is intrigued by the way anything is made, and to some extent his career has been a move away from junk-assemblage, to the re-assembling of natural and man-made shapes. His mature work is a personal mixture of sexual and erotic forms, organised with mechanistic formality. Nature, sex and machines come together in monumental, hieratic sculptures, in which human and plant verticality is conditioned by symbols of growth and procreation. They contain endless echoes and suggestions—the spiky aggression of armoured Samurai, the thrusting determination of natural growth, the urgent confrontation of male and female.

In recent years Tajiri has combined these sculptural forms with informal artistic presentations, happenings which include dance, live nude models, or photographic backgrounds.

—Charles Spencer

TAKAMATSU, Jiro.
Japanese, Born Shinpachiro Takamatsu in Tokyo in February 1936. Studied at Tokyo University of Art, 1954–58. Married Yasuko Takamatsu in 1963; child: Kei. Painter: lives and works in Tokyo. Color Designer, Tohei Animation Company, 1958–59; Industrial Designer, Silver Seikoh Company, 1960–66. Full-time Lecturer, Tokyo University of Art, 1972–75. Recipient: First Prize, *Shell Exhibition*, Tokyo, 1965; First Prize, Museum of Contemporary Art, Nagaoka, Japan, 1965; Theodoron Foundation Prize, *Biennale de Paris*, 1967; Prize, *Tokyo Biennale*, 1967; DeCarlo Cardazzo Prize, *Biennale*, Venice, 1968; Prize, *Contemporary Art Exhibition*, Museum of Ohara, Kurashiki, Japan, 1969; First Prize, *Exhibition of Prints*, Tokyo, 1972. Agent: Tokyo Gallery, 8-6-18 Ginza, Chuo-ku, Tokyo 104. Address: 2-2-27 Shimorenjaku, Mitaka, Tokyo 181, Japan.

Individual Exhibitions:

1966 Tokyo Gallery
1967 Galleria d'Arte del Naviglio, Milan
New Smith Gallery, Brussels
1969 Tokyo Gallery
1971 Tokyo Gallery
1978 Tokyo Gallery

Selected Group Exhibitions:

1967 *Biennale*, Paris
Object '67, Galerie Mathias Fels, Paris
1968 *Biennale*, Venice
1971 *International Sculpture Exhibition*, Guggenheim Museum, New York
1973 *The Art of Surface*, Art Gallery of New South Wales, Sydney
1974 *Japan: Tradition und Gegenwart*, Kunsthalle, Dusseldorf
Japanese Art in Scandinavia, Gothenburg Museum, Sweden (travelled to the Henie-Onstad Art Center, Oslo)
Japan Pa Louisiana, Louisiana Museum, Humlebaek, Denmark
1975 *A View of Japanese Contemporary Art*, Seibu Museum of Art, Tokyo
1977 *Painting in the Age of Photography*, Kunsthaus, Zurich

Collections:

Museum of Contemporary Art, Nagaoka, Japan; National Museum of Modern Art, Tokyo; Museum of Modern Art, Kanagawa, Japan; Ohara Museum of Art, Kurashiki, Japan; Australian National Gallery, Canberra.

Publications:

On TAKAMATSU: books—*Guggenheim International Exhibition*, exhibition catalogue, New York 1971; *Japan: Tradition und Gegenwart*, exhibition catalogue, by J. Harten and J. P. Love, Dusseldorf 1974; articles—"Jiro Takamatsu" in *Mizue* (Tokyo), no. 2, 1971; "Tokyo Letter" by J. P. Love in *Art International* (Lugano, Switzerland), February 1972.

In his first public showing, Jiro Takamatsu stretched twine out of the museum, stuffed twine into glass bottles, and even wound other twine around his body much like a silkworm spinning a cocoon. This "String" series was his contribution to the *Yomiuri Independent Exhibition* in 1961. It was three years after he had graduated from the faculty of oil painting at the Tokyo University of Fine Arts. Then only 25, Takamatsu has sought to materially express, at the exhibition, the concepts of line and distance. He bottled, in effect, a hundred meters "distance."

He soon teamed with Gemei Akasegawa and Natsuyuki Nakanishi to form the High Red Center, which created happenings in such places as Ginza streets. It was not until 1964, however, that he began to attract serious attention in art circles, by means of a series "Shadows." In these works, he deliberately outlined, on white canvas, the shadows of every-day objects such as jars and clothing brushes, and people in various positions. If painting since the discovery of perspective, born of the camera obscura of even longer ago, has been depicting "shadows" on two-dimensional canvas to show the three-dimensional outer world, then to merely paint shadows was to be true to that principle—moreover, it had significance as a denial of the reality. Doubt about the existence of the real world was what Takamatsu showed by painting shadows, and it was, further, a lyrical expression.

The "Perspective" series which followed was Takamatsu's essay in solidifying for our view the deception in the relationship between the real world and human beings. As the laws of perspective have it, the further an object is from the viewer the smaller it appears, but in Takamatsu's tables, in this series, the diminution is real, not merely apparent, and exaggerated beyond what the eye has been trained to perceive. Chairs too, and entire interiors, rush away from the viewer toward distant vanishing points. A culmination of this work was "Perspective Dimension—Sky" which earned Takamatsu a prize at the Venice *Biennale* in 1968. Then, in 1970, at the Festival Plaza at the *World's Fair* in Osaka, his "Perspective Construction," with its mirror surfaces which reflected the sky and created strange illusions also attracted considerable critical attention.

Having brought out the fiction of our habitual perception of the real world by means of his Shadow and Perspective works, Takamatsu since 1969 has come to be interested in how to perceive things under conditions of absolutely minimal participation by the person involved. He painted numbers on rounded river stones, and attempted other experiments in this quest. More recently, he has been cutting tree trunks in great slices and then stacking them as they had been before, or breaking a block of concrete into fragments which he would then fit into a box. One such reassembled box was included in the *International Sculpture Exhibition* at the Guggenheim in 1971, where it was praised as a fine example of conceptual art. In 1972 he received the grand prize for his arrangement of alphabetical letters at the Eighth *International Prints Biennale* in Tokyo.

In the 1980s, Takamatsu resumed painting with a completely abstract style. He was exploring the narrow possibilities of pictorial diversification via grids of entangled wavy lines overlaid with washes of vivid colors to promote and illusion of depth. The pictures sometimes have the appearance of seaweed dancing in water and reflecting the varying moods of light throughout the day; at other times, they appear as a retinal fantasy that can only be experienced deep in a forest or in the brilliance on sunlight on a white beach.

—Yoshiaki Tono

TAKIS.
Greek. Born Panayotis Vassilakis in Athens, 29 October 1925. Self-taught in art, from 1946. Married the artist, Liliane Lijn, q.v., in 1961 (divorced, 1967); son: Athanasios Thanos; married Do Koenig in 1971. Sculptor, Athens, 1945–46, in Paris and London, 1954–59, in Paris and Athens, since 1959; produced first "Signals," 1954–58; first telemagnetic sculptures, 1958; first electro-magnetic musical works, 1973. Recipient: Fellowship in Advanced Visual Studies, Massachusetts Institute of Technology, Cambridge, 1968–70; Prix de la Biennale, *Biennale de Paris*, 1985. Agents: Galerie Lelong, 13 rue de Teheran, 75008 Paris, France; Alexandre Iolas Gallery, 15 East 55th Street, New York, New York 10022. U.S.A. Addresses: 22 rue Liancourt, 75014 Paris, France; and Odos Dervenakious, Gero Vounos, Aharne, Attikis, Athens, Greece.

Individual Exhibitions:

1955 Hanover Gallery, London
Galarie Furstenberg, Paris
1958 Hanover Gallery, London
1959 Galerie Iris Clert, Paris
Alexandre Iolas Gallery, New York
1960 *L'Impossible, un homme dans l'espace*, Galerie Iris Clert, Paris
1961 Alexandre Iolas Gallery, New York
1962 *Signals and Telesculptures*, Galleria Schwarz, Milan
1963 Alexandre Iolas Gallery, New York

Takis: *Three Totems/Espace Musical*, 1981

1964 Galerie Alexandre Iolas, Paris
Signals Gallery, London
1965 Galerie Alexandre Iolas, Geneva
1966 Galerie Alexandre Iolas, Paris
Hanover Gallery, London
Indica Gallery, London
1967 Howard Wise Gallery, New York
Galerie Krikhaar, Amsterdam
Galerie Claude Givaudan, Paris
1968 Galleria Schwarz, Milan
Arts Laboratory, London
Widcombe Manor, Bath, England
1969 Howard Wise Gallery, New York
Massachusetts Institute of Technology, Cambridge (retrospective)
1970 Städtisches Museum Schloss Morsbroich, Leverkusen, West Germany (retrospective)
Howard Wise Gallery, New York
1971 Galerie Alexandre Iolas, Paris
Galerie Bama, Paris
1972 Galleria Iolas, Milan
Centre National d'Art Contemporain, Paris (retrospective)
1973 Nederlands Dans Theater, Amsterdam (decors for ballet *Elkesis*)
1974 Zoumboulakis Gallery, Athens
Musikalische Raume, Kunstverein, Hannover
Espace Cardin, Paris
1975 Galerie Fred Lanzenberg, Brussels
1976 Galerie Alexandre Iolas, Paris
1977 Galerie Artcurial, Paris
New Smith Gallery, Brussels
Trito Mati Gallery, Athens
1978 Musée d'Art Moderne de la Ville, Paris
1979 Kölnischer Kunstverein, Cologne
Galarie Reckermann, Cologne
Musée de la Ville, Calais
1981 Centre Georges Pompidou, Paris
Galerie Maeght, Paris
1983 Galerie Maeght Lelong, Paris
1985 Centre Georges Pompidou, Paris
Ecole Régionale des Beaux Arts, St. Etienne, France
1986 Musée Rath, Geneva
Galarie Hotel de ville, Villeurbanne, France

Selected Group Exhibitions:

1952 *Exposition Internationale*, Delphi, Greece
1959 *14 European Sculptors*, Staempfli Gallery, New York
1961 *Bewogen Beweging*, Stedlijk Museum, Amsterdam (toured Scandinavia)
1965 *Lumière et Mouvement*, Kunsthalle, Berne (toured Belgium and Germany)
1967 *The Machine*, Museum of Modern Art, New York
1974 *Art of the 20th Century*, Fondazione Peggy Guggenheim, Venice (toured Europe)
1977 *Documenta*, Kassel, West Germany
1981 *Machins-Machines*, Centre Culturel, Bretigny, France
1983 *Electra*, Musée d'Art Moderne de la Ville, Paris
1985 *Biennale de Paris*, Musé d'Art Moderne, Paris

Collections:

Centre Georges Pompidou, Paris; Centre National d'Art Contemporain, Paris; Städtisches Museum Schloss Morsbroich, Leverkusen, West Germany: Arts Council of Great Britain, London; Tate Gallery, London; Museum of Tel Aviv; Museum of Modern Art, New York; Guggenheim Museum, New York; Art Institute of Chicago; Art Gallery of Ontario, Toronto.

Publications:

By TAKIS: books—*Estafilades*, Paris 1961; *Poems 1942–46*, Paris 1972; *Elkesis*, Rotterdam 1973; *Musique Magnetique*, Paris 1975; articles—"Conversation dans l'Atelier," interview, with Luce Hoctin in *L'Oeil* (Paris), November 1964, "Statements by Kinetic Artists" in *Studio International* (London), February 1967; "Revelations: Interview de Takis," with Jean Clay, in *Rhobo* (Paris), Spring 1968; "Technology Against Technology = Anti-technology" in *Radical Software* (New York). no. 2, 1970; "Lignes Paralleles" in *Takis*, exhibition catalogue, Paris 1971; "Interview de Takis," with Catherine Millet, in *Chroniques de l'Art Vivani* (Paris), May 1971.

On TAKIS: books—*La Sculpture de ce Siècle* by Michel Seuphor, Paris 1959; *Takis: l'Impossible un homme dans l'espace*, exhibition catalogue, with texts by Alain Jouffroy, Gregory Corso, William Burroughs, Bryon Gysin and others, Paris 1960; *Icons and Images of the 60's* by Nicolas and Elena Calas, Paris 1961; *Takis: Signals and Telesculptures*, exhibition catalogue, with texts by William Burroughs, Alain Jouffroy, Nicolas Calas and others, Milan 1962; *Une Révolution du Regard* by Alain Jouffroy, Paris 1964; *Naissance de l'Art Cinétique* by Frank Popper, Paris 1967; *Nature and the Art of Movement* by Gyorgy Kepes, Paris 1968; *Kinetic Art: The Language of Movement* by Guy Brett, London 1968: *25 Ans d'Art Vivant* by Michel Ragon, Paris 1969; *L'Avant Garde au 20eme Siècle* by Pierre Cabanne and Pierre Restany, 1969; *L'Art Present dans la Cité* by Adam Saulnier, Paris 1969; *Focus* by Pierre Cabanne, Paris 1971; *Takis*, exhibition catalogue, with text by J. J. Lebel, Nicolas Calas, Alain Jouffroy and others, Paris 1972; *Takis: Musikalische Raume*, exhibition catalogue, with texts by Helmut R. Leppien and Christos M. Jachimides, Hannover 1974; films—*Takis* by Jean-Marie Drot, 1960; *10 Artists de Paris*, French television film, 1965; *Meet the Artist* by Colette Robert, 1967; *Takis Unlimited* by Mahmoud K. Khosrowshaki, 1967; *Takis, Chant of the Magnetic Minstre* by Richard Edelman, 1968; *Takis* by Wayne Anderson, 1969; *Takis* by ARC-New Film, 1969; *CBS-TV: 21st Century* by Keeper Poor, 1969.

I will try to put down on paper something about magnets. I have been intrigued by radar systems, and tried to find out how they function. I was told that they depend on a magnet which swings around through the full 360 degrees of the compass. The signal reported to the observer tells him of the presence of some other metallic object in space. I bought my first magnet and dreamt of using it in some way to bring about a perpetual movement by using the force of the magnet. I hoped to make some metallic object move forever. And I saw that the magnet gave me the use of a new fantastic element which I could apply to the iron-work which I had done before. (The "tiges" which I had been making were antennae to capture the force of nature in the clouds . . . electricity. In other works they had been receivers all along. This struck me as being incomplete.) Magnets, however, are not "receivers" but "senders". Yet, like radar itself a magnet "feels" out towards any passing metallic object facing the magnet. What I had been doing up until the moment I started with the magnets was making signals which merely received the electricity from the sky. Even though they moved, my sculptures seemed to me to still be static.

Up until now those who made metal sculptures had been trying to create tension by twisting iron bars. Many sculptors had been making twisted and pointed forms which were intended to create a sort of vibration between two points; the unreal made to seem real through the talent of the sculptor himself, if you like. What I wanted was to make what I felt to be really REAL. A magnet is not an idea—it is something so real that I was led to dream of making a Perpetual Motion machine with magnets. Very soon I realised that this was not really my intention. What interested me was, rather, the way in which magnetism creates a connection between two metallic objects through the magnetic waves which are a communication. When Gonzales twisted iron objects he produced only a graphic achievement such as the painters had been interested in. Many painters like Matta and Lam have worked along that line as have others who were more interested in creating an illusion of space rather than an action in space which I feel is the role of the sculpture.

When I wished to express the space-communication between an object and a magnet I was obliged to tie up the object. When I did this in order to keep an object at a distance from a magnet, I realized that I had "floated" the object. My metallic object floated in the air and vibrated. This was even further from my original intention. I had wished to communicate the two metals only symbolically but, now, they communicated realistically through the magnetic field. Immediately they gave the sensation of being alive. A new and very real force was working between the two objects which I had approached one to the other. When I attached an object by a string and floated it towards the magnet, even a breath of air started a visible vibration. In actual fact the vibration is continuous whether one sees it or not through the wave-motion of the magnetic field, working alternatively but continuously. The vibration is perpetual. What interested me was to put into iron sculpture a new, continuous, and live force. The result was in no way a graphic representation of a force but the force itself which had to be handled as one would handle any other force in nature—even an animal force. The perpetual movement aspect of it became obviously of secondary interest and I put myself to treating, guiding and dominating magnetic force itself in its aspects of real communication . . . the space communication of objects on this planet. More than that, I have wanted to bring off what the Egyptians tried to communicate through the human form in which muscles were represented in a state of tension or slack. The ancient Cycladic sculptors, too, tried to represent these forces through the action of the muscles and forms. In what I do I intend that the tension of forces shall be as visible as the nylon cord which floats an object in front of the magnet whose live force and vibration gives life to what has seemed to be dead material.

—Takis

Takis is a pioneering kinetic sculptor who has effectively fulfilled his intention of bridging the barriers between art and science by making his own art one which used or unleashes the natural forces of gravity, magnetism and electromagnetism, the movement of the tides, or light. He is an elemental sculptor in much the same sense as Turner was an elemental painter, concerned not so much with the visible surface of the world but with the underlying natural forces, which can be enormously destructive and yet have been harnessed by man to drive the Industrial Revolution, a revolution which depended on the new scientific concept of nature as the carrier of energy.

The progress of Takis' work can be seen as a constant attempt to intensify the presence of energy, to make these powerful natural forces the living core and essence of his sculpture, which with his electromagnetic works he triumphantly has done. He has told how he was fascinated as a child by the way Greek children cut vegetable roots into dolls and hang them on a string to float in the wind. But he came to kinetics only gradually, starting as a self-taught sculptor who at the age of 21 made objects in clay, then for several years from 1948–1953, carved in wood. These wooden sculptures were of the human figure, more or less in the Giacometti tradition, though from 1953–1955 they became more and more abstract, and Takis came to regard abstraction as inseparable from an objective view of the modern world of science and technology.

Since 1974 he has lived mainly in Paris, though with prolonged stays in London. Here his work crystallized, and from making bronze "idols" with flexible wire necks, or arrow-and piston-headed flower sculptures, he moved decisively into the kinetic sphere with the series of words he called "Signals". He has described how the idea germinated while he was waiting three of four hours for a train in Calais, and became fascinated by the signalization of the railways: "I drew some sketches, thinking how dramatic this signalization was, and how necessary a part of our century this was. When I came back to Paris I started making a sort of imitation of those signals, and as I used thin wires as bodies to hold the signals, accidentally they started moving, and I thought it was very fascinating." These Signals consist of modelled forms on the end of long rods of steel, an extremely pliable and light material which allows them to remain in constant vibration when set in motion. They contain suggestions not only of railway signals, but also of road signs, antennae, and all sorts of other aspects of our technological environment.

His next step of using magnetic and electrical forces instead of gravity was inspired by seeing "radar scanners moving as if directed by an invisible power." He was trying to build his own radar machine, which included piano wires in the hope that it would also make mysterious music, when one day these wires broke because of their tension and floated towards a magnet which was next to the machine. This led him to focus his attention on forces rather than on objects, trying to make visible in his sculptures the invisibly energy of magnetism. The magnetic and telemagnetic sculptures he began making in 1959, in which balls, cones or needles are suspended in a magnetic or electromagnetic field, do not exist as forms, like traditional sculptures, but an invisible energy which makes them move and change.

The idea that the locally more powerful force of magnetism could liberate objects from the earth's gravity excited him, and in November 1960 Takis put a man in space by suspending the poet Sinclair Beiles in a magnetic field. The following year he was producing his "Magnetic Ballets," which depend on combining and controlling two different forces, electromagnetism and gravity, by suspending balls over upturned electromagnets and making them swing and gyrate in a cosmic dance which makes perceptible the energy that is all around us and the forces that dominate the natural world.

An extension of this is to increase the tension at the centre of this moving kinetic energy sculpture by revealing the source of energy of the electromagnet, which is operated by a blue mercury vapour lamp. This not only used light in the sculpture, but shows that light itself is just another form of electromagnetic energy. Yet the constantly flickering mercury vapour lamp is also poetic in character, so that Takis can think of it as "cosmic flower" emitting its energy. Takis has shown constant inventiveness in finding fresh sources such as signal-lamps, aircraft instruments and fireworks for revealing the energy which is always the core of his recent sculptures. At MIT's Center for Visual Studies in 1968 he turned to yet another natural source of energy in his "Hommage a Marcel Duchamp." The original bicycle wheel exhibited by Duchamp was mounted so that it could be turned by hand, but Takis floated a similar bicycle wheel in the sea so that it was perpetual motion, driven by the motion of the tides.

Takis also offers homage to Thales of Miletus, for it was the pioneering Greek scientist who first described magnetism and electricity 2,500 years ago. And though modern science has learnt how to harness such forces, and that they are interchangable with light, heat and even matter, their ultimate nature remains as mysterious as it was when Thales first described them. Schlegel's prediction that the response to a scientifically explored universe ought to be that it is a still intractable mystery has proved true with a vengeance, and the fascination of Takis' kinetic sculptures is that they are not parodies of technological instruments but highly poetic creations which bring us into direct contact with the fundamental and still mysterious forces which power nature and life. No wonder that Takis in his own statements often seems to verge on animism when he talks about his works as cosmic flowers.

—Konstantin Bazarov

TAL-COAT, Pierre.

French. Born Pierre Jacob in Clohars-Carnoet, Finistere, 12 December 1905; adopted pseudonym "Tal-Coat" in 1926. Educated in Quimperle, 1912–18; studied at Ecole Supérieure, Quimperle, 1919–22; studied casting, Académie de la Grand Chaumière, Paris, 1924–26, and pottery moulding at a manufacturer in Sevres, 1926. Served in French Army, 1925–26, 1939–40. Married Bronislawa Lewandowska in 1927; daughter: Pierette; married Xaviere Angeli in 1950 (died, 1970). Independent artist, Paris, 1924, Brittany, 1927–39, Paris, 1931–40, Aix-en-Provence, 1940–56, and St. Pierre de Baileul, L'Eure, 1956 until his death in 1985: Founder-Member, with R. Humblot, H. Jannot, J. Lasne, A. Pellan and G. Rohner, "Forces Nouvelles," Paris, 1932–39. Recipient: Prix Paul Guillaume, 1936; Grand Prix National des Arts, 1968. Commandeur, Ordre des Arts et Lettres, 1976. Agents: Galerie Maeght, 13 rue de Teheran, 75008 Paris; Galerie Benador, rue Hotel de Ville 7, Place Saconnerie 10, Geneva 1200; and Galerie Clivages, 46 rue de l'Université, 75007 Paris. *Died* (in Saint-Pierre de Bailleul) *11 June 1985.*

Individual Exhibitions:

1927 Galerie Fabre, Paris
1930 Galerie Fabre, Paris
1933 Gallerie Billiet Pierre Vorms, Paris
1936 Galerie Renou et Colle, Paris
Julien Levy Gallery, New York
1937 Galerie Renou et Colle, Paris
1943 Galerie de France, Paris
1945 *Peintures*, Galerie de France, Paris
1946 Galerie de France, Paris
1948 Galerie de France, Paris
1950 Galerie Maeght, Paris
Galerie de France, Paris
1954 Galerie Maeght, Paris
1956 Galerie Maeght, Paris
1957 Kunsthalle, Berne, Switzerland

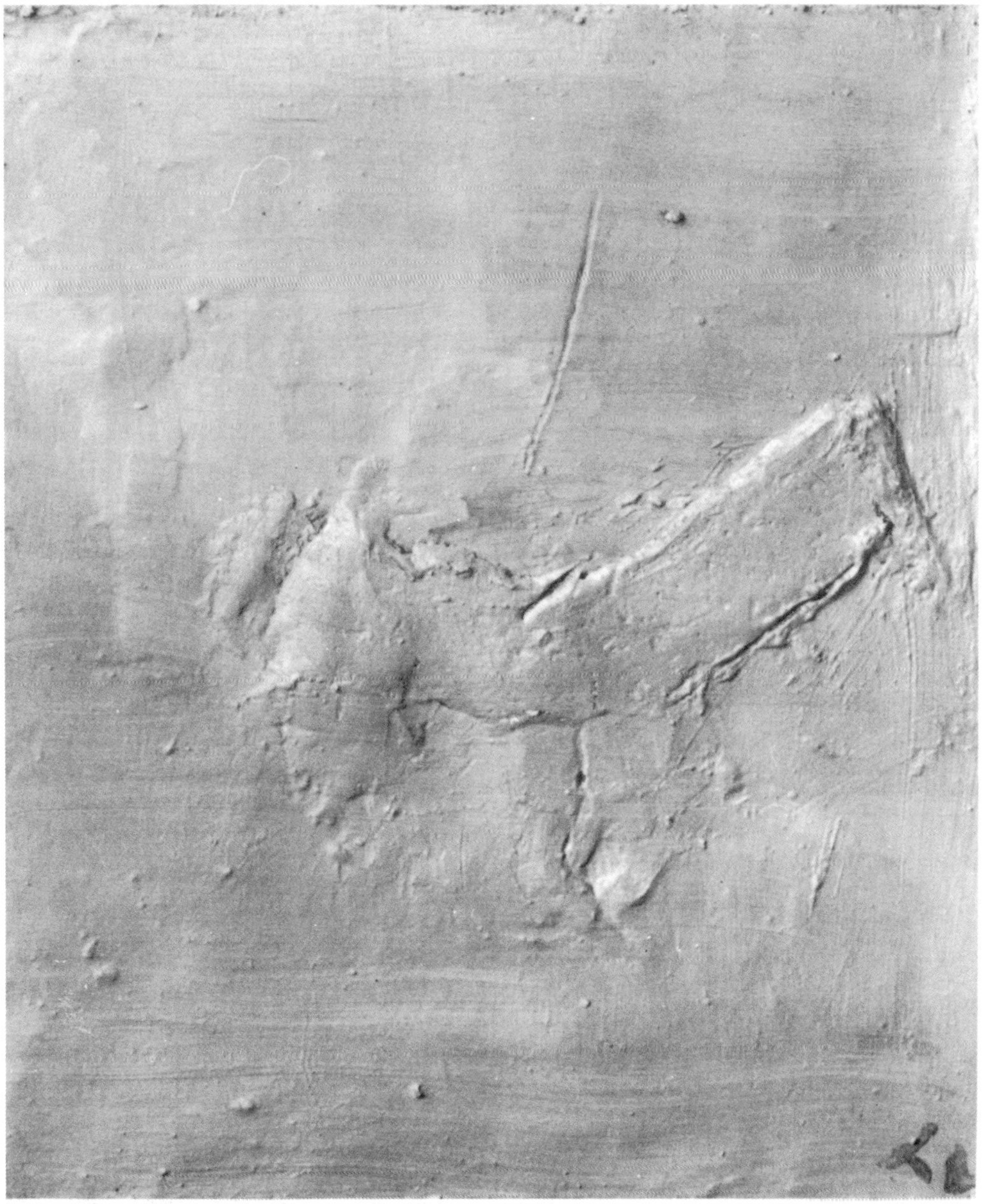

Pierre Tal-Coat: *Passage Gris*

1965 Galerie Beno d'Incelli, Paris
1968 Galerie Henri Benezit, Paris
Galerie André Schoeller, Paris
Galerie Beno d'Incelli, Paris
1969 Palais de l'Europe, Menton, France
Maison de la Culture, Le Havre, France
Maison de la Culture, Amiens, France
1970 *Ocuvres Récentes,* Galerie Benador, Geneva
1972 *Almanach de Tal-Coat,* Galerie Benador, Geneva
1973 Galerie L'Entracte, Lausanne, Switzerland
1974 Galerie Maeght, Zurich
Museée des Beaux-Arts, Metz, France
1975 Galerie Benador, Geneva
Ueno Royal Museum, Tokyo (travelled to the Hakone Open-Air Museum, Ninotaira).
1976 Grand Palais, Paris
Musée d'Art Moderne, Paris
Galerie Eveil, Marlenheim, West Germany
Galerie Shapiro, Paris
Galerie de France, Paris
Galerie du Benelux, Brussels
1978 Galerie Biren, Paris
Galerie de l'Entracte, Lausanne, Switzerland
1979 Galerie Benador, Geneva (travelled to the Galerie Karsten-Greve, Cologne)
Chateau de Ratilly, Yonne, France (with André du Bouchet)
Galerie Ditesheim, Neuchâtel, Switzerland
Bibliotenque de Lyons, France
1980 Galerie Benador, at *F.I.A.C.*, Paris
1981 Galerie Clivages, Paris
Chapelle de Locronan, Brittany, France
Centre d'Art Contemporain, Jouy-sur-Eure, France
Galerie Clivages, at *F.I.A.C.*, Paris
1982 Galerie Clivages, Paris
Grand Palais, Paris
1983 Galerie Clivages, Paris
Galerie Michel Cachoux, Paris
Galerie Patrice Trigano, Paris
1984 Centre Noiroit, Arras, France
Galerie Clivages, Paris
Galerie Sapone, Nice, France
1985 Galerie Clivages, Paris
New Museum of Contemporary Art, New York
Cabinet des Estampes, Geneva
1986 Gallery Art Point, Tokyo
Galerie Clivages, Paris
Galerie L'Entract, Lausanne
Centre Gerard Philippe, Bretigny-sur-Orge, France
1987 Maison de la Culture, Bourges, France
Musée de Valence, France
Galerie Clivages, Paris

Selected Group Exhibitions:

1934 *Bateaux et Marin,* Galerie Billiet Pierre Vorms, Paris
1935 *Forces Nouvelles,* Galerie Billiet Pierre Vorms, Paris
1949 *La Jeune Peinture Francaise,* Leicester Galleries, London
1955 *Documenta 1,* Kassel, West Germany (and *Documenta 2,* 1959)
1968 *Painting in France 1900–1967,* National Gallery of Art, Washington, D.C. (toured the United States)
1973 *Collections Genevoises: Art du 20e. Siècle,* Musée Rath, Geneva
1976 *Front Populaire,* Ancienne Gare de la Bastille, Paris
1980 *Forces Nouvelles 1935–39,* Musée d'Art Moderne de la Ville, Paris
1981 *Paris-Paris,* Centre George Pompidou, Paris
1982 *Bretons à Paris,* Grand Palais, Paris

Collections:

Centre Georges Pompidou, Paris: Musée de Grenoble, France; Fondation Maeght, Saint-Paul-de-Vence, France.

Publications:

By TAL-COAT: books illustrated—*Honore de Balzac,* Geneva 1946; *Elements de Nature,* Paris 1949; *Colle Surface,* with text by André du Bouchet, Paris 1956; *Sur le Pas,* with text by André du Bouchet, Paris 1959; *Traverse d'un Plateau,* Paris 1963; *Laisses,* with text by André du Bouchet, Lausanne 1975; *Espace Delute,* with text by Pierre Torreilles, Paris 1976; *Sous le Linteau en Forme de Joug,* with text by André du Bouchet, Lausanne 1978; *Surface d'eceuil,* with text by Philippe Denis, Paris 1980.

On TAL-COAT: books—*Pierre Tal-Coat: Peintures,* exhibition catalogue, with text by Michel Florisoone, Paris 1945; *Tal Coat,* exhibition catalogue, with text Jacques Lassaigne, Paris 1950; *Tal-Coat,* exhibition catalogue, with text by F. Meyer, Berne 1957; *Peintres Contemporains* by Georges Duthuit and others, Paris 1964; *Tal-Coat,* exhibition catalogue, with texts by Francis Palermo and E. Marze, Menton, France 1969; *Tal-Coat: Oeuvres Récentes,* exhibition catalogue, with text by Henri Maldiney, Geneva 1970; *Almanach de Tal-Coat,* exhibition catalogue, with text by Pietro Sarto, Geneva 1971; *Pierre Tal-Coat,* exhibition catalogue, with text by Raoul-Jean Moulin, Zurich 1974; *Forces Nourvelles 1935–1939,* exhibition catalogue, with text by Pierre Vorms, Paris 1980; *Tal Coat,* exhibition catalogue, with text by Jean Pascal Leger, Valence 1987.

Prior to the naming of things invisible wave sweeping us out of our cell of insistent visitation. Seized by such an awareness, beyond the dull means of pastures old, I had to proceed towards that which, from the curves, from even our stammerings, can attempt to express what otherwise escapes fair reason. I mean that which cannot be partitioned off by fluctuating edges and escapes from the filed frame, from the established patterns. And that it was the extreme precariousness of the enterprise at which every extremity gleamed a possibility of freedom which is beyond tensions.

Here, accosted by the world, overrun on all ideas, unable to claim I observe it, which always implies perception lagging behind for excess of reference. This said to explain my attempt to raise myself to the level of the experienced without the convention of the known. And the necessity to proceed forbids recapitulation, for all that belongs to the moment is its one guarantee in the ineffable of its presence.

And to yield to one's wonderment requires a necessary precariousness. But no less precarious the continuing awakening to preserve expressive harmony. To thus proceed suits me, demanding neither courage nor special gift: that which is given to each in its emerging necessity.

Thus the arid path common to all has always given out into more distance from the mirage of proximity, for always is the shackle. But also proceeding likewise, in the grip of the ungraspable.

—Pierre Tal-Coat (1983)

Son of a Breton fisherman, Pierre Tal-Coat was largely self-taught as a painter. His first stay in Paris

lasted only two years but by 1931 he was back in the French capital where he quickly became popular with liberal collectors and fellow-artists. He was figurative in his approach, and his portrait of Gertrude Stein was hailed as a fine example of his work that reflected a kind of primitive monumentality. He mixed with the avant-garde painters of his time and his experiences in the Spanish Civil War became the subject of a series "Massacres" that has been compared with Picasso's "Guernica," though Tal-Coat's treatment was more emotional and directly figurative. By about 1945 he in fact came under the influence of Picasso and then two years later André Masson introduced him to the lyrical interpretation of landscape by Chinese artists. This phase continued into the 1960's.

These landscapes represent perhaps the peak of Tal-Coat's art, for in them he aimed at a synthesis of nature that came close to a perfect analogy in its choice of motives more or less echoing reality. The pale grounds of pure tone bore patches of colour that might be held to represent clouds in the sky or boats at anchor on a sunlit bay. This Funambuliste equivocation in his compositions was invariably handled with a sensitive and delicate control of mass and spatial relationship that gave the works a great feeling of atmosphere: the transparency of air and the quivering essence of light were understated in soft-edged outlines. In other works the colours were more violently contrasted in intensity and weight with central motives taking stronger emphasis often in themes redolent of country-side. It is this lack of precision in identification of the objects suggested in his landscapes that gives Tal-Coat's work its edge of interest, for though the associations are less than exact their massing and placing on the canvas have a direct and powerful dynamic operating over the surface of the canvas. By 1974 he was still capable of painting some huge monochrome pictures such as "Bleu surgi" that seemed derivative of earlier works by Yves Klein.

His later work shows a rough and vital animation of pigment, scarring its own surface in the relief contour of a lunar landscape, certainly devoid of human habitation and having in its mineral colour something hinting at volcanic origins. "Depot 2" (1974) is a painting of this geological metaphor where a dark gesture raises its facets to reflect the light in an aerial panorama shading into the void of outer space itself. In their own terms the paintings indicate their process of maturing through periods of time in which the surface is moulded, melted, suffering fission and enduring heat and eruption. Tal-Coat has described his motivation. "As though beyond me a vision, a hand has overruled my blindness, conducting me I know not where nor cannot see."

—G. S. Whittet

TAMAYO, Rufino.

Mexican. Born in Oaxaca in 1899; moved to Mexico City, 1911. Studied at the Academia de Bellas Artes, Mexico City, 1917–20. Married Olga Flores Rivas in 1934. Painter: travelled frequently from Mexico City to New York, 1926–36; lived in New York, 1936–1954, and in Paris, 1954 until his return to Mexico, 1964; donated museum for permanent display of his Mexican Pre-Columbian art collection of more than 1000 works. Oaxaca, 1974; donated his international collection of contemporary art to the Mexican People: Museo Rufino Tamayo Arte Contemporaneo Internacional officially opened in Chapultepec Park, Mexico City, May 1981. Chairman, Department of Ethnographic Drawing, Museo Nacional de Arqueologia, Mexico City, 1921–23. Recipient: First Prize, *Carnegie International*, Pittsburgh, 1952; First Prize for Painting, *Bienal*, Sao Paulo, 1953; Guggenheim International Foundation Award, 1960; National Award for Artistic Merit, Mexico City, 1964; Calouste Gulbenkian Prize, Institut Francais, Paris, 1969; First Prize, 10th Triennale of Colour Graphics, Grenchen, Switzerland, 1985. Street named in his honor, Oaxaca, 1972. Member: Argentinian Academy of Art; Accademia Disegno, Florence; Academy of Arts, Buenos Aires, 1959; American Institute and Academy of Arts and Letters, 1961. Chevalier, 1957, Officier, 1970, and Commandeur, 1975, Légion d'Honneur, France; Comendador of the Italian Republic, 1971. Agent: Marlborough Gallery, Inc., 40 West 57th Street, New York, New York 10019, U.S.A. Address: Callejon del Santisimo 12, San Angel, Mexico D.F., Mexico.

Individual Exhibitions:

1926 Weyhe Gallery, New York
1929 Palacio de Belles Arts, Mexico City
1931 Julien Levy Gallery, New York
1937 Julien Levy Gallery, New York
1938 Galeria de Arte Mexicano, Mexico City
Catherine Kuh Gallery, Chicago
1939 Valentine Gallery, New York
1940 Valentine Gallery, New York
1942 Valentine Gallery, New York
1945 Arts Club of Chicago
1946 Valentine Gallery, New York
1947 Cincinnati Art Museum, Ohio
Pierre Matisse Gallery, New York
1948 *Retrospective of 25 Years of Painting*, Palacio de Bellas Artes, Mexico City
1950 *16 Paintings*, at the *Biennale*, Venice
Galerie des Beaux-Arts, Paris
Palais des Beaux-Arts, Brussels
Knoedler Gallery, New York
1951 Instituto de Arte Moderno, Buenos Aires
Salon de la Plastica Mexicana, Mexico City
Frank Peris Gallery, Los Angeles
Knoedler Gallery, New York
1952 individual exhibition, at the *Arte Mexicain du Pre-Columbien à nos Jours*, Musée d'Art Moderne, Paris
Fort Worth Art Museum, Texas
Pan American Union, Washington, D.C.
1953 Knoedler Gallery, New York
Frank Perls Gallery, Los Angeles
Santa Barbara Museum of Art, California
San Francisco Museum of Art
1956 Museum of Fine Arts, Houston
Knoedler Gallery, New York
1959 Kunstnernes Hus, Oslo
Felix Landau Gallery, Los Angeles
Knoedler Gallery, New York
1960 Galerie de France, Paris
1961 Gallery One, London
1962 Galeria Misrachi, Mexico City
Knoedler Gallery, New York
1963 Mainichi Newspaper, Tokyo (retrospective)
Association of Museum of Israel (travelling exhibition)
1965 Galerie Semiha Huber, Zurich
1968 Palacio de Bellas Artes, Mexico City (retrospective of 103 works)
Exhibition of 124 Works from American Collections, Phoenix Art Museum, Arizona
Biennale, Venice (retrospective of 100 works)
1971 Perls Gallery, New York
1973 Galeria Misrachi, Mexico City
Perls Gallery, New York
1974 Museo de Arte Moderno, Mexico City
Musée d'Art Moderne, Paris
1975 Palazzo Strozzi, Florence
1976 Museo de Arte Moderno, Mexico City
National Museum of Modern Art, Tokyo
1977 *Bienal*, Sao Paulo (retrospective of 134 paintings)
Marlborough Galery, New York
1978 Phillips Collection, Washington, D.C.
1979 Marion Koogler McNay Art Institute, San Antonio, Texas
Myth and Magic, Guggenheim Museum, New York
Marlborough Fine Art, London
1981 Brenner Gallery, Boca Raton, Florida
Marlborough Gallery, New York
1982 Marlborough Fine Art, London
1983 Graphische Sammlung Albertina, Vienna
1984 Marlborough Fine Art, Tokyo
1985 Marlborough Gallery, New York
1986 Marisa Del Re Gallery, New York

Collections:

Museo de Arte Moderno, Mexico City; Centre Georges Pompidou, Paris; Musée Royal, Brussels, Galleria Nazionale de Arte Moderna, Rome; Museum of Modern Art, Tokyo; Nasjonalgalleriet, Oslo; Museum of Modern Art, New York; Guggenheim Museum, New York; Albright-Knox Art Gallery, Buffalo, New York; Art Institute of Chicago.

Publications:

By TAMAYO: book—*Drawings by Tamayo*, Mexico City 1950.

On TAMAYO: books—*Tamayo* by Robert Goldwater, Mexico City 1947; *Rufino Tamayo* by Enrique Gual, Mexico City 1947; *Tamayo* by Paul Westheim, Mexico City 1957; *Tamayo en la Pintura Mexicana* by Octavio Paz, Mexico City 1959; *Tamayo* by Juan Garcia Ponce, Mexico City 1967; *Tamayo* by Octavio Paz, Mexico City 1967; *Rufino Tamayo* by Emily Genauer, New York 1974; *Rufino Tamayo: 50 Years of His Painting*, with an introduction by James G. Lynch, Jr., Washington, D.C. 1979; *Rufino Tamayo: Recent Paintings 1980–85*, exhibition catalogue, New York 1985; films-*Birth of a Mural*, Universidad Nacional de Mexico, 1965; *Rufino Tamayo*, BBC, London, 1966; *Tamayo*, directed by Max Pol Fouchet, Paris, 1970; *The Artistic Life of Rufino Tamayo*, directed by Gary Conklin, 1973.

Although it was not until 1972 that a street was named Calle Rufino Tamayo in Oaxaca City (his birthplace), like so many others, worldwide, I was already familiar with Tamayo works from the 1-man exhibition of his paintings mounted by Victor Musgrave at London's Gallery One (1961), the first showing of his work to reach British shores, but by no means his first personal exhibition. That had been at the Weyhe Gallery, New York, in 1926 and he had held at least 25 Tamayo exhibitions in Mexico, the United States, Paris, Brussels and Buenos Aires in that interim.

Tamayo, with some reservations, may be described as a kind of Expressionist (although probably not easily recognisable as such to those who have clear title to that description)—there is plenty of latent Thunder in some of his paintings, but on the whole expressionist Lightning stays muted by his personal colouration and the diminution of the flash. This in no way reduces hints of manic/magical violence when he decides such drama should enter his pictures. In its anti-hysterical manner this cool portrayal of vibrant passions is an inheritance (over the heads of North American and European modernisms) to the cultures and art products of the Ancient Mexicans—Aztec, Toltec, Mayan. Their quiet fierceness, and their placid monumentality as well, would seem naturally handed down to a *modern* artist familiar—as he is—with the ethnical ties of his country's *ur-alt* past. And it should be remembered that, not without good reason, Tamayo was appointed in 1921 for three years as Head of the Department of Ethnographic Drawing by the Museo Nacional de Arqueologia in Mexico City.

Along with all the contacts he had with contemporary art—his early years (1926–49) were frequently spent in New York interspersed with return visits to Mexico and during the succeeding ten years he was domiciled in Paris—and his special knowledge of the traditions of ancient Mexican art and their esoteric meanings, he was able to build up an important reputation as an exceptional artist.

Tamayo's painting is essentially constructed upon three foundations: a vagrant and beguiling figuration, sometimes departing from exact imagery, at others plotted with unerring potency that leaves no bewilderment—techniques of paintwork which include very careful preparations of surfaces from which a picture is to emerge coupled with elaborate mixing of tints, colours and numerous variations beautifully subtly wrought—both these fundamental

aspects are inbued with the pervading character of mystery to be expected from one steeped in occult knowledge and feeling. As can be observed, this is not an artistic talent and its attendant attributes that can be summed up in some sort of art-critical shorthand.

Rufino Tamayo has always had a strong sense of monumentality, borne out by his close attachment (in itself a particularly Mexican enthusiasm) for the opportunities to hand for mural painting (one recalls the politico-historical huge wall paintings by Siquieros—some of which led to his imprisonment as a dissident at one stage—the equally violent enormous pictorial statements produced by the—more fortunate—Orozco, and the many, many examples in his murals output by the politically unassailable Diego Rivera) but based upon (in spirit, not in copyist content) art which proceeded from the great Mexican Empires in the years before the coming of the Europeans. Not for him the towering political propaganda wall paintings from the Mexican artists of a generation before his own, busy celebrating revolution and less or more Marxist supremacy of a new-born republic. With a long look over his shoulder, he always thought back to the wall masterpieces of Pre-Columbian days and has sought to inject into his own commissioned murals (*and* his paintings) echoes of that greatness. Amongst the many Tamayo-made monuments of this kind, his work for the UNESCO Building in Paris is particularly memorable.

It can be seen that this unique artist has many ingredients with which to attract, but it should not be overlooked that there is a certain duality in much of his work so that monumentality is never supremely overwhelming because the way these works of art are fashioned besides seeking their goal of greatness reserves a direct personal approach of equal veracity for the lone viewer, admirer and collector alike.

—Sheldon Williams

TAPIÈS, Antoni.

Spanish. Born in Barcelona, 13 December 1923. Educated at the College of the Sisters of Loreto, Barcelona, 1926–29; Escuela Alemana, Barcelona, 1928–31; Colegio Balmes, Order of Christian Schools, Barcelona, 1931, 1940; Liceo Pratico, Barcelona, 1934–36; and at the Instituto Menendez y Pelayo, Barcelona, 1939; studied law at the University of Barcelona, 1943, 1945–46; studied drawing at the Academia Valls, Barcelona, 1944. Married Teresa Barba in 1954; children: Antoni, Clara and Miguel. Concentrated on painting and established his first studio, Barcelona, 1943; as independent artist, Barcelona, since 1946; Member, "Dau al Set" group of artists and writers, Barcelona, 1948–51, and Founder, with others, *Dau al Set* review, Barcelona, 1948. Recipient: French Government Scholarship, Paris, 1950; Academia Breve prize, Madrid, 1950, 1951: Acquisition Prize, Bienal, Sao Paulo, 1953; First Prize, Salon del Jazz, Barcelona, 1954; Republic of Colombia Prize, *Bienal Hispano-Americana,* Barcelona, 1955; Premio Lissone, Milan, 1957; Unesco Prize, 1958; David Bright Foundation Prize, Los Angeles, 1958; First Prize, *Carnegie International,* Pittsburgh, 1958; Ministry of Foreign Affairs Prize. *International Biennale of Graphics,* Tokyo, 1960; Providence Art Club Prize, Rhode Island, 1963; Guggenheim Foundation Award, 1964; Grand Prix, *Biennale de Menton,* France, 1966; Gold Medal, 15th Congress of Art Critics, Historians and Artists, Rimini, Italy, 1966; Grand Prize, *7th International Biennale of Graphics,* Ljubljana, Yugoslavia, 1967; Rubens Prize, City of Siegen, West Germany, 1972; British Arts Council Prize, *German International Graphics Exhibition,* 1974; Stephan-Locher Medal, Cologne, 1974; Plastic Arts Prize, City of Barcelona, 1979; Gold Medal for Fine Arts, Ministry of Culture, Madrid, 1981; Wolf Foundation Prize, with Marc Chagall, Israel, 1982. Honorary doctorate: Royal College of Art, London, 1981. Honorary Member, Akademie der Künste, West Berlin, 1979. Agent: Galeria Maeght, Calle Montcada 25, Barcelona-3, Spain. Address: Saragossa 57, Barcelona-6, Spain.

Individual Exhibitions:

1950 Galerias Layetanas, Barcelona
Museo Municipal, Barcelona
1952 Galerias Layetanas, Barcelona
1953 Marshall Field Art Gallery, Chicago
Galeria Biosca, Madrid
Martha Jackson Gallery, New York
1954 Galerias Layetanas, Barcelona
1955 Club 49, Sala Gaspar, Barcelona
1956 *Tapies et l'Oeuvre Complete,* Galerie Stadler, Paris
Club 49, Sala Gaspar, Barcelona
1957 Galerie Schmela, Dusseldorf
Martha Jackson Gallery, New York
Galerie Stadler, Paris
1958 Galleria dell'Ariete, Milan
Spanish Pavilion, at the *Biennale,* Venice
1959 Martha Jackson Gallery, New York
Galerie Stadler, Paris
1960 Sala Gaspar, Barcelona
Museo de Arte, Bilbao, Spain
Martha Jackson Gallery, New York
1961 Martha Jackson Gallery, New York
David Anderson Gallery, New York
Galerie Stadler, Paris
Instituto Torcuato di Tella-Museo Nacional, Buenos Aires
Galleri Blanche, Stockholm
Galerie Rudolf Zwirner, Essen
1962 Kestner-Gesellschaft, hannover (retrospective)
Guggenheim Museum, New York (retrospective)
Kunsthaus, Zurich
Museo Nacional de Bellas Artes, Caracas
Galleria Il Segno, Rome
Galleri Pierre, Stockholm
1963 Pasadena Art Museum, California
Galerie Berggruen, Paris
Galerie Im Erker, St. Gallen, Switzerland
International Center of Aesthetic Research, Turin
Galleria Notizie, Turin
Martha Jackson Gallery, New York
1964 Galleria La Tartaruga, Rome
Galerie Rudolf Zwirner, Cologne
Galerie Stadler, Paris
Galleri Buren, Stockholm
Moss Gallery, Toronto
Galerie Agnes Lefort, Montreal
Sala Gaspar, Barcelona
1965 Galerie Rudolf Awirner, Cologne
Galerie Van de Loo, Munich
Institute of Contemporary Arts, London
Galerie Im Erker, St. Gallen, Switzerland
Sala Gaspar, Barcelona
1966 Cercle Artistic, Manresa, Barcelona
Galeria Biosca, Madrid
Galerie Stadler, Paris
Galerie Jacques Verrière, Cannes
Galleri Buren, Stockholm
1967 Martha Jackson Gallery, New York
Kunstmuseum, St. Gallen, Switzerland (graphics retrospective)
Galerie Maeght, Paris
Sala Gaspar, Barcelona
1968 Museum des 20, Jahrhunderts, Vienna (retrospective)
Galerie Im Erker, St. Gallen, Switzerland
Librairie-Galerie La Hune, paris
Kunstverein, Hamburg (retrospective)
Kunstverein, Cologne (retrospective)
Martha Jackson Gallery, New York
Galerie Maeght, Paris
Galerie Schmela, Dusseldorf
1969 Galerie Maeght, Paris
Sala Gaspar, Barcelona
Galerie Stadler, Paris
Tapies Room, At *Biennale of Prints,* Ljubljana, Yugoslavia
Museum of Modern Art, Belgrade
Kunstverein, Kassel, West German (graphics retrospective)
1970 Galleria dell'Ariete, Milan
Galleri Blue, Stockholm
Martha Jackson Gallery, New York
Neue Galerie, Baden-Baden, West German
1971 Galleria San Luca, Bologna
Galerie Hachette, London
Galerie Maeght, Zurich
Sala Pelaires, Palma de Mallorca, Spain
Galleri Borjeson, Malmo, Sweden
Sala Gaspar, Bracelona
Galleria Il Collezionista, Rome
1972 Galerie Hans Seel, Siegen, West German
Galerie Maeght, Paris
Museo de Mataro, Spain
1973 Galleri Borjeson, Malmo, Sweden
Galerie Wünsche, Hamburg
Musée d'Art Modern, paris (retrospective)
Musee Rath, Geneva (retrospective)
Galeria As, Barcelona
Jodo Seully Gallery, Los Angeles
Galeria 42, Barcelona
Sala Gaspar, Barcelona
Daual Set-Galeria d'Art, Barcelona (retrospective)
Galeria Juana Mordo, Madrid (retrospective)
1974 Nationalgalerie, West Berlin (retrospective)
Galerie Schmela, Dusseldorf
Glynn Vivian Gallery, Swansea, Wales
Martha Jackson Gallery, New York
Galerie Maeght, Paris
Hayward Gallery, London (retrospective)
Galerie Carl Van der Voort, Ibiza, Spain
Galeria Jaun Martin, Mexico City
Louisiana Museum, Humlebaek, Denmark (retrospective)
1975 Galeria Maeght, Barcelona
Galerie Jeanne Castel, Paris
Galeria Ruiz Castillo, Madrid
Galeria La Mulassa, Barcelona
Galeria Juana de Aizpuru, Seville
Sala Pelaires, Palma de Mallorca, Spain
Galeria La Kabala, Madrid
Galerie Maeght, Zurich
Erker-Galerie, at *Art 6 75,* Kunstmesse, Basle
Galeria Kreisler 2, Madrid
Galerie Beyeler, Basle (retrospective)
Galeria Cicnto, Barcelona
Martha Jackson Gallery, New York
Galerie Le Scriptorium, Paris
1976 Galeria Carmen Durango, Valladolid, Spain
Galeria d'Art 3 i 5, Gerona, Spain
Galeria Rayuela 19, Madrid
Galerie Maeght, Paris
Galeria Joan Prats, Barcelona
Edit Art, Geneva
Fondation Maeght, St. Paul-de-Vence, France (retrospective)
Seibu Museum of Art, Tokyo (retrospective)
Fundacio Joan Miró, Barcelona (retrospective)
Galeria Maeght, Barcelona
1977 Albright-Knox Art Gallery, Buffalo, New York (retrospective)
Galeria del Banco de Granda, Spain
Galeria Yerba, Murcia, Spain
Museum of Contemporary Art, Chicago (retrospective)
Biblioteca de la Caixa de Pensions, Sant Celoni, Barcelona
Marion Koogler McNay Art Institute, San Antonio, Texas (retrospective)
Sala Celini, Madrid
Des Moines Art Center, Iowa (retrospective)
Kunsthalle, Bremen, West Germany (retrospective: works on paper)
Galeria Terra, Catellon, Spain
Galeria Cop d'Ull, Lerida, Spain
Musée d'Art Contemporain, Montreal (retrospective)
Staatliche Kunsthalle, Baden-Baden, West Germany (retrospective: works on paper)

1978 Kunstmuseum, Winterthur, Switzerland (retrospective: works of paper)
Galeria Lucas, Gandia, Spain
Martha Jackson Gallery, New York
Musée Municpal de l'Abbaye Sainte-Croix, Les Sables d'Olonne, France
Galeria Juana Mordo, madrid
Centre d'Etudes Catalans, Paris
Galeria Sen, Madrid
Galeria A, Vilafranca del Penedes, Barcelona
Galerie Amstutz, Zurich
Caixa d'Estalvis Laietana, Mataro, Barcelona
Galeria Artema, Barcelona (retrospective, 1945–54)
Galeria Im Erker, St. Gallen, Switzerland
Munro Galerie, Hamburg
Galeria Isernhagen, Burgdorf, West Germany
Galeria Maeght, Barcelona
Hating Gallery-Spanish Institute, New York
1979 Galeria Torques, Santiago de Compostela, Spain
Galeria A i B, Granollers, Barcelona
Galerie Maeght, Paris
Badischer Kunstverein, Karlsruhe (retrospective)
Galeria Atelier Hilbur, Karlsruhe
Caja de Ahorros Municipal, Pamplona, Spain
Galeria Joan Prats, Barcelona
Sala Esplai, Gerona, Spain
1980 Kunsthalle, Kiel, West Germany (retrospective)
Caja Insular de Ahorros, Las Palmas, Canary Islands
Escola Taller d'Art, Reus, Tarragona, Spain
Neue Galerie am Wolfgang Gurlitt Museum, Linz, Austria (retrospective)
Galeria de la Caixa d'Estalvis, Manresa, Barcelona
Estudio Palmo, Malaga, Spain
Studio Dueci, Rome
Museo Espanol de Arte Contemporano, Madrid (retrospective)
Stdelijk Museum Amsterdam (retrospective)
Galeria Brinkman, Amsterdam
Sala d'Art La Tralla, Vich, Barcelona
Galeria Carmen Durango, Valladolid, Spain
Galeria Maeght, Zurich
1981 *Antoni Tapiès o lárt del mon no dit,* Galerie Maeght, Barcelona
Galeria Cuatro, Valencia
Galeria Punto, Valencia
Galeria Yerba, Murcia, Spain
Ueda Gallery, Tokyo
Kasamara Gallery, Osaka
Galeria Rayuela 19, Madrid
Galeria de la Mota, Madrid
Satany Gallery, Tokyo
Fondation du Chateau de Jau, France (retrospective)
M. Knoedler Gallery, New York
Stephan Wirtz Gallery, Los Angeles
Galerie Maeght, Zurich
Galeria Ponce, Mexico City
1982 Palacio do la Lonja, Saragossa, Spain (retrospective)
Galerie Art in Progress, Munich
Escola Massana, Barcelona
Galeria Art-3, Figueres, Gerona, Spain
Marisa del Re Gallery, New York
Union des Arts Plastiques, St Etienne du Rouvray, France
Galerie Maeght, Paris
Scuola Grande San Giovanni Evangelista, at the *Biennale,* Venice
Galeria Academia, Salzburg
1983 Stadtische Galerie im Prinz-Max-Palais, Karlsruhe, West Germany
Galeria Maeght Lelong, Paris
1984 Galerie Maeght Lelong, Zurich
Fundacio Joan Miro, Barcelona
Galeria Maeght, Barcelona
1985 Musee d'Art Moderne, Brussels
Galleria Gabriele Mazzotta, Milan
1986 Kunstlerhaus, Vienna
Van Abbemuseum, Eindhoven, Netherland
Galeria Theo, Madrid
Galerie Maeght Lelong, New York
1987 Galeria Maeght, Barcelona
1988 Annely Juda Fine Art, London

Antoni Tapiès: *Gran X con Grafismo,* 1979

Selected Group Exhibitions;

1948 *1st Salon de Octubre,* Barcelona
1949 *Un Aspecto de la Pintura Catalana,* Instituto Frances, Barcelona
1950 *Carnegie International,* Pittsburgh
1951 *Dau al Set,* Sala Caralt, Barcelona
1952 *Biennale,* Venice
1953 *Bienal,* Sao Paulo
1960 *Before Picasso, after Miró,* Guggenheim Museum, New York
1964 *Documenta,* Kassel, West German
1978 *Foire Internationald'Art Contemporain/FIAC,* Paris
1985 *Painterly Visions 1940–84,* Guggenheim Museum, New York

Collections

Museo Espanol de Arte contemporaneo, Madrid; Museo de Arte Moderno, Barcelona; Centre Georges Pompidou, Paris; Tate Gallery, London; Nationalgalerie, West Berlin; Stedelijk Museum, Amsterdam; Kunsthaus, Zurich; National Gallery of Victoria, Melbourne; Musée d'Art Contemporain, Montreal; Museum of Modern Art, New York.

Publications:

By TAPIÈS: books—*El pa a la Braca,* with poems by J. Brossa, Barcelona 1963; *Album Saint-Gallen,* with J. Brossa, Barcelona 1965; *Novella,* with J. Brossa, Barcelona 1965; *La Nuit Grandissante,* with text by Jacques Dupin, Paris 1967; *Fregoli,* with J. Brossa, Barcelona 1969; *Nocturn Matinal,* with J. Brossa, Barcelona 1970; *Air,* with text by André du Bouchet, Paris 1970; *La Practica de l'Art,* Barcelona 1970; *La Clau del Foc,* with text by Gimferrer, Barcelona 1973; *Suite Catalana: Poems from de Catalan,* with poems by J. Brossa, introductory text by Arthur Terry and Roland Penrose, Barcelona 19731 *Cartes per a la Teresa,* Barcelona 1974; *L'Art contre L'Estetica,* Barcelona 1974; *Llamberec Material,* with poems by Takiguchi, Paris 1975; *Ca suit son cours,* with poems by Jean Daive, Paris 1975; *Oda a Xirinachs,* with poems by J. Brossa, Barcelona 1975; *Dialogo sobre arte, cultura y sociedad,* with Imma Julian, Barcelona 1977; *Memorial Personal,* autobiography, Barcelona 1978; *Retorno de lo vivo lejano,* with poems by Rafael Alberti, Madrid 1978; *Sinnieren über Schmutz,* with text by Alexander Mitscherlich, St. Gallen, Switzerland 1978; *U no es ningu,* with poems by Jorge Guillen, Valladolid, Spain 1980; *Conversaciones con Tapies,* with Miguel Fernandez-Brasso, Madrid 1981.

On TAPIÈS: books—*Antoni Tapiès* by Enric Jardi, Barcelona 1950: *Antoni Tapiès o el Dau Modern de Versailles* by Joan Josep Tharrass, Barcelona 1950; *Tapiès et l'Oeuvre Complete* exhibition catalogue, with text by Michel Tapie, Paris 1956; *Antoni Tapiès* by Michel Tapie, Barcelona 1959; *Tapiès* by Juan Eduardo Cirlot, Barcelona 1960; *Antonio Tapiès,* exhibition catalogue, with text by Lawrence Alloway, New York 1962; *Significacion de la Pintura de Tapiès,* Barcelona 1962; *Tapiès* by Blai Bonet, Barcelona 1964; *Antoni Tapiès: Fustas, papers, cartons i collages* by Joan Teixidor, Barcelona 1964; *Tapiès* by Joan Brossa and Francesco Vicens, Barcelona 1967; *Antoni Tapiès,* with texts by Guisepppe Gatt, Guilio Carlo Argan, Renato Barilli and others, Bologna 1967; *Grandi Monografie Pittorie Scultori d Oggi: Antoni Tapiès* by Michel Tapie, Milan 1969, *Tapiès: Testimino del silenci* by Alexandre Circi, Barcelona 1970: *Tapiès,* exhibition catalogue, with texts by Nello Ponenete and Guiseppe Gatt, Rome 1971; *Antoni Tapiès* by Vera Linhartova, Stuttgart and Barcelona 1972; *Tapiès: Obra Grafica 1947–1972* by Carl Vogel, Barcelona 1973; *Antoni Tapiès: Zeichen und Strukturen* by Werner Schmalerbach, West Berlin 1974, Barcelona 1975; *Antoni Tapiès,* exhibition catalogue, with text by Tomas Llorens, Barcelona 1976; *Tapiès: Meditaciones 1976* by José Medina, Madrid 1976; *Tapiès* by Georges Raillard, Paris 1976; *Tapiès* by Roland Penrose, Barcelona 1977; *Antoni Tapiès: Kunstlerische Herkunft und Entwicklung* by Andreas Franzke, Stuttgart 1979; *Antoni Tapiès,* exhibition catalogue, with texts by Lluis Permanyer and Jose Maria Valverde, Madrid 1980; *Antoni Tapiès o l'Art del mon no dit,* exhibition catalogue, with text by Alexander Circi, Barcelona 1981; *Tapiès* by Carmine Beninasa, Rome 1982; *Antoni Tapiès: Dipinti, Sculpture, Opere su Carta, Grafiche,* exhibition catalogue with text by Guido Ballo, Milan 1985; *Tapiès,* exhibition catalogue with text by Francesc Farreras, Barcelona 1987.

When silence manifests itself in quiet waves of meditative hues crisscrossed with deeply etched scarifications, its evocation can be spellbinding. But when energy and matter brood in contained dynamic mark-

ings spread over contemplative fields of subdued color that expand into new forms, the experience is often overwhelming. Antoni Tapiès, whose aesthetic is deeply rooted in the "matter painting" idiom of Europe's "art informel," uses silence as a symbol—a key to a private mythology in which raw materials (earth, sand, X-ray film, labels, rags, and paint in various degrees of thickness and consistency) transcend their physicality to become mute metaphors of a world in which existential passions have given way to the serenity of resignation and acquiescence. In the limelight since the early 1950's, Tapiès is one of a number of post World War II European artists who, in their attempt at breaking through the constraints of cubism and geometric abstraction, came out with revolutionary seminal styles that roughly paralleled the development of Abstract Expressionism in the United States. Although he grew up in a time of political ferment, when much of Western art focused on rebellion, struggle, and isolation, and although he was, in politics, a liberal, his forms were never totally circumscribed by radical dictates. For him, for instance, geometry was never the anathema that it was for many of his contemporaries. In fact, an intuitive, spontaneous approach tempered through geometric organization is the one factor that served as a distinguishing mark of his early works—a mark which, over the years, proved to be the fundamental variable that spurred a pattern of growth and gradual change without compromise to the integrity of his forms. Thus, what in the 50's were crude expressions of the artist's fascination with the effect of timeworn surface texturized by several generations of the clandestine graffiti of Catalonian walls, was tranformed, in the 1960's and 70's, into poetically charged statements about cosmic intelligence and the unification of all matter into infinity. And, when such words as "essence," "purity," and "reduction" were, once again, part and parcel of the artistic vocabulary of the Western world, Tapiès was able to make the transition—to accommodate his vision to the new order while, at the same time, gaining a new stature.

> . . . Everything joined together in a uniform mass. What was ardent ebullition was transformed into static silence. It was a great lesson in humility received by the haughtiness of violent passion. And one day I tried to arrive directly at silence with more resignation, giving into the fatality that governs all profound struggle. The millions of furious stabs were transformed into millions of grains of dust, of sand . . . suddenly before me a new landscape was opened, the same as the one in the story about crossing through the mirror, as if to communicate to me the most secret interior parts of all things . . .

These words, written by Antoni Tapiès, summarize the metamorphosis—describe what he calls his "qualitative jump." Underlining a lifetime of sustained creativity, they explain the poetry, the profundity of his vision, as the paintings resonate over two continents with a sense of total resolution—a feeling of attainment and completion.

—Andrée Maréchal-Workman

TATAFIORE, Ernesto.
Italian. Born in Marigliano, near Naples, in 1943. Educated at Giambattista Vico High School, Naples, 1956–60; mainly self-taught in art. Married Simonetta; son: Marco. Painter: lives and works in Naples, Address: Piazza Medaglie d'Oro 51, 80129 Naples, Italy.

Individual Exhibitions:

1969 Galleria Lucio Amelio, Naples
1970 Galleria Lucio Amelio, Naples
1972 Galerie Stampa, Basle
1973 Galleria La Salita, Rome
1974 Galleria Lucio Amelio, Naples
Studio Carla Ortelli, Milan
1975 Galleria Lucio Amelio, Naples
Galleria Lucio Amelio, at *Expo Arte Fiera*, Bari, Italy
1976 Galleria La Salita, Rome
1977 Galleria Lucio Amelio, Naples
1978 Galerie Stampa, Basle
Galleria Lucio Amelio, Naples
Galerie Paul Maenz, Cologne
1979 Studio Memini, Naples
Arte 10 79, Kunstmesse, Basle
Galerie Stampa, Basle
Galleria Fabjbasaglia, Bologna
1980 Galerie Stampa, Basle
Galerie 't Venster, Rotterdam
Incontri 1980, Spoleto, Italy
Kunsthalle, Basle
Biennale, Venice
Museum Folkwang, Essen
Stedelijk Museum, Amsterdam
1981 Annina Nosei Gallery, New York
Lisson Gallery, London
Galleria Lucio Amelio, Naples
1982 Galerie Jossevel, Zurich
Galleria Lucio Amelio, Naples
Istituto Italiano di Cultura, Madrid
Galeria Ehrhardt, Madrid
Aetatis Suae, Kunstmuseum, Lucerne
1983 Andre Emmerich Gallery, New York
Gimpel-Hanover/Andre Emmerich Galeries, Zurich
1984 Galleria Lucio Amelio, Naples
1985 Il Ponte Editrice d'Arte, Rome
Mezzanine Gallery, New York
Metropolitan Museum of Art, New York

Seclected Group Exhibitions:

1966 *Quadriennale d'Arte*, Palazzo dell'Exposizione, Rome
1967 *Arte Grafica Oggi*, Palazzo Reale, Naples
1970 *Italy II: Art Aournd 70*, Philadelphia Museum of Art
1973 *Biennale*, Paris
1978 *Der Kulturelle Unterschied*, Stuttgart
1979 *Arte Cifra*, Galerie Paul Maenz, Cologne
1980 *Kunstforum*, Städtische Galerie im Lenbachhaus, Munich
1981 *Linee della Ricerca Artistica in Italia 1960–1980*, Palazzo delle Esposizioni, Rome
1983 *Tema Celeste*, Museo di Gibellina, Sicily
1984 *Painting and Sculpture Today*, Indianapolis Museum of Art, Indiana

Publications:

On TATAFIORE: books—*Arte Cifra*, exhibition catalogue, with an introduction by Wolfgang Max Faust, Cologne 1979; *7 Junge Künstler aus Italien*, exhibition catalogue, with text by Zdenek Felix, Essen 1980; *Ernesto Tatafiore: Aetatis Suae*, exhibition catalogue, with texts by Marlis Gruterich, Michael Newman and Harald Szeeman, and an interview by Martin Kunz, Lucerne 1982; *Ernesto Tatafiore: New Work*, exhibition catalogue, with text by Martin Kunz, New York 1983; *Ernesto Tatafiore*, exhibition catalogue with introduction by Ronny Cohen, New York 1985.

I was born at Marigliano, near Naples, my mother's name was Ida and my father's Enrico.
When I was a child I played with the sea, the sand and the stones then I enjoyed painting "from life" beside my father.
When I was about ten years old my mother took my sister Maria Antonietta and me to see Rome and Florence, Giotto's tall bell-tower, thousands and thousands of steps.
Classical high school at the «Giambattista Vico».
Literature, poets, philosophy and then politics, strikes.
Medicine and art as mystery and discovery.
Meeting Simonetta and the journeys in Africa: Morocco, Tunisia, Algeria, then Turkey and Istanbul, London and Paris.
Marco is born.
Psychoanalysis tripping up the system of logic.
Painting as a game without end or purpose.

—Ernesto Tatafiore

Ernesto Tatafiore prepares free associations between selected episodes, episodes that revolve round the themes of the French Revolution and the *Titanic* disaster. Using these as an interpretative grid and as a track on which a journey is still only partly and temporarily completed, Tatafiore makes psychological use of pretexts borrowed from the reservoir of history; the mind is left free to float up and down within the area affected by the subject, an area chosen as a limiting field of associative-metaphorical forces which of course can be aroused in confrontation with the pretext.

Robespierre, Marie Antionette, Louis XVI, Charlotte Corday, Marat, the *Titanic*—all take on an emblematic quality. Robespierre presides over a dinner of dead men; the *Titanic* becomes the hopeless shipwreck following the "crisis" of scientific "presumption" (ships built with watertight compartments do sink; the iceberg does remain in its rough shape with its tip above the surface; the absence of lifeboats is further evidence of lack of precaution). The event is still, as ever, in the hands of fate, and history as such continues in its meretricious oscillation of permanent instability: illusion and madness.

The features of the cherubic faces of the actors in the scene that Tatafiore depicts hide the images of the guillotine. The venom is concealed by the grace and sensuality of the drawing; it is deliberately given to fragile, delicate figures and to such symbols as caresses; the saliva passed from mouth to mouth with a kiss starts up deadly mechanisms; the poison may even have a taste of honey. The solidity of the outlines of the historical figures evoked is turned back into a cloud of memory, and history is focussed on events that can be selected at will and used on associationistically. The correspondence between "sign-picture" and "truth of the conclusion" is then played upon by the view in his own way; only he can read the word of history as an individual story as he sees it himself. Vision will condition choice.

—Demetrio Paparoni

TÉLÉMAQUE, Hervé.
Haitian. Born in Port-au-Prince, 5 November 1937. Studied art, under Julien Levy, at the Art Students League, New York, 1957–60. Painter and graphic artist, Paris, 1961–81; in Villejuif, France, since 1982. Recipient: Ingram Merrill grant, 1972; Art Grant, Regie Renault, Paris, 1980. Agents: Gianni Schubert, Galleria Arte Borgogna, Via Borgogna 7, 20121 Milan, Italy; G. de Muga, Galeria Joan Prats, Rambla de Catalunya 54, Barcelona 7, Spain. Address: 52 Avenue de Paris (10–12 impasse Ernest Renan), 94800 Villejuif, France.

Individual Exhibitions:

1964 Galerie Mathias Fels, Paris
Hanover Gallery, London (with Gessler)
1965 Galleria L'Attico, Rome
1966 Galleria Il Punto, Turin
1967 Galerie Mathias Fels, Paris
Studio Marconi, Milan
1968 Galleria del Minotaura, Brescia, Italy
Galleria de'Foscherari, Bologna
1969 Galerie Brusberg, Hannover
Ulmer Museum, Ulm, West Germany
1970 Galerie Mathias Fels, Paris

Hervé Télémaque: *Vallie de l'Ohio*, 1986

1971 Galerie Bama, Paris
1972 Marc Gallery, Washington, D.C.
Galerie 3 rue Laplace, Paris
1973 Galleria Arte Borgogna, Milan
Galleria d'Arte San Michele, Brescia, Italy
1974 Galerie K et K, Paris
Galerie Municipale, Vitry-sur-Seine, France (with Desterac)
1975 Galerie J. Storme, Lille, France
1976 Galerie D. Blanco, Geneva
Musée d'Art Moderne de la Ville, Paris
Galerie des Ponchettes, Nice
Maison de la Culture, Rennes
1977 Galeria Joan Prats, Barcelona
1979 Galerie Maeght, Paris
Galerie Maeght, Zurich
1980 Galerie Alinea, Toulon
Galerie Atmospheres, Brussels
1981 Galerie Adrien Maeght, Paris
Galeria de Arte Moderna, Santa Domingo, Dominican Republic
1982 Galerie Convergence, Nantes, France
Galerie Adrien Maeght, at *FIAC*, Paris
1983 Galeria Maeght, Barcelona
Galeria Italia, Alicante, Spain
1985 Mairie de Fort de France, Martinique
1986 Casa de las Americas, Havana

Selected Group Exhibitions:

1964 *Documenta*, Kassel, West Germany
1965 *Biennale*, San Marino
1968 *Biennale*, Venice
Documenta, Kassel, West Germany
1976 *Biennale Internazionale d'Arte Grafico*, Florence
1977 *Paris-New York*, Centre Georges Pompidou, Paris
1979 *Le Tondo; De Monet à nos jours*, Musee de l'Abbaye de Sainte-Croix, Les Sables d'Olonne, France
1982 *De Cezanne à Aujourd'hui*, Bridgestone Museum, Tokyo
1984 *Ecritures dans la Peinture*, Villa Arson, Nice, France
1986 *Aspect de la Figuration Aujourd'hui*, Les Cordeliers, Chateauroux, France

Collections:

Fond National d'Art Contemporain, Paris; Bibliothèque Nationale, Paris; Musée d'Art Moderne de la Ville, Paris; Goteborgs Kunstmuseum, Gothenburg, Sweden; Moderna Museet, Stockholm; Hunterian Museum and Art Gallery, Glasgow; Musée d'Art Haitien, Port-au-Prince; Casa de la Americas, Havana; Museo de Bellas Artes, Caracas; University of California, Berkeley.

Publications:

On TÉLÉMAQUE: books-*Télémaque-Geissler*, exhibition catalogue, with text by John Ashbery, London 1964; *Hervé Télémaque*, exhibition catalogue, with text by Albert Boatto and José Pierre, Rome 1965; *L'Avant-Garde Internationale de Paris* by Alain Jouffroy and others, Cologne 1966; *Hervé Télémaque*, exhibition catalogue, with texts by Christopher Finch and José Pierre, Paris 1967; *Pop Art* by Lucy R. Lippard, New York 1968; *Télémaque*, exhibition catalogue, with text by Jean-Patrice Marandel, Paris 1970; *Reperes: La Peinture en France debut et fin d'un systeme visuel 1870–1970* by Dora Vallier, Paris 1976; *Depuis 1945* by Gerald Gassiot-Talabot and others, vol. 2. Brussels 1971; *Le Surréalisme* by José Pierre, Lausanne 1971, Paris 1972; *Art en France; Une nouvelle generation* by Jean Clair, Paris 1972; *Hervé Télémaque*, exhibition catalogue, with text by Gerald Gassiot-Talabot, Milan 1973; *L'Art Actuel* by Anne Tronche, Paris 1973; *Le Pop Art* by José Pierre, Paris 1975; *Hervé Télémaque*, exhibition catalogue, with text by Bernard Noel, Paris 1976; *Dictionnaire Universel de la Peinture* by R. Mayard, vol. 4, Paris 1976; *Télémaque*, exhibition catalogue, with a preface by Carlos Franqui, Barcelona 1977; *Figures d l'Art Contemporain* by M. Le Bot, Paris 1977; *Hervé Télémaque*, exhibition catalogue, with texts by Bernard Noel and Catherine Thieck, Paris 1981.

An artist is not a machine producing and immediately recuperating fine feelings. I accept objects as they are—they make up a kind of landscape of our life in the midst of a consumer society. It is interesting to see how these objects speak to us at the unconscious level. This is the reason why I have called upon familiar everyday objects—a walking stick (difficulty of locomotion)—a corset (the idea of desire)—a whistle (a scream).

My purpose is not to blame the consumer society—this invasion certainly causes me a great deal of anguish, but a certain history of human activity is contained in it. I think that the unconscious can begin to function using this collection of forms as a starting point. But it was an easy temptation to represent the objects. It is a question of relating this object to others by allusion, by a suppression of the pictorial illusion.

In the past the spectator plunged into the spatial illusion of the painting. Van Gogh's chair is very close to us. Today it is better to keep to a minimum any illusion, any manipulation of fictional space, any balancing of all these objects towards the spectator. I want to be concrete.

—Hervé Télémaque

Hervé Télémaque's work is a constant interrogation of the world of man-made objects that surround him, and he seems constantly to be asking himself about the way these objects correspond to his own intimate needs. Do they or don't they, and to what degree, and to precisely what kind of need? He looks at a shoe or a saddle or a house and asks himself how he feels about it, he asks himself how he feels about the very idea of a shoe or a saddle or a house, he asks himself how he feels about depicting the idea of a shoe or a saddle or a house. He is not a social critic since he is gifted or burdened with a penchant for a kind of emotional skepticism that goes much farther than that. He asks himself not why these things exist in society, but rather why they exist in his universe. He seems not quite sure that he should have any need of needs at all.

Télémaque works as much with collages of cutouts of colored paper as he does with paint and brush, and when he does work with paint and brush the result can easily look like collages of cut-out paper. His earlier work often created a whole community of images where real objects (ropes, or a cane or a shopping net stuffed with a ball of newspaper) existed on an entirely equal footing with painted representations of other objects (a weight, a tent, a cup of coffee, a facade). His forms are always flat and very simple, geometrically clear but never harsh: there are curves in his collages and painted images that are difficult to imagine as belonging originally to their subjects. His colors are always uniform, muted, and highly saturated with grey, even though the range of his palette runs all the way from one end of the spectrum to the other. The world, as Télémaque wants to show it to us, is a little less real, a little less up front, than we ordinarily imagine it to be, and as it recedes a step or so away from us, there is a little more room in which to think about it. Télémaque is also an excellent draughtsman, and in some of the works he has been doing since 1978, collage versions of a subject are juxtaposed to drawings of precisely the same view, but with the difference that what reads from right to left in the drawing will read from left to right in the collage; and when the subject permits (which is to say with subjects that have no clear right-side-up and up-side-down) the axis of symmetry, rather than horizontal, is vertical. These drawings are in fact the transparent stencils on the basis of which the collage

cut-outs were made, and the works of which they form a 'second' part can also be completed by still a third panel in which some of the individual collage elements that go to form the image (or scraps that fell away from the forming of the image) are presented as though free-floating and out of context. Télémaque shows us various stages in giving concreteness to an image as though to imply that the real world of humanly made objects is itself but another stage in the very same process.

—Henry Martin

THEK, Paul.

American. Born in Brooklyn, New York, 2 November 1933. Studied at Cooper Union, New York; Art Students League, New York; and Pratt Institute, New York, 1951–54. Lived in Florida, 1955–57, and Italy, 1957–62; lived in New York, 1962–68, then returned to Europe; designed sets and costumes for *Arena*, ballet, Nederlands Dance Theatre, 1969; sets for Louis Falco Dance Company, New York, 1978. Recipient: Fulbright Fellowship, 1967; National Endowment for the Arts Award, 1977. Agents: Galerie M. E. Thelen, Cologne, West Germany; and Iolas-Jackson Gallery, New York. Address: 58 East Third Street, New York, New York 10003, U.S.A.

Individual Exhibitions:

1957 Mirrell Gallery, Miami
1963 Galleria 88, Rome
1964 Stable Gallery, New York
1966 Pace Gallery, New York
1968 Institute of Contemporary Arts, London
Galerie M. E. Thelen, Cologne
1969 Stable Gallery, New York
Stedelijk Museum, Amsterdam
Moderna Museet, Stockholm
1972 Moderna Museet, Stockholm
1973 Kunstmuseum, Lucerne
Galerie Stahli, Lucerne
Wilhelm Luhmbruck Museum, Duisburg, West Germany
1975 Alexandre Iolas Gallery, New York
1976 Galerie Alexandre Iolas, Paris
1977 Il Fante di Spade, Rome
Iolas-Jackson Gallery, New York
1980 Iolas-Jackson Gallery, New York
1981 Iolas-Jackson Gallery, New York

Selected Group Exhibitions:

1967 *Carnegie International*, Carnegie Institute, Pittsburgh
1968 *The Obsessive Image*, Institute of Contemporary Arts, London
Documenta, Kassel, West Germany
1969 *Kunst der Sechziger Jahre*, Wallraf-Richartz Museum, Cologne
1972 *Documenta*, Kassel, West Germany
1976 *Biennale*, Venice
1977 *Processions*, Institute of Contemporary Art, University of Pennsylvania
1980 *Biennale*, Venice

Collections:

Stedelijk Museum, Amsterdam; Moderna Museet, Stockholm; Centre National d'Art Contemporain, Paris; Wallraf-Richartz Museum, Cologne; Smithsonian Institution, Washington, D.C.

Publications:

By THEK: book—*A Document Made by Paul Thek and Edwin Klein*, Amsterdam and Stockholm 1969; articles—"An Interview with Paul Thek," with G. R. Swenson, in *Artnews* (New York), April 1966; "Paul Thek: Entretien avec Harald Szeeman" in *Chroniques de l'Art Vivant* (Paris), April 1974.

On THEK: articles—"The New School of New York" by Lil Picard in *Das Kunstwerk* (Baden-Baden, West Germany) December 1964; "Beneath the Skin" by G. R. Swenson in *Artnews* (New York), April 1966; "In the Galleries: Paul Thek" by William Berkson in *Arts Magazine* (New York), June 1966; "In the Galleries: Paul Thek" by Mary Stewart in *Arts Magazine* (New York), November 1967; "Paul Thek: Love-Death" by William Wilson in *Art and Artists* (London), April 1968; "Before Nature Disappears, Let Us Return" by B. Sydgoff in *Domus* (Milan), March 1972; "Individuelle Mythologien" by B. Catoir in *Das Kunstwerk* (Baden-Baden, West Germany), March 1974; review by Elizabeth Frank in *Art in America* (New York), Summer 1981.

Paul Thek's works from 1964 to 1967 consisted mainly of wax facsimiles of raw, fleshy meat incased in plexiglass boxes which became more and more elegant and ornamental. These chunks of tormented fleshiness in their pristine enclosures, which look very like the artifacts we see in museums of natural history, are provocative symbols for humanity's entrapment in technologically caused boxes, sealed off artificially from the life of the spirit. Thek's "Meat Piece with Warhol Brillo Box" (1965) suggests his opinion that Pop Art, among other things, had done nothing to change or help alleviate this human condition.

In his 1967 environmental sculpture titled "The Tomb—Death of a Hippie", Thek further developed his allegorical and ritualistic intentions involving themes of survival in the secularized world of life and art. Placed within a hazy atmosphere of rosy light and incense is a large three-tiered ziggurat which houses the artist's tomb, complete with realistically detailed wax-cast effigy of Thek accompanied by the accoutrements of his past life and symbolic objects of use for his future life. Among the many things surrounding the artist's wax duplicate are the fingers missing from it, severed parts being one of Thek's recurrent images suggestive of the individual's frustrations at feeling fragmented both physically and spiritually. Accompanying "The Tomb" are a series of "offerings," boxes containing arms, hands, legs and artificial limbs and supports, all altered to evoke various states of mutilation or decay. After this surreal, fetishistic use of self in portrayal of the artist/individual's feelings of separateness from the world at large, Thek left New York for Europe in 1968.

Since then he has continually traveled throughout Europe together with a small group of collaborators, creating a series of complex, transitory environments with multifarious elements including ordinary objects and also paintings and sculptures of his own in various states of transformation and overlap. With his characteristic flair for irreverent reverence, Thek calls these works 'Processions,' a title which acts both as an allusion to the spiritualizing nature of the pieces and as a reference to process art.

Thek's major work of the next decade is this unfolding series of "Processions," loaded with signs and symbols from various historical periods of high and low culture which are combined, re-used, altered to convey mythic and religious levels. As the works move from place to place, presented when possible in correspondence with religious holidays, objects from Thek's own past work and elsewhere re-enter along with things accumulated along the "processional" route. A partial listing of the elements included in "Pyramid/A Work In Progress" (1971–72) amply communicates the extremely fetishistic complexity of Thek's works. In this work were parts from Thek's "The Artist's Co-op" (1969) such as the Coop, the worktable-bridge which carried Thek's "Fishman" (1968) and "The Tomb" (1967), the crates in which these works had been shipped, a fishing boat, old bathtubs, park benches, a piano, tissues, paint, drawings, letters, seashells, and many more. Moving through such a fantastic conglomerate of stuff, the viewer is stimulated to see these things as out-of-the-ordinary, strange indications of the mystical life-quality each component seems to possess. Thek is not nihilistic in his cryptic and theatrical narratives. His continual commitment to the "Processions" is linked to his desire to convey a spiritual life by making the ordinary and his own past work as well vehicles to insert the mystical element back into our secularized society.

It is this positive spirit, accompanied by a touch of humor, which also informs Thek's small paintings such as "Periscope" and "Hot Potatoes" (both 1979–80), which seem, at least in part, a hommage to Philip Guston's moving late pictures. Thek has received most of his attention in Europe, where he continues to spend most of his time perhaps largely because he feels the need to be "in the regions", away from the New York art world and closer to the older mystical history of Europe.

—Barbara Cavaliere

THIEBAUD, Wayne.

Born in Mesa, Arizona, 15 November 1920. Educated in California public schools; studied at San Jose State College, California, and Sacramento State College, California, B.A. 1951, M.A. 1952. Served in the United States Air Force, at Mather Army Air Field, Sacramento, and in Culver City, California, 1942–45. Married Patricia Patterson in 1943 (divorced, 1959); daughters: Twinka and Mallary Ann; married Betty Jean Carr in 1959; sons: Paul Le Baron and (adopted) Matthew Bult Carr. Painter, in Sacramento, California, from 1950, and in San Francisco from 1972: worked as sign painter, cartoonist, commercial artist, illustrator, designer and advertising art director, 1938–49; Design and Art Consultant, *California State Fair,* 1950–57; designed sets for music festivals, Sacramento City schools, 1953–55; producer of educational films, Patrician Films, Hollywood, 1954–59; co-founder, Artists' Cooperative Gallery (now Artists Contemporary Gallery), Sacramento, 1958. Instructor in Art, 1951–59, and Chairman of the Department of Art, 1954–57, Sacramento City College; Assistant Professor, 1960–63, Associate Professor, 1963–67, and Professor since 1967, University of California, Davis; Visiting Professor at numerous colleges and universities in the United States, since 1967. National Juror, National Endowment for the Arts, Washington, D.C., 1972. Recipient: Golden Reel, *American Film Festival,* Chicago, 1956; First Prize, *Art Film Festival,* at the California State Fair, 1956; Columbia Records Award, 1959; Creative Research Foundation Grant, 1961; Scholastic Art Award, for film, *Space and Design,* 1961; Creative Research Grant, 1964, Golden Apple Award, 1972, and Faculty Research Lecture Medal, 1984, University of California, Davis; Distinguished Studio Teacher Award, College Art Association of America, 1981; Award of Distinction, National Art Schools Association, 1984; Special Citation, National Association of Schools of Art and Design, 1984; Cyril Magnin Award, San Francisco Chamber of Commerce, 1987. Honorary Doctorate: California College of Arts and Crafts, Oakland, 1972; Dickinson College, Carlisle, Pennsylvania, 1983. Member, American Academy and Institute of Arts and Letters, 1985; Associate, 1986, and Academician, 1987, National Academy of Design, New York. Agent: Allan Stone Gallery, 48 East 86th Street, New York, New York 10028. Address: c/o Paul Thiebaud, 1617 Seventh Avenue, Sacramento, California 95818, U.S.A.

Individual Exhibitions:

1951 Crocker Art Gallery, Sacramento, California
1957 Artists Co-Op Gallery, Sacramento, California

1958 Artists Co-Op Gallery, Sacramento, California
1961 San Francisco Museum of Art
1962 M. H. de Young Museum, San Francisco
Allan Stone Gallery, New York
1963 Allan Stone Gallery, New York
1964 Allan Stone Gallery, New York
1965 Galleria Schwarz, Milan
Allan Stone Gallery, New York
Stanford University, California
1966 Nelson-Atkins Museum, Kansas City, Missouri
1967 Allan Stone Gallery, New York
1969 Crocker Art Gallery, Sacramento, California
1971 Whitney Museum, New York
1976 Phoenix Art Museum, Arizona (retrospective)
University of California at Santa Cruz
1977 Allan Stone Gallery, New York
University of California at Davis
Diablo Valley College, Pleasant Hill, California
1978 San Francisco Museum of Modern Art
Allan Stone Gallery, New York
1979 Allan Stone Gallery, New York
Walker Art Center, Minneapolis (retrospective)
1980 Allan Stone Gallery, New York
John Berggruen Gallery, San Francisco
1981 California State University at Hayward
Museum of Fine Arts, St. Petersburg, Florida
Honolulu Academy of Arts
Walker Art Center, Minneapolis
University of Pennsylvania, Philadelphia
Fort Worth Art Museum, Texas
1985 San Francisco Museum of Modern Art (travelled to Newport Beach, California; Milwaukee, Wisconsin; Columbus, Ohio; Kansas City, Missouri, 1985–86)

Selected Group Exhibitions:

1967 *Bienal,* Sao Paulo
1972 *Documenta,* Kassel, West Germany
1973 *25 Years of American Painting 1948–73,* Des Moines Art Center, Iowa
Separate Realities: Developments in California Representational Painting and Sculpture, Municipal Museum, Los Angeles
1987 *Made in USA,* University of California, Berkeley (travelled to Kansas City, Missouri; Richmond, Virginia)

Collections:

Museum of Modern Art, New York; Metropolitan Museum of Art, New York; Whitney Museum, New York; Albright-Knox Art Gallery, Buffalo, New York; Wadsworth Atheneum, Hartford, Connecticut; Philadelphia Museum of Art; Hirshhorn Museum, Washington, D.C.; Art Institute of Chicago; Museum of Fine Arts, Salt Lake City; San Francisco Museum of Modern Art.

Wayne Thiebaud: *Study for Apartment Hill,* 1980

Publications:

By THIEBAUD: book—*America Rediscovered,* 1963.

On THIEBAUD: books—*Documenta 5,* exhibition catalogue, Kassel, 1972; *25 Years of American Painting 1948–73,* exhibition catalogue, by Max Kozloff, Des Moines, Iowa 1973; *Separate Realities: Developoments in California Representational Painting and Sculpture,* exhibition catalogue, by Laurence Dreiband, Los Angeles 1973; *Wayne Thiebaud,* exhibition catalogue with essay by Karen Tsujimoto, San Francisco and Seattle 1985; articles—"Slice of Cake School" in *Time* (New York), May 1962; review by Thomas B. Hess in *Artnews* (New York), May 1962; "Something's Cooking" in *Life* (New York), June 1962; article in *Life* (New York), September 1963; article in *Time* (New York), April 1963; "Eros in the Cafeteria" by Diane Waldman in *Artnews* (New York), March 1966.

When Wayne Thiebaud showed his urban landscapes for the first time at the San Francisco Museum of Modern Art in 1978, the question of an essentialization ultimately leading to non-objectivity came to mind. Viewed in the context of both the prevalent trends in California art and the artist's candid acknowledgement of the influence of Richard Diebenkorn's landscapes of the 1960's, the cubes, the columns, the simplified architectonic compositions, the flat crosses, the patterns carried out in rhythmic repetitions of color seemed prophetic of a direction toward absolute abstraction. But Thiebaud's strong realist orientation proved too emphatic an impulse, and it is now obvious that the simplified forms were not indicative of a reductive sensibility, but instruments of exploration into the realist idiom. "Reduction in a realist painting is the same as reducing a sauce," he explains. "You take away by simplification, by leaving out details. But you also put in selective bits of other experiences, or perceptual nuances which enforce it, giving it more of a multi-dimension than if it were done directly as a visual recording."

Thiebaud emerged on the New York art scene in the early 60's, when the Pop movement was beginning to be recognized as the new acceptable form of American art. He did not participate in the movement, but, because of his predilection for mundane subject matter (pinball machines, dimestore lipsticks, bakery and delicatessen foodstuff), he has, at times, been identified as a Pop artist. The association was fortuitous, however, for Thiebaud's choice of imagery was then, as it is today, predicated upon formal concerns rather than identification with specific objects. An avowed realist whose roots are steeped in tradition, he is best characterized as heir to such masters as Vermeer, Chardin, and Thomas Eakins for whom the creation of a painting involved hours of scrutinizing an object in order to arrive at stylistic individualization. "For me, realist painting is an alive confrontation," he says. "If you stare at an object, as you do when you paint, there is no point at which you can stop learning things about it. You can just look and look, and, if you really are a realist painter, you finally realize that what you are doing is a tremendous amount of adoption, adaptation, and change."

"Adopting, adapting, and changing"—his subjects according to the tenets of 20th Century modernism—is precisely what Thiebaud has been doing for almost 30 years. With the sure eye of a modernist, he has

transformed cakes into circles, still-lifes and figures into arrangements of spheres, triangles, and cylinders with the same alacrity that he is, today, translating street panoramas into compositions in which arcs, cubes, and complex networks of diagonal and rectangular lines play a sophisticated game of dialectic between geometry and realism.

With the urban landscapes, however, Wayne Thiebaud has reached a new zenith. In many respects, they build on earlier Thiebaud forms and concepts, but they also bring to his vocabulary a new dramatic dimension—a feeling of pressure, a compaction, of vertigo that affect the framework of his pictorial space. In this sense, they come to the forefront of his oeuvre, and represent the upmost in the resolution of that special tension between modernism and tradition that has been his trademark since the very beginning of his career.

The retrospective that premiered at the San Francisco Museum of Modern Art in September 1985 confirmed Thiebaud's unflagging commitment to a modern traditionalist aesthetic. When asked to explain what motivated such new "dark paintings" as *Black Shoes* and *Dark Lipstick,* (1983), he replied that they were prompted by "looking at dark paintings done by a great many artists." Rembrandt, Goya, Whistler, Balthus were among those from whom he sought counsel, and if the results prove that the lessons were well learned, they also unveil an energized pictorial repertoire—reinforcing Thiebaud's often acknowledged opinion that art can never be re-invented, only refreshed through constant practise and experimentation.

Sometimes the experimentation is of a technical nature, such as the manipulation of acrylic and oil paints to create new surface characters and formulations. "If you wash into oil," he explains, "the surface of the paint is being dissolved all the time. On the other hand, the acrylic dries and creates those terrific washes which you can rework with oil, and then use the underpainting combined with oil paint later on." Such manipulations strengthened the artist's landscape idiom by changing what he feels were "pictorially dominant" compositions into visual reconstructions of such forces of nature as feelings of light, texture, rutting—thus adding structural factors to the framework of Thiebaud's dramatic vocabulary.

But the significance of the retrospective overrides considerations of style and content. A California painter of major standing, Thiebaud has been channeled into as many movements, modes, and characterizations as there are essays written about his work by critics and art historians. Pop Art, New Realism, American Realism have been cited as peer groups, and a rich, complex interpretative menu of his aesthetic has been offerred as possible identifications of his oeuvre. What the perspective of some 23 years suggested, however, is a novel interpretation which, based upon the artist's repeatedly stated views of his forms, brings into focus the theme of *abstraction* as the one consistent thread that unifies, and thus gives identity, to the entire body of his work. To be sure, it is evident that realism is a dominant element; but the picture that emerged out of the Retrospective is one in which the term "realism" is translated into "abstraction": Abstraction as reduction or essentialization; abstraction as an alteration of reality; abstraction as a conceptualized force of realism; abstraction as one source of illusionism. In short, "abstraction" in all but the non-objective sense of the word.

—Andree Marechal-Workman

TILLERS, Imants.

Australian. Born in Sydney, New South Wales, in August 1950. Studied architecture, Sydney University, 1969–72. Married Jennifer Slayter in 1972; son: Isidore. Independent painter, Sydney, since 1973. Recipient: University Architecture Medal, Sydney University, 1973. Agents: Bess Cutler Gallery, 164 Mercer Street, New York, New York 10012; Yuill/Crowley Gallery, 270 Devonshire Street, Surry Hills 2010, Sydney, New South Wales. Address: 66 Raglan Street, Sydney, New South Wales 2088, Australia.

Individual Exhibitions:

1983 Yuill/Crowley Gallery, Sydney
Matt's Gallery, London
1984 Yuill/Crowley Gallery, Sydney
Bess Cutler Gallery, New York
1985 Yuill/Crowley Gallery, Sydney
Bess Cutler Gallery, New York
1986 Yuill/Crowley Gallery, Sydney
Australian Pavilion, *Biennale,* Venice
1987 Queensland Art Gallery, Brisbane
Australian Centre for Contemporary Art, Melbourne
Art Gallery of South Australia, Adelaide
Reed College, Portland, Oregon
Bess Cutler Gallery, New York
Galerie Susan Wyss, Zurich
Yuill/Crowley Gallery, Sydney
1988 Institute of Contemporary Arts, London
Bess Cutler Gallery, New York
Yuill/Crowley Gallery, Sydney
National Gallery of Victoria, Melbourne
Wellington Art Gallery, New Zealand

Selected Group Exhibitions:

1982 *Documenta 7,* Museum Fridericianum, Kassel, West Germany
1984 *An Australian Accent,* Project Studio One, New York (travelled to Washington, D.C.; Perth; Sydney)
1985 *Two Words Collide,* Artspace, Sydney
1986 *Contemporary Issues III,* Trenton State College, New Jersey
1987 *Avant Garde in the Eighties,* Los Angeles County Museum of Art
1988 *Contemporary Australian Painting,* Auckland City Art Gallery, New Zealand (travelled to Wellington)

Collections:

Australian National Gallery, Canberra; Art Gallery of New South Wales, Sydney; Art Gallery of South Australia, Adelaide; Art Gallery of Western Australia, Perth; Queensland Art Gallery, South Brisbane; National Gallery of Victoria, Melbourne.

Imants Tillers: *Opus Pataphysicum,* 1986

Publications:

On TILLERS: books—*Imants Tillers: White Aborigines*, exhibition catalogue with text by Paul Taylor, London 1983; *Imants Tillers: Venice Biennale 1986, Australia*, exhibition catalogue edited by Kerry Crowley, Sydney 1986; *Australian Appropriations: Recent Paintings of Imants Tillers*, exhibition catalogue with essay by John S. Wber, Portland 1987; *State of Art: Ideas and Images in the 1980s* by Sandy Nairne, London 1987; *Imants Tillers*, exhibition catalogue with text by Stuart Morgan, London 1988.

TILLIM, Sidney.

American. Born in Brooklyn, New York, 16 June 1925. Studied at the College of Fine Arts, Syracuse University, New York, 1946–50, B.F.A. 1950. Served in Engineer Corps, United States Army, 1943–46. Married Muriel Sharon in 1956. Independent artist since 1950, known for historical, narrative paintings, and, more recently, abstract works: lives and works in New York. Contributing Editor, *Arts Magazine*, New York, 1959–65; Contributing Editor, *Artforum*, New York, 1965–69. Instructor, Parsons School of Design, New York, 1961–63; Instructor, Pratt Institute, Brooklyn, New York, 1964–68. Instructor, Bennington College, Vermont, since 1966. Recipient: Yaddo Fellowship, Saratoga Springs, New York, 1963; National Endowment for the Arts Grant, 1975; Painting Grant, Ingram-Merrill Foundation, 1976. Address: 17 Bleecker Street, New York, New York 10012, U.S.A.

Individual Exhibitions:

1960 Cober Gallery, New York
1965 Robert Schoelkopf Gallery, New York
1967 Robert Schoelkopf Gallery, New York
1969 Georgia State College, Atlanta
Noah Goldowsky Gallery, New York
1970 Benson Gallery, Bridgehampton, New York
1973 Edmonton Art Gallery, Alberta
1974 Noah Goldowsky Gallery, New York
1976 Edmonton Art Gallery, Alberta
1977 Tibor de Nagy Gallery, New York
1979 Meredith Long Gallery, New York
1986 Bennington College, Vermont

Selected Group Exhibitions:

1964 *Contemporary Realism in Figure and Landscape*, Wadsworth Atheneum, Hartford, Connecticut
1966 *Recent Still Life*, Museum of Art, Rhode Island School of Design, Providence
1968 *Realism Now*, Vassar College, Poughkeepsie, New York
1970 *Aspects of a New Realism*, Milwaukee Art Center
1972 *Whitney Annual*, Whitney Museum, New York
1975 *Modern Views of George Washington*, New Jersey State Museum, Trenton
1980 *Realism and Metaphor*, University of South Florida, Tampa
1981 *Contemporary American Realism since 1961*, Pennsylvania Academy of Design, Philadelphia
1984 *American Still Life 1945–83*, Contemporary Arts Museum, Houton
1986 *Artists Choose Artists*, CDS Gallery, New York

Collections:

Dana Art Center, Colgate University, Hamilton, New York; New Jersey State Museum, Trenton; Hirshhorn Museum, Washington, D.C.; City Art Museum, St. Louis; Weatherspoon Art Gallery, University of North Carolina, Greensboro; University of New Hampshire; Edmonton Art Gallery, Alberta; Alten Kurhaus, Aachen, West Germany.

Sidney Tillim: *Reassurance*, 1979

Publications:

By TILLIM: book—*Richard Lindner*, Chicago 1960; articles—"Notes on Narrative and History Painting" in *Sidney Tillim*, exhibition catalogue, Hamilton, New York 1973, revised version in *Artforum* (New York), May 1977; "The Ideal and the Literal Sublime" in *Artforum* (New York), May 1976; "Benjamin Reconsidered: The Work of Art After the Age of Mechanical Reproduction" in *Artforum* (New York), May 1983; "The Modest Greatness of Julio Gonzalez" in *Art in America* (New York), October 1983; "The View from Past 50" in *Artforum* (New York), May 1984; "Abstraction Revisited" in *Art in America* (New York), April 1986; "Criticism and Culture, or Greenberg's Doubt" in *Art in America* (New York), May 1987.

On TILLIM: books—*Neue Formen des Realismus* by Peter Sager, Cologne 1973; *Sidney Tillim*, exhibition catalogue, by Terry Fenton, Edmonton, Alberta 1973; *Artists Choose Artists*, exhibition catalogue with essay by Max Kozloff, New York 1986; articles—review by Donald Judd in *Arts Magazine* (New York), November 1960; review by Dennis Adrian in *Artforum* (New York), September 1967; "Unconventional Realists" by Gabriel Laderman in *Artforum* (New York), November 1967; "22 Realists at the Whitney Museum" by Douglas Davis in *Newsweek* (New York), February 1970; "Neuer Realismus" in *Der Spiegel* (Hamburg), August 1970; review by Jed Perl and Deborah Rosenthal in *Arts Magazine* (New York), January 1980; review by Gerrit Henry in *Art in America* (New York), January 1980; "The Representational Impulse" by Jed Perl in *The New Criterion* (New York), April 1985.

Between 1958 and 1978 I painted in a representational and ultimately narrative style. In 1979 my work became more expressionist and semi-abstract. And in 1980 it became entirely abstract. In short, I resumed the modernist style I had abandoned in 1957. There were no profoundly ideological reasons for making this change. Perhaps I had begun to feel too ideologically constrained by the ambitious history paintings I had been painting since the mid-60's. In any event, assumptions about the demise of modernism, and by extension abstract art, are now virtually commonplace, so that any abstract art has a certain ideological function imposed on it. For me, resuming an abstract style marks some sort of *return*, and in this sense I have not abandoned the nostalgic impulses that informed that aspect of my representational work that was dominated, perhaps even distorted, by ideological demands. I feel my nostalgia—which I do not feel *as* nostalgia—is more organic now and is thus a more complete embrace of art and tradition. I never consciously attempted to create something new, just something that was my own. For artists like myself, the search for a style is largely a search for something upon which to build. "We are all going to heaven," said Gainsborough on his deathbed, "and Van Dyke is of that company." On the other hand, as Marie Bashkirtseff noted in her journal, "What I require is all the recognition that has been denied me since the beginning of time."

—Sidney Tillim

After abandoning his beginnings as a geometric abstract painter more than 15 years ago, Sidney Tillim proceeded to develop a kind of stylized representationalism. In his still-lifes of the 1960's, Tillim painted random arrangements in close-up, cropped compositions which reveal connections with the photographic as antecedent. Like Lowell Nesbitt, Tillim opted for firm, unbroken contours and cooly descriptive surfaces. Next came a range of figure pictures dealing with the artist's childhood and family life. In "A Dream of Being" (1968–69), crisp, simplified, caricaturized figures are arranged in a highly formalized composition, caught in a moment of frozen activity which suggests a modern-day allegorical theme about the passage of time and life. Next, Tillim began making paintings of more generally historical themes, his subjects including the early history of the United States, the Jews and the Bible. He underwent a campaign to help revive the genre of epic history painting and became known as a "social historian" during the 1970's. Often compared with Puvis de Chavannes and Nicolas Poussin, Tillim rejected modernist canons of picture making, emphasizing communication of the narrative by negating the painterly handwriting of the expressionist artist. He created complex compositions filled with arrested action aimed at heightening the drama of an often violent moment from past history of historic myth. Of his intentions in such pictures Tillim has noted, "History painting gambles more recklessly than most on the problem of converting tastes to its own point of view." His choices of particular themes were, according to his own statements, predicated on their relevance for the present moment, and it is this symbolic and psychological connection which he wants to convey without using methods of contemporary art. Considering this desire for subjects analogous with the present, it is not surprising to find Tillim also painting themes taken from the movies and from media accounts of current events.

What is surprising is Tillim's switch in 1978–79 from anti-modernist representation to a more abstracted stylization which resembles Cubism and Vorticism. In this new work, Tillim continues to deal with social themes, now depicting them in an angular, jagged planar structuring with openly agitated brushstrokes. It is a turnaround which seems well suited for subjects such as "The Capture of Patti Hearst," "An American Tragedy" (Norman Mailer's knife attack on his wife at a party), and "Murder Hollywood Style" (scene from the movie *The Big Sleep*). In many of the pictures from this group, the vantage point is downward on an angle to view a series of overlapping triangular planes. The sharpness and frenetic energy of the rather summary stylization works well to enhance the frenetic emotiveness of the subject matter, and Tillim's confrontation with modernism in such a personal form has brought with it a rewarding effectiveness.

Among the qualities which persist throughout Tillim's development are stylization for dramatic effect and satirical edge. In these and other ways, Tillim can be compared with the American magic and Social Realists who developed during the 1930's and 1940's. Tillim's earlier works resemble the figural stylizations of George Tooker or Peter Cadmus, and it is not unenlightening to see his newer pictures in comparison with a painter such as Ben Shahn, or even with the painter of an earlier "American Tragedy," Phillip Evergood.

—Barbara Cavaliere

TILSON, Joe.

British. Born in London, 24 August 1928. Studied, with Frank Auerbach and Leon Kossoff, St. Martin's School of Art, London, 1949–52; also studied at the Royal College of Art, London, 1952–55, A.R.C.A. 1955. Served in the Royal Air Force, 1946–49. Married Joslyn Morton in 1956; children: Jake, Anna and Sophy. Worked as carpenter and joiner, London, 1944–46. Independent artist: in Italy and Spain, 1955–57; in London, 1958–72; and in Christian Malford, Wiltshire, and Italy, since 1972. Instructor, St. Martin's School of Art, London, 1958–63; Visiting Lecturer, University of Durham, Newcastle upon Tyne, 1962–63; Instructor, School of Visual Arts, New York, 1966; Visiting Lecturer, Staatliche Hochschule für Bildende Künste, Hamburg, 1971–72. Recipient: Knapping Foundation Prize, London, 1955; Rome Prize, 1955; Painting Prize, *John Moores Exhibition*, Liverpool, 1957, 1967; Painting Prize, *Gulbenkian Foundation Exhibition*, London, 1960; Gold Medal, *Biennale*, San Marino, 1963; Print Prize, *Exposition Internationale de Gravure*, Ljubljana, 1965, 1967, 1975, 1977, 1979, 1983; Grand Prize, *Graphics Biennale*, Krakow, 1974; First Prize, Bradford Print Biennale, 1984; Grand Prix d'Hon neur, *16th Biennale de la Gravure*, Liubliana, 1985. Agent: Waddington Galleries, 11 Cork Street, London W1 XPD. Address: The Old Rectory, Christian Malford, Wiltshire SN15 4BW, England.

Individual Exhibitions:

1962 Marlborough New London Gallery
1963 Hatton Gallery, Newcastle upon Tyne
Ferens Art Gallery, Hull
Walker Art Gallery, Liverpool
University of Nottingham
1964 Marlborough New London Gallery
1966 Marlborough Graphics, New York
Marlborough New London Gallery
1967 Galleria del Naviglio, Milan
Galleria del Deposito, Genoa
Galleria Fiori, Montecatini, Italy
Marlborough-Gerson Gallery, New York
Galleria Marlborough, Rome
1968 Galleria Ferrari, Verona
Galleria de'Foscherari, Bologna
Galerie Brusberg, Hannover
1970 Marlborough New London Gallery
Hausam Waldsee, West Berlin (with Gerd Winner)
1971 CAYC: Centro de Arte y Comunicacion, Buenos Aires
Waddington Galleries, London
1972 Abrams Gallery, Amsterdam (with Juan Genoves)
Galerie René Block, West Berlin
1973 Museum Boymans-van Beuningen, Rotterdam (retrospective)
1974 Musée Royal des Beaux-Arts, Antwerp
Galerie von Loeper, Hamburg
University of Parma, Italy (retospective)
1975 Studio Marconi, Milan
Galleria Marlborough, Rome
Galleria del Cavallino, Venice
1976 Galerie Espace, Amsterdam
Galleria Il Chiodo, Mantua, Italy
Galleria Il Tritone, Biella, Italy
Marlborough Fine Art, London
Galerija Krzysztofory, Cracow, Poland
Galleria Corsini, Intra, Italy
1977 Galleria Rizzardi, Milan
Galleria La Chiocciola, Padua
Galleria A, Parma, Italy
1978 Waddington-Tooth Galleries, London
Tate Gallery, London
Peterloo Gallery, Manchester
Galleria Giuli, Lecco, Italy
1979 Waddington Galleries, London
Van Straaten Gallery, Chicago
Clark Gallery, Boston
Aronson Gallery, Atlanta
Edward Tohta Gallery, London
Graphics, Vancouver Art Gallery (graphics retrospective)
1980 Galerie Espace, Amsterdam
De Vries ond Roeloff, Rotterdam
Erica Williams-Ann Johnson Gallery, Seattle
Horwitch Gallery, Scottsdale, Arizona
Galleri 22, Aarhus, Denmark
Gumps Gallery, San Francisco
Hokin Gallery, Miami
1981 Fitterman Gallery, Minneapolis
Meridan House, Washington, D.C.
University of Maryland, College Park
Schneebach Gallery, Cincinnati, Ohio
Galerie Mira Godard, Toronto (travelled to Mira Godard Gallery, Calgary)
Galleria Il Chiodo, Mantua, Italy
Galleria Il Sole, Bolzano, Italy
1982 Galleria Meta, Florence
Galleria Adelfi, Padua
University of Pittsburgh
Joseph Wolpe Gallery, Cape Town
Natalie Knight Gallery, Johannesburg
Galerie Kammer, Hamburg
1983 Galleria d'Arte, Volterra, Italy
Thorden Wetterling Gallery, Goteborg, Sweden
Galleria Dabbeni, Lugano, Switzerland
Galleria Menghelli, Florence
Galleria Rotta, Genoa, Italy
1984 Galleria Nazzari, Parma, Italy
Arnolfini Gallery, Bristol, Avon
1985 Galleria del Cavallino, Venice
1987 Art Museum of Liubliana, Yugoslavia (retrospective)
Thorden Gallery, Goteborg, Sweden

Selected Group Exhibitions:

1961 *Biennale*, Paris
1964 *Biennale*, Venice
1965 *Op and Pop*, Moderna Museet, Stockholm
1969 *Pop Art*, Hayward Gallery, London
1976 *Pop Art in England*, Kunstverein, Hamburg
1979 *Photography in Printmakling*, Victoria and Albert Museum, London
1981 *Landscape*, Tate Gallery, London
1983 *Pintura Britanica Contemporanea*, Museo Municipal, Madrid
1985 *Modern Artists' Books*, Victoria and Albert Museum, London
1987 *Pop Art USA/UK*, Metropolitan Museum, Tokyo (travelled to Osaka, Funabashi and Yokohama)

Collections:

Tate Gallery, London: Victoria and Albert Museum, London; Stedelijk Museum, Amsterdam; Museum Boymans-van Beuningen, Rotterdam; Musée Royal des Beaux-Arts, Antwerp; Kunstmuseum, Hannover; Galleria Nazionale d'Art Moderna, Rome; National Gallery of South Africa, Johannesburg; National Gallery of Australia, Canberra; Museum of Modern Art, New York.

Publications:

By TILSON: books—*A-Z Box, Fragments of an Oneiric Alphabet*, London 1970; *Alchera . . . notes for Country Works*, London 1976; *Alchera: 1970–76*, Pollenza, Italy 1977; *Wessex*, Pollenza, Italy 1977; *Alchera—Joe Tilson*, exhibition catalogue, London 1978; *Joe Tilson: Proscinemi, Oracles*, exhibition catalogue, London 1978; *Hesiod's Crown*, London 1984; *Joe Tilson: Festivals*, London 1987.

On TILSON: books—*Collage* by Harriet Janis and Rudi Blesh, New York 1962; *Contemporary = British Art* by Herbert Read, London 1964; *The Painter and the Photograph: From Delacroix to Warhol* by Van Deren Coke, Alburquerque, New Mexico 1964, 1972; *Pop as Art* by Mario Amaya, London 1965; *Pop Art* by Lawrence Alloway and Lucy Lippard, London 1966; *Pop Art Redefined* by John Russell and Suzi Gablik, London 1969; *Pop Art* by Michael Compton, London, New York, Sydney and Toronto 1970; *Tilson—Winner*, exhibition catalogue, with text by Thomas Kempas, West Berlin 1970; *Eroticism in Contemporary Art* by Volker Kahmen, London 1970; *The Moderns* by Terry Measham, London 1976; *Pop Art in England*, exhibition catalogue, with text by Uwe M. Schneede, Hamburg 1976; *Arte Inglese Oggi 1960–1976*, exhibition catalogue, by Norbert Lynton, 2 vols., London and Milan 1976; *Tilson* by Arturo C. Quintavalle, with a preface by Pierre Restany, Milan 1977; *Understanding Prints* by Pat Gilmour, London 1979; *Photography in Printmaking* by Charles Newton, London 1979; *Joe Tilson: Graphics*, exhibition catalogue, with text by Pat Gilmour, Vancouver 1979; *Maestri Contemporanei: Tilson* by Gillo Dorfles and Michael Compton, Milan 1982.

Joe Tilson: ***Trojan Door*****, 1974**

Joe Tilson is a rare example, among British artists, of a multi-media creator, not tied to technique or material, yet always able to stamp the mark of his personality and inventive constructivist manner on all his work.

In general terms it is probably easiest to label him a Pop-artist, since it is clear that what motivates his creative juices is the stimulation of every-day, urban, industrial society. On the other hand, he could be labelled a "land-scapist," with the proviso that what arrests his attention and inspires his art is the landscape of the modern city and its decorative addenda. In essence this is a non-analytical or non-critical stance; Tilson does not judge modern society and the physical or moral forms of life it produces. He is a traditionalist in the sense that the English landscape poets or painters looked at nature, analyzed its forms, produced and perfected the means of producing images based on this phenomena, and thereby expressed their relationship with nature. There was no question of "criticising" nature, since it is a non-criticisable force. Modern industrial society is, however, open to criticism or disapproval, but it is also there to be observed, to be analysed formally, to be used as the basis of design and art.

Pop-artists are not critics or philosophers; they are poets. Tilson, in fact, can be compared with the Italian Metaphysical painters, with de Chirico in particular, sharing their detachment from the symbols they chose in order to express a state of mind or spirit. Thus when Tilson builds a column of wooden blocks, whose four sides all bear the word "Yes," he is both creating a plastic form, a sculpture, and also a combination of fact and abstraction which is concerned with everyday life, yet which mysteriously, even perhaps mystically, stands apart from it. Tilson, in fact, spent two years in Italy, in the late 50's and has maintained connections with the country.

Tilson is a member of a remarkable generation of English artists who were connected with the Institute of Contemporary Arts in London when the critic Lawrence Alloway, and artists such as Richard Hamilton and Eduardo Paolozzi were attempting to work out the relationship of art to life and the public. These artists included Peter Blake, Ron Kitaj, Peter Phillips and David Hockney. The intellectual and stylistic example of Hamilton, and the brilliant inventiveness of Paolozzi, led to the special English branch of Pop-art, long before the emergence of the American brand; the younger artists, many of whom visited the United States as students and teachers, created a bridge between the continents.

Tilson, as indeed his English contemporaries, whilst impressed and affected by the remarkable American generation of Pop-artists, retained his own individuality. This is compounded by a love and use of words as symbols equally useful and powerful as images, as well as the incorporation of geometrical and three-dimensional forms as extensions of flat surfaces. He is catholic in the use of materials, used uniquely or in combination—wood, plastics, painted surfaces, photographic images, collage, screen printing, etc. As well as the abstract insertion of single words, or the serialised image of an eye, Tilson reproduces newspaper photographs, pages from magazines, references to contemporary events, as well as details of famous works of art. None of this is erratic or chance; Tilson is careful and positive in his choice and juxtaposition of conponents, even if, to the viewer, it is a total effect, either of forms, images, or even verbal messages, rather than an immediately understood philosophy, which makes its impact. Probably Tilson's finest gift is for public communication, evident in the murals he has constructed in different parts of the world.

—Charles Spencer

TINDLE, David.

British. Born in Huddersfield, Yorkshire, 29 April 1932. Educated in Coventry, Warwickshire public schools; studied at the Coventry School of Art, 1945–46. Married Janet F. Trollope in 1969; children: Saskia, Charlotte and Nathan. Painter: in London, 1951–56; in Arbroath and Wantage, 1956–58; in London, 1959–64; in Brome, Suffolk, 1964–66; in London, 1966–69; in East Hadden, Northamptonshire, 1969–80; in Clipston, Leicestershire, 1980–86; in Leamington Spa, Warwickshire, since 1986. Lecturer, Hornsey College of Art and Byam Shaw School of Painting, London, 1959–74. Part-time Lecturer, Royal College of Art, London, since 1972. Recipient: Painting Prize, *Chichester National Art Exhibition*, Sussex, 1975. Associate, 1973, Royal Academician, 1979, Royal Academy of Art, London; Associate, 1973, Fellow, 1981, and Honorary Fellow, 1984, Royal College of Art, London; Ruskin Master of Drawing and Fine Art, Oxford University, 1985. Honorary MA: St. Edmund Hall, Oxford, 1985. Agent: Fischer Fine Art, London. Address: c/o Fischer Fine Art, 30 King Street, London SW1, England.

Individual Exhibitions:

1954 Piccadilly Gallery, London (and regularly 1954 83)
Crane Gallery, Manchester, England
1957 City Art Gallery, Coventry, England
57 Gallery, Edinburgh
1958 Stone Gallery, Newcastle upon Tyne, England
1961 *New Painting*, Bear Lane Gallery, Oxford
1963 Metropole Gallery, Folkestone, England
1964 Galerie du Tours, San Francisco (travelled to Galerie du Tours, Los Angeles)
1965 Metropole Gallery, Folkestone, Kent
1968 Galleria Carbonesi, Bologna
Galleria Vinciana, Milan
1970 27 Gallery, Northampton
1972 City Art Gallery, Northampton (retrospective)
1974 Galerie XX, Hamburg
1977 Galerie XX, Hamburg
1980 Galerie XX, Hamburg
1985 Fischer Fine Art, London

Selected Group Exhibitions:

1958 *International Biennale of Realist Art*, Bruges, Belguim
1959 *John Moore's Exhibition*, Liverpool (and 1961)
1967 *Mostra Mercate d'Arte Contemporanea*, Florence
1974 *British Painting 74*, Hayward Gallery, London
1975 *Art 6 '75*, Kunstmesse, Basle
1977 *British Painting 1952–77*, Royal Academy of Art, London
1978 *English Realism*, Waddington Galleries, Montreal
1979 *The British Art Show*, toured Britain

Collections:

Tate Gallery, London; Arts Council of Great Britain, London; Department of the Environment, London; London Museum; Contemporary Art Society, London; Walker Art Gallery, Liverpool; Whitworth Art Gallery, Manchester; Wakefield Art Gallery, Yorkshire; Arts Council of Northern Ireland, Belfast.

Publications:

On TINDLE: *David Tindle*, exhibition catalogues, edited by Piccadilly Gallery, London 1957, 1963, 1965, 1966, 1968, 1971, 1973, 1976, 1979; *David Tindle: New Paintings*, exhibition catalogue, Oxford 1961; *David Tindle: Paintings 1962*, exhibition catalogue, with text by Neville Wallis, London 1962; *Exhibition of Works by David Tindle*, exhibition catalogue, Northampton 1972; *David Tindle*, exhibition catalogue with text by Marina Vaizey, London 1985.

The images I paint are of things I know best or can remember most. I try to place them in an order that expresses the feelings I have about them. It is not a question of painting them as realistically as I can, but to get the right tonality, so that memory and presence are very close.

—David Tindle

"20th-century art, now free from the intolerable burden of representation . . . "—how often has one heard that phrase! Yet, if one casts around for contemporary artists whose work asserts the enduring value of representation as a way of finding oneself in the universe, there are very few who offer visible, incontrovertible evidence. David Tindle is one of them.

Why is he so much less acclaimed than, say, Wyeth in the United States? He has been the victim of a special situation in Britain: art, and especially "modern" and abstract art, has had such an uphill task to win recognition, interest and respectability in the first half of the 20th century that sitting in front of an easel and nature, and *learning* from it by making marks and looking again, has been made to seem like a reactionary gesture. And the fact that the brightest talents of those decades chose more immediate forms of self-expression weighed the public scales even more against it.

Tindle moved from vigorous, gestural paintings of such subjects as high seas breaking on the shore, towards "every-blade-of-grass" scenes of landscape seen out of windows, or evocative still-lifes of straw hats on chairs, done in traditional tempera and much like old Roman murals in their effect; but not with that obsessional deadness that high detail so often carries, but a fine, refined, luminescent and atmospheric stillness, full of lively details of observed light, direct and reflected, as in Vermeer or de Hoogh; they have manifest presence. These are paintings which "are what they do"; some find a melancholy in them, others, the timeless repose of the suspended moment, complete in itself. In them, "representation" catches our remembering that "that is how it is"—but "how it is" includes the recognition or memory of mental and spiritual worlds beyond the physical and manifest.

From time to time, Tindle has painted very straightforward portraits of young art students; these in their directness deserve to be seen more publicly. Tindle's is a major, little-recognized contribution to 20th-century factual realism, and to art itself, as a method and also a gift of self-realization.

—Michael Shepherd

TINGUELY, Jean.

Swiss. Born in Fribourg, 22 May 1925. Educated at primary and secondary schools, in Basle, 1930–39; apprentice decorator, Globus Department Store, Basle, 1941–45; studied art at the Kunstgewerbeschule, Basle, 1941–45. Married the artist Eva Aeppli in 1951 (separated, 1958). Independent artist, in Basle, 1945–52; subsequently in Paris, Basle, and in Soisy-sur-Ecole, France; abstract paintings and kinetic assemblage-sculptures, 1945–52; first "Metamecanismes," 1952; first "Metamatics," 1959; collaborative works with artists Yves Klein, 1958–62, Niki de Saint-Phalle, from 1960, and with Bernard Luginbuhl, 1968–72. Member, Pierre Restany's "Nouveaux Réalistes" group of artists, Paris, 1960–70. Address: L'Auberge du Chéval-Blanc, 91840 Soisy-sur-Ecole, Essones, France.

Individual Exhibitions:

1954 Galerie Arnaud, Paris
Studio d'Architettura, Milan
1955 Galleri Samlaren, Stockholm

David Tindle: *Room*, 1985

1956 Galerie Denise René, Paris
1957 Galerie Edouard Loeb, Paris
Galerie Denise René, Paris
1958 Galerie Iris Clert, Paris
1959 Galerie Schmela, Dusseldorf
Kaplan Gallery, London
Galerie Iris Clert, Paris
Institute of Contemporary Arts, London (happening-event)
1960 Staempfli Gallery, New York
Museum of Modern Art sculpture garden, New York (outdoor event)
Galerie des Quatres Saisons, Paris
Museum Haus Lange, Krefeld, West Germany
Kunsthalle, Berne, Switzerland (with Bernard Luginbuhl and Norbert Kricke)
1961 Moderna Museet, Stockholm
Louisiana Museum, Humlebaek, Denmark
Staempfli Gallery, New York
Galerie Rive Droite, Paris
Galleria Schwarz, Milan
1962 Galerie Handschin, Basle
Everett Ellin Gallery, Los Angeles
Alexandre Iolas Gallery, New York
1963 Minami Gallery, Tokyo
Dwan Gallery, Los Angeles
1964 Galerie Alexandre Iolas, Geneva
Kunsthalle, Baden-Baden, West Germany
Galerie Rudolf Zwirner, Cologne
1965 *Sculpture*, Museum of Fine Arts, Houston
Palais des Beaux-Arts, Brussels
3 Sculpteurs: Cesar, Roel d'Haese, Tinguely, Musée des Arts Décoratifs, Paris
2 Kinetic Sculptors: Nicolas Schoffer and Jean Tinguely, Jewish Museum, New York (toured the United States)
Alexandre Iolas Gallery, New York
Kunsthalle, Berne
1966 Ohio State University, Columbus
Gimpel und Hanover Galerie, Zurich
Hon-en Katedral, Moderna Museet, Stockholm (with Niki de Saint-Phalle and Per Olof Ultveldt)
1967 Galerie Alexandre Iolas, Paris
Galleria Iolas, Milan
Rijksmuseum Kröller-Müller, Otterlo, Netherlands (with Bernard Luginbuhl)
Galleri Buren, Stockholm
1968 Hanover Gallery, London
Tekeningen, Stedeijk Museum, Amsterdam
Museum of Contemporary Art, Chicago
1969 Gimpel und Hanover Galerie, Zurich
Victor Loeb Department Store, Berne
1970 Galleria Iolas, Milan
Galerie Alexandre Iolas, Geneva
Galleria L'Attico, Rome
1971 *Machines de Tinguely*, Centre National d'Art Contemporain, Paris (toured Europe, 1971–72)
1974 *Debricollages*, Galerie Bischofberger, Zurich
1975 *Reliefs et Sculptures 1954–1965*, Galerie Bonnier, Geneva
1976 *Dessins et Gravures pour les Sculptures*, Musée d'Art et d'Histoire, Geneva
Tinguely in Kunstmuseum Basle, Kunstmuseum, Basle
Galerie Bischofberger, Zurich
1978 Wilhelm-Lehmbruck-Museum, Duisburg, West Germany (retrospective)
1979 *Jean Tinguely im Stadel*, Städtische Galerie, Frankfurt
1981 Galerie Bischofberger, Zurich
Abbaye de Senanque, Vaucluse, France
1982 Kunsthaus, Zurich (travelled to the Tate Gallery, London, Palais des Beaux-Arts, Brussels, and the Musée d'Art et d'Histoire, Geneva)
1983 Centre Georges Pompidou, Paris
1984 Stedelijk Museum, Amsterdam
1985 Kunsthalle der Hypo-Stiftung, Munich
1986 Louisiana Museum, Humlebaek, Denmark
Kunsthalle der Hypo-Stiftung, Munich
1987 Galerie Beyeler, Basle
Palazzo Grassi, Venice

Selected Group Exhibitions:

1955 *Le Mouvement*, Galerie Denise René, Paris
1959 *Biennale*, Paris
1961 *Le Mouvement dans l'Art*, Stedelijk Museum, Amsterdam (travelled to the Moderna Museet, Stockholm, and the Louisiana Museum, Humlebaek, Denmark)
1964 *Biennale*, Venice
1967 *French Art Today*, at *Expo 67*, Montreal

1968 *The Machine,* Museum of Modern Art, New York
1977 *Paris-New York,* Centre Georges Pompidou, Paris
1980 *Paris Paris 1937–57,* Centre Georges Pompidou, Paris
1982 *60–80: Attitudes, Concepts, Images,* Stedelijk Museum, Amsterdam
1984 *Salvaged: Altered Everyday Objects,* Project Studio One, Long Island City, New York

Collections:

Centre Georges Pompidou, Paris; Kunsthaus, Zurich; Kunstmuseum, Dusseldorf; Kaiser-Wilhelm-Museum, Krefeld, West Germany; Stedelijk Museum, Amsterdam; Stedelijk Van Abbemuseum, Eindhoven, Netherlands; Museum of Modern Art, New York; Museum of Fine Arts, Houston.

Publications:

By TINGUELY: book—*Für Statik,* manifesto, Dusseldorf 1959.

On TINGUELY: books—*Tinguely,* exhibition leaflet, with text by Pontus Hulten, Paris 1957; *3 Sculpteurs: Cesar, Roel d'Haese, Tinguely,* exhibition catalogue, with texts by Francois Mathey, Chris Yperman and James Johnson Sweeney, Paris 1965; *Jean Tinguely: Sculpture,* exhibition catalogue, with text by James Johnson Sweeney, Houston 1965; *2 Kinetic Sculptors: Nicolas Schoffer and Jean Tinguely,* exhibition catalogue, with texts by Sam Hunter and K. G. Pontus Hulten, New York, 1965; *Jean Tinguely,* exhibition catalogue, with text by Jean-Christophe Ammann, Zurich 1966; *Jean Tinguely: Tekeningen,* exhibition folder, Amsterdam 1968; *Tinguely,* exhibition catalogue, with texts by Peter F. Althaus, and others, Basle 1972; *Jean Tinguely,* exhibition catalogue, with texts by Wieland Schmied, Peter F. Althaus and others, Hannover 1972; *Jean Tinguely: 166 Fotos von Leonardo Bezzola,* with texts by Eva Aeppli, Bernard Luginbuhl, Niki de Saint-Phalle and others, Zurich 1974; *Jean Tinguely: Debricollages,* exhibition catalogue, with text by Gerald Minkoff, Zurich 1974; *Mesa* by Pontus Hulten, London 1975; *Jean Tinguely: Reliefs et Sculptures 1954–1965,* exhibition catalogue, Geneva 1975; *Jean Tinguely: dessins et gravures pour les sculptures,* exhibition catalogue, with an interview by Charles Georg and Rainer Michael Mason, Geneva 1976; *Tinguely in Kunstmuseum, Basle,* exhibition catalogue, with text by Franz Meyer, Basle 1976; *Jean TInguely im Stadel,* exhibition catalogue, with texts by Klaus Gallwitz and Willy Rotzler, Frankfurt 1979; *Der Tinguely-Brunnen in Basle* by Annemaire Monteil, Basle 1980; *Tinguely,* exhibition catalogue, with texts by Felix Baumann, and Richard Calvocoressi, Zurich 1982; *Jean Tinguely: catalogue raissone 1954–1968,* compiled by Christina Bischofberger, Zurich 1982; *Jean Tinguely,* exhibition catalogue with texts by Carla Schulz-Hoffmann and Stephanie Poley, Munich 1985; *Jean Tinguely,* exhibition catalogue with text by Gert Kaiser, Basle 1987.

Tinguely's formal artistic training was at the School of Art and Crafts in Basel from 1941–45, though his attendance was irregular. By 1945 he was painting abstract pictures and making constructions from wire, metal and other materials, influenced by the work of Kurt Schwitters. It was also at this time that he expressed interest in movement as an artistic medium.

Between 1945–53, Tinguely worked at various jobs in Basel and was attracted to the work of Paul Klee and the Bauhaus, Tanguy, Dali and Miro. He was living in Paris in 1953 and worked with Daniel Spoerri in Jean Lurcat's studio on a project for 'autotheatre', which was intended to bring action to the stage with or without actors. Tinguely spent most of the 1950's working on various series of reliefs: 1954—reliefs made up of layers of moving rods; 1954–56 "meta-mechanical" reliefs and free-standing sculptures; 1956–59 reliefs with rotating metal elements. The late 1950's to early 1960's saw the advent of Tinguely's first 'painting machines' and his involvement with *Nouveaux Realisme,* which rejected the ivory tower world of abstract painting (then the major international trend in painting), and advocated the use of real materials and found objects; all of which was a harkening back to *Dada.* Indeed, Tinguely's own constructions owed a great deal to Picabia's work of 1917–19.

In 1960 one of Tinguely's most famous series was inaugurated with the *Hommage à New York,* a sculpture which self-destructed in the garden of New York's Museum of Modern Art. By the mid-1960's the sculptures were becoming huge and were major media events, especially if they were of the self-destructing variety.

Tinguely's machines usually worked in some way, even if only just. The irony inherent in his early work, particularly the painting machines, receded though never entirely disappeared. He brought together a combination of a dadaist tradition with the fascination for humourous and outlandish machines as seen by artists such as Paul Klee and the Surrealists, adding to all this a concern for the use of cast off materials and an overwhelming interest in movement.

—Victoria Keller

TITUS-CARMEL, Gerard.

French. Born in Paris, 10 October 1941. Studied engraving at the Ecole Boulle, Paris, 1958–62. Served in the French Air Force, 1962–64. Married Joan C. Robinson in 1971; children: Jeanne and Guillaume. Independent artist, Paris, 1964–82, and in Oulchy-le-Château, Aisne, since 1982; also, filmmaker, since 1972. Recipient: First Prize, *Drawing Biennale,* Rijeka, 1970; International Art Critics Association Prize, *Biennale de Paris,* 1971; First Prize, *Biennale of Alexandria,* 1971. Agent: Galerie Lelong, Paris. Address: c/o Galerie Lelong, 13 rue de Teheran, 75008 Paris, France.

Individual Exhibitions:

1967 Galerie du Fleuve, Paris
1968 Galerie du Fleuve, Paris
1969 Galerija 212, Belgrade
1970 Galerie Daniel Templon, Paris
Galerie A.P.I.A.W., Liège, Belgium
1971 Musée d'Art Moderne de la Ville, Paris
Galerie Bama, Paris
Galleria La Salita, Rome
1972 Neue Galerie, Aachen, West Germany (retrospective)
Galerie Daniel Templon, Paris
Muzeum Sztuki, Lodz, Poland
French Pavilion, at the *Biennale,* Venice
Galerie du Fleuve, Bordeaux
Royal College of Art, London
Galleria Diagramma, Milan
1973 Galerie Godula Buchholz, Munich
Stedelijk Museum, Amsterdam
La Strategia del Disegno, Galleria Schwarz, Milan
Galerie Jalmar, Amsterdam
1974 Galerie Daniel Templon, Paris
Le Grifforme, Galerie La Hune, Paris
Galerie La Touriale, Marseilles
Galerie Birger Arnesen, Copenhagen
Galerie Vega, Liège, Belgium
1975 Galerie Graphikhuset Futura, Stockholm
Galerie Daniel Templon, Paris
Galerie Hecate, Paris
Palais des Beaux-Arts, Brussels
1976 Galerie La Hune, Paris
Galerie Therese Roussel, Perpignan, France
Galerie Baudoin Lebon, Paris
1977 Gimpel und Hanover Galerie, Zurich
Gimpel Fils, London
Kunstbandel Brinkman, Amsterdam
Galerie Art Actuel, Nancy, France
1978 Gentre Georges Pompidou, Paris
Galerija Krzysztofory, Cracow
Galerie Maeght, Paris
1979 Kunstverein für die Rheinlande und Westfalen, Dusseldorf
Galerie Maeght, Zurich
Galerie Charles Kriwin, Brussels
1980 Kunsthalle, Bielefeld, West Germany
Stadia Graphics Gallery, Sydney
Kunstverein, Kassel, West Germany
Nishimura Gallery, Tokyo
1981 Oberbeck-Gesellschaft-St. Annen Museum, Lübeck
Galerie Maeght, Paris
Kunsthalle, Nuremberg
Musée de l'Abbaye Sainte-Croix, Les Sables-d'Olonne, France
Nishimura Gallery, Tokyo
Henie-Onstad Kunstsenter, Oslo
1982 Xavier Fourcade Inc., New York
Galerie Chappe-Lautier, Toulouse
Galerie Maeght, Zurich
Galerie Maeght, Paris
1983 Galerie Elisabeth Franck, Knokke-le-Zoute, Belgium
Studio Marconi, Milan
1984 Galerie de la Cite, Luxembourg
Galerie de l'Ancienne Poste, Calais, France
Galerie Maeght Lelong, Paris
1985 Galerie des Ponchettes, Nice, France
Spaightwood Galleries, Madison, Wisconsin
Tours Narbonnaises, Carcassonne, France
Institute Francais, Stuttgart (travelled to Hamburg, Munich and Bonn)
Musee d'Art Moderne, Villeneuve d'Ascq, France
1986 Galerie Maeght Lelong, Paris
Galerie Graff, Montreal
Galerie Brinkman, Amsterdam
Galerie du Musee du Quebec, Canada
Spaightwood Galleries, Madison, Wisconsin
1987 Mucsarnok, Budapest
Fuji Television Gallery, Tokyo
Galleri Asbaeck, Copenhagen
Abbaye des Cordeliers, Chateauroux, France
Galerie La Hune, Paris
Denise Cade Gallery/Art Prospect Inc., New York
Lelong Gallery, New York

Selected Group Exhibitions:

1965 *Biennale,* Musée Municipal d'Art Moderne, Paris
1972 *Amsterdam-Paris-Dusseldorf,* Guggenheim Museum, New York (travelled to the Pasadena Art Museum, California, and Dallas Museum of Fine Arts)
1974 *Hyperréalistes Americains, Réalistes Européens,* Centre National d'Art Contemporain, Paris (travelled to the Museum Boymans-Van Beuningen, Rotterdam, and the Rotonda Besana, Milan)
1975 *Junggesellenmachinen,* Kunsthalle, Berne (travelled to the *Biennale,* Venice, and the Palais des Beaux-Arts, Brussels)
1976 *International Print Biennale,* National Museum of Modern Art, Tokyo (travelled to the National Museum, Kyoto)
1977 *Trois Villes, Tois Collections,* Musée Cantini, Marseilles (travelled to the Musée de Peinture, Grenoble; Musée d'Art et d'Industrie, St. Etienne; and the Centre Georges Pompidou, Paris)
1979 *European Dialogue,* at the *Biennale,* Art Gallery of New South Wales, Sydney (toured Australia)
1980 *Printed Art: A View of 2 Decades,* Museum of Modern Art, New York
1981 *Biennale der Europaischen Grafik,* Pavillon des Olympischen Kongress, Baden-Baden, West Germany
1982 *Statements: Leading Contemporary Artists from France,* Delahunty and Carol Taylor Gallery, Dallas (travelled to Hansen-Fuller-Golden Gallery, Dallas; Hansen-Fuller-Golden Gallery, San Francisco; and the Richard Hines Gallery, Seattle)

Collections:

Centre Georges Pompidou, Paris; Victoria and Albert Museum, London; Stedelijk Museum, Amsterdam; Musées Royaux des Beaux-Arts, Brussels; Kobbersticksamlingen ved

Gerard Titus-Carmel: *Papier Collé No. 9*, 1986

Statens Museum for Kunst, Copenhagen; Staatliche Graphische Sammlung, Munich; Kunsthaus, Zurich; Fundacio Joan Miró, Barcelona; Australian National Gallery, Canberra; Museum of Modern Art, New York.

Publications:

By TITUS-CARMEL: books—*Joaquin's Love Affair,* Paris 1971; *The Pocket Size Tlingit Coffin,* Paris 1976; books illustrated: *Pour Bramm* by Mathieu Benezet, Paris 1965; *La Porte de Nuit* by Dusan Matic, Montpellier, France 1972; *L'Humus l'Hymen* by Jean-Marc Tisserant, Montpellier, France 1973; *Matiere Premiere* by Denis Roche, Paris 1976; *Verres* by Jean-Pierre Faye, Paris 1977; *Sarx* by Pascal Quignard, Paris 1977; *Noeud* by Jean Fremon, Paris 1978; film—*Joaquin's Love Affair,* 1972.

On TITUS-CARMEL: books—*Gerard Titus-Carmel,* exhibition catalogue, with text by Jean Marc Tisserant, Liège, Belgium 1970; *Titus-Carmel,* exhibition catalogue, with texts by Mathieu Benezet, Jean-Pierre Faye, and an interview by Maurice Maurin, Paris 1971; *Gerard Titus-Carmel,* exhibition catalogue, with a preface by Wolfgang Becker, texts by others, Aachen, West Germany 1972; *Art en France: Une nouvelle generation* by Jean Clair, Paris 1972; *L'Art Actuel en France* by Anne Tronche, Paris 1973; *Gerard Titus-Carmel of het Juk van de Weegschaal,* exhibition catalogue, with text by Irmeline Lebeer, Amsterdam 1973; *La Strategia del Disegno: Gerard Titus-Carmel,* exhibition catalogue, with text by Tommaso Trini, Milan 1973; *Gerard Titus-Carmel ou le Procès du Modele* by Jean-Marc Tisserant, Paris 1974; *Gerard Titus-Carmel: Le Grifforme,* exhibition catalogue, with text by Jean-Pierre Faye, Paris 1974; *Dictionnaire Universel de la Peinture,* edited by Robert Maillard, Paris 1975; *Reperes, La Peinture en France: Debut et fin d'un systeme visuel 1870–1970* by Dora Vellier, Paris 1976; *Gerard Titus-Carmel,* exhibition catalogue, with an introduction by Willy Rotzler, London 1977; *Le Vérité en Peinture* by Jacques Derrida, Paris 1978; *Gerard Titus-Carmel,* exhibition catalogue, with texts by Jacques Derrida and Gilbert Lascault, Paris 1978; *Ecrits Timides sur le Visible* by Gilbert Lascault, Paris 1979; *Petit Larousse de la Peinture,* edited by Michel Laclotte, Paris 1979; *Dictionnaire International des Beaux-Arts,* edited by Pierre Cabanne, Paris 1979; *Gerard Titus-Carmel,* exhibition catalogue, with preface by Günter Metken, and an introduction by Karl-Heinz Hering, Dusseldorf 1979; *Great Drawings of All Times* by Genevieve Monnier and others, Tokyo 1979, New York 1980; *Titus-Carmel,* exhibition catalogue, with an introduction by Erich Franz, texts by others, Bielefeld, West Germany 1980; *Gerard Titus-Carmel,* exhibition catalogue, with a preface by Yoshiaki Tono, Tokyo 1981; *Gerard Titus-Carmel,* exhibition catalogue with preface by Jean Fremon, Chateauroux 1987; films—*Gerard Titus-Carmel* by Jacques Scandelari, 1973; *Titus-Carmel* by Angeliki Haas, 1975; *Gerard Titus-Carmel ou l'Aventure du trait* by Teri Wehn-Damisch, 1977; *Gerard Titus-Carmel* by Alain Sayag, 1978; *Gerard Titus-Carmel, un Artiste trait pour trait* by Carlos Vilardebo, 1982.

DRAWING

1. To draw: to deposit. To engrave: to remove. (idea of a work situated halfway between these two mutilations of the support: the significant maculation of the paper, the matricial groove of the metal).
2. To draw, to encroach: to cover. (Would the *image* be the *mask* of the paper?).
3. Drawing is, above all, a work on a double loss: loss of white (loss of consciousness), loss of materiality (diversion).
4. "Carta Tina." Drawing the shadows, lighting the lights: between the deaf *sanguine* and the chalky luminosity, the tinted paper is SIGNIFICANT MATTER.
5. On white paper, the brightness (the light) is the absence of drawing—the *lack;* to cease shading is to *enter into light.* On a tinted background, at the end of a stump, there is a rediscovery of the paper's matter as a designated element of form, the *interstatement,* just before the hollow shading, the countertype: the drawing of the luminosities with a white pencil.
6. Praxis of drawing, alluvia of the graphite.
7. Drawing as the practice of *outrage: to mark* the paper, to leave (plumbaginous traces).
8. Before the mark: *the image* of the mark, defined simultaneously as the striation of the void and the stigma (blemish) of its model.

—Gerard Titus-Carmel

Although he did not have his first exhibition until 1964, this artist, having completed his studies at the École Boulle in Paris, has mounted 81 one-man shows in many parts of the world during the intervening years (including 48 + prints at the Abbaye des Cordeliers, Châteauroux, 1987).

Essentially, that early training at the École Boulle has stood him in good stead largely because he has proved himself a master of linear craft with a particular understanding of the extra fulfilment he can acquire from the promise that the paper has to offer depending upon its 'character'. Evidence of this special gift has been attested on a global scale. (In point of fact, Titus-Carmel ceased to paint pictures in oils after 1969, and did not employ oil again as a medium until the huge *IX Ombres pour STC* series of 1984.)

Important enough; but this is only half of the story. From his well-established basis as an exceptional draughtsman, he has gone to the heart of 'figuration' and linked it with a controlling—in Willy Rotzler's words—conviction "of the *reflection* of the *functioning*" of subject and technique combined. What this means becomes clear and apparent in actual contact with his works. Then it can be seen that the 'figuration' is still realised even when it is clothed and engulfed by the creator's graphic and detailed techniques.

These descriptions refer to the artistic production of the 1970s when Titus-Carmel sought to swathe and tightly bandage his subjects with taut accuracy. More recently, and increasingly at the present time, his work in style and its current huge dimensions has undergone a number of fundamental changes. The devastating 'neatness' of the earlier pictures has given way to a calculated flamboyance decked out for the most part in washes of pulsating darknesses with rare flashes of brightness almost like accents in the course of some heroic oratory.

Typical instances of this transformation occur in the two collections: *Eclats* and *Caparaçons.* These began in 1980, lasting for two more years before going on show at the Galerie Maeght, Paris. All the works shown then, although they were emphasised with rich stretches of watercolour/sometimes browns or greys, sometimes a combination of both/in certain cases more varied with a colour scale ranging through blues, greens, yellows and reds/together with their colour fabrics/continued to be supported by his deft ability—even in this new approach—as a supreme draughtsman. His work now avoided his erstwhile strict linear sharpenss. The images, including their outline edges, possessed the rolling rhythm of waves—especially in the *Éclats.* They created a theatre-in-the-round (even when they gave sweeping glimpses of the half-filled glass at the Circle Bar) which could flow from stage to amphitheatre and back, whereas the *Caparaçons* concentrated on the curtain concealing the stage, or upon the stage itself alive with decor-scaffolding bric-a-brac. Swish curtains or unwriggled forefront of rich opacity, both these kinds of imagery evoke a magic of the playhouse never previously present in works of art.

After the *Éclats* and the *Caparaçons,* he became busy with work on other themes: the *Suite Chancay,* his *Boréales,* the *Compositions autour de l'X* and this year's *Interieurs.* Something of the meaning of this artist's raison-d'être development—not always easy to perceive—has yielded a part of its secrets during the past two years.

Possibly Jacques Henric who knows Titus-Carmel well has put his finger on the pulse when he looks into T-C's means and motives. Most of all he asserts that here is a creator who understands that the finest perfume always requires a fly-in-the-ointment. This does not mean that for Titus-Carmel *Perfection* is a dirty word, but rather to draw near to unsullied beauty it is necessary to introduce a soupçon of *valde malum* to offset a pervading atmosphere of *valde bonum*! More than that. As this hardening process has continued in the artist's works, so a stripping and scalping, a ripping off of some of the epidermis element has had to be introduced. It is almost as if *id quod visum placet* has needed to be debunked because under the skin real beauty lies hidden. Not that such a painful operation should be brought about in one fell swoop. Such a revealing has to be accomplished only a tiny bit at a time.

Paradoxically a suggestion of the same result can be obtained (and is obtained by Titus-Carmel) by his concern with what he modestly dubs Papiers-Collés, only in such instances (especially the most recent) these additives obscure parts and surfaces of the original washes and linear structures of his huge pictures—a sort of agreeable torture inflicted upon ideas. His is not, however, a destructive intention. On the contrary, he is seeking to find hidden realities of what his pictures have in their innermost recesses by use of a continuing subtraction of surplus avoir-dupoids until deepseated (and eternal, past and future) truths within the essence of subjects and matter come to the surface. Put another way, this artist is in a sense riding off at a tangent in the belief that the cruder aspect of original picture painting ought not to be allowed to stay in situ. Rather they should be opening doors, windows, even secret trap-doors to divulge what lies within.

Grand displays of this latest period in the artist's career have been organised by Louis-François Larnaud for Montpellier, Carcassone and the Narbonnaise area, as well as by Daniel Lelong at the Galerie Maeght Lelong in Paris, and now by the Service de la Ville de Châteauroux in the Abbaye des Cordelliers.

—Sheldon Williams

TOBEY, Mark.

American. Born in Centerville, Wisconsin, 11 December 1890. Educated in Trempealeau, Wisconsin and Hammond, Indiana; attended Saturday classes at the Art Institute of Chicago, 1906, then studied under Frank Zimmerman and Professor Reynolds at Art Institute of Chicago, 1906–08; studied calligraphy and composition under Teng Kwei, University of Washington, Seattle, 1922–25, and Chinese calligraphy, privately, under Teng Kwei, Shanghai, 1934–35. Painter: occasional illustrator for a fashion design studio, Chicago, 1909–10; lived in Chicago and New York, 1912–17; interior designer, New York, 1918–22; joined Bahai movement, c. 1918; moved to Seattle, 1922; travelled in Europe, 1925–26; visited Mexico, 1931; lived in England, 1931–38; spent a month in a Zen monastery in Kyoto and travelled in Japan, 1934; visited Ceylon, Hong Kong, and Shanghai, 1934–35; Easel Painter, Works Progress Administration, Federal Art Project, Seattle, 1938; travelled in Sweden where he associated with Pehr Hallsten, 1954; settled in Basle, in Paul Klee's former house, 1960. Lecturer, Cornish School, Seattle, 1923–29; Lecturer in Art, 1930, and Artist in Residence, 1931–38, Dartington Hall, Devon, England. Recipient: Katherine Baker Memorial Award, Seattle Art Museum, 1940; Artists for Victory Prize, 1942; Guggenheim International Award, 1956; Fine Arts Medal, American Institute of Architects, 1957; First Prize for Painting, *Biennale,* Venice, 1958; First Prize for Painting, *Carnegie International,* Pittsburgh, 1961. Honorary Member, National Institute of Arts and Letters. 1956. Commandeur de l'Ordre des Arts et des Lettres, Paris, 1968. *Died* (in Basle), *24 April 1976.*

Individual Exhibitions:

1917	M. Knoedler Gallery, New York
1928	Arts Club of Chicago
1929	Romany Marie Café Gallery, New York
1930	Cornish School, Seattle
1931	Contemporary Arts Gallery, New York
	Harry Hartman Bookstore Gallery, Seattle
	Beaux-Arts Gallery, London
1934	Paul Elder Gallery, San Francisco

1935 Stanley Rose Gallery, Hollywood
Seattle Art Museum
1940 Arts Club of Chicago
1942 Seattle Art Museum
1944 Willard Gallery, New York
1945 Arts Club of Chicago
Willard Gallery, New York
Portland Art Museum, Oregon
San Francisco Museum of Art
1946 Arts Club of Chicago
Detroit Institute of Arts
1947 Willard Gallery, New York
1949 Margret Brown Gallery, Boston
Willard Gallery, New York
1950 Willard Gallery, New York
1951 Margret Brown Gallery, Boston
California Palace of the Legion of Honor, San Francisco
Henry Gallery, Seattle
Santa Barbara Museum of Art, California
Whitney Museum, New York
Willard Gallery, New York
1952 University of Chicago
Zoe Dusanne Gallery, Seattle
1954 Willard Gallery, New York
Otto Seligman Gallery, Seattle
Margret Brown Gallery, Boston
1955 Arts Club of Chicago
Gump's Gallery, San Francisco
Gallery of Art Interpretation, Chicago
Galerie Jeanne Bucher, Paris
Paul Kantor Gallery, Los Angeles
Institute of Contemporary Arts, London
1956 Margret Brown Gallery, Boston
Contemporary Art Museum, Houston (with John Marin and Morris Graves)
1957 Willard Gallery, New York
Margret Brown Gallery, Boston
Otto Seligman Gallery, Seattle
Art Gallery of Greater Victoria, British Columbia
1958 Galerie Stadler, Paris
1959 Galerie Jeanne Bucher, Paris
St. Albans School, Washington, D.C.
Seattle Art Museum (toured the United States)
Portland Art Museum, Oregon
Fine Arts Center, Colorado Springs
Pasadena Art Center, California
M. H. de Young Memorial Museum, San Francisco
1960 Frederic Hobbs Fine Art, San Francisco
Associazione Arti Figurative, Turin
Kunsthalle, Mannheim, West Germany
1961 Musée des Arts Décoratifs, Paris (travelled to the Whitechapel Art Gallery, London)
Galerie Beyeler, Basle
Royal Marks Gallery, New York
1962 Otto Seligman Gallery, Seattle
Willard Gallery, New York
Phillips Gallery, Washington, D.C.
Museum of Modern Art, New York (travelled to the Cleveland Museum of Art and the Art Institute of Chicago)
Konstsalongen Samlaren, Stockholm (travelled to the Konstmuseum, Gothenburg, Sweden)
1963 Seattle Art Museum
Galerie Beyeler, Basle
1965 Willard Gallery, New York
Otto Seligman Gallery, Seattle
Galerie Jeanne Bucher, Paris
Galerie Alice Pauli, Lausanne, Switzerland
1966 Galerie Beyeler, Basle
Stedelijk Museum, Amsterdam
Kestner-Gesellschaft, Hannover
Kunsthalle, Berne
Kunstverein, Dusseldorf
1967 Willard Gallery, New York
Stanford University Art Gallery, California
1968 Galerie Jeanne Bucher, Paris
Museum of Fine Arts, Dallas
Hanover Gallery, London
1969 Bon Marché, Seattle
1970 *Tobey's 80: A Retrospective,* Seattle Art Museum
Galerie Beyeler, Basle
1971 Galerie Alice Pauli, Lausanne, Switzerland
Willard Gallery, New York

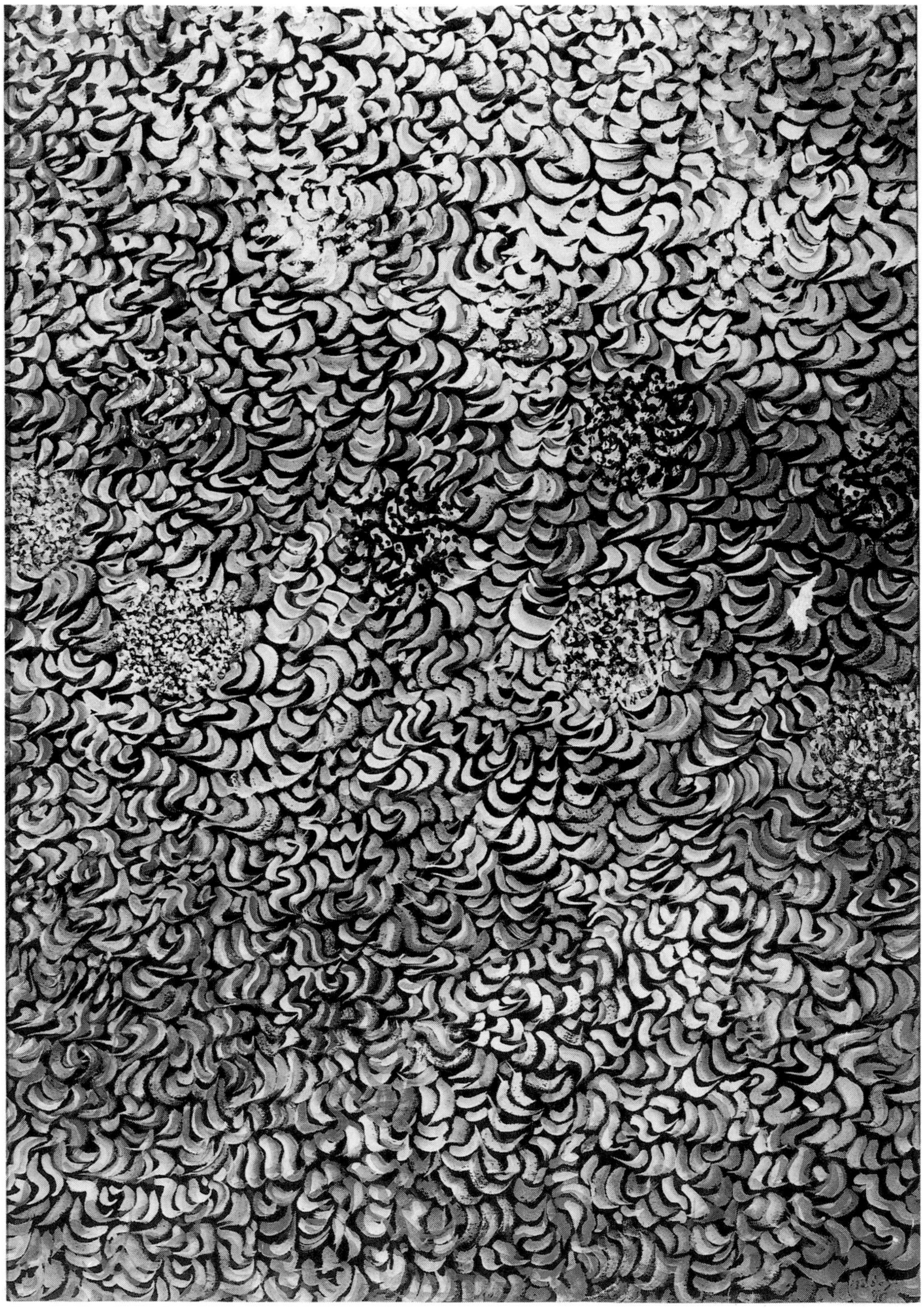

Mark Tobey: *Interspersed*, 1970

Baukunst Galerie, Cologne
Galleria dell-Ariete, Milan
Kunstkabinett, Frankfurt
Galleria Il Fauno, Turin
National Academy of Design, New York
Galerie Marbach, Paris
Whitney Museum, New York
Galerie Ursus Presse, Dusseldorf
1972 Galerie Beyeler, Basle
Willard Gallery, New York
Martha Jackson Gallery, New York
Cincinnati Art Museum, Ohio
Martha Jackson Gallery, New York
1973 Willard Gallery, New York
Martha Jackson Gallery, New York
Foster-White Gallery, Seattle
Galerie Ursus Presse, Dusseldorf
1974 *Tribute to Mark Tobey,* National Collection of Fine Arts, Smithsonian Institution, Washington, D.C. (travelled to the Seattle Art Museum and the St. Louis Art Museum)
1975 Museum Haus Lange, Krefeld, West Germany
Galerie Darthea Speyer, Paris
1978 Galleria del Naviglio, Venice
Galleria del Naviglio, Milan
1982 Galerie Jacqueline Schotland, Basle
1983 Galerie Vomel, Dusseldorf
1984 National Gallery of Art, Washington, D.C.
1986 Erker-Galerie, St. Gallen, Switzerland
1987 Baukunst-Galerie, Cologne

Selected Group Exhibitions:

1929 *Paintings by 19 Living Americans,* Museum of Modern Art, New York
1939 *World's Fair,* New York
1943 *Romantic Painting in America,* Museum of Modern Art, New York
1948 *Biennale,* Venice
1950 *American Painting Today,* Metropolitan Museum of Art, New York

1956 *50 Ans d'Art aux Etats-Unis,* Musée National d'Art Moderne, Paris
1957 *International Contemporary Art Exhibition,* New Delhi, India
1958 *Nature in Abstraction,* Whitney Museum, New York
1966 *Two Decades of American Painting,* National Museum of Modern Art, Tokyo
1973 *Futurism: A Modern Focus,* Guggenheim Museum, New York

Collections:

Museum of Modern Art, New York; Metropolitan Museum of Art, New York; Whitney Museum, New York; Albright-Knox Art Gallery, Buffalo, New York; Seattle Art Museum; Portland Museum of Art, Oregon; Tate Gallery, London; Kunstmuseum, Basle; Kunsthalle, Bremen, West Germany; Staatsgalerie, Stuttgart.

Publications:

By TOBEY: book—*Mark Tobey: The World of a Market,* Seattle 1964; articles—"Reminiscence and Reverie" in *Magazine of Art* (New York), October 1951; "Japanese Traditions and American Art" in *College Art Journal* (New York), Fall 1958; "The Painter Meets the Critic," interview with Katherine Kuh, in the *Saturday Review* (New York), July 1960; "Mark Tobey," interview, in *The Artist's Voice: Talks with 17 Artists* by Katherine Kuh, New York 1960; "Une Journée avec Mark Tobey." interview, with Denys Chevalier, in *Aujourd'hui (Paris), October, film—Mark Tobey, Artist,* with Robert Gardner, Seattle 1952.

On TOBEY: books—*Mark Tobey* by Colette Roberts, New York 1959; *Mark Tobey,* exhibition catalogue, by Edward B. Thomas, Seattle 1959; *Mark Tobey* by Francoise Choay, Paris 1961; *Mark Tobey,* exhibition catalogue, by Julien Alvard, Paris 1961; *Mark Tobey,* exhibition catalogue, by William C. Seitz, New York 1962; *Mark Tobey* by Wieland Schmied, London and Stuttgart 1966; *Tobey's 80: A Retorspective,* exhibition catalogue, Seattle 1970; *Tobey* by John Russel, New York 1971; *Tobey* by Wieland Schmied, New York 1972; *Tribute to Mark Tobey,* exhibition catalogue, by Joshua C. Taylor, Washington, D.C. 1974; *Mark Tobey: City Paintings,* exhibition catalogue with essay by Eliza E. Rathbone, Washington, D.C. 1984; *Mark Tobey: Graphische Arbeiten,* exhibition catalogue with introduction by Gunter Ott, Cologne 1987.

The calligraphic "white writing" of Mark Tobey (1890–1976) stands as his major contribution to modernism. Secondarily, his formulation of a spatially ambiguous, overall composition of repetitious and undifferentiated line heralds the "drip" paintings of Pollock. Yet his breakthrough developed not from the secular *angst* of the American Abstract Expressionists and the School of Paris painters (to whom Tobey was regarded as the foremost American painter of those post-war years). Tobey's development of an abstract mode derived from his intense beliefs in the Bahai'i faith. In that regard, he belongs to a fellowship of stylistic pioneers in modern art (Kandinsky, Malevich, Mondrian) whose adoption of pure abstraction was spiritually or metaphysically motivated.

The Bahai'i tenets of unity, humanity and "progressive revelation" are first seen in Tobey's use of its cosmological symbolism, lending to his early work a stilted romanticism and profundity. Tobey mainfested his fascination with Oriental religion, art and philosophy after visiting Asia in 1934, to study calligraphy and meditate at a Zen monastary. He abandoned a pseudo-Cubistic modeling of form for a linear description applied to representational elements in concert with purely abstract and spatial motifs. The small abstract tempera painting "Broadway Norm" (1935) announced this change with its matrix of coiling white line. The encroachment of Eastern pictorial modes propelled Tobey's art into its most genuinely individualistic and diverse phase—an inner expression of spiritual man and the city manifested as light, noise and energy.

Returning to Seattle at the eve of World War II, Tobey further developed his "white writing," which took the form of angular and curvilinear networks of line over a tonally dark and modulated ground. Figurative elements and intimations of architectural form (Gothic vaults and spires, city lights, vertically thrusting skyscrapers) were compressed and distributed across the picture plane. This formula eventually transfigured into non-hierarchial, non-objective abstract compositions: dense patterns of line expanding out to the picture edge, seeming to palpitate with a shifting focus and depth. Tobey's modified late style stemmed from experiments with *sumi* painting in the late 1950's. A broader stroke and more dabbled gesture took its place alongside his *repertoire* of anastomotic inscriptions; the "white writing" gave way to polychrome and black. Surface pattering became more chromatic and decorative, even serene. Controlled gestural surfaces superseded the spontaneous and energized calligraphy.

Tobey accepted the organic and dynamic Romantic conception of artistic creation as the proper analogue to a universal and religious interpretation of Creation. His deeply felt faith leads to the regard of his diverse art as emotionally and spiritually authentic despite stylistic and thematic fluctations and inconsistencies. "The dimension that counts for the creative person is the Space he creates within himself," Tobey once wrote. "This inner space is closer to the infinite . . ." What William Seitz has called his "world view" is Tobey's dynamic and dualistic encompassing of the inner and outer self, of internal and external space, and the synthesis of Eastern and Western thought. "At a time when experimentation expresses itself in all forms of life, search becomes the only valid expression of the spirit . . ."

—Ron Glowen

TOMASZEWSKI, Henryk.

Polish. Born in Warsaw, 10 June 1914. Studied graphics, under Mieczyslaw Kotarbinski, at the Art Academy, Warsaw, 1934–39. Graphic artist and poster designer, Warsaw, from 1946: Co-Founder, Poster Museum, Warsaw, 1968. Professor of graphic design, Art Academy, Warsaw, since 1952. Recipient: First Prize, *Polish Posters Exhibition,* Wieden, 1956; First Prize, *Bienal,* Sao Paulo, 1963; Medal, *Internationale Buchkunst Ausstellung,* Leipzig, 1965; Gold Medal, *Poster Biennale,* Warsaw, 1970; First Prize, *3rd Poster Biennale,* Lahti, Finland, 1979; First Prize, *Colorado International Poster Exhibition,* 1981; ICOGRADA Excellence Award, 1986. Honorary Royal Designer to Industry (U.K.), 1976. Address: Jazgarzewska Street 13, 00–730 Warsaw, Poland.

Individual Exhibitions:

1969 Kunstverein/Kongresshaus, Biel-Bienne, Switzerland
1972 Poster Museum, Wilanow, Poland
1984 Gallery A. and B. Wahl, Warsaw

Selected Group Exhibitions:

1948 *Miedzynarodowa Wystawa Plakatu,* Wieden, Poland
1963 *Bienal,* Sao Paulo (and 1979)
1966 *International Poster Biennale,* Warsaw (and regularly, 1968–86)
1971 *Polske Plakater,* Louisiana Museum, Humlebaek, Denmark
1978 *International Biennale of Design,* Wroclaw, Poland
1980 *Das Polnische Plakat von 1892 bis Heute,* Hochschule der Kunste, West Berlin
1981 *Colorado International Invitational Poster Exhibition*
1982 *Biennale of Graphic Arts,* Brno, Czechoslovakia
1985 *First International Poster Triennial,* Toyama, Japan
1986 *International Poster Salon,* Paris (and 1987)

Collections:

National Museum, Warsaw; Deutsches Plakat-Museum, Essen, West Germany; Kunstgewerbemuseum, Stockholm; Stedelijk Museum, Amsterdam; Kamakura Museum of Modern Art, Kamakura, Japan; Museum of Modern Art, New York; Museu de Arte Moderno, Sao Paulo.

Publications:

By TOMASZEWSKI: book—*Book of Complaints,* Warsaw 1961.

On TOMASZEWSKI: books—*Henryk Tomaszewski* by Barbara Kwiatkowska, Warsaw 1959; *International Poster Biennale,* exhibition catalogue, with text by J. Fijalkowska, Warsaw 1966; *Polski Plakat Filmowy 1947–1967,* exhibition catalogue, with text by Z. Schubert, Poznan 1969; *Polska Sztuka Plakatu* by Szymon Bojko, Warsaw 1971; *Das Polnische Plakat von 1892 bis Heute,* exhibition catalogue, West Berlin 1980; articles—"Polish Film and Theatre Posters" by Charles Robonyi in *Graphis* (Zurich), no. 63, 1956; "3rd Internationale Plakat-Biennale in Warschau 1970" by J. Spohn in *Gebrauchsgraphik* (Munich), no. 11, 1970; "Graphic Design in Poland" by Szymon Bojko in *The Penrose Annual,* London 1973; "Universal Dimensions" by Szymon Bojko in *Art and Artists* (London), September 1976; "Henryk Tomaszewski" by Jan Zielecki in *Projekt* (Warsaw), no. 4, 1985.

Thanking you, Henryk: read the eulogizing title of an exhibition held in Warsaw in 1975 by an international group of post-graduate students connected with Professor Tomaszewski's studio. In exhibiting their own works, the young graphic artists paid homage to the teacher who fascinated them by his personality. One of them wrote: "Since I have met Professor Henryk Tomaszewski, I know that the art of the poster is a moral discipline." Another student tried to sketch the Professor's stimulating way of mediating and making non-verbal comment: "With one hand, Henryk lights his 87th cigarette from the end of the 86th one, while with his other hand he puts on his spectacles No. 5; with his third hand he cuts a rectangular piece of glossy red paper which will 'play' on crumpled grey backing paper, pinned up with his fourth hand. For the 29th time he moved the edge of this paper, cuts another red rectangle, changes his spectacles to No. 2, paces back, returns, softens up a bright light, again steps back, and says 'This must sing . . . ' "

This lengthy quotation was necessary. Rare as it happens, a characteristic portrait of the artist in question is a mirror of his creative and teaching activity. Young people from various continents, desirous of moral and ethical wisdom, move to Tomaszewski's post-graduate studies, which brings to mind similar treks to Grotowski's Laboratory Institute. They rarely meet with disappointment. In Warsaw they find an impulse for spontaneous action. Freeing themselves from memorized rules and methods, they return to a happy land of free imagination. The 61-year-old dean of the Polish school of the poster is now surrounded by the legend of a man sensitive to deceit and hypocrisy. He is merciless to appearances and to sullen solemnity. With his stand and his graphic work he immunizes his fellow-countrymen to empty bureaucratic language, phraseology, and pretentiousness. He is credited with many sayings and ironic maxims, maybe once heard in the street, passed on from slang into the literary language. Resentful towards dogmas and pseudo-rationalist doctrines, intellectually independent and contrary, he has greatly influenced the artistic consciousness of a few generations of graphic artists, illustrators, and cartoonists.

Tomaszewski has originated a style of mass graphic art, demanding of the viewer some mental effort, as well as an ability to grasp rapidly the sense of abbreviations, associations, understatements, and paradoxes. Nothing should be taken seriously, verbatim, or without detachment. This work has incorporated the play element, and from child's sensitivity a kind of sophisticated infantilism. At the same time, it is opulent in subtle nuances, possessing neither cruelty, nor black humour, nor riddle. Rather irony and self-

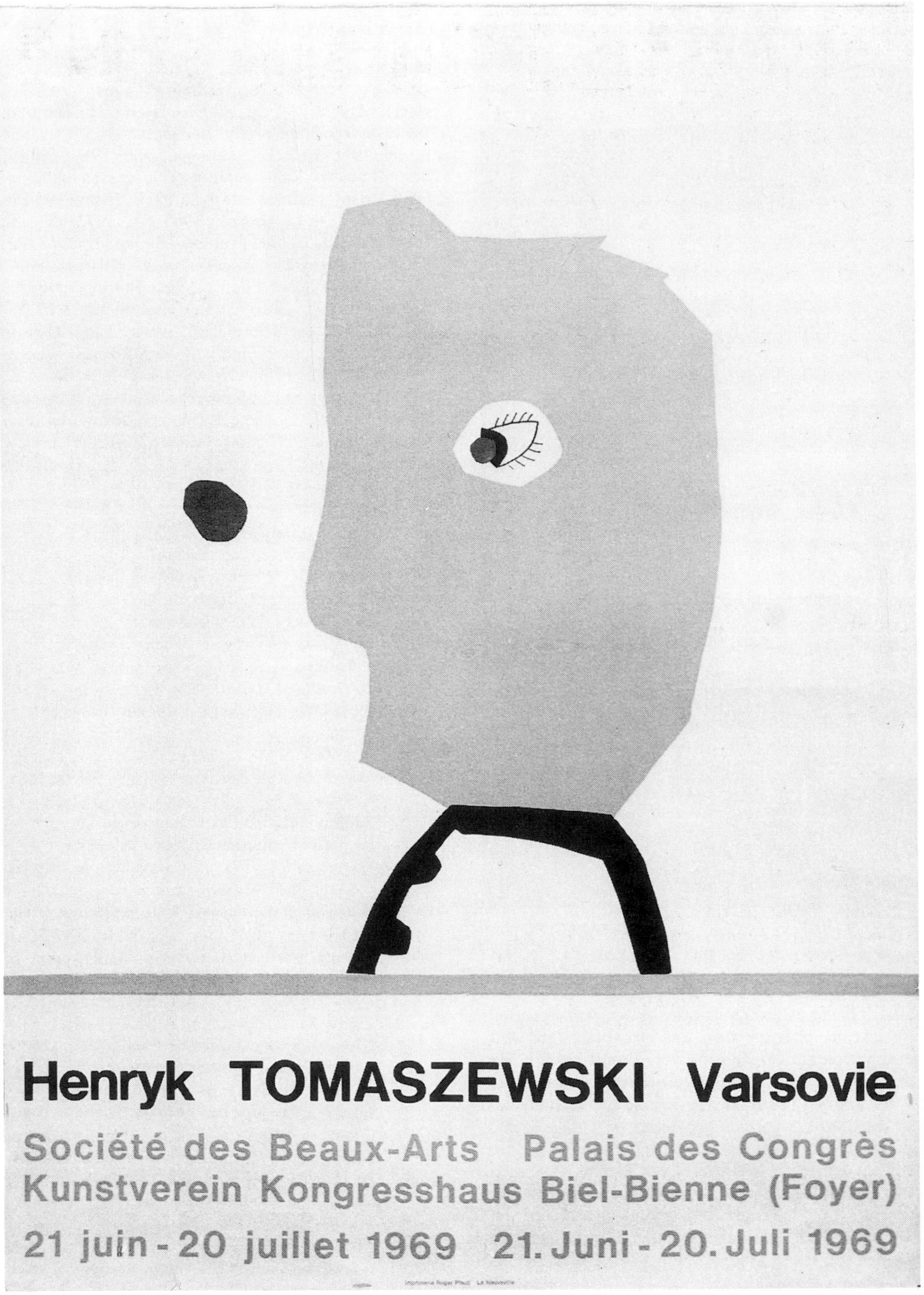

Henryk Tomaszewski: *Poster Design*, 1969

irony. Its aesthetic origin is eminently Polish and is situated in the same development line as the prose and drama of Witkiewicz, Schulz, Gombrowicz, and Mrozek, and the poetry of Tuwim and Galczynski, as well as the literary and student revues of the 1960's and earlier, headed by the Bim-Bom, crammed with grotesquerie, parody, and sneer. One may say that the posters and drawings by Tomaszewski are a mirror of popular Polish mentality. They always create an impression of handwriting, thus attaining the value of an intimate notebook, not intended for strange eyes. The line, drawn as if by a maladroit child's hand, breaks off, looses the trend on the way, and keeps scrawling. The colour plane is simultaneously undecided, and it rarely runs along the outline. It has the charm of an improvisation, and of an unconcerned scrawl. In fact, the artist prepares every line and colour patch with the greatest of care. He even brings a complicated thought or idea down to a synthesis or to a sign deriving from the drawing devoid of embellishments.

Tomaszewski has had a great moral influence in the country. Each one of his new works elicits aesthetic and social comments. In a recent interview he said that most important for him is the motive of the communication and its range of meaning: "Often on my piece of paper, there is as if nothing to be looked at, nothing beautiful. These are things unable to caress the eye." And somewhere else, in the same spirit: "I prefer a foolish proposition to mastered perfection."

The artist's poster achievement is generally known from exhibitions and publications. Many of his works have a permanent place in 20th century art, including posters for the film *La Beaute du diable* (1954), for an exhibition of sculpture by Henry Moore (1959), for the theatrical performances of *Hamlet* (1970), *Slub* (The Marriage) by Gombrowicz (1974), and *Witkacy*—a stage collage of plays by Witkiewicz (1974), and for the Theatre of the Nations session in Warsaw (1976). His drawings are dispersed among various periodicals and, apart from the album *Ksiazka zazalen* (The Book of Complaints), 1961, have not been the subject of a monograph so far.

—Szymon Bojko

TORONI, Niele.

Swiss. Born in Locarno-Muralto, 15 March 1937. Educated in Locarno. Independent artist, Locarno, subsequently in Paris; Member, with Buren, Mosset and Parmentier, Groupe BMPT, Paris 1966–68. Agent: Galerie Yvon Lambert, 5 rue Grenier Saint Lazare, 75003 Paris. Address: 73 rue Damremont, 75018 Paris, France.

Individual Exhibitions:

1969	16 rue Castagnary, Paris
1970	Galerie Yvon Lambert, Paris
	Galerie MTL, Brussels
1971	Galerie Michael Werner, Cologne
1972	Galerie Yvon Lambert, Paris
	Jack Wendler Gallery, London
	Galerie Michael Werner, Cologne
1973	Galleria Francoise Lambert, Milan
	Wide White Space Gallery, Antwerp
1974	John Gibson Gallery, New York
	Galleria Forma, Genoa
	Galleria d'Alessandro Ferranti, Rome
1975	Wide White Space Gallery, Antwerp
	Palais des Beaux-Arts, Brussels
	Galerie MTL, Brussels
	Galleria Francoise Lambert, Milan
	Galerie Yvon Lambert, Paris
1976	Galerie Paul Maenz, Cologne
	Robert Self Gallery, London
	Galerie Maier-Hahn, Dusseldorf
	Galleria Banco, Brescia, Italy
1977	Galleria Ferranti, Rome
	Galerie Yvon Lambert, Paris
	Museum Haus Kemnade, Bochum, West Germany
	Galerie MTL, Brussels
	Van Abbemuseum, Eindhoven, Netherlands
1978	Galleria Francoise Lambert, Milan
	Samngallery, Genoa, Italy
	Kunsthalle, Berne
1979	Galerie Yvon Lambert, Paris
	Galleria Ferranti, Rome
	Galerie Paul Maenz, Cologne
1980	Centre d'Art Contemporain, Geneva
	Hotel Wolfers, Brussels
1981	Galleria Banco, Brescia, Italy
	Samangallery, Genoa, Italy
	Galleria Francoise Lambert, Milan
1982	Museum van Hedendaagse Kunst, Ghent, Belgium
	Galerie M. Szwajcer, Antwerp, Belgium
	Galerie Media, Neuchatel, Switzerland

Selected Group Exhibitions:

1967	*Biennale,* Musée d'Art Moderne, Paris
1969	*Prospect 69,* Kunsthalle, Dusseldorf
1970	*18 Paris IV 70,* 66 rue Mouffetard, Paris
1972	*Actualités d'un Bilan,* Galerie Yvon Lambert, Paris
1973	*La Peinture en Question,* 16 Place Vendôme, Paris (travelled to Mönchengladbach and Antwerp)
1975	*Pour—Le/Nous,* Mesée d'Ixelles, Brussels
1977	*Europe in the Seventies,* Art Institute of Chicago
1981	*Mise en Pieces . . . ,* Maison de la Culture, Chalon-sur-Saône, France (travelled to Le Coin du Miroir, Dijon)
1982	*Documenta,* Kassel, West Germany

Collections:

Musée National d'Art Moderne/Centre Georges Pompidou, Paris; Musée de Toulon; Musée des Beaux-Arts, Ghent; Van Abbemuseum, Eindhoven; Stadtisches Museum, Monchengladbach.

Publications:

By TORONI: books—*11 Documents photographiques reunis par Niele Toroni,* Brussels 1975; *Galleria Allegria,* Paris 1981.

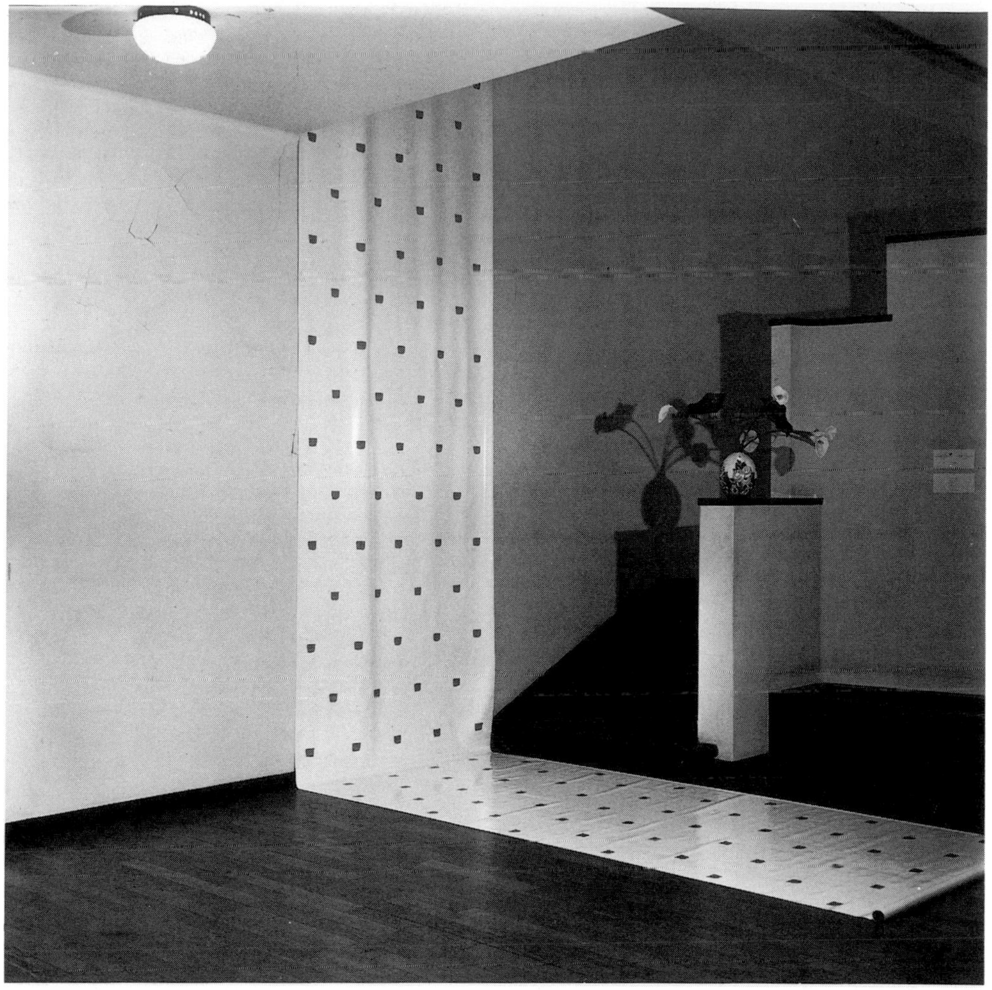

Niele Toroni: *Rouleau—toile cirée*, 1968

On TORONI: books—*18 Paris IV 70*, exhibition catalogue/book/with text by Michel Claura, Paris and New York 1970; *Actualité d'un Bilan*, exhibition catalogue, edited by Yvon Lambert, Paris 1972; *La Peinture en Question*, exhibition catalogue, with texts by Michel Claura and René Denizot, Paris 1973; *Un Empreinte n'est jamais seule* by René Denizot, Paris 1975; *Niele Toroni*, exhibition catalogue, with text by René Denizot, Eindhoven, Netherlands 1977; *Niele Toroni: 52 pages, 52 pagine, 52 seite*, exhibition catalogue, with text by Johannes Gachnang, Berne 1978; *Mise en Pieces, Mise en Place, Mise au Point*, exhibition catalogue, with an introduction by Xavier Douroux and Christian Besson, Chalon-sur-Saône, France 1981; *Documenta 7*, exhibition catalogue, 2 vols., edited by Rudi H. Fuchs, Kassel, West Germany 1982; *Formalité et Historicité* by Benjamin Buchloh, Paris 1982.

Why is it that someone who *does something* (and I underline this because there are so many very active people who never do anything at all) is continually asked "why", for a justification? Is it for reassurance?

In this instance is it because you don't have the courage to accept your reaction in front of this work? Whether negative or positive, that's not the point. The problem is this need for a "debate on", which pretends parasitically to exist in the place of that which stimulates it; this need for intermediaries; it's true that it maintains quite a lot of people, in fish, in vegetables, in art.

It's again the problem of conditioning. (There are) those who don't even dare to say "I'm fine", "I feel bad"; first they want explanations (the famous why), to know if perhaps they are unhappy because they haven't understood that they should be happy, bravo, the brave face. When you feel bad, say so, bawl it out.

To return to our story, in front of a work begin by accepting what goes through your mind (if something does, it is not an absolute necessity!). No explanation can take its place or then lots of explanations will make you admit anything. Marcel Proust wrote: "As soon as reasoning intelligence wants to judge works of art, nothing is any longer definite or indisputable: one can prove whatever one wants to". That's true enough, especially these days with the swarms of "intelligent debaters". Whoever doesn't know what to do talks painting, writes painting, understands painting . . . . but take care not to touch a brush, you could dirty your little hands or other things! It's a pity that one still doesn't know where a work of art begins and where it ends . . . . .

All this to let you know that my work/painting cannot, must not be of more or less interest depending on what I could say to you or what others might say to you about it.

It's painting and that's all.

Visible marks of a no.50 brush (typically pictural work tool), for the brush, so that it can leave its mark, is saturated with paint, paint which is colour, colour that one doesn't see as a rule because it's in a tin and is revealed by application of the brush. No. 50 brushmarks, "spots" of paint if you like, (the surface covered with colour being determined by the dimension of the hairy part of the brush, that part which is used for painting) repeated at regular intervals (30cm), occupying the chosen support while leaving it visible, legible.

Read a wall. Why not? It's up to you to see.

—Niele Toroni

TOT, Endre.

Hungarian. Born Endre Toth in Sumeg, 5 November 1937; adopted the name "Tot" in 1965. Studied at the Hungarian Academy of Applied Arts, Budapest, 1959–65. Married Teri Simon in 1969 (divorced, 1981); daughter: Bea; married Herta Paraschin in 1981. Independent artist, Budapest, 1965–78, West Berlin, 1978–79, and in Cologne, since 1980: painted first Zero and Rain works, 1971; ceased painting, 1971; first "gladness" works, 1971. Instructor, Budapest elementary school, 1965–68, 1972–75, and Technical School for Printing, Budapest, 1968–72. Recipient: Prize, *Drawing Triennale*, Wroclaw, 1974, 1977; DAAD Scholarship to West Berlin, 1978–79. Agents: Galerie Orez Mobiel, Paviljoensgracht 68/70, NL-2512 BR The Hague, Netherlands; Galerie Bama, 40 rue Quincampoix, F-75004 Paris, France; Galerie Magers, Handelstrasse 13, D-5300 Bonn 1, West Germany; and Edition Hundertmark, Brusselerstrasse 29, 5000 Cologne 1, West Germany. Address: Engelbertstrasse 55, 5000 Cologne 1, West Germany.

Individual Exhibitions:

1966 Epitök Müszaki Club, Budapest
1968 Ferenczy K. Museum, Szentendre, Hungary
1969 K.F.K.I. Club, Budapest
Mednyánszky Gallery, Budapest
1972 *My Unpainted Canvases*, Ferencvarosi Pincetariat, Budapest
1973 *10 Questions*, Galerie Adres, Lodz, Poland
Fluxus West, San Diego, California (toured California)
1974 *Zero Texts 1971–72*. Studentenhaus, Graz, Austria
One Dozen Rain Postcards 1971–73, Galerie Ecart, Geneva
1975 *Rainproof Ideas/Zero/Gladness*, Israel Museum, Jerusalem (retrospective)
1976 *Rainproof Ideas 1971–75*, Galerie Inge Baecker, Bochum, West Germany
1977 *Rainproof Ideas/Gladness Writings*, Galerie Bama, Paris
1978 *Gladness Questionary*, Studio 16 E. Turin
Nullified Questionary, Galerie A. Amsterdam
Rainy Questionary, Galleri Suburgata, Rykjavik, Iceland
1979 *Gladness Writings*, *Questions*, *TOTalJOYS*, Galerie René Block, West Berlin
Gladness Drawings, Galerie A, Amsterdam
Gladness Drawings and Writings, Galerie St. Petri, Lund, Sweden
TOTalZEROS 1973–77, Art Something, Amsterdam
1980 *Very Special Gladnesses*, Galerie Magers, Bonn
Galerie Orez Mobiel, The Hague
Stempelplaatz Galerie, Amsterdam
1981 Artothek, Cologne
1983 Galerie fur Visuelle Erlebnisse, Cremlingen, West Germany
1984 Kunstraum Kunoldstrasse 34, Kassel, West Germany
1987 Edition Hundertmark, Cologne

Tot has also presented numerous performances and actions throughout Europe since 1972.

Selected Group Exhibitions:

1971 *Biennale de Paris*, Parc Floral, Paris
1972 *Aktuelle Kunst in Ost-Europa*, Studio DuMont, Cologne (travelled to the Galerie Krauthammer, Zurich, and the Galerie Katakombe, Basle)
1974 *Artists' Stamps and Stamp Images*, Simon Fraser Gallery, Burnaby, British Columbia
1976 *Artists' Books*, Institute of Contemporary Arts, London (toured the U.K.)
1978 *L'Estampe Aujourd'hui*, Bibliothèque Nationale, Paris
Acht Kunstler stellen sich vor, DAAD Galerie, West Berlin
1980 *Ecritures*, Fondation Nationale des Arts Graphiques et Plastiques, Paris
1981 *Books by Artists*, National Gallery of Canada, Ottawa

1984 *International Kunstler Gremium Ausstellung*, Museum Fridericianum, Kassel, West Germany
1985 *Livres d'Artistes*, Centre Georges Pompidou, Paris

Collections:

Kulturministerium Nordrhein-Westfalen, Dusseldorf; Lambert Collection, Paris; Bibliothèque Nationale, Paris; Centre National d'Art Contemporain, Paris; Cabinet des Estampes, Geneva; Gemeentemuseum, The Hague; National Museum, Warsaw; Israel Museum, Jerusalem; Kunsthalle, Hamburg; Nationalgalerie, West Berlin.

Publications:

By TOT: books and cards—*My Unpainted Canvases*, Budapest 1971; *The States of Zeros*, Budapest 1971; *Incomplete Information (Verbal and Visual)*, Oldenburg, West Germany 1972; *Possessive Adjective*, Budapest 1972; *I Am Glad If I Can Write Sentences, One After the Other*, Budapest 1973; *One Dozen Rain Postcards (1971–73)*, Budapest 1973; *On the Next Page I Shall Say Something*, Budapest 1973; *Zero-Texts (1971–72)*, Graz, Austria 1974; *Night Visit to the National Gallery*, Cullompton, Devon 1974; *Zeropost*, Hinwil 1974; *Nullified Dialogue*, Hinwil 1974; *Correspondance avec John Armleder*, Geneva 1974; *TOTal Questions by TOT*, West Berlin 1974; 1/2 *Dozen Incomplete Visual Informations (1971–74)*, Budapest 1974; *One Dozen Rain Postcards (1971–73)*, Stuttgart 1974; *Rainproof Ideas (1971–74)*, Jerusalem 1975; *TOTalJOYS (1971–75)*, Geneva 1976; *Zeropost*, Geneva 1976; *Gladness Writings (1973–76)*, Liège, Belgium 1977; *TOTal Zeros (1973–77)*, Budapest 1977; 1/2/ *Dozen Berliner Gladness Postcards (1973–78)*, West Berlin 1979; *Ich freue mich, wenn ich auf Plakaten werben kann*, West Berlin 1979; *TOTalJOYS*, West Berlin 1979; *Dirty Rains*, Lund, Sweden 1979; *Some Nullified Questions*, Amsterdam 1979; *Ten Documents (1973–80)*, Amsterdam 1980; *Very Special Drawings*, West Berlin 1981; *Book of an Extremely Glad Artist*, West Berlin 1981; *From Cologne some Jecke Dinge to you, everybody and nobody*, Cremlingen 1983; *Stamps 1971– 83*, Cremlingen 1983; *Special Drawings—Private Space*, Kassel 1984. films—*One Step*, 1972; *I Am Glad If. . .* , 1974; *TOTalJOYS*, 1976; video—*I'm Glad if I Can Say Sentences, One After the Other*, 1979; *TOTalJOYS*, 1979.

On TOT: books—*Mail Art: Communication: A Distance-Concept*, edited by Jean-Marc Poinsot, Paris 1971; *Aktuelle Kunst in Osteuropa*, edited by Klaus Groh, Cologne 1972; *Stamp Activity* by Jiri H. Kocman, Brno, Czechoslovakia 1972; *An Annual of New Art and Artists 1973–74*, edited by W. Sandberg, Cologne 1974; *Art et Communications Marginale* by Hervé Fischer, Paris 1974; *Funf Osteuropaische Kunstler*, edited by Klaus Groh, Nuremberg 1975; *Visual Poetry Anthology*, edited by G. J. de Rook, Utrecht 1975; *Europe/America: The Different Avant-Gardes* by Achille Bonito Oliva, Milan 1976; *The Museum of Drawers*, edited by Herbert Distel, Berne 1978; *Fotografie als Kunst/Kunst als Fotografie* by Floris M. Neusüss, Cologne 1979; *Testuale: Le Parole e le Immagini*, exhibition catalogue, edited by F. Caroli and L. Caramel, Milan 1979; *Kunst in Sozialistischen Staaten* by J. Weichart, Oldenburg, West Germany 1980; *Books by Artists* by T. Guest and Germano Celant, Toronto 1981; *Correspondence Art*, edited by M. Cramer and M. Stofflet, San Francisco 1984; *International Artists' Postage Stamps*, edited by B. Lobach, Cremlingen 1985; *Livres d'Artistes*, edited by A. Moeglin-Delcroix, Paris 1985; *Wer hat Augst von Moholy-Nagy?*, edited by T. Straus, Cologne 1987.

I am always glad of those days, when nothing happens to me except that I wake up in the morning and go to bed in the evening.

—Endre Tot

TOUSIGNANT, Claude.

Canadian. Born in Montreal, Quebec, 23 December 1932. Studied at the School of Art and Design, Montreal Museum of Fine Arts, 1948–51; Académie Ranson, Paris, 1952. Has lived with Judith Terry since 1968; daughters: Isa and Zoe. Worked as surveyor, window-dresser, fireman and show salesman at various times; currently, independent artist. Instructor, School of Art and Design, Montreal Museum of Fine Arts, 1961–63; Instructor, École des Beaux-Arts, University of Quebec, Montreal, 1970. Recipient: First Prize (Painting), *Salon de la Jeune Peinture*, Paris 1962; First Prize (Painting), *Perspective '67*, Toronto, 1967; Italian Government Rome Prize, 1973. Addresses: (office) 3684 St. Lawrence Boulevard, Montreal, Quebec H2X 2V4; (home) 4678 St. Andre, Montreal, Quebec H2J 3A1, Canada.

Individual Exhibitions:

1955 L'Echouerie, Montreal
1956 L'Actuelle, Montreal
1957 L'Actuelle, Montreal
1961 Museum of Fine Arts, Montreal
1962 Galerie Denise Delrue, Montreal
1963 Dorothy Cameron Gallery, Toronto
1964 Galerie du Siècle, Montreal
1965 East Hampton Gallery, New York
1966 East Hampton Gallery, New York
Galerie du Siècle, Montreal
1968 Galerie du Siècle, Montreal
Gallery Moos, Toronto
1969 Galerie Sherbrooke, Montreal
1970 Galerie Jolliet, Quebec

Endre Tot: *Zero-Demonstration*, 1972

Claude Tousignant: ***420*****, 1982**

1972 Gallery Moos, Toronto
2973 National Gallery of Canada, Ottawa (retrospective)
1974 Art Gallery of Ontario, Toronto (retospective)
1976 Winnipeg Art Gallery
Waddington Gallery, Montreal
1977 Windsor Art Gallery, Ontario
1979 Graff Gallery, Montreal (prints)
1980 Musée d'Art Contemporain, Montreal
1982 Musée des Beaux-Arts, Montreal (sculptures)

Selected Group Exhibitions:

1962 *Modern Canadian Painting,* Palazzo Collicola, Spoleto, Italy
1965 *The Responsive Eye,* Museum of Modern Art, New York (toured the United States)
1968 *Canada: Art d'Aujourd'hui,* Musée National d'Art Moderne, Paris (toured Italy, Switzerland and Belgium)
7 Montreal Artists, Hayden Gallery, Massachusetts Institute of Technology, Cambridge
1969 *Form-Colour,* National Gallery of Canada, Ottawa (toured Canada)
1970 *Panorama de la Sculpture au Quebec 1945–1970,* Musée d'Art Contemporain, Montreal (travelled to the Musée Rodin, Paris)
1971 *49th Parallels: New Canadian Art,* Ringling Museum, Sarasota, Florida
1974 *Recent Canadian Painting,* Art Gallery of Ontario, Toronto
1975 *Time Canada,* Musée d'Art Contemporain, Montreal (toured Canada)
1976 *Trois Generations d'Art Quebecois,* Musée d'Art Contemporain, Montreal

Collections:

Art Gallery of Ontario, Toronto; York University, Toronto; Canada Arts Council, Ottawa; National Gallery of Canada, Ottawa; Museum of Fine Arts, Montreal; Musée d'Art Contemporain, Montreal; Musée du Quebec, Quebec City; Vancouver Art Gallery; Larry Aldrich Museum, Ridgefield, Connecticut; Phoenix Museum of Art, Arizona.

Publications:

By TOUSIGNANT: articles—"Pour une peinture evidentille" in *Art Abstract,* exhibition catalogue, Montreal 1959; "Quelques precisions essentielles" in *Peinture Canadienne Française,* Montreal 1971.

On TOUSIGNANT: books—*Modern Canadian Painting,* exhibition catalogue, by Charles Delloye, Spoleto, Italy 1962; *7 Montreal Artists,* exhibition catalogue, by Bernard Teyssedre, Cambridge, Massachusetts 1968; *Claude Tousignant,* exhibition catalogue, by Danielle Corbeil, Ottawa 1973; *Claude Tousignant: Sculptures,* exhibition catalogue with essay by Normand Theriault, Montreal 1982; articles—"La jeune peinture au Quebec" by Francois Gagnon in *Revue d'Esthetique No. 3: Art au Quebec,* Quebec 1963; "L'Illusion optique de l'Op Art" by Fernande Saint-Martin in *Vie des Arts* (Montreal), no. 39, 1965; "Le dynamisme des plasticiens de Montreal" by Fernande Saint-Martin in *Vie des Arts* (Montreal), no. 44, 1966; "Structure de l'espace pictural" by Fernande Saint-Martin in *Constantes* (Montreal), no. 17, 1968; "Claude Tousignant" by Pierre Theberge in *Canada: Art d'Aujourd'hui,* exhibition catalogue, Paris 1968; "Les Plasticiens" by Pierre Theberge in *Studio International* (London), 1970.

What I wish to do is to make painting objective, to bring it back to its source—where only painting remains, emptied of all extraneous matter—to the point at which painting is pure sensation.

—Claude Tousignant

Claude Tousignant has been painting since 1948, "and is still in transformation," he says. He admires greatly the American painter, Barnett Newman—for him the most radical of the New York school. The initial works through which he became known on the Canadian scene were, like those of other painters in Montreal, hard edged and sharp, with bright colours. In his circular paintings in particular, he used a series of rings of colour. "The hard edge was there for functional reasons."

Today Tousignant is more of a sculptor—in the sense that sculpture deals with material—"and if he paints a surface it is as a material." His large works (some are 14 feet by 8 feet), often in a series, are monochrome, flat, and in primary colours. Study of Matisse's "Dance" from the Mellon Collection in London, England, in 1968, along with a stay in Italy in 1973, led to Tousignant's later works with arches (from 1973–74 on).

The source for his more recent sculptures is a monochrome painting, *Monochrome Rangé* (Montreal Museum of Fine Arts), he painted flat, with shiny orange enamel, in 1956. (Previously his paintings had two or three divisions, horizontal or vertical). The work hung on the wall of his apartment: "I started to see it as an object in the environment." "It acted like a sculpture." Tousignant says: "If there is no image, and the object is not about something else, the viewer feels the actuality of the material, dimension, surface, colour, etc., and is physically implicated by the work."

Tousignant continues to preceive his work as non-anecdotal and non-symbolic. He is still exploring the "painting as an object", manipulating existential rather than aesthetic space.

—Joan Murray

TRBULJAK, Goran.

Yugoslav. Born in Varazdin, Croatia, 21 April 1948. Studied photography at the School of Applied Arts, Zagreb, 1963–68; studied graphics at the Academy of Fine Arts, Zagreb, 1968–72; Ecole National Supérieure des Beaux-Arts, Paris, 1974–75. Independent artist, since 1970: lives and works in Zagreb. Director of the Photography Department, Academy of Theatrical and Film Arts, Zagreb, from 1980. Recipient: Sedam Sekretara Skoja, 1972, 1979; Kodak nagrada za kameru, 1980; National Film Festival Award, Pula, 1984, 1986. Address: Djalskog 39, 41000 Zagreb, Yugoslavia.

Individual Exhibitions:

1970 Ilica 85, Zagreb
1971 Likovni Salon tribine mladih, Novi Sad, Yugoslavia
Galerie S.C., Zagreb
1972 Galerie des Locataires, Paris
Galerie S.K.C., Belgrade
1973 Likovni Salon Tibine Mladih, Novi Sad, Yugoslavia
Gallery of Contemporary Art, Zagreb
1974 Galery Remont, Warsaw
1975 Galerie 28, Paris
1976 Galery Znak, Bialystok, Poland
Atelier Milch Strasse, Freiburg, West Germany
Galerie S.K.C., Belgrade
Medvescak Library, Zagreb
1977 Galleria del Cavallino, Venice
Galleria Civica d'Arte Moderna, Moderna, Italy
Studio 16E, Turin
Gallery Nova, Zagreb
Gallery S.K.C., Belgrade

1979 Gallery of Contemporary Art, Zagreb
Hotel Dubrovnik, Zagreb
1981 Salon Muzeja savrement Umjetnosti, Belgrade
Galerija studentskog centra, Zagreb
Gallery PM, Zagreb
1986 Gallery PM, Zagreb

Selected Group Exhibitions:

1971 *Conceptual Art in Yugoslavia,* Museum of Modern Art, Belgrade
1972 *Internationale Malewochen,* Graz, Austria
1973 *Biennale de Paris*
1975 *Kunst aus Jugoslawien,* Akademie der Bildenden Künste, Vienna
1976 *Video,* Kunstmuseum, Aarhus, Denmark
1977 *Moderne Kunst in Kroatien,* Rathaus, Mainz, West Germany
1978 *Analytical Works,* Gallery S.K.C., Belgrade
1982 *Internationale Jugendtriennale,* Kunsthalle, Nuremberg
1983 *Triennale of Drawing,* Warsaw
1986 *Art and Criticism in the mid-eighties,* Sarajevo, Yugoslavia

Collections;

Gallery of Contemporary Art, Zagreb; Muzej Savremene Umjetnosti, Belgrade; Museum of Modern Art, Zagreb.

Publications:

By TRBULJAK: books—*Artiste Anonyme,* Zagreb and Belgrade 1976; *Ecrits d'un Artiste,* Zagreb 1980; *Les Pages Non-Publiés des Ecrits d'un Artiste,* Zagreb 1980; article—"Artiste Anonyme" in *Flash Art* (Milan), June 1974.

On TRBULJAK: books—*Aktuelle Kunst in Osteuropa,* edited by Klaus Groh, Cologne 1972; *Goran Trbuljak,* exhibition catalogue, with text by Jesa Denegri, Zagreb 1973; *8th Biennale de Paris,* exhibition catalogue, with texts by J. Cahen-Salvador, G. Boudaille, J-M Poinsot and others, Paris 1973.

Under the slogan, "An artist is anyone who is given the opportunity to be one", the first referendum was held on the 1st July 1972, in which ordinary citizens had to decide whether or not someone is an artist. With their choice, people were to proclaim as an artist some person whose name was previously unknown to them (the name actually printed on the ballot forms was of a person who had attended art school—and was herself passing out the ballot papers—so, for the purposes of the exercise, it was irrelevant for the recipient of votes to deal in any kind of creative activity, or even to exist at all). Out of 500 ballots, there were 259 positive decisions and 204 negative ones, the person selected as an artist being totally unknown to the voters.

—Goran Trbuljak

TREMLETT, David.

British. Born in St. Austell, Cornwall, 13 February 1945. Studied under Terry Pascoe, Falmouth School of Art, Cornwall, 1962–63; Birmingham College of Art, 1963–66; Royal College of Art, London, 1966–69. Full-time artist since 1969: travelled in Spain, Netherlands and Australia, 1969; in Malawi, Tanzania, Botswana, Mozambique, Middle East and Far East, 1970–79; in Alaska, Canada, India, Mexico and Australia, 1980–87. Agent: Hester Van Royen, Flat 3, 53 Drayton Gardens, London SW10. Address: "Broadlawns", Chipperfield Road, Bovingdon, Hertfordshire HP3 OJR, England.

Individual Exhibitions:

1969 Grabowski Gallery, London
1970 Nigel Greenwood Gallery, London
1971 Nigel Greenwood Gallery, London
Galerie Ernst, Hannover
Folker Skulima Galerie, West Berlin
1972 Nigel Greenwood Gallery, London
Tate Gallery, London
Galerie Konrad Fischer, Dusseldorf
1973 Museum of Modern Art, New York
Harold Rivkin Gallery, Washington, D.C.
Nigel Greenwood Gallery, London
1974 Nigel Greenwood Gallery, London
Museum of Modern Art, Oxford
1975 Galleria Marilena Bonomo, Bari, Italy

Goran Trbuljak: *Artiste en Crise,* 1987

David Tremlett: *Come Cani*, 1985

1976 Galerie Rolf Preisig, Basle
Nigel Greenwood Gallery, London
Art and Project, Amsterdam
Robert Self Gallery, Newcastle-on-Tyne
Galleria Marilena Bonomo, Bari, Italy
Galerie Durand-Dessert, Paris
Institute of Contemporary Arts, London
1977 Galerie Durand-Dessert, Paris
1978 Plymouth Arts Centre, Devon
Galleria Massimo Valsecchi, Milan
Zomba Road, Malawi, Africa
Art and Project, Amsterdam
1979 Galleria Marilena Bonomo, Bari, Italy
Librairie Post Scriptum, Brussels
Galleria Massimo Valsecchi, Milan
Stedelijk Museum, Amsterdam
1980 Galerie Durand-Dessert, Paris
Gordon Jetty, Tasmania
1981 John Hansard Gallery, Southampton, Hampshire
Galleria Massimo Valsecchi, Milan
Art and Project, Amsterdam
Waddington Galleries, London
Galleria Marilena Bonomo, Bari, Italy
1982 Riverside Studios, London
Galerie Durand-Dessert, Paris
1983 Galerie Durand-Dessert, Paris
Galleria Massimo Valsecchi, Milan
Galleria Marilena Bonomo, Bari, Italy
Raum fur Kunst, Hamburg
Waddington Galleries, London
1984 Waddington Galleries, London
Art and Project, Amsterdam
1985 Centre Georges Pompidou, Paris
Leicester Polytechnic, Leicestershire
Gallery 865, Aalst, Belgium
Le Crystal, Paris
Galleria Marilena Bonomo, Bari, Italy
1986 Orchard Gallery, Londonderry, Northern Ireland (with Hamish Fulton)
Waddington Galleries, London
Institute of Contemporary Arts, London
Museum Van Hedendaagse Kunst, Ghent, Belgium
1987 22 All Saints Road, London
Galerie Durand-Dessert, Paris
Galleria Massimo Valsecchi, Milan
Artek Gallery, Helsinki

Selected Group Exhibitions:

1970 *British Sculpture of the Sixties*, Institute of Contemporary Arts, London
1971 *The British Avant Garde*, New York Cultural Center
1972 *Documenta 5*, Museum Fridericianum, Kassel, West Germany
1974 *An Element of Landscape*, Mappin Art Gallery, Sheffield, Yorkshire (toured Britain)
1975 *New Media I*, Konsthall, Malmo, Sweden
1977 *03-23-03*, Institute of Contemporary Art, Montreal
1979 *Un Certain Art Anglais*, Musee d'Art Moderne de la Ville, Paris (travelled to Brussels)
1981 *British Sculpture in the Twentieth Century*, Whitechapel Art Gallery, London
1984 *The Critical Eye/1*, Yale Center for British Art, New Haven, Connecticut
1987 *L'Exotisme au Quotidien*, Musee des Beaux-Arts, Charleroi, Belgium

Collections:

Tate Gallery, London; Victoria and Albert Museum, London; Arts Council of Great Britian, London; Stedelijk Museum, Amsterdam; Museum Boymans-van Beuningen, Rotterdam; Centre Georges Pompidou/Musee National d'Art Moderne, Paris; Musee d'Art et d'Industrie, St. Etienne, France; Philadelphia Museum of Art.

Publications:

By TREMLETT: books—*Some Places to Visit*, London 1975; *On the Waterfront*, Newlyn, Cornwall 1978; *Scrub*, Bari and Paris 1978; *On the Border*, Amsterdam 1979; *Restless*, London 1983; *Old Tom and Hotel Room*, New Haven, Connecticut 1984; *Rough Ride*, Paris and London 1985; *Ruin*, Amsterdam 1987.

On TREMLETT: books—*David Tremlett: 4 Sculptures*, catalogue poster with essay by Peter Atkins, London 1969; *The British Avant-Garde*, exhibition catalogue by Charles Harrison and Donald Karshan, New York 1971; *Documenta 5: Befragung der Realitat*, exhibition catalogue edited by Harald Szeemann and others, Kassel 1972; *An Element of Landscape*, exhibition catalogue with text by Jeremy Rees, London 1974; *British Sculpture in the Twentieth Century*, exhibition catalogue by Sandy Nairne and Nicholas Serota, London 1981; *The Critical Eye*, exhibition catalogue with essay by S. Paoletti, New Haven, Connecticut 1984.

In common with Richard Long, Hamish Fulton or Lothar Baumgarten, the artist David Tremlett takes his inspiration from traditions totally outside his own. For Tremlett, it is the journey, with its transitory locations, temporary resting places and defined cultural identities, which is his stimulus. This does not mean that his language is simply 'cosmopolitan' or more international, but rather that his subject is atopical. He does not renounce that which is conventionally understood as a 'work of art', but he disrupts its traditional modes of expression and the gulf which, in our world, distinguishes the practice of the artist from that of daily life.

He has made frequent trips through Africa and Mexico where he has assimilated ideas and forms belonging to different systems of thought, in order to formulate a vocabulary which vitalizes that formal repertory inherited from Western culture. Very simplified images, latently symbolic and vaguely totemic but stripped of every connotation, become the synthetic schema which are the style of this artist.

It is not without significance that the creative process is instinctive and immediate, employing a direct physical involvement of the artist himself with his materials. Tremlett chooses media such as coloured pastels reminiscent of the organic and allusive elements of the earth, or even extracts his own pigments directly from the earth. At times, he limits himself to elementary black and white, to primary tonalities. Often, the actual wall of the gallery accommodates his images. Spreading the colour directly onto the wall with his hands, Tremlett allows a certain degree of chance in the execution of the work. The wall reveals its unpredictable qualities, its porous and pitted surface reacting in unforeseen ways with the pigment. This unpredictability does not disrupt but actually qualifies the work.

In his works on paper, the drawing signifies the concentration of the mind in the act of governing internal processes. In most cases, the act of drawing determines the dimensions of the project. The environment of the picture plane is scrupulously constructed as a rigorously two-dimensional space, while the titles of the works make reference to architectural space. The images that Tremlett adopts open a discourse on the ambiguity of traditional definitions. Each work, whilst maintaining internal references to its own fulfilment, gestures towards the work which will follow. The pigmentation reclaimed from the earth is the essential material of building and sculpting. The physical work, the action, moulding and consolidation done with the hands, result in the very material of the work.

—Giorgio Verzotti

TREVELYAN, Julian (Otto).

British. Born in Dorking, Surrey, 20 February 1910. Educated at Bedales School, Hampshire, 1922–27; studied at Trinity College, Cambridge, 1928–30; studied printmaking under S. W. Hayter at Atelier 17, Paris, 1931–34. Served as camouflage officer, Royal Engineers, British Army, 1940–43. Married Ursula Darwin in 1934 (divorced, 1950); married Mary Fedden in 1951; son: Philip. Painter and graphic artist, Hammersmith, London, from 1935; Member, London Group of painters, 1948–63. Tutor in Etching, Royal College of Art, London, 1955–63. Agent: New Grafton Gallery, 49 Church Road, Barnes, London SW13. *Died* (in London) *12 July 1988*.

Julian Trevelyan: *Harbour*, 1944

Individual Exhibitions:

1932 Bloomsbury Gallery, London (with Robin Darwin)
1934 Bloomsbury Gallery, London (with Robin Darwin)
1935 Tate Gallery, London
1936 Lefevre Gallery, London
1939 Guggenheim Gallery, London
1942 Lefevre Gallery, London
1944 Lefevre Gallery, London
1946 Lefevre Gallery, London
1948 Lefevre Gallery, London
Galerie de France, Paris
Konsthall, Gothenburg, Sweden
Galleri Fargi Form, Stockholm
1950 Gimpel Fils Gallery, London
1952 Redfern Gallery, London
1955 Zwemmer Gallery, London (with K. Allen)
1958 Zwemmer Gallery, London
1959 St. George's Gallery, London
1960 Zwemmer Gallery, London
1961 Arnolfini Gallery, Bristol
1963 Zwemmer Gallery, London
Aldgate Gallery, Farnham, Surrey
1964 Thames Gallery, Eton, Buckinghamshire
1965 Zwemmer Gallery, London
Ashgate Gallery, Farnham, Surrey
1966 Thames Gallery, Eton, Buckinghamshire
Zwemmer Gallery, London
1968 Ashgate Gallery, Farnham, Surrey
1970 Hambledon Gallery, Blandford Forum, Dorset
1973 Alexander Postan Fine Art, London
1974 Printmakers Council/Oxford Press, London
1977 Tate Gallery, London
1978 New Grafton Gallery, London
1981 Holsworthy Gallery, London
1983 Bohun Gallery, Henley-on-Thames, Oxfordshire
1985 Waterman's Arts Centre, Brentford, Middlesex
1986 Norwich School of Art, Norfolk
Bolton Museum and Art Gallery, Lancashire
Waterman's Arts Centre, Brentford, Middlesex
1987 New Grafton Gallery, London

Selected Group Exhibitions:

1936 *International Surrealist Exhibition*, New Burlington Galleries, London
1945 *A.I.A. Exhibition*, Whitechapel Art Gallery, London
1947 *English Art*, Galleri Farg i Form, Stockholm
English Art, Galerie de France, Paris
1955 *Figures in a Setting*, Tate Gallery, London
1958 *London Group*, Whitechapel Art Gallery, London
1964 *London Group: Retrospective*, Tate Gallery, London
1971 *Britain's Contribution to Surrealism of the 30's and 40's*, Hamet Gallery, London
1980 *Atelier 17*, Brooklyn Museum, New York
1982 *Peinture Surréaliste en Angleterre 1930–1960*, Galerie 1900–2000, rue Bonaporte, Paris

Collections:

Tate Gallery, London; Contemporary Art Society, London; Arts Council of Great Britain, London; City Art Gallery, Southampton, Hampshire; City Art Gallery, Aberdeen; Museum of Modern Art, New York; Brooklyn Museum, New York; Library of Congress, Washington, D.C.; Seattle Museum of Art.

Publications:

By TREVELYAN: books—*Indigo Days* (autobiography), London 1957; *The Artist and His World*, London 1960; *Etching*, London 1963; *A Place, A State*, with Kathleen Rhine, London 1974.

On TREVELYAN: books—*The Painter's Object*, edited by Myfanwy Evans, London 1937, New York 1970; *Britain's Contribution to Surealism of the 30's and 40's*, exhibition catalogue, London 1971; *Julian Trevelyan: First Retrospective*, exhibition catalogue with text by Nicholas Usherwood, Brentford 1986.

To start young with an eccentric vision of urban skylines and streets and riverbanks plus a sky hospitable to both heavenly bodies and balloons and aircraft—a sort of British Paul Klee, but one riveted in a single channel of inspiration—this can make an overnight reputation, especially if the author is capable of producing both paintings and graphics to support such a quasi-original style. It was pictures of this nature that made Julian Trevelyan's name for him, and which ensured that at the time (during the 1930's) he would be included in every up-to-date anthology of the visual arts.

What happened? Like John Piper, only not quite so decisively, he abandoned the way he had chosen and turned to something which, even if it was well made, had nothing of the bite of his initial work. Piper, following the Brighton aquatints and the commission he received from Queen Mary to do much the same for Windsor, ceased to be an abstract artist. With an ironic touch of irony the change took place just around the time when the avantgarde magazine *Transition* illustrated one of his abstract pictures. The alteration in the style of Julian Trevelyan's work was not quite so cataclysmic, but at one stage it had a terminal ring about it. He went bucolic. Bullocks replaced boats. Seagulls took over from skyscrapers.

What had once been finely executed: cobweb lines to match the skeletons of leaves pressed into service upon the paint or paper: all this was replaced by firm didactic paint, or, in the case of the graphics, by an unyielding line that framed carefully chosen areas of colour.

Was this about-face a bid for broader popularity? Maybe. Certainly with the years Trevelyan's control over his new imagery and the way in which he painted it became steadily more accomplished and resolute.

But this is not the end of the story. Late in his career, and obviously with the intention of continuing in yet another departure from what has come to be recognized as his style, the artist set about making some interesting assemblages, marine flotsam that are closer to what he was doing before the War than to what he had done since. These constructions are well finished and despite the age or nature of their component parts they have a weatherworn appearance that recalls the lichenous patina of some of the early works.

—Sheldon Williams

TROCKEL, Rosemarie.

German. Born in Schwerte, 13 November 1952. Studied at the Werkkunstschule, Cologne, 1974–78. Independent artist, Cologne, since 1979. Agent: Galerie Monika Spruth, Maria-Hilf-Strasse 17, 5000 Cologne 1. Address: Reinoldstrasse 6, 5000 Cologne 1, West Germany.

Individual Exhibitions:

1983 Galerie Monika Spruth, Cologne
Galerie Philomene Magers, Bonn
1984 Galerie Monika Spruth, Cologne
Galerie Ascan Crone, Hamburg
Gallerie Stampa, Basle
1985 Galerie Monika Spruth, Cologne
1986 Galleria Stampa, Basle (with Tatafiore and Stumpf)
Galerie Monika Spruth, Cologne
1987 Galerie Tanit, Munich
1988 Kunsthalle, Basle
Museum of Modern Art, New York

Selected Group Exhibitions:

1982 *Licht bricht sich in der oberen Fenstern,* Klapperhof 33, Cologne
1984 *Kunstlandschaft BRD,* Kunstverein, Lubeck, West Germany
Bella Figura, Wilhelm-Lehmbruck-Museum, Duisburg, West Germany
1986 *Sculptures,* Galleria Stampa, Basle
1987 *Een Keuze/A Choice,* Kunst RAI, Amsterdam
Art from Europe, Tate Gallery, London

Publications:

On TROCKEL: books—*Rosemarie Trockel: Plastiken 1982–83,* exhibition catalogue with text by Wilfried Dickhoff, Bonn and Cologne 1983; *Kunstlandschaft BRD,* exhibition catalogue with essay by Wulf Schadendorf, Lubeck 1984; *Rosemarie Trockel: Skulpturen und Bilder,* exhibition catalogue with texts by A. R. Penck and Reiner Speck, Hamburg 1984; *Bella Figura,* exhibition catalogue with essay by Karl-Egon Vester, Duisburg 1984; *Rosemarie Trockel: Bilder, Skulpturen, Zeichnungen,* with text by Wilfreid Dickhoff, Cologne 1985; *Rosemarie Trockel: Arbeiten 1980–1985,* Bonn and Cologne 1986.

Interest in Rosemarie Trockel's work has grown over the last few years due to recent abstract-geometric tendencies in painting. In fact, it could be argued that the decade of the 1980s is characterized by a predilection for cool analytical work, supplanting the earlier vogue for figurative and neo-expressionist passion. This current abstraction establishes a critical and ironic distance vis-a-vis the great tradition of abstract painting—i.e., of Malevich and Reinhardt. According to these new tendencies, the epic attempt to re-establish perspectival space falls apart, as does the attempt to achieve ultimate or 'supreme' forms.

Rosemarie Trockel aligns herself with this critical reappraisal of historical abstraction: as Klaus Ottmann has rightly pointed out, her intention is to deconstruct the aesthetic categories of modern rationalism as much as the hedonism of the Postmodernist age. She does not aim at re-establishing an up-to-date aesthetic, as Peter Halley does, neither does she intend to parody the 'fifties in the manner of John Armleder. Trockel elaborates a visual repertoire that focuses on what has been 'removed' from the realm of art by reintroducing a discussion of the categories of creativity: in doing so, she aims at positing a definition of 'feminine'.

She sees the 'feminine' as a historical dimension and an essential component of art. Typically, she expresses this idea by the device of stretching a length of knitted material onto a frame (like a painting on canvas), the material patterned with motifs akin to those in contemporary clothing. These decorative motifs, typical of feminine creativity within the domestic realm, are now presented as autonomous and formal. The result is a surprising 'pattern-painting', genetically transformed in its function and component parts. Trockel thus promotes a critique of the grand theories of abstraction by suggesting that the mundane is fundamental to all great discourses. This dimension of the mundane can be defined as 'the feminine'—a concept that the artist uses as a provocative device.

In addition to geometrical motifs, often employed as parody, Trockel has used woven wool and, more recently, fabrics printed with the most common visual stereotypes of consumerism: the Cowboy, the Hammer and Sickle, the advertising logo 'Made in West Germany'—banal or trivialized insignia of common currency which have lost any (assuming they ever possessed) original meaning.

Trockel's visual repertoire is based on ambiguity; her images are suspended between abstraction and figuration, abandoning their original meaning to appear empty. The serial form of presentation weakens their connotative power, while the elementary manner (based on pure contiguity) in which they are inserted into the visual field prevents their becoming proper structural elements. The artist explicitly talks about the 'depreciation' she intends to inflict upon the visual elements she has selected. The hammer and sickle lose their ideological significance of which they were a symbol as they become 'purified' into a geometrical motif.

This negation of the values of signs is a critique of ideologies as totalitarian world-views with their need to legitimize themselves by censoring anything that does not conform. Trockel works at what is considered to be 'insignificant' and ineffective against totalitarian ideologies. In this 'irrelevance' resides the definition of difference, and in its consecration as art lies its power to change the world.

—Giorgio Verzotti

TROOSTWYK, David.

British. Born in London. 5 August 1929. Studied at St. Albans School of Art, Hertfordshire, 1950–53; Royal College of Art, London, 1953–56, A.R.C.A. 1956. Served in the Royal Air Force, 1947–49. Married Ursula Janet Freer in 1953 (divorced, 1963); married Yvette Jean-Marie Bouzigues in 1963 (divorced, 1972); daughter: Lois. Worked as a display artist, London Display Company, 1949–50. Independent painter, London, since 1956. Visiting Lecturer, Camberwell School of Art, London, 1966–70; Chelsea School of Art, London, 1970–71; Sydney College of the Arts, 1978–79. Recipient: Painting Prize, *John Moores Exhibition,* Liverpool, 1969; First Prize, *British International Drawing Biennale,* Teesside, England, 1973. Agent: Matt's Gallery, London. Address: c/o Matt's Gallery, 10 Martello Street, London E8, England.

Individual Exhibitions:

1964 Southampton University, Hampshire
1969 R.C.A. Galleries, London
1970 Angela Flowers Gallery, London (with Alan Davie)
Axiom Gallery, London (with Ivor Abrahams)
1971 Kasmin Gallery, London
1974 Institute of Contemporary Arts, London
1977 Felicity Samuel Gallery, London
1979 Institute of Modern Art, Brisbane
Matt's Gallery, London
1980 Galerija Akumulatory, Poznan, Poland
1981 Matt's Gallery, London
1983 Holland Festival Gallery, Amsterdam
1985 Matt's Gallery, London

Selected Group Exhibitions:

1967 *4 Abstract Painters,* Institute of Contemporary Arts, London
1969 *John Moores Exhibition,* Walker Art Gallery, Liverpool
1973 *British International Drawing Biennale,*Teesside, England
1974 *International Poezie,* Rotterdam
1975 *Art 75,* Basle
1976 *Biennale,* Art Gallery of New South Wales, Sydney (and 1982)

Collections:

Tate Gallery, London; Arts Council of Great Britain, London.

Publications:

By TROOSTWYK: books and leaflets—*Imitation,* London 1977; *20 Broadsheets,* London 1979; *National Day,* London 1981; *Holiday Island,* London 1985; article—"Euan Uglow's Diagonal" in *Studio International* (London), May 1974; recording—*Advertisement of an Idea,* Audio Arts tape cassette, London 1976; *Live to Air,* Audio Arts tape cassette, London 1982.

This artist has found himself a niche amongst the painters accepted in Britain, a prizewinner and joining the elect included in the permanent collection of the Tate Gallery. But such honours do little or nothing to explain the talents of this artistic Banquo. Absent from the feast, but present in absentia. 'To make what I like and when I like may not always be easy, but what it is is what I *should do.*'

Selling antique photographs culled from sales and auction rooms to be resold in the Portobello Market reduces the financial strain on David Troostwyk, and the small profits he acquires in this way pay for canvas, stretchers and paints; but above all these monies ensure a large measure of artistic freedom so that he can pursue his ambitions as a painter relying solely upon the understanding of his works and the impact upon a public whose predilections need no cajoling of

David Troostwyk: *Mount Fuji*, 1987

any kind insofar as his coolly detached stance as an artist is concerned.

The process of artistic creation for him has been both natural and artificially encouraged. As soon as he was able to claim a pencil as his friend and companion, carefully nurtured—as he came to realise—as a child, but spiritually *relegated* by respectable parents, he filled this social gap sitting sketching on his own in a corner.

Today, this obsession to enter life through making pictures has been carefully tailored. Images, very thoughtfully selected—visual platitudes for the most part—are placed in a monochrome setting, often a black one, the white 'object' or 'statement' asserting its message against a field of black opacity. Troostwyk, who regards paint as only a *medium* (practical and necessary), steers clear of anything approaching a nuance; this is one of the reasons why he eschews the description of 'painter', preferring the title of 'artist'.

He sums up the Why and Wherefore of his creations as 'Communication'. For him, the eye of the beholder can indulge in any interpretive assessment it chooses; his wish as artist is entirely focused on telling a direct truth in absolute terms. So, the 'Empire State Building', white of course, poses with casual tilt in a stygian background or, in less audacious mood, two apples lurk in happy white purity in the midst of a black square. Painting in his Kennington studio in St. Anselm's Church Hall, he is supremely indifferent to critical reaction. These pictures are his remote exploration of finite verities into which those with a desire to investigate may delve but need never feel beholden so to do.

Troostwyk devises paper or card templates. He might make preliminary plans on paper, sketching out his eventual intentions, but he establishes these cutouts as basic aids to be placed—in scale—on his vast canvases. They are, or try to be, the exact guts of the imagery appearing in his picutres. Each of these emplacements—generally one to each picture—is a vital beginning for what will be the finalised pictorial meaning, however frequently readjusted. This is an artist who finds it difficult to persuade himself that any of his works has reached its clinching fulfilment. Many of them stand around the studio awaiting the final coup-de-grace—waiting—they may wait until their place is required in an exhibition, and only then will they receive the last coat of paint and the fine-edge finish that will gain them his personal decision that they should be allowed to go before a public.

Just to give examples of the works of this artist, who makes it a solemn contract with himself never to desert supreme symbols (immediately recognisable to the *hoi polloi,* even though the soul of such simplicity could be described as a 'slow burn' only making itself clear to the majority after long / and often returning to / contemplation) is no easy task. One needs to mentally take a stroll through the familiar in order to cross a barrier separating the obvious from the *extra* experience. A large composition like *Fuji,* a white mountain at ease (or not, depending upon mood), solid in its solitude in a surrounding total blackness is what Troostwyk calls one of my 'negatives' (in the photographic sense). Another 'negative' (and one wonders if the flavour is sardonic) is the happy-cum-alone signature of Ronald Reagan, clean and white, sprawling across the anonymous black of another work of massive dimensions. (Except in one little canvas, this painter has found it extremely difficult to extract satisfaction from painting on a small scale).

A departure from black/white occurs in his picture of the 'Ring'. The usual containing background in this case is a warm and pale brown madder broken up at casual intervals by unobtrusive glitter-spots. The Ring itself is set in innocent and not very complex curves, but if it is looked at with the aid of a simple optical appliance this unalluring sample of jewellery thrusts itself into a third-dimensional advance out of the canvas. David Troostwyk is pleased about this interference with routine vision but, at the same time, is slightly appalled that he could so easily be accused of indulging in gimmickry—the last thing such a purist should have to fear.

A more uncanny—yet typical—canvas, and one ot Troostwyk's finest, is the picture he calls *The Russian Chair* (for which he made several studies and a smaller version). This is not one of his 'negative' paintings. It portrays in a strange twisted version a variety of perspectives to form a *portrait* of a famous chair from the experimental period of the great Russian sculptor and designer Vladimir Tatlin. In a strange way the character of Tatlin's chair, despite its curious figuration typifying the acceptance of *new ideas* of the Russian Revolutionary 'Acceptance' of every break with tradition, complies with Troostwyk's determination to communicate with the public through easily digested pictorial statements (in several steps ranging from symbols to absolute realism).

It is worth mentioning here that Troostwyk is an artist who works slowly and with great deliberation. At no time can he assemble a great number of pictures in his studio. Short of the offer of a forthcoming exhibition he accepts no pressures from the outside world to perform extra feats of uncomplicated (yet haunting) painting unless suddenly inspired by a to him attractive form or feature to place in a chosen position on one of his vast canvases. The 'sections' of architecture which appear in rigid whiteness against the black background of *Heliopolis*—totalities, never randomly positioned, are a fragment of a *loge* which have not only strayed to one side (the left side of the picutre) but are quietly defying gravity.

Perhaps David Troostwyk should have the last word. He declares "Whatever sensations you receive from looking at one of my pictures are certainly enriched *after* you leave the studio with the painting still imprinted on your mind's eye"

—Sheldon Williams

TROTTA, Antonio A.

Argentinian. Born in Stio, Italy, 21 December 1937; lived in Argentina until 1968. Educated in architecture at the University of La Plata, Argentina. Independent painter and sculptor, in Buenos Aires, 1960–68, and in Milan since 1968. Recipient: Painting Prize, Mar del Plata Salon, 1966; Prize, Museum of Fine Arts, Buenos Aires, 1966; Sash of Honour, Ver y Estimar Prize, Buenos Aires, 1966 and 1967. Address: via Lamarmora 15, 20122 Milan, Italy.

Individual Exhibitions:

1965 Galeria Lirolay, Buenos Aires
1970 Galleria Lambert, Milan
1971 Galleria Christian Stein, Turin
1972 Galleria Marilena Bonomo, Bari, Italy
Studio Maddilena Carioni, Milan
1974 Galleria Christian Stein, Turin
Qui Arte Contemporanea, Rome
1976 Galleria Borgogna, Milan
1977 Galleria Christian Stein, Turin
1978 t'Venster, Rotterdam
1981 Galleria Piero Cavellini, Brescia, Italy
1982 Più due Cannaviello, Milan

Selected Group Exhibitions:

1961 *Gruppo SI,* Museo de Artas Plasticas, La Plata (travelled to Museo de Arte Moderno, Buenos Aires and Museo de Bellas Artes, Lima)
1967 *Più in là della geometria,* Istituto de Tella, Buenos Aires
1971 *Arte de Sistemas,* Museo de Arte Moderno, Buenos Aires
Understatement, Qui Arte Contemporanea, Rome
1974 *Della Falsità,* Palazzo della Pilotta, Parma
1977 *Senza Relazione: Il verosimile critico,* Palazzo Comunale, Acireale, Italy
1978 *Biennale,* Venice
1979 *L'Annunciazione di Antonello,* Museo Nazionale, Siracusa
1980 *Arte e critica 1980,* Galleria Nazionale d'Arte Moderna, Rome
1982 *La Sovrana Inattualita,* P.A.C., Milan

Publications:

By TROTTA: books—*Divagaciones,* Buenos Aires 1967; *Lo Spazio fra Me e l'Opera,* Milan 1972; *La Cruz del Sur,* Milan 1974; *Rose, Rose, Rose,* Milan 1974; *Le Finzioni Popolari,* Turin 1976; videotapes—*Punto,* Milan 1969; *Il Sogno di Coleridge,* Milan 1972; *Silbando,* Milan 1972; *Unacita,* Milan 1973.

Antonio Trotta: *La Cascata*, 1981

On TROTTA: books—*Antonio Trotta* by Romero Brest, Buenos Aires 1967; *Il corpo come linguaggio* by Lea Vergine, Milan 1974; *Antonio Trotta*, exhibition catalogue, Rome 1974; *Extra Media* by E. Crispolti, Turin 1978; *Art in Argentina* by Jorge Glusberg, Milan 1986; articles—"Letter from Buenos Aires" by G. Whitelow in *Art International* (Lugano, Switzerland), May 1969; "Antonio Trotta" by J. R. Brest in *Flash Art* (Milan), February/April 1972; "Antonio Trotta" by L. Haller in *Flash Art* (Milan), January 1973; "Antonio Trotta" in *Utopia Rivisitata*, Milan 1974; "Miracolo a Milano" by Tommaso Trini in *Data* (Milan), Spring 1975; "Antonio Trotta" in *Art Magazine Bijutsu Techo* (Tokyo), February 1975; "La Pop Art" by M. Volpi Orlandini in *L'Arte Moderna*, Milan 1975; "Antonio Trotta, lo scultore si scolpisce" in *Data* (Milan), January February 1978; "La découverte des origines" in *Art Aktuel: Skira Annual*, Geneva 1979.

Antonio Trotta has been exhibiting his work in Italy since 1970, after an extended stay in Argentina. His work is directed towards an enquiry into the rapport between the artist and the work of art—and the space that separates them. In 1972 the Toselli Gallery in Milan published a catalogue of works by Nagasawa, Salvadori and Trotta. Trotta's own preface was titled *Images Relating to the Period of the Disappearance of Giovanni Bellini's Saint Sebastian*, a title which may be understood as Trotta's declaration of an analytical view of the work of art which is internal to his own tradition. In the works which followed, Trotta revealed the ideas central to his concern with images of reality and, above all, with the superimposition of the artist's view onto the work of art. *Ricamandosi* (1974–75) is a portrait, perhaps even a self-portrait, made in embroidery. This work forms a direct link with *L'Artifice* (1977), a piece sculpted out of several different slabs of marble, and representing the sculptor at work—"a sculpture of the sculptor sculpting". This simple but effective idea demonstrates the rapport between illusion and reality which is the basis of everything.

A declaration of 1972, entitled *The Space Between Me and the Work*, indicates unequivocally where Trotta's interest lies. "The space between me and the work begins to be dissolved in that moment when it is possible to see that everything surrounding me has already been painted or sculpted. These objects are in a state of petrification, ensnared by those sensations of doubt that form our existence. In them, we observe the unreality which exists in the reality of the work."

L'Artifice reveals the artist observing his own work from the inside, the sculpture itself reflecting like a mirror the illusion of reality—a concept central to the philosophy of Borges, and perhaps developed during Trotta's time in Argentina. This work is expressed in a variety of different marbles employing quite sophisticated techniques, sometimes smooth or inlaid with a counterpoint of variously toned pieces. This sort of craftsmanship represents another aspect of Trotta, in which he participates in the tradition of the artisan, directing it towards a dialogue of invention and technique.

In June of 1976, the Turin gallery of Christian Stein published one of Trotta's works in book form under the title *Le Finzioni Popolare* (The Popular Illusion). Written the previous summer, the first part is dedicated to the window. The Window is seen from a variety of viewpoints as a screen which divides inside from outside, in a poetic sense. Thus each segment is prefaced by quotations from Mallarmé's poem *La Fenêtre*, and from Miguel Hernandez' *The Farewell is Muffled Behind the Window Pane*. The sequence comprises *La Finestra sul Vetro* (urban images superimposed onto the structure of the window), and *Dietro la Finestra sul Vetro* (external and internal images of life). The same attention, both literary and actual, is focussed onto a balcony, with a quotation from Baudelaire's *Le Balcon*. Trotta subsequently went on to make a number of works and installations on these themes.

La Trilogia: Balcone, Grata, Lampione is a work dated 1974–76 in which objects are reproduced from photographic images, but installed and illuminated in a manner that perfectly simulates that photographic

reality. Here again is one of the dominant motifs of Trotta's work—that is, the rapport between reality and appearance which exists between the artist and the work of art. The preoccupation continues to be characteristic.

—Roberto Lambarelli

TROUILLE, (Camile) Clovis.

French. Born in La Fere, Aisne, 24 October 1889. Studied painting, drawing and modelling at the Ecole des Beaux-Arts, Amiens, 1905–10. Served in the Dragoons, French Army, in Lunéville and Paris, 1910–12; active service in Champagne and Picardy, 1914–19; Gendarmerie, Picardy War Front, 1939–40. Married Jeanne Vailland in 1920 (divorced, 1922). Painter, since 1930: associated with André Breton, Salvador Dali, Louis Aragon, Paul Eluard, and other Surrealist artists and writers, Paris. Fashion design illustrator, Draeger Frères, Paris, 1912–14; wax mannequin modeller and decorator, Fabrique Pierre Imans, Paris, 1920–60. Recipient: First Prize, Collection Beaux-Arts, Amiens, 1907; Medaille d'Honneur du Travail, 19th Arrondissement, Paris, 1960. Agent: Editions Jean-Jacques Pauvert, 8 rue de Nesle, 75006 Paris. Address: 57 avenue Mathurin Moreau, Paris, France.

Individual Exhibitions:

1963 Galerie Raymond Cordier, Paris

Selected Group Exhibitions:

1930 *Salon des Artistes et Ecrivains Révolutionnaires*, Parc des Expositions, Paris
1934 *Salon des Surindépendants*, Paris
1941 *Salon des Indépendants*, Paris
1944 *Groupe Surréaliste*, at Salon d'Automne, Paris
1947 *Exposition Surréaliste*, Galerie Maeght, Paris
1959 *Exposition Internationale Surréaliste*, Galerie Daniel Cordier, Paris
1960 *Surrealist Intrusion*, D'Arcy Galleries, New York
1963 *L'An 2104*, Galerie Iris Clert, Paris
1964 *Le Surréalisme: Sources, Histoire, Affinités*, Galerie Charpentier, Paris
1965 *Salon de Mai*, Paris

Collections:

Centre Georges Pompidou, Paris.

Publications:

By TROUILLE: book illustrated—cover design for *La Clé des Songes* by Artemidore d'Ephese, Paris 1953; article—"Tout Ma Vie" in *Clovis Trouille*, Paris 1972.

On TROUILLE: books—*The History of Surrealist Painting* by Marcel Jean, Paris 1959; *Le Surréalisme: Sources, Histoire, Affinités*, exhibition catalogue, edited by Patrick Waldberg, Paris 1964; *Clovis Trouille* by Jean-Marc Campagne, Paris 1969; *Clovis Trouille* by Raymond Charmet, Paris 1972; *Antologia Grafica del surrealismo* by Maurice Henry, Milan 1972; articles—"Clovis Trouille" in *Le Surréalisme A.S.D.L.R.* (Paris), December 1931; "Chronicles of Clovis" by John Lyle in *Art and Artists* (London), February 1973; "Religion, Sex och Dod" by F. Kusan in *Paletten* (Gothenburg, Sweden), no. 1, 1978.

My parents were horticulturists in Amiens. I developed a taste for painting very early. It happened to me in a very odd way. As a child I saw a picturesque man describing his journey around the world in the bistros; he used to give away painted plates in a raffle which he organized. It was on these plates that I admired the sea, the waves "laid on thick." I saw real waves sparkling in the window of the grocer's shop-bistro where these plates ran around. There was also in Amiens Merovac, the cathedral man: wherever there were cathedrals he did drawings of them. He was dressed in a large cloak and sported a large Lavaliere cravat as well as a hat à la Rubens. His exhibition hall was the shop of the local photographer where I myself displayed caricatures of local characters.

I did my studies at the regional school in Amiens with marvellous teachers. The teachers paid a lot of attention to us. The feminine element (young ladies of good background) formed the majority of the pupils. I executed landscapes, but above all portraits. The *Child in Straw Hat* gained the admiration of my teacher: "Trouille," he said to me one day, "I shall not retouch your work. You equal the greatest." I often went off into the Picardy countryside with my fellow-students. I had two favourite artistic highspots: Amiens Cathedral and the Picardy Museum where I did copies of 17th and 18th century works. I did caricatures for the paper *Notre Picardie*. It was thanks to this paper that I was put in touch with their Paris photographer who recommended me to a fellow who specialized in fashion drawings: Berthold Mann, my first patron. I had first met him during my studies at the Académie in Amiens: he was taking advantage of his four weeks training for the military reserve to come there and draw nudes. Then I went on to become a designer for Draeger. Then came the 1914–18 war. I was a soldier for seven years. This period is very important to my work. On my return from war I went to work for the firm of Imans which made mannequins. I started by modelling faces and I placed glass eyes and sets of teeth for the "smilers." The heads were made of wax. One day, the artists of this firm held an exhibition. The management took notice then that I was a painter. They put me on to makeup (eyebrows, lips). You can't imagine the importance of makeup. How one can transform a face. For me it was of capital importance. A unique experience. This work was routine, I could think of my painting. I remained with Imans forty years. I have a long service medal for it.

Before the war my subjects were still-lifes, countrysides, portraits. A discreet type of painting. After the war, after reading Rimbaud, Sade, Lautreamont, I became an anarchist. I didn't forgive it, the war. You think it's beautiful, war? I was completely traumatised. It made me join the surrealists. Something important happened to me: the exhibition of revolutionary artists and writers at the Porte de Versailles with Aragon, Vaillant-Couturier. I exhibited there a picture which caused a sensation: "Remembrance." An anti-clerical, anti-militarist work. A German soldier and a French soldier ask what they've come to do in the war (for them it's the cross . . . the military cross); the Republic distributes decorations; the bishop blesses the shirkers and the soldiers; white rabbits symbolise the sacrifices of soldiers. I have always been against the imposture of religions. Was it in painting Amiens Cathedral that I became aware of all this "music-hall"? I remember in Amiens, a lorry passing which was distributing *Les Corbeaux*, an anti-religious humorous paper. I found it very funny. How did I become anti-religious? I don't remember. Priests have become priests because they don't feel up to working: for them, it's a sinecure. The surrealist group stopped in front of "Remembrance." Breton came to look for me outside Imans and he took me to Cyrano's, a café near the Moulin-Rouge. And Breton presented me to Eluard. Breton gave us the obligation of excluding people. It was a pain in the arse.

What interests me the most in my work is its intrinsic value: colour, the subject. Which didn't interest Breton at all; he wasn't retinal; he saw only history. What counts is composition, the subject: what I studied at the Picardy Museum in the presence of Velasquez. I place myself in a very independent way. I have never admitted cubism. It didn't move me. I like to paint feminine beauty. All my life I have looked for what was most beautiful in nature so I could express it in my pictures. I have found nothing more beautiful than the nude body of a young girl. For men who are men it is a moving spectacle. In the woman's sex, God reveals himself. I am not so attached to painting men in my pictures. You see, with men, it's no fun.

—Clovis Trouille

Who better than Clovis Trouille to paint the picture which became the design for the original poster for Kenneth Tynan's *Oh Quel cul t'as (Oh Calcutta!)*! Trouille specializes in erotic images with posteriors high on his list. Referring to him in *Eros and Surrealism*, Robert Stuart Short says "In an orgy of combative black humour, Clovis Trouille painted a whole series of lecherous festivals for pantied priests and rampant nuns, exploiting all the clichés of commercial sex mixed up with the panoply of organized religion. In 'Mes Funerailles' the fleshy buttocks of the officiants affirm the triumph of desire over death itself". This is a relatively cool assessment of the outrageous imagery of which this artist is capable. Not surprisingly he has been featured in the French magazine *Plexus* with pullouts that make anything approaching a sexy ploy by *Playboy* look demure.

Trouille works with dainty, albeit devastating, detail all carried out in bright "illustration" colours, to suggest that life, and particularly its most serious and calvanist moments, is a carnal romp. His "church" and "nunnery" pictures make "The Devils of Loudun" the rule rather than the exception.

Trouille is the most erotic of all the painters who make up the pattern of contemporary art (only Hans Bellmer comes near to him when it is a matter of *épater la bourgeoisie*). His audacity and indifference to establishment beliefs (however hypocritical they may be) have hardly been matched by any of the artists of antiquity, including the works of those kept under lock and key in the restricted collection departments of the British Museum and the Victoria and Albert Museum.

—Sheldon Williams

TRUITT, Anne.

American. Born Anne Dean in Baltimore, Maryland, 16 March 1921. Studied psychology at Bryn Mawr College, Pennsylvania, 1939–43, B.A. 1943; studied at the Institute of Contemporary Art, Washington, D.C., 1948–50. Married James McConnell Truitt in 1947 (divorced, 1971); children: Alexandra, Mary, and Samuel. Worked as a psychologist at Massachusetts General Hospital, Boston, 1943–46; full-time artist since 1950; lived in Japan, 1964–67. Lecturer, 1975–80, and since 1980 Professor in Art, University of Maryland, College Park. Recipient: Guggenheim Fellowship, 1970; National Endowment for the Arts Fellowship, 1971, 1977; Stern Foundation Grant, 1972; Australian Arts Council Fellowship, 1981. DHL: Corcoran School of Art, Washington, D.C., 1985; DFA: Kansas City Art Institute, Missouri, 1987. Agents: André Emmerich Gallery, 41 East 57th Street, New York, New York 10022; Osuna Gallery, 407 6th Street N.W., Washington, D.C. 20004. Address: 3506 35th Street N.W., Washington, D.C. 20016, U.S.A.

Individual Exhibitions:

1963 André Emmerich Gallery, New York
1964 Minami Gallery, Tokyo
1965 André Emmerich Gallery, New York
1967 Minami Gallery, Tokyo
1969 André Emmerich Gallery, New York
Baltimore Museum of Fine Arts
1971 Pyramid Galleries, Washington, D.C.

1973 Whitney Museum, New York
Pyramid Galleries, Washington, D.C.
1974 Corcoran Gallery, Washington, D.C.
Baltimore Museum of Art
1975 André Emmerich Gallery, New York
Pyramid Galleries, Washington, D.C.
1976 University of Virginia Museum of Art, Charlottesville
1977 Pyramid Galleries, Washington, D.C.
1979 Osuna Gallery, Washington, D.C.
1980 André Emmerich Gallery, New York
1981 Osuna Gallery, Washington, D.C.
1983 James Madison University, Harrisonburg, Virginia
Artemisia Gallery, Chicago
1986 Neuberger Museum, Purchase, New York
Andre Emmerich Gallery, New York
Osuna Gallery, Washington, D.C.

Selected Group Exhibitions:

1953 *8th Corcoran Annual,* Corcoran Gallery, Washington, D.C. (and 1954, 1975)
1964 *Black, White, and Grey,* Wadsworth Atheneum, Hartford, Connecticut
1966 *Color and Space,* Minami Gallery, Tokyo
Primary Structures: Younger American and British Sculptors, Jewish Museum, New York
1968 *Annual Exhibition: Contemporary American Sculpture,* Whitney Museum, New York (and 1972)
1975 *Sculpture: American Directions 1945–1975,* National Collection of Fine Arts, Washington, D.C.
1982 *Grace Hartigan/Morris Louis/Clyfford Still/Anne Truitt,* Baltimore Museum of Art
1985 *Amerikanische Zeichnungen 1930–80,* Stadtische Galerie, Frankfurt
1987 *The Hard Edge—Part I: the 60s,* Andre Emmerich Gallery, New York

Collections:

Whitney Museum, New York; Metropolitan Museum of Art, New York; Museum of Modern Art, New York; Albright-Knox Art Museum, Buffalo, New York; Hirshhorn Museum and Sculpture Garden, Washington, D.C.; National Gallery, Washington, D.C.; Museum of American Art, Washington, D.C.; St. Louis Museum of Art; Walker Art Center, Minneapolis; Museum of Fine Arts, Houston.

Publications:

By TRUITT: books—*Marcel Proust and Deliverance from Time* by Germaine Bree, translator with C. J. Hill, New Brunswick, New Jersey 1955; *Daybook: The Journal of an Artist,* New York 1982, 1984: *Turn: The Journal of an Artist,* New York 1986, 1987; article—"Interview with Anne Truitt" in *Asahi Shimbum* (Tokyo), March 1964.

On TRUITT: books—*Minimal Art: A Critical Anthology,* edited by Gregory Battcock, New York 1968; *Anne Truitt,* exhibition catalogue with essay by Walter Hopps, Washington, D.C. 1974; *Anne Truitt,* exhibition catalogue with text by E. A. Carmean, Charlottesville, Virginia 1976; *Originals: American Women Artists* by Eleanor Munro, New York 1979; articles—"Black, White and Grey" by Donn Judd in *Arts Magazine* (New York), March 1964; "Changer: Anne Truitt, American Artist Whose Painted Structures Helped to Change the Course of American Sculpture" by Clement Greenberg in *Vogue* (New York), May 1968; "Vicissitudes of Sculpture" by Peter Schjeldahl in the *New York Times,* February 1969; "Truitt's Box-Sculptures: Now You See Them" by Paul Richard in the *Washington Post,* April 1971; "Anne Truitt: The Whitney Museum" by Jeremy Gilbert-Rolfe in *Artforum* (New York), March 1974; "Anne Truitt at the Corcoran" by Gene Baro in *Art in America* (New York), July/August 1974; "New Sculptures by Anne Truitt" by John Russell in the *New York Times,* 7 March 1980; "Daybook: The Journal of an Artist" by Sara Mandelbaum in *Ms.* (New York), February 1983; "Anne Truitt" by Mary Swift in *Washington Review,* April-May 1986; "Anne Truitt at Andre Emmerich Gallery" by Nancy Princenthal in *Art in America* (New York), 1987.

Since 1961, Washington, D.C. sculptor Anne Truitt has been making austerely reductive structures of wood painted with variously hued bands of color. Truitt's simple, abstract forms resemble Minimalism's "primary structures," but her personal and intuitive application of shape and color communicate ideas associative with significative meanings beyond strictly formal ones, suggesting Truitt's connections with Abstract Expressionism, specifically with the work of Barnett Newman.

It was after Truitt saw the work of Newman during a trip to New York in 1961 that she began working in the form which was to characterize her work over the next two decades to the present. Truitt's ideological foundations had been formed through long-time friendship with Kenneth Noland, whom she had known since 1948. She had developed through the 1950's from a kind of stylized figure and landscape sculpture to geometrical works in clay which suggested primitive architectural forms. In 1961, she made a generative work titled *First,* a vertical sculptural construct resembling three sections of a picket fence. In 1962, she made a number of drawings and 32 sculptures, her first mature work. *Insurrection* (1962) consists of a vertical rectangular form rising from a small base. The column is painted in two vertical sections, half red, half maroon, in a composition very like Newman's symmetrical pictures in a color combination favored by Newman from 1949 to the early 1950's, and in a vertical configuration directly related with Newman's extremely narrow and tall series of Untitled canvases (Numbers 1 through 5) of 1950.

Like her Abstract Expressionist precursors, Truitt is an artist who finds her preferred form and proceeds consistently to find possible variations within her chosen limitations. Hers is a transposition out of painterly precedents into the more three dimensional realm. All traces of process are obliterated in her sleek, unabashedly lovely columns, sometimes leaning against the wall, mostly standing straight and tall with an aura of silent stateliness which invokes memories of the continuities and subtle changes which unfold through time and space. Truitt uses her skills as a subtly strong colorist to create a tense ambiguity between the planar and the three dimensional. In various combinations from one work to the next, vertical bands of color divide the surfaces, wrap around the corners and coexist with horizontal bands on the tops of the columns and on the thin bases. Harmonizing pastels or contrasting hues work with her diverse compositional formats to create a space which is simultaneously continuous and changing. A tense balance between gravity and weightlessness is amplified by the use of horizontal bands of color on the narrow, recessed bases. Titles, usually given when the work is nearly or totally completed, often refer to persons, places and events from Truitt's experience, reiterating her intentions for conveying associative meanings.

Truitt's sculptures are neither heroic nor monumental in scale or attitude. She developed her vocabulary alone, unusually separate from most of her contemporaries, and it is this sense of mysterious aloofness which animates her basically unitary and reductive forms. She has created a sincere and personally felt body of work which is firmly rooted in a long established line of modernist abstraction that was nearing its end by the 1950's.

—Barbara Cavaliere

TSOCLIS, Costas.

Greek. Born in Athens, 24 May 1930. Studied at the School of Fine Arts, Athens, 1948–54; University of Rome, 1957–60. Served in the Greek Army, 1954–56. Married Helen Caplanidou in 1975; daughter: Maya. Painter, Athens, 1954–57; painter and sculptor, Paris, 1960–70; in West Berlin, 1971–72; in Athens and Paris, since 1973. Recipient: Greek State Scholarship to Rome, 1957; D.A.A.D. Fellowship to West Berlin, 1971. Agent: Zomboulakis Gallery, Kriezotu 7, Athens. Address: Axiou 15, 13671 Aharnes, Greece.

Individual Exhibitions:

1965 Hilton Gallery, Athens
1969 Galerie Richard Foncke, Ghent
Galerie Michael Werner, Cologne
1970 Galerie Sonnabend, Paris
Studio Santandrea, Milan
Galerie Richard Foncke, Ghent
Galerie Defacqz, Brussels
1971 Palais des Beaux Arts, Brussels
Goethe Institut, Athens
Galerie Springer, West Berlin
Galerie Lichter, Frankfurt
Galerie Reckermann, Cologne
1972 Galerie Richard Foncke, Ghent
Ehemalige Galerie des 20 Jahrhunderts, West Berlin
Kunsthalle, Dusseldorf
1973 Galerie Iolas-Zouboulakis, Athens
Galerie Alexandre Iolas, Paris
1974 Galerie Marzona, Bielefeld, West Germany
Galerie Alexandre Iolas, Paris
1976 Studio Santandrea, Milan
Galerie New Smith, Brussels
Galerie Alexandre Iolas, Paris
Galerie Iolas-Zoumboulakis, Athems
1977 Galerie Desmos, Athens
Alexandre Iolas Gallery, New York
Galerie der Spiegel, Cologne
1978 Galerie Miranda, Hydra, Greece
Palais des Beaux-Arts, Brussels
Galerie Nothelfer, West Berlin
Axionsgalerie, West Berlin
1979 Studio Santandrea, Milan
Galerie Desmos, Athens
1980 Sala Communale d'Arte Contemporanea, Alessandria, Italy
Galerie Miranda, Athens
1981 Galerie Z.M., Thessaloniki, Greece
Galerie Oraisma, Athens
1982 Galleria Dossi, Bergamo, Italy
1983 Gallery 3, Athens
Iolas Gallery, New York
Pinacotheque Pierides, Athens
1984 Plaka Intervention, Athens
Macedonian Center of Contemporary Art, Salonika, Greece
1985 Zomboulakis Gallery, Athens
1986 Greek Pavilion, *Biennale,* Venice
1987 Castello di Rodi, Rhodes, Greece

Selected Group Exhibitions:

1963 *Biennale de Paris*
1965 *Bienal,* Sao Paulo
1969 *Avantgarde Grechenland,* Kunstverein, Stuttgart (travelled to the Haus am Lutzowplatz, West Berlin)
1970 *Surrealisme,* Moderna Museet, Stockholm
1972 *Zehn Berlin,* Kunstverein, Stuttgart
1975 *8 Artists/8 Attitudes/8 Greeks,* Institute of Contemporary Arts, London
1977 *Documenta,* Kassel, West Germany
1982 *Europalia Greece,* Palais des Beaux-Arts, Brussels
1987 *Artware,* Kunstmuseum, Hannover (travelled to Dusseldorf)

Collections:

Centre National d'Art Contemporain, Paris; Museum van Hedendaages Kunst, Ghent; Museum of Contemporary Art, Utrecht; Museum Boymans-van Beuningen, Rotterdam; Musée d'Ixelles, Brussels; Museo de Bellas Artes, Caracas; Musée d'Art Contemporain, Brussels; Fattoria di Celle, Pistoia, Italy; Pinacotheque Pierides, Athens; Vorres Museum of Modern Art, Athens.

Costas Tsoclis: *Eleni Tsoclis*, 1986

Publications:

By TSOCLIS: books—*Rue des Ecouffes*, portfolio of 8 lithos, with text by D. Analis, Paris 1973; *Anamnissis 1971–73*, portfolio of 30 lithos, Paris 1974; *Arbre, Tree, Albero, Aentpo*, book-object, Milan 1980; *Arbre*, portfolio of 8 lithos, with texts by José Pierre, C. Cafopoulos, J. P. Van Teighem and others, Paris 1982.

On TSOCLIS: books—*Art of our Time* by D. Fatouros, London and Cologne 1966; *Costas Tsoclis*, exhibition catalogue, with texts by José Pierre, Paris 1970; *Costas Tsoclis*, exhibition catalogue, with texts by Karl Geirlandt and Jean Dypreau, Brussels 1971; *Costas Tsoclis*, exhibition catalogue, with text by G. Vlachos, Ghent 1972; *Costas Tsoclis*, exhibition catalogue, with texts by Karl Ruhrberg and Peter Nestler, West Berlin 1972; *Tsoclis*, with texts by Jean Dypreau, Karl Geirlandt, José Pierre, Tony Spiteris and others, Athens 1975; *Costas Tsoclis*, exhibition catalogue, with text by M. Mauzommatis, Alessandria, Italy 1980; *An Aspect of Postwar Art in Greece* by E. Vakalo, Athens 1981; *Artware, Kunst und Electronic*, with text by N. Missirlis, Dusseldorf, Vienna and New York 1987.

As an artist, I have never selected my means of expression—no more than, as a child, I have ever devised my playthings—outside a range of "situations-objects" to which I was linked by a bond of love or necessity.

An offspring of the capital, not expecting or caring to discover my roots, I fed on facts, not myths, on things whose prior stages I was not aware of. The myths—I made them up myself from such things and facts.

It took me a long time to see the Acropolis as a vestige of a period gone for ever and not as a set of abstract and unserviceable structures, playing nevertheless a determining role in the aesthetic character of the city, and therefore in the psychology of its inhabitants.

The basements of the small houses that used to shelter my family, I considered, with no bitterness whatever, as my home, in no way inferior to the big houses, those of the rich, which I merely looked upon as the big houses of "my" neighbourhood.

Then, I was not yet trying to find out the how, or the why.

My first works recognizable as such are "objects-fragments" of that environment, both forced upon me and taken for granted, reconstructed, however, so that they should remain faithful to their inner truth, and bear the indelible mark of my own vision.

(Now, after looking for and finding that literary definition of my quest during that long period of my life, I rejoice and consider I have not worked in a barren field.)

Yet, in order to reconstruct my objects, I had to handle patiently the materials with which such objects were made. Gradually, I became familiar with a new world, the world of virgin matter and with it I began to develop bonds, memories and even secret correspondences. Thus, for a few years, the new object of my work had become the very matter of my former objects. A long series of works scattered here and there, whose theme-object is merely wood, paper, steel, colour, water, cement, testify to that boundless love for matter which has certainly not palled so far.

Now, if "love" means endeavouring to probe into the truth of the beloved object, possess oneself of its charms, finally identify oneself with it for mutual pleasure and fulfilment, then that is what I did.

And if "art" means offering a new way, a new transitory and, no doubt, incomplete code to organize, conceive and interpret facts and environments so as to attain new emotions and balances, then that is what I felt.

One day, a small revelation became the new guide of my sensibility. A tree whose fitful and phantasmal image had been imparting a touch of beauty to my life was broken by the wind and revealed to me its concrete and enduring truth: the wood, so long hidden under its transient image; and I took a fancy to that glorious wound, and I perceived an inverted continuity between the object, matter and nature and in my recent work I have endeavoured to fuse into one artistic fact the image, the source of that image and the use of that source.

As if one painted the portrait of a man not with colour but with human flesh.

—Costas Tsoclis

TUCKER, Albert.

Australian. Born in Melbourne, Victoria, 29 December 1914. Self-taught in art. Served in the Australian Army, 1942. Married Barbara Anne Bilcock in 1964. Painter: influential, with Sidney Nolan, in forging an Australian modernism; produced "Images of Modern Evil" series, 1943–47, before self-inflicted exile from Australia; lived in London, where he produced a "Thames Waterfront" series, 1947–48; travelled to Paris, with critic Lawrence Alloway, and became fascinated by the work of Jean Dubuffet, then yet unknown, in early 1948; returned shortly thereafter to Paris to live, met Alberto Giacometti and Rufino Tamayo, and made frequent trips to London, Germany, Holland, Belgium, and Italy: influenced by the work of Max Beckmann, Otto Dix, Dubuffet, and the German modernists; moved to Neu Isenburg, near Frankfurt, West Germany, 1951; returned to Paris, 1952, then travelled south, to Noli, Italy, where he lived until mid-1953; lived in Rome and Grottaferrata, 1953–56: met, and was influenced by, Alberto Burri, de Chirico, Capogrossi, and Campigli; also renewed contact with Australian compatriot Sidney Nolan, who initiated his return to interest in Australian subjects; worked on "Pan in Armour" series to parody Nolan's "Kelly" series, 1955–59; returned to London, where he met Eduardo Paolozzi and Richard Smith, 1956–57; lived in New York, where he met abstract painters of the New York School, 1958–60; his work began to receive recognition in Australia, and he returned to his native country after a 13 year absence, 1960. Recipient: Kurt Geiger Award, Australian Museum of Art, 1960; Order of Australia, 1984. Agent: Tolarno Galleries, 98 River Street, South Yarra, Victoria 3141. Address: 55 Blessington Street, St. Kilda, Victoria 3182, Australia.

Individual Exhibitions:

1951 Kunstzaal van Lier, Amsterdam
1952 Galerie Huit, Paris
1953 Galleria ai Quattro Venti, Rome
1954 Associazione della Estampa Estera, Rome (with Sidney Nolan)
1957 Imperial Institute, London
1960 Waddington Galleries, London
Hirschl and Adler Galleries, New York
1961 Australian Museum of Modern Art, Melbourne (toured the capitals of Australia, 1961–62)
1969 Poindexter Gallery, New York
Instituto Nacional de Bellas Artes, Mexico City
Galeria de Antonia Souza, Mexico City
1971 Australian National Gallery, Canberra (Australian Government travelling exhibition; toured Japan, Phillipines, Korea and Formosa)
1982 *Paintings 1945–60*, Tolarno Galleries, South Yarra, Victoria
Night Images (Images of Modern Evil) 1943–1947, Sweeney Reed Galleries, Fitzroy, Victoria
1985 *Faces I Have Met*, Tolarno Galleries, Melbourne

Selected Group Exhibitions:

1956 *Biennale*, Venice
1959 *Transferences in Art*, Smithsonian Institution, Washington, D.C. (toured the United States)
Experiences in Art, Hirschl and Adler Galleries, New York
Recent Acquisitions, Museum of Modern Art, New York
1963 *Bienal*, Sao Paulo
1964 *Australian Painting Today*, toured Europe

Collections:

Australian National Gallery, Canberra; Australian Museum of Modern Art, Melbourne; Dunedin Art Gallery, New Zealand; Museum of Modern Art, New York; Guggenheim Museum, New York; Instituto Nacional de Bellas Artes, Mexico City.

Publications:

By TUCKER: book designed and compiled—*Albert Tucker: Paintings 1945–1960*, exhibition catalogue, with William Mora, with an introduction by Richard Haese, South Yarra, Victoria 1982.

On TUCKER: books—*Albert Tucker* by Christopher Uhl, 1969; *Modern Painters 1931–1970* by James Gleeson, Melbourne 1971; *Albert Tucker* by James Mollison and Nicholas Bonham, 1982; *Albert Tucker: Night Images (Images of Modern Evil) 1943–1947*, exhibition catalogue, with text by John Henshaw, Fitzroy, Victoria 1982.

Australia during World War II felt peculiarly isolated from its cultural sources in Europe, yet it was a time which saw a most extraordinary collective achievement by certain painters working in Melbourne. Extreme individualists, Albert Tucker, Sidney Nolan and Arthur Boyd nevertheless shared both a humanist attitude and stylistic sources in Surrealism and Expressionism.

Tucker in 1950 wrote: " . . . for me the drama and tragedy of life—my feeling is quite Websterian—this 'shadow or deep pit of darkness where mankind lives.' To sing of death or disaster does not make for popularity, I'm afraid. But it's my song and I've got to sing it."

His art is the hardest from that time. It received no public praise. Its haptic forms have primitive, rock-like firmness; and after Alberto Burri introduced him to the polyvinyl acetate medium in 1954, Tucker's paintings quickly acquired a hard flinty surface, often in considerable relief. Tucker's is also an art of clear intelligence and hard statements.

As a young man on the edge of poverty in the 1930's economic depression, from a family struggling to maintain middle-class values, he had good reason to feel oppressed and humiliated by society in general. As a radical artist he soon felt oppressed by the required subservience to a common political cause. Most of all as an army conscript in 1942 he was oppressed by military authority. However, work amongst the mad and the maimed in a military hospital, drawing illustrations of wounds for plastic surgery, was an experience which supplied images to energize his art for years to come—the gaping holes below a sliced-off nose, limbless torsoes, blood-stained mouths. The following year, 1943, his extensive series of "Images of Modern Evil" began.

Apparently an indictment of social decay caused by soldiers and their mostly amateur prostitutes in wartime Melbourne, the paintings show momentarily spotlit lumps of pale naked flesh, attached to red crescent mouths, floating in the night darkness of streets and cinemas. But the vulnerability and the uninhibited freedom implied by these fleshly images might also be presented for envious admiration by a conventionally constrained society. By the way of contrast, a series of portraits, "Faces 1946," at first sight straightforward sympathetic likenesses become on second sight hauntingly ravaged souls.

Tucker left Australia in 1947 for thirteen years of expatriation in Paris, Frankfurt, Rome, New York and London. Picasso, Beckmann and Dubuffet (a new discovery in 1948) were the modern masters who most enthralled him; the exposure to old masters produced biblical subjects, Job, Judas, Lazarus. Night in the European cities was presented less hysterically than in Melbourne.

Albert Tucker: *Luna Park*, 1980

Paradoxically but not surprisingly, Tucker became an Australian artist in Rome, in 1955. Direct confrontation with Europe always makes those from transplanted European cultures intensely aware of their own non-European character. Tucker began to paint explorers and bandits from Australian history, their features ambiguously treated as Australian desert landscape, and both the figures and landscapes treated with scars, boils and wounds.

Such themes still continue in his art. They can be interpreted as an attempt to equip the Australian landscape with mythology-figures and as a comment on European disruption of the well-balanced Aboriginal ecology. But they are primarily an expression of Tucker's personal relish for flouted authority, for large-scale failures and for marks of retribution. Tragedy is a relatively uncommon mode in contemporary painting, and Tucker is one of its few masters.

—Daniel Thomas

TUCKER, William.

British. Born, of English parents, in Cairo, Egypt, in 1935. Studied history at Oxford University, 1955–58; studied sculpture at the Central School of Art and Design and St. Martin's School of Art, London, 1959–60. Worked at the Victoria and Albert Museum, London, 1961. Sculptor, working in steel, fibreglass, plastics and wood, London, since 1962. Instructor, Goldsmith's College and St. Martin's School of Art, London, 1961–62; University of Western Ontario, London, 1976; and Columbia University and New York School of Painting and Sculpture, New York, 1978. Recipient: Sainsbury Scholarship, London, 1961; Peter Stuyvesant Foundation Travel Bursary, London, 1965; Gregory Fellowship in Sculpture, University of Leeds, 1968–70; Guggenheim Fellowship, 1980. Agent: Waddington Galleries, 2 Cork Street, London W1X 1PA. Address: 102 Greencroft Gardens, London NW6, England.

Individual Exhibitions:

1962 Grabowski Gallery, London (with Michael Kidner)
1963 Rowan Gallery, London
1965 Richard Feigen Gallery, New York
1966 Rowan Gallery, London
1967 Kasmin Gallery, London
1968 Elkon Gallery, New York
1969 Leslie Waddington Prints, London
Kasmin Gallery, London
City Art Gallery, Leeds
1970 Kasmin Gallery, London
1972 British Pavilion, at the *Biennale*, Venice
1973 Kunstverein, Hamburg
Kunstmuseum, Bochum, West Germany
Galerie Müller-Wintersberger, Cologne
Serpentine Gallery, London
Waddington Galleries II, London
1974 *Drawings*, Hester van Royen Gallery, London
1976 Galerie Wintersberger, Cologne
1977 Elkon Gallery, New York
Kasmin Gallery, London
1978 Fruit Market Gallery, Edinburgh
Sable-Castelli Gallery, Toronto
1979 Elkon Gallery, New York
1980 David Reid Gallery, Sydney
Powell Street Gallery, Melbourne
Elkon Gallery, New York
1981 Galleria L'Isola, Rome
1982 Bernard Jacobson Gallery, Los Angeles
Sculpture and Drawings, Elkon Gallery, New York
1984 David McKee Gallery, New York
Galleria L'Isola, Rome
1985 Pamela Auchincloss Gallery, Santa Barbara, California
David McKee Gallery, New York
Neuberger Museum, Purchase, New York
1987 Pamela Auchincloss Gallery, Santa Barbara, California
Tate Gallery, London
David McKee Gallery, New York
Annely Juda Fine Art, London
Padiglione d'Arte Contemporanea, Milan
Galleria L'Isola, Rome

Selected Group Exhibitions:

1961 *Biennale*, Paris
1965 *London: The New Scene*, Walker Art Center, Minneapolis
1966 *Primary Structures*, Museum of Modern Art, New York
1968 *Documenta*, Kassel, West Germany

1970 *Contemporary British Painting and Sculpture*, National Museum of Modern Art, Tokyo
1975 *The Condition of Sculpture*, Hayward Gallery, London
1979 *Contemporary Sculpture*, Museum of Modern Art, New York
1981 *Il Luogo della Forma*, Museo di Castelvecchio, Verona
1983 *Monumental Drawings by Sculptors*, Long Island University, New York
1985 *Working in Brooklyn: Sculpture*, Brooklyn Museum, New York

Collections:

Arts Council of Great Britain, London: British Council, London; Tate Gallery, London; Victoria and Albert Museum, London; Rijksmuseum Kroller-Muller, Otterlo, Netherlands; Louisiana Museum, Humlebaek, Denmark; Museum of Modern Art, New York; Guggenheim Museum, New York; Walker Art Center, Minneapolis.

Publications:

By TUCKER: book—*The Language of Sculpture*, London 1974; articles—"Reflections on Sculpture" in *Tim Scott*, exhibition catalogue, London 1967; "Moore at the Tate" in *Studio International* (London), October 1968; "Anthony Caro's Work: A Symposium," with others, in *Studio International* (London), January 1969; "An Essay on Sculpture" in *Studio International* (London), January 1969; "Sidney Nolan and William Tucker Discuss Their Recent Work" in *Studio International* (London), June 1969; "The Sculptures of Matisse" in *Studio International* (London), July 1969; "4 Sculptors: Brancusi, Picasso, Matisse, David Smith" in *Studio International* (London), April, May and September 1970 and January 1971; "Notes on Sculpture, Public Sculpture and Patronage" in *Studio International* (London), January 1972; "Sculpture and Architecture: An Introduction to My Recent Work" in *Studio International* (London), June 1972; "What Sculpture Is" in *Studio International* (London), December 1974 and March/April 1975; statement in *William Tucker: Horses*, exhibition catalogue, Rome 1987.

On TUCKER: books—*William Tucker: Sculpture*, exhibition catalogue, with text by Christopher Salveson, London 1963; *36th Biennale di Venezia: British Pavilion: William Tucker*, exhibition catalogue, with text by Andrew Forge, London 1972; *William Tucker: Sculpture 1970–73*, exhibition catalogue, with text by Andrew Forge, London 1973; *William Tucker: Drawings*, exhibition catalogue, with text by Barry Martin, London 1974; *William Tucker*, exhibition catalogue, Rome 1981; *William Tucker: Sculpture and Drawings*, exhibition catalogue, with text by Andrew Forge, New York 1982; *William Tucker—Gods" Five Recent Sculptures*, exhibition ctalogue with text by Dore Ashton, London 1986.

In that group of sculptors who emerged from St. Martin's School of Art in London in the mid-60's, a group which included Phillip King, Isaac Witkin and Tim Scott, William Tucker was noted for the strongly theoretical nature of his approach to sculpture. A concern with certain qualities which he considered fundamental to sculpture—its objecthood, its literalness—has consequently informed all his works. In sculptures like "Meru I & II" he explored some of the variety of ways in which an object may be apprehended: how presence is conveyed, together with weight, mass, volume, stability and so on. Though occasionally he used unconventional materials, like resins, Tucker's aims were not iconoclastic: on the contrary, he sought to re-examine many of the crucial questions that sculptors have always faced. The rigor of his approach, however, meant that his works generally lacked the witty or playful aura found in the sculpture of many of his contemporaries.

In the late 60's Tucker turned to more attenuated forms, more nakedly structural and expressive in character, as found in the "Beulahs" and "Cat's Cradles." Still human in scale and still related to the activity of the body, these works were strictly abstract in character although individual components often had architectural associations. As Tucker explained: "the 'architectural' experience of the sculpture, that is the way in which it could be experienced with the spectator's whole body by analogy with his experience of traversing and using space, replaced the specifically 'tactile,' the experience, real or imagined, of the spectator's hands in previous sculpture."

In the 70's an increased scale, together with a greater emphasis on the mass and texture of materials, made works like "Tunnel" not only more monumental but also more architectonic than hitherto. At the same time, or perhaps as a result, they took on connotations which formerly would have been eschewed. Although not totemic objects, they are more than just structures in space, they have a new resonance or "character."

In his recent large charcoal drawings these concerns are paralleled in handsome fashion. These are not sculptor's drawings in the usual sense, for they do not simply depict a solid object in three-dimensional space; Tucker always carefully aligns the image to the format and to the surface in which it lies. Once again, that rigorous questioning which informs all his activity is apparent.

—Lynne Cooke

TURCATO, Giulio.

Italian. Born in Mantua, 16 March 1912. Studied at the Scuola d'Arte dei Carmine, Venice, 1928–31, Liceo Artistico, Venice, 1932–33, and Scuola Libera del Nudo, Venice, 1933–35. Served in the Italian Army, in Sicily, 1935–36. Married Vana Caruso in 1964. Assistant draughtsman to the architect Muzio, Milan, 1937–39. Painter and graphic artist in Milan, 1939–42, and in Rome, since 1943: Member, Corrente Group of artists, Milan, 1939; Founder Member, International Independent Artists Art Club, Rome, 1945, and, with Consagra, San Filippo, Dorazio, Guerrini and Perilli, Gruppo Arte Sociale, Rome, 1946; Co-Editor, *Forma 1* formalist art manifesto, Rome, 1947; Member, Nuovo Fronte delle Arti, Rome, 1949, Gruppo degli Otto, Rome, 1950, and, with Novelli, Perilli, Dorazio, Consagra, and Gio and Arnaldo Pomodoro, Gruppo Continuità, Rome, 1960–62. Instructor in Drawing and Design, Vocational School, Portogruaro, Italy, 1942–43. Professor, Liceo Artistico, Rome, 1953–82. Recipient: National Prize, *Biennale*, Venice, 1958; Fiorino Prize, Florence, 1962; Esso Prize, Rome, 1962; Painting Prize, *Review of Figurative Art*, Rome, 1963; Painting Prize, Termoli, 1963; First prize, *Quadriennale*, Rome, 1966; San Sofia prize, 1971; Painting Prize, Volleverede, 1972. Address: via del Pozzetto 117, 00187 Rome, Italy.

Individual Exhibitions:

1949 Galleria La Giostra, Asti, Italy
1950 Galleria del Secolo, Rome
1951 Galleria del Naviglio, Milan
1952 Galleria La Cassapanca, Rome
1953 Galleria del Naviglio, Milan
1955 Galleria La Tartaruga, Rome
Galleria del Grattacielo, Milan
1956 Galleria L'Indiano, Florence
Galleria del Grattacielo, Milan
1957 Galleria La Tartaruga, Rome
1960 Galleria del Grattacielo, Milan
1961 New Vision Centre, London
Galleria Il Canale, Venice
1962 Galerie Burdeke, Zurich
Galleria La Tartaruga, Rome
1963 Galleria Il Quadrante, Florence
1964 Galleria La Scaletta, Catania, Italy
Galleria Il Segno, Rome
Galleria La Polena, Genoa
1965 Galleria Marlborough, Rome
Galleria del Naviglio, Milan
Galleria Il Segno, Rome
1967 Galleria Arte Oggi, Pescara, Italy
Galleria Le Muse, Bologna
Galleria L'Indiano, Florence
Galleria Arco d'Alibert, Rome
1968 Galleria del Naviglio, Milan
Galleria Il Punto, Turin
Studio G30, Paris
Galleria Alfieri, Venice
Galleria L'Oca, Rome
Galleria Regis, Cadice Ligure, Italy
Galleria Ferro di Cavallo, Rome
1969 Galerie D I V , Frankfurt
Galleria L'Indiano, Florence
Galleria La Barcaccia, Montecatini, Italy
Galleria Il Capitello, Rome
Studio Santandrea, Milan
1970 Galleria Boni-Schubert, Lugano, Switzerland
Galleria del Foglio, Rome
Galleria Il Segno, Turin
Galleria La Sfera, Milan
Galleria Giovio, Lake Como, Italy
Galleria Schubert, Milan
Grafica Romero, Rome
1971 Galleria Il Segnapassi, Pesaro, Italy
Galleria La Cornice, Latina, Italy
Galleria Il Nettuno, Bologna
Galleria Barozzi, Venice
Studio Barozzi, Milan
Galleria La Bussola, Cosenza, Italy
Galleria Sinibaldi, Cagliari, Italy
Galleria Martano Due, Turin
Studio Santandrea, Milan
Galleria La Seggiola, Salerno, Italy
Galleria Duomo, Piacenza, Italy
1972 Galleria La Gradiva, Florence
Galleria Il Salotto, Como, Italy
Studio Cortina, Pescara, Italy
Galleria Editalia, Rome
Galleria Il Pozzo, Citt;a di Castello, Italy
Galleria Il Segno, Rome
Galleria Il Capricorno, Venice
Galleria Piero della Francesca, Arezzo, Italy
Square Gallery, Milan
Galleria La Sirenella, Sorrento, Italy
Galleria Nuovo Carpine, Porto Cervo, Italy
Studio d'Arte Hermes, Rome
Galleria Rotta, Milan
1973 Galleria Il Giorno, Milan
Grafica Romero, Rome
Palazzo Ancaini, Spoleto, Italy (retrospective)
1974 Galleria Editalia, Rome
Galleria i Diamante, Pescara, Italy
Palazzo delle Prigioni Vecchie, Venice
Galleria Ravagnan, Venice
Palazzo delle Esposizione, Rome (retrospective)
1975 Studio Latronica, Todi, Italy
Galleria Nuovo Saggitario, Milan
Galleria Editalia, Rome
Galleria La Gradiva, Florence
1976 Galleria Colasanti, Rome
Galleria Nuove Colonne, Trieste, Italy
1977 Galleria Il Pilastro, Milan
Galleria Lo Spazio, Naples
Galleria Ferretti, Viareggio, Italy
Galleria Pancheri, Rovereto, Italy
Galleria Ravagnan, Venice
Galleria Linea Settanta, Verona
Galleria Borghese 31, Rome
Istituto Italiano di Cultura, Cairo
1978 Istituto Italiano di Cultura, New York
Westend Galerie, Frankfurt
1979 Galleria Numerosette, Naples
Museum of Modern Art, Bucharest
Galleria del Falconiere, Ancona, Italy
1980 Agenzia d'Arte Moderna, Rome
Musee de l'Athenee, Geneva
Galleria del Milione, Milan
1981 Galleria Mazzoli, Modena, Italy
Galleria Cesarea, Genoa
Galleria Planetario, Trieste, Italy
Castello di San Giusto, Trieste, Italy
Auditorium San Lorenzo, Cento, Italy
Studio Solige C.V. 79, Rome
1982 Pinacoteca, Ravenna, Italy

Galleria De Amicis, Florence
Galleria De Crescenzo, Rome
Galleria Linea 70, Verona
Iterarte Circolo Artistico, Bologna
Galleria Pantha Arte, Como, Italy
Galleria Il Luogo, Rome
Galleria Adriano Villata, Cerrina Monferrato, Italy
1983 Galleria Nazionale d'Arte Moderna, Rome
1984 Padiglione d'Arte Contemporanea, Milan
1985 Staatsgalerie Moderner Kunst, Munich
Kunstverein, Frankfurt
1986 Galleria Nazionale d'Arte Moderna, Rome

Selected Group Exhibitions:

1945 *Associazione Artistica Internazionale Indipendente "Art Club",* Galleria San Marco, Rome
1948 *Biennale,* Venice (and 1950, 1952)
1957 *Painting in Postwar Italy,* Columbia University, New York
1959 *Documenta,* Kassel, West Germany
1963 *6 Italienska Malare,* Moderna Museet, Stockholm
1968 *Arte Italiana dal Futurismo ad Oggi,* Galleria Nazionale d'Arte Moderna, Rome
1971 *New Italian Art 1953–71,* Walker Art Gallery, Liverpool
1973 *Bienal,* Sao Paulo
1980 *Arte Astratta Italiana 1909–59,* Galleria Nazionale d'Arte Moderna, Rome
1982 *L'Immagine del Socialismo,* Palazzo delle Esposizioni, Rome

Collections:

Galleria Nazionale d'Arte Moderna, Rome; Musée d'Art Moderne de la Ville, Paris; Kunsthalle, Lund, Sweden; Konsthall, Gothenberg, Sweden; Museum of Modern Art, New York; Brooklyn Museum, New York; Museu de Arte Moderna, Sao Paulo; Galleria Civica d'Arte Moderna, Turin; Bayerische Staatsgemaldesammlungen, Munich.

Publications:

By TURCATO: articles—"Crisi della Pittura" in *Forma 1* (Rome), March 1947; "Tre Biscotti" in *Pittori che Scrivono,* Milan 1954; "Tempi di Riscatto" in *Realismo* (Milan), March 1955; "Pensiero sul Disegno" in *Civiltà delle Machine,* Rome 1956; "Declaration" in *Pittura Italiana del Dopoguerra,* edited by T. Sauvage, Milan 1957; "Le Correnti dell'Astrattismo" in *Il Punto* (Rome), April 1957; "Conformismo: Pigrizia Intellettuale" in *Arte Oggi,* Rome 1959; "Considerazione" in *Alfabeto* (Rome), February 1963; "Un Pelo dal Naso" in *Carte Segrete* (Rome), no. 3. 1967; interview, with Gerardo de Simone, in *Turcato,* exhibition catalogue, Naples 1981.

On TURCATO: books—*Giulio Turcato,* exhibition catalogue, with an introduction by Palma Bucarelli, Rome 1950; *Otto Pittori Italiani* by Luca Venturi, Rome 1952; *Dictionnaire de la Peinture Abstraite* by Michel Seuphor, Paris 1957; *Arte e Artisti d'Avanguardia in Italia 1910–1950* by Giuseppe Marchiori, Milan 1960; *Ultime Tendenze nell' Arte d'Oggi* by Gillo Doriles, Milan 1961; *Giulio Turcato,* exhibition catalogue, with an introduction by Giulio Carlo Argan, London 1961; *Turcato,* exhibition catalogue, with text by Carla Lonzi, Rome 1965; *Turcato* by Mercuri, Rome 1968; *L'Arte del XX. Secolo* by H.L. Jaffe, Florence 1970; *Turcato* by Giorgio de Marchis, Milan 1971; *New Italian Art 1953–1971,* exhibition catalogue, with text by Giovanni Carandente, Liverpool 1971; *Giulio Turcato* by Giovanna dalla Chiesa and Italo Mussa, Rome 1974; *Turcato,* exhibition catalogue, with text by Giovanni Caradente, Naples 1981; *Turcato* by Flaminio Gualdoni, Ravenna 1982; *Giulio Turcato,* exhibition catalogue with texts by Thomas Messer, Carlo Proietti and others, Rome 1986.

Giulio Turcato: *Florescenza Nucleare,* 1982

Although my works for the last 30 years can be seen as unified within the same basic aesthetical principles, their contents have differed depending upon the ideas and poetic allusions I've sought to convey. My paintings quickly developed from geometric abstractions to a more personal and dynamic form, pictorically closer to the original futurist breakthroughs of Boccioni and Balla but with contents inspired by the revolutionary enthusiasm that followed Europe's liberation from Fascism. (For example, such works as "Comizi" (Demonstration), 1948; "Rivolta" (Revolt), 1949; "Le Rovine di Varsavia" (The Ruins of Warsaw) 1949; "Fabbrica" (Factory), 1949; "Miniere" (Mines), 1950; "1 Maggio '45, a Mosca" (May 1, 1945 in Moscow), 1950.

Then, in the early 50's, I began a series of paintings whose primary concern was pure line and color—"Composizione;" "Reticolo" (Net); "La-

birinto" (Labyrinth); and a series inspired by ecological concerns—"Il Giardino de Miciurin", (The Garden of Miciurin), 1952; "Paesaggio Cosmico" (Cosmic Landscape), 1953. These concerns for pure line, color and form have remained and can be seen continuing in a series of works entitled, "Mosche Cinese" (Chinese Flies), 1957; "Arcipelago" (Archipelago), 1958; "Subacqueo", (Underwater), 1961; "Floreale" (Floral), 1961.

Two important works, "Il Deserto dei Tartari" and "Desertico" were painted after a trip in 1956 to China by plane across the vast continent of Russia and Central Asia. At about the same time I began with "Le Cavallette" (Grasshoppers) a more informal technique using colored sand surfaces that visually changed as the viewer moved his physical point of view, works such as "La Bava" (Drivel), 1960; "Astronomical", 1959; "Via Lattea" (Milky Way) 1959; "Itinerari" (Traces), 1960. Later, I would pursue this theme by using fine powdered glass that glistens or disappears depending upon the viewer's own movement in front of the painting.

Continuing this search beyond the normal confines of oil on canvas, I began in the early 60's a series of collages on surfaces of sand and asphalt using the dollar, the lire and a carbon paper whose trade-mark was the image of the Acropolis—these images of money and the Acropolis were for me polemic symbols of power. In a related manner, on the same surfaces of sand and asphalt I placed real sedatives and tranquilizers as symbols of contemporary neurosis. These collages were actually only enlargements of a painting I did in 1953 in which I painted in oil the repeated image of the lire (being much too poor to even imagine placing real money on canvas in those days). This painting, "Ricordo di S. Rocco" (Memory of Saint Rocco), shown in the Venice *Biennale* of 1954, was inspired by my seeing the poor immigrants of the village of Pisticci as they attached lire to the religious statue of Saint Rocco.

Breaking completely from canvas, in 1963, I began to work directly on rough pockmarked sheets of foam rubber that gave to me the sense of the surface of the moon, painting them in white, silver, and dark metallic browns and violet-blues with occasional dots of fluorescent and phosphorescent pigment because I believe a painting can change light within itself. Above all, with the use of phosphorescent pigment I was searching to make painting visible in the dark because, for me, it is absurd that one cannot see a painting or a wall in the dark.

Another group of paintings, interesting and for me fundamental, are those entitled "Fuori dello Spettro" (Outside of the Spectrum) since they were made to isolate colors scientifically considered not within the classified color spectrum: maroon and amaranth. I made many experiments (anticipated by a painting of the same title in 1963), and then in 1972 I showed seven paintings based purely on the color spectrum. From a quick glance around the room there remained a fleeting visual impression of maroon and amaranth. From this experiment were born other paints of monochromatic surfaces, each of a different color; each an evidence of the strength within a restraint of using only a single color on canvas.

From a desire to change the square dimensions of painting, I at first painted circular forms, later truncated triangles, until in the early 70's I created shapes in canvas and then in wood entitled "Oceanica" for their similarity to the primitive oval forms of the island civilizations of the Pacific or perhaps to the surf boards originally used by the Maori. I wanted to structuralize existing forms since I don't believe much in sculpture in its classical sense. From this came also the works entitled, "Libreria Incatenata" (Chained Library), tall wooden structures, tied in their final narrowing height by iron ropes, and painted in vivid fluorescent colors with some sections of phosphorescent pigment that can be seen in the dark. These and other objects such as the "Sarcofaghi" were intentionally painted with transparent material that gives off an illumination from inside as if by neon signs. They are the continuation of my interest in collage, but within space; adaptable to any space available—in a small space there can be one, in museum spaces I've shown 10 or 15; they can hang from the ceiling or lean on a wall or block a corridor. By being independent of any particular space, their presence underlines the very existence of free space and the artist's fundamental act of changing a previously defined ambience.

—Giulio Turcato

Everyone knows that Giulio Turcato is a born painter who lives to paint, and since early youth has done nothing else but paint. Around 1942–43 he taught drawing and design in a vocational school at Portogruaro, and from 1953 has taught figure drawing in the Liceo of Fine Arts in Rome. On the other hand, he has always found someone to buy one of his paintings. Like this, he lives. His official position and fame are much below his value because he is timid and indifferent to any public recognition, and in spite of having some difficult moments he is content in his bohemian life, the only one he considers worthy of an artist, because more than free it is anarchic. But the anarchy of Turcato is extemely gentle. It has a Venetian mood, wouldn't hurt a fly and is so disinterested that it becomes itself a work of art. If one adds that he is capable of intense work, but is desultory sometimes for great intervals, we can understand how he owes to himself the limits of his fame and of the value given to some of the great periods of his work. The last few years have been a recovery and ones of intense and happy activity. It's just the moment to speak of him.

An essential quality of Turcato, which is acknowledged by his colleagues, is his sense of the limits and an absolute lack of rhetoric. When Turcato dedicated himself to pure abstractionism, he didn't fall into it as an experiment or a joke or just for the spontaneous engagement of his painting. It never came into his mind to place a line or colour to show his ability, but only to express a feeling or to indicate an idea or to make poetic allusion. Turcato's strength often consists in his refusal to "do the painting" so that he can express a moment of his fantastic vision. Therefore, his paintings appear, and often seem to be, unfinished in spite of their authentic artistic worth. But few artists today, as in the past, are able to escape a bias to finish.

I think I have indicated here many reasons why Turcato's fame is below his value: shyness, indifference to public acknowledgement, a bohemian life, intermittent work, a sense of bounds, delicateness, and also a tenuous inspiration. He considers his art as being completely abstract. He distinguishes three types of abstraction: the American, represented by Pollock, the French and the European trend, in which he prefers Hartung. Poliakoff is too romantic for him. Matta is too surrealistic, and Manessier too tied up with impressionism. Among Italian painters he feels sympathy for Corpora, Vedova and Afro, and the young Dova and Perilli. He does not take an interest in Mondrian's constructivism because to Turcato a painting is a space charged with emotion, without a center,and without the doors of a triptych. He finds that surrealism was useful because it allowed thought to untie itself from literary tradition. What he asks of painting is for it to have an emotion that exceeds the painting, a surrealistic impulse without the need of an unconscious mind, able not to create romantic drama but colour-form. According to him, painting creates a space in eternal movement, free from any theory, that attempts to transform and modify the life of feeling.

In *Forma 1* review (April 1947) he published an article entitled "Crisis of Painting . . . " I would like readers to reflect on the fact that this text was written in 1947, and that it has prophetic value in regard to the following development of Italian painting: "Those who kept a tie with the 19th century style, or wanted to use a realistic style, or gave a small touch of Lombardic feeling to their imitative forms of Picasso, all failed . . . " Already in 1947 Turcato understood the historical condition of painting in Italy and abroad better than many eminent persons who were supposedly more learned than he. To understand the history of painting, you must understand painting. And Turcato is a born painter. Afte a show with the "Fronte Nuovo" at the Venice *Biennale* of 1948, Turcato found himself the foremost target in the condemnation of abstractionism by the Communist Party—and he was a Communist. This obstacle, arising directly in the midst of his natural development, did not leave him unaffected. On the contrary, he tried in various ways to find an accord between his convictions as a man and as an artist: he attempted figuration, symbolism, and even surrealism. But his artistic nature prevailed. Besides, he was enough of an anarchist to disregard superior orders. In facing Cagli and Guttuso, moreover, he defended his freedom with his fists. Not that Turcato refused to deal with social problems in which he believed, like in the works "Meeting," "Revolt" and "Warsaw Ruins," but he represented them in an abstract form, thereby destroying their effectiveness as propaganda in a heretical way. In the meantime, he gained a scholarship in 1950 to stay in Paris and has returned there many times. He also made other travels to Germany and as far from home as China. So, in his own way, he dominates the panorama of international art.

—Luca Venturi

TURNBULL, William.

British. Born in Dundee, Scotland, 11 January 1922. Studied at Slade School of Fine Art, London, 1946–48. Served in Royal Air Force in Canada, India, and Ceylon, 1941–46. Married Kim Lim in 1960; sons; Alexander and Jonathan. Painter and sculptor, in illustration department of D. C. Thompson magazine publishing company, Dundee, 1939–41; moved to Paris, 1948, and to London, 1950. Instructor in experimental design, 1952–61, and in sculpture, 1964–72, Central School of Arts and Crafts, London. Agent: Waddington Galleries, 11 Cork Street, London W1X, 1PD. Address: 40 Camden Square, London NW1 9XA, England.

Individual Exhibitions:

1950 Hanover Gallery, London (with Eduardo Paolozzi and Phillip King)
1952 Hanover Gallery, London
1957 Institute of Contemporary Art, London
1960 *Paintings*, Molton Gallery, London
1961 Molton Gallery, London
1963 Marlborough-Gerson Gallery, New York
Detroit Institute of Arts
1965 Bennington College, Vermont
Galerie Müller, Stuttgart
1966 *Sculpture and Paintings*, Pavilion Gallery, Balboa, California
1967 *Bienal*, Sao Paulo (toured South America)
Waddington Galleries, London
1968 Hayward Gallery, London
Museo de Arte Moderna, Rio de Janeiro
Museo Nacional de Bellas Artes, Buenos Aires
Instituto de Artes Plasticas, Santiago, Chile
1969 Waddington Galleries, London
1970 Waddington Galleries, London
1973 *Sculpture and Paintings*, Tate Gallery, London (retrospective)
1974 Scottish Arts Council Gallery, Edinburgh
Galerie Müller, Stuttgart
1976 Waddington Galleries, London
1978 Waddington Galleries, London
1981 Waddington Galleries, London
1982 Waddington Galleries, New York
Waddington Galleries, Toronto
1983 Galerie Kutter, Luxembourg
1984 National Museum Art Gallery, Singapore
1985 Waddington Galleries, London
1986 Terry Dintenfass Gallery, New York
1987 Galerie Folker Skulima, West Berlin
Waddington Galleries, London
1988 Terry Dintenfass Gallery, New York

Selected Group Exhibitions:

1952 *Biennale*, Venice (and 1957)
1958 *Carnegie International*, Pittsburgh (and 1961)
1960 *Situation*, R.B.A. Galleries, London
1964 *Guggenheim International*, Guggenheim Museum, New York
1966 *New Shapes and Forms of Colour*, Stedelijk Museum, Amsterdam
1968 *Documenta*, Kassel, West Germany
1976 *Arte Inglese Oggi*, Palazzo Reale, Milan
1982 *British Sculpture in the Twentieth Century: II*, Whitechapel Art Gallery, London
1985 *Sculptors' Drawings*, Scottish Arts Council Gallery, Edinburgh (toured Britain)
1987 *British Art in the Twentieth Century*, Royal Academy, London (travelled to Stuttgart)

Collections:

Tate Gallery, London; Victoria and Albert Museum, London; Dundee Art Gallery, Scotland; Scottish National Gallery of Modern Art, Edinburgh; Candiff Museum, Wales; Albright-Knox Art Gallery, Buffalo, New York; Hirshhorn Museum & Sculpture Garden, Smithsonian Institution, Washington D.C.; Städtisches Museum Schloss Morsbroich, Leverkusen, West Germany; Westfälischer Landesmuseum, Münster, West Germany; Teheran Museum of Contemporary Art.

Publications:

By TURNBULL: books illustrated—*Basho: The Records of a Weather Exposed Skeleton* (book/object). London 1969; *The Garden of Caresses*, translated from Arabic by Franz Toussaint, London 1970; *Der Wassermaier* by Helmut Heissenbuttel, Zurich 1976; articles—"White Text on Black Ground," with Theo Crosby, Germano Facetti, and Edward Wright, in *This is Tomorrow*, exhibition catalogue, London 1956; "William Turnbull 1949–60" in *Uppercase* (London), no. 4, 1960; "The Joining Edge" in *Gazette* (London), no. 1, 1961; "Images without Temples" in *Living Arts* (London), no. 1, 1963; "Notes on Sculpture," with others in *Studio International* (London), November 1968; "Colour in Sculpture, with Phillip King, Tim Scott and David Annesley, in *Studio International* (London), January 1969; "Statement on Sculpture," with others, in *Studio International* (London), July/August 1972; film—*83 B*, with Alan Forbes, 1953.

On TURNBULL: books—*William Turnbull*, exhibition catalogue, with text by David Sylvester, London 1950; *Sculpture of the 20th Century* by Andrew C. Ritchie, New York 1952; *William Turnbull*, exhibition catalogue, with text by Lawrence Alloway, London 1957; *The Sculpture of This Century* by Michel Seuphor, New York 1960; *Contemporary Sculpture* by Carola Giedion-Weckler, New York 1960; *Situation*, exhibition catalogue, with introduction by Roger Coleman, London 1960; *William Turnbull: Paintings*, exhibition catalogue, with text by Lawrence Alloway, London 1960; *Modern Sculpture in the Joseph H. Hirshhorn Collection*, exhibition catalogue, with introduction by H. H. Arnason, New York 1962; *A Concise History of Modern Sculpture* by Herbert Read, London 1964; *William Turnbull: Sculpture and Paintings* exhibition catalogue, with introduction by Jules Langsner, Balboa, California 1966; *IX Bienal de Sao Paulo: British Section—William Turnbull*, exhibition catalogue, with text by Alan Bowness. London 1967; *William Turnbull: Sculpture and Painting*, exhibition catalogue, with introduction by Richard Morphet, London 1973; *Turnbull*, exhibition catalogue, with introduction by Robert Kudielka. Stuttgart 1974; *The Potent Image* by Frederick S. Wight, New York 1976; *British Art* by Simon Wilson, London, 1979; *William Turnbull*, exhibition catalogue with introduction by Roger Bevan, London 1987; article—"William Turnbull—Sculptor and Painter" by Bernard Cohen in *Studio International* (London), July/August 1973.

William Turnbull: *Idol No. 5*, 1957

Although British, William Turnbull has more in common with his colleagues on the Continent than with his fellow islanders. For one thing he is equally committed to the major arts of painting and sculpture—activities typical of such continental artists as Picasso and Matisse. For another, his kinship seems closer to a sculptor like Brancusi, a painter like Albers, a draughtsman like Matisse, than to any Briton.

At the same time, his painting as it has evolved, would be hard to imagine without the precedent of the break-through Americans of the post World War II era. Rothko pre-eminently. This is not to suggest that Turnbull is merely a derivative artist—rather that he has been released into his own sensibility through an emotional tie to certain artists' work. In the formal sense, he is one of the most "serious" artists in England, producing works in wood and metal in a minimal vein which have haunting overtones of primitive art as well as an elegance which could be called oriental. His large format paintings have been "about"

fields of color in which the paint surface is handled with wonderful virtuosity being lively and rich instead of merely a flat expanse.

In recent work color-saturated, brush-inflected canvases are bordered by closely related color the hue and value of which sets up a tension between the field and its boundary, both in turn related to the actual stretcher edge. This concern with the edge/field has become a major interest to painters in the later part of our century. The "compositional" material of such paintings is often the character of the paint application itself together with whatever optical contrasts the colors provide. It is one of the extremely pure developments in modernist art and demands from the viewer a high degree of aesthetic response. As it is about the art of painting as such, it is necessary for the viewer to acquaint himself with the elements that comprise art. Except for the fact that its three-dimensionality causes it to exist in "real" space and cast "real" shadows in "real" light, thus giving us information outside of itself, much the same necessity to know its nature can be demanded by minimal sculpture as well.

Such purism can be mis-read by the impatient or lazy. A danger artists like Turnbull risk.

—Ralph Pomeroy

TURRELL, James (Archie).

American. Born in Los Angeles, California, 6 May 1943. Educated at Pasadena High School, California, 1957–61; studied at Pomona College, Claremont, California, 1961–65, B.A. in psychology 1965; University of California at Irvine, 1967; Claremont Graduate School, M.A. in Art 1973. Married Elizabeth Bartlett Elgin in 1965; children: Shana and Jennifer. Independent artist since 1967. Lecturer, University of California at Los Angeles, Summer 1968, and University of California at Riverside, 1971; Visiting Artist, Pomona College, 1971–73; Lecturer, University of California at Irvine, 1974. Recipient: National Endowment for the Arts grant, 1968; Guggenheim Fellowship, 1974; National Endowment for the Arts Matching Grant, 1975. Agent: Blum Helman Gallery, 20 West 57th Street, New York, New York 10019. Address: Box 725, Flagstaff, Arizona 86002, U.S.A.

Individual Exhibitions:

1967 Pasadena Art Museum, California
1976 Stedelijk Museum, Amsterdam
1981 Portland Center for the Visual Arts, Oregon
1982 Center for Contemporary Art, Seattle, Washington
Israel Museum, Jerusalem
1983 ARC/Musée d'Art Moderne de la Ville, Paris
1987 Kunsthalle, Basle

Selected Group Exhibitions:

1969 *Light Spaces,* Main and Hill Studio, Los Angeles
1973 *3D into 2D,* New York Cultural Center
1976 *Light Space,* Arco Center for the Visual Arts, Los Angeles
1980 *Light and Space,* Whitney Museum, New York
1982 *American Exhibition,* Art Institute of Chicago

Collections:

Stedelijk Museum, Amsterdam

Publications:

On TURRELL: books—*James Turrell,* exhibition catalogue with essay by Claude Gintz, Paris 1983; *James Turrell: Mapping Spaces/Kartographie des Raumes,* exhibition catalogue

James Turrell: ***Crater Site Plan with Survey Net,*** **1986** Courtesy Guggenheim Museum, New York

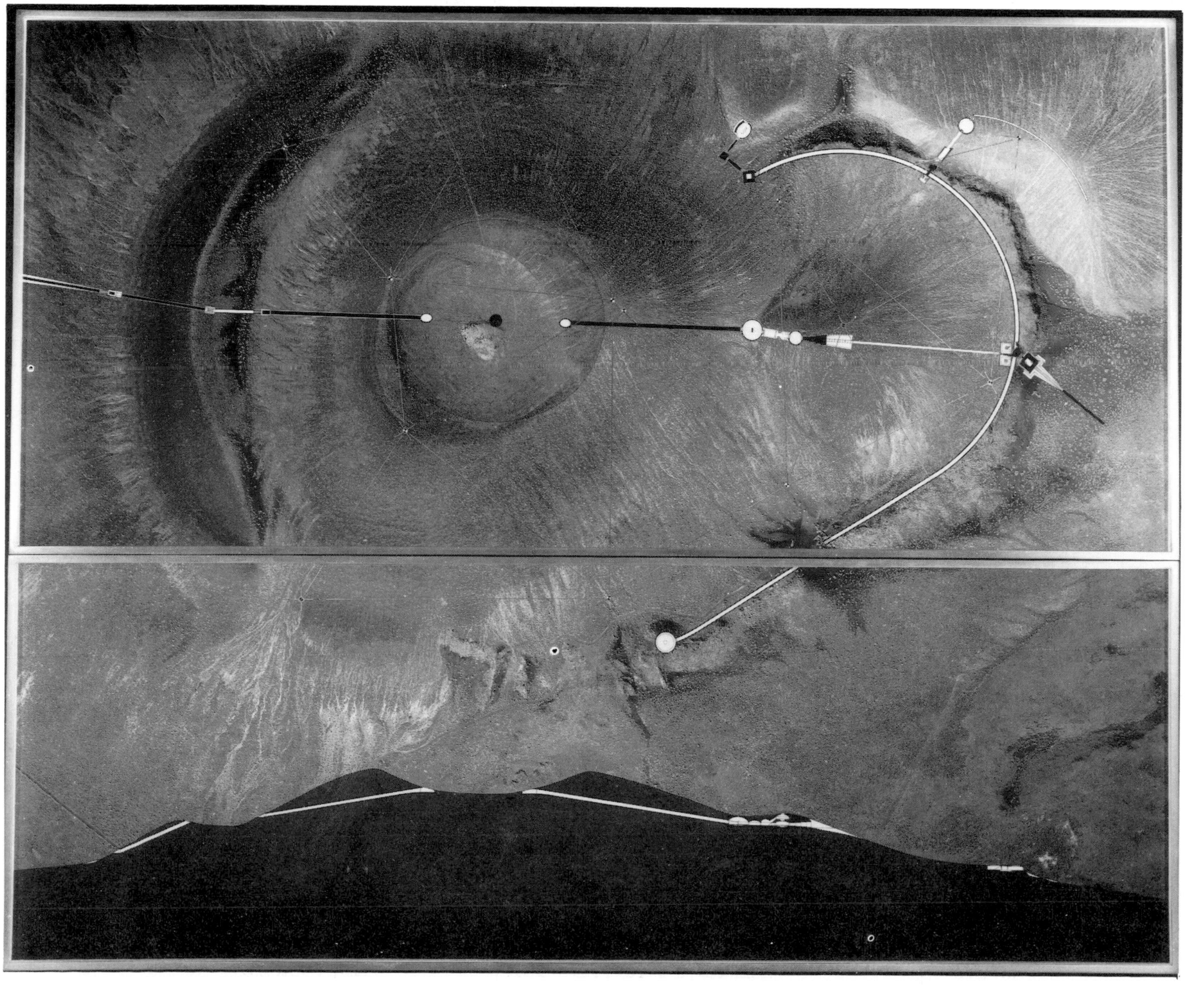

with texts by Craig Adcock, Jean-Christophe Ammann and others, New York and Basle 1987; articles—"James Turrell: Projected Light Images" by John Coplans in *Artforum* (New York), October 1967; "A Gallery Without Walls" by Barbara Rose in *Art in America* (New York), March/April 1968; "New Directions in Southern California Sculpture" in *Arts Magazine* (New York), Summer 1970; "The Talk of the Town—Light" by Calvin Tomkins in the *New Yorker,* 15 December 1980; "Poetry Out of Emptiness" by Robert Hughes in *Time* (New York), 5 January 1981; "The Art of Deception" by Nancy Marmer in *Art in America* (New York), May 1981.

TUTTLE, Richard.

American. Born in Rahway, New Jersey, in 1941. Educated at Trinity College, Hartford, Connecticut, B.A. 1963; Cooper Union, New York, 1963–64. Painter: lives and works in New York. Agent: Blum Helman Gallery, 20 West 57th Street, New York, New York 10019. Address: 734 11th Avenue, New York, New York 10019, U.S.A.

Richard Tuttle: ***Silver Mercury*, 1986** Courtesy Whitney Museum, New York

Individual Exhibitions:

1965 Betty Parsons Gallery, New York
1967 Betty Parsons Gallery, New York
1968 Betty Parsons Gallery, New York
Galerie Schmela, Dusseldorf
1969 Nicholas Wilder Gallery, Los Angeles
1970 Betty Parsons Gallery, New York
Galerie Rudolf Zwirner, Cologne
Albright-Knox Art Gallery, Buffalo, New York
1971 Museum of Fine Arts, Dallas
1972 Museum of Modern Art, New York
Galerie Yvon Lambert, Paris
Betty Parsons Gallery, New York
Galerie Rudolf Zwirner, Cologne
1973 Clocktower, Institute for Art and Urban Resources, New York
Kunstraum, Munich
Galerie Heiner-Friedrich, Munich
Daniel Weinberg Gallery, San Francisco
Galerie Annemarie Verna, Zurich
Konrad Fischer Gallery, Dusseldorf
1974 Betty Parsons Gallery, New York
Galerie Lambert, Paris
Galleria Toselli, Milan
Galleria Marilena Bonomo, Bari, Italy
Cusack Gallery, Houston
Nigel Greenwood Gallery, London
1975 Whitney Museum, New York (retrospective)
Cusack Gallery, Houston
Parsons-Truman Gallery, New York
d'Alessandro Ferranti Gallery, Rome
Wadsworth Atheneum, Hartford, Connecticut
1976 Galerie Lambert, Paris
Otis Art Institute, Los Angeles
Brooke Alexander Gallery, New York
Northwest Artists Workshop, Portland, Oregon
Fine Arts Building Gallery, New York
University of Western Ontario, London
Graeme Murray Gallery, Edinburgh
1977 Ohio State University, Columbus
Galleria Ugo Ferranti, Rome
Kunsthalle, Basle
Kunstraum, Munich
Galerie Heiner-Friedrich, Munich
Yale University, New Haven, Connecticut (with Long and Hewitt)
1978 Betty Parsons Gallery, New York
Galerie Lambert, Paris
Ugo Ferranti Gallery, Rome
Young-Hoffman Gallery, Chicago
Brown University, Providence, Rhode Island
Daniel Weinberg Gallery, San Francisco
Galleria Francoise Lambert, Milan
Musée d'Art Moderne, Ghent, Belgium
Galerie Schmela, Dusseldorf
1979 Galerie Annemarie Verna, Zurich
Galleria Marilena Bonomo, Bari, Italy
Brooke Alexander Gallery, New York
Galleria Ugo Ferranti, Rome
Stedelijk Museum, Amsterdam
Truman Gallery, New York
University of California at Santa Barbara
Centre d'Arts Plastiques Contemporains, Bordeaux
1980 Centre d'Art Contemporain, Geneva
California institute of Technology, Pasadena
1982 Blum Helman Gallery, New York (with Robert Ryman and Cy Twombly)
1983 Galerie Hubert Winter, Vienna
Blum Helman Gallery, New York
1984 Studio La Citta, Verona, italy
Galerie Yvon Lambert, Paris
Galerie Schmela, Dusseldorf
Galerie Annemarie Verna, Zurich
1985 Galerie Schmela, Dusseldorf
Galleria Toselli, Milan
Institute of Contemporary Arts, London
Galerie Yvon Lambert, Paris
1986 Victoria Miro Gallery, London
Galerie Reinhard Onnasch, West Berlin
CAPC/Musée d'Art Contemporain, Bordeaux, France
ARC/Musée d'Art Moderne de la Ville, Paris

Selected Group Exhibitions:

1968 *Other Ideas*, Detroit Institute of Arts
1970 *Using Walls*, Jewish Museum, New York
1971 *Painting Without Supports*, Bennington College, Vermont
1972 *Documenta 5*, Museum Fridericianum, Kassel, West Germany (and *Documenta 6*, 1977; *Documenta 7*, 1982)
1973 *Young American Artists*, Kunsthalle, Hamburg (travelled to the Moderna Museet, Stockholm)
1975 *14 Artists*, Baltimore Museum of Art
1976 *Drawing Now*, Museum of Modern Art, New York
1983 *Abstract Painting 1960–69*, Project Studio One, New York
1985 *New Dialogues*, Dracos Art Centre, Athens
1988 *Contemporary American Art*, Sara Hilden Museum, Tampere, Finland (travelled to Oslo)

Collections:

Museum of Modern Art, New York; Whitney Museum, New York; Albright-Knox Art Gallery, Buffalo, New York; Corcoran Gallery of Art, Washington, D.C.; St. Louis Art Museum; National Gallery of Canada, Ottawa; Stedelijk Museum, Amsterdam; Waliraf-Richartz Museum, Cologne; Kaiser-Wilhelm Museum, Krefeld, West Germany; Kunsthaus, Zurich.

Publications:

By TUTTLE: article—statement in *Richard Tuttle*, exhibition catalogue, Paris 1986.

On TUTTLE: books—*Richard Tuttle*, exhibition catalogue with text by Robert Murdock, Dallas 1971; *Contemporary American Art*, exhibition catalogue with text by Peter Schjeldahl, Tampere 1988; articles—"Reviews and Previews: Richard Tuttle at Parsons Gallery" by Scott Burton in *Artnews* (New York), January 1968; "Simple, Not Simple Minded" by John Perreault in the *Village Voice* (New York), January 1968; "Artists on Their Art" by Jeffrey Smart in *Art International* (Lugano, Switzerland), May 1968; "The Art of Richard Tuttle" by Robert Pincus-Witten in *Artforum* (New York), February 1970; "Richard Tuttle" by Robert Murdock in *Art International* (Lugano, Switzerland), May 1971; "Wire, Pencil, Shadow: Elements of Richard Tuttle" by E. Lubeel in *Arts magazine* (New York), November 1972.

Richard Tuttle's intimately scaled, fragile, awkward, eccentrically shaped works seem to question both the boundaries between the graphic/painterly and the sculptural and the heroic size and physicality which dominated during the period of Tuttle's development in the 1960's. Tuttle's work, from his ideographic wall reliefs to those composed of various combinations of pencil, wire, cloth, paper, metal and wood, is usually classified under the Postminimalist heading, and his is a particularly quirky and subtly effective variant in the range of work made by the diverse group so clustered.

In 1963–65, Tuttle was making small, paper, box constructions such as his three-inch cube *Box* (1964), using geometric shape to emphasize individual personality and also the making process. "Toy like" qualitites along with folds, slits and cuts tend toward an Arp-like anthropomorphism which carries into Tuttle's 1965 series of wood reliefs, rounded shapes painted in one color with abstract references to nature, landscape and symbolically cryptic writing. These were either hung on the wall or lain on the floor in a kind of scattering effect which heightened their personally based, intuitive nature. In 1967 Tuttle made a group of shaped canvases, shaped in irregular octagonal configurations, dyed in Tintex in a range of washy tones, hemmed and either pinned loosely on the wall or arranged on the floor. As the series progressed the shapes became more personally warped versions of the octagon, an effect achieved by Tuttle's cutting out of interior angles on different sides of the canvas. In their fusion of soaked-in paint and fragile three dimensionality, these works invoked a fusion of painting and sculpture into a tense but material coupling. In his push to achieve new levels of delicate subtlety, Tuttle made his 1972 series of wire and graphitc wall works, combining illusion and allusion through the juxtapositioning of wavey, twisting lengths of wire with nervous, straggley graphite lines. The shadows created by the wire lengths adds the third dimension, while the whole acting in concert activates the metaphorical fourth dimensional, suggesting rhythms beyond those seen with the eyes.

Throughout the past decade, Tuttle has continued to experiment with the possibilities inherent in the basic methodologies he had established during the previous decade. He has managed to achieve considerable variety and freshness by diversely combining small, simple shapes in low relief with either painted or linear elements which extend these shapes onto the wall. The works are both objects and references to drawings or paintings of objects. Their qualities of tentative whimsey and miniaturization use dephysicalized presence to intensify the personal. Because they are so odd, so attenuated and so close to becoming invisible, they draw the viewer closer to contemplate the delicate interplays between the solid and the ephemeral. Tuttle's mini-world of shadowy, elusive, and deceptively simple form offers hopeful proof that art need not be huge and heavy to achieve the strong effect.

—Barbara Cavaliere

TWOMBLY, Cy.

American. Born in Lexington, Virginia, 25 April 1929. Studied at Boston Museum School of Fine Art, 1948–49; Washington and Lee University, Lexington, 1949–50; Art Students League, New York, 1950–51; and, under Robert Motherwell and Franz Kline, at Black Mountain College, Beria, North Carolina, 1951–52. Travelled in Europe and Africa, 1952–53; moved to Rome, 1957. Head of Art Department, Southern Seminary Junior College, Buena Vista, Virginia, 1955–56. Recipient: Virginia Museum of Fine Arts Travelling Fellowship, 1952. Agent: Leo Castelli Gallery, 420 West Broadway, New York, New York 10021, U.S.A. Address: 149 via Monserrato, Rome, Italy.

Individual Exhibitions:

1951 Kootz Gallery, New York
Seven Stairs Gallery, Chicago
1953 Stable Gallery, New York
Galleria Contemporanea, Florence
Little Gallery, Princeton, New Jersey
1955 Stable Gallery, New York
1957 Stable Gallery, New York
1958 Galleria La Tartaruga, Rome
Galleria del Naviglio, Milan
Galleria del Cavallino, Venice
1960 Leo Castelli Gallery, New York
Galleria La Tartaruga, Rome
Galleria del Naviglio, Milan
Galerie 22, Dusseldorf (with Robert Rauschenberg)
1961 Galleria La Tartaruga, Rome
Galleria del Naviglio, Milan
Galerie Zwirner, Essen, West Germany
Galerie J, Paris
1962 Galerie Aujourd'hui, Brussels
Galleria del Leone, Venice
1963 Galerie Anne Abels, Cologne
Galerie Bonnier, Lausanne, Switzerland
Galerie Jacques Benador, Geneva
Galleria La Tartaruga, Rome
1964 Galerie Handschin, Basle
Galerie Friedrich und Dahlem, Munich
Leo Castelli Gallery, New York
1965 Museum Haus Lange, Krefeld, West Germany
Palais des Beaux-Arts, Brussels
Galleria Notizie, Turin
Galleria La Tartaruga, Rome
1966 Stedelijk Museum Amsterdam
Kunstverein, Freiburg, West Germany
Leo Castelli Gallery, New York
1967 Leo Castelli Gallery, New York
Galleria La Tartaruga, Rome
Galleria Notizie, Turin
1968 Galleria La Tartaruga, Rome
Milwaukee Art Center
Leo Castelli Gallery, New York
1969 Galerie Zwirner, Cologne
Nicholas Wilder Gallery, Los Angeles
1970 Galerie Neurendorf, Cologne
Modern Art Agency, Naples
Svensk-Frenska Konstgalleriet, Stockholm
Gallerie Bonnier, Geneva
1971 Galleria Sperone, Turin
Galerie Mollenhoff, Cologne
Galerie Yvon Lambert, Paris
Galleria dell'Ariete, Milan
Galerie Denise René-Hans Meyer, Dusseldorf
1972 Modern Art Agency, Naples
Dunkelman Gallery, Toronto
Locksley Shea Gallery, Minneapolis
Janie C. Lee Gallery, Dallas
Leo Castelli Gallery, New York
1973 School for Visual Arts, New York
Art in Progress, Zurich
Kunstmuseum, Basle
Kunsthalle, Berne
Städtische Galerie im Lenbachhaus, Munich
Mavor Gallery, London
Galleria Sperone, Turin
1974 Galerie Oppenheim, Brussels
Leo Castelli Gallery, New York
Modern Art Agency, Naples
1975 Modern Art Agency, Naples
Art in Progress, Munich
Galerie Karsten Greve, Cologne
Paintings, Drawings, Constructions 1951–74, Institute of Contemporary Art, Philadelphia
Galerie Jacques Benador, Geneva
Galleria Bertesca, Genoa

Cy Twombly: ***Roman Note 10*, 1970** Courtesy Anthony D'Offay Gallery, London

San Francisco Museum of Modern Art
1976 Art in Progress, Dusseldorf
Kestner-Gesellschaft, Hannover
Leo Castelli Gallery, New York
Musée d'Art Moderne, Paris
Galerie Jacques Brosser, Paris
Galleria Gian Enzo Sperone, Rome
1977 Galerie Yvon Lamberg, Paris
School of Visual Arts, New York
1978 Heiner-Friedrich Gallery, New York
Galerie Klewan, Munich
1979 Whitney Museum, New York (retrospective)
Galleria Lucio Amelio, Naples
Galleriet, Lund, Sweden
Galerie Karsten Greve, Cologne
1981 Castelli Graphics, New York
Museum Haus Lange, Krefeld, West Germany
Newport Harbor Art Museum, Newport Beach, California (travelled to Madison, Wisconsin; Richmond, Virginia; Toronto)
1982 Blum-Helman Gallery, New York (with Robert Ryman and Richard Tuttle)
Sperone Westwater Fischer, New York
Mayor Gallery, London
Galerie Karsten Greve, Cologne
Galerie Yvon Lambert, Paris
1983 Stephen Mazoh Gallery, New York
1984 Galerie Karsten Greve, Cologne
Mayor Gallery, London
Galleria Lucio Amelio, Naples
Hirschle and Adler Modern, New York
Galerie Ulysses, Vienna
CAPC/Musee d'Art Contemporain, Bordeaux, France
Kunsthalle, Baden-Baden, West Germany
Galleria Gian Enzo Sperone, Rome
Santa Barbara Contemporary Arts Center, California
1986 Larry Gagosian Gallery, New York
Hirschl and Adler Modern, New York
Dia Art Foundation, New York
Galerie Yvon Lambert, Paris
1987 Kunsthaus, Zurich
Stadtisches Kunstmuseum, Bonn
Palacio de Velazquez, Madrid
Whitechapel Art Gallery, London
Anthony D'Offay Gallery, London
Kunsthalle, Dusseldorf
1988 Centre Georges Pompidou, Paris
Galerie Klewan, Munich
Pace Gallery, New York
Anthony D'Offay Gallery, London

Selected Group Exhibitions:

1958 *Gutai 9: International Festival,* Osaka, Japan
1964 *XXXIII Biennale,* Venice
1969 *Painting and Sculpture Today,* Indianapolis Museum of Art, Indiana
1971 *The Structure of Color,* Whitney Museum, New York
1973 *Contemporanea,* Parcheggio di Villa Borghese, Rome
1976 *Drawing Now,* Museum of Modern Art, New York
1981 *A New Spirit in Painting,* Royal Academy of Arts, London
1983 *American Accents,* The Gallery, Stratford, Ontario (travelled to Toronto, Quebec City, Halifax, Windsor, Edmonton, Vancouver, Calgary and Montreal)
1986 *Hommage a Beuys,* Stadtische Galerie im Lenbachhaus, Munich
1988 *Contemporary American Art,* Sara Hilden Art Museum Tampere, Finland (travelled to Oslo)

Collections:

Museum of Modern Art, New York; Whitney Museum, New York; Rhode Island School of Design, Providence; Milwaukee Art Center; First National City Bank, Houston; Wallraf-Richartz Museum, Cologne; Hessisches Landesmuseum, Darmstadt; Neue Galerie-Sammiung Ludwig, Aachen, West Germany; Galleria Nazionale d'Arte Moderna, Rome.

Publications:

On TWOMBLY: books—*Cy Twombly,* exhibition catalogue, with notes by Robert Motherwell, Chicago 1951; *Cy Twombly: Paintings, Drawings, Constructions 1951–74,* exhibition catalogue, by Suzanne Delehanty and Heiner Bastian, Philadelphia 1975; *Drawing Now,* exhibition catalogue, by Bernice Rose, New York 1976; *Cy Twombly: Bilder/Paintings 1952–1976,* with text by Heiner Bastian, West Berlin 1978; *Cy Twombly: catalogue raisonne des oeuvres sur papier, 1973–1976,* edited by Yvon Lambert, Milan 1979; *Cy Twombly: Works on Paper 1954-1976,* exhibition catalogue with text by Susan C. Larsen, Newport Beach 1981; *Cy Twombly: Skulpturen,* exhibition catalogue with introduction by Gerhard Storck, Krefeld 1981; *Cy Twombly: retrospective,* exhibition catalogue with essay by Katharina Schmidt, Baden-Baden 1984; *Cy Twombly: A catalogue raisonne of the printed graphic work 1983–84,* with introduction by Heiner Bastian, Munich and New York 1985; *Cy Twombly,* exhibition catalogue edited by Harald Szemann, Zurich 1987.

Since the 1960's the painting/poetry of Cy Twombly has, by way of a variety of signs, fed on his own research, made prevalently of interruptions or annotations, only apparently but actually brilliantly thought out. The painting traces the poetry, while the poetry retraces the painting and defines evasive paths. Thus those different signs tell the legend, and in it stray to the infinite. It is not true, therefore, that they are something impersonal. Art is always the forbidden fruit of the imagination, and the "Roman" artist with his visual paradigms sets it out in an inestimable spatiality (that of the surface of the canvas or the sheet of paper), where there is a collection of graphic crossings and groupings so complex as to be almost impossible to follow. In Cy Twombly's works classical quotation seems more like metaphor than literary erudition. In "Empire of Flora," "School of Athens" and "Leda and the Swan" (all works of 1961) the mythological metaphor is something secretly indestructible that memory re-echoes in shapes and colours, in memory of a past splendour.

Cy Twombly evokes in his works antique myths perhaps inexplicable to contemporary sensibility. And yet, without the memory of them, the hide-and-seek of those different signs would remain as if suspended, lacking the true secrecy of that search for beauty that evokes rapture. Like marble or paint, Cy Twombly's different signs possess an immortality of their own, transforming the inexpressible into a living manifestation; the apparent chaos releases the silence, introducing incisive light and shade where there have been rare spaces in the handwriting. The beauty flows most subtly, imperceptibly; it always follows the handwriting, when it slows down or breaks off. The artist has before him, not the whirlpool, but the silence of the past which unexpectedly becomes articulate sound, dancing movement, a dream, a memory of happenings of long ago.

In Cy Twombly's painting the secret of art reveals its true mythical origin in this way; its beauty lies in the disorder, not in the polished form. Unexpectedly, those different signs appear as veiled shadows in new dress, so classical is their poetic manifestation. Hence they are not writing (unless perhaps an automatic writing); what Cy Twombly puts down on the canvas or the paper is a sort of poetically conceived composition, as in Hölderlin or Novalis. The abstraction formed by the signs may perhaps be a discourse, as we can see from the work called "Nine Discourses on Commodus" (1963). But, following Plato, it is clear that Cy Twombly knows how not to be wiser but to love wisdom; since it is only in that that the revelation of the new writing exists. Thus his work of the past 20 years is nothing less than a revelation and a concealment of a lost classical integrity.

—Italo Mussa

TWORKOV, Jack.

American. Born in Biala, Poland, 15 August 1900; emigrated to the United States, 1913: naturalized, 1928. Educated in New York City public schools; studied at Columbia University, New York (majored in English), 1920–23, and at the Art Students League, New York, 1923-26. Married Rachel Wolodarsky in 1935; daughters: Hermine and Helen. Painter: lived and worked in New York and Provincetown, Massachusetts. Teacher at the Fieldston School, New York, 1931; American University, Washington, D.C., 1948–51; Queens College, Flushing, New York, 1948–55; and Pratt Institute, Brooklyn, New York, 1955–58; Professor of Art, 1958–69, Chairman of the Art Department, 1963–69, and William C. Leffingwell Professor of Painting Emeritus, 1969–82, Yale University, New Haven, Connecticut. Visiting Professor of Painting, Cooper Union, New York 1970–72; Artist-in-Residence, American Academy in Rome, 1972; Visiting Critic, Columbia University, 1973; Artist-in-Residence, Hopkins Center, Dartmouth College, Hanover, New Hampshire, 1973; Visiting Critic, Royal College of Art, London, 1974. Recipient: William A. Clark Prize and Gold Medal, Corcoran Gallery of Art, Washington, D.C., 1963; Guggenheim Fellowship, 1971; Painter of the Year Award, Skowhegan School of Art, Maine, 1974. M.F.A.: Yale University, 1963; D.F.A.: Maryland Institute of Art, Baltimore, 1971; D.H.L.: Columbia University, 1972. Member, American Academy and Institute of Arts and Letters, 1981. Agent: Nancy Hoffman Gallery, 429 West Broadway, New York, New York 10012, U.S.A. *Died* (in Provincetown, Massachusetts) *4 September 1982.*

Individual Exhibitions:

1940 ACA Gallery, New York
1947 Egan Gallery, New York
1948 Egan Gallery, New York
Baltimore Museum of Art
1949 Egan Gallery, New York
1950 Egan Gallery, New York
1951 Egan Gallery, New York
1952 Egan Gallery, New York
1953 Egan Gallery, New York
1954 Egan Gallery, New York
University of Mississippi
Stable Gallery, New York
1955 Stable Gallery, New York
1956 Stable Gallery, New York
1957 Stable Gallery, New York
Walker Art Center, Minneapolis
1960 Holland-Goldowsky Gallery, Chicago
1962 Holland-Goldowsky Gallery, Chicago
1963 Holland-Goldowsky Gallery, Chicago
Yale University Art Gallery, New Haven, Connecticut
1965 Castelli Gallery, New York
Whitney Museum, New York (toured the United States)
1966 Castelli Gallery, New York
Gertrude Kasle Gallery, Detroit
1967 Castelli Gallery, New York
1968 Castelli Gallery, New York
1969 Gertrude Kasle Gallery, Detroit
1971 Gertrude Kasle Gallery, Detroit
Whitney Museum, New York
Toledo Museum of Art, Ohio
1972 French and Company Gallery, New York
1973 Jaffe-Friede Gallery, Dartmouth College, Hannover, New Hampshire
Gertrude Kasle Gallery, Detroit
Jack Glenn Gallery, Corona del Mar, California
Jacobs Ladder Gallery, Washington, D.C.
1974 Nancy Hoffman Gallery, New York
Denver Art Museum
Portland Center for the Visual Arts, Oregon
Reed College, Portland, Oregon
Harcus-Krakow-Rosen-Sonnabend Gallery, Boston
1975 Nancy Hoffman Gallery, New York
New Gallery, Cleveland (travelled to the Contemporary Arts Center, Cincinnati, Ohio)

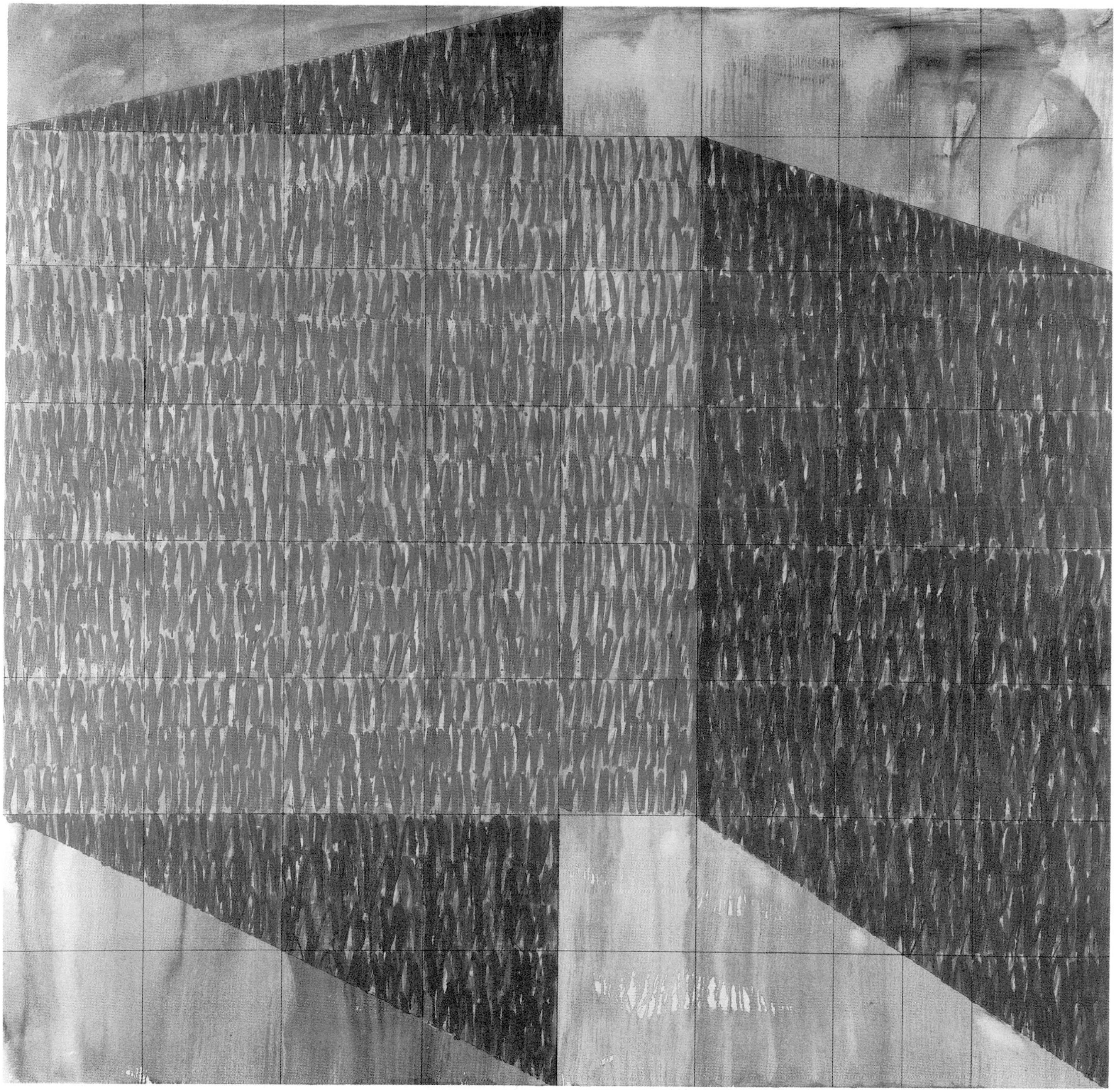

Jack Tworkov: ***Q1–75–No. 6*****, 1975**

1982 *15 Year Retrospective Exhibition*, Guggenheim Museum, New York

Selected Group Exhibitions:

1958 *New American Painting*, Museum of Modern Art, New York (toured Europe, 1958–60)
1973 *Biennial Exhibition of Contemporary Art*, Whitney Museum, New York
1974 *12 American Artists*, Virginia Museum of Fine Arts, Richmond
5 American Painters, University of California at Santa Barbara
Painting and Sculpture Today, Indianapolis Museum of Contemporary Art
Contemporary American Painting and Sculpture, Krannert Center, University of Illinois, Urbana
Contemporary American Painters, Cleveland Museum of Art
1975 *Corcoran Biennial*, Corcoran Gallery of Art, Washington, D.C.
1976 *Bicentennial Exhibition*, Hirshhorn Museum, Washington, D.C.

Collections:

Whitney Museum, New York; Guggenheim Museum, New York; Museum of Modern Art, New York; Metropolitan Museum of Art, New York; Yale University, New Haven, Connecticut; Baltimore Museum of Art; National Collection, Washington, D.C.; Cleveland Museum of Art; Detroit Institute of Arts; Indianapolis Museum of Art.

Publications:

By TWORKOV: articles—"Wandering Soutine" in *Artnews* (New York), November 1950; "Flowers and Realism" in *Artnews* (New York), May 1954; "Tworkov's Journal," excerpts, in *It Is* (New York), Spring 1958, Autumn 1958, Autumn 1959, Spring 1960; "Jack Tworkov," interview, with Phyllis Tuchman, in *Artforum* (New York), January 1971; "Notes on My Painting" in *Art in America* (New York), September 1973; "On My Outlook as a Painter" in *Leonardo* (Oxford), Spring 1974.

On TWORKOV: books—*Jack Tworkov*, exhibition catalogue, by Edward Bryant, New York 1964; *Jack Tworkov*, exhibition catalogue, with an introduction by Marcia Tucker, New York 1971; articles—"Quartered and Drawn" by Douglas Crimp in *Artnews* (New York), March 1972; "Jack Tworkov" by Kasha Linville Gula in *Art in America* (New York), September 1973.

Tworkov and his family emigrated to New York in 1913. As an undergraduate, studying English, at Columbia University (1920–23), he first saw paintings by Cezanne and Matisse. From 1923–25 he studied at the National Academy of Design and then at the Art Students' League under Guy Pené du Bois and Boardman Robinson.

During the Depression of the 1930s Tworkov was involved with the Public Works of Art Project (1934) and the Federal Art Project of the W.P.A., (1935–41). The pictures and murals of this time were mainly still-lifes, portraits and landscapes, which showed strong links with European art. He came to dismiss the work of this period as being necessary to the time but bearing little relevance to his later painting. However, during the 1930s he met William de Kooning, a friendship which was to prove very important to his mature work.

WWII proved a decisive period for Tworkov's artistic development. From 1942–45 he worked as a tool designer, cut off from the art world, except for his contact with de Kooning, and he didn't paint at all. The later 1940s was witnessing the development in New York of a strong school of abstract painting and by 1947 Tworkov was a fully committed 'Abstract Expressionist'.

Tworkov was teaching by 1948 (American University in Washington D.C.), and he was a visiting artist at Black Mountain College in North Carolina in 1952. Through the years 1948–53 de Kooning had remained an important influence as the two artists had adjoining studios. By 1949 Tworkov's painting was becoming concerned with the figure, employing a very free and energetic method.

From 1963–69 Tworkov was Chairman of the Art Department at Yale University. With the 1960's he had begun to study elementary geometry and the theories of number systems and by the 1970's his painting was moving away from Abstract Expressionism to a more disciplined and contemplative form—less gestural, more geometric and static, though by no means hardedged, as it retained its strong 'painterly' inclinations.

—Victoria Keller

U

UECKER, Günther.

German. Born in Wentdorf/Mecklenburg. 13 March 1930. Educated in Wismar; studied art at the Akademie der Künst, Berlin-Weissensee, and at the Staatliche Kunstakademie, Dusseldorf. Independent artist, Dusseldorf, since 1955: colour-structure paintings, 1955–56; first white structural objects and nail-paintings, 1957; mathematical computable structure series, 1958–59; kinetic structural discs, 1960; Member, Zero Group, with Otto Piene and Heinz Mack, 1961–66. Professor, Staatliche Kunstakademie, Dusseldorf, 1974. Recipient: Prize, *Biennale di San Marino,* 1963; Talent Prize, Landes Nordrhein-Westfalen, 1964; Prize, *Bienal,* Sao Paulo, 1971. Agent: Galerie M, Haus Weitmar, 4630 Bochum, West Germany. Address: Dusseldorferstrasse 29A, 4000 Dusseldorf II, West Germany.

Individual Exhibitions:

1959 Galleria Azimuth, Milan
1960 Galerie Schmela, Dusseldorf
1961 Galleria La Salita, Rome
1962 Galerie Ad Libitum, Antwerp
1963 *Mack/Piene/Uecker,* Museum Haus Lange, Krefeld, West Germany
1964 Howard Wise Gallery, New York
1965 Galerie Orez, The Hague
Kestner-Gesellschaft, Hanover
1967 *Flemish Landscape,* Mullen, Belgium (with Jef Verheyen)
1968 Kunsthalle, Baden-Baden, West Germany
1969 Kunsthalle, Dusseldorf
1970 Kunsthalle, Bremerhaven, West Germany
1971 *Bildobjekie 1957–1970.* Moderna Museet, Stockholm
Museum Folkwang, Essen
Galerie Zachea, Warsaw
Nationalgalerie, West Berlin
1972 Kestner-Gesellschaft, Hanover
1974 Muzeum Sztuki, Lodz, Poland
Galerie Rothe, Heidelberg
Kolnischer Kunstverein, Cologne
Kunsthalle, Cologne
1975 Museum Folkwang, Essen
Galerie im Erker, St. Galen, Switzerland
Galerie Denise René/Hans Mayer, Dusseldorf
Galerie M, Bochum, West Germany
Galerie St. Johann, Saarbrucken
Kunstmuseum, Dusseldorf (2 shows)
Wüttembergische Staatsgalerie, Stuttgart
Württembergisches Staatsheater, Stuttgart (decors for Wagner's *Parsifal)*
Antwerp Gallery
Galerie Denise René/Hans Mayer, Dusseldorf (with Heinz Mack)
1977 Forum Metall, Linz, Austria
1978 Galerie Reckermann, Cologna (travelled to Detmold, Dublin and Munich)
1979 *Bilder und Zeichnungen,* Kunstverein. Braunschweig, West Germany
Erker-Galerie, St. Gallen, Switzerland
Stüdtisches Museum Schloss Morsbroich, Leverkusen, West Germany
1981 Erker-Galerie, St. Gallen, Switzerland
1982 Galerie Walter Storms, Munich
Raumberkeilung—Bilder den Wanden zugekeht, Galerie Lohrl, Mönchengladbach, West Germany
Nationalgalerie, West Berlin
1983 Kunsthalle, Dusseldorf
Galerie Schmela, Dusseldorf
Galerie Loehrl, Monchengladbach, West Germany
Galerie Wallstrasse, Moers, West Germany
1984 Galerie Brusten, Wuppertal, West Germany
Villa Merkel, Esslingen, West Germany
Kamakura Gallery, Tokyo
Galerie im Gauserhaus, Wasserburg, West Germany
Yares Gallery, Scotsdale, Arizona
1985 Moderner Galerie, Bottrop, West Germany
Museum of Modern Art, Istanbul
Josef Albers Museum, Bottrop, West Germany
1986 Galerie Lupke, Frankfurt
1987 Vasarely Museum, Pecs, Hungary
Galerie Ronny Van de Velde, Knokke, Belgium
1988 Galerie Reckermann, Cologne

Selected Group Exhibitions:

1965 *Licht und Bewegung,* Kunsthalle, Berne
1968 *Documenta, Kassel,* West Germany (and 1977)
1972 *Amsterdam-Paris-Dusseldorf,* Guggenheim Museum, New York
1974 *Basically White,* Institute of Contemporary Arts, London
1976 *Europa/America,* Galleria d'Arte Moderna, Bologna
1978 *Elements of Drawing,* Galerie Studio, Warsaw
1979 *Zero International,* Koninklijk Museum voor Schone Kunsten, Antwerp
1981 *Schwarz,* Kunsthalle, Dusseldorf
1982 *60–80: Attitudes, Concepts, Images,* Stedelijk Museum, Amsterdam
1985 *Hundert Jahre Kunst in Deutschland 1885–1985,* Kunsthalle, Ingeleheim, West Germany

Collections:

Städtisches Kunstmuseum, Dusseldorf; Wallraf-Richartz Museum. Cologne: Kaiser-Wilhelm Museum, Krefeld, West Germany; Museum Folkwang, Essen; Stedelijk Van Abbemuseum, Eindhoven, Netherlands; Museum des 20 Jahrhunderts, Vienna; Muzeum Sztuki, Lodz Poland; Galleria Nazionale d'Arte Moderna, Rome; Tate Gallery, London; Museum of Modern Art, New York.

Publications:

By UECKER: books and pamphlets—*Projektionen von Heute,* with Otto Piene and Heinz Mack, Dusseldorf 1961; *Uecker-Zeitung,* vols. 0–9, editor, Dusseldorf 1968–82: *Der heutige kunstler . . .*pamphlet, Dusseldorf 1969; *Uber Steine: zu Skulppuren von Rolf Jorres,* pamphlet, Dusseldorf 1969; *Uecker,* portfolio of 5 lithos, with text by Lothar Wolleh, Cologne 1970; *Flamische Landschaft,* with Jef Verheyen, Dusseldorf 1970; *Einsam Gemeinsam,* book with 5 prints, text by Eugen Gomringer, Dusseldorf 1971; *Vom Licht,* with prints by Uecker and others, and an introduction by Gerhard Storck, Heidelberg 1973; *Manuelle Strukturen,* casette with 10 lithos, St. Gallen, Switzerland 1975; *Anonym,* casette with objects and 6 silkscreens, Dusseldorf 1976; *Zum Schweigen der Schrift oder die Sprachlosigkeit,* 17 silkscreens, with text by Eugen Gomringer, St. Gallen, Switzerland 1976; *Uecker: Ludwig von Beethovens Leonore,* with text by Gerhard Storck, photos by Lothar Wolleh, Stuttgart and Zurich 1978; *Schrifien, Gedichte—Projekiebeschreibungen—Reflexionen,* St. Gallen, Switzerland 1980; *Littenheid—Eine Studie . . .mit Studenien der Klasse Uecker,* with Hans Geigenmuller, St. Gallen, Switzerland 1980; *Buhnenskulpturen für Lohengrin,* with text by Guido de Werd, photos by Lothar Wolleh, Kleve and Dusseldorf 1981; films—*Eckenfilm,* 1969; *Nagelfeldzug,* 1969; *Bauchfilm,* 1970.

On UECKER: books—*Mack/Piene/Uecker,* exhibition catalogue, with foreword by Paul Wember, Krefeld, West Germany 1963; *Günther Uecker: Ten Years of a Kineticist's Work* by Willoughby Sharp, New York 1966; *Gunther Uecker* by Dietrich Helmz, Recklinghausen, West Germany 1970; *Günther Uecker: Bildobjekte 1957–1970,* exhibition catalogue, with text by K. G. Pontus Hulten, Stockholm 1971; *Günther Uecker,* exhibition catalogue/book, with texts by Wieland Schmied, Hans Strelow, Rolf-Günther Dienst and others, Hanover and St. Gallen, Switzerland 1972; *Günther Uecker,* exhibition catalogue with text by Dieter Honisch, Lodz Poland 1974; *Uecker: Bilder und Zeichnungen,* exhibition catalogue. Braunschweig, West Germany 1979; *Uecker: Raumverkeilung—Bilder den Wanden zugekehrt,* exhibition catalogue, with text by Sabine Kimpel-Fehlemann, Mönchengladbach, West Germany 1982; *Uecker* by Dieter Honisch and Marion Haedecke, Stuttgart 1983; *Gunther Uecker,* exhibition catalogue with text by Friedrich W. Heckmanns, Bottrop 1985.

The present-day artist produces and realizes ideas which could serve as examples for a new environment. The idea will come into being as a product. These real objects are clarifications of a new way of looking at things. These objects have no objective value; they have served their purpose in the instant that they are taken into consciousness. These objects can be understood as tools for thought processes.

An artist is an inventor, an inventory of ideas. Which can be realized visually. Which can serve as parables for spiritual development.

—Günther Uecker

The Zero Group was formed in 1961. For five years Otto Piene, Heinz Mack and Günther Uecker exhibited jointly as a trio the wax/soot fire-works of Piene, the silver reflections of Mack and the nail constructions and light experiments of Uecker.

Of the three Uecker was the most international in the character of his work. However different in realization and intention, his nail works use the same raw materials as those of the Canadian David Partridge, and, in their way, they imply some of the same effects of light and shade to be found in the stunted peg reliefs of the Brazilian Sergio de Camargo. But there the relationships terminate.

Uecker's use of *white* is wholly different from that of Camargo, and his understanding of the character of upstanding nails and how they can play games with chiaroscuro has nothing to do with Partridge's gleaming carpets of nail-heads. The German artist keeps sternly aloof from the decorative dangers that sometimes beset the works of both of the others. He also has a non-architectural attitude towards the transformation games he plays with "objects" like a chair or

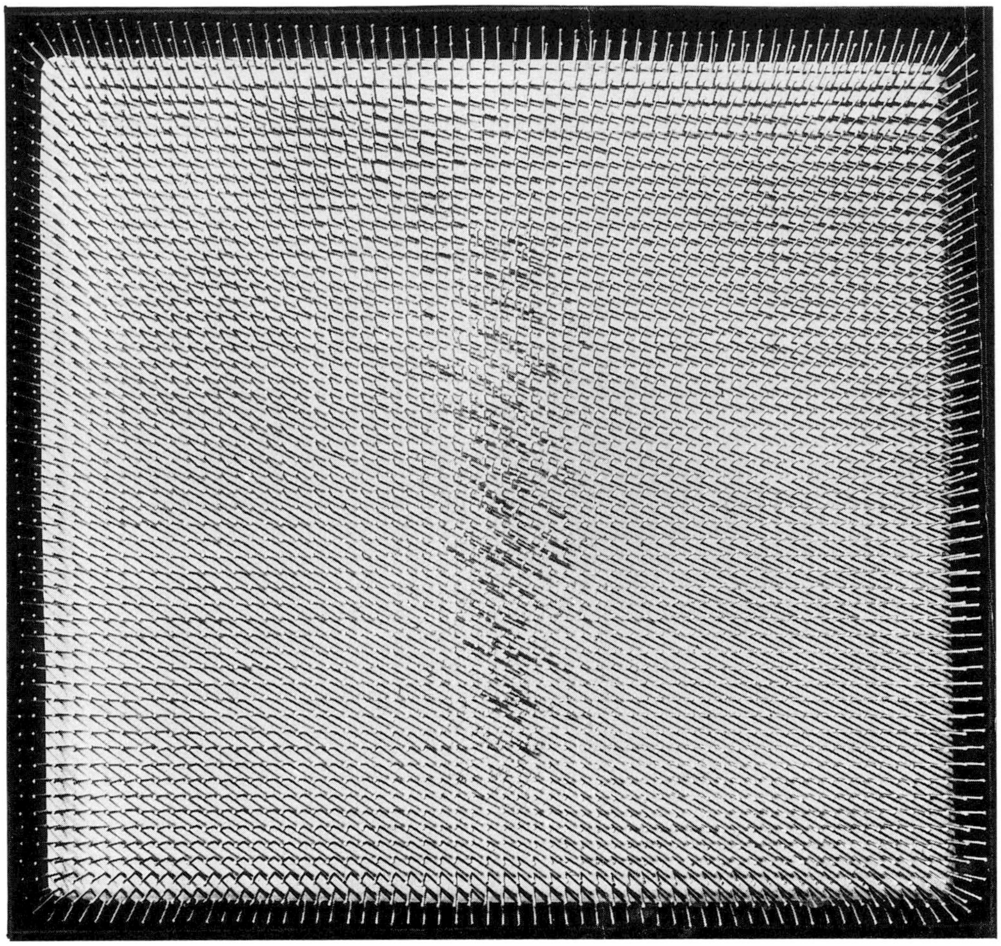

Günther Uecker: *White Work*, 1959

a picture frame. In such a mood he is demonstrating that he has the same European elan as Jean-Pierre Raynaud or Pol Bury.

Artists like Uecker are revitalising the Old World, not doing a raw survey of artistic potentialities of the New. The aggressive defiance of the Americas is not their style, and their works have no American accent, not even a mid-Atlantic one.

—Sheldon Williams

ULRICHS, Timm.

German. Born in Berlin, 31 March 1940. Educated at primary school in Bremen, 1954–59; studied architecture at the Technische Hochschule, Hannover, 1959–66; mainly self-taught in art, from 1959. Independent artist, Hannover, since 1959. Guest Professor, Hochschule für Bildende Künste, Braunschweig, 1969–70. Professor, Institut für Kunstlerzieher Münster der Staatlichen Kunstakademie. Dusseldorf, since 1972. Recipient: Literatur-Forderpreis des Niedersachsischen Kunstpresses, 1968; Kritikerpreis fur Bildende Kunst, West Berlin, 1977; Niedersachsisches Kunstlerstipendium, Hannover, 1979; Kunstpreis der Stadt Nordhorn, 1980. Address: Sodenstrasse 6, Postfach 6043, 3000 Hannover 1, West Germany.

Individual Exhibitions:

1961 Totalkunst-Zimmergalerie Ulrichs. Hannover
1964 Haus am Lutzowplatz, West Berlin
1966 Galerie Patio, Frankfurt
Bauhutte, Hannover
1967 Galleria Alpha, Modena, Italy
Galleria Il Portico, Reggio Emilia, Italy
1968 Studio di Informazione Estetica, Turin
Institut für Visuelie Kommunikation, West Berlin
Institut Autoretique, Kiel
Galerie Daedalus, West Berlin
Top-Shop, West Berlin
1969 Edition H, Hannover
Galerie Patio, Frankfurt
Galerie Kummel, Cologne
Kunstraum, Hannover
Galerie Reckermann, Cologne
1970 Kunstverein, Gottingen, West Germany
Galerie Nachst St. Stephan, Vienna
Neue Galerie, Aachen, West Germany
Kabinett für Aktuelle Kunst, Bremerhaven, West Germany
Museum Haus Lange, Krefeld, West Germany (retrospective)
Galerie Wildeshausen, Wildeshausen, West Germany
Christian-Albrechts-Universitat, Kiel
1971 Zimmertheater, Tübingen, (with Klaus Hoffmann)
Kunsthaus, Hamburg
Städtisches Museum, Wiesbaden
1972 Atelier NW8. Beindersheim, West Germany
Galerie Kummel, Cologne
Galerie Wildeshauen, Wildeshauen, West Germany
Kulturzentrum Ulrichs, Hannover
1973 Galerie Ernst, Hannover
Galerie Langer, Braunschweig, West Germany
Kunsthalle, Bielefeld, West Germany
Kunstverein, Celle, West Germany
1974 Galerie Magers, Bonn
Kunsthalle, Bremen, West Germany
Galerie Apex, Göttingen, West Germany
Stadtische Galerie, Bergkamen, West Germany
Galerie, Defet, in the Kunsthalle, Nuremberg
1975 Werkstatt Breitenbrunn, Breitennbrunn, West Germany
Kunstverein, Hannover
Westfälischer Landesmuseum, Münster, West Germany
Kunstverein, Freiburg
Konzert-Aula, Kamen, West Germany
Mobile Galerie, Frankfurt
Dierks Galleri, Aarhus, Denmark
Kunstkontor Blank, Marburg Lahn, West Germany
Restrospective 1960–1975. Kunstverein, Braunschweig, West Germany (travelled to the Karl-Ernst-Osthaus Museum, Hagen, West Germany; Kunstverein, Heidelberg; and Kunstverein, Hannover)
1976 Galleria Giurca, Modena, Italy
Galerie Wildeshauen, Wildeshauen, West Germany
Studio Kausch, Kassel, West Germany
1977 Galerie Space, Wiesbaden
Galerie und Versmolder Kunstkreis, Versmold, West Germany
Forum Kunst, Rottweil, West Germany
Galerie Gamma, Utrecht
1978 Paula Becker Modersohn Haus, Bremen, West Germany
1979 Galerie Studio M, Bamberg, West Germany
Galerie Petersen, West Berlin
Kunstmuseum, Hannover
1980 *Totalkunst*, Städisches Galerie, Ludenscheid, West Germany
Druckgraphik, Zeichnungen, Objekte. Deutsche BP Aktiengesellschaft-Clubheim, Hamburg
Städtisches Galerie, Nordhorn, West Germany
1981 Kunstraum Fuhrwerkswaage, Cologne
1982 Galerie H.C. Scheerer, Tuttlingen, West Germany
Galerie im Orangerie-Cafe, Kassel, West Germany
1984 Wilhelm-Hack-Museum, Ludwigshafen am Rhein, West Germany

Selected Group Exhibitions:

1969 *Konzeption-Conception*, Stadisches Museum, Lverkusen, West Germany
1970 *Konkrete Poesie/Visuelle Texte*, Stedelijk Museum, Amsterdam (toured Europe)
1974 *Multiples*, Neuer Berliner Kunstverein, West Berlin
1975 *Korpersprache-Bodylanguage*, Kunstverein, Hamburg (travelled to West Berlin and Frankfurt)
1977 *Documenta 6*, Neue Galerie, Kassel, West Germany
1978 *Art—Museum des Geldes*, Stadtische Kunsthalle, Dusseldorf (travelled to Eindhoven and Paris)
1980 *Monuments-Denkmal*, Kunstverein, Cologne (travelled to Karlsruhe)
1981 *Dimensionen der Plastischen*, Neuer Berliner Kunstverein, West Berlin
1982 *Momentbild: Kunstlerphotographien*, Kestner-Gesellschaft, Hannover

Collections:

Kaiser-Wilhelm-Museum, Krefeld, West Germany; Museum, Wiesbaden; Städtische Galerie, Wolfsburg, West Germany; Stadt Bergkamen, West Germany; Kunstverein, Braunschweig, West Germany; Kunstverein, Gelsenkirchen, West Germany; Kunsthalle, Hamburg; Kunstmuseum, Hannover; Städtische Galerie, Ludenscheid, West Germany.

Publications:

By ULRICHS: books—*Totalkunst: Das neue Mass aller Dinge*, Hannover 1961; *Fragment*, West Berlin 1964; *Klartecte*, Hannover 1966; *Spiel plane*, Hannover and Moderna 1967; *Beschriebene Biatter*, Hannover and Göttingen 1967; *Schriftstucke*, Munich 1967; *Ich Bin ein Gedicht*, Vienna 1968; *Lesarien und Schriebweisen*, Stuttgart 1968; *Interferenzen I*, Cologne 1968; *Interferenzen II*, Basle 1968; *Des Grossen Erfolges Wegen*, Hannover 1968; *Owertzuoipu*, Hannover 1968; *ich als Kunstfigur*, Vienna 1969; *Weiter im Text*. Hannover 1969; *Bild-Band*, West Berlin 1970; *Fernsehen in Nahsicht*, Göttingen 1970; *Kanaldeckel 1962/64*, Göttingen 1970; *Einweg-Buch*, Hannover 1972; *Die Zeitungsannonce ais Kunstwerk 1964/74* exhibition catalogue, Bonn 1974, *Uetersetzung-Translation-Traduction*, Hannover 1974; *Die Photokopie der Photokopie der Photokopie*, Hannover 1975; *1984 (Spionbuch)*, Hannover 1975; *Bilder, auf den Leib geschrieben*, Hannover 1975; *Dem Leser den Rucken zukehrend*,

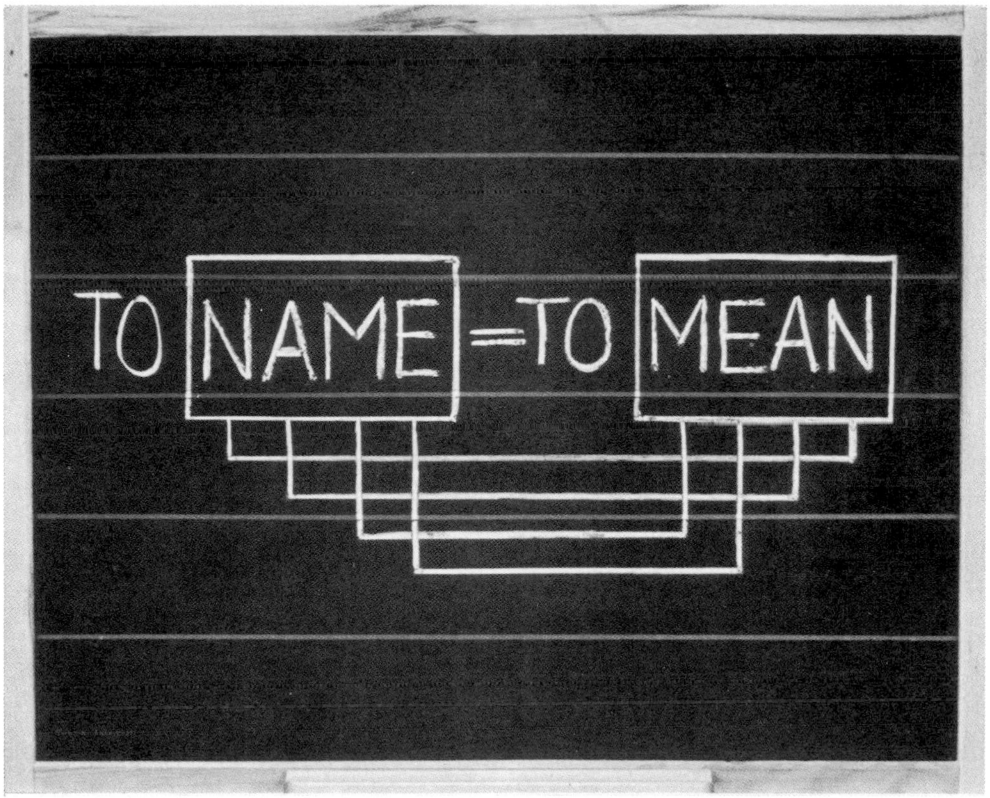

Timm Ulrichs: *To Name = To Mean*, 1968

Hannover 1976; *Ich mache (diese) Schlagzeilen,* Hannover 1977; *Ich, Gott und die Welt,* Hannover 1978; *The Infinite Book,* Hannover 1978; *Kunst: im Schweisse des Angesichts,* Hannover 1978; *Buch-(EHE)-Paar,* Hannover 1979; *Lektionen,* Frankfurt 1979; *Die Kunst des schonen Schreibens,* 2 vols., Hannover 1979.

On ULRICHS: book—*Pop und die Folgen* by Heinz Ohff, Dusseldorf 1967; *Deutsche Kunst: eine neue generation* by Rolf-Günter Dienst, Cologne 1970; *Galerie der neuen Künste* by Heinz Ohff, Gutersloh 1971; *Bis Heute* by Karin Thomas, Cologne 1971; *Konkrete Poesie* by Eugen Gomringer, Stuttgart 1972; *Kunst-im-Kopf: Aspekte der Real-Kunst* by Klaus Hoffmann, Cologne 1972: *Deutsche Kunst der 60er Jahre* by Jürgen Morschel, Munich 1972; *Il Territorio Magico* by Achille Bonito Oliva, Florence 1972; *Objekt Kunst:von Duchamp bis Kienhol:* by Willy Rotzler, Cologne 1972; *Visuelle Poesie International* by Klaus-Peter Dencker, Cologne 1973; *Selbstdarsteliung,* edited by Wulf Herzogenrath, Dusseldorf 1973; *Kunst in Krefeld* by Paul Wember, Cologne 1973; *Timm Ulrichs: Retrospektive 1960–1975,* exhibition catalogue, with texts by Margarethe Jochimsen, S.J. Schmidt and Klaus Hoffmann, Braunschweig, West Germany 1975; *Timm Ulrichs: Druckgraphik, Zeichnungen, Objekte,* exhibition catalogue, with text by Carl Vogel, Hamburg 1980; *Timm Ulrichs: Total-kunst,* exhibition catalogue, with texts by Uwe Obier, and Helmut R. Leppien, Ludenscheid, West Germany, 1980; *Vergangenheit-Gegenwart-Zukunft,* exhibition catalogue, with an introduction by Tilman Osterwold, Stuttgart 1982; *Timm Ulrichs* by Bernhard Holeczek, Bruanschweig 1982; *Timm Ulrichs: Totalkunst—Angesammelte Werke,* exhibition catalogue with text by Bernhard Holeczek, Ludwigshafen 1984.

UNCINI, Giuseppe.

Italian. Born in Fabriano, 31 January 1929. Attended Aldo Calo's lectures, Istituto Statale d'Arte, Rome, 1959; mainly self-taught in art. Served in the Italian Army, 1950. Married Marioline Delicati in 1963; son: Marzio. Worked as graphic artist and lithographer, Cartotechnica Fratelli Carmenati, Fabriano, Italy, 1948–51, and Tipolitografia Sabatini, Falconora Marittima, Ancona, 1951–53; settled in Rome where he associated with Edgardo Mannucci, Ettore Colla, Achille Perilli, and Gastone Novelli; travelled in Europe, 1956; produced jewelry for Gioiellieri Masenza from 1960; Founder, with Gastone Biggi, Nicola Carrino, Nato Frasca, Achille Pace, and Pasquale Santoro, Gruppo Uno, Rome, 1962–67. Lecturer in Mosaics, 1960–67, and since 1967 Director of the Department of Metalwork, Istituto Statale d'Arte II, Rome. Recipient: First Prize, *Mostra Concorso Ministero Pubblica Istruzione*, Rome, 1957 and 1963; First Prize, *X Premio Spoleto*, 1962; First Prize, *Premio G. B. Salvi*, Sassoferrato, 1967. Agent: Studio Marconi, via Tadino 15, 20124 Milan. Address: via Felice Cavalotti 57, 00152 Rome, Italy.

Individual Exhibitions:

1958 Chiostro Quattrocento, Fabriano, Italy
1959 Galleria La Salita, Rome (with Tano Festa and Franco Angeli)
Contemporaries Art Gallery, New York (with L. Brown)
1961 Galleria L'Attico, Rome
1963 Auditorium, l'Aquila, Italy
1967 Galleria Posto, San Remo, Italy
1968 Galleria Christian Stein, Turin
1969 Salone Annunciata, Milan
1970 Qui Arte Contemporanea, Rome
1971 Galleria Christian Stein, Turin
1973 Galleria 3B, Bolzano, Italy
Studio Marconi, Milan
1974 Galleria Godel, Rome
Galleria Ferrari, Verona
1975 Galleria La Chiocciola, Padua
Galleria Christian Stein, Turin
Galleria Seconda Scala, Rome
Galleria dei Mille, Bergamo, Italy
1976 Galleria Peccolo, Livorno
Studio Marconi, Milan
Galleria Rondanini, Rome
Galleria La Piramide, Florence
1979 Palazzo dei Consoli, Gubbio, Italy
1980 Studio Marconi, Milan
1983 Pinacoteca e Musei Conunali, Macerata, Italy

Selected Group Exhibitions:

1955 *Quadriennale*, Rome
1960 *Rome '60: 5 Pittori a Rome*, Galleria La Salita, Rome
1963 *Gruppo Uno*, Galleria Medusa, Rome
1966 *20th Century Italian Art*, Baltimore Museum of Art
1971 *Vitalità del Negativo*, Palazzo Esposizione, Rome
1972 *Progetto: Intervento: Verifica*, Palazzo Reale, Milan
1975 *Didattica*, Pinacoteca Civica, Modigliana, Italy
1977 *16 Italianse Kunstenaars*, Museum Boymans-van Beuningen, Rotterdam
1980 *Arte e Critica*, Galleria Nazionale d'Arte Moderna, Rome
1982 *Arte Italiana 1960–1982*, Hayward Gallery, London

Collections:

Galleria Nazionale d'Arte Moderna, Rome; Museo Civico, Turin; Museo d'Arte Progressiva, Livorno; Pinacoteca Civica, Termoli, Italy; Museum Boymans-van-Beuningen, Rotterdam; Nijgata Art Museum, Japan.

Publications:

By UNCINI: book—*Gruppo I*, with Nicola Carrino and Nato Frasca, Venice 1966; articles—"Dichiarizione de Poetica" in *Gruppo Uno*, exhibition catalogue, Rome 1963; "La Poetica della Percezione" in *Gruppo Uno*, exhibition catalogue, Venice 1964; "Techniche e Materiali," interview with Marisa Volpi, in *Marcatre*, (Genoa), May 1968; "Lettera a Maurizio Fagiolo" in *Didattica*, exhibition catalogue, Rome 1975.

On UNCINI: books—*Gruppo Uno* by Giulio Carlo Argan and others, Rome 1963; *Dall'Occhio al Cervello* by F. Sossi, Taranto, Italy 1965; *Gruppo Uno* by E. Marsili and Giulio Carlo Argan, Rome 1965; *Calderara e Gruppo Uno* by Giulio Carlo Argan, Milan 1966; *Le Correnti Pittoriche non Oggettive degli Anni Sessanta* by Filberto Menna, Milan 1967; *Ricerche dopo l'Informale* by Enrico Crispolti, Rome 1968; *Luce: Spazio: Strutture* by F. Sossi, Taranto, Italy 1968; *Erotismo nell'Arte Astratta* by Enrico Crispolti, Trapani, Italy 1976; *Il Artisti Italiani* by Antonio del Guercio, Verona 1976; *Uncini: La logica Fantastica*, exhibition catalogue with text by Luciano Marziano, Macerata 1983.

In Roman artistic circles in the 1960's Giuseppe Uncini (with Lo Savio, Schifano and Festa) had already progressed beyond informal painting. His first *Cementarmato* (reinforced concrete—concrete with an iron framework) has an early date—1959. It is a monochrome surface intended as an "object"—that is to say, no longer as a field of colour thick with emotive tensions—in which the grouping of the materials side by side gives the "construction" of a new dimension, more realistic than cerebral. But, in giving up spatial connexions, partly brought about by the interaction of the iron element and the monochromatic spread of the cement, the construction does not describe the period of work. It has its strong concrete presence, the presence of one who thinks with his hands, so that the cerebral dimension is absorbed by the realistic.

Undoubtedly constructive methods and mental periods are one and the same to Uncini; in practice, in the joining or dismantling, the assembling or opening/closing of the structure, which is a model on its own and not a vehicle for repetitions (visual or intellectual) with the viewer. An extreme strictness, then, which of course does not in itself exclude the unforseen manual event, the nature of which is certainly not existential. Uncini always leaves the structure of his work open; then, when the manual element does occur, its presence is immediately visible. Above all a craftsman (in the lay sense indicated by Alain), Uncini believes that thought is work and work thought—with the forthrightness of *homo faber*. Thus his works in reinforced concrete and in brick have their own meaning, leaving no margin for subjective interpretation. When that is there, it is to be found in the structure itself, with its two-dimensional or three-dimensional orders that concrete and bricks stabilize in an open space. A typical feature of Uncini's works,

Giuseppe Uncini: *Dimore No. 12*, 1982

in fact, is the spatial opening, based on constructive theories not wholly defined. His reinforced concrete and brick works are extraordinarily different forms.

With his "Room" and "Door Wall and Shadow" the spatiality, accompanied now by its shadows, becomes a symbolic structure, linked between the full and the empty (of light and shade), continually changing and unforeseeable. The spatial structure, standing by itself, is worked out in an environment whose perspectives look broken up in some way, not by creating an illusory effect but by the direct intervention of the viewer. In fact the environment is always present, insofar as the light and shade fall on the spatial construction to an equal extent. A full light framed by shadow, by means of concrete observations of the space, can be achieved in a variety of materials. A reflection that Uncini extends to the "everyday landscape" within which his works, from the 1960's to the present, have been born. In the everyday landscape he works out one of his "Theories of visibility," even seeing the possibility of a revival of classical typological forms. But he is not giving up his constructional methods; indeed he is broadening them, still in constructional style. "Vertical-Horizontal," "Columns," the "Arch," "Buttressed Wall" and the "Cloaca Maxima" are examples of works in which the classical typological form prevails, carried out in both concrete and brick together. But the artist himself declares: "They may be concrete materials and at the same time strike our cognitive consciousness as new concepts." Being in fact positive calks of what we see in negative, those historical forms show once again how light-shade-space are in real terms assumed by visibility to be actual reality, without metaphysical projection, and by iconographic recovery to be mental analysis beyond didactic proof.

Even in this last constructive fantasy Uncini remains faithful to the fact that the object must "mean" only itself—he displays the consistency of one who believes that, if visibility varies, there is only one way of representing it. The work is therefore never out of its element; everything goes back into place without ever leaving behind existential doubts.

—Italo Mussa

UNSWORTH, Ken.

Australian. Born in Richmond, Victoria, 28 May 1931. Educated at the University of Melbourne and Melbourne Teachers' College, 1952–54; studied at the National Art School, Sydney; influenced by John Passmore and Godfrey Miller, 1962–63. Married Elisabeth Crouch in 1954. Independent painter, Melbourne and Sydney, 1954–66; sculptor, Sydney, since 1966; also, performance artist since 1975. Art teacher, Victoria and New South Wales high schools, 1955–65; Lecturer in Art, Bathhurst Teachers' College, New South Wales, 1966–68; Chairman, Art Teacher Education, Tasmanian School of Art, Hobart, 1969–71. Lecturer in Sculpture, Sydney College of Advanced Education, since 1972. Executive Member, Contemporary Art Society of Australia, New South Wales, since 1972. Recipient: Captain Cook Bicentenary Sculpture Prize, Sydney, 1970; Australian-American Education Foundation Grant, to the United States, 1971; Residency, Power Studio, Cité des Arts, Paris, 1979–1980; Residency, Kunstlerhaus Bethanien, West Berlin, 1980; DAAD Artist Fellowship, West Berlin, 1987. Agent: Roslyn Oxley 9 Gallery, 13 Macdonald Street, Paddington, New South Wales. Address: 86 Paddington Street, Paddington, New South Wales 2021, Australia.

Individual Exhibitions:

1975 Institute of Contemporary Art, Sydney
1977 Institute of Contemporary Art, Sydney
1978 *Project 28,* Art Gallery of New South Wales, Sydney
Australian Pavilion, at the *Biennale,* Venice (with Robert Owen and John Davis)
1979 Institute of Contemporary Art, Sydney
Australian Embassy, Paris
1980 Kunstlerhaus Bethanien, Berlin
1981 Institute of Contemporary Art, Sydney
1982 Ivan Dougherty Gallery, Sydney
1983 Kobayashi Gallery, Tokyo
National Gallery of New Zealand, Wellington
1984 Roslyn Oxley 9 Gallery, Sydney
Art Gallery of New South Wales, Sydney
1985 Roslyn Oxley 9 Gallery, Sydney
1987 DAAD-Galerie, West Berlin
Roslyn Oxley 9 Gallery, Sydney

Ken Unsworth: *Zone of Wistful Thoughts*, 1985

Selected Group Exhibitions:

1967 *Alcorso-Sekers Sculpture Competition*, Art Gallery of New South Wales, Sydney
1968 *Flotta Lauro Sculpture Competition*, National Gallery of Victoria, Melbourne
1970 *14th Tasmanian Art Gallery Exhibition*, Hobart
1973 *Sculpturescape Triennale*, Mildura, Victoria (and 1975, 1978)
1976 *Biennale of Sydney*, Art Gallery of New South Wales, Sydney
1981 *1st Australian Sculpture Triennale*, Latrobe University, Melbourne
1982 *Biennale of Sydney*, Art Gallery of New South Wales, Sydney
1983 *Presence and Absence*, Art Gallery of Western Australia, Perth
1985 *Funf vom Funften*, DAAD-Galerie, West Berlin
1987 *ZeitBerliner*, I.F.A. Galerie, Stuttgart

Collections:

Art Gallery of New South Wales, Sydney; National Gallery of Australia, Canberra; National Capital Development Commission, Canberra; Australian National University, Canberra; National Gallery of Victoria, Melbourne; Flinders University, Adelaide, South Australia; City Art Gallery, Wollongong, New South Wales; Rijksmuseum Kröller-Müller, Otterlo, Netherlands; Museum Sztuki, Lodz, Poland.

Publications:

On UNSWORTH: books—*The Development of Australian Sculpture* by Graeme Sturgeon, London 1978; *Ken Unsworth: Project 28*, exhibition catalogue with text by Paul McGilliek, Sydney 1978; *Australian Sculptors* by Ken Scarlett, Sydney 1980; *Presence and Absence*, exhibition catalogue with essay by Jonathan Watkins, Perth 1983; articles—"The Performance Works of Ken Unsworth" by Paul McGillick in *ICA Magazine* (Sydney), January/March 1978; "The Venice Biennale: Back to Nature" by Henry Martin in *Art International* (Zurich), no. 6, 1978; "Art and Nature at the Biennale" by Milton Gendel in *Art in America* (New York), September 1978; "Australia: A Multiple Reality" by Pierre Restany in *Domus* (Milan), July 1979; "Ken Unsworth: Some Recent Works" by Paul McGillick in *Aspect* (Sydney), no. 4, 1981.

My use of technology, electronic and biomechanical, is to explore neither the dimensions of its own possibilities nor its poetic potential, but rather a subliminal, low-profile, low-key, low-technology application and adaptation in order to realise the dream—never to lose in my work the feeling of being, rather to pluck the strings of forgotten memories and emotions to invoke the sensations of the other life.

My intention is to create strange, ritualistic provocations whose outward forms and appearances implant themselves in the mind, and assert their essential inwardness by resonating with the viewer's own footsteps—sounds surrounded by sound, light caught in light, and movement in motionless movement. These visual manifestations don't happen in the real world; they are not experienced in the real world, yet happen constantly, endlessly recurring, but we only see them in that split-second of a blink of an eye, in the moment of a dream or in the sound of a door slamming.

The zone of wistful thoughts is a dimension-less space in which thought, like soft-teased skeins of solar winds, eternally streams, half-felt, half-heard, half-remembered, though the void.

The formal appearance of the installation itself perpetuates the inherent structural and perceptual ambiguities. Seemingly self-supporting, self-generating electric motors driving propellers, in whose slipstream black silken pennants constantly flutter, are held in tension in the mist of their own shadows by river stones floating several inches off the floor. Gravity is suspended, time is motionless, and the soundless sounds of energy prevail.

—Ken Unsworth

Ken Unsworth came late to his art. Not till he was about 40 did he discover that sculpture was best able to embody his feelings. In an Australian art world which especially prized subtle observation of landscape, he instead felt a need to express great human emotions, with simple directness. In 1967 his earliest venture away from painting was biomorphic soft sculpture; sensuous, even erotic, but too complicated. By 1971 he had found his personal language of forms. Surface manipulation and detail were eliminated, and at first glance purely sculptural experiences were readily apprehended: they were usually extreme states of tension, compression or balance. Although these first mature works were welded metal constructions and concrete slab constructions, they were not formalist drawing-in-space but instead had the abstract energy of a human body testing its limits.

Thus in 1975 it was perhaps inevitable that the breakthrough into art of considerable quality was Unsworth's first essay at performance art. "Five Secular Settings for Sculpture as Ritual and Burial Piece" was a series of five briefly-held static body-sculptures, in which Unsworth was suspended from various supports; followed by burial alive under shovelsful of sand while standing in an upright glass "coffin" from which he was released by a bystander smashing the glass and allowing the dry sand to drain away. In the same year the static sculptures turned to sensuous though plain materials such as worn river-stones floating from wires, or caked and sliced earth.

Music accompanied the "Five Secular Settings"..., and music or other sounds—babies crying, gun fire, night birds and wind—have been integral to subsequent performance pieces or installations. "Face to Face", 1977, was another physically demanding seven-part brief performance in which the artist, suspended upside-down, first knifed his way out of a sack, and ended lying propped on sticks.

Since then the artist has more often been a background element, endlessly replacing a mechanical crawling doll-child on a plank from which it endlessly falls, to the accompaniment of the staccato beat of a mechanical doll drummer, or sitting immobile by a doll-child and an endlessly bouncing ball.

Such pieces, contributed to *Biennales* of Sydney at the Art Gallery of New South Wales, were maintained for many weeks and (like Gilbert and George's five-day living sculpture and Marina and Ulay's 16 day static performance at the same museum in 1973 and 1981 respectively) were remarkably successful assertions of performance art as primarily a visual art properly shown in the context of a visual-arts museum. Their non-narrative character, or else their endlessly repeated brief narrative, ensured that they were not experienced as out-of-context theatre.

Unsworth's work has gained him invitations from the museum at Lodz, Poland, and the experience of a society under such stress as Poland's in turn influenced a 1982 installation, of two rooms from which humans had fled, leaving only the sense of fear and desperation, and implicit cries for help.

In his various ways—object sculpture, body sculpture, performance art, installation—Unsworth has shown that contemporary art can address itself plainly and with seriousness to the universal mysteries of birth, life, survival, death and resurrection. A body can float, stones hold themselves gracefully in the air: souls therefore may leap across voids, and meet.

—Daniel Thomas

URBAN, Janos.

Swiss. Born in Szeged, Hungary, 5 November 1934; emigrated to Switzerland, 1956: naturalized, 1976;

educated at Secondary Arts and Crafts School, Budapest, until 1953; studied art history and philosophy at Eotovos Lorand University, Budapest, 1953-56 and art at the Ecole Cantonale des Beaux-Arts, Lausanne, Switzerland, 1957-61. Married Jacqueline Nicod in 1963; son: Matthias. Independent artist, Lausanne, since 1961; mixed media work with phosphorus, UV light and radio waves, from 1967; "Memorandum Ancona" and "Lived-in Places," scripto-visual works, from 1970. Professor, Ecole des Beaux-Arts, Lausanne, since 1963. Recipient: City of Geneva Prize, *Salon de la Jeune Gravure Suisse,* 1970; Landis and Gyr-Forderungspreis, Zug, 1974. Address: 4 Chemin de Pre-Fleuri, 1006 Lausanne, Switzerland.

Individual Exhibitions:

1961 Galerie L'Entracte, Lausanne
1963 Galerie L'Entracte, Lausanne
1966 Galerie L'Entracte, Lausanne
1970 Galerie Palette, Zurich
Galerie Impact, Lausanne
Bischofsmuhle, Hildesheim, West Germany
1971 Galleria Sincron, Brescia, Italy
1973 Galerie la Fenetre, Nice
Galerie Akumulatory, Poznan, Poland
1974 Salle Patino, Geneva
Galerie der Reflektion Press, Stuttgart
1976 Galleria Civica d'Arte Moderna, Modena, Italy
1977 Galerie R + B, Fribourg, Switzerland
1980 Stempelplaats, Amsterdam
Bazillus Arts Space, Wurzburg, West Germany

Selected Group Exhibitions:

1969 *22 Jonge Switzers,* Stedelijk Museum, Amsterdam
1972 *Art Systems* 2, Museo de Arte Moderna, Buenos Aires
1973 *Biennale de l'Art Suisse,* Kunsthaus, Zurich
1978 *Sammlung der Gotthard-Bank,* Helmhaus, Zurich
1979 *International Print Biennale,* City Art Museum, Bradford, England
Art Documentation 79, California State University at San Jose
1980 *Videowochen Essen,* Museum Folkwang, Essen
22 Artistas Suicos, Galeria Nacional Belem, Lisbon
1981 *Videoarte Suizo,* Centro de Arte y Communicacion, Buenos Aires
1982 *Documenta 7,* Museum Fridericianum, Kassel, West Germany

Collections:

Musé Cantonal des Beaux-Arts, Lausanne; Cabinet des Estampes, Geneva; Kunsthaus, Zurich; City of Berne.

Publications:

By URBAN: books—*Approche des Iles—a scripto-visual work,* with others, Lausanne 1972; *Le Bateau de 13 h. 15,* with J. Monnier and L. Prebandier, Lausanne 1973; *Erlebte Erdteile,* Geneva 1974; *Praxis,* Lausanne 1978; *Poiesis,* Lausanne 1979; films—*Again . . . and Again,* 1973; *The Skating Rink,* 1973; *Cross-Talkas,* with L. Prebandier and Hans-Werner Kalkmann, 1973.

On URBAN: books—*If I Had a Mind . . . ,* edited by Klaus Groh, Cologne 1971; *Il Corpo come Linguaggio* by Lea Vergine, Milan 1974; *Cine-Graphia: 10th Festival Videoart, Locarno,* exhibition catalogue, Locarno 1980; *Schweizer Kunst 70–80,* exhibition catalogue, Lucerne 1981; *Fri-Art 81,* exhibition catalogue, Fribourg 1981; *Love/Hate/Fear/Suicide: Mail Art,* exhibition catalogue, Brussels 1981: *Bodies of Artists,* exhibition catalogue, by Carsten Schmidt-Olsen, Aalborg 1981; *A Mail Art Show,* exhibition catalogue, Detroit 1981: *Stalin: Centenaire de Joseph Djougachvili,* exhibition catalogue, Nice 1981.

Janos Urban: *Diapositive* sound and light installation

URIBURU, Nicolas (Garcia).

Argentinian. Born in Buenos Aires in 1937. Studied architecture in Buenos Aires. First Colouring project, Grand Canal, Venice, 1968; has worked on colouring natural phenomena since 1968. Lives and works in Paris. Recipient: Prix Braque, 1964; Prix Lefranc, 1967; Grand Premio Nacional, Buenos Aires, 1968; First Prize, *Biennale,* Tokyo, 1975. Address: 67 rue St. Dominique, Paris 7, France.

Individual Exhibitions:

1954 Galeria Muller, Buenos Aires
1960 Galeria Lirolay, Buenos Aires
1962 Galeria Antonio Souza, Mexico City
1963 Galeria Rubbers, Buenos Aires
1965 Galeria Guernica, Buenos Aires
1967 Galerie Iris Clert, Paris
1968 General Electric Institute, Montevideo
1972 Galerie Spectrum, Antwerp
1973 Centro de Arte y Communicacion, Buenos Aires
Musé d'Art Moderne, Paris
1974 Leo Castelli Graphics, New York
Musée Galliera, Paris
1978 Museum of American Art, Maldonado, Uruguay
1979 Salas Nacionales de Exposicion, Buenos Aires
1982 Hara Museum, Tokyo

Selected Group Exhibitions:

1967 *Salon de Mai,* Paris
1968 *Graphics Biennale,* Paris
1971 *Air, Fire, Earth and Water,* Museum of Fine Arts, Boston
Biennale, Paris
1972 *Bienal,* Medellin, Colombia
1974 *International Graphics Biennale,* Tokyo
Art and Culture in the Third World, Institute of Contemporary Arts, London
Contraste Simultane des Couleurs, Faculty of Medicine, Paris
1980 *Biennale,* Tokyo
1982 *Documenia,* Kassel, West Germany

Nicolas Uriburu: *Collage*, 1974

Publications:

On URIBURU: book—*Art in Argentina* by Jorge Glusberg, Milan 1986; articles—"Nicolas Uriburu" by John Perreault in the *Village Voice* (New York), 4 June 1970: "Art Concepts from Europe" by Pierre Restany in *Domus* (Milan). June 1970; "Nicolas Garcia Uriburu" by Jorge Glusberg in *Art and Artists* (London), January 1971: "Le marche aux Puces de l'art moderne" by Otto Hahn in *L'Express* (Paris). October 1971; "Uriburu: Coloration" by C. Bovyeure in *Lettres Francaises* (Paris), June 1972; "The World All in Green" by Pierre Restany in *Domus* (Milan), April 1973; "Une Perception Autre" by P. Borgeaud in *Pariscope,* December 1973; "Uriburu: La Vie en Vert" in *Connaissance des Arts* (Paris), February 1974; "Dix Questions sur l'Art et Les Nouveaux Media" in *Artitudes* (St. Jeannet, France), July 1974; article by Pierre Restany in *Domus* (Milan), October 1981.

My work is about ecology. I began by painting a series of trees in Argentina in 1960. In 1964 I won the Prix Braque, a scholarship to Paris. In 1968 during the Venice *Biennale* I coloured the waters of the Grand Canal in fluorescent green (about 3 kilometers): that was the beginning of a series of colourings in different waters all over the world: the East River, New York: the Seine, Paris; the Rio de la Plata, Buenos Aires—and fountains, lakes, ports, etc., always in a fluorescent green, showing my alarm about pollution. In New York in 1970 I began a series in green colours, "Antagonism Between Nature and Civilization." I have also done some body art, colouring my sexual organs, face and hair in green. In 1971 I began a defence of the trees of a park that the authorities wanted to cut; next I planted some trees in the city of Buenos Aires and also in a museum in Uruguay. I've coloured the waters of the Rhine in collaboration with the German artist Joseph Beuys and planted with him the first 7 trees (of what will eventually be about 7,000) at *Documenta 7* in Kassel. Now I am working on a series about animals that are disappearing from the world. My art defines the struggle between nature and civilization. That's why I colour my body, my genitals, and the great waters of the world. The more developed countries are destroying water, land and air, resources for the future in Latin American countries.

—Nicolas Uriburu

The relation between man and his environment has always been a matter of concern for all societies. Ecology, a discipline that began to develop at the beginning of the 20th century, is a branch of biology that deals with the relation between living things and their environment. Organisms, plants, animals, all of them perform certain activities which tend mainly to their adaptation to the surrounding medium. The three large constituent areas of ecology—vegetable, animal and human—roused successively the interest of botanists, zoologists, and lastly, of sociologists. The term "human ecology" appeared in 1921, and since then, that region has been part of the region of social sciences. Its problems are not only limited to pointing out the mutual connections between man and his environment, but emphasize the social aspects of his adaptation. If by the term eco-system is meant the universe of the elements which surround the subject as they become signs, that is to say, when man supplies them with a meaning—a topological semantics would explain the large number of forms in which man articulates space and establishes semantic relations with it. One of the manifestations of this production of meaning, born from man's relations with his environment, is the "artistic discourse," particularly that which is called "ecological art." The ecological artist develops his language in connection with two types of elements of the eco-system: the natural ones (rivers, mountains, etc.) and the artificial ones (buildings, urbanistic complexes, highways). The intersection between the artistic and what the ecologists call "natural areas" (territorial unities created and/or conditioned or not by human activity) constitutes a new phenomenon, which compels us to adopt a critical point of view in an entirely different way. Nicolas Uriburu coloured the waters of Venice Canals with green aniline in 1968, during the year's Biennial. In May and June, 1970, he coloured the East River in New York, the River Seine in Paris, once again the Grand Canal in Venice and the River Plata in Buenos Aires. In 1971, when the Paris Biennial took place, he coloured the Vincennes Lake, and he coloured himself, as a participant at a meeting (colour body work); in June, 1972, he coloured fourteen fountains at Kassel, in 1973 the Riachuelo in Buenos Aires; in 1974 the fountains in Brussels. The ecological proposals of Uriburu extend to future projects: the colouring of the fountains of Versailles, that of the snows of Mont Blanc, and of Iguazu and Niagara Falls. The project called "Cono Sur" consists of the simultaneous colouring of every river in the different countries of the southern hemisphere, by an artist from each country; through the project "Agua Nuestra" he will colour every Latin American place (Uriburu is an Argentinian architect) where water represents conflict: Panama, Iquitos, Titicaca, Puna Arenas. Uriburu's work fuses with nature and at the same time it complements her. We are, thus, in front of a different event: the artist's language inscribes itself in the space transformed by man, the signs spread over large extensions, and thus man gets himself, literally speaking, "to pervade nature with humanity." Uriburu's art refuses to adapt itself to the rules imposed by the important museums or the international galleries, but intends to take the Trojan horse out of its walls, in order to see whether the works done in the 60's are able to endure living in the open air of daily life. The protecting confinement is no longer an attraction for the vanguard, who want to operate in the reality of the profane ambits. The artist who lives in the second half of his century no longer creates new works, but new channels of sensibility, new discoveries which propose different fields of exploration of the spirit. Instead of undertaking the recreation of reality by means of imitative or decorative objects, the artist makes use of representations which do not exist as separate entities, but as elements which supply the sites where they are placed with a new definition or a new point of view. The traditional work of art has begun to be sustained by an artistic situation composed by happenings which correspond to social and ideological function, and to function related to creativeness and play, all of them belonging to the field of probability, to the world of free relation. In order to convey his sensible message, the traditional artist repeats the act of creation in a God-like manner, resorting to those tricks painters and sculptors have made use of for centuries. The ecological artists carry on with their researches in different operation levels. They are no longer interested in the space that must be filled, nor in the academic discussions about the limits between poetry and painting, nor between fullness and void, because the matter has become a situation; and this situation is communicating, is a creator of signs, and it comprises forms, ideas and being; it probably does not turn out faultless products of "good art"; it deals with the artistic event as a cultural phenomenon, as a sociological experience, as a practical work in psychology, an urbanistic project, a sort of theoretical and experimental illustration of human behaviour.

—Jorge Glusberg

V

VALENTINE, DeWain.

American. Born in Fort Collins, Colorado, 27 August 1936. Educated at University of Colorado, Boulder, 1954–60, B.F.A. 1958, M.F.A. 1960. Independent sculptor, in Colorado, 1960–65, and in Venice, California since 1965: cast polyester works, 1967–75; laminated glass works from 1976. Instructor, University of Colorado, Boulder, 1959–61; Instructor, University of California at Los Angeles, 1965–67. Recipient: Yale-Norfolk Art School Fellowship, New Haven, Connecticut, 1958; Guggenheim Fellowship, 1980; National Endowment for the Arts Fellowship, 1981. Address: 69 Market Street, Venice, California 90291, U.S.A.

Individual Exhibitions:

1958 University of Colorado, Boulder
1960 University of Colorado, Boulder
1964 The Gallery, Denver
1968 Douglas Gallery, Vancouver
Ace Gallery, Los Angeles
1969 University of British Columbia, Vancouver
Galerie Bischofberger, Zurich
University of Washington, Seattle
1970 Pasadena Museum of Art, California
1973 Denise René Gallery, New York
Walter Kelly Gallery, Chicago
1974 San Jose Museum of Art, California
Edward Thorp Gallery, Santa Barbara, California
Betty Gold Gallery, Los Angeles
1975 La Jolla Museum of Contemporary art, California
California State University at Northridge
Long Beach Museum of Art, California
1977 Santa Barbara Museum of Art, California
1979 Los Angeles County Museum of Art
1980 Malinda Wyatt Gallery, Venice, California
1981 Projects Studio One, Institute for Art and Urban Resources, New York
1982 Thomas Babeor Gallery, La Jolla, California
Malinda Wyatt Gallery, Venice, California
Missouri Botanical Garden, St. Louis
Laumeier Sculpture Park, St. Louis
1983 Madison Art Center, Wisconsin
1984 Thomas Babeor Gallery, La Jolla, California
1985 Honolulu Academy of Arts, Hawaii
Contemporary Arts Center, Honolulu, Hawaii

Selected Group Exhibitions:

1966 *Whitney Annual Sculpture Exhibition,* Whitney Museum, New York
1969 *The Industrial Edge,* Walker Art Center, Minneapolis
1973 *American Art 1948–1973,* Seattle Art Museum, Washington
1976 *Contemporary Masters,* Libra Gallery, The Claremont Colleges, California
1979 *Change, Inc. West,* Newport Harbor Art Museum, California
1980 *Sculpture in California 1975–1980,* San Diego Museum of Art
1981 *California Light and Space.* Lonny Gans and Associates, Venice, California
1983 *Urban Sculpture/Architectural Concerns,* Security Pacific National Bank Gallery, Los Angeles
1985 *California Sculpture Show,* Yorkshire Sculpture Park, Bretton Hall College
1987 *Sculpture of the Sixties,* Margo Leavin Gallery, Los Angeles

Collections:

Whitney Museum, New York: Art Institute of Chicago; Milwaukee Art Center; Los Angeles County Museum of Art; Norton Simon Museum, Pasadena, California: La Jolla Museum of Contemporary Art, California; Palm Springs Desert Museum, California; Aldrich Museum of Contemporary Art, Ridgefield, Connecticut; Contemporary Arts Center, Honolulu, Hawaii; Vancouver Art Gallery, British Columbia.

Publications:

By VALENTINE: articles—"An Interview with DeWain Valentine." with Kurt Von Meier, in *Artforum* (New York). May 1969; "DeWain Valentine: An Interview," with Melinda Wortz in *Journal* (Los Angeles), June 1974.

On VALENTINE: books—*Neue Dimensionen der Plastik* by Udo Kultermann, Tübingen. West Germany 1967; *Plastics in Arts* by Pierre Restany, Paris 1974; *A Decade of Sculpture: The 1960's* by Julia Busch. Philadelphia 1974; *Sunshine Muse* by Peter Plagens. New York 1974; *Art and Plastics* by Franco Passoni, Milan 1975: *50 West Coast Artists* by Henry Hopkins, San Francisco 1982; *Living Materials: A Sculptor's Handbook* by Oliver Andrews, Berkeley 1983; *DeWain Valentine: Recent Works* exhibition catalogue with essay by Melinda Wortz, Honolulu 1985.

Sculptor DeWain Valentine, who moved to Southern California from Colorado in 1965, has been closely identified with the so-called "L.A. Look," which during the 1960's began to attract international attention to contemporary art activity in Los Angeles. A "cool" minimalism and preoccupation with elegant

DeWain Valentine: *Triangle Gray*, 1982

surfaces was indeed characteristic of the work of artists such as Valentine, Larry Bell, Craig Kauffman, and Robert Irwin. However, despite certain mutual interests (for example, the aesthetic potential of industrial materials), neither these arts nor their works participated in a cohesive "movement." The most prominent figures associated with the emergence of contemporary Los Angeles art in fact displayed a wide variety of interests as represented by the quasi-POP imagery of Ed Ruscha and Billy Al Bengston, the tableaux assemblages of Ed Keinholz, or Irwin's optical experimentation. Nonetheless, fascination with technology, industrial materials, crafted surfaces, and visual sensuality were characteristic of one notable aspect of the creative milieu in which Valentine worked in the late 1960's. With his elegantly seductive cast-resin sculptures, Valentine played an important role in the development of what became widely regarded as the prevailing Southern California aesthetic. Furthermore, in his subsequent work he has continued to pursue the same basic concerns—mainly the exploration of light—which motivated his earlier work. Valentine's unparalleled technical virtuosity in resin casting on a monumental scale and the undeniable beauty of his work has, unfortunately, tended to obscure his important goals. Over the years Valentine has consistently developed a body of sculptural work based on geometric forms infused with subtle gradations of transparent or transluscent color "activated" (and modified) by ambient light. Consisting of polyester resin or acrylic plastic discs, wedges, rings, slabs and related shapes, Valentine's art achieves a remarkably effective fusion of physical substance and light. The installations done in the early 1970s mark an important and logical progression from these individual objects to the light environments and related work of the past decade. Throughout, his basic goal has remained the figurative and literal "illumination" of a fundamental duality: matter and phenomenon ("tonnage and ethereality," to use the artist's words) manipulated into visual harmony by technical means. Despite his use of industrial materials and techniques, these concerns place Valentine firmly within a naturalist tradition. The prismatic lenses of the late 1960's, the camera obscura pieces and photomontages of the mid 1970's, and even the concurrent planes and spectrums (cantilevered, suspended, curved), all depend upon natural phenomena to reveal their true content. In every case, there is present a view of the world that is firmly rooted in landscape. Even the delicate suspended-rod installations (such as *Catenary Light*), by introducing a curved shaft of exterior light into a dark room, deal with the experience of natural light as it responds to weather, season and time of day. The same basic perceptual concerns and interest in transparency of form underlie Valentine's recent large-scale laminated glass constructions. As always, an undeniable physical beauty and technical mastery are subservient to ideas based on nature and the almost mystical quality of light. Valentine's philosophical goals clearly separate his art from minimalist refinement and decorative formalism. His accomplishment has been the dematerialization of physicality in a way that asserts the primacy of light. Viewed in perceptual terms, Valentine's interest would appear to have more in common with French Impressionist ideas than with recent formalist theory. Nonetheless, his work does relate to that of the "environmentalists" (Irwin, Michael Asher, James Turrell) whose non-object investigations of light and perception constitute one of Southern California's significant contributions to contemporary art.

—Paul J. Karlstrom

VALOCH, Jiri.

Czechoslovakian. Born in Brno, 6 September 1946. Studied Bohemistics, Germanistics and aesthetics, J. E. Purkyně University, Brno, 1965–70. Married Mirka Antonova in 1971 (divorced, 1972). Produced first visual poems and typestracts, 1964; first photographic works, 1969; first conceptual poetry, 1970. Artist and art theoretician, House of Arts, Brno, since 1972: has organized exhibitions and written articles on numberous Czech artists. Address: Jugoslavska 46a, 61300 Brno, Czechoslovakia.

Jiri Valoch: *Sign 2 × Z*, 1987

Individual Exhibitions:

1966 Music Theatre, Ústi and Labem, Czechoslovakia
1969 Museum, Krnov, Czechoslovakia
1970 House of the Young, Jindřichuv Hradec, Czechoslovakia
1971 Regional Gallery, Jihlava, Czechoslovakia
1972 Information Centre for Events, Bielefeld, West Germany
1974 *Sculptures*, Gallery Akumulatory, Poznan, Poland
1977 *Relations*, Galleria Mercato del Sale, Milan
1978 *Relations and Haiku*, Municipal Library, Wroclaw, Poland
1979 *In, Oltre*, Centro Culturale, Monza, Italy
1984 *Werken uit 1964–82*, Het Apollohuis, Eindhoven, Netherlands
1985 *Vizuální poezie*, Kulturní středisko města Blanska, Czechoslovakia

Selected Group Exhibitions:

1966 *Uměni pisma—Poezie pisma—Visudiní poezie*, Moravian Museum, Brno
1970 *Konkrete Poezie?*. Stedelijk Museum. Amsterdam
1971 *Arte de Sistemas I*, Centro de Arte y Communicacion, Buenos Aires
1973 *Texts*, Balatonboglár, Hungary
1977 *Texty Wisualne*, Gallery Labyrint, Lublin, Poland (travelled to Lodz, 1978)
1979 *Sprachen jenseits von Dichtung*. Kunstverein, Münster, West Germany
1980 *Drawing '80, Pécz* Gallery, Hungary
1981 *Kunstlerbücher*, Kunstverein, Frankfurt
1984 *Am Anfang war das Wort*, Städtisches Galerie, Lüdenscheid, West Germany
1985 *Salut Chlebnikow*, Staatliches Lindenaumuseum, Altenburg, East Germany

Collections:

Archief voor Visuele, Concrete en Experimentele Poezie, Dutch Literary Museum. The Hague; Muzeum Sztuki, Lodz, Poland; Muzeum Narodowe, Wroclaw, Poland; Regional Gallery, Jihlava, Czechoslovakia; Moravian Gallery, Brno; Kupferstichkabinett der Staatlichen Kunstsammlungen, Dresden; Archive Hanns Sohm, Markgronimgen, West Germany; Stedelijk Museum, Amsterdam; Schlubladenmuseum Herbert Disel, Berne; Museo Laboratorio Casabianca, Malo, Italy.

Publications:

By VALOCH: books and phamphlets—*HLAS/VOICE/VOIX/STIMME*, London 1966; *9 Optical Poems*, London 1967; *Unlucky Number—13 mimeoenphamphs*, Toronto 1968; *An Interrupted Poem*, Toronto 1969; *Optical Book*, Brescia, Italy 1970; *Ga: The First and Last Collection of Sound Poems by Jiri Valoch*, London 1971; *A Minimal Monument*, Welling, Kent 1971; *Poem for Ad Reinhardt*, London 1971; *Landscapes I*, Utrecht 1972; *See Page 13*, Friedrichfehn 1973; *Hommage á Valoch*, West Berlin 1975; *12 Excercises*, West Berlin 1976; *Mobile-Two Structures-Piece III*, London 1980; *20 Works: Kunstinformatie 35*, Gorinchem 1981; *Haiku*, Toronto 1983; *Pozorování—kniha pro přátele*, Brno 1983; *Word Works*, West Berlin 1984; *Five Parts of One Piece*, Eschenau 1984; *Three Sheets*, Eschenau 1984; *Werken uit 1964–1982: Collection Herman de Vries*, Eindhoven 1984; *8 x 2 Portfolio: Czech Visual Texts*, editor, Dresden 1986; *Semantic Study*, Munich 1986.

On VALOCH: books—*Experimentalni poezie*, edited by J. Hirsal and B. Grogerova, Prague 1966; *Once Again by* Jean-Francois Bory, New York 1967; *Verso la Poesia Totale*, edited by A. Spatola, Milan 1967; *Poezie in Fuzie*, edited by Paul de Vree, Antwerp 1967; *Concrete Poetry: A World View*, edited by M. E. Solt, Bloomington, Indiana 1968: *Aktuelle Kunst in Ost Europa*, edited by Klaus Groh, Cologne 1970; *Exempla: Documents of Concrete and Visual Poetry*, edited by Maurizio Nannucci, Florence 1970; *Konkretedichtung*, edited by S. J. Schmidt, Munich 1972; *Poesia Visiva Internazionale*, edited by Galleria Il Canale, Venice 1974; *Concrete, Visual and Signalist Poetry*, edited by M. Todorovic, Belgrade 1975; *La Escritura en Liberiad*, edited by F. Millan and R. Sanchez, Madrid 1975; *Von für über—Heinz Gappmayr*, edited by Peter Weiermair, Frankfurt 1985; *Zwanzig Jahre Rainer Verlag: Eine Anthologie, Ein Almanach*, edited by R. Pretzell and T. Milch, West Berlin 1986; *Artists' Statements*, edited by Richard Kriesche, Graz 1987; *Geschichte des Fotogramms*, edited by Floris M. Neususs, Cologne 1987.

All my work has been and is motivated language—in the sixties by the possibility to isolate its elements and to create from them a purely aesthetic structure, since the break of the sixties and seventies by seeking limitations and relations that the extremely reduced language can form, either in non-verbal context/phototexts, verbal interventions in nature/or in itself. The starting point is the annihilation or at least the maximal suppression of the signifier/signified relationship. When language is released from these bonds, it is possible to work with it in another way. I am interested in semantic complications, giving evidence of the language as such, and in autonomous language structures formed by isolating the meaning or by repeating identical isolated elements. I am interested in the metamorphosis of the sign into a quasi-sign which cannot be drawn into a conventional communication system.

—Jiří Valoch

van AMEN, Woody.

Dutch. Born in Eindhoven, 26 August 1936. Studied art at the Akademie van Beeldende Kunsten, Rotterdam, 1956–58; mainly self-taught in painting. Served in Geneeskundige Troepen, Dutch Army, Amersfoort, 1956. Married Cocky Voermans in 1961; daughters: Cybele and Claudia-Nathalie. Worked as window-dresser, gardener, sailor, housepainter, docker, wood-finisher, etc., in Rotterdam, 1958–60. Independent artist, in Rotterdam, since 1960 (worked in New York City, 1961–63). Worked with Scarabee Experimental Theatre Group, Haarlem, 1967; Academie van Beeldende Kunsten, Rotterdam, 1973. Recipient: Dutch Ministry of Culture Stipend, 1967–69; Rotterdam Arts Foundation Stipend, 1969. Address: Benedenstraat 87, 3077 BA Rotterdam, Netherlands.

Individual Exhibitions:

1962 Cottage Club on the Lake, New York
1963 Galerie Delta, Rotterdam
1965 Galerie 't Venster, Rotterdam
Stedelijk Museum, Amsterdam
1966 Galerie Delta, Rotterdam
1967 Galerie 20, Amsterdam
1968 Galerie Waalkens, Finsterwolde. Netherlands
Markt 17, Enschede, Netherlands
1969 Galerie 't Venster, Rotterdam
Galerie 20, Amsterdam
Galerie Jalmar, Amsterdam
1970 Galerie De Doelen, Rotterdam (with Wim Gijzen)
Galerie Defacqz, Brussels
Galerie 't Venster, Rotterdam
1971 Galerie 20, Amsterdam
1973 Galerie Yaki Kornblit, Amsterdam
Galerie Richard Foncke, Ghent
1974 Galerie Yaki Kornblit, Amsterdam
1975 Pander Kunstcentrum, The Hague
Galerie Yaki Kornblit, Amsterdam
1978 *Moderne Kunstvoorwerpen*, Museum Boymans-van Beuningen, Rotterdam
Musée d'Art et d'Histoire, Geneva
Museum Het Prinsenhof, Delft, Netherlands
Galerie Brinkman, Amsterdam
1980 Galerie Lara Vincy, Paris
Galerie Brinkman, Amsterdam
1981 Kunstcentrum De Vaart, Hilversum, Netherlands
Buchmann Art Gallery, Antwerp
1982 Stichting Kasteel van Rhoon, Netherlands
National Museum, Singapore
Centre International d'Art Plastique, Hasselt, Belgium
Gemeentemuseum, The Hague
1983 Gallery Black Cat, Rotterdam
Centre International d'Art Plastique, Hasselt, Belgium
1984 Galerie J.L., Ostende, Belgium
1985 Van Abbemuseum, Eindhoven, Netherlands
1986 Gallery Art Action, Singapore
Le Cadre Gallery, Hong Kong
Oets Fine Art Gallery, Djakarta, Indonesia

Selected Group Exhibitions:

1964 *Neue Realisten and Pop Art*, Akademie der Künste, West Berlin
1968 *European Painters Today*. Musée des Arts Décoratifs, Paris (toured the United States)
1970 *De Metamorfose van het Objekt*, Museum Boymans-van Beuningen, Rotterdam (toured Switzerland. Germany and Italy)

Woody Van Amen: *Steenrandsel Spel*, 1972

1975 *Art Information Festival*, Middelburg, Netherlands
1976 *Biennale*, Venice
1977 *Beethoven, Music for the Millions*, Gemeentemuseum, Arnhem, Netherlands
1979 *De Jaren Zestig*, Galerie De Vries en Roeloff, Rotterdam
1981 *Not Waving*, Palais des Beaux-Arts, Brussels
1985 *Mens en Omgeving*, De Beyerd Centrum, Breda, Netherlands
1987 *Line and Image*, Muhlenberg College, Allentown, Pennsylvania (toured the United States 1988–89)

Collections:

Stedelijk Museum, Amsterdam: Peter Stuyvesant Foundation. Amsterdam; Museum Boymans-van Beuningen, Rotterdam; Centraal Museum, Utrecht; Frans Halsmuseum, Haarlém, Netherlands; Palais des Beaux-Arts, Brussels.

Publications:

By van AMEN: books and pamphlets—*Filosofie van de Nieuwe Romantiek*, Rotterdam 1973; *Book of Stamps*, with others, Amsterdam 1976; *Transit 3: Translation-Transformation*, Amsterdam 1977; *240 Days/Dagen/Jours/Tage*, with foreword by R. H. Fuchs, Amsterdam 1985; disc—*Het leven van Woody*, sound recording with Jan Donia, 1966.

On van AMEN: books—*Art Around the World* by R. W. D. Oxenaar, New York 1966; *Le Livre Rouge de la Revolution Picturale* by Pierre Restany, Milan 1968; *De Eksplosie van het Intellekt* by Jan Donia, Hilversum, Netherlands 1968; *Le Livre Blanc* by Pierre Restany, Milan 1969; *Le Pop Art* by Jose Pierre, Paris 1975; *Woody van Amen: Moderne Kunstvoorwerpen 1963–1977*, exhibition catalogue, with texts by R. Hammacher-van den Brande, Jan Donia, Pierre Restany, Goose Oosterhof and Peter Bulthuis, Rotterdam 1978; *Nieuwe Romantiek van Woody van Amen*, exhibition catalogue with texts by Rein-Arend Leeuw and Peter Bulthuis, Delft 1978; *Woody van Amen: objecten, tekeningen, grafiek*, exhibition catalogue with text by Kees Broos, The Hague 1982; *Beeldende kunst uit de verzameling van Agnes en Frits Becht*, with texts by R. H. Fuchs and Saskia Bos, Utrecht 1984.

New Romanticism

1. "New Romanticism" aims at enriching contemporary art by assigning a major role to feeling and imagination.
2. In a cool society which produces "cool art," "new romanticism" presents a form of art which meets the longings of people today for warmth, happiness and recognizable contents.
3. The need for romance has been clearly recognized in the world of films, fashion and theatre, but the plastic arts are lagging behind in this respect. New romanticism has made it its task to re-activate romanticism in the plastic arts.
4. The chief motive of "new romanticism" is to make—and make recognizable again—the ordinary things which people tend to think of as nice. 5. Socially this point of departure could prove to be of great value: it will restore the basic function of art as a means of communication intelligible to all.
6. The views of "new romanticism" will restore some balance in the chaotic and confusing multitude of art expressions of today.
7. The emphasis on feeling and imagination and the use of ordinary and familiar means of portrayal will set free the personal creativity of the "consumer." This will once again stimulate spontaneity in making and experiencing art.
8. "New romanticism" is improving the image of art.

—Woody van Amen

Camesi in Switzerland concentrates upon making art (pictures, etc.) the servant of a kind of aesthetic architecture. Pictures, like bricks, can, he has been able to show, build walls, fireplaces, houses even. At the Sao Paulo *Bienal* of 1973 he constructed a wall of self-portraits. Woody van Amen does the opposite. His *new realism* quite frequently demonstrates that architecture (and furniture), with only slight interpolations, can become pictures or *objects*. What he seeks to make clear, often with many humorous interjections, is that the world we know—from ice-block to pavingstone, from *Grande-armoire* to kitchen sink—is a natural-cum-manmade world, ripe for plunder by an artist if he knows what to do with so much valuable raw material. Not that he is suggesting a scratch round for easy-to-come-by readymades. The contrary. Whatever takes his fancy also inspires him to give it an artistic facelift. Bright colours. Aesthetic machinery. Unexpected conjunctions. Van Amen implies that the spade work performed in this field by Dada and Surrealism is already dated, and that it is time to start creating anew with materials which even if they are not raw can still be coaxed by inventive processes into the furniture and fittings of an unexplored demi-paradise.

—Sheldon Williams

VAN BUREN, Richard.

American. Born in Syracuse, New York, in 1937. Educated at San Francisco State College, the University of Mexico, and Mexico City College. Taught at the School of Visual Arts, New York. Agent: Paula Cooper Gallery, New York. Address: c/o Paula Cooper Inc., 155 Wooster Street, New York, New York 10012, U.S.A.

Individual Exhibitions:

1961 New Mission Gallery, San Francisco
1962 San Francisco Museum of Art
1964 Dilexi Gallery, San Francisco
1967 Bykert Gallery, New York
1968 Bykert Gallery, New York
1969 Bykert Gallery, New York
1970 Bennington College, Vermont
Ithaca College, Museum of Art, New York (with Benglis and Sanderson)
1972 Paula Cooper Gallery, New York
1973 112 Greene Street, New York
1974 Texas Gallery, Houston
Rice University, Houston
1975 Paula Cooper Gallery, New York
Graduate Center, City University of New York
1977 Paula Cooper Gallery, New York

Selected Group Exhibitions:

1964 *Bay Area Artists*, San Francisco Museum of Art
1967 *A Romantic Minimalism*, Institute of Contemporary Art, Philadelphia
1968 *Whitney Annual*, Whitney Museum, New York (and 1970)
1969 *Art and Process IV*, Finch College Museum of Art, New York
American Exhibition, Art Institute of Chicago (and 1972)
1970 *L'Art Vivant aux Etats-Unis*, Fondation Maeght, Vence, France
The Larry Aldrich Collection, Museum of Modern Art, New York
1972 *Eight*, Contemporary Art Museum, Houston
1973 *New American Graphic Art*, Fogg Art Museum, Cambridge, Massachusetts
1974 *Choice Dealers/Dealers' Choice*, New York Cultural Center

Collections:

Museum of Modern Art, New York; Walker Art Center, Minneapolis: Southern Texas Art Museum, Corpus Christi; National Gallery of Australia, Canberra.

Publications:

By VAN BUREN: article—"An Interview with Richard Van Buren," with Phylis Tuchman, in *Artforum* (New York), September 1969.

On VAN BUREN: articles—"In the Galleries" in *Arts Magazine* (New York), May 1967; "Reviews and Previews" by Harris Rosenstein in *Artnews* (New York), Summer 1967; "Reviews and Previews" by Harris Rosenstein in *Artnews* (New York), April 1968; "New York Commentary" by Dore Ashton in *Studio International* (London), June 1968; "In the Galleries" in *Arts Magazine* (New York), Summer 1969; "Reviews and Previews" by Stephen A. Kurtz in *Artnews* (New York), Summer 1969; "New York Letter" by Peter Schjeldahl in *Art International* (Lugano, Switzerland), September 1969; "New York" by Emily Wasserman in *Artforum* (New York), September 1969; "Reviews and Previews" by Stephen A.Kurtz in *Artnews* (New York), January 1970; "New York Letter" by Carter Ratcliff in *Art International* (Lugano, Switzerland), January 1970; "New York Commentary" by Dore Ashton in *Studio International* (London), March 1970; "New York Letter" by Carter Ratcliff in *Art International* (Lugano, Switzerland), May 1970; "New York" by Robert Pincus-Witten in *Artforum* (New York), September 1970; "Reviews and Previews" by Harris Rosenstein in *Artnews* (New York), October 1970; "Galleries" by Willis Domingo in *Arts Magazine* (New York), November 1970; "New York" by Robert Pincus-Witten in *Artforum* (New York), December 1970; "New York Letter" by Carter Ratcliff in *Art International* (Lugano. Switzerland), December 1970; "Reviews and Previews" by Bruce Wolmer in *Artnews* (New York), February 1971; "Richard Van Buren" by Susan Heineman in *Artforum* (New York), April 1975.

Richard Van Buren's eccentric abstractions are exemplary of the move to hybridize painting and sculpture which became prominent during the late 1960's and came to be placed under the heading of "Postminimalism." After a period around 1968 when he made fiberglass-covered wood beam works which resembled Minimalism's "primary structures," Van Buren shifted toward using fiberglass as his basic medium and toward making forms of a more irregular, idiosyncratic nature. In his colorfield and scatter wall reliefs of the early 1970's, Van Buren built layers of varied density, using combinations of additives in his fiberglass resin base such as charcoal, ground glass, plaster and chalk to achieve textural and chromatic effects. He made these works by a slow process in which he poured plastic on the ground, let additional materials float on or sink into the materials, and allowed the whole to congeal before hanging. There are connections with second generation color field painters, especially with Jules Olitski, in these wall reliefs, but Van Buren places deeper emphasis on the materiality of his process and materials and on the incongruity of the resulting shapes. Color becomes part of the physical properties of the material itself, its hue and intensity determined by the density of the resin in which it resides. The quirky, oddball shapes avoid notions of formal composition, stressing rather a non-hierarchical, non-ordering, emphasizing simply its physical presence, made possible by fragile looking yet solid material and process. In 1973 Van Buren began making free-standing, three-dimensional sculptures which further stretch the possibilities of his chosen medium of fiberglass and polyester resin. Strange, frail looking, skeletal structures seem in tense balance, poised precariously on fiberglass legs which jauntily support tube-like lengths. Many of these works take on anthropomorphic correspondences similar to the works from the same period by Rosemary Castoro. Van Buren's long and linear constructs seem also to allude to industrial structures gone whimsical, suggesting tough, handmade bridges or pipelines made by some knowing child. Van Buren pours polyester resin into troughs and lays fiberglass rope at regular intervals. The technical process is

purposefully allowed to remain a visible element in the finished work, acting as an integral part of the whole. Whereas in the wall pieces, colored light is often blurred by the proximity to the opaque wall, in these free-standing sculptures it is permitted to pass through translucent materials openly to achieve a glow of unhampered radiance. It is this quality of pale, watery translucence which allows Van Buren his most personal touches in a body of work which might otherwise seem simply one of many which have followed the Postminimal direction.

—Barbara Cavaliere

VAN DER HEYDEN, J(acob) C(ornelis) J(ohan). Dutch. Born in Den Bosch, 23 June 1928. Studied at the Koninklijke Akademie, Den Bosch, 1946–49; Rijksakademie, Amsterdam, 1952–53; Art School, Tilburg, 1954–55; and Jan Van Eyck Academie, Maastricht, 1955–57. Served in the Dutch Army, 1949–51. Married Johanna van Rysewyk in 1962; children: Paul, Jan and Maria. Worked at Philips Electronics, Eindhoven, 1951; drawing master in colleges at Roermond and Nijmegen, 1954–56; independent artist, Den Bosch, since 1958; paintings and prints, 1958–66; films, since 1967; computer compositions, 1968; sound and television works, 1969; calendar and time-related works, from 1973: has worked in open-air studio since 1975. Guest instructor. Jan Van Eyck Academie, Maastricht. 1971–73; Professor, State Academy, Amsterdam, since 1986. Agent: Galerie Van Gelder, Plancius Straat 9A, Amsterdam. Address: Louwse Poort 83, 5211 NE Den Bosch, Netherlands.

Individual Exhibitions:

1964 Gemeentemuseum, The Hague
1965 Galerie Swart, Amsterdam
1966 Kunststichting, Rotterdam
Prentenkabinet, Gemeentemuseum, The Hague
1967 Stedelijk Van Abbemuseum, Eindhoven, Netherlands
1971 Galerie Collection d'Art, Amsterdam
Stedelijk Van Abbemuseum, Eindhoven, Netherlands (with Kees Buurman and Carel Visser)
1977 Gemeentemuseum, The Hague (retrospective; travelled to the Van Abbemuseum Eindhoven, Netherlands)
1981 Stedelijk Van Abbemuseum, Eindhoven, Netherlands
1983 Van Abbemuseum, Eindhoven, Netherlands (retrospective)
1986 Galerie Van Gelder, Amsterdam

Selected Exhibitions:

1970 *Kontrasten,* Gemeentemuseum, The Hague
1973 *Varianten, Ministry* of Cultural Affairs, The Hague (toured the Netherlands)
1981 *Instant Fotografie,* Stedelijk Museum, Amsterdam
1982 *Contemporary Art from the Netherlands,* Museum of Contemporary Art, Chicago (travelled to Toronto and New York)
Documenta, Kassel, West Germany
1986 *Les Abstraits,* Galerie Le Consortium, Dijon, France (travelled to Nice)
1987 *Contour,* Prinsenhof, Delft, Netherlands

Collections:

Haags Gemeentemuseum, The Hague, Netherlands; Stedelijk Van Abbemuseum, Eindhoven, Netherlands; Rijksmuseum Kröller-Müller, Otterlo, Netherlands; Museum Boymans-van Beuningen, Rotterdam.

Publications:

By VAN DER HEYDEN: books—*J. C. J. Van der Heyden,* with texts by J. L. Locher and C. Blok, The Hague 1977; *Himalaya-Chomolungma,* Utrecht 1981; articles—"Child of His time" in *Konstrasten,* exhibition catalogue, The Hague 1970; "J. C. J. Van der Heyden: Essay" in *Elementary Forms,* exhibition catalogue, Amsterdam 1976; films—*Art Is Only for Beginners,* with Richard Menken and Henk van de Rijdt, 1969.

On VAN DER HEYDEN: books—*J. C. J. Van der Heyden* exhibition catalogue, with text by J. L. Locher, The Hague 1966; *Van der Heyden,* exhibition catalogue, with text by Lambert Tegenbosch, Eindhoven, Netherlands 1967; *Warning Against the Work of J. C. J. Van der Heydan* by Cor Blok, Amsterdam 1971; *Kees Buurman/Carel Visser/J. C. J. Van der Heyden,* exhibition catalogue, with text by Jaap Bremer and Hein Reedijk, Eindhoven, Netherlands 1971; *J. C. J. Van der Heyden,* exhibition catalogue, Eindhoven, Netherlands 1977; *Instant Fotografie,* exhibition catalogue, with text by Els Barents, Amsterdam 1981; *Contemporary Art from the Netherlands,* exhibition catalogue, with texts by Marianne Brouweer and others, Amsterdam 1982; *J. C. J. van der Heyden: retrospective,* exhibition catalogue, Eindhoven, Netherlands 1983; articles—"7 Dutch Artists" by R. Fuchs, B. Reise and C. Broos, in *Studio International* (London), May 1973; "J. C. J. van der Heyden" by Kees van Gelder in *Code* (Amsterdam), June 1986.

Painting before 1967 had as subject amongst others: the painting as screen and wall, appearing as image or sign (2 to 3 meters high). I had a preference for observing them together with other paintings and all of the space of the vicinity. I also made accumulations, on a smaller scale, bringing some paintings or/and prints together, as one thing. After 1966 I stopped painting. Painting had become its own subject, and by degrees I have increasingly become my own subject. I saw myself painting the painting as an artist. In 1970: "I wonder if I can go on pretending to be an artist. What I am now is an open question, not too quickly to be filled with an answer. If artists are not artists any more, they still belong to that kind of people who realize today what will be possible tomorrow. With pretentions or without, with effects or without". After 1970, I preferred a certain silence. Relationship outside/inside has become the subject in an open air studio, working with visual and non-visual things, without a direct specialization. I have, however, maintained the role of a painter. You don't have to do very much in your life, only a few things which keep on recurring.

—J. C. J. van der Heyden

J. C. J. van der Heyden's place in Dutch painting is a special one. For more than twenty years he has lived and worked in the provincial town of Den Bosch, outside the centre of artistic life. At appropriate times, he shows his works and causes a stir—in recent years, even some general appreciation. In 1968 the young

J. C. J. Van der Heyden: *Six Times Four,* 1987

art historian Rudi Fuchs wrote an article on van der Heyden's work in the serious art-historical periodical *Simiolus*. Fuchs discussed the painting *Blue Cross* (1965/66) in the light of some formal aspects of Mondrian's work. He called attention to the importance of the edges of the canvas that, in Mondrian, still belong to the realm of illusionism, but in *Blue Cross* are of a literal character. Throughout the 1970s, van der Heyden enjoyed considerable attention from the Municipal Museum in The Hague, an institution that now owns a substantial part of his early works. According to van der Heyden, the year 1970 was a turning-point. From then on, he rigorously separated himself from the outside world, including the art-world. Painting itself was not to be considered as a necessary activity. A symptom of this attitude is the manipulation of his own signature. His first name (Jacob) disappears in favour of the neutral J. C. J. that creates a distance between the painter/producer and the observer. This procedure becomes understandable if one realizes that a considerable part of van der Heyden's oeuvre consists of a re-use of his own, already executed and finished, paintings. His routine is manifold. In his studio he continuously arranges new situations with the finished canvases he has at his disposal. He observes his own paintings in various situations that he records photographically. He also uses finished compositions, usually repainted in much smaller dimensions, as part of his new paintings. Between 1967 and 1975 he made no paintings at all, only studio photos. New versions of older paintings date from after 1975. Of great importance was a trip by airplane to India in 1977. The photos taken from the inside of the plane, showing pure blue air above the white woolly clouds, have given rise to a series of convincing paintings. Van der Heyden's use of colour is very reduced and elementary (blue, yellow, black and white, and, very rarely, red). Of interest is the project *Two Cabins*, from 1972. One is dark; from the outside one sees into a closed inner space where various objects of van der Heyden's vocabulary are barely discernible. The other one, the lighter cabin, is an outdoors piece that has a roof covered in transparent plexiglass. Here, the sky is the object of meditation.

—A. F. Wagemans

VAN ELK, Ger(ard Pieter).

Dutch. Born in Amsterdam, 9 March 1941. Studied art at the Kunstnijverheidesschool, Amsterdam, 1959–61; studied art and history at Immaculate Heart College, Los Angeles, 1961–63, and art history at the Rijksuniversiteit, Groningen, Netherlands, 1965–66. Independent artist, Amsterdam, since 1961; Founder with Wim T. Schippers, Adynamic group, Amsterdam, 1961–62; with Reinier Lucassen and Jan Dibbets, International Institute for Re-Education of Artists, Amsterdam, 1968. Instructor, Ateliers 63, Haarlem, since 1972. Agent: Art and Project; Prinsengracht 785, Amsterdam. Address: Oude Zijds Achterburgwal 198, Amsterdam, Netherlands.

Individual Exhibitions:

1962 Museum Fodor, Amsterdam (with Wim T. Schippers)
Dilexi Gallery, Los Angeles
1965 Instituut voor Kunstgeschiednis, Groningen, Netherlands
1966 Galerie Swart, Amsterdam
1967 Galerie de Mangelgang, Amsterdam
Galerie Espace, Amsterdam
1968 Galleria La Nuova Loggia, Bologna (with Marinus Boezem)
Galerie Swart, Amsterdam (with Marinus Boezem and Jan Dibbets)
1969 Koninklijke Academie voor Beeldenden Kunste's, Hertogenbosch, Netherlands
Galerie Walenkamp, Leiden
Kunstkring, Rotterdam
1970 Art and Project, Amsterdam
1971 Mount San Antonio College, Walnut, California
Art and Project, Amsterdam (2 exhibitions)
De Utrechtse Kring, Neudeflat, Utrecht
Pomona Art Gallery, Los Angeles (with Ader and Leavitt)
1972 Montgomery Art Center, Claremont, California
Nova Scotia College of Art and Design, Halifax
Art and Project, Amsterdam
Kabinett Für Aktuelle Kunst, Bremerhaven, West Germany
Utrechten Ring, Utrecht
1973 Stedelijk Van Abbemuseum, Eindhoven, Netherlands
Galerie Ernst, Hannover
Wide White Space Gallery, Antwerp
Wide White Space Gallery, Brussels
Galerie Waalkens, Finsterwolde, Netherlands
Grafiek 50 VZW, Wakken, Belgium
Claire Copley Gallery, Los Angeles
1974 Art and Project, Amsterdam (2 exhibitions)
Nigel Greenwood Gallery, London
Stedelijk Museum, Amsterdam
Palais des Beaux-Arts, Brussels
1975 Museum of Modern Art, New York
Stedelijk Museum de Lakenhal, Leiden
Palais des Beaux-Arts, Brussels
Nigel Greenwood Gallery, London
Kabinett für Aktuelle Kunst, Bremerhaven, West Germany
1976 Nigel Greenwood Gallery, London
1977 Art and Project, Amsterdam
Arbeiten von 1969–1977, Badischer Kunstverein, Karlsruhe, West Germany
Rheinisches Landesmuseum, Bonn
Kunstverein, Braunschweig, West Germany
1978 Marian Goodman Gallery, New York
Hansen-Fuller Gallery, San Francisco
1979 Marian Goodman Gallery, New York
Art and Project, Amsterdam
Nigel Greenwood Gallery, London
1980 Galleria Lucio Amelio, Naples
Biennale, Venice
Kunsthalle, Basle
Musée d'Art Moderne de la Ville, Paris
Museum Boymans-van Beuningen, Rotterdam
1981 *Recent Painting and Sculpture and a Selection of Earlier Work,* Fruit Market Gallery, Edinburgh (travelled to Serpentine Gallery, London, and Arnolfini Gallery, Bristol)
1984 Art Institute of Chicago

Selected Group Exhibitions:

1967 *Beelden en Bouwen,* Plan International, Doortwerth, Netherlands
1969 *When Attitudes Become Form,* Kunsthalle, Berne (toured Europe)
1970 *Biennale,* Tokyo
1971 *Prospekt 17,* Kunsthalle, Dusseldorf
1972 *Documenta,* Kassel, West Germany (and 1977)
1976 *Reflektie en Realiteit,* Palais des Beaux-Arts, Brussels (toured Europe)
1977 *Europe in the 70s,* Art Institute of Chicago (toured the United States)
1978 *Fotografie in Nederland 1940–75,* Stedelijk Museum, Amsterdam
1979 *European Dialogue,* at the *Biennale,* Sydney
1980 *Artist and Camera,* Mappin Art Gallery, Sheffield (toured the U.K.)

Collections:

Stedelijk Museum, The Hague; Gemeentemuseum, The Hague; Museum Boymans-van Beuningen, Rotterdam; Stedelijk Van Abbemuseum, Eindhoven, Netherlands; Frans Halmsmuseum, Haarlem, Netherlands; Palais des Beaux-Arts, Brussels; Museum van Hedendaagse Kunst, Ghent; Centre Georges Pompidou, Paris; Museum of Modern Art, New York; Tate Gallery, London.

Publications:

By VAN ELK: articles—"Het Eerste (Voorlopige) A-Dynamische Manifest" in *Vrij Nederland* (Amsterdam), December 1961; "Trips voor Verzamelaars" and "Vele Landen Maken Licht Werk" in *Museumjournaal* (Amsterdam), no. 2. 1968; "The Haircut, Big Cut—Big Savings" in *Museumjournaal* (Amsterdam), July 1971; interview, with Ron Kaal, in *Ger Van Elk,* exhibition catalogue, Eindhoven, Netherlands, 1973; interview, with Antje von Graevenitz, in *Ger Van Elk: Arbeiten von 1969–1977,* exhibition catalogue, Karlsruhe, West Germany 1977; films—*The Absorption of a Shadow,* 1969; *The Fluttering Pennon,* 1969; *How Van Elk Inflates His Left Foot with His Right One,* 1969; *Self-Portrait Behind a Wooden Fence,* 1969; *Some Natural Aspects of Painting and Sculpture,* 1971; *La Pièce,* 1971; *The Well-Shaven Cactus in Identifications,* edited by Gerry Schum, 1971; *Videopiece,* 1971; *Short Play with Morandi, Klee and Kandinsky,* 1972.

On VAN ELK: books—*Arte Povera* by Germano Celant, Milan 1969; *Ger Van Elk,* exhibition catalogue, with texts by Jan Leering and Rudi H. Fuchs, Eindhoven, Netherlands, 1973; *Ger Van Elk,* exhibition catalogue, with text by Rudi H. Fuchs, Amsterdam 1974; *The Magic Image: The Genius of Photography from 1839 to the Present Day by* Cecil Beaton and Gail Buckland, London and Boston 1975; *Ger Van Elk: Arbeiten von 1969–1977,* exhibition catalogue, with texts by Rudi H. Fuchs and Michael Schwarz, Karlsruhe, West Germany, 1977; *Fotografie in Nederland 1940–1975,* exhibition catalogue, by Els Barents, Amsterdam 1977; *Ger Van Elk: La Biennale di Venezia 1980,* exhibition catalogue, with texts by Gijs Van Tuyland Wim Beeren, Amsterdam 1980; *Ger Van Elk,* exhibition catalogue, with texts by Suzanne Pagé, Jean-Christophe Ammann, and Wim Beeren, Rotterdam 1980; *Ger Van Elk: Recent Paintings and Sculpture and a Selection of Earlier Work,* exhibition catalogue, with texts by Jean Fisher and others, Edinburgh 1981.

In Ger Van Elk's work, perception is arbitrary; he manipulates facts that common sense tells us are self-evident to the perceiver. Fitting the image to an idea, he presents the image and the idea simultaneously, as a dialectical whole no longer divisible. In this way he constructs a representation played on the complexity of individual psychic activity; reality is defined as a dimension internal to the object which can be manifested only through individual subjectivity. Van Elk uses photographic pictures; he manipulates them, paints over them, distorts the dimensions, alters the perspective by shifting the vanishing point of the picture according to mental demands, removes or adds, associates the idea with the shape, deriving a representation which, while it uses techniques characteristic of surrealism (extrapolation of detail, substitutions, removal of elements, presentation of the image out of context), results in an art that is not surrealist, in that the unconscious component is associated with a definite mental planning, full of conscious, often autobiographical, references, which is legitimized through the awareness acquired from the "pre-pictorial" art of the 70's. By means of a "monumental" figuration using "exaggerated" dimensions, which brings out the tension between the opposed elements, the trick of separatism-dualism is presented as a dialectical whole. In this way the photographic image is also reintroduced into the painted picture and amplifies its evocative and allusive capacity. By forcing the lines of reality into a geometrizing figuration, the artist paradoxically geometrizes reality itself to its extreme formal effects. That leads to a situation of friction between sense and nonsense, giving rise to a suggestion of interpretation oriented in the direction of the forces internal to the field taken as the area of operative intervention; just as the artist dismantles the rules of perspective, so the viewer of the work is obliged to dismantle the rules of normal everyday interpretation. Thus we find here, in a behavior pattern area of a reality that he has adopted as internal to his own constitution, new "necessary" aspects that make of his actual "structure" a "polylegible" whole.

—Demetrio Paparoni

VAN KONINGSBRUGGEN, Rob.
Dutch. Born Rudolphus Johannes Philippus van Koningsbruggen, in The Hague, 23 September 1948. Studied at the Koninklijke Academie voor Beeldende Kunsten, The Hague, 1968; Vrije Akademie, The Hague, 1969–70; Ateliers 63, Haarlem, 1970–72. Painter, living and working in Amsterdam, since 1973. Agent: Galerie van Krimpen, Prinsengracht 629, Amsterdam. Address: Louriergracht 166, Amsterdam, Netherlands.

Individual Exhibitions:

1970 Galerie Nouvelles Images, The Hague
1971 Galerie de Mangelgang, Groningen, Netherlands
Galerie Orez, The Hague
1972 Galerie Swart, Amsterdam
Haags Gemeentemuseum, The Hague
1973 Galerie Swart, Amsterdam
1974 Galerie Waalkens, Finsterwolde, Netherlands
Galerie t'Venster, Rotterdam
Van Abbemuseum, Eindhoven, Netherlands
1975 Galerie Swart, Amsterdam
1976 Galerie Swart, Amsterdam
1977 Galerie Swart, Amsterdam
Galerie Swart, Amsterdam (with Peter Struycken)
Galerie Swart, Amsterdam (with John Duff)
1978 Galerie Swart, Amsterdam
1979 Verfindustrie Jac Eyck BV, Heerlen, Netherlands
Schilderijen/Paintings 1971–78, Stedelijk Museum, Amsterdam
1980 Galerie M, Bochum, West Germany
Galerie Swart, Amsterdam
1981 Galerie van Krimpen, Amsterdam
1982 Museum Fodor, Amsterdam
Galerie van Krimpen, Amsterdam
1983 Galerie van Krimpen, Amsterdam
1984 Galerie van Krimpen, Amsterdam
1985 Rijkschuur Acquoy, Amsterdam
Galerie van Krimpen, Amsterdam
1986 Galerie van Krimpen, Amsterdam
1987 Museum Boymans-van Beuningen, Rotterdam
Rembrandthuis, Amsterdam

Selected Group Exhibitions:

1973 *Lof der Tekenkunst,* Van Abbemuseum, Eindhoven, Netherlands
1974 *11 Dutch Artists,* Fruit Market Gallery, Edinburgh (travelled to the Aberdeen Art Gallery)
1975 *Dutch Modern Art,* Museum of Modern Art, Ghent
1976 *7 Hollandische Kunstler,* Kunstmuseum, Lucerne
1979 *Gallery Artists,* Galerie Swart, Amsterdam
1980 *Neue Malerei aus den Nederlanden,* Neue Galerie am Landesmuseum Graz, Austria
1983 *Modern Dutch Painting,* National Gallery, Athens
1985 *De Nederlandse Indentiteit in de Kunst na 1945,* Rijksmuseum Vincent Van Gogh, Amsterdam
1987 *Bienal,* Sao Paulo, Brazil

Collections:

Stedelijk Museum, Amsterdam; Haags Gemeentemuseum, The Hague; Museum Boymans-van Beuningen, Rotterdam; Groninger Museum, Groningen, Netherlands; Stedelijk Museum, Schiedam, Netherlands.

Publications:

On VAN KONINGSBRUGGEN: books—*Rob van Koningsbruggen,* exhibition catalogue, The Hague 1972; *Konstruktive Konzepte* by Willy Rotzler, Zurich 1977; *Rob van Koningsbruggen: schilderijen/Painttings 1971–78,* exhibition catalogue, with text by Rini Dippel, Amsterdam 1979; *Rob van Koningsbruggen: Schilderijen en tekening 1979–1987,* exhibition catalogue with text by Erik Beerken, Rotterdam 1987; articles—"Van Koningsbruggen schrift en breit" by Carel Blotkamp in *Vrije Nederland* (Amsterdam), 27 March 1971; "Signalement van Rob van Koningsbruggen" by T. Cruls in *Museumjournaal,* (Amsterdam), vol. 16, no. 4, 1971; "Rob van Koningsbruggen breit zeroistische avonturen" by K. Schipper in *Haagse Post* (The Hague), 21 April 1971; "Waarom Rob van Koningsburggen strafregels schreef" by Dolf Welling in *Haagsche Courant* (The Hague), 30 October 1972; "Van Koningsbruggen's debuut als schilder" by Carel Blotkamp in *Vrije Nederland* (Amsterdam), 11 November 1972; "Twee Schilders: Rob van Koningsbruggen, Toon Berhoef" by Carel Blotkamp in *Museumjournaal* (Amsterdam), vol. 24, no. 2 1979; "De modelfunctie van Rob van Koningsbruggen" by Carel Blotkamp in *Museumjournaal* (Amsterdam), no. 6, 1985.

Everything can become a mannerism, including my "shoved" paintings. When it has reached a certain point, I stop. I began making "shoved" paintings because the brushwork (in larger and larger works also became mannered. By coincidence, I noticed that my brush itself became a painting, for on the brush was reflected the same features as appeared in the painting—so it was only a small step to use my painting as a brush. Now I have abandoned also those principles. Many of my "shoved" paintings consisted of three parts: yellow, red and blue—and I discovered, that these three primary colours could produce a deep black. Making art is making discoveries—and art in itself must be renewable. So now I am using mixtures of colours—orange, purple and green, and tonal extremes—and allow them to end in black.

—Rob van Koningsbruggen

The work of the 23-year old painter Rob Van Koningsbruggen—and the motives behind it—caused something of a sensation in the Netherlands in 1971. Established critics such as Schippers and Blotkamp used his drawings and knitted objects as the point of departure for a debate about the "credibility" of the artist, although that issue had really been in the air for more than twenty years. What matters in Van Koningsbruggen's work is the action involved in painting and not the work as a finished object. The painting itself is simply the residue of an action which is a concentrated and intense as possible. Van Koningsbruggen's paintings from 1972, for example, are composed of raised horizontal streaks of paint as broad as the brush which produced them. There is no room for interpretation here: we are confronted with a simple fact (and in this respect Van Koningsbruggen's work can be compared to that of the Zero-artist, Jan Schoonhoven). Success or failure in the usual sense of those terms is irrelevant. The artist has no knowledge in advance of how his work will finally look. This tendency is emphasized even more strongly in Van Koningsbruggen's paintings after 1974. Here he uses the stretched canvas itself as a "brush." He applies paint on two canvases, on their sides or in simple geometric figures, such as circles and rectangles, painted on the surfaces; then he rubs the two canvases together for a few seconds. The results are unexpected for the painter himself, who is really no more than a machine which lets the painting create itself. There is a traditional element in Van Koningsbruggen's work, in his use of color. Because he uses only red, yellow, blue and black, he invites comparison with other painters in the mainstream of 20th century Dutch artists. His work demonstrates that pictorial quality involves more than painterly skills; for him what matters is the intelligence of the artist. Even in complex works, the presence—or absence—of this intelligence is something which the viewer can sense immediately.

Van Koningsbruggen's paintings from 1981 onwards differ considerably. He has chosen to work in small scale size, the paintings themselves usually resulting from a series of long work processes. These abstract pieces are, above all, experiments in colorism. In an unconventional (and in no respect systematic) way, verging on the naive, Van Koningsbruggen's goal each time is to achieve harmony anew.

—A. F. Wagemans

Rob Van Koningsbruggen: ***Untitled*****, 1987**

van MUNSTER, Jan.
Dutch. Born in Gorinchem, 3 July 1939. Studied at the Academie voor Beeldende Kunsten, Rotterdam, 1955–57; Instituut voor Kunstnijverheid, Amsterdam, 1957–59. Married Geertje de Stigter in 1962; daughter: Anna-Lorene. Independent artist, working with light and sound environments, in Gorinchem, 1960–66, in Rotterdam, 1967–85, and in Renesse, since 1985. Art Instructor, Ateliers 63, Haarlem, 1970–72; Academie voor Beeldende Kunsten, Rotterdam, 1973–74; Koninklijke Academie voor Kunst en

Voormgeving, 's-Hertogenbosch, since 1978. Recipient: A. Schwarz Prize for Sculpture. 1966; Travel Scholarship to London, 1967, Grant, 1969, and Film Bursary, 1973, Ministrie van Cultuur, Recreatie en Mattschappelijk, 1967; Object Prize. Salon van de Maassteden, Schiedam, 1969; Chabot-Prize, Rotterdamse Anjerfonds, 1971. Agents: Galerie Fenna de Vries, Eendrachtplein 18, Rotterdam; and Galerie Orez, Paviljoensgracht 68–70, The Hague. Address: Rampweg 24, 4326 LK Noordwelle (Renesse), Netherlands.

Individual Exhibitions:

1962 't Venster, Rotterdam (with Ad Dekkers)
1963 Galerie de Drie Hendricken, Amsterdam (with Ad Dekkers)
1964 Galerie Punt 31, Dordrecht, Netherlands (with Marinus Boezem)
Rotterdamse Kunststichting, Rotterdam (with Ad Dekkers)
1965 Galerie C. C. C., Schiedam, Netherlands
Galerie Garage, Gorcum, Netherlands
Galerie 845, Amsterdam (with Marinus Boezem)
Dromedaris, Enkhuizen, Netherlands (with Marinus Boezem)
1966 Rotterdamse Kunstkring, Rotterdam (with Nans Verweij)
De Jong-Bergers, Maastricht, Netherlands
1967 Galerie Espace, Amsterdam
Galerie Waalkens, Finsterwolde, Netherlands
Galerie C. C. C., Vlaardingen, Netherlands
1968 Market 17, Enschede, Netherlands
Galerie Julicher, Gutzenrather, West Germany
Galerie Ad Libitum, Antwerp
1969 Galerie C. C. C., Vlaardingen, Netherlands (with Mathieu Ficheroux)
Galerie Mickery, Loenersloot, Netherlands
Stedelijk Museum, Amsterdam
Internationale Galerie Orez, The Hague
1970 Dordrechts Museum, Dordrecht, Netherlands
Van Abbemuseum, Eindhoven, Netherlands
Centraal Museum, Utrecht
1971 Galerie Design, Rotterdam
Galerie Design, Rotterdam (Chabot-Prize exhibition)
1972 Museum Boymans-van Beuningen, Rotterdam (retrospective)
Galerie Fenna de Vries, Rotterdam
1973 Henie-Onstad Kunstsenter, Hovikodden, Norway (with Pieter Engels and Wim Gijzen)
Galerie Yaki Kornblit, Amsterdam
1974 Electric Gallery, Toronto
1975 Galerie Fenna de Vries, Rotterdam
1977 Galerie Orez, The Hague
1978 *Jan van Munster/David van de Kop/Wim Gijzen; Recent Werk*, Rijksmuseum Kröller-Muller, Otterlo, Netherlands
1980 Galerie Orez, The Hague
1981 Kunstcentrum Radhuis, Gorinchem, Netherlands
1982 Galerie Orez, The Hague
Kruithuis, Den Bosch, Netherlands
1983 Galerie Pictura, Dordrecht, Netherlands
1984 Galerie Orez Mobiel, The Hague
1986 Grote Kerk, Goes, Netherlands (installation)
1987 Suzanne Niederberg Galerie, Amsterdam
Galerie A. Hoffman, Friedberg, West Germany
Wilhelm-Hack-Museum, Ludwigshafen, West Germany
1988 Galerie A. Hoffmann, Friedberg, West Germany
Rijksmuseum Kroller-Muller, Otterlo, Netherlands
Museum Boymans-van Beuningen, Rotterdam

Selected Group Exhibitions:

1963 *Gorkum '63*, Nieuwe Doelen, Gorinchem, Netherlands
1964 *Stichting Nieuw Beelden*, Stedelijk Museum, Amsterdam
1965 *4th Biennale de Paris*, Musée d'Art Moderne de la Ville, Paris (and *8th Biennale*, 1973)
1967 *Science Fiction*, Kunsthalle, Berne

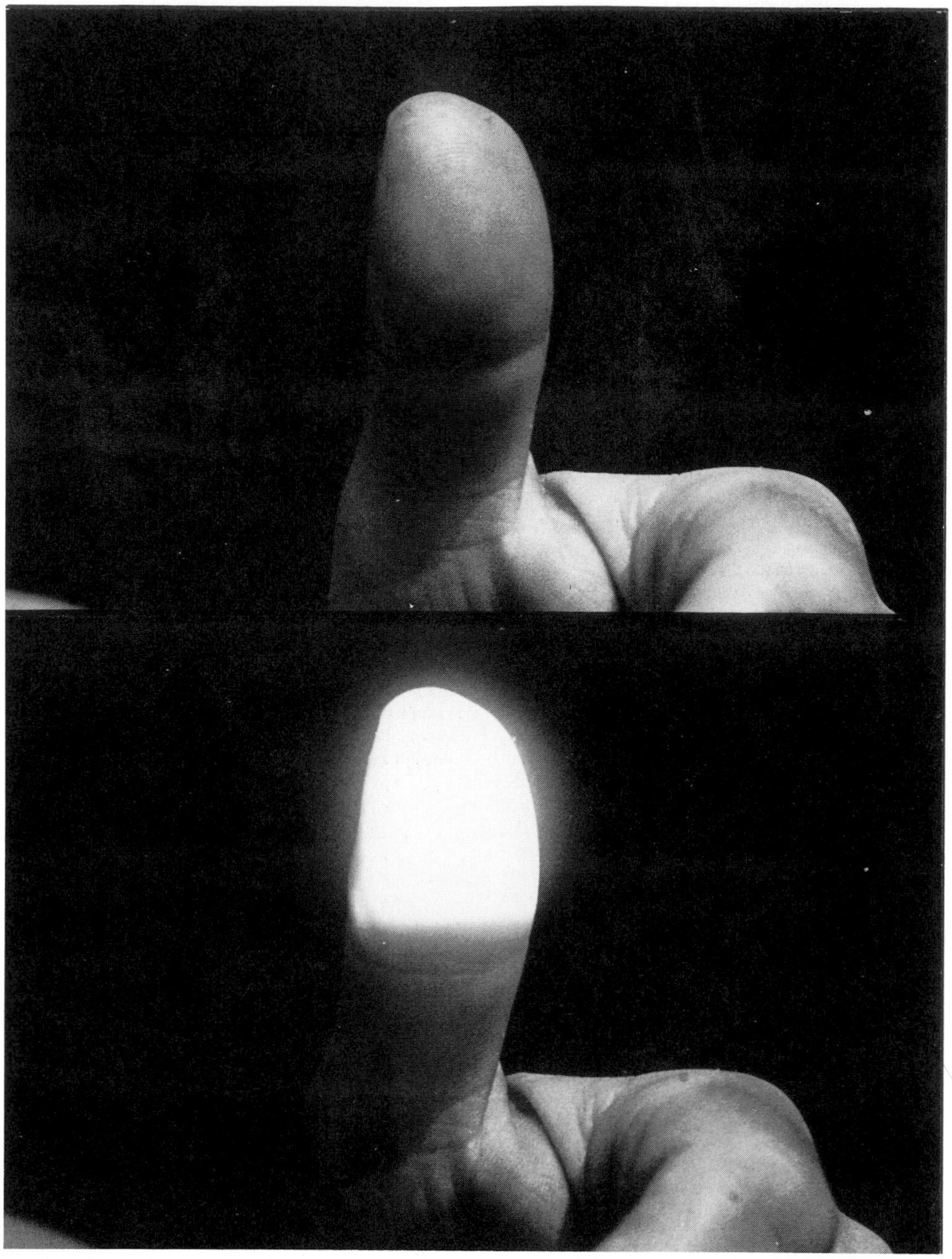

Jan Van Munster: Still from the film *Projection*, 1972

1970 *7 Rotterdam Kunstenaars*, Museum Boymans-van Beuningen Rotterdam
1972 *Van Medicijnman tot Medicus*, Frans Halsmuseum, Haarlem
1978 *Paper for Space*, Stedelijk Museum, Amsterdam
1982 *Beelden op de Berg*, Wageningen Museum, Netherlands
1984 *Kunst aus Rotterdam*, Museum Boymans-van Beuningen, Rotterdam
1986 *Von zwei Quadraten*, Wilhelm-Hack-Museum, Ludwigshafen, West Germany

Collections:

Museum Boymans-van Beuningen, Rotterdam; Stedelijk van Abbemuseum, Eindhoven, Netherlands; Stedelijk Museum, Schiedam, Netherlands; Dordrecht Museum, Dordrecht, Netherlands; Kröller-Müller, Otterlo, Netherlands; Rijks Collectie, The Hague; Stedelijk Museum, Amsterdam; Centre Georges Pompidou, Paris; Caracao Museum, Dutch Antilles.

Publications:

By van MUNSTER: articles—"Kunst Kijkt naar 2000" in *Revue*(Rotterdam), no 6, 1968; "Mijn Mechanische Mens" in *Vrije Geluiden* (Amsterdam), no 17, 1969.

On van MUNSTER: books—*De Exploisive van het Intellect* by Jan Donia, Hilversum, Netherlands 1968; *Jan van Munter*, exhibition catalogue, with text by Liesbeth Brandt-Cortius, Rotterdam 1972; *Jan van Munster*, exhibition catalogue with text by Jo-Anne Birnie Dantzker, Toronto 1974; *Paper for Space*, exhibition catalogue, with text by Gijs van Tuyl, Amsterdam 1978; *Jan van Munster, David van de Kop, Wim Gijzen: Recent Werk*, exhibition catalogue, with text by Paul Hefting. Otterlo, Netherlands 1978: *Kunst aus Rotterdam*, exhibition catalogue by Wim Beeren, Rotterdam 1984; *De eigen ruimte—Beeldhouwkunst in Nederland na 1945* by Paul Hefting, Amsterdam 1986; *Jan Van Munster: Energie Objecten, Zeichnungen, Tekeningen*, exhibition catalogue with essay by Kees Broos, Friedberg 1987; *Jan Van Munster*, 2 vols., with texts by Kees de Boer and Paul Hefting, Utrecht 1988.

I am not concerned just with the visual impression of light, but especially with the fact that it is charged with invisible energy. This involves the mystical side of the object, characterized by a kind of enclosedness. What is enclosed is brought out by a particular way of arranging the elements. This produces a tension, a radiation into space, the light seeming to burst forth. . . . The light must be on, even in the black lights: that is, compressed energy, the charge there is in me, in everyone. The light is there, even if it is not visible, just as lots of things are invisible. My work is not abstract. It is concerned with emotions, with attraction and repulsion. I want to make the tension between me and others visible in the space I am working in.

—Jan van Munster

In the catalogue of Jan van Munster's retrospective exhibition at the Boymans van Beuningen Museum, Rotterdam (1972), Liesbeth Brandt-Cortius described as follows the ways in which van Munster worked with light to produce form and specify space: "In 1972, the objects became visually less important than the shape that, from the object, via the light, is projected onto the ceiling wall and floor. The tangible objects are concentrated into small closed cubes or square poles out of which a single, very simple shape is sawn: the outline of a square with an opening on one side, a zig-zag line or a straight or dotted line. The poles or cubes stand on the floor or hang from the ceiling, and the strong bulb inside projects the sawn-out shapes, much magnified, onto the wall, floor or ceiling. In a dark room one sees first of all the light lines, and only afterwards one sees the source of light and finds the small object. The whole area seems to be dominated by insignificant objects. Each object, with its projection, forms the image." These light projections induced the Algemene Bank Nederland to give Jan van Munster a commission for its new head office building in Amsterdam, located in the Vijzelstraat between Keizersgracht and Prinsengracht. Here he was able to apply light in this form to architecture. The pavement is covered over the whole length of the building. Van Munster has applied his lightlines in this arcade, in the floors, ceiling and along the walls. As a result, some parts are concentrated, others "disappear." New space is created.

The lightlines, arranged in simple geometric patterns, definitely change the actual area in one's perception and experience of it, van Munster says: "I can make crosses, rooms and doorways from lightlines." And in this way he has given the passage under the building a new spatial function with inbuilt lightshapes in the pavement and correspondingly in the ceiling.

The shapes are: an open square, consisting of three self-expanding right angled corners—obstruction; line and dotted line—movement; parallel lines—zebra crossing; steps, seen from the side or tipped-up steps—escort (to an important point, e.g. entrance); square with openings on all sides—room or base; the same as above but in the corner of a passage—doorway; square with openings on two sides—lock; cross with double lines, signals for guiding traffic in different directions; metal benches, split in the middle, from where light shines—lighting. In these neutral geometrical shapes, van Munster has conjured up a form of "environmental design," through which this small area of a city undergoes a real, palpable experience.

Both the formal means and the materials used—the intangible light—guarantee that this experience is not forced upon one. The light suggests space and plasticity: one can follow the suggestion, one can just as easilty ignore it or put it aside, van Munster says: "It remains as a guide; it is like hopscotch, whoever want to . . . plays the game those who don't walk through it."

It is a sort of example—a guide—to a conscious experience of the environment. Nothing is enforced, as so often is the case in mental designs which compelling instruct the users how they must act, by an emphatic use of form, colour and structure.

"Too imposed," says van Munster. He limits himself; he even willingly accepts the effect to the difference between day and night. His shapes are indications; for those who want to see, they change the space from the endlessly long to a series of short distances; the light offers instruction, suggesting a narrowing or widening of the space; it helps to span distances, and helps one to experience part of the space as a room, base, lock, etc. The effect of familiarization—which is already accomplished by the use of light as a spatial and plastic element—is further emphasized by the placing of the lightlines at the same distances from each other as traffic lines on the road (to which everyone is accustomed). The idea is to call to mind plasticity by means of directed light. What van Munster made previously as a sculptor, in wood, stone and plastic, with mass and volume, it now realized with light in an exactly stipulated shape or form.

What he wants to achieve with light is clear in his object "Pressed Light" (1971). This object is of two metal sheets, clamped together, with a source of light between them. The object itself, depending on the space in which it stands, becomes relatively less important, because through the radiated beams of light on the walls the whole area is "influenced." Light as a definer of space in a controlled (dark) area—a distinct sculptor's concept, involving as it does the relationship between interior and exterior form—appears to work excellently in the arcade. In the space of 24 hours the suggested spatial differences are alternately strong or hardly noticed at all. An interaction between natural and artificial concepts maintains the tension in the experience.

—H. J. A. M. van Haaren

1966 Wallraf-Richartz Museum, Cologne
Galerie Leonhart, Munich
Galleri Birch, Copenhagen
Galerie La Balance/Galerie Stephane Janssen, Brussels
Museo Civico d'Arte Moderna, Turin
1967 Kunstnernes Hus, Oslo
1968 Galerie Knoedler, Paris
Paintings 1957–1967, Knoedler Gallery, New York
Albright-Knox Art Gallery, Buffalo, New York
1969 Galerie Benador, Geneva
Das Graphische Werk, Kunsthalle, Worpswede, West Germany (toured Europe)
1970 Galerie Stephane Janssen, Brussels
Musée d'Art Moderne, Paris
1971 Musée Rath, Geneva
Stedelijk Van Abbemuseum, Eindhoven, Netherlands
Kunsthalle, Basle
1972 Galerie Stephane Janssen, Brussels
1973 Galerie Collection d'Art, Amsterdam
Fondation Maeght, St. Paul-de-Vence, France
1974 *Oeuvre Lithographie 1923–1973*, Musée d'Art et d'Histoire, Geneva (toured Switzerland)
1975 Galerie Maeght, Paris
1976 Galerie Maeght, Zurich
1977 Galerie Collection d'art, Amsterdam
Museum de Lakenhal, Leiden, Netherlands
Apeldoorn Museum, Netherlands
Bonnefantenmuseum, Maastricht, Netherlands
Kunst Forum, Schelderode, Belgium
1978 *Retrospectiva 1908–1978*, Galeria Maeght, Barcelona
Chapelle de la Charité, Arles, France (travelled to Dordrecht, Netherlands; Randers, Denmark; Bremen and Worpswede, West Germany
Galerie Maeght, Paris
1979 Musée Rath, Geneva
1980 Galerie Collection d'Art, Amsterdam
Galerie Maeght, Paris
1982 *Bram Van Velde: 1895–1981*, Lefebre Gallery, New York
Lithographies, Galerie de la Seita, Paris
1984 Galerie Maeght Lelong, Paris

VAN VELDE, Bram.

Dutch. Born in Zoeterwoude, near Leiden, 19 October 1895. Apprenticed to Kramer painting and decorating company, The Hague, 1907–14; mainly self-taught in painting, under Kramer's sponsorship, in Munich, 1922–23, and in Worspwede, West Germany, 1923–25. After wife died, lived with Marthe Arnaud (died 1959), 1936–59, and with Madeleine Spierer, 1960–81. Painter: lived in Worpswede, West Germany, 1923–25, where he associated with Lokemar, Vogeler, Modersohn-Becker and other expressionist painters; in Paris, 1925–30; in Corsica, 1930–31; in Paris, 1931–32; in Majorca, 1932–36; in Paris, 1936–58 (ceased painting, 1940–44); in Fox, Haute-Provence, 1958–59; and in Grimaud, near Geneva, 1959–81. Recipient; Painting Prize, Heerlen, 1969; Prix National des Arts et Lettres. Paris, 1973; Prix des Belles Lettres, Geneva, 1975. *Died* (in Grimaud) *28 December 1981.*

Individual Exhibitions:

1945 Galerie Mai, Paris
1948 *Derrière Le Miroir*, Galerie Maeght, Paris
Kootz Gallery, New York
1952 Galerie Maeght, Paris
1955 Galerie Michael Warren, Paris
1957 Galerie Michael Warren, Paris
1958 Kunsthalle, Berne
1959 Stedelijk Museum, Amsterdam
1960 Galleria Notizie, Turin
1961 Galleria l'Obelisco, Rome
Galerie Knoedler, Paris
1962 Knoedler Gallery, New York
Galerie Krugier, Geneva
Walker Art Center, Minneapolis
Galleria l'Obelisco, Rome
1964 Knoedler Gallery, New York
1965 San Francisco Museum of Art
Colorado Springs Fine Art Center

Selected Group Exhibitions:

1926 *Salon des Indépendants*, Paris (and regularly thereafter)
1968 *Painting in France 1900–67*, National Gallery of Art, Washington, D.C. (toured the United States)
1953 *Elf Tijdenoten uit Parijs*, Stedelijk Museum, Amsterdam

Collections:

Stedelijk Museum, Amsterdam; Stedelijk Van Abbemuseum, Eindhoven, Netherlands; Centre Georges Pompidou, Paris; Centre National d'Art Contemporain, Paris; Musée d'Art et d'Industrie, St. Etienne, France; Fondation Maeght, St.-Paul-de-Vence, France; Musée Rath, Geneva; Musée d'Art et d'Histoire, Geneva.

Publications:

On VAN VELDE: books—*Bram Van Velde*, exhibition catalogue, with an introduction by Edouard Loeb, Paris 1945; *Derrière Le Miroir; Bram Van Velde*, exhibition catalogue, Paris 1948; *Bilan d'Art Actuel* by Georges Duthuit, Paris 1954; *Bram Van Velde*, exhibition catalogue, with texts by Samuel Beckett and Goerges Duthuit, Paris 1957; *Dictionnaire de la Peinture Abstraite* by Michel Seuphor, Paris 1957; *Bram Van Velde*, exhibition catalogue, with text by Franz Meyer, Berne 1958; *Bram Van Velde* by Samuel Beckett, Georges Duthuit, and Jacques Putman, Paris 1958, New York 1959; *Bram Van Velde*, exhibition catalogue, with text by Samuel Beckett, Amsterdam 1959; *Tendances Contemporains* by Nello Ponente, Geneva 1960; *L'Analyse Photographique d'un Tableau de Bram Van Velde* by Jean Francois Baurel, Paris 1960; *L'Image et l'Instant* by Georges Duthuit, Paris 1961; *Bram van Velde* by Jacques Putman, Turin, Paris, and New York 1961: *Bram Van Velde* by Jacques Putman, Turin, Paris, and New York 1961; *Bram Van Velde*, exhibition cata-

logue, with text by Umbro Apollonio and Xavier Fourcade, Rome 1962; *Bram Van Velde: Catalogue Raisonné 1907–62,* Turin, Paris and New York 1962; *Bram Van Velde,* exhibition catalogue, with text by Jan van der Marck, New York 1964; *Bram Van Velde,* exhibition catalogue, with text by Franz Meyer, Cologne 1966; *Bram Van Velde,* exhibition catalogue, with texts by Luigi Malle, Franz Meyer, and Jacques Putman, Turin 1966; *Bram Van Velde: Paintings 1957–1967,* exhibition catalogue, with texts by Samuel Beckett and Franz Meyer, New York 1968; *Bram Van Velde: Das Graphische Werk,* exhibition catalogue, with text by Jacques Putman, Worpswede, West Germany 1969; *Bram moi Haas* by Hubert Lucot, Paris 1969; *Bram Van Velde,* exhibition catalogue, with texts by Jean Leymarie and others, Paris 1970; *Bram Van Velde,* exhibition catalogue, with texts by Peter F. Althaus and others, Basle 1971; *Bram Van Velde,* exhibition catalogue, with text by André du Bouchet, St.-Paul-de-Vence, France 1973; *Bram Van Velde,* exhibition catalogue, with text by Jan Leering, Eindhoven, Netherlands 1971; *Bram Van Velde: Oeuvre Lithographie 1923–1973,* exhibition catalogue with text by Rainer Michael Mason, Geneva 1974, as *Bram Van Velde: Les Lithographies 1923–1973,* Paris 1974; *Bram Van Velde: Restrospective 1908–1978,* exhibition catalogue, with text by Antonio Saura, Barcelona 1978; *Bram Van Velde: 1895–1981,* exhibition catalogue, with texts by Samuel Beckett, Georges Duthuit, and Pierre Alechinsky, New York 1982; *Bram Van Velde: Lithographies,* exhibition catalogue, with text by Rainer Michael Mason, Paris 1982; *Bram Van Velde,* exhibition catalogue with preface by Yves Peyre, Paris 1984.

Bram van Velde was already 12 years old at the time of his first confrontation with the World of Art. This came about when, as a boy from a poor Dutch family, he went to work for a firm of decorators. What he saw led him to try his own hand at making pictures, the earliest of which were attempts to register straightforward realism.

It was not until some time later when he left his Zoeterwoude home and moved to Worpswede coming in touch with the works of their artists (Paula Modersohn-Becker, in particular) that the formative period of this artistic development began. At first, paintings by the Expressionists fascinated him, although in his own work he preferred to reach out for the expressionist style while at the same time rejecting the aggressive tendencies and undertones of social change often pre-eminent in the works of these artists he had come to admire. A revolutionary spirit had not as yet become a part of his art make-up.

Bram van Velde's early experiments with his own form of Expressionism signalled the beginning of much that has come to be recognised as his painting style, even if this was like a ship in a storm often tossed hither and thither by forces of circumstance, twists of life pattern and situation conditions that were to impinge upon him and his art in future years.

At the start, Bram van Velde used heavy brush strokes rapidly applied in delineating manner to surround colour areas of bright and luminous character freely established on the canvas, tints which although never haphazard possessed a kind of random liberty. "I have nothing in my pocket," he said, "How shall I look for what I seek?"

Bram van Velde left Worpswede for Paris in 1944. In the French capital he maintained his familiar fashion of painting, except that her contact with Fauvism and Cubism had their effect. From the impacts of both of these he found himself able to insert extra elements into his work, flashes of intensified colour and the introduction of unfamiliar contours, heralding a new and personal association with abstraction. This was a period of great activity for him as a painter.

Eight years later in Mallorca the pace slackened. He was able to relax on the Spanish island. His workload as artist became less exhausting, and he was at liberty to assess everything he had achieved as an artist up to that time, seeking—and finding—a synthesis that combined the essences of his early art experiments in Worpswede with the experiences and their effects that he had acquired in Paris. This contemplative period was brought to an abrupt end with the outbreak of the Spanish Civil War which drove the painter back to Paris. Once back in France, he became involved in the production of a series of huge tempera paintings, finding himself torn away from the amalgam of Worpswede peace and Paris experimentation he felt he had carefully gained during his Spanish sojourn and projected into a temperamental world of pain, anguish, protest and realisation of the physical and psychological emptiness of human sorrow.

The years of World War II for Bram van Velde broke his spirit. As they drew to a close, he felt robbed of all bodily and spiritual energies. He felt incapable of going on painting. Desperately short of food, full of depression, he could not summon up the necessary vigour to put brush to canvas. Mind, imagination, inspiration and the will to create—all seemed lost. It was not until some time later that the first glimmers of what had been his vivid artistic instinct once more reasserted itself. For the artist, it was like the sensation of rebirth. For those who remembered him and his pictures, the products of the new era were a source of amazement.

Suddenly, in the mid-forties, his pictures became resonant with happiness. Plein-d'esprit and rich, seeming kindled with a lurch towards 'abstraction' that had nothing to do with grief, suffering and despair. A key date for this revival and change came in 1945 when Pierre Loeb opened the Galerie 'Mai' and was able to include works by the 50-year-old Bram van Velde in the gallery's first exhibition. Then, in 1948 and 1952, he was exhibited at the Paris Galerie Maeght and received plaudits (written texts) from Samuel Beckett and Georges Duthuit. Throughout this renaissance, the quality of his painting became steadily invigorated. The aggression he had earlier spurned was now pressed into service in an uncompromising fashion fresh zest to joy and tragedy alike.

A grand retrospective of his paintings was organised by Franz Meier at the Berne Kunsthalle in 1958, to be repeated by Willem Sandberg at Amsterdam's Stedelijk Museum a year later. This was followed by exhibitions at the Knoedler galleries in Paris and New York with Knoedler also organising museum exhibitions for him in Minneapolis, San Francisco and Colorado Springs. Bram van Velde had acquired his international reputation as an artist of consequence, and this assessment of his qualities continued to confirm itself and was sustained in Cologne, Turin and Oslo, and so on . . . and so on . . .

In 1969, Bram van Velde from a pinacle of success could still write: "My life does not hang from any doctrine or theory. Life itself must provide my home"

—Sheldon Williams

VASARELY, Victor.

French. Born in Pecs, Hungary, 9 April 1908; emigrated to France 1930: naturalized, 1959. Educated at State School, Budapest, until 1925; studied at the Academy of Painting, Budapest, 1925–27, and at the Bauhaus School, Budapest, 1929–30. Married Claire Spinner in 1930; sons: André and Jean-Pierre (Yvaral). Worked as a graphic artist, Agence Havas, Paris, and Editions Draeger Freres, Montrouge, 1930–39. Independent graphic artist, since 1930: produced first paintings, 1944; first architectural integrations, from 1954; Yellow Manifesto, Kinetic works, films and writings, from 1955; inauguration of Vasarely Didactic Museum, Gordes Chateau, Vaucluse, 1970; Vasarely Foundation, Aix-en-Provence, 1971; Vasarely Museum, Pecs, Hungary, 1976; Vasarely Center, New York, 1978; Centre Vasarely, Oslo, 1982. Recipient: Gold Medal, *International Biennale of Graphics,* Fredrikstad, Norway, 1974; Plastic Arts Medal, Académie d'Architecture, Paris, 1975; André Bello Grand Sash of Honor, Caracas, 1977; Der Kaiserring Art Prize, Goslar, 1978; Certificate of Distinction, New York University, 1978; Medal of the Order of the Flag of the Republic, Budapest, 1978; Gold Centenary Medal, Bruckmann Verlag, Munich, 1978. D.H.: Cleveland State University, 1977. Honorary Corresponding Member, Institute of Nuclear Engineers, London. 1977; Honorary President, France-Hungary Association, 1977. Member, 1965, and Officier, 1985, Ordre des Arts et des Lettres, France; Chevalier, 1970, and Officier, 1981, Legion d'Honneur, France; Officier, 1978, and Commandeur, 1984, Ordre du Merite, France; Officier du Merite Culturel, Monaco, 1980. Address: "Les Devens", 84220 Gordes, France.

Individual Exhibitions:

1930 Kovacs Akos Gallery, Budapest
1933 Ernst Museum, Budapest
1944 Galerie Denise René, Paris
1946 Galerie Denise René, Paris
1949 Galerie Denise René, Paris
1950 Arne Bruun Rasmussen Gallery, Copenhagen
1952 Galerie Denise René, Paris
Samlaren Gallery, Stockholm
1954 Palais des Beaux-Arts, Brussels
A.P.I.A.W., Liège, Belgium
1955 Galerie Denise René, Paris
1956 Blanche Gallery, Stockholm
Galerie der Spiegel, Cologne
1958 Rose Fried Gallery, New York
Galleria del Grattacielo, Milan
Museo de Bellas Artes, Buenos Aires
Museum of Modern Art, Montevideo
1959 Galerie der Spiegel, Cologne
Galerie Denise René, Paris
Museum of Fine Arts, Caracas
1960 Galerie Denise René, Paris
Palais des Beaux-Arts, Brussels
1961 Galerie der Spiegel, Cologne
Galleria Lorenzelli, Milan
Galerie Le Point Cardinal, Paris
Artek Gallery, Helsinki
World House Galleries, New York
Hanover Gallery, London
1962 Galerie Le Point Cardinal, Paris
Artek Gallery, Helsinki
Kaare Bernsten Gallery, Oslo
Pace Gallery, Boston
1963 Taft Museum, Cincinnati
Musée des Arts Décoratifs, Paris
Kunstkabinett Klihm, Munich
Kestner-Gesellschaft, Hannover
1964 Académie des Beaux-Arts, Paris
Kunsthalle, Dusseldorf
Pace Gallery, New York
Galerie Le Point Cardinal, Paris
Kunsthalle, Berne
Hybler Gallery, Copenhagen
Brook Street Gallery, London
Haus am Waldsee, Berlin
Gemeentemuseum, The Hague
Galerie Renée Ziegler, Zurich
1965 Hanover Gallery, London
Galleria Deposito, Genoa
Galerie Handschin, Basle
Galerie Müller, Stuttgart
Pace Gallery, New York
1966 Sidney Janis Gallery, New York
Hayden Gallery, Massachusetts Institute of Technology, Cambridge
Brook Street Gallery, London
Overbeck-Gesellschaft, Lübeck
Gallery D, Prague
Galerie Denise René, Paris
Aura Krognoshuset, Lund, Sweden
L'Armitiere, Rouen
Galerie Aktuell, Berne
Galerie der Spiegel, Cologne
1967 Musée des Arts Décoratifs, Paris
De Cordova Museum, Lincoln, Massachusetts (graphics retrospective; toured the United States)
Muzeum V, Moste, Czechoslovakia
Gallery D, Prague
Stedelijk Museum, Amsterdam
Galerie Hans Meyer, Esslingen, West Germany
1968 Sidney Janis Gallery, New York
Galerie Pryzmat, Cracow

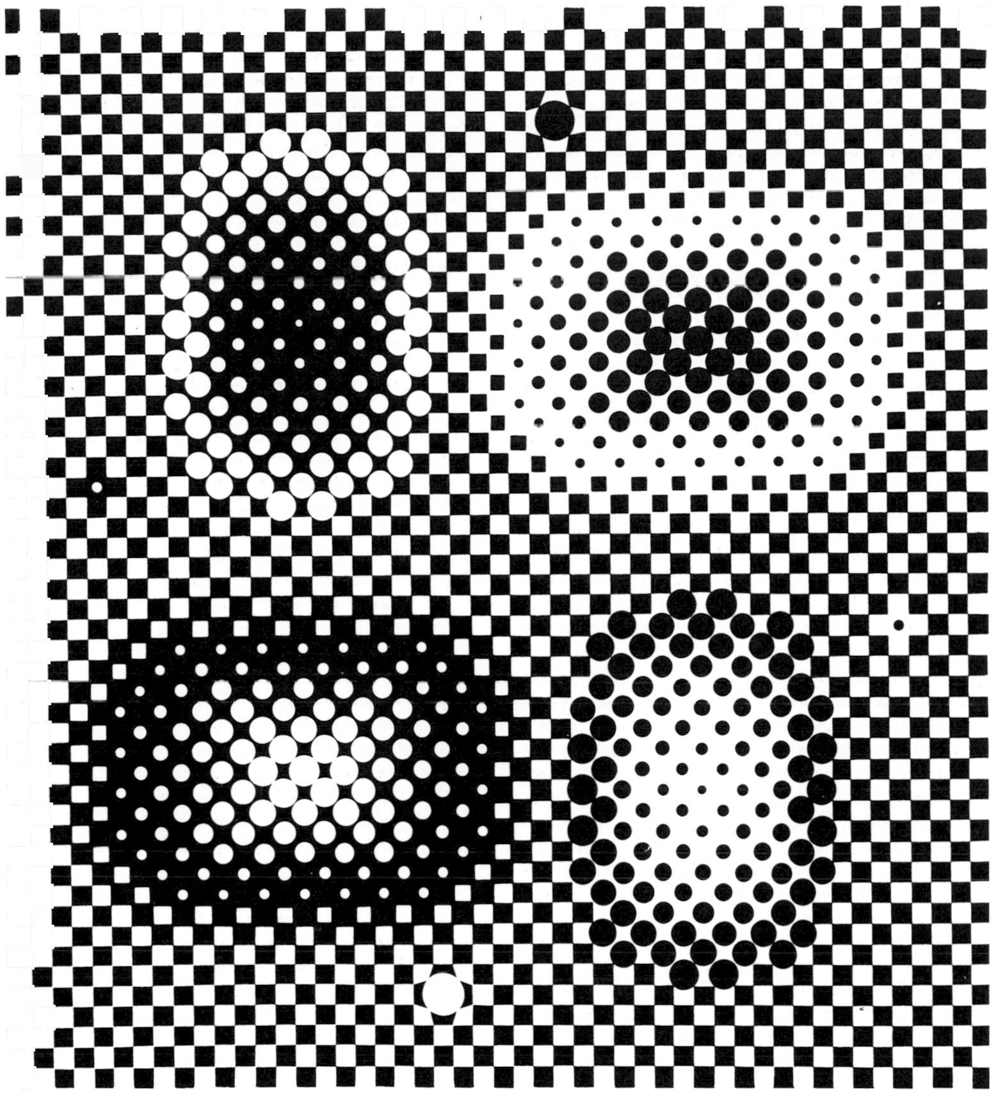

Victor Vasarely: *Metagalaxy*, 1961

Galerija Suvremene, Zagreb
Galleria del Leone, Venice
Galerie Claude Nouel, Rouen
1969 Centre de Culture, Neuchâtel, Switzerland
Galeria Rene Metras, Barcelona
Gimpel and Hanover Galerie, Zurich
Museum of Fine Arts, Pecs, Hungary
Galerie Engelberts, Geneva
Galerie Les Contards, Lacost, France
Galerie Denise René, Paris
Palace of Fine Arts, Budapest
French Institute, Budapest
1970 Galerie Veranneman, Brussels
Hungarian Institute, Paris
Knoll International, Paris
Barney Weinger Gallery, New York
Musée d'Art Moderne de la Ville, Paris (films on Vasarely)
Vision Nouvelle, Paris
1971 Galerie Suzanne Egloff, Basle
Galerie Denise René, Paris
Stratford Art Association, Ontario
Kunsthalle, Cologne
Chateau de Vacoeuil, France
Galerie Hans Mayer, Dusseldorf
Galerie Veranneman, Brussels
Minami Gallery, Tokyo
Zellweger Building, Zurich
1972 Glenbow Albert Art Gallery, Calgary (retrospective; toured Canada)
Galerie Municipale Marie-Therese Douet, Montreuil, France (toured France)
Sidney Janis Gallery, New York
Denise René Gallery, New York
Galerie Argos, Nantes, France
Galerie Charles Kriwin, Brussels
Galerie Maurel, Nimes, France
Philadelphia Museum of Art
Museum of Ludwigshafen-am-Rhein, West Germany (toured Germany, Switzerland and the Netherlands)
Galerie Formes Nouvelles, Lyons
Galerie Semiha Huber, Zurich
Galerie Schöttenring, Vienna
1973 Gallery Moos, Toronto
Galerie Veranneman, Brussels
Galerie Philippe Reichenbach, Paris
Galerie Gulliver, Paris
Ateliers d'Art Plastiques, Dieppe, France
Musée de Meaux, France
Galerie Denise René Rive Gauche, Paris
Galerie Denise René Rive Droite, Paris (retrospective)
Galerie des Arcades, Biot, France
Galerie Moser, Graz, Austria
Museo de Arte Mderno, Mexico City
1974 Goodman Gallery, Johannesburg
Galerie Semiha Huber, Zurich
Galleria Annunciata, Milan
Minami Gallery, Tokyo
French Embassy, Dakar, Senegal
Heller Gallery, London
Galerie M-L Jeanneret, Geneva
Groupe Manouchian Sports Complex, Aubervilliers, France
Tour des Echevins, Luxeuil-les-Bains, France
L'Abbaye de Gard, Acquigny, France
Galleria La Borgogna, Rome
1975 Casino-Kursaal, Ostend, Belgium
Sala della Cultura, Modena, Italy
Chateau de Cujan, Cher, France
Galeria Theo, Madrid
Galerie Bel'Art, Stockholm
Musée du Bastion Saint-André, Ramparts d'Antibes, France
Teheran Gallery, Teheran
1976 Tel-Aviv Museum
Kunstmuseum, Dusseldorf
Galerie Denise René Rive Gauche, Paris
1977 Musée Postal, Paris
Kulturforum, Bonn
Galerie des Arcades, Biot, France
Galerie Mathilde, Amsterdam
Galerie Bel'Art, Stockholm
French Institute, Stockholm
Galerie Nordenhake, Malmo, Sweden
Museo de Arte Contemporaneo, Caracas
1978 Vasarely Center, New York (opening exhibition)
Modern Art Museum, Mönchengladbach, West Germany
Städtisches Museum, Goslar, West Germany
Hilliard Collection, Munich
Centre Culturel Jacques Prévert, Villeparisis (with Yvaral)
Galerie Inard, Paris
Vasarely Center, New York
Palm Springs Desert Museum, California
1979 Phoenix Art Museum, Arizona
Chateau de Rocheshouart, Limousin, France
Centre Culturel, Villeparisis, France (with Yvaral)
Fondation Vasarely, Aix-en-Provence
Chateau de Sedieres, Correze, France
1980 Fondation Vasarely, Aix-en-Provence
Fundacao Gulbenkian, Lisbon
Konsthalle, Malmo, Sweden
Galleri Homansbyen, Oslo
Galerie Holtman, Hannover
Junior Galerie, Vienna
Chateau-de-Val, Bort-les-Orgues, France
Galleria Planetario, Trieste
Ecole des Ingenieurs, Bienne, Switzerland
Young Gallery, San Jose, California
Reading Public Museum, Pennsylvania
Nanteshi Gallery, Tokyo
1981 Royal Palace Gallery, Budapest
Badisches Landesmuseum, Karlsruhe
Jazz Academy, Budapest (toured Hungary)
Midland Center of the Arts, Michigan
Hotel de Ville, Montelimar, France
Chateau de Vassiviere, Creuse, France
1982 Vasarely Center, New York
Musee des Beaux-Arts, Chateauroux, France
Centre Vasarely, Oslo
Galeria Freites, Caracas, Venezuela
Hotel de Ville, Lucerne, Switzerland
1983 Vasarely Center, New York
Societe Hongroise de Secours Mutuel, Paris
Aktion Museum, Mistelbach, Austria
Galerie des Arcades de Blot, Alpes Maritimes, France (with Yvaral)
Museum of Karcag, Hungary
Centre Vasarely, Museum of Fine Arts, Budapest
Vasarely Center, New York
1984 Hotel de Ville, Villeurbanne, France (retrospective)
Musee de Tauroentum, St. Cyr sur Mer, France
Town Hall, Leinfelden, West Germany
Artcurial, Munich (travelled to Dusseldorf)
1985 Palais des Papes, Avignon, France
Institut Francais, Budapest
Galeria S. Dubrownik, Smobor, Yugoslavia
Hotel de Ville, Villeurbanne, France
Espace Jacques Prevert, Aulnay-sous-Bois, France
Chapelle Belloin, France
Galerie du Quesne, Castillon du Gard, France
1986 Galerie der Stadt Esslingen, Neckar, West Germany
Maison de la Lithographie, Paris
Musee National des Beaux-Arts, Algiers
Kunstkreis Sudliche Vergstrasse, Kraichgau, West Germany
Alliance Francaise, Bangkok
Heimatmuseum, Gablitzhalle, Austria
Espace Belleville, France

Galerie Schemes, Lille, France
Maison Alexandre Dumas, Marly-le-Roi, France
Abbaye St. Germain, Auxerre, France
Galerie Lahumiere, Paris

Selected Group Exhibitions:

1929 *Muhely,* Museum of Applied Arts, Budapest
1947 *1st Salon des Realities Nouvelles,* Musee d'Art Moderne, Paris
1949 *Abstract Painting,* Betty Parsons' Gallery, New York
1953 *Younger European Painters,* Guggenheim Museum, New York
1958 *50 Years of Modern Art,* at *Exposition Internationale (World's Fair),* Brussels
1961 *Le Mouvement,* Stedelijk Museum, Amsterdam
1964 *Painting and Sculpture of a Decade 1954–64,* Tate Gallery, London
1967 *Dada 1916–66,* Galleria Nazionale d'Arte Moderna, Rome
1970 *Collections Etzold,* Kolnischer Kunstverein, Cologne
1973 *The Non-Objective World 1914–55,* Annely Juda Fine Art, London (travelled to Austin, Texas)

Collections:

Centre Georges Pompidou, Paris; Tate Gallery, London; Stedelijk Museum, Amsterdam: Musée des Beaux-Arts, Brussels; Nationalgalerie, West Berlin; Israel Museum, Jerusalem; Power Gallery of Contemporary Art, Sydney; Musée d'Art Contemporain, Montreal: Museum of Modern Art, New York; Art Institute of Chicago.

Documentation of Vasarely's life and work is principally housed at the Fondation Vasarely, Aix-en-Provence: the Musée Vasarely, Vaucluse, France; the Vasarely Museum, Pecs; and the Vasarely Center, New York.

Publications:

By VASARELY: books and pamphlets—*La Forme-Couleur integrée dans la Cité par la Technique des Revetements Muraux,* Paris 1959; *Kassak-Vasarely* album of serigraphs, with an introduction by Denise René and Jean Cassou, Paris 1961; *Vasarely: Morphemes,* album of engravings with text by Imre Pan, Paris 1966; *Notes, Reflexions de Vasarely,* Paris 1964; *The Notebook of Vasarely,* Oxford 1964; *Discours de la Methode de Descartes accompagne du Discours de la Methode de Vasarely,* with a preface by Otto Hahn, Paris 1969; *Plasti-Cité,* edited by Michel Ragon, Paris 1970; *Victor-Vasarely—Notes brutes,* with a foreword by Bruno Alfiere, Venice 1970; *Folklore Planetaire—Farbwelt,* Munich 1973; *Réponses á Vasarely,* Munich and Paris 1974; *Vasarely Inconnu,* Neuchátel, Switzerland 1977; *Victor Vasarely Faabstadt/City Polychrome,* with a commentary by Eugen Gomringer, Munich 1977; *Vasarely,* Paris 1978; *Reflets,* portfolio of 4 prints, with poems by Maurice Bruzeau Paris 1979; *Vasarely Plasticien,* with William Desmond, Paris 1979; *Gea,* Paris 1982.

On VASARELY: books—*Vasarely* by Dewasne, Paris 1952; *Vasarely,* exhibition catalogue with text by Carlo Belloli, Milan 1961; *Victor Vasarely,* exhibition catalogue, with text by Wieland Schmied, Hannover 1963; *Arts Plastiques du 20e. Siecle: Vasarely,* Neuchatel, Switzerland 1965; *Vasarely* by Werner Spies, Stuttgart 1969; *Vasarely,* exhibition catalogue, with a preface by M. E. Rosta, Budapest 1969; *Vasarely II,* Neuchatel, Switzerland 1970; *Vasarely Analysen* by Axel Bruck, Hamburg 1970; *Victor Vasarely* by Werner Spies, Paris, Cologne and New York 1971; *Gesprache mit Victor Vasarely* by Jean-Louis Ferrier, Cologne 1971; *Vasarely,* exhibition catalogue, with a preface by Helmut R. Leppien, Cologne 1971; *Victor Vasarely,* exhibition catalogue, with a preface by Manfred Fath, Ludwigshafen, West Germany 1972; *Ateliers Aujourd hui: Vasarely* by Marc Hallain, Paris 1973; *J'Apprends à Peindre avec Vasarely,* Paris 1973; *Arts Plastiques du 20e. Siecle: Vasarely III,* with a preface by Marcel Joray, Neuchatel, Switzerland 1974: *Vasarely* by Marcel Joray, Neuchatel, Switzerland 1976; *Le Musée Imaginaire de Vasarely,* with a foreword by Otto Hahn, Paris 1978; *Vasarely 4,* Neuchatel, Switzerland 1979; *Vasarely, Connaissance d'un Art Moleculaire* by Bernard Dahhan, Paris 1979; *Colorier avec Vasarely,* Paris 1980.

From 1930 when he moved to Paris from Budapest, Victor Vasarely followed a course that, while it initially did not renounce realistic elements, always activated the painting surface to create its own illusions of space proper to itself, and finally to nothing beyond the confines of the picture frame. His employment as a commercial artist went hand in glove with a technical proficiency that became more and more self-centered. An early work of his pre-war period—"Chessboard" (1935)—is a forerunner of his development. It shows strength in conveying illusions of space where the surface seems to buckle and corrugate as the wavy lines swell and contract in width. His method of painting then was meticulous in its definition of form reflecting the ambivalence of Orphism and to a degree Surrealism.

In the 1940's following his first one-man show in Paris, Vasarely committed himself to a programmed system of picture making based on geometrical modules and variations in colours that went through permutations of considerable complexity. Organic forms of circles, squares, ellipses and rectangles were arranged in compositions of ordered movement and ambiguities in which colours and tonal balances set up visual tensions of alternately harmonious and disturbing elements. This calculated adjustment of solid and transparency of warm and cold hues, of stepping and breaking of linear direction was achieved with a disposition of effect harking back to the Bauhaus principles of sheer outline and immaculate profile in space, eschewing the serif and the decorative as unnecessary in terms of architectonic logic.

"Orion MC" (1963) is a typical example of Vasarely's concept. The rectangle offers a highly charged checkerboard design composed of 420 squares containing circles of different sizes alternating with ellipses also varied in size and placed on different axes relating to the picture edge. The whole picture presents a quivering screen of light intensity established by the tonal strength and juxtaposition of subtly animated areas. Nothing Vasarely does is uncomposed. In his refinement of mosaical permutations he has evolved striking effects from shades of five different colours placed in four different zones adjacent to each other. In 1959 he patented a system of "plastic unity" where he put together collages from single elements: round, oval, square, rhomboid and triangular, cut out from squares of distinctive colours and alternating them on squares of different grounds. This limitless potential and its versatility has lent itself to kinetic exploitation as well as in architectural projects as sculptures both freestanding and in relief.

Acknowledged as the originator of post-war Op Art, Vasarely had a noticeable influence on such artists as Bridget Riley without relinquishing his own authority in constructive geometric abstraction. His own belief that he had formulated a new urban folklore through a multiplicity of prototypes mechanically permutated was justified perhaps in its maturity, but its very consistency imposed an inevitable diminution in returns of aesthetic satisfaction.

—G. S. Whittet

VAUGHAN, Keith.
British. Born in Selsey Bill, Sussex, in 1912; moved with his family to London, 1916. Early education in Sussex; self-taught in art. Served as clerk and German interpreter, in the British Army, Wiltshire and Yorkshire, 1941–46. Painter: worked for Lintas Advertising Agency, while painting in his spare time, London, 1931–38; shared house with painter John Minton, St. John's Wood, London, 1946; worked on book and magazine illustrations, 1946; visited France and Italy, 1948–52; commissioned to paint mural for the Dome of Discovery, *Festival of Britain,* London, 1951; worked in studio in Hampstead, London, from 1952; spent holidays and weekends in his cottage in Essex from 1965. Part-time Lecturer, Camberwell School of Art, London, 1946–48; Lecturer, Slade School of Fine Art, London 1959; Resident Painter, State University of Iowa, Iowa City, 1959. Honorary Fellow, Royal College of Art, 1964. C.B.E. (companion, Order of the British Empire), 1965. *Died* (by suicide; in London) *4 November 1977.*

Individual Exhibitions:

1944 Reid and Lefevre Gallery, London
1946 Reid and Lefevre Gallery, London
1948 George Dix Gallery, New York
Reid and Lefevre Gallery, London
1950 instituto de Arte Moderno, Paraguay
Museo D'Arte Moderno, Buenos Aires
Redfern Gallery, London
1951 Reid and Lefevre Gallery, London
1952 Hanover Gallery, London
Reid and Lefevre Gallery, London
Redfern Gallery, London
Durlacher Brothers, New York
1953 Leicester Galleries, London
1955 Durlacher Brothers, New York
Leicester Galleries, London
1956 Hatton Gallery, Newcastle upon Tyne
Leicester Galleries, London
1957 Durlacher Brothers, New York
1958 Leicester Galleries, London
West of England Academy, Bristol
1959 Leicester Galleries, London
University of Iowa, Iowa City
1960 Bear Lane Gallery, Oxford
Matthiesen Gallery, London
1962 Whitechapel Art Gallery, London (toured the U.K.)
Matthiesen Gallery, London
1964 Mariborough Fine Art Gallery, London
1965 Bear Lane Gallery, Oxford
Mariborough Fine Art Gallery, London
1966 Redfern Gallery, London
Durlacher Brothers, New York
Hambledon Gallery, Blandford, Dorset
1967 Tib Lane Gallery, Manchester
1968 Rex Evans Gallery, Los Angeles
Marlborough Fine Art Gallery, London
1969 Mappin Gallery, Sheffield
Hamet Gallery, London
Tib Lane Gallery, Manchester
1970 Bear Lane Gallery, Oxford
Hamet Gallery, London
University of York
1971 Hambledon Gallery, Blandford, Dorset
Park Square Gallery, Leeds
1973 Waddington Galleries, London
1974 Victor Waddington, London
1976 Compass Gallery, Glasgow
1977 Mappin Gallery, Sheffield
1979 Penwith Galleries, St. Ives, Cornwall (with Tony O'Malley)
1981 *Images of Man,* Geffrey Museum, London (travelled to City Museum and Art Gallery, Birmingham)
1985 Agnew Gallery, London
1987 Austin/Desmond Fine Art, Sunninghill, Berkshire
New Grafton Gallery, London

Selected Group Exhibitions:

1943 *War Artists Exhibition,* National Gallery, London
1948 *Contemporary British Painting,* Belgrade
1950 *contemporary British Painting,* Pennsylvania Academy of Fine Arts, Philadelphia
1951 *21 Modern British Painters,* Vancouver Art Gallery
1953 *International Water-Color Exhibition,* Brooklyn Museum, New York
1960 *Guggenheim International Award Exhibition,* Guggenheim Museum, New York
1963 *Bienal,* Sao Paulo

Collections:

Tate Gallery London: Tel Aviv Museum; Calouste

Gulbenkian Foundation, Lisbon; Albright-Knox Art Gallery, Buffalo, New York; Wadsworth Atheneum, Hartford, Connecticut; Phillips Collection, Washington, D.C.; National Gallery of South Australia, Adelaide; National Gallery of New South Wales, Sydney; National Gallery of Victoria, Melbourne; Auckland Museum, New Zealand.

Publications:

By VAUGHAN: book—*Journals and Drawings 1939–1965*, London 1966; book illustrated—*Une Saison en Enfer* by Arthur Rimbaud; articles—foreword to *Keith Vaughan*, exhibition catalogue, London 1944; "Notes on Painting: August 1964," in *London Magazine*, October 1964; interview in *Conversations with Painters* by Noel Barber, London 1964.

On VAUGHAN: books—*The Changing Forms of Art* by Patrick Heron, London 1955; *Keith Vaughan*, exhibition catalogue, by David Thompson, London 1962, *Keith Vaughan: Images of Man*, exhibition catalogue, by John Nicholas Ball, London 1981; *Keith Vaughan: Paintings, Gouaches, Watercolours and Drawings 1936–1976*, exhibition catalogue with text by Robert Buhler, Sunninghill 1987; articles—"Keith Vaughan" by Benedict Nicolson in *The Observer* (London), 28 February 1960; "Keith Vaughan" by Bryan Robertson in *Studio International* (London), November 1964; "Keith Vaughan" by Anthony Carter in *Studio International* (London), January 1969; "Keith Vaughan" by Alan Ross in *London Magazine*, February 1978; "Trial of an Outsider" by C. Neve in *Country Life* (London), June 1981.

When major artists are "ahead of their time," they seem to carry their times along with them. Keith Vaughan felt at odds with his times; yet had he lived only a few years longer, the more open art scene and style of living would surely have provided a more sympathetic environment for his art, and "rediscovered" him with a major retrospective.

Self-taught while working during the 1930's in an advertising agency, and interested in ballet and photography, he illustrated his notable journal (1939–1977) during the 1939–1945 war with evocative but non-violent drawings and gouaches of soldiers off-duty; published in part in *London Magazine*, this led him to meet "neo-romantic" artists such as Sutherland, Craxton and Minton. Around 1952, De Stael's flattened and abstracted forms became an influence; around 1959, with his teaching visit to the United States, he created paintings that were even more abstracted, though their harlequin lozenges of colour scattered in space never quite lost a human presence.

But really with the examples of Cézanne's, Matisse's and Picasso's bathers and acrobats foremost, particularly Matisse's—Vaughan's prime interest was always his own resolution of that classical Greek preoccupation, the young male body as of man's birthright, power, innate harmony and aspiration—a theme dormant in art of the time, or awkwardly described as "figures in landscape," yet parallel to ballet's basic language of lyrical repose, graceful movement, significant gesture, tensions, heroism and nobility. Realism, nostalgia for remembered times of beaches and bathing before the war with companions now dead, the resolution of his own tensions in society, and the vision of an ideal, Arcadian world, all add to the emotions of these paintings, whose technical search might be described as the monumental expression of a lyrical human line in the freest space.

It could be said that Vaughan paints like a dancer and a choreographer (indeed, as they themselves might like to paint); and that would indicate the wide range of mood, gesture, expression and theme inherent in Vaughan's work beyond its lyrical physicality. In retrospect, Vaughan's courage in maintaining his artistic interests at an unsympathetic time should be praised (and he was well aware of that difficult area between eroticism and beauty too); he would have suited large public commissions, major book illustration commissions, and theatrical design. But what he describes in his eloquent, intelligent *Journal* as the ". . . constant baffling mystery—the duality of I and myself . . ." indicates the strength and enduring validity of his beautiful and memorable paintings.

—Michael Shepherd

VAUTIER, Ben.

Swiss. Born of a Swiss-French father and Irish mother in Naples, 18 July 1935. Educated in Turkey, Egypt, and Greece until 1949; mainly self-taught in art. Married Annie Baricolla in 1964; children: Eva and Francois. Independent artist in Nice since the mid-1950's; began actions and happenings and established gallery, Laboratoire 32 (32 rue Tondutti-de-l'Escarène), later re-named Galerie Ben Doute de Tout, Nice, 1958; associated with Fluxus artists in Paris and Cologne, 1962–70; established Galerie Fenetre, Nice, 1971, and Galerie La Difference, Nice, in late 1970's. Recipient: D.A.A.D. scholarship to West Berlin, 1978. Agents: Galerie Daniel Templon, 30 rue Beaubourg, 75003 Paris; Galerie Bischofberger, Buhlstrasse 7, 8700 Kussnacht, Switzerland. Address: 103 Route de Saint-Pancrace, 06100 Nice, France.

Individual Exhibitions:

1960 Laboratoire 32, Nice
1964 Amstell 47, Amsterdam
1966 La Cédille Qui Sourit, Villefranche-sur-Mer, France
1970 Galerie de la Salle, Vence, France
Galerie Yellow Now, Brussels
Galerie Daniel Templon, Paris
Galerie Hans Mayer, Dusseldorf
Galerie René Block, West Berlin
Galleria Artestudio, Macerata, Italy
1971 Galleria Sant'Andrea, Milan
Galleria Il Punto, Turin
Galerie Daniel Templon, Paris
Galerie Bischofberger, Zurich
1972 Galerie Günter Sachs, Hamburg
Galleria Lia Rumma, Naples
Galerie Grafikmeyer, Karlsrube, West Germany
Galerie Daniel Templon, Paris
1973 International Cultureel Centrum, Antwerp
Galerie Daniel Templon, Paris
Art=Ben, Stedelijk Museum, Amsterdam
Galerie Rudolf Zwirner, Cologne
Galleria La Bertesca, Milan
Neue Galerie, Aachen, West Germany
1974 Galeria Foksal, Warsaw
Galerie Yellow Now, Liège, Belgium
Neue Galerie, Aachen, West Germany
Galerie Le Flux, Perpignan, France
1975 Galleria dei Mille, Bergamo, Italy
Studio F22, Palazzolo. Italy
Centro d'Informazione Alternativa, Rome
John Gibson Gallery, New York
1976 Galerie HM, Brussels
Kunsthandel Brinkman, Amsterdam
1977 Galleria l'Uomo e l'Arte, Brescia, Italy
Galerie Baudoin Lebon, Paris
1978 Galleria Rinaldo Rotta, Genoa
Galerie Ecart, Geneva
1979 Galleri Léger, Malmo, Sweden
Berlin Inventory, DAAD-Galerie, West Berlin
1980 Musée d'Art Contemporain, Montreal
1981 *Ben Libre*. Musée d'Art et d'Industrie. St.-Etienne, France
Galerie Daniel Templon, Paris
Photos chez Stenope, Nice
Galerie Ecart, Geneva
1981 Galerie Catherine Issert, St. Paul de Vence, France
Galerie Grimaldi, Aix-en-Provence, France
Musee d'Art et d'Industrie, St. Etienne, France
Galerie Errata, Montpellier, France
1983 Galerie Beaubourg, Paris
Galerie La Hune, Paris
Galerie Donguy, Paris
Galerie Chantal Crousel, Paris
Galerie Durand-Dessert, Paris
Galerie Mollet Vieiville, Paris
Galerie Avant Premiere, Paris
Galerie Templon, Paris
Galerie Fournier, Paris
Galerie Lara Vincy, Paris
Galerie Creatis, Paris
Galerie Durand, Paris
Galerie Nez en l'Air, Nice
Galerie Catherine Issert, St. Paul de Vence, France
1984 Galerie Jollenbeck, Cologne
Galerie Ecart, Geneva
Galerie R.Z.A., Dusseldorf
Galerie Baudoin Lebon at *FIAC 84*, Grand Palais, Paris
1985 Galerie Baudoin Lebon, Paris
Galerie Bilinelli, Brussels
Galerie d'Art Contemporain, Nice
Stadtgalerie, Erlangen, West Germany
1986 Museum Ingelstad, Sweden
Sala Parpallo, Valencia, Spain
Galerie Leger, Malmo, Sweden
Galerie Daniel Templon, Paris
Galerie Semiha Huber, Geneva
Galerie Catherine Issert, St. Paul de Vence, France
Maison des artistes, Genas (Lyon), France
Galerie Schuppenhauer, Essen, West Germany
1987 Galerie Camomille, Brussels
Musee de Calais, France
Musee de Ceret, France
Centre Regional d'Art Contemporain, Lebege, France

Selected Group Exhibitions:

1962 *Festival of Misfits*, Gallery One, London
1967 *Ecole de Nice*, Galerie de la Salle, Vence, France
1970 *Happening and Fluxus*, Kunstverein, Cologne
1973 *Contemporanea*, Parcheggio Villa Borghese, Rome
1977 *A Propos de Nice*, Centre Georges Pompidou, Paris
1979 *Fluxus*, Espace Lyonnais d'Art Contemporain, Lyons (toured Europe)
1982 *Art Vivant 60/80*, Stedelijk Museum, Amsterdam
1984 *L'Ecriture dans la Peinture*, Centre Nicois des Arts Plastiques, Nice
1987 *Berlinart 1961–87*, Museum of Modern Art, New York (travelled to San Francisco)

Publications:

By BEN: books and pamphlets—*L'Esthetique de Ben*, Nice 1960; *Programme de 7 Jours de Recherche*, Nice 1964; *Tout Programme Publik*, Nice 1965; *Tout Cedille Qui Sourit*, Nice 1966; *Galerie Ben Doute de Tout Presente*, Nice 1966; *Ben Dieu (L'Art C'est les Autres)*, Nice 1966; *Propositions pour un Livre et pour des Objets Divers*, Nice 1966; *Tout Rebus*, Nice 1966; *Tout Poesis*, Nice 1966; *J'Aime et J'Attaque no. 1*, 1967; *J'Aime et J'Attaque no. 2*, Nice 1968; *tout (Musique et Cinema)*, Nice 1968; *Programme pour la Table*, Nice 1968; *Tout Moi Ben Je Signe*, Nice 1969; *Reedition de Vieux Stencils de Ben*, Nice 1969; *Capitre Idees*, Nice 1970; *Chronique Touche a Tout de Ben No. 1*, Nice 1970; *A P'Art*, Nice 1977; *Reg'Art*, Nice 1978; *Bag'Art Bay'Art*, Nice 1979; *Manuscrit pour une Premiere Internationale Ethniste*, Nice 1986; *La Verite de A a Z* , Toulouse 1987.

On BEN: books—*Aktionen, Happenings und Demonstrationen seit 1965*, edited by Wolf Vostell, Hamburg 1970; *Catalogue de Films de Ben*. Paris 1971; *Mail Art: Communication à Distance, Concept*, edited by Jean-Mare Poinsot, Paris 1971: *Documenta 5: Befragung der Realitat*, exhibition catalogue, edited by Harald Szeeman and others, Kassel, West Germany 1972; *Art = Ben*, exhibition catalogue, with an introduction by Ad Petersen, Amsterdam 1973; *Ben Vautier; Berlin Inventory*, exhibition catalogue, West Berlin 1979; *Ben Libre*, exhibition catalogue, St. Etienne, France 1981; *Ben: Encore des Mots*, exhibition catalogue, Lyon 1986.

Ben (as he signs his works) could be called the correspondence art network's Duchamp. In performance and on film he sits, or swims, or lies face down on a busy sidewalk, elevating the activity to art by giving it a title and a framework, or de-elevating art by linking it with such common actions. The notion of de-elevating art would not even arise were it not for Ben's frequent references to the questionability of the art world, the making of art and the grip that art has on him and his life.

Ben's art relies on thoughts and words; his works often contain calligraphic oneliners reflecting his humorous, reflective attitude which fluctuates between

negative and positive, sometimes in the same piece. One work shows the artist sitting on a chair with a sign on his lap which reads "Art is Useless." To the right is another message: "I sold that piece, and with the money I went on holiday for a week."

The artist is based in Nice, where he has operated a second hand record shop and maintained widespread contact with the international art scene by publishing small books, posters, brochures, and post cards. An associate of Fluxus and the nouveau realisme group, Ben has participated in Flux kits and produced memorable rubber stamp art, a medium he has used since 1949. Post cards are especially suitable for Ben's art since they function as a support for his calligraphic text and, as multiples, are able to reach a wide audience. Two of his cards, "Postman's Choice," 1965, and "Your thumb present now . . . . " 1966, are among the best known works in correspondence art.

As a participant in Mieko Shiomi's "Spatial Poem," a correspondence/response project, Ben contributed responses which reflect his philosophy about art and life and the ever changing balance between the two:

Spatial Poem No. 2 direction event. Ben Vautier was most likely in bed facing the ceiling in Nice.

Spatial Poem No. 3 falling event. After hesitating a great deal, Ben Vautier swallowed the thin piece of paper joined to the invitation letter.

Spatial Poem No. 4 shadow event. A)I found the SHADOW plastic sheet in the shadow of an envelope. B)I put the SHADOW plastic sheet 1. in the shadow of a tree 2. in the shadow of myself Ben 3. in the shadow of the moon—at night 4. in the shadow of a beautiful naked girl—my daughter 5. in the shadow of . . . Then I put it into a special file for Shiomi, and it is there in the shadow of all the documents concerning her.

Spatial Poem No. 9 disappearing event. I have come to the conclusion that my interest in art is slowly disappearing.

In September 1983, *Art News* magazine reported that Ben's Nice boutique, known as Galerie Ben Doute de Tout, is now enshrined in Paris' National Museum of Modern Art at the Centre Pompidou.

—Mary Stofflet

VEDOVA, Emilio.

Italian. Born in Venice, 9 August 1919. Educated at schools in Venice, until 1930; mainly self-taught in painting from 1935, but attended Silvio Pucci's Free School of Painting, Florence, 1939–40. Served with the Italian partisans, in northern Italy, 1944–45. Worked in a local factory, Venice, 1930–37. Independent painter, in Rome, Florence and Venice, from 1937: established studio at Dorsoduro alla Salute, Venice, 1957. Member, Corrente artists movement, Milan, 1942; founder-member, Nuova Secessione (Fronte Nuovo delle Arti), Venice, 1946; member, Gruppo degli Otto, Venice, 1952. Director, Summer Academy, Salzburg, Austria, 1965–70; Professor of Painting, Accademia di Belle Arti, Venice, from 1975. Recipient: La Colomba Prize, Venice, 1938; Volpi Prize, 1950, Drawing Prize, 1954, and Grand Prize for Painting, 1960, *Bienal de Sao Paulo,* Brazil; Guggenheim Foundation Prize for Italy, 1956; Premio Lissone, Milan, 1958; First Prize, *Drawing Biennale,* Rijeka, 1976. Agent: Galleria Giorgio Persano, Piazza Vittorio Veneto 9, 10124 Turin. Address: Dorsoduro 46, 30123 Venice, Italy.

Individual Exhibitions:

1942 Galleria Euro Romano, Genoa, Italy
1943 Galleria La Spiga e Corrente, Milan
1945 Galleria Venezia, Venice
Piccola Galleria, Venice
Galleria del Pioppo, Mantua, Italy
1946 Art Club, Rome
Galleria Del Bosco, Turin
Piccola Galleria Venezia, Venice
1947 Galleria del Cavallino, Venice
Art Club, Rome
1951 Viviano Gallery, New York
1954 Museu de Arte Moderna, Rio de Janeiro
1956 Galerie Gunther Franke, Munich (retrospective)
1957 Galerie Springer, West Berlin
1958 Zacheta Palace Museum, Warsaw (retrospective; travelled to Poznan, 1959)
Galerie Springer, West Berlin
1960 Galleria Blu, Milan (retrospective)
Galleria II Disegno, Milan (retrospective)
Kunsthalle, Hamburg
Kunstmuseum, Lucerne
1961 Palazzo della Gran Guardia, Verona, Italy (retrospective)
Galleria Annunciata, Milan
Galleri M59, Copenhagen
Museo de Ateneo, Madrid (retrospective)
Sala Gaspar, Barcelona
1962 Galleria-Libreria Einaudi, Rome
Arco Palais Galerie, Monaco
Galleri Haghfeldt, Copenhagen
Galerie Pierre, Stockholm
Kunstverein, Freiburg, West Germany (retrospective)
1963 Galleria Marlborough, Rome
Museu de Arte Moderna, Rio de Janeiro
1964 Staatliche Kunsthalle, Baden-Baden, West Germany (retrospective)
1965 Institute of Contemporary Art, Washington, D.C. (retrospective)
Kunstlerhaus, Salzburg, Austria (retrospective)
1967 Hollaru Gallery, Prague (toured Czechoslovakia)
1968 Kunstlerhaus, Salzburg, Austria (retrospective; travelled to Ferrara, Italy)
1970 Galerie Rothe, Heidelberg, West Germany
1971 Forum Gallery, Zagreb, Yugoslavia
1972 Galleria Falchi, Milan
1973 Kunstmuseum, Dusseldorf
1974 Galleria Linea 70, Verona, Italy
1975 Teatro Romano, Aosta, Italy
Castello Visconteo, Pavia, Italy (retrospective)
1976 Galleria Mariani, Ravenna, Italy
1978 Museo Castello, Portofino, Italy (retrospective)
1979 Sala Medievale di San Jacopo, Prato, Italy (retrospective; toured Australia)
1980 Galerie im Taxispalais, Innsbruck (toured Austria)
Museo Carrillo Gil, Mexico City
Galleria Planetario, Trieste, Italy
1981 Städtisches Museum, Leverkusen, West Germany
Palazzo dei Congressi, San Marino
Kunstverein, Braunschweig, West Germany
1982 Van Abbemuseum, Eindhoven, Netherlands
Galleria d'Arte Moderna, Bologna, Italy
Galerie Annemarie Verna, Zurich
Mura Aureliana, Rome
1983 Galerie Annemarie Verna 2, Zurich
Istituto Artistiche Universitario, Venice
Galleria Stevens, Padua, Italy
Galerie Thomas Borgmann, Cologne
Galerie Fred Jahn, Munich
Studio Marconi, Milan
Galerija Sebastian, Belgrade
Galerie Neuendorf, Hamburg (travelled to Venice)
1984 Galleria Loza/Galleria Meduza, Capodistria, Yugoslavia
Museo Correr, Venice
Galleria San Marco, Rome
1985 Galerie Buchmann, Basle
Galleria Giorgio Persano, Turin
Museo del Castello, Rivoli, Italy
1986 Galleria Tornabuoni, Florence
Staatsgalerie Moderner Kunst, Munich
Galerie Fred Jahn, Munich
Musée Ingres, Toulouse, France
Städtisches Museum, Leverkusen, West Germany
Galerie Ulysses, Vienna
Kunsthalle, Darmstadt, West Germany
Padiglione Arte Contemporanea, Milan
Galerie Academia, Salzburg, Austria
Galleria Niccoli, Parma, Italy
1987 Museum Wiener Secession, Vienna
Kunstmuseum, Lucerne, Switzerland
Galerie XPO, Hamburg
Museo Gorizia, Grado, Italy
Musée d'Art Contemporain, Nimes, France
Musée d'Art Contemporain, St. Etienne, France
Galerie Hannah Feldmann, Berne
1988 Galleria L'Isola, Rome (travelled to Bologna)
Fondazione Villa Celle, Santomato, Italy (installation)
Galerie Rothe, Frankfurt
Künstlerhaus, Salzburg, Austria

Selected Group Exhibitions:

1947 *Fronte Nuovo,* Galleria Cairola, Milan
1948 *Arte Astratta in Italia,* Galleria di Roma, Rome
1950 *Biennale,* Venice (and 1954, 1960, 1978)
1955 *Documenta 1,* Museum Fridericianum, Kassel, West Germany (and *Documenta 2,* 1958, *Documenta 3,* 1964)
1958 *Vitalita nell'arte,* Palazzo Grassi, Venice (travelled to Amsterdam)
1967 *Expo 67,* Montreal
1972 *Immagine per la Citta,* Museo Civico, Genoa, Italy
1977 *International Survey of Drawing,* Art Gallery of Western Australia, Perth
1985 *The European Iceberg,* Art Gallery of Ontario, Toronto
1987 *Berlinart 1961–87,* Museum of Modern Art, New York (travelled to San Francisco)

Publications:

On VEDOVA: books—*Pittura Moderna Italiana* by G. Marchiori, Trieste 1946; *Emilio Vedova* by G. Marchiori, Venice 1951; *Pittura Italiana del Dopoguerra 1945–57* by T. Sauvage, Milan 1957; *Confessions of an Art Addict* by Peggy Guggenheim, New York 1960; *New Tendencies in Art* by Aldo Pellegrini, New York 1966; *Ultime tendenze nell'arte d'oggi* by Gillo Dorfles, Milan 1973; *Emilio Vedova: Grafica e didattica,* exhibition catalogue, Aosta 1975; *Maestri Contemporanei: Vedova* by Filiberto Menna, Milan 1982; *Vedova Compresenze,* exhibition catalogue, San Marino 1981; *Emilio Vedova 1935–1984,* edited by Germano Celant and Ida Gianelli, Milan 1984; *Vedova 1986,* edited by Carla Schultz Hoffman, Munich 1986; *Vedova und Salzburg,* Salzburg 1988.

As an artist of international renown in the field of *Informel* painting, Emilio Vedova embodies one of the greatest protagonists of twentieth century Italian art. At the beginning of his career in 1935 to 1936, while still a young man, he demonstrated an extraordinary command of expressive means in a series of architectonic drawings. His elegant style has a descriptive and dynamic urgency which has become his hallmark. Up to the beginning of the 1940s, his oil paintings were clearly influenced by Tintoretto, Goya, Daumier and Rouault and by the Expressionist tradition, one of the most evident premises of Vedova's work—as in *Assassinio* (1941) and *Operaio* (1942). Vedova's expressive dynamism is also reflected in his involvement with anti-fascism and a number of social issues. He had belonged to Corrente, the group opposed to 'official' art during the 1930s. At the end of the war, he joined the Fronte Nuovo delle Arti in 1946, and took part in the debate between 'abstract' and 'realist' movements that raged through Italian art in those years. Vedova formed a close relationship with the abstract painters championed by Lionello Venturi, and between 1952 and 1954 the Gruppo degli Otto was formed.

For Vedova and other abstractionists who had been suppressed by Fascist cultural policies, abstraction

Emilio Vedova: *Image of Time (Barricade)*, 1951 Courtesy Guggenheim Museum, New York

took as a starting point the reinterpretation of Picasso and Cubist figuration. The shifting and interpenetration of different planes is articulated, in Vedova's case, by irregular geometric modules building the figures into compact and rigid forms (Vedova himself was to speak of 'automatons' or 'machines'), as in *Cucitrice No. 1* (1946). Later on, his themes become more evocative, and the painted marks tend increasingly to signify rather than to represent. *Explosion* (1948) has relaxed from the earlier rigid style into a highly dynamic and forceful language. In this work, Vedova uses signals of energy, vectors of directions, forms in which the blacks defining them are accompanied by evanescent patches of white, the function of which is to underline their dynamic rhythm.

In the 1950s Vedova relinquished the geometry which he later confessed to have obsessed and inhibited him. In such works as *Immagine del Tempo n. 1 e 2* (1951), angularity is characterized by a more lyrical brushmark. Vedova's form of cubism had by now begun borrowing from the dynamic vocabulary of early futurism to combine with the fundamental expressionism that so deeply permeated his work with a sense of tragedy. His approach to painting now oscillated between substantiating signs as a body of ideograms, and liberating that gestural fluidity in which the range of colour was highly evocative besides functioning as structure. The resolution of these diametrically opposed features in Vedova's work is evident in *Ciclo della Protesta* and *Ciclo della Natura,* both of 1953. In each of these paintings, the resolution constitutes a highly dramatic event.

Throughout his long career, the actual gesture of painting has remained of paramount importance. The gesture disturbs the surface, signifying historical man's tragedy and loneliness, isolated and unable to control unconscious impulses. In 1962, Vedova wrote: "A materic sign will never give us access to a new dimension of a universe constantly being destroyed and re-aggregated." However, still understanding the limits of his artistic language, Vedova insists that "the sign affirms itself", and that his works are "full of structures." The gestural mark is the vehicle for the violence that destroys, but always within sight of a reconstruction. Vedova's negation is full of optimism.

In the multiple images of the 1970s, Vedova's negation destroys codified two-dimensionality where marks or signs virtually dismantle the space. The painting appears to fall apart, with surface planes expanding and combining freely, so that the picture becomes an event and visual process unfolding in front of the viewer's eyes. *Absudes Berliner Tagebuch* (1964) is a work of multiple images commemorating the erection of the Berlin Wall. The 'structures' of which Vedova speaks are also the structures of conscience. The work becomes an emblem of awakened conscience, an alarm ready to expose social injustice, and thus accentuates its role as communicable testimony.

After these multiple works Vedova returned to the single canvas, where he promotes the idea of the painting as a battleground. In the painting *Lacerazioni* (1977–78), Vedova's use of both negation and affirmation is made clear by the function assigned to colours in relationship to the manner in which the paint is handled. Whereas the whites and yellows convey an aura of light and space, the reds are charged with violence. Vedova, however, balances this disruptive passion by conferring the role of regulator onto the viscous strength of his blacks. In only a few cases does Vedova yield to instinctive and informal gesture, as in *Da Dove* (1983).

Unlike Pollock, for instance, Vedova makes no attempt to match his own estangement from the world by means of an informal painting style. Through destructive and reconstructive valencies, he proclaims the world as worthy of reconquering.

—Giorgio Verzotti

VELICKOVIC, Vladimir.

Yugoslav. Born in Belgrade, 11 August 1935. Studied architecture at the University of Belgrade, 1954–60; self-taught in art, since 1960. Served as an engineer in Yugoslav Army, 1960–61. Married Maristella Matulic in 1962; children: Vuk and Marko. Independent painter, working in studio of Krsto Hegedusic in Zagreb, 1962–63, in Belgrade, 1964–66, and in Paris since 1966. Recipient: Painting Prize, *Biennale des*

Jeunes, Rijeka, 1962; Painting Prize, *October Salon*, Belgrade, 1963; Drawing Prize, *Yugoslav Triennale*, Sombor, 1963, 1966, 1975; Painting Prize, *Yugoslav Triennale*, Belgrade 1964; Painting Prize, *Biennale de Paris* 1965; Painting Prize, *Fantastique Poetique*, Sombor 1967; Painting Prize, Lignano, Italy, 1968; N. Petrovic Memorial Prize, Cacak, 1968, 1978; Prize, *International Drawings Exhibition*, Rijeka, Yugoslavia, 1970, 1974; Drawing Prize, *Internationale Grafikausstellung*, Vienna, 1970; Prize, *International Print Exhibition*, Ljubljana 1971, 1973, 1977; Painting Prize, *Momento Tangente Internazionale*, Gardone, Italy, 1971; Prize, *Yugoslav Painters 71*, Sombor, 1971; Print Prize, Belgrade Circle, 1972; Prize, *Print Biennale*, Tokyo, 1976; Painting Prize, *Bienal*, Sao Paulo, 1977; Painting Prize, 10 Anni della Galleria San Michele, Brescia, Italy, 1978; Graphics Prize, La Plume d'Or, Belgrade, 1979; Grand Prize, *Graphics Biennale*, Heidelberg, 1979; Prize, *Graphics Biennale*, Cracow, Poland 1980. Agents: Galerie du Dragon, 19 rue du Dragon, 75006 Paris France; Galerie Jan Krugier, 3 Place du Grand-Mezel, 1204 Geneva, Switzerland. Address: 7 Passage Ricaut, escalier 19/6, 75013 Paris France.

Individual Exhibitions:

1963 Museum of Modern Art, Belgrade
1964 Mala Galerija, Ljubliana, Yugoslavia
1965 Galerie Defacqz, Brussels
Zygos Gallery, Athens
1967 *Peintures, dessins*, Galerie du Dragon, Paris
1968 Galleria Il Fante di Spade, Rome
Galleria La Mutina, Modena, Italy
Galleria Il Tempo, Bologna
Dissegni 1965–1968, Galleria La Colonna, Como, Italy
1969 Museum of Modern Art, Belgrade
Gallery of Contemporary Art, Zagreb
Museum of Modern Art, Rijeka, Yugoslavia
1970 Musée d'Art Moderne de la Ville, Paris
Galerie du Dragon, Paris
Galerie T, Haarlem, Netherlands
Galerie Jalmar, Amsterdam
Hengelose Kunstzaal, Hengelo, Netherlands
1971 Galleria Vinciana, Milan
Galleria San Michele, Brescia, Italy
Art Gallery of Split, Yugoslavia
Galleria Giulia, Rome
Galleria Forni, Bologna
Galleria Goethe, Bolzano, Italy
Mala Galerija, Ljubljana, Yugoslavia
1972 Galleria Cartezius, Trieste
Galleria Eidos, Milan
Biennale, Venice
Galerie Sebastian. Dubrovnik
Maison de la Culture, Rennes, France
1973 Galerie du Dragon, Paris
Galerie Herve Odermatt, Paris
Galerie La Pochade, Paris
Galerie T., Haarlem, Netherlands
Graficki Kolektiv, Belgrade
Galerie Richard Foncke, Ghent
Galerie La Plage, Paris
1974 Galleria San Michele, Brescia, Italy
Galerie T, Haarlem, Netherlands
Galerie La Fleuve, Bordeaux
Galleria Forni, Bologna
Galleria Documenta, Turin
Pryzmat Gallery, Cracow, Poland
Galerie Sebastian, Dubrovnik
Kunsthalle, Dusseldorf
1975 Galerie Arta, Geneva
La Bijougalerie, Grenoble, France
Galleri Futura, Stockholm
1976 Konsthall, Lund, Sweden
Museum of Modern Art, Rijeka, Yugoslavia
Galleria Visconti, Milan
Konsthall, Gothenburg, Sweden
Galeria Juana de Aizpuru, Seville
Galleri Wallner, Malmo, Sweden
Galleri Borjeson, Malmo, Sweden
Kulturhuset, Stockholm
1977 Artcurial, Paris
National Museum, Leskovac, Yugoslavia
Galerie Hervé Odermatt, Paris
Galerie La Hune, Paris
Galleri Dierks, Aarhus, Denmark
Bienal, Sao Paulo
Galerie La Hune, at *FIAC 77*, Grand Palais, Paris
Galleri Leger, Malmo, Sweden
1978 Student Cultural Centre, Belgrade
Galerija Mladinska Knjiga, Ljubljana, Yugoslavia
1979 Gaerija Zagreb, Zagreb
Galerie Miroir d'Encre, Brussels
Galerie La Hune, Paris
Galerie Albert Henri, Rennes, France
Galerie 24, Novi Sad, Yugoslavia
Salon de la Tribune des Jeunes, Novi Sad, Yugoslavia
Galeria Ciento, Barcelona
Galerie Larcos, Paris
1980 Galerie Una, Geneva
Artcurial, Paris
Galerie Jan Krugier, Geneva
Galerie Krugier et Geofroy, Geneva
Galerie Sebastian, Dubrovnik
Galerie Collegium Artisticum, Sarajevo, Yugoslavia
Galerie Jean-Marie Cupillard, Grenoble, France
Galerija Nadezda Petrovic, Cacak, Yugoslavia
1981 Heni-Onstad Kunstsenter, Oslo
Peintures et Dessins, Galerie Charles Kriwin, Brussels
1982 Galerie Presence Contemporaine, Aix-en-Provence, France
Museo de Bellas Artes, Caracas
Galerie Le Point, Monte Carlo
1983 Galerie Le Dessin, Paris
Galerie de France, Paris
Galerie Athanor, Marseille, France
1984 Galleri Kaj Forsblom, Helsinki
Galleri Grafiart, Turku, Finland
Galerie Jade, Colmar, France
Stadtmuseum, Ratingen, West Germany
Galerie Pierre Huber, Geneva
1985 Espace des Cordeliers, Chateauroux, France
Galerie de l'Ancienne Poste, Calais, France
1986 Academy of Sciences and Arts, Belgrade
Atrium Gallery, Belgrade
Galerie BBL, Antwerp, Belgium
Grand Palais, Paris
Galerie Patrice Trigano, Paris

Selected Group Exhibitions:

1961 *Yugoslav Triennale*, Belgrade
1963 *Bienal*, Sao Paulo
1966 *Yugoslavia: Contemporary Trends*, Corcoran Gallery, Washington, D.C.
1968 *Contemporary Yugoslav Art*, Civic Center Museum, Philadelphia
1972 *Activite Artistique en France 1960–1972*, Grand Palais, Paris
1974 *Biennale of Prints*, National Museum of Modern Art, Tokyo
1978 *Arte Yugoslavo contemporaneo*, Fundacio Joan Miró, Barcelona (travelled to Madrid, Lisbon, London and Manchester)
1980 *20th Century Yugoslav Painting*, Museum of Modern Art, Belgrade
1984 *Ecriture dans la Peinture*, Villa Arson, Nice, France
1986 *Les Figurations*, Musee d'Art Moderne, Dunkirk, France

Collections:

Museum of Modern Art, Belgrade; Centre Georges Pompidou, Paris; Stedelijk Museum, Amsterdam; Kunstsammlung, Bochum, West Germany; Muzeum Sztuki, Lodz, Poland;

Vladimir Velickovic: *Cane No. 4*, 1970

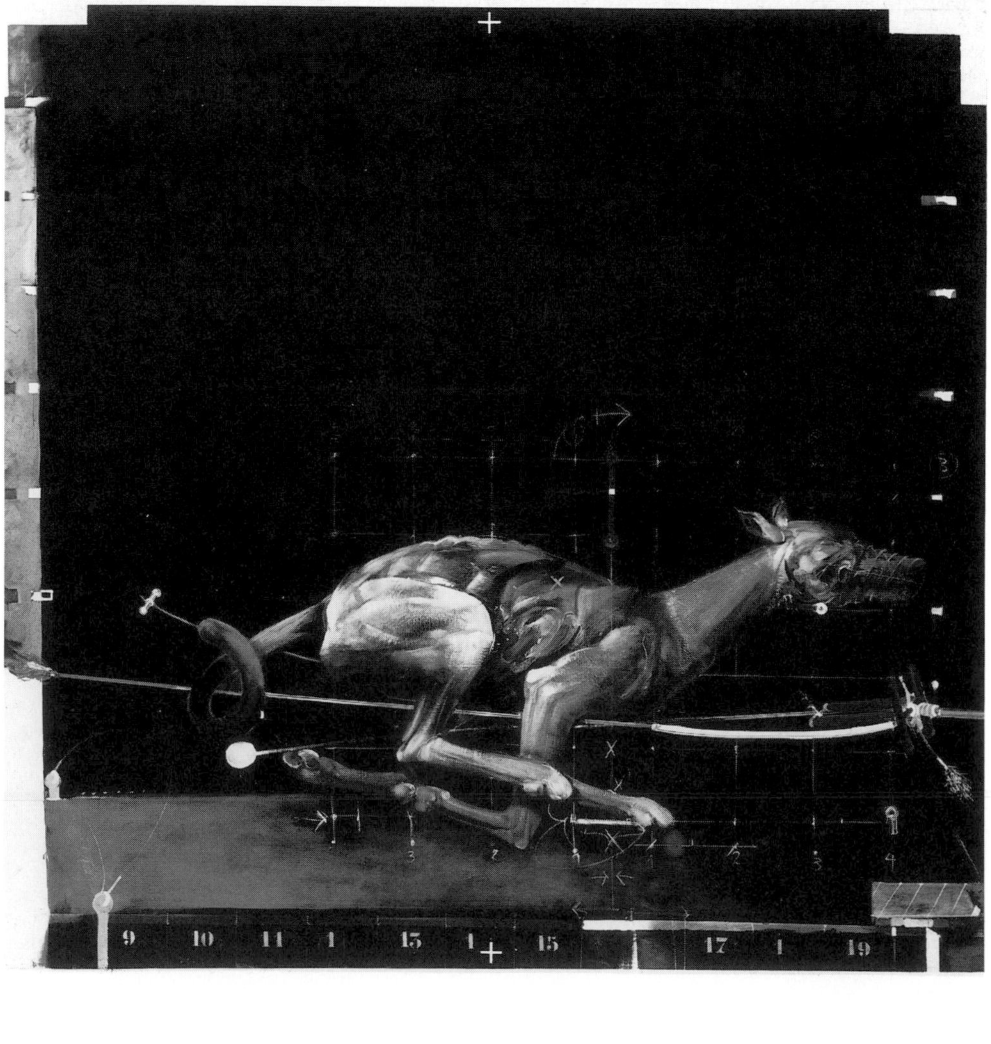

Museo Civico, Bologna; Museo Cantonal des Beaux-Arts, Lausanne, Switzerland; Museum voor Schone Kunsten, Ghent; Neue Galerie am Landesmuseum Joanneum, Graz, Austria; Museum of Modern Art, New York.

Publications:

On VELICKOVIC: books—*Velickovic: peintures, dessins,* exhibition catalogue, with text by M. Clarac-Serou, Paris 1967; *Velickovic; Dissegni 1965–1968,* exhibition catalogue, with text by I. Subotic, Como, Italy 1968: *Vladimir Velickovic: peintures, dessins 1968–1970,* exhibition catalogue, with text by Gérald Gassiot-Talabot, Paris 1970; *Velickovic,* exhibition catalogue, with text by Enrico Crispolti, Milan 1971; *Velickovic,* edited by Jean-Louis Ferrier, with texts by several authors, Paris 1976; *Vladimir Velickovic: essai sur le symbolisme artistique* by Marc Le Bot, Paris 1979; *Vladimir Velickovic: dessins et collages,* exhibition catalogue, with text by René Berger, Geneva 1980, *Vladimir Velickovic: peintures et dessins,* exhibition catalogue, with texts by Gérald Gassiot-Talabot, Jean-Pierre Faye, Alain Jouffroy and others, Brussels 1981; *Velickovic: dibujos 1958–1978/9: Veinte Anos de Agresividad* by Alain Jouffroy, Barcelona 1981: *Vladimir Velickovic,* exhibition catalogue with introduction by Marc Le Bot, Paris 1986; films—*Velickovic* by Pierre Desfons and Alain Jouffroy, 1973.

There are obvious comparisons to be made between Francis Bacon and Vladimir Velickovic, especially in the depiction of putrescent flesh, rotting or dissolving on human forms. Velickovic's paintings are less obviously autobiographic, although, in fact, the vivid images of injured, disintegrating children derive directly from memories of war-time Yugoslavia. These surrealistic nightmarish compositions, and the strange, fluid technique, would seem to derive from the Flemish masters, notably Bosch, and also Goya. Their pictorial directness is the result of an urgent need for personal exorcism and, just as important, for communication. Velickovic's brilliance as a draughtsman and painter enables him to register a disturbing imagination with extraordinary immediacy. No one seeing the work of this Yugoslav painter could ever claim indifference: the effect is either disgust, involvement, sympathy, or hatred. A more difficult-to-analyze aspect of Velickovic's work is its over sexuality, combined with a fascination for the mechanics of childbirth. Sexual allusions are already present in the paintings of mutilated children, where the positioning of the bodies, or irrational surrealistic details, permitted a wide range of interpretation. A series of paintings of reclining women, in 1972, illustrates the strange interplay of realism, sexuality, violence and nightmare in Velickovic's work; energetic images of women, with legs widespread, are alternately entitled "Birth" and "Aggression," the former suggesting the violent delivery of a screaming child, the latter showing rat-like creatures emerging from or entering the vagina. In a long series of works, rats became obsessive symbols of terror and attack, but at the same time Velickovic produced equally important, if less characteristic, images based on the famous photographs of movement by Muybridge. These paintings of running men and greyhounds develop a concern with movement already evident in the artist's earlier work and, whilst far less subjective or violent, they still convey a disturbing sense of menace.

—Charles Spencer

VENET, Bernar.

French. Born in Saint-Auban, 20 April 1941. Educated at Ecole Libre and Groupe Scolaire Paul Lapie, Saint-Auban, 1955–58; studied art at the La Villa Thiole, Nice, 1958–59. Served in the French Army, Algeria, 1961–62. Married Ella Bogval in 1971; sons: Alexander and Stephan. Worked as stage-decorator, Opera de Nice, 1959–61. Painter and "conceptual" artist, Nice, 1961–66, in New York, since 1966. Agent: Galerie Daniel Templon, 30 rue Beaubourg, 75003 Paris, France. Address: 533 Canal Street, New York, New York 10013, U.S.A.

Individual Exhibitions:

1964 Galerie Ursula Girardon, Paris
1968 Judson Church Theatre, New York
1969 Newark College of Engineering, New Jersey
1970 O. K. Harris Gallery, New York
Museum Haus Lange, Krefeld, West Germany
Kunsthaus, Hamburg
Studio Santandrea, Milan
Denise René-Hans Mayer Editions, Dusseldorf
1971 Galerie Der Spiegel, Cologne
X-One Gallery, Antwerp
Galerie Daniel Templon, Paris
Galleria Daniel Templon, Milan
1972 Galerie Bruno Bischofberger, Zurich
Galerie Daniel Templon, Paris
Galleria Daniel Templon, Milan
New York Cultural Center (retrospective)
1973 Galerie Foksal, Warsaw
1974 Galleria La Seconda Scala, Rome
Galerie Daniel Templon, Paris
Galleria Daniel Templon, Milan
1975 Galerie Hetzler und Keller, Stuttgart
Galleria Nuovi Strumenti, Brescia, Italy
French Section, at the *Bienal,* Sao Paulo
Galerie Daniel Templon, Paris
Institute of Contemporary Arts, London
Museu de Arte Moderna, Rio de Janeiro
1976 Dartmouth College, Hanover, New Hampshire
Textural Criticism, La Jolla Museum of Contemporary Art, California
1977 Galerie Bruno Bischofberger, Zurich
Musée d'Art et d'Industrie, Saint-Etienne, France
Galerie Daniel Templon, Paris
Galerie Gillespie-de Laage, Paris
Henie-Onstad Kunstsenter, Oslo
Galerie Denise René-Hans Mayer, Dusseldorf
1978 Special Project at PS 1, Long Island City, New York
Galerie Denise René-Hans Mayer, Dusseldorf
1979 Arco Center for the Visual Arts, Los Angeles
Hal Bromm Gallery, New York
Galleria Civica d'Arte Moderna, Portofino, Italy
Marianne Deson Gallery, Chicago
Galerie Daniel Templon, Paris
1981 Galerie Denise René-Hans Mayer, Dusseldorf
Galleria Unimedia, Genoa
Galerie Artline, The Hague
Galerie Daniel Templon, Paris
1982 Bonlow Gallery, New York
Malinda Wyatt Gallery, Venice, California
1984 Musée Sainte-Croix, Poitiers, France
Studio Marconi, Milan
Marianne Deson Gallery, Chicago
Centre d'Art Contemporain, Chateauroux, France
Galerie Denise Rene/Hans Mayer, at *Art 84,* Basle
Galerie ARCA, Marseille, France
Galerie Jean-Jules Bertin, Lyon, France
Musée d'Art Moderne, Villeneuve-d'Ascq, France
Galerie Daniel Templon, Paris
1985 Galerie Denise Rene/Hans Mayer, Dusseldorf
Musée Départemental des Vosges, Epinal, France
Galerie Bernard Lucas, Nice, France
Galerie Littmann, Basle
1986 Castelli Uptown, New York
Galerie Elisabeth Frank, Brussels
Daniel Templon Galerie Un, Paris
Daniel Templon Galerie Deux, Paris
1987 Galerie Pierre Huber, Geneva
Quadrat-Bottrop Moderne Galerie, Bottrop, West Germany
1988 Galerie Michèle Chomette, Paris

Selected Group Exhibitions:

1964 *Salon Comparaisons,* Musée d'Art Moderne de la Ville, Paris
1986 *Salon de la Jeune Peinture,* Musée d'Arte Moderne, Paris
1970 *Information,* Museum of Modern Art, New York
1975 *Tendencies of Contemporary Art,* Nordiyllands Kunstmuseum, Aalborg, Denmark (toured Denmark)
1977 *Documenta,* Kassel, West Germany
1979 *Construction and the Geometric Tradition,* Albright-Knox Art Gallery, Buffalo, New York (toured the United States)
1981 *Construction in Process in the Art of the 70's,* Muzeum Sztuki, Lodz, Poland
1983 *L'Art en France dans les Annees 60,* Musée d'Art et d'Industrie, St. Etienne, France
1985 *Livres d'Artistes,* Centre Georges Pompidou, Paris
1987 *Mathematik in der Kunst,* Wilhelm-Hack-Museum, Ludwigshafen, West Germany

Collections:

Centre National d'Art Contemporain, Paris; Kaiser-Wilhelm Museum, Krefeld, West Germany; Neue Galerie im Alten Kurhaus, Aachen, West Germany; Muzeum Sztuki, Lodz, Poland; Museum of Modern Art, New York; New York University; Akron Art Institute, Ohio; Georgia Museum of Art, Athens; Atlantic Richfield Company, Los Angeles; Santa Barbara Museum of Art, California.

Publications:

On VENET: books—*The Structure of Art* by Jack Burnham, New York 1970; *Bernar Venet,* exhibition catalogue, with text by Catherine Millet, Warsaw 1973; *Bernar Venet,* edited by Arthur Hubschmid, Paris and Zurich 1975; *La Linea Analitica dell'Arte Moderna* by Filiberto Menna, Turin 1975; *Dell'Informale alla Body-Art* by Lea Vergine, Turin 1976; *Bernar Venet: Textual Criticism,* exhibition catalogue, with text by Lawrence Alloway, La Jolla, California 1976; *Bernar Venet,* exhibition catalogue, with text by Bernard Ceysson, Saint-Etienne, France 1977; *A Propos de Nice,* exhibition catalogue, with text by Ben Vautier, Paris, 1977; *Biennale de Paris 1959–73,* exhibition catalogue, edited by Georges Boudaille, Tokyo 1978; *Bernar Venet,* exhibition catalogue, Portofino, Italy 1979; *Bernar Venet; Un cura di Bernar Venet,* Milan 1980; *Bernar Venet; Dessins 1963–1983,* exhibition catalogue with essay by Catherine Franklin, Poitiers 1983; *Bernar Venet,* exhibition catalogue with text by Bernard Ceysson, Epinal 1985.

Bernar Venet, born in France, worked in the late 1960's and 1970's on large photographic blow-ups of scientific equations. He then proceeded to use the look of scientific equations and diagrams in a painterly manner. He has also used segments of any number of texts, including weather reports, pages of stock market figures, and astrophysical and meteorological texts. Venet has made it his work to sell the look of contemporary science, yet in a distanced fashion. Venet has assisted in finishing the incomplete work of the scientists by presenting their work, in lieu of their own presentation, to the public. Many of his earlier projects included a number of presentations and lectures by prominent scientists. Venet's task was essentially to organize several hundred of these symposia.

Rather than repeating scientific work verbatim, Venet's canvases, such as "Calculation of the Diagonal of a Rectangle," 1966, and "Tracing of Two Complimentary Angles," 1977, expressed the look of science. Therefore, in a sense, they expressed the content of science, given the nature of belief associated with most of the contemporary sciences.

In Venet's work the contemporary need for science to hide research is revealed, and the contemporary utilization of art as decoration is proven. Perhaps the proof of art will work backwards on the contemporary mystery of science, by insisting on aesthetic reasoning along the way, reflectivity during construction. A painting on the wall, worthy of supra-scrutiny, is a misplaced aim. The scrutiny is held in the wrong area. The question is not to scrutinize the aesthetic work, but to examine the direction of the observing functions. Venet has been observing science and subjecting it, like a billboard, to the popular realm. We are supposed to be watching science, not art.

—John Robinson

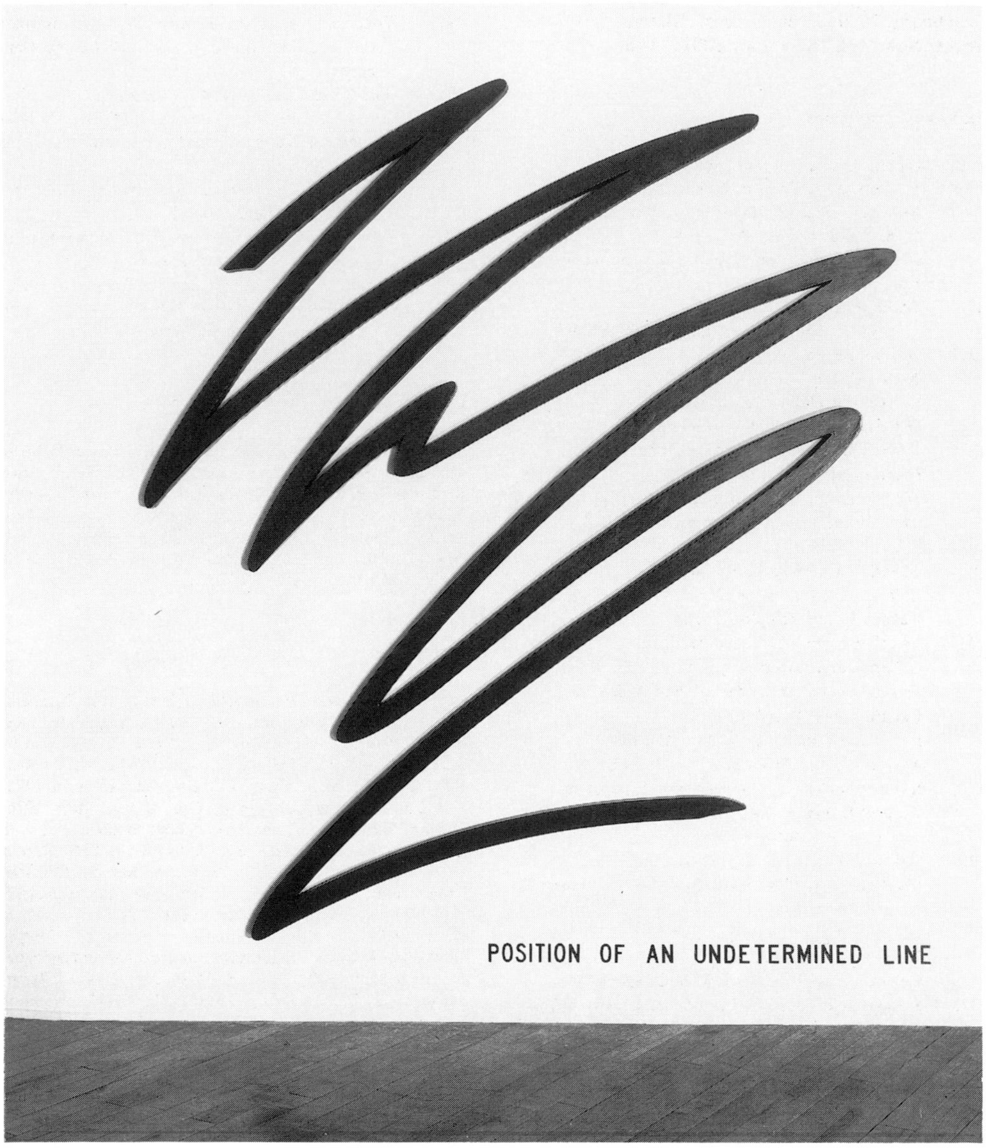

Bernar Venet: ***Position of an Undetermined Line*****, 1980**

VIALLAT, Claude.

French. Born in Aubais, Le Gard, near Nimes, 18 May 1936. Studied under Descossis, Dezeuze, and Bessil, at the Ecole des Beaux-Arts, Montpellier, 1955–59; also studied at the Ecole des Beaux-Arts, Paris, 1962–63. Served in French Army, Constantine, Algeria, 1959–61. Married Henriette Pous in 1962; daughters: Claire and Isabelle. Painter: lived in Nice, 1964–67, Limoges, 1967–69, and in Marseilles, since 1969; Member, with Louis Cane, Marc Devade, Daniel Dezeuze, Andre Valensi and others, Groupe Supports Surfaces, Paris, 1969–71. Painting Instructor, Ecole des Beaux-Arts, Nice, 1964–67; Professor of Painting, Ecole des Beaux-Arts, Limoges, 1968–1969. Professor of Painting, Ecole des Beaux-Arts, Marseilles, from 1969. Agent: Galerie Daniel Templon, Paris. Address: c/o Galerie Daniel Templon, 30 rue Beaubourg, 75003 Paris, France.

Individual Exhibitions:

1966 Galerie A, Nice
1968 Galerie Jean Fournier, Paris
Musée d'Art Moderne, Ceret, France
1971 Galerie Jean Fournier, Paris
1973 Galleria Daniel Templon, Milan
Galerie Jean Fournier, Paris
1974 Galerie Delta, Brussels
Musée d'Art et d'Industrie, St.-Etienne, France
Chez Malabar et Cunegonde (Galerie Ben), Nice
Galleria La Bertesca, Milan (with Dolla and Isnard)
Maison de la Culture, Rennes (with Dezeuze and Saytour)
1975 Galerie Athanor, Marseilles (with Tony Grand)
Galerie Jean Fournier, Paris
1976 Pierre Matisse Gallery, New York
Von-der-Heydt Museum, Wuppertal, West Germany (with J. M. Meurice)
Palais des Beaux-Arts Brussels
Galerie A.16, Perpignan, France
1977 Galerie Jean Fournier, Paris
Galerie C. M., St.-Etienne, France
Galerie Sanguine, Collioure, France
Galerie Athanor, Marseilles (with Jaccard and Pincemin)
1978 Galerie Arta, Geneva
Maison de la Culture, Orleans, France
Centre de Création Artistique, Senanque, France
Galerie Athanor, Marseilles
Traces, Musée d'Art et d'Histoire, Chambéry, France
1979 Galerie Wentzel, Hamburg
1980 Centre des Arts Plastiques Contemporains Bordeaux
Neue Galerie, Aachen, West Germany
1981 Galerie L'Atelier, Nice, France
Kamakura Gallery, Tokyo
Ace Gallery, Venice, California
1982 Galerie Wentzel, Cologne
Leo Castelli Gallery, New York
Centre Georges Pompidou, Paris
1988 Institut Francais, Cologne

Selected Group Exhibitions:

1966 *Impact*, Musée d'Art Moderne, Ceret, France
1969 *Biennale*, Paris (and 1971)
1971 *Supports/Surfaces*, Théâtre de la Cité Universitaire, Paris (travelled to Nice)
1972 *Amsterdam-Paris-Dusseldorf*, Guggenheim Museum, New York
1973 *Regarder Ailleurs*, Entrepots Laine, Bordeaux
1975 *12 x 1: Europalia 75*, Palais des Beaux-Arts, Brussels
1977 *A Propos de Nice*, Centre Georges Pompidou, Paris
1978 *Espace/Nature*, Centre des Arts Plastiques Contemporains, Bordeaux
1980 *Die Neue Wilden*, Neue Galerie, Aachen, West Germany
1982 *Du Cubisme a nos Jours*, Musée Cantini, Marseille, France

Collections:

Musée d'Art et d'Industrie, St. Etienne, France: Fonds National d'Art Contemporain, Paris: Neue Galerie-Sammlung Ludwig, Aachen, West Germany.

Publications:

On VIALLAT: books—*Claude Viallat*, exhibition catalogue, with preface by Marcelin Pleynet, Paris 1971; *Art en France: Une Nouvelle Génération* by Jean Clair, Paris 1972; *L'Enseignment de la Peinture* by Marcelin Pleynet, Paris 1972; *Amsterdam-Paris-Dusseldorf*, exhibition catalogue, with texts by Blaise Gauthier, Cor Blok, and Jürgen Harton, New York 1972; *L'Art Actuel en France* by Anne Tronche and Hervé Gloaguen, Paris 1973; *Claude Viallat*, exhibition catalogue, with text by Jacques Lepage, St. Etienne, France 1974; *Claude Viallat: Traces*, exhibition catalogue, with texts by Dominque Fourcade and others, Chambéry, France 1978; *Claude Viallat*, exhibition catalogue, with text by Bernard Ceysson, Senanque, France 1978; *Claude Viallat*, exhibition catalogue, with texts by Jean-Louis Froment and Jean-Marie Poinsot, Bordeaux 1980.

There is one single form that Claude Viallat introduced into his painting in 1966 and never again abandoned—the form of a sponge soaked in colour that one presses onto the picture surface. However, when, by this means, an impression of wealth of colour and formal exuberance appears on his canvases, it is because he knew how to effect so many variations with this single motif that it invested entire rooms/spaces as endless ornamentation.

When Viallat began his work in 1966 a radical investigation into all painting was in progress in France. What had painting ever been until then, it was asked, other than a purveyor of illusions and false dreams, in the service of the art market, bourgeois society and its ideology? If one wanted a new beginning for painting, it had to be liberated from this traditional role. This discussion was perhaps successful in the sense that it made one think about the real origins of art. Viallat was one of the younger generation who tried to trace the origin of painting back to its handcraft beginnings, that beginning where the intention was to add a non-functional dimension to the merely functional object. But he also concluded that only where one expelled all content, any statement, every subjective expression from the work and replaced this on the canvas with unchanging neutral and anonymous forms, could one be sure that painting was concentrated only on the process of its becoming, and beyond that had no further significance. Indeed, at first, Viallat had in fact begun to work with the substance, the material grounds of painting, with rope, string, thread, which in tangled knots or composed nets call to mind the matrix of the canvas to be painted. He stressed the praxis of artistic work and not the ideas which it could generate. In so doing he set himself in opposition to the art of the Ecole de Paris and also to the new tendencies of conceptual art which came from America and which provided ideas about material and form.

In France people were looking for a new aesthetic

Claude Viallat: Installation at *Regarder Ailleurs* exhibition, Bordeaux, 1974

and for a new aesthetic ethic. Each had its theoretical basis in Marxism and in the structuralist critique of language. Painting was understood as a system of signs whose forms of expression, as long as they were taken over from tradition, were charged with specific connotations and meanings. Each artist who dealt with them had to be aware that he was more or less adapting himself to the fashion, the modern myths and current ideological thought structures. So Viallat set about making visible the mechanism of such a system of signs and submitting the signs themselves to criticism. He wanted to change fundamentally the basis, the material and economic suppositions of painting so as to renew the social function of the painter and of art. He subsequently restricted himself to large unframed canvases sewn together and including also found or already printed material, on which he carried out all the possible colour variations of his special form. A "necessary materialism" was involved, it was said, in which painting is an experimentation with the material means of art, a preoccupation with the real basis and not a communication of ideas.

Painting had become a metaphor for structural thought inasmuch as it accomplished in its forms the structures of a particular social situation. "In working we have to learn," Viallat wrote. "Everything develops its own organization: to reject it would be to exclude a reality." Everything has a special language, a particular discourse, as Michel Foucault has described it. That which has no power of language expresses itself in bodies and spaces, in lines, forms and colours. The object speaks for itself, and in that moment in which it enters into a relationship with the artist's subject a corresponding composite of reality is expressed in concrete form. According to this interpretation there is no longer a difference, a separation, between subject and object, for they complement one another. In art it is important, Viallat wrote, that in working one learns from the object—or as Michel Foucault expressed it: the artist is through his body and his vision part of the visible world, and both form an inseparable essence.

Viallat wants the subject matter to intrude neither intellectually nor emotionally upon the visible but to engage with him in a process of gradual change. For that reason it is so essential in his work that with a theme which remains the same he should constantly search for fresh material, new contours and formats to whose peculiarities he has to readjust himself. From 1970 to 1971 Viallat was a member of the group Support/Surface, with which he was for a long time theoretically in agreement, but he left it when he was directing its attention less to the analysis of a situation than to direct political engagement. Art, to the group, meant intervening in historical development. Viallat's art stives for a value-free investigation of artistic means of expression, without hierarchy and differentiation between more or less "noble" activities. Everything is worthy of experience. Hence also the struggle against tasteful, academic painting and the restriction to one form, which can stand for all forms. Each impression is so similar to the next that it could be part of any picture, and in this dimension Viallat's painting also gains, over and above any theoretical, social-critical tendency, its ethical value.

—Marie Luise Syring

VIEIRA DA SILVA, Marie-Helene.

French. Born in Lisbon, Portugal, 13 June 1908; emigrated to France, 1928: naturalized, 1956. Studied drawing, under Emilia Santos Braga, in Lisbon, 1922–24; studied painting, under Armando Lucena, and sculpture, at the Academy of Fine Arts, Lisbon, 1924–27; studied painting, under Antoine Bourdelle, Académie de la Grande Chaumière, Paris, 1928–29; and engraving, under S. W. Hayter, Atelier 17, Paris. Married the painter Arpad Szenes in 1930 (died, 1985). Painter, illustrator, and fabric designer, Paris, 1929–39, Lisbon, 1939–40, Brazil, 1940–47, and again in Paris, since 1947. Recipient: Acquisition Prize, *Bienal*, Sao Paulo, 1953; Tapestry Prize, University of Basle, 1954; Grand International Prize, *Bienal*, Sao Paulo, 1961; Grand Prix des Arts, Paris, 1966; Grand Croix de Santiago da Espada, Lisbon, 1977; Medal of Honour, towns of Montargis and Montauban, France, 1983; Grand Prix Florence Gould, Académie des Beaux-Arts, Paris, 1986. Chevalier, 1960, and Commandeur, 1962, Ordre des Arts et Lettres, Paris; Member, Academy of Arts of Lisbon, 1970; Chevalier, Légion d'Honneur, Paris, 1979; Member, Académie des Sciences, des Arts et des Lettres, Paris, 1984. Address: c/o Guy Weelen, 8 Avenue Frochot, 75009 Paris, France.

Individual Exhibitions:

1933 Galerie Jeanne Bucher, Paris
1935 Galerie U.P., Lisbon
1936 Artist's Studio, Lisbon (with Arpad Szenes)
1937 Galerie Jeanne Bucher, Paris

1939 Galerie Jeanne Bucher, Paris
1942 Museu de Arte Moderna, Rio de Janeiro
1946 Galeria Askenazi, Rio de Janeiro
Palacio Municipal, Belo Horizonte, Brazil
Marian Willard Gallery, New York
1947 Galerie Jeanne Bucher, Paris
1949 Galerie Pierre, Paris
1950 Galerie Blanche, Stockholm
Galerie La Hune, Paris
1951 Galerie Pierre, Paris
Galerie Jeanne Bucher, Paris
1952 Galerie Dupont, Lille, France
1953 Redfern Gallery, London
Cadby Birch Gallery, New York
1955 Stedelijk Museum, Amsterdam (with Germaine Richier)
Galerie Pierre, Paris
1956 Saidenberg Gallery, New York
Galerie Art Moderne, Basle
1957 Galerie de Perron, Geneva
Hanover Gallery, London
Galeria Portico, Lisbon
1958 Kestner-Gesellschaft, Hannover (retrospective; travelled to Bremen and Wuppertal, West Germany)
1960 Galerie Jeanne Bucher, Paris
1961 Phillips Art Gallery, Washington, D.C.
Galerie Pierre Beres, Paris
Kunsthalle, Mannheim
Knoedler Gallery, New York
1963 Phillips Art Gallery, Washington, D.C.
Knoedler Gallery, New York
Galeria Gravura, Lisbon
Bezalel Museum, Jerusalem
Galerie Jeanne Bucher, Paris
1964 Galerie Alice Pauli, Lausanne
Musée de Peinture et Sculpture, Grenoble (retrospective)
Museo Civico, Turin (retrospective)
1965 Albert Loeb Gallery, New York
1966 Knoedler Gallery, New York
Académie des Amateurs de Musique, Lisbon
1967 Galerie Jeanne Bucher, Paris
Chateau de Ratilly, France (with Etienne Martin)
1969 Théâtre de la Comédie, Tours
Musée d'Art Moderne, Paris (retrospective)
Galerie Jeanne Bucher, Paris
Galerie Jacob, Paris
1970 Museum Boymans-van Beuningen, Rotterdam (retrospective)
Malerier 1935–1969, Kunstnernes Hus, Oslo
Kunsthalle, Basle (retrospective)
Fundacao Gulbenkian, Lisbon (retrospective)
Galeria Sao Mamede, Lisbon
Galerie 3, Lisbon
1971 *Temperas, Lithographs, Gouaches et Serigraphies*, Galerie Jeanne Bucher, Paris
Galeria Zen, Porto, Portugal
Paintings 1967–1971, Knoedler Gallery, New York
Musée Fabre, Montpellier, France
1972 Galerie Regence, Brussels
Musée Thomas Henry, Cherbourg
Musée des Beaux-Arts, Rouen
Museum Unterlinden, Colmar, France
1973 Centro Rizzoli, Milan
Musée d'Art et d'Histoire, Orleans
1974 Galerie Artel, Geneva
Gravuras e Litografias, Galeria Quadrum, Lisbon
1975 Institut Francais, Stockholm
Helsinglands Museum, Hudiksvall, Sweden
Saabskonstforening, Lingkoping, Sweden
Konsthalle, Malmo, Sweden
Galerie Monique Delcourt, Valenciennes, France
Galerie Fremond, Paris
1976 Galerie Jeanne Bucher, Paris
Maison des Arts et Loisirs, Sochaux, France
Musée de Metz, France
Musée d'Art Moderne, Paris (with Arpad Szenes)
1977 Musée de l'Etat, Luxembourg
Galerie Kutter, Luxembourg
Musée d'Art Moderne de la Ville, Paris
Pinturas a Tempera, Fundacao Gulbenkian, Lisbon
Galerie La Hune, Paris
La Galerie, Nimes, France
1978 L'Art en Dreux, France
Nordyjllands Kunstmuseum, Aalborg, Denmark (retrospective)
Ty-Kan, Locronan, France
Galerie Jeanne Bucher, Paris (with Louise Nevelson and Magdalena Abakanowicz)
1979 Musée des Beaux-Arts, Agen, France (toured France)
1980 Galeria Joan Prats, Barcelona
Centre Culturel, Dakar, Senegal
1981 Musée de Cluny, France
Bibliothèque Nationale, Paris
1982 Galerie Jeanne Bucher, Paris
Galerie de l'Information, Tunis
1983 Musée Ingres, Montauban, France
Museo de Bellas Artes, Bilbao, Spain
1984 Galeria EMI-Valentim de Carvalho, Lisbon
Centre Culturel Francais, Rome
1985 Galeria III, Lisbon
1986 Galerie Jeanne Bucher, Paris
Galeria Nasoni, Porto, Portugal (with Arpad Szenes)
Artcurial, Paris

Selected Group Exhibitions:

1930 *Salon des Surindépendants*, Paris
1946 *Salon des Réalités Nouvelles*, Paris
1950 *Biennale*, Venice
1955 *The New Decade*, Museum of Modern Art, New York
1964 *Painting and Sculpture of a Decade 1954–64*, Tate Gallery, London
1971 *Carnegie International*, Pittsburgh
1973 *L'Estampe Contemporaine*, Bibliothèque Nationale, Paris
1976 *Ratilly*, Musée des Arts Décoratifs, Paris
1978 *Portuguese Art since 1910*, Royal Academy of Arts, London
1984 *Biennale Internationale du Dessin*, Clermont-Ferrand, France

Collections:

Centre Georges Pompidou, Paris; Musée d'Art Moderne de la Ville, Paris; Tate Gallery, London; Stedelijk Museum, Amsterdam; Museum Folkwang, Essen; Kunsthaus, Zurich; Galleria d'Arte Moderna, Museo Civico, Turin; Museu de Arte Moderna, Rio de Janeiro; Museum of Modern Art, New York; Guggenheim Museum, New York.

Publications:

On VIEIRA DA SILVA: books—*Vieira da Silva* by Pierre Descargues, Paris 1949; *Le Musée de Poche: Vieira da Silva* by Rene de Solier, Paris 1956; *Vieira da Silva* by José Augusto Franca, Paris 1958; *Vieira da Silva* by Guy Weelen, Paris 1960; *Vieira da Silva*, exhibition catalogue, with text by Claude Esteban, Basle 1970; *Vieira da Silva: Malerier 1935–1969*, exhibition catalogue, with texts by Snorre Andersen and Guy Weelen, Oslo 1970; *Vieira da Silva*, exhibition catalogue, with texts by Joao Gaspar Simoes, Murilo Mendes and others, Lisbon 1970; *La Peinture de Vieira da Silva* by Dora Vallier, Paris 1971; *Vieira da Silva: Paintings 1967–1971*, exhibition catalogue, with text by John Rewald, New York 1971; *Vieira da Silva*, exhibition catalogue, with text by Georges Desmouliez, Montepellier, France 1971; *Vieira da Silva: Temperas, lithographies, gouaches et serigraphies*, exhibition catalogue, Paris 1971; *Vieira da Silva* by Guy Weelen, Paris 1973; *Vieira da Silva*, exhibition catalogue, with texts by René Char and John Rewald, Geneva 1974; *Vieira da Silva: Gravuras e Litografias*, exhibition catalogue, with text by Guy Weelen, Lisbon 1974; *Vieira da Silva: Les Estampes: Catalogue de l'Oeuvre Grave* by Guy Weelen, Paris 1976; *Vieira da Silva*, exhibition catalogue, with text by Jean-Francois Jaeger, Paris 1976; *L'Univers de Vieira da Silva* by Antoine Terrasse, Paris 1977; *Vieira da Silva: Pinturas a Tempera*, exhibition catalogue, with text by Agustina Bessa Luis, Lisbon 1977; *Vieira da Silva* by Jacques Lassaigne and Guy Weelen, Barcelona and Paris 1978; *L'Eclat de la Lumiere* by Anne Philipe, Paris 1979; *Longos dias tem cem anos: Presenca de Vieira da Silva* by Agustina Bessa Luis, Lisbon 1979; *Chemins d'approche: Vieira da Silva* by Dora Vallier, Paris 1982; *Vieira da Silva: Peintures* by Michel Butor, Paris 1983; *Vieira da Silva: Oeuvres sur Papier* by

Marie-Helène Vieira da Silva: *La Déchirure*, 1984

Guy Weelen, Paris 1983; *Vieira da Silva e Arpad Szenes ou o Castelo Surrealista* by Mario Cesariny, Lisbon 1984.

The paintings of Vieira da Silva have a timeless modernity about them but it is still hard to realize that effectively her art career began as far back as 1919. To all familiar with the dramatis personae of the Ecole de Paris, although her transformation of architecture rendered upon canvas has been almost a permanent feature for so many years, each evidence of her extraordinary talent still seems paradoxically new.

It is true that as a young girl she once had ambitions to become a sculptor and even took a course under the tutelage of Despiau. But this shortlived enthusiasm cannot in any way explain the unusual and unique control she is able to exert on her canvases across the whole fabric of architectural conception.

Even a painting like the 1939 "Les Drapeaux" shows the same grasp of the building syndrome. The fluttering flags hang down like the tails of kites from windows, and there is no doubt that these are windows of huts set on stilts by some river people. The little squares of the "flags" and the rhodoid tiles on the roofs are repeated in the fabric between the posts and the relections in the water. Already the elaborate patterning of Vieira da Silva which sets such store on the heaving chessboards of tiled vistas of which she is so fond—already this central element in nearly all her later work is plainly evident. That it was subsequently to become thicker and more tantalising to the eye, taking on the form of a gigantic art crossword puzzle, was just a matter of time.

Vieira da Silva is the supreme manipulator of perspective. Cities, promenades, floods, night, time itself are all pressed into service to act as welcome excuse for stretch after stretch of mosaic-like detail; not carefully wrought *azulejos* of Portuguese mural artists, but mosaics that have been shaken by earth tremors or frozen into noble austerity for ever.

Architectural rectitude is only disturbed by the process of time and perhaps the incursion of decay. Looking at her picturess one realizes that she is deeply conscious of what age and weathering can do to her cherished subjects.

—Sheldon Williams

VILLALBA, Dario.

Spanish. Born in San Sebastian, 22 February 1939. Educated in Boston, Massachusetts, 1950–54; studied in the Department of Fine Arts, Harvard University, Cambridge, Massachusetts, 1957–58; studied painting in the studio of André Lhote, Paris, 1968, and at the Escuela de Bellas Arte de San Fernando, Madrid, 1958–62; studied literature and philosophy, University of Madrid, 1962–64. Independent artist, concentrating on painting, Madrid, from 1957; first plexiglass-encased figures, 1966; photographic figures in plexiglass, from 1972; canvases with photo-emulsion, from 1973. Recipient: Critics prize, *Bienal of Ibiza*, Spain, 1973; International Prize, *Bienal*, Sao Paulo, 1973; International Prize, *Graphics Biennale*, Ljubljana, Yugoslavia, 1979. Agent: Galeria Vandres, Don Ramon de la Cruz 26, Madrid-1. Address: Fernandez de la Hoy 61, Madrid-3, Spain.

Individual Exhibitions:

1957 Sala Alfil, Madrid
1964 Weeden Gallery, Boston
Galeria Biosca, Madrid
Gallery 88, Miami
1966 Drian Galleries, London
Pinturas 1966, Galeria El Bosco, Cronica de Palomares, Madrid
1970 Museo Espanol de Arte Contemporaneo, Madrid
Galleria del Naviglio, Milan
Galerie Defacqz, Brussels
Spanish Pavilion, at the *Biennale*, Venice
1971 Musée d'Art et d'Histoire, Geneva
Studio C, Brescia, Italy
1972 Deson-Zaks Gallery, Chicago
Henry Mayer Gallery, Lausanne
Cité Universitaire, Neuchâtel, Switzerland
1973 Espace Pierre Cardin, Paris
Galleria del Naviglio, Milan
1974 Galeria Vandres, Madrid
Kunstverein, Frankfurt
1975 Louisiana Museum, Humlebaek, Denmark
Museum Boymans-van Beuningen, Rotterdam
Museum Bochum, West Germany
1976 *Retrospective 1972–1976*, Palais des Beaux-Arts, Brussels
Kunstverein, Heidelberg
1977 Kunstlerhaus, Vienna
Galerie Gras, Vienna
1978 Galeria Juana Mordo, Madrid
Galeria Vandres, Madrid
1980 Henie-Onstad Kunstsenter, Oslo
1981 Fondation Veranneman, Kruishoutem, Belgium
1982 Galleria del Naviglio, Milan
Charles Cowles Gallery, New York
1983 Salas Pablo Picasso, Madrid

Selected Group Exhibitions:

1963 *Contemporary Spanish Painting*, D'Arcy Galleries, New York (toured the United States)
1965 *5 Spanish Painters*, at the *Bienal*, Sao Paulo
1970 *Testimonio 70*, Museo Espanol de Arte Contemporaneo, Madrid
1971 *Erotic Art in Spain Now*, Galeria Vandres, Madrid
1972 *Grands et Jeunes d'Aujourd'hui*, Grand Palais, Paris
1973 *Salon de Mai*, Musée d'Art Moderne, Paris
1975 *Biennale of Cagnes-sur-Mer*, France
1978 *La Materia*, Galeria Rayuela, Madrid
1980 *New Images from Spain*, Guggenheim Museum, New York
1983 *International Art Fair*, Chicago

Collections:

Musée des Beaux-Arts, Ostend, Belgium; Fondation Veranneman, Kruishoutem, Belgium; Musee Royal des Beaux-Arts, Brussels; Museo de Arte Contemporaneo, Seville; Louisiana Museum, Humlebaek, Denmark; Museum Boymans-van Beuningen, Rotterdam; Musee d'Art et d'Histoire, Geneva; Musée des Beaux-Arts, Lausanne; Museo de Arte Contemporaneo, Madrid; National Gallery of Australia, Canberra.

Publications:

By VILLALBA: book—*Grupo Quince*, 4 silkscreened objects, Milan 1973.

On VILLALBA: books—*Dario Villalba: Pinturas 1966*, exhibition catalogue, with text by Angel Crespo, Madrid 1966; *Nuevos Maestros de la Pintura Espanola* by Raul Chavarri, Madrid 1972; *Dario Villalba at the Deson-Zaks Gallery*, exhibition catalogue, with text by Franz Schulze, Chicago 1972; *Villalba*, exhibition catalogue, with texts by Pierre Restany and Giancarlo Politi, Madrid 1974; *Dario Villalba*, exhibition catalogue, with text by Peter Spielmann, Hans Gercke, Titia Berlage and Michael Fehr, Bochum, West Germany 1975; *Dario Villalba: Retrospective 1972–1976*, exhibition catalogue, with texts by Titia Berlage, René Micha, Luis Gonzalez Robles and others, Brussels 1976; *Europa-America: The Different Avant-Gardes* by Achille Bonito Oliva, Milan 1976; *Diccionario de Pintores Espanoles Contemporaneos* by Ignacio De Blas, Madrid 1976; *Kunst Kommt nicht von Konnen* by Hans-Jürgen Müller, Stuttgart 1977; *Dario Villalba*, exhibition catalogue, with text by Ole Henrik Moe, Oslo 1980; *Dario Villalba: Obra Reciente 1980–1983*, exhibition catalogue with text by Eugenio de Vicente, Madrid 1983.

Man with two coverings: one
his biological skin; the other his invention,
his own industry and web.

If our skin grew outward 30 cms. from
the organic one which encloses us and
crystallized, the magic of the solitary
man, circumscribed in a transparent projection
of his silhouette would be evoked.

Glass-skins invade creation forcing
man to live with industry in a state
of hibernation.

Pathological Toys for Adults.

Fragments of reality (scratches, scars,
bruises) blown-up though mass-
media photographic emulsions create
a neo-abstractionism.
Abstraction based on cold reality.

I do not participate. I only
choose.

My mind cannot forget what my
eyes have invented.

—Dario Villalba

Dario Villalba's plastic capsules got to London in 1968. They had already caused a considerable stir at the Venice *Biennale*. At that time they were so unexpected, such a novel experience, that too few people did more than step back and marvel at them. A bad reaction because what the artist wanted from his viewers was thought rather than emotion.

Above all, Villalba is a fighter for the acceptance of human rights. That his campaigns are waged through the artistic forms that he has chosen is our good fortune, but should in no way reduce the potencies of the many messages he wishes to deliver. Villalba's ideas about human rights are basic, certainly not the application of well thought-out laws and regulations. He wants proper understanding of pain and suffering, and he wants to throw out a lifeline to the hopeless.

Effectively his career in its most pertinent sense can be divided into three periods, all of which interrelate.

From 1966 to 1971 he made life-sized flesh-coloured figures which were enclosed in plexiglass and hand-rotated at variable speeds from a plexiglass superstructure.

A year later, using the same technique and materials, he switched from his earlier fluorescent-pink figures to blow-ups from press photos. The subjects in these works were also altered. By this time Villalba had turned his attention to the area of sociological problems—a worker in overalls beset with the difficulties of the class system; a youth in jeans and T-shirt glaring at the outside world and raising his clenched fist; the face of a woman, her eyes closed, at the point of death; a patient in a psychiatric ward, his protruding feet knotted together by the wet bed-sheet. Over these images where he felt it relevant, Villalba scrawled symbols as comments.

Since then he has still further expanded the process, reproducing the figures on emulsioned canvases. To emphasize his intention, sometimes the works appear in triptych form—first the feet, then the arm, then the head. or he takes disparate elements and welds them together in a near-abstract assemblage, making the blow-up technique of the press photograph create enlargements that turn the "screen" of the original newspaper photo into an independent patterning.

Villalba is operating on two levels. On one his "man" regards nature with imperturbable calm; on the other, the same man turns a look of cold and vitriolic hatred upon the cruelties of the social system.

For the viewer, the Villalba images are also bilateral. He looks at them, but they look back at him. And not just the faces. Feet and hands have become personalized. His presentation is at one and the same time fascinating and appalling.

Does an art public, or even a public at large, want

Dario Villalba: Exhibition at the Louisiana Museum, Humlebaek, Denmark, 1975

or require such aggressive preaching? The question is an academic one. So many frightening versions of the Temptation of Saint Anthony in no way deflected praise from those who appreciate good painting. Goya's etchings of the Horrors of War are a satchel of masterpieces. Now Villalba with great technical skill hangs up his plastic bags full of the Horrors of Man.

—Sheldon Williams

VILLEGLÉ, Jacques (Mahé) de la.

French. Born in Quimper, Finistere, 27 March 1926. Educated at secondary school in Vannes-Morbihan, 1934–43; studied at the Ecole des Beaux-Arts, Rennes, 1944–46; studied architecture at the Ecole Nationale Supérieure des Beaux-Arts, Nantes, 1947–49. Married Marie-Francoise de Faultrier in 1956; daughters: Valerie, Fabienne and Adeline. Worked as architectural draughtsman, Vannes, 1943–44; in St. Malo, 1946. Independent artist, writer and film-maker, in Paris, since 1949; first decollaged poster assembly, 1949; collaborative works with Raymond Hains, 1950–53. Member, Nouveaux Realistes group of artists, Paris, 1960. Agent: Galerie Claudine Breguet, 10 passage Turquetil, 75011 Paris. Address: 15–17 rue au Maire, 75003 Paris, France.

Individual Exhibition:

1957 Galerie Colette Allendy, Paris (with Raymond Hains)
1959 Atelier Francois Dufrene, Paris
1963 Galerie J., Paris
1964 Galerie Ad Libitum, Antwerp
1967 Galerie Jacqueline Ranson, Paris
1971 Galerie Michael Werner, Cologne
Moderna Museet, Stockholm
1972 Galerie Der Spiegel, Cologne
Museum Haus Lange, Krefeld, West Germany
1974 *Temoin de Notre Temps,* Galerie Beaubourg, Paris
Galerie Semiha Huber, Zurich
Centre of Arts and Communication, Vaduz, Lichtenstein
1976 Studio Sant'Andrea, Milan
Galerie Alexandre de la Salle, St. Paul de Vence, France
Galerie Le Dessin, Paris
1978 *Ravisseur Ravi de la Réalité,* Musée des Jacobins, Morlaix, France
1979 Office d'Action Culturelle, Saint-Brieuc, France
1980 Galerie Beaubourg, Paris
Centre Noroit, Arras, France
1981 Galerie Convergence, Nantes, France
1982 Galerie J and J Donguy, Paris
Galerie Micheline Szwajcer, Antwerp
1985 Maison de la Culture Rennes, France
Espace Claudine Breguet, Paris
1986 Galerie Convergence, Nantes, France
Espace Claudine Breguet, Paris
1987 Galerie 44, Kaarst-Dusseldorf, West Germany
Galerie Reckermann, Cologne
Galerie Christian Laune, Montpellier, France
1988 Galerie d'Art Contemporain, Nice
Galerie Le Chanjour, Nice

Selected Group Exhibitions:

1959 *Biennale des Jeunes,* Musée d'Art Moderne de la Ville, Paris
1961 *The Art of Assemblage,* Museum of Modern Art, New York (toured the United States)
1965 *Pop Art, Nouveau Realisme,* Palais des Beaux-Arts, Brussels
1971 *Affiches Laceres,* Staatsgalerie, Stuttgart
1977 *Trois Villes,* Centre National d'Art Contemporain, Paris
1979 *Nouveau Realisme,* Freitags Galerie Imhof, Solothurn, Switzerland
1980 *Les Affichinistes,* Galerie Mathias Fels, Paris
1983 *Les Années 60,* Musée d'Art et d'Industrie, St. Etienne, France
1984 *Affiches,* Musée Départementale des Beaux-Arts, Valence, France
1987 *Les Nouveaux Realistes,* Musée des Beaux-Arts, Winterthur, Switzerland

Collections:

Centre Georges Pompidou, Paris; Reunion des Musée Nationaux (F.N.A.C.), Paris; Musée Cantini, Marseilles; Moderna Museet, Stockholm; Kaiser-Wilhelm Museum, Krefeld, West Germany; Hessiches Landesmuseum, Darmstadt; Von-der-Heydt Museum, Wuppertal, West Germany; Museum van Hedendaagse Kunst, Ghent; Museum Moderner Kunst, Vienna; Israel Museum, Jerusalem.

Publications:

By de la VILLEGLÉ: books—*Heperile Eclate,* with Raymond Hains and Camille Bryen, Paris 1953; *De Mathieu à Mahe,* Paris 1967; *Les Volantes du Ravisseur,* La Louvière,

Jacques de la Villeglé: *Rue Vieille du Temple*, 1980

Belgium 1974; *Lacere Anonyme*, Paris 1977; *Commemoration de la Loi du 29 Juillet 1881*, Paris 1981; *L'Innocence du Choix*, Nice 1982; *Urbi et Orbi*, Dijon 1986; *De la Manifestation Spontanée*, Cognac 1986; films—*Paris-Saint Brieuc*, 1952; *Etude aux allures*, with Raymond Hains, 1954.

On de la VILLEGLÉ: books—*Collage: Personalities, Concepts, Techniques* by Harriet Janis and Rudi Blesh, New York 1962; *Villegle*, exhibition catalogue, with text by Pierre Restany, Paris 1963; *Les Nouveaux Réalistes* by Pierre Restany, Pais 1968; *Pop Art et Cie* by Francois Pluchart, Paris 1971; *Villegle*, exhibition catalogue, with text by Otto Hahn, Stockholm 1971; *L'Art Actuel en France* by Anne Tronche, Paris 1974; *Villegle: Temoin de Notre Temps*, exhibition catalogue, with text by Pierre Restany, Paris 1974; *Les Pre-Voyants* by Alain Jouffroy, Brussels 1974; *Formalism and Historicity* by Benjamin H. D. Buchloh, Chicago 1977; *Villegle, Ravisseur Ravi de la Réalité*, exhibition catalogue, with text by Otto Hahn, Morlaix, France 1978; *Le retour de l'Hourloupe*, exhibition catalogue with text by Bernard Lamarche-Vadel, Rennes 1985; *Villeglé le chapardeur* by Jean-Phillippe Lemee, Nantes 1986; *1960: Les Nouveaux Realistes*, exhibition catalogue with text by Dieter Schwarz, Mannheim and Winterthur 1986; *Jacques Villeglé*, exhibition catalogue with text by Philippe Piquet, Montpellier 1987.

At the start of the 1950's, dislocating the square of cold abstracts which chasfised emotion, the physiological and physical powers of the artist shifted position to the profit of an element of total chance which alone was becoming and could be productive. The artist, becoming "action-painter," then, to conclude the series and by reference to the street hoarding "automobile compressor," rejected on principle all conscious intervention, all hesitation and all conscious choice. As has been stated by the author of a general aesthetic, he opposed "learnt beauty, of which he is tired, the harsh and natural beauty which man finds fully equipped beneath his feet and which owes nothing to calculation or exertion."

The lacerations, traces of the gesture in its wild state, come out of anonymity. I would have liked to see them remain there.

If, after having torn down a fragment of a hoarding, the timidity of a certain fear disheartens me it sometimes happens that I unselfconsciously give it the necessary tear to make it stand out, being unable to completely repress the common taste for producing and creating falsities.

Falsities? No, let us recall that discussion between Arp and Mondrian. The latter opposed the artificiality of art to the naturalness of nature, I think, and Arp would not contradict me, that the impulsive gesture of the street is not opposed by that natural tendency to action which more or less everybody possesses. If my hand knows how to terminate the roughed-out gesture of an unknown person, to seek for glory on account of the fact would be inane. The appropriative and selective speculation of an object must not be lowered to the level of a studio procedure, as if to return to the game of dupes which the exercise of drawing and painting has become. "It tends toward the foolish glorification of the hand. The hand is the guilty party, and how can one accept being the slave of one's own hand? It is inadmissible that drawing and painting should today still be where writing was before Gutenberg" (André Breton).

It is regrettable to sign a poster—which the worker in paint, Fernand Léger, would have considered as "having become unusable"—but it remains true that by my label I facilitate its recognition and preserve it from destruction. Beauty is a tributary of bourgeois contingencies. Nevertheless, if I sign, would it not be natural for the successive purchasers or selectors to affix their signatures also, which would simply be resuming a Chinese custom whereby the collector was invited to add his mark beside that of the artist? In sharing my merit as inventor, they would with the same stroke diminish the importance of my imprint and would bring the laceration back to the anonymity of its point of departure.

The ensemble of lacerators, ravishers and collectors will therefore be called "Lacere Anonyme," and would it be to establish the facts of activity whose author would seem to be elusive that my goal would be restricted, or rather, would it be in reconstituting the work of a collective unconscious in personalising the "Lacere Anonyme"? Giambattista Vico did not act differently when he proved that Homer was not one single person but a collective being, a symbol of the Greek people, telling of its own history in national songs.

To endorse the secret of the creation of the lacerated work, I organized in June 1959 in the atelier of Francois Dufrene a series of soirees entitled "Lacere Anonyme." With this generic title each work acquires a specific character. By anonymous gestural aggression the poster become illegible becomes one of the most outstanding manifestations "of art made by everyone and not by one alone" of our time. When Caliban becomes a painter what happens to . . . OK? the professional and traditional painter and his craft?

—Jacques de la Villéglé

The so-called *affichistes* François Dufrêne, Raymond Hains, Mimmo Rotella and Jacques Villéglé form a sort of subgroup of the group known as the Nouveaux Réalistes, since their works have a common starting point and are to some extent closely related, while the other artists in the group all tread very different paths. Along with Klein these four are also the Nouveaux Réalistes whose works, outwardly at least, most closely resemble the traditional canvas, which does not mean, however, that they are the 'painters' of the group.

Villéglé received his artistic training in Rennes, where he got to known Raymond Hains, an artist with whom he was frequently to work in the following years. While Hains was devoting his attention to photographic techniques, in 1947 Villéglé had already restricted his artistic activity to the collection of objects which he found near his home on the Breton coast: pieces of wire and other flotsam and jetsam washed up on the Atlantic coast, along with pamphlets and other fragments of printed material. He tells how in January 1947 Hains and he wandered through the Nantes docklands: during the course of that walk it became clear to him how impossible was the artistic transposition of lived reality in its entirety, with which he sought directly and objectively to confront the spectator.

Working with Hains in Paris in 1949, it was in *dé-*

collage that Villéglé found the medium for realising these ideas. The two artists worked together on their first poster abstracts. Such work was the logical consequence of the conversations revolving round the search for an alternative to the abstract art that was beginning to establish itself in Paris now the war was over. In opposition to painting, the aim of this poster abstract was to link up the avant-garde trends of the 1910s and 1920s which, in Europe, had come to an abrupt end. Not until many years later did Villéglé find a forefather for his historical researches in the person of the French Surrealist Leo Malet. Malet had coined the term *décollage* in 1938. For him *décollage* meant the tearing off of individual sections of poster in order to reveal parts of the underlying poster layers and to leave room for speculation concerning what was still concealed. It was a poetic street activity which was still fully in the service of the verbal text, and Malet did not go so far as to uproot the product of *décollage* from its immediate environment.

Hains and Villéglé removed the selected sections of poster from their backing and then mounted them on canvas; the canvas was used on account of its lightness and elasticity, not because of its association with the painted picture. In the process of mounting, the artists might in some cases introduce corrections into the selected poster section. Villéglé also mentions the 'coup de pouce' (finishing touch) which was often necessary in order to complete the insufficiently forceful works, but which was executed without destroying their overall anonymity.

Placarding, particularly that of small political placards, signifies, independently of any actual message carried by the placard, the act of occupying a public area. Under the clause 'Défense d'afficher'', the bill that was passed in France on 29 July 1881, divides public areas into display-free zones and zones reserved for the display of advertising material (*emplacements réservés*); anyone who tears down such material is guilty of a criminal offence. The sticking up or pasting over, removal or defacement of posters and placards has correspondingly become a symbol of political struggle. In contrast to wall painting and graffiti, the defacement of the writing in the poster abstract follows no subjective-aesthetic rules. It signifies above all the adoption of an attitude, 'antidote contre toute propagande', and only as an ironic afterthought can it be understood in terms of a decorative design.

By their shabby appearance poster abstracts bear witness to life in certain Parisian quarters, and in his *Le flaneur aux palissades* Villéglé describes the differences between hoardings in the various quarters depending on the degree and nature of building and renovation work going on there. The transformation of the city and especially the erection of inaccessibly high large-format advertising hoardings could mean the end of the 'era' of the poster abstract.

The selection of an object, which becomes a work of art merely by grace of the artist's decision, takes us back to Marcel Duchamp's notion of the ready-made. There are however some fundamental differences between the poster abstract and the ready-made. Poster abstracts are closer from the outset to conventional art, since they assume the conventional form of a picture. They do not merely refer to the artistic context or, as the case may be, to themselves as autonomous works of art; they have besides this a representative function: they refer to the sections of poster that were not selected, to the permanent street exhibition, and thereby step beyond the closed world of art and into that of an anonymous public.

The tradition of artistic skill is replaced by a passive, receptive strolling around, in the course of which the stroller finds and selects posters. There is equally no clear intention in the mind of the artist engaged in tearing down and shredding posters: the spontaneous, unconsidered gesture takes the place of the premeditated composition. And even if certain gestures are deliberate, their significance is lost among the multitude of other gestures whereby the poster is built up. In this way the poster abstract denies essential elements which contribute towards the value of a work of art: craftsmanship, effort and time.

A new academic style could clearly develop out of the anonymous poster abstract. Bryen had already predicted: 'Anti-painting is becoming the painting of today and even in its freedom is adopting mannerisms and styles.' Villéglé had tried to avoid that by consistently assuming the role of sociological observer and abnegating the traditional one of the creative artist. He entitles his works with the place and date of the discovery and accords thematic importance to their timing. In 1982 he thus dedicated an exhibition to the *Présidentielles 81* (the 1981 Presidential Elections), following the progress of the various election candidates: "Je n'ai aucun parti pris sur les candidats, je suis presque un historien, qui prend les faits bruts" (I have no particular bias with regard to the candidates, I am virtually a historian, merely recording the bare facts). Through his writing, moreover, he has become the historian of what he calls the *Lacéré anonyme* (the anonymous slasher), the historian of the community of anonymous 'poster slashers', the discoverer and collector of their work.

—Dieter Schwarz

VISSER, Carel (Nicolaas).

Dutch. Born in Papendrecht, 3 May 1928. Studied architecture at the Technische Hogeschool, Delft, 1948–49; studied drawing and sculpture at the Koninklijke Academie voor Beeldende Kunsten, The Hague, 1949–51. Married Margareet Donker in 1953; sons: Harm and Geert Jan. Sculptor and graphic artist, Amsterdam, since 1952, and farmer, near Culemborg, since 1968. Visiting Professor, Washington University, St. Louis, 1962; Instructor, Koninklijke Academie voor Beeldende Kunsten, The Hague, 1958–62. Instructor, Atelier 63, Haarlem, since 1962. Recipient: Dutch Government travel stipend to Mexico, 1965; David Bright Award, *Biennale*, Venice, 1968; Museum of Western Art Prize, *International Print Biennale*, Tokyo, 1972; Dutch State Prize for Sculpture and Architecture, The Hague, 1972. Agents: Galerie Espace, Keizersgracht 548, Amsterdam; Art and Project, Prinsengracht 785, Amsterdam; and Galerie Paul Maenz, Schaafenstrasse 25, 5000 Cologne 1, West Germany. Address: Prinses Margrietstraat 2, 4023AD Rijswijk, Netherlands.

Individual Exhibitions:

1954 Kunsthandel Martinet, Amsterdam
1959 Steendrukkerijk de Jong, Hilversum, Netherlands
Neue Galerie Parnass-Jaehrling, Wuppertal, West Germany
1960 Stedelijk Museum, Amsterdam
Gemeentemuseum, The Hague
1965 Galerie Espace, Amsterdam
1967 Municipal Museum, The Hague
1968 Galerie Espace, Amsterdam
1970 Galerie Espace, Amsterdam
1972 *Beelden 1969–1972*, Stedelijk Museum, Amsterdam (travelled to Gemeentemuseum, The Hague)
Galerie Espace, Amsterdam
Galerie Paul Maenz, Cologne
Galerie Fenna de Vries, Rotterdam
Sculptures, Beelden, Palais des Beaux-Arts, Brussels
1973 Form Meditation International, Amsterdam
Lucy Milton Gallery, London
1974 Art and Project, Amsterdam
Galerie Nouvelles Images, Ghent
Galerie Nouvelles Images, The Hague
1975 Art and Project, Amsterdam
Galerie Paul Maenz, Cologne
Beelden, Tekeningen, Collages, Stedelijk Van Abbemuseum, Eindhoven, Netherlands
1976 Art and Project, Amsterdam
Sperone-Westwater-Fischer, New York
1977 Art and Project, Amsterdam
Galerie Konrad Fischer, Dusseldorf
Galleria Primo Piano, Rome
Kunsthalle, Dusseldorf
1978 *Sculptor's Work by Carel Visser: Sculpture Drawings, Prints and Jewelry 1952–1977*, Whitechapel Art Gallery, London (travelled to the Arnolfini Gallery, Bristol, and the Third Eye Centre, Glasgow)
Papierbeelden, Stedelijk Museum, Amsterdam
1979 *Sculptures 1978–1979*, Groningen Museum, Netherlands
1981 Rijksmuseum Kröller-Müller, Otterlo, Netherlands
1982 Nigel Greenwood Gallery, London
1984 Groninger Museum, Groningen, Netherlands
Art and Project, Amsterdam
Galerie Plus-Kern, Brussels
1985 Institut Neerlandais, Paris
Galerie Konrad Fischer, Dusseldorf
Galerie Durand-Dessert, Paris
Kasteel Wijlre, Netherlands
1986 Galerie Durand-Dessert, Paris
Museum Boymans-van Beuningen, Rotterdam
Art and Project, Amsterdam
Galerie Fenna de Vries, Rotterdam
1987 Art and Project, Amsterdam

Selected Group Exhibitions:

1952 *Sonsbeek International Exhibition*, Sonsbeek Park, Arnhem, Netherlands
1958 *Biennale*, Venice, Italy
1961 *Carnegie International*, Pittsburgh
1969 *Biennale*, Paris
1972 *Amsterdam-Paris-Dusseldorf*, Guggenheim Museum, New York
1973 *Lof der Tekenkunst*, Stedelijk Van Abbemuseum, Eindhoven, Netherlands
1975 *Funkties van Tekeningen*, Rijksmuseum Kröller-Müller, Otterlo, Netherlands
1977 *Europe in the 70's*, Art Institute of Chicago (toured the United States)
1983 *De Statua*, Van Abbemuseum, Eindhoven, Netherlands
1986 *Geent op Bosch*, Museum Het Kruithuis, Den Bosch, Netherlands

Collections:

Stedelijk Museum, Amsterdam; Gemeentemuseum, The Hague; Rijksmuseum Kröller-Müller, Otterlo, Netherlands; Stedelijk Van Abbemuseum, Eindhoven, Netherlands; Tate Gallery, London.

Publications:

By VISSER: books—*Carel Visser*, exhibition catalogue, Amsterdam 1960; *Carel Visser: 10 Beelden*, exhibition catalogue, Otterlo, Netherlands 1981; articles—"Carel Visser in Gesprek met Jan Dibbets en Rudi H. Fuchs" in *Museumjournaal* (Amsterdam), February 1973; interview, with Ad Petersen, in *Carel Visser: Papierbeelden*, exhibition catalogue, Amsterdam, 1978.

On VISSER: books—*Art and Architecture in the Netherlands: Carel Visser* by Cor Blok, Amsterdam 1968; *34th Biennale di Venezia 1968: Olanda—Carel Visser*, exhibition catalogue, edited by R. W. D. Oxenaar, Hilversum, Netherlands 1968; *Amsterdam-Paris-Dusseldorf*, exhibition catalogue, with texts by Cor Blok, Blaise Gautier, and Jürgen Harten, New York 1972; *Carel Visser: Sculptures, Beelden*, exhibition catalogue, Brussels 1972; *Carel Visser: Beelden 1969–1972*, exhibition catalogue, Amsterdam 1972; *Lof der Tekenkunst*, exhibition catalogue, with text by Carel Blotkamp, Eindhoven, Netherlands 1973; *Carel Visser: Beelden, Tekeningen, Collages*, exhibition catalogue, with text by Rudi H. Fuchs, Eindhoven, Netherlands 1975; *Carel Visser: Papierbeelden*, exhibition catalogue, Amsterdam 1978; *Sculptor's Work by Carel Visser: Sculpture, Drawings, Prints and Jewelry 1952–1977*, exhibition catalogue, with texts by Nick Serota and Barbara Reise, London, 1978; *Carel Visser: Sculptures 1978–1979*, exhibition catalogue, with

texts by Frans Haks and Carel Blotkamp, Groningen, Netherlands 1979; *Carel Visser: Beelden 1975–1985,* exhibition catalogue with text by Wim Beeren, Rotterdam 1986.

Carel Visser is undoubtedly the most important sculptor to come into prominence in the Netherlands since the Second World War. The great tradition of constructivism, as manifested in some of Mondrian's work and in the furniture and architecture of Gerrit Rietveld, is also present in Visser's art. Not that his work represents a mere continuation of *De Stijl:* that tradition, in combination with Visser's stern Calvinistic background, simply forms the basis for his struggle against the *Kubus* and helps to explain his preference for softer constructions.

Visser's first sculptures, done in steel around 1950, include the touching "Dying Horse" and many representations of birds. In 1954 or so he became strongly interested in the problems of vertical and horizontal symmetry. "Birds," for example, from 1954, is an almost abstract piece in which the top form mirrors the form beneath it, as a bird is reflected in the calm water over which it flies. In 1959 Visser produced "Great Auschwitz," another abstract work in which linear construction and spatial openness are brought together in a tension-filled relationship. In this respect, and because of the emotion-laden title, it is more than a spatial continuation of Mondrian's Pier + Ocean paintings from 1917.

The work Visser displayed at a 1972 exhibition in the Stedelijk Museum of Amsterdam represents a particularly important point in his development. His new material, thin, malleable plastic, is in strong contrast to the massive steel of his earlier work. The sculpture "Folded Tower" (1972) is made up of four folded plates, each of which is larger than the one below it: the tower literally sighs under its own weight. "Result With a Cube" (1970) is especially significant: here a plated steel cube is held together by leather cornerbands, while stretched out in front of it is a cross made up of six metal plates identical with those which make up the cube. Visser's battle with "the cube" is clearly apparent here.

In 1979 Visser surprised his audience with the small, strongly figurative and anecdotal objects he displayed in the Groningen Museum (South African ostrich eggs, for example, bound by leather straps to a Turkish walking stick). In 1981 he exhibited ten larger constructions in the Rijksmuseum Kröller-Müller, constructions which seemed to combine his drive towards figurative work and his battle against constructivist demands for summary and clarity. These works were made out of various kinds of simple materials drawn from Visser's own recent life in the country.

Visser is also famous as a draughtsman. Especially remarkable are his drawings from 1974: totally gray, graphite backgrounds which seem as if they were made of metal, and on which Visser has attached reproductions of such objects as avocados, fish, and labels of whisky bottles.

In his works from 1982 onwards, Visser exploits his newly discovered procedures. The sculptures seem to be objects of artistic recycling, a way of conserving those things and materials that have been left behind in the fields. His exhibition at the Art and Project Gallery, Amsterdam, in 1987 consisted of two farm transport vehicles serving as pedestals for the sculptures, creating a strong contrast with the architecture of the gallery itself. In some pieces, figurative imagery is dominant as in the cardboard portrayals of his old dog.

—A. F. Wagemans

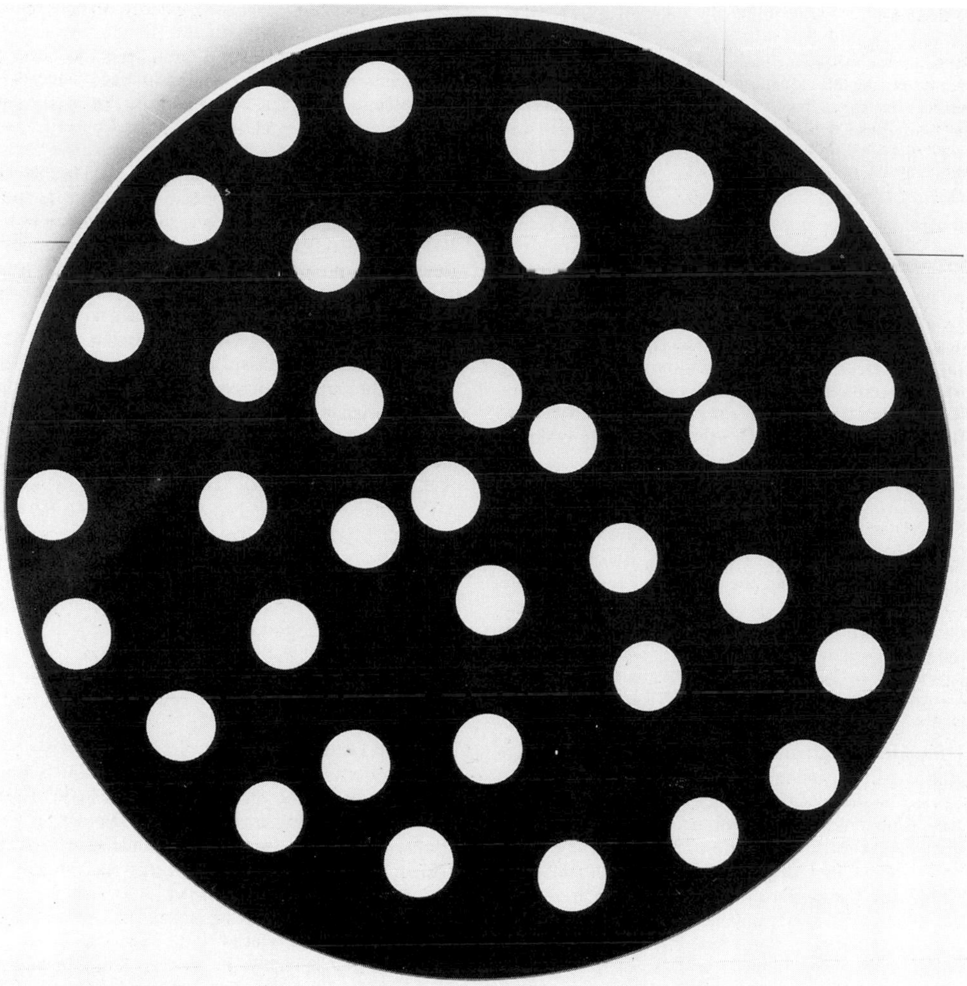

Gerhard Von Graevenitz: *Kinetic Object with White Disks*, 1965

von GRAEVENITZ, Gerhard.

German. Born in Schilde, Mark Brandenburg, 19 September 1934. Studied economics at the University of Frankfurt, 1955–56; studied art, under Ernst Geitlinger, Akademie der Schonen Künste, Munich, 1956–61: influenced by Josef Albers, Max Bill, and by Francois Morellet. Married Autje-Maria Ludwig in 1967; children: Julia and Moritz. Independent artist, concentrating on optical and kinetic works, in Munich, 1960–70, in Paris and Amsterdam, 1970 until his death in 1983: Founder-Member, Nouvelle Tendance group of artists, Paris, 1961–62. Instructor, Akademie der Schonen Künste, Kassel, 1969; Hochschule für Fernsehen und Film, Munich, 1970; and Akademie der Schonen Künste, Nuremberg, 1970; Guest-Professor, Kunstakademie, Hamburg, 1978. Editor, *Nota* magazine, Munich, 1960–61; Dutch Co-commissioner, *Biennale,* Venice, 1978; Concept and planner, *Pier Ocean* exhibition, Hayward Gallery, London, 1979–80. Agents: Galerie Reckermann, Albertusstrasse 16, 5000 Cologne 1, West Germany; Galerie Schoeller, Poststrasse 2, 4000 Dusseldorf, West Germany. *Died* (in an airplane crash in Switzerland) *in 1983.*

Individual Exhibitions:

1962 Galerie Roepcke, Wiesbaden, West Germany
1964 Galerie Wentdorf, Oldenburg, West Germany
1965 Op-Art Galerie, Esslingen, West Germany
Galerie 123, Krefeld, West Germany
Galerie Klihm, Munich
1966 Karl-Ernst-Osthaus Museum, Hagen, West Germany
Galerie im Europa-Center, West Berlin
Signals Gallery, London
1967 Galerie Klihm, Munich
1968 Museum Folkwang, Essen
Galerie M. E. Thelen, Essen
Galerie Ernst, Hannover
Galerie Swart, Amsterdam
1970 Galerie Lichter, Frankfurt
Galerie Klihm, Munich
1971 Galerie M, Bochum, West Germany
Galerie Swart, Amsterdam
1972 Studio Marconi, Milan
Galerie Swart, Amsterdam
1973 Lucy Milton Gallery, London
1974 Kunsthalle, Kiel (retrospective; toured Germany)
1976 Galerie Swart, Amsterdam
1977 Galerie Klihm, Munich
Galerie M, Bochum, West Germany
Stedelijk Museum, Amsterdam
1979 *Kinetische Objekten,* Stedelijk Van Abbemuseum, Eindhoven, Netherlands
1980 Galerie Reckermann, Cologne
Cultureel Centrum, Tilburg, Netherlands
1983 Galerie Schoeller, Dusseldorf
1984 Rijksmuseum Kröller-Müller, Otterlo, Netherlands
1985 Wilhelm-Hack-Museum, Ludwigshafen, West Germany
1986 Kunsthalle, Bremen, West Germany
Josef Albers Museum, Bottrop, West Germany

Selected Group Exhibitions:

1959 *Die neue Generation,* Kunstverein, Hannover
1964 *Nouvelle Tendance,* Musée des Arts Décoratifs, Paris
1966 *Directions in Kinetic Art,* Berkeley Museum, California
1968 *Documenta,* Kassel, West Germany
1970 *Biennale,* Venice
1973 *Kunst in Deutschland 1898–1973,* Kunsthalle, Hamburg
1979 *Zero: Bildvorstellung einer europaischen Avantgarde 1958–64,* Kunsthaus, Zurich (travelled to Antwerp)
1980 *Pier and Ocean,* Hayward Gallery, London
1985 *Kunst in der Bundesrepublik 1945–85,* Nationalgalerie, West Berlin

Collections:

Stedelijk Van Abbemuseum, Eindhoven, Netherlands; Gemeentemuseum, The Hague; Museum für Kunst und Gewerbe, Hamburg; Landesmuseum, Hannover; Städtische Galerie, Munich; Kunsthalle, Nuremberg; Westfälischer Landesmuseum, Münster, West Germany; Städtsche Museum, Bochum, West Germany; Tate Gallery, London; University of California Art Museum, Berkeley.

Publications:

By von GRAEVENITZ: articles—"Statement" in *Kunstlicht-kunst,* exhibition catalogue, Eindhoven, Netherlands 1966; "Statement" in *Directions in Kinetic Art,* exhibition catalogue, Berkeley 1966; "Statement" in *Basically White,* exhibition catalogue, London 1974; statement in *To Do With Nature,* exhibition catalogue, Amsterdam 1978; statement in *Pier and Ocean,* catalogue, London 1980; text in *Schwarz,* exhibition catalogue, Dusseldorf 1981.

On von GRAEVENITZ: books—*Constructivism: Origins and Evolution* by George Rickey, New York 1967; *Gerhard von Graevenitz,* exhibition folder, with text by Hannah Weitemeier, Munich 1967; *Naissance de l'Art Cinetique* by Frank Popper, Paris 1967; *Gerhard von Graevenitz,* exhibition catalogue, with text by Dietrich Helms and Helmut Heissenbuttel, Hannover 1968; *Wesen und Kunst der Bewegung* by Gyorgy Kepes, Brussels 1969; *Deutsche Kunst: eine neue generation* by Rolf-Günter Dienst, Cologne 1970; *Deutsche Kunst der 60er Jahre: Malerei, Collage, Op-Art, Graphik* by Juliane Roh, Munich 1971; *Basically White,* exhibition catalogue, with texts by Carel Blotkamp and Lucy Milton, London 1974; *Gerhard von Graevenitz,* exhibition catalogue, with texts by Jens Christian Jensen and Heinz Spielmann, with an interview by Frans Haks, Kiel 1974; *Gerhard von Graevenitz: Kinetische Objekten,* exhibition catalogue, with texts by J. Bremer and C. Blotkamp, Eindhoven, Netherlands 1979; *Gerhard von Graevenitz,* exhibition catalogue with texts by R. Oxenaar, A. von Graevenitz, L. Gloser and others, Otterlo 1984.

My kinetic objects are visual objects. The elements are simple. The organization is non-hierarchic (no composition). The movement is not linear (no beginning, no end). The objects are structures: networks of connections, of elements or simple processes. Because the organization is open—as it has been developed in the theory of games—there is playfulness involved. The relation of my objects to reality is not that of copies, but rather of models, i.e., I try to make the objects so simple, so logical that they take on the character of models. My round objects with disks work according to a relatively simple principle. The disks are fixed at a point on the periphery, on axes which turn at random, sometimes clockwise, sometimes counter-clockwise, and are moved by an electric motor. As all disks move, the network changes continuously and therefore the path of each disk seems to be relatively complex, while the movement of the total circle cannot be seen. The number of possible situations is so great that a repetition is very improbable.

—Gerhard von Graevenitz (1965)

Gerhard von Graevenitz belonged to that new group of artists who at the beginning of the 1960's chose as themes previously little used mediums—light, movement, mechanics—and systematically, with wide and individual variations, developed early experiments—perhaps of Calder and Gabo—into a revolutionary art form. Characteristic of the movement, which was later labelled "Kineticism," was its internationalism. Whoever looks carefully, however, soon discovers in the international groups aspects of a thoroughly regional and individual kind. In the case of Gerhard von Graevenitz a fantasy presents itself, having a basis of sober calculation, yet not exhausting itself in it. The mechanics of his objects is simple, yet the same constellations of elements, light, movements in some of his objects should, according to the law of probability, only repeat themselves every 10–20,000 years—this means that during the expected life of an object it should never precisely repeat the pattern of the passing second. The incidence of chance is thereby largely eliminated.

Graevenitz never accepted the precision of a richly incidental mechanism as an end in itself. He agreed completely with Schiller-ian maxim about art being close to a game, and about man being never more himself than when he is at play.

Graevenitz arrived at results such as the kinetic objects by virtue of consistent development. In 1959 he began to model accurate structures in slight relief, without the aid of colour, in pure white, discovering, apart from the rhythm of structure, the ambivalence of concave and convex forms in the incidence of light. After accurate structures he then worked on structures with short lines the optical interactions of which preoccupied him. Next were the kinetic objects, which consistently followed the structural images of the time around 1960/61, built from small elements—chiefly squares and circles. In their place came circular discs with flat lamellae at changing angles to each other, flat discs as well as cruciform or triangular. With the introduction of single and multi-colored light falling from the changing constellation in small areas on the turning lamellae, there began that series of objects in which the optic play gained incalculable possibilities of variation and in front of which the spectator's imagination is attracted to associations other than the merely optical perception. They can work like a glimpse into the cosmos or the microscope, like signs of scientific experiment or metaphysical symbols.

In the late 1960's Graevenitz turned from complex programmes to simple ones again. He was more and more preoccupied with the irritation caused by the slight movement of plastic elements or by the light paths. On a wall in the Gemeentemuseum in The Hague in 1969 he carried out in monumental form an example for the modification of a surface relief by a constantly changing constellation. The conscious link with his chosen tradition is made visible in the arrangement of the room of the great Stijl architects, a link which to Graevenitz went back to the mathematically-based metaphysics of Pico della Mirandola or to the play with numbers in Mesopotamia. Graevenitz always protected himself from risk of being misunderstood by virtue of the admission of such references—and because the creative fantasy of his inventions always involved a return to the simplest starting points for new ideas.

—Heinz Spielmann

VON SCHLEGELL, David.

American. Born in St. Louis, 25 May 1920. Studied engineering at the University of Michigan, Ann Arbor, 1940–42; studied painting at the Art Students League, New York, 1945–48, and with his father, William von Schlegell, 1945–50. Served in United States Army Air Corps, 1943–44. Painter, 1950–61, and sculptor since 1961; now lives and works in Connecticut. Worked as an engineer, Douglas Aircraft, Long Beach, California, 1942–43, and in an architect's office, 1944–45. Taught privately, 1950–55; Visiting Lecturer in Sculpture, University of California at Santa Barbara, 1968; Instructor in Painting, School of Visual Arts, New York, 1968–69; Visiting Instructor in Sculpture, Cornell University, Ithaca, New York 1969–70. Director of Studies in Sculpture, Yale University, New Haven, Connecticut, since 1971. Recipient: First prize for Sculpture, Colman Award, Whitney Museum, New York, 1964; Purchase Prize, *Carnegie International,* Pittsburgh, 1967; National Endowment for the Arts Grant, 1969; St. Buttolph Award, Boston, 1969; Guggenheim Fellowship, 1974; Skowhegan School Medal for Sculpture, Maine, 1978; Pollock/Krasner Foundation Grant, New York, 1986. Agent: Pace Gallery, 32 East 57th Street, New York, New York 10022. Address: c/o Department of Art/Sculpture, Yale University, 180 York Street, New Haven, Connecticut 06520, U.S.A.

Individual Exhibitions:

1956	Swetzoff Gallery, Boston
1957	Poindexter Gallery, New York
1959	Swetzoff Gallery, Boston
1964	University of New Hampshire, Durham
	Stanhope Gallery, Boston
	Museum of Art, Ogunquit, Maine (with Jack Levine)
1965	Ward-Nasse Gallery, Boston
	Institute of Contemporary Art, Boston (three-person exhibition)
1966	Royal Marks Gallery, New York
1967	Royal Marks Gallery, New York
	New York University, New York (three-person exhibition)
1968	Brandeis University, Waltham, Massachusetts (retrospective)
1969	Obelisk Gallery, Boston
	Ward-Nasse Gallery, Boston
1970	Paula Cooper Gallery, New York
1971	Reese Palley Gallery, New York
1972	Reese Palley Gallery, New York
1974	Pace Gallery, New York
1975	Pace Gallery, New York
1976	Pace Gallery, New York
	Institute of Contemporary Art, Boston
1977	Pace Gallery, New York
1981	Pace Gallery, New York

Selected Group Exhibitions:

1957	*Whitney Annual*, Whitney Museum, New York (and 1964, 1968)
1963	*New England Sculpture Today*, Boston
	5 New England Sculptors, Wadsworth Atheneum, Hartford, Connecticut
1965	*World's Fair*, New York
1966	*Primary Structures*, Jewish Museum, New York
1967	*Innovations*, Art Institute of Chicago
	Carnegie International, Pittsburgh
1971	*Sculpture for New Spaces*, Walker Art Center, Minneapolis
	Sculpture in the Park, Van Saun Park, Paramus, New Jersey
	International Biennale of outdoor Sculpture, Middelheim Museum, Antwerp

Collections:

Whitney Museum, New York; Massachusetts Institute of Technology, Cambridge; University of Massachusetts, Amherst; Addison Gallery of American Art, Andover, Massachusetts; Rhode Island School of Design, Providence; Aldrich Museum of Contemporary Art, Ridgefield, Connecticut; Carnegie Institute, Pittsburgh.

Publications:

By VON SCHLEGELL: article—"The Artist Speaks: David von Schlegell" in *Art in America* (New York), May/June 1968.

On VON SCHLEGELL: article—"David von Schlegell" by Dennis Adrian in *Artforum* (New York), December 1965.

In 1961, after he had spent over a decade painting full-time, David Von Schlegell turned his attention to sculpture. Using his previous experience in boat building design, engineering, Air Force piloting, and working for an architect, he bases his sculpture on the possibilities inherent in the materials and construction methods used in engineering structures including aircraft and boats. Von Schlegell's materials are aluminum, stainless steel and wood, which he uses with great precision and skill to invent structures which

push the limits of the material to create large yet fragile configurations which are arrived at intuitively and usually stress curved, irregular shapes. The process of design and construction is a complex one, done by Von Schlegell himself, and the resulting works are highly abstract and simplified forms.

Von Schlegell's intention is, as he stated in 1966, "to take hold of the invisible feelings one has toward form, space and motion and to make them visible." His works seem poised in a position of imminent movement, as if about to walk or fly away. In his 1966 work "Radio-Controlled Sculpture," Von Schlegell built in a complicated electronic system which enabled the twisting aluminum, three-pronged form to literally waddle away in response to radio command. Like his other sculptures, this one conveys anthropomorphic associations, which are amplified by the quality of implied motion in a gestural interaction with the surrounding environment. Titles such as "Marina" (1965) and "Voyage of Ulysses" (1977) further attest to this allusionary content level. Untitled works also refer ultimately to man-made and/or organic entities and also to the four elements. "Untitled" (1965, aluminum), consisting of a pyramid cut by a long, narrow, twisting horizontal, suggests the energy of lightning hitting this ancient symbol of mysterious and enduring architecture. "Untitled" (1978) curves and folds sensuously in vertical motion to a sharp point, transforming the dynamics of sails and wings into a 20th century icon.

Von Schlegell's most successful works have been those which harmonize with their surrounding environments, creating a sense of organic continuity with Nature's phenomena. Some use polished aluminum surfaces to reflect and warp in changing patterns dictated by time and weather. Others, such as "Storm King Project" (1972), use open, lightweight forms in tune with the lay of the land, and hover on the edge between visibility and invisibility.

Von Schlegell developed his sculpture at a time when Minimalism was coming into vogue. His inclusion in the 1966 exhibition, *Primary Structures*, mixed him with a group of sculptors most of whom were far more formally oriented. (A notable exception is Tony Smith who is also mistakenly aligned with 1960's Minimalism.) Von Schlegell stresses the abstract elements of his work, speaking against references to "some other object." Yet he often uses the word "intuitive" and speaks of a concern to make invisible feelings visible. His statements reflect a desire to avert readings which are too literal and to keep them on the level of ideas. Considering this factor, along with the underlying content visible in the sculptures themselves, and adding also Von Schlegell's previous painting in an Abstract Expressionist vein, the true nature of his work is best understood as arising out of the ideas promulgated in Abstract Expressionist painting during the 1940's and 50's.

During the early 1960's Von Schlegell stopped using wood, feeling that it aroused too many organic connotations. In recent works he has returned to wood to create horizontal configurations which are magnificently crafted and admit the loveliness of the medium as well as allusions to the sea and its crafts. At this point in time and with a large body of work behind him, Von Schlegell seems to feel freer to allow his referential content to surface. He has never been either a formalist or a depictor of specifics, and he continues to use his materials and his language of abstract forms to shape distilled visions which communicate the correspondence inherent in the nature of our industrial environment.

—Barbara Cavaliere

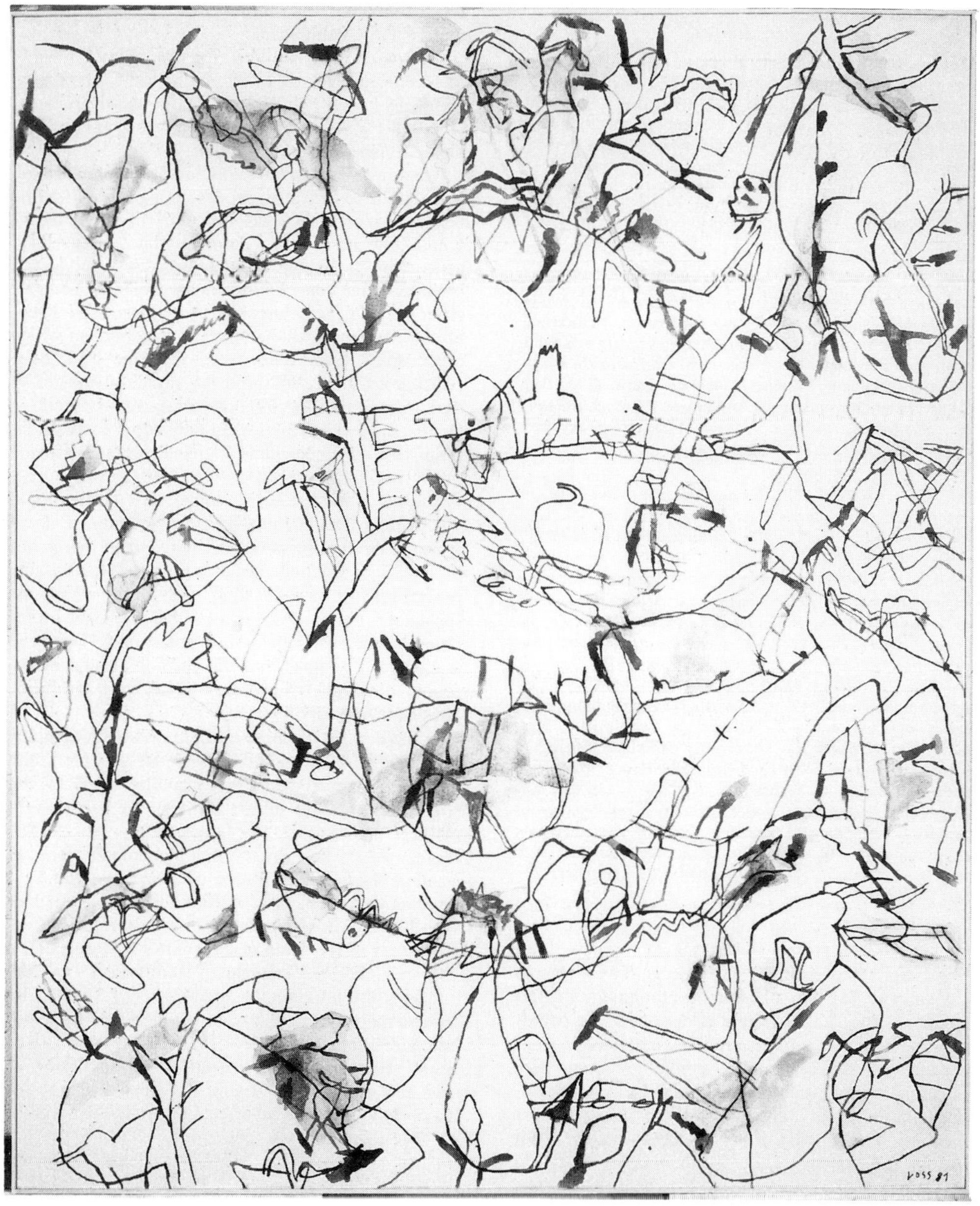

Jan Voss: *Untitled*, 1981

VOSS, Jan.

German. Born in Hamburg, 9 October 1936. Studied at the Kunstakademie, Munich, 1955–60. Independent artist, Paris, since 1960. Painting instructor, Kunstakademie, Hamburg, 1966–67. Agents: Galerie Lelong, 13/14 Rue de Teheran, 75008 Paris, France; Galerie Nothelfer, Uhlandstrasse 184, 1000 Berlin 12 (West), Germany; Galerie Moderne, Skoletorvet, 8600 Silkeborg, Denmark; Galerie Academia, Residenz, 5010 Salzburg, Austria; Galerie Satani, 4-2-6 Ginza, Chuo-ku, Tokyo, Japan. Address: 34 rue Dombasle, 75015 Paris, France.

Individual Exhibitions:

1963 Galerie Bayer, Mainz
1964 Galerie du Fleuve, Paris
1965 Galerie Lucien Durand, Paris
Galleri Birch, Copenhagen
1966 Galerie Mathias Fels, Paris
Lefebre Gallery, New York
1967 Galleria del Naviglio, Milan
1968 Galerie Brusberg, Hannover
1969 Galleri Birch, Copenhagen
1970 Galerie Van de Loo, Munich
1971 Lefebre Gallery, New York
Galleria Del Naviglio, Milan
1972 Galerie Lucien Durand, Paris
1974 Galerie Brusberg, Hannover
Galerie Buchholz, Munich
1975 Galerie Lucien Durand, Paris
Goethe Institut, Paris
1976 Galleri Birch, Copenhagen
1977 Galerie C, Paris
1978 Musée d'Art Moderne de la Ville, Paris (retrospective)
Galerie Le Dessin, Paris
Galerie Nothelfer, West Berlin
1979 Galerie Van de Loo, Munich
Centre Culturel, Toulouse
1980 Galerie Le Dessin, Paris
Leopold-Hoesch Museum, Duren, West Germany
Galerie Linssen, Bonn
1981 Kunstverein, Pforzheim, West Germany
Landesmuseum, Oldenburg, West Germany
Art Front Gallery, Tokyo
Galerie Adrien Maeght, Paris
1982 Galeria Maeght, Barcelona
Randers Museum, Denmark
Museum van Hedendaagse Kunst, Utrecht
Galerie Convergence, Nantes, France
Galerie Bel'Art, Stockholm
Centre Culturel, Bretigny-sur-Orge, France
1983 Galerie Satani, Tokyo
Galerie Academia, Salzburg, Austria
Galerie Grafica, Tokyo
Artotheque, Lyon, France
Museum van Hedendaagse Kunst, Ghent, Belgium
1984 Galerie Moderne, Silkeborg, Denmark
Galerie Ulysses, Vienna
Galerie Quaresso, Munich

Galerie Satani, Tokyo
Galerie Grafica, Tokyo
1985 Manus Presse, Stuttgart
Galerie Beaumont, Luxembourg
Galerie Wentzel, Cologne
Galerie Satani, Tokyo
Galerie Grafica, Tokyo
1986 Galerie Nothelfer, West Berlin
Galerie Academia, Salzburg, Austria
Herstand Gallery, New York
1987 Maison de la Culture, La Rochelle, France
Les Cordeliers, Chateauroux, France
Galerie Laune, Nimes, France
Galerie Satani, Tokyo
1988 Galerie Wentzel, Cologne

Selected Group Exhibitions:

1962 *Donner à Voir,* Galerie Creuze, Paris
1963 *Biennale de Paris,* Musée d'Art Moderne de la Ville, Paris
1965 *Le Merveilleux Moderne,* Konsthall, Lund, Sweden
1967 *La Bande Dessinee et la Figuration Narrative,* Musée des Arts Decoratifs, Paris
1970 *Distances,* Musée d'Art Moderne de la Ville, Paris
1972 *German Contemporary Art,* National Museum of Modern Art, Tokyo (travelled to Kyoto)
1977 *Mythologies Quotidiennes 2,* Musée d'Art Moderne de la Ville, Paris
1981 *Phoenix,* Alte Oper, Frankfurt
1984 *Ecriture dans la Peinture,* Villa Arson, Nice
1986 *Kunst Heute in Frankreich,* Sammlung Ludwig, Aachen, West Germany

Collections:

Musée d'Art Moderne de la Ville de Paris; Centre National d'Art Contemporain, Paris; Centre Georges Pompidou, Paris; Musée Cantini, Marseilles; Moderna Museet, Stockholm; Goteborgs Kunstmuseum, Sweden; Städtisches Museum, Bonn; Sammlung Ludwig-Städtische Galerie, Aachen, West Germany; Stadtische Galerie im Lenbachhaus, Munich; Museum of Modern Art, New York.

Publications:

By VOSS: articles—"Entretien avec Jan Voss," with Bernard Lamerche-Vadel, in *Artistes* (Paris), October/November 1981; "Jan Voss—Interview," with Anne Dagbert, in *Art Press* (Paris), November 1981.

On VOSS: books—*Positionen* by Rolf-Günter Dienst, Cologne 1968; *Deutsche Kunst—eine neue Generation II* by Rolf-Günter Dienst, Cologne 1970; *Deutsche Kunst der 60er Jahre* by Juliane Roh, Munich 1971; *Jan Voss,* exhibition catalogue, with text by Yves Michaud, Paris 1981; *Le Seismographe Lunatique: Jan Voss, Oeuvre Graphique 1964–1982,* exhibition catalogue with text be Anne Tronche, Paris 1982; *Jan Voss: un voyage ideal,* exhibition catalogue with essay by Katsuhiro Yamaguchi, Tokyo 1983; *Jan Voss—le presque parfait,* exhibition catalogue with text by Daniel Dobbels, Silkeborg 1984; *Trajet de Jan Voss* by Bernard Noel, Marseilles and West Berlin 1985.

Within view
Perhaps he had placed his hand against a rock and in outlining it with the help of a bit of charred wood had drawn its shape. Perhaps in this way he had recorded the beginning of history. His hand had then continued to grasp everything in sight: animals and gods, men and landscapes, objects, constructions, forms, ideas . . . .
He should never again stop taking possession of the world by marking/signing it, and we pursue this outline which connects prehistory to our decade and we observe it already overtaking us and vanishing in the vertiginous infinity like the condensation trail of an aircraft which has crossed the sound barrier.
—Jan Voss

Jan Voss has lived in Paris since 1960. Educated at a time when lyrical abstraction dominated the art schools in Germany, he sought primarily a manner of expression personal to himself and as different as possible from the aimless poesy of this tendency. From the very first he was interested in writing as a painter's gesture, not in that which it could, unwilled and uncontrolled, set free in the layers of the unconscious but in that which it can contribute to painting in its role of go-between.

In the works from the beginning of the 1960's Voss had already given it the task of making a direct statement, less by direct legibility than by the fact that painting can on the whole be conceived as writing. These pictures from 1961 and 1962 recall picture stories put together from pure and simple pictograms which are so close to scrawl that the anecdote as such finally remains incomprehensible. During the 1960's both elements became more precise: both the individual signs and the writing role of the painterly gesture. The pictures became clearer in their expression, had something to say, serve communication. The latter is indeed one of the themes around which Jan Voss's entire work will soon revolve: which sign at what time and for whom is suitable for communication?

The scrawl hardens. The picture ground and signs are from then on more radically separated from each other. The individual pictograms take on firm outlines, become discernible and recognizable and therefore even interchangeable from picture to picture. Finally Jan Voss's pictures are peopled by a number of more or less naively drawn figures and objects which are arranged across a broad unorganized area in a kind of fictional running narrative.

A synthesis of all these works was perhaps reached in 1968 in the picture which he called "Reading for Everyone." It is a challenge to the viewer to read the picture like a book and to regard the painting as a multiplicity of languages, symbols and stereotypes--and an invitation to remain conscious and critical in relation to these languages and not to surrender to them in admiration, as with secret scripts that one does not understand. What Voss was making especially visible in this instance was a critique of political emblems and ideology related symbols: from the Mao bible to Ché Guevara, they serve the individual only to adopt a political code like a fashion and not as more effective communication from man to man.

In this way Voss's work enters completely into the painterly tendencies of the 1960's in Paris, which built on a structuralist critique of language and which above all did not remain uninfluenced by Michel Foucault's writing. Instead of investigating the contents of knowledge, Foucault has begun to analyze critically the discourses, the languages of our knowledge. He had shown that we are all dependent on that discourse into which, according to our era and environment, we are born, and that it is therefore necessary above all to be vigilant in relation to the languages and forms of expression which we employ in science, literature and art so that we understand their full significance.

In 1965 and 1967 Jan Voss exhibited occasionally with painters who belonged to the so-called "Figuration Narrative." I believe, however, that he aimed less at a confrontation between figuration, or the power of the figurative picture, and abstract painting than at the preservation of a critical attitude in relation to all languages of art. Consequently, he has also, in recent years, tended towards a painting of "indecision." From the beginning of the 1970's he gave up the previously discovered language patterns in favour of imaginary signs which he arranged uniformly across empty surfaces like elementary particles. These required only to be connected with an endless line in order to arrive at current works. The world of the pictogram seemed too constricting, too didactic and too little concerned with the real problems of painting. He retained the character of the element, but it was now bound up in a kind of linear labyrinth. Even colour was banished from the plane surface back to the line. The line is led across the surface unsteadily, sometimes hesitatingly, sometimes with wilful naivete, forms a foyer here and there in which archaic figure like images take shape without ever becoming articulate forms. The line plays around them and itself; Voss liberates it from the individual object so that it may belong to all possible objects. It flies from one motif to the next; it crosses through, draws paths, horizons, mountains, in order immediately to destroy them.

Voss's pictures are thus a virtuoso example of structures which came from crossed lines. He shows without describing that one can speak neither of abstraction nor of the genesis of a picture: he has now reached an intermediate stage of landscapes without contour and distances without perspectives. He materializes a non-concentric thought, one that moves in many centres at once, that lies across the picture surface like a vibrating network which always remains incomplete and open. His pictures arise from moments of distraction—as he himself says, they arise unpremeditated from a balance between the will and the accidental, between reason and unreason.
—Marie Luise Syring

VOSTELL, Wolf.

German. Born in Leverkusen, near Cologne, 14 October 1932. Studied lithography in a printing works, Cologne, 1950–53; studied painting and typography at the Werkkunstschule, Wuppertal, 1954; studied painting, graphics and anatomy, under A. M. Cassandre, Ecole des Beaux-Arts, Paris, 1955–57; and at the Kunstakademie, Dusseldorf, 1957–58. Married Mercedes Guarado Olivenza in 1958; sons: Santiago David and Rafael Isaac. Independent artist in Paris, 1954–57, 1958–59, Dusseldorf, 1957–58, Cologne and Wuppertal, 1959–70, and in West Berlin, since 1971; and Malpartida, Spain, since 1975; produced first "décollages," Paris, 1954; first street happenings, Paris, 1958; first sculpture-actions, with cement "blockages," Cologne, 1969. Layout artist, *Neue Illustrierte,* Cologne, 1961–62; Founder-Editor, *Décoll-age,* Frankfurt, 1962–69; Founder, with George Maciunas, Jean-Pierre Wilhelm, Nam June Paik and others, Fluxus movement, Cologne, 1962–66; Founder, Happening-Archiv, West Berlin 1971; Co-Founder, Aktionen der Avantgarde (A.D.A.) foundation, West Berlin, 1973; Founder, Museo Vostell, Malpartida, Spain, 1976. Instructor in Typography, Werkkunstschule, Wuppertal, 1959–60. Agents: Galerie Van de Loo, Maximilianstrasse 27, 8000 Munich 22, West Germany; Galeria Punto, Baron de Carcer 37, Valencia, Spain. Addresses: Museo Vostell, Malpartida de Caceres (Caceres), Spain; and Giesebrechtstrasse 12, 1000 Berlin 12, West Germany.

Individual Exhibitions:

1950 Salon Educacion y Descanos, Caceres, Spain
1960 Galeria Sala Lux, Caceres, Spain
1961 Galerie Le Soleil dans la Tête, Paris
Galerie Haro Lauhus, Cologne
1962 Galerie Monet, Amsterdam
1963 Smolin Gallery, New York
Galerie Parnass, Wuppertal, West Germany
1964 Galerie Loehr, Frankfurt
1965 Galerie René Block, West Berlin
Studio F, Ulm, West Germany
1966 Something Else Gallery, New York
Verwischungen, Happening-Notationen 1961–66, Kölnischer Kunstverein, Cologne
1967 Galerie Tobies and Silex, Cologne
Galerie René Block, West Berlin
Museum of Contemporary Art, Chicago (with Allan Kaprow)
1968 Galerie Hake, Cologne
1969 Institut Dr. Gasch, Wiesbaden
Galerie Rolf Kuhn, Aachen, West Germany
Galerie Van de Loo, Munich

Wolf Vostell: ***New Yorker Chair*****, 1976**

1970 Galerie Art Intermedia, Cologne
Atelier NW 8, Beindersheim, West Germany
Elektronisch, Galerie Rolf Kuh, Aachen, West Germany
Galerie Inge Baecker, Bochum, West Germany
Galerie René Block, West Berlin
1971 Galerie Bama, Paris
Galerie Catacombe, Basle
Galerie Press, Konstanz, West Germany
Galerie Kerlikowsky und Kneiding, Munich
Galerie Inge Baecker, Bochum, West Germany
Galerie Hausdewell, Baden-Baden, West Germany
Galerie Hausdewell, Hamburg
Galerie René Block, West Berlin
Galerie Kolczynski, Stuttgart
1972 Galerie Argelander, Bonn
Rheinisches Landesmuseum, Bonn
Galerie Art in Progress, Zurich
Kunstverein, Freiburg
Galerie Van de Loo, Munich
1973 Goethe Institut, Marseilles
Galleria La Bertesca, Milan
Galerie Paramedia, West Berlin
Galerie Van de Loo, Munich
Galerie Ingo Kummel, Dusseldorf
1974 Galerie Bama, Paris
La Sala Vincon, Barcelona
Galleria La Bertesca, Milan
Galleria Multiphla, Milan
Nuovi Strumenti, Brescia, Italy
Deutsches Kulturinstitut, Madrid
Kunsthalle, Bremen, West Germany
1975 *Environments/Happenings 1958–1974,* Musée d'Art Moderne de la Ville, Paris
Galerie Van de Loo, Munich
Retrospektive 1958–1974, Nationalgalerie, West Berlin
Galleria Bocchi, Parma
Galleria Bozzi, Turin
Galleria Incontri, Rome
Galleria Area, Florence
Galerie Andre, West Berlin
Galleria Multiphla, Milan
Galerie Bama, Paris
Galerie Carsta Zellermayer, West Berlin
Galerie Inge Baecker, Bochum, West Germany
1976 Galerija Teatru-Studio, Warsaw
Städtisches Museum, Wiesbaden
Kunsthalle, Nuremberg
Galerie Pool, Graz, Austria
Galerie Kausch, Kassel, West Germany
Museo Vostell, Malpartida de Caceres, Spain (inaugural exhibitions)
Kunststation Faber, Fulda, West Germany
Galerie Andre, West Berlin
German Institute, Barcelona
1977 Galerie Kausch, Kassel, West Germany
1978 Anja Kunstsenter, Abenra, Denmark
Museo de Arte Contemporaneo, Madrid
Universitat Essen, Wset Germany
1979 Kunstlerkongress-Halle, Stuttgart
Fundacion Joan Miro, Barcelona
Fundacao Gulbenkian, Lisbon (retrospective)
Museu Nacional de Soares Dos Reis, Porto, Portugal
Museo Vostell, Malpartida de Caceres, Spain
Galerie Ars Viva, West BErlin
1980 Galleria Il Centro, Naples, Italy
Monte Video, Wuppertal, West Germany
Galerie Inge Baecker, Bochum, West Germany
Museo Vostell, Malpartida de Caceres, Spain
Kunstverein, Braunschweig, West Germany
Los Angeles Institute of Contemporary Art
1981 Galerie Ars Viva, West Berlin
Fluxus Zug, Rail Stations in Dortmund, Aachen, Cologne, Dusseldorf and other cities in West Germany
1982 Gesellschaft für neue Kunst, Bremen, West Germany
Kunstverein, Uelzen, West Germany
Museo Vostell, Malpartida de Caceres, Spain
Centre Culturel du Marais, Paris
Musee de Calais, France
DAAD-Galerie, West Berlin
1983 Palais des Beaux-Arts, Charleroi, Belgium
Centro de Arte y Comunicacion, Buenos Aires
Galerie Bama, Paris
Nationalgalerie, West Berlin
1984 Galerie Armstorfer, Salzburg, Austria
Galeria Punto, Valencia Spain
Sala Parpallo, Valencia, Spain
1985 Galerie Inge Baecker, Cologne
Galerie Wewerka, West Berlin
Galerie Muda, Hamburg
Espace Nord, Liege, Belgium
Musée d'Art Moderne, Strasbourg, France

Selected Group Exhibitions:

1961 *Salon Comparaisons,* Musée d'Art Moderne, Paris
1962 *Schrift und Bild 1,* Kunsthalle, Baden-Baden, West Germany
1967 *Pictures to Be Read—Poetry to Be Seen,* Museum of Contemporary Art, Chicago
1968 *Von der Collage zur Assemblage,* Institut für Moderne Kunst, Nuremberg
1969 *Art by Telephone,* Museum of Contemporary Art, Chicago
1970 *Happening und Fluxus,* Kölnischer Kunstverein, Cologne
1973 *Contemporanea,* Parcheggio Villa Borghese, Rome
1977 *Documenta,* Kassel, West Germany
1980 *Forms of Realism Today,* Musee d'Art Contemporain, Montreal
1982 *20 Jahre Fluxus 1962–82,* Stadtisches Museum, Wiesbaden, West Germany

Collections:

Museum am Ostwall, Dortmund, West Germany; Neuer Berliner Kunstverein, West Berlin; Berlinische Galerie, West Berlin; Nationalgalerie, West Berlin; Neue Galerie, Aachen, West Germany; Kunstmuseum, Hannover; Bundesministerium des Innern, Bonn; Gesamthochschule, Wuppertal, West Germany; Bibliothèque Nationale, Paris.

Publications:

By VOSTELL: books and pamphlets—*Tombeau de Pierre Larousse,* with poems by Francois Dufrene, Wuppertal, West Germany 1961; *Happenings, Fluxus, Pop Art, Nouveau Realisme,* editor, with Jürgen Becker, Reinbek, West Germany 1965; *24 Stunden,* Itzehoe, West Germany 1965; *Wolf Vostell: Berlin and Phenomena,* New York 1966; *Wolf Vostell: Dokumentation,* edited by René Block, West Berlin 1968; *Vostell 1: Eine Dokumentation 1954–69,* with additional text

by Sidney Simon, West Berlin 1969; *Miss Vietnam and Texts of Other Happenings*, San Francisco 1969; *Pop Architektur—Concept Art*, editor, with Dick Higgins, Dusseldorf 1969; *Wolf Vostell: Happening und Lebe*, Neuwied and West Berlin 1970; *Aktionen, Happenings und Demonstrationen seit 1965: Ein dokumentation von Wolf Vostell*, Reinbek, West Germany 1970; *Vostell: Betonierungen*, Hinwil, West Germany 1970; *Wolf Vostell: Elektronisch*, exhibition catalogue, Aachen, West Germany 1970; *Fantastic Architecture*, editor, with Dick Higgins, New York 1971; *T.O.T. (Technological Oak Tree): 310 Ideen*, Hinwil, West Germany 1973; *Wolf Vostell: Happenings Calvario*, Genoa 1973; *Vostell: Fandango*, Milan 1975; *Vostell: Zyklus Extremadura*, with interview by Maria Luisa Borras, Munich 1975; *Wolf Vostell: 10 Happeinings Knozerte 1954–1973*, Milan 1976; *Derriére l'arbre (Duchamp no ha comprendido a Rembrandt . . .): Un Video-Happening de Vostell*, Barcelona 1976; *Vostell: Projekte und Ideen meiner Medienkonzeption zu Hamlet*, Cologne 1979; *Shakespeare-Hamlet*, Cologne 1979; articles—*De-coll/ages: Bulletin aktueller ideen* (Frankfurt), nos. 1–7, 1962–69; *Postversandroman*, with Peter Faecke (Neuwied), no. 1–11, 1970–72; films—*Sun in Your Head, 1 and 2*, 1963; *Chasseur à Reaction*, 1967; *20 Juillet 1944 Aix la Chapelle*, 1967; *Notstandbordstein*, 1967; *21 Projecteurs*, 1967; *Brotvermessung*, 1969; *Circulation Bloquee*, 1969; *Vietnam 1967–71*, 1971; *Desastres*, 1972; *T.O.T.*, 1972.

On VOSTELL: books—*Postface and Jefferson's Birthday* by Dick Higgins, New York 1964; *A Primer of Happenings and Time-Space Art* by Al Hansen, New York 1965; *Assemblages, Environment and Happenings* by Allan Kaprow, New York 1976; *Pop Art* by Lucy R. Lippard, New York and Washington, D.C. 1966; *Collage: Personalities, Concepts, Techniques* by Harriet Janis and Rudi Blesh, New York, Philadelphia and London 1967; *Pop und die Folgen* by Heinz Ohff, Dusseldorf 1968; *Vostell Soziologisch* by Rainer Wick, Bonn 1969; *Wolf Vostell: Retrospektive 1958–1974*, exhibition catalogue, with text by Jorn Merket, West Berlin 1975; *Wolf Vostell: Environments/Happenings 1958–1974*, exhibition catalogue, with text by Suzanne Page, Paris 1975; *Vostell: Heuwagen*, with text by Christa Schwens, Essen 1978; *Vostell*, exhibition catalogue, with texts by Santiago Amon, Simon Marchan and Jürgen Schilling, Madrid 1978; *Vostell 1968–1979*, exhibition catalogue, with texts by Francesco Vicens, Santiago Amon and Eberhard Roters, Barcelona 1979; *Wolf Vostell: Decollagen, Verwischungen, Schichtenbilder, Bleibüder 1955–1979*, exhibition catalogue, with interview by Jürgen Schilling, Braunschweig, West Germany 1980; *LAICA-Los Angeles, Ars Viva-Berlin: Vostell*, exhibition catalogue, with text by Robert L. Smith, Los Angeles 1980; *Vostell und Berlin: Leben und Werk 1971–1981*, exhibition catalogue, with text by Wieland Schmied, West Berlin 1982; *Wolf Vostell: Estampes et Affiches*, exhibition catalogue, with text by Francoise Woimant and Anne Moeglin-Delcroix, Paris 1982; *Wolf Vostell: environment, video, peintures, dessins 1977–85*, exhibition catalogue with texts by Michael Marschall, Nadine Lehni and Michel Giroud, Strasbourg 1986.

In order to survive all the madness and craziness of daily life in a nuclear era, I have made my artwork more and more research to express more and more freedom in whatever I am doing. Art as an expression of individual freedom is the only illusion that I have developed from my work—much better than accomplishing a style, satisfying a market, or looking for a happy ending as an artist integrated with society.

The intelligence and the nervous system of the artist has to develop as far as it can; therefore, creative systems and also creative craftsmanship has to be rich and complex as it can be on all levels, far away from nature and trivial fantasy. I feel that my obligation is to concretize that which nature cannot but nature speaks through me, and I am therefore life *and* art at the same time. Every man an artwork means that before making art the artist must be complex. Anyone becomes an artist only through his work, but anyone can be an artwork through nature.

—Wolf Vostell

One of Wolf Vostell's best known Happenings was a crash between a car and a railway engine, which certainly had its intended effect of shocking and infuriating the average German consumer. And all Vostell's work is in a sense a single great composition, since it all arises from the basic idea of shocking his audience out of their normal complacency into a new critical and aesthetic awareness of the everyday world of technology and politics. Like Duchamp with his "Readymades," Vostell seizes and isolates a piece of reality and proclaims it to be a work of art. But instead of mystifying it by isolating it in a gallery stripped of its normal associations, Vostell leaves it in its normal environment, while looking at it afresh, not with the casual glance of everyday life, but with the critical and aesthetic awareness usually brought to art.

Vostell's early work was the production, alteration and destruction of images using the technique he called dé-coll/age, the opposite of the building up process of collage, since it involves tearing of posters or other printed matter. He took the word from a French newspaper headline in September 1954 which announced a plane crashing immediately after its *dé-collage*, which in this context merely means "take-off," though the general idea of "unsticking" fused with the violent event and the artistic meaning of collage to give the idea of torn posters on boardings, the resulting picture becoming a document of the violent action of tearing. The tearing away of various superimposed layers of posters on a hoarding means that bits of different posters are left, fragments of words or pictures or colours which may give each other new meaning, which however can be altered by further tearing, revealing new components.

Such pictorial dé-coll/ages already include not only the ideas of constant change and openness, but also the idea of action. So it was a short step to widen the meaning from torn posters on hoardings to actual real events, to be "torn," open actions of his dé-coll/age demonstrations. In Paris in the late 1950's Vostell collaborated with A. M. Cassandre, and the first of his demonstrations took its inspiration and its title from Cassandre's book *Das Theater ist auf der Strasse* (The Theatre Is in the Street). Vostell's demonstrations differed from the early American happenings not only in taking place out in the open in the streets, but also in relying much less on chance by giving precise instructions for action. These demonstrations had clearly defined objectives, and Vostell's aggressive attitude means that no one is allowed to be a mere passive spectator, but is involved as an actor in whatever is going on. In his TV dé-coll/ages, for instance, the viewer is unsettled by deliberately faulty pictures or sets tuned out of focus, or smeared with paint or bashed in and riddled with bullet holes.

Vostell works out illustrated "scores" with detailed instructions for his demonstrations and happenings, though without excluding chance events: "A primary characteristic of my work and that of my colleagues is that the Happening includes whatever noise, movement, object, color or psychology enters into the total work of art. Because of this I assert that people and life are art." This total work of art in which the public are performers is intended to arouse their critical and aesthetic awareness so that they "learn to live and experience in the psychological reality of their surroundings." They are to be involved in a total work of art which both arouses their sensuous and aesthetic responses and also has an intellectual impact which leads to each developing a new way of seeing, a consciousness both of himself and of his own body and of the ways in which his life is conditioned by the technological world.

From 1962 Vostell began to call his works Happenings and he became closely associated with the Fluxus movement, with such events as the group *24 Hour Happening* at Wuppertal in 1965 or Vostell's own most ambitious happening *In Ulm, round Ulm and round about Ulm* of 1964. He has called the events of May 1968 in Paris "the greatest Happening of all" because unrest supported by artistic means here moved into direct political action and the overthrow of de Gaulle. Unlike Duchamp's ready-mades, the materials Vostell selects for his happenings are not random objects but central achetypal elements of our machine age such as television, trains and cars. And unlike the futurist worship of the car as an object of beauty he emphasizes its destructive potential, seeing in the passing car "the accident too driving by." One instruction in his earliest demonstration was to make sculpture out of crashed cars by fixing the remains to the spot where the accident occurred, and the old tendency to simply clear up the mess and thrust it out of mind has indeed now given way in some countries to putting up photographs of some of the worst accidents as a grim warning. Vostell's work, whatever its creative limitations, always presents a challenge, both to extend artistic reality to all sorts of everyday events and to approach these with a new critical and aesthetic awareness.

—Konstantin Bazarov

VOULKOS, Peter.

American. Born in Bozeman, Montana, 29 January 1924. Educated at Montana State College, Bozeman, 1946–51, B.S. 1951: California College of Arts and Crafts, 1951–52, M.F.A. 1952. Served as B52 Rear Gunner, Army Air Corps, in the Pacific, 1942–45. Independent sculptor, since 1952: lives and works in Oakland, California. Taught at Archie Bray Foundation, Helena, Montana, and Black Mountain College, Beria, North Carolina, 1952–54; Otis Art Institute, Los Angeles, 1954–59; and Greenwich House Pottery, New York, Summer 1961. Instructor, 1959–63, and Professor, 1963–85, University of California, Berkeley. Recipient: Gold Medal, *International Ceramic Exhibition*, Cannes, 1955; Sculpture Prize, *Biennale*, Paris, 1959; Sculpture Prize, San Francisco, 1967; National Endowment for the Arts grant, Washington, D.C., 1976, 1986; Creative Arts Medal, Brandeis University, Waltham, Massachusetts, 1982; Guggenheim Fellowship, New York, 1984; Gold Medal, American Crafts Council, 1986. Honorary Doctorates: California College of Arts and Crafts, Oakland, 1974; Otis Art Institute, 1982. Agent: Braunstein Gallery, 254 Sutter Street, San Francisco, California 94108. Address: 951 62nd Street, Oakland, California 94608, U.S.A.

Individual Exhibitions:

1956	Felix Landau Gallery, Los Angeles
1957	University of Southern California, Los Angeles
1958	Felix Landau Gallery, Los Angeles
	Pasadena Art Museum, California
1961	Museum of Modern Art, New York
	Bonnier Gallery, New York
1964	Gallery Unlimited, San Francisco
	Primus-Stuart Gallery, Los Angeles
1965	David Stuart Gallery, Los Angeles
1968	Quay Gallery, San Francisco
1969	David Stuart Gallery, Los Angeles
1974	Quay Gallery, San Francisco
1975	Kansas City Art Institute
	Helen Drutt Gallery, Philadelphia
	Braunstein/Quay Gallery, New York
1976	Yaw Gallery, Bloomfield Hills, Michigan
	Detroit Institute of Art
	Exhibit A Gallery, Evanston, Illinois
1978	Braunstein/Quay Gallery, San Francisco
	San Francisco Museum of Modern Art (retrospective)
1979	Exhibit A Gallery, Chicago
1981	Jacksonville Art Museum, Florida
	Exhibit A Gallery, Chicago
	Thomas Segal Gallery, Boston
	Charles Cowles Gallery, New York
1982	Braunstein Gallery, San Francisco
1983	Point View Art Center, Tokyo (travelled to Nagoya and Kyoto)
	Charles Cowles Gallery, New York
1984	Magnolia Editions, Oakland, California
	University of Iowa, Ames
	Exhibit A Gallery, Chicago
	Braunstein Gallery, San Francisco
1985	Exhibit A Gallery, Chicago
1986	Braunstein Gallery, San Francisco
1987	Braunstein Gallery, San Francisco

Peter Voulkos: *Untitled*, 1959

Selected Group Exhibitions:

1958 *World's Fair*, Brussels
1962 *World's Fair*, Seattle
1963 *International Sculpture Exhibition*, Battersea Park, London
1976 *200 Years of American Sculpture*, Whitney Museum, New York
1979 *A Century of Ceramics in the USA*, Everson Museum of Art, Syracuse, New York
1981 *Ceramic Sculpture*, Whitney Museum, New York (toured the United States)
1983 *Ceramic Echoes*, Nelson-Atkins Gallery of Art, Kansas City, Missouri
1984 *Art in Clay 1950s to 1980s*, Los Angeles Municipal Art Gallery

Collections:

Museum of Modern Art, New York; Museum of Contemporary Crafts, New York; Baltimore Museum of Art; San Francisco Museum of Modern Art; Oakland Museum, California; Los Angeles County Museum of Art; Norton Simon Museum, Pasadena, California; Portland Art Museum, Oregon; Den Permanente, Copenhagen.

Publications:

On VOULKOS: books—*Objects: U.S.A.* by Lee Nordness, London 1970; *Peter Voulkos: A Dialogue with Clay* by Rose Slivka, Boston 1978; articles—"Los Angeles Letter" by M. Leopold in *Art International* (Lugano), Summer 1973; "The Art of Peter Voulkos" by Hal Fischer in *Artforum* (New York), November 1978; "Peter Voulkos: Ceramics that Transcend Art" by Thomas Albright in *San Francisco Chronicle*, 27 March 1984.

W

WADE, Robert (Shrope).
American. Born in Austin, Texas, 6 January 1943. Studied at the University of Texas at Austin, 1961–65, M.F.A. in Painting, 1965; University of California at Berkeley, 1965–66, M.A. in Painting, 1966. Married Susan Elaine Immel in 1966; daughter: Christine. Lives and works in Dallas: engaged in automobile customizing and hot-rod esthetics, 1957–62. Member, Advisory Committee, Texas Commission on the Arts and Humanities, 1975–78. Taught at McLennan College, Waco, Texas, 1966–70; Artist in Residence, Northwood Institute, Cedar Hill, Texas, 1970–72; Director, Northwood Experimental Art Institute, Dallas, 1972–73; Assistant Professor of Art, North Texas State University, Denton, 1973–77. Recipient: National Endowment for the Arts Grants, 1973 and 1974. Agent: Elaine Horwitch Galleries, Santa Fe, New Mexico. Address: c/o Elaine Horwitch Galleries, 129 West Palace Avenue, Santa Fe, New Mexico 87501, U.S.A.

Individual Exhibitions:

1967 Baylor University, Waco, Texas
1970 Chapman Kelley Gallery, Dallas
1971 Chapman Kelley Gallery, Dallas
Kornblee Gallery, New York
1972 Smither Gallery, Dallas
Temple University, Philadelphia (with Bladen)
1973 Baylor University, Waco
University of St. Thomas, Houston
Austin College, Sherman, Texas
University of California at San Diego
1974 University of Texas at El Paso
Kornblee Gallery, New York
1975 Delahunty Gallery, Dallas
Laguna Gloria Art Museum, Austin, Texas
1976 Kornblee Gallery, New York
1978 Janus Gallery, Los Angeles
1984 Cultural Activities Center, Temple, Texas

Selected Group Exhibitions:

1966 *Annual Exhibition,* Dallas Museum of Fine Arts
1969 *Biennial,* New Orleans Museum of Art
Biennial, Whitney Museum, New York
1972 *Painting and Sculpture Today,* Indianapolis Museum of Art
1974 *12 Texans,* Contemporary Arts Museum, Houston
1975 *5 Artists,* North Texas State University, Denton
Texas Tough, White Museum, San Antonio, Texas
1976 *Photo Process as Medium,* Rutgers University, New Brunswick, New Jersey
1977 *Maps,* Museum of Modern Art, New York
1983 *Showdown,* Alternative Museum, New York

Collections:

Chase Manhattan Bank, New York; Illinois Bell Telephone Company, Chicago; Oklahoma Art Center, Oklahoma City; Witte Museum, San Antonio, Texas; Mountainview College, Dallas; Longview Museum, Longview, Texas; Centre Georges Pompidou, Paris; Groningen Museum, Netherlands.

Publications:

By WADE: article—"Visions of the City" in *D Magazine* (Dallas), October 1975.

On WADE: book—*Photo Process as Media,* exhibition catalogue, by Rosanne Truxes, New Brunswick, New Jersey 1976; articles—"Houston-Dallas Axis" by Janet Kutner in *Art in America* (New York), September/October 1972; "The Young Texans" by Jan Butterfield in *Arts Magazine* (New York), March 1973; "Contemporary Art in Texas" by Henry Hopkins in *Artnews* (New York), May 1973; "The ABC's of the Oak Cliff Four" by Josie Rabyor in *Southwest Art* (Austin, Texas), September 1973; "Texas Map" by Charlotte Moser in the *Houston Post,* October 1973; "Kick That Art Off Your Boots" by Josie Rabyor in *D Magazine* (Dallas), February 1975; "Texas" by Jane Kutner in *Artnews* (New York), Summer 1975; "Texas Ball and Chain Cult—112 Greene" by Mona da Vinci in *Soho Weekly News* (New York), September 1975.

At the beginning of his career Robert Wade was linked with the loosely-associated group of "Oak Cliff" artists, all of whom lived or worked in the same area of Dallas; they included such diverse members as Jim Roche (sculptor and conceptual artist) and Jack Mims (allegorical figurative painter who works in monumental scale). Although there are no formal resemblances among any of these artists, they do share similarities in approach and allusion, most noticeably in a proudly wry celebration of the state in which they all live. Wade is particularly drawn to the peccadillos for which Texas is (rightly or wrongly) known: a massive sense of both space and architectural size, and an undercurrent of cultivated violence and rawness which deliberately harks back to the early days of the American West.

Although this emphasis is overwhelmingly obvious, it would be the most popular of clichés to let it rest there. For Wade's work demonstrates a conceptual edge that takes it beyond regionalism, one which is frequently missed—or perhaps deliberately ignored—by many critics. For instance, national attention in America was first drawn to Wade's "Jumbo U.S. Map," a project that makes a cultural, rather than an aesthetic or political, statement. It is a work that is exactly what it says it is, an enormous recreation of the United States executed in earth, plywood, concrete and water and located just beside one of Dallas' busiest freeways. This project has had a precedent. The "Map of Texas," which, when completed in 1973, measured 40' x 40'. Although both the U.S. and Texas Maps are undoubtedly the most physically ambitious, other, smaller works are more important, and rely more heavily on a mixture of laden content and innovative form.

These are Wade's photo-emulsions on canvas, which operate as images frozen in time, frequently forcing the view to confront scenes of potential or actual violence. For Wade is at his best when he gives situations form—takes it, in effect, out of the *realm* of situation and makes it imagery. The best known of this series is entitled "Criminal Wall," in which we see large photos-on-canvas, loosely tacked to the wall, of such infamous and anti-heroic characters as Lee Harvey Oswald, Bonnie and Clyde, John Wesley Harding, and Pancho Villa, all "death-bed" portraits. They are all presented without comment, and are all the more powerful for that. In others, such as his series of postcard images, accompanied by texts from grade school textbooks, interior and landscape scenes are more complex, nostalgic, not self-consciously violent in the least but somehow sinister in their evocation of a past. This is true as well in his autobiographical work, which incorporated images of inanimate objects as well as human subjects—a piece which he terms "photographic projections on paper." Wade's obsessional sense of scale is much in evidence in this work, as it measures 30 feet long and 16 feet high, and requires fifteen hours of projection: yet there is also an idiosyncratic quality to this work, and to others, a calculated irony that stops short of exuberance.

—Jane Bell

WAGEMAKER, Jaap.
Dutch. Born Adriaan Barend in Haarlem, 6 January 1906; later adopted name Janus, then Jaap. Studied decorative arts, School voor Bouwkunde, Versierende Kunsten en Kunstambachten, Haarlem, 1920; mainly self-taught in painting. Married in 1943 (divorced, 1951): subsequently married Didi van der Meer. Painter: lived and worked in Haarlem, 1922–27, in Paris, 1927–45, and in Amsterdam, 1945–72; influenced by work of Alberto Burri and Antoni Tapies, from 1955; produced assemblage paintings, from 1960. Recipient: Premio Marzotto, Milan, 1960; Talensprijs, Amsterdam, 1962; Association Internationale des Critiques d'Art Prize, Section Pays-Bas, Luxembourg, 1965; Order van Oranje-Nassau, The Hague, 1966; Staatsprijs voor Beeldende Kunsten en Architectuur, The Hague, 1966; Gold Medal, *Biennale d'Arte Premio del Fiorino,* Florence, 1969. *Died* (in Amsterdam) *28 January 1972.*

Individual Exhibitions:

1937 Kunsthandel de Schakel, Rotterdam (with Loots)
1948 Kunstzaal Eekman, Velp, Netherlands (with Fred Sieger)
1949 International Cultureel Centrum, Amsterdam (with J. L. Muler and Mark Kolthoff)
1955 Havezathe Hagen, Doetinchem, Netherlands
Galerie Le Canard, Amsterdam
1955 Kunstcentrum 't Venster, Rotterdam
1957 Galerie C.C.C., Schiedam, Netherlands
Stedelijk Museum, Amsterdam
1958 Galerie Gunar, Dusseldorf
1959 Markisches Museum, Witten, West Germany
Städtische Kunsthalle, Recklinghausen, West Germany (with Jaap Mooy)
Galerie Gunar, Dusseldorf

Robert Wade: *El Paso*, 1974

1960 Galerie Orez, The Hague
Kunstring, Rotterdam
Galerie de Boog, Willemstadt, Curacoa, Dutch Antilles (travelled Cultureel Centrum, Aruba)
Galerie Gunar, Dusseldorf (with Gust Romijn)
1961 Galerie 20, Arnhem, Netherlands
1962 Ulmer Museum, Ulm, West Germany (with Dahmen and Cimiotti)
Galerie Aujourd'hui, Brussels (with Kees van Bohemen and J. J. Schoonhoven)
1963 Kunstzaal de Mangelgang, Groningen, Netherlands
Marlborough New London Gallery (with Woty Werner and Hans Jaenisch)
1964 Galerie Cauberg, Walkenburg, Netherlands
Galerie Magdalene Sothmann, Amsterdam
1965 Haags Gemeentemuseum, The Hague
Groninger Museum, Groningen, Netherlands
1966 Galerie Delta, Rotterdam
Bilder, Städtische Kunstgalerie, Bochum, West Germany
Galerie Magdalene Sothmann, Amsterdam
1967 Stedelijk Museum, Amsterdam
1969 Galerie Rg., Curacao, Dutch Antilles
Galerie Felison, Ijmuiden, Netherlands
Galerie Magdalene Sothmann, Amsterdam
1970 Galerie Wijngaard, Groningen
Cultureel Centrum, Venlo, Netherlands
Galerie Willy Schoots, Eindhoven, Netherlands
Galerie Felix, Maastricht, Netherlands
Galerie Nouvelles Images, The Hague
1971 Drienerhoord T.H. Twente, Enschede, Netherlands
1972 *Bilder—Materialbilder,* Kunsthalle, Bremen, West Germany
Overbeck-Gesellschaft, Lübeck
1973 De Zonnewijzer, Eindhoven, Netherlands
1975 Kunstenaarscentrum, Bergen, Netherlands

Selected Group Exhibitions:

1925 *Bloemstillevens,* Frans Halsmuseum, Haarlem
1928 *Kunst zij ons Doel,* Frans Halsmuseum, Haarlem (and regularly until 1940)
1932 *Kennemer Kunstenaars Kring,* Hotel de Prins, Velsen, Netherlands
1945 *Kunst in Vrijheid,* Rijksmuseum, Amsterdam
1959 *Niederlandische Kunst seit 1945,* Westfälischer Kunstverein, Münster, West Germany
1961 *Trends in Dutch Painting since Van Gogh,* National Gallery of Victoria, Melbourne (toured Australia)
1969 *Dutch Art Today,* Smithsonian Institution, Washington, D.C.
1971 *Europalia '71,* Palais des Beaux-Arts, Brussels
1972 *Kunst van 20th eeuw,* Museum Boymans-van Beuningen, Rotterdam

Collections:

Stedelijk Museum, Amsterdam; Museum Boymans-van Beuningen, Rotterdam; Haags Gemeentemuseum, The Hague; Stedelijk van Abbemuseum, Eindhoven, Netherlands; Städtische Kunstgalerie, Bochum, West Germany; Kunsthalle, Bremen, West Germany; Kunsthalle, Dusseldorf; Städtisches Museum Schloss Morsbroich, Leverkusen, West Germany; National Gallery of Victoria, Melbourne; Museum of Modern Art, New York.

Publications:

On WAGEMAKER: books—*The Art of Assemblage* by William C. Seitz, New York 1961; *Jaap Wagemaker's Informal Art* by C. Doleman, Amsterdam 1963; *Jaap Wagemaker,* exhibition folder, London 1963; *Jaap Wagemaker: Bilder,* exhibition catalogue, with text by Albert Schulze Vellinghausen, Bochum, West Germany 1966; *Jaap Wagemaker,* exhibition catalogue, with text by Jan Wolkers, Rotterdam 1966; *Jaap Wagemaker: Bilder—Material Bilder,* exhibition catalogue, with texts by Günter Busch and Albert Schulze Vellinghausen, Bremen, West Germany 1972; *Jaap Wagemaker* by A. M. Hammacher, Didi Wagemaker and others, Amsterdam 1975.

One of the outstanding Dutch artists of his generation, Jaap Wagemaker bridged an inherited Nordic mythological paganism with the instincts of a mystic. Basic to an understanding of his career is the interest in African art, which dates from the time he developed away from the tachisme of the Cobra Group and the romantic expressionism of his early work. He was to create one of the finest collections of African sculpture, from which he learned the qualities of non-subjective drama and tension.

A slow-starter, and a slow worker, Wagemaker waited until his 49th year before holding a one-man show, but he soon emerged as a unique talent, earning a recognition outside his native land. Stylistically he can be linked to the movement of *matiere* painting which swept through Europe, notably the Italian and Spanish schools, in the post-war period. Wagemaker never displayed the violence or bitter wit or the decorative playfulness which marks many painters in this group. He always retained the vigorous earthiness of his Dutch background, allied to a poetic inventiveness and an unfailing elegance.

His work most impressively conveys a sense of meditation, despite the heaviness of his chosen technique. This consisted of a surface composed of synthetic paint and fine sand, into which he would embody stones, shells, pieces of slate, wood, nails,

tubing and miscellaneous oddments. Despite the seeming nihilism of choice, or even assemblage, there is nothing of Dadaist shock, or calculated satire, in his work. His images of a primaeval, physical world emerge as formal, sensitive messages; it is the world of *Genesis,* elementary, primitive, unoccupied by man, or, possibly, a world long after man has disappeared. It is also a private world, where the artist exposes his vision but makes no effort to impose it. Here one finds an analogy with the African art he understood so well; there is no polite effort to establish a dialogue, to reduce poetic insight to the level of conversation. The African carvings, like Wagemaker's lunar-landscapes, speak of natural forces which cannot be fed to computers or reduced to scientific formulas. Nevertheless, Wagemaker's best paintings have a marked positivism; the meaning may be obscure, but there is nothing hesitant or left unstated.

—Charles Spencer

WALKER, John.

British. Born in Birmingham, 12 November 1939. Studied at Birmingham College of Art, 1956–60, and Académie de la Grande Chaumière, Paris, 1961–63. Painter and graphic artist, in London, 1964–70, in New York, since 1970, and in Melbourne, Australia, since 1980. Professor of Painting and Drawing, Cooper Union, New York, 1974–75; Visiting Professor, Yale University, New Haven, Connecticut, 1975–77; Artist-in-Residence, St. Catherines College, Oxford, 1977–78; Painting Tutor, Royal College of Art, London, 1974–78; Visiting Artist, Columbia University, New York, 1974–78; Artist-in-Residence, Prahran Technical College, Melbourne, 1980; Dean, Victoria College of the Arts, Melbourne, 1982–86. Recipient: Drawing Prize, Arts Council of Great Britain, 1960; Edwin Abbey travel scholarship, 1960; First Prize, National Young Artists Drawing Competition, *London,* 1960; Purchase Award, Arts Council, 1967; Gregory Fellowship, University of Leeds, 1967–69; Theodoron Award, 1969; Harkness Fellowship, 1970–72; First Prize, *International Prize Biennale,* Bradford, Yorkshire, 1974; First Prize, *John Moores Exhibition,* Liverpool, 1976; Guggenheim Fellowship, 1981. Agent: Nigel Greenwood Inc., 4 New Burlington Street, London W1, England; and Knoedler Gallery, 19 East 70th Street, New York, New York, U.S.A.

Individual Exhibitions:

1967 Axiom Gallery, London
1968 Park Square Gallery, Leeds
Axiom Gallery, London
Hayward Gallery, London
1969 City Art Gallery, Leeds
1970 Nigel Greenwood Inc., London
1971 Reese Palley Gallery, New York
1972 British Pavilion at the *Biennale,* Venice
Reese Palley Gallery, New York
Studio la Città, Verona
Ikon Gallery, Birmingham
Galerie Rolf Ricke, Cologne
1973 Nigel Greenwood Inc., London (2 shows)
Kunstverein, Hamburg
Städtisches Museum, Bochum, West Germany
Cunningham Ward Gallery, New York
Park Square Gallery, Leeds
1974 Museum of Modern Art, New York
Galerie Swart, Amsterdam
1975 Nigel Greenwood Inc., London
Cunningham Ward Gallery, New York
1976 Galerie Marguerite Lamy, Paris
Cunningham Ward Gallery, New York
Reed College, Portland, Oregon
1977 Powell Street Gallery, Melbourne
1978 Cunningham Ward Gallery, New York
Phillips Collection, Washington, D.C. (toured the United States)
Museum of Modern Art, New York
Art Gallery of New South Wales, Sydney
Nigel Greenwood Inc., London

John Walker: *Labyrinth IV*, 1980

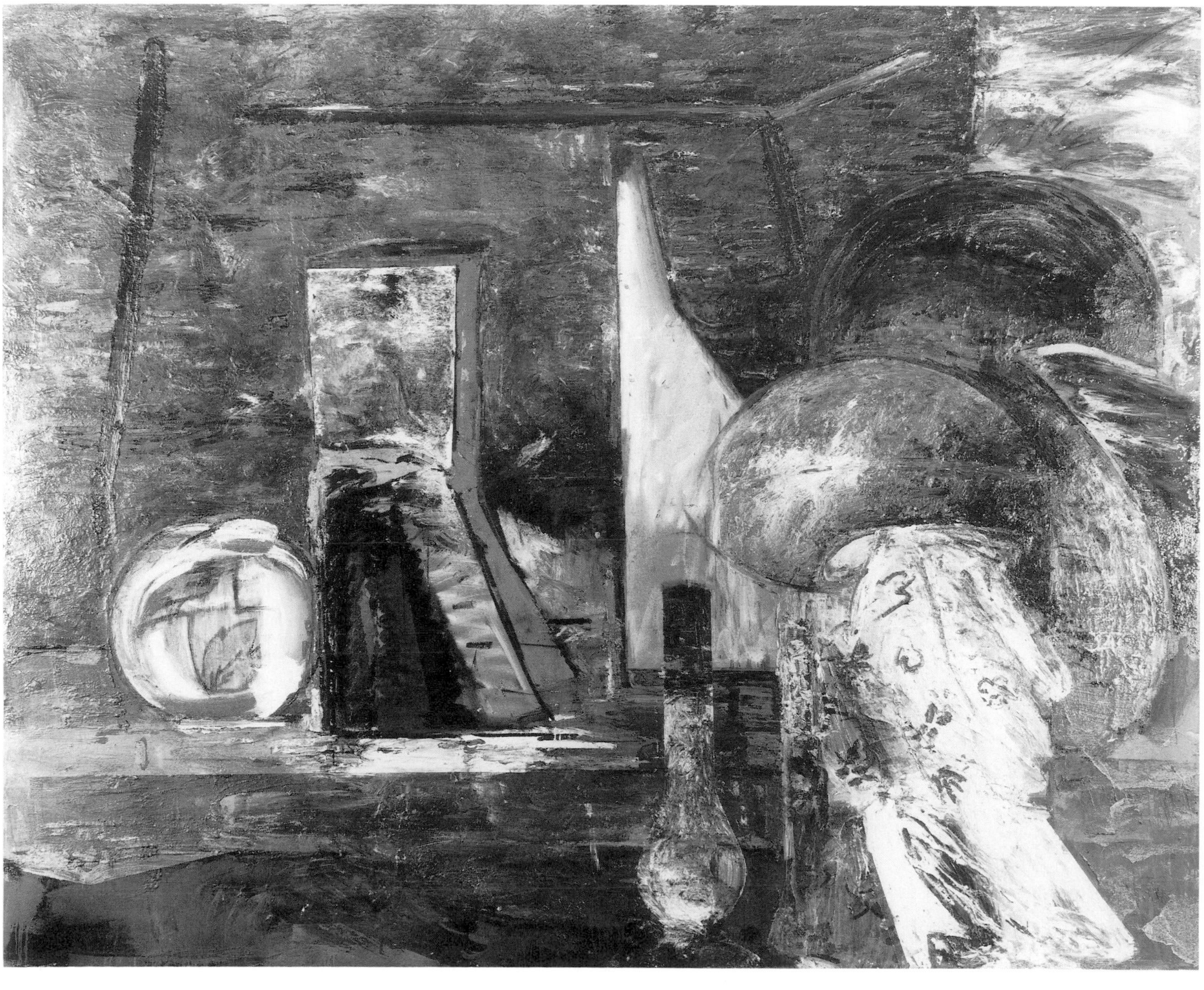

1979 University of Massachusetts, Amherst (travelled to Brown University, Providence, Rhode Island, and Brandeis University, Waltham, Massachusetts)
Powell Street Gallery, Melbourne
1980 Nigel Greenwood Inc., London (2 shows)
Betty Cunningham Gallery, New York
1981 *Drawings,* National Art Gallery, Wellington, New Zealand (travelled to Robert McDougall Art Gallery, Christchurch, Dunedin Public Art Gallery, and the City Art Gallery, Auckland)
Nigel Greenwood Inc., London
Theo Waddington Gallery, London
1982 Phillips Collection, Washington, D.C. (travelled to J. B. Speed Art Museum, Louisville, Kentucky)
1983 Madeleine Carter Gallery, Brookline, Massachusetts
M. Knoedler and Company, New York
1984 M. Knoedler and Company, New York
1985 Hayward Gallery, London (travelled to Ediburgh and Birmingham)
Tate Gallery, London
M. Knoedler, Zurich
1986 M. Knoedler and Company, New York
John Walker, at the *Adelaide Festival of Arts,* South Australia
1987 L. A. Louver Gallery, Venice, California
National Gallery of Victoria, Melbourne
Pamela Auchincloss Gallery, Santa Barbara, California
M. Knoedler and Company, New York

Selected Group Exhibitions:

1965 *John Moores Exhibition,* Walker Art Gallery, Liverpool (and 1974, 1976)
1968 *New British Painting and Sculpture,* University of California, Los Angeles
1970 *Contemporary Art in Britain,* National Museum of Modern Art, Tokyo
1973 *Towards Painting,* Tate Gallery, London
1975 *Color as Language,* Museum of Modern Art, New York (toured South America)
1977 *25 Years of British Painting,* Royal Academy of Art, London
1978 *Critic's Choice,* Institute of Contemporary Arts, London
1982 *Aspects of British Art Today,* Metropolitan Art Museum, Tokyo
1984 *The British Art Show,* City Art Gallery, Birmingham (and Ikon Gallery, Birmingham; travelled to Edinburgh, Sheffield, Southampton)
1987 *British Art 1900–80: The Modern Movement,* Royal Academy, London (travelled to Stuttgart)

Collections:

Arts Council of Great Britain, London; Tate Gallery, London; Victoria and Albert Museum, London; City Art Gallery, Leeds; Scottish National Gallery of Modern Art, Edinburgh; Ulster Museum, Belfast; Museum am Ostwall, Dortmund, West Germany; Museum of Modern Art, New York; Guggenheim Museum, New York; National Gallery of Art, Washington, D.C.

Publications:

By WALKER: article—"John Walker on His Painting: From a Conversation with Tim Hilton," in *Studio International* (London), June 1972.

On WALKER: books—*Contemporary Art in Britain,* exhibition catalogue, with text by Andrew Causey, Tokyo 1970; *36th Venice Biennale: British Pavilion—John Walker,* exhibition catalogue, with text by John Elderfield, London 1972; *Color as Language,* exhibition catalogue, with text by Kynaston McShine, New York 1975; *Arte Inglese Oggi,* exhibition catalogue, with text by Norbert Lynton and others, Milan 1976; *John Walker,* exhibition catalogue, with text by Andrew Forge, Washington, D.C. 1978; *Critic's Choice,* exhibition catalogue, with text by John McEwen, London 1978; *Drawings 1981: John Walker,* exhibition catalogue, with text by Anne Kirker, Wellington, New Zealand 1981; *John Walker,* exhibition catalogue, with text by Jack B. Flam, Washington, D.C. 1982; *John Walker: Paintings from the Alba and Oceania Series 1979–1984,* exhibition catalogue with introduction by Dore Ashton, London 1985; *John Walker: Prints 1976–84,* exhibition catalogue with text by Memory Holloway, London 1985; *John Walker: Salsipuedes Suite,* exhibition catalogue with text by Ted Gott, Melbourne 1987.

There is something powerfully disciplined about John Walker's ambitions as a painter. Conventional (in the strict modernist sense of the word), Walker's work has developed slowly over the last 15 years, re-working given sets of forms and spatial schemes bit by bit, slowly re-investing them with new expressive power. The tightness of this process of transformation, its reliance on narrow formal re-invention (or adjustment) rather than borrowing and re-working a broad-school of forms, forces criticism very much into a descriptive, defensive position. Although literary claims have been made for Walker's powerful shapes, Walker's art is more at home within modernist historicism—Manet, Cézanne, Matisse, Pollock. The artist's job is to find his place within that history, to enter into a dialogue with—to measure himself against—the best work of the past. As a modern equivalent of l'art pour l'art this assumes a kind of assertiveness against the modern world. Walker has talked about the "monastic" challenge of being an artist.

Walker's development can be divided into three phases. A period of geometric abstraction, which introduces the awkward shapes (the lozenges, the pinched-in figures) that reappear in all his work. Here the shapes free-float in an atmospheric, non-illusionist space. A period of cubist collage, represented by the monumental "Juggernauts" series, which introduces into a "built" architectural space tentative figure-ground relations. The shapes here are jagged and the surface rough, ugly, which is to become a strong feature of the later work. And a period of "illusionistic" picture building, represented by the "Numinous" balcony series (a motif borrowed from Matisse and Cézanne), the "Labyrinths" series, and the recent drawings, which introduce a quasi-figurative or fictive space.

This new work makes explicit what has been—in varying degrees—the basis of Walker's art: the tension between our awareness of paintings as containers and windows.

The key to this explicitness is Walker's self-conscious re-working of elements from certain modernist (and proto-modernist) works such as Velasquez's "Las Meninas," which, as a paradigm for the artifice of picture making, becomes the perfect model for Walker's own concerns. In Walker's latest drawings, based on "Las Meninas," the re-worked forms of the painting reappear within the work as a mirror image. Walker's figure of the artist (the dwarf in "Las Meninas") looks across at a screen/canvas containing its own image. The depth of space that Walker introduced into the "Labyrinths" is here given a further illusionistic opening out.

This opening out—the transformation of shapes into what might be called images—may not, in any crucial sense, represent a change in outlook (an opening onto the world), but it undoubtedly brings with it an increased sense of esprit or quirkiness, something that seems to be at the basis of Walker's search for shapes that "irritate" the eye, that remain in the memory long after the details of the painting have been forgotten.

—John Roberts

WALL, Brian.

British. Born in London, 5 September 1931. Studied at Luton College of Art, Bedfordshire, 1949–50. Sculptor: worked as glass-blower, 1945–50; moved to Paris, 1952, to London, 1953, and to St. Ives, Cornwall, 1955, where he worked as an assistant to Barbara Hepworth, 1955–58; visited New York, 1969, and spent several months of each year in California, 1969–73. Lecturer, Ealing College of Art, London, 1961–62; Principal Lecturer, Central School of Arts and Design, London, 1962–72. Visiting Lecturer, 1969–73, Lecturer, 1973–75, and since 1975, Assistant Professor, University of California, Berkeley. Agent: Braunstein/Quay Gallery, 560 Sutter Street, San Francisco, California 94102. Address: 52 Princedale Road, London W11, England.

Individual Exhibitions:

1958 Drian Gallery, London
1959 Woodstock Gallery, London
1960 AIA Gallery, London (with Joe Tilson and Anthony Benjamin)
1961 Drian Gallery, London
1962 Grabowski Gallery, London (with Anthony Benjamin)
1963 Manchester City Art Gallery
1964 Grabowski Gallery, London
1966 Grosvenor Gallery, London
1967 Arnolfini Gallery, Bristol
1968 Grosvenor Gallery, London
1971 William Sawyer Gallery, San Francisco
1973 San Jose State University Art Gallery, California
1974 Quay Gallery, San Francisco
St. Mary's College, Morago, California
1976 Braunstein/Quay Gallery, San Francisco
Dootson/Calderhead Gallery, Seattle
University of Nevada, Las Vegas
1981 Max Hutchinson Gallery, New York
1982 Seattle Art Museum, Washington
1983 San Francisco Museum of Modern Art

Selected Group Exhibitions:

1958 *Contemporary British Sculpture,* Arts Council Gallery, London
1961 *Biennale,* Paris
1963 *British Art Today,* San Francisco Museum of Art (toured the United States)
1965 *Sculpture in the 60's,* Tate Gallery, London
1966 *Sculpture 1960–1966,* Battersea Park, London
1971 *6 x 6 x 6,* Richmond Art Center, California
1975 *Bay Area Sculpture,* James Willis Gallery, San Francisco
1976 *American Sculptors,* University of Texas, Dallas
1979 *Apsects of Abstract,* Crocker Art Museum, Sacramento, California
1982 *One Hundred Years of California Sculpture,* Oakland Museum, California

Collections:

Tate Gallery, London; Contemporary Art Society, London; Arts Council of Great Britain, London; Whitworth Art Gallery, Manchester; Penwyth Society, St. Ives, Cornwall; Museum of Art, Dublin; Billy Rose Sculpture Garden, Jerusalem; University of California at Berkeley; Oakland Museum, California; Gallery of New South Wales, Sydney.

Publications:

By WALL: articles—statement in *Architectural Design* (London), May 1959; statement in *Brian Wall,* exhibition catalogue, Bristol 1967; statement in *Sculpture International* (Oxford), October 1969.

On WALL: book—*Brian Wall,* exhibition catalogue with texts by Peter Selz and George W. Neubert, Seattle 1982; articles—"Brian Wall: Sculpture of Simplicity" by Charles Spencer in *Studio International* (London), March 1966; "London Show Offers Brian Wall Sculpture" by Charles Spencer in *New York Times International Edition,* 30 April 1966; "Sculpture To See All At Once" by Christopher Andreae in *Christian Science Monitor* (Boston), 30 November 1966; "Question and Artist: Brian Wall" by G. S. Whittet in *Sculpture International* (Oxford), October 1969; "Unusual Art in San Francisco" by Thomas Albright in the *San Francisco Chronicle,* 7 January 1974; "Monumental Sculpture"

Brian Wall: *Kingfisher*, 1974

by Thomas Albright in the *San Francisco Chronicle,* 16 January 1974; "The Fitness of Form" by Robert McDonald in *Artweek* (Oakland, California), February 1976.

A sculptor of outstanding qualities, Brian Wall has never found his true niche in the post-war British sculptural scene. Like Caro he is a teacher of special qualifications, and in Britain and America has exerted considerable influence on younger generations. His character and work are somewhat paradoxical, typically romantic in the English sense, yet preferring to condition intuitive, gestural elements within a severe discipline. Younger than Caro and Adams (his closest English colleagues), Wall has in some sense been more radical, working on large, simple steel structures when Caro was still involved in Richier-like symbols of the human form.

Wall is virtually self-taught, having taken part-time courses in art whilst serving in the Royal Air Force. A six-month stay in Paris made a decisive impression, notably admiration for Mondrian which led to detailed study of the Russian Constructivists, the Dutch de Stijl and Moholy-Nagy. The second major step in his development was a move to St. Ives, where he first worked in restaurants. Acquaintance with the local art colony led to an introduction to the late Barbara Hepworth, who engaged him as an assistant.

By 1956 he had digested all these various influences and trained himself to work in stone, wood, plaster and metal. His work at this time was distinctly Mondrianesque (painted wood boxes), but he soon switched to metal. The ethics and aims of de Stijl have remained pre-eminent in Wall's career, hence his insistence on large-scale, and his preference for public sculpture. His strength lies in an assured capacity to handle monumental proportions without over-complicating the design, retaining an impressive sense of power and drama. The sculptures are variations on a few limited shapes—flat panels, square or circular, tubular arms, four-sided boxes; this limited vocabulary is juggled with syntactic ingenuity, never reduced to the decorative or comforting. He has never favoured colour in sculpture, preferring black or white to emphasize the shapes, to stress their simplicity.

—Charles Spencer

WALTHER, Franz Erhard.

German. Born in Fulda, 22 July 1939. Studied at the Hochschule für Bildende Künste, Frankfurt, 1959–61, and the Kunstakademie, Dusseldorf, 1962–64. Married Johanna Friess in 1964; sons: Moritz and Lehmann. Worked in soap factory, Dusseldorf, 1966–67, and in bakery, New York, 1967–69. Independent artist, Dusseldorf, 1965–67, New York 1967–71, and in Hamburg, since 1971. Professor, Hochschule für Bildenden Künste, Hamburg, since 1970. Recipient: Gunter Fruhtrunk Prize, Munich, 1986. Agents: Reinhard Onnasch, Fasanenstrasse 47, 1000 Berlin 15 (West); Galerie Achim Kubinski, Olgastrasse 109, 7000 Stuttgart 1. Address: c/o Hochschule für Bildende Künste, Lerchenfeld 2, 2000 Hamburg 76, West Germany.

Individual Exhibitions:

1966 Neue Galerie, Aachen, West Germany
1967 Galerie Heiner Friedrich, Munich
Staatliche Kunstakademie, Dusseldorf
1968 Galerie Rudolf Zwirner, Cologne
1969 Galerie Heiner Friedrich, Munich
Galerie Rudolf Zwirner, Cologne
Galerie Neuendorf, Hamburg
Studio F, Ulm, West Germany
Museum Haus Lange, Krefeld, West Germany
Kunsthalle, Dusseldorf
Museum of Modern Art, New York
1970 Kunstverein, Hamburg
1971 Hessisches Landesmuseum, Darmstadt
Galerie Heiner Friedrich, Cologne
Kunstverein, Frankfurt
Galerie Heiner Friedrich, Munich
1972 Kunsthalle, Tübingen
Videogalerie Gerry Schum, Dusseldorf
Museum Haus Lange, Krefeld, West Germany
Kaiser-Wilhelm-Museum, Krefeld, West Germany
Stedelihk Van Abbemuseum, Eindhoven, Netherlands
1973 Vanier College, Montreal
Kabinett für Aktuelle Kunst, Bremerhaven, West Germany
Kunstverein, Freiburg
Hessisches Landesmuseum, Darmstadt
Galerie Heiner Friedrich, Munich (2 exhibitions)
1974 Kaiser-Wilhelm-Museum, Krefeld, West Germany
Galerie Klein, Bonn
1975 Galerie Repassage, Warsaw
Kabinett für Aktuelle Kunst, Bremerhaven, West Germany
1976 *Diagramme zum 1. Werksatz,* Kunstraum, Munich
Städtisches Museum, Bonn
Kunstverein, Frankfurt
1977 Kunsthalle, Baden-Baden, West Germany
Heiner Friedrich Gallery, New York
Wallraf-Richartz Museum, Cologne
German Pavilion, at the *Bienal,* Sao Paulo
Centro de Arte y Comunicacion, Buenos Aires
Galerie Heiner Friedrich, Cologne
1978 *Arbeiten 1954–1963 aus der Sammlung Seng,* Städtisches Museum, Fulda, West Germany
Kabinett für Aktuelle Kunst, Bremerhaven, West Germany
Hessisches Landesmuseum, Darmstadt
1979 Stadtische Galerie im Lenbachhaus, Munich
1980 *Gegensatzpaare und Unterscheidungen im Werk,* Kunstverein, St. Gallen, Switzerland
Arbeiten 1969–1963, Kunstmuseum, Bonn
1981 *Handlung Werk,* Nationalgalerie, West Berlin
Produzentgalerie, Hamburg
1982 *Werkzeichnungen,* Museum Haus Lange, Krefeld, West Germany
Galerie Klein, Bonn
Badischer Kunstverein, Karlsruhe
Kunstraum, Munich
Galerie Schiessel, Munich
Galerie Kubinski, Stuttgart
Kunsthalle, Wilhelmshaven, West Germany
Galerie Carinthia, Klagenfurt, Austria
Overbeckgesellschaft, Lübeck
Galerie Edition E, Munich
Galerie Schiessel, Munich
Kunsthalle, Wilhelmshaven, West Germany
Galerie Carinthia, Klagenfurt, Austria
1983 Galerie Schöttle, Munich (with A. Oehlen)
Ausstellungsraum Fettstrasse, Hamburg
1984 Raum für Kunst, Hamburg
Galerie Haderek, Stuttgart
Kabinett für Aktuelle Kunst, Bremerhaven, West Germany
Galerie Onnasch, West Berlin
Galerie Lock, St. Gallen, Switzerland
Van Abbemuseum, Eindhoven, Netherlands
Ulmer Museum, Ulm, West Germany
1985 Wilhelm-Hack-Museum, Ludwigshafen, West Germany
Institut für moderne Kunst, Nuremberg, West Germany
Galerie Reckermann, Cologne
Ausstellungsraum, Fulda, West Germany
Galerie Maria Wilkens/Dorit Jacobs, Cologne
Galerie Loehrl, Mönchengladbach, West Germany
Kunstverein, Bremerhaven, West Germany
Städtische Galerie, Nordhorn, West Germany
1986 Galerie Carinthia, Klagenfurt, Austria
Kunstverein, Braunschweig, West Germany
Kunstverein, Frankfurt
Galerie Achim Kubinski, Stuttgart
Galerie Tilly Haderek, Stuttgart
Gutenbergstrasse 62, Stuttgart
Galerie Annette Gmeiner, Kirchzarten, West Germany
Galerie Desluis, The Hague
1987 Galerie Edition E, Munich
Galerie Schiessel, Munich
Galerie Hufkens-de Lathuy, Brussels
Kunsthalle, Winterthur, Switzerland
Galerie Onnasch, West Berlin

Selected Group Exhibitions:

1969 *When Attitudes Become Form,* Kunsthalle, Berne (toured Europe)
1972 *Documenta 5,* Museum Fridericianum, Kassel, West Germany (and *Documenta 7,* 1982; *Documenta 8,* 1987)
1974 *Projekt 74,* Kunsthalle, Cologne

1977 *Pejling af tysk kunst*, Louisiana Museum, Humlebaek, Denmark
1979 *30 Jahre Kunst in der Bundersrepublik Deutschland*, Kunstmuseum, Bonn
1980 *Zeichnungen der 50er, 60er und 70er Jahre*, Museum Haus Lange, Krefeld, West Germany
1981 *Art Allemagne Aujourd hui*, Musée d'Art Moderne de la Ville, Paris
1983 *Skulptur und Farbe*, Gesellschaft für Aktuelle Kunst, Bremen, West Germany
1985 *Kunst in der Bundersrepublik 1945–85*, Nationalgalerie, West Berlin
1986 *Wild, Visionary, Spectral: New German Art*, Art Gallery of South Australia, Adelaide (travelled to the New Zealand National Art Gallery, Wellington)

Collections:

Nationalgalerie, West Berlin; Kunsthalle, Hamburg; Kunstmuseum, Bonn; Kunstmuseum, Dusseldorf; City of Frankfurt; Wallraf-Richartz Museum/Museum Ludwig, Cologne; Kaiser-Wilhelm Museum, Krefeld, West Germany; Hessisches Landemuseum, Darmstadt; Staatsgalerie, Stuttgart; Stedelijk Van Abbemuseum, Eindhoven, Netherlands.

Publications:

By WALTHER: books—*Leihobjekte*, Aachen, West Germany, 1966; *Information*, Dusseldorf 1967; *Objekte, Benutzen*, with photos by Barbara Brown, Cologne and New York 1968; *Tagebuch: Museum of Modern Art, New York, 28 December 1969 bis 1 Marz 1970*, Cologne 1971; *Prozessmaterial*, Cologne and Darmstadt 1971; *Proportionen*, with Ingrid Krupka, Cologne 1971; *Frank Erhard Walther: Werkmonographie, Arbeiten 1955–1963, Material zum 1, Werksatz 1963–1969*, edited by Gotz Adriani, with an interview by Ursula Meyer, texts by others, Cologne 1972; *Franz Erhard Walther: Werksatz*, Montreal 1973; *Franz Erhard Walther: Zeitbezogen/Raumbezogen/Personenbezogen/Handlungsbezogen*, Munich 1979; *Franz Erhard Walther: Hauptworte/Werkbegriffe*, Hannover 1981; *Franz Erhard Walther: 40 Sockel*, with an interview by Michael Lingner, Munich 1982; *Franz Erhard Walther: 30 x Werkbau*, Munich 1982; *Franz Erhard Walther: 2 Arbeiten—35 Werke*, Wilhelmshaven, West Germany 1982; *Organon: Feldbuch*, Klagenfurt 1983; *Zwischen Kern und Mantel*, with Michael Lingner, Klagenfurt 1985; *Organon 2*, Klagenfurt 1987; *Gelenke im Raum*, Stuttgart 1987; *Franz Erhard Walther: Wortwerke*, Klagenfurt 1987.

On WALTHER: books—*Deutsche Kunst der 60er Jahre* by Jurgen Morschel, Munich 1972; *Franz Erhard Walther: Fruhe Arbeiten 1955–1963*, exhibition catalogue, with text by Paul Wember, Krefeld, West Germany 1972; *Bis Heute* by Karin Thomas, Cologne 1972; *Franz Erhard Walther*, exhibition catalogue, with texts by Argibald Buys, Oda den Boer, Wies Leering, and Jerven Ober, Eindhoven, Netherlands 1972; *Objekte Kunst* by Karin Thomas, Cologne 1972; *Geschichte der Collage* by Herta Wescher and Karin Thomas, Cologne 1974; *Franz Erhard Walther: Diagramme zum 1, Werksatz*, exhibition catalogue, with texts by Hermann Kern and Carl Vogel, Munich 1976; *Franz Erhard Walther: 2, Werksatz: Skulpturen, Zeichnungen*, exhibition catalogue, with texts by Evelyn Weiss and Dieter Ronte, and an interview by Georg Jappe, Cologne 1977; *International Biennale Sao Paulo: Franz Erhard Walther*, exhibition catalogue, with texts by Gotz Adriani and Carl Vogel, Cologne 1977; *Kunstlerlexicon von 1945 bis zur Gegenwart* by Karin Thomas and Gerd de Vries, Cologne 1977; *Franz Erhard Walther: Arbeiten 1954–1963 aus der Sammlung Seng*, exhibition catalogue, with texts by Gilbert Seng and Carl Vogel, Fulda, West Germany 1978; *Strukturen Zeitgenossische* Kunst by Ingrid Burgbacher-Krupka, Stuttgart 1979; *Franz Erhard Walther: Gegenstazpaare und Unterscheidungen im Werk*, exhibition catalogue, with text by Dietrich Helms, St. Gallen, Switzerland 1980; *Franz Erhard Walther: Arbeiten 1969–1963*, exhibition catalogue, with texts by Dirk Stemmler, Gisbert Seng and Karl Otto Gotz, Bonn 1980; *Franz Erhard Walther: Handlung Werk*, exhibition catalogue, with text by Michael Pauseback, West Berlin 1981; *Franz Erhard Walther*, exhibition catalogue, with text by Dietrich Helms, Hamburg 1981; *Franz Erhard Walther: Werkzeichnungen*, with a foreword by Gerhard Storck and Marianne Stockebrand, Krefeld, West Germany 1982; *Der Walther-Raum in der Hamburger Kunsthalle*, with text by Achim Lipp, Hamburg 1983; *Franz Erhard Walther: Words 1978–1984*, exhibition catalogue with text by Rudi Fuchs, Eindhoven 1984; *Der 1, Werksatz (1963–69) von Franz Erhard Walther*, with text by Barbara Grotkamp-Schepers, Darmstadt 1985; *Franz Erhard Walther: gesehen gehort gedacht*, with text by Gisbert Seng, Fulda 1985; *Franz Erhard Walther—Ort und Richtung angeben: Zeichnungen 1957–1984*, with texts by Gottfried Boehm, Marianne Stockebrand and Rudi Fuchs, Klagenfurt 1985; *Franz Erhard Walther*, exhibition catalogue by Kurt Muenger, Winterthur 1987.

From the very beginning I had an interest in work processes. In any event the emphasis on process is stronger than that on form. 1958–59: quantities of drawings arise from processes: movements like writing from the top to the bottom or from left to right. Superimpositions, coverings—yet readable as a process. The formlessness of these works had for me the character of a manifesto. From 1960 to 1963 there were extensive work composites resulting from material processes. Material and process—the material process—become decisive for the work. Material is not used for something but is itself the subject. At the same time I worked with extremely simple forms without using hierarchies and meanings. "Meaninglessness" was a challenge to oneself to construct meanings in one's activity. Therein lay the invitation to spontaneous action. This motive of operation and then action as an element of the work became the main theme. The determinant basic idea was to construct a work from action. These works originated in 1963. Action is a form of work. The operative has to answer for the work. He is involved not only optically but also with the whole body. All abilities are required. It is a total performance. Man could construct works in other, more extensive ways than were previously possible. Naturally then several people also appear in the development of the work. That is complex construction.

In the alternative work concept there are central concepts such as place, time, space, interior-exterior, body, field, direction, construction, among others, and the possibility to alter historic significance. And thereby a new concept of material has become necessary. For example language, body, space, place, action are material like wood and stone to the traditional sculptor. Spaces, performance areas, action areas, concepts and methods of work should be found which extend the dimensions of earlier means of expression.

—Franz Erhard Walther

Franz Erhard Walther: *Drei Saulen Gelb*, 1985

WARHOL, Andy.

American. Born in McKeesport, Pennsylvania, 6 August 1928. Studied at Carnegie Institute of Technology, Pittsburgh, 1945–49. Worked as illustrator for *Glamour Magazine*, New York, 1949–50, and as a commercial artist, New York, 1950–57. Independent artist, New York, 1957 until his death in 1987: concentrated on making paintings derived from strip comics and advertisements, 1960–61; first silkscreen paintings, 1962; first films, mainly with Paul Morrissey, 1963. Editor, *Inter/View* magazine, New York. Recipient: Art Directors Club of New York Medal for shoe advertisements, 1957; 6th Film Culture Award, New York, 1964; *Los Angeles Film Festival* Award, 1964. *Died* (in New York) *22 February 1987.*

Individual Exhibitions:

1952 Hugo Gallery, New York
1956 Bodley Gallery, New York (and 1957, 1958, 1959)
1962 Ferus Gallery, Los Angeles
Stable Gallery, New York
1963 Ferus Gallery, New York
1964 Leo Castelli Gallery, New York
Stable Gallery, New York
Galerie Sonnabend, Paris
1965 Leo Castelli Gallery, New York

Andy Warhol: ***Mao Tse-Tung*****, 1970**

Galerie Sonnabend, Paris
Galerie Rubbers, Buenos Aires
Galerie M. E. Thelen, Essen
Gian Enzo Sperone Arte Moderna, Milan
Institute of Contemporary Art, Philadelphia
Galerie Buren, Stockholm
Jerrold Morris International Gallery, Toronto
Gian Enzo Sperone Arte Moderna, Turin

1966 Galerie M. E. Thelen, Essen
Gian Enzo Sperone Arte Moderna, Milan
Institute of Contemporary Art, Boston
Contemporary Arts Center, Cincinnati, Ohio
Galerie Hans Neuendorf, Hamburg
Ferus Gallery, Los Angeles
Leo Castelli Gallery, New York

1957 Galerie Rudolf Zwirner, Cologne
Galerie Sonnabend, Paris

1968 Galerie Rudolf Zwirner, Cologne
Stedelijk Museum, Amsterdam
Galerie der Spiegel, Cologne
Rowan Gallery, London
Galerie Heiner Friedrich, Munich
Kunsternes, Oslo
Moderna Museet, Stockholm

1969 Neue Nationalgalèrie der Staatlichen Museen Preussischer Kulturbesitz, West Berlin
Irvin Blum Gallery, Los Angeles
Leo Castelli Gallery, New York

1970 Galerie Folker Skulima, West Berlin
Museum of Contemporary Art, Chicago
Stedelijk van Abbemuseum, Eindhoven, Netherlands
Musée d'Art Moderne de la Ville, Paris
Pasadena Museum of Art, California (toured the Untied States and Europe)

1971 Galerie Bruno Bischofberger, Zurich
Gotham Book Mart Gallery, New York
Institute of Contemporary Arts, London
Musée d'Art Moderne, Paris

1972 Castelli Downtown Gallery, New York
Multiples Gallery, New York

1973 Margo Leavin Gallery, Los Angeles

1974 Mayor Gallery, London
Musée Galliera, Paris

1975 Baltimore Museum of Art

1976 Wurttembergischer Kunstverein, Stuttgart (travelled to Kunsthalle, Dusseldorf)

1980 *Andy Warhol: Photos,* Lisson Gallery, London

1981 *Portrait Screenprints 1965–1980,* Gloucestershire College of Arts and Technology, Cheltenham, England

1982 Galerie Schellmann und Kluser, Munich
Stadtische Galerie im Lenbachhaus, Munich
Galerie Daniel Templon, Paris

1983 Fraenkel Gallery, San Francisco
American Museum of Natural History, New York
Museum of Natural History, Cleveland, Ohio

1984 Scottsdale Center for the Arts, Arizona
Edition Schellmann und Kluser, Munich
Flow Ace Gallery, Los Angeles
Judith Goldberg Gallery, New York
Galerie Kammer, Hamburg
Galerie Schellmann und Kluser, Munich

1985 Museo di Capodimonte, Naples, Italy

1986 Galerie Daniel Templon, Paris
Edition Schellmann, Munich
Anthony D'Offay Gallery, London

1987 Galerie Bernd Kluser, Munich
Galerie Thaddaeus Ropac, Salzburg, Austria
Robert Miller Gallery, New York
Waddington Galleries, London
Kunstverein, Hamburg

1988 Galerie Bernd Kluser, Munich

Selected Group Exhibitions:

1956 *Recent Drawings USA,* Museum of Modern Art, New York

1962 *New Paintings of Common Objects,* Pasadena Museum of Art, California

1964 *American Pop Art,* Stedelijk Museum, Amsterdam

1966 *11 Pop Artists: The New Image,* Galerie M. E. Thelen, Essen, West Germany

1968 *Documenta 4,* Museum Fridericianum, Kassel, West Germany

1970 *De Giotto à Warhol,* Musée d'Art Moderne de la Ville, Paris

1977 *Paris-New York,* Centre Georges Pompidou, Paris

1981 *A New Spirit in Painting,* Royal Academy of Arts, London

1983 *Modern Art in the West,* Metropolitan Art Museum, Tokyo

1985 *Painterly Visions 1940–84,* Guggenheim Museum, New York

Collections:

Museum of Modern Art, New York; Whitney Museum, New York; Coreoran Gallery of Art, Washington, D.C.; Walker Art Center, Minneapolis; County Museum of Art, Los Angeles; Norton Simon Museum of Art, Pasadena, California; Art Gallery of Ontario, Toronto; Tate Gallery, London; Moderna Museet, Stockholm.

Publications:

By WARHOL: books—*Andy Warhol's Index Book,* New York 1967; *A: A Novel,* New York 1968; *Andy Warhol: Transcript of David Bailey's ATV Documentary,* London 1972; *A to B and Back Again,* London and New York 1975; *Ladies and Gentlemen,* Milan 1975; *Andy Warhol: Photographs,* portfolio of 12 photos, New York and Zurich 1980; *Popism: The Warhol 60s,* with Pat Hackett, New York 1980, London 1981; *Andy Warhol: Schweizer Portraits,* with text by George J. Dolezal, Thun 1982; *Andy Warhol's Children's Book,* Zurich 1983; *America,* New York 1985; articles—"My Favorite Superstar: Notes of My Epic, Chelsea Girls," interview with Gerard Malanga in *Arts* (New York), February 1967; "Andy Warhol Tapes Roman Polanski" in *Inter/View* (New York), November 1973; "Andy Warhol: Interview" in *Photo* (Paris), May 1979; "Warhol: Mon Carnet Mondain" in *Photo* (Paris), March 1980; films—*Kiss,* 1973; *Tarzan and Jane Regained Sort Of,* 1963; *Dance Movie,* also known as *Roller Skate,* 1963; *Haircut,* 1963; *Eat,* 1964; *Blow Job,* 1963–64; *Batman Dracula,* 1964; *Empire,* 1964, *Henry Geldzahler,* 1964; *Soap Opera,* also known as *The Lester Persky,* 1964; *Couch,* 1964; *Shoulder,* 1964; *Mario Banana,* 1964; *Harlot,* 1964; *13 Most Beautiful Women,* 1964–65; *13 Most Beautiful Boys,* 1964–65; *30 Fantastics and 50 Personalities,* 1964–66; *Ivy and John,* 1965; *Suicide,* 1965; *Screen Test 1,* 1965; *Screen Test 2,* 1965; *The Life of Juanita Castro,* 1965; *Drunk,* 1965; *Horse,* 1965; *Poor Little Rich Girl,* 1965; *Vinyl,* 1965; *Bitch,* 1965; *Restaurant,* 1965; *Kitchen,* 1965; *Prison,* 1965; *Face,* 1965; *Afternoon,* 1965; *Beauty 2,* 1965; *Space,* 1965; *Outer and Inner Space,* 1965; *My Hustler,* 1965; *Camp,* 1965; *Paul Swan,* 1965; *Hedy,* also known as *Hedy the Shoplifter* and *The 14 Year Old Girl,* 1965; *The Closet,* 1965; *More Milk, Evette,* also known as *Lana Turner,* 1965; *Lupe,* 1965; *Bufferin,* also known as *Gerard Malanga Reads Poetry,* 1966; *Eating Too Fast,* 1966; *The Velvet Underground,* 1966; *Chelsea Girls,* 1966;****also known as *Four Stars,* 1966–67; *International Velvet,* segment of****, 1967; *Alan and Dickin,* segment of****, 1967; *Imitation of Christ,* segment of ****, 1967; *Gerard Has His Hair Removed with Nair,* segment of ****, 1967; *Alan and Apple,* segment of ****, 1967; *Bike Boy,* 1967; *Nude Restaurant,* 1967; *Lonesome Cowboys,* 1967; *Blue Movie,* 1969; *Schraff's Commercial,* 1969.

On WARHOL: books—*The Painter and the Photograph: From Delacroix to Warhol* by Van Deren Coke, Albuquerque, New Mexico, 1964, 1972; *Andy Warhol* by John Coplans, Pasadena, California 1970; *Andy Warhol* by Rainer Crone, London 1970; *The Autobiography and Sex Life of Andy Warhol* by John Wilcock, New York 1971; *Andy Warhol: Films and Paintings* by Peter Gidal, New York 1971; *Voglio essere una macchina: la fotografia di Andy Warhol* by Paolo Barozzi, Milan 1979; *Andy Warhol: Works 1962–1986,* exhibition catalogue with texts by William Milie, Stuart Morgan, David Hockney and others, Salzburg 1986; *Andy Warhol: Reversal Series,* exhibition catalolgue, London 1987; *Andy Warhol Photographs,* exhibition catalogue with text by Stephen Koch, New York 1987.

At a time when enigma is one of the most sought after of aesthetic virtues, Andy Warhol has achieved the difficult feat of remaining the most enigmatic artist of all. Since he first became known at the beginning of the Pop Art boom in the early 1960's, critics and public have argued about him, dismissed him, reinstated him again, endlessly questioned him and in the absence of any useful statement by the artist himself, declared themselves baffled by the bland success of his art.

Yet, of all post-war artists, Warhol made the most obvious breaks from past traditions and displayed the most single-minded consistency. His art can be seen for what it is only by stepping aside from our current assumptions about art and understanding the logic of his point of view.

The Pop Art movement started as a reaction against the success and high seriousness of Abstract Expressionism. As Roy Lichtenstein said, "We wanted to paint pictures so outrageous and ugly that no one would want to buy them." So the chosen subject matter was figurative (heresy!), commercial (but it's not Art) and frequently humorous (please don't laugh in the art gallery). But within two or three years, the Pop Artists found that they were as successful as their predecessors, and, what is more, that it was nice to be rich. As overdrafts disappeared though, so did invention and humour, and most of the artists settled down into comfortable lives making innumerable versions of their successful styles. But not Warhol.

Warhol was a much more sophisticated and analytical thinker than most artists, whose imaginations usually terminate at the end of their paint-brushes. He was aware of the pressure of success, of the danger of becoming an institution, but where most artists react to this by trying to fight it, Warhol decided to make success and being an institution his art form. Art had been manipulated by the art-world, the critics, dealers and collectors long enough; now Warhol was going to use them as his canvas.

His first successful work consisted of sculpture in the form of Campbell's Soup Cans and Brillo Boxes, and screenprinted paintings of contemporary icons from Elvis Presley to Jackie Kennedy, which he made with the assistance of the helpers in his Factory, as his large studio was called. These works immediately raised two important questions: did it matter that the works were not unique? and did it matter that Warhol himself had not actually made them? The critics and dealers, who were riding on the wave of newness and originality that they themselves had created, had to go along with the artist and the collectors dutifully followed.

Was his work, then, the huge confidence risk that the general public suspects all "modern art" to be? Yes, and No. Yes, because Warhol was deliberately attacking all the sacred shibboleths of art, and No, because the art itself was undeniably "good" and highly influential. The effect of Warhol pointing to commercial art as a source of visual energy and his use of violent colour overlays in his screenprints can be seen in every art college, every fashion magazine in the Western world. In purely visual terms he affected the language of art more than anyone else of his generation.

The critics would have been content to leave it at that, but Warhol was after bigger game. For one thing he realized the business potential of his painting method. Rich collectors would pay many times more for Warhol portraits of their wives than for conventional ones, even though the portrait would often be no more than a blow-up photograph screenprinted by a member of the Factory. Indeed it was the very casualness of Warhol that made his work so attractive and chic. For those with a more "concerned" view of the world he produced a series of paintings of electric chairs and wanted men. All of this work is handsome to look at and in his usual startling colour combinations, and Warhol had no lack of clients.

The Factory now became increasingly improtant and the work produced there became simply the means to its existence. To explain this next stage one must consider Warhol's personality or, to be exact, his lack of it. His nature was that of a vacuum, a void. He never made the earnest statements about his work that most artists are prone to, and apparently conversed entirely on trivialities. He condemned nothing and seemed to find any odd manifestation of human behaviour fascinating.

Because of this personality, he drew to his studio an

assortment of would be actors, failed poets, and all those, especially on the sexual fringes like transvestites, whose dreams were beyond the limits understood by normal society. "I dream, and others see my dreams," says an artist in a Cabell novel, which Warhol changes to "they dream, and I make their dreams visible."

When people are allowed to act as they wish, to be what they want to be, they create a "lifestyle," and it was to fashioning the lifestyle of the group that formed around him that Warhol now turned his attention. This he did, not by giving the lead for them to follow, but by pointing out what they were doing. He filmed them continuously, in little dramas where a man could act out the fantasy of being Jean Harlow or a woman could be high priestess and whore at the same time. He did this in a style that was deliberately rough and amateur, which left in all the mistakes, ended when the film ran out and which reflected exactly the street language and stoned lifestyle of its characters.

Early examples of this genre such as *My Hustler* were no more than home movies, but with *Chelsea Girls* came commercial success. The verbal obscenity of his characters fitted exactly the so-called "permissive society," and his works became notorious and fashionable for their sexual frankness. Warhol, who was never one to pass up a good thing, began to turn out full length films such as *Trash* and *Flesh,* and achieved the unique feat of making art films highly commercial.

Warhol's style of filmmaking has had a huge effect on the commercial cinema. While the whole weight of European "new wave" movies had failed to change Hollywood techniques, he succeeded single-handed. The casual styles of acting now fashionable, the type of wandering camera movement, the passages of apparently trivial conversation, all derive from Warhol.

To be a major influence on contemporary painting and film might have been enough for most artists, but Warhol was not yet finished. The lifestyle that he had allowed to grow around him was now becoming fashionable outside his circle. The most revolutionary aspect of this was the effect on sexual roles. At a time when the gamine mini-skirted look was de rigeur, Warhol reintroduced The Woman, via a return to 30's glamour. But the femininity did not mean weakness, for all Warhol's women are much stronger than his men; it was Jean Harlow, but without a patriarchal Clark Gable to subdue her.

Men were encouraged to express their femininity too. At the centre of the fashion were Warhol's "superstars," transvestites like Holly Woodlawn and Jackie Curtis, who had the effect of making bisexuality acceptable. This fashion has operated most strongly in the pop-rock world. There would have been no "glitter" without Warhol. Mick Jagger would have remained a blues shouter, David Bowie would not have happened at all, and it could be argued that the ubiquitous glamorous soul acts would never have happened.

Warhol opened a night-club for the "beautiful people" called The Exploding Plastic Inevitable, inventing the projected light show for it and managed the house band which was called The Velvet Underground. This band became one of the most influential in rock music, restoring in songs such as Heroin and White Light/White Heat a cutting, a poetical edge to a music that was fast drowning in the soft cotton wool of flower power.

As the influence of the lifestyle spread, Warhol changed the focus of his interests, putting out a gossip magazine called *Andy Warhol's Interview* which again furthered the effects of his ideas.

From painter to gossip magazine publisher is a big step, but in terms of Warhol's output a consistent and logical one. To consider his paintings by themselves, as most critics do, is to miss the point. Warhol's subject is society, which he manipulated in actuality as a painter manipulates his paint and for the same purpose; to create, to comment upon and to illustrate.

—Alastair Mackintosh

WATTS, Robert Marshall.

American. Born in Burlington, Iowa, 14 June 1923. Studied mechanical engineering at University of Louisville, Kentucky, 1942–44; also studied at the Art Students League, New York, 1946–48, and Columbia University, New York, 1951. Served in the United States Naval Reserve, 1942–46. Independent artist active in sculpture, performance, film and video, since 1953. Member of the Fluxus Group in new York in the early 1960's. Taught at the Institute of Applied Arts and Sciences. Brooklyn, New York, 1951–52. Professor of Art, Rutgers University, New Brunswick, New Jersey, 1953–84 (Resident Artist in Film and Mixed Media, 1964–82). Carnegie Corporation Visual Artist, University of California, 1968. Recipient: Research Council Grants, 1961–75, Faculty Fellowship, 1971, F.A.S.P. Grants, 1975, 1982, and CID Grant, 1978, Rutgers University; Experimental Workshop Award, Carnegie Corporation, 1964; Creative Artists Public Service Grant, New York State Council on the Arts, 1975; National Endowment for the Arts Fellowship, Washington, D.C., 1976. Agent: Francesco Conn, Vicolo Quadrelli 7, 37121 Verona, Italy. Address: R.D. 3, Bangor, Pennsylvania 18013, U.S.A.

Individual Exhibitions:

1960 Grand Central Moderns, New York
1966 Bianchini Gallery, New York
Ricke Gallery, Kassel, West Germany
1970 Ricke Gallery, Cologne
1971 Apple Gallery, New York
1973 La Bertesca, Milan
Galerie Baecker, Bochum, West Germany

Robert Watts: ***System with Chrome Sphere*****, 1986**

1974 Multhipla, Milan
1975 Multhipla, Milan
1976 René Block Gallery, New York
1977 Studio Morra, Naples
1978 Felius Gallery, Washington, D.C.
1982 Galleria d'Arte, Verona, Italy

Performances:

Magic Kazoo, New York City and New Jersey, 1960; *Yam Festival,* with George Brecht, in the United States and by international mail, 1962; *Yam Lecture,* with George Brecht, New York, 1963; *Yam Day,* with George Brecht, Hardware Poets Playhouse, New York, 1963; *Cake,* Kornblee Gallery, New York, 1964; *Monday Night Letter,* Cafe au Go Go, New York, 1964–65; *Performance Work/Fluxus/Body Covering,* Museum of Contemporary Crafts, New York, 1967; *Superstar,* University of California, Santa Cruz, 1969; *Communication in a Noisy Environment,* Automation House, New York, 1970; *Fluxyear/Gemini/74,* Onnasch Gallery, New York, 1974; *Performance Works for Audience,* Centro d'Informazione Alternativa, Rome, 1975; *Flux-Harpsichord Konzert,* Akademie der Kunste, West Berlin, 1976; *Oraculum,* Studio Morra, Naples, 1977; *FLuxus Concert,* Musee d'Art Contemporain, Montreal, 1980.

Selected Group Exhibitions:

1960 *New Forms, New Media,* Martha Jackson Gallery, New York
1961 *Assemblage,* Museum of Modern Art, New York
1968 *The Machine,* Museum of Modern Art, New York
1970 *Happening und Fluxus,* Kunstverein, Cologne (toured Europe)
1972 *Documenta 5,* Museum Fridericianum, Kassel, West Germany
1974 *Artists' Stamps,* Simon Fraser University, Burnaby, British Columbia
1979 *Re-Visions,* Whitney Museum, New York
1981 *Fluxus, etc.,* Cranbrook Academy of Art, Bloomfield Hills, Michigan
1985 *Festival of Fantastics,* Roskilde, Denmark
1987 *Made in USA,* University of California, Berkeley

Collections:

Albright-Knox Art Gallery, Buffalo, New York; Chrysler Art Museum, Provincetown, Massachusetts; Art Institute of Chicago; Museum of Fine Arts, Houston; Fort Worth Art Center, Texas; Los Angeles County Museum of Art; Moderna Museet, Stockholm.

Publications:

By WATTS: book—*Newspaper,* with George Brecht, New York 1963; *Postage Stamps,* New York 1963; *Fluxpost Postage Stamps,* New York 1965; *Event Cards Fluxus,* New York 1965; *The Arts on Campus,* edited by Margaret Mahoney, New York 1970; *Proposals for Art Education,* New York 1970; *S.O.S.,* 2 vols., New York 1977; *The Book As An Event,* Bangor 1978; *Notes and Sketches 1964–66,* Asolo 1979.

On WATTS: books—*AQ 16: Fluxus* by Silke Paul and Harve Wurz, Antibes 1977; *The Museum of Drawers* by Herbert Distel, Zurich 1978; *Fluxus* by Harry Rule, Amsterdam 1979; *Blam: The Explosion of Pop, Minimalism and Performance 1958–64* by Barbara Haskell, New York 1984; articles—in the *Institute of Contemporary Arts Bulletin* (London), January 1967; "Transformations from Nature" by Letty Eisenhauer in *Art and Artists* (London), November 1973.

From 1946 to 1958 I was a painter mainly in the tradition of abstract expressionism and geometric art. In 1957 I began working on pieces involving electric light, with random circuitry, incandescent wire, plants and fish. One day in July 1958 I stopped painting.

During the early '60s I exhibited works of an electro-mechanical nature guided by random or quasi-random circuits. At the same time I became interested in 16mm and 8mm film, photography, tape machines—and then I met Fluxus in 1963.

In 1960 I had produced my first event of 48 hours duration which moved from New York City to the Jersey shore, utilizing students as the primary participants, but acquiring others along the way. In a sense, Fluxus came at a time of consolidation of my ideas about art and art process; it was an exploratory forum for ideas and energy which eventually had an effect on all the arts.

Since 1970 I have continued to explore methods and attitudes toward art utilizing my knowledge and experience with past art and archaeology, esoteric information, science and technology, natural phenomena, and print technology. I work with concepts first and methods secondarily, chosen to suit the thought at hand.

—Robert Watts

WEGMAN, William.

American. Born in Holyoke, Massachusetts, 12 February 1942. Educated at Massachusetts College of Art, Boston, B.F.A. 1965; University of Illinois, Urbana, 1965–67, M.F.A. 1967. Married to Gayle Wegman; son: Man Ray. Artist and freelance photographer, California and New York. Instructor, University of Wisconsin at Wausau, 1967, and at Waukesha, 1968–69; Assistant Professor, University of Wisconsin, Madison, 1969–70; Lecturer, 1970–71, and Visiting Artist, 1978, California State University at Long Beach. Recipient: Guggenheim Fellowship, 1975; National Endowment for the Arts Grant, 1975–77, 1982; Creative Artists Public Service Grant, 1979. Agent: Holly Solomon Gallery, 724 Fifth Avenue, New York, New York 10019. Address: 27 Thames Street, New York, New York 10004, U.S.A.

Individual Exhibitions:

1971 Galerie Sonnabend, Paris
Pomona College, California
1972 Sonnabend Gallery, New York
Galerie Ernst, Hannover
Situation, London
Galerie Konrad Fischer, Dusseldorf
Courtney Sale Gallery, Dallas
1973 Galerie Sonnabend, Paris
Texas Gallery, Houston
Los Angeles County Museum of Art
Francoise Lambert and Claire Copley Gallery, Los Angeles
1974 Modern Art Agency, Naples
Galerie D. Brussels
Galeria Toselli, Milan
112 Green Street Gallery, New York
Texas Gallery, Houston
1975 Mayor Gallery, London
Galleria Alessandra Castelli, Milan
Galerie Konrad Fischer, Dusseldorf
1976 The Kitchen, New York
1977 Sonnabend Gallery, New York
Bruno Soletti Gallery, Milan
1978 Rosamund Felsen Gallery, Los Angeles
Robert Cumming/William Wegman, California Institute of Technology, Pasadena
1979 Holly Solomon Gallery, New York
Arnolfini Gallery, Bristol
Galerie Konrad Fischer, Dusseldorf
Otis Art Institute, Los Angeles
William Wegman: Retrospective, Fine Arts Galleries, University of Wisconsin at Milwaukee
1980 *William Wegman: Selected Works 1970–1979,* University of Colorado Art Galleries, Boulder (travelled to the Aspen Center for Visual Arts, Colorado)
1981 Clarence Kennedy Gallery, Cambridge, Massachusetts (with William Van Dyke and Olivia Parker)
1982 Dart Gallery, Chicago
1983 Walker Art Center, Minneapolis
12 Duke Street Gallery, London
Contemporary Arts Center, Cincinnati, Ohio
Corcoran Gallery of Art, Washington, D.C.
1984 Mackenzie Art Gallery, Regina, Saskatchewan
University of Miami, Coral Gables
1985 Albright College, Reading, Pennsylvania
1986 Daniel Wolf Gallery, New York
1988 San Francisco Museum of Modern Art

Selected Group Exhibitions:

1969 *Places and Process,* Edmonton Art Gallery, Alberta
1971 *Prospect '71,* Dusseldorf
1973 *Whitney Annual,* Whitney Museum, New York
1977 *Photography as an Art Form,* Ringling Museum of Art, Sarasota, Florida
1978 *23 Photographers,* Walker Art Gallery, Liverpool
1979 *The Altered Photograph,* Project Studio 1, Long Island City, Queens, New York
1980 *The Photograph Transformed,* Touchstone Gallery, New York
1983 *Subjective Vision,* High Museum of Art, Atlanta, Georgia
1987 *Photography and Art 1946–86,* Los Angeles County Museum of Art

Collections:

Whitney Museum, New York; Museum of Modern Art, New York; Ed Ruscha Collection, Los Angeles; International Museum of Photography at George Eastman House, Rochester, New York.

Publications:

By WEGMAN: book—*Man's Best Friend,* New York 1983; articles—"Shocked and Outraged" in *Avalanche* (New York), Winter 1971.

On WEGMAN: books—*Wegman's World,* exhibition catalogue with texts by Lisa Lyon and Kim Levin, Minneapolis 1983; *Photography and Art 1946–1986,* exhibition catalogue with essays by Andy Grundberg and Kathleen M. Gauss, Los Angeles 1987; articles—"Photography" by Ben Lifson in the *Village Voice* (New York), 9 April 1978; "Everything You Wanted to Know about William Wegman but Didn't Dare Ask" by Stuart Morgan in *Arnolfini Review* (Bristol), May/June 1979; "William Wegman" by Ian Walker in *Art Monthly* (London), no. 27, 1979; "William Wegman: Altered Photographs" in *Domus* (Milan), July 1979.

"I like to subvert the familiar, but not to put it down, or make fun of it." Wegman thus adequately described the intent and nuance of his photographs, video and films, and unpretentious graphic art; that is, until the early 1980s and the death of Man Ray, his 80 pound Weimaraner companion, with whom he had made of his domestic vaudeville and other spoof images. The dog had in a sense become Wegman's persona and allowed him the fragile, deliberately ephemeral attitude in a wide spectrum of theme. Although Wegman's recent works are still characterized by such burlesque fun (Wegman is said to have genuine disdain for "art"), there is now a more Surreal and emblematic quality in the elegantly produced Polaroid form which has come to distinguish his work.

Wegman states that he became annoyed with the utterly subjective nuance of modernity, and so was then led to jokes through the need to have his communication "complete itself." His primary metaphor formed around the rational absurdity of the joke structure; and perhaps his major role is to have brought into "high" art, the casual fun of public entertainment. (His critics have often chided him in just this regard—his "lightness" of tone.) And so there came about a long-standing attack upon artistic sincerity itself through Wegman's use of autobiographic subject matter, an improvisational spontaneity, and a

humor often centered about the nature of our reality-perception. Prevalent also throughout his work has been the theme of incapacity and the thwartedness of failure. No doubt vital to his evolution has been his continuing acquaintance with his one-time studio-mate John Baldessari, and as well the appearance in 1963 at the Pasadena Museum of Art, of the first large exhibition of the works of Marcel Duchamp.

With the present decade, Wegman has used a large format Polaroid image which perhaps contradicts the self-effacing anti-mastery so important to his statement. The easy accessibility of his earlier work ("I didn't want them to be compared to paintings, and get involved in scale, and size, and 'wall' power") has thus been lost. The recent work often exudes a commercialized air through the long use of such tableaux-like imagery in the advertising world. Wegman has e.g., focused upon a female body builder as model in order to explore sexual role cliches; and in another lengthy exploration, has used a small child to present the poignance and strangeness of the child/adult interface.

—Joshua Kind

Lawrence Weiner: Installation in the Anton Herbert Collection, Ghent, 1982

WEINER, Lawrence.
American. Born in the Bronx, New York, 10 February 1940. Educated at Stuyvesant High School, New York; self-taught as an artist. Independent artist known for conceptual works incorporating verbal elements: lives and works in New York. Recipient: Deutscher Akademische Austauschdienst (DAAD) Award, 1975–76; National Endowment for the Arts Fellowship, Washington, D.C. 1977, 1985; American Exhibition Prize, Art Institute of Chicago, 1979. Agent: Leo Castelli, 420 West Broadway, New York, New York 10012. Address: 13 Bleecker Street, New York, New York 10012, U.S.A.

Individual Exhibitions:

1964 Seth Siegelaub Gallery, New York
1965 Seth Siegelaub Gallery, New York
1968 Seth Siegelaub Gallery, New York
1969 Konrad Fischer Galerie, Dusseldorf
Nova Scotia College of Art and Design, Halifax
Wide White Space Gallery, Antwerp
Galleria Sperone, Turin
1970 Konrad Fischer Galerie, Dusseldorf
Galleria Sperone, Turin
Galerie Folker Skulima, Berlin
Art & Project Gallery, Amsterdam
Galerie Yvon Lambert, Paris
Gegenverker, Aachen, West Germany
1971 Galerie Yvon Lambert, Paris
Nova Scotia College of Art and Design, Halifax
Leo Castelli Gallery, New York
1972 Jack Wendler Gallery, London
Galleria Toselli, Milan
Wide White Space Gallery, Antwerp
Leo Castelli Gallery, New York
Konrad Fischer Galerie, Dusseldorf
Galleria Sperone, Turin
Westfälischer Kunstverein, Münster, West Germany
California Institute of the Arts, Los Angeles
1973 Project Inc., Cambridge, Massachusetts
Städtisches Museum, Mönchenglabach, West Germany
Jack Wendler Gallery, London
Wide White Space Gallery, Brussels
Galleria Sperone, Turin
Modern Art Agency, Naples
Kabinett für Aktuelle Kunst, Bremerhaven, West Germany
1974 Max Protetch Gallery, Washington, D.C.
Rolf Preisig Gallery, Basle
Galleria Toselli, Milan
Gentofte Kommunes Kunstbibliotek, Hellerup, Denmark
Galerie Yvon Lambert, Paris
Leo Castelli Gallery, New York
Claire Copley Gallery, Los Angeles
Barbara Cusack Gallery, Houston
1975 Konrad Fischer Galerie, Dusseldorf
Kabinett für Aktuelle Kunst, Bremerhaven, West Germany
Galleria Sperone, Turin
Rolf Preisig Gallery, Basel
1976 Van Abbemuseum, Eindhoven, Netherlands
Institute for Contemporary Arts, London
Robert Self Gallery, Newcastle upon Tyne
Institute for Art and Urban Resources, New York
Kunsthalle, Basle
The Kitchen, New York
Rüdiger Schöttle Galerie, Munich
1977 CEAC, Toronto
Galerie Yvon Lambert, Paris
Salle Patino, Centre d'Art Contemporain, Geneva
Konrad Fischer Galerie, Dusseldorf
Claire Copley Gallery, Los Angeles
Laguna Gloria Art Museum, Austin, Texas
Wide White Space Gallery, Antwerp
1978 Renaissance Society, University of Chicago
INK, Halle für Internationale Neue Kunst, Zurich
1979 Galleria Francoise Lambert, Milan
Leo Castelli Gallery, New York
Nova Scotia College of Art and Design, Halifax
Galerija Foksal PSP, Warsaw
Saman Gallery, Genoa
Art & Project Gallery, Amsterdam
Rüdiger Schöttle Galerie, Munich
1980 Museum of Contemporary Art, Chicago
Van Abbemuseum, Eindhoven, Netherlands
Centre d'Art Contemporain, Geneva
Anthony d'Offay Gallery, London
Galerija Akumulatory 2, Poznan, Poland
Leo Castelli Gallery, New York
Art and Project, Amsterdam
1981 A Space, Toronto
Leo Castelli Gallery, New York
David Bellman Gallery, Toronto
Kabinett für Aktuelle Kunst, Bremerhaven, West Germany
P.S. 1, New York
Konrad Fischer Galerie, Dusseldorf
1982 GEWAD, Ghent, Belgium
Galerie Media, Neuchatel, Switzerland
The Movies, Amsterdam
1983 Nordjyllands Kunstmuseum, Aalborg, Denmark (with Albert Merz)
Bleecker Street Cinema, New York
Kunsthalle, Berne
Galerie Micheline Swaczer, Antwerp
Nova Scotia College of Art and Design, Halifax
1984 David Bellman Gallery, Toronto
Ohio State University, Columbus
University of Cincinnati, Ohio
Galerie Daniel Templon, Paris
Espace Lyonnais d'Art Contemporain, Lyon, France
TTL, BRT and NOS Teletekst, Belgium (television broadcast)
1985 Art and Project Plancius Straat Gallery, Amsterdam
Art and Project Prinsegracht Gallery, Amsterdam
Galerie Konrad Fischer, Dusseldorf
Galerie Daniel Templon, Paris
Le Coin du Miroir, Dijon, France
City Thoughts, Amsterdam
ARC/Musee d'Art Moderne de la Ville, Paris
Musee St. Pierre d'Art Contemporain, Lyon, France
1986 State University of New York, Old Westbury
Pier Art Centre, Stromness, Orkney Islands
Fruitmarket Gallery, Edinburgh
AIR Gallery, London (travelled to Derry, Northern Ireland)
Anthony D'Offay Gallery, London
Galerie Micheline Szwajcer, Antwerp
Art Gallery of New South Wales, Sydney
Marian Goodman Gallery, New York
Leo Castelli Gallery, New York
1987 Galerie Daniel Templon, Paris
Le Magasin Centre d'Art Contemporain, Grenoble, France

Selected Group Exhibitions:

1969 *When Attitude Becomes Form*, Kunsthalle, Bern
1971 *6th Guggenheim International Exhibition*, Guggenheim Museum, New York
1972 *Documenta 5*, Museum Fridericianum, Kassel, West Germany (and *Documenta 7*, 1982)
1973 *Prospekt '74*, Kunsthalle, Dusseldorf

1974 *Some Recent American Art*, City of Auckland Art Gallery, New Zealand
1979 *American Exhibition*, Art Institute of Chicago
1981 *Westkunst*, Cologne
1983 *When Words Become Works*, Minneapolis College of Art and Design, Minnesota
1985 *Artists' Books*, Centre Georges Pompidou, Paris
1987 *Comic Iconoclasm*, Institute of Contemporary Arts, London

Collections:

Centre Georges Pompidou, Paris; Stedelijk Museum, Amsterdam; Museum van Hedendaagse Kunst te Gent, Ghent, Belgium; Städtisches Museum, Mönchengladbach, West Germany; Van Abbemuseum, Eindhoven, Netherlands; British Museum, London; Museum of Modern Art, New York; Art Gallery of Ontario, Toronto; Nova Scotia College of Art and Design, Halifax; National Gallery of Australia, Canberra.

Publications:

By WEINER: books—*Statements*, New York 1968; *Traces*, Turin 1970; *Art & Project/Lawrence Weiner*, Amsterdam 1971; *10 Works*, Paris 1971; *Flowed*, Halifax, Nova Scotia 1971; *Causality: Affected and/or Effected*, New York 1971; *Having Been Done at/Having Been Done to*, Turin 1972; *A Primer*, Kassel 1972; *Green as Well as Blue as Well as Red*, London 1972; *Within Forward Motion*, Bremerhaven, West Germany 1973; *Within a Reasonable Doubt*, Milan 1973; *Once Upon a Time*, Milan 1973; *Having from Time to Time a Relation to*, Amsterdam 1973; *Towards a Reasonable End*, Bremerhaven, West Germany 1975; *Relative to Hanging*, Ringkobing, Denmark 1975; *Various Manners with Various Things*, London 1976; *Art & Project*, Amsterdam 1976; *On the Rocks*, Lund, Sweden 1976; *Pertaining to a Structure*, London 1977; *Coming and Going*, Geneva 1977; *In Relation to Probable Use*, Chicago 1978; *Regarding Inscriptions (of a Sort)*, Basle 1978; *With a Touch of Pink*, Bremerhaven, West Germany 1978; *Works*, New York 1978; *Hard Light*, with Edward Ruscha, Los Angeles 1978; *The Level of Water*, Ghent, Belgium 1978; *With a Probability of Being Seen*, Warsaw 1979; *Concerning 20 Works*, London 1980; *Passage to the North*, New York 1981; *Red/As Well as Green/As Well as Yellow/As Well as Blue*, with Albert Mertz, Aalborg 1983; *Sculpture*, with interview by Suzanne Page, Paris 1985; recordings—*7*, Paris 1972; *Having Been Done At*, Rome 1973; *Nothing to Lose/Niets aan Verloren*, Eindhoven, Netherlands, 1976; *Having Been Built on Sand with Another Base (Basis) in Fact*, Munich 1978; films and videos—*Beached*, 1970; *Broken off*, 1971; *To and Fro and Fro and To and Fro and Fro and To*, 1972; *Shifted from Side to Side*, 1972; *A First Quarter*, 1973; *Affected and/or Effected*, 1974; *Done To*, 1975; *A Second Quarter*, 1975; *Do You Believe in Water?*, 1976; *Green As Well As Blue As Well As Red*, 1976; *A Bit of Matter and a Little Bit More*, 1976; *For Example Decorated*, 1977; *Altered to Suit*, 1979; *There But For*, 1980; *Passage to the North*, 1981; *Plowmans Lunch*, 1982.

On WEINER: books—*Lawrence Weiner: Eine Ausstellung*, exhibition catalogue with essay by Klaus Honnef, Aachen 1971; *Lawrence Weiner: Jahresgabe 1972*, exhibition catalogue with introduction by Klaus Honnef, Munster 1973; *Lawrence Weiner, 8–30 Juni 1974*, exhibition catalogue with essay by Jane Pedersen, Hellerup 1974; *Lawrence Weiner*, exhibition catalogue with commentary by Rudi H. Fuchs, Basle 1978; *Lawrence Weiner: Mounds + Smooth Cairns*, exhibition catalogue with text by Edward Leffingwell, Columbus, Ohio 1984; *Lawrence Weiner: Above Beyond Below*, exhibition catalogue with essays by Erlend Brown and Mark Francis, Edinburgh 1986; *Lawrence Weiner: Posters, November 1965–April 1986*, edited by Benjamin H. D. Buchloh, Halifax, Nova Scotia 1986.

Art is not a metaphor upon the relationships of human beings to objects and objects to objects in relation to human beings but a representation of an empirical existing fact.

It does not tell the potential and capabilities of an object (material) but presents a reality concerning that relationship.

Constant placation of previous aesthetics consumes present resources to the extent that as the needs and desires of a present aesthetic make themselves felt (even when the basis is in a previous aesthetic) the resources have been exhausted.

There are very few material relationships of human beings to objects that at various (some) stages have not required various (some) forms of human being to human being relationships.

The utilization of media presents these various relationships at the moment of the presentation of what in essence is a material relationship. The utilization of media as both presentation and representation seems to require no justification other than the presentation itself.

The artists' reality is no different from any other reality. It is the content that gives the perceptions and observations of an artist (within the presentation/art) a use factor within the society.

The acceptance of the need for this distancing (in fact the need itself) by a society for its art to function has led to the misconception that art and artists are apart from society unless they do not function as art and artists.

The obvious change in the relationship of art to a culture is perhaps that the explanation (not needed justification) of the existence of art has been allied to the concept of production.

This reading while obviating some form of social unease is not in fact the case: art is in relation to its society a service industry.

—Lawrence Weiner

WELCH, Roger.

American. Born in Westfield, New Jersey, 10 February 1946. Educated at Westfield Senior High School. New Jersey, 1961–64; National Music Camp, Interlochen, Michigan, Summers 1963, 1964 and 1965; studied at York Junior College, Pennsylvania, 1964–65, Miami University, Oxford, Ohio, 1965–69, B.F.A. 1969, School of the Art Institute of Chicago, 1969–71, and with the Whitney Independent Study Program, New York, 1970–71. Multi-media artist: lives and works in New York. Recipient: Ford Foundation Scholarship, 1970; New York State Council on the Arts Grant, 1973; National Endowment for the Arts Grants, 1974, 1980. Agents: Ted Greenwald Gallery, 184 Mott Street, New York, New York 10013; Elizabeth Galasso Fine Arts, 191 Main Street, Ossining, New York 10562. Address: 87 East Houston Street, New York, New York 10012, U.S.A.

Individual Exhibitions:

1971 112 Greene Street, New York
98 Greene Street Loft, New York
1972 98 Greene Street Loft, New York
Galerie 20, Amsterdam
Sonnabend Gallery, New York
1973 Galerie Konrad Fischer, Dusseldorf
Galerie Sonnabend, Paris
Nova Scotia College of Art, Halifax
John Gibson Gallery, New York
1974 University of Rhode Island, Kingston
Milwaukee Art Center
1975 Galleria Forma, Genoa
Galerie Gérald Piltzer, Paris
Stefanotty Gallery, New York
1977 Albright-Knox Art Gallery, Buffalo, New York
1980 Museo de Arte Moderno, Mexico City
1981 Museo Nacional, Havana
Museo de Bellas Artes, Carcas
1982 Whitney Museum, New York
1984 Miami University, Oxford, Ohio (retrospective)
1986 Ted Greenwald Gallery, New York
Elizabeth Galasso Fine Arts, Ossining, New York
1987 Ted Greenwald Gallery, New York

Selected Group Exhibitions:

1972 *Documenta*, Kassel, West Germany
1973 *20 Conceptual Artists*, Galerie Kriwin, Brussels
1974 *Projekt '74*, Wallraf-Richartz Museum, Cologne
1975 *Camera Art*, Lund Konsthall, Sweden
1977 *Words*, Whitney Museum, New York
Video Art, Museo de Arte Moderno, Mexico City
1981 *Alternatives in Retrospect 1969–75*, New Museum, New York
1983 *Urban Pulses: The Artist and the City*, Pittsburgh Plan for Art, Pennsylvania
1985 *Prozess und Konstruktion 1985*, Landeshauptstadt Museum, Munich
1987 *Photography and Art 1946–86*, Los Angeles County Museum of Art

Collections:

Georgia Museum of Art, University of Georgia, Athens; Milwaukee Art Center; Wallraf-Richartz Museum, Cologne; Museum Haus Lange, Krefeld, West Germany; Lund Konsthall, Sweden; Museo Rufino Tamayo, Mexico City; Museo de Bellas Artes, Caracas, Venezuela; Museum of Modern Art, New York; Chase Manhattan Bank, New York.

Publications:

By WELCH: statement in *Roger Welch*, exhibition catalogue, Milwaukee 1975; statement in *Unbuilt America*, New York 1976; statement in *The Individual in a Social World*, New York 1977; statement in *The Big Jewish Book*, New York 1978; essay in *Alternatives in Retrospect 1969–75*, exhibition catalogue, New York 1981.

On WELCH: books—*Four Artists and the Map*, exhibition catalogue, by Roberta Smith, Kansas City 1980; *A Decade of New Art*, exhibition catalogue with text by Linda Cathcart, New York 1984; *Das Automobil in der Kunst 1886–1986*, exhibition catalogue with essay by Reimar Zeller, Munich 1986; *Photography and Art 1946–86*, exhibition catalogue with text by Andy Grundberg, Los Angeles 1987; articles—"Story Art" by Margarethe Jochimsen in *Magazin Kunst* (Mainz, West Germany), September 1974; "The Post-Perceptual Portrait" by Amy Goldwin in *Art in America* (New York), January/February 1975; "After Photography" by Douglas Davis in the *Village Voice* (New York), no. 14, 1981.

Roger Welch is a multi-media artist who uses film, photographs, video, drawings, diagrams, texts and various sculptural objects in multiple combinations in his environmental installations. Since 1969–70 Welch has been using real persons and events as the bases for his investigations into the nature of our perceptions as they are sifted and shifted by the passage of time. Welch's work begins with things personally experienced and/or experienced by people around him, and he expands his themes out of the purely autobiographical and biographical realms into iconic statements of the more generally recognizable social and cultural environment which shapes the typically American experience. Welch selects and organizes various visual and verbal elements of his subject matter to make interrelated and open-ended environments, making the viewer into an active participant who, by filling in meanings by association and by making choices as to how and when to take in the parts of the multi-layered work, finds possibilities for fresh and vital insights into situations which are usually either buried in half-forgotten memories or simply ingested at face value.

In 1970 Welch began examining his own memory. First, he wrote down what he was able to recall about his own experiences at Miami University in Ohio. Subsequently, he returned to that place and photographed sites which he had mentioned in his writings. In this manner Welch had created a sequence in which memory became cause, the trigger which determined the structure of present experiencing of things past. During the same period Welch began collaborating with friends and family. In graphic works of 1971 he juxtaposed older and newer photographs of members of various generations of his family and had those who were still alive write their memories of the events pictured under each photograph. In the film *Welch* (1972), he edited from old 16mm home

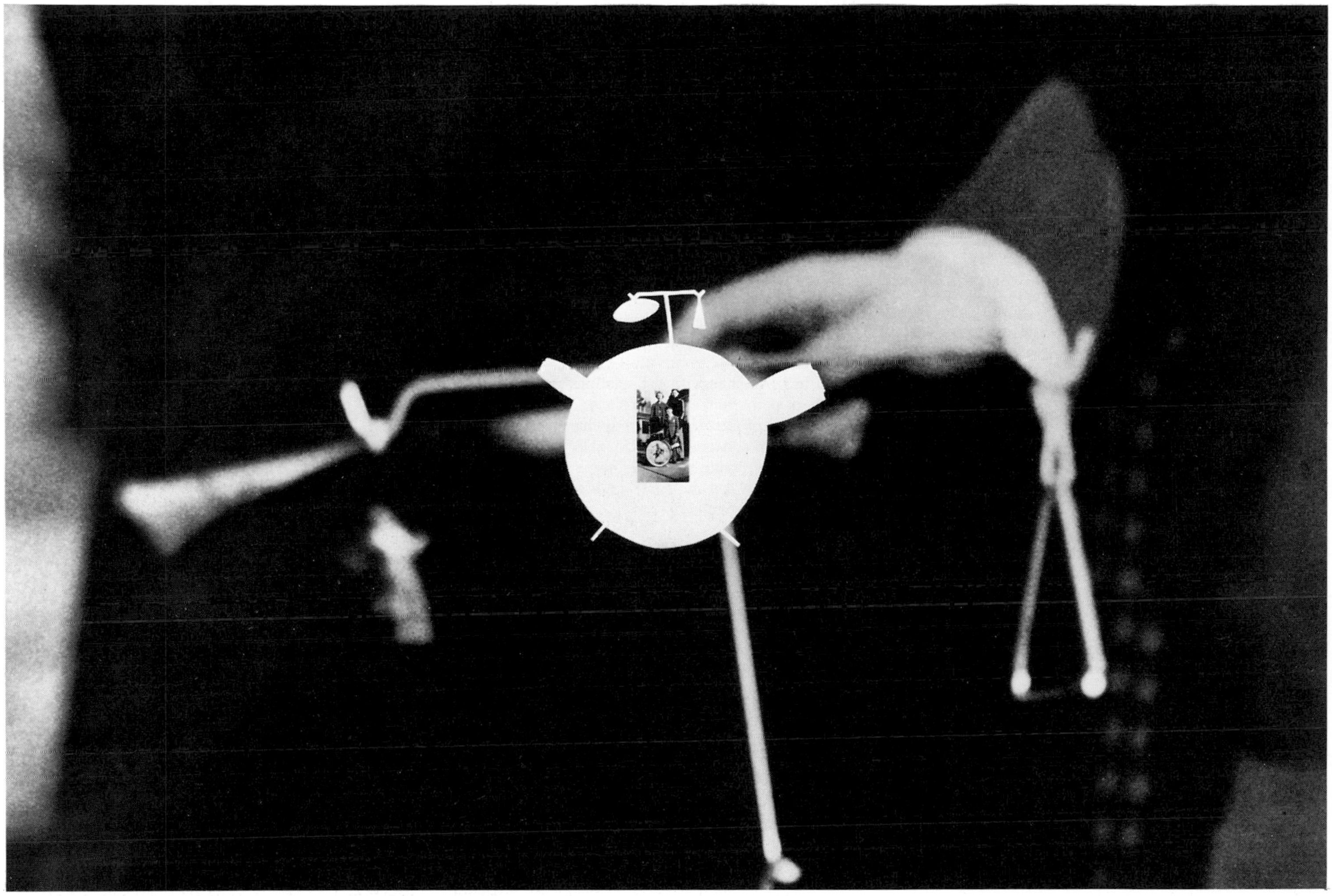

Roger Welch: ***Self-Portrait*****, 1987**

movies made from 1926 to 1972 and covering five generations of his family. In the accompanying audiotape, his father, mother, brother, brother's son and himself comment spontaneously as they watch the movies together. Past events, rearranged by the artist, are given revitalization and continuation from a new perspective and vantage point. Old and new are both experienced candidly and immediately as past and present are occurring simultaneously for the participants and for the viewers alike. In a related series of works, Welch conducted interviews with persons all born before 1890, discussing with them their recollections of their childhood home towns. Out of their descriptions, Welch constructed maps, visualizations of their almost-faded memories which make tangible that which is nearly lost from present perception. One of the most memorable of Welch's collaboration with older people is his 1976 "Alton Carter, Plains, Georgia, Memory Map," a reconstruction of Plains based on discussions with Jimmy Carter's 88-year-old uncle, Alton. Beginning with a personal collaborative effort, the artist interprets the mythology communicated by a person who has experienced a chunk of history through his own perspective and personality.

During the mid-70's Welch became involved with the American sports figure, a heroic myth of another sort. In a work such as "Preliminaries" (1976), Welch studies the different human traits underlying the image of the boxer, too often perceived as a unidimensional figure only out for blood and glory. In "Niagara Falls Project—Roger Woodward" (1975), Welch combined Panavision film of the trip to the great falls with videotaped interview of a man who, at age seven, had gone over the falls, to weave a fascinating narrative of experience and memory on another kind of heroic/mythic style. As in many of his works, portraiture and landscape are combined through various media to convey the extraordinary element in ordinary people and places.

In his sculptural installation titled "Drive In" (1980), recently remade as "Drive In: Second Feature" (1982), Welch explores an American phenomenon highly popular during the 1950's which has already become a part of the nostalgic past. The work is composed of a full-scale model of a 1958 Cadillac Eldorado made from twigs and branches tied together and of a series of "Coming Attractions Trailers" of 1950's movies interdispersed with clips taken from old drive-in intermission ads for junk food and time-left-to-the-next show. Welch himself describes it as "the product of an archaeological expedition into contemporary America," and the effect of the work is that of a half-ironic, half-reverent look at the near-past gone primitive. As you view promos for Hollywood efforts such as "Raw Wind in Eden," "The Time Machine," "Shane" and "Invaders from Mars," sending flickering light through Welch's painstakingly hand-made Caddy of twigs and branches, you realize the rapidity which now makes what was only recently stylish into a relic of nostalgia for the museum. Welch is continuing to dig into the American experience with an intuitive wit and studious understanding which promises that he will continue to unearth many more memories to be perceived as never before.

—Barbara Cavaliere

WESELER, Günter.

German. Born in Allenstein, 2 March 1930. Studied architecture at the Technische Hochschule, Braunschweig, 1953–58, Dip. Arch. 1958. Married in 1958 (separated 1970); son: Justin. Independent artist, in Braunschweig, 1953–62, in Dusseldorf since 1962: first kinetic "moving pictures," 1953–58; "hair pictures," 1962–65; "breathing music" performance, Radio Bremen, 1964; "breathing objects," since 1966. Agents: Galerie Redmann, Fasanenstrasse 30, 1000 Berlin 15 (West); Galerie Hunermann, im Ratinger Tor, 4000 Dusseldorf. Address: Bonifatiusstrasse 57, 400 Dusseldorf-Lorick, West Germany.

Individual Exhibitions:

1960 Galerie Utermann, Dortmund, West Germany
1961 Galerie Appel, Frankfurt
1962 Galerie am Bohlweg, Braunschweig, West Germany
1966 Kunsthalle, Dusseldorf
1967 Kunstverein, Hannover
Haus Ruhnau, Essen
1968 Galerie Art Intermedia, Cologne
Galerie Gunar, Dusseldorf
1969 Städtisches Museum, Leverkusen, West Germany
Kunstmuseum, Lucerne
Die Insel, Hamburg
1970 Kunstverein, Göttingen, West Germany
Edinburgh Art College
Galeria Iven Spence, Ibiza, Spain
1971 Eat-Art Galerie, Dusseldorf
1972 Galerie Magers, Bonn
Museum, Atheneum, Helsinki
1973 Turku Museum, Finland
1974 Musée d'Art Contemporain, Montreal
Werke 1964–1974, Kunstverein für Rheinland und Westfalen, Dusseldorf
Landesmuseum, Wiesbaden, West Germany
1975 Electric Gallery, Toronto

Galerie St. Johann, Saarbrucken, West Germany
Nye bella center, Copenhagen
1977 Galerie Hennemann, Bonn
Forum Kunst, Rottweil, West Germany
1978 Galerie Brinkman, Amsterdam
Electric Gallery, Toronto
Nationalgalerie, West Berlin
1979 Galerie Lang, Vienna
Galerie St. Johann, Saarbrucken, West Germany
York University, Toronto
1980 Galerie Lupke und Schonbrunn, Frankfurt
1981 Galerie Regio, Freiburg, West Germany
Alte Oper, Frankfurt
1983 Musiktheater, Gelsenkirchen, West Germany
Draier-Verlag, Frankfurt
Galerie Wunsche, Bonn
1984 Buchmesse, Frankfurt
1985 Kunstverein, Siegen, West Germany
Draier-Verlag, Frankfurt
1987 Galerie Redmann, West Berlin

Selected Group Exhibitions:

1968 *New Art from Germany,* Philadelphia Museum of Art
Science Fiction, Kunstverein für Rheinland und Westfalen, Dusseldorf
1969 *Intermedia 69,* Kunstverein, Heidelberg
1970 *New Multiple Art,* Whitechapel Art Gallery, London
1971 *Die Puppe,* Haus am Waldsee, West Berlin (toured Germany)
Kinetic Art, Goethe Institut, Athens (travelled to Ankara, Beirut and Nicosia)
1972 *Spielstrasse Olympische Spiele,* Munich
1973 *Poetry with Material,* Municipal Gallery of Modern Art, Dublin (travelled to Warsaw and Cracow)
1979 *Soft Art,* Kunsthaus, Zurich

Collections:

Kunstmuseum, Dusseldorf; Kulturministerium Nordrhein Westfalen, Dusseldorf; Kunsthalle, Bremen, West Germany; Städtisches Museum Schloss Morsbroich, Leverkusen, West Germany; Kaiser-Wilhelm Museum, Krefeld, West Germany; Institut für Auslandbeziehungen, Stuttgart; Landesmuseum, Wiesbaden, West Germany; Städtische Sammlung, Wolfsburg, West Germany; Stadtische Sammlung, Recklinghausen, West Germany; Power Gallery of Contemporary Art, Sydney.

Publications:

By WESELER: books—*Der optische Klan,* playscript, Mainz 1970; *Atemobjekte: Gunter Weseler,* Friedberg-Bruchenbrucken 1986; films—*Räume,* 1970; *Weseler, atmende Welt,* 1974.

On WESELER: books—*Raume und Environments,* Opladen, West Germany 1969; *Dusseldorfer Szene,* exhibition catalogue, with text by Jean-Christophe Ammann, Lucerne 1969; *Kunstszene Dusseldorf,* exhibition catalogue, with text by Gerhard Storck, Helsinki 1972; *Strategy—Get Arts,* exhibition catalogue, edited by Richard Demarco, Edinburgh 1970; *Bis Heute* by Karin Thomas, Cologne 1971; *Deutsche Kunst der 60er Jahr* by Jürgen Morschel, Munich 1972; *Kunstpraxis—Heute,* by Karin Thomas, Cologne 1972; *Günter Weseler: Werke 1964–1974,* exhibition catalogue, with texts by Karl Heinz Hering, Gerhard Storck, Helga Meister and others, Dusseldorf 1974; *Gunter Weseler* by Gerhard Storck and Manfred de la Motte, Bonn 1977.

The preoccupation with breathing as an artistic element was, from the beginning, an expression of a virtually neurotic sensitiveness in breathing. This coincided in those days with my conviction of the possibility to control artificially all organic processes in the body by means of chemicals, drugs, etc., and thus my inclination to influence myself by taking them in order to balance all imperfections of my own nature at will.

Hence arose (certainly based on the subconscious but as an expression of my personality) technically produced organisms whose fascination lay in breathing, in the sequence, in the pauses, in the slowness, alternating with quick phases, which no human abdomen can actually achieve.

The work with the breathing objects, the changing of relationships with respect to position, location and situation soon showed me that their character could be completely transformed, that the objects became essential symbolic figures for certain life-situations or certain fears. I noted those experiences as follows: "Actually the lattice of the crib was meant as a protection so that nobody would sit down on the reclining, breathing being . . . but at the same time I discovered that the object suddenly assumed an entirely different character: something disproportionately threatening, violent emanated from it . . . " It was the discovery that breathing objects can significantly change according to their location.

Objects which are comparatively abstract, perhaps "submarine" in the centre of the wall, appear winged when sitting on an edge; and, easily frightened, they may soon fly away again. In the corner or angle they are domestically hidden, sometimes in ambush; squatting on a log they become parasites; on the human body, possibly on the throat, they can spread terror like a malignant tumor.

This does not limit their ambiguity but gives them enigma, since a component appears which contradicts the character produced by the motion itself. The original "general metaphors of organic life" now become metaphors of parasitic growth or of the captive sufferer (in the cage) or of violent usurper (crib) and so on. The objects, the location, the room become part of a message. The breathing objects offered me the possibility to formulate a variety of environmental experiences and problems in an artistic manner.

Whereas the earlier breath-objects essentially subsisted on the contrast between artificiality and naturalness, also in the confrontation of the object with its surroundings, so to speak with its civilized environ-

Günther Weseler: *Open Mandala,* 1985

ment, recent years have brought about a distinct change toward the organic as towards the harmonic.

The tendency toward the integration of breath-objects into *mandala*-like forms has recently grown symptomatic of a harmonization and a certain re-orientation. The employment of breath-objects in *mandala*-structures corresponds to an important shift of meaning: the movement must no longer be seen as organic and animal-like but is placed in a context in which it must be understood in terms of magic and transcendence.

—Gunter Weseler

Born in Allenstein, east Prussia, in 1930 (his mother was an artist of local fame and also a pianist), Günter Weseler grew up in north Friesland/Schleswig-Holstein. His first occupation was as a farmer. He went on to train as a radio technician, studied architecture at the technical college in Braunschweig, and finally opted for the liberal arts. As a painter, Weseler tried his hand at a variety of styles that were then current, from Tachism to serial art, while, from 1962 to 1966, he also worked as an architect in Düsseldorf, where he has since lived. An increasing interest in kinetics and in musical structures brought him together with the young, experiment-crazy composer Dieter Schönbach, who was soon taking down his scores in 'graphic—painterly' fashion just as Weseler began 'composing' his pictures. Together they later produced (1964–68) 'breath music' and 'action music', predominantly for Radio Bremen, and also, in 1968 and 1971, musical theatre projects in 'breathing auditoria' in Kiel, Münster and Cologne.

Breath as a phenomenon of life fascinated Weseler increasingly; an illness which led to an 'almost neurotic respiratory disorder', since 'every physical effort made one aware of breathing', played its part in this. Around the same time Weseler gave up painting completely and began to make models out of monocoloured lumps of wax and hairs. These models, however, lacked dynamic energy, so Weseler then began experimenting with 'breathing balloons', which filled up rhythmically with compressed air and then collapsed again. What was important to him was the way objects are articulated and the way they move. His next experiment involved covering small motors with animal hides and controlling the speed and rhythm of the machines' movement with pulleys and levers. Under the guise of nature, kinetics imitated organic processes and obtained fascinating and magical effects: spherical fur-covered objects suddenly turned out to be apparently living fabulous beings that moved mysteriously and 'breathed'. Depending on position and context—we may be dealing with a bird cage, a child's bed, a cushion, or a necklace—Weseler's creations called up a multitude of other associations, including social and political ones. The addition of sound effects was provided by tape recordings. Four stuffed lion skins induced panic when they suddenly began breathing. A steel helmet complete with bullet hole moved in a macabre way.

Weseler soon began working along similar lines with foam. He made window dummies which spewed an unappetising grey-green substance due to a chemical reaction involving the combination and expansion of certain elements under the effects of heat. He also produced 'breathing walls' out of synthetic materials, as a stage set for the Cologne Opera House, for example, and increasingly vast artificial landscapes, abstract and organic at the same time, or 'post-human landscapes' with scorched trees, craters and spiny objects which breathed and rattled, or—in Edinburgh in 1970—a nauseating 'Breathing Banquet'. In 1984 Weseler designed a gently breathing 'Tidal Lake' which simulated the ebb and flow of the tide.

Since 1983 Weseler has been using grass mats for his work, making them himself by growing corn seeds on glass plates and a layer of plain-coloured humus. After a couple of months this process produces strong, naturally woven mats which gradually turn yellow. The artist then places his 'breathing objects' on top of them—fauna on top of flora—art thereby becoming one with nature.

During his investigations into breathing Weseler came across a number of ancient breathing therapies and also esoteric breathing techniques which contain possibilities for heightened physical and mental awareness, as in the case of Zen Buddhism and Tantra Yoga for example. This led him to integrate 'breathing objects' in closed structures that are inspired by Indian mandalas. "The use of breathing objects in mandala structures corresponds to an essential switch in meaning: the movement is no longer simply visible in an organic—animal sense; it exists now in a context in which it is to be understood in a magical, transcendental sense" (Weseler).

It is in this sense that one should interpret the stamp with which Weseler signs his catalogues and letters: "Weseler creates a new world—the new species."

—Werner Schulze-Reimpell

WESSELMANN, Tom.

American. Born in Cincinnati, Ohio, 23 February 1931. Educated at Hiram College, Ohio; The University of Cincinnati, Ohio, B.A. in Psychology; Art Academy of Cincinnati, Ohio; and, under Nicholas Marsicano, Cooper Union, New York. Married Claire Wesselmann in 1963; daughter: Jenny Claire. Painter. Agent: Sidney Janis Gallery, 110 West 57th Street, New York, New York 10019. Address: R.D. 1, Box 36, Long Eddy, New York 12760, U.S.A.

Individual Exhibitions:

1961 Tanager Gallery, New York
1962 Green Gallery, New York
1964 Green Gallery, New York
1965 Green Gallery, New York
1966 Sidney Janis Gallery, New York
Galerie Ileana Sonnabend, Paris
1967 Galleria Gian Enzo Sperone, Turin
1968 Sidney Janis Gallery, New York
Dayton's Gallery 12, Minneapolis (toured the United States)
1970 Sidney Janis Gallery, New York
Early Still-Lifes 1962–1964, Newport Harbor Art Museum, Balboa, California (toured the United States)
1971 Jack Glenn Gallery, Corona del Mar, California
1972 Sidney Janis Gallery, New York
Rosa Esman Gallery, New York
Galerie Aronowitsch, Stockholm
1973 Multiples Gallery, Los Angeles
1974 Sidney Janis Gallery, New York
Galerie des 4 Mouvements, Paris
The Early Years: Collages 1959–62, Ohio University, Athens (toured the United States)
1976 Sidney Janis Gallery, New York
1979 Sidney Janis Gallery, New York
1981 Hokin Gallery, Bay Harbor Islands, Florida
Hokin Gallery, Chicago
1982 Sidney Janis Gallery, New York
1985 Sidney Janis Gallery, New York
1987 Sidney Janis Gallery, New York

Selected Group Exhibitions:

1962 *Recent Painting U.S.A.: The Figure*, Museum of Modern Art, New York
1963 *Pop Goes the Easel*, Contemporary Arts Museum, Houston
1965 *Young America 1965*, Whitney Museum, New York
1966 *Art in a Mirror*, Museum of Modern Art, New York (toured the United States)
1967 *Bienal*, Sao Paulo
1968 *Documenta*, Kassel, West Germany
1974 *American Pop Art*, Whitney Museum, New York
1976 *Illusions of Reality*, Art Gallery of New South Wales, Sydney
1977 *The Dada/Surrealist Heritage*, Clark Art Institute, Williamstown, Massachusetts
1983 *Why New York?*, Futura Gallery, Stockholm

Collections:

Museum of Modern Art, New York; Whitney Museum, New York; Albright-Knox Art Gallery, Buffalo, New York; Worcester Art Museum, Massachusetts; Philadelphia Museum of Art; Cincinnati Art Museum, Ohio; Walker Art Center, Minneapolis; Minneapolis Institute of Arts; Dallas Museum of Fine Arts; Wallraf-Richartz Museum, Cologne.

Publications:

On WESSELMANN: books—*Pop Art* by Rolf Günter Dienst, Wiesbaden, West Germany, 1965; *Pop Art* by John Rublowsky, New York 1965; *Pop Art* by Lucy R. Lippard, New York 1966; *Pop Art and After* by Mario Amaya, New York 1966; *Pop Art U.S.A.* by Alberto Boatto, Milan and Rome 1967; *New York: The New Art Scene* by Ugo Mulas and Alan Solomon, New York 1967; *Art in the Age of Risk* by Nicolas Calas, New York 1968; articles—"Tom Wesselmann at Tanager" in *Arts Magazine* (New York), February 1962; "Tom Wesselmann at Green Gallery" by Jill Johnston in *Artnews* (New York), November 1962; "New Realists in New York" by Sonya Rodikoff, "Dada Then and Now" by Barbara Rose, and "Le Nouveau Realisme á la Coquete de New York" by Pierre Restany in *Art International* (Lugano, Switzerland), January 1973; "Symposium on Pop Art—Special Supplement" by Henry Geldzahler in *Arts Magazine* (New York), April 1963; "Tom Wesselmann" in *Time* (New York), February 1964; "Tom Wesselmann at Green Gallery" by Jill Johnston in *Artnews* (New York), April 1964; "The Honest Nude—Wesselmann" by Gene R. Swenson in *Art and Artists* (London), May 1966; "Tom Wesselmann and the Gates of Horn" by J. A. Abramson in *Arts Magazine* (New York), May 1966; "Paris: Wesselmann et le Nu Américain" by Jean-Louis Ferrier in *La Quinzaine* (Paris), November 1966; "Eros Presumptive" by Lucy Lippard in *Minimal Art: A Critical Anthology*, edited by Gregory Battock, New York 1968; "Images: Tom Wesselmann at Janis" in *Arts Magazine* (New York), February 1968; "Reviews: Tom Wesselmann" in *Arts Magazine* (New York), December 1972; "Reviews: Tom Wesselmann" by Carter Ratcliff in *Artforum* (New York), January 1973; "De Kinderen Kunner er 'n Joutje Van" by Tonni Burgering in *Rotterdam Nieuwsblad*, June 1973; "Art: Reading a Monumental Still Life" by John Perreault in the *Village Voice* (New York), May 1974.

If Tom Wesselmann does not tire, "The Great American Nude" will reach a thousand. This glamorous creation (*Max-Factorized*, Jean-Louis Ferrier has called her) continues her anonymous course across canvas after canvas, in and out of mixed-media set-ups, in paint, in plastic, or in any material that takes the artist's fancy. Only her personal number distinguishes her from her sisters, nearly all smiling broadly and seductively, most of them equipped with super-nubile nipples that look like erotic buttons.

And so many bathrooms . . . ! So many bathers . . . !

But it would be very wrong to think that Wesselmann never escapes from this centrally-heated eau-de-toilette inflated world of pulchritude. In her way, The Great American Nude is but one more adjunct to the late 20th-century living style. Her bosom may be bare, but her boudoir has a cassette and electric clock, her bathroom is rich with plumbing and generally a comfortable WC. And there are times when she is absent. A peep through the window shows photoch-

Tom Wesselman: *Still Life No. 39*, 1964

romatic pictures hanging on the wall above a table laid with bottle of beer and can of soda. All these appurtenances can be painted (sometimes in over-lifescale) or they can "be themselves" like Marcel Duchamp's *ready-mades,* although recruited for practical rather than surrealist purposes.

Wesselmann, supremely conscious of the mixed up world of modern times, knows full well (he is a Bachelor of Arts—Psychology) that contemporary life is based upon privately preserved classical myths in surprisingly easy concert with technical development. His girls are 20th century versions of so many sweethearts out of the past. But they live in a world of NOW. They are posed against a background that includes automobiles and TV. Their kitchens may be teeming with gadgetry, but the easy-to-serve snacks come from the supermarket and require a minimum of housewifery attention. A cardboard plate will suffice. Drinks are handy. Whoever heard of washing-up! The dishwasher will see to everything.

Lest such a coca-cola paradise be written off as trite, imagine what any other artist would make of this menu of canned lotus out of the refrigerator. Wesselmann is adept. He is able to flavour his irony with just the right amount of saccharine.

—Sheldon Williams

WESTERIK, Co.

Dutch. Born Jakobus Westerik in The Hague, 2 March 1924. Studied art, under Han van Dam, Rein Draijer, Henk Meyer, Willem Rozendaal and Willem Schrofer, Koninlijke Akademie van Beeldende Kunsten, The Hague, 1942–47. Married the painter Hens M. de Jong in 1948 (divorced, 1980); daughters: Christine, Victoria and Sophie; married gallery-director Fenna de Vries, in 1970; sons: Willem and Maurits. Painter, establishing own studio, The Hague, 1946–76, in Rotterdam, since 1971. Member, Haagsche Kunstkring artists' association, The Hague, 1946–57; Verve artists' group, The Hague, 1951–57; Pulchri Studio society of painters, The Hague, 1952. Instructor, International School, and Deutsche Schule, Scheveningen, 1953–58; Vrije Academie, The Hague, 1955–58; Koninklijke Academie van Beeldende Kunsten, The Hague, 1958–71; Ateliers 63, Haarlem, 1969–70. Recipient: Jacob Marisprijs, The Hague, 1951, 1955, 1961; Dutch Government Grant for Painting, 1953, 1954; Silver Medal, *Bienal,* Sao Paulo, 1965; Rembrandt Prize, Leiden, 1966; Dutch State Prize for Art and Architecture, 1970; Zuid-Holland Cultural Council Prize, 1987. Agent: Galerie Fenna de Vries, Rotterdam. Address: Eendrachtsplein 18, 3012 LA Rotterdam, Netherlands.

Individual Exhibitions:

1956 Museum Hofwijck, Voorburg, Netherlands
1964 Gemeentemuseum, The Hague (travelled to Vishal, Haarlem and Van Abbemuseum, Eindhoven, Netherlands)
1966 Stedelijk Museum de Lakenhal, Leiden
1968 Galerie 20, Amsterdam
Galerie Fenna de Vries, Rotterdam
Museum Boymans-van Beuningen, Rotterdam
1971 Galerie Fenna de Vries, Rotterdam
Stedelijk Museum, Amsterdam (travelled to the Groninger Museum, Groningen: Palais des Beaux-Arts, Brussels)
Galerie Escape, Amsterdam
1973 Galerie Fenna de Vries, Rotterdam
1974 Palais des Beaux-Arts, Brussels
1976 Galerie Fenna de Vries, Rotterdam
1977 Lens Fine Art, Antwerp
1978 Galerie Fenna de Vries, Rotterdam
1979 Stedelijk Museum, Amsterdam
1980 Galerie Fenna de Vries, Rotterdam
1981 Museum Boymans-van Beuningen, Rotterdam
1982 Galerie Fenna de Vries, Rotterdam
1983 Staatliche Kunsthalle, West Berlin (travelled to Saarbrucken and The Hague)

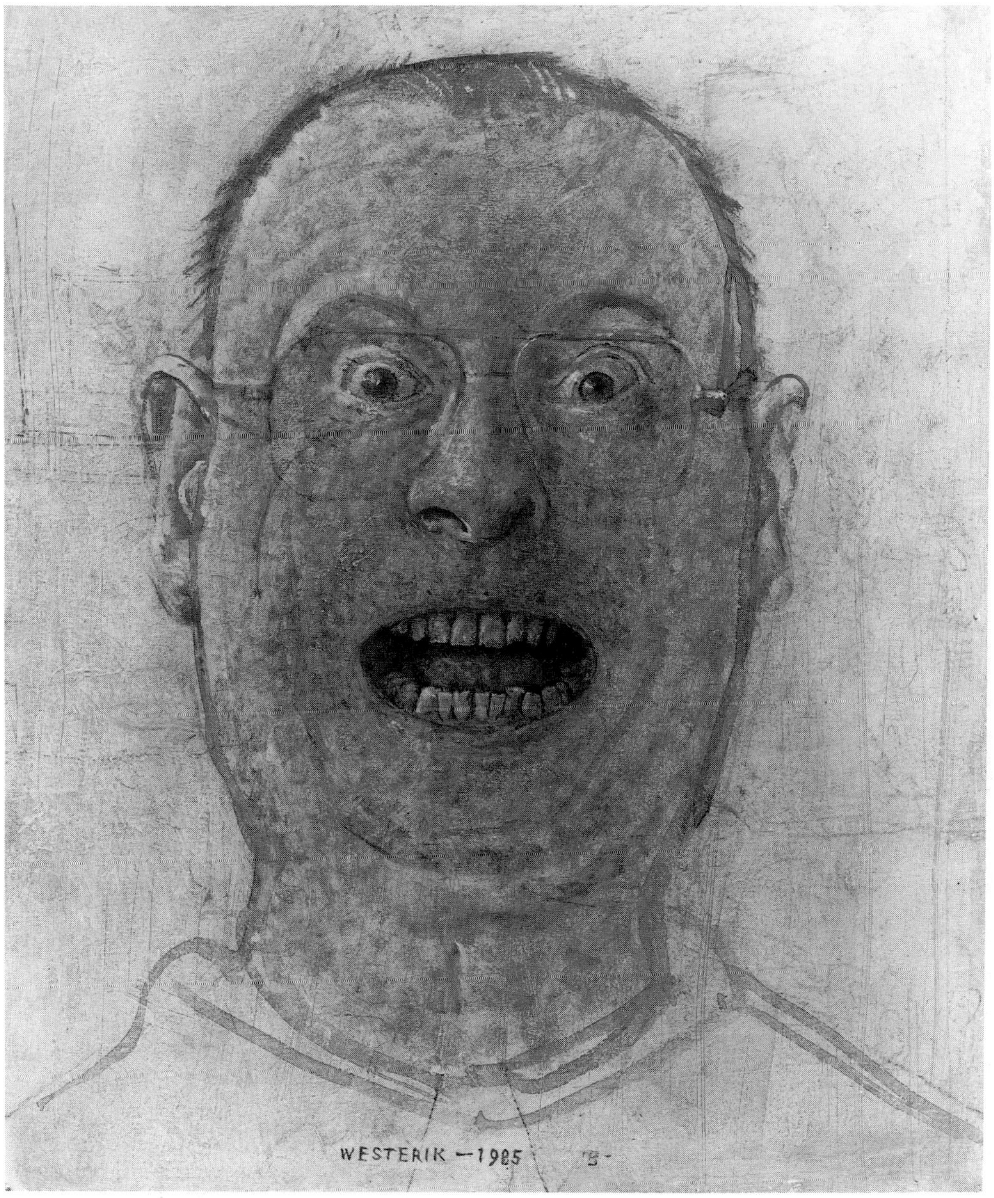

Co Westerik: ***Self Portrait with Open Mouth*****, 1985**

Selected Group Exhibitions:

1945 *Parade der Debutanten,* Lange Vijverberg, The Hague
1951 *Verve,* Kunstzaal Esher Surrey, The Hague
1954 *Irish Exhibition of Living Art,* National College of Art, Dublin
1962 *Biennale,* Venice
1964 *Carnegie International,* Pittsburgh
1966 *Tokyo International Exhibition of Art,* Keio Department Store, Tokyo
1969 *Haager Kunstler in Helmhaus,* Zurich
1974 *Verve 1951–1957,* Gemeentemuseum, The Hague
1982 *Arte come Arte,* at the *Biennale,* Venice
1985 *Nouvelle Biennale,* Paris

Collections:

Gemeentemuseum, The Hague; Museum Boymans-van Beuningen, Rotterdam; Centraal Museum, Utrecht; Frans Halsmuseum, Haarlem; Stedelijk Museum, Amsterdam; Museum Het Princessehof, Leeuwarden; Groninger Museum voor Stadt en Lande, Groningen; Gemeentemuseum, Arnhem; Museum De Lakenahl, Leiden; Stedelijk Museum, Arnhem.

Publications:

On WESTERIK: books—*Domino Book 2: Co Westerik—42 tekeningen, etsen en litho's,* with text by R. W. D. Oxenaar, Amsterdam 1961; *Co Westerik,* exhibition catalogue, with text by R. W. D. Oxenaar, The Hague 1964; *Co Westerik: Tekeningen, Grafiek, Aquarellen uit de verzameling C. Kuijman,* exhibition catalogue, with an introduction by H. R. Hoetink, Rotterdam 1968; *Co Westerik,* exhibition catalogue, with text by Wim Beeren, Amsterdam 1971; *Westerik: Drawings, Watercolours and Prints,* with text by J. L. Locher and H. R. Hoetink, Vlaardingen 1971, Amsterdam and Antwerp 1979; *Verve 1951–1957,* exhibition catalogue, with text by John Sillevis, The Hague 1974; *Co Westerik,* exhibition catalogue, with texts by R. W. D. Oxenaar and Carel Blotkamp, Brussels 1974; *Co Westerik* by W. Meewis, Schelderode, Netherlands 1979; *Co Westerik,* documentary report, by C. Withoff, Groningen, Netherlands 1979; *Co Westerik, Painter* by W. A. L. Beeren, Venlo, Netherlands 1981; *Co Westerik,* exhibition catalogue with texts by M. Eberle and J. Locher, West Berlin 1983.

Within the context of the dutch art-climate the painter Co Westerik without any doubt is a certain and constant factor. Although he never belonged to any group, although he has never been exemplary for any direction or tendency, through the years he nevertheless has held a position that is merely reflected by his work being part of all the major dutch museum collections, and countless private collections as well. Westerik's work is figurative and realistic, and miles away from the mainstreams of dutch constructivism and expressionism. Westerik's works deal with the human condition, the psychology pertaining to the individual trying and longing for another person, or thrown back at his own. His painting is convincingly humanistic and his pictures never degenerate into mere storytelling or anecdote.

Undoubtedly his best known paintings are *Fishwoman* (1951), *Schoolteacher and Child* (1961), *Cut by Grass*(1966). The last mentioned piece shows some fingers sliding through green grass. One is meanly cut by a green leaf that leaves its mark like a razorblade. The picture however has psychological impact that by far outreaches the absurdity of the event itself. One feels, here as well as in most of Westerik's paintings, a continuous hidden struggle between individuals, their lack of power and immediacy that feeds feelings of shame. On top of this, eroticism and religiosity by all means find their way through the surface. Westerik's great quality is that he always visualizes, never moralizes. The refinement of his thematic procedure corresponds with a very detailed, multi-layered painting process.

Apart from his painting, Westerik has built up a very large oeuvre of drawings and watercolors. Most of these drawings are autonomous, only part of these can be considered as preliminary studies to the paintings.

During the last two decades all his work gained in popularity, including the graphic work. In an extensive catalogue (Municipal Museum, The Hague, 1984) it is justly stated that this too deserves an autonomous status. Etching and lithography are Westerik's favourite techniques. His imagery is intimate and just as detailed and complex as his painting. The editions usually are very limited and even the prints differ.

—A. F. Wagemans

WESTERMANN, H(orace) C(lifford).

American. Born in Los Angeles, California, 11 December 1922. Studied at the Art Institute of Chicago, with Paul Weighardt, 1947–54. Served in the United States Marine Corps, 1942–45. Married Joanna Beall in 1959. Travelled widely in the Orient, and worked as an acrobat, logger, carpenter and mason. Thereafter a full-time artist. Recipient: Campana Prize, Art Institute of Chicago, 1964; National Endowment for the Arts Grant, 1967; Tamarind Fellowship, 1968; *Bienal* Prize, Sao Paulo, 1973. Agent: Xavier Fourcade Inc., 36 East 57th Street, New York, New York 10021, U.S.A. *Died in 1981.*

Individual Exhibitions:

1957 Allan Frumkin Gallery, Chicago
1961 Allan Frumkin Gallery, New York
1962 Dilexi Gallery, Los Angeles
Allan Frumkin Gallery, Chicago
1963 Dilexi Gallery, San Francisco
Allan Frumkin Gallery, New York
1965 Allan Frumkin Gallery, New York
1966 Nelson Museum, Kansas City, Missouri
1967 Allan Frumkin Gallery, Chicago
Allan Frumkin Gallery, New York
1968 Los Angeles County Museum of Art (retrospective)
Allan Frumkin Gallery, New York
1969 Museum of Contemporary Art, Chicago (retrospective)
1970 Allan Frumkin Gallery, New York
1971 Allan Frumkin Gallery, New York
Galerie Thomas Borgmann, Cologne
1974 James Corcoran Gallery, Los Angeles
Smithsonian Institution, Washington, D.C.
Allan Frumkin Gallery, New York
1976 Allan Frumkin Gallery, Chicago

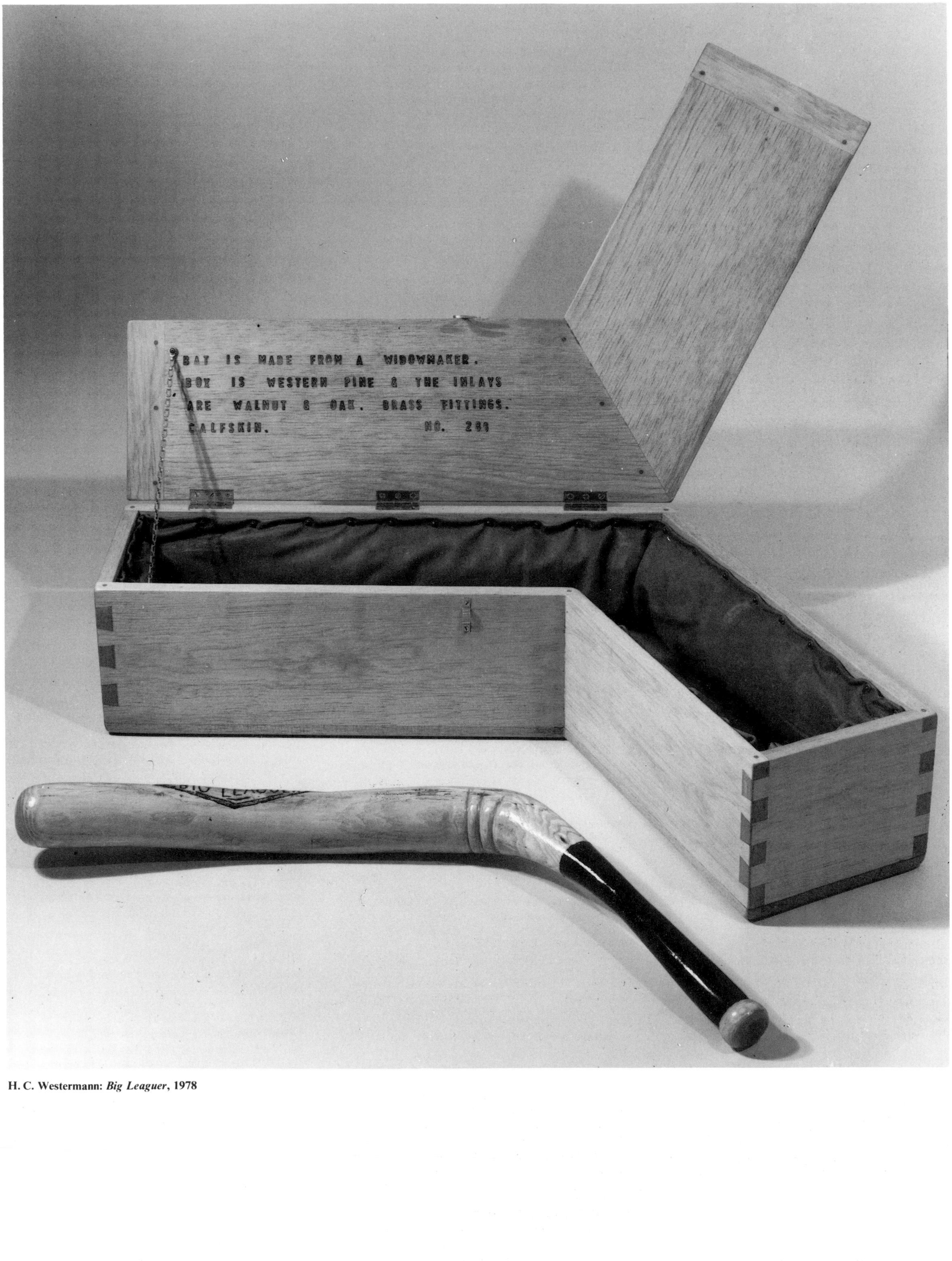

H. C. Westermann: *Big Leaguer*, 1978

1977 John Berggruen Gallery, San Francisco
1978 Whitney Museum, New York (retrospective; travelled to the New Orleans Museum of Art; Des Moines Art Center, Iowa; Seattle Art Museum; and the San Francisco Museum of Modern Art, 1978–79)
1980 Serpentine Gallery, London (retrospective)
1987 Art Institute of Chicago

Selected Group Exhibitions:

1960 *Surrealist Art*, Museum of Modern Art, New York
1964 *New Realism*, Gemeentemuseum, The Hague
1967 *American Sculpture of the 60's*, Los Angeles County Museum of Art
1968 *Documenta*, Kassel, West Germany (and 1972)
1973 *Bienal*, Sao Paulo
1974 *71st American Exhibition*, Art Institute of Chicago
1975 *Masterworks in Wood: The 20th Century*, Portland Art Museum, Oregon
1976 *200 Years of American Sculpture*, Whitney Museum, New York
1980 *One Major New Work Each*, Xavier Fourcade Inc., New York
1981 *Group Sculpture Show*, Xavier Fourcade Inc., New York

Collections:

Whitney Museum, New York; Wadsworth Atheneum, Hartford, Connecticut; Museum of Contemporary Art, Chicago; Art Institute of Chicago; Indiana University Art Museum, Bloomington; Des Moines Art Center, Iowa; Walker Art Center, Minneapolis; Los Angeles County Museum of Art; Norton Simon Art Museum, Pasadena, California; Seattle Art Museum.

Publications:

On WESTERMANN: books—*H. C. Westermann*, exhibition catalogue, by Max Kozloff, Los Angeles 1968; *Documenta 5*, exhibition catalogue, Kassel, West Germany 1972; *After Surrealism: Metaphors and Similes*, exhibition catalogue, by L. J. Ahlander, Sarasota, Florida 1972; *Fantastic Images* by Franz Schulze, Chicago 1972; *H. C. Westermann*, exhibition catalogue, by Barbara Haskell, New York 1978; *H. C. Westermann*, exhibition catalogue, by Dennis Adrian, London 1980; *H. C. Westermann: Selections from the Alan and Dorothy Press Collection*, exhibition catalogue with text by Neal Benezra, Chicago 1987.

I'm not being facetious at all—I think an artist should have very good feet!

—H. C. Westermann (1977)

H. C. Westermann was, I suppose, a sculptor. At least he worked in three dimensions and utilized such materials as wood and metal. But his work defies description. Comic strips in the round? Surrealistic statements of satire and disgust? Assemblages of hand-crafted components? His sculptures are, as the saying goes, beautifully crafted with lots of cunning detail. Quirky in the extreme and loaded with wry commentary—verbal as well as visual: here there be messages.

Westermann was from Chicago, a curious American city set on a lake which is notable for its importance as a railroad center, its slaughter houses, its grain exchange and its modern architecture. It also boasts a great art museum. Somehow all these things have helped to produce a very odd group of artists much given to the creation of a new-surrealist art involving outrageous eroticism and comic strips. Think of a marriage between George Crumb and Hieronymous Bosch. Very little of this kind of thing has come out of New York or San Francisco or Los Angeles, and one wonders what has caused it to flower in the Windy City.

Westermann fits in here but with a slight difference—his production of objects which are sculptural in implication rather than two-dimensional like comics, and the extreme fastidiousness with which he executed them. Part of their startling impressiveness is due to the beauty of their manufacture. Try to imagine a lollipop made by Hepplewhite. This "contradiction" between subject matter and technique is part of Westermann's surrealist displacement. Another contributing factor is his sly combining of images with words so that puns are put. Another is the air of fun fair about his work—things like openings to peak through, tiny doors or drawers to open, mirrors, models, abound. This in connection with the formal presentation of material so skillfully worked as to constitute a "subject" in itself.

All of it ending as a form of craziness that redefines sanity.

—Ralph Pomeroy

WHEELER, Doug.

American. Born in Globe, Arizona, 29 December 1939. Studied at Santa Monica City College, California, 1958–59; University of California at Los Angeles, 1960–64; B.F.A. Married Nancy Lee Harrison in 1965 (divorced, 1969). Instructor in Creative Studies, University of California at Santa Barbara, since 1978. Recipient: New Talent Award from the Los Angeles County Museum of Art, 1966; National Endowment for the Arts Grant, 1968, 1977; Guggenheim Fellowship, 1971. Agents: Riko Mizuno Gallery, 669 La Cienga, West Hollywood, California; Galleria Salvatore Ala, Via Mameli 3, 20129 Milan, Italy; Salvatore Ala Gallery, 32 West 20th Street, New York, New York 10011. Address: 2623 Main Street, Santa Monica, California 90405, U.S.A.

Individual Exhibitions:

1968 Pasadena Museum of Art, California
1969 Ace Gallery, Los Angeles
Fort Worth Art Center, Texas (with Robert Irwin)
1970 Artist's Studio, Venice, California
Tate Gallery, London (with Larry Bell and Robert Irwin)
1974 Riko Mizuno Gallery, Los Angeles
1975 Galleria Salvatore Ala, Milan

Selected Group Exhibitions:

1969 *Prospectus '69*, Kunsthalle, Dusseldorf
Kompas IV, Stedelijk Museum, Eindhoven, Netherlands
1973 *3D into 2D*, New York Cultural Center (toured the United States
1974 *American Exhibition*, Art Institute of Chicago
1975 *4 from 5, California*, School of Visual Arts, New York (travelled to the Corcoran Gallery of Art, Washington, D.C.)
1976 *Biennale*, Venice

Collections:

Art Institute of Chicago; Stedelijk Museum, Amsterdam.

Publications:

On WHEELER: books—*Doug Wheeler*, exhibition catalogue, by John Coplans, Pasadena, California 1968; *Wheeler/Irwin*, exhibition catalogue, by Jane Livingston, Los Angeles 1969; *Larry Bell, Robert Irwin, Doug Wheeler*, exhibition catalogue, by Michael Compton, London 1970; articles—"Place in the Sun" in *Time* (New York), 30 August 1968; "Doug Wheeler—Light Paintings" by John Coplans in *Artforum* (New York), March 1970; "Doug Wheeler—Exhibitions at Ace Gallery" by Peter Plagens in *Artforum* (New York), May 1970; "Exhibition at Ace Gallery" by Joseph E. Young in *Art International* (Lugano, Switzerland), no. 3, 1970; "Exhibition at Riko Mizuno Gallery" by Melinda Wortz in *Artweek* (Oakland, California), April 1974; "Doug Wheeler—Riko Mizuno Gallery" by Peter Plagens in *Artforum* (New York), September 1974.

WHITMAN, Robert.

American. Born in New York City in 1935. Studied at Rutgers University, New Brunswick, New Jersey, 1953–57, B.A. 1957; also studied at Columbia University, New York. Performance artist: lives and works in New York. Agent: Bykert Gallery, New York. Address: c/o Bykert Gallery, 484 Broome Street, New York, New York 10013, U.S.A.

Individual Exhibitions:

1959 Hansa Gallery, New York
Reuben Gallery, New York
Rutgers University, New Brunswick, New Jersey
1963 9 Great Jones Street, New York (with Walter De Maria)
1967 Pace Gallery, New York
1968 Jewish Museum, New York
Museum of Contemporary Art, Chicago
1973 Museum of Modern Art, New York
1974 Bykert Gallery, New York
Galleria L'Attico, Rome
1975 Bykert Downtown Gallery, New York
1976 *Theatre Works 1960–1976*, Dia Art Foundation, New York
1979 Hudson River Museum, Yonkers, New York
1980 *Outdoor Performance Work*, Snug Harbor, Staten Island, New York

Selected Group Exhibitions:

1960 *New Forms—New Media*, Martha Jackson Gallery, New York
1962 *Environments, Situations and Spaces*, Martha Jackson Gallery, New York
1964 *6 Artists*, Sidney Janis Gallery, New York
1965 *11 from the Reuben Gallery*, Guggenheim Museum, New York
1966 *Erotic Art*, Sidney Janis Gallery, New York
1967 *Projected Art*, Finch College, New York
1968 *6 Artists, 6 Exhibitions*, Walker Art Center, Minneapolis
1969 *String and Rope*, Sidney Janis Gallery, New York
1971 *Art and Technology*, Los Angeles County Museum of Art
1974 *Projected Images*, Walker Art Center, Minneapolis

Collections:

Museum of Contemporary Art, Chicago; Jewish Museum, New York

Publications:

On WHITMAN: book—*Assemblages, Environments and Happenings* by Allan Kaprow, New York 1969; articles—"Whitman Room" in *Arts and Architecture* (Los Angeles), June 1964; "7 New Artists at Janis" by Sidney Tillim in *Arts Magazine* (New York), September 1964; "Pearstein, Jagger, Whitman, Gutman" by G. Brown in *Arts Magazine* (New York), September 1967; "Mother Turn Off the Picture" by Otto Piene in *Artscanada* (Toronto), June 1968; "Magic Theatre, Une Exposition á Kansas City" by S. Bann in *Oeil* (Paris), August September 1968; "A Planned Coincidence" by Dore Ashton in *Art in America* (New York), September/October 1969; "Some Thoughts on 'Art and Technology' " by Jane Livingston in *Studio International* (London), June 1971; "Corporate Art" by Jack Burnham in *Artforum* (New York), October 1971; "Bob Whitman and Things . . . " by George Segal in *Art and Artists* (London), November 1972.

Robert Whitman is a master of visual theatre-presentational performance which cohered in terms of imagery, rather than language or narrative. He was once regarded as a sometime visual artist, who had exhibited his paintings and sculptures, but had, unlike, say, Oldenburg and Rauschenberg, abandoned those crafts to concentrate exclusively on theater; his wilful concentration was, at the time, seen as a measure of serious purpose.

His masterpiece a decade ago was *Prune Flat* (1965), which was then curiously spelled "Prune. Flat." It opens with the image of a movie projector (implicitly announcing that one theme was cinematic images) and then shows a grapefruit (that nearly fills the screen) being cut by a knife. After other images, a tomato appears, which is also cut, black egg-like objects pouring out; and when the tomato sequence is repeated, two young women dressed in white smocks and white kerchiefs in front of the screen, the filmed blade cutting through them. As the film shows the two women walking down the street, one slightly behind the other, so the same two women walk across the stage, at a perpendicular angle to their images on the screen, but in the same formation. Later in the piece, the image of a woman undressing and showering is projected directly on the full length body of one of the women performers; but once the film shuts off, the woman who appears to be undressed is suddenly revealed to be definitely besmocked. The subject of *Prune Flat* is, of course, the perceptual discrepancies between filmed image and theatrical presence, and it differs from the other mixed-means pieces not only in its precise control but in its visual beauty.

Whitman staged other mixed-means pieces at the time, including the spectacularly scaled *Two Holes of the Water* (1966): but these tended to be diffuse and temporally flaccid. I have heard of earlier pieces of his, but did not see them until a retrospective was presented in the spring of 1976. The best innovation in *American Moon* (1960) was the positioning of the audience, which is divided into groups of ten, each assigned to a cubicle within a circular structure that looks into the performance area. In other words, that is "theatre-in-the-ground" with the audience subdivided by partitions. Translucent cloth screens separated each audience from the stage before them, and film is at times projected from behind on these individual screens, so that each section sees a different part of the movie. Once the curtains are raised, the climax of the piece is a cellophane structure that is blown up from an unheard source, the plastic filling the centerspace. Two performers walk through it. As a man is suspended in a swing above the space, the piece closes. *American Moon* struck me as the best of the other works in the retrospective, which included *Flower* (1963), *Nighttime Sky* (1965), *Salad P.N.* (1974), in addition to a new work, *Light Touch* (1976). Though each of the others has stunning particulars, it is still *Prune Flat* that remains the most extraordinary of Whitman's theatrical pieces.

His work has always been uneven, and always exploratory. His forte is evocative, memorable imagery; his recurring failings include a leaden sense of theatrical time and sado-masochistic undertones.

Though I have already seen *Prune Flat* perhaps a dozen times, I would gladly see it again.

—Richard Kostelanetz

WIELAND, Joyce.

Canadian. Born in Toronto in 1931. Studied under Carl Schaeffer, Doris McCarthy, and Bob Ross, Central Technical School, Toronto. Married the artist Michael Snow, *q.v.* Painter, film-maker, and maker of quilts: lives and works in Toronto: worked for Graphic Associates, Toronto, 1956–58; lived in New York, 1963–70. Recipient: Canada Council Grants, 1966, 1968; Toronto Arts Award, 1987. Agent: Isaacs Gallery, 179 John Street, Toronto, Ontario M5T 1X3. Address: 497 Queen Street East, Toronto, Ontario M5A 1V1, Canada.

Individual Exhibitions:

1959 Isaacs Gallery, Toronto (with Gordon Rayner)
1964 Isaacs Gallery, Toronto
1967 National Gallery of Canada, Ottawa
1968 Vancouver Art Gallery (retrospective)
1971 *True Patriot Love,* National Gallery of Canada, Ottawa
1978 National Gallery of Canada, Ottawa
1979 Pauline McGibbon Art Centre, TOronto
1981 Isaacs Gallery, Toronto
1982 Forest City Gallery, London, Ontario
Yajima/Galerie, Montreal
1983 Isaacs Gallery, Toronto
1985 Concordia University, Montreal
1987 Art Gallery of Ontario, Toronto
Confederation Art Gallery, Charlottetown, Prince Edward Island
1988 Beaverbrook Art Gallery, Fredericton, New Brunswick
Mackenzie Art Gallery, Regina, Saskatchewan
Canada House Gallery, London

Selected Group Exhibitions:

1968 *Biennale of Canadian Painters,* National Gallery of Canada, Ottawa
1970 *8 Artists from Canada,* Tel Aviv Museum
1971 *49th Parallels: New Canadian Art,* Ringling Museum of Art, Sarasota, Florida
1972 *Toronto Painting 1953–1965,* National Gallery of Canada, Ottawa
1976 *Une Histoire du Cinéma,* Musée National d'Art Moderne, Paris
1977 *Canadian Tapestries 77,* Art Gallery of Ontario, Toronto
1981 *Twentieth Century Canadian Painting,* National Museum of Modern Art, Tokyo
1982 *Contemporary Outdoor Sculpture,* Guild of All Arts, Toronto
1983 *New Perceptions: Portraits,* Harbourfront Community Gallery, Toronto
1984 *Toronto Painting 84,* Art Gallery of Ontario, Toronto

Collections:

National Gallery of Canada, Ottawa; Art Gallery of Ontario, Toronto; Montreal Museum of Fine Arts; Winnipeg Art Gallery; Norman Mackenzie Art Gallery, Regina, Saskatchewan; Edmonton Art Gallery, Alberta; Vancouver Art Gallery; Museum of Modern Art, New York; Philadelphia Museum of Art; Royal Belgian Film Archives, Brussels.

Publications:

By WIELAND: article—interview, with Pierre Theberge, in *True Patriot Love,* exhibition catalogue, Ottawa 1971; films—*Larry's Recent Behaviour,* 1963; *Patriotism* (Parts 1 and 2), 1964; *Peggy's Blue Skylight,* 1964; *Barbara's Blindness,* with Betty Ferguson, 1965; *Water Sark,* 1965; *1933,* 1967; *Hand Tinting,* 1967; *Sailboat,* 1967; *Catfood,* 1968; *Rat Life and Diet in North America,* 1968; *La Raison avant la Passion,* 1969; *Dripping Water,* with Michael Snow, 1969; *Pierre Vallières,* 1972; *Solidarity,* 1973; *The Far Shore,* 1976; *A and B in Ontario,* 1984; *Birds at Sunrise,* 1985.

On WIELAND: books—*True Patriot Love,* exhibition catalogue, Ottawa 1971; *Contemporary Canadian Painting* by William Withrow, Toronto 1972; *A Concise History of Canadian Painting* by Dennis Reid, Toronto 1973; *Joyce Wieland,* exhibition catalogue with texts by Lucy Lippard, Marie Fleming and Lauren Rabinovitz, Toronto 1987; articles—"Joyce Wieland at the Isaacs Gallery" by David Donnell in *Canadian Art* (Ottawa), March/April 1964; "Joyce Wieland Retrospective, Vancouver Art Gallery: by Marguerite Pinney in *Artscanada* (Toronto), June 1968; "There Is Only One Joyce" by P. Adams Sitney in *Artscanada* (Toronto), April 1970; "True Patriot Love" by Harry Malcolmson in *Canadian Forum* (Toronto), June 1971; "True Patriot Love: The Films of Joyce Wieland" by Regina Cornwell in *Artforum* (New York), September 1971; "Wieland: An Epiphany of North" by Hugo McPherson in *Artscanada* (Toronto), August/September 1971; "True Patriot Love: The Work of Joyce Wieland" by D. Magidson and J. Wright in *Art and Artists* (London), October 1973.

Unlike most other artist members of Toronto's art community in her generation, most of whom attended the Ontario College of Art, Joyce Wieland was a graduate of the art course at Central Technical School. More important for her later development was her experimentation with film at Graphic Associates, where she worked from 1956 to 1958 as an animator. Much of Wieland's later work either uses filmic elements (as in her sequential painting referring to an unfolding of a succession of things in film strips) or is in film. It is as a movie-maker that she has secured her international reputation today, especially for her major feature film, *The Far Shore* (completed in 1976).

In her early stained paintings and collages of the late 1950's and early 1960's, Wieland often used sexual imagery, as in "Time Machine Series." By 1965 the form of her work had changed to framed or boxed constructions and serial paintings. The plastic *collages* of 1965 were stuffed and quilted movies called "home totems."

In her domestic art works she has tried to discover and explore her femininity. In the late 1960's, seeking a place for feminine work within the dominating male aesthetic, she pioneered the use of the quilt medium traditionally associated with women as a fine art form. Her quilts can hang on the wall or be used on a bed. In quilts she was able to express her spirited nationalism (she is a "cultural activist") and her love of nature. In one quilt the insert hidden under a flap reads, "Down with U.S. Imperialist Technology." Elsewhere she may examine Canadian history.

The quilt is also a vehicle for her ecological concerns. In her "Water Quilt" there is a message under the 64 cushions with their 64 embroidered flaps of the Arctic flowers—the text is from James Laxer's ecological and political study, *The Energy Poker Game.* In 109 "Views of Canada" and "Arctic Day" she examines Canada and the much-disputed ecological area of the Canadian Arctic.

From 1977 on, in Wieland's drawings in coloured pencil, she explored stories of love and catalysm, landscape and light, "drawing together all the things I care about in one place." The paintings which developed in this period, culminating with *The Artist on Fire* (1983), explored in rich colour the artist's self-image and ideals. Today, after a retrospective in 1987 at the Art Gallery of Ontario (1987), Wieland has gone back to the freedom of her early abstractions and combined it with her basic themes of growth, nature, love and life.

—Joan Murray

WILEY, William T.

American. Born in Bedford, Indiana, 21 October 1937. Educated at Columbia High School, Richland, Washington, 1952–56; studied at the San Francisco Art Institute, B.F.A. 1961, M.F.A. 1962. Independent artist incorporating verbal humor in paintings, sculpture and prints, since 1960: lives and works in California. Associate Professor, University of California at Davis, 1962–73; Instructor, San Francisco Art Institute, 1963, 1966–67; Art Instructor, University of Nevada, Reno, 1967; Art Instructor, Washington State College, Pullman, 1967; Art Instructor, University of California at Berkeley, 1967; Instructor, School of Visual Arts, New York, 1968; Art Instructor, University of Colorado, Boulder, 1968. Recipient: Painting Prize, San Francisco Art Institute, 1959; First Prize, *San Francisco Art Institute Festival,* 1960; Fletcher Award, California School of Fine

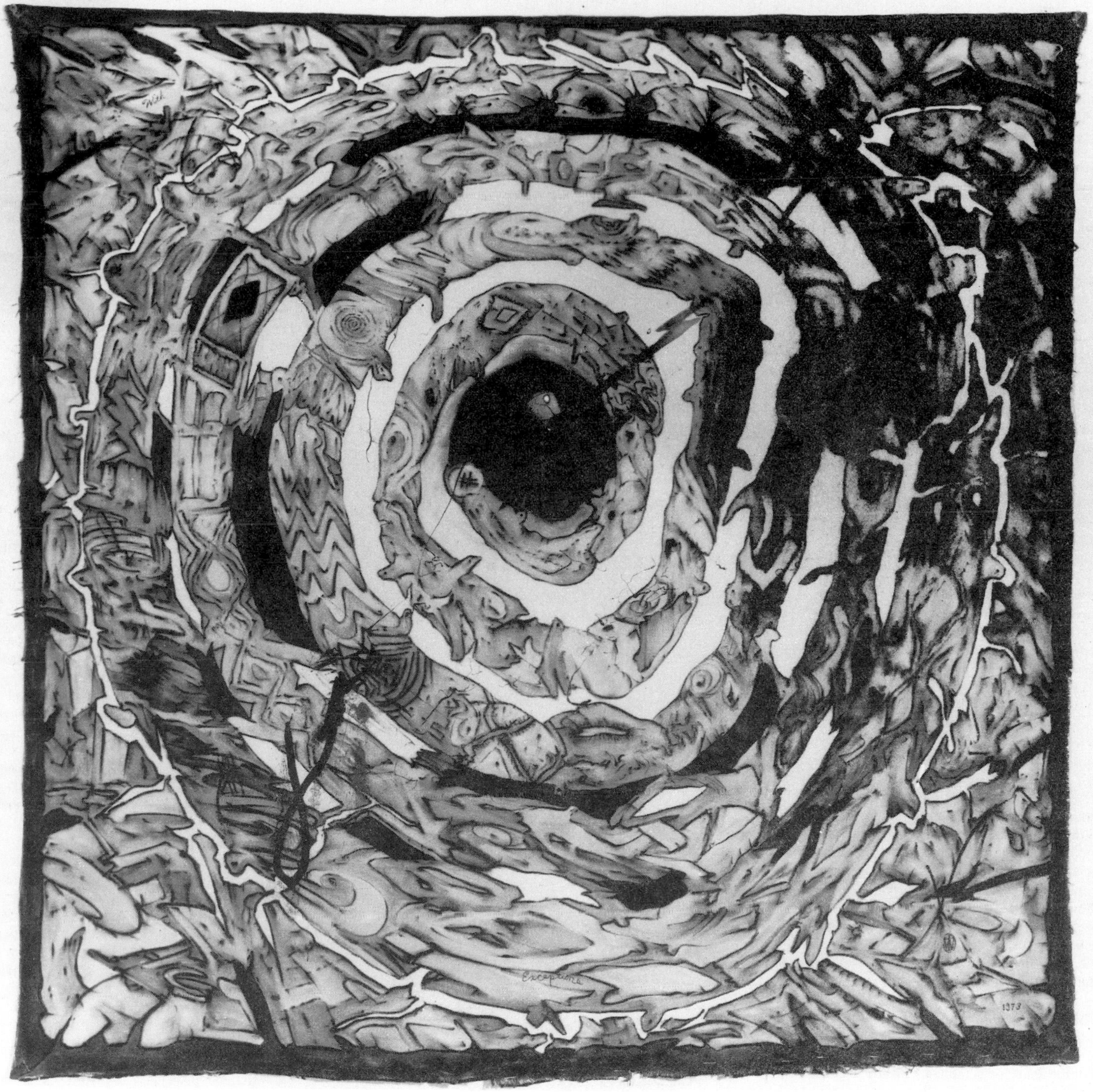

William T. Wiley: *With Few Exceptions*, 1973

Arts, 1960; First Prize, Painting, *Oakland Annual*, 1960; New Talent Award, *Art in America*, 1961; Painting Prize, *65th Annual Exhibition*, Art Institute of Chicago, 1962; Sculpture Prize, Los Angeles County Museum of Art, 1962; Creative Arts Institute Award, University of California at Davis, 1968; Purchase Prize, Whitney Museum, New York, 1968; Nealie Sullivan Award, San Francisco Art Institute, 1968; Bartels Prize, *72nd American Exhibition*, Art Institute of Chicago, 1976; Traveling Grant to Australia, Australian Arts Council, 1980. Agent: Wanda Hansen, 615 Main Street, Sausalito, California 95965. Address: P.O. Box 609, Forest Knolls, California 94933, U.S.A.

Individual Exhibitions:

1960 Staempfli Gallery, New York
San Francisco Museum of Art
1962 Staempfli Gallery, New York
1964 Staempfli Gallery, New York
1965 Lanyon Gallery, Palo Alto, California
1967 Mills College, Oakland, California
1968 Hansen Fuller Gallery, San Francisco
Allan Frumkin Gallery, New York
1969 Hansen Fuller Gallery, San Francisco
Allan Frumkin Gallery, Chicago
1970 Allan Frumkin Gallery, New York
Keel Over, Madison Art Center, Wisconsin
1971 Hansen Fuller Gallery, San Francisco
Manolides Gallery, Seattle (with Robert Arneson)
Studio Marconi, Milan
Corcoran Gallery, Washington, D.C. (travelled to the University Art Museum, University of California at Berkeley and the Art Institute of Chicago)
1972 Hansen Fuller Gallery, San Francisco
Allan Frumkin Gallery, Chicago
James Manolides Gallery, Seattle
Margo Leavin Gallery, Los Angeles
Galleria Odyssia, Rome
Galerie Richard Foncke, Ghent
1973 Allan Frumkin Gallery, New York
Van Abbemuseum, Eindhoven, Netherlands
1974 Hansen Fuller Gallery, San Francisco
Allan Frumkin Gallery, Chicago
Utah Fine Arts Museum, Salt Lake City
1975 Hansen Fuller Gallery, San Francisco
3 One-Man Shows: William T. Wiley, Dorothy Hood, Armando Morales, University of Texas at Austin
1976 Allan Frumkin Gallery, New York
Project Room, Museum of Modern Art, New York
1977 Galerie Paul Facchetti, Paris
New Publications, Landfall Press Gallery, Chicago
Suite of Daze, Art Institute of Chicago
1978 Hansen Fuller Gallery, San Francisco
Myra Morgan Gallery, Shawnee Mission, Kansas
Delahunty Gallery, Dallas, Texas
1979 *Graphics 1967–1979*, Allan Frumkin Gallery, New York and Chicago
Prints, Baltimore Museum of Art (retrospective)
1980 Hansen Fuller Goldeen, San Francisco

Prints, Illinois State University, Normal
Prints and Sculpture, San Jose Museum of Art, California
Cornish Institute of Allied Arts Gallery, Seattle
Glen Hanson Gallery, Minneapolis
Realities Gallery, Melbourne (travelled to the Institute of Modern Art, Brisbane)
Redding Museum, Redding, California

1981 Allan Frumkin Gallery, New York
Emily Carr College of Art, Vancouver
Florida State University, Tallahassee (travelled to Florida International University, Miami, and the University of South Florida, Tampa)
Wiley Territory, Walker Art Center, Minneapolis (travelled to Dallas; Denver; Des Moines; San Francisco; Phoenix)

1983 Hansen Fuller Gallery, San Francisco
Allan Frumkin Gallery, New York

1985 Alberta College of Art, Calgary (Travelled to Chicago)

1986 *Steal Witness for the Time Being*, Newport Harbor Art Museum, Newport Beach, California (travelled to Palm Springs; Boise; Seattle; San Francisco)
Moore College, Philadelphia (travelled to New York)
Fulkler Goldeen Gallery, San Francisco
Hammarskjold Plaza Sculpture Garden, New York
Marsha Mateyka Gallery, Washington, D.C.

1987 *What Is Not Music*, Galerie Grita Insam, Vienna (travelled to Frankfurt)
L.A. Louver Gallery, Venice, California

Performance: *Over Evident Falls*, with Steve Reich, Sacramento, California, 1968.

Selected Group Exhibitions:

1973 *Extraordinary Realities*, Whitney Museum, New York
1974 *Surrealität-Bildrealität 1924–1974*, Städtische Kun-Kunsthalle, Dusseldorf
1976 *3 From California*, Dalhousie Art Gallery, Halifax, Nova Scotia
1977 *Artists' Maps*, Philadelphia College of Art
1978 *Aesthetics of Graffiti*, San Francisco Museum of Modern Art
1979 *The 1970's: New American Painting*, New Museum, New York (toured Eastern Europe through 1981)
1981 *8 Funny Artists*, Institute for Art and Urban Resources, New York
1983 *Minimalism to Expressionism*, Whitney Museum, New York
1985 *Content: A Contemporary Focus 1974–84*, Hirshhorn Museum, Washington, D.C.
1987 *Bay Area Drawing*, Richmond Art Center, California

Collections:

San Francisco Museum of Modern Art; University Art Museum, University of California at Berkeley; Oakland Museum, California; Museum of Modern Art, New York; Whitney Museum, New York; Art Institute of Chicago; Fort Worth Art Center, Texas; Des Moines Art Center, Iowa; University of Kansas Art Museum, Lawrence; Van Abbemuseum, Eindhoven, Netherlands.

Publications:

By WILEY: films—*The Great Blondino*, San Francisco 1967; *Man's Nature*, San Francisco 1971.

On WILEY: books (exhibition catalogues)—*Funk* by Peter Selz, Berkeley 1967; *Wizdumb*, with introduction by Brenda Richardson, berkeley 1971; *William T. Wiley: Retrospective*, with introduction by J. Leering, Eindhoven 1973; *Wiley Territory*, with texts by Graham Beal and John Perreault, Minneapolis 1979; *William T. Wiley*, with essays by Beth Coffelt, Matthew Kangas, John Perreault and others, Tallahassee 1981; *Steal Witness for the Time Being*, with introduction by Albert Stewart, North Haven 1984; *William T. Wiley: Recent Paintings and Watercolors*, with essay by Sarah McFadden, Philadelphia and New York 1986; *What Is Not Music*, with texts by Peter Weiermair and Ben Marks, Frankfurt and Vienna 1987.

Hunger . . . For A Statement
Driven? By Something? I (We)
Don't Understand? We (I) Praise
Sing Dance Deny And Die In
The Face. Make? Pictures
Of Living, Dying, Becoming.
Knowledge Cannot Seem To Help
Much, Nor Suffering . . .
What Is Not Food?

—William T. Wiley

The surrealist elements that run through William Wiley's paintings and constructions are tempered by a kind of zany, dude dadaism and beguiling lyricism. A look at his work reveals an honest love of the land and a genuine child-like interest in minutia. This quality in turn is reflected in Wiley's style. In his two-dimensional works there are unmistakable references to comic strips, coloring books and children's book illustrations. Applied to the adult world of landscape painting, mysticism and ecology they create an off-balanced, fresh quality that is part of Wiley's distinction.

He seems very much a California artist but one who's been as they say, around. Any naivete he may display is strictly *faux*. His work abounds in visual and verbal puns. Yes, verbal. He is an artist much given to words. He likes to write all over his work—to include passages from logs, or notebooks, or fragments from letters to or from friends. He belongs to a kind of circle of like-minded fellow artists and there are constant cross-references to the work, lives, personalities, etc., of the circle.

Wiley's draughtsmanship is very fine with live, strong, *interesting* line, a little like those picture puzzles where you are supposed to locate and identify various hidden images. This incorporation of commonplace, popular material is somewhat related to Pop art—in the way, say, of relating to such things as Andy Warhol's color-me-by-numbers paintings. But Wiley's interests and direction are far more consciously "artistic" in technique than the products of most Pop artists. It can even be said that, in the end, his work has elegance.

This is related to the lyricism I spoke of and goes along with a gentleness and whimsy characteristic of much of Wiley's output. He likes to draw imaginary maps, to make charts and give directions. Besides orthodox painting on canvas he often introduces the third dimension incorporating feathers, rope, sticks, string, branches, etc., suggestive of American Indian artifacts, of camping trips, of cowboys-and-Indians. There are echoes of fetishism and secret rites, of poetry and religion, of children's games in his work and its success lies in the imaginative synthesis he has made from such complex and various subject matter. His work suggests that of a man deeply sympathetic to the American Far West and to the development of twentieth century art—a kind of pioneer who's read Proust.

—Ralph Pomeroy

WILLATS, Stephen.

British. Born in London, 17 August 1943. Studied, under Roy Ascott, at Ealing College of Art, 1952. Married Felicity Oliver in 1974; sons (from previous marriage): Justin and Nicholas. Founder, *Control* magazine, London, 1965; Founder, Centre for Behavioural Art, London, 1972–74. Lecturer, Ipswich School of Art, Suffolk, 1965–67, and Nottingham College of Art, 1968–72; Part-time Lecturer in Sculpture, Hornsey College of Art, London, 1969–71. Agents: Lisson Gallery, 68 Bell Street, London NWI; Rudiger Schöttle, Martiusstrasse 7, 8000 Munich 40, West Germany. Address: 5 London Mews, London W2, England.

Individual Exhibitions:

1964 Chester Beatty Research Institute, London
1968 Museum of Modern Art, Oxford
1971 *Man from the 21st Century*, Nottingham
1972 *Social Resource Project for Tennis Clubs*, Nottingham
West London Social Resource Project, London
Oxford Insight Development Project, Oxford
1973 Gallery House, London
Edinburgh Social Model Construction Project, Edinburgh
1974 Gallery December, Münster, West Germany
1975 Galleria Banco, Brescia, Italy
The Gallery, London (toured the U.K.)
1976 Midland Group Gallery, Nottingham
Lisson Gallery, London
Stampa Gallery, Basle
1977 *From a Coded World*, London
Attitudes within 4 Relationships, Southhampton Art Gallery
1978 *Contained Living*, Museum of Modern Art, Oxford
Questions about Ourselves, Lisson Gallery, London
1979 *Concerning Our Present Way of Living*, Whitechapel Art Gallery, London
The Lurky Place, Galerie Schweinabraden, East Berlin
Berlin Wall Drawings, Rudiger Schöttle Galerie, Munich
4 Professionals, Lisson Gallery, London
1980 *Concerning Our Present Way of Living*, Stedelijk van Abbemuseum, Eindhoven, Netherlands
4 Inseln in Berlin, Nationalgalerie, Berlin
1981 *4 Inseln in Berlin*, Gothe Institute, London
Mens en Omgeving, De Beyerd Centrum, Breda, Netherlands
1982 *Meta Filter and Related Works* Tate Gallery, London
The New Reality, Orchard Gallery, Londonderry, Northern Ireland
1983 *Angst in den Strasse*, Galerie Rudiger Schottle, Munich
Inside the Night, Lisson Gallery, London
Under Cover, Arnolfini Gallery, Bristol
1984 *Means of Escape*, Rochdale Art Gallery, Lancashire
Another City, Riverside Studios, London
1985 *Doppelganger*, Lisson Gallery, London
Double Crossing, Galerie Ralph Wernicke, Stuttgart
1986 *City of Concrete*, Ikon Gallery, Birmingham
Grusse vom modernen Lebe, Stadtische Galerie, Regensburg, West Germany
Groeten uit het moderne leven, Museum van Hedendaagse Kunst, Utrecht, Netherlands
Concepts and Models, Institute of Contemporary Arts, London
Vier Huizen in Den Haag, Gemeentemuseum, The Hague
Striking Back, Mappin Art Gallery, Sheffield, Yorkshire
Fragments of Modern Living, Galerie Tanja Grunert, Cologne
1987 *Contemporary Living*, Museum van Hedendaagse Kunst, Ghent, Belgium
Concepts and Projects Bookworks, Nigel Greenwood Books, London
Between Objects and People, Leeds City Art Gallery, Yorkshire

Selected Group Exhibitions:

1966 *Kunst Licht/Kunst*, Stedelijk van Abbemuseum, Eindhoven, Netherlands
1967 *Light and Movement*, Herbert Art Gallery, Coventry (toured the U.K.)
1970 *Kinetic Art*, Hayward Gallery, London
1972 *Cognition Control*, Midland Group Gallery, Nottingham (toured the U.K.)
1975 *Codes and Structures*, Royal College of Art, London

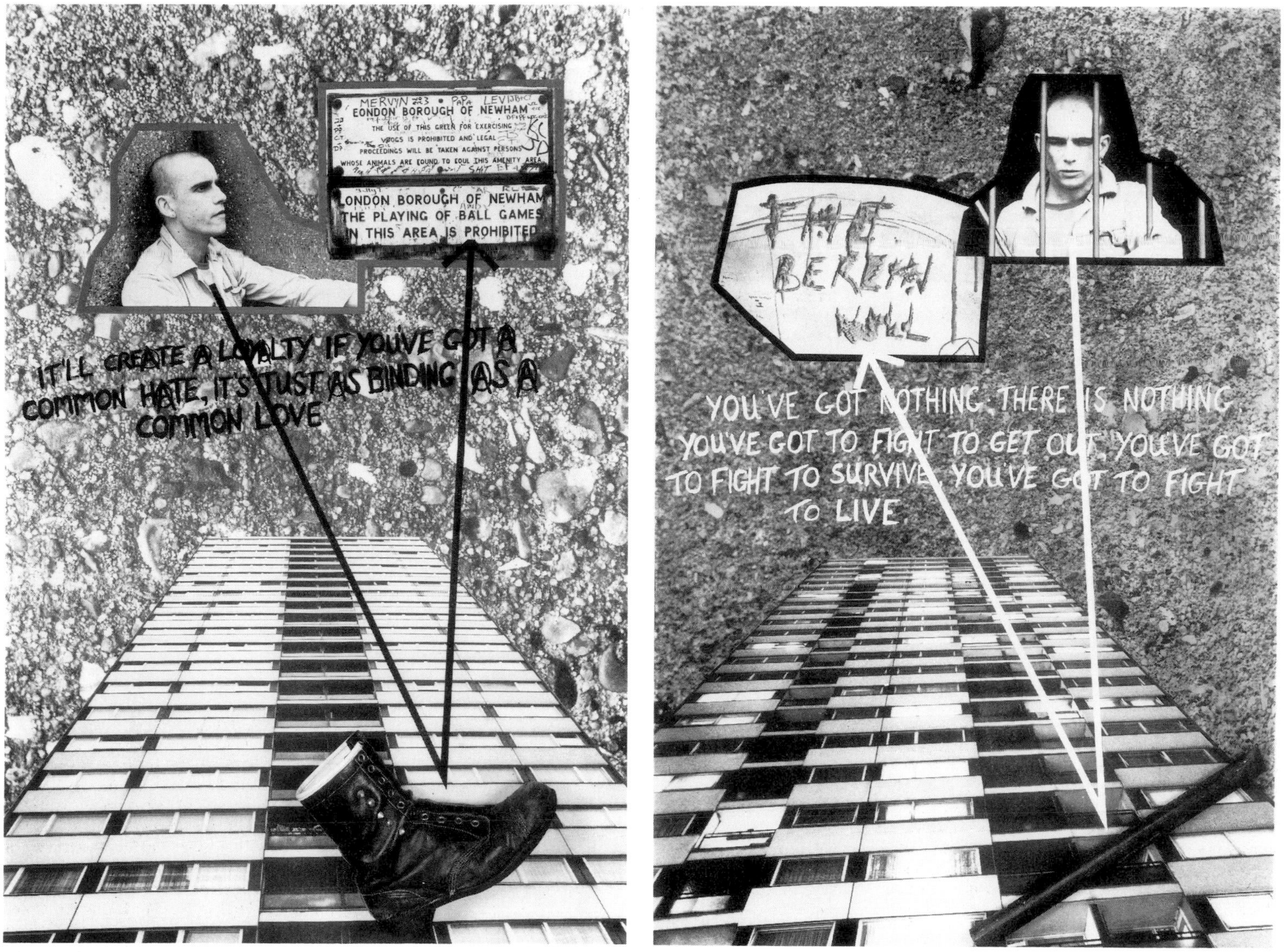

Stephen Willats: *Every Day and Every Night*, 1984

1977 *Social Criticism and Art Practice*, San Francisco Art Institute
1980 *Artist and Camera*, Mappin Art Gallery, Sheffield
1983 *The Sculpture Show*, Hayward Gallery, London
1985 *The British Show*, Art Gallery of New South Wales, Sydney
1987 *Art and Craft in the Twentieth Century*, Laing Art Gallery, Newcastel-upon-Tyne

Collections:

Tate Gallery, London; Arts Council of Great Britain, London; British Council, London; City Art Gallery, Southhampton; Gallery of Modern Art, Edinburgh; Stedelijk van Abbemuseum, Eindhoven, Netherlands; De Beyerd Museum, Breda, Netherlands.

Publications:

By WILLATS: books—*Art and Social Function*, London 1976; *Ich Lebe in Einem Betonklotz*, Cologne 1980; *Cha Cha Cha*, London 1982; *Intervention and Audience: A Synopsis*, London 1984; *Doppelganger*, London 1985; *Intervention and Audience*, London 1986; articles—statement in *Control No. 2* (London), 1966; statement in *Studio International* (London), February 1967; statement in *Control No. 3* (London), 1968; statement in *Structure No. 1* (London), October 1968; statement in *Art and Artists* (London), January 1969; "Behavioural Nets and Life Structures" in *The Paper* (Trent Polytechnic, Nottingham), 1971; statement in *Platform* (Nottingham), 1972; "West London Social Resource Project" in *Studio International* (London), January 1973; "Art and Social Function" in *Art and Artists* (London), June 1973; "The Edinburgh Project" in *Art and Artists* (London), January 1974; "Meta Filter" in *Art and Artists* (London), November 1974; "Meta Filter" in *Flash Art* (Milan), November 1974; "The West London Social Resource Project" in *Leonardo* (Oxford), 1974; "Meta Filter" in *Studio International* (London), September 1975; "A State of Agreement" and "A Survey of Distance Models of Art" in *Control No. 9* (London), 1975; "Book as Interactive Tool: The Modelling Book" in *Artists' Bookworks*, exhibition catalogue, London 1975; "Social Codes and Behaviour Parameters: An Area of Concern for Art" in *Life Codes and Behaviour Parameters*, Nottingham 1976; "Art Work as a Social Model" in *Studio International* (London), March/April 1976; "From a Coded Word" in *Studio International* (London), vol. 194, 1978; "Working with the Work of Art" in *Art Monthly* (London), April 1979; "Contained Reality" in *Art Monthly* (London), April 1979; "Contained Reality" in *Art Monthly* (London), no. 3, 1980; "Kultureller Druck" and "West Berlin als Kulturelles Symbol" in *Stephen Willats*, exhibition catalogue, Berlin 1980; "Doppelganger," interview with Antonia Payne, in *Studio International* (London), no. 1011, 1985.

On WILLATS: books—*Un Certain Art Anglais*, exhibition catalogue with text by Sandy Nairne and others, Paris 1979; *Stephen Willats: Leben in vorgegebenen Grenzen/4 Inseln in Berlin*, exhibiton catalogue with essay by Arno Hoffmann, West Berlin 1980; *The Artist as Photographer* by Marina Vaizey, London 1982; *New Art*, exhibition catalogue by Michael Compton, London 1983; *The British Show*, exhibition catalogue with texts by Richard Francis and others, Sydney 1985; *Stephen Willats*, exhibition catalogue with texts by Michael Archer and Manfred Schmalriede, London 1986.

MEANS OF ESCAPE

Throughout my work I present two states of social consciousness that are in continual cultural opposition.

There is an institutional, authoritatively mapped out social consciousness, its ramifications affect everyone, and in my work it is contrasted with a social consciousness of self-organization that expresses mutuality and personal creativity. For I see that within every person there is the potential of creative self expression, but that this is inhibited and repressed by the authoritative determinism that underpins the physical and social composition of the everyday world. Counter consciousness is the creative response of people to express their own sensibility and psychology. The presentation of these two different, and culturally opposed ways of perceiving reality, has directed both my working procedure and the visual composition of each work. The concept of self organization is not only symbolically represented in my work, but the actual process of its internalization by the audience involves them in acts of cognitive self-organization, for they construct their own means of escape.

Symbols

It is a fundamental part of my working procedure to search for and identify symbols that are residual in the culture and which will powerfully represent, to an

audience, the two opposed states of consciousness I have just described. First I look for obvious symbols of the deterministic, object-based consciousness, and then I uncover balancing expressions of people's self organization and statements of self identity. My starting point is the physical manifestations of our culture's institutional idealizations and self projections.

Contexts

At the same time as I am searching to identify symbols that represent the object-based consciousness I am revealing simultaneous, and contrasting, expressions of counter consciousness. The symbols of counter consciousness that I see as a counter balance revolve around self-organized contexts that have been established by people as a vehicle for their own expressions of creativity. Such contexts are not only hard to identify but are difficult to access as, by their very nature, they exist undercover in the inaccessible, forgotten corners of society, often directly repressed and usually alienated from their surroundings.

However, the establishing of a context or capsule is still dependent on the dominant culture, for it has to co-exist, being reliant on it as a source of material. Here lies the really creative act, which requires objects from the dominant culture, with their attendant pre-determined function, to be transformed into an agent for manifesting the counter consciousness. The set determinism given to the object by the dominant culture is broken by it being appropriated by the creators of the counter consciousness, becoming an agent for their self-organization.

Objects

Different objects have particular importance to different groups of creators of counter consciousness, and in each of my works about particular people I identify those objects that are central to them personally. These identified objects actually become part of my work so as to confront the audience with the reality they are viewing. Objects that are central to the audience's world are symbolically mirrored in the actual objects that have been incorporated into my work.

Audience

My works present the audience with a layer of references by depicting the same reality through various media forms. Each layer of references sets up disparate cues so that there is not a pre-formed, legislated, single view, but instead the disparate references are self-connected by the audience to create their own model. The audience make their own journey, their own transformations, between the cues associated with each state of consciousness; from the day to the night, the housing estate to the wasteland, from the conscious to the unconscious. My organization of the layout of the references from which the work's symbolic world is formed I consider essentially a parallel process to the audience's process of de-constructing and internalizing those disparate references into a coherent model. Thus to active, self-organization required from the audience in their cognitive relationship with a work is in itself a creative act, an expression of counter consciousness, and in this way the ideology that is its governing force is externalized. The work is the audience's means of escape.

—Stephen Willats

Stephen Willats' work is based on a critique of the isolated and elitist art practice of the 1950's and 60's and the specialist society that engendered such art. Noting the imbalance between theory and practice in much modernist art, he has tried to correct this by being especially concerned with the theory which underlies and informs his work, publishing articles and pamphlets and editing a magazine *Control* which is a forum for theoretical discussion on contemporary art. By making use of advances made in the technological and social science fields, which have begun to allow greater interaction between previously unrelated social groups, he has aimed to reach an audience not normally concerned with art, at the same time enabling them to understand the conditioning by which a manipulative society extends its controls. To reach an audience unused to according art proper attention, he had to develop ways in which to change the artist/art work/spectator relationship—away from an idea of art as commodity and decoration to one in which it is seen as a resource to be used by the whole community in a co-operative effort towards tolerance and understanding. These ideas have informed his work since the mid-1960's.

Initially the work of the late 60's and early 70's was seen as part of the Kinetic Art movement, and in so far as it made use of light and electronic systems this may have seemed appropriate, but the similarity is seen as superficial if we look at the methods and underlying meaning of such works as the "Visual Meta Language Simulation" of January 1972. This simulates the process by which separate decision-making organizations can co-operate to their mutual benefit with the minimum of antagonism. It consists of a Problem Display Box on which incomplete patterns are illuminated and two Decision Boxes on which the remainder of the pattern appears. Each Decision Box is worked by one participant. Although initially motivated by competition, the winning operator is progressively handicapped until only cooperation between operators enables completion of the game. The work enacts symbolically a decision-making process based on a system in which each unit is given equal information and effectiveness as opposed to the current pyramidal model in which information and decision-making is the prerogative of a few.

Other areas of Stephen Willats' work have had a more immediate social relevance, such as the series of Projects from 1965 in Ipswich, London, Notingham, Oxford and Edinburgh. One of the most successful was the West London Social Resource Project of 1972. This aimed to allow normally unrelated social groups to arrive at common models of their environment based on need. Four social groups were selected from areas of West London which were near enough to be visited by one another but seen as distinctly separate neighbourhoods. Using door to door techniques participants were gathered and a manual distributed. In the manual were a series of questions to be answered and tasks to be performed, the results of which were shown each day on display boards in the local library. As the complexity of the decision-making in the manual increased, so the participation between separate social groups developed. In this way people were enabled to rethink traditional ideas about their environment and to replace them with an "adaptive, self-organizing, evolutionary" social structure in which competition was replaced by cooperation. The documentation is now available in the library of Osterley used during the project and is discussed at length in Stephen Willats' book *Art and Social Function*, 1976.

"Meta Filter" 1973-75 is a direct development of the projects. It is a machine on which two participants symbolically enact the movement away from an individual, coded view of the world towards areas of common agreement. Working through a series of slides and using a thesaurus to describe the states represented, the operator, given the object of agreement attempts to understand the responses of his/her partner, to break through his restrictive perceptions to mutual understanding. The work breaks with traditional art practice; participation is not confined to an elite, for the images and language used are open to everyone. At the same time the work criticizes contemporary social divisions while offering a possible alternative.

The active participation of the spectator is necessary too for the works which take the form of panels with photographs and written descriptions. "Person A" of June 1974 is a series of six large and 12 smaller panels and a form to aid viewing. The spectator is asked to choose the most fitting description of the photograph in terms of behaviour states, attitudes etc., and is then directed to another photograph to continue the process. A narrative is built up which starts to affect responses to later panels; not only does the viewer posit how "Person A" might behave in a particular situation, but also by bringing his unique set of experiences to bear on the work he starts to comprehend how his own attitudes are achieved through a coded system which may well disguise or distort the real meaning of behaviour. The concept of relativism is used positively in this work, for though the primary meaning is constant, the process by which it is understood will depend on the experiences brought to bear.

Other panel works such as "Perceptions of a Married Couple" of June 1975, and "Attitudes Within Four Relationships" of March 1976 are more complex, making use of two or more people and presenting a more contextualised situation. The reading of these works depends on a relationship between the coded panel and the process by which the spectator decodes and then encodes the information to attain understanding.

In Stephen Willats' work the artist becomes an active instigator of social change as opposed to a passive mirror of current idealogy. His work breaks out of the isolated context of much contemporary art to reach a wider audience and the artist attains a more meaningful position in society.

—Jane Kelly

WILLENBECHER, John.

American. Born in Macungie, Pennsylvania, 5 May 1936. Educated at Mercerburg Academy, Pennsylvania, 1950–54; studied art history at Brown University, Providence, Rhode Island, 1954–58, B.A. 1958; Institute of Fine Arts, New York University, 1958–61. Independent artist, since 1962. Instructor in Painting, Philadelphia College of Art, 1972–73; Artist in Residence, Dartmouth College, Hanover, New Hampshire, 1977. Member, New York City Art Commission, since 1980. Recipient: MacDowell Colony Fellowship, New Hampshire, 1974; National Endowment for the Arts grant, 1977. Lives and works in New York. Address: 145 West Broadway, New York, New York 10013, U.S.A.

Individual Exhibitions:

1963 Feigen/Herbert Gallery, Los Angeles
Feigen/Herbert Gallery, New York
1964 Richard Feigen Gallery, Chicago
1965 Richard Feigen Gallery, New York
1966 Richard Feigen Gallery, New York
1967 Richard Feigen Gallery, Chicago
1970 Richard Feigen Gallery, Chicago
1971 Lambert 910 Gallery, New York
1973 A. M. Sachs Gallery, New York
1975 A. M. Sachs Gallery, New York
Bell Gallery, Brown University, Providence, Rhode Island
Everson Museum, Syracuse, New York
1976 Alberta College of Art, Calgary
Olympia Gallery, Philadelphia
Arts Club of Chicago
1977 Hamilton Gallery, New York
University of Massachusetts Art Gallery, Amherst
Wright State University Art Gallery, Dayton, Ohio
Jaffe-Friede Gallery, Dartmouth College, Hanover, New Hampshire
1978 Fine Arts Center, University of Rhode Island, Kingston
1979 *Day and Night*, Hamilton Gallery, New York (with Janet Stayton)
John Willenbecher 1970–1978, Allentown Art Museum, Pennsylvania (travelled to the Neuberger Museum, State University of New York at Purchase)
Dart Gallery, Chicago

John Willenbecher: *Laureate (black)*, 1982

1980 *Capriccios and Grottos*, Hamilton Gallery, New York
1981 *Susan Hall/John Willenbecher*, Hamilton Gallery, New York
1982 Hamilton Gallery, New York
1986 New York Academy of Sciences, New York

Selected Group Exhibitions:

1965 *Current Art*, Institute of Contemporary Art, Philadelphia
1967 *Contemporary American Painting and Sculpture*, Whitney Museum, New York
1968 *Annual Exhibition of Sculpture*, Whitney Museum, New York
1975 *Art in Boxes*, Monique Knowlton Gallery, New York
1977 *Contemporary Tableaux/Constructions*, University of California at Santa Barbara
1978 *Galaxies*, Taft Museum, Cincinnati, Ohio
1980 *Marking Black*, Bronx Museum of the Arts, New York
1984 *El Arte Narrativo*, Museo Rufino Tamayo, Mexico City
1986 *Olympus Revisited*, Summit Art Center, New Jersey
1987 *Faux Arts: Surface and Simulated Materials*, La Jolla Museum of Contemporary Art, California

Collections:

Guggenheim Museum, New York; Metropolitan Museum of Art, New York; Whitney Museum, New York; Chase Manhattan Bank Collection, New York; ATT Corporation Collection, New York; Neuberger Museum, State University of New York at Purchase; Museum of Art, Rhode Island School of Design, Providence; Hirshhorn Museum and Sculpture Garden, Washington, D.C.; Art Institute of Chicago; Centre Georges Pompidou, Paris.

Publications:

On WILLENBECHER: books—*John Willenbecher*, exhibition catalogue, with an essay by Ronald Onorato, Syracuse, New York 1975; *John Willenbecher*, exhibition catalogue, Philadelphia 1976; *The Commonplace Books of John Willenbecher*, Dayton, Ohio 1977; *John Willenbecher 1970–1978*, exhibition catalogue, with an essay by Jean-Louis Bourgeois, Allentown, Pennsylvania and Purchase, New York 1979; articles—"John Willenbecher" by Diane Waldman in *Artnews* (New York), February 1967; "John Willenbecher" by Max Kozloff in *Artforum* (New York), March 1975; "Through the Labyrinth: The Art of John Willenbecher" in *Art International* (Lugano, Switzerland), 20 March 1975; "John Willenbecher: Pyramids, Spheres and Labyrinths" by William Wilson in *Arts Magazine* (New York), March 1975; "The Modern Maze" by Ronald Onorato in *Art International* (Lugano, Switzerland), April/May 1976; "Janet Kardon Interviews Some Modern Maze-Makers" in *Art International* (Lugano, Switzerland), April/May 1976; "John Willenbecher" by Paul Gardner in *Arts Magazine* (New York), November 1977; "John Willenbecher's Burning Tetrahedron" by J. Kirk T. Varnedoe in *Arts Magazine* (New York), December 1978; "John WIllenbecher" by Ronny Cohen in *Artforum* (New York), April 1982; "John Willenbecher and the Riddle of Grandeur" by Dan Cameron in *Arts Magazine* (New York), September 1983.

John Willenbecher's artworks have remarkably strong iconic presence. Based on archetypal forms like the circle, square and arch, his two-and-three dimensional objects impress as richly elegant but emotive objects.

Though trained as an art historian, Willenbecher preferred the active role of making art to the passive role of studying it. In 1963 he exhibited several examples from his early series of black boxes, filled with orderly, compartmentalized arrangements of simple forms—like balls—behind glass. The theme of this series was "unknown games of chance," and the sleek and autonomous/mechanistic look of the forms reflected the then dominant Pop and Minimalism sensibilities.

Willenbecher continued to make boxes through the middle 1960's and varied the colors—"Gold and White" (1964)—and the inside contents which mostly consisted of globes and balls. Some of them even lit up. And his boxes should be viewed within the context, then, of the period's fascination with this form found also in versions, say, by Joseph Cornell, Louise Nevelson, Richard Artschwager. By the late 1960's the circle and square, the forms emphasized in the boxes, were joined by the arch. Based on "found" wooden window frames, the arches were used as the support for different mixed mediums constructed paintings.

In the late 1960's, also, he began to investigate the labyrinth. He explored both the formal and thematic aspects of this clear, but deliberately convoluted structure in many of the works through the middle 1970's. Fraught with architectural associations and psychological sensations, involving traps and enclosures, the labyrinth served as the subject of both constructed relief objects and the 2-dimensional paintings. In "The Ladder and the Labyrinth" (1970) he centered a circular shaped labyrinth from which extended a small ladder on a rectangular ground; in "Labyrinth 23.IX.72" (1972), he painted a circular labyrinth around a sphere and centered these motifs on arch-shaped masonite. The labyrinth paintings, in turn, were the source for a group of painted triptychs which consisted of schematic renderings of enclosed structures—arch within square, circle within arch—from 1974–75. Maze-like configurations also appear in another major series of works: the cenotaphs. With arched frames on which various geometric motifs were painted, the cenotaphs also contained a built-out shelf section on the lower edge upon which three-dimensional objects like spheres, tetrahedrons and even ladders were placed. Measuring about chest size, these works bring to mind the memorial function of the cenotaphs which inspired them. The group made in homage to Etienne-Louis Boullée, the 18th century Neo-classical visionary architect, in 1974 are among the most moving.

Shelves also appear in the lower edges of the constructions in the next important series named after *Das Lied ven der Erde* of Gustav Mahler, 1975–1977. In 1977 he emphasized the circle, square and the ladder in a group of large-scale, floor constructions directly inspired by designs of Dürer and Goethe. The recent works find Willenbecher returning to the contained and specific relief pieces of the cenotaph group. The series "Laureate" (1980–81) consists of arch-shaped wooden frames that each encase a masonite support, painted to simulate marble; a circle in the form of a

gold-leaf wreath adorns each surface. A tribute to creativity, the "Laureate" pictures reveal renewed interests in fine-tuning the pictorial qualities and turning them towards symbolic ends.

—Ronny Cohen

WILSON, Robert M. (Byrd Hoffman).
American. Born in Waco, Texas, 4 October 1941. Studied painting with George McNeil, Paris, 1962; studied architecture at the Pratt Institute, New York, 1962–65, B.F.A. 1965; served apprenticeship in architecture to Paolo Soleri, Phoenix, Arizona, 1965–66. Performance artist, New York, since 1966: directed theatre pieces with patients at Goldwater Memorial Hospital, New York, 1967–68; taught awareness classes, New Jersey Art Center, 1968–69, and movement classes for children, Bedford-Stuyvesant, Brooklyn, New York, 1968–69; Artistic Director, Byrd Hoffman Foundation, New York, since 1970. Recipient: Award for Best Foreign Play, Syndicat de la Critique Dramatique et Musicale, Paris, 1970; Drama Desk Award, for direction, New York, 1971; Obie Special Citation Award, for direction, New York, 1974; Lumen Award for Design, New York, 1977; Guggenheim Fellowship, 1980; Rockefeller Foundation Award, New York, 1981; Skowhegan Drawing Medal, Maine, 1987. Agent: Paula Cooper Gallery, 155 Wooster Street, New York, New York 10012. Address: 325 Spring Street, New York, New York 10013, U.S.A.

Individual Exhibitions:

1966 Byrd Hoffman Studio, New York
1967 *Theatre/Activity,* Bleecker Street Cinema, New York
1968 Grailville School, Loveland, Ohio
ByrdwoMAN, Byrd Hoffman Studio, New York
1969 *The King of Spain,* Anderson Theatre, New York
The Life and Times of Sigmund Freud, Brooklyn Academy of Music, New York
1970 *Deafman Glance,* University Theatre, Iowa City, Iowa (toured Europe and the United States)
1971 *Program Prologue Now: Overture for a Deafman,* Espace Pierre Cardin, Paris
Willard Gallery, New York (with Ann Wilson)
1972 *Overture,* Byrd Hoffman Studio, New York (toured France and Iran)
KA MOUNTAIN AND GUARDenia TERRACE, Haft Tan Mountain, Shiraz, Iran
1973 *King lyre and lady in the wasteland,* Byrd Hoffman Studio, New York
The Life and Times of Joseph Stalin, Det Ny Teater, Copenhagen, and Brooklyn Academy of Music, New York
1974 *A MAD MAN A GIANT A MAD DOG A MAD URGE A MAD FACE,* John F. Kennedy Center, Washington, D.C. (toured the United States)
Musée Galliera, Paris (with Christopher Knowles)
Prologue to a Letter for Queen Victoria, Spoleto, Italy
A Letter for Queen Victoria, Municipal Theatre, La Rochelle, France (toured France, Switzerland and the United States)
1975 *The $ Value of Man,* Brooklyn Academy of Music, New York
Einstein on the Beach, New York
1977 Multiples/Marian Goodman Gallery, New York
1978 Paul Cooper Gallery, New York
1979 Galerie Zwinger, Cologne
Multiples/Marian Goodman Gallery, New York
1980 Contemporary Arts Center, Cincinnati, Ohio
State University of New York at Purchase
1981 *Medea,* Washington Project for the Arts, Washington, D.C.
1982 Marian Goodman Gallery, New York
Galerie le Dessin, Paris
Galerie Annemarie Verna, Zurich
Stadtische Museum im Lenbachhaus, Munich
Galerie Fred Jahn, Munich
Franz Morat Institut, Freiburg, West Germany
1983 Pavillon des Arts, Paris
Galerie Brinkman, Amsterdam
Museum Boymans-van Beuningen, Rotterdam
Produzentgalerie, Hamburg
Festival Mondial du Theatre, Nancy, France
Gallery Ueda, Tokyo
Sogetsu School, Tokyo
Castelli-Feigen-Corcoran Gallery, New York
Rhode Island School of Design, Providence
1984 Paula Cooper Gallery, New York
Otis Art Institute, Los Angeles
Jones Troyer Gallery, Washington, D.C.
Walker Art Center, Minneapolis
Museo di Folklore, Rome
Centre d'Art Contemporain, Marseille, France
Kunstverein, Cologne
1985 Galleria Franca Mancini, Pesaro, Italy
Kammerspiele, Munich
Institute of Contemporary Art, Boston
1986 University of Iowa, Iowa City
Kemo Gallery, Albuquerque, New Mexico
Theater in der Kunsthalle, Hamburg
Laguna Gloria Museum, Austin, Texas (retrospective)
Grey Art Gallery, New York University
Lehman College, Bronx, New York
Carnegie-Mellon University, Pittsburgh
Kuhlenschmidt Gallery, Los Angeles
Alpha Gallery, Boston
Rhona Hoffman Gallery, Chicago
1987 Paula Cooper Gallery, New York

Selected Group Exhibitions:

1965 *World's Fair,* New York
1972 *Overture,* Musee Galliera, Paris
1980 *Further Furniture,* Marian Goodman Gallery, New York
1981 *Other Realities,* Contemporary Arts Museum, Houston
1982 *American Drawings of the Seventies,* Louisiana Museum, Humlebaek, Denmark (travelled to Basle, Munich and Ludwigshafen)
1983 *Art and Dance 1890–1980,* State University of New York, Purchase
1984 *Survey of Contemporary Painting and Sculpture,* Museum of Modern Art, New York
1985 *High Style,* Whitney Museum, New York
1986 *The Painter and the Theatre in the Twentieth Century,* Schirn Kunsthalle, Frankfurt

Collections:

Museum of Modern Art, New York; Centre Georges Pompidou, Paris; Australian National Gallery, Canberra; Fonds d'Art Contemporain, Paris; Kunstmuseum, Berne; Museum of Fine Arts, Houston; Museum Boymans-van Beuningen, Rotterdam; Museum of Fine Arts, Boston; Rhode Island School of Design, Providence.

Publications:

By WILSON: books—*The King of Spain in New American Plays,* New York 1970; *Two Conversations with Edwin Denby,* New York 1973; *A Letter for Queen Victoria,* Paris 1974; *Einstein on the Beach,* with Philip Glass, New York 1976; *I Was Sitting On My Patio This Guy Appeared I Thought I Was Hallucinating,* New York 1978; *Death Destruction and Detroit,* New York 1978, West Berlin 1979; *The Golden Windows,* Munich 1982; *The Civil Wars: A Tree Is Best Measured When It Is Down (Rotterdam section),* Amsterdam and Paris 1983; *The Civil Wars: A Tree Is Best Measured When It Is Down (Cologne section),* Frankfurt 1984; *The Civil Wars: A Tree Is Best Measured When It Is Down (Rome section),* Rome 1984; *The Civil Wars: Drawings, Models and Documentation,* Los Angeles 1984; *The Civil Wars: A Tree Is Best Measured When It Is Down (Act III Scene E; Act IV Scene A, and Epilogue),* with Heiner Muller, Cambridge, Massachusetts 1985.

On WILSON: books—*Il Teatro di Robert Wilson* by Franco Quadri, Venice 1976; *The Theater of Visions: Robert Wilson* by Stephan Brecht, Frankfurt 1979; *American Alternative Theater* by Theodore Shank, New York 1982; *Robert Wilson: The Theater of Images* by Craig Nelson, New York 1984; *New Works on Paper 3* by Bernice Rose, New York 1985; *The President of Paradise: A Traveller's Account of the Civil Wars* by Janny Donker, Amsterdam 1985; *Robert Wilson: Die lithographischen Zyklen 1984–1986 (Medea, Parsifal, Alceste)* by Fred Jahn, Munich 1986.

Robert Wilson's most noted project has been his collaboration with composer Philip Glass on *Einstein on the Beach.* Wilson's interest, like that of Gertrude Stein, is in the use of components of syntax and sound to create a new form of language. In *Einstein on the Beach,* as part of the splicing of language, he combined both understood and senseless words and phrases. Because of Wilson's language, sets, and movement patterning, each of his works have a complex world of colorful and inane artistic principles.

Wilson generally chooses performers from the world at large, paralleling the casting of non-trained performers in a number of post-modern dance productions. The movements in the plays are generally influenced by both Andy deGroat's choreography and Wilson's own background in movement sensitization. The emphasis on internal movement, rather than dancerly, external and linear movements, is an aspect that ties Wilson's work to a theatrical, rather than dance, evolution. There has always been the suggestion though, that Wilson's work is actually silent, visual dance, as well as silent, visual opera.

The sense of allowing time to slip by, but very slowly, during Wilson's dream-like performances, is his special talent. *The Life and Times of Joseph Stalin* was a 12 hour play, *Deafman Glance* was 7 hours in duration, and *Ka Mountain,* performed in Iran, 7 days and 7 nights. Rather than a Western expansionism of space, he has chosen an Eastern withdrawing of Western, linear time. As Wilson's performances continue over long periods of time, audiences begin to lose the feeling of directionality.

Wilson has chosen several 20th century aspects of scale: delayed time, disoriented language and, finally, the inclusion of quantity. *The Life and Times of Joseph Stalin* had a complete cast of 148 performers. The performance of *Ka Mountain* included 17 directors, 9 authors, and a cast of 79. Wilson described the 7-day festival as a sort of family which existed throughout the course of time, a type of performance without end. There is the sense here that art-making reaches a scale of proportion akin to other 20th century mass activities. There has also been evidence, and he uses both conventionally trained and non-conventionally trained performers now, that life in the 20th century will go on as a very intricate, well-defined, necessary and habitually organic performance.

—John Robinson

WINNER, Gerd.
German. Born in Braunschweig, 8 October 1936. Studied art, under W. Volkert, Hochschule für Bildende Künste, West Berlin, 1956–62; and at the Suomen Taide-Akatemian Konki, Helsinki (West German Study Scholarship), 1959–62. Married to Ingmar Reuter. Graphic artist and printmaker: lived and worked in West Berlin, 1963–70, London 1970–72, New York, 1972–78, and in Braunschweig, since 1978. Recipient: Kunstpreis für Graphik, Wolfsburg, 1969; British Council travel scholarship, to work at Kelpra Studio, London, 1970; Deutscher Kritikerpreis für Bildende Kunst, West Berlin, 1972; 2 prizes, *International Biennale,* Cracow, 1972; Graphics Prize, *Biennale,* Lugano, Switzerland, 1972; Graphics Prize, *Print Biennale,* Ljubljana, 1973;

Graphics Prize, World Graphics Competition, San Francisco, 1973; Graphics Prize, *International Biennale,* Cracow, 1974; Arts Council Prize, *International Print Biennale,* Bradford, Yorkshire, 1982. Agent: Galerie Mikro, Carmerstrasse 1, Berlin. Address: Finkenherd 10, 3300 Braunschweig, West Germany.

Individual Exhibitions:

1960 Galerie Fenestra, Helsinki
1965 Galerie Mikro, West Berlin
Galerie im Hailing, Goeppingen, Switzerland
Galerie Sous Sol, Giessen, Switzerland
1966 Galerie für Grafikfreunde, Frankfurt
Werkstaat Schnoor, Bremen, West Germany
Städtisches Museum, Braunschweig, West Germany
1967 Galerie Gerda Bassenge, West Berlin
Museum am Ostwall, Dortmund, West Germany
Galerie C. D. Rothe, Wolfsburg, West Germany
Schloss Wolfsburg, West Germany
1968 Galerie Mikro, West Berlin
Galerie Nos, Duisburg, West Germany
Werkstaat Schnoor, Bremen, West Germany
Kunstkreis, Hameln, West Germany
Galerie im Schinkelsaal, West Berlin
1969 Galerie Sous Sol, Giessen, Switzerland
Galerie Wildeshausen, Wildeshausen, Switzerland
Galerie Dr. Hartmann, Stuckvilla, Munich
Galerie am Rhein, Cologne
1970 Overbeck-Gesellschaft, Lübeck
Galerie Querschnitt, Braunschweig, West Germany
Tilson: Siebdruck + Winner: Workshop, Haus am Waldsee, West Berlin (with Joe Tilson)
1971 Galerie M. E. Thelen, Cologne
Staatliche Graphische Sammlung, Munich
Kunstverein, Wolfsburg, West Germany (with Joe Tilson)
1972 Herzog-Anton-Ulrich Museum, Braunschweig, West Germany
Galerie Schmucking, Braunschweig, West Germany
Galerie 2000, West Berlin
1973 Marlborough Graphics, London
Siebdruck, Kunstverein, Cologne
Galerie Schmucking, Braunschweig, West Germany
Institut für Moderne Kunst, Nuremberg
Wentzel Galerie, Hamburg
Galerie M. E. Thelen, Cologne
1974 Galerie Stangl, Munich
Galerie Domberger, Reutlingen, West Germany
Galerie Craven, Paris
Galerie Schmucking, Basle
Bundesministerium für Raumordnung, Bauwesen und Stadtebau, Bonn
Arnolfini Gallery, Bristol
Galleri Dierks, Aarhus, Denmark
Konstmuseum, Aarhus, Denmark
Galerie Wentzel, Hamburg
Galerie 2000, West Berlin
1975 Kunsthalle, Bremen, West Germany
Galerie M. E. Thelen, Cologne
1981 *Gerd Winner and Kelpra Studio,* Drumcroon Art Centre, Wigan, Lancashire
1982 University of Regina, Saskatchewan
1983 Riverside Studios, Hammersmith, London

Selected Group Exhibitions:

1961 *Grosse Berliner Kunstausstellung,* Messehallen, West Berlin (and regularly 1962–69)
1967 *20 Jahre Internationale Graphik,* Kunstverein, Wolfsburg, West Germany
1970 *International Print Biennale,* City Museum and Art Gallery, Bradford, Yorkshire
1971 *Biennale,* Musée d'Art Moderne, Paris
1974 *Print Biennale,* National Museum of Modern Art, Tokyo
1977 *Documenta,* Kassel, West Germany
1982 *Big Prints,* Southampton Art Gallery (toured the U.K.)

Collections:

Nationalgalerie, West Berlin; Kupferstichkabinett, West Berlin; Neue Galerie Sammlung Ludwig, Aachen, West Germany; Wallraf-Richartz-Museum, Cologne; Muzeum Sztuki, Lodz, Poland; Narodni Museum, Warsaw; Musée d'Art et d'Histoire, Geneva; Victoria and Albert Museum, London; Museum of Modern Art, New York; University of Iowa, Iowa City.

Publications:

By WINNER: book—*London Dockland,* West Berlin 1972; film—*Hommage à la France II,* 1969.

On WINNER: books—*Tilson: Siebdruck + Winner: Workshop,* exhibition catalogue, West Berlin 1970; *Gerd Winner,* exhibition catalogue, with text by Pat Gilmour, London 1973; *Gerd Winner: Siebdruck,* exhibition catalogue with text by Wulf Herzogenrath, Cologne 1973; *Gerd Winner and Kelpra Studio,* exhibition catalogue, with texts by R. C. Hopkinson and A. R. Taylor, Wigan, Lancashire 1981; *Gerd Winner: Paintings and Graphics 1970–1980* by Pat Gilmour, London 1981; *Gerd Winner,* exhibition catalogue, with texts by Carol A. Phillips and Maija Bismanis, Regina, Saskatchewan 1982.

In the catalogue to his 1975 Bremen Kunsthalle exhibition, Gerd Winner can be paraphrased as saying that to have people in a picture immediately imposes on that picture an interpretation, an explanation, a type of identity that it would never have acquired without people. Winner's work noticeably excludes the human figure. This makes his pictures, mostly urban landscapes, that much more haunting, for they are places where one would expect to see a figure from time to time, even if only a stray dog.

Because of his concern with photographic realism in his printmaking and his obsession with the more seamy areas of the city landscape, his series of e.g., the London dockland, the London underground or the canyons formed by New York City streets, his avoidance of human life could tend ultimately towards the depressing if it weren't for his non-descriptive use of colour. This is what takes Winner's work beyond a mere photo-realist or "pop" approach; it is his technical ability as a printmaker that keeps him from being completely typecast as one who makes "statements about deserted streets." The use of colour in his printmaking, particularly his work consequent to working with Chris Prater of Kelpra Studio, London, where he was invited by the British Council in 1970, tends to be pearly, giving an iridescent glitter to surfaces normally bereft of such delicacy.

—Victoria Keller

WINNEWISSER, Rolf.

Swiss. Born in Niedergosgoen, 5 June 1949. Educated in Lucerne, until 1965; studied graphics and design at the Kunstgewerbeschule, Lucerne, 1966–71. Served as music corps drummer in the Swiss Army, 1969. Worked as designer, Olten, 1971–72; as technical assistant on alphabetization project, Tillaberi region, River Niger, Africa, 1972–74. Independent artist, in Lucerne, since 1974; also worked in Zurich and Gambia, 1978–80, in New York, 1981–82, in Schongau, 1982–84, and in London, 1987–88. Drawing Instructor, Kunstgewerbeschule, Zurich, 1976–80, and since 1982. Recipient: Vordemberge-Gildewart Award, Rapperswil, 1984. Agent: Galerie und Edition Stahli, Bahnhof Enge, Postfach, 8027 Zurich. Address: P.O. Box 345, 6000 Lucerne 7, Switzerland.

Individual Exhibitions:

1972 Galerie Stahli, Lucerne
1973 Galerie Stahli, Lucerne
1975 Galerie Elisabeth Kaufmann, Olten, Switzerland
Galerie Stahli, Zurich (with Aldo Walker)
1976 Galerie Meier, Geneva (with Martin Disler)
Galerie Elisabeth Kaufmann, Olten, Switzerland (with Martin Disler)
Galerie Stahli, Zurich (with Martin Disler)
1977 Galerie Elisabeth Kaufmann, Basle
1978 Galerie Stahli, Zurich
1979 Kunsthalle, Basle
1980 Studio d'Arte Cannaviello, Milan (with Martin Disler)
1981 Galerie Camomille, Brussels
Galerie Stahli, Zurich
1982 Kunstverein, Mannheim (with Aldo Walker)
Galerie Stahli, Zurich
1983 Kunsthalle Waaghaus, Winterthur, Switzerland
1985 Galerie Anton Meier, Geneva
Galerie Biederberg, Amsterdam
Galerie Stahli, Zurich
1986 Galerie Pro(s)art, Lucerne

Selected Group Exhibitions:

1972 *Giovane Arte Svizzera,* Rotonda della Besana, Milan
1973 *Biennale,* Musée d'Art Moderne de la Ville, Paris
1974 *Profile 10,* Städtisches Museum, Bochum, West Germany
1975 *Beryll Cristallo,* Kunstmuseum, Lucerne
1976 *Landscapes,* Mint Museum of Art, Charlotte, North Carolina
1980 *Aperto '80,* at the *Biennale,* Venice
1981 *Schweizer Kunst '70–'80,* Kunstmuseum, Lucerne (travelled to Bologna, Genoa, Bonn and Graz)
1983 *Eight Portfolios,* Nigel Greenwood Gallery, London
1984 *Bluten des Eigensinns,* Kunstverein, Munich
1987 *Malen, Schreiben-Schreiben malen,* Kunstmuseum, Solothurn, Switzerland

Collections:

Kunstmuseum, Lucerne; Kunstmuseum, Aarau, Switzerland; Kunthaus, Zurich.

Publications:

By WINNEWISSER: books—*Aus dem Logbuch Ikons,* Zurich 1982; *Immer Wieder Zuruck,* Rome 1984; *Nil,* with texts by Theo Kneubuhler and Karl Sauter, Lucerne 1986; *Prossima volta in due volupta,* edited by Stephan Banz, Lucerne 1986; articles—"Der Geraumte Weg oder das schrecklich Personliche in Beobachtungen über das andere" in *Kunst-Bulletin* (Berne), no. 7–8, 1976; "Zeichen in Bewegung ohne Titel: Fortlaufend" in *Sondern* (Berlin/Basle), no. 1, 1976; "Uberquerungen" in *Sondern* (Berlin/Basle), no. 2, 1977; "Arabesken einer Reise nach Seltsam" in *Innerschweizer Blatter* (Lucerne), February 1978; "Split Horizon" in *Oboe* (San Francisco), no. 5, 1981.

On WINNEWISSER: books—*Kunst: 28 Schweizer* by Theo Kneubuhler, Lucerne 1972; *Rolf Winnewisser,* exhibition catalogue, with text by Theo Kneubuhler, Lucerne 1973; *An Annual of New Art and Artists* by Willem Sandberg, Amsterdam 1973; *Rolf Winnewisser,* exhibition catalogue, with texts by Jean-Christophe Ammann and Theo Kneubuhler, Basle 1979; *Rolf Winnewisser,* exhibition catalogue, Geneva 1985.

Unplanned meeting of lines, a line meets, intersects another line, annullable at that point when "formulatable" wishes can be shaped out of the vantage point of pictorial plane into which flowing, unflagging signs can flee and a monochrome, with lines winding around an acrobatic sensation, pattern for thought and sensation, where words fail in the sense of following a trail, of wanting to make a language out of the image spoken by the image itself. Deviations between what is conceivable and what is still imaginable. Whereby

Rolf Winnewisser: *Map*, 1986

the image as image no longer works, is not longer able to give for consideration designs of a sign system to current, present-day dissected, dissectable opaque, disintegrating reality and imagination, forgotten in the image state: far from me, in me.

Things, thoughts, reflections, held outwards, turned inside out, there broken and breaking other things, expanding, fanning out, suffocating and making them breathe, domain between image and intent, image as sediment, residue of this activity, an incessant flowing, breaking and being broken of the within and the outermost, the innermost and the uttered.

Because it has to begin somewhere, where was I again when I forgot the image, when I forgot to speak of the image and disappointed by the image as expectation, by the expectation as image of what has already been, meanings running away to prevent signs from catching up with them, under way from image to image, through images. Things thought in the light of the representable and the non-representable movements between mind, mental signs in their brokenness, formulas of inconclusiveness, and the inconclusiveness of a formula, things existential in the light of acting and failing to act, the mistakes, the inconclusiveness of experience, the realities of appearance, embodied signs, when signs flow from their significance, contaminations held and released again.

—Rolf Winnewisser

WINSOR, Jacqueline.

American. Born in Newfoundland, Canada, 20 October 1941. Educated at Yale Summer School of Art and Music, New Haven, Connecticut, 1964; Massachusetts College of Art, Boston, 1965, B.F.A. 1965; Rutgers University, New Brunswick, New Jersey, 1967, M.F.A. 1967. Independent artist, New York, since 1967. Art and Ceramics Instructor, Douglass College, New Brunswick, New Jersey, 1967; Art Instructor, Middlesex County College, Edison, New Jersey, and Newark State Teacher's College, New Jersey, 1968–69; Ceramics Instructor, Mills College of Education, Oakland, California, 1968, 1971; Graphics Instructor, Loyola University, New Orleans, Summer 1969; Ceramics Instructor, Greenwich House Pottery School, New York, 1969–72; Sculpture Instructor, School of Visual Arts, New York, Spring 1971 and 1975; Art Instructor, Hunter College, New York, 1972–75. Recipient: Creative Artists' Public Service Program Award, 1973; New York State Council of the Arts Grant, 1973–74; Mather Award, Art Institute of Chicago, 1974; National Endowment for the Arts Grant, 1974, 1977, 1984; Louis Comfort Tiffany Foundation Award, 1977; Guggenheim Fellowship, 1978; Creative Artist's Award, Brandeis University, Waltham, Massachusetts, 1979. Agent: Paula Cooper Gallery, 155 Wooster Street, New York, New York 10012. Address: 141 Canal Street, New York, New York 10002, U.S.A.

Individual Exhibitions:

1968 Douglass College Gallery, New Brunswick, New Jersey
1971 Nova Scotia College of Art and Design, Halifax
1973 Paula Cooper Gallery, New York
1976 Paula Cooper Gallery, New York
Contemporary Arts Center, Cincinnati, Ohio
Portland Center for Visual Arts, Oregon
1977 Museum of Modern Art, San Francisco
1978 Wadsworth Atheneum, Hartford
1979 Museum of Modern Art, New York
Art Gallery of Ontario, Toronto
Fort Worth Art Museum, Texas
1981 Virginia Museum of Fine Arts, Richmond
1982 Paula Cooper Gallery, New York
Akron Art Museum, Ohio
1983 Massachusetts Institute of Technology, Cambridge (with Barry Ledoux)
Paula Cooper Gallery, New York
1985 Margarete Roeder Fine Arts, New York (with Richard Deacon)
1986 Paula Cooper Gallery, New York

Selected Group Exhibitions:

1969 *American Abstract Artists*, Riverside Museum, New York

1972 *American Women Artists,* Kunsthaus, Hamburg
1975 *The Condition of Sculpture,* Hayward Gallery, London
1976 *The Liberation: 14 American Artists,* Aarhus Museum of Art, Denmark (toured Europe)
1977 *Biennial,* Whitney Museum, New York
1978 *Fading Bounds in Sculpture,* Stedelijk Museum, Amsterdam
1979 *The Decade in Review,* Whitney Museum, New York
1982 *Currents: A New Mannerism,* Jacksonville Art Museum, Florida (travelled to Tampa, Florida)
1985 *Tranformations in Sculpture,* Guggenheim Museum, New York
1987 *The Success of Failure,* Laumeier Sculpture Park, St. Louis (travelled to Middlebury, Vermont; Tucson, Arizona)

Collections:

Museum of Modern Art, New York; Whitney Museum, New York; Detroit Institute of Arts; Musée d'Arte Moderne, Paris; Australian National Gallery, Canberra.

Publications:

By WINSOR: book—*Jackie Winsor: Sculpture,* exhibition catalogue, text with Ellen Phelan, Cincinnati, Ohio 1976; articles—"An Interview with Jackie Winsor," with Liza Bear, in *Avalanche* (New York), Spring 1972; interview in "Artists Now Living in New York" in *Criteria* (Vancouver), November 1977; statement in *Jackie Winsor,* exhibition catalogue (New York), 1979.

On WINSOR: books—*26 Women Artists,* exhibition catalogue, by Lucy Lippard, Ridgefield, Connecticut 1971; *12 Statements Beyond the 60's,* exhibition catalogue, by Frank Kolbert, Detroit 1972; *4 Young Americans,* exhibition catalogue, by Mario Amaya, New York 1973; *8th Biennale de Paris,* exhibition catalogue, by Georges Boudaille, Paris 1973; *A Response to the Environment,* exhibition catalogue, by Jeffrey Wechsler, New Brunswick, New Jersey 1975; *The Condition of Sculpture,* exhibition catalogue, by William Tucker, London 1975; *The Liberation: 14 Women Artists,* exhibition catalogue, Aarhus and Copenhagen, 1976; *Ideas in Sculpture 1965–77,* exhibition catalogue, essay by Anne Rorimer, Chicago 1977; *A View of a Decade,* exhibition catalogue, essay by Robert Pincus-Witten, Chicago 1977; *Strata: Nancy Graves/Eva Hesse/Michelle Stuart/Jackie Winsor,* exhibition catalogue, with an essay by Lucy Lippard, Vancouver 1977; *12 From Rutgers,* exhibition catalogue, by Jeffrey Wechsler, New Brunswick, New Jersey 1977; *Matrix 38,* exhibition catalogue, with an essay by Andrea Miller-Keller, Hartford 1978, *Jackie Winsor,* exhibition catalogue, with an essay by Ellen Johnson, New York 1979; *Born in Boston,* exhibition catalogue, Lincoln, Massachusetts 1979; articles—"Jackie Winsor: Doing It the Hard Way" by Claire C. Kelly in *Artweek* (Oakland, California), 15 January 1977; "Winsor Built" by Roberta Smith in *Art in America* (New York), January/February 1977; "Winsor Knots: The Sculpture of Jack Winsor" by Robert Pincus-Witten in *Arts Magazine* (New York), June 1977; "Art: Jackie Winsor" by David Bourdon in *Vogue* (New York), February 1979; "Raw Magic" by Mark Stevens in *Newsweek* (New York), 26 February 1979; "Jackie Winsor: Eloquence of a 'Yankee Pioneer' " by John Gruen in *Artnews* (New York), March 1979; "Jackie Winsor" by Ellen Johnson in *Parachute* (Montreal), Winter 1979; "Jackie Winsor" by Badanna Zack in *Artmagazine* (Toronto), September/October 1979; "Jackie Winsor and Post Minimalism" by Alan Barkley in *Vanguard* (Vancouver), September 1979.

Winsor's particular success is best seen in her '70s production, the moment in her career when her artistic temperament matched perfectly with the evolving Minimalist idiom to achieve an authentic significance. The nature of her art in its use of primary structures such as cube, sphere, and grid, but extended into a metaphorical position through emphasis upon process, material, and craft, has been labelled second wave Minimalism.

While the very forcefully delineated hand-made aura of this work was perhaps parallel to the feminist art of that time, Winsor typically chose manufactured materials and worked towards weight and density, if not as well a fragile poignance. She said of those works: "The overall element I seek is self-containment. My aim is that the pieces not intrude on you, but that they give one time to come to them." Humbling in their often ritual-like craft repetitiveness, there may also be an essentially masochistic quality in the numbing anti-ego self-effacement implied in such work—aptly felt in the phrase "confessional formalism." (S. Westfall). Hundreds of the artist's hours are implied in the wrapping together, for instance, of the four logs of *Bound Square* (1972). Likewise in *Exploded Piece* (1980–82), a steel-reinforced concrete cube (with Winsor's signature small opening on each face presenting a view of the impacted interior space), was blown apart in order to be carefully, even lovingly reconstructed. This motif of tender repair on materials monstrous in either scale or industrial redolence is reminiscent of Grosvenor's approach in the last decade. He also comes to mind in an assessment of Winsor's pace of production: the unhurried appearance of their art betokens more than merely a private, meditative and personal aim. Both artists, among others, are at play with a puritanical American strain, testing the metaphysical implications of weight, idea, and silence within materials divided between the natural and industrial.

If there has been a selflessness in Winsor's art, it is also found in her persistent disinclination to reveal any details of her personal life; and as well in the control which she demands over the dispersal of her still small oeuvre by insisting that her of course obliging buyers sign a contract which permits Winsor to exercise exhibition and reproduction controls, and receive a percentage of the future sales of the works. In her recent sculptures, while still based upon weight, density, and aperture leading to a cubic interior, and as before constructed from industrial materials, it appears that Winsor's privacy of vision has attempted a more public self. The plaster board cubes are beveledged, and pastel hued, and the interior space is mirrored; and just so, a concrete, two-ton sphere is blue toned. For the moment, Winsor relinquished the tragic stance of the previous decade and more, and evinces a curious paradoxical decorous air.

—Joshua Kind

WODICZKO, Krzysztof.

Polish. Born in Warsaw, 16 April 1943. Studied industrial design, Academy of Fine Arts, Warsaw, 1962–68, MFA 1968. Worked as an industrial designer, Warsaw, 1969–77. Independent artist, living in Toronto and New York, since 1977. Instructor in design, Warsaw Polytechnic, 1969–77; Visiting Professor in Design, Nova Scotia College of Art and Design, Halifax, 1977–79; Part-time Professor of Drawing, Guelph University, Ontario, 1979; Part-time Professor in Design, Ontario College of Art, Toronto, 1979; Assistant Professor in Photography and Studio Art, Nova Scotia College of Art and Design, Halifax, 1980–81; Associate Professor of Design, New York Institute of Technology, Old Westbury and Columbus Circle, since 1983; Guest Professor, Cooper Union School of Art, New York, 1987; Visiting Professor in Photography, California Institute of the Arts, Valencia, 1988. Artist-in-Residence: University of Illinois, Urbana, 1975; York University, Toronto, 1976; A Space, Toronto, 1976; Nova Scotia College of Art and Design, Halifax, 1976, 1977; Artists Space, New York, 1977; South Australian School of Art, Adelaide, 1981–82. Agent: Hal Bromm Gallery, 90 West Broadway, New York, New York 10007. Address: 199 East 7th Street, Apt. 2D, New York, New York 10009, U.S.A.

Individual Exhibitions:

1970 Gallery Wspolczesna, Warsaw
1972 Gallery Wspolczesna, Warsaw
1973 Gallery Akumulatory 2, Warsaw
Gallery Foksal, Warsaw
1974 Gallery Foksal, Warsaw
1975 Gallery Akumulatory 2, Warsaw
Gallery Foksal, Warsaw
N.A.M.E. Gallery, Chicago
University of Illinois, Urbana
1976 Gallery Akumulatory 2, Warsaw
Gallery Foksal, Warsaw
Gallery St. Petri, Lund, Sweden
Vehicule, Montreal
A Space, Toronto
1977 Gallery Akumulatory 2, Warsaw
Gallery Foksal, Warsaw
Project Studio One, New York
A Space, Toronto
York University, Toronto
Eye Level, Halifax, Nova Scotia
Hal Bromm Gallery, New York
1978 Artists Space, New York
Hal Bromm Gallery, New York
1979 Eye Level, Halifax, Nova Scotia
Galerie Optica, Montreal
Gallery 76, Toronto
1980 Hal Bromm Gallery, New York
1981 Eye Level, Halifax, Nova Scotia
Great George Street Gallery, Charlottetown, Prince Edward Island
Franklin Furnace, New York
Artspace, Peterborough, Ontario
1982 South Australian School of Art, Adelaide
1983 Ydessa Gallery, Toronto
1984 Hal Bromm Gallery, New York
1985 State University of New York, Purchase
Ydessa Gallery, Toronto
Canada House, London
Robert McLaughlin Gallery, Oshawa, Ontario
Orchard Gallery, Derry, Northern Ireland
1986 49th Parallel Gallery, New York
Gallery Foksal, Warsaw
1987 Massachusetts Institute of Technology, Cambridge
Hal Bromm Gallery, New York
1988 Clocktower, New York
La Jolla Museum of Contemporary Art, California

Selected Group Exhibitions:

1969 *Biennale de Paris,* Musee d'Art Moderne, Paris (and 1975)
1977 *Documenta 6,* Museum Fridericianum, Kassel, West Germany (and *Documenta 8,* 1987)
1979 *Biennale of Sydney,* Art Gallery of New South Wales (and 1982)
1983 *Presence Polonaise,* Centre Georges Pompidou, Paris
Kunstler aus Kanada, Kunstverein, Stuttgart
1984 *Body Politic,* Tower Gallery, New York
1985 *Alles und Noch Viel Mehr,* Kunstmuseum, Berne
1986 *42nd Biennale,* Venice
Expanding Commitment, Maryland Institute of Art, Baltimore
1987 *Poetic Injury,* Alternative Museum, New York

Collections:

National Gallery of Canada, Ottawa; Art Bank, Toronto; Mininstry of External Affairs, Ottawa; Muzeum Sztuki, Lodz; Gallery Foksal, Warsaw; National Museum, Poznan; Chase Manhattan Bank, New York; La Jolla Museum of Contemporary Art, California.

Publications:

By WODICZKO: books—*On Line,* Guelph, Ontario 1976; *Projection,* Halifax, Nova Scotia 1979; *Poetics of Authority, Vehicles, Line, Images of Propaganda, Public Architecture,* with essay by Alisa Maxwell, Adelaide 1982; *Homeless Vehicle Project, Homeless Conversations,* with Rudolph Luria, New York 1988.

On WODICZKO: books—*Krzysztof Wodiczko: Line,* exhibition catalogue, Warsaw 1976; *Krzysztof Wodiczko: References,* exhibition catalogue, Warsaw 1977; *Expanding Commitment: Diverse Approaches to Socially Concerned*

Krzysztof Wodiczko: *City Projection*, Kassel, West Germany, 1987

Photography, exhibition catalogue, Baltimore 1986; *42nd Venice Biennale, Canadian Pavilion: Krzysztof Wodiczko and Melvin Charney,* with essay by Diana Nemiroff, Ottawa 1986; *Counter-Monuments: Krzysztof Wodiczko's Public Projections,* exhibition catalogue, Cambridge, Massachusetts 1987.

WOODHAM, Derrick.

British. Born in Blackburn, Lancashire, 5 November 1940. Studied at South East Essex Technical College and School of Art, 1957–60, Hornsey College of Art London, 1960–62, and the Royal College of Art, London, with Meadows, Clatworthy, Brown, Dalwood and Atkins, 1962–65. Married Irene Janusaityte in 1966; children: Anele and Alexandra. Independent sculptor, since 1965. Part-time Instructor, Royal College of Art, 1965–68; Instructor, Philadelphia College of Art, 1968–70; Associate Professor, School of Art, University of Iowa, Iowa City, 1970–73; Assistant Professor, Department of Art, University of Kentucky, Lexington, 1973–80; Professor and Director of The School of Art, University of Cincinnati, Ohio, since 1980. Junior Member, Fine Arts Advisory Panel, Arts Council of Great Britain, 1966–68. Recipient: Walter Neurath Prize for Drawing, Royal College of Art, 1964; Peter Stuyvesant Award, 1965; Group Prize, Prix de la Ville de Paris, 1965; North Jersey Cultural Council Purchase Award, Van Saun Park, Paramus, New Jersey, 1974; University of Kentucky Research Council Grants, 1974–76. Address: 1910 Bluebell Drive, Cincinnati, Ohio 45224, U.S.A.

Individual Exhibitions:

1966 Richard Feigen Gallery, New York
1968 Ad Libitum Gallery, Antwerp
1969 Jewish Museum, New York
1970 Richard Feigen Gallery, New York
1973 Rasdall Gallery, Lexington, Kentucky
1974 J.H. Duffy Gallery, New York
1976 University of Kentucky, Lexington
1980 Lexington Arts Council Gallery, Kentucky
1984 Northern Kentucky University, Frankfort

Selected Group Exhibitions:

1965 *The New Generation*, Whitechapel Gallery, London
Biennale, Paris
1966 *International Exhibition*, Sonsbeek Park, Arnhem, Netherlands
Primary Structures, Jewish Museum, New York
1968 *British Artists: 6 Painters, 6 Sculptors*, Museum of Modern Art, New York
1970 *British Sculpture of the 60's*, Institute of Contemporary Arts, London
1971 *Der Geist Surrealismus*,Baukunst, Cologne
1974 *Artists Choose Artists*, Tweed Museum, Duluth, Minnesota
1976 *National Sculpture Exhibition*, Athens, Georgia (travelled)
1985 *Midwest Sculpture Invitational*, Indianapolis, Indiana

Collections:

Arts Council of Great Britain, London; British Council, London; Peter Stuyvesant Foundation, London: Tate Gallery, London; North Jersey Cultural Council, Paramus, New Jersey; Nagaoka Museum of Art, Japan; Fort Worth Art Museum, Texas; Cincinnati Bell Collection, Ohio.

Publications:

On WOODHAM; books—*The New Generation*. exhibition catalogue, by Ian Dunlop, London 1976; *Jonge Engelse Bildhowers*, exhibition catalogue, by Christopher Finch, Amsterdam 1967; *The New Sculpture* by Udo Kultermann, New York 1968; *Form and Structure* by Teruo Fujieda, Tokyo 1971; articles—"Colour in Sculpture" by Jasia Reichardt in *Quadrum* (Brussels), no. 18, 1965; "Caro und die junge englische skulptur" by Jean-Christophe Ammann in *Werk* (Berne), vol.54, 1967; "Stage" in *Art and Artists* (London), Summer 1970; "Art: Sculpture Beside a Lake" by Hilton Kramer in the *New York Times*, 16 June 1974.

My originally recognized contribution to the dialogue amongst artists attracted to the presentation of experience in sculpture through the formal management of space, surface and colour, and our challenges to the de-sensitizing protocols of pedestal presentation, the convention of time, continues to motivate my work. I am fascinated by the expressive versatility of geometry and its propensity for organization. The mutuality of material and function.

This persistent engagement has drawn me into the realization of a variety of sets, systems, monoliths, arrangements and multiples. *Rotating Cube* is my latest example of the latter. This work, close to human scale, is intended to invite structural analysis. Each recognized cube re-orients the apparent attitude of the work (and the viewer).

—Derrick Woodham

There are striking similarities between the work that Derrick Woodham first exhibited in 1963 and his more recent pieces. Edges are clear and sharp, the surfaces are smooth, colors are muted but vibrant and volume is described with great precision. Woodham was a pioneer of what at the time was referred to as "minimal" sculpture, and it is hardly surprising that he has remained faithful to certain of the tenets he originated and exploited at the start of his career.

Derrick Woodham: ***Rotating Cube*****, 1986**

What is surprising, however, is that all of his subsequent work up to and including his more recent sculpture exemplifies a position of ideology and practice that continues to place him at the vanguard of contemporary art.

In the decade during which sculptors nurtured on Henry Moore capitulated by the dozens to the seductive embraces of technology and the fugitive dogmas of conceptualism, Woodham firmly followed a course dedicated to constantly testing the limits of expression that can be encompassed by the sculpture as object (rather than the sculpture as light, electricity, sound, printed word or invisible idea). As a teacher he has sponsored, encouraged and designed multi-media activities of radical dimensions and vital innovation. In 1972 at the University of Iowa he orchestrated a series of events that explored totally new directions for live performance possibilities. Such activities feed, rather than replace, Woodham's inspiration to create object-sculpture. These investigations suggest to him related stratagems that he anchors in solid materials. A major work of his, dated 1975 and titled "Arrangements with a Modular Group," consists of 86 units,square or oblong in shape and varying in length from six inches to eight feet. The material is Masonite, painted white. These units are arranged by the artist according to the space available. Specific preliminary settings are modified and not all the pieces need be used. The final appearance may vary from a seemingly random placement to a stacking system that looks almost symmetrical.

Although more recent work is predominantly rectilinear and contains no traces of the rounded, somewhat biomorphic, shapes of his early pieces, the human element in his work still assumes great importance. The scale of the sculpture, indoor or outdoor, is geared to stretch our normal ways of seeing. The gallery work must be explored perimetrically and looked down, into and across, much as one would have to examine a shallow valley from a hilltop. The outdoor work, three or four times human height, invites close inspection while towering above the viewer. Viewing his work makes one very conscious of one's own body scale, size and relative immobility.

His permanently installed outdoor commissions are very successful despite (or perhaps on account of) the fact that they do not self-consciously make the acquaintance of their sites. They do not suggest overtly that they have been custom-designed for the particular setting. Most of them have been erected in rural environments and they uncompromisingly resist blending into the landscape. Their severe angles and proportions are not mitigated by monochromes quite at odds with nature's friendly mix. Woodham does not try to adapt or design to accommodate a particular site because the strength of the work is implicit, not a product of its decorative suitability. Color is a very vital element in this work, and were his forms less stimulating he would still hold a very important position as a colorist. Most modern sculpture is either self-colored, the natural wood or steel exposed in a raw or rusted state or else flagrantly "painted on" with color applied so that it is impossible to eradicate the notion that two layers exist, a "skin" of paint over a quite differently colored solid. Woodham challenges both conventions by using the methods of the latter to confound the former. With the exception of "Gates," 1974, a huge outdoor work utilizing interlocking segments of identical timber frameworks, none of his colors are endemic to the materials, yet they appear so because the color is applied in such a skillful, controlled manner and the surface is so smooth and pure that the predominant sensation is that the color is completely through the material. Though they are carefully mixed and often very subtle (salmon, mauve, turquoise) the colors really seem to be *in* not *on* the sculpture. Woodham achieves a fusion of such density that even to speak of the color of his work as an issue implies a separate identity for color that simply does not exist in the work as perceived.

With physically most prepossessing results, Woodham has doggedly stuck to the notion that quite apart from the formidable range of expression he can cull with his sculpture, it should not be divorced from principles of volume. Many of his peers, on both sides of the Atlantic, now take their cues from abstract painting and try to "draw" in space using flat planes of the now orthodox and ubiquitous brown corten steel. Woodham has reached far more meaningful levels of dialogue by surrounding and containing space and exploring it from the inside out. Yet there is nothing at all "fat" about Woodham's work. It is spare and lean.

"Fields" consists of a four-layered grid of twelve narrow girders stacked horizontally in a lattice formation. Each girder is monochrome and the colors vary from white through yellow, purple and grey to black. This piece operates on the viewer with great immediacy and the clear, sensational impact of a complex and provocative statement. Woodham's intellectual grasp of his vocation is prodigious, but even rarer is his ability to create a unique visual vocabulary that is well-defined, self-sufficient, spontaneous and universal.

—Michael Alistair Findlay

WOODROW, Bill.

British. Born in Henley, Oxfordshire, 1 November 1948. Studied at Winchester School of Art, Hampshire, 1967–68; Saint Martin's School of Art, London, 1968–71; Chelsea School of Art, London, 1972. Independent sculptor, London, since 1972. Agent: Lisson Gallery, 67 Lisson Street, London NW1 5DA. Address: 44 Camberwell Grove, London SE5 8RE, England.

Individual Exhibitions:

1972	Whitechapel Art Gallery, London
1979	Kunstlerhaus, Hamburg
1980	The Gallery, Acre Lane, South London
1981	LYC Gallery, Banks, Cumbria
	New 57 Gallery, Edinburgh
	Galerie Wittenbrink, Regensburg, West Germany
1982	Lisson Gallery, London
	Stuttgarter Kunstausstellungen, Stuttgart
	Galerie Eric Fabre, Paris
	St. Paul's Gallery, Leeds, Yorkshire
	Ray Hughes Gallery, Brisbane, Queensland
	Galerie 't Venster, Rotterdam
	Galerie Michele Lachowsky, Antwerp, Belgium
1983	Galleria Toselli, Milan
	Museum van Hedendaagse Kunst, Ghent, Belgium
	Lisson Gallery, London
1984	Mercer Union, Toronto
	Musee de Toulon, France
	Galerie Paul Maenz, Cologne
1985	Kunsthalle, Basle
	Barbara Gladstone Gallery, New York
	Donald Young Gallery, Chicago
	La Jolla Museum of Contemporary Art, California (travelled to Berkeley)
1986	Galleri Nordenhake, Malmo, Sweden
	Galerie Paul Maenz, Cologne
	Butler Gallery, Kilkenny, Ireland
	Fruitmarket Gallery, Edinburgh
	Mattress Factory, Pittsburgh
1987	Kunstverein, Munich
	Lisson Gallery, London
	Cornerhouse Gallery, Manchester, Lancashire
	Barbara Gladstone Gallery, New York
1988	Galerie Paul Maenz, Cologne

Selected Group Exhibitions:

1971 *Art as an Idea in England*, Centro de Arte y Comunicacion, Buenos Aires
1972 *Platform '72*, Museum of Modern Art, Oxford
1981 *British Sculpture in the 20th Century*, Whitechapel Art Gallery, London
1982 *Lecons des Choses*, Kunsthalle, Berne (travelled to Chambery and Chalon-sur-Saone, France)
1983 *Edges and Shadows: Sculpture in Britain*, Hayward Gallery/Serpentine Gallery, London
1984 *An International Survey of Recent Painting and Sculpture*, Museum of Modern Art, New York
1985 *Space Invaders*, Norman Mackenzie Art Gallery, Regina, Saskatchewan
1986 *Nine Artists from Britain*, Louisiana Museum, Humlebaek, Denmark
1987 *A Quiet Revolution: British Sculpture Since 1965*, San Francisco Museum of Modern Art (travelled to Newport Beach, California; Washington, D.C.; Buffalo, New York
1988 *Graven Images*, Harris Museum and Art Gallery, Preston, Lancashire

Collections:

Tate Gallery, London; Imperial War Museum, London; Leeds City Art Gallery, Yorkshire; Scottish National Gallery of Modern Art, Edinburgh; Kunsthaus, Zurich; Moderna Museet, Stockholm; Museum Boymans-van Beuningen, Rotterdam; National Gallery of Canada, Ottawa; Musee d'Art Contemporain, Montreal; La Jolla Museum of Contemporary Art, California.

Publications:

On WOODROW: books—*Objects and Sculpture*, exhibition catalogue with text by Iwona Blaszczyk, London and Bristol 1981; *Lecons des Choses*, exhibition catalogue with text by Catherine Ferbos, Berne 1982; *Englische Plastik Heute*, exhibition catalogue with essay by Michael Newman, Lucerne 1982; *Bill Woodrow*, exhibition catalogue edited by Jean-Christophe Ammann, Basle 1985; *Bill Woodrow*, exhibition catalogue with essay by Lynne Cooke, Edinburgh 1986; *Bill Woodrow*, exhibition catalogue with essay by Lynne Cooke, Munich 1987; *A Quiet Revolution: British Sculpture Since 1965*, with texts by Lynne Cooke, Mary Jane Jacob and others, London 1987.

WUNDERLICH, Paul.

German. Born in Eberswalde, near Berlin, now in East Germany, 10 May 1927. Educated at High School in Eutin until 1946; studied art, under Willi Titze and Willem Grimm, Landeskunstschule, and Hochschule für Bildende Künste, Hamburg 1947–51; studied printing techniques with Desjobert, Paris, 1961–62. Served in the German Army, 1943–45: prisoner-of-war 1945. Married the photographer Karin Székessy (see *Contemporary Photographers*) in 1972; children: Oliver, Natascha and Laura. Painter, printmaker and sculptor, Hamburg, 1952–60 and since 1963, in Paris and Italy, 1961–63. Freelance instructor in graphics and printmaking, 1960–63; Professor of Graphics, Hochschule für Bildende Künste, Hamburg, 1963–67. Recipient: Cultural Circle bursary, Hamburg, 1951; Stipendium des Kulturkreises, Hamburg, 1955; Deutsche Kunstpreis der Jugend für Grafik, 1960; M. S. Collins Prize, Philadelphia, 1962; Cultural Forum Prize, Tokyo, 1964; Premio Marzotto, Milan, 1967; Graphic Art Prize, Kamakura Museum, Tokyo, 1968; Gold Medal, Florence, 1970; Gold Medal, Oslo, 1973; Medal, Cracow, 1975; Gold Medal, *Graphics Biennale*, Listowell, Ireland, 1978; Graphics Prize, Taiwan, 1984; Kunstpreis des Landes Scheswig Holstein, West Germany, 1986. Agents: Galerie Levy, Magdelenstrasse 26, 20000 Hamburg 13; Redfern Gallery 20 Cork Street, London W1, England. Address: Hayn Strasse 2, Eppendorf, 2000 Hamburg 20, West Germany.

Individual Exhibitions;

1949 Overbeck-Gesellschaft, Lübeck
1955 Kunstlerklub Die Insel, Hamburg

Bill Woodrow: *Empty Grate*, 1987

Paul Wunderlich: ***Georg, Ulrike und Daniela II*****, 1972**

1958 Galerie Nebelung, Dusseldorf
Orangerie, Eutin, West Germany
1960 Dragonerstall, Hamburg
1961 Galerie die Insel, Worpswede, West Germany
Galerie Niepel, Dusseldorf
1962 Galerie Brusberg, Hannover
Galerie Diogenes, West Berlin
Galerie Brockstedt, Hamburg
1963 Galerie Sydow, Frankfurt
Galerie Niedlich, Stuttgart
Print Club, Philadelphia
San Francisco Museum of Art
Galerie Rothe, Heidelberg
Galerie Niepel, Dusseldorf
Miami Museum of Art
Eric Locke Gallery, San Francisco
1964 *Olbilder*, Galerie Van de Loo, Munich
Galerie Brechbuhl, Grenchen, Switzerland
1965 Galleria Arco, Rome
Musee des Beaux-Arts, Mons, Belgium
Galerie Hausdewell, Baden-Baden, West Germany
Galerie Niepel, Dusseldorf
Pfalzgalerie, Kaiserslautern, West Germany
Galerie Wilbrand, Münster, West Germany
1966 Kubus-Ausstellung, Hannover
Europa-Center, West Berlin
Kunstverein, Dusseldorf
Städtische Galerie, Bochum, West Germany
Galerie Brusberg, Hannover
Kunsthalle, Mannheim
1967 Overbeck-Gesellschaft, Lübeck
Gallerie Dierks, Aarhus, Denmark
Galerie Wolfgang Ketterer, Munich
Galerie Toni Gerber, Berne
Lithographs 1949–1967, Auckland City Art Gallery, New Zealand
1968 *Paintings, Sculpture, Drawings, Graphics*, Redfern Gallery, London
Galerie Passepartout, Copenhagen
Kunstverein, Wolfsburg, West Germany
Galerie Brusberg, Hannover
Gemalde/Zeichnungen/Graphik/Plastik, Badischer Kunstverein, Karlsruhe
Galerie d'Eendt, Amsterdam
1969 Associated American Artists Gallery, New York
Minneapolis Institute of Arts
Perls Galleries, Los Angeles
Phoenix Gallery, Berkeley, California
Kovler Gallery, Chicago
1970 Galerie Brusberg, Hannover
Recent Paintings, Drawings and Sculpture, Staempfli Gallery, New York
Kunsthalle, REcklinghausen, West Germany
Kunsthalle, Gelsenkirchen, West Germany
Museum for Moderner Konst, Gothenburg, Sweden
Galleri Leger, Copenhagen
1971 Galleri Aronowitsch, Stockholm
Amos Andersonin Taidemuseo, Helsinki
Perls Galleries, Los Angeles
Kestner-Gesellschaft, Hannover
1972 Galleria Schwarz, Mulan
Galerie Berggruen, Paris
Galerie André-Francois Petit, Paris
Galleria La Bussola, Turin
1973 *Recent Oils, Gouaches and Drawings*, Staempfli Gallery, New York
Redfern Gallery, London
Galerie Levy, Hamburg
Retrospektive der Jahre 1958 bis 1973, Baukunst, Cologne
1974 Tokyo Gallery
Galerie Art Contacts, Paris
Graphischen, Radierungen, Lithographien, Plastische Werk, Kunsthalle, Kiel
1975 Wilhelm-Lehmbruck-Museum, Duisburg, West Germany
Kunstverein, Augsburg, West Germany
Galerie Cour Saint-Pierre, Geneva
Galerie Orangerie, Cologne
1976 Fondation Veranneman, Kruishoutem, Belgium
Galerie Octave Negru, Paris
Galleri Uddenberg, Gothenburg, Sweden
Galerie Berggruen, Paris
1977 Redfern Gallery, London
Gouaches, Tekeningen, Litho's en Beeldhounnerken, Centrum voor Kunst en Cultuur, Ghent
1979 Galerie Veranneman, at *FIAC 79*, Paris
1980 Seibu Art Museum, Tokyo
Kunsthalle, Kiel
Redfern Gallery, London
1981 Seibu Museum of Art, Tokyo
Staempfli Gallery, New York
Von Informel zur Figuration: Bilder, Objekte, Druckgraphik seit 1957, Baukunst, Cologne
1983 Fondation Veranneman, Kruishoutem, Belgium
1985 Le Bateau Lavoir, Paris
Sonet Galerie, Stockholm
1987 Kloster Gisma, Holstein, West Germany (retrospective)
Museum Schloss Gottorf, Schleswig, West Germany (graphics retrospective)
Redfern Gallery, London

Selected Group Exhibitions:

1955 *Farbige Grafik*, Kestner-Gesellschaft, Hannover
1962 *16 German Artists*, Corcoran Gallery, Washington, D.C.
1964 *Documenta* Kassel, West Germany
1966 *Phantastische Figuration*, Haus am Waldsee, West Berlin
1968 *Europaische Druckgraphik der Gegenwart*, Gemeentemuseum, The Hague
1970 *Malerei nach Fotografie*, Stadtmuseum, Munich
1972 *After Surrealism*, Ringling Museum of Art, Sarasota, Florida
1976 *Les Espaces Insolites*, Palais du Congres, Strasbourg
1987 *Zauber der Medusa*, Museum Moderner Kunst, Vienna

Collections:

Museum Boymans-van Beuningen, Rotterdam; Kunstverein, Darmstadt; Städtische Galerie, Bochum, West Germany; Museum of Modern Art, New York; San Francisco Museum of Modern Art; Miami Museum of Art.

Publications:

On WUNDERLICH: books—*Paul Wunderlich: Olbilder*, exhibition catalogue, Munich 1964; *Paul Wunderlich: Lithographs 1949–1967*, exhibition catalogue, with text by Edouard Roditi, Auckland 1967; *Paul Wunderlich:Gemalde/Zeichnungen/Graphik/Plastik*, exhibition catalogue, with text by G. Bussmann, Karlsruhe 1968; *Paul Wunderlich: Paintings, Sculpture, Drawings, Graphics*, exhibition catalogue, with texts by Frank Whitford and Wieland Schmied, London 1968; *Paul Wunderlich: Recent Paintings, Drawings and Sculpture*, exhibition catalogue, with text by George W. Staempfli, New York 1970; *Paul Wunderlich: Catalogue Raisonne de l'Oeuvre Graphique 1949–1971* by Max Bense, Hanns Theodor Flemming, Frank Whitford and others, West Berlin 1971; *Paul Wunderlich*, exhibition catalogue, with text by José Pierre, Paris 1972; *Paul Wunderlich: Recent Oils, Gouaches and Drawings*, exhibition folder, with text by George W. Staempfli, New York 1973; *Paul Wunderlich: Retrospektive der Jahre 1958 bis 1973*, exhibition catalogue, with text by Max Bense, Cologne 1973; *Paul Wunderlich: Skizzen 1966*, with text by Max Bense, Offenbach 1974; *Paul Wunderlich: Graphischen, Radierungen, Lithographien, Plastische Werk*, exhibition catalogue, with texts by Jens Christian Jensen, Johann Schlick and Eberhard Freitag, Kiel 1974; *Paul Wunderlich: Gouaches, Tekeningen, Litho's en Beeldhouwwerken*, exhibition catalogue, Ghent 1977; *Paul Wunderlich und Karin Szekessy: Correspondenzen*, with an introduction by Fritz J. Raddaz, Hamburg 1977; *Paul Wunderlich* by Octave Negru, Paris 1979; *Paul Wunderlich: Werkverzeichnis* by Jens Christian Jensen, Offenbach 1979; *Paul Wunderlich*, exhibition catalogue, with text by Jens Christian Jensen,Tokyo 1980; *Paul Wunderlich;Von Informel zur Figuration: Bilder, Objekte, Druckgraphik seit 1957*, exhibition folder, with text by Jens Christian Jensen, Cologne 1981; *Paul Wunderlich: Werkverzeichnis der Lithografien*, Offenbach 1981; *Paul Wunderlich: Methamorphosen*, with text by H. Hollander, Dortmund 1985; *Paul Wunderlich*, exhibition catalogue, Holstein 1987: *Paul Wunderlich: Skulpturen und Objekte* by Heinz Spielmann, Offenbach 1987.

Paul Wunderlich's pictures are frequently associated with the tradition of surrealism. While this historical aspect may appear understandable in view of the imagination and fantasy in his art, the work can be described just as well if not more accurately as an analysis of political involvement, sense of reality, Eros, violence, space—that is, of direct experiences related to the present. Wunderlich has painted portraits, paraphrases of older masters, illustrations to the *Song of Solomon* and to Joyce; he has modelled sculptures and conceived useful objects which are not exhausted by use; he is a perfectionist in his craft—in the name of perfect form; he keeps his distance but is always available for practical help; he is very articulate but refrains almost entirely from comment on his pictures. This diversity serves him, however, as a stimulus to the style with which he makes each idea and each problem his own.

Apart from some graphic works Wunderlich's oeuvre begins in 1959. Two series of lithographs at this time show two essential qualities which would always preoccupy him: the oppressed human being,susceptible to violence, whose worth is visible precisely in his destruction, and Eros as an essential human quality which Wunderlich shows as an aesthetic quality. The two series which, seen from today, appear as a key to Wunderlich's art, excited attention when they were shown in a small gallery: the first (the cycle "20 July 1944") translated the concrete political event, the assassination of the men involved in the revolt against Hitler, into a general interpretation of human sorrow; the other (the cycle "qui s'explique") became the occasion for a demonstration of anti-constitutional bigotry. The punishment of the artist for "pornography" brought his into public view, although he shuns rather than seeks publicity. The event has in no way influenced the development of his work.

In the early 1960's Wunderlich next varied the poetic, macabre, erotic themes with graphic works ("Francois Villon," "Leda," "Kleine Anatomie," among others), and then around 1964 he began an essential phase in his painting. Wunderlich strives for a painterly line away from traditional peinture by frequent use of the spray gun. The stimulus for his pictures is artificial reality, whether it be the artistic photographs of his wife Karin Szekessy or pictures by kindred spirits (Runge, the Fontainebleau school, Leonardo, Ingres, David, and later on Dürer and Manet). The pictures and coloured lithographs to the *Song of Solomon* may count as an initial high point in Wunderlich's art, soon followed by a second in the paraphrases of Dürer. It is not only concern for style and form, perfection of craft and execution that links Wunderlich to Dürer; in similar fashion, Wunderlich soon became a representative abroad of the art of his native land, mainly in Western Europe, Japan and the United States.

To the themes which are to him already classical, he added, in the 1970's, portraits in which he can demonstrate in exemplary fashion his relationship to reality. Sculpture to him is a further medium—there has not been since Max Ernst any comparable sculptural work carried out by a German painter. Wunderlich's useful objects are also sculpture that more clearly bewitches reality.

—Heinz Spielmann

WYETH, Andrew (Newell).

American. Born in Chadds Ford, Pennsylvania, 12 July 1917. Educated by private tutors; studied art with his father, N. C. Wyeth. Married Betsy Merle James in 1940; children: Nicholas and James. Painter: lives and works in Chadds Ford. Recipient: Dana Watercolor Medal. *Pennsylvania Academy Annual*, Philadelphia, 1947; Award of Merit, American Academy of Arts and Letters, 1947; Second Prize,

Andrew Wyeth: *Marsh Mawk*, 1964 Courtesy Terra Museum of American Art, Chicago

Painting in the United States, Carnegie Institute, Pittsburgh, 1948; Popular Prize, *Carnegie International*, Pittsburgh, 1958; Presidential Medal of Freedom, 1963; Annual Award, with James Johnson Sweeney, *Art in America*, 1963. D.F.A.: Harvard University, Cambridge, Massachusetts, 1955; Colby College, Waterville, Maine, 1955; Swarthmore College, Pennsylvania, 1958. Member, National Institute of Arts and Letters. Agent: Coe Kerr Gallery Inc., 49 East 82nd Street, New York 10028. Address: Chadds Ford, Pennsylvania 19317,U.S.A.

Individual Exhibitions:

1937 Macbeth Gallery, New York
1938 Macbeth Gallery, New York
Doll and Richards, Boston
1939 Macbeth Gallery, New York
1940 Doll and Richards, Boston
1941 Macbeth Gallery, New York
1942 Doll and Richards, Boston
1943 Macbeth Gallery, New York
1944 Doll and Richards, Boston
1945 Macbeth Gallery, New York
1946 Doll and Richards, Boston
1948 Macbeth Gallery, New York
1950 Macbeth Gallery, New York
1951 Currier Gallery of Art, Manchester, New Hampshire (retrospective)
William A. Farnsworth Library and Art Museum, Rockland, Maine (retrospective)
1952 Macbeth Gallery, New York
1953 M. Knoedler and Co., New York
1956 M. H. de Young Memorial Museum, San Francisco (retrospective)
Santa Barbara Museum of Art, California (retrospective)
1957 Delaware Art Center, Wilmington (retrospective)
1958 M. Knoedler and Co., New York
1960 Charles Hayden Memorial Library, Massachusetts Institute of Technology, Cambridge (retrospective)
1962 Albright-Knox Art Gallery, Buffalo, New York (retrospective)
1963 Fogg Art Museum, Harvard University, Cambridge, Massachusetts (retrospective; toured the United States)
University of Arizona Art Museum, Tucson
1966 Pennsylvania Academy of Fine Arts, Philadelphia (retrospective; toured the United States)
1970 Musuem of Fine Arts, Boston
1974 National Museum of Modern Art, Tokyo (retrospective)
Lefevre Gallery, London
National Museum of Modern Art, Kyoto, Japan
1976 Metropolitan Museum of Art, New York (retrospective)
1981 Station Gallery, Greenville, Connecticut
Delaware Art Museum, Wilmington
Brandywine River Museum, Chadds Ford, Pennsylvania
Greenville County Museum of Art, South Carolina
Galerie Claude Bernard, Paris
1982 Virginia Art Museum, Richmond
1983 Fort Lauderdale Museum of Art, Florida
Brooks Museum of Art, Memphis, Tennessee
Portland Museum of Art, Maine
1984 Brandywine River Museum, Chadds Ford, Pennsylvania
Funabashi Gallery, Tokyo
Gallery Iida, Tokyo
1985 Canton Art Institute, Ohio
1987 National Gallery of Art, Washington, D.C.
Museum of Fine Arts, Boston
1988 Houston Museum of Fine Arts, Texas
Los Angeles County Museum of Art
Fine Arts Museum, San Francisco
Detroit Institute of Arts, Michigan

Selected Group Exhibitions:

1938 *Pennsylvania Academy Annual*, Philadelphia (and frequently until 1963)
1943 *American Realists and Magic Realists*, Museum of Modern Art, New York
1947 *Painting in the United States*, Carnegie Institute, Pittsburgh (and 1948, 1949)
1950 *Carnegie International*, Pittsburgh (and 1952, 1958, 1961, 1964)
1959 *American Painting and Sculpture*, Moscow
1963 *Dunn International*, Beaverbrook Art Gallery, Fredericton, New Brunswick (travelled to the Tate Gallery, London)
1964 *Between the Fairs: 25 Years of American Art 1939–64*, Whitney Museum, New York
1965 *N. C. Wyeth and the Brandywine Tradition*, William Penn Memorial Museum, Harrisburg, Pennsylvania
1971 *The Brandywine Heritage*, Brandywine River Museum, Chadds Ford, Pennsylvania
1974 *10 Americans*, Andrew Crispo Gallery, New York

Collections:

Brandywine River Museum, Chadds Ford, Pennsylvania; Metropolitan Museum of Art, New York; Museum of Mod-

ern Art, New York; Museum of Fine Arts, Boston; Wadsworth Atheneum, Hartford, Connecticut; Currier Gallery of Art, Manchester, New Hampshire; Philadelphia Museum of Art; North Carolina Museum of Art, Raleigh; Art Institute of Chicago; Museum of Fine Arts, Houston.

Publications:

By WYETH: article—"Andrew Wyeth", interview, with George Plimpton and Donald Stewart, in *Horizon* (New York), September 1961.

On WYETH: books—*The Brandywine Tradition* by Henry C. Pitz, Boston 1969; *Andrew Wyeth from Public and Private Collections*, exhibition catalogue with introduction by M. J. Albacete, Canton, Ohio 1985; *Andrew Wyeth: The Helga Pictures* by John Wilmerding, New York 1987; articles—"Andrew Wyeth" by Lloyd Goodrich in *Art in America* (New York), October 1955; "Andrew Wyeth" by Henry C. Pitz in *American Artist* (New York), November 1958; "Andrew Wyeth" by Eliot Clark in *Studio* (London), December 1960; "The Four Seasons: Dry-Brush Drawings by Andrew Wyeth" by Lloyd Goodrich in *Art in America* (New York), no. 2, 1962; "New Light in Andrew Wyeth" by James W. Fosburgh in *Artnews* (New York). November 1962: "The Drawings of Andrew Wyeth" by Agnes Morgan in *American Artist* (New York), September 1963; "Andrew Wyeth" by E. P. Richardson in the *Atlantic* (Boston), June 1964; "Andrew Wyeth" by Brian O'Doherty in *Show* (New York), May 1965; article in *Current Biography*, New York 1981.

Not many artists in the 20th century, like their 16th century predecessors, have made good by staying home. Andrew Wyeth, born in Chadds Fork, Pennsylvania, is one such exception; his address in 1988 is still Chadds Ford. In more ways than one his fixed place of residence is symptomatic of his art. His father, N. C. Wyeth, was the pupil of Howard Pyle in that sleepy village and set up his own studio as an illustrator of the historical and romantic episodes of the Union's days of glory and struggle. Andrew, born and brought up in a home where art belonged, had no need to sever family ties to develop his own brand of imagery. His father taught him the techniques; his attitudes grew undisturbed by the pressures of the past or the competitions of the present among young artists in the cities. Pennsylvania alternated with summer sojourns in Maine and between the two localities the younger Wyeth's art grew along the parallel media of water-colour and tempera.

In water-colour the format is usually small and the landscape is the favorite motive. Often it is in the winter fields under snow where the gradual thawing presents a bonus to the artist in the metamorphosis in the changing colour of the ground and the melting tracery of frost-etched foliage.

In 1937–38 Wyeth held his first one-man shows in Boston and in New York. Since then he has exhibited all over the United States and abroad with success without ever failing, once the sterling character of his work became recognized for its consistency and unadulterated painterly quality. Never engaged in the equivocal dialogue of contemporary viability of experiment and discovery, Wyeth's accomplishments have been the seemingly archaic devotion to the search for perfection within a chosen system of conventions owing most to the native American tradition and its personal interpretation by a mind unswayed by art politics of any kind. This concentration of means and directions endows his paintings with the airless atmosphere of a studio where each brush stroke is meditated and deliberated before it takes its place in the canvas with the irrevocable logic of a segment in a jigsaw puzzle.

Sometimes there is a hint of contrived symbolism as in the picture of "Young America," the much exhibited painting of 1950. In this panel the young man rides his bicycle across the open pasture land. He wears a sundowner hat, one side clipped up by a quasi-military badge, and above his head flies a bright tricolour burgee from the long strut rising from the front hub. This mood of adolescent nostalgia for the pioneering past and the battles of adventurous frontiers seems dated now, but it is at one with the somewhat naive innocence of a genre tied firmly to sentiment and homebound associations.

In less allusive interiors and landscapes without figures Wyeth works in a restricted palette. His realism is of a totally composed scene in which every inch of surface plays its integral part towards the final impression. Its radical compass is short but magnetic. One can share the artist's serious passion in a reconstruction dictated by retinal plotting, leaving not only the memorable image but also a superlative material equivalent.

—G. S. Whittet

Y

YAMADA, Masaaki.
Japanese. Born in Tokyo in 1930. Studied with the artist Saburo Hasegawa, Tokyo, 1953; studied at Tokyo University, 1954. Independent painter, Tokyo, since 1954. Agent: Satani Gallery, Asahi Building 11 BF, 2-6, 4-chome, Ginza, Chuo-ku, Tokyo 104. Address: 1-3-16 Hikari-cho, Kokubunji, Tokyo 185, Japan.

Individual Exhibitions:

1958	Kyobunkan Gallery, Tokyo
1960	Yoseido Gallery, Tokyo (and 1962, 1963)
1964	Nantenshi Gallery, Tokyo
1965	Tsubaki Kindai Gallery, Tokyo
1966	Muramatsu Gallery, Tokyo
1968	Gallery Cristal, Tokyo
1978	Koh Gallery, Tokyo
1979	Satani Gallery, Tokyo (and 1980, 1981, 1982)
1982	Kasahara Gallery, Osaka, Japan
1983	Inoue Gallery, Tokyo
	Satani Gallery, Tokyo (and 1984, 1985)
1985	Gallery Yonetsu, Tokyo (twice)
1986	Inoue Gallery, Tokyo
	Satani Gallery, Tokyo (and 1987, 1988)
	Gallery Yonetsu, Tokyo (and 1987)
1988	Galerie Springer, West Berlin

Selected Group Exhibitions:

1949	*Yomiuri Independent Show*, Tokyo Metropolitan Museum of Art (and regularly until 1953)
1950	*Jiyu Bijutsu-ka Kyokai Association Show*, Tokyo Metropolitan Museum of Art (and regularly until 1956)
1963	*4th Ecole de Tokyo Exhibition*, Jewish Center Hall, Los Angeles
1969	*9th Contemporary Art Exhibition of Japan*, Tokyo Metropolitan Museum of Art
1972	*Modern Japanese Graphic Art*, Institute of Contemporary Arts, London
1974	*Japan: Tradition und Gegenwart*, Stadtische Kunsthalle, Dusselforf
1980	*Variations on Planar Painting*, Fukuoka Art Museum, Japan
1984	*Contemporary Art: Tokyo/Paris*, Galerie Denise Rene, Paris
1985	*Japanese Contemporary Paintings*, Museum of Modern Art, New Delhi
1987	*19th Bienal de Sao Paulo*, Brazil

Collections:

National Museum of Modern Art, Tokyo; Museum of Modern Art, Toyama; Miyagi Museum of Art; Museum of Modern Art, Shiga; Museum of Modern Art, Saitama; Kitakyushu Municipal Museum of Art; Seibu Museum, Tokyo; Ohara Museum, Kurashiki; Seibu Museum, Karuizawa; Takamatsu Municipal Museum of Art.

Publications:

On YAMADA: books—*Japan: Tradition und Gegenwart*, exhibition catalogue with texts by Jurgen Harten and Joseph Love, Dusselforf 1974; *Masaaki Yamada's Paintings 1950–1980*, exhibition catalogue with text by Takashi Hayami, Tokyo 1981; *Masaaki Yamada: Works 1985–86*, exhibition catalogue edited by the Satani Gallery, Tokyo 1986; *Yamada: Paintings of the Late 1950s*, exhibition catalogue with essay by Tazmi Shinoda, Tokyo 1986; *19th Bienal Internacional de Sao Paulo: Japan*, exhibition catalogue with text by Yoshiaki Tono, Sao Paulo 1987.

In my work during the mid-1960s, paintings were examined within certain constraints as a condensation of an autonomous structure expressed by the act of painting. The opposition to color is seen in the merging of material and method and includes the brushstrokes and use of repressed color. The objective quality, which interacts with form and content through the use of things like crosses and stripes, is looked at from a position that lies in opposition to the real world, as I sought to indicate the fundamental meaning that paintings establish. The restraint, however, cannot be traced to silence. My later works reflect a shift toward previously anticipated colors and stratified forms; selecting a certain point in the midst of the endless flow of time tells where I was at a given time. A compelling feeling of diversity is incorporated in the paintings.

—Masaaki Yamada

Ever since the 1950s, Masaaki Yamada's paintings have been the best example that shows the intellectual essence of the abstract paintings in Japan. Surprisingly enough, his marvelous achievements have not been shared with a lot of people in the art circles in Japan until the 1970s. He has remained aloof from any other artist or movement, creating high-standard substantial paintings by himself which miraculously corresponded with those of some modernist painters in America.

Yamada was born in Tokyo in 1930 and studied at Tokyo University. He studied painting with Saburo Hasegawa, one of the pioneering abstractionists in prewar Japan. However, Yamada's existent canvases retain no evidences that he made paintings under the major influence of Hasegawa. It is notable that he kept apart from any influence of not only the Japanese abstract painters in the prewar period, but also his contemporary abstractionists in Japan in the postwar era which, in a sense, was strongly affected by the idea of the *Informel* movement advocated and introduced to Japan by the French critic/painter Michel Tapié. The ideas of *Informel* and Action Painting in the United States in the '40s and '50s rapidly assimilated into Japanese avant-garde art, and evolved into the Dadaistic movement in 1960s.

Yamada stood detached and was making his analytic paintings with great subtlety which many other Japanese contemporaries were apt to ignore. He stuck to painting and explored the pictorial heritage of Cubism and Cézanne all by himself.

Early in the 1950s, he started still lifes with very limited information of Cézanne and Giorgio Morandi, but soon decomposed the subjects in analytic manner which he acquired instinctively from Cubist methodology. The surface of his painting attained the pictorial unity with flat, decomposed and geometric forms. It was 1956 when he destroyed every simplistic geometric form and began the intricate mosaic painting with numerous small broken planes. But in order to maintain stability of the painted surface, he took the constructive direction in 1957 instead of destructive. His paintings in 1958 consisted of squares and rectangles that looked like nested boxes with different colors, most of which could be regarded as the similitudes of the canvas shapes. Those works remind us of paintings by Josef Albers, but it was not until 1965 that Yamada actually saw the works by the modernist painter. Probably Yamada's idea had the affinity with not so much Albers's as Ad Reinhardt's.

The vertical and lateral elements which were introduced to stabilize the picture developed in the first half of the 1960s into the paintings of the lateral stripes in various colors. The paintings with crossed lines followed from 1965 to 1967, which actually consisted of four painted square planes in monochrome arranged at right angles, leaving the ground in a different color in the shape of the narrowest crossed lines.

From 1968 to 1973 his canvases resumed stripes, but only in two colors with the thinner surface. Next six years until 1978 was replaced by the paintings of checkered-flag pattern, retaining the thinly painted surface in two colors of adjacent values. It has been pointed out that in this period Yamada allowed his paintings to approach nearest to 'objecthood', naturally with the great affinity to the Minimalist paintings.

Liberation of free-hand drawings began in 1979 and developed into the splendid variety of strokes and colors in the paintings in the 1980s. In the first half of the eighties, his canvases retained the segmentations by square lines, limiting his free-hand drawing lines in each division with the ground of subtle but rather restrained colors. However, since 1985, the segmenting square lines have reduced to the scattering crosses, and lavish drawings in rich colors spread over the canvas, making the painting an optical ravishment. It should not be overlooked that Yamada's exuberant works have been accomplished with the excellent texture and soft-hued, creamy colors, and they could be only possible through the Japanese sensibility.

—Tazmi Shinoda

YAMAGUCHI, Takeo.
Japanese. Born in Seoul, Korea, 23 November 1902. Studied at the Tokyo School of Art, 1922–27; also studied in France, 1927–31. Independent painter, working in Seoul, 1931–45, and in Tokyo, 1945 until

Masaaki Yamada: *Work E. 277*, 1987

his death in 1983: associated with the Nikka group of artists, Tokyo, from 1938. Professor, Musashino Art College, Tokyo, 1954–74. From 1974, Honorary Instructor, Tama Art College, Tokyo. Recipient: First Prize, *Contemporary Japanese Art Exhibition*, Tokyo, 1954; Guggenheim International Award, 1958. *Died* (in Tokyo) *in 1983*.

Individual Exhibitions:

1939 Seijusha, Tokyo
1961 Minami Gallery, Tokyo
1965 Minami Gallery, Tokyo
1968 Musashino Art College, Tokyo
Minami Gallery, Tokyo
1969 Nihonbashi Gallery, New York
1972 Minami Gallery, Tokyo
1975 Minami Gallery, Tokyo
1980 National Museum of Modern Art, Tokyo (retrospective; with Masakazu Horiuti)

Selected Group Exhibitions:

1954 *Annual Exhibition*, American Artists Society, New York
Contemporary Japanese Art, Tokyo
1955 *Bienal*, Sao Paulo
1956 *Biennale*, Venice
1963 *Bienal*, Sao Paulo
1965 *New Japanese Painting and Sculpture*, travelling exhibition (toured the United States)
Modern Japanese Painting, Kunsthaus, Zurich
1970 *Expo*, Museum of Fine Arts, Osaka, Japan

Collections:

National Museum of Modern Art, Tokyo; Ohara Museum of Art, Kurashiki, Japan; Museum of Modern Art, Kamakura, Japan; Museum of Contemporary Art, Nagaoka, Japan; Museum of Modern Art, New York; Guggenheim Museum, New York.

Publications:

By YAMAGUCHI: article—"Various Confessions: Why I Use the Color Brown" in *Geijutsu Shincho* (Tokyo), October 1976.

On YAMAGUCHI: book—*Yamaguchi/Horiuti*, exhibition catalogue, with an essay by Tamon Miki, Tokyo 1980; articles— "From Wandering: Opened His Eyes to Abstract Painting" by S. Miyake in *Bijutsu Techo* (Tokyo), 1958; "The Art of Takeo Yamaguchi: The Unworldly Spirit and its Forms" by T. Uemura in *Mizue* (Tokyo), 1968.

Takeo Yamaguchi, a Japanese painter born in Seoul in Korea in 1902, was one of the leading figures in the country who plowed their way of abstraction through the postwar period up to the end of 1970s.

He left his home in Seoul for Tokyo in 1921 to study at the Tokyo School of Fine Art, the former institute of the Tokyo University of Fine Art, in which he enrolled in 1922 and took a classic training for five years. Soon after graduation in 1927, he went to France, counting on a Japanese expressionist painter in Paris, Yuzo Saeki, and stayed in and around Paris until 1930. He frequently visited the atelier of Ossip Zadkine, but there is no evident influence from the artist or other contemporary painters, for example, Picasso, Braque, Leger, Klee, Soutine, Picabia and Lipchitz, whose works Yamaguchi came to admire.

He settled in his home in Seoul again in 1931, where he was due to succeed his wealthy family business, farming and forestry. In that year, he sent the Nika Exhibition in Tokyo ten paintings, two of which were accepted. He continued, while engaging himself in the family business with tenant farmers working in the vast paddy field, to send his works to the exhibition every year until Japan's participation in the World War II in 1941 made it impossible for him to continue shipping paintings. Most of his paintings in this early stage were those in which a dozen of slow, small daubs or quick, narrow brushstrokes in yellow, blue, red, green and black were sporadically strewed over white backgrounds. (*Pond* (1936), *Garden A* (1936))

He was drafted into the army in 1945, but the war ended in that year, forcing him to abandon all the property in Seoul and be repatriated to Japan. He settled in Tokyo, resumed painting for Nika Exhibition, and became one of the important members of the group.

A new stage opened up when he introduced thick and dark, mostly black backgrounds into his postwar abstract paintings with a few oval shapes or distorted strips in yellow, white, red or brown pigment flatly overlayed with a painting knife. (*Shape* (1952)).

It is noteworthy that after 1953 he had limited his colors in a single work to only two, either yellow ochre with black or Venetian red with black. The artist had recollected that the yellow ochre reflected the characteristic color in China; on the other hand, the

red, the color in Korea. And these peculiar colors as well as the limitation of colors to two had never changed until his death in 1983.

Up to the last half of the 1950s he made his own paintings with a thick, multi-layered surface consisting of black background with clear-cut, extended series of bands in red or yellow, many of them cornered almost at right angles, sometimes curved in boomerang shape, sometimes with an isolated circle like an island, as if the bands were making flat circuit-ways on dark cosmic space. (*Composition* (1955), *Yellow Shape* (1955)).

Around 1958, the bands in red or yellow began to spread over so that they assumed large quasi-geometric color-fields, putting aside the black background to the outer edges. He advanced the development to such a degree that there were no distinctions between subject and background, and from 1966 the color-field either in yellow ochre or red had begun to dominate over the surface with an impressively small corner area in black, or with a rift painted in black. (*Red Eye* (1959), *Red* (1971), *Track* (1975)).

His paintings in his last 15 years could be associated with color-field painting in Minimalism, but the texture and the color, reminding us of the muddy field, the clay house walls or the earthenware in his birthplace, definitely differ with those in Minimalist painting.

He had been a professor at the Musashino College of Fine Art in Tokyo from 1954 to 1974. He was selected as a Japanese artist for the third São Paolo Biennial in 1955, the 7th in 1963, and the 28th Venetian Biennial in 1956.

—Tazmi Shinoda

YOKOMI, Richard (Koji).
American. Born in Denver, Colorado, 12 March 1944. Studied at the Chouinard Art Institute, Los Angeles, 1962–65, B.A. 1965. Married Shigemi Susie Sasaki. Painter: lives and works in Los Angeles. Agents: Nicholas Wilder Gallery. 8225 Santa Monica Boulevard, Los Angeles, California 90046; and Felicity Samuel Gallery, 16 Savile Row, London WIXIAE, England. Address: 3666 Division Street, Los Angeles, California 90065, U.S.A.

Individual Exhibitions:

1969 Nicholas Wilder Gallery, Los Angeles
1970 Joseph Helman Gallery, St. Louis
1971 Jill Kornblee Gallery, New York
Galerie Neuendorf, Cologne
1972 Nicholas Wilder Gallery, Los Angeles
1973 Felicity Samuel Gallery, London
1974 Nicholas Wilder Gallery, Los Angeles
1975 Seder/Creigh Gallery, Coronado, California

Selected Group Exhibitions:

1971 *Color and Scale,* Oakland Museum of Art, California
1972 *U.S.A. West Coast,* Galerie Neuendorf, Cologne
Southern California Attitudes 1972, Pasadena Museum of Art, California
1974 *15 Abstract Artists,* Santa Barbara Museum of Art, California
1975 *Current Concerns,* Los Angeles Institute of Contemporary Art
1976 *Painting and Sculpture in California: The Modern Era,* San Francisco Museum of Modern Art (travelled to the Smithsonian Institution, Washington, D.C., 1977)

Collections:

Norton Simon Museum of Art, Pasadena, California.

Publications:

On YOKOMI: articles—"Los Angeles: Richard Yokomi, Nicholas Wilder Gallery" by Peter Plagens in *Artforum* (New York, September/October 1974.

YOSHIDA, Kenji.
Japanese. Born in Osaka, 24 May 1924. Studied pedagogy, University of Osaka, 1939–44; studied with Stanley Hayter, Atelier 17, Paris, 1964–72; also influenced by the painter Hayashi Kiyoshi and the Spanish sculptor Apel-Les Fenosa. Served as an Ensign Second Class in the Japanese Marine Corps, 1943–44. Married Hiroko Uehara in 1973; daughter: Kiyoko. Teacher in Osaka, 1945–51, and Tokyo, 1952–64. Full-time artist, living and working in Paris, since 1964. Recipient: Norwegian Government Grant, Oslo, 1966. Agent: Galerie Hexagramme, 67b rue des Saints-Peres, 75006 Paris. Address: 49 rue de la Procession, 75015 Paris, France.

Individual Exhibitions:

1957 Muramatsu Gallery, Tokyo
1958 Muramatsu Gallery, Tokyo
1959 Muramatsu Gallery, Tokyo
1960 Muramatsu Gallery, Tokyo
1964 Takegawa Gallery, Tokyo
1966 Galerie Hammerlund, Oslo
1968 Museum of Japanese Art, Haifa, Israel
1971 Galerie St.-Johann, Saarbrucken, West Germany
1972 Linz Museum, Austria
1973 Seibu Gallery, Tokyo
1974 Galerie Modern-Art, Vienna
1976 Fuji Yoshi Gallery, Tokyo
1977 Galerie L'Estampille, Brussels
Galerie Point W, Gallard, France
1979 Galerie Aujourd'hui, Geneva
1982 Atelier Alma, Lyon, France
Ecole de Francais, Geneva
1983 Gallery Art-Houre, Tokyo
Gallery Beni, Kyoto, Japan
Gallery Taiken, Osaka, Japan
1984 Galerie Galise, Thonon, France
1986 Galerie Galise, Thonon, France
1987 Galerie Galise, at *FIAC 87,* Grank Palais, Paris

Selected Group Exhibitions:

1965 *Graphics Biennale,* Moderna Galerija, Ljubljana, Yugoslavia
1966 *Graphics Biennale,* Modern Museum, Cracow, Poland
Nordisk Grafik Union, Kunstforening, Oslo
1967 *Graphics Biennale,* Kunstverein, Grenchen, Switzerland
1968 *Wiener Sezession Grafika,* Wiener Sezession, Vienna
1970 *Print International,* Kunstverein, Frechen, West Germany
1974 *Graphik Klein-Plastik,* Kunstlerhaus, Vienna
1976 *Exposition International,* Maison de la Culture, Berck-Piage, France
1984 *Actu, Art 84,* Galerie Galise, Thonon, France (and 1985, 1986, 1987)
1986 *Contemporary Art:Japan/Denmark,* Konstmuseum, Copenhagen

Collections:

Bibliotheque Nationale, Paris; Ministere des Affaires Culturelles, Paris; Bibliotheque Royale, Brussels; Museum Louviers, France; Museum of Modern Art, Norrkoping, Sweden; Kunst pa Arbeidsplassen, Oslo; Bergen Art Association, Norway; Kunstverein, Frechen, West Germany; Museum of Modern Art, Skopje, Yugoslavia; Museum of Japanese Art, Haifa, Israel.

Kenji Yoshida: ***La Vie,*** **1980**

Publications:

On YOSHIDA: book—*Kenji Yoshida: La Vie,* exhibition catalogue with texts by Tadashi Fukuda, Joseph Paul Schneider and others, Thonon 1986; article—"My Friend Yoshida" by Uehara Kaza in *Sansai* (Tokyo), January 1974.

I was born in a farmhouse. I was brought up surrounded by sun, water, earth and men who knew how to work. So then I knew that man can not live without nature and can do nothing without nature . . . nature which runs according to laws on the cosmos that all things obey.

The movement of the cosmos is equal to the movement of life on a smaller scale.

The ancients called it "the voice of God".

The voice makes itself heard in nature and within me. It exists in all things.

When man moves with this voice in harmony with the movement of the cosmos, peace will come.

Therefore, we must have an attitude of moderation towards all things and all men.

I took part in the Second World War, and I found myself facing death and I saw the horrors of war. So, I had to think.

What is life? What is peace? Happily, I survived. I looked for the point of harmony of the voice within myself.

I think that it is my mission, and it is hard for me.

It is difficult to explain the spirit of Japan to a European. So I must say it on canvas.

One can only judge one's own feelings—isn't that right?

—Kenji Yoshida

Fumio Yoshimura: *Tomato*, 1987

YOSHIMURA, Fumio.

Japanese. Born in Kamakura, 22 February 1926. Studied at Tokyo National University of Art, 1941–49, M.F.A. 1949. Served as Cadet in Japanese Imperial Army, 1945. Married Yoshiko Oshima in 1951 (died, 1963); married the American writer Kate Millett in 1965 (divorced, 1986); married Carol Ann Watkinson in 1987. Independent artist, Tokyo, 1950–61, and in New York since 1962: first realist wood sculptures, 1970. Taught kite-making at Brookfield Craft Center, Connecticut during summers, 1965–70; Assistant Professor, Dartmouth College, Hanover, New Hampshire, since 1982. Recipient: Faculty Research Grant, Dartmouth College, 1984, 1985. Addresses: 5 East Third Street, New York, New York 10003; R.R. 1, Box 139, Academy Road, Thetford, Vermont 05075, U.S.A.

Individual Exhibitions:

1950 Maramatsu Gallery, Tokyo (and yearly until 1958)
1970 Pennsylvania Academy of Fine Arts, Philadelphia
1971 Wichita Art Museum, Kansas
1972 Marian Locks Gallery, Philadelphia
1973 Nancy Hoffman Gallery, New York
1974 Galerie Arneson, Copenhagen
1975 Galeriet, Lund, Sweden
1976 Squibb Gallery, Princeton, New Jersey
Nancy Hoffman Gallery, New York
1977 Marian Locks Gallery, Philadelphia
1978 Norton Gallery of Art, West Palm Beach, Florida
1979 Amherst College, Massachusetts
Nancy Hoffmen Gallery, New York
1981 Beaumont and May Gallery, Dartmouth College, Hanover, New Hampshire
1983 Nancy Hoffman Gallery, New York
1984 Mitchell Museum, Mount Vernon, Illinois
1985 Atlantic Center of the Arts, New Smyrna Beach, Florida
1986 Windsor House, Vermont
1987 Temple Gallery, Philadelphia

Selected Group Exhibitions:

1968 *Made with Paper,* Museum of Contemporary Crafts, New York
1973 *Made with Wood,* Dartmouth College, Hanover, New Hampshire
1974 *New/Photo Realism,* Wadsworth Atheneum, Hartford, Connecticut
1976 *Object as Poet,* Renwick Gallery, Smithsonian Institution, Washington, D.C.
1979 *Illusion and Material,* Paterson College, Wayne, New Jersey
1981 *Katachi,* Albuquerque Museum of Art, New Mexico
1982 *Contemporary Realism,* Pennsylvania Academy of Fine Arts, Philadelphia
1983 *Materials and Illusion/Unlikely Materials,* Taft Museum, Cincinnati, Ohio
1985 *Fine Woodwork,* Filbrook Art Museum, Tulsa, Oklahoma
1987 *Four Wood Sculptors,* Kansas City Art Institute, Missouri

Collections:

Albright-Knox Gallery, Buffalo, New York; Pennsylvania Academy of Fine Art, Philadelphia; Philadelphia Museum of Art; Taft Museum, Cincinnati, Ohio; Go Vett-Brewster Gallery, New Plymouth, New Zealand; Power Gallery of Contemporary Art, Sydney, Australia; Albuquerque Museum of Art, New Mexico; Delaware Art Museum, Wilmington; Mississippi Museum of Art, Jackson; Norton Gallery of Art, West Palm Beach, Florida.

Publications:

On YOSHIMURA: books—*New/Photo Realism,* exhibition catalogue, by Jack Cowart, Hartford, Connecticut, 1974;*Super Realism: A Critical Anthology,* edited by Gregory Battcock, New York 1975; *Super Realism* by Edward Lucie Smith, Oxford 1977; *Superrealist Painting and Sculpture* by Christine Lindsey, New York 1980; *Masters of Wood Sculpture* by Nicholas Rourkes, New York 1980; *Wood Working: The New Wave* by Dona Z. Meilach, New York 1981; *Poetry of the Physical,* exhibition catalogue by Paul Smith, New York 1986.

In 1970 Fumio Yoshimura began making illusionistic wooden sculptures using the forms of real objects covering a range of subjects from bicycles to tomato plants. Yoshimura had been a painter from around 1948, but it is for his sculpture that he became known.

Yoshimura turns readymade and organic forms into hand made simulations. The element of imitation is co-existent with an element of removal in his finely crafted, smooth wooden substitutes for the real thing. The works are both accurate to their models and modified by the translation into natural, untreated wood. (He prefers linden spruce and pine.) Yoshimura shows considerable involvement with literal depiction, but he is more concerned with close approximation than with scrupulously accurate reduplication down to the last details. This factor, along with the neutralizing colorlessness and smooth graining of the wood, place the appearance of reality at a distance. "I'm reproducing a ghost," Yoshimura has noted, and the sculptures have a disembodied quality achieved through the materials and the handmade craftsmanship which both imitate the original subject/object and simultaneously place it within a new level of artificiality.

"Motorcycle" (1973), "Typewriter" (1975), "Bicycle with Parking Meter" (1978) originate from precise working drawings, are made a part at a time and are assembled like the industrial objects they repre-

sent. The finished works are sensuously organic, solid yet soft wood, removed from the mobility and use of their models, and turned into three-dimensional objects of contemplation. There is an element of irony in Yoshimura's reversal process, a Zen-like move from the subjective particular to the objective general. He questions perception and the real nature of literal presence.

Yoshimura's work has obvious likenesses with Jasper Johns, George Segal and Claes Oldenburg. Yet, he remains closer to the literal than any of these artists, and he avoids the rough-edged wistfulness of Segal and the flamboyant Pop comedy of Oldenburg. Yoshimura's kind of Realism differs also from the deceptive mimicry central to the work of Duane Hanson or the Photo-Realists. Yoshimura reverses the Duchampian idea of the readymade, transforming it into the hand-crafted artifact. Illusionism is tempered; both organic forms and hard, metal, working objects are slowly and deliberately crafted into sleek, smooth, naturally grained presences, apparitions hovering in suspended animation on the border between becoming and being.

—Barbara Cavaliere

YOUNG, Peter (Ford).

American. Born in Pittsburgh, Pennsylvania, 2 January 1940. Studied at Chouinard Art Institute, Los Angeles, 1957; Pomona College, Claremont, California, 1958–60; Art Students League, New York, 1960; New York University, 1961–63, B.A. 1963. Influenced by Dynaton Group (Lee Mullican, Onslow Ford and Wolfgang Paalen). Independent painter practicing a formal abstraction rooted in study of primitive design and mysticism: lived and worked in New York, 1960–70, in Bisbee, Arizona, since 1970. Visiting Artist, Oberlin College, Ohio, 1970; Pima College, Tucson, Arizona, 1976. Agents: Leo Castelli, 420 West Broadway, New York, New York 10012; and Oil and Steel Gallery, 157 Chambers Street, New York, New York 10012. Address: Box 715, Bisbee, Arizona 85603, U.S.A.

Individual Exhibitions:

1968 Nicholas Wilder Gallery, Los Angeles
Galerie Ricke, Cologne
1969 *Peter Young/David Diao*, Leo Castelli Gallery, New York
1970 Goldowsky Gallery, New York
1972 Galerie Ricke, Cologne
Goldowsky Gallery, New York
Greenberg Gallery, St. Louis
1974 Goldowsky Gallery, New York
1975 Texas Gallery, Houston
1980 Cochise Fine Arts, Bisbee, Arizona
1981 Leo Castelli Gallery, New York

Selected Group Exhibitions:

1967 *Painting Annual*, Whitney Museum, New York
1968 *Documenta 4*, Kassel, West Germany
1969 *31st Biennial*, Corcoran Gallery, Washington, D.C.
9 Young Artists, Guggenheim Museum, New York
The Development of Modernist Painting: Jackson Pollock to Present, Steinberg Art Gallery, Washington University, St. Louis
One Tendency of Contemporary Art, Kunstmart, Cologne
1971 *6 Painters*, Albright-Knox Gallery, Buffalo, New York
1972 *Painting: New Options*, Walker Art Center, Minneapolis, Minnesota
1974 *8 Artists*, Art Museum of South Texas, Corpus Christi

Peter Young: *Linear Weave Painting No. 14*, 1980

Collections:

Museum of Modern Art, New York: Whitney Museum, New York: Guggenheim Museum, New York: Albright-Knox Gallery, Buffalo, New York; Allen Art Museum, Oberlin College, Ohio.

Publications:

By YOUNG: articles—"Artists on Their Art" in *Art International* (Lugano, Switzerland), March 1968; "Peter Young" in *Art Now* (New York), vol. 1, no. 5, 1969.

On YOUNG: Books—*The Triumph of American Painting* by Irving Sandler, New York 1970; *The Twentieth Century (American Painting Vol. 2)* by Barbara Rose. Cleveland 1971; *Introduction to 6 Painters*, exhibition catalogue, by James Wood, Buffalo, New York 1971; articles—"Gallery Without Walls" by Barbara Rose in *Art in America* (New York). March 1968; "David Diao, Peter Young, R. Pettibone" by J. R. Baker in *Arts Magazine* (New York), March 1969; "Diao and Young at Castelli" by Dore Ashton in *Studio International* (London), April 1969; review by Emily Wasserman in *Artforum* (New York), May 1969; "Presenting Peter Young" in *Art in America* (New York), 1969; "Notes on American Painting of the '60s" by Walter Bannard in *Artforum* (New York), January 1970; "New Informalists" by Carter Ratcliff in *Artnews* (New York), February 1970; "Color Abstractionism" by Willis Domingo in *Arts Magazine* (New York), December 1970; "The Spectrum of Monochrome" by Lawrence Alloway in *Arts Magazine* (New York), December 1970; "Peter Young: A Chronology of the Works" by Ellen Johnson in *Artforum* (New York), April 1971; "Materiality and Painterliness" by Gregoire Muller in *Arts Magazine* (New York), September 1971; review by Hayden Herra in *Artnews* (New York), November 1974.

The very greatest art is the "art" of perfecting one's Self.

—Peter Young

Peter Young's involvement with painting began in the early '60's when there seemed to be a preference for coolness and linear abstraction, a reaction fostered by young artists who felt antagonized by the decadence of such late Abstract Expressionists as Bannard, Poons, Stella and Martin—an insistence on "doing the next thing." This became the theoretical enemy of Young.

Young's work has always been involved with a rich sense of history; primitive design, and American Indian and African art are important influences. Although his early work (1963–65) seemed to respond to the linear grid work of his contemporaries, he was to develop a "dot" technique derived from Seurat.

The "dot₆ technique, applied in acrylic, is basically an ,all-over type of composition which has an edge and corner-to-corner continuity related to the formal aspects of Jackson Pollock's work. The dots are irregular, applied with the tip of a brush; the dots may be marbleized, chained or connected, clustered or fully saturated into the canvas. The dot patterns may suggest constellations or star clusters. An analogy to heavenly bodies is not inconsistent with Young's own rather mystical approach to the mid-60's work. At that time he was concerned with the investigation of light and color on large fields. Working from a white background he developed a series of color studies which achieved the primal light and became the hallmark of his work.

Young is a color painter and considers color to be the one constant in a long series of stylistic experiments from 1965 to 1969. "There are many color painters in my generation who have worked from a mathematical process. My early painting was very pale and white. This had a lot to do with living in New York, having a lot of artificial lighting, and a sort of psychedelic yogic insistence of lightness," he states. His work established a serial format of color composition which was provocative in the midst of work he felt was lacking in warmth and a sense of life.

At the peak of his popularity in 1969, Young left New York to live in a remote Indian village in Costa Rica, then in Utah and New Mexico. Back in New York in early 1970 his work showed a loosening of the dot patterning and a more intense color palette.

After a trip to Morocco and Spain in 1972, a further bread occurred in his work. He began to fold his canvas when it was wet, producing a totemic two-column figural arrangement a la Rorschach. Already the ground of his dot painting had changed from white base to patchwork color base. In these folded works the figural element takes over and is defined not as a nuance but as sculptural form. The over-painting in these folded works was applied with the Pollock splash and drip method.

At some point in the folding process Young began to fold the canvas diagonally as well as vertically. The diagonal folds produce a mandala image. "When I began to fold the canvas I was aware that the sense of lightness I was once working for was not as important," he says. The color of these mandala paintings is deep and thick, recalling tantric manuscripts. The imagery of his paintings in fully integrated with the animation of moving forms. The busy surface of the circular shape is punctuated with hand over-painting and some splash and drip work.

Now in the mandala works there is still an all-over patterning and dotting. "The essence of these works is the centrality and decentrality of the image in various states of focus. The symbol is not specific to Indian culture but to all religious art of the world."

Mysticism and art are unified concepts in a chronology of Young's work. The use of hallucinogens was an additive for Young but only tangential to his belief in universal imagery and the importance of the artist's development of his own decorative motifs.

—Adina Wingate

YOUNGERMAN, Jack.

American. Born in Louisville, Kentucky, 25 March 1926. Studied at the University of North Carolina, Chapel Hill (United States Navy Training Program), 1944–46, and University of Missouri, Columbia, 1947, B.A. 1947; studied at the Académie des Beaux-Arts, Paris, 1947–48. Married Delphine Seyrig in 1950; son: Duncan. Painter and sculptor; lived in Europe, 1947–56;has lived and worked in New York since 1956; designed stage sets for Jean-Louis Barrault's production of *Histoire de Vasco*, Paris, 1956, and *Deathwatch* by Jean Genet, New York, 1958. Artist-in-Residence, Worcester Art Museum, Massachusetts, 1965; Instructor, Yale University, New Haven, Connecticut, 1974–75, and Hunter College, New York, 1981–82. Instructor, New York University, since 1982. Recipient: New Talent Award, *Art in America*, New York, 1959; National Endowment for the Arts Award, 1972; Guggenheim Fellowship, 1976. Agent: Washburn Gallery, New York. Address: c/o Washburn Gallery, 42 East 57th Street, New York, New York 10022, U.S.A.

Individual Exhibitions:

1951 Galerie Arnaud, Paris
1958 Betty Parsons Gallery, New York
1960 Betty Parsons Gallery, New York
1960 Betty Parsons Gallery, New York
1961 Betty Parsons Gallery, New York
1962 Galerie Lawrence, Paris
1963 Galleria dell'Ariete, Milan
Everett Ellin Gallery, Los Angeles
1964 Betty Parsons Gallery, New York
1965 Betty Parsons Gallery, New York
Worcester Art Museum, Massachusetts
1966 Massachusetts Institute of Technology, Cambridge
Galerie Maeght, Paris
1967 Betty Parsons Gallery, New York
1968 Betty Parsons Gallery, New York
Phillips Collection, Washington, D.C.
1971 Pace Gallery, New York
J. L. Hudson Gallery, Detroit
1972 Pace Gallery, New York
Center for the Visual Arts, Portland, Oregon
Seattle Art Museum
1973 Arts Club of Chicago
Galerie Denise René, Paris
Pace Gallery, New York
Galerie Denise René/Hans Mayer, Dusseldorf
1974 Fendrick Gallery, Washington, D.C.
Kingpitcher Gallery, Pittsburgh
1975 Pace Gallery, New York
1976 Parrish Museum, Southampton, New York
1977 Tampa Bay Museum, Florida
1978 Truman Gallery, New York
1981 Washburn Gallery, New York
1982 Washburn Gallery, New York
1983 Alex Rosenberg Gallery, New York
1985 Washburn Gallery, New York
1986 Guggenheim Museum, New York

Selected Group Exhibitions:

1950 *Les Mains Ebouies*, Galerie Maeght, Paris
1959 *16 Americans*, Museum of Modern Art, New York
1961 *Abstract Expressionists and Imagists*, Guggenheim Museum, New York
1964 *American Drawings*, Guggenheim Museum, New York
1966 *Systemic Painting*, Guggenheim Museum, New York
1976 *Abstract Expressionists and Imagists*, University of Texas at Austin
1979 *Americans in Paris: The 50's*, California State University at Northridge
1981 *Contemporary Americans*, Guggenheim Museum, New York
1984 *The Folding Image*, National Gallery of Art, Washington, D.C.
1985 *Transformations in Sculpture*, Guggenheim Museum, New York

Collections:

Guggenheim Museum, New York; Whitney Museum, New York; Museum of Modern Art, New York; Albright-Knox Art Gallery, Buffalo, New York; Worcester Art Museum, Massachusetts; Hirshhorn Museum, Washington, D.C.; Phillips Collection, Washington, D.C.; Corcoran Gallery, Washington, D.C.; Carnegie Institute, Pittsburgh; Art Institute of Chicago.

Publications:

By YOUNGERMAN: article—"Interview with Jack Youngerman," with Barbara Rose, in *Artforum* (New York), January 1966.

On YOUNGERMAN: books—*Systemic Painting*, exhibition catalogue, by Lawrence Alloway, New York 1966; *Constructivism: Origins and Evolution* by George Rickey, New York 1967; *American Art since 1900: A Critical History* by Barbara Rose, New York 1967; *The Joys and Sorrows of Recent American Art* by A. S. Weller, Urbana, Illinois 1968; *Jack Youngerman*, exhibition catalogue with text by Diane Waldman, New York 1986.

Jack Youngerman's career has involved a continuing absorption with the formal and even psychological possibilities inherent in leaf-like form and flat and brilliantly-hued pictorial pattern. Impersonal and banal forms marked the work of many chromatic and hard-edged abstract artists of the 1960's; in strong contrast Youngerman, both then and to the present, has worked in distinctly natural-referent form. The form and color precedents of Arp and Matisse may easily be cited; yet perhaps more to the point might be the strong American symbolist precedents for such undulant and rhapsodic nature-focused art—for instance, Dove, O'Keeffe, Burchfield, and, with Gorky, the surrealist strain in American modernism. It is as if Youngerman would wish the clarity and rationalist force of the Constructivist tradition— with which he initially became conversant during his long European stay, 1947–1956—and yet also wish to imbue it with an irrepressible rhythm of nature. The emphatic urgency of Youngerman's painting and sculpture has been referred to by the artist: "We are immersed in the powerful and autonomous images of the world before these forms are possessed and diminished by names and uses—the name preempting the form. Painting involves the restoring of the image to that original primacy."

After some heavy-textured, expressionist work in the mid-1950's, Youngerman was, by the end of the decade, a post-painterly abstract artist. His images, already restricted to one or two colors, featured flat and sharp-edged forms which resolved themselves into landscape panorama. While he has restricted the internal shape and pattern of his work to natural reference, he has continuously attempted variance by his manipulation of the ground shape and the concomitant ordering of his forms in their positioning on these grounds. In 1967 he produced symmetrical works, with butterfly-like shapes on diamond shaped canvases— forms clearly influenced by beetle and fish patterning. His exhibition in 1971 featured circular, elliptical canvases. And in the following year, Youngerman detached his floral emblems from their ground and produced shaped canvases, at times in several sections whose edges conformed to the flaring edged forms. He has also exhibited stainless steel sculpture (1971), and wooden cut-outs (1972), and all white fiberglass and resin three-dimensional sculpture (1976). A recent exhibition (1978) involved the use of folding screens on which he painted his signature shapes.

Youngerman's art has been marked by an almost heroic poignance because of his insistence upon a duality—clear abstractionist idealism yet linked with the resonance of an older subjective translation of nature into pattern. If this has been a detriment for the critical acceptance of his work—the restrictiveness of his form world—it may as well have operated to deny the artist access to larger, more current, views of the mechanico-metabolic confrontation.

—Joshua Kind

YUNKERS, Adja.

American. Born in Riga, Latvia, 15 July 1900; lived in Germany, 1919–22, Havana, 1924–27, Paris, 1927–38, and Stockholm, 1939–47; emigrated to the United States in 1947; subsequently naturalized. Educated at the Art Academy of Petrograd, 1914–17. Married the art critic Dore Ashton in 1952; daughters: Alexandra and Marina. Independent graphic artist, also active as a painter, magazine editor and interior designer: lived and worked in New York, 1947 until his death in 1983. Taught at the New School for Social Research, New York, 1947–56; summer sessions at the University of New Mexico, 1948–49; Cooper Union, New York, 1956–67; Barnard College, New York, 1967–69, Visiting Artist, Academy of Art, Honolulu, 1964; Visiting Critic, Columbia University, New York, 1967–69. Recipient: Guggenheim Fellowship, 1949, 1954; Ford Foundation Grant, 1960; Gold Medal, *2nd International Print Biennial,* Norway, 1974, Agent: C D S Gallery, 13 East 75th Street, New York, New York 10021. *Died* (in New York City), *24 December 1983.*

Individual Exhibitions:

1922–46 Maria Kunde, Hamburg
Galleri Moderne, Stockholm
Galleri Per, Oslo
Galleri Tokanten, Copenhagen
1947–54 Henry Kleeman Gallery, New York
Grace Borgenicht Gallery, New York
Corcoran Gallery, Washington, D.C.
Art Alliance, Philadelphia
Art Institute of Chicago
Colorado Springs Fine Arts Center
San Francisco Museum of Art
Buchholtz Galeria, Madrid
1955 Galerie d'Art Moderne, Basle
Studio Paul Facchetti, Paris
Galleria Numero, Florence
Zwemmer Gallery, London
Konstmuseum, Gothenburg, Sweden
Grace Borgenicht Gallery, New York
1957–59 Los Angeles County Museum of Art
Rose Fried Gallery, New York
André Emmerich Gallery, New York
Howard Wise Gallery, Cleveland
Instituto de Arte Contemporaneo, Lima
1960 Baltimore Museum of Art
1962–65 Honolulu Academy of Art
Feigen Gallery, Detroit
Malmquist and Wood Gallery, Cleveland
1966 Museum Boymans-van-Boyningen, Rotterdam (organized exhibition)
1968 Rose Fried Gallery, New York
1969 Utah Museum of Art, Salt Lake City
1970 Estudio Actual, Caracas
1972 Whitney Museum, New York
Estudio Actual, Caracas
1973 Hayden Gallery, Massachusetts Institute of Technology, Cambridge
Lantern Gallery, Ann Arbor, Michigan
Mazalow Gallery, Toronto
Imprint Gallery, San Francisco
Smith-Andersen Gallery, Palo Alto, California
1974 *Bienal Internacional de Arte Grafica y Arte Seriado,* Segovia, Spain
Norwegian International Print Biennale, Frederikstad
3rd International Exhibit of Graphic Art, Frechen, Germany
Zabriskie Gallery, New York
Estudio Actual, Caracas
Lantern Gallery, Ann Arbor, Michigan
Langsam Gallery, South Yarra, Australia
Carpenter Center for the Visual Arts, Harvard University, Cambridge, Massachusetts
Phoenix Art Museum, Arizona
1975 Museo do Arte Moderno, Chapultepec, Mexico
Smith-Andersen Gallery, San Francisco
Smith-Andersen Gallery, Palo Alto, California
Nielsen Gallery, Boston
Impressions Workshop, Boston
Zabriskie Gallery, New York
Kent State University, Ohio
1976 Simsar Gallery, Ann Arbor, Michigan
Estudio Actual, Caracas
Fairweather Hardin Gallery, Chicago
Daedal Fine Arts Gallery, Baltimore
1977 Estudio Actual, Caracas
Nielsen Gallery, Boston
City Hall Gallery, Boston
Impressions Workshop, Boston
Simsar Gallery, Ann Arbor, Michigan
1978–80 Allrich Gallery, San Francisco
Galeria Juan Martin, Mexico
Philadelphia College of Art
Museo de Bellas Artes, Caracas
Smith-Andersen Gallery, Palo Alto, California
Nielsen Gallery, Boston
Simsar Gallery, Ann Arbor, Michigan
Impressions Gallery, Boston
Estudio Actual, Caracas
1981 Nielsen Gallery, Boston
1982 C D S Gallery, New York
1983 Galleria L'Isola, Rome

Selected Group Exhibitions:

1949 *Master Prints of the MOMA Collection,* Museum of Modern Art, New York
1950 *50 Years of American Painting,* Paris
1969 *The First Generation,* Museum of Modern Art, New York
1970 *L'Art Vivant aux Etats Unis,* Fondation Maeght, St.-Paul-de-Vence, France

Collections:

Museum of Modern Art, New York; Guggenheim Museum, New York; Corcoran Gallery, Washington, D.C.; Hirshhorn Museum, Smithsonian Institution, Washington, D.C.; Philadelphia Museum of Art;Museum of Fine Arts, Boston; Walker Arts Center, Minneapolis; Stadtmuseum, Hamburg; Goteborgs Konstmuseum, Sweden; Museo de Bellas Artes, Caracas.

Publications:

By YUNKERS: magazines edited and published—*Creation* (Stockholm), 1942; *Ars* (Stockholm), 1942; *Prints in the Desert* (Albuquerque, New Mexico), 1949; books illustrated—*5 Love Poems for Marie-Jose* by Octavio Paz, New York 1969; *Blanco* by Octavio Paz, New York 1974.

On YUNKERS: books—*Rio Grande Portfolios* by John Leeper, New York 1952; *Yunkers,* exhibition catalogue, by Grohman and Westholm, Gothenburg, Sweden 1955; *Perspectives, El Arte Moderno en los Estados Unidos* by William Lieberman, Barcelona 1955; *The New American Art, Western World, Volume 3* by Howard Devree, New York 1959; *Adja Yunkers,* exhibition catalogue, by Breeskin and Sawyers, Baltimore 1960; *American Art of Our Century* by John Baur, New York 1961; *50 Years of American Art 1916–1966* by Edward Henning, Cleveland 1966; *Amerikanse Skilderinen Collage* by Van Den Branden, Rotterdam 1966; *Drawings of the Masters: 20th Century Drawings* by Una Johnson, New York 1968; *Yunkers,* exhibition catalogue, by Edward Henning, Salt Lake City, Utah 1969; *Yunkers: American Graphic Artists of the 20th Century #7* by Una Johnson, New York 1969; *L'Art Vivant aux États Unis,* exhibition catalogue, by Dore Ashton, St.-Paul-de-Vence, France 1970; *Yunkers,* exhibition catalogue, by Nico Calas. New York 1972.

From the age of 18 in Germany Adja Yunkers was involved in art as his most intensive activity whether as printmaker, lecturer, interior decorator, magazine editor or painter. Best known as a graphic artist, he reflected in his prints of the 1940's something of the anguish of those years when he was in Sweden physically remote but mentally concerned with the struggles going on in mainland Europe and the Far East. Expressionist in figuration, his most poignant images echoed the harrowing sorrow of the woman as mother, wife and lover projecting something of the strong emotions of Munch and his German followers, distortions heightening the mood of strong feelings associated with the human form though this gradually came to assume less descriptive affinities and to rely more on the forcefully accented contour lines and masses.

After his move to the United States in 1947 Yunkers exploited the potential capacity of the print to emulate painting by expanding in size and colour ranges—he created one tour de force in a polyptych measuring 3 ft. 3 ins by 14 feet wide employing no fewer than 56 colours. From the self-contained area of the paper on which the impression from woodcut, silk screen and other multiple media made their effects, Yunkers proceeded to the revealing experiments with collage and the folding canvas to disrupt the even surface of his support. In one such work, "Folded Canvas I" of 1970, the mauve ground of one side is folded to form an asymmetrical pattern contrasting with the raw textures of the weave, the whole supported on a field of blue. "Yellow Form" (1971) is a collage where blue and mauve also predominate.

While in earlier prints gestural elements gave their emotional appeal, in his later works the shaped outlines in their encounters and association of linear contact produced lyrical suggestions of lovers in generous ovoid and rhythmic curves. Yunkers set himself the almost impossible task of commanding an emotional return from an investment in abstract forms that by themselves seem arbitrary without apparent correlation to the straight confines of the support. Yet such is his mastery of assembling a minimum of motives in telling relationships of outline and colour that he evokes a sense of classical economy and serene calm through such a simple means as the placing of what resembles a torn vertical strip laid across a roughly executed rectangular mass on the dark ground of the picture frame. Abstract as the works are in appearance there is also about them a strong presence of surrealist juxtaposition.

Almost defying analysis in conventional critical terms, Yunkers found the wave length of emotional communication by the mystic amalgam of surface delineation of shapes that nevertheless imply unidentified corporeal entities in space, inspiring an acceptive mood by emotively tuned harmonies of colour.

—G. S. Whittet

Adja Yunkers: ***Aegean III*****, 1967** Courtesy Whitney Museum, New York

Z

ZAPPETTINI, Gianfranco.

Italian. Born in Genoa, 16 June 1939. Studied at the Accademia di Belle Arti, Carrara. Married Gabrielle Gonfiantini in 1963; daughter: Martina. Painter: lives and works in Genoa. Address: via Aurelia 116, 16043 Chiavari, Italy.

Individual Exhibitions:

1962 Galleria Belle Arti, Genoa
1963 Galleria Pescetto, Albisola, Italy
1964 Galleria Ferrari, Verona
Galleria 2000, Bologna
1965 Galleria La Polena, Genoa
1966 Galleria L'Arco, Macerata, Italy
1967 Galleria Vismara, Milan
Galerie Du Disque Rouge, Brussels
1968 Galleria del Cavallino, Venice
1969 Galleria Il Punto, Turin
1971 Galleria Peccolo, Livorno
Galleria pourquoi pas, Genoa
1972 Galerie Loehr, Frankfurt
Galleria La Polena, Genoa
1973 Centro d'Arte Santelmo, Salo, Italy
1974 Galleria la Polena, Genoa
Galleria La Piramide, Florence
Galleria Vinciana, Milan
Galleria Peccolo, Livorno
Galerie December, Münster, West Germany
1975 Westfälischer Kunstverein, Münster, West Germany
Galerie Karsten Greve, Cologne
1976 Galleria La Seconda Scala, Rome
Galerie Peccolo, Cologne
1977 Studio Soldano, Milan
Galleria La Bertesca, Genoa
1978 International Cultureel Centrum, Antwerp
Galerie Peccolo, Cologne
Galerie Artline, The Hague
Galleria Eremitani, Padua

Selected Group Exhibitions:

1969 *Nove Tendencije 4,* Zagreb
1970 *Multiples,* Whitechapel Art Gallery, London
1971 *Triennale,* Delhi, India
Concrete Art, Westfälischer Kunstverein, Münster, West Germany
1973 *Tempi du Percezione,* Casa della Cultura, Livorno
1974 *Geplante Malerei,* Westfälischer Kunstverein, Münster, West Germany
1975 *Pittura,* Palazzo Ducale, Genoa
1976 *A proposito della Pittura,* Stedelijk Museum, Amsterdam
1977 *Documenta,* Kassel, West Germany
1978 *Abstraction Analytique,* Centre Georges Pompidou, Paris

Collections:

Westfälischer Kunstverein, Münster, West Germany.

Publications:

By ZAPPETINI: articles—"Ricerca di una Dimensione" in *Gala* (Milan), September 1974: "Per una Pittura Analitica" in *Data* (Milan), Winter 1974 and *Kunstforum* (Mainz, West Germany), October/November 1974; statement in *Gianfranco Zappettini,* exhibition catalogue, Münster, West Germany 1975; statement in *Gianfranco Zappettini,* exhibition catalogue. Antwerp 1978.

On ZAPPETTINI: book—*Gianfranco Zappettini,* exhibition catalogue, by Klaus Honnef, Münster, West Germany, 1975: article—"Gianfranco Zappettini" by Klaus Honnef in *Kunstforum* (Mainz, West Germany), October/November 1974.

The course followed by Gianfranco Zappettini in more than ten years of work might be called the "recovery of meaning," and to an extent it reflects a wider change of cultural direction than simply one of those that we are passing through at present. Zappettini started from a strictly, rigorously analytical painting, in which all the materials and other "ingredients" of pictorial work were subjected to a test both operational and conceptual. "Think in terms of painting," was his motto. The reduction of the metaphorical level to an absolute zero was obtained through an intent metonymic process, which always restrained the elements used to the same level of (non-) meaning. The "outside," the "world," anything "other than the picture" was never to be incorporated in the work; the process was vital, political, social. And this kind of process came into being by his painting exactly according to the autonomous instruments of painting, with no concession to Meaning but reinforcing the materiality of the source of Meaning.

Zappettini then moved on to a manner of painting which, while still retaining some elements typical of analysis (the breaking down of the support, for instance), nevertheless involved a more open attitude towards the world, its colours, its emotions and feelings, its power of evoking memories. But it is only in the past few years that Zappettini has completed the full, complete recovery, almost to the point of iconism, figuration, "pictorial reconciliation" (and not only pictorial) with the world.

This change has also had a great personal effect on him: he has gone to live in the country, on the Ligurian coast, where he has developed personal taste for "minor" painting, with little innovatory quotient but a high level of technique and craftsmanship. One might say that his investigation of "the painter's trade" is still going on, but with other, quite different means. The brush stroke is free, harking back to the Fauves and Impressionists (it might even be better to say, to Barbizon); the subjects are ordinary, everyday, slightly ironic, deliberately "common." In this way Zappettini displays the historicity of painting, reviving methods and processes typical to its still "heroic" past.

Most recently his work has been enriched by another aspect and other themes, always drawn from the outpouring of meaning, of metaphor, of the desire to narrate, to tell of himself. His painting has become more spectacular than ever; it has become theatrical, depicting scenes from films (with well-known actors quite recognizable) or historic scenes with famous people in them; this is the world of the Public, of kitsch, of the Myth of the Masses. With a special effect of alienation he puts himself into the scene, in poses sometimes deliberately ironic (no problem in identifying these), as if he were required to "introduce" and "present" what is going on around him, as if in one of his personal circuses. The return of the Subject (since that is basically what we are looking at) is thus completed, after an analytical period composed of total, anonymity, the disappearance of the "I" in the work processes—but it is a Subject which, despite all its bodily and concrete appearance, cannot but remain confined in the world of images, of icons, of phantasms.

—Massimo Carboni

ZORIO, Gilberto.

Italian. Born in Andorno Micca, Italy, 21 September 1944. Studied painting at the Accademia di Belle Arti, Turin, 1963–70. Lives and works in Turin. Lecturer, Liceo Artistica, Turin, since 1971. Agent: Galleria Christian Stein, Piazza San Carlo 206, 10121 Turin. Address: Via Gorizia 149, 10137 Turin, Italy.

Individual Exhibitions:

1967 Galleria Sperone, Turin
1968 Centro Calautti, Salerna, Italy
1969 Galerie Ileana Sonnabend, Paris
Galleria Sperone, Turin
1970 Galleria Toselli, Milan
1971 Galleria Flori, Florence
Galleria Sperone, Turin
Modern Art Agency, Naples
Palazzo Taverna, Rome
1973 Galleria Sperone, Turin
Galerie MTL, Brussels
1974 Galleria Toselli, Milan
Galleria Sperone, Turin
1975 Galleria dell'Ariete, Milan
1976 Kunstmuseum, Lucerne
Galleria Schema, Florence
Studio de Ambrogi Cavellini, Milan
1977 Galleria del Tritone, Biella, Italy
Studio G 7, Bologna, Italy
Studio Cesare Manzo, Pescara, Italy
1978 Galleria Cavellini, Brescia, Italy
Galerie Albert Baronian, Brussels
Galerie Eric Fabre, Paris
Galerie t'Venster, Rotterdam
Galleria del Tritone, Biella, Italy
Studio Carlo Grossetti, Milan
Galleria Cavellini, Milan
Salone Annunciata, Milan
1979 Galleria Christian Stein, Turin
Jean and Karen Bernier, Athens
Stedelijk Museum, Amsterdam
Galleria Emilio Mazzoli, Modena, Italy

Gilberto Zorio: *Star* (*to purify words*), 1980

1980 Galleria de Crescenzo, Rome
Galerie Eric Fabre, Paris
Studio G 7, Bologna, Italy
Galerie Albert Baronian, Brussels
Galerie Walter Storms, Munich (with Marco Gastini and Giuseppe Spagnulo)
1981 Galleria Salvatore Ala, Milan
Galerie Meyer-Hahn, Dusseldorf
Galerie Rudiger Schöttle, Munich
Sonnabend Gallery, New York
Galleria de Crescenzo, Rome
Galerie Appel und Fertsch, Frankfurt
1982 Galleria Cavellini, Brescia, Italy
1092 Galleria Christian Stein, Turin
Pinacoteca Comunale, Ravenna, Italy
1983 Galerie Mueller-Roth, Stuttgart
Forum Kunst, Rottweil, West Germany
Galerie Walter Storms, Munich
Center of Contemporary Art, Syracuse, Italy
1984 Galerie au Fond de la Cour a Droite, Chagny, France
Galerie Albert Baronian, Brussels
Galleria Plurima, Udine, Italy
1985 Galleria Civica d'Arte, Modena, Italy
Kunstverein, Stuttgart
1986 Galleria Christian Stein, Turin
Centre d'Art Contemporain, Geneva
Jean Bernier Gallery, Athens
Centre Georges Pompidou, Paris
1987 Galleria Christian Stein, Turin

Selected Group Exhibitions:

1969 *When Attitudes Become Form,* Kunstahalle, Berne (travelled to the Museum Haus Lange, Krefeld, West Germany, and the Institute of Contemporary Arts, London)
1970 *Biennial,* Metropolitan Museum of Art, Tokyo (toured Japan)
1971 *Biennale de Paris,* Parc Floral, Paris
1972 *Documenta,* Kassel, West Germany
1974 *Projekt 74,* Kunsthalle, Cologne
1978 *Biennale,* Venice
1981 *Identité Italienne: L'Art en Italie depuis 1959,* Centre Georges Pompidou, Paris
1982 *Italian Art Now: An American Perspective,* Guggenheim Museum, New York
1984 *International Survey of Recent Painting and Sculpture,* Museum of Modern Art, New York
1986 *Hommage a Beuys,* Stadtische Museum im Lenbachhaus, Munich

Collections:

Galleria Nazionale d'Arte Moderna, Rome: Rijksmuseum Kröler-Müller, Otterlo, Netherlands: Stedelijk Museum, Amsterdam: Stedelijk van Abbemuseum, Eindhoven, Netherlands; Museum van Hedendaagse Kunst, Ghent; Kunstmuseum, Lucerne; Staatsgalerie, Stuttgart; Guggenheim Museum, New York.

Publications:

By ZORIO: article—"Gilberto Zorio" in *Data* (Milan), Summer 1978.

On ZORIO: books—*Gilberto Zorio,* exhibition catalogue, by Tommaso Trini, Turin 1967; *Arte Povera* by Germano Celant, Milan 1969; *Europe/America: The Different Avant Gardes* by Achille Bonito Oliva, Milan 1976; *Gilberto Zorio,* exhibition catalogue, by Jean-Christophe Ammann, Ugo Castagnotto and Werner Lippert, Lucerne 1976; *Avantguardia di Massa* by Maurizio Calvesi; Milan 1978; *Schema Informazione: Politic-Art.* Florence 1978: *Gilberto Zorio,* exhibition catalogue, by Jean-Christophe Ammann, Amsterdam 1979; *Gilberto Zorio,* exhibition catalogue with essay by Werner Lippert, Frankfurt 1981; articles—"Primary Energy and the Micro-Emotive Artists" by Piero Gilardi in *Arts Magazine* (New York). September/October 1968: "Gilberto Zorio: Corpo di Energia: by Jole de Sanna in *Date* (Milan), April 1972; "La Stella di Zorio" by Mirella Bandini in *Data* (Milan), December 1976: "Zorio's Star" by Mirella Bandini *Data* (Milan), December/January 1976/77; "Gilberto Zorio" by G. S. Brizio in *D'Ars* (Milan), July 1979; "Gilberto Zorio" by Flamino Gualdoni in *G7 Studio* (Bologna), June 1981.

Energy, tension, purification: these, essentially, are the concerns which govern Gilberto Zorio's aesthetic. His works are experiments in which he investigates the principles of change in time and space, in the elements of the atmosphere and physical phenomena,

and in chemical reactions. In "Pieces of Lead" (1968), for example, two lead containers filled with chlorine and chloridic acid have produced crystalline salts on the copper bands which join the containers. In "Curtain" (1967), Zorio has placed a cloth saturated with salt water over a structure of Dalmine tubes, so that a border of salt appears as the liquid evaporates.

These works are designed to show physical and chemical changes, but also to direct our attention to the element of time in which such changes take place. In still other works the process of change itself becomes the subject matter. This is the case, for example, with "Rose/Blue/Rose" (1967), in which the color of cobalt chlorite changes according to the degree of moisture in the air produced by the presence of viewers. A little later he produced objects which may be used to print words such as "Hate" and "Radical Fluidity" on the human body. The intention here is to use words to evoke images. "Hate" was printed on the artist's forehead on one occasion; on another, it was scratched on a wall with a hatchet; and on still another occasion the word itself was modelled in terracotta.

In his search for archetypal images which can be transformed into new vistas and produce new energies, Zorio sometimes chooses a figure such as a star and constructs it out of elements which are in themselves significant—a javelin, for example, or a laser or an incandescent nickel. Like the acids, metals, leather and even the skin which he had used before, these now become part of the repertory out of which Zorio makes his poetic statements.

In all of his work, then, it is the dynamic manipulation of energy and change which plays a dominant role. The tensions and energies which are released lead to pure archetypal symbols—as is the case, for example, with "Purifying Words." Purification itself becomes the final aesthetic goal.

—Roberto G. Lambarelli

NOTES ON ADVISERS AND CONTRIBUTORS

ABADIE, Daniel. Essayist. Curator at the Centre Georges Pompidou, Paris, since 1975; Editor of *Art/ Cahiers*, Paris, since 1980. Curator, Centre National d'Art Contemporain, Paris, 1969–74; Professor, Ecole des Beaux-Arts, St.-Etienne, France, 1979–80. Author of *Bryen Abhomme; Hyperréalisme; Hélion; Klee;* and *Simonds.* **Essays:** Eddy; Moser; Stämpfli.

ALBRECHT, Dietrich (Albrecht D.). Essayist. Freelance artist and writer; Founder-Editor, Reflektion Press, Stuttgart. **Essay:** Muehl.

ALLOWAY, Lawrence. Essayist. Professor at the State University of New York at Stony Brook, since 1968. Deputy Director, Institute of Contemporary Arts, London, 1957–60; Curator, Guggenheim Museum, New York, 1962–66; Chairman, Division of Fine Arts, School of Visual Arts, New York, 1967–68. Art Editor, *The Nation*, 1968–81; Contributing Editor, *Artforum*, 1972–76. Author of *Nine Abstract Artists*, 1954; *Ettore Colla*, 1960; *The Metalization of a Dream*, 1963; *The Venice Biennale 1895-1968*, 1969; *Violent America: The Movies 1946–64*, 1970; *American Pop Art*, 1974; *Topics in American Art since 1945*, 1975. **Essay:** Sonfist.

AMMANN, Jean-Christophe. Adviser and essayist. Director of the Museum für Moderne Kunst, Frankfurt, from 1989. Director, Kunstmuseum, Lucerne, 1969–77, and Kunsthalle, Basle, 1978–88. Author of *Von Hodler zur Antiform*, with Harald Szeemann, 1968; *Louis Moilliet: Das Gesamtwerk*, 1972. **Essays:** Buthe; Erro.

ANDRAS, Ban. Essayist. Editor of *Elet es Irodalom* weekly art magazine, and art critic of *Magyar Nemzet* newspaper, Budapest. Author of *A fenykep kulturaja*, 1983; *Video*, with Beke Laszlo, 1983; *Fotoelmeleti szoveggyujtemeny*, with Beke Laszlo, 1984. **Essay:** Lupas.

BARKER, Carrie. Essayist. Freelance writer and journalist, London. **Essays:** Antonakos; Bernd and Hilla Becher; James Bishop; Bourgeois; Daphnis; Douglas Davis; De Rivera; Diehl; Robert Graham; Richard Hunt; Kushner; Lobdell; Merkin; Posen; Savelli; Sonnier; Stevenson.

BARRETT, D. C. Essayist. Reader in Philosophy at the University of Warwick, Coventry. Author of *Art*, 1970; *An Introduction to Optical Art*, 1971; *Michael Farrell: A Monograph*, 1979; *Paintings, Objects, Installations 1963–80: Peter Sedgley*, 1980; and editor of *Collected Papers on Aesthetics*, 1965, and *Ludwig Wittgenstein*, 1966. **Essays:** Baer; Baskin; Buren; Coleman; Colombo; Le Brocquy; Lijn; Riley; Steele.

BAZAROV, Konstantin. Essayist. Freelance writer and researcher, London; also, professional geologist-zoologist. Author of *Landscape Painting*, 1981. **Essays:** Clark; Indiana; Johns; Latham; Le Parc; Mack; Matta; Metzger; Neizvestny; Olitski; Picasso; Piene; Rauschenberg; Rivers; David Smith; Takis; Vostell.

BELL, Jane. Essayist. Contributing Editor. *New York Arts Journal*, since 1974; Editorial Associate, *Artnews*, since 1978; Associate Director, International Network for the Arts, since 1979; and Senior Editor, *The Art Economist*, since 1981—all New York. Associate Editor, *Art Express*, 1980–81. **Essays:** Agnetti; Askevold; Beckley; Le Gac; Ossorio; Wade.

BENINCASA, Carmine. Essayist. Art Critic for *Corriere della Serra* since 1977; also, teacher of art history in the Faculty of Architecture at the University of Rome, and Adviser to the Italian Ministry of Culture and Environment. Author of *Sul Manierismo, Come Dentro ad Uno Specchio*, 1978; *Architettura come Dis-Identita: Le Teoria delle Catastrofi in Architettura*, 1979; *Paul Klee*, 1979; *Paul Klee*, 1981; *Il Labirinto dei Sabba, L'Architettura di Riema Pietila*, 1980; *Oskar Kokoschka*, 1981; *Roland Barthes*, 1981; *André Masson*, 1981; *Antoni Tapies*, 1982; *Portale, Alle Soglie del Sapere*, 1980; *Babilonia in Fiamme*, 1978; *L'Altra-Scena*, 1979. **Essay:** Parmiggiani.

BERGER, Maurice. Essayist. Visiting Assistant Professor, and Special Projects Curator of the Karl and Bertha Leubsdorf Art Gallery, Hunter College, City University of New York. Contributor to *Artforum, Arts Magazine, New Observations*, and *Artistes.* **Essays:** Andre; Bartlett; Gottlieb; Mason; Robert Morris; Serra; Shapiro.

BEX, Florent. Essayist. Director, International Cultureel Centrum, Antwerp (has organized more than 200 exhibitions of contemporary art). Administrator of La Jeune Peinture Belge; Vice-President, Belgian Association of Art Critics; Member, International Committee for Museums and Collections of Modern Art (CIMAM). **Essay:** Romberg.

BOHN, Willard. Essayist. Assistant Professor of French, Illinois State University at Normal, since 1981. Assistant Professor of French and Comparative Literature, Brandeis University, Waltham, Massachusetts, 1972–74; Research Associate in Comparative Literature, University of California, Berkeley, 1974–79; Lecturer in French, University of California at Santa Cruz, 1979–81. Frequent contributor to *The Art Bulletin, Arts Magazine*, and the *Journal of Aesthetics and Art Criticism.* Author of *Apollinaire et l'homme sans visage: creation et evolution d'un motif moderne*, 1983, editor of *A quelle heure un train partira-t-il pour Paris?* by Apollinaire, 1982. **Essays:** Delvaux; Man Ray.

BOJKO, Szymon. Adviser and essayist. Freelance art critic and art historian, Warsaw, since 1975. Editor of *Projekt* (visual arts and design review), 1969–74; Editor-in-chief, *Polish Art Review*, 1972; Consultant to the Gmurzynska Gallery, Cologne, 1973–80; Visiting Lecturer, School of Art and Design, Lodz, 1976–79. Author of *Polish Poster Art: Its Origins and Development to 1939*, 1971; *The Polish Poster Today*, 1972; *New Graphic Design in Revolutionary Russia*, 1972; *Rot Schlägt Weiss*, 1975. **Essays:** Anuskiewicz; Cieslewicz; Lenica; Paschke; Stankiewicz; Tomaszewski.

BONITO OLIVA, Achille. Essayist. Freelance art critic, Rome. Professor, School of Architecture, Rome, since 1971; Editorial Staff Member, *Avanti*, Rome, since 1978. Author of *Il territorio magico*, 1971; *L'ideologia del traditore*, 1976; *Vita di Marcel Duchamp*, 1976; *Le avanguardie diverse*, 1976; *Passo dello strabismo*, 1978; *La transavanguardia italiana*, 1980; *La transavanguardia internazionale*, 1982. **Essay:** Jaccard.

BORDEAUX, Jean-Luc. Essayist. Professor of Art History, California State University at Northridge, since 1972 (Director of the Fine Arts Gallery, 1972–80). Visiting Curator, Department of Paintings, Musée du Louvre, Paris, 1979. Author of *Francois Le Moyne and His Generation*, 1983. **Essays:** Cooper; Lippold; McCoy.

BOURDON, David. Essayist. Art Critic for *The Village Voice*, New York. **Essay:** Christo.

BROWN, David. Essayist. Assistant Keeper of Modern Collections at the Tate Gallery, London (has written numerous catalogues for exhibitions at the Tate); also a doctor of veterinary medicine and surgery. **Essay:** Long.

BURROUGHS, William S. Essayist. Novelist and social critic. Author of *Junkie*, 1953; *The Naked Lunch*, 1959; *The Soft Machine*, 1961; *The Ticket That Exploded, 1962; Dead Fingers Talk*, 1963; *Nova Express*, 1964; *The Wild Boys*, 1971; *Exterminator*, 1973; *Short Novels*, 1978; *Blade Runner: A Movie*, 1979; *Port of Saints*, 1980; *Cities of the Red Night*, 1981; etc. **Essay:** Gysin.

CARBONI, Massimo. Essayist. Art critic, Livorno, since 1978. Sometime Lecturer, Faculty of Architecture, University of Rome. **Essays:** Boeyen; Burri; Cane; Gastini; Jaudon; Ryman; Zappettini.

CATALANO, Gary. Essayist. Freelance writer and critic, Melbourne. author of *Remembering the Rural Life* (verse), 1978; *The Years of Hope: Australian Art and Criticism 1959–1968*, 1981; *Heaven of Rags* (verse), 1982; *The Bandaged Image: A Study of Australian Artists' Books* 1982. **Essay:** Booth.

CAVALIERE, Barbara. Essayist. Contributing Editor, *Arts Magazine*, New York, since 1976. Helena Rubenstein Fellow, Whitney Museum, New York, 1975; Fellow in Art Criticism, National Endowment for the Arts, 1980. Author of the exhibition catalogue, *William Baziotes: A Retrospective*, 1978. **Essays:** Africano; Beal; Blume; Burden; Cornell; D'Arcangelo; Diebenkorn; Evergood; Ferrara; Foulkes; Gertsch; Glarner; Goings; Greene; Haacke; Hanson; Bryan Hunt; Lester Johnson; Kaprow; Kelly; Krasner; Le Va; Les Levine; Marden; Agnes Martin; McCracken; Morley; Nesbitt; Nonas; Pollock; Pousette-Dart; Rothko; Sandback; Simonds; Thek; Tillim; Truitt; Tuttle; Van Buren; Von Schlegell; Welch; Yoshimura.

COHEN, Ronny. Essayist. Editorial Associate, *Artnews*, New York. Reviewer for *Artforum*, New York. Author of *Thomas McKnight's World*, 1987; *Charles Ginnever*, 1987. **Essays:** Benglis; Bladen; Bolotowsky; Campus; Nancy Graves; Hamilton; Hicks; Ray Johnson; Kirili; Elizabeth Murray; Sugarman; Willenbecher.

COMPTON, Michael. Essayist. Director of Museum Services at the Tate Gallery, London. Author of numerous books and exhibition catalogues on contemporary art, including *Optical and Kinetic Art*, 1967; *Auguste Rodin: The Kiss*, 1967; *Pop Art*, 1970; *Art as a Thought Process*, 1974; *Art since 1945*, 1976; *Some Notes on the Work of Richard Long*, 1978; *Mark Boyle's Journey to the Surface of the Earth*, 1978; *Looking at Pictures in the Tate Gallery*, 1979; *Towards a New Art*, with others, 1980; *Howard Hodgkin's Indian Leaves*, 1982. **Essays:** Charlton; Hoyland; Milow.

COOKE, Lynne. Essayist. Lecturer in the History of Art, University College, University of London, since 1978. **Essays:** Armitage; Davies; Flanagan; Head; King; William Tucker.

CORTRIGHT, Barbara. Essayist. Art Critic for the *Scottsdale Progress*, Arizona. Contributing Editor, *Artspace*. **Essays:** Clarke; Cuevas; De Andrea.

CRICHTON, Fenella. Essayist. Art critic, London. **Essay:** Hill.

DAY, Melvin N. Adviser and essayist. Freelance writer and art historian, Wellington, New Zealand. Lecturer in Art History, University of London Extension, 1964–68; Director, National Art Gallery of New Zealand, 1968–78; Government Art Historian, New Zealand Department of Internal Affairs, 1978–87. Author of *Nicholas Chevalier, Artist*, 1980. **Essay:** Bullmore.

DORFLES, Gillo. Essayist. University Professor in Aesthetics, since 1965 (has taught at the universities of Milan, Cagliari, and Florence; also served as Director of the Institute of Fine Arts, University of Cagliari, 1970–75). Author of *Discorso tecnico delle arti*, 1951; *Barocco nell'architettura moderna*, 1952; *Bosch*, 1953; *L'architettura moderna*, 1954; *Dürer*, 1958; *Constantes tecnicas de las artes*, 1958; *Il divenire delle arti*, 1959; *Ultime tendenze dell'arte d'oggi*, 1961; *Simbolo comunicazione consumo*, 1962; *Il disegno industriale e la sua estetica*, 1963; *Nuovi riti, nuovi miti*, 1965; *L'estetica del mito*, 1967; *Il Kitsch*, 1968; *Artificio e natura*, 1968; *Le Oscillazioni del gusto*, 1970; *Introduzione al disegno industriale*, 1972; *Sentido e Insenzatez en el Arte de Hoy*, 1973; *Dal significato alle scelte*, 1973; *Czlowiek zwielokrontniony*, 1973; *Mythes et rites d'aujourd'hui*, 1975; *Il devenire della critica*, 1976, *La Body Art*, 1978; *Mode e Modi*, 1979; *L'intervallo perduto*, 1980. **Essays:** Baj; Capogrossi; Chiari; Miró; Spagnulo.

ELLIS, Mary. Essayist. Freelance critic and lecturer at the Tate Gallery, London. **Essays:** Atkinson; Deacon; Dimitrijevic; Fulton; Guston; Law; Nash; Rothenberg.

EMANUEL, Muriel. Essayist. Freelance researcher, editor and writer, London. Editor of *Israel: A Survey and Bibliography*, 1971; *Contemporary Architects*, 1980. **Essays:** Neustein; Schad.

FELIX, Zdenek. Essayist. Curator at the Museum Folkwang, Essen. **Essays:** Nordman; Palermo; Raetz.

FINDLAY, Michael Alastair. Essayist. Art writer and artist's agent, New York. **Essay:** Woodham.

FORGE, Andrew. Essayist. Dean of the School of Art, Yale University, New Haven, Connecticut. Senior Lecturer, Slade School, London, 1950–64; Head of the Department of Fine Art, Goldsmith's College, London, 1964–70. Trustee, Tate Gallery, 1964–71, 1972–74, and National Gallery, London, 1966–72. President, London Group, 1964–71. Author of *Klee*, 1953; *Vermeer*, 1954; *Soutine*, 1965; *Rauschenberg*, 1972; *Monet at Giverny*, with C. Joyes, 1975; and editor of *The Townsend Journals*, 1976. **Essay:** Stephenson.

FOURNET, Claude. Essayist. Art critic, Paris. **Essay:** Aubertin.

FRASER, Alison. Essayist. Director, Victorian College of the Arts Gallery, Melbourne, since 1979. Education Officer, Art Gallery of New South Wales, Sydney, 1974–76; Art Education Consultant, Visual Arts Board, Australia Council, Sydney, 1978–79. Author of *History of Australian Art* (slide kit with text), 1981; and co-ordinator of *Tertiary Visual Arts Education in Australia*, 1980. **Essay:** John Davis.

FRIEDMAN, B. H. Essayist. Trustee, Whitney Museum of American Art, New York, since 1961, and of the Fine Arts Work Center, Provincetown, Massachusetts, since 1968; also, Member, Advisory Council of the College of Arts and Sciences and of the Herbert F. Johnson Museum, Cornell University, Ithaca, New York; Member, Fiction Collective, since 1973. Author of the biographies *Jackson Pollock: Energy Made Visible*, 1972, and *Gertrude Vanderbilt Whitney*, 1978; has edited written or contributed to various art monographs, including *School of New York*, 1959; *Robert Goodnough*, with Barbara Guest, 1962; *Lee Krasner*, 1965; *Alfonso Ossorio*, 1973; *Salvatore Scarpitta*, 1977; and *Myron Stout*, 1979; also a novelist and short story writer. **Essays:** Copley; Scarpitta.

FRIEDMAN, Kenneth S. Essayist. Artist and writer, New York. Consultant Editor, University of Michigan Research Press, since 1978; Director, Institute for Advance Studies in Contemporary Art and Architecture, New York, since 1979. **Essay:** Kocman.

FRITSCH, Gerolf. Essayist. Professor of German Language and Literature, Chur, Switzerland. Author of *Die deutsche Ballade zwischen Herders naturaler Theorie und später Industriegesellschaft*, 1976; *Das deutsche Naturgedicht: Der fiktionale Text im Kommunikationsprozess*, 1978. **Essays:** Eggenschwiler; Giacometti.

GALE, Peggy. Essayist. Independent curator and critic, specializing in contemporary media and installation works, Toronto. Assistant Film and Video Officer, Canada Council, Ottawa, 1974; Video-Film Director, Art Metropole, Toronto, 1975–79; Executive Director, A Space, Toronto, 1979–81. Editor of *Video by Artists*, 1976; *Performance by Artists*, 1979; and *Museums by Artists*. 1983. **Essay:** General Idea.

GAZZERO, Edda. Essayist. Freelance art critic. Genoa. **Essay:** Costa.

GLOWEN, Ron. Essayist. Freelance art critic, Washington, since 1975. Contributing Editor, *Artweek*, Oakland, California, since 1976; Visual Arts Critic, *The Herald*, Everett, Washington, since 1978. **Essays:** Boyle; Bruce; Morris Graves; Kienholz; Raffael; Tobey.

GLUSBERG, Jorge. Adviser and essayist. Director, Centro de Arte y Communicacion, Buenos Aires. Author of *Towards a Topological Architecture*, with Clorindo Testa, 1977; *The Rhetoric of Latin American Art*, 1978; *Socio-Semiotic of Architecture*, 1978; *Myths and Magic of Fire, Gold and art*, 1978; *From Incan Habitat to the Lima of the Future*, 1979; *The Theory and Criticism of Architecture*, 1979. **Essays:** Benedit; Grippo; Maler; Uriburu.

GOLEAS, Janet. Essayist. Artist-in-Residence at the Sierra Nevada Museum of Art, and Fine Arts Instructor, University of Nevada, Reno, since 1980. **Essays:** Allen; Ronald Davis; Flavin; Grooms; Holland; Jensen.

GRANATH, Olle. Essayist. Freelance writer and art critic, Stockholm. Has written several books on contemporary Swedish art. **Essay:** Dietmann.

HARITHAS, James. Essayist. Art critic. Formerly: Curator, DeCordova Museum, Lincoln, Massachusetts. Director, Corcoran Gallery, Washington, D.C. **Essay:** Jimenez.

HIGGINS, Dick. Essayist and entrant. See his own entry. **Essay:** Knowles.

HOLLOWAY, John H. Essayist. British Co-Editor of *Leonardo* (international art journal), since 1971; also, Senior Lecturer in Chemistry, University of Leicester, since 1978. **Essay:** Albers.

HONNEF, Klaus. Adviser and essayist. Curator for Changing Exhibitions and the Photographic Collection, Rheinisches Landesmuseum, Bonn; also, Professor of the Theory of Photography at the University of Kassel. Director, Westfälischer Kunstverein, Münster, West Germany, 1970–74. Author of *20 Deutsche*, 1971; *Concept Art*, 1971; Gerhard Richter, 1976; *Wilhelm Schürman*, 1979 and editor of *Verkehrskultur*, 1974, and *Lichtbildnisse*, 1982. **Essays:** Darboven; Gaul; Krieg; Ruthenbeck.

JOHNSTON, Jill. Essayist. Author and art critic. Formerly, Columnist for *The Village Voice*, New York; contributor to various art journals. Author of *Marmalade Me; Lesbian Nation;* etc. **Essay:** Cage.

KARLSTROM, Paul J. Essayist. West Coast Director, Archives of American Art/Smithsonian Institution (based at the M. H. de Young Memorial Museum, San Francisco), since 1973. Assistant Curator, Grunwald Center for the Graphic Arts, University of California at Los Angeles, 1967–70; Instructor of Art History, California State University at Northridge, 1972–73; Guest Curator, Hirshhorn Museum and Sculpture Garden, Washington, D.C., 1977. Author of the monograph *Louis M. Eilshemius*, 1978, and of the catalogues, *Americans Abroad: Painters of the Victorian Era*, 1975; *The United States and the Impressionist Era*, 1979; and *Venice Panorama: Views of Venice in the Graphic Artsfrom the Late 15th Through the 18th Centuries*, 1979. **Essays:** Bechtle; Kauffman; McLaughlin; Oliveira; Valentine.

KELLER, Victoria. Essayist. Exhibitions Administrator, 369 Gallery, Edinburgh. **Essays:** Artschwager; Broodthaers; Francis; McLean; Nutt; Penck; Polke; Tinguely; Tworkov; Winner.

KELLY, Jane. Essayist. Art critic, London. **Essay:** Willats.

KEPINSKA, Alicja. Essayist. Professor, Academy of Visual Arts, Poznan, Poland. Author of *Jan Piotr Norblin: A Monograph*, 1978; *The New Polish Art 1945–1978*, 1981; *Element and Myth* (on action painting), 1983; *Ecology of Art*, 1988. **Essays:** Berdyszak; Brzozowski; Dibbets; Fischl; Fisher; Kruger; Merz; Opalka; Stazewski.

KIND, Joshua. Essayist. Professor of Art History, Northern Illinois University, DeKalb, since 1969. Instructor in Art History, Northwestern University, Evanston, Illinois, 1959–62; Instructor in the Humanities, University of Chicago, 1962–65; Visiting Professorial Lecturer, School of the Art Institute of Chicago, 1964–76; Assistant Professor of Humanities, Illinois Institute of Technology, Chicago, 1965–69. Author of *Rouault*, 1969; *Naive Painting in Illinois 1830–1976*, 1976; *Geometry as Abstract Art: The Lipschultz Collection*, 1980; and *The Geometric Impulse: The Florsheim Collection*, 1981. **Essays:** Albright; Baldessari; Bengston; Breer; Brooks; Close; Cottingham; Ferrer; Gilliam; Gorchov; Gordy; Grossman; Grosvenor; Irwin; Jenney; Judd; Lane; Robert and Sylvia Mangold; McGarrell; Catherine Murphy; Poons; Samaras; Sarkisian; Saul; Schnabel; Shields; Wegman; Winsor; Youngerman.

KINGSLEY, April. Essayist. Instructor, School of Visual Arts, New York, since 1973; Director, The Sculpture Center, New York, since 1980. Curatorial Assistant, Museum of Modern Art, New York, 1969–71; Associate Curator, Pasadena Art Museum, California, 1971–72. Secretary, American Section, International Art Critics Association, since 1978; Member, Board of Advisers, New York Feminist Art Institute, since 1978, and *Women's Art Journal*, since 1979. Author of numerous books/catalogues: *Frank Stella*, 1970; *Romare Bearden*, 1971; *Rafael Ferrer*, 1972; *Budd Hopkins*, 1973; *The Magic Circle*, 1977; *Cape Cod as an Art Colony*, 1977; *Victor Candell*, 1978; *Rudolf Baranik*, 1978; *David Shapiro/Christopher Wilmarth*, 1978; *Michael Loew*, 1979; *Richard Hunt*, 1979; *Robert Motherwell*, 1980; *Nassos Daphnis*, 1980; *Melvin Edwards*, 1981; and *Alternative Realities*, 1981. **Essay:** Motherwell.

KLEIN, Mason. Essayist. Freelance writer, New York. Formerly, lecturer at Hunter College, and Brooklyn College, New York. Contributor to *Arts Magazine* and *New Observations*. **Essays:** Acconci; Anderson; Snow.

KONTOVA, Helena. Essayist. Co-Editor of *Flash Art*, Milan, since 1977. Assistant Curator, National Gallery, Prague, 1976–77. Editor of *The International Trans-Avantgarde*, with Achille Bonito Oliva, 1982; and *Jiri Kolar*, 1982. **Essays:** Abramovic; Collins; Knizák; Pane.

KOSTELANETZ, Richard. Essayist. Poet, critic, cultural historian; Co-Founder, Assembling Press, and proprietor, The Future Press, Co-Editor, *Precisely*, and Contributing Editor, *The Humanist* and *Performing Arts Journal*. Author of several books of verse, two novels, several collections of short stories, and critical works including *The Theatre of Mixed-Means*, 1968; *The End of Intelligent Writing*, 1974; and *Twenties in the Sixties*, 1978; *John Cage Conversing*, 1987; also editor of numerous collections and anthologies. **Essays:** Higgins; Whitman.

KULTERMANN, Udo. Essayist. Ruth and Norman Moore Professor of Architecture, Washington University, St. Louis. Director, City Art Museum, Leverkusen, West Germany, 1959–64; Architecture Commission Member, Venice Biennale, 1979–82; Member of the National Humanities Faculty, Georgia, 1986–88. Author of numerous critical works, including: *Architecture of Today*, 1958; *Dynamische Architektur*, 1969; *New Japanese Architecture*, 1960, 1967; *New Architecture in Africa*, 1963; *New Architecture in the World*, 1965–1976; *History of Art History*, 1966, 1981; *The New Sculpture*, 1969, 1977; *The New Painting*, 1969, 1977; *Art and Life: The Function of Intermedia*, 1970; *New Realism*, 1972; *Architecture in the Seventies*, 1980; *Contemporary Architecture in Eastern Europe*, 1985. **Essays:** Butterfield; Deem; Jonas; Jorn; Kanovitz; Messager; Roehr; Rosenbach; Schneemann.

LAMBARELLI, Roberto G. Essayist. Art critic: Contributor to *Flash Art*, Milan, since 1977, and *Segno*, since 1978; Editor of *AMP* since 1980. Author of *Maurizio Corona*, 1982; *Pier Luigi Meneghello*, 1982; and *Razionale Decorativo*, exhibition catalogue, 1981. **Essays:** Afro; Anselmo; Battaglia; Boetti; Carrino; Castellani; Ceroli; Cucchi; de Dominicis; Greco; Griffa; Kounellis; Mauri; Nagasawa; Novelli; Paolini; Pistoletto; Trotta; Zorio.

LANCER, Sharon. Essayist. Freelance art writer and exhibition organizer, London. Curator of the Ben Uri Gallery, London. **Essay:** Gilbert and George.

LaROSE, Elise. Essayist. Freelance art writer for *Arts Magazine*, *New Art Examiner*, and *Art Express*. **Essays:** Kuehn; Schapiro; Spero.

LEARMONT, Lavinia. Essayist. Freelance writer and artist, London. **Essays:** Dine; Finlay; Marisol; Roszak; Sedgley; Sutherland.

LIQUOIS, Dominique. Essayist. Freelance art writer and researcher, Paris. Formerly worked with the Galerie Chantal Crousel, Paris, the Galeria Yvan Martin, Mexico City, and the Centre Beaubourg, Paris. **Essays:** Berni; Cragg; Holzer; Kosice.

LIVINGSTONE, Marco. Essayist. Freelance writer and art historian, London. Formerly, Deputy Director of the Museum of Modern Art, Oxford. Author of the exhibition catalogues: *Sheer Magic by Allen Jones*, 1979; *David Hockney*, 1981; *Patrick Caulfield: Paintings 1963–1981*, 1981; *Peter Phillips Retrovision*, 1982. **Essay:** Barker.

LYNTON, Norbert. Essayist. Professor of the History of Art, University of Sussex, Brighton, since 1975. Senior Lecturer, then Head of the Department of Art History, Chelsea School of Art, London, 1961–70; London Correspondent, *Art International*, 1961–66; Art Critic, *The Guardian*, London, 1965–70; Director of Exhibitions, Arts Council of Great Britain, 1970–75. Author of *Kenneth Armitage*, 1962; *Paul Klee*, 1964; *The Modern World*, 1968; *The Story of Modern Art*, 1980. **Essay:** Moon.

MACKINTOSH, Alastair. (died, 1987). Essayist. Formerly, freelance writer and teacher, London; also, Visual Arts Officer, Scottish Arts Council, Edinburgh. Author of *Symbolism and Art Nouveau*, 1975. **Essays:** Bell; Beuys; Brisley; Di Suvero; Filliou; Laing; Medalla; Neagu; Price; Saura; Schöffer; Segal; Warhol.

MARECHAL-WORKMAN, Andrée. Essayist. Curator, Berkeley Art Center, and Instructor, University of California, Berkeley. Curator, Center for Visual Arts, Oakland, California, 1977–80; Creative Growth Gallery, Oakland, California, 1984–86. Author of the catalogues, *The Siegriests: A Family of Artists and Their Work*, 1980; *Robert DeNiro: Recent Paintings and Drawings*, 1981; *Chris Ranes: A Survey of Recent Paintings*, 1983. **Essays:** Connor; Ramos; Tapies; Thiebaud.

MARTIN, Henry. Essayist. Editorial Associate, *Art International*, Lugano, Switzerland, since 1968; Milan Correspondent for *Artnews*, New York, since 1980. Author of *Arman*, 1972; *Adami*, with Hubert Damish, 1974; *Renato Mambor's Evidenziatore*, 1975; *Fragments of a Possible Apocalypse*, with Gianfranco Baruchello, 1978; *An Introduction to George Brecht's "Book of the Tumbler on Fire,"* 1978; *Notes on the Work of Teodosio Magnoni*, 1980; *Gianfranco Baruchello*, 1982. **Essays:** Arman: Baruchello; Brecht; Fahlstrom; Gnoli; Hendricks; Nannucci; Télémaque.

MAURICE, Carine. Essayist. Freelance contributor to the *London Review of the Arts*, and Consultant to L. S. Graphics, London, since 1982. **Essays:** Caulfield; Davie; Green; Jones; Kitaj; Monro; Tom Phillips; Procktor; Steinberg.

McCANN, Cecile N. Editor/Publisher of *Artweek*, Oakland, California, since 1970. **Essays:** Abakanowicz; Arneson.

McINTYRE, Arthur. Adviser and essayist. Sydney Art Critic, *The Age*, Melbourne, since 1980. Lecturer in Design and Composition, University of New South Wales, since 1979; Lecturer in Australian Art History, Rollins College Australia Programme, since 1980. Art Critic, *The Australian*, 1977–78; contributor to *Art and Australia*, 1975–87. Author of *Australian Art of the 70s*, 1980; *Resurgence and Redefinition: Australian Contemporary Drawing*, 1988. **Essays:** Coleing; Drysdale; Nolan; Parr.

MENEGUZZO, Marco. Essayist. Teacher of Art History at the Istituto Statale d'Arte, Villa Reale, Monza, Italy, since 1978. Contributor to numerous magazines, including *Flash Art*, *Segno*, *D'Ars Agency*, etc. Author of *Il Moviemento Arte Concreta*, 1981; *Michelangelo*, 1981; *Leonardo: Disegni*, 1982; *Fausto Melotti: La Dimensione del Disegno*, with F. Gualdoni, 1981; *Schifano*, 1982. **Essays:** Nigro; Olivieri.

MESSER, Thomas. Essayist. Director of the Guggenheim Museum, New York, since 1961. Director, Institute of Contemporary Art, Boston, 1957–61. President, The MacDowell colony, 1977–78. Author of *Edward Munch*, 1973. **Essays:** Kolar; Soto.

METKEN, Günter. Essayist. Freelance writer on contemporary art and photography, Paris. Author of numerous exhibition catalogues. **Essay:** Lang.

MIKI, Tamon. Essayist. Art critic, Tokyo. **Essay:** Kudo.

MOORE, Alan. Essayist. Art critic, New York. **Essay:** Scanga.

MOORE, Barbara. Essayist. Administrative Director, Archives of Experimental Art, New York. Formerly, Editor-in-Chief of Something Else Press, New York. **Essay:** Miralda.

MORRIS, Lynda. Essayist. Curator, Norwich School of Art Gallery, Norfolk, England. Formerly, Curator at the Nigel Greenwood Gallery, London, and the Midland Group Gallery, Nottingham. **Essay:** Lamelas.

MURRAY, Joan. Adviser and essayist. Director of the Robert McLaughlin Gallery, Oshawa, Ontario, since 1974. Curator of Canadian Art, Art Gallery of Ontario, Toronto, 1969–74. Author of *Letters Home: William Blair Bruce 1859–1906,* 1982; *Kurelek's Vision of Canada,* 1983; *The Best of the Group of Seven,* 1984; *The Best of Tom Thomson,* 1986; *The Best Contemporary Canadian Art,* 1987. **Essays:** Carr-Harris; Curnoe; Meredith; Prent; Tousignant; Wieland.

MUSSA, Italo. Essayist. Art critic, Rome, since 1970; Director of the Centro di Cultura Ausoni, Rome. Contributor to *Flash Art, Segno* and *L'Avanti.* Author of *L'Ipperrealismo, il vero piu vero del vero,* 1974; *Victor Vasarely,* 1975; *Il Gruppo N e la situazione dei gruppi in Europa negli anni '60,* 1976; *Wilhelm von Gloeden: Photographs,* 1979; *Carlo Maria Mariani, Pictor Philosophus,* 1980; *L'Inattualita dell'arte,* 1982; *Arnaldo Pomodoro at the Belvedere Fort,* 1986; *La Peinture de l'Avenir,* 1987. **Essays:** Calzolari; Castelli; Nicola De Maria; Lupertz; Ontani; Pisani; Salle; Twombly; Uncini.

NARAHARA, Yusuke. Essayist. Freelance art critic, Tokyo. Author of *Man-Made Nature,* 1971; *Contemporary Sculpture,* 1977; and *Akira Baba's Work,* 1980. **Essays:** Matsuzawa; Suga.

NASGAARD, Roald. Essayist. Chief Curator, Art Gallery of Ontario, Toronto, since 1978 (Curator of Contemporary Art, 1975–78). Lecturer 1971–74, and Assistant Professor, 1974–75, Department of Fine Art, University of Guelph, Ontario. Contributing Editor, *Arts Magazine,* New York, 1974–75; Secretary-General, International Association of Art Critics (Canada), 1976–78. Author of the exhibition catalogues, *Ron Martin: World Paintings,* 1976; *Peter Kolisnyk,* 1977; *Structures for Behavior,* 1978; *Garry Neill Kennedy: Recent Work,* 1979; *Yves Gaucher: A 15 Year Perspective,* 1979; *The Mystic North: Symbolist Landscape Painting,* 1984; *Gerhard Richter: Retrospective,* 1988. **Essays:** Favro; Gaucher; Ron Martin; Molinari; Richter.

NEWMAN, Michael. Essayist. Freelance art critic and historian, London. **Essay:** Coleman.

NORTH, Percy. Essayist. Freelance art critic and writer, Atlanta, Georgia; Lecturer, Emory University, Atlanta, since 1987. Formerly, instructor at the University of Minnesota, George Mason University, and James Madison University. Author of the exhibition catalogues: *Hudson D. Walker,* 1977; *Max Weber: American Modern,* 1982; *Into the Melting Pot,* 1984; *Gene Davis: Child and Man,* 1985; *Visions of an Inner Life: Will Henry Stevens,* 1988. **Essays:** Bertoia; Gene Davis; Liberman.

OSBORNE, Harold. (died, 1987). Essayist. Editor, *British Journal of Aesthetics,* 1960–78; Vice-President, International Committee for Aesthetics, 1976–87; President, British Society of Aesthetics, 1982–87. Author of *Foundations of the Philosophy of Value,* 1933; *Christ and the Early Church,* 1934; *Indians of the Andes,* 1952; *Bolivia: A Land Divided,* 1954, 3rd ed. 1964; *Aesthetics and Criticism,* 1955; *Aesthetics and Art Theory,* 1968; *South American Mythology,* 1968; *The Art of Appreciation,* 1970; *The Oxford Companion to Art,* 1970; *The Oxford Companion to the Decorative Arts,* 1975; *Abstraction and Artifice in 20th Century Art,* 1979; *The Oxford Companion to 20th Century Art,* 1981. **Essays:** Appel; Bazaine; Chamberlain; Dubuffet; Esteve; Gerstner; Marca-Relli; Meadows; Morellet; Munari.

PAPARONI, Demetrio. Essayist. Director, Centro d'Arte Contemporanea, Siracusa, Italy, since 1981. Author of numerous exhibition catalogues, including *L'Annunciazione di Antonello,* 1979; *Aljofre barroco,* 1981; *L'Altra Anatomia,* 1981; *Thinking of Europe,* 1982; and *In virtu del possesso delle mani,* 1982. **Essays:** Baselitz; Fetting; Paladino; Schifano; Tatafiore; Van Elk.

PARMESANI, Loredana. Essayist. Contributor to *Flash Art* and to other Italian art magazines since 1979. Has organized various exhibitions, including *La frase e il discorso,* Cortina d'Ampezzo, 1981, and *Registrazione di Frequenze,* Bologna, 1982. Author of *Nuova Immagine,* 1980; and *Baj: I grandi quadri,* 1982. **Essays:** Cavaliere; Pascali; Tadini.

POMEROY, Ralph. Essayist. Associate Director, Forum Gallery, New York, since 1979; Contributing Editor, *Arts Magazine,* New York, since 1981. Member, Editorial Staff, *Artnews,* New York, 1963–68, and *Art and Artists,* London, 1966–73. Author of *Stills and Movies,* 1961; *The Canaries as They Are,* 1965; *In the Financial District,* 1968; *Stamos,* 1974; *The Ice Cream Connection,* 1975; *First Things First,* 1977. **Essays:** Balthus; Bearden; Calder; Estes; Hall; Held; John Koch; Mitchell; Morandi; Noguchi; Noland; O'Keeffe; Pearlstein; Reinhardt; Richard Smith; Tony Smith; Stamos; Turnbull; Westermann; Wiley.

POPPER, Frank. Adviser and essayist. Director of the Fine Arts Department since 1970, and Professor of Aesthetics and of the Science of Art since 1975, University of Paris VIII (Assistant Professor, 1969–70; Reader, 1970–75). Author of *Naissance de l'Art Cinétique,* 1967, 1970; *Origins and Development of Kinetic Art,* 1968; *L'Arte Cinetica,* 1970; *Le Déclin de l'Objet,* 1975; *Art-Action and Participation,* 1975; *Agam,* 1976, 3rd ed. 1982; *L'Artiste et la Créativité Aujourd'hui,* 1980. **Essays:** Agam; Boto; Cruz-Diez; Demarco; Kowalski.

RICKEY, George. Essayist and entrant. See his own entry. **Essay:** Baertling.

ROBERTS, John. Essayist. Freelance writer, London; regular contributor to various art magazines. **Essays:** Brus; Burgin; Craig-Martin; Hesse; Walker.

ROBINSON, John. Essayist. Editor, Archives of American Art, San Francisco office; Lecturer, California College of Arts and Crafts, Dominican College, and Holy Names College. Contributor to *Artforum, Artweek, San Francisco Review of Books,* and *Flash Art.* **Essays:** Borofsky; DeForest; Newton Harrison; Hockney; Kaltenbach; LeWitt; Robert Smithson; Venet; Wilson.

ROBINSON, Marlee. Essayist. Personal assistant to Eduardo Paolozzi, and Lecturer at the Tate Gallery, London, since 1977. **Essays:** Buckley; Chicago; Page.

SCHIPPER, Merle. Essayist. Freelance art critic and exhibition organizer, Los Angeles. Contributing Editor, *Artweek,* Oakland, since 1983, and columnist, *Artscene,* Los Angeles, since 1987. Los Angeles Correspondent, *Artnews,* New York, 1985–87. Author of *Americans in Paris: the 50s,* 1979; *Abstract Painting and Sculpture in America 1927–44,* with others, 1983; *Jean Helion: Abstraktion und Mythen des Altags,* with others, 1984; *Susan Rankaitis,* 1988. **Essays:** Moses; Ruppersberg.

SCHULZE-REIMPELL, Werner. Essayist. Freelance journalist, West Germany, since 1977. Chief Editor of the theatre monthly *Die Deutsche Bühne* 1972–77. Author of *Structure and Development of the Theatre in the Federal Republic of Germany,* 1973, 1977. **Essays:** Grutzke; Schult; Schultze; Weseler.

SCHWARZ, Dieter. Essayist. Assistant Curator, Kunstmuseum, Winterthur, Switzerland, since 1985. Author of *Auf der Bogen Bahn: Studien zum literarische Werk von Dieter Roth,* 1981; *Camille Graeser: Zeichnungen,* 1986. Editor of *John Armleder,* 1987; *Andre Thomkins: Gesummelte Anagramme,* 1987. **Essays:** Armleder; Gosewitz; Hains; Roth; Villegle.

SELZ, Peter. Adviser and essayist. Professor of the History of Art, University of California, Berkeley, since 1965 (Director of the University Art Museum, 1965–73). Head, Graduate Program, Institute of Design, Chicago, 1949–55; Chairman of the Art Department, Pomona College, Claremont, California, 1955–58;Curator, Department of Painting and Sculpture Exhibitions, Museum of Modern Art, New York, 1958–65. Author of *German Expressionist Painting,* 1957; *New Images of Man,* 1959; *Art Nouveau,* 1960; *The Work of Jean Dubuffet,* 1962; *Emil Nolde,* 1963; *Max Beckmann,* 1964; *Ferdinand Hodler,* 1972; *Sam Francis,* 1975, 1982; *Art in Our Times: A Visual History,* 1981; *Art in a Turbulent Era,* 1985; *Chillida,* 1986. **Essay:** Denes.

SHEPHERD, Michael. Essayist. Art Critic of the *Sunday Telegraph,* London, since 1971; Consultant, Art Review, London, since 1975; Art Critic, *What's On in London,* since 1978; Postgraduate Thesis Tutor, Royal Academy of Arts, London, since 1979; London Correspondent, *Artmagazine,* Toronto since 1980. Author of *Barbara Hepworth,* 1963. **Essays:** Abrahams; Andrews; Burra; Tindle; Vaughan.

SHINODA, Tazmi. Adviser and essayist. Freelance art critic and art historian, Kanagawa, Japan. Member, Association Internationale des Critiques d' Art, since 1986.Co-author of *The Dictionary of Contemporary Art,* 1984. **Essays:** Kawara; Kitatsuji; Kusama: Nakazato; Niizuma; Onosato; Saito; Yamada; Yamaguchi.

SINZ, Dagmar. Essayist. Parisian Correspondent for Cultural Events, *Neue Zürcher Zeitung,* Zurich, since 1980, and for Saarlandischer Rundfunk/Radio Saarbrucken, West Germany, since 1981; Art Critic, *Artis,* Konstanz, West Germany, since 1977. **Essays:** Dado; Penalba; Anne and Patrick Poirier.

SMITH, Katharine. Essayist. Freelance art critic, Denver. Formerly, Colorado Editor, *Artspace* magazine. Author of numerous exhibition catalogues for museums and art centers in the western United States. **Essays:** Pepper; Ross.

SPENCER, Charles. Essayist. Freelance writer, and lecturer at various British art schools for the British Council. Formerly: Editor, *Art and Artists*, London; Art Critic for the London *Daily Mail* and the European Edition of the *New York Times*; Editor, Editions Alecto, London; and Principal Lecturer, Croydon College, Surrey. Author of *Erté*, 1970, 1981; *A Decade of Printmaking*, 1972; *The Aesthetic Movement*, 1972; *Leon Bakst*, 1973; *Cecil Beaton: Stage and Film Designs*, 1975; *The World of Serge Diaghilev*, 1978. **Essays:** Botero; Boyd; Butler; Canogar; Cascella; Chadwick; Chillida; Cohen; Consagra; Cremonini; Domela; Dorazio; Efrat; Frost; Genoves; Grau Garriga; Hilton; Hodgkin; Hoflehner; Ipousteguy; Kenny; Kossoff; Leverett; Lundquist; Morlotti; Partridge; Pasmore; Perilli; Piché; Arnaldo/Gio Pomodoro; Radice; Rotella; Sandle; William Scott; Shahn; Tajiri; Tilson; Velickovic; Wagemaker; Wall.

SPIELMANN, Heinz. Adviser and essayist. Director of the Landesmuseum Schleswig-Holstein, West Germany, since 1986. Professor at the University of Munster, since 1984. Chief Curator, Museum für Kunst und Gewerbe, Hamburg, 1960–85. Editor of *Das Fruhe Plakat in Europa und den USA*, 3 vols., 1969–75; *Oskar Kokoschka*, 4 vols., 1972–76; *Spektrum der Kunst*, 1974, 1987; *Oskar Kokoschka, Briefe*, 4 vols., 1984–88; *Die Japanische Photographie*, 1985. **Essays:** Bill; Janssen; Kokoschka; Nagel; Schumacher; von Graevenitz; Wunderlich.

STANISLAWSKI, Ryszard. Essayist. Freelance art critic and historian of contemporary art, Warsaw. Author of *Constructivism in Poland 1923–36*, 1973; etc. **Essay:** Kantor.

STOFFLET, Mary. Essayist. Curator of Education, San Diego Museum of Art, California, since 1985. Assistant Curator of Exhibitions and Cultural Programs, San Francisco International Airport, 1982–84; Instructor in Art History, Oakland Museum, California, 1977–83; Associate Editor, *Images and Issues*, Los Angeles, 1979–82; Editor, Western Association of Art Museums *Newsletter*, 1974–77. Author of *Women Artists: Sculpture*, with Karen Petersen, 1980; *Dr. Seuss from Then to Now*, 1986. **Essays:** Antin; Isabel Bishop; Cadmus; Hare; Katz; Ellen Lanyon; Leslie; Marilyn Levine; Maciunas; Marioni; Shiomi; Vautier.

SYRING, Marie Luise. Essayist. Art Critic, Paris, since 1976. Parisian Correspondent for *Du*, Zurich, and Contributing Editor, *Kunstforum*, Cologne. **Essays:** Gerz; Honegger; Viallat; Voss.

THOMAS, Daniel. Essayist. Senior Curator of Australian Art, Australian National Gallery, Canberra, since 1978. Curator of Australian Art, Art Gallery of New South Wales, Sydney, 1958–77. Author of *Outlines of Australian Art: The Joseph Brown Collection*, 1973, 1980. **Essays:** Albert Tucker; Unsworth.

TONO, Yoshiaki. Essayist. Art Critic, Tokyo; Professor, Tama University of Art; Guest Curator, Seibu Museum of Art, Tokyo, and Toyama Museum of Modern Art, Tokyo. Author of *Artists in Grotta*, 1957, 1965; *After Pollock*, 1965; *Diaries in the U.S.A.*, 1968; *Marcel Duchamp*, 1977; *Jasper Johns and/or*, 1979; *The Betrayed Regard*, 1980; *The Ambiguous Water*, 1980; *Chatting with Artists*, 1984; *Mrs. Robinson and Contemporary Art*, 1986. **Essays:** Arakawa; Ay-O; Kawaguchi; Kuwayama; Miki; Sekine; Sugai; Takamatsu.

TRINI, Tommaso. Adviser. Art critic and historian, Milan. Formerly, Editor of *Data*, Milan. Author of numerous works on 20th century art.

VAIZEY, Marina (Lady Vaizey). Advisor. Art Critic, *The Sunday Times*, London, since 1974. Art Critic, *The Financial Times*, London, 1970–74. Member of the Arts Panel, 1973–78, Member, 1976–78, and Chairman of Arts Films, 1976–78, Arts Council of Great Britain. Author of *100 Masterpieces of Art*, 1979; *Andrew Wyeth*, 1980; and *The Artist as Photographer*, 1982.

van HAAREN, H.J.A.M. Essayist. Art Critic, Rotterdam. **Essay:** van Munster.

VARIA, Radu. Essayist. Art critic, Paris and New York. Director of the International Committee of the *Biennale de Paris* in the 1970's, and Director of the International Section of the *Sao Paulo Bienal* in 1973; assisted Salvador Dali in the founding of the Dali Museum in Figueras, 1974. Has organized numerous exhibitions, particularly of the work of Horia Damian. **Essay:** Dali.

VENTURI, Luca. Freelance art critic, Milan. **Essay:** Turcato.

VERZOTTI, Giorgio. Essayist. Temporary Exhibitions Curator, Pinacoteca di Brera, Milan, since 1983; contributor to *Flash Art*, Milan, since 1979. Author of *Paesaggio Metropolitano*, 1982; and the exhibition catalogues: *Imago*, 1983; *In Labirinto*, 1983; *John Armleder/Alberto Garutti*, 1987; *Lucio Fontana*, 1987; *Presi per incantamento*, 1988. **Essays:** Bertrand; Chia; Clemente; Devade; Dias; Fabro; Immendorff; Kapoor; Mosset; Opie; Penone; Tremlett; Trockel; Vedova.

von ZITZEWITZ, Monika. Essayist. Cultural Correspondent in Italy for *Die Welt*, Bonn, since 1965. Author of *Auch so ist der Ivan*, 1953; *Verzaubert in Florenz*, 1962; *Golf von Neapel*, 1974, 1978; *Florenz und die Toskana*, 1979, 1980; *Toskana und Umbrien*, 1981. **Essays:** Guttuso; Manzù; Marini; Melotti.

WAGEMANS, A. F. Essayist. Instructor in Art Theory, State Academy, Amsterdam, since 1987. Assistant Curator, Rijksmuseum Kroller-Muller, Otterlo, 1980–81; Curator, Bonnefantenmuseum, Maastricht, 1982–84. **Essays:** Boezem; Botschuyver; Dahn; D'Armagnac; Dekkers; Dokoupil; Engels; Fernhout; Gijzen; Pyke Koch; Rajlich; Schoonhoven; Van der Heyden; Van Koningsbruggen; Visser; Westerik.

WEIL, John A. Essayist. Professor of Chemistry, University of Saskatchewan, Saskatoon, since 1971. **Essay:** Albers.

WHITTET, G. S. Essayist. Art critic and consultant, London. Assistant Editor, 1946–50, Managing Editor, 1950–58, and Editor, 1958–64, *The Studio*, London, and Editor, *Studio International*, 1964–66; London Art Correspondent, *Le Monde*, Paris, 1969–72; London Editor, *Pictures on Exhibit*, New York, 1972–80. Author of *Bouquet*, 1949; *London* (in the series "Art Centres of the World"), 1967; *Scotland Explored*, 1969; *Lovers in Art*, 1972. **Essays:** Antes; Boshier; Bury; Calderara; Cesar; Colville; Dahmen; Dewasne; Duchamp; Fraser; Freud; Goeritz; Hartigan; Hayter; Heiliger; Hepworth; Huxley; Jenkins; Jorn; Kricke; Peter Lanyon; Lichtenstein; Lipton; Manessier; Kenneth Martin; Mathieu; Mesens; Moore; Negret; Nevelson; Newman; Nicholson; Oldenburg; Paolozzi; Peter Phillips; Piper; Prassinos; Rickey; Rosenquist; Scanavino; Soulages; Frank Stella; Still; Sutton; Tal-Coat; Vasarely; Wyeth, Yunkers.

WILKIN, Karen. Essayist. Freelance curator and art critic, New York, since 1978. Chief Curator, The Edmonton Art Gallery, 1971–78. Author of *Modern Painting in Canada*, with Terry Fenton, 1978; *David Smith: The Formative Years*, 1981; *Jack Bush*, 1983; *Frankenthaler on Paper*, 1985; *Stuart Davis*, 1987. **Essays:** Bannard; Bush; Caro; Dzubas; Frankenthaler; Robert Murray; Tim Scott.

WILLIAMS, Sheldon. Essayist. English Correspondent of *L'Arte Naive*, Italy, since 1970; Artistic Adviser to RONA, London, since 1977. Editor, *Art Illustrated*, 1969–71. Author of *Situation Humaine*, 1967; *Verlon*, 1969; *A Background to Sfumato*, 1969; *Voodoo and the Art of Haiti*, 1971; *20th Century British Naive and Primitive Artists*, with Eric Lister, 1975; editor of *RONABOOK*, 1978, and *A Quiet Thunder*, 1978. **Essays:** Adami, Alechinsky; Arroyo; Auerbach; Bacon; Bayer; Bellmer; Berlewi; Biederman; Blake; Bontecou; Brauer; Bravo; Castillo; Chagall; Chryssa; Corneille; Crippa; Ad Dekkers; De Kooning; Ernst; Fangor; Fontana; Frink; Fruhtrunk; Fuchs; Furnival; Golub; Goodnough; Hajdu; Hartung; Helion; Hrdlicka; Hundertwasser; Iannone; Jacquet; Kalinowski, William King; Klapheck; Kothe; Krushenick; Lam; Lardera; Lenk; Lindner; Lindstrom; Lohse; Magritte; Masson; McWilliam; Michaux; Millares; Molinier; Monory; Mundy; Nitsch; Oiticica; Meret Oppenheim; Paik; Panamarenko; Pignon; Rainer; Raynaud; Raysse; Rebeyrolle; Rinke; Riopelle; Ruckriem; Ruscha; Saint-Phalle; Self; Seuphor; Sonderborg; Sorge; Spoerri; Tamayo; Titus-Carmel; Trevelyan; Trouille; Uecker; Van Amen; Van Velde; Vieira da Silva; Villalba; Wesselman.

WINGATE, Adina. Essayist. Development Consultant, Arizona Historical Society, Tucson, since 1980. Art Critic, *Arizona Daily Star*, Tucson, 1973–76; Public Information and Program Director, Tucson Museum of Art, 1976–79; Senior Curator, La Jolla Museum of Contemporary Art, California, 1979–80. **Essay:** Peter Young.

ZACHAREA, Chryssa. Essayist. Freelance writer and researcher, London. **Essay:** Louw.

CONTEMPORARY ARTISTS

CONTEMPORARY ARTS SERIES

Contemporary Artists
Contemporary Architects
Contemporary Photographers
Contemporary Designers
International Contemporary Arts Directory

CONTEMPORARY ARTISTS

THIRD EDITION

Editor:
Colin Naylor

Advisers:
Jean-Christophe Ammann, Szymon Bojko
Melvin N. Day, Jorge Glusberg
Klaus Honnef, Arthur McIntyre
Joan Murray, Frank Popper
Peter Selz, Tazmi Shinoda
Heinz Spielmann, Tommaso Trini
Marina Vaizey

StJ
ST. JAMES PRESS
CHICAGO AND LONDON

Front cover: Horst Antes—maquette for *Der Ring*, 1987.

ST. JAMES PRESS
233 East Ontario Street
Chicago 60611, U.S.A.
or
3 Percy Street
London W1P 9FA, England

First Published in the U.S.A. and U.K. in 1989

British Library Cataloguing in Publication Data

Contemporary artists—3rd ed.
1. Visual arts—Biographies
I. Naylor, Colin, *1944–*
709′.2′2

ISBN 0-912289-96-1

Printed and bound in Great Britain by
Butler & Tanner Ltd, Frome and London
Typeset at BookMasters, Ashland, Ohio

CONTENTS

EDITOR'S NOTE

The selection of entrants in this third edition of *Contemporary Artists* is based on the recommendations of the Advisers whose names are listed on page ix. Guidelines for selection proposed that all entrants should have worked as professional artists for at least five years, have exhibited their work in several individual exhibitions at important galleries, and have been included in large-scale museum survey shows—and be represented in the permanent collections of major museums throughout the world. In the case of young—and perhaps lesser-known—artists, one important criterion was that they should have already attracted serious critical attention in the current art media. The inclusion of deceased artists is dependent upon the continuing influence of their work on current art activity—though, for general purposes, no artist deceased prior to 1960 has been included.

Entries include: a biography; a list of individual exhibitions; a selection of up to 10 group exhibitions; a listing of those public galleries and museums that have the work of the entrant in their permanent collection (again, up to a limit of 10); and a bibliography of books and articles by and about the entrant. As well, living entrants have been invited to make a statement on their work or on contemporary art in general, and to choose a photograph of a representative work. Critical texts have been provided by 125 contributors.

Most of the information in the entries on living artists was supplied by the entrants themselves. Research was carried out mainly in the libraries of the Tate Gallery, London, the Museum of Modern Art, New York, and the Art Institute of Chicago: we are grateful to the staff at all three institutions for their unfailing co-operation and courtesy.

ADVISERS/CONTRIBUTORS

Advisers

Jean-Christophe Ammann, Szymon Bojko
Melvin N. Day, Jorge Glusberg, Klaus Honnef
Arthur McIntyre, Joan Murray, Frank Popper
Peter Selz, Tazmi Shinoda, Heinz Spielman
Tommaso Trini, Marina Vaizey

Contributors

Daniel Abadie, Albrecht D., Lawrence Alloway
Jean-Christophe Ammann, Ban Andras

Carrie Barker, D. C. Barrett, Konstantin Bazarov
Jane Bell, Carmine Benincasa, Maurice Berger
Florent Bex, Willard Bohn, Szymon Bojko
Achille Bonito Oliva, Jean-Luc Bordeaux
David Bourdon, David Brown, William Burroughs

Massimo Carboni, Gary Catalano, Barbara Cavaliere
Ronny Cohen, Michael Compton, Lynne Cooke
Barbara Cortright, Fenella Crichton

Melvin N. Day, Gillo Dorfles

Mary Ellis, Muriel Emanuel

Zdenek Felix, Michael Alastair Findlay
Andrew Forge, Claude Fournet, Alison Fraser
B. H. Friedman, Kenneth S. Friedman, Gerolf Fritsch

Peggy Gale, Edda Gazzero, Ron Glowen
Jorge Glusberg, Janet Goleas, Olle Granath

James Harithas, Dick Higgins, John H. Holloway
Klaus Honnef

Jill Johnston

Paul J. Karstorm, Victoria Keller, Jane Kelly
Alicja Kepinska, Joshua Kind, April Kingsley
Helena Kontova, Richard Kostelanetz, Udo Kultermann

Roberto G. Lambarelli, Sharon Lancer, Elise La Rose
Lavina Learmont, Dominique Linquois, Marco Livingstone
Norbert Lynton

Alastair Mackintosh, Andrée Marechal-Workman
Henry Martin, Carine Maurice, Cecile N. McCann
Arthur McIntyre, Marco Meneguzzo, Thomas Messer
Gunter Metken, Tamon Miki, Alan Moore
Barbara Moore, Lynda Morris, Joan Murray
Italo Mussa

Yusuke Narahara, Roald Nasgaard, Michael Newman
Percy North

Harold Osborne

Demetrio Paparoni, Loredana Parmesani
Ralph Pomeroy, Frank Popper

George Rickey, John Roberts, John Robinson
Marlee Robinson

Merle Schipper, Werner Schulze-Reimpell
Dieter Schwarz, Peter Selz, Michael Shepherd
Tazmi Shinoda, Dagmar Sinz, Katharine Smith
Charles Spencer, Heinz Spielmann, Ryszard Stanislawski
Mary Stofflet, Marie Luise Syring

Daniel Thomas, Yoshiaki Tono
H.J.A.M. van Haaren, Radu Varia, Luca Venturi
Giorgio Verzotti, Monika von Zitzewitz

A.F. Wagemans, John A. Weil, G. S. Whittet
Karen Wilkin, Sheldon Williams, Adina Wingate

Chryssa Zacharea

CONTEMPORARY ARTISTS

Magdalena Abakanowicz
Ivor Abrahams
Marina Abramovic
Vito Acconci
Valerio Adami
Nicholas Africano
Afro
Yaacov Agam
Vincenzo Agnetti
Josef Albers
Ivan Albright
Pierre Alechinsky
Terry Allen
Laurie Anderson
Carl Andre
Michael Andrews
Giovanni Anselmo
Horst Antes
Eleanor Antin
Stephen Antonakos
Richard Anuskiewicz
Siegfried Anzinger
Karel Appel
Shusaku Arakawa
Arman
Kenneth Armitage
John Armleder
Robert Arneson
Eduardo Arroyo
Richard Artschwager
Michael Asher
David Askevold
Conrad Atkinson
Gabor Attalai
Bernard Aubertin
Frank Auerbach
Alice Aycock
Ay-O

Francis Bacon
Jo Baer
Olle Baertling
Enrico Baj
John Baldessari
Balthus
Walter Darby Bannard
Clive Barker
Robert Barry
Jennifer Bartlett
Gianfranco Baruchello
George Baselitz
Leonard Baskin
Carlo Battaglia
Herbert Bayer
Jean Bazaine
Jack Beal
Romare Bearden
Bernhard and Hilla Becher
Robert Bechtle
Bill Beckley
Larry Bell
Hans Bellmer
Luis Benedit
Lynda Benglis
Billy Al Bengston
Jan Berdyszak
Jaap Berghuis
Henryk Berlewi
Antonio Berni
Bertholin
Jake Berthot
Harry Bertoia
Jean-Pierre Bertrand
Joseph Beuys
Charles Biederman
Max Bill
Isabel Bishop
James Bishop
Ronald Bladen
Peter Blake
Bernhard-Johannes Blume
Peter Blume
Mel Bochner
Alighiero E. Boetti

Mari Boeyen
Marinus Boezem
Ilya Bolotowsky
Christian Boltanski
Lee Bontecou
Peter Booth
Jon Borofsky
Jean Francois Bory
Derek Boshier
Fernando Botero
Martha Boto
Theo Botschuyver
Louise Bourgeois
Arthur Boyd
Mark Boyle
Erich Brauer
Claudio Bravo
George Brecht
Robert G. Breer
K.P. Brehmer
Stuart Brisley
Marcel Broodthaers
James Brooks
Stanley Brouwn
Günter Brus
Tadeusz Brzozowski
Stephen Buckley
Edward Bullmore
Chris Burden
Daniel Buren
Victor Burgin
Edward Burra
Alberto Burri
Pol Bury
Jack Bush
Michael Buthe
Reg Butler
Deborah Butterfield

Paul Cadmus
John Cage
Alexander Calder
Antonio Calderara
Pier Paolo Calzolari
Peter Campus
Louis Cane
Rafael Canogar
Guiseppe Capogrossi
Anthony Caro
Ian Carr-Harris
Nicola Carrino
Pietro Cascella
Enrico Castellani
Luciano Castelli
Jorge Castillo
Patrick Caulfield
Alik Cavaliere
Mario Ceroli
Cesar
Lynn Chadwick
Marc Chagall
John Chamberlain
Alan Charlton
Sandro Chia
Giuseppe Chiari
Judy Chicago
Eduardo Chillida
Christo
Chryssa
Roman Cieslewicz
Lygia Clark
John Clem Clarke
Francesco Clemente
Chuck Close
Bernard Cohen
Tony Coleing
James Coleman
James Collins
Gianni Colombo
Alex Colville
Bruce Conner
Pietro Consagra
Ron Cooper
William Nelson Copley

Corneille
Joseph Cornell
Claudio Costa
Robert Cottingham
Tony Cragg
Michael Craig-Martin
Leonardo Cremonini
Roberto Crippa
Carlos Cruz-Diez
Enzo Cucchi
José Luis Cuevas
Greg Curnoe
Roger Cutforth

Dado
K.F. Dahmen
Walter Dahn
Salvador Dali
Ken Danby
Nassos Daphnis
Hanne Darboven
Allan D'Arcangelo
Ben D'Armagnac
Alan Davie
John Davies
Douglas Davis
Gene Davis
John Davis
Ronald Davis
Richard Deacon
John De Andrea
Sergio de Camargo
Giorgio de Chirico
Gino de Dominicis
George Deem
Roy De Forest
Raoul de Keyser
Ad Dekkers
Ger Dekkers
Willem de Kooning
Lucio Del Pezzo
Paul Delvaux
Hugo Demarco
Nicola De Maria
Walter De Maria
Agnes Denes
José de Riva
Marc Devade
Paul de Vree
Herman De Vries
Jean Dewasne
Daniel Dezeuze
Antonio Dias
Jan Dibbets
Richard Diebenkorn
Hans-Jürgen Diehl
Erik Dietmann
Braco Dimitrijevic
Jim Dine
Mark Di Suvero
Jiri Georg Dokoupil
Noël Dolla
César Domela
Piero Dorazio
Russell Drysdale
Jean Dubuffet
Marcel Duchamp
Natalia Dumitresco
David Dye
Friedel Dzubas

Don Eddy
Benni Efrat
Franz Eggenschwiler
Pieter Engels
Max Ernst
Errò
Richard Estes
Maurice Esteve
Philip Evergood

Luciano Fabro
Oyvind Fahlstrom
Wojciech Fangor

Murray Favro
Edgar Fernhout
Jackie Ferrara
Rafael Ferrer
Rainer Fetting
Robert Filliou
Ian Hamilton Finlay
Eric Fischl
Joel Fisher
Barry Flanagan
Dan Flavin
Lucio Fontana
Llyn Foulkes
Terry Fox
Sam Francis
Helen Frañkenthaler
Donald Hamilton Fraser
Lucian Freud
Elisabeth Frink
Terry Frost
Günter Fruhtrunk
Ernst Fuchs
Hamish Fulton
John Furnival
Klaus Fussmann

Marco Gastini
Yves Gaucher
Winfred Gaul
Johannes Geccelli
General Idea
Juan Genoves
Isa Genzken
Karl Gerstner
Franz Gertsch
Jochen Gerz
Alberto Giacometti
Wim Gijzen
Gilbert and George
Sam Gilliam
Bruno Gironcoli
Fritz Glarner
Domenico Gnoli
Mathias Goeritz
Ralph Goings
Leon Golub
Joe Goode
Robert Goodnough
Ron Gorchov
Robert Gordy
Ludwig Gosewitz
Adolph Gottlieb
Dan Graham
Robert Graham
Gotthard Graubner
Josep Grau Garriga
Morris Graves
Nancy Graves
Emilio Greco
Alan Green
Gloria Greenberg
Balcomb Greene
Giorgio Griffa
Victor Grippo
Red Grooms
Nancy Grossman
Robert Grosvenor
Johannes Grützke
Philip Guston
Renato Guttuso
Brion Gysin

Hans Haacke
Raymond Hains
Etienne Hajdu
Nigel Hall
Richard Hamilton
Duane Hanson
David Hare
Helen Harrison
Newton Harrison
Grace Hartigan
Hans Ernst Hartung
Erich Hauser

Stanley William Hayter
Tim Head
Erwin Heerich
Bernhard Heiliger
Michael Heizer
Al Held
Jean Hélion
Geoffrey Hendricks
Maurice Henry
Barbara Hepworth
Patrick Heron
Eva Hesse
Sheila Hicks
Dick Higgins
Anthony Hill
John Hilliard
Roger Hilton
David Hockney
Howard Hodgkin
Rudolf Hoflehner
Tom Holland
Nancy Holt
Jenny Holzer
Gottfried Honegger
Rebecca Horn
Dom Sylvester Houedard
John Hoyland
Alfred Hrdlicka
Douglas Huebler
Friedensreich Hundertwasser
Bryan Hunt
Richard Hunt
Paul Huxley

Dorothy Iannone
Taka Iimura
Jorg Immendorff
Robert Indiana
Will Insley
Jean Ipousteguy
Robert Irwin

Christian Jaccard
Alain Jacquet
Horst Janssen
Valerie Jaudon
Paul Jenkins
Neil Jenney
Alfred Jensen
Luis Jimenez
Jasper Johns
Lester Johnson
Ray Johnson
Joan Jonas
Allen Jones
Asger Jorn
Michel Journiac
Donald Judd

Horst Egon Kalinowski
Stephen Kaltenbach
Howard Kanovitz
Tadeusz Kantor
Anish Kapoor
Allan Kaprow
Alex Katz
Craig Kauffman
Tatsuo Kawaguchi
On Kawara
Ellsworth Kelly
Michael Kenny
Anselm Kiefer
Edward Kienholz
Phillip King
William King
Alain Kirili
Per Kirkeby
R.B. Kitaj
Yoshihisa Kitatsuji
Konrad Klapheck
Milan Knízák
Alison Knowles
John Koch
Pyke Koch

J.H. Kocman
Oscar Kokoschka
Jiri Kolar
Gyula Kosice
Leon Kossoff
Joseph Kosuth
Fritz Köthe
Jannis Kounellis
Piotr Kowalski
Joyce Kozloff
Lee Krasner
Norbert Kricke
Dieter Krieg
Richard Kriesche
Barbara Kruger
Nicolas Krushenick
Tetsumi Kudo
Gary Kuehn
Yayoi Kusama
Robert Kushner
Tadaaki Kuwayama

Gerald Lang
Laszlo Lakner
Wilfredo Lam
David Lamelas
Lois Lane
Nikolaus Lang
Ellen Lanyon
Berto Lardera
John Latham
Bob Law
Jan Lebenstein
Louis Le Brocquy
Jean Le Gac
Jan Lenica
Thomas Lenk
Julio Le Parc
Alfred Leslie
Barry Le Va
David Leverett
Les Levine
Marilyn Levine
Sol LeWitt
Alexander Liberman
Roy Lichtenstein
Liliane Lijn
Richard Lindner
Christian Lindow
Bengt Lindström
Richard Lippold
Seymour Lipton
Frank Lobdell
Richard Paul Lohse
Richard Long
Antonio Lopez Garcia
Roelof Louw
Reinier Lucassen
Sven Lukin
Evert Lundquist
Ana Lupas
Markus Lupertz
Urs Lüthi
Len Lye

George Maciunas
Heinz Mack
René Magritte
Leopoldo Maler
Alfred Manessier
Robert Mangold
Sylvia Mangold
Man Ray
Giacomo Manzù
Conrad Marca-Relli
Brice Marden
Marino Marini
Tom Marioni
Marisol
Agnes Martin
Kenneth Martin
Ron Martin
John Mason
André Masson

Georges Mathieu
Yutaka Matsuzawa
Roberto Matta
Gordon Matta-Clark
Fabio Mauri
Ann McCoy
John McCracken
James McGarrell
John D. McLaughlin
Bruce McLean
F.E. McWilliam
Bernard Meadows
David Medalla
Christian Megert
Fausto Melotti
John Meredith
Richard Merkin
Mario Merz
E.L.T. Mesens
Annette Messager
Gustav Metzger
Henri Michaux
Tomio Miki
Manolo Millares
Keith Milow
Antoni Miralda
Joan Miró
Joan Mitchell
Manfred Mohr
Guido Molinari
Pierre Molinier
Jacques Monory
Nicholas Monro
Jeremy Moon
Henry Moore
Giorgio Morandi
Francois Morellet
Malcolm Morley
Ennio Morlotti
Michael Morris
Robert Morris
Wilfred Moser
Ed Moses
Olivier Mosset
Robert Motherwell
Tania Mouraud
Otto Muehl
Robert Muller
Bruno Munari
Henry Mundy
Catherine Murphy
Elizabeth Murray
Robert Murray

Hidetoshi Nagasawa
Peter Nagel
Hitoshi Nakazato
Maurizio Nannucci
David Nash
Bruce Nauman
Paul Neagu
Edgar Negret
Ernst Neizvestny
Lowell Nesbitt
Joshua Neustein
Louise Nevelson
Barnett Newman
Ben Nicholson
Mario Nigro
Minoru Niizuma
Hermann Nitsch
Constantino Nivola
Isamu Noguchi
Sidney Nolan
Kenneth Noland
Richard Nonas
Maria Nordman
Gastone Novelli
Jim Nutt

Helio Oiticica
Georgia O'Keeffe
Claus Oldenburg
Jules Olitski

Nathan Oliveira
Claudio Olivieri
Toshinobu Onosato
Luigi Ontani
Roman Opalka
Julian Opie
Dennis Oppenheim
Meret Oppenheim
Alfonso Ossorio

Robin Page
Nam June Paik
Mimmo Paladino
Pablo Palazuelo
Palermo
Panamarenko
Gina Pane
Giulio Paolini
Eduardo Paolozzi
Claudio Parmiggiani
Mike Parr
David Partridge
Ed Paschke
Victor Pasmore
Philip Pearlstein
Alicia Penalba
A.R. Penck
Giuseppe Penone
Beverly Pepper
Achille Perilli
Irving Petlin
Peter Phillips
Tom Phillips
Pablo Picasso
Roland Piché
Otto Piene
Edouard Pignon
John Piper
Vettor Pisani
Michelangelo Pistoletto
Anne and Patrick Poirier
Sigmar Polke
Arnaldo Pomodoro
Gio Pomodoro
Larry Poons
Stephen Posen
Richard Pousette-Dart
Lucio Pozzi
Mario Prassinos
Mark Prent
Kenneth Price
Patrick Procktor

Mario Radice
Markus Raetz
Joseph Raffael
Arnulf Rainer
Tomas Rajlich
Mel Ramos
Robert Rauschenberg
Jean Pierre Raynaud
Martial Raysse
Paul Rebeyrolle
Ad Reinhardt
Edda Renouf
Erich Reusch
Hans Peter Reuter
Gerhard Richter
George Rickey
Bridget Riley
Klaus Rinke
Jean-Paul Riopelle
Larry Rivers
Dorothea Rockburne
Osvaldo Romberg
Ulrike Rosenbach
James Rosenquist
Charles Ross
Theodore Roszak
Mimmo Rotella
Dieter Roth
Susan Rothenberg
Mark Rothko
Ulrich Ruckriem

Allen Ruppersberg
Edward Ruscha
Reiner Ruthenbeck
Robert Ryman

Niki de Saint-Phalle
Yoshishige Saito
David Salle
Lucas Samaras
Fred Sandback
Michael Sandle
Jean-Michel Sanejouand
Alan Saret
Sarkis
Paul Sarkisian
Peter Saul
Antonio Saura
Angelo Savelli
Henry Saxe
Emilio Scanavino
Italo Scanga
Salvatore Scarpitta
Christian Schad
Miriam Schapiro
Mario Schifano
Julius Schmidt
Julian Schnabel
Carolee Schneemann
Nicolas Schöffer
Jan J. Schoonhoven
HA Schult
Bernard Schultze
Emil Schumacher
Tim Scott
William Scott
Peter Sedgley
George Segal
Nobuo Sekine
Colin Self
Richard Serra
Pablo Serrano
Michel Seuphor
Ben Shahn
Joel Shiparo
Jeffrey Shaw
Alan J. Shields
Mieko Shiomi
Katharina Sieverding
Charles Simonds
David Smith

Richard Smith
Tony Smith
Robert Smithson
Kenneth Snelson
Michael Snow
K.R.H. Sonderborg
Alan Sonfist
Keith Sonnier
Peter Sorge
Jesus Rafael Soto
Pierre Soulages
Giangiacomo Spadari
Giuseppe Spagnulo
Nancy Spero
Daniel Spoerri
Klaus Staeck
Theodoros Stamos
Peter Stämpfli
Richard Stankiewicz
Robert Stanley
Henryk Stazewski
Jeffrey Steele
Saul Steinberg
Frank Stella
Ian Stephenson
Harold Stevenson
John Stezaker
Clyfford Still
Michelle Stuart
Kishio Suga
Kumi Sugai
George Sugarman
Graham Sutherland
Philip Sutton

Emilio Tadini
Shinkichi Tajiri
Jiro Takamatsu
Takis
Pierre Tal-Coat
Rufino Tamayo
Antoni Tapiès
Ernesto Tatafiore
Hervé Télémaque
Paul Thek
Wayne Thiebaud
Imants Tillers
Sidney Tillim
Joe Tilson
David Tindle

Jean Tinguely
Gerard Titus-Carmel
Mark Tobey
Henryk Tomaszewski
Niele Toroni
Endre Tot
Claude Tousignant
Goran Trbuljak
David Tremlett
Julian Trevelyan
Rosemarie Trockel
David Troostwyk
Antonio A. Trotta
Clovis Trouille
Anne Truitt
Costas Tsoclis
Albert Tucker
William Tucker
Giulio Turcato
William Turnbull
Jim Turrell
Richard Tuttle
Cy Twombly
Jack Tworkov

Günther Uecker
Timm Ulrichs
Giuseppe Uncini
Ken Unsworth
Janos Urban
Nicolas Uriburu

DeWain Valentine
Jiri Valoch
Woody van Amen
Richard Van Buren
J.C.J. van der Heyden
Ger Van Elk
Rob Van Koningsbruggen
Jan van Munster
Bram Van Velde
Victor Vasarely
Keith Vaughan
Ben Vautier
Emilio Vedova
Vladimir Velickovic
Bernar Venet
Claude Viallat
Vieira da Silva
Dario Villalba

Jacques de la Villegle
Carel Visser
Maurice de Vlaminck
Gerhard von Graevenitz
David Von Schlegell
Jan Voss
Wolf Vostell
Peter Voulkos

Robert Wade
Jaap Wagemaker
John Walker
Brian Wall
Franz Erhard Walther
Andy Warhol
Robert Marshall Watts
William Wegman
Lawrence Weiner
Roger Welch
Günter Weseler
Tom Wesselmann
Co Westerik
H.C. Westermann
Doug Wheeler
Robert Whitman
Joyce Wieland
William T. Wiley
Stephen Willats
John Willenbecher
Robert M. Wilson
Gerd Winner
Rolf Winnewisser
Jacqueline Winsor
Krzysztof Wodiczko
Derrick Woodham
Bill Woodrow
Paul Wunderlich
Andrew Wyeth

Masaaki Yamada
Takeo Yamaguchi
Richard Yokomi
Kenji Yoshida
Fumio Yoshimura
Peter Young
Jack Youngerman
Adja Yunkers

Gianfranco Zappettini
Gilberto Zorio

Magdalena Abakanowicz: *Katarsis*, Santomato di Pistoia, Italy, 1985

A

ABAKANOWICZ, Magdalena.

Polish. Born in Falenty, 20 June 1930. Educated at the School of Fine Arts, Sopot, 1949, and at the Academy of Fine Arts, Warsaw, 1950–55, M.A. 1955. Married Jan Kosmowski in 1956. Independent artist, Warsaw, since 1956; has concentrated on woven constructions and sculptures since 1961. Instructor, 1965–74, Associate Professor, 1974–79, and since 1979 Professor, State College of Arts, Poznan. Member, Z.A.I.K.S. Union of Polish Artists, Writers and Composers, Warsaw, 1965. Recipient: State Travel Fellowship to France, Warsaw, 1962; 1st Prize, Ministry of Culture, 1965; Gold Medal, Polish Artists' Union, 1965; Gold Medal, *Bienal,* Sao Paulo, 1965; Grand Prize of the Ministry for Foreign Affairs, 1970; State Prize of the Polish Folk Republic, Warsaw, 1972; Grand Prize, World Crafts' Council, New York, 1974; Golden Cross of Merit, Polish Folk Republic, Poznan, 1974; Special Professor's Prize, State College of Art, Poznan, 1975; Gottfried-von-Herder Prize, Vienna 1979; Cross of Polonia Restituta, Warsaw, 1980; Jurzykowski Foundation Award, New York, 1983. Honorary doctorate: Royal College of Art, London, 1974. Chevalier, Ordre des Arts et Lettres, France, 1985. Agent: Galerie Alice Pauli, 6 Avenue Rumine, 1005 Lausanne, Switzerland. Address: Al. Stanow Zjednoczonych 16/53, 03-947 Warsaw, Poland.

Individual Exhibitions:

1960 Kordegarda, Warsaw
1962 Galerie Dautzenberg, Paris
1963 Galerie Sztuki Nowoczesnej, Warsaw
1965 Galerie Zacheta, Warsaw
Biuro Wystaw Artystycznych, Zakopane, Poland
1966 Biuro Wystaw Artystycznych, Zielona Gora, Poland
1967 Galerie Alice Pauli, Lausanne
Galeria Wspolczesna, Warsaw
Kunstindustrimuseet, Oslo (travelled to Vestlandske Kunstindustrimuseum, Bergen; the Stavanger Kunstforening; and the Trondheim Kunstforening)
1968 Van Abbemuseum, Eindhoven, Netherlands (travelled to the Frans Halsmuseum, Haarlem; Groninger Museum, Groningen; and the Stedelijk Museum, Schiedam)
Helmhaus, Zurich
1969 Galerie Alice Pauli, Lausanne
Tapisserien und Raumliche Texturen, Kunsthalle, Mannheim
Stedelijk Museum, Arnhem, Netherlands
1970 Nationalmuseum, Stockholm
Textil Skulptur/Textil Environment, Konsthall, Sodertalje, Sweden
1971 Galerie Alice Pauli, Lausanne
Galeria Pryzmat, Cracow
Galeria Wspolczesna, Warsaw
Pasadena Art Museum, California
1972 Aberdeen Art Gallery, Scotland
Textile Strukturen und Konstruktionen, Environments, Kunstverein für die Rheinlande und Westfalen, Dusseldorf
1973 Arnolfini Gallery, Bristol
Galerie Alice Pauli, Lausanne (with Jagoda Buic)
Galerie des Beaux-Arts, Bordeaux
1974 Museum Sztuki, Lodz, Poland
1975 Galerie Alice Pauli, Lausanne
Galerie Zacheta, Warsaw
Whitechapel Art Gallery, London
1976 Art Gallery of New South Wales, Sydney (travelled to the National Gallery of Victoria, Melbourne)
1977 Galerie Alice Pauli, Lausanne
Konsthalle, Malmo, Sweden
Sonja Henie-Niel Onstadt Kunstsenter, Oslo
1978 Biuro Wystaw Artystyczynch, Lodz, Poland
Biuro Wystaw Artystyczynch, Bydogoszczy, Poland
1979 Galerie Alice Pauli Lausanne (retrospective)
1980 Polish Pavilion, at the *Biennale,* Venice
1981 Galerie Alice Pauli, Lausanne
1982 ARC/Musée d'Art Moderne de la Ville, Paris
Galerie Jeanne Bucher, Paris
Walter Phillips Gallery, The Banff Centre, Alberta, Canada
Museum of Contemporary Art, Chicago (toured the United States and Canada)
1983 De Cordova Museum, Lincoln, Massachusetts (retrospective)
National Academy of Sciences, Washington, D.C.
Musée d'Art Contemporain, Montreal
Visual Arts Centre of Alaska, Anchorage
1984 Dallas Museum of Arts, Texas
University of California, Los Angeles
Portland Art Museum, Oregon
1985 Galerie Alice Pauli, Lausanne
Virginia Museum of Fine Arts, Richmond
Xavier Fourcade Inc., New York
1986 Catholic University Art Gallery, Lublin, Poland
McIntosh-Drysdale Gallery, Washington, D.C.
1987 BWA Muzeum Chemitex-Stilon, Gorzow Wielkopolski, Poland
Muku Gallery, Hiroshima, Japan

Selected Group Exhibitions:

1962 *Biennale Internationale de la Tapisserie,* Musée Cantonal des Beaux-Arts, Lausanne (regularly until 1979)
1965 *Bienal,* Sao Paulo
1968 *Wall Hangings,* Museum of Modern Art, New York
1979 *Sculpture Polonaise,* Musée d'Art Moderne de la Ville, Paris
1980 *Biennale,* Venice
1981 *Malmoe,* Konsthall, Malmo, Sweden
1982 *Kunst Wirt Material,* Nationalgalerie, Berlin
1984 *Recent Painting and Sculpture,* Museum of Modern Art, New York
1986 *Eva und die Zukunft,* Kunsthalle, Hamburg
1987 *Avant-Garde in the Eighties,* Los Angeles County Museum of Art

Collections:

Muzeum Narodow, Warsaw; Muzeum Sztuki, Lodz, Poland; Stedelijk Museum, Amsterdam; Nationalmuseum, Stockholm; Henie-Onstad Kunstsenter, Oslo; Centre Georges Pompidou, Paris; Museu de Arte Moderna, Sao Paulo; National Museum of Modern Art, Kyoto; Australian Gallery of Art, Canberra; Museum of Modern Art, New York.

Publications:

On ABAKANOWICZ: books—*Abakanowicz,* exhibition catalogue, with text by André Kuenzi. Lausanne 1967; *Magdalena Abakanowicz: Tapisserien und Raumliche Texturen,* exhibition catalogue, with text by Heinz Fuchs, Mannheim 1969; *Magdalena Abakanowicz: Textil Skulptur/Textil Environment,* exhibition catalogue, with text by Eje Hogestatt and Danuta Wroblewska, Sodertalje, Sweden 1970; *Beyond Craft: The Art Fabric* by Mildred Constantine and Jack Lenor Larsen, New York 1972; *Magdalena Abakanowicz: Textile Strukturen und Konstruktionen, Environments,* exhibition catalogue, with text by Karl-Heinz Hering and Jasia Reichardt, Dusseldorf 1972; *La Nouvelle Tapisserie* by André Kuenzi, Geneva 1974; *Biennale di Venezia '80: Magdalena Abakanowicz,* exhibition catalogue, with text by Aleksander Wojciechowski, Warsaw 1980; films—*Abakany,* 1969; *Abakanowicz in Australia* 1976; *Division of Space,* 1976; *Abakanowicz,* 1976.

From the very beginning man has created myths out of his longing for the lost state of balance, for prehistoric existence called paradise which was a state without consciousness. He tried to find in religion the explanation of himself, to compensate his defects by its commandments, to justify the suffering of life by giving them purpose as does Christianity. In the practice of Tantra and yoga, man attempted to gain control over his instincts. This struggle of man with himself for control over his own nature, a struggle with a lack of internal norms of behaviour is reflected in the whole mythology, and ultimately in the vision of man seeking balance and perfection from the remotest time of the Assyrian poem "Gilgamesh" to the circular shape described by Plato of the first human being, to Balzac's book about Serafit the only one of Balzac's works not based on reality, or in Goethe's considerations about the Demon as the creator of life in his poem "Faust".

While reading about the structure and functioning of the human brain, which is formed of interdependent parts, but originating in different periods of evolution, I discovered how contradictory the factors determining behaviour are, how deeply rooted are sources of this permanent struggle. To all the most ancient fears of man I add my own. These can perhaps be glimpsed in my art as a story of the same anxieties and pains which have accompanied human existence as well as mine.

I once observed mosquitoes swarming. In gray masses. Host upon a host. Little creatures in slew of other little creatures. In incessant motion. Each preoccupied with its own spoor. Each different, distinct in details of shape. A horde emitting a common sound. Were they mosquitoes or people?

I feel overawed by quantity where counting no longer makes sense. By irrepeatabiliy within such a quantity. By creatures of nature gathered in herds, droves, species, in which each individual while subservient to the mass retains some distinguishing features. A crowd of people or birds, insects or leaves, is a mysterious assemblage of variants of certain prototype. A riddle of nature's abhorrence of exact repetition or inability to produce it. Just as a human hand cannot repeat its own gesture I invoke this disturbing law, switching my own immobile herds into that rhythm.

—Magdalena Abakanowicz

The manipulation of fiber into thread and the weaving of those threads into intricately constructed forms and surfaces are skills that can be counted among humankind's earliest and most enduring accomplishments. Those same techniques, which for all these thousands of years have produced shelters, utilitarian artifacts and garments to warm and protect human bodies, are the means by which Magdalena Abakanowicz shapes hauntingly eloquent and powerful sculptures. Many of these take possession of the spaces in which they are placed, sometimes seeming to become themselves architectural elements of the structures that enclose them; other groups of work assume more specific referential form.

In her first exhibitions Abakanowicz presented highly abstract environmental aspects, binding fibers into long, attenuated hawsers, shaping large organic forms and weaving stiff, heavy hangings or huge dark cocoons of rough jute. The alleyways and mazes created by these installations simultaneously functioned as enclosures and as impediments to free movement; their dark rough textures were pleasant to see but harsh to touch. A viewer walking among the forms could experience their impressive strengths, which offered a comforting but somewhat intimidating environment, suggesting a reference to the experience of individuals who find themselves cared for, and oppressed by, the unresponsive structures of a socialist state.

The cultural implications of Abakanowicz's work have become more explicit since the early 1970's. Burlap sacking, impregnated with glue and molded into the plaster cast of a seated male figure, became shell-like fragments, as if these were the broken, emptied husks of human bodies. Installed in mute throngs or lined up in poignant queues, they silently protested all authoritarian and suppressive regimes. A sequence of very large wrapped heads succeeded the figures, followed later by groups of hollow, burlap-covered ovoid forms, some intact and some fractured, in a wide range of sizes.

The imagery with which Abakanowicz works is as universal as her materials and techniques. It speaks to emotional responses which are even more basic and instinctive than the techniques which shape her forms. Since its earliest exhibitions, her work has been a provocative stimulus to other artists, revolutionizing our contemporary conceptions of fiber art.

—Cecile N. McCann

ABRAHAMS, Ivor.

British. Born in Wigan, Lancashire, in January 1935. Studied sculpture, St. Martin's School of Art, London 1952–53; under Karl Vogel, Camberwell School of Art, London 1953–57. Married; sons: Saul and Etienne. Worked as display artist, London, 1956–60. Full-time artist, London, since 1960. Visiting Lecturer in Sculpture, Royal College of Art, London, Goldsmith's College, London. Slade School of Art, London, and Edinburgh College of Art. Agent: Mayor Gallery, London. Address: c/o Mayor Gallery, 22a Cork Street, London W1, England.

Individual Exhibitions:

1962 Gallery One, London
1970 Richard Feigen Gallery, New York
Axiom Gallery, London
1971 Arnolfini Gallery, Bristol
1972 Felicity Samuel Gallery, London
Mappin Art Gallery, Sheffield
Aberdeen Art Gallery
1973 *Environments, Skulpturen, Zeichnungen, Komplette Graphiken*, Kunstverein, Cologne
Lijnbaan Centrum, Rotterdam
Galerie von Loeper, Hamburg
1974 Bernard Jacobson Gallery, London
Private Gallery, Munich
Galerie de la Clautre, Perigeaux, France
Galerie T., Amsterdam
Galerie Richard Foncke, Ghent
Galeria Quince, Madrid
Galerie Marzona, Bielefeld, West Germany
Natalie Stern Gallery, London
Galleri Ahlner, Stockholm
Galerie Laurent, Geneva
1975 Galerie Kummel, Cologne
Aktionsgalerie, Berne
Galleria del Cavallino, Venice
Bernard Jacobson Gallery, London
Galleri Ahlner, Stockholm
Galerie Bonnier, Geneva
1976 Mayor Gallery, London
Galleria Vinciana, Milan
Ikon Gallery, Birmingham
Galleri Nordenhake, Malmo, Sweden
Galerie Bonnier, Geneva
1977 Galleri Malgram, Gothenburg, Sweden
Galerie Ann von Horrenbeck, Brussels
Galerie Manfred Schonbrun, Frankfurt
1978 Drol-Kolbert Gallery, New York
Mayor Gallery, London
Hobson Gallery, Cambridge
1979 *Sculpture and Works on Paper*, Bernard Jacobson Gallery, London
Effigies du Pays d'Oc: Oeuvres de 1979, Galerie Bonnier, Geneva
Ferens Art Gallery, Hull England (toured Britain)
1980 St. Enoch's Gallery, Glasgow
Mayor Gallery, London
1981 Hobson Gallery, Cambridge
1982 Bernard Jacobson Ltd., Los Angeles
Warwick Arts Trust, London
1983 Mayor Gallery, London
1984 Bolton Museum and Art Gallery, Lancashire
Bluecoat Gallery, Liverpool, Merseyside
Bernard Jacobson Ltd., Los Angeles
Galerie Bonnier, Geneva
Galerie Engelberts, Geneva
Yorkshire Sculpture Park, Wakefield
1986 Bernard Jacobson Gallery, London
Mayor Gallery, London
1987 Galerie Albrecht, Munich

Selected Group Exhibitions:

1961 *La Joven Escultura Inglesa*, Salas des Exposiciones del Ateneo, Madrid
1964 *MICA Sculpture Exhibition*, City Art Gallery, Manchester
1968 *From Life*, Camden Arts Centre, London
1970 *Print Loan Show*, Museum of Modern Art, New York
1971 *Road Show*, at the *Bienal*, Sao Paulo
1973 *La Peinture Anglaise Aujourd'hui*, Musée d'Art Moderne de la Ville, Paris
1976 *Arte Inglese Oggi 1960–76*, Palazzo Reale, Milan
1979 *Museum of Drawers*, Kunsthaus, Zurich
1982 *Symbol and Imagination 1957–80*, Whitechapel Art Gallery, London
1988 *Figure It Out: Visual Body Language*, Helander Gallery, Palm Beach, Florida

Collections:

Victoria and Albert Museum, London; Arts Council of Great Britain, London; British Council, London; Museum Boymans-van Beuningen, Rotterdam; Wilhelm-Lehmbruck-Museum, Duisburg, West Germany; Museum of Modern Art, New York; Princeton University, New Jersey; Vassar College, Poughkeepsie, New York; Norton College of Art, Miami; National Gallery of Australia, Canberra.

Publications:

By ABRAHAMS: books—*Oxford Garden: A Sketchbook*, London 1977.

On ABRAHAMS: books—*The New Sculpture* by Udo Kultermann, London 1966; *Bienal de Sao Paulo: Gran Bretanha—Road Show*, exhibition catalogue, London 1971; *14 Big Prints*, with a foreword by Bernard Jacobson, London 1972; *La Peinture Anglaise Aujourd'hui*, exhibition catalogue with texts by Jacques Lassaigne and Edward Lucie Smith, Paris 1973; *Ivor Abrahams: Environments, Skulpturen, Zeichnungen, Komplette Graphiken*, exhibition catalogue, with an interview by R. J. Rees, and texts by W. Herzongenrath, M. S. Bibble and others, Cologne 1973; *Ivor Abrahams*, exhibition catalogue, with text by Richard Shone, London 1978; *Ivor Abrahams: Sculpture and Works on Paper*, exhibition catalogue, with text by Richard Shone, London 1979; *Ivor Abrahams: Effigies du Pays d'Oc: Oeuvres de 1979* exhibition catalogue, Geneva 1979; *Ivor Abrahams: The Garden Image Prints and Related Sculpture 1969–79*, exhibition catalogue with foreword by John McEwen, London 1984; *Ivor Abrahams: Models for Projects 1986*, exhibition catalogue with introduction by Bryan Robertson, London 1986.

The meeting of man and nature; the meeting of form and atmosphere; the meeting of popular art and formal art; the meeting of the present with what endures from the past—all these together sound like a great but well-nigh impossible task for 20th-century art. Add to that, a way of being English and also European. However, Ivor Abrahams has found a sly, tangential, subtle angle of approach with which to encompass all these themes, in works which give great delight. His basic ingredients are vegetation, space, and the implicit hand of man, partly able, partly unable, to control and plan. Since this embraces activities from the ordinary, vulgar and popular passion for "gardening", to the most refined and ambitious landscaping design, and from the most formally-disintegrating romantic situations, to the most severely classic, formal or even rigid, Abrahams' scope is potentially tremendous. At the same time, his actual realizations of these perceptions, ranging from glass fibre sprayed with bright green flock, with its "pop" associations, to bronzes which tend to compete with the formal and monumental which they themselves comment on, allows Abrahams a wide range of mood—comic, witty, ironic or detached. His effective drawings and lithographs should also be noted. There are many things to enjoy in Abrahams' art, from the way he catches our own childhood memories of secret corners in public parks, to elegiac and formal allusions which speak of the Europe of earlier centuries. His early training as a display artist has stood him in good stead; and his wide reading among the treatises on gardening, from popular to grand, enables him to include concept as well as precept. He is in the broadest sense an "observer"; and an observer of society as much as art: "I'm interested in the rules behind the rules," he has said; and the Brechtian "alienation effect" is important to him in his detached view of this "public aesthetic given concrete form." He has been singularly successful in making, out of passively truthful observation of man's relationship to nature, creative and witty realizations—in his earlier work, more literal, and in the later work more sculptural. One side effect of his art is that he has created a relationship between "pop" and "popular" art, and also reminded us that gardening is a real example of popular art, involving ordinary people in aesthetic judgments from blatant to subtly civilized.

—Michael Shepherd

ABRAMOVIC, Marina.

Yugoslav. Born in Belgrade in 1946. Studied at Academy of Fine Arts, Belgrade. Independent performance artist, Belgrade, from 1972; currently lives and works in Amsterdam. Address: Brouwersgracht 196, Amsterdam, Netherlands.

Ivor Abrahams: image from *Garden Suite*, 1970

Individual Exhibitions:

1974 Galerija Suvremene umjetnosti, Zagreb
Galleria Diagramma, Milan
1975 Studio Morra, Naples
1987 Centre d'Art Contemporain, Paris

Selected Group Exhibitions:

1970 *April Meeting*, Student Cultural Centre, Belgrade (and 1971, 1972)
1972 *Young Artists and Young Critics*, Museum of Modern Art, Belgrade
1973 *Post-Object Trends in Yugoslav Art*, Museum of Modern Art, Belgrade
8 Yugoslav Artists, Richard Demarco Gallery, Edinburgh
1974 *Contemporanea*, Parcheggio Villa Borghese, Rome
1975 *Contemporary Yugoslav Art*, Richard Demarco Gallery/Fruit Market Gallery, Edinburgh (toured the U.K.)
1979 *Expansion: International Biennale für Graphik und Visuelle Kunst*, Stadtpark, Vienna
1980 *ROSC '80*, University College, Dublin
1987 *Avant-Garde in the Eighties*, Los Angeles County Museum of Art

Publications:

By ABRAMOVIC: books—*Relation Work and Detour: First Complete Works*, Nijmegen, Netherlands 1980; videotapes—*Television Is a Machine*, 1972; *Rhythm 4*, 1974; *Smaile*, 1975; *I Won't . . .*, 1975.

On ABRAMOVIC: books—*Marina Abramovic*, exhibition catalogue, with text by Davor Maticevic, Zagreb 1974; *Contemporary Yugoslav Art*, exhibition catalogue, with text by Richard Demarco and others, Edinburgh 1975; *Expansion: Internationale Biennale für Graphik und Visuelle Kunst*, exhibition catalogue, with text by Horst Gerhard Haberl, Georg F. Schwarzbauer and others, Vienna 1979.

Before they met in 1975 Marina Abramovič and Ulay were both engaged in the performance of a kind of radical Body Art that took them to the limits of danger and physical resistance; that was while one of them was working in Belgrade unknown to the other, who was working in Amsterdam.

In their very first work together, the performance called "Relation in Movement" at the 1976 Venice *Biennale*, the couple expressed the special idea of performance based on interaction, the reciprocal exchange of energy effected both actually and symbolically. Their work, like their lives at that time, began to grow closer and to unite, until they became inseparable. Thus, in their performances and in their daily

life, they began to develop the possibilities of releasing and controlling their mind through forms of asceticism, creating situations of physical suffering. "You have to nearly break your body before you can free the mind," Ulay declared after one of their most punishing performances, during which both of them went without food for several days.

But unlike the ascetics, Abramovič and Ulay use the structures and elements of art, one of which is the geometric pattern, linear or circular, used to coordinate their movements. This is an idea derived from abstract art, or rather from minimal art, which in the real sense, in performance that is, suggests the concentration of energy. The circle is also a symbol of meeting and may be thought of as possessing magic powers. Each element is thus used in a number of senses. The repetitiveness of their movements or the staticness of their performances allow them to be easily interpreted in photography, video or film, media which they do in fact use for documentary purposes. Recently, in some static performances, these artists have created the illusion of a picture, almost a Tableau Vivant.

Moving as they do on the frontier between illusion and reality, between the physical and the metaphysical, Abramovič and Ulay show that our empirical world is far vaster than we can usually perceive, but that by certain practices our minds can be freed from many of its limitations.

—Helena Kontova

ACCONCI, Vito.

American. Born in New York City, 25 January 1940. Studied literature at Holy Cross College, Worcester, Massachusetts, B.A. 1962; University of Iowa, 1962–64, M.F.A. 1964. Independent poet and writer, New York, 1965–69; independent visual artist, concentrating on performance and environment works, New York, since 1969. Lecturer in Art Theory, School of Visual Arts, New York 1968–71; Instructor in post-studio art, California Institute of Art, Valencia, 1976. Formerly, Co-Editor, *0 to 9* magazine, New York. Agent: Sonnabend Gallery, 420 West Broadway, New York, New York 10013. Address: 39 Pearl Street, Brooklyn, New York 11201, U.S.A.

Individual Exhibitions:

1969 Rhode Island School of Design, Providence
Emanu-eul Midtown Y.M./Y.W.H.A., New York
Architectural League of New York
Far Broadway, New York
1970 Gain Ground Gallery, New York
Art Institute of Chicago
Nova Scotia College of Art and Design, Halifax
1971 74 Grand Street, New York
A Space, Toronto, Ontario (2 shows)
93 Grant Street, New York
Trappings, Kunstmuseum, Mönchengladbach, West Germany
Protetch-Rivkin Gallery, Washington, D.C.
Rhode Island School of Design, Providence
Museum of Conceptual Art, San Francisco
John Gibson Gallery, New York
Wisconsin State University at Whitewater
Sonnabend Gallery, New York
1972 California Institute of the Arts, Valencia
Sonnabend Gallery, New York
Galerie Sonnabend, Paris
Galleria L'Attico, Rome
1973 Modern Art Agency, Naples, Italy
Galerie D. Brussels
Galleria Schema, Florence
1974 Galleria Forma, Genoa
Galleria Alessandra Castelli, Milan
1975 Sonnabend Gallery, New York
Portland Center for the Visual Arts, Oregon
And/Or Gallery, Seattle
Carp Gallery, Los Angeles
Museum of Conceptual Art, San Francisco
Hallwalls Gallery, Buffalo, New York
Fine Arts Building, New York
Whitney Museum, New York
1976 The Kitchen, New York
Lerner-Heller Gallery, New York
Anthology Film Archives, New York
Sonnabend Gallery, New York
1977 Ohio State University, Columbus
School of Visual Arts, New York
University of Massachusetts, Amherst
Anthology Film Archives, New York
Sonnabend Gallery, New York
Modern Art Agency, Naples
Galerie D, Brussels
Institute of Art and Urban Resources, New York
Centre d'Art Contemporain, Geneva
Galeria Stampa, Basle
1978 Studio Ala, Milan
San Francisco Museum of Modern Art
Galerie Nachst St. Stephan, Vienna
International Cultureel Centrum, Antwerp, Belgium
The Kitchen, New York
Kunstmuseum, Lucerne
Stedelijk museum, Amsterdam (retrospective)
Galleria Mario Diacono, Bologna
Tampa Bay Art Center, Florida
1979 Young-Hoffman Gallery, Chicago
Sonnabend Gallery, New York
Galerie De Appel, Amsterdam (toured the Netherlands)
University of Rhode Island, Kingston
Galerie Sonnabend, Paris
1980 Muhlenberg College, Allentown, Pennsylvania
Vito Acconci: A Retrospective 1969 to 1980, Museum of Contemporary Art, Chicago (retrospective)
1981 *Machineworks: Vito Acconci, Alice Aycock, Dennis Oppenheim*, Institute of Contemporary Art, Philadelphia
Museum of Fine Arts, Montreal
Indianapolis Museum of Art, Indiana
1981 Young-Hoffman Gallery, Chicago
Institute of Contemporary Art, Philadelphia (with Alice Aycock and Dennis Oppenheim)
1982 Virginia Museum of Fine Arts, Richmond
Portland Center for the Visual Arts, Oregon
San Diego State University, California
University of Massachusetts, Amherst
1983 Miami-Dade Community College, Florida
Whitney Museum, New York
Williams College, Williamstown, Massachusetts
1984 Gallery Nature Morte, New York
University of Nebraska, Omaha
Zone Center for the Arts, Springfield, Massachusetts
1985 University of North Carolina, Chapel Hill
Carpenter and Hochmann Gallery, New York
City Hall Park, New York
Rhona Hoffman Gallery, Chicago
Brooklyn Museum, New York
Wadsworth Atheneum, Hartford, Connecticut
1986 Kent State University, Ohio
The Palladium, New York
University of South Florida, Tampa
Zone Gallery, New York
1987 International Center of Photography, New York
International with Monument, New York
La Jolla Museum of Contemporary Art, California

Selected Group Exhibitions:

1969 *Language 3*, Dwan Gallery, New York
1970 *Software*, Jewish Museum, New York (traveled to the Smithsonian Institution, Washington, D.C.)
1971 *Biennale*, Musée d'Art Moderne, Paris
1972 *Documenta 5*, Kassel, West Germany (and *Documenta 7*, 1982)
1973 *Aspects de l'Art Actuel*, Musée Galliera, Paris
1974 *Art and Image in Recent Art*, Art Institute of Chicago
1976 *Biennale*, Venice
1978 *Performance Art Festival*, Vienna
1981 *Italians and American Italians*, Crown Point Gallery, Oakland, California
1982 *Metaphor: New Projects by Contemporary Sculptors*, Hirshhorn Museum, Washington D.C.
1985 *Promenades*, Parc Lullin, Genthod, Geneva
1987 *Concrete Crisis: Urban Images of the 80s*, Exit Art, New York

Collections:

Museum of Modern Art, New York; Los Angeles County Museum of Art, California; Musée National d'Art Moderne/Centre Georges Pompidou, Paris.

Publications:

By ACCONCI: books—*Four Book*, New York 1968; *Transference: Roget's Thesaurus*, New York 1969; *Notes Toward the Development of a Show*, Hamburg 1972; *Leap/Think/Rethink/Fall*, Dayton, Ohio 1979; Films—*3 Frame Studies*, 1970; *2 Inceptions*, *3 Adaption Studies*, 1970; *2 Clearance Studies*, 1970; *Openings*, 1970; *Hand and Mouth*, 1970; *Twin Cover Studies*, 1970; *4 Studies for a Meditation Chamber* 1970; *Three Relationship Studies*, 1970; *See-Through Rubbings*, 1970; *Applications*, 1970; *Watch*, 1971; *Second Hand*, 1971; *Control Room*, 1971; *Zone*, 1971; *Combination*, 1971; *Pickup*, 1971; *Storage*, 1971; *Waterways*, 1971; *Conversions 1, 2, 3*, 1971; *Training Ground*, 1971; *Trappings*, 1971; *Dress Up*, 1971; *Directions*, 1971; *Seedbed Transference Zone*, 1972; *Supply Room*, 1972; *Cross Fronts*, 1972; *Anchors*, 1972; *Reception Room*, 1972; *Air Time*, 1972; *My Reticence*, 1972; video—*Corrections*, 1970; *Pryings*, 1971; *Centers*, 1971; *Feelers*, 1971; *Claim*, 1971; *Passes*, 1971; *Association Area*, 1971; *Trials*, 1971; *Contacts*, 1971; *Pull*, 1971; *Sound Barrier*, 1971; *Waiting Room*, 1971; *Filles*, 1971; *Focal Points*, 1971; *2 Track*, 1971; *Eyespots*, 1971; *Sounding Board*, 1971; *Remote Control*, 1971; *Projections*, 1972; *Supply Room*, 1972; *Undertone*, 1973; *Face Off*, 1973; *Home Movies*, 1973; *Walk-Over*, 1973; *Theme Song*, 1973; *Full Circle*, 1973; *Stages*, 1973.

On ACCONCI: books—*Software*, exhibition catalogue, with introduction by Jack Burnham, New York 1970; *Conceptual Art* by Ursula Meyer, New York 1972; *Documenta 5*, exhibition catalogue, edited by Harald Szeemann and others, Kassel, West Germany 1972; *Pop Art et Cie* by Francois Pluchart, Paris 1972; *6 Years: The Dematerialization of the Art Object from 1966 to 1972* by Lucy R. Lippard, London and New York 1973; *Art and Image in Recent Art*, exhibition catalogue, with text by Anne Rorimer, Chicago 1974; *Senza Titolo* by Germano Celant, Milan 1974; *Il Corpo come Linguaggio* by Lea Vergine, Milan 1974; *Vito Acconci* by Mario Diacono, New York 1976; *Vito Acconci*, exhibition catalogue, with text and interview by Martin Kunz, Lucerne 1978; *Vito Acconci: A Retrospective 1969 to 1980* exhibition catalogue, with texts by John Hallmark Neff and Judith Russi Kirshner, Chicago 1980; *Machineworks: Vito Acconci, Alice Aycock, Dennis Oppenheim*, exhibition catalogue, with texts by Janet Kardon and Kay Larson, Philadelphia 1981; *Italians and American Italians: Etchings by Francisco Clemente, Jannis Klunellis, Italo Scanga, Tom Marioni, Vito Acconci*, exhibition catalogue, with an introduction by Kathan Brown, Oakland 1981; *Metaphor: New Projects by Contemporary Sculptors*, exhibition catalogue, with text by Howard N. Fox, Washington, D.C. 1982; *Vito Acconci: Domestic Trappings*, exhibition catalogue with essay by Ronald J. Onorato, La Jolla 1987.

For many artists in the 1960s who sought to evade the cul de sac of formalism and its concomitant obsession with the art object, the continued aesthetization of art became untenable. The institutions of painting and sculpture were surpassed by other forms of advanced art and especially by photography, which offered new possibilities for a generation who grew up surrounded by the imagery of television. The artist Vito Acconci both identified and defined the very terms of his art of the 1970s—his investigations of the self within the broad scope of conceptual art—in the photographic and cinematic medium of video.

The video projects Acconci produced in the late

Vito Acconci: Performance at *Aspects de l'Art Actuel*, Paris, 1973

1960s and early '70s sought to transpose the aesthetic and philosophical terms of Minimalism and Process Art, both explorations of self-referential, temporal, and phenomenological conditions. Similar to the temporal/physical passage from one state to another experienced in Process Art, video permitted the artist to further intensify a dismantling of the myth of the subject as something given and preconstructed.

Minimalism's disavowal of structural closure and the myths of universal meaning became for Acconci a positive, liberating force. In his full-length video *The Red Tapes,* 1976–77—a trilogy reflecting the full range of his social, political and semiotic concerns—the artist, in fact, perpetuates the '60s revolutionary spirit with just such a message: "Let's make the symbols our own." Challenging the origin of the work of art in memory and *a priori* assumptions, the temporal experience of Minimalism tended to decenter our perception of the object. Attempting to exceed that movement's primary interest in formal concerns, Acconci began to exploit the dominant Minimalist aesthetic—temporal manipulations and the concomitant loss of self—as analogous to the fractured nature of consciousness as it is reproduced in video. Despite the proliferation of cultural types immediately accessible during the media-oriented '60s, a period fascinated by social change, Acconci was aware that the cooption of the self by the political economy of late-capitalism would render hopeless any search for a "new" or fixed identity.

Mirroring the reflexive nature of consciousness, video's electronic feedback allowed both the artist and viewer to dialectically explore the self as object and subject. Such a process suggested the distinction experienced by the patient in psychoanalysis between a subjectivity experienced and the conceptual projection of the self as object. Acconci contrasted one's identity as felt with one's own seen/heard projection, for example, in *Air Time,* 1973, in which the artist faces a mirror and for 35 minutes engages his own reflection in a monologue. In *Centers,* 1971, in which the artist filmed himself pointing at the center of a television monitor for 20 minutes, Acconci moved toward a condition of self-enclosure in an effort to constitute or encapsulate a self—a particularly ironic exercise, during a cultural period of sexual and psychological openness, of disillusioning futility.

It was, however, this fundamental conjunction (and consequent diffusion) of the personal by a subsuming public "other" that connects Acconci's earlier video and performance work with his more recent furniture-like sculpture. Throughout most of the last two decades, he has transgressed convention, continually challenging our standards of normalcy by relentlessly blurring the categories (landscape, architecture, site) that define the spaces we live in. Acconci's strategy of representation, based on the pragmatics of language, hinges on the latter's arbitrariness. In order to combat the rigidity of our lives, Acconci's recent work increasingly has assumed the status of "play." The notion of play—with its irreverent collapse of convention and constant assertion of new rules—is manifest in many of the artist's recent fantasy-rooted works. Pieces such as *Garden Chair* [1986], *Bad Dream House* [1984] or *Sleeping Dog Couch* [1984] have permitted Acconci to create a deceptively simple fusion of form and content, one which is *engaging* rather than alienating.

—Mason Klein

ADAMI, Valerio (Romani).

Italian. Born in Bologna, 17 March 1935. Studied painting, under A. Funi, at the Accademia de Brera, Milan, 1951–54. Married Camilla Adami in 1962. Independent painter and graphic artist since 1955, working in Milan, 1955–61, in London, 1957, 1961–62, and in Arona, Italy, since 1961, and in Paris 1962, 1963, 1964. Agent: Galerie Lelong, 13 rue de Teheran, 75008 Paris. Address: Villa Cantoni, via San Carlo 56, 28041 Arona, Italy.

Individual Exhibitions:

1958	Galleria San Fedele, Milan
1959	Galleria del Naviglio, Milan
1960	Galerie Art Bremen, Bremen, West Germany
1961	Galleria L'Attico, Rome
	Salone Annunciata, Milan
1962	Institute of Contemporary Arts, London
1963	*Disegni e Parole,* Galleria del Naviglio, Milan
1964	Galleria del Cavallino, Venice
1965	Galeria Ad Libitum, Antwerp
	Galleria Schwarz/Studio Marconi, Milan
	Galleria L'Attico, Rome
1966	Galleria Il Punto, Turin
	Galerie Aujourd'hui, Brussels
	Galleria Schwarz/Studio Marconi, Milan
1967	Studio Marconi, Milan
	Galleria L'Attico, Rome
	Galerie Aujourd'hui, Brussels
	Galleria Schwarz/Studio Marconi, Milan
1968	Institute of Contemporary Art, Boston
	Deson Gallery, Chicago
	Fondacion Mendoza, Caracas
	Privacy, Galerie B. Mommaton, Paris

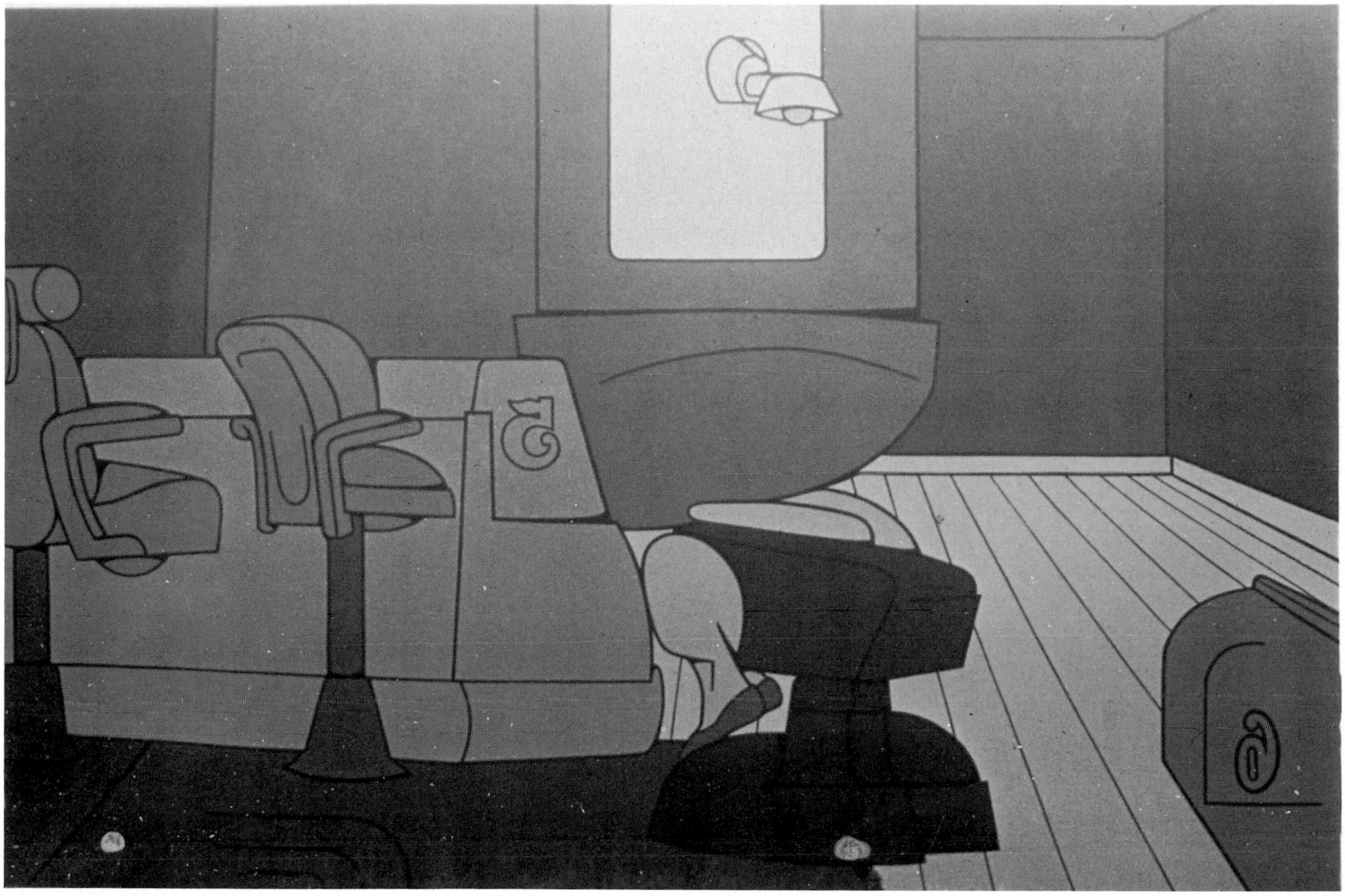

Valerio Adami: *Interno Pubblico*, 1969

Galerie Withofs, Brussels
Institute of Contemporary Arts, London
1969 Museo de Bellas Artes, Caracas
Galleria Schwarz, Milan
Studio Marconi, Milan
Galerie Withofs, Brussels
1970 Hansen Gallery, San Francisco
Musée d'Art Moderne de la Ville, Paris
Kunstverein, Ulm, West Germany
Galerie Maeght, Paris
62 Elsworthy Road, London
Galerie Wunsche, Bonn
Studio Marconi, Milan
1971 Museo de Bellas Artes, Caracas
1972 Galerie Schmela, Dusseldorf
Galerie Maeght, Zurich
Galleri Lowenadler, Stockholm
Galerie Maeght, Paris
Galerie Wunsche, Bonn
1973 Galerie Jacqueline Storme, Lille, France
Kunstverein, Hamburg
Galerie Maeght, Paris
Galerie Wunsche, Hamburg
1974 University of Wisconsin, Madison
1975 Bijou Galerie, Grenoble, France
Galerie Karl Flinker, Paris
Galerie Maeght, Paris
1976 Galerie Jacqueline Storme, Lille, France
Centre d'Arts Plastiques Contemporains, Bordeaux
Pinturas, Dibuixos, Aquarelles 1970–1975, Galeria Maeght, Barcelona
Galerie Maeght, Paris
Galerie Maeght, Zurich
1977 Musée Cantini, Marseilles
1978 Palais des Beaux-Arts, Charleroi, Belgium
Abbaye de Fontevraud, France
Galerie Maeght, Zurich
1980 Musée de Grenoble, France
1981 Galerie Maeght, Zurich
Judith Posner Gallery, Milwaukee, Wisconsin
1982 Lens Fine Art, Antwerp
Centre d'Animation Culturelle, Mulhouse, France
Galleria Stamparte, Bologna, Italy
1983 Galleria Giulia, Rome
Galerie Maeght, Paris
Fùji Television Gallery, Tokyo
Goldman Kraft Gallery, Chicago
1984 Marisa del Re Gallery, New York
Galeria Alencon, Madrid
Museo de Bellas Artes de Asturias, Oviedo, Spain
1985 Musée de la Ville, Vitry, France
Galerie Il Punto, Monte Carlo
Centre Georges Pompidou, Paris
Palazzo Reale, Milan
Galerie Les Cordeliers, Chateauroux, France
Galerie A.C.A.P., Le Touquet, France

Selected Group Exhibitions:

1956 *Premio Marzotto,* Milan
1959 *Possibilita di Relazione,* Galleria L'Attico, Rome
1960 *Young Italian Painters,* Museum of Kamakura, Japan
1962 *Italian New Figurative Painters,* Piccadilly Gallery, London
1969 *Maler und Modell,* Staatliche Kunsthalle, Baden-Baden, West Germany
1971 *Radical Realists,* D. M. Gallery, London
1977 *La Traccia del Racconto,* Villa Comunale Ormond, Sanremo, Italy
1982 *Arte Italiana 1960–82,* Hayward Gallery, London
1983 *Bonjour Monsieur Manet,* Centre Georges Pompidou, Paris
1985 *Il Cinema,* Galleria Gastaldelli, Milan

Collections:

Galleria d'Arte Moderna, Milan; Musée National d'Art Moderne, Paris; Kunstverein, Ulm, West Germany; Museo de Bellas Artes, Caracas; Rhode Island School of Design, Providence.

Publications:

By ADAMI: book—*Dix Lecons sur le Reich,* with Helmut Heissenbuttel, Munich and Paris 1974; film—*Vacances dans le Desert,* with Giancarlo Adami, 1970; record—*Concerto per un quadro di Adami,* with Henry Martin, 1970.

On ADAMI: books—*Valerio Adami: disegni e parole,* exhibition catalogue, with text by Enrico Crispolti, Milan 1963; *Le Pop Art* by Enrico Crispolti, Milan 1966; *Painting in the 20th Century* by Werner Haftmann, New York 1967; *Art of Our Time* by Will Grohmann, London 1967; *Pop Art* by Lucy R. Lippard, London 1967; *Righe per Adami* by Carlos Fuentes, Venice 1968; *Adami: Privacy,* exhibition catalogue, with text by Gerald Gassiot-Talabot and Henry Martin, Paris 1968; *Adami,* exhibition catalogue, with text by Carlos Franqui, Milan 1969; *Adami,* exhibition catalogue, with texts by Pierre Gaudibert, Henry Martin, Carlos Fuentes and others, Paris 1970; *Art Without Boundaries 1950–1970,* edited by Gerald Wood, Philip Thompson and John Williams, London 1972; *Valerio Adami,* exhibition catalogue, with texts by Hans Gerd Tuchel, Castor Seibel and Jacques Dupin, Hamburg 1973; *Adami* by Hubert Damisch and Henry Martin, Paris 1974; *Adami: pinturas, dibuixos, aquarelles 1970–1975,* exhibition catalogue, with text by Xavier Rubert de Ventos, Barcelona 1976; *Valerio Adami,* exhibition catalogue, with text by Nicolas and Elena Calas, Charleroi, Belgium 1978; *Valerio Adami,* exhibition catalogue, with text by Italo Calvino, Zurich 1981; *Valerio Adami,* exhibition catalogue, with text by Pietro Bonfiglioli, Bologna 1982; *Adami, presence contemporaine,* exhibition catalogue with texts by Nicolas and Elena Calas, Marc Le Bot and others, Aix-en-Provence, France 1984.

Arturo Schwarz of Milan lists Valerio Adami as one of the top International Avant-garde. He is certainly crisp in the Pop Art sense of the world, but he is also blessed with a tight ingredient of irony which slots comfortably into his unusual dislocated imagery. His flat colours vary between primaries and interesting tints, and generally every colour has a black edge to it.

Adami, armed with his personal style, is able to make wry comments upon sex and eroticism, intellectualism, psychology, social conditions, and art itself (as for instance in the "Surrealist Map of the World" 1972). What change there has been in his works has been a gradual drift from curious abstractions to a more formal figuration which began to take place in the late 1960's. Yet although the figuration may become steadily more and more recognizable to the unsophisticated eye, the colours continue their wayward direction; the woodwork or metal of a chair can be white, but the upholstery is straight green, the cushion red. It all sounds normal enough, but the talent of Adami transforms the three into the abstract colours of a flag or a trademark. These colours are bright, never gaudy; their message is immediate, magnetic.

In very different moods this painter has things in common with two such disparate artists as Jean-Pierre Raynaud and Tom Wesselmann. In his jigsaw-style interiors he sometimes introduces bourgeois fixtures that Raynaud might employ as adjuncts for his "objects" (one thinks of the lavatory—impersonalised by Raynaud, but sharply ludicrous in an Adami painting) or that Wesselman interpolates into his visions of "the American way-of-life." Of course the climates in the works of all three artists are entirely different but, just because their imagery can overlap at times, they can, however disconnected, be seen to belong to their own special era.

—Sheldon Williams

AFRICANO, Nicholas.

American. Born in Kankakee, Illinois, in 1948. Studied at Illinois State University, B.A. in English literature 1970, M.A. in painting, 1974, M.F.A. in painting 1975. Agent: Holly Solomon Gallery, New York. Address: c/o Holly Solomon Gallery, 724 Fifth Avenue, New York, New York 10019, U.S.A.

Individual Exhibitions:

1976 University of Illinois, Urbana
Nancy Lurie Gallery, Chicago
1977 Sheldon Memorial Art Gallery, University of Nebraska, Lincoln
Daddy's Old, Holly Solomon Gallery, New York
New Concepts Gallery, University of Iowa, Iowa City
Insulin, Holly Solomon Gallery, New York
University of Rhode Island, Kingston
Personal Information, Nancy Lurie Gallery, Chicago
1978 *The Man Who Lived in a Hat,* Walker Art Center, Minneapolis
1979 *The Battered Woman,* Holly Solomon Gallery, New York
Battered Woman Series, Mayor Gallery, London
Asher/Faure Gallery, Los Angeles
Galerie Farideh Cadot, Paris
1980 Holly Solomon Gallery, New York
Galerie 't Venster, Rotterdam
1981 *The Girl of the Golden West,* Holly Solomon Gallery, New York
The Girl of the Golden West, Middendorf/Lane Gallery, Washington, D.C.
The Girl of the Golden West, Asher/Faure Gallery, Los Angeles
1982 *The Girl of the Golden West,* Dart Gallery, Chicago
The Girl of the Golden West, Greenberg Gallery, St. Louis
1983 Asher/Faure Gallery, Los Angeles
1984 North Carolina Museum of Art, Raleigh

Nicholas Africano: ***A Passionate Man*, 1980**

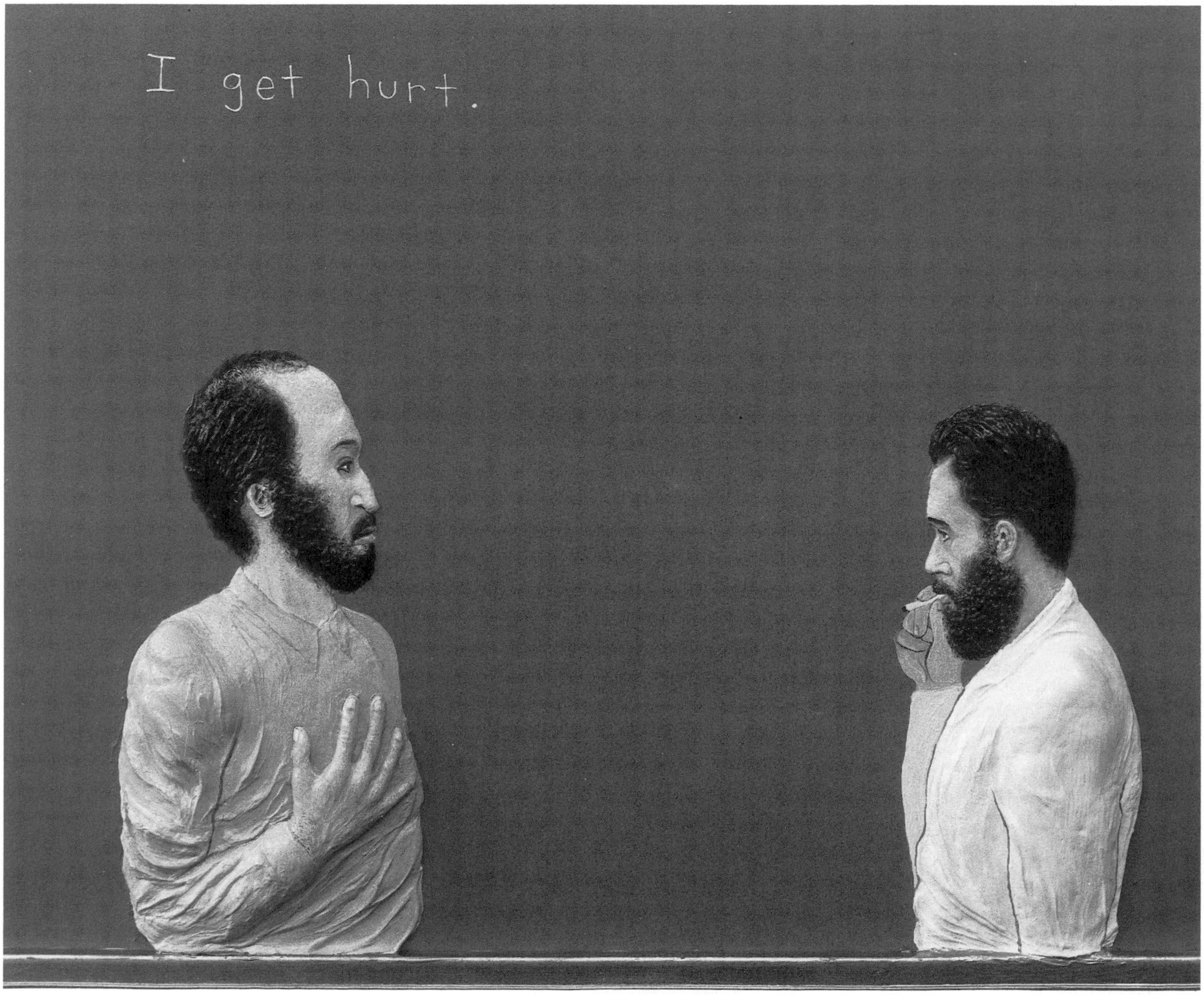

Selected Group Exhibitions:

1976 *Chicago Connection,* E. B. Crocker Gallery, Sacramento, California
1977 *American Painting '75, '76, '77,* Sarah Lawrence College, Bronxville, New York (travelled to the Museum of the American Foundation for the Arts, Miami, and the Contemporary Arts Center, Cincinnati, Ohio)
1978 *Narration,* Institute of Contemporary Art, Boston
1979 *New Image Painting,* Whitney Museum, New York
American Portraits of the 60's and 70's, Aspen Center for the Visual Arts, Colorado
1980 *The Pluralist Decade,* at the *Biennale,* Venice (toured Europe, 1980–81)
Chicago/Chicago, Contemporary Arts Center, Cincinnati, Ohio
1981 *Contemporary Drawings in Search of an Image,* University of California Art Museum, Santa Barbara
1982 *New York Now,* Kestner-Gesellschaft, Hannover
1984 *The Human Condition,* San Francisco Museum of Modern Art

Publications:

On AFRICANO: book—*Nicholas Africano: Paintings 1976–1983,* exhibition catalogue with essay by Mitchell D. Kahan, Raleigh 1983; articles—"Nicholas Africano" by Peter Frank in *The Village Voice* (New York), 7 November 1977; "Nicholas Africano" by Harold Olejarz in *Arts Magazine* (New York), April 1979; "Nicholas Africano: Responsible Relevance" by Dupuy Reed in *Arts Magazine* (New York), June 1979; "Nicholas Africano's Primitivism" by Howard Singerman in *Artweek* (Oakland, California), 29 September 1979; "New York, New York: Nicholas Africano" by Valentin Tatransky in *Flash Art* (Milan), March/April 1979; "Rodney Ripps and Nicholas Africano" by John Russell in the *New York Times,* 16 May 1980; "Art (Nicholas Africano/Rodney Ripps)" by Kay Larson in *The Village Voice* (New York), 26 May 1980; "Nicholas Africano Parables" by Joan Hugo in *Artweek* (Oakland, California), 16 May 1981.

Nicholas Africano places one or two tiny figures, molded in lumpy bas-relief, close to center in large monochrome fields or sometimes directly on the wall. His pictorial methodology makes us draw closer to focus in on the mini-people who are unattractively lumpy and primitivizing and marked by a cartoony flavor relating them with the Chicago-based group "The Hairy Who," particularly with Jim Nutt's bizarre and theatrical figures.

Africano's kind of "knowing" naiveté and true grit encourages an attitude of uncomfortable empathy toward his intimately scaled object of attention, who is characteristically poised during a moment of tension, facing some basic psychological state with tentative indecision. The ambiguously portrayed drama borders on the narrative but is never quite elaborated in specific terms. Trained as a writer, Africano wants to evade the formal element and concentrate on evoking meaning. The pictorial elements, however, are used quite effectively to lead to underlying content. Africano's uses of proportion and location place the figure at an introspective removal from the world at large, and his use of densely modeled form lends his figures a sense of physicality in their vulnerability. The primitivizing quality lies somewhere in between Africano's regard for the Italian primitives and for the cartoonist's satire. He starts, in fact, with a series of sketches like the frames of the cartoon format.

During the late 1970's, Africano produced a number of works in the autobiographical vein, such as "Nicholas Waiting" (1976, oil, acrylic, wax, linoleum shelf), which concentrated on the bearded figure of the artist himself. His 1978 series, "Battered Woman," moves away from the autobiographical, coming closer to a narrative of social implications. In a series of 10 canvases, Africano portrays the dilemmas faced by the "battered woman" in question, who is going through a set of psycho-sociological situations with an aura of dread understandable to any sympathetic viewer. The fifth in the series, "The Door," exemplifies Africano at his more effective moments. The miniaturized victim stands facing a simply rendered door, leading to the unknown, whether within or without. The moment of poignant vulnerability is captured with a rugged sensitivity which avoids sentimental melodrama successfully, though precariously.

Africano is creating humane stage settings of a contemporary tragi-comic order, locating himself on the borderline between the real and the surreal and on the fragile tightrope which aims at avoiding the literally illusionistic while realistically evoking the basic alienation felt by the young in today's society, whether they be artists or not. His is a youthful, quirky expression, and it remains to be seen how well it will serve in his future development.

—Barbara Cavaliere

AFRO (Basaldella).

Italian. Born in Udine, 4 March 1912. Educated in Florence and Venice. Served in Italian Army, 1933–34, 1940–44. Independent artist, Milan, 1930–33, 1935–36, in Rome, 1936–40, 1945–76: associated with new generation of painters, including Birolli and Morlotti, Milan, 1930–36; worked with sculptor Arturo Martini, 1932; member, Gruppo degli Otto artists' group, Rome, 1952. Guest Lecturer, Mills College, Oakland, California, 1958. Recipient: Regional Grand Prize for Painting, Udine, 1929; Prize, 1952, 1954, and Grand Prize, 1956, *Biennale,* Venice; International Painting Prize, *Bienal,* Sao Paulo, 1955. *Died* (in Zurich) *24 July 1976.*

Individual Exhibitions:

1932 Galleria del Milione, Milan
1936 Galleria La Cometa, Rome
1940 Galleria Mediterranea, Palermo
1942 Galleria Roma, Rome
1944 Galleria del Sindicato Belle Arti, Udine
1946 Galleria dello Zodiaco, Rome
Galleria Lo Scorpione, Trieste
1947 Galleria Il Camino, Milan
1948 Galleria La Saletta, Modena
Galleria dell'Obelisco, Rome
1950 Catherine Viviano Gallery, New York
Galleria del Milione, Milan
1951 Studio d'Arte Palma, Rome
1952 Catherine Viviano Gallery, New York
1953 Galleria dell'Obelisco, Rome
1955 Catherine Viviano Gallery, New York
Galleria dell'Obelisco, Rome
1956 Italian Pavilion, at the *Biennale,* Venice
1957 Catherine Viviano Gallery, New York
1959 Catherine Viviano Gallery, New York
1960 Galleria La Tartaruga, Rome
Galleria Schneider, Rome
Italian Pavilion, at the *Biennale,* Venice
Catherine Viviano Gallery, New York
Massachusetts Institute of Technology, Cambridge
1961 Galleria Blu, Milan
Galerie de France, Paris
1962 Galleria Toninelli, Milan
AMIT Gallery, Boston
1963 Catherine Viviano Gallery, New York
1964 Galerie im Erker, St. Gallen, Switzerland
Catherine Viviano Gallery, New York
1965 Galerie Rabner, Lucerne
Galerie Ricke, Kassel, West Germany
Galerie Günther Franke, Munich
Galleria La Medusa, Rome
1966 University of South Florida, Tampa
1967 Palazzina Vitelli, Cittá di Castello, Italy
1968 Galleria Toninelli, Milan
Catherine Viviano Gallery, New York
Galleria Michaud, Florence
Galleria Narciso, Turin
1969 Nationalgalerie, West Berlin
Kunstverein, Darmstadt
Galleria Civca d'Arte Moderna, Ferrara, Italy
1970 Centro Culturale Nuove Frontiere, Gaviarate, Italy
Galleria D4, Alessandria, Italy
Galleria Moretto, Brescia, Italy
Galleria Forni, Bologna
1973 Galleria Editalia, Rome
1974 Galleria del Milione, Milan
1975 Galleria 2RC, Rome
1978 Galleria Nazionale d'Arte Moderna, Rome (retrospective; travelled to the Villa Manin di Passariano, Udine)
1981 *Retrospektive 1912–1976,* Staatsgalerie Moderner Kunst, Munich (travelled to the Wilhelm-Hack-Museum, Ludwigshafen, West Germany)
1987 Palazzo Rosari Spada, Spoleto, Italy

Selected Group Exhibitions:

1936 *Quadriennale di Roma,* Galleria d'Arte Moderna, Rome
1949 *Afro/Cagli/Guttuso/Morlotti/Pizzinato,* Catherine Viviano Gallery, New York
1951 *Exhibition of Italian Art,* Museum of Modern Art, New York
1952 *Biennale,* Venice (and 1954)
1953 *Bienal,* Sao Paulo (and 1955)
1955 *The New Decade,* Museum of Modern Art, New York
1959 *Carnegie International,* Carnegie Institute, Pittsburgh
1971 *New Italian Art 1953–1971,* Walker Art Gallery, Liverpool

Collections:

Galleria Nazionale d'Arte Moderna, Rome; Museo Civico, Turin; Nationalgalerie, West Berlin; Musée des Beaux-Arts, La Chaux de Fonds, Switzerland; Tate Gallery, London; Museum of Modern Art, New York; Guggenheim Museum, New York; Museum of Fine Arts, Boston; Los Angeles County Museum of Art; Museum of Fine Arts, Montreal, Quebec.

Publications:

On AFRO: books—*Afro,* exhibition catalogue, with text by L. de Libero, Rome 1946; *Afro,* exhibition catalogue, with text by Luca Venturi, New York 1955; *Afro,* exhibition catalogue, with text by Marco Valescchi, Milan 1961; *Afro,* exhibition catalogue, with text by Cesare Brandi, New York 1963; *Afro,* exhibition catalogue, with text by Hans Platte, Munich 1965; *Afro,* exhibition catalogue, with text by Maurizio Calvesi, Rome 1965; *Afro,* exhibition catalogue, with text by Lamberto Vitali, Milan 1968; *Afro,* exhibition catalogue, with text by Werner Haftmann, and Bernd Krimmel, West Berlin 1969; *Afro,* exhibition catalogue, by Hans G. Sperlich and Bernd Krimmel, Darmstadt 1969; *New Italian Art 1953–1971,* exhibition catalogue, with text by Giovanni Caradente, Liverpool 1971; *Afro,* exhibition catalogue, with text by Cesare Brandi, Rome 1973; *Afro,* by Cesare Brandi, Rome 1977; *Afro,* exhibition catalogue with text by B. Mantura, Rome 1978; *Afro: Retrospektive 1912–1976,* exhibition catalogue, with texts by Guido Ballo, and Carla Schulz-Hoffmann, Munich 1981; *Afro,* by Alessandra Borgogelli, Milan 1986.

After completing his artistic studies in Venice, Afro moved to Rome in 1933 where he visited Corrado Cagli and the group known as the Roman School. Two years later, he participated in the Rome Quadriennale, the capital's most important public show. Included in this exhibition were the figurative paintings that were characteristic of Afro's work up to the outbreak of World War II. In 1937 he had his first one-man show at the Galleria La Cometa, which had taken on the best of the young artists.

Afro's work of the late 1930s had become luminous and baroque, as can be seen in a still life of 1937 where the picture is enriched by a surreal use of carnival masks. He frequently used such motifs to explore problems of tonality. The early 1940s brought

his first expressionist works; feeling now predominated over formal or decorative qualities, expressive pathos becoming the primary mood of the picture, as Afro profoundly felt the horror of war.

In 1944 he began his first neo-cubist works. With the end of a world conflict, a new cultural ferment swept through Italian art. Artists working with abstraction offered the possibility of international dialogue; Afro meanwhile continued exhibiting in several European Countries and in the United States while developing a new approach. In this, the form and colour are still those of his neo-cubist phase, but the composition is decidedly different. The style which was to give Afro his international status was already here in embryo. In 1952 he exhibited with the Gruppo degli Otto. The art critic and historian Lionello Venturi, co-ordinator of the group, wrote of their work: "They have adopted a pictorial language which emerges from those traditions of the period around 1910, incorporating the ideas of the cubists, expressionists and abstract artists."

Afro also took part in the show *Five Italian Painters* at the Catherine Viviano Gallery in New York in 1952, with Cagli, Guttuso, Morlotti and Pizzinato. Contact with the cultural ambiance of New York was a positive influence, leading to a series of works strongly inspired by American abstract expressionism. These works bear a strong resemblance to those of Arshile Gorky, while maintaining Afro's characteristic use of vibrant and transparent colour. For example, *Balletto*, a work of 1953, with its vertical organization arrangement of the motifs, creates a line which constructs the image and its range of blue tones. These elements are maintained unaltered throughout Afro's most extreme period of expressionism when all naturalistic references had been abandoned.

By the end of the 1960s, Afro had developed his particular style of abstraction by reducing the composition to a colossal smudge of saturated hues. The colour is now sombre, expressing the dark sentiment of the night, of the end of existence.

Afro died in Zurich in 1976.

—Roberto Lambarelli

AGAM, Yaacov.

Israeli. Born Jacob (Yaacov) Gipstein in Rishon Letzion, Palestine, now Israel, 11 May 1928; adopted name "Agam," Paris, 1953. Studied art at the Bezalel School, Jerusalem, 1947–48; architecture, under Siegfrid Giedion, at the Kunstgewerbeschule, Zurich, 1949; and art at the Atelier d'Art Abstrait, Paris, 1951. Married Clila Agam in 1956; children: Ron, Orram and Orrit. Independent artist, in Paris, since 1951; first transformable paintings, 1951; first polyphonic paintings, 1953; first sound paintings, 1961; stainless steel sculptures, from 1968. Guest Instructor, Illinois Institute of Technology, Chicago, 1961; Visiting Lecturer, Harvard University, Cambridge, Massachusetts 1968. Recipient: Painting Prize, *International Festival of Painting*, Cagnes-sur-Mer, France 1970. Agent: Galerie Denise René, 124 rue La Boetie, 75008 Paris. Address: 45 rue Castagnary, 75015 Paris, France.

Individual Exhibitions:

1953 Galerie Craven, Paris
1954 Galerie Furstenberg, Paris
1955 Doris Meltzer Gallery, New York
Galerie Denise René, Paris (with Soto and Abner)
1956 Galerie Denise René, Paris
1958 Galerie Aujourd'hui, Brussels
Tel-Aviv Museum
Galerie Denise René, Paris
1959 *Transformable Painting/Painting in Movement*, Drian Gallery, London
Galerie Suzanne Bollag, Zurich
Städtisches Museum, Leverkusen, West Germany
1962 *Peinture Transformable, Peinture Polyphonique, Peinture et Mouvement*, Galerie Suzanne Bollag, Zurich
1966 Marlborough-Gerson Gallery, New York
1969 Whitechapel Art Gallery, London (with Lifshitz and Zaritzky)
1971 *Transformables*, Galerie Denise René, New York
1972 Musée d'Art Moderne, Paris (travelled to the Stedelijk Museum, Amsterdam; Städtisches Museum, Dusseldorf; and the Tel-Aviv Museum, 1972–73)
1975 *Selected Suites*, Jewish Museum, New York
1980 Guggenheim Museum, New York

Selected Group Exhibitions:

1954 *Salon des Réalités Nouvelles*, Musée d'Art Moderne, Paris
1958 *Carnegie International*, Carnegie Institute, Pittsburgh
1961 *Bewogen Beweging*, Stedelijk Museum, Amsterdam
1963 *7th Bienal*, Sao Paulo
1965 *The Responsive Eye*, Museum of Modern Art, New York
1967 *Art and Movement*, National Gallery of Canada, Ottawa (toured Canada)
1970 *International Festival of Painting*, Cagnes-sur-Mer, France
1972 *12 Ans d'Art Contemporain en France*, Grand Palais, Paris
1973 *The Non-Objective World 1914–1955*, Annely Juda Fine Art, London (travelled to the University of Texas, Austin)

Collections:

Centre Georges Pompidou, Paris; Kaiser-Wilhelm-Museum, Krefeld, West Germany; Kunstmuseum, Dusseldorf; Julliard School, Lincoln Center, New York.

Publications:

By AGAM: films—*Recherches et Inventions*, with I. Mambush, 1956; *Le Desert Chante, Microsalon*, with I. Mambush, 1957.

On AGAM: books—*Agam: Transformable Painting/Painting in Movement*, exhibition catalogue, with texts by Michel Ragon and Eugene Kolb, London 1959; *Yaacov Agam: Peinture Transformable, Peinture Polyphonique, Peinture et Mouvement*, exhibition folder, with text by Siegfried Giedion, Zurich 1962; *Yaacov Agam* by Jasia Reichardt, London 1966; *Yaacov Agam*, exhibition catalogue, with texts by Haim Gamzu and Jasia Reichardt, New York 1966; *Neue Dimensionen der Plastik* by Udo Kultermann, Tübingen 1967; *New Tendencies in Art* by Aldo Pellegrini, London 1967; *Beyond Modern Sculpture* by Jack Burnham, New York 1968; *Origins and Development of Kinetic Art* by Frank Popper, London and New York 1968; *Movements in Art since 1945* by Edward Lucie Smith, London 1969; *Op Art* by Cyril Barrett, London 1969; *Yaacov Agam: Transformables*, exhibition catalogue, with texts by Haim Gamzu and Jean-Jacques Leveque, New York 1971; *Agam*, exhibition catalogue, with texts by Jean Leymarie, Blaise Gautier, Germain Viatte and others, Paris 1972; *Yaacov Agam: Peintures, Sculptures* exhibition catalogue with text by Haim Gamzu, Tel-Aviv 1973; *Yaacov Agam: Selected Suites*, exhibition catalogue, with text by Paul Kaniel, New York 1975; *Agam* by Frank Popper, New York 1976, 1980; *Yaacov Agam* by Günter Metken, London 1977.

Agam is one of the pioneers of Kinetic Art and in particular of the trend which is concerned with the participation of the spectator. Having begun with paintings, reliefs, play objects and sculptures, he then experimented with the forces of light, air, water and fire before reaching a stage where his works are developed on the environmental scale, sometimes with the aid of the newest technological means.

But it is impossible to dissociate Agam's plastic achievements from the metaphysical implications of his research, his religious and cosmological beliefs. Agam's search for the perceptible absence of the image, his demonstration of the irreversibility of time, and the simultaneity of significant happenings which can be found in most of his works have a biblical and epistemological origin.

All of Agam's works are "transformable," since a time sequence is implicit in their structure. But this term is reserved by the artist himself for works in which the basis of transformation lies in the possibility of modifying the pictorial structure, a research begun back in the early 1950s which has given rise to a great number of statements ranging from "polyphonic" pictures destined for the interior or the exterior of private dwellings to environmental installations like the "Salon de l'Elysée" in Paris, "Agam Space" at the Forum in Leverkusen or the "Aenaitral Tower" and the "Panoramagam" created for the artist's one-man show at the Guggenheim Museum in New York in 1980. All these transformable pictorial statements imply the spectator's participation since their chromatic structures are revealed only through his movements.

However, the movable structures and play objects of the early 50s which preceded the Tactile works and which were followed by a great variety of small-and large-scale metal sculptures provoked a still more complete participation of the spectator who was induced to freely exercise his creative powers.

The multiplicity of the pursuits of Agam and the great diversity of his works can only be measured if one also mentions his graphic works and inventions, ranging from the single print to the holograph by way of multigraphs, polymorph graphics, interspaceographs, environmental graphics, prismographics, and video graphics. Agam's other achievements include constructions with artificial light, water-fire sculptures, monumental mixed media works such as the Fountain at the Défence complex near Paris, and incursions into other domains like the theatre as well as many technological experiments and pedagogical projects.

All these endeavours show clearly the tendency of Agam's thought: his entirely optimistic and dynamic interpretation and celebration of the force of life in art and his total faith in the participation of the public in the creative process.

—Frank Popper

AGNETTI, Vincenzo.

Italian. Born in Milan, 14 September 1926. Studied at the Academy of Dramatic Art, Milan; Liceo Artistico, Accademia di Brera, Milan. Married Bruna Soletti in 1949 (divorced); daughter: Germana. Worked as actor, Piccolo Teatro, Milan, 1949–51. Concentrated on "informal painting," Milan, 1953–61; settled in Buenos Aires, 1961–67; returned to Milan, 1967–81; spent year in Rome, 1969–70; visited New York frequently, 1977–81. Lecturer in Art, Accademia di Brera, Milan; Guest Lecturer, in Art and Architecture, Universities of Rome, Milan and New York, 1974–81. Recipient: Premio Pascali, Rome, 1972. Agent: Bruna Soletti, Piazza S. Alesandro, 6 Milan. *Died* (in Milan) *1 September 1981.*

Individual Exhibitions:

1967 Palazzo dei Diamanti, Ferrara, Italy
1968 Galleria Visualità, Milan
1971 Galleria La Tartaruga, Rome
1972 Galleria Lambert, Milan
Galleria Martano, Turin
Galleria Schema, Florence
Galleria Toselli, Milan

Vincenzo Agnetti: ***Monolog in an Empty Theatre*****, 1973**

1973 Galerie Annemarie Verna, Zurich
Galleria Rumma, Naples
San Fedele Teatro, Milan
Galleria Marilena Bonomo, Bari, Italy
Galleria Nazionale d'Arte Moderna, Rome
Galleria Forma, Genoa
1974 Galleria Seconda Scala, Rome
Bolaffi Arte, Turin
Galleria Alessandra Castelli, Bergamo, Italy
Museum am Ostwall, Dortmund, West Germany
Galleria Allesandra Castelli, Milan
1975 Ronald Feldman Fine Arts, New York
Studio Canaviello, Rome
Sonnabend Galerie, Paris
Art in Progress, Munich
1976 Galleria La Tartaruga, Rome
Mercato del Sale, Milan
1977 Israel Museum, Jerusalem
Studio Guiliana de Crescenzo, Rome
Galleria Civica d'Arte Moderna, Castello di Portofino, Italy
1978 Ronald Feldman Fine Arts, New York
Galerie Wintersberg, Cologne
Arta Studio, Milan
1979 Ronald Feldman Fine Arts, New York
Palazzo Grassi, Venice
1980 Ronald Feldman Fine Arts, New York
Galleria Toselli, Milan
Padiglione d'Arte Contemporanea, Milan
1981 Galleria Bruna Soletti, Milan
1982 Galleria Comunale d'Arte Moderna, Bologna
Galleria Il Luogo di Gauss, Milan

Selected Group Exhibitions:

1969 *Principia*, Historical Archives, Biennale, Venice
1970 *Vitality of the Negative*, Palazzo delle Esposizione, Rome
1972 *Documenta 5*, Kassel, West Germany
1973 *Bienal*, Sao Paulo
1976 *Artists and Photograph*, Israel Museum, Jerusalem
1986 *Aspects of Italian Art 1960–85*, Kunstverein, Frankfurt

Collections:

Galleria Nazionale d'Arte Moderna, Rome; Galleria d'Arte Moderna, Parma, Italy; Raccolte Civiche d'Arte, Milan; Galleria d'Arte Moderna, Livorno, Italy; Galleria d'Arte Moderna, Cagliari, Italy.

Publications:

By AGNETTI: books—*Intorno alla*, Milan 1967; *Obsoleto*, Milan 1967; *Rigoree Utopia*, Milan 1968; *Tesi*, Milan 1968; *Ciclostile*, Milan 1969; *Spazio perduto e Spazio Costruito*, Marcerata, Italy 1972; *Progetto per un Amieto Politico*, Genoa 1973; *Tradotto azzerato presentato*, Milan 1974; *Image of an Exhibition*, Milan and New York 1974; *Machiavelli 30*, Milan 1978; *Lettre dal Deserto*, Milan 1981; articles—"Intervento" in *Tavole di Accertamento* by Piero Manzoni, Milan 1958; "Intervento" in *Linea* by Piero Manzoni, Milan 1959; "Non commettere atti Impuri" in *Azimuth* (Milan), 1959; "Indulgentia" in *Nuova Corrente* (Milan), March 1968; "Copia dal Vero Numero Primo" in *Domus* (Milan), nos. 495–498, 1971; "Utopia" in *Ricerca Contemporanea* (Milan), nos. 1–3, 1971; "High Fidelity" in *Documenta 5*, exhibition catalogue, Kassel, West Germany 1972; interview, with Mario Peruzzi, in *Corriere della Sera* (Milan), February 1972; video tapes—*Vobulazione e Bioloquenza: NEG*, with G. Colombo, 1970; *Documentario No. 2*, Centro Diffusione Grafica, Florence 1973; *Machiavelli 30*, with Licitra, Roselli and Pagano, 1978.

On AGNETTI: books—*Manzoni* by Germano Celant, Rome 1971; *Territorio Magico* by Achille Bonita Oliva, Florence 1972; articles—by Tommaso Trini and Pierre Restany in *Domus* (Milan), February 1973; "The Why of Things and Gestures" by Jane Bell in *Arts Magazine* (New York), October 1974; "Arte e Critica dopo l'Avanguardia" by Maurizio Calvesi in *Corriere della Sera* (Milan), February 1975; "Torniami alle Armi" by Pierre Restany in *Vincenzo Agnetti*, exhibition catalogue, Bologna 1982.

Milanese conceptual artist Vincenzo Agnetti emerged from a thoroughly European tradition, that which finds its roots in the image of the "Renaissance Man." Agnetti's studies in film, theater, philosophy, and applied engineering not only weave in and out of his work as esoteric references, but also serve as a solid foundation for his complex *oeuvre*, both visual and linguistic. This "intervention" (i.e., conscious interdisciplinary approach to an entire system) was from the beginning crucial to his work, although in no way can he be dismissed as another "multimedia" artist. Only by understanding this precept can the work be at all accessible.

There are certain obvious parallels to other artists using the conceptual mode; like *Art-Language*, Agnetti used verbal structures; like Hanna Darboven, he based a good deal of his work on numerical anti-systems; and, like Beuys, whom he most closely resembles, he used the tape-recorded dialogue format. But he attempted to carry out the conceptual premise further still, away from tautologies and freedom from (or negation of) content. In his 1975 New York exhibition he demonstrated post-Duchampian irony combined with a serious investigation of perceptual distortions, primarily of Time and Space. His work is as complex, although less formal and more free-wheeling, as that of his conceptual colleagues. What concerns him, in such works as "Herewith I Transmit a 30-Minute Tape Recording," "Architecture Translated for all the Peoples of the World," and "1870–1974," is a quest for anti-meaning, a meaning which transcends that of pure gesture, into a fundamentally eccentric world of paradox and imaginative constructs. The disciplines that he chose (whether electronic, photographic, or apparently mathematical) became catalytic tools, replacing, as he said himself, "the how it is done" by "the why it is done." Apparently analytic in method, Agnetti's work is not, in fact, analytic in intent. It differs also from other conceptual work in the fact that it is not hermetic; it is not only unselfconscious, but rarely self-absorbed. What concerned him is the *behavior* of phenomena and mental processes themselves.

Much of the value in Agnetti's investigations, perhaps best exemplified by "A's Median Age," a "translation" of a woman's face taken from photographs from different stages of her life culminating in a composite, very nearly ideational construct, lies in his critical and even admittedly prejudiced approach to his subjects. The work is in the nature of speculation, as a search for conclusions, even if he would occasionally perform an entirely unexpected about-face and negate those same conclusions; this method is used to great effect in his "Architecture Translated for all the Peoples in the World," in which his final conclusion (after an impeccably, apparently inevitably reached solution) negates his initial premise.

Agnetti's *oeuvre* is thus a combination of rigorous but potentially pliable thought and an intuitively formal elegance, concerned with the whole culture, and not simply with the strictly visual arts. As he wrote in 1974, "I am only an intuitive creator of signs who makes paintings out of philosophy by searching out shape and design in the dialogue, by looking for forms in the culture that has crystallized our common experience." It is this common experience, or what Henry Martin has termed the "*universalization* of culture and experience," that underscores the importance of Agnetti's ironic speculations.

—Jane Bell

ALBERS, Josef.

American. Born in Bottrop, Westphalia, Germany, 19 March 1888; emigrated to the United States, 1935; naturalized, 1939. Educated at Teachers College, Buren, Germany, 1905–08; studied at the Königliche Kunstschule, Berlin, 1913–15 (qualified as art teacher, 1915); Kunstgewerbeschule, Essen, 1916–19; Kunstakademie, Munich, 1919–20; Bauhaus, Weimar, 1920–23. Married Anni Fleischmann in 1925. Taught in public schools in Bottrop, 1908–13 and 1915–19; organized glass workshop and designed stained glass windows and developed one-pane glass paintings at the Bauhaus, Weimar, 1922, and conducted course in design, at the invitation of Gropius, 1923, then became Lecturer, 1923–25, Professor, 1925–33, Assistant Director, 1930, and Director of the Furniture Workshop, at the Bauhaus, Weimar, Dessau and Berlin (developed sandblasted glass painting, and designed glass, metal and wood furniture containers, Dessau, 1926). Lecturer, International Congress for Art Education, Prague, 1928; Chairman, Art Department, Black Mountain College, Beria, North Carolina, 1933–49; Head of the Art School, 1950– 58, and Visiting Professor, 1958–60, Yale University, New Haven, Connecticut (also developed special teaching methods, for basic design, drawing and color, Yale Art School, during the 1960's). Recipient: William A. Clark Prize, Corcoran Gallery, Washington, D.C., 1954; Ada S. Garrett Prize, Art Institute of Chicago, 1954; Courant von Goesch Prize, 1958; Ford Foundation Fellowship, 1959; Penwalphra Museum College of Art Award, 1962; Medal of the Year, American Institute of Graphic Arts, 1964; National Institute of Arts and Letters Award, 1968; Grand Prize, North Rhein-Westphalia, Germany, 1968; Citation, National Asso-

ciation of Schools of Art, 1971; Citation, College Art Association, 1973; Akademie der Künste Award, Berlin, 1974; Fine Arts Medal, *American Institute of Arts Convention,* Atlanta, 1975; D.F.A.: University of Hartford, Connecticut, 1957; Yale University, 1962. Benjamin Franklin Fellow, Royal Society, London, 1970; Honorary Citizen, Bottrop, West Germany, 1970. Fellow, American Academy of Arts and Sciences, 1973. Albers Museum opened in Bottrop, 1983. *Died* (in Orange, Connecticut) *24 March 1976.*

Individual Exhibitions:

1948 *Josef Albers/Hans Arp/Max Bill,* Herbert Hermann Gallery, Stuttgart
1949 Cincinnati Art Museum, Ohio
Yale University Art Gallery, New Haven, Connecticut
Museum of Fine Arts, Richmond, Virginia
Sidney Janis Gallery, New York
1950 J. B. Speed Art Museum, Louisville
1951 Contemporary Art Society, Sydney
1952 Sidney Janis Gallery, New York
Arts Club of Chicago (with Naum Gabo)
1953 Museum of Art, San Francisco
Josef and Anni Albers, Wadsworth Atheneum, Hartford, Connecticut
1954 Academy of Art, Honolulu
1955 Sidney Janis Gallery, New York
Massachusetts Institute of Technology, Cambridge
1956 Yale University Art Gallery, New Haven, Connecticut
Kunsthaus, Zurich (with Fritz Glarner and Friedrich Vordemberge-Gildewart)
1957 Galerie Denise René, Paris
Museum der Stadt, Ulm, West Germany
Karl Ernst Osthaus Museum, Hagen, West Germany
1958 Sidney Janis Gallery, New York
Kunstverein, Freiburg im Breisgau, West Germany
Landesmuseum, Münster, West Germany
1959 Sidney Janis Gallery, New York
Museum am Ostwall, Dortmund
1961 Stedelijk Museum, Amsterdam
Sidney Janis Gallery, New York
Gimpel Fils, London
1963 Sidney Janis Gallery, New York
Galerie Hybler, Copenhagen
Kunsthaus, Hamburg
Folkwangmuseum, Essen
Art Museum, Dallas
1964 Sidney Janis Gallery, New York
Museum of Modern Art, New York
Museum of Art, San Francisco
1965 Galleria Toninelli, Milan
Galerie Gimpel-Hanover, Zurich
Morgner-Haus, Soest, West Germany

Josef Albers: *Homage to the Square—Pale Autumn,* 1963 Courtesy Museum of Contemporary Art, Chicago

Gallery of Modern Art, Washington, D.C.
Museum of Modern Art, New York (toured South America, Mexico and the United States, 1965–67)
1968 Landesmuseum, Münster, West Germany (toured Germany and Switzerland, 1968–69)
Sidney Janis Gallery, New York
Galerie Denise René, Paris
1969 Kestner Gesellschaft, Hannover
Sonia Henie-Niels Onstad Foundation, Oslo
1970 Sidney Janis Gallery, New York
Kunsthalle, Hamburg
Kunstverein, Munich
Städtische Kunsthalle, Dusseldorf
1971 London Arts Gallery
University Art Museum, Princeton University, New Jersey
Metropolitan Museum of Art, New York
1973 Landesmuseum, Münster, West Germany
Kestner Gesellschaft, Hannover
Galerie Beyeler, Basle
Kunsthaus, Zurich
Galerie Gmurzynska, Cologne
Galerie Melki, Paris
Heslington Hall, York University, England
1976 Busch-Reisinger Museum, Harvard University, Cambridge, Massachusetts
1980 Galerie Christel, Stockholm
1981 Montclair Art Museum, New Jersey
1983 Josef Albers Museum, Bottrop, West Germany
1984 Sidney Janis Gallery, New York
1986 Galerie Teufel, Cologne
Sidney Janis Gallery, New York
1987 Galeria Theo, Madrid

Group Exhibitions:

1929 *Bauhaus Masters*, Kunsthalle, Basle (travelled to the Kunsthalle, Zurich)
1939 *American Abstract Artists*, Riverside Museum, New York
1951 *Contemporary American Painting*, University of Illinois, Champaign
1962 *Geometric Abstraction in America*, Whitney Museum, New York
1965 *The Responsive Eye*, Museum of Modern Art, New York
1967 *2 Decades of American Painting*, Museum of Modern Art, New York (toured Japan, India and Australia)
1972 *Geometric Abstraction 1926–42*, Museum of Fine Art, Dallas
1973 *Futurism: A Modern Focus*, Guggenheim Museum, New York
1983 *Modern Art in the West*, Metropolitan Art Museum, Tokyo
1986 *Seven Artists in Depth: The Creative Process*, San Francisco Museum of Modern Art

Collections:

Metropolitan Museum of Art, New York; Guggenheim Museum, New York; Museum of Modern Art, New York; Museum des 20. Jahrhunderts, Vienna; Centre Georges Pompidou, Paris; Bauhaus Archiv, Darmstadt; Stedelijk Museum, Amsterdam; Moderna Museet, Stockholm; Kunstmuseum, Basle; Kunsthaus, Zurich.

Publications:

By ALBERS: books—*Zeichnungen: Drawings*, New York 1956; *Poems and Drawings*, New Haven, Connecticut 1958; *Poems and Drawings: Gedichte und Zeichnungen*, New York 1961; *Despite Straight Lines*, New Haven, Connecticut 1961; *The Interaction of Color*, New Haven, Connecticut 1963; *Search Versus Re-Search: 3 Lectures by Josef Albers at Trinity College April 1965*, New Haven, Connecticut 1969; *Formulation: Articulation*, New York 1972; articles—"Werklicher Formunterricht" in *Bauhaus 2*, Dessau, Germany 1928; "Concerning Art Instruction" in *Black Mountain College Bulletin* (Beria, North Carolina), no. 2, 1934; "Modular Brick Wall Partition" in *Art in Modern Architecture* by Eleanor Bitterman, New York 1952; "Homage to the Square" in *Artnews* (New York), October 1961; "Op Art and/or Perceptual Effects" in the *Yale Scientific Magazine* (New Haven, Connecticut), November 1965; "My Courses at the Hochschule für Gestaltung at Ulm" in *Form* (Opladen, West Germany), no. 4, 1967; "Selected Writings" in *Origin* (Kyoto, Japan), January 1968; statement in *Futurism: A Modern Focus*, exhibition catalogue, New York 1973.

On ALBERS: books—*Staatliches Bauhaus: Weimar 1919–23*, Munich 1923; *Die Kunst des 19. und 20. Jahrhunderts* by Hans Hildebrandt, Potsdam 1924; *Bauhaus 1919–28* by Herbert Bayer and Walter and Ilse Gropius, New York 1938; *Erinnerungen an Sturm und Bauhaus* by Lothar Schreyer, Munich 1956; *Josef Albers, Despite Straight Lines: An Analysis of His Graphic Constructions* by Francois Bucher, New Haven, Connecticut 1961; *The Artist's Voice: Talks with 17 Artists*, New York 1962; *Josef Albers* by Eugen Gomringer, New York 1968; *The Bauhaus: Weimar, Dessau, Berlin, Chicago* by Hans Maria Wingler, Cambridge, Massachusetts 1969; *Josef Albers* by Werner Spies, London 1971; *Josef Albers 1888–1976*, exhibition catalogue with essay by Francois Boucher, Cologne 1986; *Albers*, exhibition catalogue with text by Kelly Feeney, New York 1986.

The works of Josef Albers (1888–1976) span much of the 20th century and, although seminal in generating considerable similar output by others, bear unmistakably the stamp of his strong individuality. They are part of his evolving quest for simplicity and understanding. His practical background, son of a Westphalian furniture manufacturer, gave him experience with wood, glass and other construction materials. Indeed, among his numerous interests during his early Bauhaus years was furniture design, where woodgrain and natural whorled patterns were (frustratingly?) bounded and constrained by simple rectangular shapes. His pieces feature studies in contrast (light vs. dark oak, flat-back painted vs. natural wood surfaces), as well as economy of design and rationing of decoration. Perhaps an early portent of his colored squares to come are to be found on an Albers-designed set of four hand-painted glass-topped stacking tables.

Moving from 3-dimensional to 2-dimensional artistry, for a time (1930–1950) his graphics exhibit preoccupation with the contrast between, and the not obviously reconcilable superposition of, grain patterns and geometric designs. Also evident is a struggle between and attempts at fusion of curved boundaries and straight-edged objects. With the eventual rejection of the former, which implies also a disposal of most of the demands for emotional analysis of his productions, Albers' works came to feature primarily the seemingly simple rectangle and square. The realization that even these exhibit intriguing and non-trivial complexities led to a search for simplification, to separation into studies of the effects of geometry and those of color and shading.

Albers' studies of simple lined black and white planar objects led to numerous examples of interactions of lines and of the trickery encountered when the eye views 2-dimensional information and the brain attempts a 3-dimensional interpretation of it. Here, for example, he produced a massive output of interwoven box-figures, each interpretable in multi-variate readings.

Simultaneously his quest for successful analysis and understanding and his long career in teaching led him to study interaction of colors, whereupon he produced a monumental and still much-discussed book on the topic, *The Interaction of Color* (1963). A primary idea was the use of squares of colors to minimize as much as possible the intrusion of shape and of associative, descriptive or emotional context. His celebrated series of hundreds of paintings "Homage to the Square" yields clear examples of what the physical scientist has also come to realize, that scientific method to focus on the simplest possible system is rewarding but has ultimate limitations, in that the surroundings and the presence of the observer can never be completely eliminated. Albers' Squares, and their more elaborate cousins, entitled "Variants," amply demonstrate that identical colors in different settings are perceived to be different by different observers, in different lighting, at different times.

Whatever his final place in art history, Josef Albers was a charming and exciting man; a teacher who felt that "good teaching is more a giving of right questions than a giving of right answers," a lifelong student whose "main concern [was] to remain a student looking for further problems to be solved and working for [his] own development," and an artist who produced superficially impersonal images but images which echoed the pithy quality of his written statements. His aims were simple—"My painting is meditative, is restful. . . . I seek no quick effects. . . . You see, this is what I want to create: meditation pictures of the 20th century."

—John A. Weil and John H. Holloway

ALBRIGHT, Ivan (Le Lorraine).
American. Born in North Harvey, Illinois, near Chicago, 20 February 1897. Educated at New Trier High School, Evanston, Illinois, 1911–15; Northwestern University, Evanston, 1915–16; University of Illinois, Urbana, 1916–17; Ecole des Beaux-Arts, Nantes, France, 1919; School of the Art Institute of Chicago, 1920–23, B.F.A. 1923; Pennsylvania Academy of Fine Arts, Philadelphia, 1923; National Academy of Design, New York, 1924. Served in the United States Army, 1917–18: did medical drawings at Base Hospital No. 11, Nantes, France, 1918–19. Married Josephine Medill Patterson Reeve in 1946, children: Adam Medill and Blandina Van Etten. Worked at architectural offices of Dwight Heald Perkin and did color work for advertising at Alfred Pick and Company, Chicago, 1919; independent artist, 1924 until his death in 1983: travelled to Laguna Beach and La Jolla, California, Camelback, Arizona, and Old Laguna, New Mexico, 1924–25; established studio on Cherry Street, Philadelphia, 1925–26; and in Balboa Park, California, 1927; settled in Warrenville, Illinois and established studio (also built twin studios with brother Malvin Marr Albright), 1927–46; spent summers in Maine, 1939–41; worked for Metro-Goldwyn-Mayer film studios painting a portrait for the film *The Picture of Dorian Gray*, Hollywood 1943–44; returned to Chicago in 1946; moved to New England, 1971. Visiting Artist, Dartmouth College, Hanover, New Hampshire 1971–74. Recipient: Temple Gold Medal, Pennsylvania Academy of Fine Arts, Philadelphia, 1942; First Prize and Purchase Prize (refused), *The Artists for Glory Exhibition*, Metropolitan Museum of Art, New York, 1942; Watson F. Blair Prize, Art Institute of Chicago, 1949; Centennial Award, Northwestern University, 1951; Silver Medal, Corcoran *Biennial*, Washington, D.C., 1955; Benjamin Altman Figure Prize, National Academy of Design, 1961; Award, *Dunn International Exhibition*, Beaverbrook Art Gallery, Fredericton, New Brunswick, Canada, 1963; Governor of Vermont Award for Excellence in the Arts, 1975. D.H.L.: Mundelein College, Chicago, 1969; D.F.A.: Lake Forest College, Illinois, 1972, Columbia College, Chicago, 1974, and School of the Art Institute of Chicago, 1977. Associate Academician, 1942, and Academician, 1950, National Academy of Design. Member, National Institute of Arts and Letters, 1957. Agent: Kennedy Galleries, 40 West 57th Street, New York, New York 10019. *Died* (in Woodstock, Vermont) *13 November 1983.*

Individual Exhibitions:

1930 Walden Books Shop, East Walton Place, Chicago
1931 Art Institute of Chicago
1935 Old White Art Gallery, White Sulphur Springs, West Virginia
1945 Associated American Artists Galleries, New York (with Malvin Marr Albright)
1946 Associated American Artists Galleries, Chicago (with Malvin Marr Albright)

Ivan Albright: ***Poor Room . . . ,*** **c. 1961**

1964 Roosevelt University, Chicago
Art Institute of Chicago (retrospective; travelled to the Whitney Museum, New York, 1965)
1972 *Medical Drawings*, Galleries of the Renaissance Society, University of Chicago
1975 *Ivan Albright: The Vermont Farmer*, Dartmouth College, Hanover, New Hampshire
1978 Art Institute of Chicago
Graven Image: The Prints of Ivan Albright 1931–1977, Lake Forest College, Illinois

Selected Group Exhibitions:

1923 *Annual Chicago Exhibition*, Art Institute of Chicago
1926 *Annual American Exhibition*, Art Institute of Chicago
1942 *Artists for Victory*, Metropolitan Museum of Art, New York
1963 *Dunn International Exhibition*, Beaverbrook Arts Gallery, Fredericton, New Brunswick, Canada
1975 *Selected Works from the L. Marshall Pucci Collection*, Mt. Vernon, Illinois

Collections:

Metropolitan Museum of Art, New York; Art Institute of Chicago.

Publications:

By ALBRIGHT: recorded interview—"Interview, Woodstock, Vermont" with Paul Cummings, in *Archives of American Art*, February 1972.

On ALBRIGHT: books—*For Art's Sake* by Adam Emory Albright, Chicago 1953; *The Artist's Voice: Talks with Seventeen Artists*, New York 1962; *American Realists and Magic Realists*, edited by Dorothy C. Miller and Alfred H. Barr, Jr., with statements by artists, and an introduction by Lincoln Kirstein, New York 1963; *Ivan Albright*, exhibition catalogue, by Frederick A. Sweet, with commentary by Jean Dubuffet, Chicago 1964; *Medical Drawings by Ivan Le Lorraine Albright*, exhibition pamphlet, with an introduction by Harold Haydon, Chicago 1972; *Readings in American Art 1900–1975*, edited by Barbara Rose, New York, 1975; *Selected Works from the L. Marshall Pucci Collection*, exhibition catalogue, Mt. Vernon, Illinois 1975; *Graven Image: The Prints of Ivan Albright 1931– 1977*, exhibition catalogue, compiled and edited by Gael Grayson, with an introduction by Michael Croydon, Lake Forest, Illinois 1978; *Ivan Albright* by Michael Croydon, New York 1978; film—*Unfinished Portrait of an Artist* by Lester Weinrott, Chicago 1963.

Man is not an individual
Nothing is individual in the world
Man is not a separate identity
Man is a fragment of the whole
Everything in existence makes the whole
The whole is one—and the one includes all
Man cannot be separated from his surroundings
Out doors he is part of the trees the grass the flowers
He is not separate from them—he is part of them
In—doors he is part of the room the window—the door—the chair the table—the fork—the spoon—
All that man sees becomes part of him
There is no separation of parts in the universe
Everything is part of everything else
The whole is one
Man is no more an individual than a blade of grass or a pebble
Man cannot hold onto a minute of time
And life
If life were life there would be no death
There is only light and motion in this world
And they are life
As fragments I am in you and you are in Me
And we are One
And the One is the whole.
—Ivan Albright(1982)

World wide, Albright may at present still be considered *the* Chicago artist, even as a succession of Chicago artists' groups and individuals have achieved renown since World War II. And Albright's idiosyncratic spirit might be argued as adrift in these more recent artists—of course through primitivizing, Surreal, Pop and abstract modes far removed from his expressionist realism. If he has been a "father figure," then it is not in paint quality or disposition of subject matter, but rather in his life-long absorption with an unhurried pace to produce an utterly personal if not obsessional personal art. Albright's larger works appear as a concretion of his daily life experience in time—e.g. *The Poor Room* (1962) was in his studio for 21 years (and he worked from a full-size model of a brick-surrounded window frame).

Outwardly a cheerful if shy person, Albright's pace came about partially no doubt through his life-patterns. Left a life-long income by the investments of his artist-father (as was also his twin brother Malvin Marr, an exhibiting artist who took the pseudonym 'Zsissley' so that he might be alone at the far end of an exhibition catalog), Albright married only in later middle age. Josephine Reeve was an heiress, daughter of the founder of the *New York Daily News*, and Albright expanded his subject matter to coincide with his new residences in Vermont, Wyoming, and Georgia.

All this anxiety-free existence notwithstanding, ironically there is omnipresent in perhaps all of his large scale work, in both their figures and object-world, a literal depiction of decay—the dissolution of the physicality of matter. (The older U.S. general public may still associate the Albright brothers with a well-publicized episode in Hollywood in 1943 when they painted the images used in a movie version of *The Portrait of Dorian Gray:* audiences shrieked when they were shown). But Albright's profound sense of being alive in time—perhaps with some influence from Cezanne—also moved him to dislocate elements of an image with a slight bend or twist, the more clearly to emphasize personal feeling if not moreso the transiency of art and artist. Because of his absorption with minutiae, and his long involvement with individual works, there is often still found, left over no doubt from older catalogs, his label as Magic Realist. Yet seen close, his surface touch is brusque and whatever optical presence it has, occurs only in smaller scale reproduction.

It may also be said that he practiced—however self-consciously—two manners. In his use of oils, through the layered build-up of paint in his laborious process, the constant touch returning to every part of the canvas, there appears a diminishment of the overt quality of his inherent naivete. (He had a lengthy academic training which concluded at the Pennsylvania Academy of Fine Art, where his father had been a student of Thomas Eakins.) However in his drawings and watercolors, such technique is not possible, and so the halting quality of his attack is more readily revealed. Albright's almost ingenuous earnestness, his yearning for some means to translate his sense of the melancholy immediacy of his perception, is often found in his characteristic statements such as: "After all, there is no sorrow like existence, but the thought of anything existing is so marvelous that I doubt its reality." It is no coincidence that Jean Dubuffet who was very much after some similar quality of existential actuality which would dissolve the abstraction of visual creative process, was deeply moved by Albright's work.

Many of the artist's important works are in the collections of Art Institute of Chicago, donated by Albright himself.

—Joshua B. Kind

ALECHINSKY, Pierre.
Belgian. Born in Brussels, 19 October 1927. Educated in Brussels, also studied clarinet there; studied book illustration and typography, at the Ecole Nationale Supérieure d'Architecture et des Arts Décoratifs, La Cambre, Brussels, 1944–48, and engraving, under S. W. Hayter, at Atelier 17, Paris 1952. Married Michele (Micky) Dendal in 1949; sons: Ivan and Nicolas. Painter, designer and illustrator, in Brussels, 1947–51, in Paris, since 1951. Member, Jeune Peinture Belge group, Brussels, 1947–51; Founder-Member, Les Ateliers du Marais community studios, Brussels, 1949–51; Founder-Member, with Karel Appel, Corneille, Asger Jorn, Constant, Pedersen, etc., COBRA (Copenhagen-Brussels-Amsterdam) group, 1949–51. Committee Member, October Salon, Paris 1953; Organizer, *Autour de S. W. Hayter* touring exhibition, Amsterdam, Brussels, Copenhagen and Florence, 1953; Member, Management Committee, *Salon du Mai*, Paris, 1958–70; Contributor, *Daily Bul*, La Louvière, Belgium, 1957, and *The Situationist Times* and *La Breche*, Paris 1963. Recipient: Prix Helene Jacquet, La Louvière, 1950; Prix Jeune Peinture Belge, Brussels, 1950; Special Award, *Festival du Film d'Art*, Bergamo, Italy, 1957; Hallmark Prize, New York, 1960; Diploma of Honour, *Festival of Cultural Film*, Tokyo, 1961; First Prize, *Triennale de la Gravure en Belgique*, Brussels 1966; First Prize, *Biennale Internationale de la Gravure*, Cracow 1966; Premio Marzotto, Valdagno, Italy, 1968; Andrew W. Mellon Prize, Carnegie Institute, Pittsburgh, 1976. Agent: Lefebre Gallery, 47 East 77th Street, New York, New York 10021, U.S.A. Address: 2 bis rue Henri Barbusse, 78 Bougival, Paris, France.

Individual Exhibitions:

1947 Galerie Lou Cosyn, Brussels
1948 Galerie Apollo, Brussels
1953 Kunsthandel Martinet, Amsterdam (with Shinkichi Tajiri)
1954 Galleria Schwarz, Milan
Galerie Nina Dausset, Paris
1955 Palais des Beaux-Arts, Brussels
Nabis Gallery, Tokyo
1956 Galerie du Dragon, Paris
1957 Galerie Espace, Haarlem, Netherlands
Galerie Aujourd'hui, Brussels
Galerie Michael Warren, Paris
1958 Institute of Contemporary Arts, London
1960 Galerie Benador, Geneva
1961 Carnegie Institute, Pittsburgh
Stedelijk Museum, Amsterdam (with Reinhoud; travelled to the Kunstkring, Rotterdam)
Galerie Van de Loo, Munich
1962 Galerie de France, Paris
Lefebre Gallery, New York
1963 Stedelijk Van Abbemuseum, Eindhoven, Netherlands
Librairie-Galerie La Hune, Paris
Stedelijk Museum, Amsterdam
Lefebre Gallery, New York
1964 Galerie Birch, Copenhagen
Galerie Espace, Amsterdam
Galleria Il Punto, Turin
Instituto Torcuato di Tella, Buenos Aires (with Reinhoud)
1965 Lefebre Gallery, New York
Arts Club of Chicago (travelled to University of Minnesota, Minneapolis; and the Jewish Museum, New York)
1966 Galerie de France, Paris
Stedelijk Museum, Amsterdam
Galleria La Medusa, Rome
1967 Museum of Fine Arts, Houston
Lefebre Gallery, New York
Librairie-Galerie La Hune, Paris
Galerie La Balance, Brussels
20 Jahre Impressionen, Galerie Van de Loo, Munich
1968 Galerie de France, Paris
Museum voor Schone Kunsten, Ghent
Staatliche Kunstgalerie, Bochum, West Germany (travelled to the Kunstverein, Freiburg)

Pierre Alechinsky: *Monsieur Hune*, 1974

Galerie Birch, Copenhagen
Lefebre Gallery, New York
Galleri Moderne, Silkeborg, Denmark
APIAW, Liège, Belgium
Kaleidoscoop Galerie, Ghent

1969 Palais des Beaux-Arts, Brussels
Louisiana Museum, Humlebaek, Denmark
Kunstverein, Dusseldorf
Kunsthalle, Bremen, West Germany
Galerie La Taille Douce, Brussels
International School, Brussels
Dom Galerie, Cologne
Nielsen Gallery, Boston
Galerie de Montreal
J. L. Hudson Gallery, Detroit

1970 London Arts Gallery, London
Librairie-Galerie La Hune, Paris
Israel Museum, Jerusalem
Galleria Rotta, Milan
Lefebre Gallery, New York
Galerie Birch, Copenhagen
Chez Stephane Janssen, Brussels

1971 Galerie de France, Paris
Galleri Haaken, Oslo
Galerie Espace, Amsterdam
Galerie du Fleuve, Bordeaux
Lens Fine Art, Antwerp
Grand Rapids Art Museum, Michigan (with Reinhoud)

1972 Maison des Jeunes et de la Culture, Annecy, France (toured France)
Lefebre Gallery, New York
Galerie de l'Auditorium, Brussels
Galerie Benador, Geneva
Galerie in der Blutgasse, Vienna
Galleria San Sebastianello, Rome

1973 Lefebre Gallery, New York
Galerie de France, Paris
Galerie Birch, Copenhagen
Galleria del Milione, Milan
Palazzo Municipale, Asolo, Italy
Galerie Vega, Liège, Belgium
Galerie Stephane Janssen, Brussels
Librairie-Galerie La Hune, Paris
Lens Fine Art, Antwerp
Musée d'Art Moderne, Brussels

1974 Le Miroir d'Encre, Brussels
Galerie Espace, Amsterdam
Mathildenhoehe, Darmstadt (toured Europe)

1975 Galerie Birch, Copenhagen
Galeria Turner, Madrid
Galeria 42, Barcelona
Musée Cantini Marseilles
Galerie Van de Loo, Munich
Galerie Stephane Janssen, Basle
Librairie-Galerie La Hune, Paris
Graphica Club, Milan

1976 Lefebre Gallery, New York
Maison de la Culture, Chalon-sur-Saône, France (toured Europe)
Galeria Aele, Madrid
Galerie Birch, Copenhagen
La Maison Bleue, Strasbourg

1977 Galerie Fleuve Trois, Bordeaux
Galeria Aele, Madrid
Herzog Galerie, Orleans, France
Galeria Ponce, Madrid
Halifax University, Nova Scotia
Le Miroir d'Encre, Brussels
Galerie de France, Paris (with Reinhoud)
Paintings and Writings, Carnegie Institute, Pittsburgh (retrospective; travelled to the Art Gallery of Ontario, Toronto)
Lens Fine Art, Antwerp
Lefebre Gallery, New York
Riis Gallery, Trondheim, Norway
Librairie-Galerie La Hune, Paris

1978 *Les Dessins d'Alechinsky,* Centre Georges Pompidou, Paris
Galerie de France, Paris (with Karel Appel; toured Europe)
Galerie Van de Loo, Munich (travelled to Galerie Rolf Ohse, Bremen)

1979 Lefebre Gallery, New York
Le Miroir d'Encre, Brussels

1980 Museo de Arte Moderno, Mexico City
Galerie Maeght, Paris
Galerie Maeght, Zurich
Kaneko Gallery, Tokyo
Kestner-Gesellschaft, Hannover (retrospective)
Museum of Modern Art, New York (print retrospective)

1981 Lefebre Gallery, New York

1982 Galerie Moderne, Silkeborg, Denmark
Galerie Birch, Copenhagen

1983 Galerie M, Hannover

1984 Kaneko Art Gallery, Tokyo
Lefebre Gallery, New York
Galerie Maeght Lelong, Paris

1985 Galerie Le Mejan, Arles, France
Galerie Birch, Copenhagen
Gand Gallery, Seoul, Korea
Musée d'Art et d'Histoire, Metz, France
Galerie Van de Loo, Munich

1986 Lefebre Gallery, New York
Artcurial, Paris
Galerie La Hune, Paris
Galerie Maeght Lelong, Paris

1987 Lefebre Gallery, New York
Isselbacher Gallery, New York
Guggenheim Museum, New York

Selected Group Exhibitions:

1948 *Les Mains Eblouies,* Galerie Maeght, Paris

1949 *Cobra: 1st Exhibition of Experimental Art,* Stedelijk Museum, Amsterdam

1959 *European Art Today,* Minneapolis Institute of Art

1968 *Painting in France 1900–1967,* National Gallery of Art, Washington, D.C. (toured the United States)

1976 *Daily Bul & Co.,* Fondation Maeght, St. Paul de Vence, France (travelled to Studio du Passage 44, Brussels)

1978 *Cobra 1948–78,* Statens Museum for Konst, Copenhagen

1980 *L'Affiche en Belgique,* Musée d'Affiche, Paris

1983 *Informele Kunst 1945–60,* Rijksmuseum Twenthe, Enschede, Netherlands

1985 *Painterly Visions 1945–85,* Guggenheim Museum, New York

1987 *Galerie Espace 1956–86,* Galerie Espace, Amsterdam

Collections:

Musées Royaux des Beaux-Arts de Belgique, Brussels; Centre Georges Pompidou, Paris; Stedelijk Museum, Amsterdam; Museum der Stadt, Darmstadt,; Galleria Nazionale d'Arte Moderna, Rome; Guggenheim Museum, New York; Museum of Modern Art, New York; Carnegie Institute, Pittsburgh; Musée d'Art Contemporain, Montreal, Quebec; Israel Museum, Jerusalem.

Publications:

By ALECHINSKY: books and portfolios—*Trades,* 9 etchings, with text by Luc de Heusch, Brussels 1948; *Les Poupées de Dixmunde,* Brussels 1950; *Bites,* etchings portfolio, Milan 1962; *Titres et Pains Perdus,* Paris 1965; *Ideotraces,* Paris 1966; *Le Test du Titre,* Paris 1967; *Minutes,* Venice 1967; *Indivisible Prints,* with Arman, text by Joyce Mansour, London 1969; *Vulcanologies,* lithos portfolio, Paris 1970; *Roue Libre,* Geneva 1971; *L'Avenir de la Propriété,* Paris and Geneva 1972; *Les Estampes: Pierre Alechinsky 1946–1972,* Paris 1972; *Krach,* engravings portfolio, Paris 1973; *Au Fil du Bois,* woodcuts portfolio, Paris 1973; *Blindly,* etchings portfolio, Rome 1974; *Serpent,* engravings portfolio, Paris 1977; *Far Rockaway,* Montpellier 1977; *Monument Tobacco,* with text by Marcel and Gabriel Piqueray, Paris 1978; *Encres à Deux Pinceaux,* with Karel Appel, text by Hugo Claus, Paris 1978; *Papiers Traites,* 6 lithographs, Paris 1978; *La Vie comme elle Tourne,* drawings portfolio, with text by André Frenaud, Paris 1979; books illustrated—*Le Sens des Tarots* by Marcel Lecomte, Brussels 1948; *Zonder Vorm van Proces* by Hugo Claus, Brussels 1950; *La Reine des Murs* by Christian Dotremont, Paris 1960; *Les Tireurs de Lange* by Amos Kenan, Turin 1961; *Moi Qui J'Avais* by Christian Dotremont, Paris 1961; *A la Gare* by Amos Kenan, Milan 1962; *One Cent Life* by Walasse Ting, Zurich 1964; *Carre Blanc* by Joyce Mansour, Paris 1965; *De la Mort* by Francois Nourissier, Brussels 1967; *Le Bleu des Fonds* by Joyce Mansour, Paris 1968; *Tourmente* by Michel Butor, with Bernard Dufour and Jacques Herold, Montpellier 1968; *Au Demeurant* by Achille Chavee, La Louvière, Belgium 1969; *Hoire-Voirie* by Michel Butor, Milan 1970; *Pointes* by Louis Scutenaire, Paris 1972; *Laborinthe* by Jean-Clarence Lambert, Paris 1973; *Un Mannequin sur le Trottoir* by Roger Caillois, Paris 1974; *Reve de l'Ammonite* by Michel Butor, Montpellier 1975; *Par Experience* by Yves Bonnefoy, Paris 1976; *Vacillations* by A. M. Cloran, Montpellier 1980; film—*Japanese Calligraphy,* with Francis Haar, Roger Blin and others, 1956.

On ALECHINSKY: books—*The COBRA Library: Alechinsky* by Luc de Heusch, Copenhagen 1950; *Ink* by Jean Cleinge, Paris 1963; *Pierre Alechinsky: 20 Jahre Impressionen,* exhibition catalogue, Munich 1967; *Alechinsky* by Jacques Putman, Milan and Paris 1967; *Alechinsky* by Alain Bosquet, Paris 1971; *Alechinsky à la Ligne: catalogue raisonne,* edited by Yves Riviere, Paris 1973; *Pierre Alechinsky,* exhibition catalogue, with text by Bernd Krimmel, Darmstadt 1974; *Kunstpocket no. 3: Alechinsky* by Freddy de Vree, Schelderode 1976; *Pierre Alechinsky: Paintings and Writings,* exhibition catalogue, with texts by Leon A. Arkus and Eugene Ionesco, Pittsburgh 1977; *Les Dessins d'Alechinsky,* exhibition catalogue, with text by Pierre Georgel, Paris 1978; *Pierre Alechinsky eine retrospektive,* exhibition catalogue, with text by Carl Haenlein, Hannover 1980; *Pierre Alechinsky: Bouches et Grilles,* exhibition catalogue with essay by Pierre Descargues, Paris 1986; *Pierre Alechinsky: Margin and Centre,* exhibition catalogue with texts by Michael Gibson and Octavio Paz, New York 1987.

A great debate has raged for years about what values training at an art school can bestow upon an artist in embryo. Sometimes the experience provides full knowledge of useful techniques, sometimes the bonus amounts to little more than the chance to take advantage of important contacts that will reduce the teething pains of starting an art career.

Pierre Alechinsky belongs to the first category. At the Ecole Nationale Supérieure d'Architecture et des Arts Décoratifs in Brussels he mastered "book illustration" which involves wide knowledge and experience of all kinds of graphic printing, including typography.

Today he is recognized as one of the prime graphic artists. As early as 1948 he was able to design a set of tarot cards for the Belgian surrealist Marcel Lecomte and he also made the pictures for "Les Metiers" by Luc de Heusch.

In Paris Alechinsky made contact with the surrealist movement through Max Ernst. He was also recognized by Dubuffet who saw in his works a flavour of *Art Brut.*

In 1949 he joined the COBRA group with Appel, Corneille, Constant, Dotremont, Jorn and Pedersen, and a few years later he went to work at S. W. Hayter's Atelier 17 in order to still further improve his graphic techniques. But perhaps the greatest influence he received came when he visited Japan (1955) and made a careful and professional study of the art of that country, particularly as it applied to the printed image and to calligraphy (about which he made a prize-winning film).

It is tempting to concentrate upon his graphic works because of his confident expertise in this wide field, but it should not be overlooked that Alechinsky is a good painter and an attractive collagist.

In all his works he retains his own version of COBRA imagery. Strange beasts, strange people, strange flowers; but he is also adept in the storytelling which inspires his own fantasy comicstrips—a genre he exploits both in his painting and in his prints. Good examples of this narrative painting are found in large canvases like "The Voyeur Seen," "Stars and Disasters" and "Central Park".

Whilst his colours are not those of Jorn or Appel, and certainly not those of Pedersen, they are rich with COBRA tints and toning. The rusts and cerulean blues are particularly appealing. But, as with every painting, there is always more than just the colour scheme. Alechinsky's imagery, whether solid or in

line, has a rangy-ness that makes the eye restless, makes it search for inner meanings. The composition also arouses this tatters-in-the-wind sensation (when it is not volcanic). Even so, his early experience as an illustrator has given him a well-defined sense of balance.

—Sheldon Williams

ALLEN, Terry.

American. Born in Wichita, Kansas, 7 May 1943; raised in Lubbock, Texas. Studied at Chouinard Art Institute, Los Angeles, B.F.A. 1966. Independent artist since 1968, working in a wide variety of modes including musical and theatrical performance, sculpture, painting and video. Taught drawing classes at Chouinard Art Institute, Los Angeles, 1968–69; Guest Artist, University of California at Berkeley, 1971; on faculty of California State University at Fresno, 1971–79. Recipient: National Endowment for the Arts Fellowship, 1972, 1979; Guggenheim Fellowship, New York, 1986; Bessie Award, New York, 1986. Agent: Wanda Hansen, 615 Main Street, Sausalito, California 94965. Address: 735 East Fedora, Fresno, California 93704, U.S.A.

Individual Exhibitions:

1966 Gallery 66, Los Angeles
1968 Michael Walls Gallery, San Francisco
Pasadena Art Museum, California
1970 Michael Walls Gallery, San Francisco
1971 Mizuno Gallery, Los Angeles
Museum of Contemporary Art, Chicago
1973 Michael Walls Gallery, Los Angeles
1974 Michael Walls Gallery, New York
1975 *Juarez Series*, Contemporary Art Museum, Houston
1976 Claire S. Copley Gallery, Los Angeles
Morgan Art Gallery, Kansas City, Kansas
1978 Hansen-Fuller Gallery, San Francisco
Nancy Lurie Gallery, Chicago
Landfall Press Gallery, Chicago
1979 Lubbock Lights Gallery, Texas
Morgan Art Gallery, Kansas City, Kansas
Miami-Dade Community College, Florida
1980 Baxter Art Gallery, California Institute of Technology, Pasadena
1981 Portland Center for the Visual Arts, Oregon
Ring, Nelson Gallery/Atkins Museum, Kansas City, Missouri
The Southern Voice: Terry Allen, Vernon Fisher, Ed McGowin, Fort Worth Art Museum, Texas
1983 *Rooms and Stories*, La Jolla Museum of Contemporary Art, California
University of California, San Diego
Morgan Art Gallery, Kansas City, Missouri
1984 *Sprawl/Prowl/Growl*, Espace Lyonnais d'Art Contemporain, Lyon, France
Barbara Gladstone Gallery, New York
1985 Betty Moody Gallery, Houston
China Night, Fresno Art Center, California
1986 *Revelations*, Southwest Center for Arts and Crafts, San Antonio, Texas
Ohio, Wright State University, Dayton, Ohio
John Weber Gallery, New York
Gallery Paule Anglim, San Francisco
1988 L. A. Louver Gallery, Venice, California
Santa Barbara Contemporary Arts Forum, California
Pittsburgh Center for the Arts, Pennsylvania
Moore College of Art, Philadelphia
Institute of Contemporary Arts, Boston
Madison Art Center, Wisconsin
Gallery Paule Anglim, San Francisco

Selected performances: plays and occurrences—*Dialogues in Drag . . . a Satire*, Lucille Street Theatre, Los Angeles, 1968; *The 20th Century Pronto, Arrived*, Lucille Street Theatre, Los Angeles, 1968; *The Levels* (performance for Robert Irwin), University of California at Berkeley, 1970; *The Embrace . . . Advanced to Fury*, Spinoza Arena/Theatre, Houston, 1978; *Anterabbit Bleeder (a biography)*, La Jolla Museum of Contemporary Art, 1983; *Face to Face/Back to Back*, California State University, Fullerton, 1984; *Pedal Steel*, Brooklyn Academy of Music, New York, 1985; *Leonce and Lena*, Walker Art Center, Minneapolis, 1987; music—since 1964, Allen has made numerous appearances as a solo performer in both country and western music venues and in galleries and museums; since 1978 he has frequently appeared with the Panhandle Mystery Band.

Selected Group Exhibitions:

1973 *Extraordinary Realities*, Whitney Museum, New York
1976 *The Great American Rodeo Show*, Fort Worth Art Museum, Texas
Painting and Sculpture in California: The Modern Era, San Francisco Museum of Modern Art (travelled to the National Collection of Fine Arts, Smithsonian Institution, Washington, D.C.).
1977 *10th Biennale de Paris*
The Record as Artwork, Fort Worth Art Museum, Texas (toured the United States and Canada)
1979 *Image & Object in Contemporary Sculpture*, Detroit Institute of Arts (travelled to P.S. 1, New York)

Terry Allen: *The Magic Kingdom*, 1986

1982 *Sydney Biennale,* Art Gallery of New South Wales, Australia
1984 *Content: A Contemporary Focus 1978–84,* Hirshhorn Museum, Washington, D.C.
1986 *The Texas Landscape 1900–86,* Museum of Fine Arts, Houston
1987 *Avant Garde in the Eighties,* Los Angeles County Museum of Art

Collections:

Museum of Modern Art, New York; Fort Worth Art Museum, Texas; Detroit Institute of Arts; University Art Museum, Berkeley, California; Nelson Gallery/Atkins Museum, Kansas City, Missouri; La Jolla Museum of Contemporary Art, California; The Stuart Collection, La Jolla California; Los Angeles County Museum of Art; Metropolitan Museum of Art, New York.

Publications:

By ALLEN: books—*China Night,* with Roxy Gordon, Fresno, California 1985; *Terry Allen's "Ohio",* with essay by Dave Hickey, Dayton, Ohio 1986; recordings—"Gonna California" and "Color Book" (single), Bale Creek Records, Los Angeles 1968; *Juarez* (album), Landfall Press, Chicago 1975 (re-released by Fate Records, Chicago 1980); *Lubbock (on everything)* (album), Fate Records, Chicago 1978; "Cajun Roll" and "Whatever Happened to Jesus (and Maybeline)?" (single). Fate Records, Chicago 1979; *Smokin the Dummy* (album), Fate Records, Chicago 1980; "The Arizona Spiritual" (single), 1983; *Bloodlines* (album), 1984; "Cocktail Desperado" (single), 1986.

On ALLEN: books—*Juarez Series: Terry Allen,* exhibition catalogue, by Paul Shimmel, Michael Walls and Dave Hickey, Houston 1975; *Performance Anthology,* edited by Carl Loeffler and Darlene Tong, San Francisco 1980; *Ring: Terry Allen,* exhibition catalogue, by Marcia Tucker and Sherry Cromwell-Lacy, Kansas City, Missouri 1981; *Rooms and Stories by Terry Allen,* exhibition catalogue, by Dave Hickey, Robert McDonald and Lynda Forsha, La Jolla, California 1983; *Sprawl/Prowl/Growl: A Geographic Survey of Works by Terry Allen* by Thierry Raspail, Marcia Tucker and others, Lyon, France 1984; *Terry Allen: Visual and Aural Mythologies* by Ron Gleason and Val Greenfield, Calgary, Alberta 1985; *KaChina Night* by Craig Adcock, Tallahassee, Florida 1986; articles—"Earthscapes, Landworks and Oz" by Dave Hickey in *Art in America* (New York), September/October 1971; "The Ironic L.A. Artist" by Sandy Ballatore in *Artweek* (Oakland, California), 2 November 1974; "Terry Allen's C & W Imagery at CAM" by Charlotte Moser in the *Houston Chronicle,* 16 November 1975; "The Art of Terry Allen: A Personal Evaluation" by Claire Copley in *Journal* (Los Angeles), October/November 1976; "Terry Allen's Narratives" by Robert McDonald in *Artweek* (Oakland, California), 22 April 1978; "Wrestling with Human Relationships" by Janice Ross in *Artweek* (Oakland, California), 4 November 1978; "Objecting to Image" by Kay Larson in the *Village Voice* (New York), 14 January 1980; "Dallas/Ft. Worth You Can Go Home Again" by Janet Kutner in *Artnews* (New York), December 1981; "West Texas Dada" by Jonathan Crary in *Art in America* (New York), September 1983; "Terry Allen: The Return of Vietnam" by Gregory Galligan in *Arts Magazine* (New York), April 1987.

Terry Allen is a musician and songwriter, storyteller and visual artist hailing from none other than Lubbock, Texas. Though he's spent most of his adult life in southern California, he retains his "southernness" most obviously in his compositions (a little rock 'n roll, a little country western) which tell the tale of waitresses, truckers, mobile home life, card playing and drinking whiskey on their own down home surface. It is underneath the surface, however, that Allen's writing as well as his visuals become more dense, more circuitous. In his visual art of every conceivable medium, all of the above ambitions fuse to create cryptic narratives which meander somewhat autobiographically around the conflicts and passages of his heroes and heroines.

The installations themselves combine such dramas as murder, denial, anger, love, alcoholism and confusion (to name very few) which are represented by an odd assortment of everyday objects doubling as loaded symbols which address his perplexing soap operas. Crows, playing cards, male and female silhouettes, high heels, books and rocks combine with an infinite array of materials ranging from live birds to typewritten notes to videotape and much, much more. The viewer, inevitably disoriented by these intricate tales must tug at and dig through each revolving metaphor to cull out whatever drama may reside in these abstruse worlds of passion and intrigue.

Like a scavenger, the viewer picks and pulls at details both visual and "verbal" which, though they are certainly no exercise in futility, lead to no plot and no resolution. But Allen is more than merely a perpetrator of tricky labyrinths. His circular stories catapult the viewer into a world which defines the very stuff they're made of. Each phrase, while leading into another, also confirms or denies its own identity within the context of the myth as a whole and the separate components which reveal it. There is so much happening in Allen's work at any given moment that it is difficult to assign any specific or literal "meaning" to it.

Perhaps his most renowned piece, "Ring" is a four-section, four year work of individual but ideologically connected installations, a videotape (theatre occurrence, as Allen would say) written by Allen (he does not perform in these) and several smaller pieces. The installations ("The Evening Gorgeous George Died" and "Messages from Wrestlers in Hell") include both two and three dimensional elements as well as varying typewritten narratives which partially illuminate an obscure relationship between the stars, HE and SHE. Intricate details of these participants' lives are revealed through their discussions of marriage, drinking, affairs and fantasies. Though these characters lead and acknowledge their complex existences as more than simple fictions, they remain only shadows on the wall—emblems of Allen's ruminations and not their own. Their identity is that of mythical situations rather than actual folks.

Clearly, in his work, Allen develops a mysterious dialogue in which the skeletons of a private saga are uncloaked for us all. But still, we must excavate the obscure threads with which these tales are woven to reveal the humour, intensity and reality of their games.

—Janet Goleas

ANDERSON, Laurie.

American. Born in Wayne, Illinois, in 1942. Educated at Barnard College, New York, B.A. 1969 (magna cum laude with honors in art history; Phi Beta Kappa); studied sculpture at Columbia University, New York, M.F.A. 1972. Performance artist, New York, since 1972. Instructor in art history, City College, New York, 1973–75. Recipient: New York State Council on the Arts grant, 1974, 1977; National Endowment for the Arts grant, 1974, 1977, 1979; Villager Award, 1981. Honorary doctorate: San Francisco Art Institute, 1980; Guggenheim Fellowship, New York, 1983. Agent (for visual works): Holly Solomon Gallery Inc., 724 Fifth Avenue, New York, New York 10019. Address: 530 Canal Street, New York New York 10013, U.S.A.

Individual Exhibitions:

1970 Barnard College, New York
1973 Harold Rivkin Gallery, Washington, D.C.
1974 Artists Space, New York
1977 Holly Solomon Gallery, New York
Hopkins Center, Dartmouth College, Hanover, New Hampshire
1978 And/Or Gallery, Seattle
Projects Gallery, Museum of Modern Art, New York
Matrix Gallery, Hartford Atheneum, Connecticut
1979 University of California Art Museum, Berkeley
1980 *Dark Dogs, American Dreams,* Holly Solomon Gallery, New York
1981 *Scenes from 'United States,'* Holly Solomon Gallery, New York
1982 *Retrospective,* Institute of Contemporary Arts, London
1983 Institute of Contemporary Art, Philadelphia (travelled to Los Angeles; Houston; Flushing, New York)
1984 Laforet Museum, Akasaka, Tokyo
Nihon Seinehkau, Tokyo
Sankei Hall, Osaka, Japan
Kyoto Kaikan, Tokyo

Performances: *Automotive,* Town Green, Rochester, Vermont, 1972; *O-Range,* Lewisohn Stadium, City College of New York, 1973; Artists Space, New York, 1974; The Clocktower, Institute for Urban Resources, New York, 1974; Projects Gallery, Boston, 1974; *Duets on Ice,* 5 New York City locations, 1974; *How to Yodel,* The Kitchen, New York, 1974; music, Whitney Museum Downtown Branch, New York, 1975; *Songs and Stories for the Insomniac,* Artists Space, New York, 1975; *Songs and Stories for the Insomniac . . . Continued,* Oberlin College, Ohio, 1975; *Out of the Blue,* University of Massachusetts, Amherst, 1975; *Dearreader,* Holly Solomon Gallery, New York, 1975; *Dearreader-2,* Sarah Lawrence College, Bronxville, New York, 1975; *Dearreader-3,* Rhode Island School of Design, Providence, Rhode Island, 1975; *From "For Instants,"* Whitney Museum, New York, 1976; *From "For Instants,"* Brockport College, New York, 1976; *Fast Food,* Artist Space, New York, 1976; *From "For Instants,"* Skidmore College, Saratoga, New York, 1976; *From "For Instants 3,"* Philadelphia College of Art, 1976; *From "For Instants,"* California Institute of the Arts, Valencia, 1976; *From "For Instants-4,"* University of California at San Diego, 1976; *From "For Instants-4,"* Museum of Contemporary Art, La Jolla, California, 1976; *Stereo Stories,* M. L. D'Arc Gallery, New York, 1976; *Engli-SH,* Akademie der Kunst, Berlin, 1976; *Engli-SH,* Louisiana Museum, Humlebaek, Denmark, 1976; *Road Songs,* St. Mark's Poetry Center, New York 1976; *Songs,* New School, New York, 1976; *For Instants-5: Songs for Lines, Songs for Waves,* The Kitchen, New York, 1977; *Audio Talk,* School of Visual Arts, New York, 1977; De Appel, Amsterdam, 1977; *From "For Instants,"* at *Arte Fiera,* Bologna, 1977; *Some Songs,* International Cultural Center, Brussels, 1977; *That's Not the Way I Heard It,* at *Documenta,* Kassel, West Germany, 1977; *On Dit,* at the *Biennale,* Paris, 1977; *That's Not the Way I Heard It-2,* Galleria Salvatore Ala, Milan, 1977; *For Instants—Continued,* Otis Art Gallery, Los Angeles, 1978; *Some Songs,* And/Or Gallery, Seattle, 1978; *Like a Stream,* The Kitchen, New York, 1978; reading, The Ear Inn, New York; *Like a Stream-3,* with St. Paul Chamber Orchestra, at Walker Art Center, Minneapolis, 1978; *Down Here,* Texas Opry House, Houston (sponsored by Contemporary Art Museum, Houston), 1978; *Some Songs,* Mills College, Oakland, California, 1978; *Some Songs-2,* Portland Center for the Visual Arts, Oregon, 1978; *For Instants-6,* DC Space, Washington, D.C., 1978; *A Few Are . . . ,* Art Gallery of Ontario, Toronto, 1978; *Songs for Self-Playing Violin,* Contemporary Art Center, Cincinnati, Ohio, 1978; *Songs for Self-Playing Violin,* Real Art Ways, Hartford, Connecticut, 1978; *Some Are . . . ,* benefit for Hallwalls, Buffalo, New York, 1978; *Americans on the Move—Preview,* Carnegie Recital Hall, New York, 1979; *Americans on the Move,* The Kitchen, New York, 1979; at *Theatre of Nations Festival,* Hamburg, 1979; Groningen Museum, Netherlands, 1979; International Cultural Center, Brussels, 1979; Dany Keller Gallery, Munich; Cultural Center, Bonn, 1979; CAPC, Bordeaux, 1979; Stadtparkforum, Graz, Austria, 1979; Modern Art Gallery, Vienna, 1979; Aspen Center for the Visual Arts, Colorado, 1979; *Blue Horn File,* with David van Tieghem and Peter Gordon, Mudd Club, New York, 1979; *Commerce,* with Peter Gordon, U.S. Customs House, New York, 1979; at *Cabrillo Festival,* California, 1979; at *Autumn Festival,* Paris, 1979; at *OGGImusica Festival,* Lugano, Switzerland, 1979; Real Art Ways, Hartford, Connecticut, 1979; San Francisco Art Institute, 1979; Mills College, Oakland, California, 1979; Thorne Hall, Northwestern University, Chicago, 1979; University of Virginia, Richmond, 1979; Glenbow Museum, Calgary, Alberta, 1979; *Für Augen und Ohren,* Akademie der Kunst,

Laurie Anderson photo by Chris Harris

Berlin, 1980; Santa Barbara Museum of Art, California, 1980; at *Per-for-mance Festival,* Florence, 1980; Harvard University, Cambridge, Massachusetts, 1980; at *Rome Performance Festival,* 1980; *New Music America,*Walker Art Center, Minneapolis, 1980; Parachute Magazine Performance Series, Montreal, 1980; University of Northern Iowa, Cedar Falls, 1980; Levande, Gothenburg, Sweden, 1980; Paul Klee Kunstmuseum, Berne, 1980; Kunstmuseum, Zurich, 1980; Mixage International, Rotterdam, 1980; Rust/Roost, Middleburg, Netherlands, 1980; at *ROSC,* Dublin, 1980; Benefit for Volume Magazine, Irving Plaza, New York, 1980; Lenbachhaus, Munich, 1980; Paramount Theatre, with Oakland Youth Symphony, California, 1980; Orpheum Theatre, New York (sponsored by the Kitchen), 1980; Glenbow Museum, Calgary, Alberta, 1981; Western Front, Vancouver, 1981; York University, Toronto, 1981; Kunstmuseum, Basel, 1981; Cirque Divers, Liège, Belgium, 1981; Pension Building, Washington, D.C. (sponsored by DC Space and WPA), 1981; Detroit Institute of Arts, 1981; Institute of Contemporary Art, Philadelphia, 1981; University of California at San Diego, 1981; University of California at Davis, 1981; *Privates,* New York (sponsored by Franklin Furnace), 1981; *Bonds* (sponsored by The Kitchen), New York, 1981; Riverside Studios, London, 1981; Pension Building, Washington, D.C., 1981; *It's Cold Outside,* Alice Tully Hall, New York (commissioned by American Composers Concerts), 1981; *United States,* Moore Theatre, Seattle, 1982; *United States I–IV,* Park West, Chicago (sponsored by the Museum of Contemporary Art, Chicago), 1982; *Mister Heartbreak,* toured the United States, Canada and Japan, 1984–85.

Selected Group Exhibitions:

1973 *Thought Structures,* Pace University, New York
1976 *New Work, New York,* Fine Arts Gallery, California State University at Los Angeles
1977 *Surrogates/Self-Portraits,* Holly Solomon Gallery, New York
Words at Liberty, Museum of Contemporary Art, Chicago
1978 *American Narrative Story Art,* Contemporary Art Museum, Houston (travelled to the University of California Art Museum, Berkeley)
1979 *10 Artists: Artists' Space,* Neuberger Museum, State University of New York at Purchase (travelled to the New Museum, New York)
1980 *Drawings: The Pluralist Decade,* at the *Biennale,* Venice (toured Europe; American version shown at Institute for Contemporary Art, Philadelphia)
1987 *Avant-Garde in the Eighties,* Los Angeles County Museum of Art

Publications:

By ANDERSON: books—*The Package,* New York 1971; *October,* New York 1972; *Transportation Transportation,* New York 1973; *The Rose and the Stone,* New York 1974; *Notebook,* 1976; *Typisch Frau,* Regensburg, West Germany 1981; *Artifacts at the End of a Decade,* with an essay by John Perreault, 1981; articles—"From 'For Instants' " in *Individuals,* edited by Alan Sondheim, New York 1977; "From 'Americans on the Move' " in *October* (New York), Spring 1979; interview, with Robin White, in *View* (Oakland, California), vol. II, no. 8, 1980; "Dark Dogs American Dreams" in *Hotel,* New York 1980; "Laurie Anderson: Interview," with David Sparkman, in *Washington Review,* October/November 1981; films—*14 Americans,* 1979; *Film du Silence,* 1981; records—*It's Not the Bullet That Kills You, It's the Hole,* 1977; *Airwaves,* 1977; *New Music for Electronic and Recorded Media,* 1978; *Big Ego,* 1979; *Walk the Dog, O Superman,* 1981.

On ANDERSON: book—*Variants: Drawings by Contemporary Sculptors,* exhibition catalogue, Houston 1981; articles—"Laurie Anderson" by Robert Pincus-Witten in *Art Rite* (New York), April 1974; 5–11 November 1980; "Laurie Anderson Grows as a Performance Artist" by John Rockwell in the *New York Times,* 27 October 1980; "Laurie Anderson: American on the Move: Touching, Funny, Vivid, Assured" by Gregory Sandow in the *Village Voice* (New York) 5–11 November 1980; "The United States of Laurie Anderson" in *Soho News* (New York), 5–11 November 1980; "Amplifications: Laurie Anderson" by Craig Owens in *Art in America* (New York), March 1981; "Laurie Anderson: Ephemeral turns Permanent" by Robert Palmer in the *New York Times,* 21 April 1982.

During her art historical training at Barnard College in New York, performance artist Laurie Anderson explored the proliferating critical discourse of the 1970s—the semiological and structuralist theories that formed the basis of Minimal and Conceptual Art. Anderson's early Minimalist sculpture was influenced by Process Art (especially the work of Eve Hesse), an art that questioned the non-objectivity of materials whose intrinsic qualities could elicit a range of psycho-sexual responses and whose installations often created a theatrical effect. The static modernist art object, with its authoritative ideologies that sustained belief in the universality of meaning vested in form, was no longer tenable. Moreover, a Minimalism rooted in phenomenological rather than cultural conditions precluded textual, postmodern and, most importantly, feminist discourse, ideas important to Anderson.

After a number of one-person performances, invariably accompanied by a mechanically enhanced violin, Anderson, beginning with *Americans on the Move* in 1979, enlarged her production. At first, she increased her musical accompaniment to five musicians playing electronic instruments, eventually intro-

ducing film and photographic imagery into her performances. In her seven-hour, four-part opus, *United States* ("Transportation," "Politics," "Money" and "Love," 1979–83), the artist transcended the personal and autobiographical tone of her earlier work in favor of a multimedia examination of the social codes and mythologies that pervade popular culture. With *United States,* she arrived at a basic theme in her oeuvre—a questioning of the linguistic and semiological systems by which information is transmitted and received and their concomitant ideologies. In whole or in part based on songs from *United States,* her two albums *Big Science* [1982] and *Mister Heartbreak* [1984]—the latter resulting in an international tour that formed the basis for Anderson's first movie *Home of the Brave* [1986]—allowed Anderson to reach an even larger audience.

Anderson's imagery—generalized depictions of cityscapes, highways and newscasts culled from advertising and the media—is a veritable field of semiotic signs in the form of maps, clocks, airplanes, roads and hands. Such a panoply of urban images is, of course, foreboding, and is aggressively compounded by the use of a cold, corporate voice speaking the demands of "big brother," by a radical plurality of altered voices and characters, and by a constant sense of temporal and geographic dislocation. Further denuding herself of a stable identity through the use of parody and quotation, Anderson acts as an electronic magician who both controls and receives the messages of a technocratic society.

Despite the multitude of technological and theatrical effects, which both augment her performance works and diffuse her personality, the focus rarely shifts from Anderson's finely honed persona. Exchanging the rarified aesthetics of the modernist art object for the temporal and confrontational medium of performance (in an age when the music video was first being launched), Anderson's complex media-driven persona reveals the relative purity of the Minimalist performances of Yvonne Rainer, Robert Morris and Simone Forti. In an age of cultural icons inflated by the media, Anderson presents herself in order to wryly comment on the cultural and textual nature of postmodernism.

—Mason Klein

ANDRE, Carl.

American. Born in Quincy, Massachusetts, 16 September 1935. Educated in Quincy Public Schools, 1941–50; Phillips Academy, Andover, Massachusetts, with Patrick and Maude Morgan, Hollis Frampton, Michael Chapman, Frank Stella and Harry Curtis, 1951–53. Served in the United States Army, in North Carolina, 1955–56. Married Rosemarie Castoro (divorced). Freelance artist. Worked for the Boston Gear Works, Quincy, and travelled in England and France, 1954; moved to New York, 1957; worked as an editorial assistant, New York, 1957–58; freight brakeman and conductor, Pennsylvania Railroad, 1960–64. Member, Art Workers Coalition, New York, 1967–72. Agents: Paula Cooper Inc., 155 Wooster Street, New York, New York 10012; Konrad Fischer, Platanestrasse 7, 4 Dusseldorf, West Germany. Address: Post Office Box 1001, Cooper Station, New York, New York 10003, U.S.A.

Individual Exhibitions:

1965 Tibor de Nagy Gallery, New York
1966 Tibor de Nagy Gallery, New York
1967 Dwan Gallery, New York
Dwan Gallery, Los Angeles
Konrad Fischer Gallery, Dusseldorf
1968 Stadtisches Museum, Monchengladbach, West Germany
Heiner Friedrich Gallery, Munich
Wide White Space, Antwerp
Irving Blum Gallery, Los Angeles
1969 Dwan Gallery, New York
Konrad Fischer Gallery, Dusseldorf
Wide White Space, Antwerp
Haagsgemeentemuseum, The Hague
Galleria Gian Enzo Sperone, Turin
1970 Guggenheim Museum, New York
Ace Gallery, Los Angeles
1971 St. Louis Art Museum
Dwan Gallery, New York
Konrad Fischer Gallery, Dusseldorf
Locksley-Shea Gallery, Minneapolis
Galerie Yvon Lambert, Paris
Wide White Space, Antwerp
Heiner Friedrich Gallery, Munich
1972 John Weber Gallery, New York
Konrad Fischer Gallery, Dusseldorf
Friends of Contemporary Art, Denver
Janie C. Lee Gallery, Dallas
Lisson Gallery, London
1973 John Weber Gallery, New York
Thayer Academy, Braintree, Massachusetts
Galleria Gian Enzo Sperone, Turin
Portland Center for the Visual Arts, Oregon
Addison Gallery, Phillips Academy, Andover, Massachusetts
Institute for Contemporary Art, Boston
Museum of Modern Art, New York
Konrad Fischer Gallery, Dusseldorf
Max Protetch Gallery, Washington, D.C.
1974 Wide White Space, Antwerp
Konrad Fischer Gallery, Dusseldorf
Ace Gallery, Vancouver
1975 Barbara Cusak Gallery, Houston
Ace Gallery, Vancouver
Lisson Gallery, London
Galleria Sperone, Rome
Sperone Westwater Fischer Gallery, New York
Dan Weinberg Gallery, San Francisco
Museum of Modern Art, Oxford
Sculpture 1958–1974, Kunsthalle, Berne
John Weber Gallery, New York
1976 Barbara Cusak Gallery, Houston
John Weber Gallery, New York
Ace Gallery, Venice, California
Ace Gallery, Los Angeles
Konrad Fischer Gallery, Dusseldorf
Galerie Yvon Lambert, Paris
Carl Andre/Richard Long/Barry LeVa, Corcoran Gallery, Washington, D.C.
Davidson Art Center, Wesleyan University, Middletown, Connecticut
The Clocktower, New York
Detroit Institute of Arts
Kabinet für Aktuele Kunst, Bremerhaven, West Germany
Minneapolis College of Art and Design
1977 Sperone Westwater Fischer Gallery, New York
Joseloff Gallery, Hartford Art School, Connecticut
Otis Art Institute, Los Angeles
1978 *Sculpture 1959–1977,* Sperone Westwater Fischer Gallery, New York
Sculpture 1959–78, Whitechapel Art Gallery, London
Laguna Gloria Art Museum, Austin, Texas
Contemporary Arts Center, Cincinnati
Albright-Knox Art Gallery, Buffalo, New York
Art Institute of Chicago
1979 La Jolla Museum of Contemporary Art, California
University of California Art Museum, Berkeley
Museum of Fine Arts, Dallas
Musée d'Art Contemporaine, Montreal
Musée d'Art Moderne de la Ville de Paris
1980 Institute of Contemporary Arts, Boston
Paula Cooper Gallery, New York
Lopoukhine Nayduch Gallery, Boston
David Bellman Gallery, Toronto
National Gallery of Canada, Ottawa
Portland State University, Oregon
Galerie Konrad Fischer, Dusseldorf
1981 Susan Caldwell Gallery, New York
Seagram Plaza, New York
Wurttembergischer Kunstverein, Stuttgart
Anthony D'Offay Gallery, New York
Museum Haus Lange, Krefeld, West Germany
Graeme Murray Gallery, Edinburgh
1982 Susan Caldwell Gallery, New York
Galerie Konrad Fischer, Dusseldorf
Alberta College of Art, Calgary
University of New Mexico, Albuquerque
Colorado State University, Fort Collins
University of Wyoming, Laramie
Galerie Hans Mayer, Basel
University of Miami, Coral Gables
1983 Galerie Konrad Fischer, Zurich
Paula Cooper Gallery, New York
Heath Gallery, Atlanta, Georgia
Galerie Daniel Templon, Paris
Nouveau Musee, Lyon, France
Le Coin du Miroir, Dijon, France
The Clocktower, New York
Flow Ace Gallery, Venice, California
Galerie Plus-Kerns, Brussels
1984 Broward Community College, Fort Lauderdale, Florida
Richland College, Dallas
Westfalischer Kunstverein, Munster, West Germany
Galerie Konrad Fischer, Dusseldorf
Galleria Primo Piano, Rome
Galerie im Kornerpark, Berlin-Neukolln
State University of New York at Stony Brook
Galerie Plus-Kern, Brussels
Galerie Andre, West Berlin
1985 Paula Cooper Gallery, New York
Galerie Daniel Templon, Paris
Kunstraum Munchen, Munich
Galerie Konrad Fischer, Dusseldorf
Galleria Gian Enzo Sperone, Rome
1986 Galerie Plus-Kern, Brussels
Galerie Konrad Fischer, Dusseldorf
1987 Van Abbemuseum, Eindhoven, Netherlands
Haags Gemeentemuseum, The Hague
Museo d'Arte Contemporanea, Castello di Rivoli, Italy

Selected Group Exhibitions:

1964 *Eight Young Artists,* Hudson River Museum, Yonkers, New York (and Bennington College, Vermont)
1968 *Minimal Art,* Gemeentemuseum, The Hague (travelled to Dusseldorf and Berlin)
1970 *Unitary Forms: Minimal Sculpture,* San Francisco Museum of Art
1974 *Andre / Broodthaers / Buren / Burgin / Gilbert and George / On Kawara / Long / Richter,* Palais des Beaux-Arts, Brussels
1975 *The Condition of Sculpture: A Selection of Recent Sculpture by Younger British and Foreign Artists,* Hayward Gallery, London
1976 *Drawing Now,* Museum of Modern Art, New York (toured West Germany, Israel and Norway)
1977 *Paris—New York,* Musée d'Art Moderne, Centre Georges Pompidou, Paris
1980 *Andre/Judd/Morris: Sculpture Minimal,* Galleria Nazionale d'Arte Moderna, Rome
1985 *Transformations in Sculpture,* Guggenheim Museum, New York
1987 *A Century of Modern Sculpture,* Dallas Museum of Art, Texas (and National Gallery of Art, Washington, D.C.)

Collections:

Museum of Modern Art, New York; Albright-Knox Art Gallery, Buffalo, New York; Walker Art Center, Minneapolis; National Gallery of Canada, Ottawa; Tate Gallery, London; Stedlijk Museum, Amsterdam; Kunstmuseum, Basel; Hessisches Landesmuseum, Darmstadt; Wallraf-Richartz Museum, Cologne.

Carl Andre: *Hellgate*, 1981 Courtesy Anthony D'Offay Gallery, London

Publications:

By ANDRE: books—*First 5 Poems*, New York 1961; *The Xerox Book*, with others, New York 1968; *7 Books of Poetry: Passport, Shape and Structure, A Theory of Poetry, 100 Sonnets, American Drill, 3 Operas, Lyrics and Odes*, New York 1969: *Attica Book*, with others, edited by Benny Andrews and Rudolf Barabik, New York 1972; *Quincy Book*, Andover, Massachusetts 1973; *144 Blocks and Stones*, Portland, Oregon 1973; *11 Poems*, Turin 1974; *Wood/Carl Andre*, with additional text by R. H. Fuchs, Eindhoven, Netherlands 1978; *12 Dialogues: 1962–1963*, with Hollis Frampton, New York and Halifax, Nova Scotia 1980; articles—"Frank Stella" in *Allen Memorial Art Museum Bulletin* (Oberlin, Ohio), vol. 17, no. 1, Fall 1959; "Preface to Stripe Painting (Frank Stella)" in *16 Americans*, exhibition catalogue, New York 1959; "beam . . . room" in *Primary Structures: Younger American and British Sculptors*, exhibition catalogue, New York 1966; "Art Is What We Do/Culture Is What Is Done to Us" in "Sensibility of the 60's" in *Art in America* (New York), January/February 1967; "New in New York: Line Work" in *Arts Magazine* (New York), May 1967; "Artist Interviews Himself" in *Carl Andre*, exhibition catalogue, Monchengladbach, West Germany 1968; "Flags: An Opera for 3 Voices" in *Studio International* (London), April 1969; "Carl Andre: Form, Structure, Place" in *Arts Magazine* (New York), May 1969; "A Reasonable and Practical Proposal for Artists Who Wish to Remain Free Men in These Terrible Times" in *Open Hearing: Art Workers Coalition*, New York 1969; "Questions et Responses" in *VH101* (Paris), Spring 1970; "An Interview with Carl Andre," with Phyllis Tuchman in *Artforum* (New York), June 1970; statement in "The Artist and Politics: A Symposium" in *Artforum* (New York), September 1970; "Carl Andre," interview with Jeanne Siegel, in *Studio International* (London), November 1970; "Carl Andre," interview with Willoughby Sharp, in *Avalanche* (New York), Fall 1970; "A Juror's Statement" in *Centennial Exhibition*, exhibition catalogue, San Francisco 1971; "Letters" in *Artforum* (New York), March 1972; "Interview with Carl Andre," with Achille Bonito Oliva, in *Domus* (Milan), October 1972; "A Note on Bernhard and Hilla Becher" in *Artforum* (New York), December 1972; statement in *Deurle 11/7/73*, exhibition catalogue, Brussels 1973; "Dialogues with Carl Andre," with Andrea Gould, in *Arts Magazine* (New York), May 1974; "Carl Andre," interview with Irmeline Lebeer in *L'Art Vivant* (Paris), June 1974; "Against Duchamp" in *Praxis* (Chicago), Spring 1975; "The Role of the Artist in Today's Society" in *Art Journal* (New York), Summer 1975; "8 Statements (on Matisse): in *Art in America* (New York), July/August 1975; "Versions of Witness: A Note on Sculpture and Scholarship" in *Art Journal* (New York), Winter 1975–76; "An Interview with Carl Andre," with Michael Ballou and George Morgenstern, in *Minneapolis College of Art and Design* newspaper, 1976; Billy Builder, or, The Painful Machine," chapters I–IV, in *Tracks* (New York), Spring 1976; "Public Notice" in *Artforum* (New York), April 1976; statement in "Views from the Studio" by Henry Gerrit in *Art News* (New York), May 1976; "Correspondence" in *Studio International* (London), May/June 1976; "Commodity and Contradiction; or, Contradiction as Commodity," with Jeremy Gilbert-Rolfe, in *October* (New York), Summer 1976; "Billy Builder; or, The Painful Machine," chapters V–XI, in *Tracks* (New York), Fall 1976; notes in *Bienal*, exhibition catalogue, Sao Paulo 1977; "Questions, Public? Sculpture? For Münster?" in *Skulptur Ausstellung in Münster*, exhibition catalogue, Münster, West Germany 1977; "Billy Builder, or, The Painful Machine," chapters XII–XVI, in *Tracks* (New York), Spring 1977; statement in "The 20th-Century Artists Most Admired by Other Artists" in *Art News* (New York), November 1977; interview in *Artists in Their Own Words* by Paul Cummings, New York 1979; "Interview with Carl Andre," with Ida Panicelli, in *Neue Kunst in Europa* (Munich), January/February 1985.

On ANDRE: books—*8 Young Artists*, exhibition catalogue, by C. E. Goossen, Yonkers, New York 1964; *Carl Andre*, exhibition catalogue, Monchengladbach, West Germany 1968; *Carl Andre*, exhibition catalogue, by Enno Develing, The Hague 1969; *Unitary Forms: Minimal Sculpture by Carl Andre, Don Judd, John McCracken, Tony Smith*, exhibition catalogue, by Suzanne Foley, San Francisco 1970; *Carl Andre*, exhibition catalogue, by Diane Waldman, New York 1970; *the New Avant-Garde* by Gregoire Müller, New York 1972; *Carl Andre: Sculpture 1958–1974*, exhibition catalogue, by Angela Westwater, Berne 1975; *Carl Andre: Sculpture 1959–78*, exhibition catalogue, with an essay by Nicholas Serota, London 1978; *Carl Andre: Sculpture 1959–1977*, exhibition catalogue, by David Bourdon, with a foreword by Barbara Rose, New York 1978; *Carl Andre: Sculpture 1983*, exhibition catalogue, with essay by John Howett, Atlanta, Georgia 1983; *Carl Andre* (catalogue raisonne), The Hague 1987; articles—"Carl Andre: Poems 1958–74" by Lynda Morris in *Studio International* (London), September/October 1975; "An Andre Is What It Is, Not Another Thing" by John Russell in the *New York Times*, 20 February 1976; editorial in *Studio International* (London), March/April 1976; "Carl Andre: Art Versus Talk" by Jeff Perrone in *Artforum* (New York), May 1976; "Carl Andre Has the Floor" by Thomas Hess in *New York*, 7 June 1976; "Carl Andre on

Work and Politics" by Sandy Ballatore in *Artweek* (Oakland, California), 3 July 1976; "Trivialization of Art by the Press" by Pat Gilmour in *Arts Review Yearbook*, London 1977; "Minimalism and Critical Response" by Phyllis Tuchman in *Artforum* (New York), May 1977; "Carl Andre" by David Bourdon in *Arts Magazine* (New York), December 1977; "Background of a Minimalist: Carl Andre" by Phyllis Tuchman in *Artforum* (New York), March 1978; "Andre in Retrospect" by Kenneth Baker in *Art in America* (New York), April 1980; "Bricklaying with Andre" by Waldemar Januszczak in *The Guardian* (London), 12 December 1985.

My works are not the embodiments of ideas or conceptions. My works are, in the phrase of William Blake, "Lineaments of gratified desire."

—Carl Andre

Carl Andre's minimalist work of the 1960s participated in a radical disruption of the reverential condition of traditional sculpture. His early work, wooded columns influenced by Brancusi's totemic figures, eventually yielded to austere, floorbound arrangements of ordinary, prefabricated materials such as brick, metal plates or ribbon, and wood. The promotion of a minimal esthetic, exemplified by Andre's work of the late 60s, represented a prolonged reaction against abstract Expressionism and the spiritual and utopian program of modernism in general. Andre's disenchantment with the antigravitational illusionism of 20th century sculpture led him to explore the possibilities of earthworks, stating that the "ideal piece of sculpture is a road." The artist's interest in the idea of passage, perhaps related to his employment in the early 1960s as a freight brakeman and conductor for the Pennsylvania Railroad, resulted in a rejection of the conventional model of sculpture as a closed and sanctified object. "Spill" (1968), a scatter-piece in which 800 identical plastic blocks were flung to the gallery floor, further emphasized this rejection. While "Spill" has been tenuously compared to Jackson Pollock's overall compositions, it is, on the contrary, antithetical to Pollock's painting in its tacit repudiation of the modernist preoccupation with internal paradox, structural balance, and artistic control. Instead, Andre's floorbound arrangements of magnesium, lead, copper, or steel plates aim for a continuity with their ambient space: "FORM = STRUCTURE = PLACE" Andre has written in a kind of theoretical formula for his work. Rather than possessing internal or metaphoric content, these minimalist pieces function at the level of externality; it is the temporal experience—the act of passage itself—that is at the core of Andre's work.

Engaged in a subtle dialogue with modernism, Andre's minimalist pieces, therefore, cannot be seen as entirely ahistorical. "Lever" (1966), an early and generative work composed of a single row of unattached firebricks, marked an auspicious beginning for the artist's offensive against sculptural convention. Andre's position toward modernism is suggested in a remark made in relation to "Lever": ". . . all I am doing is putting Brancusi's 'Endless Column' on the ground instead of in the air. . . . The engaged position is to run along the earth." Toppled from its "pedestal," "Lever" is representative of the postmodernist attack against the sanctity of the art object. The underlying principles of modernism, as Andre's statement indicates, were not entirely rejected; rather, they were brought to the threshold of something radical and new.

—Maurice Berger

ANDREWS, Michael.

British. Born in Norwich, Norfolk, in 1928. Educated at City of Norwich School; studied at evening classes, Norwich Art School; studied at the Slade School of Fine Art, London, 1949–53. Served in British Army, in Bicester, Oxfordshire and in Egypt, 1946–49. Painter, in London, 1953–77, and in Norfolk since 1977; participated in Lorenza Mazzetti's films *Metamorphosis*, 1952, and with Eduardo Paolozzi, *q.v.*, in *Together*, 1954. Lecturer, Norwich Art School, 1959; Chelsea School of Art, London, 1960, and Slade School of Fine Art, London, 1963–66. Recipient: Rome Scholarship in Painting, 1953; Gulbenkian Purchase Award, 1961. Agent: Anthony D'Offay, London. Address: c/o Anthony D'Offay, 9 Dering Street, London W1, England.

Individual Exhibitions:

1958 Beaux-Arts Gallery, London
1963 Beaux-Arts Gallery, London
1964 Norfolk Contemporary Arts Society, Norwich (with Bernard Meadows)
1974 Anthony D'Offay Gallery, London
1978 *Paintings 1977–78*, Anthony D'Offay Gallery, London
1980 Hayward Gallery, London (travelled to the Fruit Market Gallery, Edinburgh; and the Whitworth Art Gallery, Manchester)
1986 Anthony D'Offay Gallery, London

Selected Group Exhibitions:

1952 *Young Painters*, Institute of Contemporary Arts, London
1954 *Drawings for Pictures*, Arts Council Gallery, London
1960 *Modern British Portraits*, Arts Council Gallery, London
1964 *British Painting in the 60's*, Whitechapel Art Gallery, London
1966 *Figurative Art*, Camden Arts Centre, London
1971 *The Slade 1871–1971*, Royal Academy of Arts, London
1979 *Narrative Painting*, Institute of Contemporary Arts, London
1981 *8 Figurative Painters*, Yale Center for British Art, New Haven, Connecticut (travelled to the Santa Barbara Museum of Art, California)
1984 *Hard-Won Image*, Tate Gallery, London
1987 *A School of London*, Kunstnernes Hus, Oslo (travelled Humlebaek, Denmark; Dusseldorf)

Collections:

Tate Gallery, London; Victoria and Albert Museum, London; Arts Council of Great Britain, London; Gulbenkian Foundation, London; Slade School of Fine Art, University College, London; Norwich Castle Museum, Norfolk; Australian National Gallery, Canberra; National Gallery of Victoria, Melbourne.

Publications:

By ANDREWS: articles—"Notes and Pre-occupations" in *X: A Quarterly Review* (London), vol. 1, no. 1, 1960–61; statement in *Survey 66: Figurative Art*, exhibition catalogue, London 1966.

On ANDREWS: books—*Modern English Painters, volume III: Wood to Hockney* by John Rothenstein, London 1974; *Michael Andrews: Paintings 1977–78*, exhibition catalogue, with text by Anne D'Offay, London 1978; *Michael Andrews*, exhibition catalogue, with text by Lawrence Gowing, London 1980; *8 Figurative Painters*, exhibition catalogue, with texts by Andrew Forge and Lawrence Gowing, New Haven, Connecticut 1981; *A Partial Testament* by Helen Lessore, London 1986; articles—"Stranded Dinosaurs" by William Feaver in *London Magazine* July/August 1970; "Painter of Fact and Feeling" by Lawrence Gowing in the *Sunday Times Magazine* (London), October 1980; "Michael Andrews: Recent Paintings" by Peter Fuller in *Burlington Magazine* (London), July 1986.

At the very beginning of his career Michael Andrews was dubbed Britain's most interesting young artist by Britain's leading contemporary painter; recently it has been said of him that "he paints hardly anything but masterpieces." Yet even in this time when individuality is said to be so highly prized, there are individual artists, even of Andrews' stature, who escape attention; and it was not until his retrospective of 1980 that the general public—and much of the art public—"discovered" Andrews. This can be variously attributed to his slowish production, his figurative content, and his subtle, expansive and unfashionable preoccupations; among artists, his equal ability (shared with Bacon) with broad summary brushwork and exquisitely judged sprays and washes has incited partisan envy.

The title of one of Andrews' earliest paintings, made on passing out of the Slade School of Art in 1952, affords a valuable clue to his interests: "A Man Who Suddenly Fell Over." The individual human ego and its relation to society and to public "image"—as well as its "staying power"—has constantly preoccupied him, and one can imagine both Rembrandt and Hals being fascinated by Andrews' perceptions of the psychological undercurrents that make up a single face, or one of his several group scenes. (It reminds us how rare this once common theme, of community, has become.) His figure studies, and his studies of spatial effects such as fish in water, would grace any public gallery or museum; yet he is one of those artists whose work is best appreciated when seen in sequence. The almost oriental allusiveness of that haunting image of the *shadow* only of a balloon seen against the sand of a deserted beach with a scribble of seaweed—the equivalent of a Japanese *haiku* poem—can be recognised as a superb aesthetic achievement, vibrant with emotional meaning; but a knowledge of Andrews' earlier paintings of the ego as expanding or shrinking balloon adds to its appreciation.

British art is constantly in danger of yielding to a predominantly literate culture; but in Andrews we have an artist who can set a scene like a playwright, a novelist or a poet, yet whose exceptional skills in rapid brushwork plus refined manipulation of paint, and in condensed imagery, open a huge area of life to his potential observation, whose paintings give pleasures both popular and refined. And there is always the feeling that he could move in any direction for his subject-matter—one awaits every new painting from him with eager anticipation.

—Michael Shepherd

ANSELMO, Giovanni.

Italian. Born in Borgofranco d'Ivrea, 5 August 1934. Lives and works in Turin. Agent: Galleria Christian Stein, 206 Piazza San Carlo, 10121 Turin. Address: Via Massena 68, 10128 Turin, Italy.

Individual Exhibitions:

1968 Galleria Sperone, Turin
1969 Galleria Sperone, Turin
Galerie Sonnabend, Paris
1970 Galleria Sperone, Turin
Galleria Toselli, Milan
1971 Galleria Sperone, Turin
Galleria Multipli, Turin
1972 Galleria Sperone, Turin
John Weber Gallery, New York
1973 Galerie MTL, Brussels
Kunstmuseum, Lucerne
1974 Galleria Marilena Bonomo, Bari, Italy
Galleria Sperone-Fischer, Rome
Studio d'Arte L. Rumma, Naples
Galleria Sperone, Turin
Galerie Foksal, Warsaw

Michael Andrews: ***The Cathedral (Ayres Rock)*, 1987** Courtesy Anthony D'Offay Gallery, London

1975 Galleria Sperone, Turin
Galleria Sperone, Rome
Galleria Area, Florence
Saman Galleria, Genoa
Kabinett für Aktuelle Kunst, Bremerhaven, West Germany
1976 Galleria Ghiringelli-Sperone, Milan
Sam Galleria, Genoa
Nuovi Strumenti, Brescia, Italy
1977 Galleria Sperone, Rome
Kabinett für Aktuelle Kunst, Bremerhaven, West Germany
Galleria Il Tritone, Biella, Italy
Galleria G. de Crescenzo, Rome
1978 Galleria Salvatore Ala, Milan
Studio Tucci Russo, Turin
Galerie Paul Maenz, Cologne
Galerie Durand-Dessert, Paris
Sperone-Westwater-Fischer Gallery, New York
1979 Kunsthalle, Basle
Galerie Rudiger Schöttle, Munich
Galleria Emilio Mazzoli, Modena
1980 Stedelijk van Abbemuseum, Eindhoven
Galerie Helen van der Meij, Amsterdam
Forum Kunst, Rottweil, West Germany
Musée de Grenoble, France
Galleria Sperone, Turin
1981 Salvatore Ala Gallery, New York
1982 Galleria Christian Stein, Turin
Galerie Durand-Dessert, Paris
Galerie Helen van der Meij, Amsterdam
1983 Galleria Christian Stein, Turin
1984 Marian Goodman Gallery, New York
Galerie Michele Szwacjer, Antwerp
Castello di Rivoli, Turin
1985 ARC/Musee d'Art Moderne de la Ville, Paris
1986 Kunstnernes Hus, Oslo
Galleria Christian Stein, Milan
1987 Galerie Tanit Kunigk und Mollier, Munich

Selected Group Exhibitions:

1967 *Group Exhibition,* Galleria Sperone, Turin
1968 *9 at Castelli,* Leo Castelli Warehouse, New York
1969 *When Attitude Becomes Form,* Kunsthalle, Berne (travelled to the Museum Haus Lange, Krefeld, West Germany, and the Institute of Contemporary Arts, London)
1970 *Vitalita del Negativo nell'Arte Italiana 1960–1970,* Palazzo delle Esposizioni, Rome
1972 *Documenta 5,* Kassel, West Germany
1974 *Art and Image in Recent Art,* Art Institute of Chicago
1978 *Words,* Kunstmuseum, Bochum, West Germany (travelled to the Palazzo Ducale, Genoa)
1981 *Identite Italienne: L'Ari en Italie depuis 1959,* Centre Georges Pompidou, Paris
1983 *Presence Discrete,* Musee des Beaux-Arts, Dijon, France
1985 *The European Iceberg,* Art Gallery of Ontario, Toronto

Collections:

Stedelijk van Abbemuseum, Einhoven; Stedelijk Museum, Amsterdam; Rijksmuseum, Kroller-Muller, Otterlo, Netherlands; Groninger Museum, Groningen, Netherlands; Australian National Gallery, Canberra.

Publications:

By ANSELMO: books—*Leggere,* Turin 1972; *116 Particolari Visibili e Misurabili di Infinito,* Turin 1975.

On ANSELMO: books—*Anselmo,* exhibition catalogue, by Maurizio Fagiolo, Turin 1968; *Giovane Scultura Italiana* by Germano Celant, Casabella, Italy 1968; *Arte Povera* by Germano Celant, Salerno/Milan/Tübingen/New York 1969; *Giovanni Anselmo,* exhibition catalogue, by Jean-Christophe Ammann, Lucerne 1973; *Giovanni Anselmo,* exhibition catalogue, by Jean-Christophe Ammann and Rudi Fuchs, Basle 1979; *Giovanni Anselmo,* exhibition catalogue, by Thierry Raspail, Grenoble, France 1980; *Anselmo,* exhibition catalogue with text by Suzanne Page, Paris 1985.

By the time Giovanni Anselmo had held his first one-man show at the Galleria Sperone in Milan in 1968, the group known as Arte Povera, of which he was a member, had already been formed. In this exhibition of his work, with its balanced cubes, floating bubbles, suspended sheets of plexiglass and hanging chains, Anselmo had abandoned the traditional picture plane in an attempt to create a more direct representation of the themes of gravity and movement. He was striving for an immediate relation to the real world, both visible and invisible.

In 1966 he had made a work consisting of a small cube above which was fixed a slender baton. The work was labeled *Untitled,* but the materials employed were precisely noted: iron, wood and the force of gravity. A work of 1967/68, *Direzione,* is made of a heavy triangular granite block containing a small compass. The stone is oriented to the north as indicated by the compass needle. Anselmo thus commented on the magnetic forces residing in all natural objects.

Torsione of 1968 is made of cowhides partially embedded in a block of concrete. The lengths of hide emerging from the cement block are stretched out and secured by a sturdy piece of wood piercing and keeping the hides in tension from its position leaning against the wall.

Anselmo's work makes play with the themes of infinity and energy, and the notion that the artist intervenes in a natural order, impressing his own definition of reality on the materials at his disposal.

Giovanni Anselmo: *Direzione*, 1968

From 1970 onwards he began using projected slides together with parallelopiped prism shapes made of lead onto which words were engraved. *Infinito* is a work of 1971 in which Anselmo uses a projection, focused to infinity of the word "Infinito." In other works he projects the word "particolare" (detail) onto a wall to distinguish it from the remainder of the unlit surface. In *Invisibile,* the projection focuses the word "visibile" into an empty space so that the word *is* genuinely invisible. He uses the same idea when he engraves a parallelopiped of lead with the word "visibile": the space in which we would expect to find the prefix "in-" is missing, and all that remains is "visibile".

The different ways in which Anselmo pursues these ideas are all aimed at establishing an appropriate expressive rapport between the energies of the invisible and the infinite. His work is thus intended to be a part, or fragment, which indicates an invisible totality.

—Roberto Lambarelli

ANTES, Horst.

German. Born in Heppenheim, 28 October 1936. Educated at primary school in Heppenheim, 1942–47, and Heppenheim College, 1948–57; studied at the Staatliche Akademie der Bildenden Künste, under H. A. P. Grieshaber, Karlsruhe, 1957–59. Married Dorothea Grossman in 1961; children: Aaron and Salomea. Lived in Florence, 1962; in Rome, 1963; now lives and works in Karlsruhe. Professor of Art, Staatliche Akademie der Bildenden Künste, Karlsruhe, 1965–73; Guest Professor of Art, Academy of Fine Arts, Berlin, 1967–68. Recipient: Kunstpreis, Hannover, 1959; Pankofer prize, 1959; Stipendium des Kulturkreises im Bundesverband der Deutschen Industrie, 1960; Junger Western Fellowship, Recklinghausen, 1961; André Malraux Prize, *Biennale,* Paris, 1961; Villa Romana Prize, Florence, 1962; Villa Massimo Fellowship, Rome, 1963; Guggenheim Award, 1964; Aldegrever-Gesellschaft Fellowship, Münster, 1966; Unesco Prize, *Biennale,* Venice, 1966; Premio Marzotto-Europa, Valdango, 1968. Agents: Galerie Brusberg, Kurfürstendamm 213, 1000 Berlin 15 (West), Germany; Galerie Gunzenhauser, Maximilianstrasse 10, 8000 Munich 22, West Germany; Nishimura Gallery, 4-3-13 Ginza, Chuo-ku, Tokyo 104, Japan. Address: 11 Hohenbergstrasse, 75000 Karlsruhe 41, West Germany.

Individual Exhibitions:

1960 Galerie der Spiegel, Cologne
Galerie Richentor, Basle
Galerie Boukes, Wiesbaden, West Germany
Galerie 61, Freiburg, West Germany
1961 Kellergalerie im Schloss, Darmstadt
Galerie Baier, Mainz, West Germany
Studio for Neue Kunst, Wuppertal, West Germany
1962 Stadtheater, Remscheid, West Germany
1963 Galerie der Spiegel, Cologne
Galerie N., Bremen, West Germany
Musée d'Art Moderne, Paris
Städtisches Museum, Ulm, West Germany
1964 Städtisches Galerie, Munich
Freie Galerie, Berlin
Kurbuchhandlung and Galerie Krohn, Badenweiler, West Germany
Galerie d'Eendt, Amsterdam
Galerie Schmucking, Braunschweig, West Germany
Kleiner Raum Clasing, Münster, West Germany
1965 Deutsche Bibliothek, Brussels
Galerie der Spiegel, Cologne
Galerie Stangl, Munich
1966 Galerie Altes Theater, Ravensburg, West Germany
Kunstverein, Ulm, West Germany
Galerie Valentien, Stuttgart
Galerie Maercklin, Stuttgart
Galerie Schmucking, Braunschweig, West Germany
Städtische Kunsthalle, Mannheim
Galerie Defet, Nuremberg, West Germany
1967 Lefebre Gallery, New York
Studentenhaus, Universität Tübingen, West Germany
Kunstkabinett am Institut für Lehrerweiterbildung, Berlin Pankow
Bundesgartenschau, Karlsruhe (travelled to the Badischer Kunstverein, Karlsruhe)

Kurbuchhandlung and Galerie Krohn, Badenweiler, West Germany
Städtischer Kunstpavillon, Soest, West Germany
Kleiner Raum Clasing, Münster, West Germany
Kunstmuseum, Basle
Galerie d'Eendt, Amsterdam (with Hans Andreus)
Galerie Gimpel and Hanover, Zurich
Staatliche Kunsthalle, Baden-Baden, West Germany
Freunde Mainfränkischer Kunst und Geschicht, Wurzburg, West Germany
1968 Gimpel Fils, London
Kunstverein, Braunschweig, West Germany
Galleria d'Art del Naviglio, Milan
Galerie Lochte, Hamburg
Galerie Junge Generation, Innsbruck
Arts Studeo, Aarhus, Denmark
Galerie Junge Generation, Vienna
Worpsweder Kunsthalle, Bremen, West Germany
Galerie Stangl, Munich
Galerie Forum 67, Linz, Austria
Theater Stadt Nordhorn, West Germany
1969 Lefebre Gallery, New York
Galerie Prisma, Copenhagen
Tatkreis Kunst der Ruhr, Essen
Galerie Trost, Lippstadt, West Germany
Galerie Regio, Lorrach, Switzerland
Goethe Institut, Marseilles
Galleria d'Arte del Cavallino, Venice
1970 Galerie Valentien, Stuttgart
Sitzende Figur mit Scheibe und Ei, Gimpel and Hanover Galerie, Zurich
Gimpel Fils, London
Galerie Jesse, Bielefeld, West Germany
1971 Galerie Muchow, Freiburg, West Germany
Galerie Walther, Dusseldorf
Kunsthalle, Kiel, West Germany
Städtische Verkehrsamt, Offenburg, West Germany
Galerie Schmucking, Braunschwieg, West Germany
Bilder und Skulpturen 1965–1971, Kunsthalle, Baden-Baden, West Germany (travelled to the Gesellschaft der Kunstfreunde, Lindau; Kunsthalle, Berne; Kunsthalle, Bremen; and the Frankfurter Kunstverein)
Antes in der Sammlung Wolf und Ursula Hermann, Kabinett 2, Graphisches Kabinett, Bremen, West Germany
1972 Galerie Hoeppner, Hamburg
Kunsthalle, Wilhelmshaven, West Germany
Lefebre Gallery, New York
Kunstverein Gentofte, Copenhagen
Nordjutland Museum, Aalborg, Denmark
Galerie Stangl, Munich
Galerie Pudelko, Bonn
Galerie Defet, Nuremberg, West Germany
1973 Goethe Institut, Rome
Theater der Stadt, Schweinfurt, West Germany
Gimpel Fils, London
Gimpel and Hanover Galerie, Zurich
Kunstkreis Hameln, West Germany
1974 Ulmer Museum, West Germany
Städtisches Galerie, Rosenheim, West Germany
Lefebre Gallery, New York
Galerie Orek, Constance, West Germany
Librairie et Galerie La Hune, Paris
P and P Galerie, Zug, Switzerland
1975 Galerie Stangl, Munich
Lippische Gesellschaft für Kunst, Detmold, West Germany
1976 Gimpel Fils Gallery, London
Lefebre Gallery, New York
Arts Club of Chicago
1978 Gimpel-Hanover-André Emmerich Galleries, Zurich
Lefebre Gallery, New York
1980 Lefebre Gallery, New York
1981 Galerie Valentien, Stuttgart
Nishimura Gallery, Tokyo
1982 Galerie Brusberg, Hannover
Galerie Schloss Hardenberg, Velbert-Neviges, West Germany
Galerie Rehklau, Augsburg, West Germany
Kreissparkasse, Reutlingen, West Germany
Galerie Der Spiegel, Cologne
Galerie Schaefer, Giessen, West Germany
Galerie Bernd Lutze, Friedrichshafen, West Germany
Lefebre Gallery, New York
1983 Galerie von Loe, Konigstein, West Germany
Galerie Brusberg, West Berlin
Kunsthalle, Bremen, West Germany
Stadtische Galerie, Frankfurt
Kunstmuseum, Hannover
Galerie Gunzenhauser, Munich
Stadthalle, Weiden, West Germany
Goethe-Institut, Athens
Dada Art Gallery, Athens
Wilhelm-Hack-Museum, Ludwigshafen, West Germany
Kunstverein, Ludwigshafen, West Germany
1984 Goethe-Institut, Cairo
Goethe-Institut, Nicosia, Cyprus
Freilichtgalerie, Ludwigsburg, West Germany
Villa Franck, Ludwigsburg, West Germany
Galerie Der Spiegel, Cologne
Galerie Ilverich, Meerbusch-Ilverich, West Germany
Galerie Albrecht, Kaltern/Bozen, West Germany
Lefebre Gallery, New York
Guggenheim Museum, New York
Galerie Hor, Nuremberg, West Germany
Nishimura Gallery, Tokyo
Galerie Defet, Nuremberg, West Germany
1985 Lefebre Gallery, New York
Galerie Krohn, Badenweiler, West Germany
Kupferstichkabinett, Dresden, East Germany
Galerie Michael Neumann, Dusseldorf
Kunstverein, Bayreuth, West Germany
1986 Lefebre Gallery, New York
Kunstbuchhandlung Art Service, Karlsruhe-Durlach, West Germany
Stadtsparkasse, Gladbeck, West Germany
Galerie Reichard, Frankfurt
Galerie Funck, Mannheim, West Germany
Taimei Gallery, Tokyo
Galerie Schmucking, Archsum/Sylt, West Germany
Galerie Gunzenhauser, Munich
1987 Galerie Holbein, Lindau, West Germany
Galerie Wilbrand, Cologne
Stadtische Galerie, Villingen-Schwenningen, West Germany (and Kunstverein Hochrhein, Bad Sackingen)
Galerie K. G. Schafer, Frankfurt
Galerie Ilverich, Meerbusch-Ilverich, West Germany
Galerie Gunzenhauser, Munich

Selected Group Exhibitions:

1959 *1st Biennale des Jeunes Artistes,* Musée d'Art Moderne, Paris
1961 *Carnegie International,* Pittsburgh
1964 *Documenta 3,* Kassel, West Germany
1966 *Biennale,* Venice
1968 *European Painters Today,* Musée des Arts Décoratifs, Paris (toured the United States)
1971 *2nd Triennale of India,* New Delhi
1974 *From Picasso to Lichtenstein,* Tate Gallery, London
1982 *Torso als Prinzip,* Kunstverein, Kassel, West Germany
1985 *Kunst in der Bundesrepublik 1945–85,* Nationalgalerie, West Berlin
1987 *Fifty Years of Collecting,* Guggenheim Museum, New York

Collections:

Kunstmuseum, Basle; Neue Nationalgalerie, Berlin; Städtische Kunstsammlungen, Bonn; Wallraf-Richartz, Cologne; Musée Royaux des Beaux-Arts, Brussels; Centre Georges Pompidou, Paris; Gemeentemuseum, The Hague; museum Boymans-van Beuningen, Rotterdam; Museum des 20, Jahrhunderts, Vienna; Guggenheim Museum, New York.

Publications:

By ANTES: articles—"Interview mit Horst Antes," with Otmar Engel, in *Civis* (Bonn), no. 9–10, 1963; *Deutsche Kunst: Eine Neue Generation* by Rolf-Günter Dienst, Cologne 1970; *Noch Kunst—Neuestes aus deutschen Ateliers* by Rolf-Günter Dienst, Dusseldorf 1970; *Horst Antes: Sitzende Figur mit Scheibe und Ei,* exhibition catalogue, by Willy Rotzler and Mark Rothko, Zurich 1970; *Antes in der Sammlung Wolf und Ursula Hermann,* exhibition catalogue, Bremen, West Germany 1971; *Horst Antes,* exhibition catalogue, by Willy Rotzler, Zurich and London 1973.

On ANTES: books—*Horst Antes,* exhibition catalogue, with text by Herbert Pee, Ulm, West Germany 1963; *Vortrag zur Eroffnung der Ausstellung Horst Antes—Das graphische Werk 1959–1967* by Günther Gercken, Baden-Baden, West Germany 1967; *Kunst unserer Zeit* by Will Grohmann, Cologne 1970; *Bis Heute* by Karin Thomas, Cologne 1971; *Horst Antes: Bilder and Skulpturen 1965–1971,* exhibition catalogue, by Carlo Huber, Berne 1971; *Contemporary Prints* by Riva Castleman, New York 1973; *Antes,* exhibition catalogue, by Wolf Hermann, Rosenheim, West Germany 1974; *Horst Antes Poggibonsi 1979–1980* by Klaus Gallwitz, Frankfurt 1980; *Horst Antes Votives,* exhibition catalogue, with texts by Werner Haftmann and Thomas Messer, New York 1984; *Horst Antes—Dreiundfunfzig Bilder, Dreiunddreisig Sammler aus Suddeutschland,* edited by Volker Huber, Offenbach am Main 1987.

Though he studied at Karlsruhe and returned there to teach at the Academy of Fine Arts from 1965 to 1973, Horst Antes could be described as the explorer of a territory known only to himself, an anthropologist specialising in creatures discovered in his own imaginative experience.

His early paintings in the late 1950's were strong, highly coloured works deriving partly from the Expressionism of the previous generations of German painters and partly from the example of his professor H. A. P. Grieshaber. They were a variant of the New Figuration that was popular among German artists at the time. Antes then developed his own figuration in his "Gnome" people, massive beings who presented their profiles impassively on the canvas. Bright synthetic colours heightened the surrealist effect of these strange personages, often crippled or distorted so that a head would surmount two legs without a trunk, one arm waving in futility. Large in scale, these brooding heads sometimes with eyes set vertically one above the other recall such visual twists by Picasso while a landscape of a deserted classic temple beneath floating white clouds takes on the atmosphere of a naive Chirico.

Within a year of leaving the Karlsruhe Academy Antes had his first one-man show at the Spiegel Gallery, Cologne, and since then he has shown continuously in Europe and the U.S.A. In 1962 and 1963 he lived in Italy and now spends much of his time in Tuscany. His interest in the paintings of the Italian Primitives had its effect on his work which became more pure and simplified in colour.

Antes's "family" of art figures possess formidable sculptural elements often truncated and disjointed and painted in monochrome. On two facing figures prehensile toes of equal length and stylised hands assume schematic patterns akin to the hieratic reliefs of Assyrian wall sculpture.

The severe iconography of the pictures, their economy of colour and simplicity of motives demand a concentration upon meaning that is never clarified. Deliberate malformation of humanity carries with it some of the ominous messages transmitted by Bacon but in more mechanistic effigy and at the same time carrying something of the haunting masks of primitive societies.

Man as mask is likewise suggested in other connotations such as "Portrait with Slide" where a man looks out from the apertures in his helmet of skin. Affinities with Leger seem superficial; in the projected puzzle there is more of the early surreal drama of Max Ernst and the prehistoric imagery of Easter Island gods.

Iconic and personal, the paintings and prints of Horst Antes illustrate not a phase of art history but

the concrete externalisation of community dreams. He has created the identifiable hero of contemporary myth, conveying in each successive work satisfaction of a curiosity aroused in all sagas: what happens next? He maintains the strength of his figurative concepts by involving the spectator in the funambulist contest of his rudimentary compositions.

—G. S. Whittet

ANTIN, Eleanor.

American. Born Eleanor Fineman in New York City, 27 February 1935. Studied at the Tamara Daykarhanova School for the Stage, New York; studied creative writing at the College of the City of New York. Married the poet David Antin in 1961; child: Blaise. Worked as a professional actress, 1955–58; now a full-time artist, living and working in California. Visiting Lecturer, University of California at Irvine, 1974–75. Assistant Professor, 1975–78, Associate Professor, 1978–79, and since 1979 Professor of Visual Arts, University of California at San Diego. Recipient: National Endowment for the Arts grant, 1979; Vesta Award for Performance, 1985. Agent: Ronald Feldman Fine Arts, 31 Mercer Street, New York, New York 10013. Address: Post Office Box 1147, Del Mar, California 92014, U.S.A.

Individual Exhibitions:

1968 Long Island University, Brooklyn, New York
1970 *California Lives,* Gain Ground Gallery, New York
1971 *Library Science,* Brand Library Art Center, Los Angeles
Portraits of 8 New York Women, Chelsea Hotel, New York
1972 *Traditional Art,* Henri Gallery, Washington, D.C.
Library Science, California Institute of the Arts, Valencia, California
Library Science, University of California at San Diego
Library Science, Austin Peay State University, Clarksville, Tennessee
Traditional Art, Orlando Gallery, Los Angeles
1973 *100 BOOTS,* Museum of Modern Art, New York
Part of an Autobiography, Portland Center for the Visual Arts, Oregon
More Traditional Art, Northwood Experimental Art Institute, Dallas
I Dreamed I was a Ballerina, Orlando Gallery, Los Angeles
1974 *Several Selves,* Everson Museum, Syracuse, New York
The Ballerina and the King, Galleria Forma, Genoa
Black Is Beautiful, University of California at Irvine
1975 The Kitchen, New York (video exhibition)
2 Transformations, Stefanotty Gallery, New York
1976 *Eleanor Antin, R.N.,* The Clocktower, New York
1977 *The Angel of Mercy,* D'Arc Gallery, New York
The Angel of Mercy, La Jolla Museum of Contemporary Art, California
The Nurse and the Hijackers, Ronald Feldman Fine Arts Gallery, New York
100 BOOTS Once Again and Choreographies, Wadsworth Atheneum, Hartford, Connecticut
1978 *The Ballerina,* Whitney Museum, New York
The Nurse and the Hijackers, Long Beach Museum of Art, California
Ballerina, Los Angeles Institute of Contemporary Art
1979 *Before the Revolution,* Ronald Feldman Fine Arts Gallery, New York
100 BOOTS: Transmission and Reception, Franklin Furnace, New York
The Black Ballerina, Marianne Deson Gallery, Chicago
1980 *Recollections of My Life with Diaghilev,* Ronald Feldman Fine Arts Gallery, New York
1981 *Angel of Mercy,* Los Angeles Institute of Contemporary Art
Nova Gallery, Vancouver
Early Works, Palomar College, California
1982 *Recollections of My Life with Diaghilev,* Minneapolis College of Art and Design, Minnesota
La Mamelle, San Francisco
Rutgers University, New Brunswick, New Jersey
1983 *El Desdichado,* Ronald Feldman Fine Arts, New York
Recollections of My Life with Diaghilev, Tortue Gallery, Los Angeles
1986 *Loves of a Ballerina,* Ronald Feldman Gallery, New York

Performances: *The Ballerina Goes to the Big Apple,* Woman's Building, Los Angeles, 1974; *Eleanor 1954,* Woman's Building, Los Angeles, 1974; *The King's Meditations,* Center for Music Experiment, University of California at San Diego, 1975; *The Ballerina Goes to the Big Apple,* Stefanotty Gallery, New York, 1975; *The Battle of the Bluffs,* Fine Arts Gallery, San Diego, 1975; *The Battle of the Bluffs,* Palace of Fine Arts, San Francisco, 1975; *Escape,* Palace of the Legion of Honor, San Francisco, 1975; *The Battle of the Bluffs,* The Clocktower, New York, 1976; *The Battle of the Bluffs,* Los Angeles Institute of Contemporary Art, 1976; *The Battle of the Bluffs,* at the *Biennale,* Venice, 1976; *The Battle of the Bluffs,* at the *American Theatre Association Convention,* Los Angeles, 1976; *Escape from the Tower,* The Clocktower, New York, 1976; *It's Still the Same Old Story,* The Clocktower, New York, 1976; *The Angel of Mercy,* D'Arc Gallery, New York, 197; *The Angel of Mercy,* La Jolla Museum of Contemporary Art, California, 1977; *The Battle of the Bluffs,* Museum of Contemporary Art, Chicago, 1978; *The Battle of the Bluffs,* Contemporary Arts Museum, Houston, 1978; *The Battle of the Bluffs,* Center for Music Experiment, University of California at San Diego, 1978; *Before the Revolution,* Kitchen Center for Music, Video and Dance, New York, 1979; *Before the Revolution,* Santa Barbara Museum of Art, California, 1979; *Recollections of My Life with Diaghilev,* Ronald Feldman Fine Arts Gallery, New York, 1980; *Recollections of My Life with Diaghilev,* 80 Langton Street, San Francisco, 1980; *The Battle of the Bluffs,* at the *National Women's Caucus for Art,* New Orleans, 1980; *The Battle of the Bluffs,* performed at the Ford Theatre, at the *11th Annual International Sculpture Conference,* Washington, D.C., 1980; *Battle of the Bluffs,* College of Art, Calgary, Alberta, 1980; *The Battle of the Bluffs,* Western Front, Vancouver, 1981; *Battle of the Bluffs,* Concordia University, Montreal, 1981; *Battle of the Bluffs,* Newport Harbor Art Museum, California, 1981; *Angel of Mercy,* Los Angeles Institute of Contemporary Art, 1981; *Recollections of My Life with Diaghilev,* Contemporary Arts Museum, Houston, 1981; *Recollections of My Life with Diaghilev,* School of the Art Institute of Chicago, 1981; *Recollections of My Life with Diaghilev,* University of Regina, Saskatchewan, 1981; *Battle of the Bluffs,* La Mamelle, San Francisco, 1982; *Recollections of My Life with Diaghilev,* Oklahoma City Museum of Fine Arts, 1982; *Battle of the Bluffs,* Hofstra University, Hempstead, New York, 1982; *Recollections of My Life with Diaghilev,* California State University, Chico, 1983; *Recollections of My Life with Diaghilev,* Institute of Contemporary Art, Boston, 1984; *Student Days in Paris,* Radio Station WGBH, Boston, 1984; *Recollections of My Life with Diaghilev,* Laguna Beach Museum of Art, California, 1985; *Help! I'm in Seattle,* L.A.C.E., Los Angeles, 1986; *Help! I'm in Seattle,* Franklin Furnace, New York, 1987; *Who Cares About a Ballerina,* Bowery Theatre, San Diego, California, 1987.

Selected Group Exhibitions:

1969 *Language 3,* Dwan Gallery, New York
1975 *Video Art U.S.,* at the *Bienal,* Sao Paulo
1976 *Autobiographical Fantasies,* Los Angeles Institute of Contemporary Art
1977 *American Narrative/Story Art 1967–1977,* Contemporary Arts Museum, Houston (travelled to the Fine Arts Museum, New Orleans; Fine Arts Museum, Vancouver; University of California Museum of Art, Berkeley; and the University of California at Santa Barbara)
1979 *Directions,* Hirshhorn Museum and Sculpture Garden, Smithsonian Institution, Washington, D.C.
1981 *Persona,* New Museum, New York
1984 *Content: A Contemporary Focus,* Hirshhorn Museum, Washington, D.C.
Revising Romance: New Feminist Video, Institute of Contemporary Art, Boston (toured the United States, 1984–86)
1985 *From the Collection of Sol LeWitt,* California State University, Long Beach (toured the United States)
1986 *Photography as performance,* The Photographers' Gallery, London

Collections:

Museum of Modern Art, New york; Wadsworth Atheneum, Hartford, Connecticut; San Francisco Museum of Modern Art; Long Beach Museum of Art, California; Walker Art Center, Minneapolis.

Publications:

By ANTIN: books—*Before the Revolution,* Santa Barbara, California 1979; *Being Antinova,* Los Angeles 1983; *The Antinova Plays,* Los Angeles 1987; articles—"Women Without Pathos" in *Artnews* (New York), January 1971, reprinted in *Art and Sexual Politics,* edited by Elizabeth Baker and Thomas Hess, New York 1973; "Out of the Box" in *Art Gallery* (Ivoryton, Connecticut), June 1972; "Reading Ruscha" in *Art in America* (New York), September/October 1973; "Recollections of My Life with Diaghilev" in *Artweek* (Oakland, California), 27 October 1973; "Letter to a Young Woman Artist" in *Anonymous Was A Woman,* Valencia, California 1974; "Video as a Medium" in *Art-Rite* (New York), October 1974; photo-texts of "Ballerina and the Bum" and "Little Match Girl Ballet" in *Video Art,* edited by Ira Schneider and Beryl Korot, New York 1976; interview, with Leo Rubenfein, in *Art in America* (New York), September/October 1978; "Interview with Eleanor Antin," with Dinah Portner, in *Journal: Southern California Art Magazine* (Los Angeles), February/March 1980; interview, with Nancy Bowen, in *Profile: Eleanor Antin,* publication of the Video Data Bank, School of the Art Institute of Chicago, 1981; "Pocahontas" in *Skew* (Tucson), no. 1, 1981; "Revolutions Per Minute," interview, with Carter Ratcliff, in *Inter-View* (New York), September 1982.

On ANTIN: books—*6 Years: The Dematerialization of the Art Object from 1966–72* by Lucy Lippard, New York 1973; *Art Talk* by Cindy Nemser, New York 1975; *Angel of Mercy,* exhibition catalogue, with essays by Jonathan Crary and Kim Levin, La Jolla, California 1977; *Originals: American Women Artists* by Eleanor Munro, New York 1979; *Directions,* exhibition catalogue, with an essay by Howard Fox, Washington, D.C. 1979; *Performance Anthology: Source Book for a Decade of California Performance Art,* edited by Carl Loeffler and Darlene Tong, San Francisco 1980; *The Amazing Decade: Women and Performance Art in America 1970–1980,* edited by Moira Roth, Los Angeles 1983; articles—review by Lawrence Alloway in *The Nation* (New York), 23 February 1970;"Los Angeles 1971" by Elizabeth Baker in *Artnews* (New York), September 1971; "The Post Perceptual Portrait" by Amy Goldin in *Art in America* (New York), January/February 1975; "4 Artists of Sensuality" by Cindy Nemser in *Arts Magazine* (New York), March 1975; "When Greatness Is a Box of Wheaties" by Carol Duncan in *Artforum* (New York), October 1975; "Eleanor Antin: Wishes, Lies and Dreams" by Peter Frank in *Soho Evening News* (New York), 19 February 1976; "Eleanor Antin's Historical Daydream" by John Russell in the *New York Times,* 23 January 1977; "The Nurse and the Dandy" by John Perreault in the *Soho Evening News* (New York), 27 January 1977; "Life/Art/Life: Quentin Crisp and Eleanor Antin: Notes on Performance in the 70's" by John R. Clarke in *Arts Magazine* (New York), February 1979; "Entries: Maximalism" by Robert Pincus-Witten in *Arts Magazine* (New York), February 1981; "Antin/Antinova: The Self as Art Medium" by Sanda Agalidi in *Michigan Quarterly Review* (Ann Arbor), Winter 1984; "Antinova Dances Again" by Henry Sayre in *Artweek* (Oakland, California), 31 May 1986.

For some time I have been considering my art as an exploration of the self, which means that I have been attempting to define my self by moving out to its frontiers, where knowledge of what I cannot and will not be gradually helps shape what I am.

Apparently I have an action or acting theory of the

Eleanor Antin: image from the film *Swan Lake*, 1986

self, because I tend to think of the self as a collection of possible characteristic roles that wait in the wings for their chance to play. No actor can play all roles. A good one can play at most three or four fundamental ones, which he or she can, with effort and talent, bend, stretch and transform to satisfy the casting demands life makes on him or her. The inferior actor—the impoverished self—can play only one role over and over again, no matter what demands life makes on him. This boring and impoverished performance is considered sincerity by an equally boring and impoverished criticism, which supposes one life, one truth. I have never accepted such a trivial truth, and I have determined by empirical investigation of my soul that I am by nature typecast as a King, a Ballerina, a Nurse, and a color—Black. A King must rule or try to rule, a Ballerina must star, a Nurse must help, and as all of my selves turn Black, I transform my eccentric Blackness in a white culture into a virtue and a power.

My work has taken the course through drawing, painting, writing, photography, video and performance—of allowing these figures of my soul to play out their roles and answer to all the demands that life makes on me—an artist, a woman, an American in the last quarter of the 20th century.

—Eleanor Antin

Eleanor Antin is a small woman who looks remarkably kingly in the cape and beard she wears during performances as the King of Solana Beach. The King visits the people of Solana Beach (where Antin happens to live) and discusses politics while participating in daily activities. The real life encounters are documented in black and white slides which become part of performances such as the *Battle of the Bluffs.* The King feels that Solana Beach is a small but natural kingdom "for no kingdom should extend further than a King can walk on any given day." Although Antin is not interested in having Solana Beach revert to the 17th century, a time more familiar to a King dressed like a Van Dyck portrait, the emphasis on naturalness is significant. The "battle"refers to a confrontation between real estate developers and a band of young skateboarders and elderly citizens with shuffleboard sticks who are organized by the King to stop excessive construction in the small California beach town. There are arrests, and the King escapes down a cliff to travel around the country and alert others. "The world restored will have trees and homegrown food," says the King.

Antin's performance work is autobiographical, yet it has historical and art historical roots. As the King, Antin is pleased with her resemblance to Charles I as painted by Van Dyck, finding him to be "a very small man, like me, a stubborn romantic, and all in all, an impossible person. . . . I recognized all these things in myself. So I knew what sort of man I was, and that he was my political self because a king rules a country." As Eleanora Antinova, she presents herself as a black dancer with Diaghilev's troupe, reminiscing over her triumphs and failures. As a nurse, she occasionally uses material from the life of Florence Nightingale. At all times Antin is completely immersed not only in her part but in many parts. The *Battle of the Bluffs* is done as a narrative, and although Antin wears the King's costume and performs in front of slides of the King's activities in Solana Beach, she provides the voices for all the characters, lending a charming story hour at the library ambiance to the work.

Autobiography blends with historical allusions and the real history of Antin's characters, documented for performance in slides, or, for Eleanora Antinova, photographs of the ballerina in her greatest roles. Antin's self, therefore, manifests itself in several characters and across several centuries. She is in a position of power as the King, and in a position of powerlessness as the black dancer whose career is thwarted. She controls the performance, yet she is always a vulnerable character. As King, she travels on foot, unprotected, through her kingdom in a manner no one expects of leaders or royalty. By mingling her own vision and experiences with the past, she gives clues to the self of Eleanor Antin in a context which redefines not only the artist but some concepts about power and traditional roles for women. While she has not abandoned any of her characters, Antin has focused on Eleanora Antinova, the black ballerina, in

the 1980s. In 1983 she published *Being Antinova*, a detailed account of the twenty-day buildup and letdown of transforming herself from a performance artist living in California to Antinova, dancer in New York. The milieu is the contemporary New York art world, with an astonishing quantity of frank comments and gossip, but the artist's familiarity as a native New Yorker enables her to provide a wide-ranging commentary on class and race consciousness in the Big Apple past and present. Antinova resurfaced in 1986 in *Help! I'm in Seattle*, a performance wherein she hits the skids as a performer in vaudeville houses in the 1930s, and mourns her past with Diaghilev. Once again Antin poses seemingly unsolveable questions about the relation between theater and performance art, couching them in Antinova's own dilemma.

—Mary Stofflet

ANTONAKOS, Stephen.

American. Born in St. Nickolas, Gythion, Greece, 1 November 1926; settled with his family in the United States, 1930. Studied at the Brooklyn Community College, New York. Independent artist, New York, since 1950. Instructor in Painting, Brooklyn Museum Art School, 1965–67; Instructor, University of North Carolina, Greensboro, 1967, 1969; Artist-in-Residence, Viterbo College, LaCrosse, Wisconsin, 1968; Instructor, Yale University, New Haven, Connecticut, 1968; Instructor in Sculpture, Brooklyn College, 1970; Artist-in-Residence, University of Wisconsin, Madison, and Fresno State College, California, 1971. Recipient: Creative Artists Public Service Program Grant, New York, 1972; National Endowment for the Arts grant, 1973. Lives and works in New York. Address: 435 West Broadway, New York, New York 10012, U.S.A.

Individual Exhibitions:

1958 Avant-Garde Gallery, New York
University of Maine Art Gallery, Orono
1964 Byron Gallery, New York
Schram Galleries, Fort Lauderdale, Florida
Miami Museum of Modern Art
1967 Fischbach Gallery, New York
1968 Fischbach Gallery, New York
1970 Fort Worth Art Center Museum, Texas
Fischbach Gallery, New York
1971 Madison Art Center, Wisconsin
Fischbach Gallery, New York
Allen Priebe Art Gallery, Wisconsin State University, Oshkosh
Contemporary Arts Museum, Houston
1972 Fischbach Gallery, New York
Fresno State College Art Gallery, California
1973 State University of New York Art Galleries, Albany (toured the United States)
1974 *Drawings*, Rosa Esman Gallery, New York
4 Neon Sculptures, John Weber Gallery, New York
Recent Drawings and Sculptures, Albright-Knox Art Gallery, Buffalo, New York
Discussions: Works/Words, The Clocktower, New York
4 Incomplete Square Neons, Cusack Gallery, Houston
10 Outdoor Neons, Fort Worth Art Museum, Texas
1975 *Incomplete Blue Neon Circles*, Galleria Marilena Bonomo, Bari, Italy
Incomplete Red Neon Circles, Galerie 26, Paris
Incomplete Green Squares, Galleriaforma, Genoa
Neon for Wright State, Wright State University Art Gallery, Dayton, Ohio
Incomplete Neon Squares/Incomplete Neon Circles, John Weber Gallery, New York
1976 *Incomplete Neon Circles*, Galerie December, Dusseldorf
Packages Meant to Be Opened/Packages Meant Never to Be Opened, John Weber Gallery, New York
Incomplete Circles, Neons and Drawings, Art and Project, Amsterdam
Incomplete Circle Neons, Galerie Bonnier, Geneva
Incomplete Neon Squares/Incomplete Neon Circles, Nancy Lurie Gallery, Chicago
1977 *Neons—Stockholm—1977*, Galerie Aronowitsch, Stockholm
Neons—New York—1977, John Weber Gallery, New York
Neons-Athens—1977, Jean and Karen Bernier, Athens
1978 *Outdoor and Indoor Neons*, University of Massachusetts Art Gallery, Amherst
Drawings, Galerie Tanit, Munich
Neons/Drawings/Chicago/1978, Young Hoffman Gallery, Chicago
1979 *Neons/Paris/1979*, Galerie Nancy Gillespie/Elisabeth de Laage, Paris
1980 *Neons, Drawings, Collages, München, 1980*, Galerie Tanit, Munich
3 Neon Walls, Lowe Art Museum, Miami
1982 *New Works/1982*, Nassau County Museum of Art, Roslyn, New York
1983 *Neon for Nevers*, Maison de Culture, Nevers, France
Three Neons, Le Coin du Miroir, Dijon, France
New York/1983, Bonnier Gallery, New York
Neons, Jean Bernier Gallery, Athens
1984 *Neons and Works on Paper*, La Jolla Museum of Contemporary Art, California
1985 Sandpiper Gallery, Tacoma, Washington
Neons, Davenport Art Gallery, Iowa
1986 *Neons and Drawings*, Brandeis University, Waltham, Massachusetts
Neon Room for the Elvehjem Museum of Art, University of Wisconsin, Madison (installation)
1987 *Neons and Drawings*, Burnett Miller Gallery, Los Angeles
Neons, Drawings and Prints, Dalsheimer Gallery, Baltimore, Maryland

Selected Group Exhibitions:

1975 *Painting, Drawing and Sculpture of the 60's and 70's from the Dorothy and Herbert Vogel Collection*, Institute of Contemporary Art, Philadelphia
1976 *Soho—Downtown Manhattan*, at the *Fall Arts Festival*, West Berlin
1977 *Documenta 6*, Kassel, West Germany
1978 *A Shade of Light*, San Francisco Museum of Modern Art
1979 *Minimal Tradition*, Aldrich Museum of Contemporary Art, Ridgefield, Connecticut
1980 *Aspects of the 70's: Site Work*, Jewett Arts Center, Wellesley College Museum, Massachusetts
1981 *Summer Light*, Museum of Modern Art Penthouse, New York
1983 *Elektra*, Musee d'Art Moderne de la Ville, Paris
1984 *Intermedia Space*, Aldrich Museum of Contemporary Art, Ridgefield, Connecticut
1987 *XIX Bienal de Sao Paulo*, Brazil

Collections:

Whitney Museum, New York; Museum of Modern Art; New York; Finch College Museum of Art, New York; Newark Museum, New Jersey; Aldrich Museum of Contemporary Art, Ridgefield, Connecticut; Milwaukee Art Center; Miami Museum of Modern Art; Weatherspoon Art Gallery, University of North Carolina, Greensboro; Phoenix Art Museum, Arizona; La Jolla Museum of Contemporary Art, California.

Permanent public installations: Federal Building, Dayton, Ohio; Crown Center, Hampshire College, Amherst, Massachusetts; University of Massachusetts, Amherst; Hartsfield International Airport, Atlanta; 42nd Street, between Ninth and Tenth Avenues, New York; Charles Center Mass Transit Station, Baltimore; Center Resident Theatre; Seattle; York College, New York; Southwestern Bell Texas Headquarters, Dallas; Columbus Museum of Art, Ohio; Tacoma Dome, Washington.

Publications:

On ANTONAKOS: books—*New Forms/New Media*, exhibition catalogue, by Lawrence Alloway and Allan Kaprow, New York 1960; *Minimal Art: A Critical Anthology*, edited by Gregory Battcock, New York, 1968; *The Magic Theatre* by Ralph T. Coe, Kansas City, Missouri 1970; *Stephen Antonakos: Six Corner Neons*, exhibition catalogue, with essay by Naomi Spector, New York 1973; *Stephen Antonakos*, exhibition catalogue, with texts by Xavier Douroux, Franck Gautherot and Naomi Spector, Dijon 1983; *Neons and Works on Paper*, exhibition catalogue, with essay by Sally Yard, La Jolla 1984; articles—"New Talent" by Larry Aldrich in *Art in America* (New York), July/August 1966; "Stephen Antonakos: 5 Neons for the San Francisco Show" by Naomi Spector in *Data* (Milan), Autumn 1973; "Stephen Antonakos" by Lawrence Campbell in *Artnews* (New York), April 1974; "Stephen Antonakos" by Ellen Lubell in *Arts Magazine* (New York), April 1974; "Stephen Antonakos at the Fort Worth Art Museum" by Janet Kutner in *Art in America* (New York), September/October 1975; "Stephen Antonakos' Neons" by Hugh Davies in *Arts Magazine* (New York), January 1979; "Lights of the Night" by Michael Webb in *Sky* (New York), February 1984; "Creations in Neon" by William Zimmer in the *New York Times*, 15 March 1987.

My work concerns light, color and space: neon used in relation to architectural sites, painted canvases, and painted wood panels. My drawings, prints, books, and other projects are also very important to me in working out my ideas about placing elements in relation to each other.

Neon is endless. Its ability to change and be changed by various elements—alone, or in combination—is a continuing source of inspiration to me.

I am interested in a direct visual experience which will allow the viewer to participate fully, which will provide a feeling of heightened consciousness, or excitement.

—Stephen Antonakos

Stephen Antonakos' work has never been a search for new technical possibilities. His concern for light as a means of expression is the sole impetus for his perserverance with a potentially dated art form, neon. Yet he is no "light artist," but a sculptor and a painter. His search is rather for new ways of commanding ever more intense and refined statements from his formal vocabulary.

Born in southern Greece, Antonakos immigrated to the United States in 1930. He graduated from the New York Institute of Applied Arts and Sciences in 1947, then worked two years as a commercial artist until becoming frustrated by the restrictions of drawing in black and white. After assisting Umberto Romano in 1951, Antonakos spent nine months in Europe visiting galleries and museums. During that period he formulated an individual approach to painting in colour.

Nearly all of Antonakos' work contains the leitmotif of incompletion. In the late 40s and early 50s he developed a complicated vocabulary of forms and a penchant for natural and found materials and colours. The result was a composition of found objects and fragments glued, pinned, or sewn to the canvas called "sewlages." He devoted his energies in the late 50s to freestanding, wooden assemblages. Beginning in September 1962, Antonakos conceived all of the renowned "Pillow" series in one intense 14 month period. The pillows communicate in words, in forms, in materials, in symbols, and with real objects. They deliver themes of interruption, chaos, loss and pain, offering riddles, promising revelations, and ultimately define the struggle of an identity unable to reconcile what it wants to be with what it really is. The pillows tell a story of how they must overcome being ripped open, sewn up, and nailed down to achieve understanding and to reach wholeness.

The focus of his work shifted again in 1962 as he developed a regime of light as environment. The first

ave 3
re.
l have 5
ature.

Stephen Antonakos: ***Neon for New York College*****, 1986**

neons were fully three-dimensional sculpture forms, traditional pedestal objects whose constituent tubes emitted intense coloured light and were programmed to turn on and off in series. With the advent of environmental art during the decade following, Antonakos persistently exploited the full potential of a medium which projects colour and creates volume without sculptural mass.

The three-dimensional forms gradually evolved into neons which conspicuously hugged the plane of the wall. In this sense his work has progressed from assertively sculptural to architectural and finally to environmental painting. The latter is characterised by a dramatic increase in scale, as many neon elements are arranged across the entire two-dimensional surface in mural fashion. The painting's actual dimensions are obfuscated by deliberate perspectival distortions: the bright neon elements establish a flat plane, although the neon itself appears to float, making the depth of the rear supporting wall ambiguous.

Recently Antonakos discovered that painting the supporting walls in colours compliments the neons they entertain. Background colour defines the boundaries of the work and alters the ambient light. He reiterates his original leit-motif by painting the walls in fragments of squares or circles, incomplete shapes that suggest the language of minimalism.

Yet his work seems to adhere to no single identifiable group. Being conspicuously versatile it satisfies dogmatists of most spheres: technological utopianism, geometric reduction, grammatical vision. Because neon is so direct it seems uncomplicated at first, but even in the same piece it can be completely different in meaning; it is quiet and inconspicuous in the daylight, more alert and assertive at dusk, progressively more dominating and abstract at night. From different points of view it is a series of illusions which succeeds as an architectural statement both indoors and out.

The power of these neons rests undeniably in their ability to excite and evoke. Antonakos is particularly sensitive to the warmth and ambiance of colour—mostly reds, blues and greens—and rhythm. When the light goes off, the tubes often seem to become immaterial, and when they burst back on, the shock is extremely effective, especially in rhythmic repetition. This rhythmic quality is one of his most crucial elements. From the beginning the forms—especially the linear ones—appear in repetitive patterns hinting at rhythms of various sorts.

While the emanation of ambient light and the resulting environmental command it bears resemble artists like Flavin, the colour and composition of his neon paintings echo the works of Matisse. Indeed his work bears comparison to a range of artists and dogmas, although the constant evolution in Antonakos's work continues to avoid type-casting.

—Carrie Barker

ANUSKIEWICZ, Richard (Joseph).
American. Born in Erie, Pennsylvania, 23 May 1930. Studied at the Cleveland Institute of Art, 1948–53, B.F.A. 1953; School of Art and Architecture, Yale University, New Haven, Connecticut, 1953–55 (studied with Josef Albers), M.F.A. 1955; Kent State University, Ohio, B.S. in Education 1956. Independent artist known for hard-edge non-objective paintings and prints. Instructor, Cooper Union, New York, 1963–65; Artist-in-Residence, Dartmouth College, Hanover, New Hampshire, 1967; Visiting Artist, University of Wisconsin, Madison, Cornell University, Ithaca, New York, and Visiting Artist, Kent State University, Ohio, 1968; instructor in painting, School of Visual Arts, New York, since 1983. Recipient: Pulitzer Travelling Scholarship, National Academy of Design, 1953; Purchase Prize, Flint Institute of Arts, Michigan, 1966. Agent: Sidney Janis Gallery, 110 West 57th Street, New York, New York 10019. Address: 76 Chestnut Street, Englewood, New Jersey 07631, U.S.A.

Individual Exhibitions:

1955 Butler Art Institute, Youngstown, Ohio
1960 The Contemporaries, New York
1961 The Contemporaries, New York
1963 The Contemporaries, New York
1965 Sidney Janis Gallery, New York
1966 Cleveland Museum of Art
1967 Sidney Janis Gallery, New York
Hopkins Art Center, Dartmouth College, New Hampshire
1968 Kent State University, Ohio
1969 Sidney Janis Gallery, New York
1971 Sidney Janis Gallery, New York
1972 DeCordova Museum, Lincoln, Massachusetts
Jacksonville Art Museum, Florida
1973 Sidney Janis Gallery, New York
1974 Andrew Crispo Gallery, New York
1975 Andrew Crispo Gallery, New York
Ulrich Museum of Art, Wichita, Kansas
1976 Andrew Crispo Gallery, New York
La Jolla Museum of Contemporary Art, California
1977 University of California Art Museum, Berkeley
Columbus Gallery of Fine Arts, Ohio
1978 Ringling Museum, Sarasota, Florida
Allentown Art Museum, Pennsylvania
1979 Alex Rosenberg Gallery, New York
Clark Art Institute, Williamstown, Massachusetts
1980 Brooklyn Museum, New York
Carnegie Institute, Pittsburgh
1981 University Fine Arts Galleries, Tallahassee, Florida
Museum of Fine Arts, St. Petersburg, Florida
Lowe Art Museum, Coral Gables, Florida
Hokin Gallery, Bay Harbor Islands, Florida
1984 Butler Art Institute, Youngstown, Ohio
Hecksher Museum, Huntington, New York
Pembroke Gallery, Houston, Texas
1985 Hokin-Kaufman Gallery, Chicago
Schweyer-Galdo Galleries, Pontiac, Michigan
1986 Tampa Museum, Florida

Selected Group Exhibitions:

1962 *Geometric Abstraction in America*, Whitney Museum, New York (toured the United States)
1965 *The Responsive Eye*, Museum of Modern Art, New York
1967 *American Painting Now*, Institute of Contemporary Art, Boston
1968 *Documenta 4*, Kassel, West Germany
1971 *Color Structure*, Whitney Museum, New York
1974 *Opening Exhibition*, Hirshhorn Museum, Smithsonian Institution, Washington, D.C.
1975 *34th Biennial of Contemporary American Painting*, Corcoran Gallery, Washington, D.C.
1976 *30 Years of American Printmaking*, Brooklyn Museum
1979 *2 Decades of Printmaking*, Museum of Modern Art, New York
1980 *5 in Florida: Anuszkiewicz/Chamberlain/Olitski/Rauschenberg/Rosenquist*, University of South Florida, Tampa

Collections:

Metropolitan Museum of Art, New York; Museum of Modern Art, New York; Whitney Museum, New York; Albright-Knox Art Gallery, Buffalo, New York; Yale University Art Gallery, New Haven, Connecticut; Corcoran Gallery of Art, Washington, D.C.; Smithsonian Institution, Washington, D.C.; Art Institute of Chicago; Detroit Institute of Arts; Philadelphia Museum of Art.

Publications:

On ANUSKIEWICZ: books—*The New Art: A Critical Anthology*, edited by Gregory Battcock, New York 1966; *Purposes of Art* by Albert Elsen, New York 1967; *Constructivism: Origins and Evolution* by George Rickey, New York 1967; *Optical Art: Theory and Practice* by Rene Parola, New York 1969; *Op Art* by Cyril Barrett, New York 1970; articles—"A Theology of Hard Edge" by Edouard Roditi in *Arts Magazine* (New York), December 1963; "Art That Pulses, Quivers and Fascinates" by John Canaday in the *New York Times*, February 1965; "Anuskiewicz Sets Legs in Motion" by Bernadine Morris in the *New York Times*, May 1965; "Richard Anuskiewicz: "It's Baffling" by John Canaday in the *New York Times*, April 1969; "Graphics '70: Richard Anuskiewicz" by Donald Karshan in *Art in America* (New York), March 1970; "Trays by 10 Artists" by Mario Amaya in *Art in America* (New York), January 1971; "Portrait of the Artist: Richard Anuskiewicz" by Jay Jacobs in *Art Gallery* (Ivoryton, Connecticut), March 1971; "At Lincoln: Anuskiewicz Acrylics" by Susan Drysdale in the *Christian Science Monitor* (Boston), March 1972.

Born in 1930 of Polish emigrant parents, Richard Anuskiewicz is one of the most outstanding exponents of colorism, the movement which developed from abstract expressionism, and pop art. At first, Anuskiewicz leaned towards realism. The change took place as a result of meeting Albers at Yale while he was studying there. Albers opened his eyes to the way colours behave and to their mutual influence on each other which causes "everything to depend on everything else."

In spite of all his respect for the master, Anuskiewicz rejects total acceptance of Albers' theory. Other theories of colour also interest him—that of Paul Klee, in particular. He has found Klee less pedantic and more poetic in his perception of the world of colour.

Anuskiewicz was one of the first American painters to be interested in creating space in a picture, introducing the effect of vibrations on a flat surface. He was a pioneer in applying the technique of mixing colours optically—i.e., instead of physically mixing colours on a palette, he achieves the same impression on the retina. This, of course, was nothing new; the process had been in use since divisionism. Developed now, in terms of non-representational art, based on geometric form—it brought a new element to painting. Anuskiewicz's painting, while exploiting 19th century colour physics, Chevreul's and Helmholtz's theories of colour, also makes use of new technology. This kind of painting distinguishes itself by a specific atmosphere. Created as it is under warm light conditions, it ideally needs to be viewed in a similar light. The intensity of colour, the precision of its optical limits, the technical elegance of coloured surfaces, by rays or a regular network, the juxtaposition of complementary colours which causes after-images—all form a tight, logical system.

This system, recalling Albers' theoretical assumptions, is inherent in the structure of the square. The square forms an unlimited collection of alternatives; divisions into quadrilateral compartments are filled with ever greater or ever smaller fields of squares. These, in turn, yield not only diagonal rhombuses, networks, screens, modules, cuboid spatial variants covered by a network of lines giving the impression of being concave or convex, but also deformations of perspective. Optical illusions also arise on a flat, square surface. If a geometric shape is given by the grouping or separation of lines, the space between them is formed by a subtle gradation of chromatic shades of equal intensity.

The construction of complicated linear and interlinear structures (both inside and outside the modulated squares) has become possible from a technological point of view, thanks to industrial innovations. The fact is that, at the beginning of the 1960's, fast-drying paints (acrylics) appeared as did masking tapes—adhesive and varying in width from 0.2 cm—used hitherto in technical projects. When stuck to the surface of a painting, the tapes cover the parts already painted, thus protecting them from being covered by the next layer of paint. When the tapes are removed, the outline of the resulting image appears. Thanks to the tapes, the business of masking can be carried out with ideal precision, impossible with any other tech-

nique. Even the thinnest lines have sharp, well-defined edges. But that is not the artist's goal. "What I am trying to do," Anuskiewicz has said, "is to achieve a soft effect by means of so-called hard media." That is why his paintings, in spite of his emphasis on geometry, differ from classical geometrical abstraction by a softness, blurred forms and a chromatic subduing, despite a simultaneously bright palette. They also differ from op-art—although articles about him usually refer to Anuskiewicz as an op-artist. This kind of classification is not wholly wrong. Artists interested in optics, optical illusion and kinetics are also called perpetuators of the Bauhaus and Constructivist traditions. Thus Anuskiewicz, Vasarely, Riley and others all share a common antecedent.

Anuskiewicz proclaimed his particular view of painting in the United States, but maintained a certain independence from other American artists, retaining his own vision during two decades, the 1960's and 70's. Nothing augurs a change in his artistic attitude.

—Szymon Bojko

ANZINGER, Siegfried.

Austrian. Born in Weyer, in 1953. Educated in Steyr, until 1971; studied art, under Professor Melcher, Akademie der bildenden Kunste, Vienna, 1971–77. Married the painter Marie-Luise Lebschik. Independent painter, Vienna, since 1977, and in Cologne, since 1981. Address: Neusser Strasse 27/29, 5000 Cologne 1, West Germany.

Individual Exhibitions:

1976 Galerie Herzog, Vienna
1978 Galerie Ariadne, Vienna
1979 Osterreichische Hochschulerschaft, Vienna
1980 Galerie und Edition Sigrid Friedrich/Sabine Knust, Munich
Galerie Krinzinger, Innsbruck
Galerie Ariadne, Vienna
1981 Galerie und Edition Sigrid Friedrich/Sabine Knust, Munich
Perspektive, at *Art 12, '81*, Basel
1982 Galerie Buchmann, St. Gallen, Switzerland
Galerie t'Venster, Rotterdam (with Hubert Schmalix)
Galerie Bitterlin, Basel (with Hubert Schmalix)
Galerie Krinzinger, Innsbruck
Galerie Nachst St. Stephan, Vienna
Galerie Thaddaus J. Ropac, Lienz, Austria
1983 Galerie Sigrid Friedrich, Munich
Galeria Heinrich Ehrhardt, Madrid (with Hubert Schmalix)
Galerie Vera Munro, Hamburg
Galerie Albert Baronian, Brussels
Galerie Gugu Ernesto, Cologne
1984 Galerie Farideh Cadot, Paris (with Hubert Schmalix and Alois Mosbacher)
Holly Solomon Gallery, New York (with Hubert Schmalix)
Studio Cannaviello, Milan
Galerie Bleich-Rossi, Graz, Austria
1985 Kunstmuseum, Basel
Galerie Buchmann, Basel
ORF, Graz, Austria
Galerie Gugu Ernesto, Cologne
Burnette Mille Gallery, Los Angeles (with Hubert Schmalix)
Galerie Six Friedrich, Munich
Museum für Gegenwartskunst, Basel (travelled to Bonn and Linz 1985–86)
1986 Neue Galerie Graz, Austria
Kunsthalle, Hamburg
Galerie Krinzinger, Vienna
Kunstverein, Frankfurt
Galerie Sigma, Bregenz, Austria

Selected Group Exhibitions:

1977 *Interkunst*, Palais Liechtenstein, Vienna
1980 *Malerei 80*, Galerie Annasaule, Innsbruck
1981 *Neue Malerei in Ostereich*, Landesgalerie Joanneum, Graz, Austria
1982 *Documenta 7*, Museum Fridericianum, Kassel, West Germany
1983 *Einfach gute Malerei*, Museum des 20. Jahrhunderts, Vienna
1987 *Arco 87*, Madrid

Collections:

Kupferstichkabinett, Basel; Neue Galerie der Stadt Linz, Austria.

Publications:

By ANZINGER: books—*Laokoon Ubt*, with introduction by Peter Weiermair, Innsbruck and Vienna 1986.

On ANZINGER: books—*Siegfried Anziner: Malerei, Gouachen, Zeichnungen*, exhibition catalogue, with introduction by Dieter Ronte, Vienna and Munich 1982; *Siegfried Anzinger: Werke auf Papier 1977–1985*, exhibition catalogue with text by Dieter Koepplin, Basel 1985; *Siegfried Anzinger: Zeichnung, Malerei, Skulpture*, exhibition catalogue, by Dieter Koepplin, Innsbruck 1986.

APPEL, Karel.

Dutch. Born in Amsterdam, 25 April 1921. Educated at the Royal Academy of Fine Arts, Amsterdam, 1940–43. Met Corneille, Louis Van Lint, and Marc Mendeksin, 1946; Co-Founder of the Dutch experimental artists group "Reflex" (known as "COBRA" in Paris), Amsterdam, 1948; moved to Paris, 1950, and officially ended "COBRA"; met the avant-garde art critic Michel Tapie, Paris, 1951; first travelled to America and Mexico, 1957; established studios at the Chateau de Molesmes, Auxerre, France, 1964–72; now lives in Monaco and New York. Recipient: Unesco Prize, *Biennale*, Venice, 1954; Prize at the *Premio Lissone*, Italy, 1957; Graphics Prize, *Biennale*, Ljubljana, 1957; International Prize for Painting, *Sao Paolo Bienal*, 1959; First Prize from the Netherlands Committee, and First Prize for Painting, *Guggenheim International Exhibition*, New York, 1960. Honorary Citizen, Hamilton, Ontario, 1977. Knight of Orange Nassau, Netherlands, 1968. Agent: Marisa del Re Gallery, New York. Address: c/o Marisa del Re Gallery, 41 East 57th Street, New York, New York 10022, U.S.A.

Individual Exhibitions:

1946 Beerenhuis, Groningen, The Netherlands
1947 Guildhall, Amsterdam
1948 Santee Landweer, Amsterdam
1951 Van Lier Gallery, Amsterdam
1952 Het Venster Gallery, Rotterdam
1953 Palais des Beaux-Arts, Brussels
Bennewitz Gallery, The Hague
1954 Martha Jackson Gallery, New York
Studio Fachetti, Paris
1955 Bennewitz Gallery, The Hague
Galerie Rive Droite, Paris
Cultural Center, Schiedam, Netherlands
Stedelijk Museum, Amsterdam
1956 Galleria dell'Ariete, Milan
1957 Institute of Contemporary Arts, London
Galerie Espace, Haarlem, The Netherlands
Galleria Tartaruga, Rome
Martha Jackson Gallery, New York
1958 Galerie Claude Bernard, Paris
Galerie Anna Abels, Cologne
Palais des Beaux-Arts, Brussels
1959 Galerie Espace, Haarlem, The Netherlands
Gimpel Fils, London
Charles Lienhard Gallery, Zurich
Gendai Gallery, Tokyo
Musée d'Art, Neuchâtel, Switzerland
1960 Martha Jackson Gallery, New York
Gimpel Fils, London
Galleria Lorenzelli, Bergamo, Italy
Nova Gallery, Boston
Fairweather-Hardin Gallery, Chicago
Rudolf Zwirner, Essen
Esther Robles Gallery, Los Angeles
David Anderson Gallery, New York
Galerie Rive Droite, Paris
1961 Esther Robles Gallery, Los Angeles
David Anderson Gallery, New York
Gallery Espace, Amsterdam
Galerie d'Art Moderne, Basel
Stedelijk Van Abbe Museum, Eindhoven
Haags Gemeentemuseum, The Hague
Irving Gallery, Milwaukee
Tirca Karlis Gallery, Provinceton, Massachusetts
Galleria Le Medusa, Rome
Gallery Moos, Toronto
Gres Gallery, Washington, D.C.
Galleria Blu, Milan
Museum of Art, San Francisco (retrospective)
Pasadena Art Museum, California (retrospective)
Phoenix Art Museum, Arizona (retrospective)
Santa Barbara Art Museum, California (retrospective)
1962 Galerie Rive Droite, Paris
Gallery Moos, Toronto
La Jolla Art Museum, California
Gimpel Fils, London
Galleria dell'Ariete, Milan
Gallery Charles Lienhard, Zurich
Galerie Agnes Lefort, Montreal
Stephen Hahn Gallery, New York
Martha Jackson Gallery, New York
James Goodman Gallery, New York
Park Gallery, Detroit
Anderson-Mayer Galerie, Paris
Esther Robles Gallery, Los Angeles
1964 Gimpel Fils, London
Martha Jackson Gallery, New York
Stephen Hahn Gallery, New York
American Art Gallery, Copenhagen
Gallery Krikhaar, Amsterdam
1965 Kunsthallen, Göteborg, Sweden
Palais des Beaux-Arts, Brussels
Donald Morris Gallery, Detroit
Gallery Leger, Malmo, Sweden
Stedelijk Museum, Amsterdam (retrospective)
City Museum, Copenhagen (retrospective)
Moderna Museet, Stockholm (retrospective)
Museum of Bochum, West Germany (retrospective)
1966 Stedelijk Museum, Breda, Netherlands (retrospective)
1967 Martha Jackson Gallery, New York
Redfern Gallery, London
Galerie Agnes Lefort, Montreal
1968 Centre National d'Art Contemporain, Paris
Stedelijk Museum, Amsterdam
1969 Martha Jackson Gallery, New York
Galerie Gimpel und Hanover, Zurich
Gallery Gimpel, London
Galerie Krikhaar, Amsterdam
Kunsthalle, Basel
Palais des Beaux-Arts, Brussels
1970 Centraal Museum, Utrecht (retrospective)
Galleria La Medusa, Rome
Winterhur, Lucerne
Richard Gray Gallery, Chicago
Gallery Moos, Toronto
Galerie Nova, Spectra, The Hague
1971 Galerie Nova, Spectra, The Hague
Galerie Ariel, Paris
Martha Jackson Gallery, New York (thrice)
Galerie Teatre, Brussels
Nantensi Gallery, Tokyo (twice)
Kunstgalleri, Aarhus, Denmark
London Arts Gallery, Detroit
London Arts Gallery, London

Academy of Fine Arts, Philadelphia
Galleria d'Arte Rinaldo Rotta, Milan
1972 London Arts Gallery, Detroit
S. A. Freedman Gallery, Jamaica, New York
Rothman's of Pall Mall, Toronto (retrospective)
Rothman's Art Gallery, Stratford, Ontario (retrospective)
Musée d'Art Contemporain, Montreal (retrospective)
Art Gallery of Greater Victoria, British Columbia (retrospective)
Edmonton Art Gallery, Alberta (retrospective)
Winnipeg Art Gallery, Manitoba (retrospective)
1973 Art Gallery of Ontario, Toronto (retrospective)
Martha Jackson Gallery, New York
Dalhousie University Art Gallery, Halifax, Nova Scotia (retrospective)
London Public Library and Art Museum, London, Ontario (retrospective)
Art Gallery of Hamilton, Ontario (retrospective)
New York Cultural Center, New York (retrospective)
Miami Art Center (retrospective)
Gallery Moos, Toronto
1974 Oklahoma Art Center, Oklahoma City (retrospective)
Ft. Lauderdale Museum, Florida (retrospective)
Phoenix Art Museum, Arizona (retrospective)
Galleria La Medusa, Rome
Galerie Ariel, Paris
Gimpel Fils, London
Gimpel and Weitzenhoffer, New York
Court Gallery, Copenhagen
Gloria Lauria Gallery, Miami
1975 Gimpel and Weitzenhoffer, New York
Galerie Nova Spectra, The Hague
David Gallery, Pittsford, New York
Aberbach Fine Arts, New York
Wildenstein Gallery, London
1976 Galerie Nova Spectra, The Hague
Gallery Moos, Toronto
Modern Master Tapestries Inc., New York
1977 Galerie Ariel, Paris
Galerie Krikhaar, Amsterdam
Museo de Arte Moderno, Mexico City (retrospective)
Hamilton Museum, Ontario
Museum Terneuzen, The Netherlands
Museum 'Slot Zeist, The Netherlands
Palm Springs Desert Museum, California
Gallery Collection d'Art, Amsterdam
Lillian Heidenberg Gallery, New York
1978 Galerie Nova Spectra, The Hague
Galerie Krikhaar, Amsterdam
Museo de Bellas Artes, Caracas (retrospective)
Museo de Arte Moderno, Bogota (retrospective)
Moderne Galerie Saarlandmuseum, Saarbrucken, West Germany
Museum Van Bommel, Van Dam, Venlo, The Netherlands
Cultureel Centrum Hasselt, Belgium
Brewster Gallery, New York
1979 Vienna Museum, Austria (retrospective)
Bonn Museum, West Germany (retrospective)
Janus Gallery, Washington, D.C.
6 Scandinavian Museums (retrospective; tour)
1980 Galerie Daniel Templon, Paris
Janus Gallery, Washington, D.C.
State University of New York, Binghamton
Bede Gallery, Jarrow, County Durham
Museum Wilhelmshafen, West Germany
1981 Galerie Ariel, Paris
Gimpel Fils, London
Kunstforum, Schelderode, Belgium
Stedelijk Museum, Amsterdam
Fame Gallery, Houston, Texas
London Arts Gallery, Detroit
Fundacao Gulbenkian, Lisbon
Museu de Arte Moderna, Rio de Janeiro
Museu de Arte Moderna, Sao Paulo
1982 Biblioteca Nacional, Madrid
Gemeentemuseum, The Hague
Museum Boymans-van Beuningen, Rotterdam
Galerie Collection d'Art, Amsterdam
Staatliche Kunsthalle, Baden-Baden, West Germany

Karel Appel: *Donna Cubista*, 1968

1984 Kunstforening, Copenhagen
National Gallery of Iceland, Reykjavik
Palais des Beaux-Arts, Brussels
Galerie Collection d'Art, Amsterdam
1985 Palazzo di Medici, Florence
1986 Arnolfini Gallery, Bristol, Avon
Marisa del Re Gallery, New York
Fort Lauderdale Museum of Art, Florida
Virginia Miller Gallery, Coral Gables, Florida
1987 Galerie d'Art Contemporain, Nice, France
Douglas Hyde Gallery, Dublin
Marisa del Re Gallery, New York
1988 Galerie Beyeler, Basle

Selected Group Exhibitions:

1946 *Salon de Mai*, Paris (regularly until 1971)
1951 *2nd COBRA International*, Palais des Beaux-Arts, Liege, Belgium
1953 *2nd Biennial*, Museum of Modern Art, Sao Paolo
1955 *Expressionism 1900–1955*, Walker Art Center, Minneapolis (toured the United States)
1959 *50 Years of Research*, Stedelijk Museum, Amsterdam
1964 *Documenta 3*, Kassel, West Germany
1969 *Portraits in Contemporary Art*, Museum of Modern Art, New York
1972 *Humor, Satire, Irony*, New School for Social Research, New York
1973 *25th Anniversary Exhibition of COBRA*, Court Gallery, Copenhagen
1982 *On The Road: The Jack Kerouac Exhibit*, Boulder Center for the Visual Arts, Colorado

Collections:

Stedelijk Museum, Amsterdam; Stedelijk Van Abbe Museum, Eindhoven, Netherlands; Musée Royal des Beaux-Arts, Brussels; Centre National d'Art Contemporain, Paris; Tate Gallery, London; National Museet, Copenhagen; Museum of Modern Art, New York; Guggenheim Museum, New York; Museum of Fine Arts, Boston; Los Angeles County Museum; Hamilton Museum, Ontario; Art Gallery of Ontario, Toronto; Montreal Museum of Fine Arts.

Publications:

By APPEL: books—*A Beast-Drawn Man*, portfolio, with Bert Schierbeek, Paris 1962; *Karel Appel over Karel Appel*, with a foreword by Albert Rikmans, Amsterdam 1971; *En-*

cres à Deux Pinceaux et Leurs Poemes par Hugo Claus, with Pierre Alechinsky, Paris 1978; *Forty Years of Paintings, Sculptures and Drawings,* Paris 1987; *Nocturne de San Ildefonso,* with poems by Octavio Paz, Paris 1987.

On APPEL: books—*Art since 1945* by Marcel Brion and Samuel Hunter, New York 1958; *Karel Appel: Painter* by Hugo Claus, New York 1962; *Karel Appel: Nudes,* exhibition catalogue, by Bert Schiebeek, New York 1964; *Karel Appel: Reliefs 1964–1968,* exhibition catalogue, by Julien Alvard, Paris 1968; *Appel* by Peter Bellew, Milan 1968; *Het Tidschrift Cobra* by Anne Choisez, Brussels 1970; *Appel's Oogappels,* exhibition catalogue, by Simon Vinkenoog, Utrecht 1970; *Appel's Appels,* exhibition catalogue, by Luke Rombout, Toronto 1972; *Karel Appel: The Early 50's,* exhibition catalogue, New York 1973; *Opere di Karel Appel* by Armondo Nocentini, Florence 1973; *Karel Appel: Recent Works,* exhibition catalogue, New York 1973; *Cobra + Contrasts,* exhibition catalogue, by Willem Sandberg, Detroit 1974; *Appel,* exhibition catalogue, by Herbert Read, London 1975; *Karel Appel: Pintor de Insolita Expresividad,* exhibition catalogue, by Antonio Rodriguez, Mexico City 1977; *Visages-Payages,* exhibition catalogue, Paris 1977; *Karel Appel* by Peter Berger, Venlo, Netherlands 1977; *Pierre Alechinsky, by the Artist* by Pierre Alechinsky, New York 1977; *Het Gezicht van Appel* by Nico Koster and Edward Wingen, Venlo, Netherlands 1977; *Eloge de la Folie* by Jean-Clarence Lambert, Paris 1977; *30 Years of Painting by Appel* by Edward Wingen, Venlo, Netherlands 197; *Karel Appel,* exhibition catalogue, Bogota 1978; *Karel Appel: Works on Paper* by Jean-Clarence Lambert, with a foreword by Marshall McLuhan, New York 1980; *Karel Appel* by Alfred Frankenstein, New York 1980; *Karel Appel: Paintings 1980–85,* exhibition catalogue with introduction by Rupert Martin, Dublin and Bristol 1986; *Karel Appel: Recent Paintings,* exhibition catalogue with text by Sam Hunter, New York 1986; *Karel Appel: Recent Paintings and Sculpture,* exhibition catalogue with text by Donald Kuspit, New York 1987.

Over the years my work has changed, and the philosophy behind my thinking about my work has changed too, and still is changing today. I mean by this, that painting is always a fight with yourself and the material. The most difficult thing is the concentration and tension to be "one" with myself, my painting and my materials. It's an inner fight, and inner fight means the inner evolution that the artist can see in his work—in his paint, in his image, in his expression, in his color—that means his *inner* evolution is going on.

Take television, for instance. Television is something like the artist—a reality of our planet. The only difference is that television shows only reality and I show the future. I work on the future, and that is the most important thing for me, and thus the reason why my work started changing after the war.

When we started to paint seriously, we formed the *Cobra* group and we met people, other artists, who were busy with the same phenomena, problems and concerns. We made good comrades. *Cobra* was the only real new movement after the War in Europe. A real movement like Dada, Surrealism, Tachism and so on. All these movements existed before the War and there was nothing new about them. But the Cobra group started new, and first of all we threw away all these things we had known and started afresh, like a child—fresh and new. Sometimes my works look very childish, or child-like, schizophrenic or stupid, you know. But that was the good thing for me. Because, for me, the material is the paint itself. The paint expresses itself. In the mass of paint, I find my imagination and go on to paint it. I paint the imagination I find in the material I paint.

Karel Appel

During his COBRA period Karel Appel stood out together with the Dane Asger Jorn and the Belgian Corneille as the most extreme representatives of a wild and uncontrolled Expressionism which had more in common with the vehement impetuosity of the traditional Dutch and Flemish Expressionism than with the more sober classicism of the French. Working in very thick impasto, Appel produced swirling abstract masses of vigorously contrasting colours and clusters of contorted linear scribbling stamped with the imprint of sweeping brush-strokes. The effect was one of apparently unrestrained spontaneity which, as H. H. Arnason has said, was at first sight reminiscent of Ruskin's remark about Whistler—a pot of paint thrown in the face of the public. Or, to quote Herbert Read, when looking at Appel's pictures one has the impression of "a spiritual tornado that has left the images of its passage." Relying heavily on the evocative power of the materials when moulded into abstract shapes, his work anticipated "art informel" and represented a violent reaction from the principles of order and harmony which dominated de Stijl. In its largely automatic procedures, spontaneous brushstrokes and excited linear gestures it represented an early European parallel to American Action Painting. The aim was direct expression unguided by the intellect. Associations were aroused and the mechanism of the unconscious was set in motion by the act of painting itself. Like his fellow-countryman De Kooning in America, Appel did not eschew figuration, but his aim was to stimulate associations and set in motion the unconscious phantasy by the dramatic power and evocative force of his waves of speaking colour—as is evidenced, for example, by "Red Nude" (1960) and "Angry Landscape" (1967). His later, post-COBRA, work displayed no radical change although the pigment became somewhat more fluid and the facture smoother, while the images often emerged more explicitly as the strange faces in "Two Times" (1974) which in the words of Arnason possess "a wonderful quality of childlike madness." Appel's images are in the tradition of Bosch and Ensor: distorted vestiges of human or animal bodies, grimacing masks, strange demonic figures reminiscent of Nordic mythology and folklore. His portraits were often composed of contorted clusters of spiky lines and masses of spontaneous colour without apparent figuration, as in his "Portrait of Willem Sandberg" (1956).

In 1968 Appel began to do relief paintings, and from this he progressed to sculpture in painted wood and polychrome polyester. Of this work he said: "These materials open for me more possibilities to work in space—which is the feeling I want to achieve in my paintings." He then worked in aluminum sheet and made sculptures with movable parts, of which he said: "I hinge the ears so that you can play with them, and they move in the wind as well, which changes the whole shape of the sculpture. The toy principle, you know."

In an exhibition catalogue Herbert Read summed up the painting of Appel: "Violent as they are, I do not find terror in his images; as Christian Dotrement has said, he captures the beast but does not kill it. He then identifies himself with its animal vitality. One must always distinguish between vitality and violence. Though Appel's paintings may be said to stream with the blood of animals, they are not patches on the floor of an abattoir: they represent the physical substance of life itself. Their colors are living, moving, never coagulated or faded. They stream through the field of vision as natural forces, conveying life to hearts that are invisible only because they are hidden within our own breasts." In less poetic vein Appel himself said of the change that took place in his work: "Around 1957–58 my painting was a fight. I did not paint—I hit! . . . My red, for instance, was blood. Now my red is space. . . . My work was a war, was a fight . . . little by little I have gone over more to a magic space feeling. . . . I set my frame of mind in a child-like feeling or toy feeling. My work is like a toy for adults. I believe that through the coming atomic age there will be more time for people to express themselves and to express their own desires as a play element in life. This being the same feeling of inner joy as a child gets with its toys. This is one of the feelings I project as a sound of the future in my work."

—Harold Osborne

ARAKAWA, Shusaku.

Japanese. Born in Nagoya, 6 July 1936. Studied medicine and mathematics, in Tokyo, 1954–58. Has lived in New York since 1961. Recipient: DAAD Fellowship, West Berlin, 1972. Agent: Ronald Feldman Fine Arts, 31 Mercer Street, New York, New York 10013. Address: 124 West Houston Street, New York, New York 10012, U.S.A.

Individual Exhibitions:

1958	Museum of Modern Art, Tokyo
1961	Mudo Gallery, Tokyo
1963	Galerie Schmela, Dusseldorf
1964	Dwan Gallery, Los Angeles
	Palais des Beaux-Arts, Brussels
1965	Galerie Schmela, Dusseldorf
	Minami Gallery, Tokyo
	Galleria dell'Ariete, Milan
1966	Dwan Gallery, New York
	Dwan Gallery, Los Angeles
	Minami Gallery, Tokyo
	Galerie Schmela, Dusseldorf
	Wide White Space, Antwerp
	Württembergischer Kunstverein, Stuttgart
	Stedelijk van Abbemuseum, Eindhoven, Netherlands
1967	Von der Heydt Museum, Wuppertal, West Germany
	Dwan Gallery, New York
	Dwan Gallery, Los Angeles
	Galleria Schwarz, Milan
	Galerie Seyfried, Monaco
1968	Dwan Gallery, New York
	Galerie Lauter, Mannheim
1969	Galerie Yvon Lambert, Paris
	Galleria Schwarz, Milan
	Dwan Gallery, New York
	Minami Gallery, Tokyo
	Whitney Museum, New York (film)
1970	Musée d'Art Moderne de la Ville, Paris
	Kunstverein, Hannover
	Badischer Kunstverein, Karlsruhe
	Biennale, Venice
1971	Fendrick Gallery, Washington, D.C.
	Harcus-Krakow Gallery, Boston
	Galerie Yvon Lambert, Paris
	Galleria Schwarz, Milan
	Angela Flowers Gallery, London
	ROSC, Dublin
	CAYC, Buenos Aires
	Whitney Museum, New York (films)
1972	Kunsthalle, Hamburg National Galerie, Berlin
	Lenbachhaus, Munich
	Kunstverein, Frankfurt
	Kunsthalle, Berne
	Art in Progress, Zurich
	Galleria Bertesca, Genoa
	Ronald Feldman Fine Arts, New York
1973	Daytons Gallery 12, Minneapolis
	Margo Leavin Gallery, Los Angeles
1974	Alessandra Castelli Gallery, Milan
	Museum of Modern Art, New York
	University of Wisconsin at Eau Claire
	Ronald Feldman Fine Arts, New York
	University of Missouri-Rolla
	University of Oklahoma, Norman
	Moorhead State College, Minnesota
	Multiples Gallery, New York
	Louisiana Museum, Humleback Denmark
1975	Galerie Art in Progress, Dusseldorf
	Galerie Aronowitsch, Stockholm
	Galerie Yvon Lambert, Paris
	Isy Brachot, Brussels
	Pasquale Trisorio, Naples
	Henie Onstad Museum, Oslo
	Michael Berger Gallery, Pittsburgh
	Carl Solway Gallery, Cincinnati
1976	Ronald Feldman Fine Arts, New York
	Multiples, New York
	Galeria 42, Barcelona
	Art Gallery of Ontario, Toronto
	Rubicon Gallery, Los Altos, California
	Margo Leavin Gallery, Los Angeles
	Delahunty Gallery, Dallas

Grupo Quince, Madrid
Galerie Art in Progress, Munich
Dorothy Rosenthal Gallery, Chicago
ICC, Antwerp
University of Wisconsin Art History Gallery, Milwaukee
Stadtische Kunsthalle, Dusseldorf
Galerie Maeght, Paris
Galerie Art in Progress, Dusseldorf
Museo de Arte Moderno, Bogota
1978 Gallery Takagi, Nagoya, Japan
Stedelijk Museum, Amsterdam
Margo Leavin Gallery, Los Angeles
Galerie Maeght, Paris
Neue Galerie am Landesmuseum Johanneum, Graz, Austria
1979 Stadtische Kunstsammlungen, Ludwigshafen, West Germany
Seibu Museum of Art, Tokyo
Austrian Landesmuseum, Graz
National Museum, Osaka
Ronald Feldman Fine Arts, New York
Minneapolis Institute of Arts
Gallery Takagi, Nagoya, Japan
Dorothy Rosenthal Gallery, Chicago
1980 John Stoller and Company, Minneapolis
Gallery Luria, Palm Beach, Florida
Gallery Takagi, Nagoya, Japan
Galerie Maeght, Zurich
1981 Ronald Feldman Fine Arts, New York

Selected Group Exhibitions:

1975 *View of Japanese Contemporary Art*, Seibu Museum of Art, Tokyo
1976 *Artist-Immigrants of America 1876–1976*, Hirshhorn Museum, Washington, D.C.
1977 *Documenta 6*, Kassel, West Germany
Words: A Look at the Use of Language in Art, Whitney Museum Downtown, New York
1978 *Art about Art*, Whitney Museum, New York
Drawings of the 70's, Art Institute of Chicago
1980 *Lettres et Chiffres*, Galerie Beyeler, Basel
1981 *American Prints and Printmaking 1956–1981*, Pratt Graphics Center, New York

Collections:

Museum of Modern Art, New York; Walker Art Center, Minneapolis; Kunsthalle, Berne; Kunstmuseum, Basel; National Galerie, West Berlin; Musée d'Art Modern, Paris; Stedelijk Museum, Amsterdam; National Museum of Modern Art, Tokyo.

Publications:

By ARAKAWA: books—*Mechanismus der Bedeutung*, with Madeline H. Gins, Munich 1971; *For Example (A Critique of Never)*, with Madeline H. Gins, Milan 1974; *The Mechanism of Meaning*, with Madeline H. Gins, New York 1979; article—"Forgettance (Exhaustion Exhumed)" in *Arts Magazine* (New York), 1975; "Some Words" in *Arakawa*, exhibition catalogue, Dusseldorf 1977.

On ARAKAWA: books—*Icons and Images* by Nicolas Calas, New York 1971; *Prints of the 20th Century: A History* by Riva Castleman, New York 1976; *Constructive Concepts: A History of Constructive Art from Cubism to the Present* by Willy Rotzler, Zurich 1977; *Arakawa*, exhibition catalogue, Dusseldorf 1977; *Arakawa*, exhibition catalogue, Tokyo 1979; articles—"Arakawa's Paintings: A Reading" by Lawrence Alloway in *Arts Magazine* (New York), November 1969; "Arakawa: The Mechanism of Meaning" by Lawrence Alloway in *Art International* (Lugano), November 1972; "Art: The Universe of Arakawa" by John Russell in the *New York Times*, 7 September 1974; "Playing in the Surd" by John Loring in *Arts Magazine* (New York), February 1975; "ReTurning Points and Revolutions" by John Loring in *Print Collector's Newsletter* (New York), May/June 1977; special issue of *Derrière le Miroir* (Paris), no. 223, 1977; "Traces of the Unimaginable: On Arakawa's Recent Work" by Rolf-Dieter Hermann in *Arts Magazine* (New York), April 1978; "Arakawa" by Brian Wallis in *Arts Magazine* (New York), September 1979; "The Flourishing Art of the Print" by Ann Barry in the *New York Times*, 10 February 1980; "Arakawa: 'I Am Looking for a New Definition of Perfection' " by Paul Gardner in *Art News* (New York), May 1980; " 'Some Place Enormously Movable'—The Collaboration of Arakawa and Madeline H. Gins" by Robert Creeley in *Artforum* (New York), Summer 1980.

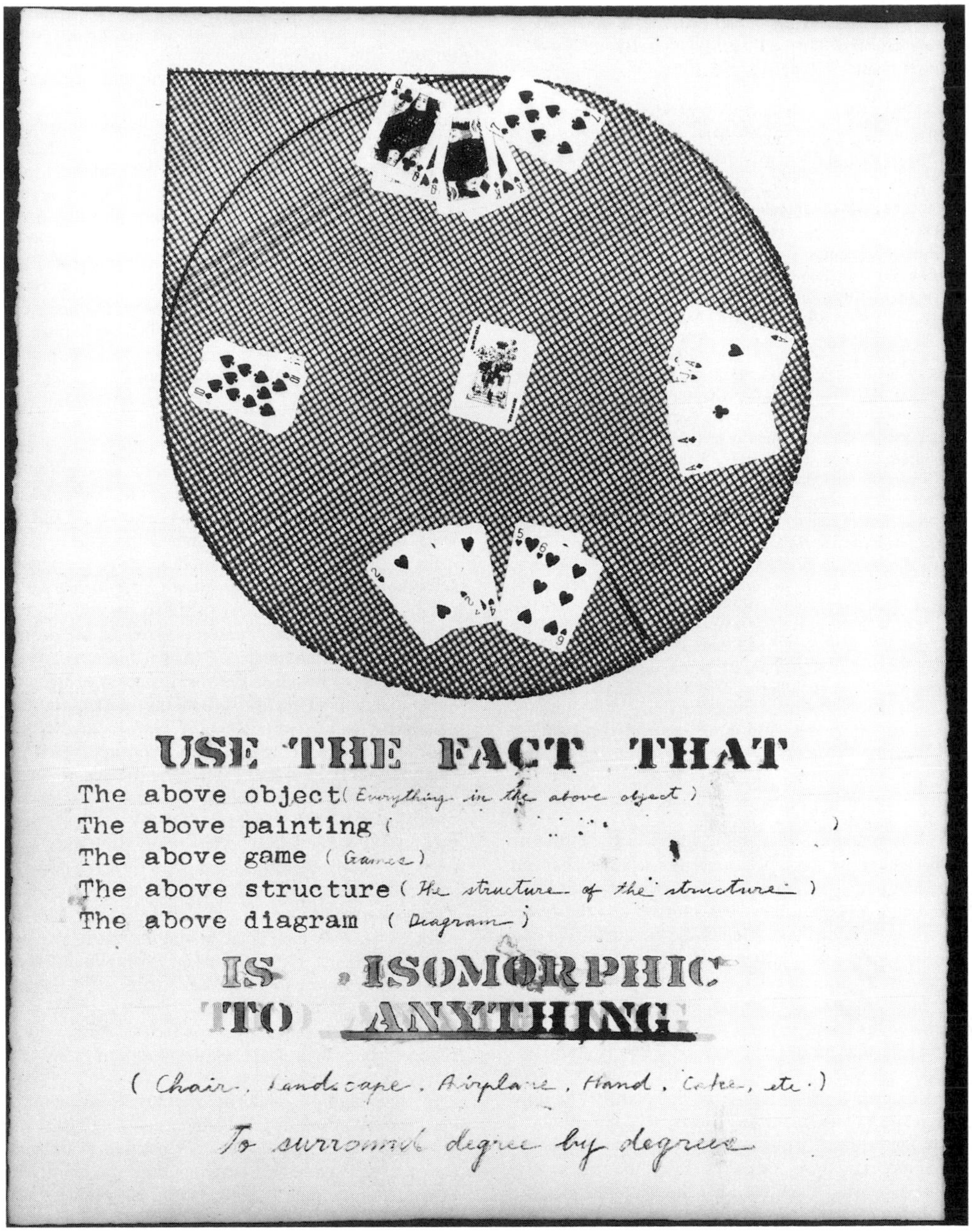

Shusaku Arakawa: *The Degrees of Meaning*, 1973

Born in Nagoya in 1936, Shusaku Arakawa left Tokyo's Musashino College of Art before completing his studies. In 1958 he began submitting paintings to the Yomiuri Independent exhibitions, and in 1960 joined the Neo-Dada Organizers group. In a happening, by placing himself in a pitchblack room in a "feigned state of death," he experimented with the physical bounds of man. In his "Box" series, which in one instance consisted of a glob of cement and cotton placed on a blanket and called "Foetus," he gave expression to fear and madness. This work attracted attention as being an original expression of the contemporary spirit of the times. In 1962 he went to the United States, and abandoned work in the "Boxes" series in favor of a new series, "Diagram." In this series of paintings on canvas he juxtaposed silhouettes of such things as tennis rackets, combs, footprints, arrows, circles and other symbols, to depict structurally the "relationship" of man to the material world.

After participating in a group show at the Sidney Janis Gallery in New York, in 1963, Arakawa had a number of one-man shows, at the Dwan Gallery in Los Angeles, at the Alfred Schmela Gallery in Dusseldorf, and elsewhere. He won the grand prize at the *Contemporary Art Exhibition of Japan* in 1968, and also showed his work at the Venice *Biennale* in 1970. From about this time, even the "silhouettes" disappeared from his paintings, and almost all his paintings were given simple names such as "Window Place" and "Room," and Arakawa painted words on the canvas. By this means, words, which are symbols of images and things, themselves became the objects painted, and the image evoked by the words was assigned a secondary place.

His new development is a series called "Mechanisms of Meaning." In 1969 he made a full-length film, *Why Not: A Serenade of Eschatological Ecology*, which became a sensation because of the way he depicted the relationship between man and object within a lifeless domain of sex. A sequel, *For Instance*, was completed in 1971. Although Arakawa's concept remains unchanged throughout the 1970s up to the present, his large paintings in the 1980s reveal more and more intricate diagrammatic vertigo with multi-directional arrow signs, indicating a conceptual relationship between the physical presence and the metaphysical contemplations.

—Yoshiaki Tono

ARMAN.

American. Born Armand Fernandez in Nice, France, 17 November 1928; relinquished surname in 1947; adopted name Arman, as a result of printing error, 1958; emigrated to the United States; naturalized, 1972. Educated at Cours Poisat School, 1934–40; studied at the Ecole du Louvre and Ecole Nationale des Arts Décoratifs, Paris. Served in the French Army, 1952. Hitch-hiked with Yves Klein and Claude Pascall in Europe, 1947; concentrated on Zen Buddhism and astrology, 1947–53; lived in New York, 1963; worked on series of assemblages in collaboration with Renault Car Company, Paris, 1967. Artist-in-Residence, University of California at Los Angeles, 1967–68. Recipient: Prize, *International Biennale, Exhibition of Prints,* Tokyo, 1964; Second Prize, Premio Marzotto, 1966. Commander, Order of Arts and Letters, France, 1984. Agent: Marisa Del Re Gallery, 41 East 57th Street, New York, New York 10022. Address: 430 Washington Street, New York, New York 10013, U.S.A.

Individual Exhibitions:

1956 Galerie du Haut Pave, Paris
1957 Galerie La Roue, Paris
1958 Galerie Iris Clert, Paris
1959 Galleria Apollinaire, Milan
Galerie St. Germain, Paris
1960 Galerie Iris Clert, Paris
Galerie Schmela, Dusseldorf
1961 Galleria Schwarz, milan
Cordier and Warren Gallery, New York
1962 Galerie Saggarah, Gstaad, Switzerland
Dwan Gallery, Los Angeles
Galerie Aujourd'hui, Brussels
Galerie Lawrence, Paris
1963 Galleria Schwarz, Milan
Galerie Lawrence, Paris
Sidney Janis Gallery, New York
Galerie ad Libitum, Antwerp
Galerie Schmela, Dusseldorf
1964 Walker Art Center, Minneapolis
Stedelijk Museum, Amsterdam
Museum Haus Lange, Krefeld, West Germany (retrospective)
Sidney Janis Gallery, New York
1965 Richard Feigen Gallery, Chicago
Galerie Bonnier, Lausanne,Switzerland
Galerie Lawrence, Paris
Galleria del Leone, Venice
1966 Galerie Saggarah, Gstaad, Switzerland
Svensk-Franska Konstgalleriet, Stockholm
Palais des Beaux-Arts, Brussels (retrospective)
Galerie La Vielle Echoppe, Saint-Paul-de-Vence, France
Musée de la Ville, Saint-Paul-de-Vence, France
1967 Galerie Ileana Sonnabend, Paris
Galleria Il Punto, Turin
Galerie Françoise Meyer, Brussels
Galerie des Ponchettes, Nice
Galleria La Bussola, Turin
Galleria Sperone, Turin
Palazzo Grassi, Venice
1968 Galleria Schwarz, Milan
Sidney Janis Gallery, New York
Biennale, Venice
1969 Galerie Bonnier, Lausanne, Switzerland
Arman: Verk frân 1964–1969, Svensk-Franska Konstgalleriet, Stockholm
Accumulations Renault, Musée des Arts Décoratifs, Paris (toured Europe)
Galerie Ileana Sonnabend, Paris
Galerie Mathias Fels, Paris
1970 Galerie Ileana Sonnabend, Paris
Städtische Kunstsammlungen, Ludwigshafen, West Germany
Ace Gallery, Los Angeles (travelled to the Ace Gallery, Vancouver)
Galerie der Spiegel, Cologne
Galleria dell'Ariete, Milan
Studio Sant'Andrea, Milan
Galerie Lambert-Monet, Geneva
Galerie Bonnier, Geneva
Galerie Jacqueline Soisson, Nice
Lawrence Rubin Gallery, New York
1971 Galerie Bonnier, Geneva
Galerie de la Salle, Saint-Paul-de-Vence, France
Lawrence Rubin Gallery, New York
Galerie Bischofberger, Zurich
Galerie Semiha Huber, Zurich
Galleria Arte Borgogna, Milan
Galerie Venise, Casablanca
1972 Galleria del Leone, Venice
Galleria Arte Borgogna, Basle
Galleria Sanluca, Bologna
Galerie Guillaume Campo, Antwerp
Galerie de l'Oeil, Paris
1973 Galerie Kriwin, Brussels
Le Tas de Echanges, Galerie Entre, Paris
Arman: Selected Activities, John Gibson Gallery, New York
Galerie Aronovich, Stockholm
White Gallery, Lausanne, Switzerland
Galleria Arte Bologna, Milan
Rosa Esman Gallery, New York
Concrete Lyrics, Andrew Crispo Gallery, New York
1974 Andrew Crispo Gallery, New York
Musée d'Arles, France
Galerie Daniel Templon, Paris
Arman: Selected Works 1958–1974, La Jolla Museum of Contemporary Art, California (travelled to Henry Art Gallery, University of Washington, Seattle; Fort Worth Art Museum, Texas; Des Moines Art Center, Iowa; and Albright-Knox Art Museum, Buffalo, New York, 1974–75)
Dartmouth College, Hanover, New Hampshire
1975 Musée d'Art Moderne de la Ville, Paris
Galerie Bonnier, Geneva
Galerie Tchou, Paris
John Gibson Gallery, New York
Lyrical Surfaces, Andrew Crispo Gallery, New York
1976 Andrew Crispo Gallery, New York
Musée d'Art Moderne de la Ville, Paris

Arman: *End of Romanticism,* 1973

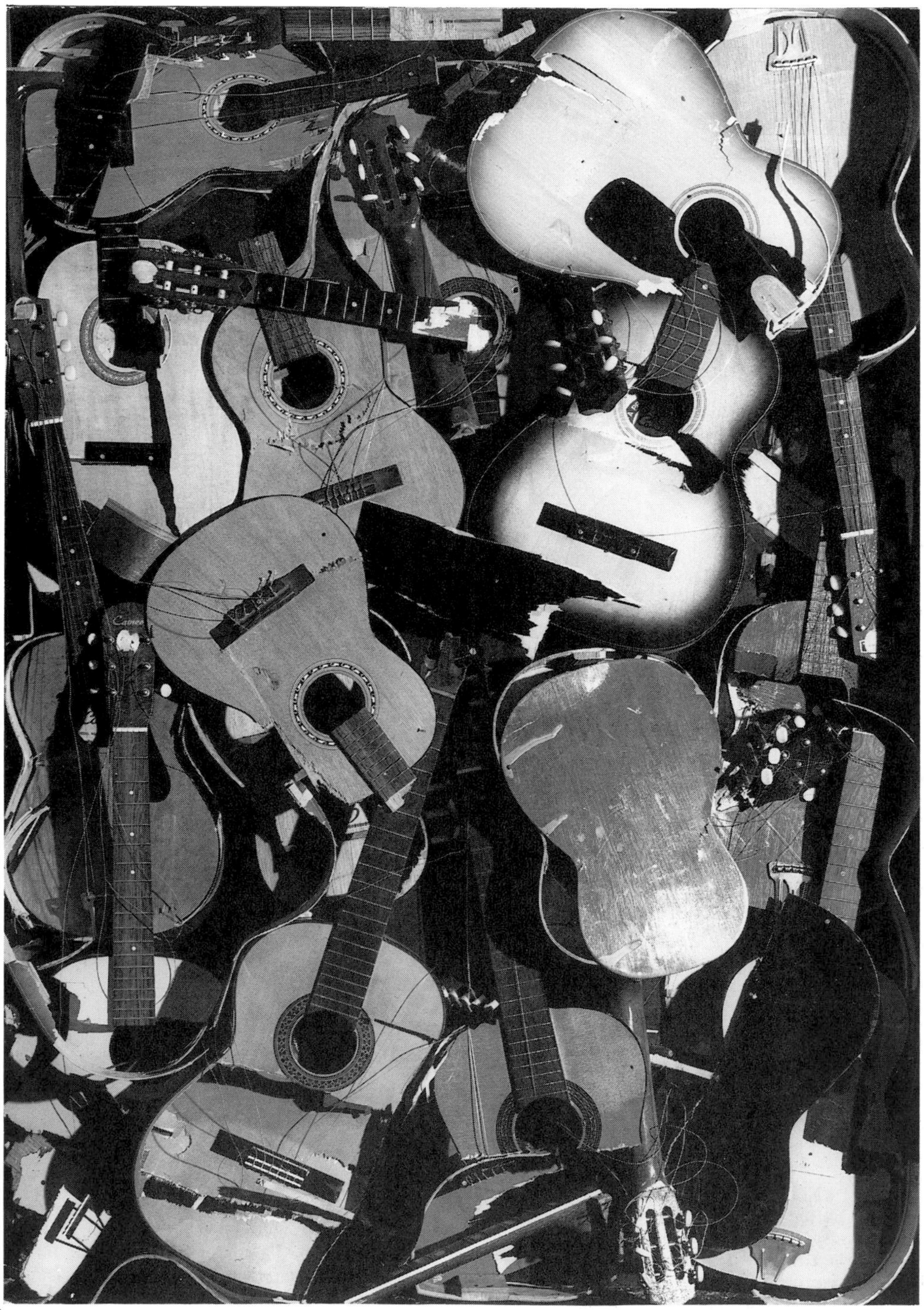

1979 André Emmerich Gallery, New York
1980 Amano Gallery, Osaka, Japan
Satani Gallery, Tokyo
1981 Galerie Beaubourg, Paris
Grand Palais, Paris
1982 Galerie Sapone, Nice, France
Galerie Beaubourg, Paris
Solomon Gallery, Dublin
1983 Goldman's Gallery, Haifa, Israel
Galerie Beaubourg, Paris
1984 Gloria Luria Gallery, Bay Harbor Islands, Florida
Galerie Reckermann, Cologne
Galerie Rene Ziegler, Zurich
Marisa Del Re Gallery, New York
1985 Seibu Museum of Art, Tokyo
1986 Marisa Del Re Gallery, New York
1988 Galerie de Poche, Paris

Selected Group Exhibitions:

1964 *International Biennale Exhibition of Prints*, Tokyo
1967 *Expo '67*, Montreal
1968 *Documenta 4*, Kassel, West Germany
1970 *Expo '70*, Osaka, Japan
1980 *From Reinhardt to Christo*, Allen Memorial Museum, Oberlin, Ohio
1984 *Salvaged: Altered Everyday Objects*, Project Studio One, Long Island City, New York

Collections:

Museum of Modern Art, New York; Albright-Knox Art Museum, Buffalo, New York; Walker Art Center, Minneapolis; Stedelijk Museum, Amsterdam; Musée Royal des Beaux-Arts, Brussels; Musée d'Art Moderne, Ghent; Louisiana Museum of Art, Humlebaek, Denmark; Museum Haus Lange, Krefeld, West Germany; Centre Georges Pompidou, Paris; Musée des Arts Décoratifs, Paris.

Publications:

By ARMAN: articles—"Interview d'Arman," with Michel Ragon, in *Chorus*, nos. 5/6/1970; "Arman Qualité Quantité," interview, with Catherine Millet, in *Art Press* (Paris), December/January 1974.

On ARMAN: books—*Arman*, exhibition pamphlet, with text by Pierre Restany, Los Angeles 1962; *Arman*, exhibition catalogue, with text by Alain Jouffroy, Milan 1963; *Arman*, exhibition catalogue, with text by Pierre Restany, and Claude Pascal, with statement by Arman, Amsterdam 1964; *Arman*, exhibition catalogue, Stockholm 1966; *Arman*, exhibition catalogue, with texts by Otto Hahn, Pierre Restany, and Michael Sonnabend, Paris 1967; *Arman*, exhibition catalogue, with text by John Ashbery, New York 1968; *Arman*, exhibition catalogue, with text by Pierre Restany, Milan 1968; *Arman: Accumulations Renault*, exhibition catalogue, with text by François Mathey, and interview of Arman with Claude Renard, Paris 1969; *Arman: Verk from 1964–1969*, exhibition catalogue, Stockholm 1969; *Arman*, exhibition catalogue, Milan 1970; *Arman*, exhibition pamphlet, with introduction by Pierre Restany, Antwerp 1972; *Arman: Ateliers d'Aujourd'hui* by Otto Hahn, Paris 1972; *Arman: Selected Activities*, exhibition catalogue, with texts by Peter Schjeldahl and Jan van der Marck, New York 1973; *Arman* by Henry Martin, New York 1973; *Arman: Concrete Lyrics*, exhibition catalogue, with text by Andrew Crispo, New York 1974; *Arman: Selected Works 1958–1974*, exhibition catalogue, with an introduction by Jan van der Marck, La Jolla, California 1974; *Arman: Lyrical Surfaces*, exhibition catalogue, New York 1975; *Arman: Objets Armés 1971–74*, exhibition catalogue, with text by Jacques Lassaigne, Paris 1975; *From Reinhardt to Christo*, exhibition catalogue, Oberlin, Ohio 1980; *Arman* by Jan van der Marck, New York 1984; *Arman*, exhibition catalogue, with text by Masashi Miura, Tokyo 1985; *Arman: Gods and Goddesses*, exhibition catalogue with essay by Henry Geldzahler, New York 1986.

Of all the "New Realists" who appeared at various places in Europe at the beginning of the 1960's, Arman ranks surely as the purest poet of the object, but he's also the artist of the group with the clearest commitment to a concept of significant form, and the power of his work depends on an almost relentless classicism. He is never sentimental. Even though he seems to allow the objects he deals with to speak entirely by themselves, he also allows his procedures a very similar sort of privilege, and it's the procedures of the artist rather than the objects of reality that finally hold the upper hand. The object is almost always reduced to a statuesque icon or an element of an all-over pattern, and the excitement of these configurations lies in the way we are invited to deal both with what the objects that go into them used to be and as well as with what they have since become. Arman keeps us spell-bound by creating an almost palpable tension between things we know with our intellect and things we see with our eyes.

Arman first came into his own around 1955 when he ceased to be what Pierre Restany has called a "Sunday painter" dedicated to " 'nice' painting in the taste of the period, a post-Cubism at first figurative and later on abstract." That was the moment at which he invented the first of a whole series of new and entirely personal genres. He began to make works that consisted of repeated stampings of the same rubber stamp (his *cachets*); he then went on to making tracings (*allures*) of objects other than rubber stamps by inking them and sending them scudding across sheets of paper or canvas; he then decided that the object itself can be a trace of itself and put a definitive end to his work with rubber stamps by sealing them all into a box and this was the beginning of the *accumulations*, which were also later to become accumulations of trash called *poubelles* (trash cans). Later still he began to work with the possibility of smashing, burning, and sectioning objects (often musical instruments, and especially violins) and these became his *colères* (rages). He has made accumulations of everything from dollar bills to crucifixes, machine-gun bullets, dolls, Kodak brownie cameras, sewing machines, cigarette butts, trombones, chess men, tea pots, gas burners from old kitchen stoves, guns, parts of automobiles, cogs and wheels for watches, tennis shoes, pencils and squeezed tubes of artist's oil paint; his way of dealing with these accumulated objects is sometimes to weld them together, at other times to nail them to a board or simply to heap them into a glass-covered box; still other accumulations, like many of the destroyed violins, are drowned in polyester or embedded in cement. With his *colères*, he has been known to take an axe to quarry as large as a grand piano and to dynamite a sports car. He once went before an audience and destroyed the entirety of the contents of a fully furnished three-room middle-class apartment that had been set up for him in a New York art gallery.

Arman's work, finally, simply isn't understood at all unless it's understood to be an always on-going ritual. He is always bending the object to his entirely personal and purely arbitrary will as though to tell us that will is what we are most truly made of; the utilitarian objects in which will is codified and limited are destroyed or accumulated into almost purely visual pattern as though to tell us that we must know how to look beyond them if we're to see the essence of the human capacity that went into pulling them into existence in the first place.

—Henry Martin

ARMITAGE, Kenneth.

British. Born in Leeds, Yorkshire, 18 July 1916. Studied at the Leeds College of Art, 1934–37; Slade School of Fine Art, London, 1937–39. Served in the British Army, 1939–46. Independent sculptor, since 1946. Visited Caracas; formed workshop, together with other Venezuelan sculptors, 1964; lived in Berlin, 1967–69. Chairman, Sculpture Department, Bath Academy of Art, Crosham, 1946–56; Visiting Professor, Boston University, 1970. Visiting Tutor, Royal College of Art, London, since 1974. Recipient: Gregory Fellowship in Sculpture, Leeds University, Yorkshire, 1953–55; First Prize International War Memorial Competition, Krefeld, West Germany, 1956; David E. Bright Foundation Award, *Biennale*, Venice 1958; Prize, *International Drawing and Engraving Exhibition*, Lugano, Switzerland, 1958; Berlin Arts Programme Fellowship, 1967–69. C.B.E. (Commander of the Order of the British Empire), 1969. Address: 22a Avonmore Road, London W14 8RR, England.

Individual Exhibitions:

1952 Gimpel Fils, London
1954 Bertha Schaefer Gallery, New York
1956 Bertha Schaefer Gallery, New york
1957 Gimpel Fils, London
1958 Paul Rosenberg Gallery, New York
Musée Nationale d'Art Moderne, Paris
Biennale, Venice (with Stanley William Hayter and William Scott; toured Europe)
1959 Whitechapel Art Gallery, London
British Council World Tour (until 1976)
1960 Kestner Gesellschaft, Hannover (with Lynn Chadwick; toured Europe and Japan, 1960–61)
1962 Paul Rosenberg Gallery, New York
Marlborough Fine Art, London
Galerie Suvremene Umjetnosti, Zagreb
1963 Galerie Charles Linehard, Zurich
Galerie Wilhelm Groshennig, Dusseldorf
Galleria Blu, Milan
1965 Marlborough Fine Art, London
Arnolfini Gallery, Bristol
1972 Castle Museum, Norwich (toured the U.K., 1972–73)
1974 Hester van Royen Gallery, London
Gallery Kasahara, Osaka
1975 New Art Centre, London
1978 Fuji Television Gallery, Tokyo (travelled to the Galerie Humanite, Nagoya, and the Gallery Kasahara, Osaka)
1980 Gimpel Fils, London
1981 City Museum and Art Gallery, Stoke-on-Trent, Staffordshire
1982 Sala Mendoza, Caracas
Taranman Gallery, London
1985 Artcurial, Paris (retrospective)

Selected Group Exhibitions:

1952 *Biennale*, Venice
1953 *Open Air Sculpture Exhibition*, Middleheim Park, Antwerp
1955 *The New Decade*, Museum of Modern Art, New York
1957 *Bienal*, Sao Paulo
1959 *New Images of Man*, Museum of Modern Art, New York
1962 *British Sculpture Today*, San Francisco Museum of Art (toured the United States)
1967 *Guggenheim International Sculpture Exhibition*, Guggenheim Museum, New York
1972 *British Sculptors 72*, Royal Academy of Art, London
1982 *British Sculpture of the 20th Century, Parts I and II*, Whitechapel Art Gallery, London
1987 *British Art of the 20th Century*, Royal Academy of Arts, London (travelled to Staatsgalerie, Stuttgart)

Collections:

Tate Gallery, London; Arts Council, London; Victoria and Albert Museum, London; Middleheim Museum, Antwerp; Musée Royale des Beaux-Arts, Brussels; Centre Georges Pompidou, Paris; Kunsthalle, Hamburg; Galleria Nazionale d'Arte Moderna, Rome; Albright-Knox Art Gallery, Buffalo, New York; Museum of Modern Art, New York.

Publications:

On ARMITAGE: books—*Artists of our Time, No. 7: Kenneth Armitage* by Sir Roland Penrose, Amriswil, Switzerland

Kenneth Armitage: *Blasted Oak*, 1986

1960; *Arts in Progress: Kenneth Armitage* by Norbert Lynton, London 1962; *Kenneth Armitage* by Charles Spencer, London 1973; *Kenneth Armitage: Sculptures and Drawings*, exhibition catalogue, with foreword by Roland Penrose, Tokyo 1978; *Kenneth Armitage: Richmond Oaks and Other Works*, exhibition catalogue, with introduction by John McEwen, London 1980; *Kenneth Armitage: New Sculptures and Collages*, exhibition catalogue, with introduction by John McEwen, London 1982; articles—"Kenneth Armitage" by John Glaves-Smith in *Artscribe* (London), no. 16, 1979; "Artists' Dialogue" by Connie Glenn in *Architectural Digest* (Los Angeles) February 1982; films—*Kenneth Armitage*, directed by John Read, BBC Television, London 1960; *5 British Sculptors Work and Talk*, directed by Warren Forma, 1964; *Armitage in Berlin*, Berlin 1969.

The character of my work divides into periods, some short, others long-lasting, in the way we tend to wear different clothes at different times. For example, the Oak Tree love affair in Richmond Park lasted non-stop from 1975 to 1986 with one or two large versions yet to be made. Others, like the attempts to combine drawing and sculpture, went no further than five or six pieces, although a ten-foot relief combining both has now started, and a residual of black pubic and head hair still occurs, The series called *Chair* (based on my bedroom chair) lasted only through four versions, Then, a time-lag can exist between forming an idea and testing it in one or several maquettes—and the full-scale realization perhaps not until several years later. Or I can finish something started long ago, like the big *Arm* made in Berlin in 1968 and cast temporarily in white resin and shown like that in Japan and London, is now receiving attention with a sprayed camouflage design based on drawings made in 1968 but never used until now. I regard it all as a body of work without much care for what was done when, and where nothing is final. A lifetime is so very short anyway, and the time-scale of art enormous. I sometimes look at a small engraving on a reindeer antler fragment in the British Museum with an age estimated at 11,000 BC—which might have been made by a good artist last week. We often hear people on television say, "way back in (say) 1985," when an Irish sense of time can range over centuries as though it was only recent. This easy communication across race, language and vast spans of time is comforting in an age when indifference to art seems general.

—Kenneth Armitage

Although he gained his international laurels as one of that group of young British sculptors that included Butler, Chadwick and Paolozzi, which showed at the Venice *Biennale* in 1952, Kenneth Armitage has generally stood aside from the prevailing ethos. Herbert Read rhetorically dubbed artists of this self-consciously angst-ridden post-war era the "geometry of fear" sculptors, but unlike many of the others Armitage stuck to the human figure rather than employing bestial or insect hybrids to serve at metaphors for the human condition. Moreover, Armitage's figures were not loaded with a tragic import; they were depicted in low-key casual situations, as seen in "People in a Wind." Their scale was usually small, the observations modest and delivered sotto voce. In these respects his work owed more to artists like Giacometti and Picasso than to Surrealism and Moore.

When he adopted a larger scale and a more public manner in such works of the later 50's as "Diarchy," Armitage invested his figures with a hieratic monumentality: the torsos are flattened into plaques or tablets from which protrude the architectonic limbs. They are static and silent images, with a rare grandeur that is free from bombast and posturing.

During the 60's he experimented with various new figurative subjects and new materials, including resins and aluminum, but recently he has returned to bronze, long his favorite material. A new richness of color and material is evident in his series of Richmond Oaks from the late 70's. Armitage has always made drawings, both sketches and presentation works; they act as aids to observation but not as blueprints for sculptures. Once again numerous studies, this time of trees in Richmond Park, accompany this group of new works. Characteristically, these sculptures are modest in scale and statement, but no less powerful for that. Armitage has abandoned the figure almost for the first time in his career, yet he never anthropomorphizes his oaks, and that elusive sense of poetic metaphor which inhabits his best works is found here too.

—Lynne Cooke

ARMLEDER, John M(ichael).

Swiss. Born in Geneva, 24 June 1948. Studied at the Ecole des Beaux-Arts, Geneva, 1966–67; with John Epstein, Glamorgan Summer School, Wales, 1969. Associated with the Groupe Luc Bois artists' group, Geneva, 1963; independent artist, from 1969; founder, with Patrick Lucchini and Claude Rychner, Groupe Ecart, Geneva, 1969; Galerie Ecart, Geneva, from 1973; Ecart Publications, Geneva, 1972; Ecart Performance Group, Geneva, 1974; Ecart/Books, Geneva, 1975; International Institutions Register, Geneva, 1976; Leathern Wing Scribble Press, 1977; Laboratorio artists' co-operative, Milan, 1977. Recipient: Graphics Prize, *Xylon VI* exhibition, Geneva, 1972; Kiefer-Hablitzel-Stipendium, Geneva, 1972, 1974, 1976; Eidgenossiche Kunststipendium, Geneva, 1977, 1978, 1979; Prize of the Banque Hypothecaire du Canton de Geneve, 1986. Agents: Ecart Books, rue Philippe, Plantamour 6, 1211 Geneva; Galerie Marika Malacorda, rue de l'Eveche 1, 1204 Geneva; Galerie Toni Gerber, Gerechtigkeitsgasse 74, 3011 Berne. Address: 3 rue des Paquis, P.O.B. 253, 1211 Geneva, Switzerland.

Individual Exhibitions:

1973	Galerie Ecart, Geneva
	Palais de l'Athenee, Geneva
	Galerie Ecart, Geneva (with Patrick Lucchini)
1975	Galerie Gaetan, Carouge, Switzerland
1976	Palais de l'Athenee, Geneva
1977	Galerie Marika Malacorda, Geneva
1980	Rue Vignier, Geneva
	Kunstmuseum, Basle
	C Space, New York (with Helmut Federle and Christoph Gossweiler)

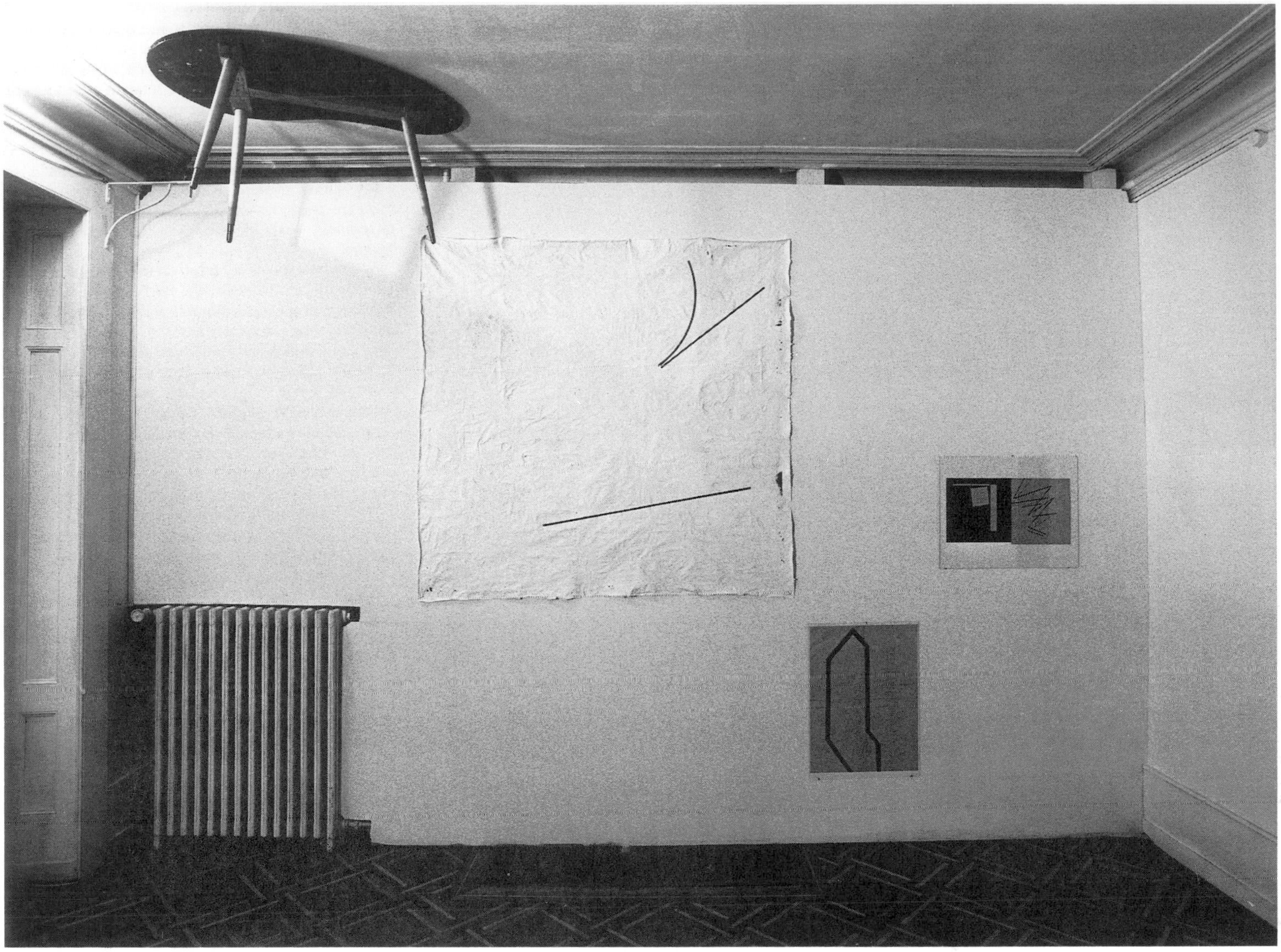

John Armleder: *1681*, installation at the Centre d'Art Contemporain, Geneva, 1981

1981 Centre d'Art Contemporain, Geneva (with Martin Disler and Helmut Federle)
1982 Musee d'Art et d'Histoire, Fribourg, Switzerland
Gangurinn/The Corridor, Reykjavik
Galerie Toni Gerber, Berne
Galerie Marika Malacorda, Geneva
Vitrine Fri-Art, Fribourg, Switzerland
Nylistasafnid/The Living Arts Museum, Reykjavik
1983 Kunstmuseum, Solothurn, Switzerland
Gymnase Cantonal du Bugnon, Lausanne
Galerie Grita Insam, Vienna
Galerie Rivolta, Lausanne
Galerie Susanna Kulli, St. Gallen, Switzerland
Le Consortium, Dijon, France
1984 Galerie Marika Malacorda, Geneva
John Gibson Gallery, New York
Galerie Claudia Knapp, Chur, Switzerland
Galerie Filiale, Basle (with Christian Floquet)
1985 Galerie Marika Malacorda, Geneva
John Gibson Gallery, New York
Galerie Media, Neuchatel, Switzerland
Galerie und Lager Rudolf Zwirner, Cologne
1986 Galerie Susanna Kulli, St. Gallen, Switzerland
Ecole Nationale d'Art Decoratif, Limoges, France
Galerie Rivolta, Lausanne
John Gibson Gallery, New York
Galerie Tanit, Munich
Swiss Pavilion, *Biennale*, Venice
Galerie Catherine Issert, St. Paul-de-Vence, FRance
Galerie Toni Gerber, Berne
Galerie Bama, Paris
Lisson Gallery, London
Musee d'Art et d'Histoire, Geneva
Verein Kunsthalle, Zurich (with Helmut Federle and Olivier Mosset)
Stadtische Galerie, Regensburg, West Germany (with Olivier Mosset)
1987 Galleria Piero Cavellini, Milan
Galerie Munro, Hamburg
Galerie Daniel Buchholz, Cologne
Galerie Nachst St. Stephan, Vienna
Galerie Susanna Kulli, St. Gallen, Switzerland
Galerie Jean-Francois Dumont, Bordeaux, France
Kunstmuseum, Winterthur, Switzerland (travelled to Paris, Dusseldorf, and West Berlin)
John Gibson Gallery, New York
Pat Hearn Gallery, New York
Daniel Newburg Gallery, New York
Musee de Peinture et de Sculpture, Grenoble, France
Galerie Marika Malacorda, Geneva
Galerie Tanit, Munich
Hoffman Borman Gallery, Santa Monica, California
Galerie Joost Declercq, Ghent, Belgium
Kunstverein, Aachen, West Germany
Maison de la Culture, St. Etienne, France (with Olivier Mosset; travelled to Nevers)
1988 Galerie Tanit Kunigk und Moller, Munich

Selected Group Exhibitions:

1972 *Xylon VI*, Musee d'Art et d'Histoire, Geneva
1974 *Ambiente 74: 28 Schweizer Kunstler*, Kunstmuseum, Winterthur, Switzerland (travelled to Geneva and Lugano)
1976 *Rubber Stamp Exhibition*, La Mamelle Arts Center, San Francisco
1978 *Artwords and Bookworks*, Los Angeles Institute of Contemporary Art
1981 *CH '70–'80*, Kunstmuseum, Lucerne (travelled to Bologna, Genoa, Bonn and Graz)
1982 *Zwitserse Avant-Garde*, Galerie Nouvelles Images, The Hague
1984 *Peinture Abstraite*, Galerie Ecart, Geneva
1986 *Tableaux Abstraits*, Villa Arson, Nice, France
1987 *Documenta 8*, Museum Fridericianum, Kassel, West Germany

Collections:

Kunstmuseum, Basle; Kunstmuseum, Lucerne; Musee d'Art et d'Histoire, Geneva; Cabinet des Estampes, Geneva; Kunsthaus,Zurich; Kunstmuseum, Winterthur; Staatsgalerie, Stuttgart; Musee Saint-Pierre, Lyon; Musee d'Art et d'Industrie, Saint-Etienne; Musee de Grenoble.

Publications:

By ARMLEDER: books—*Lezards Sauvages*, Geneva 1973; *Ayacotl*, with Patrick Lucchini, Geneva 1973; *Ayacotl-Excerpts*, Geneva 1973; *12 Portes + 1*, with Patrick Lucchini, Geneva 1973; *Correspondances avec John Armleder*, with Endre Tot, Geneva 1974; *Niente, Purtroppo*, Geneva 1975; *John Armleder*, with texts by Heinz Breloh, Jochen Gerz and others, Geneva 1975; *The John Armleder Is A Vegetarian Book*, Geneva 1975; *Une Pluie d'Etoiles Filantes*, Geneva 1975; *Dictionnaire Moderne Francais-Arabe*, Geneva

1975; *Dieu Expulse du Paradis*, with Claude Rychner, Geneva 1976; *3 x (2 x 1): A Chhjlnoruxy Production*, with Patrick Lucchini and Claude Rychner, Lucerne and Geneva 1977; *Hall*, with Dougal, Geneva 1977; *Sketches to Higgins' Intermedia Object No. 1*, with Patrick Lucchini, Geneva 1977; *Lezards Sauvages IIA: Egouttes*, Geneva 1979; *Titles Untitled*, Geneva 1979; *The D. S. Lick Nets*, with Helgi Thorgils Fridjonsson, Reykjavik 1982; *The Geneva Pond Bubbles*, with Arni Ingolfsson and others, Reykjavik 1982; *The Rex-Headed Master*, with Dadi Gudbjornsson and others, Reykjavik 1982; *One Year Lick*, with Dadi Gudbjornsson and Helgi Thorgils Fridjonsson, Reykjavik and Geneva 1983; *One Year Net*, with Helgi Thorgils Fridjonsson and Thor Vigfusson, Reykjavik and Geneva 1983; *Ecrits et Etretiens*, with Helmut Federle and Olivier Mosset, St. Etienne and Grenoble 1987; *Furniture Sculpture 1979–1986*, with texts by Nena Dimitrijevic and Christoph Schenker, Dudweiler 1987.

On ARMLEDER: books—*AMAM: Premieres Acquisitions et Donations*, exhibition catalogue with text by Rainer Michael Mason, Geneva 1976; *John M. Armleder: 891 und weitere Stucke*, exhibition catalogue with text by Dieter Koepplin, Basle 1980; *John M. Armleder/Martin Disler/Helmut M. Federle*, exhibition catalogue with texts by Christoph Schenker, Dieter Schwarz and others, Geneva 1982; *John M. Armleder: Arbeiten auf Papier 1962–83*, exhibition catalogue with texts by André Jamber and Ben Vautier, Solothurn 1983; *John Armleder*, exhibition catalogue with text by Jean-Hubert Martin, Dijon 1983; *John Armleder: Paintings and Furniture Sculpture*, exhibition catalogue with text by Stuart Morgan, London 1986; *John M. Armleder*, exhibition catalogue with text by Maurice Besset and Dieter Schwarz, Winterthur 1987.

For about seven years now the public has been seeing pictures and articles of furniture by John Armleder, an artist who had previously made a name for himself via graphics and performance art. If his first pictures still owed something to graphics, Armleder was soon elaborating a working style which, although it could not have been described as 'painterly,' was nevertheless clearly distinct from the poetic refinements of work on paper. These next works, rather than embodying a specifically subjective style, offered a neutral stage for the representation of various techniques; the drawings might incorporate traces of 'happening-activities' or they might equally follow paraconstructive lines (to use Armleder's terminology); simple designs might appear alongside designs based on complex random methods. Armleder was already playing with a variety of referents which would be evident to the acute observer: references to compositions by Cage, to graffiti, but also to Balla, Picabia and the Russian Constructivists. If there seemed to be a connection between these works and the Swiss graphic mentality of the seventies this was as a result of the intimacy of the medium rather than of a deliberate strategy. In contrast to his colleagues, Armleder was concerned with deconstructing a closed poetic universe rather than with a steady materialisation of the same; his pictures and furniture now confirm that beyond doubt.

In 1984 Armleder exhibited a large number of pictures for the first time, putting on a one-man exhibition in Geneva and contributing a selection of his work to a group exhibition which he himself had organised under the title *Peinture abstraite*. This exhibition, whose title, in a period when figurative art was in retreat, almost took on the quality of a manifesto, contained a mixture of abstract pictures of a geometric type in which Armleder's own works were completely at home. The choice of works by foreign artists was determined by circumstances and by the pressure towards improvisation; it demonstrated, not historical continuity, but abstraction as the icon of modernity. That in this exhibition concrete artists of the Zurich School (Loewensberg) hung beside Americans of the most diverse provenance (Held, Motherwell and Ryman on the one hand, minimal artists such as Lewitt and Mangold on the other), in combination with younger artists like Merz, Mosset and Armleder himself, was a clear indication that Armleder was concerned, not with a precise stylistic definition of his work, but with a practical blurring of the boundaries which the various schools of abstract art have erected. From the various processes of abstraction Armleder takes up for his own use only certain elements which point to the modernistic tradition without representing it in all its consequences.

Armleder's pictures are not painterly in the first instance, because it is not his aim to carry on working through the problems of an art radicalised by the modern approach. He avoids the formalistic tradition, which continues to preoccupy artists such as Toroni or Mosset, and concerns himself with the concept of 'modernism' as hypostatised by the avant-garde in the first half of the century. Consequently, he is not caught up in an exclusively geometric approach but takes as his theme the historical representation of this method: a rhetoric which establishes itself in an idealised sphere beyond mediation, seduction and expropriation. By distancing himself, however, from the geometric approach, Armleder has not shifted to a new form of representation. In this, he differs from artists like Schuyff or Taaffe who produce pictures which either verbally cite models from the '60s or use the geometric approach as a means to the production of a, yet again, illusionistic field of vision. In contrast too to Halley, for whom the geometric elements serve as pretext for a symbolical scenery, Armleder extracts from his simple polka dots the possibility for a dissolution of content. In denying the significance of an isolated picture and concentrating instead on its contextualisation, he abandons the sphere of pure painting. An example of this is to be found in the group exhibition Armleder organised, and also in his one-man exhibitions: each of his dot pictures relates first to the other dot pictures present, which differ from one another according to their physical composition, the materials used and variations in the organisation of the ground plan, and secondly to the whole range of dot and scanning patterns in modernist art. The dots are especially relevant to Armleder's purpose, since on the one hand they mark out a simple latticework distribution of the picture's surface, but on the other, in contrast to a quadratic arrangement, they disturb any uninterrupted perception of that surface.

In his combination of pictures and objects Armleder finds further possibilities for contextualisation. The objects, be they old pieces of furniture or newly produced consumer articles, are set, as anonymously produced decorative elements, over and against painting itself. It is not by chance that Armleder began with old drawing room furniture, sofas and dressing tables, more recently replaced by musical instruments. If the furniture devalues the picture (which furnishes the background to conversation) as part of the furnishings, the canvases on the other hand, often hung in place of mirrors, reflect the narcissistic position of the subjectively determined abstract painting, which was suppressed in the modernistic tradition by the concept of the autonomy of the painting. The musical instruments for their part repeat a popular still-life motif (compare, for example, the guitar employed by the Cubists), at the same time shifting the pictures out of the painterly tradition and into association with the contemporary entertainments industry.

Pictures and objects are not parts of a continuum. Picture and object react one upon the other: the pictorial composition turns to account formal qualities of the neighbouring object and the object defines the picture's real location. They do not interreact like parts of a surrealistic montage in which the alienating co-existence of objects very different to one another provides the key note. In contrast to Rauschenberg with his *Combine Paintings*, Armleder is not interested in the graduation of planes between painting, reproduction and real object. His so-called *Furniture Sculptures* intervene in painting, treating the picture no longer as an autonomous object but as a commodity and presenting commodities as possible extensions of painting.

—Dieter Schwarz

ARNESON, Robert.

American. Born in Benicia, California, 4 September 1930. Educated at Benicia High School, 1945–49; Marin College, Kenfield, California, 1949–51; studied art education at California College of Arts and Crafts, Oakland, 1952–54, B.A. 1954; studied art, under Antonio Prieto, Mills College, Oakland, 1957–58, M.F.A. 1958. Married Jeanette Jensen in 1955 (divorced, 1972); sons: Leif, Derek, and Kirk; married Sandra Shannonhouse in 1973. Sports cartoonist, *Benicia Herald*, 1949–52. Independent artist, since 1958; established studio with Richard McLean, East Oakland, 1961–62; lived in Doylestown, Pennsylvania and shared New York loft studio with former student Stephen Kaltenbach, 1967; established and maintains studio in old saloon, Benicia, California, since 1975; travelled to major museums in France, Belgium, Holland, and Switzerland, 1978. Art Teacher, Menlo-Atherton High School, Atherton, California, 1954–57, Santa Rosa Junior College, California, 1958–59, and Fremont High School, Oakland, 1959–60; Instructor in Design and Crafts, Mills College, Oakland, 1960–62. Assistant Professor of Art and Design, 1962–68, Associate Professor of Art, 1968–73, and Professor, since 1973, University of California at Davis. Recipient: Creative Arts Grant, University of California, 1967; Artists' Fellowship Grant, 1971, and Apprentice Fellowship Grant, 1978, National Endowment for the Arts; National Council on Education for the Ceramic Arts Award, 1979; D.F.A.: Rhode Island School of Design, Providence, 1985. Agents: Fuller-Goldeen Gallery, 228 Grant Avenue, San Francisco, California 94108; Allen Frumkin Gallery, 50 West 57th Street, New York, New York 10022. Address: c/o Art Department, University of California at Davis, Davis, California 95616, U.S.A.

Individual Exhibitions:

1960 Oakland Art Museum, California (with Tony DeLap)
1962 M. H. de Young Memorial Museum, San Francisco
Barrios Gallery, Sacramento, California
1963 Richmond Art Center, California
1964 Cellini Gallery, San Francisco
Home Economics Building, University of California at Davis
Allan Stone Gallery, New York
1967 San Francisco Museum of Art
1968 Hansen-Fuller Gallery, San Francisco
1969 Hansen-Fuller Gallery, San Francisco
Bob and Roy Ceramics, Esther Robles Gallery, Los Angeles (with Roy De Forest)
Candy Store Gallery, Folsom, California
1970 *Recent Art Works in Porcelain*, Hansen-Fuller Gallery, San Francisco
Bob and Roy Ware, Candy Store Gallery, Folsom, California (with Roy De Forest)
Fresno State College of Art Gallery, California
1971 Hansen-Fuller Gallery, San Francisco
Candy Store Gallery, Folsom, California
Manolides Gallery, Seattle (with William T. Wiley)
University of Calgary, Alberta
1972 Hansen-Fuller Gallery, San Francisco
Miami-Dade Junior College, Florida
1973 Hansen-Fuller Gallery, San Francisco
Church Fine Arts Gallery, University of Nevada, Reno
1974 Hansen-Fuller Gallery, San Francisco
Deson-Zaks Gallery, Chicago
Museum of Contemporary Art, Chicago (retrospective; travelled to the San Francisco Museum of Art)
Candy Store Gallery, Folsom, California
1975 Allan Frumkin Gallery, New York
Hansen-Fuller Gallery, San Francisco
Ruth Schaffner Gallery, Los Angeles
Dootson/Calderhead Gallery, Seattle
1976 Hansen-Fuller Gallery, San Francisco
Fendrick Gallery, Washington, D.C.
Memorial Union Art Gallery, University of California at Davis

Robert Arneson: *Ground Zero*, 1984

Allan Frumkin Gallery, Chicago
National Collection of Fine Arts, Smithsonian Institution, Washington, D.C.
1977 Hansen-Fuller Gallery, San Francisco
Allan Frumkin Gallery, New York
1978 *Works on Paper,* Allan Frumkin Gallery, New York
Allan Frumkin Gallery, Chicago
1979 *Heroes and Clowns,* Allan Frumkin Gallery, New York
Self-Portraits 1965–1978, Moore College of Art, Philadelphia
Allan Frumkin Gallery, New York
1980 Hansen-Fuller-Goldeen Gallery, San Francisco
Frumkin and Struve Gallery, Chicago
1981 Allan Frumkin Gallery, New York
1982 Foster Goldstrom Gallery, San Francisco
University of California, Davis
Fuller-Goldeen Gallery, San Francisco
1983 Allan Frumkin Gallery, New York
Landfall Press Inc., Chicago (travelled to Beloit, Wisconsin; Saginaw, Michigan; Springfield, Missouri; Tulsa, Oklahoma; Shawnee Mission, Kansas; Muncie, Indiana)
Yares Gallery, Scottsdale, Arizona
Crocker Art Museum, Sacramento, California
Triton Museum of Art, Santa Clara, California (travelled to Sacramento, California; Fresno, California; Portland, Oregon)
1984 Allan Frumkin Gallery, New York
Fuller-Goldeen Gallery, San Francisco
Frumkin and Struve Gallery, Chicago
1985 Fuller-Goldeen Gallery, San Francisco

Selected Group Exhibitions:

1964 *Ceramic National,* Everson Museum of Art, Syracuse, New York (toured the United States, 1964–66)
1967 *Funk Art,* University of California Art Museum, Berkeley
1968 *Dada-Surrealism and Their Heritage,* Museum of Modern Art, New York
1970- *Teacups, Teapots and Gorillas,* Moore College of Art, Philadelphia (with Ron Nagle, David Gilhooly, and Michael Frimkess)
1972 *A Decade of Ceramic Art 1962–1972,* San Francisco Museum of Art
1976 *Painting and Sculpture in California: The Modern Era,* San Francisco Museum of Modern Art (travelled to the National Gallery, Smithsonian Institution, Washington, D.C., 1977)
1978 *American Art since 1950,* Whitney Museum, New York
1981 *Ceramic Sculpture: Six Artists,* Whitney Museum, New York (travelled to San Francisco Museum of Modern Art, 1982)
1982 *100 Years of California Sculpture,* Oakland Art Museum, California
1984 *California Sculpture Show,* University of Southern California, Los Angeles (travelled to Bordeaux, France; Mannheim, West Germany; West Bretton, Yorkshire; Hovikodden, Norway)

Collections:

Whitney Museum, New York; Museum of Contemporary Crafts, New York; Hirshhorn Museum and Sculpture Garden, Smithsonian Institution, Washington, D.C.; Philadelphia Museum of Art; University of California at Berkeley; San Francisco Museum of Modern Art; Oakland Museum, California; E. B. Crocker Art Gallery, Sacramento, California; Stedelijk Museum, Amsterdam; Australian National Gallery, Canberra.

Publications:

By ARNESON: book—*My Head in Ceramics,* exhibition catalogue, San Francisco, 1972; articles—"About Arneson, Art and Ceramics," interview, with Cecile N. McCann, in *Artweek* (Oakland, California), 26 October 1974; "Robert Arneson in Conversation with Gwen Stone" in *Visual Dialog* (Los Altos, California), vol. 2, no. 1, 1977.

On ARNESON:books—*A Decade of Ceramic Art 1962–1972,* exhibition catalogue, with text by Suzanne Foley, San Francisco 1972; *Robert Arneson,* exhibition catalogue, with texts by Suzanne Foley and Stephen Prokopoff, Chicago 1974; *American Sculpture in Process 1930–1976* by Wayne Anderson, New York 1975; *Tradition and Change: The*

American Craftsman* by Julie Hall, New York 1977; *Painting and Sculpture in California: The Modern Era,* exhibition catalogue, San Francisco 1977; *History of American Ceramics: The Studio Potter* by Paul S. Donhauser, Dubuque, Iowa 1978; *Heroes and Clowns,* exhibition catalogue, with text by Michael McTwigan, New York 1979; *Robert Arneson: Self-Portraits 1965–1978,* exhibition catalogue, with text by Beth Coffelt, Philadelphia, 1979; *A Century of Ceramics in the United States 1878–1978,* exhibition catalogue, with texts by Garth Clark and Margie Hughto, New York 1979; articles—"Sweet Land of Funk" by Harald Paris in *Art In America* (New York), March/April 1967; "Arneson, Richardson" by Cecile N. McCann in *Artweek* (Oakland, California), 23 May 1970; "Sacramento!" by John FitzGibbon in *Art in America* (New York), November/December 1971; "Crock Art" By Douglas Davis in *Newsweek* (New York), 5 July 1971; "Arneson, Moses—Study in Contrasts" by Cecile N. McCann in *Artweek* (Oakland, California), 14 October 1972; "Arneson and Towbridge" by Cecile N. McCann in *Artweek* (Oakland, California), 20 October 1973; "Robert Arneson's Feats of Clay" by Dennis Adrian in *Art in America* (New York), September/October 1974; "Bob Arneson: Take Notice" by David Van Houten in *Artweek* (Oakland, California), 25 January 1975; "Arneson's Landscape" by R. F. Stepan in *Artweek* (Oakland, California), 24 January 1976; "The Ceramic Sculpture of Robert Arneson, Transformation of Craft into Art" by Alfred Frankenstein in *Artnews* (New York), January 1976; "Sculpture—From Boring to Brilliant" by Hilton Kramer in the *New York Times,* 15 May 1977; "Robert Arneson at Frumkin" by Sarah McFadden in *Art in America* (New York), July 1977; "A Modern Way with Clay" by Bill Marvel in *Horizon* (New York), September 1978; "57,500 Ceramics Commission" in *Ceramics Monthly* (Athens, Ohio), May 1981; "Arneson's Bust" by Robert Sommer in *Arts and Architecture* (Los Angeles), 1 August 1982; "A Monumental Side to Arneson" by Dennis Adrian in *San Francisco Chronicle,* 22 February 1984; "Arneson's Outrage" by Donald Kuspit in *Art in America* (New York), May 1985.

I think I've always been a social political artist. My art is accessible. Recently, I've done a body of work on the nuclear issue. *Ground Zero* (1984) is a typical example. It visualizes targeting of mankind through a nuclear holocaust. It's not fun to look at, but I wanted to bring my concern of the dangers of nuclear proliferation to an expanded art audience—the museum and gallery visitor—to let them know that art and life were inseparable.

—Robert Arneson

Robert Arneson's explicitly autobiographical sculptures confront his pleasures and embarrassments with a wry, self-deprecating humor that touches a responsive chord for most viewers. It is easy to identify with the blissful face that surveys a table loaded with festive foods or the ceramic head which shows the sculptor on the receiving end of a gob of clay—mud in his eye, or perhaps a metaphor for critical barbs occasionally flung at his work.

Beyond the clearly personal comments, the work contains wide-ranging art-historical references. Arneson has so thoroughly studied the history of ceramics that he has made both the concepts and techniques of the past accessible for his own uses. At one time he created a series of irreverent small sculptures that used imagery resembling fruit stand souvenirs, and made them of exquisitely finished, celadon-glazed porcelain as seductive as a Sung bowl. One homage to ancient Rome took the form of a self-portrait bust set head-high on an accurately reproduced classical column, the calm austerity of the piece punctured by male genitals protruding from the smooth cylinder at the appropriate position and bare toes lifting the column's base as if it were the hem of a toga. Pomposity and self-importance are not permitted to linger in this artist's work.

More recently Arneson has preferred low-fire white ware as a medium, indulging his painter's eye in the pleasures of skillfully handled color only possible with the brilliance of low-temperature glazes. The self-portraits continue, their good-natured jocularity reflecting the pleasanter aspects of Arneson's daily life. If the cheerfulness at times seems over-insistent, perhaps this has some connection with the long, sustained effort necessary to produce a sculpture. In the immediacy of watercolors and drawings, Arneson occasionally records darker thoughts and grim self-images, as if to purge them from his mind and let happier moods return. Happy or sad, it is himself and the small concerns that define a personality which Arneson records with detailed accuracy.

—Cecile N. McCann

ARROYO, Eduardo.

Spanish. Born in Madrid, 26 February 1937. Educated at Lycée Francais, Madrid, 1949–53; studied journalism at the Ecole Supérieure de Journalisme, Madrid, 1956–57; mainly self-taught in painting, from 1949. Served in the Spanish Infantry, 1956–57. Worked as freelance journalist, Madrid, 1957; as independent painter, Paris, 1958–68; in Milan, 1968–72; in West Berlin, 1975–76; permanently in Paris, since 1973. Instructor, Atelier Populaire, Ecole des Beaux-Arts, Paris, 1968. Worked as freelance theatre, set and costumer designer, in Milan, Bremen, Dusseldorf, Frankfurt, Berlin, and Paris, 1969–76. Recipient: Deutscher Akademischer Austauschdienst (D.A.A.D.) Grant, Berlin, 1975–76. Agent: Galerie Karl Flinker, 25 rue de Tournon, 75006 Paris. Address: 2 Passage Dantzig, 75015 Paris, France.

Individual Exhibitions:

1961	Galerie Claude Levin, Paris
1962	Crane Kalman Gallery, London
1963	Galleria Biosca, Madrid
1964	Galerie 20, Amsterdam
	Galerie 20, Arnhem, Netherlands
	Galerie Bernheim Jeune, Paris
1965	Galerie André Schoeller Jr., Paris
	Galerie 20, Amsterdam
1967	Galleria de'Foscherari, Bologna
	Galleria Mendoza, Caracas
	Galleria Il Fante di Spade, Rome
1968	Studio Marconi, Milan
	Studio Bellini, Milan
	Galleria Il Canale, Venice
	Galleria La Chiocciola, Padua
1969	Galleria La Bussola, Turin
	Galleria La Robinia, Palermo
	Galerie André Weill, Paris
1970	Galerie Withofs, Brussels
	Galleria Il Fante di Spade, Rome
	Galleria Aldina, Rome
	Galleria Arte Borgogna, Milan
	Galleria San Michele, Brescia
1971	*30 Jahre Danach,* Kunstverein, Frankfurt (travelled to the Musée d'Art Moderne de la Ville, Paris)
	Museum Hedendaagse Kunst, Utrecht
	Kunstverein, Munich
	Kunstverein, Berlin
	Palazzo del Gobernatore, Parma
	Galleria People, Turin
1972	Galerie 9, Paris
	Städtische Kunsthalle, Dusseldorf
	Galerie d'Eendt, Amsterdam
1973	Galleria d'Arte Borgogna, Milan
	Gastaldelli Arte Contemporanea, Milan
	Galleria Nuove Muse, Bologna
1974	*Portraits,* Galerie Karl Flinker, Paris
	Studio P. L., Milan
1975	Galerie Fred Lanzenberg, Brussels
	Galleria L'Aprodo, Turin
1976	D.A.A.D. Akademie der Künste, Berlin (with Grazia Eminente)
	Galerie Leger, Malmo, Sweden
1977	Galeria Maeght, Barcelona
	Galeria Juana Mordo, Madrid
	Galeria Val y 30, Valencia
1978	Fondation Nationale des Artes Graphiques et Plastiques, Paris
	Galerie Karl Flinker, Paris
1979	Galerie Karl Flinker, Basle
	Gallery Art Package, Highland Park, Illinois
1980	Galerie Maeght, Zurich
	Städtische Galerie im Lenbachhaus, Munich
	Galerie Michael Hasenclever, Munich
1981	Galerie Karl Flinker, Paris
1982	Modern Art Museum, Madrid
	Centre Georges Pompidou, Paris
	Eva Cohen Gallery, Highland Park, Illinois
1983	Leonard Hutton Galleries, New York
1984	Galerie Levy, Hamburg
	Guggenheim Museum, New York (retrospective)

Selected Group Exhibitions:

1960	*Salon de la Jeune Peinture,* Paris
1964	*Neue Realisten und Pop Art,* Akademie der Künste, Berlin
1965	*Pop Art: Nouveaux Réalistes,* Palais des Beaux-Arts, Brussels
1970	*Kunst und Politik,* Kunstmuseum, Karlsruhe, West Germany
1971	*Peintures et Objets,* Musée Galliera, Paris
1972	*Immagini per la Città,* Palazzo Reale, Genoa
1974	*L'Arte contre il Fascismo,* Palazzo della Loggia, Brescia
1976	*Realidada Social 1936–76,* at the *Biennale,* Venice
1979	*1968–79: Tendances de l'Art en France II,* Musée d'Art Moderne de la Ville, Paris
1980	*L'Art et le Sport,* Centre Culturel, Boulogne-Billancourt, France

Collections:

Musée d'Art Moderne de la Ville, Paris; Centre Georges Pompidou, Paris; Ministère de la Culture et de la Communication, Paris; Fondation Maeght, St. Paul de Vence, France; Musée des Beaux-Arts, Lausanne; National Galerie, Berlin; Hirshhorn Museum, Washington, D.C.

Publications:

By ARROYO: book—*"Panama" Al Brown 1902–1951,* Paris 1982.

On ARROYO: books—*Kunst und Politik,* exhibition catalogue, Karlsruhe 1970; *Eduardo Arroyo: 30 Jahre Danach,* exhibition catalogue, with text by Gerard Gassiot-Talabot, Frankfurt 1971; *Arroyo: Portraits,* exhibition catalogue, with text by Michel Tournier, Paris 1974; *Eduardo Arroyo,* exhibition catalogue, with text by Gilbert Lascault, Paris 1978; *Eduardo Arroyo: Blinde Maler und Exit,* exhibition catalogue, with text by Armin Zweite, Munich 1980; *Arroyo* by Pierre Astier, Paris 1982; *Eduardo Arroyo,* exhibition catalogue with texts by Dominique Bozo and Werner Spies, New York 1983.

There has always been an element of nakedness about Eduardo Arroyo's imagery. Even in early times, when the paint of his pictures was a little thicker, it was present. This is the surface effect, but below it lies an active conscience that dictates imagery. Not the sort of artist who can live comfortably in the cloying atmosphere of a dictatorship. This Spaniard with his direct approach tinted with character is a fine example of *engagierte kunst.* The Buonaparte paintings he showed in Paris made this very plain. But even politics as an inspiration for artists has not necessarily got eternal appeal.

Some of his later work has been concerned with the boxing ring, especially with coloured fighters. In these new works he is able to give a fresh and wholly unexpected dimension to the promotional side of "commercial art," although in Arroyo's case it is fine art, not the product of advertising nor some hybrid hyperrealist artist that is under consideration.

Arroyo's paint is flat. The subject (at one time he even divided his canvases into sections like a comic strip, although hardly in the same vein as those of CPLY's) is painted sparingly with the minimum of chiaroscuro. Colours tend to be block, and there is

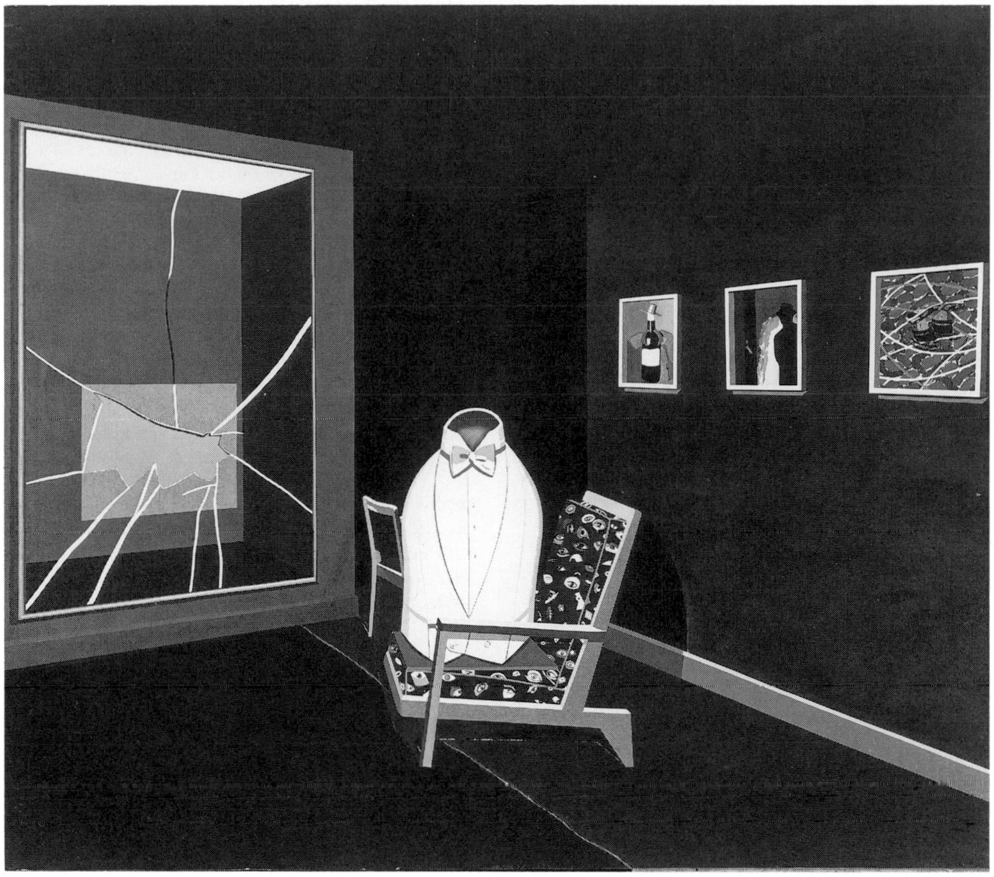

Eduardo Arroyo: ***A la Tate Gallery, José Maria Blanco White est Surveillé*, 1979**

virtually no tinting. All of his pictures have a careful, even traditional, sense of composition. Carried out by another artist, they might even have been associated with the pop image.

—Sheldon Williams

ARTSCHWAGER, Richard (Ernst).

American. Born in Washington, D.C., 26 December 1924. Studied chemistry and mathematics at Cornell University, Ithaca, New York, 1943–44, 1946–48, B.A. 1948; studied art with Amedee Ozenfant, New York, 1950. Served in the United States Army, 1944–46. Married Elfriede Wejmelka in 1947 (divorced, 1971); daughter: Eva; married Catherine Kord in 1972. Worked as a baby photographer for Stork Diaper Service, New York; lathe operator for Efrem Natkin Flexible Couplings, New York; and in export/import department, Colonial Trust Company, New York, 1950–55; operated a furniture factory, New York, 1955–65. Full-time artist, New York, since 1970. Recipient: Cassandra Award, New York, 1969; National Endowment for the Arts grant, 1973. Agent: Leo Castelli Gallery, 4 West 77th Street, New York, New York 10021. Address: 158 South Oxford Street, Brooklyn, New York 11217, U.S.A.

Individual Exhibitions:

1965 Leo Castelli Gallery, New York
1967 Leo Castelli Gallery, New York
1968 Galerie Konrad Fischer, Dusseldorf
1969 Galerie Ricke, Cologne
1970 Lo Guidice, Chicago
Eugenia Butler Gallery, Los Angeles
Onnasch Galerie, Berlin
1972 Leo Castelli Gallery, New York
Galerie Ricke, Cologne
1973 Leo Castelli Gallery, New York
Dunkelman Gallery, Toronto
Museum of Contemporary Art, Chicago
1974 Daniel Weinberg Gallery, San Francisco
Galerie Ileana Sonnabend, Geneva
1975 Leo Castelli Gallery, New York
Daniel Weinberg Gallery, San Francisco
Jared Sable Gallery, Toronto
Galerie Neuendorf, Hamburg
Galerie Sonnabend, Paris
1976 Walter Kelly Gallery, Chicago
Castelli Graphics, New York
1977 Sable-Castelli Gallery, Toronto
1978 Texas Gallery, Houston
Clocktower, New York
Institute for Art and Urban Resources, New York
Morgan Gallery, Shawnee Mission, Kansas
Kunstverein, Hamburg
1979 Leo Castelli Gallery, New York
Albright-Knox Art Gallery, Buffalo, New York
Institute of Contemporary Art, University of Pennsylvania, Philadelphia
1980 La Jolla Museum of Contemporary Art, California
Young-Hoffman Gallery, Chicago
1982 Leo Castelli Gallery, New York
1985 Kunstverein, Basel
Leo Castelli Gallery, New York
1986 CAPC Musée d'Art Contemporain, Bordeaux, France
1988 Whitney Museum, New York

Selected Group Exhibitions:

1964 *Boxes*, Dwan Gallery, Los Angeles
1966 *Primary Structures*, Jewish Museum, New York
1967 *The 1960's*, Museum of Modern Art, New York
1968 *Documenta 4*, Kassel, West Germany
1969 *When Attitudes Become Form*, Kunsthalle, Berne (toured Germany and Great Britain)
1972 *Documenta 5*, Kassel, West Germany
1974 *American Pop Art*, Whitney Museum, New York
1976 *200 Years of American Sculpture*, Whitney Museum, New York
1977 *Improbable Furniture*, Institute of Contemporary Art, University of Pennsylvania, Philadelphia
1987 *Documenta 8*, Museum Fridericianum, Kassel, West Germany

Collections:

Museum of Modern Art, New York; Whitney Museum, New York; Wadsworth Atheneum, Hartford, Connecticut; Kansas City Museum, Missouri; Detroit Institute of Arts; La Jolla Museum of Contemporary Art, California; Art Institute of Chicago; Rotterdam Museum; Wallraf-Richartz Museum, Cologne; Kunstmuseum, Basel.

Publications:

By ARTSCHWAGER: books—*Leo Castelli: 20 Years*, pamphlet, New York 1977; articles—"The Hydraulic Door Check" in *Arts Magazine* (New York), November 1967; "Statements on Art: in *N.A.M.E. Gallery, Book I*, edited by Donald Sultan and Nancy Davidson, Chicago 1977; "Actual Art" in *Skira Annual 79*, Geneva 1979; "Parade in the Face of Death: Robert Stanley" in *Galleries Magazine* (New York), September 1987.

On ARTSCHWAGER: books—*Direction I: Options*, exhibition catalogue, with introduction by Lawrence Alloway, Milwaukee 1968; *Documenta 5*, exhibition catalogue, Kassel, West Germany 1972; articles—"The Object: Still Life" by Jan McDevitt in *Craft Horizons* (New York), September/October 1965; "Artschwager's Mental Furniture" by Elizabeth C. Baker in *Art News* (New York), January 1968; "Richard Artschwager" by William Zimmer in *Arts Magazine* (New York), June 1975; "Richard Artschwager" by Noel Frackman in *Arts Magazine* (New York), January 1977; "Die Graue Tarnhulle der Wirklichkeit" by Peter Winter in *Frankfurter Allgemeine Zeitung* (Frankfurt), 2 October 1978; "The Elastic Vision of Richard Artschwager" in *Art in America* (New York), May/June 1978; article by John Russell in the *New York Times*, 8 July 1979; "The Artschwager Enigma" by Roberta Smith in *Art in America* (New York), October 1979.

It has been known since the Renaissance that art is produced by artists, and the notion has been available for more than a century that art is internal to the recipient; in a sense, "made" by the recipient. The first notion has tended to block off the availability of the second, and I think my contribution has been to make it not only available but Necessary, i.e., to force the issue of the context or, to put it in more old-fashioned terms, to make art that has no boundaries. At the beginning (around 1962) this was worked out in two steps: first make something which is "art," then insert it into a demanding, absorbent context, like inserting a garlic sliver into a joint of mutton. I have done some other things, but this certainly got the ball rolling!

—Richard Artschwager

Artschwager studied cell biology at Cornell University, with an interruption for military service, between 1941–48. In 1949–50 he studied in New York with Amadee Ozenfant. In 1953 he took up cabinet making and by 1956 he was massproducing simple furniture.

With the encouragement of his first wife he turned his energies towards actively being an artist by the early 1960s. He began to produce his 'infactory' works which were Constructivist in tone with identical sheets of plywood cut-offs joined into stacks, fans and baffles. By the mid 1960s, (when he began to exhibit with Leo Castelli Gallery), his work had become more like highly simplified furniture shapes frequently with formica or laminated surfaces. This neo-Dada type work came to be classified as "Minimalist." Barbara Rose, wrote in 1965 on Minimalist Art: "It is part of the irony of the works . . . and irony plays a large part in them—that they blatantly assert their unsaleability and functionlessness. Some, like Artschwager's pseudofurniture or Warhol's Brillo boxes, are not too unwieldy to be sold, but since they approximate real objects with actual uses, they begin

to raise questions about the utility of art, and its ambiguous role in our culture."

At the same time as he was producing the 'pseudo-furniture,' Artschwager was making grisaille pictures, frequently of highrise apartment blocks, by grid-enlarging photos and reproducing them with acrylic on celotex. In 1967 he developed an object which he termed a Blp and which he used as a kind of installation piece that could be installed anywhere, (a gallery wall, or on the sidewalk). The Blp was a long flat oval of any size, painted black. The name Blp came from a military expression Artschwager had learned during the war; it is an object connected with a sound as it moves on a radar screen.

Richard Artschwager: ***Chair*****, 1963**

In the late 1960s there came a lapse into pure Surrealism when Artschwager produced hair boxes and wall reliefs. The acrylic on celotex pictures, primarily of architectural interiors, lasted well into the 1970s.

By the early 1980s, Artschwager had become one of the sculptors involved in the U.S. government's General Services Administration's 'Art in Architecture' programme. This partnership has had a high profile with the Battery Park City development in southwestern Manhattan, where Artschwager's work will be sited.

—Victoria Keller

ASHER, Michael.

American. Born in Los Angeles, California, 15 July 1943. Studied liberal arts and sciences at Orange Coast College, Costa Mesa, California, 1961–63; anthropology and art, University of New Mexico, Albuquerque, 1963–64; New York Studio School, 1964–65; fine arts, University of California at Irvine, 1965–67, B.A. 1966. Worked as advertising sales representative for West Coast Industries, New York, 1964; worked as research assistant for use of cardboard materials in furniture, Los Angeles. Independent sculptor and environmental artist, Los Angeles, since 1966. Assistant Instructor in Sculpture, 1966–67, and Painting Instructor, 1967–68, University of California at Irvine; Instructor in Art, California Institute of Arts, Valencia, 1976. Artist-in-Residence, University of California at Irvine, 1973, California Institute of the Arts, Valencia, 1973, Nova Scotia College of Art and Design, 1974, and Otis Art Institute, Los Angeles, 1975. Recipient: Purchase Award, Contemporary Art Council, Los Angeles County Museum of Art, 1967; Short-Term Activities Fellowship Grant, National Endowment for the Arts, 1973; Guggenheim Fellowship, 1974; Artists Fellowship Grant, National Endowment for the Arts, 1975. Address: 262 Carmelina Avenue South, Apt. 6, Los Angeles, California 90291, U.S.A.

Individual Exhibitions:

1969	La Jolla Museum of Art, California
1970	Gladys K. Montgomery Art Center, Pomona College, Claremont, California
1972	Market Street Program, Venice, California
1973	Gallery A 402, California Institute of the Arts, Valencia
	Cambridge School, Weston, Massachusetts
	Lisson Gallery, London
	Galerie Heiner Friedrich, Cologne
	Galleria Toselli, Milan
1974	Claire S. Copley Gallery, Los Angeles
	Anna Leonowens Gallery, Nova Scotia College of Art and Design, Halifax
1975	Otis Art Institute, Los Angeles
1976	The Clocktower, New York
	The Floating Museum, San francisco
1977	Van Abbemuseum, Eindhoven, Netherlands
1980	*Exhibitions in Europa 1972–1977,* Van Abbemuseum, Eindhoven, Netherlands
1984	Hofhour Gallery, Albuquerque, New Mexico
1986	Hofhour Gallery, Albuquerque, New Mexico

Selected Group Exhibitions:

1967	*I Am Alive,* Los Angeles County Museum of Art
1969	*Anti-Illusion: Procedures: Materials,* Whitney Museum, New York
	Plane und Projekte als Kunst, Kunsthalle, Berne (travelled to Aktionsraum I, Munich, and the Kunsthaus, Hamburg)
1970	*Art in the Mind,* Allen Art Museum, Oberlin College, Ohio
1971	*24 Young Los Angeles Artists,* Los Angeles County Museum of Art
1972	*Documenta 5,* Kassel, West Germany
1973	*3D into 2D: Drawings for Sculpture,* New York Cultural Center
1975	*University of California, Irvine, 1965–75,* La Jolla Museum of Contemporary Art, California
1976	*Ambiente,* at *Biennale,* Venice
1977	*Skulptur,* Westfälische Landesmuseum, Münster, West Germany

Publications:

By ASHER: book—Commentary in *Michael Asher: Exhibitions in Europa 1972–1977,* exhibition catalogue, Eindhoven, Netherlands, 1980.

On ASHER: book—*Anti-Illusion: Procedures: Materials,* exhibition catalogue, with texts by James Monte and Marcia

Michael Asher: *Untitled*, installation at the Museum of Contemporary Art, Chicago, 1979

Tucker, New York 1969; *8e Biennale de Paris*, exhibition catalogue, with texts by J. Cahen-Salvador, and others, Paris 1973; *Michael Asher: Exhibitions in Europa 1972 1977*, exhibition catalogue, with essays by R. H. Fuchs and B. H. D. Buchloh, Eindhoven, Netherlands 1980; articles—"Michael Asher: La Jolla Art Museum" by T. H. Garver in *Artforum* (New York), January 1970; "Michael Asher: An Environmental Project" by B. Munger in *Studio International* (London), October 1970; "The Art of Existence: 3 Extravisual Artists, Works in Progress" by Robert Morris in *Artforum* (New York), January 1971; "Michael Asher: The Thing of It Is . . ." by Peter Plagens in *Artforum* (New York), April 1972.

I feel it is implicit, yet perhaps not immediately recognised through background information, that those activities which pertain to my art and those activities which pertain to me in general, are determined by one another.

—Michael Asher

ASKEVOLD, David.

American. Born in Conrad, Montana, 30 March 1940. Educated at University of Montana, Missoula; Brooklyn Museum School of Art, New York; Art Institute of Kansas City, Missouri. Taught at Nova Scotia College of Art and Design, Halifax, 1968–75; University of California at Irvine, 1976–77; and California Institute of the Arts, Valencia, 1977–78; instructor, Art Center College of Design, Pasadena, California, 1980–81; lecturer, York University, Downsview, Ontario, 1981–82. Agents: Studio Cannaviello, Piazza Beccaria 10, 20122 Milan, Italy; Galerie Paul Maenz, Bismarckstrasse 50, 5000 Cologne 1, West Germany. Address: P.O. Box 898, Big Sky, Montana 59716, U.S.A.

Individual Exhibitions:

1970 Nova Scotia College of Art and Design, Halifax
1971 Anna Leonowens Gallery, Nova Scotia College of Art and Design, Halifax
1972 Anna Leonowens Gallery, Nova Scotia College of Art and Design, Halifax
Galerie Paul Maenz, Cologne
Galerie Yvon Lambert, Paris
Galleria Françoise Lambert, Milan
Jack Wendler Gallery, London
1973 John Gibson Gallery, New York
1974 Anna Leonowens Gallery, Nova Scotia College of Art and Design, Halifax
Galerie Paul Maenz, Cologne
Galleria Françoise Lambert, Milan
1975 Galerie Yvon Lambert, Paris
John Gibson Gallery, New York
Art Metropole, Toronto
1976 Fine Arts Gallery, University of California at Irvine
1977 John Gibson Gallery, New York
1978 Thomas Lewallen Gallery, Los Angeles
Foundation for Art Resources, Los Angeles (with Michael Kelley)
1980 Van Abbemuseum, Eindhoven, Netherlands
Cannaviello Studio d'Arte, Milan
1981 Jancar Kuhlenschmidt Gallery, Los Angeles

Selected Group Exhibitions:

1974 Palais des Beaux-Arts, Brussels
1976 Daniel Templon Galerie, Paris
The Artist and the Photograph, Israel Museum, Jerusalem
1977 *Documenta*, Kassel, West Germany
1978 *Story, Narrative Art*, Contemporary Art Museum, Houston (travelling exhibition)
1979 *Narrative Art*, Groningen Museum, Netherlands
Text/Visual, Commune di Milano, Milan
1980 *Camerie Incantate*, Commune de Milano, Milan
Artist and Camera, Arts Council of Great Britain (travelling exhibition)

Collections:

Van Abbemuseum, Eindhoven, Netherlands; Museum of Contemporary Art, Houston, Texas.

Publications:

By ASKEVOLD: book—*Extra,* Cologne, April 1975; articles—"Liberal Art University Experiences: David Askevold in Conversations with Paul McMahon" in *Studio International* (London), April 1972; article in *Video by Artists,* edited by Peggy Gale, Toronto 1976; radio broadcast—17 Minute Tuning Fork Music Concert, K.P.F.A. Radio, Berkeley, California, April 1971.

On ASKEVOLD: books—*6 Years: The Dematerialization of the Art Object* by Lucy Lippard, New York 1973; *Individuals: Post Movement Art in America,* edited by Alan Sondheim, New York 1977; *The Artist and the Photograph #2,* exhibition catalogue No. 55, Jerusalem 1977; *Narrative Art,* exhibition catalogue, Groningen, Netherlands 1979; articles—"Artist as Film-Maker" by Annabel Nicholson in *Art and Artists* (London), December 1972; review in *Arts* (New York), February 1974; article in *Kunst Magazine* (Munich), March 1974; article in *Artforum* (New York), September 1974; article by Ronald Shuebrook in *Artscanada* (Toronto), December 1974; article in *Data* (Milan) nos. 16/17, 1975; articles in *Artweek* (Oakland, California), 4 February 1977, and 14 July 1979; article in *Kunstforum* (Cologne), Fall 1979; article in *Artweek* (Oakland, California), 13 February 1979; article in *Artforum* (New York), May 1981.

David Askevold is perhaps one of the most prolific and experimental of all the artists associated with the school of Narrative Art. In many ways he differs from them wildly: unlike Bill Beckley, he has never remained with one primary medium (the large glossy color photograph and short, pithy text); and unlike French artist Jean Le Gac, he is not concerned with the gentler aspect of a series of banal incidents and certainly does not invest his narrative with mild or startling humor. Rather, Askevold steers his work through a variety of mediums and even concerns, depending upon their appropriateness at a given time. He has, of course, made many still works (the conventional Narrative device of visual sign and quasi-expository text), but he has also made discrete films and videotapes, and ambitious film, video, and slide installations. Furthermore, these are frequently and deliberately obscure, and therefore do not share with other work in the genre an immediate and engaging sensibility.

This is not to say that there is not an active and linking sensibility throughout Askevold's oeuvre. This takes the form of a complex approach and an occasionally sinister iconography. First of all, Askevold rarely if ever follows the structural pattern of several of his colleagues, in which image and text deliberately diverge (i.e., the texts meandering while the images form a logical dramatic sequence). Instead, the combination of word and sign create, as Filiberto Menna has pointed out in a catalogue essay, "a perfect parallelism between the two terms, so that the text accompanies and comments upon the horizontal concatenation of the images . . . " (This, of course, applies specifically to Askevold's more conventionally Narrative pieces, such as "Elektra," a series of eleven photos and text, completed in 1974.) Secondly, Askevold has never felt restricted by the convention of his chosen genre, and on several occasions has used an extraordinary ambitious formal structure, as in his installation "Four Notes Through a Wall and Into the Grass" (1972–73) which used a series of 80 color slides, audiotape, drawing, and super-8 film. And, as far as Askevold's iconography is concerned, it has involved a frequent use of snakes (as in the previously mentioned "Four Notes" and "Kepler's Music of the Spheres to Be Played by Six Snakes," (1971–73), as well as paradigms from algebra and physics, and quasi-psychological experiments.

In one of his most major sequences, "Dream of Descartes," Askevold takes a theme through several media: in his still version, he uses four photographs and a number of versions of a nearly identical text (with phrases added or deleted), as well as a 16 millimeter color film, and later, a fairly ambitious installation using two super-8 film projections and scored music, combined with Kepler's "Music of the Spheres." Askevold's is, in a sense, an art of retrieval, both physical and conceptual, never linear or progressive, but continually evolving both backwards and forwards, borrowing from and expanding upon itself.

—Jane Bell

ATKINSON, Conrad.

British. Born in Cleator Moor, Cumbria, 15 June 1940. Educated in Cumbria primary schools; studied painting at the Carlisle College of Art, 1957–61, Liverpool College of Art, 1961–62, and the Royal Academy of Art Schools, London, under William Townsend, 1962–65. Married Margaret Harrison in 1967; daughter: Sophie. Printmaking Adviser, the Royal Academy of Art Schools, London, 1963–65; Exhibition Organizer, Northern Arts Gallery, Newcastle upon Tyne, 1975–76. Since 1978, Lecturer, Slade School of Fine Art, London. Member, Art Science Working Party, University of London, 1971; Member, National Committee, British Society for Social Responsibility on Science, 1972; Chairman, Artists' Union, London, 1974; Member, Visual Arts Panel, Northern Arts, Newcastle upon Tyne, 1975–76; Member, Tyneside Trade Unionists for Socialist Arts, Newcastle upon Tyne, 1975–76. Recipient: National Book League Prize, 1955; Second Prize, Northern Young Artists, Middlesborough, 1965; Leverhulme Award, 1965; Abbey Travelling Scholarship, 1965; Granada Fellowship, 1967; Churchill Fellowship, 1972. Associate, School of Advanced Studies, Manchester, 1968; Fellow in Fine Arts, Northern Arts Association, Newcastle upon Tyne, 1974–76. Agent: Ronald Feldman Fine Arts, 31 Mercer Street, New York, New York 10013, U.S.A. Address: 172 Erlanger Road, London SE14, England. Address: 96 Lyndhurst Grove, London SE15, England.

Individual Exhibitions:

1967 *2 Painters,* City Art Gallery, Manchester (with Gerald Park)
1972 Institute of Contemporary Arts, London
1974 Institute of Contemporary Arts, London (toured the U.K.)
1975 Northern Ireland's Arts Council Gallery, Belfast
1976 Art Net Gallery, London
1977 Northern Arts Gallery, Newcastle upon Tyne
1978 Serpentine Gallery, London
1979 Ronald Feldman Fine Arts, New York
The Craft of Art, Walker Fine Art Gallery, Liverpool
1980 Chapter House Gallery, Cardiff
1975–1980: Work about the North, Pentonville Gallery, London
Project Gallery, Dublin
Carlisle Museum and Art Gallery
1981 Institute of Contemporary Arts, London
Sunderland Arts Centre
1983 Power Gallery, Sydney
1985 Art Institute of Chicago
1987 Artangel Trust, London

Selected Group Exhibitions:

1965 *Northern Young Artists,* City Art Gallery, Middlesborough
1968 *Royal Academy Bicentenary,* Royal Academy of Art, London
1970 *Garbage Strike,* Sigi Krauss Gallery, London
1973 *Critics' Choice,* Tooth Gallery, London
1975 *Biennale de Paris*
1977 *British Art 77,* Newcastle upon Tyne
1978 *Art for Society,* Whitechapel Gallery, London
1979 *Un Certain Art Anglais,* Musée National d'Art Moderne, Paris
1980 *Photography into Print,* Victoria and Albert Museum, London
1981 *Landscape,* Tate Gallery, London

Collections:

City Art Gallery, Manchester; William Morris Housing Estate, Cleator Moor, Cumbria.

Publications:

By ATKINSON: books—*A Shade of Green: An Orange Edge,* exhibition catalogue, with John Hewitt and Caroline Tisdall, Belfast 1975; *Newcastle Writings,* Newcastle upon Tyne 1977; *Art for Whom,* exhibition catalogue, London 1978; statement in *The Craft of Art,* exhibition catalogue, by Edward Lucie Smith, Liverpool 1979; *Shamrock's Truth: The 1st Casualty: The British Media and Northern Ireland,* 1979; articles—"Conrad Atkinson: An Interview," with Richard Cork in *Studio International* (London), March/April 1976; "Capitalist Realism or Socialism in One Person" in *Skira Annual,* Geneva 1977; introduction to *Conrad Atkinson 1975–1980: Work about the North,* exhibition catalogue, London 1980.

On ATKINSON: books—*The Craft of Art,* exhibition catalogue, by Edward Lucie Smith, Liverpool 1979; *Art in the 70's* by Edward Lucie Smith, Oxford 1980; *Conrad Atkinson: Picturing the System,* edited by Caroline Tisdall and Sandy Nairne, London 1981; articles—"Tribute to a strike" by Laurie Flynn in *the Socialist Worker* (London), June 1972; "The Art of Work" by Caroline Tisdall in *The Guardian* (London), April 1974; "A Struggling Artist" by Bobby Campbell in *The Morning Star* (London), April 1974; "Atkinson in Northern Ireland" by Caroline Tisdall in *The Guardian* (London), 1976; film—*Atkinson,* BBC Television, 1981.

To deal with living situations and forces is obviously a difficult undertaking for an artist, fraught with pitfalls. It is an era unexplored by artists since the 1920's, and it is one in which attitudes to both form and content have a vast and unexplored potential.

One of the main problems for any artist is the necessity to isolate sections of our perceptions in order to examine and express them. Yet we have to maintain a sense of total relationships. The uneasy tug of war between these two conflicting necessities is the battleground on which the specialist and the generalist fight. In this difficult question of isolating an area of research without alienating oneself from overall problems, there is a tension which creates new solutions.

Most of my works have a potency and an impact on the social dynamic of their communities which artists trained as academic easel painters might well enjoy in its immediacy, its utilization within its community and its context. This is where art touches base. The relevance of this art is central to the philosophies and ideologies which it supports and in some cases advances. All societies lay down rules the main function of which is naturally to preserve those societies and hopefully to develop their aims and ideas. These rules tend to operate as mechanisms for preserving the status quo. Most of the citizens of societies understandably go along with these rules and laws, and artists, contrary to popular opinion, are in general no exception. Nevertheless, no matter what sort of society is involved, the values and aspirations of that society need to be constantly either affirmed, probed, developed or denied; to analyse and create a picture for these purposes is one of the important functions of art.

Artists, I think, have had a dialogue with themselves and with other artists for far too long during the course of the 20th century. I believe one must start from a belief that art is not about art, but that art is about anything which is not art, and my work should be seen as an attempt to relate to the aims and aspirations of the mass of the people, the opposite in fact to the popular view of the artist as an isolated individual committed to the exploration of his own psyche. It then follows that a whole range of subjects become open to investigation for artists from regional development to the EEC, from wage differentials to

Conrad Atkinson: Meeting at Art Net, London, 1968 (Atkinson second from left)

strikes, from minority rights to profits, from property to politics, from education to pensions, housing, factories, leisure—any human activity becomes a possible subject and open to the artist in a different way than hitherto. In this way, the artist can move towards a more central position in society, a position from which real issues, real analyses, real dialogue and real gains can be made.

It may be that art has a problem for all solutions. If that is the case, then artists in their relationship to society may reconsider another famous slogan in the attempt to break art from the magic hedonism of current art forms: "If you are not part of the solution, you must be part of the problem."

—Conrad Atkinson

Conrad Atkinson is an artist who works in a radical tradition of politics and social reality. This is, in large measure, due to his background and the formative influences of his birth and upbringing in Cleator Moor, a small mining village in a depressed industrial area which lies in a narrow strip on the western coast of Cumbria. Previously a place of heavy industry, as the coal and iron ore were exhausted a pall of unemployment and poverty enveloped the community and the men were driven away to find work. Thus the young Conrad was faced with the basic problems of life from his earliest years. During the 1950's there was a brief period of boom during the building of the nuclear power station known as Calder Hall, later to bear the ominous name of Windscale and now known as Sellafield. Atkinson himself worked for a short time for British Nuclear Fuels. The mining industry had always taken its toll annually in injuries and deaths from its workers but after the opening of the nuclear power station the local population had to learn to live with persistent and disquieting anxieties about radioacative fallout.

Conrad Atkinson studied art first at the nearby School of Art at Carlisle and then at the Royal Academy Schools in London but he has never distanced himself from the place where he was born and its people. In his art he shows his deep involvement by creating telling images of the bitter contrast between the depressed west coast industrial wasteland and the Lakeland National Park. The latter he has described as a "middle class, high income bracket, outdoor museum and playground, 'The English Lake District' in which the workers are 'invisible' or 'hidden' as were the workers in Engel's Manchester . . . "

In a major work entitled "For Wordsworth, For West Cumbria," (1980) which has since been acquired by the Tate Gallery, London, he shows these concerns in an imaginative assemblage of sixteen panels displayed in two rows of eight. They are in a mixed media of photography, acrylic, iron ore and coal. The images reveal how passionately he feels but the treatment in this cool, documentary mode creates a tension between subject matter and manner which reinforces their impact.

The upper row of eight panels which is mainly photographic are all of an outstretched hand and a daffodil flower. This row is bright and inviting with its pale yellow and pale green lettering superimposed which invites the viewer to draw nearer and read the quotation from Wordsworth, the Lakes Poet. The outstretched hand represents 'man' and the yellow daffodil stands for 'nature' and changes in scale tell of a changing imbalance between the two. The lower row is bleaker to look at; a photograph of a picket line in a long drawn out strike has a superimposed picture postcard 'scenic' view of the Lakes; a contour map of the Lake District has a tracery of the dangers and perils to which workers in the area have been and are exposed; one panel shows a lump of iron ore between two excerpts from a poem by an immigrant worker forced to leave Cleator when the iron ore and the work ran out; the record of the first acknowledged death from exposure to radioactive waste which caused a young worker to contract leukemia; disused mining machinery with nature encroaching; and under words from Wordsworth after the loss of his brother at sea in 1805 a panel commemorates the drowning of six local men in the wreck of an oil rig onto which unemployment had driven them to work.

Wordsworth is important to Atkinson who said he only really discovered him after he had grown up and realised the relevance of Wordsworth and the Romantic poets, through their commitment politically and economically, to social issues and the crucial relationship between man and the landscape—a landscape which man both helps to create and preserve and also to destroy and which may, in its turn, destroy him. Atkinson points up vividly the harsh choice that so many West Cumbrian workers have had to make between 'life and livelihood' both from the perils of mining and the unseen, insidious dangers of nuclear power. In his work Atkinson skillfully avoids the dangers inherent in strongly polemical and controversial issues of becoming either shrill or hectoring and presents his arguments with thoughtful sensitivity.

—Mary Ellis

ATTALAI, Gabor.
Hungarian. Born in Budapest, 20 November 1934. Educated at Applied Arts University, Budapest, 1953–58. Married Maria Nemes in 1961; daughter: Nora. Served as corporal in the Hungarian Infantry, in Nagykanisz and Mezotur, 1955–1956. Designer, Imparmuveszeti Vallat Company, Budapest, since 1958. Recipient: Magyar Nepkoztarsaasag Muveszeti Alap (Prize for experimental art), Budapest, 1970; Fellowship of the Neue Galerie, Graz, 1973; Yorkshire Arts Association Prize, England, 1974; Prize of the Galerie d'Art Contemporain, Zagreb, 1974. Address: Groza rkp. 11, Budapest 1013, Hungary.

Individual Exhibitions:

1963 Petrigalla Room, Budapest
1966 Modern Nordisk Konst Gallery, Gothenburg, Sweden
1970 Bank of Danube, Budapest
1972 KKI Galerie, Budapest
International Artists' Cooperation, Oldenburg, Germany
Central Administration of Artistic Environment Defence, Bad Salzdetfurth, Germany
1973 Veste Sagrada Organizacao Criativa, Rio de Janeiro
Sum Gallery, Reykjavik
1974 Galerie Remont, Warsaw
New Reform Gallery, Antwerp
1975 New Reform Gallery, Aalst, Belgium
1976 Galerie Sztuki Najnowszej, Wroclaw, Poland
Galleria Banco, Brescia
Galleria Diagramma, Milan
1977 Galerie Loa, Haarlem, Netherlands
1978 Pecsi Galerie, Pecs, Hungary
Galerie Sudurgata, Reykjavik
1979 Echnaton Gallery, Cairo

Selected Group Exhibitions:

1960 *Debrenci Tarlat,* Deryne Museum, Debrecen, Hungary
1964 *Forma '64,* Veszpremi Muzeum, Veszprem, Hungary
1969 *Plans and Projects as Art,* Kunsthalle, Berne
1970 *Mozgds,* Janus Pannonius Museum, Pecs, Hungary
1971 *"Land Art,"* Aktionsraum, Munich
1972 *3rd International Graphics Biennale,* Rijeka Museum, Rijeka, Yugoslavia
1973 *Omaha Flow Systems,* Joslyn Art Museum, Omaha, Nebraska
1974 *4th British International Print Biennale,* Cartwright Hall, Bradford
1982 *International Photo Biennale,* Vienna

Collections:

Dery Museum, Debrecen, Hungary; Iparmuveszeti Museum, Budapest; Janus Pannonius Museum, Pecs, Hungary; Saveria Museum, Szombathely, Hungary; Neue Galerie, Graz, Austria; National Museum, Stockholm; Modern Art Museum, Zagreb; Bradford City Council, England.

Publications:

By ATTALAI: books—*Future,* Budapest 1972; *Identifications,* Budapest 1972; *Time Book,* Oldenburg, Germany 1973; *Without Instruments,* Aalst, Belgium 1974; *11 Textiles,* Budapest 1978; *Photographie als Kunst,* Vienna 1979; *Texts,* Munster 1979; *Del Libro artista,* Geneva 1979; *Muveszet,* Budapest 1979–80; *Mozgo Vilag,* Budapest 1981; *Objektek szituaciok Ellenpontok Lagy anyagokkal* Budapest 1981; article—essay in *Aktuelle Kunst in Osteuropa,* edited by Klaus Groh, Cologne 1972.

On ATTALAI: books—*Mugyujto* by Janos Frank, Budapest 1972; *Gabor Attalai und die "society art"* by Klaus Groh, Nuremberg 1972; articles—"Report" by Janos Frank in *Elet Es Irodalom* (Budapest), March 1969; "Die Ungarische Avantgarde" by Jurgen Weighardt in *Nordwest Zeitung* (Oldenburg, Germany), no. 15, 1969; "Concept Makers" by A. Merckx in *Newspaper* (Brussels), February 1972; "Objects from Felt" by Gyula Rozsa in *Nepszabadsag* (Budapest), June 1972; "Andere Kreative Production in Osteurope" by Klaus Groh in *Osteurope* (Stuttgart), no. 11, 1972; review in *+-0* (Genval-Lac, Belgium), no. 9, 1975.

In the last five years I have created paintings, environments and photographs to an idea: "Red-y Made," which is the counterpoint of Duchampian Ready-Made. Red-y Mades are paintings. Yellow-y Mades are also.

—Gabor Attalai

AUBERTIN, Bernard
French. Born in Fontenay-aux-Roses, 29 July 1934. Initially self-taught in painting, studying cubist and futurist works, until 1951; studied at the Ecole des Metiers d'Art, and the Ecole du Professorat de Dessin, Paris, 1952–54. Served in the French Army, 1957–58. Married the artist Denise Demaldent in 1955; sons: Vincent and Frederic; lived with Joelle Fontaine, 1975–86; children: Julien and Solene. Painter, influenced initially by Yves Klein, Paris, since 1957; first monochrome red paintings, 1958; rednail-paintings, 1960–71; fire-paintings, 1961; burned-book works, 1962. Lived in Brest, Finistere, 1975–86. Agents: Galerie Beaubourg, 23 rue de Renard, 75004 Paris; Galerie Cical-Lefebre, 30 rue Mazarine, 75006 Paris; Galerie Spiess, 4 Avenue de Messine, 75008 Paris; Espace J. et J. Donguy, 57 rue de la Roquette, 7501 Paris. Address: 14 Villa St. Jacques, 75014 Paris, France.

Individual Exhibitions:

1962 Galerie Wulfengasse 14, Klagenfurt, Austria
1967 Galerie Weiller, Paris
Galerie M. E. Thelen, Essen
1968 Galerie des Quatre Vents, Paris
Galerie Riquelme, Paris
Kleine Galerie, Frankfurt
1969 Galerie Senatore, Stuttgart
1971 Galerie Ursula Lichter, Frankfurt
1972 Centre National d'Art Contemporain, Paris (retrospective; with Fred Deux and Otto Schauer)
1973 Galerie Toni Brechbuhl, Grenchen, Switzerland
Musée de l'Abbaye Sainte-Croix, Les Sables-d'Olonne, France
Galerie Seebacher, Vorarlberg, Austria
1974 Galerie 2, Stuttgart
Studio Brescia, Brescia, Italy
Galleria Banco, Brescia, Italy
Studio Firenze, Florence
Galleria dei Mille, Bergamo, Italy
Galleria Delta, Salerno, Italy
Studio F. 22, Palazzolo, Italy
Galleria Il Canale, Venice
1975 Studio Brescia, Brescia, Italy
Galleria Il Canale, Venice
Galleria Il Punto, Turin
1977 Galleria Rebus, Florence
1978 Palazzetto dello Sport, Abano Terme, Italy
Galerie 44, Kaarst bei Dusseldorf, West Germany
1979 Galerie Weiller, Paris
1983 Galerie J. et J. Donguy, Paris
Galerie Toni Brechbuhl, Grenchen, Switzerland
1986 Galerie Charley Chevalier, Paris
1987 Galerie Beatrix Wilhelm, Stuttgart

Selected Group Exhibitions:

1961 *Zero,* Galerie Dato, Frankfurt
1965 *Zero Avant-Garde,* Atelier de Fontana, Milan
1967 *Luminism,* George Washington Hotel, New York
1968 *Cinetisme,* Maison de la Culture, Grenoble, France
1969 *Dynamozero 1959–1969,* Galerie Ursula Lichter, Frankfurt
1971 *Sammlung Cremer: Kunst der 60er Jahre, Kunstverein, Heidelberg*
1972 *Douze Ans d'Art Contemporain en France,* Grand Palais, Paris
1976 *Kunst der 60er und 70er Jahre,* Kunstmuseum, Bonn
1985 *Eine Europaische Bewegung,* Museum Carolino Augusteum, Salzburg
1987 *Ephemerite,* Chapelle St. Louis de la Salpetriere, Paris

Collections:

Centre National d'Art Contemporain, Paris; Mobilier National, Paris,; Musée de l'Abbaye Sainte-Croix, Les Sables-d'Olonne, France; Musée de Grenoble, France; Kunstmuseum, Dusseldorf, Kunsthalle, Tübingen, West Germany; Landesmuseum Joanneum, Graz, Austria.

Publications:

By AUBERTIN: books—*Bernard Aubertin: 6 Textes,* Paris 1962; *Bernard Aubertin: 9 Textes,* Paris 1968; *Aubertin Pyromane,* Paris 1969; *Aubertin par Aubertin pour Aubertin,* Brest, France 1985; articles—"Esquisse de la situation picturale du rouge dans un concept spatial" in *Zero* (Dusseldorf), no. 3, 1961; "La Monochromie" in *Nul=0* (Arnhem, Netherlands), no. 1, 1962; "La Couleur" in *Nul=0* (Arnhem, Netherlands), no. 2, 1963; "Je suis un realiste" in *Integration* (Arnhem, Netherlands), no. 4, 1965; "L'Art dans la Société Capitaliste d'Aujourd'hui" in *Integration* (Arnhem, Netherlands), no. 7–8, 1967; "Sur Pierre Manzoni" in *Robho* (Paris), no. 3, 1968; "Yves le bleu vu par Bernard le rouge" in *La Galerie des Arts* (Paris), no. 64, 1969; "La Cage Rouge de Fumée . . . " in *Robho* (Paris), no. 5–6, 1971; "A Propos de mes Nouvelles Sculptures" in *Integration* (Eschenau, Netherlands), no. 13–14, 1972.

On AUBERTIN: books—*Bernard Aubertin,* exhibition catalogue, with text by Udo Kultermann, Essen, West Germany 1967; *Douze Ans d'Art Contemporain en France,* exhibition catalogue, with texts by F. Mathey, V. Huchard, D. Cordier and others, Paris 1972; *Aubertin/Deux/Schauer,* exhibition catalogue, with texts by Hans Haacke, Bernard Rancillac, Udo Kultermann and others, Paris 1972; *Factotum Book 5: Bernard Aubertin,* with text by Egidio Mucci, Padua 1978; *Bernard Aubertin: Le Point Zero de la Peinture,* exhibition catalogue, edited by Charley Chevalier, Paris 1986; *Bernard Aubertin,* exhibition catalogue, with essay by Gabriele Kubler, Stuttgart 1987.

I started painting in my 21st year after having studied two years in an artist's studio preparing to enter the State schools of decoration. On receiving admission I disdained returning there: I wanted to dedicate myself to painting, my vocation. Until the age of 23 I painted portraits, landscapes, still-lifes, and above all did plenty of drawing. The figurative or abstract painting I saw in the galleries did not satisfy me. In 1957 I met Yves Klein and this meeting was for me, of major importance. Under his influence I completed about 15 canvases, which were monochrome, red and very structured. I used to do this with every type of painter's knife, even the prongs of a fork, the round back of a spoon, etc. The whole painted surface was a unity composed of repeated structures. These structures didn't give me entire satisfaction: they weren't specific enough for my taste. One day I threw a handful of nails into the red colour spread on the canvas. Accidentally, I had just discovered in the nail the structure which corresponded to that precision which I was looking for. From here the idea of planting the nails one by one in the support, rather than scattering them at random on it, followed naturally. I was recreating the unity of the surface by filling it with nails. My work on nail-pictures divides into two periods: 1) the picture presents the nail head-outwards; 2) the picture presents the point of the nail, the head of the nail being the picture.

I soon had the idea of using elements other than nails in series: screws, pitons, matches. With matches, I invented fire-painting. All my researches

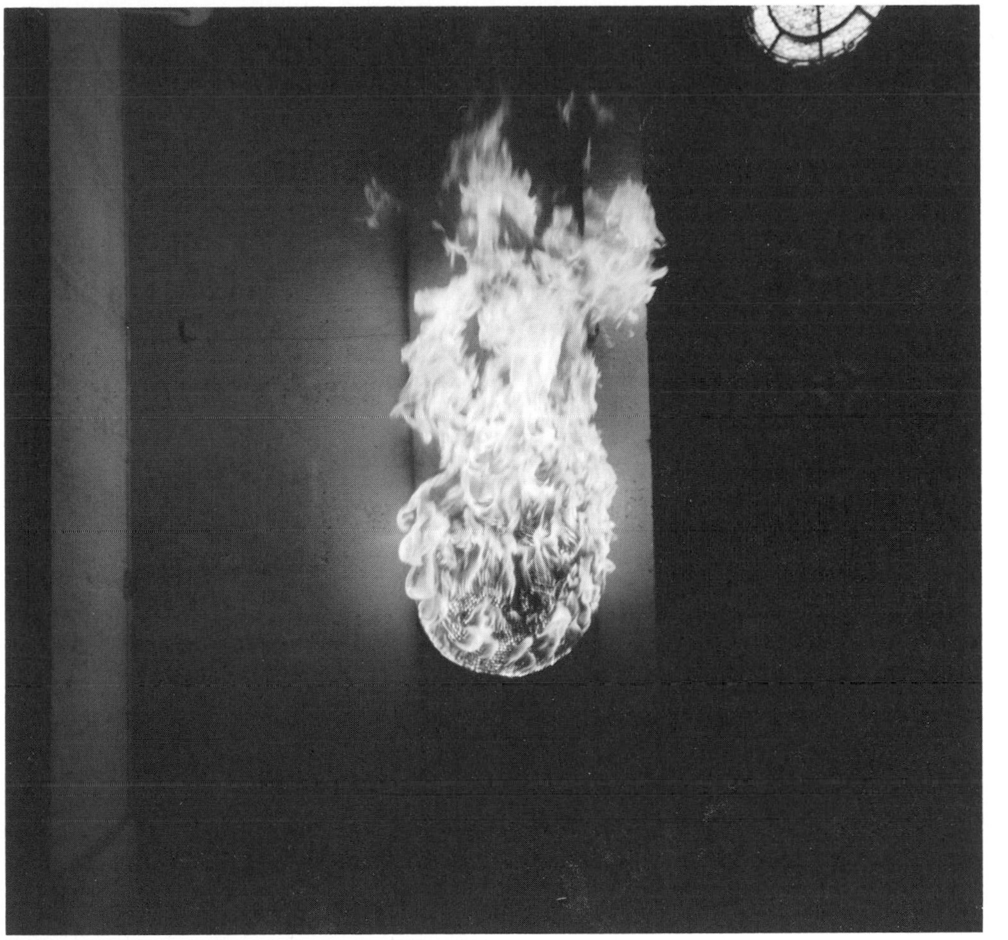

Bernard Aubertin: Rotating Fire Disk from *Ephemerité*, 1987

are inspired by one ideal: to humanise. From my own observation of what is going on in the culture of our present-day world, I have acquired the opinion that our present art expresses, for the most part, the impossibility, for man, of communicating harmoniously with his fellows. Our present art is founded on a therapy on the level of the individual, without any message for other men concerning the transformation of human nature demanded of humanity. It is the statement of the misery of a humanity in conflict with itself, dehumanised: it is journalism, news in brief; it offers itself up to the caprices of fashion, creates it, and finally reveals itself as completely incapable of exerting a vaguely spiritual influence.

The truth is that it is incumbent upon the artist, aware of the always dehumanised state of society, to base art first of all on man.

Art, in my sense, can not be envisaged except as a therapy on the collective level, which brings about the fraternisation of men and ennobles the dose of therapy inherent in all art. Our role as artists is to lead to the TOTALITY, shorn of all contradictions, of human nature. In this way, man will always be in a position to foresee the needs of humanity and to reply to them. In acting for collectivity, we liberate ourselves from nature and from our own natures.

That is why, in the field of the realisation of a plastic work, I find it necessary to reduce the role of manual execution to its dominant function: the hand is nothing else than a manufacturing tool; to entrust it with the responsibility of fixing the various tensions—emotive, instinctive, animal even—accumulated in the soul, is an error.

We must strive to take distance in comparison with nature, if we want to realise ourselves as a specific human species. The creation of a distance in the execution is the means that one finds to take distance in comparison with nature and with our own natures.

Thus, to fill the surface regularly with the help of nails, screws, pitons, matches etc. signifies, in my case, the creation of this distance in the execution. If form in art is limitation, if it corresponds, in the plastic arts, to the natural and social order in which we live (we all know that man is determined), it must not be unchanging. On the contrary, it must be constructed by means of the relief which catches the light and modifies it naturally. (Form can be rendered mobile by many other means; I'm talking here of what I do myself.) The distribution of the light on the reliefs of my pictures changes according to the times of day. In this way, the picture is never completely the same.

I am seeking to obtain greater precision in the definition of human nature. In this sense, I think I have the right to say: I am a realist.

—Bernard Aubertin

Where does Bernard Aubertin begin? One would like to reply: at the stake stripped of all his witches. To ignite things like this, by vocation, at least with a "flash in the pan" of the metaphors, would not easily resolve that linguistic impression that the world is an artifice—hence this determination to strike things which, from the blow, take fire with a mad hope: to illuminate the art of ashes.

The technique is simple: fire. The proposition "water propagates, fire reduces" is thus articulated in this way: the machinery of fire, as play of flames, starting from propositions reduced to homothetic multiplications (matches) forms a system. Hence the difficulty of any extraneous propositions: water does not extinguish fire. For the pyromaniac who Aubertin demands of himself is substituted a flamboyant fireman.

The Aubertin rises again from his ashes and explains himself historically. Use of the time where the history of art stores away its recipes. It's practically everything (the question at least, since there must be a "reader" or a "spectator" which is *the question itself,* posed to Aubertin.)

Therefore an obstinate question situated at *his* origin, towards a first glance, in a gesture which does not lack antecedents: Heraclitus the hydropic marking the rhythm of the first (philosophical) cadence, Empedocles and Etna—but this time with matches: another Ulysses, of the time of Mr. Bloom, whom one meets in the tobacconist, carrying out his provision of combustibles.

This symbol is clear (he is lighting things up); in it one forgets that "reality" does not invent itself. That it suffices to "trap" it with the means at hand: means which are objective, existing, taken as given—the setting fire as "act" not justifying an investment, but the operation which results from an excessive confrontation: burning as radicalization setting ablaze as opening out. In such a way that escaping from subjectivism comes back to risking any gesture (any breath) in a given matter. Aubertin excels at explaining it, and there is no reason not to read it. What he is showing passes beyond the fabrication of what he is applying. One can see in it what one wills: broaching the subject, as sufficient reason, when all is allowed: it suffices to know where.

In the titles first of all—for once explicit: fire-pictures, monochromes dedicated, as he writes, to the dynamism of colour. More exactly a trajectory of flame, from red to black, from burning to burnt. A brief, momentary act from which there is no reconversion. What has been used once has been used for good—in the sense that the work with fire measures its adequacy in igniting as much as possible to consume as surely as possible. Nevertheless the object resists. There are thus unexpected versions: the remains stick to the ash, support it. A new limit is shown, a new route can be hazarded. When Aubertin partially burns telephone books (which are difficult to burn, he acknowledges), "using" the debris (of the phone books) to construct his "avalanches," to constitute "series" where he arranges other fragments, the reference he is making is to the geography of an act begun more than 10 years ago. In the same way the red monochromes and the nail-pictures *imagine* the flame and the work in fire: I mean that they determine the place of an act which symbolically unites all these acts. The symbolic place, for the artist (in this case Aubertin, as will have been guessed . . .), reducing itself to a machinery where chance (including Aubertin) tests the states; the works only correspond to stratificatory moments which never add up to the entirety of the researches. In this sense, no "master works," no over-meaningful points, but a series of connotations, "object-arts," "fabrication-routes," in the very judgement which presents them as works.

One understands that Aubertin asserts himself (with obstinacy) as a realist. He is so to the scandal of all dogmatism. Because "reality" does not stop, it does not copy itself, it does not depict itself. Either it does work or it doesn't work. And it always works differently in the sense that the principal of identity, so dear to a certain rationalism, in art, designates its imposture. It is therefore to a "lesson in reality" that we invite Aubertin with all the ardour which is wasting away there.

—Claude Fournet

AUERBACH, Frank.

British. Born in Berlin, 29 April 1931; emigrated to England in 1939; naturalized, 1947. Educated in Kent primary schools; attended art classes at Hampstead Garden Suburb Institute, London, 1947; Borough Polytechnic, under David Bomberg, London, 1947–48; St. Martin's School of Art, London, 1948–52; Royal College of Art, London, 1952–55 (Silver Medal, 1955). Married Julia Wolstenholme in 1958; one son. Independent painter, London, since 1955. Lecturer, art schools in Sidcup, Kent, and London Boroughs: Ealing, Bromley and Camberwell; and Slade School of Fine Art, London, 1956–58. Recipient: Golden Lion Award, *42nd Biennale,* Venice, 1986. Agent: Marlborough Fine Art, London. Ad-

dress: c/o Marlborough Fine Art, 6 Albemarle Street, London W1X 4BY, England.

Individual Exhibitions:

1956 Beaux Arts Gallery, London
1959 Beaux Arts Gallery, London
1961 Beaux Arts Gallery, London
1962 Beaux Arts Gallery, London
1963 Beaux Arts Gallery, London
1965 Marlborough Fine Art, London
1967 Marlborough Fine Art, London
1969 Marlborough Gerson Gallery, New York
1971 Marlborough Fine Art, London
Villiers Art Gallery, Sydney
Municipal Gallery, Dublin
1972 Toorak Gallery, Melbourne
1973 University of Essex, Colchester
Galleria Bergamini, Milan
1974 Marlborough Fine Art, London
Municipal Gallery of Modern Art, Dublin
1976 Marlborough Fine Art, London (with Francis Bacon)
Marlborough Galerie, Zurich
1978 Hayward Gallery, London (travelled to the Fruit Market Gallery, Edinburgh)
1979 Bernard Jacobson, New York
1982 *Recent Paintings and Drawings,* Marlborough Gallery, New York
1983 Marlborough Fine Art, London
Anne Berthoud Gallery, London
1986 Kunstverein, Hamburg
1987 Marlborough Fine Art, London
Museum Folkwang, Essen, West Germany
Centro de Arte Reina Sofia, Madrid

Selected Group Exhibitions:

1958 *Critics' Choice,* Arthur Tooth and Sons, London
1961 *Pittsburgh International,* Carnegie Institute, Pittsburgh
1967 *Stuyvesant Foundation Exhibition,* London and Zurich
1970 *Painting and Perception,* MacRobert Centre Art Gallery, University of Stirling, Scotland
1972 *Immagine per la Città,* Palazzo dell'Accademia and Palazzo Reale, Genoa
1977 *British Painting 1952–1977,* Royal Academy of Art, London
1979 *This Knot of Life: Paintings and Drawings of British Artists,* Louver Gallery, Venice, California
1981 *A New Spirit in Painting,* Royal Academy of Art, London
1984 *The British Art Show,* City Art Gallery, Birmingham (and Ikon Gallery, Birmingham; travelled to Edinburgh, Sheffield and Southampton)
1987 *A London School,* Louisiana Museum, Humlebaek, Denmark (travelled to Oslo, Venice and Dusseldorf)

Collections:

British Museum, London, Tate Gallery, London; Scottish National Gallery of Modern Art, Edinburgh; National Gallery of Australia, Canberra; National Gallery of Victoria, Melbourne; Metropolitan Museum of Art, New York; Museum of Modern Art, New York; Los Angeles County Museum of Art; Tamayo Museum, Mexico City; Museo de Art Moderna da Bahia, Salvador, Brazil.

Publications:

By AUERBACH: articles—"7 Portraits" in *Ark 23* (London), 1958; "Fragments from a Conversation" *X Quarterly* (London), 1959; "Reply to a Letter from Michael Peppiatt" in *Cambridge Opinion,* January 1964; "Frank Auerbach Talks to Christopher Battye" in *Art and Artists* (London), January 1971; statement in *European Painting in the 70's,* exhibition catalogue, Los Angeles 1975; statement in *Frank Auerbach,* exhibition catalogue, Zurich 1976; "Conversation with Frank Auerbach," with Catherine Lampert, in *Frank Auerbach,* exhibition catalogue, London 1978; foreword to *Late Sickert Paintings,* exhibition catalogue, London 1981.

On AUERBACH: books—*Frank Auerbach,* exhibition catalogue, by William Feaver, Zurich 1976; *Frank Auerbach,* exhibition catalogue, by Leon Kossoff and Catherine Lampert, London 1978; *Frank Auerbach: Recent Paintings and Drawings,* exhibition catalogue, by Stephen Spender, New York 1982; *Frank Auerbach: XLII Venice Biennale,* exhibition catalogue, by Catherine Lampert, London 1986; articles—"A Stick in the Dark" by John Berger in *New Statesman* (London), April 1961; "Titian and Auerbach" by Richard Wollheim in *The Listener* (London), October 1973.

Frank Auerbach came to England from Berlin at the age of 8. In retrospect it is difficult to believe that he had been anywhere else than in the London in which he works and whose portrait he has painted so many times. Even harder to understand is how he somehow absorbed and subsequently recorded in his painting an Englishness that has been a kind of national art accent right through the Bloomsbury period of British culture. The scenes are right. Even the friendly contact with the subjects of the portraits is right. And so is the ungainly sprawl of nudes who seem to have come out of an age when central heating never functioned properly. The penny-in-the-slot gas fire epoch.

None of these remarks relates to the way in which Auerbach paints. They have been made because the mood or moods which invade his paintings must be accepted as "English" in a very strong way. Specially English. This anglicization is almost unique, unless one counts David Bomberg as British.

Auerbach is famous for his thick pigment. No one past maturity should attempt to lift any but the smallest canvases. If this heavy paint has not been of quite the same density in recent years, that is not to suggest that it is still not laid onto the picture like pâté. The result is a dour sort of late expressionism whose temperament is occasionally lightened by swathes of bright colour.

Where Auerbach succeeds is in his extraordinarily effective control of so much viscous material. How successful he may seem to have been with each picture may depend upon the character of the viewer. Some may reject some of the paintings as being too lumbering or opaque, while others will recognize in them the uncanny skill with which he makes the paint not only do his bidding but also turn *itself* into whatever figuration he seeks.

—Sheldon Williams

Frank Auerbach: *Head of Julia,* 1987

AYCOCK, Alice.
American. Born in Harrisburg, Pennsylvania, 20 November 1946. Educated at Douglass College, New Brunswick, New Jersey, 1964– 68, B.A. 1968; Hunter College, New York (studied under Robert Morris), 1968–71, M.A. 1971. Married Mark Segal in 1968. Independent sculptor and installation artist, since 1972, known for large-scale semi-architectural and machine-like projects. Adjunct Lecturer in Art, Hunter College, 1972–73; Visiting Sculptor and Teacher, Rhode Island School of Design, Providence, 1977; taught foundation and advanced sculpture courses at the School of Visual Arts, New York, 1977–78; Visiting Sculptor and Teacher, Princeton University, New Jersey, 1979; Visiting Sculptor and Teacher, San Francisco Art Institute, 1979. Since 1979, teacher at the School of Visual Arts, New York. Artist-in-Residence, Williams College, Williamstown, Massachusetts, 1974. Recipient: National Endowment for the Arts Fellowship, 1975, 1980, 1986; New York State Creative Artists Public Service Grant, 1976. Agent: John Weber Gallery, 142 Greene Street, New York, New York 10012. Address: 62 Greene Street, New York, New York 10012, U.S.A.

Individual Exhibitions:

1972 Nova Scotia College of Art and Design, Halifax
1974 112 Greene Street Gallery, New York
Project inc., Cambridge, Massachusetts
Williams College Museum of Art, Williamstown, Massachusetts
1976 Wheaton College, Norton, Massachusetts
1977 Projects Room, Museum of Modern Art, New York
1978 Portland Center for the Visual Arts, Oregon
John Weber Gallery, New York
University of Rhode Island, Kingston
Salvatore Ala, Milan
Projects for PCA, Philadelphia College of Art
Cranbook Academy of Art, Bloomfield Hills, Michigan
Projects and Proposals, Muhlenberg College, Allentown, Pennsylvania
1979 *Flights of Fancy,* San Francisco Art Institute
The Contemporary Art Center, Cincinnati, Ohio
Machinations, Protetch-McIntosh Gallery, Washington, D.C.
The Large Scale Disintegration of Microelectronic Memories, Art on the Beach, Battery Park Landfill, New York
Collected Ghost Stories From the Workhouse from the series *How to Catch and Manufacture Ghosts,* University of South Florida, Tampa
1980 *The Miraculating Machine in the Garden,* Douglass College, New Brunswick, New Jersey
1981 *The Savage Sparkler,* New York State University at Plattsburgh
Machineworks: Vito Acconci/Alice Aycock/Dennis Oppenheim, Institute of Contemporary Art, Philadelphia
John Weber Gallery, New York
1982 *Drawings,* Locus Solus, Genoa
Lawrence Oliver Gallery, Philadelphia
New Work, John Weber Gallery, Ne v York
1983 Museum of Contemporary Art, Chicago
Protetch McNeil Gallery, New York
Wurttembergischer Kunstverein, Stuttgart (retrospective; travelled to Cologne, Marl, The Hague and Lucerne)
1984 *New Work,* John Weber Gallery, New York
1985 Humanic Corporation Gallery, Graz, Austria
Serpentine Gallery, London
New Drawings, Insam Gallery, Vienna
1986 Sculpture Park, St. Louis, Missouri
John Weber Gallery, New York
Tel Aviv Museum, Israel
1987 Central Park, New York
Galerie Walter Storms, Munich

Selected Group Exhibitions:

1972 *Untitled V,* Museum of Modern Art, New York
1974 *Interventions in Landscape,* Massachusetts Institute of Technology, Cambridge
1977 *Documenta 6,* Kassel, West Germany
1978 *Biennale,* Venice
1979 *Whitney Biennial,* Whitney Museum, New York
1980 *International Sculpture Conference,* Washington, D.C.
1981 *Mythos & Ritual in der Kunst der 70er Jahre,* Kunsthaus, Zurich
1984 *Land Marks,* Bard College, Annandale-on-Hudson, New York
1985 *Modern Machines: Recent Kinetic Sculpture,* Whitney Museum, New York
1987 *Avant-Garde in the Eighties,* Los Angeles County Museum of Art

Alice Aycock: *Three-Fold Manifestation II,* 1987

Collections:

Museum of Modern Art, New York; Guggenheim Museum, New York; Hirshhorn Museum, Washington, D.C.; Whitney Museum, New York.

Publications:

By AYCOCK: books—*Project Entitled "The Beginnings of a Complex . . . ,"* New York 1977; *After Years of Ruminating on the Events That Led Up to This Misfortune, Alice Aycock—Projects and Proposals,* with essays by Stuart Morgan and Edward Fry, Allentown, Pennsylvania 1978; *Alice Aycock Projects 1979–1981,* with an introduction by Edward Fry, Tampa 1981; *Alice Aycock: Retrospective of Projects and ideas 1972–1983,* exhibition catalogue, Stuttgart 1983; articles—"Four 36–38 Exposures" in *Avalanche* (New York), Spring 1972; "5 Semi-Architectural Projects" in *c. 7500,* Valencia, California 1973; "New York City Orientations" in *Triquarterly* (Evanston, Illinois), Winter 1975; "Notes on Project for a Simple Network of Underground Wells and Tunnels" in *Projects in Nature,* Far Hills, New Jersey 1975; "Interviews with Some Modern Mazemakers—Interview with Alice Aycock" by Janet Kardon in *Art International* (Lugano, Switzerland), April/May 1976; "Work 1972–1974" in *Individuals: Post-Movement Art in America,* edited by Alan Sondheim, New York 1977; "Projects for My Body" in *17 Lotus International* (New York), December 1977; "An Interview with Alice Aycock" in *D.A.A. Journal* (Cincinnati, Ohio), no. 1, 1980; "2 Fantasies of a Mythical Waterworks," with James Freed, in *Artists and Architects Collaboration,* edited by Barbaralee Diamonstein, New York 1981; "A Conversation with Alice Aycock," interview with Aimee Price Brown, in *Architectural Digest* (Los Angeles), April 1983; video—*Alice Aycock,* interview with Kate Horsfield, Video Data Bank, School of the Art Institute of Chicago, 1977.

On AYCOCK: books—*6 Years: The Dematerialization of the Art Object* by Lucy R. Lippard, New York 1972; *From the Center* by Lucy R. Lippard, New York 1976; *Unbuilt America,* by Alison Sky and Michelle Stone, New York 1976;

Metaphor: New Projects by Contemporary Sculptors, by Howard N. Fox, Washington, D.C. 1982; *Avant-Garde in the Eighties,* exhibition catalogue, with introduction by Howard Fox, Los Angeles 1987; articles—"Aligned with the Nazca" by Robert Morris in *Artforum* (New York), October 1975; "Projects in Nature" by Jonathan Crary in *Arts Magazine* (New York), December 1975; "Labyrinths, Philadelphia College of Art" by April Kingsley in *Artforum* (New York), February 1976; "The Modern Maze" by Ronald Onorato in *Art International* (Lugano, Switzerland), April/May 1976; " 'Sculpture Sited' at the Nassau County Museum" by Lucy Lippard in *Arts In America* (New York), March/April 1977; "American Women Architects" by John Lobell in *Artforum* (New York), Summer 1977; "Mystery Under Construction" by Margaret Sheffield in *Artforum* (New York), September 1977; "6 Women at Work in the Landscape" by April Kingsley in *Arts Magazine* (New York), April 1978; "Alice Aycock: A Certain Image of Something I Like Very Much" by Stuart Morgan in *Arts Magazine* (New York), March 1978; "The Present Tense of Space" by Robert Morris in *Art in America* (New York, January/February 1978; "Women of the Fourth Wave; Humboldt's Daughters" by Eleanor Munro in *Originals: American Women Artists,* New York 1979; "Discovery of the Sources: Model of History" by Jean-Luc Daval in *Art Actuel: Skira Annual '79,* Geneva 1979; "Complexes: Sculpture in Nature" by Lucy Lippard in *Art in America* (New York), January/February 1979; "Ancient Places and Personal Spaces: Homage to Alice Aycock" by Elter, McCormick, McKeon and Reynolds, "Alice Aycock's Explanation, An, of Spring and the Weight of Air" by Jonathan Kamholtz, and "The Work of Alice Aycock: A Pictorial Section" in *D.A.A. Journal* (Cincinnati, Ohio), no. 1, 1980; "Aycock's Dream Houses" by Donald Kuspit in *Art in America* (New York), September 1980; "Beyond Revivalism and the Bauhaus: A New Partnership in the Arts" by Jonathan Barnett in *Artists and Architects Collaboration,* New York 1981; "Alice in Duchamp-Land" by Kay Larson in *New York,* 25 May 1981; "The Poetic Machines of Alice Aycock" by Edward Fry in *Portfolio* (Boulder, Colorado), November–December 1981; "Alice Aycock" by Antje von Graevenitz in *Museumjournaal* (Amsterdam), no. 27, 1982.

AY-O.

Japanese. Born Takao Iijima in Ibaraki Prefecture, Japan, 19 May 1931. Educated at Kyoiku University, Tokyo, B.A. 1954. Married Ikuko Yoshida in 1955; child: Hanako. Independent artist: began as engraver and lithographer, then expanded work to include painting, sculpture, environments, and happenings; joined "Demokrato" avant-garde artists group, 1954, lived in New York, 1958–66; joined "Flux" avant-garde artists group, 1962; travelled in Europe and India before returning to Japan, 1966; has concentrated on producing rainbow-hued silk-screens, since mid-1960's; again lived in New York, 1968–71; returned to Japan, 1971; travelled in Britain, Europe, and Nepal, 1973. Visiting Professor of Painting, University of Kentucky, Lexington, 1968–69. Recipient: Special Prize, *Vancouver International Prints Biennial,* 1967; Grand Prize, 1969, and Minister of Foreign Affairs Award, 1971, *Japan Art Festival;* Award, *Mainichi Modern Art Exhibition,* National Museum of Modern Art, Kyoto; Brazil Bank Prize, *Bienal,* Sao Paulo, 1969; Prize, *Tokyo International Print Biennial,* National Museum of Modern Art, Tokyo, 1970; Bridgestone Museum Prize, *Mainichi modern Art Exhibition,* Japan, 1971; Prize, *Exposition International de Dessins Originaux,* Rijeka, Yugoslavia, 1973; Grand Prize, Listowele Print Biennial, 1980; Zagreb Contemporary Art Gallery Prize, Original Drawings Exhibition, Rijeka, Yugoslavia, 1982; Warsaw National Museum Prize, International Drawing Triennale, Wroclaw, 1982. Agent: Suzuki Graphics Inc., 797 Madison Avenue, New York, New York 10021, U.S.A. Address: 2–6–38 Matsuyama, Kiyose-shi, Tokyo 100–31, Japan.

Individual Exhibitions:

1955 Takemiya Gallery, Tokyo
1956 Forme Gallery, Tokyo
1962 Gordon's Fifth Avenue Gallery, New York
1963 Gordon's Fifth Avenue Gallery, New York
1964 Smolin Gallery, New York
1965 Smolin Gallery, New York
1966 Gordon's Fifth Avenue Gallery, New York
Minami Gallery, Tokyo
1967 Gallery 669, Los Angeles
1969 Melida Gallery, Louisville, Kentucky
Hank Baum Gallery, San Francisco
1971 Minami Gallery, Tokyo
1972 Nantenshi Gallery, Tokyo
Suzuki Graphics Gallery, New York
Hank Baum Gallery, San Francisco
1973 Suzuki Graphics Gallery, New York
Museum of Modern Art, New York
1974 Suzuki Graphics Gallery, New York
1975 Suzuki Graphics Gallery, New York
1976 Suzuki Graphics Gallery, New York
Nantenshi Gallery, Tokyo
Hank Baum Gallery, San Francisco
Bonino Gallery, New York
1977 Minami Gallery, Tokyo
1978 Hank Baum Gallery, San Francisco
1979 Ikeda Museum of Contemporary Art, Japan
1980 Graphics Gallery, San Francisco
Wako Hall, Tokyo
Hank Baum Gallery, San Francisco
Suzuki Graphics Gallery, New York
1982 Fuji Television Gallery, New York
!985 Fuji Television Gallery, Tokyo

Selected Group Exhibitions:

1964 *Rainbow Happening: Flux-Orchestra Concert,* Carnegie Recital Hall, New York
Rainbow-Happening: "The Tart" by Dick Higgins, Sunny-Side Garden, New York
1965 *Rainbow Happening: Flux Concert,* Carnegie Recital Hall, New York
1966 *Rainbow Tactile Room,* at the *Biennale,* Venice
1967 *Annual Avant-Garde Festival,* New York (and 1968, 1972, 1977, 1980)
1969 *Tactile Rainbow Room,* at *Expo 70,* Tokyo (travelled to the Cincinnati Art Museum, Ohio, and the University of Kentucky, Lexington)
Modern Japanese Art, National Museum of Art, Kyoto
1971 *Bienal,* Sao Paulo
1973 *Japanese Artists in the Americas,* National Museum of Modern Art, Kyoto
1987 *FIAC '87,* Grand Palais, Paris

Collections:

National Museum of Modern Art, Tokyo; National Museum of Modern Art, Kyoto; Museum of Modern Art, New York; Metropolitan Art Museum, Tokyo; National Museum, Warsaw; Cincinnati Art Museum, Ohio; Stedelijk Museum, Amsterdam; British Museum, London.

Publications:

By AY-O: book—*Rainbow Prints: Catalogue Raisonne 1954–1979,* compiled by Sadajiro Kubo, Tokyo 1979.

On AY-O: books—*FLUXshoe,* exhibition catalogue, edited by David Mayor and Felipe Ehrenberg, Cullompton, England 1972; *Japanese Artists in the Americas,* exhibition catalogue, by T. Ogura, Kyoto 1973; *Ay-O: Arc-en-ciel,* exhibition catalogue, with introduction by Akira Asahi, Paris 1987; article—"Tokyo Letter' by J. P. Love in *Art International* (Lugano, Switzerland), March 1971.

Ay-O has nearly magical power by which he metamorphoses objects which are a part of everyday life into metaphysical, tactile objects which demand to be sensually experienced. His 1961 "Ay-O's Box," exemplifies this. It consists of a series of cubical wooden boxes snugly fitting into an attaché chase; each box has a hole through which an unexpected sensory experience is obtained by inserting a forefinger into the holes. The rainbow series on which he has been working since 1964 is nothing less than the creation of versicolored environments, of walls, furniture, utensils and other ordinary articles used in daily life. One work in this series, "Rainbow Tactile Room," was exhibited at the 1966 Venice *Biennale.*

Born Takao Iijima in Ibaraki Prefecture in 1931, the artist graduated from the art department of Tokyo's University of Arts and Science in 1954. He started as an engraver and lithographer and gradually expanded his scope of activity to include painting, sculpture, environments and happenings. In 1966 he returned to Japan after nine years overseas, and had a show at Minami Gallery, Tokyo. Since 1962 he has often been among the Japanese artists exhibiting in the Tokyo *International Biennale Exhibition of Prints.* Ay-O was awarded the JAFA Prize in the 1969 Japan Art Festival. The same year, he won the Kyoto National Museum of Modern Art Prize at the Ninth Modern Japanese Art Exhibition.

Ay-O was a member of the Fluxus movement in New York in the early 1960s, making a lot of performance events with George Maciunas and other Fluxus artists. His recent manifestation was on the Eiffel Tower in Paris. A truly astonishing effect was created in 1987 by a 300-meter long banner in rainbow colour flowing down to the ground from the tower's observation platform.

—Yoshiaki Tono

B

BACON, Francis.

British. Born, of English parents, in Dublin, Ireland, 28 October 1909. Mainly self-taught in art, from 1927. Served in Civil Defence Corps, London 1942–45. Worked in an office, London 1925; visited Berlin and Paris, 1926–27; worked as an interior decorator, London 1928–31. Independent painter, London 1929–46, Monte Carlo, 1946–50 and again in London since 1950; study-travels in South Africa 1950, in Italy 1954, with Peter Lacey in Tangier, 1956–59; visited New York and Rome, 1968; death of friend and model George Dyer, in Paris, 1971. Recipient: Painting Prize, *Carnegie International,* Pittsburgh, 1966; Rubenspreis, Siegen, West Germany 1967. Agent: Marlborough Fine Art, London. Address: c/o Marlborough Fine Art, 6 Albemarle Street, London W1X 4DY, England.

Individual Exhibitions:

1930 Bacon Studio, London (with Roy Le Maistre)
1934 Transition Gallery, London
1949 Hanover Gallery, London
1950 Hanover Gallery, London
1951 Hanover Gallery, London
1952 Hanover Gallery, London
1953 Durlacher Gallery, New York
Beaux-Arts Gallery, London
1954 Hanover Gallery, London
1955 Institute of Contemporary Arts, London
Hanover Gallery, London (with William Scott and Graham Sutherland)
1957 Galerie Rive Droite, Paris
Hanover Gallery, London
1958 Galleria Galatea, Turin, Italy (travelled to the Galleria dell'Ariete, Milan and the Galleria dell'Obelisco, Rome)
Victoria Art Gallery, Bath, Avon (with Matthew Smith and Victor Pasmore; toured Britain)
1959 Richard Feigen Gallery, Chicago
British section, at the *5th Bienal,* Sao Paulo
Hanover Gallery, London
1960 Marlborough Fine Art, London
University of California at Los Angeles (with Hyman Bloom)
1961 University of Nottingham
1962 Galleria Galatea, Milan
Tate Gallery, London (travelled to Mannheim, Turin and Zurich)
1963 Galleria Il Centro, Naples (with Graham Sutherland)
Galleria La Loggia, Bologna (with Graham Sutherland)
Granville Gallery, New York
Marlborough Fine Art, London
Guggenheim Museum, New York (travelled to Art Institute of Chicago, and the Houston Contemporary Arts Association)
1965 Kunsthalle, Hamburg (travelled to the Moderna Museet, Stockholm, and the Museum of Modern Art, Dublin)
Marlborough Fine Art, London
1966 Galleria Toninelli, Milan
Galerie Maeght, Paris (travelled to Marlborough Fine Art, London)
1967 Oberes Schloss, Siegen, West Germany
1968 Marlborough-Gerson Gallery, New York
1970 Galleria Galatea, Turin
1971 Grand Palais, Paris (travelled to the Kunsthalle, Dusseldorf)
1972 Galleria del Milione, Milan
1975 Metropolitan Museum of Art, New York
Marlborough Galerie, Zurich
1976 Musée Cantini, Marseilles
1977 Galerie Claude Bernard, Paris
Museo de Arte Moderna, Mexico City (travelled to the Museo de Arte Contemporaneo, Caracas)
1978 Fundación Juan March, Madrid (travelled to the Fundación Joan Miró, Barcelona)
1980 Marlborough Gallery, New York
Städtische Kunsthalle, Mannheim
1983 National Museum of Modern Art, Tokyo (travelled to Kyoto and Nagoya)
Marlborough Fine Art, London
1984 Galerie Maeght/Lelong, Paris
Marlborough Gallery, New York
1985 Marlborough Fine Art, London
Tate Gallery, London (travelled to Stuttgart and West Berlin)
1987 Marlborough Gallery, New York
Galerie Beyeler, Basel
Galerie Lelong, Paris

Selected Group Exhibitions:

1937 *Young British Painters,* Agnew Gallery, London
1945 *Recent Paintings: Bacon/Hodgkins/Moore/Smith/Sutherland,* Lefevre Gallery, London
1973 *Cuatro Maestros Contemporaneos: Giacometti, Dubuffet, De Kooning, Bacon,* Museo de Bellas Artes, Caracas (travelled to Sao Paulo and Rio de Janeiro)
1977 *Englische Kunst der Gegenwart,* Kunstlerhaus, Bregenz, Austria
1981 *A New Spirit in Painting,* Royal Academy of Art, London
1983 *Modern Art in the West,* Metropolitan Museum, Tokyo
1985 *Painterly Visions 1940–85,* Guggenheim Museum, New York
1987 *A School of London,* Kunstnernes Hus, Oslo (travelled to Copenhagen, Venice and Dusseldorf)

Collections:

Tate Gallery, London; Ulster Museum, Belfast; Centre Georges Pompidou, Paris; Nationalgalerie, West Berlin, Musée des Beaux-Arts, Brussels; Museum of Modern Art, New York; Guggenheim Museum, New York; Art Institute of Chicago; National Gallery of Canada, Ottawa, National Gallery of Australia, Canberra.

Publications:

On BACON: books—*Art Now* by Herbert Read, London 1933; *Francis Bacon,* exhibition catalogue, with text by M. Clarac Serou, London 1955; *Francis Bacon,* exhibition catalogue, with text by Helen Lessore, Nottingham 1961; *Francis Bacon,* exhibition catalogue, with text by John Rothenstein, London 1962; *Francis Bacon,* exhibition catalogue, with texts by Thomas Messer and Lawrence Alloway, New York 1963; *The Masters: Francis Bacon* by John Rothenstein, London and Milan 1963, Paris 1967; *Francis Bacon* (catalogue raisonne), by John Rothenstein and Ronald Alley, London 1964; *Francis Bacon* by John Russell, London, Paris and Berlin 1971; *Francis Bacon,* exhibition catalogue, with text by Michel Leiris, Paris 1971; *The Age of the Avant-Garde: An Art Chronicle of 1956–1972* by Hilton Kramer, New York and London 1974; *Interviews with Francis Bacon* by David Sylvester, London and New York 1975; *Francis Bacon* by Lorenza Trucchi, Milan and New York 1975, London 1976, rev. ed. Milan 1984; *Francis Bacon: Logique de la Sensation* by Gilles Deleuze, Paris 1981, 1984; *Francis Bacon: Full Face and in Profile* by Michel Leiris, London, New York, Paris and Munich 1983; *Francis Bacon* by Dawn Ades and Andrew Forge, London and Berlin 1985; *Francis Bacon: Vier Studien zu einem Portrait* by Wieland Schmied, Berlin 1985; *Francis Bacon: Kreuzigung* by Jorg Zimmermann, Frankfurt 1986; *Francis Bacon* by Hugh Davies and Sally Yard, New York 1986.

The two biggest names Britain has bestowed upon the contemporary art world are Moore and Bacon. Moore has moved steadily and unhesitatingly forward in world esteem, but Francis Bacon, ever since Herbert Read reproduced his "Crucifixion" (1933) in the first issue of *Art Now,* has shot up and, in recent years, with meteoric velocity.

Bacon, from being a one-time designer of "modern furniture" (actually reviewed in the *Studio* magazine, 1930), proved himself in 1966 one of the only British artists able in those days to beat Parisian chauvinism. Against all forecasts by experienced pundits his exhibition at the Galerie Maeght was a sell-out. But by then he had already made his reputation in Italy, the U.S., Brazil, Germany, Sweden, Switzerland and Ireland. The following year brought him the coveted Rubens International Prize.

Contemporary Bacon began 25 years ago. It was at that point that his style became identifiably his own. Since then he has passed through a number of specific phases and enthusiasms. Once he had overcome his fascination for the umbrella (although it certainly reoccurred), he turned to other categories like the series of near-monochrome business men (in expensive if shadowy suits), his portraits of the popes at peace or screaming, the oil collection of pictures he made based upon studies by the photographic pioneer Muybridge, the Van Gogh self-portraits, animals and sphynxes—especially the lonely dog caught in some kind of proto-Chirico piazza, and so on to the nudes like butchers' cadavers splayed or jumbled up after they have been defrozen and have been taken off the hook. Hypodermics, narcotics, addicts, all the sub-life of the seedy 60's.

How is Bacon now, compared with then?

During all this time when he has been establishing a world reputation, his style has become steady and consistent, but he has also acquired a kind of personal painterly finesse which is particularly evident in the portraits (especially the portrait studies). The brushstrokes in these display a kind of skilful instantaneous ease remote from the tortured and heavy impasto that clad many of his earlier paintings. It is as if the food has been cooked with greater expertise and experience, but has the strange exoticism of the meal lived up to the mysterious quality of those in the past? The

Francis Bacon: *Study for Self-Portrait Triptych*, 1986

world seems to think so. There will be many more Bacon Crucifixions (although nowadays they seem to spread into enormous triptychs), but will they ever revive the visual shriek of the one that Herbert Read picked to illustrate in *Art Now* more than 40 years ago?

—Sheldon Williams

BAER, Jo.

American. Born Josephine Gail Kleinberg in Seattle, Washington, 7 August 1929. Studied biology and art at the University of Washington, Seattle, 1946–49. Married television writer Richard Baer in 1953; son: Joshua; married John Wesley in 1960. Painter: worked in kibbutz in Israel, then moved to New York, 1950; worked with Graduate Faculty in Physiological Psychology, New School for Social Research, New York, 1952; moved to Los Angeles, 1953; associated peripherally with the Ferus Gallery run by Walter Hopps and Ed Kienholz, 1957; returned to New York, 1960, changing painting style from Abstract-Expressionist to a reductive, hard-edge style; began first "mature" series of work, 1962. Instructor, School of Visual Arts, New York 1969–70. Recipient: National Endowment for the Arts Grant, 1969. Agent: John Weber Gallery, 420 West Broadway, New York, New York 10012. Address: Art Galaxy, 262 Mott Street, New York, New York 10012, U.S.A.

Individual Exhibitions:

1966 Fischbach Gallery, New York
1967 *Jo Baer/David Judd/Peter Young,* Noah Goldowsky Gallery, New York
1968 *Jo Baer and Al Leslie,* Noah Goldowsky Gallery, New York
1969 Galerie Rolf Ricke, Cologne
1970 Galerie Rolf Ricke, Cologne
Gordon Locksley-Shea Gallery, Minneapolis
Noah Goldowsky Gallery, New York
1971 *Paintings from '62–'63,* School of Visual Arts, New York
1972 Lo Guidice Gallery, New York
1973 Galerie Rolf Ricke, Cologne
Nicholas Wilder Gallery, Los Angeles
1974 Galleria Toselli, Milan
Paintings 1962–1972, Daniel Weinberg Gallery, San Francisco
1975 Whitney Museum, New York

Selected Group Exhibitions:

1964 *11 Artists,* Kaymar Gallery, New York
1966 *Systematic Painting,* Guggenheim Museum, New York
1967 *Annual Exhibition of Contemporary American Painting,* Whitney Museum, New York (and 1969)
1968 *Documenta 4,* Kassel, West Germany
1969 *Eine Tendenz Zeitgenössischer Malerei,* Kölnischer Kunstverein, Cologne
1971 *Drawings,* Art Institute of Chicago
1973 *Options and Alternatives,* Yale University of Art Gallery, New Haven, Connecticut
1974 *5 Artists: A Logic of Vision,* Museum of Contemporary Art, Chicago
1975 *14 Artists,* Baltimore Museum of Art
Hand Colored Prints, travelling exhibition organized by Brooke Alexander, Inc., New York

Collections:

Museum of Modern Art, New York; Guggenheim Museum, New York; Albright-Knox Art Museum, Buffalo, New York; University of North Carolina at Greensboro; University of Texas at Austin; Kölnischer Kunstverein, Cologne; Suermondt Museum, Aachen, West Germany; Australian National Gallery, Canberra.

Publications:

By BAER: book—*Cardinations,* portfolio of 9 screenprints, New York 1974; articles—"Letters" in *Artforum* (New York), September 1967; "Edward Kienholz: A Sentimental Journeyman" in *Art International* (Lugano, Switzerland), April 1968; "Letters" in *Artforum* (New York), April 1969; "The Artist and Politics: A Symposium" in *Artforum* (New York), September 1970; "Mach Bands: Art and Vision: and "Xerography and Mach Bands: Instrumental Model" in *Aspen Magazine* (Colorado), Fall/Winter 1970; "Art and Politics" and "On Painting" in *Flash Art* (Milan), November 1972.

On BAER: books—*Systematic Painting,* exhibition catalogue, with text by Lawrence Alloway, and statement by Baer, New York 1966; *Minimal Art: A Critical Anthology,* edited by Gregory Battcock, New York 1968; *American Art of the 20th Century* by Sam Hunter, New York 1972; *5 Artists: A Logic of Vision,* exhibition catalogue, with an introduction by Stephen Prokopoff, Chicago 1974; *American Art since 1900* by Barbara Rose, revised edition, New York 1975; *Jo Baer,* exhibition catalogue, with text by Barbara Haskell, New York 1975; *Hand Colored Prints,* exhibition catalogue, with an introduction by Carter Ratcliff, New York 1975; articles—"Jo Baer" by Will Insley in *Art International* (Lugano, Switzerland), 20 February 1969; "Diversity in Unity: Recent Geometricizing Styles in America" by Lucy Lippard in *Abstract Art since 1945,* New York 1971; "Jo Baer: Playing on the Senses" by Peter Schjeldahl in the *New York Times,* 14 May 1972; "Once More with Feeling" by Carter Ratcliff in *Artnews* (New York), Summer 1972; "Baer's Painterly Elegance" by Elena Karina Canavier in *Artweek* (Oakland, California), 28 April, 1973; "Jo Baer: Peintre Traditionel et 'Radical' " by Serge Guilbaut and Michael Sgan-Cohen in *Art Press* (Paris), May 1974.

Jo Baer began her career, in the 1950's, as an abstract expressionist. But with the advent of hard-edge abstraction in the 1960's she found a style more to her liking. The brand of hard-edge abstraction which she adopted came to be called "minimal," as practised by Judd and Le Witt. The principle was reductionist—less is more. It is no coincidence that at the time she came under the influence of Samuel Beckett, whose work, always reductive, was then reaching the *ne plus ultra* of reductionism, as in *Come and Go,* where three female characters literally come and go, and hardly a word is spoken. (It was my pleasure to open Jo Baer's exhibition on the occasion of the inauguration of the Douglas Hyde Gallery, Trinity College, Dublin, which, appropriately, contains a Beckett room.)

It might be said that Baer did for painting what Beckett did for drama, that is, pare everything down to an absolute minimum, so exiguous that with one more stroke there would be nothing left.

Even in her abstract expressionist days she had been interested in contrasts of light and darkness. This contrast persists in her minimal paintings. There is black round the edges and white or grey in the centre. Some are completely surrounded by black, like mortuary cards; others, of a somewhat later vintage, on the vertical sides only (given the equestrian name "Doublebar"). They are square or rectangular; sometimes vertical (V), sometimes horizontal (H). In the earlier works there is often a contrasting lightly coloured motif, like art deco decoration, which makes them even more like mortuary cards. They are usually arranged in groups of two (diptychs) or three (triptychs). And, most important of all, there is always a thin band of colour in or beside the black border.

It is this band of colour—blue, orange, green, lavender, red and aluminum being the favourite colours—which gives the richness and vibrancy to her work: the more added to the less. Where the thin line of colour is in the black, a reaction takes place which enhances the colour; where the colour is on the boundary of the black and white, the reaction is ambiguous, since the black tends to enhance and the white to bleach the band of light colour; but the result is always an effect of vibrancy. Further complexities are introduced by juxtaposing canvases, whether vertical or horizontal, into groups of diptychs or triptychs. In this way the blacks, whites and coloureds not only react with each other internally within a canvas, but react with their neighbours in the juxtaposed canvases.

It should, perhaps, be mentioned that Baer studied physiological and Gestalt psychology, and, in particular, the work of the 19th century physicist Ernst Mach (famous for his work on the relationship of a projectile to the speed of sound). She refers to the bands of colour in relationship to the black and white as "Mach Bands"; they, as it were, break the colour barrier by a sudden acceleration of light intensity.

While other minimalists, such as Judd and Le Witt, abandoned the flat surface in favour of the third dimension, on the grounds that two dimensional painting is allusionistic, Baer, who disagreed, quite rightly persisted in painting flat surfaces. However, in the late 1960's, she succumbed. At first she merely distanced the canvas from the wall by deepening the stretcher. But she soon evolved what she called "Wraparounds" in which the bands continue round the side of the stretcher. At the same time the severity of the bands of black was eased by making them taper and by breaking them up or making them intersect. By the early 1970's the black was replaced by bands of colour and the rectilinear shapes by curved ones. They even took on an Art Deco appearance. The white central area had been invaded. She also gave them invented Latin names such as "Pandurata," "Eutopicus," "Orbitaster" and "Arcuata" (extended, twisted, curved) derived from the names of orchids, a flower particularly dear to Jo Baer.

By the end of the 1970's the curve had become dominant and Jo Baer's painting underwent a radical change. From being starkly and geometrically abstract, it became figurative, sensual and, at times, erotic; from being ordered and closely knit, it became fragmented: drawings of anatomical parts, predominantly, human and animal buttocks, studies of seated nudes, etc. These latest "drawings," mostly in black on white (still the contrast), look like entries in a sketchbook or the fragmented drawings on caves. The drawings are sensitive in line; colour, when it is used, is sensuous. In spite of the fragmented appearance of these works, they are highly, if covertly, ordered.

It is hard, as yet, to assess these works in relation to the earlier ones, but one thing is certain: Jo Baer is among the most perspective of contemporary artists, one who makes demands on the perceptive powers of those who look at her work. Even her description of her work—"percepts become precepts, precepts become percepts"—might elude the casual or superficial reader.

—D. C. Barrett

BAERTLING, Olle.

Swedish. Born in Halmstead, 6 December 1911. Educated at State Secondary Grammar School, Halmstead, 1922–28; studied business administration at the School of Economics and Trade, Stockholm, 1928–29; also studied English, French and German, 1929–40; studied painting, under André Lhote and Fernand Léger, Paris, 1948. Married Lisa Maria von Roxendorff in 1939. Worked as branch manager and publicity manager, Skandinaviska Enskilda Banken, Stockholm, 1929–47, and part time, 1949–55; independent artist, in Paris and Stockholm, 1949–81:associated with painter Auguste Herbin, Paris from 1950; Member, Réalités Nouvelles artists group, Paris, 1950–56; Co-Founder, Groupe Espace, Paris, 1952–59. Recipient: Painting Prize, *Bienal,* Sao Paulo, 1963; National Swedish Art Award, 1964. *Died* (in Stockholm) *2 May 1981.*

Olle Baertling: *Yoyan*, 1970

Individual Exhibitions:

1949 Galerie Samlaren, Stockholm
1951 Galerie Brinken, Stockholm (with Auguste Herbin)
1952 Galerie Birch, Copenhagen
1953 Konsthall, Uppsala, Sweden
1954 Galerie Denise René, Paris (with Breer and Bitran)
Galerie Samlaren, Stockholm (open-air exhibition)
1955 Galerie Samlaren, Stockholm
Skanska Konstmuseum, University of Lund, Sweden (with Mortensen)
1956 Liljevalchs Konsthall, Stockholm (with Jacobsen and Mortensen)
Royal Academy of Fine Art, Copenhagen (with Jacobsen and Mortensen)
1957 Galerie Samlaren, Stockholm (3 exhibitions)
1958 *Dramaturge des Formes,* Galerie Denise René, Paris
Musée des Beaux-Arts, Liège, Belgium (with Matisse and Kylberg)
1960 Galerie Samlaren, Stockholm
Konstnarshuset, Stockholm (retrospective)
1961 Galerie Samlaren, Stockholm (with Matisse and Léger)
1962 Galerie Denise René, Paris
Galerie Observatorium, Stockholm
1963 Galerie Hybler, Copenhagen
Swedish Pavilion, at the *Bienal,* Sao Paulo
1964 Galerie Samlaren, Stockholm
Columbia University, New York (retrospective; toured the United States and Sweden, 1964–66)
1966 Galerie Samlaren, Stockholm
1967 Rose Fried Gallery, New York (retrospective)
S.D. Gallery, New York
Galerie Lowendahl, Uppsala, Sweden
1968 Galerie Aronowitsch, Stockholm (retrospective)
Galerie Bleue, Stockholm
Musée des Arts Décoratifs/Palais du Louvre, Paris
1969 Galerie Plus-Kern, Ghent
Royal Academy of Fine Arts, Stockholm (retrospective)
New York University (retrospective)
Esther Robles Gallery, Los Angeles (retrospective)
1970 Rose Fried Gallery, New York (retrospective)
Axiom Gallery, London (retrospective)
1971 Galerie Larsson, Gavle, Sweden, (retrospective)
1972 Galerie Denise René, Paris (retrospective)
Galerie 66–H. G. Krupp, Hofheim/Taunus, West Germany
Obrebro Museum, Sweden (retrospective)
Norrkoping Museum, Sweden (retrospective)
1973 Vasteras Museum, Sweden (retrospective)
Galerie Samlaren, Stockholm
University of Stockholm (Baertling Collection)
Le Disque Rouge, Brussels
Galleria Lorenzelli, Milan (retrospective)
1974 Galleria della Trinita, Rome
Galerie Samlaren, Stockholm
Galerie Denise René, Paris (retrospective)
Galerie Ferm, Malmo, Sweden
1975 Galerie Denise René, Paris
Galleriet, Lund, Sweden
Baertling: Creator of Open Form, Junior Galerie, Copenhagen (travelled to the Junior Galerie, Zurich)
1976 Contemporary Royale, Vancouver
Galerie Denise René, Paris
Galerie Denise René Rive Gauche, Paris
Galerie Royal, Calgary, Alberta
Galerie Nordenhake, Malmo, Sweden
Konstsalongen Samlaren, Stockholm
Galerie Fabian Carlsson, Gothenburg, Sweden
1977 Nordenhaken Rykken Galleri, Oslo
Gemalde, Skulpturen 1950–1975, Kunsthalle, Dusseldorf
Galerie Karsten Greve, Cologne (retrospective)
1978 Galerie Karin Fesel, Wiesbaden, West Germany (retrospective)
Galerie von Bartha, Basle (retrospective)
Galleri Christel, Helsinki
1979 Galerie von Bartha, at the *Internationale Kunstmesse,* Basel (retrospective)
1981 *Baertling 1911–1981: Creator of Open Form,* Konsthall, Malmo, Sweden (travelled to Moderna Museet, Stockholm)
Galerie Nordenhake, Malmo, Sweden
Galerie Bel'Art, Stockholm
1982 Henie-Onstad Kunstsenter, Hovikodden, Norway
Galerie Konstruktiv Tendens, Stockholm
Moderna Museet, Stockholm

Selected Group Exhibitions:

1950 *Salon des Réalités Nouvelles,* Musée d'Art Moderne Paris
1960 *Construction and Geometry in Painting,* Galerie Chalette, New York (toured the United States)
1967 *Art et Mouvement,* Musée d'Art Contemporain, Montreal
1972 *Swedish Art 1972,* Museum of Modern Art, Tokyo (travelled to the Museum of Modern Art, Kyoto)
1974 *Konstruktivt 1974,* Moderna Museet, Stockholm (travelled to the Amos Andersonin Taidemuseo, Helsinki)
1976 *Creative Sweden,* Northwestern National Bank of Minnesota, Minneapolis
1978 *Museo Nacional de la Resistencia Salvador Allende,* Moderna Museet, Stockholm
1979 *Constructivism and the Geometric Tradition,* Albright-Knox Art Gallery, Buffalo, New York (toured the United States)
1980 *Dansk-Svensk Grafik,* Jonkopings Lans Museum, Sweden
1981 *Hommage à Baertling,* Liljevalchs Konsthall, Stockholm

Collections:

National Museum, Stockholm; Konsthall, Malmo, Sweden; Tate Gallery, London; Centre Georges Pompidou, Paris; Galleria Nazionale d:Arte Moderna, Rome; Nationalgalerie, West Berlin; Stedelijk Museum, Amsterdam; Museum of Modern Art, Tokyo; Museum of Modern Art, New York; Hirshhorn Museum, Washington, D.C.

Publications:

By BAERTLING: books—*Document-Aspect-61,* exhibition catalogue, with others, Stockholm 1961; *Nytt Svenskt Konstnarsgalleri,* exhibition catalogue, with others, Malmo, Sweden 1966; *Baertling: precurseur de la Forme Ouverte,* exhibit catalogue, with others, Paris 1968; *The Angles of Baertling,* exhibition catalogue, New York 1969; *Baertling: precurseur de la forme ouverte,* with others, Stockholm, Paris and New York 1971, 1974; *Olle Baertling,* exhibition catalogue, with others, Milan 1973; *Open Form,* Stockholm 1978; articles—"Mortensen" in *Aujourd'hui* (Paris), March 1955; "Konkret Realism", in *Konstperspektiv* (Gothenburg, Sweden), February 1956; "Den aktuella konstens problematik" in *Konstperspektiv* (Gothenburg, Sweden), January 1958; "Angreppet ar ovasentglit" in *Fonstret* (Stockholm), July 1959; "Estetisk rum—immateriell rymd" in *Konstperspektiv* (Gothenburg, Sweden), February 1960; "Om den

konstruktiva konsten" in *Svenska Dagbladet* (Stockholm), 4 March 1963; "Konstruktive konst—framtids miljo" in *Arkitektur* (Stockholm), June 1965; "Aben Form—uendligt rum" in *Kunst* (Odense), November 1969.

On BAERTLING: books—*Baertling: Dramaturge des Formes*, exhibition catalogue, with text by Oscar Reutersvard, Paris 1958; *Abstract Painting: 50 Years of Accomplishment from Kandinsky to the Present* by Michel Seuphor, New York 1961; *History of Modern Art: Painting, Sculpture, Architecture* by H. H. Arnason, New York 1969; *Aesthetics: An Introduction* by Ruth Saw, New York 1971; *Alla Trinita—Baertling*, exhibition catalogue, with text by Lorenza Trucchi, Rome 1974; *Another Light: Swedish Art since 1945* by Olle Granath, Stockholm 1975; *Baertling: Creator of Open Form*, exhibition catalogue, with text by Teddy Brunius, Copenhagen 1975; *Konstruktive Konsepte: Eine Geschichte der Konstruktivier Kunst von Kubismus bis Heute* by Willy Rotzler, Zurich 1977; *Olle Baertling: Gemalde, Skulpturen 1950–1975*, exhibition catalogue, with text by Karl-Heinz Heing, Teddy Brunius and Oscar Reutersvard, Dusseldorf 1977; *Olle Baertling*, exhibition catalogue, with text by Friedrich W. Heckmanns, Wiesbaden, West Germany 1978; *Baertling 1911–1981: Creator of Open Form*, exhibition catalogue, with texts by Teddy Brunius, Oscar Reutersvard and Gunnar Berefelt, Malmo and Stockholm 1981.

In 1953, Olle Baertling introduced into a vertical-horizontal world (of landscape, of gravity, of architects, of the written or printed page, of the reference co-ordinates of human measurement of space, of Mondrian) images of great clarity, positiveness, and vitality, made up entirely of diagonal lines which marked out acutely tapered triangles. For three decades Baertling continued to reveal this diagonal world, a little at a time, not to ingratiate or to win confidence or friends, but to create and populate a world of his own, not comfortable in its topography, not ingratiating in the colors of its landscape, but hard and real and challenging to the explorer.

Baertling's lines made space—in two senses: the *space between* rigid dividers (whether in his sculpture of his painting) and the *space generated* behind and in front of the picture plane by illusion, through the perspective effect of converging lines and the advance-recession stimulus of flat colors in combination. Using both these kinds of space as a plastic material, modelled and modified by a knowing mind and eye and a powerful and decisive hand, he developed what he called "open form." This was a modest label, for the forms Baertling opened were not the blooming of a flower but an explosion which burst through the frame of the painting.

Between the lines there are his colors. In maps only enough are used to give each country a chromatic autonomy. Three will do. Baertling's economical linear assertions succeed with black and a single color. He often used only two colors, rarely three and almost never four. Color, especially when it is unmodulated, separates and emphasizes; any distinguishable hues suffice. But Baertling knew that color is sensation and aesthetic in its fundamental meaning of "feeling." He used it to provide sensation, but not necessarily pleasure. He used it for visibility, for stimulus, for impact. His colors are as awkward as his discordant, unbalanced triangles, and as forceful. So in the face of a strong personality, we modify our aesthetics and begin to take pleasure in these colors. As so often happens in art we come to like those qualities which at first we most disliked.

In Baertling's world we find confirmed that rules are made *by* works of art not *for* them. To allow converging lines to meet at or near the picture's edge used to be compositional blunder; it is Baertling's principal compositional theme. Directing diagonals into the corner of a picture was worse; it drew the eye away from the center of interest; it caused visual traffic jams. Such traffic jams at the edge, or even projected outside the center of the painting, are precisely what Baertling wanted to confront us with. Concomitant with these hard, sharp, punching vertices are the unadjusted, unmodulated, disharmonious, blatant colors. Having got to know them, one can miss them like a departed friend, with whom one liked to argue.

Baertling repeated himself. He took from his small bundle of lines, from his bundle of narrow, sharp, scalene triangles, from his tiny handful of sharp colors, only what he needed for each successive painting; and for his sculptures, he took only the lines. The repertoire is small; the performance is in a long, narrow rectangular space, two by one or two and half by one. Over and over again he played out the variations in that squeezed space, with vertices spilling out of it. Like a conscientious detective story writer, he had certain rules for himself. Not only did diagonals never cross inside the rectangle but also he never allowed an island to establish itself in his space; nor would he allow a compositional idea to complete itself within his frame—the action was always resolved off stage.

The effect of this repetition has been that each painting, each sculpture, reasserted and at the same time expanded, by a small increment, the world which Baertling had made his own and had ruled without compromise.

—George Rickey

BAJ, Enrico.

Italian. Born in Milan, 31 October 1924. Educated in Milan: studied law, 1937–39; painting, at the Accademia de Brera, 1945–48. Married Gigliola Olivieri in 1954; daughter; Lucilla; married Roberta Cerini de Castegnate in 1966; children: Angelo, Andrea, Pietro and Marianna. Independent painter, writer and graphic artist, since 1948. Founder Member, with Sergio Dangelo, Nuclear Art Movement, Milan, 1951; Founder, with Asger Jorn, International Movement for an Imaginary Bauhaus, Albissola, Italy, 1953; Founder Editor, with Sergio Dangelo, *Il Gesto* magazine, Milan, 1955–1959; produced first collages and assemblages, Milan, 1956; contributed regularly to avant-garde magazines *Phases, Boa, Edda, Direzioni* and *Bokubi*, Milan, 1956–60; associated with the Nouveau Realiste group, Milan, 1959; Founder, with Raymond Queneau, Institute of Pataphysics, Milan, 1963; friendly with Max Ernst, Marcel Duchamp and André Breton, Paris, 1963–66; produced first pointilliste works, Milan, 1971. Spazio Baj permanent exhibition centre established by the city of Milan, 1987. Agent: Studio Marconi, Milan. Address: Via delle Ville 18, 21029 Vergiate, Italy.

Individual Exhibitions:

1951 Galleria San Fedele, Milan (with Sergio Dangelo)
1954 Galleria l'Asterisco, Rome
Galleria Schettini, Milan
1956 Galleria Schettini, Milan
Kunstkredsen, Copenhagen
1957 Gallery One, London
Galleria Il Prisma, Turin
1958 Galleria Gruppo, Bergamo (with Lucio Fontana and Piero Manzoni)
Galerie Daniel Cordier, Paris
1959 Gallery One, London
Galerie Rive Gauche, Paris
1960 Galleria del Naviglio, Milan
1961 Galerie Raymond Cordier, Paris
Galeria du Fleuve, Paris
Galleria Schwarz, Milan
1962 Sevenarts Gallery, London
Galerie Berggruen, Paris
1963 Cordier and Ekstrom Gallery, New York
1964 Galerie Alice Pauli, Lausanne
Palazzo Reale, Milan
1965 Galerie Pierre, Stockholm
Castello Spagnolo, L'Aquila, Italy
Galerie Berggruen, Paris
1966 Galleria Odyssia, Rome
Arts Club of Chicago
1967 Studio Marconi, Milan
Gemeentemuseum, The Hague
Museum voor Schone Kunsten, Ghent
Galerie Francoise Mayer, Brussels
Galleria del Minotauro, Brescia, Italy
1968 Studio Condotti, Rome
1969 Studio Marconi, Milan
Galerie Creuzevault, Paris
1970 Studio Condotti, Rome
Galerie Georges Moos, Geneva
1971 Musée de l'Athenée, Geneva
Palazzo Grassi, Venice
Museum of Contemporary Art, Chicago
1972 Galleria Michaud, Florence
1973 Museum Boymans-van-Beuningen, Rotterdam
Moderna Museet, Stockholm
Kunsthalle, Dusseldorf
1974 Koninklijk Museum voor Schone Kunsten, Antwerp
Palazzo Reale, Milan (travelled to the Kunsthalle, Dusseldorf, and the Palais des Beaux-Arts, Brussels)
Musée d'Art et d'Histoire, Cabinet des Estampes, Geneva
Galleria Spagnoli, Florence
Galerie Spectrum, Vienna
1975 Galleria San Benedetto, Brescia, Italy
Studio Marconi, Milan
Centre Design, Lugano, Switzerland
Galerie Christel, Helsinki (toured Sweden)
Museo Progressivo d'Arte Contemporanea, Livorno, Italy
Galleria della Piazza, Varese, Italy (with Lucio Del Pezzo and Emilio Scanavino)
1976 Galleria Il Centro, Naples
Galerie Friebe, Cologne (travelled to Galerie Volker Huber, Frankfurt)
Arras Gallery, New York
Arte Contacto, Caracas
Galleria Pancheri, Rovereto, Italy
Gallerie Ostermalm, Stockholm
Castello Sforzesca, Milan
1977 Arras Gallery, New York
Galerie Actu-Art, Helsingor, Denmark
Palazzo dei Diamanti, Ferrara, Italy
Centro Congressi La Sera, Ivrea, Italy
Galeria Gerhild Grolitsch, Munich
1978 Galleria Schettini, Milan
Arras Gallery, New York
Indianapolis Museum of Art
Palais de l'Europe, Menton, France
1979 Studio Marconi, Milan
Dartmouth College, Hanover, New Hampshire
1980 Galerie l'Ile de France, Paris
1981 Studio Marconi, Milan
1982 Palazzo della Ragione, Mantua, Italy
1983 Studio Marconi, Milan
1985 Center of Fine Art, Miami, Florida
Castello di Bard, Val d'Aosta, Italy
FIAC, Paris
1987 Palazzo Bellini, Comacchio, Italy

Selected Group Exhibitions:

1952 *Arte Nucleare*, Amici della Francia, Milan
1957 *Phasen*, Stedelijk Museum, Amsterdam
1961 *The Art of Assemblage*, Museum of Modern Art, New York
1963 *Schrift en Beeld*, Stedelijk Museum, Amsterdam
1968 *Recent Italian Painting and Sculpture*, Jewish Museum, New York
1971 *Metamorphase de l'Objet*, Palais des Beaux-Arts, Brussels
1977 *Italienische Druckgraphic des 20. Jahrhunderts*, Kunsthalle, Darmstadt
1980 *Arte Nucleare 1951–1957*, Galleria San Fedele, Milan
1984 *Primitivism in 20th Century Art*, Museum of Modern Art, New York
1987 *Lo specchio e il doppio*, Mole Antonelliana, Turin

Enrico Baj: *Generale "Generale"*, 1961

Collections

Centre Georges Pompidou, Paris; Museum Boymans-van Beuningen. Rotterdam; Stedelijk Museum, Amsterdam; Moderna Museet, Stockholm; Museum des 20. Jahrhunderts. Vienna; Tate Gallery, London; Lodz Museum, Poland; Galleria d'Arte Moderná, Milan; Museum of Contemporary Art, Chicago; National Gallery, Washington, D.C.

Publications:

By BAJ: books—*Manifeste de la Peinture Nucleaire*, with Sergio Dangelo, Brussels 1952; *Contro lo Stile*, with others, Milan 1957; *Arte Interplanetaria*, with others, Pianeta Terra, Italy 1959; *Manifeste de Naples*, with others, Naples 1959; *A Proposito de Coesistenza e Modificazione*, Naples 1959; *Pittura e Realtà*, Milan 1959; *Alternativi Attuali*, exhibition catalogue, L'Aquila, Italy 1962; *Testa a Testa*, with Umberto Geo, Padua 1980; *Autodanse*, Bologna 1980; articles—"Pop Napoli" in *Marcatre* (Milan), June 1965; "Milano Caves" in *Marcatre* (Milan), December 1965; "La Vita e l'Uomo" in *Del Pezzo*, exhibition catalogue, Milan 1966; "Parigi: FON 2104" in *Marcatre* (Milan), April 1966; "Ho visto Dio" in *Marcatre* (Milan), June 1966; "L'affaire des Generaux" in *L'Ultimo dei Generali*, Gallarate, Italy 1968; "Deflorando" in *Guido Biasi*, exhibition catalogue, Turin 1969; "L'Australia ha sete" in *Corriere della Sera* (Milan), May 1969; "Da Breton alla Luna" in *Corriere della Sera* (Milan), August 1969; "Baj da San Francisco" in *Flash Art* (Milan), no. 13, 1969; "Lattuga a Porno" in *Corriere della Sera* (Milan), October 1970; "Buzzati sexpittore" in *Dino Buzzati: Un Caso a Porte*, Rome, 1971; "Milano Cinquanta" in *Milano 70 / 70 Un Secolo d'Arte*, Milan 1972; "Sonnenstern" in *Multiplicata Internationale*, Stockholm and Zurich 1972; "Venne la Crisi e fu la Catastrofe" in *Corriere della Sera* (Milan), 25 May 1975; "Signorno all Autoritarismo" in *Doppiovu* (Milan), December 1976; "Pompidou chez Baj: Baj chez Pompidou" in *La Nuova Rivista Europea* (Trento, Italy), September / October 1977; "Baj on Baj," interview with Ellen Wardwell Lee in *Baj*, exhibition catalogue, by Joanne Muller Kuebler, Indianapolis 1978.

On BAJ: books—*Baj* by Jan van der Marck, Milan 1962; *Baj: Catalogue de l'Oeuvre et des Multiples*, 2 vols., by Jean Petit, Geneva 1970, 1974; *Baj* by Alain Jouffroy, Paris 1972; *Catalogo Generale Bolaffi Opere di Baj* by Enrico Crispolti, Turin 1973; *Enrico Baj, Dada Impressionist* by Herbert Lust, Turin 1973; *Enrico Baj, Apocalisse*, edited by Umberto Eco, Milan 1979; *Enrico Baj* by Jean Baudrillard, Paris 1980; *Testa a Testa* by Umberto Eco, Padua 1980; *Baj, dal generale al particolare* by Italo Calvino, Gerard G. Lemaire and Jan van der Marck, Milan 1985; *Baj: graphic works—catalogue raisonné*, edited by Roberto Sanesi and Jan van der Marck, Milan 1986; *Baj, nostalgia del futuro* by J. Baudrillard, P Bellasi and others, Milan 1987.

On other occasions, I have put forward a distinction between art-as-invention, i.e. art capable of affecting the current vision of things, and art-as-representation—which is to say, art which simply records and is more or less descriptive or analytical. At the ultimate level of ignominy is to be found commemorative art, seen without question in the art so dear to Stalin and Hitler, and at the Museum of Modern Art when engaged in the defence of Campbell's Soup or Coca-Cola. Celebrative art is art that does not content itself with merely representing power or is extreme in it homogenising degenerations, but even glorifies with marble monuments and kitsch imagery the commandant-bosses and / or the flavour of the month—be it neon lights, cartoons and plastic packages or any of the variety of junk with which we identify our finer feelings.

Today, more than ever, in our landscape made of conditioned and computerised responses, art as invention anticipates the new systems of communication in new visual languages capable of confronting an all-embracing robotization.

The spaces of the gallery Studio Marconi in Milan lend themselves to this type of research. There, space, which is everything for the painter, allows the exhibition of large canvases and the organization of the exhibit as the manifestation of different states of mind. I do have a system for filling such spaces—in fact, for some time I returned wholeheartedly to the technique of the 'fifties: action painting, dripping, gesture and sign. These methods of mine between 1951 and 1959 were constrained within the walls of small (not to say minimal) studio spaces in Milan; the constraints of the place inhibited my gesture and my dance around the canvas placed on the floor.

Living now in the countryside and the open air, I have recovered a completely different dimension. Onto a fine green meadow—a green I've always loved—I lay out a fresh canvas (which looks like an airport runway) and there my action begins, my own way of making pictures, which is the ultimate in the exultation, continuation and mega-inflation of painting 'au plein air'. Man must return to nature. Never again should he fight it, if he is to survive! This is the message of Georgescu Roegen and the message of the hope of a solar civilization. A new message and a new hope—new because they are given to us in highly philosophical and scientific terms, and not just to satisfy a naturalistic urge. At times, I work only with black on a white canvas, and I retrieve signs, symbols and scribbles reminiscent of the famous Rorschach test. At other times, I have abandoned black to give myself over to the manic and overwhelming joy of colour, I grind it, splash it, dilute it with turpentine and various solvents, or allow it to coagulate in the sun until concentrated, stringy and viscous to the touch before using it to create contrasts with other chromatic dilutions. Sometimes, I work with a kind of abstract drawing or pointillism, attracting me into a vacuum made up of a thousand colours. On other occasions, mindful of the cultural revolution of May 1968, when everybody spraycanned on walls the slogan of his own political failures, I try to produce ancestral languages and figures precisely in spraypaint, a sign language similar to the man of Altamira. The feelings we experience, the messages we intercept, the materials at our disposal are by now extremely varied, manifold and often contradictory, so that my exhibition will include a dual series of watercolours and drawings. The watercolours are reminiscent of a kind of cubo-futurism I practised at the time of my Manifesto for Static Futurism. Pastel drawings, on the other hand, emerged together with my use of the big spray green canvases. Finally, other canvases incorporate the symbolic transposition of bits and pieces of wood collected off the ground during the construction of my new studio.

Such wooden fragments, due to their humble, ephemeral and weathered look, have a charge which I would define as archaeological. They imply an ancient discourse redolent of the gesture of the carpenter's or bricklayer's art. Effectively, our houses are already archaeological. We live in archaeology as is

demonstrated by the continual restoration of old farm houses and decaying city centres. Today, the streets where brothels operated, the Fossati cinema building and the industrial premises are precious relics that we should clean up and restore.

Some of the canvases with wooden fragments are used to represent my family, whereas another is freely inspired by Pythaogras' theorem. One is a study for Voltaire's Micromegas. The famous conversation between the inhabitants of Sirio and Saturno reverberates in my latest works, as in the Citta del Sole for which I am indebted to another great Utopianist (T. Campanella).

'Megalizzazione' and 'miniaturizzazione' face one another in everyday life. It should not be difficult to understand that, faced with grand general projects (and their frequent failure), we opt for the cure of the particular.

—Enrico Baj

What we might regard as a new iconology, combining the influence of popular and of cultured iconology and reviving the mytho-poetical qualities of present-day man, has always been present in Enrico Baj's work. Ever since 1951—the time of the *Movimento Nucleare*, of which he was a member—Baj has understood the importance of those mocking creatures that fill the popular horizon and in the end can be heard breathing within the "cultured" painting, and he has press-ganged them into his paintings and *assemblages*. Thus we have seen the first clumsy sketches of the "ultrabodies" or of the flying saucers, and after them those of the Generals and the Dames: a whole gallery teeming with people and events which are beginning to be organized and which the artist has used as a background against which to compose his pictures.

In Baj's case, in addition to the readymade material constituted by the *objet trouvé*, used just as it is as an emotional and fanciful starting point, there is always the desire to give life to the shapeless, to find the right relationship between forms and colours. Ever since his first grotesque drawings, the artist has been able to combine his sense of humour with his feeling for experiment, his narrative ability with his eagerness for research into materials; thus he has worked with stained cloth from mattresses or tapestries, for use as background to his "monsters"; he has borrowed our grandfathers' looking-glasses, but in order to create an ambiguous medium that would reflect the image of the past and that of the future together.

While almost all American and British pop art used "found objects" as symbols of everyday life, Baj took a completely opposite line. The wide use he made of old, out-of-date materials, of old 19th-century trimmings, of ancient medals, of our great-grandparents' ribbons and lace, tells us how the artist has pointed out the importance of creating a "kingdom of memory," haunted by the ghosts of an age already far away from us but in which we can still recognize our origins. When Baj invented his "Dames" and "Generals," the Pop adventure was still a long way off; it was too easy, later, to lump his pictures together with those of other masters of United States pop.

If, then, we want to analyse the signs and symbols in some of Baj's figures and collages, we must notice the subtle metaphorical game that he plays with the heteroclitic materials he uses; we must notice that it is no accident that the discs he uses for eyes are buttons, the nipples are skittles, the sexes are rough brushes.

There are too many examples to quote here, but they show us how there nearly always exists in these works a Concept side by side with an Object; a linguistic search (for a visual-verbal metaphor) side by side with a plastic search. And it is this that, in the last years, has enabled Baj to tackle the great socio-political themes depicted in some of his gigantic works like "Watergate," "The Anarchic Pinelli" and "The Apocalypse," in which the same humorous elements from the past have been used for a more exacting, more austere purpose: to put in relief the sins of our civilization and draw attention to the threats that supreme political power can exert on present and future society.

—Gillo Dorfles

BALDESSARI, John.

American. Born in National City, California, 17 June 1931. Educated at Sweetwater High School, National City, 1945–49; studied painting at San Diego State College, California, 1949–53, 1954–57, B.A. 1953, M.A. 1957. Married Carol Wixom in 1962; children: Anna Marie and Antonio. Professional artist since 1957. Instructor, Fine Arts Gallery, San Diego, 1953–54, San Diego city schools, 1956–57, San Diego State College, 1956, 1959–61, and Southwestern College, Chula Vista, California, 1962–68; Assistant Professor of Art, University of California at San Diego, 1968–70; also, Instructor, La Jolla Museum of Art, California, 1966–70. Professor, California Institute of Arts, Los Angeles, since 1970. Visiting Instructor, Hunter College, New York, 1971. Recipient: National Endowment for the Arts Grant, 1973, 1974–75. Agents: Sonnabend Gallery, New York; and James Corcoran Gallery, 8223 Santa Monica Boulevard, Los Angeles, California 90046. Lives and works in Santa Monica, California. Address: c/o Sonnabend Gallery, 420 West Broadway, New York, New York 10012, U.S.A.

Individual Exhibitions:

1960 La Jolla Museum of Art, California
1962 Southwestern College, Chula Vista, California (and 1964)
1966 La Jolla Museum of Art, California
1968 Molly Barnes Gallery, Los Angeles
1970 Richard Feigen Gallery, New York
Eugenia Butler Gallery, Los Angeles
1971 Galerie Konrad Fischer, Dusseldorf
Art and Project, Amsterdam
Nova Scotia College of Art and Design, Halifax
1972 Galerie MTL, Brussels
Art and Project, Amsterdam
Galleria Franco Toselli, Milan
Jack Wendler Gallery, London
1973 Sonnabend Gallery, New York
Galerie Sonnabend, Paris
Galleria Schema, Florence
Galerie Konrad Fischer, Dusseldorf
1974 Galerie Folker Skulima, West Berlin
Jack Wendler Gallery, London
Galleria Franco Toselli, Milan
Art and Project/Galerie MTL, Antwerp
1975 Galerie Felix Handschin, Basle
Galerie MTL, Brussels
Saman Gallery, Genoa
Sonnabend Gallery, New York
Stedelijk Museum, Amsterdam
Modern Art Agency, Naples
Galerie Sonnabend, Paris
Southwestern College, Chula Vista, California
The Kitchen, New york
University of California at Irvine
1976 Ewing Gallery, University of Melbourne, Australia
Auckland Art Gallery, New Zealand
University of Akron, Ohio
Ohio State University, Columbus
Cirrus Editions Gallery, Los Angeles
James Corcoran Gallery, Los Angeles
1977 Galleria Massimo Valsecchi, Milan
Matrix, Hartford Atheneum, Connecticut
John Baldessari: Films, Fox Venice Theatre, Venice, California
Robert Self Gallery, London
Julian Pretto Gallery, New York
1978 Portland Center for the Visual Arts, Oregon
Sonnabend Gallery, New York
Recent Films, Theatre Vanguard, Los Angeles
Films by Baldessari, Artists' Space, New York
3 Films, Pacific Film Archives, Berkeley, California
Baldessari: New Films, Whitney Museum, New York
1979 Halle für Internationale Neue Kunst, Zurich
1980 *Fugitive Essays*, Sonnabend Gallery, New York
1981 *Werken 1966–1981*, Stedelijk Van Abbemuseum, Eindhoven, Netherlands
John Baldessari/Deborah Turbeville, Sonnabend Gallery, New York
Wright State University, Dayton, Ohio
1982 Stedelijk Van Abbemuseum, Eindhoven, Netherlands
Museum Folkwang, Essen, West Germany
CEPA Gallery, Buffalo, New York
Albright-Knox Art Gallery, Buffalo, New York
Galerie Rudiger Schottle, Munich
Sonnabend Gallery, New York
Samangallery, Genoa, Italy
Contemporary Art Center, Cincinnati
Wright State University, Dayton, Ohio
Contemporary Arts Museum, Houston, Texas
1983 Galerie Stampa, Basle
Marian Deson Gallery, Chicago
Galerie Arte Viva, Basle
1984 Sonnabend Gallery, New York
Margo Leavin Gallery, Los Angeles
Galerie Peter Pakesch, Vienna
Galerie Gillespie-Laage-Salomon, Paris
1985 Le Consortium Centre d'Art Contemporain, Dijon, France
De Vleeshal, Middelburg, Netherlands
1986 Sonnabend Gallery, New York
University of California, Berkeley
University of California, Santa Barbara
Margo Leavin Gallery, Los Angeles

Selected Group Exhibitions:

1960 *The Uncommon Denominator: 13 San Diego Painters*, La Jolla Art Center, California (toured the United States)
1969 *Pop Art Redefined*, Hayward Gallery, London
1976 *Painting and Sculpture in California: The Modern Era*, San Francisco Museum of Modern Art (travelled to the National Collection of Fine Arts, Smithsonian Institution, Washington, D.C.)
1977 *Photography as Means*, Center for Photographic Art, La Jolla, California
1978 *Narration*, Institute of Contemporary Art, Boston
Art about Art, Whitney Museum, New York
1979 *American Photography in the 70's*, Art Institute of Chicago
1981 *Westkunst*, Messehallen, Cologne
1985 *Extending the Perimeters of 20th Century Art*, San Francisco Museum of Modern Art
1987 *Avant-Garde in the Eighties*, Los Angeles County Museum of Art

Collections:

Museum of Modern Art, New York; Los Angeles County Museum of Art; La Jolla Museum of Art, California; Wallraf-Richartz Museum, Cologne; Stedelijk Museum, Amsterdam; Kunstmuseum, Basle.

Publications:

By BALDESSARI: books—*Ingres and Other Parables*, London 1972; *Choosing: Green Beans*, Milan 1972; *Throwing 3 Balls in the Air to Get a Straight Line (Best of 36 Attempts)*, Milan 1973; *Throwing a Ball Once to Get 3 Melodies and 15 Chords*, Irvine, California 1975; *4 Events and Reactions*, Amsterdam 1975; *Artists and Photographers*, portfolio, with others, New York 1975; *Raw Prints*, portfolio, Los Angeles 1976; *Brutus Killed Caesar*, Akron, Ohio 1976; *A Sentence of 13 Parts (with 12 Alternative Verbs) Ending in Fable*, Hamburg 1977; articles—"Photography and Language," interview, in *John Baldessari*, exhibition catalogue, Los Angeles

John Baldessari: *Vanitas Series—With Hair and Bubbles*, 1981

1976; "John Baldessari: Interview," with Diane Spodarek, in *Detroit Artists' Monthly*, June 1976; interview with Leo Rubinfein in *Art in America* (New York), September/October 1978; also, interview for the Video Data Bank, School of the Art Institute of Chicago, 1973.

On BALDESSARI: books—*Pop Art Redefined* by John Russell and Suzi Gablik, London and New York 1969; *Conceptual Art* by Ursula Meyers, New York 1971; *Video Visions: A Medium Discovers Itself* by Jonathan Price, New York 1972; *Video Art* by Ira Schneider and Beryl Korot, New York 1976; *John Baldessari*, exhibition catalogue, with texts by Marcia Tucker and Robert Pinsuc-Witten, and an interview by Nancy Drew, Dayton, Ohio 1981; articles—"John Baldessari, Sonnabend Gallery" by Nancy Foote in *Artforum* (New York), September 1976; "When Is a Book Not a Book?" by Grace Glueck in the *New York Times*, 18 March 1977; "Pictures and Picture Books" by April Kingsley in the *Soho Weekly News* (New York), 21 April 1977; "John Baldessari and Daniel Buren" by Jeff Perrone in *Artforum* (New York), September 1977; "Making Light of Heavy Art" by Kenneth Baker in the *Boston Phoenix*, 10 January 1978; review by Paul Stimson in *Art in America* (New York), March/April 1979; "John Baldessari's Blasted Allegories" by Hal Foster in *Artforum* (New York), October 1979; "Well Hung" by Ben Lifson in the *Village Voice* (New York), 5 November 1980; review by Joan Casademont in *Artforum* (New York), January 1981.

WHAT THINKS ME NOW.
I want to re-enchant and remythologize.
I want to drill a hole deep-down in art to discover the mythic infrastructure.
(I am less interested in the form art takes than the meaning an image evokes.)
(I am interested in myth as a way of knowing.)
I want to express myself in archetypal imagery.
I want to stand at the edge rather than the center.
I want to recall what I always knew. (I am interested in what thinks me.)
(I would rather discover the memory of the soul than to be correct in thought.)
I want to move away from racial amnesia.
I want to produce images that startle one into recollection.
I want to think of history so that it is not a record of events but is a method of release.
I want to see the world as something else than serial progression.
I want to know the matrix of events in history.
(What appears to be trivial in a fairy tale, etc. could be the lingering remnant of the memory of the soul.)
I want to engage in the spiritualization of matter and the materialization of the spirit.
I want to think of time as synchronic.
I want to see all variants of a myth in a single imaginary space w/o regard to historical context.
I want to sift information from noise.
I want to avoid the tedium of sectarianism and dogma.
I want to consider language as an articulation of the limited to express the unlimited.
I want to be at home with the paradoxical, the ambiguous, and the random.
I want to eroticize time, consciousness, and human culture.
I want to blur the boundaries between truth and fiction.

—John Baldessari

Baldessari is a Californian who—like his long-time friend William Wegman—rejected a '60s modernism become too self-important and aloofly formalist. He will for long be known for his declaration *I will not make any more boring art*, and the burning in 1970 of his earlier work, the ashes ending up in a book-shaped urn marked with his name and the dates 1953–1967. Although Baldessari is more broadly classed a conceptual artist and has worked with photography, video, film and texts, through his use of media imagery, he can be held a pioneer "image appropriator." (Salle and Brauntuch number among his students.) His work harbors ambiguity, yet its mystery is not that of modernist symbolism and ego-centered stream-of-consciousness. Instead Baldessari can be said to be a post-modernist in his casual and good-natured didacticism; and thus a post-structuralist in his dissection of signs and their information bearing dimensions. His pervasive flavor has then been an enigmatic conjunction of imagery, often with text to influence the nature of the viewer's perception, and most often pointing to some semantic issue: the cliches of perception a constant focus. Such an overriding philosophical reflection in his work bespeaks his long-time absorption with spiritual relationships in the world, perhaps evinced by his church membership into early adulthood. While in his earliest such work, in the later 1960s and on into the following decade, the construct was achieved through his own photography, he then became a collector of literature and images. When he turned to the popular media, and for instance came to use television imagery as a major source, he positioned three cameras to face three soundless TV screens; within the past decade, his most important source came to be still photographic scenes from the history of film, thus tacitly acknowledging their ready availability and his residence in Los Angeles. Through his wit and intelligence, Baldessari has not permitted himself to become a mere illustrator of theoretical premises—he retains his position as major representative of a cerebral-founded visual art.

—Joshua B. Kind

BALTHUS.

French. Born Comte Balthazar Klowssowski de Rola, of Polish parents, in Paris, 29 February 1908. Studied in Paris in 1924, but mainly self-taught in art. Served in the French Army in Morocco, 1929–33; recalled, Paris, 1939, but demobilized shortly thereafter because of ill health. Married in 1937. First book of drawings published, Geneva, 1920; worked on frescoes, Church of Beatenburg, Bernese Oberland, 1928; designed sets and costumes for *The Cenci* by Antonin Artaud, Paris, 1935; during Occupation, lived in Switzerland; returned to Paris, 1945; designed sets and costumes for *Cosi fan Tutti*, Aix-en-Provence, 1950; settled in Morvan, France, 1954. Director, French Academy, Rome, since 1961. Recipient: Premio Via Condotti, Rome, 1983. Address: Viale Trinite dei Monti 1, Villa Medicis, 00187 Rome, Italy.

Individual Exhibitions:

1934	Galerie Pierre, Paris
1938	Pierre Matisse Gallery, New York
1943	Galerie Moos, Geneva
1946	Wildenstein Galerie, Paris
1949	Pierre Matisse Gallery, New York
1952	Lefevre Gallery, London
1956	Wildenstein Galerie, Paris
	Museum of Modern Art, New York
1961	Galleria Civica d'Arte Moderna, Turin
1962	Pierre Matisse Gallery, New York
1963	E. V. Thaw and Company, New York
1964	Arts Club of Chicago
	Massachusetts Institute of Technology, Cambridge
1966	Casino Municipal, Knokke-le-Zoute, Belgium
	Pierre Matisse Gallery, New York
	Musée des Arts Decoratifs, Paris
	Galerie Henriette Gomes, Paris
1967	Pierre Matisse Gallery, New York
1968	Tate Gallery, London
1969	Donald Morris Gallery, Detroit
1971	*Dessins et Aquarelles*, Galerie Claude Bernard, Paris
1973	Musée Cantini, Marseilles
1977	Pierre Matisse Gallery, New York

1978 Pierre Matisse Gallery, New York
1980 Scuola Grande di San Giovanni Evangelista, Venice
1982 Museo d'Arte, Spoleto, Italy
1983 Musée d'Art Moderne, Paris

Selected Group Exhibitions:

1976 *Group Exhibition*, Galerie Jacques Benador, Geneva
1980 *Biennale*, Venice
1981 *The New Spirit in Painting*, Royal Academy of Arts, London
1982 *A Century of Modern Drawing*, British Museum, London

Collections:

Centre National d'Art Contemporain, Paris; Tate Gallery, London; Museum of Modern Art, New York; Hirshhorn Museum and Sculpture Garden, Smithsonian Institution, Washington, D.C.; Wadsworth Atheneum, Hartford, Connecticut; Institute of Art, Minneapolis; Art Institute of Chicago; National Gallery of Victoria, Melbourne.

Publications:

On BALTHUS: books—*Balthus*, exhibition catalogue, by James Thrall Soby, New York 1938; *Balthus*, exhibition catalogue, by Albert Camus, New York 1949; *Balthus and a Selection of French Paintings* by Cyril Connolly, London 1952; *Balthus*, exhibition catalogue, by James Thrall Soby, New York 1956; *Balthus*, exhibition catalogue, by John Russell, London 1968; *Balthus: Dessins et Aquarelles*, exhibition catalogue, by Jean Leymarie, Paris 1971.

Nearly unique in this century in his allegiance to the traditions of figurative art, Balthus has worked aloof from the torrents of abstraction. He has contributed at least three great portraits to those traditions—of the painters Derain and Miró and of the art patron Marie Laure, Vicomtesse de Noilly. He has added luminous, direct landscapes as well, and, perhaps most importantly of all, a series of narrative compositions centering on young girls.

If the portraits contain a little of the doll-like quality sometimes produced by Goya, the large compositions of Paris streets recall the arrested drama that charges the frozen figures of Seurat—also, in another way, doll-like. And of course these unexplained, "plotless" dramas raise many questions, chiefly: who are these people? and what are they doing? We are made uneasy in the presence of gesturing orientals, misshapen children, streets without traffic, forms smoothed down as though carved from wood. The isolation of each figure—though caught forever in reaction to others—reminds us of Piero della Francesca. Like that painter, Balthus stops time, "correcting reality" to use the marvellous phrase Camus once wrote in an essay about him.

Again and again it is evident how much Balthus has learned from the painters of the past. Even the "awkwardly" posed adolescents—forever at their games, or reading, sprawled on couch or floor for which he is most famous—can be seen echoed, say, in the posture of Noah, passed-out, in "The Drunkenness of Noah" by Giovani Bellini. And yet the formal power of these paintings, with their close-value browns, greys and reds, their light-struck whites, and their elaborate design, cannot displace the force of their subject matter: young nudes with heads thrown back in Mannerist transport; girls with legs raised in invitation, arms behind their heads provocatively; girls kneeling uncomfortably over books; girls arched over chairs—all, usually, occupying rooms of stifling respectability and often accompanied by disturbing, unclear—in the sense of who or what they are—dwarf-like figures busy pulling back curtains or lighting fires. Many compositions feature a cipher cat sometimes sitting sphinx-like, sometimes actively involved wearing a cunning, even satanic expression.

It is all a bit like the world of Lewis Carroll taken several extreme steps further. No wonder Balthus has been able to create a superbly apt set of illustrations for *Wuthering Heights* and that Picasso, a master of erotic games, kept one of Balthus' paintings nearby until his death.

—Ralph Pomeroy

BANNARD, Walter Darby.

American. Born in New Haven, Connecticut, 23 September 1934. Educated at Phillips Exeter Academy, Exeter, New Hampshire, 1950–52; Princeton University, New Jersey, 1952–56, B.A. 1956. Married Mya Hay in 1977; son: William. Independent artist, Princeton, since 1956. Visiting Critic, Columbia University Art School, New York, 1968; Visiting Professor, Princeton University Creative Arts Program, 1974; Visiting Artist, Kent State University, Ohio, 1974; Visiting Artist and Lecturer, University of Texas at Austin, 1975; Visiting Critic, Brooklyn Museum Art School, New York, 1975; Instructor in Painting, San Francisco Art Institute, 1979. Contributing Editor, *Artforum*, New York, 1973–74. Juror, Davidson National Print and Drawing Competition, North Carolina, 1974; Adviser, *The Flowering of American Folk Art*, exhibition at the Whitney Museum, New York, 1974; Curator, *Hans Hofmann* exhibition, Hirshhorn Museum, Washington, D.C., 1976. Member, Art Advisory Committee, Phillips Exeter Academy, since 1977; Co-Chairman, International Panel on the Visual Arts, National Endowment for the Arts, Washington, D.C., since 1979. Recipient: Guggenheim Fellowship, 1968; National Endowment for the Arts Award, 1968; Purchase Award, New Jersey State Museum, 1971; Francis J. Greenburger Foundation Award, 1986. Agent: Knoedler Contemporary Art, 19 East 70th Street, New York, New York 10021. Address: Box 1157, Princeton, New Jersey 08540, U.S.A.

Individual Exhibitions:

1965 Tibor de Nagy Gallery, New York
Kasmin Gallery, London
1966 Tibor de Nagy Gallery, New York (twice)
Richard Feigen Gallery, Chicago
1967 Nicholas Wilder Gallery, Los Angeles
Tibor de Nagy Gallery, New York
1968 Kasmin Gallery, London
Tibor de Nagy Gallery, New York
1969 Kasmin Gallery, London
Tibor de Nagy Gallery, New York
New Gallery, Bennington College, Vermont
David Mirvish Gallery, Toronto
1970 David Mirvish Gallery, Toronto
Lawrence Rubin Gallery, New York
Joseph Helman Gallery, St. Louis
1971 Neuendorf Gallery, Cologne
1972 Lawrence Rubin Gallery, New York
Newport Harbor Art Museum, Newport Beach, California
Kasmin Gallery, London
David Mirvish Gallery, Toronto
1973 Lawrence Rubin Gallery, New York
Pasadena Art Museum
Walter Darby Bannard, 1957–1973, Baltimore Art Museum (retrospective; toured the United States)
Tibor de Nagy Gallery, Houston (opening show)
1974 Knoedler Contemporary Art, New York (twice)
1975 Tibor de Nagy Gallery, Houston
Douglas Drake Gallery, Kansas City, Kansas
David Mirvish Gallery, Toronto
Olympia Gallery, Philadelphia
Knoedler Contemporary Art, New York
1976 Knoedler Contemporary Art, New York
1977 Knoedler Contemporary Art, New York
Watson/de Nagy Gallery, Houston (twice)
Lamont Gallery, Phillips Exeter Academy, New Hampshire
Greenberg Gallery, St. Louis
1978 Knoedler Contemporary Art, New York
David Mirvish Gallery, Toronto
1979 Knoedler Contemporary Art, New York
Watson/de Nagy Gallery, Houston
Miami University, Oxford, Ohio
1980 Knoedler Contemporary Art, New York
Douglas Drake Gallery, Kansas City, Kansas
Ulrich Art Museum, Wichita
State University of Kansas, Wichita
Gallery 700, Milwaukee
Knoedler Gallery, New York
Wichita State University, Kansas
Douglas Drake Gallery, Kansas City, Kansas
Gallery 700, Milwaukee, Wisconsin
1981 Watson/de Nagy Gallery, New York
Knoedler Gallery, New York
1982 Martin Gerard Gallery, Edmonton, Alberta
Knoedler Gallery, New York
Watson/de Nagy Gallery, New York
James Madison University, Harrisonburg, Virginia
Clayworks Studio Workshop, New York
Virginia Technical University, Blacksburg
1983 Mint Museum of Art, Charlotte, North Carolina
Martin Gerard Gallery, Edmonton, Alberta
Edmonton Art Gallery, Alberta
1984 Knoedler Gallery, New York
Watson/de Nagy Gallery, New York
1986 Salander-O'Reilly Gallery, New York
1987 St. Lawrence University, Canton, New York

Selected Group Exhibitions:

1965 *The Responsive Eye*, Museum of Modern Art, New York (toured the United States)
1968 *Art of the Real*, Museum of Modern Art, New York (toured the United States and Europe)
1970 *Color and Field 1890–1970*, Albright Knox Art Gallery, Buffalo, New York (toured the United States)
1974 *The Great Decade of American Abstraction: Modernist Art 1960 to 1970*, Museum of Fine Arts, Houston
1977 *Private Images: Photographs by Painters*, Los Angeles County Museum of Art
1979 *Art in America After World War II*, Guggenheim Museum, New York
1980 *Aspects of the 70's: Painterly Abstracolor*, Brockton Art Museum, Massachusetts
1983 *Touch*, Laguna Gloria Art Museum, Austin, Texas
1985 *PrePostmodern*, St. Lawrence University, Canton, New York
1987 *Luminous Impressions*, Mint Museum of Art, Charlotte, North Carolina

Collections:

Guggenheim Museum, New York; Metropolitan Museum of Art, New York; Whitney Museum, New York; Museum of Modern Art, New York; Albright-Knox Art Gallery, Buffalo, New York; Princeton University, New Jersey; Newark Museum, New Jersey; Fogg Art Museum, Cambridge, Massachusetts; Baltimore Museum of Art; Museum of Fine Arts, Houston; University of Texas at Austin.

Publications:

By BANNARD: books—*The Structure of Color*, exhibition catalogue, New York 1971; *Hans Hofmann*, exhibition catalogue, Washington D.C. 1976; articles—"Color, Paint and Present-Day Painting" in *Artforum* (New York), April 1966; "Present-Day Art and Ready-Made Styles" in *Artforum* (New York), December 1966; "Cubism, Abstract Expressionism and David Smith" in *Artforum* (New York), April 1968; "Willem de Kooning's Retrospective at the Museum of Modern Art" in *Artforum* (New York), April 1969; review of *Beyond Modern Sculptures* by Jack Burnham, in *Artforum* (New York), May 1969; "Hofmann's Rectangles" in *Artforum* (New York), Summer 1969; "Notes on American Painting of the 60's" in *Artforum* (New York), January 1970; "Color Painting and the Map Problem" in *Artforum* (New York), March 1970; "The Artist and Politics" in *Artforum* (New York), September 1970; "Notes on An Auction" in *Artforum* (New York), September 1970; "Touch and Scale:

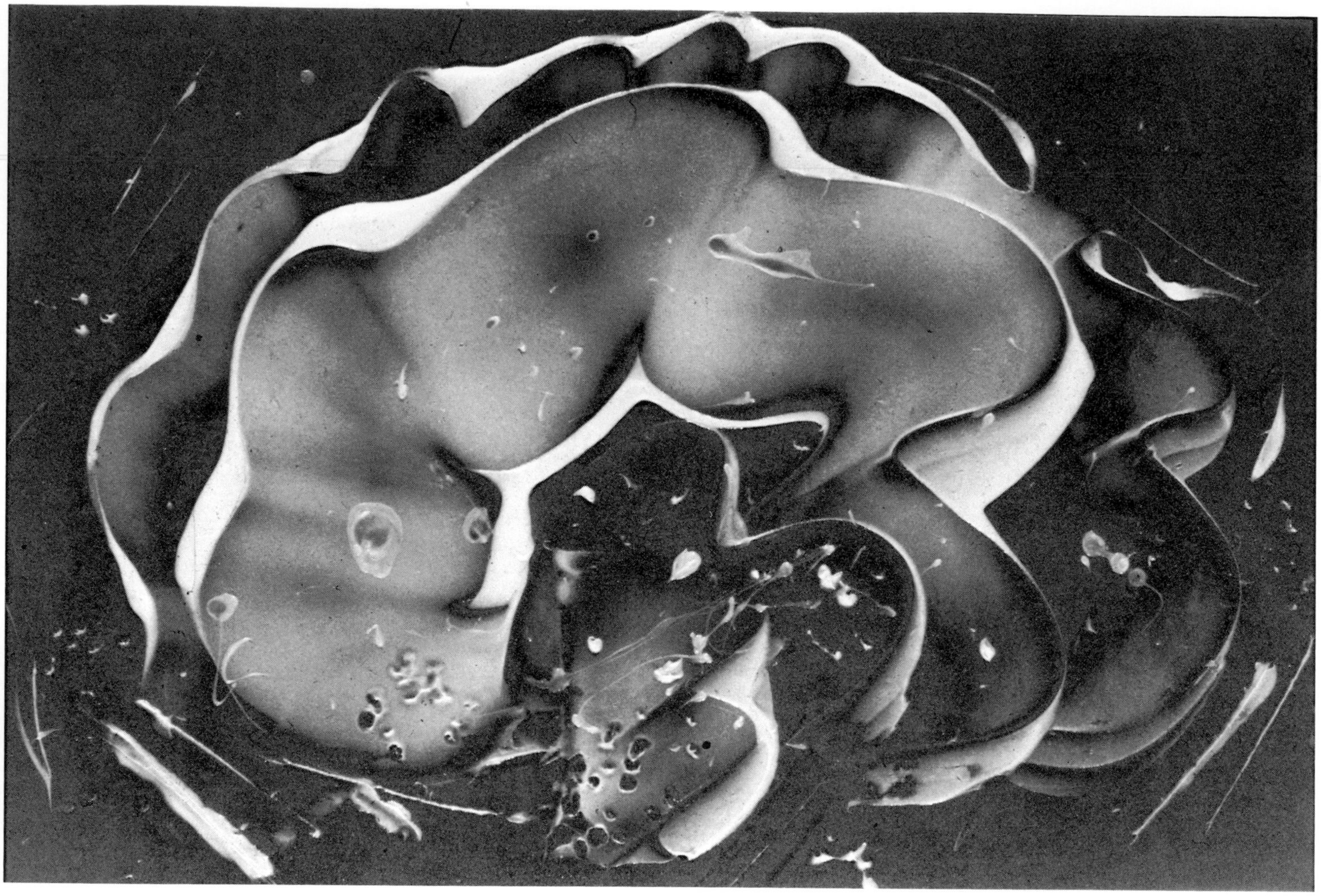

Walter Darby Bannard: ***The Flurry*, 1982**

Cubism, Pollock, Newman and Still" in *Artforum* (New York), September 1970; review of Michael Fried's *Morris Lewis* in *The Print Collector's Newsletter* (New York), July/August 1971; "Noland's New Paintings" in *Artforum* (New York), November 1971; *The Structure of Color,* exhibition catalogue (New York), June 1972; review of Thomas B. Hess' *Barnett Newman,* in the *Paint Collector's Newsletter* (New York), July/August 1972; "The War Against the Good in Art" in the *New York Times,* 6 August 1972; "Quality, Style and Olitski" in *Artforum* (New York), October 1972; statement in *Walter Darby Bannard,* exhibition catalogue, Newport Beach, California 1972; "He Comes to Praise the Net" in the *New York Times,* 1 July 1973; "Morris Louis and the Restructured Picture" in *Studio International* (London), July/August 1974; "The Museum and the Living Artist," essay in *On Understanding Art Museums,* New York 1974; "Art Quality and the Formalist Controversy" in *Quadrille* (Vermont), Fall 1974; "On Postmodernism" in *Arts* (New York), February 1984; "The Art Glut" in *Arts* (New York), December 1986.

On BANNARD: books—*The Development of Modern Painting: Jackson Pollock to the Present,* exhibition catalogue, with text by R. T. Buck Jr., St. Louis 1969; *The Structure of Color,* exhibition catalogue, with an essay by Marcia Tucker, New York 1971; *6 Painters,* exhibition catalogue, by G. Smith, New York 1971; *Walter Darby Bannard,* exhibition catalogue, with an essay and interview by J. H. Cone, Baltimore 1973; *Walter Darby Bannard,* exhibition catalogue, with text by Terry Fenton, Edmonton, Alberta 1983; articles—"Darby Bannard: The Possibilities of Color" by David Bourdon in *Art International* (New York), May 1967; "London Commentary: Bannard at Kasmin" by J. Mashek in *Studio International* (London), November 1969; "Walter Bannard at Kasmin Gallery" by John Eiderfeld in *Studio International* (London), November 1972; "Walter Darby Bannard at the Baltimore Museum" by David Bourdon in *Art in America* (New York), March/April 1974; "Third Generation Abstraction" by K. Carpenter in *Arts Magazine* (New York), February 1975; "The Impasto World of Walter Darby Bannard" by V. Raynor in the *New York Times,* 29 May 1981; "Walter Darby Bannard's New Pictures" by J. Walsh in *Arts* (New York), September 1982; "Walter Darby Bannard" by J. Link in *Arts* (New York), October 1986.

Like everybody else, I just keep working and try to do the best I can.

—Walter Darby Bannard

Walter Darby Bannard is probably as well known for his perceptive writings about art as he is for his economical abstract paintings. A frequent contributor to art journals, he is also the author of, among other essays, an important critical study of the work of Hans Hofmann. Bannard, however, considers himself first and foremost a painter and feels that being a practitioner gives him special insight as a critic.

His reputation was first established as a painter, soon after he turned 30, when he began to exhibit spare color abstractions that marked him as one of the most thoughtful and original young artists of the mid-60s. By then, Bannard had been painting seriously for about a decade, since his student days at Princeton. Frank Stella had been a fellow student and a friend, but the two young painters worked in quite different ways. Unlike Stella, Bannard was unaffected by the seductions of minimalism. His earliest paintings often seemed to allude, albeit distantly, to landscape motifs or floating figures, and while he soon radically simplified these pictures, it was to clarify what they were about, not to conform to theory.

During his first years of concentrated paintings, Bannard realized that his primary concern was color and stripped his imagery down to allow himself to focus on how colors affected one another when set side by side. Like many of the best young painters of the period, he arrived at simplified, clear formats that resolved, for the moment, issues of where to put color. Bannard's paintings from about 1959 through 1961 were usually symmetrical, often square, with narrow framing borders and centralized disc shapes. Thinly painted, with no sense of anything having been concealed, they demonstrated Bannard's opposition to the layered, gestural de Kooning-inspired version of Abstract Expressionism of the time. Yet even the most severe of his "band" and "framed circle" pictures of these years was conspicuously handmade and intuitive. Bannard may have dissected painting into what he saw as essential components of field, figure and edge, but he did so in the service of making color as eloquent as possible, not as a demonstration of a system.

In the 1960s and '70s, Bannard seemed primarily a colorist. His distinctive palette of odd, chalky pastels was unmistakeable and criticism of the time frequently praised him for having managed to detach cosmetic, candy hues from their conventional associations. Bannard, on the other hand, claims simply to have liked the colors and to have had no particular associations with them. His primary concern remained the unexpected juxtaposition of the disparate. The extreme close-valuing of his palette brought even the most unlikely pairings into tonal unity and at the same time, made the smallest nuances of differences in hue or surface of overmastering importance. Bannard's sensibility was so subtle that, on occasion, the chief distinction between areas of identical color could be the difference between mat and gloss.

Bannard has never hesitated to change the look of his pictures quite dramatically, in order to explore his changing ideas of what a painting could be. During the '60s and '70s, his compositions remained essentially geometric, but became increasingly complex, as though he had expanded his reach. The pared-down, centered band and framed circle layouts gave way to arrangements of hard-edged intersecting arcs

and later to "checkerboards" and floating rectangles. He seemed to rely less on predetermined placement of colors or, at least, on predetermined *areas* in which to set colors, and by the late '60s, he seemed more willing to let the making of the picture dictate its structure rather than to rely on a simplified and preconceived format. His profound understanding of Hofmann's ability to construct with color is apparent in these paintings, particularly in a series that juxtaposed relatively solidly painted rectangles against multicolored grounds. They could be described as "Hofmann disembodied", a translation of Hofmannesque attitudes into then current notions about color as pure optical experience, richly evocative and expressive, but as detached from any material presence as possible.

Bannard's pictures of the late '60s and early '70s are remarkable for their complex structure: overlapping layers of color, repeated passes of a spreading tool, create intricate intersecting color shapes. Only Bannard's meticulous orchestration of pale values keeps these canvases unified and makes one's experience of them that of all-over painting rather than of violent polychromy. The tension between their deadpan surfaces—an overwhelming sense of a flat, uninterrupted expanse—and their notably broad color range—which breaks that expanse into smaller units—constitutes part of these pictures' strength and part of Bannard's originality.

Bannard's next series, made in the early '70s, appears, in retrospect, like a deliberate effort to explore completely opposite notions to those examined in the pale, flat color paintings of the previous few years. Each of the series has a single, dominant, startling hue—off-white, poison green or funky lavender, for example—distributed in thick, aggressively scraped strokes. Paint is piled and trowelled in broad bands that fold around one another; underlying colors are glimpsed between strokes. The act of moving the paint across the surface of the canvas is what *makes* the image, literally and metaphorically. It is a logical extension of the attitude that led to Bannard's checkerboards of the preceeding years, but all vestiges of preconception have been banished. The checkerboards and their fellows were made very directly, but still depended upon a tacit acknowledgement of the given vertical and horizontal dimensions of the canvas. In Bannard's best paintings of the series that followed, there is no sense of a preexisting rectangle's having been divided. Instead, the expanse and dimension of the painting seem to have been created by the momentary coalescence of the broad, juicy strokes of paint.

Bannard relaxed his innate sense of the geometric in his subsequent series, while giving free rein to his growing taste for materiality. Like many of his colleagues, he was fascinated with the expanded properties of the acrylic paints and gels beginning to be commonly available in the late '70s and early '80s: thickeners and additives that allowed greater surface advantage of these possibilities, exploiting gel-thickened acrylic's ability to retain the mark of a tool or the rhythm of a gesture. A group of pictures from the early '80s depended upon his typically surprising color sensibility, but presented in new ways; underlying layers of color were revealed by the pulling back of a superimposed layer of thicker, shinier paint in a contrasting hue. For the first time, drawing and surface inflection—here a playful scalloping—seemed as important as color itself. The danger was that Bannard's method could be a little insistent, but in the most successful of the series, inventive color and exuberant drawing made considerations of how the pictures were made seem irrelevant.

The next series was still more complex, as Bannard layered a variety of paint applications, masking and reexcavating buried courses of color. As surfaces grew more elaborate, however, color became more restrained, so that the series is characterized by a range of greys, silvers and unnameable neutrals. As if in reaction to the density and complexity of these pictures, Bannard's most recent paintings are as direct and pared down as those of 20 years ago. They are once again transparent and made, apparently, by a single campaign of over-scaled sweeps and passes. The best seem to happen as we look, drawing, painting and structure having magically and instantaneously fused. Bannard has, for the moment, abandoned the high chroma that preoccupied him until a few years ago, but paradoxically, the subtle metallic greys, greens, sepias and the like of his 1987 pictures seem closer, in their clarity, to the pastels of his earlier palette than to the "off" shades of the thick, worked pictures that preceeded them. In the earlier, thickly painted canvases, neutral hues appeared to have been the result of many different colors' cancelling each other out; by contrast, Bannard's newer pictures have a limpid, monochrome transparency.

Of course, the monochrome, textured, all-over picture is not unique to Bannard, any more than paintings based on thinly applied and various colors were unique to him in the 1960s. He shares common attitudes with, for example, his older colleagues, Kenneth Noland and Jules Olitski, and his contemporary, Lawrence Poons. All take as their point of departure the assumption that a painting is a flat surface whose raw materials can be both expressive and communicative in themselves and the carriers of the painter's deepest feelings. In a period riddled with trend, dictated by fashion, Bannard takes his place among the uncompromising American artists who have remained faithful to these notions. In his more than 25 years of painting, Bannard's work has provided intense pleasure and, at the same time, it has been a rigorous examination of the implications of post-war abstraction. He has been described as a lyrical painter, but his lyricism depends on considerable toughness. The intelligence manifest in Bannard's writing is equally present in his art.

—Karen Wilkin

BARKER, Clive.
British. Born in Luton, Bedfordshire, 29 August 1940. Educated in Luton primary schools; studied at the Luton College of Technology and Art, 1951–56. Married the artist, Rose Bruen, in 1961; sons: Tad and Erasmus. Worked at Vauxhall Motors, Luton, 1960–61; as a pawnbroker, in London, 1962–64; began creating art objects, 1962; worked on series of 12 bronze studies of Francis Bacon, 1978; moved to Malvern, Worcestershire, 1978. Lecturer, Maidstone School of Art, Kent, 1965; Croydon School of Art, 1971. Recipient: Arts Council Purchase Prize, London, 1978; Elephant Trust Award, London, 1983. Address: 6 The Clock Tower, Heath Street, London NW3, England.

Individual Exhibitions:

1968 Robert Fraser Gallery, London
1969 Hanover Gallery, London
1974 Anthony d'Offay Gallery, London
1978 Felicity Samuel Gallery, London (with Francis Bacon)
1981 *Sculpture, Drawings and Prints,* Mappin Art Gallery, Sheffield (toured the U.K., 1981–82)
1983 Imperial War Museum, London
1985 Wolverhampton Art Gallery, Staffordshire
1987 National Portrait Gallery, London

Selected Group Exhibitions:

1962 *Young Contemporaries,* FBA Galleries, London
1968 *Young British Artists,* Museum of Modern Art, New York
1969 *Pop Art,* Hayward Gallery, London
1971 *Metamorphose de l'Objet,* Palais de Beaux-Arts, Brussels (toured Europe)
1975 *Bienal,* Sao Paulo
1977 *British Artists of the '60s,* Tate Gallery, London
1981 *British Sculpture in the 20th Century,* Whitechapel Art Gallery, London
1984 *British Pop Art,* Robert Fraser Gallery, London
1986 *Contrariwise Surrealism and Britain 1930–86,* Glynn Vivian Art Gallery, Swansea (travelled to Bath, Newcastle and Llandudno)
1987 *Pop Art—UK, USA,* Odakyu Grand Gallery, Tokyo (travelled to Osaka and Yokohama)

Collections:

Arts Council of Great Britain, London; Imperial War Museum, London; Victoria and Albert Museum, London; Tate Gallery, London; Kunsthalle, Mannheim; Smithsonian Institution, Washington, D.C.; National Portrait Gallery, London; Wolverhampton Art Gallery, Staffordshire; Ferens Art Gallery, Hull, Yorkshire.

Publications:

On BARKER: books—*Pop Art* by Christopher Finch, London 1968; *Pop Art Redefined* by John Russell, London 1969; *Image as Language* by Christopher Finch, London 1969; *Art in Britain 1969–1970* by Edward Lucie-Smith, London 1971; *Heads and Chariots,* exhibition catalogue, by Sir Roland Penrose, London 1974; *Clive Barker: Sculpture, Drawings and Prints,* exhibition catalogue, by George Melly, Sheffield, Yorkshire 1981; *Clive Barker: Portraits,* exhibition catalogue, with introduction by Norbert Lynton, London 1987.

Clive Barker initially made his name in the late 1960s with chromeplated sculptures of steel, bronze and brass both of objects from everyday life—including buckets, Coca Cola bottles, cowboy boots, a newspaper and even a set of false teeth—and of artefacts conceived as materializations from the work of famous painters such as Magritte, Picasso and Soutine. Of all these homages the most Pop in flavour were undoubtedly *Van Gogh's Chair* (chrome-plated bronze, 1966) and *Van Gogh's Sunflowers* (bronze, 1969), both of them devoted to images which had entered the public domain through an incessant reproduction by which the aura of the originals had been replaced by their status as icons of modern art. Barker's habit of coating his objects in a uniform shiny surface had the effect both of distancing them from reality and of creating for them a new identity as symbols of another level of experience. As Christopher Finch remarked in the catalogue to Barker's 1968 exhibition at the Robert Fraser Gallery, 'The banal is metamorphosed into the perfect . . . Their perfection is not an end in itself but acts as a foil for . . . an irony of affirmation. The perfection of an *objet d'art* is intrinsically prosaic since it contains no ambiguities . . . Barker's objects, by contrast, are lyrical in themselves—charged by the ambiguities that exist between banality and perfection.' The two *Art Boxes* that Barker produced in 1967—one in chrome-plated steel, the second in gold-plated brass—are quintessential Pop sculptures that bring together Barker's favoured theme of art about art with his innate feeling for objects. The irony of a sculptor producing a three-dimensional replica of the tools of a painter—rendering them passive and useless—is compounded by means of the simple tactic of casting actual brushes and tubes of paint. Although the human head has occupied Barker's attention at intervals since the early 1970s—notably in the threatening group of gas masks shown in 1974 and in a series of portraits of Francis Bacon, beginning with a life mask in 1969 and elaborated in a group of studies in 1978—it is from other art that he has continued to draw the most sustenance. *Venus Escargot* is his latest mutation of the Venus de Milo, that fragment of classical perfection which has exerted such a powerful hold over the collective imagination.

—Marco Livingstone

Clive Barker: *Venus Escargot*, 1987

BARRY, Robert.
American. Born in the Bronx, New York, 9 March 1936. Studied at Hunter College, New York, B.F.A., 1957, M.A. 1963. Agent: Sperone-Westwater-Fischer Inc., 142 Greene Street, New York, New York 10012. Address: c/o Hunter College, 695 Park Avenue, New York, New York 10021, U.S.A.

Individual Exhibitions:

1964 Westerly Gallery, New York
1969 Seth Siegelaub Gallery, Los Angeles
Galleria Sperone, Turin
Art and Project, Amsterdam
1970 Eugenia Butler Gallery, Los Angeles
Galleria Sperone, Turin
1971 Galerie Yvon Lambert, Paris
Galerie Paul Maenz, Cologne
Leo Castelli Gallery, New York
Galleria San Fedele, Milan
Art and Project, Amsterdam
Eugenia Butler Gallery, Los Angeles
1972 Galleria Toselli, Milan
Jack Wendler Gallery, London
Galerie M.T.L., Brussels
Tate Gallery, London
Galerie Paul Maenz, Cologne
Leo Castelli Gallery, New York
Art and Project, Amsterdam
1973 Galleria Sperone and Fischer, Rome
Galeria Foksal, Warsaw
Kabinett für Aktuelle Kunst, Bremerhaven, West Germany
1974 Galerie Yvon Lambert, Paris
Leo Castelli Gallery, New York
Jack Wendler Gallery, London
Galerie Paul Maenz, Cologne
Art and Project-M.T.L., Antwerp
Kunstmuseum, Lucerne
Stedelijk Museum, Amsterdam
1975 Gian Enzo Sperone Gallery, New York
Cusack Gallery, Houston
1976 Leo Castelli Gallery, New York
Galerie Rolf Preisig, Basle
Galerie Paul Maenz, Cologne
Galleria Enzo Sperone, Rome
Portrait: Part I, Julian Pretto Gallery, New York
Portrait: Part II, P.S. 1 Gallery, Long Island City, New York
1977 Stedelijk Van Abbemuseum, Eindhoven, Netherlands
Robert Self Gallery, London
Galerie Yvon Lambert, Paris
Galerie Rudiger Schöttle, Munich
1978 Museum Folkwang, Essen
Galerie M.T.L., Brussels
Leo Castelli Gallery, New York
Museum of Conceptual Art, San Francisco
University of Colorado, Boulder
1979 Leo Castelli Gallery, New York
Galleria François Lambert, Milan
Galerie Rolf Preisig, Basle
Galerie Paul Maenz, Cologne
1980 Joslyn Art Museum, Omaha, Nebraska
1987 Glynn Vivian Art Gallery, Swansea, Wales
Camarthen Museum, Abergwili, Wales
Oriel Gallery, Cardiff, Wales
Galleria Christian Stein, Turin (with Lawrence Weiner)
1988 Galerie Schiessel, Munich

Selected Group Exhibitions:

1968 *8 New Artists*, Hudson River Museum, New York
1966 *Systematic Painting*, Guggenheim Museum, New York
1969 *Barry/Huebler/Kosuth/Weiner*, Seth Siegelaub Gallery, New York
When Attitudes Become Form, Stedelijk Museum, Amsterdam (travelled to the Museum Folkwang, Essen)
1970 *Conceptual Art, Arte Povera, Land Art*, Galleria Civica d'Arte Moderna, Turin
Nirvana, Kyoto Municipal Museum of Fine Arts, Japan
1971 *Artist, Theory and Work*, Kunsthalle, Nuremberg, West Germany
1973 *Documenta 5*, Kassel, West Germany
1974 *Concept Art*, Kunstverein, Braunschweig, West Germany
1980 *Music, Sound, Language, Theater: John Cage, Tom Marioni, Robert Barry, Joan Jonas*, Cowell College, University of California at Santa Cruz (toured the United States)

Publications:

By BARRY: books-*An Untitled Book*, Turin 1970; *One Billion Dots*, Turin 1971; *30 Pieces as of 14 June 1971*, Cologne 1971; *Two Pieces*, Turin 1972; *It Is . . . It Isn't . . .* , Paris 1972; *Changes and Disappearences*, portfolio of 5 etchings, 1979; articles—interview, with Arthur Rose, in *Arts Magazine* (New York), February 1969; interview, with Achille Bonito Oliva, in *Domus* (Milan), August 1973; film—*Scenes 1967*, New York 1967.

On BARRY: books—*Systematic Painting*, exhibition catalogue, with text by Lawrence Alloway, New York 1966; *Arte Povera* by Germano Celant, Milan, 1969; *Conceptual Art* by Ursula Meyes, New York 1972; *6 Years: The De-Materialization of the Art Object from 1966 to 1972* by Lucy R. Lippard, New York 1973; *Idea Art* by Gregory Battcock, New York 1973; *Robert Barry*, exhibition catalogue, with text by Jean-Christophe Ammann, Lucerne 1974; *Robert Barry*, exhibition catalogue, Eindhoven, Netherlands 1977; *Robert Barry*, exhibition pamphlet, with text by Holliday T. Day, Omaha, Nebraska 1980; *Music, Sound, Language, Theater: John Cage, Tom Marioni, Robert Barry, Joan Jonas*, exhibition catalogue, edited by Robin White, with essays by Kathan Browne and others, Oakland, California 1980; articles—"Systematic Painting" by Robert Pincus-Witten in *Artforum* (New York), November 1966; "Painting Is Obsolete" by Gregory Battcock in *New York Free Press*, January 1969; "Impossible Art" by David Shirey in *Art in America* (New York), May/June 1969; "Art after Philosophy" by Joseph Kosuth in *Studio International* (London), November/December 1969; "Concept Art" by Klaus Honnef in *Kunst* (Mainz, West Germany), 1970; "Book as Artwork" by Germano Celant in *Data 1*, Milan 1971.

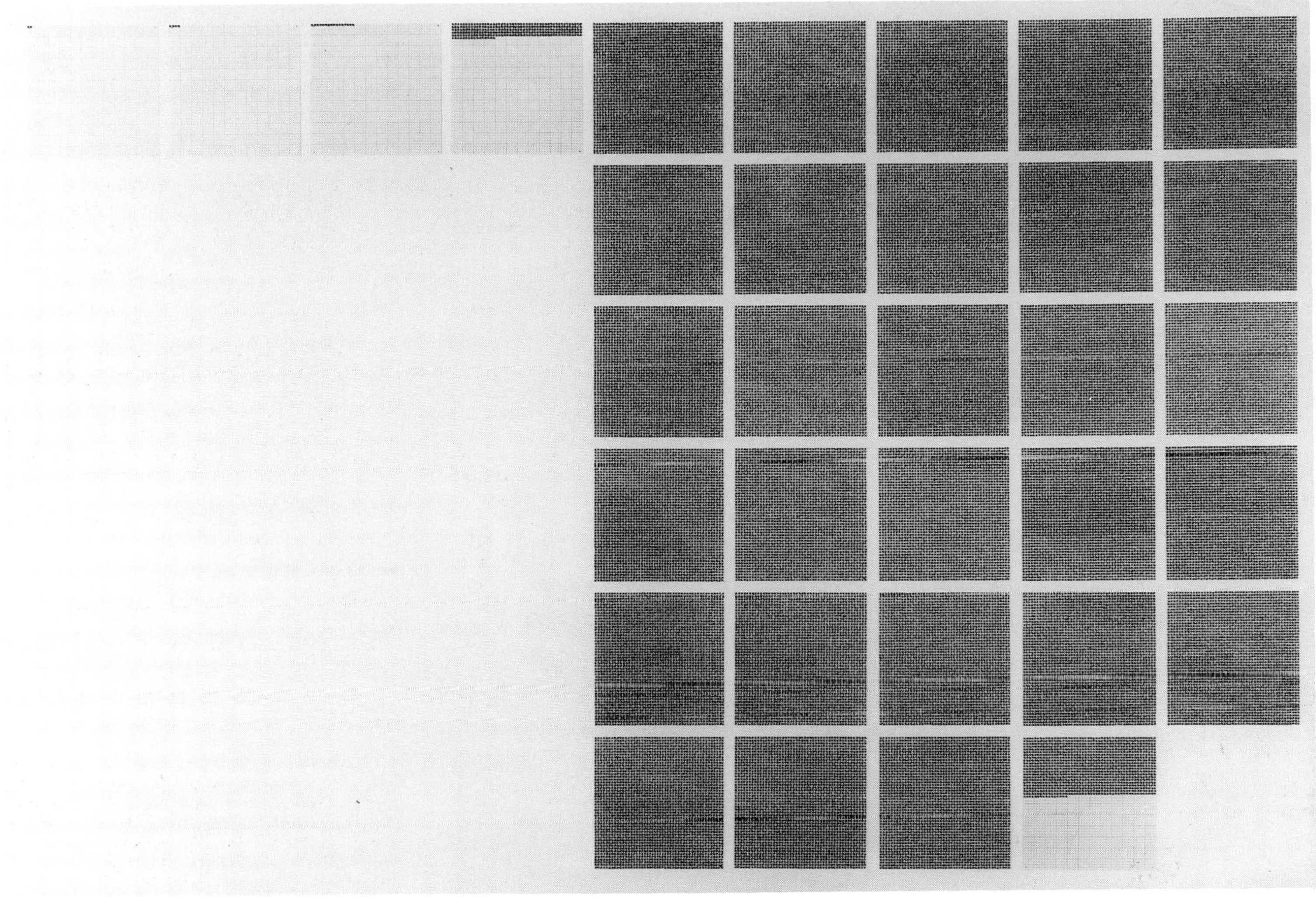

Jennifer Bartlett: *Squaring—2/4/16/256/65,536*, 1974

BARTLETT, Jennifer (Losch).
American. Born in Long Beach, California, 14 March 1941. Educated at Mills College, Oakland, California, 1961–63, B.A. 1963; Yale School of Art and Architecture, New Haven, Connecticut, with Jack Tworkov, James Rosenquist, Al Held and Jim Dine, 1963–65, B.F.S. 1964, M.F.A. 1965. Instructor, University of Connecticut, Storrs, 1968–72; Visiting Artist, Art Institute of Chicago, 1962. Instructor in Painting, School of Visual Arts, New York, 1972–77. Recipient: Creative Artist Public Services Fellowship, 1974; Harris Prize, Art Institute of Chicago, 1976; Lucas Visiting Lecture Award, Carleton College, Northfield, Minneapolis, 1979; Creative Arts Award, Brandeis University, Waltham, Massachusetts, 1983; American Institute of Arts and Letters Award, New York, 1983; Harris Prize and M. V. Konstamm Award, Art Institute of Chicago, 1986; American Institute of Architects Award, New York, 1986. Agent: Paula Cooper Gallery, New York. Address: c/o Paula Cooper Gallery, 155 Wooster Street, New York, New York 10012, U.S.A.

Individual Exhibitions:

1963 Mills College, Oakland, California
1970 119 Spring Street Gallery, New York
1972 Reese Palley Gallery, New York
1973 Jacob's Ladder, Washington D.C. (with Jack Tworkov)
1974 Paula Cooper Gallery, New York
Saman Galleria, Genoa
1975 John Doyle Gallery, Chicago
Garage, London (with Joel Shapiro)
1976 Paula Cooper Gallery, New York
Dartmouth College, Hanover, New Hampshire
Contemporary Art Center, Cincinnati, Ohio
1977 Wadsworth Atheneum, Hartford, Connecticut
Paula Cooper Gallery, New York
1978 Saman Galleria, Genoa
University of California at Irvine
San Francisco Museum of Modern Art
Hansen-Fuller Gallery, San Francisco
Art Museum of South Texas, Corpus Christi
Baltimore Art Museum
1979 Margo Leavin Gallery, Los Angeles
The Clocktower, New York
University of Akron, Ohio
Carleton College, Northfield, Minnesota
Heath Gallery, Atlanta
Paula Cooper Gallery, New York
1980 Galerie Mukai, Tokyo
Akron Art Institute, Ohio
Hallwall, Buffalo, New York
Albright-Knox Art Gallery, Buffalo, New York
1981 Paula Cooper Gallery, New York
Margo Leavin Gallery, Los Angeles
1982 Joslyn Art Museum, Omaha
Paula Cooper Gallery, New York
Tate Gallery, London
McIntosh/Drysdale Gallery, Houston
1983 Margo Leavin Gallery, Los Angeles
Gloria Luria Gallery, Harbor Islands, Florida
Heath Gallery, Atlanta, Georgia
Paula Cooper Gallery, New York
1984 Brandeis University, Waltham, Massachusetts
Long Beach Museum of Art, California
University of California, Berkeley
1985 Paula Cooper Gallery, New York
Lowe Art Museum, Coral Gables, Florida
Knight Gallery, Charlotte, North Carolina
Carpenter + Hochman Gallery, Dallas
Hodges Taylor Gallery, Charlotte, North Carolina
Walker Art Center, Minneapolis (travelled to Kansas City, Missouri; Brooklyn, New York; La Jolla, California; Pittsburgh)
1986 Cleveland Museum of Art, Ohio
Greg Kucera Gallery, Seattle, Washington
1987 Harvard Graduate School of Design, Cambridge, Massachusetts
Paula Cooper Gallery, New York

Selected Group Exhibitions:

1975 *37th Corcoran Biennial*, Corcoran Gallery, Washington, D.C.
1976 *The Liberation: 14 American Artists*, Aarhus Museum of Art, Denmark (toured Europe)
1977 *Documenta 6*, Kassel, West Germany
1978 *New Image Painting*, Whitney Museum, New York
1979 *Corner*, Hayden Gallery, Massachusetts Institute of Technology, Cambridge
1980 *Urban Encounters*, Institute of Contemporary Art, University of Pennsylvania, Philadelphia
Printed Art: A View of 2 Decades, Museum of Modern Art, New York
1981 *Biennial Exhibition*, Whitney Museum, New York
1983 *Back to the U.S.A.*, Rheinisches Landesmuseum, Bonn (travelled to Lucerne and Stuttgart)
1987 *The Monumental Image*, Sonoma State University, Rohnert Park, California (toured the United States)

Collections:

Museum of Modern Art, New York; Metropolitan Museum of Art, New York; Whitney Museum, New York; Albright-Knox Gallery, Buffalo, New York; Yale University Art Gal-

lery, New Haven, Connecticut; Philadelphia Museum of Art; Allen Memorial Art Museum, Oberlin, Ohio; Walker Art Center, Minneapolis; Museum of Fine Arts, Dallas.

Publications:

By BARTLETT: books—*Cleopatra I-IV,* poems, New York 1971; *Autobiography,* New York 1973; *History of the Universe* New York 1973; texts in *The World: Autobiography Issue,* edited by Lewis Warsh, New York 1973.

On BARTLETT: books—*Painting and Sculpture Today,* exhibition catalogue, Indianapolis 1972; *Arts Without Limits,* exhibition catalogue, by Ira Licht, New York 1972; *Painting: New Options,* exhibition catalogue, Minneapolis 1972; *Art in Evolution,* exhibition catalogue, by Anthony Sorce, New York 1973; *Jennifer Bartlett and Jack Tworkov,* exhibition catalogue, Washington, D.C. 1973; *34th Biennial of Contemporary American Painting,* exhibition catalogue, Paris 1975; *72nd American Exhibition,* exhibition catalogue, by Anne Rorimer, Chicago 1976; *New Work/New York,* exhibition catalouge, Los Angeles 1976; *Matrix* by Andrea Miller Keller, Hartford, Connecticut 1977; *Painting '75, '76, '77,* exhibition catalogue, New York 1977; *Documenta 6,* exhibition catalogue, Kassel, West Germany 1977; *Critics' Choice,* exhibition catalogue, New York 1977; *New Image Painting,* exhibition catalogue, New York 1978; *New York Now,* exhibition catalogue, Phoenix, Arizona 1979; *Corners,* exhibition catalogue, Cambridge, Massachusetts 1979; *Printed Art: A View of 2 Decades,* exhibition catalogue by Riva Castleman, New York 1980; *Extensions: Jennifer Bartlett/Lynda Benglis/Robert Longo/Judy Pfaff,* exhibition catalogue, Houston 1980; *Aspects of the 70's: Painterly Abstractions,* exhibition catalogue, by Marilyn Friedman Hoffman, Brockton, Massachusetts 1980; *Drawings: The Pluralist Decade,* exhibition catalogue, with an introduction by Janet Kardon, Philadelphia 1980; *Jennifer Bartlett: Selected Works,* exhibition catalogue, Buffalo, New York 1980; *20 Artists: Yale School of Art 1950–1970,* exhibition catalogue, New York 1981; articles—"Jennifer Bartlett" by Sally Webster in the *Feminist Art Journal* (Brooklyn, New York), Vol. 5, no. 3, 1976; "Jennifer Bartlett: Artist Who Keeps Pushing" by Caroline Drewes in the *San Francisco Examiner,* 24 May 1978; "The Abstract Image" by Roberta Smith in *Art in America* (New York), March/April 1979; "Les nouvelle images de la peinture Americaine" by Thomas B. Hess in *Art Press International* (Paris), May 1979; "Jennifer Bartlett" by Barbara Schreiber in *Atlanta Art Workers' Coalition,* January/February 1980; "Young Artists New Yorkers Are Talking About" by Lee Wohlfett in *Town and Country* (London), September 1980; "Adding Up Jennifer Bartlett" by Diane Bertolo in the *Buffalo Evening News,* 30 Novmeber 1980; "Bartlett's Pairs" by Kim Levin in the *Village Voice* (New York), 4 February 1981; "She's Got Style" by Jeff Perone in *Arts Magazine* (New York), April 1981.

"The series," Jennifer Bartlett has said, "permits a range of possibilities; it reminds us that things can change." Since 1968, the series has constituted the central theme of Barlett's work. "Rhapsody" (1975–76), a series of 987 gridded, one-foot square enameled plates, represents a monumental exploration of serial structure. Like most of the artist's work, "Rhapsody" juxtaposes the raw and the cooked, examining the way the world is filtered through the human mind and is encoded into cultural conventions or sign systems. The work offers a succinct discourse on the strategies of representation: a sophisticated "botanical" drawing of a tree is matched with a naive rendering of the same subject, or a simple geometric form (a square or a triangle) is contrasted by a signifying one (a house). On another level, Bartlett locates the work historically, advancing a subtle commentary on the paradoxical situation of modernism (e.g. the integrity of abstraction over decoration). In the end, "Rhapsody" is about transition and stasis, continuity and discontinuity suspended in a matrix of resonant formal and intellectual values.

Mapped onto a field of facts, images, and associations, Bartlett's serial structure is often analogous to conventional systems for organizing the world. A "pointillist" map of the United States (from "Series XIV", 1971–72) is further subdivided into 15 parts, establishing a parallel relationship between the formal conditions of Bartlett's serial projection and cartographic apportionment based on real political boundaries. The artist's recurrent use of points, dot, or dashes to compose her imagery creates a situation in which each unit serves as a node within a network of scale systems. Bartlett's fascination with the series extends even to her large-scale public work "Swimmers Atlanta" (1979), a 9-painting series commissioned by the General Services Administration for the lobby of a federal court building in Georgia's capital city. While the obsessive interest in serial form has subsided in Bartlett's most recent work, the seemingly arbitrary scale relationships of "Up the Creek" and "To the Island" (1981–82), two 10-part multimedia works, appear to be governed by a personal, internal logic. Concentrating on problems of condition and place (the syntax of the present work hinges on locative prepositions), these paintings are neither fully autonomous nor serial; in their indecisiveness, they fail to obtain a convincing balance.

The historian Michel Foucault, in his brilliant *The Archaeology of Knowledge,* has explored the shift in historical methodologies from a continuous to a discontinuous view of events and monuments. As attention has turned away from "vast unities like 'periods' or 'centuries' to the phenomena . . . of discontinuity," Foucault argues that an internal organizing structure must come into play to make "relevant" an otherwise ungrouped mass of elements: "The problem now is to constitute series," he writes, "to define elements proper to each series, to fix its boundaries, to reveal its own specific type of relations, to formulate its laws, and beyond this, to describe the relations between different series." Postmodernism has produced a similar challenge for the artist at a time when the continuities of modernist thought have yielded to a more pluralistic attitude. In her most resolute exploration of the series, Jennifer Bartlett has clearly understood the dynamics of this challenge.

—Maurice Berger

BARUCHELLO, Gianfranco.

Italian. Born in Livorno, 29 August 1924. Studied in Rome. Married to Agnese Naldoni; daughter: Paolina. Lives and works in Rome. Agent: Galleria Schwarz, Via Gesu 17, 20121 Milan. Address: Via di Santa Cornelia, km. 6,5 (prima porta), Rome, Italy.

Individual Exhibitions:

1963 Galleria La Tartaruga, Rome
1964 Cordier and Ekstrom Gallery, New York
1965 Galleria Schwarz, Milan
1966 Galleria Il Punto, Turin
Cordier and Ekstrom Gallery, New York
IOIOMISS, Galleria Schwarz, Milan
1967 Palais des Beaux-Arts, Brussels
Galerie Yvon Lambert, Paris
1968 Galleria Schwarz, Milan
Galleria Roma, Chicago
1969 Studio Condotti 85, Rome
Galerie Schmela, Dusseldorf
Galerie Lauter, Mannheim
1970 Galleria Schwarz, Milan
1971 Galerie Buchholz, Munich
1972 Studio Condotti 85, Rome
Centro d'Arte Europa, Naples
Galleria La Bertesca, Genoa
1973 Galleria L'Uomo e L'Arte, Milan
Galerie Der Spiegel, Cologne
Galerie Craven, Paris
1975 Galleria Schwarx, Milan
Galleria L'Arcipelago, Turin
Galleria Etrusculudens, Rome
1976 Italian Pavilion, at the *Biennale,* Venice
Galleria Valsecchi, Milan
Galerie Fred Lansenberg, Brussels
Galerie Gilbert Delorme, Paris
1977 Galleria Il Mercato del Sale, Milan
Galleria Margherita, Rome
Galerie Arta, Geneva
Galerie Bama, Paris
1981 Galleria Milano, Milan
1983 Galerie Reckermann, Cologne
1987 Galleria Milano, Milan

Selected Group Exhibitions:

1962 *Collage et Objet,* Galerie du Cercle, Paris
1963 *4th Biennale,* San Marino (and *6th Biennale,* 1967)
1966 *European Drawings,* Guggenheim Museum, New York
1967 *Pictures to Be Read, Poetry to Be Seen,* Museum of Contemporary Art, Chicago
1968 *Le Collage,* Kunstverein, Frankfurt (travelled to the Kunstgewerbemuseum, Zurich)
1969 *Al di la della Pittura,* Galleria Pilota, Modena, Italy
1970 *Il Cocodrillo,* Teatro dell'Opera, Rome (deoors for V. Bucchi opera)
1975 *Baruchello/Erro/Fahlstrom/Liebig,* Musée d'Art Moderne de la Ville, Paris
Let's Mix All Feelings Together, Städtische Galerie im Lenbachhaus, Munich (travelled to Frankfurt and Paris)
1978 *La Traccia del Racconto,* Villa Comunal Ormond, Sanremo, Italy

Collections:

Museum of Modern Art, New York; Guggenheim Museum, New York.

Publications:

By BARUCHELLO: books—*Mi Vione in Mente,* Milan 1966; *Enonce Impossible,* Milan 1967; *In Cold Fact,* Milan 1968; *La Quindices,* Rome 1968; *Avventure nell'Armadio di Plexiglass,* Milan 1968; *Fragments of a Possible Apocalypse,* with Henry Martin, Milan 1978; *Agricola Cornelia S.P.A. 1973- 81,* Milan 1981; *Faraone dei Sentimenti,* Milan 1987; films and videos—*La Verifica Incerta,* with Alberto Grifi, 1964; *Costretto a Scomparire,* 1968; *Perforce,* 1968; *Complete di Colpa,* 1968; *Norme per gli Olocausti,* 1969; *Per una Giornata de Malumore Nazionale,* 1969; *Non Accaduto,* 1969; *Limbosigne,* 1969; *A Little More Paranoid,* 1969; *I Giorni di Lun,* 1969; *In Quarantasette Secondi,* 1969; *La de'Gringolade,* 1970; *Pietro Bessone en Renato Ghittoni, due gemme della Lotta di Liberazione,* 1970; *LAP,* 1971; *Deep Sea Show,* 1971; *Beaufort no. 2,* 1971.

On BARUCHELLO: books—*Gianfranco Baruchello,* exhibition catalogue, with text by Giorgio Manganelli, Milan 1965; *Gianfranco Baruchello: IOIOMISS,* exhibition catalogue, Milan 1966; *Gian Franco Baruchello,* exhibition catalogue, with text by Italo Calvino, New York 1966; *Baruchello,* exhibition catalogue, with interview by Arturo Schwarz, Milan 1968; *Introduzione a Baruchello* by Tomasso Trini, Milan 1975; *Let's Mix All Feelings Together,* exhibition catalogue, Munich 1975; *La Traccia del Racconto,* exhibition catalogue, Sanremo, Italy 1978.

Between 1959 and 1963 Gianfranco Baruchello's investigations into art moved through a series of widely differing but interconnected problems and experiences. His first works were a kind of super-cold abstract expressionism; these works were abandoned in favor of found objects that seem a little reminiscent of Dada; the found objects turned into assemblages or constructions and also furnished images for drawings that have the flavor of a harsh and expressive surrealism. These assemblages then simplified themselves and entered into a kind of New Realism while the drawings turned into paintings full of an internal debate about the relative weight and importance of paint quality and personally significant imagery. The decision went clearly, after not too long, to personally significant imagery, and Baruchello began to work on large squares of aluminum sheet metal, first primed white and then sprinkled with miniscule drawings of schematic trees, imaginary monsters, non-existent machines, arrows, words, sentences and paragraphs written in various languages, tiny representations of

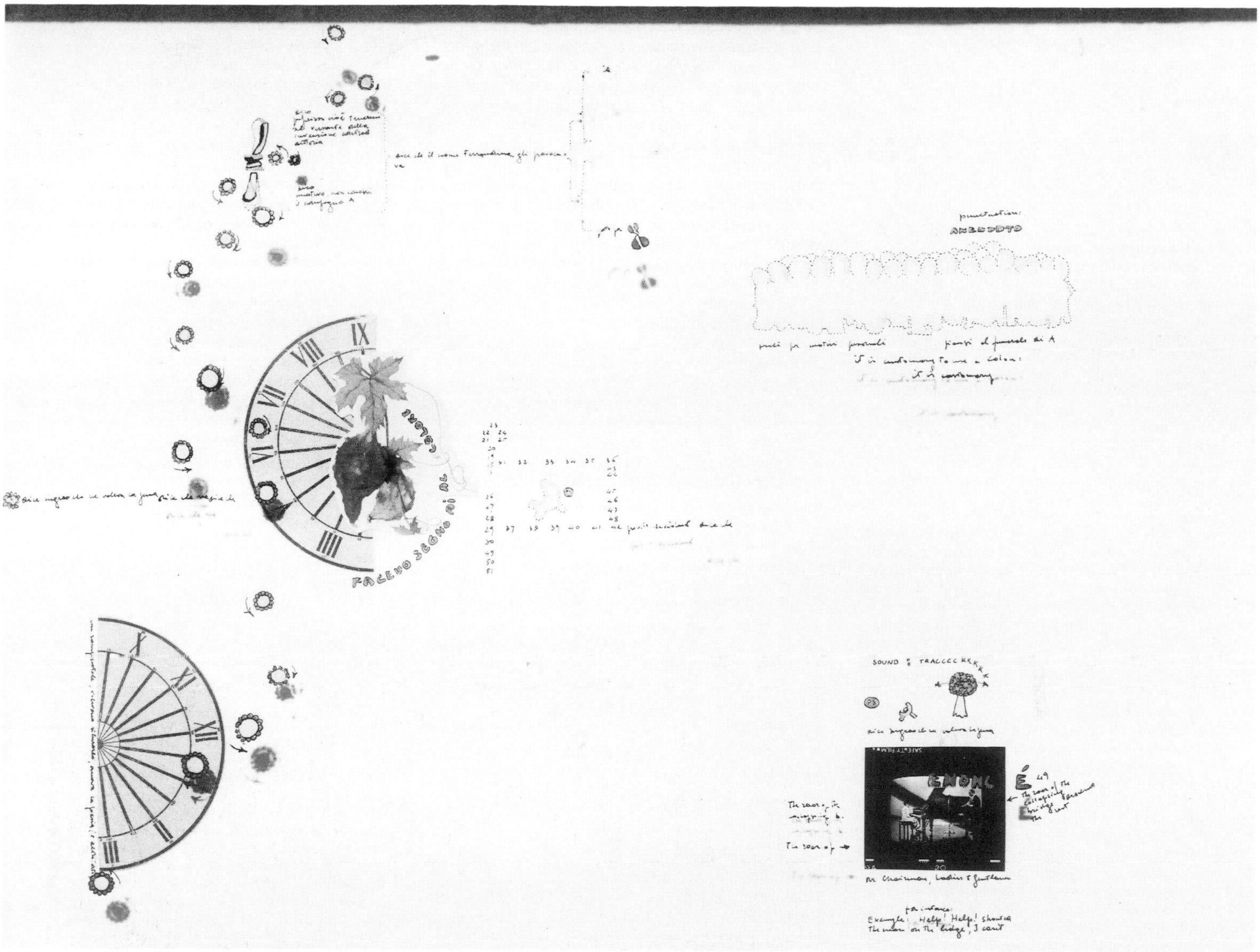

Gianfranco Baruchello: ***The Roar of the Collapsing Bridge Drowned the Rest*****, 1967**

the various organs of the body, patches of hair, diagrams, articles of clothing, splotches of numbers, a veritable convention of erudite references to a host of personal mysteries at the point where they encounter public and political confusions.

And just as Baruchello's paintings have not always been what they are today, they are also a part of a vaster series of aesthetic activities that include objects, films, theater pieces, books, video tapes, stage sets, postal happenings, sound tracks, sculptures, narrative series of drawings, assemblages of odds and ends and cardboard cut-outs in plexiglass cases and wooden boxes, and he has also reported on the experience of running a farm as though it were a work of art. The relationship between the paintings and these other activities is a fairly curious relationship: the themes of these other activities frequently find their source in the paintings and the "results" of these activities are usually reintroduced into the paintings.

Painting for Baruchello is the Queen of the Sciences just as theology was the Queen of the Sciences for the Scholastics of the Middle Ages: his paintings always seem to want to do more than what any rigorously materialistic definition of the act of painting would allow him to do, and his excursions into other media help him to define more clearly the impossible tasks to which his paintings must be put. His paintings, for Baruchello, are what all of reality must be reduced to; they're the crucible in which reality, as Phoenix, is to be experimentally incinerated and then resurrected as myth. The intention is to deal with all of reality in a way that will make all of reality coherent, self-reflexive, and emotionally meaningful. Baruchello's technique is to work by themes, each of which, as it exhausts itself, is responsible for spawning another. It's as though he were trying to discover the myth that's the source of all myth, and he is always interrogating the facts of his daily experience to see what sort of a place they can have within it.

—Henry Martin

BASELITZ, Georg.

German. Born Georg Dern in Deutschbaselitz, Saxony, now East Germany, 23 January 1938; adopted name "Baselitz" in 1956. Educated at Volksschule and Gymnasium, Kamenz, until 1955; studied art at the Kunstakademie, East Berlin, 1956–57; under Hann Trier, Akademie der Künste, West Berlin, 1957–64. Married Elke Kretzschmar in 1962; sons: Daniel and Anton. Painter, in West Berlin, 1964–66, in Osthofen bei Worms, 1966–70, in Forst, 1970–73, in Mussbach, 1973–75, in Derneburg, Lower Saxony, since 1975; associated with artist Ralf Winckler (A. R. Penck), West Berlin, 1961; published "Pandemonium" manifestos, with Eugen Schönebeck, West Berlin, 1961, 1962. Instructor, 1977–78, and Professor, 1978–83, Staatliche Akademie der bildenden Kunste, Karlsruhe; Professor, Hochschule der Kunste, West Berlin, since 1983. Recipient: Villa Romana Scholarship, Florence 1965; Kulturpreis der Deutsche Industrie, 1968; Kaiserring-Prize, City of Goslar, 1986; Kunstpreis der Nord/LB, Hannover, 1986. Agents: Galerie Neuendorf, Feldstrasse, Hochhaus 1, Hamburg; Galerie Michael Werner, Friesenstrasse 50, Cologne. Address: Schloss Derneburg, 3201 Holle bei Hildesheim, West Germany.

Individual Exhibitions:

1961	*Pandemomnium,* Schaperstrasse 22/Fasanenplatz, West Berlin (with Eugene Schönebeck)
1963	Galerie Werner und Katz, West Berlin
1964	Greie Galerie, West Berlin
	Galerie Werner, West Berlin
1965	Galerie Friedrich + Dahlem, Munich
	Galerie Krohn, Badenweiler, West Germany
	Galerie Werner, West Berlin
1966	Galerie Springer, West Berlin
1967	Galerie Obere Zaune, Zurich
	Galerie Beck, Erlangen, West Germany
1969	Galerie Beck, Erlangen, West Germany
1970	*Zeichnungen,* Kunstmuseum, Basle
	Galerie Berner, Stuttgart
	Franz Dahlem Galeriehaus, Cologne
	Tekeningen en Schilderijen, Wide White Space Gallery, Antwerp
1971	Galerie Rothe, Heidelberg
	Galerie Borgmann, Cologne
	Galerie Tobies & Silex, Cologne
1972	Galerie Grafikmeyer, Karlsruhe
	Gemalde und Zeichnungen, Kunsthalle, Mannheim
	Kunstverein, Hamburg

Staatliche Graphische Sammlung, Munich
Galerie Loehr, Frankfurt
Galerie im Goethe-Institut, Amsterdam
Galerie Rudolf Zwirner, Cologne
1973 *Bilder, Objekte, Filme, Konzepte,* Galerie Heiner Freidrich, Munich
Galerie Loehr, Frankfurt
Galerie Grunangergasse, Vienna
Ein neuer Typ, Galerie Neuendorf, Hamburg
1974 Galerie Heiner Friedrich, Cologne
Radierungen 1963–1974/Holzschnitte 1966–1967, Städtisches Museum Schloss Morsbroich, Leverkusen, West Germany
Städtisches Galerie Altes Theater, Ravensburg, West Germany
1975 Galerie Heiner Friedrich, Munich
Galerie Michael Werner, Cologne
Galerie Loehr, Frankfurt
1976 Staatsgalerie Moderner Kunst, Munich
Malerei, Handzeichnungen, Druckgraphik, Kunsthalle, Berne
Galerie Heiner Friedrich, Cologne
Kunsthalle, Cologne
1977 Galerie Heiner Friedrich, Cologne
Galerie Heiner Friedrich, Munich
1978 Galerie Helen van der Meij, Amsterdam
Galerie Heiner Friedrich, Cologne
1979 Galerie Gillespie/De Laage, Paris
Bilder 1977–78, Stedelijk van Abbenuseum, Eindhoven, Netherlands
32 Linolschnitte aus den Jahren 1976 bis 1979, Josef-Haubrich-Kunsthalle, Cologne
Tekeningen/Zeichnungen, Groninger Museum, Groningen, Netherlands
1980 Galerie Heiner Friedrich, Cologne
Galerie Gillespie/De Laage, Paris,
Galerie Rudolf Springer, West Berlin
Whitechapel Art Gallery, London (with Max Backmann)
Centre d'Arts Plastiques Contemporains, Bordeaux (with A. R. Penck and Joseph Beuys)
1981 Kastrupgardsamlingen, Kastrup, Denmark
Galerie Michael Werner, Cologne
Stedelijk van Abbemuseum, Eindhoven, Netherlands
Kunsthalle, Dusseldorf (with Gerhard Richter)
Kunstverein, Braunschweig, West Germany
Das Strassenbild, Stedelijk Museum, Amsterdam
Galerie Annemarie Verna, Zurich
Galerie Fred Jahn, Munich
Xavier Fourcade Inc., New York
1982 *Zeichnungen,* Galerie Michael Werner, Cologne
Sonnabend Gallery, New York
Waddington Galleries, London
Galerie Fred Jahn, Munich
Galerie Rudolf Zwirner, Cologne
Anthony D'Offay, London
Galerie Helen van der Meij, Amsterdam
Galerie Springer, West Berlin
Xavier Fourcade Inc., New York
Young Hoffman Gallery, Chicago
Galerie Nachst St. Stephan, Vienna
Kunstverein, Gottingen, West Germany
1983 Galerie Michael Werner, Cologne
CAPC Musee d'Art Contemporain, Bordeaux, France
Galerie Albert Baronian, Brussels
Galerie Springer, West Berlin
Galerie am Markt, Schwabisch Hall, West Germany
Galerie Gillespie-Laage-Salomon, Paris
Xavier Fourcade Inc., New York
Sonnabend Gallery, New York
Galerie Neuendorf, Hamburg (twice)
Akron Art Museum, Ohio (with Julian Schnabel)
Whitechapel Art Gallery, London
Galerie Folker Skulima, West Berlin
Galerie Fred Jahn, Munich
Los Angeles County Museum of Art
1984 Van Abbemuseum, Eindhoven, Netherlands (drawings retrospective)
University of California, Berkeley
Kunstmuseum, Basel
Kunsthalle, Basel
Mary Boone/Michael Werner Gallery, New York
Neue Pinakothek, Munich (graphics retrospective)
Galerie Borgmann, Cologne
Stadtische Kunstmuseum, Bonn
Mussee d'Art et d'Histoire, Geneva
Kunstverein, Freiburg, West Germany
Galerie Meyer-Ellinger, Frankfurt
Kunsthalle, Nuremberg, West Germany
Artotheque, Lyon, France
Waddington Galleries, London
Vancouver Art Gallery, British Columbia
Deweer Art Gallery, Zwevegem-Otegem, Belgium
Galerie Michael Werner, Cologne
1985 Galerie Fred Jahn, Munich
Stadtisches Museum Simeonstift, Trier, West Germany
DAAD-Galerie, West Berlin
Kunstverein, Hannover
Galerie Gillespie-Laage-Salomon, Paris
Bibliotheque Nationale, Paris (print and sculpture retrospective)
Galerie Collection d'Art, Amsterdam
Galerie-Lager Rudolf Zwirner, Cologne
Galerie Joachim Becker, Cannes, France
Anthony d'Offay, London
Haus am Waldsee, West Berlin
Kunsthalle, Bielefeld, West Germany
Galerie Thomas Borgmann, Cologne
Ernst Barlach Haus, Hamburg
Alpha Gallery, Boston
Kunstverein, Oldenburg, West Germany
1986 Kunstmuseum, Winterthur, Switzerland
Mary Boone/Michael Werner Gallery, New York
Galerie Beyeler, Basel
Muzej Savremene Umetnosti, Belgrade
Obalne Galerije, Piran, Yugoslavia
Galerija Loza, Koper, Yugoslavia
Cankarjev Dom, Liubliana, Yugoslavia
Galerija Grada, Zagreb, Yugoslavia
Galerija Suvremene Umjetnosti, Zagreb, Yugoslavia
Galerie Beuamont, Luxembourg
Galerie Thaddaeus Ropac, Salzburg, Austria
Galerie Chobot, Vienna
Sonja Henie/Nils Onstads Stifelser, Oslo
Monchehaus Museum fur moderne Kunst, Goslar, West Germany
Wiener Secession, Vienna
Galerie Heike Curtze, Vienna
Galerie Springer, West Berlin
1987 Maximilian Verlag/Sabine Knust, Munich
Meine kleine Galerie, Hildesheim, West Germany
Galleria Christian Stein, Milan
Galerie Collection d'Art, Amsterdam
Kestner-Gesellschaft, Hannover
Galerie Buchmann, Basel
Museum Ludwig, Cologne
Galerie Neuendorf, Frankfurt
Anthony D'Offay Gallery, London

Georg Baselitz: *Untitled,* 1967 Courtesy Anthony D'Offay Gallery, London

Selected Group Exhibitions:

1968 *14 x 14*, Kunsthalle, Baden-Baden, West Germany
1969 *Kunst und Kritik*, Städtisches Museum, Wiesbaden, West Germany
1971 *Zeichen und Farbe*, Staatsgalerie, Stuttgart
1972 *Documenta 5*, Kassel, West Germany (and *Documenta 7*, 1982)
1973 *Prospekt '73*, Städtische Kunsthalle, Dusseldorf
1975 *Bienal*, Sao Paulo
1980 *Biennale*, Venice
1981 *A New Spirit in Painting*, Royal Academy of Art, London
1985 *The European Iceberg*, Art Gallery of Ontario, Toronto
1987 *Berlinart 1961–87*, Museum of Modern Art, New York (travelled to San Francisco Museum of Modern Art)

Collections:

Kunsthalle, Hamburg; Städtisches Museum, Braunschweig, West Germany; Hessisches Landesmuseum, Darmstadt; Sammlung Ludwig, Cologne; Stedelijk Museum, Amsterdam; Museum Boymans-van Beuningen, Rotterdam; Centre Georges Pompidou, Paris.

Publications:

By BASELITZ: books and pamphlets—*Pandemonium: First Manifesto*, with Eugen Schönebeck, West Berlin 1961; *Pandemonium: Second Manifesto*, with Eugen Schönebeck, West Berlin 1962; *Warum das Bild 'Die grossen Freunde' ein gutes Bild ist*, manifesto and poster, West Berlin 1966; *Comte de Lautreamont: Die Gesange des Maldoror*, gouache illustrations, Munich 1976; articles—"Liber Herr W." in *Die Schastrommel* (Berlin/Bolzano), March 1972; "Vier Wande und Oberlicht" in *Kunstforum International* (Mainz), no. 4, 1979; "George Baselitz", special monograph issue of *Lo Spazio Umano* (Milan), January/March 1983.

On BASELITZ: books—*Baselitz*, exhibition catalogue, with text by Martin G. Butler, Herbert Read and Edouard Roditi, West Berlin 1963; *Baselitz: Zeichnungen*, exhibition catalogue, with text by Dieter Koepplin, Antwerp 1970; *Georg Baselitz: Zeichnungen und Radierungen*, exhibition catalogue, with text by Herbert Poe, Munich 1972; *George Baselitz: Gemalde und Zeichnungen*, exhibition catalogue, with text by Heinz Fuchs, Mannheim 1972; *George Baselitz: Ein neuer Typ*, exhibition catalogue, with text by Günther Gercken, Hamburg 1973; *Bilder, Objekte, Filme, Konzepte*, exhibition catalogue, Munich 1973; *Georg Baselitz: Radierungen 1963–1974/Holzschnitte 1966–1967*, exhibition catalogue, with text by Rolf Wedewer, Fred Jahn and Mircea Eliade, Leverkusen, West Germany 1974; *13. Bienal de Sao Paulo: George Baselitz*, exhibition catalogue with text by Evelyh Weiss, Cologne 1975; *Baselitz: Malerei, Handzeichnungen, Druckgraphik*, exhibition catalogue, with text by Theo Kneubuhler, Berne 1976; *Georg Berlitz*, exhibition catalogue, with text by Carla Schulz-Hoffman, Günther Gercken and Johannes Gachnang, Munich 1976; *Georg Baselitz: Bilder 1977–78*, exhibition catalogue, with text by Rudi Ruchs, Eindhoven, Netherlands 1979; *Georg Baselitz: 32 Linolschnitte aus den Jahren 1976 bis 1979*, exhibition catalogue, with texts by Siegfried Gohr and Fred Jahn, Cologne 1979; *Georg Baselitz: Tekeningen/Zeichnungen*, exhibition catalogue with texts by Frans Haks and Johannes Gachnang, Groningen, Netherlands 1979; *Georg Baselitz: Biennale de Venezia 1980*, exhibition catalogue, with texts by Johannes Gachnang, Theo Kneubuhler and Klaus Gallwitz, Stuttgart 1980; *Georg Baselitz: Das Strassenbild*, exhibition catalogue, with text by A. van Grevenstein, Amsterdam 1981; *George Baselitz: Zeichnungen*, exhibition catalogue, with text by H. Heere, Cologne 1982; *Georg Baselitz: Holzplastiken*, exhibition catalogue, with texts by A. Franzke, R. H. Fuchs and S. Gohr, Cologne 1983; *Baselitz: Paintings 1960–83*, exhibition catalogue with texts by N. Serota and R. Calvocoressi, London 1983; *Georg Baselitz: Das malerische Werk 1960–83, Linolschnitte 1976–79*, exhibition catalogue, with texts by J. C. Ammann and R. Calvocoressi, Basel 1984; *Georg Baselitz: Selected Prints 1963–85*, exhibition catalogue, with text by J. E. Fink, Boston 1985; *Georg Baselitz: Baume*, exhibition catalogue, with texts by E. Kob, O. Rychlik and H. Hrachovec, Vienna 1986; *Georg Baselitz: Skulpturen und Zeichnungen 1979–1987*, exhibition catalogue, with texts by C. Haenlein, A. M. Hammacher and others, Hannover 1987.

From the end of the 1960's, in a search for a new equilibrium—new, but still within the dimension of painting, clarifying the control of the actual picture through well thought analytical premises—Georg Baselitz has continually explored the modalities of a procedure which, while making use of recognizable images, refutes the classical conceptions—the sense of space, composition, perspective, the idea of style, etc. What we see is thus the continuous and constant presentation of the negation of exposition, of meaning, of the subject-object relationship that makes reality manifest as if reflected in a mirror.

Baselitz's painting tends to confuse the viewer, distorting the organized mechanisms of visual perception. It repudiates sensuousness, the quality of traditionally accepted painting, the subject and all those other elements that show it to be a reference to something. The picture, the work, thus becomes just a picture, a work—an enquiry into painting filtered through a complex pre-established mental process and a play of arbitrary elaborations.

What is exceptional in Georg Baselitz's methods lies in the fact that his works repudiate "painting with images" by actually using recognizable images which are presented directly as themselves, with no suggestion of story or description. The picture thus has to be looked at, not as a mirror on the world, but as a world in itself, self-sufficient.

It is as if these works had been executed with a technique such as might be used to build a boat actually in the sea during a shipwreck. Painting that does not have to flirt with structuralism, but is rather looked at casually, establishes an equilibrium of its own; the boat will not sink provided there are eyes to be sure of being present at the shipwreck—that of the modern age. The artist is building rafts with his pictures, fragments at a time of the recent past which, despite everything, are still in our present time and fragments of the present projected into the next moment, fragments which together (deliberately or not, it matters little) build a bridge towards "that which has been."

—Demetrio Paparoni

BASKIN, Leonard.
American. Born in New Brunswick, New Jersey, 15 August 1922. Educated at a yeshiva, Brooklyn, New York, 1929–38; studied at New York University of School of Architecture and Allied Arts, 1939–40; Yale University School of Fine Arts, 1941–42; Académie de la Grande Chaumière, Paris, 1950; Accademia di Belle Arte, Florence, 1951. Served in the United States Navy, 1943–46. Independent artist active in sculpture, painting and printmaking as well as calligraphy, design and illustration. Instructor in Printmaking, Worcester Art Museum, Massachusetts, 1952. Has taught at Smith College, Northampton, Massachusetts, since 1953. Recipient: Honorable Mention for Sculpture, Prix de Rome, 1940; Tiffany Foundation Fellowship for Sculpture, 1947; Guggenheim Fellowship, 1953; Ohara Prize, National Museum of Tokyo, 1954; National Institute of Arts and Letters Grant, 1961; Mather Prize, Art Institute of Chicago, 1961; Widener Medal, Pennsylvania Academy of Fine Arts, 1965; Special Medal of Merit, American Institute of Graphic Arts, 1965; Medal, National Institute of Arts and Letters, 1969; Agent: Kennedy Galleries, New York. Address: c/o Kennedy Galleries, 40 West 57th Street, New York, New York 10019, U.S.A.

Individual Exhibitions:

1952 Mount Holyoke College, South Hadley, Massachusetts
1957 Worcester Art Museum, Massachusetts
1961 Museum Boymans-van Beuningen, Rotterdam
Le Centre Culturel Américain, Paris
University of Minnesota, Minneapolis
1962 Royal Watercolor Society Galleries, London
Bowdoin College Museum of Art, Brunswick, Maine
1963 Maxwell Galleries, San Francisco
1966 Peale House, Pennsylvania Academy of the Fine Arts, Philadelphia
1968 Stockholm National Museum (travelled to Oslo, Norway and Gothenburg, Sweden)
1970 *Leonard Baskin: The Graphic Work 1950–1970*, FAR Gallery, New York
Smithsonian Institution, Washington, D.C.
Illustrations for the Divine Comedy of Dante by Leonard Baskin, Yale University, New Haven, Connecticut
1971 Kennedy Galleries, New York
1972 *Indian Drawings*, Amon Carter Museum, Fort Worth, Texas
Brookhaven National Laboratory, Associated Universities, Upton, New York
1973 Kennedy Galleries, New York
1974 Kennedy Galleries, New York
Summit Art Center, New Jersey
Museum of Fine Arts, Springfield, Massachusetts
1975 Kennedy Galleries, New York
Watercolors for a Passover Haggadah, Fine Arts Museums of San Francisco
1976 Kennedy Galleries, New York
Indianapolis Museum of Art
Towson State College Art Gallery, Baltimore, Maryland
1977 Prince Arthur Galleries, Toronto
Port Washington Public Library, New York
Lockhaven Art Center, Orlando, Florida
1978 *Images of Man*, Washington University Gallery of Art, St. Louis
Recent Works, Kennedy Galleries, New York
1980 Kennedy Galleries, New York
1981 Cottage Gallery, London
Leonard Baskin's West, Amon Carter Museum, Forth Worth, Texas (toured the Western United States)
1982 *Sculpture and Watercolors*, Kennedy Galleries, New York

Selected Group Exhibitions:

1961 *Bienal*, San Paulo
1962 *American Paintings and Drawings from Michigan Collections*, Detroit Institute of Arts
1969 *The Figurative Tradition in Recent American Art*, at the *Biennale*, Venice (travelled to National Collection of Fine Arts, Washington, D.C. and Sheldon Gallery, University of Nebraska, Lincoln)
1979 *The American View*, MacNider Museum, Mason City, Iowa
1980 *Sculpture in the 70s: The Figure*, Pratt Manhattan Center Gallery, New York
A Penthouse Aviary, Museum of Modern Art, New York

Collections:

Museum of Modern Art, New York; Whitney Museum, New York; Hirshhorn Collection, Smithsonian Institution, Washington, D.C.; National Gallery of Art, Washington, D.C.; Museum of Fine Arts, Boston; Art Institute of Chicago; Detroit Institute of Arts; Amon Carter Museum of Art, Fort Worth, Texas; Vatican Museum, Rome.

Publications:

By BASKIN: books—*To Color Thought*, New Haven, Connecticut 1967; *Figures of Dead Men*, Amherst, Massachusetts 1968; *5 Addled Etchers*, Hanover, New Hampshire 1969; *Baskin: Sculpture, Drawings, Prints*, New York 1970; books illustrated—*Creatures of Darkness* by Esther Baskin, Boston 1962; *The Iliad of Homer*, translated by Richmond Lattimore, Chicago 1962; *The Poppy and Other Deadly*

Plants by Esther Baskin, New York 1967; *The Divine Comedy* by Dante Alighieri, translated by Thomas Bergin, New York 1969; *Hosie's Alphabet* by Hosea, Tobias and Lisa Baskin, New York 1972; *Selected Poems 1957–1967* by Ted Hughes, New York 1973; *A Passover Haggadah*, New York 1974; *Season Songs* by Ted Hughes, New York 1975; *Hosie's Aviary* by Tobias, Hosea, Lucretia and Lisa Baskin, New York 1979; *Chosen Days* by David Rosenberg, New York 1980; *Hosie's Zoo* by Tobias, Hosea, Lucretia and Lisa Baskin, New York 1981; *Under the North Star* by Ted Hughes, New York 1981; articles—"New Talent in the USA: with Note by the Artist" in *Art in America* (New York), February 1956; "The Necessity for the Image" in *Atlantic Monthly* (Boston), April 1961; "To Wear Blood Stain with Honor" in *Judaism* (New York), vol. 10, 1961; "On the Nature of Originality" in *Show* (New York), August 1963; "Of Roots and Veins: A Testament" in *Atlantic Monthly* (Boston), September 1964; "Studio Talk . . . Industrial Sand Casting in Bronze: An Interview with Leonard Baskin" in *Arts* (New York), February 1967.

On BASKIN: books—*Conversations with Artists* by Selden Rodman, New York 1961; *The Sculpture of Leonard Baskin* by Irma Jaffe, New York 1980; *Profiles of American Artists Represented by Kennedy Galleries* by Gloria-Gilda Deak, New York 1981; articles—"Art: Baskin's Foreboding Reflections" by Dore Ashton in the *New York Times*, 2 April 1958; "Nouvelles Images de L'Homme" by Peter Selz in *L'Oeil* (Paris), February 1960; "Leonard Baskin" by Brian O'Doherty in *Art in America* (New York), Summer 1962; "Leonard Baskin" by Brian O'Doherty in *Art in America* (New York), August 1963; "Baskin and the Sooty God" by John Canaday in the *New York Times*, 9 February 1964; "Leonard Baskin: Printer, Teacher, Affluent Artist—The Pleasant Pariah" by Jane Howard in *Life* (New York), 24 January 1964; "Leonard Baskin's Gehenna Press" by D. R. Roylance in *Art in America* (New York), November 1966; "Baskin—His Graphic Work" by J. T. Butler in *Connoisseur* (London), May 1970; "Art's Poet Laureate" by Douglas Davis in *Newsweek* (New York), 29 June 1970; "Images of Man" by Alfred Werner in *Art and Artists* (London), October 1976; "FDR Memorial: A Monument to Politics, Bureaucracy and the Art of Accommodation" by M. N. Carter in *Artnews* (New York), October 1978; "History and Fate in Leonard Baskin's Sculpture" by J. Deckert in *Arts* (New York), June 1980.

Leonard Baskin is one of those anomalies of contemporary art, though more complex than most. He belongs to the 20th century, to a certain extent is of it, yet repudiates it. He has not received the recognition he deserves, simply because he is not and does not want to be in the so-called mainstream of modern art. It is hard to say whether the neglect of this major artist is due to his own intransigence or to the myopia of art critics and art historians. There is another element: for me, at least, his output is uneven; that is, one could defend the neglect with reference to certain works. This makes an assessment of Baskin's achievement difficult.

Although his reputation rests on his sculpture, to my mind his chief title to fame is as a draughtsman and watercolourist and, secondly, as a printer, engraver, maker of wood-cuts and lithographs, in that order. His illustrations for Ted Hughes's poem *Crow* are masterly, the equal of any studies of birds by Picasso.

Even in his sculpture he is unfailingly successful in his treatment of birds, some pathetic, some menacing. His treatment of the human form is not quite so successful. Some works have the simplicity, if not the charm, of Barlach, whom Baskin much admired—he even did a head of Barlach in 1959; most impressive. His "Seated Woman" and "Seated Man with Owl" have the simple eloquence of the best of 20th century sculpture, well worthy of Barlach. Like Barlach, Baskin has been in search of humanistic, spiritual and religious values in sculpture which reach back beyond the Renaissance, to the late Middle Ages, to the simple expression of Tino do Camaino, particularly the sinister Counsellors of Pisa.

Baskin's themes are mostly drawn from the Bible and classical mythology, with some symbolic representations of abstract ideas—expulsion, thought, silence. The human figure, usually cast in bronze, sometimes nude, sometimes elaborately swathed in garments, is central to his work, as it was to the sculptors of the Renaissance and to Rodin, whom, in

Leonard Baskin: *Medea*, 1980

his more elaborate works, he closely resembles—there is the same malleability of material, the sensuousness of moulding of garments, etc.

At his best Baskin can produce powerful and impressive sculptural images. But he has a tendency to over-dramatize and to be highly emotional, when restraint would have been more effective, as in his "Prodigal Son" (compare it with Barlach's version of the same subject). And, at times, his fantastical works make very little impact and seem to belong to a private, eccentric vision, rather than to one which can be shared.

But his versatility, not only in the variety of media in which he is supremely competent, but also in the variety of visual ideas, is remarkable. I have mentioned his studies of birds (and other animal studies must be added); add his treatment of the human form, of legendary and symbolic subjects (to which one

must add subjects from European and American literature, Dante, Shakespeare, etc), and his fantasies. There are also his portraits of artists (Géricault, Corot, Velasquez) and of literary figures (Melville, Blake, John Skelton). And there are excellent pastiches, such as his "Homage to August Saint-Gaudens."

Baskin will probably not be seen for what he is—an artist in the European tradition, who continued that tradition, while being open, in part, to new developments in the visual arts, artist of individual, original, if sometimes eccentric, vision—until the dust of 'modernism' settles.

—D. C. Barrett

BATTAGLIA, Carlo.

Italian. Born La Maddalena, Sardinia, 28 January 1933. Studied at the Accademia delle Belle Arti, Rome, 1952–57. Served in the Italian Air Force, 1958–59. Married Anna Paparetti in 1959 (divorced, 1962); married Carla Panicali in 1972. Designed scenery for *La Merce Esclusa* by Elio Pagliarani, at the Teatro Parioli, Rome, 1965. Visited New York, 1967. Assistant Professor of Scenography, Accademia delle Belle Arti, Rome, 1970–72. Lives alternately in Rome and New York, since 1980. Agent: Galleria L'Isola, Via Gregoriana 5, 00187 Rome. Address: Via di Monserrato 111, 00186 Rome, Italy.

Individual Exhibitions:

1964 Galleria La Salita, Rome
1965 Galleria La Metopa, Bari, Italy
1968 Galleria Salone Annunciata, Milan
1968 Galleria Editalia, Rome (with Nicola Carrino)
Galleria Salone Annunciata, Milan
Galleria Arco d'Alibert Rome
Galleria Qui Arte Contemporanea, Rome
1969 Galleria Flori, Florence
Galleria Qui Arte Contemporanea, Rome
Galleria Editalia, Rome
1970 Galleria Salone Annunciata, Milan
Biennale, Venice
1971 Deson-Zaks Gallery, Chicago
Galleria Salone Annunciata, Milan
1972 Galleria Editalia, Rome
Galleria Peccolo, Livorno
Galleria Qui Arte Contemporanea, Rome
Westend Galerie, Frankfurt
Studio 3Bi, Bolzano, Italy
1973 Galleria Godel, Rome
Galleria Nova Arte Moderna, Prato, Italy
1974 Galleria Salone Annunciata, Milan
Elementi per Carlo Battaglia, Palazzo Grassi, Venice
Studio Soldano, Milan
1975 Studio 3Bi, Bolzano, Italy
Galleria Il Sole, Bolzano, Italy
Galleria Il Segnapassi, Pesaro, Italy
Galerie Daniel Templon, Paris
Galleria La Bertesca, Genoa
1976 Galeria Arnessen, Copenhagen
Galleria Salone Annunciata, Milan
Galeria La Bertesca, Dusseldorf
Palazzo dei Diamante, Ferrara
1977 Studio 3Bi, Bolzano, Italy
Galleria Il Sole, Bolzano, Italy
Galleria La Bertesca, Rome
Studio Ennesse, Milan
1978 Galleria E Tre, Rome
Kunsthalle, Dusseldorf
1980 Studio 3Bi, Bolzano, Italy
Sergio Tosi, New York
Galleria Civica, Alessandria, Italy
Galleria E Tre, Rome
Studio Grossetti, Milan
Ann Jacob Gallery, Atlanta
Biennale, Venice
Galleria Il Sole, Bolzano, Italy
1981 Lo Spazio, Naples
1983 Galleria Il Sole, Bolzano, Italy
Galeria Albrecht, Caldaro, Bolzano, Italy
Galleria L'Isola, Rome
Studio Carlo Grossetti, Milan
1984 Ann Jacob Gallery, Atlanta, Georgia
1985 Galleria Arte Duchamp, Cagliari, Italy
Galleria L'Isola, Rome
1986 Galleria Forzani, Terni, Italy
Museo Civico d'Arte Contemporanea, Gibellina, Italy
Studio Marconi, Milan
1987 Galleria Ellequadro, Genoa, Italy

Selected Group Exhibitions:

1964 *Arte Nuova*, Konsthall, Lund, Sweden
1966 *Peintures Italiennes d'Aujourd'hui*, Teheran
1968 *6th Biennale Romana*, Palazzo Esposizioni, Rome
1972 *Proposta a Quattro*, Galleria del Milione, Milan
1975 *Tendensen Moderne Kunst*, Nordjylands Kunstmuseum, Aalborg, Denmark (travelled to Stifts Museum, Odense, Denmark)
1978 *Biennale*, Venice
1980 *Arte e Critice*, Museo Nazionale d'Arte Moderna, Rome
1982 *Arte Italiana 1960–82*, Hayward Gallery, London
1984 *Art from Italy*, Hirshhorn Museum, Washington, D.C.
1986 *Arte e Scienza-Colore*, at the *Biennale*, Venice

Collections:

Museo Nazionale d'Arte Moderna, Rome; Boymans-van Beuningen Museum, Rotterdam; Louisiana Museum, Humlebaek, Denmark; Museo Soto, Ciudad Bolivar, Venezuela; Hirshhorn Museum and Sculpture Garden, Smithsonian Institution, Washington, D.C.

Publications:

By BATTAGLIA: articles—statement in *Carlo Battaglia*, exhibition catalogue, Milan 1968; statement in *Flash Art* (Milan), February 1972; "3 Artists: Ryman, Marden and Bell" in *Qui Arte Contemporanea* (Rome), June 1973; "Come Dipingono," interview with Griffa Verna, in *Data* (Milan), Summer 1973; "La Pittura come Disciplina," with Maurizio Fagiolo, in *Bolaffi Arte* (Turin), April 1975; "L'Immagine parallela" in *L'Immagine parallela ed altre congetture*, Genoa 1976; "Dialogo tra Carlo Battaglia, Giampaolo Prearo e Nino Soldano" in *Casa Arredamento e Giardino* (Milan), April 1979; "Arshile Gorky al Guggenheim" in *Flash Art* (Milan), no. 105, 1981; "Marginalia" in *Carlo Battaglia*, exhibition catalogue, Rome 1985.

On BATTAGLIA: books—*Carlo Battaglia* by Tommaso Trini, Milan 1974; *Elementi per Carlo Battaglia*, exhibition catalogue, by Roberto Sanesi, Venice 1974; *Carlo Battaglia*, exhibition catalogue, by Filiberto Menna, Dusseldorf 1978; *Carlo Battaglia*, exhibition catalogue, by Dore Ashton, New York 1980; *Il corpo della pittura: critici e nuovi pittori in Italia 1972–76* by Claudio Caritelli, Turin 1986; articles—"La Pittura come Paesaggio" by Gabriella Otudi in *Data* (Milan), May 1972; "Carlo Battaglia: Ambiguita Visionaria" by Guido Ballo in *Arte Milano* (Milan), March 1973; "Carlo Battaglia" by Filiberto Menna in *Opus International* (Paris), September 1974; "Carlo Battaglia a Palazzo Grassi, Venezia" by Gianni Contessi in *Nac* (Milan), December 1974; "Il

Carlo Battaglia: ***Imbre*****, 1986**

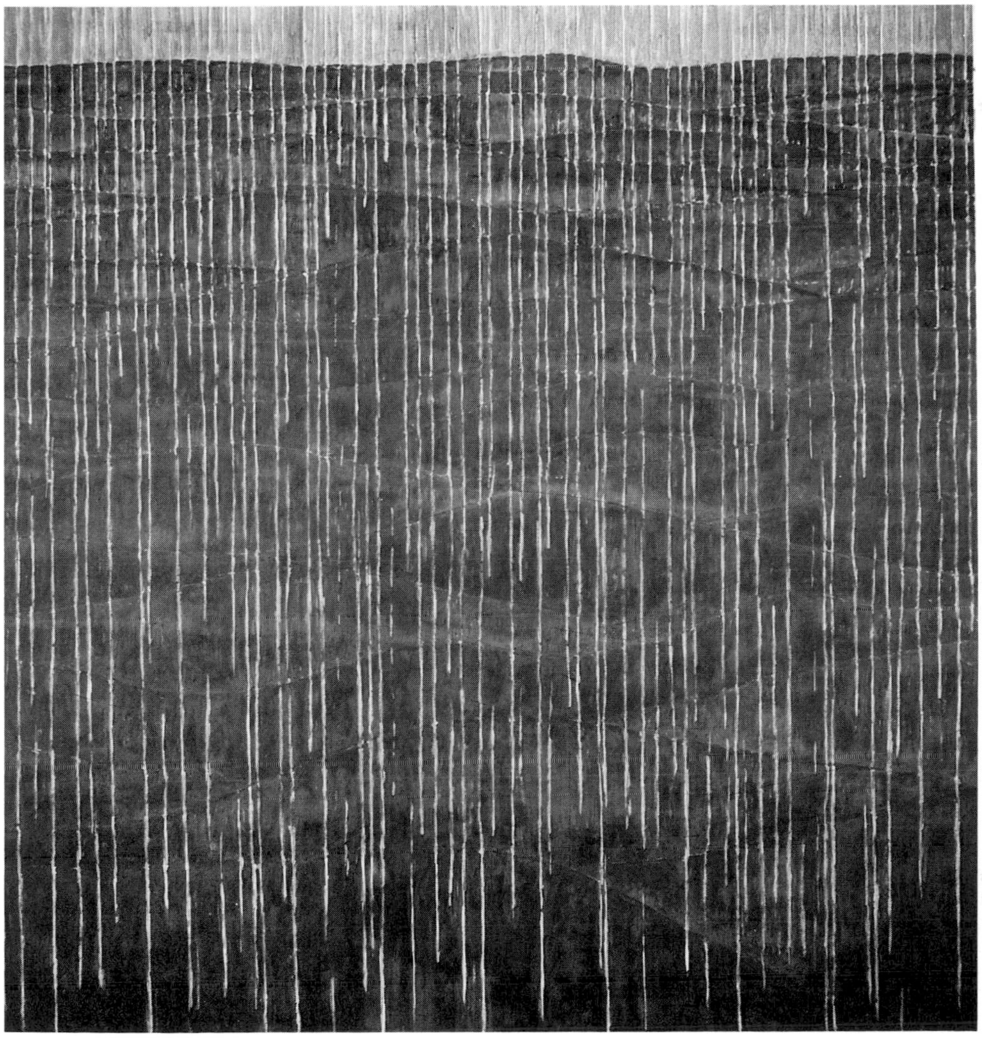

quadro di Carlo Battaglia" by Vittorio Fagone in *Data* (Milan), July / September 1976; "Incontro col pittore Carlo Battaglio" by Maurizio Fagiolo in *Il Messaggero* (Rome), 18 April 1977; "Carlo Battaglia, La metrica del mare" by Vito Apuleo in *I Messaggero* (Rome), 7 June 1983; "I paesaggi di Carlo Battaglia" by Enzo Bilardello in *Corriere della Sera* (Milan), 16 December 1985.

"My aspiration is to catch everyone's attention, even those people who know nothing about painting. The idea of landscapes, which obsesses me at the moment, could also be this: the vague discernment of a common need for contemplation. Contemplating is a fundamentally irrational act. I want to pursue this gratuitous impulse until I attain the mutable visionariness of landscapes which escapes the control of logic, but is conveyable by virtue of its very obviousness. I see the risks I am running: the idolatry of the mists of emotions or the unconditional surrender to popular banality. Two blind alleys for anyone who is tempted to nullify the enigma of expression. Except I have already made my choice, beyond the point of no return. I say so without hesitation.

This is an excerpt from an article by Gabriella Drudi about my work in 1972, entitled "Painting as Landscape," and article which, miming a series of conversations we had, put words into my mouth that are much more specific than I was able to formulate at that time. The result of that remote and still vague motive are these pictures. I don't know if I have surmounted those risks, doubt is always the only certainty, but I am relieved to know that I have carried out what I felt obliged to do: this is the only conceit I allow myself. Observation and love lie at the root of these paintings. Identification between painting and landscape, landscape as a place of memory, dreamy distance, timeless portrayal. The reflections in perpetual motion in the clear pure light of the archipelago, the shadows, mysterious abstract clippings, summon up memories, fragments, pictures loved to the point of becoming a part of me, presences, awareness. The "Madonna Enthroned with Child and Saints" at S. Zaccaria, the giddy interplay of countless sources of light, sublime challenge of the "Martyrdom of St. Lawrence" at the Jesuits, the gold ground no longer a flat emblematic surface but a glowing atmosphere of light-space in the polyptych of the Misericordia in Sansepolcro, the appearance of the city of Delft in Den Haag as the sudden, unexpected materialization of those islands suspended between cobalt blue and ultramarine, murky with green, haloed with pink and violet. An ancient landscape, the presence of the sacred in the absence of man, a landscape that already in itself is structure, archetype.

So I haven't painted rocks and shrubs as such. They are tokens, essential traits shaped by the age-old erosion of wind and sea, precious traces for reinventing a pictorial structure free of imitation or representation, a "parallel code". I have sought to paint the air between object and obiect, island and island, foreground and distances inside a spherical space. The sea, crazed anamorphosis of a checkerboard. To pinpoint the eternal in the prime elements, earth, water, air. Not a specific landscape but the place of universal landscapes. I don't feel like, nor up to, giving theoretical explanations of my work. I am also aware of its probable unactuality was well as its ineluctability. What I can say is that I have attempted to do something that exists once and for all.

As to feelings, passions, expectations and dramas I choose not to speak of them. If I have been capable of expressing them they are contained in the pictures, hence visible to all.

—Carlo Battaglia

Carlo Battaglia's first one-man show was in 1964 at the La Salita gallery in Rome. At that time, his work was based on the rapport between space and colour. The show heralded a significant change in his work which, as noted by Milton Gendel in 1966, signified "the end of his research between the School of Paris and of New York". In *Spazio Ambiguo* of 1966, a large rectangle occupies the central part of the canvas in the manner of a window across which an orthogonal takes on the character of a road moving to infinity until interrupted by a horizontal line.

From 1967 his painting changed, in accordance with that particular tendency characterised by Argan as the transition of Cubism from Mondrian to Constructivism. In this year, after a brief stay in Paris, Battaglia moved to New York for some time. The works of this period convey a strong geometric character. Between 1967 and 1968, he produced a series of works forming the cycle Misterioso in which he organized the picture plane in different perspectival planes to create an advancing and receding space. Our attention is directed around an ordered geometrical space of outlines and blocks of form to create a perspectival illusion.

The year 1969 was marked by a new departure. *Light Visionario* and *Solitario* both make their impact as large monochrome canvases with soft and hazy mood. Libertated from any geometric reference these works have become like large windows open to a sky of visionary light. In 1970, the year he took part in the Venice Biennale, Battaglia produced the first works based on two opposing characters, one geometric, and the other evocative and visionary. By now, he had arrived at his personal poetic style. The structure of the surface is abbreviated to horizontal marks or isolated strokes of geometric form overlaying the visionary field of colour and light. Out of this period come *Cadmus, Calypso, Renir, Spargi, Diaspro*—all works of 1970—that confirm the artist's declaration: "What I have sought to do is to imbue the picture with as much significance as possible, including signifiers whose origin seems quite obscure, to give force to this garden of images." Gradually, the geometric shapes give way to the colour-light field which has now assumed a dominant role. Having abandoned geometric rigour, Battaglia releases the picture, free to evoke a natural world.

Grande immagine parallela (1976), a large work of ten metres length, constitutes a poetic introduction to the work which will follow. In this parallel image of the natural world, Battaglia attempts to overcome the anachronistic dichotomy between figuration and abstraction, a position that is to become clearer in later work. Emblematic of this intention is *Grande Oceana Blu* of 1980 / 81. An area of sea (as evinced by the title) is painted as an arrangement of wavey marks in chiaroscuro. This work recalls those made ten years earlier which evoked a luminescent blue sky, while the most recent works, such as the series *Oltremare* (1982 / 83), the reference is to the ocean depths.

In this most recent work, references to the natural world are more pronounced. By means of a highly refined technique, Battaglia continually inserts an element of ambivalence, making the meaning difficult to grasp—as in *Gli dei a Gibellina* of 1985, where the landscape continually moves between land and sea. In this way Battaglia stresses his need to put in every significance possible.

—Roberto Lambarelli

BAYER, Herbert.

American. Born in Haag, Austria, 5 April 1900; emigrated to the United States, 1938; naturalized, 1944. Educated at gymnasium, Linz, Austria, 1911–17; apprentice in architecture and decorative arts, under architect George Schmidthammer, Linz, 1919; graphic design and typography assistant to architect Emanuel Margold, Darmstadt, Germany, 1920; studied mural painting and design, with Vasily Kandinsky, at the Staatliche Bauhaus, in Weimar, 1921–23, and in Dessau, 1925–28. Served in Infantry Regiment 14, Austrian Army, 1917–19. Married Irene Hecht in 1925 (divorced); daughter: Julia; married Joella Haweis Levy in 1944. Young Master of Typography and Graphic Design, Staatliche Bauhaus, Dessau, 1925–28; Director, Dorland Studio of Design, and active as painter, photographer, graphic designer and exhibition architect, Berlin 1928–30; painter, photographer, graphic designer, and exhibition architect, New York, 1938–45; Director, Dorland International design company, New York, 1945; Consultant Designer, 1945–56, and Chairman of Department of Design, 1956–65, Container Corporation of America, Chicago. Consultant and Architect, Aspen Institute of Humanistic Studies, Colorado, 1946–85; Art and Design Consultant, Atlantic Richfield Company, Los Angeles, 1966–85. Visiting Artist, Jerusalem Foundation, 1977; Artist-in-Residence, American Academy, Rome, 1978. Recipient: First Prize, *Foreign Advertising Photography* exhibition, New York, 1931; Medal, City of Salzburg, Austria, 1936; Gold Medal, Art Directors Club of Philadelphia, 1961; Trustees Award, Aspen Institute for Humanistic Studies, Colorado, 1965; Ambassador's Award for Excellence, London, 1968; Kulturpreis for Photography, Cologne, 1969; Gold Medal, American Institute of Graphic Arts, 1970; Adalbert Stifter Preis für Bildende Kunst Verliehen, Linz, Austria, 1971; Austrian Cross of Honor for Art and Science, 1978. Honorary Doctorate: Technische Hochschule, Graz, Austria, 1973; D.F.A.: Philadelphia College of Art, 1974. Honorary Member, Alliance Graphique Internationale, 1975; Honorary Fellow, Royal Academy of Fine Art, The Hague, Netherlands, 1975. Fellow, American Academy of Arts and Sciences, 1979. Agent: Marlborough Gallery, 40 West 57th Street, New York, New York 10019. *Died* (in Montecito, California) *30 September 1985.*

Individual Exhibitions:

1929 Kunstverein Marz, Linz, Austria
Galerie Povolotsky, Paris
1931 Staatliche Bauhaus, Dessau, Germany
1936 Kunstverein, Salzburg, Austria
1937 London Gallery
1939 Black Mountain College, North Carolina
P.M. Gallery, New York
1940 Yale University, New Haven, Connecticut
1943 Willard Gallery, New York
North Texas State Teachers College, Denton
1944 Outline Gallery, Pittsburgh
1947 *The Way Beyond Art,* Brown University, Providence, Rhode Island (retrospective; toured the United States, 1947–49)
1952 Cleveland Institute of Art
1953 Hans Schaeffer Galleries, New York
1954 Kunstkabinett Klihm, Munich
Galleria del Milione, Milan
1955 Aspen Institute for Humanistic Studies, Colorado
1956 *33 Years of Herbert Bayer's Work,* Germanisches Nationalmuseum, Nuremberg, West Germany (retrospective; travelled to Munich, Zurich, Berlin, Braunschweig and Vienna, 1956–57)
1957 Kunstkabinett Klihm, Munich
1958 *Recent Works,* Fort Worth Art Center, Texas (travelled to the Walker Art Center, Minneapolis)
1959 Kunstkabinett Klihm, Munich
1960 Städtische Kunsthalle, Dusseldorf
Museum am Ostwall, Dortmund, West Germany
1961 Bauhaus Archiv, Darmstadt, West Germany
1962 Stadtisches Kunstmuseum, Duisberg, West Germany (retrospective; toured the United States, Germany and Italy)
1963 Andrew Morris Gallery, New York
Neue Galerie, Linz, Austria
1964 Aspen Institute for Humanistic Studies, Colorado
5207 Galleries, Oklahoma City
1965 Byron Gallery, New York
Esther Robles Gallery, Los Angeles
Boise Art Association, Idaho
1966 University of New Hampshire, Durham
1967 Galerie Klihm, Munich
Galerie Conzen, Dusseldorf
Philadelphia Art Alliance
1968 Marlborough New London Gallery

Herbert Bayer: ***Aging Star*, 1968** Courtesy Museum of Contemporary Art, Chicago

1969 University of California at Santa Barbara
Two Visions of Space: Herbert Bayer and Ingeborg ten Haeff, Hudson River Museum, Yonkers, New York
1970 Dunkelman Gallery, Toronto
Germanisches Nationalmuseum, Nuremberg
Galerie Conzen, Dusseldorf
1971 Marlborough Gallery, New York
Centre Culturel Allemand, Paris
Goethe-Institut, Paris
Die Neue Sammlung, Munich
Österreichisches Museum für Angewandte Kunst, Vienna
1972 Marlborough Gallery, Montreal
Mer-Kup Galerias, Mexico City
1973 Landesbildstelle, Hamburg (travelled to Krefeld and Leverkusen)
Saarland Museum, Saarbrücken
Herbert Bayer: A Total Concept, Denver Art Museum (retrospective)
1974 Marlborough Galerie, Zurich
Galerie Klihm, Munich
Galerie Nächst St. Stephan, Vienna (travelled to Innsbruck and Graz)
Marlborough Graphics, New York (toured the United States, 1974–75)
Das Druckgrafische Werk bis 1971, Haus Deutscher Ring, Hamburg (retrospective; toured Germany, Switzerland, Portugal and Spain), 1974–76)
1975 Marlborough Gallery, Toronto
Arte Contacto Galeria, Caracas
1976 *Beispiele aus dem Gesamtwerk 1919–1974,* Neue Galerie, Linx, Austria
Graphics and Small Sculptures, Marlborough Gallery, New York
Photomontages, Marlborough Gallery, New York
1977 Marian Locks Gallery, Philadelphia
From Type to Landscape, Hopkins Center, Dartmouth College, Hanover, New Hampshire (American Federation of Art show; toured the United States)
Photographic Works, Arco Center for Visual Art, Los Angeles (toured the United States)
1978 *Tapestries and Environmental Designs,* Galerie Klihm, Munich
Museum Bochum, West Germany (retrospective)
1979 *Recent Works,* Marlborough Gallery, New York
Photographic Exhibition, Galerie Breiting, West Berlin
1980 *Inaugural Exhibition of the Herbert Bayer Archive,* Denver Art Museum
Neue Gallery, Linz, Austria
Galerias Mer-Kup, Mexico City
1981 *A Selected Survey,* Grapestake Gallery, San Francisco
Centre Georges Pompidou, Paris (with Umbo)
University of California, Santa Barbara
1982 Bauhaus Archiv, West Berlin (travelled to Basle)
1983 Galerie Thomas, Munich
1984 Galerie Lopes, Zurich
Saidenberg Gallery, New York
1986 Museum fur Gestaltung, West Berlin
1987 Quadrat Moderne Galerie, Bottrop, West Germany
Kunsthaus, Zug, Switzerland
Oberosterreichisches Landesmuseum, Linz, Austria

Selected Group Exhibitions:

1923 *Kunst and Technik: Eine neue Einheit,* Bauhaus und Staatliches Landesmuseum, Weimar
1929 *Film und Foto,* Stuttgart
1936 *Entartete Kunst,* Haus der Deutschen Kunst, Munich
1959 *V Bienal,* São Paulo
1964 *Documenta,* Kassel, West Germany
1966 *Les Années 25,* Musée des Art Décoratifs, Paris
1967 *50 Jahre Bauhaus,* Württembergische Kunstverein, Stuttgart (toured Europe, the United States, Canada, Argentina and Japan)
1978 *Paris-Berlin 1900–1933,* Centre Georges Pompidou, Paris
1980 *Avant-Garde Photography in Germany 1919–1939,* San Francisco Museum of Modern Art (toured the United States)
1985 *Das Aktfoto,* Fotomuseum im Stadtmuseum, Munich

Collections:

Museum of Modern Art, New York; Fogg Art Museum, Cambridge, Massachusetts; Denver Art Museum, Colorado (Archives); Santa Barbara Museum of Art, California; San Francisco Museum of Modern Art; Neue Galerie der Stadt Linz, Austria; Museum Folkwang, Essen; Bauhaus Archiv, Berlin; Nationalgalerie, Berlin; Nazionale d'Arte Moderna, Rome

Publications:

By BAYER: books—*Fotomontagen,* portfolio of 11 photomontages, Berlin 1932; *Fotoplastiken,* portfolio of 10 photos, Berlin 1937; *Bauhaus 1919–1928,* with Ise and Walter Gropius, New York 1938, 1959, 1975; *Seven Convolutions,* portfolio of lithographs, Colorado Springs 1948; *World Geo-Graphic Atlas,* Aspen, Colorado 1953; *Book of Drawings,* Chicago 1961; *Eight Monochrome Suite,* portfolio of lithographs, Los Angeles 1965; *Herbert Bayer: Paintings,* portfolio of reproductions, Chicago 1965; *Herbert Bayer: Painter/Designer/Architect,* New York, Ravensburg, London and Tokyo 1967; *Herbert Bayer,* portfolio of 6 silkscreens, with introduction by Dieter Honisch, Stuttgart 1968; articles—"Reflections from One of the Sculptors Who Contributed to the 'Route of Friendship' " in *Architecture Formes et Fonctions* (Lausanne), 1969; "Typography and Design" in *Concepts of the Bauhaus: Busch-Reisinger Museum Collection,* exhibition catalogue, Cambridge, Massachusetts 1971; foreward to *The Graphic Design of Yusaka Kamekura* by Masuro Katsumi, New York 1973; "Herbert Bayer," interview, in *Dialogue with Photography,* edited by Paul Hill and Thomas Cooper, London 1979; "Many Paths from the Bauhaus," interview, in *Darkroom Photography* (San Francisco), January/February 1981.

On BAYER: books—*The Way Beyond Art: The Work of Herbert Bayer* by Alexander Dorner, New York 1947; *Fotoauge Herbert Bayer,* exhibition catalogue, edited by Jan Tschichold, Munich 1967; *Herbert Bayer,* exhibition catalogue, with text by Ludwig Grote, London 1968; *50 Jahre Bauhaus,* exhibition catalogue, by Wulf Herzongenrath, Stuttgart and London 1968; *Two Visions of Space: Herbert Bayer and Ingeborg ten Haeff,* exhibition catalogue, with introduction by Carl Black, Jr., New York 1969; *The Bauhaus* by Hans M. Wingler, Cambridge, Massachusetts 1969; *Painters of the Bauhaus* by Eberhard Roters, New York 1969; *Bauhaus and Bauhaus People,* edited by Eckhard Neumann, New York 1970; *Herbert Bayer: A Total Concept,* exhibition catalogue, with introduction by Karl Otto Bach, Denver 1973; *Herbert Bayer: Das Druckgraftsche Werk bis 1971,* with text by Hans M. Wingler and Peter Hahn, Berlin 1974; *Herbert Bayer,* exhibition catalogue, with introductions by Ida Rodriguez Prampolini, Zurich 1974; *Photographie als Kunstlerisches Experiment* by Willi Rotzler, Lucerne and Frankfurt 1974; *Herbert Bayer: Un Concepta Total* by Ida Rodriguez Prampolini, Mexico City 1975; *Beispiele aus dem Gesamtwerk 1919–1974,* exhibition catalogue, with introduction by Peter Baum, Linz 1976; *Photomontage* by Dawn Ades, London and New York 1976; *Herbert Bayer: From Type to Landscape,* exhibition catalogue, with text by Jan van der Marck, New York 1977; with text by Leland Rice and Beaumont Newhall, Los Angeles, 1977; *Kunstlerphotographie im XX. Jahrhundert,* exhibition catalogue, edited by Carl-Albrecht Haenlein, Hannover 1977; *Neue Sachlichkeit and German Realism of the Twenties,* exhibition catalogue, by Wieland Schmied and Ute Eskildsen, London 1978; *Das Experimentelle Photo in Deutschland 1918–1940* by Emilio Bertonati, Munich 1978; *Paris-Berlin 1900–1933,* exhibition catalogue, by Herbert Molderings, Werner Spies, Günter Metken and others, Paris 1978; *Photographen der 20er Jahre* by Karl Steinorth, Munich 1979; *Film und Foto der 20er Jahre,* exhibition catalogue, by Ute Eskildsen and Jan Christopher Horak, Stuttgart 1979; *Internationale Ausstellung des Deutschen Werkbundes "Film und Foto" 1929,* facsimile reprint, edited by Karl Steinorth, Stuttgart 1979; *Herbert Bayer: Recent Works,* exhibition catalogue, New York 1979; *Herbert Bayer: Das kunstlerische Werk 1918–1938,* exhibition catalogue, West Berlin 1982; *Herbert Bayer: The Complete Work* by Arthur A. Cohen, Cambridge, Massachusetts 1984.

I believe in a totality of art and design integrated with the life of our time. I have extensively collaborated with industry and other institutions toward the visual improvements in life.

—Herbert Bayer (1983)

Of all the artists who taught at the Bauhaus, Herbert Bayer was the most prone to the non-figurative-design way of life promoted by that institution. He himself was particularly active in the field of design, and much of what he produced at that time still influences the works of contemporary lay-out and functional design (and craft) as it is found in the notepaper, packaging and kindred requirements in bureaux of industry, commerce and trade today.

Something of this commercial "awareness" percolated through to his art works. Accuracy is exact. Almost over-exact. Techniques are manifold and he is the master of all of them. Neatness is the key-word to the entire oeuvre. The shapes and the compositions in which they find themselves cannot be faulted. Colours are chosen with unyielding care but not with love. Any one of Bayer's pictures could grace the boardroom without affront and without distracting attention from business. The words "modern art" would not pass through the head of any of the directors. Bayer is "safe," efficient, and burdened with good taste, a kind of glyptothek taste that wounds none, however up-to-date in accent.

Can he claim a place in the ranks of Contemporary Artists? As a stylist and one whose influence on design is far from moribund—Yes.

In the words of Will Grohmann, "Bayer was first and foremost a graphic designer, and secondly a painter who, with patterns and metal foil, succeeded in transcending reality."

—Sheldon Williams

BAZAINE, Jean.

French. Born in Paris, 21 December 1904. Educated in the Ile-de-France, 1914–20; studied sculpture with Landowski, Paris, 1920–24; mainly self-taught in painting, from 1924. Independent painter, Paris, since 1924; associated with artists Pierre Bonnard and Marcel Gromaire, from 1932; executed stained glass windows for church of Assy, 1943–47, for Chateau de la Chaux, Morvan, 1954, for church of Villaparisis 1958, and murals for church of Audincourt, 1951, Unesco Building, Paris, 1960, Maison de la Radio, Paris, 1963, and windows for Saint Severin, Paris, 1966. Recipient: Prix Blumenthal, Paris 1938; Grand Prix National des Arts, 1964. Address: c/o Editions de Seuil, 27 rue Jacob, 75006 Paris, France.

Individual Exhibitions:

1932 Galerie Van Leer, Paris
1934 Galerie Van Leer, Paris
1941 Galerie Jeanne Bucher, Paris
1945 Galerie Louis Carre, Paris (with Esteve and Lapicque)
1946 Stedelijk Museum, Amsterdam (with Esteve and Lapicque; travelled to the Statens Museum for Konst, Copenhagen, and the Foreningen for Nutida Konst, Stockholm)
1949 Galerie Maeght, Paris
1950 Galerie Blanche, Stockholm
1953 Galerie Maeght, Paris
1957 Galerie Maeght, Paris
1958 Galerie Benador, Geneva
1959 Kunsthalle, Berne, Switzerland (retrospective; travelled to Van Abbemuseum, Eindhoven, Netherlands, and the Stedelijk Museum, Amsterdam)
1963 Kestner-Gesellschaft, Hannover (retrospective; travelled to the Kunsthaus, Zurich, and the Kunstnernes Hus, Oslo)
1964 Galerie Blanche, Stockholm (travelled to the Konstmuseum, Gothenburg)
1965 Musée d'Art Moderne, Paris (retrospective)
Galerie Louis Carre, Paris
1968 Galerie Maeght, Paris
1975 *Aquarelles*, Villand-Galanis, Paris
1976 Galerie Maeght, Zurich
1979 Galerie Moderner Kunst, Frankfurt
1980 *Paintings and Watercolours 1970–1979*, Talbot Rice Art Centre, Edinburgh (travelled to the Institut Francais, London)

Selected Group Exhibitions:

1937 *L'Art Indépendant: Maitres d'Aujourd'hui*, Petit Palias, Paris
1941 *20 Jeunes Peintres de Tradition Francaise*, Galerie Braun, Paris
1942 *Bazaine/Esteve/Lapicque/Villon*, Galerie Louis Carre, Paris
1948 *Biennale*, Venice
1951 *Bienal*, San Paulo
1952 *Biennale*, Venice
1953 *Bienal*, Sao Paulo
1955 *Documenta*, Kassel, West Germany
1958 *World's Fair*, Brussels
1959 *Documenta*, Kassel, West Germany

Collections:

Centre Georges Pompidou, Paris; Stedelijk Museum, Amsterdam

Publications:

By BAZAINE: books—*La Noce Noire*, illustrations to poem by André Frenaud, Paris 1947; *Notes sur la peinture d'aujourd'hui*, Paris 1948, 1953, 1960; *Hollande*, with text by Jean Tardieu, Paris 1962; *Entre Savoir et Croire*, illustrations to text by Pierre Lecomte du Nouy, Paris 1964.

On BAZAINE: books—*Bazaine, Esteve, Lapicque*, exhibition catalogue, with text by André Frenaud, Paris 1945; *Peintres d'Aujourd'hui* by Pierre Courthion, Geneva 1952; *Jean Bazaine* by Jean Leymarie, Paris 1959; *Jean Bazaine*, exhibition catalogue, with text by Franz Meyer, Berne 1959; *Jean Bazaine*, exhibition catalogue, with text by Ole Henrik Moe, Oslo 1963; *Jean Bazaine*, exhibition catalogue, with text by Werner Schmalenbach, Hannover and Zurich 1963; *Jean Bazaine*, exhibition catalogue, with text by Bernard Dorival, Paris 1965; *Bazaine: Aquarelles*, exhibition catalogue, with text by Jean-Claude Schneider, Paris 1975; *Bazaine: Paintings and Watercolours 1970–1979*, exhibition catalogue, with text by Jean-Claude Schneider, Edinburgh and London 1980.

During the 1930's Jean Bazaine painted in a manner of expressive Naturalism in which the impact of the late Impressionism of Monet and Bonnard combined with influences from the Naturalism of Gromaire. Always sensitive to the value of tradition, he acknowledged his debt to both Fauvism and Cubism although he was never a convert to either style. He painted still lifes and landscapes, striving to come ever closer to the expressive individuality of his theme as in the "Nageur dans les roseaux" of 1943. During the 1940's he became increasingly discontent with the reproduction of expressive appearances and made it his aim to present the mysterious inner reality which lies behind the visible and external, what he called the "interior geometry of forms"—the secret rhythms and structure which in his view unite each individual thing with the totality of things while at the same time endowing it with its separate particularity for human feeling. Thus he evolved a non-objective mode of expression which had little in common with the "psychic improvisation" of Wols and Hartung or with the "automatism" of Riopelle but brought him within the ambit of the group of artists around Roger Bissière who wished to display the expressive structure of things without fidelity to appearances. His style at this time had affinities with that of the Tachists Charles Lapique, Alfred Manessier and Jean le Moal.

His essay *Notes sur la peintre d'aujourd'hui*, first published in 1948, gives an illuminating insight into his own artistic outlook and is perhaps the best statement ever made of the philosophy which animated painters of this school. In it he says: "A tree, a landscape, even a human face, I see these through their complex network of directions, their lines of force." He denies that his work was abstract in any other sense than that in which all art is necessarily abstract, but claimed that "the object must disappear as object to find its justification as form" and that in painting "an essential quality of the object devours the object." He also said that it was his aim "to retrieve the essential by violent means, the passion for expression relying on the choice of elementary colours and forms." His work at this period consisted typically of a lattice of firm and criss-cross lines in glowing, semi-transparent colours on several planes and distantly reminiscent of the stained glass technique in which he also worked. An example is "La Messe de l'Homme armé" (1944, illustrated in colour in Bernard Dorival's *Les Peintres du Vingtième Siècle*).

It was because of his belief in the unity of the whole universe and man, the oneness of form and feeling, that he understood his own style to represent a continuation and culmination of the main tradition of French painting. "True sensibility," he wrote, "begins when the painter discovers that the eddies of a tree and the bark of the water are kin, that the stones and his own face are twins, and when as the whole world thus shrinks together he gradually sees arise under this rain of appearances those great essential signs which are at once his own truth and the truth of the universe. For more than half a century we have shared the efforts of French painting to give ever new shape to its incarnation, to realize this interpretation, this great common structure, this profound resemblance between man and the world without which no living form exists."

From the mid 1950's his style became somewhat less rectilinear, as in the painting "Rochetaillée" (1955, illustrated in colour in Marcel Brion: *Art Abstrait*) and more free in the manner of Robert Lapoujade or Pierre Dmitrienko, as in "The Sea at Noon" (1960, illustrated in colour in H. Osborne: *The Oxford Companion to Twentieth-Century Art*).

—Harold Osborne

BEAL, Jack.

American. Born in Richmond, Virginia, 25 June 1931. Educated at the Norfolk Division of William and Mary College, Virginia, 1950–53; studied at the Art Institute of Chicago, under Briggs Dyer, Isobel MacKinnon and Kathleen Blackshear, 1953–56; University of Chicago, 1955–56. Painter: lives and works in New York. Artist-in-Residence/Visiting Lecturer, University of Indiana, Bloomington, 1966; Purdue University, Lafayette, Indiana, 1967; University of Wisconsin, Madison, 1967; and Cooper Union, New York, 1968. Recipient: First Prize, *University of Chicago Arts Festival*, 1955; Wild Award, *70th American Exhibition*, Art Institute of Chicago, 1972; National Endowment for the Arts Grant, 1972. Agent: Allan Frumkin Gallery, 50 West 57th Street, New York, New York 10019. Address: 67 Vestry Street, New York, New York 10013; and 83-A Delhi Stage, Oneonta, New York 13820, U.S.A.

Individual Exhibitions:

1965 Allan Frumkin Gallery, New York (2 exhibitions)
1966 Allan Frumkin Gallery, Chicago

Jack Beal: *The Painting Lesson*, 1981

1967 Allan Frumkin Gallery, New York
1968 *Recent Paintings by Jack Beal,* Allan Frumkin Gallery, New York
1969 Allan Frumkin Gallery, Chicago
1970 Allan Frumkin Gallery, New York
1972 Allan Frumkin Gallery, New York
Miami-Dade Junior College, Florida
1973 Allan Frumkin Gallery, New York
Galerie Claude Bernard, Paris
Virginia Museum, Richmond (retrospective; travelled to Boston University, and the Museum of Contemporary Art, Chicago, 1974)
1974 Allan Frumkin Gallery, Chicago
1975 Allan Frumkin Gallery, New York
1978 Allan Frumkin Gallery, New York
1980 Allan Frumkin Gallery, New York
Reynolds' Minor Gallery, Richmond, Virginia

Selected Group Exhibitions:

1968 *Whitney Annual,* Whitney Museum, New York (and 1969)
1969 *Aspects of a New Realism,* Milwaukee Art Center (toured the United States)
1971 *New Realism,* Art Gallery of the State University of New York at Potsdam (travelled to the Delaware Art Museum, Wilmington)
1973 *American Realism: Post Pop,* Oakland University, Rochester, Michigan
1975 *Drawings: Techniques and Types,* William Benton Museum of Art, University of Connecticut, Storrs
Portrait Painting 1970–1975, Allan Frumkin Gallery, New York
1976 *America 1976,* United States Department of the Interior travelling Exhibition (toured the United States, 1976–78)
1979 *100 Artists/100 Years: Alumni of the School of the Art Institute of Chicago,* Art Institute of Chicago
1981 *Contemporary American Realism since 1960,* Pennsylvania Academy of Fine Arts, Philadelphia
1985 *American Realism,* San Francisco Museum of Modern Art (travelled to Lincoln, Massachusetts; Austin, Texas; Evanston, Illinois; Williamstown, Massachusetts; Akron, Ohio; Madison, Wisconsin)

Collections:

Whitney Museum, New York; Museum of Modern Art, New York; Neuberger Museum, Purchase, New York; University of Vermont, Burlington; Delaware Art Museum, Wilmington; University of North Carolina, Chapel Hill; Art Institute of Chicago; Minneapolis Institute of Art; Walker Art Center, Minneapolis; Museum of Modern Art, San Francisco.

Publications:

On BEAL: books—*Recent Painting by Jack Beal,* exhibition catalogue, with an introduction by R. C. Kenedy, New York 1968; *Aspects of a New Realism,* exhibition catalogue, with texts by Sidney Tillim and William Wilson, Milwaukee 1969; *22 Realists,* exhibition catalogue, New York 1970; *Jack Beal,* exhibition catalogue, with text by Mark Strand, Paris 1973; *Jack Beal,* exhibition catalogue, with text by Peter Schjeldahl, Norfolk, Virginia 1973; *Jack Beal,* exhibition catalogue, with text by Gerrit Henry, New York 1975; *100 Artists/100 Years: Alumni of the School of the Art Institute of Chicago,* Chicago 1979; articles "Is Jack Beal Still a Figurative Painter?" by Scott Burton in *Art Scene* (Chicago), April 1969.

Make art like life—make life like art—that's become my motto. As a student my training was confined to modernist aesthetics and practices, which I finally found too restrictive. I began to paint from Life, and realized that I could use everything I had learned from modernism, *and* all that study of great representational art had taught me, to make paintings about the best of life as we live it. This purpose grew as I understood that the arts had influenced my own life at least as much as the experience of life itself had done. I hope to contribute to that tradition.

—Jack Beal

Among the diverse painters who arose during the late 1960's under the banner of 'New Realism,' Jack Beal lies somewhere towards the middle. Over the years his work has been more closely aligned with that of Philip Pearlstein and Alfred Leslie than that of the Photo-Realists. Beal concentrates on tightly controlled organization, structuring his complex composition with clarity of detail, intricate articulation of contour, color and light in a manner which implies the mentality of a post-Pop, post-formalist abstraction context. He is most noted for his compositions of the figure (many of them nudes) in interior environments filled with complexly patterned fabrics, which stress a dynamically diagonal thrust and a point of view slightly below eye level.

Among the best of these is Beal's "Danae" (1972) which skillfully incorporates flesh, figure, pattern and sharp light and shadow in an intimate interior, conveying a sense of presence yielded by its deliberately dispassionate ordering. Beal, like Pearlstein, stresses the objectivity of his analysis which treats the figure as one element among the many in the composition. Yet despite the sense of distancing and the antinarrative leaning, there is always a psychological element which reads as content beyond the formal in Beal's pictoral analyses. It is evoked by the very openness of the forms whose blank, nonjudgmental qualities constitute a state of mind as concrete as it is aesthetic. The title, "Danae," is suggestive of Beal's involvement with Renaissance to Baroque themes and structures which have lately come even more into the forefront of his painting.

In 1977 Beal completed a series of four murals commissioned by the General Services Administration for the Department of Labor Building in Washington, D.C. on the given theme of the History of American Labor. For help in accomplishing this complex task, Beal turned to the art historical past, specifically to Caravaggio, the Italian Mannerists and Benjamin West, for various elements of dramatic realism, composition and figure drawing. The murals, titled "Settlement," "Colonization," "Industry" and "Technology," are 12 by 12 foot, monumental statements of a sweeping moral nature which have earned Beal the position of being called the most prominent Social Realist in America since the 1930's generation.

Although Beal continues to paint his more intimate studies of figures and textured surroundings, he has also produced works of a more directly traditional thematic kind. In a series titled "Vices and Virtues" (Envy, Sloth, Prudence, Avarice, Lust, Anger, Justice, Fortitude), Beal makes his contemporary models into allegorical figures who symbolize the traditionally moral themes. As always, the compositions are tight and complex, stressing diagonal motion which is more violent in the painting of "Anger" and more meditatively dynamic in "Fortitude." In his large paintings "The Farm" (1979) and "Harvest" (1980), Beal takes on a more bucolic subject matter. Painted on his farm in Oneonta, New York, these two pictures combine two figures in a rural setting which is highly idealized. The man and woman in "The Farm" are painting some pigs in the company of a dog/companion and in a setting filled with some flowers and sun and blue skies. People, animals, art and nature working in harmony, the details of which are given tender loving care which is reminiscent of the Hudson River School painters and, even more, of the Pre-Raphaelite William Holman Hunt. However, there is the basic difference of context, relevance and artifice, and, although Beal is a master technician, the pictures come across as a kind of adaptation from the past which remains more in the realm of the formal than the social real or meaningful real, whether as art or as nature.

—Barbara Cavaliere

BEARDEN, Romare (Howard).

American. Born in Charlotte, North Carolina, 2 September 1914. Educated at Public School 139, New York, until 1925; Peabody High School, Pittsburgh, Pennsylvania, 1925–29; New York University, 1932–35, B.S. 1935; studied under George Grosz, at the Art Students League, New York, 1936–37; studied advanced mathematics at Columbia University, New York, 1943, and philosophy and art history at the Sorbonne, Paris, 1951. Served in the 372nd Infantry, United States Army, 1942–45. Married Nanette Rohan in 1954. Case Worker, New York City Department of Social Services, 1938–42, 1946–49, and 1952–66. Travelled in Italy, Switzerland, Algiers, and Morocco, 1950; concentrated on song writing, 1951–54; established studio on Canal Street, New York, 1956; Art Director, Harlem Cultural Council, New York, since 1964; Co-Founder, with Norman Lewis and Ernest Crichlow, Cinque Gallery in New York Public Theater, 1969; Set and Costume Designer for Alvin Ailey Ballet Company, New York, 1977. Artist-in-Residence, Spelman College, Atlanta, 1968; Visiting Lecturer in African and Afro-American Art, Williams College, Williamstown, Massachusetts, 1969; Artist-in-Residence, University of Delaware, Newark, 1970; Instructor, Yale College, New Haven, Connecticut, 1980. Recipient: American Academy of Arts and Letters Painting Award, 1966; National Institute of Arts and Letters Grant, 1966; Guggenheim Fellowship, 1970; Ford Foundation Fellowship, 1973; Medal of the State of North Carolina, 1976; Frederick Douglas Medal, New York Urban League, 1978; James Weldon Johnson Award, Atlanta Chapter of the National Association for the Advancement of Colored People (NAACP), 1978. Honorary Doctorates: Pratt Institute, New York, 1973; Carnegie Mellon University, Pittsburgh, 1975; Maryland Institute of Art, Baltimore, 1976; North Carolina Central University, Durham, 1977; Davidson College, North Carolina, 1978. Member, American Academy of Arts and Letters. Agent: Cordier and Ekstrom Inc., 980 Madison Avenue, New York, New York 10021. Address: 357 Canal Street, New York, New York 10013, U.S.A.

Individual Exhibitions:

1935 "G" Place Gallery, Washington, D.C.
1940 A. D. Bates Studio, New York
1944 *10 Hieroglyphic Paintings,* "G" Place Gallery, Washington, D.C.
1945 Galerie John Duvuloy, Paris (with Pietro Lazzari)
"G" Place Gallery, Washington, D.C.
Samuel Kootz Gallery, New York
1946 Samuel Kootz Gallery, New York
1947 Samuel Kootz Gallery, New York
1948 Niveau Gallery, New York
1955 Barone Gallery, New York
1960 Michel Warren Gallery, New York
1961 Cordier and Ekstrom Gallery, New York
1964 *Projections,* Cordier and Ekstrom Gallery, New York
1966 Carnegie Institute, Pittsburgh
6 Panels on a Southern Theme, Bundy Art Gallery, Waitsfield, Vermont
Corcoran Gallery, Washington, D.C.
1967 Fine Arts Building, Spelman College, Atlanta
Collages, J. L. Hudson Gallery, Detroit
Cordier and Ekstrom Gallery, New York
1968 *Paintings and Projections,* State University of New York at Albany
1969 Williams College, Williamstown, Massachusetts
Iowa State University, Iowa City
1970 Cordier and Ekstrom Gallery, New York
Tricia Karliss Gallery, Provincetown, Massachusetts
The Prevalence of Ritual, Museum of Modern Art, New York (retrospective; toured the United States, 1971–72)
Cordier and Ekstrom Gallery, New York
1973 Cordier and Ekstrom Gallery, New York
1974 Galerie Albert Loeb, Paris
Madison Art Museum, Wisconsin
Everson Museum, Syracuse, New York
Of the Blues, Cordier and Ekstrom Gallery, New York
1976 Firehouse Gallery, Nassau College, New York
Graphics Gallery, Toronto
Cordier and Ekstrom Gallery, New York
1977 Union College, Cranford, New Jersey
Odysseus: Collages, Cordier and Ekstrom Gallery, New York
1978 Cordier and Ekstrom Gallery, New York
Davidson College, North Carolina
1980 *Retrospective: 1970–1980,* Mint Museum, Charlotte, North Carolina (travelled to the Mississippi Museum of Art, Jackson; Baltimore Museum of Art; and the Virginia Museum of Fine Arts, Richmond, 1981)
1981 *Collages: Profile: The 30's,* Cordier and Ekstrom Gallery, New York

Selected Group Exhibitions:

1945 *Annual Exhibition,* Whitney Museum, New York (and 1946, 1955, 1969)
1948 *6 American Painters,* Galerie Maeght, Paris
Abstract and Surrealist American Art, Art Institute of Chicago
1951 *Survey of American Art,* Metropolitan Museum of Art, New York
1968 *30 Contemporary Black Artists,* Minneapolis Institute of Art (toured the United States, 1968–70)
1969 *New American Painting and Sculpture,* Museum of Modern Art, New York
1970 *5 Famous Black Artists,* Museum of the National Center of Afro-American Arts, Boston
1981 *6 Black Americans,* New Jersey State Museum, Trenton
The Human Form, Maryland Institute College of Art, Baltimore
24 Black American Artists, Goucher College, Baltimore

Collections:

Metropolitan Museum of Art, New York; Museum of Modern Art, New York; Whitney Museum, New York; Rochester Memorial Art Gallery, New York; Museum of Fine Arts, Boston; Princeton University, New Jersey; Newark Museum, New Jersey; Philadelphia Museum of Art; High Museum of Art, Atlanta; Madison Art Center, Wisconsin.

Publications:

By BEARDEN: books—*The Painter's Mind,* with Carl Holty, New York 1969; *6 Black Masters of American Art,* with Harry Henderson, New York 1972; *Prevalence of Ritual,* portfolio of 5 silkscreens, New York 1977; articles—"The Negro Artist and Modern Art" in *Opportunity,* December 1934; "Problems of the Negro Artists" in *Critique,* October 1948; "Rectangular Structure in My Montage Paintings" in *Leonardo* (Paris), January 1969; "The Artist and His Education" in *Harvard Art Review* (Cambridge, Massachusetts), Spring 1969.

On BEARDEN: books—*Romare Bearden: Paintings and Projections,* exhibition catalogue, with text by Ralph Ellison, Albany, New York 1968; *Romare Bearden: The Prevalence of Ritual,* exhibition catalogue, with an introduction by Carroll

Greene, New York 1971; *The Art of Romare Bearden* by John Williams and Bundie Washington, New York 1974; *Of the Blues,* exhibition catalogue, with text by Albert Murray, New York 1975; *Romare Bearden: Odysseus: Collages,* exhibition catalogue, with an introduction by Calvin Tomkins, New York 1977; *Romare Bearden: Collages: Profile: The 30's,* exhibition catalogue, edited by Albert Murray, New York 1981; articles—"Romare Bearden—Projections" by Dore Ashton in *Quadrum* (Brussels), no. 17, 1965; "Black Persephone" by Ralph Pomeroy in *Artnews* (New York), October 1967; "Romare Bearden—Paintings and Projections" by Ralph Ellison in *Crisis* (New York), March 1970; "Profile: by Calvin Tomkins in *New Yorker,* 28 November 1977; "Romare Bearden: 'I Paint Out of the Tradition of the Blues' " by Avis Berman in *Artnews* (New York), December 1980; "Romare Bearden" in *Vogue* (New York), February 1981; "Romare Bearden" in *Smithsonian* (Washington, D.C.), March 1981; "Romare Bearden" in *Newsweek* (New York), 30 March 1981; "Romare Bearden: Rites and Riffs" by M. S. Campbell in *Art in America* (New York), December 1981.

Part of Romare Bearden's originality lies in his application of the formal means discovered by the Cubist masters at the beginning of the century to the world of the American black. Negro himself, he simply rethought the subject matter that interested and involved him most in such a way that he was able to "distance" it as an artist and, instead of some negative form of protest, to take the history and life of his race and present it anew in works of high artistic sophistication. He has looked fully and found Aphrodite in a vegetable patch, "The Three Musicians" in the apartment next door.

His themes run to jazz and folk music, urban and rural Negro life, rituals of baptism and voodoo, home life and street action. He prefers the archetypal and the not-too-specific image. He combines fragments of photostats and torn and cut paper which he has painted and mounts them on canvas. Usually he draws the composition beforehand in charcoal in the traditional manner. There is something especially "right" about his large collages in their mix of African imagery with Cubist space—a moving backwards as it were through art history past the discoveries of African art that led to the invention of Cubism. It is this formal strength that sets Bearden apart from many of his contemporaries. He is not afraid of the strong traditional qualities in his pictures. In fact he strives for them. By being so much a part of something already established in terms of time he is able to surmount the merely fashionable and enter a larger span of time. It is also a way of placing at the proper distance whatever it is he wants to show us. His sense of the largeness of his themes enables him not only to equate a field hand with a god, but to mix the races: it is no surprise in his work to come upon, say, a hand that has both black and white fingers. This way he avoids being pinned down to the over-simplified and the over-stressed. Because he has taken unexpected routes, he has succeeded in arriving at new realms of dignity.

—Ralph Pomeroy

BECHER, Bernhard and Hilla.

German. Bernhard Becher born in Siegen, 20 August 1931; studied painting and lithography at the Staatlichen Kunstakademie, Stuttgart, 1953–56, and typography at the Staatlichen Kunstakademie, Dusseldorf, 1957–61. Hilla Becher born Hilla Wobeser in Potsdam 2 September 1934; studied photography in Potsdam, and painting at the Staatlichen Kunstakademie, Dusseldorf. Bernhard and Hilla Becher married in 1961; they have worked together as freelance photographic artists, concentrating on industrial photography, Dusseldorf, since 1959. Both are instructors in photography at the Staatlichen Kunstakademie, Dusseldorf. Recipients: British Council Photo Study Grant, 1966; Fritz-Thyssen-Stiftung grant, West Germany, 1967–68. Agents: Galerie Konrad Fischer, Platanenstrasse 7, Dusseldorf; Nigel Greenwood Inc., 4 New Burlington Street, London W1X 1FE, England; and Sonnabend Gallery, 420 West Broadway, New York, New York 10012, U.S.A. Address: Wittlauer 4, Am Muhlenkamp 16, Dusseldorf, West Germany.

Individual Exhibitions:

1963 Galerie Ruth Nohl, Siegen, West Germany
1965 Galerie Pro, Bad Godesburg, West Germany
1966 Staatliche Kunstakademie, Dusseldorf
1967 Staatliches Museum, Munich
Technische Hochschule, Karlsruhe
Bergbau-Museum, Bochum, West Germany
Kunstakademie, Copenhagen
1968 Wachsman Institute, University of Southern California, Los Angeles
Goethe Center, San Francisco
Stedelijk Van Abbemuseum, Eindhoven, Netherlands
Galerie Ruth Nohl, Siegen, West Germany
Städtisches Museum, Monchengladbach, West Germany
1969 Städtische Kunsthalle, Dusseldorf
1970 Städtisches Museum, Ulm, West Germany
Form genom Funktion, Moderna Museet, Stockholm
Galerie Konrad Fischer, Dusseldorf
1971 Kabinett für Aktuelle Kunst, Bremerhaven, West Germany
Gegenverkehr, Aachen, West Germany
1972 Sonnabend Gallery, New York
Bennington College, Vermont
1973 Galleria Forma, Genoa
Nigel Greenwood Inc., London
Sonnabend Gallery, New York
1974 Institute of Contemporary Arts, London (toured the U.K.)
LaJolla Museum of Contemporary Art, California
Sonnabend Gallery, New York
1975 *Fotografien* 1957–1975, Rheinisches Landesmuseum, Bonn
Galleria Castelli, Milan
Museum of Modern Art, New York
Sonnabend Gallery, New York
1976 Kunsthalle, Tübingen, West Germany
1977 Sonnabend Gallery, New York
1978 Sonnabend Gallery, New York
Milwaukee Art Center, Wisconsin
Von der Heydt Museum, Wuppertal, West Germany
1979 Galerie Sonnabend, Paris
Kunstbibliothek Tranegarden, Copenhagen
Galleria Massimo Valsecchi, Milan
Kunstraum Munich
1981 Stedelijk Van Abbemuseum, Eindhoven, Netherlands (Retrospective)
Kunstverein, Siegen, West Germany
Sonnabend Gallery, New York
Carl Taylor Gallery, Dallas
1982 Sonnabend Gallery, New York
1985 Museum Folkwang, Essen, West Germany
Musée d'Art Moderne, Paris
Musée d'Art Moderne, Liège, Belgium
1986 Architekturmuseum, Basle

Selected Group Exhibitions:

1969 *Prospekt '69,* Städtische Kunsthalle, Dusseldorf
1970 *Information,* Museum of Modern Art, New York
1974 *Art and Image in Recent Art,* Art Institute of Chicago
1975 *New Topographics: Photographs of a Man-Altered Landscape,* International Museum of Photography, George Eastman House, Rochester, New York (travelled to the Otis Art Institute, Los Angeles, and Princeton University Art Museum, New Jersey)
1977 *Documenta 6,* Museum Fridericianum, Kassel, West Germany
1979 *Photographie als Kunst 1879–1979/Kunst als Photographie 1949–1979,* Tiroler Landesmuseum Ferdinandeum, Innsbruck, Austria (travelled to the Neue Galerie am Wolfgang Gurlitt Museum, Linz, Austria; Neue Galerie am Landesmuseum Joanneum, Graz, Austria; and Museum des 20. Jahrhunderts, Vienna)
Concept, Narrative, Document, Museum of Contemporary Art, Chicago
1981 *Photos der 70er Jahre,* Galerie Wilde, Cologne
1983 *The Medium is Photography,* San Francisco Museum of Modern Art
1987 *Photography and Art 1946–86,* Los Angeles County Museum of Art

Collections:

Wallraf-Richartz Museum, Cologne; Moderna Museet, Stockholm; Tate Gallery, London; Museum of Modern Art, New York; Metropolitan Museum of Art, New York; Allen Memorial Art Museum, Oberlin College, Ohio; Art Gallery of Ontario, Toronto.

Publications:

By the BECHERS: books—*Anonyme Skulpturen: Eine Typologie Technische Bauten,* Dusseldorf 1970; *Die Architektur der Förder-und Wasser-Türme,* with text by W. Schoenberg, J. Werth and T. Aachen, Munich 1971; *Industrial Buildings,* portfolio of 14 photos, Munich 1975; *Framework Houses of the Siegen Industrial Region,* Munich 1977; articles—interview, with Lynda Morris, in *Berhard and Hilla Becher,* exhibition catalogue, London 1974; "Photographing Industrial Architecture," interview, with Angela Graverholz and Anne Ramsden, in *Parachute* (Montreal), Spring 1981.

On the BECHERS: books *Bernhard och Hilla Becher: form genom Funktion,* exhibition catalogue, Stockholm 1970; *Visuelle Kommunikation,* edited by Hermann K. Ehmer, Cologne 1971; *Bernhard and Hilla Becher,* exhibition catalogue, edited by Lynda Morris, London, 1974; *Berhard and Hilla Becher,* exhibition catalogue, with text by Germano Celant, LaJolla, California 1974; *Bernhard and Hilla Becher: Fotografien 1957–1975,* exhibition catalogue, with text by Klaus Honnef, Bonn 1975; *New Topographics: Photographs of a Man-Altered Landscape,* exhibition catalogue, with text by William Jenkins, Rochester, New York 1975; *Documenta 6/Band 2,* exhibition catalogue, edited by Klauf Honnef and Evelyn Weiss, Kassel and Cologne 1977; *Geschichte der Fotografie im 20. Jahrhundert/Photography in the 20th Century* by Petr Rausk, Cologne 1977, London 1980; *Typologien Industrieller Bau 1963–1975,* exhibition catalogue, Sao Paulo 1977; *Photographie als Kunst 1879–1979/Kunst als Photographie 1949–1979,* exhibition catalogue, 2 vols., by Peter Weiermair, Innsbruck, Austria 1979; *Bernd und Hilla Becher,* Exhibition catalogue, Essen 1985; *Photography and Art 1946–86,* exhibition catalogue by Andy Grundberg and Kathleen M. Gauss, Los Angeles 1987.

The age of industrialization brought with it vast collections of documentation which depicted all the elements of mechanical subjects in the clearest detail. Towards the 18th Century when smokestacks, factories and bridges became an almost inseparable part of the landscape, this documentation, once a singular expression of scientific reality, had also become a statement of new sociological and human realities. Since 1959 Hilla and Bernd Becher, upholding a tradition of archeological-industrial documentation, have salvaged testimonies of past developments for future cultural historians.

Their medium is photography, one that ignores every expressionistic component and concentrates on the real subject. The anonymous nature of photography gives the viewer the possibility of perceiving the reality of a rational and conceptual process, which produces two results: the first, the industrial monument, and the second, an artistic composition. This monument will derive a decorative value because it exists as a testimony of itself without the artists in any way adding a personal setting. It was with great perserverance that the Bechers traced a variety of objects, simply because they existed. They began photographing in Germany, then travelled to the industrial regions of Belgium, France, Luxemborg, Holland, England and the United States. Their artistic endeavours were propelled as much by their interest in the technical qualities of these areas as by the

Bernhard and Hilla Becher: ***Blast Furnaces*****, 1970–1980**

strange fascination of the "anonymous" buildings, many of which, having been recently demolished, remain only as a visual record.

To organise the overwhelming quantity of their work, the Bechers developed a consistent, methodological photographic approach. Irrespective of the photograph's subject, a certain legibility had to be maintained. The photographs had to be pure images rather than the artists' interpretation. Each shot was equal in light intensity: greyish, overcast, even skies, no dramatic cloud effects producing photographs at once factual and objective and simultaneously enhanced by the details unfolding around the subject. Equally important to the Bechers' approach was the concept of comparability, since the true character of an object gains explicitness when compared with other objects of the same kind. Thus by means of a comparison of all available structures of a particular type and by means of offering different angles and different points of view, they reveal their subject.

The visual association of the same subjects, specifically industrial monuments, provides a "reading system" for visual comparison, enabling artifacts of apparent anonymity and banality to be seen in terms of notable decorative and typological differences. The Bechers are chiefly interested in photographing a sequence of heavy drills, silos, gas tanks, water towers and other structures. Each structural "family" disposes itself throughout the sequences of illustrations to form typological catalogues whose variations are grouped according to their material and formal similarities. But these are presented in a way that offers contrasting images characterized by symbols and ornamentation of different styles. Thus the visual result (in the same category of object) glows with differences, paradoxes and contradictions, likening it to sculpture.

The Bechers' photographs, along with their other capabilities, underline environmental and social differences between the cultures. They show the industrial monuments of England as being cold, resolved to mere practical uses and devoid of aesthetic value. Those of Continental Europe, however, are quietly symbolic as if to negate their function by masquerading as buildings either Romanesque or Renaissance. The typological correlation of different structures of different periods or countries has become not just a source of information of different areas of knowledge (history, technology), but also a new kind of vision. In this sense Bernd and Hilla Becher are making significant visual and intellectual contributions to our knowledge of the environment.

—Carrie Barker

BECHTLE, Robert (Alan).

American. Born in San Francisco, California, 14 May 1932. Studied graphic design at the California College of Arts and Crafts, Oakland, 1950–54, 1956–58, B.A. 1954, M.F.A. 1958; education and literature, University of California at Berkeley, 1960–61. Served in the United States Army, 1954–56. Married Nancy Elizabeth Dalton in 1963; children: Max, Robert, and Anne Elizabeth. Worked part-time as Graphic Designer for Kaiser Industries, Oakland, California, 1956–59; travelled in Europe, 1961–62;

Robert Bechtle: *'61 Pontiac*, 1969

established studio in Oakland, 1966. Instructor, 1957–61, and Associate Professor, 1962–65, California College of Arts and Crafts, Oakland; Lecturer in Design, University of California at Berkeley, 1965–66; Associate Professor, San Francisco State University, now California State University, since 1968. Visiting Artist, University of California at Davis, 1967–68. Recipient: James D. Phelan Award for Painting, San Francisco, 1965; National Endowment for the Arts Grant, Washington, D.C., 1977, 1982. Agents: O. K. Harris Gallery, 383 West Broadway, New York, New York 10012; John Berggruen Gallery, 228 Grant Avenue, San Francisco, California 94108. Address: 4250 Horton Street, Apartment 14, Emeryville, California 94608, U.S.A.

Individual Exhibitions:

1959 Museum of Art, San Francisco
1965 Berkeley Gallery, San Francisco
Richmond Art Center, California
1966 E. B. Crocker Art Gallery, Sacramento, California
1967 University of California at Davis
Berkeley Gallery, San Francisco
San Francisco Museum of Art
1969 Achenbach Foundation for Graphic Arts, San Francisco
1971 O. K. Harris Gallery, New York
1973 E. B. Crocker Art Gallery, Sacramento, California (retrospective; travelled to the Fine Arts Gallery, San Diego)
John Berggruen Gallery, San Francisco (retrospective; travelled to Jack Glenn Gallery, San Diego)
1974 O. K. Harris Gallery, New York
O. K. Harris Gallery, New York
1977 O. K. Harris Gallery, New York
1980 Matrix Gallery, University of California Art Museum, Berkeley

Selected Group Exhibitions:

1968 *Realism Now*, Vassar College, Poughkeepsie, New York
1970 *22 Realists*, Whitney Museum, New York
1971 *Radical Realism*, Museum of Contemporary Art, Chicago
1972 *Documenta 5*, Kassel, West Germany
1975 *Image, Color and Form: Recent Paintings by Americans*, Toledo Museum of Art, Ohio
1976 *Super Realism*, Baltimore Museum of Art
1977 *30 Years of American Art 1945–1975*, Whitney Museum, New York
1980 *Photo-Realistic Painting in California: A Survey*, Santa Barbara Museum of Art
1985 *American Realism*, San Francisco Museum of Modern Art (travelled to Lincoln, Massachusetts; Austin, Texas; Evanston, Illinois; Williamstown, Massachusetts; Akron, Ohio; Madison, Wisconsin)
1988 *Figure It Out: Visual Body Language*, Helander Gallery, Palm Beach, Florida

Collections:

Guggenheim Museum, New York; Museum of Modern Art, New York; Chase Manhattan Bank, New York; Library of Congress, Washington, D.C.; Caollection of Fine Arts, Smithsonian Institution, Washington, D.C.; High Museum of Art, Atlanta; Oakland Museum, California; Mills College, Oakland; San Francisco Museum of Modern Art; Arts Council of Great Britain, London.

Publications:

By BECHTLE: articles—interview, with Brian O'Doherty, in *Art in America* (New York), November/December 1972; interview, with P. J. Karlstrom, in *Archives of American Art Journal* (Washington, D.C.), vol. 20, no. 2, 1980.

On BECHTLE: books—*Realism Now*, exhibition catalogue, with an introduction by Linda Nochlin, Poughkeepsie, New York 1968; *The Highway*, exhibition catalogue, with an introduction by Denise Scott Brown and Robert Venturi, Philadelphia 1970; *22 Realists*, exhibition catalogue, New York 1970; *Robert Bechtle: A Retrospective Exhibition*, catalogue, with text by Susan McKillop, Sacramento, California 1973; *Neue Formen des Realismus* by Peter Sager, Cologne 1973; *Super Realism* by Gregory Battcock, New York 1975; *Superrealist Painting and Sculpture* by C. Lindey, New York 1980.

I first started to work in a realistic manner as a way of avoiding many of the problems of style that were troubling me in the early 1960's. I was interested in the use of subject matter, and Realism, paradoxically,

seemed the only direction that was relatively open and free of recent precedent. It offered the prospect of solving painting problems without being overly aware of how others had solved them or even knowing what the problems and possibilities might be.

My inclination toward the use of subject matter goes back to the Bay Area Figurative tradition of the late 50's. My drift to realism came partly as a reaction against the more obvious expressionist attitudes of the tradition and partly as an acceptance of the implications of using subject matter for its own sake.

It became important for me to try for a kind of neutrality or transparency that hides the more artful evidences of the painter's craft and that causes the subject to be the first thing encountered in the picture. Of course my painting is no more neutral than any other. It involves choice, decision, emotion, etc., but hopefully in a way that is not overly apparent. I choose to paint the things I do—cars, suburban street, etc., because they seem to offer the greatest opportunity of looking without reminding me of other art.

—Robert Bechtle

One of America's leading Photo-Realists, Robert Bechtle has systematically explored the possibilities of the realist style for more than two decades. Like many other young California art students in the late 1950's, he first experimented with Abstract Expressionism before coming under the influence of Bay Area figurative painters such as Richard Diebenkorn and Nathan Oliveira. During and immediately following a trip to Europe his interests became more objective and, as a consequence, his style tighter and less expressionistic. Stimulated by a growing desire to record the appearances of things, and his concurrent exposure to the work of Larry Rivers and the British Pop artists, Bechtle began to look with fresh eyes at his suburban California environment as a possible subject for serious painting.

By 1963 Bechtle had abandoned the Bay Area figurative style in a favor of a far more literal treatment of common-place subjects within the context of contemporary formalist issues. At the same time, he became interested in Pop Art's use of commercial art techniques—notably photography. Initially concentrating on objects within the studio—pictures, mirrors, furniture—depicted straight-forwardly but within a rigidly controlled format, he soon turned his attention outside to the still-life framed by the studio window. It was at this point that the parked automobile accidentally entered Bechtle's *oeuvre* in "'56 Plymouth" (1963). A subsequent painting depicting another car through a window, "'61 Pontiac" (1963), began the series of automobile portraits that occupied him through the mid-70's and for which he is probably best known. Typical and important examples are "'61 Pontiac," 1969 (Whitney Museum) and "'60 T-Bird," 1967–68 (University Art Museum, Berkeley).

Bechtle's approach to his subjects—parked automobiles, snapshot vignettes of middle-class life, abandoned streets in suburban neighborhoods, or family and friends gethered on decks and patios (e.g. "Stinson Beach Cookout," 1979)—is that of a sympathetic but neutral observer: sympathetic in that he is depicting the world in which he grew up and neutral in his lack of overt commentary. His frequently banal subjects are chosen precisely because they are unremarkable. Presented within a fine art context, they challenge the established ways we look at our surroundings. Above all, Bechtle (like most of his fellow Photo-Realists) strives to avoid symbolic and literary content. He selects familiar, nondescript objects to allow the viewer to respond directly to the painting without interference on the part of the artist.

Bechtle's methodology involves the basic Photo-Realist practice of creating compositions from projected slides (the "models") with a minimum adjustment of elements. The practice is laborious, time-consuming, and far from spontaneous. Another area of Bechtle's creative activity, one in which he is an accomplished master, allows for the immediacy his large oil paintings deny him. Bechtle's watercolor views of sunwashed stucco facades and neat suburban lawns convey the precise temperature and time of day in a manner that brings to mind Edward Hopper or even Winslow Homer. "Ingleside House" of 1975 (Oakland Museum) perfectly embodies the sensitive and contemplative observation which distinguishes Bechtle's softened Photo-Realism. Breathing life into sharp-focus literalism, he maintains a humanistic warmth missing in the glittering, reflective and artificial surfaces of many of his colleagues' more dramatic images. In Bechtle's paintings, humble and familiar subjects are skillfully transformed into convincing and imposing works of art.

—Paul J. Karlstrom

BECKLEY, Bill.

American. Born in Hamburg, Pennsylvania, 11 February 1946. Educated at Kutztown State College, Pennsylvania, 1964–68, B.A. 1968; studied under Italo Scanga and Steven Green, Temple University, Philadelphia, 1968–70, M.F.A. 1970. Instructor, School of Visual Arts, New York, since 1971. Committee Member, New York State Council of Arts Grants, 1975. Recipient: Creative Artists Program Service Grant, New York, 1972, 1973, 1974, 1975; National Endowment for the Arts Grant, Washington, D.C., 1979; New York Foundation of the Arts Grant, 1987. Agent: Hans Mayer, Grabbeplatz 2, 4000 Dusseldorf, West Germany. Address: 155 Wooster Street, New York, New York 10012, U.S.A.

Individual Exhibitions:

1969 Wabash Transit Gallery, Chicago
1971 93 Grand Street, New York (performance)
1972 98 Green Street, New York (performance)
112 Green Street, New York (installation)
Galerie Rudolf Zwirner, Cologne (performance)
Galerie 20, Amsterdam
Galleria Françoise Lambert, Milan
1973 John Gibson Gallery, New York
Nigel Greenwood Gallery, London
Galerie Conrad Fischer, Dusseldorf
1974 Galerie 20, Amsterdam
Galleria François Lambert, Milan (performance)
John Gibson Gallery, New York
1975 Galerie Yvon Lambert, Paris
Galerie Patric Verelst/Marc Poitier, Antwerp
Galleria François Lambert, Milan
Steinway Hall, New York (performance)
Galerie 20, Amsterdam
1976 Galleria d'Allessandro-Ferranti, Rome
Narrational Imagery: Beckley, Ruscha, Warhol, University of Massachusetts, Amherst
John Gibson Gallery, New York
Galleria Lucio Amelio, Naples
1977 Nigel Greenwood Gallery, London
Galerie Denise René/Hans Mayer, Dusseldorf
1978 Galerie Daniel Templon, Paris
1979 Museum of Modern Art, New York
1980 Hal Bromm Gallery, New York
Bill Beckley and Philip Greenwood, Nigel Greenwood Gallery, London
1981 Annina Nosei Gallery, New York
Marian Deson Gallery, Chicago
Galerie Daniel Templon, Paris
International Center of Photography, New York
1982 Studio Cannaviello, Milan
Brownlow Gallery, New York
1983 John Gibson Gallery, New York
Galerie Denise Rene/Hans Mayer, Dusseldorf
1984 Freidus/Ordover Gallery, New York
Stadtisches Museum, Monchengladbach, West Germany (retrospective)
1986 Galerie Daniel Templon, Paris
John Gibson Gallery, New York
Galleria Pasquale Trisorio, Naples
1987 Toni Shafrazi Gallery, New York
Galerie Hans Mayer, Dusseldorf

Selected Group Exhibitions:

1969 *Art in the Mind,* Allen Memorial Art Museum, Oberlin, Ohio
1971 *Projects Piers 18,* Museum of Modern Art, New York
1972 *Actualité d'un Bilan,* Galerie Yvon Lambert, Paris
1973 *"7",* Museum of Modern Art, New York
Biennale, Paris
1976 *Biennale,* Venice
1977 *Documenta 6,* Kassel, West Germany
Pier + Ocean, Hayward Gallery, London (travelled to the Rijksmuseum Kroller-Muller, Otterlo, Netherlands)
1983 *Kunst mit Photographie,* Nationalgalerie, West Berlin (travelled to Cologne, Munich and Kiel)
1985 *A New Beginning,* Hudson River Museum, Yonkers, New York
1987 *Large Scale Photography,* Los Angeles County Museum of Art

Collections:

Museum of Modern Art, New York; Guggenheim Museum, New York; Whitney Museum, New York; Kunstmuseum, Basel; Stadtisches Museum, Monchengladbach; Victoria and Albert Museum, London; La Jolla Art Museum, California; Cincinnati Art Museum, Ohio; Morton Neuman Collection, Chicago.

Publications:

On BECKLEY: books—*Art in the Mind,* exhibition catalogue, by Athena Spear, Oberlin, Ohio 1969; *Narrative Art,* exhibition catalogue, Brussels 1974; *In Progress 5,* exhibition catalogue, with text by Achille Bonita Oliva, Livorno, Italy 1975; *Modern Art* by Sam Hunter, New York 1979; *Bill Beckley,* exhibition catalogue, Monchengladbach, West Germany 1984; *Bill Beckley,* exhibition catalogue, Paris 1986; articles—"Story Art" by James Collins in *Artforum* (New York), September 1973; "Bill Beckley" in *Heute Kunst* (Dusseldorf), July/August 1973; "Bill Beckley" in *Interfunctionen* (Cologne), no. 10, 1973; "Bill Beckley" by M. Jochimsen in *Kunst* (Mainz, West Germany), September 1974; "Story Art" by James Collins in *New York Magazine,* October 1974; "Narrative Art" in *Arti* (Milan), January 1975; "Story Art" by Barbara Radice in *Data* (Milan), June 1975; "Narrative Art" by Peter Schjeldahl in *Domus* (Milan), February 1976; "Bill Beckley's Lies" by E. Cameron in *Artforum* (New York), February 1977; "Bill Beckley: L'Archeologie du Tableau" by Anne Dagbert in *Art Press* (Paris), June 1985.

Born in 1946, Bill Beckley is not only one of the youngest proponents of the new "Narrative Art," but also one who has produced one of the most solid bodies of work in a relatively short time. Like other artists whose work has been linked to the grass-roots "Story Art" movement, such as James Collins, William Wegman, and even John Baldessari, Beckley concerns himself with three interrelationships; time, relationships between objects, humans, animals and natural or urban phenomena, and process. Also like them, Beckley spices his technically brilliant, sleek series of photographs and texts with a gleeful wit ranging from the subtly self-deprecating to the patently absurd. As a result, his work tends to be more immediately accessible than, for example, David Askevold's or Peter Hutchinson's.

Formerly, Beckley presented his stories in a shaggy dog style, beginning and ending with deliberately pointless incidents—sometimes an encounter between a young man (the artist) and a groundhog, sometimes an erotic encounter more obviously based in fantasy than in reality, though the confessional spirit seems to be an underlying thematic device. Beckley's "shaggy

dog stories" have been from his first shows immensely popular (though never populist), because they never propound theory but present faintly ridiculous incidents via one or two mysteriously selected photographs and a dead-pan, non-editorializing simple text. Because of this tersely poetic presentation, his stories frequently take on the characteristics of entertaining myths or children's tales once told to prove an otherwise, unpalatable point.

Beckley's work since 1975 shares this mythologizing aspect, but has become less accessible and perhaps consequently stronger in its formal aspects. It has become, in fact, a work hinging more directly on the manipulation of mood in a progressively more theatrical (or contrived) context. Beckley depends less on the unconscious and more on establishing a formal situation, while replacing the explicit story/subject with an implicit one. The "characters" in his stories—which rely almost entirely on large panels of color prints—now tend to be almost exclusively domestic objects, engaged in an anthropomorphic visual dialogue. Two color-coded faucets, for example, drip and meet in a single stream down a yellow drain; a broom relentlessly follows a dustball until it is, literally, swept "under the rug"; two equally lovely professional photographic models wordlessly enact the vainglorious theme of Snow White, in his panel, "The Fairest of Them All"; even a hamburger and its condiments are "actors" in a Beckley scenario. Because of the increased visualization of Beckley's narrations, the trick ending so frequently used to effect in his shaggy dog period has been deliberately sacrificed for a harder, more sophisticated statement; the slyly innocent inanities in the early work are making way for greater formal impact in the exquisite staging of objects photographed in lush flat colors, and an increasingly mysterious iconographic power.

—Jane Bell

BELL, Larry.

American. Born in Chicago, Illinois, 6 December 1939. Educated at Birmingham High School, Eureka, California, 1953–57; Chouinard Art Institute, Los Angeles, 1957–59. Married Gloria Jean Neilsen in 1967 (divorced, 1971); daughter: Zara Augusta; has lived with Janet Ruth Burns, since 1973. Worked as a bowling alley maintenance engineer, truck driver and picture framer, Los Angeles, 1957–59; general manager, The Unicorn saloon-cabaret, Hollywood, 1957–65. Full-time artist since 1965. Instructor, University of California, Berkeley, 1972, and University of South Florida, Tampa, 1973. Founder-Member, with Bob Irwin, Newton Harrison, Joshua Young, Ed Wirtz, and Frank Geary, Don Quixote Collective, California, 1974. Recipient: William Noma Copley Foundation Prize, 1963; Guggenheim Fellowship, 1969. Address: Box 4101, Taos, New Mexico 87571, U.S.A.

Individual Exhibitions:

1962 Ferus Gallery, Los Angeles
1963 Ferus Gallery, Los Angeles
1965 Ferus Gallery, Los Angeles
Pace Gallery, New York
1967 Galerie Sonnabend, Paris
Pace Gallery, New York
Stedelijk Museum, Amsterdam
1969 Mizuno Gallery, Los Angeles
1970 Pace Gallery, New York
Ace Gallery, Los Angeles
1971 Pace Gallery, New York
Helman Gallery, St. Louis
Mizuno Gallery, Los Angeles
Ace Gallery, Los Angeles
Galerie Rudolf Zwirner, Cologne
1972 Pace Gallery, New York
Felicity Samuel Gallery, London
Pasadena Art Museum, California
Wilmaro Gallery, Denver
1973 Oakland Art Museum, California
Pace Gallery, New York
Bonython Gallery, Sydney
1974 Marlborough Galleria d'Arte, Rome (toured Italy)
Galleria La Cittá, Verona
Galleria Il Cavallino, Venice
Salone Annunciata, Milan
1975 Marlborough Galleria d'Arte, Rome (toured Italy)
Galleria Il Cavallino, Venice
Tally Richards Gallery, Taos, New Mexico
Recent Works, Fort Worth Art Museum, Texas
1976 Washington University, St. Louis
Santa Barbara Museum of Art, California
Art Museum of South Texas, Corpus Christi
1977 Hayden Gallery, Massachusetts Institute of Technology, Cambridge
University of Massachusetts, Amherst
Federal Reserve, Boston
Fort Worth Art Museum, Texas (with Eric Orr)
1978 Multiples Gallery, New York
Delahunty Gallery, New York
Texas Gallery, Houston
Erica Williams-Anne Johnson Gallery, Seattle
University of New Mexico, Albuquerque
Roswell Museum and Art Center, New Mexico
Tally Richards Gallery, Taos, New Mexico
1979 Roswell Museum and Art Center, New Mexico
Multiples Gallery, New York
Sebastian-Moore Gallery, Denver
Hill's Gallery of Contemporary Art, Santa Fe, New Mexico
Hansen Fuller Gallery, San Francisco
Tally Richards Gallery, Taos, New Mexico
Janus Gallery, Venice, California
Marian Goodman Gallery, New York
1980 Sebastian-Moore Gallery, Denver
Hill's Gallery of Contemporary Art, Santa Fe, New Mexico
Tally Richards Gallery, Taos, New Mexico
Marion Goodman Gallery, New York
1981 Hudson River Museum, Yonkers, New York
Marion Goodman Gallery, New York
Ann Jacob Gallery, Atlanta, Georgia (with Eric Orr)
L. A. Louver Gallery, Venice, California
Wildine Galleries, Albuquerque, New Mexico
Tally Richard Gallery, Taos, New Mexico
University of Ohio, Athens
1982 Newport Harbor Art Museum, Newport Beach, California
Marion Goodman/Multiples Gallery, New York.
Ruth S. Schaffner Gallery, Santa Barbara, California
Erica Williams/Anne Johnson Gallery, Seattle, Washington
Milwaukee Art Museum, Wisconsin
Museum of Fine Arts, Santa Fe, New Mexico
Tally Richards Gallery, Taos, New Mexico
Detroit Institute of Arts, Michigan
1983 University of Nebraska, Lincoln
Advanced Art Gallery, Riconada, New Mexico
Arco Center for Visual Art, Los Angeles
Wildine Gallery, Albuquerque, New Mexico
1984 Colorado springs Fine Arts Center, Colorado
Museum of Contemporary Art, Los Angeles
The Works Gallery, Long Beach, California
1985 Dord Fitz Gallery, Amarillo, Texas (with Lee Mullican)
The Works Gallery, Long Beach, California
L. A. Louver Gallery, Venice, California
1986 Braunstein Gallery, San Francisco
Boise Gallery of Art, Idaho
The New Gallery, Houston
Amarillo Art Center, Texas
1987 Galerie Gilbert Brownstone, Paris
Braunstein/Quay Gallery, San Francisco (with Peter Voulkos)

Selected Group Exhibitions:

1964 *California Hard-Edge Painting*, Pavilion Gallery, Balboa, California
1966 *Primary Structures*, Jewish Museum, New York
1972 *USA West Coast*, Kunstverein, Hamburg (travelled to Hannover, Cologne and Stuttgart)
1976 *200 Years of American Sculpture*, Whitney Museum, New York
1977 *Painting and Sculpture in California: The Modern Era*, Washington Collection of Fine Arts, Smithsonian Institution, Washington D.C.
1979 *Contemporary Sculpture: Selections from the Collection of MOMA*, Museum of Modern Art, New York
1980 *Beyond Object*, Aspen Center for the Visual Arts, Colorado
1982 *One Hundred Years of California Sculpture*, Oakland Museum, California
1984 *Americans in Glass*, Woodson Art Museum, Wausau, Wisconsin (toured Europe)
1987 *Art and the West*, University of Wyoming, Laramie

Collections:

Whitney Museum, New York; Guggenheim Museum, New York; Museum of Modern Art, New York; National Collection of Fine Arts, Smithsonian Institution, Washington, D.C.; Fort Worth Art Center, Texas; Museum of New Mexico, Santa Fe; Roswell Museum and Art Center, New Mexico; Los Angeles County Museum of Art; Norton Simon Art Museum, Pasadena, California; Tate Gallery, London; Stedelijk Museum, Amsterdam.

Publications

By BELL: articles—statement in "Saint Andy" by Philip Leider in *Artforum* (New York), 1965; statement in *A New Esthetic*, exhibition catalogue, Washington, D.C. 1967; interview in *Los Angeles 6*, exhibition catalogue, by John Coplans, Vancouver 1968; interview in *Transparency, Reflection, Light, Space*, exhibition catalogue, by Frederick S. Wight, Los Angeles 1971; "Larry Bell," interview with Alastair Mackintosh, in *Art and Artists* (London), January 1972; "The Iceberg" in *Vision* (Oakland, California), September 1975.

On BELL: books—*Larry Bell*, exhibition catalogue, with texts by Raphael Sorin and Annette Michelson, Paris 1967; *American Art since 1900* by Barbara Rose, London 1967; *6 Artists: 6 Exhibitions*, exhibition catalogue, Milwaukee 1968; *West Coast 1945–1969*, exhibition catalogue, by John Coplans, Pasadena, California 1969; *Kompas IV-West Coast U.S.A.*, exhibition catalogue, Amsterdam 1969; *Larry Bell, Robert Irwin, Doug Wheeler*, exhibition catalogue, by M. Compton and N. Reid, London 1970; *Larry Bell*, exhibition catalogue, by Barbara Haskell, Pasadena, California 1972; *USA West Coast*, exhibition catalogue, Hamburg 1972; *Possibilities for Glass Sculpture*, exhibition catalogue, Sydney 1973; *Larry Bell*, exhibition catalogue, Rome 1974; *Sunshine Muse: Contemporary Art on the West Coast* by Peter Plagens, New York 1974; *Readings in America Art 1900–1975*, edited by Barbara Rose, New York 1975; *Larry Bell: Recent Works*, exhibition catalogue, Fort Worth, Texas 1975; *Larry Bell. New Work*, exhibition catalogue with introduction by Robert Creeley, New York 1981; articles—"A Lot of Talent . . ." by Henry J. Seldis in the *Los Angeles Times*, 21 October 1973; "American in Paris: 1974" by Melinda Wortz in *Arts Magazine* (New York), 1975; "Larry Bell" in *Art News* (New York), March 1975; "A Hotbed of Advanced Art" by E. Perlmutter in *Art News* (New York), January 1976; "Larry Bell on New York" by David Rush in *Artweek* (Oakland, California), 15 May 1976; "The Grip of the Iceberg" by Kenneth Baker in the *Boston Phoenix*, 8 February 1977; "A Glass Menagerie" by R. Talor in the *Boston Globe*, 16 June 1977; "Larry Bell and Eric Orr" by Gerrit Henry in *Art News* (New York), April 1978; article by Gerrit Henry in *Art News* (New York), May 1979; "Larry Bell" by Jon Meyer in *Arts Magazine* (New York), September 1982; "Art Vapor Made" by Jody Jacobs in the *Los Angeles Times*, 14 October 1985; "Larry Bell's Lights" by Kenneth Baker in the *San Francisco Chronicle*, 14 June 1986; film—*A Video Portrait: Larry Bell*, directed by John Hunt, Venice, California 1976.

I used to think that a person got what he wanted, and that was all he got, 'cause that's all there was. Everything was very simple. If you didn't know what you wanted, you still got what you set up for yourself, but you may not know that you got what you wanted. In a recent conversation with a friend, he suggested that

Larry Bell: *Triangles on Grid*, 1984

maybe you get what your character dictates, and you spend most of your life trying to make sense out of the chaos of your character; finding your rational explanation to yourself, of what it's all about. I like to look at it like this. And I am responsible for my acts, for the things I say and do, just like everybody else. My rational mind is fighting the same chaotic battle that everyone fights every day, who either thinks that they know what they want, or don't think about it at all. I think it's a terrible delusion to believe that a person is the master of his character.

—Larry Bell

In all the art capitals of the world, the artists jostle for their place in the hierarchy of reputation, eyeing the other contenders and marshalling their supporting forces of critics and other hangers-on: in all the capitals except Los Angeles, where Larry Bell is undisputed king.

There are of course many West Coast artists with high reputations and an international following, and it would be foolish to pretend at this stage of history that one could say who will or will not be remembered. Anyway, status has little to do with quality; it stems rather from the stance or image of the artist, and the consistency and self-confidence of the work.

Bell has achieved his position of pre-eminence by matching his work exactly to the ethos of Los Angeles. Art from New York tends to have an intellectual and slightly paranoid edge, that from San Francisco a colourful messiness associated with psychedelia—the art matches the city from whence it grows. L.A. is the blandest, least intellectual and most stylish of American cities, the worst place on earth to be poor. Economic extravagance is an aesthetic quality in L.A., and nothing matters more than effect.

This may sound like a condemnation, but any quality can become a virtue in the hands of a skilful artist, and there is no denying Bell's skill. His art may depend on great technical ability based upon a high cost of production, but it is also successful. Who complains at the cost of a high budget movie as long as it succeeds at box office, and Bell's work has certainly done that.

His work, since it first became widely known in 1964, has all been variations on a single idea. The earlier examples were glass cubes with 15–30 cm sides, upon which were imposed pattersn by an aluminising process, which caused delicate interference when one side was seen against another. Soon, however, Bell was finding this technique too crude, and he switched to vacuum coating, which allowed him to introduce extremely subtle variations of transparent colour onto the surface of the glass. After experimenting with various colour effects, he settled mainly on the use of greys, some of which were so slight as to be almost non-existent.

The reductive quality of these works has led to Bell's being associated with minimalism, an essentially East Coast school of art. But the differences are far greater than the similarities. Minimalism is an intellectual system; art is reduced to the bare essentials for theoretical reasons and any visual impact is a subsidiary bonus. Bell's work is extremely sensuous and the reduction is made to increase the sensuality, not for any theoretical reason. It is minimal only in the sense that the whiteness of Jean Harlow's satin dresses is minimal, as an increase of visual impact.

In 1968, Bell started to work on a large scale, evolving techniques that would allow him to make pieces big enough for the viewer to walk through. The equipment necessary to achieve this was very expensive, and this had a concomitant effect on Bell's prices. On the East Coast there is still a feeling that art should cost little to make (whatever price it is sold for) and that blatantly industrial techniques are somehow cheating; but in Los Angeles this attitude is considered absurd. In a city where you can buy a gold-plated toothbrush, vacuum coated sculpture is perfectly logical.

There is no denying that Bell's work is possibly the most sheerly beautiful and elegant of the post-war period. Its flawless finish combined with great simplicity makes it seductively attractive compared to the "unfinished" aesthetic of most contemporary art. Critics have tended to underrate Bell because there is no theory to his art for them to bite on; it is there, you look at it and that is that, and in a period where art is weighed down by the verbiage that surrounds it, this is a highly satisfactory quality.

Bell's best pieces are probably those constructed in the form of simple mazes. The sheets of glass, six feet high, are coated with grey, and this is further treated with a mirroring process which fades evenly top to bottom. The viewer finds himself in a web of reflections, sometimes seeing himself in a mirrorized part of the glass and sometimes seeing through the surface to a further series of reflections beyond. It is like entering a multiple exposure photograph. The effect is not at all disturbing, but rather of pure visual pleasure, in which the analytical part of the mind becomes servant to the sensuous, and problems of form and content do not exist; a Los Angeles aesthetic par excellence, and one that is perfectly legitimate for that.

—Alastair Mackintosh

BELLMER, Hans.

German. Born in Katowice, Silesia, Germany/Poland border (now in Poland), 13 March 1902. Studied engineering, Technische Hochschule, Berlin, 1923–24; drawing and perspective studies with artist George Grosz, Berlin, 1924. Married Margarete Bellmer in 1927 (died, 1937); 2 daughters; married again in 1942 (separated, 1946); twin daughters: Doraine and Beatrice; lived with poetess Nora Mitrani, 1946–51, and with writer Unica Zurn, 1953–70 (died, 1970). Worked as coal-miner, Katowice, 1920–23; designer, typographer and illustrator, for Malik Publishing Company, Berlin, 1924–25; independent painter and designer, Berlin, 1926–36, in Paris, 1936–39; interned in prison camp, Aix-en-Provence, France, 1940; independent painter and designer, Toulouse, France, 1941–45, and Paris, 1946 until his death, 1975; worked on photographs of puppet doll (Die Puppe), Berlin, 1934–36, and in Paris, 1936–39, 1946–75. Recipient: William and Noma Copley Foundation Prize, Chicago, 1958. *Died* (in Paris) *23 February 1975.*

Individual Exhibitions:

1943 Galerie Trentin, Toulouse
1945 Galerie du Luxembourg, Paris
1963 Galerie Daniel Cordier, Paris
1966 Robert Fraser Gallery, London
Galerie Sydow, Frankfurt
Robert Self Gallery, London
Ulmer Museum, Ulm, West Germany
Galerie Benador, Geneva
Galerie Gmurzynska, Cologne
1967 Galerie A. F. Petit, Paris
Kestner Gesellschaft, Hannover (retrospective)
Galerie Wolfgang Ketterer, Munich
Galleria d'Arte Moderna, Turin
Galerie Thomas, Munich and Cologne
1969 Galerie A. F. Petit, Paris
1970 Stedelijk Museum, Amsterdam
Galerie La Pochade, Paris
1971 Centre National d'Art Contemporain, Paris (retrospective)
Von der Heydt Museum, Wuppertal, West Germany
1971 Lerner-Misrachi Gallery, New York
Sidney Janis Gallery, New York
Editions Graphiques, London
1974 Sidney Janis Gallery, New York
Galerie Schindler, Berne
1975 Museum of Contemporary Art, Chicago
Galerie A. F. Petit, Paris
1976 Galerie A. F. Petit, Paris
1980 *Les Jeux de la Poupée,* Vision Gallery, Boston
1983 Centre Georges Pompidou, Paris
1984 Kestner-Gesellschaft, Hannover
1985 Barbara Gladstone Gallery, New York

Selected Group Exhibitions:

1935 *Exposicion Surealista,* Galeria Ateneo, Tenerife, Canary Islands
1936 *International Surrealist Exhibition,* Museum of Modern Art, New York
1947 *Exposition Internationale du Surrealisme,* Galerie Maeght, Paris
1960 *Exposition Internationale du Surrealisme,* Galerie Daniel Cordier, Paris
1977 *Künstlerphotographien im 20. Jahrhundert,* Kestner Gesellschaft, Hannover
1978 *Dada and Surrealism Reviewed,* Hayward Gallery, London
1979 *Photographic Surrealism,* New Gallery of Contemporary Art, Cleveland, Ohio (travelled to Dayton Art Institute, Ohio; and Brooklyn Museum, New York)
1980 *Masks, Mannequins and Dolls,* Prakapas Gallery, New York
1981 *Germany: The New Vision,* Fraenkel Gallery, San Francisco

Hans Bellmer: ***Pay-sage 1800*****, 1942**

1985 *L'Amour Fou: Photography and Surrealism,* Corcoran Gallery of Art, Washington, D.C., (travelled to San Francisco, Paris and London)

Collections:

Centre Georges Pompidou, Paris; Ulmer Museum, Ulm, West Germany; Galerie Brusberg, Hannover; Museum of Modern Art, New York; Institute for Sex Research, University of Indiana, Bloomington; Art Institute of Chicago.

Publications:

By BELLMER: books—*Die Puppe,* Karlsruhe 1934, Paris 1936, revised edition, Berlin 1962; *The Story of Eve,* with text by Georges Bataille, Paris 1944; *Les Jeux de la Poupée,* with text by Paul Eluard, Paris 1949; *L'Anatomie de l'Image,* Paris 1957; *A Sade,* Paris 1967; *Madame Edwarda,* with text by Georges Bataille, Paris 1965; *Mode d'Emploi,* Paris 1967.

On BELLMER: books—*Hans Bellmer* by Christian d'Orgeix, Paris 1950; *Hans Bellmer* by Alain Jouffroy, Chicago and London 1959; *Les Dessins de Hans Bellmer,* edited by Constantin Jelenski, Paris 1966; *Hans Bellmer: Oeuvre Gravé* by André Pieyre de Mandiargues, Paris 1969; *CNAC Archives 1: Hans Bellmer,* exhibition catalogue, by Paul Eluard and others, Paris 1971; *The Drawings of Hans Bellmer,* edited by Alex Grall, London 1972, New York 1973; *Hans Bellmer* by Sarane Alexandrian, Paris 1972, New York 1973; *Photography as Art* by Volker Kahmen, London 1974; *The Erotic Arts* by Peter Webb, London 1975; *Künstlerphotographien im XX. Jahrhundert,* exhibition catalogue, by Carl-Albrecht Haenlein, Hannover 1977; *Geschichte der Fotografie im 20. Jahrhundert/Photography in the 20th Century* by Petr Tausk, Cologne 1977, London 1980; *Dada and Surrealism Reviewed,* exhibition catalogue, by Dawn Ades, London 1978; *Le Trésor Cruel de Hans Bellmer* by André Pieyre de Mandiargues, Paris 1979; *Photographic Surrealism,* exhibition catalogue, by Nancy Hall-Duncan, Cleveland 1979; *Avant-Garde Photography in Germany 1919–39,* exhibition catalogue, by Van Deren Coke, Ute Eskildsen and Bernd Lohse, San Francisco 1980; *L'Amour Fou: Photography and Surrealism* by Rosalind Krauss and Jane Livingston, Washington, D.C. and New York 1985.

Hans Bellmer was the prince of image therapy. His dolls, reconditioned like pieces of fractured antique sculpture, were expertly reincarnated except that he re-assembled their parts according to the dictates of his own pleasure rather than as an archeologist would have attempted to make repairs in order to restore figurative realism. For Bellmer, time and erosion had nothing to do with it. He did his own disjointing and subsequent realignment. He made toys for grown-ups which could be accounted art products (whether they were exhibited in the forms in which he fashioned them, whether they were made the subject of alarming photographs—some of them crowding several poses into one frame, others enlarged to the extent of being over lifesize—or whether they were used as the inspirations for his pictures of physical reconstruction).

This artist had dual gifts of imagination and craft, both to an exceptional degree. Whatever he set out to achieve was so exquisitely made that even his most hysterical critics could not fail to be abashed. The same expertise that he employed in his portraits would also appear with identical accuracy in the pictures he made of carnal romps or sexual adventures.

Faced by such doughty accomplishment, moral censors find it difficult to make much of a case against Bellmer on grounds of erotic licence (or—for the most passionately outraged—pornography). Those who would like the portrayal of physical licentiousness to be kept under lock and key, or at least to be refrigerated, have always discovered themselves to be in an awkward position when the creator of what they are attacking is so obviously a consummate artist. One remembers Savonarola's problems with Botticelli, the unbreachable popularity of the Gavarni prints, Stanley Spencer's tangles with the Royal Academy and the Establishment in Britain.

Bellmer exhibited with the surrealists, and he was certainly on the best of terms with many of the movement's members, but his own art could never have been described as definitively surrealist. Nor could he be seen as some kind of contemporary descendant of Felicien Rops and clearly not as a companion of Horst Janssen. Sex as a subject for Bellmer is not so much a private investigation of adult personal habits (way-out habits even, in the instance of an artist like the Marquis von Bayros) as a corporeal re-creation which may suddenly burst into flame at the bureau desk of a secretary or, in another mood, captures the most venal recesses of thought in the mind of a little girl, secrets that even Graham Ovenden can scarcely have pondered upon. And talking of Ovenden, it is interesting to find Bellmer making his own "translation" of *Alice in Wonderland,* a new interpretation in that Alice has lifted the billows of her Edwardian skirt and petticoats in order to vaunt her unveiled sex.

Hans Bellmer saw the female body as raw material for creativity. Its natural configuration for him was no more than a chance series of juxapositions by Nature. Legs, arms, breasts, buttocks and primary sexual characteristics could find fresh patterns of relationship, and the way in which he made these rearrangements always seemed to have a biological and physical viability, however bizarre the resulting assembly. It would never, for instance, have occurred to Bellmer to embark upon cubist experiments in the manner of Picasso. The waistline might be discovered in an unexpected divorce from hips and belly, but eyes, nose and lips belonged to the face and Bellmer kept them there.

—Sheldon Williams

BENEDIT, Luis Fernando.

Argentinian. Born in Buenos Aires, Argentina, 12 July 1937. Educated at the Facultad de Arquitectura, Universidad de Buenos Aires, 1956–63, Diploma Arquitecto 1963; studied popular architecture, Instituto de Cultura Hispanica, Madrid, 1964–65; drawing and landscape, Facoltà d'Architettura, Rome, 1967–68. Served in the Argentine Air Force, Buenos Aires, 1958. Married Monica Prebisch in 1963; children: Juana, Pedro, Rosita, and Tomas. Architect, Estudio Prebisch, Buenos Aires, 1969–71. Recipient: Premio Ver y Estimar, Buenos Aires, 1962; Premio Rosa Galisteo, *Salón de Santa Fé,* Argentina, 1962; Premio en el Arte, San Isidro, Argentina, 1968; Premio de la Critica, *Salón Nacional,* Buenos Aires, 1968. Agents: Galeria Bonino, Marcelo T. de Alvear 636, Buenos Aires, Argentina; Spectrum Gallery, Leopoldstraat 10, 2000 Antwerp, Belgium; Galerie Buchholz, Maximilianstrasse 29, Munich 22, West Germany. Address: Ingeniero Huergo 1191, Buenos Aires, Argentina.

Individual Exhibitions:

1961 Galeria Lirolay, Buenos Aires
1962 Galeria Lirolay, Buenos Aires
1963 Galeria Rubbers, Buenos Aires
1964 Galeria Lirolay, Buenos Aires
1965 Galerie Europe, Paris
1966 Galerie La Balance, Brussels
1967 Galeria Rubbers, Buenos Aires
1968 Galeria Rubbers, Buenos Aires
1969 Pan American Union, Washington, D.C.
1972 *3-Labyrinthe von Luis F. Benediti Ein Versuch über der Displazierung,* Galerie Buchholz, Munich
1973 C.A.Y.C., Buenos Aires
1975 Spectrum Gallery, Antwerp
Galeria Bonino, Buenos Aires
Whitechapel Gallery, London
Galerie Buchholz, Munich

Selected Group Exhibitions:

1961 *3 Nuevos Rostros,* Galeria Lirolay, Buenos Aires
1966 *Salón des Jeunes,* Musée d'Art Moderne, Paris
1967 *Surrealismo en la Argentina,* Instituto Di Tella, Buenos Aires
1968 *Materiales, Nuevas, Técnicas, Nuevas Expresiónes,* Museo de Bellas Artes, Buenos Aires
1969 *Biennale des Jeunes,* Musée de Arte Moderno, Buenos Aires
Argentinische Kunst der Gegenwart, Kunsthalle, Basle (toured Europe)
1972 *Toys by Artists,* Musée des Arts Décoratifs, Paris (and world tour)
1975 *International Exhibition of Prints,* Museum of Modern Art, Tokyo

Collections:

Museo de Arte Moderno, Buenos Aires; Museo de Bellas Artes, Buenos Aires; Museo de Bellas Artes, La Plata, Argentina; Museo Rosa Galisteo de Rodrizuez, Santa Fé, Argentina; Museo de Bellas Artes, Tandil, Argentina; Museum of Modern Art, New York; Museum of Rhode Island, Providence; Museum of the Organization of American States, Washington, D.C.; Braniff Collection, University of Texas at Austin.

Publications:

By BENEDIT: article—prologue in *Bienal de Arte Coltejer,* exhibition catalogue, Medellin, Colombia 1970; film—editor, *4,000 Abejas en Venezia* by Pedro Roth, Venice, Italy 1970.

On BENEDIT: book—*3-Labyrinthe von Luis F. Benedit: Ein Versuch über die Kunst der Displazierung,* exhibition catalogue, by A. M. Battro, Munich 1972; article—"Intra-Functional Modules" by Jorge Glusberg in *Art and Artists* (London), July 1970.

I am interested in designing physical spaces which can be inhabited, explored or observed, and where the major evidence is a certain sort of behavior, individual or collective. I use persons, animals or physical phenomena simply as protagonists. My aim is to force culturally the aesthetic participant of my works: I consider my work justified if I am able to provoke just one reflection out of the daily routine about his inner self.

These works are *experiences* in the field of art, but if their mechanism is operated by a scientist they can be transformed into real *experiments* with consequences outside the field of aesthetics.

—Luis Benedit

Luis Benedit shows how every plant constitutes by itself a laboratory. By means of a process of osmosis their roots obtain the possibility of elaborating the food substances which could be either in the earth or in the inert substances in which they arrive; a nutritive solution. Furthermore, the roots separate out the acids which help out in the dissolution of the minerals existent in the earth or in the plastic material. The roots also serve as deposits of the assimilated products. The stem and the branches act as a system to transport the liquids, and the fibrovasculars work like small channels. It isn't until the food substances which have been absorbed by the roots and converted into sap (solutions which circulate inside the plants) get into the leaves that they can be utilized, by means of a process called chlorophyllous synthesis, in which by utilizing solar light the plant obtains the energy which it needs for its subsistence and reproduction.

In the works of Benedit the plants find the same environmental conditions which nature offers them, and the artificial nutritive solution is the basis of his experiment: with that system the artist models along

Luis Benedit: ***Project Cancer Pagurus,*** **1975**

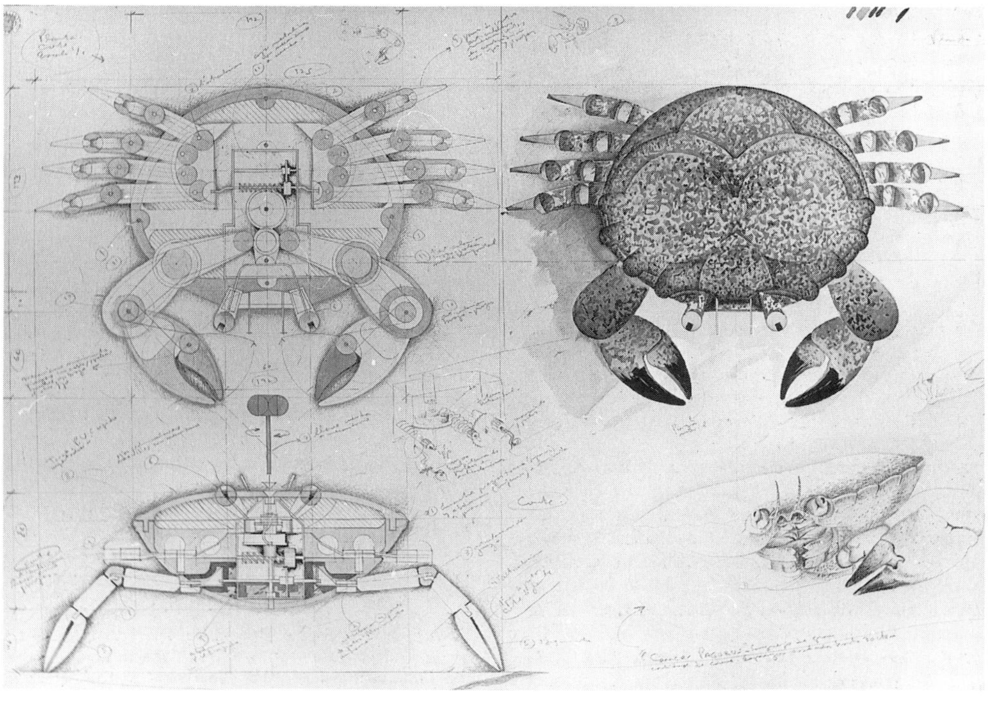

with the scientist the conditions which the earth offers to the vegetables.

The botanical experiments of Benedit, architect and painter, who studied the drawing of landscapes with the Italian master Francesco Fariello, are surely a result of the lessons he was allowed to enjoy from European gardens. The elements of landscape painting are precisely the plants, the birds, water and the sun, all of which are elements which Benedit utilizes in his investigations: the presentation of natural facts, their representation, the relation between the works of art and animals, their functions; without a scientific explanation, but simply showing what is observable.

From "Biotron," his most important work with animals (an experiment with 4,000 bees), Benedit went on to present the behaviour of plants, varying the parameters and conditioning them in accordance with scientific experiments, such as hydroponics.

In the "Phitotron" Benedit puts the spectator in front of a natural system of live organisms which develops, and modifies, allowing in addition a direct observation of the growth and change, during a determined length of time.

The proposal is not a direct scientific observation of the phenomenon, but rather the developments which could grow out of his proposal. Adhering to and developing the ideas of Duchamp, Benedit thinks that the observation of these natural phenomena, in terms of the different context in which he proposes them, produce a different effect in the spectator.

Every science not only uses models of other sciences, but also uses them on distinct levels of abstraction in order to anticipate kinds of happenings or realities. The models serve as objects of representation, as constructions which reproduce phenomena in such a way as to make them more accessible or easier to investigate.

In the case of Benedit's botanical experiments, the marks of reference elected are the investigations by means of vegetable models, a kind of scientific laboratory where collective behaviour in a vegetable community is studied. Benedit operates as a social anthropologist; he has elaborated a series of interesting models which, although exhibited as artistic facts, go beyond the purely descriptive or documental study. In August of 1968 Benedit made his first "Animal Habitat" in the Buenos Aires Fine Arts Museum; and in December of that year, in the Rubbers Gallery, he worked painstakingly with cats, lizards, fish, turtles, birds, a hive of bees in full activity and botanical experiments in fecundation and germination.

The objects of his studies are not industrial or folkloric structures, as are the objects of Marcel Duchamp; rather, they are located at a level in which the object nearly tends to disappear due to its being used, something like an object which carries its presence to the limit of perception. He does not establish a cultural dialogue with the spectator, but rather liberates activity and existence in the animal and vegetable world, in a process in which every possible intellectual intervention is reduced. He puts in the forefront the elements of reality and makes them react among themselves, in order to investigate their own expressive charges.

—Jorge Glusberg

BENGLIS, Lynda.

American. Born in Lake Charles, Louisiana, 25 October 1941. Educated at Newcomb College, New Orleans, with Zoltan Buki, Harold Carney, Ida Kolhmeyer, Patrick Trivigno, 1960–64, B.F.A. 1964; Yale Summer School, Norfolk, Connecticut, 1963; Brooklyn Museum Art Achool, Max Beckmann Scholarship Class, 1964–65. Assistant Professor of Sculpture, University of Rochester, New York, 1970–72; Assistant Professor, Hunter College, New York, 1972–73; Visiting Professor, California Institute of the Arts, Valencia, 1974; Visiting Professor, Princeton University, New Jersey, 1975; Visiting Professor, California Institute of the Arts, Valencia, 1976; Visiting Artist, Kent State University, Ohio, 1977; Visiting Artist, Skowhegan School of Painting and Sculpture, Maine, 1979. Recipient: Guggenheim Fellowship, 1975; Artpack Grant, 1976; Australian Arts Council Award, 1976; National Endowment for the Arts Grant, 1979; Avery Distinguished Professor Award, Bard College, Annandale-on-Hudson, New York, 1987. Agent: Paula Cooper Gallery, 155 Wooster Street, New York, New York, 10012. Address: 222 Bowery, New York, New York, 10012, U.S.A.

Individual Exhibitions:

1969 University of Rhode Island, Kingston
1970 Paula Cooper Gallery, New York
Janie C. Lee Gallery, Dallas
Virginia Polytechnic Institute, Rockwell
1971 Kansas State University, Manhattan
Paula Cooper Gallery, New York
Hayden Gallery, Massachusetts Institute of Technology, Cambridge
1972 Hansen-Fuller Gallery, San Francisco
1973 Hansen-Fuller Gallery, San Francisco
Portland Center for the Visual Arts, Oregon
The Clocktower, New York
1974 Hansen-Fuller Gallery, San Francisco
Texas Gallery, Houston
Paula Cooper Gallery, New York
1975 Texas Gallery, Houston
Physical and Psychological Monuments in Time, State University of New York, at Oneonta (retrospective)
The Kitchen, New York
Paula Cooper Gallery, New York
1976 Paula Cooper Gallery, New York
1977 Margo Leavin Gallery, Los Angeles
Hansen-Fuller Gallery, San Francisco
Douglas Drake Gallery, Kansas City
1978 Paula Cooper Gallery, New York
1979 Texas Gallery, Houston
Dart Gallery, Chicago
Real Art Ways, New Haven, Connecticut
Hansen-Fuller Gallery, San Francisco
Georgia State University, Atlanta
Galerie Albert Baronian, Belgium
Suzanne Hilberry Gallery, Birmingham, Michigan (with Ron Gorchov)
1980 Galerie Albert Baronia, Belgium
Texas Gallery, Houston
Lynda Benglis: 1968–1979, University of South Florida, Tampa
Lowe Art Museum, Miami
Margo Leavin Gallery, Los Angeles
Portland Center for the Visual Arts, Oregon
Paula Cooper Gallery, New York
David Heath Gallery, Atlanta
Chatham College, Pittsburgh
Suzanne Hilberry Gallery, Birmingham, Michigan
1981 University of Arizona, Tucson
Galerie Albert Baronian, Brussels
Dart Gallery, Chicago
Texas Gallery, Houston
Jacksonville Art Museum, Florida
1982 Okun-Thomas Gallery, St. Louis, Missouri
Margo Leavin Gallery, Los Angeles
Paula Cooper Gallery, New York
Fuller Goldeen Gallery, San Francisco
1983 Susan Hillberry Gallery, Birmingham, Michigan
Dart Gallery, Chicago
1984 Paula Cooper Gallery, New York
Texas Gallery, Houston
Tilden-Foley Gallery, New Orleans
1985 Margo Leavin Gallery, Los Angeles
Dart Gallery, Chicago
Susan Hillberry Gallery, Birmingham, Michigan
Heath Gallery, Atlanta, Georgia
1986 Fuller Goldeen Gallery, San Francisco
Tilden-Foley Gallery, New Orleans
1987 Paula Cooper Gallery, New York

Selected Group Exhibitions:

1977 *Recent Acquisitions*, Guggenheim Museum, New York
1978 *Art at Work: Recent Art from Corporate Collections*, Whitney Museum, Downtown Branch, New York
1979 *Contemporary Sculpture: Selections from the Collection of The Museum of Modern Art*, Museum of Modern Art, New York
1980 *Extensions: Jennifer Bartlett/Lynda Benglis/Robert Longo/Judy Pfaff*, Contemporary Arts Museum, Houston
1981 *Decorative Sculpture*, Whitney Museum, New York
1982 *Postminimalism*, Aldrich Museum of Contemporary Art, Ridgefield, Connecticut
1983 *Back to the U.S.A.*, Rheinisches Landesmuseum, Bonn (travelled to Lucerne and Frankfurt)
1984 *American Art Since 1970*, Whitney Museum, New York
1985 *New York Now: Correspondences*, Laforet Museum, Tokyo (travelled to Tochigi and Kobe, Japan)
1986 *Between Geometry and Gesture*, Palacio de Velazquez, Madrid

Collections:

Museum of Modern Art, New York; Guggenheim Museum, New York; Philadelphia Museum of Art, Detroit Institute of Arts; Walker Art Center, Minneapolis; Milwaukee Art Center; National Gallery of Australia, Canberra.

Publications:

By BENGLIS: articles—"Interview 99/Lynda Benglis," with Karen Edwards, in the *Sunday Herald* (New York), 13 June 1971 "Lynda Benglis in Conversation with France Morin" in *Parachute* (Montreal), Spring 1977; videotapes—*Totem 1971*, New York, 1971; *Document 1972*, Castelli-Sonnabend exhibition catalogue, New York, 1972; *Collage*, Castelli-Sonnabend exhibition catalogue, New York, 1973; *Female Sensibility*, Castelli-Sonnabend exhibition catalogue, New York, 1974.

On BENGLIS: books—*Physical and Psychological Monuments in Time*, exhibition catalogue, by Robert Pincus-Witten, Oneonta, New York, 1975; *Video Art*, exhibition catalogue, with essays by David Antin, Lizzie Borden, Jack Burnham, and John McHale, Philadelphia 1975; *From the Center* by Lucy Lippard, New York, 1976; *American Artists '76: A Celebration*, exhibition catalogue, with an essay by Alice Simkins, San Antonio, Texas 1976; *The 1976 Biennale of Sydney*, exhibition catalogue, Sydney 1976; *Artculture* by Douglas Davis, New York, 1977; *Video-Visions: A Medium Discovers Itself* by Jonathan Price, New York 1977; *Postminimalism* by Robert Pincus-Witten, New York 1977; *5 from Louisiana*, exhibition catalogue, supplement to the *Times-Picayune* (New Orleans), 30 January 1977; *A View of a Decade* exhibition catalogue, Chicago 1977; *Made by Sculptors*, exhibition catalogue, Amsterdam 1978; *American Portraits of the 60's and 70's*, exhibition catalogue, Aspen, Colorado 1979; *Painting: 5 Views*, exhibition catalogue, Wayne, New Jersey 1979; *Contemporary Sculpture: Selections from the Collection of the Museum of Modern Art*, exhibition catalogue, New York 1979; *Extensions: Jennifer Bartlett/Lynda Benglis/Robert Longo/Judy Pfaff*, exhibition catalogue, Houston 1980; *Sculpture on the Wall* exhibition catalogue, Amherst, Massachusetts 1980; *Lynda Benlis: 1968–1979*, exhibition catalogue, Tampa, Florida 1980; *Current/New York*, exhibition catalogue, Syracuse, New York 1980; *Painting in Relief*, exhibition catalogue, New York 1980; *Painting in Environment*, exhibition catalogue, Milan 1980; *Drawing: The Pluralist Decade*, exhibition catalogue, introduction by Janet Kardon, Philadelphia 1980; *With Paper, About Paper*, exhibition catalogue, with an essay by Charlotta Kotik, Buffalo, New York 1980; *Lynda Benglis: Works in Glass*, exhibition catalogue, with essay by David Shapiro, Los Angeles, 1985; articles—"Lynda Benglis: The Frozen Gesture" by Robert Pincus-Witten in *Artforum* (New York), November 1974; "The New Sexual Frankness: Good-bye to Hearts and Flowers" by Dorothy Seiberling in *New York Magazine*, 17 February 1975; "Lynda Benglis: Sculptural Knots" by Suzanne Muchnic in *Artweek* (Oakland, California), 4 June 1977; "Artpeople" by John Russell in the *New York Times*, 17 February 1975; "Lynda Benglis" by Ellen Lubell in *Arts Magazine* (New York), January 1979; "Cosmetic Transcendentalism: Surface Light in John Torreano, Rodney Ripps and Lynda Benglis" by Donal Kuspit in *Artforum* (New York), October 1979; "Painting in New York: An Illustrated Guide"

Lynda Benglis: *The Wave*, 1984

by Thomas Lawson in *Flash Art* (Milan), October/November 1979; "Women Artists" by John Gruen in *Working Women* (New York), July 1980; "Ramshackle Kennels Glimpsed by Moonlight" by John Ashbery in *New York Magazine*, 6 October 1980; "Lynda Benglis" by Douglas Welch in *Arts Magazine* (New York), November 1980; "Knot-Theme Sculptures by Lynda Benglis" by Vivien Raynor in the *New York Times*, 26 November 1982; "A Girl of the Zeitgeist" by Janet Malcolm in *The New Yorker*, 20 October 1986; "Lynda Benglis at Paula Cooper" by Holland Cotter in *Art in America* (New York), July 1987.

I am interested in work that depends on technology, that is visually exciting, and that hasn't been experienced in art or technology. Through genetic engineering, science is re-creating nature. Artists also do this. Only recently has science been able to understand nature in order to re-create it (e.g., using fusion research to create a star and genetic engineering to create new forms of life). Art ideas that are really inventive do not repeat each other. They re-create the nature of art.

The allusion to and the imitation of nature are the substance of art. I like to think that I mime the spirit of nature in re-creating it. Adjustments to gravity, weightlessness, hardness, softness, and motion are felt. Painting led me to sculpture; I wanted to free color of its flat form on canvas or board and to free form of much-used flat planes. I work with the probable and stretch it to the possible by using contradictions in material and context. Each work exists in its right scale and motion within the contextual rules I've set up.

Perhaps these rules exist as I make them (that's my illusion), or perhaps they exist as they have always existed and I only allude to them. I am definitely bound by traditional concepts of classicism and beauty, while using technology, and wish to enter the contemporary spirit with this personal game.

—Lynda Benglis

Lynda Benglis' interests in a wide range of materials, structures and modes of presentation have produced some of the most sensuous and provocative sculpture in contemporary American art. With the first execution of the organic latex and foam floor pieces in the late 1960's that boasted blob-like and spreading structures and intensely garish colors, she began the explorations of an issue that proved to be a major concern of hers in the 1970's and that continues to occupy many artists in the 1980's: the relationship of painting and sculpture. Benglis created these works by pouring the liquid substances onto the floor and mixing in fluorescent tones; this method, by the late 1960's was associated with the "poured" paintings, say, of Morris Louis. In the early 1970's the forms moved off the floor onto the wall and took on more specific shapes. Made of various combinations of materials they offered a more concentrated experience of color and form. Two examples are "Sparkle Totem" (1971–72), a narrow tube consisting of cotton bunting, plaster, pigment and sparkles; and "Valencia" (1972) a vertical bar with a corrugated surface of beeswax and damar resin on masonite. Staying on the wall, the works that followed explored various formats. Some of them continued to develop the narrow tubular shape; they include the cord-like "Zulu" (1970) a mixed mediums piece that features a central knot and the columnar-like "Volt" (1977), gold leaf and mixed mediums. Among the others that explored eccentric gestural shapes are "Pinto" (1971), the serial, polyurethane foam piece whose wing-like, curved appendages appear to fly-off-the-wall and penetrate the viewer's space, and "Omega" (1973), an asymmetrical multiple layered surface, containing folds and various protuberances.

In the middle 1970's Benglis also made videos in which she focused on female sexuality. Perhaps her most controversial statement on this subject was the announcement card she did for the May 1985 show she had at the Paula Cooper Gallery in New York. It featured a color photograph of the artist herself nude except for the jeans dropped to below her knees and a pair of platform shoes. With head turned toward the viewer and back-side aimed at the same, she is offering a provocative take-off on the "classic" pin-up pose.

Benglis is continuing to explore the issue of the female in the abstract relief sculptures she has done

since the late 1970s. The sensual curves of the female body are brought to mind in a number of the gold leaf pieces whose volumetric sections swell out at top and bottom from a narrow center. Figure #2 (1978) is an example. In the cast metal pieces with repetitive elements reminiscent of pleats and fanning structures there is strong reference made to the tradition of the draped female figure in classical sculpture. In Essex (1986) and Lozier (1985) the vivid sensations of movement produced by the contrasting rhythms of each composition's dynamic parts are heightened by the intensely reflective metallic surfaces to give the illusion of glorious presence.

—Ronny Cohen

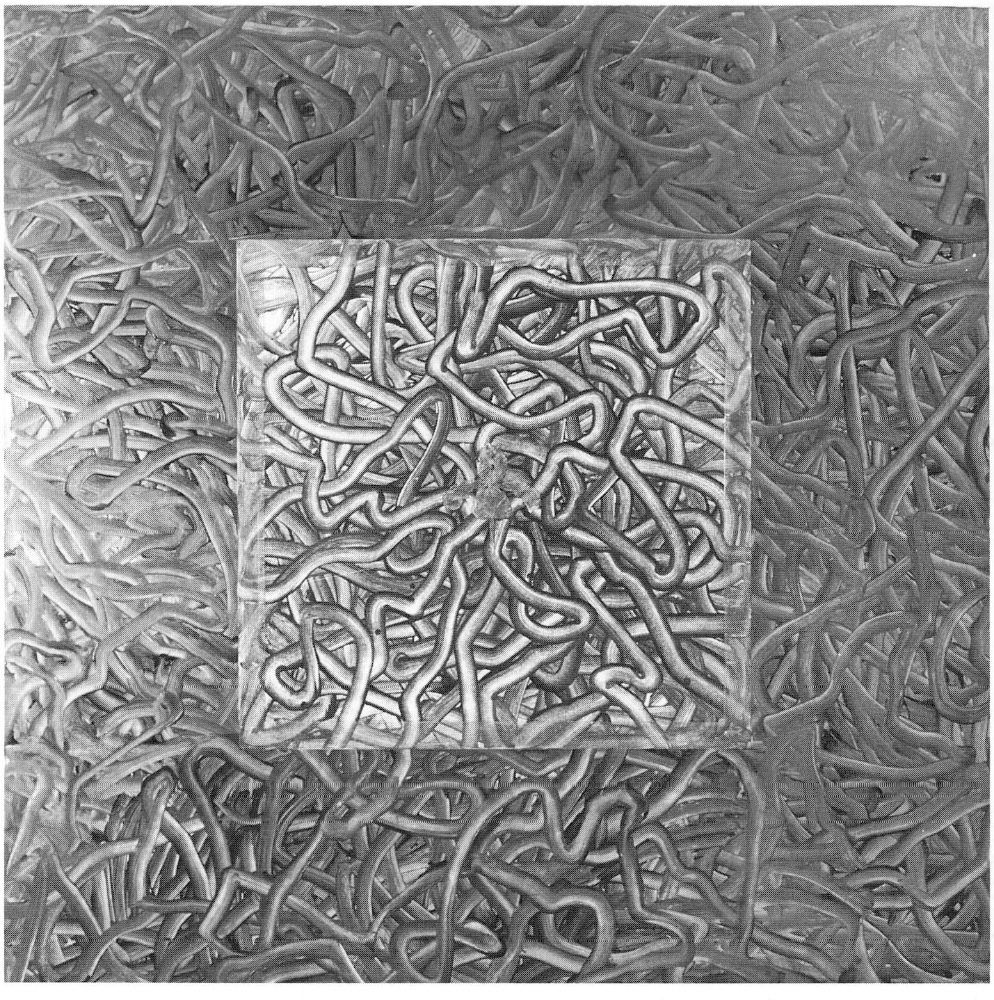

Billy Al Bengstom: *Bolognese Dracula* (*A. R.*), 1972

BENGSTON, Billy Al.

American. Born in Dodge City, Kansas, 7 June 1934. Educated at Los Angeles City College, 1953–54; Los Angeles State College, 1954–55; California College of Arts and Crafts, San Francisco, 1955–56; and Los Angeles County Art Institute, 1956–57. Independent Artist since 1957. Founder of Artist Studio, Venice, California, 1960. Instructor, Chouinard Art Institute, Los Angeles, 1961; Lecturer, University of California at Los Angeles, 1962–63; Guest Artist, University of Oklahoma, Norman, 1967; Guest Professor, University of Colorado, Boulder, 1969; Guest Instructor, in Ceramics and Painting, University of California at Irvine, 1973. Recipient: National Foundation for the Arts Grant, 1967; Tamarind Fellowship, Tamarind Lithography Workshop, Los Angeles, 1968, 1982; Guggenheim Fellowship, 1975. Agent: James Corcoran Gallery, 8223, Santa Monica Boulevard, Los Angeles, California 90046. Address: 100 Mildred Avenue, Venice, California 90291, U.S.A.

Individual Exhibitions:

1958 Ferus Gallery, Los Angeles
1960 Ferus Gallery, Los Angeles
1961 Ferus Gallery, Los Angeles
1962 Martha Jackson Gallery, New York
Ferus Gallery, Los Angeles
1963 Ferus Gallery, Los Angeles
1968 *Motel Dracula,* San Francisco Museum of Art (toured America and Canada)
1969 Utah Museum of Fine Arts, Salt Lake City
1970 Santa Barbara Museum of Art, California
Mizuno Gallery, Los Angeles
Galerie Neuendorf, Hamburg
Galerie Neuendorf, Cologne
1971 Margo Leavin Gallery, Los Angeles
La Jolla Museum of Art, California
Contract Graphic Associates, Houston
Galerie Neuendorf, Cologne
1972 Felicity Samuel Gallery, London
Galerie Neuendorf, Hamburg
1973 Corcoran and Corcoran Gallery, Miami
Nicholas Wilder Gallery, Los Angeles
Pollock Gallery, Southern Methodist University, Dallas
Contemporary Arts Museum, Houston
Texas Gallery, Houston
1974 John Berggruen Gallery, San Francisco
Jared Sable Gallery, Toronto
Texas Gallery, Houston
Nicholas Wilder Gallery, Los Angeles
1975 Pyramid Gallery, Washington, D.C.
Seder/Creigh Gallery, Coronado, California
Tortue Gallery, Santa Monica, California
Dootson-Calderhead Gallery, Seattle
1976 Texas Gallery, Houston
Dobrick Gallery, Chicago
Portland Center for the Visual Arts, Oregon
1977 Texas Gallery, Houston
University of Montana, Missoula
James Corcoran Gallery, Los Angeles
1978 James Corcoran Gallery, Los Angeles
Security Pacific Bank Building, Los Angeles
John Berggruen Gallery, San Francisco
Sarah Campbell Blaffer Gallery, University of Houston
Texas Gallery, Houston
Mizuno Ceramics Gallery, Los Angeles
1979 James Corcoran Gallery, Los Angeles
Texas Gallery, Houston
Conejo Valley Art Museum, Thousand Oaks, California
Acquavella Contemporary Art Gallery, New York
Cantor-Lemberg Gallery, Birmingham, Michigan
1980 James Corcoran Gallery, Los Angeles
Malibu Art and Design, California
Honolulu Academy of Arts
1981 Corcoran Gallery, Washington, D.C.
Acquavella Contemporary Art, New York
San Diego University, California
Thomas Babeor Gallery, La Jolla, California
James Corcoran Gallery, Los Angeles
Texas Gallery, Houston
1982 James Corcoran Gallery, Los Angeles
Thomas Babeor Gallery, La Jolla, California
Linda Farris Gallery, Seattle, Washington
1983 James Corcoran Gallery, Los angeles
John Berggruen Gallery, San Francisco
Thomas Babeor Gallery, La Jolla, California
Acquavella Contemporary Art, New York
1984 Smith Anderson Gallery, Palo Alto, California
Douglas Drake Gallery, Kansas City, Kansas
James Corcoran Gallery, Los Angeles
Thomas Babeor Gallery, La Jolla, California
Texas Gallery, Houston
1985 James Corcoran Gallery, Los Angeles
Angles Gallery, Santa Monica, California
Thomas Babeor Gallery, La Jolla, California
1986 James Corcoran Gallery, Los Angeles
Thomas Babeor Gallery, La Jolla, California
Smith Anderson Gallery, Palo Alto, California

Selected Group Exhibitions:

1957 *Los Angeles Annual,* Los Angeles County Museum of Art
1963 *Pop Art USA,* Oakland Art Museum, California
1969 *New Media: New Methods,* Museum of Modern Art, New York (toured the United States)
1972 *Working in California,* Albright-Knox Art Gallery, Buffalo, New York
1976 *The Last Time I Saw Ferus,* Newport Harbor Art Museum, Newport Beach, California
1979 *1979 Biennal Exhibition,* Whitney Museum, New York
1980 *Fabrications,* Lowe Art Museum, University of Miami
1983 *On and Off the Wall,* Oakland Museum, California (toured the United States)
1985 *Poly-Eclecticism,* Humano Institute, Tokyo
1986 *Tamarind Impressions: Recent Lithographs,* Tamarind Institute, Albuquerque, New Mexico

Collections:

Los Angeles County Museum of Art; Newport Harbor Art Museum, Newport Beach, California; La Jolla Museum of Contemporary Art, California; University of California at Los Angeles; San Francisco Museum of Modern Art; Guggenheim Museum, New York; Museum of Modern Art, New York; Whitney Museum, New York; Museum of Fine Arts, Houston; Art Institute of Chicago.

Publications:

By BENGSTON: book—*Business Cards*, with Ed Ruscha, Los Angeles 1968; articles—"Late 50's at the Ferus" in *Artforum* (New York), January 1969; "Los Angeles Artists' Studios" in *Art in America* (New York), November/December 1970; interview with William Robinson in *Art in America* (New York), March/April 1973; "Billy Al Bengsten Framed by Joan Quinn", interview, in *Interview* (New York), October 1979.

On BENGSTON: books—*Pop Art*, by Lucy Lippard, New York 1966; *Billy Al Bengston*, exhibition catalogue, by James Monte, Los Angeles 1968; *Sunshine Muse*, by Peter Plagens, New York 1974; *Billy Al Bengston*, exhibition catalogue, Los Angeles 1977; *Billy Al Bengston: Paintings of the 70's*, exhibition catalogue, by Fredericka Hunter, Los Angeles 1978; articles—"Billy Al Bengston" by John Coplans in *Artforum* (New York), June 1965; "Billy Al Bengston's Dentos" by Fidel Danieli in *Artforum* (New York), May 1967; "Bengston in Los Angeles" by James Monte in *Artforum* (New York), November 1968; "Billy Al Bengston, Vancouver Art Gallery" by Charlotte Townsend in *Artscanada* (Toronto), August 1969; "Billy Al Bengston, Felicity Samuel Gallery" by Peter Fuller in *Connoisseur* (London), December 1972; "Bengston's Recent Work" by R. H. MacDonald in *Artweek* (Oakland, California), March 1974; "Billy Al Bengston's New Paintings" by Peter Piagens in *Artforum* (New York), March 1975; "The Decorative Impulse" by Jeff Perrone in *Artforum* (New York), November 1979; "Billy Al Bengston" by Ruth Bass in *Artnews* (New York), November 1979; "Billy Al Bengston: Sensuality and Structure" by Susie Kahil in *Artweek* (Oakland), 22 December 1979; "Billy Al Bengston" by Elise Miller in *San Diego Magazine*, May 1981; "New Editions" in *Artnews* (New York), October 1983; "Los Angeles: The New Mecca" by Barnaby Conrad III in *Horizon* (New York), January/February 1987.

It's the best I can do.

—Billy Al Bengston

Undeservedly, there may yet hover about Bengston's works a "tough guy" image. If so, it remains from the textbook use, to illustrate early 1960s Pop art, of his paintings which prominently featured a centralized motif of chevron bars. Of course these were taken, as in *Buster* (1962) as military iconography. What was forgotten is that the chevrons were centered on a gently hazy sprayed lacquer surface surrounded by glowing balls of light. While Bengston himself is a physical person, with life-long interests in gymnastics, surfing, and motorcycle racing, his art has always been, like Los Angeles Pop art, easy-going and non-aggressive. His oeuvre may in fact be taken as almost a cliche of California Art: light-filled, vaporously-hued, Japanese influenced both in calligraphic concerns, and more importantly in the wider sense of elegant finesse. (His memory of the on-set of the chevron bar element is simply a personal fascination with the motif-pattern; and such thinking has permeated his art since, as he continues to fasten upon a particular shape or object—for no outward reason and with no intent to indicate and incisive daily life involvment.) And so there appear in his body of works, long series of paintings which show bars, circles, fish, the Iris, et. al. In their decorative, collaged-like flat pattern, his paintings in recent years have come to resemble silk-screened fabrics. Bengston clearly foreshadows the Pattern and Decoration movement and may be linked to those artists who coalesced that idiom through contact with the Art Department at the University of California at San Diego—M. Schapiro, Kushner, Zakanitch, and MacConnel.

—Joshua Kind

BERDYSZAK, Jan.

Polish. Born in Zawory, 15 June 1934. Educated at State College of Plastic Arts, Poznan, 1952–58, sculpture diploma 1958. Married Maria Mrozek in 1958; son: Marcin. Served as a Lieutenant in the Polish Army, 1953–56. Artist working in sculpture, painting, graphics, ephemeral media and stage design; lives in Poznan. Director of Sculpture, State Academy of Plastic Arts, Poznan, since 1965; Director, Department of Architecural Painting and Sculpture, since 1970. Recipient: Design Prize, *3rd International Puppet Theatre Exhibition*, Bucharest, 1965; Honorable Mention, *International Education Year Exhibition*, Unesco, Paris, 1970; Third Art Prize, Ministry of Culture and Art, Warsaw, 1971; First Prize, *International Triennale of Drawings*, Wroclaw, 1974; First Prize, *Art Biennale for Children*, Poland, 1977; Jan Cybis Prize, Warsaw 1978; Gold Medal, *Quadriennale*, Prague 1979; Third Prize, *Polish Print Exhibition*, Warsaw, 1981. Address: U1. Augustowska 17, 61–051 Poznan, Poland.

Individual Exhibitions:

1960 Klub Od Nowa, Poznan
Klub Zwiazku Polskich Artystow Plastykow, Poznan
1962 Biuro Wystaw Artystycznych, Poznan
1964 Galerie Zwiazku Polskich Artystow Plastykow, Poznan
Biuro Wystaw Artystycznich Arsenal, Poznan
1965 Galerie Krzystofory, Cracow
Stowarzyszenie Polskich Artystow Muzykow, Warsaw
1966 Akiyama Gallery, Tokyo
Biuro Wystaw Artystycznych Arsenal, Poznan
State College of Plastic Arts, Poznan
1967 Galerie in der Biberstrasse, Vienna
Galerie A. Gniezno, Poland
1968 Panstowa Opera il Filharmonia Baltycka, Danzig
Biuro Wystaw Artystycznych Arsenal, Poznan
1969 Central Biuro Wystaw Artystycznych Zacheta, Warsaw
Galerie Od Nowa, Poznan
Grabowski Gallery, London
Galerie Krzysztofory, Cracow
1970 Biuro Wystaw Artystycznych, Sopot, Poland
1971 Biuro Wystaw Artystycznych Arsenal, Poznan
House of Arts, Brno, Czechoslovakia
Galerie 70, Zielona Gora, Poland
1972 Lengyel Kultura, Budapest
Galerie Arkady, Cracow
Klub Zwiaskow Tworczych, Wroclaw
1973 Krytykow, Lublin
1974 Muzeum Narodow, Poznan
1975 Galerie Teatru Studio, Warsaw
1976 Osrodek Propogandy Sztuki, Lodz
1977 Galerie Koregarda, Warsaw
Galerie Sztuki Najnowszej, Wroclaw
1978 Biuro Wystaw Artystycznych, Poznan
Galerie Kordegarda, Warsaw
Biuro Wystaw Artystycznych, Radom, Poland
Biuro Wystaw Artystycznych, Jelenia Gora, Poland
Dom Artysty Plastyka, Warsaw
1979 Galerie Aut, Gdansk
Biuro Wystaw Artystycznych, Szczecin, Poland
Biuro Wystaw Artystycznych, Pila, Poland
1980 Galerie Foto, Medium Art, Wroclaw
Galerie Krytykow, Warsaw
Biuro Wystaw Artystycznych, Koszalin, Poland
Galerie Zapiecek, Warsaw
1981 Biuro Wystaw Artystycznych, Lublin
Galerie GN, Gdansk
Galerie Krzysztofory, Cracow
Galerie Foto, Medium Art, Wroclaw
Biuro Wystaw Artystycznych, Bialystok, Poland
1982 Biuro Wystaw Artystycznych, Poznan
Galerie Kubus, Hannover
Galerie Tolerance, Hamburg
1983 Galerie ON, Poznan
Biuro Wystaw Artystycznych, Jelenia Gora, Poland
1984 Galerie ON, Poznan
Galerie MPiK, Torun, Poland
Mala Galeria, Gorzow, Poland
1985 Biuro Wystaw Artystycznych, Leszno, Poland
Galerie Wschodnia, Lodz
Galerie Rysunku, Gdynia, Poland
Biuro Wystaw Artystycznych, Lublin, Poland
1986 Biuro Wystaw Artystycznych, Torun, Poland
Biuro Wystaw Artystycznych, Bydgoszcz, Poland
Biuro Wystaw Artystycznych, Lodz

Selected Group Exhibitions:

1969 *Biennale*, Paris
1971 *3rd Triennale Rysunku*, Museum Architektury, Wroclaw
1972 *Modern Legnyel Muveszet*, Mucsarnok, Budapest
1973 *Polkst Moderne Kunst*, Nordyllands Kunstmuseum, Aalborg, Denmark
1974 *10th Biennale d'Art*, Palais de l'Europe, Menton, France
1975 *Polish Painting Today*, Mall Galleries, London
1978 *7th International Contemporary Art Exhibition*, New Delhi
1980 *International Print Biennale*, Cracow
1983 *Biennale der Europaischen Grafik*, Baden-Baden, West Germany
1985 *International Open-Air Sculpture Biennale*, Athens

Publications:

By BERDYSZAK: articles—"Calosc Monumentalna i synteyczna" in *Nurt* (Poznan), February 1968; "Kreaja Przestrzeni Spolecznej: Lagow wrzesien 1974," with Stefan Papp, in *Madodrze* (Zielona Gora), November 1975; "Emptiness as a Sense of Individual Creations" in *The Aspects of Polish Modern Arts*, exhibition catalogue, Warsaw 1975; "Pytanie o Poznanie" in *Jan Berdyszak*, exhibition catalogue, Wroclaw 1977; "Wieloobraz porownawczy" in *Berdyszak*, exhibition catalogue, Jelenia Gora, Poland 1978; "Varied Media . . . " in *Jan Berdyszak*, exhibition catalogue, Wroclaw 1980; "Obszary koncentrujace" in *Jan Berdyszak*, exhibition catalogue, Lublin 1981.

On BERDYSZAK: books—*Jan Berdyszak*, exhibition catalogue, Poznan 1964; *Jan Berdyszak*, exhibition catalogue, by Tadeusz Czrzanowski, Cracow 1965; *Jan Berdyszak*, exhibition catalogue, by Teresa Kostyrko, Griezno, Poland 1967; *Jan Berdyszak*, exhibition catalogue, by Bozena Kowalska, Sopot, Poland 1970; *Jan Bedryszak*, exhibition catalogue, with text by Bozena Kowalska, Frno, Czechoslovakia 1971; *Problemy Sztuki Wspolczesnei* by Teresa and Krzysztof Kostyrkowie, Poznan 1972; *Jan Berdyszak*, exhibition catalogue, by Adam Radajewski, Lublin 1973; *Katalogu Wystawy Jana Berdyszak*, exhibition catalogue, with text by Kazimierz Malinowski and Maria Berdyszakova, Poznan 1974; *Polska Awangarda Malarska 1945– 1970* by Bozena Kowalska, Warsaw 1975; *Jan Berdyszak*, exhibition catalogue, by Bozena Kowalska, Lodz 1976; *Jan Berdyszak*, exhibition catalogue, with text by Alicja Kepinska, Torun, Poland 1986.

Art, unlike philosophy, never allows the possibility of "arrangement." Art is natural; it remains a general value even when declaring, for example, some perceptible construction. Art has always aimed to be, was and is COGNITION. Cognition is contrary to recognition, regardless of whether it is based on an object, situation, happening, energy, plurality of reality, homogeneity of language, or analogous abstraction.

External order, then, is either distorted or tolerated by the necessary as long as it does not make creative needs impossible.

There is no order in cognition; there are wishful guesses. It seems to be most important to sense plurality without order, leading us to possibilities of forming "breaks" in our sense of reality, which, perhaps, will allow us to look at hitherto existing concepts and senses of existence and our fellow creatures in some other way. By "look at" I do not mean either seeing, saying or knowing but communication of self-communication from the area between naming and recognizability. Understanding is less; experiencing is more.

Experiencing, unlike experience, does not permit the repetition of phenomena, therefore does not resolve to elements, perceptible processes or values; at the same time, it is also impossible to define whole

states and intervalues—supplementary values. Experiencing does not exist non-personally; it is not homogeneous, so inheres potentially.

Art is experiencing. Experiencing is a one-fold possibility, and I perceive one-foldedness as the most important feature of continuous eternity.

—Jan Berdyszak

For Jan Berdyszak art is a cognitive activity: cognition through art is a specific kind of active thought, a kind of total cognition, covering the whole experience—intuition and knowledge—of the creator, yet not "total" or "apart" or "complete." The artist calls it "cognition among cognitions," an awakening of the senses through art; simultaneously, it builds its own content.

This kind of act differs from other kinds of cognition—for example, academic—and gives rise to the question which provokes Berdyszak's attention: what conditions are necessary for the creation of art?

This is, at the same time, a question about the ontological status of art. It doesn't suggest a definitive answer but points to the possibility of an infinite number of approaches to the problem. Berdyszak builds successive models of approximation. Each model takes on the character of the cycle in the frame: as such, as a mutation of the end product, it becomes an instrument of cognition. In the process of examining the creative potential of the artist's imagination, he compares it with "emptiness," the primary state. It is a special area, referred to variously as "unknown place" or "area to question" or "area for contemplation" or "concentrated region" to be filled in and pondered in order that the reality of art may appear in the process. The boundaries of these regions are delineated with the help of the shape and colour of their shells, and as such are given the name "painting." The real picture, however, is the emptiness, that which does not exist.

This emptiness makes the existence of the "potential painting" possible: the onus is on the actual possibility of existence. These dealings simultaneously concern the whole history of the occurrence of "painting," revealing its basic construction, the "shell" (frame) and "that which is inside." Examples are "Models of the Value of a Picture" (1975), where the indispensable elements are maintained but always threatened by some process of disturbance. On the other hand, "Multi-Image" (1977), consisting of three paintings superimposed, shows three aspects of a painting: its "record," "statement" and "essence."

The delineation of the potential areas of construction of art which are so important to the artist sometimes takes place through the adaptation of the rule of uncertainty concerning the boundaries of the region. For example, there are "areas of reflection"—discs of metaplex covered with a thickening white substance that gradually blots out their transparency. Sheets of glass, also, are laid on top of each other until they lose their transparency.

The awareness of the unlimited potential of art causes the problem of infinity to be an important one in Berdyszak's work. The artist constructs various models of understanding of the infinite: one of them treats the infinite as that which is "apart"; another treats it as a centric value—i.e., conditioned by something. In the "Great" and the "Small Circle of Infinity," the object, which has been split up as far as possible, he tries to bring the actual concept of infinity closer to us. Infinity—a term used in mathematics and logic—also inheres in the idea of "boundary." In Berdyszak's work, this idea appears in two ways—in the sense of the boundary of regions that call forth the construction of art and as a question having to do with the possibility of filling these areas—their individual penetration.

The ever-present problem of "potential regions" appears in the cycle "Projects of Conception" (since 1977). Here, the artist poses the problem of his own

Jan Berdyszak: ***Die Durchsichtige VI*****, 1974**

question. He ignores our conditioned response, that a question must necessarily involve awaiting an answer. In order to focus on the meaning of the actual question as a value in itself, he introduces the term "negative question." For example, in a number of works, "negative painting" is that which exists between "painting" and that which is no longer the painting and which can be called, for want of a better word, "space."

From the question so considered come "Studies After" from the period 1975–79. They are graphics obtained by the artist's throwing the shapes of old sculptures onto a lit offset plate. These statues are thought of as creating a picture of continuity; it is a way of proceeding "after" and not "to"—a question of the importance of what it was that follows man like a shadow.

In the 1980s, he rendered the series "Concentrating Areas", "Ontological Areas" and "Radical Wholes". All of them deal with the possibilities of existence rather than existence itself. In fact, Berdyszak's art evolves in the direction of seeking possibilities instead of fulfilment.

The artist ever more readily uses transparent material—panes of glass. Transparent planes do not close anything, do not remove anything from vision and do not define anything ultimately. On the other hand, placed on the floor, stood by the wall, suspended in the air, sticking from among rocks they show places where we can ponder over art, that is change our behavior. Therefore, these places become potential areas as they focus our attention and open themselves up to us, revealing ways to unexpected destination.

In recent years also the role of drawing has been growing in Berdyszak's art, as if in keeping with Bachelard's statement: "If a metaphysician did not draw, would he be able to think? Openings and closures become ideas for him".

The artist formulates his ideas also in his numerous texts. In one of them he writes: "Most doubts are raised whatever is determined and "recognized". The expressed springs from the hope called by uncertainty. Searching for the potential is an attempt to bring back the conscience of the beginning or to become aware of special states and forms of existence. Differentiation and discrimination of the potential makes one come closer to the pre-initial which as form is not to be replaced while approaching the beings and their personal experience."

—Alicja Kępińska

BERGHUIS, Jaap.

Dutch. Born in Smilde, 15 August 1945. Studied interior architecture at the Instituut voor Kunstnijverheidsonderwijs, Amsterdam, 1963–67; painting, at Atelier 63, Haarlem, 1969–71. Married Annette Fehrmann in 1971; son: Thomas. Worked as interior architect, Nielson and Spruit, Amsterdam, 1967–69, and with D. van Shedregt and J. Rietveld, Amsterdam, 1969. Independent artist, concentrating on painting, Amsterdam, since 1969. Recipient: Dutch Government Study Grant, 1968, 1976, 1979. Agent: Art and Project, Prinsengracht 785, Amsterdam. Addresses: Javastraat 126, 1094 HP Amsterdam; Wilhelminastraat 57, 1054 VW Amsterdam, Netherlands.

Individual Exhibitions:

1969 Galerie Siau 1, Amsterdam
1970 Galerie Booker, Amsterdam
1974 Art and Project, Amsterdam
1975 Kabinett für Aktuelle Kunst, Bremerhaven, West Germany
Art and Project, Amsterdam
Westfalischer Kunstverein, Münster, West Germany (with Rajlich and Rous)
1976 Art and Project, Amsterdam
1977 Kabinett fur Aktuelle Kunst, Bremerhaven, West Germany
Galleria La Bertesca, Genoa, Italy
Galerie Waalkens, Finsterwolde, Netherlands
Galleria La Bertesca, Dusseldorf
Galleria La Bertesca, Milan
Art and Project, Amsterdam
1979 Museum Fodor, Amsterdam
Art and Project, Amsterdam (with J. Commandeur and T. Rajlich)
1980 Art and Project, Amsterdam
1981 Art and Project, Amsterdam (with A. Blom and J. Commandeur)
1982 Art and Project, Amsterdam

Selected Group Exhibitions:

1970 *Utrechtse Kring,* Neudeflat, Utrecht
1972 *Multiples,* Kunststichting, Amsterdam
1973 *Prospect 73,* Städtische Kunsthalle, Dusseldorf
1974 *Somer 74,* Art and Project, Amsterdam
1975 *Fundamentele Schilderkunst,* Stedelijk Museum, Amsterdam
1976 *Sovrastruttura e Metapittura,* University of Palermo, Sicily
1977 *Bilder ohne Bildhauer,* Rheinisches Landesmuseum, Bonn
1980 *Neue Malerei aus den Niderlanden,* Neue Galerie, Graz, Austria
1982 *Amsterdam 60–80,* Museum Fodor, Amsterdam

Collections:

Stedelijk Museum, Amsterdam; Frans Halsmuseum, Haarlem, Netherlands; Dienst voor Rijks Verspreide Kunstvoorwerpen, The Hague; Museum Boymans-van Beuningen, Rotterdam; PTT Collection, The Hague.

Publications:

By BERGHUIS: articles—texts in *Art and Project Bulletin* (Amsterdam), nos. 77, 78, 1974; interview, with Dorine Mignot, in *Fundamentele Schilderkunst,* exhibition catalogue, Amsterdam 1975; interview, with Gijs Van Tuyl, in *Elementarformen,* exhibition catalogue, Bonn 1975.

On BERGHUIS: books—*Berghuis/Rajlich/Rous,* exhibition catalogue, with text by Klaus Honnef, Münster, West Germany 1975; *Elementarformen,* exhibition catalogue, with texts by Hans Sizoo, Klaus Honnef and others, Bonn 1975; *Berghuis/Dibbets/van Elk,* exhibition catalogue with text by R. Hammacher-van den Brande, Belgrade 1977; articles "Debuten" by Lambert Tegenbosch in *De Volkskrant* (Amsterdam), September 1969; "Erotiek en Humor" by Fanny Kelk in *Het Parool* (Amsterdam), October 1969; "Jaap Berghuis" by M. van Emde Boas in *NRC-Handelsblad* (Amsterdam), October 1969; "Seizoenbegin in de Amsterdamse Kunstzalen" by M. van Emde Boas in *NRC-Handelsblad* (Amsterdam), September 1970; "Anonymous—Art & Project" in *Flash Art* (Milan), December 1974; "Fordert zur Kunst aug" by Hannelore Ahorn in *Nordsee-Zeitung* (Bremerhaven, West Germany), January 1975; "Jaap Berghuis" by Klaus Honnef in *Art Press* (Paris), September 1975; "Jaap Berghuis" by Betty van Gerrel in *NRC Handelsblad* (Amsterdam), 29 October 1982.

Jaap Berghuis: *Pieces for Schumann VII*, 1980

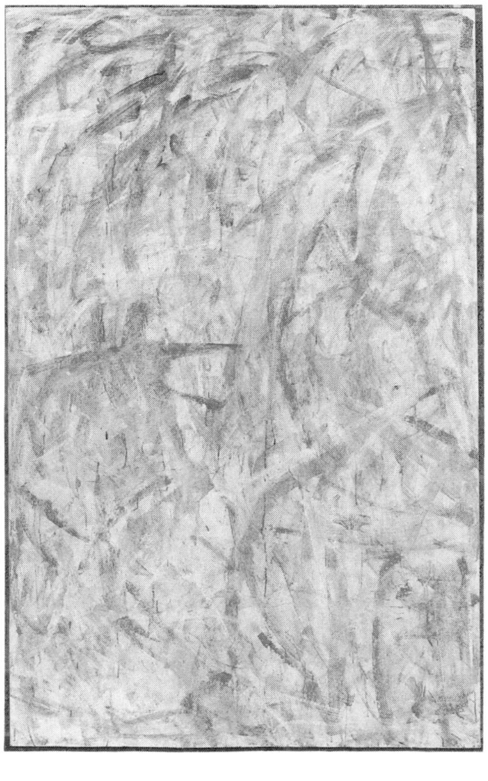

BERLEWI, Henryk.

Polish. Born in Warsaw, 30 October 1894. Educated in schools in Warsaw; attended art classes, Warsaw, 1904–09, and Antwerp, 1909–10; studied at the Ecole des Beaux-Arts, Paris, 1911–12. Lived in Warsaw, 1913–21; settled in Berlin, 1921: participated in Group "G" with Hans Richter, Werner Graeff, Sacha Stone and Mies van der Rohe; Member, Novembergruppe, Berlin, 1922; experimented with Mecano-Faktura theory, publishing his manifesto, 1923–24; returned to Warsaw, 1923: Co-Founder, Blok. 1923; worked as a theatre designer and art critic. 1926; settled in Paris, 1928: returned to Mecano-Faktura theory, 1957; founded Archives of *Abstract Art and International Avant-Garde,* Paris, 1960; continued development of Mecano-Faktura theory; experimented with cinematographic representation, Akademie der Künste, Berlin, 1962. *Died* (in Paris) *2 August 1967.*

Individual Exhibitions:

1934 Austro-Daimler Automobilsalon, Warsaw
Galerie der Sturm, Berlin
1950 Galerie Petrides, Paris
1963 Galerie Situationen 60, Berlin
1964 Maison de France, Berlin
1965 Centre d'Art Cybernetique, Paris
1966 Fine Art Society, Warsaw (toured Poland)
1967 Galerie Rewolle, Bremen
1978 Helen Serger, La Boetie, New York

Selected Group Exhibitions:

1914 *4th Jack of Diamonds*, Moscow
1915 *Zacheta*, Warsaw (and regularly until 1921)
1916 *Futurist Exhibition 0.10*, Petrograd
1923 *Novembergruppe*, Berlin
1954 *Zeitgenossische Kunst aus Hannoverschem Prvatbesitz*, Kestner Gesellschaft, Hannover
1958 *De Renaissance der 20th Eeuw*, Stedelijk Museum, Amsterdam
1961 *The Art of Assemblage*, Museum of Modern Art, New York
1963 *Schrift und Bild*, Kunsthalle, Baden-Baden
1965 *Signale: Manifest: Proteste im 20 Jahrhundert*, Stadtische Kunsthalle, Recklinghausen
1966 *Von Impressionismus zum Bauhaus*, Kunstverein, Frankfurt

Collections:

Sztuki Museum, Lodz, Poland; Musée d'Art Moderne de la Ville, Paris.

Publications:

By BERLEWI: book—*Temoignages*, Paris 1965; articles—"Mecano Faktura Manifesto" in *Der Sturm* (Berlin), 1924; "Michel Larionov und Natalie Goncharova und der Rayonismus" in *Das Werk* (Winterthur, Switzerland), October 1961.

On BERLEWI: books—*Constructivism in Poland*, exhibition catalogue, Essen 1973; *Henryk Berlewi*, exhibition catalogue, by Helen Serger, New York 1978; article—"Berlewi et les Maccano-Factures" by C. Estienne in *XXe Siècle* (Paris), May 1966.

Henryk Berlewi's paintings of the 1960's give very little clue of how important this emigré Pole was to the development of non-figurative painting after his involvement with Dada during the First World War. It was in the early 1920's that his personal contribution to non-figurative art began. Through Lissitzky he was to become associated with the "New Poland," albeit at some distance removed. A year later he joined the Novembergruppe in Berlin and started his own version of abstract art which he called Mecano-Faktura (details of which were published in *Der Sturm* in 1924), ideas and theories which, however remote from the AR activities of Strzeminski and Kobro in Lodz, still made him eligible as an innovator in their eyes. In fact, so successful was Berlewi when he returned to Warsaw that he became the founder member of yet another group of abstract artists—Blok.

The Stalinist period in Poland meant that there was no room for artists like Berlewi, and he left his homeland yet again for the West. The absurd political interruption in the progress of contemporary Polish culture had a devastating effect upon a great number of Polish creative talents (in some cases actually lethal—a terrible situation after the culmination of the Nazi occupation during which men like the gifted artist Karol Hiller went to their deaths).

For Berlewi it meant the start of one more new life. The hard-edge perfection of geometricized Kandinsky (in pianissimo mood) in rich colours, all of which had passed comfortably from Mecano-Faktura to Blok, gave way to the old man's translations of the Mediterranean. Fine paintings, but not to be compared for quality with what had gone before.

—Sheldon Williams

BERNI, Antonio.

Argentinian. Born in Rosario, 14 May 1905. Educated in Roldan, Santa Fe Province, 1915, 1917–20; apprenticeship in a stained-glass workshop and drawing studies at the Catala Centre, Rosario, 1916; studied in Madrid, 1925, and under André Lhote and Othon Friesz at the Grand Chaumière, Paris, 1926 (on Santa Fé Government Scholarship). Married Paule Cazenave in 1930; daughter: Hélène; married Nelida Gerino in 1950; son: José Antonio. Lived with peasants in the Pampas, painting landscapes, 1921–24; lived in Madrid, 1925, in Paris, 1926, and in Arcueil, near Paris, also travelling to Italy, Belgium, and Holland, 1927–30; influenced by Surrealists and Marxists while in Europe, and began making photomontages, collages, drawings, and paintings in surrealistic style, 1929; returned to Argentina, 1930; worked as a municipal employee, Rosario, 1931; co-founder with other young painters of "New Realism" movement in Argentina, and organized group productions of larger canvases, Buenos Aires, 1932–40; travelled to the Pacific Coast, 1946; lived for long periods of time with cotton harvesters and woodcutters, and painting popular subjects, Santiago del Estero, 1947–56; resumed collage and assemblage techniques of the 1930's, 1957–60; concentrated on engravings, 1960–64. Instructor, National School of Fine Arts, Buenos Aires, 1935–45. Recipient: Prix, 1925, Premier Prix, 1940, and Grand Prix, 1943, *Salon Nacional*, Buenos Aires: Prix d'Honneur, *Salon Internacional*, Buenos Aires, 1960; Grand Prix International de la Gravure, *Biennale*, Venice, 1962; Prix de la Commission Culturelle, *Biennale Internationale de la Gravure*, Ljubljana, 1965; Prix, *Biennale Internationale de la Gravure*, Cracow, 1966; Prix Intergrafik, Berlin, 1967. *Died* (in Buenos Aires) *13 October 1981*.

Individual Exhibitions:

1928 Salon Nancy, Madrid
1932 Galeria Amigos del Arte, Buenos Aires (surrealistic works)
1938 Galeria Amigos del Arte, Montevideo
1952 Galeria Viau, Buenos Aires
1954 Teatro del Pueblo, Buenos Aires
1955 Galeria Creuze, Paris
1957 Galeria Witcomb, Buenos Aires
1958 Galeria Serra, Buenos Aires
1961 Galeria Peuser, Buenos Aires
Galeria Witcomb, Buenos Aires
1963 Galeria du Passeur, Paris
Museo de Arte Moderno, Buenos Aires
1964 Museo de Arte Moderno, Santiago de Chile (retrospective)
Galeria Rubbers, Buenos Aires
1965 Instituto Di Tella, Buenos Aires (retrospective; travelled to Cordoba and Santa Fe)
1966 Galleria Due Mondi, Rome
1967 Galeria Rubbers, Buenos Aires
1968 Galeria Rubbers, Buenos Aires
1969 Galeria El Taller, Buenos Aires
1970 Galeria Exposhow, Buenos Aires
1971 ARC / Musée d'Art Moderne de la Ville, Paris
Galeria Rubbers, Buenos Aires
1973 Atelier Jacob, Paris
Galeria Rubbers, Buenos Aires
1974 Wells Gallery, Ottawa
Galeria del Mar, Buenos Aires
Galeria Imagen, Buenos Aires
Galeria Rubbers, Buenos Aires
1975 Galleria Zunini, Rome
Galeria Rubbers, Buenos Aires
1976 Galeria Carmen Waugh, Buenos Aires
Galeria Imagen, Buenos Aires
1977 Museo de Bellas Artes, Caracas (retrospective)
Bonino Gallery, New York
1978 Galeria Bonino, Buenos Aires
Galeria Imagen, Buenos Aires
1980 Galeria Arte Nuevo, Buenos Aires
Fundacion San Telmo, Buenos Aires
Museo de Arte Contemporaneo, Mar del Plata (retrospective)

Selected Group Exhibitions:

1955 *Hommage à Machado*, Maison de la Pensée, Paris
1962 *Biennale*, Venice
Art Latino-Américain, Centre Georges Pompidou, Paris (and 1965)
1965 *Mythologies Quotidiennes*, Centre Georges Pompidou, Paris
Biennale Internationale de la Gravure, Ljubljana, Yugoslavia
1967 *Le Monde en Question*, Musée d'Art Moderne de la Ville, Paris
La Nature Moderne, Palais de Glace, Paris
1969 *Art et Cybernétique*, Galeria Bonino, Buenos Aires (travelled to Caracas, 1970)
1972 *Encuentro de Artistas Plasticas del Cono Sur*, Santiago de Chile
1980 *Biennale of Contemporary Art*, Tokyo

Collections:

Museo Nacional de Bellas Artes, Buenos Aires; Museo de Arte Moderno, Buenos Aires; Museum of Modern Art, New York; Musée Municipal, Saint-Denis, France.

Publications:

By BERNI: articles—"Siqueiros et l'Art des Masses" in *Nueva Revista* (Buenos Aires), 1935; "Le Peintre Colonial Melchor Perez de Holquin" in *Prensa* (Buenos Aires), 15 February 1942; "Goribar, Peintre de Quito" in *Prensa* (Buenos Aires), 31 May 1942; "La Culture de Quito a l'Epoque Coloniale" in *Prensa* (Buenos Aires), 25 April 1943; "El arte como experiencia" in *Continente* (Buenos Aires), 16 April 1952; "Persecucion a la Inteligencia" in *Propositos* (Buenos Aires) 18 December 1957; "El arte, su desarrollo, promocion y mercado" in *La Opinion* (Buenos Aires), 9 June 1972.

On BERNI: books—*Antonio Berni* by Geo-Dorival, Buenos Aires, 1944; *Antonio Berni* by Roger Pla, Buenos Aires 1945; *Biennale di Venezia*, exhibition catalogue with text by Jorge Romero Brest, Venice 1962; *Naissance d'un Art Nouveau* by Michel Ragon, Paris 1963; *Antonio Berni*, exhibition catalogue, with text by Gérald Gassiot-Talabot, Buenos Aires 1965; *Ramona Montiel* by E. Sabato and E. Schoo, Buenos Aires 1966; *Panorama de la Pintura Argentina Contemporanea* by Aldo Pellegrini, Buenos Aires 1967; *Berni* by Rafael Squirru, Montevideo 1968; *Vingt-Cinq Ans d'Art Vivant* by Michel Ragon, 1969; *A History of Latin American Art and Architecture* by Leopoldo Castedo, London 1969; articles—"Antonio Berni" by Rafael Squirru in *Journal of Inter-American Studies* (Washington, D.C.) July 1965; "Antonio Berni" by Gérald Gassiot-Talabot in *Depuis 45*, vol. 2, Brussels 1970; "Antonio Berni" by Michel Troche in *Opus International* (Paris), May 1971.

"The most thought-provoking human drama in Latin America in our century is that of those nations suffering under the yoke of colonialism with its burden of poverty and backwardness . . . . To seek to draw our artists away from the essential truth in order to direct them towards other secondary truths is equivalent to depriving them of all possibility of achieving the great art to which every man of progress aspires", wrote Antonio Berni in 1952, himself a fellow-traveller on this artistic journey dictated by political commitment. Eschewing all aesthetic and formal apriority, Berni's art is above all an art of the real, an art whose concern is to emphasise and denounce the excess of social injustices weighing down the Argentinian nation.

Berni was born in 1905 in Santa Fé. As in the case of the majority of his fellow Argentinians, many of his ancestors were Italian emigrés. Berni studied painting and drawing from an early age at the Centro Catala de Rosario, the capital of the province and second major city of Argentina. A scholarship from the Jockey Club gave him the opportunity to complete his studies in Europe. This trip, an inevitable 'return to one's roots' for any Latin American artist eager to seek out aesthetic models from the continent of his origin, took Berni first to Madrid, then to Paris, where he became familiar with various currents of

avant-garde thinking. In 1926 he began studying painting at the Grande Chaumière under the direction of Othon Friesz and André Lhote, but his taste for realism, intense colours and architectural decors was to find in De Chirico, rather than in the Cubists whom he nevertheless admired, a source of inspiration which accorded with his artistic sensibilities. This influence is manifest in the self-portrait of 1929 showing the painter in a garish light which accentuates the angular lines of the face and the austerity of a poverty-stricken urban environment. His meeting with the Surrealists in 1928, his relations with Max Jacob, Louis Aragon and various intellectuals of the period, far from seducing him into accepting the easy and frivolous life style of a certain Parisian intellectual milieu, were to drive him to take a stand against oppression and social injustice and to deepen his political convictions by familiarising himself with the theories of Marx, Lenin and Engels, theories which would form the mainstay henceforth of his artistic work.

On his return to Argentina in 1930 he exhibited a collection of works which were regarded as the first example of Surrealist art realised by an artist from the American continent. This series of paintings and collages, which have been described as 'fantastic metaphysical' art, present everyday objects with symbolical associations—keys, screws, locks, pins—invading neo-classic landscapes and architecture with their nightmarish presences abounding in references to torture, imprisonment and repression.

But this incursion into the world of objects and dreams, still conditioned by European influences, was to be suddenly invested with all the emotional force of a direct human crisis when Berni confronted the situation that had arisen in his own country. For he could not have remained indifferent to the particularly alarming political and economic crisis which overtook Argentina at the beginning of the 'thirties. During his 'realist period', which lasted approximately from 1934 to 1957, the Argentine artist introduced into his large pictorial compositions various aspects of the harsh existence endured by an urban rural proletariat which he daily frequented in Buenos Aires and during his numerous trips into the country. With their violent colours, massive outlines and the almost 'cinematographic' structure of the different parts of the image, Berni's paintings inevitably remind one of certain aspects of Mexican 'Muralismo' (Berni met the 'muralista' D. Alfaro Siqueiros during the latter's stay in Buenos Aires) and of Expressionism, but they exaggerate still further the dramatic intention, the working-class, specifically Third World, character of their themes by their pathetic rendering of faces, their choice of nuances and sordid accentuation of details. Painted from photographs or from straighforward observation, these scenes showing work in the fields, popular manifestations of anger or impotence in face of an inflexible social system, unemployment and poverty, function as political denunciations purely through the evocative power of the evidence contained in the choice of subject matter.

The Second World War produced a radical change in the formal orientation of Berni's work and the innovative character of his researches was soon to bring him international renown, crowned by the prize for engraving at the Venice Biennale in 1962. Although the social theme remained central to his work, Berni became absorbed in new technical processes based on assemblage, discovering the rich plasticity of reject materials and the naiveté of popular urban art. In his compositions the recycling of used objects, picked up in the streets of the Argentine capital or in the Parisian flea markets, seems to have nothing to do with either the 'cult of the object' in the manner of Pop Art, or with a fad for assembling disparate objects for its own sake, but, as Gerald Gassiot-Talabot supposes, tends to underline "the relationship which is established between the reject and the social organisation which has produced it". And, in order to denounce even more firmly the aberrations of the social organisation, Berni was to retrace in the course of his work the urban epic of the life of a small boy, Juanito Laguna, a stereotype for the lives of all the thousands of inhabitants of those 'villa misérias', the shanty town homes sprawling on the periphery of Buenos Aires. In these large-format collages the decor, worked without attention to perspectives, is comprised of objects deriving from the very place they represent; the figures are set off and unified by the pictorial matter and their faces have coarse, roughly executed, almost caricatured faces which are movingly expressive.

These chapters of Juanito's life relate trivial incidents and scenes in the naive manner of children but in which the intrusion of elements symbolising progress or science (cosmonauts, the bomb . . .) only renders all the more insupportable the anachronistic situation in which the characters find themselves. Then, through Ramona Montiel, a woman torn between her romantic ideals and the sordid experience of prostitution, Berni describes the corrosive, degrading world of money, corruption and power. As if himself seduced by the charms of his Ramona, the artist deploys all his skill in assembling, all his engraving talents, to dress her in lace cut from cake wrappings, to coif her with buttons and artificial flowers, and to surround her with all the kitsch imagery of a shanty town Madame Bovary. So emotive are these works that the characters of Berni's 'pictorial novel' have been reintegrated into popular Argentinian culture, giving rise, for example, to numerous songs.

During the last years of his life Berni put together a collection of sculptural pieces: assemblages of three-dimensional objects characterised by a mixture of a baroque and the science fictional, the humorous and the horrific, in order to represent in the form of monsters and dragons nightmarish visions of maleficient powers, of death, vice, power and terror, in other words, all man's ancestral fears. Some of these sculptures were to inhabit 'Ramona's cavern', a huge site of a son et lumière, which was presented in 1968.

From his first Surrealist paintings to his final sculptures, via his realist period and the large series of assemblages which have often been associated—because of their chronological simultaneity and their political bias—with the 'Nouvelle Figuration' in Europe, Berni's œuvre, which has achieved a formal diversity of astonishing richness (including painting, sculpture, engraving, xylography and collages), stands out above all for the commitment and acuteness of observation which puts it at the service not of the aesthetic demands of its age, but of a reality which, beneath its wretched exterior, is full of the tragic grandeur of the objects and feelings which are its offspring.

—Dominique Liquois

BERTHOLIN.

French. Born Maurice Bertholin in Granges-sur-Vologne, Vosges, 20 April 1936. Mainly self-taught in art, since 1952. Served in Service de Santé, French Army, in Nancy, France, 1956–58; Oran and Ain Sefra, Algeria, 1958. Married Francoise Andreux in 1959; children: Jacques, Veronique, Elisabeth. Nurse in Saint-Die Hospital, France, since 1959. Professor, Ecole des Beaux-Arts, since 1977. Agent: Galerie Baudoin Lebon, 34 rue des Archives, 75004 Paris, France. Address: 42 rue Eau de Robec, 76000 Rouen, France.

Individual Exhibitions:

1972 Galerie Sonnabend, Paris
Galerie Handschin, Basle
1974 Musée d'Art Moderne de la Ville, Paris
1975 Galerie Maenz, Cologne
Galerie Germain, Paris
Galerie Art in Progress, Munich
1976 Galerie Isy Brachot, Brussels
International Cultural Centrum, Antwerp
Galerie Germain, Paris
Galerie Paul Maenz, Cologne
1977 *La Matière Inavouable*, Musée de Saint-Etienne, France
Galerie Germain, Paris
1978 *Bertholin-Objekte*, Bädischer Kunstverein, Karlsruhe
Galerie Art Actuel, Nancy
Stèles de Bertholin, Galerie Isy Brachot, Brussels
Galerie Baudoin Lebon, Paris
1979 Kunst Forum, Rottweil, West Germany
L'Infinito Intrattenimento con le Cose, Galleria Unimedia, Genoa
1980 Galleria Cenobio Visualita, Milan
Ray Hughes Gallery, Brisbane
Galerie Baudoin Lebon, Paris
Galleria Il Gabbiano, La Spezzia, Italy
1981 Galleria Villa Romana, Florence
Galleria Unimedia, Genoa
Musée Départmental des Vosges, Epinal, France
1982 Musée du Fer, Jarville, Nancy, France
Musée d'Art Moderne, Strasbourg, France
1983 ARC/Musée d'Art Moderne de la Ville, Paris
Centre d'Art Contemporain, Chateauroux, France
1984 Espace Lyonnais d'Art Contemporain, Lyon, France
Galerie Baudoin Lebon, Paris
1987 Musée de la Cohue, Vannes, France

Selected Group Exhibitions:

1971 *Biennale des Jeunes*, Paris
1972 *Salon de Mai*, Musée d'Art Moderne, Paris
1973 *5 Musées Personnels*, Musée de Grenoble, France
1974 *L'Art du 20th Siècle: Les Courants Historiques, Les Tendances de l'Art Actuel*, Musée d'Art Moderne, Paris
1975 *Today, Together*, Galerie Paul Maenz, Cologne
1977 *Documenta 6*, Kassel, West Germany
1978 *La Creazione Volgeva alla Fine*, Galleria Unimedia, Genoa
1984 *Les écritures dans la peinture*, Villa d'Arson, Nice, France
1985 *Livres d'Artistes*, Centre Georges Pompidou, Paris
1978 *Les Années Mémoire*, Centre d'Art Contemporain, Meymac, France

Collections:

Centre National d'Art Contemporain, Paris; Centre Georges Pompidou, Paris; Musée de Grenoble, France; Musée Cantini, Marseilles; Musée de Ceret, France; Musée de Strasbourg, France; Musée d'Epinal, France; Musée de Martiques, France; Queensland Art Gallery, Brisbane; Power Gallery of Contemporary Art, Sydney.

Publications:

By BERTHOLIN: books—*Impact II*, exhibition catalogue, Caret, France 1972; *5 Musees Personnels*, exhibition catalogue, Grenoble 1973; *Pour Mémoires*, exhibition catalogue, Bordeaux 1973; articles—article in *Flash Art* (Milan), July/August 1977; statement in *Documenta 6*, exhibition catalogue, Kassel, West Germany 1977; statement in *Bertholin-Objekte*, exhibition catalogue, Karlsruhe 1978; "Emtretien avec Eddy Devolder" in *Jalons et actualités des Arts* (Paris), May 1978; "On ne peut que parler dans l'ombre . . ." in *Cahier* (Paris), Autumn 1987.

On BERTHOLIN: books—*Bertholin et La Matière Inavouable*, exhibition catalogue, with text by Gilbert Lascault, Saint-Etienne 1977; *Bertholin-Objekte*, exhibition catalogue, with text by Andreas Franzke, Karlsruhe 1978; *Steles de Bertholin*, exhibition catalogue, with text by André Jocou, Brussels 1978; *Bertholin: L'Infinito Intrattenimento con le Cose*, exhibition catalogue, with text by Antonio D'Avossa, Genoa 1979; *Bertholin*, exhibition catalogue, with text by Bernard Noel, Paris 1980; *Le Bout des Bordes: les choses pensantes de Bertholin* by Jean-Luc Parant, Paris 1980; *Bertholin: Les choses mêmes*, exhibition catalogue by Philippe Lacoue-Lbarthe, Paris 1983; *Bertholin: Les choses, l'utopie*, exhibition catalogue by Alain Cueff, Lyon 1984;

Bertholin: Works of 1971–1983 at the ARC, Paris, 1984

Bertholin—un fragmentaire qui s'assemble, exhibition catalogue by Valerie Chanut, Vannes 1987; articles—"Bertholin" by Bernard Borgeaud in *L'Art Vivant* (Paris), January 1972; "Fevrier à Paris" by Francois Pluchart in *Artitudes* (Saint Jeannet, France), March 1972; "Une Avant-Garde Clandestine" by Jean Clair in *L'Art Vivant* (Paris), September 1972; "Art en France: Une Nouvelle Generation" by Jean Clair in *Chêne* (Paris), 1973; "L'Art de Masse n'Existe Pas" by Jean Clair in *L'Art Vivant* (Paris), 1974; "Aux Entrepots de la Mémoire" by Pierre Schneider in *L'Express* (Paris), 30 September 1974; "Un Rituel Fétichiste" by Alain Macaire in *Artitudes* (Saint Jeannet, France), March 1976; "Bertholin" by Jacques Memis in *Libre Belgique* (Brussels), 19 May 1978; "Bertholin Aides-Mémoires" by Thierry Chabanne in *Art Press* (Paris), January 1979; "Bertholin et la Communication différée" in *Art Press* (Paris), December 1980; "Bertholin: Le papier est à l'intérieur" by Bernard Huin in *Kanal* (Paris), January 1985.

It was working out something very modest but definitely of my own that I was seized by a profound need to fabricate, using an artisan's method of working, some "things" which would possess something of the history of men and of myself.

Begotten like life itself at the price of infinite care, all these "things" are fashioned from the same material and retain the mark of fire and the trace of varied manipulations. This "substance" is transformed from several worn-out materials recovered from refuse consigned to destruction, so that in transmuting them into this new "paste" I tear them, momentarily, from their inexorable annihilation as if for an ultimate celebration of the perishable.

From the most complex pieces to the pellets formed in the hollows of my hand, all these "things"—tangible witness of the ephemeral activity of man—are in harmony with my intimate life or are disinterred from the furthest recesses of my memory of the world. If their form is, in the first instance, copied from objects from everyday life, it becomes, as the work is amplified and enlarged, more complex not to say even in certain cases fragmentary and destructured.

As for the dimensions of the pieces, they have sprung from two currents which co-exist in the work: on the one hand all those which can be held in the hand, on the other hand those which are to be proportions of the human body. It is according to the latter tendency that the dimensions are, more and more, copied from the height of my children or the size of a part of their body. If each piece becomes the witness of a moment of their growth, this aleatory—established through chance—system of measurement recalls that the origin of measurements is to be found in the measurements of the human body while thus transgressing the fixed systems of measurement imposed by societies.

It must be noted that a number of pieces present themselves as a sort of prolongation of the hand—rediscovery of the primordial tool—but where the place and the function of these "tools," like moreover the corporal gestures which accompany them, escape all elucidations.

Other pieces—the large chests for example—comparable to types of "furniture," can it seems contribute to the furnishing of a habitable place. In fact many pieces present surfaces which retain the mark of a wear and tear due to the work of man.

Each piece is repeated untiringly in order to take from it whatever it might conserve of the unique, the rare and the precious, but also to lead to a greater perfecting through gestures which have become familiar. This repetition is also felt as a need to win over this "thing," to seize from it its hidden forces and its relations with the world.

Nevertheless, it becomes more and more apparent that these works are the fruit of a visceral and organic activity in which are mixed the rational and the irrational, rigour and approximation, precision and imprecision. Work that is open, not allowing the loss of any "accident" or artefact (it is in looking for India that one finds America). This production—so to speak physiological—with its pulsations and its phantasms seeks not to exhaust but to maintain in me a certain power of invention. This process of auto-production—always on the edge of disaster—oscillates between memory and invention, imitation and creation, experiment and practice . . .

Each piece invokes another or its contrary, thus adding them to one another in an endless movement, a perpetually unfinished work—far from all references—and with almost infinite combinations.

In exile whatever the place which receives them, all these unindexed "things," without evident link between themselves, unless it be their epidermis, come to accumulate, letting one perceive that they derive from a coherent whole but one which would have existed far away. Nevertheless, it seems that each of these "things" only becomes clear by the relations which link it to the others, and one can not therefore decipher each piece except with regard to the whole, as one can not seize the whole except by starting out from each piece.

Thus, all these "vestiges" of the history of men and of myself have finally no meaning but that of allowing me to play a role in it.

With some stubborn materials and long manual work, this production becomes a function of life, a mania to produce to kill the anguish, an effort to escape from an unbearable solitude, a last bridge between man and the indistinct forces which surround him, an ultimate interrogation of the human condition

and aesthetic practice, and, derisory though it may seem, a wish to leave some traces of my passing.

—Bertholin

BERTHOT, Jake.

American. Born in Niagara Falls, New York, 30 March 1939. Studied at the New School for Social Research, New York, 1960–61; Pratt Institute, Brooklyn, New York, 1960–62. Independent artist, New York, since 1962. Artist-in-Residence, Yale University, New Haven, Connecticut, 1982. Recipient: Guggenheim Fellowship, 1981. Agent: David McKee Gallery, 41 East 57th Street, New York, New York 10022. Address: 105 Bowery, New York, New York 10002, U.S.A.

Individual Exhibitions:

1970 O.K. Harris Gallery, New York
1971 Michael Walls Gallery, San Francisco
1972 O.K. Harris Gallery, New York
Michael Walls Gallery, San Francisco
1973 Portland Center for the Visual Arts, Oregon
Galerie de Gestlo, Hamburg
Cunningham Ward Gallery, New York
1974 Locksley-Shea Gallery, Minneapolis
1975 O.K. Harris Gallery, New York
Daniel Weinberg Gallery, San Francisco
1976 David McKee Gallery, New York
1977 Galerie de Gestlo, Hamburg
Brandeis University, Waltham, Massachusetts
1978 David McKee Gallery, New York
1979 Nigel Greenwood Gallery, London
Nina Nielsen Gallery, Boston
1982 David McKee Gallery, New York
1983 David McKee Gallery, New York
1984 University of California, Berkeley
Nina Nielsen Gallery, Boston
1985 Southern Methodist University, Dallas
David McKee Gallery, New York

Selected Group Exhibitions:

1972 *8 New York Painters,* University of California Art Museum, Berkeley
1974 *Recent Abstract Painting,* Pratt Institute, Brooklyn, New York
1976 *Critical Perspectives in American Art,* at the *Biennale,* Venice
1977 *8 Abstract Painters,* Institute of Contemporary Art, Philadelphia
1979 *New Painting/New York,* Hayward Gallery, London
1980 *L'Amerique aux Indépendents 1944–1980,* Grand Palais, Paris
1981 *New Works on Paper,* Museum of Modern Art, New York (travelled to the Museum of Fine Arts, Houston; La Jolla Art Museum, California; and the Art Museum of South Texas, Corpus Christi)
1984 *International Survey of Recent Painting and Sculpture,* Museum of Modern Art, New York
1985 *Landscape and Abstract Art,* Colby College, Waterville, Maine
1988 *Contemporary American Art,* Sara Hilden Art Museum, Tampere, Finland (travelled to Oslo)

Collections:

Museum of Modern Art, New York; Whitney Museum, New York; Guggenheim Museum, New York; Fogg Art Museum, Harvard University, Cambridge, Massachusetts; Museum of Art, Carnegie Institute, Pittsburgh; Philadelphia Museum of Art; High Museum of Art, Atlanta; Dallas Museum of Fine Arts; Australian National Gallery, Canberra.

Publications:

By BERTHOT: article—comment in "Points of View: A Taped Conversation with 4 Painters" by Willoughby Sharp in *Arts Magazine* (New York), December 1971.

On BERTHOT: books—*Jake Berthot,* exhibition catalogue, with text by Dore Ashton, Minneapolis 1974; *Painting Endures,* exhibition catalogue, Boston 1975; *Critical Perspectives in American Art,* exhibition catalogue, Venice 1976; *Jake Berthot,* exhibition catalogue, with text by Bonnie Saulnie, Waltham, Massachusetts 1977; *8 Abstract Painters,* exhibition catalogue, with text by Dore Ashton, Philadelphia 1977; *Silence and Slow Time,* exhibition catalogue, by Robin Karson, South Hadley, Massachusetts 1977; *New Painting/New York,* exhibition catalogue, with text by C. Lampert, London 1979; *New Works on Paper,* exhibition catalogue, New York 1981; *American Art Since 1945* by Dore Ashton, New York 1984; articles—"Jake Berthot Paints Quietness" by Dore Ashton in *Arts Magazine* (New York), November 1971; "Jake Berthot" by C. Beret in *Art Press* (Paris), September/October 1973; "Jake Berthot: Recent Works" by Stephen Kasher in *Artforum* (New York), September 1978; "Jake Berthot" by Dore Ashton in *Arts Magazine* (New York), January 1979; "Jake Berthot" by Oswell Blakeston in *Arts Review* (London), 27 April 1979; "Jake Berthot" by B. Lemarche-Vadel in *Artistes* (Paris), April 1981; "Jake Berthot's Order" by Dore Ashton in *Arts Magazine* (New York), March 1982; "Jake Berthot" by Grace Glueck in the *New York Times,* 25 November 1983; "A Return to the Basics: Jake Berthot's Recent Paintings" by John Yau in *Arts* (New York), March 1984.

BERTOIA, Harry.

American. Born in San Lorenzo, Udine, Italy, 10 March 1915; moved to the United States, 1930. Educated at Cass Technical High School, Detroit, 1932–36; studied, on scholarship, at the Society of Arts and Crafts, Detroit, 1936, and at the Cranbrook Academy of Art, Bloomfield Hills, Michigan, 1937–39. Married Brigitta Valentiner in 1943; children: Mara, Val, Celia. Set up metal shop and taught metalwork, Cranbrook Academy, 1939–43; produced molded plywood products for the war effort at the Evans Products Company, Venice, California, 1943–46 (later designed chairs with Charles Eames for the same company); did graphic work at the Point Loma Naval Electronics Laboratory, 1947–49; settled in Pennsylvania, 1950, setting up studio there, with support of Knoll Associates of New York: Bertoia Chair introduced by Knoll, 1952. Recipient: Fine Arts Medal, 1955, and Craftsmanship Medal, 1956, American Institute of Architects; Graham Foundation Grant, for European travel, 1957; Fine Arts Medal, American Institution of Architects, Pennsylvania Chapter, 1963, 1967; Gold Medal, American Institute of Architects, 1973. Honorary doctorate: Muhlenberg College, Allentown, Pennsylvania, 1971. Agent: Staempfli Gallery, 47 East 77th Street, New York, New York, U.S.A. *Died 6 November 1978.*

Individual Exhibitions:

1940 Karl Nierendorf Gallery, New York
1943 Karl Nierendorf Gallery, New York
Museum of Non-Objective Art, New York
Smithsonian Institution, Washington, D.C. (toured the United States)
1947 Karl Nierendorf Gallery, New York
1951 Knoll Associates, New York
1956 Fairweather-Hardin Gallery, Chicago
1959 Staempfli Gallery, New York
1961 Fairweather-Hardin Gallery, Chicago
Staempfli Gallery, New York
1963 Staempfli Gallery, New York
1964 Knoll International, Paris
1967 Knoll International, Amsterdam
1968 Fairweather-Hardin Gallery, Chicago
Staempfli Gallery, New York
Knoll International, Zurich
1970 Staempfli Gallery, New York
1972 K.B. Gallery, Oslo
1974 *Sensations in Sculpture,* Wadsworth Atheneum, Hartford, Connecticut
1975 K.B. Gallery, Oslo
Fairweather-Hardin Gallery, Chicago
Art Institute of Chicago
Sculpture and Graphics, Allentown Art Museum, Pennsylvania (restrospective)
1976 Staempfli Gallery, New York
1978 Staempfli Gallery, New York
1981 Staempfli Gallery, New York
1982 Robert Kidd Associates, Birmingham, Alabama
Community College, Lancaster, Pennsylvania
1983 Benjamin Mangel Gallery, Philadelphia
1986 Allentown Art Museum, Pennsylvania
1987 Michigan State University, East Lansing

Selected Group Exhibitions:

1943 *Non-Objective Painting Exhibition,* Guggenheim Foundation, New York
1945 *Graphics,* San Francisco Museum of Art
1958 *World's Fair,* Brussels
1963 *London Triennial Exhibition of Sculpture in the Open Air,* Battersea Park, London
1970 *The Modern Chair 1918–70,* Whitechapel Art Gallery, London
1974 *Sensations in Sculpture,* Wadsworth Atheneum, Hartford, Connecticut
1983 *Design Since 1945,* Philadelphia Museum of Art

Collections:

Museum of Modern Art, New York; Albright-Knox Art Gallery, Buffalo, New York; Munson-Williams-Proctor Institute, Utica, New York; Massachusetts Institute of Technology, Cambridge; Virginia Museum of Fine Art, Richmond; Joslyn Art Museum, Omaha, Nebraska; Denver Art Museum; Colorado Springs Fine Art Center; Dallas Public Library; San Francisco Museum of Modern Art.

Numerous commissions in public buildings and plazas throughout the United States.

Publications:

On BERTOIA: books—*Form and Space: Sculpture in the 20th Century* by Eduard Trier, New York 1968; *The Sculptural Idea* by James J. Kelly, Minneapolis 1970; *Harry Bertoia: Sculptor* by June Kompass Nelson, Detroit 1970; *The Technique of Kinetic Art* by John Torvey, New York 1971; *Bertoia,* Copenhagen 1972; *Science and Technology in Art Today* by Jonathan Benthall, New York 1972; *Art and the Future: A History/Prophecy of the Collaboration Between Science, Technology and Art* by Douglas Davis, New York 1973; *Harry Bertoia: An Exhibition of His Sculpture and Graphics,* exhibition catalogue, by Beverly H. Twitchell, Allentown, Pennsylvania 1975; *Design Since 1945,* exhibition catalogue edited by Kathryn B. Hiesinger and George H. Marcus, Philadelphia 1983; articles—"Harry Bertoia" by Jules Langsner in *Arts and Architecture* (Los Angeles), January 1953; "Sculpture Alive" by John Canaday in the *New York Times,* 19 March 1961; "Song and Dance Man" in *Time* (New York), 31 March 1961; "Creative Casting" by Lawrence Campbell in *Craft Horizons* (New York), November/December 1963; article in *Art International* (Lugano), April 1973; "Harry Bertoia: An American Sculptor with an Extended Concept of His Art" by Stig Anderson in *Kunsteg Idag* (Oslo), no. 1, 1973; film—*Harry Bertoia's Sculpture* by Clifford B. West, 1965.

People sometimes ask me how I do it, how I get my ideas, and I tell them by working like hell. I'm in this studio every day from 9 to 5. I know that runs against people's notions of creativity—you know, the midnight bursts of inspiration—but I don't think there is such a thing as a moment of inspiration. You get an idea and you try it out and it doesn't work, so you try something else until you discover something which pleases you.

I believe I'm getting to something of great importance. I think of the excitement of Picasso, Braque

Harry Bertoia: *Metal Sculpture*, c. 1962

and Gris when they began their experiments in cubism. What they did was to introduce a new dimension into painting—the dimension of time—revealing all sides of an object simultaneously. I believe sound is a dimension which could have great consequences. I know it's more meaningful to me now than the dimensions of color intensity or spatial relations. I don't hold onto terms like music and sculpture anymore. Those old distinctions have lost their meaning.

If I had to sum up my 40 years as an artist I'd say my intent has always been the enrichment of life. I've avoided that which would depress man's mood or being. There's plenty in the newspapers of that. I want to show what's positive and joyful in the world. I like to see the beauty of a flower before I admit it will vanish in three days.

—Harry Bertoia (from the 1st edition)

Well known as the designer of the wire shell chair produced by Knoll Associates that bears his name. Harry Bertoia had a multifaceted career which included the production of woodcuts, monoprints, biomorphic shaped silver jewelry, kinetic sculpture he referred to as "sculptural soundings," stationary sculpture including fountains, and environmental metal screens that are a combination of sculpture and architecture.

Born in Italy, Bertoia came to the United States with his father during his adolescence and he studied art and design at Cranbrook Academy in Bloomfield Hills, Michigan. After graduation he taught in the department of metalcraft and graphic arts from 1939 to 1943. Bertoia's training at America's premier institution of design nurtured his conception of himself as a craftsman rather than as a fine artist, which conditioned his habit of leaving his works unsigned and largely untitled. Florence Knoll, one of his associates at Cranbrook, encouraged his turn to furniture design for her husband's firm, Knoll Associates. In 1952 Knoll Associates introduced the Bertoia chair, a grid of welded metal wires in a diamond shape with a curved indentation molded to fit the contours of a seated human form. Routinely upholstered or padded, the chair reflects modern industrial design technology adapted for domestic interiors to enhance comfort, utility, and durability.

Bertoia designed a high backed chair, an ottoman, a side chair, and bench by 1953 when he turned his attention to more monumental architectural projects. During the late 1940s Bertoia had begun welding abstract metal sculpture from metal rods and wire and this technique precipitated his initial architectural collaboration with his Cranbrook classmate Eero Saarinen. His first major welded metal work and the first of his numerous public commissions was designed for Saarinen's General Motors Technical Center in Warren, Michigan in 1953. To designate a division between an entryway and a cafeteria, Bertoia structured a screen wall from a series of layered metal rectangles that demonstrate an artistic use of the techniques and materials utilized in the company's car making facility. Two years later Saarinen and Bertoia worked together on a non-denominational chapel for Massachusetts Institute of Technology. Bertoia designed an altar screen of rectangular bits of metal welded to a row of thin metal wires to hang behind the altar. Illuminated from above by a skylight, the only natural lighting in the circular chapel, the irregular metal shapes appear to float in space and they reflect on the water in the moat surrounding the chapel lending it an especially mystical presence. For their final artistic association, Bertoia made a mural of poured bronze panels for Saarinen's Dulles Airport in Chantilly, Virginia that was installed in 1963 after the architect's death.

Bertoia's other major public screen sculptures can be found in the Dallas Public Library (1955), Lambert/St. Louis Airport (1955), and the Southdale Shopping Center in Minneapolis (1956). One of Bertoia's fountains of welded rods radiating from a central core that sprays water in a spherical patter is also in Minneapolis as is his only major sculpture to be named. *Sunlit Straw,* a monumental sculpture comprised of brass coated steel rods hangs in the lobby of Minoru Yamasaki's National Life Insurance Company building.

During the 1960s Bertoia began exploring kinetic sculpture in his "sculptural soundings," made of bronze rods welded to a stationary base. When brushed against or activated by wind currents the rods resonate with ringing that expands into the surrounding space. For Bertoia welded metal was the material most representative of modern technology and he exploited its possibilities in sculpture, furniture, and interior design. His innovative range of creative endeavors designates him as a leading designer of his generation—a master of modern materials and environmental concerns.

—Percy North

BERTRAND, Jean-Pierre.

French. Born in Paris, 11 January 1937. Studied filmmaking at the Ecole Technique du Cinéma, Paris, 1955–57; mainly self-taught in drawing. Served in film section, French Army, in Senegal, Algeria and West Germany, 1958–60. Married Christa Anna Seidl in 1963 (divorced, 1975); daughter: Viana. Worked as cameraman in several film productions in France, 1960–63; television cameraman, O.R.T.F., Paris, 1963–69; freelance cameraman, in Buenos Aires, Rome, Hamburg and Madrid, 1969–72; independent artist, Paris, since 1972. Address: 27 rue Titon, 75011 Paris, France.

Individual Exhibitions:

1970	Kunstsammlungen, Ludwigshafen, West Germany
1972	Galerie Sonnabend, Paris
1975	Galerie Eric Fabre, Paris
1976	Chapelle de la Salpetriere, Paris
	Fine Arts Building, New York
1977	Galerie Eric Fabre, Paris
1978	Galleria Nuovi Strumenti, Brescia, Italy
1979	C Space, New York
	Galerie Jacques Donguy, Bordeaux
1980	Galerie Eric Fabre, Paris
1981	Musée de Toulon, France
1982	Galleria Luigi Deambrogi, Milan
	Galerie Camomille, Brussels
1983	Galerie de France, Paris

Selected Group Exhibitions:

1972	*International Art Festival,* Spoleto, Italy
1973	*Contemporanea,* Parcheggio Villa Borghese, Rome
1974	*Pour Memoires,* Entrepots Laine, Bordeaux
1975	*Photography as a Medium,* Maison de la Culture, Rennes, France
	Memoire d'un Pays Noir, Musée des Beaux Arts, Charleroi, Belgium
1978	*Boites,* Musée d'Art Moderne de la Ville, Paris
	Aspects de l'Art en France, at *Art 9, '78,* Basle
1979	*Europa 79,* Stuttgart
1982	*Trente Ans de Cinema Experimentale en France,* Centre Georges Pompidou, Paris

Collections:

Centre Georges Pompidou, Paris; Musée de Toulon, France.

Publications:

On BERTRAND: *Pour Memoires,* exhibition catalogue, with text by Jean Clair and others, Bordeaux 1974; *Jean-Pierre Bertrand,* exhibition catalogue, Toulon, France 1981;

Jean-Pierre Bertrand: *The Fifty Four Days of Robinson Crusoe*, 1974

articles—"Jean-Pierre Bertrand" by C. Bouyere in *Opus International* (Paris), June 1974; "In Memoriam" by Effie Stephano in *Art and Artists* (London), July 1974; "L'obscure Clarté de J. P. Bertrand" by Michel Nuridsany in *Le Figaro* (Paris), 19 June, 1981; "Jean Pierre Bertrand in Milano" in *Domus* (Milan), June 1982.

Perhaps my work began during this summer morning when, entering in my room, I saw a book opened in front of the window, between outside and outside, sun and darkness. With the sun, the two pages seemed to be white for a short time I was in the whiteness; the magic world revealed in His absence-presence. The book was the memorandum of Robinson Crusoe in the island. During fifty-four days I began to copy each day a day of Crusoe at the present form (the original text is at past) and took each day a photo of the book opening more and more to the end laying by the window. A few years after I noticed that Crusoe left the island when he was fifty-four years old. My last show was a sentence of which Crusoe has a strange relation with my own life.

I try to be available and vigilant with the magic world. Sometimes art makes me wink. Sometimes I wink at art. As Defoe says "serious reflections during the life and surprising adventures of Robinson Crusoe." The solitary man is between the "real" man and his emblematic original.

—Jean-Pierre Bertrand

The art of Jean-Pierre Bertrand recalls attitudes typical of the 'seventies. This aspect of his work appears spontaneously and without inhibition in his choice of materials—a choice which ultimately makes way for the unpredictable and extra-artistic element. Objects, natural products, photographs, paper drawings or ready-mades all provide the ideal vehicle for the realization of Bertrand's concepts, through which the chemical components intrinsic to these materials find their expression.

Bertrand's works and installataions thus become a theatre of phenomena, revelations of nature and hidden decay, which at the same time are visualizations of the artist's attention to those materials through which he can find the most appropriate metaphor. Here we have honey or lemon juice sprinkled onto paper, and, in time, changing back to their original colour; salt placed in a metal box will corrode, or may be used to form a star on the floor of a room; a dark area drawn around the edge of a sheet of white paper, then covered by a pane of glass (which then protects it) takes on the character of the missing frames from around drawings in series of diptychs, and thus becomes a part of the work.

In certain respects, Bertrand's work has similarities to those processes typical of 'Arte Povera', in particular those of Gilberto Zorio, where the work is an event occurring within the duration of the time taken to construct it. In other respects, he recalls Beuys, who employed every means available, even his own body, to expound his own ideology and elaborate symbolism. Bertrand also institutes the symbolic language of the Cabala, which for this French artist redefines and renews specific aspects of Hebraic mysticism. This complex system transforms the work—canvases or performances—resulting in a freedom and sensibility which is essentially contemporary while contributing a timeless and precise significance.

—Giorgio Verzotti

BEUYS, Joseph.

German. Born in Krefeld, 12 May 1921. Educated in Rindern, near Kleve, 1930–39; preparatory medical studies, Kleve, 1940; studied art, under Joseph Enseling and Ewald Matare. Staatliche Kunstakademie, Dusseldorf, 1947–51. Served as a radio-operator and fighter pilot, German Air Force, in Posen, Erfurt and Pardobitz, 1940–45; injured in plane crash in Russia, 1943; prisoner-of-war, Cuxhaven, 1945. First concentrated on art, Kleve, 1946; independent artist, Dusseldorf and Kleve, 1951, until his death in 1986: first "actions" and contact with Fluxus artists, Dusseldorf, 1962–65. Professor of Sculpture, Staatliche Kunstakademie, Dusseldorf, 1961–72; Guest Professor, Hochschule für Bildende Kunste, Hamburg, 1974–75. Founder, German Students Party, Dusseldorf, 1967, and Non-Voting Free Referendum Party for Direct Democracy, Dusseldorf, 1970; Candidate, Joint Action Party for Independent Germans, Dusseldorf, 1976; Candidate for the Green Party, West Germany, 1979. Recipient: Lichtwark-Preis, Hamburg, 1977; Thorn-Prikker-Ehrenplakette, Krefeld, 1978; Kaiserring Award, Goslar, 1979; Honorary Citizen Award, Bolognano, 1984; Wilhelm-Lehmbruck Prize, Duisburg, 1986. Honorary doctorate, Nova Scotia College of Art and Design, 1976; Member, Akademie der Kunste, West Berlin, 1978; Member, Royal Academy of Fine Arts, Stockholm, 1980. *Died* (in Dusseldorf) *23 January 1986.*

Individual Exhibitions:

1952 Kunstmuseum, Wuppertal, West Germany
1953 Kunstmuseum, Nijmegen, Netherlands
1961 Städtische Museum, Kleve, West Germany
1963 Staatliche Kunstakademie, Dusseldorf
Haus van der Grinten, Kranenburg, West Germany
1965 Galerie Schmela, Dusseldorf
1966 *Joseph Beuys . . . mit Braunkreuz,* Galerie René Block, West Berlin
Galerie St. Stephan, Vienna
Galerie Schmela, Dusseldorf
1967 Galerie Franz Dahlem, Darmstadt
Wide White Space Gallery, Antwerp
Beuys und das weisse Kreuz von Malewitsch, Städtische Museum, Mönchengladbach, West Germany
1968 Stedelijk Van Abbemuseum, Eindhoven, Netherlands
Kunstmuseum, Hamburg
Neue Pinakothek, Munich
Intermedia Galerie, Cologne
Staatliche Kunstakademie, Dusseldorf
1969 Galerie Schmela, Dusseldorf
Galerie René Block, West Berlin
Nationalgalerie, West Berlin
Akademie der Künste, West Berlin
Städtisches Museum, Mönchengladbach, West Germany
Werk aus der Sammlung Stroher, Kunstmuseum, Basle
1970 Galerie Nachst, St. Stephan, Vienna
Herzog Anton-Ulrich Museum, Braunschweig, West Germany
Louisiana Museum, Humlebaek, Denmark
Kunsthalle, Dusseldorf
Zeeuws Museum, Middleburg, Netherlands
Kunstmuseum, Lucerne
Kunstverein, Ulm, West Germany
1971 *Sammlung Hans und Franz Josef van der Grinten,* Galerie im Taxispalais, Innsbruck
Zeichnungen und Objekte 1937–1970 aus der Sammlung van der Grinten, Moderna Museet, Stockholm
Galerie Schellmann, Munich
Von-der-Heydt Museum, Wuppertal, West Germany
Kunsthalle, Kiel, West Germany
Galerie Schmela, Dusseldorf
Galerie Seebacher, Nuziders, Austria
1972 Staatliche Graphische Sammlung, Munich
Galerie René Block, West Berlin
Art Information Agency, Naples
Harcus-Krakow Gallery, Boston
Museum Folkwang, Essen
Tate Gallery/Whitechapel Art Gallery, London
"Friedenfeier," Mönchengladbach, West Germany
Centro d'Informazione Alternativa, Rome
Videogalerie Gerry Schum, Dusseldorf
Galerie Schmela, Dusseldorf
Hessisches Landesmuseum, Darmstadt
Galleria L'Attico, Rome
Tate Gallery, London

Joseph Beuys: *Plight* (detail), 1958–1985 Courtesy Anthony D'Offay Gallery, London

1973 Ronald Feldman Fine Art, New York
John Gibson Gallery, New York
Galerie Loehr, Frankfurt
Studio Marconi, Milan
Galerie Klein, Bonn
Galerie Grafikmeyer, Karlsruhe, West Germany
Eat-Art Galerie, Dusseldorf
Daytons Gallery 12, Minneapolis
Kaiser-Wilhelm-Museum, Krefeld, West Germany
Galerie René Block, West Berlin
1974 Ronald Feldman Fine Art, New York
René Block Gallery, New York
John Gibson Gallery, New York
Centre d'Art Contemporain, Bordeaux
The Secret Block for a Secret Person in Ireland, Museum of Modern Art, Oxford, (travelled to National Gallery of Modern Art, Edinburgh; Institute of Contemporary Arts, London; Municipal Gallery of Modern Art, Dublin; Arts Council Gallery, Belfast)
Zeichnungen 1946–1971, Museum Haus Lange, Krefeld, West Germany
Galerie Bama, Paris
Galleria Lucrezia De Domizio, Pescara, Italy
1975 Studio Brescia, Brescia, Italy
Galleria Lucrezia De Domizio, Pescara, Italy
René Block Gallery, New York
Ronald Feldman Fine Art, New York
Schwarzes Kloster, Freiburg, West Germany
Kestner-Gesellschaft, Hannover
Kunstverein, Kassel, West Germany
Fecoman Gallery, New York
1976 Kunstforum, Munich
Galerij Albert Baronian, Brussels
Kaiser-Wilhelm-Museum, Krefeld, West Germany
Wasserfarben 1936–1963, Kunstverein, Frankfurt
1977 Galerie Bama, Paris
Galleria Lucrezia De Domizio, Pescara, Italy
Museum Folkwang, Essen
Richtkrafte, Nationalgalerie, West Berlin
Kunstmuseum, Basle
Galerie Marika Malacorda, Geneva
Galerie Konrad Fischer, Dusseldorf
Galerie Schellmann und Kluser, Munich
Tekeningen, Aquarellen, Gouaches, Collages, Olieverven, Museum van Hedendaagse Kunst, Ghent
Galleria Saman, Genoa, Italy
1978 Kleine-Grafik-Galerie, Bremen, West Germany
Museo Diego Aragona Pignatelli Cortes, Naples
Galleria Ferrari, Verona, Italy
Kunstverein, Bremerhaven, West Germany
Galerie Polit-Art/o42, Nijmegen, Netherlands
University of California, Riverside
Studio Cavalieri, Bologna, Italy
Galerie Cuenca, Ulm, West Germany
Universitatsmuseum, Marburg, West Germany
Landesmuseum Joanneum, Graz, Austria
Galerie Schmela, Dusseldorf
1979 Galerie Nachst St. Stephan, Vienna
Kunstverein, Gottingen, West Germany
Galerie Puschel, Bielefeld, West Germany
Monchehaus-Museum, Goslar, West Germany
Galleri Per Sten, Copenhagen
Museum Boymans-van Beuningen, Rotterdam (travelled to Berlin, Bielefeld and Bonn)
Guggenheim Museum, New York
Galerie Schmela, Dusseldorf
1980 Galerie Schellmann and Kluser, Munich
Galleria Piero Cavellini, Brescia, Italy
Galleria Delta, Salerno, Italy
Anthony D'Offay Gallery, London
Richard Demarco Gallery, Edinburgh
Stadtisches Kunstmuseum, Bonn
Badischer Kunstverein, Karlsruhe, West Germany
Galerie Holtmann, Cologne
Stadtische Galerie, Erlangen, West Germany
1981 Ink Halle fur internationale Kunst, Zurich
Kunstverein, Mannheim, West Germany
Heath Gallery, Atlanta, Georgia
Kunstraum, Munich
Galleria del Cortile, Rome
Galleria Schellmann und Kluser, Munich
Stadtische Galerie im Lenbachhaus, Munich
Museum Commanderie van St. Jan, Nijmegen, Netherlands (travelled to Dusseldorf and Ulm)
Sammlung Ulbricht, East Berlin

1982 Ronald Feldman/Schellmann und Kluser, New York
Galerie Durand-Dessert, Paris
Forum fur aktuelle Kunst/Galerie Krinzinger, Innsbruck, Austria
Henie-Onstad Kunstsenter, Hovikodden, Norway
Galerie Klein, Bonn
1983 City Art Gallery, Leeds, Yorkshire (travelled to Cambridge and London)
Galerie Konrad Fischer, Dusseldorf
Galerie Schmela, Dusseldorf
Europaisches Forum, Alpbach, Austria
Stadelschen Kunstinsitut, Frankfurt
Anthony D'Offay Gallery, London
Galerie Stahlberger, Weil am Rhein, West Germany
Musee Cantonal des Beaux-Arts, Lausanne (travelled to Winterthur; Calais; St. Etienne; Linz; Oslo; Marseille)
1984 Galerie Konrad Fischer, Dusseldorf
Galerie Durand-Dessert, Paris
Stadtsparkasse, Wuppertal, West Germany
Galerie Schellmann und Kluser, Munich
Mittelrhein-Museum, Mainz, West Germany
Busch-Reisinger Museum, Harvard University, Cambridge, Massachusetts
Seibu Museum of Art, Tokyo
Kunsthalle, Tubingen, West Germany
Kunstlerhaus Eisenturm, Mainz, West Germany
Neue Galerie der Stadt Linz, Austria
Stadtische Galerie, Wurzburg, West Germany
1985 Galerie Beaubourg, Paris
Galerie Cuenca, Ulm, West Germany
Edition Schellmannn, Munich
Nassauischer Kunstverein, Wiesbaden, West Germany
Museum und Museumsverein, Aachen, West Germany
Commanderie van St. Jan, Nijmegen, Netherlands
Suermondt-Ludwig-Museum, Aachen (travelled to Ratingen)
Museum am Ostwall, Dortmund, West Germany
John Gibson Gallery, New York
Galerie Bernd Kluser, Munich
Anthony D'Offay Gallery, London
Edizione Lucio Amelio, Naples (travelled to New York)
Fundacion Caja de Pensiones, Madrid
Museo di Capodimonte, Naples
1986 Stadtische Galerie im Lenbachhaus, Munich
Galerie Gogger und Murrer, Munich

Selected Group Exhibitions:

1963 *Festum Fluxorum Fluxus,* Staatliche Kunstakademie, Dusseldorf
1964 *Documenta 3,* Museum Fridericianum, Kassel, West Germany (and *Documenta 4,* 1968; *Documenta 5,* 1972; *Documenta 7,* 1982)
1973 *Contemporanea,* Parcheggio Villa Borghese, Rome
1974 *Projekt 74,* Kunsthalle, Cologne
1976 *Biennale,* Venice
1977 *Art of the 60s.* Städtisches Kunstmuseum, Bonn
1982 *Arte Povera et Anti-Form,* Centre d'Arts Plastiques Contemporains, Bordeaux
1983 *Museums by Artists,* Art Gallery of Ontario, Toronto
1985 *Kunst in der Bundesrepublik 1945–85,* Nationalgalerie, West Berlin
1987 *Berlinart 1961–87,* Museum of Modern Art, New York (travelled to San Francisco)

Collections:

Stroher Collection, Hessisches Landesmuseum, Darmstadt; Kaiser-Wilhelm-Museum, Krefeld, West Germany; Städtisches Museum, Mönchengladbach, West Germany; Louisiana Museum, Humlebaek, Denmark; Kunstmuseum, Basle; Centre Georges Pompidou, Paris.

Publications:

By BEUYS: books—*I a gebraten Fischgrate,* West Berlin 1972; *Die Leute sind ganz prima in Foggia,* Naples 1973; *Lotta Poetica; 3 Pots Action, Edinburgh,* Brescia 1975; *Zeichnungen zu "Codices Madrid" von Leonardo da Vinci,* Stuttgart 1975; *Joseph Beuys: Series of 90 Paintings,* Munich 1976; articles—"Plastik und Zeichnung" in *Kunst* (Mainz), 1965; "Winterlager" in *Christ und Welt* (Dusseldorf), no. 37, 1968; "Direkte Demokratie: Joseph Beuys Talking at Documenta 5" in *Avalanche* (New York), 1972; "Joseph Beuys: Public Dialogue" in *Avalanche* (New York), May/June 1974.

On BEUYS: books—*Joseph Beuys . . . mit Braunkreuz,* exhibition catalogue, edited by René Block, West Berlin 1966; *Beuys und das weisse Kreuz von Malewitsch,* exhibition catalogue, with text by Johannes Cladders, Mönchengladbach, West Germany 1967; *Wat Bedoelt Beuys?* by Tom-Frenken, Eindhoven, Netherlands 1968; *Beuys' Boys* by Per Kirkeby, Copenhagen 1968; *Beuys,* exhibition catalogue, with text by Otto Maurer, Eindhoven, Netherlands 1968; *Joseph Beuys: Werk aus der Sammlung Stroher,* exhibition catalogue, with text by Dieter Koepplin, Basle 1969; *Joseph Beuys* by Gotz Adriani, Winfried Konnertz and Krain Thomas, Cologne, 1970; *La Rivoluzione siamo noi* by Achille Bonito Oliva, Naples 1971; *Joseph Beuys: Sammlung Hans und Franz Josef van der Grinten,* exhibition catalogue, with an introduction by Hans van der Grinten, Innsbruck 1971; *Uber Beuys* by Rolf Wedewer and Lothar Romain, Dusseldorf 1972; *Joseph Beuys: Zeichnungen 1947–1959,* with text by Hagen Lieberknecht, Cologne 1972; *Joseph Beuys: Bleistiftzeichnungen aus den Jahren 1946–1964* by Franz Josef and Hans van der Grinten, West Berlin 1973; *Tod im Leben, gedicht für Joseph Beuys* by Heiner Bastian, Munich 1972; *Joseph Beuys: Zeichnungen 1946–1971,* exhibition catalogue, with text by Paul Wember, Krefeld, West Germany 1974; *Joseph Beuys: The Secret Block for a Secret Person in Ireland,* exhibition catalogue, with foreword by Nick Serota, Oxford 1974; *Joseph Beuys, Jeder Mensch ein Kunstler* by Clara Bodenmann-Ritter, Frankfurt, West Berlin and Vienna 1975; *Joseph Beuys,* exhibition catalogue, with text by Paul Wember, Hannover 1975; *Joseph Beuys: Wasserfarben 1936–1963,* exhibition catalogue, with text by Franz Josef and Hans van der Grinten, Frankfurt 1976; *Soziale Plastik, Materialen zu Joseph Beuys* by Volker Harlan, Rainer Rappmann and Peter Shata, Achberg 1976; *Joseph Beuys: Coyote,* with text by Caroline Tisdall, Munich 1976; *Joseph Beuys: Tekeningen, Aquarellen, Gouaches, Collages, Olieverven,* exhibition catalogue, with text by R. Vandenwege, Jan Hoet and Clair van Damme, Ghent 1977; *Prophete rechts, Prophete links: Joseph Beuys* by Ingrid Burgbacher-Krupka, Stuttgart 1977; *Joseph Beuys: Richtkrafte,* exhibition catalogue, West Berlin 1977; *Joseph Beuys: Multiples—catalogue raisonne,* Munich 1977; *Beuys tracce in Italia* by Germano Celant, Naples 1978; *Joseph Beuys: Spuren in Italien,* exhibition catalogue, with text by Martin Kunz, Lucerne 1979; *Joseph Beuys,* exhibition catalogue, with text by Caroline Tisdall, New York 1979; *Beuys/Burri,* exhibition catalogue, edited by Italo Tomassoni, Perugia, Italy 1980; *Joseph Beuys: Multiplizierte Kunst 1965– 1980* with text by Willi Bongard, Dusseldorf 1980; *Joseph Beuys: Zeichnungen Begleitende Texte,* with foreword by Ulrich Weisner, text by Heribert Heere, Bielefeld, West Germany 1980; *Joseph Beuys: Zeichnungen, Bildobjekte, Holzschnitte,* exhibition catalogue, with texts by Michael Schwarz and Dieter Koepplin, Karlsruhe 1980; *Joseph Beuys: Dernier Espace avec Introspecteur 1964–1982* by Caroline Tisdall, London 1982; *Joseph Beuys: Is It About A Bicycle?,* exhibition catalogue with text by Bernard Lamarche-Vadel, New York 1985.

Of all the hagiographies of 20th century art, none has seemed more secure than that of Marcel Duchamp. It has been argued that the style and subject matter of most post-war art can be traced to his influence, that he set up the pieces of the game which everybody else is now playing. To question Duchamp's status is like attacking the Pope if you're Catholic.

Yet Duchamp's influence has been largely negative. There was nothing forward looking in his art; rather, it was an attempt to close the book before the barbarians arrived. He belonged to the old European tradition of artists—elegant, sensitive, aristocratic. If the language of art were tainted, then the only thing a gentleman could do was lapse into enigmatic silence. Duchamp's art is one of defeat.

So it is apt that it was a barbarian who called this deadly silence. One thinks of Luther nailing his theses on the church door: enough of this southern pomp and circumstance, enough of this Frenchness. So the barbarian, dressed like a poacher, bearing the scars of a war that destroyed Duchamp's country writes in chalk across a blackboard:

THE SILENCE OF DUCHAMP
IS OVERRATED.

Joseph Beuys was not interested in enigma; come to that he was not interested in Dada, Happenings, Situations, Environments, Performances or any of that Latinate epicenity. I suspect he had suffered too much to think that art was anything else but a life and death matter.

Duchamp had destroyed the language of art; Beuys would create a new one; one that was based, as are all languages of art in their new born state, on the emotions used raw, on pain and pleasure, on the senses used as reasoning devices, on the mind used as a sense.

In Dusseldorf, he sat in a bar room, surrounded by the salient textures of his universe: felt, fat, wires, wood, cradling in his arms a dead hare. The piece was called "How to explain art to a Dead Hare." The urgent whispering shattered Duchamp's silence, and here, for those prepared to follow him was a solution; go back to your own experience, to your own agony if necessary, for there the fountainhead of art was still bubbling.

The art of Beuys then is, like all great developments, a move towards realism. In recent years, that word has been much in vogue, but it has usually been applied to painting of a clearly revisionist tendency, or to the rather shallow use of "real" objects à la Duchamp. Beuys used reality in the form of his favourite textures and objects, or his own body and personality—not for theoretical or stylistic reasons, but for honesty. They were important to him, as important as perspective was to Piero or chiaroscuro to Caravaggio, and I think he believed that they are important also to everyone else. We may not all be felt freaks or butter fetishists, but we all have our obsessions. Upon these, Beuys suggests, our humanity rests.

Robert Morris also uses felt in large rolls, but for their abstract, sculptural quality. Beuys reacts against abstraction; he used such materials because they made up his world, his real world, a world in which theory has become debased but in which real people still live and die, as happy or miserable as they have always done.

One must not hope to understand Beuys if one has seen him only in the centres of culture, the great museums, the private dealers. One had to catch him somewhere where people still talk to each other, still get drunk to forget, where they couldn't give a damn about modern art. There he made sense, there people would warm to him, but not in New York, Paris or London.

I saw him first in Scotland, home of last stands and hopeless causes. In a huge bare room he went through a series of motions, sitting, drawing, sticking globs of fat to a wall and picking them off again, finally standing motionless. The first day he spent three hours doing this, by the fifth and last the whole procedure took nearer five. Yet people looked in and stayed. He had the ability to convince one of the significance of his actions. Each of his moves seemed like an element of meaning and by putting them together he was creating a new syntax. The resulting sentence was not written in any existing syntax, and its meaning can not be exactly transcribed, but as far as I am able to put it into words, I would say that its basic ingredients were to do with passion, courage and nobility, not exactly words one would associate with most contemporary art.

There was a moment when it seemed as if Beuys was destined to become a cult figure with a pathetic band of imitators trailing behind him. He refused, however, to act in the way expected of him, and frequently offended his defenders by offering unfashionable views. He remains, though, the most avant-garde of artists, in the true sense of the word, the one who most convincingly forged a new language, and a new method. His real influence has been to suggest that artists must rely upon themselves rather than upon any one style. One cannot imitate Beuys, but one can follow his method.

—Alastair Mackintosh

BIEDERMAN, Charles.

American. Born in Cleveland, Ohio, 23 August 1906. Educated at the Art Institute of Chicago, 1926–29; has studied semantics privately, since 1938. Married Mary K. Moore in 1941; daughter: Anna. Travelled and lived in New York and Paris, 1930–37; now lives and works in Minnesota. Member, Advisory Committee, Artists, Composers and Authors Caucus, Minnesota, 1972. Recipient: Sikkens Award, Sikkens Paint Company, Amsterdam, 1962; Ford Foundation Purchase Award, 1964; Minnesota State Arts Council Award, 1969; Fine Arts Award, Minnesota Branch, American Institute of Architects, 1971; National Endowment for the Arts Award, 1973. D.F.A.: Minneapolis College of Art and Design, 1973. Agent: Grace Borgenicht Gallery, 1018 Madison Avenue, New York, New York 10021. Address: Route 2, Red Wing, Minnesota 55066, U.S.A.

Individual Exhibitions:

1936 Pierre Matisse Gallery, New York
1941 Arts Club of Chicago
1954 St. Paul Gallery, Minnesota
1963 Columbia University School of Architecture, New York (toured the United States)
1965 Walker Art Center, Minneapolis (retrospective)
1967 Rochester Art Center, Minnesota
1969 Hayward Gallery, London (retrospective, toured England)
1971 Dayton's Gallery, 12, Minneapolis
1976 Minneapolis Institute of Arts (retrospective; toured the East Coast of America, 1976–77)
1980 Borgenicht Gallery, New York
1985 Borgenicht Gallery, New York

Selected Group Exhibitions:

1936 *5 Peintres Americains*, Galerie Pierre, Paris
1962 *Experiment in Constructie*, Stedelijk Museum, Amsterdam (travelled to Kunstgewerbemuseum, Zurich)
1964 *Mondrian, De Stijl and Their Impact*, Marlborough Gallery, London
1966 *Reliefs, Sculpture*, Marlborough New London Gallery, London
1968 *Relief/Construction/Relief*, Museum of Contemporary Art, Chicago (toured the United States)
1972 *Geometric Abstraction: 1926–42*, University Museum, University of Texas at Austin
1973 *The Non-Objective World 1914–1955*, Annely Juda Fine Art, London
1979 *Vanguard American Sculptors, 1913–1939*, Rutgers University Art Gallery, New Jersey
1983 *Abstract Painting and Sculpture in America 1927–1944*, Carnegie Institute, Pittsburgh
1987 *Twentieth Century Drawings*, Whitney Museum, New York

Collections:

Museum of Modern Art, New York; Whitney Museum, New York; Metropolitan Museum of Art, New York; Albright-Knox Art Gallery, Buffalo, New York; Art Institute of Chicago; Dallas Museum; High Museum, Atlanta; Minneapolis Institute of Art; Walker Art Center, Minneapolis; Tate Gallery, London.

Publications:

By BIEDERMAN: books—*Art as The Evolution of Visual Knowledge*, Red Wing, Minnesota 1948; *Letters on The New Art*, Red Wing, Minnesota 1951; *The New Cezanne*, Red Wing, Minnesota 1958; *An Art Credo*, Lanark, Scotland 1965; *Search for New Arts*, Red Wing, Minnesota 1979; articles—"Art and Science as Creation" in *Parnas* (Amsterdam), no. 5, 1956; "Nature and Art" in *Structure* (Amsterdam), series 2, No. 2, 1957; "Symmetry, Nature and the Plane" in *Structure* (Amsterdam), series 3, No. 1, 1960; "Dialogue on Art as Imitation or Creation" in *Main Currents* (New York), March/April 1962; "A Non-Aristotelian Creative Reality" in *Structure* (Amsterdam), series 4, No. 2, 1962; "The Sphere and The Cube" in *Structure* (Amsterdam), series 6, No. 1, 1964; "The Visual Revolution of Structurist Art" in *Artforum* (New York), April 1965; "Art in Crisis" in *Studies in the 20th Century*, Troy, New York 1968; "Dialogue II: Creative or Conditioned Vision" in *DATA* (London), 1968; "Note on New Arts" in *Studio International* (London), 1970.

On BIEDERMAN: books—*Charles Biederman*, exhibition catalogue, Minneapolis, 1965; *Charles Biederman: A Retrospective*, London 1969; *Experimental Painting* by Stephen Bann, New York and London 1970; *Documents of 20th Century Art: The Tradition of Constructivism*, edited by Stephen Bann, New York 1974; *Charles Biederman: A Retrospective*, Minneapolis 1976; articles—"Biederman and the New Art" by Frank Getlein in the *New Republic* (New York), February 1963; "Biederman's Structurism: Its Influence" by Leif Sjoberg in *Art International* (Lugano), March 1966; "Charles Biederman and The Structurist Direction in Art" by Jan van der Marck in *Feestbundel* (Amsterdam), 1966; "The Centrality of Charles Biederman" by Stephen Bann in *Studio International* (London), September 1969; "The Un-American Activist" by Norbert Lynton in *The Guardian* (London), September 1969; "American Geometric Abstraction in the Late 30's" by John Elderfield in *Artforum* (New York), December 1972; "Biedermans Konst Och Evolution" by Leif Sjoberg in *Kunst Og Kuttur* (Oslo), 1978; "Charles Biederman's Art of Complicity" by David Craven in *Arts* (New York), March 1980; "Charles Biederman and the English Constructionists" in *The Burlington Magazine* (London), February 1984.

Charles Biederman: *Number 34*, 1972

After passing through the influence of nearly all the major aspects of 20th century European art, I con-

cluded that the post-Cezannian condition of art (and architecture) has been one of confusion and desperation. I understood that all the much lauded "diversity" (Read) of modern art, purportedly exemplifying a great liberation, was simply a mask for the retreat of each artist to his own personal world. The artist had not only lost a coherent relation to the whole of the past human effort at art, but had sealed in his isolation completely by severing himself from the perceptual life of nature.

After many years I arrived at a view of new art that was not uniquely American, that is, not in the sense of the futile New York chauvinism, nor a uniquely European view, however that might be considered. Hence, European critics would note the "American" characteristics of my art and theory, while Americans (New York) regarded my work as "un-American." What escaped notice was that my art was the result of both America and Europe, but in the sense of the uniquely American temperament allowing for a wholly new perception of the uniquely European achievements.

The new art I pursue brings to a conclusion the "research" which Cezanne felt he would not live to "realize" and answers his hope for a "continuator" of his efforts. I realized this goal, not by "going back" to Cezanne, but rather by experiencing an American evolution in my art which opened the way for the continuance of Cezanne's extraordinary achievements in the spatial world of light. This became possible because, like Monet and Cezanne, I sought solutions in the visual study of nature, and like them was able to extend my perception of the structural process of nature. This permitted a truly genuine non-mimetic creation of the artist's art (bereft of confusion and compromise with the now obsolete vision of mimesis), according to the creative potentialities inherently given in the creative structural process of nature—the only structural possibilities available to the artist. The alternative is the artist's false assumption of superiority to nature, his denial of nature and his arrogant claim of being "his own nature." This alternative confuses and confounds the structural world of nature, and so art, by a naive appeal to an unlimited freedom purportedly residing in the subconscious.

It is precisely out of this attitude that the post-Cezannian chaos has arisen in which art is *reduced* to the "puny" (Cezanne) concern of revealing the questionable value of the artist's personal "inner world." The new art I advocate, in the line of Monet-Cezanne, acts in the very opposite way. That is, not "reducing" but extending the past evolution of human art by ceasing any form of imitating what nature has already created, ceasing the limitation of imitating light as in painting and ceasing the limited notion of form as in sculpture. The new art liberates the artist to create his own art in the full dimensions of the actualities of spatial reality. The artist is freed from conditioning to the biological creations of nature to adopt what is uniquely suited to human creation—geometric structuring. This mode of structuring, however, is submitted to the potentialities as given by the creative process of nature. It then becomes evident why neither the brush nor the chisel but rather the machine is now the ideal medium which enables the artist to engage the exactitude of geometric structuring in the spatial world of light and thus secure the full reality experience inherent in the new art of creation.

—Charles Biederman

To be an eminent theoretician and one who withdraws from the art scene of life in cities is to risk international obscurity. Charles Biederman has written extensively about his theory of "structurism," and his works have been read and to some extent heeded by a narrow echelon of cultured cognoscenti. In this wise his reputation has thrived, albeit to a limited capacity. He chose to live and work—since 1942—in Red Wing, Minnesota. It was in that remote area that he evolved his principles of "structurism," and it was at that address that he wrote and prepared his most famous book, *Art as the Evolution of Visual Knowledge,* which influenced the development of a number of artists—not always as a result of accurate understanding of its contents. These included Victor Pasmore, Kenneth Martin, Mary Martin, and Anthony Hill, all of whom entered into correspondence with the American.

Before settling in Red Wing, Biederman had been influenced by a number of artists and art movements of the Old World, most notably Mondrian and de Stijl, but structurism, and particularly its concern with the pure and natural character of colour(s), cut him adrift from all but his own admirers.

It seems a far cry from the days when Biederman was best known for the illustration of his button collage which appeared in Alfred Barr's *Cubism and Abstract Art*—a picture which at the time of publication looked as if it was the work of an unknown but interesting "newcomer," perhaps a fluke or perhaps a signal of even better things to come. But thereafter, outside the United States, his fame was severely curtailed. A few isolated works were exhibited in London (across the decades!), but it was not until the Arts Council exhibition at London's Hayward Gallery—when the artist was in his 60's—that Londoners had a proper opportunity to see Biederman structural reliefs. Enthusiasm was moderate. Perhaps structurism is an acquired taste, or even more likely, most of those who came to stand and stare were not prepared to read and absorb Biederman's intellectual arguments.

—Sheldon Williams

BILL, Max.

Swiss. Born in Winterthur, 22 December 1908. Trained as silversmith, Kunstgewerbeschule, Zurich, 1924–27; studied art, Staatliche Bauhaus, Dessau, Germany, 1927–29. Served in the Swiss Army, 1939–45. Married Bibia Spoerri in 1931; son: Johann. Independent architect, painter, sculptor and graphic artist, Zurich, since 1929, and industrial designer, since 1944. Lecturer on the Theory of Form, Kunstgewerbeschule, Zurich, 1944–45; Co-Founder and Rector, Hochschule für Gestaltung, Ulm, Germany, 1951–56; Professor of Environmental Design, State Institute of Fine Arts, Hamburg, 1967–74. Member of the Communal Council, City of Zurich, 1961; National Councillor, Swiss Parliament, 1967–74. Member of the Central Board, Schweizerische Werkbund, 1952–62; Member, Swiss Federal Art Commission, 1961–69; Member of the Board, Geschwister-School Foundation, Ulm, 1964; Member of the Superior Council (Creation Esthetique Industrielle), French Ministry of Industrial and Scientific Development, 1971–73. Member: Abstraction-Creation group, Paris, 1932–36; Allianz, Zurich 1937; CIAM (Congrès Internationaux d'Architecture Moderne), 1938; UAM (Union des Artistes Modernes), Paris 1949; Deutscher Werkbund 1956. Recipient: Grand Prize, *Triennale di Milano,* Milan, 1936, 1951, 1954; Kandinsky Prize, 1949; First Prize for Sculpture, *Bienal,* Sao Paulo, 1951; Gold Medal, Verucchio, Italy, 1966; City of Zurich Art Prize, 1968. Honorary Fellow, American Institute of Architects, 1964; Extraordinary Member, Akademie der Künste, West Berlin, 1972; Honorary Member, Royal Flemish Academy of Sciences, Literature and Arts, 1973. Agent: Marlborough Fine Art, 6 Albemarle Street, London WIX 3HF, England. Address: Albulastrasse 39, 8048 Zurich, Switzerland.

Individual Exhibitions:

1928 Staatliche Bauhaus, Dessau, Germany (with Albert Braun)
1929 Atelier des Kunstlers, Zurich
1939 Kunstmuseum, Basle
1946 Galerie des Eaux-Vives, Zurich
1948 Herber Hermann Galerie, Stuttgart (with Josef Albers and Jean Arp)
1949 Galerie d'Art Moderne, Basle
Kunsthaus, Zurich (with Antoine Pevsner and Georges Vantongerloo)
1950 Museu de Arte Moderna, Sao Paulo
1951 Kunstverein, Freiburg im Breisgau, West Germany (with Julius Bissier and Georges Vantongerloo)
1956 Ulmer Museum, Ulm, West Germany (toured Germany)
1957 Helmhaus, Zurich
1958 Galerie Suzanne Bollag, Zurich
1959 Galerie Gelbes Haus, St. Gallen, Switzerland
Städtisches Museum, Leverkusen, West Germany
Studio F., Ulm, West Germany
1960 Staatsgalerie, Stuttgart
Kunstmuseum, Winterthur, Switzerland
Galerie Suzanne Bollag, Zurich
Galerie im Ronca-Haus, Lucerne
1961 Galerie du Perron, Geneva
Galerie Anna Roepke, Wiesbaden, West Germany
1962 Galerie Hilt, Basle
1963 Galerie Suzanne Bollag, Zurich
Gimpel & Hanover Galerie, Zurich
Staempfli Gallery, New York
Pace Gallery, Boston
Studio F., Ulm, West Germany
1964 Galleria Cadario, Milan
Galleria del Deposito, Genoa
Galleria dell'Accademia, Rome
Galleria Suzanne Bollag, Zurich
1965 Galerie Aktuell, Berne
Op-Art Galerie, Esslingen, West Germany
Galleria Flaviana, Locarno, Switzerland
Galerie 58, Rapperswil, Switzerland
Gemeindehaus, Uster, Switzerland
Galerie Suzanne Bollag, Zurich
1966 Staempfli Gallery, New York
Galerie Hilt, Basle
Hanover Gallery, London
Galerie Suzanne Bollag, Zurich
1967 Galerie im Erker, St. Gallen, Switzerland
1968 Kunsthalle, Berne
Kestner-Gesellschaft, Hannover
Kunstverein für die Rheinland und Westfalen, Dusseldorf
Haags Gemeentemuseum, The Hague
Musée des Beaux-Arts, La Chaux de Fonds, Switzerland
Kunsthalle, Nuremberg, West Germany
Kunsthaus, Zurich
Galerie Suzanne Bollag, Zurich
1969 Arts Club of Chicago
Galleria La Bertesca, Genoa
Galleria La Polena, Genoa
Galleria Vismara, Milan
Galerie Godard Lefort, Montreal
Staempfli Gallery, New York
Galerie Denise Renè, Paris
Galleria Martano/Due, Turin
Galerie Bischofberger, Zurich
Centre National d'Art Contemporain, Paris
Musée de Peinture et de Sculpture, Grenoble, France
1970 Galerie Bischofberger, Zurich
Galerie Loeb, Berne
Galerie im Weissen Haus, Winterthur, Switzerland
San Francisco Museum of Art
Galerie Appel und Fertsch, Frankfurt
Galleria del Cavallino, Venice
White Gallery, Lutry, Switzerland
Galleria Arte Studio, Macerata, Italy
Galerie Design II, Hamburg
Galleria d'Arte Peccolo, Livorno, Italy
Galleria del Cortile, Rome
Galerie Kludschule, Zurich
Staempfli Gallery, New York
1971 Galerie Reckermann, Cologne
Galerie Denise René, Paris
Galerie Suzanne Bollag, Zurich
Galerie im Erker, St. Gallen, Switzerland

1972 Musée Rath, Geneva
Galleria Lorenzelli, Milan
Marlborough Galerie, Zurich
Kunstmuseum, Aarhus, Denmark
Galerie Hausdewell, Baden-Baden, West Germany
Marlborough-Godard Gallery, Toronto (travelled to the Marlborough Gallery, Montreal)
1973 Galerie 58, Rapperswil, Switzerland
Galerie Ziegler, Geneva
1974 Marlborough Fine Art, London
Galleria Lorenzelli, Bergamo, Italy
Galerie Media, Neuchâtel, France
Galleria Medea, Milan
Marlborough Galerie, Zurich
Watari Gallery, Tokyo
Albright-Knox Art Gallery, Buffalo, New York (toured the United States)
1975 Comsky Gallery, Los Angeles
Art Institute, San Francisco
Marlborough Gallery, New York
Galleria Effereridi, Bologna
1976 Museum für Kunst und Gewerbe, Hamburg (toured Germany)
Akademie der Künste, West Berlin
Galleria Lorenzelli, Milan
1977 Universita di Parma, Italy
1978 Moderne Galerie, Bottrop, West Germany
1979 *Pinturas, Esculturas, Grafica,* Museo de Bellas Artes, Caracas
Galerie Bossin, West Berlin
Gallery Watari, Tokyo
1980 Galerie Seestrasse, Rapperswil, Switzerland
Galerie Bossin, West Berlin
Artline, The Hague
1981 Galerie Buhler, Biel, Switzerland
Gallery Watari, Tokyo
1982 Galerie Bossin, West Berlin
Galerie Denise Rene, Paris
Gimpel-Hanover-Andre Emmerich Galerie, Zurich
1983 Galleria Narciso, Turin
Galerie Bertram, Burgdorf, Switzerland
Gimpel-Hanover-Andre Emmerich Galerie, Zurich
1984 Galerie Henz, Munich
Galleria Narciso, Turin
Deutsche Bank, Hamburg
1985 Galerie Wolfgang Ketterer, Munich
Galerie Teufel, Cologne
Galleria Lorenzelli, Milan
Galerie Edith Wahlandt, Stuttgart
1986 Mucsarnok Art Gallery, Budapest
1987 National Gallery, Belgrade
Kunsthalle, Frankfurt

Selected Group Exhibitions:

1930 *Bill/Valloton/Probst/Steck/Von May,* Kunsthalle, Berne
1944 *Konkrete Kunst,* Kunsthalle, Basle
1951 *Bienal,* Sao Paulo
1952 *Monument to the Unknown Political Prisoner,* Institute of Contemporary Arts, London
1958 *Biennale,* Venice
1960 *Concrete Art: 50 Years of Development,* Kunsthaus, Zurich
1971 *La Peinture Non-Objective 1924–1939,* Galerie Jean Chauvelin, Paris (travelled to Annely Juda Fine Art, London, and Galleria Milano, Milan)
1972 *Konstruktivismus,* Galerie Gmurzynska + Bargera, Cologne
1973 *Kunst in Deutschland 1898–1973,* Kunsthalle, Hamburg (travelled to Städtisches Galerie im Lenbachhaus, Munich)
1982 *Acquisition Priorities: Postwar European Painting,* Guggenheim Museum, New York

Collections:

Kunsthaus, Zurich; Kunstmuseum, Winterthur, Switzerland; Musée d'Art et d'Histoire, Geneva; Musées Royaux des Beaux-Arts, Brussels; Centre Georges Pompidou, Paris; Wilhelm-Lehmbrock Museum, Duisburg, West Germany; Galleria Nazionale d'Arte Moderna, Rome; Art Institute of Chicago; Albright-Knox Art Gallery, Buffalo, New York; Hirshhorn Museum and Sculpture Garden, Washington, D.C.

Max Bill: ***Albert Einstein Memorial, Ulm,* 1982**

Bill's architectural works, including his own house and studio at Zumikon/Zurich, are extant throughout Europe in Aargau, Ulm, Rhinfall, Leverkusen, Cologne, Tamins, Dusseldorf and Esbly.

Publications:

By BILL: books—*Quinze Variations sur un meme Theme,* Paris 1938; *Le Corbusier: Oeuvre Complete,* volume 3, editor, Zurich 1939, London 1964; *5 Konstruktionen + 5 Kompositionen,* Zurich 1941; *10 Original Lithos,* Zurich 1941; *X + X,* Zurich 1942; *Leo Luppi: 10 Kompositionen,* Zurich 1943; *Konkrete Kunst,* exhibition catalogue, with others, Basle 1944; *Hans Arp: 11 Configurations,* with others, Zurich 1945; *Wiederaufbau,* Zurich 1945; *Wassily Kandinsky: 10 Farbige Reproduktionen,* Basle 1949; *Robert Maillart: Brucken und Konstruktionen,* Zurich 1949, New York 1969; *Moderne Schweizer Architektur 1925–1945,* Basle 1950; *Wassily Kandinsky,* editor, Paris 1951; *Form: A Balance Sheet of Mid-20th Century Trends in Design,* Basle 1952; *Uber des Geistige in der Kunst,* editor, Berne 1952; *Mies van der Rohe,* Milan 1955; *Essays über Kunst und Kunstler,* editor, Stuttgart 1955, Berne 1963; *Die Gute Form,* Winterthur 1957; *Punkt und Linie zu Flache,* editor, Berne 1959; *Enzo Mari,* with Bruno Munari, Milan 1959; *Konkrete Kunst: 50 Jahre Entwicklung,* exhibition catalogue, Zurich 1968, 1969; *11 x 4,* Zurich 1970; *Jahresgabe 1972,* Berne 1972; *System mit funf vierfarbigen Zentren,* St. Gallen Switzerland 1972; *8 = (2 x 4/4) = 8,* Neuchâtel, Switzerland 1974; *16 Constellations,* Paris 1974; *7 Twins,* Neuchâtel, Switzerland 1977.

On BILL: books—*Max Bill,* Buenos Aires 1955; *Max Bill* by Max Bense and others, Teufen, Switzerland 1958; *Max Bill* by Margit Staber, St. Gallen, Switzerland 1971; *Max Bill* by Eduard Huttinger, Zurich 1977, 1978; *Max Bill,* exhibition catalogue, edited by Arturo Carlo Quintavalle, Parma 1977; *Max Bill: Pinturas, Esculturas, Grafica,* exhibition catalogue, by Carlos Silva and Ricardo Axel Stein Nunex, Caracas 1979; *Contemporary Architects,* edited by Muriel Emanuel, London and New York 1980.

One often speaks of the mathematics, the structure, the systems in art. I also did so. Looking for a non-individualistic approach to so-called art problems. I did different kinds of research, and I wrote a few statements which were publicized and interpreted worldwide.

As life—and so ideas and art as one of the human activities—is in constant motion, and we hope permanent development, my ideas have also developed and become clearer. This because of more experience and an accumulation of knowledge.

When I wrote a quarter of a century ago about "the mathematical approach in contemporary art" this was a new way to see art which until then had been considered mostly as the more or less uncontrolled experience of an individual.

Today I know better that mathematics are only a part of the methods to be adapted for the regulation of so-called works of art. I know that a concept has to conform to its inner organization and its visual existence. This means that a concept and the finally executed work have to be a unity. This unit is the result of the logical approach to the solution of the problem and its realization.

I prefer today to describe this process as the logical approach to the problems of art. This means that every part of the creative process consciously follows step by step a logical analysis and feedback. This is the way I hope to best realize my vision.

—Max Bill

Among the painters of the 20th century Max Bill is one of the few who represents and puts into effect the Renaissance principle of the *uomo universale.* It is true that he is presented officially as an architect, but his painting and sculptural work is at least as important as his buildings. He is equally instigator and publicist, organizer, man of letters and teacher; he is versed in philosophy and involves himself in the cultural politics of his country. Judgment—the balance between rationalism and emotion—and order—the demonstration of law in the world—form the basis of his multiple activities. As an artist he became the most important representative of "concrete art" which he himself defined as follows: "We call those works of art concrete art which have arisen by virtue of their original means and laws—without external support from natural appearances or their transformation, therefore without abstraction . . . they are of that sharp, unequivocal and perfect nature as must be expected from works of the human intellect." The striving after perfection evident in the definition marks all Bill's creative work. In the realization of his buildings, sculptures and pictures, mathematics is, to him, not the only but the most important medium. A large part of his work could be understood as mathematics become visible, although not exhaustively. Bill himself speaks of an "application of logical thought processes in the organization of rhythms and relationships, of laws that have individual origins . . . . " In this emphasis on the individual is hidden the allusion to creative fantasy which Bill develops as much in purpose-free as in purposeful problems, perhaps in the design of a poster or a memorial.

His life's work presents itself as an explanation of the aesthetic principles he has himself defined. It possesses a chronology, yet hardly any development in the sense that no stylistic groups or periods are discernable in his work. A theme which preoccupies the artist can again be taken up by him after a number of years and varied with new methods of realization without any apparent breach.

Bill's work stands in a tradition which follows directly on Stijl and the Bauhaus. It continues this tradition in that it systematically and methodically pursues the experiments which had begun there. This aim was also served by the "Design School" in Ulm, which despite its short life after 1945 gained greater international influence than all other didactic art institutes of the last decades.

When in 1975/76 a comprehensive retrospective of Bill's pictures, sculpture, graphics and models was mounted in the USA and Germany, he himself spoke of certain modifications to his principles in the sense that he described the "design process as that of logical method" and made a clear differentiation between purposeful and purpose free activity: "while the problems of building, of the form of an object, of education or political decision must be solved in relation to their complex functions, the function of painting and sculpture is unequivocal: their usefulness rests on their intellectual/spiritual usefulness."

—Heinz Spielmann

BISHOP, Isabel.

American. Born in Cincinnati, Ohio, 3 March 1902. Studied illustration at the New York School of Applied Design for Women, 1918–20; painting, under Kenneth Hayes Miller and Guy Pène du Bois, at the Art Students League, New York, 1920–24; engraving, under Stanley William Hayter, at the New School for Social Research, New York, 1941. Married the neurologist Harold G. Wolff in 1934; son: Remsen. Established loft studio at 9 West 14th Street, New York, 1926; established and maintains studio in Union Square, New York, since 1934. Instructor, Art Students League, New York, 1936–37; Instructor, 1956–58, and Guest Lecturer, 1963, Skowhegan School of Painting and Sculpture, Maine; Visiting Artist, Yale University School of Fine Arts, New Haven, Connecticut, 1963. Recipient: Isaac N. Maynard Portrait Prize, 1936, Adolph and Clara Obrig Prize, 1942, Andrew Carnegie Prize, 1945, Benjamin Altman Prize, 1955, 1967, Joseph S. Isidor Medal, 1957, Samuel Finley Breeze Morse Medal, 1966, and Purchase Prize, 1973, National Academy of Design, New York; Newport Art Association Prize, Rhode Island, 1937, First Prize, 1940, and Noyes Memorial Prize, 1947, American Society of Etchers: Watercolor Prize, Butler Art Institute, Youngstown, Ohio, 1941; American Academy of Arts and Letters and National Institute of Arts and Letters Grant, 1943; William A. Clark Prize, *Corcoran Biennial Exhibition,* Washington, D.C., 1945; First Pennell Purchase Award, *Library of Congress National Exhibition of Prints,* Washington, D.C., 1946; Walter Lippincott Prize, *Pennsylvania Academy Annual,* Philadelphia, 1953; Gold Medal, 1968, and Best of Show Award, 1973, National Arts Club, New York; Purchase Prize, National Prints and Drawings Exhibition, Mount Holyoke College, Hadley, Massachusetts, 1974; Outstanding Achievement in the Arts Award, from President Carter, 1979. D.F.A.: Moore Institute of Art, Science and Industry, Philadelphia, 1954. Associate Member, 1940, and Academician, 1941, National Academy of Design; Member, 1944, and Vice-President, 1946, National Institute of Arts and Letters; Member, American Academy of Arts and Letters, 1944. Benjamin Franklin Fellow, Royal Society of Arts, London, 1964. Agent: The Midtown Galleries, 11 East 57th Street, New York, New York 10022. Addresses: (studio) 33 Union Square, New York, New York 10003; (home) 355 West 246th Street, New York, New York 10471, U.S.A.

Individual Exhibitions:

1932 *Paintings,* Midtown Galleries, New York
1935 *Drawings and Etchings,* Midtown Galleries, New York
1936 *Paintings, Drawings, and Etchings,* Midtown Galleries, New York.
1939 *Paintings and Drawings,* Midtown Galleries, New York
1940 Herbert Institute, Atlanta
1942 *Drawings,* Midtown Galleries, New York
1945 *Drawings,* Smithsonian Institution, Washington, D.C.
1948 American-British Art Center, New York (with Augustus John)
1949 *Paintings and Drawings,* Midtown Galleries, New York
1955 *Paintings and Drawings,* Midtown Galleries, New York
1957 Berkshire Museum, Pittsfield, Massachusetts
1960 *Paintings and Drawings,* Midtown Galleries, New York
Judge the Jury: Perry T. Rathbone/Isabel Bishop/Richard Lippold, Virginia Museum of Fine Arts, Richmond
1967 *Paintings and Drawings,* Midtown Galleries, New York
1970 *Paintings, by Isabel Bishop/Sculptures by Dorothea Greenbaum,* New Jersey State Museum, Trenton
1971 *3 Figurative Painters,* Midtown Galleries, New York
1972 *Drawings and Prints,* Wood Art Gallery, Montpelier, Vermont
1974 *A Selection of Drawings and Prints,* Midtown Galleries, New York
Isabel Bishop: The First Retrospective Exhibition Held in American Museums of Paintings, Drawings, Etchings, and Aquatints. University of Arizona Museum of Art, Tucson (travelled to the Wichita State University Art Museum, Kansas, and the Whitney Museum, New York, 1975)
1979 Midtown Galleries, New York
1980 *Prints.* Associated American Artists Gallery, Philadelphia (with Miller and Marsh)
1981 *Paintings and Drawings,* Midtown Galleries, New York
Isabel Bishop: Etchings and Aquatints. Associated American Artists Gallery, New York (retrospective)

Selected Group Exhibitions:

1936 *Biennial Exhibition: Part I: Sculpture, Drawings, and Prints,* Whitney Museum, New York
1947 *American Printmaking 1913–1947,* Brooklyn Museum, New York.
1957 *Golden Years of American Drawings 1905–1956,* Brooklyn Museum, New York
1963 *Contemporary American Painting and Sculpture,* Krannert Art Museum, University of Illinois, Urbana (and 1967)
1966 *79 Original Drawings by 20th Century American Artists,* Storm King Art Center, Mountainville, New York
1971 *Boston Printmakers' Annual,* De Cordova Museum, Lincoln, Massachusetts
Celebrate Ohio: 50th Anniversary Exhibition, Akron Art Institute, Ohio
1973 *Drawings U.S.A.,* Minnesota Museum of Art, St. Paul
1974 *National Prints and Drawings Exhibition,* Mount Holyoke College, South Hadley, Massachusetts

Collections:

Metropolitan Museum of Art, New York; Brooklyn Museum, New York, Museum of Fine Arts, Boston; Fogg Art Museum, Harvard University, Cambridge, Massachusetts; Pennsylvania Academy of Art, Philadelphia; Baltimore Museum of Art; Corcoran Gallery of Art, Washington, D.C.; Virginia Museum of Fine Arts, Richmond; British Museum, London.

Publications:

By BISHOP: books—*8 Etchings I, 1938–1959,* portfolio, New York 1978; *8 Etchings II, 1936–1959,* portfolio, New York 1981; articles—"Concerning Edges" in *Magazine of Art* (Washington, D.C.), May 1945; "Kenneth Hayes Miller" in *Magazine of Art* (Washington, D.C.) April 1953; "Isabel Bishop Discusses Genre Drawings" in *American Artist* (New York), Summer 1953; "Drawing the Nude" in *Art in America* (New York), December 1963; 2 essays in *Isabel Bishop: Prints and Drawings 1925–1964,* Brooklyn New York 1964.

On BISHOP: books—*Biennial Exhibition: Part I: Sculpture, Drawings, and Prints,* exhibition catalogue, New York 1936; *American Printmaking 1913–1947,* exhibition catalogue, with an introduction by Jean Charlot, Brooklyn, New York 1947; *Painting in America: The Story of 450 Years* by E. P. Richardson, New York 1956; *Golden Years of American Drawings 1905–1056,* exhibition catalogue, with text by Una E. Johnson, Brooklyn, New York 1957; *A History of American Art* by D. M. Mendelowitz, New York 1961; *Isabel*

Isabel Bishop: *Variations on a Theme of Walking*, 1979

Bishop: Prints and Drawings 1925–1964, with text by Una E. Johnson, Brooklyn, New York 1964; *American Art since 1900: A Critical History* by Barbara Rose, New York 1967; *Paintings by Isabel Bishop/Sculpture by Dorothea Greenbaum*, exhibition catalogue, with an introduction by Suzanne Corlette, Trenton, New Jersey 1970; *Isabel Bishop*, exhibition catalogue, with a foreword by John I. H. Baur, introduction by Martin H. Bush, and text by Sheldon Reich, Tucson, Arizona 1974; *Isabel Bishop* by Karl Lunde, New York 1975; *Isabel Bishop: Etchings and Aquatints*, exhibition catalogue, compiled and edited by Susan Teller, New York 1981; articles—"Isabel Bishop" by Elaine de Kooning in *Artnews* (New York), May 1949; "Isabel Bishop" by Lawrence Campbell in *Artnews* (New York), November 1955; "Isabel Bishop" by George Dennison in *Arts Magazine* (New York), May 1960; "Light as the Beginning: The Art of Isabel Bishop" by Ernest Harms in *American Artist* (New York), February 1961; "Is There Discrimination Against Women Artists?" in *American Artist* (New York), May 1978; "American Realists of the 1930's: The 14th Street School" by M. S. Young in *Apollo* (London), March 1981.

For more than 40 years, from 1934 to 1978, Isabel Bishop occupied a painting studio which overlooked Union Square in New York City, Union Square is a busy area; below ground several subway lines converge in a labyrinthine station and above ground shoppers and shopkeepers walk to a multitude of discount stores of every description while street people conduct their own business in the Square. Isabel Bishop watched, drew, and painted the people of Union Square, and rode the subway with them morning and evening. Throughout her career, her paintings have contained metaphors about life above and below ground from "Dante and Virgil in Union Square," 1932, to the most recent, ethereal people rushing to the next chapter of their city lives. The presence of Dante and Virgil in such an unlikely setting immediately establishes a connection with hell and souls, and Bishop's use of architectonic space typical of the Renaissance increases the association with otherworldly, or at least religious, experience. In the recent paintings Bishop succeeds in putting figures on canvas without immobilizing them, and in so doing, fills them with strokes of light colored paint. She has expressed an interest in the mobility of figures, but what she appears to have captured is souls in transit.

Bishop, who studied with Kenneth Hayes Miller at the Art Students League in the 1920's, can be linked with other realist painters of city life—Guy Pène du Bois or Reginald Marsh—but it would be a great mistake to interpret Bishop's paintings as nothing more than city genre scenes. Even when her paintings contain only a few figures, Bishop conveys information about the masses in urban life. In an outdoor setting, a city square, even such details as clothing do not establish individuality; any park bench can be vacated and refilled within a few seconds. Since everyone in the square is a transient, the mobility of the figure is implied by the situation as well as suggested by Bishop's flitting brush style. City life in Bishop's paintings, even during the Depression, is not entirely a cement-bound, grimy affair but a multilayered existence of continuous motion.

Bishop also painted female nudes until the early 1970's, when, she has said, she felt no new impulse toward the subject. The nudes are often in the act of dressing or undressing, sometimes on a bed, and are among the least self-conscious nudes in art history. Perhaps they reflect Bishop's respect for comfortable relationships among women, evident in such paintings as "Two Girls," 1935 or "Lunch Hour," 1939. Non-competitive friendship between women is a rare subject in painting, yet Bishop has found and captured many relaxed acquaintanceships among her urban subjects. Although Bishop has cited Union Square as a long time source of artistic nourishment, clearly she has added many layers of meaning to 40 years of city life.

—Mary Stofflet

BISHOP, James.

American. Born in Neosho, Missouri, 7 October 1927. Educated at Syracuse University, New York, 1946–50, B.A. 1950; Washington University, St. Louis, Missouri, 1951–54; studied under Esteban Vicente, Black Mountain College, North Carolina, 1953; Columbia University, New York, 1955–56. Independent artist: lived and travelled in France, 1957–66; now lives and works in New York. Editorial Associate, *Artnews*, New York, 1969–70. Artist-in-Residence, Cooper Union, New York, 1969–70; University of California at Irvine, 1970; Carnegie-Mellon University, Pittsburgh, 1971; School of Visual Arts, New York, 1972. Recipient: Guggenheim Fellowship, 1970. Agent: Fourcade, Droll Inc. 36 East 75th Street, New York, New York 10021. Address: 5 Lispenard Street, New York, New York 10013, U.S.A.

Individual Exhibitions:

1963 Galerie Lucien Durand, Paris
Galerie Smith, Brussels
1964 Galerie Lawrence, Paris

1966 Fischbach Gallery, New York
Galerie Fournier, Paris
1968 Fischbach Gallery, New York
1970 Fischbach Gallery, New York
1971 Galerie Fournier, Paris
1972 Fischbach Gallery, New York
1973 Galerie Fournier, Paris
The Clocktower, New York
1974 Rosa Esman Gallery, New York
1975 Galleria D'Alessandro-Ferranti, Rome
1976 Galerie Annemarie Verna, Zurich
Galerie Fournier, Paris
1979 Droll/Kolbert Gallery, New York

Selected Group Exhibitions:

1965 *Promesses Tenues,* Musée Galliera, Paris
1967 *L'Art Vivant,* Fondation Maeght, St.-Paul-de-Vence, France
Expo '67 Montreal
1968 *Preview '68,* Trinity College, Hartford, Connecticut
Painting Annual, Whitney Museum, New York
1970 *One Man's Choice,* Dallas Museum of Fine Arts
L'Art Américain, Foundation Maeght, St.-Paul-de-Vence, France
1971 *Award Invitational,* National Institute of Arts and Letters, New York
1972 *Zeichnungen Amerikanischer Künstler,* Galerie Annemarie Verna, Zurich
1973 *Options and Alternatives: Some Directions in Recent Art,* Yale University Art Museum New Haven, Connecticut

Collections:

San Francisco Museum of Modern Art; Centre Georges Pompidou, Paris

Publications:

On BISHOP: book—*Options and Alternatives: Some Directions in Recent Art,* exhibition catalogue, with texts by Anne Coffin Hanson, Klaus Kertess, and Annette Michelson, New Haven, Connecticut 1973; articles—"An Experiment in Reality: The Painting of James Bishop" by Marcelin Pleynet in *Art and Literature* (Paris), March 1964; "La Peinture et Son Sujet?" by Philippe Sollers in *Tel Quel* (Paris), Winter 1965; "Paris Letter" by Annette Michelson in *Art International* (Lugano, Switzerland), March 1965; "Post-Painterly Quattrocento" by John Ashbery in *Artnews* (New York), December 1966; "Symbol Lurking in the Wings" by Dore Ashton in *Studio International* (London), February 1967; "James Bishop: Reason and Impulse" by Robert Rosenblum in *Artforum* (New York), February 1967; "A Dying Style?" by Peter Schjeldahl in the *New York Times,* 3 May 1970; "New York Letter" by Carter Radcliff in *Art International* (Lugano, Switzerland), Summer 1970; "Pourquoi la Peinture?" by Marcelin Pleynet and "Peinture sur Peinture: James Bishop" by Philippe Sollers in *Peinture Cahiers Théoriques* (Paris), Winter 1972; "Le Couleur au Carré—Les Rides—Le Dessin" by Marcelin Pleynet in *Art International* (Lugano, Switzerland, 20 March 1972; "James Bishop" by Kenneth Baker in *Artforum* (New York), June 1972; "Once More, With Feeling" by Carter Radcliff in *Artnews* (New York), Summer 1972; "Towards A Theory and Practice of Painting: Abstract Expressionism and the Surrealist Discourse" by P. Rogers in *Artforum* (New York), March 1980; "Mostly Monochrome" by Carter Radcliff in *Art in America* (New York), April 1981.

Since the Second World War the character of art and artists has changed dramatically. Kandinsky's semi-abstract and abstract work of the years 1911–14 provided a major impetus for the rediscovery of Abstract Expressionism in the 50s. This rediscovery also served as a response to the horrors made so familiar by the war: the destruction of cities and individuals, the barbarity of concentration camps and mass annihilation, found expression in paintings that spoke of violence and wounds. What started as an imperative art of protest developed into a style, or rather a whole range of styles unified by being more or less abstract or expressionist in its free, almost vehement handling of paint and colour.

American James Bishop was among the first generation of post-war abstract expressionists who, though under the auspices of his group, is not without individual sensibility or the diversity of vision which affirms the vitality of contemporary art. Having studied at the famous Black Mountain College, Bishop was exposed to the leading figures in every domain of the avant-garde. He was also familiar with the latest artistic developments from first-hand experience in New York which were then labeled "Abstract Expressionism." During the late 50s in New York, he attempted to assimilate the important elements of Abstract Expressionism to modern art whilst avoiding the flamboyant splashes and dribbles of the de Kooning followers. As a result Bishop developed a pictorial organisation derived from the structure of the painting as a means of both controlling the flamboyance and to anchor his painting more firmly in the formal properties of its material. A contributing factor to his success is his strict insistence on using oil paint during a period when his contemporaries were relying on ubiquitous acrylics.

Bishop's method of painting is clearly his own. He first pours the oils onto a canvas placed flatly on the ground; then he tilts the stretcher so that the paint runs up to, and encroaches on, the painting's pictorial organisation, spilling over its delineations. After the paint has been applied in this manner, he reverts to a more traditional method of brushwork which allows him to control his surface, building up successive coats and paying meticulous attention to underpainting. The delicate tidal interaction between free-moving paint and the boundaries of pictorial organisation shows how Bishop plays off the gestural manner of abstract Expressionism against the more linear and structural approach of later painting.

Bishop distinguishes himself from his contemporaries by placing the crucial issue of "automatism" at the centre of his art. The notion of "psychic automatism," introduced by Breton from his reading of Freud, is the process of purging the unconscious, a preoccupation found in virtually all art, music and literature in the 20th century. Automatism plays a key role in Bishop's paintings because it answers for the mysterious disappearance in his subject matter, indeed in that of most modern art. Ironically, a close survey of his work reveals a new "subject" in the unravelled line of the classical figure.

The Surrealist provided Bishop with the necessary technique to unveil the new "subject." According to this method, the painter begins his picture with an automatic gesture in an effort to make contact with the world of his unconscious mind. First, his canvas is marked by the spontaneous impulse of the artist. Next, he uses this mark to prompt associations in his imagination so that the subject of the picture emerges in an embellishment of vivid imagery. Thus Bishop's subject seems to emanate from the interior of his painting.

In all of Bishop's paintings, his central preoccupation falls in his manipulation of rich and subtle tones of colour in a discreetly changed flow of liquid energy resulting in an intimate and withdrawn art. Collectively, these elements seem to hint at the perception of an underlying presence. The result, ironically, likens him to de Kooning, an artist primarily concerned with making and confronting an image. For Bishop, subject and image were one. Being an abstract expressionist in the 1950s meant working without apparent constraints whilst retaining something of a brand image that separated his work from another's. His art proved itself capable of remarkable refinement noting the marks made and the materials used.

—Carrie Barker

BLADEN, Ronald.

Canadian. Born in Vancouver, British Columbia, 13 July 1918. Studied at Vancouver School of Arts, and California School of Fine Arts, San Francisco. Sculptor: lives and works in New York. Awards: Rosenberg Fellowship from the San Francisco Art Association, California; National Arts Council Grant; Guggenheim Fellowship, 1970. Agent: Max Hutchinson Gallery, 138 Greene Street, New York, New York 10012. Address: 5 West 21st Street, New York, New York 10010, U.S.A.

Individual Exhibitions:

1953 Brata Gallery, New York
1955 University of British Columbia, Vancouver
1956 Six Gallery, San Francisco
1962 Green Gallery, New York
1967 Fischbach Gallery, New York
Emily Lowe Gallery, Hofstra University, Hempstead, New York
1970 *Ronald Bladen/Robert Murray,* Vancouver Art Gallery
Fischbach Gallery, New York
1971 Fischbach Gallery, New York
1972 Pasadena Art Museum, California
Tyler School of Art, Philadelphia
University of Wisconsin, Madison
Fischbach Gallery, New York

Selected Group Exhibitions:

1963 *Paintings, Drawings and Prints Owned by Local Collectors,* The Wilmington Sociiety of the Fine Arts, Delaware Art Center
1965 *Concrete Epressionism,* Loeb Student Center, New York University
1966 *Sculpture Annual,* Whitney Museum, New York
Primary Structures: Younger British and American Sculptors, Jewish Museum, New York
1967 *Scale as Content,* Corcoran Gallery of Art, Washington, D.C.
1968 *Minimal Art,* Gemeentemuseum, The Hague (travelled to the Akademie der Künste, Berlin; and Dusseldorf, 1968–69)
1970 *American Sculpture,* Sheldon Memorial Art Gallery, University of Nebraska Art Galleries, Lincoln
1973 *Art in Space,* Detroit Institute of Arts
1974 *Outdoor Sculpture 1974,* Merriwold West Gallery, New Jersey
1975 *Monumental Sculpture,* Janie C. Lee Gallery, Houston

Collections

Museum of Modern Art, New York; Los Angeles County Museum of Art; Albright-Knox Art Gallery, Buffalo, New York; La Jolla Museum of Art, California; South Albany Mall, New York; King Saud University, Riyadh, Saudi Arabia.

Publications:

On BLADEN: books—*Minimal Art* by Lucy Lippard and Enno Develing, Dusseldorf 1969; *Ronald Bladen/Robert Murray,* exhibition catalogue, Vancouver 1970; *Icons and Images of the 60's* by Nicolas and Elena Calas, New York 1971; articles—"Aspects of Art Called Minimal" in *Studio International* (London), April 1969; "The Artist Speaks" by Corinne Robins in *Art in America* (New York), September 1969, "Ronald Bladen/Robert Murray" by D. Cameron in *Artscanada* (Toronto), June 1970; "Bladen and Murray: The Giants of Canadian Sculpture" by J. Lowndes in *Vie des Arts* (Montreal), Summer 1970; "New York Letter: Ronald Bladen" by G. Henry in *Art International* (Lugano, Switzerland), June 1971; "New York: Ronald Bladen" by K. Linville in *Artforum* (New York), June 1971; "Ronald Bladen" by K. Jürgen-Fischer in *Kunstwerk* (Baden-Baden, West Germany), March 1972; "Ronald Bladen" by K. Baker in *Artforum* (New York), April 1972.

Ronald Bladen has long been in the forefront of those artists seeking to realize the full potentials of abstract sculpture. Bladen was an established and exhibiting painter before he turned exclusively to sculpture in 1963. Before then he had evolved a thick, lush style of painting, influenced by Abstract Expressionism, first in San Francisco, where he lived and worked until 1957 and had maintained close connections with the city's burgeoning poetry movement of the 1950's, and then in New York City. In the last group of paintings, the "bas-reliefs", a growing concern with the physicality and object presence of these pictures that came off-the-wall is found. After some experimentation with three-dimensional paper collages. Bladen executed the first painted wood sculptures: "Untitled Construction" (1963–65) and "Untitled Construction No. 2" (1964). Like the later examples, they focused attention on the act and perception of construction. Each one offered a clear-cut presentation of the act of construction in the formation of a whole made from hard-edged geometric units like boxes, columns, and rectangular slabs joined together in an additive structure. Each one, also, focused attention on the perception of the different spaces, both the solid and void constructed by the sculptural structure. And even in these early examples is found a desire to activate the internal space of the sculpture, defined by the grid-oriented structure in "Untitled Constructivism" or the cantilevered structure in "Untitled Construction II."

Movement, whether real—in the case of the single kinetic piece "The Rockers" (1965)—or implied in the others is always a discrete matter of the precise and provocative integration of the placement, scale and contours. Bladen is able to impart strong dynamic sensations to massive and weighty forms by coordinating these factors. With "The X" (1967), these sensations invest this 23 foot high x-shaped sculpture with a tremendously forceful presence.

During the 1970's, Bladen became involved in public art, an activity that has necessitated the translation of the work, which he continues to build himself in wooden forms/models, into steel or aluminum. *Black Lightning* (1981), a black painted steel sculpture 24 foot long is based on a model executed in 1979. Its asymmetrical and sharply rhythmical forms and structures are representative of this period of the late 1970's and 1980's in his work.

An exciting recent development for Bladen is what he calls "private sculpture," a term used in acknowledgment of the speciific set of concerns distinguishing this body of work from the publiic commission pieces. Bladen has dedicated these aluminum and wood structures to the challenging task of illuminating space through the capturing of light.

The definitive way light is held its energy reflected on the shaped surfaces of the metal parts makes the sculptures like *Monarch* (1984) and *Moment* (1985) into genuinely moving experiences. Bladen here is using the objective face of the world of materials to get at the inner core of symbolic values animating the universe.

—Ronny H. Cohen

BLAKE, Peter (Thomas).

British. Born in Dartford, Kent, 25 June 1932. Studied at Gravesend Technical College, and Gravesend School of Art, Kent, 1946–51; and Royal College of Art, London, 1953–56. Served in the Royal Air Force, 1951–53. Married the artist Jann Haworth. Painter and graphic artist, London, since 1956. Recipient: Leverhulme Research Award, 1956; Guggenheim Painting Award, 1958; First Prize, *John Moores Exhibition,* Liverpool, 1961. Agent: Waddington Galleries, 2 Cork Street, London W1. Address: 8 Esmond Road, London W4, England.

Individual Exhibitions:

1962 Portal Gallery, London
1965 Robert Fraser Gallery, London
1967 *3 Painters: Peter Blake/Jim Dine/Richard Hamilton,* Midlands Arts Centre, Birmingham (travelled to Arts Council Gallery, Cambridge)
1969 Bristol City Art Gallery
Portal Gallery, London
Robert Fraser Gallery, London
Leslie Waddington Prints, London
1970 Waddington Galleries, London
Ashgate Gallery, Farnham, Surrey
1971 Peter M. David Gallery, Minneapolis
1972 Waddington Galleries, London
1973 Stedelijk Museum, Amsterdam (travelled to the Gemeentemuseum, The Hague, and the Gemeentemuseum, Arnhem, Netherlands)
Kunstverein, Hamburg
Palais des Beaux-Arts, Brussels
1974 Hayward Gallery, London
Festival Gallery, Bath (with Jann Haworth)
1977 Waddington/Tooth Galleries, London
1979 Bohun Gallery, Henley-on-Thames, Oxfordshire
1980 Galleria Documenta, Turin
1983 Tate Gallery, London
Kestner-Gesellschaft, Hannover
Olympus Gallery, London
1984 Galerie Claude Bernard, Paris

Selected Group Exhibitions:

1954 *Summer Exhibition,* Royal Academy of Art, London
1958 *5 Painters,* Institute of Contemporary Arts, London
1964 *Carnegie International,* Carnegie Institute, Pittsburgh (and 1967)
1969 *Pop Art,* Hayward Gallery, London
1970 *Contemporary British Art,* National Museum of Modern Art, Tokyo
1976 *Arte Inglese Oggi 1960–76,* Palazzo Reale, Milan
1977 *British Painting 1952–1977,* Royal Academy of Art, London
1980 *Prints of the 70's by 6 British Artists,* National Art Gallery, Wellington (toured New Zealand)
1981 *The Brotherhood of Ruralists,* Arnolfini Gallery, Bristol (toured the U.K.)
1988 *The British Picture,* L.A. Louver Gallery, Venice, California

Collections:

Arts Council of Great Britain, London; British Council, London; Tate Gallery, London; Victoria and Albert Museum, London; Whitworth Art Gallery, Manchester; Bristol City Art Gallery; Museum Boymans-van Beuningen, Rotterdam; Wallraf-Richartz Museum, Cologne; Baltimore Museum of Art; Museum of Modern Art, New York.

Publications:

On BLAKE: books—*Peter Blake,* exhibition catalogue, with text by Robert Melville, London 1965; *3 Painters: Peter Black/Jim Dine/Richard Hamilton,* exhibition catalogue, with text by John English, Birmingham 1967; *Image as Language; Aspects of British Art 1950–1968* by Christopher Finch, London 1969; *Movements in Art since 1945* by Edward Lucie-Smith, London 1969; *Peter Blake,* exhibition catalogue, with text by Roger Coleman, Bristol 1969; *Pop Art Redefined* by John Russell and Suzi Gablik, London 1969; *Pop Art* by Michael Compton, London 1970 *English Pop Art: Figurative Art since 1945* by Robert Melville, London 1971; *Peter Blake,* exhibition catalogue, with text by Rainer Crone, Amsterdam 1973; *Peter Blake,* exhibition catalogue, with text by Uwe M. Schneede, Hamburg 1973; *Prints of the 70's by 6 British Artists,* exhibition catalogue, with text by Anne Kirker, Wellington 1980; *The Brotherhood of Ruralists* by Nicholas Usherwood, London 1981; *The British Picture,* exhibition catalogue with essays by Marina Vaizey, Catherine Lampert and William Feaver, Venice, California 1988.

The small panel surfaced with gold-leaf sheets never quite all in juxtaposition, the caparison-richness of which is also occasionally disturbed by small abrasions betraying undercoating, is in no way typical, however early its creation date, of the actual enduring character of the British painter Peter Blake and the essence of his works. "Painted" possibly as a Pop-art spoof, it was offered to a dealer in barter for a picture by a naïve fantasist that had caught Blake's fancy.

Yet in a way this anecdote unveils the dichotomy that invades the spirit (itself hydra-headed) of this artist's talent and personalised brilliance.

In his day Blake has given a tinpot (I was tempted to say tinsel) glitter to Pop Art at a time when it was reaching its English zenith. Not necessarily goldplated it is true, but none the less buoyant as he was neatly painting pop-realist images in carefully arresting colours on plaques of metal (seemingly tin, but probably copper) so as to meet art half-way between deliberate naivety and the echo of the old metal-based ads that used once to adorn sites where they were allowed to be nailed up (many decades before Blake was born), while at the same moment he was underlining the abiding simplicity that is the beguiling factor of so much "innocent" art.

One of the earliest of his paintings to catch the attention of the public had for subject a much-bemedalized self-portrait (again rendered in super-real honest exactitude), but this along with the sheets of metal in no fashion could place any limit on his inventiveness and the extent to which it could progress. If each of these avenues, taken together or apart, suggested an extraordinary marriage between Pop and Naïve—not Naïve in its true Art sense of course, because here was a highly sophisticated and fully-trained artist—such a quaint circumstance was to be still further expanded in near 3-dimensional setups with his *furniture* (Blake has always taken exceptional pleasure in the point-of-sale straightforwardness of children's toys), and perhaps even more so with his decorated doors and their incorporated nooks and crannies alive with pin-ups, grafitti, scrappy press-cuttings even—all the pathetic short-lived enthusiast desiderata of the "with-it" poor.

In style and manner Blake had a culture breakthrough to population millions and was able to speak in visual terms in a voice that was at once direct, without art complications, and "popular."

Comes the interim . . . Since the heady days of *Swinging Britain* the artist has cooled down and, in doing so, he has joined the ranks of approved British Artists, acquiring all the rights, respect and relevance such acceptance implies. Career success assured, the quality of his works, the infusions of "reality" into them, the spontaneous innuendos (paradoxically subtle yet obvious) are untrammelled. Blake and his gifts have not been dislocated; it is the Times and the People who are out of joint.

—Sheldon Williams

BLUME, Bernhard-Johannes.

German. Born in Dortmund, in 1937. Trained as a decorative painter and graphic artist, Dortmund, 1956–60; liberal studies, under Joseph Fassbender, Kunstakademie, Dusseldorf, 1960–65; studied philosophy and art, Cologne, 1967–71. Independent painter and photo-artist, in Cologne, 1960–71, and in Bedburg, since 1971; collaborative photo-works with Anna Blume, since 1984. Agent: Galerie Philomene Magers, Handelstrasse 13, 5300 Bonn. Address: Gutenbergstrasse 10, 5000 Cologne 30, West Germany.

Individual Exhibitions:

1961 Galerie Hella Nebelung, Dusseldorf
1969 Kunstakademie, Dusseldorf
1970 Galerie Thelen/Jollenbeck, Cologne

1971 Galerie Thelen, Essen, West Germany (with Anna Blume)
1973 Galerie Thelen/Jollenbeck, Cologne
1974 Galerie Magers, Bonn
1975 Galerie Jollenbeck, Cologne
1976 Galerie Magers, Bonn (with Anna Blume)
Galerie Vor Ort, Hamburg
1977 Artothek der Stadtbucherei, Cologne
1978 Galerie Herta Klang, Cologne
Galerie AK, Frankfurt (with Maria Blume)
1979 Galerie Jollenbeck, Cologne
1980 Galerie Petersen, West Berlin (twice)
Galerie A, Amsterdam
Stedelijk Museum, Breda, Netherlands
Produzentengalerie, Hamburg
Galerie Klewan, Munich
Galerie Dany Keller, Munich
Galerie Magers, Bonn
1981 Kunstforum, Rottweil, West Germany
1982 Galerie Petersen, West Berlin
Galerie Magers, Bonn
Museum Folkwang, Essen, West Germany
Produzentengalerie, Hamburg
Galerie Krinzinger, Innsbruck, Austria
Galerie Dany Keller, Munich
1983 Galerie Peter Noser, Zurich
Kunstverein, Bonn
1984 Galerie Schurr, Stuttgart
Kunstlerhaus, Stuttgart (with Anna Blume)
Galerie Wilde, Cologne
Kunstfonds, Bonn (with Anna Blume)
Galerie AK, Frankfurt
1985 Galerie Dany Keller, Munich
1986 Galerie Magers, Bonn (with Anna Blume)
1987 Kunsthalle, Basle (with Anna Blume)
Galerie Klaus Littmann, Basle
Galerie Schiessel, Munich
1988 Portikus, Frankfurt (with Anna Blume; travelled to Cologne)
Landesmuseum, Bonn (retrospective)

Selected Group Exhibitions:

1964 *Fluxusaktionen*, Hochschule fur bildende Kunste, Dusseldorf
1969 *Anstrengungen zur Herbeibringung des Kreuzes*, Kunstakademie, Dusseldorf
1973 *Between*, Kunsthalle, Dusseldorf (travelled to London)
1976 *6 Kolner Kunstler*, Kunstverein, Cologne
1979 *Story Art*, Bonner Kunstverein, Bonn
1981 *Die Absage an das Einzelbild*, Museum Folkwang, Essen, West Germany
1982 *Mit Fotografie*, Museum Ludwig, Cologne
1984 *Kunstlandschaft Bundesrepublik*, Kunstverein, Wilhelmshaven, West Germany
1986 *Behind the Eves: 8 German Artists*, San Francisco Museum of Modern Art
1987 *Een keuze/A choice*, Kunst RAI, Amsterdam

Publications:

By BLUME: books—*Anweisungen zum seligen Leben*, Cologne 1970; *Ideoplastie*, Cologne 1971; *Ich sehe die Gegenstande immer vor mir*, Cologne 1973; *Die vierte Dimension*, Dusseldorf 1974; *Schizo*, Cologne 1981; *Heilsgebilde*, Cologne 1983; *Naturlich, quasiphilosophisch-ideoplastischer Diavortrag*, Munich c. 1984; *Hellsehen als Schwarzsehen*, Munich 1986; *Heilig, heilig, heilig*, Munich 1986.

On BLUME: books—*Bernhard-Johannes Blume*, exhibition catalogue with texts by Gunther Schulte and Horst Walter, Bonn 1976; *Ideografien Bernhard Johannes Blumes*, exhibition catalogue with essay by Kurt Hamburger, Cologne 1977; *Polaroid Sofortbildfotografie*, exhibition catalogue with text by Johann Gerhardt Lischka, Berne 1977; *Von hier aus*, exhibition catalogue by Peter Weibel, Dusseldorf 1984; *Der vergessliche Engel* by Walter Grasskamp, Munich 1986; *Anna und Bernhard Blume: Fotos aus dem wirklichen Leben*, exhibition catalogue with introduction by Jean-Christophe Ammann, Basle 1987.

BLUME, Peter.

American. Born in Russia, 26 October 1906; emigrated to the United States, 1911: naturalized, 1919. Educated in Brooklyn public schools, and at the Educational Alliance School of Art, New York, until 1921; studied at the Art Students League, and the Beaux-Arts Academy, New York, 1921–24. Married Grace Douglas Craton in 1931. Worked briefly for a jewelry firm and a lithographic and engraving company, New York, 1920. Independent painter since 1924: established studio on 13th Street, New York, and subsequently in Patterson, New York, 1925; travelled in New England, 1926–27, and in Pennsylvania and South Carolina, 1930; established and maintains studio in Sherman, Connecticut, since 1930; travelled in Italy, France, and England, 1932; commissioned by United States Government to paint murals for Post Offices in Geneva, New York and Cannonsburg, Pennsylvania, and by local government to paint mural for the Court House in Rome, Georgia, 1941; travelled in Mexico, 1949, and in Italy and Sicily, 1952, 1956. Artist-in-Residence, American Academy, Rome, 1956, 1962, 1973. Recipient: Guggenheim Fellowship, 1932–1936; First Prize, *International Exhibition of Painting and Sculpture*, Carnegie Institute, Pittsburgh, 1934; Artists for Victory Prize, Museum of Modern Art, New York, 1942; National Institute of Arts and Letters Grant, 1947. Associate, National Academy of Design; Member, National Institute of Arts and Letters Grant, 1947. Associate, National Academy of Design; Member, National Institute of Arts and Letters. Agent: Terry Dintenfass Gallery, 50 West 57th Street, New York, New York 10019. Address: Route 1, Box 185, Sherman, Connecticut, 06784, U.S.A.

Individual Exhibitions:

1930 *Paintings*, Daniel Gallery, New York
1936 Julien Levy Galleries, New York
1941 The Downtown Gallery, New York
1947 The Downtown Gallery, New York
Durlacher Brothers Inc., New York
1949 Durlacher Brothers Inc., New York
1954 Durlacher Brothers Inc., New York
1958 Durlacher Brothers Inc., New York
1964 *Paintings and Drawings in Retrospect 1925–1964*, Currier Gallery of Art, Manchester, New Hampshire (travelled to the Wadsworth Atheneum, Hartford, Connecticut)
1968 Kennedy Galleries, New York
Recollections of the Flood and Related Works, Danenberg Gallery, New York
1970 Danenberg Gallery, New York
1975 *Bronzes about Venus*, Coe Kerr Gallery, New York
1976 *A Retrospective Exhibition*, Museum of Contemporary Art, Chicago
New Britain Museum, Connecticut (retrospective)
1980 *"From the Metamorphoses": Recent Paintings and Drawings*, Terry Dintenfass Gallery, New York

Selected Group Exhibitions

1933 *Century of Progress Exhibition I*, Art Institute of Chicago
1934 *Century of Progress Exhibition II*, Art Institute of Chicago
International Exhibition of Painting and Sculpture, Carnegie Institute, Pittsburgh
1938 *American Painting and Sculpture Annual*, Art Institute of Chicago

Collections:

Metropolitan Museum of Art, New York; Museum of Modern Art, New York; Whitney Museum, New York; Museum of Fine Arts, Boston; Williams College, Williamstown, Massachusetts; Fogg Art Museum, Harvard University, Cambridge, Massachusetts; Wadsworth Atheneum, Hartford, Connecticut; Newark Museum, New Jersey; Randolph-Macon College, Lynchburg, Virginia; Gallery of Fine Arts, Columbus, Ohio.

Publications:

By BLUME: articles—statements in *Peter Blume: Recollections of the Flood and Related Works*, exhibition catalogue, New York 1970; statement in *Peter Blume: A Retrospective Exhibition*, catalogue, Chicago 1976; *Peter Blume: Paintings and Sculpture*, New York 1987.

On BLUME: books—*Painting in America: The Story of 450 Years* by E. P. Richardson, New York 1956; *Modern Art and the New Past* by James Thrall Soby, Norman, Oklahoma 1957; *From Realism to Reality in Recent American Painting* by Virgil Barker, Lincoln, Nebraska 1959; *Mainstreams of Modern Art* by John Canaday, New York 1959; *Paintings in the 20th Century* by Werner Haftman, 2 vols., New York 1960; *A History of American Art* by Daniel M. Mendelowitz, New York 1961; *Art: U.S.A.: Now*, edited by Lee Nordness, 2 vols., Lucerne 1962; *Peter Blume: Paintings and Drawings in Retrospect 1925–1964*, exhibition catalogue, with an introduction by Charles E. Buckley, Manchester, New Hampshire 1964; *American Art since 1900: A Critical History* by Barbara Rose, New York, 1967; *Peter Blume*, exhibition catalogue, with text by Frank Getlein, New York 1968; *Peter Blume: Recollections of the Flood and Related Works*, exhibition catalogue, New York 1970; *Peter Blume: Bronzes about Venus*, exhibition catalogue, with an introduction by Gordon Hendricks, New York 1974; *Peter Blume: A Retrospective Exhibition*, catalogue, with text by Dennis Adrian, Chicago 1976; *Peter Blume: "From the Metamorphoses": Recent Paintings and Drawings*, exhibition catalogue, with text by John Paul Driscoll, New York 1980.

During the 1930s Peter Blume produced four major paintings, and it is for these Magic Realist works that he is still best known. "Parade" (1930), "South of Scranton" (1931), "Light of the World" (1932) and "The Eternal City" (1934–37) invest contemporary scenes with a bizarre allegorical element of surreality. They are painted with a highly precise, meticulously detailed technique, using smooth contours and clear outlines, which is related with the illusionistic surrealism of Dali. Blume's earlier work had been closer to the American Precisionist vein, and his subsequent painting continued to be characterized by a detailed preparation and long term experimentation carried on with numerous sketches. Blume pursues complicated compositional schema and dramatically heightened imagery to portray humanity's struggles with a hostile world. The narrative element is unabashedly present in his works, and reality tends toward the horror/science fiction levels, especially those types of the genres which make the real into the animistic.

Most of Blume's paintings are on a rather generalized level, such as that in "Light of the World" (1932) which is a critical statement about the new technology as symbolized in the foreground and about the dark, church dominated past as depicted in the background. "The Eternal City" is Blume's most overtly political painting, directly portraying the ruthless menace of Fascism with an attitude of passionate hostility and very specific protest. In a wildly perverse and complicated setting which combines ancient Roman ruins with contemporary Roman ruins, the jack-in-the-box head of a green faced Mussolini with scowling red lips arises on his accordion-pleated "body". It is a purposefully dissonant visualization of the perversities of Italian Fascism, including two people looking toward the grotesque effigy of their leader as they come out of a primitive bomb shelter. Blume spent nearly four years exclusively developing this picture, whose combination of powerful human drama and highly skilled technique shows him at his best level of pictorial satire.

After "The Eternal City," Blume concentrated on more general human themes of struggle, always pursuing the long, slow route which produces fastidiously composed and executed paintings, in a relatively small number because each is the result of sustained periods of preparation. "The Rock" (1948) becomes the symbol of life and death, with man before it as if in judgment. "Man of Sorrows" (1951) communicates the sufferings of war.

Peter Blume: ***Recollection of the Flood*****, 1969**

Subsequent paintings portray Blume's more and more fervent involvement with Quattrocento techniques, and, in works such as "Hadrian's Villa" (1957), he lapses dangerously into dependence on the past, losing much of the potent satirical edge he had achieved earlier and remaining more in the realm of the mundane despite his always thoughtfully well-composed execution. This kind of prosaic pastorale quality continues to plague Blume's works, even in his most ambitious compositions such as "Recollection of the Flood" (1967) which, although it is skillfully composed in every detail, remains more sentimental than socially relevant, more an exercise in formal prowess than a conveyor of the human struggle. Perhaps there is a certain frustration underlying Blume's move to sculpture in the early 70's, but his series of "Bronzes About Venus" remain virtuoso displays of the classic Greek theme, refined and elegant, but beneath the level of Blume's achievements of earlier times.

—Barbara Cavaliere

BOCHNER, Mel.

American. Born in Pittsburgh, Pennsylvania, in 1940. Studied painting and philosophy at the Carnegie Institute of Technology, Pittsburgh, B.F.A. 1962. Now lives and works in New York. Instructor, School of Visual Arts, New York, since 1965. Agent: Sonnabend Gallery, 420 West Broadway, New York, New York 10012. Address: c/o School of Visual Arts, 209 East 23rd Street, New York, New York U.S.A.

Individual Exhibitions:

1966	Visual Arts Gallery, New York
1968	Galerie Konrad Fischer, Dusseldorf
	Bykert Gallery, New York
1969	Galerie Heiner Friedrich, Munich
	Ace Gallery, Los Angeles
	Yale University, New Haven, Connecticut
1970	Art and Project, Amsterdam
	Galleria Sperone, Turin
	Galleria Toselli, Milan
1971	112 Green Street Gallery, New York
	University of Rhode Island, Kingston
	Centro de Arte y Comunicacion, Buenos Aires
	Museum of Modern Art, New York
1972	Galerie Sonnabend, Paris
	Sonnabend Gallery, New York
	Lisson Gallery, London
	Hartford Art School, Connecticut
	Galerie MTL, Brussels
	Galleria Bonomo, Bari, Italy
	Galleria Toselli, Milan
1973	Galerie Sonnabend, Paris
	Sonnabend Gallery, New York
1974	Galerie Sonnabend, Paris
	Galleria Schema, Florence
	University of California Art Museum, Berkeley
1975	Sonnabend Gallery, New York
	Galerie Ricke, Cologne
1976	Sonnabend Gallery, New York
	Number and Shape, Baltimore Museum of Art

1977 Bernier Gallery, Athens
Acconci/Bochner/LeVa, Sonnabend Gallery, New York
1978 Sonnabend Gallery, New York
Daniel Weinberg Gallery, San Francisco
Galleria Schema, Milan
Galleria Schema, Florence
Gallerie Sonnabend, Paris
1979 Galerie Art in Progress, Dusseldorf
1980 Sonnabend Gallery, New York
Mel Bochner/Richard Serra, Massachusetts Institute of Technology, Cambridge
1981 Texas Gallery, Houston
Daniel Weinberg Gallery, San Francisco
1982 Sonnabend Gallery, New York
Centre de Creation Artistique, Abbaye de Senanque, Gordes, France
Med a Mothi Galerie, Montpellier, France
1983 Sonnabend Gallery, New York
Yarlow/Salzman Gallery, Toronto
Daniel Weinberg Gallery, Los Angeles
Pace Editions, New York
Carol Taylor Gallery, Dallas, Texas
1984 Roger Ramsay Gallery, Chicago
1985 Sonnabend Gallery, New York
Carnegie-Mellon University, Pittsburgh

Selected Group Exhibitions:

1970 *Information,* Museum of Modern Art, New York
1974 *Art and Image in Recent Art,* Art Institute of Chicago
1975 *Bochner/LeVa/Rockburne/Tuttle,* Contemporary Arts Center, Cincinnati, Ohio
1976 *Drawing Now,* Museum of Modern Art, New York
1977 *Whitney Biennale,* Whitney Museum, New York
1978 *Contemporary Drawing/New York,* University of California Museum, Santa Barbara
1979 *The Decade in Review,* Whitney Museum, New York
1981 *Murs,* Centre Georges Pompidou, Paris
1983 *Minimalism to Expressionism,* Whitney Museum, New York
1985 *New Abstraction,* Milwaukee Art Museum, Wisconsin

Collections:

Los Angeles County Museum of Art; Musée National d'Art Moderne, Paris.

Publications:

By BOCHNER: books—*Working Drawings and Other Visible Things on Paper,* New York 1966; *The Singer Notes,* New York 1968; *10 Misunderstandings (A Theory of Photography),* New York 1970; *Notes on Theory,* Kingston, Rhode Island 1971; *11 Excerpts,* Paris 1972; *Primer,* Milan 1973; *(Toward) Axiom of Indifference,* New York 1975; articles—"Less is Less (for Dan Flavin)" in *Art and Artists* (London), 1966; "Primary Structures" in *Art Magazine* (New York), June 1966; "Domain of the Great Bear (Hayden Planetarium)" in *Art Voices* (New York), Summer 1966; "Art in Process" in *Arts* (New York), October 1966; "The Beach Boys—100%" in *Arts Magazine* (New York), March 1967; "Serial Art (Systems: Solipsism)" in *Arts Magazine* (New York), Summer 1967, reprinted in *Minimal Art,* edited by Gregory Battcock, New York 1968; "The Serial Attitude" in *Artforum* (New York), December 1967; "Compilation for Robert Mangold" in *Art International* (Lugano), April 1968; "Alphaville, Godard's Apocalypse" in *Art International* (New York), May 1968; "7 Discrete Tiers" in *Aspen Magazine* (Colorado), June 1968; "Background Is Not the Margin" in *Art in Process* (New York), no. 4, 1969; "No Thought Exists . . . " in *Arts Magazine* (New York), April 1970; "Excerpts from Speculation" in *Artforum* (New York), May 1970; "3 Conditions" in *Art and Project Bulletin 27* (Amsterdam), September 1970; "10 Hypotheses de Travail" in *VH* (Paris), Fall 1970; "Bullshit" in *Artforum* (New York), October 1970; "Mental Exercise: No. 1 Counting" in *Data* (Milan), February 1972; "Concerning the Art of Dorothea Rockburne" in *Artforum* (New York), March 1972; "Parenthetical Reflections on 5 Earlier Statements" in *Flash Art* (Milan), May 1972 and in *Arts Magazine* (New York), Summer 1972; statement in *Some Recent American Art,* exhibition catalogue, by Jennifer Licht, New York 1973; "Interview", with L. Haller, in *Flash Art* (Milan), June 1973; "Book Review" in *Artforum* (New York), June 1973; "On Malevich", interview with John Coplans, in *Artforum* (New York), June 1974; "Statement on My Prints" in *Prints,* exhibition catalogue, Toronto 1975; films—*Walking a Straight Line Through Grand Central Station,* 1965; *NYC Windows,* 1965; *Dorothea in 15 Positions Stasis,* 1970.

On BOCHNER: books—*Mel Bochner,* exhibition catalogue, Milan 1971; *Mel Bochner,* exhibition catalogue, Buenos Aires 1972; *Line as Language: 6 Artists Draw,* exhibition catalogue, by Rosalind Krauss, Princeton, New Jersey 1974; *Mel Bochner/Barry LeVa/Dorothea Rockburne/Richard Tuttle,* exhibition catalogue, Cincinnati, Ohio 1975; *Drawing Now,* exhibition catalogue, by Berenice Rose, New York 1976; *Mel Bochner: Number and Shape,* exhibition catalogue, by Brenda Richardson, Baltimore 1976; *Mel Bochner 1973–1985,* exhibition catalogue, Pittsburgh 1985.

BOETTI, Alighiero E.

Italian. Born in Turin, 16 December 1940. Married Anne Marie Sauzeau; children: Matteo and Agata. Independent artist, Turin, 1965–72, and in Rome since 1972. Established the "One Hotel", Kabul, Afghanistan, 1971–73. Agent: Galleria Christian Stein, Via Lazzaretto 15, 20124 Milan. Address: Via del Pantheon 57, 00186 Rome, Italy.

Individual Exhibitions:

1967 Galleria Christian Stein, Turin
Galleria La Bertesca, Turin
1968 Galleria De Nieuborg, Milan
Galleria Sperone, Turin
Galleria Christian Stein, Turin
1970 Galleria Toselli, Milan
Galleria Acme, Brescia, Italy
Aktionsraum I, Munich
1971 Galerie Konrad Fischer, Dusseldorf
Galleria Sperone, Turin
1972 Galleria Toselli, Milan
1973 Galleria Marilena Bonomo, Bari, Italy
John Weber Gallery, New York
Galleria Sperone-Fischer, Rome
Galerie MTL, Brussels
Art and Project, Amsterdam
Galleria Toselli, Milan
1974 Kunstmuseum, Lucerne
Galleria Sperone, Turin
1975 John Weber Gallery, New York
Galerie Annemarie Verna, Zurich
Galleria Sperone, Rome
Galleria Pascuala Trioprio, Naples
Galleria Area, Florence
Zwei Area Galerie, Munich
Saman Gallery, Genoa
1976 Studio Marconi, Milan
Galleria Lia Rumma, Naples
Galleria d'Alessandro Ferranti, Rome
Galleria Banco, Brescia, Italy
1977 Galleria Marlborough, Rome
Galleria dell'Ariete, Milan
Centre d'Art Contemporain, Geneva
Galerie Annemarie Verna, Zurich
1978 Kunsthalle, Basle
Galleria Christian Stein, Turin
Galleria Mario Diacono, Bologna
Galerie Paul Maenz, Cologne
Galleria il Cortile, Rome
Galleria Giuliana de Crescenzo, Rome
1979 Chiostro di Voltorre, Gavirate, Italy
1980 Salvatore Ala Gallery, New York
Art Agency Gallery, Tokyo
Galleria Banco, Brescia, Italy
1981 Galerie Chantal Crousel, Paris
Galleria LP220, Turin (twice)
Galleria Banco, Brescia, Italy
1982 Galleria Mario Diacono, Rome
Galerie Annemarie Verna, Zurich
Galleria Franco Toselli, Milan
1983 Galleria Mario Pieroni, Rome
Galleria LP 220, Turin
Galleria Giorgio Persano, Turin
Galleria Enzo Cannaviello, Milan
1984 Faculty of Architecture, University of Rome
Galerie Eric Franck, Geneva
Galleria LP 220, Turin
John Weber Gallery, New York
Pinacoteca di Ravenna, Italy
1985 Galleria Il Cortile, Rome
Galleria Marilena Bonomo, Bari, Italy
Galleria Pero, Miozawo, Italy
Galleria Chisel, Genova
1986 Le Nouveau Musée, Lyon, France
Galerie Pietro Sparta, Chagny, France
Michael Klein Inc., Amsterdam
Galerie Susan Wyss, Zurich
Van Abbemuseum, Eindhoven, Netherlands
Villa Arson, Nice, France
1987 Galleria Lucio Amelio, Naples
Galleria Christian Stein, Milan
Galleria Sergio Casoli, Milan
Galleria Alessandra Bonomo, Rome

Selected Group Exhibitions:

1967 *Arte Povera,* Galleria La Bertesca, Genoa (toured Italy)
1968 *Prospect 68,* Städtische Kunsthalle, Dusseldorf (and *Prospect 69*)
1969 *When Attitudes Become Form,* Kunsthalle, Berne (toured Europe)
1970 *Conceptual Art/Arte Povera/Land Art,* Galleria Civica d'Arte Moderna, Turin
1972 *Documenta 5,* Kassel, West Germany
1974 *8 Contemporary Artists,* Museum of Modern Art, New York
1978 *La Traccia del Racconto,* Villa Comunale Ormond, San Remo, Italy
1981 *Identité Italienne,* Centre Georges Pompidou, Paris
1984 *Il Modo Italiano,* California State University, Northridge
1987 *Arte Povera,* Galerie Durand Dessert, Paris

Collections:

Museo Sperimentale, Turin; Galleria Civica d'Arte Moderna, Turin; Stedelijk Museum, Amsterdam; Museum of Modern Art, New York.

Publications:

By BOETTI: books—*Insicuro Noncurante,* Genoa 1976; *Classifying the thousand longest rivers in the world,* with Anne Sauzeau Boetti, Rome 1977; *Alighiero Boetti,* exhibition catalogue, with Guido Fuaga, Rome 1977; *Alighiero & Boetti,* exhibition catalogue, Milan 1979; *Da uno a dieci,* edited by Rosellina Archinto, Milan 1980.

On BOETTI: books—*Alighiero Boetti,* exhibition catalogue, with texts by Henry Martin, Germano Celant and Tomasso Trini, Turin 1967; *Nuove Dimensioni della Scultura* by Udo Kultermann, Milan 1968; *7th Paris Biennale: Italy,* edited by Achille Bonito Oliva, Rome 1971; *Documenta 5: Befragung der Realität,* edited by Harald Szemann and others, Kassel, West Germany 1972; *Art Annual 73–74,* edited by Willem Sandberg, Cologne 1973; *6 Years: The Dematerialization of the Art Object* by Lucy R. Lippard, New York 1973; *8 Contemporary Artists,* exhibition catalogue, New York 1974; *Alighiero E. Boetti,* exhibition catalogue, with text by Jean-Christophe Ammann, Lucerne 1974; *Segni e disegni: Alighiero e Boetti 1976,* exhibition catalogue, Rome 1977; *Alighiero Boetti, La festa dell'immaginario visivo,* exhibition catalogue, edited by Tommaso Trini, Gavirate 1979; *Boetti,* exhibition catalogue, edited by Alberto Boatto, Ravenna 1984.

In 1969 Alighiero Boetti produced his "Little Traced Squares," a work which epitomizes his basic princi-

Alighiero Boetti: *Untitled*, 1985

ples as an artist. Here he has taken a sheet of paper and traced on it, in pencil, a series of squares, thereby giving us an elemental situation which invites an endless series of interpretations, each with its own formal effect.

In all of his work Boetti uses this basic device of a minimalist whole with functional parts. Each work contains a secret, but a secret which is full of mysteries and possibilities. He has given us "Ping Pong," two signs placed close to each other which light up in turn and read, first "ping," then "pong." The spaces opened up by such works permit the perception of different units which are infinitely suggestive; and his works also set up elaborate cross-references among themselves which we are meant to recognize.

Different rhythms, gestures, repetitions, deliberate artifice—all of these are the basic elements of Boetti's experiments, and each work is designed to reflect a certain kind of mental operation or thought-process; for him art *is* really the manifestation of these processes.

In some instances the results are analytical and follow the pattern of elementary mathematical operations. This is the case, for example, with his "Alternating From 1 to 100" (1970) and "The Four Operations" (1980), in which the play of numbers and letters is reduced to a minimum: the end result is always the same, whether the process involved is addition, subtraction or multiplication. In other works—"Producing the World," for example, or "Other and Disorder"—he suggests an underlying creative, cosmic force. The basic elements remain the same but they now contain a much broader range of implications.

Recently Boetti has perfected a technique which synthesizes his earlier, more abstract concerns with a new regard for colour and subject matter. By incorporating bits of pre-existing objects (coins, stamps, and so forth) he has produced collages which give us a new, experessive symbolic language.

—Roberto G. Lambarelli

BOEYEN, Mari.
Dutch. Born in Mook, Limbourg, 17 February 1951. Studied at Koninklijke Academie voor Kunst en Vormgevings, Hertogenbosch, 1968–71; Ateliers '63, Haarlem, 1971–73. Married Manny Kol in 1973 (divorced). Travelled in France and Germany, 1973, 1974 and 1975. Film Board Member, Ministry of Culture, The Hague, 1973. Address: Jacobijnestraat 21, Haarlem, Netherlands.

Individual Exhibitions:

1974 Groninger Museum voor Stad en Lande, Groningen, Netherlands
Galerie het Venster, Rotterdam
Galerie Yaki Kornblitt, Amsterdam
1975 Galerie Waalkens, Finsterwolde, Netherlands
1976 *Werken 1974–1976*, Van Abbemuseum, Eindhoven, Netherlands
Hal Bromm Gallery, New York
1978 P.I.A.C., Amsterdam
1979 Galleria Peccolo, Livorno, Italy
Museum Fodor, Amsterdam
1981 Galleria Peccolo, Livorno, Italy
1983 Haags Gemeentemuseum, The Hague
Galerie Felison, Velzen, Netherlands (with R. de Vries)
1984 Frans Hals Museum, Haarlem (with S. Buisman and F. Benjamins)
K.C.B. Gallery, Bergen, Norway
Kruithuis, Den Bosch, Netherlands
1985 Galerie Suzanne Biederberg, Amsterdam

Selected Group Exhibitions:

1973 *Einde, Begin . . .*, Noord Brabants Museum, Hertogenbosch, Netherlands
8th Biennale de Paris, Musée d'Art Moderne, Paris
1974 *11 Dutch Artists*, Fruit Market, Edinburgh (travelled to the Aberdeen Museum, Scotland)
Film als Beeldend Medium, Kunsthistorisch Institut, Groningen, Netherlands
1975 *9th Biennale de Paris*, Musée d'Art Moderne, Paris
1976 *Photography as an Artwork*, Belgrade (toured Yugoslavia)
1978 *A Photo*, Studio Marconi, Milan (travelled to Rome and Antwerp)
10 Jonge Nederlandse Kunstenaars, Stedelijk Museum, Amsterdam
1979 *Beelden van de eigen werkelijkheid*, Van Reekum Galerie, Apeldoorn, Netherlands
1980 *Camere Incantate*, Palazzo Reale, Milan
1983 *Ruimtelijk werk*, Gemeentemuseum/Akademie, Arnhem, Netherlands
1985 *Bienale van Noord Holland*, De Vaart, Hilversum, Netherlands

Collections:

Frans Hals Museum, Haarlem; Stedelijk Museum, Amsterdam.

Publications:

By BOEYEN: films—*Door I*, 1972; *Door II*, 1972; *Tripod*, 1972; *Sheet*, 1972; *Glasses*, 1973; *Turning Around*, 1973; *Self-Portrait Painting*, 1974; *The Expression of the Square*, 1974.

On BOEYEN: books—*Mari Boeyen*, exhibition catalogue, by Poul ter Hofstede, Groningen, Netherlands 1974; *11 Dutch Artists*, exhibition catalogue, by Caroline Tisdall, Edinburgh 1974; *Film als Geeldend Medium*, exhibition catalogue, by Lon de Vries-Robbe, Groningen, Netherlands 1974; *Mari Boeyen: Werken 1974–1976*, exhibition catalogue, introduction by R. H. Fuchs, Eindhoven, Netherlands 1976; *Europe—America: The Different Avant-Garde* by Achille Bonita Oliva, Milan 1976; *A Photo*, exhibition catalogue, Milan 1978; *10 Jonge Nederlandse Kunstenaars*, exhibition catalogue, Amsterdam 1978; *Beelden van de eigen werkelijkheid*, exhibition catalogue, Apeldoorn 1979; *Camere Incantate*, ex-

Mari Boeyen: *Ode I*, 1986

hibition catalogue, Milan 1980; *De eigen Ruimte* by P. Hefting, Amsterdam 1986; articles—"Intelligent spel me fotos" by Rudi Fuchs in *Niewe Rotterdamse Courant* (Rotterdam), July 1974; "Mari Boeyen" in *Flash Art* (Milan), February/March 1975.

The formula "art as reflection on art" covered both Conceptual and analytical painting. However (since every formula prefers definition to "nuance"), one basic fact was still left in the shade. While the reflection in Conceptual art was actuated only on the level of mental abstraction, putting forward for instance logical propositions on the general terms of art and regarding the importance of the material inscription of the work as superfluous, in the practice of analytical painting the reflection on the actual artistic operation was explained by means of investigation of the intrinsic potentialities of the material. Thus the material, the "basis" of the work of art, is not used with a view to the construction of definite "pictures" and a higher level of internal articulation; it does not "disappear in use"; on the contrary, it is made the object of an analysis that tests out its resistances and its possibilities.

Heir of the illustrious Dutch tradition of the period after the first World War, Mari Boeyen puts into his works the precision, the mental sharpness and the intrinsic rationality of a logical syllogism. When he made so many photographs of a pavement (this was in one of his old works) by setting them in rows, he cut and arranged them so that the connections between the tiles result in a form of detailed inscription. A demonstration, no more and no less, that it is possible to produce layers of codified meaning even starting from the phenomenal chaos of random everyday things. That it is possible therefore to prime the rational project not only by means of purely mental data but also by emphasizing the meaning by withdrawing it from the immediate living reality. "The material employed" could then take on the quality of Mari Boeyen's work.

The concreteness of the subject does not vanish; it is not volatilized by being concealed in a purely mental sphere, but is "displayed," "made clear" together with the psychological process which the artist has practised on it. It may be that the broad sector of artistic experimentation descended from rationalism, from a wholly European analytical process, does not respond today to the current pressures of a return to Significance and Metaphor. But its heredity is not disregarded; it is not possible today, in the 1980s, for us to reconstruct a virginity—neither of feelings nor of intellect.

—Massimo Carboni

BOEZEM, Marinus.

Dutch. Born in Leerdam, 28 January 1934. Educated at the Akademie Artibus, Utrecht; Vrije Akademie, The Hague. Married Maria-Rosa Busato in 1966; daughter: Natasia. Discovered air as a plastic material, 1963; the shadow as suggestion of light, time and space, 1968; "artificial natureimpressions," 1968; Member, Council of Art of the Government of the Netherlands, 1976–80. Professor of Art, Architecture Section, Technical University of Delft, since 1979. Agent: Art and Project, 36 Willemsparkweg, Amsterdam 1007. Address: Bellinkstraat 25, 4331 gv Middelburg, Netherlands.

Individual Exhibitions:

1964 *Hommage à Marilyn Monroe*, Galerie Leiden, Netherlands
Galerie Punt 31, Dordrecht, Netherlands (with Jan van Munster)
1965 Galerie 845, Amsterdam (with Jan van Munster)
Dromedaris, Enkhuizen, Netherlands (with Jan van Munster)
1968 *Air Environment*, Galerie Swart, Amsterdam
Boezem/Van Elk, Galleria Nuova Loggia, Bologna (with Ger Van Elk)
1969 *Korenveld*, Kunstkring, Rotterdam (with Ger Van Elk)
1970 Studium Generale, Economics High School, Rotterdam
Modern Art Agency, Naples
Art and Project, Amsterdam
Boezem/Panamarenko, Stedelijk Van Abbemuseum, Eindhoven, Netherlands
1971 Yellow Now Gallery, Liège, Belgium
1975 Galerie Het Badhuis, Gorinchem, Netherlands
1976 Gemeentemuseum, The Hague
1978 Galerie Media, Neuchâtel, Switzerland
Art Fair, Bologna
Multi Art Points, Amsterdam
Galleria Ferrari, Verona
1979 *Space Sculptures*, De Vleeshal, Middelburg, Netherlands
1980 Kunstcentrum Het Badhuis, Gorinchem, Netherlands
1981 Galerie Media, Neuchâtel, Switzerland
1982 Provinciaal Museum, Hasselt, Belgium
De Vleeshal, Middelburg, Netherlands
Musée Grenoble, France
1983 *Toren-Project*, at the *Festival De Stad*, Arnheim, Netherlands
Galerie Media, Neuchatel, Switzerland
1984 Galerie Muller-Roth, Stuttgart
1985 Galerie Peter van Beveren, Rotterdam
Anthony Reynolds Gallery, London
Galerie Waalkens, Finsterwolde, Netherlands
1986 Galerie Muller-Roth, Stuttgart
1987 Wilhelm-Hack-Museum, Ludwigshafen, West Germany

Selected Group Exhibitions:

1968 *Les Structures Gonflables*, Musée d'Art Moderne de la Ville, Paris
1969 *Op Losse Schroeven*, Stedelijk Museum, Amsterdam
When Attitudes Become Form, Kunsthalle, Berne
1970 *Between Man and Matter*, at the *Biennale*, Metropolitan Museum of Modern Art, Tokyo (travelled to the Kyoto Municipal Art Museum, and the Aichi Prefectural Art Gallery, Nagoya)
1979 *L'estetico e il selvaggio*, Galleria Civica, Modena
1981 *Contemporary Art from the Netherlands*, Museum of Contempory Art, Chicago (travelled to the Brooklyn Museum, New York; Little Rock Museum, Arkansas; La Jolla Museum, California; and the Art Gallery of Ontario, Toronto)
1983 *Ruimtelijk Werk*, Gemeentemuseum, Arnhem, Netherlands
1986 *Tu es Pierre*, Fonds Regional d'Art Contemporain, Limoges, France
1987 *Flags of 12 Artists*, Musée d'Art et d'Hisoire, Geneva

Collections:

Museum Boysmans van Beuningen, Rotterdam; Haags Gemeentemuseum, The Hague; Stedelijk Museum, Amsterdam; Van Abbemuseum, Eindhoven, Netherlands; Kunsthaus, Zurich; Musée Cantonal des Beaux Arts, Lausanne, Switzerland; Musée de Grenoble, France.

Publications:

By BOEZEM: books—*Boezem Airobjects*, 1966; *Paper-Events*, Antwerp 1970; *Anti-Art and Visual Education*, photo book, The Hague 1970; *Press-Art-Project*, Gorinchem, Netherlands 1974; *Podio del Mondo per l'Arte*, Middelburg, Netherlands 1975; films—*Sand-Fountain*, 1969; *Project Hoogland Church*, 1971; *A Little Breeze in May*, 1974.

On BOEZEM: books—*Boezem/Van Elk*, exhibition catalogue, with text by Renato Barilli, Bologna 1968; *Op Losse Schroeven*, exhibition cagalogue, text by W. Beeren, Amsterdam 1969; *Von Hodler zur Antiform* by Harold Szeeman, Berne 1970; *Boezem-Panamarenko*, exhibition catalogue, Eindhoven, Netherlands 1970; *Contemporary Art from the Netherlands*, exhibition catalogue, Chicago 1981; *Marinus Boezem*, exhibition catalogue, Grenoble, France 1982; *Marinus Boezem: La Lumière Cistercienne Clairvaux*, exhibition catalogue, Ludwigshafen 1987; articles—"Dall 'Olanda' " by Piero Gilardi in *Flash Art* (Milan), June 1968; "Primary Energy and the Micromotive Artists" by Piero Gilardi in *Artsmagazine* (New York), September/October 1968; "Imagination Takes Command" by Tommaso Trini in *Domus* (Milan), February 1969; "Dutch Artists on Television" by Carel Blotkamp in *Studio International* (London), June 1971; "Education and Art" by Frans Haks in *Museumjournaal* (Amsterdam), December 1974; "Narrative Art" by Liesbeth Brandt Corstius in *Museumjournaal* (Amsterdam), March 1975.

Marinus Boezem: *Untitled*, 1984

The world as the complement of the work of art.

In the course of years an image of my work has grown which cannot be described on formal grounds of conformity of form and/or material. The basic theme of these works is, over and over again, the search for a new concept in which art becomes art: the context of the work of art as its necessary complement.

The works all have much in common; they evoke a new "environment," interacting with the work. Both components thus form the work of art. The works do not refer to themselves. They endeavor to formulate a new context. As such, I do not make a "profile" of reality to reach a specialization of it, but place the spectator himself in the process of searching for that reality.

The works that originated in the 60's already point in this direction: both "Wind-Tables" (1968) and the photographic work "To Sign the Sky by an Aeroplane" (1968).

In the more recent works, this idea of interaction between the work and the spectator is materialized again, such as in the mirror-project "space-sculpture" (1978), in which two large mirrors are placed in the center of the exhibition room, the reflecting sides facing each other. Space and time are here expressed in themselves, not dependent on the surrounding architecture. This work, on the one hand, is a materially space-determining sculpture: dividing the physical space; on the other hand, it creates its own context as a concept.

The "wallpaper-project" (1970), later realized at the Gemeentemuseum in The Hague, also reacts to the physical quality of the museum room. For me, this means searching for expression and significance in the classical conception of sculpture as illustrated in a later work titled "Jump" (1981), in which I try to epitomize a classical socle.

This socle, placed in space with only my shoes on it, is in front of a wall which has a life-size photograph of myself, seen as background. Here, then, is a connection between plastic art and flat level. Hopefully, a dimension is created out of the shoes to the wall to sculpture.

In recent years, I was also engaged in studying gothic space, which apart from its specific form and rhythm, develops its own mythology as a metaphor. Such metaphors are used as a datum to suggest new spaces and to evoke new dimensions of them. The ground-plan as a given structure is used here to attain a new interpretation of sculpture.

My works try to illustrate a process of research in which the staging and interim results are shown by means of the works of art. That is why these works lack the stamp of a trademark. They attempt to approximate my own obsessions with relation to reality from a plural point of view, as if answers could be found.

—Marinus Boezem

From the very start, Marinus Boezem has made clear that his artistic activities were not to be hampered by the traditional painter's and sculptor's materials. In the year 1966, in a privately published booklet, he states that already in 1963 he discovered air 'as a purification, as a reality, as a conquest of space'. Boezem identifies air with freedom and he considers man himself 'as an object of art'.

In 1968 he shows his famous *Windtables,* covered with lightweight white cloth that is moved to wave by a ventilator. The atmosphere created by these Tables is poetically suggestive and, because of the empty cloth, brings some good painterly associations to the fore. During these years, around 1970, Boezem's work can be seen at international exhibitions like *Op Losse Schroeven* (Stedelijk Museum, Amsterdam, 1969). For this show he proposed to give a number of gigantic white sheets some airing by opening the huge first floor windows of the museum and let these hang over the window-sill out in the open.

Contrary to his colleagues Jan Dibbets and Ger van Elk, Boezem's work has retained a process-like character; he has not chosen a production of traditionally framed objects. Already in 1969 he demonstrated the expansive but at the same time substantially non-permanent status of an individual signature in a piece called *Sign the sky above the port of Amsterdam with an areoplane.* Another piece, dating from 1967 and realised in 1981, illustrates the possibility of combining a heavy, unmovable form with a never ending process. Boezem measures the outline of the shadow of a given tree, at a certain time of a certain day, and fills this with a black granite. As the tree in the course of time grows and changes, and correspondingly the shadow, the granite form becomes autonomous as a three-dimensional piece of sculpture.

From 1980 onwards Boezem has concentrated on a new project, the 'Etude Gothique'. At its starting point is the groundplan of a gothic cathedral, a continuously recurrent motif that functions as the vehicle for various images, including many self-portrayals. A recent manifestation is the planting of poplars litterally following the lines of a cathedral plan. Within a number of years the trees will touch the sky and sheep will graze among its pillars. This project has been realised in the newly developed Ysselmeerpolders, where one will find some other large-scale works of art, for instance Robert Morris' Observatorium, originally proposed for the important outdoor exhibition *Sonsbeek buiten de Perken* in 1971.

Boezem works at the fringe of the artistic scene in Holland, in the quiet provincial town of Middelburg in Zealand. In this city, together with his wife Maria-Rosa, he yearly organizes a symposium where artists, critics and audience meet in a well motivated and concentrated atmosphere.

—A. F. Wagemans

BOLOTOWSKY, Ilya.

American. Born in Petrograd, Russia, 1 July 1907; emigrated to the United States 1923: naturalized, 1929. Educated at the College of St. Joseph, Istanbul, 1921–23, and the National Academy of Design, New York, 1924–30. Travelled in Europe, 1932; influenced by the Mondrians in the Gallatin Collection, and the Mirós at the Pierre Matisse Gallery, leading to first abstract work, 1933; Member of *The Ten* with Rothko, Gottlieb and others, in the mid-1930s; active member of the WPA Federal Arts Project Program, 1935–40; co-founder and charter member of American Abstract Artists, 1936; co-founder of Federation of Modern Painters and Sculptors, 1939; began collecting North West Coast Indian and Eskimo art 1942; emergence of Mondrian-influenced Neo-Plastic style, 1945. Acting Head of Department, Black Mountain College, North Carolina, 1946–48; Associate Professor of Art, University of Wyoming, Laramie, 1948–57; Adjunct Professor, Brooklyn College, New York, 1954–56; Professor of Art, State Teachers' College, New Paltz, New York, 1957–65; Adjunct Professor of Art, Hunter College, New York, 1963–64; Professor Art, University of Wisconsin at Whitewater, 1965–71; Visiting Professor of Art, University of New Mexico, Albuquerque, 1969; Lecturer, Graduate School of Fine Arts, Columbia University, New York, 1970; Adjunct Professor, graduate honors course, Queens College, New York, 1973; retired from teaching 1976; Artist-in-Residence, Fort Wayne Museum of Art, Indiana, 1978. Recipient: 1st Prize for Drawing, 1925, 1926, and Hallgarten Prize for Painting, National Academy of Design, New York, 1929–30; Scholarship, Tiffany Foundation, New York, 1929–30; Fellowship, Yaddo Foundation, Saratoga Springs, New York, 1933; Grant, Museum of Non-Objective Painting, New York, 1941; Grant for Experimental Film Work, University of Wyoming Graduate School, Laramie, 1953–54; First Prize for Painting, Sharon Creative Arts Foundation, Connecticut, 1959; First Prize for Metanoia, *Midwest Film Festival,* University of Chicago, 1963; Abstract Painting Prize, National Institute of Arts and Letters, 1971; Guggenheim Foundation Grant, 1973. Agent: Grace Borgenicht Gallery, 1018 Madison Avenue, New York, New York 10021. *Died* (in New York City) *22 November 1981.*

Individual Exhibitions:

1930 G.R.D. Studios, New York
1946 New Art Circle, J. B. Neumann, New York

1947 The Pinacotheca, New York
1950 The Rose Fried Gallery (The Pinacotheca), New York
1952 New Art Circle, J. B. Neumann, New York
1954 Grace Borgenicht Gallery, New York
1956 Grace Borgenicht Gallery, New York
1958 Grace Borgenicht Gallery, New York
1959 Grace Borgenicht Gallery, New York
1959 Grace Borgenicht Gallery, New York
1960 State University College, New Paltz, New York
1961 Grace Borgenicht Gallery, New York
1963 Grace Borgenicht Gallery, New York
1964 Art Depot Gallery, La Grangeville, New York
1966 Grace Borgenicht Gallery, New York
East Hampton Gallery, New York
1967 Gorham State College Art Gallery, Maine
1968 Grace Borgenicht Gallery, New York
George Gershwin College, Stony Brook, New York
1970 Grace Borgenicht Gallery, New York
Painting and Columns, University Art Museum, University of New Mexico, Albuquerque (toured the United States)
Art Harris Gallery, Los Angeles
1971 London Arts Gallery
1972 Grace Borgenicht Gallery, New York
David Barnett Gallery, Milwaukee
1973 Wichita Art Museum, Kansas
1974 Grace Borgenicht Gallery, New York
Guggenheim Museum, New York (retrospective; travelled to The National Collection, Washington, D.C.)
1976 Grace Borgenicht Gallery, New York
1978 Grace Borgenicht Gallery, New York
Fort Wayne Art Gallery, Indiana
1980 Grace Borgenicht Gallery, New York
1981 Salt Lake Art Center, Utah
1982 Yares Gallery, Scottsdale, Arizona
1983 *Bolotowsky and His Circle*, Grey Art Gallery, New York University
1984 Washburn Gallery, New York
Il Punto Blu Gallery, Southampton, New York
River Gallery, Irvington-on-Hudson, New York
Pembroke Gallery, Houston, Texas
1987 Washburn Gallery, New York

Selected Group Exhibitions:

1942 *2nd Annual Federation of Modern Painters and Sculptors*, Wildenstein Galleries, New York (and annually in New York until 1971)
1946 *10th Annual Exhibition, American Abstract Artists*, American-British Center, New York until 1972)
1950 *Whitney Annual*, Whitney Museum, New York (and regularly until 1972)
1971 *The Non-Objective World*, Galerie Jean Chauvelin, Paris (toured Europe)
1972 *Geometric Abstraction—1930's*, Zabriskie Gallery, New York (toured the United States)
Post-Mondrian Abstraction in America, Museum of Contemporary Art, Chicago
1978 *Painting and Sculpture Today*, Indianapolis Museum of Art
1979 *Recent Acquisitions*, Metropolitan Museum of Art, New York

Collections:

Metropolitan Museum of Art, New York; Museum of Modern Art, New York; Guggenheim Museum, New York; Whitney Museum, New York; Albright-Knox Art Gallery, Buffalo, New York; Art Institute of Chicago; Walker Art Center, Minneapolis; The Phillips Collection, Washington, D.C.; National Collection of Fine Arts, Washington, D.C.; Hirshhorn Museum and Sculpture Garden, Washington, D.C.

Publications:

By BOLOTOWSKY: book—*Russian/English Dictionary of Painting and Sculpture*, New York 1962; articles—in *Réalitiés Nouvelles* (Paris), no. 4, 1950; *Réalitiés Nouvelles* (Paris), no. 6, 1952; "Russian Constructivism: An Interview with Ilya Bolotowsky," with Ibram Lassaw, in *The World of Abstract Art*, New York 1957; "On Neoplasticism and My Own Work, A Memoir," in *Leonardo* (London), no. 2, 1969; "Concerning My Tondo Paintings" in *Art Now* (New York), vol. 2, no. 2, 1970; statement in *Bolotowsky*, exhibition catalogue, New York 1972; "Moholy Nagy, ed. Richard Kostelanetz" (book review) in *Leonardo* (London), vol. 6, no. 1, 1973; interview, with Louise A. Svendsen and Mimi Poser, in *Ilya Bolotowsky*, exhibition catalogue, New York 1974; statement in *Paintings and Columns*, exhibition catalogue, New York 1974; "Going Abstract in the 30's, "interview with Susan Carol Larsen, in *Art in America* (New York), September/October 1976; films—*Bolotowsky Shows* (various dates); early shorts; western shorts, 1953–57; *David Smith*, 1953; *Haunted House*, 1954; *Broadway*, 1955; *Constant*, 1955; *Dead End*, 1955; *Gabo*, 1955; *Highways*, 1955; *George L. K. Morris*, 1955; *The Museum of Modern Art*, 1955; *The National Gallery*, 1955; *The Philadelphia Museum*, 1955; *Zceron*, 1955; *Ruth Asawa*, 1955; *Avery*, 1956; *Nell Blaine*, 1956; *Rhys Caparn*, 1956; *Wolf Kahn Paints a Picture*, 1956; *Nevelson*, 1956; *David Smith*, 1956; *Knute Stiles*, 1956; *Sand Creek*, 1956–57; *DeRivera*, 1958; *Subways*, 1958; *Andrew Winter*, 1958; *Narcissus in a Gothic Mood*, 1959–60; *Positive Negative* (Metanoia), 1961; *Metanoia*, 1961–62; *The Last Orpheus*, 1961; *Walking Dream*, 1967; *Afternoon of a Fawn*, 1968; *The Eye*, 1968; *The Ambassadors*, 1969; *Torreon*, 1969; *The Parnassian*, 1971; also, numerous plays and stories.

On BOLOTOWSKY: books—*Ilya Bolotowsky*, exhibition catalogue, New York 1947; *Ilya Bolotowsky*, exhibition catalogue, New York 1950; *Abstract Painting and Sculpture in America* by Andrew Carnduff Ritchie, New York 1951; *Ilya Bolotowsky*, exhibition catalogue, with text by George L. K. Morris, New York 1952; *Dictionary of Contemporary American Artists* by Paul Cummings, New York 1966 and subsequent editions; *Constructivism: Origins and Evolutions* by George Rickey, New York 1967; *American Art since 1900: A Critical History* by Barbara Rose, New York and Washington 1967; *Ilya Bolotowsky: Paintings and Columns*, exhibition catalogue, text by Robert M. Ellis, Albuquerque, New Mexico 1970; *Bolotowsky*, exhibition catalogue, New York 1972; *Geometric Abstraction 1926–1942*, exhibition catalogue, Dallas 1972; *The New York School: A Cultural Reckoning* by Dore Ashton, New York 1972; *Ilya Bolotowsky*, exhibition catalogue, New York 1974; *Paintings and Columns*, exhibition catalogue, with notes by J. D. Cohn, New York 1974; *Ilya Bolotowsky*, exhibition catalogue, by John Krushenick, Fort Wayne, Indiana 1978; *Ilya Bolotowsky—WPA Murals*, exhibition catalogue, New York 1980; articles—"Towards A Plastic Revolution" by Brie Taylor in *Art News* (New York), March 1964; "Ilya Bolotowsky" by Leif Sjoberg in *Konstrevy* (Stockholm), vol. 4, no. 2/3, 1964; "The Growing IInfluence of Mondrian" by Robert Welsh in *Canadian Art* (Toronto), January 1966; "Squaring the Circle and Vice-Versa" by Lawrence Campbell in *Art News* (New York), February 1970; "American Geometric Abstraction in The Late 30's" by John Elderfield in *Artforum* (New York), December 1972; "Noland" by Kenworth Moffett in *Art International* (Lugano), Summer 1973; "Mondrian's American Circle" by J. Burnham in *Arts Magazine* (New York), September 1973; review by Thomas B. Hess in *New York*, 22 April 1974; "Ilya Bolotowsky" by J. Tannenbaum in *Arts Magazine* (New York), October 1974; "Ilya Bolotowsky: Pure Precise Loveliness" by H. Herrera, in *Art News* (New York), November 1974.

Ilya Bolotowsky is best known for having developed a uniquely personal brand of expression influenced by the rigorous and purist Neo-Plastic approach of Mondrian. After acquiring a solid academic background, Bolotowsky began the difficult task for an American artist in the early 1930's of becoming a modernist. His investigative assimilation of the melange of European sources popular then—Picasso, Braque, Miró, Kandinsky, Mondrian—are evident in paintings of the 1930's. For example, both the analytical geometric structures of Cubism and the biomorphic forms of Surrealism can be found in the abstract mural he designed for the Williamsburg Housing Project in New York in 1936. Also, in 1936, he became a founding member of the American Abstract Artists, a group dedicated to the discussion and the pursuit of abstraction. Unlike others of his colleagues, Bolotowsky did not abstract from nature and aimed, instead, towards a pure pictorial expression.

The strong influence of Mondrian is detectable in his paintings executed after World War II. In such examples as *Upright in Gold and Violet* (1945) a new and confident orderliness is present in the color-planar composition that, also, featured the thick, scaffolded lines which were a signature in Mondrian's painting. By the late 1940's Bolotowsky had limited his forms to right angle relationships. Like Mondrian, he decided to banish the diagonal because this element disturbed the equilibrous spatial tension he aimed to achieve. At this time, also, Bolotowsky introduced the diamond shaped format in which he would do many of his most complex and challenging pictures. Some examples are *Configuration Within a Diamond* (1951), a wondrously rhythmical composition that features a complicated interplay of many, variously sized and shaped color bars; *Large Cobalt Diamond* (1957), a composition with fewer and larger color shapes where the angles of the picture's edges balance the linear movements of the image; *Deep Blue Diamond* (1973), an elegant composition in blue, black, red and white in which the various sections are made to work together by pulling against each other.

In 1961, his paintings which had already began to spill over the edges of the canvas, led him to develop three-dimensional, columnar sculptures. The painted imagery on the surface of the sculpture echoed the paintings. Other shaped formats that Bolotowsky mastered include the ellipse and tondo: *Light Yellow Tondo* (1981) and *Open Space Blue Tondo* (1981) are outstanding examples of the high degree of control he had in the late work. It allowed Bolotowsky to create what he called "ideal, balanced harmony" out of the dynamic interplay of the building blocks of art: line, color and plane.

In addition to painting, Bolotowsky made films and wrote plays in which he dealt with the kinds of subjective and emotional issues that he had consciously eliminated from his Neo-Plastic pictorial expression.

—Ronny Cohen

BOLTANSKI, Christian.

French. Born in Paris, 6 September 1944. Self-taught in art. Professional photographer and artist, Paris, since 1969. Agent: Sonnabend Gallery, 420 West Broadway, New York, New York 10012, U.S.A.; and Galerie Sonnabend, 12 Rue Mazarine, 75005 Paris. Address: 746 Boulevard Camelinat, 92240 Malakoff, France.

Individual Exhibitions:

1970 Galerie Templon, Paris (with Jean Le Gac)
Musée d'Art Moderne, Paris
1971 Galerie Sonnabend, Paris
Galerie M. E. Thelen, Cologne
1972 Galerie Folker Skulima, Berlin
Studio Santandrea, Milan
1973 Galleria Lucio Amelio, Naples
Kunsthalle, Baden-Baden, West Germany
Sonnabend Gallery, New York
Museum of Modern Art, Oxford
Israel Museum Jerusalem
1974 *Saynette Comique*, Westfalischer Kunstverein, Münster, West Germany
Louisiana Museum, Humlebaek, Denmark
Centre National d'Art Contemporain, Paris (with Jacques Monory)
1975 Sonnabend Gallery, New York
Kunsthalle, Kiel, West Germany
Centre d'Art Contemporain, Geneva
Württembergische Kunstverein, Stuttgart
Galerie Seriaal, Amsterdam
1976 Musée d'Art Moderne, Paris
Rheinisches Landesmuseum, Bonn
1977 Museum of Contemporary Art, La Jolla, California
Galleria Bruno Soletti, Milan
Galerie Sonnabend, Paris

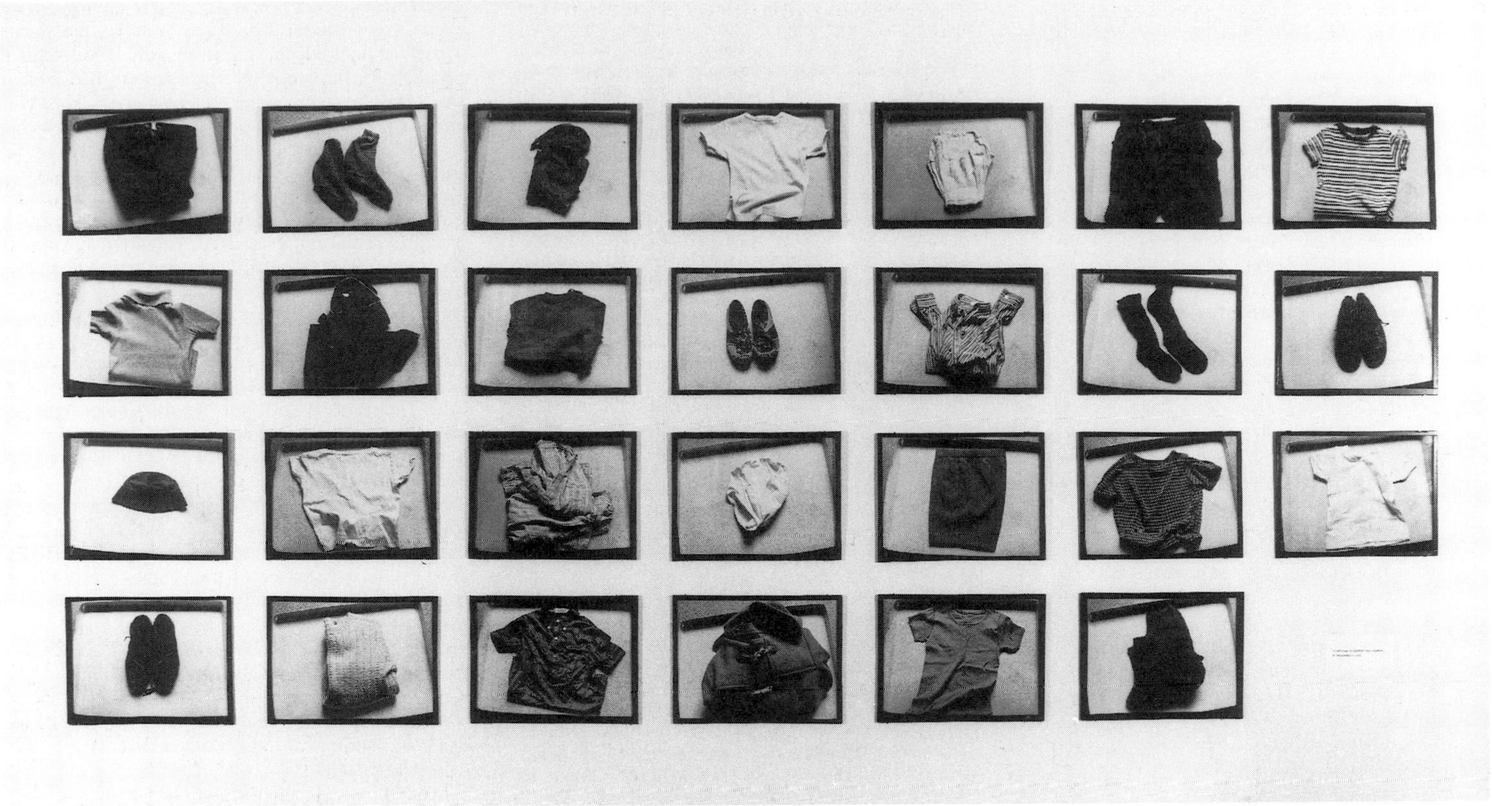

Christian Boltanski: ***29 Apparels de François C.*****, 1972**

1978 Badischer Kunstverein, Karlsruhe, West Germany
Galerie Jollenbeck, Cologne
Galerie Malacorda, Geneva
Galerie Foksal, Warsaw
1979 *Compositions,* Musée de Peinture, Calais
Galerie Sonnabend, Paris
Carpenter Art Center, Harvard University, Cambridge, Massachusetts
1981 Musée d'Art Moderne, Paris (retrospective)
1982 Sonnabend Gallery, New York
Le Nouveau Musée, Lyon, France
1983 Aldrich Museum of Contemporary Art, Ridgefield, Connecticut
1984 Centre Georges Pompidou, Paris
Kunsthaus, Zurich
Staatliche Kunsthalle, Baden-Baden, West Germany
Galerie 't Venster, Rotterdam
1985 Galerie Optica, Montreal
Galerie Crousel-Hussenot, Paris
Le Consortium Centre d'Art Contemporain, Dijon, France
1986 Galerie Elisabeth Kaufmann, Zurich
Galerie Crousel Hussenot, Paris
Galerie des Ponchettes, Nice, France
Kunstverein, Munich

Selected Group Exhibitions:

1969 *Biennale de Paris,* Musée d'Art Moderne, Paris
1971 *Prospekt 71,* Kunsthalle, Dusseldorf
1972 *Documenta 5,* Museum Fridericianum, Kassel, West Germany (and *Documenta 6,* 1977)
1974 *Pour Memoire,* Centre d'Art Plastique Contemporain, Bordeaux, France (travelled to Paris)
1977 *Malerei und Photographie im Dialog,* Kunsthaus, Zurich
1979 *3rd Biennale of Sydney,* Art Gallery of New South Wales, Sydney
1980 *Artist and Camera,* Mappin Art Gallery, Sheffield, Yorkshire (travelled to Stoke, Durham and Bradford)
1983 *Kunst mit Photographie,* Nationalgalerie, West Berlin
1986 *Photography as Performance,* Photographers' Gallery, London

Collections

Musée d'Art Moderne, Paris; Musée d'Art, Dijon, France; Kunsthalle, Hamburg; Kunsthalle, Kiel, West Germany; Neue Galerie, Aachen, West Germany; Louisiana Museum, Humlebaek, Denmark; Boymans-van Beuningen Museum, Rotterdam; Museum of Fine Arts, Lodz, Poland; Israel Museum, Jerusalem; Art Institute of Chicago.

Publications:

By BOLTANSKI: books—*Tous ce que reste de mon enfance,* Paris 1969; *Reconstitutions des Gestes,* Paris 1971; *10 Portraits Photographiques,* Paris 1972; *Album Photographique,* Hamburg 1972; *Inventaire,* Münster, West Germany 1973; *Quelques Interpretations,* Paris 1974; *20 Regles et Technique,* Copenhagen 1975; *Les Morts pour Rire,* Antibes, France 1975; *Modellbilder,* with others, Bonn 1976; film—*La Vie Impossible de Christian Boltanski,* 1968.

On BOLTANSKI: books—*L'Art en France: Une Nouvelle Generation* by Jean Clair, Paris 1973; *Saynette Comique,* exhibition catalogue, by Klaus Honnef, Münster, West Germany 1974; *Reconstitution* by Andreas Franke, Paris 1978; *Les Modeles* by Paull-Hervé Würz, Paris 1979; *Spurensicherung* by Günter Metken, Cologne 1979. *Compositions,* exhibition catalogue, by Dominique Vieville, Calais 1980; *Christian Boltanski,* exhibition catalogue, Baden-Baden 1984; *Christian Boltanski: Lecon des Tenebres,* exhibition catalogue, Munich 1986.

BONTECOU, Lee.

American. Born in Providence, Rhode Island, 15 January 1931. Educated at the Arts Students League, New York, 1952–55; Skowhegan School of Art, Maine, 1954 (on scholarship); studied in Rome, 1956, 1958 (on Fulbright Scholarships). Independent sculptor and printmaker. Recipient: Lewis Comfort Tiffany Award, 1959; Competition Award, *Biennial Exhibition,* Corcoran Gallery of Art, Washington, D.C., 1963; First Prize, *Annual Invitational,* National Institute of Arts and Letters, 1966. Agent: Leo Castelli Gallery, 4 East 77th Street, New York, New York 10021. Address: Post Office Box 1290, East Hampton, New York 11937, U.S.A.

Individual Exhibitions:

1959 *Sculpture,* "G" Gallery, New York
1960 Leo Castelli Gallery, New York
1962 Leo Castelli Gallery, New York
1965 Galerie Ileana Sonnabend, Paris
1966 Leo Castelli Gallery, New York
1968 *Sculpturen, Tekeningen, Lithos,* Museum Boymans-van Beuningen, Rotterdam
Städtisches Museum Schloss Morsbroich, Leverkusen, West Germany (travelled to Kunstverein, Haus am Waldsee, West Berlin)
1971 Leo Castelli Gallery, New York
1972 Museum of Contemporary Art, Chicago
1974 *Prints and Drawings,* Davison Art Center, Wesleyan University, Middletown, Connecticut

Selected Group Exhibitions:

1960 *New Media—New Forms I + II,* Martha Jackson Gallery, New York
1963 *Biennial,* Corcoran Gallery of Art, Washington, D.C.
1964 *Painting and Sculpture of a Decade 1954–1964,* Tate Gallery, London
1966 *Flint Invitational,* Flint Institute of Arts, Michigan
1967 *Sculpture: A Generation of Innovation,* Art Institute of Chicago
1970 *L'Art Vivant,* Fondation Maeght, St.-Paul-de-Vence, France
1971 *Works on Paper,* University of North Carolina at Chapel Hill
1973 *American Drawing 1970–1973,* Yale University, New Haven, Connecticut
1975 *Recent American Etching,* Davison Art Center, Wesleyan University, Middletown, Connecticut (travelled to the National Collection of Fine Arts, Smithsonian Iinstitution, Washington, D.C., 1977)

1976 *American Artists 76: A Celebration,* Marion Koogler McNay Art Institute, San Antonio, Texas

Collections:

Whitney Museum, New York; Museum of Modern Art, New York; Chase Manhattan Bank, New York; Corcoran Gallery of Art, Washington, D.C.; Washington Gallery of Modern Art, D.C.; Art Institute of Chicago; Museum of Fine Arts, Houston; Museum of Fine Arts, Dallas; Stedelijk Museum, Amsterdam.

Publications:

On BONTECOU: books—*Lee Bontecou,* exhibition catalogue, with texts by Gillo Dorfles, Gérald Gassiot-Talabot, and Annette Michelson, Paris 1965; *New Art Around the World: Painting and Sculpture,* edited by Sam Hunter, New York 1966; *Lee Bontecou: Sculpturen, Tekeningen, Lithós,* exhibition catalogue, with text by Dore Ashton, Rotterdam 1968; *Lee Bontecou,* exhibition catalogue, with texts by Rolf Günter Dienst, Rolf Wedewer, Wibke von Bonin, and Dore Ashton, Leverkusen, West Germany 1968; *Minimal Art: A Critical Anthology,* edited by Gregory Battcock, New York 1968; *Lee Bontecou,* exhibition catalogue, with text by Carter Ratcliff, Chicago 1972; *Lee Bontecou: Prints and Drawings,* exhibition catalogue, with text by Richard S. Field, Middletown, Connecticut 1974; *Recent American Etching,* exhibition catalogue, with text by Richard S. Field, Middletown, Connecticut 1975; *American Artists 76: A Celebration,* exhibition catalogue, with text by Alice C. Simkins, San Antonio, Texas 1976; articles—"Lee Bontecou's Aquatints" by R. S. Field in *Art International* (Lugano, Switzerland), November 1970; "Lee Bontecou" by Lil Picard in *Kunstwerk* (Baden-Baden, West Germany), Summer 1971; "A Diversity of Approaches in Contemporary Art: Rauschenberg, Bontecou, and Noland" by Lincoln Johnson in *Honolulu Academy of Arts Journal,* vol. 1, 1974.

The bulky constructions by Lee Bontecou loom out from the walls upon which they have been hooked and invite the eyes to go down into the mirky depth of a central orifice whose sexual connotations have been happily dwelt upon by a number of professional critics. But is the sense of a boiler-room sex the natural and immediate reaction of those who have never seen her works before? After initial surprise-coupled-with-consternation, they are far more likely to lay about them in the upper recesses of their minds looking for a visual twinship with something less emotional, something more matter-of-fact. The emotion, in any case, has been provided by the constructions themselves. Everyday eyes are less inclined to light upon the factor of sexuality, however implicit; they will equate the "hole" with the hollow shaft that once acted as the protuberance to hold an airplane propeller in the days before jets. The taut stretched canvas facets stitched to their wire framework enhance this image of early aircraft and the variations of grey and rusts which colour the entire construction do nothing to reduce this offbeat identification.

These comments are made because as well as being pertinent in the context of a first introduction to Lee

Lee Bontecou: *Untitled Sculpture*, 1961

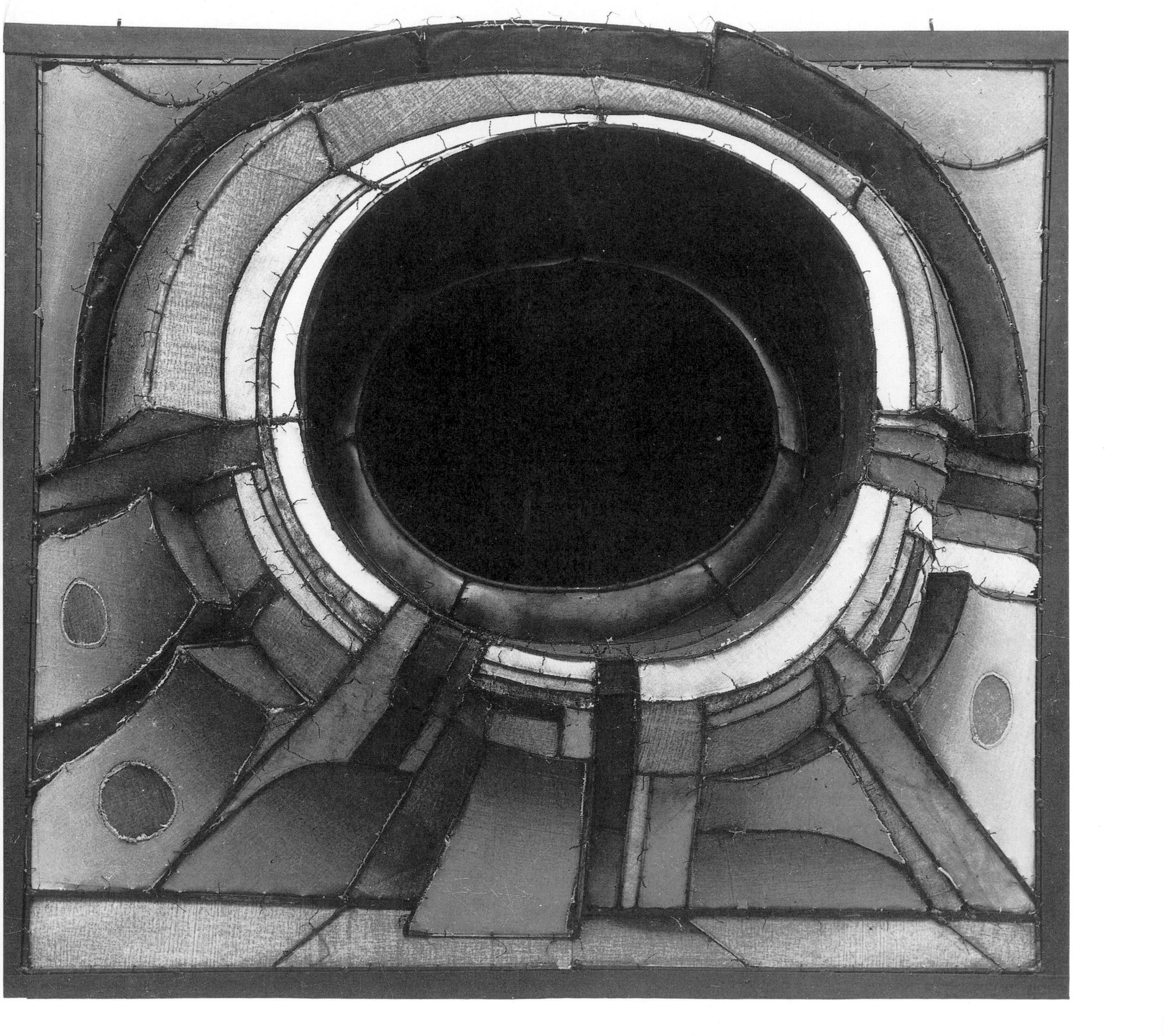

Bontecou's work, they also help to place it in its proper chronological setting which is somewhere between the mid-20th Century and now.

What is left? It needs asserting that this artist is telling a terrible story, oft repeated, that we live in self-destructive times and that they have somehow harnessed the power of the machine (or something very like it) to act, not with us, but virtually independently to proliferate a state of sado-masochism that is fundamentally corrupt. Not perhaps for sado-masochists, but clearly for everyone else. Grim warnings are maybe unappealing, but this in no way reduces their relevance.

On the credit side, Lee Bontecou's constructions and drawings are original, striking and possessed of a personal beauty that translates them, without psychological hang-ups, into the world of art where they belong.

—Sheldon Williams

BOOTH, Peter.

Australian. Born in Sheffield, England, in 1940; emigrated to Australia in 1958. Studied at the Sheffield College of Art, 1956–57, and National Gallery School, Melbourne, 1962–65. Painter: lives and works in Melbourne. Agent: Pinacotheca, Richmond. Address: c/o Pinacotheca, 10 Waltham Place, Richmond, Victoria 3121, Australia

Individual Exhibitions:

1969 Pinacotheca, Melbourne
Central Street Gallery, Sydney
1970 Pinacotheca, Melbourne
1972 Pinacotheca, Melbourne
1973 Chapman Powell Gallery, Melbourne
1974 Chapman Powell Gallery, Melbourne
1975 Pinacotheca, Melbourne
1976 Monash University Gallery, Melbourne
Project 12: Peter Booth, Art Gallery of New South Wales, Sydney
Pinacotheca, Melbourne
1977 Pinacotheca, Melbourne
1978 Pinacotheca, Melbourne
1979 Pinacotheca, Melbourne
1980 Pinacotheca, Melbourne
1981 Pinacotheca, Melbourne
1982 *Works by Peter Booth and Rosalie Gascoigne,* at the *Biennale,* Venice
1984 Museum of Modern Art, New York
Guggenheim Museum, New York
1987 CDS Gallery, New York

Selected Group Exhibitions:

1968 *The Field,* National Gallery of Victoria, Melbourne (travelled to the Art Gallery of New South Wales, Sydney)
1973 *Recent American Art,* Art Gallery of New South Wales, Sydney
1976 *Minimal Art,* National Gallery of Victoria, Melbourne
Drawing: Some Definitions, Ewing and George Paton Galleries, University of Melbourne
1979 *Third Biennale of Sydney: European Dialogue,* Art Gallery of New South Wales, Sydney
1981 *Australian Perspecta 1981: A Biennial Survey of Contemporary Australian Art,* Art Gallery of New South Wales, Sydney
1982 *Eureka! Artists from Australia,* Serpentine Gallery, London

Collections:

Australian National Gallery, Canberra; National Gallery of Victoria, Melbourne; Monash University Art Gallery, Melbourne; Geelong Art Gallery, Victoria; Ballarat Fine Art Gallery, Victoria; Bendigo Art Gallery, Victoria; Mornington Peninsula Art Gallery, Mornington, Victoria; Art Gallery of South Australia, Adelaide; Art Gallery of New South Wales, Sydney; Queen Victoria Museum and Art Gallery, Launceston, Tasmania.

Publications:

On BOOTH: books—*Project 12: Peter Booth,* catalogue broadsheets, with text by Frances Lindsay, Sydney 1976; *Australian Perspecta 1981,* exhibition catalogue, with text by Bernice Murphy, Sydney 1981; *Australia: Venice Biennale 1982: Works by Peter Booth and Rosalie Gascoigne,* exhibition catalogue, with an essay by Gary Catalano, Sydney 1982; *Eureka! Artists from Australia,* exhibition catalogue, with essays by Nancy D. H. Underhill, Ian Burn and Paul Taylor, London 1982; articles—"Peter Booth" by Frances Lindsay in *Art and Australia* (Sydney), vol. 16, no. 1, 1978; "Images of Tradition" by Gary Catalano in *The Australian Arts Today,* edited by John Colmer, London 1980.

I feel that my work has to speak for itself, and that the viewer should be free to make his/her own interpretations.

—Peter Booth

Like those of many Australian artists who began to exhibit in the late 1960's, Peter Booth's early works were decidedly minimal in appearance. Characteristically his paintings of the time often contained nothing more than a black rectangle bounded on its upper horizontal and two vertical sides by a thin strip of lighter-toned canvas. During the past 6 or 7 years the

Peter Booth: ***Untitled*****, 1982**

Jonathan Borofsky: Installation at the Museum Boymans-van Beuningen, Rotterdam, 1982

appearance of his work has greatly altered. Figurative images are now to the fore. Yet in one important sense Booth's concerns have not changed, for human society is still the major theme of his work. While the blank facades of his early paintings gave symbolic form to the alienating power of society, his more recent paintings present a more direct image of society's tensions and conflicts.

This change has certainly been facilitated by his obsessive graphic activity. Born in the English industrial city of Sheffield, Booth has continually sketched the industrial landscapes of his adopted Melbourne. Even an unpractised eye can see the similarities between the proportions of his early minimal paintings and those found in the facades of the factories and warehouses which he has sketched. A further influence on his work stems from his interest in certain romantic and symbolist writers of the 19th century. William Blake is of particular importance to him. The influence of Blake's graphic illustrations can be discerned in Booth's drawings of the mid-1970's. In these drawings Booth first unveiled many of the specific images to be found in his current paintings—the winding roads, the fire-engulfed monoliths, the totemic symbols.

For a number of years now Booth has recorded his dreams in pictorial form. His recent paintings can often be traced back to these dream images. By combining such material with scenes or incidents directly experienced, Booth attempts to show what it is like to be alive in our day and age. His is the ambition of most romantic artists: to be true to one's self, to be true to one's time.

—Gary Catalano

BOROFSKY, Jon(athan).

American. Born in Boston, Massachusetts, in 1942. Educated at Carnegie Mellon University, Pittsburgh, B.F.A. 1964; Ecole de Fontainebleau, France, Summer 1964; and Yale School of Art and Architecture, New Haven, Connecticut, M.F.A. 1966. Independent artist, New York, and now California, since 1966. Teacher, School of Visual Arts, New York, 1969–77, and California Institute of the Arts, Valencia, since 1977. Agent: Paula Cooper Gallery, New York. Address: c/o Paula Cooper Gallery, 155 Wooster Street, New York, New York 10012, U.S.A.

Individual Exhibitions:

1975 Paula Cooper Gallery, New York
1976 *Matrix 18,* Wadsworth Atheneum, Hartford, Connecticut
Paul Cooper Gallery, New York
1977 University of California at Irvine
1978 Protetch-McIntosh Gallery, Washington, D.C.
Thomas Lewallen Gallery, Los Angeles
University of California Art Museum, Berkeley
Corps de Garde, Groningen, Netherlands
Projects Gallery, Museum of Modern Art, New York
1979 Paula Cooper Gallery, New York
INK: Halle für Internationale Neue Kunst, Zurich
Portland Center for the Visual Arts, Oregon
1980 Paula Cooper Gallery, New York
Hayden Gallery, Massachusetts Institute of Technology, Cambridge
1981 Contemporary Arts Museum, Houston
Galerie Rudolf Zwirner, Cologne
Kunsthalle, Basel
Institute of Contemporary Arts, London
1982 Museum Boymans-van Veuningen, Rotterdam
Museum van Hedendaagse Kunst, Ghent, Belgium
Paula Cooper Gallery, New York
Gemini G.E.L., Los Angeles
Friedrich Gallery, Berne
1983 Kunstmuseum, Basel
Galleria dell'Ariete Grafica, Milan
Akron Art Museum, Ohio
Paula Cooper Gallery, New York
Gemini G.E.L., Los Angeles

1984 University of Miami, Coral Gables
Louisiana Museum, Humlebaek, Denmark
Israel Museum, Jerusalem
Moderna Museet, Stockholm
Kunsthalle, Bielefeld, West Germany
Carl Solway Gallery, Cincinnati
Seattle Art Museum, Washington
Philadelphia Museum of Art, Pennsylvania
Gallery Watari, Tokyo
Galerie Susanna Kulli, St. Gallen, Switzerland
1985 Philadelphia Museum of Art, Pennsylvania (travelled to New York; Berkeley, California; Minneapolis; Washington, D.C.; Los Angeles, 1985–86)
Gemini G.E.L., Los Angeles
1986 St. Louis Art Museum, Missouri
Gemini G.E.L., Los Angeles
Harvard University Art Museum, Cambridge, Massachusetts
Paula Cooper Gallery, New York
Heath Gallery, Atlanta, Georgia
Milwaukee Art Museum, Wisconsin (travelled to Des Moines Art Center, Iowa)
1987 Cathedral of St. John the Divine, New York
Metropolitan Museum of Art, Tokyo (travelled to Shiga, Japan)
Galerie Yvon Lambert, Paris
Gallery Watari, Tokyo

Selected Group Exhibitions:

1974 *Drawing and Other Work,* Paula Cooper Gallery, New York
1976 *Soho,* Akademie der Kunste, West Berlin (travelled to the Louisiana Museum, Humleback, Denmark)
1977 *New York: The State of Art,* New York State Museum, Syracuse
Surrogates/Self-Portraits, Holly Solomon Gallery, New York
1978 *Contemporary Drawing, New York,* University of California Art Museum, Santa Barbara
1979 *Visionary Images,* Renaissance Society, University of Chicago
10 Artists: Artists Space, Neuberger Museum, State University of New York at Purchase
1983 *Back to the USA,* Rheinisches Landesmuseum, Bonn (travelled to Lucerne and Stuttgart)
1985 *Modern Machines: Recent Kinetic Sculpture,* Whitney Museum, New York
1987 *Berlinart,* Museum of Modern Art, New York (travelled to San Francisco Museum of Modern Art)

Collections:

Whitney Museum, New York; Museum of Modern Art, New York; BankAmerica Corporation, San Francisco; Philadelphia Museum of Art, Pennsylvania; Commodities Corporation, Princeton, New Jersey; Tate Gallery, London.

Publications:

On BOROFSKY: books—*6 Years: The Dematerialization of the Art Object from 1966 to 1972* by Lucy Lippard, New York 1973; *Jon Borofsky: Matrix 18,* exhibition catalogue, with text by Mark Rosenthal, Hartford, Connecticut 1976; *Contemporary Drawing, New York,* exhibition catalogue, Santa Barbara, California 1978; *Drawings: A Contemporary Approach* by Claudia Betti and Teel Sale, New York 1980; *Drawing: The Pluralist Decade,* with an introduction by Janet Kardon, Philadelphia 1980; *20 Artists: Yale School of Art 1950–1970,* exhibition catalogue, by Irving Sandler, New Haven, Connecticut 1981; *Jonathan Borofsky: Dreams 1973–81,* exhibition catalogue with essay by Joan Simon, London and Basel 1981; *Jonathan Borofsky: Zeichnungen 1960–1983,* exhibition catalogue with texts by C. Geelhaar and D. Koepplin, Basel 1983; *Jonathan Borofsky,* exhibition catalogue with essays by Mark Rosenthal and Richard Marshall, Philadelphia and New York 1984; *Jonathan Borofsky: New Works,* exhibition catalogue with introduction by Peter Nisbet, Cambridge Massachusetts 1986; *Jonathan Borofsky: Dreams,* Tokyo 1987; *Borfosky: Drawings, Printings and Multiples,* exhibition catalogue with essay by Mark Rosenthal, Tokyo 1987; articles—"Jonathan Borofsky at 2,096,974" in *Artforum* (New York), November 1974; "Before the Reason of Images: The New Work of Jon Borofsky" in *Arts* (New York), October 1976; "Jon Borofsky's Dream Language" in *Artweek* (Oakland, California), 23 April 1977; "Jon Borofsky" by Philip Smith in *Arts Magazine* (New York), March 1978; "Energism: An Attitude" by Ronny H. Cohen in *Artforum* (New York), September 1980; "Art: Transformations of Jonathan Borofsky" by John Russell in the *New York Times,* 24 October 1980; "Strike: A Project by Jonathan Borofsky" in *Artforum* (New York), February 1981; "A Walk Through Borofsky's Brain" by Nancy Grimes in *Artnews* (New York), Summer 1985.

Jonathan Borofsky's installation at the L.A. County Museum, 1981, included a large figure painted on both wall and ceiling. The image had giant rabbit ears, a haunted face, and eyes which were circled in a deadened, exacerbated state. He presented a flying man at Basel's Kunsthalle, and a running man in the Hayden Gallery, M.I.T. At Paula Cooper Gallery he painted legions of black-streaked humans which hurried over the wall. Also installed was a ping-pong table set in the middle of the space, along with assorted debris, a stopped black human form, large scissors, and 80 to 100 other strewn objects attached to the installation. Also at Basel: a 26 foot high, two-dimensional planar sculpture, which is Borofsky's hammering man, with a hand-held object, head-hung, feet plodding, a techno-cave man, an emblematic cut-out.

Borofsky's work is shadowy. At first one thinks the work could be a mistake, since the painting is often done on the gallery walls. Even in his sculptural work, objects generally appear awry. Soon, though, the relationship between the clear, interior lit gallery space becomes apparent against the underlife of Borofsky's mammoth figures. The images and the people are private possessions of Borofsky's; therein lies their unfocused dream-like reference. They are exposed interior beings in which a particular imagination chooses as it wants, rather than as it dreams.

For years Borofsky worked with numbers, counting incessantly. He literally wrote out numbers onto pieces of paper, reaching over two million in several years. He still occasionally counts and is now past three million. This pile of sheets of numbers was exhibited in Borofsky's first New York show at Artists Space. Later Borofsky learned to use numbers as numerical signification, as a "signature" next to his imagery. This impersonal quality of signature assisted in placing his imagery within a larger opus, similar to the type of posthumous textual studies usually written and catalogued by scholars. In a sense Borofsky was creating the categorization of his work, if not the analysis, at an early stage.

Most of Borofsky's work belies bourgeois scale and therefore "civilized" dwellings. The rooms and buildings are appropriately the wrong size for the work: either they are too small or misshaped for the quantity of strewn objects exhibited. The work is not hesitant, though obviously the sign of odd inward intelligence, a fulfilled combination of form turning into crazed function. The rational mind explains itself inside out in Borofsky's work. "Self-Portrait in Closet at 2490197" was shown at the Morgan Thomas Gallery in Los Angeles, painted over and also inside of a closet, with the closet door ajar. The blunt, dark markings picture Borofsky with a downcast gaze, a hat and its brim, closed and tight lips, and the closet door which opens and closes through the portrait, suggesting certain transparencies. The portrait is softer in tone than the rest of the work.

—John Robinson

BORY, Jean-Francois.

French. Born in Paris, 2 May 1938. Studied animal physiology at the Université de Paris, 1956 58. Served as infantryman in the 54th Battalion of the French Army, in Ouarsenis, Algeria, 1958–61. Worked as a barman, Paris 1962, as re-writer, Association Francais du Presse, Paris 1963. Independent artist, Paris since 1964. Agent: Galerie Lara Vincy, 41 rue de Seine, 75007 Paris. Address: 85 rue St. Dominique, 75007 Paris, France.

Individual Exhibitions:

1970 Galleria Il Canale, Venice
Galleria Santandrea, Milan
Galleria Studio Brescia, Brescia, Italy
1972 Gallerie Les Mains Libres, Paris
Galerie Lara Vincy, Paris
1985 Galerie J. et J. Donguy, Paris
1986 Galerie J. et J. Donguy, Paris

Selected Group Exhibitions:

1967 *Biennale de Paris,* Musée d'Art Moderne, Paris (and 1969, 1971)
1972 *Biennale,* Venice
Concrete Poetry, Stedielijk Museum, Amsterdam
Contemporanea, Parcheggie Villa Borghese, Rome
1986 *Biennale,* Venice

Collections:

Centre Georges Pompidou, Paris; Stedelijk Museum, Amsterdam; Museo d'Arte Moderna, Bologna, Italy.

Publications:

By BORY: books—*Once Again,* New York 1967; *Post-Scriptum,* Paris 1970; *Made in Machine,* Brescia, Italy 1970; *Logorinthe,* Rome 1970; *Untitled,* Paris 1973; *Un Auteur sous Influence,* Paris 1986; articles—"Proposition pour une lecture de Jean-Francois Bory" in *Artitudes* (St. Jeannet), July/September 1972; "La Poésie Visuelle dans le Monde" in *Opus International* (Paris), January 1973; "Hommage à Pavlov" in *Artitudes International* (St. Jeannet), February/March 1973; "Le dechet du festa" in *Artitudes International* (St. Jeannet), June/September 1975.

On BORY: book—*Bory, L'Anarchiste,* exhibition catalogue, with text by Alain Borer, Paris 1986; articles—"Portrait of Bory as a Young Bory" by Richard Kostelanetz in *Art International* (Lugano, Switzerland), August/September 1971; "J. F. Bory: un classico" by G. Lista in *NAC* (Milan), February 1973; "Jean-Francois Bory" in *Chroniques de l'Art Vivant* (Paris), March 1973; "Jean-Francois Bory ou l'Ubiquite" by P. Bourgeade in *Opus International* (Paris), September 1973; "Jean-Francois Bory" by S. Dupey in *Art Press* (Pariis), September 1973; "Logique de Jean-Francois Bory" by P. Bourgeade in *Artitudes International* (St. Jeannet), December 1973/March 1974; "Jean-Francois Bory" in *Opus International* (Paris), April 1975.

End of the book, end of the world, of the work, of the world.

—Jean-Francois Bory

BOSHIER, Derek.

British. Born in Portsmouth, Hampshire, in 1937. Studied at the Yeovil School of Art, Somerset, 1953–57; Royal College of Art, London, 1959–62. Served in the British Army, 1957–59. Lecturer, Central School of Art and Design, and Hornsey College of Art, London, since 1963. Visiting Lecturer, University of Victoria, 1975; and University of Houston, 1980–81. Recipient: Arts Council Young Contemporaries Award, 1961; Indian Government Scholarship, 1962; Peter Stuyvesant Foundation Travel Bursary to the United States, 1964; British Government Cultural

Jean-Francois Bory: *Opera*, 1986

Exchange Programme Grant, 1968; Minister of Affairs Prize, *7th Print Biennale,* Tokyo, 1970; Film Grant, Arts Council of Great Britain, 1970. Agents: Angela Flowers, London; Robin Cronin, Houston, Texas. Address: 25 Ladbroke Gardens, London W11, England.

Individual Exhibitions:

1962 *Image in Revolt,* Grabowski Gallery, London (with Frank Bowling)
1965 Robert Fraser Gallery, London
Galerie Aujourd'hui, Brussels
1967 Galerie Bischofberger, Zurich
1968 Robert Fraser Gallery, London
1970 Edizioni O, Milan
Nigel Greenwood Gallery, London
Galerie Bucholtz, Munich
Galerie Varenne, Paris
1971 Hayward Gallery, London
1972 Arnolfini Gallery, Bristol (toured the U.K., 1972–73)
1974 Angela Flowers Gallery, London
1975 Art Net, London
Whitworth Art Gallery, Manchester
Angela Flowers Gallery, London
1976 Angela Flowers Gallery, London
1977 Peterloo Gallery, Manchester
1979 Felicity Samuel Gallery, London
1980 Angela Flowers Gallery, London
1981 Angela Flowers Gallery, London
Painting 1980–81, Contemporary Art Museum, Houston
Muzeum Sztuki, Lodz, Poland
1982 Cronin Gallery, Houston, Texas
Institute of Contemporary Arts, London
1983 Bluecoat Gallery, Liverpool, Merseyside
Texas Gallery, Houston
1985 Edward Totah Gallery, London
Texas Gallery, Houston
1986 Totah-Stelling Art, New York
1987 Edward Totah Gallery, London
Texas Gallery, Houston

Selected Group Exhibitions:

1963 *3rd Biennale des Jeunes,* Paris
1964 *The New Generation,* Whitechapel Art Gallery, London
1967 *New Shapes of Color,* Stedelijk Museum, Amsterdam (toured the Netherlands)
1969 *12 British Artists,* Kunstlerhaus Galerie, Vienna
1973 *Henry Moore to Gilbert and George,* Victoria and Albert Museum, London
1977 *British Painting 1952–1977,* Royal Academy of Art, London
1979 *A Generation,* Scottish National Gallery of Modern Art, Edinburgh
1982 *The Human Figure,* Contemporary Arts Center, New Orleans
1984 *Content: A Contemporary Focus,* Hirshhorn Museum, Washington, D.C.
1987 *Still-Life: Theme and Variation,* Glassel School of Art, Houston, Texas

Collections:

Arts Council of Great Britain, London; Victoria and Albert Museum, London; City Art Gallery, Manchester, National Museum of Wales, Cardiff; Museum of Modern Art, New York.

Publications:

By BOSHIER: books—*16 Situations,* London 1971; *6 Cities* (series of postcards), London 1972; articles—"Derek Boshier on His Constructed Prints: A Suite of Three, in Conversation with Christopher Fox" in *Studio International* (London), December 1970; statement in *Studio International* (London), November 1973; films—*Link,* 1970; *Circle,* 1971; *Reel,* 1973; *Watch,* 1975.

On BOSHIER: books—*Derek Boshier,* exhibition catalogue, London 1973; *Boshier,* exhibition catalogue, Manchester 1975; *Lives: An Exhibition of Artists Whose Work Is Based on Other People's Lives,* selected by Boshier, exhibition catalogue, London 1979; *Derek Boshier: Painting 1980–81,* exhibition catalogue, by Cheryl Brutvan, Houston 1981; articles—"Derek Boshier: Hayward Gallery" by Eddie Wolfram in *Arts Review* (London), December 1970; "Derek Boshier Situations" in *Creative Camera* (London), June 1971; "The Impossibility of Scùlpture" by Paul Overy in *The Times* (London), June 1973.

Of the class of 1962 at the Royal College of Art, taking his diploma with David Hockney and Peter Phillips, Derek Boshier was one of the successes of the Pop movement in England. With Frank Bowling he showed under the title *Image in Revolt* at the Grabowski Gallery, London, in the same year. In large canvases he expressed his personal rejection of the conventional format for pictures. Chiefly the motives were those of printed symbols, many of them from commercial packaging and cheap comics.

This employment of ready-made and widely known characters from the media aligned the work with the proletarian connection in Pop art, though this aspect was bent by Boshier to narrative content concerned with S.F. and a fanciful quasi-surrealist effect. Large-scale compositions emphasized the repetitive elements, mostly tiny figures representing mankind in situations of symbolic compulsive direction or motivation.

Fascinated by ambiguities, Boshier saw some of his earlier Pop paintings as embodying social comment based on autobiographical experience, though this was not always explicit. Strangely enough, after he had gone to India for a year on a scholarship, he completely rejected the figurative element in his painting. In *The New Generation* exhibition at the Whitechapel Gallery in 1964, Boshier's post-Indian paintings echoed more the eye-dazzling stripes and hard-edge patterns of Bridget Riley and Frank Stella than any assimilated visual data from the East. The use of shaped stretchers for surfaces that projected beyond the usual rectangular enclosure implied a possible allegorical meaning in the shape of the canvas. The colour bands, stepped and curbed, alternately straight and diagonal, embody a symbolism more subtle than any exercise in abstract Op organization. The Pop allusion (that of a giant table game akin to "Monopoly") is played down in a cool context, but the metaphors can be no less than intentional. Traffic signs, painted wall and street insignia and directions—these are all part of the universal eye-reaction vocabulary.

In common with several of his generation, Boshier is concerned less with a medium for its own character than for its capacity to carry the message he loads into it. Experiments in plastic constructions, though inconclusive, indicated his versatility and adaptability

Derek Boshier: ***Frightened Cowboy*, 1986**

in approach. He says: "Art is about ideas, and your medium is the medium that is best suited to your ideas." As a friend of poets and writers, he is interested in film-making and in writing for communication—e.g., fiction. He has written a novel, and—as he demonstrates—his approach to art is open-ended.

G. S. Whittet

BOTERO, Fernando.

Colombian. Born Fernando Botero Angulo in Medellin, Antioquia, 19 April 1932. Educated at primary and secondary schools in Medellin, 1938–49; Liceo de la Universidad de Antioquia, Medellin, 1950, baccalaureate; studied at the Real Academia de Bellas Artes, San Ferdinando, Spain, and copied paintings of Goya, Veláquez, and others at the Museo del Prado, Madrid, 1952; studied fresco painting at the Accademia San Marco, and art history, under Roberto Longhi, at the Università degli Studi, Florence, 1953. Married Gloria Zea in 1955 (divorced, 1960); children: Fernando, Lina, and Juan Carlos; married Cedilia Zambrano in 1964 (divorced, 1975); son: Pedro (died in auto crash, 1974). Worked as an illustrator for the Sunday Literary Supplement of *El Colombiano*, Medellin, 1948– 51; worked briefly as a set designer for the Compania Lope de Vega touring Spanish theatre group, 1950. Independent artist since 1951: lived in Bogota, then moved to Tolú on the Gulf of Morrosquillo, also painting at Coveñas and the islands of San Bernardo, 1951; returned to Bogota, then travelled to Barcelona, and lived in Madrid, 1952–53; spent summers in Paris, 1953–54; lived and established studio in Florence, and travelled throughout northern Italy to study fresco sites, 1953–54; influenced strongly by exhibition of the works of Piero della Francesca, Paolo Uccello, Andrea del Castagno, and Domenico Veneziano, Florence, 1954; returned to Bogota, 1955; lived in Mexico City, 1956–57; travelled to New York and Washington, D.C., 1957, 1958; lived in Bogota, 1957–60; commissioned by Banco Central Hipotecario to paint a fresco in its Medellin branch, 1960; lived in New York, 1961–73: rented a loft studio at MacDougal and Third Streets in Greenwich Village, 1961–64, moved to Tomkins Square on Lower East Side, 1963–71, built summer house and studio on Stephen's Hand Pass Road, Easthampton, Long Island, and established a studio at 214 West 14th Street, 1964–72, moved to 30 Fifth Avenue, 1971; rented an apartment in Paris, and established studio in Bogota, 1971; rented studio on rue Monsieur-le-Prince, Paris, and bought house in which to spend summers in Cajicá, north of Bogota, 1972; has lived in Paris since 1973; concentrated almost entirely on sculpture, 1976 77; established Sala Pedro Botero, with 16 of his works, at the Museo de Zea, Medellin, 1977; established and maintains studio on rue du Dragon in building formerly housing the Académie Julian, Paris, since 1978. Professor of Painting, Escuela de Bellas Artes, Universidad Nacional, Bogota, 1958–60. Recipient: First Prize for Painting, *Salon Anual de Artistas Colombianos*, Bogota, 1958; Colombian Section Award, *Guggenheim International Award Exhibition*, New York, 1960; Andrés Bello Award, President of Venezuela, 1975. Cruz de Boyacá for service to Colombia, Government of Antioquia, 1977. Agent: Marlborough Fine Art, New York. Address: c/o Marlborough Fine Art, 40 West 57th Street, New York, New York 10019, U.S.A.

Individual Exhibitions:

1951 Galerias de Arte Foto-Estudio Leo Matiz, Bogota
1952 Galerias de Arte de Leo Matiz, Bogota
1955 Biblioteca Nacional, Bogota (travelled to Club de Profesionales, Medellin, Colombia)
1957 Galeria Antonio Souza, Mexico City
Fernando Botero of Colombia, Pan American Union, Washington, D.C.
1958 *Oleos*, Galeria Antonio Souza, Mexico City
Recent Oils, Watercolors, Drawings, Gres Gallery, Washington, D.C.
1959 *Obras Recientes*, Biblioteca Nacional, Bogota
1960 Gres Gallery, Washington, D.C.
1961 Galeria de Arte El Callejón, Bogota
1962 Gres Gallery, Chicago
The Contemporaries, New York
1964 *Obras Recientes*, Museo de Arte Moderno, Bogota
Bosquejos Realidades, Galeria Arte Moderno, Bogota
1965 *Recent Works*, Zora Gallery, Los Angeles
1966 Staatliche Kunsthalle, Baden-Baden, West Germany (travelled to the Galerie Buchholz, Munich)
Ölbilder und Zeichnungen, Galerie Brusberg, Hannover
Recent Works, Milwaukee Art Center
1968 Galeria Juana Mordó, Madrid
Paintings by Fernando Botero and Leopold Richter, Walter Engel Gallery, Toronto
Galerie Buchholz, Munich
1969 Center for Inter-American Relations, New York
Peintures, Pastels, Fusains, Galerie Claude Bernard, Paris
1970 *Bilder 1962–1969*, Staatliche Kunsthalle, Baden-Baden, West Germany (travelled to Haus am Waldsee, Berlin; Städtische Kunsthalle, Dusseldorf; Kunstverein, Hamburg; and Kunsthalle, Bielefeld)
Botero/Coronel/Rodon, Museo de la Universidad de Puerto Rico
Hanover Gallery, London
Botero/Cuevas: Paintings, Drawings. Walter Engel Gallery, Toronto

1971 *Botero/Lindner/Wesselmann: Ausgewähte Bilder, Zeichnungen und Grafik.* Galerie Brusberg, Hannover
1972 Marlborough Gallery, New York
Bleisiftzeichnungen, Sepiazeichnungen, Aquarelle, Galerie Buchholz, Munich
Pastels, Fusains, Sanguines, Galerie Claude Bernard, Paris
1973 *Retrospectiva 1948–1972,* Colegio San Carlos, Bogota
Marlborough Galleria d'Arte, Rome
Botero/Akawie, Pyramid Galleries, Washington, D.C.
1974 *Aquarelle und Zeichnungen,* Galerie Brusberg, Hannover
Sala de Arte, Biblioteca Publica Piloto, Medellin, Colombia
Marlborough Galarie, Zurich
1975 Museum Boymans-van Beuningen, Rotterdam
Galeria Adlec Castillo, Caracas
Marlborough Gallery, New York (travelled to Marlborough Godard, Toronto; and Marlborough Godard, Montreal, 1976)
1976 *Aquarelles et Dessins,* Galerie Claude Bernard, Paris
Museo de Arte Contemporaneo, Caracas
Pyramid Galleries, Washington, D.C.
Arte Independencia, La Galeria de Colombia, Bogota
1977 *Las Sala Pedro Botero,* Museo de Arte Medellin, Colombia
Sculptures, at *FIAC,* Grand Palais, Paris
1978 *Das Plastische Werk,* Galerie Brusberg, Hannover (travelled to Skulpturenmuseum der Stadt Marl, West Germany)
1979 Galerie Isy Brachot, Knokke, Belgium
Musée d'Ixelles, Brussels (travelled to Konsthall, Lund, Sweden; and Sonja Henie-Neils Onstad Foundations, Oslo)
Galerie Claude Bernard, Paris
Galerie Brusberg, Hannover
Hirshhorn Museum and Sculpture Garden, Smithsonian Institution, Washington, D.C. (travelled to the Art Museum of South Texas, Corpus Christi, 1980)
1980 *Aquarelles, Dessins, Sculptures,* Galerie Beyeler, Basle
1981 Marlborough Gallery, New York
Betsy Rosenfield Gallery, Chicago
1982 *Sculpture and Drawings,* Hokin Gallery, Chicago
1983 Galerie Beyeler, Basle
Thomas Segal Gallery, Boston
1984 Proctor Institute, Utica, New York
Everhart Museum, Scranton, Pennsylvania
Cornell University, Ithaca, New York
Purdue University, Lafayette, Indiana
Botero, at the *International Art Expo,* Chicago
1985 National Museum, Bogota, Colombia
Museo de Ponce, Puerto Rico
Marlborough Gallery, New York
1986 Museum of Contemporary Art, Caracas, Venezuela
Kunsthalle der Hypo-Kulturstiftung, Munich
Kunsthalle, Bremen, West Germany
Tokyo Art Gallery, Tokyo
Daimaru Museum, Osaka, Japan
City Art Museum, Niigata, Japan

Selected Group Exhibitions:

1948 *Exposición de Pintores Antioqueños,* Instituto de Bellas Artes, Medellin, Colombia
1952 *Salón Anual de Artistas Colombianos,* Biblioteca Nacional, Bogota (and 1957, 1958, 1959)
1956 *Gulf-Caribbean Art Exhibition,* Museum of Fine Arts, Houston (toured the United States, 1956–57)
1958 *Guggenheim International Award,* Guggenheim Museum, New York (and 1960)
1959 *Botero/Grau/Obregón/Ramirez/Villegas,/Wiedemann,* Galeria de Arte Callejón, Bogota
Arte de Colombia, Galleria Nazionale d'Arte Moderna, Rome (travelled to Liljevalchs Konsthall, Stockholm; Rautenstrauch-Joest-Museum, Cologne; Staatliche Kunsthalle, Baden-Baden; and the Sociedad Española de Amigos del Arte, Madrid)
1965 *The Emergent Decade: Latin American Painting,* Guggenheim Museum, New York (toured the United States and Canada, 1965–67)
1970 *Latin American Paintings and Drawings from the Collection of John and Barbara Duncan,* Center for Inter-American Relations, New York (toured the United States, 1970–72)
1971 *12 Artists from Latin America,* Ringling Museum of Art, Sarasota, Florida
1977 *Recent Latin American Drawings 1969–1976: Lines of Vision,* Center for Inter-American Relations, New York (toured the United States and Philippines, 1977–79)

Collections:

Museo de Zea, Medellin, Colombia; Museo de Arte Moderno, Bogota; Museo de Bellas Artes, Santiago; Museum of Modern Art, New York; Guggenheim Museum, New York; New York University; Baltimore Museum of Art; Neue Pinakothek, Munich; Museo d'Arte Moderno del Vaticano, Rome; Museo de Arte Contemporaneo, Madrid.

Publications:

By BOTERO: books—*Botero,* portfolio of 20 black-and-white reproductions, with an introduction by Walter Engel, Bogota 1952; articles—"Picasso y la Inconformidad en el Arte" in *El Colombiano* (Medellin), 17 July 1949; "Anatomia de Una Locura" in *El Colombiano* (Medellin), 7 August 1949; interview, with Wibke von Bonin, in *Fernando Botero,* exhibition catalogue, New York 1972; interview, with Titia Berlage, in *Fernando Botero,* exhibition catalogue, Rotterdam 1975.

On BOTERO: books—*Fernando Botero,* exhibition catalogue, Bogota 1951; *Botero,* exhibition catalogue, Bogota 1952; *Botero* by Walter Engel, Bogota 1952; *Gulf-Caribbean Art Exhibition,* catalogue, with foreword by Lee Malone and an introduction by José Gómez-Sicre, Houston 1956; *Fernando Botero of Colombia,* exhibition catalogue, Washington, D.C. 1957; *Fernando Botero: Recent Oils, Watercolors, Drawings,* exhibition catalogue, Washington, D.C. 1958; *Botero: Obras Recientes,* exhibition catalogue, Bogota, 1959; *Botero,* exhibition catalogue, Chicago 1962; *Botero: Recent Works,* exhibition catalogue, Los Angeles 1965; *Fernando Botero,* exhibition catalogue, with text by Daniel Robbins, Baden-Baden, West Germany 1966; *Fernando Botero: Recent Works,* exhibition catalogue, with a foreword by Tracy Atkinson, Milwaukee 1966; *The Emergent Decade: Latin American Painters and Painting in the 1960's,* Ithaca, New York 1966; *Paintings by Fernando Botero and Leopold Richter,* exhibition catalogue, Toronto 1968; *Fernando Botero,* exhibition catalogue, with foreword by Stanton Catlin, and essay by Klaus Gallwitz, New York 1969; *Botero: Peintures, Pastels, Fusains,* exhibition catalogue, with text by Fernando Arrabal, Paris 1969; *Botero* by Klaus Gallwitz, Munich 1970; *Botero: Pastels, Fusains, Sanguines,* exhibition catalogue, with an introduction by Jean paget, Paris 1972; *Fernando Botero: Retrospectiva 1948–1972,* exhibition catalogue, with text by Tracy Atkinson, Bogota 1973; *Botero* by Marta Trata, Mexico City 1973; *Fernando Botero* by German Arciniegas, Madrid 1973, translated by Gabriela Arciniegas, New York 1977; *Botero,* exhibition catalogue, by Antonio Hernandez Barrera, Medellin, Colombia 1974; *Fernando Botero,* exhibi-

Fernando Botero: *Man on Horseback,* 1982

tion catalogue, with an introduction by R. Hammacher-van den Brande, Rotterdam 1975; *Fernando Botero*, exhibition catalogue, with an introduction by Sam Hunter, New York 1975; *Los Intocables: Botero, Grau, Negret, Obregón, Ramirez V.* by Fausto Panesso, Bogota 1975; *Botero: Aquarelles et Dessins*, exhibition catalogue, with an introduction by Severo Sarduy, Paris 1976; *Fernando Botero*, exhibition catalogue, with an introduction by Sofia Imber, Caracas, Venezuela 1976; *Botero*, exhibition catalogue, with text by Robert Pinzón, Bogota 1976; *Fernando Botero* by Klaus Gallwitz, New York, London, and Stuttgart 1976; *Modern Art* by Sam Hunter and John Jacobus, New York 1976; *La Sala Pedro Botero*, exhibition catalogue, with text by Belisario Betancur, Medellin, Colombia 1977; *Recent Latin American Drawings 1969–1979: Lines of Vision*, exhibition catalogue, with essays by Barbara Duncan and Damián Bayón, New York 1977; *Fernando Botero: Das Plastische Werk* by Ursula Bode, Hannover 1978; *Fernando Botero*, exhibition catalogue, with text by Marie-Françcoise Carolus-Barré, Brussels 1979; *Fernando Botero*, exhibition catalogue, by Cynthia Jaffee McCabe, with foreword by Abram Lerner, Washington, D.C. 1979; *Fernando Botero: Malerier, Tegninger, Skulpturer*, exhibition catalogue, with texts by Marianne Nanne-Brahammar and Ole Henrik Moe, Oslo 1979; *Botero: Aquarelles, Dessins, Sculptures*, exhibition catalogue, with an introduction by Ernst Beyeler, Basle 1980; *Botero* by Carter Ratcliff, New York 1980.

Fernando Botero is one of those fortunate artists whose subject or style becomes immediately recognizable. His pneumatic nudes and overdressed, adipose children form a personal, fantasy world of undeniable conviction. The combination of obese, exaggerated, human forms, elaborately decorative costumes and the oversweet colours of South American peasant art results in images in which wit and sympathy are undermined by an aggressive irreverence.

It must be noted that the two major influences in Botero's art are Goya and Veláquez. Born in the industrial centre of Colombian life, Medellin, he moved to to Bogota, where he held his first exhibitons, and then entered the Academia in San Ferdinando, Spain. Here the work of the two great Spanish masters had their effect; from Goya he absorbed a critical view of the human comedy, whilst in the meticulously painted, realistic still-lifes, one recognizes the influence of Velázquez. In Europe Botero also studied fresco techniques in Florence, especially impressed by the famous series of wall paintings by Piero della Francesca in Arezzo. These disparate forces in his development were bound into an artistic whole by Botero's love for his native Colombia, whose daily life, religious myths and folk art, descended from the Indians, remain his basic subjects.

The resultant images are curiously enigmatic; he is neither as open a commentator as Goya, nor as willing a participant as Velázquez. On the other hand, nor is he merely a recording camera. Whilst the real world is Botero's point of departure, he feels at liberty to use anti-natural devices common to native art—or to the "primitive" painters of Christian Europe—his own depiction as a tiny figure, carrying palette and brushes, beside a full-length portrait, or his self-portrait on Communion Day, with two tiny devils whispering into his ear.

—Charles Spencer

BOTO, Martha.

Argentinian. Born in Buenos Aires, 27 December 1925. Studied drawing, Academy Prilidiano Pueyrredon, Buenos Aires, 1942–43; Ernesto de la Cracova Superior Academy of Fine Arts, Buenos Aires, 1944–46. Married to Gregorio Vardanega. Independent artist since 1946, producing kinetic sculptures and installations that alter light: has lived and worked in Paris since 1959. Founding Member, Groupe Artistes non-Figurative Argentins, 1956. Recipient: Painting Prize, Museo Quinquella Martin, Buenos Aires, 1947. Agent: Galerie Denise Rene, 196 Boulevard Saint-Germain, 75007 Paris. Address: Atelier 127, 21 rue de l'Admiral-Roussin, 75015 Paris, France.

Individual Exhibitions:

1951	Galerie van Riel et Krayd, Paris (and each year through 1955)
1957	Galeria Galatea Pizarro, Buenos Aires
1960	Galerie H. Buenos Aires
1969	Galerie Denise René, Paris
1970	Galerie Thelen, Essen
1972	La Belle Epine, Val de Marne, France
1976	Centre Culturel, Sceaux, France

Selected Group Exhibitions:

1962	*Trente Argentins de la nouvelle generation*, Galerie Creuze, Paris
1963	*L'Art Lationamericain*, Musée d'Art Moderne, Paris
1964	*Chromocinétisme*, Maison des Beaux-Arts, Paris
1968	*Art Cinétique*, Maison de la Culture, Greenoble, France
1970	*Denise René in London*, Hayward Gallery, London
1971	*Art Argentin*, Kunsthalle, Basel
1973	*Art Cinétique*, Bagneaux, France
1981	*Grands et Jeunes d'Aujourd'hui*, Grand Palais, Paris
1983	*Electra*, Musée d'Art Moderne de la Ville, Paris
1987	*Féerie Cinetique*, Monte Carlo, Monaco

Collections:

Centre Georges Pompidou, Paris; Prefecture of Paris; Museo Nacional de Bellas Artes, Buenos Aires; Torcuato di Tella, Buenos Aires; Recklinghausen Museum, West Germany; Tel-Aviv Museum, Israel.

Martha Boto: *Vallée*, 1982

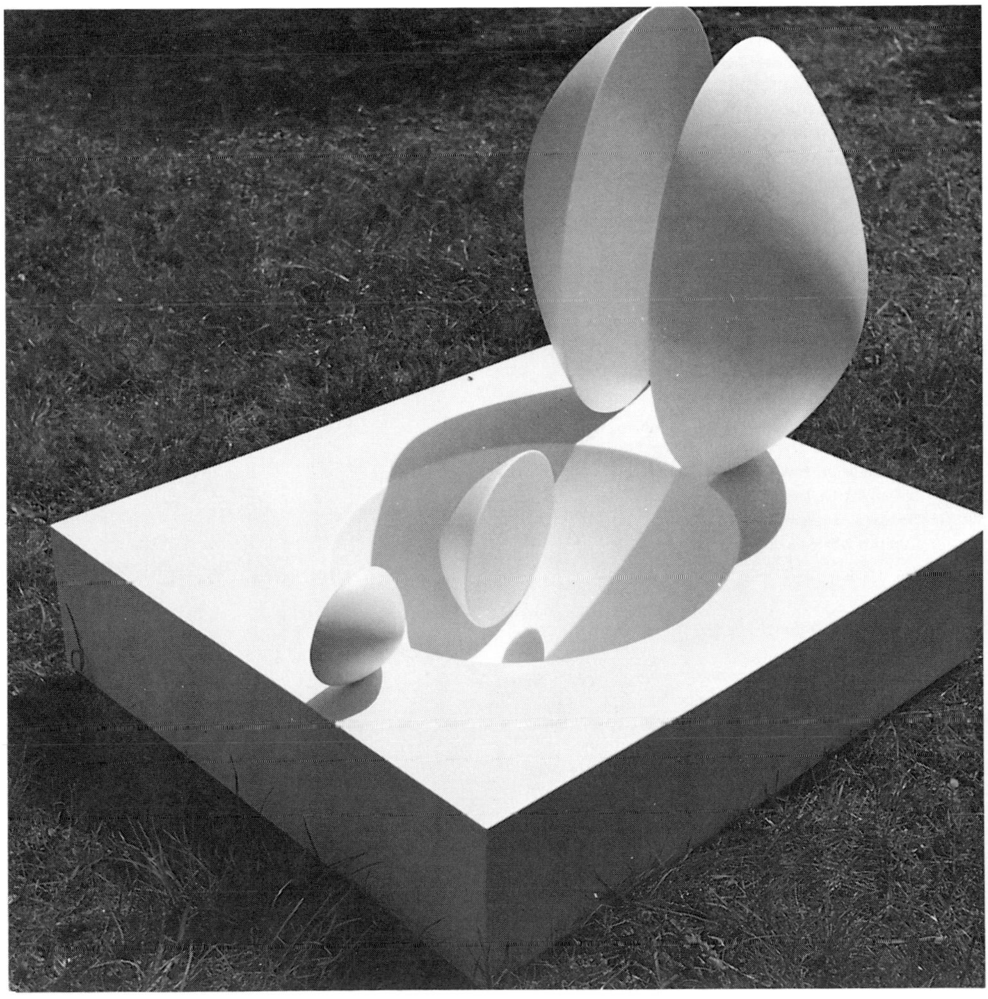

Publications:

On BOTO: books—*Artes y Letras Argentinas* by Cordova Iturburu, Buenos Aires 1961; *Naissance de l'Art cinétique* by Frank Popper, Paris 1966; *Art et Mouvement*, exhibition catalogue, by Denys Chevalier, Montreal 1967; *Martha Boto*, exhibition catalogue, by Michael Ragon, Paris 1969; *L'Art Actuel* by Tronche, Paris 1973; *L'Art Abstrait*, vol. 4, by Michel Ragon and Michel Seuphor, Paris 1975; articles—"L'Art de la lumiére artificielle" by Frank Popper in *L'Oeil* (Paris), December 1966; "Buenos Aires, nouvelle capitale artistique" by Michel Ragon in *Jardin des Arts* (Paris), April 1967; "Dalla Francia con amore" by Ettore Sottsas in *Domus* (Milan), July 1967; "Lumiére et mouvement" by Frank Popper in *Art Cinétique à Paris*, exhibition catalogue, Paris 1967.

Ever since we evolved into true human beings, we have been able to perceive or intuit the relationships which govern the cosmos, with its mysterious systems of energy and equilibrium. We are part of this evolving whole, and the interplay of permanence and change forms the very basis of our lives. The artist is the person who recognizes his place in this system and is able to reveal it to others.

From the very beginning, when I did my first impressionistic paintings of the natural world, I was fascinated by motion, color and light, and have always tried to reveal their sensuousness and evanescent rhythms. During my surrealist period, which was a natural reaction to my slavery to realism, I abandoned representation and sought to express the irrational and unconscious by means of symbolic figures. Thus by a more or less logical progression, I was drawn towards abstraction and a concern for spatial relationships.

I now became eager to escape from flat surfaces. I experimented with mobiles moving in space and with transparent construction which contained moving, colored water. The impulse to control light, color and

motion, and to see natural movements in their relationship to space and time brought me to new aesthetic horizons. With my kinetic works I am now trying to create analogies to the underlying processes of cosmic motion.

I have tried to achieve this by two primary means. First, I have projected shifting forms on flat surfaces, thereby creating a sense of sudden changes, of appearances and disappearances, of transformations and luminous disclosures of changing rhythmic motions. Second, I have created various kinds of tubes, discs and mirrored surfaces—over which lights are programmed to play—in order to produce shimmering labyrinths and color and movement. A fixed structure is thus dissolved and diffused into a myriad of images, sometimes by means of mirrors placed on its sides or along its curved surfaces.

I have also experimented with translucent columns and mobiles, producing groups of reflections which once again express the relationships which exist between forms and space and between forms and time. I have sometimes used little steel balls which move through transparent structures at different rates of speed and with different kinds of natural rhythms. All of these attempts to integrate movement, light, color and space give my work a kind of instability which is sometimes hypnotic for viewers, sometimes pleasant—and sometimes disquieting. At the moment I am working with related groups of shapes, combining different volumes and white polygraphisms to suggest figures which have in themselves a principle of motion or seem to be moved by wind and water. What dominates my work is a sense of free forms, joyous, expressive, humanized; I have created my kinetic and illuminated structures to vitalize the urban spaces in which they are placed.

—Martha Boto

Martha Boto belongs to the tradition of South American Constructivism and has taken a prominent part in its conversion into kinetic art. Light and movement appear in all their purity and dynamism in her art, but there is always an underlying formal structure which can be seen or sensed.

Boto's works concentrate upon such features as rapid movement, circular forms and intense luminous effects. The light source itself is constantly moving in many of her works, and this results in a strong impression of contraction and expansion in the interplay of circles and planes, as well as a tendency for forms to appear and disappear, ranging from intensity to diffusion.

Martha Boto's investigation leads from the principle of repetition into the world of reflection and the progressive transformation of the image. In her "chromokinetic" works she has rarely used more than one colour, usually an ultramarine blue or a transparent rose. But the variations of the hues are many. They allow her to add an individual sense of completeness to the distinctive arrangements of movement through the manipulation of transparent light and enable the graphic properties inherent in the circle to emerge.

Boto's environment works realized since 1971 in and around Paris reflect all the accomplishments of the earlier research, yet in these works the sensuality of the rhythm, the hypnotizing variations of speeds, the subtle programmation of form transformation and the original treatment of colour and space take on a new dimension and most clearly demonstrate the interrelationship between the artist's technical/aesthetic achievements and her distinctive personality.

—Frank Popper

BOTSCHUYVER, Theo.

Dutch. Born in Rotterdam, 8 January 1943. Studied at the Academie voor Industriele Vormgeving, Eindhoven, 1960–65. Independent artist, Amsterdam, since 1967: Founder, with Jeffrey Shaw, Eventstructure Research Group (E.R.G.), Amsterdam 1967–82 (with the participation of Sean Wellesley-Miller 1967–69). Guest Lecturer, Department of Architecture, University of Eindhoven, 1970–71. Recipient: Grant from Arts Council, Amsterdam, 1967; Grants from Dutch Ministry of Culture, The Hague, 1970–75. Address: 126 Javastraat, Amsterdam 1094 HP, Netherlands.

Individual Exhibitions: (with E.R.G.)

1967 Sigma Projects, Amsterdam
Sigma Projects, Rotterdam
Casino Communal, Knokke, Belgium
1968 Museum of Modern Art, Oxford
Open-Air display, at the *Brighton Festival*, Sussex
Open-Air display, at the *City of London Festival*
1969 Institute of Contemporary Arts, London
Six Events display, Amsterdam
Six Events display, Rotterdam
St. George's Art Center, Liverpool (with John Latham)
1970 Stedelijk Museum, Amsterdam
1972 National Gallery of Victoria, Melbourne
1973 Pinacotheca Gallery, Melbourne
Tolarno Gallery, Melbourne
1974 Stedelijk Museum, Amsterdam
De Lantaren, Rotterdam
Drama Institute Theatre, Amsterdam
1975 National Bus Company, London (with Artist Placement Group)
1976 Genesis World Tour (with Genesis rock group)
1978 Stitching de Appel, Amsterdam
1979 Koopwaarders Plantsoen, Amsterdam Noord (permanent installation)
1980 De Hoogeberg, Velsen, Netherlands (permanent installation)
1981 Frascati Theatre, Amsterdam (permanent installation)
1982 Scholengemeenschap, Tilburg, Netherlands (permanent installation)

Selected Group Exhibitions:

1968 *Structure Gonfables*, Musée d'Art Moderne, Paris
Contemporary Art from Holland, Kunsthalle, Berne
1969 *Kinetic Objects*, Frans Halsmuseum, Haarlem, Netherlands
1970 *Street Art Programme*, Hannover
1971 *Between 5*, Kunsthalle, Dusseldorf
1972 *British Avant-garde*, Gallery House, London
1974 *Tabarka Festival*, Tunisia
1975 *9th Biennale de Paris*, Musée d'Art Moderne de la Ville, Paris

Collections:

Dutch National Collection, The Hague; City Collection, Haarlem, Netherlands; City Collection, Amsterdam.

Publications:

By BOTSCHUYVER: books—*Evenstructures*, with E.R.G., Delft 1972; *Prospectus for the Strombeeld Foundation*, with E.R.G., Amsterdam 1980; articles—"Inflatable Structures and Participation," with E.R.G., in *Robho* (Paris), Spring 1968; "Concepts for an Operational Art," with E.R.G., in *Arts and Artists* (London), January 1969.

On BOTSCHUYVER: books—*Arthropods* by Jim Burns, New York 1971; *Kunst van Nu*, Amsterdam 1971; *Sonsbeek 71 Report*, Arnhem 1972; *9e Biennale de Paris*, exhibition catalogue, Paris 1975; articles—"Evenstructures" by Albrecht Kwast in *Pneutube*, exhibition catalogue, London 1969; "Evenstructure Research Group" by Ruud Englander in *Mickery Mouth* (Amsterdam), no. 11, 1971; "E.R.G. in Australia" by Terry Smith in *Studio International* (London), October 1972; "Diadrama" by Max Adrian in *Toneel Teatral* (Amsterdam), no. 1, 1974.

In 1980 the Museum Boymans-van Beuningen in Rotterdam published a catalogue with the very meaningful title: *Action, reality and fiction in the arts of the sixties in The Netherlands*. It is a detailed report, put together by students of the Institute of Arthistory, Groningen University. It is a well-documented overview of a roaring period that brought about a lot of good art.

Fluxus and Happening, as well as a typical Dutch phenomenon like the Provo-movement, short-lived collaborations between artists who later would occupy leading, individual positions in a more traditionally oriented artclimate, the whole repertory of artistic expressions that move out of the well-established boundaries, have been put in the correct chronological order. Theo Botschuyver's activities were closely related with this general atmosphere of cultural liberation that reigned during the sixties. They take place at the end of the period and they are, in a way, its closing end because of the organizational dimensions and applied technical facilities.

The first documented project (together with Jeffrey Shaw and Tjebbe van Tijen) was a hundred meter air-filled tube that meandered through a labyrinth-like space that formed the setting for a Happening-like party entitled *Hommage a Clovis Trouille* (1965). This project still had an improvised character, the next one demanded extensive preparation and organization. The title of the project was Corpocinema, executed in Rotterdam and Amsterdam in 1967. From a thirty meter distance slides and films were projected over a large polythene construction that was transparent and that moved, not only in form but in color as well. The audience had access to this moving form and formed part of its totality, overwhelmed. At the same time, for those remaining outside, one was a moving element in this continuously changing form. Five nights different pieces were performed with meaningful titles like *Smokespawn*, *Fluidomatics*, *Jellyquake*, *Foamswell*, *Splattersplode*. In the Amsterdam version a beatband performed a program inside entitled the *Dolly Pond Church of Cacophony*. Corpocinema has been one of the projects coordinated by the Sigma-centre, also responsible for the famous Continuous Drawing (1967) leading from London through Amsterdam to Rotterdam and the *Concerto for three grinding-organs* (1967) on Dam Square, Amsterdam. Together with Jeffrey Shaw, in 1969 Botschuyver initiated the Eventstructure Research Group that recapitulates some elements of the Corpocinema. Large air-filled objects are placed in the streets, as play-things, inviting the people to participate by crawling over them.

—A. F. Wagemans

BOURGEOIS, Louise.

American. Born in Paris, France, 25 December 1911; moved to New York, 1938. Educated at the Lycée Fenelon, Paris, 1932; Sorbonne, Paris, 1932–35; Ecole de Louvre, Paris, 1936–37; Académie des Beaux-Arts, Paris 1936–38; Atelier Bissière, Paris, 1936–37; Académie Julian, Paris, 1938; Atelier Fernand Léger, Paris, 1938; also studied with Marcel Duchamp in New York. Married Robert Goldwater in 1938; children: Michel, Jean-Louis and Alain. Independent artist, New York, since 1938. Taught at the Academie de la Grande Chaumière, Paris, 1937–38; Great Neck Public Schools, New York, 1960; Brooklyn College, New York, 1963, 1968; and Pratt Institute, New York, 1965–67. Professor of Sculpture, School of Visual Arts, New York; Lecturer, Lebanon College, New York University; Critic, New York Studio School. Recipient: National Endowment for the Arts Grant, 1973; Outstanding Visual Arts Achievement Award, Women's Caucus for Art, New York, 1980; Skowhegan Medal, Skowhegan School of Painting and Sculpture, Maine, 1984. Honorary doctorate: Yale University, New Haven, Connecticut,

Louise Bourgeois: *Nature Study—Velvet Eyes*, 1984

1977; Bard College, Annandale-on-Hudson, New York, 1981; Massachusetts College of Art, Boston, 1983; Maryland Art Institute, Baltimore, 1984; The New School, New York, 1987. Agent: Xavier Fourcade Inc., New York; and Max Hutchinson Gallery, 138 Greene Street, New York, New York 10012. Address: c/o Xavier Fourcade Inc., 36 East 75th Street, New York, New York 10021, U.S.A.

Individual Exhibitions:

1945 Bertha Schaefer Gallery, New York
1947 Norlyst Gallery, New York
1949 Peridot Gallery, New York
1950 Peridot Gallery, New York
1953 Peridot Gallery, New York
Allan Frumkin Gallery, Chicago
1959 Cornell University, Ithaca, New York
1964 The Stable Gallery, New York
Rose Fried Gallery, New York
1974 112 Greene Street Gallery, New York
1975 Stable Gallery, New York
1978 *Structures*, Xavier Fourcade Inc., New York
Confrontations, Hamilton Gallery, New York
1979 *Sculptures 1941–53*, Xavier Fourcade Inc., New York
Art Museum, University of California, Berkeley
1980 *The Iconography of Louise Bourgeois*, Max Hutchinson Gallery, New York
Sculpture: The Middle Years 1955–1970, Xavier Fourcade Inc., New York
1981 University of Chicago
1982 Robert Millery Gallery, New York
Museum of Modern Art, New York (retrospective; travelled to Chicago and Akron, Ohio, 1983)
1984 Daniel Weinberg Gallery, Los Angeles
Daniel Weinberg Gallery, San Francisco
Robert Miller Gallery, New York
1985 Serpentine Gallery, London
Galerie Maeght-Lelong, Zurich
Galerie Maeght-Lelong, Paris (retrospective)
1986 Eyes Gallery, Doris Freedman Plaza, New York
Texas Gallery, Dallas
1987 Robert Miller Gallery, New York
Yares Gallery, Scottsdale, Arizona
Taft Museum, Cincinnati (toured the United States, 1987–90)

Selected Group Exhibitions:

1945 *Whitney Annual*, Whitney Museum, New York (and regularly until 1973)
1969 *International Sculpture Biennale*, Carrara, Italy
1975 *200 Years of American Sculpture*, Whitney Museum of American Art, New York
1977 *Permanent Collection of American Art*, Whitney Museum, New York
1980 *The Originals: Women in Art*, Graham Gallery, New York
1981 *Decade of Transition 1940–50*, Whitney Museum, New York
1982 *Sculpture 1982: 20 American Artists*, San Francisco Museum of Modern Art
1983 *Portrait Sculpture*, State University of New York, Buffalo
1985 *Traces: Sculpture and Monuments*, Kunsthaus, Zurich
1987 *Von Chaos und Ordnung der Seele*, Universität Mainz, West Germany

Collections:

Museum of Modern Art, New York; Whitney Museum, New York; New York University; Storm King Arts Center, Mountainville, New York; Rhode Island School of Design, Providence; Detroit Institute of Arts; Musée d'Art Moderne, Paris; National Gallery of Australia, Canberra; Kunstmuseum, Lucerne, Switzerland.

Publications:

By BOURGEOIS: articles—"Louise Bourgeois: A Search for

Gravity," interview with Marcia Pels, in *Art International* (Lugano), October 1979.

On BOURGEOIS: books—*Nature in Abstraction* by John Baur, New York 1958; *American Art of Our Century*, exhibition catalogue, by Lloyd Goodrich and John Baur, New York 1961; *Form and Space; Sculpture in the 20th Century* by Eduard Trier, New York 1968; *The Iconography of Louise Bourgeois*, exhibition catalogue. New York 1980; *Louise Bourgeois* by Deborah Wye, New York 1982; articles—"Some Reflections Prompted by the Recent Work of Louis Bourgeois" by William S. Rubin in *Art International* (Lugano), April 1969, "Louise Bourgeois" by J. P. Marandel in *Art International* (Lugano), December 1971; "Louise Bourgeois from the Inside Out" By Lucy Lippard in *Artforum* (New York), March 1975; "Louise Bourgeois" by Carter Ratcliff in *Art International* (Lugano), November/December 1978; "The Discreet Charm of Louise Bourgeois" in *Art News* (New York), February 1980; "Louise Bourgeois" by Carter Ratcliff in *Vogue* (New York), October 1980.

A study of Louise Bourgeois' work from the late thirties to the present indicates that style and the evolution thereof are not fundamental to her character as an artist. Rather, it reveals the struggle of an individual actively attempting to define herself through her art. Bourgeois looks to herself for inspiration; consequently her work is personal and deeply autobiographical in content. Art functions for her as a psychological outlet, for making art is the process of giving tangible form to, and thus exorcising, the gripping, subconscious states of being that fill one with anxiety. Bourgeois' greatest achievement has been her ability to capture—and animate—the depth of the human psyche within a wide range of inventive and meaningful images.

Most of her prominent themes can be traced back to her years in France when a series of unresolved psychological conflicts governed her imagination. Her art belies the tension of her family life as created by the opposition of a clear-thinking, calm, and nurturing mother, and a powerful, volatile, and oppressive father. The polarity exacted anxiety, pain and anger, emotions that became the sources of Bourgeois's art. The psychological trauma of the war years, during which time her father was wounded, also had an impact on her work. After the war an English tutor caused the Bourgeois family additional problems because of her eventual liaison with Louise's father. The complications inherent in that triangle, the betrayals and primordial jealousies, seem to constitute a convincing origin for the violence in a significant part of her oeuvre.

Bourgeois' career began to take form in the mid-1940's after studying at several schools in France, including the Academie Ransom, the Academie Julian, the Academie de la Grande-Chaumiere, and the Ecole des Beaux-Arts, from 1934 to 1938. Stylistically, by the end of 1944 a grid scheme began to dominate the compositions of her paintings. She has related her use of this surface structure to her early family connections with tapestries and the delineation of their weave. During this period she developed an interest in balancing the formal issues of abstraction with the depiction of symbolic subject matter, a concern which she shared with the Abstract Expressionist tradition. As the decade progressed, Bourgeois' painting began to evolve toward a more personal, quasi-figurative imagery, with an underlying spirit of Surrealism. Her work moved toward the exploration of the reality of the subconscious. In effect, Surrealism encouraged her to tap the complex texture of her personal life as a source for her art.

Not to be overlooked in these early years is Bourgeois' involvement with feminism. The "Femme-Maison" paintings of 1947, portrayals of women with houses perched on their bodies in place of heads, are among her most powerful images. They are also symbols, moving in thematic directions that preoccupy the rest of her career. In them, a woman's sign of identity, her face, has been replaced by a house, implying that domesticity becomes the very definition of these women, since they have no other means by which to speak. Interestingly, the feminist dimension of her early imagery was not recognised until 30 years later.

In 1949 Bourgeois abandoned painting as a medium and began to explore the possibilities of sculpture, with the greatest level of substantiality and physical impact afforded by its three-dimensional nature. By 1950 she had made over thirty sculptures and had achieved a surprising breadth of emotion through an increasingly formal sophistication. Her 1953 piece "Foret" embodied a new sculptural concept that would characterize her formal and thematic development of wood sculpture in the fifties. In this piece Bourgeois crowded a large assemblage of unusual elements together on a single base, suggesting a primordial group of plants. Due to the group's placement on the floor, it seems to be growing, as sprouting seeds or pods. Furthering the theme of growth, Bourgeois exhibited "One and Others" in 1955. With its colourful, separate spools, this piece appears as a garden or bouquet. Yet viewed from certain angles, it takes on the form of a single flower whose blooming petals crate an organic symbol of health and burgeoning fecundity. The title, however, brings the sculpture back to the human world, suggesting individuals of various shapes and sizes huddling in mutual support and interdependence. This technique of clustering and crowding elements on a base is one that Bourgeois has employed persistently as a visual counterpart or symbol for the interactions of groups.

After 1953, Bourgeois participated in no solo shows until 1964 in New York. The highly politicized atmosphere of the 60s may have contributed to the transition of her formal development, as she was actively involved with certain issues. Her work was still an investigation of psychological and symbolic meaning. Yet the entire decade represented a time of wide experimentation with plaster, cement, rubber, latex, plastics, marble, and bronze. She toyed with twisted arrangements, labyrinthine formations, and amorphous masses of plaster or cement. With these eccentric pieces she tried to animate such psychological states as fear, vulnerability, and loss of control. She revived her favourite themes of withdrawl, hiding, protection, sheltering and nurturing. "Lairs," cavernous plaster structures resembling cocoons, illustrate these themes. The 1967 "Landscape" series expanded the format of "Lair," yet they bear the suggestions of human contours which are the beginnings of the sexual works that follow.

During the 60s and 70s, when feminism was gathering strength, sexuality finally emerged explicitly in her work. Her previous definition of woman—that of being helpless, expendable, and utterly without identity—gradually gave way to a new conception tending toward a greater aggressiveness, sophistication, and elegance.

Her work in the 70s seemed to fill a distinct aesthetic need for personal content and meaning well beyond her earlier achievements. "The Destruction of the Father," 1974, a continuation of her earlier preoccupation with the hidden recesses of the plaster "Lairs," was the loudest personal statement of her career. This piece was the reincarnation of a childhood fantasy in which the members of her family dismembered and devoured its self-important, domineering father.

The wide interest in and new recognition of Bourgeois's work in the late 70s and early 80s were demonstrated by several distinguished awards and a series of four exhibitions that focused on earlier periods of her work. She received an honorary degree from Yale University in 1977; an outstanding achievement award from the Women's Caucus for Art in 1980; and a secondary honourary degree from Bard College in 1981. The exhibitions of her early wood figures, her early paintings, and her middle-period sculpture in 1980 allowed Bourgeois to further explore and interpret her former imagery and themes. In conjunction with this work, she continued making new sculpture.

Bourgeois's work is best understood when it is looked at as a significant, singular entity its distinctive features identified, and its essence revealed. This approach defies the intellectual framework of contemporary art history, for it does not progress logically in the development of style. The independent course of Bourgeois's work, its variety of forms, limits the results of this traditional approach.

—Carrie Barker

BOYD, Arthur (Merrick Bloomfield).
Australian. Born in Murrumbeena, near Melbourne, Victoria, 24 July 1920. Educated at State School, Murrumbeena 1927–35; mainly self-taught in art from 1935, but influenced initially by the painter Jo Bergner, Melbourne, 1937–38. Served as cartographic field surveyor, Australian Army, in Melbourne and Bendigo, 1940–43. Married Yvonne Hartland Lennie in 1945; children: Polly, Jamie and Lucy. Worked in paint factory, Melbourne, 1934–36; as potter, Melbourne, 1943–48; independent artist, concentrating exclusively on painting, Melbourne 1948–55, in Beaumaris, Victoria 1955–59, in Nowra, New South Wales, and in London and Woodbridge, Suffolk, since 1959: first theatre decors, Edinburgh, 1963. Recipient: *Encyclopedia Britannica* Award, 1971; Fellowship in Creative Arts, Australian National University, Canberra, 1971–72. Officer, Order of the British Empire (O.B.E.), 1970; Officer, Order of Australia (A.O.), 1979. Agent: Fischer Fine Art, 30 King Street, St. James, London S.W.1. Address: c/o The Commercial Bank of Australia, 34 Piccadilly, London W 1, England; or Box 343, North Nowra, New South Wales 2540, Australia.

Individual Exhibitions:

1937	Westminster Gallery, Melbourne
1939	Royden White Library, University of Melbourne (with Jo Bergner)
1940	Athenaetum Gallery, Melbourne
1949	Kozminsky Galleries, Melbourne
1950	David Jones Gallery, Sydney (retrospective)
1951	Princes Gallery, Melbourne (retrospective, travelled to the Marodian Gallery, Brisbane)
	John Martin's Gallery, Adelaide
1952	Princes Gallery, Melbourne
	Peter Bray Galleries, Melbourne
	Macquarie Galleries, Sydney
1953	Peter Bray Galleries, Melbourne (retrospective)
	Johnstone Gallery, Brisbane
1954	Peter Bray Galleries, Melbourne
1958	Australian Galleries, Melbourne
	South Australian Society of Arts, Adelaide
	Terry Clune Gallery, Sydney
	David Jones Gallery, Sydney
1960	Zwemmer Gallery, London
1962	Whitechapel Art Gallery, London (retrospective)
1963	Australian Galleries, Melbourne
	Terry Clune Gallery, Sydney
	Ceramic Paintings by Arthur Boyd, Zwemmer Gallery, London
1964	National Gallery of South Australia, Adelaide (retrospective)
	Museum of Modern Art and Design, Melbourne (retrospective)
	Bear Lane Gallery, Oxford
1965	Skinner Gallery, Perth
	Australian Galleries, Melbourne
1966	Hungry Horse Art Gallery, Sydney
1969	*Retrospective Exhibition*, Richard Demarco Gallery, Edinburgh
	Arthur Tooth & Sons, London
	Hamet Gallery, London
	Maltzahn Gallery, London
1971	Australian National University, Canberra Skinner Gallery, Perth
1973	*Recent Paintings*, Fischer Fine Art, London
1977	Fischer Fine Art, London

1980 Folkstone Arts Centre, Kent
Fischer Fine Art, London
1981 Britten-Pears School, Aldeburgh, Suffolk
1982 Queensland University, Brisbane
Australian Galleries, Melbourne
1983 Fischer Fine Art, London
1984 Art Gallery of South Australia, Adelaide
1986 Fischer Fine Art, London

Selected Group Exhibitions:

1942 *Contemporary Art Society,* Athenaeum Gallery, Melbourne (and annually until 1946)
1953 *12 Australian Artists*, New Burlington Galleries, London (toured the U.K.)
1955 *Australian Contemporary Painting.* National Gallery of Victoria, Melbourne (toured Australia)
1958 *Biennale*, Venice
1963 *Australian Painting and Sculpture in Europe Today,* New Metropole Arts Centre, Folkstone, Kent (toured West Germany and the Netherlands)
1966 *Australian Painters 1964–66.* Corcoran Gallery, Washington, D.C.
1972 *Australian Prints,* Victoria and Albert Museum, London
1981 *Australian Drawings of the 30s and 40s,* Victoria and Albert Museum, London
1983 *The Boyd Family,* Arts Council Gallery, Canberra
1985 *Representations Abroad,* Hirshhorn Museum, Washington, D.C.

Collections:

Department of External Affairs, Canberra; Australian National University, Canberra; National Gallery of Victoria, Melbourne; Art Gallery of New South Wales, Sydney; National Gallery of Queensland, Brisbane; National Gallery of South Australia, Adelaide; Art Gallery of Western Australia, Perth; Museum and Art Gallery of Tasmania, Hobart; Contemporary Art Society, London; Rhodes House Trust, Oxford.

Publications:

By BOYD: books—*Saint Francis of Assisi*, with text by T. S. R. Boase, London 1968; *Nebuchadnezzar: 34 Paintings and 18 Drawings by Arthur Boyd,* with text by T. S. R. Boase, London 1972; *Jonah*, with poems by Porter, London 1973.

On BOYD: books—*Arthur Boyd*, exhibition catalogue, with text by Bryan Robertson, London 1960; *Australian Painting* by Bernard Smith, Melbourne 1962, rev. ed. as *Australian Painting 1788–1970*, Melbourne 1971; *Arthur Boyd,* exhibition catalogue, with text by Bryan Robertson, London 1962; *Ceramic Paintings by Arthur Boyd,* exhibition catalogue, with text by T. S. R. Boase, Oxford 1964; *Day of My Delight* by Martin Boyd, Melbourne 1965; *Arthur Boyd* by Franz Philipp, London 1967; *Encyclopaedia of Australian Art* edited by Alan MacCulloch, Melbourne 1968; *Arthur Boyd: Retrospective Exhibition* catalogue with texts by T. G. Rosenthal and Cordelia Oliver, Edinburgh, 1969; *Art in Britain 1969–1970* by Edward Lucie-Smith and Patricia White, London 1970; *Arthur Boyd: Etchings and Lithographs* by Imre von Maltzahn, London 1971; *Arthur Boyd: Drawings 1934–1970*, with a foreword by Laurie Thomas, London 1973; *Arthur Boyd: Recent Paintings,* exhibition catalogue, with text by Robert Melville, London 1973; *Outlines of Australian Art: The Joseph Brown Collection* by Daniel Thomas, Melbourne and Sydney 1973, London 1974; *Arthur Boyd,* exhibition catalogue, with an introduction by Robert Melville, Folkestone, Kent 1980; *The Art of Arthur Boyd* by Ursula Hoff, London 1986.

Arthur Boyd: ***Australian Landscape with Pond,*** **1976**

Arthur Boyd is a distinguished member of the remarkable generation of Australian artists who transferred to Britain in the post-war period and made a profound impact on European art. He also typifies the curious phenomenon (discernible in many other artists who move away physically from their origins) whereby aspects of native culture and subject-matter become more profoundly realised as a result of transplantation. Thus as with Sidney Nolan, Boyd remains deeply influenced by the richly diverse landscape of his native country and the equally strange mythology rooted in the original settlement of the country by criminals and other exotic characters.

Boyd comes from a long line of Australian artists; his parents and grandparents included popular painters, and various aunts and uncles are also represented in national collections. His brother David Boyd is a successful painter, also resident in England.

Arthur Boyd's first important paintings, in the immediate post-war period, depicted the charming Victorian architecture of Melbourne, but soon after, as a result of his admiration for the Flemish masters Breugel and Bosch, a series of religious paintings emerged, subjects such as "The Assumption" and "The Prodigal Son" being used in architectural murals, and also on a brilliant series of ceramic tiles. Pottery led to sculpture, still on religious themes, re-interpreting Flemish expressionism in the new medium. Picasso and Chagall influenced this period of Boyd's career, coinciding with his earliest absorption with the Australian folk hero, Ned Kelly.

The Chagallian strain then emerged to dominate Boyd's series of "Bride" paintings in which a small white-faced female figure accompanies her aboriginal husband. Whilst residence in England has heightened the painter's involvement in Australian themes, the urgency of the "Bride" series, with their anatomy of inter-racial problems, has never been repeated or surpassed.

Boyd's technical control remains impressive, and his versatility has extended to designing for theatre, lithography and etching.

—Charles Spencer

BOYLE, Mark
British. Born in Glasgow, Scotland, 11 May 1934. Studied law at the Glasgow University 1955–56;

mainly self-taught in art, from 1956. Served in the British Army, 1950–53. Has lived with the artist Joan Hills since 1958; children: Sebastian and Georgia. Worked as labourer, Stewarts and Lloyd steelyard, Parkhead, Glasgow, 1953–54; as park keeper, office clerk, barman and head-waiter, all London, 1955–58. Independent artist, London, since 1958; collaborated on light environments for theatrical events, 1960–65; Co-Director, with Joan Hills, Sensual Laboratory, London, since 1966; light-shows for U.F.O. Club, London, 1967; light-environments for music groups Jimi Hendrix Experience and Soft Machine, U.S.A., 1968–69; has worked on Earth Pieces since 1964, and Journey to the Surface of the Earth since 1967. Instructor, Waterford School of Art, 1966–67. Recipient; Painting Prize, *5th Biennale de Paris,* 1967; Painting Prize, *15th Premio Lissone,* Italy, 1967; Painting Prize, *Zagreb International,* Yugoslavia 1968. Agent: A Notional Gallery, Greenwich, London. Address: c/o A Notional Gallery, Hillside House, Crooms Hill, Greenwich, London SE10, England.

Individual Exhibitions:

1963 Woodstock Gallery, London
Traverse Gallery, Edinburgh
Citizens' Gallery, Glasgow
1964 *Suddenly Last Supper,* South Kensington, London (event)
Richard Demarco Gallery, Edinburgh
Exit Music, Strand Electric Theatre, London (with Ken Dewey and Charles Marowitz)
The Street, London (event)
1965 *O, What A Lovely Whore,* Institute of Contemporary Arts, London (event)
Any Plan or No Play, Theatre Royal, Stratford East, London (event)
1966 Indica Gallery, London
Dig, Shepherd's Bush, London (event)
Son et Lumiére for Earth, Air, Fire and Water, Cochrane Theatre, London (event)
Son et Lumiére for Insects, Reptiles and Water Creatures. Cochrane Theatre, London (event)
Bodily Fluids and Functions, Roundhouse, London (event)
1967 Bluecoat Gallery, Liverpool
1969 Institute of Contemporary Arts, London
1970 Gemeentemuseum, The Hague
Bela Centre, Copenhagen
Institute of Contemporary Arts, London
1971 Henie-Onstad Kunstsenter, Oslo
Requiem for an Unknown Citizen, Rotterdam (event)
Galerie Paul Maenz, Cologne
1972 Henie-Onstad Kunstsenter, Oslo
Galerie Paul Maenz, Cologne
1973 Kelvin Hall, Glasgow
Galerie Müller, Stuttgart
McRoberts Centre, Stirling, Scotland
1974 Galerie Paul Manez, Cologne
1975 Serpentine Gallery, London
1977 Felicity Samuel Gallery, London
1978 British Pavilion, at the *Biennale,* Venice
Kunstmuseum, Lucerne
Kulturhuset, Stockholm
Seattle Museum of Art
Henie—Onstad Kunstsenter, Oslo
1979 Louisiana Museum, Humlebaek, Denmark
Museum am Ostwall, Dortmund, West Germany (with Joan Hills)
1980 Charles Cowles Gallery, New York
Kunstmuseum, Lucerne
Art Gallery of South Australia, Adelaide
Richard Hines Gallery, Seattle, Washington
1981 Seattle Art Museum, Washington
Newport Harbor Art Museum, Newport Beach, California
1982 Institute of Contemporary Art, Boston
San Francisco Museum of Modern Art
1983 Nishimura Gallery, Tokyo
1985 Henie-Onstad Kunstsenter, Hovikodden, Norway
A Notional Gallery, London
1986 Cornerhouse Arts Centre, Manchester, Lancashire
Hayward Gallery, London
1987 City Art Gallery, Southampton, Hempshire
Glasgow Art Gallery and Museum, Scotland
Museum of Modern Art, Oxford
Muzeum Sztuki, Lodz, Poland (travelled to Sopot)
British Pavilion, *Bienal de Sao Paulo,* Brazil
Gardner Centre, Brighton, Sussex
Warwick Arts Centre, Warwickshire
Turske und Turske Galerie, Zurich
Turske and Whitney Gallery, Los Angeles
1988 Galerie Lelong, Paris
Paco Imperial, Rio de Janeiro

Selected Group Exhibitions:

1967 *Biennale de Paris,* Musee d'Art Moderne de la Ville, Paris
1968 *International Exhibition,* Zagreb, Yugoslavia
1973 *Magic and Strong Medicine,* Walker Art Gallery, Liverpool
1976 *Arte Inglese Oggi 1960–76,* Palazzo Reale, Milan
1980 *British Art 1940–80,* Hayward Gallery, London
1981 *Approaches to Landscape,* Tate Gallery, London
1983 *Aspects of British Art,* Metropolitan Art Museum, Tokyo (toured Japan)
1985 *Exhibition Dialogue,* Fundaco Calouste Gulbenkian, Lisbon
1986 *Between Object and Image: British Contemporary Sculpture,* Palacio de Velazquez, Madrid (trevelled to Barcelona and Bilbao)
1987 *British Art in the Twentieth Century,* Royal Academy, London (travelled to Stuttgart)

Collections:

Tate Gallery, London; British Council, London; Ulster Museum, Belfast; Scottish National Gallery of Modern Art, Edinburgh; Städtisches Museum, Bochum, West Germany; Kaiser-Wilhelm Museum, Krefeld West Germany; Gemeensemuseum, The Hague; Sonja Henie-Nils Onstad Kunstsenter, Oslo; Australian National Gallery, Canberra; Seattle Museum of Art.

Publications:

By BOYLE: books—*Journey to the Surface of the Earth: Mark Boyle's Atlas and Manual,* with introduction by J. L. Locher, The Hague 1970; *Boyle Family Archives,* Oslo 1985; *Familia Boyle: 19a, Bienal de Sao Paulo,* Sao Paulo 1987.

On BOYLE: books—*Art in Britain 1969–70* by Edward Lucie-Smith and Patricia White, London 1970; *Art Without Boundaries 1950–1970* by G. Woods, P. Thompson and J. Williams, London 1972; *Magic and Strong Medicine,* exhibition catalogue, with text by Norbert Lynton, Liverpool 1973; *Projekt 74: Aspekte Internationaler Kunst am Anfang der 70er Jahre,* exhibition catalogue, with texts by Dieter Rönte, Evelyn Weiss, Marlis Gruterich and others, Cologne 1974; *Venice Biennale: Mark Boyle,* exhibition catalogue, with text by Michael Compton, London 1978; *Mark Boyle's und Joan Hills' Reise um die West 3: Schweizer Serie,* exhibition catalogue, with text by Martin Kunz, Lucerne 1980.

Mark Boyle: *Broken Path with Tiles (West London),* 1983

In a condition of adamant doubt you are asked for explanations when all you want is for someone to explain anything. And you are asked for purposes when you are learning to accept that a purpose is not going to emerge ever. And you are asked for a statement of intent when the head seethes with all your fluctuating statements of the past instantly and meticulously taken down and which you use constantly, with increasing derision, in evidence against yourself. And you remember years ago deciding that art, if the work had any meaning, should be waged like war and how, according to all the strategists, you had to locate the enemy and evaluate your own forces and assess the terrain and clarify your objectives and work out your strategy and your tactics and, whatever you do, do not forget your logistics, and how after months of thinking you succeeded with point one and it's not the dealers or the critics or the intellectuals or the government or the rich or the bourgeoisie or "them" and it's not even like Father Xmas your father all the time but the only enemy is yourself and maybe it doesn't matter too much whether you win or lose.

—Mark Boyle

Journey to the Surface of the Earth is the unwavering conceptual excursion of Mark Boyle and his collaborator/wife, Joan Hills. This "journey" is Boyle's ongoing series of "earthprobes," the literal mapping in every minute detail of 6-ft. square sections of the earth's surface.

In 1970 Boyle handed visitors to his studio a dart to throw at a large Mercator projection map of the world. Eventually a thousand sites were randomly selected for the Boyles to document. A closely guarded and painstaking procedure lifts topographical surface texture, extraneous natural or man-caused materials, and whatever surface deformations are present (shifting beach sands, tire tracks, railroad ties, ploughed fields, ablating rock formations, etc.), onto a molded fiberglass shell. Real and ersatz materials are added to achieve versimilitude. Full documentation includes the surface casting, a cast vertical sampling of the substrata, and photographic enlargements of microscopic details of plants and insects gathered on-site, hair, and fluid wastes from the artist's body, all revealed as crustaceous or crystalline molecular patterns of structure.

The meticulous factuality of these relief panels are presented in the rarified space of the gallery. They demand and invite scrutiny. The works are not intended as abstractions of nature, though formal relationships of texture, shape and compositional balance can be readily ascertained in the patterns of wave-tossed sand, tilled soil and geologic outcroppings. Rather, the viewer is re-sensitized by the direct immediacy of these panels, to look at nature in terms of Boyle's process, product and attitude. The moral and ethical imperative is to heighten and engage, in a non-militant yet forceful way, a greater sensitivity to ecological matters. The "grand scheme" of nature merges in the macro-and micro-cosmic units of reality: the flecks of stone, the crusty exoskeleton of a mite, the kaleidoscopic rainbow colors of crystals and molecules. The world beneath one's feet seems more real, more solid and palpable, after seeing the work of Mark Boyle.

—Ron Glowen

BRAUER, Erich or Arik.

Austrian. Born in Vienna, 4 January 1929. Educated in elementary schools in Vienna, 1935–42; studied art, under Robin Anderson and Albert Paris Gütersloh, Academy of Fine Arts, Vienna, 1945–51; also studied singing at the City Conservatory, Vienna, 1949–53. Married Naomi Dahabany in 1955; daughters: Timma, Talija and Ruth. Served in underground resistance, Vienna, 1942–45. Bicycled to Paris to work as folk singer; travelled to Algeria, stayed in Sahara Desert, 1950; travelled to France, Spain, Greece, Israel and Austria, earned living as folk-singer, 1951–58; settled in Paris, performed as folk-singer, with wife Naomi, 1958; former friendship, with Hundertwasser, Paris, 1958. Has painted full time in Vienna, since 1960, and in Ein Hod, Israel, since 1964; has also worked as a costume and set designer for operas, in Zurich, Vienna and Paris, since 1970. Agent: Joram Harel Management, Vienna. Address: c/o Joram Harel Management, Colloredogasse 32, 1180 Vienna, Austria.

Individual Exhibitions:

1956	Neue Gallerie, Vienna
1957	Artist's House, Jerusalem
1958	Galerie Ernst Fuchs, Vienna
	Galerie Wolfgang Gurlitt, Munich
1959	Galerie La Cour d'Ingres, Paris
	Artist's House, Jerusalem
1960	Galerie Delta, Basle
1961	Galerie Brochstedt, Hamburg
	Galerie Sydow, Frankfurt
	Galerie Raymond Cordier, Paris
1963	Galerie Karl Flinker, Paris
1964	Galerie Sydow, Frankfurt
	Galerie Karl Flinker, Paris
1965	Galerie Peithner-Lichtenfels, Vienna
	Felix Landau Gallery, Los Angeles
1966	Galerie Sydow Fine Art, Frankfurt
1967	Felix Landau Gallery, Los Angeles
	Landau Gallery, New York
1968	Galerie 3 + 2, Paris
	Kunstlerhaus Peithner, Vienna
	Galerie Sydow, Frankfurt
	Galerie Sydow, West Berlin
1969	Marlborough New London Gallery
	Galerie Haas, Vaduz, Lichtenstein
	Galerie Passepartout, Copenhagen
	Galerie 3 + 2, Paris
	Galleria La Vetrina, Rome
	Galerie Wolfgang Ketterer, Munich
1970	Galerie Wendtorf, Dusseldorf
	Buhler Graphics, Stuttgart
	Galerie Le Grenier d'Art, Geneva
	Galleria Vicotti, Turin
1971	Galerie des 20, Jahrhunderts, Vienna
	Galerie Peithner-Lichtenfels, Vienna
	Galerie d'Halluin, Dusseldorf
	Galerie Hartmann, Munich
	Oils, Goaches, Watercolors and Etchings, Marlborough-Gerson Gallery, New York
1973	Galerie Hartmann, Munich
	Galerie Wolfrum Vienna
	Galerie Lochte, Hamburg
	Marlborough Galerie, Zurich
1974	*Das Graphische Werk 1951–1974,* Die Graphische Sammlung Albertina, Vienna (toured Norway, Yugoslavia and Latin America 1977–78, Turkey, 1979, Germany 1980–81, and France, 1982)
1975	Museum for Culture and Fine Arts, University of Marburg, West Germany
1976	Kurpfalzisches Museum Heidelberg
	Kunst und Kulturverein, Esslingen, West Germany
	Museum Mazowiecki, Plock, Poland (toured Poland)
	Galerie Facchetti, Paris
	Städtische Galerie, Rosenheim, West Germany
	Osterreichische Galerie im Oberen Belvedere, Vienna
	Oberbach Fine Art, New York
1977	St. Mary's University Art Gallery, Halifax
	Galerie Facchetti, Paris
	Galerie in der Staatsoper, Vienna
1978	Goldmann Fine Art, Basie
	Beethovenhaus, Schwenningen, West Germany
	Kunstverein Hochrhein, Sackingen, West Germany
1979	*Austria Presents Brauer to the Continents*, The Jewish Museum, New York (and world tour, 1979–83)
1985	Jack Rutberg Gallery, Los Angeles

Selected Group Exhibitions:

1961	*Micro Salon*, Tokyo Gallery
	Der Gegenstand in Der Osterreichischen Malerei und Plastik Secession, Vienna
1962	*Surrealismus, Phantastiche Malerei der Gegenwart*, Kunslerhaus, Vienna
	Graphik aus Osterreich, Ljubljana, Yugoslavia
1963	*Grands et Jeunes d'Aujourd'hui*, Musée d'Art Moderne de la Ville, Paris
1964	*Salon de Mai*, Paris
1965	*Bienal*, Sao Paulo
1968	*Die Entwicklung der Wiener Schule*, Kunstlerhaus, Vienna
1972	*Die Wiener Schule des Phantastischen Realismus*, Museum des 20, Jahrhunderts, Vienna
1975	*22nd Biennale Premia Del Fiorina*, Palazzo Strozzi, Florence

Collections:

Albertina, Vienna; Historisches Museum der Stadt Wien, Vienna; Osterreichische Galerie des 19th and 20th, Jahrhunderts, Vienna; City of Vienna; Moderne Galerie und Graphische Sammiung Rupertinum, Salzburg; Des Moines Art Center, Iowa; The Jewish Museum, New York; Tel Aviv Museum, Israel

Publications:

By BRAUER: books—*Human Rights*, portfolio, New York, London and Paris 1975, *Die Zigeunerziege*, Munich 1976; *Das Runde Fliegt*, Munich 1983; *Monography*, Harenberg, West Germany 1984; records—*Arik Brauer*, Vienna 1971; *Alles was Flugel Hat Fliegt*, Vienna 1974; *Poesie mit Krallen*, Vienna 1984; television show—*Alles was Flugel Hat Fliegt*, Vienna 1973.

On BRAUER: books—*Brauer*, exhibition catalogue by Wieland Schmied, Frankfurt 1964; *Brauer: Malerei des Phantastischen Realismus*, Munich 1968; *Brauer*, exhibition catalogue, London 1969; *Art in Britain 1969–70* by Edward Lucie-Smith and Patricia White, London 1970; *Brauer: Oils Goaches, Watercolors and Etchings*, exhibition catalogue, by Wolfgang Fischer, New York 1971; *Brauer: Monographie mit Werkkatalog* by Wieland Schmied, Vienna 1972; *Erich Brauer: Morgenrot, Morgengrau*, Vienna 1972; *Brauer*, exhibition catalogue, by Gustav Rene Hocke, Zurich 1973; *Brauer Small Monography*, Salzburg 1973; *Malerei aus Bereichen des Unbewussten; Kunstler experimenteeren unter LSD* by Richard P. Hartmann, Cologne 1974; *Brauer: Das Graphische Werk 1951–1974* by Walter Koschatzky, Vienna 1974; *Die Wiener Schule des Phantastischen Realismus* by Johann Muschik, Vienna and Munich 1974; *Brauer's Bunte Mauer* by Erich Lessing, Munich 1975; *Brauer: New York*, Glarus, Switzerland 1975; *Brauer: Paris*, Glarus, Switzerland 1976; *Austria Presents Brauer to the Continents*, Glarus, Switzerland 1979; articles—"Erich Brauer" in *Mizue* (Tokyo), 1969; "Brauer" by Wieland Schmied in *Graphis* (Zurich), December 1973/January 1974.

I have been painting ever since I can remember, and I have done so from 7 to 8 hours a day over the past 30 years. Even though I painted more or less always the same, painting has never lost its fascination for me.

My first studio was the windowsill in my father's workshop. He was a bootmaker. The window was on the ground floor and I could thus sit astride, one leg inside the shop and the other dangling outside into the street. It gave me a grand feeling of commanding the crossroads of two worlds.

On the other side of the street lived a charcoal-dealer. His door was decorated with faggots and coalsacks. There were many cats around his place. I believe that those cats made me understand movement and sequences of motion. For years I drew the cats and admired their well-rounded grace. I even played at cats myself and prowled around on all fours between the bundles of leather. I slid down the big pile of solo-leather and mewed. I understood the cats. My father hummed yiddish songs and asked: "And what are you today?" He did not ask: "What do you paint today?" My movements and my painting had become as one.

Erich Brauer: ***Fehdehandschuh—Friedehandschuh*****, 1971**

Next to motion, my painting's second base is colour. I discovered my true colours rather late and quite suddenly, from one day to the next. I had finished my studies at the Academy in Vienna and was on my first visit to Israel. One evening I sat on the beach and looked at a small shell. In a flash I suddenly realized that a colour appears luminous when it is enhanced by a second colour: a reddish-brown leaf, for example, turns red at the edge, a yellow ball turns white around the middle.

To know and to realize are not the same in painting. My "realization" of this intensification of colour was certainly not new then and is known to every better commercial artist. But I alone can make use of it in my own way. The sudden realization found me ready, encountered a subjective inclination, which changed mere knowledge into creative understanding. There and then I went home and started painting. My head grew hot, and I understood what impact the little shell had had upon my life.

For the next twenty years, the cat's movements and the shimmering shell were my spiritual baggage. Sometimes, and out of mere curiosity, I tried different styles of painting, perhaps a plainer surface, or a harder contour, but all such attempts ended in crisis. I have now understood that one man can do one painting only, even if he seems to pass through different periods. Other paintings, other painters.

My own painting has always been figurative and literary. In my graphic work in particular, I have often illustrated stories or followed a theme. Every artist has certain objects and forms suited to his style. The topics of his paintings may therefore quite often grow out of these objects. When painting a given subject, the situation is reversed: the painter is confronted with the difficult but exciting task of fitting the literary content to his personal forms. If, for instance, a painter's style is particularly apt for the representation of plants, an interesting tension ensues if he tries to do buildings or machinery. I do not believe that the theme can enhance the quality of a painting, but I do believe that a subject can provide an added impetus and trigger the artist's best effort.

Among the many ways which lead towards painting, one passes through story-telling. Jewish history has almost never been painted. Those who should have created the images did not do so for religious reasons. Only the future will show whether I was big enough to fill that gap.

The history of oppression and persecution of a minority is the same for all nations. I have therefore quite often used the symbols and signs of other oppressed nations. I do not care whether the stories and contents of all the details and all the backdrops are seen my way. The subjects are unequivocal, but my paintings are resilient and open to interpretation. They ought to stimulate the imagination. Every spectator should continue to think them to their very conclusion.

Painting is influenced by so many unconscious, subconscious processes that it really cannot be learnt. It will always remain an exciting, risky endeavour, full of attraction for a lifetime. In painting there are no recognizeable, generally valid laws. One painter's quality is the other's weakness. The art of painting cannot be stolen. The purloined artistic gold turns to pitch in the hands of the thief. This holds equally true for the painter who steals from his own painting, that is who tries to repeat his own, old ideas over and over without inner need. It is impossible to fake an idea and even untrained spectators can tell an artist's living work from his empty, barren products. A visitor who approaches an exhibit with a total lack of understanding, even with disgust, will nevertheless arrive at a relatively correct judgement of the works of art. Painting is a veritable hour of truth, and one may lie with words but not with images.

The idea that strikes the artist is at the core of every work of art. The word "strike" suggests something which hits one from the outside, as if an artist could not do anything by himself but would have to wait until "art" comes to him. This is not so. I am convinced that nothing ever comes from waiting alone. I believe, on the contrary, that "being struck" is a spiritual act which a gifted person can bring about by concentration. These basic ideas, the very essence of a painting, of its forms and colours, are usually so simple that, once executed, they seem self-evident, almost two-dimensional eggs of Columbus.

Painting, unlike language, knows no frontiers in space and time. Looking at works of art created many thousand years ago, one can still re-live the artists' efforts and feelings. One can experience the same, deep understanding for the works of foreign cultures, for Chinese or African art. The fine arts seem to express something that is common to all mankind, something everybody can understand. Potentates and dictators of all kind react to painting with astounding irritability. The poetic world of forms and colours may be a closed book to them; but with the heightened senses of the wrongdoer they understand the psychological and, even more so, the political impact of painting. It is not the light-hearted art it might seem at first glance.

Painting must become a mass-activity, like speaking. Professional painters should stop feeling like miracle-workers whose magic is inaccessible to the average person. They should become examples and stimuli, almost like top-athletes in sport. The painting on houses and public institutions should not be forbidden, but should be promoted and rewarded. Industry ought to produce objects of daily use with a surface that lends itself to colouring. Children in particular should be encouraged to paint their schools inside and out.

Painting is a mysterious and singular activity that cannot be replaced by anything else and may well have the power to solve problems of our time.

—Erich Brauer

There is a school in Vienna, a school with very few pupils. It is dedicated to the teaching of *misch-technik,* a kind of melding of the ancient painting craft (from the times before oils and canvases became the natural raw materials for aspiring artists) and its mysteries—some of them far from easy to comprehend and then be able to harness effectively—together with antique lore and alchemies. Ernst Fuchs could be regarded as a champion of this "other" art; but the misch-technik school is not the only source of painted magic in contemporary Vienna. It is quoted here because it is an important part of his magico-medieval cultural atmosphere in which so many exotic flowers bloom. Side by side with these unexpected outcrops of archaic imagination and learning there is the Vienna School of Phantastic Realism of whose artists perhaps the best known is Erich Brauer, painter and erstwhile lute-player, folk-singer and dancer.

The fluttering petals that invade so many of Brauer's pictures recall in imagery some of the details in paintings by Naumowski, except that the Yugoslav has none of the finesse of the Austrian, nor does he impart any of the same romantic strangeness.

Even though the majority of Brauer's paintings, watercolours and etchings tend to have titles that have an everyday ring about them like "Naomi on Friday Evening," this picture suggests a parallel unreality with "The Angel Tree" or "The Flying Saucers Weep." In all three can be found a kindred iridescence. The cuffs of Naomi's dress are like the flowers of "The Redheaded King." The Orpheus-figure in "Looking Back" is accompanied by a dog whose ears are like diaphanous wings. Every image sprouts vegetally, whether through its limbs or its garments or out of the landscape itself. A world of articulated Turkish delight, except that everything is more delicately rendered and the colours are not the pale evanescences of pastel, but the burnished hues expanded in an imaginative furnace.

These are narrative pictures. The stories they tell are in a visual language for the sensitive eye. They are beguiling, a natural mirror for children's dreams. Brauer treats luxury with respect.

—Sheldon Williams

BRAVO, Claudio.

Chilean. Born in Valparaiso, Chile, 8 November 1936. Studied with Miguel Venegas, 1947–48. Lived in Spain, 1961–72. Has lived in Tangier since 1972. Agents: Galeria Vandres, Don Ramon de la Cruz 26, Madrid 1, Spain; Marlborough Fine Art, 40 West 57th Street, New York, New York 10019, U.S.A. Address: 49 rue du Village. Marshan, Tangier, Morocco.

IIndividual Exhibitions:

1970 Gallery Staempfli, New York
1971 Galeria Egam, Madrid
1972 Gallery Staempfli, New York
Galeria Vandres, Madrid
1980 F.I.A.C, Paris
1981 Marlborough Gallery, New York
1982 Marlborough Gallery, New York
Museum of Monterrey, Mexico
1983 Marlborough Fine Art, London
1984 Marlborough Gallery, New York
Galeria Quintana, Bogota, Colombia
1985 Marlborough Gallery, New York

Claudio Bravo: *Still Life*, 1970

Selected Group Exhibitions:

1972 *Documenta 5,* Kassel, West Germany
Relativerend Realisme Stedelijk Van Abbemuseum, Eindhoven, Metherlands
1973 *Artistes Hyper-realistes,* Galerie des Quatre Mouvements, Paris
1974 *Ars 74: Alternatives of Realism,* Fine Arts Academy of Finland, Helsinki
1976 *Modern Portraits: The Self and Others,* Wildenstein Galleries, New York
1981 *International Contemporary Art,* Museo Rufino Tamayo, Mexico City
1983 *48th Carnegie International,* Carnegie Institute, Pittsburgh
1984 *The Classic Tradition in Painting and Sculpture,* Aldrich Museum of Contemporary Art, Ridgefield, Connecticut
1985 *Contemporary Narrative Figure Painting,* Moravian College, Bethlehem, Pennsylvania

Collections:

University of Pennsylvania Art Museum, Philadelphia; Princeton University Art Museum, New Jersey; Ponce Art Museum, Puerto Rico; Museo de Arte Abstracto, Cuenca, Spain; Museum Boymans-van Beuningen, Rotterdam; Museum of Art, Helsinki.

Publications:

On BRAVO: books—*Documenta 5,* exhibition catalogue, Kassel, West Germany 1972; *Relativerend Realisme,* exhibition catalogue, Eindhoven, Netherlands 1972; articles—"Lettre de New York: Claudio Bravo, Staempfli Gallery" by J. P. Marandel in *Art International* (Lugano, Switzerland), January 1971; "Flashback su Kassel" in *Flash Art* (Milan), September/October 1972; "The New Spanish Realists" by W. Dyckes in *Art International* (Lugano, Switzerland), September 1973.

At present nothing interests me except the resurrection. I don't want movements or fashions. Art is something so subtle that these things do not last. They are poor flowers that test the brightness and quickly fade.

One has to be forgotten, and work as an honest labourer, perhaps for some years, not to be mistaken as the follower of a trend. Neither Leonardo nor Vermeer knew anything about tendencies; they did what they had to do and what they believed in—alone, very alone and quietly.

One has to be forgotten, like the dead—to disappear.

I live beside a Moroccan cemetery that I see every morning when I open my window to let the sun into my place on the bed. My experiences each day are so long and serene that I don't have even a moment to think of the neurotic involvements of other artists in big cities. I am apart from time in my beautiful Arabian palace, quiet and white like a dove sitting next to a rose.

Hyperealism, realism, superrealism and other isms will pass; they fly far above my studio and only come to visit. I am shut in, painting, and don't open my windows to them: like Abel with the Angel I will fight to be alone.

One day will come the resurrection.

—Claudio Bravo

Claudio Bravo is a painter, draughtsman, sculptor and lithographer of exhaustive accurate realism. Although it is hard to believe that some of the subjects of his works could—in real life—exist with the same dust-free stillness, this in no way invalidates the effect of his achievement. Quite rightly he holds himself to be aloof from all art movements past and present. His work is carried out in a condition of seclusion that might well be compared with that of an anchorite, and perhaps like the more successful hermits, who found both lack of company and the failure of the world to impinge upon their solitude was conducive to practical meditation, perhaps like them Claudio Bravo has been able to create a distillation (of vision, in his case) that would be difficult for an actively involved member of human society to imitate.

The "artificiality" of Bravo's works might be said

to measure up to the improbability of a character without stain; the famous ointment has no fly in it.

And yet, with all this respectable attitude of withdrawal, Bravo slots neatly into place amongst contemporary artists. He might not like his exquisitely packed and strung parcels, marvels of painted observation, to be hung beside the packages of Christo and Manzoni, yet—for all their difference in construction—they would be fit companions. He would be appalled if his elegant drawings of boots shared exhibition with pop-art metal castings of the same subject, and yet both are part of the modern art scene.

Works by Bravo have been shown in the black museum at Cuenca, normally a venerated show-place for nonfigurative art, but such an action merely underlies the proof, if underlining were necessary, that the accomplished artist ought never to be hidebound by the dictates of contemporary taste. The unrecognisable can be the ineffable just as easily as can exact representation. Claudio Bravo might not agree with such a statement, but to substantiate it the whole history of mankind's creativity ought to be enough.

—Sheldon Williams

BRECHT, George

American. Born in New York City, 7 March 1926. Studied at the Philadelphia College of Pharmacy and Science, 1946–50, B.Sc. 1950; New School for Social Research, New York, 1958–59. Served in the United States Army, 1943–45. Married Marceline Allemand in 1951 (divorced); son: Eric. Worked as analytical chemist and quality control supervisor, Chas. Pfizer and Co., Brooklyn, New York; Quality control supervisor, research chemist, engineer and inventor, Johnson and Johnson, New Brunswick, New Jersey; research inventor, chemist and engineer, Mobil Chemicals, New Brunswick, New Jersey. Independent artist active in areas including performance, artists' writings and conceptual art; early associate of Fluxus group; founded *Sight Unseen* journal: has lived and worked in Cologne since 1972. Research Fellow, Leeds College of Art, England, 1968–69. Agent: Renate Fassbender, Pienzenauerstr. 98, 8000 Munich 81. Address: Wildenburgstrasse 9, 5 Cologne-Sulz, West Germany.

Individual Exhibitions:

1959 *Toward Events*, Rueben Gallery, New York
1965 *The Book of the Tumbler on Fire*, Fischbach Gallery, New York
1967 Galleria Schwarz, Milan
1969 Galleria Schwarz, Milan
1970 Galerie Michael Werner, Cologne
Galerie Hansjörg Mayer, Stuttgart
Los Angeles County Museum of Art
1973 Galerie Onnasch, New York
1978 *Beyond Events*, Kunsthalle, Bern

Selected Group Exhibitions:

1961 *The Art of Assemblage*, Museum of Modern Art, New York
1962 *Fluxus International Festival*, New York
1965 *11 From the Reuben Gallery*, Guggenheim Museum, New York
1967 *Poems to be Seen, Paintings to be Read*, Museum of Contemporary Art, Chicago
1968 *Chemistry of Music*, Moderna Museet, Stockholm
1969 *La Cedille Qui Sourit*, Städtisches Museum, Mönchengladbach, West Germany
1970 *Art in the Mind*, Allen Art Museum, Oberlin College, Ohio
1972 *Documenta 5*, Kassel, West Germany
1984 *Salvaged: Altered Everyday Objects*, Project Studios One, Long Island City, New York
1986 *Europa-Amerika*, Museum Ludwig, Cologne

Collections:

Museum of Modern Art, New York; Städtisches Museum, Mönchengladbach, West Germany; Archiv Sohm, Markgroningen, West Germany; Staatsgalerie, Berlin; Centre Georges Pompidou, Paris.

Publications:

By BRECHT: books—*Chance Imagery*, New York 1966; *Games at the Cedillas or the Cedilla Takes Off*, with Robert Filliou, New York 1967; *Vicious Circles and Infinity*, with Patrick Hughes, New York 1975; *Hsin-hsin-ming*, Cologne 1987; articles—"3 Dances" in *New Departures* (London), no 4, 1962; "Chance Imagery" in *Collage* (Palermo, Italy), December 1964; "Conversation sur Autre Chose," with Ben Vautier, in *Identities* (Nice, France), no. 11–12, 1965; "Dances, Events and Other Poems" in *Something* (New York), vol. 1, no. 2, 1965; "An Inteview," with Henry Martin in *Art International* (Lugano, Switzerland), November 1967; "From the Brecht/Lovell Motto Board" in *Big Venus* (London), no. 3, 1969; "George Brecht: An Interview" by Robin Page and others in *Art and Artists* (London), October 1972.

On BRECHT: books—*Postface* by Dick Higgins, New York 1964; *Assemblage, Environments and Happenings* by Allan Kaprow, New York 1966; *An Introduction to George Brecht's Book of the Tumbler on Fire* by Henry Martin, Milan 1978; articles—"Environments, Situations, Spaces at Martha Jackson Gallery" by J. Kroll in *Artnews* (New York), September 1961; "The Value of Didactic Art" by Barbara Rose in *Artforum* (New York), August 1967; "Non-Games" by Jasia Reichardt in *Studio International* (London), March 1968; "An Art of Multiple Dimensions" by Jan van der Marck in *Art in America* (New York), July/August 1974.

To paraphrase Satie: "I was born unborn into a very young world."

—George Brecht

George Brecht is always mentioned as one of the original members of the Fluxus group, and like many of the others he had participated in the composition course that John Cage held at New York's New School for Social Research in 1958 and 1959. But Brecht's own attitude to the movement (or "non-movement") that claims him is, "I say, let it go. After all, FLUXUS is a Latin word Maciunas dug up. I never studied Latin. If it hadn't been for Maciunas nobody would ever have called it anything. We would all have gone our separate ways like the man crossing the street with his umbrella, and a woman walking a dog in another direction."

After an initial period of splashing liquid paint on canvases that he then folded up so as to allow the colors to blot and bleed, Brecht went on to begin to work with the idea of the "event." Some of his events are performance pieces, and some of them are not, and with some it is a little difficult to say. A 100 or so of these events were all printed on small squares of paper and published in 1962 in a box called "Water Yam." One card, for example, says "Three aqueous events: ice, water, steam." Another says "Table: on a white table, glasses, a puzzle, and (having to do with smoking)." Still another requires a performer to make a vertical pile of playing blocks on the strings of an open grand piano until one or more of the blocks fall off.

Many of these events were later to find a more physical and permanent form as assemblages, and as such they entered that continuing and ever-growing collection of experiences that's entitled *The Book of the Tumbler on Fire*. Though later dated retroactively to include certain works from as early as 1962, it was begun in 1964 and contains almost all the work that Brecht has done since. Its various chapters consist of series of assemblages of odds and ends in shallow cotton-filled specimen boxes (like the ones for presenting collections of butterflies), other assemblages in deeper boxes that allow the objects in them to move, various arrangements of chairs or tables with specific objects placed upon them (a glove, for example, or a pepper-mill, or a blind man's black-and-white cane and an orange) and sometimes associated as well with quotations from the *Guinness Book of Records*. One chapter consists of signs that say things like "No Smoking," or "Sans Issue," or "Silence" spelled out in cork letters on canvas; another is dedicated to an aerodynamic redesigning of the letters of the alphabet; another is a translation of a book by Robert Filliou. There's also a collection of paradoxes (the first in the history of philosophy) done in collaboration with Patrick Hughes and published by Doubleday and Company: this is Part III of Volume III of the *Book* . . . Part I is a work called "Donna dei Nodi": a full-sized reclining figure of a naked woman

George Brecht: *Void*, Munster, West Germany, 1987

carved in marble by a tomb-stone sculptor and holding in her hand a large monkey's paw knot at the end of a rope the strands of which separate to end in a series of other knots at her side and feet. The artist has also made maps containing proposals for the displacement of various land-masses from one part of the earth to another. Other works are crystals grown in Petri dishes and housed in leather boxes that may also have a row of smaller lateral compartments for objects such as keys, dice, pieces of wood, and tiny spheres of marble. He has also done an English translation of the Chinese original of Seng-ts'an's *Hsing-Hsing Ming,* the first of the classical texts of Zen Buddhism. Some of Brecht's most recent works have been stones, large and small, inscribed with the word "Void."

The internal logic of George Brecht's work is entirely impossible to describe, since his problem as an artist is always and only to work towards an intuitive grasp of the problems of knowledge and awareness that are central to his own individual being in the universe. He has written, "Science tells us that the universe is what we conceive it to be, and chance enables us to determine what we conceive it to be (for the conception is only partly conscious). The receptacle of forms available to the artist thus becomes open-ended, and eventually embraces all of nature, for the recognition of significant form becomes limited only by the observer's self." His works, then, are simply things that he has *done* in the course of trying to clarify his relationship to the rest of existence, and they don't try to posit themselves as symbolic expressions with which the artist has established any simple kind of psychological identification. Brecht's works, like many of Marcel Duchamp's, seem marvellously arbitrary. They're about that experience of inner freedom that *allows* an individual to be arbitrary—arbitrary with respect to any and all previous conditioning. This is to say that Brecht stands behind his work much as we can stand in front of it: he, the work, and we are all a part of a larger arrangement in which both artist and spectator have the potential to realize a condition in which they're of entirely equal status. We can do with Brecht's works whatever we like: but to discover that they are beautiful is not to fall in line with an artist's revelation of a definition of beauty; it's rather to discover that the discovery of beauty is itself an entirely personal event of which all of us are individually capable.

—Henry Martin

BREER, Robert C.

American. Born in Detroit, Michigan, 30 September 1926. Educated at the Detroit University School, 1932–43; Stanford University, California, 1943–45, 1947–49, B.A. 1949. Served in the United States Army, 1945–47. Married Frances Foote in 1955; children: Julia, Emily, and Harriet. Lived in Paris, 1949–59, now resident in New York State. Adjunct to Carnegie Professor, Films and Kinetics, Cooper Union, New York City, since 1972. Member, Board of Directors, Filmmakers Cooperative, New York 1967–72; Co-Designer, Pepsi-Cola Pavilion, *Expo'70,* Osaka, Japan, 1970. Recipient: Annual Painting Award, Stanford University, 1949; Creative Film Foundation Award, 1957–61; Diplome Speciale, Bergamo, Italy, 1962; Max Ernst Award, Oberhausen, West Germany, 1968; Film Culture Award, New York, 1972; Guggenheim Fellowship, 1978. Agents: Cinegate Ltd., 70 Portobello Road, London W11, England; Projection Galerie Ursula Wevers, Am Rinkenpfulh 20–26, 5000 Cologne 1, West Germany; and Filmmakers Cooperative, 175 Lexington Avenue, New York, New York 10016. Address: 80 Sparkill Avenue, Tappan, New York 10983, U.S.A.

Individual Exhibitions:

1956 Palais des Beaux-Arts, Brussels
American Students and Artists Center, Paris
1960 Gallery Mayer, New York
1961 Charles Cinema, New York (film retrospective)
1962 Bleecker Cinema, New York
1963 Dwan Gallery, Los Angeles (film retrospective)
1965 Galeria Bonino, New York
1966 Galeria Bonino, New York
1968 Galerie Ricke, Cologne
1969 Museum of Contemporary Art, Chicago
1970 Galeria Bonino, New York
Museum of Modern Art, New York
1972 J. L. Hudson Gallery, Detroit
Millenium Film Workshop, New York
1973 Hammarskjold Plaza, New York
1974 IBM Plaza, New York
Michael Berger Gallery, Pittsburgh
1975 Film Forum, New York (film retrospective)
Museum of Modern Art, New York (film retrospective)
Whitney Museum, New York (film retrospective)
1977 Whitney Museum, New York
1979 St. Louis Art Museum
Walker Art Center, Minneapolis
1980 Whitney Museum, New York (film retrospective)
Albright Knox Art Gallery, Buffalo, New York
Art Institute of Chicago
1981 Exterior Film Forum, New York (mural painting)

Selected Group Exhibitions:

1976 *Une Histoire du Cinema,* Centre Beaubourg, Paris
1977 *Paris-New York,* Centre Beaubourg, Paris
1978 *Filmex: American Independent Animation,* Hollywood, California
1979 *Contemporary Sculpture,*Museum of Modern Art, New York
Film as Film, Arts Council of Great Britain, London
Biennial Exhibition, Whitney Museum, New York
Americans in Paris: The 50's, California State University at Northridge
1980 *The Pleasure Dome: American Experimental Film 1939–79,* Moderna Museet, Stockholm
1981 *Biennial Exhibition,* Whitney Museum, New York

Collections:

Museum of Modern Art, New York; New York Public Library; Anthology Film Archives, New York; Institute of Contemporary Art, London; Musée National d'Art Moderne, Paris; Austrian Film Archives, Vienna; Moderna Museet, Stockholm; National Film Archives, Canberra, Australia.

Publications:

By BREER: articles—"On 2 Films" in *Film Culture* (New York), Summer 1961; "What Happened" in *Film Culture* (New York), Fall 1962; "Interview with Robert Breer," with Guy Cote, in *Film Culture* (New York), Winter 1962; "A Statement" in *Film Culture* (New York), Summer 1963; films—*Form Phrases I,* 1952; *Form Phrases II,* 1953; *Form Phrases III,* 1953; *Form Phrases IV,* 1954; *Images by Images I,* 1954; *Un Miracle,* 1955; *Image by Images II,* 1955; *Image by Images III,* 1955; *Image by Images IV,* 1966; *Cats,* with Frances Breer, 1956; *Recreation I,* with spoken text by Noel Burch, 1956–57; *Recreation II,* 1956–57; *Jamestown Baloos,* 1957; *A Man and His Dog Out for Air,* 1957; *Par Avion,* 1958; *Eyewash,* 1958–59; *Homage to Jean Tinguely's Hommage to New York',* 1960; *Blazes,* 1961; *Horse Over a Tea Kettle,* 1962; *Pat's Birthday,* 1962; *Breathing,* 1963; *Fistfight,* 1964; *66,* 1966; *69,* 1968; *OBL No. 2,* 1968; *70,* 1970; *Gulls and Buoys,* 1972; *Fuji,* 1974; *Rubber Cement,* 1975; *77,* 1977; *LMNO,* 1978; *TZ,* 1979.

On BREER: books—*Robert Breer* by Michel Seuphor, Paris 1956; *Hard Center* by Nicholas and Elena Calas, New York 1964; *Film: A Montage of Theories* by Richard Dyer, New York 1966; *Animation in the Cinema* by Ralph Stephenson, London 1967; *An Introduction to the American Underground Film* by Sheldon Renan, New York 1967; *The New American Cinema* by Gregory Battcock, New York 1967; *Art of Time* by Michael Kirby, New York 1969, *The American Independent Film* by P. Adams Sitney, Boston 1971; *Experimental Cinema* by David Curtis, New York 1971; *Pavilion* by Nilo Lindgreen, Barbara Rose, and Calvin Tomkins, New York 1972; *Experimental Animation* by Robert Russett, New York 1976; *Robert Breer* by Sandra Moore, Minneapolis 1980; *Robert Breer: A Study of His Work in the Context of the Modernist Tradition* by Louis Mendelson, Ann Arbor, Michigan 1981; articles—"4 Artists as Film-Makers" by Adrienne Mancia and Willard Van Dyke in *Art in America* (New York), January 1967; "The Experience of Kinesis" by Michael Kirby in *Art News* (New York), February 1968; "Onward and Upward with the Arts," by Calvin Tomkins, in *The New Yorker,* October 1970; "Gulls and Buoys" by Scott Hammen in *Afterimage* (Rochester, New York), December 1974; notes by Lucy Fischer in *Museum of Modern Art Circulating Films,* exhibition catalogue, New York 1976; "The Other Cinema" by Noel Carroll in *Soho Weekly News* (New York), 25 January 1979; "Robert Breer's LMNO" by Elena Simons in *Millenium Film Journal* (New York), nos. 4 and 5, 1979; "On A Breer Day" by Amy Taubin in *Soho Weekly News* (New York), 28 May 1980; "Robert Breer's Animated World" by J. Hoberman in *American Film* (Washington, D.C.), September 1980; "Robert Breer, Whitney Museum" by Amy Taubin in *Artforum* (New York), September 1980.

. . . is my major contribution, these big things I call floats—other people call them creepies—these large dome-shaped objects. They're motorized underneath by batteries to move very, very slowly. We are talking about film, the way I got these floats, or at least the connection to film, is obviously one of motion. Ironically enough, these things move, the speed is so slow it's almost barely perceptible. When you're standing there one bumps into you, you don't really notice it, and, of course, with the films, they're ultra fast my films—so fast, there again, you almost don't realize that they're moving, it breaks up the motion so much. In looking back at what I've done, I guess, there is a connection there. I play with thresholds of perception very closely, I think, and in the case of the concrete object, here is something improbable, that it would move, looking at it, and lo and behold, it does. With cinema, it's the other way round.

—Robert Breer

The art of traditional animation—with very modest means—has been the medium in which Robert Breer has invented filmic language paralleling the evolution of recent attitudes towards form and content in the visual arts. His oft-quoted statement best approaches the long-evolved, and even anti-animation, effect of his films: "I'm interested in the domain between motion and still pictures . . . the single frame is the basic unit of film, just as bricks are the basic unit of brick houses." And thus his films have generally offered a sense of the sequence of separate images that compose the film rather than a continuous flow. His art has been described as an animated film variant comprising the Pop art use of everyday accessories, especially as in Dine and Oldenburg; the color fields and geometric hard edge of Ellsworth Kelly; pictorial collage and stream-of-consciousness flow as in Rauschenberg; and cubist-like line found in the paintings of Stuart Davis.

The son of an engineering prodigy then working in Detroit, Breer himself first studied engineering. In 1949 he went to Paris intending to be a painter, but soon became interested in documenting the process by which his final work was achieved. With his father's borrowed Bolex, he began to construct films as geometric abstraction paralleling and reviving the pre-World War II graphic cinema tradition of Richter and Eggeling—with which Breer was then only little acquainted. In 1954 he began a loop work *Image by Image,* which became a series where single framing became the structural and ideational base. In this manipulation, although unknown to one another at that time, Breer has been likened to the Viennese Peter Kubelka. With *Recreation I* (1956–57), Breer began his use of the collage of actual objects, and thus referred to the type of graphic cinema originated in Léger's *Le Ballet Mechanique;* and then a year after, Breer began to produce film based upon a combina-

Robert Breer: Self-Propelled Sculptures in Osaka, 1970

tion of literal figure collage and abstract geometric patterns as in *Jamestown Baloos*. During the years 1957–64, he produced essentially animated cartoons in this manner, including *Man and His Dog Out for Air* (1957) which through long commercial run in New York spread his reputation beyond the avant-gardist film community. At that time, he also began to use 3 by 5 inch flip cards to construct his films, and has since offered mutoscopes—a device that permits the hand-cranking of these flip cards—in his public exhibitions, e.g.,his retrospectives at the Whitney Museum of American Art in 1977 and 1980.

Breer returned to the U.S. in 1959, and absorbed at first the open vulgarity of Pop—perhaps best felt in the autobiographical *Fist Fight* (1964); and then the abstract vigor of Minimalism. Under the influence of the latter, he reworked his earliest films *Form Phases* (1952–3), and then went on to create his finest abstract films, each setting itself specific problems of color, illusion, and image control, *66* (1966), *69* (1969), and *70* (1970). At this time, which coincided with a strong rise of interest in the United States in a Tech-art, Breer also became known as the maker of extremely slow-moving abstract geometric, motorized, sculptures; less well-known were the violently moving mylar sheet constructions. In the next decade Breer's films made more liberal use of literal content as he began the use of the rotoscope which permits a frame-by-frame tracing of live action footage. With it, he continued his exploration of the connections between figuration and abstraction through retarded movement and figure-dissolution. His most recent works, such as *LMNO* and *T.Z.* (1978 and 1980), continue his long-time synthesis of literal subject and geometric pattern.

—Joshua Kind

BREHMER, K. P.

German. Born in Berlin, 12 September 1938. Studied applied graphics at the Werkkunstschule, Krefeld, West Germany, 1959–60, and printmaking at the Staatliche Kunstakademie, Dusseldorf, 1961–63. Married Monika Aich in 1963; children: Sebastian and Jelle. Worked as photographic technician, Carl Lange Verlag publishers, Duisburg, West Germany, 1957–59. Independent graphic artist, Dusseldorf, 1963–71, Hamburg, 1971–74, and in West Berlin, since 1974; also filmmaker, since 1959. Professor, Hochschule für Bildende Künste, Hamburg, 1971–74. Lives in West Berlin, Hamburg and Vietze an der Elbe, West Germany. Agent: Galerie René Block, Schaperstrasse 11, 1000 Berlin 12. Addresses: Lerchenfeld 2, 2000 Hamburg 76, West Germany; Regensburgerstrasse 27, 1000 Berlin 30, West Germany.

Individual Exhibitions:

1964 Graphisches Kabinett der Freien Galerie, West Berlin
1965 Galerie René Block, West Berlin
1966 Galerie Patio, Frankfurt
1967 Galerie Rudolf Zwirner, Cologne
Galerie René Block, West Berlin
1969 Galerie René Block, West Berlin
1970 Goethe-Institut, Athens
Galerie Centro, Oldenburg, West Germany
Deutsch Bibliothek, Rome
1971 *Produktion 1962–1971*, Kinstverein, Hamburg (retrospective)
1972 Galerie Bama, Paris
1973 Galerie René Block, West Berlin
Galerie Magers, Bonn
Galerie Inge Baecker, Bochum, West Germany
1975 René Block Gallery, New York
1976 René Block Gallery, New York
Museum Wiesbaden, West Germany
1977 Galerie René Block, West Berlin
1985 DAAD-Galerie, West Berlin
1986 Stadtgalerie Saarbrucken, West Germany
Buro Orange, Munich
1987 Galerie Vorsetzen, Hamburg

Selected Group Exhibitions:

1964 *Kapitalistischer Realismus*, Galerie René Block, West Berlin
1966 *Kritische Kunst*, Dum panu z kunstatu, Brno, Czechoslovakia
1968 *Ars Multiplicata*, Kunsthalle, Cologne
1970 *Information*, Museum of Modern Art, New York
1972 *Documenta 5*, Kassel, West Germany
1974 *Art into Society/Society into Art*, Institute of Contemporary Arts, London
1979 *Kunstler/Sozialarbeiter/Eremit/Forscher*, Kunstverein, Hamburg
1981 *Art Allemagne Aujourd'hui*, ARC/Musee d'Art Moderne, Paris
1984 *Der Mang zum Gesamtkunstwerk*, Akademie der Kunste, West Berlin
1987 *Berlinart*, Museum of Modern Art, New York (travelled to San Francisco Museum of Modern Art)

Collections:

Kaiser-Wilhelm Museum, Krefeld, West Germany; Museum of Modern Art, New York; DAAD-Buro, West Berlin.

Publications:

By BREHMER: films—*Madame Butterfly*, 1969; *Ideale Landschaft*, 19679; *Musikfilm—Stumm*, 1969; *Die ges-*

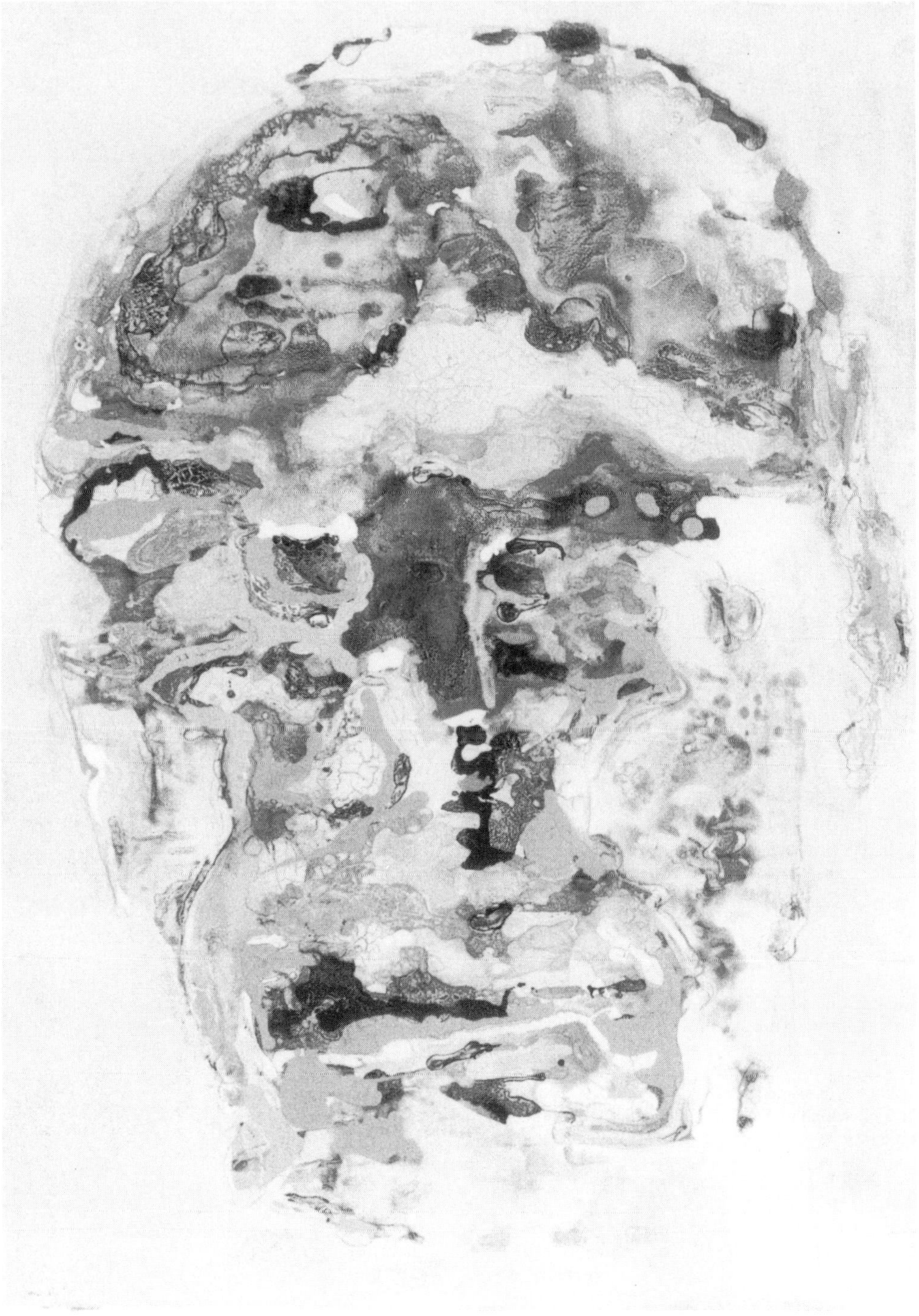

K. P. Brehmer: *Wie mich die Schlange sieht*, 1985

chiedene Frau, 1969; *Walkings*, 1969; *Nr. 1 (Sieg)*, 1969; *Nr. 2 (Mauer)*, 1969; *Nr. 3 (Stanley Brouwn)*, 1969; *Nr. 4 (Passer)*, 1969; *Nr. 5 (Parallel/Identitat)*, 1969; *Nr. 6 (Out/In—Imaginar)*, 1969; *Die Welt im Kopf—Skala*, 1970; *Helmut von Florenz*, 1970; *MA MA*, 1970; *Fernsehoper*, 1970.

On BREHMER: books—*Ars Multiplicata*, exhibition catalogue, Cologne 1968; *K. P. Brehmer: Produktion 1962–1971*, exhibition catalogue, with an interview by Werner Rohde, Hamburg 1971, *Documenta 5. Befragung der Realitat*, exhibition catalogue, edited by Harald Szeemann and others, Kassel, West Germany 1972; *Kunst im Politischen Kampf*, exhibition catalogue, Hannover 1973; *Art into Society/Society into Art*, exhibition catalogue, London 1974; *Tampons d'Artistes*, edited by Herve Fischer, Paris 1974; *K. P. Brehmer: Wie mich die Schlange sieht*, exhibition catalogue, with text by Bernd Schulz, Munich 1986.

It is my view that the only progress achieved by art is that represented by the transference of its whole intensity from "I" to "we." Through ideological kleptomania, so to speak, we must intervene in bourgeois culture, whereby the value of personal possessions, which is inherent in artistic creation, is reduced. This is possible by withholding "creativity" and substituting "imitation." This modification consists of the reduction of "artistic language" to apparent theft and adoption of collective symbols.

The transformation of art from the ideology of self to a social plane signifies stepping away from the private act of individual creation in favour of a collective and anonymous stance, in order to recognize reality through a frame of reference and to provide an orientation for oneself and the on-looker.

In this way the artist develops from a lone hero to an active participant.

—K. P. Brehmer

BRISLEY, Stuart.

British. Born in Haslemere, Surrey, in 1933. Studied at Guildford School of Art, Surrey, 1949–54; Royal College of Art, London, 1956–59; Akademie der Bildenden Künste, Munich, 1959–60; and Florida State University, Tallahassee, 1960–62. Independent artist, concentrating on performance and installation works, London since 1963: Artist in Residence, Imperial War Museum, London, 1987. Founder-Member, Arts Information Registry, London, 1967, and Artists' Union, London, 1972; Member, Artists Placement Group, London, 1967–71. Recipient: Bavarian State Stipendium, 1959–60; Fulbright Travel Award, to Florida, 1960–64; Deutscher Akademischer Austauschdienst (D.A.A.D.) Scholarship, West Berlin, 1973; British Council grant, 1976, 1977. Address: 28 Oakhill Road, London SW15, England.

Individual Exhibitions:

1960	Galerie Deutscher Bucherbund, Munich
1961	Studio F. Ulm, West Germany
1962	Cornell University, Ithica, New York
1963	Washington and Jefferson College, Washington, Pennsylvania
	Cornell University, Ithica, New York
1965	New Vision Centre, London
1966	McRoberts and Tunnard Gallery, London
1967	Museum of Modern Art, Oxford (with Bill Culbert)
	Herbert Art Gallery, Coventry (with Bill Culbert; travelled to Trinity College, Dublin, and the University of Bristol)
1968	*Bromsgrove Festival*, Worcestershire (with Bill Culbert)
	Tate Gallery, London (with Peter Sedgeley)
	Camden Arts Centre, London (with Bill Culbert)
	Madame Tussaud's Waxworks, London (with Bill Culbert)
1969	Camden Arts Centre, London
1970	*Guest of Honour*, New Arts Laboratory, London
	Sigi Krauss Gallery, London
1971	Centro de Arte y Communicacion, Buenos Aires
1972	*You Know It Makes Sense*, Ikon Gallery, Birmingham
	Zl656395C, Gallery House, London
	Artist as Whore, Gallery House, London
1973	*10 Days*, Paramedia Editions, West Berlin
1975	*12 Days*, Kunsforum, Rottweil, West Germany
	Moments of Decision/Indecision, Palac Kultury i Nauki, Warsaw
1976	Battersea Arts Centre, London
	Northern Arts Gallery, Newcastle upon Tyne
1981	Institute of Contemporary Arts, London (travelled to Ikon Gallery, Birmingham)
	Acme Gallery, London (with Iain Robertson)
1986	Orchard Gallery, Derry, Northern Ireland
1987	Imperial War Museum, London

Selected Group Exhibitions:

1953	*Young Contemporaries*, R.B.A. Galleries, London (and 1957, 1958, 1959)
1960	*Grosse Sommer Ausstellung Neue Gruppe*, Haus der Kunst, Munich
1965	*The London Group*, Art Federation Galleries, London
1968	*Artists for Czechoslovakia*, Camden Arts Centre, London
1970	*Come Together*, Royal Court Theatre, London
1972	*A Survey of the Avant-Garde in Britain*, Gallery House, London
1973	*Magic and Strong Medicine*, Walker Art Gallery, Liverpool
1976	*Arte Inglese Oggi 1960–76*, Palazzo Reale, Milan
1978	*Spring Show 2*, Serpentine Gallery, London
1982	*Group Exhibition*, Lewis Johnstone Gallery, London

Publications:

By BRISLEY: articles—"Wanted: A New Deal in Art Schools?" in *Penrose Annual*, London 1969; "Environ-

ments" in *Studio International* (London), June 1969; "Physical Situations," interview with Simon Field, in *Art and Artists* (London), August 1971; "No, It Is Not On" in *Studio International* (London), March 1972; "Anti-Performance Art" in *Arte Inglese Oggi 1960–76*, exhibition catalogue, Milan 1976; "Stuart Brisley," interview with John Roberts, in *Artlog* (London), April/May 1981.

On BRISLEY: books—*Play Orbit*, edited by Jasia Reichardt, with texts by several authors, London 1969; *Art Event and Happenings* by Udo Kultermann, London 1971; *A Survey of the Avant-Garde in Britain*, volume 1, with an introduction by Rosetta Brooks, London 1972; *Magic and Strong Medicine*, exhibition catalogue, with text by Norbert Lynton, Liverpool 1973; *Stuart Brisley*, exhibition catalogue, with texts by Paul Overy and John Roberts, London 1981.

The work of Stuart Brisley is concerned with pain.

In a period when art has upped stakes and moved from its position of lofty detachment to set up its own stall at the Vanity Fayre, when painters celebrate the latest fashions in automobiles, ladies' shoes or pop singers in a joyful and colourful discord, when sculptors rush to imitate the recent inventions of a mechanical age, when artists of all persuasions are glad to see their work sold to the highest bidder with all the television and champagne razzmatazz of the big gallery opening, Brisley has taken it upon himself to be the conscience of the art world, reminding it that art also contains a more somber tradition of horror and disgust, protest and pain.

Such a role is difficult to sustain; it could easily become strident or embarrassing, which is possibly why Brisley has always been meticulous about his techniques, about what is and what is not permissible, and is certainly why in his work the pain is transmitted to the audience via himself. To paint pictures of the ills of society could easily become mere preaching, but to use himself as the illustration safeguards the artist from such a tendency.

A typical Brisley piece, and one of his best, was his "Bath" performance at Gallery House in London. This, now sadly defunct, avant-guard gallery invited Brisley to take part in a survey of recent British art and followed its usual policy of allowing the artists to choose their own space. The gallery had once been a private house and Brisley choose the bathroom.

On the day the exhibition opened, visitors, drawn to the location by the gathering crowd, could see Brisley lying fully clothed in the bath with only his nose and mouth above water. He had put dye in the water which gave it a stagnant look and had not attempted to clean the room, which had been unused for sometime. On the floor were scattered pieces of raw meat.

The image was powerful, with overtones of police state torture or lonely suicide. It worked as well as a photograph of the real thing might do and clearly had a strong effect on the spectators. But Brisley was not yet finished: the exhibition ran for three weeks and every day he spent lying in the bath just able to breathe. After about three days the flies in the neighborhood woke up to the fact that a magnificent free meal was available to them in the form of the now rotting flesh; after 10 the stench was unbearable, and Brisley's fellow artists had to ask him to terminate the performance.

The effect of such a work is shock, but because Brisley is careful to do work slowly and submit his own mind and body to far greater pressure than he inflicts on his audience, it avoids being mere shock and becomes instead archetypal and thought provoking.

Brisley's earliest performances took place in gridlike sculptural settings and featured large casts dressed in white medical-looking clothes and bandages. This phase of working with others reached its culmination in an exhibition in Edinburgh where the artist worked in a disused car saleroom on one of the main streets. In this the grid was replaced by wrecked cars, some of which still were capable of movement, and Brisley spent the exhibition driving them headlong into each other until the whole area was littered with wreckage. He eventually had to stop this when affected by carbon monoxide poisoning from the exhaust fumes.

Since that time Brisley has realized that he cannot ask others to take part in his art and has worked alone. In one recent piece he had himself locked for five days in a room containing just one chair and one lightbulb continuously burning; the floor was swimming in water. Visitors to the exhibition could see him through a small barred window.

There are other artists who are working in similar fields of self-inflicted pain and humiliation, but only Brisley brings to this highly questionable type of activity a dignity and an ability to relate the images he creates to the wider issues of society. Where others indulge in exhibitionistic masochism, Brisley by carefully removing his individuality from the situation and by using his own body as if it were inert sculpture, often achieves the difficult feat of enabling the spectator to overcome his feelings of shock and embarrassment and, in their place, to contemplate the creepy-crawlies that still lurk under the stone of our affluent and somewhat complacent society.

—Alastair Mackintosh

BROODTHAERS, Marcel.

Belgian. Born in Brussels, 28 January 1924. Studied chemistry briefly; mainly self-taught in art. Married Maria Bilessen; daughter: Marie-Pucke. Worked as a book dealer and guide in art museums, Brussels; as writer and poet; became artist in 1964; settled in London in the late 1960s. *Died* (in Cologne) *28 January 1976.*

Individual Exhibitions:

1964	Galerie Smith, Brussels
	Galerie St. Laurent, Brussels
1965	Palais des Beaux-Arts, Brussels
1966	Galerie J., Paris
	Wide White Space Gallery, Antwerp
1967	Palais des Beaux-Arts, Brussels
1968	Galerie 44, Brussels
	Wide White Space Gallery, Antwerp
	Librarie Saint Germain des Pres, Paris
1969	Wide White Space Gallery, Antwerp
	Galerie R. Roucke, Ghent
	Galerie Basenge-Katz, Berlin
1970	Galerie Michael Werner, Cologne
	Galerie MTL, Brussels
	Galerie Skulima, Berlin
1971	Wide White Space Gallery, Antwerp
	Galerie Michael Werner, Cologne
	Städtisches Museum, Mönchengladbach, West Germany
	Galerie Yvon Lambert, Paris
1972	Wide White Space Gallery, Antwerp
	Galerie Heiner Friedrich, Munich
	Modern Art Agency, Naples
	Städtische Kunsthalle, Dusseldorf
	Galerie Grafikmeyer, Karlsruhe
	Jack Wendler Gallery, London
1973	Galerie Michael Werner, Cologne
	Galerie Heiner Friedrich, Munich
	Galerie Francoise Lambert, Milan
	Cinema Arsenal, Berlin
	Galerie Loehr, Frankfurt
	Art and Project, Amsterdam
	Galerie Rudolf Zwirner, Cologne
	Galerie Yvon Lambert, Paris
1974	Palais des Beaux-Arts, Brussels
	Wide White Space Gallery, Antwerp
	Galerie MTL, Brussels
	Cinema Melville, Paris
	Kunstmuseum, Basle
	Galerie René Block, Berlin
	Petersberg Press, London
1975	Galerie Grafikmeyer, Karlsruhe
	Nationalgalerie, Berlin (travelled to Museum of Modern Art, Oxford, and the Centre Georges Pompidou, Paris)
	Kunsthalle, Dusseldorf
	Institute of Contemporary Arts, London
	Nigel Greenwood Gallery, London
1977	Nigel Greenwood Gallery, London
	Hester van Royen Gallery, London
	Tate Gallery, London
	New 57 Gallery, Edinburgh
1978	Galerie Heiner Friedrich, Munich
	Galerie Isy Brachot, Brussels
1980	Galerie Michael Werner, Cologne
	Tate Gallery, London
	Museum Ludwig, Cologne
1981	Museum Boymans-van Beuningen, Rotterdam
1982	Kunsthalle, Berne
	Moderna Museet, Stockholm
1983	Galerie Michael Werner, Cologne
1984	Mary Boone Gallery, New York

Selected Group Exhibitions:

1958	*Films Experimentaux*, Knokke-le-Zoute, Belgium
1964	*Jeune Sculpture Belge*, Palais des Beaux-Arts, Brussels
1965	*Pop Art, Nouveau Realisme, etc.*, Palais des Beaux-Arts, Brussels
1969	*Language 3*, Dwan Gallery, New York
1972	*Documenta 5*, Kassel, West Germany
1973	*Bilder: Objekte: Film: Konzepte*, Städtische Galerie Lenbachhaus, Munich
1975	*Functions of Drawing*, Rijksmuseum Kröller-Müller, Otterio, Netherlands
1976	*Biennale*, Venice
1980	*Printed Art: A View of Two Decades*, Museum of Modern Art, New York
1983	*Der Hang zum Gesamtkunstwerk*, Kunsthaus, Zurich

Collections:

Musée des Beaux-Arts, Brussels; Städtisches Museum, Mönchengladbach, West Germany; Sammlung Hahn, Cologne.

Publications:

By BROODTHAERS: books—*Mon Livre d'Ogre*, Ostend 1957; *Minuit*, Brussels 1960; *La Bete Noire*, Brussels 1962; *Pense-Bete*, Brussels 1963; *Phantomas*, Brussels 1966; *Le Corbeau et le Renard*, book and film, Antwerp 1968; *Un Coup de Des Jamais n'Abolira le Hasard*, Antwerp and Cologne 1969; *Vingt ans Après, Brussels*, Brussels 1969; *Plan Vert*, Cologne 1972; *Magie (Art et Politique)*, Paris 1973; *Je hais le Mouvement qui Deplace les Lignes*, Hamburg 1973; *Jeter due Poisson sur le Marche de Cologne*, Cologne 1973; *Un Jardin d'Hiver*, London 1974; *A Voyage on the North Sea*, London, Hamburg, and Cologne 1974; *Rascisme Vegetal*, Cologne 1974; *Pauvre Belgique*, Brussels 1974; *En lisant la Lorelei oder wie ich die Lorelei gelesen habe*, Paris and Munich 1975. films—*La Clef de l'Horloge (Kurt Schwitters)*, 1957; *Le Corbeau et le Renard*, 1967; *Section 29th Siècle (Musée d'Art Moderne, department des Aigles)*, 1968; *La Signature*, 1970; *La Pluie (Projet pour un Texte)*, 1970; *La Pipe (René Magritte)*, 1970; *Un Film de Ch. Baudelaire*, 1971; *Histoire d'Amour (Dr. Huysmans)*, 1971; *Le Poisson*, 1971; *Paris*, 1971; *Au dela de cette Limite*, 1972; *Chere petite soeur*, 1972; *Voyage en mer du Nord*, 1973; *Ah, que la chasse soit le plaisir des rois*, 1972; *Un Jardin d'Hiver*, 1974; *Eau de Cologne*, 1974; *Berlin oder ein Traum mit Sahne*, 1974; *Jeremy Bentham*, 1974; *The Battle of Waterloo*, 1975–76.

On BROODTHAERS: books—*Marcel Broodthaers*, exhibition catalogue, Paris 1975; *Marcel Broodthaers* by Freddy de Vree, Antwerp 1979; *Marcel Broodthaers*, exhibition catalogue, London 1980; *Marcel Broodthaers*, exhibition catalogue, Cologne 1980 (with complete bibliography).

Broodthaers was raised in French speaking Belgium and was persuaded to study chemistry rather than art which he had wanted to study. He subsequently worked in a bank and then as a bookdealer. Before

1964 his interest in writers and in books as objects had led him to become a poet with excursions into photography and film-making.

Early on in his life Broodthaers had been fascinated by the work of Rene Magritte, Belgium's most famous twentieth century artist, and his major works, produced in the last ten years of his life, were to reflect similar preoccupations with puzzles, hidden messages and irony and the use of the written word as an element in visual art. His first film, *La Clef de l'Horloge*, produced in 1957, was a cinematographic poem in honor of Kurt Schwitters

In 1963 Broodthaers was introduced to the Pop Art of Jim Dine, Roy Lichtenstein and Claus Oldenberg, which prompted him to write an article on Magritte's influence on Dine. Broodthaers' link with Magritte was strongest in the use of literary and visual puns—a concept dear to the heart of 1930s Surrealism which sprang from poetry in the first instance.

Between 1967–75 Broodthaers produced films, books, works using words, photography, sound tapes and slides, and during this time established his position in the visual art world with *Musée d'Art moderne, Départment des Aigles*. This was a 'museum' with 'departments' of 'many sections' which Broodthaers erected in houses and galleries between 1968 and 1974. Behind it was the idea of the worker who takes over his workplace, and though it was a parody, it was not a parody of the museum, but a comment upon the sociology of the museum or the curator who usurps the role of the creator—the artist—a very elaborate piece of irony.

Though Broodthaers could be seen as a sort of latter day Dadaist or Surrealist, in his use of 'found' imagery, his aggregation of objects tended to reflect the 'good life'—European style, food, wine, literature, etc. Like the Surrealists who preceded him, Broodthaers' visual art rests heavily on a poetic base. This base, in Broodthaers' case, relies for its strucure on "metonymy," which is a term of rhetoric meaning, (according to the *Shorter Oxford English Dictionary)*, "A figure in which the name of an attribute or adjunct is substituted for that of the thing meant, e.g., sceptre for authority."

Though he remained, in his time, very much on the fringes of the art world, (at a time of Pop Art he was almost a throwback to Surrealism), his work was acknowledged by the art world in the 1970s with the rise of interest in Conceptual and Performance Art.

—Victoria Keller

BROOKS, James.

American. Born in St. Louis, Missouri, in 1906. Studied at Southern Methodist University, Dallas, 1923–25; Art Students League, New York, under K. Nicolaides and Boardman Robinson, 1927–30. Served in the United States Army, as an Art Correspondent, in the Middle East, 1942–45. Married Mary MacDonald in 1938; married the artist Charlotte Park in 1947. Full-time artist, New York and East Hampton, New York. Taught at Columbia University, New York, 1946–48, and Pratt Institute, New York, 1948–55; Visiting Critic in Advanced Painting, Yale University, New Haven, Connecticut, 1955–60; Artist-in-Residence, American Academy, Rome, 1963; Visiting Critic, New College, Sarasota, Florida, 1965–67; Professor of Art, Queens College, New York, 1966–69; Visiting Critic, University of Pennsylvania, Philadelphia, 1972–75; Andrew Carnegie Visiting Professor of Art, Cooper Union, New York, 1975. Recipient: First Painting Prize and Logan Medal, 1957, and Normal Waite Harris Silver Medal and Prize, 1961, Art Institute of Chicago; Ford Foundation Purchase Award, Pennsylvania Academy of Fine Arts, 1962; Guggenheim Fellowship, 1969; National Endowment for the Arts Grant, 1973. Member, American Academy and Institute of Arts and Letters, 1973. Agent: Gruenebaum Gallery, 415 West Broadway, New York, New York 10012. Address: 128 Neck Path, The Springs, East Hampton, Long Island, New York 11937, U.S.A.

Individual Exhibitions:

1950 Peridot Gallery, New York
1951 Peridot Gallery, New York
1952 Miller-Pollard Gallery, Seattle
Peridot Gallery, New York
1953 Peridot Gallery, New York
1954 Grace Borgenicht Gallery, New York
1957 Stable Gallery, New York
1959 Stable Gallery, New York
1961 Kootz Gallery, New York
1962 Kootz Gallery, New York
1963 Whitney Museum, New York (retrospective; toured the United States, 1963–64)
1965 Kootz Gallery, New York
1966 Philadelphia Art Alliance
1968 Martha Jackson Gallery, New York
Southampton College, Southampton, Long Island, New York
1969 Berenson Gallery, Miami
1970 The Century Association, New York
1971 Martha Jackson Gallery, New York
1972 Museum of Fine Arts, Dallas (retrospective)
Martha Jackson Gallery, New York
1975 Martha Jackson Gallery/Finch College Museum of Art, New York (retrospective of paintings and drawings; travelled to Guild Hall Museum, East Hampton, New York; Flint Institute of Arts, Michigan; Grand Rapids Art Museum, Michigan; Cranbrook Academy of Art, Bloomfield Hills, Michigan; and University of Connecticut, Storrs)
Galleria Lorenzelli, Milan
Works in Progress, Cooper Union, New York
1976 Summit Art Center, New Jersey (retrospective)
Robinson Galleries, Houston
Martha Jackson Gallery, New York
Foire International d'Art Contemporain, Paris
1977 Carone Gallery, Fort Lauderdale, Florida
Himelfarb Gallery, Watermill, New York
1978 Lerner-Heller Gallery, New York
Himelfarb Gallery, Watermill, New York
1979 Montclair Museum, New Jersey
Gruenebaum Gallery, New York (with Giorgio Cavalion)
1981 Gruenebaum Gallery, New York
Himelfarb Gallery, Watermill, New York

Selected Group Exhibitions:

1958 *Jong Amerika Schildert*, Stedelijk Museum, Amsterdam
1960 *60 American Painters*, Walker Art Center, Minneapolis
1961 *American Abstract Expressionists and Imagists*, Guggenheim Museum, New York
1967 *200 Years of Watercolor Painting in America*, Metropolitan Museum of Art, New York
1969 *The New American Painting and Sculpture: The First Generation*, Museum of Modern Art, New York
1973 *Exhibition of Newly Elected Members*, American Academy and Institute of Arts and Letters, New York
American Art Mid-Century Exhibition, National Gallery of Art, Washington, D.C.
1980 *Arte Americana Contemporanea*, Civic Museum, Udine, Italy
1981 *American Painting 1930–1980*, Haus der Kunst, Munich
1982 *5 Distinguished Alumni: The WPA Federal Art Project*, Hirshhorn Museum, Washington, D.C. (with DeKooning, Neel, Bolotowski and Lassaw)

Collections:

Guggenheim Museum, New York; Metropolitan Museum of Art, New York; Museum of Modern Art, New York; Whitney Museum, New York; Fogg Art Museum, Harvard University, Cambridge, Massachusetts; Hirshhorn Museum, Washington, D.C.; Detroit Institute of Art; Art Institute of Chicago Museum of Fine Arts, Houston; Tate Gallery, London.

Publications:

On BROOKS: books—*The Story of Modern Art* by Sheldon Cheney, New York 1958; *Art Since 1945* by Sam Hunter New York 1959; *American Painting in the 20th Century* by Henry Geldzahler, New York 1960; *The Unknown Shore* by Dore Ashton, Boston 1962; *James Brooks* by Sam Hunter New York 1963; *History of Modern Art* by H. H. Arnason New York 1969; *James Brooks*, exhibition catalogue, by Merrill Ruepple, Dallas 1972; *A History of American Art* by George M. Cohen, New York 1973; *James Brooks*, exhibition catalogue, by Elayne H. Varian, New York 1975, articles—"James Brooks and the Abstract Inscape" by Irving Sandler in *Artnews* (New York), February 1963; "James Brooks" by H. H. Arnason in *Art International* (Lugano Switzerland), March 1963; "James Brooks: Stain into Image" by April Kingsley in *Artnews* (New York), December 1972; "James Brooks: The Man and His Art" by Barbara Delatiner in the *New York Times*, 29 June 1975; "James Brooks at Finch College and Martha Jackson Gallery" by Phyllis Derfner in *Art in America* (New York, July/August 1975; "The Paintings of James Brooks" by Carter Ratcliff in *Arts Magazine* (New York), September 1978.

I work under these assumptions. That a private symbolism is not possible; that my work will occupy others as it has me; that whether it does, and how soon, depends on things we can not know—the ultimate power of the painting and the need felt for it; that manipulation of form to assure an audience would destroy the reality of the work and debase the concept of communication; that good painting, as always, is a door opened to man's spirit; that it will not repel because of its obscurity, but may because of its directness.

—James Brooks

Like Guston, Frankenthaler, and his own long-time friend Bradley Walker Tomlin, Brooks stands with those New York School artists who, about the onset of the 1950s, took the overtly emotive and tactile-based improvisatory flow of Pollock and DeKooning, and made it a more meditative, slow-paced gesture, an even cherishing kind of paintery act. Before his military service in World War II, where he was a combat artist, Brooks had been a commercial artist, and had then, from 1936 until 1942, worked with the Federal Art Project, a subdivision of the Works Progress Administration (WPA). A major portion of his time was devoted to the creation of a 235 feet long mural *Flight* in the rotunda of the Marine Terminal at LaGuardia Airport in New York City. Admired as an important work at the time, and overpainted in the 1950s, the painting has recently been restored to revived acclaim. With his return to New York in 1946, Brooks met Guston and Pollock (with whom he would be in close contact in the last years of the 1940s), and found the push towards a new confidence and a new style in American art already well underway. Yet he remained a Cubist, who needed the painterly epiphany of an intimate personal confrontation with abstraction to move him unhesitatingly into that mode. It is said to have occurred only in 1948 when Brooks saw the glue seepage of a collage on the reverse canvas side. In a sense, he is still that artist, surprised by the elegance of chance and the softer dispersion of paint into the canvas surface. He has been claimed (A. Kingsley) as the first American artist to stain pigment directly into raw canvas: and thus the premier American to grasp the wider-ranging significance of Pollock's drip techniques. (T. Hess remarked, in 1951, that Brooks' forms "stayed in the weave of the canvas.")

The general aura of his work appears a genial disorder, with a lyricism based upon essentially organic terrain the guiding force since the 1950s' close. Before then, during his first decade of non-representational art, there may have been a more easily detected rhythm still infused with the pattern of

James Brooks: *Ealand*, 1973

Cubism. More and more, Brooks gave into the automatist influence of Surrealism—although that mode has never been easily assignable to his art—to achieve a pulse quite his own with wire-like linearities and fluctuating biomorphic shapes. (A part of his acknowledged success is the only momentary sense of reference to Arp or Miro that surfaces in his many works.) His creative methods have always been canted towards improvisation, so that he will frequently turn the canvas while engaged in the painting process; just so, he has used blotting techniques and paint randomly dispersed in the effort to achieve a personally authentic significance. It is also known that he, quite self-consciously, will work on but one painting at a time, so as to avoid any carryover of form and pattern invention in a successive image. Still active at the onset of this penultimate decade of the modernist century, Brooks may well be hailed as "an old master of modernism" in his continual and enlivening manipulation of these once-radical precepts. Such continual self-challenge has moved him as well into the position of "father of recent lyrical abstraction."

—Joshua B. Kind

BROUWN, Stanley.

Dutch. Born in Paramaribo, Surinam, in 1935. Educated in Paramaribo; self-taught in art. Independent artist, Amsterdam, since 1960; first "This Way Brouwn" works, Amsterdam, 1960; associated with the Fluxus performance artists, Amsterdam, from 1962. Address: Willem de Zwygerlaan 60–1, Amsterdam, Netherlands.

Individual Exhibitions:

1970 Stedelijk Museum, Schiedam, Netherlands
Städtisches Museum, Mönchenglabach, West Germany
1971 Zentrum fur Aktuelle Kunst, Aachen, West Germany
1976 Van Abbemuseum, Eindhoven, Netherlands (travelled to the Kunsthalle, Berne)
1977 Whitechapel Art Gallery, London

Selected Group Exhibitions:

1970 *18 Paris iv 70*, Paris
1972 *Documenta*, Kassel, West Germany
1978 *Werke aus der Sammiung Crex*, Ink, Zurich (travelled to the Louisiana Museum, Humieback, Denmark, Städtische Galerie in Lenbachhaus, Munich, and the Van Abbemuseum, Eindhoven, Netherlands)
1979 *Mit Zeichnerischen Mittein gemacht*, Stadtschloss, Fulda, West Germany

Collections:

Van Abbemuseum, Eindhoven, Netherlands; Stedelijk Museum, Amsterdam; Kunsthalle, Berne.

Publications:

By BROUWN: books—*This Way Brouwn*, Cologne and New York 1971; *Afghanistan/Zambia*, Aachen, West Germany 1971.

On BROUWN: books—*18 Paris iv 70*, edited by Michel Claura, Paris 1970; *Concept Art* by Klaus Honnef, Cologne 1971; *Documenta 5: Befragung der Realiat Bildwelten huete*, exhibition catalogue, edited by Harald Szeeman and others, Kassel, West Germany 1972; *Stanley Brouwn*, exhibition catalogue, edited by Coosje van Bruggen and Rudi H. Fuchs, Eindhoven, Netherlands 1976; *Werke aus der Sammlung Crex*, exhibition catalogue, by Cristel Sauer and Urs Raussmuller, Zurich 1978; *Mit Zeichnerischen Mitteln gemacht*, exhibition catalogue, with text by Michael Lingner, Fulda, West Germany 1979; articles—"Dutch Artists on Television" by Carel Blotkamp in *Studio International* (London), June 1971; "Stanley Brouwn: Door Kosmischestralen Lopen" by J. Cladders in *Museumjournaal* (Amsterdam), July 1971; "Stanley Brouwn: Steps" in *Avalanche* (New York), Spring 1972.

BRUS, Günter.

Austrian. Born in Ardning, 27 September 1938. Educated at Volkschule and Hauptschule, Mureck, 1944–50, and Hauptschule, Stainz, 1950–56; studied at the Kunstgewerbeschule, Graz, 1953– 57; Akademie fur Angewandte Kunst, Vienna, 1957–60. Served in the Austrian Federal Army, 1961. Married Anni Steiner

in 1962; daughter: Diana. Independent artist; has lived and worked in Vienna, 1960–69, West Berlin, 1969–79, and in Graz, Austria, since 1979; produced first action works and self-painting works, Vienna, 1964; Founder Member, with Hermann Nitsch, Otto Muehl and Rudolf Schwarzkogler, Wiener Aktionismus group, Vienna, 1964; Founder, with Otto Muehl, Institut fur Direkte Kunst, Vienna, 1966; Founder, with Arnulf Meifert, *Deutsche Trivialeum,* West Berlin, 1974; Founder Editor, with Arnulf Meifert, *Die Schastrommel,* later *Die Drossel* newspaper of the Osterreichische Exilregierung, West Berlin, 1969–76. Recipient: Wurdignungspreis des Ministeriums fur Unterricht und Kunst, Vienna, 1981, 1982; Kunstpreis, City of Graz, 1986; Kunstpreis, City of Vienna, 1986. Agent: Galerie Heike Curtze, Citadellstrasse 11, 4000 Dusseldorf 1, and Seilerstatte 15/14, 1010 Vienna. Address: Einspinnergasse 3, 8010 Graz, Austria.

Individual Exhibitions:

1961 *Aktionsmalerei,* Galerie Junge Generation, Vienna (with Alfons Schilling)
1965 *Malerie-Selbstbemalung-Selbstverstümmelung,* Galerie Junge Generation, Vienna
1971 *Handzeichnungen,* Galerie Michael Werner, Cologne
1973 *Zeichnungen,* Galerie Grünangergasse 12, Vienna
Fotos von Aktionen, Galleria Diagramma, Milan
1974 *Zeichnungen,* Galerie Krauthammer, Zurich
Fotos von Aktionen, Studio Morra, Naples
Der Vollschmerz, Galerie Springer, Berlin
1975 *Das Namenlos,* Galerie Wiener and Würthle, Berlin
Der Vollschmerz und Arbeiten von 1973 und 1975, Galerie Van de Loo, Munich
Nachtfreudenwalzer, Galerie Grünangergasse 12, Vienna
1976 *Nachtfreudenwalzer,* Galerie Stummer und Hubschmid, Zurich
Auszüge aus dem Laufenden Werk, Galerie Gaetan, Carouge, Geneva
Zeichnungen, Galerie Klein, Bonn
Das Aulicht, Rathaus, Mureck, Austria
Brus: Werke, Galerie Kalb, Vienna
Zeichnungen und Schriften, Kunsthalle, Berne
1977 *Zeichnungen, Bücher und Mappenwerke,* Galerie A. Amsterdam
Bilder aus Gebenedeitanien, Galerie Springer, Berlin
Die Gärten in der Exosphäre, Galerie Van de Loo, Munich
Herzeigung, Galerie Jörg Stummet, Zurich (travelled to the Galeriei Gysin, Dübendorf, Switzerland)
1978 *Die Pracht der Hellsten Freude,* Goethe-Institut, Amsterdam
Amorphophallus Titanum, Studio Morra, Naples
1979 *Franz Schreker: Die Gazeichneten,* Frankfurt Oper
Reizfluten, Galerie Heike Curtze, Vienna
Franz Schreker: Die Gezeichneten, Staatsoper, Vienna
Bild-Dichtungen, Galerie Heike Curtze, Dusseldorf
Das Knaben Wunderhorn, DAAD Galerie, Berlin
Abendwerke und Nachtarbeiten, Galerie Jörg Stummer, Zurich
1980 *Bild-Dichtungen,* Whitechapel Art Gallery, London (travelled to the Kunstverein, Hamburg, and the Kunstmuseum, Lucerne)
Schadelschrei-Romantik, Galerie Van de Loo, Munich
Augenmusik, Galerie Heike Curtze, Dusseldorf
Augenmusik: Trugschattengewächse, Galerie Bloch, Innsbruck
1981 *Bild-Dichtungen,* Kulturhaus, Graz, Austria
Traumentiziehungskur, Galerie Heike Curtze, Vienna
Weisser Wind, Gallerie Jörg Stummer, Zurich
1982 *Unruhe nach dem Sturm,* Galerie A, Amsterdam
Blaues Herz im Nerveninfernal, Galerie Zell am See, Austria
Zyankal-Zyklamen, Galerie Van de Loo, Munich

Günter Brus: *Der Fruchtentkerner*, 1979

1983 *Rasende Geduld,* Maximilianverlag Sabine Knust, Munich
Lichtsprache—Le Langage de la Lumière, Galerie Farideh Cadot, Paris
Die Gärten in der Exosphäre und andere Bild-Dichtungen, Rupertinum, Salzburg
Blindes Brot, Petersen Galerie, West Berlin
Trunkene Triebe, Galerie Heike Curtze, Dusseldorf
1984 *Morchposten des Pulsschlags,* Galerie Jörg Stummer, Zurich
Sonata Domestica, Galerie Bleich-Rossi, Graz, Austria
Augensternstunden, Van Abbemuseum, Eindhoven, Netherlands
Franz Schreker: Die Gezeichneten, Rupertinum, Salzburg
La Croce del Veneto, Galerie Heike Curtze, Vienna
Eisblut, blauer Frost, Edition Hundertmark, Cologne
1985 *Astres de la nuit—Nachtgestirne,* Galerie Maeght Lelong, Paris
Eisblut, blauer Frost, Galerie A, Amsterdam
Bühnebild-und Kostümentwürfe zu G. Roth, Kulturhaus, Graz, Austria
1986 *Der Ausblick,* Galerie Heike Curtze, Vienna (and Galerie Zell am See, Austria)
Stichproben, Maximilianverlag Sabine Knust, Munich
Stumme Gewitter, Galerie Jörg Stummer, Zurich
1987 *Ballungsträume,* Galerie Thaddaeus Ropac, Salzburg

Selected Group Exhibitions:

1966 *Ornament ist ein Verbrechen,* Galerie Dvorak, Vienna (with Otto Muehl, Loos-Villa and Wien-Hietzig)
1967 *Direct Art Festival,* Porrhaus, Vienna
1972 *Documenta 5,* Kassel, West Germany
1975 *Body Works,* Museum of Contemporary Art, Chicago
1978 *11 Artists Working in Berlin,* Whitechapel Art Gallery, London
1980 *Kunst der Siebziger Jahre,* at the *Biennale,* Venice
1981 *Westkunst,* Rheinhallen, Cologne
1983 *New Art* Tate Gallery, London
1985 *Rennweg,* Castello di Rivoli, Turin, Italy

1987 *Berlinart 1961-87,* Museum of Modern Art, New York (travelled to San Francisco Museum of Modern Art)

Collections:

Uno-City, Vienna; Tate Gallery, London; Museum of Modern Art, New York; Musee d'Art Moderne, Paris; Van Abbemuseum, Eindhoven, Netherlands; Kunsthalle, Hamburg; Kunstmuseum, Winterthur, Switzerland; Festspielhaus, Bregenz; Landessammlungen Rupertinum, Salzburg; Staatsgalerie, Stuttgart.

Publications:

By BRUS: books—*Malerei-Selbstemalung-Selbstverstrümmelung,* Vienna 1965; *b & m—direkte kunst,* with Otto Muehl, Vienna 1967; *Burs/Muehl: Direkte' Theatre,* Vienna 1967; *Patent Urinoir,* Vienna 1968; *Patent Merde,* Vienna 1968; *Unter dem Ladentisch,* Berlin 1969; *Die Schastrommel* no. 1-11, Berlin 1969-73; *Burs: Bausch-und-Bogen-Scheisse,* Cologne 1970; *Korperanalyse,* Berlin 1970; *Handzeichnungen,* Cologne/New York 1971; *Irrwisch* Frankfurt 1971; *Der Balkon Europas,* Berlin 1972; *Die Neue Dekadenz,* Berlin 1972; *Art des Giftes, Dauer der Vergiftung, Sitz der Schmerzer,* Berlin 1973; *Zereissprobe,* Berlin 1974; *Nacht freudewalzer,* Berlin 1975; *Das Namelos, Die Drossel, Nr. 14,* Berlin 1975; *Circannual, Die Drossel Nr. 16,* Berlin 1976; *Die Lachende Verwesung,* Berlin 1976; *Hohes Gebrechen,* Altona and Hohengebraching 1976; *Der Frackzwang,* Altona and Hohengebraching 1976; *Das Aulicht,* Stuttgart 1977; *Jeden jeden Mittwoch,* with D. Steiger, Berlin 1977; *Farbige Zeichnungen aus dem Jahren 1970-77,* Altona and Hohengebraching 1977; *Phantom-Palaste,* Berlin 1978; *Gestirn-Abzeichan,* Altona and Hohengebraching 1978; *Die Falter des Vorschlafs,* Altona and Hohengebraching 1978; *Die Gärten in der Exosphäre,* Altona and Hohengebraching 1979; *Das Rufwort,* Altona and Hohengebraching 1979; *Die Herbsttrompete,* Vienna and Munich 1981; *Zyankal-Zyklamen,* Munich 1982; *Rasende Geduld,* Munich 1983; *Stillstand der Sonnenuhr,* Vienna and Munich 1983; *Die Geheimnistrager,* Salzburg 1984; *Die Wundharmonika,* Eindhoven 1984; *Die Ruine,* Paris 1985; *Stumme Gewitter,* Zurich 1986; *Amor und Amok,* Salzburg 1986; *Gebrauchsmystik,* Vienna and Munich 1986; films—*Ana,* with Kurt Kren, 1964; *Selbstbemalung,* Vienna 1964; *Selbstverstümmelung,* with Wiener Spaziergang, Vienna 1965; *Transfusion,* Vienna 1965; *Gut and Gerne,* 1966; *10 Rounds,* with Otto Muehl and Kurt Kren, 1966; *20 September,* Vienna 1967; *Einatmen und Ausatem,* 1967; *Direct Art Festival,* Vienna 1967; *Aktion mit Diana,* Vienna 1967; *Mit Schwung ins Meue Jahr,* with Otto Muehl and Rudolf Schwartzkogler, 1967; *Kunst und Revolution,* Vienna 1968; *Satisfaction,* Vienna 1968; *Der Helle Wahnsinn,* Aachen, West Germany 1968; *Direkte Kunst,* Dusseldorf 1968; *Strangulation,* Vienna 1968; *Impudenz im Grunewald,* Berlin 1969; *Blummenstuck, nach einem Gedicht von G. Ruhm,* Berlin 1969; *Intelligenztest,* Berlin 1969; *Korperanalyse, Zerreissprobe,* Munich 1970; *Psycho-Dramolett,* Munich 1970.

On BRUS: books—*Günter Brus: Zeichnungen und Schriften,* exhibition catalogue, with text by Johannes Gachnang and Arnulf Meifert, Berne 1976; *Die Gärten in der Exosphäre,* exhibition catalogue, Munich 1977; *Die Pracht der hellsten Freude,* exhibition catalogue, Amsterdam 1978; *Amorphophallus Titanum,* exhibition catalogue, Naples 1978; *11 Artists Working in Berlin,* exhibition catalogue, London 1978; *Franz Schreker: Die Gezeichneten,* exhibition catalogue, Frankfurt 1979; *Reizfluten,* exhibition catalogue, Vienna 1979; *Des Knaben Wunderhorn,* exhibition catalogue, with text by Wieland Schmied and Arnulf Meifert, Berlin 1979; *Kunst der 70er Jahre,* exhibition catalogue, Venice 1980; *Günter Brus: Bild-Dichtungen,* exhibition catalogue, with text by Arnulf Meifert, London 1980; *Gunter Brus: Arbeiten auf Papier 1987,* exhibition catalogue, with introduction by Helga Kocher, Salzburg 1987.

It is perhaps no great surprise that the vehemence of Gunter Brus's art has generated a good deal of extreme commentary. On the one hand he has been called neurotic, obsessive; on the other, a hero, an artist of "titanic temperament." As an unashamed Romantic, Brus would no doubt claim that the former was in some way bound up with the latter.

Brus gave up live work in 1970 for the state of his own mental health after being hounded out of Austria by the police for offending public decency. Threats were also made against his life. Exiled in West Berlin, he began to draw and paint and write poetry. The self-image of the outcast, which in the "Aktions" took the extreme form of public purging (the "Suffering Servant") today is reflected in work which is uncompromisingly conventional. In rejecting modernism Brus has turned to traditional forms of representation (the fairy tale) as a form of Aktionismus.

The tradition of the seer or visionary is very important to him. Blake, Munch, Bosch. It is Blake who has been the most direct influence. The unity of word and image. The mythic struggle between good and evil. The utopianism. Brus's first drawings, coming directly after the Aktions and his work with Nitsch, Muehl and Schwarzkogler, were very much retaliatory, Sadian fantasies of unremitting horror and degradation. "A successful drawing . . . shocks the sufferer back into life." In the fairytale drawings this Nietzchian combativeness (in a world without religion, it is the artist who must take on the ills of the world) takes on an obverse, festive side. If the earlier drawings showed the horror that prevents beauty, the new drawings, or "Soul Screens" as he calls them, celebrate the creation of new worlds—an idyllic vision of arbours and gardens, peopled by weird and wonderful creatures (pixies, homuncules) from his vivid imagination.

Brus's creation of a "world apart," like Blake's, is a moral stand. Nostalgia doesn't come into it. Whatever one thinks of Brus's millenarianism (in a sense it is only by accepting such extremes that Brus can create such an "extreme" art), he has created a formidable body of work.

—John Roberts

BRZOZOWSKI, Tadeusz (Alexander).

Polish. Born in Lvov, now U.S.S.R., 1 November 1918. Studied at the Academy of Fine Arts, Krakow, 1936-39, and, under Fryderyk Pautsch, at the School of Decorative Arts, Cracow, 1940-42. Married Barbara Gawdzik in 1952; sons: Lawrence and Joachim. Painter, in Cracow, 1944-54, in Zakopane, 1954 until his death in 1987. Member, Tadeusz Kantor's underground theatre group, 1943-45; Association of Polish Artists, Cracow, since 1945; Grupa Krakowska artists' group, Cracow, 1954; "Phases" international artists' group, Zakopane, from 1957. Assistant Design Instructor, Faculty of Architecture, Technical University, Cracow, 1945-54; Design Instructor 1954-69, and Director 1959- 61, Kenar's School of Art Technics, Zakopane. Professor, Academy of Fine Arts, Poznan, 1962-87; Professor 1979-81, and Professor Emeritus 1981-87, Academy of Fine Arts, Krakow. Recipient: 5th International Hallmark Award, 1960; Francesco Nullo Award, Venice *Biennale,* 1962; Chivalric Cross 1969, and Commander's Cross 1980, Order of Polonia Restituta; Acquisition Prize, *2nd International Exhibition of Design,* Rijeka, 1969; Ministry of Culture and Arts Prizes, Warsaw, 1970, 1975, 1980; Gold Medal Association of Polish Artists, 1974. Agent: Desa Gallery, Jana 3, 31-017 Cracow. *Died* (in Zakopane) *in 1987.*

Individual Exhibitions:

1956 Desa Gallery, Warsaw
1960 Krzywe Kolo Gallery, Warsaw
Galerie Lambert, Paris
1963 Mpik Gallery, Torun, Poland
13 Muz Gallery, Szszecin, Poland
National Museum, Poznan, Poland
1964 S.P.A.M. Gallery, Warsaw
1965 Od Nowa Gallery, Poznan, Poland
1966 Galerie Yvon Lambert, Paris
Desa Gallery, Cracow
1968 Galerie Wspolczesna, Warsaw
1969 Azyl Club, Torun, Poland
1970 Galerie PSP-ZPAP, Katowice, Poland
Desa Gallery, Cracow
Galeria Em, Wroclaw, Poland
1974 National Museum, Poznan, Poland (retrospective)
1976 Museum of Wschowa, Poland
1978 Desa Gallery, Warsaw
1979 Museum of Rzeszow, Poland
1980 BWA Gallery, Bialystock, Poland
Desa Gallery, Cracow
1981 *Tadeusz Brzozowski: His Friends, His Disciples,* BWA Gallery, Poznan, Poland

Selected Group Exhibitions:

1959 *5th Bienal,* Sao Paulo (and *13th Bienal,* 1975)
1961 *15 Polish Painters,* Museum of Modern Art, New York
1962 *Biennale,* Venice
1965 *Arte Actual de Polonia,* Museo de Arte Moderna, Buenos Aires (toured Uruguay, Mexico and Cuba)
1970 *1,000 Years of Art in Poland,* Royal Academy of Art, London
1976 *Contemporary Polish Painting,* Fundacao Gulbenkian, Lisbon (travelled to Madrid and Valencia)

Collections:

National Museum, Warsaw; National Museum, Cracow; National Museum, Wroclaw, Poland; National Museum, Poznan, Poland; Muzeum Sztuki, Lodz, Poland; Tatra Museum, Zakopane, Poland; Muzei na Sovremena Umetnost, Skopje, Yugoslavia; Stedelijk Museum, Amsterdam.

Publications:

On BRZOZOWSKI: books—*Artisti Polacchi d'Oggi* by Giuseppe Marchiori, Venice 1967; *Ricerche dopo Informale* by Enrico Crispolti, Rome 1968; *Tadeusz Brzozowski,* exhibition catalogue, Poznan, Poland 1974; articles—"5 Pittori Polacchi d'Oggi" by Giuseppe Marchiori in *Il Milione* (Milan), no. 25, 1958; "Polish Art: The Younger Figurative Painters" by Aleksander Wojciechowski in *The Studio* (London), no. 79, 1959; "Quatra Peintres Polonais d'Aujourd'hui" by Juliusz Starzynski in *Quandrum* (Brussels), no. 8, 1960; "La Face Inconnue de la Terra" by Eduard Jager in *Phases* (Paris), January 1960; "Romantik-Expression-Emotion" by Aleksander Wojciechowski in *Das Kunstwerk* (Baden-Baden, West Germany), no. 8, 1961; "The Younger Generation in Polish Painting" by Aleksander Wojciechowski in *Polish Art Review* (Warsaw), no. 1, 1971; films—*Interpretacje* by J. Brzozowski, 1964; *Tadeusz Brzozowski* by M. Szczepanski and Franci Slak, 1978; *Brzuch* by A. Papuzinski, 1979; *Tadeusz Brzozowski* by Cz. Kruszelnicki, 1980.

I steal blood and sweat tar milk and salt and I paint pictures with them that is but a joke I just paint my pictures with . . . paints.

—Tadeusz Brzozowski (1983)

Tadeusz Brzozowski started as an artist in the mid-1930s, being at that time associated with the then radical "Cracow group," seeking to break down conventional ways of thinking in art. This attitude was adopted by a movement of young artists in Cracow, which developed clandestine activity during the Nazi occupation. Tadeusz Brzozowski also belonged to that circle. Among other things, he was an actor in the clandestine theatre of Tadeusz Kantor, where the expressive treatment of the motifs of reality and the use of "ready made" were combined with the surrealisticizing aspect. At the same time, the artist passionately studies painting technology—secrets of dyes, binders, primers, glazings and varnishes. He did it in a conviction that a picture transmits its message primarily through its being saturated with paint substance; that was how his private philosophy of a picture as a specific form of the existence of matter was born.

Immediately after the end of the war Tadeusz Brzo-

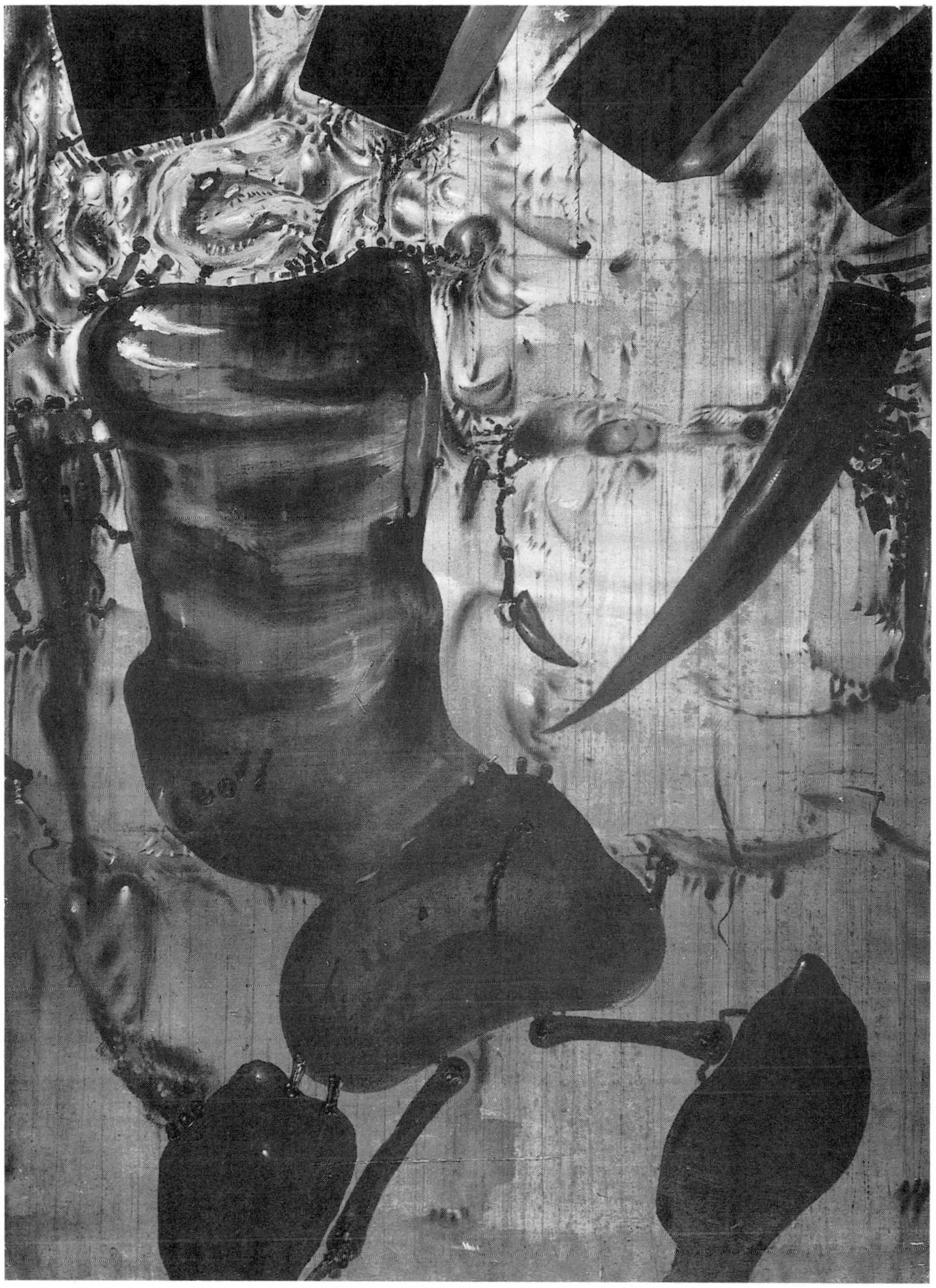

Tadeusz Brzozowski: *Misericordia*, 1982

zowski associated himself with a young "Modern group" in Cracow, one of the most dynamic groups in Polish art at that time. The group was dominated by the tone of surrealisticizing metaphor, which has also become a significant element of Brzozowski's art. The artist expresses himself in painting and in drawing, which has become for him an autonomous field, equally important as painting, sometimes even dominating. It is in the drawing technique that he executes characteristic figures with traits of vexing grotesque. Their soul-penetrating existence has accompanied the artist throughout his lifetime.

These figures are transposed into painting and with time change into semi-abstract creatures, torn with expressive, thorny drawing. The lines of black drawing sometimes painfully injures the substance of colour patches, emphasizing its intensity and brightness.

Brzozowski's pictures are always given specific titles, virtually impossible to be expressed in any other language but Polish. ("Dygi", "Kuszer", "Mecyje", "Kretes", etc.). These names draw on the colloquial language, popular sayings, parables, that is "genius loci". There are also universal names, such as "Fraucymer", "Sakwojaz", "Antichambre", etc.; none of them directly explains the presented motif but supplement the climate of this art by spotting unexpected images of the world. In any case, titles are here equally important as in the surrealist art.

Because of this integral melting of the element of metaphor with painting expression in the 1960s Brzozowski's art reaches the peak of its splendour. The matter of pictures thickens and shines, clashing with the neurons of drawing. Brightness and translucency of liquid colour patches reminds one of sensual qualities of old Flemish masters. It is an effect of constant improvement of technological alchemy. The artist uses resin, rubber and distemper binders, applies paints in several thin layers, freely applies glittering varnishes. This painting glamour, which clashes with perfidious titles, is accompanied by Brzozowski's statements disclosing actual intentions of this art: "I make colour maximally intensive, and then suddenly tone it down. It is just like our experiences fade away. Like contrasts of human fate are born. I always have in mind beautiful people stained with dirt". Thus, this painting is a constant metaphor of the fate of man in his dialectical struggle with his own condition.

In the 1970s, the role of drawing, usually executed in pen and ink, increased (i.e., the series of Self-portraits). The lines become simpler, but lose nothing of their expression. They are still full of pen's "staggerings" and sudden turns. They move like in a grotesque revealing what is truly dramatic in a grotesque. In their essence, the drawings are pictures of a dialogue with one's own inner self, which throws outside its anxieties and whims. Through those acts of externalization the artist overcomes his solipsism and goes beyond his individual fate, showing how individual drama is human drama in general.

At the time when Tadeusz Brzozowski's art was developing, Poland, just like the whole of Europe, was swept with the waves of informel, painting of the matter and many other currents. Brzozowski's art resists classification in any of them, although informel was probably the one which became close to the artist owing to its painting generosity. However, the temptation of gestural freedom has never lured Brzozowski. Even using floating patches of paint he has always remained faithful to his "Flemish" precision and his own painting technique. His art remains personal, just like personal is one's creed.

Brzozowski used to say: "I am trying to be faithful to myself—although it's not too fashionable. That is why I am digging the same whole ever deeper, wanting my art to be ever deeper, ever more perfect, although I don't know whether I do succeed in it. In this way I am seeking contact with other people, as I would like to tell them important things—truth about man, about human condition, its lameness—and that we are able to overcome this lameness. Of course, I do not tackle this problem, the most important one in my art, directly . . ."

—Alicja Kepinska

BUCKLEY, Stephen.

British. Born in Leicester, 5 April 1944. Educated at the University of Newcastle, 1962–67; University of Reading, 1967– 69. Married Stephanie Buckley in 1973; children: Scarlet, Matilda and Felix. Independent painter, London, since 1969. Part-time Lecturer, Canterbury College of Art, Kent, 1969–71; and Leeds College of Art, Yorkshire, 1969–71; Visiting Artist, Chelsea School of Art, London, 1971–80; Artist-in-Residence, King's College, Cambridge, 1972–74. Recipient: Painting Prize, *John Moores Exhibition*, Liverpool, 1974; Prize, Chichester National Art Exhibition, 1975; Painting Prize, Tolly-Cobbold Exhibition 1977; Agents: Brooke Alexander, 20 West 57th Street, New York, New York 10019; and Knoedler Gallery, London. Address: c/o Knoedler Gallery, 22 Cork Street, London W1X 1HB, England.

Individual Exhibitions:

1966 University of Durham
1970 Nigel Greenwood Gallery, London
1972 Galerie Neuendorf, Cologne
Kasmin Gallery, London
1973 Galleria dell'Ariete, Milan
1974 Kettles Yard Gallery, Cambridge
Garage Art, London
1975 Galerie Jacomo Santivero, Paris
Museum of Modern Art, Oxford
1976 Waddington Galleries, London
1977 Arnolfini Gallery, Bristol (travelled to the Aberdeen Art Gallery, Scotland, and the Turnpike Gallery, Leigh, Lancashire)
1978 Knoedler Gallery, London
Robert Alkon Gallery, New York
Gallery Malmgran, Gothenburg, Sweden
Hobson Gallery, Cambridge
Arnolfini Gallery, Bristol

Stephen Buckley: *Dredger*, 1986

1980 Knoedler Gallery, London
Amano Gallery, Osaka, Japan
Bernard Jacobson Gallery, London
1981 Brooke Alexander Gallery, New York
Knoedler Gallery, London
1982 L. A. Louver Gallery, Los Angeles
Knoedler Gallery, London
1983 Brooke Alexander, New York
Knoedler Gallery, London
1984 Thorden-Wetterling Galleries, Goteborg, Sweden
1985 Museum of Modern Art, Oxford
Walker Art Gallery, Liverpool
Brooke Alexander, New York
Clock Tower, New York
Yale Center for British Art, New Haven, Connecticut

Selected Group Exhibitions:

1969 *6 at the Hayward,* Hayward Gallery, London
1972 *Objects and Documents,* Arts Council Gallery, London (toured the U.K.)
1973 *La Peinture Anglaise d'Aujourd'hui,* Musée National d'Art Moderne, Paris
1975 *3rd Triennale—India,* La Kit Kala Akademi Rabindra Bhavan, New Delhi
1976 *The Human Clay,* Hayward Gallery, London (toured the U.K.)
1977 *British Painting 1952–1977,* Royal Academy of Art, London
1979 *Un Certain Art Anglais,* Musée d'Art Moderne de la Ville, Paris
1981 *Baroques '81,* Musée d'Art Moderne de la Ville, Paris
1983 *Twentieth-Century Art from the Metropolitan Museum,* Queens Museum, Flushing, New York
1985 *14th John Moores Exhibition,* Walker Art Gallery, Liverpool, Merseyside

Collections:

Tate Gallery, London; Arts Council of Great Britain, London; Victoria and Albert Museum, London; Walker Art Gallery, Liverpool; Cambridge University; Aberdeen Art Gallery, Scotland; National Art Gallery of New Zealand, Wellington; Metropolitan Museum of Art, New York.

Publications:

On BUCKLEY: books—*Objects and Documents,* exhibition catalogue, London 1972; *La Peinture Anglaise Aujourd'hui,* exhibition catalogue, by Edward Lucie-Smith, Paris 1973; articles—"London Letter" by William Feaver in *Art International* (Lugano, Switzerland), January 1973; "Stephen Buckley" by L. Morris in *Art Press* (Paris), September 1973; "Profile of Stephen Buckley" by Peter Fuller in *Arts Review* (London), 3 May 1974; "Buckley in Midstream" by John McEwan in *The Spectator* (London), 11 October 1975; "Who Will Be Who in the 1980s" in *Sunday Times Magazine* (London), 2 April 1978; "Four British Painters" by John McEwan in *Artforum* (New York), December 1978; "Serenity and Restlessness" by Neal Menzies in *Artweek* (Oakland), 24 April 1982.

As an art student in the 1960's Stephen Buckley came under the influence of surrealism, pop art (through Richard Hamilton) and abstract expressionism. Today one sees traces of this background in the grand scale of much of his work, the willingness to let chance take a part in the creation of his objects and in the use of discarded "popular" items. There are also elements of the "L.A. Look" as seen in the work of, for example, Charles Christopher Hill, who weaves together found materials, then buries, washes or pounds them.

Drawing upon these influences but keeping strongly to his own view of his environment, Stephen Buckley selects raw materials autobiographically. Discarded stretchers from a friend's attic, his mother's curtains, paintings by himself or others, his own personal clothing are transformed and renewed in his hands.

Once selected, Buckley does not treat these things gently. They are torn, scorched, twisted or stretched to their limits, then woven or stitched together. The actual process of creation is important enough to Buckley for him to share it with us so the worked-upon materials are often partially turned over to show the back side of the work. The stretchers—whether found or made—are also revealed or even placed on the front of the painting. And it is important to remember that Buckley sees himself specifically as a painter. Having provided himself with sensuously textured surfaces, he works in warm, earthy colours. A conservationist's nightmare, he also may add plaster, floor polish, wax or even yoghurt to his oils, acrylics, watercolours and enamels.

Since 1977 Buckley has created several sets of etchings, building the finished image with several plates arranged for printing on one sheet—using the medium with a painter's rather than merely a printmaker's eye—a continuation of his exploration into colours, textures and materials.

—Marlee Robinson

BULLMORE, Edward (Aaron Alexander).
New Zealander. Born in Lumsden, Southland, 6 July 1933. Educated at Christchurch Boys High School, 1947–50 (open champion in boxing); School of Fine Arts, Canterbury University College, Christchurch, 1951–55 (Canterbury Rugby Football Union Representative, 1953–55); Auckland Teachers Training College, 1956. Married Jacqueline Anne La Roche in 1958. Painter; taught art at Tauranga Boys College, 1957–59; travelled to Italy, and studied in Florence, 1959; settled in London, 1960, and worked as a scene shifter at the Royal Court Theatre, London, for a number of years, also taught at various secondary schools and art schools, including Ravensbourne College of Art and Design, Epsom School of Art, and Brixton School of Building; elected member of the London Group, 1965; returned to New Zealand and settled in Rotorua, 1969, and taught full-time, then part-time at Rotorua Boys High School. *Died* (in Rotorua) *15 November 1978.*

Individual Exhibitions:

1959 Williston Gallery, Wellington
Tauranga Art Society
1969 Tama Gallery, London
1971 *A Decade in London,* Barry Lett Galleries, Auckland
1972 Rotorua Art Society
1974 Wellington Settlement Gallery
1977 *Mamaku Bush and Farmland Exhibition,* Rotorua Art Society
1978 *Icons,* Barry Lett Galleries, Auckland
1979 *Edward Bullmore Memorial Exhibition,* Rotorua Art Gallery

Selected Group Exhibitions:

1964 *New Zealand Artists Exhibition,* Qantas Gallery, London
1965 *Biennale of Abstract Art,* Commonwealth Institute, London
1967 *Edinburgh Open 100*
The Enchanted Domain, Exeter City Gallery, Devon
1968 *From the Human Form,* Grosvenor Gallery, London
London Group, Royal Institute Galleries, London
1971 *Contemporary New Zealand Painting,* National Art Gallery, Wellington
1975 *New Zealand Society of Sculptors and Painters Exhibition,* Barry Lett Galleries, Auckland
1979 *Images of Women,* Rotorua Art Gallery
1981 *Drawing from Life,* Rotorua Art Gallery

Collections:

National Art Gallery, Wellington; Victoria University, Wellington; Dowse Gallery, Lower Hutt, New Zealand; Rotorua Art Gallery, New Zealand.

Publications:

On BULLMORE: books—*Edward Bullmore,* exhibition catalogue, with an introduction by Mario Amaya, London 1967; *New Zealand Drawing '76,* exhibition catalogue, Auckland 1976; *New Zealand Painting since 1960: A Study in Themes and Developments* by Peter Cape, Auckland 1979; articles—"Second Commonwealth Biennale Exhibition" in *Arts Review* (London), 13 November 1965; "London Group Exhibition" in *Arts Review* (London), 18 February 1967; "Edward Bullmore Exhibition" in *Art and Artists* (London), May 1967; "Edward Bullmore Exhibition" in *Studio International* (London), May 1967.

In retrospect Edward Bullmore's work falls rather neatly into two groups: work up to 1959, and work from 1960 until his death. Such a division makes for comparative ease in observing the great changes that occurred in his work and at the same time, in noting the characteristic qualities which remained as constant factors throughout his working life.

In the early New Zealand period his work was comparatively academic which can be seen in the impressive and dominant figure studies he produced. From c. 1957, however, it is clear that his artistic horizons were broadening and his painting reflected an awareness of contemporary Australian artists such as Dobell and Drysdale.

The desire to enrich and broaden his artistic life led to his travelling overseas, first to Florence where he stayed for six months. This was a period of assimilation and transition during which time he came to terms with the art of the Renaissance. In so doing he modified his painting considerably, with the result that he developed a type of painting which was nostalgic and romantic, with a touch of De Chirico thrown in for good measure.

Bullmore's arrival in London coincided with the emergence of a very fluid and affluent society, despite the pessimism engendered by the Cuba crisis. The intellectual stimulation he received provided the catalyst which projected Bullmore into what was to become his mature style of painting. He rapidly discarded the literalness of his previous work and began a series of gloomy abstract works, based around the Cuban confrontation. These works were dark and relied greatly for effect on collage and objets trouvés—like leaves and scraps of cloth. This was but an interlude, however, and as he was supporting himself by working as a stage hand for the Royal Court Theatre he was permitted to use scraps of canvas from scenery and floor coverings which he incorporated into his own canvas. The torn fragments were repaired by neat stitching (a skill he had acquired as a farmer's son) and around this necessity he formed the genesis of his highly original form of expression. The first works in his new vein were a series of landscape inspired constructions (Hiku-rangi series) in which he developed a very sculptural fecund female form which could be interpreted as a writhing and convulsing landscape. The pieces of torn canvas, wooden chair frames, padded leather and painted sections were literally stitched together with coarse leather thongs with the result that the completed work was a disturbing, yet compelling, three-dimensional construction evoking memories of a certain region of New Zealand which in his words depicted "a sort of mythological idea about the sky and earth being male and female!"

This series prepared the way for the next, the Astroform series, shaped canvases in which female and erotic connotations are much more explicit. In retrospect it was, perhaps, Bullmore's reaction to the rapidly changing mores of the 1960's. As such, they are remarkably successful. His work now began to draw the attention of some critics, and his showings in such exhibitions as the *Young Commonwealth Artists, London Group* and *Biennale of Commonwealth Abstract Art* led to his most important invitation to participate in the Surrealist exhibition, *The Enchanted Domain.*

His return to New Zealand after the absence of 10 years meant a considerable change in style of life and subject matter, and at the time of his death he was again concerning himself with aspects of the landscape.

His vision was highly personal and his work was marked by a fastidious craftsmanship. These two factors stamped his work with a quality which, while overly erotic, was never prurient, and, as Kenneth Coutts-Smith observed, his work was far removed "from the sophisticated eroticism of . . . Bellmer, Jones or Wunderlich." His work had a primeval equality, an animal vigour which was disturbing. Yet beyond this, his creations are stamped with a sensitivity and awareness that have given him a unique place in New Zealand art.

—Melvin N. Day

BURDEN, Chris.

American. Born in Boston, Massachusetts, 11 April 1946. Educated at Pomona College, Claremont, California, B.F.A. 1969; University of California at Irvine, 1970–71, M.F.A. 1971. Conceptual artist and sculptor. Instructor in Avant-Garde Art, LaVerne College, California, 1973–74; Visiting Artist, Fresno State University, California, 1974. Recipient: New Talent Award, Los Angeles County Museum of Art, 1973; National Endowment for the Arts Grant, 1974. Agent: Ronald Feldman Fine Arts, New York. Address: c/o Ronald Feldman Fine Arts, 31–33 Mercer Street, New York, New York 10013, U.S.A.

Individual Exhibitions:

1971 *Five Day Locker Piece,* University of California at Irvine
Bicycle Piece, University of California at Irvine
1972 *Bed Piece,* Market Street, Venice, California
Match Piece, Pomona College, Claremont, California
Jaizu, Newport Harbor Art Museum, Newport Beach, California
Riko Mizuno Gallery, Los Angeles
1973 *Movie on the Way Down,* Oberlin College, Ohio
Through the Night Softly, Main Street, Los Angeles
1974 Riko Mizuno Gallery, Los Angeles
Ronald Feldman Fine Arts, New York
Hansen-Fuller Gallery, San Francisco
1975 Riko Mizuno Gallery, Los Angeles
Ronald Feldman Fine Arts, New York
1979 Ronald Feldman Fine Arts, New York
1983 Ronald Feldman Fine Arts, New York
1984 Rosamund Felsen Gallery, Los Angeles
Art Park, New York

Selected Group Exhibitions:

1985 *Modern Machines: Recent Kinetic Sculpture,* Whitney Museum, New York

Collections:

Museum of Modern Art, New York; Long Beach Arts Museum, California.

Publications:

On BURDEN: articles—"Church of Human Energy" by Sharp and Bear in *Avalanche,* Summer/Fall 1973; "Young Sadhu" in *Time Magazine* (New York), 24 February 1975; "Through the Night Softly" by Jan Butterfield in *Arts Magazine* (New York), March 1975.

Chris Burden did his first Performances in 1971 while still a graduate student in Southern California. It was one of those rare cases when an artist going through the art educational system arrived at an individualistic, perceptive grasp of his own direction. In "Five-Day Locker Piece," Burden interred himself in locker "number 5" for five days below five gallons of bottled water and above an empty five gallon bottle. It was the beginning of an artistic output which was to cause mixed feelings of consternation, attention, misinterpretation and praise over the next decade which brought more than 60 works from Burden's head.

Burden's performances and sculptures are about the fears and anxieties faced by the individual in the midst of the complex psychological and social context of the late 20th century. Many earlier works, such as his (overly) notorious "Shoot" (1971, in which he had a friend shoot him in the arm) and "220" (which involved real dangers of electrocution for the participants), were rather overtly "macho" in attitude, but the vast majority of Burden's pieces which suggest real danger are very much under the artist's control. "Transfixed" (1974), for example, in which Burden had himself "crucified" on the back end of a Volkswagen with nails driven through his hands, was well researched and caused little real physical pain, expressing, rather, the symbolic element behind our attachments to the objects of our industrial environment.

In a number of works, Burden has used his body as sculptural form to express the tensions we feel in trying to maintain our individuality as artists or as anybody else dealing with our already post-industrial age. In "Bed Piece" (1972) and in "White Light/ White Heat" (1975), among other works, Burden placed himself in a state of isolation for long periods of time, assuming states of mental/physical deprivation with elements of withdrawal from contact and sight which both showed the benefits of introspective meditative states and caused anxious moments for viewers and friends in the process. Among his most seductively and frighteningly alluring works is "Through the Night Softly" (1973) in which Burden crawled through broken glass, incurring multiple small cuts on his almost naked body. Burden's quiet, controlled attitude, not unlike that of the Zen master, portrays more centrally the idea of risk sacrifice and

atonement and the mental capacity to get through danger than it does a masochistic self-destruction.

Works since the mid-70's have tended to be less dramatic, though no less involved in using self as conveyor of anxious mental states. In many, Burden opens up elements of his private life to prolong/dispel the personal "myth" of the artist built up over the past years of work. In his second television "commercial" (1976), Burden adds his own name to the list of the five most well-known (from survey) artists, in a listing which reads "Leonardo da Vinci, Michaelangelo, Rembrandt, Van Gogh, Picasso, Chris Burden." Continuing in his continually dialectical fashion, Burden, in the same year, acted as unidentified "Garcon" throughout the duration of a gallery group show, and also charged admission for a tour of his studio in Venice, California.

Along with the issues of confinement, time, fear, threat and control, Burden has also concerned himself with the state of the individual in relationship to technology and to the threat of nuclear war. In "Art and Technology" (1975) and "Death Valley Run" (1976), he created vehicles of transportation for one person which were fuel efficient, lightweight and capable of practical transport through space and, suggestively through personalized technology, into the mind. "C.B.T.V." (1977) reconstructed the primitive television precursor of 1915 in an effort to show us the nature and origin of the medium which dominates us in the present.

Among Burden's recent works are those which are concerned with the weapons of war so imminently upon us. In an exposition of another prevalent anxiety, "The Reason for the Neutron Bomb" (1979) is a grid of 50,000 nickels, each with a match on top, emblematic of the number of tanks the Soviets have on the border between Eastern and Western Europe. It is a fascinating prediction of subsequently current events and a potent visual symbol as well. Burden's recent sculptural mini-environment, "A Tale of Two Cities," incorporates a variety of toys. Medieval castles, modern buildings, airplanes and weapons of varied vintage, warriors including knights, soldiers and futuristic robots interact to create a tiny panorama of the persistence of human war, which shows no sign of abating in the foreseeable future. Looking at it through the spyglasses provided by Burden, one is forced to see us as we really are and as science fiction predicts the future. As always, there is a sardonic wit and topical pertinence in Burden's continual portrayals of our personae in this post-industrial time, in which there is more trouble than ever in dealing with psychological and sociological basics.

—Barbara Cavaliere

BUREN, Daniel.

French. Born in Boulogne-Billancourt, 25 March 1938. Educated at Lycée Condorcet, Paris, 1946–56; studied at the Ecole Nationale Supérieuire des Métiers d'Art, Paris, graduated 1960. Independent artist, Paris. Member, Buren, Mosset, Parmentier (Michel) and Toroni association, 1967. Address: 21 rue de Navarin, 75009 Paris, France.

Individual Exhibitions:

1967 *Buren o Toroni o Chichessia,* Galleria Flaviana, Lugano, Switzerland
1968 Musée d'Art Moderne de la Ville, Paris
Galleria Apollinaire, Milan
1969 Wide White Space Gallery, Antwerp
Interruption, Galerie Yvon Lambert, Paris
Position/Proposition, Galerie Konrad Fischer, Dusseldorf
Galerie Eva Buren, Stockholm
1970 Galleria Francoise Lambert, Milan
Art and Project, Amsterdam
Une pièce/peinture, Bradford College, Massachusetts
Galerie MTL, Brussels
Galerie Yvon Lambert, Paris
1971 Wide White Space Gallery, Antwerp
Galerie Folker Skulima, Berlin
Galerie Michael Werner, Cologne
Städtisches Museum, Mönchengladbach, West Germany
1972 Modern Art Agency, Naples
Jack Wendler Gallery, London
Galleria Sperone, Turin
Peinture Affichée/Pittura Affissa, Incontri Internazionali d'Arte, Rome
Theatre de la Ville, Belgrade
Wide White Space Gallery, Antwerp
1973 New Theatre, New York
Sanction of the Museum, Museum of Modern Art, Oxford
Fragment I, II and III, Mezzanine Gallery and Anna Leonowens Gallery, Halifax, Nova Scotia
Part 2, John Weber Gallery, London
California Institute of Art, Valencia
3 Paintings, Galerie Konrad Fischer, Dusseldorf
Within and Beyond the Frame, John Weber Gallery, New York
Démultiple, Städtisches Museum, Monchengladbach, West Germany
1974 *Trasposizione,* Galleria Toselli, Milan
Triptyque, Galerie Rolf Preisig, Basle
Transparency, Art and Project, Antwerp
3 Passages, Galerija Grada, Zagreb
Wide White Space Gallery, Antwerp
Transparency-Opacity, Max Protetch Gallery, Washington, D.C.
Between and Through, Cusack Gallery, Houston
On the Hang Up, 11501 West Rico, Los Angeles
Passage Between Inside and Outside, Portland Center for Visual Arts, Oregon
1975 Kunstmuseum, Lucerne
Akademie der Künste, Berlin
Galerie Folker-Skulima, Berlin
Städtisches Museum, Mönchengladbach, West Germany
1976 *Hier,* Stedelijk Museum, Amsterdam
Rijksmuseum Kröller-Müller, Otterlo, Netherlands
Ailleurs/Elders, Stedelijk van Abbemuseum, Eindhoven, Netherlands
Institute of Contemporary Arts, London
1977 *3 Installationem,* Galerie Paul Maenz, Cologne
1978 Galerie Yvon Lambert, Paris
John Weber Gallery, New York
1979 National Galerie of Victoria, Melbourne
1980 *Il Est Encore Une Fois—Toile, Toile/Voile,* Kunstmuseum, Lucerne
Art Institute of Chicago
1981 Stedelijk van Abbemuseum, Eindhoven, Netherlands
1982 Krefeld Museum, West Germany
1984 Galerie Gewad, Ghent, Belgium
Galeria Zona, Florence
Galerie Arca, Marseille, France
Galerie Arca, Paris

Selected Group Exhibitions:

1968 *Prospect '68,* Galerie Apollinaire, Dusseldorf
1970 *Conceptual Art and Conceptual Aspects,* New York Cultural Center
1971 *Situation Concepts,* Galerie Nächst St. Stephan, Vienna
1972 *Documenta 5,* Kassel, West Germany
1973 *Contemporanea,* Villa Borghese, Rome
Bilder: Objekte: Filme: Konzepte, Städtische Galerie, Munich
1974 *Political Art,* Max Protetch Gallery, Washington, D.C.
Projekt '74, Kunsthalle, Cologne
1975 *Corridor Passage,* Museum of Modern Art, New York
12 x 1, Palais des Beaux-Arts, Brussels

Collections:

Centre Georges Pompidou, Paris; Van Abbemuseum, Eindhoven; Netherlands; Stedelijk Museum, Amsterdam; Kunstmuseum, Lucerne.

Publications:

By BUREN: books—*Daniel Buren: Legend, Vol. 1 and II,* London 1973; *5 Texts,* New York 1973; *Daniel Buren: Voile/Toile, Toile/Voile,* with Bernd Mahr and Horst Merten, Berlin 1975; articles—"Beware" in *Studio International* (London), March 1970; "Mise en Garde No. 3" in *Vh 101* (Paris), Spring 1970; "Extrait de Position-Proposition" in *VH 101* (Paris), Spring 1971; "Art Is Not Free" in *Studio International* (London), June 1973; "Daniel Buren: An Interview with Jean-Marc Poinsot" in *Art and Artists* (London), July 1973; "The Function of the Museum" in *Artforum* (New York), September 1973; "The Function of an Exhibition" in *Studio International* (London), December 1973; film—*Identification,* London 1973.

On BUREN: books—*Daniel Buren,* exhibition catalogue, by Jean-Christophe Ammann, Lucerne 1975; *Daniel Buren: Hier,* exhibition catalogue, with text by E. de Wilde, Michel Claura and Germano Celant, Amsterdam 1976; *Daniel Buren: 3 Installationen,* exhibition catalogue, Cologne 1977; *Daniel Buren: Il est Encore Une Fois—Voile/Toile, Toile/Voile,* exhibition catalogue, with text by Martin Kunz, Lucerne 1980; articles—"Paris Commentary: Buren at Prospect '68, Dusseldorf" by Michel Claura in *Studio International* (London), January 1969; "La Proposition de Buren" by G. Gassiot-Talabot in *Opus International* (Paris), June 1969; "Lettre de Paris: Daniel Buren" by M. Pleynet in *Art International* (Lugano, Switzerland), February 1971; "Daniel Buren" by Jean Clair in *Chroniques de l'Art Vivant* (Paris), April 1971; 1973; "On Daniel Buren" by R. Smith in *Artforum* (New York), September 1973; "Das Prinzip der Wiederholung" by Georg F. Schwarzbauer in *Magazin Kunst* (Mainz), no. 4, 1974; "Le Groupe BMPT" by Otto Hahn in *Art Press* (Paris), June 1974.

I have often been criticized for the almost absolute "reductionism" of my work. That was the criticism leveled at me when I began, and continues even now. The main reason of these criticisms, which is particularly revealing about those who express them, is that people are accustomed to looking at a painting or an object in an exhibit as the be all and end all. In other words, they look at the visual materials that I used as if they were a painting. I never have and never will respond to such absurd comments, for I have the impression that they are talking about something other than my work. Why should I have to defend something that is not being attacked? It is as though I were being criticized under the pretext that for the opening of every one of my shows, it rains . . .

Right from the start I have always tried to show as clearly as I could that indeed a thing never exists in itself, in a kind of *"en soi."* A fortiori, this is true of all my work. Nothing that I show—the materials I use, to begin with—exists unrelated to something else that is clearly refined. Anyone who experiences my work directly—provided he agrees to make the minimum of effort required, of course—perceives that the "reduction" is in fact the widening of one's field of vision. Widening of such dimension that—for the very first time—what is being challenged in fact is the entire field of painting itself—nothingless—as being a reducing factor in art. From this stems the whole debate on art (criticism and history), based on the autonomy of a work of art; a debate which has also perforce a reducing effect, being simplistic and too good to be true. To reconsider works and their contexts, in fact to realize that their autonomy in a fable supported by an idealistic proportion, is not only to challenge the proposition itself but also, to a great extent, the works which it supports, that is, art in general.

The Marxist label, used by some who believe it offers a way to escape this debate, obviously does not change a thing. On the other hand, the concept of the non-autonomy of a work of art opens new doors to a field of study and work that is very vast and unexplored. Of course, this field has nothing to do with

Daniel Buren: Work for the *Salon de Mai*, Paris, 1968

any sociological art nor a sociology of art. It is only with plastic means—to be completely overhauled—that it is possible to question and deal seriously with plastic problems and their implications.

—Daniel Buren

Daniel Buren is a painter, but since the 1960s he has become an environmental artist, and it is on his environmental art that his fame has rested ever since. He is a painter in that he paints his environments rather than, say, covering them, as Christo does.

To say that he is a geometrical abstract painter is somewhat of an understatement. For nearly two decades he has confined himself to painting parallel black and white or coloured and white stripes. They resemble some of the structures of Bridget Riley, but, unlike hers and those of other optical artists, his stripes are broad and the optical effect is kept to a minimum, though it may operate at a distance.

Restricted, repetitious, and seemingly unpromising though this material may be, Buren manages to put it to an almost inexhaustible number of original uses. With these simple means he can produce all manner of visual effects.

In a gallery space or other interior he will adapt his stripes to the space and transform it. Sometimes this will mean exploiting the possibilities of an interesting and complex space, as, for instance, a succession of receding rooms opening on to one another. Here perspective plays a part, alters the stripes, and may even give an overall two-dimensional effect.

At other times he will take an uninteresting gallery space and enhance it to the point of distorting its size and shape (as usually perceived).

These works he calls 'installations,' with the usual implication that they have to be installed and will later be taken away. In other words, they are ephemeral. This attitude to art—among others—he holds in common with Christo.

Like Christo, he is also concerned with the great outside. His contacts with it is various. One of his practices is to paint steps or frieses or plinths of columns or parts of solemn buildings with black and white stripes. Another is to fly striped flags on important buildings, such as the Louvre or that ancient emporium, La Samaritaine, or drape striped banners around them. The point of this, as with Christo's wrapped buildings, is to draw attention to the building, to make it conspicuous, to draw attention to aspects of it, to make us look at it anew and to transform it. He even invades the streets with sandwich-boards in black and white stripes (a change from 'Prepare To Meet Your Doom' but possibly no less disturbing)

Buren has made installations the world over: Chicago, 1977, 'Step by Step, Up and Down, In and Out'; Sydney, 1979, 'Upside Down' (!), and, the same year, in Los Angeles, 'Frost and Defrost', and so on till the present day.

Though most of these works are ephemeral, Buren, like Christo, carefully records them. He has done so since the 1960s with his 'photo/souvenirs'.

His most recent, most ambitious, most controversial and most prestigious work has just (1987) been installed—and permanently, not ephemerally (unless certain elements of the public get their way)—in, of all places, the Cour d'Honneur of the Palais Royal, Paris. It is, by any standards, a spectacular work. Called 'Deux plateaux', which I take to mean 'two levels or plains', it consists of columns of various heights, partly above ground, partly below (but still visible through a grating) and, of course, with black and white stripes, forming the most elaborate patterns as one walks around the courtyard. It has outraged many Parisians who walk through it to the beautiful gardens beyond. There is certainly a note of incongruity. But with what? The Palais Royal was destroyed by the Commune in 1971; what we have now is a 19th century reconstruction. There the matter rests at present.

—D. C. Barrett

BURGIN, Victor.

British. Born in Sheffield, Yorkshire, 24 July 1941. Studied at the Royal College of Art, London, 1962–65, A.R.C.A. (1st class) 1965; Yale University, New Haven, Connecticut, 1965–67, M.F.A. 1967. Artist based in London, since 1967. Lecturer, Department of Fine Art, Trent Polytechnic, Nottingham, 1967–73. Senior Lecturer in the History and Theory of the

Visual Arts, School of Communication, Polytechnic of Central London, since 1973. Picker Professor of Fine Arts, Colgate University, Hamilton, New York, 1980. Recipient: U.S./U.K. Bicentennial Arts Exchange Fellowship, 1976–77; Deutscher Akademischer Austauschdienst (DAAD) Fellowship, Berlin, 1978–79. Agents: John Weber Gallery, 420 West Broadway, New York, New York 10012, U.S.A.; Liliane and Michel Durand-Dessert, 43 rue de Montmorency, 75003 Paris, France. Address: 25 St. Mary-le-Park Court, Albert Bridge Road, London SW11 4PJ, England.

Individual Exhibitions:

1970 Camden Arts Centre and Swiss Cottage Library, London (with Art and Language and Keith Arnatt)
1974 Galleria Banco, Brescia, Italy
1975 Musée d'Art et d'Industrie, St. Etienne, France (with Art and Language)
1976 Institute of Contempoary Arts, London
Robert Self Gallery, London
1977 *Victor Burgin: Work,* Stedelijk van Abbemuseum, Eindhoven, Netherlands (travelled to the John Weber Gallery, New York)
1978 Museum of Modern Art, Oxford
1979 Deutscher Akademischer Austauschdienst, Berlin (travelled to the John Weber Gallery, New York; Liliane and Michel Durand-Dessert Gallery, Paris; and Max Hetzler Gallery, Stuttgart)
1980 *Victor Burgin: US 77/ZOO 78,* Picker Art Gallery, Colgate University, Hamilton, New York
1981 Zwigzek Polskich Artstow Fotografikow, Warsaw
Musée de la Ville, Calais, France
1982 John Weber Gallery, New York
1983 National Gallery of Canada, Ottawa
1984 Galerie Durand-Dessert, Paris

Selected Group Exhibitions:

1969 *When Attitudes Become Form,* Institute of Contemporary Arts, London
1970 *Idea Structures,* Camden Arts Center, London
Information, Museum of Modern Art, New York
1971 *6th Guggenheim International,* Guggenheim Museum, New York
1972 *Documenta,* Kassel, West Germany
The New Art, Hayward Gallery, London
1976 *Arte Inglese Oggi,* Palazzo Reale, Milan
1977 *Aspects of European Art in the 70's,* Art Institute of Chicago (toured the United States, 1977–79)
1980 *Kunst im Sozialen Kontext,* Badischer Kunstverein, Karlsruhe, West Germany
1987 *Berlinart 1961–87,* Museum of Modern Art, New York (travelled to San Francisco)

Collections:

Tate Gallery, London; Victoria and Albert Museum, London; Arts Council of Great Britain, London; British Council, London; Walker Art Gallery, Liverpool; Graves Art Gallery, Sheffield; Museum of Modern Art, Oxford; Centre Georges Pompidou, Paris; Bibliothèque Nationale, Paris; Van Abbemuseum, Eindhoven, Netherlands.

Publications:

By BURGIN: books—*Work and Commentary,* London 1973; *Two Essays on Art, Photography, and Semiotics,* London 1976; *Family,* New York 1977; *Newcastle Writings,* with others, London 1977; *Thinking Photography: Essays in the Theory of Photographic Representation,* editor, London 1981; *Essays: Interview: Work,* Berlin 1981; articles—"Art Society Systems" in *Control* (London), no. 4, 1968; "Situational Aesthetics" in *Studio International* (London), October 1969; reprinted in *Conceptual Art,* edited by Ursula Meyer, New York 1972; "Thanks for the Memory" in *Architectural Design* (London), August 1970; "Rules of Thumb" in *Studio International* (London), May 1971; "Interview with Varsity" in *Varsity* (Cambridge), October 1971; "Margin Note" and "Interview" in *The New Art,* exhibition catalogue, edited by Anne Seymour, London 1972; "In Reply" in *Art-Language* (Leamington Spa, Warwickshire), Summer 1972; "Photographic Practice and Art Theory" in *Studio International* (London), July/August 1975; "Socialist Formalism" in *Studio International* (London), July/August 1975; "Socialist Formalism" in *Studio International* (London), March/April 1976; "Art, Common-Sense and Photography" in *Camerawork* (London), no. 3, 1976; "Modernism in the Work of Art" in *20th Century Studies* (Canterbury, Kent), no. 15/16, 1976; "Looking at Photographs" in *Screen Education* (London), Autumn 1977; "Images of People" in *Studio International* (London), no. 2, 1978; "Seeing Sense" in *Artforum* (New York), February 1980; "Photography, Fantasy, Function" in *Screen* (London), Spring 1980.

On BURGIN: book—*Victor Burgin: Work,* exhibition catalogue, Eindhoven, Netherlands 1977; articles—"Victor Burgin: La Representation par le Text" by A. Pacquement in *Art Press* (Paris), no. 5, 1973; "Victor Burgin" by E. Tynan in *Studio International* (London), September/October 1976; "Victor Burgin in Oxford" by D. Reed in *British Journal of Photography* (London), March 1978.

From the early photo-essay *Work and Commentary* (with its rather formalist foray into semiotics) to the recent captioned advertisement style documentary panels, Vic Burgin has been involved with photography as a *signifying* practice, with its inseparability—as with all visual images—from language. In the 1970's this was called conceptualism. Today it offers—for Burgin at least, who has never found the artworld conducive to his own needs—the possibility of a wholly new practice. "I feel I'm working across the fringe areas—for example . . . where "art," ad-

Victor Burgin: image from ***US 77,*** **1977**

vertising, "documentary," "theory" etc. overlap." Burgin in fact makes no hierarchical distinction between his writing (which has been extensive) his activities as a teacher and lecturer and his photography; all are part of the same *political* education—Burgin's role as an artist is, in an old fashioned sense, pedagogic.

Burgin's involvement with photography as a language has been a critique of the notion of the "purely visual," which art-historically has come to mean Greenberg's modernism, but which in reality covers a whole range of what Burgin sees as academic pre-photographic art teaching. Like many artists who questioned the primacy of painting (or rather the primacy of post-war American painting), Burgin has attempted to give back image-making certain cultural responsibilities, to "interfere," albeit peripherally, with dominant forms of representation. In the early 70's—when the Art and Society debates were at their height—Burgin attempted a populist approach, putting his images into circulation in the community itself. His poster campaign in Newcastle upon Tyne (the poster showed a young attractive couple embracing, underneath the slogan: 7% of the population own 84% of the wealth) came in for a good deal of criticism for its cosmeticism and somewhat condescending airs. It was not a success. Burgin's recent work though has been less tendentious. Series such as "US 77" and "Zoo" (shown at the *Hayward Annual* in 1979) show Burgin moving towards allegory; captions, almost poetic in their scansion, are superimposed over single shot photographs of predominantly urban scenes, some sparse and barren, some a welter of signs, symbols and narrative fragments.

Burgin's attempt to work on the margins of mainstream visual culture represents an important shift in thinking towards re-engagement with *culture as a whole*; the problem, though, still remains one of finding a broad audience for that engagement. Burgin's decision to work outside of what is notionally known a the "artworld" can only help to promote it.

—John Roberts

BURRA, Edward.

British. Born in London, 29 March 1905. Educated in London schools, 1910–18; studied at the Chelsea Polytechnic, London, 1921–23, and the Royal College of Art, London, 1923–24. Suffered poor health from rheumatic fever in childhood. Lived with his parents until 1967. Visited Paris with William Chappell, 1923, and with Paul Nash, 1930; Member, Unit One, group of architects, painters and sculptors, founded by Nash, London, 1933; visited Spain, 1935, and travelled in the United States, 1934, 1937, 1948, 1955; set and costume designs for the ballets, *Barbau,* 1938, and *Miracle in the Gorbals,* 1944, for the Sadlers Wells Ballet Company, London. C.B.E. (Commander, Order of the British Empire), 1971. Agent: Lefevre Gallery, 30 Bruton Street, London WIX8JD, England. *Died* (in Rye, Sussex) *22 October 1976.*

Individual Exhibitions:

1929	Leicester Galleries, London
1932	Leicester Galleries, London
1937	Springfield Museum of Fine Art, Massachusetts
1942	Redfern Gallery, London
1947	Leicester Galleries, London
1949	Leicester Galleries, London
1952	Lefevre Gallery, London
1955	Lefevre Gallery, London
	Swerzoff Gallery, Boston
1957	Lefevre Gallery, London
1959	Lefevre Gallery, London
	Whiteworth Art Gallery, Manchester (with Greaves and Dalwood)
1961	Lefevre Gallery, London
1963	Lefevre Gallery, London
1965	Lefevre Gallery, London
1967	Lefevre Gallery, London
1970	Hamet Gallery, London
1971	Hamet Gallery, London
	Nicholas Treadwell Gallery, London
	Lefevre Gallery, London
1972	Postan Gallery, London
1973	Tate Gallery, London
	Lefevre Gallery, London
1975	Lefevre Gallery, London
1976	Towner Art Gallery, Eastbourne, Sussex
1977	Lefevre Gallery, London
1979	Blond Fine Art, London
1980	Anthony D'Offay Gallery, London
	Lefevre Gallery, London

Selected Group Exhibitions:

1934	*Unit One,* Mayor Gallery, London
1936	*London Surrealist Exhibition,* Burlington Galleries, London
	Fantastic Art, Dada, Surrealism, Museum of Modern Art, New York
1939	*Exhibition of Contemporary British Art,* National Gallery of Canada, Ottawa
1942	*Contemporary British Art,* Toledo Museum of Art, Ohio
1948	*La Jeune Peinture en Grande Bretagne,* Galerie René Drouin, Paris
1951	*21 Modern British Painters,* Vancouver Art Gallery (toured Canada and western United States)
1963	*Mixed Modern Paintings,* Lefevre Gallery, London
1971	*Britain's Contribution to Surrealism of the 30's and 40's,* Hamet Gallery, London
1972	*John Banting and his Friends,* Rye Art Gallery, Sussex

Contributions:

National Gallery of Victoria, Melbourne; Art Gallery of New South Wales, Sydney; National Gallery of New Zealand, Wellington; Beaverbrook Gallery, New Brunswick, Canada; Museum of Modern Art, New York.

Edward Burra: ***Snowdonia No. 2*****, 1974**

Publications:

By BURRA: articles—"Letters and Postcards" in *Edward Burra,* exhibition catalogue, by John Rothenstein, London, 1973.

On BURRA: books—*Edward Burra* by John Rothenstein, London 1945; *Edward Burra,* exhibition catalogue by John Rothenstein, London 1973; *Modern English Painters: Wood to Hockney* by John Rothenstein, London 1974; articles—"Edward Burra" by J. Burr in *Apollo* (London), October 1971; "Style and Ideology in British Art and Photography" by Ian Jeffrey and David Mellor in *Studio International* (London), July 1975; "Edward Burra," obituary, in *The Times* (London), October 1976.

"He had a wicked eye . . . ," we say, chuckling. This seems to express the essence of an artist who has yet to achieve the international recognition that his art deserves—not least as an "honorary American," whose recently-unearthed paintings of Boston bars and suchlike scenes in the 1930's and 1940's are a major contribution to "American Scene" painting.

Chronic ill health in early childhood left Edward Burra a semi-invalid, yet he overcame his perpetual near-exhaustion with an iron will, conserving his powers by social isolation, but travelling widely; and his magnificent facility for memorising every detail of a scene without any visual note-taking enabled him to re-create those cheap, vulgar, debased but vigorous scenes of low-life which he uncritically enjoyed, with a stimulating accuracy which is bracing, witty and humane. Believing, wrongly, that his painting in oils was not appreciated, he developed a technique of repeated overpainting of his huge, resonant watercolours so that they have all the stature of oils on the wall.

The first sight of a typical early Burra looks like something between the savage perceptions of George Grosz and the witty economics of a social cartoonist. Burra shares with Grosz and Bacon an eye for the demonic in the 20th century, but more from the standpoint of an uninvolved observer. From private works of indulgent—but highly talented—fantasy, Burra's work opened out to include elements of social realism and many aspects of landscape, one where surrealist creatures disturbingly invade the scene; and he extended, particularly in the latter part of his life, this view of the demonic into the vegetable world: his flower forms, his vegetation and his landscapes all partake of an indefinable menace. He might have been an ideal illustrator for Evelyn Waugh; in fact, he was a major stage-designer between 1932 and 1958—six ballets, one opera and a musical play.

The "amused eye" is a surface aspect of deep feelings in Burra's act, and its surrealism is the natural breakthrough of emotion and inner vision through outer form. Burra had strong feelings of affinity with Spain, Mexico and Spanish America, long before visiting (and his remarkable affinities with Rivera have yet to be studied), and his concern with these countries' troubles produced some intense religious scenes. He learned much, too, from acute observation of the visual forms in film. Burra's perceptions of the 20th century (little known in Britain until his retrospective of 1973) deserve a place on museum walls beside those of Grosz, Beckmann and Rivera.

—Michael Shepherd

BURRI, Alberto.

Italian. Born in Città di Castello, Umbria, 12 March 1915. Studied medicine in Perugia 1934–39; mainly-self-taught in art, from 1944. Served as medical officer in the Italian Army, in North Africa, 1940–43; prisoner-of-war, Camp Hereford, Texas, 1943–45. Married Minsa Craig in 1945. Independent artist, Perugia, 1945–48, and in Rome, 1948–53; lived in the United States, 1953–69; returned to Rome, 1960; first abstract paintings, 1949; Member, with Colla, Capogrossi and Balloco, "Gruppo Origine," Rome 1951. Recipient: International Award, *Carnegie International,* Pittsburgh, 1958; Premio dell' Ariete, Milan 1959; Unesco Prize, *5th Biennal de Sao Paulo,* 1959; Critics' Prize, *Biennale,* Venice, 1960; Premio Marzotto, 1964; Grand Prix, *8th Bienal de Sao Paulo,* 1965; Feltrinelli Prize, Milan 1972. Agent: Galleria Marlborough, Rome. Address: c/o Galleria Marlborough, Via Gregoriana 5, 00187 Rome, Italy.

Individual Exhibitions:

1947 Galleria La Margherita, Rome
1948 Galleria dell'Angelo, Città di Castello, Italy
Galleria Margherita, Rome
1949 Galleria dell'Angelo, Città di Castello, Italy
1952 Galleria dell'Obelisco, Rome
Galleria d'Arte Contemporanea, Florence
1953 Fondazione Origine, Rome
Allan Frumkin Gallery, Chicago
Stable Gallery, New York
1954 Galleria dell'Obelisco, Rome
Allan Frumkin Gallery, Chicago
1955 Stable Gallery, New York
Colorado Springs Fine Arts Center
Oakland Art Museum, California
1956 Seligmann Gallery, Seattle
Galleria del Cavallino, Venice
Galerie Rive Droite, Paris (with Cesar)
1957 Galleria Del Naviglio, Milan
Galleria dell'Obelisco, Rome
Galleria La Loggia, Bologna
Galleria La Bussola, Turin
Carnegie Institute, Pittsburgh
1958 Arts Club of Chicago
Albright-Knox Art Gallery, Buffalo, New York
San Francisco Museum of Art
Galleria La Salita, Rome
Galleria Blu, Milan
Galleria Alberti, Brescia, Italy
1959 Galerie d'Art Moderne, Basle
Palais des Beaux-Arts, Brussels
Galleria La Loggia, Bologna
Galleria La Tartaruga, Rome
Museum Haus Lange, Krefeld, West Germany
Galerie Beyeler, Basle
Galerie Wiener Sezession, Vienna
Museum am Ostwall, Dortmund, West Germany
1960 Martha Jackson Gallery, New York
Hanover Gallery, London
Museo Nacional de Bellas Artes, Buenos Aires
Galerie Anne Abels, Cologne
1961 Galleria La Medusa, Rome
Galerie de France, Paris
1962 Castello Cinquecentesco, L'Aquila, Italy
Galleria Marlborough, Rome
1963 Marlborough New London Gallery
Museum of Fine Arts, Houston
1964 Walker Art Center, Minneapolis
Albright-Knox Art Gallery, Buffalo, New York
Pasadena Art Museum, California
Marlborough-Gerson Gallery, New York
1965 Galleria La Bussola, Turin
Galleria Toninelli, Milan (with Marino Marini and Afro)
1966 Galleria Il Segno, Rome
1967 Kunsthalle, Darmstadt
Museum Boymans-van Beuningen, Rotterdam
Museum of Modern Art, New York (with Lucio Fontana)
Galleria La Tartaruga, Rome
Palazzo Vitelli, Città di Castello, Italy
1968 Galleria Blu, Milan
1969 Galleria Notizie, Turin
Galleria Giussi, Turin (With Marini and Moreni)
Galleria San Luca, Bologna
1970 Galleria La Tartaruga, Rome
Galleria Acme, Brescia, Italy
Qui Arte Contemporanea, Rome
Transart, Milan
1971 Galleria Il Margutta, Rome
Galleria Civic d'Arte Moderna, Turin
Modern Art Agency, Naples
Libreria Stampatori, Turin
Libreria-Galleria Congrande, Verona
1972 Musée d'Art Moderne, Paris
1973 Galleria San Luca, Bologna
1974 Galerie Jacques Benador, Geneva
Galleria Grafica Oggi, Milan
1975 Sacro Convento di San Francesco, Assisi, Italy
Disegni, Tempere e Grafica, Galleria Il Segnapassi, Pesaro, Italy
1976 Galleria Nazionale d'Arte Moderna, Rome
1977 Fundacao Calouste Gulbenkian, Lisbon
Santa Barbara Museum of Art, California (toured the United States)
1978 P & P Galerie, Zurich
Marion Koogler McNay Institute, San Antonio, Texas
Milwaukee Art Center
Museo di Capodimonte, Naples
Guggenheim Museum, New York
1979 Galleria Lorenzelli, Milan
Studio Marconi, Milan
J. Corcoran Gallery, Los Angeles
Galleria D'Ascanio, Rome
Essiccatoio del Tabacco, Città di Castello, Italy
1980 Rocco Paolina, Perugia, Italy (with Joseph Beuys)
Staatsgalerie Moderner Kunst, Munich
Instituto Italiano di Cultura, New York
Instituto Italiano di Cultura, Madrid
Orsanmichele, Florence
1981 Galleria L'Isola, Rome
1982 Desert Museum, Palm Springs, California
Galleria San Luca, Bologna, Italy
Brooklyn Museum, New York
Columbus Museum of Art, Ohio
San Francisco Museum of Modern Art
1983 Cantieri Navali alla Guidecca, Venice
Galerie Sapone, Nice, France
Galerie des Ponchettes, Nice, France

Selected Group Exhibitions:

1947 *Art Club of Rome,* Galleria Nazionale d'Arte Moderna, Rome
1951 *Gruppo Origine,* Fondazione Origine, Rome
1952 *Biennale,* Venice (and 1956, 1966, 1968, 1983)
1953 *Younger European Painters,* Guggenheim Museum, New York
1959 *Bienal,* Sao Paulo (and 1965)
1967 *Contemporary Italian Art,* Ulster Museum, Belfast (toured the U.K.)
1971 *New Italian Art: 1953–1971,* Walker Art Gallery, Liverpool
1980 *Arte Astratta Italiana 1909–1959,* Galleria Nazionale d'Arte Moderna, Rome
1982 *Documenta 7,* Museum Fridericianum, Kassel, West Germany
1985 *The European Iceberg,* Art Gallery of Ontario, Toronto

Collections:

Galleria Nazionale d'Arte Moderna, Rome; Nationalgalerie, West Berlin; Centre Georges Pompidou, Paris; Carnegie Institute, Pittsburgh.

Publications:

On BURRI: books—*Burri* by James Johnson Sweeney, Rome 1955; *Burri* by Enrico Crispolti, Milan 1961; *I Ferri di Burri* by G. Marchiori and M. Drudi Gambillo, Rome 1961; *Ottocento e Novecento* by A. M. Brizio, Turin 1962; *Alberto Burri* by Cesare Brandi, Rome 1963; *Le Due Avantguardi,* 2 vols., by Maurizio Calvesi, Milan 1966, 1971; *New Italian Art 1953–1971,* exhibition catalogue, with text by Giovanni Carandente, Liverpool 1971; *Alberto Burri* by Maurizio Calvesi, Milan 1971; *Alberto Burri,* exhibition catalogue, with texts by Enrico Crispolti, Nello Poente, Giuseppe Marchiori and others, Rome 1971; *Art Without Boundaries 1950–1970,* edited by Gerald Woods, Philip Thompson and John

Williams, London 1972; *Alberto Burri,* exhibition catalogue, with texts by Jean Leymarie, Aldo Passoni and others, Paris 1972; *Burri* by Vittorio Rubiu, Turin 1975; *Burri: Disegni Tempere e Grafica,* exhibition catalogue, with text by Maurizio Calvesi, Pesaro 1975; *Burri,* exhibition catalogue, with text by Bruno Mantura, Lisborn 1977; *Alberto Burri: Prints 1959–1977* by Vittorio Rubin and others, Rome 1977; *Burri: La Forma e l'Informe* by Flavio Caroli, Milan 1979; *Alberto Burri: Il Viaggio,* with text by Nemo Sarteanesi and Erich Steingraber, Milan 1980; *Arte Astratta Italiana 1909–1959,* exhibition catalogue, with text by Giorgio de Marchis, Rome 1980; *Burri: Sestante,* edited by Vanni Bramanti, with introduction by Giulio Carlo Argan, Milan 1983.

The work of Alberto Burri—one of the greatest artists of this century—is an endless game with material. Sacks, wood, iron, plastics, Cellotex; he burns these materials, twists them, tears them, or else gently arranges them into amazing, calm 15th century compositions. And sometimes, dramatically, both these things are combined in a single design. With Burri the material is identified with space; it becomes pure presence, the affirmation of existence; first of all, it *is*. But (and this is a paradox to be found only in art) it is only when a human works it, forces it, building up an eminently, wholly erotic relationship with it, that it reaches the essential state. Memory, a great memory of impressionist and tonal painting, informs the whole of Burri's work, alive like no others to delicate shading (even when the material is most crushed and contaminated), to the spreading of tone within a particular colour—as in the "sacks," where the splits, the stitching, the holes, the patches that stretch the coarse stuff to its limits tell of nothing but the violence and pain of the material (and the material is the World), yet also of the chromatic chances by which everything creates colour: the shadows, the protrusions, the different tissues of the texture and the broken lines they follow.

In his different series of works there is always a strong tension between the defined space of the picture's surface and the irruptions on one side and another made by the "wounds" in these materials, natural or artificial, always poor but redeemed in the passage from quantity to quality. The "irons" of the later 1950's, for example, jammed hard together against each other so as to cover the whole rectangular frame given them, at once respect and transgress the surface of the pictorial design. They respect it because they are bent by main force to conform with it, ruled by the formal command to adhere to the design; they transgress it because, being forced in this way, they protrude in menacing spikes which encroach on the space and create a volume with the shadows they project on the others still held at the level of the surface. The burns on plastic—in which we may see a "baroque" in Burri—and on wood relate to the primordial power of fire, seat and symbol of life and so also of destruction, of biological poetry. From the subtle ambiguities between abstraction and *trompe-l'oeil,* between artifice and nature in the "cracks" (like coagulated streams of lava in which there are endless splits and fissures), to the clear, bright oblong shapes and patches of colour in the gerat impaginations of the series in Cellotex (a compound derived from the scission of cellulose). Burri's journey remains unique. And here, stupendously incarnate, breathes the absolute.

—Massimo Carboni

BURY, Pol.

Belgian. Born in Haine-Saint-Pierre, 26 April 1922. Studied painting, drawing and decoration under Louis Buisseret and Louis Navez, Academie des Beaux-Arts, Mons, 1938–39. Served in the Belgian resistance movement, Brussels, 1943. Painter and sculptor, living and working in Belgium, La Louviére, 1939–61, in Fontenay-Aux-Roses, near Paris, 1961–65, in Saulx-les-Chartres, France, 1965–73, and in Perdreauville, Yvelines, France, since 1973: produced first abstract paintings, 1947; first mobile-kinetic sculptures, 1957. Founder-member, with Archille Chavée and André Lorent, Group Rupture, La Louvière, 1939–40; Young Belgian Painters group, Brussels, 1947; member, with Christian Dotremont and Pierre Alechinsky, COBRA (Copenhagen-Brussels-Amsterdam) group, Brussels, 1949–51; member, Art Abstrait group, Brussels, 1952; founder, with André Balthazar, Academie de Montbliart and Verlag de Montbliart publishing house, Brussels, 1953. Designed sets for ballet *Der Spiegel;* also involved in filmmaking, since 1970. Instructor in Sculpture, University of California, Berkeley, 1970; Minneapolis College of Art and Design, 1973; Professor of Monumental Sculpture, Ecole Nationale Supérieure des Beaux-Arts, Paris, 1983. Recipient: Marzotto Prize, 1964; Grand Prix National de Sculpture, Paris, 1985. Honorary Doctorate: Minneapolis College of Art and Design, 1973. Agent: Lefebre Gallery, 47 East 77th Street, New York, New York 10021. Addresses: Vallée de la Taupe-Perdreauville, 78200 Mantes-La-Jolie, France; 236 boulevard Raspail, 75014 Paris, France.

Individual Exhibitions:

1953 Galerie Apollo, Brussels
1955 Galerie Les Contemporains, Brussels
1957 Galerie du Verseau, Brussels
1959 Galerie St. Laurent, Brussels
1960 Galerie St. Laurent, Brussels
1961 A.P.I.A.W., Liège, Belgium
1962 Galerie Iris Clert, Paris
1963 Galerie Iris Clert, Paris
1964 Lefebre Gallery, New York
1965 Felix Landau Gallery, Los Angeles
1966 *Twice Pol Bury: Cinetizations, Moving Sculptures,* Lefebre Gallery, New York
Galerie La Hune, Paris
1967 Kasmin Gallery, London
1968 Lefebre Gallery, New York
1969 Galerie Pierre, Stockholm
Galerie Maeght, Paris
1970 University of California, Berkeley (toured the United States)
1971 *A Way Out,* Lefebre Gallery, New York
Estudio Actual, Caracas
Gallery Moos, Toronto
Kestner-Gesellschaft, Hannover (travelled to the Nationalgalerie, West Berlin and the Kunsthalle, Dusseldorf)
1972 Palais des Beaux-Arts, Charleroi, Belgium (travelled to Centre National d'Art Contemporain, Paris)
Kunsthalle, Dusseldorf
1973 Museum Boymans-van Beuningen, Rotterdam
Louisiana Museum, Humlebaek, Denmark
1974 *25 Tonnes de Colonnes,* Foundation Maeght, St. Paul de Vence, France
1976 Musée d'Art Moderne, Brussels
Woodprints, Lefebre Gallery, New York
1977 Museo de Arte Moderno, Mexico City
1978 F.S. Wright Art Galleries, University of California at Los Angeles
University of Texas at Austin
Portland Art Museum, Oregon
University of Georgia, Athens
1979 Musée Saint-Georges, Liége, Belgium
Oeuvres de 1963 à 1978, Cloitre Saint-Trophime, Arles, France
1980 Guggenheim Museum, New York
1981 Herning Museum, Denmark (with Pablo Palazuelo)
1982 Musée d'Art Moderne de la Ville, Paris (retrospective)

Selected Group Exhibitions:

1945 *Surrealisme,* Galerie des Editions La Boetie, Brussels
1955 *Le Mouvement,* Galerie Denise René, Paris
1959 *Breer, Bury, Klein, Mack, Munari, etc.,* Hussenhuis, Antwerp
1964 *Biennale,* Venice
Documenta 3, Kassel West Germany
1967 *Dix Années de l'Art Vivant 1955–65,* Galerie Maeght, Paris
1972 *Douze Ans d'Art Contemporain en France,* Grand Palais, Paris
1973 *Hommage à Picasso,* Kestner-Gesellschaft, Hannover

Collections:

Neue Nationalgalerie, West Berlin; Kaiser Wilhelm Museum Krefeld, West Germany; Kunstmuseum, Dusseldorf; Stedelijk Museum, Amsterdam; Belgian State Collection, Brussels; Museum of Modern Art, New York; Guggenheim Museum, New York; Albright-Knox Art Gallery, Buffalo, New York; Menil Foundation, Houston.

Publications:

By BURY: books—illustrations for *L'Aventure devorante,* with COBRA group, Brussels 1950; illustrations for *La Main Heureuse,* Brussels 1950; *Dix Sérigraphies de Pol Bury,* with an introduction by R. V. Gindertael, La Louviére, Belgium 1955; *La Boule et le Trou,* Brussels 1961; *Le Petit Commencement,* La Louviére, Belgium 1965; *La Boule et le Cube,* Brussels 1967; *Milano, cinetizzazioni,* Venice 1967; *Derrière le Miroir,* Paris 1969; *Décalcomanies,* La Louviére, Belgium 1970; *L'Art à bicyclette et la Revolution à cheval,* Paris 1972; *Art is too serious to be left in the hands of artists . . . ,* Minneapolis 1973; *Douze Ramollissements du Président Mao,* Paris 1973; *Ramollissements de 17 corps,* Paris 1973; *Le petits Moutons blancs qui sorten en rang du Lavoir,* Montpellier 1976; *Infracritique de l'Oeuvre plastique de Prof, Froeppel,* La Louvière, Belgium 1976; *Le Vélo de Joseph Staline et le Circuit idéologique,* La Louvière, Belgium 1976; *Le Sexes des Anges et celui des Géomètres,* Paris 1976; *Léon III, l'Isaurien, dit l'Iconomaque, Essai d'Iconophobie,* Brussels 1976; *Les Horribles mouvements de l'immobilité* (collected writings), Paris 1977; *L'Art inopiné dans les Collections publiques,* La Louvière 1982; *Les Gaietés de l'Esthétique,* Paris 1984; article—"Tribune Libre" in *Chroniques de l'Art Vivant* (Paris), December 1970; films—*Tour Eiffel,* with Clovis Prevost , 1971; *8,500 Tonnes de Fer,* with Clovis Prevost, 1971; *Une Lecon de Geometrie plane,* with Clovis Prevost, 1972; *135 kilometres-heure,* with Clovis Prevost, 1972; *25 Tonnes de Colonnes,* with Clovis Prevost, 1973; *L'Art illustre,* 1975; *L'Oeuvre plastique du Professeur Froeppel,* with Claude Gaspari, 1976.

On BURY:—*Pol Bury,* exhibition catalogue, with texts by Roger Bordier and André Balthazar, New York 1964; *Twice Pol Bury: Cinetizations, Moving Sculptures,* exhibition catalogue, with text by Eugene Ionesco, New York 1966; *Pol Bury* by André Balthazar, Milan 1967; *Pol Bury,* exhibition catalogue, with interview by Peter Selz, introduction by Eugene Ionesco, essay by André Balthazar, Berkeley 1970; *Pol Bury* by Dore Ashton, Paris 1970; *Pol Bury,* exhibition catalogue, with text by Clara Diament de Sizo, Caracas 1971; *Pol Bury,* exhibition catalogue, edited by André Balthazar, Hannover 1971; *Icons and Images of the 60's* by Nicolas and Elena Calas, New York 1971; *Pol Bury,* exhibition catalogue, edited by Andr3 Balthazar, Paris 1972; *Douze Ans d'Art Contemporain en France,* exhibition catalogue, Hannover 1973; *Pol Bury: 25 Tonnes de Colonnes,* exhibition catalogue, with an interview by André Balthazar, St. Paul de Vence, France 1974; *Pol Bury: Oeuvres de 1963 à 1978,* exhibition catalogue, with texts by Michel Moutashar, Anne Tronche, Roger Brodier, Dore Ashton and others, Arles, France 1979; *Les Fontaines de Pol Bury* by Pierre Descargeus, La Louvière 1986.

Until 1953 when he gave up easel painting completely, Pol Bury was one of the most enterprising young Belgian painters. He studied at the Mons Academy of Art from 1938 to 1939, when he joined the experimental surrealist group formed locally by two poets. He was a member of the Jeune Peinture Belge group, and until 1951 was associated with the COBRA group. His first experiments with mobile constructions were exhibited at Galerie Apollo, Brussels, in 1953, a series of *plans mobiles,* flat planes of black and white that could be fitted together to pro-

Pol Bury: *Stainless Steel Hydraulic Sculpture*, 1987

duce a variety of patterns. With Calder, Soto, Tinguely and Vasarely, Bury showed in the 1955 "Mouvements" exhibition at Galerie Denise René in Paris.

Electric motors were first used in Bury's works in 1957. *Multiplans,* flat rectangles set edge to edge, were painted with an overall abstract design that changed by minute degrees when moved by the power. These were succeeded in 1959 by his "Ponctuations" shown at the Galerie St. Laurent, Brussels, where perforated black and white discs performed constantly changing patterns and rigid and pliable stems rose and fell according to their phasing by the current. His show at Galerie Iris Clert showed a further development in "Entités erectiles" of 1963, where the spheres and globes appeared for the first time setting up subtle and almost imperceptible shudders. This contrast with rapid movement imposed its own intrinsic character in the work. Bury described it: "Speed limits space, slowness multiplies it." The sensuous associations suggested by the nudging of the globes are summarised by Bury: "Two slownesses gently grazing each other even go so far as to rub against each other. We dare henceforward speak of such activity no longer in terms of geometry but almost in the language of the boudoir."

From kinetics Bury progressed to constructions of finely carved and painted wooden objects comprising balls, cylinders and other cubes assembled in apparent disarray on flat ramps. Other works of hammered copper in freely curving arabesques fixed in panels carried hints of shock in their end tremors. Such is the reputation acquired by Bury's almost immobile mobiles that a structure of his designed for permanent static life can produce an hallucinatory effect on the onlooker, who easily imagines that it *does* move. As Bury insists, the difference is so slight.

Following representations at the Venice *Biennale* in 1964 and at exhibitions in the U.S.A. and Europe, Bury is to be seen in most major museums of the world. Swerving of bodies in space and the frailty of seemingly fixed galactic systems is further illustrated by analogy in Bury's "Cinematisations" where photographs and reproductions have circular details cut out and replaced in collages only slightly awry so that the Eiffel Tower or a Gothic cathedral seems ominously out of true, less obviously than the Tower of Pisa, but on that account all the more nerve-tingling.

—G. S. Whittet

BUSH, Jack.

Canadian. Born in Toronto, 20 March 1909. Educated in Montreal primary schools; studied evenings under Edmund Byonnet and Adam Sherriff Scott while an apprentice in the art department of Rapid Grid Company of Montreal, 1926–28; continued study of art in evening classes at the Ontario College of Art, Toronto, under Frederick Challender, John Alfsen and Charles Comfort, while working as a commercial artist for Rapid Grid in Toronto, 1928. Married Mabel Teackle in 1934; had 3 sons. Independent artist, Toronto. Co-Founder, with Bill Ronald, Hortense Gordon and others, Painters Eleven, 1953; travelled extensively in Europe, 1962; Member, Canadian Group of Painters, 1964. Visiting Artist, Michigan State University, East Lansing, 1965, and Cranbrook Academy of Art, Bloomfield Hills, Michigan, 1968. President, Canadian Society of Painters in Watercolor, 1964. Recipient: Ralph Clark Stone Award, Ontario Society of Artists, 1946; Arts Directors Club of Toronto Medal, 1951, 1954; J. W. L. Forster Award, Ontario Society of Artists, 1953; First Prize, Canadian Sports Hall of Fame, 1957; Canada Council Senior Fellowship, 1962; Grand Award, *Montreal Museum of Fine Arts Spring Exhibition,* 1965; Albert H. Robinson Prize, Montreal Museum of Fine Arts, 1967; Guggenheim Fellowship, 1968. Associate, Royal Canadian Academy; Fellow, Ontario College of Art, 1976. O.C. (Officer, Order of Canada), 1976. *Died* (in Toronto) *24 January 1977.*

Individual Exhibitions:

1945 Hart House, Toronto (with William Winter)
1946 Trinity College, Toronto
1949 Gavin Henderson Galleries, Toronto
1952 Roberts Gallery, Toronto
1958 Park Gallery, Toronto
1959 Park Gallery, Toronto
1961 Park Gallery, Toronto
1962 Robert Elkon Gallery, New York
Gallery Moos, Toronto
1963 Robert Elkon Gallery, New York
Museum of Fine Arts, Montreal (with Francoise Sullivan Ewen)
1964 Norman Mackenzie Art Gallery, Regina, Saskatchewan
Bennington College, Vermont
Robert Elkon Gallery, New York
Gallery Moos, Toronto
Waddington Galleries, London
1966 André Emmerich Gallery, New York
David Mirvish Gallery, Toronto
Trinity College, Toronto (with Ina Meares and James Gordancer)

1967 Waddington Galleries, London
André Emmerich Gallery, New York
David Mirvish Gallery, Toronto
1968 David Mirvish Gallery, Toronto
1969 Galerie Godard-Lefot, Montreal
Waddington Galleries, London
1970 Norman Mackenzie Art Gallery, Regina, Saskatchewan
André Emmerich Gallery, New York
Edmonton Art Gallery, Alberta
Harcus Krakow Gallery, Boston
1971 Waddington Galleries, London
Nicholas Wilder Gallery, Los Angeles
Harcus Krakow Gallery, Boston
1972 Museum of Fine Arts, Boston
André Emmerich Gallery, New York
David Mirvish Gallery, Toronto
1973 André Emmerich Gallery, New York
Edmonton Art Gallery, Alberta
1974 André Emmerich Gallery, Zurich
André Emmerich Gallery, New York
David Mirvish Gallery, Toronto
Waddington Galleries, London
1975 David Mirvish Gallery, Toronto
Jack Pollock Gallery, Toronto
Prints on Prince Street, New York
1976 Waddintgon Galleries, London
Theo Waddington Gallery, Montreal
Jack Bush: A Retrospective, Art Gallery of Ontario, Toronto (toured Canada, 1976–77)
1978 Waddington Galleries, London
Waddington Galleries, Toronto
1979 Theo Waddington Gallery, Montreal
Waddington Galleries, Toronto
1980 Theo Waddington Gallery, Montreal
André Emmerich Gallery, New York
University of Edinburgh (travelled to the Serpentine Gallery, London, and the Ikon Gallery, Birmingham)

Selected Group Exhibitions:

1952 *1st Canadian All Abstract Exhibition*, Oshawa, Ontario
1954 *Painters Eleven*, Roberts Gallery, Toronto (travelled to Ottawa)
1956 *20th Annual Exhibition of American Abstract Artists, with Painters Eleven of Canada*, Riverside Museum, New York
1958 *Painters Eleven*, Ecole des Beaux-Arts, Montreal (toured Canada)
1963 *5th Biennale of Canadian Painting*, Tate Gallery, London
1967 *Bienal*, Sao Paulo
1968 *Canada: Art d'Aujourd'hui*, National Gallery of Canada, Ottawa (toured Europe)
1970 *Color and Field*, Albright-Knox Art Gallery, Buffalo, New York (toured the United States)
1974 *The Great Decade of American Abstraction: Modernist Art 1960–1970*, Museum of Fine Arts, Houston
1976 *Changing Visions: The Canadian Landscape*, Art Gallery of Ontario, Toronto (toured North America)

Publications:

By BUSH: articles—"Letter to the Editor" in *Artscanada* (Toronto), June 1969; "Some Thoughts on His Painting" and "Reminiscences of His Earlier Career" in *Jack Bush*, exhibition catalogue, London 1980.

On BUSH: books—*Contemporary Canadian Painting* by William Withrow, Toronto 1972; *Jack Bush: A Retrospective*, exhibition catalogue, by Terry Fenton, Toronto 1976; *Jack Bush*, exhibition catalogue, London 1980; articles—"In Terms of Color: Jack Bush" by Terry Fenton in *Artforum* (New York), May 1969; "Jack Bush" by Carter Ratcliff in *Artnews* (New York), December 1970; "A Balanced Judgment" by J. Burr in *Apollo* (London), October 1971; "A Garden for the Eye: The Paintings of Jack Bush" in *Artscanada* (Toronto), December 1980/January 1981; film—*Jack Bush* by Murray Battle, National Film Board of Canada, 1979.

Jack Bush is Canada's most important contemporary painter, not only because of the quality of his work in relation to his Canadian colleagues, but also because he is the only one of his generation to take his place, on merit alone, beside his international contemporaries. Nevertheless, Bush's position in the history of recent Canadian art is significant. In the '20s and '30s he was a young painter at a time when a nationalistic movement of landscape painters, the Group of Seven, set standards of approved Canadian modernism with their stylized views of untouched nature. Bush's early works echo the Group's example in many ways, but they remain resolutely unlike the paintings they attempt to emulate. In later years Bush said that he had been troubled, at the time, by this apparent failure, but eventually realized that it was part of his strength. In the 1940's he experimented with a personal brand of expressionism, populating his paintings with anguished, white robed figures, who eventually became more and more generalized, until they disappeared. By the early '50's, Bush had discovered American Abstract Expressionism, at first through reproductions and later through visits to New York. His rapid assimilation of the possibilities of gestural abstraction set him apart from the majority of his colleagues. He and ten like-minded painters, in fact, banded together to exhibit as Painters Eleven because their atypical commitment to abstraction set them apart from the rest of the art community in conservative Toronto.

Bush's paintings of the '50s are noteworthy for their energy and for gestures which anticipate his later drawing, but their layered construction and reliance on strong contrasts of dark and light often obscure his real gifts. Bush's economical, simplified watercolors of the period, however, serve as models of what was to come.

Bush's mature work begins in the late '50s. Following the suggestions of his watercolors, he gradually evolved a personal way of using the legacy of Matisse, painting with a remarkable range of thin, radiant colors, presented in clear, discrete shapes. Bush's expansive compositions, after about 1955, similarly owe a debt to Matisse, although it's apparent from works of the early '60's that he learned a great deal from Miró and Adolph Gottlieb as well. By this time he had established friendships with many of his American colleagues, such as Noland and Olitski, and these contacts proved stimulating.

The earliest well-developed series, the "Thrusts," set the pattern for the amalgamation of color and generous drawing which remains characteristic of Bush's best work. His imagery varies from stacks of colored bars, in the "Sashes" of the '60s and their variations, to the unconfined calligraphy of the "Garden" pictures of the early '70's, and the floating color strokes of the last two years of his life. Bush often spoke of his dependence upon his garden as a source of images and colors, but it is clear from clues provided in titles and notebooks that he was capable of finding stimulus in even the most banal aspects of his surroundings. Neckties, women's clothing, wallpaper, giftwrap, road signs and the like could all serve as visual triggers, and be translated into typical "Bush" configurations, wrenched from any literal meaning and transformed into his idiosyncratic, deliberately ungratiating handwriting.

These eccentric shapes are simply the carriers of Bush's remarkable color, and are improvised jazz-fashion from things seen. The analogy is an apt one, since Bush loved jazz and was an accomplished jazz pianist. There is even some indication that in his late works he attempted some kind of visual equivalence for sounds. In some instances, the scale, positioning and color of floating strokes seem to have been provoked by specific musical compositions.

Whatever their intention, however, it is evident that Bush's last paintings, those of 1975 and '76, are among his best. Their richly inflected, sponged-on grounds, fluttering shapes and dark, sonorous color assure Bush's pre-eminence in Canada and his position among his colleagues anywhere.

—Karen Wilkin

BUTHE, Michael.

German. Born in Sonthofen, Allgau, 1 August 1944. Studied at the Werkkunstschule, Kassel, 1962–64; under Arnold Bode, Hochschule fur bildende Kunste, Kassel, 1964–66. Independent painter and environmental artist, in Kassel, 1966–68, in Cologne since 1969, and in Marrakesh since 1970: adopted pseudonym Michel de la Sainte Beaute, 1971. Professor, Akademie der Kunste, Dusseldorf, 1982 (resigned, 1982). Recipient: Villa Romana Prize, Florence, 1976. Agents: Moderne Kunst Dietmar Werle, Spichernstrasse 44, 5000 Cologne 1; Galerie Bama, 40 rue Quincampoix, 75004 Paris; Galerie Toni Gerber, Gerechtigkeitsgasse 74, 3011 Berne. Address: Drb al Hammam 52, Marrakech-Mouazzin, Morocco.

Individual Exhibitions:

1968 Galerie Ricke, Kassel, West Germany
1969 Galerie Ricke, Cologne
Von-der-Heydt-Museum, Wuppertal, West Germany
1970 Galerie Kuhn, Aachen, West Germany
Kabinett für Aktuelle Kunst, Bremerhaven, West Germany
Galerie Renée Ziegler, Zurich
Galerie Ernst, Hannover
1971 Galerie Toni Gerber, Berne
Galerie Renée Ziegler, Zurich
1972 Galerie Mollenhoff, Cologne
1973 Galerie Onze, Brussels
Kunstverein, Cologne
Kunstmuseum, Lucerne
Galerie Pablo Stahli, Lucerne
Galerie Oppenheim, Cologne
1974 Galerie Loeb, Berne
Galeria Vandres, Madrid
Galerie Oppenheim, Cologne
1975 Galerie Magers, Bonn
Oppenheim-Studio, Cologne
1976 Atelier des Kunstlers, Cologne
1977 Galerie AK, Frankfurt
Tarahumaras, Stadtisches Museum Schloss Morsbroich, Leverkusen, West Germany
Kunstmuseum, Dusseldorf
1978 Galerie Gerhild Grolitsch, Munich
Galerie Toni Gerber, Berne
Stadtisches Galerie, Ravensburg, West Germany
1979 Galerie Bama, Paris
Galerie 't Venster, Rotterdam
Galerie Harlekin Art, Wiesbaden, West Germany
1980 *Die endlose Reise der Bilder*, Museum Folkwang, Essen
Kunstverein, Kassel, West Germany
1981 Galerie Munro, Hamburg
Galerie Bernier, Athens
Galerie Bama, Paris
Galerie Toni Gerber, Berne
Galerie Nachst St. Stephan, Vienna
1982 Galerie Krinzinger, Innsbruck, Austria
Galerie Art in Progress, Munich
Galerie Baronian/Lambert, Ghent, Belgium
Villa Romana, Florence
Holly Solomon Gallery, New York
1983 Galerie Toni Gerber, Berne
1984 Galerie Munro, Hamburg
Galerie Bama, Paris
Museum Villa Stuck, Munich
1987 Moderne Kunst Dietmar Werle, Cologne

Selected Group Exhibitions:

1968 *Programm I*, Galerie Ricke, Kassel, West Germany
1969 *When Attitudes Become Form*, Kunsthalle, Berne (toured Europe)
1970 *14 x 14*, Staatliche Kunsthalle, Baden-Baden, West Germany
1972 *Documenta 5*, Museum Fridericianum, Kassel, West Germany (and *Documenta 6*, 1977; *Documenta 7*, 1982)
1973 *Yes, Sir, That's My Baby(etween)*, Gallery House, London

Michael Buthe: *Lucrezia Borgia*, 1981

1975 *Dessins: Beuys/Biel/Buthe/Filliou/Polke*, Gallerie Bama, Paris
1978 *Hammer I*, Galerie Handschin, Basle
1979 *Soft Art*, Kunsthaus, Zurich
1981 *Art Allemagne Aujourd'hui*, ARC/Musee d'Art Moderne de la Ville, Paris
1983 *Sculpture from Germany*, San Francisco Museum of Modern Art (toured the United States)

Collections:

Kunstmuseum, Dusseldorf; Kunstmuseum, Lucerne; Centre Georges Pompidou, Paris; Museum des 20. Jahrhunderts, Vienna; Museum der Stadt, Linz; Museum Ludwig, Cologne; Von-der-Heydt-Museum, Wuppertal; Stadtisches Museum, Ulm; Kunsthalle, Kiel; Nationalgalerie, West Berlin.

Publications:

By BUTHE: books—*Freunde/Friends*, Dusseldorf 1971; *Lukretia bagann damals gerade von der Kuste weg zu ziehen*, Zurich 1971; *Die Wunderlose Reise des Saladin Ben Ismael*, Cologne 1977; *Der Vortrag uber die Schonheit des absoluten Positivismus: le dernier Empire*, Essen 1980.

On BUTHE: books—*Deutsche Kunst: eine neue Generation* by Rolf-Günter Dienst, Cologne 1970; *Bis Heute* by Karin Thomas, Cologne 1971; *Michael Buthe: Le Dieux de Babylon*, exhibition catalogue box with pamphlets, Cologne 1973; *Michael Buthe: Tarahumaras*, exhibition catalogue, with text by Rolf Wedewer, Leverkusen, West Germany 1977; *Weich und Plastiche/Soft-Art*, exhibition catalogue edited by Erika Billeter, Zurich 1979; *Michael Buthe: Die endlose Reise der Bilder*, exhibition catalogue, with text by Zdenek Felix, Essen 1980.

Chronologically, one could say that Michael Buthe's work has covered three areas: space, stories, journeys. Thematically these areas overlap and flow transparently into each other. The drawings of 1967–69 are almost all imaginary ground plans for spatial projects or designs for torn fabrics; whatever is revealed as "autonomous" work, as immediate in the level of perception of the figurative drawing, is seen from its starting point, a localization of a relationship game in which are woven particular experiences, or "stories" as Buthe calls them. Line movement is direct emotion and afterthought, and is experienced as process and recollection; in the drawing, objects are a deliberate "disturbance" and intentional permanent peculiarities which, as ciphers, express the object experienced. While Michael Buthe lived in his studio, it also shaped his world, and the many people who came and went were its protagonists. The fabrics, torn with delicate aggression, later sewn together and coloured with dogged tenacity, are, in the physical and psychical sense, a journey within the material itself.

The first Moroccan journey of 1970 brought about the invasion of colour. With it the points are switched for a considerable alteration in the expresion of adventure contained in Buthe's work. Travel introduced spatial expansion, colour transforms the drawing, indeed, often, by maintaining an intense significance, takes its place.

Work carried out since 1970 stands now exclusively in relation to several periods spent in Africa (Benin) and Persia.

An erupting consciousness of form and color produces simultaneously impressions sensed under completely new circumstances.

"Journey" becomes journey via myth; "stories" are stories of demons, angels, gods, and witch doctors. Buthe remains close to them because for him they are beings whose realm of experience he wishes to make his own. It is significant that Buthe does not use myth as an example, as a catch-phrase as it were "for a better future." He experiences it through people and transforms it into reality; and this capacity for experience is also found in his work, as in the scenery of "The God of Babylon" and "Zarathustra." Materials are brought together to evoke a crocodile or a ship; they are not there with a representative function but are primarily particular sculptural forms which the function of crocodile or ship approaches. The canvas stretched over a massive circular frame, coated with beeswax and scattered with splashes of gold, is picture/object *and* "sun"; the vast red-coloured fabrics are painting *and* firmament, roof of heaven and home; the rectangular structure built from strong branches, covered with wax and rose leaves, is sculpture *and* bed. In other words, the significance of the objects ensues first from something produced by the artist not in any particular context, even though they apparently fix seamlessly into it.

It is a great temptation to join, in words and in imagination, in the "journeys" of Michael Buthe, but one runs the risk thereby of considering scenery, objects, and drawings—which on their own mark out a time in boundless groups—too much under the aspect of his overwhelming sense of fantasy, fantasy which even throws out of balance the related mythologies which move very freely among themselves.

Michael Buthe's work is primarily a convincing performance of creative intelligence, born from a commitment which today can in no way be presumed to be self-evident.

—Jean-Christophe Ammann

BUTLER, Reg(inald Cotterell).
British. Born in Buntingford, Hertfordshire, 28 April 1913. Studied architecture, 1937; self taught in art. Produced first sculptures, 1920; worked as architect and industrial technologist, 1937–50; blacksmith, during the war, Sussex, 1941–45; full-time sculptor from 1950. Studio Master, Architectural Association, London, 1937–39; Lecturer, Slade School of Fine Art, London 1950; Visiting Artist, University of Leeds (Gregory Fellow), 1950– 53. Recipient: Grand Prize, International Competition for Monument to "The Unknown Political Prisoner," London, 1953. *Died 23 October 1981.*

Individual Exhibitions:

1949 Hanover Gallery, London

Reg Butler: *Nude*, 1977

1953 Curt Valentin Gallery, New York
1954 Hanover Gallery, London
1955 Curt Valentin Gallery, New York
1956 *Biennale*, Venice
1957 Hanover Gallery, London
Kunstkring, Rotterdam
Galerie Springer, Berlin
1958 Galerie Alex Vomel, Dusseldorf
1959 Pierre Matisse Gallery, New York
1960 Hanover Gallery, London
Pierre Matisse Gallery, New York
Kunstmuseum, Gothenburg, Sweden
Gummessons Konstgalleri, Stockholm
1961 Galleria Obelisco, Rome
1962 Pierre Matisse Gallery, New York
1963 Hanover Gallery, London
J. B. Speed Art Museum, Louisville, Kentucky
1964 New Metropole Arts Centre, Folkstone, Kent
Queens Square Gallery, Leeds
1967 Welsh Arts Council Gallery, Cardiff
1973 Pierre Matisse Gallery, New York
1983 Galeria Freite, Caracas, Venezuela
1986 Tate Gallery, London

Selected Group Exhibitions:

1952 *Biennale*, Venice
1955 *Young British Sculptors*, Arts Club of Chicago (toured the United States and Canada)
1958 *Pittsburgh International*, Carnegie Institute, Pittsburgh
1961 *Biennale*, Middelheim, Antwerp
1964 *Contemporary British Sculpture*, Cannon Hill Park, Birmingham (toured the U.K.)
1974 *12 Views of Mankind*, MacRobert Centre Art Gallery, University of Stirling, Scotland
1977 *Greater London Parks Exhibition*, London

Collections:

Tate Gallery, London; Arts Council of Great Britain, London; City Art Gallery, Aberdeen, Scotland; City Art Gallery, Bristol; Konstmuseum, Gothenburg, Sweden; Galleria d'Arte Moderna, Venice; Museum of Modern Art, New York; Albright-Knox Art Gallery, Buffalo, New York; Museum of Fine Arts, Boston; City Art Museum, St. Louis, Missouri.

Publications:

By BUTLER: book—*Creative Development: 5 Lectures to Art Students*, London 1962.

On BUTLER: books—*The Hand and Eye of the Sculptor* by Paul Waldo Schwartz, London 1969; *Reg Butler*, exhibition catalogue, by John Russell, New York 1973; *12 Views of Mankind*, exhibition catalogue, by Douglas Hall, Stirling, Scotland 1974; articles—"Objectified Images" by E. Wolfram in *Art and Artists* (London), June 1974; "Obituary" in *The Times* (London), 24 October 1981.

Reg Butler came to public prominence as the winner of the International Sculpture Competition "The Unknown Political Prisoner" in 1953, when, in fact, his model was destroyed by a protesting member of the public. His work at this time represented elongated, female figures, involved in strenuous energetic movements, sometimes in the process of dressing and undressing. There were similarities with the work of Giacometti, without any of that master's highly individual, stylised and disciplined view of mankind; there were also elements in common with the post-war English figurative school of sculptors, partly reacting to Moore and Hepworth's lyrical abstraction, in which the human form was used as the basis for emotional, nervous expression. Butler, however, was no tragedian, nor indeed a moralist. The early figure studies gave way to a more monumental, abstract style, ranging from the Calderesque wire constructions of the Unknown Prisoner maquette, to solid, heaving, cruciform bronze towers, which possibly reflected the influence of Henry Moore, whom Butler had assisted at one period.

In his *Concise History of Modern Sculpture*, Herbert Read linked Butler with what he termed the "vitalist tradition" (including Giacometti, Richier, Chadwick), which seeks images arising from the unconscious as the means of imposing order on chaos. It is a rather too generalised theme, since it could be said to apply to art of all periods and all styles. In the 60's Butler appeared in the forefront of British sculpture, having been presented at the Venice *Biennale* as early as 1952, which led to international attention. He also established a reputation as a teacher and theoretician, publishing *Creative Development: Five Lectures to Art Students* in 1962, in which he attempted to define the aims of modern art: "Recognition of the quality of things; their hardness and softness, heaviness and lightness, tautness and slackness, smoothness and roughness. Recognition of unities and similarities, rhythms and analogues, differences. The character of space, the definition of space, the penetration of things into space. The nature of illumination, its determination of what we see (as opposed to what we know otherwise than by vision from a static point in space). The news value of colour. The way our reading of experience is controlled by the means by which we perceive." This concern for the "essence" of things, the relationship between perception and creation, made Butler a remarkable teacher.

A common feature of British art history is the seeming impossibility of maintaining a public debate; the public, on the whole, is totally uninterested in aesthetic theories or social manifestos, and artists, even when in youth they show concern for group activities and theoretical debate, eventually revert to isolated individualism. The pattern, whether collectively or singly, is always the same. Similarly in English art is it rare to find the saintly or the disciplined, sacrifice for the sake of art and mystical experience; no Van Goghs, Maleviches, Mondrians, and the like. The English artist is usually a romantic poet, and at his worst a compromiser. In his last years Butler almost totally withdrew from the public art scene in England, rarely exhibiting, never publicly expressing his views. He abandoned abstract, didactic, public sculpture for the female nude, usually posed in strange positions, personal, erotic, even, some might say, self-indulgent.

—Charles Spencer

BUTTERFIELD, Deborah (Kay).

American. Born in San Diego, California, 7 May 1949. Educated at San Diego State College, 1966–68; University of California at Davis, 1969–73, B.A. 1972, M.F.A. 1973; studied at the Skowhegan School of Painting and Sculpture, Maine, 1972. Independent artist, concentrating on assemblages and sculpture, since 1973. Assistant Professor of Sculpture, University of Wisconsin at Madison, 1975–76, and at Montana State University, Bozeman, since 1979.

Recipient: Guggenheim Fellowship, 1980. Agents: Zolla/Lieberman Gallery, 368 West Huron Street, Chicago, Illinois 60610; O. K. Harris Gallery, 383 West Broadway, New York, New York 10012. Address: 11229 Cottonwood Road, Bozeman, Montana 59715, U.S.A.

Individual Exhibitions:

1969	Zolla/Lieberman Gallery, Chicago
1974	*2 Sculptors,* University of California, Berkeley
1976	Zolla-Lieberman Gallery, Chicago
1978	O. K. Harris Gallery, New York
1979	Hansen-Fuller-Goldeen Gallery, San Francisco
	Zolla/Lieberman Gallery, Chicago
1980	O. K. Harris Gallery, New York
	Open Gallery, Eugene, Oregon
	Hansen-Fuller-Goldeen Gallery, San Francisco
1981	*Jerusalem Horses,* Israel Museum, Jerusalem
	Arco Center for Visual Art, Los Angeles
1982	Mayor Gallery, London
	Dallas Museum of Fine Art, Texas
1983	Oakland Museum, California
1986	Contemporary Art Center, Honolulu

Selected Group Exhibitions:

1979	*Biennial,* Whitney Museum, New York
	The Decade in Review, Whitney Museum, New York
1980	*8 Sculptors,* Albright-Knox Gallery, Buffalo
	Painting and Sculpture Today, Indianapolis Museum of Art

Collections:

Whitney Museum, New York; Museum of Modern Art, New York; San Francisco Museum of Modern Art; Walker Art Center, Minneapolis; Hirshhorn Museum, Washington, D.C.; Metropolitan Museum of Art, New York; Israel Museum, Jerusalem.

Publications:

On BUTTERFIELD: books—*Painting and Sculpture Today,* exhibition catalogue, Indianapolis 1980; *Deborah Butterfield: Jerusalem Horses,* exhibition catalogue, Jerusalem 1981; articles—"Unique Balance of Realism, Art" by Thomas Albright in the *San Francisco Chronicle,* 15 June 1974; "Butterfield's Horses Surface Sensationally" by Alan G. Artner in the *Chicago Tribune,* 27 August 1976; "An Unusual Look at Nature" by Judith L. Dunham in *Artweek* (Oakland, California), 11 November 1978; "Sculptor Butterfield Plunges Deeper into a Substantial Body of Work" by Alan G. Artner in the *Chicago Tribune,* 18 May 1979; "Critic's Choice" by Franz Schulze in the *Chicago Sun-Times,* 17 June 1979; "Behold a Pale Horse (or Two)" by Kay Larsen in the *Village Voice* (New York), 28 November 1979; "Deborah Butterfield" in *Artnews* (New York), March 1980; "Explicit Horses" by J. Kelley in *Artweek* (Oakland, California), 19 December 1981.

The dominant theme in the work of Deborah Butterfield is the contemporary creative expression of the horse. She finds endless and new variations of this old motif using handmade steel, chicken-wire armature, and a variety of found materials which are all channelled to define the emotional qualities of individual horses. Even though the materials are rough, they, nevertheless, result in a most delicate definition of spatial gestures and underlying emotions of the individual horse with whom she identifies: "I first used the horse image as a metaphorical substitute for myself—it was a way of doing a self-portrait one step removed from the specificity of Deborah Butterfield."

Butterfield's horse sculptures are different from the classical image given to the horse in art. Hers constitute a completely new sculptural figuration which is a meaningful drawing in space with found materials. The theme carefully depicts specific animals in a specific moment with all the inherent individuality and vulnerability equal to that of a human being.

The artist's horses are expressions of a contemporary attitude toward life in general: "The horses in this exhibition are the most recent in a progression of work using found materials, all having their own 'history' and diverse visual qualities. These horses are no longer hollow shells but are built up from within and reveal the interior space. The gesture is continued and internalized while the posture is quiet and still. Action becomes anticipated rather than captured. Each horse represents a framework of presence which defines a specific energy at a precise moment."

Butterfield's horses have been interpreted as meditations on death, as symbols of suffering, and as signs of death and survival. These are fragmentary analogies of her work when considering the preciseness of an imagery which touches on human value and human endurance in terms of a gentle and delicate proposition of life in general.

Udo Kultermann

C

CADMUS, Paul.

American. Born in New York, 17 December 1904. Educated at Townsend Harris High School, New York, 1917–19; studied at the National Academy of Design, New York, with Charles Hawthorne, Charles Curran and William Auerbach-Levey, 1919–26; Art Students League, New York, with Joseph Pennell and Charles Locke, 1928. Worked for Blackman and Company advertising agency, New York, 1928–31; lived and worked with Jared French, who was an important influence, Majorca, and travelled in Europe, 1931–33; returned to the United States, and worked for the Public Works of Art Project, New York, 1933; designed costumes and set for the ballet *Filling Station,* New York, 1938. Vice-President, Arts Students League, New York, 1935. Recipient: Witkowsky prize, Art Institute of Chicago, 1945; National Institute of Arts and Letters grant, 1961. Member, National Institute of Arts and Letters, 1975; Associate Member, 1979, and Academician, 1980, National Academy of Design. Agent: Midtown Galleries, 11 East 57th Street, New York, New York 10022. Address: Post Office Box 1255, Weston, Connecticut 06883, U.S.A.

Individual Exhibitions:

1937 Midtown Galleries, New York
1942 *3 American Painters,* Baltimore Museum of Art
1945 Midtown Galleries, New York
1949 Midtown Galleries, New York
1956 Midtown Galleries, New York
1967 Palm Beach Galleries, Florida
1968 Midtown Galleries, New York (retrospective)
1976 Midtown Galleries, New York
1977 Midtown Galleries, New York
1979 *75th Birthday Exhibition,* Midtown Galleries, New York
1981 *Paul Cadmus: Yesterday and Today,* Miami University Art Museum, Oxford, Ohio (retrospective; travelled to the Ulrich Museum of Art, Wichita, Kansas; Gribbes Art Gallery, Charleston, South Carolina; and the William Benton Museum of Art, Storrs, Connecticut, 1981–82)
1983 Midtown Galleries, New York
1985 *Eightieth Birthday Celebration,* Midtown Galleries, New York
1986 Louis Newman Galleries, Beverly Hills, California

Selected Group Exhibitions:

1935 *Whitney Annual,* Whitney Museum, New York
1936 *Murals in Federal Art,* Corcoran Gallery, Washington, D.C.
1939 *Art in Our Time,* Museum of Modern Art, New York
1942 *20th Century American Portraits,* Museum of Modern Art, New York
1950 *American Symbolic Realism,* Institute of Contemporary Arts, London
1966 *Art of the United States 1670–1966,* New York Cultural Center
1972 *Collectors Anonymous,* New York Cultural Center
1975 *Work by Newly Elected Members,* National Institute of Arts and Letters, New York
1986 *Treasures from the National Museum of American Art,* Seattle Art Museum, Washington (travelled to Minneapolis, Fort Worth, Atlanta and Washington, D.C.)
1987 *Twentieth Century American Art,* Whitney Museum at the Equitable Center, New York

Collections:

Metropolitan Museum of Art, New York; Whitney Museum, New York; Museum of Modern Art, New York; Sara Roby Foundation Collection, New York; Fogg Art Museum, Harvard University, Cambridge, Massachusetts; National Museum of American Art, Smithsonian Institution, Washington, D.C.; Library of Congress, Washington, D.C.; J. B. Speed Art Museum, Louisville, Kentucky; Georgia Museum of Art, Atlanta; Los Angeles County Museum of Art.

Publications:

By CADMUS: book—*Ballet Alphabet: A Primer for Laymen,* with Lincoln Kirstein, New York 1939.

On CADMUS: books—*Art U.S.A. Now,* edited by Nordness, Lucerne 1962; *Paul Cadmus: Prints and Drawings* by Una E. Johnson, New York, 1968; *Paul Cadmus: Yesterday and Today,* exhibition catalogue, by Philip Eliasoph, Oxford, Ohio 1981; *Paul Cadmus* by Lincoln Kirstein, New York 1984; articles—"Paul Cadmus: Enfant Terrible" by Harvey Salpeter in *Esquire* (Chicago), July 1937; "Paul Cadmus: Etcher" by Childe Reece in *Magazine of Art* (New York), November 1937; "Paul Cadmus of Navy Fame Has His First Art Show" in *Life* (New York), March 1937; "Paul Cadmus Continues" by Ralph Pomeroy in *After Dark* (New York), December 1970; "The Figure Drawings of Paul Cadmus" by Diane Casella Hines in *American Artist* (New York), November 1972; "Profile on Paul Cadmus" by Raymond J. Steiner in *Art Times* (Woodstock, New York), May 1986; "Paul Cadmus" in *American Artist* (New York), February 1987; film—*Paul Cadmus: Enfant Terrible at 80* by David Sutherland, 1984.

A poet is not expected to give an exegesis of a poem. I don't think that a painter should do one of a painting. (*Aims* differ with each work.) I have made statements in the past, now I know better. Let art majors, art historians, etc. say their says.

In 1987 a continuing aim is clarity, a clarity that does not preclude mystery but does eschew mystification; also a technique that is delicate, precise and unobtrusive—no matter what the subject matter be.

—Paul Cadmus

Before he was 10 years old, Paul Cadmus had decided to become an artist. Although he produced a number of paintings in the 1930's and 40's, it is an interest in drawing which began as a teenager that Cadmus has sustained throughout his career. Working in a tightly rendered style, using masses of figures in motion and perspective schemes akin to those of the Italian Renaissance, Cadmus concentrated on contemporary social issues in his paintings, drawings, and etchings. The effects of densely populated city life on human behavior particularly interested the artist during the 1930's, and he chose to paint social interaction among the sexually promising.

A scandal arose in 1934 when a Cadmus painting, "The Fleet's In!," attracted negative attention from the U.S. Navy. Done as a Public Works of Art Project, "The Fleet's In!" depicted sailors smoking, drinking, and carousing with women who were behaving similarly. The Navy was outraged by Cadmus' satirical view and denounced the painting as "undignified, sordid, and depraved." Newspapers nationwide covered the incident. Cadmus, wise to the ways of Renaissance artists in pre-photography days, made an etching of the painting, pulled 50 prints, and thereby disseminated the image through his own devices, a fortunate move since the painting itself was "misplaced." Cadmus was not deterred from satire and social realism, however, and went on to paint "Hinkey-Dinkey Parlez-Vous" and "Sailors and Floosies," perhaps his best known work.

In keeping with his interest in artistic concerns of the Renaissance, Cadmus occasionally painted in egg tempera, and when he turned primarily to drawing in the mid 1950's he again used Renaissance methods—light colored strokes on toned paper. Cadmus takes his drawing seriously, regarding it as a fulfilling discipline rather than a casual study. His style and content have changed, however. "To the Lynching," 1935, for example, shows a swirling mass of horseflesh and humanity at its ugliest, while more recent drawings emphasize a single nude figure, carefully modeled. The interest in muscular tensions and dramatic foreshortening remains although the view of humanity has grown gentler.

—Mary Stofflet

CAGE, John.

American. Born in Los Angeles, California, 5 September 1912. Educated at primary schools and Los Angeles High School, until 1928 (class valedictorian); studied piano privately, 1920–28; studied at Pomona College, Claremont, California, 1928–30; studied architecture, and piano under Lazare Levy, Paris, 1930–31; studied composition, under pianist Richard Bühlig, Los Angeles, and under composers Adolph Weiss and Henry Cowell, New York, 1931–34; studied counterpoint and analysis, under Arnold Schönberg, at the University of Southern California, Los Angeles, and at the University of California at Los Angeles, 1934; studied philosophy and traditional music of India, under Gita Sarabhai, and attended lectures on Zen Buddhism by Daisetz T. Suzuki, Columbia University, New York, 1945–47. Married Xenia Andreyevna Kashevaroff in 1934 (separated, 1945). Independent composer, painter, printmaker, and writer, since 1931; travelled to Paris, Biskra, Majorca, Madrid and Berlin, painting and writing poetry, also began to compose music, 1930–31; composed chromatic music, and became increasingly interested in percussion music and rhythmic structure, 1935–36; Composer-Accompanist, dance

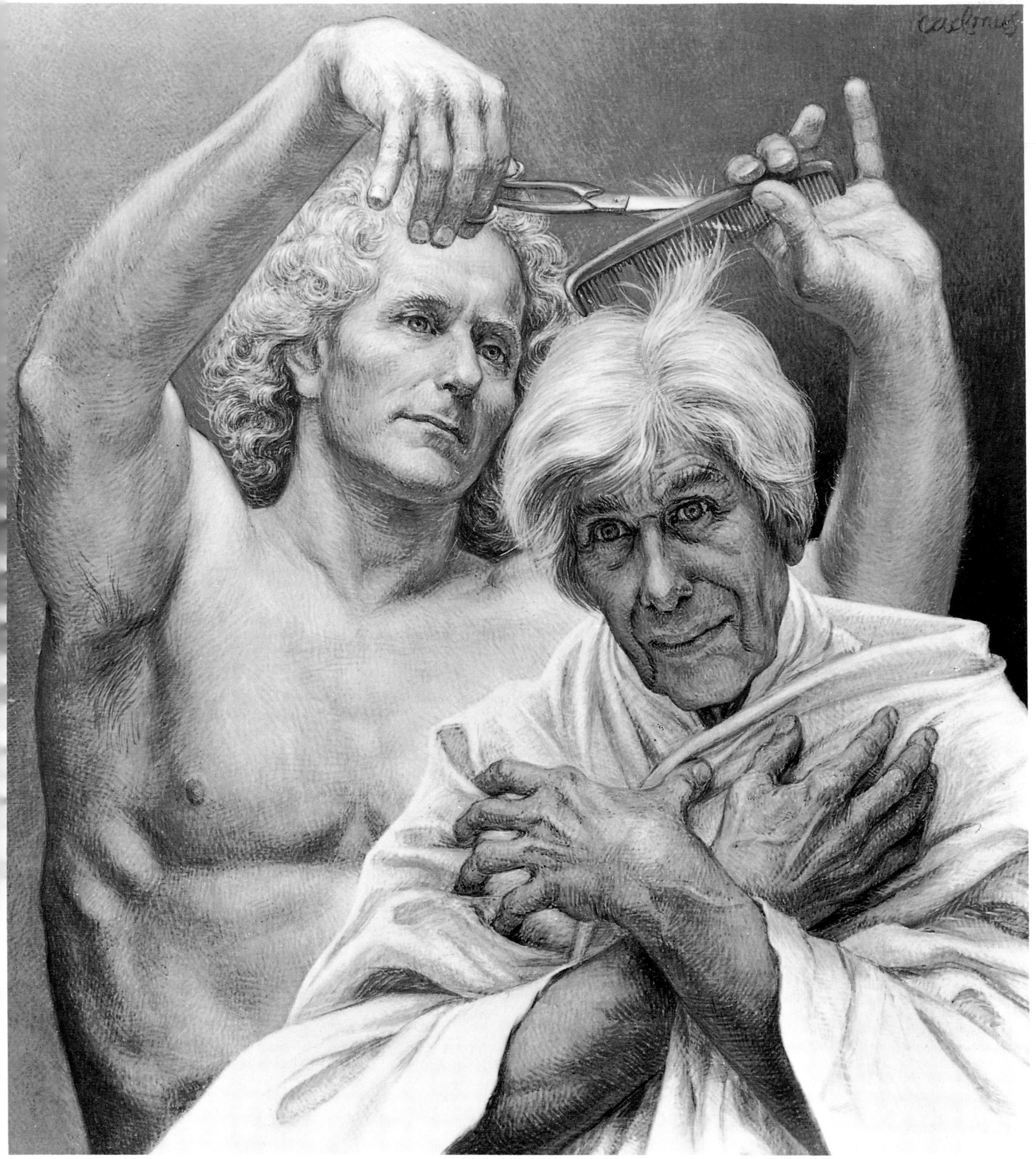

Paul Cadmus: *Haircut*, 1986

classes of Bonnie Bird, Cornish School, Seattle, where he met Merce Cunningham, then a student at the school, also composed and performed percussion music with groups and performed percussion music with groups that he organized, collecting various types of instruments, including "junk" objects, 1937–39; commissioned by CBS-Radio to create a score, *The City Wears a Slouch Hat*, with the poet Kenneth Patchen, Chicago, 1941; moved to New York and began a lifelong collaboration with Merce Cunningham, 1942; commissioned by the New York Ballet Society to score *The Seasons*, with choreography by Cunningham and sets by Isamu Noguchi, 1947; influenced by the thought of R. Buckminster Fuller, 1948; travelled to Europe, 1949; began collaboration with pianist David Tudor on many performances and projects, 1950; worked with Tudor, and composers Morton Feldman, Christian Wolff, and later, Earle Brown, to free sounds from memory, taste and fixed relationship to each other, making experiments and discoveries in the area of electronic music, 1950; influenced by Abstract Expressionist painters, 1950; introduced to the *I Ching* (Chinese *Book of Changes*), which became very important to the composition of his music and printmaking, 1951; moved with friends to a small cooperative community near Stony Brook, New York, where he became interested in nature, and concentrated on the study of mushrooms, 1954–72; made European concert tour with David Tudor, which influenced experimental music abroad, 1954; travelled to Europe with David Tudor, 1958; commissioned by the Montreal Festival Society to write major orchestral work, *Atlas Eclipticalis*, composed with astronomical charts, 1961; travelled to Japan on concert tour with David Tudor, 1962; travelled with Merce Cunningham on world tour, 1964; became interested in working with language: letters, syllables, words, and phrases free from syntax and meaning, 1969; became interested in lecture/performance for voice and tape, influenced by the writings of Mao Tse-Tung, 1971; moved back to New York, 1972; commissioned by Canadian Broadcasting Corporation to create a work related to the Bicentennial, *Lecture on the Weather*, 1975; commissioned by Seiji Ozawa and the Boston Symphony Orchestra to create a work for the Bicentennial, *Renga*, and *Apartment House 1776*, 1976; became intensely preoccupied with *Finnegans Wake*, 1976; invited by Kathan Brown to begin printmaking sessions at Crown Point Press, Oakland, California, 1978; devised way of "translating" any book into music, which he put to use on *Finnegans Wake*, 1979. Musical Director, Cunningham Dance Company, 1944–66, and President, Cunningham Dance Foundation, since 1965. Co-Founder, New York Mycological Society, 1962; Director, Foundation for Contemporary Performance Arts, since 1965. Visiting Instructor of Experimental Music, at invitation of László Moholoy-Nagy, Institute of Design, Chicago, 1941; Black Mountain College, North Carolina, 1948, 1952; New School for Social Research, New York, intermittently 1956–60; Darmstadt, West Germany, 1958; University of Hawaii, Honolulu, 1964; Fellow, 1960–61, 1970, and Associate, 1968–69, Center for Advanced Studies, Wesleyan University, Middletown, Connecticut; Composer-in-Residence, University of Cincinnati, 1967; Artist-in-Residence, University of California at Davis, 1969. Recipient: Guggenheim Fellowship, 1949; Award, American Academy of Arts and Letters and National Institute of Arts and Letters, 1949; Grand Honor, *International Biennial of Prints*, Tokyo, 1979. Member, American Academy of Arts and Sciences, 1979. Agent: Margarete Roeder Fine Arts, 545 Broadway, New York, New York 10012. Address: 101 West 18th Street, New York, New York 10011, U.S.A.

Individual Exhibitions:

1958 Stable Gallery, New York
1971 Galleria Schwarz, Milan
1977 *Renga*, Museum of Modern Art, New York (score)
1978 Museum Folkwang, Essen
Städtisches Museum, Mönchengladback, West Germany
Kunstverein, Cologne
1979 Kunstforum, Bonn
1982 *John Cage: Scores and Prints*, Whitney Museum, New York (travelled to the Albright-Knox Art Gallery, Buffalo, New York and the Philadelphia Museum of Art)

Performances:

1937 *The Future of Music: Credo*, Seattle (lecture)
1943 Museum of Modern Art, New York (concert of percussion music)
1944 Joint recital, Merce Cunningham Dance Company, New York
1950 *Lecture on Nothing*, Artist's Club, New York
1952 untitled "event," Black Mountain College, North Carolina (with Merce Cunningham, Robert Rauschenberg, David Tudor, and poets Charles Olson and Mary Caroline Richards)
1955 Joint recital, Clarktown High School, New York City (with Merce Cunningham)
1958 *Concert for Piano and Orchestra*, Town Hall, New York (retrospective)
Lecture on Indeterminacy, at *World's Fair*, Brussels (30 "amusing" stories, read 1/minute)
Water Walk, Milan (concert of theatre and music)
Sounds of Venice, Milan (concert of theatre and music)
1963 *Vexations, With 840 Repetitions*, by Erik Satie, New York (director)
1967 *1st Musicircus*, University of Illinois, Urbana (simultaneous performances of as much unrelated music as possible)
1968 *Reunion*, Toronto (with others; game of chess on an amplified board in which moves activate sound systems created by various musicians)
1969 *HPSCHD*, Assembly Hall, University of Illinois, Urbana (multi-media audio-visual performance)
1970 *Musicircus*, at *Paris Music Week*
1972 *Mesostics* and *Mureau*, European tour (with David Tudor; latter is mix of writings of Thoreau, superimposed on electronic music of Tudor)
1974 *12 Haiku*, Stony Brook, New York
1975 *Lecture on the Weather*, Canadian Broadcasting Corporation studios, Toronto (chanted texts derived from Thoreau with film and recordings of breeze, rain, and thunder)
1976 *Renga* and *Apartment House 1776*, Boston (with Boston Symphony, conducted by Seiji Ozawa; incorporated live or recorded songs, calls, and hollers)
1978 *Roaratorio: An Irish Circus on Finnegans Wake*, IRCAM recording studios, Paris (uses several thousand sounds found in *Finnegans Wake*)
1981 *Empty Words*, National Public Radio, United States
Compositions in Retrospect, at *Computer Music Conference*, Denton, Texas
30 Pieces for 5 Orchestras, Pont-á-Mousson, France
1982 *Roarotorio*, Toronto
several works, at *New Music America Festival*, Chicago

Selected Group Exhibitions:

1979 *International Biennial of Prints*, National Museum of Modern Art, Tokyo
1980 *Print Publishing in America*, Stedelijk Museum, Schiedam, Netherlands

Collections:

Metropolitan Museum of Art, New York; Museum of Modern Art, New York; Whitney Museum, New York; Museum of Fine Arts, Houston; San Francisco Museum of Modern Art; Stedelijk Museum, Amsterdam.

Compositions:

For piano—*Music for Xenia*, 1934; *2 Pieces*, 1935; *Metamorphosis*, 1938; *A Room*, 1943; *Experiences I*, 1945–48; *Ophelia*, 1946; *2 Pieces*, 1946; *Dream*, 1948; *In a Landscape*, 1948; *Suite for Toy Piano*, 1948; *Music of Changes*, 1951; *For M. C. and D. T.*, 1952; *Music for Piano I*, 1952; *7 Haiku*, 1952; *Waiting*, 1952; *Music for Piano 2*, 1953; *Music for Piano 3*, 1953; *Music for Piano 4-19*, 1953; *Music for Piano 20*, 1953; *Music for Piano 21-36, 37-52*, 1955; *Music for Piano 53-68*, 1956; *Music for Piano 69-84*, 1956; *For Paul Taylor and Anita Dencks*, 1957; *Winter Music*, 1957; *TV Koeln*, 1958; *Electronic Music for Piano*, 1964; *Cheap Imitation*, 1969; *Etudes Australes*, 1974–75; for prepared piano—*Bacchanale*, 1938; *Amores*, 1943; *Meditation*, 1943; *Totem Ancestor*, 1943; *A Book of Music*, 1944; *The Perilous Night*, 1944; *Prelude for Meditation*, 1944; *Root of an Unfocus*, 1944; *A Valentine out of Season*, 1944; *Daughters of the Lonesome Isle*, 1945; *Mysterious Adventure*, 1945; *3 Dances*, 1945; *Sonatas and Interludes*, 1946–48; *Music for Marcel Duchamp*, 1947; *2 Pastorales*, 1951; for voice—*20 Years After*, 1932; *Is It as It Was*, 1932; *At Eat and Ingredients*, 1932; *5 Songs for Contralto*, 1938; *Forever and Sunsmell*, 1942; *The Wonderful Widow of 18 Springs*, 1942; *Experiences II*, 1945–48; *A Flower*, 1950; *Aria*, 1958; *Solo for Voice 1*, 1958; *Solo for Voice 2*, 1960; *Song Books 1 & 2*, 1970; *Litany for the Whale*, 1980; *Empty Words*, 1981; for strings—*Nocturne for Violin and Piano*, 1947; *6 Melodies for Violin and Keyboard (Piano)*, 1950; *String Quartet in 4 Parts*, 1950; *Freeman Etudes*, 1977; for winds—*Sonata for Clarinet (Solo)*, 1933; *3 Pieces for Flute Duet*, 1935; *Music for Wind Instruments*, 1938; for harp—*In a Landscape*, 1948; for carillon—*Music for Carillon No. 1*, 1952; *Music for Carillon No. 2*, 1954; *Music for Carillon No. 3*, 1954; *Music for Carillon No. 4*, 1961; *Music for Carillon No. 5*, 1967; for various solos and ensembles—*6 Short Inventions*, 1933; *Solo with Obbligato Accompaniment of 2 Voices in Canon, and 6 Short Inventions on the Subject of the Solo*, 1933; *Sonata for 2 Voices*, 1933; *Composition for 3 Voices*, 1934; *3 Pieces for Flute Duet*, 1935; *She is Asleep*, 1943; *16 Dances*, 1951; *4'33"*, 1952; *59½ for a String Player*, 1953; *31'57.9864" for a Pianist*, 1954; *34'46.776" for a Pianist*, 1954; *26'1.499" for a String Player*, 1955; *27'10.554" for a Percussionist*, 1956; *Variations I*, 1958; *Variations II*, 1961; *0'00"*, 1962; *0'00" No. 2*, 1968; *Sound Anonymously Received*, 1969; *Score (40 Drawings by Thoreau) and 23 Parts*, 1974; *12 Haiku*, 1974; for orchestra and chamber orchestra—*The Seasons*, 1947; *Concerto for Prepared Piano and Chamber Orchestra*, 1951; *Concerto for Piano and Orchestra*, 1957–58; *Atlas Eclipticalis*, 1961–62; *30 Pieces for 5 Orchestras*, 1981; *Atlas Borealis* (with chorus), 1982; for percussion (and electronic devices)—*Quartet*, 1935; *Trio*, 1936; *First Construction (in Metal)*, 1939; *Imaginary Landscape No. 1*, 1939; *Living Room Music*, 1940; *Second Construction*, 1940; *Double Music*, with Lou Harrison, 1941; *Third Construction*, 1941; *Credo in Us*, 1942; *March (Imaginary Landscape No. 2)*, 1942; *Imaginary Landscape No. 3*, 1942; *Imaginary Landscape No. 4 (March No. 2)*, 1951; *Imaginary Landscape No. 5*, 1952; *Speech*, 1955; *Radio Music*, 1956; *Cartridge Music*, 1960; *Music for Amplified Toy Pianos*, 1960; *Variations III*, 1963; *Variations IV*, 1964; *Variations VI*, 1967; *Variations VII*, 1967; *Variations VIII*, 1968; *Child of Tree*, 1975; *Branches*, 1976; *Renga*, 1976; *Apartment House 1776*, 1976; *A Dip in the Lake*, 1976; *Roaratorio, An Irish Circus on Finnegans Wake*, 1979; for magnetic tape—*Williams Mix*, 1952; *Fontana Mix*, 1958; *Music for "The Marrying Maiden,"* 1960; *WBAI*, 1960; *Rozart Mix*, 1965; for audio-visuals—*Water Music*, 1952; *Music Walk*, 1958; *Sounds of Venice*, 1959; *Water Walk*, 1959; *Theatre Piece*, 1960; *Variations V*, 1965; *Musicircus*, 1967; *Newport Mix*, 1967; *Reunion*, 1968; *HPSCHD*, with Lejaren Hiller, 1969; *Lecture on the Weather*, 1975. Many of these scores have been published by Henmar Press, New York; over 40 recordings of various works have been made since 1933.

Publications:

By CAGE: books—*Virgil Thomson*, with Kathleen Hoover, New York, 1959; *Silence*, Middletown, Connecticut 1961; *A Year from Monday*, Middletown, Connecticut, 1967; *Diary: How to Improve the World (You Will Only Make Matters Worse) Continued 1967*, pamphlet, New York 1967; *Diary: Part III*, New York 1967; *Diary: Part IV*, New York 1968; *Notations*, with Alison Knowles, New York 1969; *To Describe the Process of Composition Used in Not Wanting to Say Anything about Marcel*, Cincinnati 1969; *Mushroom Book*, with Lois Long at Alexander H. Smith, New York 1972; *Writings '67-'72*, Middletown, Connecticut 1973; *Writing Through Finnegans Wake*, New York 1978; *Empty Words: Writings '73-'78*, Middletown, Connecticut 1979; *Changes and Disappearances*, portfolio of prints, New York 1982; *On the Surface*, portfolio of prints, New York 1982;

The Mud Book, with Lois Long, New York 1982; articles—"Goal: New Music, New Dance" in *Dance Observer*, December 1939; "Chavez and the Chicago Drouth" in *Modern Music*, March/April 1942; "For More New Sounds" and "South Winds in Chicago" in *Modern Music* May/June 1942; "Grace and Clarity" in *Dance Observer*, November 1944; "Summer Music: The Parks" in *Modern Music* November/December 1944; "Dreams and Dedications of George Antheil" in *Modern Music*, January 1946; "East in the West" in *Modern Music* April 1946; "Forerunners of Modern Music" in *Tiger's Eye*, March 1949; "Contemporary Music Festivals Held in Italy" in *Musical America*, June 1949; "Satie Controversy" in *Musical America*, December 1950; "A Few Ideas about Music and Films" in *Film Music News*, January/February 1951; "Letters to the Editors: More Satie" in *Musical America*, 1 April 1951; "Manifesto on Music" in *Living Theatre Program* (New York), 1952; "Letter to Peter Yates" in *Arts and Architecture* (Los Angeles), November 1953; "Manifesto on Painting of Bob Rauschenberg" in the *New York Herald Tribune*, 27 December 1953; "Music Lover's Field Companion" in *United States Lines Parts Review*, 1954; "Experimental Music" in *The Score*, June 1955; "In This Day . . ." in *Dance Observer*, January 1957; "2 Pages, 122 Words on Music and the Dance" in *Dance Magazine*, November 1957; "To Describe the Process of Composition Used in 'Music for piano 21-52' " in *Die Reihe*, vol. 3, 1957; "Morris Graves," introduction to exhibition catalogue, Ogunquit, Maine 1957; "Erik Satie" in *Art News Annual*, New York, 1958; "Composition as Process: Interdeterminacy" in *Das Neue Forum*, vol. 8, nos. 4, 6, 8, 1958; "Composition as Process: Communication" in *The Village Voice* (New York), April 1958; "Roster on Varèse" in *Nutida Musik* (Stockholm), Fall 1958; "History of Experimental Music in the United States" in *Beiträge zur Neuen Musik* (Darmstadt), vol. 4, 1959; "Unbestimmtheit" in *Die Reihe*, vol. 5, 1959; "Lecture on Nothing" in *Incontri Musicali*, August 1959; "Lecture on Something" in *It Is*, 1959; "Form Is a Language" in *Artnews* (New York), April 1960; "On Robert Rauschenberg, Artist, and His Work" in *Metro* (Milan), May 1961; "Where Are We Going? and What Are We Doing?" in *Ring des Arts*, Summer 1961; "Where Do We Go from Here?" in *Dance Perspectives*, vol. 16, 1962; "26 Statements re Duchamp" in *Mizue* (Tokyo), September 1962; "Jasper Johns: Stories and Ideas" in *Jasper Johns* by Alan R. Solomon, New York 1964; "Nam June Paik: A Diary" in *Nam June Paik*, exhibition catalogue, Rio de Janeiro 1965; interview, with Michael Kirby and Richard Schechner in *Tulane Drama Review* (New Orleans), Winter 1965; interview, with Ilhan Mimaroglu in *Discoteca*, November 1965; "Diary: Emma Lake Music Workshop 1965" in *Canadian Art*, January 1966; "Letters to the Editor: Electronic Souls" in the *Village Voice* (New York), 20 January 1966; "Seriously Comma" in *Preuves* (Paris), March 1966; "Rhythm" in *Module, Proportion, Symmetry, Rhythm*, edited by Gyorgy Kepes, New York 1966; "Diary: How to Improve the World (You Will Only Make Matters Worse) 1965" in *Joglars*, vol. 1, no. 3, 1966; "A Lethal Measurement," interview, with Michael Zwerin, in the *Village Voice* (New York), 6 January 1966; "Diary: How to Improve the World (You Will Only Make Matters Worse) 1966" in *Paris Review*, Spring 1967; "Diary: Audience 1966" in *Arts: Planning for Change*, 1967; "Remarks about Merce Cunningham" in *Dance Perspectives*, Summer 1968; "John Cage," interview, with Richard Kostelanetz, in *The Theatre of Mixed Means*, New York 1968; "HPSCHD," interview, with Larry Austin, in *Source*, vol. 2, no. 2, 1968; "Soixante Résponses à Trente Questions," interview, with Daniel Charles, in *Revue d'Esthétique* (Paris), 1968; "How to Improve the World (You Will Only Make Matters Worse) 1968 (Revised 1969)" in *Tri-Quarterly* (Evanston, Illinois), no. 18, 1970; essay in *Sound on Paper: Music Notation in Japan*, exhibition catalogue, New York 1981.

On CAGE: books—*Zen and American Thought* by Van Meter Ames, Honolulu, Hawaii 1962; *Happenings*, edited by Jürgen Becker and Wolf Vostell, Hamburg 1965; *The Bride and the Bachelors: 5 Masters of the Avant-Garde (Duchamp, Tinguely, Cage, Rauschenberg, Cunningham)* by Calvin Tomkins, New York 1965; *The New Art*, edited by Gregory Battock, New York 1966; *Die Unvermeidliche Musik des John Cage* by Werner Bartsch and others, Kolb, Switzerland 1969; *The New Music*, edited by Gregory Battcock, New York 1970; *Print Publishing in America*, exhibition catalogue, Schiedam, Netherlands 1980; *John Cage: Scores and Prints*, exhibition pamphlet, New York 1982; articles—"Cage, Composer, Shows Calligraphy of Note" by Dore Ashton in the *New York Times*, 6 May 1959; "Figure in an Imaginary Landscape" by Calvin Tomkins in *The New Yorker*, 28 November 1964; "Poets and Kings" by Jill Johnston in the *Village Voice* (New York), 8 November 1967; "Social Concern" by Calvin Tomkins in the *New York Times Book Review*, 21 January 1968; "Cage—Wissenschaftlich Betrachlet" by Hans Rudolf Zeller in *Zur Theorie der Offenen Form*, edited by Konrad Boehmer, Frankfurt 1968; "The American Avant-Garde, Part II: John Cage" by Richard Kostelanetz in *Stereo Review* (New York), May 1969; "John Cage: Some Random Remarks" by Richard Kostelanetz in *Denver Quarterly*, Winter 1969.

John Cage was born September 5, 1912, in Los Angeles. In his long career as composer he has encompassed many interests, delighted many people and enraged or antagonized a number of others. Best known as a guiding force of the avant-garde in America since the end of World War II, Cage's influence on composers, poets, dancers and painters has been as extensive as his work output has been prolific. Yet people at large are not so familiar with his music. His reputation for levity and eccentricity has served to obscure the seriousness of his inventions and perhaps limited the audience for his teachings.

Central to Cage's teaching is the view that art should imitate nature in its multiplicity and synchronous operations. He sees his music as a means of awakening people to the world around them; he has exhorted people to listen to the sounds, or noises of their everyday lives, as worthy of attention in themselves, not just as they might be structured in a composition, where they tend to lose their inherent self-sufficient value. One of Cage's most infamous pieces, called 4' 3", consisted of the performer or performers playing nothing—the sounds of the piece were the sounds of the audience and the environment. But Cage has deployed a number of methods in serving his phenomenological interests.

His earliest acclaimed invention was the "prepared piano"—a piano turned into a kind of percussion orchestra (played by one) by the placement of screws and other materials between the strings. By then, in the 40's, Cage's deviant concern for "noise" as proper material for music had been established. As a young man in California he had studied with Arnold Schoenberg whose traditional base for musical structure, dividing the whole into parts by means of tonality and harmony, provided a point of departure for the independent Cage. To include noises in his work Cage first devised rhythmic structures, which also resulted from his work with dancers. Since the early 50's Cage has worked closely with dancer/choreographer Merce Cunningham, as composer, mentor, friend and performer.

In the 40's Cage moved to New York, becoming interested in Zen Buddhism and Indian aesthetic theory. He studied with D. T. Suzuki at Columbia, an association that led him to his lifelong obsession with removing his ego (conscious taste and memory) from his work. His introduction to the *I Ching*, or *Chinese Book of Changes*, gave him the tool for implementing this removal of self, as he saw it, from composition. Since 1950 he has used the *I Ching* continuously, though not exclusively, to determine, by tossing coins, the sequence of events or specific order of sounds, and sometimes even materials, in his work. It is these "chance operations" that have impressed so many other artists in their own quests for the unfamiliar. Akin to them are the various methods of Indeterminacy by which Cage has left or instructed his performers to supply aspects of his compositions that he has not himself. Things left to the performer's discretion, however, are not to be confused with improvisation, which remains dependent on personal likes and dislikes, taste and memory, etc: rather they are determined by the performers in advance of performance, in the creation of the score.

During the 70's Cage united his chance methodology with his admiration for Henry Thoreau and James Joyce, creating literary Dada-like variations on the famous texts: *Walden* and *Finnegans Wake*.

He has also pioneered the use of tape and electronic music, and is known for producing the prototypical "happening"—at Black Mountain College in 1952.

—Jill Johnston

CALDER, Alexander.

American. Born in Philadelphia, Pennsylvania, 22 July 1898. Educated in primary school in Berkeley, California; studied mechanical engineering, Stevens Institute of Technology, Hoboken, New Jersey, 1915–18, M.E. 1918; studied drawing and painting at the Art Students League, New York, with Boardman Robinson, 1923–25, and at the Academie de la Grande Chaumière, Paris, 1926–27. Married Louisa James in 1931; children: Sandra and Mary. Served in the United States Navy, 1918. Worked as engineer, Rutherford, New Jersey, 1919; draftsman and engineer, West Coast logging camps, 1919–23; lived and worked in New York, 1923–30; contributed sketches to *National Police Gazette*, New York, 1925–26; joined cargo boat crew, travelled to England and Paris, 1926; worked on wood sculpture, produced miniature circus, Paris, 1927–28; first performance of *The Circus*, Paris, 1927; travelled in Europe and settled in Paris, 1930; member, *Abstraction-Creation* group, Paris, 1930–31; created first mobiles, Paris, 1931; purchased farm in Roxbury, Connecticut, 1933; house in Sache, near Tours, France, 1953, and spent much time there after 1960; added workshop, 1961. Set Designer, Martha Graham ballets, and *Socrate*, by Erik Satie, 1935; set designer, *Provocation*, by Pierre Halet, 1963; first performance of his ballet, *Work in Progress*, Rome Opera House, 1968; set designer, *Metaboles*, Odeon, Paris, 1969; *Eppur si muove*, opera, by Francis Miroglio, 1971. Recipient: First Prize, Plexiglass Sculpture Competition, Museum of Modern Art, New York, 1939; First Prize for Sculpture, *Biennale*, Venice, 1952; Outstanding Citizen Award, Philadelphia, 1955; First Prize, *Carnegie International*, Pittsburgh, 1958; Gold Medal, Architectural League of New York, 1960; Creative Arts Award, Brandeis University, Waltham, Massachusetts, 1962; Gold Medal, American Academy of Arts and Letters, 1971; Grand Prix, National des Arts et Lettres, Paris, 1974; Honors Award, 2nd Biennal Awards Program of the United States General Services Administration, 1975; United Nations Peace Medal, 1975. Honorary doctorates: Grand Valley State College, Allendale, Michigan, 1969; Stevens Institute of Technology, Hoboken, New Jersey, 1969; University of Hartford, Connecticut, 1973. Commandeur, Legion d'Honneur, 1968. *Died* (in New York) *11 November 1976.*

Individual Exhibitions:

1928	Weyhe Gallery, New York
	Salon des Indépendants, New York
1929	Galerie Billet, Paris
	Galerie Neumann and Nierendorf, Berlin
	Elizabeth Hawes Showroom, New York
	56th Street Gallery, New York
	Weyhe Gallery, New York
1930	Harvard University, Cambridge, Massachusetts
1931	Galerie Percier, Paris
1932	Galerie Vignon, Paris
	Madison Avenue Gallery, New York
	Julien Levy Gallery, New York
1933	Galerie Pierre Loeb, Paris
	Galerie Pierre Colle, Paris
1934	Pierre Matisse Gallery, New York
1935	University of Chicago Arts Club
	Pierre Matisse Gallery, New York
1936	Vassar College, Poughkeepsie, New York
	Pierre Matisse Gallery, New York
1937	Freddie Mayor Gallery, London
	Pierre Matisse Gallery, New York
1938	Pierre Matisse Gallery, New York
1939	Pierre Matisse Gallery, New York
1940	Pierre Matisse Gallery, New York
1941	Pierre Matisse Gallery, New York
	Wallace K. Harrison House, Huntington, Long Island, New York
	Marian Willard Gallery, New York
1942	Pierre Matisse Gallery, New York (with Yves Tanguy)
1943	Museum of Modern Art, New York

1944 Buchholz Gallery, New York
1945 Samuel Kootz Gallery, New York
Buchholz Gallery, New York
1946 Galerie Louis Carre, Paris
1947 Portland Art Museum, Oregon
Buchholz Gallery, New York
Stedelijk Museum, Amsterdam (with Fernand Leger)
1948 Buchholz Gallery, New York
Ministry of Education, Rio de Janiero (travelled to the Museo do Arte, Sao Paulo)
Gallery of Contemporary Art, Washington, D.C.
1949 Buchholz Gallery, New York
Margaret Brown Gallery, Boston
Richmond Museum of Fine Arts, Virginia
1950 Galerie Blanche, Stockholm
Massachusetts Institute of Technology, Cambridge
Galerie Maeght, Paris
1952 Curt Valentin Gallery, New York
Galerie Parnasse, Wuppertal
Galerie der Spiegel, Cologne
Galerie Otto Stangl, Munich (with Joan Miró)
1953 Frank Perls Gallery, Beverly Hills, California
Wadsworth Atheneum, Hartford (with Naum Gabo)
Galerie Christian Zervos, Aix-en-Provence, France
Walker Art Center, Minneapolis
1954 Galerie Maeght, Paris
Cahiers d'Art, Paris
1955 Curt Valentin Gallery, New York
Kunsthalle, Basle
Museo de Bellas Artes, Caracas
Reid and Lefevre Gallery, London
1956 Frank Perls Gallery, New York
Galleria dell'Obelisco, Rome
Galerie Lucie Weill, Paris
Musée Grimaldi, Antibes
1957 Kunsthalle, Basle
1958 Galerie Blanche, Stockholm (travelled to the Frank Perls Gallery, New York)
1959 Galerie Maeght, Paris
Museo do Arte Moderno, Rio de Janeiro
Stedelijk Museum, Amsterdam (toured Germany)
Haus der Jugend, Wuppertal-Barmen, West Germany
Kunstverein, Wuppertal, West Germany
Kunstgewerbe Museum, Zurich
Palais des Beaux-Arts, Brussels
1960 Frank Perls Gallery, New York
Museo do Arte Moderno, Rio de Janeiro
1961 Museo de Bellas Artes, Caracas
Frank Perls Gallery, New York
Lincoln Gallery, London
Stedelijk Museum, Amsterdam
Moderna Museet, Stockholm
Louisiana Museum, Humlebaek, Denmark
1962 Frank Perls Gallery, New York
Tate Gallery, London
Brook Street Gallery, London
Galerie Blanche, Stockholm
Galerie La Hune, Paris
Musée de Rennes, France
1963 Galerie Maeght, Paris
Frank Perls Gallery, New York
Galerie Alex Vomel, Dusseldorf
1964 Frank Perls Gallery, New York
Museum of Fine Arts, Houston
Guggenheim Museum, New York (toured the United States)
1965 Musée National d'Art Modern, Paris
1966 Galerie Krugier et Cie, Geneva
Galerie Maeght, Paris
Frank Perls Gallery, New York
Galerie Francoise Mayers, Brussels
Institute of Contemporary Arts, London
1967 Frank Perls Gallery, New York
Akademie der Künste, Berlin
Middleheim Promoters, Antwerp
Galleria Arco d'Alibert, Rome
1968 Frank Perls Gallery, New York
Galerie Maeght, Paris
Wittenborn Gallery, New York
Dayton's Gallery 12, Minneapolis
Maison de la Culture, Bourges, France (travelled to Musée des Augustins, Toulouse)

Alexander Calder: *The River—Chicago*, 1974 Courtesy Museum of Contemporary Art, Chicago

Art et Culture Festival, Noisy-le-Sec, France
1969 Frank Perls Gallery, New York
Gimpel Fils Gallery, London
Fundacion Eugenio Mendoza, Caracas
Fondation Maeght, St. Paul de Vence, France (travelled to Louisiana Museum, Humlebaek, Denmark)
Grand Rapids Museum, Michigan
Donald Morris Gallery, Detroit
Grand Valley State College, Allendale, Michigan
Museum of Modern Art, New York
1970 Long Beach Museum of Art, California (travelled to San Diego and Phoenix, Arizona)
Frank Perls Gallery, New York
Galerie Blanche, Stockholm
Chateau de Ratilly, Treigny, France (with Jean Bazaine)
Kovler Gallery, Chicago
1971 Frank Perls Gallery, New York
Galleria dell'Obelisco, Rome
Galerie Maeght, Paris
American Academy of Arts and Letters, New York
Whitney Museum, New York (toured the United States)
Studio Marconi, Milan
Musée Toulouse Lautrec, Albi, France (travelled to the Maison des Arts et Loisirs, Sochaux, France)
Taft Museum, Cincinnati, Ohio
Society of the 4 Arts, Palm Beach, Florida (with Louise Nevelson and David Smith)
Brook Street Gallery, London
Galerie d'Art Moderne, Basle
John Berggruen Gallery, San Francisco
Musco Nacional de Belas Artes, Buenos Aires
1972 Leonard Hutton Gallery, New York
Frank Perls Gallery, New York

Galerie Veerière, Paris
Sala Pelaires, Palma de Majorca
Galerie Bollack, Strasbourg
Fuji Television Company Gallery, Tokyo (with Joan Miró; travelled to Galerie Beyeler, Basle)

1973 Frank Perls Gallery, New York
Galerie Maeght, Paris
Kunsthalle, Bielefeld, West Germany
Galerie T. Roussel, Perpignan, France
Palais des Beaux-Arts, Charleroi, Belgium
Detroit Institute of Arts
University of Hartford, Connecticut
Galleria Delta, Rome
Sala Gaspar, Barcelona
Guggenheim Museum, New York
Galerie Maeght, Zurich
Whitney Museum, New York (with Louise Nevelson and David Smith)

1974 Frank Perls Gallery, New York
Esther Robles Gallery, Los Angeles
Katonah Gallery, New York
Centre Culturel de St. Pierre des Corps, France
Galerie Jeanne Albeille, Toulouse
Musée Municipal, Cluny, France
Calder Festival, Chicago
Museum of Contemporary Art, Chicago
Galerie Cour St. Pierre, Geneva
Galerie Denise René-Hans Meyer, Dusseldorf

1975 Frank Perls Gallery, New York
Galerie Maeght, Paris
Pace Gallery, New York
Haus der Kunst, Munich (travelled to the Kunsthaus, Zurich)
Galerie Parallele, Geneva
Center for the Arts Gallery, Wesleyan University, Middletown, Connecticut (toured the United States)
Bhirasi Institute of Modern Art, Bangkok
Mitchell Sewall Gallery, New York

1976 Frank Perls Gallery, New York
Pennsylvania Academy of Fine Arts, Philadelphia
Calder Festival, Philadelphia
Makler Gallery, Philadelphia
Whitney Museum, New York (toured the United States)

1977 Margaret Fisher Gallery, London

1978 Centre Georges Pompidou, Paris

1980 Kettles Yard, Cambridge, England

1981 Manor Gallery and Waddington Galleries, London
Whitney Museum, New York

1984 Whitney Museum, New York

Selected Group Exhibitions:

1927 *Salon des Humoristes*, Paris
1929 *Salon des Indépendants*, Paris
1934 *Art in Our Time*, Museum of Modern Art, New York
1938 *Trois Siècles d'Art aux Etats-Unis*, Jeu de Paume, Paris
1952 *Biennale*, Venice
1958 *Carnegie International*, Carnegie Institute, Pittsburgh
1964 *Documenta 3*, Kassel, West Germany
1966 *Trois Siècles de Tapisseries*, Gobelins and Centre Municipal, toulouse

Collections:

Metropolitan Museum of Art, New York; Museum of Modern Art, New York; Addison Gallery of American Art, Andover, Massachusetts; Philadelphia Museum of Art; Museum of Fine Arts, Dallas; Stedelijk Museum, Amsterdam; National Museum, Stockholm; Louisiana Museum, Humlebaek, Denmark; Musee National d'Art Moderne, Paris; Neue Nationalgalerie, Berlin.

Commissioned sculptures in public plazas and buildings in Europe and the United States.

Publications:

By CALDER: books—*Animal Sketching*, New York 1926, 1973; *Fables of Aesop*, Paris 1931, New York 1967; *Calder's Circus*, New York 1964; *An Autobiography with Pictures*, New York 1966; *Calder at the Zoo*, Washington, D.C. 1974; illustrated books—*3 Young Rats*, edited by James Johnson Sweeney, New York 1944; *The Rhyme of the Ancient Mariner* by Samuel Taylor Coleridge, New York 1946; *Jean de la Fontaine's Selected Fables*, New York 1948; *A Bestiary*, edited by Richard Wilbur, New York 1955; *Fêtes*, with Jacques Prévert, New York 1955, Paris 1971; *La Proue de la Tables* by Yves Elleouet, Paris 1967; *Santa Claus* by D. Jon Grossman, Paris 1974; article—"What Abstract Art Means to Me" in *Museum of Modern Art Bulletin* (New York), 1951; ballet—*Work in Progress*, 1968.

On CALDER: books—*Alexander Calder* by James Johnson Sweeney, New York 1951; *The Changing Forms of Art* by Patrick Heron, London 1955; *Essays in Aesthetics* by Jean Paul Sartre, New York 1963; *Alexander Calder*, exhibition catalogue, by Jean Cassou, Paris 1965; *Calder: A Study of the Works* by H. H. Arnason and Pedro E. Guerraro, Princeton, New Jersey 1966; *Calder: Mobiles and Stabiles* by Michel Ragon, New York and Paris 1967; *Calder* by Peter Bellow, Dusseldorf 1969; *Alexander Calder: A Pictorial Essay* by Bernice Winslow Mancewitz, Grand Rapids, Michigan 1969; *Calder* by James Johnson Sweeney, Paris 1971; *Calder's Circus*, edited by Jean Lipman and Nancy Foot, New York 1972; *Hommage to Alexander Calder*, edited by G. di San Lazzaro, special edition of *20th Siècle* (Paris), 1972; *Calder*, exhibition catalogue, New York 1984; *Alexander Calder and His Magic Mobiles* by Jean Lipman and Margaret Aspinall, London 1987;films—*Alexander Calder*, directed by Hans Aerlis, Berlin 1929; *Alexander Calder: Sculpture and Constructions* by Agnes Rindge Claflin, New York 1944; *Dreams That Money Can Buy* by Hans Richter, New York 1948; *Works of Calder* by Burgess Meredith, New York 1951; *Cirque Calder* by Carlos Vilardebo, Paris 1961; *Alexander Calder: From the Circus to the Moon* by Hans Richter, New York 1963; *Mobiles* by Carlos Vilardebo, Paris 1966; *The Great Sail* by Robert Gardner, New York 1966; *Alexander Calder: The Creation of a Stabile*, New York 1967; *Calder: un Portrait* by Charles Chaboud, Paris 1969; *Les Gouaches de Sandy* by Carlos Viladebo, Paris 1973.

There seems to be something peculiarly American about the combination in Alexander Calder of Yankee humor, pioneering inventiveness, down-to-earth tinkering, and pie-in-the-sky poetry. The playful, the practical, the dare-devil originality have deepened and broadened throughout his long career into a body of sculpture that stands high in the range of "delectable mountains" (e. e. cummings' phrase) thrown up by sculptors in our time.

The son of a distinguished academic sculptor, Calder caught the imagination of the *avant-garde* in Paris before the Second World War with his mad, funny, touching sinister, lyrical little circus—a hodge podge of wires, wheels, string, cloth with which he put on a show that revealed all his best qualities—or nearly all: his genius for capturing the individuality of things—a horse or clown or high wire performer—along with his fascination for the way things move.

Somewhere along the way his interest in movement lead to the creation of sculptures that move. Dubbed "mobiles," they have found their way into the mainstream of 20th century art. Usually painted in bold, basic colours—black, red and white is a favorite combination—they turn, bob and rotate to the whims of the slightest wind, natural or man-made. Some of them play tunes as well, either unexpectedly or by design: one work has a gong so arranged that it is the climax to the rotating "petals" as they wind or unwind.

These works are rather like trees with their "leaves" and "twigs," their extending "branches" and "limbs." Another series, the paradox-opposite one might say, are static as stone. Understandably called "stabiles," they resemble inanimate crabs or spiders, their large forms arching like claws or legs. These latter works have attained very large scale—as much as fifty feet or more in height—and have a grand, heroic effect. No wonder they have found their way into public squares and plazas.

No wonder either that Calder painted a series of actual airplanes—objects that move on a grand scale. It seems both logical and inevitable.

—Ralph Pomeroy

CALDERARA, Antonio.

Italian. Born in Abbiategrasso, 28 October 1903. Studied engineering at the Politenico, Milan, 1921–24. Served as a corporal in the Infantry Battalion, Rome, 1924–25. Married Carmela Finnati in 1933. Full-time painter from 1926; first abstract works, 1959. Recipient: Gold Medal, Ente Provinciale del Turismo di Novata, 1974. *Died* (in Vacciago) *27 June 1978.*

Individual Exhibitions:

1923 Alberto Maulini, Vacciago, Italy
1933 Nuova Vita, Milan
1934 Galleria Bolaffio, Milan
1944 Galleria Como, Italy
1947 Galleria della Spiga, Milan
1948 Galleria Del Camino, Milan
1949 Galleria del Grattecielo, Legnano, Italy
1950 Instituto di Cultura Italiana, Lisbon
1953 Galleria Obelisco, Rome

1955 Schettini Galleries, New York
Galleria Spotorno, Milan

1956 Galleria Campana, Milan

1960 Studio F., Ulm-Doneau, West Germany
Galleria Gruppo Enne, Padua

1961 Galerie Charles Lienhard, Zurich
1962 Galleria Cadario, Milan

1963 Galleria Gavana, Trieste
Galleria Gritti, Venice

1964 Galleria Levi, Milan
Galleria La Polena, Genoa

1965 2000 Galleria d'Arte, Bologna
Centro Proposte, Florence
Museo d'Arte Moderna, Rio de Janeiro
Cenobio di Milano, Milan
Op Art Galerie, Esslingen, West Germany
Galerie 132, Krefeld, West Germany
Studio Und, Munich

1966 Galerie H., Hannover
Galerie Toni Gerber, Berne
Galleria Milano, Milan

1967 Studio Und, Munich
Galerie Toni Gerber, Berne

1968 Kestner Gesellschaft, Hannover
Kunst-Centrum t'Venster, Rotterdam
Stedelijk Museum, Schiedam, Netherlands
Documenta, Kassel, West Germany
Udstillingen Ved, Charlottenborg, Copenhagen

1969 Galleria La Polena, Genoa
Studio Und, Munich
Galleria Milano, Milan
Galerie Appelbaum, Karlsruhe
Ommagio a Calderara, Galleria Alberti, Omegna, Italy
Galerie Defet, Nuremberg
Galleria Barozzi, Venice
Kunstmuseum, Lucerne
Galerie Nachst St. Stephan, Vienna
Galerie Anne Marie Verna, Zurich

1970 Studio Berggemende, Frankfurt
Kozmopolitan Gallery, New York
Zimmergalerie, Detmold-Hiddesen, West Germany
Galerie Reckermann, Cologne
Galerie Berner, Stuttgart
Galerie M, Bochum, West Germany
Stadtische Galerie Die Fahre, Salgau, West Germany

1971 Galerie Nachst St. Stephan, Vienna
Galerie Anne Marie Verna, Zurich
Galerie Diogenes in Cubus, Berlin
Hofhauspresse Hans Moller, Hubbelrath, West Germany
Galerie Francoise Mayer, Brussels
Galerie im Taxispalais, Innsbruck
Aargauer Kunsthaus, Aarau, Switzerland
Galerie Denise René, Paris

1972 Galleria Milano, Milan
Galerie Anne Marie Verna, Zurich
Galerie M, Bochum, West Germany
Galerie Interior, Frankfurt
Galerie Ubu, Karlsruhe

Galerie Regio, Friburg Lorrach, West Germany
Galerie Drosche, Hamburg
Galerie Thomas Keller, Starnburg, West Germany
Galleria Peccolo, Livorno, Italy
Badische Kunstverein, Karlsruhe
Galerie Zodiaque, Geneva
Galerie Collection d'Art, Amsterdam
Kunstmuseum, Dusseldorf
Galerie Schottle, Munich
Studio Eyck, Heerlen, Netherlands

1973 Galleria Milano, Milan
Galerie Anne Marie Verna, Zurich
Galerie Thomas Keller, Starnburg, West Germany
Kunstmuseum, Dusseldorf
Galerie Schottle, Munich
Galerie Club 44, La Chaux de Fonds, Switzerland
Galleria Godel, Rome
Galerie Lens Fine Art, Antwerp
Galleria l'Incontro, Borgomanero, Italy
Salone Annunciata, Milan
Galleria Marlborough, Rome
Kunstmuseum, Solingen, West Germany
Galleria Schettini, Milan

1974 Galleria Schottle, Munich
Galleria Schubert, Milan
Studio V, Vigevano, Italy
Castello Svevo, Termoli, Italy
Museo de Arte Contemporaneo, Cuidad Bolivar, Venezuela

1975 Galleria La Polena, Genoa
Galleria Milano, Milan
Galerie Anne Marie Verna, Zurich
Arte Contacto, Caracas
Galleria Pellegrino, Bologna
Piura Edizioni, Milan
Galleria E., Bolzano, Italy
Galerie Nouvelle Images, The Hague
Galleria de Arte Centro El Bosque, Caracas
Palazzo dell'Arengario, Monza, Italy
Galleria Team Colore, Milan
Galleria Grazia Bosser, Turin

1976 Galerie Reckermann, Cologne
Galerie Thomas Keller, Starnburg, West Germany
Annely Juda Fine Art, London
Kunstverein, Freiburg, West Germany (travelled to the Kunstverein, Brunswick, West Germany)
Stadtische Galerie, Villengen-Schwenningen, West Germany

1977 Galerie Schottle, Munich
Salone Annunciata, Milan
Museum of Modern Art, Bottrop, West Germany
Stedelijk Museum, Amsterdam
Museum des 20, Jahrhunderts, Vienna
Kunstcentrum Badhuis, Gorinchem, Netherlands

1978 Stedelijk Museum, Schiedam, Netherlands
Studio La Città, Verona
Ohio State University Gallery of Fine Arts, Columbus
Galerie Dorothea Loehr, Frankfurt
Galleria Martano, Turin
Palazzo Municipale, Novara, Italy

1979 Galleria La Polena, Genoa
Galleria Vismara, Milan
Galerie Bossin, Berlin

1980 Galerie Schottle, Munich
Galerie 44 Kaarst, Dusseldorf
Galleria Spriano, Omegna, Italy

1981 Studio La Città, Verona
Padiglione d'Arte Contemporanea, Parco Mazzari, Ferrara, Italy
Galerie Christel, Stockholm
Parco Massari, Ferrara, Italy
Studio La Città, Verona, Italy

1982 Wilhelm-Hack-Museum, Ludwigshafen, West Germany

Selected Group Exhibitions:

1929 *Gallery Group*, Galleria del Naviglio, Milan
1934 *Biennale di Brera*, Milan
1936 *Mostra Nazionale della Promotrice*, Turin
1945 *Esposizione Fondo Natteotti*, Milan
1948 *Biennale*, Venice
1956 *Biennale*, Venice
1962 *Moderne Italiensk Malerei*, Kunstbiblioteket Nikolay Kiske, Copenhagen
1966 *International Exhibition of Engraving*, Museum of Modern Art, Tokyo
1967 *Art and Movement*, Museum of Contemporary Art, Montreal
1969 *Les Grandes et les Jeunes d'Aujourd'hui*, Musée d'Art Moderne de la Ville, Paris

Publications:

By CALDERARA: illustrated books—*Tempo Spazio Luce*, music score, by Bruno Canino, Milan 1963; *Misura di Luce*, edited by Umberto Eco, Milan 1964; *Il Numero Cromatico* by Andries van Onck, Milan 1965; *Frequenze Ortogonali* by Carlo Guilio Argan, Milan 1965; *Sequenzen* by Herbert August Haseke, Munich 1968.

On CALDERARA: books—*Antonio Calderara* by Rafaello Giolli, Milan 1946; *Antonio Calderara* by Giorgio Nicodemi, Milan 1947; *Antonio Calderara: Disegni* by Agnoldomenico Pica, Milan 1955; *Antonio Calderara e Gruppo I* by Guilio Carlo Argan, Milan 1966; *Omaggio a Calderara*, exhibition catalogue, by Reimer Jochims, Starnburg, West Germany 1972; *Gli Acquerelli di Antonio Calderara* by Carlo Belloli, Milan 1975; *Antonio Calderara: Acquerelli dal 1958 al 1975* by Tommaso Trini, Milan 1975; *Antonio Calderara*, exhibition catalogue, by Bernhard Holezzek, Freiburg, West Germany 1976; *Antonio Calderara 1903–1978* by Friedrich W. Heckmanns, Cologne 1982.

Though he held his first exhibition in 1923, it was not until 1959 that Antonio Calderara made his first abstract painting: he exhibited it in the following year. It is perhaps significant that in the intervening years the lists of his shows have lengthened with an almost equal division of venues between his native Italy and Germany and Switzerland. His popularity in the latter two countries is readily understandable in the light of his style and format.

In appearance these works bear a strong affinity to those of Josef Albers, the German-born painter whose apt phrase, "homage to the square," summarized his work. The selection of the colour field that set the mood of paintings and watercolours was for Calderara the dominant effect. His choice of body hue was usually on the warm side—quivering cadmium reds, strong yellows that by their proportions within square and rectangular boundaries set up equations of vibrating chords tuned to the scale of the areas covered and the distance separating them from the spectator.

Mostly small in format, the works took on their appropriate range of radiation when hung in juxtaposition on a gallery wall. In general, while the immediate response seemed to form a complete saturation from edge to edge, closer examination revealed the note of comparison, sometimes as a tiny square on the border deeper in tone than the even spread of the whole yet in its concentration echoing the dimensions of the larger ground. In other words, the suggestion of a paler halation of open rectangles overpainted by the general red gave more than a hint of Rothko's colour vibrations but within a rigid geometric base subtly subdued by the elimination of contrast. This marriage of emotional stimulation from colour fields of evocative hues and the classic ratio of height to width was consummated by the nicely judged relationships of size with the carrying power of the design.

Eminently rare for his capacity of self-generated warmth and balance in small formats, Calderara is a supreme miniaturist in the abstract idiom whose calculations are as precise in terms of visual engineering. Strictly speaking, nothing is left to chance, for all that was placed on the canvas or on paper was preceded by the artist's experimental testing of values—the vibratory sensation of pigment surface obscuring interior straight edges by the slightest change in weight. Delicate though the differences are, Calderara's works maintain something ineluctably Italian in their certainty of execution, preserving historic vitality through a high chromatic key and a sense of architectural order expressed in small and two-dimensional limits. Yet, by their projection of their quivering shadows in a given section of the spectrum, Calderara's paintings operate most powerfully through the variable and magic third dimension that radiates between their surface and the eye of the beholder.

—G. S. Whittet

CALZOLARI, Pier Paolo.

Italian. Born in Bologna in 1943. Studied at the Accademia di Belle Arti, Urbino, 1967. Married; has one child. Independent artist, Bologna, since 1967. Agent: Sonnabend Gallery, 420 West Broadway, New York, New York 10012, U.S.A. Address: Via San Felice 13, 40122 Bologna, Italy.

Individual Exhibitions:

1965 Sala Studio Bentivoglio, Bologna
1967 Sala Studio Bentivoglio, Bologna
1969 Galleria Sperone, Turin
1970 Galerie Sonnabend, Paris
Galleria Sperone, Turin

1971 Sonnabend Gallery, New York
Galerie Sonnabend, Paris
Modern Art Agency, Naples

1973 Galerie Skulima, Berlin
1975 Galleria de Domizio, Pescara, Italy
1976 Galleria Toselli, Milan
1977 Galleria Tucci Russo, Turin
1978 Galleria San Ala, Milan
1979 Galerie Jean und Karen Bernier, Cologne
Galerie Tucci Russo, Cologne

1980 Stanze, Genazzano, Italy
LP 220, Turin
Galleria Paludetto, Turin
Cantieri Navali/Luigi De Ambrogi, Venice
Galleria di Capricorno, Naples

1981 Galerie Eric Fabre, Paris
Galerie Eric Schurr, Stuttgart

1982 Galerie Knoedler, Zurich
1983 Galleria Luigi De Ambrogi, Milan
1984 Galerie de France, Paris
Galerie Bernier, Athens
Galerie Pakesch, Vienna

Selected Group Exhibitions:

1968 *Teatro delle Mostra*, Galleria La Tartaruga, Rome
1969 *Square Pegs in Round Holes*, Stedelijk Museum, Amsterdam
When Attitudes Become Form, Kunsthalle, Berne
1970 *Conceptual Art/Arte Povera/Land Art*, Galleria Civica d'Arte Moderna, Turin
1971 *Biennale des Jeunes*, Paris
1974 *Projekt 74*, Cologne
1975 *Americans in Florence/Europeans in Florence*, Long Beach Museum of Art, California
1978 *Biennale*, Venice (and 1980)
1981 *A New Spirit in Painting*, Royal Academy of Art, London
1986 *Aspects of Italian Art 1960–85*, Kunstverein, Frankfurt

Publications:

On CALZOLARI: books—*Calzolari*, exhibition catalogue, by Alberto Boatta, Bologna 1967; *Teatro delle Mostra*, exhibition catalogue, by Maurizio Calvesi, Rome 1968; *Documenta 5*, exhibition catalogue, Kassel, West Germany 1974; *Pierpaolo Calzolari*, exhibition catalogue with essay by Dieter Ronte, Vienna 1984; *Pier Paolo Calzolari*, exhibition

catalogue with text by Denys Zacharopoulos, Paris 1984; articles—"Nuovo al Fabeto per Corpo e Materia" by Tommaso Trini in *Domus* (Milan), no. 470, 1969, "Pier Paolo Calzolari" by Germano Celant in *Studio International* (London), July 1970; "Pier Paolo Calzolari" by Gregory Battcock in *Arts Magazine* (New York), February 1972; "Pier Paolo Calzolari" by Denys Ropp-Zacharopoulos in *Artistes* (Paris), October/November 1980.

After some work in the field of "poor art," in which he showed his main interest in ephemera and in fairytales (some significant works of the period were "The Filter," "Welcome to the Angel" and "Horoscope," 1967), Pier Paolo Calzolari moved on to painting. His first works in this field date from the 1970's. He did not abandon the object all at once; it is present as dramatic "comment" both in and outside the painting. He adds to the materiality of the painting, so that his all-embracing spatiality is also full of existential meanings. But what emerges most of all is the grandeur of the surface, abounding in grotesque multicoloured material. There is a sort of love-hate relationship between the object, essentially poor, and the positively opulent painting, as if the artist were struggling against the imaginativeness of his experience. For Pier Paolo Calzolari, art proceeds by metamorphoses; it faces destiny rather than the project, so that his work is always somewhat unfinished. His art is above all possessed of a violent gesturality, which unites differing significances; enigmatic symbols of a vitality that breaks down the whole surrounding reality, which is constantly changing and so seems unpredictable. Thus the artist is the one who meets reality in the space of an essay open to the shifting play of the elements between object and painting. If in his "poor art" he was exalting the contradiction of the ephemeral, in his recent painting he demonstrates the deflagration of the material of art. His fulfillment is achieved only in the gesture, through which he completes the picture's destiny.

Calzolari's painting distorts itself. A material in expansion and contraction dramatizes its striking quality, which takes in also the space outside the picture. The material of painting consists of paints—soft, mellow paints, responding to the light. It is their coagulation that is informal. The material colours are firmly obedient to the urgency of the gesture.

In his big pictures Calzolari's creative gesture has a primordial fury which breaks up the material, and with it any possible figuration. The abstraction is powerful, incontrovertible, hermetically closed/opened. It brings out obvious surprise effects in the wide surface of the picture. Calzolari thus comes near to a painting made by continual, striking attacks which break down the growth of the abstraction. It is only in appearance that this approaches the informal. But Calzolari is not a post-informal artist, and he possesses a creative density too firm to be channelled into the flow of the new painting. If anything he is looked on as the initiator of a "diverse" materiality of painting. In fact, his work, at once noble and terrifying, shows how painting can be liberated (especially from the material point of view). A movement prevails on the surface that spreads out in all directions (interrupted only by external elements—a dagger, for instance, thrust into the canvas). Calzolari is thus a "visionary" artist who materializes the secret magma contained in the creative gesture.

—Italo Mussa

CAMPUS, Peter.

American. Born in New York City, 19 May 1937. Educated at Ohio State University, Columbus, 1955–60, B.Sc. 1960. Served in the United States Army, 1960–62. Associated with artist Robert Grosvenor; began informal art studies, New York, 1960–62. Worked as production assistant and film editor, with William Shatner, on the television series *For The People*, Plantus Productions, New York; *Trials of O'Brien*, with Peter Falk, Filmways Inc., New York, 1962–70. Influenced by the work of Ian Wilson, Charles Ross, Robert Smithson, Nancy Holt, Yvonne Rainer and Joan Jonas, New York, 1962–70. First art works, New York, 1970. Video Consultant, Education Department, Metropolitan Museum of Art, New York, 1970–72. Instructor, Massachusetts Institute of Technology, Cambridge, 1976–80; Rhode Island School of Design, Providence, 1982–83. Recipient: Guggenheim Fellowship, 1975–76; Advanced Visual Studies Fellowship, Massachusetts Institute of Technology, Cambridge 1975–76; National Endowment for the Arts Grant, 1976. Agent: Paula Cooper Gallery, New York. Address: c/o Paula Cooper Gallery, 155 Wooster Street, New York, New York 10012, U.S.A.

Individual Exhibitions:

1972 Bykert Gallery, New York
1973 Bykert Gallery, New York
1974 *Closed Circuit Video*, Everson Museum of Art, Syracuse, New York
1975 Bykert Gallery, New York
1976 Leo Castelli Gallery, New York
Hayden Gallery, Massachusetts Institute of Technology, Cambridge
Projects Gallery, Museum of Modern Art, New York
1977 The Kitchen, New York
Ohio State University, Columbus
1978 Whitney Museum, New York
Sarah Lawrence College, Bronxville, New York
Atlantic Gallery, Boston
1979 Akron Art Institute, Ohio
Paula Cooper Gallery, New York
Protetch-McIntosh Gallery, Washington, D.C.
Kölnischer Kunstverein, Cologne
Neuer Berliner Kunstverein, West Berlin
1980 Centre Pompidou, Paris
1981 Paula Cooper Gallery, New York
McIntosh-Drysedale Gallery, New York
1982 Paula Cooper Gallery, New York
1983 Paula Cooper Gallery, New York
Hayden Gallery, Massachusetts Institute of Technology, Cambridge (with David Deutsch)
1985 Paula Cooper Gallery, New York
1986 Paula Cooper Gallery, New York
1987 Albright College, Reading, Pennsylvania (travelled to the Institute of Contemporary Art, Philadelphia)

Selected Group Exhibitions:

1973 *Circuit: A Video Invitational*, Everson Museum of Art, Syracuse, New York (toured the United States and travelled to the Kunstverein, Cologne)
1975 *Bienal*, Sao Paulo
1976 *Autogeography*, Whitney Museum, New York
1977 *Documenta 6*, Kassel, West Germany
1978 *Biennale*, Venice
1979 *Art on Paper 1979*, Weatherspoon Art Gallery, University of North Carolina, Greensboro
1980 *Lynda Benglis/Jon Borofsky/Peter Campus/Michael Hurson*, Paula Cooper Gallery, New York
1982 *PostMinimalism*, Aldrich Museum of Contemporary Art, Ridgefield, Connecticut
1984 *Content: A Contemporary Focus 1974–84*, Hirshhorn Museum, Washington, D.C.
1987 *Photography and Art 1946–86*, Los Angeles County Museum of Art (travelled to Fort Lauderdale, Florida; Flushing, New York)

Publications:

By CAMPUS: articles—statement in *Peter Campus: Closed Circuit Video*, exhibition catalogue, Syracuse, New York 1974; in *Studio International* (London), May/June 1976; essay in *Peter Campus*, exhibition catalogue, Cologne 1979; in *Studio International* (London), no. 1008, 1985.

On CAMPUS: books—*Peter Campus: Closed Circuit Video*, exhibition catalogue, with an introduction by Jane Harithas, essay by David A. Ross, Syracuse, New York 1974; *Video Art*, exhibition catalogue, by Susan Delehanty, Philadelphia 1975; *Peter Campus*, exhibition catalogue, Cologne 1979; *5 Artists, 5 Technologies*, exhibition catalogue, Grand Rapids, Michigan 1979; *The Elusive Image*, exhibition catalogue, Minneapolis 1979; *Peter Campus Photographs/David Deutsch Paintings and Drawings*, exhibition catalogue, with essay by Kathy Halbreich and Katy Klein, Cambridge, Massachusetts 1983; articles—"Video Is Being Invented" by Bruce Kurtz in *Arts Magazine* (New York), December 1972; "Fields: Peter Campus" by Bruce Kurtz in *Arts Magazine* (New York), May 1973; "Video Art by Peter Campus" by John Perreault in the *Village Voice* (New York), 11 October 1973; "Inference and Actuality" by Robert Pincus-Witten in *Projected Images*, exhibition catalogue, Minneapolis 1974; "Beyond Flashing Lights" by Mike Steele in *Art News* (New York), December 1974; "Epistemological TV" by Joseph Lorber in *Art Journal* (New York), Winter 1974–75; "Video: The Aesthetics of Narcissism" by Rosalind Krauss in *October* (New York), Spring 1976; "The Ins and Outs of Video" by Jeff Perrone in *Artforum* (New York), June 1976; "About Faces: The New Work of Peter Campus" by Roberta Smith in *Art in America* (New York), March/April 1977; "Galleries: A Dark Seriesof Portraits" by Benjamin Forgey in the *Washington Star*, 28 March 1979; "Inside Out: Peter Campus" by Ingrid Sischy in *Artforum* (New York), March 1985; "Peter Campus" by Hearne Pardee in *Arts Magazine* (New York), May 1985.

I work in both closed circuit video installations and video tape. The closed circuit installations include viewer participation where his/her image is projected in front of him/her in some altered state. This work concerns itself with: projections and confrontation of self, light, space and accumulations in time. My videotapes generally have me performing some activity that continuously alters the image. These tapes are more concerned with narrative, utilizing questions of figure-ground, surface, illusion, time and space.

—Peter Campus

Peter Campus is an artist who knows how to create psychologically charged visual fields. After working in commercial films and television, he decided in the late 1960's to change careers and become an artist. Video remained the dominant concern during the 1970's. He produced both videotapes and video environments in which a superbly precise and efficient mastery of this electronic technique was channeled to the creative investigations of the perceptual and emotional politics of seeing and knowing the self. In each medium time is an active and aggressive element.

Structured episodically, the videotapes, though of short duration, took the individual as the subject. Many of them featured a deep, dark spatially ambiguous background before which close-ups of faces, often in emotively laden split and repetitive structures, were highlighted. "Three Transitions" (1973) and "East Ended Tapes" (1976), both six minutes in length, are examples. In the video environments, time is a direct factor of the viewing, which, in turn, depends on the presence and participation of the audience. Usually composed of a basic set-up consisting of one or more video cameras and infrared lights, projectors and monitors in a darkened room, they are closed-circuit installations, "closed" or activated by the viewer's entry into the boundaries of the designated situation. Once in a camera view, the viewer, in essence, the viewer's image, is the piece. Each environment/installation is designed to reveal different aspects of the complex relationship involving the self and the image of the self. The image of the self is manipulated, for example in "Interface" (1972) to offer a confrontation between the projected video image and a reflected mirror image, and in "Num," "lus" and "aen" (1976–77) the imagery consisted of enlarged, expressionistically shadowed and inverted pictures of the viewer's head.

In 1979, a projected slide-piece signalled a turning away from video towards photography. This development was a natural one dictated by the work in response to a lessening interest in time and a growing interest in what Campus has called "tangible image."

Peter Campus: *Mem* (closed circuit TV installation), 1974

Photography has been the central concern since 1980.

In the silverpoint photographs he has done of various landscape subjects, reality is being reconstituted in the concreteness of the illusion these images give. Campus' careful modulation of light and dark values allows him to create a composition that conveys the material essence of forms. In *Slow Tide* (1987), a close-up of a rock on a pebble-covered ground, the luminous intensity of the surface is suggestive of metaphorical concerns.

—Ronny Cohen

CANE, Louis.

French. Born in Beaulieu-sur-Mer, Alpes-Maritimes, 13 December 1943. Studied at the Ecole Nationale des Arts Décoratifs, Nice, 1961–64; Ecole Nationale Supérieure des Arts Décoratifs, Paris, 1964–68. Independent painter, Paris, since 1968. Co-Founder and Director of the review *Peinture*, Paris, from 1971. Agent: Galerie Daniel Templon, 30 rue Beaubourg, Paris 3. Address: 37 rue d'Enghein, 75010 Paris, France.

Individual Exhibitions:

1969 Galerie Givaudan, Paris
1970 Galerie Daniel Templon, Paris
1971 Galerie Yvon Lambert, Paris
Galleria Francoise Lambert, Milan
1972 Galerie Yvon Lambert, Paris
1973 Galerie Daniel Templon, Paris
Institute of Contemporary Arts, London
Galleria Daniel Templon, Milan
Galleria Lia Rumma, Naples
1974 Galerie Rudolf Zwirner, Cologne
Galleria del Cortile, Rome
1975 Galerie D., Brussels
Galerie Daniel Templon, Paris
Galleria Daniel Templon, Milan
Galerie Konrad Fischer, Dusseldorf
1976 Galerie Bischofberger, Zurich
Louisiana Museum, Humlebaek, Denmark
Musée d'Art Contemporain, Montreal
Kunstverein, Frankfurt
1977 Galerie Daniel Templon, Paris
Galleria Spagnoli, Florence
Leo Castelli Gallery, New York
Galerie Arnessen, Copenhagen
Centre Georges Pompidou, Paris
1978 Galleria del Milione, Milan
Galerie Daniel Templon, Paris
Louis Cane 1968–1978: The First 10 Years of a Painter, Israel Museum, Jerusalem
Art 9'78, Basle
Kunsthalle, Bielefeld, West Germany
1979 Galerie Art in Progress, Dusseldorf
Galerie Art Line, The Hague
Galerie Charles Kriwin, Brussels
Musée d'Art Moderne, Strasbourg
Galleria Mantra, Turin
Galerie Daniel Templon, Paris
1980 Galerie Art in Progress, Munich
Galerie Artline, La Haye, Netherlands
1981 Galerie Daniel Templon, Paris
Galerie Ressle, Stockholm
Galerie Art in Progress, Dusseldorf
F.I.A.C., Grand Palais, Paris
1982 Leo Castelli Gallery, New York
Galerie Art in Progress, Munich
Inoue Gallery, Tokyo
Ecole National Superieure des Beaux-Arts, Paris
1983 Galerie J. Giraud, Toulouse, France
Fondation Maeght, St. Paul de Vence, France
1986 Galerie Reckermann, Cologne

Selected Group Exhibitions:

1968 *Salle Rouge pour le Vietnam,* Musée d'Art Moderne de la Ville, Paris
1969 *ABC Production,* Maison de la Culture, Montpellier, France
1971 *Biennale,* Paris
1973 *Réalité-Réalité,* Musée de Saint Etienne, France
Biennale, Paris
1975 *Fundamental Painting,* Stedelijk Museum, Amsterdam
Europalia, Palais des Beaux-Arts, Brussels
1976 *Europa-America,* Bologna
1977 *Documenta 6,* Kassel, West Germany
1979 *Biennale,* Sydney

Collections:

Centre Georges Pompidou, Paris; Musée d'Art Moderne de

la Ville, Paris; Musée de Saint-Etienne, France; Musée de Grenoble, France; Louisiana Museum, Humlebaek, Denmark; Kunstmuseum, Basle; Ghent Museum; Musée d'Art Contemporain, Montreal; Museum of Modern Art, New York.

Publications:

By CANE: book—*Paroles sur l'Art Moderne,* exhibition catalogue with Camille Saint-Jacques, St. Paul de Vence 1983; articles—"Pour un programme théorique pictural," with Daniel Dezeuze, in *Peinture* (Paris), June 1971; "Le peintre sans modèle" and "Vivela Chine révolutionnaire" in *Peinture* (Paris), January 1972; "Louis Cane," interview with Catherine Millet, in *Art Press* (Paris), March/April 1973; "Sur le sol, pliée, avec lacouleur," introduction to a Don Judd interview with John Coplans, and "Sur la peinture d'Alain Kirili" in *Peinture* (Paris), April 1973; "La Mort de Germanicus" and "Sur James Bishop" in *Peinture* (Paris), February 1974; "Marc Devade, piongée dans la couleur" in *Art Press* (Paris), February 1974; "Robert Ryman, peinture à tempera" in *Art Press* (Paris), March/April 1975; "Peinture fondamentale, une exposition au Stedelijk Museum d'Amsterdam" in *Art Press* (Paris), July/August 1975; "Le métier de peintre" in *Peinture* (Paris), November 1975; "James Bishop: Savoir le près pour voir le loin" in *Art Press* (Paris), March/April 1976; "L'Hétérogènesous gène" in *Peinture* (Paris), March 1977; "A propos de Rubens" in *Art Press* (Paris), January 1978; "Philipe Sollers: Interview" in *Peinture* (Paris), May 1978; "Un peintre en analyse," interview with Catherine Millet, in *Art Press* (Paris), January 1979; "Ce qui ira" in *Skira Annuel,* Geneva 1980; "L'age mur de l'avant-garde," interview with Catherine Millet, in *Art Press* (Paris), January 1981; "Cy Twombly" in *Art Press* (Paris), March 1981; "L'Art Moderne" in *Spirali* (Milan), June 1982; "Yves Klein" in *art Press* (Paris), February 1983.

On CANE: articles—"Notes sur un peintre opérant dans de beaux draps" by Marc Devade and "Les toiles systématiquement temponnées de Louis Cane" by Daniel Dezeuze in *Louis Cane,* exhibition catalogue, Paris, 1971; "L'intervention picturale de Louis Cane" by Marcelin Pleynet in *Art Vivant* (Paris), April 1971; "Quelques problèmes de la peinture moderne: Louis Cane" by Marcelin Pleynet in *Louis Cane,* exhibition catalogue, Paris 1972; "Forme et couleur découpées de la peinture de Louis Cane" by Marcelin Pleynet in *Art Press* (Paris), March/April 1973; "Louis Cane" by Claire Stoulig in *Cimaise* (Paris), May-August 1974; *Louis Cane,* exhibition catalogue, with text by Marcelin Pleynet, Paris 1977; *Louis Cane 1968–1978: The First 10 Years of a Painter,* exhibition catalogue, with interview by Michael Pauseback, Jerusalem 1978; "La rupture de l'avant-garde" by Catherine Millet in *Connaissance des Arts* (Paris), January 1981; "Louis Cane: la peinture et la loi" by Michel Brandeau in *Art Press* (Paris), no. 70, 1983.

To tell the truth, I think that for the most part the type of painting which can be seen in galleries today is deliberately deluding itself. Sunk in ignorance, it pretends there is nothing to know. It shows nothing because there is nothing to show. Simplicity turns out to be over-simplification.

It is a fact, and I think a true one, that drawing and lines result in composition: i.e., a set of forms well adjusted together and also adjusted into a kind of unitary relation with my desire to paint. Adjusted so that the desire I cast into it will correspond to the desire I expect from it. In this sense, composition can't be but a compromise: even unfinished paintings cannot invalidate this. As a "composer" I am a subject who is calling upon and summoning himself as Another to be identified in the lines of the drawing. And I call myself into it to thwart somehow, to undo what unconsciously forces me to be me and not, if only for a moment, possessing the other. Drawing which orders form is the first stage in a process of identification of this Other whom painting displays. More precisely, I think I have a certain conception of painting but finally "Painting" is nothing else than a certain conception I have of the "other." The "other" could be the recollection of something: I remember an old art teacher used to give me the following piece of advice: "Keep hold of forms with the lines and you'll have composition!"

The simple question today is to know whether our painter's means and ways, in a word our painter's craft, correspond to the end of naturalism or whether, in the making of abstract painting, there's not still a conception of painting which comes too close to the old naturalist school.

In his notes on painting, Shi Tao (1641–1717) says about receptivity and knowledge that receptivity comes first and knowledge follows. I think that Shi Tao is right. He is right not only because his statement has the truthfulness of practice but also because he seems to suggest that I give more attention to my own receptivity so that my knowledge be not limited to the knowledge of others. This is how, for me, time spent painting can become time spent learning.

—Louis Cane

The fundamental characteristic of every *avant-garde* movement has always been the trying out of new languages, of unfamiliar cultural situations, the production of subjects or ideas that, in their deepest significance, would violate the traditional orders to which the artistic experience of the time was subject. "A drive towards the new" is a phrase often used to describe this characteristic, with its significant Freudian references. For a painter like Louis Cane, the *avant-garde* coincided with the Support/Surface period, during which material features of painting were subjected to a rigorous critical-ideological analysis which tended to disclose things in them which had been kept quiet but which, for that very reason, were still operative. Later, the French artist—whose work as a painter has a strong background of theory—took up the history of art as a subject on which to set down his working reflections. This history became a really authoritative source, taking in all the multiple and contradictory interpretations of current artistic practice; the work was based essentially on an inextricable round of reading (of the sources) and writing (the production of a new authoritative text on painting). The architecture of Brunelleschi, 14th and 15th century Tuscan painting and the non-objective painting of the United States were the great reference points of these masterly paintings, evident in the pictorial quality and in the formal layout, always complex and thick with references.

More recently, making a decision which, for him, evidently cloaked a great, profound and "philosophical" significance, Louis Cane rediscovered the figure, the image, and there appeared his series of women in which we can see the influence of Picasso and Giacometti, of De Kooning and of primitive rock paintings. Here Man appears in his essential pristine nakedness—the anthropological body untouched by any cultural transformation belonging to the times. He appears as in Matisse (though the two men's methods and rhythms of composition are fundamentally different), isolated in a solitary expanse of colour which is neither background nor surroundings, and he assumes primitive, sometimes indecent, poses. But it is still the pictorial significance that is final and conclusive, arising as it does from the history of art which Louis Cane is still rewriting, taking on himself the responsibilities of the present time and its dramatic, neurotic conflicts.

—Massimo Carboni

Louis Cane: *Untitled Painting*, 1975

CANOGAR, Rafael (Gomez).

Spanish. Born in Toledo, 17 May 1935. Educated at Madrid High School, 1945–50; studied with the painter Daniel Vazquez-Diaz, in Madrid, 1948–53, Married Ann Jane McKenzie in 1960; children Susana, Daniel, Diego and Robert. Independent painter, Madrid, since 1956. Founder-member, El Paso group, Madrid, 1957. Visiting Professor of Art, Mills College, Oakland, California, 1965–66; Guest artist, Tamarind Lithography Workshop, Los Angeles, 1969. Recipient: Third Prize, *2nd International Festival of Painting,* Gagnes-sur-Mer, France, 1970; Grand Prize, *Bienal,* Sao Paulo, 1971; D.A.A.D. Artist in Residence, Berlin, 1972 and 1974; Grand Prize, International Triennial of Painting, Sofia, 1982; National Prize for Plastic Arts, Madrid, 1982. Chevalier, Ordre des Arts et des Lettres, France, 1985. Address: Ronda de la Abubilla 31, Parque Conde de Orgaz, Madrid 28043, Spain.

Individual Exhibitions:

1954	Galeria Altamira, Madrid
1955	Galeria Fernando Fe, Madrid
1956	Galerie Arnaud, Paris
	Galleria Numero, Florence

Rafael Canogar: ***Cabeza*****, 1987**

1959 Galleria L'Attico, Rome
Galleria Blu, Milan
1960 Galerie Aujourd'hui, Brussels
1961 Galleria L'Attico, Rome
Galerie Rive Gauche, Paris
1962 Galerie Anne Abels, Cologne
Galleria Naviglio, Milan
Galleria Il Cancello, Bologna
1963 Galerie Rive Gauche, Paris
Galeria Biosca, Madrid
1964 Galleria L'Attico, Rome
1965 Galeria Juana Mordo, Madrid
1966 Mills College Art Gallery, Oakland, California
De Young Memorial Museum, San Francisco
Salle Communali del Palazzo Constanzi, Trieste
Galleria 3, Pescara, Italy
1967 Bertha Schaefer Gallery, New York
1968 Galeria Grises, Bilbao, Spain
Galeria Juana Mordo, Madrid
1969 Silvan Simone Gallery, Los Angeles
Deson-Zaks Gallery, Chicago
Galleria Senior, Rome
Galerie Withofs, Brussels
Galleria Sanluca, Bologna
1970 Galerie Klang, Cologne
Galerie Poll, Berlin
1971 Istituto di Storia dell'Arte, Parma
Galeria Tolmo, Toledo
1972 Museo Espanol de Arte Contemporaneo, Madrid
Galeria Rayuela, Madrid
Silvan Simone Gallery, Los Angeles
Galleria Naviglio, Milan
Galerie Poll, Berlin
Galeria Punto, Valencia
Galeria Adria, Barcelona
Galeria Luzaro, Bilbao
1973 Galeria Alcoiart, Altea, Spain
Galeria Juana Mordo, Madrid
1974 Galeria Arte-Contacto, Caracas
Galerie Poll, Berlin
Galleria Bocchi, Milan
Galleria Bocchi, Parma, Italy
Galleria Brazia Bosser, Turin
1975 Silvan Simone Gallery, Los Angeles
Musée d'Art Moderne de la Ville, Paris
Sonia Henie Foundation, Oslo
Kunsthalle, Lund, Sweden
Galleria d'Art San Michele, Brescia, Italy
Pirkanpohja-75, Nykytaidetta, Ah-Tarissa, Finland
1976 Galeria Juana Mordo, Madrid
Galerie Christel, Stockholm
1977 Galerie Nordenhake, Malmo, Sweden
Galerie Nordenhake Rykken, Oslo
Galerie Benet Malmgram, Gothenburg, Sweden
1978 Galerie Nouvelles Images, The Hague
Galeria Punto, Valencia
1979 Galleria Esse Arte, Rome
Galeria San Diego, Bogota
1980 Galeria 3i5, Gerona, Spain
Colegio Oficial de Arquitectos, Canary Islands
Sala Luzan, Zaragoza, Spain
1981 Casa Municipal de Cultura, Aviles, Spain
1982 National Library of Spain, Madrid
Galeria Punto, Valencia
Caja de Ahorros, Alicante (travelled to Murcia)
1983 Casa de los Caballos, Caceres, Spain
Galeria Cadaques, Gerona, Spain
1984 Contemporary Art Museum, Madrid
Galeria Juana Mordo, at *Art 15/84*, Basel
1985 Galeria Bronda, Helsinki
Galeria Sala Gaspar, Barcelona
Galerie Poll, West Berlin
1986 Galeria Cadaques, at *Arco 86*, Madrid
Municipal Cultural Centre, Alcoy, Valencia (retrospective)
1987 Paris Art Center, Paris (retrospective; travelled to Museum Bochum, West Germany)

Selected Group Exhibitions:

1955 *3rd Biennale Hispano-Americana*, Barcelona
1956 *Biennale*, Venice
1959 *13 Peintres Espagnois*, Musée Des Arts Décoratifs, Paris
1960 *Junge Spanische Kunst*, Kunsthalle, Berne (toured Europe)
1971 *Bienal*, Sao Paulo
1973 *Tra Rivolta e Rivoluzione*, Museo Civico, Bologna
1977 *Exposition International des Arts Plastiques*, Modern Art Museum, Belgrade
1980 *Printed Art: A View of Two Decades*, Museum of Modern Art, New York
1984 *Arte Espanol Contemporaneo*, Pinacoteca Nacional, Athens
1986 *Spagna: 75 anni di protagonisti nell'arte*, Villa Malpensata, Lugano, Switzerland

Collections:

Galleria Civica d'Arte Moderna, Turin; Galleria Civica d'Arte Moderna, Bologna; Museo de Arte Contemporaneo, Barcelona; Museo de Arte Contemporaneo, Seville; Contemporaneo de la Universidad, Sao Paulo; Staatliche Museum, Berlin; Haags Gemeentemuseum, The Hague; Carnegie Institute, Pittsburgh; Museum of Modern Art, New York; Art Institute of Chicago.

Publications:

On CANOGAR: books—*Rafael Canogar* by Enrico Crispolti, Madrid 1959; *Neue Kunst nach 1954* by U. Apollonio, Cologne 1959; *Canogar* by J. Dypreau, Cirlot and others, Rome 1962; *Canogar* by J. Castro Arines, Barcelona 1964; *Pintura Espanola: La Ultima Vanguardia* by J. Moreno Galvan, Madrid 1969; *Arte Dopo II 1945 "Spagna"* by U. Aguilera Cerni, Bologna 1970; *Canogar*, exhibition catalogue, Parma 1971; *Treinta Anos de Arte Espanol* by Carlos A. Arean, Madrid 1972; *Canogar* by A. Garcia-Tizon, Madrid 1973; *Rafael Canogar: Evolution dans la Synthese*, exhibition catalogue, with essay by J. M. Ballester, Paris 1975; *Rafael Canogar, pintor*, exhibition catalogue by Daniel Giralt-Miracle, Madrid 1976; *Rafael Canogar*, with texts by Ante Glibota, Peter Spielmann and Gerard Xuriguera, Paris 1987; articles—"Still und Entwicklung bei R. Canogar" by Juan Eduardo Cirlot in *Musee Labirinthe* (Aschaffenburg, Germany), no. 1, 1963; "Reality and Silence" by U. Aguilera Cerni in *Art International* (Lugano, Switzerland), January 1969; "Rafael Canogar" by D. W. Case in *Art and Artists* (London), February 1970; special Canogar issue of *Nueva Forma* (Madrid), December 1971; "La Aventura Plastica de Rafael Canogar" by F. Calvo Serraller in *El Pais* (Madrid), 25 September 1982; "Rafael Canogar: Beyond Modernism" by Keith Patrick in *Studio International* (London), no. 1007, 1984; "Rafael Canogar, Sala Gaspar" by Gloria Moure in *Artforum* (New York), September 1985.

My present position is above all eclectic, and at the same time a synthesis, a resume of many things from my earlier periods; an encounter between abstraction and figuration. I am not particularly interested in figurative images *per se*, but they do give the work its structure or framework, the spinal column to which the painting adheres. The images are totemic, mental, emblematic: large heads or masks, a flower, a bottle—like elements out of cubism. An excuse for painting and painting freely, as a means of communication and self-realization. Painting as the ultimate subject and the expressiveness of brush strokes, texture, color, all vital elements.

—Rafael Canogar

Before 1962 Rafael Canogar's paintings and graphics bore a strong resemblance to the passionate churned-up images of Saura, and the matière painting of the gifted, post-war Spanish school. He was then 27, and had developed from meticulous depictions of his native Toledo (following in the footsteps of El Greco), to Miro-like linear compositions. The powerful abstracts of the 60's, with their flashing, cutting, brush strokes, sombre colours, and sense of urgency, expressed a frustration with Spanish life. Saura, Millares and other compatriots were involved in similar imagery and similar situations.

By 1966 a return to figuration tentatively concerned itself with intimate, domestic matters, although there was already evidence in the gestural dominance of limbs, of the dramatic narrative manner of Canogar's now celebrated political paintings. In 1967 he began to use a mixture of media, both to encrust, so to speak, reality onto his canvas, and convey a sense of shock. Photography, often newspaper images of accidents or police confrontations, would be used, with isolated elements emerging from a solid black background, emphasized by collage, so that a pair of real trousers would be used with a drawn or painted figure.

Gradually the collage method developed into full-scale sculptural relief, so that the insistent gesture, present in all Canogar's work, became the movement of a simulated hand or leg. The protagonists were now openly political; demonstrating mobs versus uniformed members of the state; sometimes a group of raised hands symbolizing the demand for freedom and liberty; the titles "Protest," "Arrest," "Desolation," "Aggression," "The Escape," "Tumult," making no effort to disguise the inspiration or purpose of the impassioned images.

They are, of course, in the great tradition of Goya, sufficiently generalized to include all forms of state violence and denial, to be applicable to governmental systems and methods in many parts of the world. For this reason, perhaps, Canogar has been able to function and exhibit in his native Spain, as well as winning respect internationally.

—Charles Spencer

CAPOGROSSI, Giuseppe.

Italian. Born in Rome, 7 March 1900. Educated at the University of Rome, 1919–23; Instituto Massimiliano Massimo, Rome, 1915–17; studied painting privately with Felice Carena, Rome, 1926. Served as a Second Lieutenant in the Mountain Regiment, Adamello, Italy, 1918. Married Costanza Menney in 1956; daughters: Beatrice and Olga. Lived in Paris, 1927–33, then returned to Rome; Co-Founder, with Mario Ballocco, Alberto Burri and Ettore Colla, Gruppo Origine, Rome, 1951; Co-Signer, with Lucio Fontana, Emilio Scanavino, Roberto Crippa and others, *3rd Manifesto dello Spazialismo*, Milan, 1952. Lecturer in Painting, Liceo Artistico, Rome, 1946–55, and Academia di Belle Arti, Naples, 1965–70. Recipient: Premio Einaudi, 1954, and Grand Prize, 1962, *Biennale*, Venice; Etching Prize, *Graphics Biennale*, Venice, 1959; First Prize, *International Etching Exhibition*, Ljubljana, 1969; 20th Anniversary Prize, *Bienal*, Sao Paulo, 1971; Prix d'Honneur, *International Exhibition of Engraving*, Ljubljana, 1971; Cultural Merit Medal, Ministero di Pubblica Istruzione, Italy, 1971. *Died* (in Rome) *9 October 1972.*

Individual Exhibitions:

1946 Galleria San Marco, Rome
1950 Galleria del Secolo, Rome
Galleria Il'Milione, Milan
Galleria del Cavallino, Venice
1951 Galleria del Naviglio, Milan
Galleria Numero, Florence
1952 Zimmergalerie Franck, Frankfurt
Galleria del Cavallino, Venice
Galleria del Naviglio, Milan (with Roberto Crippa and Gianni Dova)
1953 Galleria del Naviglio, Milan
Circolo della Cultura e delle Arti, Trieste
1954 Galleria del Cavallino, Venice
1955 Galleria del Naviglio, Milan
1956 Galleria Selecta, Rome
Galleria del Cavallino, Venice
Galleria del Naviglio, Milan
Galerie Rive Gauche, Paris

Università degli Studi di Milano, Gargnano sul Garda, Italy
1957 Institute of Contemporary Arts, London
Galleria del Naviglio, Milan (with Giacomo Balla and Robert Crippa)
1958 Galleria del Cavallino, Venice
Leo Castelli Gallery, New York
Galleria Casanuova, Trieste
1959 Palais des Beaux-Arts, Brussels
1960 Galerie 22, Dusseldorf
Galleria Tornabuoni, Florence
Galeria Sistina, Sao Paulo
1961 Galerie du 20th Siècle, Paris
Galleria Santacroce, Florence
1962 Galleria La Bussola, Turin
Assetto/Capogrossi/Scanavino, Joachim Gallery, Chicago
Galleria L'Attico, Rome
1963 Galerie Handschin, Basel
Galleria del Naviglio, Milan
Galerie Schmela, Dusseldorf
Tokyo Gallery
Capogrossi/Sangregorio, Galerie Muller, Stuttgart
1964 Galleria del Cavallino, Venice
Galleria Rotta, Genoa
Galleria La Medusa, Rome
Capogrossi/Fontana, Gutai Pinacotheca, Osaka, Japan
1965 Galerie im Erker, St. Gallen, Switzerland
1966 Galleria 3, Pescara, Italy
Galleria Il Segno, Rome
1967 Staatliche Kunsthalle, Baden-Baden, West Germany (travelled to the Kunsthalle, Nuremberg, and the Europa Centre, Berlin)
Mala Galerija, Ljubljana, Yugoslavia
Kunstverein, Kassel, West Germany
1968 Galleria del Cavallino, Venice
Galleria del Naviglio, Milan
1969 Galleria Marlborough, Rome
Galleria d'Arte La Nuova Loggia, Bologna
Arte Studio, Macerata, Italy
1970 Galleria Martano, Turin
Erker-Presse, St. Gallen, Switzerland
Galerie George Moos, Geneva
1971 Galleria Il Centro, Naples
1972 Studio LD, Pescara, Italy
1973 Galleria Qui Arte Contemporanea, Rome
Galleria Bon a Tirer, Milan
1974 Galleria Nazionale d'Arte Moderna, Rome
1975 Galleria Santoro, Rome
Galleria Nazionale d'Arte, Rome (retrospective)
1976 Galleria dello Scudo, Verona, Italy
1977 Galleria Trimarchi, Bologna, Italy
Westend Galerie, Frankfurt
Galleria 72, Bergamo, Italy
1979 Galleria del Naviglio, at the *Arte Fiera,* Bologna, Italy
Centro Iniziative Culturali, Pordenone, Italy
1980 Galleria Civica d'Arte Moderna, Ferrara, Italy
Galleria Images, Padua, Italy
1982 Galleria l'Isola, Rome

Selected Group Exhibitions:

1932 *Mostra del Sindacato Fascistà Belle Arti,* Rome
1950 *Mostra Annuale dell'Art Club,* Galleria Nazionale d'Arte Moderna, Rome
1953 *Younger European Painters,* Guggenheim Museum, New York
1957 *Trends in Watercolors Today,* Brooklyn Museum, New York
1960 *Contemporary Italian Art,* Illinois Institute of Technology, Chicago
1964 *Painting and Sculpture of a Decade 1954–64,* Tate Gallery, London
1967 *Contemporary Italian Art,* Museum of Modern Art, Tokyo (toured Poland, Germany and Sweden)
1969 *Contemporary Art: Dialogue Between East and West,* Museum of Modern Art, Tokyo
1972 *5 Maestri,* Galleria La Medusa, Rome
1974 *L'Arte della Stampa,* Galleria d'Arte Moderna, Rome

Collections:

Galleria Nazionale d'Arte Moderna, Rome; Galleria Comunale d'Arte Moderna, Rome; Museum of Fine Arts, Houston.

Publications:

By CAPOGROSSI: book—*Callo e Formiche: Pittori che scrivono,* edited by L. Sinisgalli, Milan 1946; articles—statement in *Galleria San Marco* (Rome), January 1946; statement in *The New Decade,* exhibition catalogue, New York 1955.

On CAPOGROSSI: books—*Capogrossi* by Michel Seuphor, Venice 1954; *Capogrossi* by M. Tapie, Venice 1962; *Capogrossi* by Giulio Carlo Argan, Rome 1967; *Giuseppe Capogrossi,* exhibition catalogue, by Palma Bucarelli, Rome 1974; *Giuseppe Capogrossi,* exhibition catalogue edited by Galleria L'Isola, Rome 1982; *Capogrossi fino al 1948* by Bruno Mantura, Spoleto 1986.

The case of Giuseppe Capogrossi is undoubtedly a very unusual one in postwar Italian painting: an isolated artist who had neither master nor followers, who took no part in "manifestos" and who was over 40 when he began his rapid ascent in the world of contemporary painting with a renewed creative adolescence.

The Roman artist, who already had a long, busy experience of painting behind him, begun with the Roman expressionist group of Scipione, Mafai, Pirandello, found himself unexpectedly at the centre of interest and attention in the artistic world after he adopted an expressive language that was quite new and quite different from that of his earlier work. It was in about 1950 that Capogrossi exhibited his new abstract canvases for the first time, the result of some two years' meditation and of assiduous efforts to free himself from the naturalistic object and work out a new pictorial grammar. It was in the first exhibition, at the Galleria del Secolo in Rome, that there appeared in his paintings that unique, mysterious factor, that emblematic sign which some people soon came to describe as a "comb" or "fork", a sign that had in it not only an undeniable plastic and compositional effectiveness but also a mysterious, cryptic nature, almost as if it had been drawn from the reappearance of an ancient symbol taken from a Hermetic head or an alchemist's formula.

We need not analyze Capogrossi's "sign" from a semeiological point of view. What matters is that Capogrossi, making use almost exclusively of his personal graphico-pictorial alphabet, has succeeded in building up an immensely complex and dense *oeuvre* of undoubted expressive value. The artist, in fact, once having taken over his "alphabet," has been able to make surprising use of it, with no need for recourse to other modes of expression. If we look at the vast amount of pictorial and graphic material he has produced, we can see what a range of different "variations" can be obtained from a single "graphic" theme. Sometimes the symbolical elements are minutely small, superimposed or set apart, but always forming a unity of composition; sometimes they are used rhythmically in widely spaced groups, leaving a good deal of empty space; sometimes again they are single elements of giant size that cover the whole canvas.

Capogrossi, once related from the refined atmospheric tonalism that characterized the Roman school, no longer needed to return to the dubious support of chromatic tonalism, and always used essentially timbric colouring. That is why he was able from the very first days of his new creative phase to start firmly on a new line of "symbolic" (even if decidedly "asemantic") art, in which a single ideogram—or, better, "pictogram"—has enabled him to express himself with a precision and certainty that make his case one of the most remarkable events in the painting of our times.

—Gillo Dorfles

CARO, Anthony (Alfred)

British. Born in London, 8 March 1924. Educated in Hampshire and Surrey primary schools; apprenticed to the sculptor Charles Wheeler during school vacations, 1937–42; studied engineering at Christ's College, Cambridge, 1942–44; attended Farnham School of Art, 1944; studied sculpture, then drawing at the Royal Academy Schools, London, under Charles Wheeler, 1947–53. Served in the Fleet Air Arm, 1944–45. Married the artist Sheila Girling in 1949; son: Tim. Worked as a part-time assistant to Henry Moore, Much Hadham, Hertfordshire, 1951–53; settled in Hampstead, London, 1954; produced first abstract welded, bolted steel and aluminum works, 1959; visited Mexico and the United States, 1959; and continued working visits to the U.S. from 1965; worked in Kenneth Noland's studio, Shaftsbury, Vermont, 1970; worked with James Wolfe, Ripamonte Factory, Verduggio, Italy, 1972–73; worked on York Sculptures, York Steel Corporation, Ontario, Spring and Summer 1974. Part-time Lecturer, St. Martin's School of Art, London, 1952–53; Lecturer in Sculpture, Bennington College, Vermont, 1963–65; and St. Martin's School of Art, London, 1964–72; Artist-in-Residence, Summer Workshop, University of Saskatchewan, Emma Lake, 1977; Lecturer, Slade School of Fine Art, London, since 1982; Founder/Lecturer, Triangle Summer Sculpture Workshops, Pine Plains, New York, since 1982. Council Member, Royal College of Art, London, 1981–83; Trustee, Tate Gallery, London, since 1982; Recipient: Ford Foundation Travel Grant, 1959; Prize for Sculpture, *Paris Biennale,* 1959; David Bright Sculpture Prize, *Biennale,* Venice, 1966; Prize for Sculpture, *Bienal,* Sao Paulo, 1969. Honorary Fellow, Christ's College, Cambridge, 1979; honorary doctorate: University of East Anglia, 1979; University of York, 1979; Brandeis University, Waltham, Massachusetts, 1981; Cambridge University, 1985; Honorary Fellow: Royal College of Art, London, 1986; honorary degree: University of Surrey, Guildford, 1987. C.B.E. (Commander, Order of the British Empire), 1969; Knight Bachelor, 1987. Address: 111 Frognal, London NW3, England.

Individual Exhibitions:

1956 Galleria del Naviglio, Milan
1957 Gimpel Fils, London
1963 Whitechapel Art Gallery, London
1964 André Emmerich Gallery, New York
1965 Gallery of Modern Art, Washington, D.C.
Kasmin Gallery, London
1966 André Emmerich Gallery, New York
David Mirvish Gallery, Toronto
Galerie Bischofberger, Zurich
1967 Kasmin Gallery, London
David Mirvish Gallery, Toronto (with Kenneth Noland)
Rijksmuseum Kröller-Müller, Otterlo, Netherlands
1968 André Emmerich Gallery, New York
Metropolitan Museum of Art, New York (with Kenneth Noland and Morris Louis)
1969 Hayward Gallery, London
Dayton's Gallery 12, Minneapolis (with Kenneth Noland and Frank Stella)
1970 André Emmerich Gallery, New York
1971 David Mirvish Gallery, Toronto
Kasmin Gallery, London
1972 André Emmerich Gallery, New York
Kasmin Gallery, London
1973 *Norfolk and Norwich Triennial Festival,* Norwich
André Emmerich Gallery, New York
1974 André Emmerich Gallery, New York
Kenwood House, London
David Mirvish Gallery, Toronto
Galleria dell'Ariete, Milan
1975 Museum of Modern Art, New York (toured the United States)
Watson de Nagy Gallery, Houston
1976 Richard Gray Gallery, Chicago
Lefevre Gallery, London

Anthony Caro: *Veduggio Sound*, 1973

Galerie Wentzel, Hamburg
Museum of Fine Arts, Boston
1977 Galerie Piltzer-Rheims, Paris
Waddington and Tooth Galleries, London
Tel Aviv Museum (toured New Zealand, Australia and travelled to Ottawa, 1977–79)
1978 Knoedier Gallery, London
Galerie André Emmerich, Zurich (with Ben Nicholson)
Harcus-Krakow Gallery, Boston
Richard Gray Gallery, Chicago
Galerie Wentzel, Hamburg
Ace Gallery, Venice, California
Antwerp Gallery
1979 Kunstverein, Brunswick, West Germany
Gallery Kasahara, Osaka, Japan
Ace Gallery, Vancouver
Stadt Galerie im Lenbachhaus, Munich
Kunstverein, Frankfurt
Kunsthalle, Mannheim
1980 *The York Sculptures*, Christian Science Center, Boston
Aquavella Contemporary Art, New York
Galerie André, Berlin
1981 Kenwood House, London
1982 Hunterian Art Gallery, Glasgow (toured the U.K., 1982–83)
1983 Knoedler Gallery, London
Waddington Galleries, London
Galerie de France, Paris
1984 Knoedler Gallery, London
Galerie Wentzel, Cologne
Martin Gerard Gallery, Edmonton, Alberta
Andre Emmerich Gallery, New York
Acquavella Galleries, New York
Serpentine Gallery, London
Whitworth Art Gallery, Manchester
Leeds City Art Gallery, Yorkshire
Ordrupgaard Samlingen, Copenhagen
1985 Kunstmuseum, Dusseldorf
Fondacion Joan Miro, Barcelona
Galerie Wentzel, Cologne
Galerie Andre Emmerich, Zurich
Grimaldis Gallery, Baltimore, Maryland
Gallery One, Toronto
Galerie Blanche, Stockholm
Galleri Lang, Malmo, Sweden
Galerie Artek, Helsinki
Harcus Gallery, Boston
Galleria Stendhal, Milan
Norrkopings Kunstmuseum, Sweden
1986 Richard Gray Gallery, Chicago
Andre Emmerich Galery, New York
Acquavella Galleries, New York
Galeria Joan Prats, Barcelona
Comune di Bogliasco, Genoa, Italy
Knoedler Gallery, London
Waddington Galleries, London
Iglesia de San Esteban, Murcia, Spain
1987 La Lonja, Valencia, Spain
Galeria Soledad Lorenzo, Madrid
Grimaldis Gallery, Baltimore, Maryland

Selected Group Exhibitions:

1955 *New Sculptors and Painter-Sculptors*, Institute of Contemporary Arts, London
1958 *Pittsburgh International*, Carnegie Institute, Pittsburgh
1959 *1st Biennale des Jeunes*, Musée d'Art Moderne, Paris
1954 *Painting and Sculpture of a Decade: 1954–1964*, Tate Gallery, London
1968 *New British Sculpture and Painting*, University of California, Berkeley (toured the United States and Canada)
1970 *Contemporary British Art*, Museum of Modern Art, Tokyo
1974 *The Great Decade of American Abstract Art*, Museum of Fine Arts, Houston
1980 *Hayward Annual*, Hayward Gallery, London
1983 *Aspects of British Art*, Guggenheim Musuem, New York
1987 *British Painting and Sculpture in the 1980s*, Museum of Modern Art, Oxford (toured Hungary, Poland, Czechoslovakia)

Collections:

Tate Gallery, London: Arts Council of Great Britain, London; Kunsthaus, Zurich; Museum of Modern Art, New York; National Gallery of Art, Washington, D.C.

Publications:

By CARO: articles—"The Master Sculptor" in *The Observer* (London), 27 November 1960; "Conversation with Anthony Caro, Ken Noland and Jules Olitski" by David Thompson in *Nonad* (London), January 1964; statement in *Art Now* (New York), September 1969; "Some Thoughts after Visiting Florence" in *Art International* (Lugano, Switzerland), May 1974; "An Interview with Anthony Caro," with Phyllis Tuchman, in *Anthony Caro* by Richard Whelan and others, London 1974; "Conversations with Anthony Caro" by Lutz Haufschile in *Arts Magazine* (New York), June 1978; interview, with Christopher Andreae, in the *Christian Science Monitor* (Boston), August 1980; "A Conversation with Anthony Caro," with Yorick Blumenfeld, in *Architectural Digest* (Los Angeles), September 1981.

On CARO: books—*Anthony Caro*, exhibition catalogue, by Michael Fried, London 1969; *Anthony Caro* by Richard Whelan and others, London 1974; *Anthony Caro* by William Rubin, New York and London 1975; *The York Sculptures*, exhibition catalogue, Boston 1980; *Anthony Caro*, exhibition catalogue, New York 1980: *The Sculpture of Anthony Caro: Catalogue Raisonné*, 5 vols., edited by Dieter Blume, Cologne 1981–86; *Anthony Caro: Sculptures*, exhibition catalogue with text by Karen Wilkin, New York 1981; *Anthony Caro* by Diane Waldman, Oxford and New York 1982 (includes bibliography); *Anthony Caro Sculpture 1969–84*, exhibition catalogue with foreword by Joanna Drew and Catherine Lampert, London 1984; *Anthony Caro* by Terry Fenton, London and Barcelona 1986.

You cannot explain abstract art in ten minutes, and you cannot expect yourself to like it on the very first

glance, any more than you'll like a piece of unfamiliar serious music on the first hearing. It takes a lot of listening and a lot of looking to get the rewards of difficult art, but it is worthwhile in the end.

—Anthony Caro

Anthony Caro's reputation was established by his superb welded steel pieces of the 1960's. He is rightly acclaimed as having pushed sculpture even further into abstraction, by eliminating any lingering figurative references and by freeing it completely from the constraints of the pedestal.

Caro's works of the '60's usually develop horizontally, appropriating the viewer's own space. They claim and animate that space simply by looking like nothing other than themselves. They are built of industrial materials—I-beams, stock angles, expanded metal mesh and the like—but in spite of the literal strength and weight of their components, they appear weightless, like disembodied drawings which hover above the floor rather than resting heavily upon it. This is partly due to the thinness of their members; they are sculptures of plane, edge, and line, not of mass. It results, too, from Caro's practice of painting these works in uniform, often rather light colors, which homogenizes the disparate components and makes the sculptures declare themselves as single, unified objects. More importantly, the apparent weightlessness of Caro's work depends on his habit of deliberately confusing supporting and pictorial elements. He often establishes elevated surrogate horizon planes, and disposes forms above and below them, so that these elements appear to float freely.

Caro's sculptures of the '60's expanded our notions of what sculpture could be, picking up, as they did, the implications of Picasso and Gonzalez's metal constructions as well as those of David Smith's work, and making them still more abstract and more optical. For once, the over-used term "drawing in space" seems apt. Caro's sculptures of the period were conceived as transparent three-dimensional objects. Their eloquent gestures and comfortable human scale made us aware of our own bodies" ability to move, yet at the same time, they were purely visual structures.

The small scale Table sculptures of more or less the same time were equally remarkable. In these, Caro at first established scale by incorporating real grips and handles (in ungraspable positions) to instantly give a sense of the hand. Later, perhaps to contradict this reference to ordinary objects on a table, which were distinguished because they *could* be picked up, Caro eliminated the handles. Instead, he established scale through positioning. The Table Pieces often spring over the edges of their supporting bases, appearing as weightless and animated as their larger counterparts, but perceived differently because of their small size. We tend to see each of their component parts as something of great importance, since we are so close to them.

If Caro had done nothing but the linear painted pieces and the Table Pieces, his place in the history of contemporary sculpture would still be secure, but in the '70's and early '80's, he has retained his preeminence with a body of inventive work which explores new territory and new materials. In the early '70's, Caro seemed to fall in love with the properties of his chosen material, with the surface inflections of steel, its weight and mass, after years of dissembling. A series of extremely painterly, relatively massive sculptures, made of rolled sheets, revelled in the particularities of magnificent pieces of metal. As if to emphasize his pleasure in the individual sheet, Caro often presented them vertically, for the viewer's inspection, rather than horizontally, as in earlier works. Works of this type began with the Verduggio series, made in Italy, and continued with the Durham series, after Caro found a British rolling mill which could provide him with the irregular sheets and folded slabs which come at the end of a run, or when the mill makes a mistake. They culminated in the York Pieces of 1974–75, Caro's first very large scale works. Previously, his improvisatory approach demanded that his sculptures be kept within a scale which he could manipulate himself, or with a minimum of assistance. Larger scale implied using maquettes or fabricators, intermediaries antithetical to his working methods. But in making the York Pieces, he had at his disposal, for the first time, men and equipment which allowed him to work on big sculptures without altering his approach. The York series, for all their size and the sheer weightness of their tilted, layered slabs, have all the immediacy of his early work, albeit with a new solemnity and dignity.

Similarly, Caro had not worked in bronze since abandoning figuration in the late '50's. Again, the medium seemed too indirect, to require too much preconception. In the early '70's, however, an invitation to make sculpture in clay at Syracuse University led Caro back to bronze without forcing him to give up his usual collage method. By having forms made in clay (or other equally manipulable material) which he could then alter and have cast in bronze, Caro assembled a lexicon of eccentric personal elements. He used these in combination with brass rods and sheets, to make bronzes as directly and spontaneously as he did works in steel, assembling and constructing unique works, rather than preparing maquettes for casting. The resulting sculptures have ranged from intimate Table Pieces which evoke Chinese temple bronzes as much as they do the tradition of modernism, to large scale "Screens" built of cascading planes which spring against vertical walls in the same way that the horizontal drawing of earlier works skimmed the floor.

Despite his interest in new formal concerns, such as verticality and mass, and new materials, such as lead, silver and bronze. Caro has continued to make expressive linear sculptures in steel. The Emma Lake pieces of 1977–78 are large scale, drawing-like works which recall earlier sculptures but are developed in the round in ways relatively new to Caro. It is as though their slender configurations had been informed by the density and substance of his painterly "slab" pieces of the early '70's. The Writing Pieces, small calligraphic works of 1978, and a recent series of larger, rather densely packed steel sculptures, both make free use of found objects from small tools to bollards. In the recent steel pieces, as well as the bronzes. Caro has begun to make use of color in new ways, varying tones and patinas to enhance structure and emphasize form, rather than applying a uniform and unifying skin of color.

Small calligraphic sculptures continued this linear vein well into the 1980s, while the most extreme examples of the persistence of this mode were a group of sculptures made at an international artists' workshop in Barcelona, in 1987, perhaps as a response to the omnipresent Catalan ironwork balconies and railings.

Yet mass and implied volume, along with an intense physical presence, have characterized much of Caro's sculpture since 1980. His steel constructions, whether polychromed or unpainted, are often very large, (within the context of his preference for human scale), massive accretions of thick members; some incorporate huge, sliced marine floats that, because of their size and hollowness, have inevitable associations with architecture and shelter. Caro acknowledges that he has been looking hard at medieval and Renaissance churches, in recent years, but as always, his best works declare themselves independently of literal allusions.

Most surprisingly, the man who long maintained that, for him, sculpture had to be abstract if was to be "real"—that is, to have the same intensity and authority as anything in the existing world—has been working from the model since the early '80s. His richly inflected cast bronze figures are a clear homage to Matisse, but they owe as much to Caro's own abstract sculpture as to any of the figurative sculptors whose work interests him; certainly they are articulated in ways that have little to do with Caro's thickest figures of the 1950s, made before he began to work abstractly in steel. The bronze figures seem to have, in turn, influenced a recent series of abstract bronzes whose swelling, sensuous forms are abutted in a manner that is typical of Caro—whose work always depends upon placement—and at the same time, evokes classic Indian sculpture, which Caro admires greatly.

Knighted in 1987, at 63, in recognition of his past achievement, Caro continues to make challenging and original sculpture. Most impressive is his enduring ability to respond to new notions and to reexamine his conception of what sculpture can be.

—Karen Wilkin

CARR-HARRIS, Ian.

Canadian. Born in Victoria, British Columbia, 12 August 1941. Studied modern history, Queen's University, Kingston, Ontario, 1959–63; library science, University of Toronto, 1963–64; sculpture, Ontario College of Art, Toronto, 1967–71. Married in 1966 (divorced); daughter: Lisa Renee. Independent sculptor, Toronto, since 1971. Director of Library Services since 1972, and Instructor in Art Theory and Practice since 1975, Ontario College of Art, Toronto. Board Member, A Space Gallery, Toronto, 1970–71, 1982–83, and The Power Plant (formerly, The Art Gallery at Harbourfront), Toronto, 1983–87; Member of the Contemporary Acquisitions Committee, Art Gallery of Ontario, Toronto, 1987–88. Contributor to the periodicals *Parachute, Vanguard* and *C Magazine,* since 1975. Member, Royal Canadian Academy, 1976. Agent: Carmen Lamanna Gallery, 988 King Street West, Toronto, Ontario M5V 1N6. Address: 68 Broadview Avenue, 4th floor, Toronto, Ontario M4M 2E6, Canada.

Individual Exhibitions:

1971 A Space, Toronto
1972 Nova Scotia College of Art and Design, Halifax
1973 Carmen Lamanna Gallery, Toronto (and annually, since 1973)
1981 Yajima/Galerie, Montreal
1982 Dalhousie University, Halifax, Nova Scotia
Scarborough College, Toronto
1983 49th Parallel Centre, New York
1987 London Regional Art Gallery, Ontario
1988 Art Gallery of Ontario, Toronto

Selected Group Exhibitions:

1970 *Concept '70,* Nightingale Gallery, Toronto
1974 *Investigations,* Mount Allison University, Sackville, New Brunswick
1977 *Another Dimension,* National Gallery of Canada, Ottawa
1978 *Kanadische Kunstler,* Kunsthalle, Basle
1979 *Confrontations,* Vancouver Art Gallery, British Columbia
1981 *Canada in Birmingham,* Ikon Gallery, Birmingham, England
1984 *41st Biennale,* Venice
1986 *Luminous Sites,* Western Front and Video Inn, Vancouver
1987 *Documenta 8,* Museum Fridericianum, Kassel, West Germany

Collections:

Art Gallery of Ontario, Toronto; Canada Council, Ottawa; National Gallery of Canada, Ottawa.

Publications:

By CARR-HARRIS: articles—"John Greer" in *Parachute*

Ian Carr-Harris: ***Reconstruction of the View From My Room*****, 1987**

(Montreal), December/February 1982–83; "Museums in the 80s", with Goldie Rans, in *Vanguard* (Vancouver), March 1983; "Philip Monk, Sentences on Art" and "Vincent Tangredi" in *Parachute* (Montreal), March/May 1983; "A. R. Penck" in *Parachute* (Montreal), June/August 1983; "From Here to Zero: Stephen Horne" in *C Magazine* (Toronto), no. 1, 1983; "Sex and Representation" in *Vanguard* (Vancouver), November 1984; "Women's Work" in *Vanguard* (Vancouver), December 1987.

On CARR-HARRIS: books—*Art in Boxes* by A. Mogelin and N. Laliberte, New York 1974; *Another Dimension*, exhibition catalogue with text by Mayo Graham, Ottawa 1977; *Confrontations*, with text by Ann Pollock, Vancouver 1979; *Ian Carr-Harris: Recent Work*, exhibition catalogue with text by Linda Milrod, Halifax 1982; *Visions: Contemporary Art in Canada* by Diana Nemiroff, Toronto 1983; *Ian Carr-Harris/Liz Magor: Canada, XLI Biennale di Venezia 1984*, exhibition catalogue with text by Jessica Bradley, Ottawa 1984; *Toronto: A Play of History*, exhibition catalogue with text by Louise Dompierre, Toronto 1987.

I have a number of concerns about what artworks can accomplish, and they fall roughly into two intersecting categories. These have to do on the one hand with their suggestiveness and the meanings they can construct dialectically in the imagination of the viewer by virtue of their permissiveness; and on the other hand with the intentions of the artist—who at least holds responsibility for the existence of the work—in directing meaning and presenting to the social consciousness of the viewer particular codes of value. When taken together—and all artworks exhibit both these categories—they act to define and to counter our own individual productions of meaning. They both produce and deny those productions: this is what artworks accomplish.

—Ian Carr-Harris

CARRINO, Nicola.

Italian. Born in Taranto, 15 February 1932. Educated in Taranto primary schools; self-taught in art. Served in the Italian Army, 1955–56. Married Angela Colacicco in 1960; children: Veneranda and Velentina. Concentrated on painting, 1952–62; has worked as a sculptor since 1962. Founder, with G. Biggi, N. Frasca, A. Pace, P. Santoro and G. Uncini, Gruppo I. Rome, 1962–67. Professor of Drawing, Istituto d'Arte, Grottagie, Italy, 1961; Professor of Figure-drawing, Liceo Artistico, Lecce, Italy, 1962–64, and Liceo Artistico, Rome, 1965–77; Professor in Visual Studies, ISIA, Rome, 1966–70 and 1975; Professor of Painting, Accademia delle Belle Arti, Bari, Italy, 1978; Professor of Sculpture, Accademia delle Belle Arti, Frosinone, Italy, 1979, 1983, 1986, Accademia di Belle Arti, Lecce, 1980–82, and Accademia di Belle Arti, Bari, 1984–85. Recipient: 2nd Prize, with Gruppo 1, *Biennale di San Marino*, 1963; Premio In-

ternacional, *11th Bienal de Sao Paulo*, 1971. Agent: Studio Carlo Grossetti, Via dei Piatti 9, 20123 Milan. Address: Via Ippolito Pindemonte 32, 00152 Rome, Italy.

Individual Exhibitions:

1960 Galleria Taras, Taranto, Italy
1961 Galleria Taras, Taranto, Italy
Galleria Numero, Prato, Italy
1962 Galleria Numero, Milan
1966 Galleria Space and Time, Spoleto, Italy
1968 Galleria Qui Arte Contemporanea, Rome
1969 Galleria Christian Stein, Turin
Galleria Il Segno, Rome
1970 Salone Annunciata, Milan
Nicola Carrino, at the *Biennale*, Venice
1972 Street Sculpture, Milan
Galerie Defet, Nuremberg
Galleria Godel, Rome
1973 Salone Annunciata, Milan
Forum Kunst, Rottweil, West Germany
Galleria Primo Piano, Rome
Studio 3Bi, Bolzano, Italy
Nicola Carrino, at the *Biennale del Metallo*, Gubbio, Italy
1974 Galerie Arges, Brussels
Galleria d'Arte di Porta Ticinese, Milan
Circolo Italsider, Taranto, Italy
1975 Salone Annunciata, Milan
Galleria Primo Piano, Rome
1976 Marlborough Galleria d'Arte, Rome
Galeria M., Bochum, West Germany
Salone Annunciata, Milan
1977 Galeria Denise René-Hans Mayer, Dusseldorf
Gallerie Civica d'Arte Contemporanea, Suzzara, Italy
1979 Salone Annunciata, Milan
Galeria Denise René, New York
1980 Galleria Comunale d'Arte Contemporanea, Taranto, Italy
Galerie Walter Storms, Munich
Galleria E Tre, Rome
1981 Studio Carriere, Martina Franca, Italy
Galleria Il Centro, Naples
Studio Carlo Grossetti, Milan
1982 Galerie Schissel, Munich
1983 Galleria Plurima, Udine, Italy
1984 Studio Carlo Grossetti, Milan
1985 Galleria Primo Piano, Rome
1986 *Nicola Carrino*, at the *Biennale*, Venice
Galleria Comunale d'Arte Contemporanea, Arezzo
Centro Culturale Dune, Molfetta, Italy
1987 Torre di Santa Caterina, Nardo, Italy

Nicola Carrino: Installation at the *XLII Biennale*, Venice, 1986

Selected Group Exhibitions:

1960 *Mostra Internazionale d'Arte Astratta*, Palazzo Pretoria, Prato, Italy
1966 *Biennale*, Venice
1969 *Zwolf Italienische Bildauer*, Kunstverein, Hamburg
1971 *Bienal*, Sao Paulo
1977 *Zestien Italiaanse Kunstenaars*, Museum Boymans-van Beuningen, Rotterdam
1978 *Metafisica del Quotidiano*, Galleria d'Arte Moderna, Bologna
1981 *Linea della Ricerca Artistica in Italia, 1960–1980*, Palazzo delle Esposizioni, Rome
1982 *Arte italiana 1960–82*, Hayward Gallery, London
1984 *Carte Blanche a Denise Rene*, Paris Art Center, Paris
1986 *Arte Astratta 1952–81*, Galleria Nazionale d'Arte Moderna, Rome

Collections:

Galleria Nazionale d'Arte Moderna, Rome; Museo Sperimentale d'Arte Contemporanea, Turin; Museum of Modern Art, Skopje, Yugoslavia; Museum of Modern Art, Haifa, Israel; Potsdam Art Galerie, Germany; Ruhr Universität Museum, Bochum, West Germany; Museum Art, Ciudad Bolivar, Venezuela.

Publications:

By CARRINO: books—*Costruttivi Grasformabili 1969–70*, Rome 1970; *Costruttivi/Testo 4*, exhibition catalogue, Milan 1973; *Costruttivo 74 Module L*, with J. de Sanna, Milan 1974; *Costruttivi Trasformabili/Processi I-10 di Trasformazione*, exhibition catalogue, Rome, 1976; *Costruttivo Trasformabile I-10 T-77/Intervention*, exhibition catalogue, New York 1978; *Opere e Interventi 1959–1979*, exhibition catalogue, Taranto, Italy 1979; *Azione e Trasformazione 1957–1985*, exhibition catalogue, Arezzo, Italy 1986; *Costruttivi Trasformabili 1969–1975*, exhibition catalogue, Nardo, Italy 1987; articles—several texts in *Dall'Occhio al Cervello*, Gruppo I, edited by F. Sossi, Taranto, Italy 1963; "Nicola Carrino" in *Flash Art* (Milan), March/April 1970; "Costrutti/Testo 1 e 2" in *Progetto, Intervento e Verifica*, exhibition catalogue, Milan 1972; "Didattica come Conoscenza e Comportamento" in *Rassegna dell'Istruzione Artistica* (Urbino, Italy), vol. 7, nos. 3–4, 1972; "Costruttivi/Testo 3" in *Faites votre Jeu*, Venice 1974; "Costruttivi/Testo 5" in *Dal Progetto al Opera*, exhibition catalogue, Verona 1974; "Nicola Carrino" in *Flash Art* (Milan), no. 48–49, 1974; "Costruttivi/Testo 10" in *Art Essata: Approcci di Critica Analitica*, edited by F. Torriani, Turin 1974; "Costruttivi/Testo 8" in *La Ricerca Scientifica come Modello Estetico in Architettura*, edited by F. Facilla, Rome 1975; "Costruttivi/Testo 11" in *R2*, Rome 1975; "Unformbare Construtionselemente/Transformationen" in *Heute Kunst* (Milan), no. 14/15, 1976; "Die Konstruktivien" in *Magazine Kunst* (Mainz), no. 3, 1976; "La Creatività Sociale e Rivoluzione Continuà" in *Qui Arte Contemporanea* (Rome), no. 17, 1977; "Costruttivi Trasformabili/Trasformazione dello Spazio" in *L'Opera dei Celebranti*, exhibition catalogue, Ancona, Italy 1981; "Critica dell'Arte" in *La Critica dell'Arte*, exhibition catalogue, Ancona, Italy 1981; "L'Arte e il Pensiero dell'Arte" in *Taide* (Salerno, Italy), no. 1, 1981; "Forma e Luogo" in *Il Luogo della Forma*, exhibition catalogue, Verona 1981; "Trasformazione dello Spazio/Ellissi" in *G7 Studio* (Bologna), vol. 6, no. 3/4, 1981; "Nicola Carrino" in *Al Vivo*, edited by S. Lux, Rome 1981; "Auto-interview" in *Neue Kunst in Europa* (Munich), no. 8, 1985.

On CARRINO: book—*Calderara e Gruppo I* by Guilio Carlo Argan, Milan 1966; articles—"Carrino" by R. Sanesi in *Opus International* (Paris), no. 35, 1972; "Nicola Carrino" by J. de Sanna in *Opus International* (Paris), no. 59, 1976; "Nicola Carrino" by J. Tannenbaum in *Arts Magazine* (New York), June 1978; "Le Ricerche di Arte Ottico-Visiva nei Gruppi Romani" in *L'Arte in Italia nel Secondo Dopoguerra*, edited by R. Barilli, Bologna 1979; "The Italian Art Scene" by Henry Martin in *Art News* (New York, vol. 80, no. 3, 1981; "Nicola Carrino" by M. Vescovo in *XLII Biennale di Venezia*, exhibition catalogue, Venice 1986.

The idea of transformation is the base of my work. In the 'sixties, I used three-dimensional iron modules that I called "Costruttivi Trasformabili". With them I

made transformations of form and of environmental spaces in which they inhabited in a dynamic and dialectical time-continuous between built-up and destroyed form, project and randomness, personal and collective actions.

Since 1980, the "Construttivi Ellissi" are formal systems consisting of several sets of modules as ellipsis, ellipses-circle, ellipsis-serrated modules, ellipsis-circle-square and as did previously the "Costruttivi Transformabili" suggest the idea of transformation and combining in that they can be arranged together in different ways depending upon the environment and the method of analysis used. The "Costruttivi Ellissi" can be realized as sculptures, iron or painted-wood reliefs or as a wall-painting, but are defined by environmental space.

The perception of such systems should not be limited to the work itself but completely inhering in the environmental space that the work measures and defines. Thus the space of the gallery as well as the methods of analysis used to visualize it together with the sculpture are the basic elements of my artistic work. I am also convinced that sculpture should spring from the need of the space and identify itself with it. Therefore, environment and sculpture are an organic whole which I call environment-sculpture.

Geometry and project are only a means and not the end of the artistic work. Nothing that controls or that makes the formal systems stiffen but only means of analysis, of checking and controlling the possibilities of the project itself. I may affirm that geometry and project constitute the methodological rigour that justifies the essential arbitrariness of research. Geometric form represents itself. There is no image problem. Every form is figure and every figure, though geometrical, is image. Thus, the formal whole determined by "Costruttivo Ellissi" may also express a cosmic, galactic aspect. In this case I would affirm that the "Costruttivi", as finite systems, investigate situations of infinite order. In modern research a project like Ellissi, taken as a critical and dialectical concept, is a necessity to express creatively a freedom of imagination, a consciousness of reality. "Progetto Ellissi", then, is not only use of form according the archetype, but behaviour of the form and the being, both free and conscious, expressed with projectual rigour and necessity of intervention.

Actually, my idea is that it should be possible to develop research in art directly in the social contexts in which the project is the media between the social demand and the individual proposal of the artist. I also believe that in such interventions it is possible to go through the aestetics of an artistic operation in order do determine more productive moments to the social aims of art.

Nicola Carrino

Artistic development in Italian art of the 'fifties followed a direct route. To begin with, the debate was predominantly between abstract and figurative, followed by (for some artists) the cubist deconstruction of the picture plane, and finally pure abstraction.

Nicola Carrino was born in 1932. In his twenties, he tried out a variety of styles. But between 1959 and 1962 he arrived at a form in which the picture plane became an arena for expressions of a geometric nature, but executed in modest materials such as wood or metal sheet. In this mode he produced, between 1959 and 1960, the series *Realta*. In the works which followed (until mid-1962) he mastered the canvas, arriving at a result similar to the tendencies then current in Europe and the United States and typified by the work of Gotz, Kline and Pollock.

In the second half of 1962 Carrino made a complete break from the pictorial to the constructive. The new works were constructed of geometric units, organized and mounted on a surface as in *Costruttivo Alta* (1963). In the same year he co-ordinated the group known as Gruppo 1, together with Biggi, Frasca, Pace, Santoro and Uncini. They disbanded in 1967. Concurrent with this period were the works *Struttura Plastica* (1964) and the series *Spaziostruttura* (1965–67). This work resulted from the modulation of geometric forms used not only for their formal potential but also for their capacity to influence surrounding space. The series *Costruttivi* moved in both these directions. *Costruttivo 1* (1963) belongs to the initial phase in which Carrino used geometric elements on a flat surface. *Costruttivo 3*, of the same year, employs elements of geometric form (in this case, concave rectangles) organized as a self-supporting structure in space.

But it is in 1969, after a number of advances in this direction, that Carrino crystallized the concept of *Costruttivo* into its final formulation. The *Costruttivo* then became based on a module and realized in iron and steel. The component modules, when combined with all the others, make up the complete artistic object. What is of interest to the artist is the constructive and deconstructive quality of the work contained within the limits of the work itself, rather than the final formal result. Through these works he conveys meanings which become on occasion performances, creative interventions demanding social participation.

Carrino wrote in 1974 of the *Costruttivi*: "It is the fruit of its message. The artist re-enters the arena with a plausible system that is not an end in itself, but an instrument for a liberal and creative intervention applicable both to the work of art and to reality."

Between 1978 and 1979 Carrino made a series of *Trasformazioni dello spazio*, that is, a harnessing of environment within colour fields of black. The use of varnish over these blacks fields emphasies the spatial quality. Amongst this group of eorks are *Ellissi* or *Costruttivi/Ellissi*, made of iron, canvas or wood which, among a variety of readings, determine a constructive rapport with space. This theme remains constant in all Carrino's recent work, from *Trasformazione dello spazio* to *Interventi nell'architettura*.

—Roberto Lambarelli

CASCELLA, Pietro.

Italian. Born in Pescara, Italy, 2 February 1921. Studied with his father Tommaso, and at the Accademia di Belle Arti, Rome. Married; children: Benedetta, Tommaso, Susanno and Jacopo. Sculptor. Recipient: First Prize, Monument to Auschwitz Competition, 1960; Prize Prize, *Biennale di Carrara*, 1967. Address: Castello della Verrucola, Fivizzano, Italy.

Individual Exhibitions:

1950 Galleria l'Obelisco, Rome (with Andrea Cascella)
1954 Galleria del Naviglio, Milan
1955 Galleria Cavallino, Venice
1957 Galleria Selecta, Rome
1960 Galleria del Milione, Milan
1962 Galleria l'Obelisco, Rome
1963 Galerie du Dragon, Paris
1965 Bonino Gallery, New York
Galleria Milano, Milan
1966 *Biennale*, Venice
Galleria Milano, Milan
1967 Galleria Milano, Milan
1968 Galerie du Dragon, Paris
Galleria Milano, Milan
Musée d'Ixelles, Brussels
1969 Galleria Arte Borgogna, Milan
Galleria Nuova Pesa, Rome
1971 Palais des Beaux-Arts, Brussels
Galleria Arte Borgogna, Milan
Musée d'Art Moderne de la Ville, Paris
Rotonda di via Besana, Milan
1972 *Biennale*, Venice
1973 Galleria Goethe, Bolzano, Italy
Galleria Etrusculundens, Rome
1974 Galleria Forni, Bologna
Galleria Giulia, Rome
1975 Galleria Forum, Trieste
1976 Galleria Nizzoli, Parma, Italy
Kloster Camiore di San Lazzaro, Italy
Galleria Salotto, Como, Italy
Galleria Nove Colonne, Trento, Italy
1977 Galleria Stendhal, Milan
Grafica Club, Milan
Centro Arte Moderna, Pisa
Centro Storico, Rimini, Italy
1979 Galerie Godula, Buchholz, West Germany
1980 Galleria del Naviglio, Milan
1983 Galleria Bergamini Diarte, Milan
1984 Galleria Gian Ferrari, Milan

Selected Group Exhibitions:

1948 *Biennale*, Venice
1950 *Consorso Internazionale*, Rome
1952 *Consorso per il Monumento di Albisola*, Italy
1960 *Auschwitz Monument Competition Exhibition*, Auschwitz, Poland
1964 *Pittsburgh International*, Carnegie Institute, Pittsburgh
1973 *Middelheim Sculpture Biennale*, Antwerp
1975 *Disegni di 34 Scultori*, Salone delle Conference, Milan
1977 *Arte in Italia 1960–77*, Galleria Civica d'Arte Moderna, Turin
1981 *Linee della Ricerca Artistiche in Italia 1960–80*, Palazzo delle Esposizioni, Rome
1983 *Memoria dell'Uomo: La Grande Metafora*, Villa Pacchiani, Santa Croce sull'Arno, Italy

Collections:

Museo d'Arte Moderna, Bologna; Middelheim Museum, Antwerp.

Commissions include: War Memorial, Albissola, Italy, 1956; Auschwitz Memorial, with Andrea Cascella and the architect Lafuente, Auschwitz, Poland 1960; Mazzini Monument, Piazza della Republica, Milan 1974.

Publications:

On CASCELLA: books—*Il Monumento di Auschwitz*, exhibition catalogue, by Mario de Michel, Milan 1960; *Pietro Cascella* by Cesare Vivaldi, Milan 1966; *Mostra dell Besana* by Guido Ballo, Milan 1971; *Pietro Cascella* by Guido Vegani, Milan 1974; *Maestri Contemporanei: Pietro Cascella* by Roberto Sanesi, Milan 1983; *Pietro Cascella* by Enrico Crispolti, Florence 1984.

From a distinguished family of sculptors, Pietro Cascella and his brother Andrea have emerged as two of the most gifted practitioners in contemporary Italian art. The two brothers are similar in their media preference and imagery, but Pietro can be identified principally for his choice of more monumental conceptions, in which scale, simplicity, and in particular rough unfinished marble are basic components.

Stone carvers are comparatively rare in modern art but for an Italian it is both a challenge and a reference to national history and the natural scene. Cascella has said that one cannot consider the process "in terms of the consumer society; the method of working, and the time required, belongs to a former age; it is an art of patience." He prefers to confront a huge block of marble (à la Michelangelo, perhaps).

Two distinct forms emerge in Pietro Cascella's work; rounded, feminine, sexual shapes, similar in a generalised way to the shapes found in Henry Moore's reclining females; but with Cascella there is no evocative comparison of the nude body to a gentle, rolling landscape. He is more involved in the complexities of the body, sexually curious, isolating and examining details, so that the emergent sculptures are enlarged combinations of rounded forms and orifices. They do not resemble landscape, or indeed nature in general, except that their organic nature evokes memories and references. Enormously enlarged, physically dominating, and abstracted beyond original

inspiration, they manage to promote the idea of intimacy and inevitability.

His sculptures neither provoke nor disturb. More open to doubt is the development from these organic, intimate, sensual conceptions, to extended public monuments, some of which he has worked on with his brother Andrea. These include the "Auschwitz Monument," the "Gate of Peace" at Tel Aviv, the "National Congress Monument" at Strasbourg and the Mazzini commemoration in Milan. Once can see the reason for such commissions since it is difficult to think of other modern sculptors who can undertake such portentous requests. Individual characteristic works by sculptors are often commissioned as public monuments, and no doubt enhance the space they occupy; Cascella, in the great Mediterranean tradition, produces massive public celebrations, partly architecture, part landscape, partly sculpture. They inevitably lack the personal involvement of the more intimate works, combining with the intimate rounded forms, the more architectural details of flat pavements and geometrical intersections.

—Charles Spencer

CASTELLANI, Enrico.

Italian. Born in Castelmassa, Rovigo, Italy, 4 August 1930. Educated in Novara and Milan; studied painting and sculpture at the Académie Royale des Beaux-Arts, Brussels, 1952–56, and architecture at the Ecole Nationale Supèrieure de la Cambre, Belgium, 1956. Has lived and worked in Milan since 1956: Founder, with Piero Manzoni, *Azimuth* journal, Milan, 1959; associated with the Zero Group, Milan, 1962. Recipient: Painting Prize, Nagaoka Museum, Tokyo, 1967; Gold Medal, *Biennale di San Marino,* 1967. Agent: Galerie M, Haus Weitmar, Bochum, West Germany. Address: 01010 Cellere, Vitterbo, Italy.

Individual Exhibitions:

1959 Galerie Kasper, Lausanne, Switzerland
1960 Galleria Azimut, Milan
1961 New Vision Centre, London
Galleria La Tartaruga, Rome
1962 Galerie Aujourd'hui, Brussels
1963 Galleria dell'Ariete, Milan
1964 Galleria La Polena, Genoa
Galleria Notizie, Turin
Galleria del Leone, Venice
Galerie Wulfengasse, Klagenfurt, Austria
1965 Galleria La Tartaruga, Rome
Galerie Lawrence, Paris
1966 Galleria Notizie, Turin
Betty Parsons Gallery, New York
Tokyo Gallery
1968 *Documenta,* Kassel, West Germany
1970 Galerie M. Bochum, West Germany
1971 Artestudio, Macerata, Italy
1972 Galleriaforma, Genoa

Selected Group Exhibitions:

1960 *Monochrome Malerei,* Städtisches Museum, Leverkusen, West Germany
1961 *Nove Tendencije I,* Zagreb
1962 *Zero,* Stedelijk Museum, Amsterdam
1964 *Guggenheim International,* Guggenheim Museum, New York
1965 *The Responsive Eye,* Museum of Modern Art, New York
1966 *Third Exhibition,* Nagaoka Museum, Tokyo
1968 *Many Italian Artists,* Jewish Museum, New York
1971 *11 Italiener Heute,* Museum am Ostwall, Dortmund, West Germany
1981 *Artee Critica,* Galleria Nazionale d'Arte Moderna, Rome
1986 *Aspects of Italian Art 1960–85,* Kunstverein, Frankfurt

Collections:

Galleria Nazionale d'Arte Moderna, Rome.

Publications:

On CASTELLANI: books—*Visites d'Atelier* by Giulia Veronesi, Lausanne, Switzerland 1959; *La Linea dell'Arte Italiana* by Guido Ballo, Milan 1964; *Testo del Libro Castellani Pittore* by Vincenzo Agnetti, Milan 1968; *Op Art* by Cyril Barrett, London 1970; articles—"La Peinture Objet dans l'Art Italien Contemporain" by Gillo Dorfles in *L'Oeil* (Paris), no. 121, 1965; "Il Purismo di Castellani" by M. F. dell Arco in *L'Avanti* (Milan), no. 6/8, 1966.

By 1956, when he and Piero Manzoni founded the review *Azimuth,* Enrico Castellani had already worked out the basic principles which have governed his artistic experiments ever since. The monochromatic surfaces which he now began to produce were essentially reactions against his earlier irrationalist exercises, with their explosive colors and violent imagery. Thus his later work is basically abstract in character: in intensity and aim he comes close to the conceptualism of an artist like Lucio Fontana.

In his monochromatic surfaces Castellani has explored new areas of painting, yet he also wishes to work within the tradition which leads back to the neoplastic origins of art, as Gestalt psychological theory defines them. These red, yellow, blue, white and silver canvases are hung over projecting nails of varying lengths, so that the surface is contoured. And over these surfaces lights play, half-lights corresponding to the convexities, shadows to the concavities. These chiaroscuro effects give his work some affinity with of the early Op-Art of the early 1960's, but the intensity of Castellani's work goes far beyond those cold experiments.

At the corner of his work lies the quintessentially modern concern with space and time. He expresses the problem by means of his contoured surfaces—"spatial modulators," as Dorfles calls them—which both contain and liberate space. Castellani wishes us to grasp the flexibility of space; and the lights which play over the surfaces at varying rates of speed are designed to express the continuity of time and the relationship which exists between time and space themselves. His experiments have opened up new vistas.

—Roberto G. Lambarelli

CASTELLI, Luciano.

Swiss. Born in Lucerne, 28 September 1951. Studied at the School of Art and Design, Lucerne, 1969. Lived and worked in Lucerne until 1977, Rome, 1977–78, and in Berlin since 1978. Recipient: Kiefer Hablitzel Stipendium, 1970–71; Bundes Stipendium, 1973–75. Agents: Galerie Stahli, 39 Gruezgasse, Zurich 8008, Switzerland; Galerie de Appel, 196 Brouwersgracht, Amsterdam, Netherlands. Address: Reckenbuhlstrasse 17, 6005 Lucerne, Switzerland.

Individual Exhibitions:

1971 Galerie Toni Gerber, Berne
1975 Galerie Stahli, Zurich
Galerie de Appel, Amsterdam
Galerie t'Venster, Rotterdam
Salle Municipal Palino, Geneva
1978 Galerie Handschin, Basle
1979 Galerie Stahli, Zurich
1981 Centre d'art contemporain, Geneva
Galerie Farideh Cadot, Paris
Annina Nosei Gallery, New York
1983 CAPC/Musee d'Art Contemporain, Bordeaux, France (with Fetting and Salome)
1984 Galerie Farideh Cadot, Paris

Selected Group Exhibitions:

1971 *Biennale des Jeunes,* Paris
1972 *Documenta 5,* Museum Fridericianum, Kassel, West Germany
1974 *Transformer-Aspekte der Travestie,* Kunstmuseum, Lucerne
1975 *Biennale des Jeunes,* Paris.
1980 *Biennale,* Venice
1981 *Schweizer Kunst '70–'80.* Kunstmuseum, Lucerne
Im Westen nichts Neues, Kunstmuseum, Lucerne
12 Kunstler aus Deutschland, Kunsthalle, Basle
1982 *A l'Ouest rien de Nouveau,* Centre d'Art Contemporain, Geneva
1987 *Berlinart 1961–87,* Museum of Modern Art, New York (travelled to San Francisco)

Collections:

Kunstmuseum, Basle, Kunstmuseum, Lucerne.

Publications:

By CASTELLI: articles—interview by Jean-Christophe Ammann in *Rapport der Innerschweiz,* exhibition catalogue, Zurich 1974; interview by Jean Christophe Amman in *Transformer-Aspekte der Travestie,* exhibition catalogue, Lucerne 1974; interview by Jacques Clayssen in *Identité/Identifications,* exhibition catalogue, Paris 1976.

On CASTELLI: books—*Visualierte Denkprozesse,* exhibition catalogue, by Jean-Christophe Ammann, Lucerne 1971; *Giovanne Arte Svizzera,* exhibition catalogue, by W. Schonenberger and Theo Kneubuhler, Milan 1972; *Aspekte der Travestie,* exhibition catalogue, Lucerne 1974; *9th Biennale,* exhibition catalogue, Paris 1975; *Fundatie,* exhibition catalogue, Amsterdam 1979; *Schweizer Kunst '70–'80,* exhibition catalogue, Lucerne 1981; *12 Kunstler aus Deutschland,* exhibition catalogue, Basle 1982; *A l'Quest rien de Nouveau,* exhibition catalogue, with texts by Martin Kunz and Eberhard Roters, Geneva 1982.

—How is the link accomplished between objects and the work on the body?

My work is much too closely linked to my life for me to be able to disassociate objects, either from the sculptures or from the photographic works. Photography is the most direct means. Objects such as the handkerchief, the motorcycle helmet, are everyday objects but they have become pipes, which is to say personal objects. As the act of smoking was very important during this period, I reconstructed that importance around objects; I found it more interesting to occupy myself with objects which concerned me and which, as a result, taught me more about myself. The link is probably to be found in the treatment of the body in my work: I use it as an object.

—The perception of the body is [put at one remove] by the photo, but do you use a mirror to realize these photographs?

I use the mirror uniquely to control the appearance; the image of the mirror is not a partner.

—You don't seek the help of a photographer?

No, it's simply a question of independence. I can get up at two o'clock in the morning to work if I want to. I use an automatic release to give me greater freedom.

—Would the voyeurism of a photographer irritate you?

I work at certain moments in very precise conditions; any person not directly involved in my work would therefore be an irritation.

Luciano Castelli: *Hund I*, 1981

—What are the origins of what you represent in a sculpture such as the oyster with a body coiled in the shell?

I made the figure first. Then, while doing so, I thought of mother of pearl, and its sweetness preoccupied me. And in Roxy Music the phrase "mother of pearl" rose up so strongly that I made the oyster shell. I plan to continue along these lines with sculptures, water-colours, objects. I don't want to use photos any more.

—Transvestism is no longer a preoccupation?

It's not really preoccupation any more. Transvestism was the provocative form of an ambiguity which I have within me, between the masculine and the feminine, but the complementary feminine element always forms part of my work. I always dealt with this feminine element in my earlier objects, notably in my drawings. When I'd had very long hair, I had done a drawing after smoking some hashish and, suddenly, I had had the impression that my trousers were becoming a dress and that I was like a woman—an optical illusion.

—At a certain moment, in your photo's, you use some very unusual garments, animal skins . . . .

There's no special scheme in the use of this type of clothing. The arrangement came about fortuitously; luck and the concordance with the spirit in which I was working brought it about that I used them.

—In the most recent works, it is no longer a question of transvestism by garments, but the accent is put on poses, expressions. There are in fact no more garments?

No.

—It's the poses which denote a certain pattern of femininity?

I gave up transvestism by make-up and clothing to try to show one of its resultants, which is aggressivity, provocation transformed into a more animal characteristic. I have done several series on this theme.

—Animal in the pose?

Yes, but I consider that the term animal, of animal appearance, is as much masculine as feminine. The animal side is aggressivity and, perhaps, brutality. But the female side masks a little of this approach.

—The pose is lascivious?

Yes, it's the feline side that I feel in myself.

—The transvestism established itself in terms of provocation, of aggression against the exterior world, but on the artistic plane?

When I use make-up, I satisfy an interior necessity. There is make-up and there is make-up; on the one hand, a make-up which is banal and entirely superficial, on the other a more considered form which, at the moment when it is confronted with the exterior by the form adopted and the context in which one presents it, becomes provocation.

—Make-up is a discourse.

Yes, absolutely.

—Can one talk of auto-analysis?

I think that this continual working has taught me a lot about myself. I have learnt from my experiments insofar as they have allowed me to see, to visualize certain elements which I carry within myself. All these images come from me, but for myself, I don't know if I get from them anything but the pleasure of seeing them.

—Your work remains a method of artistic expression.

I expressed at a certain moment the masculine-feminine side in the field of art by insisting on that which touches me closely, and I think that in this type of work it's the masculine side which is emphasized. Art is the last link of a chain; my activity expresses itself as a work which shows the ambivalence and allows me to assume it as a strategy. It is not without problems that I have accepted this ambivalence in my work. But in itself transvestism is not a problem; one must differentiate between transvestite and transvestism.

—So one can say that you are not transvestite except during the transvestism?

Yes, one can put it that way. I consider this moment as the expression of the masculine-feminine bipolarity. My works are my life, my [region of the] imaginary.

—Luciano Castelli,
from an interview with Jacques Clayssen

Luciano Castelli's painting is painting for effect; it shows off its colours with unbridled eroticism and aestheticism. Between the rapid brush-strokes there appear fragments or details of an image, a "prisoner" of the swift play set in motion by the colour-shape itself. The result is a surface abstraction/figuration, with no spatial depth. It is the emotive effect of an instant projected towards a chance pleasure. The artist gives free rein to the gesture, to the sensual peacefulness of his becoming, to the eclecticism of his deviations. The artist has only love of himself; his "inner emotions" last only a moment and are therefore exploited to the full. It would be sheer hypocrisy to emerge from this perverted state of grace; he has rather to enter freely into it, to make clearer the duration of the gestural orgasm.

Castelli is an artist by vocation; his daily prayers are made to beauty and to exhausting pleasure. Hedonism is the unknown, to be violated, to be gratified. Hence the screaming density of the colour-shape, the fragments of image exposed in the grip of excitement. The surface, crowded in this way, looks like a film show which we attend as *voyeur.* The artist, moving within the transient multicoloured light, creates unexpected situations; his movements (posed or dancing), charged with exhibitionism, let that self-love shine through above all.

Castelli's painting (like that of Rainer Fetting, Helmut Middendorf and Salomè) is pervaded with auto-erotism. With or without the self-portrait, the artist always portrays a little of himself. Painting is thus a marvellous, exhilarating, freethinking, ambiguous medium to exalt or satisfy the call to be an artist. It does not aim at surprise effects; any that are produced are only apparent. It is actually the appearance, and the wonderful melancholy of it, that attract and seduce the artist. In the self-portrait he seems to see how deviation changes aspect, obedient to an implacable fate that inexorably deforms the reality. But the self-portrait is disconcerting to anyone who looks for the logic of the likeness in it. Instead, the artist thirsts for extravagance; he is filled with an urge to follow the irreverent, shocking path of his narcissism in order to hide the true, fleeting image. Luciano Castelli disguises himself in order to fling out something disturbing through the medium of a painting whose very facility makes it pungent and enigmatic. It may be that his painting reflects a tendency to déjà vu, and why ever should it represent the invisible? An enervating scepticism does not consort with the art of the self-portrait.

—Italo Mussa

CASTILLO, Jorge.

Spanish. Born in Pontevedra, Galicia, 16 July 1933. Educated in Argentina, until 1940; studied at the School of Fine Arts, Buenos Aires, 1941–45; influenced by artist Raquel Ferrer. Served in the Spanish Army, 1956–57. Married Maria-Helena Castillo (died, 1963); daughter: Ruth; married Marienza Castillo in 1966; son: Taggio. Independent artist, Buenos Aires, 1945–55, in Madrid and Barcelona, 1957–63, in Paris, Geneva and Barcelona, 1963–66, in Loano, Italy, 1966–69, in West Berlin, and Barcelona, 1970–74, in Barcelona, since 1975: first sculptures, 1965. Recipient: International Drawing Prize, Darmstadt 1964; D.A.A.D. Fellowship, West Berlin 1969–70. Agent: Galerie Calart, Geneva. Address: c/o Galerie Calart, 4 bis Rue Prevost-Martin, Place des Philosophes, 1205 Geneva, Switzerland.

Individual Exhibitions:

1959 Galeria Altamira, Madrid
1960 Galeria Abril, Madrid
Galeria San Jorge, Madrid
1961 Bodley Gallery, New York
Galeria Diario de Noticias, Lisbon
Galeria Mediterraneo, Madrid
1962 Galeria Mediterraneo, Madrid
1963 Galerie Andrè Schoeller, Paris
Galerie Raymond Cordier, Paris
1964 Kunstverein, Dusseldorf
1965 Galerie Andrè Schoeller, Paris
Galleria Galatea, Turin
Galeria Belarte, Barcelona
Galerie Brusberg, Hannover
Musée d'Art et d'Histoire, Fribourg, Switzerland
1966 Musée de l'Athenée, Geneva
Paintings and Drawings, Richard Demarco Gallery, Edinburgh
1967 Loeb and Krugier, New York
Gallery of Modern Art, Scottsdale, Arizona
1968 *Vers un Peinture Generative,* Galerie Krugier, Geneva
1969 Frankfurter Kunstkabinett, Frankfurt
1970 Galerie Contemporaine, Geneva
Galeria Iolas-Velasco, Madrid
Galeria Seiquer, Madrid
Nationalgalerie, West Berlin
Galerie Rudolf Springer, West Berlin
1971 Galerie Krugier, Geneva
Galerie Ariadne, Cologne
Galerie Ariadne, Vienna
Traverse Art Gallery, Edinburgh
Galerie Herbert Meyer-Ellinger, Frankfurt
Musée d'Art et d'Histoire, Geneva
1972 Galeria Adria, Barcelona
Gemalde/Aquarelle/Zeichnungen/Druckgraphik, Kunstverein, Darmstadt
Galerie Pels-Leusden, West Berlin
Galerie Richard P. Hartmann, Munich
1973 *Radierungen,* Kestner-Gesellschaft, Hannover
1974 Galerie Stephane Janssen, Brussels
Galeria 42, Barcelona
Werke 1973/74, Galerie Michael Hertz, Bremen, West Germany
1976 Galeria Joan Prats, Barcelona
1977 Lefebre Gallery, New York

Selected Group Exhibitions:

1959 *El Bodega Espanol,* Galeria Darro, Madrid
1960 *20th Century Drawings and Graphics,* Galeria Darro, Madrid
1961 *Bienal,* Sao Paulo
1962 *Grands et Jeunes d'Aujourd'hui,* Grand Palais, Paris
1963 *Salon de Mai,* Musée d'Art Moderne, Paris
1964 *Internationale der Zeichnung,* Darmstadt
1973 *Hommage à Picasso,* Kestner-Gesellschaft, Hannover
1987 *Arco 87,* Madrid

Collections:

Musée Cantonal des Beaux-Ars, Lausanne, Switzerland; Kunstmuseum, Essen; Kunstmuseum, Bochum, West Germany; Kunstverein, Darmstadt; Nationalgalerie, West Berlin; Museum am Ostwall, Dortmund, West Germany; Museum des 20, Jahrhunderts, Vienna.

Publications:

On CASTILLO: books—*Castillo,* exhibition catalogue, with text by Luigi Carluccio, Turin 1965; *Jorge Castillo: Paintings and Drawings,* exhibition catalogue, with text by Jean-Luc Daval, Edinburgh 1966, *Jorge Castillo: Vers un Peinture Generative,* exhibition catalogue, with text by Jean-Luc Daval, Geneva 1968; *Jorge Castillo,* exhibition catalogue, with text by Werner Haftmann, West Berlin 1970; *Jorge Castillo: Citations,* exhibition catalogue, Geneva 1971; *Jorge Castillo: Gemalde/Aquarelle/Zeichnungen/Druckgraphik,* exhibition catalogue, with texts by G. Hofmann and B. Krimmel, Darmstadt 1972; *Hommage à Picasso,* exhibition catalogue, with texts by Wieland Schmied, Werner Haftmann and Daniel Kahnweiler, Hannover 1973; *Jorge Castillo: Radierungen,* exhibition catalogue, with texts by Wieland Schmied and Werner Haftmann, Hannover 1973; *Castillo: Werke 1973/74,* exhibition catalogue, with text by Werner Haftmann, Bremen, West Germany 1974; *Jorge Castillo,* exhibition catalogue, with text by Werner Haftmann, New York 1977.

At the *Basel International Art Fair,* three dealers—a German, a Russian (out of Spain) and a Frenchman—were involved in a complicated multiway enterprise to try to exchange five of Dali's San Francisco coloured etchings for a painting by Jorge Castillo. After four days of maneuvering and intense plotting and counterplotting the Frenchman won the day, but he had to throw in still more ballast to clinch the bargain. No money changed hands, but equity on both sides was regarded as considerable. Reference is made to this small commercial episode to indicate that from 1970 onwards Castillo has come to be reckoned as viable art market currency.

He was born in 1933 which makes him a comparatively young man to have his works high-financed in such a sub-rosa fashion. And yet his reputation has somehow managed to outstrip cognizance of his work, all too little known to the art world at large, although German collectors, during the 1970's, became specially interested in his paintings and only slightly less in his graphics.

What are the qualities that have combined to give him a particular place and consideration in the crowded corridors of contemporary art?

Castillo is essentially a Latin painter; perhaps galloromantic would be a better description in view of his quirky illogicality and personalised invention. It is as if he had painlessly digested all the twists of 20th century figurative art and then found a contemporary accent with which to make the old new, and the new old in a manner never likely to prove disruptive to those aware of the way in which modern figurative art has developed.

His is the voice of Hispañola, not España. Nobility in his oeuvres is never allowed to blot out cleverness; and cleverness is never permitted to make his imagery over-literary. His colours do not shout. They murmur. But their quiet tones in no way reduce the validity of the messages they clothe.

The impression of a contained version of collage (or, in the case of the watercolours, drawings, aquatints and etchings, maybe the underlying expression of assemblage would be a more opposite implication) could be a clue to the subliminal reason of his mysterious appeal. In plain language, it means that Castillo "builds" his pictures. However perverse the imagery of a drawing like "La petite dormeuse" of 1970, the compositional architecture is there even if he takes liberties with it. The fauteuil is enormous and the little figure is half swathed in the shadow which has somehow crept across part of the back of the chair, slipped through into the seat beyond and engulfed the figure. This is a sort of "imaginary" collage of the kind of referred to above.

Nor is Castillo limited to traditional methods. He has made some interesting experiments with mischtechnik. "The Group of Figures" he made in Barcelona in 1965 shows what an astonishing range of tonality and perspective he can achieve with media-alchemy on a sheet of drawing paper.

So Castillo is a technician as well as an artist. That in itself is not a unique position to hold in the field of visual arts. What this combination adds to his stature is that it is wedded to an offbeat mind. "Our Lady of the Sorrows" (1973) sits against a background of two goalposts and a storm-tossed tree. "Flight from the Monster" (1960) is like a cross between a circus and a ballet. The foreground figure looks as if he is going to curve into a pirouette, and the monster is sulking anyway.

Castillo is a master of surprise. All his shocks have the immediacy of wit. Sometimes sardonic, sometimes closer to the belly laugh. All his non-shocks have a curious monumentalism made paradoxical because they so often appear to be momentary.

—Sheldon Williams

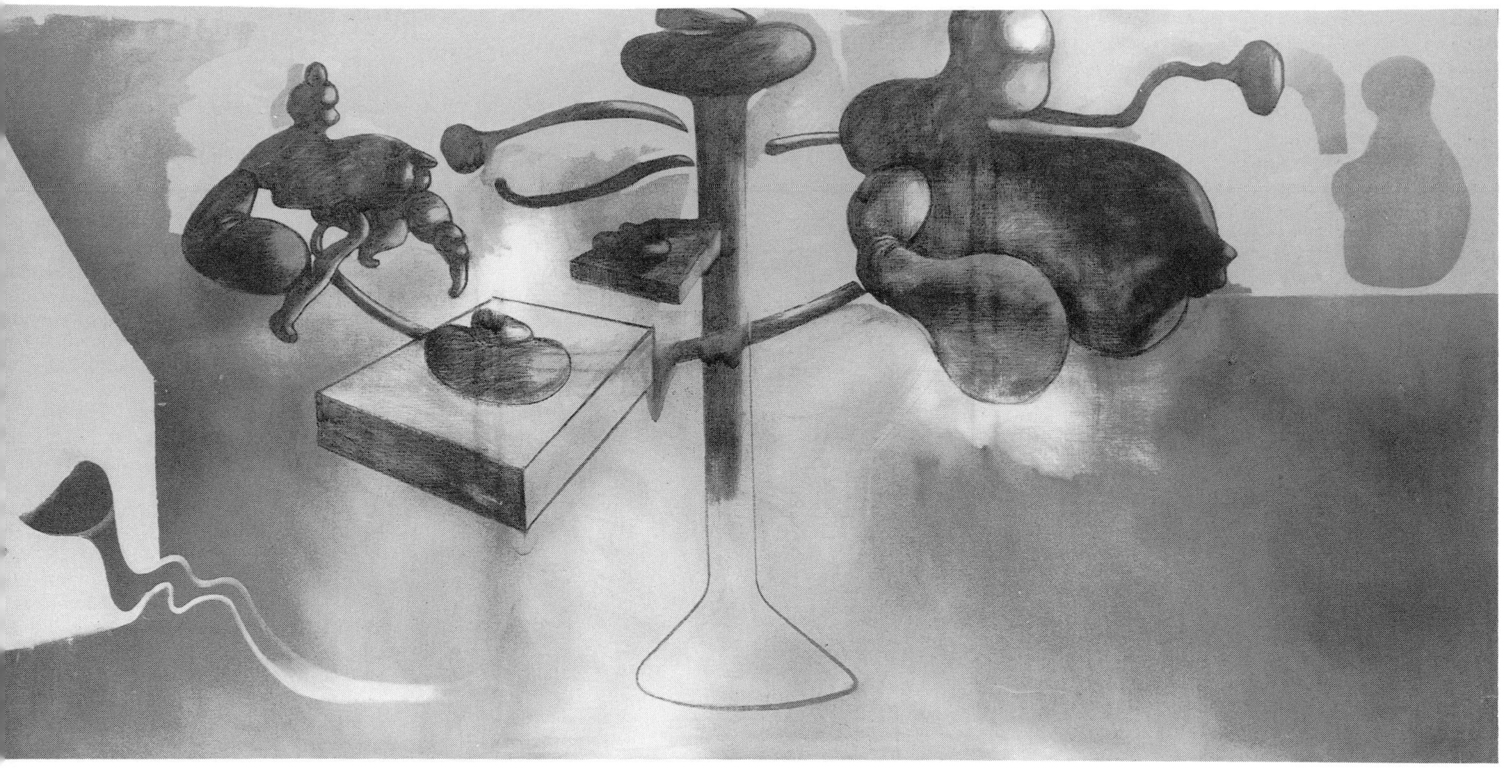

Jorge Castillo: *Jardin de Boissano*, 1970

CAULFIELD, Patrick.

British. Born in London in 1936. Studied at the Chelsea School of Art, London, under Jack Smith, 1956–60, and at the Royal College of Art, London, 1960–63. Painter and printmaker: lives and works in London. Lecturer, Chelsea School of Art, 1963–71. Recipient: Prix de Jeunes Artistes (graphics), 1965. Agent: Waddington Galleries, London. Address: c/o Waddington Galleries, 11 Cork Street, London W1, England.

Individual Exhibitions:

1965 Robert Fraser Gallery, London
Galerie d'Aujourd'hui, Brussels (with Derek Boshier)
1966 Robert Elkon Gallery, New York
1967 Studio Marconi, Milan
Robert Fraser Gallery, London
1968 Robert Elkon Gallery, New York
1969 Waddington Galleries, London
1971 D. M. Gallery, London
Waddington Galleries, London
1972 Galerie Stadler, Paris (with Howard Hodgkin and Michael Moon)
Sweeney Reed Galleries, Victoria, Australia
1973 Waddington Galleries, London
Europalia, Brussels
1974 O. K. Harris Gallery, New York
Kinsman Morrison Gallery, London
1975 Waddington Galleries, London
Scottish Arts Council Gallery, Edinburgh
1976 Arnolfini Gallery, Bristol
1977 Tortue Gallery, Santa Monica, California
1978 Tate Gallery, London
1979 Waddington Galleries, London
1980 Hughes Gallery, Brisbane
IAC, Basle
Tolarno Galleries, Melbourne
Gardner Centre for the Arts, University of Sussex, Brighton (travelled to the Oriel Gallery, Cardiff, and the Midland Group Gallery, Nottingham)
1981 Walker Art Gallery, Liverpool (travelled to the Tate Gallery, London, 1982)
Waddington Galleries, London
1982 Nishimura Gallery, Tokyo
1983 Arnolfini Gallery, Bristol
1985 Waddington Galleries, London
Bernardelli Gallery, Rio de Janeiro (toured South America, 1985–87)

Selected Group Exhibitions:

1964 *The New Generation*, Whitechapel Art Gallery, London
1965 *Biennale des Jeunes*, Musée National d'Art Moderne, Paris
1966 *Recent Still Life*, Rhode Island School of Design, Providence
1967 *Jeunes Peintres Anglais*, Palais des Beaux-Arts, Brussels
1969 *Marks on a Canvas*, Museum am Ostwall, Dortmund, West Germany
1971 *Junge Englander*, Kunststudio Westfalen, Bielefeld, West Germany
1974 *British Painting 74*, Hayward Gallery, London
1976 *Arte Inglese Oggi*, Palazzo Reale, Milan
1982 *Aspects of British: Art Today*, Metropolitan Art Museum, Tokyo (toured Japan)
1984 *British Artists' Books 1970–83*, Atlantis Gallery, London

Collections:

Arts Council of Great Britain, London: Tate Gallery, London; Walker Art Gallery, Liverpool; Whitworth Art Gallery, Manchester; Hirshhorn Museum and Sculpture Garden, Washington, D.C.: Virginia Museum of Fine Arts, Richmond; Art Gallery of Ontario, Toronto.

Publications:

By CAULFIELD: articles—"Why Do Artists Make Prints?" in *Studio International* (London), June 1967; "Questionnaire" in *London Magazine*, April/May 1979.

On CAULFIELD: books—*Paintings by Patrick Caulfield*, exhibition catalogue, London 1967; *Patrick Caulfield* by Christopher Finch, London 1971; *Patrick Caulfield*, exhibition catalogue, London 1975; *Patrick Caulfield: Paintings and Prints*, exhibition catalogue, by Norbert Lynton, Edinburgh 1975; *Patrick Caulfield Print Retrospective: Complete Works 1964–1976*, exhibition catalogue, Santa Monica, California 1977; *Patrick Caulfield: Paintings 1963–81*, exhibition catalogue by Marco Livingston, London 1981; *Patrick Caulfield*, exhibition catalogue edited by the Waddington Galleries, London 1985; *Patrick Caulfield* by John McEwan, London 1987; articles—"From Illusion to Allusion" by Christopher Finch in *Art and Artists* (London), April 1966; "Comic Strip Pop" by John Loring in *Arts Magazine* (New York), September 1974; "Patrick Caulfield" by William Feaverin *The Observer* (London), 30 November 1975; "A Talent in English Painting" by James Burr in *Apollo* (London), July 1979.

Patrick Caulfield is a deceptive artist. At first glance his work looks easy, unimaginative, almost childlike. When you examine it more closely, things look very different. The comparisons with Lichtenstein and other "Pop" artists are ridiculous. Caulfield is a profoundly European painter who never seeks to glamourise or depict American merchandise. Caulfield selects everyday objects and sometimes juxtaposes them with exotic ones. In "Still Life with Dagger" a dull jug stands next to an exotic turquoise dagger from the Victoria and Albert Museum. Banality is linked with sophistication such as in "Still Life on a Table." Highly decorative china is placed against a background of a parody of modern art. In "Pony" the horse has taken an imposing Stubbs pose but looks as though it had been painted by numbers. In "Still Life with Candle" the vanitas theme without the skull appears. The candle is burnt out, the bread is being eaten by a mouse and the glass has fallen over. In "View of the Rooftops" Caulfield has become romantic. The flame red background is reminiscent of the great fire in "Gone with the Wind." In the successful "Bend in the Road" the bend is executed in the corniest of ways by leading the viewers' eye into the canvas—similar to the children walking down the road into the sunset advertising Start Rite shoes. Sometimes Caulfield makes perverse subject choices such as the "Smokeless Coal Fire" or the room divider.

Humans are rarely present but their presence is felt. In "Window at Night" a window is open and a light is on. The contrast between the warm glow of the room and the blackness of the night is superbly portrayed. Caulfield makes little attempt at shading or modelling, but the familiar black lines create vitality. In the painting "Inner Office" there is again a contrast between the external and internal world. The

Patrick Caulfield: *Thus She Would Come, Escaped, Half Dead to My Door*, 1973

desk is silhouetted, and the objects lying on it are highly defined—the little bronze picture of the wife and so on. In "Paradise Bar" it looks as though one would never have to go outside. Plastic vines cascade from the ceiling, food and wine are plentiful, art is present in the form of a mural—nothing else is needed, except real life maybe. In "Office Party" the traces of life can certainly be seen. Empty Verdicchio bottles and wine glasses are placed against the background of Spoleto Cathedral. Against a background of such grandeur the objects would normally seem meaningless but Caulfield has turned the tables.

Caulfield has said that "nothing is stranger than life itself." In his brilliantly executed visions he certainly proves it.

—Carine Maurice

CAVALIERE, Alik.

Italian. Born in Rome, 5 August 1926. Studied at the University of Milan, and at the Accademia di Belle Arti, Milan, 1956. Sculptor: lives and works in Milan. Lecturer and assistant to Marino Marini, later Professor of Sculpture, Accademia di Belle Arti, Milan. Address: Via Foppa 49a, 20144 Milan, Italy.

Individual Exhibitions:

1951 Galleria Colonna, Milan
1953 Galleria La Bussola, Turin
1955 Galleria Il Pincio, Rome
1959 Galleria Bergamini, Milan
Galleria Il Pincio, Rome
1962 Piemonte Artistico e Culturale, Turin
1963 Galleria Levi, Milan
1964 Galleria Schwarz, Milan
1965 Gallery 12, Minneapolis
Galerie Ad Libitum, Antwerp
Martha Jackson Gallery, New York
1966 Galleria Narciso, Turin
Galerie Aujourd'hui, Brussels
Palais des Beaux-Arts, Brussels
1967 Galleria del Minotauro, Brescia, Italy
Gallerie de Foscherari, Bologna
Galleria La Medusa, Rome
Gemeentemuseum, The Hague
Galleria Schwarz, Milan
Galleria Laminima, Turin
1968 Galleria Schwarz, Milan
Castello dell'Aquilla, Italy
Kunstammlungen, Nuremberg
1969 Galerie Withofs, Brussels
Studio Condotti 85, Rome
1970 Galleria de Foscherari, Bologna
Galleria Il Segnapassi, Pesaro, Italy
1971 Galleria Caprotti, Monza, Italy
Museo de Bellas Artes, Caracas
3 Environments, Galleria Schwarz, Milan

Selected Group Exhibitions:

1955 *Premio Internazionale*, Varese, Italy
1956 *Quadriennale*, Rome
1964 *Pittsburgh International*, Carnegie Institute, Pittsburgh
1965 *Neue Realisten und Pop Art*, Akademie der Kunst Berlin
1966 *Italian Artists of Today*, Bucharest
1971 *New Italian Art 1953–1971*, Walker Art Gallery Liverpool
1972 *Scultori Italiani Contemporanei*, Palazzo Reale, Milan
1977 *La Traccia del Raconto*, Villa Comunale Ormond San Remo, Italy
1982 *Arte Italiana 1960–82*, Hayward Gallery, London

Collections:

Galleria Nazionale d'Arte Moderna, Rome; Gemeentemuseum, The Hague; Carnegie Institute, Pittsburgh.

Publications:

By CAVALIERE: article—"Notes for a Dialogue Beyond the Work" in *Alik Cavaliere: 3 Environments*, exhibition catalogue, Milan 1971.

On CAVALIERE: books—*Alik Cavaliere*, exhibition catalogue, by Enrico Crispolti, Milan 1967; *Alik Cavaliere*, by Guido Ballo, Turin/Milan, 1967; *New Italian Art 1953–1971* exhibition catalogue, by Giovanni Carandente, Liverpool 1971; article—"Cavaliere" by Guido Ballo in *Art and Artists* (London), May 1971.

Alik Cavaliere thinks of sculpture as entertainment Sculpture to him is an inversion of reality, a variant repetition that thumbs its nose at the world of experience. His aim is to reconstruct a habitat that fits the technique. Art remarks the world, and remakes it as a false construction, a nihilist deception.

Cavaliere does not want to erect monuments, to use form to celebrate events; his works are rather real life experiences, able to stage events. So his sculpture is no longer a restricted form, defined and complete, no longer a super-object to be gazed at; it has become a stage technique able to act its own plays and its own tricks.

For Cavaliere, the sculptor's work is not a formally enclosed territory, a formal event crystallized, but a mini-world made by the play of skilled hands; it is the space where the performance takes place.

The works comprised in the 1959/1962 series called "The Adventures of G. B." are all carried out on multiple levels of interpretation. They give life to little things, to a number of happenings, using scenery made up from simple elements, very small but still essential, as are the people that populate them. They look to us like little stage plays in which the producer—the sculptor, in this case—has amused himself by directing a theatre made up of random extracts, familiar happenings punctuated by continual surprises.

At the time he was producing these works Cavaliere occupied a studio in an area of ill repute at the heart of Milan—an area that has now disappeared. The room where he worked was like a maze, a network of doors and windows, dark areas and light areas; and it may be that this extraordinary place is to some extent reflected in his work, for that too is all played out in a space with a great many scenes.

Later that artist moved into a sort of oasis, still in Milan; his studio is completely surrounded by a huge, luxuriant garden in which nature seems to produce every known plant. Cavaliere's interest in nature, its theatricality and the manifold formal possibilities that it offers, dates from this time.

The tree and the forest became then, and still are, the dominant themes of all works. First he examined the roots (and it was a surprise to Cavaliere to discover how spectacular those hidden parts, the basis of

his sculpture in some ways, can be), then the trunk, the leaves and the fruit.

Playing as they do on the artificiality of nature, these works, carried out in bronze like the earlier ones, do not try to take over the natural element; they do not want to play with the actual properties but to play a game of substitution and repetition.

Interest in theatrical invention is evident in these works too; falsehood is introduced, and with it purely theatrical mechanisms are activated. Nature becomes artifice, opening itself up to complex combinations, to endless games.

—Loredana Parmesani

CEROLI, Mario.

Italian. Born in Castelfrentano, Chieti, Italy, 17 May 1938. Worked in a studio with Leoncillo, Ettore Colla and Pericle Fazzini. Served in the Italian Army, 1961. Designed scenery for Pier Paolo Pasolini's *Orgia*, Teatro Stabile, Turin, and Giordano Bruno's *Candelaio*, Festival Theatre, Venice, 1962–64. Independent sculptor and performance artist, Rome since 1964. Recipient: Prize, *Mostra Nazionale di Termoli*, Italy, 1964; Third Prize, *Biennale d'Arte Metallo*, Gubbio, Italy, 1965; Gollin Prize, *Biennale*, Venice, 1966; Bolaffi Prize, Turin, 1972. Agent: Galleria Il Naviglio, via Manzoni 45, Milan. Address: Via della Pisana 1138, Rome, Italy.

Individual Exhibitions:

1964 Galleria La Tartaruga, Rome
1965 Galleria La Tartaruga, Rome
1966 Galleria del Naviglio, Milan
1967 Galleria del Naviglio, Milan
Modern Art Agency, Naples
Bonino Gallery, New York
Galleria Sperone, Turin
Galerie Thomas, Munich
Galerie Schmela, Dusseldorf
Galleria de Foscherari, Bologna
Mana Art Market, Rome
1969 Galleria del Naviglio, Milan
Modern Art Agency, Naples
Kunstverein, Karlsruhe, West Germany
Galerie René Block, Berlin
Galerie Brusberg, Hannover
Salone delle Scuderie, Parma, Italy
Kunsthalle, Hannover
Palais des Beaux-Arts, Brussels
Palazzo Ducale, Pesaro, Italy
Albright-Knox Art Gallery, Buffalo, New York (with Michelangelo Pistoletto)
1970 Galleria La Tartaruga, Rome
Galleria de Foscherari, Bologna
Galleria Ferrari, Verona
Museum Folkwang, Essen
1971 Kunstverein, Frankfurt
Museum am Ostwall, Dortmund, West Germany
Galleria Colophon, Milan
Galleria La Tartaruga, Rome
Haus am Waldsee, Berlin
1972 Galleria Forma, Genoa
Palazzo Ducale, Pesaro, Italy
1974 Betty Parsons Gallery, New York
Studio Marconi, Milan
Galleria Plurima I, Udine, Italy
1975 Galleria Graziussi, Venice
Galleria de'Foscherari, Bologna
1976 Centro Colombo Americano, Bogota, Colombia
Nova Arte Moderna, Prato, Italy
Galleria La Tartaruga, Rome
Galleria Marin, Turin
Fundacion Eugenio Mendoza, Caracas, Venezuela
1977 Galeria Sandiego, Bogota, Colombia
1978 Galleria Plurima I, Udine, Italy
1979 Galleria Il Centro, Naples
Galleria Aries, Bari, Italy
Galleria de'Foscherari, Bologna
Galleria San Soaze, Treviso, Italy
Galleria Franca Mancini, Pesaro, Italy
1980 Galleria Mario Diacono, Rome
Galleria Torbandena, Trieste, Italy
1981 Galleria Editalia, Rome
Galleria La Chiocciola, Padua, Italy
Galleria Meta, Florence
1982 Galleria La Tartaruga, Rome
Galleria de'Foscherari, Bologna
Studio Marconi, Milan
Mario Ceroli, at the *Biennale*, Venice
1983 Banco di Santo Spirito, Rome
Forte Belvedere, Florence
1984 *Mario Ceroli*, at the *Biennale*, Venice
1985 Galleria de'Foscherari, Bologna
1986 Palazzo degli Alessandri, Viterbo, Italy
Galleria 2RC, Milan

Selected Group Exhibitions:

1960 *Quadriennale*, Galleria Nazionale d'Arte Moderna, Rome
1965 *8 Italienischer Kunstler*, Kunsthaus, Zurich
1968 *Young Italians*, Institute of Contemporary Art, Boston
1971 *New Italian Art 1953–71*, Walker Art Gallery, Liverpool
1973 *Il Ritratto Oggi*, Villa Faraggiana, Albissola, Italy
1977 *XIV Bienal de Sao Paulo*, Brazil
1980 *One Hundred Years of Italian Art*, Museum of Modern Art, Tokyo
1982 *Arte Italiana 1960–82*, Hayward Gallery, London
1985 *Italia Oggi*, Villa Arson, Nice, France
1986 *Aspekte Italienischen Kunst 1950–85*, Kunstverein, Frankfurt

Collections:

Galleria Nazionale d'Arte Moderna, Rome; Kaiser-Wilhelm Museum, Krefeld, West Germany; Kunstmuseum, Dusseldorf.

Publications:

On CEROLI: books—*Ceroli*, exhibition catalogue with text by Gillo Dorfles, Milan 1966; *4 Artistes Italiens plus que*

Mario Ceroli: *Giove*, 1983

Nature, exhibition catalogue by Maurizio Calvesi, Paris 1969; *Ceroli*, exhibition catalogue with essay by Arturo Carlo Quintavalle, Parma 1969; *Mario Ceroli / Michelangelo Pistoletto*, exhibition catalogue with text by Robert M. Murdock, Buffalo, New York 1969; *New Italian Art 1953–1971*, exhibition catalogue by Giovanni Carandente, Liverpool 1971; *Le Due Avanguardie*, 2 vols., by Maurizio Calvesi, Bari 1971; *Kunst um 1970*, edited by Wolfgang Becker, Aachen 1972; articles—"Mario Ceroli" by G. Schoenenberg in *Art International* (Lugano), June 1968; "Ceroliade" by Tommaso Trini in *Domus* (Milan), April 1969; "Ceroli", special issue of *Flash Art* (Milan), January 1971; "Mario Ceroli a Pesaro" in *Data* (Milan), Summer 1972.

Following a brief period of works characteristic of the 'informal' movement after his military service, Mario Ceroli produced the first work marking his personal style. From this first period lasting little more than four years from 1956 to 1961 comes the sculpture *Legno con Chiodi* (1958), constructed out of a tree trunk pierced by large nails. This work in some respects anticipates Arte Povera, the movement with which Ceroli was briefly associated.

From 1962 comes the piece *Lettere*, whose title is decriptive of the row of letters roughly hewn out of wood: A.S.O.Z., a partial alphabet in which is anchored in a poetry opposed to the then ubiquitous informal. *Lettere* formulates the ideas soon to be seen in his best works. *Adam and Eve* and *Leonardo's Man* are explicitly based on classical themes or the artistic culture of the past. At the same time, Ceroli created works which refer to objects of daily use, as in *Clock* and *Telephone*. In these and successive works we see his poetry ripen as his techniques reach full maturity.

Maurizio Calvesi has written of *Adam and Eve* and the related works: "The plastic marquetry is complicated by the employment of empty spaces where shadows are modelled as if they were solid matter, and settle into a cunning play of relationships between empty and full areas; the first Cerolian silhouettes occur springing and taut, produced through a system of alternating projections of image or shadow." The works which follow attain a formal coherence. The rhythms of fullness and emptiness and of light and dark are intensified, as in *Casa di Dante* (1965), which, like subsequent pieces, reveals a new element. This element is a ladder which extends forward as an invitation to climb in and enter the sculpture. Not only does this element aspire to involve the spectator, as in *La Scala* (1965), but its three-dimensionality adds a new constituent to the work's expressive possibilities. In *Casa Sistina* (1966), the diverse tendencies of the preceding works are clarified. From the outside, the work looks like a huge packing case with two small doors located on opposite walls, inviting the spectator to enter the interior whose walls are covered with silhouettes and woodcut figures standing erect at balconies. This work, a prize-winner at the Venice Biennale, is indubitably one of Ceroli's most important creations to date. Here, contemporary and historical memories meet to become one with the space and the spectator.

This creative period is followed by another phase which takes on a conceptual accent. In a 1967 exhibition, *Lo Spazio dell'Immagine*, Ceroli exhibited the piece *Centoucelli*. Three cubes inserted into one another recall early works of abstraction and minimalism, a trend which was to continue into successive works, such as *Primavera di Daria* (1968), where the juxtaposition of an infinite number of wooden poles, each square in section, were built up to form a large, tightly-packed, parallelopiped structure. It was during this phase that Ceroli took part in the first Arte Povera exhibition, and in this climate is to be found his work produced for the cultural fair *Teatro delle mostre* promoted in 1968 by the Galleria La Tartaruga. This work, entitled *Dal caldo al freddo*, was conceived as the experience of travelling through a series of wooden doors until one arrived in front of a wall of ice.

Very soon, Ceroli was to turn to re-working and inventing themes with that originality that has always been his distinguishing mark. Additionally, his work as a scenographer, notably for Luca Ronconi's production of *Richard III* in 1968, has brought him recognition most importantly for his vocation as a sculptor.

—Roberto Lambarelli

CESAR (Baldaccini).

French. Born in Marseilles, 1 January 1921. Studied at Ecole des Beaux-Arts, Marseilles, 1935–43; Ecole des Beaux-Arts, Paris, 1943–50. Served in French Army 1939–40. Married Rosine Groult in 1960; daughter: Anna. Sculptor, Paris, since 1950: first "compressions", 1960; first polyester "expansions", 1967. Instructor in Sculpture, Ecole Nationale Supérieure des Beaux-Arts, Paris, 1968–86. Recipient: Prix des trois arts, Ecole des Beaux-Arts, Marseilles, 1954; Sculpture Prize, *Biennale of Carrara,* Italy 1957; Silver Medal, *Exposition Universal,* Brussels, 1958; Grand Prix National de Sculpture, France, 1980. Chevaliere de la Legion d'Honneur, 1976; Officier de l'Ordre National du Merite, France, 1982; Commandeur de l'Ordre des Arts et Lettres, France, 1984. Address: 10 bis, Rue Roger, 75014 Paris, France.

Individual Exhibitions:

1954 Galerie Lucien Durand, Paris
1955 Galerie Rive Droite, Paris
1957 Galerie Creuzevalt, Paris
Hanover Gallery, London
1959 Galerie Claude Bernard, Paris
1960 *Recent Sculpture,* Hanover Gallery, London
1961 Saidenberg Gallery, New York
Galleria Apollinaire, Milan
1966 Stedelijk Museum, Amsterdam (travelled to the Wilhelm-Lehmbruck-Museum, Duisburg, West Germany)
Outdoor Expansions, Kunstmuseum, Munich (travelled to Sao Paulo, Rio de Janeiro, and Montevideo)
Musée Cantini, Marseilles (retrospective)
Galleria Il Fante di Spade, Rome
Galleria Galatea, Turin
1968 Galleria Buren, Stockholm (travelled to the Konstmuseum, Gothenburg)
Outdoor Expansions, Tate Gallery, London (and European tour)
1969 Musée des Arts Décoratifs, Paris
Galerie Mathias Fels, Paris
1970 Centre National d'Art Contemporain, Paris
Galerie Creuzevalt, Paris
Galleria del Leone, Venice (travelled to Galleria Schwarz, Milan)
Galleria del Naviglio, Milan
Galleria Victor Emmanuel, Milan
Galerie Rive Gauche, Brussels
Galerie Argos, Nantes, France (with Pavlos and Miralda)
Galerie Soisson, Nice (with Farhi and Arman)
1971 Palais des Beaux-Arts, Brussels
Kunsthalle, Hamburg
Galerie Semiha Huber, Zurich
Galerie Rive Gauche, Brussels
Eat-Art Gallerie, Dusseldorf
Galerie Municipale A. M. Douet, Montreuil, France
Galleria Il Centro, Naples
Henie-Onstad Kunstsenter, Oslo
Galerie Creuzevalt, Paris
Maison de la Culture, Rennes, France
1972 Musee Cantini, Marseilles
Galerie Mathias Fels, Paris
Galerie Lucien Durand, Paris
Cesar à Nice, Galerie des Ponchettes, Nice
Galerie Fred Lanzenberg, Brussels
1973 *Tête á Tête,* Galerie Creuzevalt, Paris
Cesar en Arles, Cloitre Saint Trophine, Arles, France
Galerie Semiha Huber, Zurich
Theatre Municipal, Angers, France
Centre Culturel, Romainville, France
1974 Rotonda della Besana, Milan (travelled to the Galerie L'Expression, Strasbourg)
Galleria Il Fauno Due, Turin
1975 Galerie Sapone, Nice
1976 *Retrospective des Sculptures,* Musee Rath, Geneva (travelled to the Musée des Beaux-Arts, Grenoble, France; Casino Communal, Knokke, Belgium; Museum Boymans-van Beuningen, Rotterdam; and the Musée d'Art Moderne de la Ville, Paris)
Galerie Semiha Huber, Zurich
Galerie Beaubourg, Paris
1977 Galerie Kriwin, Brussels
1978 Musee Picasso, Antibes, France
Galerie Sapone, Nice
Galerie Bornand, Marseilles
1979 Chateau de Jau, Perpignan, France (with Arman)
Les Expansions, Galerie Daniel Templon, Paris
Galerie Olga, Stockholm
1980 Galerie Beaubourg, Paris
Galerie Kriwin, Brussels
1981 Fondation Veranneman, Kruishoutem, Belgium
Musée de Cabriès-en-Provence, France (retrospective; travelled to Brest and Roubaix)
Musée d'Art Moderne, Liège, Belgium
Galerie Zanetacci, Geneva
1982 Espace nicois d'art et de culture, Nice, France (retrospective)
Fondation Seibu, Tokyo (retrospective)
Museum of Ohara, Japan (retrospective)
Yoshibi Gallery, Tokyo
Galerie Beaubourg, Paris
Musée de Villetaneuse, France
Galerie Asbaeck, Copenhagen
1983 Musée Picasso, Antibes, France
Pavillon des Arts, Paris (retrospective)
Christian Fayt Art Gallery, Knokke-le-Zoute, Belgium
Galerie Verrière, Lyon, France
Galerie Cupillard, Saint-Tropez, France
1984 Musée de la Poste, Paris
Galleria Forni, Bologna, Italy
Fondation Cartier, Jouy en Josas, France
Palazzo Grassi, Venice
1985 Musée d'Art Contemporain, Dunkerque, France
Galerie Artio, Athens
Galerie Beaubourg, Paris
Chateau de Brecey, France
1986 Art Centre, Hong Kong
Fondation Cartier, Jouy en Josas, France
Galerie Zanetacci, Geneva
1987 Musée d'Aix en Provence, France (retrospective)
Musée de Montbélliard, France
Cesar, at the *Salon d'Automne,* Brive, France
Galerie Beaubourg, at *FIAC 87,* Paris
Musée de Middelheim, Antwerp, Belgium

Selected Group Exhibitions:

1956 *Biennale,* Venice
1957 *Bienal,* Sao Paulo
1958 *Carnegie International,* Carnegie Institute, Pittsburgh
1959 *Documenta 2,* Kassel, West Germany
1961 *L'Objet,* Musée des Arts Décoratifs, Paris
1967 *Superlund,* Konsthall, Lund, Sweden
1974 *Jewelry as Sculpture as Jewelry,* Institute of Contemporary Art, Boston
1976 *L'Animal—de Lascaux à Picasso,* Musée d'Histoire Naturelle, Paris
1984 *Peinture en France,* Palazzo Sagredo, Venice
1986 *Les Nouveaux Realistes,* Musee d'Art Moderne Paris

Collections:

Centre Georges Pompidou, Paris; Musée Cantini, Marseilles; Tate Gallery, London; Scottish National Gallery of Modern

Cesar: *Centaure—Hommage à Picasso*, 1983

Art, Edinburgh; Rijksmuseum Kröller-Müller, Otterlo, Netherlands; Musée Royal des Beaux-Arts, Brussels; Moderna Museet, Stockholm; Galleria Nazionale d'Arte Moderna, Rome; Museum of Modern Art, New York; Carnegie Institute, Pittsburgh.

Publications:

By CESAR: book—*Cesar par Cesar,* edited by Pierre Cabanne, Paris 1971.

On CESAR: books—*Cesar,* exhibition catalogue, with text by John Russell, London 1957; *Cesar: Recent Sculpture,* exhibition catalogue, with text by Pierre Restany, London 1960; *Cesar* by Douglas Cooper, St. Gallen, Switzerland 1960; *Cesar,* exhibition catalogue, with text by Gerhard Handler, Duisberg, West Germany 1966; *Cesar,* exhibition catalogue, with texts by Francois Mathey and Douglas Cooper, Marseilles 1966; *Cesar Balaccini,* exhibition catalogue, with text by Luigi Carluccio, Rome 1966; *Cesar,* exhibition catalogue, with texts by Luigi Carluccio, Turin 1966; *Cesar,* exhibition catalogue, with text by Francois Mathey, Amsterdam 1966; *Cesar: Compressions,* exhibition catalogue, with text by Pierre Restany, Paris 1969; *Cesar Expansions Controlées,* exhibition catalogue, with text by Pierre Restany, Gothenburg 1969; *Cesar: Plastiques,* exhibition catalogue, with texts by Francois Mathey and Pierre Restany, Paris 1970; *Cesar,* exhibitjon catalogue, with text by Pierre Restany, Milan 1970; *Cesar à Nice,* exhibition catalogue, with texts by Jacques Medecin and Daniele Giraudy, Nice 1972; *Cesar,* exhibition catalogue, with text by Daniele Giraudy, Marseilles 1972; *Cesar en Arles,* exhibition catalogue, with texts by Douglas Cooper, Arles, France 1973; *Tête à Tête,* exhibition catalogue, with text by Pierre Restany, Paris 1973; *Cesar: Compressions d'Or,* with text by J. Baldwin, Paris, 1973; *Cesar,* exhibition catalogue, with text by Janus, Turin 1974; *Cesar,* exhibition catalogue, with text by Pierre Restany, Milan 1974; *Cesar* by Pierre Restany, Munich and New York 1975; *Cesar: Retrospective des Sculptures,* exhibition catalogue, edited by Rainer Michaed Mason, Geneva 1976; *Cesar: Les Expansions,* exhibition catalogue, with text by Catherine Millet, Paris 1979; *Cesar,* exhibition catalogue, with text by Pierre Restany, Tokyo 1982; *Les Fers de Cesar,* exhibition catalogue, by Marie-Claude Beaud, Pierre Restany and Catherine Franchlin, Jouy en Josas, France 1984; *Cesar 1955–1985,* exhibition catalogue, Dunkerque 1985.

I would say that I am, above all, a man in love with art, and yet I can't explain what I do since one doesn't explain art. It's a question of feeling and sensibility. What I can explain are practical things: how to make a mould, what glue to use, different techniques. I am not an intellectual artist, but I create my own bit of culture. I have my own deep-rooted culture with respect to my experiences, to the life I have led, to the training I have undergone, to the work I have executed. People may identify me with "Compressions", but curiosity has led me to make other discoveries too, to use a whole variety of materials: leather, iron, steel, bronze, marble, crystal, polyurethane, gold . . . . But behind every material there's the same person at work. Each day one can start the same piece of work again and each day it can be different.

There's also the question of conviction: if you believe in it, you don't make a product, you're aiming at creating something. But what does create mean? Is one creative because one has a lot of imagination? Am I creative because I've compressed cars? People will tell me that I've got imagination, but sometimes it seems to me that I haven't got any at all. I think physically and I feel a physical need to sculpt. I'm not a person who can think abstractly, who can foresee or make plans. Circumstances, events, encounters with the material, 'accidents' sometimes make me look at my work differently. But then, nobody creates anything in fact! We simply receive the heritage of one person or another, of all those who were here before us. As far as I am concerned it's the work of, among others, Duchamp and Picasso which has enabled me to progress. I should add that sculpture today is a confused notion. Anything that occupies a place in space is called sculpture. But just because it's three-dimensional an object isn't necessarily a piece of statuary. I think of my compressions, for example, as objects and not as sculptures. I've simply quoted this example at random, but it brings us back to the sculptor/artist debate, for a sculptor isn't necessarily a creator of statuary and may in fact never reach that level. A sculptor may make a torso and if it reaches the level of statuary, that torso will be enough in itself, will need no explanation, no story. The work will exist like a piece of sculpture dug up in Greek soil. It may be a fragment of a human body, without head or legs. No one will ever know who made it or when, but it will have the evocative power of Greek sculpture. It will be useless to restore it or to attach a story to it. It exists and that is enough, whereas a section of my 'compressions', for example, cannot be elaborated on by being read about. My *Venus de Villetaneuse,* in contrast, even without a head lacks nothing, and nothing can be added to it. Even if my signature is removed, and even if it's mutilated by an earthquake, my *Centaure* will continue to exist. I disown nothing that I've done, I ask simply that my work be given several 'readings'.

—Cesar

Cesar is the sculptor's sculptor. After his long studies, like many of his fellows, he was forced into another activity in order to earn his living while continuing to pursue his art in his spare time as far as possible. Which was not very far, for materials were not only difficult to obtain, they were also expensive. His choice of ready-made scraps of metal that he welded together was forced on him by economic necessity, yet at the same time the method of construction had its provocative challenge. His early constructions of insects, animals and fish are rich in improvised invention and humorous in their juxtaposition of diverse parts. His unique combination of passionate and pawky styles developed from the consistent forming of elements into a work such as the

life size "Seated Nude" (1954) where the skeletal figure has a skin of emaciated iron strips.

By 1956 the sensitive modelling of the human prototype had made evident the underlying humanism of Cesar. It was humanism that not only showed itself of the tactile shaping of the torso, in the plastic tributes to birdman Leo Valentin, but also in the symbolic winged men and central figures against a background of facetted metal akin to the placing of a statue of a saint against a stained glass window in an old chapel. His use of screens lent mystic, almost religious, presence to universal imagery.

His temporary detour into the sphere of "compressions" when he enjoyed the new sensation of surface obtained by crushing cars in an hydraulic press was but one of his investigations into the possibilities available in the treatment of the ready-made. Its significance rested in this explosive moulding of the metal in an exciting exploratory system rather than arriving at an end product of sculptural finality; they represent milestones instead of wayside shrines built in celebration of life. The same could be said of his plastic works when the liquid hardens to its ultimate form in three minutes. Captivated by the accidental results possible, similar to Jackson Pollock's poured pigment, Cesar enjoyed the speed in which a form would arrive in brilliant colour. Plastic expansions like "The Thumb," as large as its creator, marked further steps in the continuous quest, though in retrospect some appear as self-indulgence. Cesar has defended their appearance as examples of automatic and subconscious gestalts.

For Cesar the 1960's were shadowed by personal setbacks, but his ebullient spirit was not to be subdued for long, and he returned to the fray with elan and resource. His reliefs of metal junk and scrap were full of quirky formal jokes like "Portrait of Patrick Waldberg" (1961). Some of the early welded figures were now translated in bronze casts that reflected in the sympathetic metal the rigidity and angularity of the movements of cocky chickens and poised insects. His self-identification and his commitment to material came through with characteristic vitality in the series of 30 masks in bright bronze he called "Tête à tête". Self-portraits: he shows himself in them as an actor of roles having their formal roots in art history from the Roman senatorial to the caricatural; by turns he is the clown, the tragic fate-doomed sufferer, yet each work has its thumbmark of mercurial, almost primitive, power. It is scarcely accidental that, of the race of Michelangelo and Donatello, Cesar also reflects in his sculpture much of the droll worldly humour of his birthplace: Marseilles.

—G. S. Whittet

CHADWICK, Lynn (Russell).

British. Born in London, 24 November 1914. Educated at schools in London; trained as an architectural draughtsman; mainly self-taught in art. Served as a pilot in the Fleet Air Arm, 1941–44. Married Charlotte Ann Secord in 1942; one son: Frances Mary Jamieson in 1959 (died, 1964): two daughters; Eva Reiner in 1965: one son. Sculptor since 1948: in private practice as architectural draughtsman, 1946; worked with the architect Rodney Thomas, 1947, settled in Upper Coberley, 1947; made first metal mobiles in the early 1950's; executed three works commissioned for the *Festival of Britain*, London, 1951; now lives and works in Gloucestershire. Recipient: Prize, International Competition for Unknown Political Prisoner, 1953; International Sculpture Prize, *Biennale*, Venice, 1956; First Prize, *Consorso Internazionale del Bronzetto*, Padua, 1959; Prize, *International Exhibition of Drawings and Engravings*, Lugano, Switzerland, 1960. C.B.E. (Commander, Order of the British Empire), 1964; Officier, Ordre des Arts et Lettres, France, 1986. Address: Lypiatt Park, Stroud, Gloucestershire, England.

Individual Exhibitions:

1950 Gimpel Fils, London
1952 Gimpel Fils, London
1956 *Biennale*, Venice (with Ivon Hitchens; toured Europe, 1956–57)
1957 Saidenberg Gallery, New York
Palais des Beaux-Arts, Brussels (travelled to the Arts Council Gallery, London)
1958 Galerie Daniel Cordier, Paris
1959 Galerie Charles Lienhard, Zurich
Galerie Daniel Cordier, Frankfurt
1960 Kestner-Gesellschaft, Hannover (with Kenneth Armitage)
1961 Marlborough Fine Art, London
Knoedler Galleries, New York
Bienal, Sao Paulo
1963 Forum Gallery, Bristol
Carborundum Company, New York
1964 Galerie Wilhelm Grosshennig, Dusseldorf
1965 Knoedler Galleries, New York
Sunsvall Museum, Hasten, Sweden
1966 Galerie Grosshennig, Dusseldorf
Marlborough Fine Art Gallery, London
Galerie Günther Franke, Munich
1968 Galerie Gerald Cramer, Geneva
Galleria Blu, Milan
Waddington Gallery, Montreal
Galerie d'Eendt, Amsterdam
1969 Dorsky Gallery, New York
Galerie Withofs, Brussels
1970 Galerie d'Eendt, Amsterdam
Court Gallery, Copenhagen
Galerie Blu, Stockholm
Louisiana Museum, Humlebaek, Denmark
1971 Dorsky Gallery, New York
Galerie Zodiac, Geneva
1972 Gallery Moos, Toronto
Galerie Zodiac, Geneva
Gloucester City Museum
Galleria Blu, Milan
Waddington Gallery, Montreal
1974 Marlborough Fine Art Gallery, London
Galerie Farber, Brussels
Marlborough Galerie, Zurich
Marlborough Galleria d'Arte, Rome
1975 Galleria Toninelli, Milan
Galleria Contacto, Caracas
Marlborough-Godard Gallery, Toronto
Hokin Gallery, Chicago
Wolpe Gallery, Cape Town
Goodman Gallery, Johannesburg
Court Gallery, Copenhagen
Galerie Carlssen, Gothenburg, Sweden
1976 Galerie d'Eendt, Amsterdam
Galerie Farber, Brussels
JPL Fine Arts, London
1978 Court Gallery, Copenhagen
Marlborough Fine Art, London (travelled to the Marlborough Galerie, Zurich)
1979 Galerie 99, Bay Harbor Island, Florida
Century Gallery, Henley-on-Thames, Oxfordshire
The Keys Gallery, Londonderry, Northern Ireland
Arts Council Gallery, Belfast
Galerie D'Eendt, Amsterdam
1980 Galerie Regards, Paris
Galerie Farber, Brussels
Waddington/Shell Galleries, Toronto
Fondation Veranneman, Kruishoutem, Belgium
1981 Galeria Freites, Caracas, Venezuela
Theo Waddington Galleries, Montreal
1982 Christie's Contemporary Art, New York (with Victor Pasmore)
1983 Mercury Gallery, Edinburgh
Gallery Ueda, Tokyo (with Victor Pasmore)
Galerie Herbage, Cannes, France
Artcurial, Paris
Margaret Fisher Gallery, London
1984 Theo Waddington Galleries, Montreal
Marlborough Fine Art, London

Selected Group Exhibitions:

1947 *Building Trades Exhibition*, London
1951 *International Open-Air Exhibition of Sculpture*, Bat-tersea Park, London
1952 *Biennale*, Venice
1955 *The New Decade*, Museum of Modern Art, New York
1958 *10 Young British Sculptures*, Museo de Arte Mo-derno, Rio de Janeiro
1962 *British Art Today*, San Francisco Museum of Art
1964 *Painting and Sculpture of a Decade 1954–1964*, Tate Gallery, London
1967 *Expo '67*, Montreal
1982 *Chadwick/Cuevas/Manzu/Matta/Moore*, Tasende Gallery, La Jolla, California
1983 *International Art Exposition*, Navy Pier, Chicago

Collections:

Tate Gallery, London; Victoria and Albert Museum, London; Musée Royaux des Beaux-Arts, Brussels; Middelheim Sculpture Park, Antwerp; Rijksmuseum Kröller-Müller, Otterlo, Netherlands; Centre Georges Pompidou, Paris; Kunsthaus, Zurich; Louisiana Museum, Humlebaek, Denmark; Museum of Modern Art, New York; Art Institute of Chicago.

Publications:

By CHADWICK: articles—"A Sculptor and His Public" in *The Listener* (London), October 1954; statement in *The New Decade*, exhibition catalogue, New York 1955.

On CHADWICK: books—*Contemporary Sculpture: An Evolution in Volume and Space* by Carola Giedion-Welcker, London 1956; *Lynn Chadwick*, exhibition catalogue, by Robert Melville, Venice 1956; *Lynn Chadwick* by Herbert Read, Amriswill, Switzerland 1960; *Sculpture of This Century: Present-Day Sculpture in Great Britain* by Michel Seuphor, London 1960; *Lynn Chadwick* by J. P. Hodin, Amsterdam and London 1961; *Lynn Chadwick* by Alan Bowness, London 1962; *Chadwick*, exhibition catalogue edited by Marlborough Fine Art, London 1984.

Lynn Chadwick was one of the prominent group of young British sculptors who were enthusiastically acclaimed, internationally, following the discovery that in Henry Moore Britain had produced a major sculptor. Like many artists of this generation, his studies and activities were delayed by war-time service, so that he was 36 years old before he held a one-man exhibition at Gimpel Fils. With Moore winning the Venice *Biennale* Sculpture Prize in 1948, the British Council promoted the younger generation, and in the group exhibition at the 1952 *Biennale* launched a large group of new sculptors, including Armitage, Butler, Paolozzi, Turnbull, on to exciting international careers. Chadwick was in some senses the most successful of them all, returning to Venice in 1956 to win the International Sculpture Prize. His exhibition was then toured throughout Europe, with Chadwick showing his work in the leading museums in Vienna, Munich, Paris, Amsterdam, Brussels, as well as in London. There followed important international contracts, and for the next ten years Chadwick's work continued to excite wide-spread attention.

It is, however, significant that in recent years he has rarely exhibited in London. His work, in fact, has shown little development. Like a number of modern sculptors, Chadwick's roots lie in architecture, and there is also reason to assume that his experience as a war-time pilot influenced his sculpture. Movement in space, the example of Calder, inspired his earliest efforts, and his work in defining space took on menacing, animalistic forms with spiky legs and antennae. Eventually more recognisable, though still aggressive, bird-like creatures emerged, and the bleak desperation of their stance seemed to symbolise the experience of war and its aftermath. Gradually the dramatic, worrying aspects of these forms were weakened in the employment of smoother surfaces and less aggressive extensions, and by the evolution of human

or animal forms less in conflict with themselves, or us.

Stylistic formulas of pyramid shapes or wingspans have now been reduced to anecdotal, almost sentimental symbols; seated couples, walking figures, or standing forms, reminiscent of the gentler imagery of his contemporary, Kenneth Armitage.

—Charles Spencer

CHAGALL, Marc.

Russian. Born Moisei Segal in Vitebsk, Russia, 7 July 1887. Studied privately with the painter Jehuda Pen, Vitebsk, 1906; studied at the Imperial School for the Protection of Arts, St. Petersburg, 1907, and privately with Saidenberg and Leon Bakst, St. Petersburg, 1908–09. Married Bella Rosenfeld in 1915 (died, 1944); daughter: Ida; married Vava Brodsky in 1957. Lived in St. Petersburg, 1907–10, returning frequently to Vitebsk; lived in Paris, 1910–13, St. Petersburg, 1915–17, and Vitebsk, 1918–29; Commissar for Art, Vitebsk, 1918; Founder Director, Vitebsk Academy, with El Lissitsky, Jean Pougny and Kasimir Malevich as members of staff, 1919–20 (resigned following quarrel with Suprematists); settled in Moscow, 1920, and created first stage designs for the Kameray State Jewish Theatre; lived in Berlin, 1922, then settled in Paris, 1923 until the Occupation, when he moved to New York: associated with Leger, Mondrian, Zadkine and other emigre artists in New York; lived in Sag Harbor and High Falls, New York, 1945–46; returned to France, 1948, and lived in Oregeval, Saint-Germaine-en-Laye; lived in St. Paul-de-Vence from 1950; visited Israel and worked on first sculptures, 1951; worked with the glass painter Charles Marq from 1957, and continued to work on designs for opera and ballet, murals, tapestries, and stained glass windows. Visiting Lecturer, University of Chicago, 1958. Recipient: Carnegie Prize, Pittsburgh, 1939; Erasmus Prize, with Oskar Kokoschka, Copenhagen, 1960. Honorary doctorate: University of Glasgow, 1959; Brandeis University, Waltham, Massachusetts, 1960; Notre Dame University, Indiana, 1965. Honorary Member, American Academy of Arts and Letters, 1959. Honorary Citizen, St. Paul-de-Vence, 1962; City of Jerusalem, 1977. Grand Cross of the Legion of Honour, France, 1977. *Died* (in Saint-Paul-de-Vence) *28 March 1985.*

Individual Exhibitions:

1914 Galerie der Sturm, Berlin
1924 Galerie Barbazange-Hodebert, Paris
Graphisches Kabinett, Munich (with Lyonel Feininger)
1926 Reinhart Galleries, New York
1928 Galerie Le Portique, Paris
1930 Galerie Bernheim-Jeune and Galerie Le Centaure, Paris
Galerie Flechtheim, Berlin
1932 Stedelijk Museum, Amsterdam
1933 Kunsthaus, Basle
1934 Galerie Dra Feigla, Prague
1935 Leicester Galleries, London
1938 Palais des Beaux-Arts, Brussels
Lilienfeld Galleries, New York
1940 Pierre Matisse Gallery, New York
1946 Museum of Modern Art, New York (travelled to the Art Institute of Chicago)
1947 Musée National d'Art Moderne, Paris
Pierre Matisse Gallery, New York
Stedelijk Museum, Amsterdam
1948 Tate Gallery, London
Pierre Matisse Gallery, New York
1949 Galerie Rosengart, Lucerne
1950 Galerie Maeght, Paris
Kunsthaus, Zurich
Kunsthalle, Berne
Galerie Samlaren, Stockholm
Israel Museum, Jerusalem (toured Israel)
1952 Curt Valentin Gallery, New York
Galerie des Ponchettes, Nice
Galerie Maeght, Paris
Galleria dell'Obelisco, Rome
1953 Museo Civico d'Arte Moderna, Turin
1954 Galerie Maeght, Paris
1955 Kestner Society, Hannover
1956 Kunsthalle, Basle
Kunsthalle, Berne
Stedelijk Museum, Amsterdam
1957 Palais des Beaux-Arts, Brussels
Kunstmuseum, Basle
Bibliothèque Nationale, Paris
Galerie Welz, Salzburg
Cercle Royal, Charleroi, Belgium (with Paul Delvaux)
Art Club, Hamburg
1959 Haus der Kunst, Munich
Musée des Arts Décoratifs, Paris
Staedel Institute of Art, Frankfurt
1960 Musée des Beaux-Arts, Reims, France
Grosvenor Gallery, London
1961 Casino Communal, Knokke-le-Zoute, Belgium
Galerie Klipstein und Kornfeld, Berne
O'Hana Gallery, London
Musée des Arts Décoratifs, Paris
1962 Musée Massena, Nice
Musée Rath, Geneva
Galerie Madoura, Cannes
1963 Museum of Western Art, Tokyo (travelled to the Municipal Museum, Kyoto)
Musée des Beaux-Arts, Rouen
1965 Israel Museum, Jerusalem
1967 Kunsthaus, Zurich
Musée du Louvre, Paris
Fondation Maeght, St. Paul-de-Vence, France
Kunsthalle, Cologne
Musée des Augustins, Toulouse
Galerie Rosengart, Lucerne
1968 Pierre Matisse Gallery, New York
1969 *Hommage à Marc Chagall,* Grand Palais, Paris
1971 Galerie Maeght, Zurich
1972 Galerie Rosengart, Lucerne
1973 Los Angeles County Museum of Art
Pierre Matisse Gallery, New York
1975 Guggenheim Museum, New York
Pierre Matisse Gallery, New York
1976 National Museum of Modern Art, Tokyo (toured Japan)
1977 Musée du Louvre, Paris
Pierre Matisse Gallery, New York
1978 Palazzo Pitti, Florence
Museum of Modern Art, New York
Haus der Kunst, Munich
1979 Pierre Matisse Gallery, New York
1980 Musée Rath, Geneva
Redfern Gallery, London
Galerie Matignon, Paris
Galerie Maeght, Paris
Galerie Maeght, Zurich
1982 Moderna Museet, Stockholm
Galerie Patrick Cramer, Geneva
Pierre Matisse Gallery, New York
1984 Fondation Maeght, St. Paul de Vence, France
Centre Georges Pompidou, Paris
Museo Capitolino, Rome
Musee National Message Biblique Marc Chagall, Nice, France
1985 Royal Academy of Art, London
Kestner-Gesellschaft, Hannover
Philadelphia Museum of Art, Pennsylvania
1987 Jewish Museum, New York

Selected Group Exhibitions:

1912 *Salon des Independants,* Paris
1915 *Year 1915,* Salon d'Art de Michailova, Moscow
1916 *Knave of Diamonds,* Moscow
1917 *Exposition de Peintures et Sculptures d'Artistes Juifs,* Galerie Lemercier, Moscow
1948 *Biennale,* Venice
1958 *Pittsburgh International,* Carnegie Institute, Pittsburgh
1970 *Russian Art of the Revolution,* Andrew Dickson White Museum of Art, Cornell University, Ithaca, New York (travelled to the Brooklyn Museum, New York)
1971 *The Russian Avant-Garde,* Leonard Hutton Galleries, New York
1977 *40 Modern Masters,* Guggenheim Museum, New York
1982 *Guggenheim, Venezia/New York: 60 Opere 1900–1950,* Pinacoteca Capitolina in Campidoglio, Rome and the Guggenheim Museum, New York

Collections:

Centre Georges Pompidou, Paris; Musée de Peinture et Sculpture, Grenoble, France; Kunstmuseum, Basle; Nationalgalerie, Berlin; Wallraf-Richartz Museum, Cologne; Russian Museum, Leningrad; Tel Aviv Museum, Israel; Guggenheim Museum, New York; Museum of Modern Art, New York; Los Angeles County Museum of Art.

Principal commissions: stained glass windows, Metz Cathedral, France, 1960; synagogue of the Hadassah Medical Centre, Jerusalem, 1962; ceiling, Paris Opera House, 1964; murals/facade, Metropolitan Opera House, New York, 1965.

Publications:

By CHAGALL: books—*Marc Chagall: My Life,* Paris, 1957; *Chagall,* edited by Charles Sorlier, London 1979; illustrated books—*Dead Souls* by Gogol, 1925; *The Fables of La Fontaine,* 1931; *Arabian Nights,* 1948; *Daphnis and Chloe,* 1977; etc.; articles—"Reflections on Art" in *Witebskvi Listok* (Vitebsk, Russia), January 1919; "The Revolution in Art" in *Revoluzionnoje Iskustwo* (Vitebsk, Russia), no. 1, 1919; "Reflections on the People's Fine Arts Academy, Vitebsk" in *Schkola Revoluzia* (Vitebsk, Russia), August 1919; "Chez Marc Chagall," interview, with Georges Charensol, in *Paris-Journal,* May 1924; "Marc Chagall," interview, with Jacques Guenne in *L'Art Vivant* (Paris), December 1927; "My Work in the Jewish Theatre of Moscow" in *Di Idiscze Welt* (Vilna, Poland), 1938; "Delacroix" in *L'Intransigeant* (Paris), June 1930; "Marc Chagall," interview, with Pierre Courthion, in *Les Nouvelles Litteraires,* (Paris), April 1932; "Pouvez-vouz dire quelle est la Rencontre Capitale de Votre Vie?" in *Minotaure* (Paris), nos. 3–4, 1933; "Sur l'Art Aujourd'hui" in *Cahiers d'Art* (Paris), nos. 1–4, 1935; "Interview with Marc Chagall," with Raymond Abel, in *The League* (New York), April 1942; "In Honor of Jacques Maritain" in *Jewish Frontier* (New York), February 1943; "Message aux Peintres Francais" in *Le Spectateur des Arts* (Paris), December 1944; "An Interview with Marc Chagall," with James Johnson Sweeney, in *Partisan Review* (New York), Winter 1944; "Quelques Impressions sur la Peinture Francais" in *Renaissance Revue Trimestrielle des Hautes Etudes de New York,* vols. 2 and 3, 194–45; "L'Art de la Recitude et de la Clarte" in *Naje Lehn* (New York), June 1945; preface to *Di Ershte Bagegenish* by Bella Chagall, New York 1947; "Letter to S. Rosengart" in *Chagall,* exhibition catalogue, Lucerne 1949; "5 Poems" in *Di Goldene Keyt,* Tel Aviv 1951; "Visite á Chagall," interview, with Gisele d'Assailly, in *Le Figaro Litteraire* (Paris), March 1952; "Hommage à Matisse" in the *Yale Library Magazine* (New Haven, Connecticut), 1955.

On CHAGALL: books: *La Fontaine par Chagall,* exhibition catalogue, by Ambroise Vollard, Paris, 1930; *Chagall et l'Ame Juive,* Paris 1930; *Marc Chagall* by Raissa Maritain, New York, 1943; *Marc Chagall* by Lionello Venturi, New York 1945; *Chagall: Paintings* by Leon Degand and Paul Eluard, London 1947; *Chagall; ou L'Orage Enchante,* Geneva 1948; *Chagall* by Michael Ayrton, London 1950; *Marc Chagall: His Life and Work* by J. Kloomok, New York 1951; *Marc Chagall* by Jacques Lassaigne, Geneva 1952; *Chagall: A Biographical and Critical Study* by Lionello Venturi, Geneva 1956; *The Jerusalem Windows by Marc Chagall* by Jean Laymarie, New York 1962; *Chagall* by Jean Cassou, London 1965; *The World of Chagall* by Izis and Roy McMullen, New York 1968; *Hommage à Marc Chagall,* exhibition catalogue, by Jean Leymarie, Paris 1969; *Marc Chagall,* 4 vols., Monte Carlo and Boston 1969–74; *The Lithographs of Chagall 1962–68* by Fernand Moulot and Charles Sorlier, Boston 1969; *The Ceramics and Sculptures of Chagall* by André Malraux and others, Monaco 1972; *Marc Chagall* by Werner Haftmann, New York 1972; *Marc Chagall: Life and Work* by Horst Keller, New York 1978; *Marc Chagall* by Ernest Raboff, London 1980; *Marc Chagall: Arbeiten auf Papier,* exhibition catalogue edited by the Kestner-Gesellschaft, Hannover

Marc Chagall: *I and the Village*, c. 1925 Courtesy Guggenheim Museum, New York

1985; *Chagall* by Francois le Targat, Barcelona 1985, London 1987; *Marc Chagall: Druckgraphik*, Mainz 1986; *Chagall and the Bible* by Jean Bloch Rosensaft, New York 1987.

"I don't understand them at all," Chagall is claimed to have once said about his paintings; "they are not literature. They are only pictorial arrangements of images that obsess me . . . ."

He began making drawings when he was 13. It was an enthusiasm he was never to lose. What he tried to paint in Vitebsk before he left for his first visit to Paris was part the outcome of this love of making pictures, part the abortive results from attempts to become an art student in St. Petersburg. Yet those early paintings and those he made in the years following and leading up to the outbreak of the Second World War are the essence of the great Chagall, sometime cubist, pre-surrealist and restorer of the figurative image to a respected place in art appreciation between the two wars. All the elements of his best work came out of this period and, if they have been repeated since, the quality of those painted before 1940 has never been surpassed.

The big projects since the war—the Jerusalem windows or the redecoration of the Paris Opera House cannot compare with the great Chagalls like "Portrait of My Fiancee in Black Gloves" (1910), "The Poet" (1911), "I and the Village" (1911), "Paris Through the Window" (1913), the Rabbi paintings of 1914 (and 1933!), the 1917 "Promenade" still in the State Russian Museum in Leningrad, and "Lovers in the Flowers" (1931), to make only a random selection.

And during those 30 years Chagall's work was constantly developing. Quickly losing the hint of perspective he had had before leaving Vitebsk for the first time, he let the picture veer towards a kind of flatness which was not to be disturbed until he became involved with his own personal version of cubism. Altitude and distance had, in any case, never perturbed him very much. It was no chance that his fiddler sat on the roof in his earliest painting ("La Mort," 1908). And since then there have been many eccentricities to be observed in the early self-portrait with so many fingers, the train proceeding along upside down past the Eiffel Tower in "Paris Through the Window," the cow that plays the violin and the man who *is* a violin . . . .

Bright colours enflame all these visions, especially the keepsake moments, pictures of Vitebsk, or of a Vitebsk that once was. The cluttered Jewish upbringing permeates so much of the imagery, although Chagall went on to add the New Testament to his original repertoire.

Gravity is just a scientific whim. Perspective may have returned in pictures like "Time Is a River Without Banks" (1930–39), but this does not prevent the fish equipped with a practical pair of wings from perching on a pendulum clock whose top and bottom are identical and whose pendulum, in any case, has its swinging circle attached at each end of the rod—the clock is in mid-air anyway.

Time is a River without Banks? Did Chagall find the riverside after 1940? Perhaps his lexicon of images was by then complete. The colours might get prettier. Instead of bright lights, candyfloss.

—Sheldon Williams

CHAMBERLAIN, John (Angus).
American. Born in Rochester, Indiana, 16 April 1927. Studied at the Art Institute of Chicago, 1950–52; University of Illinois; and Black Mountain College, North Carolina, 1955–56. Independent artist, New York and Florida. First works used crushed automobile motor and body parts, 1957–63; moved next to painting, urethane, galvanized metals and later plexiglass. Recipient: Guggenheim Fellowship, 1966, 1977; Art in Architecture Award, United States General Services Administration, 1978. Agent: Xavier Fourcade Inc., 36 East 75th Street, New York, New York 10021. Address: Ten Coconut Inc., 1315 Tenth Street, Sarasota, Florida 33577, U.S.A.

Individual Exhibitions:

1957	Wells Street Gallery, Chicago
1958	Davida Gallery, Chicago
1960	Martha Jackson Gallery, New York
1962	Leo Castelli Gallery, New York (with Frank Stella)
	Dilexi Gallery, Los Angeles
	Dilexi Gallery, San Francisco
1963	Robert Fraser Gallery, London (with Richard Stankiewicz)
1964	Leo Castelli Gallery, New York
	Galerie Ileana Sonnabend, Paris
	Pace Gallery, Boston
1965	Leo Castelli Gallery, New York
1966	Dwan Gallery, Los Angeles
1967	Cleveland Museum of Art
	Galerie Rudolf Zwirner, Cologne
1968	Contemporary Arts Center, Cincinnati
1969	Leo Castelli Warehouse, New York
	Mizuno Gallery, Los Angeles
1970	Lo Giudice Gallery, Chicago
	Locksley-Shea Gallery, Minneapolis
1971	Leo Castelli Gallery, New York
	Guggenheim Museum, New York
1972	Taft Museum, Cincinnati, Ohi (with Peter Alexander)
1973	Leo Castelli Gallery, New York
	Dag Hammarskjolk Sculpture Plaza, New York
1974	Walter Kelly Gallery, Chicago
1975	Contemporary Art Center, Houston
	Ronald Greenberg Gallery, St. Louis
	Locksley-Shea Gallery, Minneapolis (with Cy Twombly)
	Minneapolis Institute of Art
1976	Leo Castelli Gallery, New York

1977 Margo Leavin Gallery, Los Angeles
Dia Art Foundation Installation, Ward's Island, New York
Heiner Freidrich Gallery, New York
1979 Kunsthalle, Berne
Galerie Heiner Friedrich, Cologne
1980 Van Abbemuseum, Eindhoven, Netherlands
1982 Leo Castelli Gallery, New York
1983 Ringling Museum of Art, Sarasota, Florida
Butler Institute of American Art, Youngstown, Ohio
Robert L. Kidd Galleries, Birmingham, Michigan
Dia Art Foundation, New York
Multiples/Marian Goodman Gallery, New York
L.A. Louver Gallery, Los Angeles
1984 Palacio de Cristal, Madrid
Xavier Fourcade Inc., New York
Marian Goodman Gallery, New York
University of California, Santa Barbara (with Alan Saret)
1985 Margo Leavin Gallery, Los Angeles
1986 Galerie Fred Jahn, Munich (travelled to Cologne and New York)
Museum of Contemporary Art, Los Angeles
1987 Xavier Fourcade Inc., New York
Galerie 10, Munich
Fabian Carlsson Gallery, London
Fruit Market Gallery, Edinburgh
De Menil Foundation, Houston, Texas
Albright Knox Art Gallery, Buffalo, New York

Selected Group Exhibitions:

1959 *Recent Sculpture: USA,* Museum of Modern Art, New York
1964 *Painting and Sculpture of a Decade,* Tate Gallery, London
1969 *New Media: New Methods,* Museum of Modern Art, New York
1973 *Whitney Biennial: Painting and Sculpture,* Whitney Museum, New York
1975 *Painting, Drawing, and Sculpture of the 60's and 70's from the Collection of Dorothy and Herbert Vogel,* The Clocktower, New York (toured the United States)
1978 *Art About Art,* Whitney Museum, New York (toured the United States)
1980 *Sculpture on The Wall: Relief Sculpture of the 70's.* Fine Arts Center, University of Massachusetts, Amherst
1982 *Documenta 7,* Museum Fridericianum, Kassel, West Germany
1984 *Indiana Influence,* Fort Wayne Museum of Art, Indiana
1986 *American Renaissance,* Fort Lauderdale Museum of Art, Florida

Collections:

Museum of Modern Art, New York; Whitney Museum, New York; Guggenheim Museum, New York; Albright-Knox Art Gallery, Buffalo, New York; Hirshhorn Museum, Washington, D.C.; Dallas Museum of Fine Arts; Fort Worth Museum, Texas; Los Angeles County Museum; Pasadena Art Museum, California; Gallery of Modern Art, Rome; Moderna Museet, Stockholm.

Publications:

By CHAMBERLAIN: articles—"Conversation Between Elizabeth C. Baker, John Chamberlain, Donn Judd and Diane Waldman," (excerpts) in *John Chamberlain,* exhibition catalogue, New York 1971; "Interview with John Chamberlain," by Phyllis Tuchman, in *Artforum* (New York), January 1972; "An Interview with John Chamberlain", with Michael Auping, in *Art Papers* (Atlanta, Georgia), January/February 1983; films—*Wedding Night,* 1967; *The Secret Life of Hernando Cortez,* 1968; *Wide Point,* 1968; *Thumbsuck,* 1971.

On CHAMBERLAIN: books—*The New Art Scene* by Alan Soloman and Ugo Mulas, New York 1967; *A Report on the Art and Technology Program of the Los Angeles County Museum of Art 1967–1971* by Maurice Tuchmann, Los Angeles 1971; *John Chamberlain: A Retrospective Exhibition,* exhibition catalogue, by Diane Waldman, New York 1971; *John Chamberlain,* exhibition catalogue, by Johannes Gachnang and R. H. Fuchs, Berne 1979; *John Chamberlain: A Catalogue Raisonne of the Sculpture, 1954–1985* by Julie Sylvester, New York and Los Angeles 1986; *Structure to Resemblance* by Michael Auping, New York 1987; *Sculpture: John Chamberlain 1970s and 1980s* by Walter Hopps, Houston 1987; articles—"Chamberlain: Another View" by Brian O'Doherty and "How To Look at John Chamberlain's Sculpture" by Barbara Rose in *Art International* (Lugano), January 1964; "John Chamberlain" by Robert Creely in *Recent American Sculpture,* exhibition catalogue, New York 1964; "A New Medium for John Chamberlain" by Phillip Leider in *Artforum* (New York), February 1967; "The Secret Life of John Chamberlain" by Elizabeth C. Baker in *Art News* (New York), April 1969; "The Vicissitudes of Sculpture" by Peter Schjeldahl in the *New York Times,* February 1969; "Fashions in Living: John Chamberlain's Environments" in *Vogue* (New York), April 1970; "John Chamberlain's Sculptures" by John Canaday in the *New York Times,* April 1971; "The Chamberlain Crunch" by Elizabeth C. Baker in *Art News* (New York), February 1972; "An Important Sculpture by John Chamberlain" by E. B. Henning in *Bulletin of The Cleveland Museum of Art,* October 1973; "Die Schönheit liegt im Auge des Betrachters," by Jürg Federspeil in *Tages-Anzeiger Magazin* (Zurich), 20 May 1978; "Berichteiner Reise" by Johannes Gachnang in *Kunst-Bulletin* (Berne), April 1979; "In the Heart of the Tinman: an essay on John Chamberlain" by Duncan Smith in *Artforum* (New York), January 1984; "His Sculpture Transforms Scrap into Steel Poems" by John Russell in the *New York Times,* 17 August 1986.

Towards the end of the 1950's John Chamberlain exhibited sculptures fashioned largely from steel pipes and noticeably under the influence of David Smith. He next used bent and welded metal sheets from old discarded automobiles. In the 1960's he found his place within the ambit of the movement for which the critic Lawrence Alloway coined the term "Junk art." In order to avoid any suggestion of deliberate craftsmanship the artists in this movement drew their materials from demolition yards, junk piles and refuse tips of urban waste. In this they followed a trend which had its origins in the "hautes pâtes" of Dubuffet and was exemplified in the "combines" of Robert Rauschenberg. Within this aesthetic context Chamberlain, like the Italian artist César, made his specialty polychrome "sculptures" from crushed automobile bodies.

Analogies are often made between the techniques of "Junk" sculpture, those of Chamberlain in particular, and the free brushstrokes of Willem de Kooning. But there is a world of difference between the apparently random but controlled effects of Action Painting and the deliberate randomization of Richard Stankiewicz and Chamberlain.

Much has been written, too, about the social and philosophical implications of putting to aesthetic use the discarded materials and scrap of modern urban civilisation. But the interest of Chamberlain himself was usually in the formal qualities of his finished work rather than in any implicit social comment. Although the element of serendipity inevitably features largely in an art which relies on mechanical crushing, Chamberlain in most of his works allowed suggestions from the shapes of his metal sheets to guide the composition and structure of his work. This is evident in such pieces as "Sweet William" (1962). About the mid-1950s Chamberlain also began to use new and brightly painted pieces of automobiles brand new from the factory. Later he worked with such materials as urethane, transparent plastic and fibreglass, moving on to galvanized steel and aluminium. Examples in these techniques are "Héng" (1967, urethane) and "Tippecanoe" (1967, galvanized steel and aluminium).

—Harold Osborne

CHARLTON, Alan.

British. Born in Sheffield, Yorkshire, 26 February 1948. Studied at the Sheffield School of Art, 1965–66, Camberwell School of Art, London, 1966–69, and the Royal Academy Schools, London, 1969–72. Married in 1966. Painter: lives and works in London. Agent: Konrad Fischer, Dusseldorf. Address: c/o Konrad Fischer, Platanenstrasse 7, 4 Dusseldorf, West Germany.

Individual Exhibitions:

1972 Galerie Konrad Fischer, Dusseldorf
Nigel Greenwood Inc., London
Whitechapel Art Gallery, London
1973 Galerie Konrad Fischer, Dusseldorf
Nigel Greenwood Inc., London
1974 Galleria Gian Enzo Sperone, Turin
Sperone-Fischer Gallery, Rome
Art and Project, Amsterdam
1975 Galerie Konrad Fischer, Dusseldorf
Galerie Bischofberger, Zurich
Museum of Modern Art, Oxford (travelled to the Stedelijk van Abbemuseum, Eindhoven, Netherlands, 1976)
1976 Leo Castelli Gallery, New York
1981 Lisson Gallery, London
1982 Stedelijk van Abbemuseum, Eindhoven, Netherlands
1985 John Hansard Gallery, Southampton, Hampshire
1988 Victoria Miro Gallery, London

Selected Group Exhibitions:

1972 *Drawings,* Museum of Modern Art, Oxford
1973 *7 aus London,* Kunsthalle, Berne
Prospekt 73, Kunsthalle, Dusseldorf
Exposition de Peinture Reunissant Certains Peintres qui Mettraient la Peinture en Question, Place Vendome, Paris (toured Europe)
1974 *Painting Exhibition,* Scottish Arts Council Gallery, Edinburgh
1975 *Fundamental Paintings,* Stedelijk Museum Amsterdam
1977 *Group Exhibition,* Lisson Gallery, New York
1982 *Documenta,* Kassel, West Germany

Collections:

Arts Council of Great Britain, London; Stedelijk Museum, Amsterdam.

Publications:

On CHARLTON: book—*Alan Charlton,* exhibition catalogue, Eindhoven, Netherlands 1982; *Alan Charlton,* exhibition catalogue edited by the John Hansard Gallery, Southampton 1985; articles—"Alan Charlton" by Lynda Morris in *Art Press* (Paris), July/August 1973; "European Cool Paiting" by Germano Celant in *Domus* (Milan), October 1973; "Alan Charlton" by H. Einzig in *Arts Review* (London), July 1981.

Curiously, the uniform monochrome painting appeared in caricatures of modern art before the 1914 war, some years before it appeared in art itself with Rodchenko in 1918. However, the evolving traditions of art resurrected this form of the medium in the late 1950's with Klein and Manzoni, later, for quite different reasons, Ryman and Marden.

The problem of a painting which is to be abstract to the point of eliminating any illusion whatever is to put a second colour, layer, or texture on any part of the surface. The reductionist tendency of art must lead to this crux.

Alan Charlton's painting has been monochrome, but it is not reductive in this way. His works have consisted now for many years of canvases painted uniformly grey. The precise shade of grey varies from work to work and may relate to the scale and configuration of the work. Very often rectilinear slots appear in the canvas, lined with a separate stretcher corres-

ponding in depth to the main stretcher, which is about two inches deep—that is, deep enough to give the canvas the air of being an object. It is also deep enough to produce a distinct shadow on the wall in normal conditions of lighting. Canvases may be adjoined, or arranged in such a way that they form an overall configuration which includes the wall space between them. In certain cases a slot may form a complete margin in a canvas so that an island canvas remains in the centre. In each case the treatment of the inner and outer returns of the canvas over the stretcher are the same, so that the enclosure of an inner space implies the exclusion of the outer wall space. I hope it will not appear a paradox if I assert that this has the effect of comprising the outer space in the definition of the work just as the sea around it is necessary to define an island.

This discrimination deals with the formal characteristics of Charlton's work, but his is not a purely formal art—it is not tautological, like that of Lewitt or Andre, for example. It seems rather to be an art of feeling—closer in spirit to that of Rothko.

Charlton's painting, like the art of several of his contemporaries, has been much more highly estimated in continental Europe and the United States than in Britain.

—Michael Compton

CHIA, Sandro.
Italian. Born in Florence, 20 April 1946. Studied at the Accademia di Belle Arti, Florence, 1965–69. Divorced: has 2 children. Independent painter, in Ronciglione, near Rome, 1970–85, in New York since 1980, and in Montalcino, near Siena since 1985; worked in Monchengladbach, West Germany, 1980–81. Agent: Galerie Daniel Templon, 30 rue Beaubourg, 75003 Paris, France. Addresses: Castello Romitorio, Montalcino, Siena, Italy; 521 West 23rd Street, 9th floor, New York, New York 10011, U.S.A.

Individual Exhibitions:

1971	Galleria La Salita, Rome (and 1972, 1973, 1975)
1975	Galleria Lucrezia de Domizio, Pescara, Italy
	Galleria L'Attico, Rome
1976	Galleria Paolo Marinucci / Tucci Russo, Turin
	Galleria La Salita, Rome (and 1977)
1977	Galleriaforma, Genoa, Italy
	Galleria Gian Enzo Sperone, Rome
1978	Galleria dell'Oca, Rome
	Galleria Guiliana de Crescenzo, Rome
	Studio Antonio Tucci Russo, Turin
	Framart Studio, Naples
	Galerie Paul Maenz, Cologne (and 1979)
1979	Galleria Mario Diacono, Bologna, Italy
	Galleria Gian Enzo Sperone, Rome
1980	Art and Project, Amsterdam
	Galerie Paul Maenz, Cologne
	Sperone Westwater Fischer, New York (and 1981)
1981	Galerie Bruno Bischofberger, Zurich
	Galleria Mario Diacono, Rome
	Anthony D'Offay / Gian Enzo Sperone, London
1982	James Corcoran Gallery, Los Angeles
	Sperone Westwater, New York
1983	Stedelijk Museum, Amsterdam
	Galleria Mario Diacono, Rome
	Leo Castelli Gallery, New York
	Palazzo Grassi, Venice
	Galerie Bruno Bischofberger, Zurich
	Fruitmarket Gallery, Edinburgh
	Galerie Daniel Templon, Paris
	Galerie Natalie Seroussi, Paris
	Galleri Five, Stockholm
	Galerie Silvia Menzel, West Berlin
	Stadtische Museum, Monchengladbach, West Germany
	Kestner-Gesellschaft, Hannover
1984	Staatliche Kunsthalle, West Berlin
	Musée d'Art Moderne de la Ville, Paris
	Mathildenhohe, Darmstadt, West Germany
	Kunstverein, Dusseldorf
	Akira Ikeda Gallery, Tokyo
	Metropolitan Museum of Art, New York
	Galerie Schellmann und Kluser, Munich
	Galerie Daniel Templon, Paris
	Galleria Sima, Venice
	Museum des 20. Jahrhunderts, Vienna
	Galerie Ascan Crone, Hamburg
	James Corcoran Gallery, Los Angeles
1985	Galerie Michael Haas, West Berlin
	Leo Castelli Gallery, New York
	Galerie Bruno Bischofberger, Zurich
	Galerie Thaddaus Ropac, Salzburg, Austria
1986	Staatsgalerie moderne Kunst, Munich
	Akira Ikeda Gallery, Tokyo
	Kunsthalle, Bielefeld, West Germany
1987	Akira Ikeda Gallery, Tokyo
	Sperone Westwater, New York
	Fischer Fine Art, London
1988	Galerie Daniel Templon, Paris
	Sperone Westwater, New York

Selected Group Exhibitions:

1977	*10e. Biennale de Paris*, Musée d'Art Moderne de la Ville, Paris
1979	*XV Bienal de Sao Paulo*, Brazil
1980	*The Cut-Off Hand*, Kunstverein, Bonn (travelled to Wolfsburg and Groningen)
1981	*A New Spirit in Painting*, Royal Academy of Arts, London
1982	*Aspects of Italian Art Now*, Guggenheim Museum, New York
1983	*La Transavanguardia*, Caja de Pensiones, Madrid
1984	*Six in Bronze*, Williams College, Williamstown, Massachusetts
1985	*700 Eichen*, Kunsthalle, Tubingen, West Germany (travelled to Bielefeld)
1986	*40 Ans: Une Generation Mondiale*, Palais de l'UNESCO, Paris

Collections:

Museum of Modern Art, New York; Guggenheim Museum, New York; Hirshhorn Museum, Washington, D.C.; Tate Gallery, London; National Gallery of Scotland, Edinburgh; Stadtisches Museum, Monchengladbach; Kunsthalle, Bielefeld; Stedelijk Museum, Amsterdam; Groninger Museum, Groningen; Musée d'Art Moderne / Centre Georges Pompidou, Paris.

Publications:

By CHIA: book—*Monchengladbach Journal*, with afterword by Johannes Cladders, Monchengladbach 1983.

On CHIA: books—*La Transavantgarde Italienne* by Achille Bonito Oliva, Milan 1980; *The Draught of Dr. Jekyll: An Essay on the Work of Sandro Chia* by Anne Seymour, London 1981; *Sandro Chia / Enzo Cucchi: Scultura Andata / Scultura Storna*, edited by Emilio Mazzoli, Modena 1982; *Sandro Chia*, exhibition catalogue with introduction by Carter Ratcliff, Edinburgh 1983; *Sandro Chia*, exhibition catalogue edited by Edy de Wilde and Alexander von Gravenstein, Amsterdam 1983; *Sandro Chia: Bilder 1976–1983*, exhibition catalogue with texts by Henry Geldzahler, Carl Haenlein and Anne Seymour, Hannover 1983; *Sandro Chia: New Paintings*, exhibition catalogue edited by Akira Ikeda Gallery, Tokyo 1984; *Sandro Chia*, exhibition catalogue with text by Heiner Bastian, Salzburg 1985.

Sometimes I ask myself which artists of the past have had an influence on my work and the answer that comes to mind is that any true artist would have to make his own the theoretical revolutionary statement from the beginning of this century: "It is necessary to burn the museums".

In fact the artist must not for anything in the world lose his sense of this spirit of revolt and of freedom because it is the essence of art. Free of all restriction and submission the artist participates in the conquest of this lost universe. Since the time when a man's skin ceased to be his limit, the soul has never again been the prisoner of death nor has beauty of aesthetics.

Even though today the museums are asking for nothing but to be "burned", and the spreading of freedom constitutes a new order, without the realization of the great alchemical or artistic dream coming true, it is imperative that the artist consider in a more subtle and sophisticated manner the concept of ancestry, the concept of autonomy and the concept of rebellion if he wants to be something other than the ape of modernity. In these years of intensive work, of torment and of joy, I have learned the truth of some things in metaphysics and in physics which I could also call "the passion for art".

Every man has two kinds of memory: the exterior memory of the things of the world and the interior memory of the things of the spirit, but the spirit is not, and even less are the angels, capable of seeing the world with their own eyes. If one really wants to know the reason for those eyes in spiral form on the face of the sculpture, the answer is that if works of art are not the eyes of the spirit and of the angels, at least they are their eyeglasses! The angel, a free thinking artist, looks, remembers and learns through the spectacles of art, but art, which has never been an objective instrument, obsessively weaves itself into civil, moran and strategic thinking. It is the struggle between the eyes and the head: the eyes are the superior party for looking at this civilization of the head, which the more it advances the more it deteriorates. There is a given definition of rebellion against which the angel rebels. Let us listen to his song in peace and avoid the damnation of prejudice: the soul of the whole world will reap the profit.

I think about what kind of thing art really is, and time stands still and slowly turns backwards. Yesterday Joseph Beuys died. Twenty-five years ago I decided in the glory of one night to consecrate my life to painting and to art. Meanwhile the enigmatic faces of a hundred artists are emerging from the density of time. They are a group of men fleeing from conventional history in order to attempt another way, and however much the world strives to capture them, they are beacons, they are lights, they are something which can in no way be completely hidden. To be born and to die are the same thing, to merge and to separate are the same thing, but man was not made to bear the burden of being bound for a long time without suffering or losing heart. The passion for art is identical with the passion for separation, for difference and for divorce, and if necessary I am aware that I must also be ready to divorce myself from the conventions of this contemporary art.

We were made for the plough, for hunting, for music, and for God, and instead we find ourselves with a pile of photographs in our hands, and a mistaken idea of success insists on wanting to govern us. Conscious neither of having received from nature, nor of having subsequently acquired any superior quality, I have only the love of art, and on this absolute premise, I have believed it legitimate to negotiate my existence with my contemporaries, but I have never lied, nor have I ever sought to spare myself by choosing the easiest way.

Nevertheless, it is as if I had forgotten to do something important, like killing the pig which is inside me and which dictates to me certain actions, certain formal solutions. Experience alone will teach me if my complex testimony is anything other than the dominance of mind over matter or of matter over sensuality or of sensuality over logic. Anyway one thing is certain, art can probably do without the beautiful, but not without the sublime.

This coming April twentieth I will be forty years old and in pain I would be able to write a treatise on how to break up friendships, to offend those one holds dear and perhaps to be ruined. After all, what was to be expected from someone who educated himself by reading the life of Cellini. But that is not suffi-

Sandro Chia: ***The Pharmacist's Son*****, 1981**

cient, and does not explain for example this real pain provoked by something only a phantom.

It is clear that the voices which come from the world—be they those of censure or of praise—proceeding from either friendship or enmity, are phantoms. Sometimes these phantoms have the power to cause real suffering: An unbearable inhuman suffering, which lacerates the soul to its depths and devours the body with remorse. One decides then to change, but not even the will seems to have the power to break the stone of which we are made. If to understand, to repent, to suffer, to lose, is of absolutely no use and does not teach anything, so be it!

—Sandro Chia

In the first half of the 1980s, the Italian transavantgarde formed and imposed a style and taste on an entire epoch. It was the vital energy of this explosive pictorial figuration that was responsible for the outpouring of expressionism that rapidly spread and became an international style. Its success is based on the fact that the transavantgarde corresponds to a current need—the necessity to reconsider traditional ways of making art and to posit questions centred on disquiet.

Sandro Chia has taken radical steps within this movement. Arising from his experience related to concept and performance art and reminiscent of precedents set by Merz and Kounellis, around 1978 Chia turned to the pictorial, to design and sculpture of a rigorous figuration. His figuration, however, is not that of the Realists. Any conflict between realism and abstraction in his pictures dissolves. In no way does Chia share any ideological element forming the cornerstone of that Realism whose role is to re-present the 'real'. Chia operates with an awareness that the picture is a system of self-referential signs which find their own truth in their own reality. He is particularly concerned to accentuate this character of *hortus conclusus* pertinent to the picture, while dismantling the idea of an external reality. The picture is the language of its history.

Chia's work adopts the role of "citationist": that is, the work is the fruit of a reflection on the pictures of the past. These he reads with a freely elective affinity and sentiment—an approach to the history of painting which is, of consequence, a purely ideological project. The explicit citation or quotation is evident only in rare cases—for example in *Bar Tintoretto* and *Natura Morta*, both of 1981. In the first picture, Chia reproduces not only the dominant chromatic green (precisely recording the Tintoretto original), the broken line and the fiery reds of the enflamed clouds which hang suspended above two mysterious figures in the foreground, but is also similar to certain features of Boccioni. In the distance, however, Chia has painted sketchy, agitated silhouettes which are inevitably associated with the dynamic dynamic figures of *Rissa in galleria*. In the second picture, quotation from Morandi is more openly declared, although the original lacks Chia's warm and enveloping light. In general, while Chia often retains a dynamic rhythm of broken and whirling Futurist marks, he does so without deconstructing the composition. Rather, Chia's marks form a foundation of tiny particles like a tissue of molecules, which is an irrestistible cosmic force going so far as to contaminate the image, thereby rendering it uncertain and difficult to recognize.

In Chia's iconography where the protagonist is the human figure, we also find that the ancestry is derived from something between the Metaphysical painters and those of the 1900s, between the coloration of Matisse and the structure of a Picasso. Carra, De Chirico, and—above all—Savinio appear to be the preferred sources of his inspiration. Chia shares with Savinio a certain ironic (when not completely satirical) character which, while shrouding the images with mystery, at the same time de-dramatizes them. If Savinio gave the heads of flamingoes to his noblewomen, Chia paints his people with a cartoonist's humour, though without diminishing their enigmatic nature.

The dominant literary and cultural references in Chia's work are expressed with a certain flavour of disenchantment. As Bonito Oliva has noted, Chia's thoughts are organically linked to the present. He doesn't forget that he lives in a world under continual bombardment by the mass-media and "images of the masses"; in this way he introduces into his work an omnivorous desire for signs that are iconic and heterogenous. The picture becomes a meeting-ground for images from high culture, stereotypes from pop culture and products of an industrial culture.

Chia in fact reveals the expression of the epoch's needs that he himself is answering to. Following the neo-avantgarde's break with tradition, and the dematerialization of the object as in conceptual art, art today measures up to the values of a subjectivity immersed in a high technology where sensuality is being reclaimed as a vehicle for a new and uninhibited sensibility.

—Giorgio Verzotti

CHIARI, Giuseppe.

Italian. Born in Florence, 26 September 1926. Studied mathematics and engineering at the University of Florence, 1946–51; also studied piano: concentrated on musical composition, 1950. Married Victoria Chiari in 1957; son: Mario. Artist and composer, Florence, since 1960. Founder, with Pietro Grossi, Vita Musicale Contemporanea Associazione, Florence, 1961; associated with New York Fluxus artists, 1962; worked with composer Sylvano Busotti, Florence, 1962; associated with Gruppo 70, Concrete Poets, Florence, 1964; visited Paris: worked with the Centre de Musique, 1965. Lecturer, Seminario di Musica d'Avanguardia, *Biennale*, Venice, 1969. Address: via Chiarugi 12, 50136 Florence, Italy.

Individual Exhibitions and Concert Performances:

1962 Galleria Blu, Milan
Fluxus Festival, Centre de Musique, Paris
Galleria Numero, Rome
Fluxus Festival, Wiesbaden, West Germany
Conservatorio Cherubini, Florence
Teatro Verdi, Trieste
1963 Galleria La Salita, Rome
Auditorium Società Aquilana dei Concerti, L'Aquilla, Italy
Forte Belvedere, Florence
Arte Viva, Trieste
4th Settimana Internazionale Nuova Musica, Palermo
1964 Centre de Musique, Paris
Neue Musik, München, Munich
Avant-Garde Festival, Judson Hall, New York
Forte Belvedere, Florence
Ensemble Die Reihe, Vienna
Institute of Contemporary Arts, London
Galleria Blu, Milan
Staatstheater, Oldenburg, West Germany
Kölner Kurse für Neue Musik, Cologne
1965 Musica Nova, Reykjavik, Iceland
Galerie René Block, Berlin
Goethe Universität, Frankfurt
Galleria Numero, Florence
Philadelphia College of Art
Festival de la Libre Expression, Paris
Galerie Zwirner, Cologne
Ford Foundation, Berlin
Centre de Musique, Paris
Roverto Vezzosi, Florence
La Scaletta, Matera, Italy
5th Settimana Internazionale Nuova Musica, Palermo
Centre de Musique, Paris
Creative and Performing Arts Center, Buffalo
Teatro delle Arti, Rome
Musikalskur Leikur, Reykjavik, Iceland
Biennale, Zagreb, Yugoslavia
Fluxus Festival, Washington Square Gallery, New York
Museum des 20, Jahrhunderts, Vienna
Galerie Parnass, Wuppertal, West Germany
1966 Casa della Cultura, Livorno
Academia Filarmonica Romana, Rome
University of Madrid
Liberia Feltrinelli, Rome
Avant-Garde Festival, New York
Galerie Zwirner, Cologne
1967 *Vita Musicale Contemporanea*, Florence
Galleria Feltrinelli, Rome
Unione Culturale, Turin
Teatro dei Satiri, Rome
St. Paul's American Church, Rome
Avant-Garde Festival, Central Park, New York
Art Total, Lugano, Switzerland
1968 Institute of Contemporary Arts, London
Film Studio, Rome
Teatro Verdi, Trieste
Film und Fernsehakademie, Berlin
Teatro Politeama, Palermo
Palazzo Strozzi, Florence
Cafe Gebler, Berlin
Premio Masaccio, San Giovanni Valderno, Italy
1969 Galleria Milano, Milan
Galleria Il Centro, Naples
Teatro Verdi, Trieste
8th Biennale d'Arte, San Benedetto del Tronto, Italy
Autunno Musicale, Como, Italy
Unione Culturale, Turin
Unione Goliardica, Mantua, Italy
1970 Warszawska Jesien, Warsaw
Palazzo Grassi, Venice
Centro Techne, Florence
Film Studio, Rome
University of Rome
Filarmonica Landuna Messina, Sicily
Sendesaal Rasio, Bremen, West Germany
Teatro La Fede, Rome
1971 Rondo di Bacco, Florence
Associazione Musicale Lucchese, Lucca, Italy
Istituto Italiano di Cultura, Cologne
Palazzo Strozzi, Florence
Chalet I Tigli, Florence
Autunno Musicale, Como, Italy
1972 Galleria Toselli, Milan
LP 220, Turin
Staatstheater, Kassel, West Germany
Bitef, Belgrade
Modern Art Agency, Naples
Istituto Italiano di Cultura, Strasbourg
Teatro Verdi, Pisa
Istituto Italiano di Cultura, Budapest
Arte Viva, Trieste
Contemporanea, Rome
Centro Lepetit, Milan
Palazzo Pitti, Florence
1973 Galleria Il Cortile, Rome
Kunstmuseum, Lucerne
Galerie 11, Paris
Kunstverein, Hannover
Spot, Kiel, West Germany
Quadriennale, Rome
University of Florence
Galerie René Block, Berlin
1974 Galerie Baecker, Bochum, West Germany
Royal College of Art, London
Lucrezia de Comizio, Pescara
Galleria Martano, Turin
Projekt 74, Cologne
1975 Art Tapes 22, Florence
Galerie Stampa, Basle
Galleria Schema, Florence
Studio Carla Ortelli, Milan
Maud Center, Varese, Italy
Situation Gallery, London
1976 ARC, Paris
1977 Chantal Pontbriand, Montreal
Instituto Italiano di Cultura, Tokyo
Centre Art Contemporaine, Geneva
1978 *Biennale*, Venice
1979 Centre Georges Pompidou, Paris
1980 Musée St. Georges, Liége, Belgium
1981 Galerie René Block, Berlin
Light-Concert, Antwerp, Belgium
Fluxus Festival, Enschede, Netherlands
1982 *Fluxus 1962–82*, Wiesbaden, West Germany
Kunstverein, Cologne
Universidad de Bellas Artes, Madrid
Kunstler Haus, West Berlin
1983 *Piano Concert*, Valencia, Spain
Modern Art Galerie, Vienna
Villa Romana, Florence
1984 Galleria N2, Bologna, Italy
Galleria Dada, Florence
1985 Silbermann Gallery, Chicago
1986 Galleria Milano, Milan
Galleria Vivita, Florence
Piano Concert, Middelburg, Netherlands
1987 Galleria Chisel, Milan (with Ben Vautier)
Piano Concert, Pratolino, Florence
Carl Solway Gallery, Chicago

Collections:

Centro Di, Florence; Kunstmuseum, Lucerne.

Publications:

By CHIARI: books—*Giuseppe Chiari: Extra*, exhibition catalogue, Florence 1986; *Chiari: Aesthetik*, Frankfurt 1987; article—"Interview mit Giuseppe Chiari" with Giancarlo Politi, in *Heute Kunst* (Dusseldorf), July/August 1973; musical scores—*Intervalli; Studi su una Sola Frequenza: Gesti sul Piano; Per Arco; Teatrino; Il Silenzio; Play What You Like; Rompere; La Strada; Whisky; Don't Trade Here;* since 1960.

On CHIARI: books—*Il Territorio Magico* by Achille Bonito Oliva, Florence 1971; *Projekt 74*, exhibition catalogue, Cologne 1974; *Il Metodo per suonare di Giuseppe Chiari* by Gillo Dorfles, Turin 1976; *Aktions-kunst* by Jürgen Schilling, Frankfurt 1978; *Identité Italienne* by Germano Celant, Paris 1981; *Giuseppe Chiari: Music is Easy*, exhibition catalogue with text by Enrico Pedrini, Florence 1983; *Fluxus: An Anthology of Chance Operations* by Marco Meneguzzo, Genoa 1987; articles—"Giuseppe Chiari" by Gillo Dorfles in *Nuovi Miti, Nuovi Riti*, Turin 1969; "Chiari" by John Cage in *Notations*, New York 1970; "What's Music?" in *Data* (Milan), no. 2 1972; "Music and Teaching" by Tommaso Trini in *Data* (Milan), no. 13, 1973; "Fluxus" by Tommaso Trini in *Data* (Milan), no. 18, 1976.

Art is easy; music is easy.

—Giuseppe Chiari

The visual quality of Giuseppe Chiari's works results directly from their morphological-syntactical quality; it never comes from graphic tricks or arbitrary flourishes and arabesques. The "symbols" that Chiari has often used are spare and functional, never given any "picturesque" or graphic emphasis. What is it, then, that accounts for the remarkable interest that these works ("scores," one might perhaps call them) have aroused in the past ten years, particularly in the field of visual art rather than the musical field? I believe that their success—like that of Chiari's other activities (actions on the keyboard, "playing" different objects and so on)—is due mainly to their conceptual placing, to their starting from a precise formative idea applied to definite situations, to definite musical (and non-musical) processes, acoustic and gestural; in short, to the fact that Chiari has understood—ever since his "Teatrino" of 1965 and his "Gestures on the Piano," performed in 1962 at the *Fluxus Festival* in Paris—the importance of an analysis of the actions that were appropriate long before western art was overwhelmed by the powerful wave of Concept Art. That is probably why Chiari's works have been associated with those—very different in themselves and in their background—of some Concept artists who used words (Art and Language), gestures and the body itself (Body Art) to express themselves.

The revolt against the object in visual art corresponds closely with the re-utilization of the object itself, no longer as something ready-made but as something "to be played"; to be used, that is, for its form and its structural characteristics in the musical field.

The main task that Chiari set himself was that of disclosing the inner quality of the form of objects and of instruments so as to be able to "play" them by making use of all their morphological features. Even when Chiari speaks of "playing the chair" (1969), what he means is that he has studied the possibilities of handling the object, acoustically if not musically, for long months.

The case of the pianoforte is similar but more complex; here too it is not just a matter of producing certain sounds from the keyboard, but of studying the whole structure of the instrument, of weighing up the morphologically expressive possibilities it has in addition to the production of sounds, even through a symbiosis with the player's body.

It remains to add some observations on the artist's presentation of himself as the author of the performances. This aspect of his art came after the strictly musical and the "graphic" aspects; it is only since 1964 that the artist has taken to performing his own works and so inaugurated a new phase of his work.

Some of his performances inevitably remind us of Beuys, Ben or Palestine. In all those artists, as in

Giuseppe Chiari: ***Music Is Easy*, 1982**

Chiari, the element most specifically present is that of Body Art. But in Chiari the self-presentation, the narcissistic gestures, that mark the Body Art artists is always subordinated to a precise end: to bring out the "action" qualities of his musical compositions or of his actions through the objects handled, which are the medium through which he expresses himself. This puts him in the forefront of those who have identified the most authentic matrix of an aesthetic activity in the manipulation of the substance of their own bodies.

—Gillo Dorfles

CHICAGO, Judy.

American. Born Judy Cohen in Chicago, Illinois, 20 July 1939. Educated at the University of California at Los Angeles, 1960–64, B.A. 1962, M.F.A. 1964; influenced by the work of Emily Carr, Georgia O'Keeffe, Barbara Hepworth, and Louis Nevelson. Married Jerry Gerowitz in 1961 (died, 1963); married Lloyd Hamrol in 1969. Instructor, University of California Extension, Los Angeles, 1963–69; Painting Instructor, University of California Institute Extension, Irvine, 1966–69; Assistant Professor, California State University at Fresno (started first women's art program), 1969–71; Faculty Member and Co-Founder, Feminist Art Program, California Institute of Arts, Valencia, 1971–73; Artist-in-Residence, Western Washington State College, Bellingham, 1973. Co-Director, Womanhouse, Los Angeles, 1972; Co-Founder, Woman-Space Art Gallery, Los Angeles, 1972; Co-Founder and Instructor, Feminist Studio Workshop, Los Angeles, 1973–74; Co-Founder, Woman's Building, Los Angeles, 1974. Recipient: Woman of the Year Award, *Mademoiselle* magazine, New York, 1973; Individual Artist Grant, 1976, and Services to the Field Grant, 1977, National Endowment for the Arts. Agents: Kenmore Galleries, 122 South 18th Street, Philadelphia, Pennsylvania 19103; and JPL Fine Arts, 23 Grafton Street, London W1X 31D, England. Address: Post Office Box 834, Benicia, California 94510, U.S.A.

Individual Exhibitions:

1966 Rolf Nelson Gallery, Los Angeles
1969 Pasadena Art Museum, California
1970 Faculty Club, California State College, Fullerton
Fresno State College, California
1972 Jack Glenn Gallery, Corona de Mar, California
1973 Grandview Gallery, Woman's Building, Los Angeles
1974 Kenmore Galleries, Philadelphia
Artemisia Gallery, Chicago
Coe College, Cedar Rapids, Iowa
Judy Chicago and Lloyd Hamrol, Western Washington State College, Bellingham
1975 College of St. Catherine, St. Paul, Minnesota
Fe/Vision, Los Angeles
JPL Fine Arts, London
1976 Quay Ceramics, San Francisco
1977 Schaffner Gallery, Los Angeles
1979 Schaffner Gallery, Los Angeles
Anhalt-Barnes Gallery, Los Angeles
The Dinner Party, San Francisco Museum of Modern Art (toured the United States and Canada)
1980 Hadler-Rodriguez Gallery, Houston
Parco Gallery, Tokyo
Parco Gallery, Osaka

Selected Group Exhibitions:

1967 *Sculpture of the 60's*, Los Angeles County Museum of Art (Travelled to the Philadelphia Museum)
1972 *Color as Structure,* Whitney Museum, New York
1974 *16 Los Angeles Women Artists,* Cerritos College, Norwalk, California
1975 *Woman as Viewer,* Winnipeg Art Gallery
1976 *Painting and Sculpture in California: The Modern Era,* San Francisco Museum of Modern Art
1977 *Frauen machen Kunst,* Galerie Magers, West Germany
Overglaze Imagery: Cone 019 to 016, California State University at Fullerton Art Gallery
1979 *Works on Paper,* Institute of Contemporary Art, Boston
The 1970's: New American Painting, organized by the New Museum, New York (toured Eastern Europe)
Creativity, A Human Resource, Academy of Sciences, San Francisco (toured the United States and Canada)

Collections:

Museum of Modern Art, New York.

Publications:

By CHICAGO: books—*Through the Flower: My Struggle as a Woman Artist,* New York 1975; *The Dinner Party: A Symbol of Our Heritage,* New York 1979; *Embroidering Our Heritage: The Dinner Party Needlework,* New York 1980; *The Birth Project,* New York 1985; articles—statement in *Everywoman Newspaper* (Los Angeles), 7 May 1971; statement and introduction, with Miriam Shapiro, in *Womanhouse,* exhibition catalogue, Los Angeles 1972; introduction to *Invisible/Visible,* exhibition catalogue, Long Beach, California 1972; "Let Sisterhood Be Powerful" in *Womanspace Journal* (Los Angeles), February/March 1973; "Female Imagery," with Miriam Shapiro, in *Womanspace Journal* (Los Angeles), Summer 1973; "Letter to A Young Woman Artist," with Arlene Raven, in *Anonymous Was A Woman,* Valencia, California 1974; "2 Artists Interview Each Other," with Lloyd Hamrol, in *Criteria* (Vancouver), 1974; "Interview with Judy Chicago," with Arlene Raven and Susan Rennie, in *Chrysalis* (Los Angeles), no. 4, 1977; films—*Judy Chicago and The California Girls,* with J. Dancoff, Los Angeles 1971; *Womanhouse,* with Johanna Demetrakis, Los Angeles 1972.

On CHICAGO: books—*Primary Structures,* exhibition catalogue, by Kynaston McShine, New York 1966; *Painting, Sculpture, Photographs of Judy Chicago,* by Dextra Frankel, Fullerton, California 1970; articles—"Thru The Feminist Loking Glass with Judy Chicago" by Susan Stocking in the *Los Angeles Times,* July 1972; "Woman's Art: A Theoretical

Judy Chicago: *The Dinner Party*, 1979

Perspective" by Arlene Raven in *Womanspace Journal* (Los Angeles), February/March 1973; "Judy Chicago at Kenmore" by Judy Stein in *Art in America* (New York), July/August 1974; "Judy Chicago Talking to Luch R. Lippard" in *Artform* (New York), September 1974; "Judy Chicago and Trials of 'Dinner Party' " by Grace Glueck in the *New York Times*, 30 April 1977; "Judy Chicago: World of China Painter" in *Ceramics Monthly* (Columbus, Ohio), May 1978.

I organized the first feminist art program in America in 1970 and have been instrumental in developing the Women's Building in Los Angeles, which is committed to a feminist perspective in art-related professions. I am a feminist artist, interested in making the female experience stand for an aspect of the human condition which has been shrouded in mythology and fantasy. I am committed to expanding the perspective of my world through breaking the historical silence of women. I believe in art that is connected to real human feeling, that extends itself beyond the limits of the art world to embrace all people who are striving for alternatives in an increasingly dehumanized world. I am trying to make art that relates to the deepest and most mythic concerns of human kind and I believe that, at this moment of history, feminism is humanism. I believe that art, if authentic, can reach across all gaps between people and create understanding.

—Judy Chicago

"I wanted to wed my skills to my real ideas and to aspire to the making of art that could clearly reveal my values and point of view as a woman . . . integrating my art and my feminism."

—Judy Chicago
from *Through the Flower*

Painter, sculptor, teacher, director, organizer, political activist, writer. Judy Chicago is all these.

She originally studied traditional painting and sculpture. Later—struggling for male acceptance—she learned spray painting in an auto body shop, taught herself carpentry, discovered how to use machinery in an industrial arts shop, studied pyrotechnology, made a lithograph—"toughing it out". Her autobiography, *Through the Flower,* is partly an attempt to escape that search for masculine approval and to resolve the conflict of how to be a woman *and* an artist.

Chicago's early work was often labelled "Judy's cunts," but she soon hid her aggressive female imagery in minimalism. In painting series whe explored "hard" and "soft" interactions through colour relationships. In sculpture three-domed shapes represented both her physical self and the family of mother/father/child.

Driven to share her experiences, Chicago initiated an art class for women in Fresno, California, then created "Womanhouse" with a group of working female artists. "Womanhouse" involved renovating a dilapidated house—so learning "male" skills and crafts—then transforming it into environmental statements. The women, working alone or in teams on individual rooms, emerged stretched emotionally mentally and artistically. Chicago grew and learned with them.

"Womanhouse" taught Chicago that a woman's art benefits from being shown with art of other women—in context, so to speak. It also stimulated her to "wave a red flag" at the bull of the male-dominated art community with renewed emphasis in her work on recognizable female imagery. "Red Flag" is the title of her first lithograph—an overt highly-coloured image of a used Tampax being withdrawn from a woman.

In 1973 Chicago began a major five-year project—"The Dinner Party." A "symbolic history of women's achievements and struggles," it is an evolutionary summation of Chicago's own achievements begun with the inspiration of a single hand-painted plate. Thirty-nine women are honoured with a full place at Chicago's triangular-shaped table. Each place setting is marked by an embroidered runner and a ceramic plate. The strong three-dimensional plate designs, reminiscent of Chicago's early specific imagery, fight to rise from their bases—trapped butterflies straining for freedom. The entire work stands on a porcelain floor of triangles painted in gold with names of 999 "supporting" women. A feminist statement is made using traditional female crafts and activities.

"The Dinner Party," which has been travelling since its completion, is both a celebration and a challenge—a celebration of accomplishments from the primordial goddess of ancient religions to Katherine Hepburn. It celebrates women's successes in art, politics, science and religion. "The Dinner Party" would, however, be a beautiful failure if it did not also challenge, demanding of men and women a better knowledge of and interest in contributions of women to every facet of life—and a demand that women continue to answer the challenge. That is the reason for "The Dinner Party"—and for the art and life of Judy Chicago.

—Marlee Robinson

CHILLIDA, Eduardo.
Spanish. Born in San Sebastian, 10 January 1924. Educated at Classical High School, San Sebastian, 1930–42; studied architecture at the University of Madrid, 1943–47, and painting at a private art school, Madrid, 1947. Married Pili de Belzunce in 1950; children: Guiomar, Pedro, Ignacio, Carmen and Suzanna. Independent artist, in Paris, 1948–49, in Villaines-sous-Bois, France, 1950, in Hernani, Spain, 1951–58, in San Sebastian, since 1959. Visiting Professor, Carpenter Center, Harvard University, Cambridge, Massachusetts 1971. Recipient: Diploma of Honour, *Triennale di Milano,* 1954; Sculpture Prize, Comune di Venezia, 1958; Graham Foundation Award, Chicago 1958; Kandinsky Prize, 1960; Carnegie Sculpture Prize, Pittsburgh, 1964; Nord-Rhein Prize, Dusseldorf, 1966; Wilhelm-Lehmbruck Sculpture Prize, Duisburg, West Germany, 1966; Rembrandt Prize, San Sebastian, 1975; Engraving Prize, Japanese Ministry of Culture, 1976; Peach Prize, Victor Seix Institute, 1978; Andrew W. Mellon Prize, with Willem de Kooning, Carnegie Institute, Pittsburgh, 1978; Gold Medal of Merit for Fine Arts, Madrid, 1981; European Plastic Arts Prize, Strasbourg, 1983; Grand Prix des Arts et des Lettres, Paris, 1984; Wolf Foundation Prize, Herzlia, Israel, 1985; Kaiserring Award, Goslar, West Germany, 1985; *Revista Euzkadi* Prize, Bilbao, Spain, 1986; Premio de Asturias, Madrid, 1987; Premio Lorenzo il Paris Magnifico, Florence, 1987; Order of Merit for Science and Art, Bonn, 1987. Agents: Sala Gaspar, Consejo de Ciento 323, Barcelona, and Galerie Maeght, 13 rue do Tehran, 75008 Paris, France. Address: Intzenea—Paseo del Faro 26, 20008 San Sebastian, Spain.

Individual Exhibitions:

1954 Galeria Clan, Madrid
1956 Galerie Maeght, Paris
1961 Galerie Maeght, Paris
1962 Kunsthalle, Basle
1964 McRoberts and Tunnard Gallery, London
1966 Galerie Maeght, Paris
Wilhelm-Lehmbruck-Museum, Duisburg, West Germany
Galerie Buchholz, Munich
Museum of Fine Arts, Houston
1967 Munson-Williams-Proctor Institute, Utica, New York
City Art Museum, St. Louis
Alex Galerie, Dusseldorf
Konstsalongen Samlaren, Stockholm
1968 Galerie Maeght, Paris
Galerie Im Erker, St. Gallen, Switzerland
1969 Kunstmuseum, Basle
Kunsthaus, Zurich
Stedelijk Museum, Amsterdam
Galerie-Verein München e.V, Munich
Galerie Buchholz, Munich
Galerie im Erker, St. Gallen, Switzerland
1970 Kunstkabinett, Frankfurt
Galerie Maeght, Paris
Librairie-Galerie La Hune, Paris
Galerie Renée Ziegler, Zurich
1971 Sala Gaspar, Barcelona
1972 Galeria Iolas-Velasco, Madrid
Konsthall, Lund, Sweden
Ulmer Museum, Ulm, West Germany
1973 Galerie Maeght, Paris
Caja de Ahorros, Pamplona, Spain
Caja de Ahorros, Sorguesa, Spain
Caja de Ahorros, Estella, Spain
Galerie Wünsche, Hamburg
1974 Hastings Gallery/Spanish Institute, New York
Galeria 42, Barcelona
Galeria Juana de Aizpuru, Seville
Galeria Turner, Madrid
Chateau de Ratilly, France
Galleria d'Art Serfontana, Morbio Inferiore, Italy
Galerie d'Art Moderne, Basle
1975 Galerie Nouvelle Images, The Hague
Galerie Numaga, Neuchâtel, Switzerland
Galeria Internacional de Arte, Madrid
1976 Kulturhuset, Hellerup, Denmark
1977 Galeria Iolas-Velasco, Madrid
Museo de Durango, Spain
Caja de Ahorros, Pamplona, Spain
FIAC 77, Grand Palais, Paris
Carpenter Center, Harvard University Cambridge, Massachusetts
Galerie Art in Progress, Munich
1978 Staatliche Kunsthalle, Baden-Baden, West Germany
Galerie Maeght, Zurich
Galerie Schmela, Dusseldorf
Galerie Artek, Helsinki (with Luginbuhl and Tinguely)
1979 Landau-Alexander Gallery, Los Angeles
National Gallery, Washington, D.C.
Carnegie Institute, Pittsburgh
1980 Galerie Maeght, Paris
Guggenheim Museum, New York (retrospective)
Palacio de Valezquez, Madrid
Esculturas/Obra Grafica, Galeria Maeght, Barcelona
Galerie Maeght, Paris
1981 Museo de Bellas Artes, Bilbao
Skulpturen, Kestner-Gesellschaft, Hannover
Galerie Maeght, Zurich
Frances Aronson Gallery, Atlanta, Georgia
Galerie Marghescu, Hannover
Galerie Hans Ostertad, Frankfurt
1982 Galerie Beyeler, Basle
Galerie Maeght, Zurich
1983 Maison de Goya, Bordeaux, France
Galeria Maese Nicolas, Leon, Spain
Erker Galerie, St. Gallen, Switzerland
Galerie Herbert Meyer-Ellinger, Frankfurt
1984 Sala Celini, Madrid
Galerie Kaj Forsblom, Helsinki
Galerie Grariart, Turku, Finland
Galerie Brusberg, Hannover
Galerie Adrien Maeght, Paris
M. A. Martin Gallery, New York
Tasende Gallery, La Jolla, California
1985 Caja Ahorros Municipal, Elgoibar, Spain
Anne Berthoud Gallery, London
Galerie Biedermann, Munich
Caja Laboral Popular, Portugalete, Spain
Caja Laboral Popular, Algorta, Spain
Galerie Beaumont, Luxembourg
Abadia Montmajour, Arles, Franch
Musee d'Art Moderne, Brussels
Galerie Maeght-Lelong, Zurich
1986 Fondacion Miro, Barcelona
Caja Laboral Popular, Aretxabaleta, Spain (toured Spain)

Eduardo Chillida: ***Peine del Viento*****, 1976**

Centro de Arte Reina Sofia, Madrid
Neue Galerie der Stadt, Linz, West Germany
Galerie Meyer-Ellinger, Frankfurt
Dresdner Bank, Frankfurt
Museo de Bellas Artes, Bilbao, Spain
Tasende Gallery, La Jolla, California
Ospedale degli Innocente Florence
Fondacion Miro, Barcelona
1987 Galeria Joan Prats, Barcelona
Galerie Ulysses, Vienna
Galeria Ederti, Bilbao, Spain
Stadtmuseum, Pforzheim, West Germany

Selected Group Exhibitions:

1949 *5th Salon de Mai*, Musée d'Art Moderne, Paris
1954 *10th Triennale di Milano*
1958 *Biennale*, Venice
1964 *Documenta 3*, Kassel, West Germany (and *Documenta 4*, 1968; *Documenta 6*, 1977)
1967 *Guggenheim International*, Guggenheim Museum, New York
1974 *9th Biennale of Prints*, National Museum of Modern Art, Tokyo (travelled to the Museum of Modern Art, Kyoto)
1975 *Contemporary Spanish Painters*, Cultural Center, New York
1979 *L'Univers d'Aime Maeght*, Maison de la Culture, Rennes, France
1983 *Arte abstracto espanol*, Fundacion Juan March, Madrid
1987 *Monumenta*, Middelheim Museum, Antwerp, Belgium

Collections:

Wilhelm-Lehmbruck-Museum, Duisburg, West Germany; Kunstmuseum, Basle; Kunsthaus, Zurich; Tate Gallery, London; Galleria, Nazionale d'Arte Moderna, Rome; Museo Civico, Turin; Museum of Modern Art, New York; Guggenheim Museum, New York; Art Institute of Chicago; Museum of Fine Arts, Houston.

Publications:

By CHILLIDA: books—*Hommage à Georges Braque*, Paris 1964; *Chillida*, portfolio, with foreword by Carola Giedion-Welcker, Paris 1964; *Chillida: Sculptures*, with foreword by Juan Daniel Fullaondo, Paris 1968; books illustrated—*Le Chemin des Devins/Menerges* by André Frenaud, Paris 1966; *Meditationen in Kastillien* by Max Holzer, St. Gallen, Switzerland 1968; *Die Kunst und der Raum* by Martin Heidegger, St. Gallen, Switzerland 1969; *Poetes-Peintres-Sculpteurs*, Paris 1960; *Mas alla* by Jorge Guillen, Paris 1973; *Die Penser* by Aeschylus, Madrid 1978.

On CHILLIDA: books—*Dictionary of Modern Sculpture* by Micel Seuphor, Neuchâtel, Switzerland 1959; *Contemporary Sculpture: An Evolution in Volume and Space* by Carola Giedion-Welcker, London 1961; *Chillida*, exhibition catalogue, with text by Franz Meyer, Basle 1962; *Eduardo Chillida*, exhibition catalogue, with text by James Johnson Sweeney, Houston 1966; *Chillida* by Pierre Volboudt, Paris 1967; *Form and Space* by Eduard Trier, London 1968; *Vingt-Cing Ans d'Art Vivant* by Michael Ragon, Paris 1968: *The Eye and the Hand of the Sculptor* by Paul Waldo Schwartz, London 1969; *Chillida* by Claude Esteban, Paris 1971; *Los Espacios de Chillida* by Gabriel Celaya, Barcelona 1974; *Hablando con Chillida,escultor vasco* by Marin de Ugalde, San Sebatian 1975; *Chillida* by Luis Figuerola-Ferretti, Madrid 1976; *Cuaderno Chillida*, edited by Revista de Occidente, Madrid 1976; *Eduardo Chillida: Akte-Hande-Formen* by Werner Schmalenbach, West Berlin 1977; *Chillida:Oeuvre Graphique* by Julien Clay, Paris 1978; *Chillida* by Octavio Paz, Paris 1979; *Chillida*, exhibition catalogue, with text by Octavio Paz, New York 1980; *Chillida: Esculturas/Obra Grafica*, exhibition catalogue, with text by Santigo Amon, Barcelona 1980; *Eduardo Chillida; Skulpturen*, exhibition catalogue, with text by Carl-Albrecht Haenlein, Hannover 1981; *Chillida*, exhibition catalogue, with text by Octavio Paz, Zurich 1981; *Eduardo Chillida: Graphic Works*, exhibition catalogue with text by R. Hohl, La Jolla, California 1984; *Eduardo Chillida*, exhibition catalogue by Michael Semff, Pforzheim, West Germany 1987.

Since the deaths of Gonzalez and Picasso, Eduardo Chillida is the most distinguished living Spanish sculptor. He is, however, a Basque, and does not share with those two great compatriots, and many other Spanish artists, a concern for surrealistic fantasy or narrative necessity. Cubism and the Constructivism seem to be part of his formal inheritance, but from his native background he also brings the influence of artianship, in the use of heavy metals and the making of positive, forged shapes. A slow, contemplative artist, Chillida has always preferred to live and work away from international centres.

It was not until the early 60's that Chillida established a positive style. Earlier work in wood and forged iron, elaborated from heavy, gestural, twisted forms, is reminiscent, at times of Gonzalez, but, in the eclectic change of manner, clearly searching for a final, personal form. Since then Chillida's sculptures have become more and more ascetic and controlled, the twisted, writhing, interlocking forms, carefully articulated into rhythmic definitions of space. This maturity is the result of a return, both physically and emotionally, to his native soil. His drawings, on paper, or the lead-inlaid marble calligraphy, as well as the attenuated sculptures, are deeply involved in the landscape of a mountainous country which plunges into a turbulent ocean. The division and meeting of these natural elements are vigorously delineated by Chillida, with a mixture of energy and elegance which brings to mind the stylised images of Japanese landscape painting. His sculptures further explore natural forces, through a medium which has roots in

Spanish artisanship. They are concerned with flow, not conflict; he avoids intersections which interfere with the monumental rhythms of his forms.

Chillida says his subject is the relationship between time and space, defined by three-dimensionality: ". . . the two elements of space, one which might be called negative, the other positive, are in a relationship which I call a dialogue." This dialogue is concerned with poetic values, not scientific definitions, and derives from the observation of nature.

—Charles Spencer

CHRISTO. (Christo Javacheff).
American. Born in Gabrovo, Bulgaria, 13 June 1935; emigrated to the United States, 1964: naturalized, 1973. Educated at Fine Arts Academy, Sofia, Bulgaria, 1952–56; Burian Theatre, Prague, 1956; Fine Arts Academy, Vienna, 1957. Married Jeanne-Claude de Guillebon in 1960; son: Cyril. Lived in Paris 1958–64; moved to New York, 1964; designed first packages and wrapped objects, 1958; first showcases, 1963; first storefronts, 1964, and first packaged public buildings, 1968. Recipient: Cassandra Award, Bill and Noma Copley Foundation, Chicago, 1966; Colorado Award for Engineering Excellence, 1973; Sonoma-Marin County Ranchers Award, California, 1976; Honarary Citizenship, City of New Orleans, 1977; Process and Environment Award, Skowhegan School of Painting and Sculpture, Maine, 1979; Royal Danish Academny of Art Award, Copenhagen, 1979; Award of Excellence, Chelterham Art Center, Pennsylvania, 1980; Admiral's Award of the Fleet of Miami, Florida, 1986; Liberty Award, New York, 1986; Menotti Artist in Residence Award, College of Charleston, South Carolina, 1987; Kaiser Ring Award, Goslar, West Germany, 1987. DHL: College of Saint Rose, Albany, New York, 1986. Agent: Jeanne-Claude Christo, 48 Howard Street, New York, New York 10013. Adress: 48 Howard Street, New York, New York 10013, U.S.A.

Individual Exhibitions:

1961 Galeria Haro Lauhus, Cologne
1962 Galerie J. Paris
1963 Galerie Schmela, Dusseldorf
Galleria Apollinaire, Milan
Galleria de Leone, Venice
1964 Gallerie Schmela, Dusseldorf
Galleria del Leone, Venice
Galerie Ad Libitum, Antwerp
Galleria G.E. Sperone, Turin
Galleria La Salita, Rome
1966 Stedelijk van Abbemuseum, Eindhoven, Netherlands
Leo Castelli Gallery, New York
1967 Wide White Space Gallery, Antwerp
Galerie Der Spiegel, Cologne
1968 John Gibson Gallery, New York
Museum of Modern Art, New York
Galleria del Leone, Venice
1969 John Gibson Gallery, New York
Lo Giudice Gallery, Chicago
Wide White Space Gallery, Antwerp
Central Street Gallery, Sydney
National Gallery of Victoria, Melbourne
Galerie der Spiegel, Cologne
1970 The New Gallery, Cleveland
Galerie Francoise Lambert, Milan
Galerie Rene Ziegler, Zurich
Kaiser-Wilhelm Museum, Krefeld, West Germany
1971 Annely Juda Gallery, London
Galerie Yvon Lamberg, Paris
Haus Lange Museum, Krefeld, West Germany
Museum of Fine Arts, Houston
Kunstsammlungen-Stadt Nurnberg, Nuremberg
Galerie Victor Loeb, Berne
Kunsthaus, Hamburg
Colophon Galleria, Milan
Centro La Capella, Trieste
Ars Studeo, Copenhagen
Galerie Mikro, Berlin
Centro de Arte y Comunicacion, Buenos Aires
1972 The New Gallery, Cleveland
La Jolla Museum of Contemporary Art, California
Santa Barbara Museum of Art, California
The Friends of Contemporary Art, Denver
Joslyn Art Museum, Omaha, Nebraska
Contemporary Arts Center, Cincinnati, Ohio
The Morgan Gallery, Kansas City
1973 Stedelijk Museum, Amsterdam
Seriaal Galerie, Amsterdam
Alan Frumkin Gallery, New York
Miami Dade Junior College
Ball State University, Muncie, Indiana
University of Washington Art Museum, Seattle
La Rotonda, Milan
Galeria Francoise Lambert, Milan
Galerie Charles Kriwin, Brussels
Neue Pinakoteck, Munich
Max Protetch Gallery, Washington, D.C.
Museu La Tertulia, Cali, Columbia
Kalamazoo Institute of Arts, Michigan
Rosa Esman Gallery, New York
Kunsthaus, Zurich
Kunsthalle, Dusseldorf
Kroller-Muller Museum, Otterlo, Netherlands
Kansas State University, Manhattan
Galleria d'Arte Vinciana, Milan
1974 *The Wall Wrapped,* Rome
Ocean Front, Newport, Rhode Lsland
Louisiana Museum, Humleback, Denmark
Sonja Henie-Niels Onstad Foundation, Oslo
Galerie W. Aronowitsch, Stockholm
Millersville State College, Pennsylvania
Annely Juda Gallery, Ondon
Hatton Gallery, University of Newcastle-upon-Tyne, England
Musée de Peinture et de Sculpture, Grenoble, France
1975 Musée Rath, Geneva
White Gallery, Lutry, Switzerland
Galeria Conkreight, Caracas
Galerie Gimpel Hanover, Zurich
Princeton University Art Museum, New Jersey
Galleria d'Alesandro-Ferranti, Rome
Galerie J. Benador, Geneva
La Jolla Museum of Contemporary Art, California
Oakland Museum, California
Institute of Contemporary Art, Boston
Musée Jenisch, Vevey, Switzerland
M. H. de Young Memorial Museum, San Francisco
Alberta College of Art Gallery, Calgary
Memorial Union Art Gallery, University of California at Davis
Grinnell College, Iowa
Galeria Ciento, Barcelona
Fabian Fine Arts, Cape Town
Harcus-Krakow-Rasoen-Sonnabend Gallery, Boston
Galerie Der Spiegel, Cologne
Galleria Buonaparte, Milan
1976 Foundation Veranneman, Kruishoutem, Belgium
Museum des 20. Jahrhunderts, Vienna
San Francisco Museum of Modern Art
Museum of Contemporary Art, La Jolla, California
Pasadena City College, California
Fine Arts Center, University of Massachusetts, Amherst
Broxton Gallery, Los Angeles
Art Association, Newport, Rhode Island
1977 Colorado Springs Fine Arts Center
Galeria Juan Prats, Barcelona
Galeria Trece, Barcelona
Israel Museum, Jerusalem
Newcomb College Art Department, Tulane University, New Orleans
Metropolitan Museum, Miami
Museum Boymans-van-Beuuingen, Rotterdam
Landische Museum, Bonn
Kestner Gesellschaft, Hannover
Minami Gallery, Tokyo
Annely Juda Fine Arts, London
American Center, Kyoto
1978 Louisiana Museum, Humlebaek, Denmark
Sonja Henie-Niels Onstad Foundation, Oslo
The American Foundation for the Arts, Miami
Western Michigan University, Kalamazoo
Murray State University, Kentucky
Galerie Art in Progress, Munich
Kunstgewerbe Museum, Zurich
Palais des Beaux-Arts, Brussels
Musée de Grenoble, France
Atkins Museum, Nelson Gallery of Art, Kansas City, Missouri
Wadsworth Atheneum, Hartford, Connecticut
University of Arkansas, Little Rock
1979 Weiner Secession, Vienna
Appalachian State University, Boone, North Carolina
Greenville County Museum of Art, South Carolina
Institute of Contemporary Arts, London
Institute of Contemporary Art, Boston
Kunstverein, Freiburg, West Germany
Annely Juda Fine Arts, London
Wright State University, Dayton, Ohio
Hunter Museum of Art, Chattanooga, Tennessee
Laguna Gloria Museum, Austin, Texas
Corcoran Gallery, Washington, D.C.
Appalachian State University, Boone, North Carolina
Nash Gallery, University of Minnesota, Minneapolis
Galerie Catherine Issert, Saint Paul de Vence, France
1980 Newport Harbor Museum, Newport Beach, California
The New Gallery, Cleveland
Swen Parson Gallery, Northern Illinois University, DeKalb
Midwest Museum of American Art, Elkhart, Indiana
Mississippi Museum of Art, Jackson
Winnipeg Art Gallery
Hatton Gallery, Colorado State University, Fort Collins
French Cultural Center-Alliance Francaise, Abu Dhabi
Artspace, Peterborough, Ontario
Cabrillo College Gallery, Apros, California
Sonoma Arts Council, Santa Rosa, California
1981 American Graffiti Gallery, Amsterdam
Hokin Gallery, Miami, Florida
Metropolitan Museum, Miami, Florida
Tennessee Tech University, Cookeville
Albuquerque Museum, New Mexico
Musee d'Art Contemporain, Montreal
Santa Monica City College, California
Community College of Lancaster, Pennsylvania
University of Texas, El Paso
Museum Ludwig, Cologne
Juda-Rowan Gallery, London
Portland Center for the Visual Arts, Oregon
La Jolla Museum of Contemporary Art, California
Madison Art Center, Wisconsin
Conejo Valley Art Museum, Thousand Oaks, California
1982 Nickle Arts Museum, University of Calgary, Alberta
University of Maine, Orono
Colby College Museum of Art, Waterville, Main
Stadel Museum, Frankfurt
Kunstlerhaus Bethanian, West Berlin
Biuro Wystaw Artystycznych, Krakow, Poland
Art Gallery of Hamilton, Ontario
Miami-Dade Public Library, Florida
Galerie Catherine Issert, St. Paul de Vence, France
Elvehjem Museum of Art, University of Wisconsin, Madison
Dumont-Landis Gallery, New Brunswick, New Jersey
Hara Museum of Contemporary Art, Tokyo
1983 Snite Museum of Art, University of Notre Dame, Indiana
Fukuoka Municipal Museum of Art, Japan
National Museum of Osaka, Japan
Contemporary Arts Center, Cincinnati, Ohio

Christo: *Valley Curtain*, Rifle, Colorado, 1972

Art Museum of Santa Cruz County, Soquel, California
Delahunty Gallery, Dallas
Galleria Pero, Milan
1984 Hartnell College, Salinas, California
Luther Burbank Center for the Arts, Santa Rosa, California
Harron School of Art, Indiana University, Indianapolis
Satani Gallery, Tokyo
Nationalgalerie, West Berlin
Annely Juda Fine Art, London
Sun Valley Center for the Arts and Humanities, Idaho
Henie-Onstad Foundation, Oslo
Westport-Weston Arts Council, Connecticut
Boston Atheneum, Massachusetts
1985 University of West Florida, Pensacola
Kunsthalle, Hamburg
New Britain Museum of American Art, Connecticut
Fondation Maeght, St. Paul de Vence, France
Rijksmuseum Kroller-Muller, Otterlo, Netherlands
Carpenter + Hochman Gallery, Dallas
1986 Florida State University, Tallahassee
Fundacion Caja de Pensiones, Madrid
Galeria Joan Prats, Barcelona
Southern Illinois University, Carbondale
Bass Museum, Florida
Alternative Work Site, Omaha, Nebraska
Barrett Art Gallery, Utica College, New York
Satani Gallery, Tokyo
Real Art Ways, Connecticut
1987 Musee Cantonal des Beaux-Arts, Lausanne, Switzerland
Lehman College, Bronx, New York
Aldrich Museum of Contemporary Art, Ridgefield, Connecticut
Elizabeth Galasso Fine Art, Ossining, New York
Halsey Gallery, College of Charleston, South Carolina
Museum van Hedendaagse Kunst, Ghent, Belgium
Seibu Museum of Art, Takanawa, Japan
Museo de Arte Moderno, Bogota, Colombia
1988 Seibu Museum of Art, Tokyo
Schneider Museum, Southern Oregon State College, Ashland
Annely Juda Fine Art, London

Selected Realized Projects:

1961 *Stacked Oil Drums*, Cologne Harbour, West Germany
1962 *Iron Curtain*, Rue Visconti, Paris
Stacked Oil Drums, Gentilly, Paris
Wrapping a Girl, London
1966 *42,390 Cubic Feet Package*, Walker Art Center, Minneapolis
1968 *Packaged Fountain and Tower*, Spoleto, Italy
1,240 Oil Drums/2 Tons of Stacked Hay, Philadelphia Institute of Contemporary Art
1969 *Packed Museum of Contemporary Art/Wrapped Floor*, Chicago
Wrapped Coast, Little Bay, Australia
1971 *Valley Curtain*, Grand Hogback, Rifle, Colorado
1974 *The Wall Wrapped*, Rome
Ocean Front, Newport, Rhode Island
1975 *Running Fence*, Sonoma-Marin County, California
1977 *Wrapped Walkways*, Kansas City, Missouri
1980 *Surrounded Islands*, Biscayne Bay, Florida
1985 *Pont Neuf Wrapped*, Paris
1986 *Wrapped Reichstag*, West Berlin

Collections:

Museum of Modern Art, New York; Whitney Museum, New York; Philadelphia Museum of Fine Arts, Pennsylvania; Stedelijk Museum, Amsterdam; Kunsthaus, Zurich; Moderna Museet, Stockholm; Rheinisches Landesmuseum, Bonn; Tate Gallery, London; Hara Museum of Contemporary Art, Tokyo; National Gallery of Art, Canberra.

Publications:

By CHRISTO: books—*Christo*, text by David Bourdon, Otto Hahn and Pierre Restany, Milan 1965; *Christo: 5600 Cubic Meter Package*, Munich 1968; *Christo*, text by Lawrence Alloway, New York 1969; *Christo: Wrapped Coast, One Million Square Feet*, Minneapolis 1969; *Christo*, text by David Bourdon, New York 1970; *Christo: Valley Curtain*, New York 1973; *Christo: Ocean Front*, texts by Sally Yard and Sam Hunter, Princeton, New Jersey 1975; *Christo: Running Fence*, text by Calvin Tomkins and David Bourdn, New York 1978; *Christo: Wrapped Walk Ways*, New York 1978; *Christo, Surrounded Islands, Biscayne Bay, Greater Miami, Florida, 1980–83*, with essay by Jonathan Fineberg, New York 1986.

On CHRISTO: books—*Christo*, exhibition catalogue, with text by Pierre Restany, Cologne 1961; *Christo*, exhibition catalogue, with text by Lawrence Alloway, Eindhoven, Netherlands 1966; *Christo*, exhibition catalogue with text by William Rubin, New York 1968; *Christo*, exhibition catalogue, with text by S. Prokopoff, Philadelphia 1968; *Christo*, exhibition catalogue, with text by Jan van Der Marck, Melbourne 1969; *Christo*, exhibition catalogue, with text by Paul Wember, Krefeld, West Germany 1971; *Christo*, exhibition catalogue, with text by John Matheson, Dusseldorf 1973; *Christo*, exhibition catalogue, with text by Maurice Besset, Grenoble, France 1974; *Christo*, exhibition catalogue, with text by Alexandre Cirici, Barcelona 1975: *Christo: The Running Fence* by Werner Spies, New York 1977; *Christo*, exhibition catalogue, with text by Yusuke Nakahara, Tokyo 1977; *Christo*, exhibition catalogue, with text by Wieland Schmied and Tilmann Buddensieg, London 1977; *Christo*, exhibition catalogue, with text by Carl Albrecht Haenlein, Munich 1978; *Christo*, exhibition catalogue, with an introduction by R. Oxenaar, text by Ellen Joosten, Otterio, Netherlands 1978; *Christo*, exhibition catalogue with an introduction by H. J. Painitz, text by Werner Spies, Vienna 1979; *Christo: Complete Editions 1964–82*, with introduction by Per Hovdenakk, Munich and New York 1982; *Christo: Works 1958–83*, with text by Yusuke Nakahara, Tokyo 1984; *Christo: Surrounded Islands, Biscayne Bay, Greater Miami, Florida, 1980–83*, with text by Werner Spies, Cologne 1984, New York 1985; *Christo—Der Reichstag*, compiled by Michael Cullen and Wolfgang Volz, Frankfurt 1984; *Christo*, with text by Dominique Laporte, Paris 1985, New York 1986; films—*Wrapped Coast*, Blackwood Productions 1969; *Christo's Valley Curtain*, Maysles Brothers and Ellen Giffard 1972; *Running Fence*, Maysles Brothers and Charlotte Zwerin 1977; *Wrapped Walk Ways*, Blackwood Productions 1978; *Islands*, Maysles Brothers and Charlotte Zwerin 1985; *The Pont Neuf*, Maysles Brothers 1986.

In all of his packages, Christo transforms familiar objects into ambivalent presences, sometimes rendering them unrecognizable and often raising doubts about their past, present, and future identity and function. In his more epic endeavors, he questions the relationship of art at both the urban and natural environments. In a materialistic age, his art is a profound comment on the chronic expectations and frustrations aroused by the increasing number of consumer products and services that are "enhanced" through packaging.

No other artist so fully illuminates the 20th century's preoccupation with packaging. By appropriating and wrapping familiar objects, buildings and sites, making them visible in a new way, he has created a wide range of disturbing and strangely beautiful art works that collectively call for a double take.

—David Bourdon

CHRYSSA.

American. Born in Athens, Greece, 31 December 1933. Educated at Académie de la Grande Chaumière, Paris, 1953–54; California School of Fine arts, San Fransciso, 1954–55. Has lived and worked in New York since 1955. Recipient: Guggenheim Fellowship, 1973. Address: c/o Albright-Knox Art Gallery, 1285 Elmwood Avenue, Buffalo, New York 14222, U.S.A.

Individual Exhibitions:

1961 Betty Parsons Gallery, New York
Guggenheim Museum, New York
1962 Cordier and Ekstrom, New York
1963 Museum of Modern Art, New York
1965 Institute of Contemporary Arts, Philadelphia
1966 Pace Gallery, New York
1968 Pace Gallery, New York
Harvard University, Cambridge, Massachusetts
Walker Art Center, Minneapolis
Galerie Rive Droite, Paris
1969 Galerie der Spiegel, Cologne
Obelisk Gallery, Boston
1970 Graphics Gallery, San Francisco
Galleria d'Arte Contemporenea, Turin
1973 Galerie Denise René, New York
Galerie Denise René-Hans Mayer, Dusseldorf
1974 Galerie Denise René, Paris
Musée d'Art Contemporain, Montreal
Andre Emmerich Galerie, Zurich
1976 Galerie Denise René, New York
1978 Galerie Denise René, New York
1979 *Oeuvres Recentes*, Musèe d'Art Moderne de la Ville de Paris
1980 National Pinacotheque Museum Alexander Soutsos, Athens
1982 Albright-Knox Art Gallery, Buffalo, New York

Selected Group Exhibitions:

1966 *68th American Exhibition*, Art Institute of Chicago
1967 *Light-Motion-Space*, Walker Art Center, Minneapolis
Art of the 60's, Los Angeles County Museum of Art (travelled to Philadelphia Museum of Art)
1968 *Documenta 4*, Kassel, West Germany
1969 *Bienal*, Sao Paulo
1970 *Annual Exhibition of Contemporary American Sculpture*, Whitney Museum, New York
1971 *Annual Exhibition of Contemporary American Sculpture*, Whitney Museum, New York
1972 *Biennale*, Venice

Collections:

Museum of Modern Art, New York; Guggenheim Museum, New York; Whitney Museum, New York; Albright-Knox Art Gallery, Buffalo, New York; Walker Art Center, Minneapolis; Corcoran Gallery of Art, Washington D.C.; Hirshhorn Museum and Sculpture Garden, Washington D.C.; Musée d'Art Contemporain, Montreal; Tate Gallery, London; Pinacotheque Nationale, Athens.

Publications:

By CHRYSSA: articles—statement in "The Artists Say—Chryssa" in *Art Voices* (New York), Fall 1965; interview with John Gruen in the *New York Herald Tribune*, 27 March 1968.

On CHRYSSA: books—*Pop Art* by Lucy Lippard, New York 1966; *Chryssa*, exhibition catalogue, New York 1966; *Chryssa*, exhibition catalogue, with text by Pierre Restany, Paris 1968; *Minimal Art: A Critical Anthology*, edited by Gregory Battcock, New York 1968; *Chryssa: Selected Works 1955–1957*, exhibition catalogue, New York 1968; *Icons and Images of the 60's* by Nicolas and Elena Calas, New York 1971; *Art Without Boundaries 1950–1970*, edited by Gerald Woods, Philip Thompson and John Williams, London 1972; *Chryssa*, exhibition catalogue, New York 1973; *Chryssa* by Sam Hunter, London and New York 1974; *Chryssa* by Pierre Restany, New York 1977; *Chryssa: Oeuvres Récentes*, exhibition catalogue, Paris 1979; articles—"The Role of the Inscription in Painting" by James Reaney in *Canadian Art* (Toronto), October 1966; "Chryssa" by Don Cyr in *School Arts* (Cherry Hill, New Jersey), March 1967; "Light Art" by Nan R. Piene in *Art in America* (New York), May/June 1967; "Torino: Chryssa" in *NAC* (Milan), February 1971; "New York Letter" by Carter Ratfliff in *Art International* (Lugano), December 1972; "Chryssa" by Sam Hunter in *Art News* (New York), 3 May 1973; "Chryssa: Some Observations: by V. Campbell in *Art International* (Lugano), April 1973; "Chryssa Sculptures with Neon Tubes" by James Mellow in th *New York Times*, 21 April 1973; "Mysteries of Neon" by Robert Hughes in *Time* (New York), 4 June 1973.

Birthright and nationality are not necessarily built in to the thumbprint of an artist, Chryssa, for all her Hellenic origins, cannot claim—as she does, and as others have done for her—to have inherited a cultural legacy from Ancient Greece. This is sheer lunacy. If she wants a public to be impressed with the classical Greek accent of her "Cycladic Books" (sculpture which she made in the 1950s), then she could expect that public to trace the same influence in Brancusi's "Kiss". Of course the Greek civilization (and the Roman) left its mark on Europe, but it was a mark not a last-will-and-testament.

This point needs to be established because if Chryssa the artist is not *typically Greek*, neither can she claim to have become Americanized after naturalization. For all her New World methods and media, this sculptor/constructor/luminator retains a European character. After she abandoned her early experiments with lay-out moulds on newsprint scale or blown up even larger and began investigating the optentialities of the alphabetical confusion of shop signs, she was continuing the coutcome of the cubist papier-collé rather than exploring variants of Jasper Johns' interest in the same field. From the refuse dumps and demolition years, like many European artists before her, she was able to extract and reassemble material of more than objet-trouvé stature. Scrap of this kind can be on a large scale and at this time of her development her works often had a monumentality that derived their

dimensions more from origins than from invention.

The change, in size as well as importance, came when she started examining the opportunities afforded by neon lighting. If at first this new medium came about as the result of chance encounter, it was soon to be a matter of far less casual concern. Chryssa studied the nature of neon and how it could be made subservient to her will. Today, a brilliant technician, she is capable of discussing the science of illuminated signs with people whose entire business lies in that field.

Her neon works she calls *luminates*, but she is not wholly concerned with light and colour. She parallels her views with those of a maker of mobiles. If an Alexander Calder mobile looks beautiful when it is still and in repose, why cannot a luminate claim just as fine an appearance when the lights have been extinguished as when it blazes with colour? This is an issue she takes up with anyone who complains about the limited longevity of neon tubing. Either have the tube replaced or live with your Chryssa in the dark.

—Sheldon Williams

CIESLEWICZ, Roman.

French. Born in Lvov, Poland, now U.S.S.R., 13 January 1930; emigrated to France, 1963; naturalized, 1971. Studied at the Academy of Fine Arts, Cracow, Independent graphic artist, working for several magazines and book publishers, Warsaw, 1955–62, in Paris since 1963; Art Director, *Elle* magazine 1964, 1966–69, *Vogue* magazine 1966, and M.A.F.I.A. publicity agency, 1969–72; Designer, *Opus International* magazine, 1967–69, *Kitsch* magazine, 1970–71, *Musique en Jeu* magazine, 1970–73, *CNAC-Archives* publications, 1971–74, *Kamikaze* magazine 1976, and *XX Siècle* magazine, 1976; Graphics Designer, *Festival d'Automne*, 1976–77. Instructor, Ecole Nationale Supérieure des Arts Graphiques, Paris, 1973–75; Ecole Supérieure des Arts Graphiques, Paris, from 1975. Recipient: Trepkowski Prize, Poland 1955; Grand Prix, Czech Cinema Posters Awards, 1964; Grand Prix, *4th Biennale of Posters*, Warsaw, 1972; Special Prize for Cinema Poster, Cannes, 1973; Grand Prix, *4th Biennale of Photomontage*, Poland, 1979; Grand Prix, *Affiche Francaise*, Paris, 1980. Address: c/o *Elle*, 100 rue Réaumur, 75002 Paris, France.

Individual Exhibitions:

1959 Salon d'Ecran, Warsaw
1960 Salon CBWA—ZPAP, Cracow
1961 Galerija Likovnih Umjetnosti, Rijeka, Yugoslavia
1963 Goethe-Institut, Frankfurt
Librairie Mandragore, Paris
1964 Club Synergie, Paris
1965 Théâtre de la Cité, Villeurbanne, France
Salon CBWA—ZPAP, Szczecin, Poland
Galerie in der Biberstrasse, Vienna
1967 Salon CBWA—ZPAP, Warsaw
1968 Galerie Aurora, Geneva
1971 *Wystawa Foto-grafiki 1962–1971*, Muzeum Sztuki, Lodz, Poland
Galerie Aurora, Geneva
1972 *Graphismes*, Musée des Arts Décoratifs, Paris
Musée du Grenoble, France
1973 Stedelijk Museum, Amsterdam
Hotel de Ville, Dieppe, France
Galerija Suvremene Umjetnosti, Zabreg
Razstavno Salon Ratzovz, Maribor, Yugoslavia
1974 Galerie l'Oeil de Boeuf, Paris
Musée de l'Affiche, Vilanov, Poland
Galerie Saluden, Quimper, France
1975 Salon G.V.N., Amsterdam
Mala Galeria, Wroclaw, Poland
Galerie Baumeister, Munich
Galerie Aurora, Geneva
Galerie 13/Theatre Municipal, Angers, France
1976 Centre Jean Prevost, Saint-Etienne-du-Rouviray, France
Cantieri Navali, at the *Biennale*, Venice
1977 Galerie l'Oeil de Boeuf, Paris
Martinischule am Rhein, Emmerich, West Germany
French Institute, Stockholm
1978 Konsthall, Lund, Sweden
Galeria Stu, Teatr Stu, Wroclaw, Poland
Galeria Fotografii, Wroclaw, Poland
B.W.A. Salon Krytykow, Lublin, Poland
Palais Rihour, Lille, France
Galerie Baumeister, Munich
Stedelijk Museum, Amsterdam
1979 Maison de la Culture, Grenoble, France
Librairie-Galerie La Hune, Paris
Maison du Tourisme, Auxerre, France
1980 Centre Choreographique, Nancy, France
House of Culture, Legnica, Poland
Teatr Narodowy, Warsaw
FNAC—Montparnasse, Paris
Centre Dramatique, Nanterre, France
Théâtre National Populaire, Villeurbanne, France
Centre Dramatique, Nice
FNAC, Toulouse
Photomontages, Maison de la Culture, Grenoble, France
1981 *Photomontages*, Chelsea School of Art, London

Selected Group Exhibitions:

1962 *International Poster Exhibition*, Smithsonian Institution, Washington, D.C.
1963 *Bienal*, Sao Paulo
1964 *Documenta 3*, Kassel, West Germany
1965 *Internationale Buchkunstausstellung*, Messehaus, Leipzig
1967 *Affischer ur Tekniska Museet*, Fagersta Stadsbibliothek, Fagersta, Sweden
1968 *Experimental 4*, Casino, Knokke-le-Zoute, Belgium
1970 *4th Biennale of Graphic Arts*, Moravska Galerie, Brno, Czechoslovakia
1971 *Word and Image*, Museum of Modern Art, New York (toured the United States)
1972 *Biennale*, Venice
International Graphic Exhibition Arkcenter, London

Collections:

Stedelijk Museum, Amsterdam, Moderna Museet, Stockholm, Umelecko-Proumyslove Muzeum, Prague; Musée des Arts Décoratifs, Paris; Museum Narodowe, Warsaw; Museum Narodowe, Poznan, Poland; Muzeum Sztuki, Lodz, Poland; Museo de Arte Moderna, Sao Paulo; Museum of Modern Art, New York; Library of Congress, Washington, D.C.

Publications:

On CIESLEWICZ: books—*Polnische Plakatkunst* by Jozek Mroszczak, Dusseldorf 1962; *Das Plakat* by Anton Sailer, Munich 1965; *Roman Cieslewicz* by Aleksander Wojciechowski, Warsaw 1966; *Roman Cieslewicz: Wystawa Fotografiki 1962–1971*, exhibition catalogue, with text by Ursula Czartoryska, Lodz, Poland 1971; *Les Chefs-d'Oeuvre du Kitsch* by Jacques Sternberg, Paris 1971; *Roman Cieslewicz: Graphismes*, exhibition catalogue, with text by Alain Jouffroy, Paris 1972; *Histoire Concise de l'Affiche* by John Barnicoat, Paris 1972; *Roman Cieslewicz*, exhibition catalogue, with text by Roland Topor, Amsterdam 1973; *Roman Cieslewicz: Photomôntages*, exhibition brochure, with text by Yann Pavie, Grenoble, France 1980; *Roman Cieslewicz: Photomontages*, exhibition brochure, with text by Nick Wadley, London 1981.

Roman Cieslewicz, the Polish graphic artist who has lived in Paris since 1963, operates on the "borderline" between two areas of artistic exploration—popular art addressed to the consumer of mass media and art with cognitive pretensions, that of creating images of modern man's spiritual experiences.

Since his debut in 1955 Cieslewicz has succeeded in appealing both to the man in the street and to an elitist audience. At the same time as his work appeared at the 1976 Venice *Biennale*, every passerby in Paris (and perhaps elsewhere) carried his shopping in a bag or paper decorated with a Cieslewicz collage. With the help of Cieslewicz and a few more artists of similar ilk, the graphics of mass media was ennobled into a tool—a tool that would spread the visions of today.

Cieslewicz had several revelations along his artistic path: they made a great impression on everything that lay within his sphere of capability. While still in Warsaw, he discovered the possibilities that collage offered to 20th century art, in particular expressionist and surrealist collages as understood by Max Ernst. As a result, he decided to part with all traditional graphical equipment—brushes, paint, pen and ink. Instead, he began to use scissors, glue, a rule, photographic paper and a darkroom. Under what came to be called photomechanical technique, his dramatic theatrical and operatic posters came to life. The collage, in fact, remains the basis of Cieslewicz's artistry, though it now appears in many forms.

Another result of the time spend in the darkroom was a series of experiments with photographic materials. "I am trying," he said, "to obtain something that has nothing to do with photographic technique—a screen, the network of thread that is . . . the polygon which opens all possibilities." By means of this work without a camera, the joint structures of photographics (the separation of the two words is important) were born. Rooted in photography, these structures laid the foundations for the pictures that were to appear. A few methods worthy of mention were: the separation of an image by the use of a screen with a varied gradation of points; the use of contrast with no half-shades; reflections and rotations; multiple images; plain colour (grounds) and other sallies by colour into black-and-white photography.

His next artistic adventure was the discovery of the originality of expression of a repeated image. These images were an offshoot of his photo-graphical work. Developed in an epoch of mass media, they revealed man's lack of defense against the aggression of his visual surroundings.

His last revelation came as a result of contact and identification with Pop Art as a universal style. "I not only thought, but was quite certain," he said in an interview, "that this would be a never ending style. That it would register reality forever." This, course, was not to be. But—until it fizzled out—Pop, which added the whole of consumer life to art—mass production, fashion, sex, amusements, advertisements, the lights and shadows of the great metropolis, rape, kitsch and horror—all became Cieslewicz's sources of ideas and inspiration. He was infected by Pop's dynamism—as were most young people keen on rock and pop music. He acted as Artistic Director of *Elle* and *Vogue*, edited such exclusive periodicals as *Kitsch* and *Kamikaze* and *Opus International*, designed theatrical posters and programmes (for Arabal, among others), and founded a new kind of visual publication.

The second half of the 1970's saw a "change of climate" in Cieslewicz's work. This is the title that he gave to the cycle of photomontage exhibited at the Galerie l'Oeil de Boeuf in Paris. The critics pointed to the artist's spriitual evolution, his tendency toward contemplation and metaphysics. As shown in these colorful pictures reminiscent of the old masters, the world is full of peace and harmony. The artist no longer interferes with it as brutally as before but offers a modern interpretation, a new and possible way of reading the representational.

—Szymon Bojko

Lygia Clark: *Superficie Modulada*, 1965

"De Kunst ur Lygia Clark" by Frans Haks in *Vroumbiar Huis* (Hilversum, Netherlands), September 1969.

From the *Beasts* to the *Tramping* to the silent thought, the author climbs as a precursor the slope which leads from the manipulable object, which does not exist other than by participation, to pure gestural experience, untrammelled by any objective support, where the artist is no more than a catalyst, part creator, part group leader, part therapist.

My work has always consisted, at least since 1954, of a changing of the relationship artist/work/spectator, or rather of a displacement and a deconstruction of these concepts. Certainly, the radical overthrow of these classical notions (genius, frozen and predetermined object, passive contemplation) has come about in fits and starts, through successive crises, in proportion as I became aware of the implications of my experiments. But the key to my research is, from the origin, the *participation* of the public: the breaking of the barrier separating the spectator from the work and from its "creator". From it I also arrived 8 years ago, at collective experiences in which the object abolishes itself and where man, a cell in a biological architecture constituted by his own body, becomes the object of his own sensation. These propositions, sorts of elastic spider webs stretched by the participants whose every gesture is more or less determined by those of the others—and vice versa—or indeed sorts of plastic tunnels where man is the support and which the participants support and cross through by turns—these propositions have a tribal and initiatory character. It is in truth a matter of a *rite without the myth:* mythology, the metaphysics exterior to man, is abandoned so that man can replace it in assuming his own myth in these ritual gestures.

This outcome—for me essential because, leaving the field of "art", it issues forth upon life—has a very old origin: it is a matter of the *Beasts.* Since 1954 the problem of the frame, of the plan of the limits of the picture, has preoccupied me.

—Lygia Clark

CLARK, Lygia.

Brazilian. Born Lygia Pimentel Lins in Belo Horizonte, Minas Gerais, Brazil, 23 October 1920. Educated at Ecole Normale, Belo Horizonte, 1934–37, Teaching Certificate, 1937; studied art, under Roberto Burle-Marx, Rio de Janeiro, 1947; with Arpad Szenes and Dobrinsky, under Fernand Léger, Paris, 1948–50. Married Aloizio Clark in 1939 (died, 1968); children: Elisabeth, Alvaro, and Eduardo. Lived in Paris and Stuttgart, 1964, in Venice and Paris, 1968, in California, 1969, and in Paris since 1970. Instructor, Institute for the Deaf and Dumb, Rio de Janeiro, 1950–55. Professor of Nostalgy of the Body, Sorbonne, Paris, since 1972. Recipient: Frederico Schmidt Prize, Rio de Janeiro, 1952; Prize, *Bienal,* Sao Paulo, 1957, 1961; Revelation Artistique de l'Année, Rio de Janeiro, 1962; Grand Prize, *Bienal,* Bahia, Brazil, 1966. Addresses: 67 Boulevard Brune, 75014 Paris, France; 16 Hueuida Prado Junior, Apartment 801, 6 Jacebana, Rio de Janeiro, Brazil.

Individual Exhibitions:

1952 Galerie Institut End Plastique, Paris
Ministere de L'Education et la Culture, Rio de Janeiro
1960 Galeria Bonino, Rio de Janeiro
1963 Luis Alexander Gallery, New York
Museu de-Arte Moderna, Rio de Janeiro
1964 Technische Hochschule, Stuttgart
1965 Signals Gallery, London
1966 *Bienal,* Bahia, Brazil (retrospective)
1968 Museu de Arte Moderna, Rio de Janeiro
Galerie M.E. Thelen, Essen
Biennale, Venice (retrospective)
1970 Galerie Camargo, Sao Paulo

Selected Group Exhibitions:

1953 *Bienal,* Sao Paulo (and 1955, 1959)
1963 *Biennale,* Venice (and 1962)
1963 *Arte Neoconcrete,* Museu de Arte Moderna, Rio de Janeiro
1964 *Festival of Modern Art in Latin America,* Signals Gallery, London
1965 *Mouvement 2,* Galerie Denise René, Parie
Art et Mouvement, Galerie Denise René, Paris (toured the U.K.)
1969 *Symposium of Survival Art,* at *International Tactile Sculpture Symposium,* California State University at Long Beach
1970 *Kunstmarkt,* Cologne

Collections:

Museu de Arte Moderna, Rio de Janeiro: Museu de Arte Moderna, Sao Paulo; Museo de Arte Moderno, La Paz, Bolivia; Museum of Modern Art, New York; Arts Council of Great Britain, London; Centre National d'Art Contemporain, Paris.

Publications

By CLARK: articles—several articles in *Signals* (London), April/May 1968; several articles in *Robho* (Paris), no.4, 1968; "Le Corps Est la Mai'sm" in *Robho* (Paris), nos. 5/6, 1971; "L'art c'Est le Corps" in *Preuves* (Paris), 1973; "Tote Kultur—Lebende Kultur," with Adviniula, in *Heute Kunst* (Dusseldorf), no. 9, 1975.

On CLARK: book—*Kinetic Art* by Guy Brett, London 1968; articles—"La IX Biennale de Sao Paulo" by Pierre Restany in *Domus* (Milan), no 457, 1967; "Lygia Clark and Spectator Participation" by C. Barrett in *Studio International* (London), no. 173, 1967; special issue of *Robho* (Paris), 1968;

The essence of Lygia Clark's art is spectator participation, for her kinetic works are not mechanically operated by motors but have to be touched and manipulated. Her works are in fact primitivistic rather than technological, luring the participants into play which has sensual and erotic implications, often needing two people in collaboration to join in, and giving them a heightened awareness of their bodies and their physical surroundings. Her art has constantly been directed to the rediscovery of the sensual and instinctive sides of life, which have been suppressed both by the social constraints of civilized life and by the ever-increasing dominance of the intellect, even in art.

And in evolving new and ever simpler means of getting people involved in sensual games she has moved further and further from the art object for its own sake. In 1959 she was a co-founder of the Brazilian neo-concrete group MAM, which was inspired by the discoveries of abstract artists, above all Mondrian. At that time she was making reliefs which were symmetrical and elementary in form and colour, with shallow changes of level. These "modulated surfaces" developed into her "counter-reliefs," consisting of two superimposed planes, the upper of which could be folded back like a shutter, thus allowing different compositions according to how far it was folded. It was from this idea of folding that she developed in 1960 the articulate aluminium sculptures she called *animals.* These have hinged planes, which enable the spectator to fold them into different shapes, and are often suspended, giving an additional range of movements. They were called animals because she stressed their *organic* aspect: each has his own, well-defined cluster of movements which react to the promptings of the spectator. He is not made of isolated static forms which can be manipulated at random as in a game; no, his parts are functionally related to each other, as if he were a living organism; and the movements of these parts are interlinked. The

interlinking of the spectator's action and the "animal's" immediate answer is what forms this new relationship, made possible precisely because the "animal" moves—i.e., has a life of its own.

Thus the "animals" do enable the spectator to be not merely a passively receptive observer of works of art, but to become an active partner with forces which develop of their own accord. There is no longer a static work of art to be passively contemplated. This resembles the development in avant-garde music which leaves the performer free to interpret the work within a certain range of possibilities, and Lygia Clark herself sees the spectator's act in co-operating with the artist to move the work as a moment of self-awareness. Her aim is to make this a rewarding experience, an intensification of the faculties, and her later works are all further developments of the idea of sensual interplay between art object and spectator or participant. The works she calls *bichos* (a Portuguese word referring to animals without backbones, from worms to caterpillars, which have a generally wriggly motion) are ribbon forms cut out of completely flexible materials such as rubber, so that playing with them reveals their elasticity and marvellous freedom from constraint. These led on to her "dialogue of hands" with her fellow-Brazilian artist Helio Oiticaca, in which the "art object" as such is reduced to a band which links the two participants' hands while they explore each other in a sensual dialogue.

One of her unrealized projects is an *Architecture fantastique*, an articulated architecture capable of taking on an almost limitless number of shapes as people move about inside it. At the Venice *Biennale* in 1968 she did realize a labyrinth called "The House Is the Body," where participants went through a series of cells which were designed to give them the feeling of conception and birth, from the copulatory act of entering, through ovulation and fertilization to expulsion from the womb at the other end. Her TUNNELS are further developments of this idea that "art is the body," plastic tunnels which are brought to life by being crossed and held in position by the participants who move in and through them. She has used all sorts of other objects such as nets, sacks, air-filled plastic bags and pebbles, to evoke complex sensations of life, from breathing to sex, with very simple but concrete means. They often involve several participants working together, for instance with her large shaped sheets of transparent plastic where one person has to lie on the ground while another manipulates the sheets. In such works she aims at a tribal, initiatory quality which she describes as "a question of *ritual without myth:* mythology, which is a metaphysic external to man, is abandoned in order that man may take his place and perform his own myth in these ritual gestures."

Lygia Clark is a highly articulate artist whose writings on spectator participation and the metaphysical implications she sees in it are among the best things so far written on movement in time and space. Her own work has consistently aimed at the withering away of the venerated and valuable art object towards simple means of making the participant use his own energy to give a heightened awareness of himself, his body and his senses. Thus her art, which has been among the most successful of those aiming to encourage active and creative participation, is a contribution to making contemporary man more aware of that disastrous split between intellect and emotions which has been one of the main concerns of artists ever since the Romantic Movement rebelled against the shallow and superficial rationalization of life.

—Konstantin Bazorov

CLARKE, John Clem.

American. Born in Bend, Oregon, 6 June 1937. Studied at Oregon State University, Corvallis; Mexico City College; University of Oregon, Eugene, B.F.A. 1960. Lives and works in New York. Agent: O.K. Harris Gallery, 383 West Broadway, New York, New York 10012, U.S.A.

John Clem Clarke: *Abstract No. 5*, 1973

Individual Exhibitions:

1968 Kornblee Gallery, New York
1969 Franklin Siden Gallery, Detroit
1970 O.K. Harris Gallery, New York
Michael Walls Gallery, San Francisco
Galerie M.E. Thelen, Essen
1971 Kornblee Gallery, New York
Phyllis King Gallery, Chicago
Pyramid Gallery, Washington, D.C.
Galerie de Gestlo, Hamburg
1972 Jack Glenn Gallery, Corona del Mar, California
O.K. Harris Gallery, New York
Carl Solway Gallery Cincinnati, Ohio
1974 D.M. Gallery, London
1981 O.K. Harris Gallery, New York
Morgan Gallery, New York

Selected Group Exhibitions:

1969 *New Aspects of Realism*, Milwaukee Art Center (toured the United States)
1970 *22 Realists*, Whitney Museum, New York
1971 *New Realism*, State University of New York at Potsdam
Radical Realism, Museum of Contemporary Art, Chicago
1972 *Realism Now*, New York Cultural Center
1973 *New York Avant-Garde 74*, Saidye Bronfman Centre, Montreal
Hyperrealisme, Galerie Lsy Brachot, Brussels
1974 *Biennale*, Tokyo
Contemporary Painting from the Lewis Collection, Delaware Art Museum, Wilmington
New Realism Revisited, State University of New York at Potsdam

Collections:

Museum of Modern Art, New York; Whitney Museum, New York; Metropolitan Museum of Art, New York; Hirshhorn Museum, Washington, D.C.; Flint Institute, Michigan; Milwaukee Arts Center; Nelson Museum of Art Kansas City; Museum of Fine Arts, Dallas; University of California, Berkeley; Security Pacific National Bank Collection, Los Angeles.

Publications:

On CLARKE: books—*Neue Formen des Realismus* by Peter Sager, Cologne 1973; *Selection 3: Contemporary Graphics from the Museum's Collection*, catalogue, by D. L. Johnson, Providence, Rhode Island 1973; articles—"An Art of Transmission: John Clem Clarke at Kornblee" by Jeanne Siegel in *Arts Magazine* (New York), Summer 1969; "John Clem Clarke Transmits a Picture" by William S. Wilson in *Artnews* (New York), Summer 1969; "Oedipus and the Sphinx" in *Art Now: New York*, vol. 2, no. 5, 1970; "Bar Area Survey: John Clem Clarke, Michael Walls Gallery" by B. Richardson in *Arts Magazine* (New York), November 1970; "San Francisco: John Clem Clarke, Michael Walls Gallery" by J. Tarshis in *Artforum* (New York), December 1970; "New York Letter: John Clem Clarke, Kornblee Gallery" by Carter Ratcliff in *Art International* (Lugano, Switzerland). March 1971; "The Deductive Image" by J. P. Marendel in *Art International* (Lugano, Switzerland). September 1971; "Szene Rhein-Ruhr" by B. Kerber in *Art International* (Lugano, Switzerland). Summer 1972.

In a century which has focused on the question, what is real? John Clem Clarke is often classed with the Super Realists. His illusionary paintings of wood and wood grain, for example, the convoluted meshes of the transistor, are certainly kin to their concern with the photograph as a means of transmitting subjects, but Clarke's real subject is more the camera as a means of seeing than the subjects it transmits, more how did it get there? than what is it?

Anything, then, can serve Clarke as subject, including the paintings already painted by artists of the past. He has even exhibited numbered versions of replays of the same painting, their subtle differences derived from the subtle differences between one slide of the painting and the next. For the observer this seems subtle indeed, though, apparently, to the artist the differences are clear.

Apparent differences are what the story is, the emphasis being on this apparentness and not its primal subject. All of this recognizes that modern recognition, a formalist concern which goes back at least to Denis, that the painting in itself, since it is a 2-dimensional representation of what exists in 3, is an illusion. Clarke points out the illusion of painting through the medium of paint. If, then, the medium is the message, as by his example he appears to agree, he succeeds in presenting it through the sheer virtuos-

ity of his *trompe l'oeil* technique, dazzlingly illusionistic paintings about painting. He recreates, for example, not only the grain of wood, but even the way rough stroked lettering soaks into it, and can take on the way other artists painted, from obscure Dutch masters to Grant Wood. But in so doing, another element enters, in for, say, in his sly replicas of Bougereau, Clarke not only offers a representation, he criticizes it. There is irony in this. Irony is an attitude, and artists have always painted in the context of the attitudes of the age, inevitably present in any work. But this conscious painting of attitude, of perception, is a specifically twentieth century point of view. Wittingly or otherwise, artists have always quoted artists who have gone before, but before Kant and then the phenomenologists art did not raise the question how do we perceive? Now in the last years of the century it has become a concern handled through the medium of paint.

In painting modes of transmission, Clarke is dealing with a very old opposition as well, the opposition of content versus form. Clarke says, through his art, as do some others in the present, that content can be anything. Yet in this decade, the heyday of formalism having, for now, passed, there is a new interest in content, and content is something transmitted by the artist to the person who sees the work. This raises, then, another question, for if Clarke's paintings come off as paintings about painting, as pictured modes of picturing, what does the person who sees the work receive? Does the observer remain simply an observer or is he involved?

—Barbara Cortright

CLEMENTE, Francesco.

Italian. Born in Naples in 1952. Married to Alba Clemente; has two children. Independent painter, since 1973: lives and works in New York, Rome and Madras. Agents: Galerie Daniel Templon, 30 rue Beaubourg, 75003 Paris, France; Anthony D'Offay Gallery, 9 Dering Street, New Bond Street, London W1, England; Sperone Westwater, 142 Greene Street, New York, New York 10012, U.S.A. Address: Via dei Riari 59, 00165 Rome, Italy.

Individual Exhibitions:

1974 Galleria Area, Florence
1975 Galleria Gian Enzo Sperone, Rome
Galleria Gian Enzo Sperone, Turin
Galleria Massimo Minini, Brescia, Italy
Galleria Franco Toselli, Milan
1976 Galleria Gian Enzo Sperone, Rome
Galleria Lucrezia de Domizio, Pescara, Italy
1977 Galleria Paolo Betti, Milan
1978 Centre d'Art Contemporain, Geneva
Art and Project, Amsterdam
Galerie Paul Maenz, Cologne
1979 Gian Enzo Sperone, Turin
Art and Project, Amsterdam
Galerie Paul Maenz, Cologne
Lisson Gallery, London
Galerie Annemarie Verna, Zurich (with Mimmo Paladino and Nicola de Maria)
Galleria Emilio Mazzoli, Modena, Italy
Galleria Guiliana de Crescenzo, Rome
Galleria Lucio Amelio, Naples
1980 Galleria Gian Enzo Sperone, Rome
Art and Project, Amsterdam
Galerie Paul Maenz, Cologne
Sperone Westwater Fischer Gallery, New York
Padiglione d'Arte Contemporanea, Milan
Galleria Mario Diacono, Rome
1981 Vereniging voor het Museum van Hedendaagse Kunst, Ghent
Anthony d'Offay Gallery, London
Sperone Westwater Fischer Gallery, New York
Galerie Bruno Bischofberger, Zurich
University of California, Berkeley (travelled to Long Beach, California; Hartford, Connecticut)
1982 Galerie Daniel Templon, Paris
Galerie Paul Maenz, Cologne
Galleria Mario Diacono, Rome
Galerie Bruno Bischofberger, Zurich
1983 Whitechapel Art Gallery, London (travelled to Groningen, Karlsruhe, Stockholm and Nice)
Anthony D'Offay / Gian Enzo Sperone, London
Galerie Ascan Crone, Hamburg
Galleria Mario Diacono, Rome
A Space, Toronto
Sperone Westwater / Mary Boone Gallery, New York
Akira Ikeda Gallery, Tokyo and Nagoya, Japan
Kunsthalle, Basle
James Corcoran Gallery, Los Angeles
Fruitmarket Gallery, Edinburgh
Arts Council Gallery, Belfast
1984 Nationalgalerie, West Berlin (travelled to Essen, Amsterdam and Tubingen)
Kestner-Gesellschaft, Hannover
Akira Ikeda Gallery, Tokyo
Riverside Studios, Hammersmith, London
1985 Sperone Westwater / Leo Castelli Gallery, New York
Mary Boone / Michael Werner Gallery, New York
Galerie Bruno Bischofberger, Zurich
Metropolitan Museum of Art, New York
Ringling Museum of Art, Sarasota, Florida (travelled to Minneapolis, Dallas, Berkeley, Buffalo and Los Angeles)
Museum fur Gegenwartskunst, Basle
1986 Akira Ikeda Gallery, Tokyo
Anthony D'Offay Gallery, London
Sperone Westwater, New York
Museum of Modern Art, New York
1987 Galerie Ascan Crone, Hamburg
Museum fur Gegenwartskunst, Basle
Galerie Bruno Bischofberger, Zurich (twice)
Fundacion Caja de Pensiones, Madrid
Art Institute of Chicago
Galerie im Taxispalais, Salzburg, Austria
Ulmer Museum, Ulm, West Germany
Kunstmuseum, Basle (travelled to Groningen, Ulm, Cologne, Lausanne, Frankfurt and Nice)

Francesco Clemente: *Two Men*, 1981 Courtesy Anthony D'Offay Gallery, London

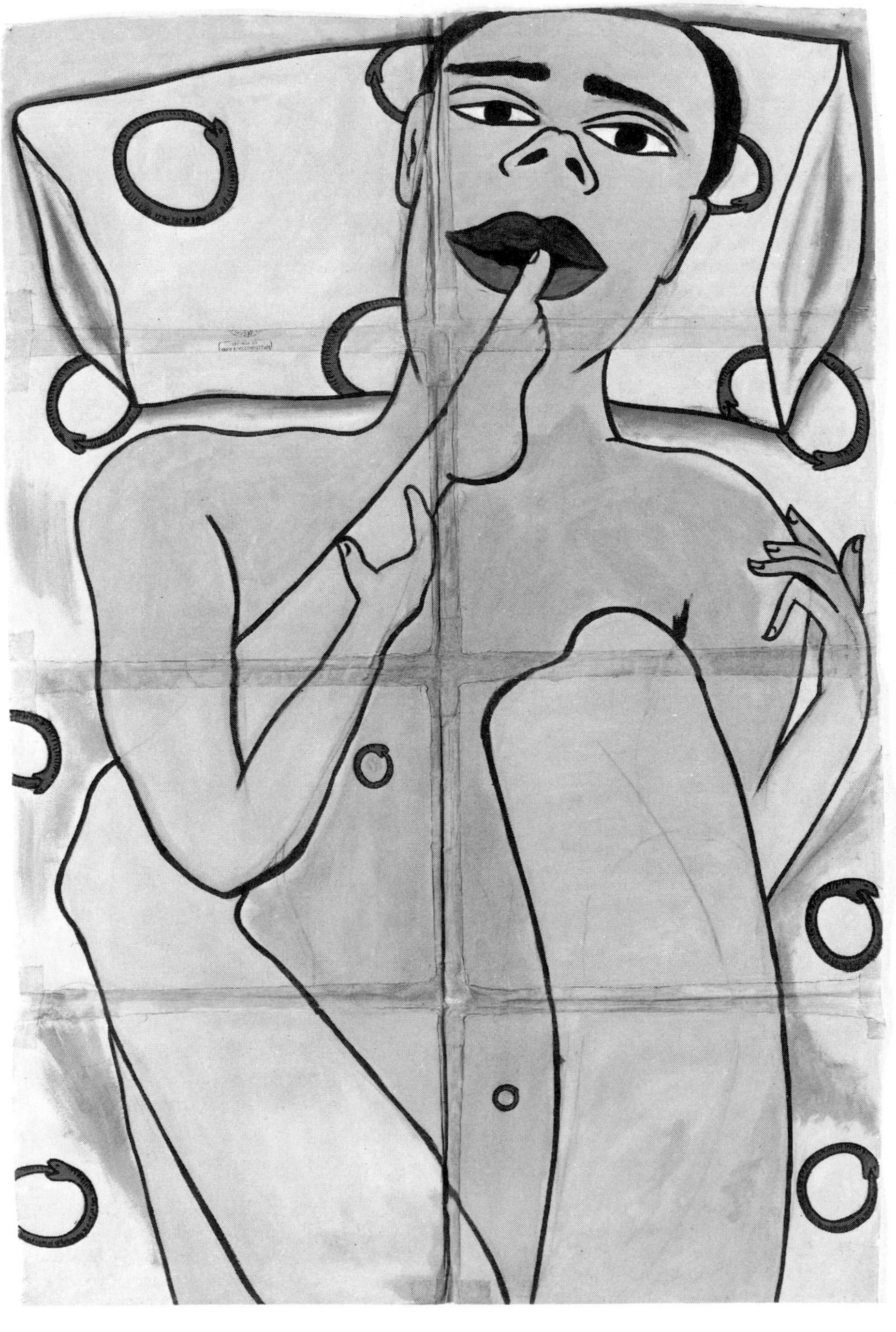

Selected Group Exhibitions:

1973 *Italy Two*, Civic Center Museum, Philadelphia
1975 *Bienal*, Sao Paulo
1977 *X Biennale de Paris*, Musée National d'Art Moderne, Paris
1979 *Europa '79*, Stuttgart
1980 *Die Enthauptete Hand: 100 Zeichnungen aus Italien*, Kunstverein, Bonn
1981 *Westkunst*, Cologne
1982 *Documenta 7*, Kassel, West Germany
1984 *Content: A Contemporary Focus 1974–84*, Hirshhorn Museum, Washington, D.C.
1985 *India and the Contemporary Artist*, Museum of Modern Art, New York
1987 *Avant-Garde in the Eighties*, Los Angeles County Museum of Art

Publications:

By CLEMENTE: books—*The Pondicherry Pastels*, London and Madras 1986; *India*, with John Wieners, Altadena, California 1987; articles—"An Interview with Francesco Clemente", with Achille Bonito Oliva, in *Flash Art* (Milan), Summer 1980; "Francesco Clemente at the Metropolitan", interview with Danny Berger, in *Print Collector's Newsletter* (New York), March / April 1982; "Francesco Clemente", interview with Edit deAk, in *Interview* (New York), April 1982; "Samtale me Francesco Clemente", interview with Heiner Bastian, in *Louisiana Revy* (Humlebaek), June 1983; "A Project for Artforum", in *Artforum* (New York), March 1987.

On CLEMENTE: books—*The Different Avantgarde: Europe / America*, by Achille Bonito Oliva, Milan 1976; *The Italian Trans Avantguarde* by Achille Bonito Oliva, Milan 1980; *Francesco Clemente: il viaggiatore napoletano*, exhibition catalogue with essay by Rainer Crone, Cologne 1982; *Francesco Clemente: The Fourteen Stations*, exhibition catalouge edited by Mark Francis, London 1983; *Currents: Francesco Clemente*, with text by Elisabeth Sussman, Boston 1984; *Francesco Clemente: Pastelle 1974–83*, with texts by Rainer Crone, Zdenek Felix and Lucius Grisebach, Munich 1984; *Francesco Clemente*, exhibition catalogue with texts by Mark Ormond and Marianna Adams, Sarasota 1985; *Francesco Clemente* by Michael Auping, New York 1985; *Francesco Clemente CVIII*, with text by Dieter Koepplin, Basle 1987.

Francesco Clemente has made an impression as one of the most significant personalities in the panorama of "new tendencies" characterized by the renewed interest in the image and in traditional painting techniques. The pre-eminence of the concept in art, with the consequent tendency to dematerialism, is being seriously re-examined in the work of the younger artists, those whose work began to take shape at the end of the 1970's. The optimistic, evolutionist theory of *avant-garde* ideology starts to decline; together with the revival of techniques hitherto regarded as obsolete, artists are trying out the end of ideologies as a theory of a new cultural orientation, pointing to a reinterpretation of the past and a revival of local cultures. There is an established international movement which no longer wants to model itself on a parallel "international style," but prefers to stimulate the differences between one culture and another in a free cross-fertilization of ideas.

Clemente has adopted the stylistic eclecticism that is the most significant outcome of these tendencies and the consequence of an aesthetic attitude that argues the case for the values of subjectivity. Like a number of others, the artist has moved on from photographic media and has abandoned them in favour of manual techniques (collages, oil painting, pastels, tempera, fresco, mosaic, drawing . . .) giving more immediate access to the objects of an ambiguously expressed expressiveness. Clemente's pictures are, as it were, intrinsically ambivalent; they allude to an explicit perverted erotic phantasmagoria, yet at the same time escape from recognizability, closed in the blazons of a private heraldry ("emblems" is the title of a series of works by Clemente). Clemente has often expressed a lively interest in esoteric ideas, in astrology, the history of religion and Indian civilization, from whose symbolism he has drawn inspiration for his own pictorial language. In addition, his painting explicitly recalls the world of late Roman culture, an era of surprising cultural and stylistic eclecticism. This purpose can be recognized especially in Clemente's self-portraits, which have become a recurrent theme with him. A common enough theme in the pictorial tradition, here the self-portrait becomes an elaboration of the idea of self through a self-denigrating rhetoric with a literary flavour, near to the influence of an Egon Schiele, near in short to an "accursed" nature, strongly intellectualized.

The identity loses its familiar features and becomes an unreal, iridescent apparition, organically degenerate, connected with the world of impulses. The artist depicts himself as a convulsed body, an eroticized object ready for any metamorphosis. The image in Clemente springs from the encounter between the this body, this cheerful intensity, and objects and entities transformed by a similar tension into emblems, enigmatic fragments, already completely detached from the totality. The figures are flattened on to the surfaces, suspended in an irrationally defined spatiality. With no depth, a caricature of itself, the picture no longer tries to come to terms with reality, and the painting becomes an example of excess. The excess lies in the recourse to ambiguity. It even dictates the selection of forms: sometimes the drawing looks ugly, crude, like "anti-graceful" graffiti, deliberately elementary, but at other times its studied elegance and surprising fastidiousness are astonishing. The painting fluctuates between a "neo-savage," aggressively *brut* style, even in the choice of colours, and a style that is courtly and sumptuous, with backgrounds of delicately evanescent colour.

The painter's knowledge is there to see in his virtuoso skill, or else lies hidden in coprophilia; it becomes clear in the stylistic polymorphism of one who, in his painting, wishes not to find an identity but to lose himself. As Edit deAk has written, Clemente is a clever chamaeleon cynically content with his own state of grace.

—Giorgio Verzotti

CLOSE, Chuck.

American. Born in Monroe, Washington, 5 July 1940. Educated at Everett Community College, Washington, 1958–60; University of Washington, Seattle, 1960–62, B.A. 1962; Yale Summer School of Art and Music, Norfolk, Connecticut, 1961; Yale University, New Haven, Connecticut, 1962–64, B.F.A. 1963, M.F.A. 1964; Akademie der Bildenden Künste, Vienna, 1964–65. Married Leslie Rose in 1967; daughters: Georgia Molly and Maggie Sarah. Independent artist, since 1966: has lived and worked in New York since 1967. Instructor, University of Massachusetts, Amherst, 1965–67; School of Visual Arts, New York, 1967–71; New York University, 1970–73; University of Washington, Seattle, Summer 1970; Yale Summer School of Art and Music, Norfolk, Connecticut, 1971, 1972. Recipient: Fulbright Grant, 1964; National Endowment for the Arts Grant, 1973. Agent: Pace Gallery, 32 East 57th Street, New York, New York 10022. Addresses: (studio) 75 Spring Street, New York, New York 10012; (home) 271 Central Park West, New York, New York 10024, U.S.A.

Individual Exhibitions:

1967 University of Massachusetts Art Gallery, Amherst
1970 Bykert Gallery, New York
3 Young Americans: A Biennial, Allen Memorial Art Museum, Oberlin College, Ohio (with Ron Cooper and Neil Jenney)
1971 *Recent Work*, Los Angeles County Museum of Art
Bykert Gallery, New York
1972 Museum of Contemporary Art, Chicago
1973 Museum of Modern Art, New York
Akron Art Institute, Ohio
Bykert Gallery, New York
1974 *3 Realists: Close, Estes, Raffael*, Worcester Art Museum, Massachusetts
1975 Edwin Ulrich Museum, Wichita State University, Kansas
Mint Museum of Art, Charlotte, North Carolina
Ball State University Art Museum, Muncie, Indiana
Phoenix Art Museum, Arizona
Laguna Gloria Art Museum, Austin, Texas
Texas Gallery, Houston
Art Museum of South Texas, Corpus Christi
Minneapolis Institute of Arts
Center for Visual Arts, Portland, Oregon
San Francisco Museum of Modern Art
Bykert Gallery, New York
1976 Contemporary Art Center, Cincinnati, Ohio
Baltimore Museum of Art
Richard Artschwager/Chuck Close/Joe Zucker, David Weinberg Gallery, San Francisco (travelled to the La Jolla Museum of Art, California, and the University of California at Davis)
1977 *Matrix 35*, Wadsworth Atheneum, Hartford, Connecticut
Recent Work, Pace Gallery, New York
1979 Kunstraum, Munich
New Painting of Mark and Recent Drawings, Pace Gallery, New York
1980 *Close Portraits*, Walker Art Center, Minneapolis (retrospective 1968–80; travelled to the St. Louis Art Museum, Missouri; Museum of Contemporary Art, Chicago; and the Whitney Museum, New York, 1981)
1982 *Photographs*, California Museum of Photography, Riverside (travelled to Berkeley, California)
Paperworks, Richard Gray Gallery, Chicago (travelled to Minneapolis; Jacksonville; St. Louis)
1983 *Recent Work*, Pace Gallery, New York
1984 *Paper Works*, Herbert Palmer Gallery, Los Angeles (travelled to Cheney, Washington; Milwaukee; DeKalb, Illinois: Columbia, South Carolina)
1985 *Works on Paper*, Contemporary Arts Museum, Houston
Fuji Television Gallery, Tokyo
Photographs, Pace/MacGill Gallery, New York
Large Scale Photographs, Fraenkel Gallery, San Francisco
1986 *Maquettes*, Pace/MacGill Gallery, New York
Recent Works, Pace Gallery, New York
1987 *Polaroids*, Aldrich Museum of Contemporary Art, Ridgefield, Connecticut

Selected Group Exhibitions:

1969 *Annual Exhibition*, Whitney Museum, New York
1970 *22 Realists*, Whitney Museum, New York
1971 *Prospect 71*, Städtische Kunsthalle, Dusseldorf
1972 *Documenta 5* Kassel, West Germany (and *Documenta 6*, 1977)
1974 *Hyperréalistes Américains/Réalistes Européens*, Centre National d'Art Contemporain, Paris (toured Europe)
1978 *American Painting of the 1970's*, Albright-Knox Art Gallery, Buffalo, New York
1980 *Printed Art: A View of 2 Decades*, Museum of Modern Art, New York
1982 *Great Big Drawings*, Massachusetts Institute of Technology, Cambridge
1984 *Drawings 1974–84*, Hirshhorn Museum, Washington, D.C.
1986 *Nude, Naked, Stripped*, Massachusetts Institute of Technology, Cambridge

Collections:

Museum of Modern Art, New York; Whitney Museum, New York; Allen Memorial Art Museum, Oberlin College, Ohio; Walker Art Center, Minneapolis; National Museum of Can-

Chuck Close: *Fanny (fingerpainting)*, 1985

ada, Ottawa; Art Gallery of Ontario, Toronto; Neue Gallery, Aachen, West Germany; Museum Boymans-van Beuningen, Rotterdam; Australian National Gallery, Canberra.

Publications:

By CLOSE: articles—"An Interview with Chuck Close," with Cindy Nemser, in *Artforum* (New York), January 1970; interview, in "Photo-Realists: 12 Interviews" by Linda Chase and Ted McBurnett in *Art in America* (New York), November/December 1972; statement in "The Artist and the Face: A Modern American Sampling: by Gerrit Henry in *Art in America* (New York), January 1975; statement in "The Art of Portraiture in the Words of 4 New York Artists" in the *New York Times,* 31 October 1976; interview in "The 20th Century Artists Most Admired by Other Artists" by Grace Glueck in *Artnews* (New York), November 1977; "An Interview with Chuck Close," with Barbara Harshman, in *Arts Magazine* (New York), June 1978; interview, with Barbaralee Diamonstein, in *Inside New York's Artworld,* New York 1979; "An Interview with Chuck Close", with Jane Cottingham, in *American Artist* (New York), May 1983; "New York in the Eighties: A Symposium" in *The New Criterion* (New York), Summer 1986.

On CLOSE: books—*22 Realists,* exhibition catalogue, with text by James Monte, New York 1970; *3 Young Americans: A Biennial,* exhibition catalogue, with text by Athena Spear, Oberlin, Ohio 1970; *Chuck Close: Recent Work,* exhibition catalogue, with text by Gail R. Scott, Los Angeles 1971; *The Painter and the Photography* by Van Deren Coke, Albuquerque, New Mexico 1972; *American Art since 1900* by Barbara Rose, New York 1972; *Neue Formen des Realismus* by Peter Sager, Cologne 1973; *Photo-Realism: The Ludwig Collection,* exhibition catalogue, London 1973; *3 Realists: Close, Estes, Raffael,* exhibition catalogue, Worcester Massachusetts 1974; *Super Realism: A Critical Anthology,* edited by Gregory Battcock, New York 1975; *History of Modern Art* by H. H. Arnason, New York 1977; *Chuck Close/Matrix 35,* exhibition catalogue, Hartford, Connecticut 1977; *Chuck Close: Recent Work,* exhibition catalogue, New York 1977; *Malerei und Photographie im Dialog* by Erika Billeter, Zurich 1977; *Super-Realism* by Edward Lucie-Smith, New York 1979; *What Is Art?* by John Canaday, New York 1980; *Printed Art: A View of 2 Decades,* exhibition catalogue, New York 1980; *Close Portraits,* exhibition catalogue, with texts by Lisa Lyons and Martin Friedman, Minneapolis 1980; *Contemporary American Realism Since 1960* by Frank H. Goodyear, Jr., New York 1981; *Realists at Work* by John Arthur, New York 1983; *Chuck Close,* exhibition catalogue with text by John Perreault, New York 1983; *The Revenge of the Philistines: Art and Culture 1972–1984* by Hilton Kramer, New York 1985; *Chuck Close: Recent Work,* exhibition catalogue with text by Arnold Glimcher, New York 1986; *50 New York Artists* by Richard Marshall and Robert Mapplethorpe, San Francisco 1986; *Chuck Close* by Lisa Lyons and Robert Storr, New York 1987.

Portraiture is very important to my work, but not for what would seem like the most obvious reasons. Everyone knows something about the way people look—we have certain ideas about what's right and what's wrong. If the complexion is too green, all of a sudden it's not acceptable—whereas, if I were painting a tree, and it were a little too green or too red, no one but a botanist would know or care. I wanted to paint something that people cared about—a face contains very specific information that people can sense is either right or wrong. That keeps me on my toes, keeps me from letting well enough alone, or saying, this is close enough—no pun intended.

Likeness is an important by-product of what I do, but only to the extent that if the photograph I paint from looks like the person, the painting will look like the photograph. But the photograph may not look like the person and if it doesn't, it can be bothersome. I suppose I'd like to make the image like the person, but I've always felt it necessary to maintain a certain distance from the subject. When I painted myself, I always referred to it as "him"—I somehow couldn't deal with the fact that it was me and whether I looked ugly or handsome or whatever.

I have a hard time dealing with my work in terms of the history of portraiture—I don't know how it fits. A lot of great paintings, when I think about it, happen to be portraits, but I have a hard time with it—when I think of something called portrait painting. I think of how all portraits by Rembrandt look like paintings by Rembrandt—that would seem to be a shortcoming of portraiture.

I'm not really interested in photograph, but one thing I like about photographs is the snapshot or mugshot quality of a California driver's license. It's got such an immediacy and a strong reason to exist in terms of mailing down what a certain driver looks like. It doesn't have anything to do with vanity, it doesn't have anything to do with the ego of the sitter or whatever. I've never done commissioned portraits because I never wanted to get involved with those ego problems. If somebody wants a nine-foot-high picture of their head, they must be involved with how they look. I'd hate to have the feeling that I needed to straighten teeth.

As to sitters, I just photograph my friends. Most of the people are relatively anonymous when I photograph them; sometimes they don't stay too anonymous, but I don't try and paint art stars or anything like that.

I never see someone and say, oh, you'd be great to paint. What I do is, get together a whole bunch of people and shoot them, and some of them turn out to be interesting photographs. I don't really think about interesting *people.* I scan a contact sheet and try to imagine what it would be like to paint from that photograph. Some of them seem better than others, not in terms of the overall iconography but in terms of what kind of painting experience they would be—how sharp and how blurry.

But I do care that they are people. I think sometimes it sounds like I don't care, or for that matter, that I don't think they're people. But if you're going to spend three to six months on a painting, you can't just worry about the image and say, gee, I just want this to be a picture of so-and-so. The workaday problems of making a painting tend to take over in my mind. Of course, for the last six or seven years, at least, I haven't really felt like painting anything else, so there must be something there.

—Chuck Close

A key to the work of Chuck Close lies in his statement: "I liked the fact that I wasn't thinking of the cheek in relation to the ear and trying to decide which was closer and which farther away . . . if a person were simply panning across or scanning the cheek and some informational change took place, he would realize that he was moving back and forth in space . . . ." It is such disattachment from his subject—through the huge scale that breaks free of the normal human facial confrontation; through his success at the challenge to keep the visage impersonal yet of course recognizable; through the tight-'sandwich' of clear focus that Close established when he blurred the nose tip in the frontally positioned heads which he himself photographs with a 190mm/. lens so that clarity reigns only in a zone ending at the back of the cheeks; through the melange of non-gestural marks that comprise all his works both the very large and small; through the grids left visible in the watercolors, pastels, and prints, but not present in the large paintings ("By breaking—the grid—down this way, I can make the act of painting exactly the same all the way through."); all such attitudes and processes have led to Close quite suitably being labelled a Minimalist and Conceptualist—his subject matter thus disregarded.

Close appeared at a time when a photographic style in painted art was ostensibly logical because of the triumph of Pop Art and photography's importance there. He had worked on Big Nude, a 20-feet long, black-and-white canvas based on his photograph, but found that he had to avoid 'hot subject matter.' And so as he worked, in the late 1960s, to develop an anthology of techniques to avoid any gestural pictorialism and subjective color, he worked with his spray painting, rag smearing, and razor markings. ("My invention is an invention of means, rather than an invention of shape and other things.") Close then was a pioneer Photo-Realist, used only his own features in these early large works, and remains one of the few Photo-Realists to use the figure. When be began to use color in the early 70s—on the basis of his pleasure with the previous monochromatic images where no color mixing was involved as the black was diluted on the white picture surface—Close wished to continue without palette. From his color photographs, as the image of the icon-like frontal head has remained unvaried, Close had three color separation prints made which he then matched in three painting campaigns (magenta, cyan, yellow) across the canvas from the top down. He thus avoided traditional paint-mixing necessities as he himself produced a handicrafted image based upon the chemical-mechanical photographic process. At this time as well, since he wished neither to change his image nor his a-subjective approaches, he changed the nature of his studio practice in order to maintain his interest in the experience of the technical process. He developed the use of a grid which allowed him to present the same kind of marking unit throughout the image: i.e., the title of the work gave the specific number of grid points, even when as in large works, *Robert 104,072,* 1973–74, 108 by 84 inches, they are not visible as a grid. With smaller works, where they might be but 2760 grid points and they were left clearly distinct as individual, unblended marks, there is a striking resemblance to computer-generated, so-called digital images. In yet another variant of such attempts at a relatively depersonalized creative process, Close more recently has used dyed paper pulp, cut into tiny curved-edged chips, glued onto the picture surface to produce the most tactile work of his mature career.

Perhaps Close is easily appreciated as a hybrid in his fusion of Pop Art and Mimimalism: his image, while by no means sentimental, does of course force the introduction of species-recognition and its concommitant instantaneous search for sentiment; and more cogently his subject choice of the human face (as seen by the camera), led the artist of necessity to invent a pictorial means to achieve both the image and his Minimalist, purist and anti-sentimental surface. He has then used the camera image to establish—in his larger works—a phenomenological reduction to the emblem of consciousness. In his smaller works, where a grid remains, Close may appear a skeptic who does not understand the contents of his consciousness and thus relies upon a photograph for the source of his attempt at "mimicry" of the non-imaginative and neuro-chemical constructive processes of appearance.

—Joshua B. Kind

COHEN, Bernard.

British. Born in London, 28 July 1933. Educated at schools in London; studied shorthand and typing at Clark's College, Leytonstone, London, 1947, and art at South West Essex Technical College and School of Art, 1949–50, St. Martin's School of Art, London, 1950–51, and Slade School of Fine Art, London 1951–54. Married Jean Britton in 1959. Painter: lives and works in London: lived in Paris and travelled in France, 1954–56, and spent several months in Rome, 1956; lived in Hertfordshire, 1959; returned to London, and shared house with William Turnbull, 1961–63, then settled in Putney, South London, 1963; worked on design for stage curtain, Theatre Royal, Stratford, East London, 1965; built studio in Kingston-on-Thames, Surrey, 1967. Part-Time Lecturer, Hammersmith School of Art, London, 1957–60; Lecturer, Ealing School of Art, London, 1961–64; Guest Lecturer, St. Martin's School of Art, London 1963–64; Lecturer, Chelsea School of Art, London, 1966–68, and Slade School of Fine Art, 1967–73 and since 1977. Visiting Professor, Department of Art, University of New Mexico, Albuquerque, 1969–70. Recipient: French Government Travel

Bernard Cohen: *Home Territory*, 1979

Scholarship, 1954; Boise Scholarship, University of London, 1955. Address: 17 Leyborne Park, Kew, Surrey, England.

Individual Exhibitions:

1958 Gimpel Fils, London (with James Tower)
Midland Group Gallery, Nottingham
1960 Gimpel Fils, London
1962 Molton Gallery, London
1963 Kasmin Gallery, London
1964 Kasmin Gallery, London
1967 Kasmin Gallery, London
Arnolfini Gallery, Bristol
Betty Parsons Gallery, New York
Lady Margaret Hall, Oxford
1972 Arnolfini Gallery, Bristol
Hayward Gallery, London
Waddington Galleries, London
Studio LaCitta, Verona
Hester van Royen Gallery, London
1973 Galleria Annunciata, Milan
Waddington Galleries, London
1974 Waddington Galleries, London
1977 Waddington Galleries, London
1979 Waddington Galleries, London
1980 Amano Gallery, Osaka, Japan

Selected Group Exhibitions:

1958 *Abstract Impressionism*, Arts Council Gallery, London
1960 *Situation*, Federation of British Arts Galleries, London
1964 *Painting and Sculpture of a Decade*, Tate Gallery, London
1965 *London: The New Scene*, Walker Art Center, Minneapolis
1967 *Jeune Peintres Anglais*, Palais des Beaux-Arts, Brussels
1969 *Marks on Canvas*, Museum am Ostwall, Dortmund, West Germany
1970 *British Painting*, National Gallery, Washington, D.C.
1973 *New British Painting*, Musée National d'Art Moderne, Paris
1976 *Arte Inglese Oggi*, Palazzo Reale, Milan
1982 *Carnegie International*, Pittsburgh

Collections:

Tate Gallery, London; Arts Council of Great Britain, London; Whitworth Art Gallery, Manchester; Museum am Ostwall, Dortmund, West Germany; Museum of Modern Art, New York; Walker Art Center, Minneapolis; Museum of Modern Art, Caracas.

Publications:

By COHEN: articles—"Gesture and Style" in *Gazette* (London), no. 2, 1961; "International Union of Architects Congress Buildings, South Bank, London" in *Architectural Design* (London), November 1961; "Observations about the Photograph of the Painting Generation" in *Cambridge Opinion*, January 1964; interview, with Denis Bower, in *Arts Review* (London), December 1964; "The Art That Launched a Thousand Ships" in the *Sunday Times Colour Magazine* (London), November 1965; statement in *Bernard Cohen*, exhibition catalogue, Bristol 1967; statement in *Recent British Painting* by Alan Bowness, London 1968; statement in *Arte Inglese Oggi*, exhibition catalogue, Milan 1976.

On COHEN: book—*Bernard Cohen: Paintings and Drawings 1959–71*, exhibition catalogue, by Richard Morphet, London 1972; articles—"Bernard Cohen and Harold Cohen: From Gesture to Symbol: in *London: The New Scene*, exhibition catalogue by Martin Friedmann, Minneapolis 1965; "Bernard Cohen" by David Thompson in *5 Young Painters*, exhibition catalogue, Vence, France 1966; "Bernard Cohen" by Andrew Forge in *The Listener* (London), April 1972; "The Work of Bernard Cohen" by B. Bernstein in *Studio International* (London), June/July 1972.

There has been a dramatic change in Bernard Cohen's paintings; in the 1960s they resembled highly coloured spaghetti, arranged on the canvas in a mixture of meticulous care and free association. One could see why he pointed to their narrative quality, since, in Klee's immortal phrase, they were rather like taking a line, or a tube, for a walk. The churned-up, intestinal association of the imagery also suggested intense, emotional elements, and there were indications that the paintings were, so to speak, graphs of both the process of painting and the physical experience before the canvas.

Cohen is a member of that English generation of artists whose greatest influences came from the United States; whilst he refers to his admiration for such artists as Fontana, Dubuffet, Miró and Dali—and one certainly notes the mixture of informality and surrealism in this early period—there can be little doubt that the most relevant example is Jackson Pollock. The American painter's famous drip paintings are precisely images which record the effort of creation, as well as being monuments to that creativity: they are facts and sequences of time. Cohen's narratives clearly sought to experience the same direct intensity of creation, and to record that experience on canvas. He also refers to his liking for *art nouveau*, which relates to the sinuous convolution of these painted linear graphs.

More recently he has pushed his way through the morass of neo-organic matter, into the fresh air, into uncluttered space; the result is a series of almost white canvases, arranged in a series of oblong areas, against acid-coloured backgrounds, in which pale, distantly burning, lunar symbols float in corners of space. Meticulously conceived and painted, this new phase is immediately more elegant and sophisticated, suggesting a search for idealistic physicality, for a meditative stance through which to reflect metaphysical notions of the physical world and human life. Most recently Cohen has returned to the undisturbed space of a single canvas, in which the clinically white surface is broken not by single sums, but galaxies of coloured spots, floating, drifting rhythmically through space. Perhaps they suggest the smallness of individual man, the non-uniqueness of the earth, the remote mystery of the universe.

—Charles Spencer

COLEING, Anthony.
Australian. Born in Warrnambool, Victoria, in 1942. Studied at the National Art School, Sydney, 1958–59. Recipient: First Prize, Kolotex Competition, 1968; Flotta Lauro Prize, 1971; Australian Visual Arts Board Grant, 1973, 1976, and Studio Grant in New

Tony Coleing: *If the Tyre Fits . . .*, 1979

York, 1987; Mussellbrook Art Prize, 1986; Patron Print Award, Print Council of Australia, 1987. Agent: Ray Hughes Gallery, Brisbane. Address: c/o Ray Hughes, 11 Enoggera Terrace, Red Hill, Brisbane, Queensland, Australia.

Individual Exhibitions:

1969	Gallery A, Melbourne (and Sydney)
1971	Gallery A, Sydney
1974	Watters Gallery, Sydney (and 1975)
1977	Ray Hughes Gallery, Brisbane (and 1978, 1980)
1980	Australian Pavilion, *39th Biennale*, Venice
1981	Institute of Modern Art, Brisbane
	123 Charlotte Street, Brisbane (with Kevin Mortensen)
1982	Roslyn Oxley 9 Gallery, Sydney
	Tony Coleing/Margaret Dodd, at the *Adelaide Festival*, South Australia
	123 Charlotte Street, Brisbane (with Adrian Hall)
1983	Ray Hughes Gallery, Brisbane
1984	Ray Hughes at Reconnaissance, Melbourne
1985	Ray Hughes Gallery, Brisbane
	Ray Hughes Gallery, Sydney

Selected Group Exhibitions:

1968	*Young Commonwealth Artists*, Whitechapel Art Gallery, London
1969	*Mildura Sculpture Triennial*, Mildura, Victoria
1973	*Object and Idea*, National Gallery of Victoria, Melbourne
1975	*Survival Kits*, Melbourne University, Victoria
1976	*Contemporary Australian Sculpture*, Art Gallery of South Australia, Adelaide
1980	*The Queensland Connection*, Contemporary Art Society, Adelaide
1982	*A Photographer's Choice*, Darling Downs Institute of Advanced Education, Toowoomba, Queensland (travelled to Brisbane)
1984	*International Survey of Painting and Sculpture*, Museum of Modern Art, New York
1986	*Biennale of Sydney*, Art Gallery of New South Wales, Sydney
1987	*Urban Anxieties*, Australian National Gallery, Canberra

Collections:

Australian National Gallery, Canberra; Art Gallery of New South Wales, Sydney; National Gallery of Victoria, Melbourne; Art Gallery of South Australia, Adelaide; Queen Victoria Museum and Art Gallery, Launceston, Tasmania; Mildura Arts Centre, Victoria; Ballarat Fine Art Gallery, Victoria; Museum of Contemporary Art, Brisbane; Darling Down Art Gallery, Queensland; National Gallery of New Zealand, Wellington.

Publications:

On COLEING: books—*Tony Coleing: Venice Biennale 1980*, exhibition catalogue by Robin Wallace-Crabbe, Canberra 1980; *The Development of Australian Sculpture* by Graeme Sturgeon, Sydney 1983.

Tony Coleing is a mid-career artist with a pronounced collage sensibility which expresses itself in both two dimensional and three dimensional forms.

A major survey of Australian collage pursuits entitled 'The Age of Collage', held in Sydney during 1987, gave us some insight into Coleing's experiments with two dimensional works on paper since his schooldays. The pattern-making pursuits of a youngster were gradually replaced by photo-collages (many combined with other media) expressing an increasingly ironic view of man and the world.

Some would condemn Coleing as a pessimist; that is a man who lacks faith. I see him as a realist who can penetrate beneath the surface of things and perceive the truths of the human condition. Coleing delights in conveying those insights which can be achieved through the intelligent juxtaposition of unlikely images. From strange bedfellows revealing truths are born.

Much of his work is autobiographical, confronting issues dealing with sexuality, mortality and greed. Personal elements are reinforced by those of a more objective nature. Social concerns show a healthy disrespect for conventional party political philosophies and a cynical acknowledgement of the more ruthless aspects of human endeavour. There is little room for any form of idealism in Coleing's scenario, although his activities as an artist possess a sense of outrage which seems to propel him as a kind of 'noble' prophet and philosopher.

By shunning many of the 'niceties' of the art-making process and electing, instead, for a more brutally sparse approach, Coleing, is, in his own way, offering us a role-model for human survival. Who needs high technology, uranium and Star Wars? Not the likes of Coleing and those who reject the propaganda of political leaders, industrial magnates and newspaper and television moguls.

Coleing's art during the past two decades has embraced formats which have enabled him to extend his flair for juxtaposition in installation formats (as at the Venice Biennale in 1980) and in large canvases dealing with international military confrontations. A series of 'Pope Cards' mocked the hypocrisy of the Roman Catholic church.

A 1980 Venice Biennale installation analysed Australia's role as a producer of 'yellowcake' for the production of uranium and the ruthless exploitation by overseas interests of a uniquely isolated and extraordinary environment. In his catalogue notes for this Venice Biennale piece, Robin Wallace Crabbe observed that one of Coleing's major achievements was his "avoidance of the chic of radicalism. His art protests but offers no fringe luxuries, no 'my god that was worth doing but really . . . . waiter! another scotch on the rocks.' Instead the statement remains unavoidable in its simplicity, relentless, and with seedy comedy, tragically uncomic."

Much of Coleing's best work faces up to issues which are simultaneously regional and universal in significance. Some critics attacked an installation work of Coleing's at Venice 1980 as being too parochial, because it incorporated jars of an Australian bread and butter spread called Vegemite and two mounted Kangaroo heads. They missed the point. Does Australia actually *own* its own Vegemite, or yellowcake, or anything else for that matter? What price becoming a fully-fledged, paid-up member of the global community?

—Arthur McIntyre

COLEMAN, James.
Irish. Born in Ballaghaderreen, County Roscommon,

July 1941. Studied at the Ecole des Beaux-Arts, Paris, 1960–61, Central School of Arts and Crafts, London, 1961–63, National College of Art and Design, Dublin, 1963–66, and Accademia di Belle Arti, Milan, 1966–71. Lives and works in Dublin and Milan. Recipient: Arts Council of Ireland grant, 1968, 1970; Irish-American Cultural Institute Award for the Arts, 1977; Irish Arts Council Award, 1979. Agents: Studio Marconi, via Tadino 15, 20124 Milan; David Hendricks, 119 St. Stephen's Green, Dublin, Ireland; and Nigel Greenwood Inc., 4 New Burlington Street, London W1, England. Address: 189 Emmet Road, Inchicore, Dublin 8, Ireland.

Individual Exhibitions:

1965 Molesworth Gallery, Dublin
1967 Design Studio, Amsterdam
1970 Studio Marconi, Milan
1972 *Projections*, Galleria Toselli, Milan
1973 *Habitual Object*, David Hendricks Gallery, Dublin
Habitual Object, Studio Marconi, Milan
1974 Ulster Museum, Belfast
Slide Piece, Studio Lia Rumma, Naples
Installation Made for Location and Slide Piece, Galerie t'Venster, Rotterdam
2 Seagulls; or, One Seagull Twice, Cork Arts Society, Ireland
1975 *Clara and Dario*, Studio Marconi, Milan
1978 *Strongbow*, Project Arts Centre, Dublin
1979 *Box*, Galleria Schema, Florence
Box, Nigel Greenwood Inc., London (with Marc Chaimowicz)
1980 *Connemara Landscape*, University College Art Gallery, Galway, Ireland
So Different . . . and Yet, Nigel Greenwood Inc., London
Douglas Hyde Gallery, Dublin
1981 *Now and Then, So Different . . . and Yet*, Project Arts Centre, Dublin
So Different . . . and Yet, Franklin Furnace, New York
1982 *Slide Piece*, John Hansard Gallery, Southampton, England
Nigel Greenwood Inc., London
Douglas Hyde Gallery, Trinity College, Dublin (travelled to the Arts Council of Northern Ireland Gallery, Belfast)
Ignotum per Ignotius, Lantaren Theatre, Rotterdam (toured Netherlands)
1983 Whitechapel Art Gallery, London
Orchard Gallery, Derry, Northern Ireland
Teatro Estudio Citac, Coimbra, Portugal (travelled to Lisbon)
1984 Douglas Hyde Gallery, Dublin
David Bellman Gallery/Art Metropole, Toronto
1985 Dungaire Castle, County Clare, Ireland
Renaissance Society, Chicago (retrospective; travelled to Institute of Contemporary Arts, London)
1987 Galerie Rudiger Schottle, Munich
Galeria Johnen und Schottle, Cologne

Selected Group Exhibitions:

1972 *Living Art*, Project Arts Centre, Dulbin
1973 *Biennale de Paris*, Musée d'Art Moderne de la Ville, Paris
1976 *Living Art*, National Gallery of Ireland, Dublin
1977 *ROCS '77*, Hugh Lane Municipal Gallery of Modern Art, Dublin
1978 *Milano '80*, Palazzo Reale, Milan
Biennale, Venice
1980 *Without the Walls*, Institute of Contemporary Arts, London
1982 *Biennale*, Sydney
1986 *In De Maalstroom*, Palais des Beaux-Arts, Brussels
1987 *From the Europe of Old*, Stedelijk Museum, Amsterdam

Collections:

Ulster Museum, Belfast; Arts Council of Northern Ireland, Belfast; Municipal Gallery of Dublin.

Publications:

By COLEMAN: articles—statement in *VIII Biennale de Paris*, exhibition catalogue, Paris 1973; article in *Art Press* (Paris), September 1973; articles in *Prospect* (Milan), March/April 1973; "Essay from Coleman" in *Art in Ireland* (Dublin), vol. II, no. 3, 1974; article in *Data* (Milan), Summer 1974; "Flash Piece 1970 and Slide Piece 1972/73" in *Bolaffi Selected Artists*, Turin 1974; statement in *Rotterdam Art News*, September/October 1974.

On COLEMAN: books—*Installation Made for Location and Slide Piece*, exhibition catalogue, by Achille Bonito Oliva, Rotterdam 1974; *Europe-America: The Different Avant Gardes* by Achille Bonito Oliva, Milan 1976; *James Coleman*, exhibition catalogue, by Jean Fisher, Dublin 1982; *The Enigma of the Hero in the Work of James Coleman* by Jean Fisher, Londonderry 1983; *James Coleman: Selected Works*, exhibition catalogue with essays by Anne Rorimer and Michael Newman, Chicago and London 1985; articles—"James Coleman à la Tête de l'Avant-garde à la Biennale de Paris" by George Astalos in *Nouvelle Europe* (Paris), no. 6, 1973; "Causality and the Interpretation of Information" by Ricardo Luccio in *Data* (Milan), May/June 1976; "Review from Dublin" by Dorothy Walker in *Art Monthly* (London), November 1978; "Installations and Performances in Ireland" by Dorothy Walker in *Flash Art* (Milan), October/November 1979.

In the theatre the audience interpret what they see and hear to reconstruct the narrative and its meaning. James Coleman foregrounds this process of interpre-

James Coleman: *Living and Presumed Dead*, tape/slide installation, Toronto, 1986

tation in his work which has taken a variety of forms since the early 1970s including slide projection, tape-slide, film, video, installation, and performance using actors. By constructing the work as an enigma, by fragmenting the narrative and making the relation of images to text not an obvious or illustrative one, Coleman draws attention to the way in which the viewer or audience is drawn into the work by the interpretative act. The way in which images and text intersect to constitute the position of the interpreter becomes a subject of the work. Through the process of interpretation the subject—the interpreter—is constituted within Language.

Coleman builds into his works allusions to different codes. The slide projection *Connemara Landscape* (1980) deconstructs the implications of romantic depictions of the Irish landscape by simultaneously providing clues for and frustrating interpretation. The video work *So Different . . . and Yet* (1980) could be interpreted according to the discourse of psychoanalytic theory: this would focus on the fetishistic pose of the woman, and the fetishism of the green dress and woman as an object of desire in the fragmented romantic-fiction narrative. For those familiar with the code of Irish national and literary history the green dress and the proper names of the characters take on additional symbolic functions. Yet another interpretation, this time according to the code of mythology, is hinted at by the horns on the head of the pianist in the video image—a possible reference to Cernunnos, the horned god of pre-Christian Irish myth—as well as the structural relationships within the narrative. Yet while the act of interpretation is continually provoked it is never allowed to be conclusive, to terminate in a "transcendental signified." The fragmentation of the linear chain of the narrative—where one thing would otherwise lead smoothly to another—opens the space for the "vertical" metaphorical substitutions of interpretation. Yet, like the needle of a record player which jumps to another track, these possible interpretations don't lead outside Language to the signified as thing-in-itself, whether artist's intention, viewer's experience, or enclosing context. One signifier only leads to another, and yet another. The title invites completion: "So different, and yet—the same." But this "same" is suspended as absence, as an identity that cannot be provided, as the void or lack which instigates the desire which motivates the play of signifiers.

One of the features which contributes to the extraordinary richness of Coleman's work is that it involves a modern reworking of age-old themes. While he employs contemporary media and techniques of handling text and images, Coleman draws on such central texts of the Western tradition as Sophocles' *Oedipus the King* and the Irish epic the *Táin Bó Cuailnge.* Not only do his works thematize interpretation, they are also reinterpretations of tradition—interpretations in terms of the interpretative act itself. In this sense they are reflexive—analytical—allegories of the theatrical scent of interpretation with the interpreter—the viewer or member of the audience—as protagonist, both victim and murderer.

To see identity as something which is constituted in a process and involved with interpretation is to prise it away from what is often taken to be its natural relation to the fully rounded character. Coleman uses theatricality to deconstruct the identification of the actor with character as if he or she were a real person. Rather the figures in the narrative of *So Different . . . and Yet* and in the tableaux of *Living and Presumed Dead* (1983–85) serve as what V. Propp in *The Morphology of the Folktale* called "functions" in a narrative structure. Just as the figures in a dream are not real characters but elements in a structure which expresses, in a distorted form, a repressed unconscious wish, so the functions in *So Different . . . and Yet* and *Living and Presumed Dead* only become interpretable (in a way that is always problematic and reflexive) in terms of their interrelationship and, in this process of allegorical reading, construct a position for the interpreter.

In *Living and Presumed Dead* the narrative of identity is also a story of a secret discovered, of a search for the father or the hero, of murder and of revenge. The murderer turns out to be an obscure figure without face who is unnamed in the action and listed only as "Mr." This designation functions linguistically as a shifter, like "I" or "you," a syntactical position filled by whoever performs the utterance or is designated by it. This is the point where the act of enunciation encounters the symbolic order, where the living speaker assumes a position within language, in a sense "dying" into representation. It could be said that the interpreter is both the murderer and the victim of the interpretation, in that he or she both constructs a symbolic order and takes a position within it, freezing being—the living flow of desire—into meaning.

—Michael Newman
(from *The Analytical Theatre,*
Independent Curators Inc., 1987)

COLLINS, James.

British. Born in Northampton, England, 1939; emigrated to United States, 1970. Studied at St. Martins School of Art, London, 1959–63; Hornsey School of Art, London, 1963–64. Independent artist: lives and works in both New York and London. Taught at London College of Printing, High Wycombe and Epsom Schools of Art, England, 1964–69; taught at New York University, 1970–75; taught at Hartford University, Connecticut, 1976–77. Recipient: Prix de Rome Scholarship (Painting), 1964; National Endowment for the Arts Fellowship, 1977. Address c/o Max Protetch Gallery, 37 West 57th Street, New York, New York 10019, U.S.A.

Individual Exhibitions:

1975 Galleria Françoise Lambert, Milan
Galerie Gaetan, Geneva
John Gibson Gallery, New York
Patrick Verelst Gallery, Antwerp
1976 Galleria Il Capricorno, Venice
York University Gallery, Toronto
Galleria Renzo Spagnoli, Florence
Galerie Folker Skulima, Berlin
Galleria Piergiorgio Firinu, Turin
Galleria Pasquale Trisorio, Naples
Galerie Ingrid Oppenheim, Cologne
1977 Palomar College, San Marcos, California
Galerie Isy Brachot, Brussels
Galleria Pasquale Trisorio, Naples
Galerie Tanit, Munich
Akron University, Ohio
Galerie Krinzinger, Innsbruck, Austria
Galeria Stampa, Basel
Western Front Gallery, Vancouver
Galleria Cicconi, Macerata, Italy
Galleria Ginevra Grigolo, Bologna
A Space Gallery, Toronto
Galleria Arte Verso, Turin
University of California at Santa Barbara
1978 Arnolfini Gallery, Bristol
Institute of Contemporary Arts, London
University of Wisconsin, Menomonie
Emily Carr College, Vancouver
1979 Washington Project for the Arts, Washington, D.C.
University of South Florida, Tampa
University of Iowa, Iowa City
Max Protetch Gallery, New York
Galleria Paolo Tonin, Truin
Glen Hanson Gallery, Minneapolis
University of Florida, Miami
Galleria Arte Borgogna, Milan
1980 Pallazzo dei Diamanti, Ferrara, Italy
Galerie Linssen, Bonn
Galleria Arte Borgogna, Milan
Galleria Pasquale Trisorio, Naples
L'Incontro Galleria d'Arte, Imola, Italy
1981 Hans Redman Gallery, Berlin
'123' Gallery, Antwerp
Galleria Anna D'Ascanio, Rome
Mississippi Museum of Art, Jackson
1982 Anne van Horenbeeck Gallery, Brussels
Galleria Paolo Tonin, Turin
Galleria Pasquale Trisorio, Naples

Selected Group Exhibitions:

1976 *Foto & Idea,* Comune di Parma, Italy
1977 *Documenta 6,* Kassel, West Germany
Contemporary Figuration, Ohio State University, Columbus
1979 *AA on Paper,* University of North Carolina, Greensboro
Concept, Narrative, Document, Museum of Contemporary Art, Chicago
1980 *Presences The Figure and Man-Made Environments,* Albright College, Reading, Pennsylvania
Refigurations, Max Protetch Gallery, New York
1981 *Genius Loci,* Ferrara, Italy
1982 *Façons de Peindre,* Chalon-sur-Saône, France

Publications:

By COLLINS: book—*Narrative Art,* exhibition catalogue, Brussels, 1974; articles—"Things and Theories" in *Artforum* (New York), May 1973; "Pointing, Hybrids and Romanticism: John Baldessari" in *Artforum* (New York), October 1973; "Remarks on Romanticism" in *Flash Art* (Milan), June 1975; "The Importance of Not Being Earnest About Photography" in *Skira 76,* Geneva 1976; "The Rise of Europe" in *Flash Art* (Milan), October 1981.

On COLLINS: books—*6 years* by Lucy Lippard, New York 1973; *Europa/America* by Achille Bonita Oliva, Milan 1979; *James Collins,* edited by Giancarlo Politi and Helena Kontová, with an essay by Sarah Kent, Milan 1978; articles—"The Semantics of Concept Art" by Gopnik in *Artscanada* (Toronto), April 1970; review by David Bourdon in the *Village Voice* (New York), September 1975; review by Romano Giachetti in L'Express (Paris), October 1975: "The Boulevard of Soho Dreams" by Mona Da Vinci in the *Soho Weekly News* (New York), 18 September 1975; review by Walter Robinson in *Art in America* (New York), December 1975; "The Erotic and the Didactic" by Robert Pincus-Witten in *Arts Magazine* (New York), January 1976; "James Collins Voyeuredonista" by Angelo Calabrese in *Documentioggi* (Naples), March 1976; "Photography: A Specific Communication for Artistic Research" by Ilaria Bignamini in *Flash Art* (Milan), June 1976; "New Movements in Conceptual Art" by Margaret Sheffield in *Studio International* (London), November/December 1976; "James Collins" by Werner Lippert in *Kunstforum* (Mainz), June 1976; "James Collins Double Portraits" by Margaret Sheffield in *Artforum* (New York), April 1977; review by A. A. Bronson in *Artscanada* (Toronto), May 1977; review by Anne-Sargent Wooster in the *New York Arts Journal,* no. 15, 1979; review by John Russell in the *New York Times,* July 1979.

My 1973 essay, "Things and Theories" was really a corrective attack against the extremes of conceptual art and a defense of then beleagured "painting," and I say painting in inverted commas because at that time I was interested in the idea of promoting a very open kind of situation, and I've always looked at my photographs as just one kind of painting, but I must say recently I'm interested in painting in perhaps more traditional terms—some kind of mark.

When I started photographs in late 1968, it was an avant-garde activity—at least as a kind of painting. The history of people using photographs in fine arts was short, and photographs seemed a new area not explored. I didn't know the history of photography, and it was an interesting new way of working. Now the whole art world is full of people using photographs, and it no longer has those avant-garde ramifications. This is one complaint. My other complaint is the limited visual things you can do with photographs; it's a kind of "a priori" activity. You set the situation up, you photograph it, you can manipulate the photograph afterwards to some extent, but you can't manipulate it the same way you can manipulate

James Collins: *And There She Goes Just Walking Down the Street*, 1981

a drawing or an image. What I like about drawing particularly, for example, is that it's a kind of fiction where you can bring together very disparate elements, whereas in a photograph you have to actually get hold of the elements and then photograph them. It's a different kind of activity.

I started off as a painter, and I still consider myself a painter. And what's interesting about painting is its limitations: all you have is a surface and marks to move people with. That's it! What puts me off about so many other art areas is the apparatus. Never could I image myself being a film-maker just because of the Mickey Mouse organization stuff. You have to orchestrate the lives of 50 people for 6 months, raise money, etc., etc. Activities interesting perhaps sociologically—but they are not my main interests. I'm an image maker: my passion is making images to move people. Photography was merely a way to make those images quickly. Now I'm finding that photographs do move people, but they move them within certain limitations.

You run into big problems any time you make marks on canvas, however you make those marks. I'm interested in trying to find visual equivalent to the speed of photography—images almost like handwriting, having some reference to the world, having the speed of handwriting, but getting information across quickly. I wouldn't mind mixing the sensuousness of Morris Louis with the subjects of Richard Pryor.

—James Collins

James Collins's work is comprehensively characterized by the intermixed use of the media, from abstract and figurative painting to conceptual photography. Even if the changes of media are often caused by external events and by artistic fashions, there is a persisting continuity around which his work is built. He has in fact been concentrating for the past ten years on a single theme, "Watching Women," a sort of intellectual voyeurism which is presented in a number of variations: on the beach, on the grass, in bed or in the artist's studio, but always as observer. The only one who can observe the girl is in fact someone at the front, in front of the picture.

Voyeurism, which the artist says has been a lifetime obsession, has since 1973 become his basic poetry.

As early as 1969–1971 his "Introduction Pieces" were based on his introducing himself to unknown people whom he had met casually. All that was necessary was to change the situation from one of sexual indifference to one of eroticism to bring about the different result. His photography, which looked at first like something from the newspapers or the police records, turned into a photography directly executed by the artist, becoming much more evocative and esthetic.

Later works left simple photo-documentation even further behind and moved towards formal solutions, such as the segmentation of the panels, symmetry between objects and persons (i.e. the woman and the artist), the use of a monochromatic background, and painting. The situations photographed became increasingly artificial and composed until they formed a meticulous design.

The pastels of girls or of voyeuristic situations done in the last years are mostly based on photographic portraits collected from time to time during a journey, in the street or in an art gallery. Certain details in the figure, standing out against the monochrome field, are highly focused so as to emphasize the eroticism of the model. The extremely elegant and controlled painting, like that of Balthus or Klossowski, whom Collins greatly admires, with its startling contrasts of light and colour, succeeds in maintaining the tension of an aloof eroticism.

—Helena Kontova

COLOMBO, Gianni.

Italian. Born in Milan, 1 January 1937. Self-educated in art. Began artwork using various materials, 1954; produced first monochrome reliefs, 1958; first changeable objects, 1959. Co-Founder, with Giovanni Anceschi, Davide Boriani and others, Gruppo T, 1959. Organized Nouvelle Tendance, 1963. Lecturer, Faculty of Architecture, University of Berlin, 1982. Recipient: Gold Medal for Industrial design, *13th Triennale*, Milan, 1964; Gold Medal, *14th Covegno Internazionale Artisti*, Rimini, 1964; 1st Prize, *34th Biennale*, Venice, 1968; Giolli Prize, 1980; First Prize, *Kunst am Bau* competition, West Berlin, 1981. Address: Via Giacosa 52, 20127 Milan, Italy.

Individual Exhibitions:

1960	Galleria Pater, Milan
1965	Galleria Vismara, Milan
	Galleria La Salita, Rome
1966	Galerie Loehr, Frankfurt
1967	Galleria del Deposito, Genoa
	Galleria Flaviana, Locarno, Switzerland
1968	Galleria Schwarz, Milan
	Galleria L'Attico, Rome
	Galleria Guida, Naples
	Biennale, Venice
	Galerie Tony Gerber, Berne
	Studio di Informazione Estetica, Turin
1969	Galleria del Leone, Venice
1970	Studio Marconi, Milan
	Kunstlersiedlung Halfmannshof, Gelsenkirchen, West Germany
	Galerie Suzanne Bollag, Zurich
	Galleria La Città, Verona
1971	Galerija Suvermeni Umjetnosti, Zagreb
	Galleria La Polen, Genoa
	Neue Galerie am Landesmuseum, Graz, Austria
	Plus-Kern, Ghent (with Morellet and Stein)
1972	Galerie Thomas Keller, Munich
	Palazzo dei Diamanti, Ferrara, Italy
	Galerie M., Bochum, West Germany
	Galerie Suzanne Bollag, Zurich
1973	Sineron, Brescia, Italy
	Studio Marconi, Milan
	Studio Casati, Merate, Italy
1974	Galerie Swart, Amsterdam
	Galerie Lydia Megert, Berne
	Centro Serre Ratti, Como, Italy
1975	Studio V., Vigevano, Italy
	Galleria Giuli, Lecco, Italy
	Galerie Media, Neuchâtel, Switzerland
	Galleria Uxa, Novara, Italy
	Studio Marconi, Milan
	Galerie Muller-Roth, Stuttgart
	Städtisches Museum, Leverkusen, West Germany
1976	Kunsthalle, Baden-Baden, West Germany
	Kunsthalle, Kiel, West Germany
	Galleria G7, Bologna
	Galleria A, Parma, Italy
1977	Studio Marconi, Milan
	Galleria Solferino, Milan
1978	Arte Struktura, Milan
	Galleria 2000, Bologna
	Centro Culturale, Fara d'Adda, Italy
1981	Van Abbemuseum, Eindhoven, Netherlands
	Studio Grosetti, Milan
	Centro Serre Ratti, Como, Italy
1982	Nuovo Spazio Metropolitano, Milan
	Raad Galerie, West Berlin
1983	Galleria Civica d'Arte Contemporanea, Suzzara, Italy
1984	Padiglione d'Arte Contemporanea, Milan
	Italian Pavilion, *XLI Biennale*, Venice
1985	Galleria Pero, Milan
	Galerie Hoffman, Friedberg, West Germany
	Galerie Scholler, Dusseldorf

Selected Group Exhibitions:

1960	*Contemporary Italian Art*, Institute of Design, Chicago
1965	*Licht und Bewegung*, Kunsthalle, Berne (toured Europe)
1966	*Kunst-Licht-Kunst*, Stedelijk van Abbemuseum, Eindhoven, Netherlands
1970	*Kinetic Art*, Hayward Gallery, London
1974	*Fotomedia*, Museum am Ostwall, Dortmund, West Germany

1976 *Biennale*, Sydney
1978 *Metafisica del Quotidiano*, Galleria d'Arte Moderna, Bologna
1980 *Pier and Ocean*, Hayward Gallery, London (travelled to the Rijksmuseum Kröller-Müller, Otterlo, Netherlands)
1983 *Electra*, Musée d'Art Moderne de la Ville, Paris
1987 *Mathematik in der Kunst*, Wilhelm-Hack-Museum, Ludwigshafen, West Germany

Collections:

Galleria Nazionale d'Arte Moderna, Rome; Museo Sperimentale, Turin; Museum des 20, Jahrhunderts, Vienna; Städtisches Museum, Bochum, West Germany; Museum of Modern Art, New York; Columbia University, New York.

Publications:

By COLOMBO: books—*Miriorama I*, Milan 1960; *After Structures*, exhibitions catalogue, Genoa 1967; *Lo Spazio dell'Immagine*, Foligno, Italy 1967; articles—"Im Elastichen Raum" in *Trigon*, exhibition catalogue, Graz 1967; "Spazioelastico-Ambiente" in *Studio V* (Vigevano, Italy), 1975; films—*Vobulazione e Bieloquenza Neg*, with Vicento Agnetti, Milan 1970; *Arte programmata*, Milan 1972.

On COLOMBO: books—*Nature and Art of Motion* by Gyorgy Kepes, New York 1965; *Gianni Colombo* by Gillo Dorfles, Rome 1965; *Rapporto 60* by Maurizio Fagiolio dell'Arco, Rome 1966; *L'Art Cinetic* by Frank Popper, Paris 1967; *Constructivism: Origins and Evolution* by George Rickey, New York 1967; *Gianni Colombo*, exhibition catalogue, by Guido Balla, Venice, 1968; *Gianni Colombo*, exhibition catalogue, by Rolf Wedewer, Gelsenkirchen, West Germany 1970; *Gianni Colombo*, exhibition catalogue, by Guilio Carlo Argan, Ferrara, Italy 1972; *Gianni Colombo*, exhibition catalogue, by Antije von Graevenitz, Eindhoven, Netherlands 1981; *Gianni Colombo*, exhibition catalogue, by Marco Meneguzzo, Suzzara, Italy 1983; *Gianni Colombo*, exhibition catalogue, by Jean Louis Scheffer, Milan 1984.

To construct is that particular dimension of a work (not only the work of art) that implies a coming into contact with the manifold inventory of materials. It is work carried out through a 'culture of materials' which technology continuously develops through time. It is the universe of technologies that consigns to us not only materials but also the ways to put them together in order to concretise 'the construction'.

Once we understand art as something to do with construction, materials, and technology as the 'working supervisor', does the presentation of such materials represent a 'technological universe'?

As far as the relationship with the technological is concerned, in may case it it is just a question of multiplying the usage of different techniques toward concentrating on the opposite ends of technology—i.e., the impact it has on man's behaviour. My art means placing the notion of behaviour within the operation of environmental planning, where 'environment' is understood as he visualization of the specific condition of planning itself.

—Gianni Colombo

Gianno Colombo's earliest works (1954) were nonfigurative, 'multimaterial' (sort of collage) pieces. From these he went on to make monochrome pieces, reliefs composed of rectangles arranged vertically in rows. By 1959 these had become mobile. They were either moveable by the spectator or on their own account. In either case they moved rhythmically, the rectangular elements coming out and going in: *In and Out* or *Pulsating Structures*. This was the beginning of his interest in kinetic art. In that year he became a founder member of Gruppo T and four years later the group joined the Nouvelle Tendence.

The next year, 1960, he began to make 'Fluid Structures'. These consisted of moving, transparent plastic tapes that writhed within an enclosed space. In 1964, like many of the Nouvelle Tendence, he turned to optical-kinetic and environmental art. This began with his 'Roto-optic' work which produced strange moving luminous forms, like X-rays of organs pulsating with life. Pulsation and rhythmic, organic movement means much to him and he finds various ways of displaying it.

But his most adventures light structures were his 'Elastic Spaces', begun in the mid-1960s. These consisted of cubes of elastic florescent cords, subdivided into regular sections and lit by ultra-violet light. The cords either distort themselves rhythmically or are distorted by the spectator walking through them.

In the 1970s Colombo turned from kinetic and light works to lopsided structures of various kinds, mostly interiors. These seem to have been inspired by a house built by Buster Keaton in the film *A Week* (1920). Everything about the house—roofs, windows the door—is askew, but it holds together; and Keaton stands back, saw in hand, looking at it admiringly. Colombo sometimes uses pillars arranged at odd angles and looking like the ruins of an ancient city that had been struck by earthquake. At other times he constructs interiors rather on the lines of the rooms constructed by the psychologist, Ames (*Ames room*) to illustrate illusions of space. The floor is tilted, possibly the ceiling also, in consequence the walls are inevitably out of kilter. He calls these works 'Topestesia' or 'Architettura Cacogonimetrica', which loosely translates as fruitfully bad architecture, but the words themselves are lopsided and strictly meaningless.

These are among the most original works to come from Colombo's fertile imagination. The source of inspiration he acknowledges, but he alone exploited it. Hitherto he had tended to swim with the tide that flowed: kinetic-optical-light art. But in these later works he has struck out on his own. Not that he was not original when swimming with the tide. He invariably was. Three things seem to obsess him: a striving for purity and clarity of expression, characteristic of the Nouvelle Tendence; a feeling for and love of the fluctuations and pulsations and the rhythms of living forms; and the oddness of our perception of the world around us.

—D. C. Barrett

COLVILLE, Alex.

Canadian. Born David Alexander Colville in Toronto, Ontario, 24 August 1920. Studied, under Stanley Royle, at Mount Allison University, Sackville, New Brunswick, 1938–42, B.F.A. 1942. Served in Canadian Infantry, 1942–46: Lieutenant, then Captain; War Artist, 1944–46. Married Rhoda Wright in 1942; children: Graham, John, Charles, and Ann. Independent painter, Nova Scotia, since 1963. Commissioned to Design Canadian Centennial Coinage, 1967. Assistant to Associate Professor, Mount Allison University, 1946–63. Visiting Artist, University of California at Santa Cruz, 1967–68; Künstler Program, West Berlin, 1971. Member, Canada Council, 1966–72. Recipient: Dunn International Award, 1963; Canada Council Award, 1975. Honorary degrees: Trent University, Peterborough, Ontario; Dalhousie University, Halifax, Nova Scotia; Simon Fraser University, Burnaby, British Columbia; University of Windsor, Ontario; Acadia University, Wolfville, Nova Scotia; Officer, 1967, and Companion, 1982, Order of Canada. Agents: Mira Godard Gallery, 22 Hazelton Avenue, Toronto, Ontario M5R 2E2; Galerie Claude Bernard, 9 Rue des Beaux-Arts, 75006 Paris, France. Address: Box 550, Wolfville, Nova Scotia, Canada.

Individual Exhibitions:

1951 New Brunswick Museum, St. John
1953 Hewitt Gallery, New York
1955 Hewitt Gallery, New York
1963 Banfer Gallery, New York
1966 Hart House, University of Toronto
1969 Kestner Gesellschaft, Hannover
1970 Marlborough Fine Art Gallery, London
1971 *Serigraphs*, University of Moncton, New Brunswic[k] (toured Canada, 1971–73)
1976 Fischer Fine Art, London
Norman Mackenzie Art Gallery, Regina, Saskatche[wan]
Lynnwood Arts Center, Simcoe, Ontario
1977 *Bilder und Zeichnungen 1970–1977*, Kunsthalle, Dusseldorf (travelled to Fischer Fine Art, London)
1978 Mira Godard Gallery, Toronto
1983 Art Gallery of Ontario, Toronto
Staatliche Kunsthalle, West Berlin
Museum Ludwig, Cologne
1984 Museum of Fine Arts, Montreal
Dalhousie Art Gallery, Halifax, Nova Scotia
Vancouver Art Gallery, British Columbia
Exhibition Hall, Beijing, China
1985 University of Hong Kong
Teien Art Museum, Tokyo
Canada House, London

Selected Group Exhibitions:

1964 *Canadian Painting*, Tate Gallery, London
1967 *Statements: 18 Canadian Artists*, Norman Mackenzie Art Gallery, Regina, Saskatchewan
1973 *Kunst nach Wirklichkeit*, Kunstverein, Hannove[r] (toured Europe)
Ekstrem Realisme, Louisiana Museum, Humleback Denmark
1974 *Hyperréalists Américains/Réalistes Européens*, Centre National d'Art Contemporain, Paris (toured Europe)
1975 *Realismus und Realität*, Kunsthalle, Darmstadt
Der Einzelne und die Masse, Städtische Kunsthalle Recklinghausen, West Germany
1976 *Aspects of Realism*, Rothman's of Pall Mall travelling exhibition, Stratford Art Gallery, Ontario (toured Canada, 1976–78)

Collections:

National Gallery of Canada, Ottawa; Art Gallery of Hamilton, Ontario; Art Gallery of London, Ontario; Montreal Museum of Fine Arts; New Brunswick Museum, St. John Beaverbrook Museum, Fredericton, New Brunswick; Museum of Modern Art, New York; Kestner Gesellschaft, Hannover; Museum Boymans-van Beuningen, Rotterdam; Centre National d'Art Contemporain, Paris.

Publications:

On COLVILLE: books—*Statements: 18 Canadian Artists*, exhibition catalogue, Regina Saskatchewan 1967; *Neue Formen des Bildes* by Udo Kultermann, Tübingen, 1969; *The Art of Alex Colville* by Helen J. Dow, Toronto 1972; *Neue Formen des Realismus* by Peter Sager, Cologne 1973; *Der Neue Realismus in Amerika* by Linda Chase, Berlin 1973; *High Realism in Canada* by Paul Duval, Toronto 1974; *Hyperréalistes Américains/Réalistes Européens*, exhibition catalogue, Paris 1974; *Colville* by David Burnett, Toronto 1983; articles "Realism, Surrealism and Celebration: The Paintings of Alex Colville in the National Gallery of Canada" by Patrick Hutchings in *National Gallery of Canada Bulletin* (Ottawa), vol. 4, no. 2, 1966; "For Real" by Robert Melville in *New Statesman* (London), January 1970; "Alex Colville" by Peter Kipphoff in *Die Zeit* (Hamburg), October 1970; "Alex Colville as Image Maker" by Helen J. Dow in *The British Journal of Aesthetics* (London), Summer 1972; "Alex Colville: La Perfection dans le Realisme" by Virgil G. Hammock in *Vie des Arts* (Montreal), Autumn 1976; "Modes of Representational Art" by Micheal Greenwood in *Artscanada* (Toronto), December 1976/January 1977.

Born in Toronto and brought up in the salty atmosphere of the Maritimes, Alex Colville studied at the Mount Allison University School of Fine Art until 1942, when he joined the Canadian Army. He served in Europe as a war artist, painting and drawing scenes

Alex Colville: *Western Star*, 1985

and action in Belgium, Holland and Germany. On demobilization, Colville returned to Mount Allison as professor of painting, though now he paints only professionally.

Colville is a realist painter who aims at epitomising Jung's definition by attempting a synthesis of total experience. Details from life are observed and noted; then they are articulated within a setting composed for the purpose of making evident a sensation of fact.

"Magic Realism" is the term that covers Colville's approach, but though it verges on a noncommital lack of emphasis common to Photo-Realism, its precise definition and lighting, together with the purposeful focus on individuals and objects, create an irresistible atmosphere of significance. The square of canvas reveals a segment of actuality, often of the most common place aspect, and it paradoxically endows this chosen viewpoint with a signal intensity. Unlike Impressionism, his intention is not to capture light in the division of the spectrum. Colville imposes a universality of tone across the whole field of vision.

Often there is an implied aura of loneliness akin to some of Andrew Wyeth's works such as "Christina's World." "Hound in a Field" of 1958 shows Colville's grasp of drama in the selection of an incident or a moment of time, freezing it within the framework of the canvas. Sometimes the realism is as airless as a still life *trompe l'oeil,* but the scale again distorts its presence.

The freezing may take place on a large oil-on-masonite, such as "Elm Tree at Horton Landing" of 1965, representing its own environmental tragedy. This once handsome tree standing alone is now flawed and damaged, some of its branches stricken and bleached. It nonetheless retains some original dignity in its upright stance. Viewed from ground level, it becomes more than a tree preserved for its lost beauty. It has the pathetic note of a graceful creation singled out for accidental violation; whether by vandalism or act of God is unknown. The effect, however, is endowed with Colville's unique paint touch, immaculate in strength and balance of tone.

Often the import is meteorological. The cold sterility of a winter day clarifies a landscape of snow in one even tone of whiteness, shadowed and pocked by changes of contour. The sky is a level blue, and the chill almost strikes our bones. In the human figures, the blood seems frozen too, as they stand immersed in suspended action. One aspect runs through Colville's painting; it is the stillness of the final scene. No words pass between his people, mute in the trivial

commonplaces of the day, silent evidence of the unremarkable, miraculously immobilized in clinical antiseptic objectivity.

—G. S. Whittet

CONNER, Bruce.

American. Born in McPherson, Kansas, 18 November 1933. Educated at Kansas City Art Institute, Missouri, and Wichita State University, Kansas, 1951–52; University of Nebraska, Lincoln, 1952–56, B.F.A. 1956; Brooklyn Museum, with Reuben Tam, 1956–57; University of Colorado, Boulder, 1957. Married Jean Connor in 1957; son: Robert. Independent painter and filmmaker, since 1957. Taught 8mm film-making, California College of Arts and Crafts, Oakland, 1965; life drawing, 1966 67, and painting and sculpture, 1972, at the San Francisco Art Institute; taught "The Art of Assemblage" at UCLA Extension, 1973; beginning and advanced painting, San Jose State University, California, 1974; film-making, San Francisco State University, 1976. Recipient: Ann Bremer Award, San Francisco Art Association, 1958; Second Prize, Church Art Today, San Francisco Episcopal Diocese, 1960; First Prize, Art Competition of the National Council of Churches, 1960; Neallie Sullivan Award, San Francisco Art Association, 1963; Ford Foundation Fellowship, 1964; Tamarind Lithography Workshop Fellowship Grant, 1965; Copley Foundation Award 1965; Gold Medal, *Sesta Biennale D'Arte,* San Marino 1967; National Endowment for the Arts Grant 1973; American Film Institute Grant, 1974; Francis Scott Key Award, 1975; Guggenheim Fellowship, 1975; Citation in Film, Brandeis University Creative Awards, Waltham, Massachusetts, 1979. Agents: Fraenkel Gallery, 55 Grant Avenue, San Francisco, California 94108; and Smith-Andersen Gallery, 200 Homer Street, Palo Alto, California 94301. Address: 45 Sussex Street, San Francisco, California 94131, U.S.A.

Individual Exhibitions:

1956 Rienzi Gallery, New York
1958 East West Gallery, San Francisco
Designers Gallery, San Francisco
1959 Spatsa Gallery, San Francisco
1960 Alan Gallery, New York
Batman Gallery, San Francisco
1961 Alan Gallery, New York
1962 Batman Gallery, San Francisco
Glantz Gallery, Mexico City
Antonio Souza Gallery, Mexico City
1963 Neallie Sullivan Award Show, San Francisco
Wichita Art Museum, Kansas
Alan Gallery, New York
Swetzoff Gallery, Boston
1964 Batman Gallery, San Francisco
Alan Gallery, New York
George Lester Galleria, Rome
Robert Fraser Gallery, London
1965 University of British Columbia Art Gallery, Vancouver
Rose Art Museum, Brandeis University, Waltham, Massachusetts
Galerie "J", Paris
Alan Gallery, New York
1966 Quay Gallery, San Francisco
1967 Institute of Contemporary Art, Philadelphia
San Francisco Art Institute
1971 San Francisco Art Institute
Molly Barnes Gallery, Los Angeles
Reese Palley Gallery, San Francisco
1972 Reese Palley Gallery, San Francisco
Martha Jackson Gallery, New York
Willis Gallery, San Francisco
Texas Gallery, Houston
Nicholas Wilder Gallery, Los Angeles
1973 Texas Gallery, Houston
1974 Quay Gallery, San Francisco
Tyler Art Museum, Texas
Gallerie Smith-Anderson, Palo Alto, California
DeYoung Museum, San Francisco (retrospective toured United States)
1980 North Point Gallery, San Francisco
1984 Smith-Andersen Gallery, Palo Alto, California
1986 Smith-Andersen Gallery, Palo Alto, California

Selected Group Exhibitions:

1967 *Funk Art,* University of California Art Museum, Berkeley
Sculpture of the 60's, Los Angeles County Museum of Art

Bruce Conner: *Ink Blot,* 1975

1969 *Human Concern/Human Torment,* Whitney Museum, New York
1972 *Family Show of Work by Robert, Jean and Bruce Conner,* Quay Gallery, San Francisco
1973 *Family Show of Work by Robert, Jean and Bruce Conner,* Jacqueline Anhalt Gallery, Los Angeles
1975 *Poets of the Cities,* Museum of Fine Arts, Dallas (travelled to San Francisco Museum of Modern Art, and the Wadsworth Atheneum, Hartford, Connecticut)
1976 *The Modern Era: California Painting and Sculpture,* San Francisco Museum of Modern Art (travelled to National Collection of Fine Art, Washington, D.C.)
1979 *Biennial Exhibition,* Whitney Museum, New York
1981 *Remember It's Only Art,* Civic Arts Gallery, Walnut Creek, California
1986 *Seven Artists in Depth: The Creative Process,* San Francisco Museum of Modern Art

Collections:

Museum of Modern Art, New York; Whitney Museum, New York; Los Angeles County Museum of Art; San Francisco Museum of Modern Art; Oakland Art Museum, California; University Art Museum, University of California, Berkeley; Norton Simon Museum of Art, Pasadena, California; Rockhill Nelson Gallery, Kansas City, Missouri; Art Institute of Chicago; Centre Georges Pompidou, Paris.

Publications:

By CONNER: articles—"Bruce Conner Makes a Sandwich" in *Artforum* (New York), September 1967; "Bruce Conner: A Discussion at the 1968 Flaherty Film Seminar" in *Film Comment* (New York), No. 4, 1969; films—*A Movie,* 1958; *Cosmic Ray,* 1961; *Looking for Mushrooms,* 1961–67; *Report,* 1963–67; *Vivian,* 1964; *Breakaway,* 1966; *White Rose,* 1967; *Permian Strata,* 1969; *5 X Marilyn,* 1973; *Crossroads,* 1976; *5:10 to Dreamland,* 1976; *Valse Triste,* 1977; *Mongoloid,* 1978; *America Is Waiting,* 1981.

On CONNER: books—*Bruce Conner,* exhibition catalogue, New York 1960; *Bruce Conner,* exhibition catalogue, New York 1965; *Bruce Conner,* exhibition catalogue, with text by Thomas Garver, Waltham, Massachusetts 1965; *Bruce Conner,* exhibition catalogue, with text by Joan C. Siegfried and Stephen S. Prokopoff, Philadelphia 1967; *Assemblage in California: Works from the Late 50's and Easly 60's,* exhibition catalogue, with texts by John Coplans, Walter Hopps, Philip Leider, and Hal Glicksman, Irvine, California 1968; *Bruce Conner: Drawings 1955–1975,* exhibition catalogue, San Francisco 1974; *Bruce Conner* by Anthony Reveaux, St. Paul, Minnesota 1981; articles—"Bruce Conner" by Cecile McCann in *Artweek* (Oakland, California), March 1974; "The Artist as Dactylographer" by Peter Selz in *Art in America* (New York), July/August 1974; "Bruce Conner's Cinematic Drawings" by A. Flanagan in *Artweek* (Oakland, California), November 1974; "Fallout: Some Notes on the Films of Bruce Conner" by W. Moritz and B. O'Neill in *Film Quarterly* (Berkeley, California), Summer 1978.

Bruce Conner has long been acknowledged as a seminal force behind the collage and assemblage movement of the early 1960's. Yet, he is probably one of the most misunderstood and underexposed artists of his generation. Although drawing has been his primary form of artistic expression since 1964, he is still recognized mainly for his collages and small sculptures and for the films that grew out of his collage sensibility. At times, even they are overlooked because of their iconoclastic content, or dismissed on the basis of their heterodoxy, when they could best be appreciated in stylistic terms—for example, "Last Supper," (1961), or "Couch," (1963), two sculptures whose mordantly satirical subject matter obscured their fundamental contribution to an expressionistic tradition that reaches back to Bosch, Bruegel, Goya, Daumier and, more recently, George Grosz.

In 1974–75, in recognition of Conner's skill with the medium, San Francisco's de Young Museum organized a traveling exhibition of his drawings, highlighting the various factors that influenced their development over a period of some 17 years. Unfortunately, by focusing entirely on the drawings instead of showing them in the context of his other works, and despite a comprehensive catalog essay stressing the connection, the exhibition isolated the drawings visually instead of emphasizing their relationship to other aspects of the artist's repertoire. Since then, he has been included in many museum group shows but, save for a limited retrospective at the North Point Gallery (San Francisco), the totality of his oeuvre has never been fully explored or documented. As a result, the significance of his contribution to the history of American art in the realm of mysticism has been greatly diluted. For, by taking a separative rather than combinative approach, curators have missed the opportunity to demonstrate both the correlation that exists between his handling of various media and the continuity of his style over a period of some 25 years.

That mysticism is at the core of Bruce Conner's vision is obvious from the entire body of his drawings and from the photograms and paintings of the 1970's. Drawn from such variant sources as religious symbolism, ethnic mythology, and private spiritual experience, their iconography often alludes to the cosmos—to distant stars and galaxies whose suggested forms seem to be undergoing visionary transmutations into geometrical and metaphysical shapes. The mystical implications of the collages and assemblages of the 60's are not as readily apprehensible. More intellectual than visual, their content is based upon philosophically esoteric notions that portend cataclysmic events and challenge our concepts of God, life, and death.

The seeds of an expressionist revival scattered in the late 70's throughout the art scene of Western Europe and the United States are currently being nurtured by the depressing financial condition of the world. Talented young artists anxious to ride the wave of avant-garde breakthroughs are, in increasing numbers, trading ultimate objectivity for emotionally-charged subjectivity. But it takes time and experience to become a master—someone who not only understands the lessons of the past, but who also has the ability to press those lessons into service of the present. Bruce Conner is such an artist. A veteran expressionist, he has demonstrated his ability to grow and change within the continuity of a highly mystical vocabulary. In his custody, the future of the medium is in good hands.

—Andrée Maréchal-Workman

CONSAGRA, Pietro.

Italian. Born in Mazara del Vallo, Sicily, in 1920. Studied at the Accademia di Belle Arti, Palermo, 1938–44. Sculptor: lives and works in Rome, since 1944; Founder, with Piero Dorazio, Achille Perilli, Giulio Turcato and others, Forma I, Rome, 1947. Recipient: Second Prize, *Biennale del Bronzetto,* Padua, 1955; Metallurgica Prize, *Bienal,* Sao Paulo, 1955; Premio Einaudi, *Biennale,* Venice, 1956; Belgium Critics Prize, 1958; First Prize for Sculpture, *Biennale,* Venice, 1960. Agent: Marlborough Galleria d'Arte, via Gregoriana 5, 00187 Rome. Address: Via Cassia 1162, 00189 Rome, Italy.

Individual Exhibitions:

1947 Galleria Mola, Rome
1948 Galleria Sandri, Venice
1949 Galleria del Secolo, Rome
1951 Galleria del Pincio, Rome
1953 Galleria del Naviglio, Milan
1956 *Biennale,* Venice
1958 Palais des Beaux-Arts, Brussels
Galleria Tartaruga, Rome
1959 Galerie de France, Paris
Bienal, Sao Paulo
1960 *Biennale,* Venice
1961 Galleria Blu, Milan
Mostra di Disegni di Pietro Consagra, Galleria Odyssia, Rome
Galerie Charles Lienhard, Zurich
1962 Staempfli Gallery, New York
Bonino Gallery, Buenos Aires
1963 Pace Gallery, Boston
1964 Odyssia Gallery, New York
1965 Galleria dell'Ariete, Milan
1966 Marlborough Galleria d'Arte, Rome
1967 Galleria dell'Ariete, Milan
Boymans van Beuningen Museum, Rotterdam
Marlborough-Gerson Gallery, New York
1969 Marlborough Galleria d'Arte, Rome
Galleria dell'Ariete, Milan
Galleria Rampa, Naples
Grafica Romera, Rome
1971 Galleria dell'Ariete, Milan
1972 Marlborough Galleria d'Arte, Rome
Galleria Peccolo, Livorno
1973 Galleria Editalia, Rome
Palazzo dei Normanni, Palermo
Qui Arte Contemporanea, Rome
Salone Annunciata, Milan
1974 Galleria del Bibliofili, Milan
Marlborough Galleria d'Arte, Rome
Galleria Ferrari, Treviglio, Italy
1975 Galleria Annunciata, Milan
1976 Marlborough Galleria d'Arte, Rome
1977 *Disegni 1945–1977,* Galleria Stendhal, Milan
Museo di Castelvecchio, Verona
Galleria Il Disegno, Rome
Studio L'Arco, Rome
1981 Galleria Editalia, Rome
Palazzo dell'Arengo, Rimini
Museo d'Arte Grafica, Gibellina, Italy
1984 Bottega dell'Incisione, Turin
1985 Qui Arte Contemporanea, Rome

Selected Group Exhibitions:

1946 *Group Exhibition,* Rome
1950 *Biennale,* Venice
1953 *Junge Italienische Kunst,* Kunsthaus, Zurich
1959 *European Art Today,* Minneapolis Museum of Art (toured the United States)
1964 *Decade 1954–1964,* Tate Gallery, London
1966 *Moderne Kunst aus Italien,* Museum am Ostwall, Dortmund, West Germany
1971 *New Italian Art 1953–71,* Walker Art Gallery, Liverpool
1977 *Disegni 1945–77,* Galleria Scheiwiller, Milan
1981 *Omaggio a Serpotta,* Galleria dell'Arco, Rome
1983 *Giornale di Manovra,* Galleria della Cometa, Rome

Collections:

Galleria Nazionale d'Arte Moderna, Rome: Tate Gallery, London; Musée Royaux des Beaux-Arts, Brussels; Centre Georges Pompidou, Paris; Middelheim Sculpture Park, Antwerp; Galerija Suvremene Umjetnosti, Zagreb; Museo d'Arte Moderna, Sao Paulo; Museum of Modern Art, New York; Guggenheim Museum, New York; Art Institute of Chicago.

Publications:

By CONSAGRA: books—*Necessita della Scultura,* Rome 1952; *L'Agguato c'e,* Rome 1960; *LaCitta Frontale,* exhibition catalogue, Rome, Milan and Bari, Italy 1969; *Poema Frontale,* Milan 1973; *Fotografia L'Arte,* Milan 1973; *Malumore,* Milan 1974; *Welcome to Italy,* MIlan 1974; *La Ruota Quadrata,* Milan 1976; *Approssimativamente,* Milan 1977; *Vita Mia,* Milan 1980; articles—"Teorema dell Scultura" in *Forma I* (Rome), March 1947; "Disegno" in *Traits* (Paris), no. 6, 1947; "Mangeri" in *Noi Donne* (Rome), July 1951; "Scultura" in *Domus* (Milan), no. 2, 1951; "Plastico" in *Spazlo* (Milan), December 1951; "In Difesa dell'Astratismo" in *Calendario del Popolo* (Milan), September 1951; "Design for Sculpture" in *Contemporary Drawings from 12 Countries,* exhibition catalogue, Chicato 1952; "Autoritratto" in *Arte Libera* (Naples), October 1952; "La

Fiamma Issidrica" in *Paese Sera* (Rome), March 1953; "Der Eiserne Arm" in *Junge Italienische Kunst*, exhibition catalogue, Zurich 1953; "Inchieste sull-Arte Contemporanea" in *Il Nuovo Corriere* (Florence), February 1954; "Colloqui" in *Paese* (Rome), January 1955; "Uno Scultore guidica l'Architettura" in *L'Architettura* (Rome), May 1956; "Intervista a Pietro Consagra," with Lonzi, in *Pietro Consagra*, exhibition catalogue, Milan and Rome 1967; "Una Lezione di Scultura" in *Civilta delle Macchine* (Rome), vol. XVIII, 1970; "L'Ogetto" in *Consagra*, exhibition catalogue, Milan 1971; "Avere di me: in *Consagra*, exhibition catalogue, Rome 1972; statement in *Pietro Consagra*, exhibition catalogue, Rome 1974; "Io Consagra" in *Bolaffiarte* (Turin), October 1980.

On CONSAGRA: books—*Pietro Consagra* by Umbro Apollione, Rome 1956; *Mostra di Disegne Pietro Consagra*, exhibition catalogue, by Marisa Volpi Orlandini, Rome 1961; *Pietro Consagra* by Giulio Carlo Argan, Neuchâtel, Switzerland 1962; *Consagra*, exhibition catalogue, by Giovanni Carandente and others, Palermo 1973; *Pietro Consagra* by Marisa Volpi Oraldini, Milan 1977; *Pietro Consagra: Disegni 1945–1977*, Milan 1977; *Pietro Consagra*, exhibition catalogue, by Guido Ballo, Rimini, Italy 1981; *Consagra*, exhibition catalogue with essay by Lorenza Trucchi, Rome 1985.

One of Pietro Consagra's distinctions is that unlike most Italian sculptors of his generation, he originates from Sicily, arriving in Rome at the age of 24; it is however interesting to note that the painter Guttuso, his senior by eight years, was also born in Sicily. In some senses the term sculptor does not quite fit Consagra; he is a maker of icons rather than an investigator of three-dimensional space, a manufacturer of screens rather than sculptural volumes. Whilst there may be some original preoccupation with Sicilian Baroque architecture, or the richly decorated mosaic walls of some of the island's famous chapels, Consagra's more obvious influence derives from Cubist definition of space.

Consagra belongs to the important post-war movement in Italian sculpture which sought a new language, a renewal in the face of the relaxed inheritance of classical forms which marked the older generation, Marini, Manzu, Greco, or the achievements of the Futurists. It is one of the fascinations of modern Italian art that in addition to brilliant craftsmanship, inventive form, striking intelligence and undeniable elegance and taste, many of the most gifted artists have felt the need to adopt mannerisms or styles which suggest violence or self-hatred. It is as though they distrust the very gifts which Italian civilization and taste have given them; hence the violation of space and form in Fontana, the torn and scratched techniques of Burri, the satire of Baj, the aggressive calligraphy of Capogrossi, Colla's spiky gestures, and the variations of bruised bronze surfaces or penetrated images found in Cavaliere, Arnaldo Pomodoro and Mastroianni.

Consagra is of this school. His standing screens, often brightly coloured, are images of aggression and destruction, giving the impression of torn fabric scarred wood, or disintegrated matter. The starting point is a simple square, manipulated out of all recognition. Consagra is a brilliant technician, working in every variety of material, bronze casting, welded steel, oxidizing, aluminium forms either cut into strange, oriental patterns, or elaborating a Calderesque hanging manner, each misshapen petal suspended by wire. Consagra is more organic than his fellow Italians, sometimes building up webbed or comb-like structures, patterned on some natural system of growth or development. His famous polemical manner—the author of numerous essays and manifestos on sculpture—is evident in the sculptures, and saves them from the more obviously over-designed decorativeness of some of his compatriots.

—Charles Spencer

COOPER, Ron(ald).

American. Born in Venice, California, 24 July 1943. Studied at the Chouinard Art Institute, Los Angeles, 1963–65. Environmental artist and photographer, Los Angeles, since 1965. Commissioned by Library of Congress to do *Floating Volume Atmosphere*, Washington, D.C., 1968; travelled in the United States and Europe, 1969–70; and in Central America, 1971. Director, Los Angeles Institute of Contemporary Art, since 1981. Board Director, Artist's Equity Association, 1980–81. Recipient: Purchase Award, Los Angeles County Museum of Art, 1968; National Endowment for the Arts Award, 1970; Theodoron Purchase Award, Guggenheim Museum, New York 1971. Agent: Galerie Alfred Schmela, Mutter-Ey-Strasse 3, 4000 Dusseldorf, West Germany. Address: 1310 Main Street, Venice, California 90291, U.S.A.

Individual Exhibitions:

1969 Ace Gallery, Los Angeles
1970 Michael Walls Gallery, San Francisco
Pomona College Art Gallery, Claremont, California
Galerie Schmela, Dusseldorf
3 Young Americans: A Biennal, Allen Memorial Art Museum, Oberlin College, Ohio (with Chuck Close and Neil Jenney)
1972 Pasadena Art Museum, California
Ace Gallery, Los Angeles
1973 Galerie Folker Skulima, West Berlin
1974 Galerie Alfred Schmela, Dusseldorf
1979 Rosamund Felsen Gallery, Los Angeles

Selected Group Exhibitions:

1967 *Arp to Artschwager*, Goldowsky Gallery, New York
1969 *Annual Exhibition*, Whitney Museum, New York
1970 *Prospect '69*, Städtische Kunsthalle, Dusseldorf
1970 *Permutations: Light and Color*, Museum of Contemporary Art, Chicago
1971 *10 Young Artists*, Guggenheim Museum, New York
Theodoron Awards Invitational, Guggenheim Museum, New York
1972 *Art in Progress*, Kunsthaus, Zurich
Documenta 5, Kassel, West Germany
1974 *Light*, Lang Art Gallery, Scripps College, Claremont, California
1979 *California Perceptions: Light and Space*, California State University at Fullerton

Collections:

Whitney Museum, New York; Guggenheim Museum, New York; Art Institute of Chicago; Los Angeles County Museum of Art; Kaiser Wilhelm Museum, Krefeld, West Germany; Stedelijk Museum, Amsterdam.

Publications:

On COOPER: books—*3 Young Americans: A Biennial*, exhibition catalogue, with text by Athena Spear, Oberlin, Ohio 1970; *California Perceptions: Light and Space*, exhibition catalogue, Fullerton, California 1979; articles—"Ronald Cooper" by Jane Livingston in *Artforum* (New York), Summer 1969; "Reflections of Close, Cooper and Jenny: 3 Young Americans at Oberlin" by Athena Spear in *Arts Magazine* (New York), May 1970; "Ronald Cooper" by Peter Plagens in *Artforum* (New York), April 1971; "Ronald Cooper" by M. Terbell in *Arts Magazine* (New York), April 1971; "Ronald Cooper" by M. Hartman in *Glass Art Magazine* (Oakland, California), October 1973.

Since the late 1960's the career of Ron Cooper has reflected two main tendencies, the first being the experimental research with and manipulation of light, the second being either an attempt to reproduce honestly the physical properties of the material or to exact the pictorial qualities of the characteristics of the process involved.

That his career began in the late 1960's is demonstrated by his early work: he began by painting transparent vertical bars, which was followed by his making large square fiberglass and polyester resin paintings which acted as light traps. Later, he eliminated the object altogether and simply dealt with volumes of light which he documented with a camera—and particularly since 1974 Cooper has totally devoted himself to exploring the possibilities of making art with the camera.

Like that of several of his peers from the Los Angeles school (Robert Irwin, Larry Bell, etc.), Cooper's art focuses on how we perceive things and illustrates the perennial theme of how deceptive is our appearance-reflecting world. His goal is to pose or propose a perceptual dilemma rather than make a beautiful object capturing the poetic discourse of the ever-changing sunlight. Cooper is, of course, like Irwin, concerned with the process of perception though he is not concerned like him—as it seems—with meditation and emptiness.

He has also become more and more interested in the problem-solving ability of the camera rather than in the technique of photography which he practices from a painter's "point of view," His most recent works are series of photographs entitled "What It Is" and "Torsos."

—Jean-Luc Bordeaux

COPLEY, William Nelson. (CPLY).

American. Born in New York City, 24 January 1919. Educated at Phillips Academy, Andover, Massachusetts, until 1938; Yale University, New Haven, Connecticut, 1938–42. Served in the United States Army, in Africa, Sicily, and Italy, 1942–46. Married Chuang-Hua. Began painting in 1946; Director, with John Ployardt, Copley Galleries, showing the work of Magritte, Cornell, Matta, Tanguy, Man Ray, and Ernst, Beverly Hills, California, 1946–48; lived in Paris, associating with Max Ernst, Man Ray, and Marcel Duchamp, 1951–64; returned to the United States and has lived in New York since 1964. Agent: Phyllis Kind Gallery, New York and Chicago. Address: c/o Phyllis Kind Gallery, 136 Greene Street, New York, New York 10012, U.S.A.

Individual Exhibitions:

1947 Royer's Bookstore, Los Angeles
1953 Galerie Nina Dausset, Paris
1954 Galerie Monte Napoleone, Milan
1956 *Peintures Récentes*, Galerie du Dragon, Paris
Iolas Gallery, New York
1958 Iolas Gallery, New York
1959 Galerie Furstenberg, Paris
1960 Galleria Naviglio, Milan
Galleria Cavallino, Venice
Iolas Gallery, New York
1961 *Recent Paintings by CPLY*, Institute of Contemporary Arts, London
Galleria Schwarz, Milan
Galerie Iris Clert, Paris
1963 *Paintings*, Hanover Gallery, London
Les Suffragettes Erotiques, Galerie Iris Clert, Paris
Iolas Gallery, New York
1964 David Stuart Gallery, Los Angeles
1965 Louisiana Gallery, Houston
Southwestern College, Chula Vista, California
Allan Frumkin Gallery, Chicago
1966 *Projects for Monuments to the Unknown Whore*, Galerie Iolas, Paris (travelled to the Iolas Gallery, New York)
Entertainment for Men, Stedelijk Museum, Amsterdam
1967 *Homage to Robert W. Service*, Iolas Gallery New York (travelled to the Galerie Iolas, Paris)
1968 Bodley Gallery, New York
1969 Merida Gallery, Louisville, Kentucky

970 Galerie Neuendorf, Cologne
Project for a Dictionary of Platitudes, Galleria Iolas, Milan (travelled to Iolas Gallery, New York)
CPLY, Magritte and Brauner, Louisiana Gallery, Houston
972 Galerie Springer, West Berlin
Galerie Aspects, Brussels
David Stuart Gallery, Los Angeles
Mail Order, Galleria Iolas, Milan (travelled to the Iolas Gallery, New York)
973 *CPLY*, Galeria Anselimo, Turin
974 *X—Rated*, New York Cultural Center
Western Songs, Onnasch Gallery, New York (retrospective; travelled to Moore College of Art, Philadelphia, and Galerie Onnasch, Cologne)
Galerie Iolas, Paris
Nounes, Galleria Iolas, Milan (travelled to the Iolas Gallery, New York)
975 Erik Nord Gallery, Nantucket, Massachusetts
976 Iolas Gallery, New York
978 Iolas Gallery, New York
Galerie Fassbinder, Munich
Galerie Springer, West Berlin
Galerie Zwirner, Cologne
979 Iolas Gallery, New York
Reflections on a Past Life, Institute for the Arts, Rice University, Houston
980 Iolas Gallery, New York
Museum of Fine Arts, St. Petersburg, Florida
Kunsthalle, Berne (travelled to the Centre Georges Pompidou, Paris, and the Stedelijk Van Abbemuseum, Eindhoven, Netherlands)
981 Iolas Gallery, New York
Sierra Nevada Museum of Art, Reno
Colorado Springs Fine Arts Center
982 Phyllis Kind Gallery, Chicago
983 Reinhard Onnasch Ausstellungen, West Berlin
985 Galerie Susanna Kulli, St. Gallen, Switzerland

Selected Group Exhibitions:

962 *Collage out of California*, Pasadena Art Museum, California
L'Antagonisme de l'Objet, Musée des Arts Décoratifs, Paris
1964 *New Directions in American Painting*, Brandeis University, Waltham, Massachusetts
Surrealism: Sources/History/Affinities, Galerie Charpentier, Paris
1966 *Surrealist Exhibition*, University of California at Santa Barbara
1972 *Humor in Art*, New School for Social Research, New York
1973 *Erotic Art*, New School for Social Research, New York
1975 *3 Generations of American Nudes*, New York Cultural Center
1977 *Artists' Rendering of Paintings*, Brera Museum, Milan (travelled to Le Louvre, Paris)

Collections:

Museum of Modern Art, New York; Whitney Museum, New York; New York Cultural Center; Philadelphia Museum of Art; Art Institute of Chicago; Los Angeles County Museum of Art; Tate Gallery, London; Centre Georges Pompidou, Paris; Stedelijk Museum, Amsterdam; Nagaoka City Museum, Japan.

Publications:

By COPLEY: books—*The Evil Story of My Life by CPLY*, New York 1965; *CPLY: Project for a Dictionary of Platitudes*, exhibition catalogue, Milan and New York 1970; *Notes on a Project for a Dictionary of Ridiculous Images*, Cologne and New York 1972; *Variations on a Theme by Francis Picabia*, New York 1979; articles—"Introducing the Paintings of Serge Charchoune" in *Artnews* (New York), March 1960; "Man Ray: The Dada of Us All: in *Portfolio* (New York), Winter 1963.

On COPLEY: books—*Copley: Peintures Récentes*, exhibition catalogue, with text by Patrick Waldberg, Paris 1956; *William Copley: 470, Mostra del Cavallino*, exhibition catalogue, with text by Roberto Rossellini, Venice 1960; *History of Surrealist Painting* by Marcel Jean, New York 1960; *Recent Paintings by CPLY*, exhibition catalogue, London 1961; *Bill Copley*, exhibition catalogue, with text by Roland Penrose, Milan 1962; *W.N. Copley: Paintings*, exhibition catalogue, with text by Robert Melville, London 1963; *Les Suffragettes Erotiques de Bill Copley*, exhibition catalogue, with texts by Marcel Duchamp and others, Paris 1963; *CPLY: Projects for Monuments to the Unknown Whore*, exhibition catalogue, with text by Julien Levy, Paris and New York 1966; *Copley: Entertainment for Men*, exhibition catalogue, with text by Roland Renrose, Amsterdam 1966; *CPLY:Homage to Robert W. Service*, exhibition catalogue, New York and Paris 1967; *Pop Art* by Lucy Lippard, New York 1967; *CPLY: Mail Order*, exhibition catalogue, Milan and New York 1972; *CPLY*, exhibition catalogue, with text by Janus, Turin 1973; *CPLY: Nounes*, exhibition catalogue, Milan and New York 1974; *CPLY: X-Rated*, exhibition catalogue, with an introduction by Sam Hunter, New York 1974; *CPLY: Western Songs*, exhibition catalogue, Cologne 1974; *CPLY: Reflections on a Past Life*, exhibition catalogue, Houston 1979; *William N. Copley*, exhibition catalogue, with texts by Johannes Gachnang and Marianne Schmidt, with an introduction by R. H. Fuchs, Berne 1980; *William N. Copley*, exhibition catalogue with essay by Ilona Lindenburg, West Berlin 1983.

Though born a full generation after the original Surrealists, William Copley—a.k.a. CPLY—calls himself a Surrealist, lives as a Surrealist, paints as a Surrealist, in fact, is a Surrealist. At first glance this may seem a retrogressive role for a post-World War II American artist. But the important paradox in Copley's career is that he saw and, without chauvinism, *admitted* the influence of classic European Surrealism on American art while simultaneously his own work anticipated some of the directions in which American art has grown from these historic roots.

As early as 1946 Copley (with a brother-in-law) was running a Surrealist gallery in Los Angeles. There, the first Surrealist they met was Man Ray, who said, "There's more Surrealism rampant in Hollywood than all the Surrealists could invent in a lifetime." Through Man Ray, Copley met Duchamp in New York, Max Ernst in Arizona, and gradually other surviving Dadaists, Surrealists, and modern masters. He bought their work—first for the gallery, then for himself, for pleasure and as sort of visual reference library. At the same time, he taught himself to paint innocently and playfully, absorbing the Surrealists' improvised, free-associative spirit and abandoning (as they did) aesthetic and moral prejudices.

Copley's theme was, is, and, presumably, always will be sex—sex in its most cheerful, anxiety-free form, dirty but not filthy, erotic but not pornographic. By the late 40's he developed an iconography of curvy, cartoon-like women who cavort through his paintings, often being chased, kissed, ogled, mounted, etc. by a small man in a derby who is not only closely related to Copley himself but to the Keystone Cops and other heroes of silent film, and to the bourgeois males in the work of Magritte. Authority, when it appears, is an equally playful and cartoon-like French cop (un flic). As Duchamp said, "Cops pullulate, Copley copulates." A painting like Copley's "Capella sextina" (1961) makes Delacroix' "Le bain turque" look spare and monogamous.

While raiding the zaniness of comic strips and Hollywood (Mae West, W. C. Fields, and the Marx Brothers are other Copley favorites), he also reinvented popular images from advertising (THINK), newspapers (the crossword puzzle), Robert Service's ballads (the Yukon bars and whorehouses), patriotic symbols (the flag, the Liberty Bell), slogans (BEAT YALE, Copley's university), etc. All of his very large production of drawings and paintings are flat, nonillusionistic, "American." As Julien Levy said, Copley was "a Pop of Pop in 1948." That's true, and so is the fact, which Copley is the first to acknowledge, that the grandparents of Pop (and Abstract Expressionism) were Dada and Surrealism. In recent years, Copley has shown regularly at the Phyllis Kind Gallery in New York City and Chicago, in addition to travelling shows in the United States and abroad.

—B. H. Friedman

CORNEILLE.

Dutch. Born Cornelis Guillaume Beverloo, in Liège, Belgium. 3 July 1922; emigrated to the Netherlands 1940; subsequently naturalized. Studied drawing at the Rijksakademie, Amsterdam, 1940–43, etching, under S. W. Hayter, at Atelier 17, Paris, 1953, and ceramics, with Mazzotti, at Albisola Mare, Italy, 1954–55. Independent painter and graphic artist, Amsterdam, 1943–53, and in Paris since 1950: Co-Founder, Dutch Experimental Group, Amsterdam 1948, and COBRA (Copenhagen-Brussels-Amsterdam) group, with Appel, Jorn, Constant, Alechinsky, Pedersen, etc., 1949–51; worked in Mallorca and Cadaques, Spain, 1961–66. Recipient: Guggenheim Netherlands Prize, 1956; Graphics Prize, Ibiza, 1972. Agent: Galerie Krikhaar, Spuistraat 330, 1012 VX Amsterdam, Netherlands. Address: 58 Rue Vieille du Temple, 75003 Paris, France.

Individual Exhibitions:

1946 Het Beerenhuis, Groningen, Netherlands
1947 Europai Iskola, Budapest
1950 Galleri Birch, Copenhagen
1951 Martinet en Michels, Amsterdam
Galerie t'Venster, Rotterdam
1953 Kunstkabinett Horemans, Antwerp
1954 Galerie Colette Allendy, Paris
1956 Galerie Craven, Paris
Palais des Beaux-Arts, Brussels
Stedelijk Museum, Amsterdam
Stedelijk Museum, Schiedam, Netherlands
1957 Museum of Curacao, Dutch Antilles
1959 Galerie Espace, Haarlem, Netherlands
Galerie Le Gendre, Paris
1960 *Tekening van Corneille*, Stedelijk Museum, Amsterdam
1961 Galerie Ariel, Paris
Haags Gemeentemuseum, The Hague
Stedelijk Van Abbemuseum, Eindhoven, Netherlands
Brook Street Gallery, London
K.B. Galleri, Oslo
1962 Lefebre Gallery, New York
Galerie Mathias Fels, Paris
1963 Galleria del Naviglio, Milan
Musée d'Antibes, France
Galleri Blanche, Stockholm
Galerie Le Point Cardinal, Paris
Galerie Creuzevalt, Paris
1964 Galeria Souza, Mexico city
Lefebre Gallery, New York
Galleria Schwarz, Milan, Italy
1965 Cultureel Centrum, Hilversum, Netherlands
Galerie Stangl, Munich
Lefebre Gallery, New York
1966 Stedelijk Museum, Amsterdam
Kunsthalle, Dusseldorf
Galeria Relevo, Rio de Janeiro
1967 Galerie Kaleidoskoop, Ghent
Lefebre Gallery, New York
1968 Galerie Espace, Amsterdam
Galerie Casse, Paris
1969 Galerie Stangl, Munich
Galeria Ivan Spence, Ibiza, Spain
1970 Galerie Ariel, Paris
Galerie La Pochade, Paris
Lebebre Gallery, New York
Galeria Ivan Spence, Ibiza, Spain
1971 Galerie Rive Gauche, Paris
Palais Walderdorf, Trier, West Germany
Galeria Ivan Spence, Ibiza, Spain
Galleria d'Arte, Trieste
Kunstverein, Salzburg
Lefebre Gallery, New York
1972 Galleria 70, Potenza, Italy
Schillerhof, Graz, Austria
1974 Galleria La Medusa, Rome
The Quartier Rose of Amsterdam, Lefebre Gallery, New York
Galerie Montjoie, Brussels
Palazzo Buonacorsi, Macerata, Italy
Palais des Beaux-Arts, Charleroi, Belgium

	Retrospective Tentoonstelling: Corneille, Museum voor Schone Kunsten, Ghent
	Studio Erre, Rome
	Galleria La Medusa, Rome
1975	Galleria del Cavallino, Rome
	Petite Galerie, Rio de Janeiro
	Galerie l'Oeil de Boeuf, Paris
	Meseu de Arte Moderno, Sao Paulo
	Galerie Espace, Amsterdam
	Institut Neerlandais, Paris
	Galleria Gian Ferrari, Milan
	Galerie Krikhaar, Amsterdam
	Galleria M. Arte, Milan
	Galleria C.M., Rome
	Carnegie Institute, Pittsburgh
	Lefebre Gallery, New York
	Galleria Gregory, Rome
1976	Galleri Documenta, Copenhagen
	Centro d'Arte, Sarono, Italy
	Galerie Riis, Trondheim, Norway
	Galerie Fabien Boulakia, Paris
	Galerie Moderne, Silkeborg, Denmark
	Lefebre Gallery, New York
1977	Galerie Espace, Amsterdam
	Galleri Documenta, Copenhagen
	Maison Bernard, Caracas, Venezuela
1978	Galerie Orientale, Geneva
	Galleri Kanda Malare, Jonkoping, Sweden
	Galleria Bonaparte, Milan
1979	Galerie Fabien Boulakia, Paris
	Galerie L'Oeil de Boeuf, Paris
	New Gallery, Jabbeke, Belgium
	Galerij Maeyaert, Ostend, Belgium
1980	Galerie Delta, Rotterdam
	Galerie Michel Casse, Paris
	Galerie Reflex, Amsterdam
1981	Galerie Fabien Boulakia, Paris
	Galleri Hammerlunds, Osla
	Galerie de Kuil, The Hague
	Galerie Jas, Utrecht, Netherlands
1982	Galerie Krikhaar, Amsterdam

Selected Group Exhibitions:

1946	*Junge Schilders,* Stedelijk Museum, Amsterdam
1949	*COBRA,* Stedelijk Museum, Amsterdam
1951	*Salon de Mai,* Musée d'Art Moderne, Paris
1953	*Bienal,* Sao Paulo
1956	*Carnegie International,* Carnegie Institute, Pittsburgh
1959	*Documenta 2,* Kassel, West Germany (and *Documenta 3,* 1964)
1964	*Guggenheim International,* Guggenheim Museum, New York
1973	*Hommage à Picasso,* Kestner-Gesellschaft, Hannover
1978	*Cobra 1948–78,* Statens Museum for Konst, Copenhagen
1983	*Cobra 1948–51,* Musée d'Art Moderne, Paris

Collections:

Stedelijk Museum, Armsterdam; Stedelijk Museum, Schiedam, Netherlands; Stedelijk Van Abbemuseum, Eindhoven, Netherlands; Palais des Beaux-Arts, Brussels; Musée de Liège, Belgium; Collection de la Ville de Paris; Museum Charlottenborg, Copenhagen; Nasjonalgalleriet, Oslo; Brooklyn Museum, New York; Museum of Djakarta, Indonesia.

Corneille: *Le Grand Oiseau de l'Eté,* 1981

Publications:

By CORNEILLE: book—*Journal de la Tour,* Paris 1981.

On CORNEILLE: books—*Corneille,* exhibition catalogue, with text by Charles Estienne, Paris 1954; *Corneille,* exhibition catalogue, with text by Edouard Jaeger, Amsterdam 1956; *Tekening van Corneille,* exhibition catalogue, with text by Imre Pan, Amsterdam 1960; *Corneille,* exhibition catalogue, with texts by Lawrence Alloway and E. L. L. de Wilde, London 1961; *Corneille,* exhibition catalogue, with text by A. M. Hammacher, The Hague 1961; *Corneille,* exhibition catalogue, with text by Karl K. Ringstrom, Oslo 1961; *Corneille,* exhibition catalogue, with text by Lawrence Alloway, New York 1961; *Corneille,* exhibition catalogue, with text by Willem Sandburg, New York 1964; *Corneille,* exhibition catalogue, with text by Werner Haftmann, New York 1965; *Corneille,* exhibition catalogue, with text by Max Loreau, Amsterdam 1966; *Corneille,* exhibition catalogue, with an interview by Christian Bussy, New York 1967; *Ariel 17: Corneille,* exhibition catalogue, with texts by D. H. Lawrence, Octavio Paz and Malcolm Lowry, Paris 1970; *Corneille,* exhibition catalogue, with text by André Laude, New York 1970; *Corneille,* exhibition catalogue, with text by Gunnar Jespersen, New York 1971; *Hommage à Picasso,* exhibition catalogue, with texts by Wieland Schmied, Werner Haftmann and Daniel H. Kahnweiler, Hannover 1973; *Corneille Le Roi—Image* by André Laude, Paris 1973; *Corneille et la Vie* by Elvirio Maurizi, Macerata, Italy 1974; *Corneille: The Quartier Rose of Amsterdam,* exhibition catalogue, New York 1974; *Corneille,* exhibition catalogue, with text by Elvirio Maurizi, Rome 1974; *Retrospective Tentoonstelling: Corneille,* exhibition catalogue, Ghent 1974; *Corneille Aujourd'hui* by Andre Laude, Stockholm 1978; *Corneille* by Daniel Marchesseau, Paris 1980.

COBRA was a nest of poets as well as artists. Corneille, a co-founder of the group, even if he is now wholly concerned with painting, injects into all his work the haunting suggestion of halfheard verse.

In his way he is a cyclic artist. Starting, as so many COBRA painters did, with what Lawrence Alloway has described as a "hectic display of birds and moonheads in free-fall," he later departed from this

style of imagery and concentrated on a series of compacted landscapes, pictures in which every tiny facet of colour was bounded by a rugged edge of paint in contrasting tone. All these areas of colour came together in a crowded amalgam like a delicious many-hued fruit of random shape. These paintings were veritable banquets.

Yet about 15 years ago he came back to his figures and figuration, albeit retaining the painted outline of every fragment of the picture. Colour areas increased in size. The sheer glutinous gravity of the landscapes was replaced by puckish humour. Mankind and the other creatures met once again, and they would be seen to be in a world which, if not real in the orthodox recognizable way, was still a world sprouting grass and trees and flowers under the canopy of a sky (however quirkily populated).

With or without COBRA affiliations, he stands out as an important artist of Northern Europe. His rejection of latin geometry and equal disinterest in a classical devotion to composition and style, has left him free to let the gamut of emotion in figures—or landscapes—run riot.

—Sheldon Williams

CORNELL, Joseph.

American. Born in Nyack, New York, 24 December 1903. Educated at Phillips Academy, Andover, Massachusetts, 1917–21; self-taught in art. Worked for the Whitman Textile Company, summer vacations, as salesman for woolen goods, New York, 1921–30; lived and worked in Flushing, New York, 1929 until his death, 1972; began painting and making assemblages, 1932, films, 1939; associated with the New York Surrealists, 1939–45. Recipient: Copley Foundation grant, 1954; Ada S. Garsh Prize, Art Institute of Chicago, 1959; Merit Award, American Academy of Arts and Letters, 1968. *Died* (in Flushing) *29 December 1972.*

Individual Exhibitions:

1932 Julien Levy Gallery, New York
1939 Julien Levy Gallery, New York
1940 Julien Levy Gallery, New York
1942 *Objects by Joseph Cornell/Box-Valise by Marcel Duchamp/Bottles by Lawrence Vail,* Art of This Century, New York
Ayer Galleries, Philadelphia
Wakefield Gallery, New York
1946 Park Lane Hotel, New York
Arthur A. Everts, Dallas
Hugo Gallery, New York
1948 Julien Levy Gallery, New York (with Marcel Duchamp and Yves Tanguy)
Copley Galleries, Beverly Hills, California
1949 Egan Gallery, New York
1950 Egan Gallery, New York
New York Public Library
1953 Egan Gallery, New York
Allan Frumkin Gallery, Chicago
Walker Art Center, Minneapolis
1955 Stable Gallery, New York
1956 Wittenborn and Company, New York
1957 Stable Gallery, New York
1959 New Gallery, Bennington College, Vermont
1962 Ferus Gallery, Los Angeles
1963 Loeb Student Center, New York University
1965 J. L. Hudson Gallery, Detroit
1966 Robert Schoelkopf Gallery, New York
Cleveland Museum of Art
Alan Stone Gallery, New York
Pasadena Art Museum, California
1967 Guggenheim Museum, New York
Walker Art Center, Minneapolis
1968 Rose Art Museum, Brandeis University, Waltham, Massachusetts
Queens College, Flushing, New York
1970 Cosmopolitan Club, New York
Metropolitan Museum, New York
1971 Galleria Galatea, Turin
1972 Gimpel and Hanover Galerie, Zurich
Cooper Union, New York
Alan Stone Gallery, New York
Albright-Knox Art Gallery, Buffalo, New York
Kestner-Gesellschaft, Hannover
1973 Queens County Art and Cultural Center, New York
Hopkins Center and Galleries, Dartmouth College, Hanover, New Hampshire
National Collection of Fine Arts, Smithsonian Institution, Washington, D.C.
1974 Museum of Contemporary Art, Chicago
1975 Pyramid Galleries, Washington, D.C.
ACA Galleries, New York
College of Creative Studies, University of California at Santa Barbara
1976 James Corcoran Gallery, Los Angeles
Leo Castelli Gallery, New York
Rice Museum, Houston
John Berggruen Gallery, San Francisco
1977 James Corcoran Gallery, Los Angeles
Edward Hopper House, Nyack, New York
L'Attico, Rome
Akron Art Institute, Ohio
1978 James Corcoran Gallery, Los Angeles
Gatodo Gallery, Tokyo
1979 Institute of Contemporary Arts, Boston
University of California Art Museum, Berkeley
1980 Baudoin Lebon, Paris (travelled to Musée de Toulon, France)
Castelli/Feigen/Corcoran Galleries, New York
Sierra Nevada Museum, Reno
Ulrich Museum of Art, Wichita State University, Kansas
Museum of Modern Art, New York (travelled to Whitechapel Art Gallery, London)
1986 Pace Gallery, New York
1987 Waddington Galleries, London

Selected Group Exhibitions:

1932 *Surrealist Group Exhibition,* Julien Levy Gallery, New York
1936 *Fantastic Art, Dada and Surrealism,* Museum of Modern Art, New York
1938 *Exposition International du Surrealisme,* Galerie Beaux-Arts, Paris
1944 *Abstract and Surrealist Art in the United States,* Denver Art Museum (toured the United States)
1958 *The Disquieting Muse: Surrealism,* Contemporary Art Museum, Houston
1961 *The Art of Assemblage,* Museum of Modern Art, New York (travelled to Museum for Contemporary Arts, Dallas, and the Museum of Art, San Francisco)
1964 *Painting and Sculpture of a Decade 1954–1964,* Tate Gallery, London
1970 *New York Painters and Sculptors,* Metropolitan Museum of Art, New York
1985 *Transformations in Sculpture,* Guggenheim Museum, New York
1986 *Seven Artists in Depth: The Creative Process,* San Francisco Museum of Modern Art

Collections:

Museum of Modern Art, New York; Whitney Museum, New York; Museum of Fine Arts, Boston; Walters Art Gallery, Baltimore, Hirshhorn Museum, Washington, D.C.; Norton Simon Museum of Art, Pasadena, California; Tate Gallery, London; Musée National d'Art Moderne, Paris; Kaiser Wilhelm Museum, Krefeld, West Germany.

Publications:

By CORNELL: articles—"M. Phot," scenario, in *Surrealism,* edited by Julien Levy, New York 1936; "Enchanged Wanderer" in *View* (New York), December 1941; "Recorded Conversations with Belle Krasne" in *Design Quarterly* (Minneapolis), no. 30, 1954; films—*Rose Hobart,* with Stan Brakhage, 1939; *Gnir Rednow,* with Stan Brakhage, 1955; *Centuries of June,* with Stan Brakhage, 1955; *Aviary,* with Rudy Burckhardt, 1955; *What Mozart Saw on Mulberry Street,* with Rudy Burckhardt, 1956; *A Fable for Fountains,* with Rudy Burckhardt, 1957; *Angel,* with Rudy Burckhardt, 1957; *Nymphlight,* 1959; *Cotillion,* with Larry Jordan, 1969; *The Children's Party,* with Larry Jordan, 1969; *The Midnight Party,* with Larry Jordan, 1969.

On CORNELL: books—*The History of Surrealist Painting* by Marcel Jean, New York 1960; *Joseph Cornell,* exhibition catalogue, by Diane Waldman, New York 1967; *Joseph Cornell,* exhibition catalogue, Pasadena, 1967; *Art Works and Packages* by Harold Rosenberg, London 1969; *A Joseph Cornell Album* by Dore Ashton, New York 1974; *Joseph Cornell Portfolio,* edited by Sandra Leonard Starr, New York 1976; *Joseph Cornell* by Diane Waldman, New York 1977; *Joseph Cornell,* exhibition catalogue, by Kynaston McShine, New York 1980; *Joseph Cornell: Art and Metaphysics* by Sandra Leonard Starr, New York 1982; *Joseph Cornell,* exhibition catalogue with text by Brian O'Doherty, New York 1986.

Joseph Cornell: *Cassiopeia No. 3*, c. 1954

During the 1930's Joseph Cornell began arranging found objects in glass and wooden boxes, creating three-dimensional collage constructions which are the immediate forerunners of Assemblage, an art form highly popularized in America during the 1950's and 1960's. Over a span of about 40 years, Cornell fashioned a magical miniature world by arranging the trivia and memorabilia he retrieved from antique and secondhand shops, on beaches and in backyards.

Maps, balls, butterflies, figurines, springs, printed cards and papers, jars, glass, glasses, photo-engravings and reproductions of famous people and art from the historical past, compasses, feathers, marbles, toys, pipes, dried flowers, counters—Cornell juggled so much so tenaciously, to convey his message of time, mortality and the infinite. He was early in using mirrors, movement and sound, and he was also early in using series. He often used astronomical maps and astrological charts, alluding to our fateful destiny in the hands of the sun, moon and planets. He often used images out of the past, making the Medici or dancers, for example, participants in his obsession to create a historical present which sees through the cultural past. Alongside the gentleness there is an element of warning, seducing with no nostalgic sentimentality but always with a sense of intelligent intimacy with the accumulated treasures he collected from nature, from culture and from the industrial world.

Cornell questioned what's real and what's artificial, what's precious and what's mundane. Sometimes apothecary jars are arranged in grid-cabinets, filled with a variety of things, like some inexplicable medicine, like spices and equally like some inexplicable warning of impending encapsulation. Cornell's dioramas convey the wonderment in all aspects of life, using juxtaposition to heighten consciousness of the interconnectedness of so many things and of the past and the present. And always the magic is informed by a highly refined formal prowess, both when the compositions are filled and when they are more spare, as in the later years.

Cornell's transformation of the ordinary into the extraordinary is related to the methods of the Surrealists, and he did find inspiration from the likes of Max Ernst, Miró and Duchamp. He was, however, concerned with seduction rather than with surrealist shock, and he chose his repertoire as treasures in a spirit vastly differing from the more tough and junky castaways preferred by Kurt Schwitters. Cornell does not fit comfortably into any "ism" and is best understood as one of the independents in art history who, like Redon, Ryder, Poe and Klee, is basically a hermetic spell caster, small in scale but monumental in magic, and is endowed with an ingenuous imagination capable of reshaping the modest into the wondrous symbol as mysterious as life itself.

—Barbara Cavaliere

COSTA, Claudio.

Italian. Born in Tirana, Albania, 22 June 1942; moved with his family to Italy, 1944. Studied architecture at the Polytechnico, Milan, 1963–65; studied engraving, Atelier Hayter, Paris, 1965–67. Married Anita Zeiro in 1967; daughter: Marisol. Independent artist, Genoa, since 1967. Agents: Galleria Massimo Valsecchi, Via S. Marta II, Milan; Galleria Unimedia, Vico dei Garibaldi I, Genoa. Address: Vico dei Garibaldi 1, 16123 Genoa, Italy.

Individual Exhibitions:

1969 Galleria La Bertesca, Genoa
1970 Galleria Modulo, Milan
1971 *Il Cervello sul Muro*, Modern Art Agency, Naples
Galleria Barozzi, Venice
Produzenten Galerie, Berlin
Tele Acide: Tele Acidate, Galleria Ferrari, Verona
1972 Galleria Duemila, Bologna
Galleria del Leone, Venice
1973 Galleria La Bertesca, Genoa
1974 *In the Company of the Human Brain and Prehistoric Man*, Neue Galerie, Aachen, West Germany
Galerie Klang, Cologne
Galleria Nuovi Strumenti, Brescia, Italy
1975 Galleria Massimo Valsecchi, Milan
Foundation of the Museum of Anthropology, Monteghirfo, Genoa
1976 Galleria Arteverso, Genoa
Galleria Civica, Moderna, Italy
1977 Galleriaforma, Genoa
Studio di Via Crugoni, Genoa
Studio Torelli, Ferrara, Italy
1978 Galleria Arte Moderna, Portofino, Italy
Fabjbasaglia Galleria, Bologna
Galleria Arte Moderna, Alessandria, Italy
Galleria Nuova 13, Alessandria, Italy
1979 Galleria Nuovi Strumenti, Brescia, Italy
Galleria R. Rotta, Genoa
Galleria Unimedia, Genoa
Galleria Arco d'Alibert, Rome
Galleria Il Luogo di Gauss, Milan
1980 Galleria De Amicis, Florence
Galleria Il Gabbiano, La Spezia, Italy
Studio Cesare Manzo, Pescara, Italy
Salone Villa Romana, Florence
1981 Galleria Massimo Valsecchi, Milan
Galeria Andata-Ritorno, Geneva
1982 Galleria R. Rotta, Genoa
Galleria del Cavallino, Venice
Galleria Unimedia, Genoa

Selected Group Exhibitions:

1969 *Rassegna Biennale*, Galleria di Tendenza, Modena, Italy
1973 *8th Biennale*, Paris
1974 *Spruensicheerung: Archaelogie und Erinnerung*, Hamburg and Munich
1976 *Identitè: Identification*, CAP, Bordeaux
1978 *Arte e Cinema negli Anni 70*, Pinacoteca Civica, Ravenna, Italy
1979 *Metafisica del Quotidiano*, Galleria d'Arte Moderna, Bologna
1980 *Work in Progress*, Galleria Arte Moderna, Genoa
1981 *Mythos and Ritual*, Kunsthaus, Zurich
1982 *Deserto*, Comune di Bergamo, Italy

Collections:

Neue Galerie, Aachen, West Germany

Publications:

By COSTA: books—*Interpretazione Intera*, Genoa 1970; *Sintomi di un Lavoro*, Naples 1971; *Evolution: Involution*, Berlin and Genoa 1971; *Due Esercizi di Antropologia*, Brescia, Italy 1974; *Materiale e Metaforico*, Genoa 1979; *Sublimato Potabile*, Milan 1981.

On COSTA: books—*Il Cervello sul Muro*, exhibition catalogue, by Corrado Maltese, Naples 1971; *Tele Acide: Tele Acidate*, exhibition catalogue, by Renato Barilli, Verona 1971; *In the Company of the Human Brain and Prehistoric Man*, exhibition catalogue, by Wolfgang Becker, Aachen, West Germany 1974; *Maori's Eyes Reflect the Latent Colours of the Forest* by Lorenza Trucchi, Rome 1974; articles—"Metodologia del fare" by Edda Gazzerro in *Due Esercizi di Antropoliga*, Brescia, Italy 1974; "Noi i Primitivi" by Franco Torriani in *Gala* (Milan), February 1975.

After a period of quite general activity, I turned to experimentation in the most difficult means of expression: I slowly acquired the use of the "substance" as a means referring to itself and to its history. At that time I worked particularly on acid and acidified canvas.

In the meantime I had acquired a consciousness of a precise interest in man. I then ideally reconstructed the brain and the brain-pan, assimilating it to the polar skull-cap: this interest produced a big file of engravings and of other works.

My intention was the definition of an "absolute" geographical place as an ambiguous sign of existence. At that time I began to make use of chalk and afterwards of raw clay.

And I also worked, at that time, on research into man's memory. Works such as "portraits by heart" are of this category.

To be more exact, the work about man's evolution began in 1971. The book *Evolution: Involution* is of this period too. In it I also tried to present the idea, which I consider as fundamental, of recovering the past in a critical perspective: I started the work as research into the "possibilities of space and of time" which man has altered and lost during his evolution.

I studied pre-historic man, and I extracted and reproduced his peculiar traits. The casts of living persons, reconstructed according to the different periods of evolution, belong to this period. Then I studied primitive cultures that have preserved their original way of life and original tools. I have also been interested in man's "habitat," and some of my works have to be considered as studies of its changes.

Afterwards I recognized in the objects used by man signs of his way of life: the object reveals the relationship it has with man. The reconstructions on which I work or the appropriation of certain objects, inserted into the works, have precisely this purpose: they are a sign of reality; they propose it again as directly as possible.

In the work of reconstruction of the "Active Museum of Monteghirfo" it was my intention to collect and preserve in their original setting these objects of use—signs of a culture crushed by our consumer civilization.

Through this work I have identified things, persons, places, nuclei of families, the human aggregate and the environment—an exact and fated living mosaic. A certain number of document-works have been the result of this interest. In these works the materials used are photographic enlargements of environments or of objects and the objects themselves, which I have covered with clay.

I make use of anthropology as a means of knowing, but in my work it is only a tool aiding my intuition and emotion, which more decidedly are the means to urge me to operate and perform.

I believe that man, as all the things on earth, must be perceived in himself, in what he is in his totality beyond and outside scientific knowledge, which ends by concealing, by darkening our lives and the existence of things.

—Claudio Costa

In the making of a work, Claudio Costa behaves according to a methodology of "doing," which is typical of that kind of contemporary conceptual art of which he is certainly a prominent practitioner. His work consists of perfectly identifiable images or objects, and they can "placed" historically: they are documents (both real and faithfully reconstructed) of periods prior to contemporary life. Annotations explaining the cultural references are inserted into the works. Thus, the construction has form and functions as a channel for communication in a typically contemporary particularization of inquiry and expression.

However, this description is not sufficient to convey the fundamental characteristics of his art. Costa's work is not complete within itself or within the conceptual/rational reference in which it places itself as praxis (which is, more or less, the characteristic of the art-concept), for it is his intention to establish a relationship of knowledge as from the objects as facts. A relationship of this kind, as realized by Costa, does not exhaust itself in mere rational fact; it aims to go further, to become a kind of feedback on man facing his history—in a process analogous in its psychic mechanism to that of the emotional, nonformal genesis of classic expressionism.

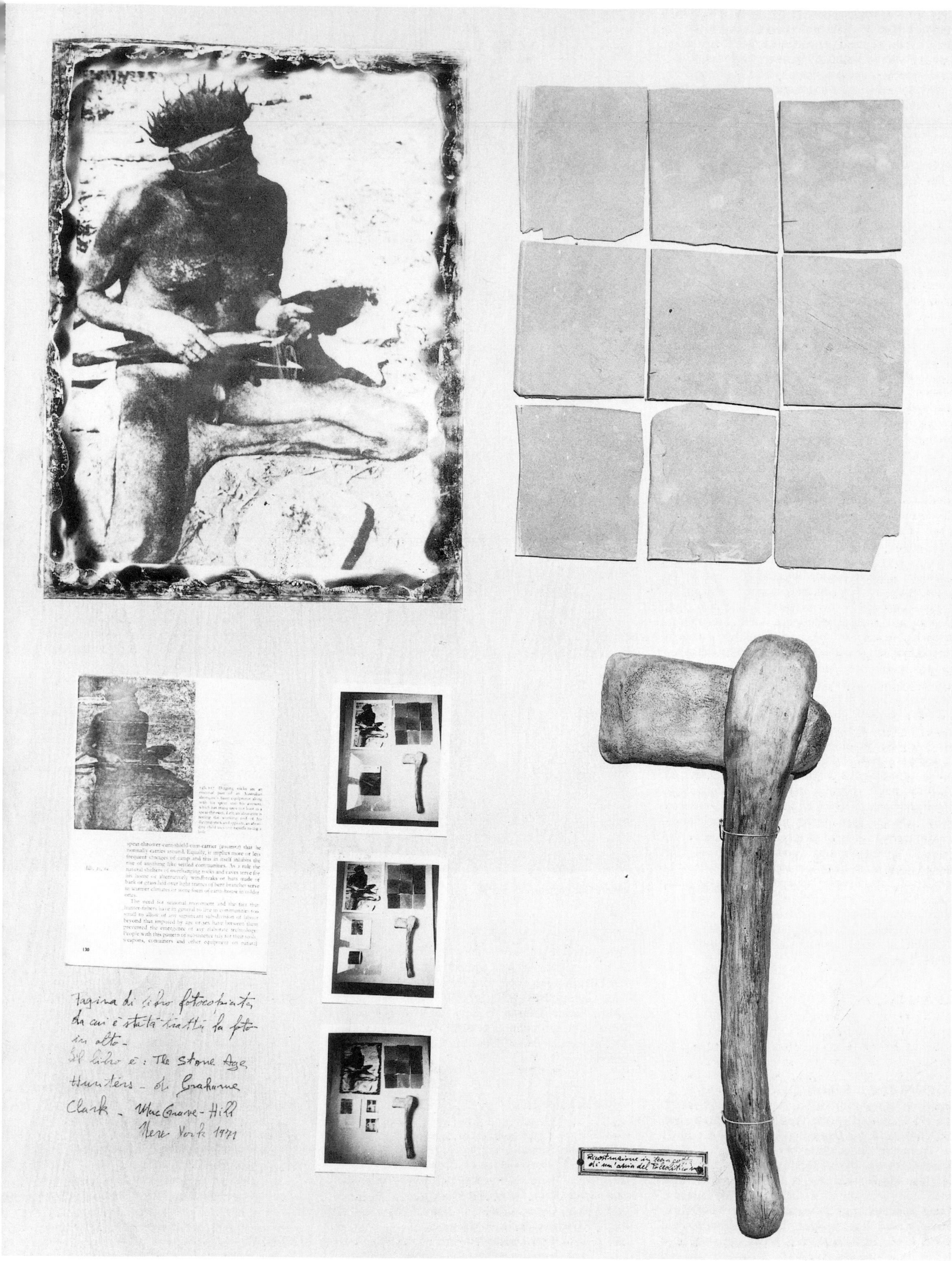

Claudio Costa: *Old Making of Man*, 1975

As for the composition of the work: the chosen object—identified, indicated—is not used for the image it offers of itself, nor as an indication, a reference, of external reality to be analyzed for ethical or social values. Claudio Costa's "object" is, as it were, a laboratory finding, a cognitive moment in itself, to be regarded as such. In this sense the artist is a kind of anthropologist—not only in his interests but also in his methods. He reports his findings without loading them with symbols or myths; he does not report according to some basic cultural perspective.

His form of analysis is a propaedeutic methodology, and therefore neutral. And his work should be regarded in its entirety, so as to differentiate it from that of those contemporaries who also use historical, archaeological or anthropological findings in their works. For Costa such findings do not involve an occasional fact or a chance discovery of an unusual source of images and objects. Rather, they are the result of a constant "observation" of man and his natural habitat.

In the past Costa has edited the memory of man; he has proposed a relation with Cromus; he has analyzed "lived" space in relation to "possible" space. He has investigated the materiality, the availability, the modifications of habitat. From the relationship between man and space-time, as well as habitat, he has extracted the "object"—an object which, however, does not report on itself but on something other than itself.

If for most artists one can speak of the object-as-code or the sign-as-code, for Costa one must speak perhaps of some primary, preliminary code in the sense that the significant means are external to the object and to its meaning. These "means" rest between object and observer, and they are constituted not as conventional signs but as evocations of a relationship. It is a code composed of object/man means, in which the sign is not the object nor the man but the action occurring between the two and modified (i.e., further codified) by the remote, philogenetic, and consequently, present experience. Costa uses this relationship as an art object, an intuitive means of knowledge, and, paradoxically, his work is characterized by the absence of real time: what he proposes is proposed always in the present, without temporal references.

Costa's analysis proceeds synchronically (that is, descriptively); the sign juxtapositions of another type which he also uses do not actuate a diachronism (that is, comparison with different systems) but are notes in a thought progress within the work, which thus are taken for single cognitive moments: he proceeds by simple elements to which he juxtaposes in a differentiated and conscious manner more complex cultural indications, which are, however, always placed *a posteriori* as regards the single cognitive moment. Thus Costa injects himself, by a route of his own, into the context of contemporary thought, which recognizes man's sources of knowledge as contingent and contained within himself as well as within his biologically delimited being. Through his work Costa creates a cognitive, intuitive/emotional, biologically recognizable moment.

—Edda Gazzerro

Robert Cottingham: *Nite*, 1986

COTTINGHAM, Robert.

American. Born in Brooklyn, New York, 26 September 1935. Studied at the Pratt Institute, Brooklyn, 1959–64, Associate Degree in Advertising Art 1962. Served in the United States Army, in Com-Z Unit, Orleans, France, 1955–58: Specialist 3rd Class. Married Jane Marie Weismann in 1967; daughters: Reid Ann, Molly Jane and Kyle Annie Bliss. Art Director, Young and Rubicam Advertising Inc., New York, 1959–64, and Los Angeles, 1964–68. Independent painter, since 1968. Instructor, Art Center College of Design, Los Angeles, 1969–70. Recipient: National Endowment for the Arts Grant, 1974; Artist of the Year Award, Fairfield Chamber of Commerce, Connecticut, 1988. Agents: Gimpel and Weitzenhoffer, 724 Fifth Avenue, New York, New York 10019; Fendrick Gallery, 3059 M Street NW, Washington, D.C. 20007; Roger Ramsay Gallery, 212 West Superior Street, Chicago, Illinois 60610. Address: P.O. Box 604, Blackman Road, Newton, Connecticut 06470, U.S.A.

Individual Exhibitions:

1968 Molly Barnes Gallery, Los Angeles
1969 Molly Barnes Gallery, Los Angeles
1970 Molly Barnes Gallery, Los Angeles
1971 O.K. Harris Gallery, New York
1974 O.K. Harris Gallery, New York
1975 D.M. Gallery, London
Galerie de Gestlo, Hamburg
1976 O.K. Harris Gallery, New York
John Berggruen Gallery, San Francisco
1977 Landfall Press Gallery, Chicago
1978 Morgan Gallery, Kansas City, Missouri
Bethel Art Gallery, Connecticut
O.K. Harris Gallery, New York
1979 Aldrich Museum, Ridgefield, Connecticut
Beaver College, Glenside, Pennsylvania
Landfall Press Gallery, Chicago
Galerie de Gestlo, Cologne
Delta Gallery, Rotterdam
Getler-Pall Gallery, New York
Dean Junior College, Franklyn, Massachusetts
1980 University of Bridgeport, Connecticut
Thomas Segal Gallery, Boston
Ball State University, Muncie, Indiana
Madison Art Center, Wisconsin
1981 Fendrick Gallery, Washington, D.C.
Mattatuck Museum, Waterbury, Connecticut
Swain School of Design, New Bedford, Massachusetts
1982 Coe Kerr Gallery, New York
1983 Signet Arts, St. Louis, Missouri
Modernism Gallery, San Francisco
Wichita Art Museum, Kansas

1984 Coe Kerr Gallery, New York
Fendrick Gallery, Washington, D.C.
Springfield Art Museum, Missouri
Palace Theatre, New Haven, Connecticut
1985 The Art Guild, Farmington, Connecticut
Abilene Christian University, Texas
Roger Ramsay Gallery, Chicago
Reynolda House Museum of American Art, Winston-Salem, North Carolina
Arkansas Arts Center, Little Rock (travelled to Washington, D.C.; St. Louis, Missouri; Odessa, Texas)
1986 Signet Arts, St. Louis, Missouri
Museum of Art, Science and Industry, Bridgeport, Connecticut
Gallery Karl Oskar, Westwood Hills, Kansas
Brenda Kroos Gallery, Columbus, Ohio
Springfield Art Museum, Missouri (travelled to Chattanooga, Tennessee; Kansas City, Missouri; Joplin, Missouri; Norman, Oklahoma; Cedar Rapids, Iowa)

Selected Group Exhibitions:

1970 *The Highway,* Institute of Contemporary Art, University of Pennsylvania, Philadelphia (travelled to the Institute for the Arts, Rice University, Houston, and the Akron Art Institute, Ohio.)
1971 *Radical Realism,* Museum of Contemporary Art, Chicago
1972 *Documenta 5,* Kassel, West Germany
1973 *Photo-Realism: The Ludwig Collection,* Serpentine Gallery, London
1974 *Hyperréalistes Américains/Réalistes Européens,* Centre National d'Art Contemporain, Paris (toured Europe)
1978 *Art about Art,* Whitney Museum, New York (travelled to the North Carolina Museum of Art, Raleigh; Frederick S. Wright Art Gallery, University of California at Los Angeles; and the Portland Museum, Oregon)
1981 *Contemporary American Realism since 1960,* Pennsylvania Academy of Fine Arts, Philadelphia
1983 *Painting New York,* Museum of the City of New York
1985 *American Realism: The Precise Image,* Isetan Museum, Tokyo (travelled to Osaka and Yokohama, Japan)
1986 *Hollywood: Legend and Reality,* Smithsonian Institution, Washington, D.C. (toured the United States)

Collections:

Whitney Museum, New York; Syracuse University, New York; Hirshhorn Museum and Sculpture Garden, Smithsonian Institution, Washington, D.C.; Indianapolis Museum of Art; Honolulu Academy of Art; Museum of Modern Art, New York; Art Institute of Chicago; Arts Council of Great Britain, London; Boymans-van Beuningen Museum, Rotterdam.

Publications:

By COTTINGHAM: article—interview in "Photo-Realists: 12 Interviews" by Linda Chase and Ted McBurnett in *Art in America* (New York), November/December 1972.

On COTTINGHAM: books—*New Realism* by Udo Kultermann, Tübingen, West Germany 1972; *Photo-Realism: The Ludwig Collection,* exhibition catalogue, London 1973; *Hyperréalistes Américains/Réalistes Européens,* exhibition catalogue, Paris 1974; *Realists at Work* by John Arthur, New York 1983; *Robert Cottingham—A Print Retrospective 1972–86,* edited by John Arthur, Springfield, Missouri 1986; articles—"Too Easy to Be Art" by Peter Schieldahl in the *New York Times,* May 1974; "Robert Cunningham: The Capers of the Signscape" by Toni del Renzio in *Art and Artists* (London), February 1975; "Cottingham's Air: Letter Perfect" in *New Art Examiner* (Chicago), December 1985.

For more than twenty years now I have been painting and drawing a uniquely American subject—the neon signs, shop fronts and movie marquees of our cities and downtown neighborhoods.

My interest in these cultural icons seems to derive from my Brooklyn upbringing, my fascination with letter forms as symbols and my interest in society's use of language as a means of persuasion.

During the four year period from 1983 through 1986, I became particularly intrigued by a row of shop fronts that included such diverse commercial establishments as a barber shop, a hotel, a bar, a newsstand, a liquor store, and a Mexican restaurant named Barrera-Rosa's. This panorama of facades and messages struck me as an image rich with aesthetic possibilities, not only as a singular, unified vision, but as a network of separate and overlapping compositional fragments. I began an extensive exploration of this image, dissecting and analysing its parts, in an attempt to reveal its abstract underpinnings. This pictorial foray resulted in an output of 45 individual works executed in a multitude of media, including watercolor, acrylic, gouache, ink, graphite, woodcut, linoleum cut, etching, lithography and oil.

The three prints in the *Barrera-Rosa* portfolio played an important part in this exploration. Each deals with a specific means of visual expression: line(dry-point etching), mass(linoleum cut), and color(lithograph). Each print, while a finished graphic work in its own right, contributes significantly to the overall investigation of the image's substructure; its abstract patterns, the formal relationships of interlocking shapes, the nuances of line, value and color—in short, the fundamental components of composition.

And beyond these formal issues there is, of course, the subject matter itself. I like to think of these prints and my work in general as a celebration of the signs and urban iconography that have given American cities their peculiar energy. Monumental, poignant, absurd, and surreal, these structures stand as vivid testimony to the vitality and variety of contemporary American life.

—Robert Cottingham

Robert Cottingham ascribes to Pop Art the essential permissiveness that allowed him to paint images of mundane urban reference, with an emphasis upon a display of letter types in commercial signs, and clearly based upon the photograph. Although Cottingham has always used photographs—which he himself takes in carefully planned forays to various American cities—he has likewise always handpainted his images without the use of compressed air spray techniques. He thus joins Richard Estes and others among prominent "Photo-Realists" who ironically enough combine the traditional liking for the handicraft and brushed facture of easel painting with the apparently antithetical feel of the mechanically-produced photographic print. His etchings and lithographs are also handwork, and not photo-transcriptions of painted works.

After an earlier career in advertising and a move from the East Coast to California, Cottingham's first exhibition in Los Angeles, in 1968, already presented the themes and compositional orderings which have remained constant throughout his career.

These early works, of city landmarks from the pre-World War II era, such as "Ralph's Market" and the "Pan Pacifica Auditorium" (the latter still one of his largest works at 10 feet in width), presented a passerby's view of the building's upper parts; while lettering was already a clear intent in these works, the structures were seen broadly against the sky. At the onset of the next decade, Cottingham had painted one of his most often reproduced works, "Art," 1971: a closely-cropped—the photo terminology clearly appropriate—view of a theatre marquee which goes on beyond the picture frame. Although the light bulbs are missing and have been replaced by neon light strips and the letter character is clearly inter-war, nostalgia and good-humored wordplay are only infrequently the clear goal of the artist. More pointedly, these paintings are intended as brilliantly hued, abstracted plays of line and movement.

Cottingham himself has affirmed that it is not the social character of the letters as much as their visual interest that led him initially to those parts of American cities (sections which he has found often changed in his subsequent returns). In interviews he has spoken of his calculated use of three lenses on the cameras with which he gathers materials for his studio production. And his paintings have easily reflected this photographic practice—the use of telephoto lenses with their close-up, "zoom" focus. Although Cottingham's best-known works have been signage seen at sharp angles from below, he has also produced more relaxed, less camera-referential and more personal, perceptual. The omnipresence of the photographic image in our culture has neither diminished his productivity nor style qualities. His mid-decade work is still based upon the "fading" urban neighborhood. There may now more often appear a dazzling, even mannered, interplay of a multitude of elements, but perhaps more often presented both more parallel and more perpendicular to the picture plane. A touch of the long American love for *trompe l'oeil* has been added to another Populist tradition—the neighborhood realism of the Ash Can School of the early twentieth century—and modernist abstraction is likewise touched with pre-modern attitudes. Cottingham has said of his particular poignant formalism: "I'm not primarily interested in documentation, although I think there is a certain documentary aspect to my work. It's unavoidable because of the degree of realistic depiction involved and by the nature of the subject matter. It's a vision exclusive to the century and is fading fast."

—Joshua Kind

CRAGG, Tony.
British. Born in Liverpool, Merseyside, in 1949. Studied art, Gloucestershire College of Arts and Technology, Cheltenham, 1968–70; painting, Wimbledon School of Art, London, 1970–73; sculpture, Royal College of Art, London, 1973–77, MA 1977. Married Ute Uberste-Lehn in 1977; sons: Daniel and Thomas. Worked as a laboratory technician, Natural Rubber Producers Research Association, Liverpool, 1966–68. Independent sculptor, in Wuppertal, West Germany, since 1977. Instructor in sculpture, Ecole des Beaux-Arts, Metz, France, 1976; instructor, Kunstakademie, Dusseldorf, since 1979. Agents: Galerie Crousel-Robelin, 40 rue Quincampoix, 75004 Paris, France; and Lisson Gallery, London. Address: c/o Lisson Gallery, 67 Lisson Street, London NW1, England.

Individual Exhibitions:

1979 Lisson Gallery, London (and 1980)
Lutzowstrasse Situation, West Berlin
Kunstlerhaus Weidenallee, Hamburg
1980 Arnolfini Gallery, Bristol
Galerie Konrad Fischer, Dusseldorf
Galerie Chantal Crousel, Paris
Lutzowstrasse Situation, Buro Berlin
Galleria Lucio Amelio, Naples
Galleria Franco Toselli, Milan
Saman Galleria, Genoa, Italy
1981 Galerie Schellmann und Kluser, Munich
Musee d'Art et d'industrie, St. Etienne, France
Whitechapel Art Gallery, London
Front Room, London
Nouveau Musee, Lyon, France (and 1982)
Von der Heydt Museum, Wuppertal, West Germany
Galerie Vacuum, Dusseldorf
1982 Badischer Kunstverein, Karlsruhe, West Germany
Kanransha Gallery, Tokyo
Nisshin Gallery, Tokyo
Marian Goodman Gallery, New York (and 1983)

Tony Cragg: *Instinctive Reactions*, 1987 Courtesy Lisson Gallery, London

Galerie Chantal Crousel, Paris
Buro Berlin
Lisson Gallery, London
Galerie Konrad Fischer, Dusseldorf
Museum Kroller-Muller, Otterlo, Netherlands
Galerie Schellmann und Kluser, Munich
1983 Galleria Lucio Amelio, Naples
Kunsthalle, Berne
Art and Project, Amsterdam
Galeria Thomas Cohn, Rio de Janeiro
Galleria Franco Toselli, Milan
Galerie Buchmann, St. Gallen, Switzerland
1984 Yarlow and Salzmann, Toronto
De Vleeshal, Middelburg, Netherlands
Louisiana Museum, Humlebaek, Denmark
Galerie Schellmann und Kluser, Munich
Marian Goodman Gallery, New York
Kanransha Gallery, Tokyo
Galerie Crousel-Hussenot, Paris
Kunstverein, Cologne
Galleria Tucci Russo, Turin
1985 Kunsthalle Waghaus, Winterthur, Switzerland
Staatsgalerie Moderner Kunst, Munich
Donald Young Gallery, Chicago
Lisson Gallery, London
Art and Project, Amsterdam
Palais des Beaux-Arts, Brussels
ARC/Musee d'Art Moderne de la Ville, Paris
1986 Kestner Gesellschaft, Hannover
Galerie Bernd Kluser, Munich
Galerie Joost Declercq, Ghent, Belgium
Brooklyn Museum of Art, New York
Galerie Pierre Huber, Geneva
University of California, Berkeley
1987 Hayward Gallery, London
Galleria Tucci Russo, Turin
Marian Goodman Gallery, New York
1988 Galeria Marga Paz, Madrid
Galerie Buchmann, Basle
Galerie Crousel-Robelin, Paris

Selected Group Exhibitions:

1977 *RCA Degree Show*, Royal College of Art, London
1980 *Kunst in Europa na '68*, Museum van Hedendaagse Kunst, Ghent, Belgium
1981 *British Sculpture in the 20th Century*, Whitechapel Art Gallery, London
1982 *Kunst wird Material*, Nationalgalerie, West Berlin
1983 *Edges and Shadows: Sculpture in Britain*, Hayward Gallery, London (and Serpentine Gallery, London)
1984 *The British Art Show*, City Art Gallery, Birmingham (and Ikon Gallery, Birmingham; travelled to Edinburgh, Sheffield and Southamption)
1985 *Mobel—Objekte und Installationen*, Von der Heydt Museum, Wuppertal, West Germany
1986 *Beuys zu Ehren*, Stadtische Galerie in Lenbachhaus, Munich
1987 *A Quiet Revolution: British Sculpture since 1965*, San Francisco Museum of Modern Art (travelled to Newport Beach; Washington, D.C.; Buffalo)
1988 *Brittanica: Vingt-cinq ans de sculpture*, Musee des Beaux Arts, Le Havre, France (travelled to Evreux, Rouen and Antwerp, 1988–89)

Collections:

Tate Gallery, London; British Council, London; Arts Council of Great Britain, London; Museum of Modern Art, New York; Fonds Regional d'Art Contemporain Rhone-Alpes, France.

Publications:

By CRAGG: books—*Tony Cragg: Skulpturen*, exhibition catalogue, with others, Hannover 1985; *Tony Cragg*, exhibition catalogue, with Lynne Cooke, London 1987.

On CRAGG: books—*Tony Cragg*, exhibition catalogue with foreword by Bernard Ceysson, St. Etienne 1981; *Tony Cragg*, exhibition catalogue with text by Ursula Peters, Wuppertal 1981; *Tony Cragg: Skulpturen*, exhibition catalogue with essay by Michael Newman, Karlsruhe 1982; *Tony Cragg*, exhibition catalogue with text by Nobuo Nakamura, Tokyo 1982; *Tony Cragg*, exhibition catalogue with texts by Jean-Hubert Martin and Germano Celant, Berne 1983, *Tony Cragg. Zwei Landschaften*, exhibition catalogue with text by Armin

Wildermuth, St. Gallen 1984; *Tony Cragg*, exhibition catalogue with essay by Armin Wildermuth, Cologne 1984; *Tony Cragg*, exhibition catalogue with texts by Anneliese Pohlen and Demosthenes Davvetos, Brussels and Paris 1985.

Tony Cragg is a part of that generation of artists who, following Philip King, Richard Long and Barry Flanagan, have renewed the scope of English sculpture by insisting on a critical rereading and one sensitive to the value of the object in the contemporary plastic arts. Though close to the trends of the seventies, Cragg's work nevertheless departs from the rigorous formulas and strictly 'objectual' criteria of minimal art in order to address itself to the crisis of our modern consumer society.

Cragg, who has lived in West Germany since 1979, trained as a biologist and then worked in a research laboratory, which taught him to consider "art as an extension of science" (T. C.) From the time of his first artistic creations, while he was still a student at London's Royal College of Art, it was as an 'archaeologist' of the technological era that he discovered and utilised the formal, emotional and narrative potential of the industrial object.

All the products-throwouts of consumption, used and discarded, those reject materials which clutter our daily world, are retrieved by the artist near his place of work, then 'staged' in the exhibition area. The materials are displayed without modifications according to a system of accumulation which demonstrates the complex interactions that take place between man and his creations, the object being the projection and the receptacle of socio-economic interests and of individual pretensions. "I think that objects have the capability to carry valuable information for us, to be important to us, but the fact is that most objects are made in ways which are irresponsible and manipulative. Irresponsible because people—the makers of this or that—don't really consider in any metaphysical way the meanings of the objects that they are making: and manipulative because things are made for a variety of commercial and power based reasons" (T. C.). In his work Tony Cragg ignores the functional side of objects; the plastic unity of his assemblages is subjectively determined by the preliminary choice of a form (one of his first pieces, *Stapel*, 1977, is made up of planks, stones and diverse other materials which together build up a perfect cube) or of a colour (for *Spectrum*, 1984, the materials have been put together in series of blues, reds, yellows and greens). For his first compositions Cragg primarily used plastic objects that had been worn out by time or use, and bits and pieces of artificially coloured synthetic materials, placing them one beside the other so that they filled out the human figures which he had outlined on walls or ground. A veritable critical cartography of society and of the object's vocabulary, these assemblages represent life-size human silhouettes (self-portraits, groups, *Britain seen from the north*, 1981, *Polizist*, 1981, *Riot*, 1987 . . .) which have the quality of historical and metaphysical symbols. Some of the figures take on the magnified shape of one of the objects of the composition (*Green bottle*, 1980) or of a natural element (*Red skin*, 1979), or of an object-type in the artistic (*Palette*, 1982) or poetic vocabulary (*Blue moon*, 1980).

From 1982 Cragg's working methods became more diversified. By covering objects with a uniform layer of white or speckled paint and thereby obscuring the qualities themselves of the material, he accorded particular importance to the form and to the equilibrium of the work as a whole (*Lens*, 1985, *No place for a rabbit*, 1985, *Aquaduct*, 1986).

From 1982 Cragg also developed an interest in organic objects and in hand-crafted objects, in a pre-technological mode of production where manual work plays a direct part in the transformation of the material. *Axe*, for example, in which an axe figures as part of the overall image, brings into contact with one another certain wooden objects of varying volume and complexity which, in view of the means of their production, carry within themselves this very axe.

The tool, symbol of man's creative capacities and of his control over matter, became the object of a number of Cragg's sculptures. Chosen for the purity of their volumes, various tools were magnified and worked in wood, glass or steel in works which underline the interaction between form and function (*Mortar and pestle*, 1986, *Eye bath*, 1986).

With the series entitled *Landscape* (1982, 1983) Cragg distances himself once again from industrial society in order to linger over the organisation of natural elements, in the face of which man abandons rationalism and returns to his ancient role as creator of images and inventor of myths. The austere compositions of *Landscape* seem to be insisting still on the arbitrary forms and structures of stones, the result of fractures to the original block from which they have split. Certain compositions in which crude materials are assembled are then exploded by the introduction of a geometric shape symbolising the intrusion of architecture into the landscape (*Installation in Cadillac*, 1985, *Jurassic landscape*, 1986). With *Echo*, 1984, a piece which is made up of large geometric volumes uniformly covered with repetitive and depersonalising graffiti, the artist analyses urban architecture. The degradation and dehumanisation of the natural or city environment occupy a prominent place in Cragg's work as a whole.

In some of his latest works (*The Worm Returns*, 1986, *DNA-Molecule*, *Bacchus Drops*, 1985, *Inverted Sugar Crop*, 1987 . . .) Cragg demonstrates his interest in science, alluding to chemical processes upon which the manufacture of certain food products like sugar and wine is based. From a preoccupation with the manufacturing techniques of various objects, via an interest in the modifications directly imposed on the molecular structure of natural elements and the material changes resulting therefrom, Cragg was naturally led to reconsider the creative function (in both artistic and scientific terms) in its primary alchemical acceptation as a transforming power.

Besides the diversity of its scientific, social and historical associations and the constant reappraisal of its plastic solutions, the work of Tony Cragg should be regarded above all as a sensitive and frequently philosophical approach to the human situation, as testified by the following extract from an interview with Cragg: "In a sense, it's obvious that in terms of the physical world scientists make the more fundamental statements, but artists and philosophers don't have a less important job. They humanize, they find out what the significance of science is for human beings . . . . I think you have to make images of objects which are like thinking models to help you get through the world."

—Dominique Liquois

CRAIG-MARTIN, Michael.

British. Born in Dublin in 1941; moved with his family to the United States, 1946; returned to Britain, 1966. Educated at Yale University, New Haven, Connecticut, 1961–63; studied at the Yale School of Art and Architecture, 1964–66. Divorced; has one daughter. Settled in Corsham, Wiltshire, 1966–68; lived in London, 1968–70, and since 1972. Lecturer, Bath Academy of Art and Canterbury College of Art, 1970–72; Principal Lecturer, Goldsmiths' College, London, 1973. Agent: Waddington Galleries, London. Address: c/o Waddington Galleries, 2 Cork Street, London WIX 1PA, England

Individual Exhibitions:

1969	Rowan Gallery, London
1970	Rowan Gallery, London
1971	Arnolfini Gallery, Bristol
	Richard Demarco Gallery, Edinburgh
1972	Rowan Gallery, London
1973	Rowan Gallery, London
1974	Rowan Gallery, London
	Galerie December, Münster, West Germany
1975	Rowan Gallery, London
1976	Rowan Gallery, London
	Selected Works 1966–1975, Turnpike Gallery, Leigh, Lancashire (toured the U.K.)
1977	Third Eye Centre, Glasgow
	Oliver Dowling Gallery, Dublin
1978	Galerie December, Dusseldorf
	Institute of Modern Art, Brisbane (toured Australia)
	Rowan Gallery, London
1979	Galerie Foksal, Warsaw
	Galerie Akmulatory, Poznan, Poland
	Oliver Dowling Gallery, Dublin
1980	Rowan Gallery, London
	Galerie BaMa, Paris
1981	Galerija Suvremene Umjetnosti, Zagreb
1982	Waddington Galleries, London
1983	Waddington and Shiell Galleries, Toronto
1985	Waddington Galleries, London
1988	Waddington Galleries, London

Selected Group Exhibitions:

1966	*First II*, Jewish Community Center, New Haven, Connecticut
1970	*Critics' Choice*, Tooths Gallery, London
1972	*The New Art*, Hayward Gallery, London
1973	*Henry Moore to Gilbert and George*, Palais des Beaux-Arts, Brussels
1974	*Idea and Image in Recent Art*, Art Institute of Chicago
1975	*Bienal*, Sao Paulo
1976	*Sydney Biennale*, Art Gallery of New South Wales, Sydney
1979	*Un Certain Art Anglais*, Musée d'Art Moderne de la Ville, Paris
1980	*ROSC*, University College Gallery, Dublin (travelled to the Crawford Gallery, Cork)
1982	*Aspects of British Art Today*, Metropolitan Art Museum, Tokyo (toured Japan)
1984	*When Attitudes Became Form 1965–72*, Kettle's Yard Gallery, Cambridge (travelled to Edinburgh)
1986	*Esculturas sobre la Pared*, Galerie Juana de Aizpuru, Madrid

Collections:

Tate Gallery, London; Arts Council of Great Britain, London; Victoria and Albert Museum, London; Fitzwilliam Museum, Cambridge; Australian National Gallery, Canberra; Baltimore Museum of Art; City Art Gallery, Southhampton, Hampshire; Allen Art Museum, Oberlin College, Ohio; Swindon Art Gallery, Wiltshire.

Publications:

By CRAIG-MARTIN: articles—"Acquisitions" in *The Tate Gallery Biennial Report 1968–70*, London 1970; "A Procedural Proposition: Selection, Repetition, Extension, Exchange" in *Studio International* (London), September 1971; "An Interview with Simon Field" in *Art and Artists* (London), May 1972; "Acquisitions" in *The Tate Gallery Biennial Report 1970–71*, London 1972; interview with Anne Seymour in *The New Art*, exhibition catalogue, London 1972; "Acquisitions" in *The Tate Gallery Biennial Report 1972–74*, London 1974; statement in *Michael Craig-Martin*, exhibition catalogue, Zagreb 1981.

On CRAIG-MARTIN: books—*Michael Craig-Martin: Selected Works 1966–75*, exhibition catalogue, by Anne Seymour, Leigh, Lancashire 1976; *Michael Craig-Martin*, exhibition catalogue with text by Richard Stone, London 1985; articles—"Michael Craig-Martin" by Merete Bates in *The Guardian* (London), March 1976; "Best of British" by Marina Vaizey in the *Sunday Times* (London), 31 July 1977; "Sculptor's Visit Is Bound to Have an Impact" by Gertrude Langer in *Courier Mail* (Brisbane), 17 February 1978; "The State of British Art: It's a Bewilderment" by William Feaver in *Art News* (London), January 1980.

I have a thought, not clearly formulated, but a sense of the possibility of a particular meaning.

I am focusing my attention, seeking the words to express this thought, to give it form. I am using words I know. (My vocabulary is not static, new words enter it, others fall from use.)

These words are in common usage. They have immediacy and flexibility. Each word carries great associative resonance.

I am employing the grammar I know, putting the words together to make phrases and sentences, simple and complex.

I am stating facts, expressing opinions, making allusions, drawing comparisons, revealing values.

I have used these words many times, but this is the first time I have used them to express this thought in this way.

This is how I do my drawings.

—Michael Craig-Martin

Like a number of other "post-object" artists (to use the then-fashionable phrase) who took part in the *New Art* show at the Hayward Gallery in 1972, Michael Craig-Martin has been preoccupied with how we see and judge the veracity of a picture. What constitutes a picture? In what ways do words anchor or interfere with images? During the 1970's, of course, these concerns were for the most part the basis for reflections on photography. Craig-Martin's work, though, has had little to do—in any formal sense—with photography.

Trained as a sculptor, Craig-Martin's investigations into "ways of seeing" have been based—until recently—on the manipulation of objects and words. In an early installation work he involved the spectator in a simple experiment on the limits of our field of perception (what we take in, what we lose). Using numerous mirrors, Craig-Martin re-presented a composite view of the spectator. Craig-Martin has been called an illusionist. These powers are perhaps no better illustrated than by a piece he did in 1973. A glass of water was exhibited on a shelf as an oak tree. Here our partial or subjective perception of things is troubled by an obvious conflict between the sign and the signifier. But besides acting as a kind of visual example of Sausserian linguistics, the work achieved something else. In the most simple of ways it tapped the transforming powers that artists claim as magic (or rather the institutions from within which artists operate, label magic). It is charming work and takes its place alongside other object-pieces of the same period which test the limits of the real.

In the recent work (post-78) this gap between a present and an absent object, or rather the gap between picture and pictured, has shifted away from objects to images—isometric drawings of domestic objects projected onto the gallery wall. These large scale objects are superimposed over each other, creating a dense jungle of projecting lines. Ambiguity here is based on a static simultaneity of objects. In the mirror piece, simultaneity was the result of the break-up of a single image; the mirrors acted very much like a camera, panning around the object. In these drawings, the play between absence and presence becomes a kind of half-way house. Objects hover in and out of view. The eye can only take in one object at a time. Although visible, the other objects remain half-hidden, submerged. This has a lot to do with the scale of the objects. All the objects are uniform in size. We are therefore unable to read off objects according to their normal scale.

Picturing for Craig-Martin has nothing to do with interpretation, but rather with establishing a framework for inquiry. Each set of works adopts (adapts) a perceptual model which decentres the single and unitary vantage point of the viewer. In principle, Craig-Martin's work could be said to be structuralist in origin. It works on the interstices between things, between names, pictures and signs.

—John Roberts

CREMONINI, Leonardo.

Italian. Born in Bologna, 26 November 1925. Studied at the Accademia delle Belle Arti, Bologna, under the painters Alfred Protti and Giuglielmo Pizzirani and sculptor Luciano Minguzzi, 1932–36; attended art classes, Paris, 1951. Moved to Milan, 1945; settled in Paris, 1951, but worked often in Forio d'Ischia, until 1955; spent time in Douarnenez, Finistere, 1956; lived in Panarea, Eolian Islands, 1958–59. Professor, Ecole des Beaux-Arts, Paris, Lives in Florence and Paris. Agent: Galerie Claude Bernard, 7 rue des Beaux-Arts, 75006 Paris. Address: 11 rue de Buci, 75006 Paris, France.

Individual Exhibitions:

1951 Centre d'Art Italien, Paris
1952 Catherine Viviano Gallery, New York
1954 Galleria dell'Obelisco, Rome
Frank Perls Gallery, Beverly Hills, California
Catherine Viviano Gallery, New York
1955 Hanover Gallery, London
1957 Catherine Viviano Gallery, New York
1960 Galleria del Milione, Milan
Galleria Galatea, Turin
Galerie du Dragon, Paris
Galerie Lacloche, Paris
1962 Catherine Viviano Gallery, New York
Galerie du Dragon, Paris
1963 Gallerie Galatea, Turin
1964 Galerie du Dragon, Paris
Biennale, Venice
1966 Galerie du Dragon, Paris
1967 Galleria Il Fante di Spade, Rome
1969 Palais des Beaux-Arts, Brussels
National Gallery, Prague
Kunsthalle, Basle
Konsthall, Lund, Sweden
Museum Civico, Bologna (retrospective)
Galleria Il Bisonte, Florence
Musée d'Art Moderne de la Ville, Paris
1970 Kunsthalle, Darmstadt
1971 Galleria Giulia, Rome (toured Italy, Brussels, Paris)
1972 Galerie du Dragon, Paris
Galleria dei Lanzi, Milan
Galleria Il Gabbiano, Rome
1973 Galerie du Dragon, Paris
Maison des Arts et Loisirs, Montbeliard, France
Maison de la Culture, Rennes
Musée d'Art Moderne, Strasbourg
1974 Galerie du Dragon, Paris
Galleria Il Portico, Cesena, Italy
Maison de la Culture, Grenoble
Galleria Eidos, Milan
Maison de la Culture, Amiens, France
1975 Galerie Jan Krugier, Geneva
1976 Galerie Forni, Amsterdam
Maison de la Culture, Gretil, France
Maison de la Culture, Corbeil, France
1977 Galleria Il Gabbiano, Rome
Galleria Forni, Bologna
Galleria Santacroce, Florence
Galleria Adelphi, Padua
1978 Galleria Santacroce, Florence
Galleria Communale, Prato, Italy
Galleria Communale, San Gimignano, Italy
1979 Galerie Claude Bernard, Paris
1980 Galleria Forni, Bologna
Seibu Museum, Tokyo
Galerie La Hune, Paris
Musée Dechelette, Roanne, France
1982 Centre Culturel Le Parvis, Tarbes, France
La Chartreuse, Villeneuve-les-Avignon, France
1983 Galerie Claude Bernard, Paris
Musée de Grenoble, France
Tours Narbonnais, Carcassonne, France
Galerie Jean Claude David, Grenoble, France
1984 Palazzo Racani-Arroni, Spoleto, Italy
1985 Palazzo Pubblico, Siena, Italy
1986 Galleria Tentadue, Milan
Institut Culturel Francais, Athens
Spedale di Santa Maria della Scala, Siena, Italy
Castello Aragonese, Ischia, Italy
1987 Galerie Claude Bernard, at *FIAC 87*, Grand Palais, Paris

Selected Group Exhibitions:

1952 *Pittsburgh International*, Carnegie Institute, Pittsburgh
1956 *Modern Italian Art*, Tate Gallery, London
1961 *Italian Contemporary Art*, Museum of Kamakura, Japan
1967 *Le Monde en Question*, Musée National d'Art Moderne, Paris
1971 *Aspetti della Nuova Figurazione*, Palazzo Reale, Naples
1977 *Arte in Italia 1960–1977*, Galleria d'Arte Moderna Turin
1978 *Biennale*, Venice
1981 *Il Materiale delle Arte*, Castello Sforzesco, Milan
1984 *L'Immagine e il suop Doppio*, Palazzo Bagatti Valsecchi, Milan (travelled to Galleria Rondanini Rome)
1986 *Il Viaggio del Dialogo*, Villa Medici, Rome

Collections:

Museum of Modern Art, New York; Albright-Knox Art Gallery, Buffalo, New York; Carnegie Institute, Pittsburgh Hirshhorn Museum and Sculpture Garden, Smithsonian Institution, Washington D.C.; Princeton University, New Jersey Israel Museum, Jerusalem; Galleria d'Arte Moderna, Bologna; Galleria d'Arte Moderna, Milan; Centre Georges Pompidou, Paris; Musee d'Art Moderne de la Ville, Paris

Publications:

By CREMONINI: articles—"Artisanat Populaire et Artisana Colonise" in *Revolution* (Paris), no. 3, 1963; "Picasso? 13 Peintres Répondent" in *Le Jardin des Arts* (Paris), October 1970; "Dialogue avec Michel Troche" in *La Nouvelle Critique* (Paris), December 1970; "Nature bien ordonnee," with Marc le Bot, in *Traverses* (Paris), October 1976; "Art et Machine: Entretien à propos du Multiple avec Cremoni et Cueco" in *ATAC Informations* (Paris), April 1978; "La Commande Sociale dans les Arts Plastiques Seminaire du Creusot" in *Cracap Informations* (Le Creusot), May 1978; "Biennale '78: Il Pluralism o la Cattava Coscienza dell Avanguardia" in *La Loggia dei Mercanti* (Milan), May 1978; "La Pudeur n'est pas Parole: L'Image Autobiographique" in *Skira Annuel*, Geneva 1978; "Modeles de l'Histoire" in *Skira Annuel*, Geneva 1979.

On CREMONINI: books—*Cremonini* by Marco Valsecchi, Milan 1962; *Cremonini* by Franco Solmi, Michel Butor and Louis Althusser, Bologna 1969; *Cremonini: 80 Dessigni* by Giuliano Briganti, Florence 1970; *Leonardo Cremonini* by Jacques Brosse and others, Bologna and Paris 1979 (includes bibliography); *Das kritische Engagement in Leonardo Cremoninis Malerei 1965–1980*, thesis by Petra Spatazza, Ruprecht Karl University, Heidelberg 1981; *Approche des peintures et dessins (1953–1978) de Leonardo Cremonini et des discours du peintre*, thesis by Jean Louis Fauthoux, University of Toulouse Le Mirail 1981; *Om relationemmellan rummet, objekten och Manniskan i Leonardo Cremoninis Maleri*, thesis by Carina Heden, University of Goteborg 1981; *Leonardo Cremonini*, with texts by William Rubin, Italo Galvino, Alain Jouffroy and others, Geneva 1987; films—*Grand Portrait: Leonardo Cremonini ou les jeux sans regle* by Jean Louis Roy, 1973; *Peintre de notre temps: Cremonini* by Georges Paumier, 1977.

Leonardo Cremonini is one of the group of Italian artists who were influenced and inspired by Picasso's "Guernica" to develop a dramatic, realistic style, enabling them to translate a concern for everyday life and human tragedy into a stylized, illustrative manner. It is no wonder, therefore, that in 1951, in his mid-30's, Cremonini transferred himself to Paris, where he has remained ever since, though he maintains regular contact with Italy; in 1969 he was honoured with a major retrospective at the Museo Civico in his native Bologna.

His work, apart from the example of Picasso, reveals the profound influence of such Renaissance art-

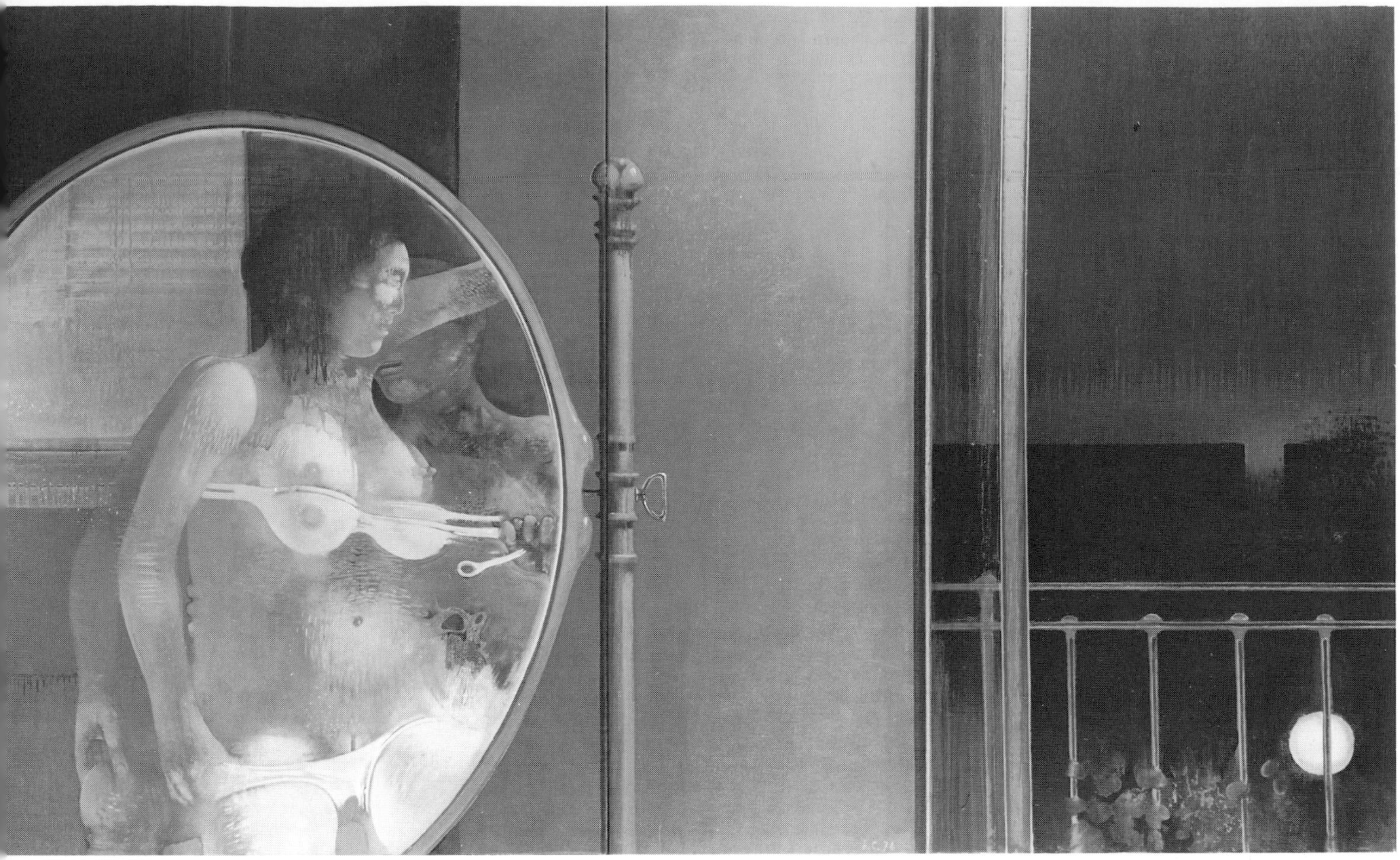

Leonardo Cremonini: ***Le Silence du Désir*****, 1976**

ists as Giotto, Masaccio and Piero della Francesca, especially in the balance that he has struck between rounded, almost sculptural human depiction, and an anti-natural, linear, geometrical form of composition. His preoccupations, however, have always been more dramatic and tense than these masters, almost theatrical in the investigation of torture, accidents, and the like, at the same time investing even the most innocent setting (figures in the interiors of autobuses, children at play, lovers in a park, or the wall furniture of a bathroom) with strange, nervous overtones. Cremonini is a brilliant draughtsman, and there are aspects of his figures, in their doll-like rounded stylization, which are reminiscent of such fellow Italians as Campigli and Manzu. His stated subject is "l'homme social," or man in existentialist relationship to the world. Certainly there is usually present a sense of uncertainty, as though one were waiting for the catastrophe to occur.

In his earlier work, often landscapes, isolating vegetation as huge, fleshy forms, he used paint in deep impasto with bright, brash colour. Gradually, as he adopted the idea of the figure in landscape, albeit urban landscape, he refined both his draughtsmanship and thinned down his palette. The early 1960's saw violent subjects, tortures, road accidents, often involving children (reminiscent of the Yugoslav painter Velickovic). Although the superficial drama of these subjects was eventually abandoned, precisely the same sense of unease is contained in the interior views of buses, with the bulbous heads barely in view, or in the beach-scenes and domestic interiors. There is something cinematic in Cremonini's visual definitions, as if he were seeking to place his figures at odd angles to their architectural settings. Throwing them, and us, so to speak, off balance.

—Charles Spencer

CRIPPA, Roberto.

Italian. Born in Monza in 1921. Studied at the Accademia di Brera, Milan, under Carpi, Funi and Carra. First Italian artist to practice action painting, 1947–52; signed, with Lucio Fontana, Emilio Scanavino, Gianni Dova and Giuseppe Capogrossi, *3rd Manifesto dello Spazialismo,* Milan, 1952. Also internationally renowned acrobatic pilot; represented Italy at the world championship air acrobatics, Hullavington, Wiltshire, England. Recipient: Premio Leonardo da Vinci, 1947; Premio Sipra, 1947; Premio Giani, 1952; Premio Graziano, 1956; Premio di Scultura, Città di Carrara,1957; Premio Viterbo, 1958; Premio Giovane Pittura Europea, Menton, 1960; Gran Premio, *Triennale di Milano,* 1963; Premio Nazionale Umberto Biacamana, 1970; Premio Einaudi, 1970. *Died* (in flying accident, near Milan) *in 1972.*

Individual Exhibitions:

1947 Galleria Bergamini, Milan
1948 Galleria di Pittura,Milan
1949 Galleria San Fedele, Milan
1950 Galleria San Fedele, Milan
1951 Alexander Iolas Gallery, New York
1952 Alexander Iolas Gallery, New York
Galleria del Cavallino, Venice
Stable Gallery, New York
Galleria del Naviglio, Milan
Galleria d'Arte Contemporanea, Florence
Galleria del Cavallino, Venice (with Gianni Dova)
1953 Alexander Iolas Gallery, New York
Hugo Gallery, New York
Galerie d'Arte Latine, Stockholm
Galleria del Naviglio, Milan (with Gianni Dova and Giuseppe Capogrossi)
1954 Galleria del Cavallino, Venice
Galleria del Naviglio, Milan
1955 Galleria del Cavallino, Venice
Galleria del Naviglio, Milan
Obelisk Gallery, Washington, D.C.
1956 Galleria del Naviglio, Milan
Galerie du Dragon, Paris
Galleria Selecta, Rome
1957 Alexander Iolas Gallery, New York
Galleria del Naviglio, Milan (with Giuseppe Capogrossi and Giacomo Balla)
Galeria du Dragon, Paris
1958 Alexander Iolas Gallery, New York
Galleria del Cavallino, Venice
Galleria del Naviglio, Milan
Galerie Bernard, Arrau
1959 Galleria del Naviglio, Milan
Arts Council Gallery, Edinburgh (with Lucio Fontana and Gianni Dova)
Palais des Beaux-Arts, Brussels (travelled to Concertgebouw, Bruges, and the Palais des Beaux-Arts, Charleroi, Belgium)
Galerie Bernard, Grenchen, Switzerland
1960 Alexander Iolas Gallery, New York
Städtisches Museum, Leverkusen, West Germany
Stone Gallery, Newcastle upon Tyne
Galerie d'Art Moderne, Basle
Galerie Smith, Brussels
1961 Galleria del Naviglio, Milan
Galleria del Cavallino, Venice
Tokyo Gallery
1962 Alexander Iolas Gallery, New York
Gallery One, London
Galleria Schwarz, Milan
Galleria Toninelli, Milan
1963 Alexander Iolas Gallery, New York
Galerie Alice Pauli, Lausanne
Museum Haus Lange, Krefeld, West Germany
1964 Galleria Schwarz, Milan
Palazzo Reale, Milan
Galleria S. Rocco, Scregno, Italy
Biennale, Venice
1965 Museum am Ostwall, Dortmund, West Germany
Kunsthalle, Mannheim
Galerie Argos, Nantes, France

	Galleria Carlevaro, Genoa
1966	Alexander Iolas Gallery, New York
	Galleria del Naviglio, Milan
	Galerie Alice Pauli, Lausanne
	Daytons, Minneapolis
	Galleria Blu, Milan
1967	Galerie Alexandre Iolas, Paris
	Galleria La Bussola, Turin
	Galleria Il Salotto, Como, Italy
	Aspects, Chexbres, Switzerland
	Galerie Alexandre Iolas, Geneva
	Galleria Blu, Milan (with Gianni Dova)
	Galleria Iolas Galatea, Rome
1968	Galleria Il Cosmo, Bergamo, Italy
	Galleria Lo Zodiaco, Genoa
	Galleria Tassoni, Modena, Italy
	Palais des Beaux-Arts, Brussels
	Galleria Lo Scudo, Verona
	Galeria Iolas Velasco, Madrid
	Galleria Cortina, Milan
	Galleria Giraldi, Livorno
1969	Palais des Beaux-Arts, Brussels
	Galleria Cortina, Milan
	Galleria Stefanoni, Lecco, Italy
	Galleria Schreiber, Brescia, Italy
	Galleria Sylvia, Rome
1970	Galleria Cortina, Milan
	Galleria Giraldi, Ivorno
	Galleria Schettini, Milan
	Galleria Gissi, Turin
	Galleria Torbandena, Trieste
	Galleria Cecchini, Perugia, Italy
	Palazzo delle Prigioni, Venice
	Galleria Il Centro, Naples
1971	Galerie Alexandre Iolas, Paris
	Galleria Cortina, Milan
	Alexander Iolas Gallery, New York
	Galleria Iolas, Milan
	Palazzo Reale, Milan

Selected Group Exhibitions:

1948	*Biennale,* Venice
1951	*Arte Astratta e Concretea in Italia,* Galleria Nazionale d'Arte Moderna, Rome
1955	*Pittura Italiana Contemporeanea,* Palacio de la Vierreina, Barcelona
1958	*Pittsburgh International,* Carnegie Institute, Pittsburgh
1960	*Sculpture Italienne Contemporaine,* Musée Rodin, Paris
1961	*The Art of Assemblage,* Museum of Modern Art, New York (travelled to Museum for Contemporary Arts, Dallas, and the Museum of Art, San Francisco)
1966	*L'Art dans l'Usine,* Musée du Louvre, Paris
1968	*7th Biennale dell'Incisione Italiana Contemporanea,* Venice
1970	*Biennale de Menton,* Palais de la Mediterranée, Menton

Collections:

Moderna Museet, Stockholm; Galleria d'Arte Moderna, Rome; Museum am Ostwall, Dortmund, West Germany; Museum Haus Lange, Krefeld, West Germany; Palais des Beaux-Arts, Brussels; Tate Gallery, London; Centre Georges Pompidou, Paris; Museum of Modern Art, New York.

Publications:

By CRIPPA: articles—"Lo Spazio Ovunque" in *Corriere d'Informazione* (Milan), December 1968; "Dippinge le Sue Poesie" in *Corriere d'Informazione* (Milan), May 1969; "Ricordando Victor Brauner, Alchimista Vittorioso" in *Corriere d'Informazione* (Milan), June 1969; "Il Teorema di Rubini" in *Corriere d'Informazione* (Milan), June 1969; "Tony Dallara in una Mostra alla 'Cortina' " in *Il Miliardo* (Carrara-Avenza), June 1969; "Affamato di Cielo" in *Corriere d'Informazione* (Milan), July 1969; "Principessa Rispondi . . ." in *Corriere d'Informazione* (Milan), July 1969; "Vede il sole durante e la Terra che gli Gira Attorno" in *Bolaffiarte* (Turin), February 1972.

On CRIPPA: books—*Lo Spazialismo* by G. Giani, MIlan 1955; *Manifesto per Crippa* by Alain Jouffroy, Milan 1962; *Crippa,* exhibition catalogue by Robert Lebel and Franco Russoli, Rome 1967; *Roberto Crippa,* exhibition catalogue, Perugia, Italy 1970; articles—"Crippa sui Valori della Rhodesia" by Ugo Longho in *Tempo* (Milan), May 1967; "Personale di Roberto Crippa" in *Le Arti* (Milan), February 1969; "Roberto Crippa" by Guido Ballo in *D'Ars Agency* (Milan), November 1969/April 1970; "Visita alla studio di Crippa" by Enzo Fabiana in *Notizie d'Arte* (Milan), 1970; "La Morte di Roberto Crippa" in *Bolaffiarte* (Turin), April 1972.

That Roberto Crippa came to regard himself as a Spatialist, along with his friend Fontana, is at first hard to digest. How could the man who brought his own version of action painting (his spiral vortexes) to Italy have anything in common with the maker of anonymous ceramic urns and slashed canvases? But this is to overlook the stern nature of the development which so much of his work was subsequently to take, and it is to fail to understand the urgency of his non figurative assemblages, bereft of messages but not of meaning.

Crippa's art changed at the time of the Hungarian revolution when Imre Nagy was deposed and a European bloodbath took place. For him, art is close to life, not close to the career-conscious pirouetting of quasi-successful artists. It is significant that he renamed the Venice *Biennale,* the "Banale." So it is not surprising to find his dedicating his cork and wood bark offerings to "Man of Hiroshima" and Caryl Chessman ("I died innocent").

All his work was the outcome of an interior *coup de force.* He did not regard his pictures as opportunities to demonstrate his undeniable dexterity with mixed media. He had the same passion for the renaissance of scraps and tatters that Kurt Schwitters lavished upon his *merz.*

Roberto Crippa was not concerned with *making pictures:* for him his works were doorways which will yield to the touch of a true friend.

Always so sober? No. In his last years he was able to indulge himself a little by making large-scale collages in flippant colours, but it is the great assemblages of the early 1960s that stay in the mind's eye.

—Sheldon Williams

CRUZ-DIEZ, Carlos.

Venezuelan. Born in Caracas, 17 August 1923. Studied at the School of Plastic and Applied Arts, Caracas, 1940–45, Diplomas in Artistic Education and Manual Arts, 1945; studied advanced techniques of art and publicity, New York, 1947. Publications Designer, Creole Petroleum Corporation, 1944–45; Art Director McCann-Erickson Advertising Agency, Venezuelan Subsidiary, 1946–51; Illustrator, *El Nacional,* Caracas, 1953–55; travelled to Barcelona, and to Paris to study physical qualities of color, 1955–56; Designer of Publications, Ministry of Education, and Designer, *El Disco Anaranjado,* Caracas, from 1957; lived in Paris, 1960–80, before returning to Caracas. Teacher, 1953–55, Professor and Assistant Director, School of Arts, Caracas, 1958– 60; Professor, School of Journalism, Central University of Venezuela, Caracas, 1959–60; Professor, 1972–73, and Juror, 1973–80, Ecole Supérieur des Beaux-Arts, Paris. Recipient: First Prize, Alphabetization Poster Contest, Caracas, 1946; José Loreto Arismendi Prize, 1950, Artistides Rojas Prize, 1952, and Enrique Otero Vizcarrando Prize, 1953, *Official Exhibition of Venezuelan Art;* Emilio Boggio Prize, *Ateneo de Valencia Exhibition,* Venezuela, 1950; First Prize, *Bienal,* Cordoba, Argentina, 1966; Subsecretaria de la Cultura Award, Cordóba, 1966; International Painting Prize, *Bienal,* Sao Paulo, 1967; First Prize, *Nacional de Artes Plasticas,* Venezuela, 1971; Premio de Intervención del Arte en la Arquitectura, *Bienal de Arquitectura,* Venezuela, 1976. Agents: Galerie Denise René, 124 rue de la Boetie, 75008 Paris, France; Galeria Adler Castillo, Edificio Galipan Avenida Francisco de Miranda, Caracas 106. Address: Qta. Romali, Avenida Berlin La California Norte, Caracas, Venezuela.

Individual Exhibitions:

1947	Instituto Venezolana Americano, Caracas
1955	Museum of Fine Arts, Caracas
1956	Galeria Buchholz, Madrid
1960	Faculty of Architecture, Central University of Venezuela
	Museum of Fine Arts, Caracas
1965	Galleria La Polena, Genoa
	Galleria Il Punto, Turin
	Signals Gallery, London
	Physichromies de Cruz-Diez: Oeuvres do 1954 à 1965, Galerie Kerchache, Paris
1966	Galerie M.E. Thelen, Essen
	Galeria Fundacion Mendoza, Caracas
1967	Galeria Corkright, Caracas
1968	Galerie Art Intermedia, Cologne
	Galerie Accent, Brussels
	Gallerie K.B., Oslo
	Museum am Ostwall, Dortmund, West Germany
1969	*Cruz-Diez et les 3 Etapes la Couleur Moderne,* Galerie Denise René, Paris (Rive Droite and Rive Gauche)
	Galeria Corkright, Caracas
1970	Galerie Ursula Lichter, Frankfurt
	Artestudio Macerata, Macerata, Italy
1971	*Physichromies, Couleur Additive, Induction Chromatique, Chromointerferences,* Galerie Denise René, New York
	Galeria Corkright, Caracas
1972	Galerie Buchholz, Munich
	Galerie Formes et Muraux, Lyons
1973	Galleria Falchi, Milan
	Galerie Denise René, Paris
	Galleria Christian Stein, Turin
	Galeria Cadafe, Caracas
1974	Galleria Trinita, Rome
	Génesis, Eclosión y Absoluto del Color, Galeria Corkright, Caracas
1975	Galeria Aele, Madrid
	Galerie Denise René, Paris
	Museo de Arte Contemporáneo, Bogota
	Galeria Barbie, Barcelona
	Museo La Tertulia, Cali, Colombia
	Artiste et Ville, Caracas
1976	Galeria de Arte Mikeldi, Bilbao, Spain
	Museo de Arte Moderno, Mexico City
	Pabellón de Arte de la Ciudadela, Pamplona, Spain
	Galerie Denise René, New York
	Musée de la Chaux des Fonds, Switzerland
1977	Galerie Latzer, Kreuzlingen, Switzerland
	Allianza Francesa, Caracas
	Galerie Venezuela, New York
	Galerie Noroit, Arras, France
	Art in the Street, Imperial College, London
1978	*Art in the Street,* University of Reading
	Ausbildungszentrum USB, Wolfsberg, Switzerland
	Pavillon Werd, Zurich
	Umjetnik i Grad, Galerija Suvremene, Zagreb
	Ibero-Amerikansiches Institut, West Berlin
1979	Arte Contacto, Caracas
	Galerija Zgraf, Sarajevo, Yugoslavia
1980	Universidad Simon Bolivar, Caracas
	Art in the Street, University of Liverpool
	Casa de las Americas, Havana
1981	*Didactica y Diálectica del Color,* at *Triennale,* Caens (travelled to the Museo de Bellas Artes, Pordenone, Italy; and Museo de Arte Contemporáneo, Caracas)

Selected Group Exhibitions:

1950	*Official Exhibition of Venezuelan Art,* Caracas (and 1952, 1953)
1953	*Bienal,* Sao Paulo (and 1963, 1967, 1979)

Carlos Cruz-Diez: *Induction Chromatique*, Plaza de la Pastora, Caracas, 1981

1962 *Biennale, Venice*
1964 *Mouvement II,* Galerie Denise René, Paris
1965 *Anthology of Kinetic Sculpture and Perceptual Art,* Signals Gallery, London
1966 *Licht und Bewegung,* Kunstverein, Dusseldorf
1968 *Art Vivant,* Foundation Maeght, St.-Paul-de-Vence, France
1972 *12 Ans d'Art Contemporain en France,* Grand Palais, Paris
1977 *3 Villes, 3 Collections,* Centre Georges Pompidou, Paris
1979 *Modern Latin American Art,* Lowe Art Museum, University of Miami

Collections:

Museo de Bellas Artes, Caracas; Casa de la Cultura, Havana; Museum of Modern Art, New York; Museum of Contemporary Art, Chicago; Musée d'Art Contemporain, Montreal; Victoria and Albert Museum, London; Städtisches Museum, Leverkusen, West Germany; Museum des 20. Jahrhunderts, Vienna; Centre National d'Art Contemporain, Paris, Musée d'Art Moderne de la Ville, Paris.

Publications:

On CRUZ-DIEZ: books—*Physichromies de Cruz-Diez: Oeuvres de 1954 à 1965,* exhibition catalogue, with text by Frank Popper, Paris 1965; *Carlos Cruz-Diez,* exhibition catalogue, with text by Carlos Dorante, Caracas 1967; *Cruz-Diez et les 3 Etapes de la Couleur Moderne,* exhibition catalogue, with text by Jean Clay, Paris 1969; *Relief and 3-Dimensional Structures* by Cyril Barrett, London 1970; *An Introduction to Opitcal Art* by Cyril Barrett, London 1971; *The Techiques of Kinetic Art* by John Tobey, New York 1971; *12 Ans d'Art Contemporain en France,* exhibition catalogue, with text by Jean-Luc Allerant, Paris 1972; *Carlos Cruz-Diez: Génesis, Eclosión y Absoluto del Color,* exhibition catalogue, with text by Roberto Guevara, Caracas 1974; *Cruz-Diez* by Alfredo Boulton, Caracas 1975; *Cruz-Diez: Didactia y Dialectica del Color,* exhibition catalogue, with text by Umbro Apollonio, Caracas 1981.

Cruz-Diez's main preoccupation is to set up "situations" of various kinds which in their turn give rise to certain sequences of events whose interest lies in an intense experience of colour. These "chromatic events" are obtained by transforming "concepts" into sensory phenomena and in this way colour, which is traditionally subordinate to subject or form, acquires an existence of its own and pursues its own evolution in space and time.

All of Cruz-Diez's chromatic propositions—*Physichromies, Chromointerferences, Chromosaturations, Transchromies*— are based on this particular theoretical position, but the artist expresses a different aspect of the problem in each type of work.

The *Physichromies* are changing structures which project colour from a surface into space. They set up an atmosphere of coloured light which varies with the intensity and the position of the light source and with the position and the distance of the spectator. These statements combine three modalities of colour: addition, reflection and subtraction. The *Chromointerferences* are formal networks which bring into the foreground the phenomenon of chromatic waves produced by interference. While these works are based in general on a plane surface, the *Chromosaturations,* on the contrary, are conceived in terms of the appropriation of three-dimensional space for the purpose of bringing the experience of pure colour into the foreground. The *Transchromies* differ from the other colour experiments by Cruz-Diez through the use of effects which derive from the superimposition of various different chromatic scales and the accent is placed specifically on transparency, on optical mixture and the instability of the chromatic vision.

All of these researches by Carlos Cruz-Diez have given rise to large-scale architectural and environmental applications in-and outside private dwellings, industrial plants, administrative buildings and town squares in his native Venezuela and in Europe.

The artist has also undertaken a number of chromatic "actions" in public places involving the spectator both physically and psychologically in the creative process. In fact, in all his statements involving space and taking place in time, Cruz-Diez aims through the intermediacy of the public, to achieve perpetual transformation of both event and colour.

—Frank Popper

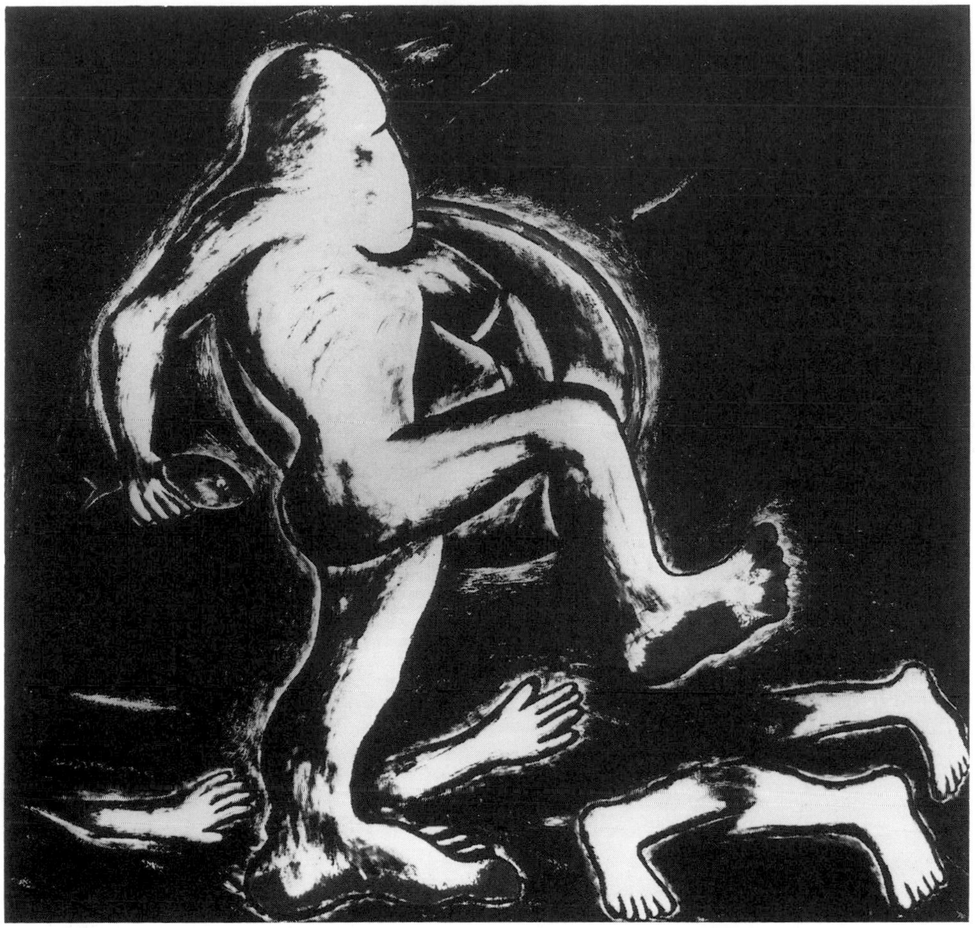

Enzo Cucchi: *Under the Wind*, 1982

CUCCHI, Enzo.

Italian. Born in Morra d'Alba, near Ancona, in 1950. Married to Brunella Cucchi. Independent painter, living and working in Ancona. Agents: Anthony D'Offay Gallery, 9 Dering Street, London W1; Galerie Paul Maenz, Bismarckstrasse 50, 5000 Cologne 1; and Galleria Lucio Amelio, Naples. Address: c/o Galleria Lucio Amelio, Piazza dei Martiri 58, 80121 Naples, Italy.

Individual Exhibitions:

1977 Incontri Internazionali d'Arte, Rome
1978 Galleria de Crescenzo, Rome
1979 Galleria Mario Diacono, Bologna
Galleria Tucci Russo, Turin
Galleria Mozzoli, Modena, Italy
1980 Galerie Paul Maenz, Cologne
1981 Gallery Sperone/Westwater/Fischer, New York
Galleria Sperone, Rome
Galerie Bruno Bischofberger, Zurich
Galleria Mario Diacono, Rome
Galerie Paul Maenz, Cologne (travelled to Art and Project, Amsterdam, 1982)
1982 Galerie Beyeler, Basle
Kunsthaus, Zurich (travelled to the Groningen Museum, Netherlands)
1983 Museum Folkwang, Essen, West Germany
Galerie Schellmann und Kluser, Munich
Sperone-Westwater, New York
1984 Akira Ikeda Gallery, Tokyo
Anthony D'Offay Gallery, London
Sperone-Westwater, New York
Kunsthalle, Basle
1985 Galerie Daniel Templon, Paris
Galerie Bernd Kluser, Munch
Kunstmuseum, Dusseldorf
Louisiana Museum, Humlebaek, Denmark
1986 CAPC/Musee d'Art Contemporain, Bordeaux, France
Guggenheim Museum, New York
Centre Georges Pompidou, Paris
1987 Galerie Beyeler, Basle

Selected Group Exhibitions:

1979 *Alternativa del Nuovo*, Palazzo delle Esposizioni, Rome
1980 *Die Enthauptete Hand: 100 Zeichnungen aus Italien*, Kunstverein, Bonn (travelled to the Städtische Galerie, Wolfsberg, West Germany, and the Groningen Museum, Netherlands)
1981 *Westkunst: Zeitgenossiche Kunst seit 1939*, Rheinhallen, Cologne
1982 *'60-'80: Attitudes, Concepts, Images*, Stedelījk Museum, Amsterdam
1983 *New Art*, Tate Gallery, London
1984 *International Survey of Recent Painting and Sculpture*, Museum of Modern Art, New York
1985 *The European Iceberg*, Art Gallery of Ontario, Toronto
1987 *Avant-Garde in the Eighties*, Los Angeles County Museum of Art

Publications:

By CUCCHI: books—*Treo Quattro Artisti Secchi*, exhibition catalogue, Modena, Italy 1979; *Canzone*, Modena, Italy 1979, *Enzo Cucchi*, exhibition catalogue, Basle 1981; *Enzo Cucchi: Italia*, London 1984; articles—"Designo Finto" in *Enzo Cucci*, exhibition catalogue, Rome 1978; "Die Hauser fullen sich alle bis auf halbe Höne" in *Sieben Junge Kunstler aus Italien*, exhibition catalogue, Basle 1980; "Di Certo Communque ce che l'Immagine" in *Enzo Cucchi*, exhibition catalogue, Cologne 1981.

On CUCCHI: books—*Enzo Cucchi*, exhibition catalogue, Rome 1978; *Enzo Cucchi*, exhibition catalogue, Cologne 1981; *Die Enthaupieie Hand: 100 Zeichnungen aus Italien*, exhibition catalogue, with W. M. Faust, Bonn 1980; *The Italian Trans-Avantgarde* by Achille Bonito Oliva, Milan 1980; *Seiben Junge Kunstler aus Italien*, exhibition catalogue, by Jean-Christophe Ammann, Basle 1980; *Mythe/Drame/Tragedie*, exhibition catalogue, by Achille Bonito Oliva and others, Saint-Etienne, France 1982; *Enzo Cucchi: Zeichnungen*, exhibition catalogue with texts by Ursula Perucchi and Frans Haks, Zurich 1982; *Baldessari/Borofsky/Chia/Clemente/Cucchi/Disler/Penck/Winnewisser*, with foreword by Frans Haks, introduction by Steven Kolsteren, New York and Groningen 1982; *Enzo Cucchi*, exhibition catalogue with essay by Diane Waldman, New York 1986.

Towards the end of the 1970's there were a number of Italian painters who were looking for new foundations for their work, new horizons, and new ways of dealing with the artistic problems of the recent past. By using some of their experiments Enzo Cucchi was able to realize a poetic style of his own, although his debt to these artists is apparent in those first works of his which clearly reveal a kind of tension between form and content. These are works which bear his own personal signature and yet still reflect a general preoccupation with the problematic relationship between a work of art and the space it occupies. More precisely, Cucchi is interested in the conflicts which characterize such relationships.

Two of his exhibitions are particularly relevant here. In the first of these, *Alla lontana alla francese* (January, 1979), Cucchi gave us a canvas, loosely hung from the wall, which depicted an ordered series of houses in silhouette. In the foreground is a large cane, curved at the top, and a white-enamel ceramic form. And further away is another canvas, bearing the artist's signature, which depicts a series of repeated animal forms. In the second exhibition, *Lucavalla, Azzura* (February, 1979), there is an unbleached canvas, thickly overlaid with earthy, red-orange pigment, one corner of which has been curled up to reveal a large terracotta ladle, resting on two easels below. The aim here is to establish a rapport among the canvas, the paint, and the objects themselves.

After these two exhibitions, Cucchi turned his attention to the pictorial image, which until now had played a secondary role in his work. There is a kind of transitional period, in which he moves from his earlier concern for relationships to works in which the images themselves carry the full burden of his meaning. Here we have paintings in which the object to be represented is tied to the canvas or placed nearby. And now, in his recent work, the depicted object becomes the primary vehicle of his sensibility—a sensibility nourished by the mountains and valleys and forests of rural Italy and its villages and the traditions behind them.

—Robert G. Lambarelli

CUEVAS, José Luis.

Mexican. Born in Mexico City, 26 February 1934. Studied at the School of Painting and Sculpture, La Esmeralda, Mexico City, 1944–47; studied engraving with Lola Cueto, Mexico City, 1948. Married Bertha Lilian in 1961; children: Mariana, Zimena and Marie-Jose. Independent painter and graphic artist, Mexico City and New York. Professor of Drawing, Latin American University, Mexico City, 1956–57; Artist-in-Residence, Philadelphia Museum School of Art, 1957–58, San Jose State College, California, 1970, and Fullerton College, Los Angeles, 1975. Recipient: First International Drawing Award, *Bienal*, Sao Paulo, 1959; First Prize, *Mostra Internazionale di Bianco e Nero*, Lugano, Switzerland, 1962; "Madeco" Prize, *Bienal de Santiago*, Chile, 1965; First International Award, *Triennale*, New Delhi, 1968; First Prize, *Bienal de Grabado Latinoamericano*, San Juan, Puerto Rico, 1977; National Fine Arts Award,

Mexico, 1981. Agents: Galeria de Arte Mexicano, Milan 18, Mexico City; Marisa Del Re Gallery, 41 East 57th Street, New York, New York 10019; Tasende Gallery, 820 Prospect Street, La Jolla, California 92037. Address: Galeana 109, San Angel, Mexico City 20, Mexico; and 14 West 17th Street, New York, New York 10011, U.S.A.

Individual Exhibitions:

1953 Galeria Prisse, Mexico City
1954 Pan American Union, Washington, D.C.
1955 Galerie Edouard Loeb, Paris
1956 Galeria Proteo, Mexico City
Palacio de Bellas Artes, Havana
1957 Aenille Gallery, New York
1958 Instituto de Arte Contemporáneo, Lima, Peru
Galeria de Arte Contemporáneo, Caracas
1959 Galeria Bonino, Buenos Aires
1960 David Herbert Gallery, New York
Silvan Simone Gallery, Los Angeles
Fort Worth Art Center, Texas (retrospective)
1961 Galleria L'Obelisco, Rome
University of Texas at Austin
Santa Barbara Museum of Art, California
1962 Galleria Sixtina, Milan
Jerrold Morris Gallery, Toronto
Occidental College, Toronto
1963 Pan American Union, Washington, D.C. (graphic works retrospective, 1947–62)
Andrew Morris Gallery, New York
228 Gallery, St. Louis
Galeria Antonio Souza, Mexico City
1964 Galleria Profili, Milan
Silvan Simone Gallery, Los Angeles
Biblioteca Luis Angel Arango, Bogota
1965 Grace Borgenicht Gallery, New York
Munson-Williams-Proctor Institute, Utica, New York
Cuevas antes de Cuevas, Galeria Mer-Kup, Mexico City
1966 Galeria Misrachi, Mexico City
Silvan Simone Gallery, Los Angeles
1967 Walter Engel Gallery, Toronto
1969 Glade Gallery, New Orleans
1970 Galeria Misrachi, Mexico City
San Francisco Museum of Art
University Museum, Ciudad Universitaria, Mexico City
1971 Grace Borgenicht Gallery, New York
La Sala Nacional de Exposiciones, San Salvador
Galeria El Morro, San Juan, Puerto Rico
Museo de Bellas Artes, Toluca, Mexico
1972 Michael Wyman Gallery, Chicago
Museo de Arte Moderno, Mexico City
1973 Rothman Galleries, Toronto
Museo de Arte Moderno, Bogota
Galeria Aele, Madrid
Galeria Pecanins, Barcelona
1974 Palais de Beaux Arts, Brussels
Galeria Multipla, Sao Paulo
Museo de Arte Contemporáneo, Caracas
1975 San Diego Museum of Fine Arts, California
Phoenix Art Museum, Arizona
Palace of the Legion of Honor, San Francisco
Fullerton College, Los Angeles
Bienal, Sao Paulo
Museum of Modern Art, Gothenburg, Sweden
1976 Museo de Arte Moderno, Mexico City
Musée d'Art Moderne, Paris (retrospective)
1977 Galeria Estudio Actual, Caracas
Musée des Beaux-Arts, Chartres, France
Galeria Misrachi, Mexico City
Galerie de Seine, Paris
1978 Grace Borgenicht Gallery, New York
1979 Museo de Arte Moderno, Mexico City
Tasende Gallery, San Diego, California
1980 Museo de Monterrey, Mexico (retrospective)
1981 Meeting Point Gallery, Miami
Galeria Joan Prats, Barcelonia
Museo de Ponce, San Juan, Puerto Rico
1982 Marisa del Re Gallery, New York

Selected Group Exhibitions:

1957 *Quatre maitres de la ligne: José Luis Cuevas, Alexander Calder, Stuart Davis and Morris Graves*, Napoule Museum, Napoule, France
1967 *Rosc 67*, Dublin
1970 *Collection of José Gómez Sicre*, College Art Gallery, State University of New York at New Paltz
1972 *Biennale*, Venice
1978 *Documenta*, Kassel, West Germany

Collections:

Museum of Modern Art, New York; Hirshhorn Museum, Smithsonian Institution, Washington, D.C.; Pan American Union art Collection, Washington, D.C.; Munson Williams-Proctor Institute, Utica, New York; Fine Arts Gallery of San Diego, California; Art Gallery of Ontario, Canada; Museo de Arte Moderno, Mexico City; Museo de Bellas Artes, Caracas; Museo de Arte Moderno, Bogota; Museum of Art, Tel Aviv.

Publications:

By CUEVAS: books—*Cuevas por Cuevas*, Mexico City 1965; *Cuevario*, Mexico City 1973; books illustrated—*The World of Kafka and Cuevas*, Philadelphia 1959; *Recollections of Childhood*, Los Angeles, 1962; *Cuevas-Charenton*, Los Angeles 1966; *Crime by Cuevas*, New York 1968; *Homage to Quevedo*, San Francisco 1969; *Cuevas Comedies*, San Francisco 1972; *La Rue des Mauvais Garcons*, Paris 1972; *Cuaderno de Paris*, Mexico City 1977; *Zarathustra*, Milan 1979; *Les obsesions noires de J.-L. Cuevas*, Paris 1982; *Letters to Tasende*, San Diego 1982.

On CUEVAS: books—*José Luis Cuevas* by Jean Cassou, Philippe Soupault, and Flores Sanchez, Paris 1955; *José Luis Cuevas* by Carlos Valdes, Mexico City 1967; *El Mundo de José Luis Cuevas* by Carlos Fuentes, Mexico City 1969; *Confesiones de José Luis Cuevas* by Alaide Foppa, Mexico City 1975; *Revelando a José Luis Cuevas* by Daisy Ascher, Mexico City 1979; *Cuevas: Ipotesi per una lettura* by Roberto Sanesi, Milan 1979; *Cartas para una exposicion*, Mexico City 1981; *José Luis Cuevas* by José Gomez Sicre, Barcelona 1982.

I hate accident, improvisation, play with materials for their own sake. I believe in "originality" only when it comes from the very essence of tradition. I believe an artist is original only when he shows his own accent or his full voice through materials given by his predecessors.

Today my main interest is the work of the great artist of the past: Van Eyck, Hals, Velazquez, Zurbaran, etc., and above all the great Chinese draftsmen of the 16th and 17th centuries.

—José Luis Cuevas

Jose Luis Cuevas is one of this century's most expressive draftsmen. His expressive power stems from a tension between the monstrous crudeness of the people he portrays, deformed, distorted, seamed and ridged, and an extreme delicacy of touch and technical skill. Like Leonardo, he sets down the line very swiftly, and, should the stroke in a slightly different place seem better to him, leaves the first and adds the second, to produce an impression of the artist's hand, sure and immediate. His line, most often done with the pen, combines with a system of washes in greys and blacks, or a spectrum of watered down hues, pale, evoking faded things like dried flowers under glass, lavender in keepsakes, whatever has no juice. The vital elixir is drained. By choosing to work in the dessicated colors of the funeral wreath, the artist calls up sensations of mortality, a modern day *memento mori*, which fixes the moment before transition to another stage.

The presence of death has been constant with Cuevas since, at the age of 9, he was bedridden for a year with rheumatic fever. During that time he read intensely in European literature, which gave him a background in that culture and an understanding of its history coupled with respect, and he drew. His images have, ever since, reflected that background and the hallucinatory quality of the fevered sickbed.

They reflect as well his familiarity with the life of the miserable poor. Born himself in a poor quarter of Mexico City, living in rooms above his grandfather's pencil factory, he came to know intimately the lives of people society has trained us not to see: the old and sick, the cripple, the prostitute, the criminal. Through the remarkable compelling quality of his art he brings the observer to a headon confrontation with these subjects, at once marvelous and grotesque.

The frequency of the *autoretrato* in his oeuvre makes it clear that it was the artist himself who was first forced to this confrontation and to this fascination, in the end. As with the image of death, which he has often, through continuing ill health, been forced to contemplate, his contemplation ends in an erotic embrace: "When the last heartbeat stops pounding, my good lady will bend down and give me a kiss." Death the Sweet Sister.

This attitude is very much in tune with the Mexican obsession with death, evident in the ritual festivities in the cemetery, the sweet candy skulls of the Day of the Dead, the cult of mutilation and sacrifice in the ancient religions of Mexico. Indeed, the bulbous heads in his drawings hark back to Olmec ancestors, yet Cuevas is no Mexican nationalist in his art. He abhors "the Cactus Curtain" and insists that art must build on the European tradition which has gone before, feeling a special affinity to many of the European masters, especially Rembrandt and Velasquez. This affinity has much to do with the international staus which has always been accorded him, and much of his art has to do with European cities as well as his own.

But neither the European past nor echoes from ancient Mexico really determine his choice of subject, but rather the present day reality of the streets, the jails, cafes, brothels, where the struggle from day to day is all too real. It is this continual, brooding concern with the tragedy of life in this century, the conviction that life is not only absurd but a waste, a conviction born of experience, which makes his art ring true.

—Barbara Cortright

CURNOE, Greg.
Canadian. Born in London, Ontario, 19 November 1936. Educated at Wortley Road Public School, London, 1940–50; South Collegiate Institute, London, 1950–54; studied art at H.B. Beal Technical School, London, 1954–56; Doon School of Art, Ontario, 1956; Ontario College of Art, Toronto, 1957–60. Married Sheila Curnoe in 1965; children: Owen, Galen, and Zoe. Worked with Survey Crew, City of London, 1957–60; worked as a trucker for Coca Cola Company, London, 1961. Independent artist in London since 1960: established studio on Richmond Street, 1960–63, on King Street, 1963–68, and on Weston Street, since 1968. Founder-Member, Garrett Gallery artists' cooperative, Toronto, 1957–59; Region Gallery, London, 1961–63; 20/20 Gallery, London, 1966–70; and Forest City Art Gallery, London, since 1973. Founder-Editor, *Region* magazine, London, 1961–78; Contributing Editor, *20 Cents Magazine*, London, 1967–70. Member, Société pour l'Etude du Mouvement Dada, London, 1954; President, Nihilist Party of Canada, since 1961; kazoo manufacturer, and member, Nihilist Spasm Band, since 1966; member, and former Racing Secretary, London Centennial Wheelers Club, since 1971; Founder-Member, Association for the Documentation of Neglected Aspects of Culture in Canada popular culture group, since 1972; Spokesman, Canadian Artists Representation, Ontario, 1974–75. Artist-in-Residence, University of Western Ontario, London, 1975–76. Agents: Isaacs Gallery, 832 Yonge Street,

Toronto 5, Ontario; Forest City Art Gallery, 432 Richmond Street, London, Ontario. Address: 38 Weston Street, London, Ontario, Canada.

Individual Exhibitions:

1964 *Exhibition of Things,* Richard E. Crouch Branch Library, London, Ontario
Isaacs Gallery, Toronto
McIntosh Memorial Art Gallery, London, Ontario
Region Gallery, London, Ontario
1962 *Greg Curnoe/Larry Russell,* Region Gallery, London, Ontario
McIntosh Memorial Art Gallery, London, Ontario
1963 McIntosh Memorial Art Gallery, London, Ontario
Greg Curnoe/Brian Dibb, Region Gallery, London
1964 *Imports and Local Works: Curnoe/Urquhart,* McIntosh Memorial Art Gallery, London, Ontario
David Mirvish Gallery, Toronto
Norman MacKenzie Art Gallery, Regina, Saskatchewan
1965 David Mirvish Gallery, Toronto
1966 *Paintings by Greg Curnoe,* Vancouver Art Gallery (travelled to Edmonton Art Gallery)
New York from Sowesto Greg Curnoe, Isaacs Gallery, Toronto
Recent Collages, New Design Gallery, Vancouver
1967 *Series,* 20/20 Gallery, London, Ontario
Time Series, Isaacs Gallery, Toronto
Chambers/Curnoe, McIntosh Memorial Art Gallery, London, Ontario
1969 *Bienal,* Sao Paulo
1970 *Drawings,* McIntosh Memorial Art Gallery, London, Ontario
Collages 1961–70, Isaacs Gallery, Toronto
Views of Victoria Hospital and Wings over the Atlantic, Isaacs Gallery, Montreal
1971 Waddington Galleries, Montreal
1972 *Display of Water Colours, Measurements and Clockings,* London House, Ontario
1973 Isaacs Gallery, Toronto
Watercolours and Drawings, Polyglot Gallery, London, Ontario
1974 *The Great Canadian Sonnet,* Drawings, National Gallery, Ottawa (toured Canada)
Watercolours, Forest City Art Gallery, London, Ontario
1975 *Recent Watercolours,* Isaacs Gallery, Toronto
Some Lettered Works 1961–69, London Art Gallery, Ontario
1976 *Biennale,* Venice

Selected Group Exhibitions:

1967 *Statements: 18 Canadian Artists,* Norman Mackenzie Art Gallery, Regina, Saskatchewan
1969 *Canada: Art d'Aujourdhui,* Centre Georges Pompidou, Paris (toured Europe)
The Heart of London, National Gallery of Canada, Ottawa (toured Canada, 1968–69)
Canada 101, at the *Edinburgh Festival*
1973 *Realism: Emulsion and Omission,* Kingston, Ontario
1974 *Bienal Americana de Arts Graphics,* at *Colombia Art Mart.* Kitchener-Waterloo Art Gallery, Ontario

Collections:

University of Western Ontario, London; London Public Library and Art Gallery, Ontario; The Canada Council, Ottawa; National Gallery of Canada, Ottawa; Art Gallery of Ontario, Toronto; Art Institute of Ontario, Toronto; Museum of Fine Arts, Montreal; Vancouver Art Gallery; City Trust, Vancouver, Norman Mackenzie Art Gallery, Regina Saskatchewan.

Publications:

On CURNOE. books—*Paintings by Greg Curnoe,* exhibition catalogue, Vancouver 1966; *Chambers and Curnoe,* exhibition catalogue, London, Ontario 1967; *Statements: 18 Canadian Artists,* exhibition catalogue, Regina, Saskatchewan 1967; *Canada; Art d'Aujourdhui,* exhibition catlogue, Paris 1968; *The Heart of London,* exhibition catalogue, Ottawa 1968; *Greg Curnoe: Canada,* exhibition catalogue, Sao Paulo 1969; *Canadian Art Today* by William Townsend, London 1970; *Realism: Emulsion and Omission,* exhibition catalogue, with text by M. Kluyver-Cluysenaer, Kingston, Ontario 1973; *Greg Curnoe,* exhibition catalogue, Venice 1976; articles "More Words on Curnoe's Worldly World" by John Chandler in *Artscanada* (Toronto), April 1969; "The Language of the Eyes: Windows and Mirror" by Ross Mendes in *Artiscanada* (Toronto), October 1969; "Painting from Life: Greg Curnoe at the Isaacs Gallery" by J. N. Chandler in *Artscanada* (Toronto), June 1971; "Knowing: The Surface" by V. Coleman in *Artscanada* (Toronto), February 1972; "Sources, Resources: Greg Curnoe" by J. N. Chandler in *Artscanada* (Toronto), February 1973.

Greg Curnoe: *The Way It Is*, 1980

I frequently work in series, but what I do does not come from any general concept or framework of ideas. I work with people, places and things. Any ideas that I have and conclusions that I make come from the people, places and things I know.

I assemble all kinds of material. Assembling, sorting, listing and collecting has been the basis of most of my work.

I have strong feelings: about where I was born, about living in a relatively small city slightly over 200km away from a large one, about living in a sparsely populated large country beside a heavily populated large one. I live in an extended family and that makes me think a lot about the shared culture in my community contrasted with other cultural activities that only a small number of people are aware of. My work operates in both of these contexts. I also think a lot about eroticism and pornography and about how they relate to community and individual tastes.

My work is about resisting as much as possible the tendency of American culture to overwhelm other cultures. I also resist, as much as possible, any attempt to elevate what I do to the level of high art.

—Greg Curnoe

"The world is your own backyard," says Greg Curnoe. More important, he might add, your own background is your world. For Curnoe, a sense of Regionalism is the key to authentic work. His is based on London, Ontario (he was born there in 1936), more humid in summer and colder in winter

than other parts of southern Ontario. It's a place with its own confident, dynamic creative milieu, to some extent associated with the University of Western Ontario. It's a breeding-ground for artists, most of whom, like Curnoe, receive a firm foundation at H. B. Beal Technical School where he studied from 1954 to 1956.

Curnoe first came into contact with Dada through his teachers at Beal in 1954. In 1961, he participated with Michael Snow and Joyce Wieland in a Neo-Dada exhibition. His work is remarkable for its bold design sense, bright primary flat colours, clean outlines, a complete rejection of modelling. His work is spare and deft.

From 1964, Curnoe has expressed his concerns in works like "Springs on the Ridgeway," using words to describe the real world around the edge, and in the picture space, a real curtain, metal rod and yoyo. Combined with these "real" objects are a cut-out of a radio and a lushly painted and flat nude seen from the back. In later works, like his masterpiece, the mammoth "View of Victoria Hospital, Second Series," 1969–1971, Curnoe adds wires and electric lights. Here, his fine, harmonious colour is modelled on Robert Delaunay and county town carnivals, strident oranges and greens or rainbow tints.

In works expanded from his journals, wordscapes, he records what he sees in lettered words that seem almost compulsive. At times, the results are bland and overly earnest, but they are personal documents too, perhaps even the most personal, recording the pattern of his life, his trips, his thoughts, his conversations.

Curnoe is an original. Today, he may paint his wife Sheila, Toronto's C. N. Tower, or his Maraposa or Doc Morton bikes—he's an amateur competitive cyclist. But his kind of painting always has the feel of the real, "Made in Canada." "I am afraid of art," he once said. "It could still kill me."

—Joan Murray

CUTFORTH, Roger.
British. Born in Sleaford, Lincolnshire, 29 October 1944. Studied at the Nottingham College of Art, 1962–63; and the Ravensbourne College of Art, England, 1963–66. Independent conceptual artist and photographer, since 1966: moved to New York City in 1968, concentrated on making films of women in landscapes, 1973–75; now lives and works in Texas. Recipient: National Endowment for the Arts Photography Fellowship, Washington, D.C., 1984. Agent: Hal Bromm Gallery, 170 Avenue A at Eleventh, New York, New York 10009. Address: Box 375, Terlingua, Texas 79852, U.S.A.

Individual Exhibitions:

1969	Pinacotheca Gallery, Melbourne
1971	Lisson Gallery, London
	Nova Scotia College of Art, Halifax
1972	Pinacotheca Gallery, Melbourne
1974	John Gibson Gallery, New York
	Galerie Kornblit, Amsterdam
	Studio Cannaviello, Rome
1975	Galerie Kornblit, Amsterdam
1976	Galerie Gaetan, Geneva
	John Gibson Gallery, New York
	Studio Cannaviello, Rome
1977	Galleria II Diaframma, Milan
	Studio 46, Turin
1978	John Gibson Gallery, New York
	Studio Cannaviello, Milan
1979	Unimedia, Genoa
	Studio Cannaviello, Milan
1981	Hal Bromm Gallery, New York
1983	Hal Bromm Gallery, New York
1986	Dos Amigos Gallery, Terlingua, Texas
	Hal Bromm Gallery, New York
1987	University of Texas, El Paso
	AIR Gallery, Austin, Texas

Selected Group Exhibitions:

1970	*Art in the Mind,* Allen, Memorial Art Museum, Oberlin College, Ohio
	Information, Museum of Modern Art, New York
1971	*Prospect 71,* Studtische Kunsthalle, Dusseldorf
1972	*Artists Using Photographs,* Inhibodress, Sydney
1975	*Artists' Bookworks,* British Council travelling exhibition, London (toured West Germany)
1976	*Photo as Art,* Contemporary Art Museum, Zagreb, Yugoslavia
1977	*Artists Super 8 Film Exposition,* Artists Space, York
1979	*New Acquisitions,* Wallraf-Richartz Museum, Cologne
1980	*Printed Art,* Museum of Modern Art, New York
1981	*Biennale,* Sydney
1987	*This is Not A Photograph,* Ringling Museum, Sarasota, Florida

Collections:

Museum of Modern Art, New York; Metropolitan Museum of Art, New York; Wallraf-Richartz Museum, Cologne; Stadtisches Museum Abteiberg, Monchengladbach.

Publications:

By CUTFORTH: books—*The Empire State Building: A Reference Work,* New York 1969; *The Visual Book,* New York 1970; *Cleopatra's Needle/Eiffel Tower/Empire State Building,* London 1971.

On CUTFORTH: books—*Situation de l'Art Conceptual* by Catherine Millet, Paris 1970; *Conceptual Art* by Ursula Meyer, New York 1971; *6 Years: The Dematerialization of the Art Object* by Lucy Lippard, New York 1973; *La Linea Analitica de Arte Moderna* by Menna Filiberto, Turin 1975; *Skira Annuel,* Geneva 1977; *Skira Annuel,* Geneva 1980; *The Gallery of World Photography: New Directions,* edited by Weston Naef, New York 1984; *Thought Objects,* edited by Barbara Ess and Glenn Branca, New York 1987; articles—"Personal Spaces" by James Collins in *Artforum* (New York), September 1973; "Roger Cutforth" by Valentin Tatransky in *Arts Magazine* (New York). September 1978; article by Loredana Parmesani in *Segno* (Pescara, Italy), no. 13, 1979, "Roger Cutforth" by Jean Fisher in *Aspects* (Newcastle upon Tyne), no. 13, 1981.

My portrait work began as a group of experimental photographic works in 1984. They grew out of a feeling of frustration with conventional photography, i.e., the single image lying behind a glasslike surface in which any presence of the artist is excluded. For me, photography was always a sequence of images connected either in time, or in the consciousness of the person who had taken them. What follows is an outline of some of the problems I saw in photography. The notes begin by referring to painting. I was, and still am, a painter, though I've worked mainly in photography for the last fifteen years.

In painting it is not so much an issue about how things look as about how things feel. Photography is almost exclusively about how things look. I'm cutting up photographs and sticking them together so that I can get details from different frames all into one picture. The photographs are portraits of people I know. One thing can be said in favor of photography in this respect: it is revealing. Most of us have lots of trouble with photographs of ourselves. I search all the frames of the films for details that really interest me. These details of various images become a key for me as to

Roger Cutforth: *Portrait of Kim Gordon,* 1983

what is interesting about this medium. Thoughts on the portrait of Kim Gordon work fast so that ideas stay ahead of the medium. By this I mean, what interests me in the images should stay ahead of any consideration of them as photographs. Think about the irrational. Is it possible to subvert the rational construction of the world, that the camera constantly hands to us? One of the things wrong with conventional photography is that the medium speaks for itself and tells us next to nothing. Yet, another picture of the world (the direct photography of the nineteenth century, where the world was seen freshly through photographs) only exists for us today in the family snap-shot album. I think it was Carl Andre who once said, "Photographs are like rumors" (i.e. unverified information of uncertain origin). What I want from photography is the possibility of working creatively with the medium after the pictures have been taken. I want the process by which a picture is constructed to show in the end result. Photography, as a mechanical means of reproduction, naturally avoids this issue. This, plus the fact that there's no visible presence of the artist, is the reason photography has such a shaky footing as an artform.

I want the work to reveal something that was not previously known. The psychology of the photographer or artist must come forward and play a role in the finished work. "Sometimes you can hide behind a photograph but you can't hide behind a line." (Paulette Nenner)

Man Ray set us a good example but we have regressed.

What the world doesn't need is another pretty picture.

Some friends are rephotographing photographs. I see this not only as a comment on our media-based culture, but also as a reflection of the fact that everything has been photographed a hundred times over. Photographs no longer bear any relationship to anything other than an endless, ongoing series of visual statements. The issue of photography is a false track. The medium is invisible, forget it. Lift from the film whatever interests you and follow your intuition; it's the only route to whatever power there is left in the process in its relation to life. I tell Dan Graham I know what I'm trying to do with photography. I want to show a certain kind of truth about it that's contained in what I consider the dross of my existence, test strips. The strips, made of the most interesting part of the image, accumulate in piles on my floor. I catch myself thinking that they probably contain a more interesting picture than the finished print on the wall. Bethany Jacobson asks me why I don't use the test strips? Because I think I may hate what the work made up of them looks like. I think I may hate what really interests me. I constantly have to tell myself to go ahead and make a mess, to subvert the idealized perfection of the photographic image. "Photographs are always presented as if the photographer doesn't exist. You are reinstating the photographer in the picture." (Jean Fisher) The portrait work is becoming even more unpredictable, the result of a performance between the person photographed, myself, and the camera. I want the finished work to reflect these aspects. It's odd that we think portraits can reveal something hidden about the person portrayed, yet do not see that they speak just as much of the person who made the portrait. It's impossible for me not to see the portraits as mirroring my own desire, of being equally that which I want to see, as well as that which is shown to me. Photographing women the camera obviously becomes a phallic extension through which I am intimate with them and take what I wish. But what about the men? The portrait with Jean Fisher makes me realize that the missing element in the construction of these works is myself. Jean plays me off against myself. Before the camera she displays an embarrassed prostituted image of femininity, then turning the camera on me, forces me into beng a parody of my own expectations of her. This work is hard for me to take. I feel I am naked in it both physically and symbolically.

From this work I realize I can no longer handle the images I collect without being aware that they are also references to an unconscious meaning that is demanding to be brought out.

—Roger Cutforth

D

DADO.
Yugoslav. Born Miodrag Djuric in Cetinjie, Montenegro, 4 October 1933. Studied at School of Fine Art, Hercognovi, Montenegro, 1947-52; Academy of Fine Arts, Belgrade, 1952-56. Worked as a lithographic printer, Paris, 1956-58. Independent painter, draughtsman and printmaker, Paris and Courcelles, France, since 1958. Agent: Galerie Jeanne Bucher, Paris. Address: c/o Galerie Jeanne Bucher, 53 rue de Seine, 75006 Paris, France.

Individual Exhibitions:

1958 Galerie Daniel Cordier, Paris
1960 Galerie Daniel Cordier, Frankfurt
1962 Galerie Daniel Cordier, Paris
1964 Galerie Daniel Cordier, Paris (2 shows)
1965 Cordier and Ekstrom Gallery, New York
1967 Galerie d'Aujourd'hui, Brussels
1970 Byron Gallery, New York
Centre National d'Art Contemporain, Paris (retrospective)
1971 Galerie Jeanne Bucher, Paris
Galerie Therese Roussel, Perpignan, France
1973 Galerie Jeanne Bucher, Paris
1974 Museum Boymans-van Beuningen, Rotterdam (retrospective)
Aberbach Fine Art, New York
Galerie Jeanne Bucher, Paris
1975 Galerie Isy Brachot, Brussels
Galerie Jeanne Bucher, Paris
1976 Aberbach Fine Art, New York
1978 *Dessins,* Galerie Isy Brachot, Paris
Malningar teckningar grafik, Konsthall, Lund, Sweden
1979 Galerie Isy Brachot, Knokke, Belgium
Galerie Isy Brachot, at *Art 10, '79,* Basle
1979 Fondation Veranneman, Kruishoutem, Belgium
Aberbach Fine Art, New York
Galerie Isy Brachot, Paris
1981 Galerie André-Francois Petit, Paris
1982 Centre Georges Pompidou, Paris

Selected Group Exhibitions:

1960 *Antagonismes,* Musée des Arts Décoratifs, Paris
1963 *Carnegie International,* Carnegie Institute, Pittsburgh (and 1967)
1964 *Documenta 3, Kassel,* West Germany
1965 *European Drawings,* Guggenheim Museum, New York
1968 *The Obsessive Image,* Institute of Contemporary Arts, London
1969 *Malerei des Surrealismums,* Kunstverein, Hamburg
1972 *Creation Artistique en France 1960-72,* Grand Palais, Paris
1976 *Les Espaces Insolites,* Palais des Congress. Strasbourg
Contemporains IV, Musée d'Art Moderne, Paris
1978 *FIAC 78,* Grand Palais, Paris

Collections:

Centre Georges Pompidou, Paris; Centre National d'Art Contemporain, Paris; Stedelijk Museum, Amsterdam; Museum Boymans-van Beuningen, Rotterdam; Guggenheim Museum, New York; Art Institute of Chicago.

Publications:

On DADO: books—*Dado,* exhibition catalogue, with text by Georges Limbour, Frankfurt 1960; *Dado,* exhibition catalogue, with text by Patrick Waldberg, Paris 1967; *Dado,* exhibition catalogue, with text by Daniel Cordier, Paris 1970; *Dado,* exhibition catalogue, with text by Gaeton Picon, Paris 1971; *Dado,* exhibition catalogue, with text by Richard E. Friedman, New York 1974; *Dado,* exhibition catalogue, with an introduction by R. Hammacher-van den Brande, text by Francois Mathey, Rotterdam 1974; *Dado,* exhibition catalogue, with text by Michael Peppiatt, Paris 1975; *Dado: Dessins,* exhibition catalogue, with text by Bernard Noel, and an interview by Michael Peppiatt, Paris 1978; *Dado: Malningar teckninger grafik,* exhibition catalogue, with texts by Marianne Nanne-Brahammer and Jacques Adelin Brutaru, Lund, Sweden 1978; *Dado; L'Exasperation du Trait,* exhibition catalogue, with texts by Christian Derouet and others, Paris 1981.

Dado cannot be classified, neither in his times and its isms of art, nor in a country, nor in a culture. He cites Martin Schongauer, Konrad Witz and Dürer as his great ideals and loves the Renaissance painting of the North. From the richly historical Montenegrin alpine landscape of his native country the artist has withdrawn—with occasional excursions to the pygmies in Africa and to New York—to a Norman watermill in France, as far away as possible from the Parisian art world; he prefers to maintain contact with his surroundings through his children.

Dado came at an early stage to his own style—in the manner of the old masters—which achieved its perfect expression in the graphic works. To him, drawings are always of specific value; they are never sketches or designs for paintings whose themes they in any case share. The impetus to Dado's creative activity starts from obsessions which are so intense that only extreme precision in their portrayal is able to liberate the artist from them momentarily. In 1973/74 Dado destroyed a large number of earlier drawings in order to form the pieces into an assemblage showing in one picture the total horror of his vision. Since 1973 his frightening images have grown ever larger. In correlation to the consequent slow down in the production of paintings, there is a simultaneous intensification of graphic activity. From 1976, as the paintings were undergoing a stylistic change, the most remarkable feature of which is in a new distribution of light, the drawings also show larger free zones in front of which on various planes and in detail passing images unite to form an exciting style.

The fascinating effect of Dado's style lies in the juxtaposition of detailed realistic images and indefinable fantastic scenes. The viewer is attracted by a seemingly hazy painting which often seems bathed in luminous rosy colours—and is deceived by the changing play on perception, appearance and reality. Behind the delicate haze graphic elements appear in various places, and on closer inspection one sees them condense to form gruesome images. Yet the details cannot be identified precisely. If one thinks that one sees pictures of the atrocities of concentration camps or Hiroshima, after longer inspection one finds that the scenery blurs to a vision of unutterable horror which as yet has no name in contemporary art and which perhaps as a vision of the future constitutes the originality of Dado's work. There one discovers children "in limbo" to whom no life is allotted and an "ancestral gallery" of old people who have outlived themselves, drawn by one who "above all sees in nature not life but death" and who dreads one day the loss of the seeing eye. Idyllically painted children are disfigured with repulsive hydrocephalus, animals with bodies torn open turn into hideous legendary creatures, plants are destructively rampant, and poisonous mushrooms develop dangerous explosive matter. Walls and buildings crumble away beneath the spectator's gaze and fall in ruins. In the midst of putrefaction arise monstrosities, terrifying mutants are born of dislocated and mutilated beings. The Book of Job, the interpretation of which Dado has pursued since the 1950's, always with a fresh technical approach, gains in his hands an added contemporary dimension. Mankind's frightful primeval visions couple with contemporary anxieties about organ transplants in living bodies, the fear of cancer and the bomb—without any hope of salvation.

Dado produces pictures of anxiety, superbly crafted with the precision of an old master, on which the eye cannot rest but in confusion wanders from one scene to another. It is only at first sight that one thinks to have discovered the work of a modern Brueghel (he has, after all, an acquaintance with Hans Bellmer, Max Ernst, Magritte and Dali). Yet Dado does not see the world with the same eyes as the old masters in the Christian Occident; he also does not view it with the profound psychologically acute vision of a contemporary adult, who perhaps delights in cruelties; he looks with the wide open eyes of a terrified child who sometimes (with the help of diluted ink) artificially "ages" his drawings so that he is relieved of his visions, a child who refuses to learn to suppress the dread of being devoured or turned to stone, who regards the old and the sick with dread and mortal terror, who stares with horror at deformity, a child who perhaps frightens others with terrifying spiders but does not himself tear off the legs of insects.

—Dagmar Sinz

DAHMEN, K(arl) F(red).
German. Born in Stolberg, 4 November 1917. Studied at the Kunstschule, Aachen, West Germany, 1931–33. Served in the Light Anti-Aircraft Artillery Division 84, German Army, in France, the Balkans and Russia, 1939–45. Married Ursula Hesse in 1940; son: Volker. Associated with Raoul Ubac and Serge Poliakoff, 1950–54; travelled regularly in Spain, 1960–67, in the United States, 1974. Guest Professor,

Kunstschule, Bremen, 1963–64; Professor, Akademie der Bildenden Künste, Munich, from 1967. Recipient: Swiss International Art Prize, Lausanne, 1959; Karl-Ernst-Osthaus Prize, Hagen, 1966; Graphics Prize, Ibiza, Spain, 1972. Agents: Galerie Gunther Franke, Maximilianstrasse 22, 8000 Munich 22; Galerie Muller-Wintersberger, Lindenstrasse 20, 5000 Cologne; Galerie Rothe, Werderplatz 17, 6900 Heidelberg; and Galerie Albert Verbeke, 7 Place Furstenberg, Paris. *Died* (in Preinderdorf, West Germany) *12 January 1981.*

Individual Exhibitions:

1946 Suermondt Museum, Aachen, West Germany
1948 Suermondt Museum, Aachen, West Germany
Galerie Leithauser, Wuppertal, West Germany
1949 Suermondt Museum, Aachen, West Germany
1951 Galerie Kasper, Ascona, Switzerland
1955 Galerie Arnaud, Paris
1956 Galerie La Roue, Paris
1957 *Ölbilder—Wachsmalerei*, Galerie Vertico, Bonn
Zimmergalerie Franck, Frankfurt
Galerie Arnaud, Paris
Galerie CCC, Schiedam, Netherlands
1958 Leopold-Hoesch Museum, Düren, West Germany
Galerie 22, Dusseldorf
Galerie La Roue, Paris
Galerie Behr, Stuttgart
1959 Galerie Aujourd'hui, Brussels
Kunsthalle, Mannheim
Galerie Parnass, Wuppertal, West Germany
1960 Galerie Hella Nebelung, Dusseldorf
Insel Galerie, Hamburg
Kabinett Grisebach, Heidelberg
Galerie d'art Moderne, Stuttgart
Studio F, Ulm, West Germany
Galerie Boukes, Wiesbaden, West Germany
1961 Galerie Anne Abels, Cologne
Galleria Pater, Milan
Galerie Baier, Milan
Galerie La Roue, Paris
1962 Galerie Günther Franke, Munich
Städtisches Museum, Ulm, West Germany
1963 Galerie Rothe, Heidelberg
Galeria Ivan Spence, Ibiza, Spain
Lefebre Gallery, New York
Galerie Haaken, Oslo
Galerie Delta, Rotterdam
Von-der-Heydt Museum, Wuppertal, West Germany
1964 Galerie Widman, Bremen, West Germany
Galerie Prestel, Frankfurt
Galerie Günther Franke, Munich
1965 Suermondt Museum, Aachen, West Germany
Kleine Grafik Galerie, Bremen, West Germany
Landolinshof, Esslingen, West Germany
Galerie Brechbühl, Grenchen, Switzerland
Kölnischer Kunstverein, Cologne
Galleria Flaviana, Locarno, Switzerland
Museum, Mönchengladbach, West Germany
Galerie Hammerlund, Oslo
Galerie La Roue, Paris
1966 Galerie Les Trois Feuilles d'Or, Beirut
Galeria Ivan Spence, Ibiza, Spain
Galerie Raeber, Lucerne
Galerie Lauter, Mannheim
Galerie Numaga, Neuchâtel-Auvernier, Switzerland
1967 Galerie Regio, Lörrach, West Germany
1969 Kunstverein, Augsburg, West Germany
Galerie 66, Hofheim, West Germany
Galeria Ivan Spence, Ibiza, Spain
Galerie Regio, Lörrach, West Germany
Galerie Lauter, Mannheim
Galerie Günther Franke, Munich
1970 Kunstverein, Kassel, West Germany
Kunstverein, Freiburg, West Germany
Galerie Raeber, Lucerne
Kunstverein, Ravensburg, West Germany
1971 Galerie Hardenstein, Bremen, West Germany
Forum Kunst, Rottweil, West Germany
Städtisches Museum, Ulm, West Germany
1972 Kleine Galerie, Bremen, West Germany
Galerie Lauter, Mannheim
Galerie 66, Hofheim, West Germany
Galerie Schneider, Karlsruhe
Galerie Kessler, Bad Godesberg, West Germany
Galerie 2, Stuttgart
Galerie Merian, Krefeld, West Germany
Kunstverein, Munich
1973 Galerie Schottenring, Vienna
Kunstverein, Aachen, West Germany
Galerie Kuhn, Aachen, West Germany
Galerie Regio, Kunstmesse Basle, Switzerland
Galerie Schlieper und Busch, Hagen, West Germany
Galerie Dr. Vogel, Augsburg, West Germany
Kulturkreis, Berg-Neustadt, West Germany
Galerie Kuhn, Dusseldorf
Galerie Rothe, Heidelberg
1974 BMW Galerie, Munich
Galerie Jaeschke, Braunschweig, West Germany
Galerie Vonderbank, Frankfurt
Galerie Lometsch, Kassel, West Germany
Studio Kausch, Kassel, West Germany
Galerie Riis, Trondheim, Norway
Galerie im Zilemp, Olten, Switzerland
Kunstverein, Darmstadt
1975 Galerie Hennermann, Bonn
Galerie Nothelfer, Berlin
Galerie Limited, Munich
Galerie Hermanns, Fürstenfeldbruk, West Germany
Galerie Rothenstein, Bremen, West Germany
Galerie Moderne, Silkeborg, Denmark
Galerie Hennemann, Dusseldorf
Galerie Loehrle, Schiefbahn bei Dusseldorf
Galerie Günther Franke, Munich
Junior Galerie, Dusseldorf
Galerie Rothe, Heidelberg
Junior Galerie, Cologne
1976 Neue Galerie der Stadt, Linz, Austria
Junior Galerie, Zurich
Kunstverein, Salzburg
Galerie Verbeke, Paris
Galerie Golong, St. Paul de Vence, France
Junior Galerie, Copenhagen
Galerie BLA, Oslo
Museum Duren, West Germany
Galerie Rohklan, Augsburg, West Germany

Karl Fred Dahmen: *Reduktion einer Landschaft*, 1975

Selected Group Exhibitions:

1948 *Neue Aachener Gruppe*, Suermondt Museum, Aachen, West Germany
1955 *Beteiligung an den Manifestationen bei den Ausstellungen "Divergence" 3, 4, and 5*, Galerie Arnaud, Paris
1963 *German Artists* touring exhibition (toured United States)
1966 *13 Aspekte deutscher* touring exhibition (toured West Germany)
1967 *Deutsch Kunst im 20 Jahrhundert*, Suermondt Museum, Aachen, West Germany
1970 *Internationale Kunstmesse*, Basle
1972 *1st International Graphic Biennale*, Fredrikstad, Norway
1973 *Sammlung Dobermann*, Landesmuseum, Münster, West Germany
1974 *25 Jahre Kunst in der Bundesrepublik Deutschland*, Kunstmuseum, Bonn
1976 *Salon des Réalités Nouvelles*, Paris

Collections:

Suermondt Museum, Aachen, West Germany; Sammlung Ludwig, Aachen, West Germany; Städtisches Museum, Bonn; Kunsthalle, Bremen, West Germany; Staatsgalerie, Stuttgart; Kunsthalle, Hamburg; Städtisches Museum, Mönchengladbach, West Germany; Städtisches Museum, Wup-

pertal, West Germany; Nationalgalerie, Oslo; Museo de Arte Moderna, Caracas.

Publications:

By DAHMEN: books—*Tradition und Gegenwart*, exhibition catalogue, Leverkusen, West Germany 1966; *Depot Schloss Morsbroich*, Leverkusen, West Germany 1969.

On DAHMEN: books—*K. F. Dahmen: Olbilder—Wachsmalerei*, exhibition catalogue, Bonn 1957; *K. F. Dahmen*, exhibition catalogue, with texts by Rolf Wedewer, Carl Linfert, Jacques Lassaigne and others, Cologne 1965; *Geschichte der modernes Kunst* by H. Harvard Arnason, Bremen, West Germany 1971; *K. F. Dahmen: Das malerische Werk 1950–72*, Munich 1972; articles—"K. F. Dahmen" by Roger von Gindertael in *Cimaise* (Paris), no. 5, 1955; "K. F. Dahmen" by Karl-Heinz Goerres in *Das Kunstwerk* (Baden-Baden, West Germany), no. 5, 1956–57; "Der Maler K. F. Dahmen" by Karl-Heinz Goerres in *Quadrum* (Brussels), no. 5, 1958; "K. F. Dahmen" by Günther Ladstetter in *Deutsche Zeitung* (Stuttgart), April 1959; "Present Day German Painting" by Stefan Munsing in *Art News and Review* (London), vol. II, no. 4, 1959; "Bilder und Collagen von K. F. Dahmen" by J. A. Thwaites in *Deutsche Zeitung* (Stuttgart), November 1960; "K. F. Dahmen" by Marco Valsecchi in *Il Giorno Milano*, May 1961; "K. F. Dahmen" by Charlotte Weidler in *Arts Magazine* (New York), November 1963; "The Informal and the Surreal in New German Art" by Hanns Th. Flemming in *Studio International* (London), June 1964; "K. F. Dahmen" by Jacques Michel in *Le Monde* (Paris), March 1965; "K. F. Dahmen" by Hanns Th. Flemming in *Studio International* (London), August 1965; "Neue Material montegan von West Germany" by Kramer-Badoni in *Die Welt* (Bonn), no. 106, 1969; film—*K. F. Dahmen* by Rolf Wiesselmann, 1958.

By one of those strange combinations of impulses that are as likely to occur in art as in other forms of self-expression, it was in the 1950's that Tapies, Burri, Dubuffet and others began the styles of object making that became known as Tachisme and Informal Art. In Germany the chief exponent was Karl Fred Dahmen, and the works he made are among the most powerful in the category, having force and cathartic shock capable of penetrating the inertia of the casual onlooker to cause a definite reaction.

1950 was for Dahmen the point of departure in an abstract style. Landscapes and townscapes gradually became submerged in masses owing some of their structure to Cubism. Space-plan pictures evolved in which the motive became sublimated within the material. Free play of creative means was given its head so that in the end his earth-crust pictures are truly described; the coruscating colour and the irregular surface take on a volcanic rocky contour. This extreme indentation and irregularity of the surface raised in relief carries in it a history of mural and vegetable deterioration and organic change: dilapidated walls gleam in a strange patina of damp and fungus, rotting bark, petrified lava and the porosity of pumice stone. Beyond this engrossment in the texture and skins of the canvas's camouflage, the marking of the graffiti and the linear design is man-formed in hieroglyph and pictograph, suggesting evidence of ancient civilization brought now to life by archaeological discovery. The surprise of historic recall is alternated by traces of a new Pompeii in a collage of a newspaper partially obliterated and scrawled with some runic note.

For Dahmen chance was not a prerequisite of composition. His choice was wide and the random sources were selected with care for nuances of colour and texture in each picture. He had a painterly concern for effect, though the pure pigment and its ordered synthesis in colour design had no attraction to compare with the object itself, the ready-made that took its place in works of intense presence and direct attack. This unconventional vocabulary would be vapid without the existence of the catalysing talent. Dahmen belonged to the rare band of artists who, despising the demands for pedantic purity, reap from the bountiful crop of improvisation, and the unexpected, exotic fruit to adorn his creations. Unlike Archimboldo's proficient transmutations by paint worked in figurative idiom, Dahmen produced a severe organic tremor by surrealist juxtaposition. History-laden materials from many places combine to exude, under the artist's hands, a palpable spirit of primitive and magic complexity.

—G. S. Whittet

DAHN, Walter.

German. Born in St. Tonis bei Krefeld, 8 October 1954. Studied art, under Joseph Beuys, Kunstakademie, Dusseldorf, 1971–77. Painter, in Cologne, since 1976. Agent: Galerie Paul Maenz, Bismarckstrasse 50, 5000 Cologne 1. Address: Klapperhof 33, 5000 Cologne 1, West Germany.

Individual Exhibitions:

1982 Galerie Paul Maenz, Cologne (and 1983)
Galerie Helen van der Meij, Amsterdam
Galerie 't Venster, Rotterdam (with Georg Dokoupil)
Galerie Hetzler, Stuttgart
1983 Galerie Chantal Crousel, Paris
Produzentengalerie, Hamburg (with Georg Dokoupil)
Galerie Six Friedrich, Munich (with Georg Dokoupil)
Mary Boone Gallery, New York
1984 Galerie Six Friedrich, Munich (and 1985)
Groninger Museum, Groningen, Netherlands (with Georg Dokoupil)
Galerie Paul Maenz, Cologne (and 1985)
Marian Goodman Gallery, New York
Galerie Crousel-Hussenot, Paris (and 1985)
1985 Galerie Barbara Jandrig, Krefeld, West Germany
Galerie Paul Maenz, Cologne (with Georg Dokoupil)
Galerie Vera Munro, Hamburg (with Georg Dokoupil)
Gallery Paule Anglim, San Francisco
Asher/Faure, Los Angeles
Rheinisches Landesmuseum, Bonn
Groninger Museum, Groningen, Netherlands
1986 Museum fur Gegenwartskunst, Basle
Kaiser Wilhelm Museum, Krefeld, West Germany
Kunsthalle, Basle
Museum Folkwang, Essen, West Germany
Galerie Paul Maenz, Cologne
Galerie Six Friedrich, Munich
1987 Van Abbemuseum, Eindhoven, Netherlands
Galerie Roger Pailhac, Marseille, France
Neuer Aachener Kunstverein, Aachen, West Germany
Galerie Luis Campana, Stuttgart
1988 Galerie Paul Maenz, Cologne
Galerie F. C. Gundlach, Hamburg
Galerie Six Friedrich, Munich

Selected Group Exhibitions:

1980 *Auch wenn das Perlhuhn leise weint,* Hahnentorburg, Cologne
1981 *Phoenix,* Alte Oper, Frankfurt
1982 *La Giovane Pittura in Germania,* Galleria d'Arte Moderna, Bologna
1983 *Expressionisten—Neue Wilde,* Museum am Ostwall, Dortmund, West Germany
1984 *International Survey of Recent Painting and Sculpture,* Museum of Modern Art, New York

Walter Dahn: ***Mann am baum*, 1982** Courtesy Museum of Contemporary Art, Chicago

1985 *Koln-Kunst*, Kunsthalle, Cologne
1987 *Avant-Garde in the Eighties*, Los Angeles County Museum of Art

Collections:

Museum Folkwang, Essen; Hessisches Museum, Darmstadt; Bonnefantenmuseum, Maastricht; Groninger Museum, Groningen; Van Abbemuseum, Eindhoven; Staatsgalerie, Stuttgart; Kaiser Wilhelm Museum, Krefeld; Museum fur Gegenwartskunst, Basle; Museum am Ostwall, Dortmund.

Publications:

On DAHN: books—*10 Junge Kunstler aus Deutschland*, exhibition catalogue with text by Zdenek Felix, Essen 1982; *Walter Dahn*, exhibition catalogue with text by Patrick Frey, Cologne 1982; *Dahn und Dokoupil: Die Afrika-Bilder*, exhibition catalogue with text by Wilfried Dickhoff, Groningen 1984; *Walter Dahn: Zeichnungen, 12 Skulpturen*, exhibition catalogue with text by Dieter Koepplin, Basle 1986; *Walter Dahn: Gemalde 1981–1985*, exhibition catalogue edited by Wilfried Dickhoff, Basle 1986.

The first unequivocal manifestation of Walter Dahn's independent position was his painting, in 1981, *Maler ohne Idee* (Painter without Idea), undoubtedly a self-portraiture. This title is a paradox that, for those who do not recognize it as such, seemed to confirm the common presumption that Dahn, as well as his former Mullheimer Freiheit colleagues (Adamski, Bommels, Dokoupil, Kever, Naschberger) were merely a bunch of naive 'wild painters'. It is important to realize that these Cologne-based artists were very keen to distinguish themselves from the group of Berlin expressionists that included among others Fetting and Salome.

After the dissolution of Mullheimer Freiheit, Dahn went his own way, although he regularly worked together with Georg Dokoupil. In 1982–83 both did the series of Ricki-paintings, based on the motif of a shower splashing water over various objects such as an oven, a transistor radio, a pair of gloves, an armchair. These paintings might be considered as playful ironies of Fetting's expressionist Dusche-Bilder. However, the following collaboration project is of a different character. These Afrika-paintings from the end of 1983 show a sincere respect towards the visual qualities of primitive painting.

Like Dokoupil, Dahn produces in considerable quantity, although in less chameleontic fashion. While Dokoupil, above all, seems to be involved with continuous comment and irony concerning the artworld's codes and conventions, Dahn, on the other hand, concentrates on his own personal impulse in relation to the relics of other cultures. He tries to balance direct emotional response with the reproduction techniques through which we learn about the existence of these relics. For him there exists a correlation between his own imagery and the things from the past, not in terms of subconscious mythology but in those of potential subject-matter to be painterly reproduced.

From 1985 onwards he has put a lock to his spontaneous way of painting by complicating his procedure. This resulted in a series of monotype silkscreens on cloth, where there is no relief in the paint at all, a technique also employed by the American artist Robin Winters in his Bonaparte's Party series (1984).

From 1986-87 dates a group of large paintings, among these a painting that shows the figure of an Australian native. On a monochrome ground there is a multitude visible of massive black forms, blow-ups of photographic mass-reproduction. This painting demonstrates two complementary ways of seeing and enjoying. Nearby the expression is a painterly one. It is only at a distance that the image appears. The subject-matter is not anecdotal and, by its archaism, brings the viewer in a state that conflicts with his sheer esthetic pleasure.

Dahn has also done a group of small bronzes with subject-matter that includes a large number of self-portrayals. He also shows photopieces taking his friends, street life and shop windows for subjects. Altogether Dahn seems to grow as a painter, as an artist who does not depend on the circumstantial evidence of the current art world.

—A. F. Wagemans

DALI, Salvador.

Spanish. Born Salvador Felipe Jacinto Dali y Domenech, in Figueras, Gerona, 11 May 1904. Educated at Marist Friars School, Figueras, 1914–18; studied at San Fernando Academy of Fine Arts, Madrid, 1921–25. Married Gala Eluard in 1930. Worked as book and magazine illustrator, Figueras, 1919–21; independent artist, in Sitges, 1925–30, Paris, 1930–40, Pebble Beach, California, 1940–48, and in Port-Lligat, Spain, since 1948; worked on films with Luis Bunuel, 1929; member, André Breton's Surrealist Group of artists and writers, Paris, 1930–34; first theatre decors, 1939; first classical and religious paintings, 1948; first 3-dimensional works, 1964; established Dali Museum, Figueras, 1973. Editor, *L'Amic des Arts* magazine, Sitges, 1926–29, and *Manifest Groc*, with S. Gasch and L. Montanya, Sitges, 1928. Agent: Knoedler and Co., 21 East 70 Street, New York, New York 10021, U.S.A. Address: Port-Lligat, Cadaques, Spain.

Individual Exhibitions:

1925 Galeria Dalmau, Barcelona
1927 Galeria Dalmau, Barcelona
1929 Galerie Goemans, Paris
1931 Galerie Pierre Colle, Paris
1932 Julien Levy Gallery, New York
Galerie Pierre Colle, Paris
1933 Galeria d'Art Catalunya, Barcelona
Julien Levy Gallery, New York
Galerie Pierre Colle, Paris
1934 Julien Levy Gallery, New York
Galeria d'Art Catalunya, Barcelona
Zwemmer Gallery, London
Galerie Quatre Chemins, Paris
Galerie Jacques Bonjean, Paris
1936 Alex Reid and Lefevre Gallery, London
Julien Levy Gallery, New York
1939 Dali Studio, Paris
Julien Levy Gallery, New York
1941 Museum of Modern Art, New York
Julien Levy Gallery, New York
Julien Levy Gallery, Hollywood, California
1942 Museum of Modern Art, New York
1943 M. Knoedler and Co., New York
1945 Bignon Gallery, New York
1946 M.Knoedler and Co., New York
1947 Cleveland Museum of Art
Bignon Gallery, New York
1948 Bignon Gallery, New York
1950 Carstairs Gallery, New York
1951 Galerie David Weill, Paris
Alemany and Ertman, New York
Lefevre Gallery, London
1952 Carstairs Gallery, New York
Alemany and Ertman, New York
1953 Santa Barbara Museum of Art, California
1954 Palazzo Pallaricini-Rospigliosi, Rome
Carstairs Gallery, New York
1955 Philadelphia Museum of Art
Denver Art Museum
1956 Casino Communal, Knokke, Belgium
Carstairs Gallery, New York
1958 M. Knoedler and Co., New York
Carstairs Gallery, New York
1959 French and Co., New York
1960 Musée Galliera, Paris
Finch Gallery, New York
Carstairs Gallery, New York
1963 M. Knoedler and Co., New York
1964 Prince Hotel Gallery, Tokyo (travelled to Prefectural Museum of Art, Nagoya and the Municipal Art Gallery, Kyoto)
Los Angeles Municipal Art Gallery
1965 M. Knoedler and Co., New York
Phyllis Lucas Gallery, New York
1966 Gallery of Modern Art, New York
1967 Hotel Meurice, Paris
Galerie D, Prague
Staempfli Gallery, New York
1968 Palais des Beaux-Arts, Charleroi, Belgium
London Graphic Art Gallery
Phyllis Lucas Gallery, New York
1969 Galerie Les Heures Claires, Paris
Hiram College, Ohio
Galerie Knoedler, Paris
Zachary Walker Gallery, Los Angeles
1970 Museum Boymans-van Beuningen, Rotterdam (retrospective)
M. Knoedler and Co., New York
Galleria Guissi, Turin
Musée de l'Athenée, Geneva
Galerie Andre-Francois Petit, Paris
M. Knoedler and Co., New York
Karl-Ernst-Osthaus Museum Hagen, West Germany
1971 *Gemalde, Zeichnungen, Objekte Schmuck*, Staatliche Kunsthalle, Baden-Baden, West Germany
Art-in-Jewels Exhibition, Whitechapel Art Gallery, London
Museum Boymans-van Beuningen, Rotterdam
1972 *Holograms Conceived by Dali*, M. Knoedler and Co., New York
Museum Boymans-van Beuningen, Rotterdam
Galerie Isy Brachot, Brussels
1974 Städtisches Galerie/Stadelsches Kunstinsitut, Frankfurt
1977 *Bilder, Gouachen, Zeichnungen, Skulpturen*, Sammlung Levy, Hamburg
1979 *Retrospective 1920–1980*, Centre Georges Pompidou, Paris
1980 Tate Gallery, London
1982 *Obra Grafica*, Caja de Ahorros, Madrid
1984 Galeria Surrealista, Barcelona
1987 Galerie 1900–2000, Paris

Selected Group Exhibitions:

1921 *Group Exhibition*, Galeria Dalmau, Barcelona
1933 *Exposition Surrealiste*, Galerie Pierre Colle, Paris
1936 *Fantastic Art, Dada & Surrealism*, Museum of Modern Art, New York
1940 *Exposicion Internacional del Surrealismo*, Galeria de Arte Mexicano, Mexico City
1951 *Surrealisme en Abstractie*, Stedelijk Museum, Amsterdam
1959 *Exposition Internationale du Surrealisme*, Musée d'Art Moderne, Paris
1965 *Bienal*, Sao Paulo
1968 *Dada, Surrealism and Their Heritage*, Museum of Modern Art, New York
1970 *Surrealism*, Moderna Musset, Stockholm
1982 *A Century of Modern Drawing*, British Museum, London (travelled to the Boston Museum of Fine Arts, and the Cleveland Museum of Art)

Collections:

Salvador Dali Museum, Figueras, Spain; Centre Georges Pompidou, Paris; Nationalgalerie, West Berlin; Stedelijk Museum, Amsterdam, Museum Boymans-van Beuningen, Rotterdam; Kunsthaus, Zurich; Tate Gallery, London; Museum of Modern Art, New York; Guggenheim Museum, New York; Cleveland Museum of Art (A guide to Dali's work in public museums is published by Cleveland Museum of Art, 1974)

Publications:

By DALI: books and pamphlets—*La Femme Visible*, Paris 1930; *L'Amour et al Memoire*, Paris 1931; *Conquest of the*

Salvador Dali: ***The Hallucinogenic Toreador*****, 1970** Courtesy Salvador Dali Museum, St. Petersburg, Florida

Irrational, Paris 1935; *The Metamorphosis of Narcissus*, 1937; *Declaration of the Independence of the Imagination and the Rights to His Own Madness*, 1938; *Hidden Faces*, New York 1944; *The Secret Life of Salvador Dali*, London 1948; *Mystical Manifesto*, 1951; *Dali's Moustache*, 1954; *The Cuckolds of Old Modern Art*, 1956; *The Tragic Myth of Millet's Angelus*, 1963; *Diary of a Genius*, 1964; *Dali de Draeger*, Paris 1968; *Dali by Dali*, New York 1970; *Les Diners de Gala*, New York 1963; *The Unspeakable Confessions of Salvador Dali*, New York 1976; films—*Un Chien Andalou*, with Luis Bunuel, 1929; *L'Age d'Or*, with Luis Bunuel, 1930; *The Prodigious History of the Laceworker and the Rhinoceros*, with Robert Descharnes, 1954.

On DALI: books—*Dickens, Dali and Others: Studies in Popular Culture* by George Orwell, New York 1946; *Salvador Dali* by James Thrall Soby, New York 1946; *Catalogue of Works by Salvador Dali* by A. Reynolds Morse, Cleveland 1956; *Dali* by Michel Tapie, Paris 1957; *Dali*, edited by Linda Livingstone, Greenwich, Connecticut 1959; *The Case of Salvador Dali* by Fleur Cowles, London 1959; *A New Introduction to Salvador Dali* by A. Reynolds Morse, Cleveland 1960; *The Salvador Dali Museum* by A. Reynolds Morse, Cleveland 1962; *Dali Exhibition-Japan 1964*, exhibition catalogue, edited by Shuzo Takiguchi, Yoshiaki Tono and Shin Ohoka, Tokyo 1964; *Salvador Dali 1910–1965*, exhibition catalogue, with an introduction by Carl J. Weinhardt Jr., New York 1965; *Dali: Miró* by Paul Walton, New York 1967; *Dali*, edited by Max Gerard, New York 1968; *In Quest of Dali* by C. Lake, New York 1969; *Dada and Surrealist Art* by William S. Rubin, London 1970; *Dali*, exhibition catalogue, with texts by Patrick Waldberg, Robert Descharnes and Gerrit Komrij, Rotterdam 1970; *Dali: Paintings and Drawings 1965–1979*, exhibition catalogue, with text by Thomas B. Hess, New York 170; *A Short Survey of Surrealism* by David Gascoyne, London 1970; *Deli: The Masterworks* by A. Reynolds Morse, Cleveland 1971; *Dali: Gemalde, Zeichnungen, Objekte, Schmuck*, exhibition catalogue, with a foreword by Klaus Gallwitz, texts by Patrick Waldberg, Gerrit Komrij and others, Baden-Baden, West Germany 1971; *Dali: Art-in-Jewels Exhibition*, exhibition catalogue, London 1971; *The Surrealists* by William Gaunt, London 1972; *Antologie Grafica del Surrealismo* by Maurice Henry, Milan 1972; *Holograms Conceived by Dali*, exhibitoin catalogue, with an introduction by Dennis Gabor, New York 1972; *Salvador Dali: Catalogue of a Collection—93 oils 1917–1970*, edited by A. Reynolds Morse, Cleveland 1972; *The World of Salvador Dali* by Robert Descharnes, London 1972; *The History of Surrealism* by Maurice Nadeu, London 1973; *Salvador Dali/ Pablo Picasso* by A. Reynolds Morse, Cleveland 1973; *Surrealisme et Sexualité* by Xaviere Gauthier, Paris 1971; *Dictionnaire de la Peinture Surrealiste* by Sarane Alexandrian, Paris 1973; *Malerei des Surrealismus* by Uwe M. Schneede, Cologne 1973; *A Dali Primer* by A. Reynolds Morse, Cleveland 1970; *The Draftsmanship of Dali*, with an introduction by A. Reynolds Morse, Cleveland 1970; *Dali*, edited by David Larkin, with an introduction by J. G. Ballard, London 1974; *Dali: A Guide to His Works in Public Museums* by A. Reynolds Morse, Cleveland 1974; *Salvador Dali*, exhibition catalogue, with a foreword by Klaus Gallwitz, texts by several authors, Frankfurt 1974; *Salvador Dali: Bilder, Gouachen, Zeichnungen, Skulpturen* exhibition catalogue, Hamburg 1977; *Salvador Dali: Retrospective 1920–1980*, exhibition catalogue, with texts by Daniel Abadie and others, Paris 1979; *Salvador Dali*, exhibition catalogue, with text by Simon Wilson, London 1980; *Dali: Obra Grafica*, exhibition catalogue, with texts by Javier Tusell, Ramon Gomez de la Serna and others, Madrid 1982; *Salvador Dali*, exhibition catalogue with essay by Robert Descharnes, Paris 1987.

After faltering Impressionist and then Cubist beginnings, Salvador Dali settled rapidly on a world and language of his own and on a style of painting not unlike that of the old masters. At the age of 25, in 1929, he was in full control of his art. It is for that reason that he went through the entire Surrealist era an absolute master. Furthermore, the theory he had just developed, labeled "paranoiac critical method," made it possible for him to present all his erotic, libidinous and scabrous obsessions in a fairy-tale-like context, thus transcribing visually everything Freud had expressed in words. André Breton wrote that in this method, Dali had provided the Movement with "an instrument of the utmost importance." Dali was to apply it with equal care and success to painting, to poetry, to film-making *(Un Chien Andalou, L'Age d'Or,* made with Luis Bunuel), to the construction of the familiar surrealist objects (the telephone with receiver in the shape of a lobster, the Venus of the drawers, the sofa in the shape of Mae West's lips), to fashion (he designed for Elsa Schiapparelli) and to any sort of exegesis (for instance, his theories on the emperor Trajan and Romania). Later on, Dali maintained that the greatest of his discoveries was doubtless still the paranoiac critical method. He doesn't know exactly what the term means, but he's sure it has brought him millions and millions of dollars.

All joking aside, it is the Surrealist period which clearly dominates his works, and which gives us a master of the art of painting: "The Great Masturbator" (1929), "The Enigma of Desire" (1929), "The Persistence of Memory: Limp Watches" (1933); watches can be anything, even limp, provided they show the correct time, says the artist. The power of words (reinforcing as they do the pictorial image, while the image sends us back to the title) nearly take us outside the limits of painting: the artist becomes a medium. This period is also that of Dali's historical intuitions represented by such magnificent canvases as The "Enigma of William Tell" (1933), showing a figure with tentacle-like legs and a raw chop on one knee, and the *shapka* (Russian hat) picture, held up by a crutch, showing a Lenin who had already sacrificed the children of his Revolution. There are also works foretelling the Spanish Civil War: "Prémonition de la Guerre Civile" (1936).

The 1950's marked the gradual disappearance of this emotion-filled, profoundly upsetting a content, so full of eccentricities, sadism, solitude, and those complexes necessarily a part of Dali's erotically-based universe. The images of Christ, where Dali is trying to leave the spectator breathless through his panoramic, plunging views, are the reflection of a different world.

As everybody knows, Dali did more than anyone else to make himself an object of discussion, giving a tragic example to the new generations. "I want people to talk about me, even if they say nice things" he declared in that period of his youth when he was already formulating the following principle: "Painter, if you wish to take your place in society, you must at a very tender age launch a terrific kick at its left leg." Such violence began as instinctive and was later refined; Dali was, doubtless, the first to evaluate to the status of doctrine a notion which was to become one of the signs of our times. Increasingly "different," increasingly eccentric, forever doing the opposite of what others did in order to set himself apart, and forever calling into question his position as madman or genius, Dali left a lifeless and declining bourgeoisie increasingly astounded; and he made them pay the outrageous price for his psychological maneuverings.

The story of his eccentricities is a long one, and has been brilliantly told by Dali himself in his books. The most important of them is a literary masterpiece, as well as one of the most entertaining pieces one could hope to encounter: *The Secret Life of Salvador Dali* by Salvador Dali. Its first chapter is cleverly entitled "Am I a genius?", a question which he answers repeatedly throughout the book, and which is treated again in a sequel. Of course he's a genius. The title of the second volume, by the way, is highly revelatory: *Diary of a Genius* by Salvador Dali. What can we learn from these books concerning the most celebrated of living artists? At six years of age, he wanted to be a cook, and at seven, Napoleon. Since then, he assures us, his ambition has never ceased to grow; nor his megalomania.

Dali has gone about building his universal kingdom and temple of "genius" in a number of different ways. He has been doing so in his mind since his birth on May 11, 1904, or perhaps even before if one takes into account the intrauterine memories he has continued to describe in minute detail right up to present day. Along more concrete lines he has built, ten years ago, a theater-museum in his birthplace, Figueras, for the self-glorification of his genius.

The persistent nature of Dali's torment has led to a curious identification with the ultimate incarnations of power, be they Lenin, Stalin, Hitler, Mao, Franco, King Juan Carlos; money (the Dollar) or Science. But, the same Dali who tried to assimilate all new discoveries, all forms of power, and who never hesitated to use extravagant forms of provocation to establish his position as "genius," has at the same time, as a rule, been obsessively strict when it came to painting. In painting he is against "freedom" and for restraint. He favors form. "Classicism stood for integration, synthesis, cosmogony, instead of breakup, experimentation on scepticism" wrote this enemy of the "old modern art."

The specter of Picasso constantly confronts Dali. It is undeniable that just as the former revolutionized painting, the latter revolutionized the behavior of the painter. Seeing the two juxtaposed in this way, we can notice how very different their work has been. "Picasso," says Dali, "pushed ugliness to its furthest extreme." Breaking up the shape of reality and yet continually clashing with objects, Picasso remained a prisoner to his perceptions. Having broken up the universe, with his tireless worker's hands, he put it back together, using the smashed pieces. Dali did just the opposite. The two geniuses are mutally exclusive in their fundamental approach. Interested rather in beauty and in the hidden harmony of things, Dali stands as the great manipulator of myths in our time—of myths and not simply of media. That is perhaps the most interesting thing about him, and certainly the most important as well, at a period in history when people are satisfied with myths which have been debased or made caricatures, which are useless in helping us to live.

In person, Dali is touching, serious, well-informed. He is infinitely charming. The persona he has created for himself, on the other hand, demonstrates an egotistical inflation without parallel, and is devouring, cruel, extravagant and provocative. Now if this persona has been able to endure and to continue to be identified with the notion of *genius* for more than 50 years, it is because Dali has simultaneously cultivated a second art—that of *galateo,* the art of laughing at oneself invented in 16th century Tuscany, of finding one's weaknesses, of publicly identifying them and of blowing them up to such proportions that we are forced to regard him with tenderness and humor rather than with what might have been hatred. For we will have recognized something of ourselves in this hero who up till then had seemed sublime and without weakness.

The concept of *genius,* peculiar to the 19th century, was applied above all to the *artist*—that person who could not prove his place in society and who was subject to both divine grace and disgrace. He was chosen by the gods and damned by society, whence the helpless rebellion expressed his Alfred de Vigny in *Moise:*"—Why me?" However, no one has done as much as Dali to amass unto himself the advantages of being *chosen.*

The notion of *genius* has suffered a loss of favor since 1930, but has remained in use from Napoleon right up through Dali. (Remember that he wanted to be Napoleon as a child.) We have learned from Zielsel and Isac Kapuano that the concept of *genius* cannot exist without that of flaw or Achilles heel. Dali seems to have sensed this instinctively in his perpetual effort to call attention to his own weaknesses ("How cowardly I am," "At any rate, I'm completely impotent," "I used to read Kant and understand nothing"). One might also conclude that *genius* is necessarily eccentric, that is *ex-centric.* But it remains to be known whether genius can coexist in the same person as the initiate who, by definition, is supposed to be *the center.*

—Radu Varia

DANBY, Ken.

Canadian. Born in Sault Sainte Marie, Ontario, 6 March 1940. Studied under Jock MacDonald, Ontario College of Art, Toronto, 1957–60. Married Judith E. Harcourt in 1965; sons: Sean, Ryan, Noah. Worked in mining tower construction, Wawa, Canada, 1958; Set Designer, CJIC-TV, Toronto, 1960;

ken Danby: *Acapulco*, 1985

Promotions Designer, *The Telegram* newspaper, Toronto, 1960–62. Independent artist: influenced by Andrew Wyeth exhibition, New York, 1962; moved to Speed River, Guelph, Ontario, 1967; commissioned to design Series III Olympic Coinage, 1976. Member, Canada Council, 1985. Recipient: Purchase Award, *Four Seasons Exhibition,* Toronto, 1962; Jessie Dow Best Painting Award, Museum of Fine Arts, Montreal, 1964; Drawing Award, *Hadassah Exhibition,* Toronto, 1965; R. Tait McKenzie Chair for Sport Award, National Sport and Recreation Centre and Labatt Breweries, Ottawa; Ontario Arts Council Award, 1976; Queen's Canadian Silver Jubilee Medal, 1977. Member, Royal Canadian Academy of Arts, 1976. Agent: Gallery Moos Ltd., 136 Yorkville Avenue, Toronto, Ontario M5R 1C2. Address: R.R. 4, Guelph, Ontario NIH 5JI, Canada.

Individual Exhibitions:

1964	Gallery Moos, Toronto
1965	Gallery Moos, Toronto
1966	Gallery Moos, Toronto
	Galerie Agnes Lefort, Montreal
1967	Gallery Moos, Toronto
1968	Gallery Moos, Toronto
1969	*Kunstmarkt,* Cologne
	Gallery Moos, Toronto
1970	Gallery Moos, Toronto
1971	Gallery Moos, Toronto
1972	William Zierler Gallery, New York
	Gallery Moos, Toronto
	Images Gallery, Toledo, Ohio
1973	Galerie Allen, Vancouver
	Fleet Gallery, Winnipeg
	Continental Art Agencies, Vancouver
	William Zierler Gallery, New York
1974	*Brown/Danby/Forrestall,* Canadian Consulate, New York
	Gallery Moos, Toronto
	Wallack Gallery, Ottawa
	Galerie Moos, Montreal
	Kitchener-Waterloo Gallery, London, Ontario (retrospective; toured Southern Ontario)
1975	*Algoma Arts Festival,* Sault Ste. Marie, Ontario
	Galerie Allen, Vancouver
	Gallery Moos, Toronto
1976	Gallery Moos, Toronto
1977	Canadian Consulate, New York
	Arras Gallery, New York
	de Vooght Galleries, Vancouver
	Gallery Moos, Toronto
1978	Gallery Moos, Toronto
1979	Gallery Moos, Toronto
1980	*Ken Danby: The Graphic Work: Lithographs and Serigraphs,* Art Gallery of Hamilton, Ontario (toured Canada, 1980–82)
	De Vooght Galleries, Vancouver
1982	Gallery Moos, Toronto
1983	Galerie Mihalis, Montreal
	Americas Cup Gallery, Newport, Rhode Island
1985	Gallery Moos, Toronto
	Kenneth G. Heffel Fine Art, Vancouver

Selected Group Exhibitions:

1964	*Drawings and Watercolours,* National Gallery of Canada, Ottawa
1966	*Magic Realism in Canadian Art,* London Art Gallery, Ontario
1970	*Survey 70: Realisms,* Art Gallery of Ontario, Toronto (travelled to the Museum of Fine Arts, Montreal)
1971	*Biennale,* Paris
1972	*Silk Screen: History of a Medium,* Philadelphia Museum of Art
1974	*Canadian Realists,* Canadian Cultural Centre, Paris (toured Europe)
1976	*Aspects of Realism,* Rothman's of Pall Mall travelling exhibition, Stratford Art Gallery, Ontario (toured Canada, 1976–78)
1980	*Canadian high Realism,* Bayard Gallery, New York
1981	*Champions of American Sports,* National Portrait Gallery, Washington, D.C. (travelled to Los Angeles, Chicago, New York)
1985	*A Celebration of Amateur Sport,* Queen's Park, Toronto

Collections:

National Gallery of Canada, Ottawa; Visual Arts Bank, Canada Council, Ottawa; Museum of Fine Arts, Montreal; Art Gallery of Vancouver; Mendel Art Gallery, Saskatoon, Saskatchewan; Museum of Modern Art, New York; Museum of Fine Arts, Indianapolis; Art Institute of Chicago; University of California, Berkeley; Bradford City Art Gallery and Museum, England.

Publications:

By DANBY: article—interview, with Andrew J. Oka, in *Ken Danby: The Graphic Work: Lithographs and Serigraphs,* exhibition catalogue, Hamilton, Ontario 1980.

On DANBY: books—*Ken Danby,* exhibition catalogue, with texts by Russell J. Harper and Paul Duval, Toronto 1967; *Ken Danby,* exhibition pamphlet, by Mario Amaya, New York 1972; *4 Decades* by Paul Duval, Toronto 1972; *High Realism in Canadian Art* by Paul Duval, Toronto 1974; *Neue Formen des Realismus* by Peter Sagel, Cologne 1974; *Ken Danby* by Paul Duval, Toronto, deluxe edition 1974, trade edition 1976; *Danby Images of Sport* by Hubert de Santana, Toronto 1978;

Super Realism by Edward Lucie-Smith, London 1979; *Siebdruck: Technik, Praxis, Geschichte* by Wolfgang Hainke, Cologne 1979; *Ken Danby: The Graphic Work: Lithographs and Serigraphs,* exhibition catalogue, with a foreword by Glen E. Cumming, Hamilton, Ontario 1980; *Contemporary Canadian Art,* by David Burnett and Marilyn Schiff, Toronto 1983; *Ken Danby: The New Decade* by Paul Duval, Toronto 1984; film—*Ken Danby,* produced by Rex Bromfield, Toronto 1971.

Throughout the history of art, we have witnessed a great metamorphosis taking place, which continues to alter and expand our appreciation of art. A constant exploration, into the various elements of the visual world, together with individual interpretation, has always been at the core of fine art.

As important discoveries and insights have been offered, the posture of the "art community" has been unsettled and then adjusted over a period of time, according to the degree of accommodation necessary. For example, for centuries, a great effort was made to resolve the applications of simple perspective, in drawing and painting. Equally so, was the attempt to create form and dimension through the use of strong light and shade; chiaroscuro.

While acknowledging that continued experimentation is essential, I also feel that it is time to integrate that which we have learned; in a cohesive and constructive manner, as well as in an experimental one. The individual entities of art; colour, shape, light, dimension, texture, etc., are but the pieces of the whole. Rather than continue the procedure of assessing these elements separately, I prefer to utilize their particular assets collectively, in creating a complete statement—a total integration of all I have learned and am learning. Only in this way, can I hope to communicate successfully, and be satisfied with the results.

—Ken Danby

Born in Sault Ste. Marie, Ontario, Ken Danby studied at the Ontario College of Art in Toronto from 1958 to 1960 with the well-known abstractionist, J. W. G. (Jock) MacDonald, and began his own career as an abstract painter, but soon returned to his first love, realism. The palette of his early abstractions with their colours of coral, grey and brown set the tone for later work. Nor did he forget the techniques he'd learned as an abstract artist—he used them later. But in the meantime, the subjects of his paintings changed to carefully posed, snapshot like views, often of rural Ontario. In 1962 a visit to an Andrew Wyeth exhibition at Buffalo, N. Y., confirmed for Danby that a realist artist could be respected. In his maturity as an artist Danby enjoyed painting personal friends and family, and anonymous sports figures. In his *At the Crease* (1972), the masked ice-hockey goalie recalls knights of an earlier day. For many in Canada that painting has become something of a national symbol.

In its mix of abstraction and realism, Danby's work recalls that of Christopher Pratt, but Danby's atmosphere is not so rarefied and cerebral. He did not hesitate to deal with almost Caravaggesque low-life, as in *Motel* (1971) which recounts the cigarettes, coffee, and crumpled pillow of the lonely motel room. Over the last decade, he has increasingly sought poetic, simple, effects; the almost invisible division between water and land in *The Sculler* (1976); the way the water in *Acapulco* (1985) is abstractly treated while the woman seated on the diving board, and the setting, are realistic. "The symmetrical design was challenging, as was the need to create a sensuous and luminous light," said Danby of *Acapulco*. "I was intrigued by the fact that the work combines both a confrontational thrust with a peaceful calm."

—Joan Murray

Nassos Daphnis: *101–71*, 1971

DAPHNIS, Nassos.

American. Born a United States citizen, in Krokeai-Sparta, Greece, 23 July 1914; settled in the United States, 1930. Studied at the Art Students League, New York 1946–49; Académie Frochot, Paris, 1950–51; Institute Statale d'Arte, Florence, 1951–52. Served in the United States Army, 1942–45. Married Helen Avlonitis in 1956; children: Artemis, Demetrios. Independent artist, New York, since 1938. Member, American Abstract Artists, New York, since 1957. Member of the Board, City Walls Incorporated, New York, since 1969. Recipient: Ford Foundation Award, 1962; Purchase Award, Whitney Museum, New York, 1962; National Foundation of Art and Humanities Award, 1966; National Endowment of the Arts grant, 1971; Prize, *New England 350th Celebration Exhibition,* 1972; A. P. Saunders Medal 1973; Tree Peony Award 1973; Guggenheim Fellowship, New York, 1977; Francis J. Greenburger Foundation Award, New York, 1987; Pollock/Krasner Foundation grant, New York, 1987. Agent: Leo Castelli Gallery, 4 East 77th Street, New York, New York 10021. Address: 362 West Broadway, New York, New York 10013, U.S.A.

Individual Exhibitions:

1938 Contemporary Arts Gallery, New York
1947 Contemporary Arts Gallery, New York
1949 Contemporary Arts Gallery, New York
1950 Colette Allendy Galerie, Paris
1959 Leo Castelli Gallery, New York
1960 Leo Castelli Gallery, New York
1961 Leo Castelli Gallery, New York
Toninelli Arte Moderna, Milan
1962 Galerie Iris Clert, Paris
1963 Leo Castelli Gallery, New York
1965 Leo Castelli Gallery, New York
1967 Franklin Siden Gallery, Detroit
1968 Leo Castelli Gallery, New York
1969 Albright-Knox Museum, Buffalo, New York (retrospective)
Everson Museum, Syracuse, New York
1970 Brockton Art Center, Massachusetts
1971 Leo Castelli Gallery, New York
1973 Leo Castelli Gallery, New York
1974 Ande Zarre Gallery, New York
1975 Leo Castelli Gallery, New York
1980 *Paintings of the 50's.* Leo Castelli Gallery. New York
Phillips Gallery, Salt Lake City
Eaton-Shoen Gallery, San Francisco
1983 Leo Castelli Gallery, New York
Andre Zarre Gallery, New York
1985 Kouros Gallery, New York
Leo Castelli Gallery, New York
Eaton-Shoen Gallery, San Francisco
Andre Zarre Gallery, New York
1986 Leo Castelli Gallery, New York

Selected Group Exhibitions:

1960 *International Art of a New Era,* Museum of Fine Arts, Osaka, Japan
American Abstract Expressionists and Imagists, Guggenheim Museum new York
1963 *Formalists,* Washington Gallery of Modern Art, Washington, D.C.
1965 *White on White,* DeCordova Museum, Lincoln, Massachusetts
1967 *10 Years,* Leo Castelli Gallery, New York
1969 *Color in Control,* Museum of Fine Arts, St. Petersburg, Florida
1972 *Monoprints.* Trica Karlis Gallery, Provincetown, Massachusetts

974 *Drawings.* Leo Castelli Gallery Downtown, New York
987 *Leo Castelli y sus Artistas,* Centro Cultural Arte Contemporaneo, Mexico City

Collections:

Whitney Museum, New York Museum of Modern Art, New York; Guggenheim Museum, New York; Albright-Knox Gallery; Buffalo, New York; Everson Museum, Syracuse, New York; Baltimore Museum of Art; Museum of Art, Pittsburgh: Akron Art Institute, Ohio; Utah Art Museum Salt Lake City; Tel Aviv Museum, Israel.

Publications:

On DAPHNIS: books—*Nassos Daphnis: Paintings of the '0's,* exhibition catalogue, by April Kingsley, New York 1980; *Nassos Daphnis: Biomorphic Paintings 1947-48,* exhibition catalogue with essay by John Gruen, New York 1985; articles—"Nassos Daphnis: A Perennial Order" by James R. Mellow in *Art International* (Lugano, Switzerland) March 1969; "Nassos Daphnis" by A. Brunelle in *Art News* New York). April 1973; "Nassos Daphnis: Wall Painting at 620 West 47th Street, New York" in *Art Now: New York* (New York), 1973; review in *Artforum* (New York), June 1973, "New York" by April Kingsley in *Art International* (Lugano, Switzerland), Summer 1973; Nassos Daphnis at Leo Castelli" by Elizabeth Frank in *Art in America* (New York), Summer 1980; "Nassos Daphnis" by Mary Anne Staniszewski in *Art News* (New York). Summer 1980; *Organic Geometry''* by Blair T. Birmelin in *Art in America* (New York), October 1985.

For the past few years, I have been searching for images which convey the energies that permeate the universe. I try to portray the forces of energy itself, its wavelengths, its movement through space and its interaction with other waves as their paths intersect. While the visual patterns of color which I use are free of content, my intention is to express creative, life-giving forces, although, from time to time, more violent, ambiguous forces come into play.

Since 1952, I have used geometric forms to express my ideas. I have concentrated on pure color, using only the primaries—blue, red, yellow, white and black. By so doing, I can achieve the most vibrant qualities inherent in each color. It is also extremely important for me to try to liberate color from form. In my paintings, color is an element in and of itself, eloquent and independent in its presentation.

In 1957, I developed my own color theory, according to which each color exists relative to the planal space which it occupies. I order colors according to their characteristic spatial depth. This permits me to create visual space without using perspective or modelling, and contributes simultaneously to the complex interactions of forces in conjunction or tension with each other.

—Nassos Daphnis

When Nassos Daphnis began hybridizing exotic tree peonies, crossing rare Chinese species with hardy native varieties, he had to outsmart the nearly insurmountable sterility of the hybrid to reestablish the line of offspring that may extend into the future. This need to circumvent dead ends, to predate dogmatic trends, has characterized Daphnis' work since the beginning of his career. Paying homage to the pure and simple during the freewheeling period of expressionism in the 50s, he precociously hybridizes a blunt forthrightness to create a strain of geometric abstraction that has borne fruit ever since.

More than a painter, Daphnis is a pioneer. His work has been a succession of experiments, surviving complex alterations to achieve the degree of simplification encompassed in his recent paintings. Yet through each phase, his attention to purity of colour and image has remained consistent. In 1938 Daphnis began painting landscapes that made direct, legible statements in bold, intense colours neatly bound within hard edges. In 1947 critics noticed a change in style when he exhibited quasi-surrealistic representations of charred trees in barren landscapes. His work in camouflage and relief maps during the war years may have been responsible for the new forms and textures in his paintings. His 1950 travels to Greece, where the light "flattened everything," slanted his perspective towards abstraction. The effect eliminated texture and surface incident, prompting Daphnis to research optical properties of colour and the activities of planes.

His commitment to "pure" colour resulted in a colour theory which has sustained the basic structure of his subsequent work. Visualizing an arbitrary scale of 1 to 100, he gave each colour a value: black, the most intense colour, occupies planes 0–10; blue from 10–70 followed by red, yellow and finally white, being "without substance but an expanding essence" from 90–100. The colour planes extend back to infinity behind the picture plane. A colour becomes a tonal value and loses the energy of pure colour whenever it goes beyond its limit.

Around 1955 his painting became highly complex in design in efforts to overcome the strict limitations of "pure" art. The adherence to his colour theory nevertheless remained tenacious. Yet the seeming arbitrary change from one approach to the next suggests a consistent trend which moves cyclically—and cathartically—from complex design to simplified, reductive purity. In 1958 he discovered acrylic paints. First by applying the paint consistently with rollers, then by masking and spraying his canvases, Daphnis achieved effects of uniformity and geometric precision while maintaining pure bands of colour. He increased his scale, creating nearly wall-sized surfaces, and engendered a feeling of absorption into the paintings by choosing red for its intensity and strength. The viewing experience bore obvious comparisons to that of Abstract Expressionist work, though Daphnis himself is reluctant to acknowledge any analogy to the gestural approach of this school.

Daphnis added another variable to his work with the introduction of wood reliefs, physical planes which compliment and augment the painted ones. Plastics, which succeeded this phase in 1962, included the elements of translucency and transparency to the now three-dimensional bands. The interaction between actual and painted elements produced colour vibrations and spatial constituencies stronger than those in earlier paintings. This relief method allowed Daphnis to incorporate colour into sculpture. His red and black column is best known in this series. Large in scale, it commands space and absorbs light. The core of the piece is clear plastic which calls attention away from its mass creating spatial ambiguity and intensifying colour contrasts. It suggests change, and is an architectural statement of structure and continuation.

In pursuit of pure abstraction, his ingenuity captured critical attention around 1960 with his invention of a large, compass-like instrument used to delineate arcs with perfect precision. The arcs appear to continue on their great trajectories out of the picture space on either side indefinitely with the same exactitude. Yet the unsettling behavior of the arc's position on the canvas within the soothing geometric order creates the vital energy of his paintings.

Having earned a place in recent history, Daphnis is also likely to receive exposure as an important artist of the future. His devotion to purity predicted '60s Minimalism, his systematic approach predated systematic painting. Now, another phase of his work completed, he is ever exploring new possibilities. His art resists stagnation, for it is still developing, still anticipating new experiments.

—Carrie Barker

DARBOVEN, Hanne.
German. Born in Munich, 29 April 1941. Studied art at the Hochschule für Bildende Kunst, Hamburg. Independent artist, working with number-concepts, Hamburg and New York, since 1966. Agent: Leo Castelli Gallery, 420 West Broadway, New York, New York 10012. Address: Am Burgberg 20,2000 Hamburg 90, West Germany.

Individual Exhibitions:

1967 Galerie Konrad Fischer, Dusseldorf
1968 Galerie Konrad Fischer, Dusseldorf
1969 Städtisches Museum, Mönchengladbach, West Germany
Galerie Heiner Friedrich, Munch
1970 Galerie Michael Werner, Cologne
Galerie Konrad Fischer, Dusseldorf
Art & Project, Amsterdam
Galleria Sperone, Turin
1971 Westfälischer Kunstverein, Münster, West Germany
Galerie Konrad Fischer, Dusseldorf
1972 Galerie Heiner Friedrich, Cologne
Galerie M. T. L. Brussels
Galleria Toselli, Milan
Galleria Marilena Bonomo, Bari, Italy
Studio Lia Rumma, Naples
Kabinett für Aktuelle Kunst, Bremerhaven, West Germany
Museum für Kunst und Gewerbe, Hamburg
1973 Galerie Yvon Lambert, Paris
Leo Castelli Gallery, New York
1974 Art & Project/M. T. L., Antwerp (travelled to Amsterdam and Brussels)
Palais des Beaux-Arts, Brussels
Museum of Modern Art, Oxford
Kabinett für Aktuelle Kunst. Bremerhaven, West Germany
Leo Castelli Gallery, New York
Ein Monat, ein Jahr, ein Jahrhundert: Arbeiten von 1968 bis 1974, Kunstmuseum, Basle
Sonnabend Gallery, New York
1975 *Een Maand, een Jaar, een Eeuw: Werken van 1968 tot en met 1974,* Stedelijk Museum, Amsterdam
Leo Castelli Gallery, New York
Leo Castelli Gallery, New York
Kunstmuseum, Lucerne
1976 *For Jean-Paul Sartre,* Leo Castelli Gallery, New York
1978 Leo Castelli/Sperone-Westwater-Fischer, New York
1988 Kunstraum Munchen, Munich

Selected Group Exhibitions:

1967 *Normal Art,* Lannis Museum of Normal Art, New York
1968 *Language II,* Dwan Gallery, New York
1969 *When Attitudes Become Form,* Kunsthalle, Berne (toured Europe)
1970 *Conceptual Art/Arte Povera/Land Art,* Galleria Civica, Turin
1971 *7th Biennale de Paris,* Musée d'Art Moderne de la Ville, Paris
Guggenheim International, Guggenheim Museum, New York
1972 *Documenta 5,* Kassel, West Germany (and *Documenta 7,* 1982)
1973 *Bienal,* Sao Paulo
1974 *Projekt 74,* Kunsthalle, Cologne
1985 *The European Iceberg,* Art Gallery of Ontario, Toronto

Collections:

Stedelijk Museum, Amsterdam; Kaiser-Wilhelm-Museum, Krefeld, West Germany

Publications:

By DARBOVEN: book—*Ein Jahrhundert.* Amsterdam 1971; articles—"6 Manuskripte '69" with others, in *Kunstzeitung* (Dusseldorf), no. 3, 1969, "Words" in *Avalanche* (New York), Spring 1972; film—*6 books, 68-6,* 1971.

On DARBOVEN: books—*Arte Povera* by Germano Celant, Milan, Tübingen and New York 1970; *Hanne Darboven* by Ingrid Krupka, Cologne 1972; *Hanne Darboven,* exhibition catalogue with texts by Klaus Honnef and Johannes Cladders, Münster, West Germany 1971; *Guggenheim International Exhibition 1971,* catalogue with texts by Thomas M. Messer, Diane Waldman and Edward F. Fry, New York 1971; *Was Die Schonheit sei, das Weiss ich Nicht, Kunstler, Theorie, Werk,* Nuremberg 1971; *Documenia 5: Befragung der Realiät,* exhibition catalogue, edited by Harald Szeemann and others, Kassel, West Germany 1972; *Six Years: The Dematerialization of the Art Object* by Lucy R. Lippard, London and New York 1973; *Bilder, Objekie, Filme, Konzepte,* exhibition catalogue, with texts by J. Herbig, M. Petzet and A. Sweite, Munich 1973; *Projekt 74: Aspekte internationaler Kunst am Anfang der 70er Jahe,* exhibition catalogue, with texts by Dieter Ronte, Evelyn Weiss, Marlis Gruterich and others, Cologne 1974; *Hanne Darboven: ein Monat, ein Jahr, ein Jahrhundert: Arbeiten von 1968 bis 1974,* exhibition catalogue, with text by Franz Meyer, Basle 1974; *Hanne Darboven: Een Maand, een Jaar, een Eeuw: werken van 1968 tot en met 1974,* exhibition catalogue, with text by Franz Meyer, Amsterdam 1975; *Hanne Darboven: For Jean-Paul Satre,* exhibition folder, New York 1976; *Hanne Darboven,* exhibition folder, New York 1978.

Whatever the function in which numbers crop up, they are at all times subordinated to definite ends. Economic ends, political, practical and sometimes even mystical ends. Because of this, in a bourgeois society such as ours, which is conditioned to accept the use value of any-and everything, the idea of a completely purpose-free, so to say frivolous, operation with numbers must seem decidedly nonsensical, if not indeed shocking and dangerous.

All this is relevant to Hanne Darboven, an artist who, in common with Joseph Beuys, the other great mythologue of the younger art world in Germany, impresses herself on the general consciousness ever more commandingly as one of the really challenging figures of the contemporary art world. Hanne Darboven takes the numeral at its word, as it were. She takes numbers as pure numbers, concretely: letters. She writes texts with numbers, and those texts have no more, and no other, content than numbers signify in a type-face. In her texts numbers do not represent—they present. They present themselves.

Herein lies the provocativeness of her work. Numbers are stripped bare in an orderly manner. They are relieved of the task of serving as a symbol for something exterior. In Hanne Darboven's artistic programme they retain also none of the almost mystical qualities which appear involuntarily when one is confronted by the vertiginous totalling up of numbers.

Their poetic qualities are equally little played-with. As for example the letter in the clutches of "concrete poetry". Gertrude Stein's pretty manifestation: "A rose is a rose is a rose" is not allowed in Hanne Darboven's work to be twisted back into a number is a number is a number and nothing more than a number. That would be concrete poetry. An analogous formation might rather read: "1 is 1 is 1" or "One is one is one" or even "One plus one is two ones". This hardly evokes associations.

Speech and the object of speech are identical. Hanne Darboven does not describe—she scribes.

Hanne Darboven came to numbers by way of geometrical drawing. In the mid 1960's she began to occupy herself with geometric constructions. These constructions were placed on millimetre graph paper. The finely-graven squares of the millimetre paper made a good reference structure for the graphic projections. Drawn construction and the structure of the paper always stand in a reciprocal relationship to each other.

Later on Hanne Darboven did without the diagrammatic exposition. Instead of this she created constructions from pure accumulations of numbers. For years she came to terms with the problems of the calendar in a sheer endless series. She produced a century calendar, in which every conceivable date is recorded. The date of birth of so-and-so, as well as the date of his death. The date of death of the actual user crops up side by side with the date of Shakespeare's death. Hanne Darboven transposed her calendar-sequences into drawings which were regulated according to a definite system. This system consisted of a code, which prevented the numerical quantities from developing towards infinity. At the same time the code was so chosen that the drawings should not forfeit their clarity. The solution offered a mathematical method which was founded on the insight that only the numbers from one to nine are pure numbers. Consequently several digits ranked one behind the other are not looked at as a homologous number, but as isolated quantities. In the mathematical process of cross-addition the single digits are added. Hence 71 produces 7 plus one which gives 8.

Because Hanne Darboven sets forth series of dates in her calendar drawings, instead of isolated individual dates, she succeeds in representing visually the course of time. Time is seen as a continual and inexorable advance. On account of this, it is striking that the passing of time is accomplished by virtue of the systematising of the series of dates as a circular movement.

Hanne Darboven, moreover, in an intelligent and illuminating way overcomes the old artists' problem of "Representation" and "Articulation." Art has settled this problem at least since the statement of Theo van Doesburg that nothing is more concrete than a line or a right angle. Hanne Darboven's drawings are concrete, because they concretise an abstract material—which is what numbers really are. "Representation" and "Articulation," that which is "depicted" via artistic articulation, just as speech itself is articulated, are no longer separated in her works.

The same is true of Hanne Darboven's recent drawings. These are handwritten translations of literary texts. She has translated Sartre's novel *Les Mots.* Through the exact transcription of a "text," a report composed of and expressed in words, she lends it a new perceptual dimension, behind which its original content dwindles into insignificance.

Hanne Darboven does not seek to illustrate; she tries to aim at a visualization of the essence of the text by graphical means. In this Hanne Darboven is a significant artist. She makes strange what is familiar, opens our eyes to its hidden strictures, or allows it to appear in a new light. And at the same time she incorporates her objects into her original universe, which, mystical though it may seem, is the universe of all men.

—Klaus Honnef

D'ARCANGELO, Allan.

American. Born in Buffalo, New York, 16 June 1930. Studied history and government, University of Buffalo, New York, 1948–53. B.A. 1953; also studied at City College of New York and New School for Social Research, New York, 1953–54; privately with Boris Lurie, New York, 1955–56; and at Mexico City College, under John Golding and Fernando Belain, 1957–59. Painter: lives and works in New York. Instructor, School of Visual Arts, New York 1963–68; Professor of Art, Cornell University, Ithaca, New York, 1968. Professor of Art, Brooklyn College, New York, since 1973; Graduate Instructor, School of Visual Arts, New York, since 1983. Artist-in-Residence, Aspen Institute, Colorado, 1965, 1967; Visiting Artist, Yale University, New Haven, Connecticut, 1969; University of Syracuse, New York, 1971; University of Alabama 1972; St. Cloud State University, Minnesota, 1972; University of Wisconsin 1972; Skowhegan School of Art, Maine, 1974; Memphis Academy of Art, 1975; Minneapolis College of Art and Design, 1977. Recipient: First Purchase Prize, University of Omaha, 1966; First Prize, First Annual Exhibition, Hofstra University, Hempstead, New York, 1967. Address: P.O. Box 33, Kenoza Lake, New York 12750, U.S.A.

Individual Exhibitions:

1961	Long Island University, New York
1963	Thibaud Gallery, New York
	Fischbach Gallery, New York
1964	Fischbach Gallery, New York
1965	Fischbach Gallery, New York
	Galerie Ileana Sonnabend, Paris
	Galerie Zwirner, Cologne
	Galerie Neuendorf, Hamburg
	Galerie Muller, Stuttgart
1966	Dwan Gallery, Los Angeles
1967	Fischbach Gallery, New York
	Württembergischer Kunstverein, Stuttgart
	Galerie Rolf Ricke, Kassel, West Germany
	The Highway Painter, Minami Gallery, Tokyo
1968	Franklin Siden Gallery, Detroit
	Lambert Galerie, Paris
1969	Fischbach Gallery, New york
1971	*Paintings 1963–70,* Institute of Contemporary Art, Philadelphia
	Paintings 1963–70, Albright-Knox Art Gallery, Buffalo, New York
1972	Marlborough Gallery, New York
1974	Schact Fine Art Center, Russell Sage College, Troy, New York
	Patricia Moore Gallery, Aspen, Colorado
	Hokin Gallery, Chicago
1975	Marlborough Gallery, New York
	Gallery Kingpitcher, Pittsburgh
1977	Contemporary Art Forms, Encino, California
	Fiterman Gallery, Minneapolis
1978	Neuberger Museum, State University of New York at Purchase
1979	Virginia Museum of Fine Arts, Richmond
	Art Package, Highland Park, Illinois

Selected Group Exhibitions:

1964	*American Landscape Painting,* Museum of Modern Art, New York (travelled to the *Spoleto Festival,* Italy)
1965	*The New American Realism,* Worcester Art Museum, Massachusetts
1966	*Sculpture and Painting Today,* Museum of Fine Arts, Boston
	2 Decades of American Painting, Museum of Modern Art, New York (toured Japan, Australia and India)
1967	*New Forms,* Stedelijk Museum, Amsterdam
	Environment USA: 1957–1967, at the *Bienal,* Sao Paulo
	Premio International, Instituto Torquato dei Tella, Buenos Aires
1976	*In Priase of Space: The Landscape in American Art,* Corcoran Gallery of Art, Washington, D.C.
	American Art Since 1945, Museum of Modern Art, New York
1977	*Private Images: Photograph by Painters,* Los Angeles County Museum of Art

Collections:

Museum of Modern Art, New York; Guggenheim Museum, New York; Whitney Museum, New York; New York University Art Collection; Albright-Knox Art Gallery, Buffalo, New York; Wadsworth Atheneum, Hartford, Connecticut; Hirshhorn Museum, Smithsonian Institution, Washington, D.C.; Wallraf-Richartz Museum, Cologne; Museum of Contemporary Art, Nagaoka, Japan.

Publications:

By D'ARCANGELO: articles—"Landscape" in *Art Now: New York* (New York), February 1969; interview in *Allan D'Arcangelo: Paintings 1963–1970,* Buffalo, New York 1971.

On D'ARCANGELO: books—*D'Arcangelo,* exhibition catalogue, with an essay by Nicolas Calas, Paris 1965; *The Highway Painter,* exhibition catalogue, with an introduction by Yoshiaki Tono, Tokyo 1967; *Art and the Age of Risk,* by Ni-

colas Calas, New York 1968; *Icons and Images of the 60's* by Nicolas Calas, New York 1971; *Allan D'Arcangelo: Paintings 1963–1970*, exhibition catalogue, Philadelphia 1971; *Allan D'Arcangelo*, exhibition catalogue, New York 1975; *Topics in American Art since 1945* by Lawrence Alloway, New York 1975; articles—"D'Arcangelo and the New Landscape" by David Antin in *Art and Literature* (Lausanne), Summer 1966; "Highway Culture: Man at the Wheel" by Lawrence Alloway in *Arts Magazine* (New York), February 1967; "The Subject at His Own Uneasiness" by Peter Schjeldahl in the *New York Times*. 4 November 1971; "Highway Cultures" by Gregory Battcock in *Art and Artists* (London), January 1972, "The Terror of a Wooden Match" by John Perreault in the *Village Voice* (New York), January 1972; review by Mona DaVinci in *Soho News* (New York), 23 January 1975; "Allan D'Arcangelo" by Jane Bell in *Arts Magazine* (New York) March 1975; "In Search of America" by Ralph Grier in the *Christian Science Monitor* (Boston), June 1976.

During the early 1960s, Allan D'Arcangelo was linked with Pop Art, and naturally so, considering pictures such as "Marilyn" (1962) and "Madonna and Child" (1963). "Marilyn" depicts an illustrative head and shoulders on which the facial features are marked by lettered slits to be "fitted" with the eyebrows, eyes, nose and mouth which appear off to the right in the composition. In "Madonna and Child," the featureless faces of Jackie Kennedy and Caroline are ringed with haloes, enough, for the period, to make their status as contemporary icons perfectly clear.

D'Arcangelo is better known for his pictures of highways and roadblocks made during the 1960's. The first of these pictured deep perspectival vistas in a simplified, flat plane, the view as seen from the driver's seat as one zooms along the seemingly never-ending American highway in most any state. Next came a series called "Barriers," in which cropped, abstracted imagery of road barriers were superimposed over the one-point perspectival highway vistas. These were a move further toward concern with abstract, two-dimensionality without negating the element culled from seen aspects of the American landscape. The series called "Constellations" (there are 120 in all) further abstracted the view of road barriers into perspectival, jutting patterns thrusting across the canvas against a white ground. The element of the seen is never obliterated and always primary in D'Arcangelo's dialectic, as amply evidenced in his return to highway imagery more directly in the 1970's.

For several years during that decade, D'Arcangelo slowed down his formerly prolific output. In the Spring of 1982, he had his first one-man exhibition in New York in five years. The new pictures are rather scenic landscape vistas, simplified and showing his ongoing concern with jutting perspectival space, now inhabited by flatly painted images of highway overpasses, a jet wing, grain field, electric lines. Indications of the American industrial scene seem more related to the hand-painted, pristine look of Charles Sheeler than to the Pop of, say, Roy Lichtenstein. In form, there is also a reminiscence of field painting in the simplicity and emblematic quality of these new works. Now, as before, the main element in D'Arcangelo's pictures is the post-abstraction search for, as he has put it, "icons that matter," monumental archetypes of the contemporary American expansive landscape highway.

—Barbara Cavaliere

d'ARMAGNAC, Ben.

Dutch. Born Bernard Jean Jacques d'Armagnac, in Antwerp, Belgium, 28 March 1940; later settled in the Netherlands. Studied painting at the Kunstnijverheidsschool, Amsterdam, 1960-63, and with the artist Anton Heyboer, Den Ilp, Netherlands, 1965. Married Joke Lingmont in 1967. Independent artist, working mostly with Gerrit Dekker, in Amsterdam, 1966-67, in Lewedorp, Zeeland, 1967-73, in Zuid-Limburg, 1973-77, and again in Amsterdam, 1977-78: first environmental works, 1972; first performance work, 1973. *Died* (in Amsterdam) *28 September 1978.*

Individual Exhibitions:

1966 Galerie de Sfinx, Amsterdam (with Gerrit Dekker)
1967 Galerie J34, Terneuzen, Netherlands (with Gerrit Dekker)
Zeeuws Museum, Middelburg, Netherlands (with Anton Heyboer and Gerrit Dekker)
1968 Municipal Gardens, Terneuzen, Netherlands (with Gerrit Dekker)
Galerie J34, Terneuzen, Netherlands (with Gerrit Dekker)
1969 Wide White Space, Antwerp (with Gerrit Dekker)
Galerie Mickery, Loenersloot, Netherlands (with Gerrit Dekker)
Galerie Mickery, Loenersloot, Netherlands
Stedelijk Museum, Schiedam, Netherlands (with Gerrit Dekker)
Galerie Mickery, Loenersloot, Netherlands (with Gerrit Dekker)
1970 Galerie Mickery, Loenersloot, Netherlands
1971 Galerie Mickery, Loenersloot, Netherlands
Opbouwhuis Bickerseiland, Amsterdam
1974 Bonnefantenmuseum, Maastricht, Netherlands
Galerie Seriaal, Amsterdam (with Gerrit Dekker)
Galerie De Appel, Amsterdam (with Gerrit Dekker)
1975 Galerie de Mangelgang, Groningen, Netherlands (with Gerrit Dekker)
Galerie de Mangelgang, Groningen, Netherlands
Galerie De Appel, Amsterdam
Gemeentemuseum, Roermond, Netherlands
1976 Jan Van Eyck Academie, Maastricht, Netherlands
Stedelijk Museum, Amsterdam
Universiteit van Maastricht, Netherlands
1977 Bonnefantenmuseum, Maastricht, Netherlands
Ontmoetin scentrum Schaapoord, Knokke, Belgium
1978 112 Greene Street, New York
1981 Stedelijk Museum, Amsterdam (retrospective; travelled to the Kunsthalle, Wilhelmshaven, Gemeentelijke van Reekumsgalerijk, Apeldoorn, and De Vleeshal, Middelburg, Netherlands)

Selected Group Exhibitions:

1968 *Jonge Zeeuws Talent*, Zeeuws Museum, Middelburg, Netherlands
1969 *Op losse schroeven*, Stedelijk Museum, Amsterdam
Prospekt '69, Städtische Kunsthalle, Dusseldorf
1970 *Binnen en Buiten het Kadar*, Stedelijk Museum, Amsterdam
1971 *Sonsbeek Buitende Perken*, Sonsbeek Park, Arnheim Netherlands (travelled to the Kunstkring de Waag, Almelo)
1974 *II Dutch Artists*, Fruit Market Gallery, Edinburgh
1975 *Biennale de Paris*, Musée d'Art Moderne de la Ville, Paris
1977 *K45: International Art Fair*, Kunstlerhaus, Vienna
Documenta, Kassel, West Germany
1978 *European Performance*, Brooklyn Museum, New York

Publications:

By d'ARMAGNAC: books—*Negen Dagboekbladen*, Deventer, Netherlands 1970; *d' Armagnac/Dekker 1968–1973*, with Gerrit Dekker, Amsterdam and Zurich 1973; *Twee Bladen*, Amsterdam 1974; *Een Blad*, Amsterdam 1975.

On d'ARMAGNAC: books—*Biennale de Paris*, exhibition catalogue, with texts by Georges Boudaille, Günter Metken, Lucy Lippard and Douglas Davis, Paris 1975; *Documenta 6, Band I: Malerei, Plastik, Performance*, exhibition catalogue, with texts by Arnold Bode, Günter Metken, Klaus Honnef and others, Kassel, West Germany 1977; *Ben d'Armagnac*, exhibition catalogue, with a foreword by Edy de Wilde, compiled by Jan Brand, Gerrit Dekker, Alexander van Grevenstein, Louwrien Wetjers and Erna Donker, Amsterdam 1981; articles—"Houtstapels van Ben d'Armagnac en Gerrit Dekker" by Piet van Daalen in *Gazet van Antwerpen*, 28 February 1969; "d'Armagnac en Dekker" by Louwrien Weijers in *Museumjournaal* (Amsterdam), August 1969; "Weer Beeldende Kunst in Mickery: Dramatisch Project van Ben d'Armagnac" by Tom Frenken in *Eindhovens Dagblad*, 2 December 1970; "Mentaliastraum I: Kunstler in Holland; by Johannes Gachnang in *Kunst Bulletin* (Zurich), May 1974; "d'Armagnac en Dekker" by Liesbeth Brand Corstius in *Museumjournaal* (Amsterdam), October 1974; "Ben d' Armagnac" by Antje van Graeveintz in *Dutch Art + Architecture Today* (Amsterdam), November 1978; "Ben d'Armagnac: Eentekstcollage" by Antje van Graevenitz in *Museumjournaal* (Amsterdam), December 1978.

In his short life, the performance-artist Ben d'Armagnac has made an intense and lasting impression on those people who have witnessed his work. The photographic documentation and videoregistrations that remain of his performances only give an idea of the dramatic, extremely personal but at the same time, strangely enough, objective expressiveness. The audience present felt as if in a mentally unavoidable grip. Retrospectively seen in the light of his sudden and unexpected death—he drowned—his last performance seems of an almost cruel character. During a full hour d'Armagnac lay on his back on the ground, outside of the Brooklyn Museum, with a powerful beam of cold water aimed at his heart.

Most of his performances consisted of a combination of physical and mental exhaustion that brought the artist in a sumblime and tranquil state. D'Armagnac has been one of those rare performers who, despite long and monotonous repetitive movements, imposed himself visually, whose concentrated determination radiated from his sober, white-clad figure.

Around 1965 his first teacher was the artist Anton Heyboer, an artist who proclaimed the unity of art and life. From this period dates a series of monumental etchings on paper on zinc on wood, with titles like *Making Connections, Equilibrium, The Protection of Joke*. At the present moment these impressive works are in the Bonnefantenmuseum, Maastricht.

Between 1967 and 1969 d'Armagnac lived in the quiet province of Zealand, away from artistic centres, together with his friend Gerrit Dekker and both their wives. With Dekker he built huge pieces of sculpture out of material that belonged to the local ambiance, like 'Chincilla Cages' and 'Oystersieves' used by breeders and cultivators from the villages. These improvised sculptures were not to live long.

In 1969 both artists developed for Ritsaert ten Cate's Galerie Mickery (Loenersloot) the *Project for a bathroom, bedroom, kitchen, diningroom, toilet and some non-specified spaces*. From 1973 to 1977 d'Armagnac lives and works in Maastricht, in the southern part of The Netherlands, a city that during these years has been a centre for media-oriented activities and performances, largely due to the Agora-studio and Jan van Eyck-academy. In his last years d'Armagnac was closely associated with the program of the Amsterdam-based Foundation De Appel.

—A. F. Wagemans

DAVIE, Alan.

British. Born in Grangemouth, Scotland, in 1920. Studied at the Edinburgh College of Art, 1937–40. Married Janet Gaul in 1947; daughter: Jane. Served in the Royal Artillery, 1941–46. Worked as a jazz musician, 1947; travelled extensively in Europe, 1947–49; worked as a jeweller, 1949–53; visited New York, 1956; Gregory Fellow, University of Leeds, 1956–59; Lecturer, Central School of Arts and Crafts, London, 1959–60; performed at public recital, Gimpel Fils Gallery and Tate Gallery, London:

first record issued, 1971; Member, Tony Oxley group: gave concerts and broadcasts, 1973–75; travelled in the West Indies, 1976; now lives in Hertfordshire and in St. Lucia, West Indies. Recipient: Guthrie Award, Royal Scottish Academy, Edinburgh, 1942; Prize, *Bienal,* Sao Paulo, 1953; Critics' Choice Award, London, 1956, 1958, 1960; Prix Guggenheim, Musée d' Art Moderne, Paris, 1956; First Prize, *International Graphics Exhibition,* Cracow, 1966; Saltine Award, Edinburgh, 1976. Honorary Royal Scottish Academician, 1976. C. B. E. (Commander, Order of the British Empire), 1972. Agent: Gimpel Fils, London. Address: Camels Studio, Rush Green, Hertford, Hertfordshire, England.

Alan Davie: *Magic Fountain No. 7*, 1987 Courtesy Gimpel Fils, London

Individual Exhibitions:

1946 Grant's Bookshop, Edinburgh
1948 *Art and Inspiration,* Galleria Michelangelo, Florence
The Forest, Galleria Sandri, Venice
1950 Gimpel Fils, London
1951 Gimpel Fils, London
1952 Gimpel Fils, London
1954 Gimpel Fils, London
1955 Gimpel Fils, London
1956 Catherine Viviano Gallery, New York
1957 Catherine Viviano Gallery, New York
1958 Wakefield City Art Gallery, Yorkshire (travelled to Whitechapel Art Gallery, London, and the Walker Art Gallery, Liverpool)
University of Nottingham
1960 Gimpel Fils, London
Galerie Charles Lienhard, Zurich
1961 Gimpel Fils, London
Galleria del Naviglio, Milan
Galerie Rive Droite, Paris
Martha Jackson Gallery, New York
Carnegie Institute, Pittsburgh
Esther Robles Gallery, Los Angeles
1962 FBA Gallery, London (travelled to the Stedelijk Museum, Amsterdam)
Carnegie Institute, Pittsburgh
Esther Robles Gallery, Los Angeles
Kunstnernes Hus, Oslo
1963 Galleria La Medusa, Rome
Gimpel Fils, London
Commercial Centre of the Brazilian Embassy, London
Kunsthalle, Berne
Kunsthalle, Baden-Baden, West Germany
1964 Gimpel and Hanover Galerie, Zurich
Crestline Galerie, Edinburgh
1965 Gimpel Fils, London
Martha Jackson Gallery, New York
Galerie Rudolf Zwirner, Cologne
Graves Art Gallery, Sheffield (toured the U.K.)
Court Gallery, Copenhagen
Galerie d'Aujourd'hu, Brussels
1966 Gimpel Fils, London
Commonwealth Institute Gallery, Edinburgh
Castle Museum, Norwich
Kunstkring, Rotterdam
Usher Gallery, Lincoln
Queen Square Gallery, Leeds
1967 Gimpel Fils, London
Gimpel and Hanover, Zurich
Galerie de France, Paris
Arts Club of Chicago (travelled to University of Minnesota, Minneapolis)
Kestner-Gesellschaft, Hannover
1968 Kunstverein, Dusseldorf
Galerie Overbeck-Gesellschaft, Lübeck
Richard Demarco Gallery, Edinburgh
Hudson Gallery, Detroit
1969 Gimpel Fils, London
Kunstmuseum, Basle
Galleria La Medusa, Rome
Gimpel Fils, New York
1970 Gimpel Fils, London
Galleria La Medusa, Rome
Galerie Stangl, Munich
1971 Gimpel Fils, London
Galerie Lambert Monet, Geneva
Gimpel and Hanover Galerie, Zurich
1972 Gimpel Gallery, New York
Gimpel and Weitzenhoffer Gallery, New York
Royal Scottish Academy Edinburgh (travelled to the Kunstverein, Brunswick, and the Bädischer Kunstverein, Karlsruhe, West Germany)
1973 Gimpel Fils, London
Galleria d'Arte Rotta, Genoa
1974 Gimpel Fils, London (travelled to Gimpel and Hanover Galerie, Zurich)
Gimpel and Weitzenhoffer Gallery, New York
Playhouse Gallery, Harlow, Essex
1975 Gimpel Fils, London
Galleria d'Arte Rotta, Milan
Galerie de France, Paris
Arte '75, Basle
Comskey Gallery, Los Angeles
1976 Galleria La Medusa Rome
Chateau de Lucens, Switzerland
Allan Rubiner Gallery, Royal Oak, Michigan
Hokin Gallery, Chicago
1977 Gimpel Fils, London
Zoumbarakis Galleria, Athens
Caronne Gallery, Fort Lauderdale, Florida
Le Demeure, Paris
Art Galerie and Museum, Aberdeen, Scotland
1978 Kunsthandel Brinkman, Amsterdam
Gimpel and Hanover Galerie, Zurich (travelled to the Galerie am Palmengarten, Frankfurt, and Gimpel Fils, London)
Maercklin Galerie, Stuttgart
Galerie Cour St. Pierre, Geneva
Lister Gallery, Perth. Western Australia (travelled to the Art of Man Gallery, Sydney, and the Ray Hughes Gallery, Brisbane)
1979 Aitken Dott, The Scottish Gallery, Edinburgh
Gimpel Fils, London
Galerie Ado, Bonheiden, Belgium
1980 Gimpel and Weitzenhoffer, New York
Gimpel and Hanover, Zurich
Lister Gallery, Perth, Western Australia
1981 Gimpel Fils, London
Galerie van Loe, Frankfurt
1982 Rosenberg Fine Art, Toronto
The Scottish Gallery, Edinburgh
Arcade Gallery, Harrogate, Yorkshire
Arts Centre, Hong Kong
Galerie de Raam, Breda, Netherlands
Gimpel Fils, at *FIAC 82,* Grand Palais, Paris
1983 Galerie de'Eendt, Amsterdam
Gimpel Fils, London
1984 Festival Gallery, Bath, Avon
Community Arts Centre, Windsor, Berkshire
Galerie Van Loe, Frankfurt
Bede Gallery, Jarrow, Durham
Loft Gallery, Ware, Hertfordshire

985 Galerie Apicella, Bonn
Gimpel Fils, London
Yares Gallery, Scottsdale, Arizona
986 Gimpel and Weitzenhoffer, New York
987 Gimpel Fils, London
Moray House Gallery, Edinburgh
Galerie Louis Carre, Paris
Gimpel Fils, at *FIAC 86*, Grand Palais, Paris

Selected Group Exhibitions:

950 *Aspects of British Art*, Institute of Contemporary Arts, London
958 *50 Ans d'Art Moderne*, Palais des Beaux-Arts, Brussels
960 *British Painting 1720–1960*, Pushkin Museum, Moscow (travelled to The Hermitage, Leningrad)
961 *Pittsburgh International*, Carnegie Institute, Pittsburgh
966 *International Graphics Exhibition*, Cracow
970 *British Painting and Sculpture 1960–1970*, National Gallery of Art, Washington, D.C.
973 *Hommage à Picasso*, Kestner Gesellschaft, Hannover
977 *British Painting 1952–1977*, Royal Academy of Art, London
985 *Recalling the Fifties*, Serpentine Gallery, London
987 *British Art in the 20th Century*, Royal Academy, London

Collections:

Tate Gallery, London; Victoria and Albert Museum, London, Stedelijk Museum, Amsterdam; Museum des 20. Jahrhunderts, Vienna; Museum of Modern Art, Tel Aviv; Museum of Modern Art, New York; Albright-Knox Art Gallery, Buffalo, New York; Carnegie Institute, Pittsburgh; Museum of Fine Arts, Boston.

Publications:

By DAVIE: book—*Alan Davie: Major Works of the Fifties*, exhibition catalogue, London 1987; articles—statement in *Art and Inspiration*, exhibition catalogue, Florence 1948; statement in *The Forest*, exhibition catalogue, Venice 1948; statement in *Statements: British Abstract Art in 1956*, London 1957; statement in *Notes by the Artists*, exhibition catalogue, London 1958; "Notes on Teaching" in *The Developing Process*, exhibition catalogue, London 1959; "Towards a New Definition of Art: Some Notes on Now Painting" in *New Departures* (London), April 1960; "Personal Thoughts" in *Times Educational Supplement* (London), June 1960; "I Confess" in *Visone Colore*, exhibition catalogue, Venice 1963.

On DAVIE: books—*Contemporary British Art* by Herbert Read, London 1951: *Space in Colour*, exhibition catalogue, by Patrick Heron, London 1953; *Private View* by Bryan Robertson, John Russell and Lord Snowdon, London 1965; *Alan Davie* by Alan Bowness, London 1967; *The Art Scene* by Barrie Stuart-Penrose, London 1967; *Alan DAvies*, exhibition catalogue, by Alan Bowness, London 1972; *Alan Davie*, catalogue with text by Dore Ashton, London 1984; *Alan Davie*, exhibition catalogue with essay by Jacques Roche-Villiers, Paris 1987.

Writing about Alan Davie's painting makes you feel like Sisyphus pushing that huge boulder up the mountain. Just when you think you have attained a certain understanding, something else catches your eye, and you are thrown off balance yet again. This is what is so fascinating and at the same time frustrating about Davie's art. In many ways his work is reminiscent of a jam session by the saxophonist John Surman: constant improvisation, then settling down on one particular theme, then suddenly changing tracks.

Davie has made up his own world of signs and symbols. Each viewer is bound to have varying interpretations. Various images remain firmly embedded in the mind—such as the highly defined scarab which represents resurrection, the ankh which symbolises life or royal authority; dragons, serpents and birds are also always present. The influence of early Christian art can clearly be seen, and Davie's admiration for Bosch, Brueghel and Uccello is also very clear.

Davie's style is wild, exuberant, free. He paints just as if he were gliding—swooping here and there finally reaching destination. Life is seen amid a flurry of colours: reds, mauves, pinks, greens and yellows go hand in hand in "Feathers for a Serpent" of 1963. In "Phantom in the Room" a wonderful vibrant red, pink and green room is set alight; the chessboard and hand of Fatima symbolise fate and the game of life.

Davie paints almost as if he were guided by some mysterious force. Some of his paintings give the impression that they were painted in a trance: images cascaded into his mind and he could not get them down quickly enough. In fact, Davie has said, "We must confront a painting empty and open-hearted"—but not completely empty, as when a Japanese monk enquired of his Zen master, "What would you advise if a man came to you with nothing." The master immediately replied: "Throw it away." Davie has also said that he practises art for enlightenment and that a picture "must happen in spite of me rather than because of me."

After long and meticulous preparation Davie puts on his painting boots and sets off into the canvas. He is not one of the self satisfied group who sits back and thinks that is another canvas finished. One senses that he worries endlessly and returns to past works—for him they are alive, still part of him, and it is this concern that gives the paintings their vitality. For Arp art was "a fruit grown on the tree of man." For Davie the fruit never stops growing.

There is no doubt that much of Davie's imagination and vision springs from his Celtic heritage. As one wanders about Scotland, one sees many of Davie's images, but they are usually seen against a dour grey backcloth. Davie has surrounded them with brilliant colour, which remain in the mind. "Like a bird I shall take up my colour and my brush, and I shall paint as the bird sings"—and so he does.

—Carrie Maurice

DAVIES, John.

British. Born in Cheshire, 14 July 1966. Studied painting at Hull and Manchester Colleges of Art, 1963–67; studied sculpture, Slade School of Fine Art, London, 1967–69; Gloucestershire College of Art and Design, Cheltenham (Sculpture Fellowship), 1969–70. Sculptor, London and Kent, since 1970, Recipient: Sainsbury Award, 1970. Agent: Marlborough Fine Art Ltd., London. Address: c/o Marlborough Fine Art (London) Ltd., 6 Albemarle Street, London WLX 4BY, England.

Individual Exhibitions:

1972 Whitechapel Art Gallery, London
1975 Whitechapel Art Gallery, London
1980 *Recent Sculpture and Drawings*. Marlborough Fine Art, London
1981 Kunstverein, Hamburg (travelled to the Wilhelm Lehmbruck Museum, Duisburg, and the Kunstverein, Karlsruhe, 1981–82)
1982 Ferens Art Gallery, Hull, Yorkshire
1984 Marlborough Fine Art, London
1985 Sainsbury Centre, University of East Anglia, Norwich, Norfolk

Selected Group Exhibitions:

1973 *Biennale des Jeunes*, Musée National d'Art Moderne, Paris
1974 *12 Views of Mankind*, MacRobert Centre, University of Stirling, Scotland
1976 *Biennale*, Venice
1977 *Documenta*, Kassel, West Germany
1979 *Europaische Realistische Plastik*, Kunsthalle, Bremen, West Germany
1981 *British Sculpture since 1900: Part II, 1950–1980*, Whitechapel Art Gallery, London
1982 *Aspects of British Art Today*, Metropolitan Museum of Art, Tokyo (toured Japan)
1984 *The British Art Show*, Museum and Art Gallery, Birmingham (and Ikon Gallery, Birmingham; toured Britain)

Collections:

Tate Gallery, London; Arts Council of Great Britain, London; Contemporary Arts Society, London; Sainsbury Centre for the Visual Arts, Norwich; Wigan Art Gallery, Lancashire; Ulster Museum, Belfast; Wilhelm Lehmbruck Museum, Duisburg; McCrory Corporation, New York; Queensland Museum, Brisbane, Australia.

Publications:

By DAVIES: article—discussion with Nicholas Wadley in *John Davies: Recent Sculpture and Drawings*, exhibition catalogue, London 1980.

On DAVIES: books—*John Davies: Recent Sculpture and Drawings*, exhibition catalogue, London 1980; articles—"A Show to be Seen" by Edward Lucie-Smith in the *Sunday Times* (London), 25 June 1972; "The Human Condition" by Robert Melville in *Architectural Review* (London), September 1972; "The Sculpture of John Davies" by Nicholas Wadley in *Art International* (Lugano, Switzerland), February 1980; "The Bald Facts" by Michael Shepherd in the *Sunday Telegraph* (London), 23 November 1980.

In his search to create 'something very real' John Davies soon found that mimeticism was not the answer: something, and often something drastic, had to be done to the figures in order to wrench them from the realm of art, from looking too much like sculpture and too little like human beings:

"I used to think that there was no limit to what I'd have to make the figures do to get something out of them, anything that extraordinary or novel, which—however strange it might have seemed—created something very real: making sense."

In an effort to secure this quality he placed 'devices', nose-bags or other kinds of masks or wire-mesh cones over his carefully modelled or life-cast heads. The attention required to by-pass the mask in order to 'read' the head better brings the face into sharper focus, making it more vivid than otherwise. This approach is closer to Francis Bacon's distorting of the sitter's features in an attempt to capture the truth than it is to a surrealist delight in the bizarre or shocking.

Since Davies found that the gaze was a key ingredient in eliciting the sense of animation and presence he desired, he sought to establish contact with the viewer by displaying these life-size heads on thin poles, at eye-level.

Recently he has eliminated the devices without losing the intense vitality. The heads have become tiny, often not more than a couple of inches high and the coloring less naturalistic, yet they are more potent. Given their size, the scrutiny normally accorded art objects does not reveal an excess of detail, like that found in a photograph: what is revealed is all that is given in just looking—the content of any ordinary glance.

In those works which contain life-size figures engaged in activities ranging from the extreme to the ordinary, Davies has sought a similar kind of reality:

"There is always a conflict for me between the qualities of made sculpture and what one might see on the street, but I strive to make the figures display the qualities of a human being rather than those of sculpture."

Yet the means by which this is achieved clearly belong to the realm of art. For example, the figures

John Davies: *Figures and Railings*, 1981

often have a frozen quality, but this is very different from that found in snap-shots. They seem much closer to Egyptian sculpture where movement is conveyed through stasis. As one concentrates on these figures the props and other devices which accompany them gradually dissolve and the figures take on the immediacy and immutability of ancient sculpture. They are never merely genre or anecdotal works.

—Lynne Cooke

DAVIS, Douglas (Matthew).

American. Born in Washington, D.C., 11 April 1933. Studied at the Abbott Art School, Washington, D.C., 1948–50; American University, Washington, D.C., 1952–56, B.A. 1956; Rutgers University, New Brunswick, New Jersey, 1956–58, M.A. 1958. Married Mary Virginia Miller (divorced, 1967); Children: Laura and Mary; married the art critic Jane Bell in 1970. Painter until 1969; since then has concentrated on video-performance work. Teaching Fellow in English, Douglass College, 1957–60; freelance editor and writer, 1961–67; Art Critic, *National Observer*, Silver Spring, Maryland, 1965–69; Contributing Editor, *Art in America*, New York, 1968–70; Art Critic, *Newsweek*, New York, 1970–76 (now Senior Writer), Visiting Artist in Video, Corcoran Gallery, Washington, D.C., 1970–71; Artist-in-Residence, Television Laboratory, WNET-TV, New York, 1972; Visiting Artist, Northwood Experimental Art Institute, Dallas, 1972. Artistic Director, International Network for the Arts. Recipient: New York State Council on the Arts grant, 1970; National Endowment for the Arts grant, 1971, 1975; DAAD Exchange Fellowship, Berlin, 1977; National Endowment for the Arts grant, Washington, D.C., 1981. Agents: Galleria Forma, Largo San Giuseppe 18, 16121 Genoa, Italy; Ronald Feldman Fine Arts, 33 East 74th Street, New York, New York 109012; and Electronic Arts Intermix, 100 Fifth Avenue, New York, New York 10011. Address: 80 Wooster Street, New York, New York 10012, U.S.A.

Individual Exhibitions:

1970 Reese Palley Gallery, New York
1972 *Events, Drawings, Objects, Videotapes 1967–72*, Everson Museum of Art Syracuse, New York
1973 DeSaisset Museum, University of Santa Clara, California
1975 *Videotapes*, San Francisco Museum of Modern Art
1976 *3 Silent and Secret Acts*, The Kitchen Center for Video and Music, New York
1977 *4 Places, 2 Figures, 1 Ghost*, Whitney Museum, New York
1978 *Arbeiten 1970–77*, Neue Berliner Kunstverein and Kunstlerhaus Bethanien, Berlin (travelled to Basel and Essen)
1979 *Drawings, Objects and Soundboxes*, PS 1, New York
1980 *Double Entendre*, Whitney Museum, New York (objects and drawings, accompanied by satellite telecast between the Whitney and the Centre Georges Pompidou, Paris, broadcast on WNYC-TV and via satellite to National Public Radio Stations in the United States)
1981 *The Wizard of Malta and The Moving Obscura* (3-screen film and room-sized installation), Ronald Feldman Fine Arts, New York
1982 *Video, Objects, Graphics*, Museum Sztuki, Lodz, Poland (retrospective)
1986 Guggenheim Museum, New York

Selected Group Exhibitions:

1971 *10 Videotape Performances*, Finch College Museum of Contemporary Art, New York
1974 *L'Art Video*, Musée de l'Art Moderne de la Ville de Paris
1975 *Video Art*, Institute of Contemporary Art, Philadelphia
Projected Video, Whitney Museum, New York
Questions: Moscow-NY-NY-Moscow, San Francisco Museum of Modern Art
Bodyworks, Museum of Contemporary Art, Chicago
1976 *Biennale*, Venice
1977 *Documenta*, Kassel, West Germany (installation and satellite telecast, "The Last 9 Minutes," with Nam June Paik and Joseph Beuys, broadcast to 25 countries)
1982 *Counterparts: Form and Emotion in Photography*, Metropolitan Museum of Art, New York

Collections:

Metropolitan Museum of Art, New York; Everson Museum of Art, Syracuse, New York; DeSaisset Museum, University of Santa Clara, California; Museo de Arte Contemporaneo, Caracas; Wallraf-Richartz Museum, Cologne; Museum Sztuki, Lodz, Poland; Centre Georges Pompidou, Paris

Publications:

By DAVIS: books—*Art and the Future*, New York and Lon-

don 1973, Cologne 1975; *Fragments for a New Art of the 70's*, with Robert Stefanotty, Los Angeles 1975; *Artculture: Essays on the Post-Modern*, New York 1977; *Photography as Fine Art*, New York 1983; articles—numerous critical essays in the *National Observer, Art in America*, and particularly *Newsweek* (since 1970), and "For a New Esthetic" in *American Scholar* (Washington, D.C.), March/April 1966; "Media Art Media" in *Arts Magazine* (New York), April 1972; "A Conversation with Douglas Davis," with Marc Sapporta, in *Information and Documents* (Paris), May 1973; "Filmgoing/Videogoing: Making Distinctions" in *American Film Institute Journal* (Washington, D.C.), May 1973; "What Is content? Notes Toward an Answer" in *Artforum* (New York), October 1973; "Time! Time! Time! The Context of Immediacy" in the *Museum of Modern Art Newsletter* (New York), January 1974; "Interview with Douglas Davis," with David Ross, in *Flash Art* (Milan), May 1975; "Artpolitics: Thoughts Against the Prevailing Fantasies" in the *New York Arts Journal*, May 1975; "Video in the Mid-70's: Prelude to an End/Future" in *Video Art*, edited by Beryl Korot and Ira Schneider, New York 1976; "The Idea of a 21st Century Museum" in *Art Journal of the College Art Association* (New York), January 1976; "The Size of Non-Size" in *Art-forum* (New York), December 1976; "The End of Video: Black Death/White Vapor" in *Video End*, edited by Horst Gerhard Haberl, Graz, Austria 1976; "Die Euro American Generation" in *Favored-Forever?*, edited by Werner Hofer, Dusseldorf 1976; "Post-Modern Form: Stories Real and Imagined/Toward a Theory" in the *New York Arts Journal*, January/February 1978; "The Post-Modernist Dilemma," dialogue with Suzi Gablik, in the *Village Voice* (New York), 27 March 1978, 3 April 1978 and 10 April 1978; "How to Make Love to Your Television Set" in the *New York Arts Journal*, May/June 1979; "Post Post-Art Where Do We Go from Here?" in the *Village Voice* (New York), 25 June 1979; "Post Post-Art II: Symbolismo, Come Home" in the *Village Voice* (New York), 13 August 1979; "Post Post-Art III: Symbolismo Meets the Faerie Queen" in the *Village Voice* (New York), 17 December 1979; "Dialogue with David Schapiro" in the *New York Arts Journal*, February 1980; "Post-Everything" in *Art in America* (New York), February 1980; "After Photography" in the *Village Voice* (New York), February 1981; "Post-Performance ISM" in *Artforum* (New York), October 1981.

On DAVIS: books—*Douglas Davis: Events, Drawings, Objects, Videotapes 1967–72*, exhibition catalogue, by James Harithes, Nam June Paik and David Rose, Syracuse, New York 1972; *The Videotapes of Douglas Davis* by John Hanhardt, New York 1977; *Video Art*, edited by Beryl Korot and Ira Schneider, New York 1977; *Douglas Davis: Arbeiten 1970–77*, exhibition catalogue, with essays by Wulf Herzogenrath, Wieland Schmied and Ann Sargent-Wooster, Berlin 1978; *Douglas Davis: Video, Objects, Graphics*, with essays by Ryszard Stanislawski, Ursula Czartoryska, Irving Sandler, and John G. Hanhardt, Lodz, Poland 1982; articles—"Explorations in Video" by Gregory Battcock in *Art and Artists* (London), February 1973; "The Davis tapes" by Alfred Frankenstein in the *San Francisco Chronicle*, 6 October 1973; "Douglas Davis: Video Against Video" by David Ross in *Arts Magazine* (New York), January 1974; "Douglas Davis" by Walter Robinson in *Art-Rite* (New York), Autumn 1974; "Fragments for a New Art of the 70's" by Pierre Restany in *Domus* (Milan), December 1975; "Douglas Davis" by Cynthia Nadelman in *Artnews* (New York), May 1980; "Douglas Davis" by Jean-Paul Fargier in *Art Press* (Paris), July 1981.

The medium (video) is at once of no importance and of the greatest importance. It is simply the latest tool to be adopted by contemporary art, which has been since Duchamp reaching for new means of expression. Video is thus like film, light, sound, movement, linguistics. But it is far more profound in its implication than these tools because it can communicate instantly, everywhere. And it is related to the social-power complex, very directly. Art in a gallery or a museum, or even in a film theatre, is confined. Art on television is loose, free, and dangerous.

I think that the central problems that are attached to my work are two: 1) how to communicate on a very intense, private and personal level through a public medium (videotape is public whether broadcast or seen in a gallery); and 2) how to engage in a two-way dialogue with the eye and the mind of the viewer that goes beyond Duchamp—who simply said first that art needs the viewer to complete itself.

From these two points, it is clear that the overall direction in my work is "against video" in the sense that I am assaulting what the medium *is* and *has been* (that is, bland, stupid, silly, and stiff). Video is simply the latest step in a process that is destroying the spectator ritual in art—the going-out to the temple to see it—but by no means the last. The next step is to get rid of the intervening structure, the cameras, the monitors, and telecasting circuitry.

My first thought about the television set was to activate it, as a link in a live sending as well as receiving link. We are almost blind to the two-way nature of television. Bertold Brecht wrote an astounding essay, "Theory of Radio," in 1929. He correctly pointed out that the decision to manufacture radio sets as receivers only was a political decision, not an economic one. The same is true of television. It is a conscious (and subconscious) decision that renders it one way. My attempt was and is to inject two-way metaphors—via live telecasts—into our thinking process. All my early two-way telecasts were structural invasions, then, very different from work I am doing now, though I hope that the two kinds of investigation will finally merge.

I don't even think of video as a medium anymore, but as an extension of myself, like drawing or speaking. The ideas expressed in my prints, drawings, performances and writings are all present in my work in television—and vice-versa.

Unless you use the camera as you use your hand, or a pencil—poking it wherever you want it to poke—the work will never come out like a drawing can, that is, close to your primal self. Art is a two-way process for me, whether it is printmaking, performance, drawing or video—knowing that I am involved in the evolution of a deeper, more diversified system of communication, between myself and the world and back.

—Douglas Davis

Television is the most influential mass medium of the modern world and a major icon of our culture. It has also managed to isolate and pacify a great majority of its target markets as a direct result of its de facto one-way nature. On the other hand, television has motivated a number of American, Asian and European visual artists, poets and writers towards the redevelopment of the video form and the re-structuring of the world information network. Douglas Davis is one of these contemporary artists whose refined ideas and philosophy has changed the face of mass communications.

Important to the understanding of Davis' work is the artistic and social climate out of which he developed. He was born and raised in Washington, D.C., a city whose informational system involves global communication. His videotaping began in 1970 after he moved to New York City where media-orientation is thoroughly insular. These tapes emerged from the City's increasingly open-minded techniques. His first tape, "Look Out" (1970), documented exchanges with large numbers of people he met on the streets for 24 hours. In 1971 he produced "Electronic Hokkadim," in which thousands of viewers participated in a telephone to television direct access experiment, and "Talk-Out!" an open input dialogue allowing the artist both to send and receive messages from the viewing public.

Davis regarded the television as an archetypal form projecting light radiation in such a way as to reach primary levels of communication. At the same time what interested him about the screen is that it constitutes a barrier between him and the viewer, between his image in the television space and the viewer sitting in front of the screen. Consequently we see the theme "Breaking the Barrier" recurring in his work whether it be the television screen, the Iron Curtain, or Outer Space. Sometimes the barrier is the difficulty of communication itself. In making these videotapes, Davis' goal has been to relate, interpenetrate, juxtapose, and oppose different spaces at different times in a different media.

His performances explore the illusionistic properties of video space and time both by recording actions in different locations and by manipulating stored (taped) and real (live) time. Further, they offer the process of broadcast and reception as a tactile, visual and aural experience that the viewer completes before his own television set in the perception of the work. The television becomes the viewer's medium of self-awareness. For instance, in the "Austrian Tapes" (1974) Davis asks each viewer: "Please come to the television set in front of you. Place your hands against my hands. Think about our touching each other." The viewer is then asked to touch cheeks, lips, and so on, bringing him or her to the screen. In another work Davis succeeds in arranging a conversation between his own "live" person and his own "pre-recorded" person (a ghost).

Again in 1981 he treated the public perception of broadcast and reception by exploiting the ambiguities and myths of live transmission when he carried out a "long-distance" dialogue with a female performer speaking from the Centre Pompidou in France. The work entitled "Double Entendre: Two Sites Two Times (for Roland Barthes)" incorporated live and taped audio and video linked by satellite. The dia-

Douglas Davis: *Three Silent and Secret Acts*, performance/video, New York, 1976

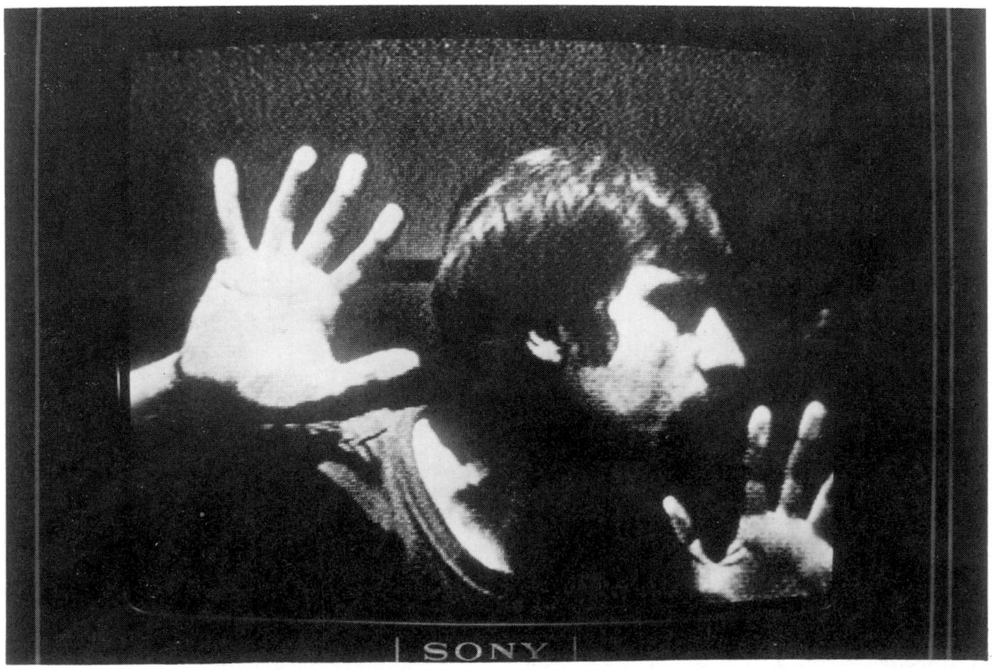

logue plied with the duality of the sexes and sites, with the difference in language, with radio and television, and with living persons. Both the paradoxes and the ultimate achieving of unity in spite of the distance constitutes the strength of the performance. The point at which the two merge summarizes Davis' concern and vision for re-shaping the television medium, as they declare in their own and each other's language: "Male and female, left and right, New York and Paris seem to become one figure, one line." By actively engaging the viewer in the work, by utilizing the ambiguity and complexity of real-time transmission, and lastly, by layering images and sound tracks, Davis' work becomes a multiple discourse, an unfolding narrative in which the self of the artist is expanded in the collective presence of the viewers.

—Carrie Barker

DAVIS, Gene.

American. Born in Washington, D.C., 22 August 1920. Educated at the University of Maryland, College Park, 1938-40; Wilson Teacher's College, Washington, D.C., 1941. Married Florence Coulson in 1960. White House correspondent, Transradio Press, Washington, D.C., 1942–52; worked as copy boy for the *New York Times*, reporter for United Press International, Jacksonville, Florida, Congressional correspondent for Newhouse Newspapers, and as a sports writer for the *Washington Daily News*, 1952–66. Assistant Professor, Corcoran Gallery School of Art, Washington, D.C., 1967–68, 1970–85; Instructor in Painting, American University, Washington, D.C., 1968–70; Artist-in-Residence, Skidmore College, Saratoga Springs, New York, Summer 1969; Artist-in-Residence, University of Virginia, Charlottesville, 1972. Recipient: Bronze Medal, *Biennial Exhibition of American Painting*, Corcoran Gallery of Art, Washington, D.C., 1965; National Endowment for the Arts grant, 1967; Guggenheim Fellowship, 1974–75. Agent: Charles Cowles Gallery, 420 West Broadway, New York, New York 10012. *Died* (in Washington, D.C.) *6 April 1985.*

Individual Exhibitions:

1952 Dupont Theatre Gallery, Washington, D.C.
1953 Catholic University, Washington, D.C.
1955 American University, Washington, D.C.
1956 Jefferson Place Gallery, Washington, D.C.
1961 Jefferson Place Gallery, Washington, D.C.
1963 Jefferson Place Gallery, Washington, D.C.
Poindexter Gallery, New York
1964 Corcoran Gallery of Art, Washington, D.C.
1965 Poindexter Gallery, New York
1966 Poindexter Gallery, New York
Hofstra University, Hempstead, New York
1967 Poindexter Gallery, New York
Jefferson Place Gallery, Washington, D.C.
Massachusetts Institute of Technology, Cambridge
Galerie Ricke, Cologne
Art Center, Des Moines, Iowa
Fischbach Gallery, New York (and yearly until 1975)
1968 Corcoran Gallery of Art, Washington, D.C.
Museum of Art, San Francisco
Washington Gallery of Modern Art, Washington, D.C.
Jewish Museum, New York
Henri Gallery, Washington, D.C.
Kunstmarkt 68, Cologne
1969 Atelier Chapman Kelley, Dallas
Henri Gallery, Washington, D.C.
Axiom Gallery, London
Boymans Museum, Rotterdam
Yale University, New Haven, Connecticut
1970 Early Paintings 1950–60, Corcoran Gallery, Washington, D.C.
Fendrick Gallery, Washington, D.C.
Nova Scotia College of Art, Halifax
1970 Annamaria Verna Galerie, Zurich
Dunkelman Gallery, Toronto
1972 Dunkelman Gallery, Toronto
J. L. Hudson Gallery, Detroit
Museum of Fine Arts, University of Utah, Logan
Friends of Contemporary Art, Denver
Joslyn Art Museum, Omaha, Nebraska
Max Protetch Gallery, Washington, D.C.
1973 Michael Berger Gallery, Pittsburgh
Quay Gallery, San Francisco
1974 New Gallery, Cleveland
Tibor de Nagy Gallery, Houston
1975 Reed College, Portland, Oregon
1976 Harcus-Krakow Gallery, Boston
1977 Corcoran Gallery of Art, Washington, D.C.
Fischbach Gallery, New York
Max Protetch Gallery, Washington, D.C.
Paris Art Fair
1978 Corcoran Gallery of Art, Washington, D.C.
Fischbach Gallery, New York
Walker Art Center, Minneapolis
Dayton Art Institute, Ohio
Protetch-McIntosh Gallery, Washington, D.C.
1979 Droll-Kolbert Gallery, New York
1980 Droll-Kolbert Gallery, New York
Protetch-McIntosh Gallery, Washington, D.C.
Arts Gallery, Baltimore, Maryland
1981 Frank Kolbert Gallery, New York
Feldman Galleries, Sarasota, Florida
McIntosh/Drysdale Gallery, Washington, D.C.
1982 Charles Cowles Gallery, New York
Brooklyn Museum, New York
1983 Middendorf/Lane Gallery, Washington, D.C.
Delaware Art Museum, Wilmington
Washington Project for the Arts, Washington, D.C.
1984 Charles Cowles Gallery, New York
U.M.K.C. Gallery of Art, Kansas City, Missouri
Middendorf Gallery, Washington, D.C.
Charles Cowles Gallery, New York
1986 Charles Cowles Gallery, New York
1987 National Museum of American Art, Washington, D.C. (memorial exhibition)

Selected Group Exhibitions:

1967 *The 60's*, Museum of Modern Art, New York
1971 *The Structure of Color*, Whitney Museum, New York

Gene Davis: *Dr. Peppercorn*, 1967

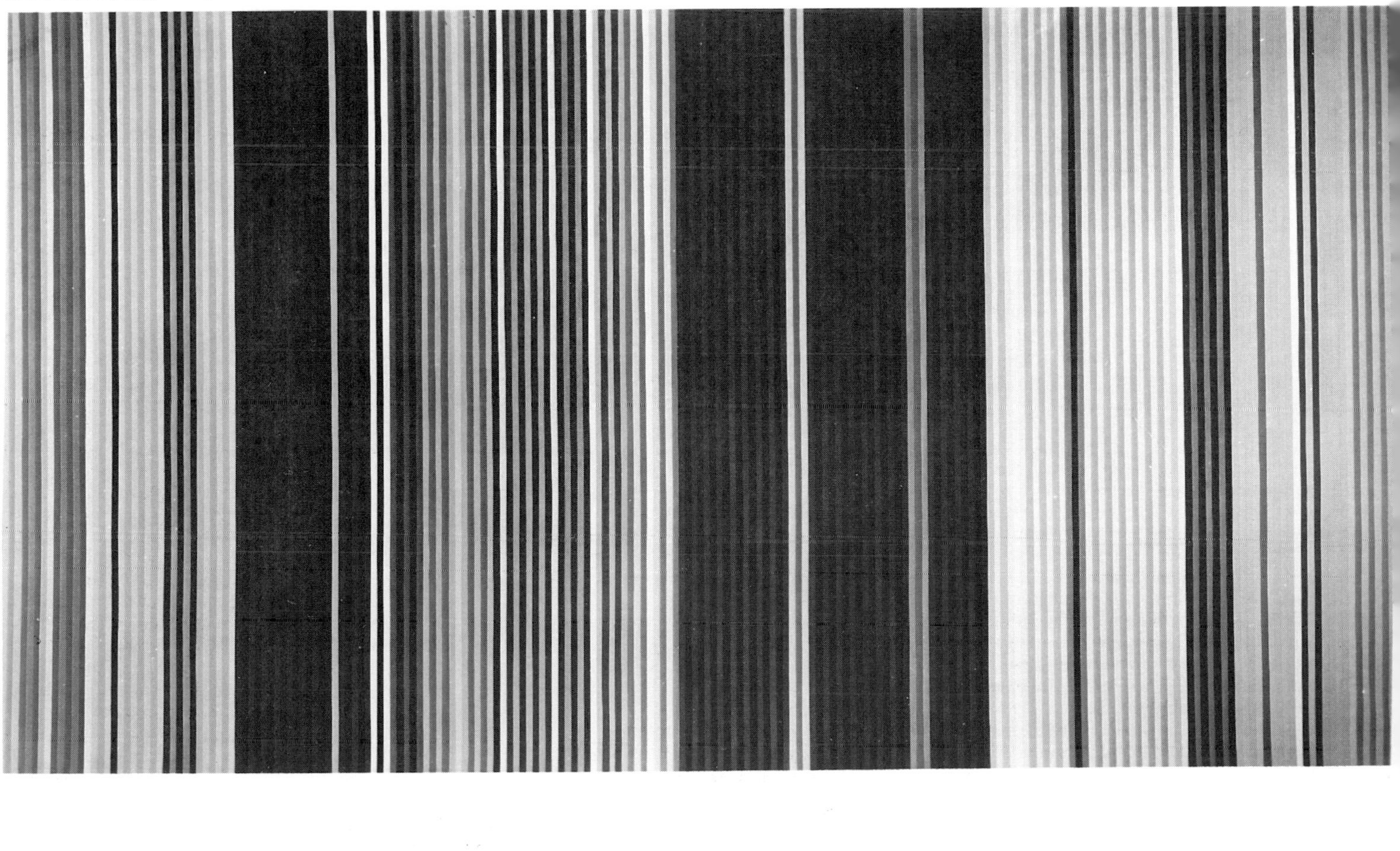

1974 *Within the Decade*, Guggenheim Museum, New York
1975 *34th Biennial of American Painting*, Corcoran Gallery of Art, Washington, D.C.
1977 *Summer Exhibition of the Permanent Collection*, Guggenheim Museum, New York
1979 *Selections from the Permanent Collection*, Museum of Modern Art, New York
1980 *American Art 1900-1980*, Guggenheim Museum, New York
1982 *Thirty Painters: Given and Promised*, Metropolitan Museum of Art, New York
1984 *Generations of the Washington Color School*, George Washington University, Washington, D.C.
1986 *The Window in Twentieth Century Art*, Neuberger Museum, State University of New York, Purchase

Collections:

Museum of Modern Art, New York; Whitney Museum, New York; Metropolitan Museum of Art, New York; Guggenheim Museum, New York; Albright-Knox Art Gallery, Buffalo, New York; National Gallery of Art, Washington, D.C.; Hirshhorn Museum, Washington, D.C., Corcoran Gallery, Washington, D.C.; Art Institute of Chicago; Walker Art Center, Minneapolis; Tate Gallery, London.

Publications:

By DAVIS: articles—"Preoccupation with Colour: Conversations with Gene Davis and Albert Stadler" by Gene Baro in *Studio International* (London), November 1967; "Statement by the Artist" in *Art Now* (New York), February 1970; "A Conversation with Gene Davis" by Barbara Rose in *Artforum* (New York), March 1971; "Random Thoughts on Art" in *Art International* (Lugano, Switzerland), November 1971; "Gene Davis on Gene Davis," in collaboration with Donald Wall, in *Art in America* (New York), May 1973; "Gene Davis and the Stripe as Subject Matter," interview with Walter Hopps, in *Art News* (New York), February 1975; "Painter's Reply" in *Artforum* (New York), September 1975; "Gorky Taught Me That—A Remembrance of Arshile Gorky" in *Art Magazine* (New York), March 1976; "Starting Out in the 50's" in *Art in America* (New York), July/August 1978; interview, with David Tannous, in *Art in America* (New York), July/August 1978; "Of Stripes on Canvas: A Conversation with Gene Davis" by Jean Lawlor Cohen in the *Washington Star* (Washington, D.C.), 17 December 1978; "An Interview with Gene Davis" by Mary Swift in *Washington Review* (Washington, D.C.), December/January 1979/80; interview, with Percy North, in *Abstractions from the Phillips Collection*, exhibition catalogue, Fairfax, Virginia 1983.

On DAVIS: books—*Gene Davis: New Paintings and Drawings*, exhibition catalogue with essay by Tom Haulik, Baltimore 1980; *Gene Davis Drawings* by Gene Baro, New York 1982; *Gene Davis* by Steven W. Naifeh, New York 1982; *Gene Davis: The Random and the Ordered*, exhibition catalogue, with essay by Pinky Kase, Kansas City 1984; *Gene Davis*, exhibition catalogue with essay by Jacquelyn Days Serwer, Washington, D.C. 1987; articles—"Gene Davis" by Ralph Pomeroy in *Arts Magazine* (New York), March 1970; "Gene Davis: New paintings" by Donald Wall in *Arts Magazine* New York), "Gene Davis: The Drawn Image" by Gene Baro in *Arts Magazine* (New York), September/October 1976; "Gene Davis at the Corcoran and the Protetch" by Davis Tannous in *Art in America* (New York), May/June 1977; "Gene Davis: A Review" by Norman Turner in *Arts Magazine* (New York), September 1977; "Art: New Drawings by Gene Davis" by Hilton Kramer in the *New York Times*, 9 March 1979; "Classical Shoppers" by William Zimmer in *The Soho Weekly News* (New York), 15 March 1979; "Out of Left Field" by John Ashbery in *New York Magazine*, 2 April 1979; "Single-Idea Art, Singularly Filmed" by Benjamin Forgey in *Washington Star News* (Washington, D.C.), 6 January 1980.

As an artist renowned for his majestic paintings of stripes, Gene Davis has left an impressive legacy of works, including early abstract expressionist oils, collages, gestural drawings, and prints. In the early 1960's, Davis emerged as a prominent member of the Washington Color School, whose artists explored painting's basic elements and the technique of straining raw canvas with thin washes of color. Like many painters of his generation, Davis fathomed the essential properties of color and space as the subject, form, and content of his work.

In creating his broad repertoire of stripe paintings, Davis likened himself to a jazz musician, "playing by eye". He felt the music of the stripes and painted them intuitively. Davis' complex and expansive investigation of the stripe format yielded numerous series, among which are hard-edge, free-hand or "bleed" stripes and broad, narrow, or pin-striped bands. Intrigued by the impact of scale, Davis challenged established perceptions of architectural space by creating minuscule "micro" paintings in 1967, countered by two monumental "street" paintings, one in front of the Philadelphia Museum in 1977 and the other at New York's Artpark in 1979. He also designed a pattern of colored tubes of water for a solar wall at the College of William and Mary's Muscarelle Museum in Williamsburg, Virginia. In the early 1980's, Davis exhibited a provocative series of large black silhouette self-portrait heads (in conjunction with "micro" replicas of the same) and offered a new investigation of interval in contrast with his brilliant stripe palette.

Davis' remarkable versatility is highlighted by a vast number of works on paper (ink, collage, colored pencil, pastel, and crayon), which were produced as drawings in themselves rather than painting studies. Among his late works are a collaborative project in 1983 which juxtaposes a series of his drawings with those of children, and a number of drawings which combine his pattern of stripes with pictographs, symbols, and collage, bringing together all the components of his artistic expression.

—Percy North

DAVIS, John.

Australian. Born in Ballarat, Victoria, in 1936. Educated at Melbourne State College, Caulfield Institute of Technology, Melbourne University, and Royal Melbourne Institute of Technology, 1955-57; studied sculpture, under Lenton Parr and Vincent Jomantis, R. M. I. T., 1963-66. Married Shirley Heberle in 1961; children: Penelope and Martin. Lives and works in Victoria. Instructor in Art, Queenscliff High School, 1958; instructor in Woodcraft, Numurkah High School, 1959-60; instructor in Art, Mildura High School, 1961-62; instructor, Highett High School, 1963-66; Lecturer in 3D Design and Sculpture, Caulfield Institute of Technology, 1967-71; Tutor in Sculpture, Summer School, Monash University, 1969-70; Lecturer in Charge of Sculpture and 3D Design, Prahan College of Advanced Education, 1973-80; Senior lecturer in charge of sculpture, 1975-80, and Co-ordinator of Post-graduate Studies, Victorian College of the Arts, 1981. Recipient: Comalco Invitation Award, Melbourne, 1970. Agents: Art Projects, 566 Lonsdale Street, Melbourne; Watters Gallery, 109 Riley Street, East Sydney. Address: 41 Crisp Street, Hampton, Victoria 3188, Australia.

Individual Exhibitions:

1969 Strines Gallery, Melbourne
1971 Watters Gallery, Sydney
1972 Gallery One Eleven, Melbourne
1974 Pinacotheca Gallery, Melbourne
C. A. S. Gallery, Adelaide
1977 Watters Gallery, Sydney
1978 National Gallery of Victoria, Melbourne
Art Gallery of New South Wales, Sydney
1979 Art Projects, Melbourne
Watters Gallery, Sydney
1980 Institute of Modern Art, Brisbane
Wollongong City Gallery, New South Wales
Q Space Annex, Brisbane
1981 Art Projects, Melbourne
Watters Gallery, Sydney
1984 Cettenball Gallery, Wolverhampton, Staffordshire

Selected Group Exhibitions:

1970 *Comalco Invitation Sculpture Competition*, Melbourne
1973 *Recent Australian Art*, Art Gallery of New South Wales, Sydney
1976 *Biennale of Sydney*
1978 *4th Indian Triennial*, New Delhi
Biennale, Venice
1981 *Landscape Art: Two-way reaction*, Australian National Gallery, Canberra
1st Australian Sculpture Triennial, Latrobe University, Melbourne
Perspecta '81, Art Gallery of New south Wales, Sydney
Relics and Rituals, National Gallery of Victoria, Melbourne
Patrick White's Choice, Art Gallery of New South Wales, Sydney

Collections:

Australian National Gallery, Canberra; Art Gallery of New South Wales, Sydney; Shepparton City Art Gallery, Victoria; Geelong City Art Gallery, Victoria; Mildura City Art Gallery, Victoria; National Gallery of Victoria, Melbourne; Hobart Art Gallery, Tasmania; Brisbane Art Gallery; Art Gallery of Western Australia, Perth; Wollongong City Art Gallery, New South Wales.

Publications:

On DAVIS: books—*Place*, exhibition catalogue, by Noel Hutchison, Melbourne 1975; *Skira Annual Special Issue 1970-1980*, Geneva 1980; articles—article by Elwyn Lynn in *Art International* (Lugano, Switzerland), July 1977; "Quadrant" in the *Venice Biennale*, exhibition catalogue, Venice 1978; "The Venice Biennale" by Henry Martin in *Art International* (Lugano, Switzerland), October 1978; article by Elwyn Lynn in *Art International* (Lugano, Switzerland), vol. XXLL/5-6, 1978; "Report from Australia" by Suzi Gablik in *Art in America* (New York), "Mildura Rides Again" by Graeme Sturgeon in *Art and Australia* (Sydney), Summer 1981; "Report from Australia, part 1, by Suzi Gablik in *Art and Australia* (Sydney), Autumn 1981; "In" in *Exchange of Contemporary Art* (Tokyo), December 1981.

A Sense of Place

In 1976 I rediscovered an informal education in the Australian Bush denied to me through urbanization and formal education. It is as relevant to my understanding of what it is to be an Australian in 1982 as is my interpretation of European and Aboriginal histories. In other words, I have attempted to establish within myself a sense of place and of time, eventually transferring this into the work.

And like all people, I am bound to carry certain aspects of history about with me. In my response to the impulse to make art, I refer to this consciously and subconsciously so that whatever evolves in the "work space" is somehow an amalgamation of that which is ancient and that which is a new experience.

The beginning is in the tying of two twigs. Then it takes its own direction, full of inconsistencies, contradictions, ambiguities and alliances, moving as nature does; or how Australia country towns eventuate; or how themes in music or poetry evolve into metaphor. Each piece is part of a larger on-going work, a specific and at the same time general occurrence, a mass of detail demanding close scrutiny because of its close approximation and juxtaposing; it demands that the viewer step back to encompass 'the view'.

Like all things in nature, it is fragile and subject to easy destruction; each part is dependent on another for its identity and difference, eventually indicating its position in another place, moving into or retreating from the location where it finds itself.

—John Davis

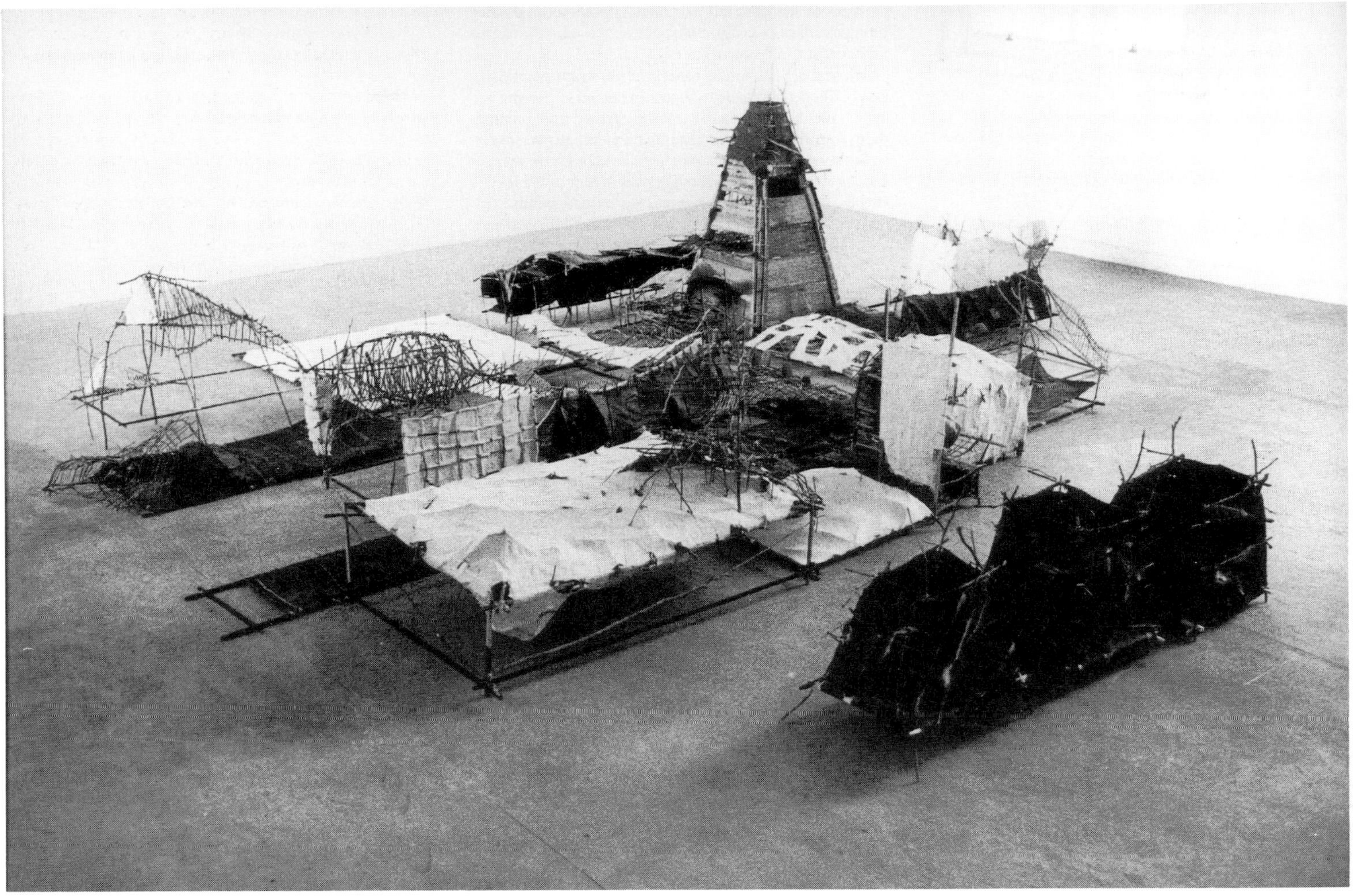

John Davis: *Region*, 1981

John Davis is an Australian. He inhabits, with the majority of his fellow Australians, the small crescent of coastal land in the south-eastern corner of a massive continent. He lives in a pleasant house in a residential suburb of Melbourne. He is married, with children. He is a convivial man, who loves the bush and the sea and believes in the sanctity of Saturdays. John Davis is in many ways a very typical Australian.

In other respects, John Davis belongs to a wider community. He is idealistic, humanist, passionate, socialist and, in the very best sense of the word, nationalistic. Most atypical of all, he chooses to make manifest his beliefs, his hopes and, often, his fears in sculptures that are at one and the same time delicate and monolithic. The fragile bindings of twigs and paper, into brooding towers and mountains or spaced marks on an endless plain, echo the fragility of the environment. The spatial relationships which characterise Davis's sculptures reflect his awareness of and empathy with landscape on a monumental scale. Davis's sculptures may not be physically large, but emotionally and conceptually they embrace the dimensions of a continent.

Davis's sculptures grow, like living organisms. In this sense too, Davis is concerned with nature. But this concern is devoid of romantic notions. Australia is a difficult and complex land from a Western standpoint. The Australian Aborigines learned, in the Dreamtime, that the means by which man might live in this contradictory land was by accepting and accommodating nature rather than trying to improve upon it. Many of the political conflicts that exist in contemporary Australia are conflicts between ecologically conservative forces and those which would seek to perpetuate the exploitative philosophies of the Industrial Revolution. Davis believes in the possibilities of a harmony (of sorts) between these two attitudes.

The Melbourne critic, Robert Rooney, coined the deathless phrase "twiggery folkery" in response to the work of John Davis and other artists who employ natural materials in their art. In so doing, Rooney was revealing a commonly held fear of a sentimental response to the Australian landscape, and a parochial sense of identity, rather than making serious critisism. The fear is that a cloying romanticism towards the landscape (perhaps a hangover from the champagne days of Tom Roberts et al) will reveal Australians as intellectually barren land-lovers. The gum-tree school of painting is an embarrassment: we often seek to legitimise our artistic status by adopting a preference for international modes in art and in rejecting that which smacks of the "pretty" or of sources closely identified with heroic concepts of landscape art. "Nature," in Australian art terms, can often appear to be a euphemism for cliché and corn. Yet the "natural" pattern of Australia is a violent one—fire is needed for the germination of some plant seeds, drought and floods re-occur, often within one season. Balance does exist, but often between extremes. John Davis's sculptures are a lucid and loving attempt to recreate not only the balances and relationships that exist in this most unorthodox of climes, but also, through his own experience, the balances and relationships of those who live in the environment and who choose to be affected by it.

In so doing Davis transcends his "Australianness" and offers concepts and statements that can be recognized and understood on an international level. By embracing an accessible specific, Davis speculates on the universal.

—Alison Fraser

DAVIS, Ronald (Wendel).

American. Born in Santa Monica, California, 29 June 1937. Studied engineering, University of Wyoming, Laramie, 1955–56; art, San Francisco Art Institute, 1960–64, under Philip Guston, Yale University Summer School of Music and Art, Norfolk, Connecticut, 1962. Worked as a sheet metal machinist, Cheyenne, Wyoming, 1956–58; and as a radio announcer, Cheyenne, 1958. Independent painter since 1959; has lived in Greeley, Colorado, 1959–65, in Pasadena, then Los Angeles, 1965–73, and in Malibu, California, since 1973. Instructor, University of California at Irvine, 1966. Recipient: National Endowment for the Arts Grant, 1968, 1972. Agent: Nicholas Wilder Gallery, 8225 1/2 Santa Monica Boulevard, Los Angeles, California 99046. Address: 29715 Cuthbert Road, Malibu, California 90265, U.S.A.

Individual Exhibitions:

1965 Nicholas Wilder Gallery, Los Angeles
1966 Tibor de Nagy Gallery, New York
1967 Nicholas Wilder Gallery, Los Angeles
1968 Leo Castelli Gallery, New York
Vancouver Art Gallery
Kasmin Gallery, London
1969 University of Saskatchewan, Saskatoon
Nicholas Wilder Gallery, Los Angeles
Leo Castelli Gallery, New York
1970 Albright-Knox Art Gallery, Buffalo, New York
Leo Castelli Gallery, New York
Paintings Never Before Exhibited, David Mirvish Gallery, Toronto
Joseph Helman Gallery, St. Louis
Kasmin Gallery, London
Gemini Gallery, Los Angeles

Pasdena Museum of Art, California
1972 Walker Art Center, Minneapolis
Galleria dell'Ariete, Milan
Joseph Helman Gallery, St. Louis
1973 Nicholas Wilder Gallery, Los Angeles
John Berggruen Gallery, San Francisco
1974 Gemini Gallery, Los Angeles
Western Galleries, Cheyenne, Wyoming
Leo Castelli Gallery, New York
1975 Mirvish Gallery, Toronto
John Berggruen Gallery, San Francisco
Boise State University, Idaho
Greenberg Gallery, St. Louis
Leo Castelli Gallery, New York
Ronald Davis/Tom Holland: Works from the Collection of Mr. and Mrs. Robert A. Rowan, Los Angeles Municipal Art Gallery, Barnsdall Park
1976 Aspen Gallery of Art, Colorado
Seder-Creigh Gallery, Coronado, Colorado
Paintings 1962–1976, Oakland Museum, California
1977 Church Fine Arts Gallery, University of Nevada, Reno
1979 Blum-Helman Gallery, New York

Selected Group Exhibitions:

1968 *Documenta 4*, Kassel, West Germany
1969 *Corcoran Biennal*, Washington, D.C. (and 1973)
1970 *Annual American Exhibition*, Art Institute of Chicago
1971 *6 Painters*, Fine Arts Academy, Buffalo, New York
1972 *Biennale*, Venice
1973 *25 Years of American Painting*, Des Moines Art Center, Iowa
1975 *Current Concerts Part 1*, Institute of Contemporary Art, Los Angeles
1976 *Painting and Sculpture in California*, San Francisco Museum of Modern Art (travelled to Washington, D.C.)
1978 *4 Contemporary Painters: Arakawa/Bruce Boice/Ronald Davis/Agnes Martin*, Cleveland Museum of Art
1979 *Reality of Illusion*, University of Southern California, Los Angeles (travelled to the Honolulu Academy of arts; Oakland Museum, California; and the University of Texas at Austin, 1980)
1984 *Olympian Gestures*, Los Angeles County Museum of Art

Collections:

Museum of Modern Art, New York, Albright-Knox Art Gallery, Buffalo, New York; Baltimore Museum of Art; Los Angeles County Museum of Art; San Francisco Museum of Modern Art; Tate Gallery, London; National Gallery of Victoria, Melbourne.

Publications:

On DAVIS: books—*Ron Davis*, exhibition catalogue, with text by Charles Kessler, Los Angeles 1970; *Ron Davis*, exhibition catalogue, with text by Barbara Rose, Milan 1973; *Ronald Davis/Tom Holland: Works from the Collection of Mr. and Mrs. Robert A. Owen*, exhibition catalogue, Los Angeles 1975; *Ronald Davis: Paintings 1962–1976*, exhibition catalogue, with text by Charles Kessler, Oakland, California 1976; *Ronald Davis*, exhibition catalogue, with text by John McCracken, Reno, Nevada 1977; *4 Contemporary Painters: Arakawa/Bruce Boice/Ronald Davis/Agnes Martin*, exhibition catalogue, with an introduction by Tom E. Hinson, Cleveland 1978; articles—"Ronald Davis: Surface and Illusion" by Michael Fried in *Artforum* (New York), April 1967; "Ron Davis" by J. Livingston in *Artforum* (New York), January 1968; "New Paintings by Ron Davis" by John Eiderfield in *Artforum* (New York), March 1971; "Imagine a Space, a Form, a World: The paintings of Ron Davis" by S. C. Larsen in *Artnews* (New York), January 1980.

The most commonly asked question about my plastic paintings has been, "How do you make them?" My reply usually has been, "The same way one makes a fiberglass boat or car body." In case you have never built a boat in your backyard, here is my attempt at a more technical explanation.

In 1966 I began to substitute polyester resin plus pigments and dyes for traditional painting media. Fiberglass cloth and mat replaced canvas as reinforcement and support for the colored resin (paint). These plastic paintings were painted with a brush face down, on a flat, waxed Formica mold. The mold itself was table height, and the preliminary drawings I had made for these paintings were cartooned up to scale on the mold. The illusionary plane *nearest* the viewer was masked out with tape and painted *first;* the planes further away from the viewer were painted last. The rapid chemical heatcuring properties of resin (about thirty minutes) allowed me to apply layer behind layer of colored resin until the painting was completed. Layers of fiberglass impregnated with resin were then laminated to the back of the painting, giving it a support, and a wood stretcher bar the shape of the image was attached to the painting. The completed painting was peeled from the waxed mold and polished. It was then that I viewed the painting for the first time.

On later plastic paintings, i.e. "Eleven Colors," 1967, the wood was eliminated and instead the sides were molded onto the painting as one piece, and a backing sheet of resin and fiberglass was added for structural support. In 1970 I began to use a flexible type resin, i.e. "Single Sawtooth," 1971, eliminated the sides entirely, and attached the painting directly to the wall with Velcrotape.

For health and aesthetic reasons I discontinued the use of resin and fiberglass in 1972.

—Ronald Davis

Ron Davis emerged on the art scene in the turbulent 60's winning critical acclaim afforded few west coast artists of the era. Though his first exhibition in New York City was coolly received, it was not long before formalist art critic Michael Fried heralded his paintings in *Artforum* as being ". . . among the most significant produced anywhere during the last few years . . ." which propelled Davis on to the honor roll of American art. Clearly, he proposed a new alternative to the growing notion of sculpture as painting or vice-versa.

An admirer of the perspectival illusionism of Renaissance painters, most notably Uccello, Davis resurrected the long discarded principles of two-point perspective. By slicing the illusion free from a rectangular format, the images (geometric donut shapes, squares within squares, etc.) hovered independently and illogically on gallery walls. Illogically, because not only was their uncanny sense of depth disarming, but also, although one viewed them at eye level, they depicted objects as would be seen perspectively from above. This seductive contradiction, coupled with Davis's use of polyester resins and fiberglass, lent a real sense of freshness to the work and to an art world drenched with minimalism.

Though they satisfied many of the more traditional requirements of painting, using resins freed Davis to manipulate the thin skin of his plastic paintings in a new way. Juxtaposing translucent resins with opaque pigment, which was often laced with pearlessence and buffed until glossy, somehow liberated the surface, making it appear to teasingly float apart from the imagery. Davis is undeniably a painter, but was and continues to be fed by an emphatically sculptural aesthetic.

For various reasons, not the least of which was health, Davis discontinued his use of resins in 1972. He began a series of small-scale canvases which seemed almost to deify varying arrangements of sundry geometric shapes. Like tiny two-dimensional Stonehenges, each grouping of shapes was bathed in dramatic light and shadow and saturated with rich, jewel-like color.

Towards the late 70's Davis's scale and his application of paint once again both changed drastically. The new paintings were so large that they easily overwhelmed entire walls or even rooms. These acrylic paintings defined a fictitious environment distorted by dramatically foreshortened spatial planes. The objects, often sitting on checkerboard surfaces or sim-

Ron Davis: *Diamond in a Box*, 1975

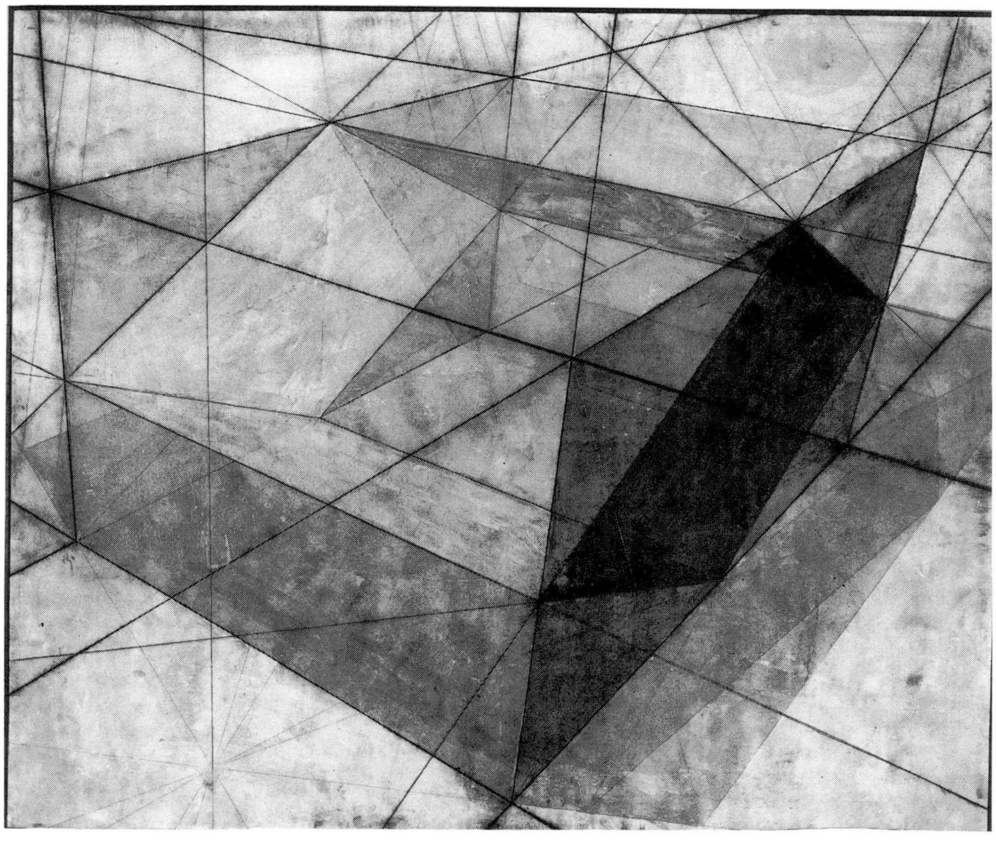

ply dangling in space, changed too. Now they were more tent-like, their form fully described by a complex network of perspectival chalk snap-lines which elucidated the infra-structure of each structural component. Splashy, rhoplex laden paint lent an element of expressioniam to the pieces which had been only hinted at in earlier pieces.

Davis continues to paint irregular geometric shapes in space today. He also pursues, on a less professional level, a keen interest in musical composition.

—Janet Goleas

DEACON, Richard.

British. Born in Bangor, Caernarvonshire, Wales, in 1949. Studied at Somerset College of Art, Taunton, 1968–69; Saint Martin's School of Art, London, 1969–72; Royal College of Art, London, 1974–77; part-time, Chelsea School of Art, London, 1977–78. Independent sculptor, London, since 1978. Instructor, Central School of Art, London, 1978. Recipient: Turner Prize, Tate Gallery, London, 1987. Agent: Lisson Gallery, London. Address: c/o Lisson Gallery, 67 Lisson Street, London NW1 5DA, England.

Individual Exhibitions:

1975 Royal College of Art, London
1976 Royal College of Art, London
1978 Acre Lane Studio, Brixton, London
1980 Acre Lane Studio, Brixton, London
1981 City Polytechnic, Sheffield
1983 Lisson Gallery, London
Orchard Gallery, Londonderry, Northern Ireland
1984 Riverside Studios, Hammersmith, London
Chapter Gallery, Cardiff, Wales
Fruitmarket Gallery, Edinburgh
Le Nouveau Musee, Lyon-Villeurbanne, France
1985 Donald Young Gallery, Chicago (with Tony Cragg)
Israel Museum, Jerusalem (with Julian Opie and Richard Wentworth)
Tate Gallery, London
Centre International du Verre, Aix-en-Provence, France
Margarete Roeder Fine Arts, New York (with Jackie Winsor)
Serpentine Gallery, London (with Richard Rogers and John Tchalenko)
1986 Marian Goodman Gallery, New York
Interim Art, London
Galerie Artlogos, Nantes, France
Aberystwyth Arts Centre, Wales (toured Britain)
1987 Lisson Gallery, London
Bonnefanten Museum, Maastricht, Netherlands (travelled to Lucerne, Madrid, Antwerp)
1988 Lisson Gallery, London
Ecole des Beaux Arts, Macon, France
Marian Goodman Gallery, New York

Selected Group Exhibitions:

1978 *Staff Sculpture*, Central School of Art, London
1980 *Lambeth Summer Festival*, Winchester School of Art, Hampshire
1981 *Objects and Sculpture*, Institute of Contemporary Arts, London (travelled to Bristol)
1982 *Englische Plastik Heute*, Kunstmuseum, Lucerne
1983 *The Sculpture Show*, Hayward Gallery/Serpentine Gallery, London
1984 *The British Art Show*, City Museum/Ikon Gallery, Birmingham (travelled to Edinburgh; Sheffield; Southampton)
1985 *Transformations in Sculpture*, Guggenheim Museum, New York
1986 *Skulptur: 9 Kunstnere fra Storbrittanien*, Louisiana Museum, Humlebaek, Denmark
1987 *A Quiet Revolution: British Sculpture Since 1968*, Museum of Contemporary Art, Chicago (travelled to San Francisco; Newport Beach, California; Washington, D.C.; Buffalo, New York)
1988 *All That Matters*, Art Gallery of Windsor, Ontario (travelled to Saskatoon and Montreal)

Richard Deacon: *Blind, Deaf and Dumb A*, 1985 Courtesy Lisson Gallery, London

Collections:

Tate Gallery, London; British Council, London; Arts Council of Great Britain, London; Fonds Regional d'Art Contemporain des Pays de la Loire, France; Fonds Regional d'Art Contemporain Rhone-Alpes, France; Le Nouveau Musee, Lyon-Villeurbanne; Museum of Modern Art, New York.

Publications:

By DEACON: books—*Stuff Box Object*, London 1972, Cardiff 1984; *Jacqui Poncelet: New Ceramics*, exhibition catalogue, London 1981; *Carol McNicoll*, exhibition catalogue, London 1985; *For Those Who Have Ears No. 2*, London 1985; *For Those Who Have Eyes*, exhibition catalogue, Aberystwyth 1986.

On DEACON: books—*Objects and Sculpture*, exhibition catalogue with texts by Iwona Blaszcwyk, Lewis Biggs and Sandy Nairne, London 1980; *Englische Plastik Heute*, exhibition catalogue with texts by Martin Kunz and Michael Newman, Lucerne 1982; *Richard Deacon: Sculpture*, exhibition catalogue with text by Lynne Cooke, Londonderry 1983; *Making Sculpture: Richard Deacon*, broadsheet edited by the Tate Gallery, London 1983; *Richard Deacon: The Face of Things*, exhibition catalogue with text by Michael Newman, Edinburgh 1984; *Richard Deacon*, exhibition folder with text by Richard Francis, London 1985; *Richard Deacon: Recent Sculpture*, exhibition catalogue with text by Charles Harrison, Maastricht 1987; *Richard Deacon*, exhibition catalogue with text by Peter Schjeldahl, New York 1988.

Richard Deacon is one of the younger generation of British sculptors who have won international acclaim in the last few years. He himself prefers the term 'fabricator' as a more accurate description of what he does as he is neither a modeller nor a carver. The materials he works with, such as laminated wood, linoleum or galvanised steel or aluminium, are chosen primarily for their structural potential rather for any intrinsic value or sensual properties.

As an undergraduate at St. Martin's School of Art in the 'seventies he was much involved in Performance Art, but even then he was not using his own body as the basic material as had his immediate predecessors, Bruce McLean or Gilbert and George. In Deacon's performances he used materials which underwent a transformation or were resolved into a final object, so though he was accepted for the experimental post-graduate course at the Royal College of Art on the basis of his performance art, process became of much less importance than the object in mind. The works he made about this time were strong, architectonic shapes with emphasis on integration of surface and structure. There is no hidden armature in these works, no distraction of surface detail from the spare, angular shapes. Already the young artist seems to be pondering on the centuries-old pre-occupations of sculptors—the relationships of skin and structure, inner and outer surfaces, mass and volume and edge conditions, and this exploration continued when he went to the United States in 1978 /9. After his return from America his ideas start to cohere in a series of confident and mature constructions. Some of Deacon's work is reminiscent of the moving parts of machinery—of mills and steam engines and others are evocative of propellors and conic sections. There is often the suggestion of potential movement. There are forms which remind one of navigation aids in preradar days—those spherical, open basket shapes on top of high poles at harbour mouths. (Interestingly, for Deacon has never mentioned them as source material, one of these round open basket forms is entitled *For Those Who Have Eyes*). Other works indicate that Deacon enjoyed and was inspired by the geometry of conic sections—the ellipse, the circle, the parabola and the hyperbola—but he then became increasingly interested in organic and biomorphic forms and the expressive content of his work deepened accordingly.

Whilst he was in the States he had made a series of drawings entitled *Orpheus When There's Singing* which were inspired by *Sonnets to Orpheus* by Rainer Maria Rilke. Deacon says that these drawings started with a geometric figure with parts linked by a spiral. "A series of arcs and curves build up a network or ground against which specific shapes are allowed to emerge." That is an accurate description of the series *For Those Who Have Ears*. The Orpheus myth is about music, both the making of music and the hearing of music. In *For Those Who Have Ears No. 2 1983*, which is made of curving loops of laminated wood, the shapes can suggest both ears and also lyres—the ears to hear and the lyres to make music. The forms in this work are open, generous and flowing; the luxuriant curves are sensuous and suggest sexual imagery. It is a large sculpture, 9×13×13 feet, but Deacon can handle large scale works which never become monumental. It sits lightly on the ground and is particularly pleasing in its balance and poise and its subtle delineation of shifting forms expressed in a linear context. The process of the making is indicated by the glue which oozed out when the strips of wood were pressed together.

His later work seems to have certain basic themes which deal with growth processes and with a continuing concern with orifices where the sexual imagery and the penetration of the forms becomes more evident. Works which appear initially to have a limpid simplicity develop a haunting and mysterious presence. The titles with their references to poetry and literature remind us of the artist's recurrent dilemma of the balance between form and content and the need to synthesise abstraction and nature.

Interestingly, Richard Deacon has recently collaborated with a Dance Company, designing and making objects which can be moved about the stage by the dancers, demonstrating once again the wide variety of arenas in which the 20th century artist is not only mixing his media but also moving freely in other modes of artistic expression.

—Mary Ellis

DE ANDREA, John (Louis).
American. Born in Denver, Colorado, 24 November 1941. Educated at the University of Colorado, Boulder, 1961-65, B.F.A. 1965; University of New Mexico, Albuquerque, 1966-68 (on art assistantship). Sculptor: lives and works in Denver. Agent: O.K. Harris Gallery, 465 West Broadway, New York, New York 10013. Address: 4646 Grove Street, Denver, Colorado 80211, U.S.A.

Individual Exhibitions:

1970 O. K. Harris Gallery, New York
1971 O. K. Harris Gallery, New York
1972 Wilmaro Gallery, Denver
1973 O. K. Harris Gallery, New York
1976 O. K. Harris Gallery, New York
1981 Tortue Gallery, Santa Monica, California
1982 Aspen Center for the Visual Arts, Colorado

Selected Group Exhibitions:

1970 *Annual Exhibition*, Whitney Museum, New York
1971 *Biennale*, Paris
1972 *Documenta 5*, Kassel, West Germany
1973 *Amerikansk Realism*, Lunds Konsthall, Sweden
1974 *Hyperréalistes Américains/Réalistes Européens*, Centre National d'Art Contemporain, Paris (toured Europe)
1976 *Aspects of Realism*, Rothman's of Pall Mall travelling exhibition, Stratford Art Gallery, Ontario (toured Canada, 1976-78)
1977 *The Nude: Avery and the European Masters*, Borgenicht Gallery, New York
1979 *7 on the Figurine*, Pennsylvania Academy of Fine Arts, Philadelphia
1981 *Contemporary American Realism Since 1960*, Pennsylvania Academy of Fine Arts, Philadelphia
1982 *Real, Really Real, Super Real*, San Antonio Museum of Art, Texas (travelled to Indianapolis, Tucson and Pittsburgh)
1988 *Figure It Out: Visual Body Language*, Helander Gallery, Palm Beach, Florida

Collections:

Everson Museum, Syracuse, New York; Neue Galerie, Aachen, West Germany.

Publications:

By DE ANDREA: article—"The Verist Sculptors: 2 Interviews: Duane Hanson and John De Andrea," with J. Masheck, in *Art in America* (New York), November/December 1972.

On DE ANDREA: books—*Hyperréalistes Américans/Realistes Européens*, exhibition catalogue, Paris 1974; *Aspects of Realism*, exhibition catalogue. Stratford, Ontario 1976; *Neue Formen des Realismus* by Peter Sager, Cologne 1974; *John De Andrea: Sculptures 1978-81*, exhibition catalogue with essay by Philip Yenaivine, Aspen, Colorado 1982; articles—"A New Realism in Sculpture" by Grace Glueck in *Art in America* (New York), November/December 1971; "Downtown Uptown, Not 10th Street" by John Perreault in the *Village Voice* (New York), December 1971; "Art in the Artist" by Emily Genauer in the *New York Post*, December 1971; "Neutral Style" by Edward Lucie-Smith in *Art and Artists* (London), August 1975; "Hyper-Realistic Dreiklang" in *Du* (Zurich), July 1979.

John De Andrea casts his figures straight from life, and equivalent of Photo Realism in 3-D. Still, however much his painted polyvinyl seems at first like living flesh, one would never take them for the people in the street. The people in the street are not young, untarnished, gracefully formed nudes. They have, besides, a beauty of gesture; they present a dynamic, rhythmic, harmonious composition of torso and limb as they leave or enter an embrace, play ball, lie easily asleep. It is this carefully caught grace of body and motion which has led to the classification of De Andrea's nudes as classic and ideal, in spite of his disclaimer: "How can you idealize from casts?"

It is true that he practices total honesty. Every fold of skin, every pore, every broken capillary, shows, yet in the models that he chooses there are few of these. By opposing the present, transitory beauty of the model's flesh to the imagined beauty of the classic past, the work comes off as emphasizing a transcendent loveliness in the here and now. The idealization lies in selection, of gesture and of model, just as with Pheidias the ideal form, the ideal act, was the one portrayed.

Seemingly unposed, these figures appear as studiedly dispassionate, objectified. They never address the observer directly through the gaze of their real-seeming eyes, and by this means a distance is created which sets off the work as art, not life, even more effectually than a frame would do. They are not nature caught as if by the camera, with all the attendant out-of-jointedness which accident, while freezing motion, can create, but something based on life, distilled and offered as apart from it.

As his work has developed in recent years, De Andrea has widened it to include, beside the recreation of single figures, the figure in dialog with another, sometimes as becoming itself, as for example in the artist—De Andrea complete with spattered jeans and beard—painting the sculpted model, Pygmalion catching himself in the act. There are also quotations from other works, like the *Déjeuner sur l'herbe*, into which the artist enters, a tableau in which the author joins.

By this means De Andrea has allied himself with the twentieth century tradition of offering the work of

John De Andrea: *Seated Man and Woman*, 1981

art as comment on art, as in, say, Duchamp, but the difference seems to be that De Andrea still believes in and affirms the beauty of the human form.

—Barbara Cortright

de CAMARGO, Sergio.

Brazilian. Born in Rio de Janeiro, Brazil, 8 April 1930. Educated at Santo Inacio-Rio Champagnat, Buenos Aires, 1935–47; Faculty of Law, Buenos Aires, 1947–48; Faculté de Lettres, Paris, 1948–51; studied sociology and art, under Pierre Francastel, Ecole Pratique de Haute Etudes, Paris, 1961–64. Married Marie-Louise Berthodin in 1950; children: Cristovao, Carlos, and Maria; married Aspasia Brasiliero Alcantra in 1970. Recipient: Hors Concours, *Salón Nacional de Arte Moderna,* Rio de Janeiro, 1954; Acquisition Prize, *Salao Paulista de Arte Moderna,* Sao Paulo, 1954; International Sculpture Prize, *Biennale,* Paris, 1963; Gold Medal, Bienal, Sao Paulo, 1965; Stern Prize, Rio de Janeiro, 1965. Agents: Galeria Luis Buarque de Hollanda and Paulo Bittencourt, Rio de Janeiro; Gimpel Fils, 50 Davies Street, London W1, England; Gimpel and Hanover Galerie, Claridenstrasse 35, Zurich, Switzerland; Gimpel and Weitzenhoffer, 1040 Madison Avenue, New York, New York 10020, U.S.A. Address: c/o Galerie Luis Buarque de Hollanda and Paulo Bittencourt, 19 rua das Palmerias, Rio de Janeiro, Brazil.

Individual Exhibitions:

1958 Galerie GEA, Rio de Janeiro
Galeria de Arte das Folhas, Sao Paulo
1964 Signals Gallery, London
1965 Museu de Arte Moderna, Rio de Janeiro
1966 *Biennale,* Venice
1967 Galleria del Naviglio, Milan
Galleria del Obelisco, Rome
Galleria La Polena, Genoa
1968 Gimpel Fils Gallery, London
Galleria Notizie, Turin
Galerie Buchholz, Munich
1969 Gimpel and Weitzenhoffer Gallery, New York
1970 Gimpel Fils Gallery, London
Artestudio, Macerata, Italy
Artestudio, Brescia, Italy
Gallerie Grumholt, Oslo
Galerie Buchholz, Munch
Galerie M. Bochum, West Germany
1972 Estudio Actual, Caracas
Galeria Collectio, Sao Paulo
Petite Galeria, Rio de Janeiro
1974 Gimpel Fils Gallery, London
Gallerie Gromholt, Oslo
Museo de Arte Moderno, Mexico City
1975 Museu de Arte Moderna, Rio de Janeiro
Galeria Luis Buarque de Hollanda and Paulo Bittencourt, Rio de Janeiro
Galerie de Arte Global, Sao Paulo
1982 Gimpel Fils Galery, London

Selected Group Exhibitions:

1955 *Bienal,* Sao Paulo (and 1957, 1965)
1957 *Arte, Moderno Brasileo,* Buenos Aires (toured South America)
1963 *Biennale,* Paris
1965 *Mouvement II,* Gallerie Denise René, Paris
1966 *White Structures,* Kunsthalle, Bern
1967 *Structures et Mouvement,* Galerie Denise René, Paris
Lumière et Mouvement, Musé d'Art Moderne, Paris
1968 *Documenta 4,* Kassel, West Germany
1969 *Vision 24,* Instituto Italo Americano, Rome
1974 *Basically White,* Institute of Contemporary Arts, London

Sergio de Camargo: ***Carrara Marble Piece*, 1972** Courtesy Gimpel Fils, London

Collections:

Museu Nacional de Belas Artes, Rio de Janeiro: Pinacoteca do Estadio, Sao Paulo; Museu de Arte Moderna, Sao Paulo; Museu de Arte Moderno, Mexico City; Albright-Knox Art Gallery, Buffalo, New York; Contemporary Art Society, London; Tate Gallery, London; Ulster Museum, Belfast; Galleria Nazionale d'Arte Moderna, Rome; Rijksmuseum Kröller-Müller, Otterlo Netherlands

Publications:

On de CAMARGO: books—*Camargo,* exhibition catalogue, by Jean Clay, London 1967; *Naissance de l'Art Cinetique* by Frank Popper, Paris 1967; *Optical and Kinetic Art* by Michael Compton, London 1967; *New Brazilian Art* by Pietro Maria Bardi, London 1970; *Sergio de Camargo,* exhibition catalogue with essay by Ronaldo Brito, London 1982; articles—"Sept Brasiliens de l'Ecole" by Georges Boudaille in *XX Siécle* (Paris), no. 22, 19634; "Camargo" by Denys Chevalier in *Aujourd-nui* (Paris) no 46, 1964; "Sergio de Camargo" by Stuart Penrose in *Arts Review* (London), no 28, 1965; "Camargo: Unica Gestaldo"; by Jaimé Mauricio in *Correio de la Manha* (Rio de Janeiro), November 1972; "Camargo" by Jasia Reichardt in *Architectural Design* (London), no. 3. 1974; "Camargo: Juegos Luminicos . . ." by Juan Acha in *Plural* (Mexico City), July 1975.

DE DOMINICIS, Gino.

Italian. Born in Ancona, Italy, in 1947. Settled in Rome, 1965. Address: c/o Galleria L'Attico, via del Babuino 114, 00187 Rome, Italy.

Individual Exhibitions:

1969 Galleria L'Attico, Rome
1970 Galleria Toselli, Milan
Galleria L'Attico, Rome
1971 Galleria L'Attico, Rome
1979 Galleria Mario Pieroni, Rome (with Jannis Kounellis and Ettore Spalletti)

Selected Group Exhibitions:

1970 *Biennale d'Arte Contemporanea,* Bologna
Group Exhibition, Galleria L'Attico, Rome
1971 *Comportamento e cose di 13 Uomini che invecchiano e muoiano,* Munich
1978 *Biennale,* Venice
1982 *Documenta,* Kassel, West Germany

Collections:

Stedelijk Museum, Amsterdam.

Publications:

On DE DOMINICIS: book—*L'Arte Moderna* by Renato Barilli, Milan 1975.

As one critic has observed, by 1970 Gino De Dominicis had become the most important "find" of the Galleria L'Attico where a year before he had held his one-man exhibition of "invisible" objects. "Invisible Pyramid" may serve as an example: here we have the square base of a pyramid drawn on the floor, while nearby there is a placard which gives the title of the work and the date. In 1970, at the same gallery, he exhibited "The Zodiac," a large work which demonstrates his own particular imaginative powers: here he has provided a very literal and concrete version of the zodiac in which a lion stands for Leo, a young woman for Virgo, and so forth. And in the same year De-

Dominicis participated in two group shows and made a statement which sums up his aesthetic: "To have true existence, things must be eternal and immortal. "Invisibility" and "ubiquity" are also key concepts rendered in mythic terms: it is immortality which is the greatest attribute of the gods, and as was the case with "The Zodiac," artistic representation involves a kind of anthropomorphism. He asserted his position once again in the Venice *Biennale* of 1972 and caused a scandal by placing a mongoloid on display as the symbol of a particular attitude towards death. This goes to the center of De Dominicis' work: the victory over death which proves man's genuine existence. His basic assumption is that without immortality there is no true life. Thus the mongoloid became a symbol of the triumph of life over death: he is indifferent to fate or change or death: he simply exists.

The boundaries of De Dominicis' art are the cosmic and the mythic. He uses archetypal images to provoke esoteric sensations and emphasizes once again the ability to overcome the laws of nature. To this end he also uses the discoveries of technology and the efforts of science to conquer death. In "Greeting Card" (1971) he seems to be wishing immortality of the body for everyone. For him immortality means the capacity to overcome nature, in terms drawn from myth and evolutionary struggle. "Attempt at Flight," for example, is a video-tape produced by Gerry Schum in 1970 in which the artist makes repeated attempts to fly. Once more De Dominicis is struggling to overcome the natural order and limits of things: the laws of nature are what bind man to one place and time, and force him to grow old. To transcend even one of these limitations would be to prove the possibility of attaining the great goal of immortality.

—Roberto G. Lambarelli

DEEM, George.
American. Born in Vincennes, Indiana, 18 August 1932. Studied, under Paul Wieghardt and Boris Margo, at the School of the Art Institute of Chicago, 1950–51, 1953–57, B.F.A. 1957; under Willi Baumeister, Stuttgart. 1951–52. Served in the United States Army. 1951–53. Restoration Assistant, Metropolitan Museum of Art, New York, 1958–60; Assistant to Josef Albers, School of Fine Arts, Yale University, New Haven, Connecticut, 1960–61. Independent artist since 1960; lives and works in New York; spent 1970 living and working in Cortana and Arezzo, Italy. Painting Instructor, College of Art and Technology, Leicester, England, 1966–67, and University of Pennsylvania, Philadelphia. 1968–69; Visiting Artist, Illinois State University, Normal, 1982. Agents: Nancy Hoffman Gallery, 429 West Broadway, New York, New York 10012; Merida Gallery, 2007 Frankfort Avenue, Louisville, Kentucky 40206. Address: 10 West 18th Street, New York, New York 10011, U.S.A.

Individual Exhibitions:

1962 Allan Stone Gallery, New York
1963 Allan Stone Gallery, New York
1964 Allan Stone Gallery, New York
Merida Gallery, Louisville, Kentucky
1965 Goodman Gallery, Buffalo, New York
Allan Stone Gallery, New York
1966 Allan Stone Gallery, New York
1968 Allan Stone Gallery, New York
Merida Gallery, Louisville, Kentucky
1969 Ferrier Gallery, Houston
Allan Stone Gallery, New York
1974 *Paintings and Drawings,* Indianapolis Museum of Art (travelled to the Witte Memorial Museum, San Antonio, Texas)
1975 Allan Stone Gallery, New York
1979 *The Making of a Masterpiece: Recent Paintings.* Evansville Museum of Arts and Sciences, Indiana

Selected Group Exhibitions:

1964 *Nieuwe Realisten,* Gemeentemuseum, The Hague (toured the Netherlands and West Germany)
4 American Painters, Yale University, New Haven, Connecticut
1968 *New Realism,* Walker Art Center, Minneapolis
1969 *Painting and Sculpture Today,* Indianapolis Museum of Art
1972 *Recent Accessions 1966–1972,* Indianapolis Museum of Art
1974 *Contemporary American Painting and Sculpture 1974,* University of Illinois, Urbana
1978 *Artists Look at Art,* Spencer Museum of Art, University of Kansas, Lawrence
Art about Art, Whitney Museum, New York
1981 *Contemporary American Realism since 1960,* Pennsylvania Academy of Fine Arts, Philadelphia

Collections:

Memorial Art Museum, Rochester, New York; Albright-Knox Art Gallery, Buffalo, New York; Hirshhorn Museum and Sculpture Garden, Washington, D.C.; J. B. Speed Museum, Louisville, Kentucky; Oberlin College, Ohio; Indianapolis Museum of Art; Museum of Art, Houston; San Francisco Museum of Modern Art; Neue Galerie, Aachen, West Germany.

Publications:

By DEEM: books—*Bruna Seviri, Sun and Moon,* with Ronald Vance, 1978; *Aanababcac, Sun and Moon,* 1979; *Mona Lisa Washington, Zone,* 1980; *Extra Genre, White Walls,* 1981.

On DEEM: books—*The New Realism* by Udo Kultermann, New York 1972; *Recent Accessions 1966–1972,* exhibition catalogue, Indianapolis 1972; *Deem: An Exhibition of Paintings and Drawings,* exhibition catalogue, Indianapolis, 1974; *The New Painting* by Udo Kultermann, Tübingen, West Germany 1975; articles—"Painting Lists" by Ronald Vance in *Art and Artists* (London), February 1968; "George Deem" by Edgar Buenaquiro in *Arts Magazine* (New York), November 1977; "Vermeer and Contemporary American Painting" by Udo Kultermann in *American Art Review* (Los Angeles), November 1978.

Back home in Indiana, some of the women back home in Indiana give remnants of fabric that could be useful for making quilts to their friends, and the women are made very happy who receive the scraps of cloth and who give them. Reproductions of my paintings are satisfying. My paintings are paintings of reproductions, and when my paintings in turn become reproductions a circuit is completed. It is now Thursday. Two people have come to my loft this week and between them bought three drawings and what up until now was a lost week of too many things to do and of too many people is not a lost week after all but just a week wearing a different face from the weeks when all I do is paint. Tomorrow I am going to Philadelphia to visit the art museum and a friend. Other friends I have been seeing now it is summer are come to dinner and meet new people friends, and I go to dinners and I meet new people and the cooking is usually good and the vodka and tonic everybody offers this year and going to Fire Island every few weeks for a few days and coming home to my loft where everything is as usual and I realize again that all the play world I have been visiting in is like a Saturday afternoon movie when I was a boy that I thought of all the next week on the farm and I could never really get to to the movie again not even when I went back and saw it again. One has always a style and an attitude to work with or against. Archaic: A time when everything that had been taken as given breaks up. Some artists

George Deem: *Still Life with Rug,* 1970

continue by trying to pour new wine into broken bottles. Archaic. There may be several pockets of space but the one we are in is the one we know. When Marcel Duchamp went to look out of the window he used to bump his forehead against the pane. Every work of art calls upon the spectator to continue it. Most of the time it is this way: I have worked harder on paintings that are merely inevitable than on paintings that are miraculously unforeseeably themselves; and if one is ever to paint any unforeseen paintings it does seem one has to work hard to complete a very large number of merely inevitable paintings until one comes at last no longer to think about any such thing at all.

—George Deem

The paintings of George Deem are devoted to the exploration and rediscovery of prefigurated themes of art from the past. He uses images of paintings by artists such as Vermeer, Caravaggio, Rubens and Rogier van der Weyden as subject matter to express a contemporary sensibility revitalizing and translating the themes of the old masters. It is, therefore, necessary for the viewer to have a pre-knowledge of the original work in order to fully appreciate the fresh adaptation. The re-cycling and complexity of dealing with the source is a serious form of contemporary painting and reflects the historic dimension in contemporary art.

One of the major thematic sources for Deem is the work of Vermeer van Delft, whose paintings are often used by Deem as a point of departure from which new and exciting results are achieved. Vermeer's images are transformed to a contemporary level which finds an equivalent in Deem's masterly painting technique. In several of his works Deem identifies with the artist from the past by translating past centuries into the 20th century. Through this identification new aspects of the content are introduced, thereby constituting the earlier work into a more complex one in which old and new are combined.

In other paintings by Deem new aspects of serial art have emerged. Following the pioneering examples by Jasper Johns and Andy Warhol, Deem added a new variation to the theme in paintings such as "Eight Women" (1967). Another innovative aspect of his work can be seen in a complex combination of historic images. One such example is "Mona Lisa Washington" of 1972, which is a combination of two images from different sources painted into one new complex form inaugurating an interpersonal figuration. The dimension of this complex image has yet to be fully appreciated.

The work of George Deem between 1960 and 1982 is of consistent character in its exploration of thematic prefigurations which relate art of our time to art of the past. His work transcends the concept of the avantgarde and is one of the many parallels in the spectrum of contemporary art.

—Udo Kultermann

DE FOREST, Roy (Dean).

American. Born in North Platte, Nebraska, 11 February 1930. Educated at Yakima Junior College, Washington, 1948–50, A.A. 1950; studied painting, drawing, astrology and meteorology, California School of Fine Arts, San Francisco, with Edward Corbett, Hassel Smith, Elmer Bischoff, James Budd Dixon and David Park, 1950–52; San Francisco State College, with Alexander Nepote, Seymour Locks, Dr. May Byrce, 1952–53, 1956–58, B.A. 1953, M.A. 1958. Served as a Specialist 3rd Class, 3rd Engineering Regiment, United States Army, Fort Lewis, Washington, 1953–55. Married Gloria Scott in 1974; daughter: Oriana. Children's Painting Instructor and Gallery Assistant, San Francisco Museum of Art, 1955–58; Instructor, and Director of the Larson Gallery, Yakima Junior College, Washington, 1958–60; Art Instructor, Contra Costa Junior College, San Pablo, California, 1960–61; Painting Instructor, San Francisco State College, 1961–62; Art Instructor, Junior Center of Arts and Sciences, Oakland, California 1963, and San Quentin Prison, California 1964; Painting Instructor, California College of Arts and Crafts, Oakland 1964–65. Lecturer and Associate Professor, University of California at Davis, since 1965. Chairman, Artists Council, San Francisco Art Association, 1964. Recipient: San Francisco Art Association Award, 1954; Purchase Prize, Bay Printmakers' Society, Oakland Art Museum, California, 1956; Nealie Sullivan Award, San Francisco Art Institute, 1962; Purchase Prize, La Jolla Museum of Art, California, 1965; National Endowment for the Arts Fellowship, 1972. Agents: Allan Frumkin Gallery Inc., 50 West 57th Street, New York, New York 10019; Hansen Fuller Gallery, 228 Grant Avenue, San Francisco, California 94569, U.S.A. Address: P.O. Box 47, Porta Costa, California 94569, U.S.A.

Individual Exhibitions:

1955 East and West Gallery, San Francisco
1958 East and West Gallery, San Francisco
1959 Stone Court Gallery, Yakima, Washington
1960 Stone Court Gallery, Yakima, Washington
Dilexi Gallery, San Francisco
1962 Dilexi Gallery, Los Angeles
San Francisco Art Association
1963 Dilexi Gallery, San Francisco
1966 Allan Frumkin Gallery, New York
Peninsula Gallery, Menlo Park, California
Dilexi Gallery, San Francisco
1967 Dilexi Gallery, San Francisco
City College of Sacramento
1968 Candy Store Gallery, Folsom, California
1969 San Francisco Art Institute
Cowell College, University of California at Santa Cruz
1971 Gallery Marc, Washington, D.C.
The Fantasy Watercolors of Roy De Forest/The Sculpture World of David Gihooly, Leadville Galleries, Sun Valley, Idaho
Candy Store Gallery, Folsom, California
Manolides Gallery, Seattle
California Palace of the Legion of Honor, San Francisco
Hansen Fuller, Gallery, San Francisco
1972 Manolides Gallery, Seattle
Allan Frumkin Gallery, New York
1973 Hansen Fuller Gallery, San Francisco
Allan Frumkin Gallery, Chicago
1974 San Francisco Museum of Modern Art (retrospective; travelled to Fort Worth Art Center Museum, Texas; Utah Museum of Fine Art, Salt Lake City; and Whitney Museum, New York)
Galerie Darthea Speyer, Paris
Glenbow-Alberta Gallery, Calgary
1975 Hansen-Fuller Gallery, San Francisco
Allan Frumkin Gallery, New York
1976 Hansen Fuller Gallery, San Francisco
Fendrick Gallery, Washington, D.C.
1977 Galerie Darthea Speyer, Paris
Allan Frumkin Gallery, New York
Clark-Benton Gallery, Sante Fe, New Mexico
Institute of Contemporary Arts, Boston (with Robert Hudson)
1978 Hansen Fuller Gallery, San Francisco
1979 Fresno City College Art Space Gallery, California
1980 Crocker Art Museum, Sacramento, California

Selected Group Exhibitions:

1968 *West Coast Now*, Portland Art Museum, Oregon
1971 *California Works on Paper 1950–1971*, University of California Art Museum, Berkeley
1973 *Extraordinary Realities*, Whitney Museum, New York
1975 *Painting and Sculpture in California: The Modern Era*, San Francisco Museum of Modern Art
1976 *3 from California*, Dalhousie Art Gallery, Halifax
1977 *New in the 70's*, University of Texas Art Museum, Austin
Recent Works on Paper, Madison Art Center, Wisconsin
1978 *West Coast Artists*, New Gallery of Contemporary Art, Cleveland
Late 20th Century Art, Virginia Commonwealth University, Richmond
1984 *The Human Condition*, San Francisco Museum of Modern Art

Collections:

California College of Arts and Craft, Oakland; Oakland Art Museum; University of California Art Museum, Berkeley; San Francisco Museum of Modern Art; Crocker Art Gallery, Sacramento, California; Stanford University Museum of Art, California; Arizona State University, Tempe; Art Institute of Chicago; Weatherspoon Gallery, University of North Carolina; Philadelphia Museum of Art.

Publications:

On DE FOREST: books—*Roy De Forest*, exhibition catalogue, San Francisco 1963; *Roy De Forest: Retrospective*, exhibition catalogue, San Francisco 1974; *Roy De Forest: Retrospective*, exhibition catalogue, by John Humphrey, New York 1975; *Roy De Forest*, exhibition catalogue with essay by Roger D. Clisby, Sacramento, 1980; articles—"San Francisco" by David Zack in *Art News* (New York), September 1969; "Stepped-up Pitch, Color in Roy De Forest Art" in *San Francisco Chronicle*, 21, November 1969; "Another Part of De Forest" by Charles Johnson in the *Sacramento Bee* (Sacramento, California), 21 March 1971; "De Forest Is De Forest Is De Forest" by Juris Prudence in *Artweek* (Oakland, California), 27 November 1971; "Art" by Hilton Kramer in the *New York Times*, 22 January 1972; "A Master of Fantasy" by Alfred Frankenstein in the *San Francisco Chronicle*, 8 March 1973; "The National Scene: San Francisco" by Jerome Tarshish in *Art News* (New York), May 1973; "Smutty Jokes by Sophisticated Yokels" by Hilton Kramer in the *New York Times*, October 1973; "De Forest Amuses with His Fantasy Art" by Hilton Kramer in the *New York Times*, 29 March 1975; review by Da Vinci in *Soho Weekly New* (New York), 10 April 1975.

One day while talking to an obscure poet, I expressed my belief in the artificer as an eccentric individual creating fantasy art with the amazing intention of totally building a miniature cosmos into which the artful alchemist could retire with all his friends, animals and paraphernalia.

And so said we, "The work of peculiar and eccentric, fastidious being can truly be described as the mechanic and conductor of the convoluted, rambling, roundabout vehicle of journey to central Tibet in the company of a French Count and his constant companion, a mangy sheepdog of Lombardy. The mechanical artificer travels in a phantasmagoric micro-world, small and infinitely compact, as the light of a dwarf star imploding inward as it collapses paradise and hell to one vanishing whole, while we are forever with our joys, sorrows and unrequited love. A black hole in the reconstructed night is mysterious and hermetic in the darkness, slyly cunning and opulent in the firelight."

"Furthermore," wrote an obscene hyena, "Maniacal art is a squirrel in the forest of visual delights." "Scenic nature art constitutes a scarlet robot striding forward immune to the light of distant street lamps," announced the horse of a different color. "Tinted canvas beckons the dogmatic fellow to antisocial aristocracy," shouted Rover, a domesticated but still recalcitrant Dingo. "I give a howl to the phantasmagoric artist," barked Samuel Johnson, distinguished short-haired poet of the Terriers. He growled, "Oh how I abhor the fond lap dogs, the surly spaniels—those clever thieves of current taste. And what is current taste but old desires made palatable by present boredom."

All of us, obscure poet, myself (obscure visual

Roy De Forest: *On the Sea Wall*, 1976

constructor of mechanical delights), a travelling French Count and his mangy sheepdog, a black mongrel of the night, an obscene hyena, Samuel Johnson (distinguished Terrier), and Rover (domesticated Dingo) shouted, barked and howled, "Picturesque art is now and forever the hope of the future as well as the dream of the past."

"All too true," lisped the horse of a different color as he stood marking the earth with his translucent hooves. Would that I could have read the significance of those abstract channels chiselled in the moist earth.

—Roy De Forest

"See Through Jane," 1970, has a vacant-looking woman, with animals placed in a television set occupying her mind. Dabs of paint are placed on the edges of the frame, remaining stiffened and upright. These characteristic dabs of Roy De Forest are like circus lights framing our arrival at the carnival. All of De Forest's paintings are circus-colored and candy-treated. De Forest's animals serve as testament to a double-edged appreciation. They both haunt and please.

These worlds of De Forest, peculiar to themselves, having few people we know who inhibit them, directly treat our imaginative life and our sense of how we travel in the internal world. A number of recent color drawings have no titles, yet are easily distinguishable from each other because of certain standoffish figures. A woman with a pink face appears to be spitting. A man with a red and yellow face, with musical hieroglyphic notes on his face, appears to have x-ray vision. Other untitled drawings include a population of spitters, cylindrical robot-like men, tall-hatted men, and rabbits, horses and coyotes. All the animals look out at the viewer through the window of the canvas. As in one drawing, there is an attenuated excursion through the desert mountains with a friend and dog.

De Forest has worked in the color art land of the University of California at Davis, where, with his, the careers of Thiebaud, Nauman and Arneson were also developing. Strangely enough, color appears masked in the real countryside of Davis, and all the animals appear hidden to general, immediate observation. Always, delightful miscalculations of crisscrossed people and animals, party hats, over-sized glasses, long shoes.

—John Robinson

DE KEYSER, Raoul.

Belgian. Born in Deinze, 29 August 1930. Studied art at the Academie of Deinze, 1963. Served as adjunct in the welfare section, Belgian Army, in West Germany, 1950–51. Married Dina Baudoneq in 1952; children: Luc, Piet and Jan. Independent painter, Deinze, since 1963. Non-teaching Adjunct Advisor, University of Ghent, since 1970. Recipient: Jeune Peinture Belge Prize, Brussels, 1967. Address: Kouterlosstraat 118, 9800 Deinze, Belgium.

Individual Exhibitions:

1965 Galerie Drieghe, Wetteren, Belgium
Kaleidoskoop, Ghent
1966 Galerie Les Contemporains, Brussels
3 Vlaamse Schilders, Groninger Museum, Groningen, Netherlands (with Elias and Raveel)
1967 Celbeton, Dendermonde, Belgium
M.A.S., Deinze, Belgium
1968 Galerie Contour, Brussels
Galerie Kaleidoskoop, Ghent
1969 Galerie Les Contemporains, Brussels
1970 Galerie Denise-Emmanual, Brussels
Korrekelder, Bruges
Galerie Richard Foncke, Ghent
Museum, Antwerp
Groninger Museum, Groningen, Netherlands
Museum, Haarlem, Netherlands
Museum, 'sHertogenbosch, Netherlands
1971 Galerie de Vaart, Hilversum, Netherlands
Galerie Plus-Kern, Ghent
1972 Galerie Ado, Bonheiden, Belgium
Galerie Grafiek 50, Wakken, Belgium
Galerie Plus-Kern, Ghent
1973 Galerie Aksent, Waregem, Belgium
Provinciaal Begijnhof, Hasselt, Belgium
1974 Van Abbemuseum, Eindhoven, Netherlands (with Amedée Cortier)
Galerie de Mangelgang, Groningen, Netherlands
1975 Galerie Aksent, Waregem, Belgium
E v H Loringhoven Galerie, Ghent
Neue Galerie, Aachen, West Germany (with Norbert Heyers)
1976 Galerie de Mangelgang, Groningen, Netherlands
Galerie Grafiek 50, Wakken, Belgium
1977 Galerie Drieghe, Wetteren, Belgium
Wittepoppetoren, Hasselt, Belgium (with Hugo Duchâteau)
1978 Galerie Jeanne Buytaert, Antwerp

Galerie Jean Leroy, Paris
Museum van Hedendaagse Kunst, Ghent
1979 Galerie Waalkens, Finsterwolde, Netherlands
Bilder 1976–1978, Belgisches Haus, Cologne
1980 Galerie Declercq, Knokke, Belgium
Galerie Jeanne Buytaert, Antwerp
International Cultureel Centrum, Antwerp
1982 Kunsthandel Lambert Tegenbosch, Heusden aan de Maas, Netherlands
Galerie Richard Foncke, Ghent, Belgium
1983 Vereniging Aktuele Kunst Gewad, Ghent, Belgium
1984 Villa des Roses, Ghent, Belgium
1985 Dam 43, Middelburg, Netherlands
Galerie Drieghe, Wetteren, Belgium
Ado, Bonheiden, Belgium
1986 Museum Mw. J. Dhondt-Dhaenens, Deurle, Belgium
Paleis voor Schone Kunsten, Brussels
1987 Vereniging voor het Museum van Hedendaagse Kunst, Ghent, Belgium
Villa des Roses, Ghent, Belgium

Selected Group Exhibitions:

1967 *Premio Lissone*, Milan
1968 *Alternative Attuali 3*, L'Aquila, Italy
1971 *D'Après*, Museo Civico, Lugano, Switzerland
Bienal, Sao Paul
1973 *Fortunately There Is Still Some Grass*, Camden Arts Centre, London
1974 *3rd Triennale*, Bruges
1975 *Concerning Painting*, Museum van Bommel—Van Dam, Venlo, Netherlands (toured the Netherlands)
1980 *Beervelde 1966—nu*, De Vieeshal, Middelburg, Netherlands
Belgie-Nederland: Kunst na '45, Palais des Beaux-Arts, Brussels (travelled to the Museum Boymans-van Beuningen, Rotterdam)
1986 *Een keuze/un choix*, KunstRAI, Amsterdam

Collections:

Museum van Hedendaages Kunst, Ghent; Groeninge Museum, Bruges; Museum voor Schone Kunsten, Courtrai, Belgium; Provinciaal Museum, De Lakenhalle, Ypres, Belgium; Gemeentekrediet van Belgie, Brussels; Museum, Dienze, Belgium; Groninger Museum, Groningen, Netherlands; Museum voor Moderne Kunst, Brussels.

Publications:

By DE KEYSER: book—*More Is Less*, with Roland Jooris, Deinze, 1972.

On DE KEYSER: books—*Raoul De Keyser*, exhibition catalogue, with text by Roland Jooris and Paul Vries, Groningen, Netherlands 1970; *Raoul De Keyser: Het samengaan van gegeven en schilderij* by Roland Jooris, Wakken, Belgium 1972; *Raoul De Keyser: Nota najaar 73*, by Roland Jooris, Deinze, Belgium 1973; *Amedée Cortier and Raoul De Keyser*, exhibition catalogue, with text by Yves De Smet and Roland Jooris, Eindhoven, Netherlands 1974; *Raoul De Keyser* with text by Roland Jooris, Antwerp 1978; *Raoul De Keyser*, exhibition catalogue, with texts by Jan Hoet, Marc Callewaert and Roland Jooris, Ghent 1978; *Raoul De Keyser: Bilder 1976–1978*, exhibition catalogue, with text by Roland Jooris, Cologne 1979; *Raoul De Keyser*, exhibition catalogue, with text by Roland Jooris, Heusden, Netherlands, 1982; *Raoul De Keyser*, exhibition catalgoue with text by Bart De Baere, Deurle 1986; *Raoul De Keyser*, exhibition catalogue with text by Olivier Hamerlynck, Ghent 1987.

Raoul De Keyser: *Knauw*, 1984

DEKKERS, Ad(rian).

Dutch. Born in Nieuwpoort, Netherlands, 21 March 1938. Studied at the Art Academy, Rotterdam, 1954–58. Married; had one child. Independent full-time painter and sculptor, Gorcum, from 1960. *Died* (in Gorcum, Netherlands) *27 February 1974.*

Individual Exhibitions:

1961 Galerie t'Venster, Rotterdam (with van Munster)
1962 Galerie de Drie Hendricken, Amsterdam (with van Munster)
1964 De Bijenkorf, Rotterdam
Galerie de Nieuwe Doelen, Gorinchem, Netherlands (with Joost Balijeu)
Kunststichtung de Lijnbaan, Rotterdam
1965 Galerie Walenkmap, Leiden
Galerie Swart, Amsterdam
1966 Galerie Reflex, Hilversum, The Netherlands
Galerie Swart, Amsterdam
Stedelijk Museum, Schiedam, The Netherlands (with Koetsier)
1967 Stedelijk Museum, Amsterdam
Technical College, Delft, Netherlands
Galerie Orez, The Hague
1968 Museum voor Stad en Lande, Groningen, The Netherlands
Galerie Walenkmap, Leiden
Stedelijk Museum, Amsterdam
Galerie Orez, The Netherlands
Galerie der Spiegel, Cologne
Galerie ad Libitum, Antwerp
1969 Galerie Dorothea Loehr, Frankfurt
1970 Stedelijk van Abbemuseum, Eindhoven, Netherlands
Plus Kern, Ghent
1971 Galerie Swart, Amsterdam
Galerie M, Bochum, West Germany
1972 Gemeentemuseum, The Hague
1973 Lucy Milton Gallery, London
1974 Stedelijk van Abbemuseum, Eindhoven, Netherlands
Rosa Esman Gallery, New York
Kunsthalle, Dusseldorf
1977 Rijksmuseum Kröller-Müller, Otterlo, Netherlands
1982 Staatliche Kunsthalle, Baden-Baden, West Germany

Selected Group Exhibitions:

1964 *Stichting Liga Nieuwe Beelden*, Stedelijk Museum, Amsterdam
1965 *4th Biennal des Jeunes Artistes*, Musée d'Art Moderne de la Ville, Paris
1966 *Weiss auf Weiss*, Kunsthalle, Berne
1967 *Dutch Contemporary Art*, at the *Expo '67*, Montreal
1968 *Kleur Object*, Middelheim Open Air Museum, Antwerp
1968 *10 Dutch Artists*, Midland Group Gallery, Nottingham (toured the U.K.)
1970 *Sammlung Etzold*, Kunstverein, Cologne, West Germany

1971 *Tendances Constructivistes dans l'Art Hollandais aprés 1945*, Musée des Beaux-Arts, Liége, Belgium
1972 *Amsterdam/Paris/Dusseldorf*, Guggenheim Museum, New York
1973 *Lof der Tekenkunst*, Stedelijk van Abbemuseum, Eindhoven, Netherlands

Collections:

Stedelijk Museum, Amsterdam; Stedelijk van Abbe Museum, Eindhoven, Netherlands; Rijksmuseum Kröller-Müller, Otterlo, Netherlands; Museum voor Stad en Lande, Groningen, Netherlands; Gemeentemuseum, The Hague; Museum Boymans van Beuningen, Rotterdam; Stedelijk Museum, Schiedam, Netherlands; Tate Gallery, London; McCrory Corporation, New York.

Publications:

By DEKKERS: articles—"Statement on My Work" in *Structure* (Amsterdam), no. 6, 1964; *Inleiding*, exhibition catalogue, Utrecht 1969; "Over de Lijn" in *Museumsjournaal* (Amsterdam), December 1971.

On DEKKERS: books—*Dekkers* by Jean Leering, Frankfurt 1973; *Ad Dekkers*, exhibition catalogue with texts by Siegmar Holtzen and Katharina Schjmidt. Baden-Baden 1982; articles—"Modern Dutch Art" by Enno Develing in *Art and Artists* (London), October 1969; "Dutch Commentary Drawings in Holland" by Carol Blotkamp in *Studio International* (London), December 1970; "Shifted Squares and Quartering by a Left to Right Sawn Groove" by M. Vos in *Studio International* (London), May 1973; "Ad Dekkers," obituary, by Liesbeth Brandt Corstius in *Studio International* (London), May 1974.

The early death of Dekkers robbed the world and Holland in particular of one of the most successful sculptors in the constructivist vein. In terms of association it has been suggested that he is a natural descendant aesthetically of the de Stijl experimentalist Van Doesburg (not in the early distortions of figuration—like Van Doesburg's famous canvases of the cow, starting with semi-realism and winding up in subtle sotto-voce abstract symbols—but rather in that artist's excursions into unreal architectural design); and, in the late fifties and early sixties a degree of style-contact in Dekkers' work of that time can also be discerned which shows a kinship with methods employed by the Swiss artists Lohse and Max Bill. Development leading to his final stage of uncomplicated and absolutist reliefs went through a gradual refinement over the years.

First serious art works from Dekkers had taken the form of exact realism. But when this ceased to satisfy his artistic intentions, he allowed these images to become modulated and eventually to go increasingly geometric in concept. Internationally, it is the ultimate parting from any form of realistic imagery that this artist took which made his final style most familiar to the global framework of contemporary modern art.

There had come a time in the progress of his creativity when he abandoned painting 'pictures' altogether, settling instead for flat reliefs and other low-level reliefs where the only variant would be a straightline incision (carved into the wood at a rising or falling level). Literally his output had become confined to rectangles, squares, triangles and circles. (towards the end of his life Dekkers switched from 'working drawings' to graphic work which could stand on its own rather than act as a guide to creation of a new relief. Sometimes as plain in character as the reliefs themselves, on occasions he did also investigate the promises extended by straightline shading, maybe dividing the square with a diagonal line, but shading the resultant triangles in different straightline intensities and in so doing evoking a visual attraction, magnetic and magic in its compulsion).

Reliefs—and drawings—were the constructed fulfilment to his demanding ambition: total clarity. Perhaps this clarity was still further emphasised after 1968 by the same principles being extended to free-standing sculptures, not in tandem with but also not disassociated from the purity of the reliefs.

The largest, and probably most formidable, of his major works in the field of construction, completed only a few years before his death, was the commission he undertook for the Kröller-Müller Museum in Otterlo. Working from his designs, he built a pair of reliefs for the two walls chosen for the Museum's new extension wing. The logical advance of refined economy that is observed here in a 14-year-long art career, beginning with true and careful recording of visible reality and ending with spatial construction of tireless precision editing, does not give the background out of which this artist's mastery proceeded. His gradual shredding of realism and the vicissitudes through which it passed were seemingly out of context with the prevailing taste for Dutch artistic modernism at the time, veering as it did towards forms of romantic and undisciplined non-figuration and abstraction, distinctly at odds with the clean geometric elements in the pictures painted by Dekkers. True, he had the stern unyielding hard geometry practised by the de Stijl artists running parallel with his other kind of Abstract painting, but Mondrian and his colleagues were not at that period at the centre of modern Dutch Art, interest in their theories and conclusions was far more prominent outside Holland and, whilst admiring Piet Mondrian for much of what he was achieving, Dekkers found his rejection of the triangle and the circle incompatible just because triangle and circle in the conception of the de Stijl ran contrary to total pictorial harmony.

In consequence, to find agreeable encouragement for the way in which Dekkers wanted to pursue his own artistic intentions, he had to find consolation from abroad in the quiet seclusion of Dutch museums of which the Kröller-Müller was a prime example; places where he could see examples of works by Ben Nicholson and Hans Arp. He was also aware in this way of oeuvres of Biederman, Baljeu, Judd, LeWitt and Morris. It was the performance of artists like these, carried out in complete contrast to the indifference to his careful approach to geometric nonfiguration which he had experienced from the teachers when he was attending Rotterdam Art Academy effectively making him a loner during his student days, which helped provide comfort to him in cultural isolation, gladdened his heart and steeled his patience while he pressed on for ultimate recognition.

—Sheldon Williams

DEKKERS, Ger(rit Hendrik).

Dutch. Born in Borne, 21 August 1929. Educated at secondary school in Hangelo, 1942-46; studied graphics at the Academie voor Kunst en Industrie, Enschede, 1950-54. Served in the Dutch Army, in Indonesia, 1948-50. Married Hilda Hartsuiker in 1954; children: Henriette and Jose. Freelance artist and photographer, Enschede, 154-73, and in Giethoorn, since 1973. Member, Photo Section, Gebonden Kunstenfederatie (GKf), since 1969. Recipient: Dutch Ministry of Culture Grant, 1970, 1971, 1975, 1976; City of Amsterdam Stipendium, 1976. Agents: Galerie M., Haus Weitmar, 463 Bochum-Weitmar, West Germany; and Galerie Nouvelles Images, Westeinde 22, The Hague, Netherlands. Address: Dwarsgracht 31, 8355 CV Giethoorn, Netherlands.

Individual Exhibitions:

1972 *Landscape Perception*, Rijksmuseum Kröller-Müller, Otterlo, Netherlands.
1973 *Landscape Perception*, Museum Bochum-Kunstsammlung, Bochum, West Germany.
Landscape Perception, Neue Galerie-Kunstsammlung Ludwig, Aachen, West Germany
1974 *Landscape Perception*, Stedelijk Museum, Amsterdam
Landscape Perception 1968-1975, Gemeentemuseum, The Hague
1975 *Landscape Perception*, Palais des Beaux-Arts, Brussels
Landscape Perception, Galleria del Cavallino, Venice
1976 *Landscape Perception*, Kunstmuseum, Aarhus, Denmark
Landscape Perception, Print Gallery Peiter Brattinga, Amsterdam
Landscape Perception, Galerie M. Bocum, West Germany
1977 *Planned Landscapes*, Rijksmuseum Kröller-Müller, Otterlo, Netherlands
Plastic, Museum Boymans van Beuningen, Rotterdam
1978 *Plastic*, Gemeentemuseum, Arnhem, Netherlands
Planned Landscapes, De Vishal, Haarlem, Netherlands
1979 *New Dutch Landscape*, Hayden Gallery, Massachusetts Institute of Technology, Cambridge
Planned Landscapes, Print Gallery Pieter Brattinga, Amsterdam
Planned Landscapes, Provincial Begijnhof, Hasselt, Belgium
1980 *Planned Landscapes*, Kunstcentrum Markt 17, Enschede, Netherlands
Planned Landscapes, Rijksplanologische Dienst, The Hague
1981 *Planned Landscapes*, Stadium Generale, Wageningen, Netherlands
Planned Landscapes, Städtische Galerie, Nordhorn, West Germany

Selected Group Exhibitions:

1969 *Atelier 6*, Stedelijk Museum, Amsterdam
1971 *Sonsbeek 71*, Central Station, Amsterdam
1974 *Projekt 74*, Kunsthalle, Cologne
1977 *Sequenzen*, Kunstverein, Hamburg
Documenta 6, Kassel, West Germany
Museum of Drawers, Kunsthaus, Zurich (now permanent installation)
1978 *Fotografie in Nederland 1940-75*, Stedelijk Museum, Amsterdam
Fotografie als Kunst/Kunst als Fotografie 2, Fotoforum der Gesamthochschule, Kasel, West Germany (toured Germany, Poland, Portugal, Spain and the United States)
1979 *To Do With Nature*, travelling exhibition (toured the Netherlands, Sweden, Belgium, West Germany, Denmark, and Portugal)
Kunst als Fotografie 1949-79, Tiroler Landesmuseum Ferdinandeum, Innsbruck (travelled to the Neue Galerie am Wolfgang Gurlitt Museum, Linz, Austria; Neue Galerie am Landesmuseum Joanneum, Graz, Austria; and the Museum des 20. Jahrhunderts, Vienna)

Collections:

Rijksmuseum Kröller-Müller, Otterlo, Netherlands; Stedelijk Museum, Amsterdam; Frans Halsmuseum, Haarlem, Netherlands; Museum Boymans van Beuningen, Rotterdam; Gemeentemuseum, The Hauge; Gemeentemuseum, Arnhem, Netherlands; Ministry of Culture, The Hague; Sammlung Ludwig, Cologne; Kunsthalle, Hamburg; Museum Bochum-Kunstsammlung, Bochum, West Germany.

Publications:

By DEKKERS: book—*Planned Landscapes: 25 Horizons*, with an introduction by R. W. D. Oxenaar, Amsterdam 1977; *Graven en begrave in Overijssel*, editor, with H. Schelhaas and B. Molenaar, Zwolle 1980.

On DEKKERS: books—*Ger Dekkers: Landscape Perceptions*, exhibition catalogue, with text by R. W. D. Oxenaar, Otterlo, Netherlands 1972; *Ger Dekkers: Landscape Perceptions*, exhibition catalogue, with text by Peter Spielmann, Bochum, West Germany 1973; *Ger Dekkers: Landscape Perceptions*, exhibition catalogue, with text by Wolfgang Be-

cker, Aachen, West Germany 1973; *Ger Dekkers: Landscape Perceptions 1968–1975,* exhibition catalogue, with text by J. L. Locher and Manfred Schneckenburger, The Hague 1974; *Fotografie in Nederland 1940–1975,* exhibition catalogue, with text by Els Barents, Ingeborg Leyerzapf and others, The Hague 1978; *New Dutch Landscape,* exhibition catalogue, by Marc S. Gerstein, Cambridge, Massachusetts 1979; *The Artist as Photographer* by Marina Vaizey, London 1982; articles—"Ger Dekkers" in *Flash Art* (Milan), December 1974/January 1975; "Ger Dekkers" by A. Van Berswordt-Wallrabe in *M-Bochum* (Bochum, West Germany), no. 3, 1976, "Ger Dekkers" by Betty van Garrel in *Volker Post* (Rotterdam), no. 4, 1978; "Ger Dekkers" by Dolf Welling in the *Holland Herald* (Amsterdam), July 1979; "Ger Dekkers" by Fred Hazelhoff in *Foto* (Hilversum, Netherlands), September 1980; "Ger Dekkers" by Herman v. Buuren in *Bijvoorbeeld* (Amsterdam), no. 2. 1981.

My actual subject is the effect that our culture has on landscape. The Dutch landscape with its polders provides an excellent example.

I am aware that my work is a personal expression, in which my personality is one factor. My principal action—to record a situation that I encounter—I experience myself as an intruder.

My concern with the subject and its surroundings does not go further than emotionally choosing the angle of the camera and focussing it, and later on making a selection and carefully completing the process.

The horizon acts as a middle line in the square pictures: this gives a continuous line that runs throughout the series and thus the whole project.

The medium I use is another factor.

I find only a limited number of phototechnical possibilities important. It is not the gimmicks of photography that mean most to me but its very irrevocability, its inevitability. From these factors, but mainly, I hope, from its essence, my work derives its validity.

—Ger Dekkers

In his works Ger Dekkers makes visible the way in which the Dutch landscape reveals itself to the observer as a continuous series of organized data—although a simple disclosure itself is not necessarily an ordered achievement. Thus it is no accident that around 1972 the color photographs of Ger Dekkers were at the center of a debate about the differences between photography as a means of recording reality and as a plastic art.

Dekkers' large exhibition at the Rijksmuseum Kröller-Müller gave the distinguished critic Rudi Fuchs an occasion to consider the nature of photography. For Fuchs, the most important elements of photography are the possibilities afforded by direct manipulation, especially by the deliberate placing of objects and the process of excision. But he goes on to accuse Dekkers of using the medium in an unnatural way, of denying the history of photography and structuring his work according to the aesthetic of a particular trend of the moment, in this case Minimal Art. He accuses Dekkers of going beyond the bounds of his medium, of borrowing from the plastic arts without giving anything in return: Dekkers does not even bother to acknowledge that the boundaries are problematic. On another occasion Fuchs defended those works by Jan Dibbets in which there is a living relationship between an impersonal medium and the artist's individuality. But in general Dekkers is an artist because he *makes,* and Dibbets, because he merely *registers,* is not.

The importance of Ger Dekkers work is that its quality is apparent whether it is a photograph, a slide or a book. For example, in cooperation with the Art Animation in Groningen (since 1977 the Corps de Garde) he produced a series of carefully planned catalogues. These are particularly relevant to the question raised by Conceptual Art: is plastic art necessarily confined to particular forms and occasions? No doubt the particular qualities of the Dutch landscape are especially suited to the point of view of constructivism and minimalism. That Dekkers has been influenced by them is itself unimportant: what matters is what he has done with dikes, the forests and fields of grain and playgrounds. The special realms of the gallery and museum are not for him. Much more appropriate, in fact, are busy public buildings—the Netherlands railway stations, for example, where some of his photographs now appear.

—A. F. Wagemans

de KOONING, Willem.

American. Born in Rotterdam, Netherlands, 24 April 1904; emigrated to the United States as stowaway on a ship, 1927. Studied at the Akademie voor Beeldende Kunsten en Techischen Wetenschappen, Rotterdam, 1916–24, 1926–27. Married Elaine Marie Catherine Fried in 1943; daughter: Lisa. Apprentice to the commercial artists Jan and Jaap Gidding, Rotterdam 1916; assistant to Bernard Romein, art director of a Rotterdam department store, 1920–23; worked as house painter, Hoboken, New Jersey 1927; moved to New York and held various commercial art jobs, 1927–28; met John Graham, Arshile Gorky and Stuart Davis, New York, 1928–29; full time painter from 1935; shared studio with Arshile Gorky, New York 1937; designed and painted murals, Federal Arts Project, New York, 1935-39. Instructor, Black Mountain College, Beria, North Carolina, 1948, and Yale University, New Haven, Connecticut, 1950–51, 1959–60. Recipient: Logan Medal and Purchase Prize, Art Institute of Chicago, 1951; President's Freedom Award Medal, 1964; Talens Prize International, Amsterdam 1968; Gold Medal, American Academy of Arts and Letters, New York, 1975; Artist of the Year Award, Fairfield Arts Festival, Connecticut, 1978; Mellon Prize (with Eduardo Chillida), Carnegie Institute, Pittsburgh, 1979; Max Beckman Prize, Frankfurt, 1984; Kaiser Ring Award, Goslar, 1984; National Medal of Arts, Washington, D.C., 1986; Mayor's Liberty Medal, New York, 1986. Member, National Institute of Arts and Letters, 1960; Member, Royal Academy of Fine Arts, Stockholm, 1986. Agent: Xavier Fourcade Inc., New York. Address: c/o Xavier Fourcade Inc., 36 East 75th Street, New York, New York 10021, U.S.A.

Individual Exhibitions:

1948	Charles Egan Gallery, New York
1951	Charles Egan Gallery, New York
	De Kooning/Pollock/Shahn, Arts Club of Chicago
1943	Sidney Janis Gallery, New York
	Boston Museum Art School (retrospective; travelled to the Workshop Art Center, Washington, D.C.)
1955	Martha Jackson Gallery, New York
1956	Sidney Janis Gallery, New York
1959	Sidney Janis Gallery, New York
1961	Paul Kantor Gallery, Beverly Hills, California
1962	*Barnett Newman and Willem de Kooning,* Allan Stone Gallery, New York
1964	Allan Stone Gallery, New York
	'Woman' Drawings by Willem de Kooning, James Goodman Gallery, Buffalo, New York
1965	Paul Kantor Gallery, Beverly Hills, California
	Smith College Museum of Art, Northampton, Massachusetts (retrospective; travelled to the Massachusetts Institute of Technology, Cambridge)
1966	*De Kooning's Women,* Allan Stone Gallery, New York
1967	M. Knoedler and Company, New York
	Allan Stone Gallery, New York
1968	*Peintures Récentes,* M. Knoedler et Cie, Paris
	Stedelijk Museum, Amsterdam (retrospective; travelled to the Tate Gallery, London)
1969	Museum of Modern Art, New York (retrospective)
	M. Knoedler and Company, New York
1971	M. Knoedler and Company, New York
	Allan Stone Gallery, New York
1972	Allan Stone Gallery, New York
	Baltimore Museum of Art
	Sidney Janis Gallery, New York
1974	University of Alabama, University (toured the United States)

Willem De Kooning: *Untitled VI*, 1985

Walker Art Center, Minneapolis (toured the United States and Canada)
Richard Gray Gallery, Chicago

1975 *New Works: Paintings and Sculpture*, Xavier Fourcade Inc., New York
Paintings, Drawings, Sculpture 1967–75, Norton Gallery of Art, Palm Beach, Florida

1976 Seattle Art Museum
Stedelijk Museum, Amsterdam
Collection d'Art, Amsterdam
Gimpel Fils, London
Gimpel Fils, Zurich
New Paintings 1976, Xavier Fourcade Inc., New York
Blaffer Gallery, University of Houston

1977 Collection d'Art, Amsterdam
Xavier Fourcade Inc., New York
Wilheim Lembruck Museum, Duisburg, West Germany
Musée de Grenoble, France
The Sculpture of de Kooning with Related Paintings, Drawings and Lithographs, Arts Council of Great Britain, London
Galerie Templon, Paris
Museum of Modern Art, Belgrade
Museum of Modern Art, Ljubljana, Yugoslavia

1978 *Willem de Kooning in East Hampton*, Guggenheim Museum, New York
Museum of Art, Science and Industry, Bridgeport, Connecticut
Romanian National Museum of Art, Bucharest
Branch Post, Cracow
Helsinki National Museum of Art
America House, East Berlin
University of California Art Museum, Berkeley
De Kooning 1969–1978, University of Northern Iowa, Cedar Falls

1979 St. Louis Art Museum
Contemporary Arts Center, Cincinnati, Ohio
Akron Art Institute, Ohio
March Foundation, Alicante, Spain
Fundación Juan March, Madrid
Norwegian National Gallery of Art, Oslo
Dordrechts Museum, The Netherlands
Pittsburgh International Series, Museum of Art, Pittsburgh

1980 Richard Hines Gallery, Seattle
Richard Gray Gallery, Chicago
Galerie Hans Strelow, Dusseldorf

1981 Janie C. Lee Gallery, Houston
Guild Hall, East Hampton, New York

1982 C. Grimaldis Gallery, Baltimore
Xavier Fourcade Inc., New York

1983 *The North Atlantic Light 1960–63*, Stedelijk Museum, Amsterdam (travelled to Denmark and Sweden)
Xavier Fourcade Inc., New York
De Kooning Drawings, Whitney Museum, New York (travelled to West Berlin and Paris)
Retrospective Exhibition, Whitney Museum, New York (travelled to West Berlin and Paris)
De Kooning Sculpture, Josef-Haubrich-Kunsthalle, Cologne
Sculpture Court, Philip Morris, New York
Galerie Maeght LeLong, New York

1984 Colorado State University, Fort Collins
Intimate Gallery, Lincoln Center, Fort Collins, Colorado
Stadelsches Kunstinstitut, Frankfurt
Xavier Fourcade Inc., New York
Das Moenchehaus Museum, Goslar, West Germany
Galerie Daniel Templon, Paris
Galerie Hans Strelow, Dusseldorf
Anthony D'Offay Gallery, London

1985 Studio Marconi, Milan
Xavier Fourcade Inc., New York
Margo Leavin Gallery, Los Angeles

1986 Fabian Carlsson Gallery, London
Anthony D'Offay Gallery, London

1987 Margo Leavin Gallery, Los Angeles
C. Grimaldis Gallery, Baltimore
Richard Gray Gallery, Chicago

Selected Group Exhibitions:

1945 *Group Show*, Charles Egan Gallery, New York
1950 *Biennale*, Venice
1951 *60th Annual of American Painting and Sculpture*, Art Institute of Chicago
1954 *Biennale*, Venice
1969 *Festival of 2 Worlds*, Spoleto, Italy
1978 *Sculpture and Works on Paper from the 1930's and 1940's*, Washburn Gallery, New York
1981 *A New Spirit in Painting*, Royal Academy, London
1982 *New York School: Four Decades*, Guggenheim Museum, New York
1985 *Flying Tigers: Painting and Sculpture in New York 1939–46*, Brown University, Providence, Rhode Island (travelled to Worcester, Massachusetts; Southampton, New York)
1987 *L'Epoque, la mode, la morale, la passion*, Centre Georges Pompidou, Paris

Collections:

Museum of Modern Art, New York; Metropolitan Museum of Art, New York; Guggenheim Museum, New York; Whitney Museum, New York; Art Institute of Chicago; Carnegie Institute, Pittsburgh; National Gallery, Washington, D.C., Centre Georges Pompidou, Paris; Tate Gallery, London; Stedelijk Museum, Amsterdam; Bayerische Staatsgemaldesammlung, Munich

Publications:

By de KOONING: articles—letter to the editor, on Arshile Gorky in *Art News* (New York), January 1949; interview, with Martha Boudrez, in *The Knickerbocker* (New York) May 1950; "Artists' Sessions at studio 35 (1950)" in *Modern Artists in America*, edited by Robert Motherwell and Ad Reinhardt, New York 1951; "The Renaissance and Order" in *Transformation* (New York), vol. 1, no. 2, 1951; "What Abstract Art Means to Me" in *Museum of Modern Art Bulletin* (New York), Spring 1951; interview in *Conversations with Artists* by Selden Rodman, New York 1957; "Is Today's Artist with or Against the Past?", interview, with Thomas B. Hess, in *Artnews* (New York), June 1958; film-script in *Sketchbook No. 1:3 Americans*, (New York), 1960; "Content is a Glimpse . . ." interview, with David Sylvester, in *Location* (Easthampton, New York), 1963; interview, with James T. Valliere, in *Partisan Review* (New York), Fall 1957; interview in *Vrij Nederland* (Amsterdam), 5 October 1968; "A Desperate View" in *Willem de Kooning* by Thomas B. Hess, New York 1969; "Interview with Willem de Kooning," with Harold Rosenberg, in *Artnews* (New York), September 1972.

On de KOONING: books—*De Kooning Retrospective*, exhibition catalogue, with a foreword by Clement Greenberg, Boston 1953; *De Kooning*, exhibition catalogue, New York 1955; *Willem de Kooning* by Thomas B. Hess, New York 1959; *De Kooning* by Harriet Janis and Rudi Blish, New York and London 1960; *Willem de Kooning*, exhibition catalogue, with text by Clifford Odets, Beverly Hills, California 1961; *Willem de Kooning*, 3 volume unpublished collections of photographs, critical commentaries and annotations, compiled by William C. Agee, New York 1962; *De Kooning-Newman*, exhibition catalogue, with comments by Allan Stone, New York 1962; *'Woman' Drawings by Willem de Kooning*, exhibition catalogue, with a preface by Merle Goodman, Buffalo, New York 1964; *Willem de Kooning*, exhibition catalogue , with preface by William Inge, Beverly Hills, California 1965; *De Kooning's Women*, exhibition catalogue, New York 1966; *De Kooning: Recent Paintings*, exhibition catalogue, by Thomas B. Hess, New York 1967; *De Kooning: Peintures Récentes*, exhibition catalogue, Paris 1968; *Willem de Kooning*, exhibition catalogue, with an introduction by Thomas B. Hess, Amsterdam 1968; *De Kooning: January 1968—March 1969*, exhibition catalogue by Thomas B. Hess, New York 1969; *Drawings of Willem de Kooning* by Thomas B. Hess, Greenwich, Connecticut 1972; *Willem de Kooning* by Gabriella Drudi, Milan 1972; *De Kooning* by Harold Rosenberg, New york 1974; *American Masters: The Voice and the Myth* by Brian O'Doherty, New York 1974; *De Kooning: Paintings, Drawings, Sculpture 1967–1975*, exhibition catalogue, Palm Beach, Florida 1975; *De Kooning: New Works, Paintings and Sculpture*, exhibition catalogue, New York 1975; *Willem de Kooning*, exhibition catalogue, Amsterdam 1976; *De Kooning: New Paintings, 1976*, exhibition catalogue, New York 1976; *The Sculpture of de Kooning with Related Paintings, Drawings and Lithographs*, exhibition catalogue, with text by Andrew Forge, foreword by David Sylvester, London, 1977; *American Art at Mid-Century: The Subjects of the Artist* by E. A. Carnean, Jr. and Eliza R. Rathbone, Washington, D.C. 1978; *Willem de Kooning in East Hampton*, exhibition catalogue, by Diane Waldman, New York 1978; *De Kooning 1969–1978*, exhibition catalogue, edited by Sanford Shman, with text by Jack Coward, Cedar Falls, Iowa 1978; *Willem de Kooning: Pittsburgh International Series*, exhibition catalogue, Pittsburgh 1979; *Willem de Kooning: The North Atlantic Light 1960–83*, exhibition catalogue, Amsterdam 1983; *Willem de Kooning: Skulpturen*, exhibition catalogue, Cologne 1983; *Willem de Kooning: Drawings, Paintings, Sculpture*, exhibiiton catalogue, New York 1983; *Willem de Kooning: Retrospective*, exhibition catalogue, West Berlin and Paris 1984.

The de Kooning style of work has spread itself across a variety of influences, not all of them comfortable bedfellows.

His successful childhood apprenticeship with the commercial artists' company run by the decorators Jan and Jaap Gidding in Holland prompted Jaap to arrange for him to enter the Rotterdam Academy of Fine Arts and Techniques where he remained a student for eight years absorbing the breadth of a wide curriculum which was nevertheless strict in its determination to give every aspirant a stern academic training in the arts and a mastercraftsman's proficiency in craft techniques. During this time he also became aware of what the de Stijl group of Mondrian and van Doesburg believed creative art should achieve.

Later on when, after several vain attempts, he left Holland behind and entered the United States, he was able to bring with him the balance of a training that gave him an aptitude for both painting and making things. He was practical as well as accomplished.

When he started to paint seriously—as an artist—his first development was in the direction taken by Arshile Gorky (in his early portraits), but these de Kooning paintings of the 1930s were in double-harness with untitled, non-figurative works which may have owed something to de Stijl (but had none of the hard-edge of the Dutch School) and something also to the later and more fantastic Gorky. At all events, in both categories there lurked a strong flavour of the United States.

In the mid-1940s the character of his paintings took on two other aspects. A number of them (generally based on figures and usually those of women) seemed to transmute at least a part of what Jackson Pollock had discovered. Rarely with Pollock's random attack (most of them, but by no means all, were very carefully strung together in professionally correct composition), they still inspired the same effect of splintered or sprawling confusion—an emotional confusion rather than a visual one. For all their frequent and decorous attention to expert tailoring, these pictures—full of pastel tints and black outlines or dark areas edged with white—were moving proof that here was an artist who combines taste with passion.

Side by side with them, and with increasing frequency, appeared the figure studies. No hint of early Gorky this time. These paintings are a fascinating mixture of picassoid distortions with Cobra School vehemence and vibrant colouring (a curious, if long delayed legacy from the Netherlands where he was born). The Spaniard's part in all this alchemy at the hands of a contemporary art apothecary has been gradually phased out, but the Cobra element remains and has since entered the near-abstract landscapes and pictures of atmosphere like "Rosy-Fingered Dawn at Louse Point."

Without question Willem de Kooning is a well-organised modern artist. He works steadily and never totally rejects what he has been able to glean from experience. His newest development has been to try his hand—with some success—at sculpture. He can make things.

—Sheldon Williams

DEL PEZZO, Lucio.

Italian. Born in Naples in 1933. Studied land surveying at the Accademia di Belle Arti, Naples, 1954–58; mainly self-taught. First paintings, 1954; full-time artist, Milan, 1958–64, and in Paris, since 1965; Founder, with Alberto Biasi, Mario Persico, Sergio Fergola and others, Gruppo 58, Naples, 1958; regular contributor to the avant-garde periodical *Documento Sud,* Naples and Milan, 1958-59. Agent: Studio Marcomi, Milan. Address: c/o Studio Marconi, Via Tadino 15, 20124 Milan, Italy.

Individual Exhibitions:

1960 Galerie Senatore, Stuttgart
1961 Galleria Schwarz, Milan
1962 Knapik Gallery, New York
1963 Gallerie Schwarz, Milan
Alexandre Iolas Gallery, New York
Galerie J., Paris
1964 Galleria Il Cavallino, Venice
1965 Galleria L'Arco d'Alibert, Rome
Rijksmuseum Kröller-Müller, Otterlo, Netherlands
Stadtische Museum Schloss Morsbroich, Leverkusen, West Germany
Galleria Odyssia, Rome
1966 Galleria Il Centro, Naples
Il Costruttore di Quadri Moderni, Studio Marconi, Milan
Italian Pavilion, at the *Biennale,* Venice
Galleria del Deposito, Genoa
1967 Studio Marconi, Milan
1968 Galerie Blumenthal-Mommaton, Paris
Galleria de Foscherari, Bologna
Galleria del Minotauro, Brescia, Italy
1969 Galleria La Chiocciola, Padua
Studio Marconi, Milan
1970 Galerie Germain, Paris
Galerie Brusberg, Hannover
Galerie Foncke, Ghent
Palais des Beaux-Arts, Brussels
La Pilotta, Istituto di Storia dell'Arte, University of Parma
1971 Marlborough Galleria d'Arte, Rome
Studio Marconi, Milan
1972 Galerie Ostermaim, Stockholm
1973 Galerie Lucien Durand, Paris
Galerie Visat, Paris
1974 Studio Marconi, Milan
Rotonda de Via Besana, Milan

Selected Group Exhibitions:

1962 *Kunst von 1960 bis Heute,* Museum des 20. Jahrhunderts, Vienna
1963 *Biennale de Paris,* Musée National d'Arte Moderne, Paris
1964 *Biennale,* Venice
1966 *Dada 1906–1966,* Museo d'Arte Moderna, Milan
1968 *International Exhibition of Drawings,* University of Puerto Rico
1970 *Salon de Mai,* Paris
1971 *Biennale,* Tokyo
Art et Anti-Art 1910–1979, Palais des Beaux-Arts, Brussels
1973 *Kunst Markt,* Cologne
1982 *Arte Italiana 1960–82,* Hayward Gallery, London

Collections:

Galleria Nazionale d'Arte Moderna, Rome; Centre Georges Pompidou, Paris; Centre National d'Art Contemporain, Paris; Stedelijk Museum, Amsterdam; Victoria and Albert Museum, London; Museum of Modern Art, New York; Guggenheim Museum, New York; Carnegie Institute, Pittsburgh; Museum of Fine Art, Montreal; Art Gallery of Ontario, Toronto.

Publications:

On DEL PEZZO: books—*Del Pezzo,* exhibition catalogue, with text by Giorgio Kaisserlain, Milan 1961; *Lucio Del Pezzo,* exhibition catalogue, Milan 1963; *Lucio Del Pezzo: Techiche Miste su Cartone,* exhibition catalogue, with text by Cesare Vivaldi, Rome 1965; *Lucio Del Pezzo,* exhibition catalogue, with text by Roberto Sanesi, Genoa 1966; *Lucio Del Pezzo: Il Costruttore di Quadri Moderni,* exhibition catalogue, with texts by Enrico Baj, Gillo Dorfles and Alain Jouffroy, Milan 1966; *Del Pezzo,* exhibition catalogue, with text by Gillo Dorfles, Brescia, Italy 1968; *Lucio Del Pezzo,* exhibition catalogue, with text by Tommaso Trini, Rome 1971; *Lucio Del Pezzo,* exhibition catalogue, with text by Guido Ballo, Milan 1974.

DELVAUX, Paul.

Belgian. Born in Antheit, near Huys, 23 September 1897. Educated in Brussels; studied architecture, 1916–17, then painting under Constant Montald and Jean Delville, 1919–21, Academie des Beaux-Arts, Brussels. Served in the Belgian Army, Brussels, 1920–21. Married Anne-Marie (Tam) DeMartelaere in 1952. Painter from 1921: established studio in Brussels, 1924; visited Paris, 1926; travelled in Italy, 1938, 1939; worked in seclusion during the German occupation, 1940–44; worked on designs for *Adame Mirroir,* ballet by Jean Genet, Theatre Marigny, Paris, 1948; lived in Choisel, France, 1949. Professor of Painting, Ecole Nationale Supérieure d'Art et d'Architecture, Brussels, 1950–62. President, Académie Royale des Beaux-Arts, Brussels, 1965. Recipient: Prix de l'Académie Picard, Brussels, 1938; Prix de Reggio Emilio, 1955; Grand Prize for Painting, Province of Liège, 1961; Rembrandt Prize, Amsterdam, 1969; Prix Septemnnal, Province of Liège, 1987. Honorary Doctorate: Free University of Brussels, 1979. Member, Institut de France, 1977; Honorary Citizen, Town of Furnes, 1978. Foundation Paul Delvaux established, 1980; Musée Paul Delvaux, Saint-Idesbald, established, 1982. Address: Foundation Paul Delvaux, 42 Kabouterweg, 8460 Saint-Idesbald, Belgium.

Individual Exhibitions:

1925 Galerie Breckpot, Brussels (with Robert Giron)
1926 Galerie Manteau, Brussels
1927 Galerie Manteau, Brussels
1928 Galerie Manteau, Brussels (with Robert Giron)
Palais des Beaux-Arts, Brussels
1929 Galerie Manteau, Brussels
1939 Palais des Beaux-Arts, Brussels
1933 Atelier de la Grosse-Tour, Brussels
1934 Palais des Beaux-Arts, Brussels
1936 Palais des Beaux-Arts, Brussels (with Rene Magritte)
1937 Palais des Beaux-Arts, Brussels
Galerie Esher Surrey, The Hague
1938 Palais des Beaux-Arts, Brussels
London Gallery
1940 Palais des Beaux-Arts, Brussels
1943 Galerie Lou Cosyn, Brussels
1944 Palais des Beaux-Arts, Brussels
1946 Julien Levy Gallery, New York
Redfern Gallery, London
1948 Julien Levy Gallery, New York
APIAW, Liège, Belgium
Galerie René Drouin, Paris
Sidney Janis Gallery, New York
1949 Palais des Beaux-Arts, Brussels
Société Royale des Beaux Arts, Verviers, Belgium
1952 Casino Communal, Knokke-le-Zoute, Belgium (with Rene Magritte)
1955 Atelier Veranneman, Courtrai, Belgium
Het Atelier, Deurne, Antwerp
1956 Atelier Veranneman, Courtrai, Belgium
1957 Maison Haute, Boitsfort, Belgium
Cercle Royal, Charleroi, Belgium (with Marc Chagall)
1959 Staempfli Gallery, New York
1962 APIAW, Liège, Belgium
Musée des Beaux-Arts, Ostende, Belgium
Renée Lachowsky and Lou Cosyn, Brussels
1963 Staempfli Gallery, New York
1964 Galerie Helikon, Hasselt, Belgium
Staempfli Gallery, New York
1965 Musée des Beaux-Arts, Mons, Belgium
Galerie Luttece, Paris
1966 Galleria del Naviglio, Milan
Gallerie del Naviglio, Turin
Gallerie Krugier, Geneva
Palais des Beaux-Arts, Lille, France
1967 Galerie Bateau-Lavoir, Paris
New Smith Galerie, Brussels
Musée d'Ixelles, Brussels
1968 Société Royale des Beaux Arts, Verviers, Belgium
Belgisches Haus, Cologne
1969 Staempfli Gallery, New York
Musée des Arts Décoratifs, Paris
1970 Musée de Peinture et de Sculpture, Grenoble, France
1971 Staempfli Gallery, New York
1972 Atelier Veranneman, Courtrai, Belgium
1973 Casino Knokke-Heist, Belgium
Museum Boymans-van-Beuningen, Rotterdam
1974 Art Salon Ginza Nova, Tokyo
Museo de Arte Moderno, Mexico City (with James Ensor and Rene Magritte)
Cultural Center, New York
Galerie Isy Brachot, Brussels (with Domenico Gnoli and Rene Magritte)
1975 Museum of Modern Art, Tokyo (travelled to the Museum of Modern Art, Kyoto)
Galerie Isy Brachot, Brussels
Palais des Beaux-Arts, Brussels (with James Ensor)
1976 Palais de l'Europe, Menton, France
1977 Galerie Isy Brachot, Brussels
Galerie Isy Brachot, Basle
Ilot St. Georges, Liège, Belgium
Musée Royaux des Beaux-Arts, Brussels
1978 Galerie Isy Brachot, Paris
1980 Gentre Cultural de la Communaute Francaise de Belgique, Paris
San Francisco Museum of Modern Art
Museum of Fine Art, Montreal
1981 Museum of Art, Newport Beach, California
La Chataigneraie, Flemalle, Liège, Belgium
Bienal, Sao Paulo
1982 Museum of Modern Art, Rio de Janeiro
Museum of Modern Art, Caracas

Selected Group Exhibitions:

1924 *Le Sillon,* Brussels
1935 *Exposition Internationale d'Art Moderne,* Brussels
1938 *Exposition Internationale du Surrealisme,* Galerie des Beaux-Arts, Paris
1942 *Surrealist Exhibition,* 451 Madison Avenue, New York
1948 *Biennale,* Venice
1952 *Contemporary Belgian Art,* Mitsikoshi Department Store, Tokyo
1961 *Midwestern Exhibition of Belgian Painters,* Arts Club of Chicago (toured the Midwestern states)
1968 *Dada, Surrealism and Their Heritage,* Museum of Modern Art, New York
1972 *Peintures de l'Imaginaire: Symbolistes et Surrealists Belge,* Grand Palais, Paris
1982 *A Century of Modern Drawing,* British Museum, London

Collections:

Delvaux Museum, St. Idesbald, Belgium; Musee Royaux des Beaux-Arts, Brussels; Musee Royaux des Beaux-Arts, Antwerp; Musee d'Art Moderne, Brussels; Musee des Beaux-Arts, Charleroi, Belgium; Gemeentemuseum, The Hague; Tate Gallery, London; Centre Georges Pompidou, Paris; Museum of Modern Art, New York; Art Institute of Chicago.

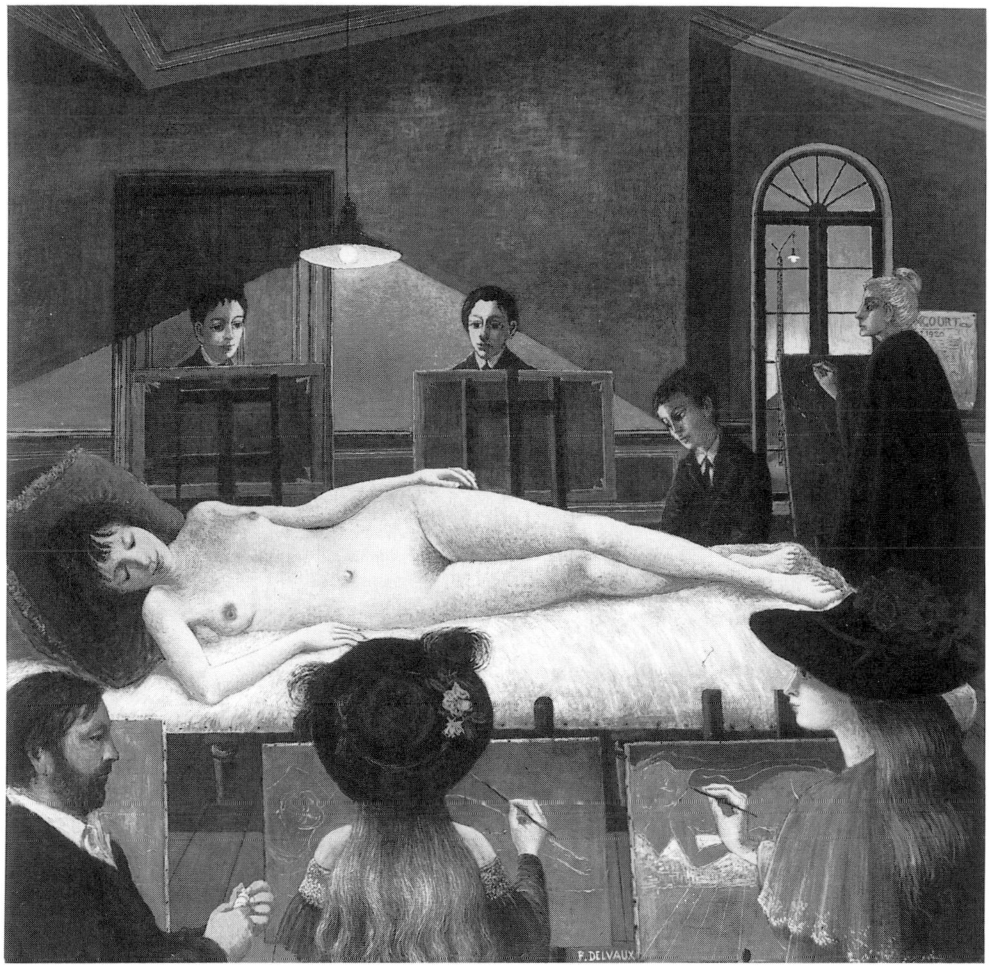

Paul Delvaux: *La Pose*, **1979**

Publications:

By DELVAUX: book—*Sept Dialogues avec Paul Delvaux, Accompagnes de Sept Lettres Imaginaires*, with Jacques Meuris, Paris 1971; articles—"Notice sur James Ensor" and "Notice sur Alfred Bastien" in *Annuaire de l'Académie Royale de Belgique*, Brussels 1963; "A propos d'un Voyage en Grece" in *Bulletin de l'Academie Royale de Belgique*, Brussels 1965.

On DELVAUX: books—*Paul Delvaux ou les Rêves Eveillés* by René Gaffe, Brussels 1945; *Paul Delvaux* by Claude Spaak, Antwerp 1948; *Paul Delvaux: Der Mensch, her Maler* by Paul Aloise de Bock, Hamburg 1965, as *Paul Delvaux: L'Homme. Le Peintre: Psychologie d'Un Art*, Brussels 1967; *Cahiers Paul Delvaux I: Premières Lithographies*, Paris 1969; *Paul Delvaux II: L'Oeuvre Grave 1966–69*, Paris 1969; *Paul Delvaux* by Antoine Terrasse, Paris 1972; *Paul Delvaux: Catalogue Raisonne* by Michel Butor and Jean Clair, Brussels 1974; *Paul Delvaux: Catalogue de l'Oeuvre Peint* by Michel Butor, Jean Clair and Suzanne Houbart-Wilken, Brussels 1975; *Paul Delvaux, Graphic Work* by Mira Jacob, Paris 1976; *Delvaux* by P. Emerson, Antwerp 1985.

Paul Delvaux' earliest paintings belong to the Post Impressionist mode. "Holy Cross Square" (1923) is a typical cityscape in the style of Utrillo, while "Promenade on the Isle of Huy" (1926) derives from Cézanne's landscape studies. In the late 1920's Delvaux adopted a primitive style reminiscent of Henri Rousseau. Depicting stylized nude figures in sylvan settings, "Figures in the Forest" (1928) and "Pink and White" (1929) achieve a remarkable serenity through simplicity of line and color. Over the next few years this style became increasingly expressionistic, focusing on crowd scenes in urban settings and culminating in "Sleeping Venus" (1932) and "The Spitzner Museum" (1933). In both works a supine female nude is juxtaposed with clothed figures in a museum environment of skeletons and display cases. As the artist later explained, their source was a bizarre exhibit he had encountered at the *Brussels Fair*. "I was struck by an extraordinary display by the Spitzner Museum," he noted, "with red velvet draperies at the window, two skeletons and a mechanical sleeping Venus . . . which was very sad and strange amid the hubbub of the merry-go-rounds and the frantic fun-seeking characteristic of such large carnivals." That this display deeply affected him is evidenced by the many skeletons and sleeping Venuses in his later work.

Toward 1934, fortified by his experience at the Museum, Delvaux discovered Giorgio de Chirico—an encounter that was to leave a lasting impression on his work. Among other things, it precipitated his conversion to Surrealism which was to occupy him for the rest of his life. To some extent his preexisting iconography was superimposed on de Chirico's. His sleeping Venuses resemble the latter's reclining Ariadnes, while his skeletons correspond to various de Chirico statues and mannequins. In general he borrows freely from the Italian master, appropriating his vast, deserted public squares, his architectural settings, his claustrophobic interiors ("The Mirror," 1936), and his old-fashioned trains. Like the latter, and pursuant to Surrealist doctrine, he devotes himself to the "marvelous"—revelatory experience springing from the unconscious. Whence the supreme importance of mystery and enigma.

Drawing on this background and on his own experience, Delvaux creates paintings that are profoundly original, exerting a strange hypnotic power on the viewer. His scenes, which often take place at twilight, are essentially dramas of the mind in which figures, objects, and settings are juxtaposed according to the processes of dream. In this context his aesthetics revolve around inconguity and contradiction. Delvaux' characters are also uniquely his own. To some extent the skeleton illustrates the traditional mortality theme, especially in the late 1940's and 1950's when it appears in a series devoted to Christian subjects. In many cases, however, it simply represents the armature of the body and as such acquires a purely architectural significance. Beginning in 1939 the artist introduced a character taken from Jules Verne's *Journey to the Center of the Earth,* the heroic scientist Prof. Otto Liedenbrock (Prof. von Hardwigg in the English translations). In painting after painting, including "The Phases of the Moon" (1939), we see the good professor intent on examining a mineral specimen, totally oblivious to the bevy of nude beauties surrounding him. This is a frequent theme in his work: the impossibility of significant connection between the sexes. Certainly it reflects the artist's own ambivalence toward women, springing from a childhood shaped by a domineering mother. This explains why all the women in his paintings look the same—they are all equally seductive, all equally threatening. Part of the fascination of a Delvaux painting resides in its violation of the taboo against public nudity. Typically he places his nude-or semi-nude female protagonists in a public setting where they remain totally unaffected by the experience, distracted, even aloof. Undeniably attractive, they seem impervious to our stares. In the last analysis Delvaux specializes in tantalizing his audience—and himself—with unattainable dreams. Above all, he is the master of frigid eroticism.

—Willard Bohn

DEMARCO, Hugo.

Argentinian. Born in Buenos Aires, 13 July 1932. Married Amalia Aguirre in 1959; Children: Marcello, Paula and Valerie. Painter. Professor of Painting, Drawing and Engraving, National School of Fine Art, Buenos Aires. Recipient: French Government Grant, to work in Paris, 1960. Address: 24 rue de Pressoir, Paris 20, France.

Individual Exhibitions:

1967	Op-Art Galerie, Esslingen, West Germany
1968	Galerie Denise René, Paris
	Galerie Grises, Bilbao, Spain
	Galerie Denise René/Hans Meyer, Dusseldorf
1969	Galerie Rubbers, Buenos Aires
1970	Estudio Actual, Caracas
	Hayward Gallery, London
1972	Galeria Antonona, Carcas
	Galleria del Naviglio, Milan
1973	Galleria La Polena, Geneva
	Galleria Sincron, Brescia, Italy
1974	Galleria Proposte, Cuneo, Italy
	Galleria A. Parma, Italy
	Galleria Zen, Milan

Selected Group Exhibitions:

1963	*Latin American Art*, Musée d'Art Moderne, Paris
1965	*The Responsive Eye*, Museum of Modern Art, New York
	Lumiére Mouvement et Optique, Palais des Beaux-Arts, Brussels
1967	*Biennale*, Paris
	Lumière Mouvement et Optique, Palais des Beaux-Musée d'Art Moderne, Paris
1968	*Documenta*, Kassel, West Germany
1971	*Art Argentin Contemporain*, Kunsthalle, Basle
1972	*Biennale*, Venice
1974	*Latin American Painters*, at the *Festival Royan*, Royan, France

Collections:

Museo Nacional de Bellas Artes, Buenos Aires; Collection di

Tella, Buenos Aires; Museo Bellas Artes, Caracas; Museo de Arte Contemporaneo, Caracas; Museo Soto, Ciudad Bolivar, Venezuela; Centre Georges Pompidou, Paris; Peter Stuyvesant Collection, Amsterdam; Kunsthalle, Recklinghausen, West Germany; Tel Aviv Museum.

Publications:

By DEMARCO: book—*La Prisionière*, with Crouzot, Paris 1967.

On DEMARCO: books—*Art cinetique* by Frank Popper, Paris 1967; *Kinetic Art* by Cyril Barrett, London 1968; *Encyclopedia Universalis*, Paris 1970; articles—Kineticists Working in Paris" in *Studio International* (London), October 1970; "Lettera da Milano" in D'Ars (Milan), March/April 1973.

Hugo Demarco is one of the Kinetic artists who has developed his research meticulously and surely from basic plastic problems such as colour in its most essential form to environmental integrations with their spatial, temporal, luminous and chromatic components.

In his "Dynamisations," "Superpositions spatiales" and "Réflexions changeantes" he has first reduced colour to pure vibration and set it off in a series of different planes. By introducting metal surfaces in space ans sometimes adding a transparent plane of perspex with a certain number of geometrical forms marked in translucent colours, he obtains transformations of structure and new intensities of light and colour. From the basis of this experience, real movement is integrated with the elements or reflecting bodies which are provided as a mechanical basis, and possibilities of combinations of movement, interrelations of speeds and directions emerge. In this way Demarco has managed to transpose harmonically problems connected with "optical art" into lumino-kinetic areas which he enriches by a series of works utilizing "black" or ultraviolet light in view of creating strong vibratory effects and in order to intensify the relationship between form, space, and motion.

More recently Demarco has turned again to his research into "space dynamisations" which follow the intuitions of the earliest Kinetic artists like Gabo (wtih his "Virtual Kinetic Volume" of 1920) by carrying them into the environmental sphere. In these constructions, which he calls "Relations," Demarco studies the spatial relationships between the movement and the relexions of metal rods and structures in such a way as to bring into focus the dematerialisation of the art object while at the same time creating a climate in which the spectator becomes aware of the basic qualities and the aesthetic implications not only of space but also of light, form and colour.

In fact all of Demarco's endeavours are directed towards the intensification and the diversification of the image, the dynamisation of the perceptive field of the spectator and the creation of plastic forms demonstrating the properties of time and, above all, its immaterialness.

—Frank Popper

Hugo Demarco: *Relations H. g. V.*, 1973

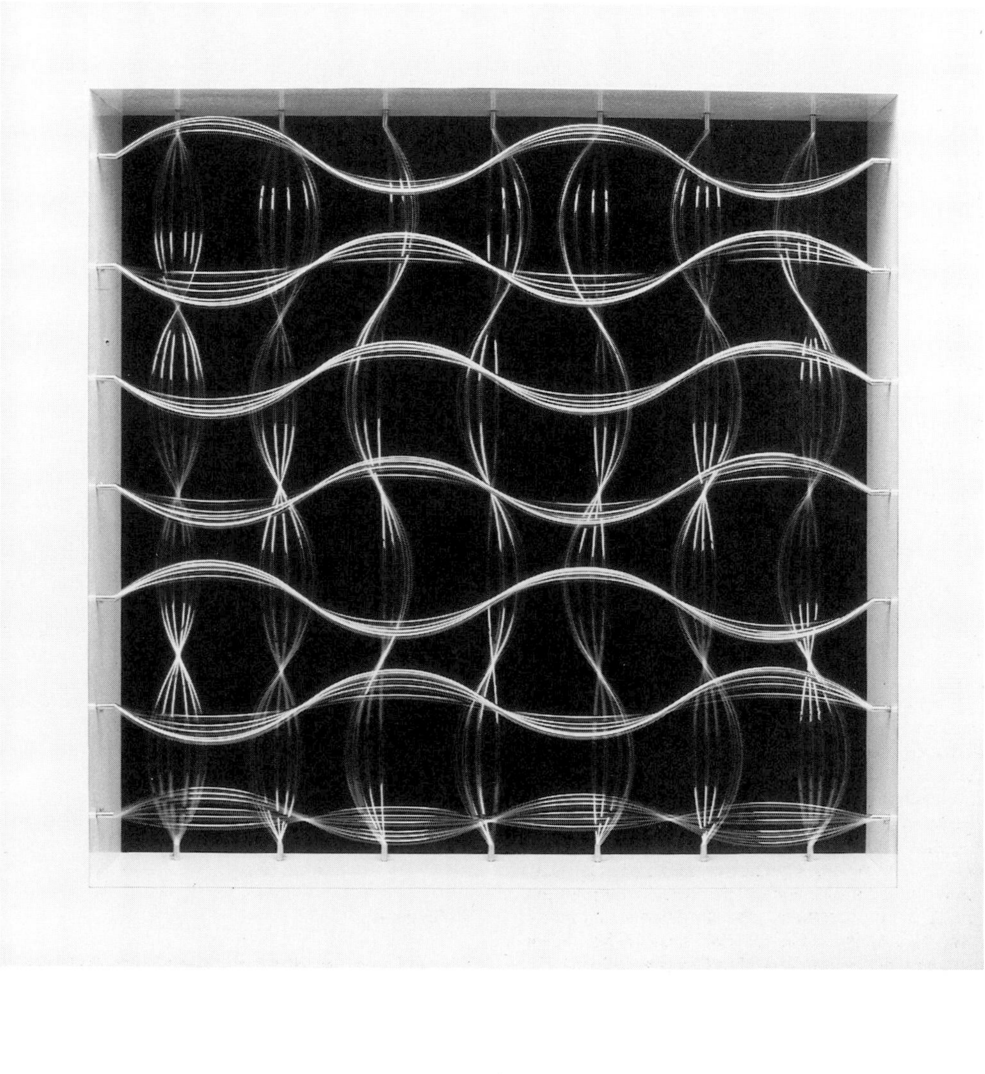

DE MARIA, Nicola.

Italian. Born in Foglianise, near Benevento, Italy, 6 December 1954. Lives and works in Turin. Address: Corso G. Agnelli 46/12, 10137 Turin, Italy.

Individual Exhibitions:

1975	Galleriaforma, Genoa
1976	Galleria Amelio, Naples
1977	Galleria Toselli, Milan
1978	Galleria Toselli, Milan
	Galerie Maenz, Cologne
	Galleria Persano, Turin
1979	Galleria Mario Diacono, Bologna
	Galerie Annemarie Verna, Zurich (with Francesco Clemente and Mimmo Paladino)
1980	Galleria Toselli, Milan
	Galerie Maenz, Cologne
	Galleria Persano, Turin
	Galerie Annemarie Verna, Zurich
1983	Kunsthalle, Basle

Selected Group Exhibitions:

1980	*Arte e Critica 1980*, Galleria Nazionale d'Arte Moderna, Rome (and 1981)
1981	*Identité Italienne*, Centre Georges Pompidou, Paris
1985	*The European Iceberg*, Art Gallery of Ontario, Toronto
1986	*Aspects of Italian Art 1960–85*, Kunstverein, Frankfurt

Publications:

On DE MARIA: book—*The Italian Trans-Avantgarde* by Achille Bonito Oliva, Milan 1980; *Nicola De Maria*, exhibition catalogue with text by Jean-Christophe Ammann, Basle 1983; articles—"Nicola de Maria" by M. Bandini in *Data* (Milan), October/November 1976; "Espansivo Eccessivo: Osservazioni sulla Giovane ARte Italiana" by Jean-Christophe Ammann in *Domus* (Milan), April 1979; "Il Primo Catalogo degli Artisti Nuovi" by F. Alinovi, R. Barilli and R. Daolio in *Bolaffiarte* (Turin), March 1980.

Among the artists of the *Transavantgarde*, Nicola De Maria certainly has the least recourse to "quotation." His pictorial lyricism is extravagant, devoid of figuration and abstraction and relative designs. Nearly always conceived in relation to the surroundings (and so beyond the borders of the picture), his painting, always annotated in a symbolic writing, is wholly manifested in a space that seems as far distant as the heavenly vault. The space of his painting, a vision of the void, is crowded with moments of colour, very thin forms and evanescent shapes freely interwoven and generating rich "contaminations." In this respect Nicola De Maria comes close to the compositional balances of Paul Klee, particularly to those that alternate the visible and the invisible.

As early as 1978, in a work with the significant title of "Philosophy of Magic and of Works of Art," De Maria had stressed his rapport with the liberation of painting. The form and colour indicated a vision made of distances, of chromatic improvisations. Their spatiality was something enigmatic and impalpable.

Ut pictura poesis might be De Maria's motto. Painting as a poetry of silence, of something constantly changing in the infinity of light, animates his noble work through beauty of design and colour. The artist paints as if he was digging in the transcendental splendour of an eternal sunset. But the sunset—not the decline—of art presages a new dawn. Its own shadow or reflection, De Maria's changeful painting is the most complete manifestion of that. He concentrates regard on it until it is lost, for the changing of the colours is at once visible and hidden.

De Maria loves the unaccustomed and the exotic: indeed, one of his works is called "I Am African, I Am Asian" (1980).

In another work, "Quore" (1982), he portrays an environment that might be called a (provisional) exposition of the work of art, a study of the rich path taken by responses between the single parts of a work and the spatiality of the work as a whole. The single elements of which it is composed (a big painted card,

a handbag also painted, and a series of little squares) have a clear meaning in themselves and, of course, in the context in which they are found. In "Quore" the spatiality of the colours expands their specificity, setting the real significant symbols of the painting at an almost unattainable distance. The inimitable visual evolution seems to take place somewhere else, somehow outside the visual range of the eye. It is a magical moment, coloured by painting that continually changes even when it displays subtle material thicknesses and spontaneous writing. The ensemble is in unstable equilibrium, which extends the moment in contemplative rapture. Invisible at the centre of the work, there dominates the fantasy of the artist (or the heart of art); the shifts of his imagination recognizable in the colours and the writing can be vaguely seen. The effect of the writing, the handmaid of the work, leads to the heart of art, to the rediscovery of an unsullied grace of colour and symbol. But it is the existential abyss that gives them their beauty; to paraphrase Ungaretti, when Nicola De Maria finds a colour or a symbol it is as if it was discovered in the abyss of the starry heavens. Thus his work, an esoteric work, is a sort of maze, not walled at all but open to the far distance of an interior light, visible only to the veiled eye of poetry.

—Italo Mussa

DE MARIA, Walter (Joseph).

American. Born in Albany, California, 1 October 1935. Studied at the University of California, Berkeley, 1953–59, B.A. in history 1957, M.A. in art 1959. Organized "happenings" at the University of California and at the California School of Art, San Francisco, 1959–60; drummer with the group Velvet Underground, 1965. Now lives and works in New York. Recipient: Guggenheim fellowship, 1969; Mathew Sculpture Prize, Art Institute of Chicago, 1976. Agent: Xavier Fourcade Inc., New York. Address: c/o Xavier Fourcade Inc., 26 East 57th Street, New York, New York 10021, U.S.A.

Individual Exhibitions:

1963 9 Great Jones Street, New York
1965 Paula Cooper Gallery, New York
1966 Cordier Ekstrom Gallery, New York
1968 Nicholas Wilder Gallery, Los Angeles
Galerie Heiner Friedrich, Munich
1969 Dwan Gallery, New York
1972 Kunstmuseum, Basel
1974 Heinrich Friedrich Inc., New York
Hessisches Landesmuseum, Darmstadt
1977 *The New York Earth Room/The Equal Area Series*, Heiner Friedrich Gallery, New York
1979 *The Broken Kilometer*, Heiner Friedrich Gallery, New York
1981 *360° I Ching/64 Sculptures*, Centre Georges Pompidou, Paris
1982 Centre Georges Pompidou, Paris
1986 Xavier Fourcade Inc., New York

Selected Group Exhibitions:

1968 *Directions 1: Options*, Milwaukee Art Center
1969 *When Attitudes Become Form*, Kunsthalle, Berne (toured Europe)
1970 *Information*, Museum of Modern Art, New York
1971 *Guggenheim International*, Guggenheim Museum, New York
1972 *Diagrams and Drawings*, Kunstverein, Stuttgart (toured Switzerland and the Netherlands)
1973 *Medium Fotografie*, Stadisches Museum, Leverkusen, West Germany
1975 *Masterworks in Wood: The 20th Century*, Portland Art Museum, Oregon
1976 *Rooms*, P.S. 1: Institute for Art and Urban Resources, New York
1977 *Biennale*, Venice

Walter De Maria: *Lightning Field*, 1977

Collections:

Museum of Modern Art, New York; Whitney Museum, New York; Dia Art Foundation, New York; Kunstmuseum, Basel.

Publications:

By DE MARIA: articles—text in *The New Avant-Garde*, New York and London 1972; "Project for Munich" in *Domus* (Milan), Aguust 1973; "The Lightning Field" in *Artforum* (New York), April 1980.

On DE MARIA: books—*Changing: Essays in Art Criticism* by Lucy Lippard, New York 1971; *The New Avant-Garde* by Gregoire Muller, New York and London 1972; *6 Years: The Dematerialization of the Art Object* by Lucy Lippard, New York and London 1973; *Walter De Maria*, exhibition catalogue, with text by H. H. Schmidt, Darmstadt 1974; *Walter De Maria*, exhibition catalogue edited by Xavier Fourcade, New York 1986; articles—"Walter DeMaria" by Jill Johnston in *Artnews* (New York), February 1963; "Walter De Maria: Word and Thing" by Dennis Adrian in *Artforum* (New York), January 1967; "A Sedimentation of the Mind: Earth Projects" by Robert Smithson in *Artforum* (New York, September 1968; "Walter De Maria: The Singular Experience" by David Bourdon in *Art International* (Lugano, Switzerland), December 1968; "Walter De Maria" by Germano Celant in *Casabella* (Milan), March 1969; "Drawing Lines in the Desert" by Eric Cameron in *Studio International* (London), October 1970; "Artworks on the Land" by Elizabeth C. Baker in *Art in America* (New York), January 1976; "De Maria: Elements" by Roberta Smith in *Art in America* (New York), May 1978; "Walter De Maria's 'The Broken Kilometer' " by Brian Wallis in *Arts Magazine* (New York), February 1980; "Walter De Maria: Les Danger de l'Art" by Jean-Marc Poinsot in *Art Press* (Paris), May 1981; "Exerzitien in der Wüste: Eine Reise zu Walter De Maria's 'Biltzfeld' nach Neu-Mexiko" by Günter Metken in *Die Zeit* (Hamburg), 9 April 1982.

I feel proud to have started minimal art and land art.
—Walter De Maria

DENES, Agnes (Cecilia).
American. Born in Budapest, Hungary, 31 May 1938; left Hungary with parents to live in Stockholm, 1948; moved to the United States, 1954. Studied at the New School for Social Research, New York, 1959-63; City College of New York, 1961-62; Columbia University, New York (M. L. Robinson Scholar), 1964-66. Lives and works in New York. Lecturer, School of Visual Arts, New York, 1971-79; Skowhegan School of Painting and Sculpture, Maine, 1979; University of Genoa, Italy, 1986. Recipient: Creative Artists Public Service Grant, New York, 1972, 1974; National Invitational Purchase Award, Albion College, Michigan, 1973; National Endowment for the Arts Fellowship, 1974, 1975, 1981; National Invitational Purchase Award, Rutgers University, New Brunswick, New Jersey, 1975; DAAD Fellowship, West Berlin, 1978; Berthe Von Moschzisker Prize, 1980, and McPhail Award, 1982, Print Club of Philadelphia; Sponsored Grant, New York State Council of the Arts, 1984; Purchase Award, American Academy and Institute of Arts and Letters, New York, 1985. Agent: Associated American Artists, 663 Fifth Avenue, New York, New York. Address: 595 Broadway, New York, New York 10012, U.S.A.

Individual Exhibitions:

1965 Columbia University, New York
1966 Granite Gallery, New York
1967 New Masters Gallery, New York
1968 Ruth White Gallery, New York
1972 A.I.R. Gallery, New York
1974 Ohio State University, Columbus
Perspectives, Corcoran Gallery, Washington, D.C. (toured the United States)
1975 Stefanotty Gallery, New York
Galleria Forma, Genoa
Sawyer Gallery, San Francisco
University of California Art Museum, Berkeley
Long Beach Art Museum, California
1976 Douglass College, Rutgers University, New Brunswick, New Jersey
University of Akron, Ohio
1977 Tyler School of Art, Temple University, Philadelphia
112 Greene Street Gallery,New York
Rice/Tree/Burial, Artpark, Lewiston, New York (installation)
1978 Amerika Haus, West Berlin
Ikon Gallery, Birmingham, England
Franklin Furnace, New York
Centre Culturel Americain, Paris
1979 Institute of Contemporary Arts, London
Studio d'Arte Cannaviello, Milan
Time Capsule I, Artpark, Lewiston, New York (installation)
Great Ideas, Container Corporation of America, Chicago (installation)
1980 Hayden Gallery, Massachusetts Institute of Technology, Cambridge
Lund Galleriet, Sweden
Galerie Aronowitsch, Stockholm
Elise Meyer Gallery, New York
1981 Elise Meyer Gallery, New York (print retrospective)
1982 Kunsthalle, Nuremberg, West Germany
Wheatfield—A Confrontation, Downtown Manhattan, New York (installation)
1985 University of Hawaii, Honolulu
Northern Illinois University, Evanston
1986 Ricardo Barreto Arte Contemporaneo, Guadalajara, Mexico
Stelae, Department of Cultural Affairs, Genoa, Italy (installation)
1987 *Hypersphere*, Equitable Tower, New York (installation)
Flying Pyramids for the Twenty-Second Century, Tamiami Airport, Florida (installation)

Selected Group Exhibitions:

1970 *Software*, Jewish Museum, New York
1971 *New Acquisitions*, Whitney Museum, New York
Art Systems, Museum of Modern Art, Beunos Aires (toured South America)
1972 *American Women Artists*, Kunsthaus, Hamburg
1973 *American Drawings 1963-1973*, Whitney Museum, New York
1974 *Painting and Sculpture Today*, Indianapolis Museum of Art (toured the United States)
1977 *Documenta*, Kassel, West Germany
1980 *From Reinhardt to Christo*, Allen Memorial Art Gallery, Oberlin College, Ohio
1986 *V Bienal Americana de Artes Graficas*, Museo de Arte Moderno, Cali, Colombia
1988 *Making Their Mark*, Cincinnati Art Museum, Ohio (toured the United States)

Collections:

Museum of Modern Art, New York; Whitney Museum, New York; Neuberger Museum, State University of New York at Purchase; University of Massachusetts, Amherst; National Collection of Fine Arts, Washington, D.C.; National Air and Space Museum, Washington, D.C.; Corcoran Gallery, Washington, D.C.; Allen Memorial Art Museum, Oberlin College, Ohio; Albion College, Michigan; Israel Museum, Jerusalem.

Publications:

By DENES: books—*Sculptures of the Mind*, Akron, Ohio 1976; *Paradox and Essence*, Rome 1977; *Isometric Systems in Isotropic Space*, Rochester, New York 1979; *Book of Dust: The Beginning and the End of Time, and Thereafter*, Rochester, New York 1988; articles—statement in *Software*, exhibition catalogue, New York 1970; "Psychographic" in *Duration Piece No. 8* by Douglas Huebler, New York and Turin 1973; "Study of Distortions" in *Flash Art* (Milan), July/August 1977; "Wheatfield—A Confrontation" in *Reaktion* (Alsbach), no. 7, 1983.

On DENES: books—*6 Years: The Dematerialization of the Art Object* by Lucy Lippard, New York 1973; *Agnes Denes: Perspectives*, exhibition catalogue, with texts by Roy Slade, Lawrence Alloway, and Susan Collins, Washington, D.C. 1974; *Agnes Denes: Sculptures of the Mind*, exhibition catalogue, with an introduction by Thomas Deecke, West Berlin 1978; *Agnes Denes: Drawings, Objects, Graphics, Photos*, exhitibion catalogue, Lund, Sweden 1980; *Agnes Denes 1968-1980*, exhibition catalogue with text by Garry Garrels, Cambridge, Massachusetts 1980; *Art in a Turbulent Era* by Peter Selz, Ann Arbor, Michigan 1985; articles—"Agnes Denes" by Barbara Reise in *Studio International* (London), December 1974; "A Visual Presentation of Meaning: The Work of Agnes Denes" by Peter Selz in *Art in America* (New York), March 1975; "Agnes Denes: The Ironies of Comprehension" by D. B. Kuspit in *Arts Magazine* (New York), December 1981; "Agnes Denes: The Triumph of the Will" by Ronny Cohen in *Print Collectors Newsletter* (New York), November 1982.

All my work up to now seems to culminate in my environmental art. From the early poetry to the philosophical drawings, from the abandonment of painting to working without color for eleven years (a self-imposed discipline that allowed concepts to dictate the mode of presentation), this complex body of work I have created; the art put out into the world is the most fully realized.

My work that always reached beyond the boundaries of the art area (to bring about a flow of communication among alien disciplines) now addresses controversial global issues questioning the status quo and the endless contradictions we seem to accept into our lives. It touches on ecological, territorial, social and cultural issues, celebrating our achievements, calling attention to our misconceptions and the most endearing of all human traits—our follies.

It's important to put art out into the world where it loses its preciousness but not its beauty, so it can touch all levels; it can elevate, communicate, be mysterious, provocative, ask disturbing questions and have a conscience. And it can be realized on a monumental scale when necessary. The art is freed to be true to itself. Before, I allowed it to dictate the mode of presentation; now I let it breathe and touch people's lives. Whether permanent or temporary, these are fully realized works that live and evolve in the environment.

—Agnes Denes

Although her work bears no likeness to Moholy-Nagy's. Agnes Denes shares his awareness that science and philosophy can be used in the service of art for the purpose of sensitizing the individual and society. Like the brilliant earlier modernist, Denes does not fit into any art movement or school. Although she has been described as a Conceptual artist by some critics, and although like certain Conceptualists she deals with a variety of intellectual problems, she gives palpable form and specific aesthetic beauty resulting from the visual clarification of complexity to her scientific and/or philosophic probes. Her work brings new thoughts and insights into the art arena, stretching its boundaries, toward a new breadth of thought and vision.

Increasingly, as many artists have rejected formalist aesthetics, they have absorbed and appropriated material from other disciplines for art (or non-art) purposes and Denes has turned to philosophy and science. But this is where we may easily misunderstand her. Denes is not interested in providing new scientific information. What she does rather is use the latest stages of scientific knowledge for the enrichment of artistic possibilities. She extends art, which traditionally had dealt with life and nature, into the realms of science; she is drawn to the enormous significance and creative energy in scientific thought.

Agnes Denes: *Wheatfield—A Confrontation*, Downtown Manhattan, 1982

She also sees parallels between the structure of science and the structure of art.

At first encounter with Denes' work, one wonders about the relationship between X-ray photographs of the underlayers of famous paintings, diagrammatic studies of time and truth, the visualization of Pascal's triangle, concern with dust and bones, a visual presentation of human evolution, the exploration of organic cells through extreme magnification, a psychograph of artists' "Profiles" based on questionnaires, various "abstract" studies of the meaning of language and communications, and many other such analytical works. Yet a certain unity of concept and form slowly emerges.

In all her forays, Denes is attracted to the most basic of questions—the structure of matter and idea, the void, the meaning of life, the place of humanity in the world, the mysteries of human existence. It may be useful to point out that while her subject matter is essentially a unified one when viewed in terms of her broadest concerns, it is expressed in several different ways. Like much new and innovative art, some of it may be difficult to grasp. We are not accustomed to art which is presented in a philosophical/mathematical form. Her physical investigations (X-rays of paintings, magnifications of cell tissue, etc) or those which use anthropological and psychological material are, of course, more immediately accessible.

In 1968-69 Denes created her first major environmental project when she planted rice seeds to represent life and growth, chained trees to indicate interference with life and imply death, and buried her own Haiku poetry to symbolize the dialectical synthesis: human intellectual power. Since that time she has continued with important outdoor projects, outstanding among which was *Wheatfield—A Confrontation* (1982): the planting of a two-acre wheatfield at Battery Park in Lower Manhattan and the harvesting of 1,000 pounds of wheat. In 1987 she embarked on a commission for the Tamiami Airport in Florida of three large fields of green shrubs, wild flowers and poured concrete in the shape of *Flying Pyramids.* Also in 1987 she completed *Hypersphere—The Earth in the Shape of the Universe,* a lobby environment in New York's Equitable Tower of 144 panels of carved, frosted glass to form the ceiling which represents one of her earlier map projections.

Denes brings new philosophic insight into the abundance of available information, dealing with man's "importance or insignificance in the universe". Her work is analytic in the Kantian sense. Her singular contribution is in the fact that her symbols remain visual, her attitude romantic, her approach intuitive. Denes' unique position in today's art is at the place where systematic and intuitive knowledge intersect.

—Peter Selz

de RIVERA, José.

American. Born in West Baton Rouge, Louisiana, 18 September 1904. Studied drawing with John W. Norton, Chicago, 1926; mainly self-taught in sculpture. Served as an armorer with the United States Army, 1942-43, and as a designer of training aids for the United States Navy, 1943-46. Married Rose Covelli in 1926 (divorced); son: Joseph; married Lita Jeronimo in 1955. Worked as a draftsman, designer, etc. in foundries and the machine tool industry, Chicago, 1924-32; independent sculptor, living in New York, 1930 until his death in 1985: worked on the WPA Federal Art Project, New York, 1937-38. Instructor in Sculpture, Brooklyn College, New York, 1953; Critic in Sculpture, Yale University, New Haven, Connecticut, 1953-55; Instructor in Sculpture, School of Design, North Carolina State College, Raleigh, 1957-60. Recipient: Watson F. Blair Prize, Art Institute of Chicago, 1957; National Institute of Arts and Letters grant, 1959; Creative Arts Medal, Brandeis University, Waltham, Massachusetts, 1969. D.F.A.: Washington University, St. Louis, 1974. Agent: Grace Borgenicht Gallery, 724 Fifth Avenue, New York, New York 10019. *Died* (in New York) *18 March 1985.*

Individual Exhibitions:

1946	Mortimer Levitt Gallery, New York
1952	Grace Borgenicht Gallery, New York
1955	Grace Borgenicht Gallery, New York
1957	Walker Art Center, Minneapolis (retrospective)
	Grace Borgenicht Gallery, New York
1959	Grace Borgenicht Gallery, New York
1960	Grace Borgenicht Gallery, New York
1961	Whitney Museum, New York (retrospective; toured the United States)
1969	Grace Borgenicht Gallery, New York
1972	Whitney Museum, New York (retrospective)
	Isaac Delgado Museum, New Orleans
	Retrospective Exhibition 1930–1971, La Jolla Museum of Contemporary Art, California
	Grace Borgenicht Gallery, New York (retrospective)
1975	Grace Borgenicht Gallery, New York
1978	Grace Borgenicht Gallery, New York
1980	Grace Borgenicht Gallery, New York
1983	Grace Borgenicht Gallery, New York
1985	Grace Borgenicht Gallery, New York (memorial exhibition)

Selected Group Exhibitions:

1930 *Annual Exhibition*, Art Institute of Chicago (and 1931)
1934 *Whitney Annual*, Whitney Museum, New York (and regularly until 1968)
1939 *Worlds Fair*, New York
1946 *Contemporary Sculpture, Objects, Constructions*, Yale University, New Haven, Connecticut
1951 *American Sculpture*, Metropolitan Museum of Art, New York
1956 *Abstract Sculpture*, Galerie Denise René, Paris
1959 *Contemporary Sculpture*, Museum of Modern Art, New York (toured the United States)
1960 *Konkrete Kunst*, Kunsthaus, Zurich
1963 *Sculpture of Our Time*, Gallery of Modern Art, Washington, D.C.
1967 *Sculpture of the 60's*, Los Angeles County Museum of Art (travelled to the Philadelphia Museum of Art)

Collections:

Museum of Modern Art, New York; Whitney Museum, New York; Metropolitan Museum of Art, New York; Memorial Art Gallery, Rochester, New York; Newark Museum Association, New Jersey; Hirshhorn Museum and Sculpture Garden, Smithsonian Institution, Washington, D.C.; Museum of Fine Arts, Richmond, Virginia; Art Institute of Chicago; Tate Gallery, London.

Publications:

On de RIVERA: books—*José de Rivera*, exhibition catalogue, with text by John Gordon, New York 1961; José de Rivera: Retrospective Exhibition 1930–1971, exhibition catalogue, with text by Thomas S. Tibbs, La Jolla, California 1972; *The Non-Objective World*, exhibition catalogue, with text by George Rickey, London, 1972; *The Age of the Avant-Garde: An Art Chronicle of 1956–1972* by Hilton Kramer, New York and London 1974; *José de Rivera: Constructions* by Dore Ashton and Joan M. Marter, Madrid 1980.

Art for me is a creative process of individual plastic production without immediate goal of finality. The prime function is the total experience of production. The social function: the communication of that experience. In the attempt to find plastic harmony in my work, I am conscious always of the necessary for a prime, visual, plastic experience. The content, beauty and source of excitement is inherent in the interdependence and relationships of the space, material and light, and is the structure.

—José de Rivera (1983)

Each piece of work by José de Rivera reflects the impeccable craftsmanship of an individual who achieves a fluid balance of opposite tensions by using four elements; light, space, time, and material. The result—heavy, sensuous, flawlessly smooth metal sculptures, in which time and space go hand in hand. Whether one moves around the sculpture or stands in place as it slowly revolves, the line continues unbroken by the slightest hesitancy. The skillfully refined curvilinear forms dissolve into tracings of light or liquid, while the voids within become the forms themselves, swelling and diminishing with such ease as to belie the complex geometry of their being.

De Rivera's strength as a sculptor rests not only in his ability to produce a body of work as endlessly subtle in variation and nuance as time and space suggest, but also in his use of light. Each sculpture is polished through many gradations of abrasion to a brilliant, gleaming surface. Final polishing is achieved with jeweler's rouge and wood felt buffer. Whereas in traditional sculpture light causes shadows to fall on the piece, in de Rivera's case the material used—be it aluminium, copper, bronze or stainless steel—is transformed into light by reflections from the surface of the piece. When set in rotation, beams of light are cast out into the distance with the points of cross-over constantly changing. This produces the optical effect of sudden deflections of light, a process eloquently illustrated by de Rivera's 1955 "Construction 1: Homage to the world of Minkowski", a piece dedicated to the Russian mathematician and physicist Herman Minkowski, whose philosophy of an inseparable time and space inspired de Rivera's career.

Born in 1904 in Louisiana, USA, the son of a sugar mill engineer, de Rivera acquired skills at an early age which provided a base for a future sculptor. He was an adept blacksmith and capable of repairing machinery. After graduating from high school in 1922, he moved to Chicago where his knowledge of pipe-fitting and the making of tools and dies secured him employment in machine shops almost immediately. Between 1928 and 1931 de Rivera studied drawing under the painter John W. Norton at the studio school in Chicago. During these years he was influenced by Mondrian, Brancusi, and Georges Vantongerloo, a Belgian artist and theorist. Finally, after a year of travelling through Europe visiting galleries and museums in 1932, de Rivera re-affirmed his decision to be a sculptor.

He released his first pieces in 1930, "Owl", "Form Synthesis", and "Bust", three works of highly polished metal, gleaming with purity and simplicity. From 1938 to 1940 he worked on a cavalry monument for El Paso, Texas. Finding this type of commission too restricting, he devoted himself to the type of work which allowed him the freedom he required. In 1938 he constructed the aluminium "Flight" for the Newark Airport, a work which became the highlight of the Federal Art Project Sculp-

José De Rivera: ***Construction No. 199*****, 1983**

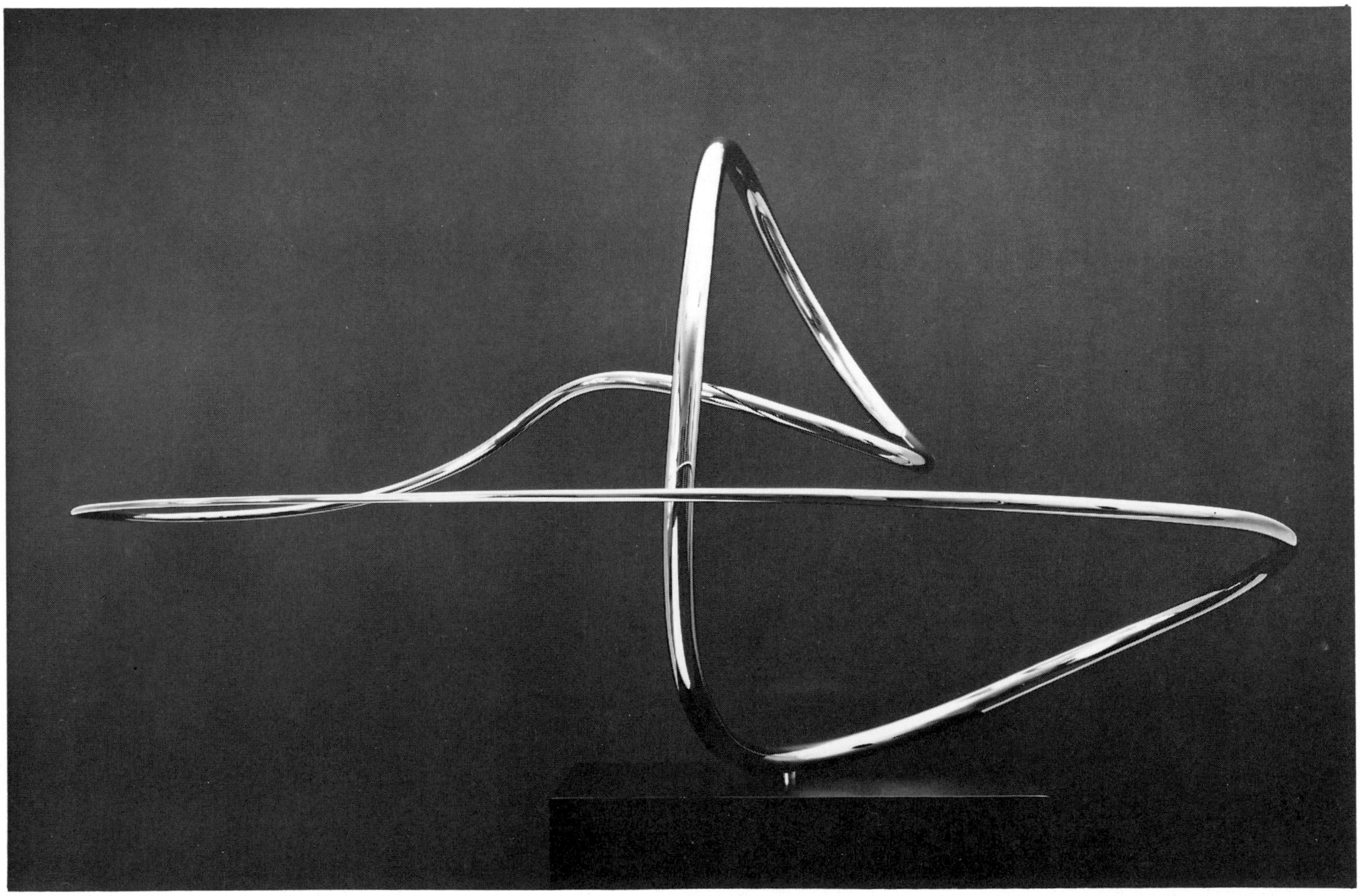

ture Division Show in New York that year. Simple, human in scale, it was a beautiful symbol of aviation.

That year proved to be an important one for his development as a sculptor. His construction "Black and Red, Double Element" began an abstract analysis of space, form and material with the addition of colour. It consisted of two shaped and painted aluminium sheets mounted in opposing positions and attached to the same base. The desired shape was then cut out of a flat sheet of metal, the surface filed and rubbed with abrasives, and was then painted with primary colours. De Rivera's reputation as an internationally acclaimed sculptor was enhanced yet again the following year in 1939 when his designs for stainless steel reliefs for the Soviet Pavilion were exhibited at the New York World's Fair.

Working in collaboration with architect William Lescaze and builder William Kaufman in 1955, de Rivera produced the relief "Continuum" for the stainless steel lobby wall 711 Third Avenue in New York City. Following that success he was commissioned by the Hotel Statler-Hilton in Dallas to construct a flashing steel and cadmium yellow piece which revolved once every six minutes in an open courtyard. The late 50's and 60's marked the highlight of his career; his major works were exhibited at the Brussel World Fair in 1958, he was featured at the New York World Fair in 1964, and the spectacular piece "Infinity" of 1966, which was installed in front of the Smithsonian Institution in Washington D.C., earned him further critical attention.

Throughout his career José de Rivera has engaged himself in an analytical and unrelenting search for elemental values. The fruits of his labours have been borne out by his wide acclaim as a contemporary sculptor, whose works are sublimely endowed with perfect fluid gestures, gently ebbing and flowing in timeless revolution.

—Carrie Barker

DEVADE, Marc.

French. Born in Paris, 5 November 1943. Painter: lives and works in Paris. Founder-Member, with Daniel Dezeuze, Vincent Bioules, Patrick Saytour, Louis Cane, Claude Viallat and Andre Valensi, Supports-Surfaces group, Paris. Editor of *Peinture: Cahiers Théoriques*, Paris. Address: 10 rue Toullier, 75005 Paris, France.

Individual Exhibitions:

1970 Galerie Le Haut Pavé, Paris
1972 Galerie Daniel Templon, Paris
1973 Galleria Daniel Templon, Milan
Institute of Contemporary Arts, London
1974 Galerie Daniel Templon, Paris
Maison de la Culture, Rennes, France
1975 Galleria Daniel Templon, Milan
Galleria Lia Rumma, Naples
Galerie D, Brussels
Galerie Le Flux, Perpignan, France
Galerie Piltzer, Paris
1976 Galleria Lia Rumma, Rome
Galleria Daniel Templon, Milan
Galerie Quadrum, Lisbon
1977 Galerie Piltzer, Paris
Galleria La Bertesca, Genoa
Galleria Mantra, Turin
Galerie C. M., Saint-Etienne, France
Galerie La Bertesca, Dusseldorf
Galerie Arnesen, Copenhagen
Centre International de Création Artistique de Sénanque, France
Galerie Lavunn, Ghent
Galerie N. R. A., Paris
1978 Galerie Le Dépot, Bourges, France
Galerie Gerald Piltzer, Paris
Musée d'Art Moderne de la Villa, Paris
1979 Galerie Lavuun, Ghent
Galerie Quadrum, Lisbon
1981 *Peintures 1979–1981*, Galerie Blancs-Monteaux Espace Expositions, Paris

Selected Groups Exhibitions:

1970 *Support-Surface*, Musée d'Art Moderne de la Ville, Paris
1971 *Peinture, cahiers théoriques*, Galerie Yvon Lambert, Paris
1974 *L'art au present*, Galerie Daniel Templon, Paris
1975 *Analitische Malerei*, Galerie La Bertesca, Dusseldorf
1976 *I colori della pittura*, Galleria del Milione, Milan
Tendenser I Europaeisk Kunst, Galerie Arnesen, Copenhagen
1977 *Biennale*, Paris
1978 *Biennale*, Venice
1979 *Tendances de l'art en France 68–78*, Musée de la Ville, Paris
1981 *Tel Quel*, Galerie La Hune, Paris

Publications:

By DEVADE: articles—"Poème" in *Tel Quel* (Paris), no. 18, 1964; "Réponse à un questionnaire sur l'art abstrait" in *Lettres Francaises* (Paris), no. 41, 1970; "Note pour la théorie materialiste de la pratique picturale" in *Support-Surface*, exhibition catalogue, Paris 1970; "Notes sur une peinture operant dans de beaux draps" in *Louis Cane*, exhibition catalogue, Paris 1971; "Pourquoi une revue" in *V. H. 101* (Paris), 1971; "Comment voir la Chine en peinture" in *Peinture: Cahiers Théoriques* (Paris), no. 2–3, 1972; "On va partir de Cézanne," interview, with Francois Pluchart in *Artitudes* (St. Jeannet, France), no. 6, 1972; "La peinture et son double" in *Peinture: Cahiers Théoriques* (Paris), no. 4–5, 1972, partially reprinted in *Tracks* (New York), April 1976; "Dates, repères, références et commentaires" in *Peinture: Cahiers Théoriques* (Paris), no. 6–7, 1973; "Comment me vient la peinture" in *Promesse* (Paris), no. 34–35, 1973; "La peinture vue d'en-bas" in *Peinture: Cahiers Théoriques* (Paris), no. 8–9, 1974; "Note sur la Chine et la modernité" in *Peinture: Cahiers Théoriques* (Paris), no. 8–9, 1974; "La situation ideologique et politique en peinture" in *Peinture: Cahiers Théoriques* (Paris), no. 8–9, 1974; *Passages, programme théorique et graphique*, exhibition catalogue, Paris 1974, partially reprinted in *Data* (Milan), no. 16–17, 1975; interview with Catherine Millet, in *Art Press* (Paris), no. 9. 1974 and *Flash Art* (Milan), no. 54–55, 1975; article in *Les uns-postures ou quand la sculpture se colore*, exhibition catalogue, Paris 1975; "La matière du sujet de la peinture" in *Peinture: Cahiers Théoriques* (Paris), no. 10–11, 1975; "Théorie ou les figures de la peinture" in *Peinture: Cahiers Théoriques* (Paris), no. 12, 1977; responses to a questionnaire in *Bilder öhne Bilder*, exhibition catalogue, Bonn 1977; "May 1968, May 1978—Peinture, l'impossible quotidien" in *Art Press International* (Paris), 1978; "Picasso nous regarde" in *Documents sur* (Paris), October 1978; "L'après coup de pinceau," interview, with Klaus Honnef in *Peintures: Cahiers Théoriques* (Paris), May 1979; "La peinture au plus près" in *Peinture: Cahiers Théoriques* (Paris), no. 14–15, 1979; "Une architectonique de plaques" in *Tony Long*, exhibition catalogue, Paris 1979; "Dix ans, encore, toujours", interview, with Catherine Millet, in *Art Press International* (Paris), October 1979; "La peinture en excès" in *Peinture: Cahiers Théoriques* (Paris), no. 1, 1980; "Une peinture en personne," interview, with Marcelin Pleynet, in *Peinture: Cahiers Théoriques* (Paris), no. 16, 1981; interview with Catherine Millet and Jacques Henrie in *Art Press* (Paris), June 1981.

On DEVADE: books—*Quelques Problèmes de la Peinture Moderne* by Marcelin Pleynet, Paris 1972; *Art en France* by Jean Clair, Paris 1974; *L'art actuel en France* by Anne Tronche and Hervé Gloaguen, Paris 1974; *Marc Devade: Peintures 1979–1981*, exhibition catalogue, with a preface by Philippe Sollers, and an interview by Marcellin Pleynet, Paris 1981; articles—"Des idées, des critiques, de la peintures et des galeries . . . Marc Devade" by Marcelin Pleynet in *Art International* (Lugano, Switzerland), Summer 1971; "Vio-

Marc Devade: *Peinture*, 1973

lence Feutrée et Attention Flouttant" by Bernard Lamarche-Vadel in *Art Press* (Paris), no. 18, 1975; "Effet Devade" by Bernard Lamarch-Vadel in *Cimaise* (Paris), no. 125–126, 1976; "Waiting for Gloire" by Nancy Marmer in *Artforum* (New York), February 1977; "Le risque du geste et celui du regard" by Catherine Millet in *Art Press International* (Paris), October 1977; "Matière, geste et hasard" by Marc Le Bot in *XXe Siècle* (Paris), no. 49, 1977; "La nuova pittura" by Filiberto Menna in *L'arte Moderna* (Milan), no. 110, 1978; "Contemporary Painting in France" by Paul Rodgers in *Artscribe* (London) August 1978; "Toward a Theory/Practice of Painting in France" by Paul Rodgers in *Artforum* (New York), April 1979; "Le Parti du parti pris" by Geneviève Breerette in *Le Monde* (Paris), 22 September 1979.

Marc Devade has been a member of the French group 'Supports/Surface', and it is within this context that he has worked as a painter. Members of the group included such artists as Dezeuze, Cane, Viallat, Dolla and Saytour. The group's primary aim was to state the problems of art—or, more specifically, painting—at a structuralist level, following Althusser's Marxist interpretation and some Freudian theories enriched by the ideas of Lacan. It was therefore a kind of practice which constantly matched itself to theory. From its formation in 1971, the group expressed its views in the journal *Peinture-Cahiers Theoriques* which represented an up-to-date analysis of the painting of the 'seventies. Far from being dogmatic (and particularly far from any kind of Marxist dogmatism), the group—and Devade in particular—employed a dialectical method of analysis. Devade wrote: "To act and think stand in a dialectical relationships, within which the one term works as a reference point for the other, in a never-ending movement. The unity of theory and praxis is neither a compromise nor an appeal for order; it is rather the safest means to induce transformation in either field".

Furthermore, Devade made use of psychoanalytic theory to establish an enquiry into the pictorial event, not merely limited to the analysis of its media, constituent elements or pertinence, but extending beyond these areas to stress the problem of the place of the Subject vis-a-vis Language. What displaces the positivist position of the subject is the element of sexuality which is expressed as rhythm in the painting prior to becoming formalised and institutionalised. Devade applies himself to the problems of colour, to the extent that it 'produces' the painting as it drives the needs of the subject engaged in the act of painting.

Devade is inspired by American experiences such as Kenneth Noland's, by a kind of practice that locates painting in its own physical field and self-referentiality. Devade's analysis, however, was not limited to this. His analysis also succeeded in grasping and expressing the movement between the poles of geometry and colour—a rhetoric of impulses. His structure of painting-within-the-painting during 1968–69 (of the square frame within which the painting is enclosed) became a code within which the moment a construction made possible a rational reading of the work it also posited itself as one of the dialectical poles.

The other critical element was colour, with its quasi-evocative values—a kind of colour that imposed on the painting autonomous values of the chromatic surface. In later works (1972), the artist eliminated the geometrical linear grid that delimited the organization of the colour; at the same time, he substituted inks for acrylic colours, as the fluidity of ink allows the artist to deal with the surface as a field of events quite independent of his own will. In this way, he obtains layered effects, more or less saturated areas and haloes of colour. For the earlier preconceived structure, he substituted a fragile and aleatory system, sometimes splitting the canvas in two to form a diptych. In certain cases, Devade applied strips of wood as enclosures to delimit particular areas of the canvas. These areas would be free of colour, creating more or less rectangular white spaces. At times, such areas would appear to the viewer as the mnemonic relics of a geometric universe which by then had disintegrated.

By thus interrupting the surface, Devade actually acted upon the structural, signifying a differentiation between design and colour. At this stage, colour is no longer a complement to line, mark or form; on the contrary, it comes to indicate form as an absence, meaning that the formal hypothesis appeared within the visual field of the work as a pointer to the beyond and to the void.

—Giorgio Verzotti

de VREE, Paul.

Belgian. Born in Antwerp, 13 November 1909. Educated at l'Ecole Normale, Antwerp, 1924–28, and at the University of Ghent, 1934–38. Served as a Reserve Lieutenant, Belgian Army, 1929–47; mobilized, 1939–40. Married Charlotte Marie Versterren, 1932; son: Frits. Visual poet; lives and works in Antwerp. Primary School Teacher, Antwerp, 1932–41; Professor of Secondary Instruction, Antewerp, 1941–44, and at the Athenaeum, Lier, Belgium, 1951–69. Editor, *De Brug* magazine, Antwerp, 1944–51. Recipient: Poetry Prize, Province of Antwerp, 1935; Order of Knighthood, Brussels, 1974; Prize for complete works, Province of Antwerp, 1981. Agent: Studio Brescia, Italy. Address: 46 Camille Huysmanslaan, 2020 Antwerp, Belgium.

Paul De Vree: *Lady Chatterley*, 1972

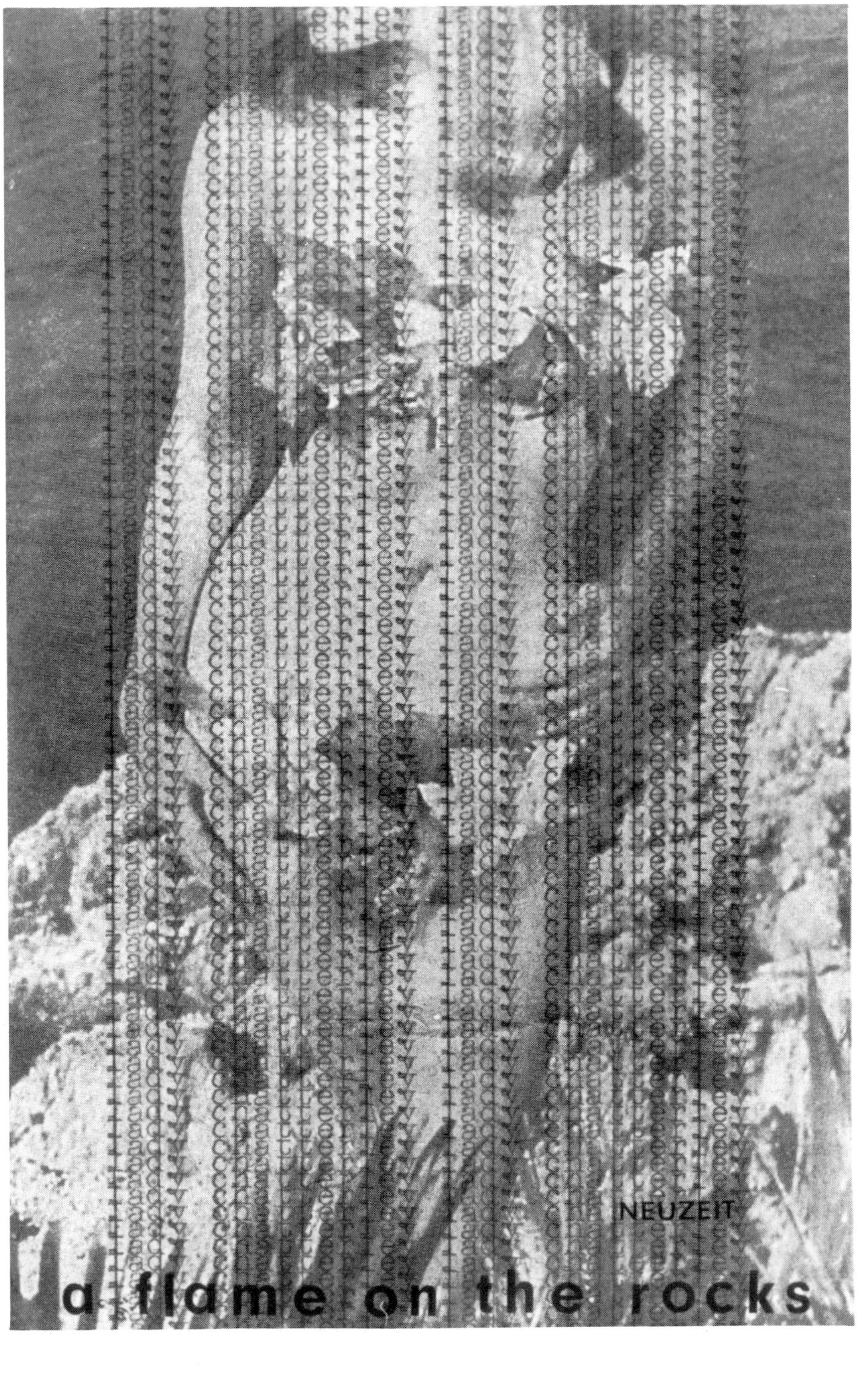

Individual Exhibitions:

1971 Galleria S. Chiara, Brescia, Italy
DeVaart Galerie, Hilversum, Netherlands
1972 Museum Van Vlaamse Letterkunde, Antwerp
Studio Santandrea, Milan
1973 Studio Brescia, Brescia, Italy
1974 Galleria Il Canale, Venice
Museum Van Schone Kunsten, Antwerp
1975 Galerie Au Quai, Liège, Belgium
Galleria Santelmo, Salo, Italy
1976 Galerie Richard Foncke, Ghent
1977 Galerie Artel, Antwerp
Galerie Drieghe, Wetteren, Belgium
1979 Galerie Candid, Ghent
Galerie Buytaert, Antwerp
1981 Provinciaal Begijnhof, Hasselt, Belgium
Galerie De Brakke Grond, Amsterdam

Selected Group Exhibitions:

1971 *Konkrete Poezie,* Stedelijk Museum, Amsterdam (travelled to the International Cultureel Centrum, Antwerp)
1972 *Poesia Visiva,* travelling exhibition (toured Italy, Germany and Gellgium, until 1974)

Collections:

Museum of Fine Arts, Antwerp; Museum of Modern Arts, Ieper, Belgium; Ministry of Culture, Brussels.

Publications:

By de VREE: books—*Posia Visiva,* Rome 1975; *Verzamelde Gedichten,* Bruges 1978; *De Brandwonden,* Verona 1979; *The Street Tells the Truth,* Verona 1979; *Naar het einde,* Hilversum, Netherlands 1979; articles—"Zimprovisaties" in *De Tafelronde* (Antwerp), 1968; "Poezie in Fusie" in *De Balden Voor de Poezie* (Lier), 1968; article in *Konkrete Poezie,* exhibition catalogue, Amsterdam 1970; "Verbaal Gelaat" in *De Tafelronde* (Antwerp), 1970; "Poezien" in *Amodula* (Brescia, Italy), 1971; "Maskers" in *De Tafelronde* (Antwerp), 1973; article in *Jozef Peeters,* exhibition catalogue, Antwerp 1973; "De Visule Poezie in Belgie en Nederland" in *De Tafelronde* (Antwerp), no. 4, 1973.

On de VREE: books—*10 huize van . . . 13* by Joos Florquin, Louvain 1977; *Monographie Paul De Vree* by Henri Floris Jespers, Antwerp 1977; *Paul de Vree,* exhibition catalogue, Hasselt, Belgium 1981; articles—"Poesia Visiva-Visuelle Poezie" by Urs Graf in *Werk* (Berne), LIX 1972; "Paul de Vree" by Erik Salgter in *Litareir Lustrum* (Amsterdam), no. 2, 1973; "Monography Paul de Vree" by Sarenco in *Lotto Poetica* (Brescia, Italy), no. 37–38, 1974.

The texture and structure of my poetry have, as a whole, evolved from the audio-visual phase to that of visual poetry, pure synglossy: the indivisible unity of the work and image. The spirit of this poetry is not born from the desire to amuse myself with letters, nor from the need to employ graphics, mechanical means and collage to attain aesthetic effects. The new methods, by which since Mallarmé, the futurists and the dadaists have restored to poetry its freshness and its striking power, these methods I have applied, above all since the revolutionary days of May 1968, to find with several spiritual companions a poetry which fitted the demands which communication poses in relation to the recoil that consciousness undergoes when information is manipulated by the authorities.

—Paul de Vree

DE VRIES, Herman.

Dutch. Born in Alkmaar, 11 July 1931. Studied at the Ecole des Beaux-Arts, Montpellier, France, 1949–52. Married in 1956 (divorced 1968); children: Mirgam, Marc, Dirk, Merik and Herman Vincent. Worked in the plant protection service, at the Institute for Applied Biological Research in Nature, Alkmaar, 1952–68. First art activities, Alkmaar, 1953; first mobile works, 1954; first monochrome paintings and collages, 1956; participated in Zero group exhibitions, 1961–63; researched random systems, 1962–75; experimental language and poetry, 1965; chance and change processes, 1970. Published *NUL=Zero* magazine, Amsterdam, 1961–64; *Revue Integration,* Amsterdam, 1965–72; and Eschenau Summer Press (temporary travelling press), since 1974. Agents: Antoinette Hilgemann, Havendijk 40, Gorinchem, Netherlands; Galerie Muller-Roth, Blumentstrasse 15, Stuttgart; and Galerie Lydia Megert, Munstergasse 6, Berne, Switzerland. Address: 8729 Eschenau nr. 8, Knetzgau bei Hassfurt/Main, West Germany.

Individual Exhibitions:

1959 Galerie 31, Dordrecht, Netherlands
1960 Mensa, Delft
1963 Galerie Wulfengasse 14, Klagenfurt, Austria
Metz and Company, Amsterdam
1964 Galerie D., Frankfurt
1965 Galerie Knoll, Basle
Galerie Akruell, Berne
Galerie Loehr, Frankfurt (with Colombo)
1967 'tVenster, Rotterdam
't Ouwe Tientje, Arnhem
Galerie Julicher, Mönchengladbach, West Germany
Galerie Hansjorg Mayer, Stuttgart
1968 Gemeentemuseum, The Hague
Nederlandse Kunststichting, Zeist, Netherlands
Felison, Ijmuiden, Netherlands
1969 Art Academy, Copenhagen
1970 Galerie Swart, Amsterdam
Galerie Swart, Amsterdam (with Frieder Nake)
Kunsthistorisch Instituut, Amsterdam
Galerie M., Bochum, West Germany
1971 Utrechtse Kring, Utrecht
Galerie Swart, Amsterdam
Galerie Lichter, Frankfurt
I.K.I., Dusseldorf
1972 Galerie Teufel, Koblenz
Aktionsgalerie, Berne (with Sarenco)
I.K.I./Modern Art Galerie, Dusseldorf
1973 Galerie Swart, Amsterdam
1974 Lucy Milton Gallery, London
Galerie Swart, Amsterdam
Galerie Lydia Megert, Berne
Galerie am Wochenende, Feldkirchen, West Germany
1975 Galerie Hermanns, Furstenfeldbruck, West Germany
Stedelijk Museum, Amsterdam
1976 *At Random,* Kunstcentrum Badhuis, Gorinchem, Netherlands
Galerie Swart, Amsterdam
1977 Galerie Lydia Megert, Berne
Galerie Muller-Roth, Stuttgart
Galerie Magazijn, Groningen, Netherlands
1978 Lieftinghsbroek Nature Reserve, Groningen, Netherlands
1979 De Vleeshal, Middelburg, Netherlands
Galerie Lydia Megert, Berne
Galerie Muller-Roth, Stuttgart
1980 *Werken 1954–1980,* Groninger Museum, Groningen, Netherlands
Galerie Swart, Amsterdam
Galerie Magazijn, Groningen, Netherlands
Kunsthistorisch Instituut, Groningen University Netherlands
1981 Van Reckum Museum, Apeldoorn, Netherlands
Het Apollonius, Eindhoven, Netherlands
1982 Gemeentemusuem, The Hague
Gomera, Canary Islands

Selected Group Exhibitions:

1957 *Natuur en Kunst,* Stedelijk Museum, Amsterdam
1962 *Nul,* Stedelijk Museum, Amsterdam
1965 *Licht und Bewegung,* Kunsthalle, Berne
1970 *Konkrete Poesie,* Stedelijk Museum, Amsterdam
1974 *Basically White,* Institute of Contemporary Arts, London
1975 *Poesia Concreta 1952–1967,* Biblioteca Nazionale, Florence
1976 *System + Program,* Patac Kulturyi Nanki, Warsaw
1979 *Zero,* Kunsthaus, Zurich
1980 *Pier + Ocean,* Hayward Gallery, London
1981 *Lapidar,* Galerie Muller-Roth, Stuttgart

Collections:

Sammlung Albertina, Vienna; Haggs Gremeentemuseum, The Hague; Stedelijk Museum, Amsterdam; Van Abbemuseum, Eindhoven, Netherlands; Kröller-Müller Museum, Otterlo, Netherlands; Kunstmuseum, Dusseldorf; Staatsgalerie, Stuttgart; Kunsthaus, Zurich; Museum Sztuki, Lodz, Poland; Museum of Modern Art, New York.

Publications:

By DE VRIES: books—*Wit is overdaad,* Amsterdam 1960; *Manifest van de gecastreerde werkelijkheid,* Amsterdam 1960; *Wit,* with introduction by J. C. Van Schagen, Amsterdam 1962; *Permutierbard Text,* Stuttgart 1967; *Wit/Weiss,* Stuttgart 1967; *Change,* Amsterdam 1970; *Ramdom Objectivations,* Brescia, Italy 1972; *Chance-fields/Chancefelder: An Essay on the Topology of Randomness,* Dinkelscherben 1973; *The Wittgenstein Paper, I and II,* Berne 1974; *To Be All Ways to Be,* Katmandu 1974; *Vijf Manifesten over Taal—en een Gedicht,* Berne 1975; *Asiatische und Eschenauer Texte,* portfolio, Berne 1975; *October, February, June,* Eschenau 1977; *The Dust of Some Roads and Leaf from a Tree,* Eschenau 1977; *Some Early Change Projects/Einige fruhe anderungs Projekte 1963–1967,* portfolio with tape cassette, Berne 1977; *16 dm2, an Essay,* Berne 1979; *Concept,* Eschenau 1981; *Documents of a Stream,* Eindhoven, Netherlands 1981; *From Here,* Gorinchem, Netherlands 1982; articles—"Nul=0" in *Nul=0* (Amsterdam), vol 1, no. 10, 1962; "Random Objectivations" in *Nul=0* (Amsterdam), vol. 2, no. 34–35, 1963; "Objektivitat und Wirklichkeit" in *Nul=0* (Amsterdam). vol. 4, no. 83–85; "Visuel Informatie/Visual Information/Visuelle Information/Information Visuelle" in *Revue Integration* (Amsterdam), vol. 1, 1965; "Wit/White/Blanc" in *Revue Integration* (Amsterdam), vol 9, 1967; "Fragmentarische Argumenten: in *Felison—Kahier* (Ijmuiden), no. 10, 1968; "Notes for a Random Reader" in *Panel 13 Information* (Copenhagen), no. 1, 1968; "The Lines of Life and Love" in *Bulletin Festival 200* (Copenhagen), no. 1, 1969; "Chance and Change" in *Prospectus Galerie Swart,* exhibition catalogue, Amsterdam 1974; "The Wittgenstein Papers—framentarische argumenten" in *Taal Beeld Taal* (Brummen), no. 1, 1975; "A Line" in *Museumjournaal* (Amsterdam), no. 6, 1976; films—*Look Out of any Window,* 1972; *100 Ansichten von grossen Knetzberg,* 1972; *Chance and Change,* 1973; *A Letter from James,* 1977; *The Flower-Sutra,* 1979; *Film-Notes,* 1979; *Water Pictures,* 1980; sound-recordings—*Natura Artis Magistra,* tape-cassette, 1967; *Humanae Vitae,* tape-cassette, 1967; *Natura Artis Magistra and Humanae Vitae,* tape-cassette with drawing, 1971; *Water—The Music of Sound,* 1977.

On DE VRIES: books—*Herman De Vries* by Walter Aue, Cologne 1966; *Constructivism: Orgins and Evolution* by George Rickey, New York 1967; *Herman De Vries,* exhibition catalogue, with text by Herbert V. Franke, Bochum, West Germany, 1970; *Konkret Dichtung* by Siegfried J. Schmidt, Munich 1972; *Asthetik als Informationsverarbeitung* by Frieder Nake, Vienna and New York 1974; *Programmi Sistematici* by Jean Leering, Milan 1975; *Herman De Vries: At Random,* exhibition catalogue, with an introduction by Antoinette Hilgemann-de Stiger, Gorinchem, Netherlands 1976; *Konstruktive Konzepte* by Willy Rotzler, Zurich 1977; *Nederlandse Kunstenarsboeken* by Flip Bool and G. J. de Rook, The Hague 1978; *Herman De Vries: Werken 1954–1980,* exhibition catalogue, with an introduction by Frans Haks, and essays by Urs and Ros Graf, Groningen, Netherlands 1980.

Around 1960, my grey-white informal paintings changed slowly to empty white canvases under the influence of the Buddhist thought of emptiness.

Some years later, I was looking for structure without giving up the objectivity, the emptiness of limited

Herman De Vries: *Das grosse Rasenstuck*, 1979

and limiting meaning I had gained in the white paintings with homogenous surfaces.

In my biological work I used randomness as a means for leaving out the influence of the researcher in the research series, and discovered that this system was very useful to come to form again and not to have to say anything. In the following 14 years I was mainly occupied with "random objectivations"—researching visual relationships in random programs. During this work, I became interested in the nature of randomness and chance: the existing definitions were not satisfying nor did they coincide with the results of my work. By following definitions of randomness and of art and always having to change them again and again, I realized that there are limits to the intellect. In this period, I also found that the patterns of *chance* were connected to *change:* they were all around in everyday reality. I tried to document them, first in photo-series at the beginning of the 70's, and later in the facts of reality itself—works which I now call "actuality as a document of itself."

Last year I crossed the border between art and non-art, between art and actuality, so becoming free of an important contradiction. My parallel ongoing preoccupations with philosophy and poetry all became integrated.

A final statement is not possible to give. When I say "all," I include the negation "not all"; so I prefer to leave it open.

—Herman de Vries

From 1949 to 1952 Herman de Vries was a student at the Montpellier Ecole des Beaux-Arts. Even that was for him a period when he was intensely caught up with the patterning wrought by geometric fragments hanging together as mobiles, but subsequently conjured into monochrome oil paintings which proved a short step to collages of the same character.

In 1965 he made his first experiments with *concrete poetry* and by 1968 had become an active contributor to the Edition Hansjörg Mayer's great anthology exhibition at the Hague's Gemeentemuseum with a number of exhibits which (besides unnumbered blank or patterned pages) included a wild conglomeration of interwoven linear triangles with title: "empty space for an empty space prepared for you by herman de vries this one is for him".

Ten years after found him at work upon pocket-multiples (white squares each with ten black spots, dots would be a more accurate description of them, in quasi-casual disarray on their surfaces) and—rather larger—1 decimeter^2 in dimension and when fully assembled stretching 16 decimeters in extent. These were not only bigger than the pocket-multiples, the black images set central on each part of the full assembly of squares were non-fugurative, of course, but more complicated than those of the pocket-multiples and were richly different, each from each.

Herman de Vries, in his casual economy of means, with a predominant desire to establish what imagery he does employ in implied boundless space, has somehow translated the freedom of the mobile onto a two-dimensional surface. In doing so he has endowed his works with an enduring character of liberty.

—Sheldon Williams

DEWASNE, Jean.

French. Born in Lille, 21 May 1921. Studied music, the classics and architecture, at the Ecole des Beaux-Arts, Paris. Produced first abstract paintings, Paris, 1943; Member, Abstract art group, with Hartung, Schneider, de Staël, Poliakoff and Deyrolle, Paris, 1945; Founder-Member, with Jean Arp, Antoine Pevsner, Sonia Delaunay and others, Salon des Réalités Nouvelles, Paris, 1945; painted first large mural commission, Paris, 1948; Founder-Director, Studio of Abstract Art, Paris, 1950–53. Has travelled and lectured extensively in Europe and America, since 1951. Recipient: Kandinsky Award, Paris, 1945. Address: 18 rue du Bourg-Tibourg, 75004 Paris, France.

Individual Exhibitions:

1949 Arne Bruun-Rasmussen Galerie, Copenhagen
1955 Palais des Beaux-Arts, Brussels
Arne Bruun-Rasmussen Galerie, Copenhagen
1956 Galerie Cordier, Paris
1959 Palais des Beaux-Arts, Brussels
1961 Galleria Lorenzelli, Milan
1962 Carrefour Galerie, Brussels
1963 Galerie Cordier, Paris
Galerie Hybler, Copenhagen
Esbjerg Museum, Denmark
1965 Cordier-Ekstrom Gallery, New York
1966 Kunsthalle, Berne (retrospective)
1967 Galleria Lorenzelli, Bergamo, Italy
1969 Musée d'Art Moderne, Paris
Palais des Beaux-Arts, Brussels
1971 Galerie Creuzevalt, Paris
1972 Lefebre Gallery, New York
Galerie Janssen, Brussels
1973 Galerie Francoise Tournier, Paris
Galerie Artel, Geneva
Soto Museum, Ciudad Bolivar, Venezuela
1974 Louisiana Museum, Humlebaek, Denmark
Nordyllands Kunstmuseum, Aalborg, Denmark
Orly Airport, Paris
1975 Galerie Mark, Zurich
Centre d'Art et Loisirs, Privas, France

Jean Dewasne: Mural at the Musée de Grenoble, France, 1970

Maison des Arts et Loisirs, Sochaux, France (toured France)
Musée d'Art Moderne de la Ville, Paris
Carnegie Institute, Pittsburgh (toured the United States)
Musée d'Art Moderne, Paris
Galerie Remarque, Trans en Provence, France
Esbjerg Kunstforening, Denmark (toured Denmark)
Idées Contemporaines, Pontaven, France
Galerie Attali, Paris
Jean Dewasne, Muraliste, Kunstverein, Hannover
Centre Culturel Pablo Neruda, Corbeil, France
Centre Action Culturel, Macon, France
1976 Centre d'Art et Communication, Vaduz, Liechtenstein
Galeria d'Arte Contacto, Caracas
1977 *Gouches et Dessins,* Galerie Asbaek, Copenhagen
Galerie Groninger, Groningen, Netherlands
Antisculptures et Gouaches, Nordjyllands Kunstmuseum, Aalborg
1978 *Antisculptures, Maxi-Peintures, Gouaches,* Henie Onstad Museum, Oslo
Conceptions, Institut Francais, Stockholm
1979 Galerie Sapone, Nice
Museum of Modern Art, Caracas
1980 Grand Palais, Paris
1981 *La Longue Marche,* Centre Georges Pompidou, Paris

Selected Group Exhibitions:

1945 *Salon des Réalités Nouvelles,* Paris
1968 *Biennale,* Venice
1972 *The Non-Objective World 1939–1955,* Annely Juda Fine Art, London (toured Europe)
Douze Ans d'Art Contemporain en France, Grand Palais, Paris
1975 *Kunstmesse Art 6/75,* Basle
Art Fair, Cologne
1976 *Artists from France,* Covent Garden, London
1981 *Paris—Paris 1937–1957,* Centre Georges Pompidou, Paris

Collections:

Nordyllands Kunstmuseum, Aalborg, Denmark; Louisiana Museum, Humlebaek, Denmark; Boymans van Beuningen Museum, Rotterdam; Musée des Beaux-Arts, Brussels; Centre Georges Pompidou, Paris; Musée de Grenoble, France, Carnegie Institute, Pittsburgh; Guggenheim Museum, New York; Museum of Modern Art, New York.

Publications:

By DEWASNE: books—illustrations for *Preface to a Future Book* by Lautreamont, Copenhagen 1949; *Robert Jacobsen,* Copenhagen 1950; *Vasarely,* Paris 1952: *Traité de la peinture* (written in 1949), Paris 1972; articles—"Mathematical Space and Abstract Art" in *20th Siècle* (Paris) no. 2, 1952; "The Paintings of the Cuzco School" in *Lettres Francaises* (Paris), September/October 1952; "Visit to the Secret City of Macchu-Picchu" in *Lettres Francaises* (Paris), March 1956; "Romanesque Paintings and Gothic Painting in Denmark" in *Lettres Francaises* (Paris), October 1956; "Andrea del Castagno" and "The Gods of Saint Augustine" in *Letters Francaises* (Paris), August 1957; "What Is Avant-Garde in 1958" in *Lettres Francaises* (Paris), June 1958; "Reflections on Abstract Art in *Quadrum* (Brussels), no. 7, 1959; "Abstract Art and Objectivity" in *Nouvelle Critique* (Paris), September 1968; "The Problem of the Wall" in *L'Oeil* (Paris), September/October 1971; "De la Théorie au Concept" with E. Mavrommatis, in *Opus* (Paris), no. 37, 1972; "Dedie au spectateur" in *Galerie des Arts* (Paris), March 1977; "Une création mathématisée" in *Gazette des Beaux-Arts* (Paris), September 1977.

On DEWASNE: books—*Jean Dewasne* by Pierre Descargues, Paris 1952; *Jean Dewasne,* exhibition catalogue, with texts by several authors, Milan 1961; *Dewasne,* exhibtion catalogue, with text by Daniel Cordier, New York 1965; *Dewasne,* exhibition catalogue, with text by Daniel Cordier, New York 1972; *The Mondial Art 1960–1975,* edited by Germain Viatte, Geneva 1975; *From Thorvaldsen to the Atomic Age,* edited by Sigurd Schultz, Copenhagen 1975; *Art Actuel: Skira Annuel 75,* Geneva 1975.

Here is a general theory of aesthetic creation:

The artist begins by formulating dynamic currents in order to express the drama of plastic happenings. Because of this, the assemblies cannot be isolated from their liaisons. The rhythm of these liaisons gives the work its main meanings. The dynamic currents and the filiations impose the sittings and the positions.

The positions, within the currents, give rise to other plastic assemblies which momentarily hold the spectator's attention. This period of contemplation and analysis permits the spectator to experience mental speculations which can ensure and multiply his pleasure. They prepare him to then throw himself into the torrent of the current; this, in its turn, can be considered as a significant assembly, one that can be analysed, a detectable one. The relative positions, the situations, the combinations triumph over the form-colour elements that were visible at first. The structures of association will liberate from the